THE OFFICIAL
MAJOR LEAGUE
BASEBALL
1991 STAT BOOK

THE OFFICIAL
MAJOR LEAGUE
BASEBALL
1991 STAT BOOK

COMPILED BY

Major League Baseball Properties, Inc.
and the editors of *The Baseball Encyclopedia*

COLLIER BOOK/MACMILLAN PUBLISHING COMPANY • NEW YORK

COLLIER MACMILLAN CANADA • TORONTO

Collier Books
Macmillan Publishing Company
866 Third Avenue, New York, NY 10022

Collier Macmillan Canada, Inc.
1200 Eglinton Avenue East, Suite 200
Don Mills, Ontario M3C 3N1

ISBN 0-02-063381-5

Macmillan books are available at special discounts for bulk purchases for sales promotions, premiums, fund-raising, or educational use. For details, contact:

Special Sales Director
Macmillan Publishing Company
866 Third Avenue, New York, NY 10022

First Collier Books Edition 1991

10 9 8 7 6 5 4 3 2 1

Printed in the United States of America

Designed by Robert Bull Design

CONTENTS

Acknowledgments

Macmillan gratefully acknowledges the efforts of the following people without whose help *The Official Major League Baseball 1991 Stat Book* could not have been produced. From Major League Baseball: Steven D. Nordman, Fred Coseglia, Julio Carbonell, Cindy McManus, Dave Alworth, and Steve Adamus. From Black Dot Graphics: Glenn Soltau, Randall Zubow, Amy Melichar, and Darlene Wesemann. And from Macmillan: John Ball, Andrew Attaway, Janet Tingey, Bob Bull, Ken Samelson, Jeanine Bucek, Rick Wolff, publisher Bill Rosen, who came up with the idea for the book, and a special tip of the cap to Camillo Lo Giudice, who really engineered the entire project from the drawing board to finished books.

THE OFFICIAL
MAJOR LEAGUE
BASEBALL
1991 STAT BOOK

INTRODUCTION

How to Use Your *Major League Baseball 1991 Stat Book*

This book was designed to be easy for all baseball fans to use, from the professional sportswriter or sportscaster in the press box to the casual fan at home to the diehard fantasy baseball league player. Macmillan, in conjunction with Major League Baseball and IBM, has produced a unique statistical analysis of the top players and pitchers in the game, as well as the complete and official record of the 1990 Major League Baseball season. The *Stat Book* features

- The complete season's record of every player and pitcher who appeared in a major league game in 1990.
- The complete career record of every player and pitcher in the 1990 season who has played in the majors for more than one season.
- Statistical analyses and graphic comparisons of the top players and pitchers according to widely used fantasy league criteria.
- The complete records of all the managers who managed a major league team in 1990.
- A detailed recap of the League Championship Series and the World Series, including game-by-game and composite box scores.

For the most part, the *Stat Book*'s contents are self-explanatory. The *Stat Book* serves as *The Baseball Encyclopedia*'s annual update, and fans of the *Encyclopedia* will find the presentation of much of the material familiar. Each entry includes the ballplayer's full name, his nickname, personal data such as his birthplace and birthdate, height, weight, and complete season and career record.

You will also find complete statistical analyses of all of 1990's top pitchers and players. The *Stat Book* divides all pitchers into two categories: starters and relievers. While we recognize that some pitchers do perform both functions on some major league teams, most pitchers are used either as starters or in relief. For each starting pitcher who faced at least 300 batters in 1990, we have provided a breakdown of that pitcher's performance by month, in day as opposed to night games, versus right- or left-handed hitters, at home and on the road, and on grass and artificial turf. There's even a breakdown of how the pitcher did against each opposing team in his club's division. A complete analysis is also provided for each relief pitcher who made at least 20 relief appearances during the year.

The *Stat Book* presents an equally thorough analysis for all batters with 250 or more plate appearances in 1990. Each batter's hitting is broken down by month, against left-handed pitchers and right-handers, during night as opposed to day games, on grass and on artificial turf, on the road and at home. There is also a breakdown of how a player hit against other teams in his division, and how he hit with a man on third and less than two outs.

In addition to the statistical analysis, the *Stat Book* provides graphic comparisons for the top pitchers and players. These graphs enable you to compare a pitcher's or player's 1990 performance with the league average for his position.

Hitters with 250 or more plate appearances are compared to all the players in their league at their position in home runs, batting average, runs batted in, and stolen bases. For example, take a look at the graphic analysis of Steve Sax of the New York Yankees. In the four boxes you will see two bars: one represents the American League average for second basemen in each of the four categories; the other bar in each box show Sax's statistics. Thus the collective batting average of American League second basemen in 1990 was .260. Sax, in fact, hit .260. But the average number of stolen bases for AL second basemen was 12; Sax stole 43. The same comparisons are made for home runs and RBI.

Starting pitchers who faced 300 or more batters in 1990 are compared with league averages for wins, earned run average, strikeouts per nine innings, and ratio (which is defined as hits plus walks per nine innings pitched). Here again, the bar columns in each box represent the league average and the individual pitcher's performance respectively.

Relief pitchers who made twenty or more appearances in 1990 are compared against the league in wins, saves, earned run average, and ratio. Comparisons can easily be made between the bar representing the league average and that representing the individual reliever's performance.

In certain rare instances, the editorial staff of Major League Baseball and Macmillan have decided how a player or pitcher should be classified. For instance, in 1990 Bob Ojeda of the Mets qualified as both a starting pitcher and a relief pitcher. But in our judgment, Ojeda is better known and recognized as a starting pitcher, and as such, his National League comparisons are with other starting pitchers.

The Teams and Their Players

The Teams and Their Players lists, for the 1990 season, each team, its manager and record, the regulars at each position, the pitchers, and the leading substitutes. The teams are presented in the order of the standings of the division. Substitutes are listed if they had at least 162 at bats or 20 runs batted in; pitchers are listed if they pitched 162 innings or had 9 or more decisions (including saves).

Fielding statistics listed for regulars are for the indicated position only. The position listed for substitutes may vary. If a substitute played 70 percent of his games at one position, that is the only position listed for him. If he did not play 70 percent of his games at one position, but played 90 percent of his games at two positions, he is listed with a combination position, such as "S2" for shortstop and second base, or "CO" for catcher and outfield. In such cases, the fielding statistics listed are combined for both positions. All outfield positions are considered one position for these purposes. If a player failed to meet either the 70 percent or 90 percent requirement listed above, he is listed as a utility player ("UT").

Any statistic that appears in boldface print is a league-leading total for that category. An asterisk (*) next to a particular statistic indicates that the player led the league, but since he was traded during the season, the figure listed there is not necessarily his league-leading final total or average. For batting averages or percentages, a batter must have 502 plate appearances to qualify for the title. Pitchers must have pitched 162 innings to qualify in any pitching average. Fielders must have appeared in 100 games at the position to qualify.

NATIONAL LEAGUE 1990

	POS	Player	AB	BA	HR	RBI	PO	A	E	DP	TC/G	FA	Pitcher	G	IP	W	L	SV	ERA
East																			
Pittsburgh	1B	S. Bream	389	.270	15	67	971	104	8	80	7.6	.993	D. Drabek	33	231	22	6	0	2.76
	2B	J. Lind	514	.261	1	48	330	449	7	74	5.2	.991	J. Smiley	26	149	9	10	0	4.64
W-95 L-67	SS	J. Bell	583	.254	7	52	260	459	22	85	4.7	.970	N. Heaton	30	146	12	9	0	3.45
Jim Leyland	3B	J. King	371	.245	14	53	58	215	18	15	2.5	.938	B. Walk	26	130	7	5	1	3.75
	RF	B. Bonilla	625	.280	32	120	289	8	12	1	2.1	.961	B. Patterson	55	95	8	5	5	2.95
	CF	A. Van Slyke	493	.284	17	77	326	6	8	0	2.6	.976	B. Landrum	54	72	7	3	13	2.13
	LF	B. Bonds	519	.301	33	114	338	14	6	2	2.4	.983	B. Kipper	41	63	5	2	3	3.02
	C	LaValliere	279	.258	3	31	478	36	5	6	5.5	.990	S. Belinda	55	58	3	4	8	3.55
	3B	W. Backman	315	.292	2	28	34	104	12	5	2.1	.920	T. Power	40	52	1	3	7	3.66
	C	D. Slaught	230	.300	4	29	345	36	8	4	5.0	.979							
	1B	G. Redus	227	.247	6	23	447	35	6	29	6.8	.988							
	OF	R. Reynolds	215	.288	0	19	102	3	3	0	1.8	.972							
New York	1B	D. Magadan	451	.328	6	72	830	71	2	52	8.0	.998	F. Viola	35	250	20	12	0	2.67
	2B	G. Jefferies	604	.283	15	68	219	278	12	49	4.3	.976	D. Gooden	34	233	19	7	0	3.83
W-91 L-71	SS	K. Elster	314	.207	9	45	159	251	17	42	4.6	.960	D. Cone	31	212	14	10	0	3.23
	3B	H. Johnson	590	.244	23	90	52	159	20	11	2.5	.913	S. Fernandez	30	179	9	14	0	3.46
Davey Johnson	RF	Strawberry	542	.277	37	108	268	10	3	4	1.9	.989	R. Darling	33	126	7	9	0	4.50
W-20 L-22	CF	D. Boston	366	.273	12	45	203	3	3	1	1.9	.986	B. Ojeda	38	118	7	6	0	3.66
	LF	McReynolds	521	.269	24	82	237	14	3	2	1.8	.988	A. Pena	52	76	3	3	5	3.20
Bud Harrelson	C	M. Sasser	270	.307	6	41	498	43	14	4	6.4	.975	J. Franco	55	68	5	3	33	2.53
W-71 L-49	OF	K. Miller	233	.258	1	12	146	1	3	1	2.5	.980							
	OF	M. Carreon	188	.250	10	26	87	1	0	0	1.5	1.000							
	UT	T. Teufel	175	.246	10	24	141	58	4	16	—	.980							
	1B	M. Marshall	163	.239	6	27	277	24	2	19	7.2	.993							
Montreal	1B	A. Galarraga	579	.256	20	87	1,300	94	10	93	9.1	.993	D. Martinez	32	226	10	11	0	2.95
	2B	D. DeShields	499	.289	4	45	236	371	12	65	4.8	.981	O. Boyd	31	191	10	6	0	2.93
W-85 L-77	SS	S. Owen	453	.234	5	35	216	340	6	52	3.8	.989	K. Gross	31	163	9	12	0	4.57
Buck Rodgers	3B	T. Wallach	626	.296	21	98	128	309	21	23	2.8	.954	M. Gardner	27	153	7	9	0	3.42
	RF	L. Walker	419	.241	19	51	249	12	4	5	2.1	.985	Z. Smith	22	139	6	7	0	3.23
	CF	D. Martinez	391	.279	11	39	257	6	3	1	2.5	.989	B. Sampen	59	90	12	7	2	2.99
	LF	T. Raines	457	.287	9	62	239	3	6	1	2.0	.976	T. Burke	58	75	3	3	20	2.52
	C	Fitzgerald	313	.243	9	41	560	41	6	10	6.2	.990	D. Hall	42	58	4	7	3	5.09
	OF	M. Grissom	288	.257	3	29	165	5	2	0	2.0	.988	S. Frey	51	56	8	2	9	2.10
	OF	O. Nixon	231	.251	1	20	149	5	1	0	1.8	.994	D. Schmidt	34	48	3	3	13	4.31
	UT	T. Foley	164	.213	0	12	80	123	5	26	—	.976							
	C	Santovenia	163	.190	6	28	264	24	6	7	5.8	.980							
Chicago	1B	M. Grace	589	.309	9	82	1,324	180	12	116	9.9	.992	G. Maddux	35	237	15	15	0	3.46
	2B	R. Sandberg	615	.306	40	100	278	469	8	81	4.9	.989	M. Harkey	27	174	12	6	0	3.26
W-77 L-85	SS	S. Dunston	545	.262	17	66	255	392	20	77	4.6	.970	M. Bielecki	36	168	8	11	1	4.93
Don Zimmer	3B	L. Salazar	410	.254	12	47	55	136	10	12	2.2	.950	S. Wilson	45	139	4	9	1	4.79
	RF	A. Dawson	529	.310	27	100	250	10	5	4	1.9	.981	L. Lancaster	55	109	9	5	6	4.62
	CF	J. Walton	392	.263	2	21	247	3	6	0	2.6	.977	Assenmacher	74	103	7	2	10	2.80
	LF	D. Dascenzo	241	.253	1	26	174	2	0	1	1.6	1.000	S. Boskie	15	98	5	6	0	3.69
	C	J. Girardi	419	.270	1	38	653	61	11	5	5.5	.985	J. Pico	31	92	4	4	2	4.79
	OF	D. Smith	290	.262	6	27	139	4	2	2	1.8	.986	M. Williams	59	66	1	8	16	3.93
	3B	D. Ramos	226	.265	2	17	23	46	5	2	1.1	.932	J. Nunez	21	61	4	7	0	6.53
	3B	C. Wilkerson	186	.220	0	16	25	62	11	4	1.9	.888	B. Long	42	56	6	1	5	4.37
	OF	M. Wynne	186	.204	4	19	108	3	1	2	1.7	.991							
	OF	D. Clark	171	.275	5	20	60	2	0	0	1.6	1.000							
Philadelphia	1B	R. Jordan	324	.241	5	44	743	37	4	65	9.3	.995	P. Combs	32	183	10	10	0	4.07
	2B	T. Herr	447	.264	4	50	240	290	5	79*	4.7	.991	Mulholland	33	181	9	10	0	3.34
W-77 L-85	SS	D. Thon	552	.255	8	48	222	439	25	86	4.6	.964	B. Ruffin	32	149	6	13	0	5.38
Nick Leyva	3B	C. Hayes	561	.258	10	57	121	324	20	30	3.2	.957	D. Cook	42	142	8	3	1	3.56
	RF	V. Hayes	467	.261	17	73	272	8	6	0	2.3	.979	J. DeJesus	22	130	7	8	0	3.74
	CF	L. Dykstra	590	.325	9	60	439	7	6	5	3.0	.987	K. Howell	18	107	8	7	0	4.64
	LF	J. Kruk	443	.291	7	67	141	2	2	0	1.7	.986	D. Akerfelds	71	93	5	2	3	3.77
	C	D. Daulton	459	.268	12	57	683	70	8	10	5.5	.989	R. McDowell	72	86	6	8	22	3.86
	02	R. Ready	217	.244	1	26	78	86	2	18	—	.988	J. Parrett	47	82	4	9	1	5.18
	OF	D. Murphy	214	.266	7	28	113	4	1	1	2.1	.991	J. Boever	34	46	2	3	6	2.15
	10	C. Martinez	198	.242	8	31	350	25	2	31	—	.995							
St. Louis	1B	P. Guerrero	498	.281	13	80	1,083	73	13	74	8.9	.989	J. Magrane	31	203	10	17	0	3.59
	2B	J. Oquendo	469	.252	1	37	285	393	3	65	4.5	.996	J. DeLeon	32	183	7	19	0	4.43
W-70 L-92	SS	O. Smith	512	.254	1	50	212	378	12	66	4.3	.980	J. Tudor	25	146	12	4	0	2.40
	3B	T. Pendleton	447	.230	6	58	91	248	19	18	3.1	.947	B. Tewksbury	28	145	10	9	1	3.47
Whitey Herzog	RF	M. Thompson	418	.218	6	30	232	4	7	0	2.1	.971	B. Smith	26	141	9	8	0	4.27
W-33 L-47	CF	W. McGee	501	.335	3	62	341	13	16	4	3.0	.957	F. DiPino	62	81	5	2	3	4.56
	LF	V. Coleman	497	.292	6	39	244	12	5	2	2.2	.981	K. Hill	17	79	5	6	0	5.49
Red Schoendienst	C	T. Zeile	495	.244	15	57	533	56	7	3	5.7	.988	K. Dayley	58	73	4	4	2	3.56
W-13 L-11	C	T. Pagnozzi	220	.277	2	23	334	39	4	4	6.0	.989	S. Terry	50	72	2	6	2	4.75
	UT	R. Hudler	217	.281	7	22	158	42	5	9	—	.976	L. Smith	53	69	3	4	27	2.10
Joe Torre																			
W-24 L-34																			

NATIONAL LEAGUE 1990, *cont.*

West — Cincinnati (W-91 L-71, Lou Piniella)

POS	Player	AB	BA	HR	RBI	PO	A	E	DP	TC/G	FA	Pitcher	G	IP	W	L	SV	ERA
1B	T. Benzinger	376	.253	5	46	707	52	6	58	8.1	.992	T. Browning	35	228	15	9	0	3.80
2B	M. Duncan	435	.306	10	55	245	287	15	51	4.8	.973	J. Rijo	29	197	14	8	0	2.70
SS	B. Larkin	614	.301	7	67	254	469	17	86	4.7	.977	J. Armstrong	29	166	12	9	0	3.42
3B	C. Sabo	567	.270	25	71	70	273	12	17	2.4	.966	N. Charlton	56	154	12	9	2	2.74
RF	P. O'Neill	503	.270	16	78	271	12	2	0	2.0	.993	R. Mahler	35	135	7	6	4	4.28
CF	E. Davis	453	.260	24	86	257	11	2	1	2.2	.993	D. Jackson	22	117	6	6	0	3.61
LF	B. Hatcher	504	.276	5	25	308	10	1	2	2.4	.997	R. Dibble	68	98	8	3	11	1.74
C	J. Oliver	364	.231	8	52	686	59	6	8	6.4	.992	R. Myers	66	87	4	6	31	2.08
1B	H. Morris	309	.340	7	36	589	53	3	50	8.1	.995	T. Layana	55	80	5	3	2	3.49
OF	G. Braggs	201	.299	6	28	110	10	4	3	2.1	.968	S. Scudder	21	72	5	5	0	4.90
C	J. Reed	175	.251	3	16	358	26	5	1	5.6	.987							

Los Angeles (W-86 L-76, Tom Lasorda)

POS	Player	AB	BA	HR	RBI	PO	A	E	DP	TC/G	FA	Pitcher	G	IP	W	L	SV	ERA
1B	E. Murray	558	.330	26	95	1,180	113	10	88	8.7	.992	R. Martinez	33	234	20	6	0	2.92
2B	J. Samuel	492	.242	13	52	194	258	13	47	4.3	.972	M. Morgan	33	211	11	15	0	3.75
SS	A. Griffin	461	.210	1	35	221	382	26	63	4.5	.959	Valenzuela	33	204	13	13	0	4.59
3B	Sharperson	357	.297	3	36	70	153	12	10	2.2	.949	T. Belcher	24	153	9	9	0	4.00
RF	H. Brooks	568	.266	20	91	255	9	10	2	1.8	.964	T. Crews	66	107	4	5	5	2.77
CF	K. Gibson	315	.260	8	38	191	4	1	1	2.4	.995	M. Hartley	32	79	6	3	1	2.95
LF	K. Daniels	450	.296	27	94	207	13	3	2	1.8	.987	J. Howell	45	66	5	5	16	2.18
C	M. Scioscia	435	.264	12	66	842	58	10	9	6.9	.989	J. Gott	50	62	3	5	3	2.90
32	L. Harris	431	.304	2	29	139	203	11	24	—	.969							
OF	S. Javier	276	.304	3	24	204	2	0	1	2.4	1.000							
OF	C. Gwynn	141	.284	5	22	39	1	0	0	0.9	1.000							

San Francisco (W-85 L-77, Roger Craig)

POS	Player	AB	BA	HR	RBI	PO	A	E	DP	TC/G	FA	Pitcher	G	IP	W	L	SV	ERA
1B	W. Clark	600	.295	19	95	1,456	119	12	118	10.4	.992	J. Burkett	33	204	14	7	1	3.79
2B	R. Thompson	498	.245	15	56	287	441	8	94	5.2	.989	S. Garrelts	31	182	12	11	0	4.15
SS	J. Uribe	415	.248	1	24	182	373	20	73	4.3	.965	D. Robinson	26	158	10	7	0	4.57
3B	M. Williams	617	.277	33	122	140	306	19	33	2.9	.959	T. Wilson	27	110	8	7	0	4.00
RF	M. Kingery	207	.295	0	24	126	7	3	2	1.4	.978	R. Reuschel	15	87	3	6	1	3.93
CF	B. Butler	622	.309	3	44	420	4	6	0	2.7	.986	J. Brantley	55	87	5	3	19	1.56
LF	K. Mitchell	524	.290	35	93	295	9	9	3	2.3	.971	S. Bedrosian	68	79	9	9	17	4.20
C	T. Kennedy	303	.277	2	26	390	38	4	3	4.2	.991	M. LaCoss	13	78	6	4	0	3.94
C	G. Carter	244	.254	9	27	323	31	3	2	4.5	.992							
OF	K. Bass	214	.252	7	32	88	2	3	0	1.7	.968							
UT	G. Litton	204	.245	1	24	90	43	1	10	—	.993							
OF	R. Leach	174	.293	2	16	86	3	1	0	1.7	.989							
UT	E. Riles	155	.200	8	21	53	105	3	14	—	.981							

Houston (W-75 L-87, Art Howe)

POS	Player	AB	BA	HR	RBI	PO	A	E	DP	TC/G	FA	Pitcher	G	IP	W	L	SV	ERA
1B	G. Davis	327	.251	22	64	796	55	4	56	9.4	.995	J. Deshaies	34	209	7	12	0	3.78
2B	B. Doran	344	.288	6	32	170	265	5	43	4.4	.989	M. Scott	32	206	9	13	0	3.81
SS	R. Ramirez	445	.261	2	37	190	321	25	57	4.2	.953	M. Portugal	32	197	11	10	0	3.62
3B	K. Caminiti	541	.242	4	51	118	243	21	22	2.6	.945	Gullickson	32	193	10	14	0	3.82
RF	G. Wilson	368	.245	10	55	225	12	6	6	2.3	.975	D. Darwin	48	163	11	4	2	2.21
CF	E. Yelding	511	.254	1	28	230	5	7	2	2.6	.971	J. Agosto	82	92	9	8	4	4.29
LF	F. Stubbs	448	.261	23	71	112	1	1	0	1.6	.991	J. Clancy	33	76	2	8	1	6.51
C	C. Biggio	555	.276	4	42	546	54	9	4	5.4	.985	L. Andersen	50	74	5	2	6	1.95
UT	C. Candaele	262	.286	3	22	147	120	3	20	—	.989	D. Smith	49	60	6	6	23	2.39
OF	E. Anthony	239	.192	10	29	124	5	4	0	1.9	.970							

San Diego (W-75 L-87; Jack McKeon W-37 L-43; Greg Riddoch W-38 L-44)

POS	Player	AB	BA	HR	RBI	PO	A	E	DP	TC/G	FA	Pitcher	G	IP	W	L	SV	ERA
1B	J. Clark	334	.266	25	62	855	69	6	72	8.5	.994	E. Whitson	32	229	14	9	0	2.60
2B	R. Alomar	586	.287	6	60	311	392	17	73	5.3	.976	B. Hurst	33	224	11	9	0	3.14
SS	G. Templeton	505	.248	9	59	214	367	26	74	4.5	.957	A. Benes	32	192	10	11	0	3.60
3B	Pagliarulo	398	.254	7	38	79	200	13	16	2.5	.955	D. Rasmussen	32	188	11	15	0	4.51
RF	T. Gwynn	573	.309	4	72	327	11	5	2	2.4	.985	G. Harris	73	117	8	8	9	2.30
CF	J. Carter	634	.232	24	115	385	13	5	4	2.7	.988	E. Show	39	106	6	8	1	5.76
LF	B. Roberts	556	.309	9	44	160	8	3	1	2.3	.982	C. Schiraldi	42	104	3	8	1	4.41
C	B. Santiago	344	.270	11	53	538	51	12	6	6.1	.985	C. Lefferts	56	79	7	5	23	2.52
OF	F. Lynn	196	.240	6	23	92	1	0	0	1.7	1.000							
C	M. Parent	189	.222	3	16	324	31	3	6	6.0	.991							
OF	S. Abner	184	.245	1	15	108	1	1	0	1.8	.991							
1B	Stephenson	182	.209	4	19	345	36	1	33	6.4	.997							

Atlanta (W-65 L-97; Russ Nixon W-25 L-40; Bobby Cox W-40 L-57)

POS	Player	AB	BA	HR	RBI	PO	A	E	DP	TC/G	FA	Pitcher	G	IP	W	L	SV	ERA
1B	D. Justice	439	.282	28	78	488	38	10	43	7.8	.981	J. Smoltz	34	231	14	11	0	3.85
2B	J. Treadway	474	.283	11	59	241	360	15	72	5.0	.976	T. Glavine	33	214	10	12	0	4.28
SS	J. Blauser	386	.269	8	39	141	257	16	47	4.5	.961	C. Leibrandt	24	162	9	11	0	3.16
3B	J. Presley	541	.242	19	72	101	231	25	19	2.7	.930	M. Clary	33	102	1	10	0	5.67
RF	D. Murphy	349	.232	17	55	208	3	4	0	2.2	.981	S. Avery	21	99	3	11	0	5.64
CF	R. Gant	575	.303	32	84	357	7	8	2	2.5	.978	P. Smith	13	77	5	6	0	4.79
LF	L. Smith	466	.305	9	42	254	6	12	2	2.2	.956	Lilliquist	12	62	2	8	0	6.28
C	G. Olson	298	.262	7	36	501	43	7	3	5.7	.987	K. Mercker	36	48	4	7	7	3.17
OF	O. McDowell	305	.243	7	25	134	2	4	0	1.9	.971	J. Boever	33	42	1	3	8	4.68
SS	A. Thomas	278	.219	5	30	103	193	10	41	4.3	.967							
1B	T. Gregg	239	.264	5	32	334	34	5	31	7.5	.987							
32	M. Lemke	239	.226	0	21	90	192	4	29	—	.986							
C	E. Whitt	180	.172	2	10	296	42	3	1	5.8	.991							
1B	F. Cabrera	137	.277	7	25	264	19	3	15	6.0	.990							

NATIONAL LEAGUE 1990, *cont.*

BATTING AND BASE RUNNING LEADERS

Batting Average
W. McGee, STL	.335
E. Murray, LA	.330
D. Magadan, NY	.328
L. Dykstra, PHI	.325
A. Dawson, CHI	.310

Slugging Average
B. Bonds, PIT	.565
R. Sandberg, CHI	.559
K. Mitchell, SF	.544
R. Gant, ATL	.539
A. Dawson, CHI	.535
D. Justice, ATL	.535

Home Runs
R. Sandberg, CHI	40
D. Strawberry, NY	37
K. Mitchell, SF	35
B. Bonds, PIT	33
M. Williams, SF	33

Total Bases
R. Sandberg, CHI	344
B. Bonilla, PIT	324
R. Gant, ATL	310
M. Williams, SF	301
T. Wallach, MON	295

Runs Batted In
M. Williams, SF	122
B. Bonilla, PIT	120
J. Carter, SD	115
B. Bonds, PIT	114
D. Strawberry, NY	108

Stolen Bases
V. Coleman, STL	77
E. Yelding, HOU	64
B. Bonds, PIT	52
B. Butler, SF	51
O. Nixon, MON	50

Hits
L. Dykstra, PHI	192
B. Butler, SF	192
R. Sandberg, CHI	188

Bases on Balls
J. Clark, SD	104
B. Bonds, PIT	93
B. Butler, SF	90

Home Run Percentage
D. Strawberry, NY	6.8
K. Mitchell, SF	6.7
R. Sandberg, CHI	6.5

Runs Scored
R. Sandberg, CHI	116
B. Bonilla, PIT	112
B. Butler, SF	108

Doubles
G. Jefferies, NY	40
B. Bonilla, PIT	39
C. Sabo, CIN	38

Triples
M. Duncan, CIN	11
T. Gwynn, SD	10

PITCHING LEADERS

Winning Percentage
D. Drabek, PIT	.786
R. Martinez, LA	.769
J. Tudor, STL	.750
D. Darwin, HOU	.733
D. Gooden, NY	.731

Earned Run Average
D. Darwin, HOU	2.21
Z. Smith, MON, PIT	2.55
E. Whitson, SD	2.60
F. Viola, NY	2.67
J. Rijo, CIN	2.70

Wins
D. Drabek, PIT	22
R. Martinez, LA	20
F. Viola, NY	20
D. Gooden, NY	19
T. Browning, CIN	15
G. Maddux, CHI	15

Saves
J. Franco, NY	33
R. Myers, CIN	31
L. Smith, STL	27
D. Smith, HOU	23
C. Lefferts, SD	23

Strikeouts
D. Cone, NY	233
D. Gooden, NY	223
R. Martinez, LA	223
F. Viola, NY	182
S. Fernandez, NY	181

Complete Games
R. Martinez, LA	12
D. Drabek, PIT	9
B. Hurst, SD	9
G. Maddux, CHI	8

Fewest Hits/9 Innings
S. Fernandez, NY	6.53
J. Rijo, CIN	6.90
R. Martinez, LA	7.34

Shutouts
B. Hurst, SD	4
M. Morgan, LA	4

Fewest Walks/9 Innings
D. Darwin, HOU	1.72
E. Whitson, SD	1.86
C. Leibrandt, ATL	1.94

Most Strikeouts/9 Inn.
D. Cone, NY	9.93
S. Fernandez, NY	9.10
D. Gooden, NY	8.65

Innings
F. Viola, NY	250
G. Maddux, CHI	237
R. Martinez, LA	234

Games Pitched
J. Agosto, HOU	82
P. Assenmacher, CHI	74
G. Harris, SD	73

							Batting						Fielding				Pitching				
		W	L	GB	R	OR	2B	3B	HR	AVG	SLG	SB	E	DP	PCT	CG	BB	SO	SHO	SV	ERA
East	Pittsburgh	95	67	—	733	619	**288**	42	138	.259	.405	137	134	125	.979	18	413	848	8	43	3.40
	New York	91	71	4.0	775	613	278	21	**172**	.256	**.408**	110	132	107	.978	18	444	**1,217**	**14**	41	3.43
	Montreal	85	77	10.0	662	598	227	43	114	.250	.370	235	110	134	.982	18	510	991	11	**50**	**3.37**
	Chicago	77	85	18.0	690	774	240	36	136	.263	.392	151	124	136	.980	13	572	877	7	42	4.34
	Philadelphia	77	85	18.0	646	729	237	27	103	.255	.363	108	117	**150**	.981	18	651	840	7	35	4.07
	St. Louis	70	92	25.0	599	698	255	41	73	.256	.358	221	130	114	.979	8	475	833	13	39	3.87
West	Cincinnati	91	71	—	693	597	284	40	125	**.265**	.399	166	102	126	**.983**	14	543	1,029	12	**50**	3.39
	Los Angeles	86	76	5.0	728	685	222	27	129	.262	.382	141	130	123	.979	**29**	478	1,021	12	29	3.72
	San Francisco	85	77	6.0	719	710	221	35	152	.262	.396	109	107	148	.983	14	553	788	6	45	4.08
	Houston	75	87	16.0	573	656	209	32	94	.242	.345	179	131	124	.978	12	496	854	6	37	3.61
	San Diego	75	87	16.0	673	673	243	35	123	.257	.380	138	141	141	.977	21	507	928	12	35	3.68
	Atlanta	65	97	26.0	682	**821**	263	26	162	.250	.396	92	**158**	133	.974	17	**579**	938	8	30	4.58
					8173	8173	2967	405	1521	.256	.383	1787	1516	1561	.980	200	6221	11164	116	476	3.79

AMERICAN LEAGUE 1990

		POS	Player	AB	BA	HR	RBI	PO	A	E	DP	TC/G	FA	Pitcher	G	IP	W	L	SV	ERA
East	**Boston**	1B	C. Quintana	512	.287	7	67	1,188	137	17	116	9.1	.987	R. Clemens	31	228	21	6	0	**1.93**
		2B	J. Reed	598	.289	5	51	215	374	6	82	5.0	.990	M. Boddicker	34	228	17	8	0	3.36
	W-88 L-74	SS	L. Rivera	346	.225	7	45	186	310	18	69	4.6	.965	G. Harris	34	184	13	9	0	4.00
	Joe Morgan	3B	W. Boggs	619	.302	6	63	108	241	20	18	2.4	.946	D. Kiecker	32	152	8	9	0	3.97
		RF	T. Brunansky	461	.267	15	71	267	7	5	1	2.3	.982	T. Bolton	21	120	10	5	0	3.38
		CF	E. Burke	588	.296	21	89	324	7	2	0	2.3	.994	D. Lamp	47	106	3	5	0	4.68
		LF	M. Greenwell	610	.297	14	73	287	13	7	1	1.9	.977	W. Gardner	34	77	3	7	0	4.89
		C	T. Pena	491	.263	7	56	864	74	5	13	6.6	.995	R. Murphy	68	57	0	6	7	6.32
		DH	D. Evans	445	.249	13	63							J. Reardon	47	51	5	3	21	3.16
														J. Gray	41	51	2	4	9	4.44
	Toronto	1B	F. McGriff	557	.300	35	88	1,246	126	6	119	9.4	.996	D. Stieb	33	209	18	6	0	2.93
		2B	M. Lee	391	.243	6	41	259	286	4	65	4.9	**.993**	Stottlemyre	33	203	13	17	0	4.34
	W-86 L-76	SS	T. Fernandez	635	.276	4	66	297	480	9	93	4.9	.989	D. Wells	43	189	11	6	3	3.14
	Clarence Gaston	3B	K. Gruber	592	.274	31	118	123	280	19	21	2.9	.955	J. Key	27	155	13	7	0	4.25
		RF	J. Felix	463	.263	15	65	244	11	9	3	2.1	.966	J. Cerutti	30	140	9	9	0	4.76
		CF	M. Wilson	588	.265	3	51	370	5	3	2	2.7	.992	D. Ward	73	128	2	8	11	3.45
		LF	G. Bell	562	.265	21	86	226	4	5	1	2.2	.979	F. Wills	44	99	6	4	0	4.73
		C	P. Borders	346	.286	15	49	515	46	4	6	4.9	.993	T. Henke	61	75	2	4	32	2.17
		DH	J. Olerud	358	.265	14	48													
		OF	G. Hill	260	.231	12	32	115	4	2	0	2.0	.983							
		C	G. Myers	250	.236	5	22	411	30	3	4	5.1	.993							
		2B	N. Liriano	170	.212	1	15	93	132	4	26	4.7	.983							
	Detroit	1B	C. Fielder	573	.277	**51**	132	1,190	111	14	**137**	9.2	.989	J. Morris	36	250	15	18	0	4.51
		2B	L. Whitaker	472	.237	18	60	286	372	6	98	5.1	.991	F. Tanana	34	176	9	8	1	5.31
	W-79 L-83	SS	A. Trammell	559	.304	14	89	232	409	14	102	4.6	.979	D. Petry	32	150	10	9	0	4.45
	Sparky Anderson	3B	T. Phillips	573	.251	8	55	69	200	20	16	2.8	.931	J. Robinson	27	145	10	9	0	5.96
		RF	C. Lemon	322	.258	5	32	209	7	6	1	2.3	.973	P. Gibson	61	97	5	4	3	3.05
		CF	L. Moseby	431	.248	14	51	288	9	5	5	2.6	.983	M. Henneman	69	94	8	6	22	3.05
		LF	G. Ward	309	.256	9	46	157	2	2	1	1.9	.988	J. Gleaton	57	83	1	3	13	2.94
		C	M. Heath	370	.270	7	38	585	54	13	7	5.6	.980	E. Nunez	42	80	3	1	6	2.24
		DH	D. Bergman	205	.278	2	26							W. Terrell	13	75	6	4	0	4.54
		OD	L. Sheets	360	.261	10	52	98	7	2	1	1.9	.981							
		3B	T. Fryman	232	.297	9	27	23	95	11	12	2.7	.915							
		OF	J. Shelby	222	.248	4	20	138	5	4	3	2.2	.973							
		C	M. Salas	164	.232	9	24	227	14	7	3	4.4	.988							

AMERICAN LEAGUE 1990, *cont.*

Cleveland
W-77 L-85
John McNamara

POS	Player	AB	AVG	HR	RBI	PO	A	E	DP	TC/G	FA	Pitcher	G	IP	W	L	SV	ERA
1B	D. James	248	.274	1	22	228	17	i	21	7.0	.996	G. Swindell	34	215	12	9	0	4.40
2B	J. Browne	513	.267	6	50	286	382	10	69	4.9	.985	T. Candiotti	31	202	15	11	0	3.65
SS	F. Fermin	414	.256	1	40	213	421	16	81	4.4	.975	B. Black	29	191	11	10	0	3.53
3B	B. Jacoby	553	.293	14	75	44	158	4	14	2.1	.981	S. Valdez	24	102	6	6	0	4.75
RF	C. Snyder	438	.233	14	55	224	11	6	2	2.0	.975	D. Jones	66	84	5	5	43	2.56
CF	M. Webster	437	.252	12	55	330	1	3	0	2.8	.991	J. Orosco	55	65	5	4	2	3.90
LF	C. Maldonado	590	.273	22	95	293	9	2	1	2.3	.993							
C	S. Alomar	445	.290	9	66	686	46	14	6	5.8	.981							
DH	C. James	528	.299	12	70													
3S	C. Baerga	312	.260	7	47	57	142	12	19		.943							
OF	A. Cole	227	.300	0	13	145	3	6	1	2.6	.961							
32	T. Brookens	154	.266	1	20	49	99	6	18		.961							

Baltimore
W-76 L-85
Frank Robinson

POS	Player	AB	AVG	HR	RBI	PO	A	E	DP	TC/G	FA	Pitcher	G	IP	W	L	SV	ERA
1B	R. Milligan	362	.265	20	60	846	87	9	94	9.6	.990	P. Harnisch	31	189	11	11	0	4.34
2B	B. Ripken	406	.291	3	38	250	366	8	84	4.9	.987	D. Johnson	30	180	13	9	0	4.10
SS	C. Ripken	600	.250	21	84	242	435	3	94	4.2	.996	B. Milacki	27	135	5	8	0	4.46
3B	Worthington	425	.226	8	44	90	218	18	28	2.5	.945	J. Ballard	44	133	2	11	0	4.93
RF	J. Orsulak	413	.269	11	57	267	5	3	2	2.5	.989	B. McDonald	21	119	8	5	0	2.43
CF	M. Devereaux	367	.240	12	49	281	4	5	1	2.8	.983	J. Mitchell	24	114	6	6	0	4.64
LF	P. Bradley	289	.270	4	26	149	3	2	0	2.2	.987	Williamson	49	85	8	2	1	2.21
C	M. Tettleton	444	.223	15	51	425	37	4	3	5.2	.991	G. Olson	64	74	6	5	37	2.42
DH	S. Horn	246	.248	14	45													
OF	S. Finley	464	.256	3	37	298	4	7	1	2.3	.977							
C	B. Melvin	301	.243	5	37	364	25	1	2	5.1	.997							
OF	B. Anderson	234	.231	3	24	149	3	2	1	2.4	.987							

Milwaukee
W-74 L-88
Tom Trebelhorn

POS	Player	AB	AVG	HR	RBI	PO	A	E	DP	TC/G	FA	Pitcher	G	IP	W	L	SV	ERA
1B	G. Brock	367	.248	7	50	885	63	5	89	8.3	.995	T. Higuera	27	170	11	10	0	3.76
2B	J. Gantner	323	.263	0	25	164	220	7	54	4.9	.982	M. Knudson	30	168	10	9	0	4.12
SS	B. Spiers	363	.242	2	36	159	326	12	72	4.5	.976	J. Navarro	32	149	8	7	1	4.46
3B	G. Sheffield	487	.294	10	67	98	254	25	16	3.0	.934	R. Robinson	22	148	12	5	0	2.91
RF	R. Deer	440	.209	27	69	243	14	8	7	2.3	.970	C. Bosio	20	133	4	9	0	4.00
CF	R. Yount	587	.247	17	77	422	3	4	0	2.7	.991	B. Krueger	30	129	6	8	0	3.98
LF	G. Vaughn	382	.220	17	61	195	8	7	1	2.0	.967	T. Edens	35	89	4	5	2	4.45
C	B. Surhoff	474	.276	6	59	615	53	10	10	5.4	.985	C. Crim	67	86	3	5	11	3.47
DH	D. Parker	610	.289	21	92							D. Plesac	66	69	3	7	24	4.43
21	P. Molitor	418	.285	12	45	461	215	9	64		.987							
OF	M. Felder	237	.274	3	27	165	8	5	6	1.6	.972							
SS	E. Diaz	218	.271	0	14	101	163	14	36	4.3	.950							

New York
W-67 L-95

Bucky Dent
W-18 L-31

Stump Merrill
W-49 L-64

POS	Player	AB	AVG	HR	RBI	PO	A	E	DP	TC/G	FA	Pitcher	G	IP	W	L	SV	ERA
1B	D. Mattingly	394	.256	5	42	800	78	3	81	9.9	.997	T. Leary	31	208	9	19	0	4.11
2B	S. Sax	615	.260	4	42	292	457	10	102	4.9	.987	D. LaPoint	28	158	7	10	0	4.11
SS	A. Espinoza	438	.224	2	20	268	447	17	100	4.9	.977	A. Hawkins	28	158	5	12	0	5.37
3B	R. Velarde	229	.210	5	19	43	128	10	11	2.4	.945	C. Cary	28	157	6	12	0	4.19
RF	J. Barfield	476	.246	25	78	305	16	9	3	2.2	.973	G. Cadaret	54	121	5	4	3	4.15
CF	R. Kelly	641	.285	15	61	420	5	5	0	2.7	.988	M. Witt	16	97	5	6	0	4.47
LF	O. Azocar	214	.248	5	19	105	4	1	1	1.9	.991	Guetterman	64	93	11	7	2	3.39
C	B. Geren	277	.213	8	31	487	55	4	5	5.1	.993	D. Righetti	53	53	1	1	36	3.57
DH	S. Balboni	266	.192	17	34													
DO	M. Hall	360	.258	12	46	70	2	2	0	1.5	.973							
3B	J. Leyritz	303	.257	5	25	43	101	11	5	2.2	.929							
1B	K. Maas	254	.252	21	41	486	35	9	45	9.3	.983							
CD	M. Nokes	240	.238	8	32	181	27	1	5	4.5	.995							
3B	M. Blowers	144	.188	5	21	26	63	10	4	2.2	.899							

West Oakland
W-103 L-59
Tony LaRussa

POS	Player	AB	AVG	HR	RBI	PO	A	E	DP	TC/G	FA	Pitcher	G	IP	W	L	SV	ERA
1B	M. McGwire	523	.235	39	108	1,329	95	5	126	9.3	.997	D. Stewart	36	267	22	11	0	2.56
2B	W. Randolph	292	.257	1	21	148	240	7	62	4.7	.982	B. Welch	35	238	27	6	0	2.95
SS	W. Weiss	445	.265	2	35	194	373	12	77	4.2	.979	S. Sanderson	34	206	17	11	0	3.88
3B	C. Lansford	507	.268	3	50	100	194	9	22	2.4	.970	M. Moore	33	199	13	15	0	4.65
RF	J. Canseco	481	.274	37	101	182	7	1	2	2.2	.995	C. Young	26	124	9	6	0	4.85
CF	D. Henderson	450	.271	20	63	319	5	4	1	2.8	.988	G. Nelson	51	75	3	3	5	1.57
LF	R. Henderson	489	.325	28	61	289	5	5	0	2.5	.983	D. Eckersley	63	73	4	2	48	0.61
C	T. Steinbach	379	.251	9	57	396	31	5	1	5.2	.988	R. Honeycutt	63	63	2	2	7	2.70
UT	M. Gallego	389	.206	3	34	207	379	13	78		.978							
OF	F. Jose	341	.264	8	39	212	5	5	1	2.4	.977							
C	R. Hassey	254	.213	5	22	307	18	5	2	5.5	.997							
UT	J. Quirk	121	.281	3	26	168	18	5	4		.974							

Chicago
W-94 L-68
Jeff Torborg

POS	Player	AB	AVG	HR	RBI	PO	A	E	DP	TC/G	FA	Pitcher	G	IP	W	L	SV	ERA
1B	C. Martinez	272	.224	4	24	632	38	8	50	8.3	.988	G. Hibbard	33	211	14	9	0	3.16
2B	S. Fletcher	509	.242	4	56	305	436	9	115	5.0	.988	J. McDowell	33	205	14	9	0	3.82
SS	O. Guillen	516	.279	1	58	252	474	17	100	4.7	.977	M. Perez	35	197	13	14	0	4.61
3B	R. Ventura	493	.249	5	54	116	268	25	32	2.8	.939	E. King	25	151	12	4	0	3.28
RF	S. Sosa	532	.233	15	70	315	14	13	1	2.3	.962	W. Edwards	42	95	5	3	2	3.22
CF	L. Johnson	541	.285	1	51	353	5	10	3	2.5	.973	B. Thigpen	77	89	4	6	57	1.83
LF	I. Calderon	607	.273	14	74	268	7	7	1	2.2	.975	A. Fernandez	13	88	5	5	0	3.80
C	C. Fisk	452	.285	18	65	660	63	4	14	6.3	.995	D. Pall	56	76	3	5	2	3.32
DH	D. Pasqua	325	.274	13	58							B. Jones	65	74	11	4	1	2.31
D1	R. Kittle	277	.245	16	43	150	5	2	18	6.3	.987	S. Radinsky	62	52	6	1	4	4.82
1B	F. Thomas	191	.330	7	31	428	26	5	53	9.0	.989							
C	R. Karkovice	183	.246	6	20	296	31	2	4	5.1	.994							

AMERICAN LEAGUE 1990, *cont.*

	POS	Player	AB	AVG	HR	RBI	PO	A	E	DP	TC/G	FA	Pitcher	G	IP	W	L	SV	ERA
Texas	1B	R. Palmeiro	598	.319	14	89	1,215	91	7	123	9.0	.995	B. Witt	33	222	17	10	0	3.36
	2B	J. Franco	582	.296	11	69	310	444	19	101	5.1	.975	C. Hough	32	219	12	12	0	4.07
W-83 L-79	SS	J. Huson	396	.240	0	28	157	254	17	69	3.6	.960	N. Ryan	30	204	13	9	0	3.44
Bobby Valentine	3B	S. Buechele	251	.215	7	30	70	157	8	7	2.7	.966	K. Brown	26	180	12	10	0	3.60
	RF	R. Sierra	608	.280	16	96	283	7	10	1	2.0	.967	M. Jeffcoat	44	111	5	6	5	4.47
	CF	G. Pettis	423	.239	3	31	285	10	2	4	2.3	.993	J. Moyer	33	102	2	6	0	4.66
	LF	Incaviglia	529	.233	24	85	290	12	8	2	2.1	.974	K. Rogers	69	98	10	6	15	3.13
	C	G. Petralli	325	.255	0	21	599	43	6	5	5.5	.991	B. Arnsberg	53	63	6	1	5	2.15
	DH	H. Baines	321	.290	13	44							J. Russell	27	25	1	5	10	4.26
	UT	J. Daugherty	310	.300	6	47	225	22	3	21		.988							
	UT	J. Kunkel	200	.170	3	17	101	172	11	34		.961							
	UT	M. Stanley	189	.249	2	19	261	25	4	2		.986							
	3B	S. Coolbaugh	180	.200	2	13	42	118	10	12	2.6	.941							
California	1B	W. Joyner	310	.268	8	41	727	62	4	78	9.6	.995	C. Finley	32	236	18	9	0	2.40
	2B	J. Ray	404	.277	5	43	241	295	7	82	5.4	.987	M. Langston	33	223	10	17	0	4.40
W-80 L-82	SS	D. Schofield	310	.255	1	18	170	318	17	77	5.1	.966	J. Abbott	33	212	10	14	0	4.51
Doug Rader	3B	J. Howell	316	.228	8	33	70	193	17	18	2.7	.939	K. McCaskill	29	174	12	11	0	3.25
	RF	D. Winfield	414	.275	19	72	165	7	2	1	1.6	.989	B. Blyleven	23	134	8	7	0	5.24
	CF	D. White	443	.217	11	44	302	11	9	4	2.6	.972	M. Eichhorn	60	85	2	5	13	3.08
	LF	L. Polonia	381	.336	2	32	142	3	3	2	1.7	.980	W. Fraser	45	76	5	4	2	3.08
	C	L. Parrish	470	.268	24	70	760	88	6	15	6.5	.993	B. Harvey	54	64	4	4	25	3.22
	DH	C. Davis	412	.265	12	58													
	UT	D. Hill	352	.264	3	32	194	255	11	64		.976							
	OF	D. Bichette	349	.255	15	53	183	12	7	5	1.9	.965							
	1B	L. Stevens	248	.214	7	32	597	36	4	62	9.5	.994							
	OF	M. Venable	189	.259	4	21	112	3	3	1	1.5	.975							
Seattle	1B	P. O'Brien	366	.224	5	27	850	76	5	68	9.6	.995	E. Hanson	33	236	18	9	0	3.24
	2B	H. Reynolds	642	.252	5	55	330	499	19	110	5.3	.978	M. Young	34	225	8	18	0	3.51
W-77 L-85	SS	O. Vizquel	255	.247	2	18	103	239	7	48	4.3	.980	R. Johnson	33	220	14	11	0	3.65
Jim Lefebvre	3B	E. Martinez	487	.302	11	49	89	259	27	16	2.6	.928	B. Holman	28	190	11	11	0	4.03
	RF	H. Cotto	355	.259	4	33	194	4	2	1	1.7	.990	B. Swift	55	128	6	4	6	2.39
	CF	K. Griffey	597	.300	22	80	330	8	7	1	2.3	.980	M. Jackson	63	77	5	7	3	4.54
	LF	J. Leonard	478	.251	10	75	118	0	2	0	1.5	.983	M. Schooler	49	56	1	4	30	2.25
	C	D. Valle	308	.214	7	33	631	44	2	9	6.5	.997	K. Comstock	60	56	7	4	2	2.89
	DH	A. Davis	494	.283	17	68													
	OF	G. Briley	337	.246	5	29	177	4	2	1	1.7	.989							
	C	S. Bradley	233	.223	1	28	349	24	2	4	6.0	.995							
	OF	J. Buhner	163	.276	7	33	55	1	2	0	1.5	.966							
Kansas City	1B	G. Brett	544	**.329**	14	87	865	66	7	89	9.2	.993	T. Gordon	32	195	12	11	0	3.73
	2B	F. White	241	.216	2	21	142	218	8	51	4.7	.978	K. Appier	32	186	12	8	0	2.76
W-75 L-86	SS	K. Stillwell	506	.249	3	51	181	350	24	79	3.9	.957	Saberhagen	20	135	5	9	0	3.27
John Wathan	3B	K. Seitzer	622	.275	6	38	100	262	18	31	2.5	.953	S. Farr	57	127	13	7	1	1.98
	RF	Eisenreich	496	.280	5	51	261	6	1	3	1.9	.996	S. Davis	21	112	7	10	0	4.74
	CF	B. Jackson	405	.272	28	78	230	8	12	2	2.6	.952	Montgomery	73	94	6	5	24	2.39
	LF	D. Tartabull	313	.268	15	60	81	1	3	0	1.6	.965	M. Gubicza	16	94	4	7	0	4.50
	C	Macfarlane	400	.255	6	58	660	23	6	9	6.2	.991	S. Crawford	46	80	5	4	1	4.16
	DH	G. Perry	465	.254	8	57							M. Davis	53	69	2	7	6	5.11
	OF	W. Wilson	307	.290	2	42	187	2	0	1	1.8	1.000							
	UT	B. Pecota	240	.242	5	20	160	195	5	44	—	.986							
	UT	P. Tabler	195	.272	1	19	101	10	2	7	—	.982							
	OF	B. McRae	168	.286	2	23	120	1	0	0	2.7	1.000							
Minnesota	1B	K. Hrbek	492	.287	22	79	1,057	81	3	100	**9.5**	**.997**	A. Anderson	31	189	7	18	0	4.53
	2B	A. Newman	388	.242	0	30	118	173	2	48	3.3	.993	K. Tapani	28	159	12	8	0	4.07
W-74 L-88	SS	G. Gagne	388	.235	7	38	184	377	14	62	4.3	.976	R. Smith	32	153	5	10	0	4.81
Tom Kelly	3B	G. Gaetti	577	.229	16	85	102	**318**	18	**36**	2.9	.959	D. West	29	146	7	9	0	5.10
	RF	S. Mack	313	.326	8	44	230	8	3	1	2.2	.988	M. Guthrie	24	145	7	9	0	3.79
	CF	K. Puckett	551	.298	12	80	354	9	4	3	2.6	.989	S. Erickson	19	113	8	4	0	2.07
	LF	D. Gladden	534	.275	5	40	286	12	6	3	2.3	.980	J. Berenguer	51	100	8	5	0	3.41
	C	B. Harper	479	.294	6	54	672	53	11	5	6.1	.985	R. Aguilera	56	65	5	3	32	2.76
	DH	G. Larkin	401	.269	5	42							Candelaria	34	58	7	3	4	3.39
	OF	J. Moses	172	.221	1	14	103	2	0	0	1.2	1.000							
	2B	F. Manrique	228	.237	5	29	104	155	7	40	4.0	.974							
	2B	N. Liriano	185	.254	0	13	83	128	7	27	4.4	.968							
	OD	R. Bush	181	.243	6	18	52	1	0	0	1.7	.981							
	C	J. Ortiz	170	.335	0	18	247	25	0	6	4.0	1.000							

AMERICAN LEAGUE 1990, *cont.*

BATTING AND BASE RUNNING LEADERS

Batting Average
G. Brett, KC	.329
R. Henderson, OAK	.325
R. Palmeiro, TEX	.319
A. Trammell, DET	.304
W. Boggs, BOS	.302
E. Martinez, SEA	.302

Slugging Average
C. Fielder, DET	.592
R. Henderson, OAK	.577
J. Canseco, OAK	.543
F. McGriff, TOR	.530
G. Brett, KC	.515

Home Runs
C. Fielder, DET	51
M. McGwire, OAK	39
J. Canseco, OAK	37
F. McGriff, TOR	35
K. Gruber, TOR	31

Total Bases
C. Fielder, TOR	339
K. Gruber, TOR	303
F. McGriff, TOR	295
K. Griffey, SEA	287
E. Burks, BOS	286

Runs Batted In
C. Fielder, DET	132
K. Gruber, TOR	118
M. McGwire, OAK	108
J. Canseco, OAK	101
R. Sierra, TEX	96

Stolen Bases
R. Henderson, OAK	65
S. Sax, NY	43
R. Kelly, NY	42
A. Cole, CLE	40
G. Pettis, TEX	38

Hits
R. Palmeiro, TEX	191
W. Boggs, BOS	187
R. Kelly, NY	183

Bases on Balls
M. McGwire, OAK	110
M. Tettleton, BAL	106
T. Phillips, DET	99

Home Run Percentage
C. Fielder, DET	8.9
J. Canseco, OAK	7.7
M. McGwire, OAK	7.5

Runs Scored
R. Henderson, OAK	119
C. Fielder, DET	104
H. Reynolds, SEA	100

Doubles
G. Brett, KC	45
J. Reed, BOS	45
I. Calderon, CHI	44
W. Boggs, BOS	44

Triples
T. Fernandez, TOR	17
S. Sosa, CHI	10

PITCHING LEADERS

Winning Percentage
B. Welch, OAK	.818
R. Clemens, BOS	.778
D. Stieb, TOR	.750
E. King, CHI	.750
B. Jones, CHI	.733

Earned Run Average
R. Clemens, BOS	1.93
C. Finley, CAL	2.40
D. Stewart, OAK	2.56
K. Appier, KC	2.76
D. Stieb, TOR	2.93

Wins
B. Welch, OAK	27
D. Stewart, OAK	22
R. Clemens, BOS	21
D. Stieb, TOR	18
C. Finley, CAL	18
E. Hanson, SEA	18

Saves
B. Thigpen, CHI	57
D. Eckersley, OAK	48
D. Jones, CLE	43
G. Olson, BAL	37
D. Righetti, NY	36

Strikeouts
N. Ryan, TEX	232
B. Witt, TEX	221
E. Hanson, SEA	211
R. Clemens, BOS	209
M. Langston, CAL	195

Complete Games
J. Morris, DET	11
D. Stewart, OAK	11

Fewest Hits/9 Innings
N. Ryan, TEX	6.04
R. Johnson, SEA	7.14
D. Stewart, OAK	7.62
R. Clemens, BOS	7.62

Shutouts
R. Clemens, BOS	4
D. Stewart, OAK	4

Fewest Walks/9 Innings
A. Anderson, MIN	1.86
G. Swindell, CLE	1.97
R. Clemens, BOS	2.13

Most Strikeouts/9 Innings
N. Ryan, TEX	10.23
B. Witt, TEX	8.96
R. Clemens, BOS	8.25

Innings
D. Stewart, OAK	267
J. Morris, DET	250
B. Welch, OAK	238

Games Pitched
B. Thigpen, CHI	77
D. Ward, TOR	73
J. Montgomery, KC	73

		W	L	GB	R	OR	2B	3B	HR	AVG	SLG	SB	E	DP	PCT	CG	BB	SO	SHO	SV	ERA
East	Boston	88	74	—	699	664	298	31	106	**.272**	.395	53	123	154	.980	15	519	997	13	44	3.72
	Toronto	86	76	2.0	**767**	661	263	**50**	167	.265	**.419**	111	86	144	**.986**	6	445	892	9	48	3.84
	Detroit	79	83	9.0	750	754	241	32	**172**	.259	.409	82	131	178	.979	15	**661**	856	12	45	4.39
	Cleveland	77	85	11.0	732	737	266	41	110	.267	.391	107	117	146	.981	12	518	860	10	47	4.26
	Baltimore	76	85	11.5	669	698	234	22	132	.245	.370	94	93	151	.985	10	537	776	5	43	4.04
	Milwaukee	74	88	14.0	732	**760**	247	36	128	.256	.384	164	149	152	.976	23	469	771	13	42	4.08
	New York	67	95	21.0	603	749	208	19	147	.241	.366	119	126	164	.980	15	618	909	6	41	4.21
West	Oakland	103	59	—	733	570	209	22	164	.254	.391	141	87	152	.986	18	494	831	**16**	64	**3.18**
	Chicago	94	68	9.0	682	633	251	44	106	.258	.379	140	124	169	.980	17	548	914	10	**68**	3.61
	Texas	83	79	20.0	676	696	257	27	110	.259	.376	115	133	161	.979	**25**	623	997	9	36	3.83
	California	80	82	23.0	690	706	237	27	147	.260	.391	69	142	**186**	.978	21	544	944	13	42	3.79
	Seattle	77	85	26.0	640	680	251	26	107	.259	.373	105	130	152	.979	21	606	**1,064**	7	41	3.69
	Kansas City	75	86	27.5	707	709	**316**	44	100	.267	.395	107	122	161	.980	18	560	1,006	8	33	3.93
	Minnesota	74	88	29.0	666	729	281	39	100	.265	.385	96	101	161	.983	13	489	872	13	43	4.12
					9746	9746	3559	460	1796	.259	.388	1503	1664	2231	.981	229	7631	12689	144	637	3.91

Player Register

The Player Register is an alphabetical listing of the career records of every man who appeared in a game in the 1990 season, with the exception of players who are primarily pitchers. Pitchers who have appeared in a minimum of 25 non-pitching games (pinch-hitting, pinch-running, or playing other positions) are listed in this section; all others have abbreviated batting records listed in the Pitcher Register.

Any statistics that appear in boldface type indicate that the player led his league in that category that year. Where there is a tie for the league lead, all tied leaders are listed with boldface figures. If a superscript "1" appears next to a statistic, as with Rickey Henderson's stolen base total in 1982, it indicates that the player is the all-time single-season leader in the category. Figures appearing in bold beneath a player's career totals mean that the player ranks in the top ten in baseball history in that category. Career leaders are also highlighted underneath the World Series totals.

Additional statistical and graphic analyses are provided for all batters with 250 or more plate appearances in 1990. See the Introduction for more information about these features.

Year	Team		Games	BA	SA	AB	H	2B	3B	HR	HR%	R	RBI	BB	SO	SB	PINCH HIT AB	H	PO	A	E	DP	TC/G	FA	G by Pos

Shawn Abner

ABNER, SHAWN WESLEY
B. June 17, 1966, Hamilton, Ohio
BR TR 6' 1" 190 lbs.

Year	Team		Games	BA	SA	AB	H	2B	3B	HR	HR%	R	RBI	BB	SO	SB	AB	H	PO	A	E	DP	TC/G	FA	G by Pos
1987	SD	N	16	.277	.511	47	13	3	1	2	4.3	5	7	2	8	1	3	1	23	2	2	1	1.7	.926	OF-14
1988			37	.181	.289	83	15	3	0	2	2.4	6	5	4	19	0	0	0	55	1	1	1	1.5	.982	OF-35
1989			57	.176	.275	102	18	4	0	2	2.0	13	14	5	20	1	8	1	67	0	0	0	1.2	1.000	OF-51
1990			91	.245	.310	184	45	9	0	1	0.5	17	15	9	28	2	27	5	108	1	1	0	1.8	.991	OF-62
4 yrs.			201	.219	.320	416	91	19	1	7	1.7	41	41	20	75	4	38	7	253	4	4	2	1.3	.985	OF-162

Troy Afenir

AFENIR, MICHAEL TROY
B. Sept. 21, 1963, Escondido, Calif.
BR TR 6' 4" 185 lbs.

Year	Team		Games	BA	SA	AB	H	2B	3B	HR	HR%	R	RBI	BB	SO	SB	AB	H	PO	A	E	DP	TC/G	FA	G by Pos
1987	HOU	N	10	.300	.350	20	6	1	0	0	0.0	1	1	0	12	0	1	0	35	2	1	1	3.8	.974	C-10
1990	OAK	A	14	.143	.143	14	2	0	0	0	0.0	0	2	0	6	0	6	1	13	0	0	0	1.1	1.000	C-12, DH-1
2 yrs.			24	.235	.265	34	8	1	0	0	0.0	1	3	0	18	0	7	1	48	2	1	1	2.1	.980	C-22, DH-1

Mike Aldrete

ALDRETE, MICHAEL PETER
B. Jan. 29, 1961, Carmel, Calif.
BL TL 5' 11" 180 lbs.

Year	Team		Games	BA	SA	AB	H	2B	3B	HR	HR%	R	RBI	BB	SO	SB	AB	H	PO	A	E	DP	TC/G	FA	G by Pos
1986	SF	N	84	.250	.389	216	54	18	3	2	0.9	27	25	33	34	1	16	4	317	36	1	34	4.2	.997	1B-37, OF-31
1987			126	.325	.462	357	116	18	2	9	2.5	50	51	43	50	6	25	6	328	18	3	21	2.8	.991	OF-79, 1B-33
1988			139	.267	.329	389	104	15	0	3	0.8	44	50	56	65	6	29	11	272	8	4	3	2.0	.986	OF-125
1989	MON	N	76	.221	.316	136	30	8	1	1	0.7	12	12	19	30	1	26	8	109	9	1	8	1.6	.992	OF-37, 1B-10
1990			96	.242	.317	161	39	7	1	1	0.6	22	18	37	31	1	36	9	160	12	1	16	3.1	.994	OF-38, 1B-18
5 yrs.			521	.272	.374	1259	343	66	7	16	1.3	155	156	188	210	15	132	38	1186	83	10	82	2.5	.992	OF-310, 1B-98

LEAGUE CHAMPIONSHIP SERIES

Year	Team		Games	BA	SA	AB	H	2B	3B	HR	HR%	R	RBI	BB	SO	SB	AB	H	PO	A	E	DP	TC/G	FA	G by Pos
1987	SF	N	5	.100	.100	10	1	0	0	0	0.0	0	1	0	2	0	2	0	5	0	0	0	1.0	1.000	OF-3

Beau Allred

ALLRED, DALE LeBEAU
B. June 4, 1965, Mesa, Ariz.
BL TL 6' 190 lbs.

Year	Team		Games	BA	SA	AB	H	2B	3B	HR	HR%	R	RBI	BB	SO	SB	AB	H	PO	A	E	DP	TC/G	FA	G by Pos
1989	CLE	A	13	.250	.375	24	6	3	0	0	0.0	0	1	2	10	0	8	2	11	1	0	1	0.9	1.000	OF-5, DH-2
1990			4	.188	.438	16	3	1	0	1	6.2	2	2	2	3	0	0	0	5	0	1	0	1.5	.833	OF-4
2 yrs.			17	.225	.400	40	9	4	0	1	2.5	2	3	4	13	0	8	2	16	1	1	1	1.1	.944	OF-9, DH-2

Roberto Alomar

ALOMAR, ROBERTO
Born Roberto Alomar y Velasquez. Son of Sandy Alomar.
Brother of Sandy Alomar.
B. Feb. 5, 1968, Ponce, Puerto Rico
BB TR 6' 184 lbs.

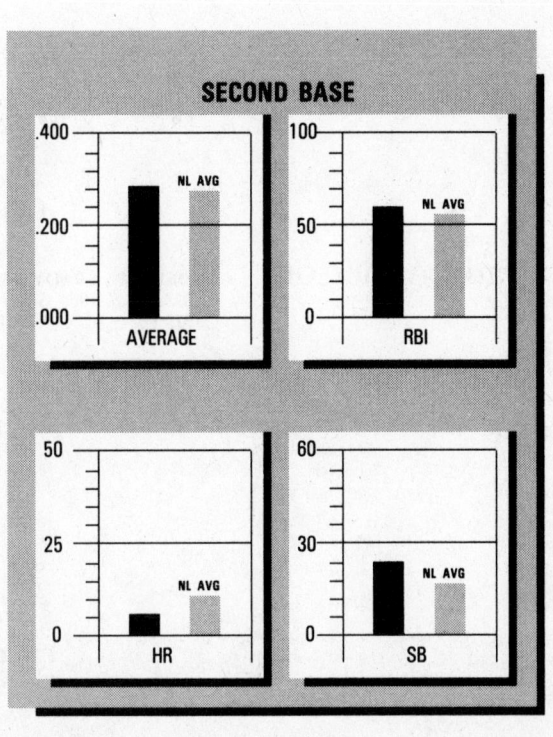

SECOND BASE

	Games	BA	SA	AB	H	2B	3B	HR	HR%	R	RBI	BB	SO	SB
April	18	.301	.370	73	22	0	1	1	1.4	9	8	6	10	4
May	27	.343	.426	108	37	9	0	0	0.0	10	13	9	10	3
June	26	.315	.459	111	35	9	2	1	0.9	18	13	10	10	4
July	29	.241	.296	108	26	1	1	1	0.9	16	10	9	17	2
Aug	28	.250	.325	120	30	6	0	1	0.8	17	8	9	18	3
Sept/Oct	19	.273	.424	66	18	2	1	2	3.0	10	8	5	7	8
Day	42	.325	.399	163	53	9	0	1	0.6	14	20	18	19	11
Night	105	.272	.374	423	115	18	5	5	1.2	66	40	30	53	13
vs. Left		.260	.377	204	53	13	1	3	1.5	22	17	21	38	3
vs. Right		.301	.382	382	115	14	4	3	0.8	58	43	27	34	21
On Grass	108	.289	.381	425	123	19	4	4	0.9	60	45	33	52	19
On Turf	39	.280	.379	161	45	8	1	2	1.2	20	15	15	20	5
Home	76	.285	.383	298	85	9	4	4	1.3	43	36	23	37	12
Road	71	.288	.378	288	83	18	1	2	0.7	37	24	25	35	12
Division Rivals														
vs. ATL	14	.345	.500	58	20	6	0	1	1.7	15	8	9	6	4
vs. CIN	15	.333	.367	60	20	2	0	0	0.0	9	4	5	6	3
vs. HOU	18	.333	.458	72	24	2	2	1	1.4	16	9	5	9	2
vs. LA	14	.333	.463	54	18	4	0	1	1.9	6	5	2	6	3
vs. SF	15	.164	.180	61	10	1	0	0	0.0	7	5	4	7	3
On 3B < 2 Out		.278	.278	18	5	0	0	0	0.0	0	13	0	4	

Year	Team		Games	BA	SA	AB	H	2B	3B	HR	HR%	R	RBI	BB	SO	SB	PINCH HIT AB	PINCH HIT H	PO	A	E	DP	TC/G	FA	G by Pos

Roberto Alomar *Continued*

Year	Team		Games	BA	SA	AB	H	2B	3B	HR	HR%	R	RBI	BB	SO	SB	AB	H	PO	A	E	DP	TC/G	FA	G by Pos
1988	SD	N	143	.266	.382	545	145	24	6	9	1.7	84	41	47	83	24	0	0	319	459	16	88	5.6	.980	2B-143
1989			158	.295	.376	623	184	27	1	7	1.1	82	56	53	76	42	1	0	341	472	28	91	5.3	.967	2B-157
1990			147	.287	.381	586	168	27	5	6	1.0	80	60	48	72	24	3	0	316	404	19	77	5.2	.974	2B-137, SS-5
3 yrs.			448	.283	.379	1754	497	78	12	22	1.3	246	157	148	231	90	4	0	976	1335	63	256	5.3	.973	2B-437, SS-5

Sandy Alomar

ALOMAR, SANTOS, JR.
Born Santos Alomar y Velasquez. Son of Sandy Alomar.
Brother of Roberto Alomar.
B. June 18, 1966, Salinas, Puerto Rico
BR TR 6′ 5″ 200 lbs.

	Games	BA	SA	AB	H	2B	3B	HR	HR%	R	RBI	BB	SO	SB	AB	H	PO	A	E	DP	TC/G	FA	G by Pos
April	18	.281	.386	57	16	3	0	1	1.8	9	9	3	6	0									
May	21	.304	.464	69	21	3	1	2	2.9	10	13	4	13	2									
June	24	.287	.333	87	25	2	1	0	0.0	6	8	6	11	0									
July	22	.265	.426	68	18	5	0	2	2.9	8	11	4	3	0									
Aug	23	.259	.383	81	21	4	0	2	2.5	13	10	5	6	2									
Sept/Oct	24	.337	.518	83	28	9	0	2	2.4	14	15	3	7	0									
Day	33	.284	.431	109	31	7	0	3	2.8	20	22	6	8	1									
Night	99	.292	.414	336	98	19	2	6	1.8	40	44	19	38	3									
vs. Left		.376	.470	117	44	5	0	2	1.7	19	18	8	13	1									
vs. Right		.259	.399	328	85	21	2	7	2.1	41	48	17	33	3									
On Grass	110	.303	.427	370	112	21	2	7	1.9	49	50	21	34	4									
On Turf	22	.227	.373	75	17	5	0	2	2.7	11	16	4	12	0									
Home	70	.300	.419	227	68	12	0	5	2.2	33	30	13	22	3									
Road	62	.280	.417	218	61	14	2	4	1.8	27	36	12	24	1									
Division Rivals																								
vs. BAL	10	.324	.486	37	12	3	0	1	2.7	4	7	1	5	0									
vs. BOS	11	.316	.421	38	12	1	0	1	2.6	3	4	4	4	1									
vs. DET	12	.372	.465	43	16	2	1	0	0.0	7	3	0	5	1									
vs. MIL	10	.267	.333	30	8	2	0	0	0.0	5	6	4	1	0									
vs. NY	11	.324	.471	34	11	0	1	1	2.9	4	8	4	0	0									
vs. TOR	12	.125	.225	40	5	1	0	1	2.5	5	4	1	6	0									
On 3B < 2 Out		.476	.667	21	10	4	0	0	0.0	0	23	0	1										

CATCHER — AVERAGE / RBI / HR / SB (with AL AVG)

Year	Team		Games	BA	SA	AB	H	2B	3B	HR	HR%	R	RBI	BB	SO	SB	AB	H	PO	A	E	DP	TC/G	FA	G by Pos
1988	SD	N	1	.000	.000	1	0	0	0	0	0.0	0	0	0	1	0	1	0	0	0	0	0	0.0	—	
1989			7	.211	.421	19	4	1	0	1	5.3	1	6	3	3	0	1	0	33	1	0	1	4.9	1.000	C-6
1990	CLE	A	132	.290	.418	445	129	26	2	9	2.0	60	66	25	46	4	9	2	686	46	14	6	5.8	.981	C-129
3 yrs.			140	.286	.417	465	133	27	2	10	2.2	61	72	28	50	4	11	2	719	47	14	7	5.6	.982	C-135

Moises Alou

ALOU, MOISES ROJAS
Son of Felipe Alou.
B. July 3, 1966, Atlanta, Ga.
BR TR 6′ 3″ 185 lbs.

Year	Team		Games	BA	SA	AB	H	2B	3B	HR	HR%	R	RBI	BB	SO	SB	AB	H	PO	A	E	DP	TC/G	FA	G by Pos
1990	2 teams		PIT N (2G — .200)			MON N (14G — .200)																			
"	total		16	.200	.300	20	4	0	1	0	0.0	4	0	0	3	0	5	1	9	1	0	0	1.4	1.000	OF-7

Brady Anderson

ANDERSON, BRADY KEVIN
B. Jan. 18, 1964, Silver Spring, Md.
BL TL 6′ 1″ 170 lbs.

Year	Team		Games	BA	SA	AB	H	2B	3B	HR	HR%	R	RBI	BB	SO	SB	AB	H	PO	A	E	DP	TC/G	FA	G by Pos
1988	2 teams		BOS A (41G — .230)			BAL A (53G — .198)																			
"			94	.212	.286	325	69	13	4	1	0.3	31	21	23	75	10	7	0	243	4	4	1	2.7	.984	OF-90
1989	BAL	A	94	.207	.312	266	55	12	2	4	1.5	44	16	43	45	16	6	1	191	3	3	0	2.1	.985	OF-79, DH-8
1990			89	.231	.308	234	54	5	2	3	1.2	24	24	31	46	15	18	6	149	3	2	1	2.4	.987	OF-63, DH-11
3 yrs.			277	.216	.301	825	178	30	8	8	1.0	99	61	97	166	41	31	7	583	10	9	2	2.2	.985	OF-232, DH-19

Year	Team		Games	BA	SA	AB	H	2B	3B	HR	HR%	R	RBI	BB	SO	SB	PINCH HIT AB	H	PO	A	E	DP	TC/G	FA	G by Pos

Dave Anderson

ANDERSON, DAVID CARTER
B. Aug. 1, 1960, Louisville, Ky.
BR TR 6′ 2″ 185 lbs.

Year	Team		Games	BA	SA	AB	H	2B	3B	HR	HR%	R	RBI	BB	SO	SB	PH AB	H	PO	A	E	DP	TC/G	FA	G by Pos
1983	LA	N	61	.165	.261	115	19	4	2	1	0.9	12	2	12	15	6	2	1	56	100	5	19	2.6	.969	SS–53, 3B–1
1984			121	.251	.329	374	94	16	2	3	0.8	51	34	45	55	15	5	0	176	359	19	67	4.6	.966	SS–111, 3B–11
1985			77	.199	.281	221	44	6	0	4	1.8	24	18	35	42	5	4	2	61	187	9	20	3.3	.965	3B–51, SS–25, 2B–2
1986			92	.245	.301	216	53	9	0	1	0.5	31	15	22	39	5	4	1	77	159	11	21	2.7	.955	3B–51, SS–34, 2B–5
1987			108	.234	.313	265	62	12	3	1	0.4	32	13	24	43	9	6	2	103	207	7	33	2.9	.978	SS–65, 3B–35, 2B–5
1988			116	.249	.319	285	71	10	2	2	0.7	31	20	32	45	4	7	2	139	244	5	53	3.3	.987	SS–82, 3B–12, 2B–11
1989			87	.229	.264	140	32	2	0	1	0.7	15	14	17	26	2	25	4	61	73	1	15	1.6	.993	SS–33, 3B–18, 2B–7
1990	SF	N	60	.350	.450	100	35	5	1	1	1.0	14	6	3	20	1	13	6	33	59	1	10	2.0	.989	SS–29, 2B–13, 1B–3, 3B–2
8 yrs.			722	.239	.312	1716	410	64	10	14	0.8	210	122	190	285	47	66	18	706	1388	58	238	3.0	.973	SS–432, 3B–181, 2B–43, 1B–3

LEAGUE CHAMPIONSHIP SERIES

Year	Team		Games	BA	SA	AB	H	2B	3B	HR	HR%	R	RBI	BB	SO	SB	PH AB	H	PO	A	E	DP	TC/G	FA	G by Pos
1985	LA	N	4	.000	.000	5	0	0	0	0	0.0	1	0	3	1	0	0	0	3	4	0	0	1.8	1.000	SS–3, 3B–1

WORLD SERIES

Year	Team		Games	BA	SA	AB	H	2B	3B	HR	HR%	R	RBI	BB	SO	SB	PH AB	H	PO	A	E	DP	TC/G	FA	G by Pos
1988	LA	N	1	.000	.000	1	0	0	0	0	0.0	0	0	0	1	0	1	0	0	0	0	0	0.0	—	DH–1

Kent Anderson

ANDERSON, KENT McKAY
Brother of Mike Anderson.
B. Aug. 12, 1963, Florence, S. C.
BR TR 6′ 1″ 180 lbs.

Year	Team		Games	BA	SA	AB	H	2B	3B	HR	HR%	R	RBI	BB	SO	SB	PH AB	H	PO	A	E	DP	TC/G	FA	G by Pos
1989	CAL	A	86	.229	.265	223	51	6	1	0	0.0	27	17	17	42	1	3	0	102	233	10	56	4.0	.971	SS–70, 2B–7, 3B–5, OF–2, DH–1
1990			49	.308	.385	143	44	6	1	1	0.6	16	5	13	19	0	0	0	75	129	9	26	4.4	.958	SS–28, 3B–16, 2B–5
2 yrs.			135	.260	.311	366	95	12	2	1	0.3	43	22	30	61	1	3	0	177	362	19	82	4.1	.966	SS–98, 3B–21, 2B–12, OF–2, DH–1

Eric Anthony

ANTHONY, ERIC TODD
B. Nov. 8, 1967, San Diego, Calif.
BL TL 6′ 2″ 195 lbs.

	Games	BA	SA	AB	H	2B	3B	HR	HR%	R	RBI	BB	SO	SB
April	2	.200	.200	5	1	0	0	0	0.0	2	0	1	1	0
May	27	.243	.446	74	18	3	0	4	5.4	8	8	11	24	4
June	22	.215	.415	65	14	4	0	3	4.6	9	9	6	20	1
July	13	.056	.056	36	2	0	0	0	0.0	4	3	4	18	0
Aug				0	0	0	0	0		0	0	0	0	0
Sept/Oct	20	.186	.356	59	11	1	0	3	5.1	3	9	7	15	0
Day	22	.156	.281	64	10	2	0	2	3.1	7	7	12	24	3
Night	62	.206	.377	175	36	6	0	8	4.6	19	22	17	54	2
vs. Left		.214	.357	84	18	3	0	3	3.6	9	10	8	23	2
vs. Right		.181	.348	155	28	5	0	7	4.5	17	19	21	55	3
On Grass	24	.145	.333	69	10	1	0	4	5.8	6	12	10	23	1
On Turf	60	.212	.359	170	36	7	0	6	3.5	20	17	19	55	4
Home	38	.218	.391	110	24	4	0	5	4.5	15	14	13	34	3
Road	46	.171	.318	129	22	4	0	5	3.9	11	15	16	44	2
Division Rivals														
vs. ATL	4	.200	.400	15	3	0	0	1	6.7	1	3	2	3	0
vs. CIN	10	.167	.208	24	4	1	0	0	0.0	2	0	5	12	0
vs. LA	8	.167	.389	18	3	1	0	1	5.6	1	5	2	7	0
vs. SD	9	.233	.400	30	7	2	0	1	3.3	3	4	4	6	1
vs. SF	11	.161	.355	31	5	0	0	2	6.5	5	4	2	6	0
On 3B < 2 Out		.000	.000	3	0	0	0	0	0.0	0	6	2	1	

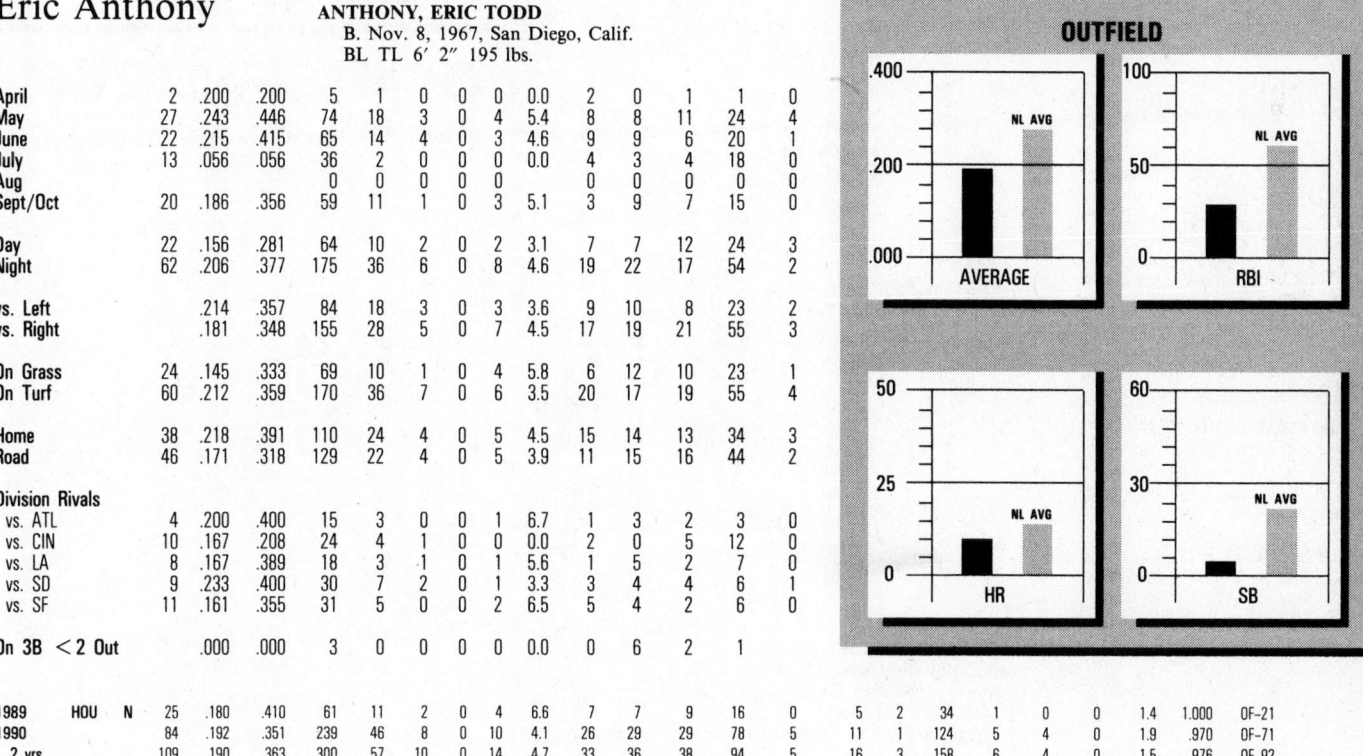

OUTFIELD

AVERAGE — NL AVG
RBI — NL AVG
HR — NL AVG
SB — NL AVG

Year	Team		Games	BA	SA	AB	H	2B	3B	HR	HR%	R	RBI	BB	SO	SB	PH AB	H	PO	A	E	DP	TC/G	FA	G by Pos
1989	HOU	N	25	.180	.410	61	11	2	0	4	6.6	7	7	9	16	0	5	2	34	1	0	0	1.4	1.000	OF–21
1990			84	.192	.351	239	46	8	0	10	4.1	26	29	29	78	5	11	1	124	5	4	0	1.9	.970	OF–71
2 yrs.			109	.190	.363	300	57	10	0	14	4.7	33	36	38	94	5	16	3	158	6	4	0	1.5	.976	OF–92

Year	Team	Games	BA	SA	AB	H	2B	3B	HR	HR%	R	RBI	BB	SO	SB	PINCH HIT AB	H	PO	A	E	DP	TC/G	FA	G by Pos

Oscar Azocar

AZOCAR, OSCAR GREGORIO
Born Oscar Gregorio Azocar y Azocar.
B. Feb. 21, 1965, Soro, Venezuela
BL TL 6′ 1″ 170 lbs.

Year	Team	Games	BA	SA	AB	H	2B	3B	HR	HR%	R	RBI	BB	SO	SB	AB	H	PO	A	E	DP	TC/G	FA	G by Pos
1990	NY	A	65	.248	.355	214	53	8	0	5	2.3	18	19	2	15	7	8	3	105	4	1	1	1.9	.991	OF–57, DH–1

Wally Backman

BACKMAN, WALTER WAYNE
B. Sept. 22, 1959, Hillsboro, Ore.
BB TR 5′ 9″ 160 lbs.

THIRD BASE

	Games	BA	SA	AB	H	2B	3B	HR	HR%	R	RBI	BB	SO	SB	AB	H	PO	A	E	DP	TC/G	FA	G by Pos
April	11	.372	.465	43	16	2	1	0	0.0	7	2	4	10	0									
May	17	.328	.443	61	20	4	0	1	1.6	15	10	8	8	1									
June	19	.188	.328	64	12	4	1	1	1.6	8	5	5	12	3									
July	19	.283	.370	46	13	4	0	0	0.0	10	3	11	11	0									
Aug	15	.209	.279	43	9	3	0	0	0.0	4	4	8	5	1									
Sept/Oct	23	.379	.483	58	22	4	1	0	0.0	18	4	6	7	1									
Day	23	.337	.422	83	28	3	2	0	0.0	15	4	5	13	1									
Night	81	.276	.388	232	64	18	1	2	0.9	47	24	37	40	5									
vs. Left		.194	.226	31	6	1	0	0	0.0	9	3	7	9	0									
vs. Right		.303	.415	284	86	20	3	2	0.7	53	25	35	44	6									
On Grass	25	.368	.529	87	32	6	1	2	2.3	17	11	9	14	0									
On Turf	79	.263	.346	228	60	15	2	0	0.0	45	17	33	39	6									
Home	53	.279	.370	154	43	12	1	0	0.0	30	12	21	28	4									
Road	51	.304	.422	161	49	9	2	2	1.2	32	16	21	25	2									
Division Rivals																							
vs. CHI	12	.387	.452	31	12	2	0	0	0.0	10	1	6	5	1									
vs. MON	16	.163	.245	49	8	4	0	0	0.0	9	2	5	9	3									
vs. NY	8	.323	.548	31	10	0	2	1	3.2	5	2	0	7	0									
vs. PHI	10	.304	.478	23	7	2	1	0	0.0	6	3	5	4	1									
vs. STL	11	.273	.333	33	9	2	0	0	0.0	4	2	3	6	0									
On 3B < 2 Out		.250	.333	12	3	1	0	0	0.0	0	11	1	1										
1980	NY	N	27	.323	.355	93	30	1	1	0	0.0	12	9	11	14	2	0	0	62	55	1	11	4.4	.992	2B–20, SS–8
1981			26	.278	.333	36	10	2	0	0	0.0	5	0	4	7	1	15	3	14	21	2	2	1.4	.946	2B–11, 3B–1
1982			96	.272	.372	261	71	13	2	3	1.1	37	22	49	47	8	5	0	173	209	16	30	4.1	.960	2B–88, 3B–6, SS–1
1983			26	.167	.214	42	7	0	1	0	0.0	6	3	2	8	0	16	3	16	15	2	2	1.3	.939	2B–14, 3B–2
1984			128	.280	.339	436	122	19	2	1	0.2	68	26	56	63	32	11	3	223	307	10	73	4.2	.981	2B–115, SS–7
1985			145	.273	.344	520	142	24	5	1	0.2	77	38	36	72	30	15	6	273	370	7	76	4.5	.989	2B–140, SS–1
1986			124	.320	.385	387	124	18	2	1	0.3	67	27	36	32	13	15	5	186	290	17	56	4.0	.966	2B–113
1987			94	.250	.287	300	75	6	1	1	0.3	43	23	25	43	11	12	2	131	210	6	44	3.7	.983	2B–87
1988			99	.303	.344	294	89	12	0	0	0.0	44	17	41	49	9	6	1	128	219	4	36	3.5	.989	2B–92
1989	MIN	A	87	.231	.284	299	69	9	2	1	0.3	33	26	32	45	1	4	0	146	187	6	37	3.9	.982	2B–84, DH–1
1990	PIT	N	104	.292	.397	315	92	21	3	2	0.6	62	28	42	53	6	15	3	56	136	12	10	2.4	.941	3B–71, 2B–15
11 yrs.			956	.279	.343	2983	831	125	19	10	0.3	454	219	334	433	113	114	26	1408	2019	83	377	3.7	.976	2B–779, 3B–80, SS–17, DH–1

LEAGUE CHAMPIONSHIP SERIES

Year	Team		Games	BA	SA	AB	H	2B	3B	HR	HR%	R	RBI	BB	SO	SB	AB	H	PO	A	E	DP	TC/G	FA	G by Pos
1986	NY	N	6	.238	.238	21	5	0	0	0	0.0	5	2	2	4	1	0	0	9	18	0	4	4.5	1.000	2B–6
1988			7	.273	.318	22	6	1	0	0	0.0	2	2	2	5	1	0	0	7	19	2	1	4.0	.929	2B–7
1990	PIT	N	3	.143	.286	7	1	1	0	0	0.0	1	0	1	3	1	1	0	1	3	0	0	2.0	1.000	3B–2
3 yrs.			16	.240	.280	50	12	2	0	0	0.0	8	4	5	12	3	1	0	17	40	2	5	3.7	.966	2B–13, 3B–2

WORLD SERIES

Year	Team		Games	BA	SA	AB	H	2B	3B	HR	HR%	R	RBI	BB	SO	SB	AB	H	PO	A	E	DP	TC/G	FA	G by Pos
1986	NY	N	6	.333	.333	18	6	0	0	0	0.0	4	1	4	2	1	0	0	9	13	0	1	3.7	1.000	2B–6

Carlos Baerga

BAERGA, CARLOS OBED
Born Carlos Obed Baerga y Ortiz.
B. Nov. 4, 1968, San Juan, Puerto Rico
BB TR 5′ 11″ 165 lbs.
See Player Register Supplement for complete graphic analysis.

Year	Team		Games	BA	SA	AB	H	2B	3B	HR	HR%	R	RBI	BB	SO	SB	AB	H	PO	A	E	DP	TC/G	FA	G by Pos
1990	CLE	A	108	.260	.394	312	81	17	2	7	2.2	46	47	16	57	0	31	11	79	164	17	27	2.6	.935	3B–50, SS–48, 2B–8

Year	Team	Games	BA	SA	AB	H	2B	3B	HR	HR%	R	RBI	BB	SO	SB	PINCH HIT AB	PINCH HIT H	PO	A	E	DP	TC/G	FA	G by Pos

Kevin Baez

BAEZ, KEVIN RICHARD
B. Jan. 10, 1967, Brooklyn, N. Y.
BR TR 6' 160 lbs.

Year	Team		Games	BA	SA	AB	H	2B	3B	HR	HR%	R	RBI	BB	SO	SB	AB	H	PO	A	E	DP	TC/G	FA	G by Pos
1990	NY	N	5	.167	.250	12	2	1	0	0	0.0	0	0	0	0	0	0	0	5	7	0	1	3.0	1.000	SS-4

Mark Bailey

BAILEY, JOHN MARK
B. Nov. 14, 1961, Springfield, Mo.
BB TR 6' 5" 195 lbs.

Year	Team		Games	BA	SA	AB	H	2B	3B	HR	HR%	R	RBI	BB	SO	SB	AB	H	PO	A	E	DP	TC/G	FA	G by Pos
1984	HOU	N	108	.212	.343	344	73	16	1	9	2.6	38	34	53	71	0	0	0	629	56	12	4	6.5	.983	C-108
1985			114	.265	.398	332	88	14	0	10	3.0	47	45	67	70	0	2	1	566	52	13	6	5.5	.979	C-110, 1B-2
1986			57	.176	.288	153	27	5	0	4	2.6	9	15	28	45	1	5	2	322	33	4	3	6.3	.989	C-53, 1B-1
1987			35	.203	.219	64	13	1	0	0	0.0	5	3	10	21	1	8	3	126	7	2	0	3.9	.985	C-27
1988			8	.130	.130	23	3	0	0	0	0.0	1	0	5	6	0	0	0	48	3	1	0	6.5	.981	C-8
1990	SF	N	5	.143	.571	7	1	0	0	1	14.2	1	3	0	2	0	5	0	3	0	0	0	3.0	1.000	C-1
6 yrs.			327	.222	.341	923	205	36	1	24	2.6	101	100	163	215	2	20	6	1694	151	32	13	5.7	.983	C-307, 1B-3

Harold Baines

BAINES, HAROLD DOUGLAS
B. Mar. 15, 1959, Easton, Md.
BL TL 6' 2" 175 lbs.

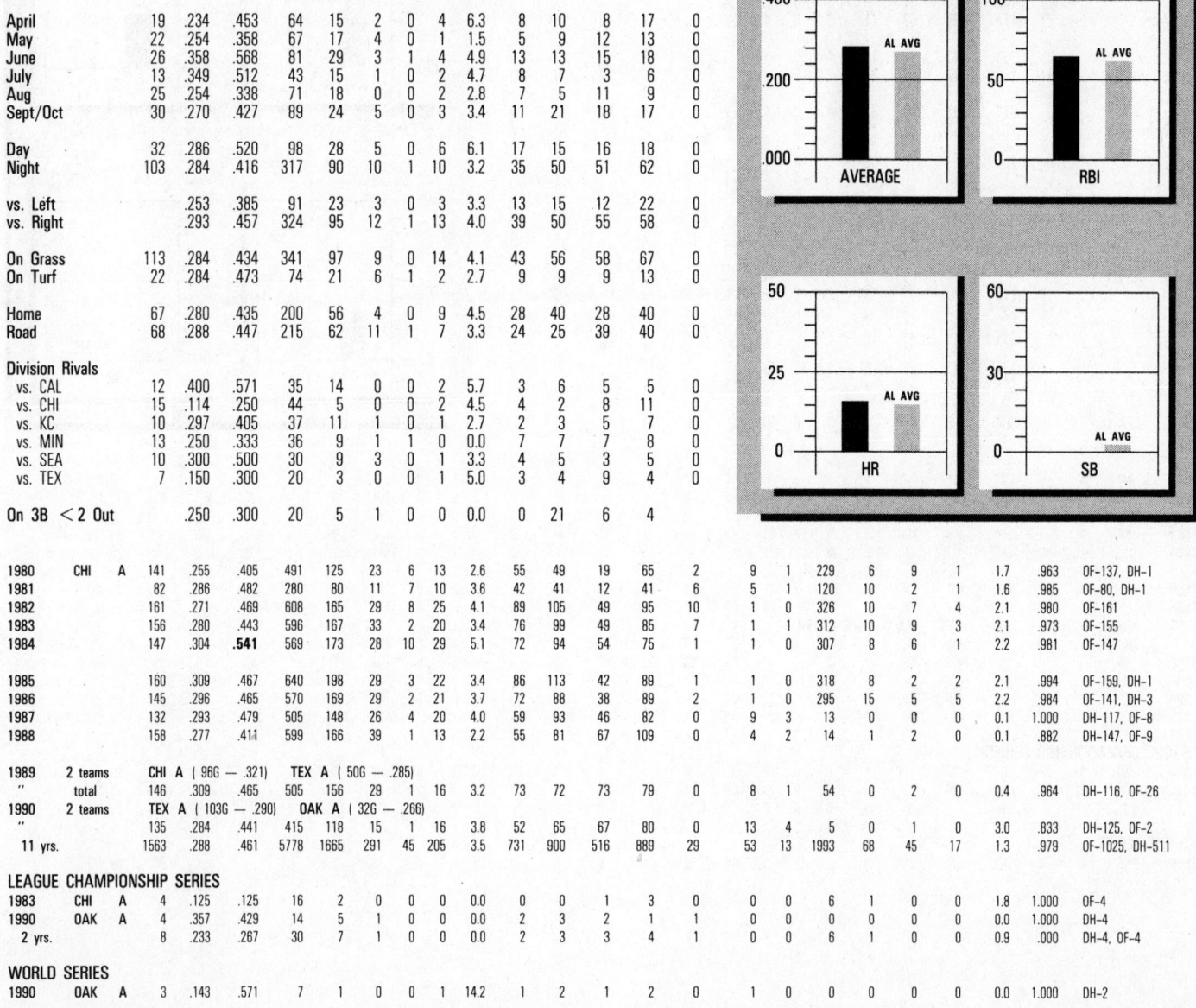

DESIGNATED HITTER

		Games	BA	SA	AB	H	2B	3B	HR	HR%	R	RBI	BB	SO	SB
April		19	.234	.453	64	15	2	0	4	6.3	8	10	8	17	0
May		22	.254	.358	67	17	4	0	1	1.5	5	9	12	13	0
June		26	.358	.568	81	29	3	1	4	4.9	13	13	15	18	0
July		13	.349	.512	43	15	1	0	2	4.7	8	7	3	6	0
Aug		25	.254	.338	71	18	0	0	2	2.8	7	5	11	9	0
Sept/Oct		30	.270	.427	89	24	5	0	3	3.4	11	21	18	17	0
Day		32	.286	.520	98	28	5	0	6	6.1	17	15	16	18	0
Night		103	.284	.416	317	90	10	1	10	3.2	35	50	51	62	0
vs. Left			.253	.385	91	23	3	0	3	3.3	13	15	12	22	0
vs. Right			.293	.457	324	95	12	1	13	4.0	39	50	55	58	0
On Grass		113	.284	.434	341	97	9	0	14	4.1	43	56	58	67	0
On Turf		22	.284	.473	74	21	6	1	2	2.7	9	9	9	13	0
Home		67	.280	.435	200	56	4	0	9	4.5	28	40	28	40	0
Road		68	.288	.447	215	62	11	1	7	3.3	24	25	39	40	0
Division Rivals															
vs. CAL		12	.400	.571	35	14	0	0	2	5.7	3	6	5	5	0
vs. CHI		15	.114	.250	44	5	0	0	2	4.5	4	2	8	11	0
vs. KC		10	.297	.405	37	11	1	0	1	2.7	2	3	5	7	0
vs. MIN		13	.250	.333	36	9	1	1	0	0.0	7	7	7	8	0
vs. SEA		10	.300	.500	30	9	3	0	1	3.3	4	5	3	5	0
vs. TEX		7	.150	.300	20	3	0	0	1	5.0	3	4	9	4	0
On 3B < 2 Out			.250	.300	20	5	1	0	0	0.0	0	21	6	4	

Year	Team		Games	BA	SA	AB	H	2B	3B	HR	HR%	R	RBI	BB	SO	SB	AB	H	PO	A	E	DP	TC/G	FA	G by Pos
1980	CHI	A	141	.255	.405	491	125	23	6	13	2.6	55	49	19	65	2	9	1	229	6	9	1	1.7	.963	OF-137, DH-1
1981			82	.286	.482	280	80	11	7	10	3.6	42	41	12	41	6	5	1	120	10	2	1	1.6	.985	OF-80, DH-1
1982			161	.271	.469	608	165	29	8	25	4.1	89	105	49	95	10	1	0	326	10	7	4	2.1	.980	OF-161
1983			156	.280	.443	596	167	33	2	20	3.4	76	99	49	85	7	1	1	312	10	9	3	2.1	.973	OF-155
1984			147	.304	.541	569	173	28	10	29	5.1	72	94	54	75	1	1	0	307	8	6	1	2.2	.981	OF-147
1985			160	.309	.467	640	198	29	3	22	3.4	86	113	42	89	1	1	0	318	8	2	2	2.1	.994	OF-159, DH-1
1986			145	.296	.465	570	169	29	2	21	3.7	72	88	38	89	2	1	0	295	15	5	5	2.2	.984	OF-141, DH-3
1987			132	.293	.479	505	148	26	4	20	4.0	59	93	46	82	0	9	3	13	0	0	0	0.1	1.000	DH-117, OF-8
1988			158	.277	.411	599	166	39	1	13	2.2	55	81	67	109	0	4	2	14	1	2	0	0.1	.882	DH-147, OF-9
1989	2 teams		CHI A (96G — .321)			TEX A (50G — .285)																			
"	total		146	.309	.465	505	156	29	1	16	3.2	73	72	73	79	0	8	1	54	0	2	0	0.4	.964	DH-116, OF-26
1990	2 teams		TEX A (103G — .290)			OAK A (32G — .266)																			
"			135	.284	.441	415	118	15	1	16	3.8	52	65	67	80	0	13	4	5	0	1	0	3.0	.833	DH-125, OF-2
11 yrs.			1563	.288	.461	5778	1665	291	45	205	3.5	731	900	516	889	29	53	13	1993	68	45	17	1.3	.979	OF-1025, DH-511

LEAGUE CHAMPIONSHIP SERIES

Year	Team		Games	BA	SA	AB	H	2B	3B	HR	HR%	R	RBI	BB	SO	SB	AB	H	PO	A	E	DP	TC/G	FA	G by Pos
1983	CHI	A	4	.125	.125	16	2	0	0	0	0.0	0	0	1	3	0	0	0	6	1	0	0	1.8	1.000	OF-4
1990	OAK	A	4	.357	.429	14	5	1	0	0	0.0	2	3	2	1	0	0	0	0	0	0	0	0.0	1.000	DH-4
2 yrs.			8	.233	.267	30	7	1	0	0	0.0	2	3	3	4	0	0	0	6	1	0	0	0.9	1.000	DH-4, OF-4

WORLD SERIES

Year	Team		Games	BA	SA	AB	H	2B	3B	HR	HR%	R	RBI	BB	SO	SB	AB	H	PO	A	E	DP	TC/G	FA	G by Pos
1990	OAK	A	3	.143	.571	7	1	0	0	1	14.2	1	2	1	2	0	0	0	0	0	0	0	0.0	1.000	DH-2

Year	Team		Games	BA	SA	AB	H	2B	3B	HR	HR%	R	RBI	BB	SO	SB	PINCH HIT AB	H	PO	A	E	DP	TC/G	FA	G by Pos

Doug Baker

BAKER, DOUGLAS LEE
B. Apr. 3, 1961, Fullerton, Calif.
BB TR 5′ 9″ 160 lbs.

Year	Team		Games	BA	SA	AB	H	2B	3B	HR	HR%	R	RBI	BB	SO	SB	PH AB	PH H	PO	A	E	DP	TC/G	FA	G by Pos
1984	DET	A	43	.185	.241	108	20	4	1	0	0.0	15	11	7	22	3	1	1	56	86	5	20	3.4	.966	SS-39, 2B-5
1985			15	.185	.222	27	5	1	0	0	0.0	4	1	0	9	0	3	0	12	12	1	2	1.7	.960	SS-12, 2B-1
1986			13	.125	.167	24	3	1	0	0	0.0	1	0	2	7	0	1	0	17	21	1	5	3.0	.974	SS-10, 2B-2, DH-1
1987			8	.000	.000	1	0	0	0	0	0.0	0	0	0	1	0	1	0	2	8	0	1	1.3	1.000	SS-6, 2B-1, 3B-1
1988	MIN	A	11	.000	.000	7	0	0	0	0	0.0	1	0	0	5	0	0	0	5	7	0	3	1.1	1.000	SS-9, 2B-1, 3B-1
1989			43	.295	.385	78	23	5	1	0	0.0	17	9	9	18	0	4	1	42	63	2	9	2.5	.981	2B-25, SS-19, DH-1
1990			3	.000	.000	1	0	0	0	0	0.0	0	0	0	0	0	0	0	1	2	0	0	1.0	1.000	2B-3
7 yrs.			136	.207	.268	246	51	11	2	0	0.0	38	21	18	62	3	10	2	135	199	9	40	2.5	.974	SS-95, 2B-38, DH-2, 3B-2

LEAGUE CHAMPIONSHIP SERIES

Year	Team		Games	BA	SA	AB	H	2B	3B	HR	HR%	R	RBI	BB	SO	SB	PH AB	PH H	PO	A	E	DP	TC/G	FA	G by Pos
1984	DET	A	1	—	—	0	0	0	0	0	—	0	0	0	0	0	0	0	0	0	0	0	0.0	—	SS-1

Steve Balboni

BALBONI, STEPHEN CHARLES (Bye-Bye)
B. Jan. 16, 1957, Brockton, Mass.
BR TR 6′ 3″ 225 lbs.

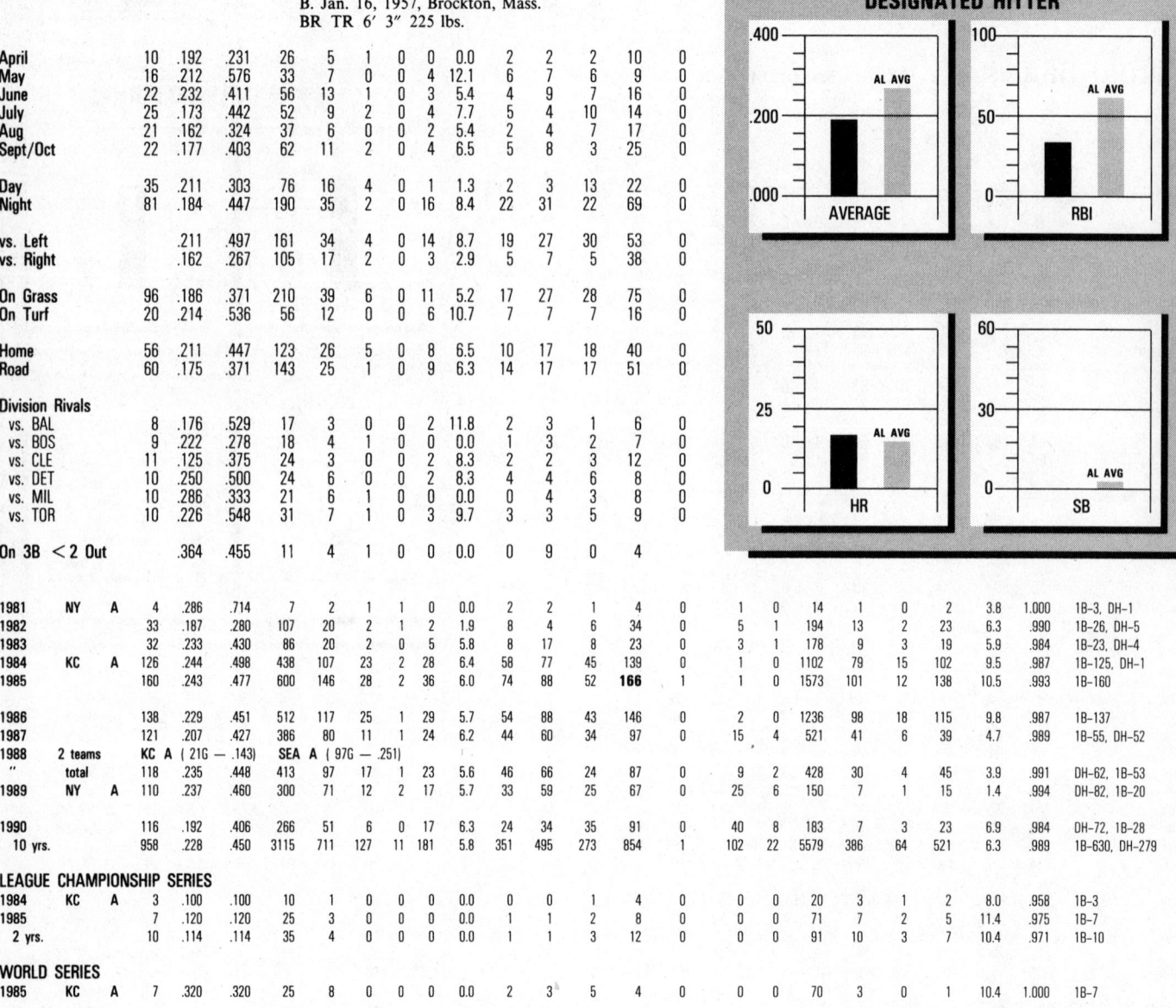

DESIGNATED HITTER (AVERAGE, RBI, HR, SB charts with AL AVG comparisons)

Split	Games	BA	SA	AB	H	2B	3B	HR	HR%	R	RBI	BB	SO	SB
April	10	.192	.231	26	5	1	0	0	0.0	2	2	2	10	0
May	16	.212	.576	33	7	0	0	4	12.1	6	7	6	9	0
June	22	.232	.411	56	13	1	0	3	5.4	4	9	7	16	0
July	25	.173	.442	52	9	2	0	4	7.7	5	4	10	14	0
Aug	21	.162	.324	37	6	0	0	2	5.4	2	4	7	17	0
Sept/Oct	22	.177	.403	62	11	2	0	4	6.5	5	8	3	25	0
Day	35	.211	.303	76	16	4	0	1	1.3	2	3	13	22	0
Night	81	.184	.447	190	35	2	0	16	8.4	22	31	22	69	0
vs. Left		.211	.497	161	34	4	0	14	8.7	19	27	30	53	0
vs. Right		.162	.267	105	17	2	0	3	2.9	5	7	5	38	0
On Grass	96	.186	.371	210	39	6	0	11	5.2	17	27	28	75	0
On Turf	20	.214	.536	56	12	0	0	6	10.7	7	7	7	16	0
Home	56	.211	.447	123	26	5	0	8	6.5	10	17	18	40	0
Road	60	.175	.371	143	25	1	0	9	6.3	14	17	17	51	0
Division Rivals														
vs. BAL	8	.176	.529	17	3	0	0	2	11.8	2	3	1	6	0
vs. BOS	9	.222	.278	18	4	1	0	0	0.0	0	1	3	7	0
vs. CLE	11	.125	.375	24	3	0	0	2	8.3	2	2	3	12	0
vs. DET	10	.250	.500	24	6	0	0	2	8.3	4	4	6	8	0
vs. MIL	10	.286	.333	21	6	1	0	0	0.0	0	4	3	8	0
vs. TOR	10	.226	.548	31	7	1	0	3	9.7	3	3	5	9	0
On 3B < 2 Out		.364	.455	11	4	1	0	0	0.0	0	9	0	4	

Year	Team		Games	BA	SA	AB	H	2B	3B	HR	HR%	R	RBI	BB	SO	SB	PH AB	PH H	PO	A	E	DP	TC/G	FA	G by Pos
1981	NY	A	4	.286	.714	7	2	1	1	0	0.0	2	2	1	4	0	1	0	14	1	0	2	3.8	1.000	1B-3, DH-1
1982			33	.187	.280	107	20	2	1	2	1.9	8	4	6	34	0	5	1	194	13	2	23	6.3	.990	1B-26, DH-5
1983			32	.233	.430	86	20	2	0	5	5.8	8	17	8	23	0	3	1	178	9	3	19	5.9	.984	1B-23, DH-4
1984	KC	A	126	.244	.498	438	107	23	2	28	6.4	58	77	45	139	0	1	0	1102	79	15	102	9.5	.987	1B-125, DH-1
1985			160	.243	.477	600	146	28	2	36	6.0	74	88	52	**166**	1	1	0	1573	101	12	138	10.5	.993	1B-160
1986			138	.229	.451	512	117	25	1	29	5.7	54	88	43	146	0	2	0	1236	98	18	115	9.8	.987	1B-137
1987			121	.207	.427	386	80	11	1	24	6.2	44	60	34	97	0	15	4	521	41	6	39	4.7	.989	1B-55, DH-52
1988	2 teams		KC A (21G — .143)			SEA A (97G — .251)																			
"	total		118	.235	.448	413	97	17	1	23	5.6	46	66	24	87	0	9	2	428	30	4	45	3.9	.991	DH-62, 1B-53
1989	NY	A	110	.237	.460	300	71	12	2	17	5.7	33	59	25	67	0	25	6	150	7	1	15	1.4	.994	DH-82, 1B-20
1990			116	.192	.406	266	51	6	0	17	6.3	24	34	35	91	0	40	8	183	7	3	23	6.9	.984	DH-72, 1B-28
10 yrs.			958	.228	.450	3115	711	127	11	181	5.8	351	495	273	854	1	102	22	5579	386	64	521	6.3	.989	1B-630, DH-279

LEAGUE CHAMPIONSHIP SERIES

Year	Team		Games	BA	SA	AB	H	2B	3B	HR	HR%	R	RBI	BB	SO	SB	PH AB	PH H	PO	A	E	DP	TC/G	FA	G by Pos
1984	KC	A	3	.100	.100	10	1	0	0	0	0.0	0	0	1	4	0	0	0	20	3	1	2	8.0	.958	1B-3
1985			7	.120	.120	25	3	0	0	0	0.0	1	1	2	8	0	0	0	71	7	2	5	11.4	.975	1B-7
2 yrs.			10	.114	.114	35	4	0	0	0	0.0	1	1	3	12	0	0	0	91	10	3	7	10.4	.971	1B-10

WORLD SERIES

Year	Team		Games	BA	SA	AB	H	2B	3B	HR	HR%	R	RBI	BB	SO	SB	PH AB	PH H	PO	A	E	DP	TC/G	FA	G by Pos
1985	KC	A	7	.320	.320	25	8	0	0	0	0.0	2	3	5	4	0	0	0	70	3	0	1	10.4	1.000	1B-7

Year	Team	Games	BA	SA	AB	H	2B	3B	HR	HR%	R	RBI	BB	SO	SB	PINCH HIT AB	PINCH HIT H	PO	A	E	DP	TC/G	FA	G by Pos

Jeff Baldwin

BALDWIN, JEFFERY ALLEN
B. Sept. 5, 1965, Milford, Del.
BL TL 6′ 1″ 180 lbs.

Year	Team	Games	BA	SA	AB	H	2B	3B	HR	HR%	R	RBI	BB	SO	SB	PINCH HIT AB	PINCH HIT H	PO	A	E	DP	TC/G	FA	G by Pos
1990	HOU N	7	.000	.000	8	0	0	0	0	0.0	1	0	1	2	0	6	0	1	0	0	0	0.3	1.000	OF-3

Jesse Barfield

BARFIELD, JESSE LEE
B. Oct. 29, 1959, Joliet, Ill.
BR TR 6′ 1″ 200 lbs.

	Games	BA	SA	AB	H	2B	3B	HR	HR%	R	RBI	BB	SO	SB
April	15	.224	.510	49	11	3	1	3	6.1	7	8	8	17	1
May	27	.259	.471	85	22	3	0	5	5.9	11	17	11	28	1
June	27	.271	.469	96	26	7	0	4	4.2	17	13	13	32	1
July	25	.243	.400	70	17	5	0	2	2.9	8	7	9	21	0
Aug	30	.193	.458	83	16	2	1	6	7.2	11	16	20	22	1
Sept/Oct	29	.269	.441	93	25	1	0	5	5.4	15	17	21	30	0
Day	38	.238	.438	105	25	7	1	4	3.8	16	14	24	35	2
Night	115	.248	.461	371	92	14	1	21	5.7	53	64	58	115	2
vs. Left		.259	.543	162	42	7	0	13	8.0	31	25	33	51	3
vs. Right		.239	.411	314	75	14	2	12	3.8	38	53	49	99	1
On Grass	128	.234	.444	401	94	17	2	21	5.2	57	66	67	129	4
On Turf	25	.307	.520	75	23	4	0	4	5.3	12	12	15	21	0
Home	74	.218	.410	239	52	10	0	12	5.0	34	35	33	79	2
Road	79	.274	.502	237	65	11	2	13	5.5	35	43	49	71	2
Division Rivals														
vs. BAL	12	.425	.900	40	17	2	1	5	12.5	10	14	10	7	1
vs. BOS	13	.105	.158	38	4	2	0	0	0.0	6	2	8	19	1
vs. CLE	13	.222	.306	36	8	3	0	0	0.0	5	1	7	13	0
vs. DET	13	.327	.592	49	16	2	1	3	6.1	9	12	8	15	0
vs. MIL	13	.261	.500	46	12	2	0	3	6.5	6	10	4	14	0
vs. TOR	12	.170	.255	47	8	1	0	1	2.1	6	2	7	13	0
On 3B < 2 Out		.200	.250	20	4	1	0	0	0.0	0	15	3	9	

OUTFIELD

Year	Team	Games	BA	SA	AB	H	2B	3B	HR	HR%	R	RBI	BB	SO	SB	PINCH HIT AB	PINCH HIT H	PO	A	E	DP	TC/G	FA	G by Pos
1981	TOR A	25	.232	.368	95	22	3	2	2	2.1	7	9	4	19	4	0	0	71	2	0	1	2.9	1.000	OF-25
1982		139	.246	.426	394	97	13	2	18	4.6	54	58	42	79	1	21	6	217	15	9	4	1.7	.963	OF-137, DH-1
1983		128	.253	.510	388	98	13	3	27	7.0	58	68	22	110	2	16	6	213	16	8	4	1.9	.966	OF-120, DH-5
1984		110	.284	.466	320	91	14	1	14	4.4	51	49	35	81	8	20	8	190	9	10	5	1.9	.952	OF-88, DH-9
1985		155	.289	.536	539	156	34	9	27	5.0	94	84	66	143	22	1	0	349	22	4	8	2.4	.989	OF-154
1986		158	.289	.559	589	170	35	2	**40**	6.8	107	108	69	146	8	1	0	368	20	3	8	2.5	.992	OF-157
1987		159	.263	.458	590	155	25	3	28	4.7	89	84	58	141	3	4	1	341	17	3	4	2.3	.992	OF-158
1988		137	.244	.425	468	114	21	5	18	3.8	62	56	41	108	7	4	1	325	12	4	4	2.5	.988	OF-136, DH-1
1989	2 teams	TOR A (21G — .200)							NY A (129G — .240)															
"	total	150	.234	.415	521	122	23	1	23	4.4	79	67	87	150	5	2	0	340	20	10	4	2.5	.973	OF-150
1990	NY A	153	.246	.456	476	117	21	2	25	5.2	69	78	82	150	4	13	3	305	16	9	3	2.2	.973	OF-151
10 yrs.		1314	.261	.473	4380	1142	202	30	222	5.1	670	661	506	1127	64	82	25	2719	149	60	45	2.2	.980	OF-1276, DH-16

LEAGUE CHAMPIONSHIP SERIES

Year	Team	Games	BA	SA	AB	H	2B	3B	HR	HR%	R	RBI	BB	SO	SB	PINCH HIT AB	PINCH HIT H	PO	A	E	DP	TC/G	FA	G by Pos
1985	TOR A	7	.280	.440	25	7	1	0	1	4.0	3	4	3	7	1	0	0	21	0	1	0	3.1	.955	OF-7

Marty Barrett

BARRETT, MARTIN GLENN
Brother of Tom Barrett.
B. June 23, 1958, Arcadia, Calif.
BR TR 5′ 11″ 175 lbs.

Year	Team	Games	BA	SA	AB	H	2B	3B	HR	HR%	R	RBI	BB	SO	SB	PINCH HIT AB	PINCH HIT H	PO	A	E	DP	TC/G	FA	G by Pos
1982	BOS A	8	.056	.056	18	1	0	0	0	0.0	0	0	0	1	0	0	0	11	21	0	4	4.0	1.000	2B-7
1983		33	.227	.295	44	10	1	1	0	0.0	7	2	3	1	0	0	0	32	28	1	8	1.8	.984	2B-23, DH-5
1984		139	.303	.383	475	144	23	3	3	0.6	56	45	42	25	4	1	0	245	417	9	67	4.8	.987	2B-136
1985		156	.266	.343	534	142	26	6	5	0.9	59	56	56	50	7	0	0	355	479	11	110	5.4	.987	2B-155
1986		158	.286	.381	625	179	39	4	4	0.6	94	60	65	31	15	0	0	303	450	14	101	4.9	.982	2B-158
1987		137	.293	.351	559	164	23	0	3	0.5	72	43	51	38	15	0	0	320	438	9	108	5.6	.988	2B-137
1988		150	.283	.337	612	173	28	1	1	0.2	83	65	40	35	7	1	0	312	402	7	97	4.8	.990	2B-150
1989		86	.256	.318	336	86	18	0	1	0.3	31	27	32	12	4	2	1	152	245	10	53	4.7	.975	2B-80, DH-4
1990		62	.226	.252	159	36	4	0	0	0.0	15	13	15	13	4	0	0	90	148	2	28	3.9	.992	2B-60, DH-1, 3B-1
9 yrs.		929	.278	.347	3362	935	162	9	17	0.5	417	311	304	206	56	4	1	1820	2628	63	576	4.9	.986	2B-906, DH-10, 3B-1

Year	Team	Games	BA	SA	AB	H	2B	3B	HR	HR%	R	RBI	BB	SO	SB	PINCH HIT AB	H	PO	A	E	DP	TC/G	FA	G by Pos

Marty Barrett *Continued*

LEAGUE CHAMPIONSHIP SERIES

Year	Team	Games	BA	SA	AB	H	2B	3B	HR	HR%	R	RBI	BB	SO	SB	AB	H	PO	A	E	DP	TC/G	FA	G by Pos
1986	BOS	A	7	.367	.433	30	11	2	0	0	0.0	4	5	2	2	0	0	0	19	21	0	4	5.7	1.000	2B-7
1988			4	.067	.067	15	1	0	0	0	0.0	2	0	1	0	0	0	0	6	8	0	1	3.5	1.000	2B-4
1990			3	.000	.000	0	0	0	0	0	0.0	0	0	0	0	0	0	0	2	0	0	0	0.7	1.000	2B-3
3 yrs.			14	.267	.311	45	12	2	0	0	0.0	6	5	3	2	0	0	0	27	29	0	5	4.0	.000	2B-14

WORLD SERIES

Year	Team	Games	BA	SA	AB	H	2B	3B	HR	HR%	R	RBI	BB	SO	SB	AB	H	PO	A	E	DP	TC/G	FA	G by Pos
1986	BOS	A	7	.433	.500	30	13	2	0	0	0.0	1	4	5	2	0	0	0	13	25	0	5	5.4	1.000	2B-7

Kevin Bass

BASS, KEVIN CHARLES
B. May 12, 1959, Redwood City, Calif.
BB TR 6' 183 lbs.

Year	Team	Games	BA	SA	AB	H	2B	3B	HR	HR%	R	RBI	BB	SO	SB	AB	H	PO	A	E	DP	TC/G	FA	G by Pos
1982	2 teams	MIL A (18G — .000)				HOU N (12G — .042)																			
"	total		30	.030	.030	33	1	0	0	0	0.0	6	1	1	9	0	1	0	18	0	1	0	0.6	.947	OF-21, DH-2
1983	HOU	N	88	.236	.333	195	46	7	3	2	1.0	25	18	6	27	2	43	11	68	1	4	1	0.8	.945	OF-52
1984			121	.260	.360	331	86	17	5	2	0.6	33	29	6	57	5	44	13	149	4	4	2	1.3	.975	OF-81
1985			150	.269	.427	539	145	27	5	16	3.0	72	68	31	63	19	12	4	328	10	1	1	2.3	.997	OF-141
1986			157	.311	.486	591	184	33	5	20	3.4	83	79	38	72	22	2	2	303	12	5	4	2.0	.984	OF-155
1987			157	.284	.449	592	168	31	5	19	3.2	83	85	53	77	21	2	1	287	11	4	2	1.9	.987	OF-155
1988			157	.255	.390	541	138	27	2	14	2.6	57	72	42	65	31	16	6	267	7	6	2	1.8	.979	OF-147
1989			87	.300	.435	313	94	19	4	5	1.6	42	44	29	44	11	2	1	186	6	3	0	2.2	.985	OF-84
1990	SF	N	61	.252	.402	214	54	9	1	7	3.2	25	32	14	26	2	5	1	88	2	3	0	1.7	.968	OF-55
9 yrs.			1008	.274	.418	3349	916	170	30	85	2.5	426	428	220	440	113	127	39	1694	53	31	12	1.8	.983	OF-891, DH-2

LEAGUE CHAMPIONSHIP SERIES

Year	Team	Games	BA	SA	AB	H	2B	3B	HR	HR%	R	RBI	BB	SO	SB	AB	H	PO	A	E	DP	TC/G	FA	G by Pos
1986	HOU	N	6	.292	.375	24	7	2	0	0	0.0	0	0	4	4	2	0	0	16	0	1	0	2.8	.941	OF-6

Billy Bates

BATES, WILLIAM DERRICK
B. Dec. 7, 1963
BL TR 5' 7" 155 lbs.

Year	Team	Games	BA	SA	AB	H	2B	3B	HR	HR%	R	RBI	BB	SO	SB	AB	H	PO	A	E	DP	TC/G	FA	G by Pos
1989	MIL	A	7	.214	.214	14	3	0	0	0	0.0	3	0	0	1	2	1	1	14	16	2	7	4.6	.938	2B-7
1990	2 teams	MIL A (14G — .103)				CIN N (8G — .000)																			
"	total		22	.088	.118	34	3	1	0	0	0.0	8	2	4	9	6	1	0	18	34	2	6	3.6	.963	2B-15
2 yrs.			29	.125	.146	48	6	1	0	0	0.0	11	2	4	10	8	2	1	32	50	4	13	3.0	.953	2B-22

LEAGUE CHAMPIONSHIP SERIES

Year	Team	Games	BA	SA	AB	H	2B	3B	HR	HR%	R	RBI	BB	SO	SB	AB	H	PO	A	E	DP	TC/G	FA	G by Pos
1990	CIN	N	2	.000	.000	0	0	0	0	0	0.0	1	0	0	0	0	0	0	0	0	0	0	0.0	1.000	

WORLD SERIES

Year	Team	Games	BA	SA	AB	H	2B	3B	HR	HR%	R	RBI	BB	SO	SB	AB	H	PO	A	E	DP	TC/G	FA	G by Pos
1990	CIN	N	1	1.000	1.000	1	1	0	0	0	0.0	1	0	0	0	0	1	1	0	0	0	0	0.0	1.000	

Bill Bathe

BATHE, WILLIAM DAVID
B. Oct. 14, 1960, Downey, Calif.
BR TR 6' 2" 200 lbs.

Year	Team	Games	BA	SA	AB	H	2B	3B	HR	HR%	R	RBI	BB	SO	SB	AB	H	PO	A	E	DP	TC/G	FA	G by Pos
1986	OAK	A	39	.184	.359	103	19	3	0	5	4.9	9	11	2	20	0	0	0	211	11	2	1	5.7	.991	C-39
1989	SF	N	30	.281	.313	32	9	1	0	0	0.0	3	6	0	7	0	26	6	13	0	0	0	0.4	1.000	C-7
1990			52	.229	.458	48	11	0	1	3	6.2	3	12	7	12	0	39	9	10	1	0	1	1.4	1.000	C-8
3 yrs.			121	.213	.377	183	39	4	1	8	4.4	15	29	9	39	0	65	15	234	12	2	2	2.0	.992	C-54

LEAGUE CHAMPIONSHIP SERIES

Year	Team	Games	BA	SA	AB	H	2B	3B	HR	HR%	R	RBI	BB	SO	SB	AB	H	PO	A	E	DP	TC/G	FA	G by Pos
1989	SF	N	2	.000	.000	1	0	0	0	0	0.0	0	0	0	1	0	1	0	0	0	0	0	0.0	—	

WORLD SERIES

Year	Team	Games	BA	SA	AB	H	2B	3B	HR	HR%	R	RBI	BB	SO	SB	AB	H	PO	A	E	DP	TC/G	FA	G by Pos
1989	SF	N	2	.500	2.000	2	1	0	0	1	50.0	1	3	0	0	0	2	1	0	0	0	0	0.0	—	

Kevin Belcher

BELCHER, KEVIN DONNELL
B. Aug. 8, 1967, Waco, Tex.
BR TR 6' 170 lbs.

Year	Team	Games	BA	SA	AB	H	2B	3B	HR	HR%	R	RBI	BB	SO	SB	AB	H	PO	A	E	DP	TC/G	FA	G by Pos
1990	TEX	A	16	.133	.200	15	2	1	0	0	0.0	4	0	2	6	0	0	0	12	0	0	0	1.3	1.000	OF-9

Year	Team		Games	BA	SA	AB	H	2B	3B	HR	HR%	R	RBI	BB	SO	SB	PINCH HIT AB	H	PO	A	E	DP	TC/G	FA	G by Pos

George Bell

BELL, JORGE ANTONIO
Born Jorge Antonio Bell y Mathey.
Brother of Juan Bell.
B. Oct. 21, 1959, San Pedro de Macoris,
Dominican Republic
BR TR 6′ 1″ 190 lbs.

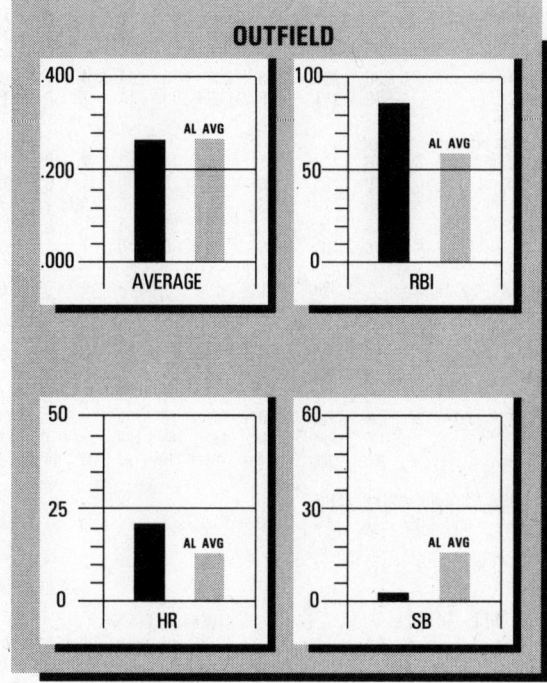

OUTFIELD

Period	Games	BA	SA	AB	H	2B	3B	HR	HR%	R	RBI	BB	SO	SB
April	20	.265	.506	83	22	2	0	6	7.2	12	16	2	6	0
May	28	.266	.367	109	29	5	0	2	1.8	12	14	8	10	1
June	28	.316	.614	114	36	7	0	9	7.9	21	26	9	16	1
July	17	.254	.413	63	16	4	0	2	3.2	7	7	5	12	0
Aug	24	.231	.297	91	21	3	0	1	1.1	7	14	4	10	0
Sept/Oct	25	.245	.314	102	25	4	0	1	1.0	8	9	4	18	1
Day	42	.311	.478	161	50	9	0	6	3.7	23	22	14	22	0
Night	100	.247	.399	401	99	16	0	15	3.7	44	64	18	58	3
vs. Left		.248	.389	149	37	6	0	5	3.4	20	22	15	17	0
vs. Right		.271	.433	413	112	19	0	16	3.9	47	64	17	63	3
On Grass	57	.266	.428	222	59	12	0	8	3.6	25	35	16	31	2
On Turf	85	.265	.418	340	90	13	0	13	3.8	42	51	16	49	1
Home	70	.255	.420	274	70	12	0	11	4.0	36	41	16	41	0
Road	72	.274	.424	288	79	13	0	10	3.5	31	45	16	39	3

Division Rivals

	Games	BA	SA	AB	H	2B	3B	HR	HR%	R	RBI	BB	SO	SB
vs. BAL	13	.275	.392	51	14	0	0	2	3.9	7	6	2	9	0
vs. BOS	12	.182	.205	44	8	1	0	0	0.0	1	4	2	15	0
vs. CLE	9	.205	.333	39	8	2	0	1	2.6	5	4	2	6	0
vs. DET	11	.214	.357	42	9	3	0	1	2.4	8	4	5	4	0
vs. MIL	10	.442	.721	43	19	3	0	3	7.0	9	11	2	2	2
vs. NY	13	.353	.745	51	18	5	0	5	9.8	13	12	8	7	0
On 3B < 2 Out		.344	.563	32	11	1	0	2	6.3	2	30	3	5	

Year	Team		Games	BA	SA	AB	H	2B	3B	HR	HR%	R	RBI	BB	SO	SB	AB	H	PO	A	E	DP	TC/G	FA	G by Pos
1981	TOR	A	60	.233	.350	163	38	2	1	5	3.1	19	12	5	27	3	5	3	92	3	3	2	1.6	.969	OF-44, DH-8
1983			39	.268	.438	112	30	5	4	2	1.8	5	17	4	17	1	3	1	61	0	3	0	1.7	.954	OF-34, DH-2
1984			159	.292	.498	606	177	39	4	26	4.3	85	87	24	86	11	8	3	289	13	9	1	2.0	.971	OF-147, DH-7, 3B-3
1985			157	.275	.479	607	167	28	6	28	4.6	87	95	43	90	21	0	0	320	14	11	3	2.2	.968	OF-157, 3B-2
1986			159	.309	.532	641	198	38	6	31	4.8	101	108	41	62	7	1	1	270	17	10	1	1.9	.966	OF-147, DH-11, 3B-1
1987			156	.308	.605	610	188	32	4	47	7.7	111	**134**	39	75	5	1	0	249	14	11	1	1.8	.960	OF-148, 2B-1, 3B-1
1988			156	.269	.446	614	165	27	5	24	3.9	78	97	34	66	4	2	0	253	8	15	1	1.8	.946	OF-149, DH-7
1989			153	.297	.458	613	182	41	2	18	2.9	88	104	33	60	4	0	0	258	4	10	1	1.8	.963	OF-134, DH-19
1990			142	.265	.422	562	149	25	0	21	3.7	67	86	32	80	3	0	0	226	4	5	1	2.2	.979	OF-106, DH-36
9 yrs.			1181	.286	.486	4528	1294	237	32	202	4.5	641	740	255	563	59	20	8	2018	78	77	11	1.8	.965	OF-1066, DH-90, 3B-7, 2B-1

LEAGUE CHAMPIONSHIP SERIES

Year	Team		Games	BA	SA	AB	H	2B	3B	HR	HR%	R	RBI	BB	SO	SB	AB	H	PO	A	E	DP	TC/G	FA	G by Pos
1985	TOR	A	7	.321	.429	28	9	3	0	0	0.0	4	1	0	4	0	0	0	13	0	0	0	1.9	1.000	OF-7
1989			5	.200	.350	20	4	0	0	1	5.0	2	2	0	3	0	0	0	3	1	0	0	0.8	1.000	DH-3, OF-2
2 yrs.			12	.271	.396	48	13	3	0	1	2.1	6	3	0	7	0	0	0	16	1	0	0	1.4	.000	OF-9, DH-3

Jay Bell

BELL, JAY STUART
B. Dec. 11, 1965, Pensacola, Fla.
BR TR 6′ 1″ 180 lbs.

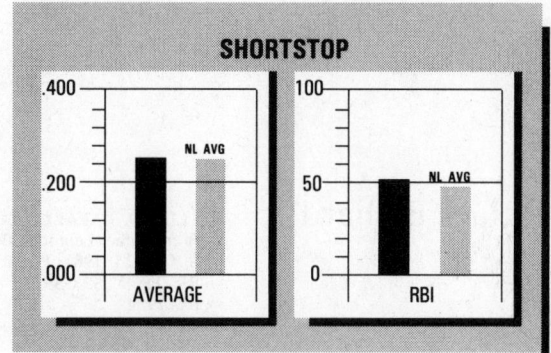

SHORTSTOP

Period	Games	BA	SA	AB	H	2B	3B	HR	HR%	R	RBI	BB	SO	SB
April	19	.261	.348	69	18	3	0	1	1.4	9	7	8	18	3
May	26	.283	.414	99	28	9	2	0	0.0	13	7	8	15	1
June	26	.261	.402	92	24	4	3	1	1.1	13	8	10	22	1
July	26	.272	.350	103	28	2	0	2	1.9	16	12	6	10	3
Aug	30	.264	.355	121	32	3	1	2	1.7	18	8	6	18	0
Sept/Oct	32	.182	.303	99	18	7	1	1	1.0	24	10	27	26	2
Day	42	.281	.431	153	43	11	0	4	2.6	28	18	14	35	4
Night	117	.244	.337	430	105	17	7	3	0.7	65	34	51	74	6
vs. Left		.275	.382	251	69	13	4	2	0.8	46	17	34	42	3
vs. Right		.238	.346	332	79	15	3	5	1.5	47	35	31	67	7

Year	Team		Games	BA	SA	AB	H	2B	3B	HR	HR%	R	RBI	BB	SO	SB	PINCH HIT AB	H	PO	A	E	DP	TC/G	FA	G by Pos

Jay Bell *Continued*

Year	Team		Games	BA	SA	AB	H	2B	3B	HR	HR%	R	RBI	BB	SO	SB	PINCH HIT AB	H	PO	A	E	DP	TC/G	FA	G by Pos
On Grass			41	.242	.342	149	36	6	0	3	2.0	26	14	16	31	4									
On Turf			118	.258	.369	434	112	22	7	4	0.9	67	38	49	78	6									
Home			80	.261	.348	287	75	14	4	1	0.3	42	17	31	56	2									
Road			79	.247	.375	296	73	14	3	6	2.0	51	35	34	53	8									
Division Rivals																									
vs. CHI			16	.259	.389	54	14	3	2	0	0.0	17	2	10	12	0									
vs. MON			18	.265	.368	68	18	5	1	0	0.0	8	6	5	16	2									
vs. NY			18	.220	.322	59	13	3	0	1	1.7	9	3	11	18	1									
vs. PHI			18	.263	.316	76	20	4	0	0	0.0	10	4	2	12	0									
vs. STL			18	.182	.309	55	10	0	2	1	1.8	11	9	13	15	3									
On 3B < 2 Out				.368	.579	19	7	2	1	0	0.0	0	16	3	4										
1986	CLE	A	5	.357	.714	14	5	2	0	1	7.1	3	4	2	3	0	1	0	1	6	2	1	1.8	.778	DH–2, 2B–2
1987			38	.216	.352	125	27	9	1	2	1.6	14	13	8	31	2	0	0	67	93	9	22	4.4	.947	SS–38
1988			73	.218	.280	211	46	5	1	2	0.9	23	21	21	53	4	0	0	103	170	10	37	3.9	.965	SS–72
1989	PIT	N	78	.258	.351	271	70	13	3	2	0.7	33	27	19	47	5	3	1	109	197	10	41	4.1	.968	SS–78
1990			159	.254	.362	583	148	28	7	7	1.2	93	52	65	109	10	2	1	260	459	22	85	4.7	.970	SS–159
5 yrs.			353	.246	.348	1204	296	57	12	14	1.2	166	117	115	243	21	6	2	540	925	53	186	4.3	.965	SS–347, DH–2, 2B–2

LEAGUE CHAMPIONSHIP SERIES

Year	Team		Games	BA	SA	AB	H	2B	3B	HR	HR%	R	RBI	BB	SO	SB	PINCH HIT AB	H	PO	A	E	DP	TC/G	FA	G by Pos
1990	PIT	N	6	.250	.450	20	5	1	0	1	5.0	3	1	4	3	0	0	0	4	22	1	2	4.5	.963	SS–6

Juan Bell

BELL, JUAN
Born Juan Bell y Mathey. Brother of George Bell.
B. Mar. 29, 1968, San Pedro de Macoris, Dominican Republic
BR TR 5′ 11″ 172 lbs.

Year	Team		Games	BA	SA	AB	H	2B	3B	HR	HR%	R	RBI	BB	SO	SB	PINCH HIT AB	H	PO	A	E	DP	TC/G	FA	G by Pos
1989	BAL	A	8	.000	.000	4	0	0	0	0	0.0	2	0	0	1	1	0	0	2	6	0	1	1.0	1.000	DH–4, 2B–2, SS–2
1990			5	.000	.000	2	0	0	0	0	0.0	1	0	0	1	0	0	0	1	1	0	0	2.0	1.000	DH–1, SS–1
2 yrs.			13	.000	.000	6	0	0	0	0	0.0	3	0	0	2	1	0	0	3	7	0	1	0.8	.000	DH–5, SS–3, 2B–2

Mike Bell

BELL, MICHAEL ALLEN
B. Apr. 22, 1968, Lewiston, N. J.
BL TL 6′ 1″ 175 lbs.

Year	Team		Games	BA	SA	AB	H	2B	3B	HR	HR%	R	RBI	BB	SO	SB	PINCH HIT AB	H	PO	A	E	DP	TC/G	FA	G by Pos
1990	ATL	N	36	.244	.467	45	11	5	1	1	2.2	8	5	2	9	0	11	2	97	9	2	6	4.5	.981	1B–24

Albert Belle

BELLE, ALBERT JOJUAN (Joey)
B. Aug. 25, 1966, Shreveport, La.
BR TR 6′ 1″ 190 lbs.

Year	Team		Games	BA	SA	AB	H	2B	3B	HR	HR%	R	RBI	BB	SO	SB	PINCH HIT AB	H	PO	A	E	DP	TC/G	FA	G by Pos
1989	CLE	A	62	.225	.394	218	49	8	4	7	3.2	22	37	12	55	2	2	1	92	3	2	1	1.6	.979	OF–44, DH–17
1990			9	.174	.304	23	4	0	0	1	4.3	1	3	1	6	0	2	0	0	0	0	0	0.0	.960	DH–6, OF–1
2 yrs.			71	.220	.386	241	53	8	4	8	3.3	23	40	13	61	2	4	1	92	3	2	1	1.4	.979	OF–45, DH–23

Rafael Belliard

BELLIARD, RAFAEL LEONIDAS
Born Rafael Leonidas Belliard y Matias.
B. Oct. 24, 1961, Puerto Nuevo Mao, Dominican Republic
BR TR 5′ 9″ 139 lbs.
BB 1982

Year	Team		Games	BA	SA	AB	H	2B	3B	HR	HR%	R	RBI	BB	SO	SB	PINCH HIT AB	H	PO	A	E	DP	TC/G	FA	G by Pos
1982	PIT	N	9	.500	.500	2	1	0	0	0	0.0	3	0	0	0	1	1	1	2	2	0	0	0.4	1.000	SS–4
1983			4	.000	.000	1	0	0	0	0	0.0	1	0	0	1	0	0	0	1	3	0	1	1.0	1.000	SS–3
1984			20	.227	.227	22	5	0	0	0	0.0	3	0	0	1	4	0	0	12	13	3	4	1.4	.893	SS–12, 2B–1
1985			17	.200	.200	20	4	0	0	0	0.0	1	1	0	5	0	2	0	13	23	2	3	2.2	.947	SS–12
1986			117	.233	.262	309	72	5	2	0	0.0	33	31	26	54	12	4	0	147	317	12	50	4.1	.975	SS–96, 2B–23
1987			81	.207	.271	203	42	4	3	1	0.5	26	15	20	25	5	1	0	113	191	6	31	3.8	.981	SS–71, 2B–7
1988			122	.213	.241	286	61	0	4	0	0.0	28	11	26	47	7	1	0	134	261	9	51	3.3	.978	SS–117, 2B–3
1989			67	.214	.240	154	33	4	0	0	0.0	10	8	8	22	5	1	0	71	138	3	20	3.2	.986	SS–40, 2B–20, 3B–6
1990			47	.204	.259	54	11	3	0	0	0.0	10	6	5	13	1	10	2	37	36	2	8	2.1	.973	2B–21, SS–10, 3B–5
9 yrs.			484	.218	.253	1051	229	16	9	1	0.1	115	72	85	168	35	20	3	530	984	37	168	3.2	.976	SS–365, 2B–75, 3B–11

Year	Team	Games	BA	SA	AB	H	2B	3B	HR	HR%	R	RBI	BB	SO	SB	PINCH HIT AB	PINCH HIT H	PO	A	E	DP	TC/G	FA	G by Pos

Mike Benjamin

BENJAMIN, MICHAEL PAUL
B. Nov. 22, 1965, Euclid, Ohio
BR TR 6' 3" 195 lbs.

Year	Team	Games	BA	SA	AB	H	2B	3B	HR	HR%	R	RBI	BB	SO	SB	PH AB	PH H	PO	A	E	DP	TC/G	FA	G by Pos
1989	SF	N 14	.167	.167	6	1	0	0	0	0.0	6	0	0	1	0	1	1	4	4	0	0	0.6	1.000	SS-8
1990		22	.214	.411	56	12	3	1	2	3.5	7	3	3	10	1	2	0	29	53	1	10	4.0	.988	SS-21
2 yrs.		36	.210	.387	62	13	3	1	2	3.2	13	3	3	11	1	3	1	33	57	1	10	2.5	.989	SS-29

Todd Benzinger

BENZINGER, TODD ERIC
B. Feb. 11, 1963, Dayton, Ky.
BB TR 6' 1" 185 lbs.

	Games	BA	SA	AB	H	2B	3B	HR	HR%	R	RBI	BB	SO	SB
April	16	.339	.441	59	20	3	0	1	1.7	9	9	9	6	0
May	26	.274	.349	106	29	6	1	0	0.0	8	14	1	16	3
June	28	.264	.385	91	24	2	0•	3	3.3	9	16	6	20	0
July	15	.119	.143	42	5	1	0	0	0.0	1	0	1	13	0
Aug	19	.235	.373	51	12	2	1	1	2.0	7	5	0	7	0
Sept/Oct	14	.185	.185	27	5	0	0	0	0.0	1	2	2	7	0
Day	36	.280	.383	107	30	6	1	1	0.9	12	6	8	22	2
Night	82	.242	.323	269	65	8	1	4	1.5	23	40	11	47	1
vs. Left		.285	.360	172	49	7	0	2	1.2	15	17	6	15	1
vs. Right		.225	.324	204	46	7	2	3	1.5	20	29	13	54	2
On Grass	31	.218	.241	87	19	2	0	0	0.0	2	6	5	16	0
On Turf	87	.263	.370	289	76	12	2	5	1.7	33	40	14	53	3
Home	62	.258	.374	190	49	8	1	4	2.1	21	23	10	30	2
Road	56	.247	.306	186	46	6	1	1	0.5	14	23	9	39	1
Division Rivals														
vs. ATL	15	.327	.418	55	18	2	0	1	1.8	4	8	1	4	0
vs. HOU	15	.200	.300	40	8	1	0	1	2.5	3	4	4	11	0
vs. LA	11	.321	.464	28	9	1	0	1	3.6	4	5	4	5	0
vs. SD	7	.091	.091	22	2	0	0	0	0.0	2	1	5	6	0
vs. SF	13	.161	.323	31	5	0	1	1	3.2	3	3	2	6	0
On 3B < 2 Out		.542	.583	24	13	1	0	0	0.0	0	25	2	5	

FIRST BASE — AVERAGE (NL AVG) · RBI (NL AVG) · HR (NL AVG) · SB (NL AVG)

Year	Team	Games	BA	SA	AB	H	2B	3B	HR	HR%	R	RBI	BB	SO	SB	PH AB	PH H	PO	A	E	DP	TC/G	FA	G by Pos
1987	BOS	A 73	.278	.444	223	62	11	1	8	3.6	36	43	22	41	5	8	2	155	7	2	2	2.2	.988	OF-61, 1B-2
1988		120	.254	.425	405	103	28	1	13	3.2	47	70	22	80	2	7	3	602	38	6	47	5.4	.991	1B-85, OF-48, DH-1
1989	CIN	N 161	.245	.381	628	154	28	3	17	2.7	79	76	44	120	3	3	1	1417	73	7	96	9.3	.995	1B-158
1990		118	.253	.340	376	95	14	2	5	1.3	35	46	19	69	3	15	0	733	52	6	58	7.5	.992	1B-95, OF-10
4 yrs.		472	.254	.391	1632	414	81	7	43	2.6	197	235	107	310	13	33	6	2907	170	21	203	6.6	.993	1B-340, OF-119, DH-1

LEAGUE CHAMPIONSHIP SERIES

Year	Team	Games	BA	SA	AB	H	2B	3B	HR	HR%	R	RBI	BB	SO	SB	PH AB	PH H	PO	A	E	DP	TC/G	FA	G by Pos
1988	BOS	A 4	.091	.091	11	1	0	0	0	0.0	0	0	1	3	0	1	0	21	1	0	2	5.5	1.000	1B-3
1990	CIN	N 5	.333	.333	9	3	0	0	0	0.0	0	0	2	0	0	2	2	17	0	0	0	8.5	1.000	1B-2
2 yrs.		9	.200	.200	20	4	0	0	0	0.0	0	0	3	3	0	3	2	38	1	0	2	4.3	.000	1B-5

WORLD SERIES

Year	Team	Games	BA	SA	AB	H	2B	3B	HR	HR%	R	RBI	BB	SO	SB	PH AB	PH H	PO	A	E	DP	TC/G	FA	G by Pos
1990	CIN	N 4	.182	.182	11	2	0	0	0	0.0	1	0	0	0	0	1	0	24	0	0	1	8.0	1.000	1B-3

Dave Bergman

BERGMAN, DAVID BRUCE
B. June 6, 1953, Evanston, Ill.
BL TL 6' 1 1/2" 185 lbs.

Year	Team	Games	BA	SA	AB	H	2B	3B	HR	HR%	R	RBI	BB	SO	SB	PH AB	PH H	PO	A	E	DP	TC/G	FA	G by Pos
1975	NY	A 7	.000	.000	17	0	0	0	0	0.0	0	0	2	4	0	0	0	10	1	1	1	1.7	.917	OF-6
1977		5	.250	.250	4	1	0	0	0	0.0	1	1	0	0	0	0	0	8	0	0	0	1.6	1.000	OF-3, 1B-2
1978	HOU	N 104	.231	.269	186	43	5	1	0	0.0	15	12	39	32	2	16	2	328	16	4	26	3.3	.989	1B-66, OF-29
1979		13	.400	.600	15	6	0	0	1	6.7	4	2	0	3	0	10	5	8	0	0	1	0.6	1.000	1B-4
1980		90	.256	.359	78	20	6	1	0	0.0	12	3	10	10	1	24	4	187	16	1	23	2.3	.995	1B-59, OF-5
1981	2 teams	HOU N (6G — .167)		SF N (63G — .255)																				
"	total	69	.252	.391	151	38	9	0	4	2.6	17	14	19	18	2	23	4	255	25	3	21	4.1	.989	1B-34, OF-15
1982	SF	N 100	.273	.413	121	33	3	1	4	3.3	22	14	18	11	3	21	5	321	20	4	18	3.5	.988	1B-69, OF-6
1983		90	.286	.457	140	40	4	1	6	4.3	16	24	24	21	2	31	11	299	27	2	20	3.6	.994	1B-50, OF-6
1984	DET	A 120	.273	.417	271	74	8	5	7	2.6	42	44	33	40	3	21	6	658	75	8	63	6.2	.989	1B-114, OF-2
1985		69	.179	.257	140	25	2	0	3	2.1	8	7	14	15	0	24	6	306	25	3	25	4.8	.991	1B-44, DH-5, OF-1
1986		65	.231	.315	130	30	6	1	1	0.8	14	9	21	16	0	22	5	255	29	4	30	4.4	.986	1B-41, DH-8, OF-2
1987		91	.273	.453	172	47	7	3	6	3.5	25	22	30	23	0	21	4	357	29	3	33	4.3	.992	1B-65, DH-7, OF-7
1988		116	.294	.394	289	85	14	0	5	1.7	37	35	38	34	0	24	3	386	37	4	31	3.7	.991	1B-64, DH-30, OF-13
1989		137	.268	.361	385	103	13	1	7	1.8	38	37	44	44	1	18	1	912	85	7	88	7.3	.993	1B-123, DH-7, OF-1

Year	Team		Games	BA	SA	AB	H	2B	3B	HR	HR%	R	RBI	BB	SO	SB	PINCH HIT AB	PINCH HIT H	PO	A	E	DP	TC/G	FA	G by Pos

Dave Bergman *Continued*

1990			100	.278	.366	205	57	10	1	2	0.9	21	26	33	17	3	33	6	203	13	1	19	6.8	.995	DH-51, 1B-27, OF-5
15 yrs.			1176	.261	.372	2304	602	87	15	46	2.0	272	250	325	288	17	288	62	4493	398	45	399	4.2	.991	1B-762, DH-108, OF-101

LEAGUE CHAMPIONSHIP SERIES

1980	HOU	N	4	.333	1.000	3	1	0	1	0	0.0	0	2	0	0	0	0	0	8	2	1	0	2.8	.909	1B-4
1984	DET	A	2	1.000	1.000	1	1	0	0	0	0.0	1	0	0	0	1	0	0	5	0	0	0	2.5	1.000	1B-1
1987			4	.250	.250	4	1	0	0	0	0.0	0	2	0	1	0	2	1	6	0	0	0	1.5	1.000	DH-1, 1B-1
3 yrs.			10	.375	.625	8	3	0	1	0	0.0	1	4	0	1	1	2	1	19	2	1	0	2.2	.955	1B-6, DH-1

WORLD SERIES

1984	DET	A	5	.000	.000	5	0	0	0	0	0.0	0	0	0	1	0	0	0	22	4	0	0	5.2	1.000	1B-5

Geronimo Berroa

BERROA, GERONIMO EMILIANO
B. Mar. 18, 1965, Santo Domingo, Dominican Republic
BR TR 6′ 165 lbs.

1989	ATL	N	81	.265	.338	136	36	4	0	2	1.5	7	9	7	32	0	47	11	67	1	2	0	0.9	.971	OF-34
1990			7	.000	.000	4	0	0	0	0	0.0	0	0	1	1	0	3	0	1	0	0	0	0.3	1.000	OF-3
2 yrs.			88	.257	.329	140	36	4	0	2	1.4	7	9	8	33	0	50	11	68	1	2	0	0.8	.972	OF-37

Sean Berry

BERRY, SEAN ROBERT
B. Mar. 22, 1966, Santa Monica, Calif.
BR TR 5′ 11″ 200 lbs.

1990	KC	A	8	.217	.348	23	5	1	1	0	0.0	2	4	2	5	0	0	0	7	10	1	2	2.3	.944	3B-8

Damon Berryhill

BERRYHILL, DAMON SCOTT
B. Dec. 3, 1963, South Laguna, Calif.
BR TR 6′ 205 lbs.

1987	CHI	N	12	.179	.214	28	5	1	0	0	0.0	2	1	3	5	0	1	0	37	3	4	0	3.7	.909	C-11
1988			95	.259	.395	309	80	19	1	7	2.3	19	38	17	56	1	6	1	448	54	9	5	5.4	.982	C-90
1989			91	.257	.341	334	86	13	0	5	1.5	37	41	16	54	1	6	2	473	41	4	4	5.7	.992	C-89
1990			17	.189	.321	53	10	4	0	1	1.8	6	9	5	14	0	1	0	87	3	2	0	6.1	.978	C-15
4 yrs.			215	.250	.358	724	181	37	1	13	1.8	64	89	41	129	2	14	3	1045	101	19	9	5.4	.984	C-205

Dante Bichette

BICHETTE, ALPHONSE DANTE
B. Nov. 18, 1963, West Palm Beach, Fla.
BR TR 6′ 3″ 215 lbs.

	Games	BA	SA	AB	H	2B	3B	HR	HR%	R	RBI	BB	SO	SB
April	19	.280	.453	75	21	4	0	3	4.0	6	10	3	12	3
May	26	.283	.457	92	26	7	0	3	3.3	12	15	4	17	0
June	18	.130	.259	54	7	1	0	2	3.7	5	6	2	18	0
July	18	.212	.455	66	14	1	0	5	7.6	9	14	5	18	1
Aug	16	.371	.514	35	13	0	1	1	2.9	5	6	2	7	0
Sept/Oct	12	.296	.481	27	8	2	0	1	3.7	3	2	0	7	1
Day	24	.160	.333	81	13	2	0	4	4.9	7	9	6	24	1
Night	85	.284	.463	268	76	13	1	11	4.1	33	44	10	55	4
vs. Left		.274	.445	146	40	8	1	5	3.4	14	21	7	30	0
vs. Right		.241	.424	203	49	7	0	10	4.9	26	32	9	49	5
On Grass	91	.262	.446	298	78	14	1	13	4.4	37	44	12	66	5
On Turf	18	.216	.353	51	11	1	0	2	3.9	3	9	4	13	0
Home	50	.258	.447	159	41	6	0	8	5.0	21	26	6	33	1
Road	59	.253	.421	190	48	9	1	7	3.7	19	27	10	46	4
Division Rivals														
vs. CHI	8	.308	.538	26	8	0	0	2	7.7	6	4	1	4	0
vs. KC	6	.000	.000	5	0	0	0	0	0.0	0	0	1	3	0
vs. MIN	10	.270	.405	37	10	2	0	1	2.7	6	5	1	6	1
vs. OAK	7	.350	.700	20	7	1	0	2	10.0	3	7	3	3	1
vs. SEA	9	.226	.419	31	7	0	0	2	6.5	2	6	4	6	0
vs. TEX	8	.154	.308	26	4	1	0	1	3.8	2	4	1	7	0
On 3B < 2 Out		.261	.391	23	6	0	0	1	4.3	1	16	1	4	

OUTFIELD

AL AVG — AVERAGE — .400 / .200 / .000

AL AVG — RBI — 100 / 50 / 0

AL AVG — HR — 50 / 25 / 0

AL AVG — SB — 60 / 30 / 0

Year	Team		Games	BA	SA	AB	H	2B	3B	HR	HR%	R	RBI	BB	SO	SB	PINCH HIT AB	H	PO	A	E	DP	TC/G	FA	G by Pos

Dante Bichette *Continued*

Year	Team		Games	BA	SA	AB	H	2B	3B	HR	HR%	R	RBI	BB	SO	SB	AB	H	PO	A	E	DP	TC/G	FA	G by Pos
1988	CAL	A	21	.261	.304	46	12	2	0	0	0.0	1	8	0	7	0	0	0	44	2	1	0	2.2	.979	OF-21
1989			48	.210	.326	138	29	7	0	3	2.2	13	15	6	24	3	9	0	95	6	1	2	2.1	.990	OF-40, DH-1
1990			109	.255	.433	349	89	15	1	15	4.2	40	53	16	79	5	8	2	183	12	7	5	1.9	.965	OF-105
3 yrs.			178	.244	.394	533	130	24	1	18	3.4	54	76	22	110	8	17	2	322	20	9	7	2.0	.974	OF-166, DH-1

Craig Biggio

BIGGIO, CRAIG ALAN
B. Dec. 14, 1965, Smithtown, N. Y.
BR TR 5′ 11″ 185 lbs.

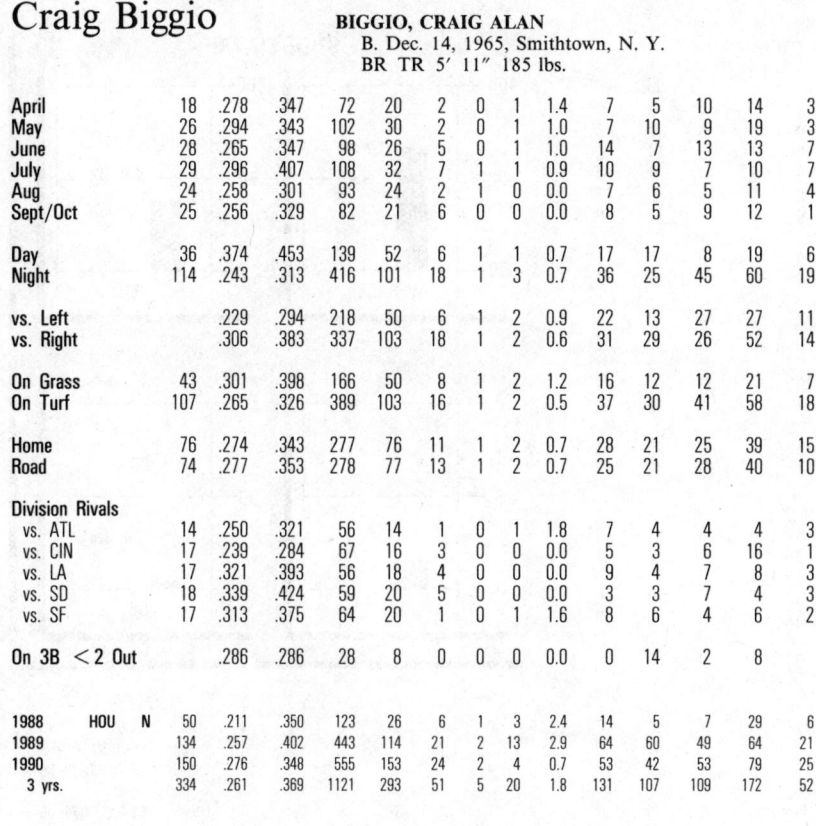

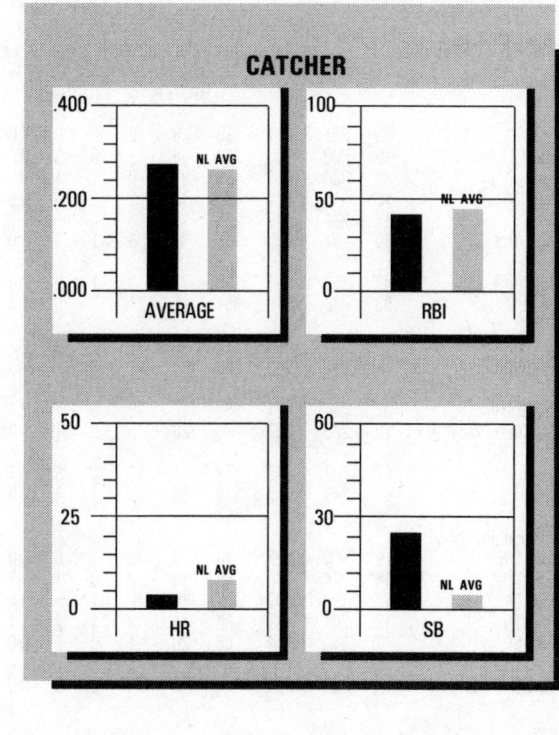

	Games	BA	SA	AB	H	2B	3B	HR	HR%	R	RBI	BB	SO	SB
April	18	.278	.347	72	20	2	0	1	1.4	7	5	10	14	3
May	26	.294	.343	102	30	2	0	1	1.0	7	10	9	19	3
June	28	.265	.347	98	26	5	0	1	1.0	14	7	13	13	7
July	29	.296	.407	108	32	7	1	1	0.9	10	9	7	10	7
Aug	24	.258	.301	93	24	2	1	0	0.0	7	6	5	11	4
Sept/Oct	25	.256	.329	82	21	6	0	0	0.0	8	5	9	12	1
Day	36	.374	.453	139	52	6	1	1	0.7	17	17	8	19	6
Night	114	.243	.313	416	101	18	1	3	0.7	36	25	45	60	19
vs. Left		.229	.294	218	50	6	1	2	0.9	22	13	27	27	11
vs. Right		.306	.383	337	103	18	1	2	0.6	31	29	26	52	14
On Grass	43	.301	.398	166	50	8	1	2	1.2	16	12	12	21	7
On Turf	107	.265	.326	389	103	16	1	2	0.5	37	30	41	58	18
Home	76	.274	.343	277	76	11	1	2	0.7	28	21	25	39	15
Road	74	.277	.353	278	77	13	1	2	0.7	25	21	28	40	10
Division Rivals														
vs. ATL	14	.250	.321	56	14	1	0	1	1.8	7	4	4	4	3
vs. CIN	17	.239	.284	67	16	3	0	0	0.0	5	3	6	16	1
vs. LA	17	.321	.393	56	18	4	0	0	0.0	9	4	7	8	3
vs. SD	18	.339	.424	59	20	5	0	0	0.0	3	3	7	4	3
vs. SF	17	.313	.375	64	20	1	0	1	1.6	8	6	4	6	2
On 3B < 2 Out		.286	.286	28	8	0	0	0	0.0	0	14	2	8	

Year	Team		Games	BA	SA	AB	H	2B	3B	HR	HR%	R	RBI	BB	SO	SB	AB	H	PO	A	E	DP	TC/G	FA	G by Pos
1988	HOU	N	50	.211	.350	123	26	6	1	3	2.4	14	5	7	29	6	0	0	292	28	3	0	6.5	.991	C-50
1989			134	.257	.402	443	114	21	2	13	2.9	64	60	49	64	21	4	3	742	56	9	6	6.0	.989	C-125, OF-5
1990			150	.276	.348	555	153	24	2	4	0.7	53	42	53	79	25	3	2	657	60	13	4	4.9	.982	C-113, OF-50
3 yrs.			334	.261	.369	1121	293	51	5	20	1.8	131	107	109	172	52	7	5	1691	144	25	10	5.6	.987	C-288, OF-55

Dann Bilardello

BILARDELLO, DANN JAMES
B. May 26, 1959, Santa Cruz, Calif.
BR TR 6′ 185 lbs.

Year	Team		Games	BA	SA	AB	H	2B	3B	HR	HR%	R	RBI	BB	SO	SB	AB	H	PO	A	E	DP	TC/G	FA	G by Pos
1983	CIN	N	109	.238	.389	298	71	18	0	9	3.0	27	38	15	49	2	5	0	494	72	5	4	5.2	.991	C-105
1984			68	.209	.280	182	38	7	0	2	1.1	16	10	19	34	0	5	2	323	34	3	3	5.3	.992	C-68
1985			42	.167	.196	102	17	0	0	1	1.0	6	9	4	15	0	1	0	198	20	3	1	5.3	.986	C-42
1986	MON	N	79	.194	.283	191	37	5	0	4	2.1	12	17	14	32	1	2	1	391	38	8	3	5.5	.982	C-77
1989	PIT	N	33	.225	.375	80	18	6	0	2	2.5	11	8	2	18	1	0	0	150	14	5	1	5.1	.970	C-33
1990			19	.054	.054	37	2	0	0	0	0.0	1	3	4	10	0	0	0	69	9	0	0	4.1	1.000	C-19
6 yrs.			350	.206	.307	890	183	36	0	18	2.0	73	85	58	158	4	13	3	1625	187	24	12	5.2	.987	C-344

Lance Blankenship

BLANKENSHIP, LANCE ROBERT
B. Dec. 6, 1963, Portland, Ore.
BR TR 6′ 190 lbs.

Year	Team		Games	BA	SA	AB	H	2B	3B	HR	HR%	R	RBI	BB	SO	SB	AB	H	PO	A	E	DP	TC/G	FA	G by Pos
1988	OAK	A	10	.000	.000	3	0	0	0	0	0.0	1	0	0	1	0	2	0	1	1	0	0	0.2	1.000	2B-4
1989			58	.232	.312	125	29	5	1	1	0.8	22	4	8	31	5	4	0	69	49	1	11	2.1	.992	OF-25, 2B-24, DH-10
1990			86	.191	.213	136	26	3	0	0	0.0	18	10	20	23	3	12	2	66	69	5	9	1.9	.964	3B-28, OF-28, 2B-20, DH-6, 1B-1
3 yrs.			154	.208	.258	264	55	8	1	1	0.4	41	14	28	55	8	18	2	136	119	6	20	1.7	.977	OF-53, 2B-48, 3B-28, DH-16, 1B-1

LEAGUE CHAMPIONSHIP SERIES

Year	Team		Games	BA	SA	AB	H	2B	3B	HR	HR%	R	RBI	BB	SO	SB	AB	H	PO	A	E	DP	TC/G	FA	G by Pos
1989	OAK	A	1	—	—	0	0	0	0	0	—	0	0	0	0	0	0	0	1	0	0	0	1.0	1.000	2B-1
1990			3	.000	.000	0	0	0	0	0	0.0	1	0	0	0	1	0	0	0	0	0	0	0.0	.900	DH-3
2 yrs.			4	.000	.000	0	0	0	0	0	—	1	0	0	0	1	0	0	1	0	0	0	0.3	.000	DH-3, 2B-1

Year	Team	Games	BA	SA	AB	H	2B	3B	HR	HR%	R	RBI	BB	SO	SB	PINCH HIT AB	PINCH HIT H	PO	A	E	DP	TC/G	FA	G by Pos

Lance Blankenship *Continued*

WORLD SERIES

Year	Team	Games	BA	SA	AB	H	2B	3B	HR	HR%	R	RBI	BB	SO	SB	PINCH HIT AB	PINCH HIT H	PO	A	E	DP	TC/G	FA	G by Pos
1989	OAK A	1	.500	.500	2	1	0	0	0	0.0	1	0	0	0	0	1	1	1	0	0	0	1.0	1.000	2B-1
1990		1	.000	.000	1	0	0	0	0	0.0	0	0	0	1	0	1	0	0	0	0	0	0.0	1.000	
2 yrs.		2	.333	.333	3	1	0	0	0	0.0	1	0	0	1	0	2	1	1	0	0	0	0.5	.000	2B-1

Jeff Blauser

BLAUSER, JEFFREY SCOTT
B. Nov. 8, 1965, Los Gatos, Calif.
BR TR 6′ 170 lbs.

	Games	BA	SA	AB	H	2B	3B	HR	HR%	R	RBI	BB	SO	SB	PINCH HIT AB	PINCH HIT H	PO	A	E	DP	TC/G	FA	G by Pos
April	12	.211	.211	38	8	0	0	0	0.0	1	0	4	8	0									
May	10	.300	.700	30	9	3	0	3	10.0	6	6	5	12	0									
June	27	.320	.454	97	31	8	1	1	1.0	16	11	6	14	0									
July	19	.210	.274	62	13	2	1	0	0.0	6	5	8	11	2									
Aug	17	.224	.328	58	13	3	0	1	1.7	8	5	5	8	1									
Sept/Oct	30	.297	.485	101	30	8	1	3	3.0	9	12	7	17	0									
Day	27	.259	.388	85	22	3	1	2	2.4	8	9	9	19	1									
Night	88	.272	.415	301	82	21	2	6	2.0	38	30	26	51	2									
vs. Left		.294	.463	136	40	12	1	3	2.2	23	17	16	20	1									
vs. Right		.256	.380	250	64	12	2	5	2.0	23	22	19	50	2									
On Grass	87	.264	.424	288	76	19	3	7	2.4	39	36	32	51	2									
On Turf	28	.286	.367	98	28	5	0	1	1.0	7	3	3	19	1									
Home	52	.297	.442	172	51	12	2	3	1.7	25	21	19	25	1									
Road	63	.248	.383	214	53	12	1	5	2.3	21	18	16	45	2									
Division Rivals																							
vs. CIN	18	.400	.557	70	28	9	1	0	0.0	5	6	2	11	0									
vs. HOU	14	.244	.378	45	11	3	0	1	2.2	3	3	1	6	1									
vs. LA	17	.190	.362	58	11	2	1	2	3.4	7	6	3	11	0									
vs. SD	18	.241	.431	58	14	3	1	2	3.4	9	12	7	13	0									
vs. SF	17	.345	.414	58	20	4	0	0	0.0	10	4	8	6	0									
On 3B < 2 Out		.250	.250	8	2	0	0	0	0.0	0	5	2	2										

Year	Team	Games	BA	SA	AB	H	2B	3B	HR	HR%	R	RBI	BB	SO	SB	PINCH HIT AB	PINCH HIT H	PO	A	E	DP	TC/G	FA	G by Pos
1987	ATL N	51	.242	.352	165	40	6	3	2	1.2	11	15	18	34	7	1	0	65	166	9	28	4.7	.963	SS-50
1988		18	.239	.403	67	16	3	1	2	3.0	7	7	2	11	0	1	0	35	59	4	8	5.4	.959	2B-9, SS-8
1989		142	.270	.410	456	123	24	2	12	2.6	63	46	38	101	5	9	4	137	254	21	28	2.9	.949	3B-78, 2B-39, SS-30, OF-2
1990		115	.269	.409	386	104	24	3	8	2.0	46	39	35	70	3	4	2	169	288	16	54	4.2	.966	SS-93, 2B-14, 3B-9, OF-1
4 yrs.		326	.264	.400	1074	283	57	9	24	2.2	127	107	93	216	15	15	6	406	767	50	118	3.8	.959	SS-181, 3B-87, 2B-62, OF-3

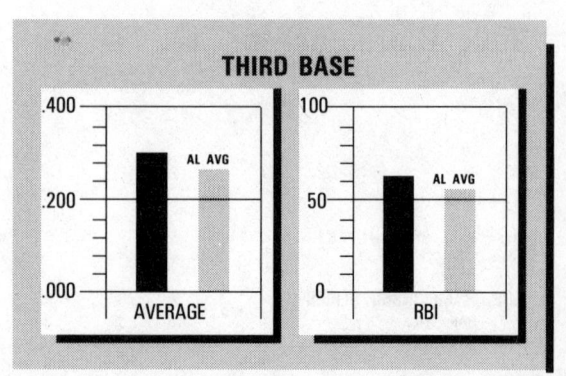

SHORTSTOP — AVERAGE (NL AVG), RBI (NL AVG), HR (NL AVG), SB (NL AVG)

Mike Blowers

BLOWERS, MICHAEL ROY
B. Apr. 24, 1965, Wurzburg, West Germany
BR TR 6′ 2″ 190 lbs.

Year	Team	Games	BA	SA	AB	H	2B	3B	HR	HR%	R	RBI	BB	SO	SB	PINCH HIT AB	PINCH HIT H	PO	A	E	DP	TC/G	FA	G by Pos
1989	NY A	13	.263	.263	38	10	0	0	0	0.0	2	3	3	13	0	1	0	9	14	4	3	2.1	.852	3B-13
1990		48	.188	.319	144	27	4	0	5	3.4	16	21	12	50	1	3	0	26	63	10	4	2.2	.899	3B-45, DH-2
2 yrs.		61	.203	.308	182	37	4	0	5	2.7	18	24	15	63	1	4	0	35	77	14	7	2.1	.889	3B-58, DH-2

Wade Boggs

BOGGS, WADE ANTHONY
B. June 15, 1958, Omaha, Neb.
BL TR 6′ 2″ 190 lbs.

	Games	BA	SA	AB	H	2B	3B	HR	HR%	R	RBI	BB	SO	SB
April	19	.333	.458	72	24	6	0	1	1.4	14	12	18	7	0
May	24	.240	.354	96	23	6	1	1	1.0	11	5	16	13	0
June	27	.320	.505	103	33	8	1	3	2.9	17	12	18	9	0
July	29	.311	.418	122	38	9	2	0	0.0	15	12	9	12	0
Aug	27	.333	.385	117	39	6	0	0	0.0	16	11	12	14	0
Sept/Oct	29	.275	.404	109	30	9	1	1	0.9	16	11	14	13	0
Day	50	.319	.430	207	66	14	0	3	1.4	39	22	24	27	0
Night	105	.294	.413	412	121	30	5	3	0.7	50	41	63	41	0
vs. Left		.274	.365	230	63	14	2	1	0.4	29	30	21	39	0
vs. Right		.319	.450	389	124	30	3	5	1.3	60	33	66	29	0

THIRD BASE — AVERAGE (AL AVG), RBI (AL AVG)

Year	Team		Games	BA	SA	AB	H	2B	3B	HR	HR%	R	RBI	BB	SO	SB	PINCH HIT AB	H	PO	A	E	DP	TC/G	FA	G by Pos

Wade Boggs *Continued*

On Grass			133	.309	.442	530	164	42	5	6	1.1	79	62	75	63	0									
On Turf			22	.258	.281	89	23	2	0	0	0.0	10	1	12	5	0									
Home			80	.359	.492	309	111	30	1	3	1.0	51	32	52	42	0									
Road			75	.245	.345	310	76	14	4	3	1.0	38	31	35	26	0									
Division Rivals																									
vs. BAL			12	.360	.520	50	18	5	0	1	2.0	7	6	4	4	0									
vs. CLE			12	.283	.391	46	13	2	0	1	2.2	8	4	10	5	0									
vs. DET			12	.340	.460	50	17	6	0	0	0.0	10	9	5	4	0									
vs. MIL			13	.283	.396	53	15	4	1	0	0.0	4	5	5	5	0									
vs. NY			12	.267	.422	45	12	3	2	0	0.0	10	2	8	8	0									
vs. TOR			13	.300	.460	50	15	2	0	2	4.0	8	7	6	3	0									
On 3B < 2 Out				.440	.760	25	11	3	1	1	4.0	2	24	4	2										
1982	BOS	A	104	.349	.441	338	118	14	1	5	1.5	51	44	35	21	1	13	4	489	168	8	51	6.4	.988	1B-49, 3B-44, DH-3, OF-1
1983			153	**.361**	.486	582	210	44	7	5	0.9	100	74	92	36	3	0	0	118	368	27	40	3.4	.947	3B-153
1984			158	.325	.416	625	203	31	4	6	1.0	109	55	89	44	3	1	0	141	330	20	30	3.1	.959	3B-155, DH-2
1985			161	**.368**	.478	653	**240**	42	3	8	1.2	107	78	96	61	2	0	0	134	335	17	30	3.0	.965	3B-161
1986			149	**.357**	.486	580	207	47	2	8	1.4	107	71	**105**	44	0	0	0	121	267	19	30	2.7	.953	3B-149
1987			147	**.363**	.588	551	200	40	6	24	4.4	108	89	105	48	1	1	0	112	277	14	37	2.7	.965	3B-145, DH-1, 1B-1
1988			155	**.366**	.490	584	214	**45**	6	5	0.9	**128**	58	**125**	34	2	1	1	122	250	11	17	2.5	.971	3B-151, DH-3
1989			156	.330	.449	621	205	**51**	7	3	0.5	**113**	54	107	51	2	1	0	123	264	17	29	2.6	.958	3B-152, DH-3
1990			155	.302	.418	619	187	44	5	6	0.9	89	63	87	68	0	0	0	108	241	20	18	2.4	.946	3B-152, DH-3
9 yrs.			1338	.346 4th	.472	5153	1784	358	41	70	1.4	912	586	841	407	14	17	5	1468	2500	153	282	3.1	.963	3B-1262, 1B-50, DH-15, OF-1

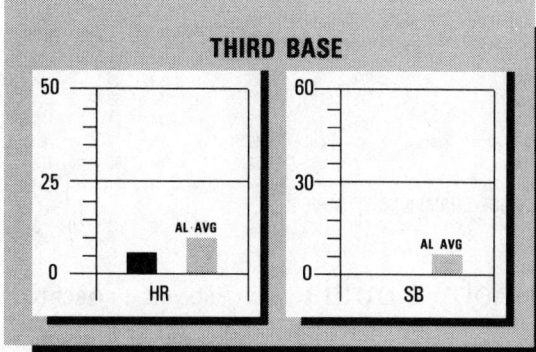

THIRD BASE

LEAGUE CHAMPIONSHIP SERIES

Year	Team		Games	BA	SA	AB	H	2B	3B	HR	HR%	R	RBI	BB	SO	SB	PINCH HIT AB	H	PO	A	E	DP	TC/G	FA	G by Pos
1986	BOS	A	7	.233	.333	30	7	1	1	0	0.0	3	2	4	1	0	0	0	7	14	2	1	3.3	.913	3B-7
1988			4	.385	.385	13	5	0	0	0	0.0	2	3	3	4	0	0	0	6	6	0	1	3.0	1.000	3B-4
1990			4	.438	.688	16	7	1	0	1	6.2	1	1	0	3	0	0	0	6	10	0	2	4.0	1.000	3B-4
3 yrs.			15	.322	.441	59	19	2	1	1	1.7	6	6	7	8	0	0	0	19	30	2	4	3.4	.961	3B-15

WORLD SERIES

Year	Team		Games	BA	SA	AB	H	2B	3B	HR	HR%	R	RBI	BB	SO	SB	PINCH HIT AB	H	PO	A	E	DP	TC/G	FA	G by Pos
1986	BOS	A	7	.290	.387	31	9	3	0	0	0.0	3	3	3	2	0	0	0	4	15	0	1	2.7	1.000	3B-7

Barry Bonds

BONDS, BARRY LAMAR
Son of Bobby Bonds.
B. July 24, 1964, Riverside, Calif.
BL TL 6' 1" 185 lbs.

			Games	BA	SA	AB	H	2B	3B	HR	HR%	R	RBI	BB	SO	SB
April			18	.317	.617	60	19	4	1	4	6.7	14	13	8	10	6
May			23	.307	.614	88	27	7	1	6	6.8	19	24	14	18	8
June			24	.369	.607	84	31	9	1	3	3.6	17	16	11	10	7
July			26	.326	.547	86	28	4	0	5	5.8	18	22	22	13	14
Aug			30	.248	.505	101	25	5	0	7	6.9	21	22	20	17	8
Sept/Oct			30	.260	.530	100	26	3	0	8	8.0	15	17	18	15	9
Day			43	.283	.601	138	39	8	0	12	8.7	36	30	31	17	15
Night			108	.307	.551	381	117	24	3	21	5.5	68	84	62	66	37
vs. Left				.304	.592	240	73	14	2	17	7.1	46	58	31	41	16
vs. Right				.297	.541	279	83	18	1	16	5.7	58	56	62	42	36
On Grass			39	.349	.644	146	51	13	0	10	6.8	29	40	21	22	12
On Turf			112	.282	.534	373	105	19	3	23	6.2	75	74	72	61	40
Home			76	.276	.515	239	66	9	0	14	5.9	50	46	50	43	26
Road			75	.321	.607	280	90	23	0	19	6.8	54	68	43	40	26
Division Rivals																
vs. CHI			17	.200	.473	55	11	1	1	4	7.3	9	12	10	11	4
vs. MON			18	.344	.672	64	22	3	0	6	9.4	15	10	12	10	11
vs. NY			16	.362	.517	58	21	6	0	1	1.7	9	13	5	6	5
vs. PHI			17	.212	.462	52	11	4	0	3	5.8	10	10	7	7	3
vs. STL			16	.268	.536	56	15	1	1	4	7.1	10	12	10	9	3
On 3B < 2 Out				.481	.593	27	13	3	0	0	0.0	0	25	5	3	

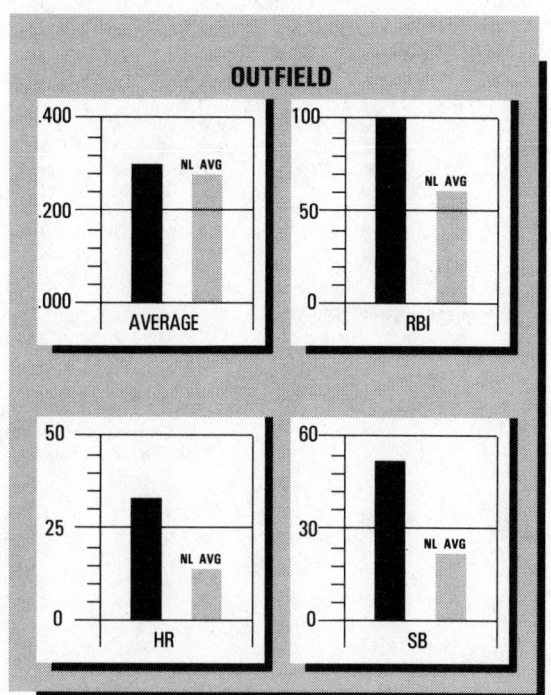

OUTFIELD

Year	Team		Games	BA	SA	AB	H	2B	3B	HR	HR%	R	RBI	BB	SO	SB	PINCH HIT AB	PINCH HIT H	PO	A	E	DP	TC/G	FA	G by Pos

Barry Bonds *Continued*

Year	Team		Games	BA	SA	AB	H	2B	3B	HR	HR%	R	RBI	BB	SO	SB	AB	H	PO	A	E	DP	TC/G	FA	G by Pos
1986	PIT	N	113	.223	.416	413	92	26	3	16	3.9	72	48	65	102	36	3	1	280	9	5	2	2.6	.983	OF-110
1987			150	.261	.492	551	144	34	9	25	4.5	99	59	54	88	32	7	1	330	15	5	3	2.3	.986	OF-145
1988			144	.283	.491	538	152	30	5	24	4.5	97	58	72	82	17	11	2	292	5	6	0	2.1	.980	OF-136
1989			159	.248	.426	580	144	34	6	19	3.3	96	58	93	93	32	8	3	365	14	6	1	2.4	.984	OF-156
1990			151	.301	**.565**	519	156	32	3	33	6.3	104	114	93	83	52	2	0	338	14	6	2	2.4	.983	OF-150
5 yrs.			717	.265	.479	2601	688	156	26	117	4.5	468	337	377	448	169	31	7	1605	57	28	8	2.4	.983	OF-697

LEAGUE CHAMPIONSHIP SERIES

Year	Team		Games	BA	SA	AB	H	2B	3B	HR	HR%	R	RBI	BB	SO	SB	AB	H	PO	A	E	DP	TC/G	FA	G by Pos
1990	PIT	N	6	.167	.167	18	3	0	0	0	0.0	4	1	6	5	2	0	0	13	0	0	0	2.2	1.000	OF-6

Bobby Bonilla

BONILLA, ROBERTO MARTIN ANTONIO
B. Feb. 23, 1963, New York, N. Y.
BB TR 6' 3" 210 lbs.

OUTFIELD — AVERAGE, RBI, HR, SB (bar charts comparing player to NL AVG)

		Games	BA	SA	AB	H	2B	3B	HR	HR%	R	RBI	BB	SO	SB
April		20	.279	.570	86	24	4	0	7	8.1	17	21	2	16	0
May		26	.320	.621	103	33	8	4	5	4.9	21	19	7	16	1
June		26	.211	.421	95	20	5	0	5	5.3	19	14	6	17	1
July		26	.240	.433	104	25	8	0	4	3.8	18	14	11	19	0
Aug		30	.357	.688	112	40	6	2	9	8.0	24	23	15	15	2
Sept/Oct		32	.264	.392	125	33	8	1	2	1.6	13	29	4	20	0
Day		44	.289	.584	173	50	13	1	12	6.9	33	37	9	37	1
Night		116	.277	.493	452	125	26	6	20	4.4	79	83	36	66	3
vs. Left			.261	.493	280	73	19	2	14	5.0	48	48	20	32	3
vs. Right			.296	.539	345	102	20	5	18	5.2	64	72	25	71	1
On Grass		41	.333	.690	171	57	13	3	14	8.2	45	44	11	32	1
On Turf		119	.260	.454	454	118	26	4	18	4.0	67	76	34	71	3
Home		81	.261	.461	310	81	19	2	13	4.2	47	52	17	44	3
Road		79	.298	.575	315	94	20	5	19	6.0	65	68	28	59	1
Division Rivals															
vs. CHI		18	.338	.690	71	24	7	0	6	8.5	17	25	3	9	0
vs. MON		18	.097	.139	72	7	3	0	0	0.0	2	3	2	27	0
vs. NY		18	.296	.479	71	21	5	1	2	2.8	16	10	4	11	1
vs. PHI		17	.292	.508	65	19	3	1	3	4.6	10	13	5	8	0
vs. STL		18	.246	.449	69	17	5	0	3	4.3	11	13	3	6	0
On 3B < 2 Out			.333	.619	42	14	3	0	3	7.1	3	44	1	10	

Year	Team		Games	BA	SA	AB	H	2B	3B	HR	HR%	R	RBI	BB	SO	SB	AB	H	PO	A	E	DP	TC/G	FA	G by Pos
1986	2 teams		CHI A (75G — .269)			PIT N (63G — .240)																			
"	total		138	.256	.333	426	109	16	4	3	0.7	55	43	62	88	8	19	2	451	38	5	29	3.6	.990	OF-94, 1B-34, 3B-4
1987	PIT	N	141	.300	.481	466	140	33	3	15	3.2	58	77	39	64	3	17	6	142	139	16	13	2.1	.946	3B-89, OF-46, 1B-6
1988			159	.274	.476	584	160	32	7	24	4.1	87	100	85	82	3	0	0	121	336	32	17	3.1	.935	3B-159
1989			163	.281	.490	616	173	37	10	24	3.9	96	86	76	93	8	1	0	190	334	35	37	3.4	.937	3B-156, 1B-8, OF-1
1990			160	.280	.518	625	175	39	7	32	5.1	112	120	45	103	4	1	0	315	35	15	2	2.3	.959	OF-149, 3B-14, 1B-3
5 yrs.			761	.279	.467	2717	757	157	31	98	3.6	408	426	307	430	26	38	8	1219	882	103	98	2.9	.953	3B-422, OF-290, 1B-51

LEAGUE CHAMPIONSHIP SERIES

Year	Team		Games	BA	SA	AB	H	2B	3B	HR	HR%	R	RBI	BB	SO	SB	AB	H	PO	A	E	DP	TC/G	FA	G by Pos
1990	PIT	N	6	.190	.238	21	4	1	0	0	0.0	0	1	3	1	0	0	0	4	5	1	1	1.7	.900	OF-5, 3B-3

Rod Booker

BOOKER, RODERICK STEWART
B. Sept. 4, 1958, Los Angeles, Calif.
BL TR 6' 175 lbs.

Year	Team		Games	BA	SA	AB	H	2B	3B	HR	HR%	R	RBI	BB	SO	SB	AB	H	PO	A	E	DP	TC/G	FA	G by Pos
1987	STL	N	44	.277	.340	47	13	1	1	0	0.0	9	8	7	7	2	18	4	25	28	2	5	1.3	.964	2B-18, 3B-4, SS-1
1988			18	.343	.429	35	12	3	0	0	0.0	6	3	4	3	2	6	2	3	15	2	0	1.1	.900	3B-13, 2B-1
1989			10	.250	.250	8	2	0	0	0	0.0	1	0	0	1	0	2	0	4	9	2	2	1.5	.867	2B-5, 3B-1
1990	PHI	N	73	.221	.290	131	29	5	2	0	0.0	19	10	15	26	3	13	2	57	74	4	15	2.4	.970	SS-27, 2B-23, 3B-10
4 yrs.			145	.253	.321	221	56	9	3	0	0.0	35	21	26	37	7	39	8	89	126	10	22	1.6	.956	2B-47, 3B-28, SS-28

Year	Team		Games	BA	SA	AB	H	2B	3B	HR	HR%	R	RBI	BB	SO	SB	PINCH HIT AB	H	PO	A	E	DP	TC/G	FA	G by Pos

Bob Boone

BOONE, ROBERT RAYMOND
Son of Ray Boone.
B. Nov. 19, 1947, San Diego, Calif.
BR TR 6' 2 1/2" 195 lbs.

Year	Team	Lg	Games	BA	SA	AB	H	2B	3B	HR	HR%	R	RBI	BB	SO	SB	PH AB	PH H	PO	A	E	DP	TC/G	FA	G by Pos
1972	PHI	N	16	.275	.353	51	14	1	0	1	2.0	4	4	5	7	1	3	0	66	7	5	1	4.9	.936	C-14
1973			145	.261	.365	521	136	20	2	10	1.9	42	61	41	36	3	0	0	868	89	10	16	6.7	.990	C-145
1974			146	.242	.322	488	118	24	3	3	0.6	41	52	35	29	3	1	1	825	77	22	7	6.3	.976	C-146
1975			97	.246	.329	289	71	14	2	2	0.7	28	20	32	14	1	6	1	459	48	5	7	5.3	.990	C-92, 3B-3
1976			121	.271	.366	361	98	18	2	4	1.1	40	54	45	44	2	12	4	587	39	6	5	5.2	.991	C-108, 1B-4
1977			132	.284	.436	440	125	26	4	11	2.5	55	66	42	54	5	1	0	654	83	8	9	5.6	.989	C-131, 3B-2
1978			132	.283	.425	435	123	18	4	12	2.8	48	62	46	37	2	5	1	650	55	8	7	5.4	.989	C-129, 1B-3, OF-1
1979			119	.286	.422	398	114	21	3	9	2.3	38	58	49	33	1	1	0	527	66	8	8	5.1	.987	C-117, 3B-2
1980			141	.229	.338	480	110	23	1	9	1.9	34	55	48	41	3	4	1	741	88	18	7	6.0	.979	C-138
1981			76	.211	.295	227	48	7	0	4	1.8	19	24	22	16	2	4	0	365	32	6	1	5.3	.985	C-75
1982	CAL	A	143	.256	.337	472	121	17	0	7	1.5	42	58	39	34	0	0	0	650	87	8	8	5.2	.989	C-143
1983			142	.256	.353	468	120	18	0	9	1.9	46	52	24	42	4	0	0	606	83	14	12	5.0	.980	C-142
1984			139	.202	.262	450	91	16	1	3	0.7	33	32	25	45	3	2	2	660	71	12	10	5.3	.984	C-137
1985			150	.248	.317	460	114	17	0	5	1.1	37	55	37	35	1	2	2	670	71	10	15	5.0	.987	C-147
1986			144	.222	.305	442	98	12	2	7	1.6	48	49	43	30	1	0	0	812	84	11	16	6.3	.988	C-144
1987			128	.242	.311	389	94	18	0	3	0.8	42	33	35	36	0	1	1	684	56	13	11	5.9	.983	C-127, DH-1
1988			122	.295	.386	352	104	17	0	5	1.4	38	39	29	26	2	1	1	506	66	8	9	4.8	.986	C-121
1989	KC	A	131	.274	.323	405	111	13	2	1	0.2	33	43	49	37	3	1	0	752	64	7	6	6.3	.991	C-129
1990			40	.239	.265	117	28	3	0	0	0.0	11	9	17	12	1	0	0	243	19	4	0	6.7	.985	C-40
19 yrs.			2264	.254	.346	7245	1838	303	26	105	1.4	679	826	663	608	38	44	14	11325	1185	183	155	1.2	.932	C-2225, 1B-7, 3B-7, DH-1, OF-1

DIVISIONAL PLAYOFF SERIES

Year	Team	Lg	Games	BA	SA	AB	H	2B	3B	HR	HR%	R	RBI	BB	SO	SB	PH AB	PH H	PO	A	E	DP	TC/G	FA	G by Pos
1981	PHI	N	3	.000	.000	5	0	0	0	0	0.0	0	0	0	0	0	0	0	10	2	0	0	4.3	1.000	C-3

LEAGUE CHAMPIONSHIP SERIES

Year	Team	Lg	Games	BA	SA	AB	H	2B	3B	HR	HR%	R	RBI	BB	SO	SB	PH AB	PH H	PO	A	E	DP	TC/G	FA	G by Pos
1976	PHI	N	3	.286	.286	7	2	0	0	0	0.0	0	1	1	0	0	0	0	8	2	0	0	3.3	1.000	C-3
1977			4	.400	.400	10	4	0	0	0	0.0	1	0	0	0	0	0	0	18	2	0	1	5.0	1.000	C-4
1978			3	.182	.182	11	2	0	0	0	0.0	0	0	0	1	0	0	0	16	2	1	0	6.3	.947	C-3
1980			5	.222	.222	18	4	0	0	0	0.0	1	2	1	2	0	0	0	22	3	0	1	5.0	1.000	C-5
1982	CAL	A	5	.250	.438	16	4	0	0	1	6.3	3	4	0	2	0	0	0	30	3	0	0	6.6	1.000	C-5
1986			7	.455	.591	22	10	0	0	1	4.5	4	2	1	3	0	0	0	35	4	0	0	5.6	1.000	C-7
6 yrs.			27	.310	.381	84	26	0	0	2	2.4	9	9	3	8	0	0	0	129	16	1	2	5.4	.993	C-27

WORLD SERIES

Year	Team	Lg	Games	BA	SA	AB	H	2B	3B	HR	HR%	R	RBI	BB	SO	SB	PH AB	PH H	PO	A	E	DP	TC/G	FA	G by Pos
1980	PHI	N	6	.412	.529	17	7	2	0	0	0.0	3	4	4	0	0	0	0	49	3	0	0	8.7	1.000	C-6

Pat Borders

BORDERS, PATRICK LANCE
B. May 14, 1963, Columbus, Ohio
BR TR 6' 2" 190 lbs.

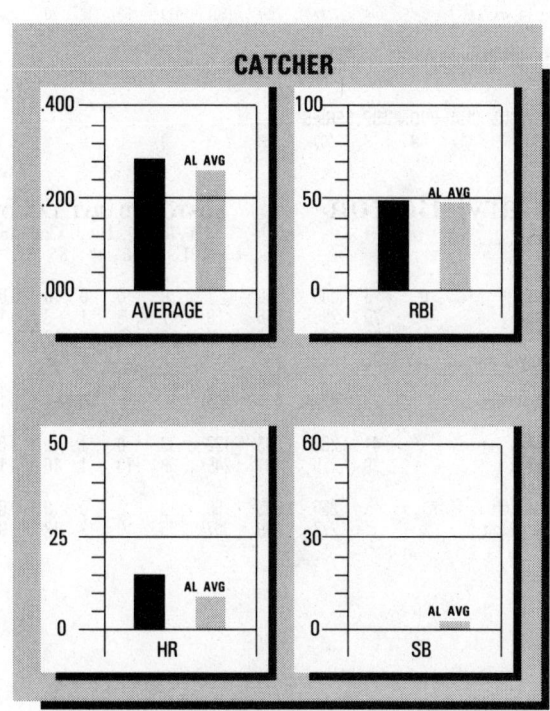

CATCHER

	Games	BA	SA	AB	H	2B	3B	HR	HR%	R	RBI	BB	SO	SB
April	14	.355	.710	31	11	2	0	3	9.7	4	4	1	5	0
May	24	.274	.500	84	23	7	0	4	4.8	8	10	3	17	0
June	19	.296	.574	54	16	4	1	3	5.6	6	13	2	4	0
July	20	.304	.500	56	17	5	0	2	3.6	6	9	3	9	0
Aug	25	.277	.415	65	18	3	0	2	3.1	8	8	6	9	0
Sept/Oct	23	.250	.393	56	14	3	1	1	1.8	4	5	3	13	0
Day	39	.307	.561	114	35	9	1	6	5.3	15	15	3	23	0
Night	86	.276	.466	232	64	15	1	9	3.9	21	34	15	34	0
vs. Left		.285	.554	186	53	16	2	10	5.4	22	27	15	29	0
vs. Right		.288	.431	160	46	8	0	5	3.1	14	22	3	28	0
On Grass	48	.297	.406	138	41	7	1	2	1.4	7	14	6	24	0
On Turf	77	.279	.558	208	58	17	1	13	6.3	29	35	12	33	0
Home	63	.274	.549	164	45	13	1	10	6.1	24	28	12	23	0
Road	62	.297	.451	182	54	11	1	5	2.7	12	21	6	34	0
Division Rivals														
vs. BAL	10	.423	.731	26	11	2	0	2	7.7	4	7	1	4	0
vs. BOS	9	.111	.167	18	2	1	0	0	0.0	1	2	1	2	0
vs. CLE	10	.323	.484	31	10	2	0	1	3.2	1	3	2	5	0
vs. DET	12	.353	.706	34	12	3	0	3	8.8	7	8	3	6	0
vs. MIL	8	.182	.455	22	4	1	1	1	4.5	2	4	2	3	0
vs. NY	12	.324	.471	34	11	3	1	0	0.0	4	3	2	5	0
On 3B < 2 Out		.267	.333	15	4	1	0	0	0.0	0	9	2	3	

Year	Team		Games	BA	SA	AB	H	2B	3B	HR	HR%	R	RBI	BB	SO	SB	PINCH HIT		PO	A	E	DP	TC/G	FA	G by Pos
																	AB	H							

Pat Borders *Continued*

Year	Team		Games	BA	SA	AB	H	2B	3B	HR	HR%	R	RBI	BB	SO	SB	AB	H	PO	A	E	DP	TC/G	FA	G by Pos
1988	TOR	A	56	.273	.448	154	42	6	3	5	3.2	15	21	3	24	0	15	5	205	19	7	0	4.1	.970	C-43, 2B-1, 3B-1
1989			94	.257	.349	241	62	11	1	3	1.2	22	29	11	45	2	20	5	261	27	6	1	3.1	.980	C-68, DH-18
1990			125	.286	.497	346	99	24	2	15	4.3	36	49	18	57	0	25	5	515	46	4	6	4.9	.993	C-115, DH-1
3 yrs.			275	.274	.439	741	203	41	6	23	3.1	73	99	32	126	2	60	15	981	92	17	7	4.0	.984	C-226, DH-19, 2B-1, 3B-1

LEAGUE CHAMPIONSHIP SERIES
| 1989 | TOR | A | 1 | 1.000 | 1.000 | 1 | 1 | 0 | 0 | 0 | 0.0 | 0 | 1 | 0 | 0 | 0 | 1 | 1 | 1 | 0 | 0 | 0 | 1.0 | 1.000 | C-1 |

Mike Bordick

BORDICK, MICHAEL TODD
B. July 21, 1965, Marquette, Mich.
BR TR 5' 11" 170 lbs.

Year	Team		Games	BA	SA	AB	H	2B	3B	HR	HR%	R	RBI	BB	SO	SB	AB	H	PO	A	E	DP	TC/G	FA	G by Pos
1990	OAK	A	25	.071	.071	14	1	0	0	0	0.0	0	0	1	4	0	4	1	9	8	0	0	0.7	1.000	3B-10, SS-9, 2B-7

WORLD SERIES
| 1990 | OAK | A | 3 | .000 | .000 | 0 | 0 | 0 | 0 | 0 | 0.0 | 0 | 0 | 0 | 0 | 0 | 0 | 0 | 0 | 2 | 0 | 0 | 0.7 | 1.000 | SS-3 |

Thad Bosley

BOSLEY, THADDIS
B. Sept. 17, 1956, Oceanside, Calif.
BL TL 6' 3" 175 lbs.

Year	Team		Games	BA	SA	AB	H	2B	3B	HR	HR%	R	RBI	BB	SO	SB	AB	H	PO	A	E	DP	TC/G	FA	G by Pos
1977	CAL	A	58	.297	.363	212	63	10	2	0	0.0	19	19	16	32	5	4	2	130	1	5	0	2.3	.963	OF-55
1978	CHI	A	66	.269	.329	219	59	5	1	2	0.9	25	13	13	32	12	1	0	155	3	4	0	2.5	.975	OF-64
1979			36	.312	.390	77	24	1	1	1	1.3	13	8	9	14	4	7	1	57	2	2	1	1.7	.967	OF-28, DH-1
1980			70	.224	.279	147	33	2	0	2	1.4	12	14	10	27	3	25	8	91	1	4	0	1.4	.958	OF-52
1981	MIL	A	42	.229	.248	105	24	2	0	0	0.0	11	3	6	13	2	4	0	55	1	2	0	1.4	.966	OF-37, DH-1
1982	SEA	A	22	.174	.196	46	8	1	0	0	0.0	3	2	4	8	3	3	0	12	1	0	0	0.6	1.000	OF-19
1983	CHI	N	43	.292	.458	72	21	4	1	2	2.8	12	12	10	12	1	18	4	27	1	0	1	0.7	1.000	OF-20
1984			55	.296	.418	98	29	2	2	2	2.0	17	14	13	22	5	23	6	39	2	1	0	0.8	.976	OF-33
1985			108	.328	.511	180	59	6	3	7	3.9	25	27	20	29	5	60	**20**	84	0	1	0	0.8	.988	OF-55
1986			87	.275	.350	120	33	4	1	1	0.8	15	9	18	24	3	51	16	31	0	1	0	0.4	.969	OF-41
1987	KC	A	80	.279	.357	140	39	6	1	1	0.7	13	16	9	26	0	**42**	**12**	28	0	1	0	0.4	.966	OF-28, DH-13
1988	2 teams			KC A (15G — .190)			CAL A (35G — .280)																			
"	total		50	.260	.313	96	25	5	0	0	0.0	10	9	8	18	1	10	3	59	0	2	0	1.2	.967	OF-32, DH-6
1989	TEX	A	37	.225	.350	40	9	2	0	1	2.5	5	9	3	11	2	28	7	12	1	0	1	0.4	1.000	OF-8, DH-5
1990			30	.138	.241	29	4	0	0	1	3.4	3	3	4	7	1	19	3	4	0	0	0	0.4	1.000	OF-9, DH-4
14 yrs.			784	.272	.357	1581	430	50	12	20	1.3	183	158	143	275	47	295	82	784	13	23	3	1.0	.972	OF-481, DH-30

DIVISIONAL PLAYOFF SERIES
| 1981 | MIL | A | 1 | — | — | 0 | 0 | 0 | 0 | 0 | — | 0 | 0 | 0 | 0 | 0 | 0 | 0 | 0 | 0 | 0 | 0 | 0.0 | — | DH-1 |

LEAGUE CHAMPIONSHIP SERIES
| 1984 | CHI | N | 2 | .000 | .000 | 2 | 0 | 0 | 0 | 0 | 0.0 | 0 | 0 | 0 | 2 | 0 | 2 | 0 | 0 | 0 | 0 | 0 | 0.0 | — | |

Daryl Boston

BOSTON, DARYL LAMONT
B. Jan. 4, 1963, Cincinnati, Ohio
BL TL 6' 3" 185 lbs.

	Games	BA	SA	AB	H	2B	3B	HR	HR%	R	RBI	BB	SO	SB
April	5	.000	.000	1	0	0	0	0	0.0	0	0	0	0	1
May	20	.288	.576	59	17	6	1	3	5.1	11	9	5	4	3
June	23	.274	.425	73	20	5	0	2	2.7	16	10	8	13	3
July	22	.319	.486	72	23	4	1	2	2.6	13	8	2	13	3
Aug	27	.260	.344	96	25	5	0	1	1.0	13	6	4	11	5
Sept/Oct	23	.227	.424	66	15	1	0	4	6.1	12	12	9	9	4
Day	41	.262	.393	122	32	8	1	2	1.6	15	16	9	13	6
Night	79	.278	.461	245	68	13	1	10	4.1	50	29	19	37	13
vs. Left		.250	.283	60	15	2	0	0	0.0	5	8	7	11	1
vs. Right		.277	.469	307	85	19	2	12	3.9	60	37	21	39	18

OUTFIELD

Year	Team		Games	BA	SA	AB	H	2B	3B	HR	HR%	R	RBI	BB	SO	SB	PINCH HIT AB	H	PO	A	E	DP	TC/G	FA	G by Pos

Daryl Boston *Continued*

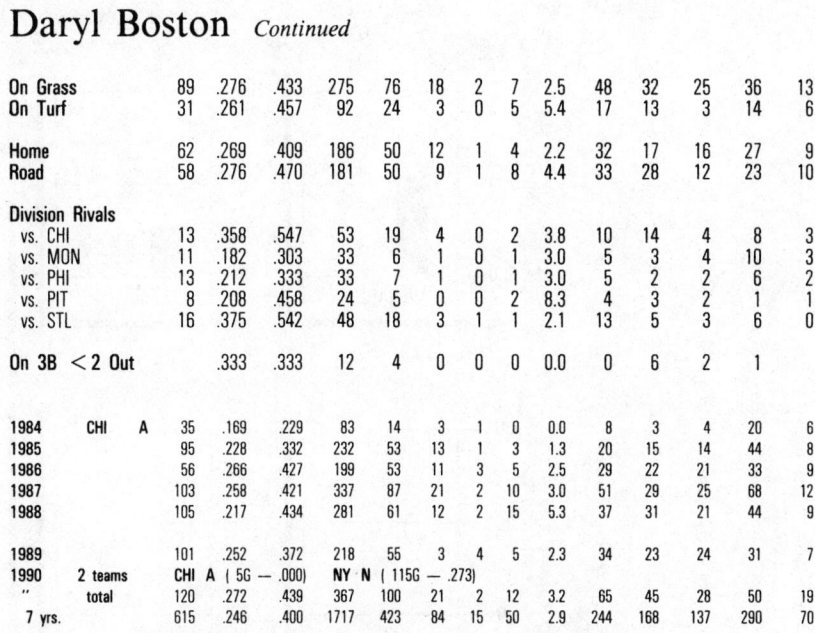
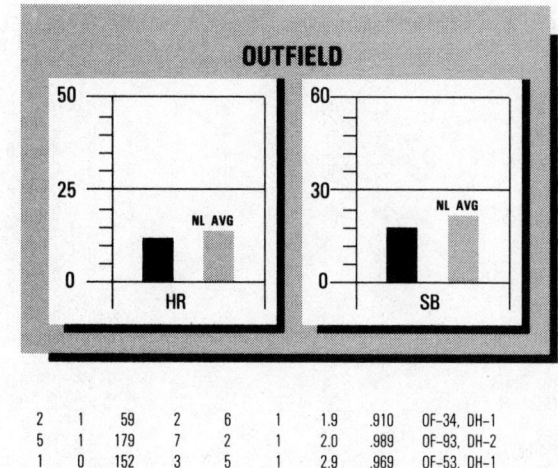

OUTFIELD

			Games	BA	SA	AB	H	2B	3B	HR	HR%	R	RBI	BB	SO	SB
On Grass			89	.276	.433	275	76	18	2	7	2.5	48	32	25	36	13
On Turf			31	.261	.457	92	24	3	0	5	5.4	17	13	3	14	6
Home			62	.269	.409	186	50	12	1	4	2.2	32	17	16	27	9
Road			58	.276	.470	181	50	9	1	8	4.4	33	28	12	23	10
Division Rivals																
vs. CHI			13	.358	.547	53	19	4	0	2	3.8	10	14	4	8	3
vs. MON			11	.182	.303	33	6	1	0	1	3.0	5	3	4	10	3
vs. PHI			13	.212	.333	33	7	1	0	1	3.0	5	2	2	6	2
vs. PIT			8	.208	.458	24	5	0	0	2	8.3	4	3	2	1	1
vs. STL			16	.375	.542	48	18	3	1	1	2.1	13	5	3	6	0
On 3B < 2 Out				.333	.333	12	4	0	0	0	0.0	0	6	2	1	

Year	Team		Games	BA	SA	AB	H	2B	3B	HR	HR%	R	RBI	BB	SO	SB	AB	H	PO	A	E	DP	TC/G	FA	G by Pos
1984	CHI	A	35	.169	.229	83	14	3	1	0	0.0	8	3	4	20	6	2	1	59	2	6	1	1.9	.910	OF-34, DH-1
1985			95	.228	.332	232	53	13	1	3	1.3	20	15	14	44	8	5	1	179	7	2	1	2.0	.989	OF-93, DH-2
1986			56	.266	.427	199	53	11	3	5	2.5	29	22	21	33	9	1	0	152	3	5	1	2.9	.969	OF-53, DH-1
1987			103	.258	.421	337	87	21	2	10	3.0	51	29	25	68	12	10	2	207	3	2	3	2.1	.991	OF-92, DH-5
1988			105	.217	.434	281	61	12	2	15	5.3	37	31	21	44	9	13	3	190	4	10	2	1.9	.951	OF-85, DH-5
1989			101	.252	.372	218	55	3	4	5	2.3	34	23	24	31	7	16	4	134	2	4	0	1.4	.971	OF-75, DH-9
1990	2 teams		CHI A (5G — .000)			NY N (115G — .273)																			
"	total		120	.272	.439	367	100	21	2	12	3.2	65	45	28	50	19	18	3	203	3	3	1	1.9	.986	OF-110, DH-3
7 yrs.			615	.246	.400	1717	423	84	15	50	2.9	244	168	137	290	70	65	14	1124	24	32	9	1.9	.973	OF-542, DH-26

Phil Bradley

BRADLEY, PHILIP POOLE
B. Mar. 11, 1959, Bloomington, Ind.
BR TR 6' 185 lbs.

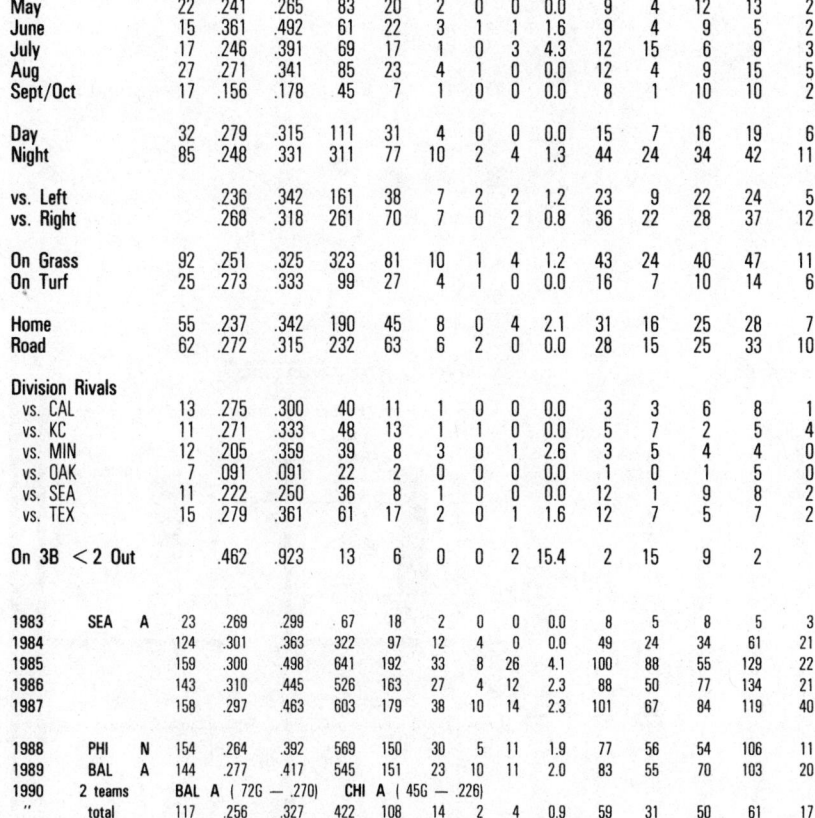
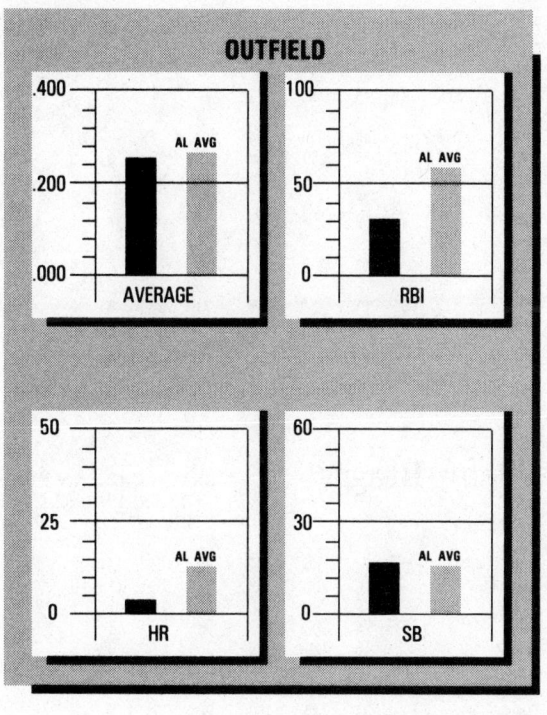

OUTFIELD

			Games	BA	SA	AB	H	2B	3B	HR	HR%	R	RBI	BB	SO	SB
April			19	.241	.278	79	19	3	0	0	0.0	9	3	4	9	3
May			22	.241	.265	83	20	2	0	0	0.0	9	4	12	13	2
June			15	.361	.492	61	22	3	1	1	1.6	9	4	9	5	2
July			17	.246	.391	69	17	1	0	3	4.3	12	15	6	9	3
Aug			27	.271	.341	85	23	4	1	0	0.0	12	4	9	15	5
Sept/Oct			17	.156	.178	45	7	1	0	0	0.0	8	1	10	10	2
Day			32	.279	.315	111	31	4	0	0	0.0	15	7	16	19	6
Night			85	.248	.331	311	77	10	2	4	1.3	44	24	34	42	11
vs. Left				.236	.342	161	38	7	2	2	1.2	23	9	22	24	5
vs. Right				.268	.318	261	70	7	0	2	0.8	36	22	28	37	12
On Grass			92	.251	.325	323	81	10	1	4	1.2	43	24	40	47	11
On Turf			25	.273	.333	99	27	4	1	0	0.0	16	7	10	14	6
Home			55	.237	.342	190	45	8	0	4	2.1	31	16	25	28	7
Road			62	.272	.315	232	63	6	2	0	0.0	28	15	25	33	10
Division Rivals																
vs. CAL			13	.275	.300	40	11	1	0	0	0.0	3	3	6	8	1
vs. KC			11	.271	.333	48	13	1	1	0	0.0	5	7	2	5	4
vs. MIN			12	.205	.359	39	8	3	0	1	2.6	3	5	4	4	0
vs. OAK			7	.091	.091	22	2	0	0	0	0.0	1	0	1	5	0
vs. SEA			11	.222	.250	36	8	1	0	0	0.0	12	1	9	8	2
vs. TEX			15	.279	.361	61	17	2	0	1	1.6	12	7	5	7	2
On 3B < 2 Out				.462	.923	13	6	0	0	2	15.4	2	15	9	2	

Year	Team		Games	BA	SA	AB	H	2B	3B	HR	HR%	R	RBI	BB	SO	SB	AB	H	PO	A	E	DP	TC/G	FA	G by Pos
1983	SEA	A	23	.269	.299	67	18	2	0	0	0.0	8	5	8	5	3	3	0	36	1	1	0	1.7	.974	OF-21, DH-1
1984			124	.301	.363	322	97	12	4	0	0.0	49	24	34	61	21	3	0	235	3	2	1	1.9	.992	OF-117, DH-3
1985			159	.300	.498	641	192	33	8	26	4.1	100	88	55	129	22	0	0	336	10	5	3	2.2	.986	OF-159
1986			143	.310	.445	526	163	27	4	12	2.3	88	50	77	134	21	2	0	250	11	1	0	1.8	.996	OF-140
1987			158	.297	.463	603	179	38	10	14	2.3	101	67	84	119	40	0	0	273	13	5	1	1.8	.983	OF-158
1988	PHI	N	154	.264	.392	569	150	30	5	11	1.9	77	56	54	106	11	2	0	298	14	3	2	2.0	.990	OF-153
1989	BAL	A	144	.277	.417	545	151	20	8	11	2.0	83	55	70	103	20	4	0	284	4	3	0	2.0	.990	OF-140, DH-2
1990	2 teams		BAL A (72G — .270)			CHI A (45G — .226)																			
"	total		117	.256	.327	422	108	14	2	4	0.9	59	31	50	61	17	6	1	219	4	4	0	2.1	.982	OF-108, DH-9
8 yrs.			1022	.286	.421	3695	1058	179	43	78	2.1	565	376	432	718	155	20	1	1931	60	24	7	2.0	.988	OF-996, DH-15

Year	Team	Games	BA	SA	AB	H	2B	3B	HR	HR%	R	RBI	BB	SO	SB	PINCH HIT AB	H	PO	A	E	DP	TC/G	FA	G by Pos

Scott Bradley

BRADLEY, SCOTT WILLIAM
B. Mar. 22, 1960, Glen Ridge, N. J.
BL TR 5' 11" 175 lbs.

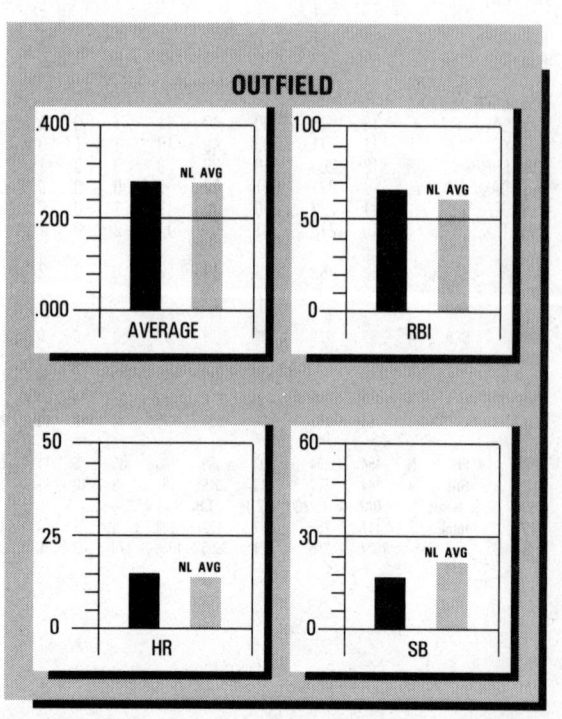

Year	Team	Games	BA	SA	AB	H	2B	3B	HR	HR%	R	RBI	BB	SO	SB	AB	H	PO	A	E	DP	TC/G	FA	G by Pos
April		11	.300	.450	20	6	3	0	0	0.0	2	4	0	1	0									
May		23	.222	.254	63	14	2	0	0	0.0	5	5	3	9	0									
June		19	.200	.280	50	10	1	0	1	2.0	2	8	4	3	0									
July		15	.290	.290	31	9	0	0	0	0.0	1	6	2	1	0									
Aug		17	.211	.289	38	8	3	0	0	0.0	1	4	3	2	0									
Sept/Oct		16	.161	.161	31	5	0	0	0	0.0	0	1	3	4	0									
Day		25	.281	.359	64	18	2	0	1	1.6	4	13	3	4	0									
Night		76	.201	.243	169	34	7	0	0	0.0	7	15	12	16	0									
vs. Left			.160	.160	25	4	0	0	0	0.0	2	4	3	2	0									
vs. Right			.231	.288	208	48	9	0	1	0.5	9	24	12	18	0									
On Grass		38	.204	.247	93	19	4	0	0	0.0	5	8	2	6	0									
On Turf		63	.236	.293	140	33	5	0	1	0.7	6	20	13	14	0									
Home		52	.250	.321	112	28	5	0	1	0.9	4	19	9	12	0									
Road		49	.198	.231	121	24	4	0	0	0.0	7	9	6	8	0									
Division Rivals																								
vs. CAL		5	.000	.000	6	0	0	0	0	0.0	0	1	0	1	0									
vs. CHI		9	.250	.250	20	5	0	0	0	0.0	0	2	1	3	0									
vs. KC		9	.217	.348	23	5	0	0	1	4.3	1	4	0	3	0									
vs. MIN		8	.250	.313	16	4	1	0	0	0.0	1	1	3	1	0									
vs. OAK		7	.143	.143	14	2	0	0	0	0.0	0	2	0	1	0									
vs. TEX		6	.200	.300	10	2	1	0	0	0.0	1	2	0	1	0									
On 3B < 2 Out			.250	.500	4	1	1	0	0	0.0	0	8	0	0										
1984	NY A	9	.286	.333	21	6	1	0	0	0.0	3	2	1	1	0	1	0	10	0	0	0	1.1	1.000	OF-5, C-3
1985		19	.163	.245	49	8	2	1	0	0.0	4	1	1	5	0	7	1	12	0	1	0	0.7	.923	DH-9, C-3
1986	2 teams					CHI A (9G — .286)					SEA A (68G — .302)													
"	total	77	.300	.432	220	66	8	3	5	2.3	20	28	13	7	1	17	5	281	21	3	5	4.0	.990	C-59, DH-9, OF-1
1987	SEA A	102	.278	.371	342	95	15	1	5	1.5	34	43	15	18	0	12	4	438	39	8	4	4.8	.984	C-82, 3B-8, OF-2
1988		103	.257	.349	335	86	17	1	4	1.2	45	33	17	16	1	12	2	543	42	6	7	5.7	.990	C-85, DH-4, OF-4, 3B-3, 1B-2
1989		103	.274	.367	270	74	16	0	3	1.1	21	37	21	23	1	25	9	400	26	4	6	4.2	.991	C-70, DH-6, 1B-2, OF-1
1990		101	.223	.275	233	52	9	0	1	0.4	11	28	15	20	0	35	10	354	30	2	4	5.8	.995	C-63, DH-6, 3B-5, 1B-1
7 yrs.		514	.263	.354	1470	387	68	6	18	1.2	138	172	83	90	3	109	31	2038	158	24	26	4.3	.989	C-365, DH-34, 3B-16, OF-13, 1B-5

Glenn Braggs

BRAGGS, GLENN ERICK
B. Oct. 17, 1962, San Bernardino, Calif.
BR TR 6' 3" 210 lbs.

Year	Team	Games	BA	SA	AB	H	2B	3B	HR	HR%	R	RBI	BB	SO	SB	AB	H	PO	A	E	DP	TC/G	FA	G by Pos
April		13	.265	.441	34	9	3	0	1	2.9	9	5	4	5	1									
May		20	.265	.368	68	18	1	0	2	2.9	6	8	7	13	4									
June		19	.295	.443	61	18	1	1	2	3.3	6	7	4	16	1									
July		24	.303	.439	66	20	6	0	1	1.5	7	10	10	17	1									
Aug		16	.194	.194	36	7	0	0	0	0.0	5	4	6	4	1									
Sept/Oct		17	.327	.571	49	16	3	0	3	6.1	6	7	7	9	0									
Day		32	.244	.456	90	22	7	0	4	4.4	11	13	4	22	2									
Night		77	.295	.402	224	66	7	1	5	2.2	28	28	34	42	6									
vs. Left			.289	.456	149	43	5	1	6	4.0	23	19	26	26	3									
vs. Right			.273	.382	165	45	9	0	3	1.8	16	22	12	38	5									
On Grass		50	.229	.347	144	33	8	0	3	2.1	21	18	17	32	5									
On Turf		59	.324	.476	170	55	6	1	6	3.5	18	23	21	32	3									
Home		56	.280	.435	161	45	8	1	5	3.1	21	25	20	37	1									
Road		53	.281	.399	153	43	6	0	4	2.6	18	16	18	27	7									
Division Rivals																								
vs. ATL		12	.378	.595	37	14	0	1	2	5.4	5	7	4	9	1									
vs. HOU		6	.417	1.000	12	5	1	0	2	16.7	2	3	3	3	0									
vs. LA		4	.250	.500	12	3	0	0	1	8.3	1	1	3	2	0									
vs. SD		13	.195	.268	41	8	3	0	0	0.0	3	4	2	7	0									
vs. SF		8	.200	.240	25	5	1	0	0	0.0	1	1	3	8	1									
On 3B < 2 Out			.462	.538	13	6	1	0	0	0.0	0	13	3	4										

Year	Team		Games	BA	SA	AB	H	2B	3B	HR	HR%	R	RBI	BB	SO	SB	PINCH HIT AB	PINCH HIT H	PO	A	E	DP	TC/G	FA	G by Pos

Glenn Braggs *Continued*

Year	Team		Games	BA	SA	AB	H	2B	3B	HR	HR%	R	RBI	BB	SO	SB	PINCH HIT AB	PINCH HIT H	PO	A	E	DP	TC/G	FA	G by Pos
1986	MIL	A	58	.237	.349	215	51	8	2	4	1.9	19	18	11	47	1	0	0	116	5	12	0	2.3	.910	OF-56, DH-2
1987			132	.269	.430	505	136	28	7	13	2.6	67	77	47	96	12	3	0	301	6	9	1	2.4	.972	OF-123, DH-8
1988			72	.261	.423	272	71	14	0	10	3.7	30	42	14	60	6	0	0	134	1	3	0	1.9	.978	OF-54, DH-18
1989			144	.247	.370	514	127	12	3	15	2.9	77	66	42	111	17	1	0	267	6	8	1	2.0	.972	OF-132, DH-13
1990	2 teams		MIL A (37G — .248)				CIN N (72G — .299)																		
"	total		109	.280	.417	314	88	14	1	9	2.8	39	41	38	64	8	14	4	191	11	7	3	2.3	.967	OF-92, DH-2
5 yrs.			515	.260	.400	1820	473	76	13	51	2.8	232	244	152	378	44	18	4	1009	29	39	5	2.1	.964	OF-457, DH-43

LEAGUE CHAMPIONSHIP SERIES

Year	Team		Games	BA	SA	AB	H	2B	3B	HR	HR%	R	RBI	BB	SO	SB	PINCH HIT AB	PINCH HIT H	PO	A	E	DP	TC/G	FA	G by Pos
1990	CIN	N	2	.200	.200	5	1	0	0	0	0.0	0	0	0	1	0	0	0	2	0	0	0	1.0	1.000	OF-2

WORLD SERIES

Year	Team		Games	BA	SA	AB	H	2B	3B	HR	HR%	R	RBI	BB	SO	SB	PINCH HIT AB	PINCH HIT H	PO	A	E	DP	TC/G	FA	G by Pos
1990	CIN	N	2	.000	.000	4	0	0	0	0	0.0	0	2	1	0	0	2	0	0	0	0	0	0.0	.903	OF-1

Sid Bream

BREAM, SIDNEY EUGENE
B. Aug. 3, 1960, Carlisle, Pa.
BL TL 6′ 4″ 215 lbs.

	Games	BA	SA	AB	H	2B	3B	HR	HR%	R	RBI	BB	SO	SB
April	17	.233	.326	43	10	1	0	1	2.3	3	4	3	10	0
May	22	.274	.468	62	17	6	0	2	3.2	7	12	10	14	0
June	23	.313	.469	64	20	2	1	2	3.1	6	11	4	9	3
July	25	.232	.464	69	16	1	0	5	7.2	9	18	11	9	2
Aug	30	.333	.533	75	25	9	0	2	2.7	7	12	11	11	1
Sept/Oct	30	.224	.421	76	17	4	1	3	3.9	7	10	9	12	2
Day	40	.275	.422	102	28	4	1	3	2.9	10	17	12	20	3
Night	107	.268	.467	287	77	19	1	12	4.2	29	50	36	45	5
vs. Left		.260	.427	96	25	8	1	2	2.1	8	12	6	16	0
vs. Right		.273	.464	293	80	15	1	13	4.4	31	55	42	49	8
On Grass	34	.226	.377	106	24	4	0	4	3.8	12	16	14	23	2
On Turf	113	.286	.484	283	81	19	2	11	3.9	27	51	34	42	6
Home	74	.276	.481	181	50	11	1	8	4.4	19	36	21	26	3
Road	73	.264	.433	208	55	12	1	7	3.4	20	31	27	39	5
Division Rivals														
vs. CHI	16	.273	.386	44	12	2	0	1	2.3	4	8	5	6	2
vs. MON	18	.326	.581	43	14	0	1	3	7.0	5	8	7	8	2
vs. NY	12	.258	.484	31	8	1	0	2	6.5	3	8	3	6	2
vs. PHI	17	.282	.590	39	11	4	1	2	5.1	5	8	7	4	0
vs. STL	17	.224	.347	49	11	3	0	1	2.0	3	5	1	8	0
On 3B < 2 Out		.467	.467	15	7	0	0	0	0.0	0	15	3	2	

FIRST BASE — AVERAGE, RBI, HR, SB (NL AVG)

Year	Team		Games	BA	SA	AB	H	2B	3B	HR	HR%	R	RBI	BB	SO	SB	PINCH HIT AB	PINCH HIT H	PO	A	E	DP	TC/G	FA	G by Pos
1983	LA	N	15	.182	.182	11	2	0	0	0	0.0	0	2	2	2	0	10	2	8	0	0	1	0.5	1.000	1B-4
1984			27	.184	.245	49	9	3	0	0	0.0	2	6	6	9	1	11	1	95	11	0	9	3.9	1.000	1B-14
1985	2 teams		LA N (24G — .132)				PIT N (26G — .284)																		
"	total		50	.230	.399	148	34	7	0	6	4.1	18	21	18	24	0	10	2	367	35	3	29	8.1	.993	1B-41
1986	PIT	N	154	.268	.450	522	140	37	5	16	3.1	73	77	60	73	13	5	1	1320	166	17	107	9.8	.989	1B-153, OF-2
1987			149	.275	.411	516	142	25	3	13	2.5	64	65	49	69	9	7	2	1236	127	17	109	9.3	.988	1B-144
1988			148	.264	.409	462	122	37	0	10	2.2	50	65	47	64	9	16	6	1118	140	6	88	8.5	.995	1B-138
1989			19	.222	.306	36	8	3	0	0	0.0	3	4	12	10	0	2	0	111	7	1	5	6.3	.992	1B-13
1990			147	.270	.455	389	105	23	2	15	3.8	39	67	48	65	8	14	2	971	104	8	80	7.6	.993	1B-142
8 yrs.			709	.263	.421	2133	562	135	10	60	2.8	249	307	242	316	40	75	16	5226	590	52	428	8.3	.991	1B-649, OF-2

LEAGUE CHAMPIONSHIP SERIES

Year	Team		Games	BA	SA	AB	H	2B	3B	HR	HR%	R	RBI	BB	SO	SB	PINCH HIT AB	PINCH HIT H	PO	A	E	DP	TC/G	FA	G by Pos
1990	PIT	N	4	.500	1.000	8	4	1	0	1	12.5	1	3	2	3	0	1	0	26	3	0	3	7.3	1.000	1B-4

Year	Team	Games	BA	SA	AB	H	2B	3B	HR	HR%	R	RBI	BB	SO	SB	PINCH HIT AB	PINCH HIT H	PO	A	E	DP	TC/G	FA	G by Pos

George Brett

BRETT, GEORGE HOWARD
Brother of Ken Brett.
B. May 15, 1953, Glen Dale, W. Va.
BL TR 6' 185 lbs.

Split	Games	BA	SA	AB	H	2B	3B	HR	HR%	R	RBI	BB	SO	SB
April	18	.217	.246	69	15	2	0	0	0.0	9	5	8	12	2
May	27	.286	.400	105	30	5	2	1	1.0	16	10	12	14	0
June	18	.250	.283	60	15	2	0	0	0.0	4	7	8	6	2
July	28	.388	.716	116	45	18	1	6	5.2	27	24	12	13	2
Aug	27	.369	.602	103	38	11	2	3	2.9	14	24	9	11	1
Sept/Oct	24	.396	.648	91	36	7	2	4	4.4	12	17	7	7	2
Day	36	.307	.536	140	43	12	1	6	4.3	20	28	10	24	2
Night	106	.337	.507	404	136	33	6	8	2.0	62	59	46	39	7
vs. Left		.316	.487	187	59	11	3	5	2.7	23	28	16	26	3
vs. Right		.336	.529	357	120	34	4	9	2.5	59	59	40	37	6
On Grass	56	.325	.565	209	68	21	1	9	4.3	32	34	27	31	3
On Turf	86	.331	.484	335	111	24	6	5	1.5	50	53	29	32	6
Home	75	.319	.448	288	92	18	5	3	1.0	40	46	27	27	4
Road	67	.340	.590	256	87	27	2	11	4.3	42	41	29	36	5
Division Rivals														
vs. CAL	10	.333	.576	33	11	2	0	2	6.1	4	9	3	2	0
vs. CHI	13	.288	.385	52	15	5	0	0	0.0	6	7	6	7	0
vs. MIN	7	.320	.440	25	8	1	1	0	0.0	4	3	3	3	0
vs. OAK	13	.313	.396	48	15	4	0	0	0.0	7	3	3	7	1
vs. SEA	7	.370	.519	27	10	4	0	0	0.0	3	5	1	4	1
vs. TEX	13	.391	.543	46	18	2	1	1	2.2	6	8	8	3	5
On 3B < 2 Out		.360	.520	25	9	1	0	1	4.0	1	26	8	2	

FIRST BASE

[Bar charts: AVERAGE, RBI, HR, SB — each showing black bar vs AL AVG]

Year	Team		Games	BA	SA	AB	H	2B	3B	HR	HR%	R	RBI	BB	SO	SB	AB	H	PO	A	E	DP	TC/G	FA	G by Pos
1973	KC	A	13	.125	.175	40	5	2	0	0	0.0	2	0	0	5	0	1	0	9	28	1	2	2.9	.974	3B-13
1974			133	.282	.363	457	129	21	5	2	0.4	49	47	21	38	8	2	0	102	279	21	16	3.0	.948	3B-132, SS-1
1975			159	.308	.456	634	195	35	13	11	1.7	84	89	46	49	13	0	0	132	356	26	27	3.2	.949	3B-159, SS-1
1976			159	.333	.462	645	215	34	14	7	1.1	94	67	49	36	21	0	0	146	350	26	23	3.3	.950	3B-157, SS-4
1977			139	.312	.532	564	176	32	13	22	3.9	105	88	55	24	14	3	1	115	325	21	33	3.3	.954	3B-135, DH-3, SS-1
1978			128	.294	.467	510	150	45	8	9	1.8	79	62	39	35	23	0	0	104	289	16	25	3.2	.961	3B-128, SS-1
1979			154	.329	.563	645	212	42	20	23	3.6	119	107	51	36	17	0	0	176	378	31	34	3.8	.947	3B-149, 1B-8, DH-1
1980			117	.390	.664	449	175	33	9	24	5.3	87	118	58	22	15	3	1	107	256	17	29	3.2	.955	3B-112, 1B-1
1981			89	.314	.484	347	109	27	7	6	1.7	42	43	27	23	14	0	0	74	170	14	7	2.9	.946	3B-88
1982			144	.301	.505	552	166	32	9	21	3.8	101	82	71	51	6	0	0	130	295	17	23	3.1	.962	3B-134, OF-12
1983			123	.310	.563	464	144	38	2	25	5.4	90	93	57	39	0	1	1	210	192	25	34	3.5	.941	3B-102, 1B-14, OF-13, DH-1
1984			104	.284	.459	377	107	21	3	13	3.4	42	69	38	37	0	3	1	59	201	14	18	2.6	.949	3B-101
1985			155	.335	.585	550	184	38	5	30	5.5	108	112	103	49	9	2	0	107	339	15	33	3.0	.967	3B-152, DH-1
1986			124	.290	.481	441	128	28	4	16	3.6	70	73	80	45	1	1	0	97	218	16	17	2.7	.952 *	3B-115, DH-7, SS-2
1987			115	.290	.496	427	124	18	2	22	5.2	71	78	72	47	6	0	0	805	69	9	72	7.7	.990	1B-83, DH-21, 3B-11
1988			157	.306	.509	589	180	42	3	24	4.1	90	103	82	51	14	0	0	1126	70	10	105	7.7	.992	1B-124, DH-33, SS-1
1989			124	.282	.431	457	129	26	3	12	2.6	67	80	59	47	14	3	0	898	80	2	71	7.9	.998	1B-104, DH-17, OF-2
1990			142	.329	.515	544	179	45	7	14	2.5	82	87	56	63	9	1	0	880	67	7	89	8.7	.993	1B-102, DH-32, OF-9, 3B-1
18 yrs.			2279	.311	.502	8692	2707	559	127	281	3.2	1382	1398	964	697	184	20	4	5277	3962	288	658	4.2	.970	3B-1689, 1B-436, DH-116, OF-36, SS-11

DIVISIONAL PLAYOFF SERIES

Year	Team		Games	BA	SA	AB	H	2B	3B	HR	HR%	R	RBI	BB	SO	SB	AB	H	PO	A	E	DP	TC/G	FA	G by Pos
1981	KC	A	3	.167	.167	12	2	0	0	0	0.0	0	0	0	0	0	0	0	0	0	1	0	0.3	—	3B-3

LEAGUE CHAMPIONSHIP SERIES

Year	Team		Games	BA	SA	AB	H	2B	3B	HR	HR%	R	RBI	BB	SO	SB	AB	H	PO	A	E	DP	TC/G	FA	G by Pos
1976	KC	A	5	.444	.778	18	8	1	1	1	5.6	4	5	2	1	0	0	0	3	7	3	1	2.6	.769	3B-5
1977			5	.300	.500	20	6	0	2	0	0.0	2	2	1	0	0	0	0	5	12	2	2	3.8	.895	3B-5
1978			4	.389	1.056	18	7	1	1	3	16.7	7	3	0	1	0	0	0	3	8	1	1	3.0	.917	3B-4
1980			3	.273	.909	11	3	1	0	2	18.2	3	4	1	0	0	0	0	2	7	0	1	3.0	1.000	3B-3
1984			3	.231	.231	13	3	0	0	0	0.0	0	0	0	2	0	0	0	2	7	0	1	3.0	1.000	3B-3
1985			7	.348	.826	23	8	2	0	3	13.0	6	5	7	5	0	0	0	7	8	2	0	2.4	.882	3B-7
6 yrs.			27	.340	.728	103	35	5	4	9	8.7	22	19	11	9	0	0	0	22	49	8	5	2.9	.899	3B-27

WORLD SERIES

Year	Team		Games	BA	SA	AB	H	2B	3B	HR	HR%	R	RBI	BB	SO	SB	AB	H	PO	A	E	DP	TC/G	FA	G by Pos
1980	KC	A	6	.375	.667	24	9	2	1	1	4.2	3	3	2	4	1	0	0	4	17	1	1	3.7	.955	3B-6
1985			7	.370	.407	27	10	1	0	0	0.0	5	1	4	7	1	0	0	10	19	1	1	4.3	.967	3B-7
2 yrs.			13	.373	.529	51	19	3	1	1	2.0	8	4	6	11	2	0	0	14	36	2	2	4.0	.962	3B-13

Year	Team		Games	BA	SA	AB	H	2B	3B	HR	HR%	R	RBI	BB	SO	SB	PINCH HIT AB	H	PO	A	E	DP	TC/G	FA	G by Pos

Rod Brewer

BREWER, RODNEY LEE
B. Feb. 24, 1966, Eustis, Fla.
BL TL 6′ 3″ 210 lbs.

Year	Team		Games	BA	SA	AB	H	2B	3B	HR	HR%	R	RBI	BB	SO	SB	AB	H	PO	A	E	DP	TC/G	FA	G by Pos
1990	STL	N	14	.240	.280	25	6	1	0	0	0.0	4	2	0	4	0	5	0	46	6	1	5	5.9	.981	1B-9

Greg Briley

BRILEY, GREGORY
B. May 24, 1965, Greenville, N. C.
BL TR 5′ 9″ 175 lbs.

	Games	BA	SA	AB	H	2B	3B	HR	HR%	R	RBI	BB	SO	SB	PO	A	E	DP	TC/G	FA
April	17	.216	.333	51	11	6	0	0	0.0	4	2	2	4	1						
May	24	.269	.397	78	21	4	0	2	2.6	9	11	6	11	5						
June	20	.283	.396	53	15	6	0	0	0.0	4	3	4	9	4						
July	20	.271	.354	48	13	1	0	1	2.1	7	7	6	8	1						
Aug	21	.169	.338	65	11	1	2	2	3.1	9	6	11	9	1						
Sept/Oct	23	.286	.286	42	12	0	0	0	0.0	7	0	8	7	4						
Day	34	.132	.165	91	12	1	1	0	0.0	5	5	5	15	3						
Night	91	.289	.427	246	71	17	1	5	2.0	35	24	32	33	13						
vs. Left		.212	.242	33	7	1	0	0	0.0	4	3	4	7	0						
vs. Right		.250	.368	304	76	17	2	5	1.6	36	26	33	41	16						
On Grass	51	.243	.340	144	35	9	1	1	0.7	19	9	18	19	4						
On Turf	74	.249	.368	193	48	9	1	4	2.1	21	20	19	29	12						
Home	62	.247	.380	166	41	8	1	4	2.4	20	17	17	23	9						
Road	63	.246	.333	171	42	10	1	1	0.6	20	12	20	25	7						
Division Rivals																				
vs. CAL	10	.353	.412	17	6	1	0	0	0.0	4	1	3	3	0						
vs. CHI	10	.095	.095	21	2	0	0	0	0.0	0	1	2	2	0						
vs. KC	7	.188	.250	16	3	1	0	0	0.0	0	1	2	5	0						
vs. MIN	8	.235	.412	17	4	1	1	0	0.0	0	1	0	2	0						
vs. OAK	13	.163	.233	43	7	3	0	0	0.0	4	1	0	5	1						
vs. TEX	12	.324	.432	37	12	2	1	0	0.0	9	1	4	7	5						
On 3B < 2 Out		.333	.667	9	3	0	0	1	11.1	1	9	0	2							

Year	Team		Games	BA	SA	AB	H	2B	3B	HR	HR%	R	RBI	BB	SO	SB	AB	H	PO	A	E	DP	TC/G	FA	G by Pos
1988	SEA	A	13	.250	.389	36	9	2	0	1	2.8	6	4	5	6	0	3	0	13	0	1	0	1.1	.929	OF-11
1989			115	.266	.442	394	105	22	4	13	3.3	52	52	39	82	11	11	3	197	38	9	7	2.1	.963	OF-105, 2B-10, DH-2
1990			125	.246	.356	337	83	18	2	5	1.4	40	29	37	48	16	18	4	177	4	2	1	1.7	.989	OF-107, DH-4
3 yrs.			253	.257	.402	767	197	42	6	19	2.5	98	85	81	136	27	32	7	387	42	12	8	1.7	.973	OF-223, 2B-10, DH-6

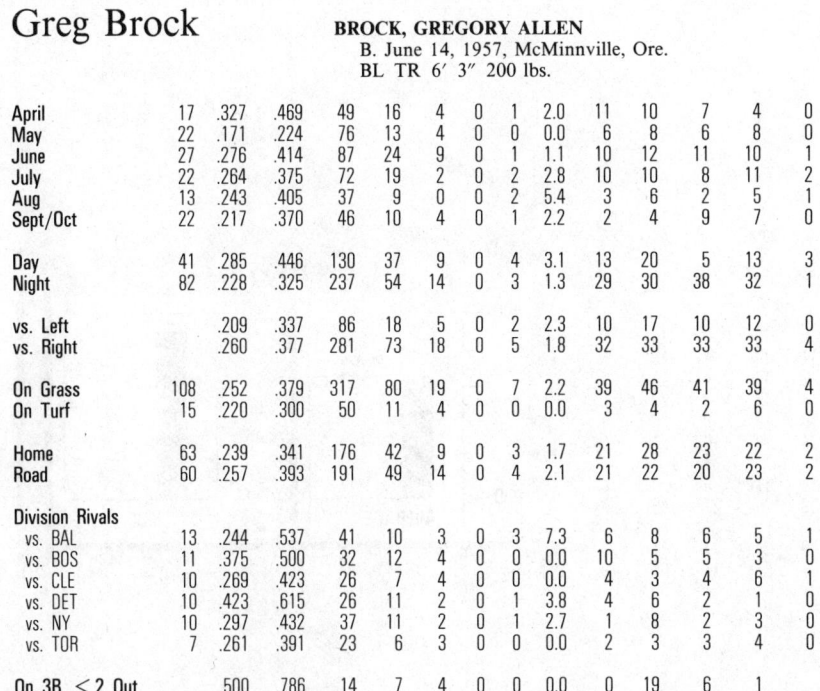

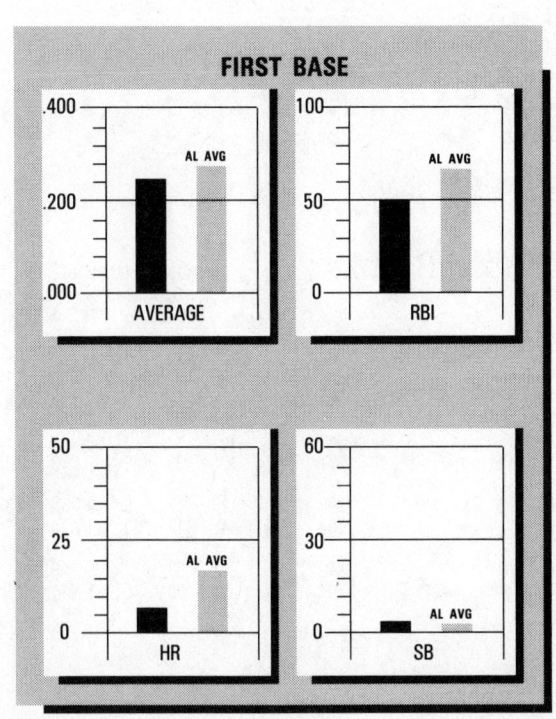

Greg Brock

BROCK, GREGORY ALLEN
B. June 14, 1957, McMinnville, Ore.
BL TR 6′ 3″ 200 lbs.

	Games	BA	SA	AB	H	2B	3B	HR	HR%	R	RBI	BB	SO	SB
April	17	.327	.469	49	16	4	0	1	2.0	11	10	7	4	0
May	22	.171	.224	76	13	4	0	0	0.0	6	8	6	8	0
June	27	.276	.414	87	24	9	0	1	1.1	10	12	11	10	1
July	22	.264	.375	72	19	2	0	2	2.8	10	10	8	11	2
Aug	13	.243	.405	37	9	0	0	2	5.4	3	6	2	5	1
Sept/Oct	22	.217	.370	46	10	4	0	1	2.2	2	4	9	7	0
Day	41	.285	.446	130	37	9	0	4	3.1	13	20	5	13	3
Night	82	.228	.325	237	54	14	0	3	1.3	29	30	38	32	1
vs. Left		.209	.337	86	18	5	0	2	2.3	10	17	10	12	0
vs. Right		.260	.377	281	73	18	0	5	1.8	32	33	33	33	4
On Grass	108	.252	.379	317	80	19	0	7	2.2	39	46	41	39	4
On Turf	15	.220	.300	50	11	4	0	0	0.0	3	4	2	6	0
Home	63	.239	.341	176	42	9	0	3	1.7	21	28	23	22	2
Road	60	.257	.393	191	49	14	0	4	2.1	21	22	20	23	2
Division Rivals														
vs. BAL	13	.244	.537	41	10	3	0	3	7.3	6	8	6	5	1
vs. BOS	11	.375	.500	32	12	4	0	0	0.0	10	5	5	3	0
vs. CLE	10	.269	.423	26	7	4	0	0	0.0	4	3	4	6	1
vs. DET	10	.423	.615	26	11	2	0	1	3.8	4	6	2	1	0
vs. NY	10	.297	.432	37	11	2	0	1	2.7	1	8	2	3	0
vs. TOR	7	.261	.391	23	6	3	0	0	0.0	2	3	3	4	0
On 3B < 2 Out		.500	.786	14	7	4	0	0	0.0	0	19	6	1	

Year	Team		Games	BA	SA	AB	H	2B	3B	HR	HR%	R	RBI	BB	SO	SB	PINCH HIT AB	H	PO	A	E	DP	TC/G	FA	G by Pos

Greg Brock *Continued*

Year	Team		Games	BA	SA	AB	H	2B	3B	HR	HR%	R	RBI	BB	SO	SB	AB	H	PO	A	E	DP	TC/G	FA	G by Pos
1982	LA	N	18	.118	.176	17	2	1	0	0	0.0	1	1	1	5	0	13	2	9	0	0	0	0.5	1.000	1B-3
1983			146	.224	.396	455	102	14	2	20	4.4	64	66	83	81	5	6	1	1162	106	12	94	8.8	.991	1B-140
1984			88	.225	.402	271	61	6	0	14	5.2	33	34	39	37	8	8	0	703	65	4	61	8.8	.995	1B-83
1985			129	.251	.438	438	110	19	0	21	4.8	64	66	54	72	4	9	2	1113	84	7	86	9.3	.994	1B-122
1986			115	.234	.422	325	76	13	0	16	4.9	33	52	37	60	2	23	4	726	87	3	46	7.1	.996	1B-99
1987	MIL	A	141	.299	.438	532	159	29	3	13	2.4	81	85	57	63	5	0	0	1065	109	8	111	8.4	.993	1B-141
1988			115	.212	.310	364	77	16	1	6	1.6	53	50	63	48	6	1	0	915	102	7	89	8.9	.993	1B-114, DH-1
1989			107	.265	.405	373	99	16	0	12	3.2	40	52	43	49	6	1	1	850	58	5	86	8.5	.995	1B-100, DH-7
1990			123	.248	.368	367	91	23	0	7	1.9	42	50	43	45	4	8	1	885	63	5	89	8.3	.995	1B-115
9 yrs.			982	.247	.399	3142	777	137	6	109	3.5	411	456	420	460	40	69	11	7428	674	51	662	8.3	.994	1B-917, DH-8

LEAGUE CHAMPIONSHIP SERIES

Year	Team		Games	BA	SA	AB	H	2B	3B	HR	HR%	R	RBI	BB	SO	SB	AB	H	PO	A	E	DP	TC/G	FA	G by Pos
1983	LA	N	3	.000	.000	9	0	0	0	0	0.0	1	0	0	3	0	0	0	13	0	0	3	4.3	1.000	1B-3
1985			5	.083	.333	12	1	0	0	1	8.3	2	2	2	2	0	1	0	35	4	0	2	7.8	1.000	1B-4
2 yrs.			8	.048	.190	21	1	0	0	1	4.8	3	2	2	5	0	1	0	48	4	0	5	6.5	.000	1B-7

Tom Brookens

BROOKENS, THOMAS DALE
B. Aug. 10, 1953, Chambersburg, Pa.
BR TR 5' 10" 165 lbs.

Year	Team		Games	BA	SA	AB	H	2B	3B	HR	HR%	R	RBI	BB	SO	SB	AB	H	PO	A	E	DP	TC/G	FA	G by Pos
1979	DET	A	60	.263	.374	190	50	5	2	4	2.1	23	21	11	40	10	0	0	76	141	11	21	3.8	.952	3B-42, 2B-19, DH-1
1980			151	.275	.418	509	140	25	9	10	2.0	64	66	32	71	13	4	1	127	307	29	38	3.1	.937	3B-138, 2B-9, DH-1, SS-1
1981			71	.243	.343	239	58	10	1	4	1.7	19	25	14	43	5	1	0	58	139	10	13	2.9	.952	3B-71
1982			140	.231	.352	398	92	15	3	9	2.3	40	58	27	63	5	6	2	119	276	20	27	3.0	.952	3B-113, 2B-26, SS-9, OF-1
1983			138	.214	.325	332	71	13	3	6	1.8	50	32	29	46	10	10	1	97	254	22	34	2.7	.941	3B-103, SS-30, 2B-10, DH-1
1984			113	.246	.397	224	55	11	4	5	2.2	32	26	19	33	6	3	2	98	187	12	35	2.6	.960	3B-68, SS-28, 2B-26, DH-1
1985			156	.237	.375	485	115	34	6	7	1.4	54	47	27	78	14	1	1	135	277	24	28	2.8	.945	3B-151, SS-8, 2B-3, DH-1, C-1
1986			98	.270	.356	281	76	11	2	3	1.1	42	25	20	42	11	7	1	106	144	7	26	2.6	.973	3B-35, 2B-31, DH-14, SS-14, OF-3
1987			143	.241	.376	444	107	15	3	13	2.9	59	59	33	63	7	2	0	119	256	19	33	2.8	.952	3B-122, SS-16, 2B-11
1988			136	.243	.351	441	107	23	5	5	1.1	62	38	44	74	4	5	1	101	235	17	16	2.6	.952	3B-136, SS-3, 2B-1
1989	NY	A	66	.226	.333	168	38	6	0	4	2.4	14	14	11	27	1	11	3	27	85	7	7	1.8	.941	3B-51, SS-7, 2B-5, DH-3, OF-3
1990	CLE	A	64	.266	.357	154	41	7	2	1	0.6	18	20	14	25	0	9	0	57	104	6	20	2.9	.964	3B-35, 2B-21, SS-3, 1B-2, DH-1
12 yrs.			1336	.246	.367	3865	950	175	40	71	1.8	477	431	281	605	86	59	12	1120	2405	184	298	2.8	.950	3B-1065, 2B-162, SS-119, DH-23, OF-7, 1B-2, C-1

LEAGUE CHAMPIONSHIP SERIES

Year	Team		Games	BA	SA	AB	H	2B	3B	HR	HR%	R	RBI	BB	SO	SB	AB	H	PO	A	E	DP	TC/G	FA	G by Pos
1984	DET	A	2	.000	.000	2	0	0	0	0	0.0	0	0	0	1	0	0	0	0	2	1	0	1.5	.667	2B-1, 3B-1
1987			5	.000	.000	13	0	0	0	0	0.0	0	0	0	3	0	0	0	3	15	0	0	3.6	1.000	3B-5
2 yrs.			7	.000	.000	15	0	0	0	0	0.0	0	0	0	4	0	0	0	3	17	1	0	3.0	.952	3B-6, 2B-1

WORLD SERIES

Year	Team		Games	BA	SA	AB	H	2B	3B	HR	HR%	R	RBI	BB	SO	SB	AB	H	PO	A	E	DP	TC/G	FA	G by Pos
1984	DET	A	3	.000	.000	3	0	0	0	0	0.0	0	0	0	1	0	2	0	0	3	0	0	1.0	1.000	3B-3

Hubie Brooks

BROOKS, HUBERT, JR.
B. Sept. 24, 1956, Los Angeles, Calif.
BR TR 6' 178 lbs.

	Games	BA	SA	AB	H	2B	3B	HR	HR%	R	RBI	BB	SO	SB
April	21	.232	.427	82	19	4	0	4	4.9	7	12	3	14	0
May	26	.240	.385	96	23	3	1	3	3.1	11	10	4	19	0
June	22	.266	.418	79	21	3	0	3	3.8	12	12	4	14	1
July	26	.277	.386	101	28	5	0	2	2.0	14	19	4	20	0
Aug	30	.349	.557	106	37	7	0	5	4.7	16	19	8	20	1
Sept/Oct	28	.221	.365	104	23	6	0	3	2.9	14	19	10	21	0
Day	35	.296	.504	125	37	8	0	6	4.8	15	17	6	20	0
Night	118	.257	.402	443	114	20	1	14	3.2	59	74	27	88	2
vs. Left		.240	.419	217	52	12	0	9	4.1	28	34	17	41	2
vs. Right		.282	.427	351	99	16	1	11	3.1	46	57	16	67	0

OUTFIELD

AVERAGE — NL AVG

RBI — NL AVG

Hubie Brooks *Continued*

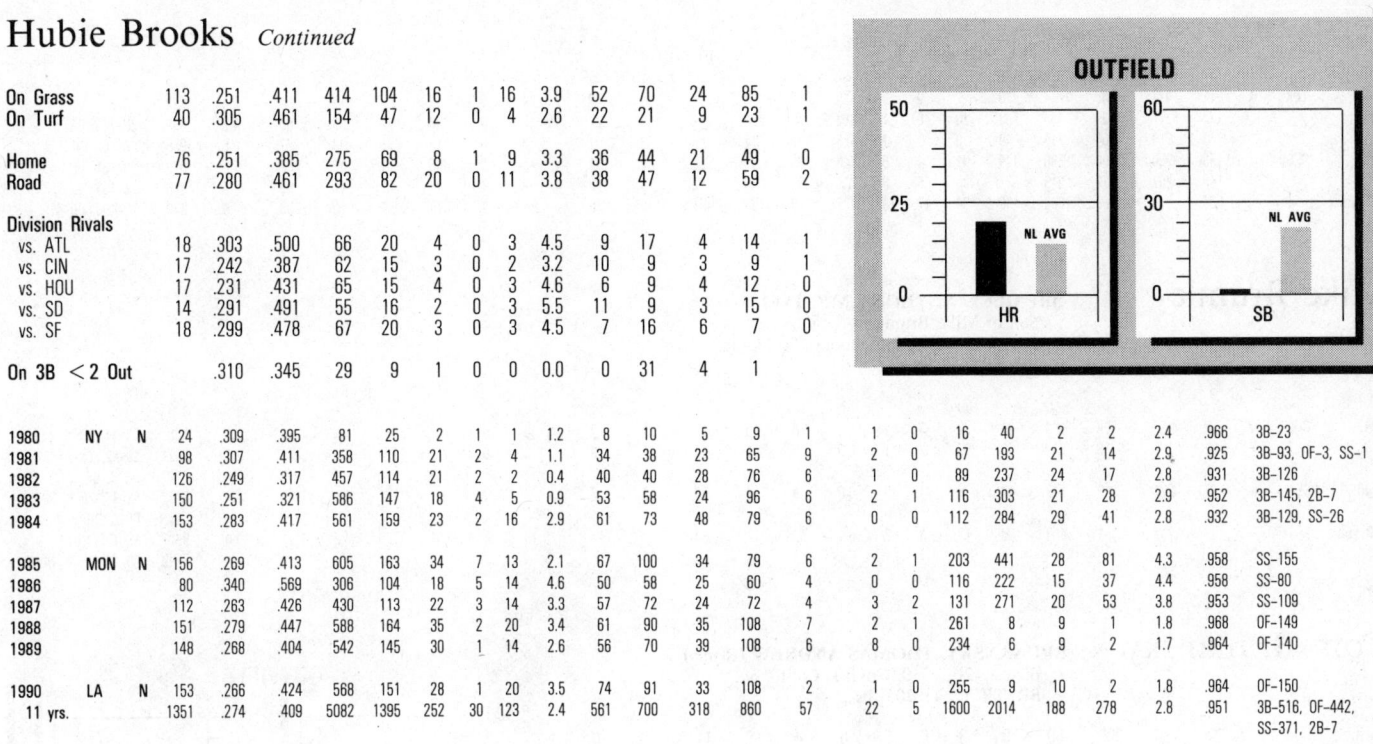

OUTFIELD

Year	Team		Games	BA	SA	AB	H	2B	3B	HR	HR%	R	RBI	BB	SO	SB	PINCH HIT AB	H	PO	A	E	DP	TC/G	FA	G by Pos
On Grass			113	.251	.411	414	104	16	1	16	3.9	52	70	24	85	1									
On Turf			40	.305	.461	154	47	12	0	4	2.6	22	21	9	23	1									
Home			76	.251	.385	275	69	8	1	9	3.3	36	44	21	49	0									
Road			77	.280	.461	293	82	20	0	11	3.8	38	47	12	59	2									
Division Rivals																									
vs. ATL			18	.303	.500	66	20	4	0	3	4.5	9	17	4	14	1									
vs. CIN			17	.242	.387	62	15	3	0	2	3.2	10	9	3	9	1									
vs. HOU			17	.231	.431	65	15	4	0	3	4.6	6	9	4	12	0									
vs. SD			14	.291	.491	55	16	2	0	3	5.5	11	9	3	15	0									
vs. SF			18	.299	.478	67	20	3	0	3	4.5	7	16	6	7	0									
On 3B < 2 Out				.310	.345	29	9	1	0	0	0.0	0	31	4	1										
1980	NY	N	24	.309	.395	81	25	2	1	1	1.2	8	10	5	9	1	1	0	16	40	2	2	2.4	.966	3B-23
1981			98	.307	.411	358	110	21	2	4	1.1	34	38	23	65	9	2	0	67	193	21	14	2.9	.925	3B-93, OF-3, SS-1
1982			126	.249	.317	457	114	21	2	2	0.4	40	40	28	76	6	1	0	89	237	24	17	2.8	.931	3B-126
1983			150	.251	.321	586	147	18	4	5	0.9	53	58	24	96	6	2	1	116	303	21	28	2.9	.952	3B-145, 2B-7
1984			153	.283	.417	561	159	23	2	16	2.9	61	73	48	79	6	0	0	112	284	29	41	2.8	.932	3B-129, SS-26
1985	MON	N	156	.269	.413	605	163	34	7	13	2.1	67	100	34	79	6	2	1	203	441	28	81	4.3	.958	SS-155
1986			80	.340	.569	306	104	18	5	14	4.6	50	58	25	60	4	0	0	116	222	15	37	4.4	.958	SS-80
1987			112	.263	.426	430	113	22	3	14	3.3	57	72	24	72	4	3	2	131	271	20	53	3.8	.953	SS-109
1988			151	.279	.447	588	164	35	2	20	3.4	61	90	35	108	7	2	1	261	8	9	1	1.8	.968	OF-149
1989			148	.268	.404	542	145	30	1	14	2.6	56	70	39	108	6	8	0	234	6	9	2	1.7	.964	OF-140
1990	LA	N	153	.266	.424	568	151	28	1	20	3.5	74	91	33	108	2	1	0	255	9	10	2	1.8	.964	OF-150
11 yrs.			1351	.274	.409	5082	1395	252	30	123	2.4	561	700	318	860	57	22	5	1600	2014	188	278	2.8	.951	3B-516, OF-442, SS-371, 2B-7

Marty Brown

BROWN, MARTY LEO
B. Jan. 23, 1963, Lawton, Okla.
BR TR 6' 1" 190 lbs.

Year	Team		Games	BA	SA	AB	H	2B	3B	HR	HR%	R	RBI	BB	SO	SB	PINCH HIT AB	H	PO	A	E	DP	TC/G	FA	G by Pos
1988	CIN	N	10	.188	.250	16	3	1	0	0	0.0	0	2	1	2	0	4	1	1	9	0	0	1.0	1.000	3B-8
1989			16	.167	.200	30	5	1	0	0	0.0	2	4	4	9	0	3	0	2	19	2	2	1.4	.913	3B-11
1990	BAL	A	9	.200	.200	15	3	0	0	0	0.0	1	0	1	7	0	2	1	1	3	0	0	0.8	1.000	DH-4, 2B-3, 3B-2
3 yrs.			35	.180	.213	61	11	2	0	0	0.0	3	6	6	18	0	9	2	4	31	2	2	1.1	.946	3B-21, DH-4, 2B-3

Jerry Browne

BROWNE, JEROME AUSTIN
B. Feb. 13, 1966, Christiansted, Virgin Islands
BB TR 5' 10" 140 lbs.

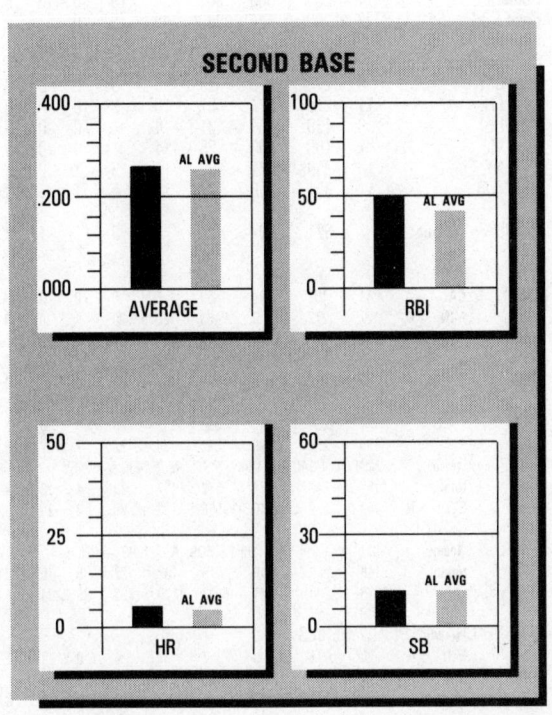

SECOND BASE

Period	Games	BA	SA	AB	H	2B	3B	HR	HR%	R	RBI	BB	SO	SB
April	13	.154	.173	52	8	1	0	0	0.0	7	0	1	7	1
May	27	.250	.308	104	26	1	1	1	1.0	14	8	6	8	1
June	26	.291	.398	103	30	5	0	2	1.9	24	8	17	6	6
July	28	.284	.431	102	29	6	3	1	1.0	16	8	17	9	2
Aug	18	.344	.547	64	22	5	1	2	3.1	15	13	9	9	0
Sept/Oct	28	.250	.341	88	22	8	0	0	0.0	16	13	22	7	2
Day	41	.252	.306	147	37	6	1	0	0.0	24	13	22	8	7
Night	99	.273	.399	366	100	20	4	6	1.6	68	37	50	38	5
vs. Left		.281	.388	139	39	9	3	0	0.0	25	14	26	8	3
vs. Right		.262	.366	374	98	17	2	6	1.6	67	36	46	38	9
On Grass	118	.282	.398	425	120	23	4	6	1.4	77	48	62	40	10
On Turf	22	.193	.250	88	17	3	1	0	0.0	15	2	10	6	2
Home	70	.272	.376	250	68	12	4	2	0.8	48	22	40	20	5
Road	70	.262	.369	293	69	14	1	4	1.5	44	28	32	26	7
Division Rivals														
vs. BAL	11	.409	.659	44	18	2	0	3	6.8	11	11	8	4	2
vs. BOS	13	.245	.265	49	12	1	0	0	0.0	7	4	7	6	1
vs. DET	7	.333	.458	24	8	3	0	0	0.0	5	1	4	2	1
vs. MIL	13	.327	.469	49	16	4	0	1	2.0	13	8	8	2	3
vs. NY	8	.250	.350	20	5	2	0	0	0.0	3	2	7	2	1
vs. TOR	13	.154	.192	52	8	2	0	0	0.0	5	2	2	7	1
On 3B < 2 Out		.222	.278	18	4	1	0	0	0.0	0	18	3	0	

Year	Team		Games	BA	SA	AB	H	2B	3B	HR	HR%	R	RBI	BB	SO	SB	PINCH HIT AB	H	PO	A	E	DP	TC/G	FA	G by Pos

Jerry Browne *Continued*

Year	Team		Games	BA	SA	AB	H	2B	3B	HR	HR%	R	RBI	BB	SO	SB	PH AB	PH H	PO	A	E	DP	TC/G	FA	G by Pos
1986	TEX	A	11	.417	.500	24	10	2	0	0	0.0	6	3	1	4	0	1	0	9	15	2	4	2.4	.923	2B-8
1987			132	.271	.339	454	123	16	6	1	0.2	63	38	61	50	27	5	0	258	338	12	66	4.6	.980	2B-130, DH-1
1988			73	.229	.304	214	49	9	2	1	0.5	26	17	25	32	7	3	0	112	139	11	27	3.6	.958	2B-70, DH-1
1989	CLE	A	153	.299	.390	598	179	31	4	5	0.8	83	45	68	64	14	2	0	305	380	15	67	4.6	.979	2B-151, DH-2
1990			140	.267	.372	513	137	26	5	6	1.1	92	50	72	46	12	3	1	286	382	10	69	4.9	.985	2B-139
5 yrs.			509	.276	.363	1803	498	84	17	13	0.7	270	153	227	196	60	14	1	970	1254	50	233	4.5	.978	2B-498, DH-4

Mike Brumley

BRUMLEY, ANTHONY MICHAEL
Son of Mike Brumley.
B. Apr. 9, 1963, Oklahoma City, Okla.
BB TR 5' 10" 165 lbs.

Year	Team		Games	BA	SA	AB	H	2B	3B	HR	HR%	R	RBI	BB	SO	SB	PH AB	PH H	PO	A	E	DP	TC/G	FA	G by Pos
1987	CHI	N	39	.202	.288	104	21	2	2	1	1.0	8	9	10	30	7	3	0	43	93	5	24	3.6	.965	SS-34, 2B-1
1989	DET	A	92	.198	.255	212	42	5	2	1	0.5	33	11	14	45	8	3	0	80	160	12	24	2.7	.952	SS-42, 2B-24, 3B-11, DH-8, OF-4
1990	SEA	A	62	.224	.313	147	33	5	4	0	0.0	19	7	10	22	2	7	2	63	123	5	26	3.4	.974	SS-47, 2B-6, 3B-3, OF-2, DH-1
3 yrs.			193	.207	.281	463	96	12	8	2	0.4	60	27	34	97	17	13	2	186	376	22	74	3.0	.962	SS-123, 2B-31, 3B-14, DH-9, OF-6

Tom Brunansky

BRUNANSKY, THOMAS ANDREW (Bruno)
B. Aug. 20, 1960, Covina, Calif.
BR TR 6' 4" 205 lbs.

	Games	BA	SA	AB	H	2B	3B	HR	HR%	R	RBI	BB	SO	SB
April	17	.180	.300	50	9	3	0	1	2.0	4	2	11	7	0
May	24	.236	.427	89	21	5	0	4	4.5	13	13	10	23	1
June	25	.326	.489	92	30	8	2	1	1.1	12	13	14	16	0
July	29	.210	.305	105	22	3	2	1	1.0	9	14	14	26	2
Aug	26	.270	.382	89	24	4	0	2	2.2	14	11	7	24	2
Sept/Oct	27	.280	.570	93	26	4	1	7	7.5	14	20	10	19	0
Day	42	.270	.493	148	40	6	0	9	6.1	22	31	13	34	2
Night	106	.249	.389	370	92	21	5	7	1.9	44	42	53	81	3
vs. Left		.285	.480	179	51	11	3	6	3.4	27	29	16	32	3
vs. Right		.239	.386	339	81	16	2	10	2.9	39	44	50	83	2
On Grass	115	.270	.459	403	109	21	5	15	3.7	57	66	51	84	5
On Turf	33	.200	.278	115	23	6	0	1	0.9	9	7	15	31	0
Home	71	.333	.603	252	84	19	5	13	5.2	43	52	27	47	3
Road	77	.180	.244	266	48	8	0	3	1.1	23	21	39	68	2
Division Rivals														
vs. BAL	8	.276	.379	29	8	3	0	0	0.0	3	3	2	1	0
vs. CLE	11	.270	.324	37	10	2	0	0	0.0	7	2	8	10	0
vs. DET	9	.129	.194	31	4	2	0	0	0.0	2	4	5	7	0
vs. MIL	7	.160	.200	25	4	1	0	0	0.0	2	1	3	8	1
vs. NY	13	.359	.641	39	14	3	1	2	5.1	6	10	6	8	0
vs. TOR	11	.351	.865	37	13	2	1	5	13.5	8	11	5	7	0
On 3B < 2 Out		.321	.607	28	9	3	1	1	3.6	1	27	8	6	

OUTFIELD — AVERAGE / RBI / HR / SB (AL AVG)

Year	Team		Games	BA	SA	AB	H	2B	3B	HR	HR%	R	RBI	BB	SO	SB	PH AB	PH H	PO	A	E	DP	TC/G	FA	G by Pos
1981	CAL	A	11	.152	.424	33	5	0	0	3	9.1	7	6	8	10	1	0	0	27	3	2	1	2.9	.938	OF-11
1982	MIN	A	127	.272	.471	463	126	30	1	20	4.3	77	46	71	101	1	0	0	343	8	5	0	2.8	.986	OF-127
1983			151	.227	.445	542	123	24	5	28	5.2	70	82	61	95	2	2	0	375	16	6	8	2.6	.985	OF-146, DH-4
1984			155	.252	.459	567	143	21	0	32	5.6	75	85	57	94	4	2	0	304	13	5	6	2.1	.984	OF-153, DH-1
1985			157	.242	.448	567	137	28	4	27	4.8	71	90	71	86	5	3	1	300	14	5	2	2.0	.984	OF-155
1986			157	.256	.423	593	152	28	1	23	3.9	69	75	53	98	12	5	1	315	10	6	1	2.1	.982	OF-152, DH-2
1987			155	.259	.489	532	138	22	2	32	6.0	83	85	74	104	11	1	1	273	10	3	1	1.8	.990	OF-138, DH-17
1988	2 teams		MIN A (14G — .184)			STL N (143G — .245)																			
"	total		157	.240	.414	572	137	23	4	23	4.0	74	85	86	93	17	0	0	286	10	4	0	1.9	.987	OF-156, DH-1
1989	STL	N	158	.239	.410	556	133	29	3	20	3.6	67	85	59	107	5	6	0	291	9	7	2	1.9	.977	OF-155, 1B-1
1990	2 teams		STL N (19G — .158)			BOS A (129G — .267)																			
"	total		148	.255	.419	518	132	27	5	16	3.0	66	73	66	115	5	6	2	304	8	7	2	2.3	.978	OF-138, DH-7
10 yrs.			1376	.248	.441	4943	1226	232	25	224	4.5	659	712	606	903	63	25	5	2818	101	50	23	2.2	.983	OF-1331, DH-32, 1B-1

LEAGUE CHAMPIONSHIP SERIES

Year	Team		Games	BA	SA	AB	H	2B	3B	HR	HR%	R	RBI	BB	SO	SB	PH AB	PH H	PO	A	E	DP	TC/G	FA	G by Pos
1987	MIN	A	5	.412	1.000	17	7	4	0	2	11.8	5	9	4	3	0	0	0	10	0	0	0	2.0	1.000	OF-5
1990	BOS	A	4	.083	.083	12	1	0	0	0	0.0	0	1	1	3	0	0	0	13	0	0	0	3.3	1.000	OF-4
2 yrs.			9	.276	.621	29	8	4	0	2	6.9	5	10	5	6	0	0	0	23	0	0	0	2.6	.000	OF-9

Year	Team	Games	BA	SA	AB	H	2B	3B	HR	HR%	R	RBI	BB	SO	SB	PINCH HIT AB	H	PO	A	E	DP	TC/G	FA	G by Pos

Tom Brunansky *Continued*

WORLD SERIES
1987	MIN	A	7	.200	.200	25	5	0	0	0	0.0	5	2	4	4	1	0	0	14	0	0	0	2.0	1.000	OF-7

Bill Buckner

BUCKNER, WILLIAM JOSEPH (Billy Bucks)
B. Dec. 14, 1949, Vallejo, Calif.
BL TL 6′ 185 lbs.

Year	Team		Games	BA	SA	AB	H	2B	3B	HR	HR%	R	RBI	BB	SO	SB	AB	H	PO	A	E	DP	TC/G	FA	G by Pos
1969	LA	N	1	.000	.000	1	0	0	0	0	0.0	0	0	0	0	0	1	0	0	0	0	0	0.0	—	
1970			28	.191	.265	68	13	3	1	0	0.0	6	4	3	7	0	8	2	37	1	0	1	1.4	1.000	OF-20, 1B-1
1971			108	.277	.366	358	99	15	1	5	1.4	37	41	11	18	4	17	3	235	11	1	4	2.3	.996	OF-86, 1B-11
1972			105	.319	.410	383	122	14	3	5	1.3	47	37	17	13	10	11	3	434	22	4	28	4.4	.991	OF-61, 1B-35
1973			140	.275	.351	575	158	20	0	8	1.4	68	46	17	34	12	9	2	981	50	3	93	7.4	.997	1B-93, OF-48
1974			145	.314	.412	580	182	30	3	7	1.2	83	58	30	24	31	9	1	284	5	7	2	2.0	.976	OF-137, 1B-6
1975			92	.243	.358	288	70	11	2	6	2.1	30	31	17	15	8	19	3	138	4	2	0	1.6	.986	OF-72
1976			154	.301	.389	642	193	28	4	7	1.1	76	60	26	26	28	1	1	315	7	5	0	2.1	.985	OF-153, 1B-1
1977	CHI	N	122	.284	.425	426	121	27	0	11	2.6	40	60	21	23	7	22	7	966	58	10	75	8.5	.990	1B-99
1978			117	.323	.419	446	144	26	1	5	1.1	47	74	18	17	7	12	2	1075	83	6	85	9.9	.995	1B-105
1979			149	.284	.437	591	168	34	7	14	2.4	72	66	30	28	9	8	3	1258	124	7	118	9.3	.995	1B-140
1980			145	**.324**	.457	578	187	41	3	10	1.7	69	68	30	18	1	6	0	916	78	8	69	6.9	.992	1B-94, OF-50
1981			106	.311	.480	421	131	**35**	3	10	2.4	45	75	26	16	5	2	1	996	81	17	92	10.3	.984	1B-105
1982			161	.306	.441	**657**	201	34	5	15	2.3	93	105	36	26	15	0	0	1547	159	12	89	10.7	.993	1B-161
1983			153	.280	.436	626	175	**38**	6	16	2.6	79	66	25	30	12	2	1	1391	161	13	132	10.2	.992	1B-144, OF-15
1984	2 teams		CHI N	(21G — .209)		BOS A	(114G — .278)																		
"	total		135	.272	.392	482	131	21	2	11	2.3	54	69	25	39	2	12	3	1045	102	15	80	8.6	.987	1B-120, OF-2
1985	BOS	A	162	.299	.447	673	201	46	3	16	2.4	89	110	30	36	18	0	0	1384	184	12	140	9.8	.992	1B-162
1986			153	.267	.421	629	168	39	2	18	2.9	73	102	40	25	6	0	0	1067	157	14	104	8.1	.989	1B-138, DH-15
1987	2 teams		BOS A	(75G — .273)		CAL A	(57G — .306)																		
"	total		132	.286	.365	469	134	18	2	5	1.1	39	74	22	26	2	15	8	640	60	6	54	5.3	.992	1B-79, DH-39
1988	2 teams		CAL A	(19G — .209)		KC A	(89G — .256)																		
"			108	.249	.330	285	71	14	0	3	1.1	19	43	17	19	5	28	**8**	161	13	1	12	1.6	.994	DH-53, 1B-22
1989	KC	A	79	.216	.267	176	38	4	1	1	0.6	7	16	6	11	1	**38**	10	181	13	3	19	2.5	.985	1B-24, DH-19
1990	BOS	A	22	.186	.256	43	8	0	0	1	2.3	4	3	3	2	0	11	2	75	6	0	6	5.4	1.000	1B-15
22 yrs.			2517	.289	.408	9397	2715	498	49	174	1.9	1077	1208	450	453	183	231	60	15126	1366	146	1203	2.6	.978	1B-1555, OF-644, DH-126

LEAGUE CHAMPIONSHIP SERIES
1974	LA	N	4	.167	.222	18	3	1	0	0	0.0	0	0	0	2	0	0	0	6	0	0	0	1.5	1.000	OF-4
1986	BOS	A	7	.214	.250	28	6	1	0	0	0.0	3	3	0	2	0	0	0	51	5	0	4	8.0	1.000	1B-7
2 yrs.			11	.196	.239	46	9	2	0	0	0.0	3	3	0	4	0	0	0	57	5	0	4	5.6	.000	1B-7, OF-4

WORLD SERIES
1974	LA	N	5	.250	.450	20	5	1	0	1	5.0	1	1	0	1	0	0	0	11	0	0	0	2.2	1.000	OF-5
1986	BOS	A	7	.188	.188	32	6	0	0	0	0.0	2	1	1	3	0	0	0	53	7	1	5	8.7	.984	1B-7
2 yrs.			12	.212	.288	52	11	1	0	1	1.9	3	2	1	4	0	0	0	64	7	1	5	6.0	.986	1B-7, OF-5

Steve Buechele

BUECHELE, STEVEN BERNARD
B. Sept. 26, 1961, Lancaster, Calif.
BR TR 6′ 2″ 190 lbs.

	Games	BA	SA	AB	H	2B	3B	HR	HR%	R	RBI	BB	SO	SB
April	12	.290	.645	31	9	2	0	3	9.7	5	7	5	4	0
May	6	.133	.200	15	2	1	0	0	0.0	1	0	2	6	0
June	17	.154	.192	52	8	2	0	0	0.0	5	3	4	16	0
July	11	.265	.441	34	9	3	0	1	2.9	7	6	8	7	0
Aug	18	.264	.396	53	14	1	0	2	3.8	6	10	3	14	0
Sept/Oct	27	.182	.242	66	12	1	0	1	1.5	6	4	5	16	1
Day	16	.256	.372	43	11	2	0	1	2.3	8	5	8	10	0
Night	75	.207	.332	208	43	8	0	6	2.9	22	25	19	53	1
vs. Left		.275	.488	80	22	5	0	4	5.0	11	12	12	18	0
vs. Right		.187	.269	171	32	5	0	3	1.8	19	18	15	45	1

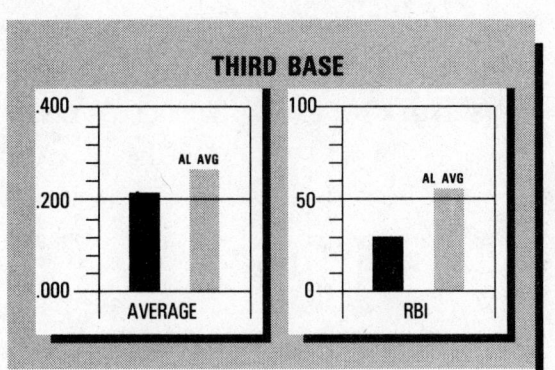

THIRD BASE

AVERAGE   RBI

Year	Team		Games	BA	SA	AB	H	2B	3B	HR	HR%	R	RBI	BB	SO	SB	PINCH HIT AB	H	PO	A	E	DP	TC/G	FA	G by Pos

Steve Buechele *Continued*

Year	Team		Games	BA	SA	AB	H	2B	3B	HR	HR%	R	RBI	BB	SO	SB	AB	H	PO	A	E	DP	TC/G	FA	G by Pos
On Grass			72	.238	.371	202	48	9	0	6	3.0	25	24	20	45	1									
On Turf			19	.122	.204	49	6	1	0	1	2.0	5	6	7	18	0									
Home			47	.243	.397	136	33	6	0	5	3.7	14	21	13	28	1									
Road			44	.183	.270	115	21	4	0	2	1.7	16	9	14	35	0									
Division Rivals																									
vs. CAL			11	.061	.091	33	2	1	0	0	0.0	3	2	1	9	0									
vs. CHI			6	.278	.278	18	5	0	0	0	0.0	0	1	1	5	0									
vs. KC			7	.136	.136	22	3	0	0	0	0.0	2	0	0	8	0									
vs. MIN			3	.000	.000	7	0	0	0	0	0.0	0	0	0	0	0									
vs. OAK			9	.304	.478	23	7	1	0	1	4.3	2	3	1	5	0									
vs. SEA			7	.167	.167	18	3	0	0	0	0.0	1	2	4	9	0									
On 3B < 2 Out				.222	.556	9	2	0	0	1	11.1	1	9	1	4										
1985	TEX	A	69	.219	.356	219	48	6	3	6	2.7	22	21	14	38	3	0	0	52	138	6	17	2.8	.969	3B-69, 2B-1
1986			153	.243	.410	461	112	19	2	18	3.9	54	54	35	98	5	2	1	174	292	12	42	3.1	.975	3B-137, 2B-33, OF-2
1987			136	.237	.399	363	86	20	0	13	3.6	45	50	28	66	2	2	1	89	211	9	20	2.3	.971	3B-123, 2B-18, OF-2
1988			155	.250	.404	503	126	21	4	16	3.2	68	58	65	79	2	2	0	114	300	16	25	2.8	.963	3B-153, 2B-2
1989			155	.235	.387	486	114	22	2	16	3.3	60	59	36	107	1	1	0	128	288	12	29	2.8	.972	3B-145, 2B-18, DH-1, SS-1
1990			91	.215	.339	251	54	10	0	7	2.7	30	30	27	63	1	2	0	72	160	8	7	2.7	.967	3B-88, 2B-4
6 yrs.			759	.237	.389	2283	540	98	11	76	3.3	279	272	205	451	14	9	2	629	1389	63	140	2.7	.970	3B-715, 2B-76, OF-4, DH-1, SS-1

THIRD BASE — HR / SB (AL AVG)

Jay Buhner

BUHNER, JAY CAMPBELL
B. Aug. 13, 1964, Louisville, Ky.
BR TR 6′ 3″ 205 lbs.

Year	Team		Games	BA	SA	AB	H	2B	3B	HR	HR%	R	RBI	BB	SO	SB	AB	H	PO	A	E	DP	TC/G	FA	G by Pos
1987	NY	A	7	.227	.318	22	5	2	0	0	0.0	0	1	1	6	0	0	0	11	1	0	1	1.7	1.000	OF-7
1988	2 teams		NY A (25G — .188)			SEA A (60G — .224)																			
"	total		85	.215	.421	261	56	13	1	13	5.0	36	38	28	93	1	4	1	186	9	3	3	2.3	.985	OF-81
1989	SEA	A	58	.275	.490	204	56	15	1	9	4.4	27	33	19	55	1	0	0	106	6	4	3	2.0	.966	OF-57
1990			51	.276	.479	163	45	12	0	7	4.2	16	33	17	50	2	3	0	55	1	2	0	1.5	.966	OF-40, DH-10
4 yrs.			201	.249	.454	650	162	42	2	29	4.5	79	105	65	204	4	7	1	358	17	9	7	1.9	.977	OF-185, DH-10

Eric Bullock

BULLOCK, ERIC GERALD
B. Feb. 16, 1960, Los Angeles, Calif.
BL TL 5′ 11″ 185 lbs.

Year	Team		Games	BA	SA	AB	H	2B	3B	HR	HR%	R	RBI	BB	SO	SB	AB	H	PO	A	E	DP	TC/G	FA	G by Pos
1985	HOU	N	18	.280	.360	25	7	2	0	0	0.0	3	2	1	3	0	12	3	6	0	2	0	0.4	.750	OF-7
1986			6	.048	.048	21	1	0	0	0	0.0	0	1	0	3	2	0	0	7	0	1	0	1.3	.875	OF-6
1988	MIN	A	16	.294	.294	17	5	0	0	0	0.0	3	3	3	1	1	10	3	7	0	1	0	0.5	.875	OF-4, DH-2
1989	PHI	N	6	.000	.000	4	0	0	0	0	0.0	1	0	0	2	0	3	0	2	0	0	0	0.3	1.000	OF-3
1990	MON	N	4	.500	.500	2	1	0	0	0	0.0	0	0	0	0	0	2	1	0	0	0	0	0.0	.995	
5 yrs.			50	.203	.232	69	14	2	0	0	0.0	7	6	4	9	3	27	7	22	0	4	0	0.5	.000	OF-20, DH-2

Ellis Burks

BURKS, ELLIS RENA
B. Sept. 11, 1964, Vicksburg, Miss.
BR TR 6′ 2″ 175 lbs.

Year	Team		Games	BA	SA	AB	H	2B	3B	HR	HR%	R	RBI	BB	SO	SB	AB	H	PO	A	E	DP	TC/G	FA	G by Pos
April			19	.213	.275	80	17	0	0	0	0.0	7	8	6	12	2									
May			26	.319	.585	94	30	7	3	4	4.3	18	16	9	11	1									
June			27	.337	.615	104	35	7	2	6	5.8	18	16	8	11	3									
July			21	.338	.451	71	24	5	0	1	1.4	12	10	6	11	2									
Aug			28	.319	.534	116	37	6	2	5	4.3	18	22	12	17	1									
Sept/Oct			31	.252	.415	123	31	3	1	5	4.1	16	17	7	20	0									
Day			49	.296	.455	189	56	10	1	6	3.2	29	29	21	22	6									
Night			103	.296	.501	399	118	23	7	15	3.8	60	60	27	60	3									
vs. Left				.298	.452	188	56	10	2	5	2.7	33	24	20	26	1									
vs. Right				.295	.503	400	118	23	6	16	4.0	56	65	28	56	8									

OUTFIELD — AVERAGE / RBI (AL AVG)

Year	Team	Games	BA	SA	AB	H	2B	3B	HR	HR%	R	RBI	BB	SO	SB	PINCH HIT AB	PINCH HIT H	PO	A	E	DP	TC/G	FA	G by Pos

Ellis Burks *Continued*

Year	Team	Games	BA	SA	AB	H	2B	3B	HR	HR%	R	RBI	BB	SO	SB	PINCH HIT AB	PINCH HIT H	PO	A	E	DP	TC/G	FA	G by Pos
On Grass		130	.297	.495	505	150	28	6	20	4.0	78	78	38	74	6									
On Turf		22	.289	.434	83	24	5	2	1	1.2	11	11	10	8	3									
Home		78	.306	.502	297	91	20	4	10	3.4	44	48	23	39	4									
Road		74	.285	.471	291	83	13	4	11	3.8	45	41	25	43	5									
Division Rivals																								
vs. BAL		13	.373	.529	51	19	2	0	2	3.9	8	6	4	5	1									
vs. CLE		13	.386	.842	57	22	3	1	7	12.3	11	19	3	10	0									
vs. DET		13	.321	.434	53	17	3	0	1	1.9	9	5	5	9	1									
vs. MIL		11	.167	.214	42	7	2	0	0	0.0	3	3	2	6	1									
vs. NY		12	.350	.750	40	14	2	1	4	10.0	12	10	7	4	1									
vs. TOR		12	.200	.289	45	9	2	1	0	0.0	6	2	5	8	1									
On 3B < 2 Out			.250	.464	28	7	0	0	2	7.1	2	14	3	6										
1987	BOS A	133	.272	.441	558	152	30	2	20	3.6	94	59	41	98	27	0	0	320	15	4	2	2.5	.988	OF-132
1988		144	.294	.481	540	159	37	5	18	3.3	93	92	62	89	25	0	0	370	9	9	0	2.7	.977	OF-142, DH-2
1989		97	.303	.471	399	121	19	6	12	3.0	73	61	36	52	21	0	0	245	7	6	3	2.7	.977	OF-95, DH-1
1990		152	.296	.486	588	174	33	8	21	3.5	89	89	48	82	9	3	1	324	7	2	0	2.3	.994	OF-143, DH-6
4 yrs.		526	.291	.470	2085	606	119	21	71	3.4	349	301	187	321	82	3	1	1259	38	21	5	2.5	.984	OF-512, DH-9

LEAGUE CHAMPIONSHIP SERIES

Year	Team	Games	BA	SA	AB	H	2B	3B	HR	HR%	R	RBI	BB	SO	SB	PINCH HIT AB	PINCH HIT H	PO	A	E	DP	TC/G	FA	G by Pos
1988	BOS A	4	.235	.294	17	4	1	0	0	0.0	2	1	0	3	0	0	0	10	0	0	0	2.5	1.000	OF-4
1990		4	.267	.400	15	4	2	0	0	0.0	1	0	1	1	1	0	0	9	1	0	0	2.5	1.000	OF-4
2 yrs.		8	.250	.344	32	8	3	0	0	0.0	3	1	1	4	1	0	0	19	1	0	0	2.5	.000	OF-8

Randy Bush

BUSH, ROBERT RANDALL
B. Oct. 5, 1958, Dover, Del.
BL TL 6′ 1″ 190 lbs.

Year	Team	Games	BA	SA	AB	H	2B	3B	HR	HR%	R	RBI	BB	SO	SB	PINCH HIT AB	PINCH HIT H	PO	A	E	DP	TC/G	FA	G by Pos
1982	MIN A	55	.244	.412	119	29	6	1	4	3.4	13	13	8	28	0	25	3	7	0	0	0	0.1	1.000	DH-26, OF-6
1983		124	.249	.418	373	93	24	3	11	2.9	43	56	34	51	0	19	4	21	3	0	1	0.2	1.000	DH-103, 1B-3
1984		113	.225	.392	311	70	17	1	11	3.5	46	43	31	60	1	20	8	5	0	0	1	0.0	1.000	DH-89, 1B-2
1985		97	.239	.449	234	56	13	3	10	4.3	26	35	24	30	3	32	4	79	0	2	1	0.8	.975	OF-41, DH-28, 1B-1
1986		130	.269	.420	357	96	19	7	7	2.0	50	45	39	63	5	30	13	182	2	4	2	1.4	.979	OF-102, DH-6, 1B-3
1987		122	.253	.413	293	74	10	2	11	3.8	46	46	43	49	10	30	7	164	5	4	4	1.4	.977	OF-75, DH-9, 1B-9
1988		136	.261	.434	394	103	20	3	14	3.6	51	51	58	49	8	19	6	206	5	4	1	1.6	.981	OF-115, DH-17
1989		141	.263	.435	391	103	17	4	14	3.6	60	54	48	73	5	18	1	339	14	3	14	2.5	.992	OF-109, 1B-25, DH-5
1990		73	.243	.387	181	44	8	0	6	3.3	17	18	21	27	0	12	2	64	3	0	1	1.9	1.000	OF-32, DH-29, 1B-6
9 yrs.		991	.252	.420	2653	668	134	24	88	3.3	352	361	306	430	32	205	48	1067	32	17	25	1.1	.985	OF-480, DH-312, 1B-49

LEAGUE CHAMPIONSHIP SERIES

Year	Team	Games	BA	SA	AB	H	2B	3B	HR	HR%	R	RBI	BB	SO	SB	PINCH HIT AB	PINCH HIT H	PO	A	E	DP	TC/G	FA	G by Pos
1987	MIN A	4	.250	.417	12	3	0	1	0	0.0	4	2	3	2	3	0	0	0	0	0	0	0.0	—	DH-4

WORLD SERIES

Year	Team	Games	BA	SA	AB	H	2B	3B	HR	HR%	R	RBI	BB	SO	SB	PINCH HIT AB	PINCH HIT H	PO	A	E	DP	TC/G	FA	G by Pos
1987	MIN A	4	.167	.333	6	1	1	0	0	0.0	1	2	0	1	0	3	0	0	0	0	0	0.0	—	DH-2

Brett Butler

BUTLER, BRETT MORGAN
B. June 15, 1957, Los Angeles, Calif.
BL TL 5′ 10″ 160 lbs.

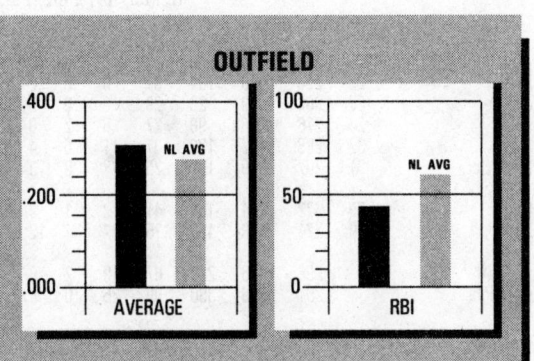

Year	Team	Games	BA	SA	AB	H	2B	3B	HR	HR%	R	RBI	BB	SO	SB	PINCH HIT AB	PINCH HIT H	PO	A	E	DP	TC/G	FA	G by Pos
April		20	.366	.488	82	30	5	1	1	1.2	16	7	13	4	4									
May		28	.182	.182	110	20	0	0	0	0.0	14	3	16	15	12									
June		26	.293	.333	99	29	4	0	0	0.0	15	8	20	9	8									
July		27	.346	.458	107	37	3	3	1	0.9	20	10	12	11	6									
Aug		28	.311	.369	103	32	4	1	0	0.0	16	9	14	10	7									
Sept/Oct		31	.364	.488	121	44	4	4	1	0.8	27	7	15	13	14									
Day		63	.294	.367	248	73	9	0	3	1.2	48	17	39	32	16									
Night		97	.318	.396	374	119	11	9	0	0.0	60	27	51	30	35									
vs. Left			.302	.355	245	74	6	2	1	0.4	49	20	33	28	18									
vs. Right			.313	.403	377	118	14	7	2	0.5	59	24	57	34	33									

Year	Team		Games	BA	SA	AB	H	2B	3B	HR	HR%	R	RBI	BB	SO	SB	PINCH HIT AB	H	PO	A	E	DP	TC/G	FA	G by Pos

Brett Butler *Continued*

Year	Team		Games	BA	SA	AB	H	2B	3B	HR	HR%	R	RBI	BB	SO	SB	AB	H	PO	A	E	DP	TC/G	FA	G by Pos
On Grass			119	.323	.409	464	150	19	6	3	0.6	86	35	69	42	39									
On Turf			41	.266	.310	158	42	1	3	0	0.0	22	9	21	20	12									
Home			81	.337	.410	312	105	12	1	3	1.0	59	25	50	28	27									
Road			79	.281	.358	310	87	8	8	0	0.0	49	19	40	34	24									
Division Rivals																									
vs. ATL			17	.328	.475	61	20	2	2	1	1.6	12	7	15	4	10									
vs. CIN			18	.262	.277	65	17	1	0	0	0.0	13	4	15	10	1									
vs. HOU			18	.266	.281	64	17	1	0	0	0.0	12	3	14	8	11									
vs. LA			18	.411	.534	73	30	5	2	0	0.0	16	4	6	6	8									
vs. SD			18	.342	.479	73	25	3	2	1	1.4	13	5	8	5	3									
On 3B < 2 Out				.261	.261	23	6	0	0	0	0.0	0	21	2	2										
1981	ATL	N	40	.254	.317	126	32	2	3	0	0.0	17	4	19	17	9	2	1	76	2	1	0	2.0	.987	OF–37
1982			89	.217	.225	240	52	2	0	0	0.0	35	7	25	35	21	6	1	129	2	0	0	1.5	1.000	OF–77
1983			151	.281	.393	549	154	21	**13**	5	0.9	84	37	54	56	39	6	1	284	13	4	4	2.0	.987	OF–143
1984	CLE	A	159	.269	.355	602	162	25	9	3	0.5	108	49	86	62	52	3	0	448	13	4	3	2.9	.991	OF–156
1985			152	.311	.431	591	184	28	14	5	0.8	106	50	63	42	47	1	0	437	19	1	5	3.0	.998	OF–150, DH–1
1986			161	.278	.375	587	163	17	**14**	4	0.7	92	51	70	65	32	1	0	434	9	3	3	2.8	.993	OF–159
1987			137	.295	.425	522	154	25	8	9	1.7	91	41	91	55	33	0	0	393	4	4	2	2.9	.990	OF–136
1988	SF	N	157	.287	.398	568	163	27	9	6	1.1	**109**	43	97	64	43	2	0	395	3	5	1	2.6	.988	OF–155
1989			154	.283	.354	594	168	22	4	4	0.7	100	36	59	69	31	0	0	407	11	6	3	2.8	.986	OF–152
1990			160	.309	.384	622	**192**	20	9	3	0.4	108	44	90	62	51	1	0	420	4	6	0	2.7	.986	OF–159
10 yrs.			1360	.285	.379	5001	1424	189	83	39	0.8	850	362	654	527	358	22	3	3423	80	34	21	2.6	.990	OF–1324, DH–1
LEAGUE CHAMPIONSHIP SERIES																									
1982	ATL	N	2	.000	.000	1	0	0	0	0	0.0	0	0	0	0	0	1	0	0	0	0	0	0.0	—	OF–1
1989	SF	N	5	.211	.211	19	4	0	0	0	0.0	6	0	3	3	0	0	0	9	0	0	0	1.8	1.000	OF–5
2 yrs.			7	.200	.200	20	4	0	0	0	0.0	6	0	3	3	0	1	0	9	0	0	0	1.3	.000	OF–6
WORLD SERIES																									
1989	SF	N	4	.286	.357	14	4	1	0	0	0.0	1	1	2	1	2	0	0	9	0	0	0	2.3	1.000	OF–4

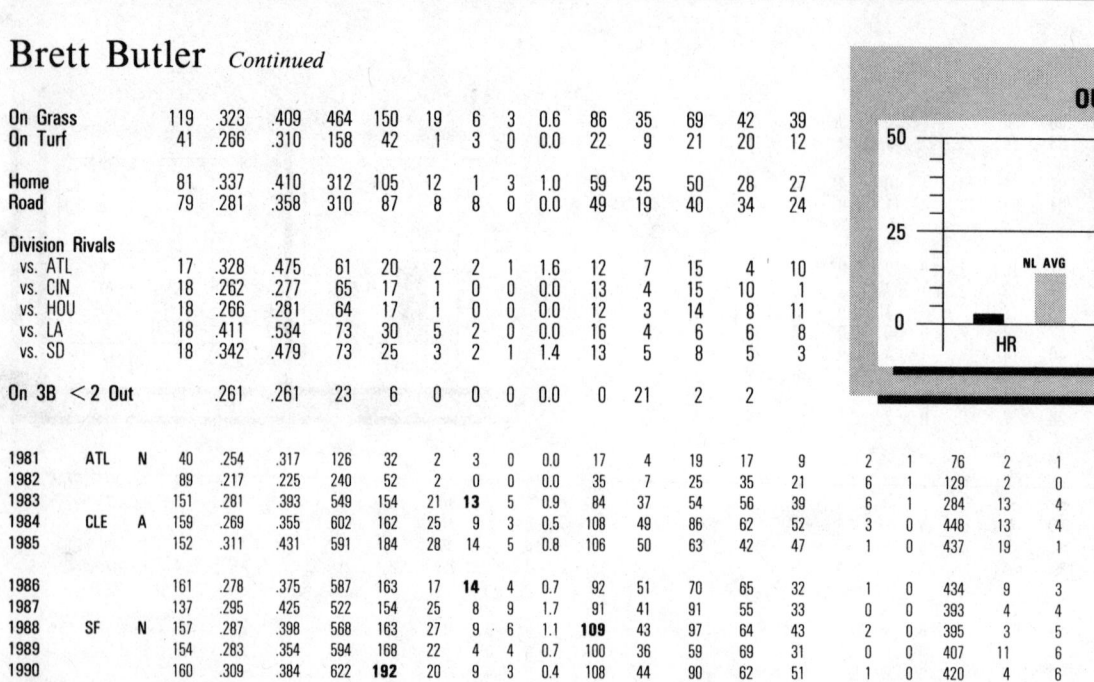

OUTFIELD

HR — NL AVG

SB — NL AVG

Francisco Cabrera

CABRERA, FRANCISCO
Born Francisco Cabrera y Paulino.
B. Oct. 10, 1966, Santo Domingo, Dominican Republic
BR TR 6′ 4″ 195 lbs.

Year	Team		Games	BA	SA	AB	H	2B	3B	HR	HR%	R	RBI	BB	SO	SB	AB	H	PO	A	E	DP	TC/G	FA	G by Pos
1989	2 teams		TOR A (3G — .167)			ATL N (4G — .214)																			
"	total		7	.192	.308	26	5	3	0	0	0.0	1	0	1	6	0	1	0	27	1	1	1	4.1	.966	DH–3, 1B–2, C–1
1990	ATL	N	63	.277	.482	137	38	5	1	7	5.1	14	25	5	21	1	21	6	269	19	3	15	5.8	.990	1B–48, C–3
2 yrs.			70	.264	.454	163	43	8	1	7	4.3	15	25	6	27	1	22	6	296	20	4	16	4.6	.988	1B–50, C–4, DH–3

Ivan Calderon

CALDERON, IVAN
Born Ivan Calderon y Perez.
B. Mar. 19, 1962, Fajardo, Puerto Rico
BR TR 5′ 11″ 160 lbs.

Period			Games	BA	SA	AB	H	2B	3B	HR	HR%	R	RBI	BB	SO	SB
April			16	.293	.500	58	17	6	0	2	3.4	9	13	7	12	5
May			28	.298	.413	104	31	6	0	2	1.9	18	12	12	15	9
June			27	.302	.479	96	29	8	0	3	3.1	11	14	11	15	7
July			24	.276	.378	98	27	6	2	0	0.0	14	10	8	9	6
Aug			32	.285	.462	130	37	11	0	4	3.1	18	16	4	10	2
Sept/Oct			31	.207	.339	121	25	7	0	3	2.5	15	9	9	18	3
Day			39	.272	.404	151	41	12	1	2	1.3	16	14	16	21	10
Night			119	.274	.428	456	125	32	1	12	2.6	69	60	35	58	22
vs. Left				.295	.478	227	67	19	2	6	2.6	32	27	21	25	14
vs. Right				.261	.389	380	99	25	0	8	2.1	53	47	30	54	18

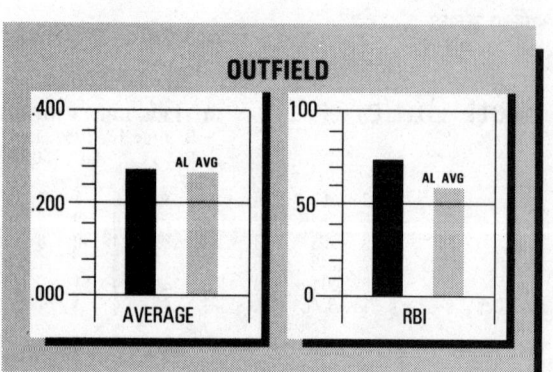

OUTFIELD

AVERAGE — AL AVG

RBI — AL AVG

Year	Team	Games	BA	SA	AB	H	2B	3B	HR	HR%	R	RBI	BB	SO	SB	PINCH HIT AB	H	PO	A	E	DP	TC/G	FA	G by Pos

Ivan Calderon *Continued*

Year	Team	Games	BA	SA	AB	H	2B	3B	HR	HR%	R	RBI	BB	SO	SB	AB	H	PO	A	E	DP	TC/G	FA	G by Pos
On Grass		132	.295	.451	508	150	39	2	12	2.4	76	66	41	61	29									
On Turf		26	.162	.273	99	16	5	0	2	2.0	9	8	10	18	3									
Home		77	.306	.468	284	87	24	2	6	2.1	45	40	30	37	19									
Road		81	.245	.381	323	79	20	0	8	2.5	40	34	21	42	13									
Division Rivals																								
vs. CAL		13	.333	.510	51	17	6	0	1	2.0	5	5	3	4	0									
vs. KC		13	.275	.392	51	14	3	0	1	2.0	6	7	5	9	2									
vs. MIN		13	.292	.458	48	14	5	0	1	2.1	6	4	2	6	3									
vs. OAK		13	.280	.340	50	14	0	0	1	2.0	8	8	5	3	2									
vs. SEA		12	.154	.282	39	6	2	0	1	2.6	5	3	7	8	1									
vs. TEX		13	.308	.404	52	16	5	0	0	0.0	5	4	5	8	1									
On 3B < 2 Out			.345	.483	29	10	1	0	1	3.4	1	24	5	4										

Year	Team		Games	BA	SA	AB	H	2B	3B	HR	HR%	R	RBI	BB	SO	SB	AB	H	PO	A	E	DP	TC/G	FA	G by Pos
1984	SEA	A	11	.208	.375	24	5	1	0	1	4.2	2	1	2	5	1	0	0	22	0	0	0	2.0	1.000	OF-11
1985			67	.286	.514	210	60	16	4	8	3.8	37	28	19	45	4	10	3	108	5	2	3	1.7	.983	OF-53, DH-3, 1B-2
1986	2 teams		50	SEA A (37G — .237)		CHI A (13G — .303)																			
"	total		50	.250	.341	164	41	7	1	2	1.2	16	15	9	39	3	7	2	64	4	5	1	1.5	.932	OF-37, DH-6
1987	CHI	A	144	.293	.526	542	159	38	2	28	5.2	93	83	60	109	10	1	0	295	8	5	3	2.1	.984	OF-139, DH-3
1988			73	.212	.424	264	56	14	0	14	5.3	40	35	34	66	4	1	0	141	5	7	1	2.1	.954	OF-67, DH-3
1989			157	.286	.437	622	178	34	9	14	2.3	83	87	43	94	7	2	0	384	17	9	24	2.6	.978	OF-103, DH-36, 1B-26
1990			158	.273	.422	607	166	44	2	14	2.3	85	74	51	79	32	2	1	269	7	7	1	2.2	.975	OF-130, DH-27, 1B-2
7 yrs.			660	.273	.451	2433	665	154	18	81	3.3	356	323	218	437	61	23	6	1283	46	35	33	2.1	.974	OF-540, DH-78, 1B-30

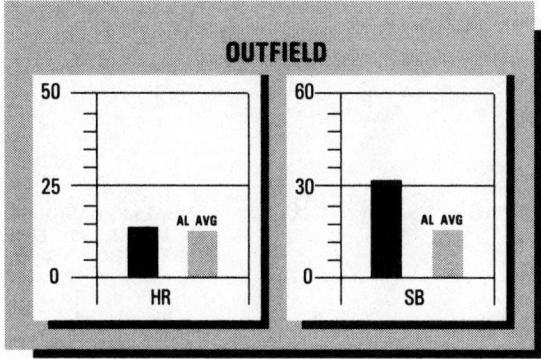

OUTFIELD

Ken Caminiti

CAMINITI, KENNETH GENE
B. Apr. 21, 1963, Hanford, Calif.
BB TR 6' 3" 200 lbs.

Year	Team	Games	BA	SA	AB	H	2B	3B	HR	HR%	R	RBI	BB	SO	SB	AB	H	PO	A	E	DP	TC/G	FA	G by Pos
April		19	.266	.297	64	17	2	0	0	0.0	5	4	6	17	1									
May		27	.302	.396	96	29	3	0	2	2.1	12	13	8	13	1									
June		28	.206	.237	97	20	3	0	0	0.0	5	9	6	15	2									
July		23	.276	.322	87	24	4	0	0	0.0	14	8	10	15	0									
Aug		26	.226	.301	93	21	5	1	0	0.0	5	6	8	19	0									
Sept/Oct		30	.192	.298	104	20	3	1	2	1.9	11	11	10	18	5									
Day		38	.250	.352	128	32	3	2	2	1.6	14	13	13	23	3									
Night		115	.240	.295	413	99	17	0	2	0.5	38	38	35	74	6									
vs. Left			.246	.317	240	59	9	1	2	0.8	23	23	13	35	3									
vs. Right			.239	.302	301	72	11	1	2	0.7	29	28	35	62	6									
On Grass		45	.195	.252	159	31	4	1	1	0.6	13	10	15	33	1									
On Turf		108	.262	.332	382	100	16	1	3	0.8	39	41	33	64	8									
Home		81	.288	.361	285	82	15	0	2	0.7	34	31	27	47	4									
Road		72	.191	.250	256	49	5	2	2	0.8	18	20	21	50	5									
Division Rivals																								
vs. ATL		17	.254	.305	59	15	3	0	0	0.0	6	5	5	10	1									
vs. CIN		18	.200	.323	65	13	0	1	2	3.1	4	7	3	13	4									
vs. LA		18	.250	.317	60	15	4	0	0	0.0	7	6	4	15	1									
vs. SD		18	.230	.279	61	14	3	0	0	0.0	4	7	6	8	0									
vs. SF		17	.188	.219	64	12	2	0	0	0.0	2	5	5	8	1									
On 3B < 2 Out			.368	.421	19	7	1	0	0	0.0	0	18	6	4										

Year	Team		Games	BA	SA	AB	H	2B	3B	HR	HR%	R	RBI	BB	SO	SB	AB	H	PO	A	E	DP	TC/G	FA	G by Pos
1987	HOU	N	63	.246	.335	203	50	7	1	3	1.5	10	23	12	44	0	9	2	50	98	8	11	2.5	.949	3B-61
1988			30	.181	.241	83	15	2	0	1	1.2	5	7	5	18	0	5	0	12	43	3	2	1.9	.948	3B-28
1989			161	.255	.369	585	149	31	3	10	1.7	71	72	51	93	4	2	0	126	335	22	27	3.0	.954	3B-160
1990			153	.242	.309	541	131	20	2	4	0.7	52	51	48	97	9	10	1	118	243	21	22	2.6	.945	3B-149
4 yrs.			407	.244	.334	1412	345	60	6	18	1.3	138	153	116	252	13	26	3	306	719	54	62	2.7	.950	3B-398

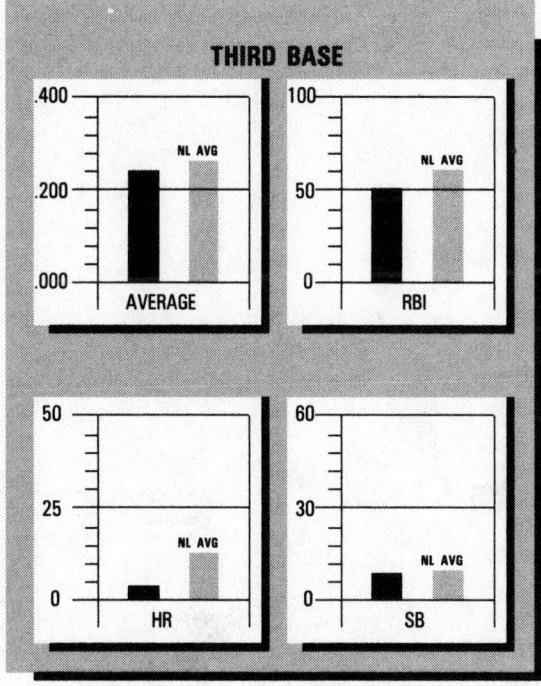

THIRD BASE

Sil Campusano

CAMPUSANO, SILVESTRE
Born Silvestre Campusano y Diaz.
B. Dec. 31, 1965, Santo Domingo, Dominican Republic
BR TR 6' 160 lbs.

Year	Team		Games	BA	SA	AB	H	2B	3B	HR	HR%	R	RBI	BB	SO	SB	AB	H	PO	A	E	DP	TC/G	FA	G by Pos
1988	TOR	A	73	.218	.359	142	31	10	2	2	1.4	14	12	9	33	0	2	0	111	2	8	0	1.7	.934	OF-69, DH-2
1990	PHI	N	66	.212	.318	85	18	1	1	2	2.3	10	9	6	16	1	16	2	40	1	1	0	0.9	.976	OF-47
2 yrs.			139	.216	.344	227	49	11	3	4	1.8	24	21	15	49	1	18	2	151	3	9	0	1.2	.945	OF-116, DH-2

Year	Team	Games	BA	SA	AB	H	2B	3B	HR	HR%	R	RBI	BB	SO	SB	PINCH HIT AB	H	PO	A	E	DP	TC/G	FA	G by Pos

George Canale

CANALE, GEORGE ANTHONY
B. Aug. 11, 1965, Memphis, Tenn.
BL TR 6' 1" 190 lbs.

Year	Team	Games	BA	SA	AB	H	2B	3B	HR	HR%	R	RBI	BB	SO	SB	PINCH HIT AB	H	PO	A	E	DP	TC/G	FA	G by Pos
1989	MIL A	13	.192	.346	26	5	1	0	1	3.8	5	3	2	3	0	0	0	86	4	1	4	7.0	.989	1B-11
1990		10	.077	.154	13	1	1	0	0	0.0	4	0	2	6	0	1	1	32	4	0	1	6.0	1.000	1B-6, DH-3
2 yrs.		23	.154	.282	39	6	2	0	1	2.6	9	3	4	9	0	1	1	118	8	1	5	5.5	.992	1B-17, DH-3

Casey Candaele

CANDAELE, CASEY TODD
B. Jan. 12, 1961, Lompoc, Calif.
BB TR 5' 9" 160 lbs.

Split	Games	BA	SA	AB	H	2B	3B	HR	HR%	R	RBI	BB	SO	SB
April	8	.273	.545	11	3	0	0	1	9.1	2	1	1	3	0
May	26	.238	.238	42	10	0	0	0	0.0	2	1	7	8	4
June	23	.240	.640	25	6	0	2	2	8.0	6	4	4	5	0
July	24	.370	.478	46	17	1	2	0	0.0	8	1	7	10	1
Aug	19	.243	.405	37	9	4	1	0	0.0	6	6	3	5	0
Sept/Oct	30	.297	.347	101	30	3	1	0	0.0	6	9	9	11	2
Day	32	.241	.310	58	14	2	1	0	0.0	8	6	10	9	2
Night	98	.299	.422	204	61	6	5	3	1.5	22	16	21	33	5
vs. Left		.341	.444	126	43	3	2	2	1.6	17	10	14	12	5
vs. Right		.235	.353	136	32	5	4	1	0.7	13	12	17	30	2
On Grass	41	.347	.480	75	26	2	1	2	2.7	9	10	10	10	2
On Turf	89	.262	.364	187	49	6	5	1	0.5	21	12	21	32	5
Home	61	.286	.413	126	36	3	5	1	0.8	18	12	17	18	4
Road	69	.287	.382	136	39	5	1	2	1.5	12	10	14	24	3
Division Rivals														
vs. ATL	12	.300	.467	30	9	1	2	0	0.0	3	6	3	4	1
vs. CIN	13	.263	.316	38	10	0	1	0	0.0	3	3	1	9	0
vs. LA	13	.370	.741	27	10	1	0	3	11.1	5	7	3	3	0
vs. SD	14	.250	.450	20	5	0	2	0	0.0	3	0	3	5	0
vs. SF	17	.242	.273	33	8	1	0	0	0.0	3	0	5	0	1
On 3B < 2 Out		.300	.300	10	3	0	0	0	0.0	0	3	3	2	

OUTFIELD — AVERAGE, RBI, HR, SB (with NL AVG comparisons)

Year	Team	Games	BA	SA	AB	H	2B	3B	HR	HR%	R	RBI	BB	SO	SB	PINCH HIT AB	H	PO	A	E	DP	TC/G	FA	G by Pos
1986	MON N	30	.231	.288	104	24	4	1	0	0.0	9	6	5	15	3	3	1	45	74	2	13	4.0	.983	2B-24, 3B-4
1987		138	.272	.347	449	122	23	4	1	0.2	62	23	38	28	7	12	3	237	176	8	28	3.1	.981	2B-68, OF-67, SS-25, 1B-1
1988	2 teams		MON N (36G — .172)			HOU N (21G — .161)																		
"	total	57	.170	.238	147	25	8	1	0	0.0	11	5	11	17	1	7	1	79	126	2	21	3.6	.990	2B-45, OF-5, 3B-1
1990	HOU N	130	.286	.397	262	75	8	6	3	1.1	30	22	31	42	7	30	10	147	120	3	20	2.5	.989	OF-58, 2B-49, SS-13, 3B-1
4 yrs.		355	.256	.338	962	246	43	12	4	0.4	112	56	85	102	18	52	15	508	496	15	82	2.9	.985	2B-186, OF-130, SS-38, 3B-6, 1B-1

John Cangelosi

CANGELOSI, JOHN ANTHONY
B. Mar. 10, 1963, Brooklyn, N. Y.
BB TL 5' 8" 150 lbs.

Year	Team	Games	BA	SA	AB	H	2B	3B	HR	HR%	R	RBI	BB	SO	SB	PINCH HIT AB	H	PO	A	E	DP	TC/G	FA	G by Pos
1985	CHI A	5	.000	.000	2	0	0	0	0	0.0	2	0	0	1	0	0	0	1	0	0	0	0.2	1.000	OF-3, DH-2
1986		137	.235	.299	438	103	16	3	2	0.5	65	32	71	61	50	1	0	276	7	9	1	2.1	.969	OF-129, DH-3
1987	PIT N	104	.275	.418	182	50	8	3	4	2.2	44	18	46	33	21	50	10	74	3	3	0	0.8	.963	OF-47
1988		75	.254	.305	118	30	4	1	0	0.0	18	8	17	16	9	42	12	52	0	2	0	0.7	.963	OF-24, P-1
1989		112	.219	.269	160	35	4	2	0	0.0	18	9	35	20	11	**68**	12	71	1	2	0	0.7	.973	OF-46
1990		58	.197	.224	76	15	2	0	0	0.0	13	1	11	12	7	36	8	24	0	0	0	2.0	1.000	OF-12
6 yrs.		491	.239	.310	976	233	34	9	6	0.6	160	68	180	143	98	197	42	498	11	16	1	1.1	.970	OF-261, DH-5, P-1

Year	Team	Games	BA	SA	AB	H	2B	3B	HR	HR%	R	RBI	BB	SO	SB	PINCH HIT AB	H	PO	A	E	DP	TC/G	FA	G by Pos

Jose Canseco

CANSECO, JOSE
Born Jose Canseco y Capas.
Brother of Ozzie Canseco.
B. July 2, 1964, Havana, Cuba
BR TR 6' 3" 185 lbs.

OUTFIELD

	Games	BA	SA	AB	H	2B	3B	HR	HR%	R	RBI	BB	SO	SB	AB	H	PO	A	E	DP	TC/G	FA	G by Pos
April	19	.300	.514	70	21	0	0	5	7.1	15	12	18	22	6									
May	27	.353	.765	102	36	3	0	13	12.7	24	35	14	30	5									
June	9	.161	.355	31	5	0	0	2	6.5	4	3	3	16	1									
July	29	.300	.673	110	33	3	1	12	10.9	21	27	11	30	3									
Aug	22	.212	.365	85	18	4	0	3	3.5	9	11	10	28	1									
Sept/Oct	25	.229	.373	83	19	4	1	2	2.4	10	13	16	32	3									
Day	48	.285	.588	165	47	6	1	14	8.5	28	38	29	56	5									
Night	83	.269	.519	316	85	8	1	23	7.3	55	63	43	102	14									
vs. Left		.276	.610	123	34	3	1	12	9.8	26	28	15	41	3									
vs. Right		.274	.520	358	98	11	1	25	7.0	57	73	57	117	16									
On Grass	112	.267	.518	409	109	11	1	30	7.3	68	80	64	131	17									
On Turf	19	.319	.681	72	23	3	1	7	9.7	15	21	8	27	2									
Home	64	.258	.539	217	56	7	0	18	8.3	40	43	45	71	10									
Road	67	.288	.545	264	76	7	2	19	7.2	43	58	27	87	9									
Division Rivals																								
vs. CAL	13	.413	.826	46	19	1	0	6	13.0	9	19	11	12	2									
vs. CHI	7	.217	.261	23	5	1	0	0	0.0	0	2	3	11	0									
vs. KC	8	.231	.385	26	6	1	0	1	3.8	3	2	5	15	0									
vs. MIN	13	.306	.714	49	15	2	0	6	12.2	11	10	8	15	3									
vs. SEA	13	.163	.265	49	8	0	1	1	2.0	9	5	10	23	3									
vs. TEX	10	.206	.324	34	7	1	0	1	2.9	3	6	4	10	1									
On 3B < 2 Out		.278	.528	36	10	0	0	3	8.3	3	26	8	15										
1985 OAK A	29	.302	.490	96	29	3	0	5	5.2	16	13	4	31	1	4	1	56	2	3	1	2.1	.951	OF-26
1986	157	.240	.457	600	144	29	1	33	5.5	85	117	65	175	15	1	1	319	4	14	1	2.1	.958	OF-155, DH-1
1987	159	.257	.470	630	162	35	3	31	4.9	81	113	50	157	15	1	0	263	12	7	3	1.8	.975	OF-130, DH-30
1988	158	.307	**.569**	610	187	34	0	**42**	**6.9**	120	**124**	78	128	40	1	0	304	11	7	3	2.0	.978	OF-144, DH-13
1989	65	.269	.542	227	61	9	1	17	7.5	40	57	23	69	6	3	1	119	5	3	2	2.0	.976	OF-56, DH-5
1990	131	.274	.543	481	132	14	2	37	7.6	83	101	72	158	19	2	1	182	7	1	2	2.2	.995	OF-88, DH-43
6 yrs.	699	.270	.510	2644	715	124	7	165	6.2	425	525	292	718	96	12	4	1243	41	35	12	1.9	.973	OF-599, DH-92
LEAGUE CHAMPIONSHIP SERIES																								
1988 OAK A	4	.313	.938	16	5	1	0	3	18.8	4	4	1	2	1	0	0	6	0	0	0	1.5	1.000	OF-4
1989	5	.294	.471	17	5	0	0	1	5.9	1	3	3	7	0	1	0	6	1	1	0	1.6	.875	OF-5
1990	4	.182	.182	11	2	0	0	0	0.0	3	1	5	5	2	0	0	14	0	0	0	3.5	1.000	OF-4
3 yrs.	13	.273	.568	44	12	1	0	4	9.1	8	8	9	14	3	1	0	26	1	1	0	2.2	.964	OF-13
WORLD SERIES																								
1988 OAK A	5	.053	.211	19	1	0	0	1	5.3	1	5	2	5	1	0	0	8	0	0	0	1.6	1.000	OF-5
1989	4	.357	.571	14	5	0	0	1	7.1	5	3	4	3	1	0	0	6	0	0	0	1.5	1.000	OF-4
1990	4	.083	.333	12	1	0	0	1	8.3	1	2	2	3	0	1	0	4	0	0	0	1.3	1.000	OF-3, DH-1
3 yrs.	13	.156	.356	45	7	0	0	3	6.7	7	10	8	11	2	1	0	18	0	0	0	1.4	.000	OF-12, DH-1

Ozzie Canseco

CANSECO, OSVALDO
Born Osvaldo Canseco y Capas. Brother of Jose Canseco.
B. July 2, 1964, Havana, Cuba
BR TR 6' 3" 220 lbs.

Year	Team	Games	BA	SA	AB	H	2B	3B	HR	HR%	R	RBI	BB	SO	SB	AB	H	PO	A	E	DP	TC/G	FA	G by Pos
1990	OAK A	9	.105	.158	19	2	1	0	0	0.0	1	1	1	10	0	5	1	3	0	0	0	1.5	1.000	DH-4, OF-2

Chuck Carr

CARR, CHARLES LEE GLENN
B. Aug. 10, 1968, San Bernardino, Calif.
BB TR 5' 10" 155 lbs.

Year	Team	Games	BA	SA	AB	H	2B	3B	HR	HR%	R	RBI	BB	SO	SB	AB	H	PO	A	E	DP	TC/G	FA	G by Pos
1990	NY N	4	.000	.000	2	0	0	0	0	0.0	0	0	0	2	1	2	0	0	0	0	0	0.0	1.000	OF-1

Year	Team		Games	BA	SA	AB	H	2B	3B	HR	HR%	R	RBI	BB	SO	SB	PINCH HIT AB	PINCH HIT H	PO	A	E	DP	TC/G	FA	G by Pos

Mark Carreon

CARREON, MARK STEVEN
Son of Camilo Carreon.
B. July 19, 1963, Chicago, Ill.
BR TL 6′ 170 lbs.

Year	Team		Games	BA	SA	AB	H	2B	3B	HR	HR%	R	RBI	BB	SO	SB	PH AB	PH H	PO	A	E	DP	TC/G	FA	G by Pos
1987	NY	N	9	.250	.250	12	3	0	0	0	0.0	0	1	1	1	0	5	1	4	0	1	0	0.6	.800	OF-5
1988			7	.556	1.111	9	5	2	0	1	11.1	5	1	2	1	0	2	0	1	0	0	0	0.1	1.000	OF-4
1989			68	.308	.489	133	41	6	0	6	4.5	20	16	12	17	2	27	10	57	0	1	0	0.9	.983	OF-39
1990			82	.250	.473	188	47	12	0	10	5.3	30	26	15	29	1	24	4	87	1	0	0	1.5	1.000	OF-60
4 yrs.			166	.281	.488	342	96	20	0	17	5.0	55	44	30	48	3	58	15	149	1	2	0	0.9	.987	OF-108

Gary Carter

CARTER, GARY EDMUND (Kid)
B. Apr. 8, 1954, Culver City, Calif.
BR TR 6′ 2″ 205 lbs.

Split	Games	BA	SA	AB	H	2B	3B	HR	HR%	R	RBI	BB	SO	SB
April	14	.194	.278	36	7	3	0	0	0.0	3	1	6	6	0
May	18	.262	.381	42	11	2	0	1	2.4	2	4	5	2	0
June	16	.326	.609	46	15	4	0	3	6.5	9	6	8	5	0
July	9	.438	.719	32	14	0	0	3	9.4	4	10	0	3	0
Aug	24	.134	.179	67	9	0	0	1	1.5	5	3	5	13	1
Sept/Oct	11	.286	.476	21	6	1	0	1	4.8	1	3	1	2	0
Day	33	.284	.511	88	25	5	0	5	5.7	11	17	9	10	0
Night	59	.237	.346	156	37	5	0	4	2.6	13	10	16	21	1
vs. Left		.236	.362	127	30	7	0	3	2.4	13	11	16	13	1
vs. Right		.274	.453	117	32	3	0	6	5.1	11	16	9	18	0
On Grass	67	.298	.497	181	54	9	0	9	5.0	20	24	18	20	1
On Turf	25	.127	.143	63	8	1	0	0	0.0	4	3	7	11	0
Home	48	.307	.504	127	39	7	0	6	4.7	13	19	9	13	0
Road	44	.197	.299	117	23	3	0	3	2.6	11	8	16	18	1
Division Rivals														
vs. ATL	9	.423	.500	26	11	2	0	0	0.0	4	3	1	2	0
vs. CIN	13	.194	.306	36	7	1	0	1	2.8	2	4	4	6	0
vs. HOU	10	.192	.346	26	5	1	0	1	3.8	2	2	2	3	0
vs. LA	9	.143	.286	21	3	0	0	1	4.8	1	1	5	5	0
vs. SD	8	.412	.882	17	7	2	0	2	11.8	4	3	6	2	0
On 3B < 2 Out		.167	.167	12	2	0	0	0	0.0	0	5	1	2	

CATCHER

(Bar charts: AVERAGE, RBI, HR, SB — each showing player value vs. NL AVG)

Year	Team		Games	BA	SA	AB	H	2B	3B	HR	HR%	R	RBI	BB	SO	SB	PH AB	PH H	PO	A	E	DP	TC/G	FA	G by Pos
1974	MON	N	9	.407	.593	27	11	0	1	1	3.7	5	6	1	2	2	1	1	28	4	0	1	3.6	1.000	C-6, OF-2
1975			144	.270	.416	503	136	20	1	17	3.4	58	68	72	83	5	5	1	430	38	9	7	3.3	.981	OF-92, C-66, 3B-1
1976			91	.219	.309	311	68	8	1	6	1.9	31	38	30	43	0	2	0	364	42	2	8	4.5	.995	C-60, OF-36
1977			154	.284	.525	522	148	29	2	31	5.9	86	84	58	103	5	6	3	813	101	9	14	6.0	.990	C-146, OF-1
1978			157	.255	.422	533	136	27	1	20	3.8	76	72	62	70	10	6	0	787	83	10	9	5.6	.989	C-152, 1B-1
1979			141	.283	.485	505	143	26	5	22	4.4	74	75	40	62	3	3	0	751	88	9	12	6.0	.989	C-138
1980			154	.264	.486	549	145	25	5	29	5.3	76	101	58	78	3	4	0	822	108	7	8	6.1	.993	C-149
1981			100	.251	.444	374	94	20	2	16	4.3	48	68	35	35	1	0	0	515	58	4	12	5.8	.993	C-100, 1B-1
1982			154	.293	.510	557	163	32	1	29	5.2	91	97	78	64	2	3	0	954	104	10	6	6.9	.991	C-153
1983			145	.270	.444	541	146	37	3	17	3.1	63	79	51	57	1	2	0	855	108	5	15	6.7	.995	C-144, 1B-1
1984			159	.294	.487	596	175	32	1	27	4.5	75	**106**	64	57	2	2	0	990	78	7	25	6.8	.993	C-143, 1B-25
1985	NY	N	149	.281	.488	555	156	17	1	32	5.8	83	100	69	46	1	2	0	987	70	8	13	7.1	.992	C-143, 1B-6, OF-1
1986			132	.255	.439	490	125	14	2	24	4.9	81	105	62	63	1	1	0	943	70	9	18	7.7	.991	C-122, 1B-9, OF-4, 3B-1
1987			139	.235	.392	523	123	18	2	20	3.8	55	83	42	73	0	4	0	886	70	9	14	6.9	.991	C-135, 1B-4, OF-1
1988			130	.242	.358	455	110	16	2	11	2.4	39	46	34	52	0	7	4	842	58	10	8	7.0	.989	C-119, 1B-10, 3B-1
1989			50	.183	.275	153	28	8	0	2	1.3	14	15	12	15	0	4	1	266	31	6	6	6.1	.980	C-47, 1B-1
1990	SF	N	92	.254	.400	244	62	10	0	9	3.6	24	27	25	31	1	19	4	348	31	3	5	4.6	.992	C-80, 1B-3
17 yrs.			2100	.265	.445	7438	1969	339	30	313	4.2	979	1170	793	934	37	71	14	11581	1142	117	181	1.4	.959	C-1903, OF-137, 1B-61, 3B-3

DIVISIONAL PLAYOFF SERIES

Year	Team		Games	BA	SA	AB	H	2B	3B	HR	HR%	R	RBI	BB	SO	SB	PH AB	PH H	PO	A	E	DP	TC/G	FA	G by Pos
1981	MON	N	5	.421	.895	19	8	3	0	2	10.5	3	6	1	1	0	0	0	21	5	0	0	5.2	1.000	C-5

LEAGUE CHAMPIONSHIP SERIES

Year	Team		Games	BA	SA	AB	H	2B	3B	HR	HR%	R	RBI	BB	SO	SB	PH AB	PH H	PO	A	E	DP	TC/G	FA	G by Pos
1981	MON	N	5	.438	.500	16	7	1	0	0	0.0	3	0	4	2	0	0	0	27	3	0	0	6.0	1.000	C-5
1986	NY	N	6	.148	.185	27	4	1	0	0	0.0	1	2	2	5	0	0	0	42	5	0	0	7.8	1.000	C-6
1988			7	.222	.333	27	6	1	0	0	0.0	0	4	1	3	0	0	0	58	1	0	0	8.4	1.000	C-7
3 yrs.			18	.243	.314	70	17	3	0	0	0.0	4	6	7	10	0	0	0	127	9	0	0	7.6	1.000	C-18

WORLD SERIES

Year	Team		Games	BA	SA	AB	H	2B	3B	HR	HR%	R	RBI	BB	SO	SB	PH AB	PH H	PO	A	E	DP	TC/G	FA	G by Pos
1986	NY	N	7	.276	.552	29	8	2	0	2	6.9	4	9	0	4	0	0	0	57	1	0	0	8.3	1.000	C-7

Year	Team	Games	BA	SA	AB	H	2B	3B	HR	HR%	R	RBI	BB	SO	SB	AB	H	PO	A	E	DP	TC/G	FA	G by Pos

Joe Carter

CARTER, JOSEPH CHRIS
B. Mar. 7, 1960, Oklahoma City, Okla.
BR TR 6' 3" 210 lbs.

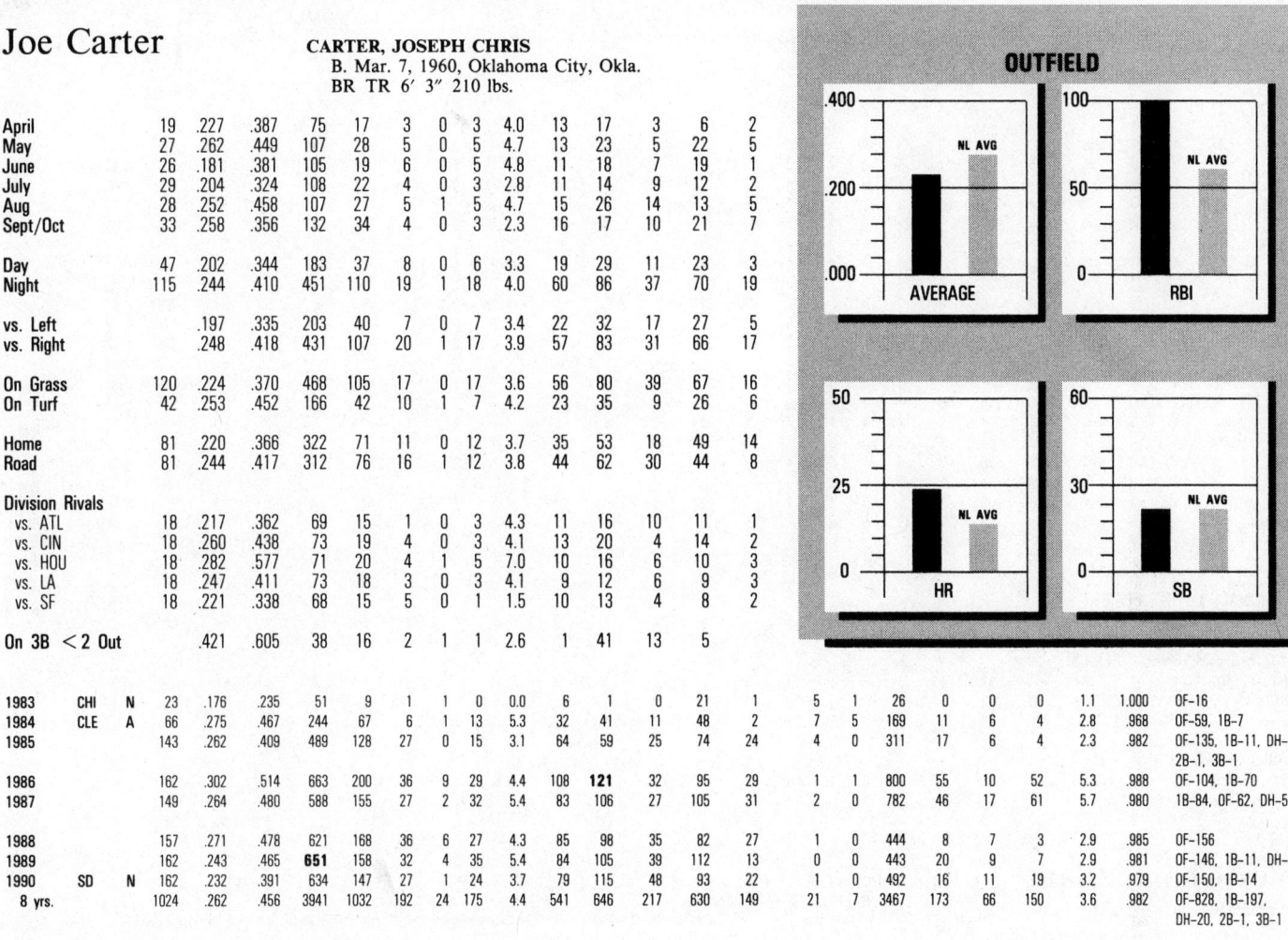

OUTFIELD

AVERAGE — .400 / .200 / .000, NL AVG
RBI — 100 / 50 / 0, NL AVG
HR — 50 / 25 / 0, NL AVG
SB — 60 / 30 / 0, NL AVG

Split	Games	BA	SA	AB	H	2B	3B	HR	HR%	R	RBI	BB	SO	SB
April	19	.227	.387	75	17	3	0	3	4.0	13	17	3	6	2
May	27	.262	.449	107	28	5	0	5	4.7	13	23	5	22	5
June	26	.181	.381	105	19	6	0	5	4.8	11	18	7	19	1
July	29	.204	.324	108	22	4	0	3	2.8	11	14	9	12	2
Aug	28	.252	.458	107	27	5	1	5	4.7	15	26	14	13	5
Sept/Oct	33	.258	.356	132	34	4	0	3	2.3	16	17	10	21	7
Day	47	.202	.344	183	37	8	0	6	3.3	19	29	11	23	3
Night	115	.244	.410	451	110	19	1	18	4.0	60	86	37	70	19
vs. Left		.197	.335	203	40	7	0	7	3.4	22	32	17	27	5
vs. Right		.248	.418	431	107	20	1	17	3.9	57	83	31	66	17
On Grass	120	.224	.370	468	105	17	0	17	3.6	56	80	39	67	16
On Turf	42	.253	.452	166	42	10	1	7	4.2	23	35	9	26	6
Home	81	.220	.366	322	71	11	0	12	3.7	35	53	18	49	14
Road	81	.244	.417	312	76	16	1	12	3.8	44	62	30	44	8
Division Rivals														
vs. ATL	18	.217	.362	69	15	1	0	3	4.3	11	16	10	11	1
vs. CIN	18	.260	.438	73	19	4	0	3	4.1	13	20	4	14	2
vs. HOU	18	.282	.577	71	20	4	1	5	7.0	10	16	6	10	3
vs. LA	18	.247	.411	73	18	3	0	3	4.1	9	12	6	9	3
vs. SF	18	.221	.338	68	15	5	0	1	1.5	10	13	4	8	2
On 3B <2 Out		.421	.605	38	16	2	1	1	2.6	1	41	13	5	

Year	Team	Lg	Games	BA	SA	AB	H	2B	3B	HR	HR%	R	RBI	BB	SO	SB	AB	H	PO	A	E	DP	TC/G	FA	G by Pos
1983	CHI	N	23	.176	.235	51	9	1	1	0	0.0	6	1	0	21	1	5	1	26	0	0	0	1.1	1.000	OF-16
1984	CLE	A	66	.275	.467	244	67	6	1	13	5.3	32	41	11	48	2	7	5	169	11	6	4	2.8	.968	OF-59, 1B-7
1985			143	.262	.409	489	128	27	0	15	3.1	64	59	25	74	24	4	0	311	17	6	4	2.3	.982	OF-135, 1B-11, DH-7, 2B-1, 3B-1
1986			162	.302	.514	663	200	36	9	29	4.4	108	121	32	95	29	1	1	800	55	10	52	5.3	.988	OF-104, 1B-70
1987			149	.264	.480	588	155	27	2	32	5.4	83	106	27	105	31	2	0	782	46	17	61	5.7	.980	1B-84, OF-62, DH-5
1988			157	.271	.478	621	168	36	6	27	4.3	85	98	35	82	27	1	0	444	8	7	3	2.9	.985	OF-156
1989			162	.243	.465	651	158	32	4	35	5.4	84	105	39	112	13	0	0	443	20	9	7	2.9	.981	OF-146, 1B-11, DH-8
1990	SD	N	162	.232	.391	634	147	27	1	24	3.7	79	115	48	93	22	1	0	492	16	11	19	3.2	.979	OF-150, 1B-14
8 yrs.			1024	.262	.456	3941	1032	192	24	175	4.4	541	646	217	630	149	21	7	3467	173	66	150	3.6	.982	OF-828, 1B-197, DH-20, 2B-1, 3B-1

Steve Carter

CARTER, STEVEN JEROME
B. Dec. 3, 1964, Charlottesville, Va.
BL TR 6' 4" 201 lbs.

Year	Team	Lg	Games	BA	SA	AB	H	2B	3B	HR	HR%	R	RBI	BB	SO	SB	AB	H	PO	A	E	DP	TC/G	FA	G by Pos
1989	PIT	N	9	.125	.375	16	2	1	0	1	6.3	2	3	2	5	0	2	0	4	0	0	0	0.4	1.000	OF-5
1990			5	.200	.200	5	1	0	0	0	0.0	0	0	0	1	0	2	0	4	0	0	0	1.3	1.000	OF-3
2 yrs.			14	.143	.333	21	3	1	0	1	4.8	2	3	2	6	0	4	0	8	0	0	0	0.6	.000	OF-8

Carmen Castillo

CASTILLO, MONTE CARMELO
B. June 8, 1958, San Pedro de Macoris, Dominican Republic
BR TR 6' 1" 180 lbs.

Year	Team	Lg	Games	BA	SA	AB	H	2B	3B	HR	HR%	R	RBI	BB	SO	SB	AB	H	PO	A	E	DP	TC/G	FA	G by Pos
1982	CLE	A	47	.208	.292	120	25	4	0	2	1.7	11	11	6	17	0	3	0	91	0	2	0	2.0	.978	OF-43, DH-2
1983			23	.278	.472	36	10	2	1	1	2.8	9	3	4	6	1	2	0	23	3	2	1	1.2	.929	OF-19, DH-1
1984			87	.261	.464	211	55	9	2	10	4.7	36	36	21	32	1	18	3	123	2	9	0	1.5	.933	OF-70, DH-2
1985			67	.245	.462	184	45	5	1	11	6.0	27	25	11	40	3	9	1	101	0	5	0	1.6	.953	OF-51, DH-9
1986			85	.278	.439	205	57	9	0	8	3.9	34	32	9	48	2	21	3	58	4	4	1	0.8	.939	OF-37, DH-35
1987			89	.250	.477	220	55	17	0	11	5.0	27	31	16	52	1	29	5	29	3	0	0	0.4	1.000	DH-43, OF-23
1988			66	.273	.386	176	48	8	0	4	2.3	12	14	5	31	6	16	4	69	1	5	0	1.1	.933	OF-45, DH-9
1989	MIN	A	94	.257	.454	218	56	13	3	8	3.7	23	33	15	40	1	29	8	119	3	3	1	1.3	.976	OF-67, DH-16
1990			64	.219	.248	137	30	4	0	0	0.0	11	12	3	23	0	22	5	24	0	2	0	1.2	.923	DH-35, OF-21
9 yrs.			622	.253	.419	1507	381	71	7	55	3.6	190	197	90	289	15	149	29	637	16	32	3	1.1	.953	OF-376, DH-152

Andujar Cedeno

CEDENO, ANDUJAR
Born Andujar Cedeno y Encarnacion.
B. Aug. 21, 1969, La Romana, Dominican Republic
BR TR 6' 1" 170 lbs.

Year	Team	Lg	Games	BA	SA	AB	H	2B	3B	HR	HR%	R	RBI	BB	SO	SB	AB	H	PO	A	E	DP	TC/G	FA	G by Pos
1990	HOU	N	7	.000	.000	8	0	0	0	0	0.0	0	0	0	5	0	2	0	3	2	1	0	2.0	.833	SS-3

Year	Team		Games	BA	SA	AB	H	2B	3B	HR	HR%	R	RBI	BB	SO	SB	PINCH HIT AB	PINCH HIT H	PO	A	E	DP	TC/G	FA	G by Pos

Rick Cerone

CERONE, RICHARD ALDO
B. May 19, 1954, Newark, N. J.
BR TR 5′ 11″ 192 lbs.

Year	Team		Games	BA	SA	AB	H	2B	3B	HR	HR%	R	RBI	BB	SO	SB	PH AB	PH H	PO	A	E	DP	TC/G	FA	G by Pos
1975	CLE	A	7	.250	.333	12	3	1	0	0	0.0	1	0	1	0	0	0	0	18	1	0	0	2.7	1.000	C-7
1976			7	.125	.125	16	2	0	0	0	0.0	1	1	0	2	0	1	1	25	1	1	1	3.9	.963	C-6, DH-1
1977	TOR	A	31	.200	.270	100	20	4	0	1	1.0	7	10	6	12	0	0	0	146	15	1	1	5.2	.994	C-31
1978			88	.223	.298	282	63	8	2	3	1.1	25	20	23	32	0	4	1	426	44	4	7	5.4	.992	C-84, DH-2
1979			136	.239	.358	469	112	27	4	7	1.5	47	61	37	40	1	2	0	560	68	13	10	4.7	.980	C-136
1980	NY	A	147	.277	.432	519	144	30	4	14	2.7	70	85	32	56	1	0	0	800	73	9	9	6.0	.990	C-147
1981			71	.244	.342	234	57	13	2	2	0.9	23	21	12	24	0	2	2	353	26	3	1	5.4	.992	C-69
1982			89	.227	.310	300	68	10	0	5	1.7	29	28	19	27	0	0	0	509	25	6	5	6.1	.989	C-89
1983			80	.220	.272	246	54	7	0	2	0.8	18	22	15	29	0	2	0	412	18	4	2	5.4	.991	C-78, 3B-1
1984			38	.208	.283	120	25	3	0	2	1.7	8	13	9	15	1	0	0	230	9	1	1	6.3	.996	C-38
1985	ATL	N	96	.216	.280	282	61	9	0	3	1.1	15	25	29	25	0	7	1	384	48	6	4	4.6	.986	C-91
1986	MIL	A	68	.259	.380	216	56	14	0	4	1.9	22	18	15	28	1	0	0	391	44	4	2	6.5	.991	C-68
1987	NY	A	113	.243	.335	284	69	12	1	4	1.4	28	23	30	46	0	6	2	542	38	1	6	5.1	.998	C-111, P-2, 1B-2
1988	BOS	A	84	.269	.360	264	71	13	1	3	1.1	31	27	20	32	0	4	1	471	28	0	4	5.9	1.000	C-83, DH-1
1989			102	.243	.345	296	72	16	1	4	1.4	28	48	34	40	0	7	3	579	41	10	5	6.2	.984	C-97, DH-1, OF-1
1990	NY	A	49	.302	.388	139	42	6	0	2	1.4	12	11	5	13	0	14	2	179	14	1	1	5.5	.995	C-35, DH-6, 2B-1
16 yrs.			1206	.243	.341	3779	919	173	15	56	1.5	365	413	287	421	4	49	13	6025	493	64	59	5.5	.990	C-1170, DH-11, P-2, 1B-2, 2B-1, 3B-1, OF-1

DIVISIONAL PLAYOFF SERIES

Year	Team		Games	BA	SA	AB	H	2B	3B	HR	HR%	R	RBI	BB	SO	SB	PH AB	PH H	PO	A	E	DP	TC/G	FA	G by Pos
1981	NY	A	5	.333	.611	18	6	2	0	1	5.6	1	5	0	2	0	0	0	42	1	1	0	8.8	.977	C-5

LEAGUE CHAMPIONSHIP SERIES

Year	Team		Games	BA	SA	AB	H	2B	3B	HR	HR%	R	RBI	BB	SO	SB	PH AB	PH H	PO	A	E	DP	TC/G	FA	G by Pos
1980	NY	A	3	.333	.583	12	4	0	0	1	8.3	1	2	0	1	0	0	0	14	4	0	0	6.0	1.000	C-3
1981			3	.100	.100	10	1	0	0	0	0.0	1	0	0	0	0	0	0	23	2	0	1	8.3	1.000	C-3
2 yrs.			6	.227	.364	22	5	0	0	1	4.5	2	2	0	1	0	0	0	37	6	0	1	7.2	.000	C-6

WORLD SERIES

Year	Team		Games	BA	SA	AB	H	2B	3B	HR	HR%	R	RBI	BB	SO	SB	PH AB	PH H	PO	A	E	DP	TC/G	FA	G by Pos
1981	NY	A	6	.190	.381	21	4	1	0	1	4.8	2	3	4	2	0	0	0	42	4	0	0	7.7	1.000	C-6

Wes Chamberlain

CHAMBERLAIN, WESLEY POLK
B. Apr. 13, 1966, Chicago, Ill.
BR TR 6′ 2″ 210 lbs.

Year	Team		Games	BA	SA	AB	H	2B	3B	HR	HR%	R	RBI	BB	SO	SB	PH AB	PH H	PO	A	E	DP	TC/G	FA	G by Pos
1990	PHI	N	18	.283	.478	46	13	3	0	2	4.3	9	4	1	9	4	8	0	23	0	1	0	2.4	.958	OF-10

Dave Clark

CLARK, DAVID EARL
B. Sept. 3, 1962, Tupelo, Miss.
BL TR 6′ 2″ 200 lbs.

Year	Team		Games	BA	SA	AB	H	2B	3B	HR	HR%	R	RBI	BB	SO	SB	PH AB	PH H	PO	A	E	DP	TC/G	FA	G by Pos
1986	CLE	A	18	.276	.448	58	16	1	0	3	5.2	10	9	7	11	1	0	0	26	0	0	0	1.4	1.000	OF-10, DH-7
1987			29	.207	.368	87	18	5	0	3	3.4	11	12	2	24	1	6	0	24	1	0	0	0.9	1.000	OF-13, DH-12
1988			63	.263	.359	156	41	4	1	3	1.9	11	18	17	28	0	19	4	36	0	2	0	0.6	.947	DH-27, OF-23
1989			102	.237	.379	253	60	12	0	8	3.2	21	29	30	63	0	29	7	27	0	1	0	0.3	.964	DH-55, OF-21
1990	CHI	N	84	.275	.409	171	47	4	2	5	2.9	22	20	8	40	7	42	11	60	2	0	0	1.6	1.000	OF-39
5 yrs.			296	.251	.386	725	182	26	3	22	3.0	75	88	64	166	9	96	22	173	3	3	0	0.6	.983	OF-106, DH-101

Jack Clark

CLARK, JACK ANTHONY (The Ripper)
B. Nov. 10, 1955, New Brighton, Pa.
BR TR 6′ 2″ 205 lbs.

	Games	BA	SA	AB	H	2B	3B	HR	HR%	R	RBI	BB	SO	SB
April	18	.204	.444	54	11	1	0	4	7.4	12	9	20	21	0
May	4	.462	.846	13	6	2	0	1	7.7	2	1	4	3	0
June	21	.190	.413	63	12	2	0	4	6.3	5	11	13	16	1
July	27	.310	.621	87	27	0	0	9	10.3	17	20	17	20	2
Aug	16	.350	.675	40	14	5	1	2	5.0	12	9	18	10	0
Sept/Oct	29	.247	.468	77	19	2	0	5	6.5	11	12	32	21	1
Day	33	.235	.529	85	20	1	0	8	9.4	15	15	29	27	1
Night	82	.277	.534	249	69	11	1	17	6.8	44	47	75	64	3
vs. Left		.377	.667	114	43	4	1	9	7.9	23	21	41	29	3
vs. Right		.209	.464	220	46	8	0	16	7.3	36	41	63	62	1

FIRST BASE

(Bar chart: AVERAGE — black bar near .280, NL AVG slightly higher, scale .000–.400)

(Bar chart: RBI — black bar near 60, NL AVG slightly higher, scale 0–100)

Year	Team		Games	BA	SA	AB	H	2B	3B	HR	HR%	R	RBI	BB	SO	SB	PINCH HIT AB	PINCH HIT H	PO	A	E	DP	TC/G	FA	G by Pos

Jack Clark *Continued*

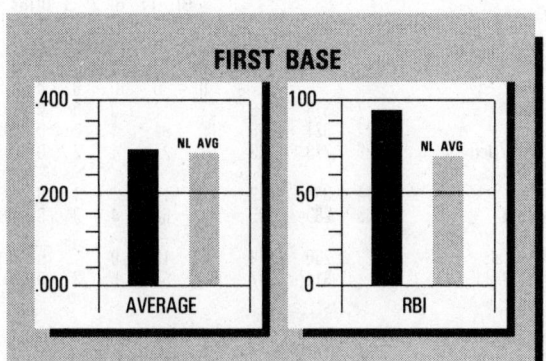

FIRST BASE — HR / SB charts (NL AVG)

On Grass			91	.260	.532	265	69	10	1	20	7.5	44	50	76	72	2									
On Turf			24	.290	.536	69	20	2	0	5	7.2	15	12	28	19	2									
Home			61	.256	.568	176	45	5	1	16	9.1	34	39	50	53	2									
Road			54	.278	.494	158	44	7	0	9	5.7	25	23	54	38	2									
Division Rivals																									
vs. ATL			13	.368	.711	38	14	4	0	3	7.9	7	8	18	4	1									
vs. CIN			16	.410	.667	39	16	1	0	3	7.7	13	5	23	13	1									
vs. HOU			14	.238	.571	42	10	2	0	4	9.5	7	15	8	8	1									
vs. LA			17	.157	.275	51	8	0	0	2	3.9	4	5	13	19	0									
vs. SF			17	.188	.417	48	9	2	0	3	6.3	9	8	13	15	0									
On 3B < 2 Out				.318	.545	22	7	2	0	1	4.5	1	11	11	5										
1975	SF	N	8	.235	.235	17	4	0	0	0	0.0	3	2	1	2	1	3	0	8	1	0	0	1.1	1.000	OF-3, 3B-2
1976			26	.225	.382	102	23	6	2	2	2.0	14	10	8	18	6	0	0	71	3	1	1	2.9	.987	OF-26
1977			136	.252	.407	413	104	17	4	13	3.1	64	51	49	73	12	29	11	226	11	6	2	1.8	.975	OF-114
1978			156	.306	.537	592	181	46	8	25	4.2	90	98	50	72	15	6	2	320	16	6	5	2.2	.982	OF-152
1979			143	.273	.476	527	144	25	2	26	4.9	84	86	63	95	11	2	0	262	13	5	7	2.0	.982	OF-140, 3B-2
1980			127	.284	.517	437	124	20	8	22	5.0	77	82	74	52	2	5	0	229	7	8	1	1.9	.967	OF-120
1981			99	.268	.460	385	103	19	2	17	4.4	60	53	45	45	1	2	0	193	14	4	4	2.1	.981	OF-98
1982			157	.274	.481	563	154	30	3	27	4.8	90	103	90	91	6	4	1	281	10	6	2	1.9	.980	OF-155
1983			135	.268	.441	492	132	25	0	20	4.1	82	66	74	79	5	1	0	262	20	9	5	2.2	.969	OF-133, 1B-2
1984			57	.320	.537	203	65	9	1	11	5.4	33	44	43	29	1	1	0	120	9	2	3	2.3	.985	OF-54, 1B-4
1985	STL	N	126	.281	.502	442	124	26	3	22	5.0	71	87	83	88	1	1	0	1128	66	14	102	9.6	.988	1B-121, OF-12
1986			65	.237	.422	232	55	12	2	9	3.9	34	23	45	61	1	1	1	623	35	3	66	10.2	.995	1B-64
1987			131	.286	**.597**	419	120	23	1	35	**8.4**	93	106	**136**	139	1	4	0	1152	77	14	116	9.5	.989	1B-126, OF-1
1988	NY	A	150	.242	.433	496	120	14	0	27	5.4	81	93	113	141	3	12	3	129	8	5	8	0.9	.965	DH-112, OF-19, 1B-10
1989	SD	N	142	.242	.459	455	110	19	1	26	5.7	76	94	**132**	145	6	1	1	1157	89	15	99	8.9	.988	1B-131, OF-12
1990			115	.266	.533	334	89	12	1	25	7.4	59	62	**104**	91	4	4	1	855	69	6	72	8.5	.994	1B-109
16 yrs.			1773	.270	.483	6109	1652	303	38	307	5.0	1011	1060	1110	1221	76	76	20	7016	448	104	493	4.3	.986	OF-1039, 1B-567, DH-112, 3B-4

LEAGUE CHAMPIONSHIP SERIES

Year	Team		Games	BA	SA	AB	H	2B	3B	HR	HR%	R	RBI	BB	SO	SB	PINCH HIT AB	PINCH HIT H	PO	A	E	DP	TC/G	FA	G by Pos
1985	STL	N	6	.381	.524	21	8	0	0	1	4.8	4	4	5	5	0	0	0	55	0	0	3	9.2	1.000	1B-6
1987			1	.000	.000	1	0	0	0	0	0.0	0	0	0	1	0	1	0	0	0	0	0	0.0	—	
2 yrs.			7	.364	.500	22	8	0	0	1	4.5	4	4	5	6	0	1	0	55	0	0	3	7.9	.000	1B-6

WORLD SERIES

Year	Team		Games	BA	SA	AB	H	2B	3B	HR	HR%	R	RBI	BB	SO	SB	PINCH HIT AB	PINCH HIT H	PO	A	E	DP	TC/G	FA	G by Pos
1985	STL	N	7	.240	.320	25	6	2	0	0	0.0	1	4	3	9	0	0	0	49	4	0	6	7.6	1.000	1B-7

Jerald Clark

CLARK, JERALD DWAYNE
B. Aug. 10, 1963, Crockett, Tex.
BR TR 6' 4" 189 lbs.

Year	Team		Games	BA	SA	AB	H	2B	3B	HR	HR%	R	RBI	BB	SO	SB	PINCH HIT AB	PINCH HIT H	PO	A	E	DP	TC/G	FA	G by Pos
1988	SD	N	6	.200	.267	15	3	1	0	0	0.0	0	3	0	4	0	3	1	10	1	0	0	1.8	1.000	OF-4
1989			17	.195	.317	41	8	2	0	1	2.4	5	7	3	9	0	4	1	16	2	1	0	1.1	.947	OF-14
1990			53	.267	.475	101	27	4	1	5	4.9	12	11	5	24	0	28	8	102	6	1	3	4.4	.991	1B-15, OF-13
3 yrs.			76	.242	.414	157	38	7	1	6	3.8	17	21	8	37	0	35	10	128	9	2	3	1.8	.986	OF-31, 1B-15

Will Clark

CLARK, WILLIAM NUSCHLER (The Natural, The Thrill)
B. Mar. 13, 1964, New Orleans, La.
BL TL 6' 2" 190 lbs.

FIRST BASE — AVERAGE / RBI charts (NL AVG)

			Games	BA	SA	AB	H	2B	3B	HR	HR%	R	RBI	BB	SO	SB									
April			20	.310	.488	84	26	4	1	3	3.6	10	17	3	13	0									
May			27	.209	.400	110	23	3	0	6	5.5	16	17	10	15	1									
June			27	.345	.545	110	38	5	1	5	4.5	29	24	13	17	5									
July			25	.305	.379	95	29	3	2	0	0.0	11	10	13	18	1									
Aug			25	.277	.394	94	26	3	1	2	2.1	10	10	10	20	0									
Sept/Oct			30	.327	.477	107	35	7	0	3	2.8	15	17	13	14	1									
Day			61	.263	.388	232	61	6	1	7	3.0	36	33	31	42	2									
Night			93	.315	.486	368	116	19	4	12	3.3	55	62	31	55	6									
vs. Left				.317	.486	249	79	7	4	9	3.6	36	47	22	35	5									
vs. Right				.279	.422	351	98	18	1	10	2.8	55	48	40	62	3									

Will Clark *Continued*

Year	Team		Games	BA	SA	AB	H	2B	3B	HR	HR%	R	RBI	BB	SO	SB	PINCH HIT AB	H	PO	A	E	DP	TC/G	FA	G by Pos
On Grass			113	.308	.458	439	135	21	3	13	3.0	67	73	48	71	7									
On Turf			41	.261	.422	161	42	4	2	6	3.7	24	22	14	26	1									
Home			77	.318	.459	296	94	14	2	8	2.7	42	44	37	49	6									
Road			77	.273	.438	304	83	11	3	11	3.6	49	51	25	48	2									
Division Rivals																									
vs. ATL			17	.348	.522	69	24	3	0	3	4.3	18	19	6	9	1									
vs. CIN			18	.310	.535	71	22	4	0	4	5.6	15	10	9	16	2									
vs. HOU			18	.406	.453	64	26	3	0	0	0.0	4	8	10	9	3									
vs. LA			13	.408	.612	49	20	7	0	1	2.0	6	12	4	10	0									
vs. SD			18	.274	.479	73	20	2	2	3	4.1	11	11	3	10	1									
On 3B < 2 Out				.250	.406	32	8	2	0	1	3.1	1	25	6	7										
1986	SF	N	111	.287	.444	408	117	27	2	11	2.7	66	41	34	76	4	9	6	942	72	11	76	9.2	.989	1B-102
1987			150	.308	.580	529	163	29	5	35	6.6	89	91	49	98	5	11	3	1253	103	13	130	9.1	.991	1B-139
1988			162	.282	.508	575	162	31	6	29	5.0	102	**109**	**100**	129	9	5	0	1492	104	12	126	9.9	.993	1B-158
1989			159	.333	.546	588	196	38	9	23	3.9	**104**	111	74	103	8	1	0	1445	111	10	117	9.8	.994	1B-158
1990			154	.295	.448	600	177	25	5	19	3.1	91	95	62	97	8	1	0	1456	119	12	118	10.4	.992	1B-153
5 yrs.			736	.302	.507	2700	815	150	27	117	4.3	452	447	319	503	34	27	9	6588	509	58	567	9.7	.992	1B-710
LEAGUE CHAMPIONSHIP SERIES																									
1987	SF	N	7	.360	.560	25	9	2	0	1	4.0	3	3	3	6	1	0	0	63	7	1	10	10.1	.986	1B-7
1989			5	.650	1.200	20	13	3	1	2	10.0	8	8	2	2	0	0	0	43	6	0	6	9.8	1.000	1B-5
2 yrs.			12	.489	.844	45	22	5	1	3	6.7	11	11	5	8	1	0	0	106	13	1	16	10.0	.992	1B-12
WORLD SERIES																									
1989	SF	N	4	.250	.313	16	4	1	0	0	0.0	2	0	1	3	0	0	0	40	2	0	2	10.5	1.000	1B-4

Bobby Coachman

COACHMAN, BOBBY DEAN
B. Nov. 11, 1961, Cottonwood, Ala.
BR TR 5' 9" 175 lbs.

Year	Team		Games	BA	SA	AB	H	2B	3B	HR	HR%	R	RBI	BB	SO	SB	PINCH HIT AB	H	PO	A	E	DP	TC/G	FA	G by Pos
1990	CAL	A	16	.311	.378	45	14	3	0	0	0.0	3	5	1	7	0	3	0	6	23	2	4	2.8	.935	3B-9, DH-2, 2B-2

Dave Cochrane

COCHRANE, DAVID CARTER
B. Jan. 31, 1963, Riverside, Calif.
BB TR 6' 2" 180 lbs.

Year	Team		Games	BA	SA	AB	H	2B	3B	HR	HR%	R	RBI	BB	SO	SB	PINCH HIT AB	H	PO	A	E	DP	TC/G	FA	G by Pos
1986	CHI	A	19	.194	.274	62	12	2	0	1	1.6	4	2	5	22	0	0	0	10	31	6	1	2.5	.872	3B-18, SS-1
1989	SEA	A	54	.235	.382	102	24	4	1	3	2.9	13	7	14	27	0	17	5	78	41	5	14	2.3	.960	SS-30, 1B-9, 3B-9, 2B-4, OF-3, C-2
1990			15	.150	.150	20	3	0	0	0	0.0	0	0	0	8	0	9	2	8	10	0	0	1.6	1.000	SS-5, 1B-3, 3B-3, C-1
3 yrs.			88	.212	.321	184	39	6	1	4	2.2	17	9	19	57	0	26	7	96	82	11	15	2.1	.942	SS-36, 3B-30, 1B-12, 2B-4, C-3, OF-3

Alex Cole

COLE, ALEXANDER, JR.
B. Aug. 17, 1965, Fayetteville, N. C.
BL TL 6' 2" 170 lbs.

	Games	BA	SA	AB	H	2B	3B	HR	HR%	R	RBI	BB	SO	SB
April				0	0	0	0	0		0	0	0	0	0
May				0	0	0	0	0		0	0	0	0	0
June				0	0	0	0	0		0	0	0	0	0
July	7	.318	.318	22	7	0	0		0.0	2	0	0	3	3
Aug	27	.321	.396	106	34	4	2	0	0.0	23	9	14	22	19
Sept/Oct	29	.273	.323	99	27	1	2	0	0.0	18	4	14	13	18
Day	14	.389	.472	36	14	1	1	0	0.0	9	2	11	6	9
Night	49	.283	.335	191	54	4	3	0	0.0	34	11	17	32	31
vs. Left		.250	.288	52	13	0	1	0	0.0	14	4	10	11	13
vs. Right		.314	.377	175	55	5	3	0	0.0	29	9	18	27	27

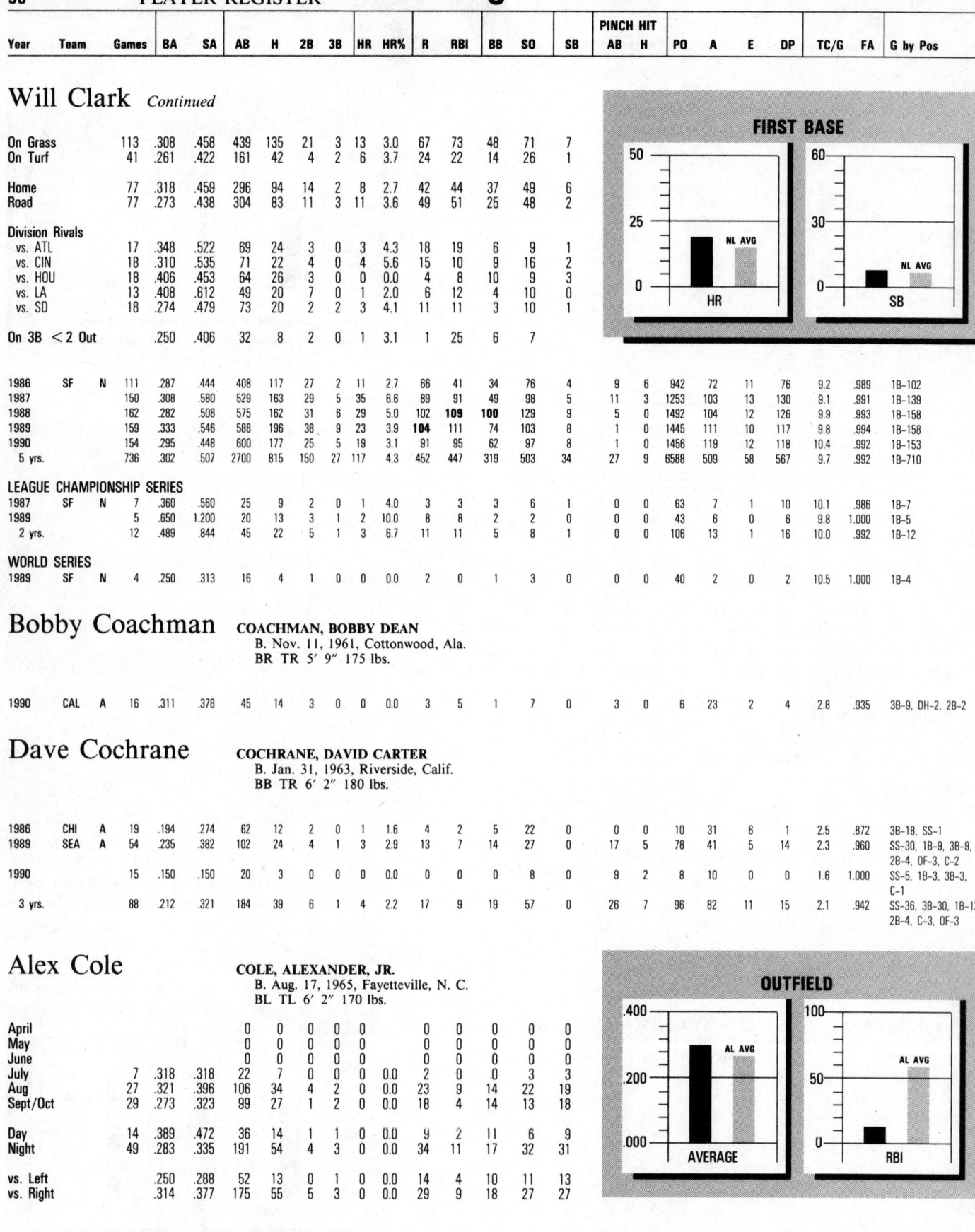

FIRST BASE — HR (NL AVG), SB (NL AVG)

OUTFIELD — AVERAGE (AL AVG), RBI (AL AVG)

Year	Team	Games	BA	SA	AB	H	2B	3B	HR	HR%	R	RBI	BB	SO	SB	PINCH HIT AB	PINCH HIT H	PO	A	E	DP	TC/G	FA	G by Pos

Alex Cole *Continued*

Year	Team	Games	BA	SA	AB	H	2B	3B	HR	HR%	R	RBI	BB	SO	SB	AB	H	PO	A	E	DP	TC/G	FA	G by Pos
On Grass		54	.309	.371	194	60	4	4	0	0.0	40	11	26	34	37									
On Turf		9	.242	.273	33	8	1	0	0	0.0	3	2	2	4	3									
Home		35	.306	.372	121	37	2	3	0	0.0	24	9	18	23	22									
Road		28	.292	.340	106	31	3	1	0	0.0	19	4	10	15	18									
Division Rivals																								
vs. BAL		5	.200	.360	25	5	2	1	0	0.0	4	1	1	4	2									
vs. BOS		6	.250	.333	24	6	0	1	0	0.0	2	1	3	6	3									
vs. DET		7	.407	.407	27	11	0	0	0	0.0	5	3	4	6	7									
vs. MIL		6	.238	.238	21	5	0	0	0	0.0	5	0	1	1	3									
vs. NY		10	.375	.375	32	12	0	0	0	0.0	10	0	5	5	9									
vs. TOR		5	.333	.333	15	5	0	0	0	0.0	0	0	4	2	1									
On 3B < 2 Out			.200	.200	10	2	0	0	0	0.0	0	4	0	4										
1990	CLE A	63	.300	.357	227	68	5	4	0	0.0	43	13	28	38	40	0	0	145	3	6	1	2.6	.961	OF–59, DH–1

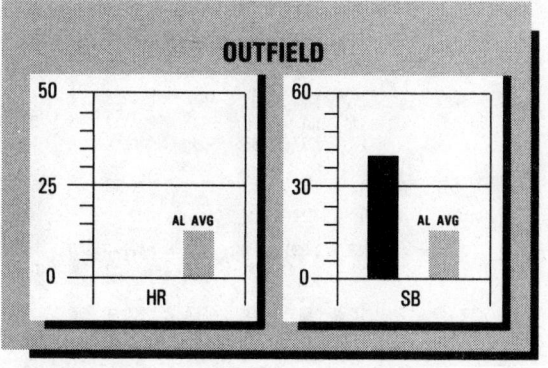

Vince Coleman

COLEMAN, VINCENT MAURICE
B. Sept. 22, 1960, Jacksonville, Fla.
BB TR 6′ 170 lbs.

Year	Team	Games	BA	SA	AB	H	2B	3B	HR	HR%	R	RBI	BB	SO	SB	AB	H	PO	A	E	DP	TC/G	FA	G by Pos
April		20	.300	.325	80	24	2	0	0	0.0	14	3	5	9	13									
May		27	.307	.455	101	31	1	4	2	2.0	14	10	8	23	10									
June		27	.297	.407	118	35	8	1	1	0.8	15	8	6	29	24									
July		20	.260	.403	77	20	3	1	2	2.6	13	4	5	10	9									
Aug		23	.337	.474	95	32	4	3	1	1.1	16	12	10	12	20									
Sept/Oct		7	.115	.115	26	3	0	0	0	0.0	1	2	1	5	1									
Day		33	.285	.401	137	39	3	2	3	2.2	15	12	10	22	17									
Night		91	.294	.400	360	106	15	7	3	0.8	58	27	25	66	60									
vs. Left			.262	.450	191	50	13	4	5	2.6	24	18	9	37	29									
vs. Right			.310	.369	306	95	5	5	1	0.3	49	21	26	51	48									
On Grass		35	.273	.324	139	38	5	1	0	0.0	14	6	7	27	14									
On Turf		89	.299	.430	358	107	13	8	6	1.7	59	33	28	61	63									
Home		63	.297	.440	259	77	10	6	5	1.9	44	21	22	48	50									
Road		61	.286	.357	238	68	8	3	1	0.4	29	18	13	40	27									
Division Rivals																								
vs. CHI		13	.404	.574	47	19	1	2	1	2.1	12	2	4	11	11									
vs. MON		10	.205	.256	39	8	2	0	0	0.0	2	3	3	7	5									
vs. NY		13	.226	.302	53	12	4	0	0	0.0	5	2	4	9	11									
vs. PHI		12	.327	.449	49	16	6	0	0	0.0	11	8	2	10	9									
vs. PIT		13	.291	.473	55	16	2	1	2	3.6	8	7	2	9	7									
On 3B < 2 Out			.353	.529	17	6	0	0	1	5.9	1	13	3	2										
1985	STL N	151	.267	.335	636	170	20	10	1	0.2	107	40	50	115	110	1	0	305	16	7	1	2.2	.979	OF–150
1986		154	.232	.280	600	139	13	8	0	0.0	94	29	60	98	107	2	1	300	12	9	2	2.1	.972	OF–149
1987		151	.289	.358	623	180	14	10	3	0.5	121	43	70	126	109	1	0	274	16	9	3	2.0	.970	OF–150
1988		153	.260	.339	616	160	20	10	3	0.5	77	38	49	111	81	2	0	290	14	9	1	2.0	.971	OF–150
1989		145	.254	.334	563	143	21	9	2	0.4	94	28	50	90	65	5	2	247	5	10	1	1.8	.962	OF–142
1990		124	.292	.400	497	145	18	9	6	1.2	73	39	35	88	77	5	0	244	12	5	2	2.2	.981	OF–120
6 yrs.		878	.265	.339	3535	937	106	56	15	0.4	566	217	314	628	549	16	3	1660	75	49	10	2.0	.973	OF–861
LEAGUE CHAMPIONSHIP SERIES																								
1985	STL N	3	.286	.286	14	4	0	0	0	0.0	2	1	0	2	1	0	0	8	0	0	0	2.7	1.000	OF–3
1987		7	.269	.308	26	7	1	0	0	0.0	3	4	4	6	1	0	0	9	1	0	0	1.4	1.000	OF–7
2 yrs.		10	.275	.300	40	11	1	0	0	0.0	5	5	4	8	2	0	0	17	1	0	0	1.8	.000	OF–10
WORLD SERIES																								
1987	STL N	7	.143	.214	28	4	2	0	0	0.0	5	2	2	10	6	0	0	10	2	0	0	1.7	1.000	OF–7

Year	Team		Games	BA	SA	AB	H	2B	3B	HR	HR%	R	RBI	BB	SO	SB	PINCH HIT AB	H	PO	A	E	DP	TC/G	FA	G by Pos

Darnell Coles

COLES, DARNELL
B. June 2, 1962, San Bernardino, Calif.
BR TR 6′ 1″ 185 lbs.

Year	Team		Games	BA	SA	AB	H	2B	3B	HR	HR%	R	RBI	BB	SO	SB	PH AB	PH H	PO	A	E	DP	TC/G	FA	G by Pos
1983	SEA	A	27	.283	.391	92	26	7	0	1	1.1	9	6	7	12	0	1	0	17	47	4	8	2.5	.941	3B-26
1984			48	.161	.196	143	23	3	1	0	0.0	15	6	17	26	2	0	0	31	63	8	10	2.1	.922	3B-42, DH-3, OF-3
1985			27	.237	.356	59	14	4	0	1	1.7	8	5	9	17	0	3	0	25	44	6	10	2.8	.920	SS-15, 3B-7, DH-2, OF-2
1986	DET	A	142	.273	.453	521	142	30	2	20	3.8	67	86	45	84	6	1	0	111	242	23	23	2.6	.939	3B-133, DH-7, SS-2, OF-2
1987 "	2 teams	DET A (53G — .181)	PIT N (40G — .227)																						
	total		93	.201	.369	268	54	13	1	10	3.7	34	39	34	43	1	9	2	123	87	20	6	2.5	.913	3B-46, OF-34, 1B-10, DH-3, SS-1
1988 "	2 teams	PIT N (68G — .232)	SEA A (55G — .292)																						
	total		123	.261	.438	406	106	23	2	15	3.7	52	70	37	67	4	11	0	166	3	3	0	1.4	.983	OF-102, DH-7, 1B-2, 3B-1
1989	SEA	A	146	.252	.359	535	135	21	3	10	1.9	54	59	27	61	5	8	1	317	76	12	20	2.8	.970	OF-89, 3B-26, 1B-18, DH-12
1990 "	2 teams	SEA A (37G — .215)	DET A (52G — .204)																						
	total		89	.209	.293	215	45	7	1	3	1.3	22	20	16	38	0	27	8	69	42	9	3	2.5	.925	DH-31, OF-31, 3B-14, 1B-4
8 yrs.			695	.243	.381	2239	545	108	10	60	2.7	261	291	192	348	18	60	11	859	604	85	80	2.2	.945	3B-295, OF-263, DH-65, 1B-34, SS-18

Dave Collins

COLLINS, DAVID SCOTT
B. Oct. 20, 1952, Rapid City, S. D.
BB TL 5′ 10″ 175 lbs.

Year	Team		Games	BA	SA	AB	H	2B	3B	HR	HR%	R	RBI	BB	SO	SB	PH AB	PH H	PO	A	E	DP	TC/G	FA	G by Pos
1975	CAL	A	93	.266	.361	319	85	13	4	3	0.9	41	29	36	55	24	5	4	159	3	2	2	1.8	.988	OF-75, DH-12
1976			99	.263	.334	365	96	12	1	4	1.1	45	28	40	55	32	2	0	160	3	1	0	1.7	.994	OF-71, DH-22
1977	SEA	A	120	.239	.313	402	96	9	3	5	1.2	46	28	33	66	25	7	4	124	6	2	2	1.1	.985	OF-73, DH-40
1978	CIN	N	102	.216	.225	102	22	1	0	0	0.0	13	7	15	18	7	**64**	14	30	1	1	0	0.3	.969	OF-24
1979			122	.318	.402	396	126	16	4	3	0.8	59	35	27	48	16	28	9	223	3	4	8	1.9	.983	OF-91, 1B-10
1980			144	.303	.370	551	167	20	4	3	0.5	94	35	53	68	79	3	1	337	5	5	1	2.4	.986	OF-141
1981			95	.272	.381	360	98	18	6	3	0.8	63	23	41	41	26	1	0	167	4	4	2	1.8	.977	OF-94
1982	NY	A	111	.253	.330	348	88	12	3	3	0.9	41	25	28	49	13	7	1	498	28	7	30	4.8	.987	OF-60, 1B-52, DH-1
1983	TOR	A	118	.271	.328	402	109	12	4	1	0.2	55	34	43	67	31	18	5	270	9	3	3	2.4	.989	OF-112, 1B-5, DH-1
1984			128	.308	.444	441	136	24	**15**	2	0.5	59	44	33	41	60	14	6	237	11	2	7	2.0	.992	OF-108, 1B-6, DH-4
1985	OAK	A	112	.251	.346	379	95	16	4	4	1.1	52	29	29	37	29	17	4	221	·1	5	0	2.0	.978	OF-91
1986	DET	A	124	.270	.329	419	113	18	2	1	0.2	44	27	44	49	27	11	1	211	2	1	1	1.7	.995	OF-94, DH-24
1987	CIN	N	57	.294	.353	85	25	5	3	0	0.0	19	5	11	12	9	35	8	36	0	0	0	0.6	1.000	OF-21
1988			99	.236	.293	174	41	6	2	0	0.0	12	14	11	27	7	58	12	66	2	4	2	0.7	.944	OF-35, 1B-3
1989			78	.236	.274	106	25	4	0	0	0.0	12	7	10	17	3	55	10	41	0	0	0	0.5	1.000	OF-16
1990	STL	N	99	.224	.241	58	13	1	0	0	0.0	12	3	13	10	7	25	6	89	0	1	5	1.5	.989	1B-49, OF-12
16 yrs.			1701	.272	.351	4907	1335	187	52	32	0.7	667	373	467	660	395	350	85	2869	78	42	63	1.8	.986	OF-1118, 1B-125, DH-104

LEAGUE CHAMPIONSHIP SERIES

Year	Team		Games	BA	SA	AB	H	2B	3B	HR	HR%	R	RBI	BB	SO	SB	PH AB	PH H	PO	A	E	DP	TC/G	FA	G by Pos
1979	CIN	N	3	.357	.429	14	5	1	0	0	0.0	0	1	0	2	2	0	0	5	0	0	0	1.7	1.000	OF-3

Jeff Conine

CONINE, JEFFREY GUY
B. June 27, 1966, Tacoma, Wash.
BR TR 6′ 1″ 205 lbs.

Year	Team		Games	BA	SA	AB	H	2B	3B	HR	HR%	R	RBI	BB	SO	SB	PH AB	PH H	PO	A	E	DP	TC/G	FA	G by Pos
1990	KC	A	9	.250	.350	20	5	2	0	0	0.0	3	2	2	5	0	0	0	39	4	1	7	4.9	.977	1B-9

Scott Coolbaugh

COOLBAUGH, SCOTT ROBERT
B. June 13, 1966, Binghamton, N. Y.
BR TR 5′ 10″ 185 lbs.

Year	Team		Games	BA	SA	AB	H	2B	3B	HR	HR%	R	RBI	BB	SO	SB	PH AB	PH H	PO	A	E	DP	TC/G	FA	G by Pos
1989	TEX	A	25	.275	.412	51	14	1	0	2	3.9	7	7	4	12	0	0	0	7	39	2	3	1.9	.958	3B-23, DH-2
1990			67	.200	.267	100	36	6	0	2	1.1	21	13	15	47	1	2	1	42	118	10	12	2.6	.941	3B-66
2 yrs.			92	.216	.299	231	50	7	0	4	1.7	28	20	19	59	1	2	1	49	157	12	15	2.4	.945	3B-89, DH-2

Year	Team		Games	BA	SA	AB	H	2B	3B	HR	HR%	R	RBI	BB	SO	SB	PINCH HIT AB	H	PO	A	E	DP	TC/G	FA	G by Pos

Scott Cooper

COOPER, SCOTT KENDRICK
B. Oct. 13, 1967, St. Louis, Mo.
BL TR 6′ 3″ 200 lbs.

Year	Team		Games	BA	SA	AB	H	2B	3B	HR	HR%	R	RBI	BB	SO	SB	AB	H	PO	A	E	DP	TC/G	FA	G by Pos
1990	BOS	A	2	.000	.000	1	0	0	0	0	0.0	0	0	0	1	0	1	0	0	0	0	0	0.0	.857	

Joey Cora

CORA, JOSE MANUEL
Born Jose Manuel Cora y Amaro.
B. May 14, 1965, Caguas, Puerto Rico
BR TR 5′ 7″ 150 lbs.

Year	Team		Games	BA	SA	AB	H	2B	3B	HR	HR%	R	RBI	BB	SO	SB	AB	H	PO	A	E	DP	TC/G	FA	G by Pos
1987	SD	N	77	.237	.282	241	57	7	2	0	0.0	23	13	28	26	15	8	2	123	200	10	32	4.3	.970	2B-66, SS-6
1989			12	.316	.368	19	6	1	0	0	0.0	5	1	1	0	1	0	0	11	15	2	3	2.3	.929	SS-7, 3B-2, 2B-1
1990			51	.270	.300	100	27	3	0	0	0.0	12	2	6	9	8	8	0	59	49	11	15	3.3	.908	SS-21, 2B-15, C-1
3 yrs.			140	.250	.292	360	90	11	2	0	0.0	40	16	35	35	24	16	2	193	264	23	50	3.4	.952	2B-82, SS-34, 3B-2, C-1

Henry Cotto

COTTO, HENRY
B. Jan. 5, 1961, Bronx, N. Y.
BR TR 6′ 2″ 180 lbs.

OUTFIELD — AVERAGE, RBI, HR, SB (with AL AVG comparisons)

	Games	BA	SA	AB	H	2B	3B	HR	HR%	R	RBI	BB	SO	SB
April	14	.259	.333	27	7	2	0	0	0.0	3	1	1	3	2
May	22	.329	.367	79	26	0	0	1	1.3	7	5	5	14	5
June	22	.319	.464	69	22	3	2	1	1.4	10	10	4	9	8
July	24	.229	.337	83	19	6	0	1	1.2	11	8	4	14	3
Aug	18	.079	.079	38	3	0	0	0	0.0	2	1	4	7	1
Sept/Oct	27	.254	.390	59	15	3	1	1	1.7	7	8	4	5	2
Day	34	.253	.368	95	24	5	0	2	2.1	11	8	5	19	3
Night	93	.262	.342	260	68	9	3	2	0.8	29	25	17	33	18
vs. Left		.260	.349	192	50	7	2	2	1.0	25	19	13	25	10
vs. Right		.258	.350	163	42	7	1	2	1.2	15	14	9	27	11
On Grass	49	.254	.303	122	31	4	1	0	0.0	12	12	8	19	9
On Turf	78	.262	.373	233	61	10	2	4	1.7	28	21	14	33	12
Home	61	.260	.358	173	45	7	2	2	1.2	21	15	13	21	10
Road	66	.258	.341	182	47	7	1	2	1.1	19	18	9	31	11
Division Rivals														
vs. CAL	9	.313	.406	32	10	3	0	0	0.0	6	3	3	5	5
vs. CHI	10	.292	.583	24	7	0	2	1	4.2	3	8	0	4	0
vs. KC	10	.227	.273	22	5	1	0	0	0.0	1	1	1	2	2
vs. MIN	12	.297	.405	37	11	4	0	0	0.0	5	2	2	5	1
vs. OAK	9	.200	.200	10	2	0	0	0	0.0	1	1	3	1	0
vs. TEX	9	.292	.417	24	7	0	0	1	4.2	4	6	1	4	4
On 3B < 2 Out		.200	.200	15	3	0	0	0	0.0	0	9	1	3	

Year	Team		Games	BA	SA	AB	H	2B	3B	HR	HR%	R	RBI	BB	SO	SB	AB	H	PO	A	E	DP	TC/G	FA	G by Pos
1984	CHI	N	105	.274	.308	146	40	5	0	0	0.0	24	8	10	23	9	13	3	117	3	2	1	1.2	.984	OF-88
1985	NY	A	34	.304	.375	56	17	1	0	1	1.8	4	6	3	12	1	4	1	41	2	1	0	1.3	.977	OF-30
1986			35	.213	.288	80	17	3	0	1	1.3	11	6	2	17	3	2	0	59	1	0	0	1.7	1.000	OF-29, DH-1
1987			68	.235	.403	149	35	10	0	5	3.4	21	20	6	35	4	11	0	89	2	1	0	1.4	.989	OF-57
1988	SEA	A	133	.259	.373	386	100	18	1	8	2.1	50	33	23	53	27	7	1	253	6	2	0	2.0	.992	OF-120, DH-2
1989			100	.264	.407	295	78	11	2	9	3.1	44	33	12	44	10	19	7	153	9	2	3	1.6	.988	OF-90, DH-2
1990			127	.259	.349	355	92	14	3	4	1.1	40	33	22	52	21	29	8	194	4	2	1	1.7	.990	OF-118, DH-3
7 yrs.			602	.258	.366	1467	379	62	6	28	1.9	194	139	78	236	75	85	20	906	27	10	5	1.6	.989	OF-532, DH-8

LEAGUE CHAMPIONSHIP SERIES

Year	Team		Games	BA	SA	AB	H	2B	3B	HR	HR%	R	RBI	BB	SO	SB	AB	H	PO	A	E	DP	TC/G	FA	G by Pos
1984	CHI	N	3	1.000	1.000	1	1	0	0	0	0.0	1	0	0	0	0	0	0	2	0	0	0	0.7	1.000	OF-3

Milt Cuyler

CUYLER, MILTON
B. Oct. 7, 1968, Macon, Ga.
BB TR 5′ 10″ 175 lbs.

Year	Team		Games	BA	SA	AB	H	2B	3B	HR	HR%	R	RBI	BB	SO	SB	AB	H	PO	A	E	DP	TC/G	FA	G by Pos
1990	DET	A	19	.255	.353	51	13	3	1	0	0.0	8	8	5	10	1	0	0	38	2	1	0	2.4	.976	OF-17

Year	Team	Games	BA	SA	AB	H	2B	3B	HR	HR%	R	RBI	BB	SO	SB	PINCH HIT AB	H	PO	A	E	DP	TC/G	FA	G by Pos

Kal Daniels

DANIELS, KALVOSKI
B. Aug. 20, 1963, Vienna, Ga.
BL TR 5′ 11″ 195 lbs.

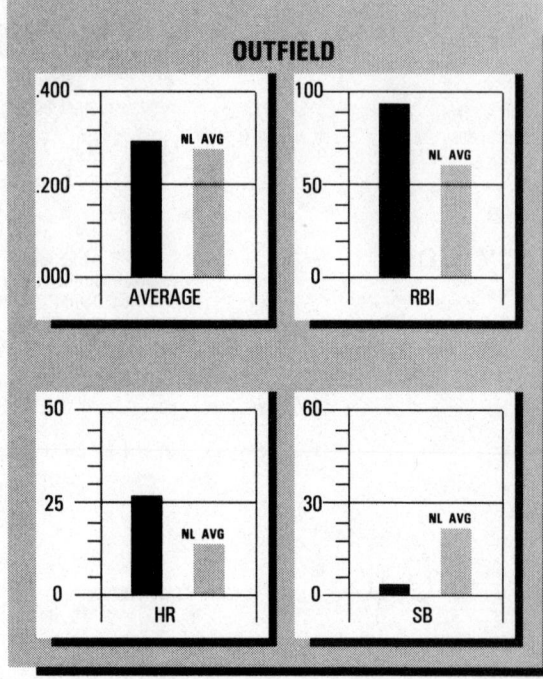

OUTFIELD

April		18	.346	.481	52	18	4	0	1	1.9	7	6	13	8	1
May		24	.311	.611	90	28	3	0	8	8.9	15	23	6	21	0
June		16	.250	.429	56	14	4	0	2	3.6	8	7	10	13	0
July		25	.293	.489	92	27	6	0	4	4.3	14	16	15	12	1
Aug		23	.222	.407	81	18	1	1	4	4.9	17	11	13	29	1
Sept/Oct		24	.354	.722	79	28	5	0	8	10.1	20	31	11	21	1
Day		29	.266	.532	94	25	7	0	6	6.4	16	21	16	30	1
Night		101	.303	.531	356	108	16	1	21	5.9	65	73	52	74	3
vs. Left			.285	.444	151	43	6	0	6	4.0	19	30	25	33	1
vs. Right			.301	.575	299	90	17	1	21	7.0	62	64	43	71	3
On Grass		97	.299	.530	334	100	18	1	19	5.7	62	72	51	79	3
On Turf		33	.284	.534	116	33	5	0	8	6.9	19	22	17	25	1
Home		67	.290	.498	231	67	10	1	12	5.2	38	43	35	48	3
Road		63	.301	.566	219	66	13	0	15	6.8	43	51	33	56	1
Division Rivals															
vs. ATL		14	.367	.571	49	18	1	0	3	6.1	14	8	17	14	0
vs. CIN		16	.280	.620	50	14	2	0	5	10.0	9	12	11	14	1
vs. HOU		15	.396	.623	53	21	3	0	3	5.7	9	15	6	6	1
vs. SD		12	.243	.459	37	9	5	0	1	2.7	5	7	5	10	1
vs. SF		15	.333	.479	48	16	4	0	1	2.1	12	8	7	11	1
On 3B < 2 Out			.379	.966	29	11	2	0	5	17.2	5	30	5	5	

Year	Team		Games	BA	SA	AB	H	2B	3B	HR	HR%	R	RBI	BB	SO	SB	AB	H	PO	A	E	DP	TC/G	FA	G by Pos
1986	CIN	N	74	.320	.519	181	58	10	4	6	3.3	34	23	22	30	15	23	11	88	0	3	0	1.2	.967	OF-47
1987			108	.334	.617	368	123	24	1	26	7.1	73	64	60	62	26	12	2	178	5	6	0	1.8	.968	OF-94
1988			140	.291	.463	495	144	29	1	18	3.6	95	64	87	94	27	1	0	256	10	5	2	1.9	.982	OF-137
1989	2 teams		CIN N (44G — .218)				LA N (11G — .342)																		
"	total		55	.246	.392	171	42	13	0	4	2.3	33	17	43	33	9	5	0	88	4	0	1	1.7	1.000	OF-49
1990	LA	N	130	.296	.531	450	133	23	1	27	6.0	81	94	68	104	4	3	2	207	13	3	2	1.8	.987	OF-127
5 yrs.			507	.300	.514	1665	500	99	7	81	4.9	316	262	280	323	81	44	15	817	32	17	5	1.7	.980	OF-454

Doug Dascenzo

DASCENZO, DOUGLAS CRAIG
B. June 30, 1964, Cleveland, Ohio
BB TL 5′ 7″ 150 lbs.

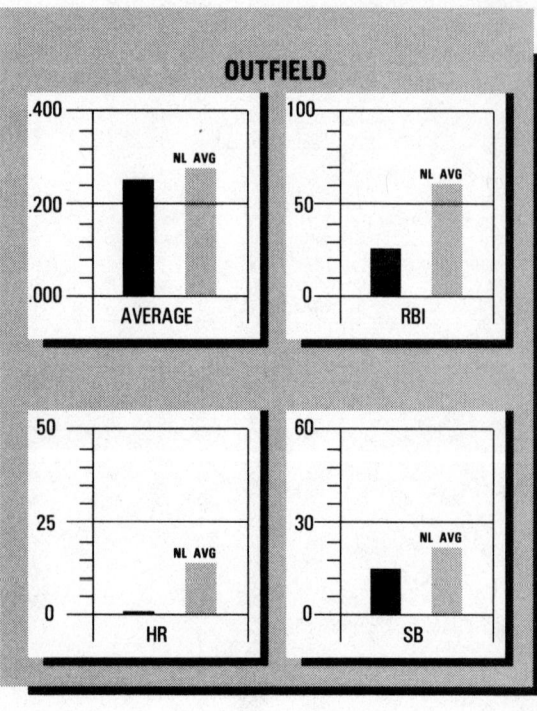

OUTFIELD

April		9	.182	.455	11	2	0	0	1	9.1	2	2	1	0	1
May		21	.212	.303	33	7	1	1	0	0.0	4	7	1	3	1
June		17	.273	.455	22	6	2	1	0	0.0	2	2	2	3	2
July		22	.269	.313	67	18	3	0	0	0.0	7	4	1	1	2
Aug		20	.352	.481	54	19	3	2	0	0.0	7	6	8	4	7
Sept/Oct		24	.167	.204	54	9	0	1	0	0.0	5	5	8	7	2
Day		58	.252	.341	123	31	6	1	1	0.8	14	15	8	9	4
Night		55	.254	.347	118	30	3	4	0	0.0	13	11	13	9	11
vs. Left			.279	.368	136	38	9	0	1	0.7	12	19	9	11	5
vs. Right			.219	.314	105	23	0	5	0	0.0	15	7	12	7	10
On Grass		77	.277	.376	173	48	6	4	1	0.6	18	21	13	13	11
On Turf		36	.191	.265	68	13	3	1	0	0.0	9	5	8	5	4
Home		55	.277	.387	119	33	4	3	1	0.8	13	13	11	6	6
Road		58	.230	.303	122	28	5	2	0	0.0	14	13	10	12	9
Division Rivals															
vs. MON		14	.160	.200	25	4	1	0	0	0.0	0	1	2	2	1
vs. NY		9	.250	.321	28	7	2	0	0	0.0	1	4	1	6	0
vs. PHI		12	.261	.478	23	6	0	1	1	4.3	7	3	7	2	0
vs. PIT		11	.107	.107	28	3	0	0	0	0.0	0	1	0	2	0
vs. STL		11	.095	.143	21	2	1	0	0	0.0	1	0	0	0	0
On 3B < 2 Out			.455	.545	11	5	1	0	0	0.0	0	11	2	0	

Year	Team		Games	BA	SA	AB	H	2B	3B	HR	HR%	R	RBI	BB	SO	SB	AB	H	PO	A	E	DP	TC/G	FA	G by Pos
1988	CHI	N	26	.213	.253	75	16	3	0	0	0.0	9	4	9	4	6	5	0	55	1	0	0	2.2	1.000	OF-20
1989			47	.165	.194	139	23	1	0	1	0.7	20	12	13	13	6	0	0	96	0	0	0	2.0	1.000	OF-45
1990			113	.253	.344	241	61	9	5	1	0.4	27	26	21	18	15	6	0	174	2	0	1	1.6	1.000	OF-107, P-1
3 yrs.			186	.220	.284	455	100	13	5	2	0.4	56	42	43	35	27	11	0	325	3	0	1	1.8	.000	OF-172, P-1

Year	Team		Games	BA	SA	AB	H	2B	3B	HR	HR%	R	RBI	BB	SO	SB	PINCH HIT AB	H	PO	A	E	DP	TC/G	FA	G by Pos

Jack Daugherty

DAUGHERTY, JOHN MICHAEL
B. July 3, 1960, Hialeah, Fla.
BB TL 6′ 188 lbs.

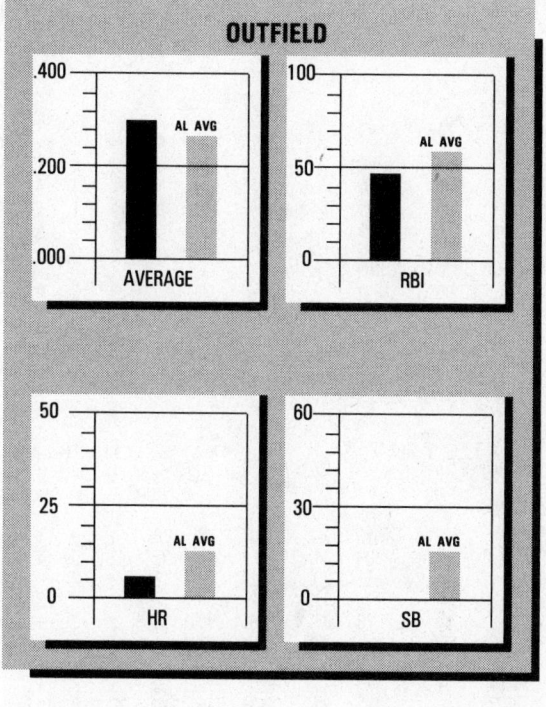

OUTFIELD

	Games	BA	SA	AB	H	2B	3B	HR	HR%	R	RBI	BB	SO	SB
April	11	.200	.267	15	3	1	0	0	0.0	2	1	2	2	0
May	20	.281	.333	57	16	3	0	0	0.0	3	5	3	5	0
June	23	.348	.500	46	16	5	1	0	0.0	6	8	2	10	0
July	24	.333	.506	81	27	8	0	2	2.5	12	12	7	18	0
Aug	19	.220	.293	41	9	3	0	0	0.0	3	3	2	5	0
Sept/Oct	28	.314	.514	70	22	0	1	4	5.7	10	18	6	9	0
Day	26	.289	.474	76	22	6	1	2	2.6	13	12	7	16	0
Night	99	.303	.423	234	71	14	1	4	1.7	23	35	15	33	0
vs. Left		.273	.312	77	21	3	0	0	0.0	7	10	7	20	0
vs. Right		.309	.476	233	72	17	2	6	2.6	29	37	15	29	0
On Grass	105	.290	.424	269	78	16	1	6	2.2	31	41	21	41	0
On Turf	20	.366	.512	41	15	4	1	0	0.0	5	6	1	8	0
Home	62	.311	.470	164	51	9	1	5	3.0	20	25	13	24	0
Road	63	.288	.397	146	42	11	1	1	0.7	16	22	9	25	0
Division Rivals														
vs. CAL	10	.188	.188	16	3	0	0	0	0.0	2	0	0	4	0
vs. CHI	11	.130	.217	23	3	2	0	0	0.0	2	2	1	5	0
vs. KC	10	.375	.594	32	12	2	1	1	3.1	7	8	3	3	0
vs. MIN	10	.429	.667	21	9	3	1	0	0.0	3	5	0	2	0
vs. OAK	11	.143	.429	21	3	0	0	2	9.5	3	4	4	5	0
vs. SEA	10	.450	.500	20	9	1	0	0	0.0	2	4	3	4	0
On 3B < 2 Out		.500	.500	14	7	0	0	0	0.0	0	13	1	3	

Year	Team		Games	BA	SA	AB	H	2B	3B	HR	HR%	R	RBI	BB	SO	SB	AB	H	PO	A	E	DP	TC/G	FA	G by Pos
1987	MON	N	11	.100	.200	10	1	1	0	0	0.0	1	1	0	3	0	9	1	1	1	0	0	0.2	1.000	1B-1
1989	TEX	A	52	.302	.406	106	32	4	2	1	0.9	15	10	11	21	2	18	7	132	14	0	12	2.8	1.000	1B-23, DH-8, OF-5
1990			125	.300	.435	310	93	20	2	6	1.9	36	47	22	49	0	45	10	225	22	3	21	3.5	.988	OF-42, 1B-30, DH-21
3 yrs.			188	.296	.423	426	126	25	4	7	1.6	52	58	33	73	2	72	18	358	37	3	33	2.1	.992	1B-54, OF-47, DH-29

Darren Daulton

DAULTON, DARREN ARTHUR
B. Jan. 3, 1962, Arkansas City, Kans.
BL TR 6′ 185 lbs.

CATCHER

	Games	BA	SA	AB	H	2B	3B	HR	HR%	R	RBI	BB	SO	SB
April	16	.234	.319	47	11	4	0	0	0.0	2	4	9	11	0
May	21	.188	.219	64	12	2	0	0	0.0	10	4	16	11	0
June	27	.253	.392	79	20	5	0	2	2.5	8	5	9	10	0
July	22	.266	.532	79	21	7	1	4	5.1	14	16	9	12	1
Aug	28	.314	.500	102	32	7	0	4	3.9	22	11	19	13	4
Sept/Oct	29	.307	.432	88	27	5	0	2	2.3	6	17	10	15	2
Day	35	.299	.458	107	32	8	0	3	2.8	17	18	16	20	0
Night	108	.259	.403	352	91	22	1	9	2.6	45	39	56	52	7
vs. Left		.257	.354	113	29	8	0	1	0.9	15	9	22	23	1
vs. Right		.272	.436	346	94	22	1	11	3.2	47	48	50	49	6
On Grass	39	.287	.388	129	37	7	0	2	1.6	19	14	20	25	2
On Turf	104	.261	.427	330	86	23	1	10	3.0	43	43	52	47	5
Home	71	.250	.384	224	56	15	0	5	2.2	26	24	34	31	3
Road	72	.285	.447	235	67	15	1	7	3.0	36	33	38	41	4
Division Rivals														
vs. CHI	17	.292	.417	48	14	3	0	1	2.1	4	7	5	7	1
vs. MON	14	.190	.333	42	8	3	0	1	2.4	3	3	12	10	0
vs. NY	17	.327	.596	52	17	2	0	4	7.7	8	9	7	13	0
vs. PIT	16	.192	.346	52	10	2	0	2	3.8	7	9	6	7	1
vs. STL	16	.360	.480	50	18	3	0	1	2.0	12	4	10	3	2
On 3B < 2 Out		.348	.609	23	8	3	0	1	4.3	1	15	2	5	

Year	Team		Games	BA	SA	AB	H	2B	3B	HR	HR%	R	RBI	BB	SO	SB	AB	H	PO	A	E	DP	TC/G	FA	G by Pos
1983	PHI	N	2	.333	.333	3	1	0	0	0	0.0	1	0	1	1	0	0	0	8	0	0	0	4.0	1.000	C-2
1985			36	.204	.369	103	21	3	1	4	3.9	14	11	16	37	3	5	0	160	15	1	1	4.9	.994	C-28
1986			49	.225	.428	138	31	4	0	8	5.8	18	21	38	41	2	1	0	244	21	4	6	5.5	.985	C-48
1987			53	.194	.310	129	25	6	0	3	2.3	10	13	16	37	0	12	3	210	13	2	6	4.2	.991	C-40, 1B-1
1988			58	.208	.271	144	30	6	0	1	0.7	13	12	17	26	2	15	4	205	15	6	1	3.9	.973	C-44, 1B-1
1989			131	.201	.310	368	74	12	2	8	2.2	29	44	52	58	2	11	2	627	56	11	8	5.3	.984	C-126
1990			143	.268	.416	459	123	30	1	12	2.6	62	57	72	72	7	10	2	683	70	8	10	5.5	.989	C-139
7 yrs.			472	.227	.359	1344	305	61	4	36	2.7	147	158	212	272	16	54	11	2137	190	32	32	5.0	.986	C-427, 1B-2

Year	Team		Games	BA	SA	AB	H	2B	3B	HR	HR%	R	RBI	BB	SO	SB	PINCH HIT AB	H	PO	A	E	DP	TC/G	FA	G by Pos

Mark Davidson

DAVIDSON, JOHN MARK
B. Feb. 15, 1961, Knoxville, Tenn.
BR TR 6' 2" 180 lbs.

Year	Team		Games	BA	SA	AB	H	2B	3B	HR	HR%	R	RBI	BB	SO	SB	AB	H	PO	A	E	DP	TC/G	FA	G by Pos
1986	MIN	A	36	.118	.162	68	8	3	0	0	0.0	5	2	6	22	2	2	1	48	0	1	0	1.4	.980	OF-31, DH-3
1987			102	.267	.327	150	40	4	1	1	0.7	32	14	13	26	9	6	3	102	3	0	0	1.0	1.000	OF-86, DH-9
1988			100	.217	.311	106	23	7	0	1	0.9	22	10	10	20	3	9	4	103	3	5	1	1.1	.955	OF-91, 3B-1
1989	HOU	N	33	.200	.308	65	13	2	1	1	1.5	7	5	7	14	1	12	2	36	0	0	0	1.1	1.000	OF-23
1990			57	.292	.369	130	38	5	1	1	0.7	12	11	10	18	0	9	1	103	1	2	0	2.1	.981	OF-51
5 yrs.			328	.235	.310	519	122	21	3	4	0.8	78	42	46	100	15	38	11	392	7	8	1	1.2	.980	OF-282, DH-12, 3B-1

LEAGUE CHAMPIONSHIP SERIES

Year	Team		Games	BA	SA	AB	H	2B	3B	HR	HR%	R	RBI	BB	SO	SB	AB	H	PO	A	E	DP	TC/G	FA	G by Pos
1987	MIN	A	1	—	—	0	0	0	0	0	0	0	0	0	0	0	0	0	0	0	0	0	0.0	—	

WORLD SERIES

Year	Team		Games	BA	SA	AB	H	2B	3B	HR	HR%	R	RBI	BB	SO	SB	AB	H	PO	A	E	DP	TC/G	FA	G by Pos
1987	MIN	A	2	.000	.000	1	0	0	0	0	0.0	0	0	0	0	0	1	0	0	0	0	0	0.0	—	OF-1

Alvin Davis

DAVIS, ALVIN GLENN
B. Sept. 9, 1960, Riverside, Calif.
BL TR 6' 1" 190 lbs.

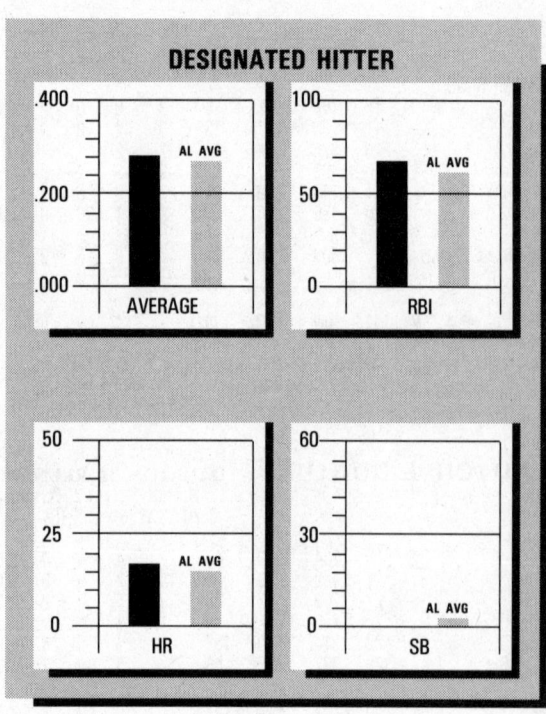

DESIGNATED HITTER

	Games	BA	SA	AB	H	2B	3B	HR	HR%	R	RBI	BB	SO	SB
April	20	.265	.368	68	18	4	0	1	1.5	7	5	16	8	0
May	26	.347	.485	101	35	2	0	4	4.0	18	9	14	10	0
June	21	.227	.253	75	17	2	0	0	0.0	4	8	10	9	0
July	18	.288	.492	59	17	3	0	3	5.1	8	14	14	10	0
Aug	28	.327	.510	98	32	6	0	4	4.1	15	14	20	13	0
Sept/Oct	27	.226	.430	93	21	4	0	5	5.4	11	18	11	18	0
Day	33	.268	.339	112	30	5	0	1	0.9	14	9	23	18	0
Night	107	.288	.455	382	110	16	0	16	4.2	49	59	62	50	0
vs. Left		.256	.405	168	43	7	0	6	3.6	23	29	28	24	0
vs. Right		.298	.442	326	97	14	0	11	3.4	40	39	57	44	0
On Grass	52	.258	.346	182	47	7	0	3	1.6	13	20	32	22	0
On Turf	88	.298	.478	312	93	14	0	14	4.5	50	48	53	46	0
Home	72	.278	.464	252	70	11	0	12	4.8	42	40	47	38	0
Road	68	.289	.393	242	70	10	0	5	2.1	21	28	38	30	0
Division Rivals														
vs. CAL	11	.226	.258	31	7	1	0	0	0.0	1	2	7	7	0
vs. CHI	13	.204	.429	49	10	2	0	3	6.1	5	13	3	8	0
vs. KC	10	.382	.529	34	13	2	0	1	2.9	6	7	6	5	0
vs. MIN	13	.354	.625	48	17	7	0	2	4.2	7	7	5	11	0
vs. OAK	13	.277	.383	47	13	2	0	1	2.1	6	3	8	3	0
vs. TEX	12	.275	.425	40	11	3	0	1	2.5	4	9	7	5	0
On 3B < 2 Out		.500	.750	16	8	1	0	1	6.3	1	23	6	1	

Year	Team		Games	BA	SA	AB	H	2B	3B	HR	HR%	R	RBI	BB	SO	SB	AB	H	PO	A	E	DP	TC/G	FA	G by Pos
1984	SEA	A	152	.284	.497	567	161	34	3	27	4.8	80	116	97	78	5	0	0	1271	94	11	108	9.1	.992	1B-147, DH-7
1985			155	.287	.441	578	166	33	1	18	3.1	78	78	90	71	1	1	1	1438	103	13	131	10.0	.992	1B-154
1986			135	.271	.426	479	130	18	1	18	3.8	66	72	76	68	0	4	0	880	82	14	112	7.2	.986	1B-101, DH-32
1987			157	.295	.516	580	171	37	2	29	5.0	86	100	72	84	0	0	0	1386	96	9	133	9.5	.994	1B-157
1988			140	.295	.462	478	141	24	1	18	3.8	67	69	95	53	1	1	1	980	65	6	111	7.5	.994	1B-115, DH-25
1989			142	.305	.496	498	152	30	1	21	4.2	84	95	101	49	0	3	1	1106	81	10	119	8.4	.992	1B-125, DH-14
1990			140	.283	.429	494	140	21	0	17	3.4	63	68	85	68	0	1	1	435	31	3	41	9.0	.994	DH-87, 1B-52
7 yrs.			1021	.289	.468	3674	1061	197	9	148	4.0	524	598	616	471	7	10	4	7496	552	66	755	7.9	.992	1B-851, DH-165

Chili Davis

DAVIS, CHARLES THEODORE
B. Jan. 17, 1960, Kingston, Jamaica
BB TR 6' 3" 195 lbs.

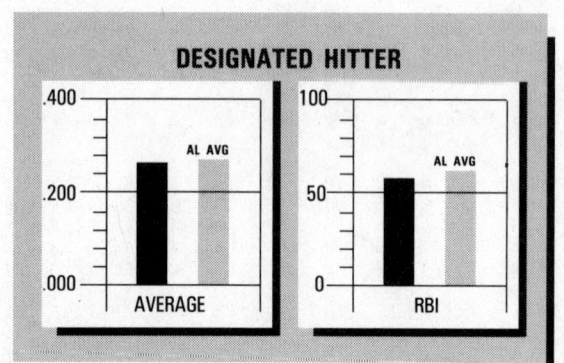

DESIGNATED HITTER

	Games	BA	SA	AB	H	2B	3B	HR	HR%	R	RBI	BB	SO	SB
April	19	.257	.405	74	19	5	0	2	2.7	9	8	10	17	0
May	29	.295	.410	105	31	4	1	2	1.9	14	16	12	16	1
June	26	.275	.516	91	25	4	0	6	6.6	19	16	18	23	0
July	9	.219	.219	32	7	0	0	0	0.0	3	0	4	6	0
Aug	17	.258	.379	66	17	2	0	2	3.0	8	14	8	15	0
Sept/Oct	13	.227	.273	44	10	2	0	0	0.0	5	4	9	12	0
Day	27	.237	.299	97	23	3	0	1	1.0	9	11	17	25	0
Night	86	.273	.429	315	86	14	1	11	3.5	49	47	44	64	1
vs. Left		.254	.389	126	32	5	0	4	3.2	14	20	18	29	0
vs. Right		.269	.402	286	77	12	1	8	2.8	44	38	43	60	1

Year	Team		Games	BA	SA	AB	H	2B	3B	HR	HR%	R	RBI	BB	SO	SB	PINCH HIT AB	H	PO	A	E	DP	TC/G	FA	G by Pos

Chili Davis *Continued*

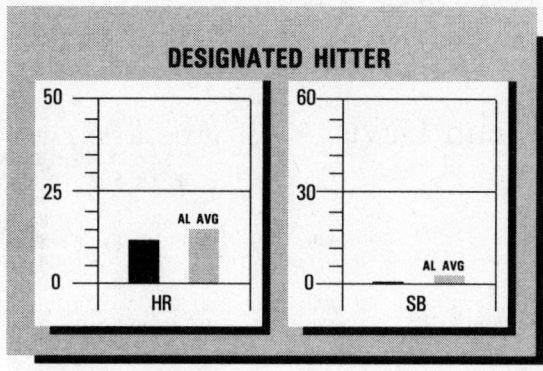

DESIGNATED HITTER

On Grass			97	.265	.403	355	94	14	1	11	3.1	52	48	50	80	0									
On Turf			16	.263	.368	57	15	3	0	1	1.8	6	10	11	9	1									
Home			59	.306	.495	216	66	9	1	10	4.6	38	39	30	46	0									
Road			54	.219	.291	196	43	8	0	2	1.0	20	19	31	43	1									
Division Rivals																									
vs. CHI			11	.275	.300	40	11	1	0	0	0.0	4	6	7	10	0									
vs. KC			9	.235	.471	34	8	2	0	2	5.9	5	8	4	9	0									
vs. MIN			9	.333	.394	33	11	2	0	0	0.0	5	4	6	7	0									
vs. OAK			2	.250	.625	8	2	0	0	1	12.5	2	2	1	0	0									
vs. SEA			9	.265	.382	34	9	1	0	1	2.9	5	3	5	10	0									
vs. TEX			9	.167	.267	30	5	0	0	1	3.3	6	4	8	6	0									
On 3B < 2 Out				.290	.452	31	9	2	0	1	3.2	1	24	6	8										
1981	SF	N	8	.133	.133	15	2	0	0	0	0.0	1	0	1	2	2	3	1	7	0	0	0	0.9	1.000	OF-6
1982			154	.261	.410	641	167	27	6	19	3.0	86	76	45	115	24	1	1	404	16	12	4	2.8	.972	OF-153
1983			137	.233	.352	486	113	21	2	11	2.3	54	59	55	108	10	4	1	357	7	9	1	2.7	.976	OF-133
1984			137	.315	.507	499	157	21	6	21	4.2	87	81	42	74	12	15	6	292	9	9	2	2.3	.971	OF-123
1985			136	.270	.412	481	130	25	2	13	2.7	53	56	62	74	15	9	2	279	10	6	2	2.2	.980	OF-126
1986			153	.278	.416	526	146	28	3	13	2.5	71	70	84	96	16	7	1	303	9	9	2	2.1	.972	OF-148
1987			149	.250	.442	500	125	22	1	24	4.8	80	76	72	109	16	20	3	265	6	7	2	1.9	.975	OF-135
1988	CAL	A	158	.268	.432	600	161	29	3	21	3.5	81	93	56	118	9	1	0	299	10	19	1	2.1	.942	OF-153, DH-3
1989			154	.271	.436	560	152	24	1	22	3.9	81	90	61	109	3	2	0	270	5	6	0	1.8	.979	OF-147, DH-6
1990			113	.265	.398	412	109	17	1	12	2.9	58	58	61	89	1	2	0	77	5	3	1	1.6	.965	DH-60, OF-52
10 yrs.			1299	.267	.422	4720	1262	214	25	156	3.3	652	659	539	894	108	64	15	2553	77	80	15	2.1	.970	OF-1176, DH-69

LEAGUE CHAMPIONSHIP SERIES

Year	Team		Games	BA	SA	AB	H	2B	3B	HR	HR%	R	RBI	BB	SO	SB	AB	H	PO	A	E	DP	TC/G	FA	G by Pos
1987	SF	N	6	.150	.200	20	3	1	0	0	0.0	2	0	1	4	0	0	0	11	1	1	1	2.2	.923	OF-6

Eric Davis

DAVIS, ERIC KEITH
B. May 29, 1962, Los Angeles, Calif.
BR TR 6' 3" 175 lbs.

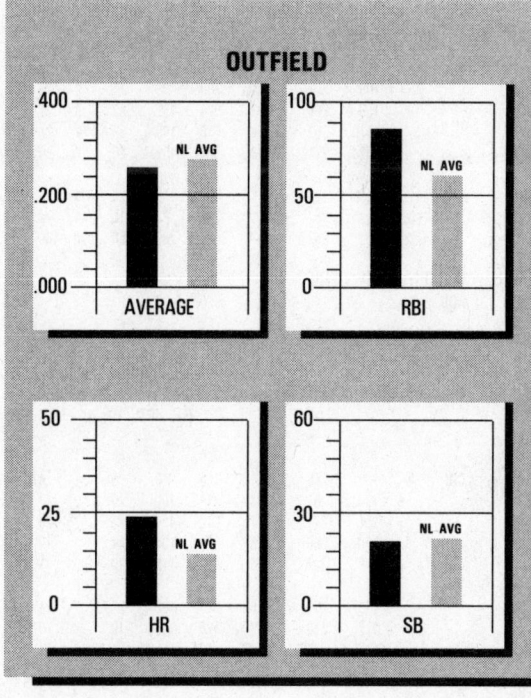

OUTFIELD

April			11	.186	.349	43	8	2	1	1	2.3	5	8	6	11	5									
May			8	.179	.321	28	5	1	0	1	3.6	3	4	6	8	0									
June			28	.292	.635	96	28	4	1	9	9.4	21	22	18	19	3									
July			28	.194	.344	93	18	5	0	3	3.2	15	16	14	21	3									
Aug			26	.263	.432	95	25	7	0	3	3.2	14	12	6	22	2									
Sept/Oct			26	.347	.633	98	34	7	0	7	7.1	26	24	10	19	8									
Day			32	.295	.549	122	36	8	1	7	5.7	24	20	8	29	4									
Night			95	.248	.462	331	82	18	1	17	5.1	60	66	52	71	17									
vs. Left				.287	.520	150	43	11	0	8	5.3	32	36	19	32	6									
vs. Right				.248	.469	303	75	15	2	16	5.3	52	50	41	68	15									
On Grass			44	.292	.515	171	50	11	0	9	5.3	32	40	18	42	9									
On Turf			83	.241	.468	282	68	15	2	15	5.3	52	46	42	58	12									
Home			58	.233	.487	193	45	8	1	13	6.7	38	34	32	42	7									
Road			69	.281	.485	260	73	18	1	11	4.2	46	52	28	58	14									
Division Rivals																									
vs. ATL			18	.254	.458	59	15	4	1	2	3.4	11	12	12	14	4									
vs. HOU			16	.254	.603	63	16	2	1	6	9.5	13	13	5	9	5									
vs. LA			18	.227	.485	66	15	5	0	4	6.1	11	14	7	18	2									
vs. SD			15	.304	.464	56	17	3	0	2	3.6	15	14	10	9	4									
vs. SF			15	.264	.415	53	14	2	0	2	3.8	7	6	8	12	2									
On 3B < 2 Out				.242	.515	33	8	3	0	2	6.1	2	24	9	8										
1984	CIN	N	57	.224	.466	174	39	10	1	10	5.7	33	30	24	48	10	6	1	125	4	1	2	2.3	.992	OF-51
1985			56	.246	.516	122	30	3	3	8	6.6	26	18	7	39	16	8	1	75	3	1	1	1.4	.987	OF-47
1986			132	.277	.523	415	115	15	3	27	6.5	97	71	68	100	80	4	0	274	2	7	0	2.1	.975	OF-121
1987			129	.293	.593	474	139	23	4	37	7.8	120	100	84	134	50	1	0	380	10	4	4	3.1	.990	OF-128
1988			135	.273	.489	472	129	18	3	26	5.5	81	93	65	124	35	3	1	300	2	6	0	2.3	.981	OF-130
1989			131	.281	.541	462	130	14	2	34	7.4	74	101	68	116	21	3	1	298	2	5	1	2.3	.984	OF-125
1990			127	.260	.486	453	118	26	2	24	5.2	84	86	60	100	21	6	1	257	11	2	1	2.2	.993	OF-122
7 yrs.			767	.272	.522	2572	700	109	18	166	6.5	515	499	376	661	233	31	5	1709	34	26	9	2.3	.985	OF-724

LEAGUE CHAMPIONSHIP SERIES

Year	Team		Games	BA	SA	AB	H	2B	3B	HR	HR%	R	RBI	BB	SO	SB	AB	H	PO	A	E	DP	TC/G	FA	G by Pos
1990	CIN	N	6	.174	.217	23	4	1	0	0	0.0	2	2	1	9	0	0	0	12	1	0	0	2.2	1.000	OF-6

Year	Team		Games	BA	SA	AB	H	2B	3B	HR	HR%	R	RBI	BB	SO	SB	AB	H	PO	A	E	DP	TC/G	FA	G by Pos
																	PINCH HIT								

Eric Davis *Continued*

WORLD SERIES

Year	Team		Games	BA	SA	AB	H	2B	3B	HR	HR%	R	RBI	BB	SO	SB	AB	H	PO	A	E	DP	TC/G	FA	G by Pos
1990	CIN	N	4	.286	.500	14	4	0	0	1	7.1	3	5	0	0	0	0	0	4	0	0	0	1.0	1.000	OF-4

Glenn Davis

DAVIS, GLENN EARLE
B. Mar. 28, 1961, Jacksonville, Fla.
BR TR 6′ 3″ 205 lbs.

	Games	BA	SA	AB	H	2B	3B	HR	HR%	R	RBI	BB	SO	SB
April	19	.343	.671	70	24	5	0	6	8.6	11	14	9	21	3
May	28	.215	.383	107	23	6	0	4	3.7	12	18	6	13	2
June	17	.211	.737	57	12	1	1	9	15.8	10	16	10	14	0
July				0	0	0	0	0		0	0	0	0	0
Aug	2	.000	.000	4	0	0	0	0	0.0	0	0	1	0	0
Sept/Oct	27	.258	.461	89	23	3	3	3	3.4	11	16	20	6	3
Day	26	.274	.583	84	23	6	1	6	7.1	14	22	12	21	5
Night	67	.243	.502	243	59	9	3	16	6.6	30	42	34	33	3
vs. Left		.252	.569	123	31	6	0	11	8.9	23	27	21	11	3
vs. Right		.250	.495	204	51	9	4	11	5.4	21	37	25	43	5
On Grass	26	.315	.826	92	29	4	2	13	14.1	15	30	14	13	1
On Turf	67	.226	.404	235	53	11	2	9	3.8	29	34	32	41	7
Home	50	.217	.349	175	38	7	2	4	2.3	19	22	21	35	7
Road	43	.289	.724	152	44	8	2	18	11.8	25	42	25	19	1
Division Rivals														
vs. ATL	8	.276	.517	29	8	2	1	1	3.4	4	7	2	7	1
vs. CIN	17	.241	.448	58	14	3	0	3	5.2	7	8	13	10	0
vs. LA	15	.226	.491	53	12	1	2	3	5.7	8	10	11	12	0
vs. SD	7	.227	.636	22	5	0	0	3	13.6	3	4	5	2	1
vs. SF	9	.346	.923	26	9	0	0	5	19.2	5	11	5	7	0
On 3B < 2 Out		.294	.353	17	5	1	0	0	0.0		10	3	4	

FIRST BASE

Year	Team		Games	BA	SA	AB	H	2B	3B	HR	HR%	R	RBI	BB	SO	SB	AB	H	PO	A	E	DP	TC/G	FA	G by Pos
1984	HOU	N	18	.213	.393	61	13	5	0	2	3.3	6	8	4	12	0	2	0	151	15	2	13	9.3	.988	1B-16
1985			100	.271	.474	350	95	11	0	20	5.7	51	64	27	68	0	4	1	766	57	12	76	8.4	.986	1B-89, OF-9
1986			158	.265	.493	574	152	32	3	31	5.4	91	101	64	72	3	2	0	1253	111	11	90	8.7	.992	1B-156
1987			151	.251	.458	578	145	35	2	27	4.7	70	93	47	84	4	1	0	1283	112	12	89	9.3	.991	1B-151
1988			152	.271	.478	561	152	26	0	30	5.3	78	99	53	77	4	2	0	1355	103	6	104	9.6	.996	1B-151
1989			158	.269	.492	581	156	26	1	34	5.9	87	89	69	123	4	3	1	1347	113	12	101	9.3	.992	1B-156
1990			93	.251	.523	327	82	15	4	22	6.7	44	64	46	54	8	4	2	796	55	4	56	9.4	.995	1B-91
7 yrs.			830	.262	.483	3032	795	150	10	166	5.5	427	518	310	490	23	18	4	6951	566	59	529	9.1	.992	1B-810, OF-9

LEAGUE CHAMPIONSHIP SERIES

1986	HOU	N	6	.269	.423	26	7	1	0	1	3.8	3	3	1	3	0	0	0	62	3	1	2	11.0	.985	1B-6

Jody Davis

DAVIS, JODY RICHARD
B. Nov. 12, 1956, Gainesville, Ga.
BR TR 6′ 4″ 192 lbs.

Year	Team		Games	BA	SA	AB	H	2B	3B	HR	HR%	R	RBI	BB	SO	SB	AB	H	PO	A	E	DP	TC/G	FA	G by Pos
1981	CHI	N	56	.256	.361	180	46	5	1	4	2.2	14	21	21	28	0	0	0	274	44	9	4	5.8	.972	C-56
1982			130	.261	.404	418	109	20	2	12	2.9	41	52	36	92	0	1	0	598	89	11	11	5.4	.984	C-129
1983			151	.271	.480	510	138	31	2	24	4.7	56	84	33	93	0	2	0	730	75	13	7	5.4	.984	C-150
1984			150	.256	.419	523	134	24	2	19	3.6	55	94	47	99	5	4	1	811	89	15	9	6.1	.984	C-146
1985			142	.232	.400	482	112	30	0	17	3.5	47	58	48	83	1	11	2	694	84	8	7	5.5	.990	C-138
1986			148	.250	.428	528	132	27	2	21	4.0	61	74	41	110	0	4	0	885	105	8	14	6.7	.992	C-145, 1B-1
1987			125	.248	.418	428	106	12	2	19	4.4	57	51	52	91	1	3	0	749	79	9	11	6.7	.989	C-123
1988	2 teams				CHI N (88G — .229)		ATL N (2G — .250)																		
"	total		90	.230	.346	267	60	9	0	7	2.7	21	36	29	52	0	13	1	396	34	2	1	4.8	.995	C-76
1989	ATL	N	78	.169	.242	231	39	5	0	4	1.7	12	19	23	61	0	8	1	376	40	6	4	5.4	.986	C-72, 1B-2
1990			12	.071	.071	28	2	0	0	0	0.0	0	1	3	3	0	4	0	64	6	0	4	7.8	1.000	1B-6, C-4
10 yrs.			1082	.245	.403	3585	877	163	11	127	3.5	364	490	333	712	7	50	5	5577	645	81	72	5.8	.987	C-1039, 1B-9

LEAGUE CHAMPIONSHIP SERIES

1984	CHI	N	5	.389	.833	18	7	2	0	2	11.1	3	6	0	3	0	0	0	23	4	0	0	5.4	1.000	C-5

Year	Team	Games	BA	SA	AB	H	2B	3B	HR	HR%	R	RBI	BB	SO	SB	PINCH HIT AB	H	PO	A	E	DP	TC/G	FA	G by Pos

Andre Dawson

DAWSON, ANDRE FERNANDO (The Hawk)
B. July 10, 1954, Miami, Fla.
BR TR 6′ 3″ 180 lbs.

Split	Games	BA	SA	AB	H	2B	3B	HR	HR%	R	RBI	BB	SO	SB
April	17	.339	.610	59	20	2	1	4	6.8	7	15	2	9	1
May	28	.350	.710	100	35	7	1	9	9.0	19	28	10	7	5
June	27	.283	.515	99	28	8	0	5	5.1	14	9	14	10	2
July	22	.355	.434	76	27	3	0	1	1.3	9	10	7	8	3
Aug	23	.236	.382	89	21	3	2	2	2.2	5	12	1	15	2
Sept/Oct	30	.311	.547	106	33	5	1	6	5.7	18	26	8	16	3
Day	76	.326	.562	267	87	12	3	15	5.6	38	56	24	31	8
Night	71	.294	.508	262	77	16	2	12	4.6	34	44	18	34	8
vs. Left		.298	.508	181	54	10	2	8	4.4	23	25	14	19	3
vs. Right		.316	.549	348	110	18	3	19	5.5	49	75	28	46	13
On Grass	106	.303	.537	376	114	16	3	22	5.9	55	77	37	45	11
On Turf	41	.327	.529	153	50	12	2	5	3.3	17	23	5	20	5
Home	77	.316	.534	266	84	10	3	14	5.3	31	51	27	26	9
Road	70	.304	.536	263	80	18	2	13	4.9	41	49	15	39	7
Division Rivals														
vs. MON	17	.311	.541	61	19	6	1	2	3.3	4	15	3	9	3
vs. NY	14	.306	.571	49	15	1	0	4	8.2	10	8	5	8	2
vs. PHI	15	.375	.750	48	18	6	0	4	8.3	12	12	4	4	0
vs. PIT	17	.359	.625	64	23	1	2	4	6.3	9	12	4	6	0
vs. STL	17	.246	.311	61	15	1	0	1	1.6	3	6	5	11	2
On 3B < 2 Out		.429	.679	28	12	4	0	1	3.6	1	34	4	2	

OUTFIELD

Charts: AVERAGE, RBI, HR, SB (with NL AVG comparisons)

Year	Team		Games	BA	SA	AB	H	2B	3B	HR	HR%	R	RBI	BB	SO	SB	AB	H	PO	A	E	DP	TC/G	FA	G by Pos
1976	MON	N	24	.235	.306	85	20	4	1	0	0.0	9	7	5	13	1	0	0	61	1	2	1	2.7	.969	OF-24
1977			139	.282	.474	525	148	26	9	19	3.6	64	65	34	93	21	5	0	352	9	4	1	2.6	.989	OF-136
1978			157	.253	.442	609	154	24	8	25	4.1	84	72	30	128	28	5	2	411	17	5	2	2.8	.988	OF-153
1979			155	.275	.468	639	176	24	12	25	3.9	90	92	27	115	35	0	0	394	7	5	1	2.6	.988	OF-153
1980			151	.308	.492	577	178	41	7	17	2.9	96	87	44	69	34	3	1	410	14	6	3	2.8	.986	OF-147
1981			103	.302	.553	394	119	21	3	24	6.1	71	64	35	50	26	0	0	327	10	7	1	3.3	.980	OF-103
1982			148	.301	.498	608	183	37	7	23	3.8	107	83	34	96	39	0	0	419	8	8	2	2.9	.982	OF-147
1983			159	.299	.539	633	**189**	36	10	32	5.1	104	113	38	81	25	1	1	435	6	9	2	2.8	.980	OF-157
1984			138	.248	.409	533	132	23	6	17	3.2	73	86	41	80	13	4	0	297	11	8	2	2.3	.975	OF-134
1985			139	.255	.444	529	135	27	2	23	4.3	65	91	29	92	13	9	3	248	9	7	1	1.9	.973	OF-131
1986			130	.284	.478	496	141	32	2	20	4.0	65	78	37	79	18	3	1	200	11	3	2	1.6	.986	OF-127
1987	CHI	N	153	.287	.568	621	178	24	2	**49**	7.9	90	**137**	32	103	11	2	1	271	12	4	0	1.9	.986	OF-152
1988			157	.303	.504	591	179	31	8	24	4.1	78	79	37	73	12	8	2	267	7	3	1	1.8	.989	OF-147
1989			118	.252	.476	416	105	18	6	21	5.0	62	77	35	62	8	5	2	227	4	3	0	2.0	.987	OF-112
1990			147	.310	.535	529	164	28	5	27	5.1	72	100	42	65	16	7	2	250	10	5	4	1.9	.981	OF-139
15 yrs.			2018	.283	.490	7785	2201	396	88	346	4.4	1130	1231	500	1199	300	52	15	4569	136	79	23	2.4	.983	OF-1962

DIVISIONAL PLAYOFF SERIES

Year	Team		Games	BA	SA	AB	H	2B	3B	HR	HR%	R	RBI	BB	SO	SB	AB	H	PO	A	E	DP	TC/G	FA	G by Pos
1981	MON	N	5	.300	.400	20	6	0	1	0	0.0	1	0	1	6	2	0	0	12	1	1	0	2.8		OF-5

LEAGUE CHAMPIONSHIP SERIES

Year	Team		Games	BA	SA	AB	H	2B	3B	HR	HR%	R	RBI	BB	SO	SB	AB	H	PO	A	E	DP	TC/G	FA	G by Pos
1981	MON	N	5	.150	.150	20	3	0	0	0	0.0	2	0	0	4	0	0	0	12	0	0	0	2.4	1.000	OF-5
1989	CHI	N	5	.105	.158	19	2	1	0	0	0.0	0	3	2	6	0	0	0	4	0	0	0	0.8	1.000	OF-5
2 yrs.			10	.128	.154	39	5	1	0	0	0.0	2	3	2	10	0	0	0	16	0	0	0	1.6	.000	OF-10

Steve Decker

DECKER, STEVEN MICHAEL
B. Oct. 25, 1965, Rock Island, Ill.
BR TR 6′ 3″ 205 lbs.

Year	Team		Games	BA	SA	AB	H	2B	3B	HR	HR%	R	RBI	BB	SO	SB	AB	H	PO	A	E	DP	TC/G	FA	G by Pos
1990	SF	N	15	.296	.500	54	16	2	0	3	5.5	5	8	1	10	0	0	0	75	11	1	2	5.8	.989	C-15

Year	Team	Games	BA	SA	AB	H	2B	3B	HR	HR%	R	RBI	BB	SO	SB	PINCH HIT AB	PINCH HIT H	PO	A	E	DP	TC/G	FA	G by Pos

Rob Deer

DEER, ROBERT GEORGE
B. Sept. 29, 1960, Orange, Calif.
BR TR 6′ 3″ 215 lbs.

OUTFIELD

	Games	BA	SA	AB	H	2B	3B	HR	HR%	R	RBI	BB	SO	SB	AB	H	PO	A	E	DP	TC/G	FA	G by Pos
April	15	.216	.514	37	8	3	0	3	8.1	7	9	9	12	1									
May	21	.197	.424	66	13	3	0	4	6.1	10	11	14	29	1									
June	22	.224	.487	76	17	2	0	6	7.9	10	18	10	21	0									
July	21	.211	.434	76	16	2	0	5	6.6	9	10	13	24	0									
Aug	27	.245	.551	98	24	4	1	8	8.2	13	17	11	37	0									
Sept/Oct	28	.161	.218	87	14	2	0	1	1.1	8	4	7	24	0									
Day	42	.152	.288	132	20	6	0	4	3.0	11	13	20	50	1									
Night	92	.234	.494	308	72	9	1	23	7.5	46	56	44	97	1									
vs. Left		.293	.671	140	41	5	0	16	11.4	26	34	25	40	1									
vs. Right		.170	.320	300	51	10	1	11	3.7	31	35	39	107	1									
On Grass	115	.214	.447	378	81	14	1	24	6.3	49	59	55	120	2									
On Turf	19	.177	.339	62	11	1	0	3	4.8	8	10	9	27	0									
Home	67	.187	.374	214	40	7	0	11	5.1	24	30	35	67	1									
Road	67	.230	.487	226	52	8	1	16	7.1	33	39	29	80	1									
Division Rivals																							
vs. BAL	9	.167	.333	24	4	1	0	1	4.2	3	2	5	8	0									
vs. BOS	10	.125	.313	32	4	0	0	2	6.3	4	5	8	8	0									
vs. CLE	13	.220	.540	50	11	1	0	5	10.0	6	10	1	15	0									
vs. DET	12	.389	1.000	36	14	2	1	6	16.7	9	14	9	8	0									
vs. NY	10	.176	.529	34	6	3	0	3	8.8	6	6	6	13	0									
vs. TOR	11	.222	.222	36	8	0	0	0	0.0	4	5	4	13	0									
On 3B < 2 Out		.111	.444	18	2	0	0	2	11.1	2	11	6	7										
1984 SF N	13	.167	.542	24	4	0	0	3	12.5	5	3	7	10	1	3	0	19	0	2	0	1.6	.905	OF-9
1985	78	.185	.377	162	30	5	1	8	4.9	22	20	23	71	0	30	5	127	2	2	4	1.7	.985	OF-37, 1B-10
1986 MIL A	134	.232	.494	466	108	17	3	33	7.1	75	86	72	179	5	1	1	312	8	8	3	2.4	.976	OF-131, 1B-4
1987	134	.238	.456	474	113	15	2	28	5.9	71	80	86	186	12	2	0	304	16	8	7	2.4	.976	OF-123, 1B-12, DH-4
1988	135	.252	.441	492	124	24	0	23	4.7	71	85	51	153	9	1	0	284	10	3	3	2.2	.990	OF-133, DH-1
1989	130	.210	.425	466	98	18	2	26	5.6	72	65	60	158	4	1	1	267	10	8	1	2.2	.972	OF-125, DH-5
1990	134	.209	.432	440	92	15	1	27	6.1	57	69	64	147	2	6	1	373	25	10	19	3.1	.975	OF-117, 1B-21, DH-1
7 yrs.	758	.225	.446	2524	569	94	9	148	5.9	373	408	363	904	33	44	8	1686	71	41	37	2.4	.977	OF-675, 1B-47, DH-11

Rick Dempsey

DEMPSEY, JOHN RIKARD
B. Sept. 13, 1949, Fayetteville, Tenn.
BR TR 6′ 180 lbs.

Year	Team	Games	BA	SA	AB	H	2B	3B	HR	HR%	R	RBI	BB	SO	SB	AB	H	PO	A	E	DP	TC/G	FA	G by Pos
1969 MIN A	5	.500	.667	6	3	1	0	0	0.0	1	0	1	0	0	1	0	5	0	1	0	1.2	.833	C-3
1970	5	.000	.000	7	0	0	0	0	0.0	1	0	1	1	0	1	0	12	0	1	0	2.6	.923	C-3
1971	6	.308	.385	13	4	1	0	0	0.0	2	0	1	0	0	0	0	30	4	2	0	6.0	.944	C-6
1972	25	.200	.225	40	8	1	0	0	0.0	0	0	6	8	0	2	1	67	5	1	0	2.9	.986	C-23
1973 NY A	6	.182	.182	11	2	0	0	0	0.0	0	0	1	3	0	0	0	9	0	2	0	1.8	.818	C-5
1974	43	.239	.321	109	26	3	0	2	1.8	12	12	8	7	1	12	2	152	22	4	0	4.1	.978	C-31, OF-2, DH-1
1975	71	.262	.338	145	38	8	0	1	0.7	18	11	21	15	0	23	5	92	9	3	1	1.5	.971	C-19, DH-18, OF-8, 3B-1
1976 2 teams	NY A (21G — .119)			BAL A (59G — .213)																			
" total	80	.194	.204	216	42	2	0	0	0.0	12	12	18	21	1	6	1	308	40	4	8	4.4	.989	C-67, OF-7
1977 BAL A	91	.226	.315	270	61	7	4	3	1.1	27	34	34	34	2	1	1	416	52	11	10	5.3	.977	C-91
1978	136	.259	.356	441	114	25	0	6	1.4	41	32	48	54	7	4	1	636	79	11	14	5.3	.985	C-135
1979	124	.239	.351	368	88	23	0	6	1.6	48	41	38	37	0	39	11	615	81	7	13	5.7	.990	C-124
1980	119	.262	.425	362	95	26	3	9	2.5	51	40	36	45	3	9	1	544	55	8	10	5.1	.987	C-112, OF-6, 1B-2, DH-1
1981	92	.215	.335	251	54	10	1	6	2.4	24	15	32	36	0	7	0	384	35	1	6	4.6	.998	C-90, DH-1
1982	125	.256	.349	344	88	15	1	5	1.5	35	36	46	37	0	8	3	491	46	5	8	4.3	.991	C-124, DH-1
1983	128	.231	.323	347	80	16	2	4	1.2	33	32	40	54	1	7	0	591	65	2	7	5.1	.997	C-128
1984	109	.230	.364	330	76	11	0	11	3.3	37	34	40	58	1	0	0	453	43	4	5	4.6	.992	C-108
1985	132	.254	.406	362	92	19	0	12	3.3	54	52	50	87	0	6	1	575	49	8	5	4.8	.987	C-131
1986	122	.208	.379	327	68	15	1	13	4.0	42	29	45	78	1	9	1	659	53	7	9	5.9	.990	C-121
1987 CLE A	60	.177	.270	141	25	10	0	1	0.7	16	9	23	29	0	2	1	293	18	5	3	5.3	.984	C-59
1988 LA N	77	.251	.455	167	42	13	0	7	4.2	25	30	25	44	1	8	1	333	29	4	4	4.8	.989	C-74
1989	79	.179	.305	151	27	7	0	4	2.6	16	16	30	37	1	24	5	265	35	5	4	3.9	.984	C-62
1990	62	.195	.281	128	25	5	0	2	1.5	13	15	23	29	1	16	1	213	27	2	3	4.6	.992	C-53
22 yrs.	1697	.233	.347	4536	1058	218	12	92	2.0	508	450	567	715	20	185	36	7143	747	98	110	4.7	.988	C-1569, OF-23, DH-22, 1B-2, 3B-1

Year	Team	Games	BA	SA	AB	H	2B	3B	HR	HR%	R	RBI	BB	SO	SB	PINCH HIT AB	H	PO	A	E	DP	TC/G	FA	G by Pos

Rick Dempsey *Continued*

LEAGUE CHAMPIONSHIP SERIES

Year	Team	Games	BA	SA	AB	H	2B	3B	HR	HR%	R	RBI	BB	SO	SB	PH AB	PH H	PO	A	E	DP	TC/G	FA	G by Pos
1979	BAL A	3	.400	.600	10	4	2	0	0	0.0	3	2	1	0	1	0	0	10	1	0	0	3.7	1.000	C-3
1983		4	.167	.167	12	2	0	0	0	0.0	1	0	1	1	0	0	0	29	5	1	1	8.8	.971	C-4
1988	LA N	4	.400	.800	5	2	2	0	0	0.0	1	2	1	0	0	1	0	7	0	0	0	1.8	1.000	C-3
3 yrs.		11	.296	.444	27	8	4	0	0	0.0	5	4	3	1	1	0	0	46	6	1	1	4.8	.981	C-10

WORLD SERIES

Year	Team	Games	BA	SA	AB	H	2B	3B	HR	HR%	R	RBI	BB	SO	SB	PH AB	PH H	PO	A	E	DP	TC/G	FA	G by Pos
1979	BAL A	7	.286	.381	21	6	2	0	0	0.0	3	0	1	3	0	0	0	38	2	0	0	5.7	1.000	C-6
1983		5	.385	.923	13	5	4	0	1	7.7	3	2	2	2	0	0	0	27	4	0	0	6.2	1.000	C-5
1988	LA N	2	.200	.400	5	1	1	0	0	0.0	0	1	1	2	0	0	0	13	1	0	0	7.0	1.000	C-2
3 yrs.		14	.308	.564	39	12	7	0	1	2.6	6	3	4	7	0	0	0	78	7	0	0	6.1	.000	C-13

Delino DeShields

DeSHIELDS, DELINO LAMONT
B. Jan. 15, 1969, Seaford, Del.
BL TR 6' 1" 170 lbs.
See Player Register Supplement for complete graphic analysis

Year	Team	Games	BA	SA	AB	H	2B	3B	HR	HR%	R	RBI	BB	SO	SB	PH AB	PH H	PO	A	E	DP	TC/G	FA	G by Pos
1990	MON N	129	.289	.393	499	144	28	6	4	0.8	69	45	66	96	42	4	0	236	371	12	65	4.8	.981	2B-128

Mike Devereaux

DEVEREAUX, MICHAEL
B. Apr. 10, 1963, Casper, Wyo.
BR TR 6' 195 lbs.

Split	Games	BA	SA	AB	H	2B	3B	HR	HR%	R	RBI	BB	SO	SB
April	14	.143	.143	35	5	0	0	0	0.0	4	0	3	4	1
May	8	.226	.323	31	7	3	0	0	0.0	4	5	0	1	1
June	15	.240	.400	50	12	2	0	2	4.0	8	7	5	9	2
July	25	.333	.531	96	32	5	1	4	4.2	18	17	6	15	6
Aug	19	.177	.274	62	11	3	0	1	1.6	4	9	8	10	3
Sept/Oct	27	.226	.441	93	21	5	0	5	5.4	10	11	6	9	0
Day	30	.297	.475	101	30	6	0	4	4.0	14	20	7	6	3
Night	78	.218	.361	266	58	12	1	8	3.0	34	29	21	42	10
vs. Left		.231	.406	160	37	7	0	7	4.4	19	22	10	15	5
vs. Right		.246	.382	207	51	11	1	5	2.4	29	27	18	33	8
On Grass	89	.250	.429	296	74	15	1	12	4.1	43	44	25	40	11
On Turf	19	.197	.239	71	14	3	0	0	0.0	5	5	3	8	2
Home	51	.233	.400	150	35	7	0	6	4.0	23	21	16	25	7
Road	57	.244	.387	217	53	11	1	6	2.8	25	28	12	23	6
Division Rivals														
vs. BOS	12	.172	.172	29	5	0	0	0	0.0	5	6	4	7	2
vs. CLE	13	.314	.569	51	16	4	0	3	5.9	6	9	5	6	2
vs. DET	8	.250	.643	28	7	0	1	3	10.7	6	8	2	2	1
vs. MIL	4	.500	1.286	14	7	2	0	3	21.4	3	6	2	1	0
vs. NY	6	.190	.429	21	4	2	0	1	4.8	2	1	1	2	0
vs. TOR	13	.167	.229	48	8	0	0	1	2.1	3	2	1	4	2
On 3B <2 Out		.143	.143	14	2	0	0	0	0.0	0	10	2	2	

OUTFIELD

AVERAGE — AL AVG
RBI — AL AVG
HR — AL AVG
SB — AL AVG

Year	Team	Games	BA	SA	AB	H	2B	3B	HR	HR%	R	RBI	BB	SO	SB	PH AB	PH H	PO	A	E	DP	TC/G	FA	G by Pos
1987	LA N	19	.222	.278	54	12	3	0	0	0.0	7	4	3	10	3	5	0	21	1	0	0	1.2	1.000	OF-18
1988		30	.116	.140	43	5	1	0	0	0.0	4	2	2	10	0	7	1	29	0	0	0	1.0	1.000	OF-26
1989	BAL A	122	.266	.379	391	104	14	3	8	2.0	55	46	36	60	22	14	0	288	1	5	0	2.4	.983	OF-112, DH-5
1990		108	.240	.392	367	88	18	1	12	3.2	48	49	28	48	13	6	3	281	4	5	1	2.8	.983	OF-104, DH-3
4 yrs.		279	.244	.366	855	209	36	4	20	2.3	114	101	69	128	38	32	4	619	6	10	1	2.3	.984	OF-260, DH-8

Carlos Diaz

DIAZ, CARLOS FRANCISCO
B. Dec. 24, 1964, Jersey City, N. J.
BR TR 6' 3" 190 lbs.

Year	Team	Games	BA	SA	AB	H	2B	3B	HR	HR%	R	RBI	BB	SO	SB	PH AB	PH H	PO	A	E	DP	TC/G	FA	G by Pos
1990	TOR A	9	.333	.333	3	1	0	0	0	0.0	1	0	0	2	0	0	0	13	3	0	0	1.8	1.000	C-9

Year	Team		Games	BA	SA	AB	H	2B	3B	HR	HR%	R	RBI	BB	SO	SB	PINCH HIT AB	H	PO	A	E	DP	TC/G	FA	G by Pos

Edgar Diaz

DIAZ, EDGAR
Born Edgar Diaz y Serrano.
B. Feb. 8, 1964, Santurce, Puerto Rico
BR TR 6' 165 lbs.

Year	Team		Games	BA	SA	AB	H	2B	3B	HR	HR%	R	RBI	BB	SO	SB	AB	H	PO	A	E	DP	TC/G	FA	G by Pos
1986	MIL	A	5	.231	.231	13	3	0	0	0	0.0	0	0	1	3	0	0	0	6	8	2	2	3.2	.875	SS-5
1990			86	.271	.298	218	59	2	2	0	0.0	27	14	21	32	3	2	2	125	197	17	43	3.9	.950	SS-65, 2B-15, 3B-7, DH-1
2 yrs.			91	.268	.294	231	62	2	2	0	0.0	27	14	22	35	3	2	2	131	205	19	45	3.9	.946	SS-70, 2B-15, 3B-7, DH-1

Mario Diaz

DIAZ, MARIO RAFAEL
Born Mario Rafael Diaz y Torres.
B. Jan. 10, 1962, Humacao, Puerto Rico
BR TR 5' 10" 145 lbs.

Year	Team		Games	BA	SA	AB	H	2B	3B	HR	HR%	R	RBI	BB	SO	SB	AB	H	PO	A	E	DP	TC/G	FA	G by Pos
1987	SEA	A	11	.304	.391	23	7	0	1	0	0.0	4	3	0	4	0	1	0	10	25	1	6	3.3	.972	SS-10
1988			28	.306	.375	72	22	5	0	0	0.0	6	9	3	5	0	3	1	31	47	1	11	2.8	.987	SS-21, 2B-4, 1B-1, 3B-1
1989			52	.135	.176	74	10	0	0	1	1.4	9	7	7	7	0	3	1	35	54	5	10	1.8	.947	SS-37, 2B-14, 3B-3
1990	NY	N	16	.136	.182	22	3	1	0	0	0.0	0	1	0	3	0	7	2	5	18	1	1	2.2	.958	SS-10, 2B-1
4 yrs.			107	.220	.277	191	42	6	1	1	0.5	19	20	10	19	0	14	4	81	144	8	28	2.2	.966	SS-78, 2B-19, 3B-4, 1B-1

Gary Disarcina

DISARCINA, GARY THOMAS
B. Nov. 19, 1967, Malden, Mass.
BR TR 6' 1" 170 lbs.

Year	Team		Games	BA	SA	AB	H	2B	3B	HR	HR%	R	RBI	BB	SO	SB	AB	H	PO	A	E	DP	TC/G	FA	G by Pos
1989	CAL	A	2	—	—	0	0	0	0	0	—	0	0	0	0	0	0	0	0	0	0	0	0.0	—	SS-1
1990			18	.140	.193	57	8	1	1	0	0.0	8	0	3	10	1	1	0	17	57	4	9	4.6	.949	SS-14, 2B-3
2 yrs.			20	.140	.193	57	8	1	1	0	0.0	8	0	3	10	1	1	0	17	57	4	9	3.9	.949	SS-15, 2B-3

Bill Doran

DORAN, WILLIAM DONALD
B. May 28, 1958, Cincinnati, Ohio
BB TR 5' 11" 175 lbs.

	Games	BA	SA	AB	H	2B	3B	HR	HR%	R	RBI	BB	SO	SB
April	19	.222	.333	63	14	4	0	1	1.6	6	7	8	10	1
May	25	.286	.338	77	22	4	0	0	0.0	11	11	13	9	4
June	23	.290	.333	69	20	3	0	0	0.0	9	2	18	13	7
July	16	.269	.538	52	14	3	1	3	5.8	8	7	13	8	2
Aug	26	.349	.530	83	29	7	1	2	2.4	15	5	19	13	4
Sept/Oct	17	.373	.559	59	22	8	0	1	1.7	10	5	8	5	5
Day	35	.361	.549	122	44	17	0	2	1.6	21	17	15	19	12
Night	91	.274	.384	281	77	12	2	5	1.8	38	20	64	39	11
vs. Left		.268	.408	142	38	12	1	2	1.4	17	12	35	19	7
vs. Right		.318	.448	261	83	17	1	5	1.9	42	25	44	39	16
On Grass	44	.312	.461	141	44	15	0	2	1.4	21	15	29	20	8
On Turf	82	.294	.420	262	77	14	2	5	1.9	38	22	50	38	15
Home	60	.332	.482	199	66	14	2	4	2.0	32	18	38	26	14
Road	66	.270	.387	204	55	15	0	3	1.5	27	19	41	32	9
Division Rivals														
vs. ATL	14	.389	.574	54	21	5	1	1	1.9	10	5	4	6	1
vs. HOU	5	.389	.556	18	7	0	0	1	5.6	4	2	2	2	1
vs. LA	16	.392	.588	51	20	7	0	1	2.0	9	7	9	11	2
vs. SD	13	.282	.410	39	11	2	0	1	2.6	4	3	9	4	2
vs. SF	15	.327	.510	49	16	6	0	1	2.0	5	5	14	5	5
On 3B < 2 Out		.250	.333	12	3	1	0	0	0.0	0	9	5	2	

SECOND BASE

Year	Team		Games	BA	SA	AB	H	2B	3B	HR	HR%	R	RBI	BB	SO	SB	AB	H	PO	A	E	DP	TC/G	FA	G by Pos
1982	HOU	N	26	.278	.309	97	27	3	0	0	0.0	11	6	4	11	5	0	0	41	78	3	17	4.7	.975	2B-26
1983			154	.271	.364	535	145	12	7	8	1.5	70	39	86	67	12	3	1	347	461	17	109	5.4	.979	2B-153
1984			147	.261	.356	548	143	18	11	4	0.7	92	41	66	69	21	2	0	274	440	12	90	4.9	.983	2B-139, SS-13
1985			148	.287	.434	578	166	31	6	14	2.4	84	59	71	69	23	2	1	345	440	16	108	5.4	.980	2B-147
1986			145	.276	.373	550	152	29	3	6	1.1	92	37	81	57	42	1	0	262	329	16	62	4.2	.974	2B-144

Year	Team	Games	BA	SA	AB	H	2B	3B	HR	HR%	R	RBI	BB	SO	SB	PINCH HIT AB	PINCH HIT H	PO	A	E	DP	TC/G	FA	G by Pos

Bill Doran *Continued*

Year	Team	Games	BA	SA	AB	H	2B	3B	HR	HR%	R	RBI	BB	SO	SB	AB	H	PO	A	E	DP	TC/G	FA	G by Pos
1987		162	.283	.406	625	177	23	3	16	2.6	82	79	82	64	31	0	0	300	432	7	70	4.6	.991	2B-162, SS-3
1988		132	.248	.333	480	119	18	1	7	1.5	66	53	65	60	17	2	1	260	371	8	73	4.8	.987	2B-130
1989		142	.219	.323	507	111	25	2	8	1.6	65	58	59	63	22	8	0	254	345	12	64	4.3	.980	2B-138
1990	2 teams	HOU	N	(109G	—	.288)		CIN	N	(17G	—	.373)												
"	total	126	.300	.434	403	121	29	2	7	1.7	59	37	79	58	23	9	2	198	306	8	49	4.5	.984	2B-111, 3B-4
9 yrs.		1182	.269	.377	4323	1161	188	35	70	1.6	621	409	593	518	196	27	5	2281	3202	99	642	4.7	.982	2B-1150, SS-16, 3B-4

LEAGUE CHAMPIONSHIP SERIES

Year	Team	Games	BA	SA	AB	H	2B	3B	HR	HR%	R	RBI	BB	SO	SB	AB	H	PO	A	E	DP	TC/G	FA	G by Pos
1986	HOU N	6	.222	.333	27	6	0	0	1	3.7	3	3	2	2	2	0	0	10	17	0	1	4.5	1.000	2B-6

Brian Dorsett

DORSETT, BRIAN RICHARD
B. Apr. 9, 1961, Terre Haute, Ind.
BR TR 6′ 3″ 215 lbs.

Year	Team	Games	BA	SA	AB	H	2B	3B	HR	HR%	R	RBI	BB	SO	SB	AB	H	PO	A	E	DP	TC/G	FA	G by Pos
1987	CLE A	5	.273	.545	11	3	0	0	1	9.1	2	3	0	3	0	2	1	12	0	0	0	2.4	1.000	C-4
1988	CAL A	7	.091	.091	11	1	0	0	0	0.0	0	2	1	5	0	0	0	19	3	0	1	3.1	1.000	C-7
1989	NY A	8	.364	.409	22	8	1	0	0	0.0	3	4	1	3	0	0	0	29	3	0	1	4.0	1.000	C-8
1990		14	.143	.200	35	5	2	0	0	0.0	2	0	2	4	0	2	0	31	0	0	1	3.4	1.000	C-9, DH-5
4 yrs.		34	.215	.291	79	17	3	0	1	1.3	7	9	4	15	0	4	1	91	6	0	3	2.9	.000	C-28, DH-5

Brian Downing

DOWNING, BRIAN JAY
B. Oct. 9, 1950, Los Angeles, Calif.
BR TR 5′ 10″ 170 lbs.

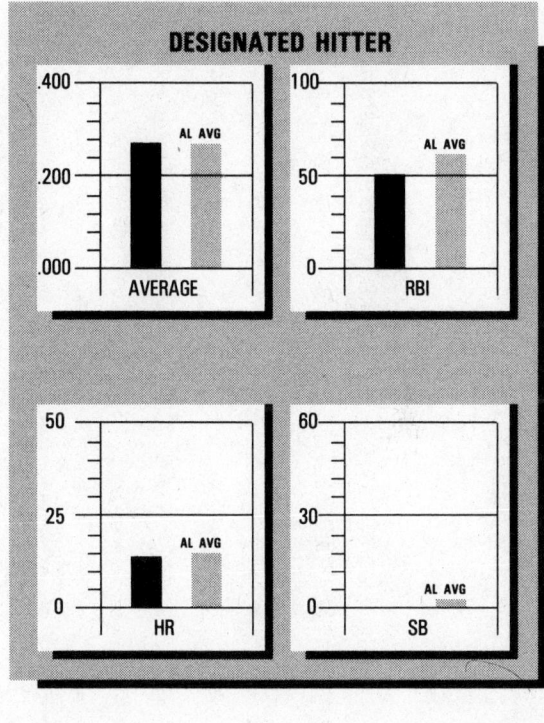

DESIGNATED HITTER

	Games	BA	SA	AB	H	2B	3B	HR	HR%	R	RBI	BB	SO	SB
April	12	.186	.279	43	8	1	0	1	2.3	2	6	4	5	0
May	7	.208	.458	24	5	0	0	2	8.3	3	4	3	1	0
June	12	.289	.474	38	11	4	0	1	2.6	6	2	2	1	0
July	23	.313	.542	83	26	5	1	4	4.8	15	13	13	12	0
Aug	19	.338	.615	65	22	6	0	4	6.2	13	18	16	11	0
Sept/Oct	23	.234	.364	77	18	2	1	2	2.6	8	8	12	15	0
Day	31	.243	.350	103	25	3	1	2	1.9	10	16	17	9	0
Night	65	.286	.520	227	65	15	1	12	5.3	37	35	33	36	0
vs. Left		.345	.555	119	41	8	1	5	4.2	28	16	25	14	0
vs. Right		.232	.417	211	49	10	1	9	4.3	19	35	25	31	0
On Grass	83	.269	.479	286	77	14	2	14	4.9	39	45	40	38	0
On Turf	13	.295	.386	44	13	4	0	0	0.0	8	6	10	7	0
Home	48	.302	.562	162	49	9	0	11	6.8	28	26	24	14	0
Road	48	.244	.375	168	41	9	2	3	1.8	19	25	26	31	0
Division Rivals														
vs. CHI	7	.190	.190	21	4	0	0	0	0.0	1	1	3	5	0
vs. KC	9	.143	.250	28	4	0	0	1	3.6	3	1	5	2	0
vs. MIN	10	.242	.303	33	8	2	0	0	0.0	5	6	7	3	0
vs. OAK	10	.242	.364	33	8	2	1	0	0.0	1	4	6	6	0
vs. SEA	7	.318	.455	22	7	0	0	1	4.5	5	4	5	4	0
vs. TEX	8	.267	.467	30	8	3	0	1	3.3	4	3	2	5	0
On 3B < 2 Out		.381	.571	21	8	1	0	1	4.8	1	16	7	3	

Year	Team	Games	BA	SA	AB	H	2B	3B	HR	HR%	R	RBI	BB	SO	SB	AB	H	PO	A	E	DP	TC/G	FA	G by Pos
1973	CHI A	34	.178	.274	73	13	1	0	2	2.7	5	4	10	17	0	8	2	72	17	5	0	2.8	.947	OF-13, C-11, 3B-8
1974		108	.225	.375	293	66	12	1	10	3.4	41	39	51	72	0	5	0	337	30	2	5	3.4	.995	C-63, OF-39, DH-9
1975		138	.240	.324	420	101	12	1	7	1.7	58	41	76	75	13	0	0	730	84	8	5	6.0	.990	C-137, DH-1
1976		104	.256	.328	317	81	14	0	3	0.9	38	30	40	55	7	3	1	450	38	6	4	4.8	.988	C-93, DH-11
1977		69	.284	.402	169	48	4	2	4	2.4	28	25	34	21	1	3	1	325	28	6	5	5.2	.983	C-61, OF-3, DH-2
1978	CAL A	133	.255	.342	412	105	15	0	7	1.7	42	46	52	47	3	3	1	681	82	5	6	5.8	.993	C-128, DH-2
1979		148	.326	.462	509	166	27	3	12	2.4	87	75	77	57	3	3	1	669	35	11	5	4.8	.985	C-129, DH-18
1980		30	.290	.419	93	27	6	0	2	2.2	5	25	12	12	0	2	0	69	6	0	0	2.5	1.000	C-16, DH-13
1981		93	.249	.379	317	79	14	0	9	2.8	47	41	46	35	1	2	0	237	18	2	2	2.8	.992	OF-56, C-37, DH-5
1982		158	.281	.482	623	175	37	2	28	4.5	109	84	86	58	2	1	0	321	9	0	0	2.1	1.000	OF-158
1983		113	.246	.429	403	99	15	1	19	4.7	68	53	62	59	1	3	1	160	9	1	0	1.5	.994	OF-84, DH-26
1984		156	.275	.462	539	148	28	2	23	4.3	65	91	70	66	0	3	1	272	5	0	0	1.8	1.000	OF-131, DH-21
1985		150	.263	.427	520	137	23	1	20	3.8	80	85	78	60	0	7	0	244	5	2	0	1.7	.992	OF-121, DH-25
1986		152	.267	.452	513	137	27	4	20	3.9	90	95	90	84	4	8	0	267	5	3	0	1.8	.989	OF-138, DH-10
1987		155	.272	.487	567	154	29	3	29	5.1	110	77	**106**	85	5	4	0	47	2	0	0	0.3	1.000	DH-118, OF-34
1988		135	.242	.442	484	117	18	2	25	5.2	80	64	81	63	3	3	1	0	0	0	0	0.0	—	DH-132
1989		142	.283	.414	544	154	25	2	14	2.6	59	59	56	87	0	1	0	0	0	0	0	0.0	—	DH-141
1990		96	.273	.467	330	90	18	2	14	4.2	47	51	50	45	0	0	0	0	0	0	0	0.0	1.000	DH-87
18 yrs.		2114	.266	.424	7126	1897	325	26	248	3.5	1059	985	1077	998	48	67	9	4881	373	51	32	2.5	.990	OF-777, C-675, DH-621, 3B-8

Brian Downing *Continued*

LEAGUE CHAMPIONSHIP SERIES

Year	Team		Games	BA	SA	AB	H	2B	3B	HR	HR%	R	RBI	BB	SO	SB	PINCH HIT AB	H	PO	A	E	DP	TC/G	FA	G by Pos
1979	CAL	A	4	.200	.200	15	3	0	0	0	0.0	1	1	1	1	0	0	0	27	0	0	2	6.8	1.000	C-4
1982			5	.158	.211	19	3	1	0	0	0.0	4	0	3	2	0	0	0	5	0	0	0	1.0	1.000	OF-5
1986			7	.222	.333	27	6	0	0	1	3.7	2	7	4	5	0	0	0	18	0	0	0	2.6	1.000	OF-7
3 yrs.			16	.197	.262	61	12	1	0	1	1.6	7	8	8	8	0	0	0	50	0	0	2	3.1	.000	OF-12, C-4

Rob Ducey

DUCEY, ROBERT THOMAS
B. May 24, 1965, Toronto, Ontario, Canada
BL TR 6′ 2″ 175 lbs.

Year	Team		Games	BA	SA	AB	H	2B	3B	HR	HR%	R	RBI	BB	SO	SB	PINCH HIT AB	H	PO	A	E	DP	TC/G	FA	G by Pos
1987	TOR	A	34	.188	.271	48	9	1	0	1	2.1	12	6	8	10	2	3	1	31	0	0	0	0.9	1.000	OF-28
1988			27	.315	.426	54	17	4	1	0	0.0	15	6	5	7	1	0	0	35	1	0	0	1.3	1.000	OF-26
1989			41	.211	.263	76	16	4	0	0	0.0	5	7	9	25	2	6	0	56	3	0	2	1.4	1.000	OF-35, DH-1
1990			19	.302	.396	53	16	5	0	0	0.0	7	7	7	15	1	0	0	37	0	0	0	1.9	1.000	OF-19
4 yrs.			121	.251	.333	231	58	14	1	1	0.4	39	26	29	57	6	9	1	159	4	0	2	1.3	.000	OF-108, DH-1

Mariano Duncan

DUNCAN, MARIANO
Born Mariano Duncan y Nolasco.
B. Mar. 13, 1963, San Pedro de Macoris,
Dominican Republic
BB TR 6′ 165 lbs.

SECOND BASE

	Games	BA	SA	AB	H	2B	3B	HR	HR%	R	RBI	BB	SO	SB
April	15	.408	.776	49	20	4	1	4	8.2	13	14	8	5	3
May	12	.349	.442	43	15	2	1	0	0.0	9	1	3	5	3
June	27	.235	.367	98	23	5	1	2	2.0	16	6	1	13	1
July	19	.317	.500	60	19	4	2	1	1.7	9	7	2	8	3
Aug	29	.321	.459	109	35	4	4	1	0.9	9	13	5	15	2
Sept/Oct	23	.276	.447	76	21	3	2	2	2.6	11	14	5	21	1
Day	35	.281	.496	121	34	3	7	3	2.5	17	18	10	19	2
Night	90	.315	.468	314	99	19	4	7	2.2	50	37	14	48	11
vs. Left		.410	.606	188	77	17	4	4	2.1	31	27	10	22	5
vs. Right		.227	.377	247	56	5	7	6	2.4	36	28	14	45	8
On Grass	34	.291	.444	117	34	7	4	1	0.9	21	14	9	26	3
On Turf	91	.311	.487	318	99	15	7	9	2.8	46	41	15	41	10
Home	66	.309	.470	230	71	12	5	5	2.2	31	30	13	30	6
Road	59	.302	.483	205	62	10	6	5	2.4	36	25	11	37	7
Division Rivals														
vs. ATL	15	.268	.411	56	15	3	1	1	1.8	14	8	4	6	1
vs. HOU	15	.250	.500	44	11	2	0	3	6.8	7	6	1	7	0
vs. LA	14	.250	.396	48	12	0	2	1	2.1	8	5	4	12	2
vs. SD	15	.500	.741	54	27	8	1	1	1.9	8	12	2	8	1
vs. SF	12	.227	.295	44	10	1	1	0	0.0	3	5	1	10	0
On 3B < 2 Out		.333	.429	21	7	2	0	0	0.0	0	19	0	2	

Year	Team		Games	BA	SA	AB	H	2B	3B	HR	HR%	R	RBI	BB	SO	SB	PINCH HIT AB	H	PO	A	E	DP	TC/G	FA	G by Pos
1985	LA	N	142	.244	.340	562	137	24	6	6	1.1	74	39	38	113	38	2	1	224	430	30	64	4.8	.956	SS-123, 2B-19
1986			109	.229	.305	407	93	7	0	8	2.0	47	30	30	78	48	2	0	172	317	25	46	4.7	.951	SS-106
1987			76	.215	.322	261	56	8	1	6	2.3	31	18	17	62	11	1	0	101	213	21	40	4.4	.937	SS-67, 2B-7, OF-2
1989	2 teams			LA N	(49G — .250)				CIN N	(45G — .247)															
"	total		94	.248	.357	258	64	15	2	3	1.2	32	21	8	51	9	18	7	101	155	14	30	2.9	.948	SS-60, 2B-13, OF-7
1990	CIN	N	125	.306	.476	435	133	22	**11**	10	2.2	67	55	24	67	13	5	0	265	303	18	55	4.9	.969	2B-115, SS-12, OF-1
5 yrs.			546	.251	.363	1923	483	76	20	33	1.7	251	163	117	371	119	28	8	863	1418	108	235	4.4	.955	SS-368, 2B-154, OF-10

LEAGUE CHAMPIONSHIP SERIES

Year	Team		Games	BA	SA	AB	H	2B	3B	HR	HR%	R	RBI	BB	SO	SB	PINCH HIT AB	H	PO	A	E	DP	TC/G	FA	G by Pos
1985	LA	N	5	.222	.444	18	4	2	1	0	0.0	2	1	1	3	1	0	0	7	16	1	3	4.8	.958	SS-5
1990	CIN	N	6	.300	.450	20	6	0	0	1	5.0	1	4	0	8	0	0	0	6	11	1	0	3.0	.944	2B-6
2 yrs.			11	.263	.447	38	10	2	1	1	2.6	3	5	1	11	1	0	0	13	27	2	3	3.8	.952	2B-6, SS-5

WORLD SERIES

Year	Team		Games	BA	SA	AB	H	2B	3B	HR	HR%	R	RBI	BB	SO	SB	PINCH HIT AB	H	PO	A	E	DP	TC/G	FA	G by Pos
1990	CIN	N	4	.143	.143	14	2	0	0	0	0.0	1	1	2	2	1	0	0	9	9	0	2	4.5	1.000	2B-4

Shawon Dunston

DUNSTON, SHAWON DONNELL (Thunder Pup)
B. Mar. 21, 1963, Brooklyn, N. Y.
BR TR 6′ 1″ 175 lbs.

Year	Team	Games	BA	SA	AB	H	2B	3B	HR	HR%	R	RBI	BB	SO	SB	PH AB	PH H	PO	A	E	DP	TC/G	FA	G by Pos
April		19	.288	.466	73	21	4	0	3	4.1	7	7	1	12	3									
May		26	.343	.545	99	34	3	1	5	5.1	16	16	1	10	3									
June		26	.216	.330	97	21	5	0	2	2.1	7	14	4	23	1									
July		23	.318	.545	88	28	3	4	3	3.4	15	16	5	13	4									
Aug		25	.271	.458	96	26	5	2	3	3.1	17	11	2	12	11									
Sept/Oct		27	.141	.217	92	13	2	1	1	1.1	11	2	2	17	3									
Day		74	.274	.448	281	77	14	1	11	3.9	47	34	10	50	14									
Night		72	.250	.402	264	66	8	7	6	2.3	26	32	5	37	11									
vs. Left			.287	.505	188	54	6	4	9	4.8	33	23	3	24	7									
vs. Right			.249	.384	357	89	16	4	8	2.2	40	43	12	63	18									
On Grass		105	.260	.435	400	104	17	4	15	3.8	57	50	10	73	17									
On Turf		41	.269	.400	145	39	5	4	2	1.4	16	16	5	14	8									
Home		72	.250	.403	268	67	12	4	7	2.6	39	25	7	46	11									
Road		74	.274	.448	277	76	10	4	10	3.6	34	41	8	41	14									
Division Rivals																								
vs. MON		18	.254	.413	63	16	2	4	0	0.0	6	10	4	9	4									
vs. NY		15	.172	.310	58	10	2	0	2	3.4	10	5	0	13	3									
vs. PHI		15	.204	.259	54	11	0	0	1	1.9	4	5	2	10	2									
vs. PIT		18	.277	.338	65	18	1	0	1	1.5	6	4	2	9	1									
vs. STL		15	.233	.383	60	14	5	2	0	0.0	4	5	0	13	0									
On 3B < 2 Out			.263	.368	19	5	0	1	0	0.0	0	15	1	6										
1985	CHI N	74	.260	.388	250	65	12	4	4	1.6	40	18	19	42	11	0	0	144	248	17	39	5.5	.958	SS-73
1986		150	.250	.410	581	145	36	3	17	2.9	66	68	21	114	13	2	1	320	465	32	96	5.4	.961	SS-149
1987		95	.246	.358	346	85	18	3	5	1.4	40	22	10	68	12	1	0	160	271	14	54	4.7	.969	SS-94
1988		155	.249	.357	575	143	23	6	9	1.6	69	56	16	108	30	3	0	257	455	20	76	4.7	.973	SS-151
1989		138	.278	.403	471	131	20	6	9	1.9	52	60	30	86	19	1	0	213	379	17	76	4.4	.972	SS-138
1990		146	.262	.426	545	143	22	8	17	3.1	73	66	15	87	25	0	0	255	392	20	77	4.6	.970	SS-144
6 yrs.		758	.257	.392	2768	712	131	30	61	2.2	340	290	111	505	110	7	1	1349	2210	120	418	4.9	.967	SS-749

LEAGUE CHAMPIONSHIP SERIES

Year	Team	Games	BA	SA	AB	H	2B	3B	HR	HR%	R	RBI	BB	SO	SB	PH AB	PH H	PO	A	E	DP	TC/G	FA	G by Pos
1989	CHI N	5	.316	.316	19	6	0	0	0	0.0	2	0	1	1	1	0	0	10	14	1	1	5.0	.960	SS-5

Jim Dwyer

DWYER, JAMES EDWARD
B. Jan. 3, 1950, Evergreen Park, Ill.
BL TL 5′ 10″ 165 lbs.

Year	Team	Games	BA	SA	AB	H	2B	3B	HR	HR%	R	RBI	BB	SO	SB	PH AB	PH H	PO	A	E	DP	TC/G	FA	G by Pos
1973	STL N	28	.193	.246	57	11	1	1	0	0.0	7	0	1	5	0	8	1	32	0	0	0	1.1	1.000	OF-20
1974		74	.279	.360	86	24	1	0	2	2.3	13	11	11	16	0	41	10	31	3	0	2	0.5	1.000	OF-25, 1B-3
1975	2 teams	STL N (21G — .194)		MON N (60G — .286)																				
"	total	81	.272	.364	206	56	8	1	3	1.5	26	21	27	36	4	21	6	104	8	4	1	1.4	.966	OF-61
1976	2 teams	MON N (50G — .185)		NY N (11G — .154)																				
"		61	.181	.229	105	19	3	1	0	0.0	9	5	13	11	0	38	6	35	0	1	0	0.6	.972	OF-21
1977	STL N	13	.226	.258	31	7	1	0	0	0.0	3	2	4	5	0	2	1	16	0	0	0	1.2	1.000	OF-12
1978	2 teams	STL N (34G — .215)		SF N (73G — .225)																				
"	total	107	.223	.366	238	53	12	2	6	2.5	30	26	37	32	7	24	5	216	15	3	14	2.2	.987	OF-58, 1B-29
1979	BOS A	76	.265	.381	113	30	7	0	2	1.8	19	14	17	9	3	22	7	167	16	4	15	2.5	.979	1B-25, OF-19, DH-4
1980		93	.285	.438	260	74	11	1	9	3.5	41	38	28	23	3	11	2	143	15	4	9	1.7	.975	OF-65, DH-12, 1B-9
1981	BAL A	68	.224	.306	134	30	0	1	3	2.2	16	10	20	19	0	6	0	97	2	2	2	1.5	.980	OF-59, 1B-3, DH-1
1982		71	.304	.493	148	45	4	3	6	4.1	28	15	27	24	2	23	6	87	0	2	0	1.3	.978	OF-49, DH-1, 1B-1
1983		100	.286	.505	196	56	17	1	8	4.1	37	38	31	29	1	33	8	123	2	4	4	1.3	.969	OF-56, 1B-4
1984		76	.255	.360	161	41	9	1	2	1.2	22	21	23	24	0	27	7	83	3	3	1	1.2	.966	OF-52, DH-3
1985		101	.249	.399	233	58	8	3	7	3.0	35	36	37	31	0	26	4	131	4	1	0	1.3	.993	OF-78, DH-3
1986		93	.244	.488	160	39	13	1	8	5.0	18	31	22	31	0	42	9	33	4	0	1	0.4	1.000	DH-24, OF-24, 1B-1
1987		92	.274	.498	241	66	11	1	15	6.2	54	33	37	57	4	24	7	57	1	0	0	0.6	1.000	DH-41, OF-30
1988	2 teams	BAL A (35G — .226)		MIN A (20G — .293)																				
"	total	55	.255	.330	94	24	1	0	2	2.1	9	18	25	19	0	24	6	3	0	0	0	0.1	1.000	DH-30, OF-2
1989	2 teams	MIN A (88G — .316)		MON N (13G — .300)																				
"		101	.315	.404	235	74	12	0	3	1.3	35	25	29	24	2	29	8	0	0	0	0	0.0	—	DH-74, OF-1
1990	MIN A	37	.190	.238	63	12	0	0	1	1.5	7	5	12	7	0	15	6	2	0	0	0	1.0	1.000	DH-23, OF-2
18 yrs.		1327	.260	.398	2761	719	115	17	77	2.8	409	349	401	402	26	416	100	1360	73	28	49	1.1	.981	OF-634, DH-216, 1B-75

Year	Team		Games	BA	SA	AB	H	2B	3B	HR	HR%	R	RBI	BB	SO	SB	PINCH HIT AB	H	PO	A	E	DP	TC/G	FA	G by Pos

Jim Dwyer *Continued*

LEAGUE CHAMPIONSHIP SERIES

Year	Team		Games	BA	SA	AB	H	2B	3B	HR	HR%	R	RBI	BB	SO	SB	AB	H	PO	A	E	DP	TC/G	FA	G by Pos
1983	BAL	A	2	.250	.500	4	1	1	0	0	0.0	1	0	1	0	0	1	0	4	0	0	0	2.0	1.000	OF-1

WORLD SERIES

Year	Team		Games	BA	SA	AB	H	2B	3B	HR	HR%	R	RBI	BB	SO	SB	AB	H	PO	A	E	DP	TC/G	FA	G by Pos
1983	BAL	A	2	.375	.875	8	3	1	0	1	12.5	3	1	0	0	0	0	0	2	0	0	0	1.0	1.000	OF-2

Len Dykstra

DYKSTRA, LEONARD KYLE (Nails)
B. Feb. 10, 1963, Santa Ana, Calif.
BL TL 5' 10" 160 lbs.

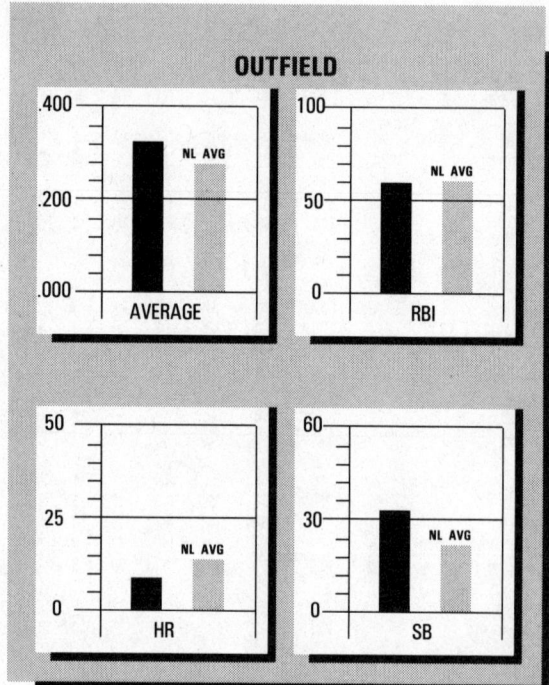

OUTFIELD

AVERAGE (NL AVG) · RBI (NL AVG) · HR (NL AVG) · SB (NL AVG)

	Games	BA	SA	AB	H	2B	3B	HR	HR%	R	RBI	BB	SO	SB
April	14	.328	.466	58	19	5	0	1	1.7	11	7	3	7	2
May	25	.431	.569	102	44	9	1	1	1.0	24	12	16	5	5
June	27	.339	.431	109	37	4	0	2	1.8	18	11	21	10	7
July	27	.287	.404	94	27	6	1	1	1.1	22	6	24	11	8
Aug	28	.316	.453	117	37	10	0	2	1.7	16	11	11	6	7
Sept/Oct	28	.255	.336	110	28	1	1	2	1.8	15	13	14	9	4
Day	36	.370	.543	138	51	16	1	2	1.4	26	14	27	9	7
Night	113	.312	.409	452	141	19	2	7	1.5	80	46	62	39	26
vs. Left		.290	.345	200	58	6	1	1	0.5	26	17	29	20	11
vs. Right		.344	.490	390	134	29	2	8	2.1	80	43	60	28	22
On Grass	39	.301	.425	153	46	14	1	1	0.7	23	19	27	11	8
On Turf	110	.334	.446	437	146	21	2	8	1.8	83	41	62	37	25
Home	74	.339	.464	280	95	15	1	6	2.1	56	27	52	23	13
Road	75	.313	.419	310	97	20	2	3	1.0	50	33	37	25	20
Division Rivals														
vs. CHI	14	.358	.491	53	19	2	1	1	1.9	7	9	10	6	0
vs. MON	14	.213	.377	61	13	1	0	3	4.9	8	6	9	7	4
vs. NY	18	.366	.521	71	26	8	0	1	1.4	15	9	12	9	3
vs. PIT	17	.279	.309	68	19	2	0	0	0.0	9	2	7	2	6
vs. STL	14	.333	.460	63	21	5	0	1	1.6	13	9	4	4	3
On 3B < 2 Out		.684	.789	19	13	2	0	0	0.0	0	18	5	0	

Year	Team		Games	BA	SA	AB	H	2B	3B	HR	HR%	R	RBI	BB	SO	SB	AB	H	PO	A	E	DP	TC/G	FA	G by Pos
1985	NY	N	83	.254	.331	236	60	9	3	1	0.4	40	19	30	24	15	9	3	165	6	1	2	2.1	.994	OF-74
1986			147	.295	.445	431	127	27	7	8	1.9	77	45	58	55	31	14	4	283	8	3	2	2.0	.990	OF-139
1987			132	.285	.455	431	123	37	3	10	2.3	86	43	40	67	27	18	5	239	4	3	1	1.9	.988	OF-118
1988			126	.270	.385	429	116	19	3	8	1.9	57	33	30	43	30	12	5	270	3	1	0	2.2	.996	OF-112
1989	2 teams		NY N (56G — .270)			PHI N (90G — .222)																			
"	total		146	.237	.356	511	121	32	4	7	1.4	66	32	60	53	30	9	3	332	10	4	0	2.4	.988	OF-139
1990	PHI	N	149	.325	.441	590	**192**	35	3	9	1.5	106	60	89	48	33	1	0	439	7	6	5	3.0	.987	OF-149
6 yrs.			783	.281	.408	2628	739	159	23	43	1.6	432	232	307	290	166	63	20	1728	38	18	10	2.3	.990	OF-731

LEAGUE CHAMPIONSHIP SERIES

Year	Team		Games	BA	SA	AB	H	2B	3B	HR	HR%	R	RBI	BB	SO	SB	AB	H	PO	A	E	DP	TC/G	FA	G by Pos
1986	NY	N	6	.304	.565	23	7	1	1	1	4.3	3	3	2	4	1	2	1	10	0	0	0	1.7	1.000	OF-6
1988			7	.429	.857	14	6	3	0	1	7.1	6	3	4	0	0	0	0	9	0	0	0	1.3	1.000	OF-7
2 yrs.			13	.351	.676	37	13	4	1	2	5.4	9	6	6	4	1	2	1	19	0	0	0	1.5	.000	OF-13

WORLD SERIES

Year	Team		Games	BA	SA	AB	H	2B	3B	HR	HR%	R	RBI	BB	SO	SB	AB	H	PO	A	E	DP	TC/G	FA	G by Pos
1986	NY	N	7	.296	.519	27	8	0	0	2	7.4	4	3	2	7	0	1	1	14	0	0	0	2.0	1.000	OF-7

Jim Eisenreich

EISENREICH, JAMES MICHAEL
B. Apr. 18, 1959, St. Cloud, Minn.
BL TL 5' 11" 175 lbs.

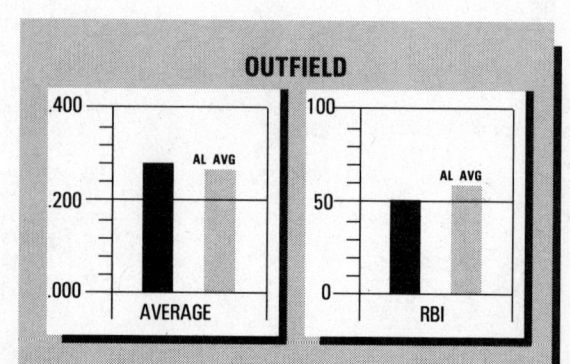

OUTFIELD

AVERAGE (AL AVG) · RBI (AL AVG)

	Games	BA	SA	AB	H	2B	3B	HR	HR%	R	RBI	BB	SO	SB
April	13	.235	.392	51	12	3	1	1	2.0	6	5	2	9	2
May	26	.330	.400	100	33	7	0	0	0.0	11	15	7	10	1
June	26	.262	.369	84	22	4	1	1	1.2	7	7	12	8	4
July	29	.291	.464	110	32	11	4	0	0.0	18	8	11	8	4
Aug	26	.322	.460	87	28	1	1	3	3.4	16	13	6	7	1
Sept/Oct	22	.188	.234	64	12	3	0	0	0.0	3	3	4	9	0
Day	32	.345	.517	116	40	7	2	3	2.6	14	18	15	7	4
Night	110	.261	.361	380	99	22	5	2	0.5	47	33	27	44	8
vs. Left		.224	.327	156	35	9	2	1	0.6	15	16	10	18	4
vs. Right		.306	.429	340	104	20	5	4	1.2	46	35	32	33	8

Year	Team	Games	BA	SA	AB	H	2B	3B	HR	HR%	R	RBI	BB	SO	SB	PINCH HIT AB	PINCH HIT H	PO	A	E	DP	TC/G	FA	G by Pos

Jim Eisenreich *Continued*

Year	Team	Games	BA	SA	AB	H	2B	3B	HR	HR%	R	RBI	BB	SO	SB	PH AB	PH H	PO	A	E	DP	TC/G	FA	G by Pos
On Grass		55	.302	.407	189	57	12	1	2	1.1	21	13	16	27	4									
On Turf		87	.267	.391	307	82	17	6	3	1.0	40	38	26	24	8									
Home		70	.258	.377	236	61	12	5	2	0.8	30	29	25	19	5									
Road		72	.300	.415	260	78	17	2	3	1.2	31	22	17	32	7									
Division Rivals																								
vs. CAL		11	.308	.462	26	8	2	1	0	0.0	2	0	5	2	1									
vs. CHI		11	.270	.297	37	10	1	0	0	0.0	4	1	4	4	0									
vs. MIN		11	.333	.405	42	14	3	0	0	0.0	5	6	1	4	3									
vs. OAK		12	.316	.605	38	12	0	1	3	7.9	4	8	8	1	0									
vs. SEA		11	.184	.211	38	7	1	0	0	0.0	3	2	1	3	1									
vs. TEX		10	.250	.361	36	9	1	0	1	2.8	2	7	0	5	0									
On 3B < 2 Out			.136	.136	22	3	0	0	0	0.0	0	16	4	3										
1982	MIN A	34	.303	.424	99	30	6	0	2	2.0	10	9	11	13	0	3	1	72	0	2	0	2.2	.973	OF-30
1983		2	.286	.429	7	2	1	0	0	0.0	1	0	1	1	0	0	0	6	1	0	0	3.5	1.000	OF-2
1984		12	.219	.250	32	7	1	0	0	0.0	1	3	2	4	2	3	1	5	0	0	0	0.4	1.000	DH-6, OF-3
1987	KC A	44	.238	.467	105	25	8	2	4	3.8	10	21	7	13	1	15	5	0	0	0	0	0.0	—	DH-26
1988		82	.218	.282	202	44	8	1	1	0.5	26	19	6	31	9	9	1	109	0	4	0	1.4	.965	OF-64, DH-13
1989		134	.293	.448	475	139	33	7	9	1.9	64	59	37	44	27	6	2	273	4	3	0	2.1	.989	OF-123, DH-10
1990		142	.280	.397	496	139	29	7	5	1.0	61	59	42	51	12	8	4	261	6	1	3	1.9	.996	OF-138, DH-2
7 yrs.		450	.273	.402	1416	386	86	17	21	1.5	173	162	106	157	51	44	14	726	11	10	3	1.7	.987	OF-360, DH-57

Kevin Elster

ELSTER, KEVIN DANIEL
B. Aug. 3, 1964, San Pedro, Calif.
BR TR 6′ 2″ 180 lbs.

Year	Team	Games	BA	SA	AB	H	2B	3B	HR	HR%	R	RBI	BB	SO	SB	PH AB	PH H	PO	A	E	DP	TC/G	FA	G by Pos
April		18	.097	.194	62	6	1	1	1	1.6	6	5	6	15	1									
May		23	.238	.438	80	19	4	0	4	5.0	11	13	12	11	1									
June		27	.270	.427	89	24	11	0	1	1.1	10	16	6	16	0									
July		22	.190	.354	79	15	4	0	3	3.8	9	11	5	11	0									
Aug		2	.250	.250	4	1	0	0	0	0.0	0	0	1	1	0									
Sept/Oct					0	0	0	0	0		0	0	0	0	0									
Day		31	.132	.245	106	14	6	0	2	1.9	10	15	8	19	0									
Night		61	.245	.423	208	51	14	1	7	3.4	26	30	22	35	2									
vs. Left			.227	.336	119	27	7	0	2	1.7	9	8	10	16	0									
vs. Right			.195	.379	195	38	13	1	7	3.6	27	37	20	38	2									
On Grass		65	.206	.363	223	46	15	1	6	2.7	28	38	23	39	2									
On Turf		27	.209	.363	91	19	5	0	3	3.3	8	7	7	15	0									
Home		47	.196	.313	163	32	11	1	2	1.2	17	24	15	30	1									
Road		45	.219	.417	151	33	9	0	7	4.6	19	21	15	24	1									
Division Rivals																								
vs. CHI		6	.095	.143	21	2	1	0	0	0.0	3	3	2	6	0									
vs. MON		11	.205	.333	39	8	2	0	1	2.6	2	6	1	6	0									
vs. PHI		6	.167	.167	18	3	0	0	0	0.0	2	0	2	4	0									
vs. PIT		10	.235	.382	34	8	5	0	0	0.0	4	4	4	8	0									
vs. STL		8	.308	.538	26	8	3	0	1	3.8	1	3	2	2	0									
On 3B < 2 Out			.357	.429	14	5	1	0	0	0.0	0	16	2	3										
1986	NY N	19	.167	.200	30	5	1	0	0	0.0	3	0	3	8	0	0	0	16	35	2	6	2.8	.962	SS-19
1987		5	.400	.600	10	4	2	0	0	0.0	1	1	0	1	0	2	2	4	6	1	0	2.2	.909	SS-3
1988		149	.214	.313	406	87	11	1	9	2.2	41	37	35	47	2	1	0	196	345	13	61	3.7	.977	SS-148
1989		151	.231	.360	458	106	25	2	10	2.2	52	55	34	77	4	0	0	235	374	15	63	4.1	.976	SS-150
1990		92	.207	.363	314	65	20	1	9	2.8	36	45	30	54	2	0	0	159	251	17	42	4.6	.960	SS-92
5 yrs.		416	.219	.343	1218	267	59	4	28	2.3	133	138	102	187	8	3	2	610	1011	48	172	4.0	.971	SS-412

LEAGUE CHAMPIONSHIP SERIES

Year	Team	Games	BA	SA	AB	H	2B	3B	HR	HR%	R	RBI	BB	SO	SB	PH AB	PH H	PO	A	E	DP	TC/G	FA	G by Pos
1986	NY N	4	.000	.000	3	0	0	0	0	0.0	0	0	0	1	0	0	0	2	3	0	0	1.3	1.000	SS-4
1988		5	.250	.375	8	2	1	0	0	0.0	1	1	3	0	0	0	0	7	7	2	2	3.2	.875	SS-5
2 yrs.		9	.182	.273	11	2	1	0	0	0.0	1	1	3	1	0	0	0	9	10	2	2	2.3	.905	SS-9

WORLD SERIES

Year	Team	Games	BA	SA	AB	H	2B	3B	HR	HR%	R	RBI	BB	SO	SB	PH AB	PH H	PO	A	E	DP	TC/G	FA	G by Pos
1986	NY N	1	.000	.000	1	0	0	0	0	0.0	0	0	0	0	0	0	0	3	3	1	1	7.0	.857	SS-1

OUTFIELD

HR — AL AVG
SB — AL AVG

SHORTSTOP

AVERAGE — NL AVG
RBI — NL AVG
HR — NL AVG
SB — NL AVG

Year	Team		Games	BA	SA	AB	H	2B	3B	HR	HR%	R	RBI	BB	SO	SB	PINCH HIT AB	H	PO	A	E	DP	TC/G	FA	G by Pos

Jim Eppard

EPPARD, JAMES GERHARD
B. Apr. 27, 1960, South Bend, Ind.
BL TL 6' 2" 180 lbs.

Year	Team		Games	BA	SA	AB	H	2B	3B	HR	HR%	R	RBI	BB	SO	SB	PH AB	PH H	PO	A	E	DP	TC/G	FA	G by Pos
1987	CAL	A	8	.333	.333	9	3	0	0	0	0.0	2	0	2	0	0	5	3	1	0	0	0	0.1	1.000	OF-1
1988			56	.283	.327	113	32	3	1	0	0.0	7	14	11	15	0	26	8	63	4	2	2	1.2	.971	OF-17, DH-10, 1B-6
1989			12	.250	.250	12	3	0	0	0	0.0	0	2	1	4	0	9	2	12	0	0	2	1.0	1.000	1B-4
1990	TOR	A	6	.200	.200	5	1	0	0	0	0.0	0	0	0	2	0	5	1	0	0	0	0	0.0	.983	
4 yrs.			82	.281	.317	139	39	3	1	0	0.0	9	16	14	21	0	45	14	76	4	2	4	1.0	.976	OF-18, DH-10, 1B-10

Nick Esasky

ESASKY, NICHOLAS ANDREW
B. Feb. 24, 1960, Hialeah, Fla.
BR TR 6' 3" 190 lbs.

Year	Team		Games	BA	SA	AB	H	2B	3B	HR	HR%	R	RBI	BB	SO	SB	PH AB	PH H	PO	A	E	DP	TC/G	FA	G by Pos
1983	CIN	N	85	.265	.450	302	80	10	5	12	4.0	41	46	27	99	6	1	0	53	133	13	11	2.3	.935	3B-84
1984			113	.193	.348	322	62	10	5	10	3.1	30	45	52	103	1	12	0	220	137	18	19	3.3	.952	3B-82, 1B-25
1985			125	.262	.465	413	108	21	0	21	5.1	61	66	41	102	3	10	4	169	106	8	16	2.3	.972	3B-62, OF-54, 1B-12
1986			102	.230	.403	330	76	17	2	12	3.6	35	41	47	97	0	5	1	585	33	5	14	6.1	.992	1B-70, OF-42, 3B-1
1987			100	.272	.529	346	94	19	2	22	6.4	48	59	29	76	0	6	1	773	41	6	72	8.2	.993	1B-93, 3B-1, OF-1
1988			122	.243	.412	391	95	17	2	15	3.8	40	62	48	104	7	11	0	982	52	6	70	8.5	.994	1B-116
1989	BOS	A	154	.277	.500	564	156	26	5	30	5.3	79	108	66	117	1	4	0	1319	107	6	129	9.3	.996	1B-153, OF-1
1990	ATL	N	9	.171	.171	35	6	0	0	0	0.0	2	0	4	14	0	0	0	79	5	5	7	9.9	.944	1B-9
8 yrs.			810	.250	.446	2703	677	120	21	122	4.5	336	427	314	712	18	49	6	4180	614	67	338	6.0	.986	1B-478, 3B-230, OF-98

Alvaro Espinoza

ESPINOZA, ALVARO ALBERTO
Born Alvaro Alberto Espinoza y Ramirez.
B. Feb. 19, 1962, Valencia, Venezuela
BR TR 6' 160 lbs.

	Games	BA	SA	AB	H	2B	3B	HR	HR%	R	RBI	BB	SO	SB
April	17	.200	.255	55	11	3	0	0	0.0	2	4	2	11	0
May	25	.197	.211	76	15	1	0	0	0.0	3	4	2	6	0
June	26	.244	.333	78	19	2	1	1	1.3	5	1	3	9	0
July	27	.276	.329	76	21	1	0	1	1.3	6	4	4	10	0
Aug	28	.159	.207	82	13	2	1	0	0.0	7	3	1	10	0
Sept/Oct	27	.268	.310	71	19	3	0	0	0.0	8	4	4	8	1
Day	39	.190	.219	105	20	1	1	0	0.0	5	8	5	12	0
Night	111	.234	.291	333	78	11	1	2	0.6	26	12	11	42	1
vs. Left		.250	.299	144	36	2	1	1	0.7	12	9	9	13	1
vs. Right		.211	.262	294	62	10	1	1	0.3	19	11	7	41	0
On Grass	128	.208	.251	370	77	9	2	1	0.3	25	15	15	44	1
On Turf	22	.309	.397	68	21	3	0	1	1.5	6	5	1	10	0
Home	74	.215	.265	219	47	7	2	0	0.0	14	9	9	21	0
Road	76	.233	.283	219	51	5	0	2	0.9	17	11	7	33	1
Division Rivals														
vs. BAL	11	.133	.133	30	4	0	0	0	0.0	1	0	0	4	0
vs. BOS	12	.103	.207	29	3	0	0	1	3.4	1	2	0	3	0
vs. CLE	11	.207	.241	29	6	1	0	0	0.0	3	4	0	1	0
vs. DET	12	.200	.200	40	8	0	0	0	0.0	5	0	4	8	0
vs. MIL	13	.351	.486	37	13	3	1	0	0.0	6	1	1	2	1
vs. TOR	12	.256	.349	43	11	2	1	0	0.0	5	2	1	5	0
On 3B < 2 Out		.214	.214	14	3	0	0	0	0.0	0	8	2		0

SHORTSTOP

AVERAGE — AL AVG · RBI — AL AVG · HR — AL AVG · SB — AL AVG

Year	Team		Games	BA	SA	AB	H	2B	3B	HR	HR%	R	RBI	BB	SO	SB	PH AB	PH H	PO	A	E	DP	TC/G	FA	G by Pos
1984	MIN	A	1	—	—	0	0	0	0	0	—	0	0	0	0	0	0	0	0	0	0	0	0.0	—	SS-1
1985			32	.263	.298	57	15	2	0	0	0.0	5	9	1	9	0	0	0	25	69	5	15	3.1	.949	SS-31
1986			37	.214	.238	42	9	1	0	0	0.0	4	1	1	10	0	1	0	23	52	4	11	2.1	.949	2B-19, SS-18
1988	NY	A	3	.000	.000	3	0	0	0	0	0.0	0	0	0	0	0	0	0	5	2	0	1	2.3	1.000	2B-2, SS-1
1989			146	.282	.332	503	142	23	1	0	0.0	51	41	14	60	3	0	0	237	471	22	114	5.0	.970	SS-146
1990			150	.224	.274	438	98	12	2	2	0.4	31	20	16	54	1	0	0	268	447	17	100	4.9	.977	SS-150
6 yrs.			369	.253	.301	1043	264	38	3	2	0.2	91	71	32	133	4	1	0	558	1041	48	241	4.5	.971	SS-347, 2B-21

Year	Team		Games	BA	SA	AB	H	2B	3B	HR	HR%	R	RBI	BB	SO	SB	PINCH HIT AB	H	PO	A	E	DP	TC/G	FA	G by Pos

Cecil Espy

ESPY, CECIL EDWARD
B. Jan. 20, 1963, San Diego, Calif.
BB TR 6′ 3″ 190 lbs.

1983	LA	N	20	.273	.364	11	3	1	0	0	0.0	4	1	1	2	0	2	1	11	0	0	0	0.6	1.000	OF-15
1987	TEX	A	14	.000	.000	8	0	0	0	0	0.0	1	0	1	3	2	1	0	8	1	0	1	0.6	1.000	OF-8
1988			123	.248	.349	347	86	17	6	2	0.6	46	39	20	83	33	13	5	200	11	7	0	1.8	.968	OF-98, DH-12, SS-3, C-2, 1B-1, 2B-1
1989			142	.257	.331	475	122	12	7	3	0.6	65	31	38	99	45	13	6	281	5	3	2	2.0	.990	OF-133, DH-3
1990			52	.127	.127	71	9	0	0	0	0.0	10	1	10	20	11	6	0	56	1	0	0	1.5	1.000	OF-39, DH-4, 2B-1
5 yrs.			351	.241	.319	912	220	30	13	5	0.5	126	72	70	207	91	35	12	556	18	10	3	1.7	.983	OF-293, DH-19, SS-3, C-2, 2B-2, 1B-1

Dwight Evans

EVANS, DWIGHT MICHAEL (Dewey)
B. Nov. 3, 1951, Santa Monica, Calif.
BR TR 6′ 2″ 180 lbs.

Split			Games	BA	SA	AB	H	2B	3B	HR	HR%	R	RBI	BB	SO	SB
April			19	.243	.392	74	18	2	0	3	4.1	9	12	8	18	0
May			26	.253	.352	91	23	6	0	1	1.1	12	11	15	14	0
June			28	.226	.441	93	21	3	1	5	5.4	17	17	20	16	1
July			10	.179	.282	39	7	1	0	1	2.6	5	4	6	7	0
Aug			22	.310	.476	84	26	3	1	3	3.6	16	11	12	9	0
Sept/Oct			18	.250	.328	64	16	3	1	0	0.0	7	8	6	9	2
Day			40	.285	.521	144	41	4	0	10	6.9	25	34	18	25	1
Night			83	.233	.329	301	70	14	3	3	1.0	41	29	49	48	2
vs. Left				.265	.422	147	39	10	2	3	2.0	23	16	25	29	0
vs. Right				.242	.376	298	72	8	1	10	3.4	43	47	42	44	3
On Grass			105	.247	.379	380	94	14	3	10	2.6	58	52	58	62	3
On Turf			18	.262	.462	65	17	4	0	3	4.6	8	11	9	11	0
Home			60	.252	.413	218	55	10	2	7	3.2	41	31	30	42	3
Road			63	.247	.370	227	56	8	1	6	2.6	25	32	37	31	0
Division Rivals																
vs. BAL			10	.294	.588	34	10	1	0	3	8.8	4	8	6	1	0
vs. CLE			12	.295	.432	44	13	3	0	1	2.3	11	6	12	7	0
vs. DET			8	.484	.677	31	15	3	0	1	3.2	6	10	3	2	0
vs. MIL			6	.167	.292	24	4	0	1	1	4.2	3	1	1	8	0
vs. NY			10	.226	.387	31	7	0	1	1	3.2	4	5	5	5	0
vs. TOR			11	.237	.368	36	9	2	0	1	2.6	5	6	4	6	2
On 3B < 2 Out				.267	.433	30	8	2	0	1	3.3	1	27	5	5	

DESIGNATED HITTER

AVERAGE (.000–.400) — player vs. AL AVG
RBI (0–100) — player vs. AL AVG
HR (0–50) — player vs. AL AVG
SB (0–60) — player vs. AL AVG

1972	BOS	A	18	.263	.404	57	15	3	1	1	1.8	2	6	7	13	0	1	1	25	3	0	0	1.6	1.000	OF-17
1973			119	.223	.383	282	63	13	1	10	3.5	46	32	40	52	5	3	0	178	4	1	0	1.5	.995	OF-113
1974			133	.281	.421	463	130	19	8	10	2.2	60	70	38	77	4	12	2	294	8	3	2	2.3	.990	OF-122, DH-7
1975			128	.274	.456	412	113	24	6	13	3.2	61	56	47	60	3	6	0	281	15	4	8	2.3	.987	OF-115, DH-7
1976			146	.242	.431	501	121	34	5	17	3.4	61	62	57	92	6	2	1	324	15	2	4	2.3	.994	OF-145, DH-1
1977			73	.287	.526	230	66	9	2	14	6.1	39	36	28	58	4	7	1	126	2	1	0	1.8	.992	OF-63, DH-17
1978			147	.247	.449	497	123	24	2	24	4.8	75	63	65	119	8	4	1	305	14	6	2	2.2	.982	OF-142, DH-4
1979			152	.274	.456	489	134	24	1	21	4.3	69	58	69	76	6	5	1	307	15	4	5	2.1	.988	OF-149
1980			148	.266	.484	463	123	37	5	18	3.9	72	60	64	98	3	5	0	268	11	5	7	1.9	.982	OF-144, DH-2
1981			108	.296	.522	412	122	19	4	**22**	5.3	84	71	**85**	85	3	0	0	259	9	2	1	2.5	.993	OF-108
1982			162	.292	.534	609	178	37	7	32	5.3	122	98	112	125	3	0	0	346	9	10	3	2.3	.973	OF-161, DH-1
1983			126	.238	.436	470	112	19	4	22	4.7	74	58	70	97	3	5	2	222	6	3	1	1.8	.987	OF-99, DH-21
1984			162	.295	.532	630	186	37	8	32	5.1	**121**	104	96	115	3	0	0	311	7	2	2	2.0	.994	OF-161, DH-1
1985			159	.263	.454	617	162	29	1	29	4.7	110	78	**114**	105	7	0	0	291	9	3	1	1.9	.990	OF-152, DH-7
1986			152	.259	.476	529	137	33	2	26	4.9	86	97	97	117	3	1	0	280	10	5	3	1.9	.983	OF-149, DH-1
1987			154	.305	.569	541	165	37	2	34	6.3	109	123	**106**	98	4	2	0	753	46	13	72	5.3	.984	1B-79, OF-77, DH-4
1988			149	.293	.487	559	164	31	7	21	3.8	96	111	76	99	5	2	1	611	34	9	39	4.4	.986	OF-85, 1B-64, DH-6
1989			146	.285	.463	520	148	27	3	20	3.8	82	100	99	84	3	0	0	153	5	3	1	1.1	.981	OF-77, 1B-69
1990			123	.249	.391	445	111	18	3	13	2.9	66	63	67	73	3	0	0	0	0	0	0	0.0	.946	DH-122
19 yrs.			2505	.272	.473	8726	2373	474	72	379	4.3	1435	1346	1337	1643 10th	76	55	10	5334	222	76	151	2.2	.987	OF-2079, DH-270, 1B-143

LEAGUE CHAMPIONSHIP SERIES

1975	BOS	A	3	.100	.200	10	1	1	0	0	0.0	1	1	1	2	0	0	0	7	0	0	0	2.3	1.000	OF-3
1986			7	.214	.357	28	6	1	0	1	3.6	2	4	3	3	0	0	0	11	0	0	0	1.6	1.000	OF-7
1988			4	.167	.250	12	2	1	0	0	0.0	1	1	3	5	0	0	0	11	0	0	0	2.8	1.000	OF-4
1990			4	.231	.308	13	3	1	0	0	0.0	1	0	0	1	0	0	0	0	0	0	0	0.0	1.000	OF-4
4 yrs.			18	.190	.302	63	12	4	0	1	1.6	4	6	6	13	0	0	0	29	0	0	0	1.6	.000	OF-14, DH-4

Year	Team	Games	BA	SA	AB	H	2B	3B	HR	HR%	R	RBI	BB	SO	SB	PINCH HIT AB	H	PO	A	E	DP	TC/G	FA	G by Pos

Dwight Evans *Continued*

WORLD SERIES

Year	Team	Games	BA	SA	AB	H	2B	3B	HR	HR%	R	RBI	BB	SO	SB	AB	H	PO	A	E	DP	TC/G	FA	G by Pos
1975	BOS A	7	.292	.542	24	7	1	1	1	4.2	3	5	3	4	0	0	0	23	1	0	1	3.4	1.000	OF-7
1986		7	.308	.615	26	8	2	0	2	7.7	4	9	4	3	0	0	0	16	1	1	0	2.6	.944	OF-7
2 yrs.		14	.300	.580	50	15	3	1	3	6.0	7	14	7	7	0	0	0	39	2	1	1	3.0	.976	OF-14

Paul Faries

FARIES, PAUL TYRELL
B. Feb. 20, 1965, Berkeley, Calif.
BR TR 5′ 10″ 165 lbs.

Year	Team	Games	BA	SA	AB	H	2B	3B	HR	HR%	R	RBI	BB	SO	SB	AB	H	PO	A	E	DP	TC/G	FA	G by Pos
1990	SD N	14	.189	.216	37	7	1	0	0	0.0	4	2	4	7	0	1	0	21	34	2	8	4.8	.965	2B-7, SS-4, 3B-1

Mike Felder

FELDER, MICHAEL OTIS
B. Nov. 18, 1961, Vallejo, Calif.
BB TR 5′ 8″ 160 lbs.

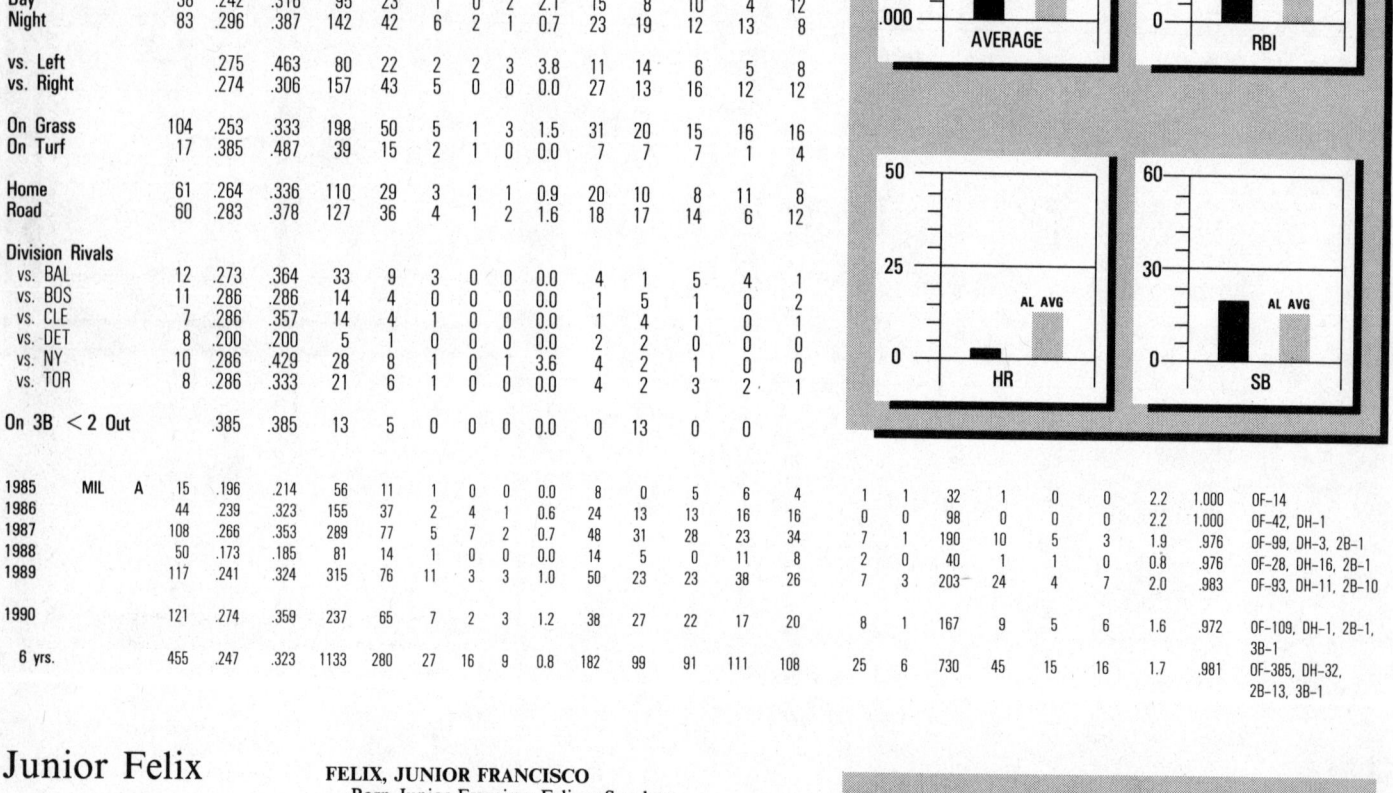

OUTFIELD

AVERAGE — AL AVG
RBI — AL AVG
HR — AL AVG
SB — AL AVG

Split	Games	BA	SA	AB	H	2B	3B	HR	HR%	R	RBI	BB	SO	SB	AB	H
April	16	.250	.250	12	3	0	0	0	0.0	3	2	2	2	1		
May	20	.172	.172	29	5	0	0	0	0.0	2	2	4	0	4		
June	23	.292	.354	65	19	4	0	0	0.0	7	6	7	3	3		
July	21	.224	.347	49	11	0	0	2	4.1	8	3	2	5	4		
Aug	21	.324	.486	37	12	1	1	1	2.7	8	9	2	3	2		
Sept/Oct	20	.333	.422	45	15	2	1	0	0.0	10	5	5	4	6		
Day	38	.242	.316	95	23	1	0	2	2.1	15	8	10	4	12		
Night	83	.296	.387	142	42	6	2	1	0.7	23	19	12	13	8		
vs. Left		.275	.463	80	22	2	2	3	3.8	11	14	6	5	8		
vs. Right		.274	.306	157	43	5	0	0	0.0	27	13	16	12	12		
On Grass	104	.253	.333	198	50	5	1	3	1.5	31	20	15	16	16		
On Turf	17	.385	.487	39	15	2	1	0	0.0	7	7	7	1	4		
Home	61	.264	.336	110	29	3	1	1	0.9	20	10	8	11	8		
Road	60	.283	.378	127	36	4	1	2	1.6	18	17	14	6	12		
Division Rivals																
vs. BAL	12	.273	.364	33	9	3	0	0	0.0	4	1	5	4	1		
vs. BOS	11	.286	.286	14	4	0	0	0	0.0	1	5	1	0	2		
vs. CLE	7	.286	.357	14	4	1	0	0	0.0	1	4	1	0	1		
vs. DET	8	.200	.200	5	1	0	0	0	0.0	2	2	0	0	0		
vs. NY	10	.286	.429	28	8	1	0	1	3.6	4	2	1	0	0		
vs. TOR	8	.286	.333	21	6	1	0	0	0.0	4	2	3	2	1		
On 3B < 2 Out		.385	.385	13	5	0	0	0	0.0	0	13	0	0			

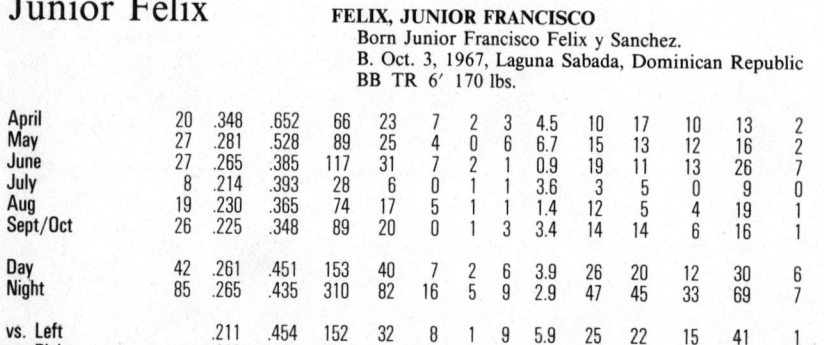

Year	Team	Games	BA	SA	AB	H	2B	3B	HR	HR%	R	RBI	BB	SO	SB	AB	H	PO	A	E	DP	TC/G	FA	G by Pos
1985	MIL A	15	.196	.214	56	11	1	0	0	0.0	8	0	5	6	4	1	1	32	1	0	0	2.2	1.000	OF-14
1986		44	.239	.323	155	37	2	4	1	0.6	24	13	13	16	16	0	0	98	0	0	0	2.2	1.000	OF-42, DH-1
1987		108	.266	.353	289	77	5	7	2	0.7	48	31	28	23	34	7	1	190	10	5	3	1.9	.976	OF-99, DH-3, 2B-1
1988		50	.173	.185	81	14	1	0	0	0.0	14	5	0	11	8	2	0	40	1	1	0	0.8	.976	OF-28, DH-16, 2B-1
1989		117	.241	.324	315	76	11	3	3	1.0	50	23	23	38	26	7	3	203	24	4	7	2.0	.983	OF-93, DH-11, 2B-10
1990		121	.274	.359	237	65	7	2	3	1.2	38	27	22	17	20	8	1	167	9	5	6	1.6	.972	OF-109, DH-1, 2B-1, 3B-1
6 yrs.		455	.247	.323	1133	280	27	16	9	0.8	182	99	91	111	108	25	6	730	45	15	16	1.7	.981	OF-385, DH-32, 2B-13, 3B-1

Junior Felix

FELIX, JUNIOR FRANCISCO
Born Junior Francisco Felix y Sanchez.
B. Oct. 3, 1967, Laguna Sabada, Dominican Republic
BB TR 6′ 170 lbs.

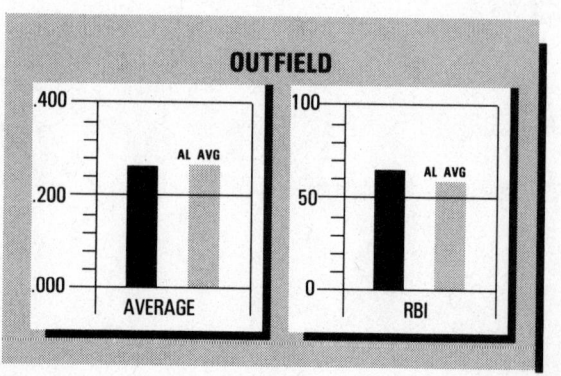

OUTFIELD

AVERAGE — AL AVG
RBI — AL AVG

Split	Games	BA	SA	AB	H	2B	3B	HR	HR%	R	RBI	BB	SO	SB
April	20	.348	.652	66	23	7	2	3	4.5	10	17	10	13	2
May	27	.281	.528	89	25	4	0	6	6.7	15	13	12	16	2
June	27	.265	.385	117	31	7	2	1	0.9	19	11	13	26	7
July	8	.214	.393	28	6	0	1	1	3.6	3	5	0	9	0
Aug	19	.230	.365	74	17	5	1	1	1.4	12	5	4	19	1
Sept/Oct	26	.225	.348	89	20	0	1	3	3.4	14	14	6	16	1
Day	42	.261	.451	153	40	7	2	6	3.9	26	20	12	30	6
Night	85	.265	.435	310	82	16	5	9	2.9	47	45	33	69	7
vs. Left		.211	.454	152	32	8	1	9	5.9	25	22	15	41	1
vs. Right		.289	.434	311	90	15	6	6	1.9	48	43	30	58	12

Year	Team		Games	BA	SA	AB	H	2B	3B	HR	HR%	R	RBI	BB	SO	SB	PINCH HIT AB	PINCH HIT H	PO	A	E	DP	TC/G	FA	G by Pos

Junior Felix *Continued*

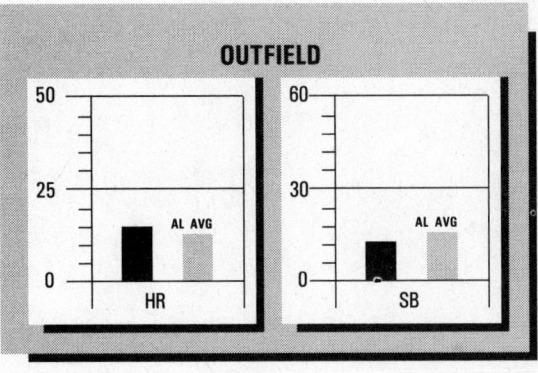

On Grass			46	.262	.424	172	45	8	1	6	3.5	27	23	17	37	5									
On Turf			81	.265	.450	291	77	15	6	9	3.1	46	42	28	62	8									
Home			67	.246	.441	236	58	13	6	7	3.0	35	29	24	50	6									
Road			60	.282	.441	227	64	10	1	8	3.5	38	36	21	49	7									
Division Rivals																									
vs. BAL			10	.258	.419	31	8	0	1	1	3.2	5	3	6	5	0									
vs. BOS			12	.286	.469	49	14	1	1	2	4.1	9	5	1	10	4									
vs. CLE			12	.279	.535	43	12	5	0	2	4.7	7	7	4	8	0									
vs. DET			11	.162	.324	37	6	1	1	1	2.7	6	3	4	7	1									
vs. MIL			10	.231	.410	39	9	5	1	0	0.0	6	2	5	12	0									
vs. NY			11	.196	.283	46	9	1	0	1	2.2	6	3	5	5	2									
On 3B < 2 Out				.238	.286	21	5	1	0	0	0.0	0	18	1	6										
1989	TOR	A	110	.258	.395	415	107	14	8	9	2.2	62	46	33	101	18	2	0	243	9	9	0	2.4	.966	OF-107, DH-2
1990			127	.264	.441	463	122	23	7	15	3.2	73	65	45	99	13	2	0	244	11	9	3	2.1	.966	OF-125, DH-1
2 yrs.			237	.261	.419	878	229	37	15	24	2.7	135	111	78	200	31	4	0	487	20	18	3	2.2	.966	OF-232, DH-3

LEAGUE CHAMPIONSHIP SERIES

Year	Team		Games	BA	SA	AB	H	2B	3B	HR	HR%	R	RBI	BB	SO	SB	AB	H	PO	A	E	DP	TC/G	FA	G by Pos
1989	TOR	A	3	.273	.364	11	3	1	0	0	0.0	0	3	0	2	0	0	0	8	0	0	0	2.7	1.000	OF-3

Felix Fermin

FERMIN, FELIX JOSE
Born Felix Jose Fermin y Minaya.
B. Oct. 9, 1963, Mao Valverde, Dominican Republic
BR TR 5′ 11″ 160 lbs.

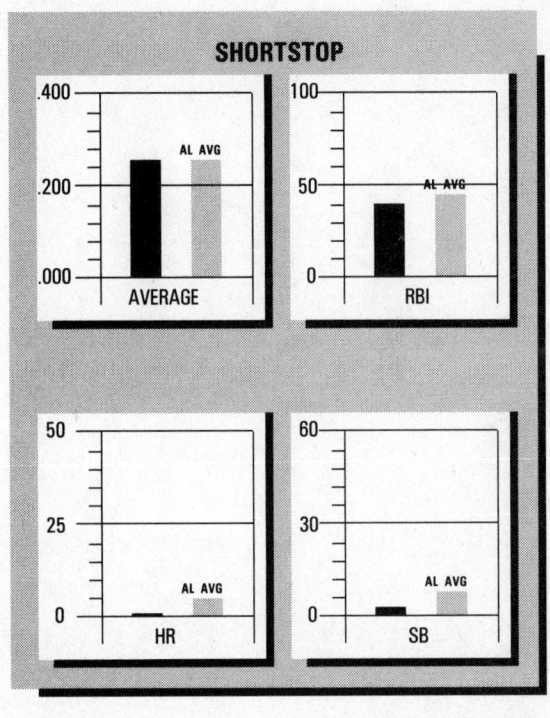

April			17	.250	.417	36	9	1	1	1	2.8	5	4	1	1	0									
May			22	.203	.254	59	12	1	1	0	0.0	6	4	4	6	0									
June			28	.238	.298	84	20	5	0	0	0.0	10	6	4	3	1									
July			29	.221	.233	86	19	1	0	0	0.0	5	5	1	3	0									
Aug			27	.306	.375	72	22	5	0	0	0.0	10	12	7	3	1									
Sept/Oct			25	.312	.312	77	24	0	0	0	0.0	11	9	9	6	1									
Day			41	.298	.377	114	34	4	1	1	0.9	15	14	6	7	2									
Night			107	.240	.277	300	72	9	1	0	0.0	32	26	20	15	1									
vs. Left				.262	.285	130	34	3	0	0	0.0	11	15	9	4	0									
vs. Right				.254	.313	284	72	10	2	1	0.4	36	25	17	18	3									
On Grass			125	.245	.296	351	86	13	1	1	0.3	40	32	21	18	2									
On Turf			23	.317	.349	63	20	0	1	0	0.0	7	8	5	4	1									
Home			74	.278	.361	205	57	12	1	1	0.5	27	24	8	13	1									
Road			74	.234	.249	209	49	1	1	0	0.0	20	16	18	9	2									
Division Rivals																									
vs. BAL			12	.256	.333	39	10	3	0	0	0.0	5	3	3	3	1									
vs. BOS			13	.194	.222	36	7	1	0	0	0.0	1	4	3	6	0									
vs. DET			12	.286	.321	28	8	1	0	0	0.0	5	6	4	0	0									
vs. MIL			13	.304	.326	46	14	1	0	0	0.0	5	3	1	0	1									
vs. NY			13	.206	.206	34	7	0	0	0	0.0	4	0	4	1	0									
vs. TOR			12	.286	.371	35	10	1	1	0	0.0	4	6	2	0	0									
On 3B < 2 Out				.250	.250	20	5	0	0	0	0.0	0	11	1	2										
1987	PIT	N	23	.250	.250	68	17	0	0	0	0.0	6	4	4	9	0	0	0	36	62	2	13	4.3	.980	SS-23
1988			43	.276	.322	87	24	0	2	0	0.0	9	2	8	10	3	1	0	51	76	6	14	3.1	.955	SS-43
1989	CLE	A	156	.238	.260	484	115	9	1	0	0.0	50	21	41	27	6	0	0	253	517	26	84	5.1	.967	SS-153, 2B-2
1990			148	.256	.304	414	106	13	2	1	0.2	47	40	26	22	3	0	0	214	423	16	81	4.4	.976	SS-147, 2B-1
4 yrs.			370	.249	.282	1053	262	22	5	1	0.1	112	67	79	68	12	1	0	554	1078	50	192	4.5	.970	SS-366, 2B-3

Year	Team	Games	BA	SA	AB	H	2B	3B	HR	HR%	R	RBI	BB	SO	SB	PINCH HIT AB	H	PO	A	E	DP	TC/G	FA	G by Pos

Tony Fernandez

FERNANDEZ, OCTAVIO ANTONIO
Born Octavio Antonio Fernandez y Castro.
B. Aug. 6, 1962, San Pedro de Macoris,
Dominican Republic
BB TR 6' 1" 160 lbs.

Split	Games	BA	SA	AB	H	2B	3B	HR	HR%	R	RBI	BB	SO	SB	PH AB	PH H	PO	A	E	DP	TC/G	FA	G by Pos
April	21	.310	.425	87	27	3	2	1	1.1	13	15	6	11	2									
May	28	.216	.288	111	24	3	1	1	0.9	9	3	17	17	5									
June	28	.255	.396	106	27	5	5	0	0.0	18	14	15	15	2									
July	26	.228	.356	101	23	3	5	0	0.0	14	8	11	11	3									
Aug	28	.297	.446	101	30	6	3	1	1.0	15	15	13	5	2									
Sept/Oct	30	.341	.434	129	44	7	1	1	0.8	15	11	9	11	12									
Day	49	.292	.400	195	57	9	3	2	1.0	29	17	18	23	7									
Night	112	.268	.386	440	118	18	14	2	0.5	55	49	53	47	19									
vs. Left		.238	.302	202	48	6	2	1	0.5	21	13	31	18	5									
vs. Right		.293	.432	433	127	21	15	3	0.7	63	53	40	52	21									
On Grass	62	.241	.316	237	57	5	5	1	0.4	30	20	33	26	11									
On Turf	99	.296	.435	398	118	22	12	3	0.8	54	46	38	44	15									
Home	81	.308	.455	321	99	17	12	2	0.6	46	38	31	36	12									
Road	80	.242	.325	314	76	10	5	2	0.6	38	28	40	34	14									
Division Rivals																							
vs. BAL	13	.269	.385	52	14	4	1	0	0.0	6	7	6	10	2									
vs. BOS	13	.327	.442	52	17	2	2	0	0.0	6	7	4	10	3									
vs. CLE	13	.364	.473	55	20	1	1	1	1.8	6	6	0	5	3									
vs. DET	13	.240	.320	50	12	1	0	1	2.0	8	4	8	3	3									
vs. MIL	13	.400	.580	50	20	4	1	1	2.0	9	7	7	6	2									
vs. NY	13	.152	.239	46	7	2	1	0	0.0	5	2	6	1	3									
On 3B < 2 Out		.440	.800	25	11	2	2	1	4.0	1	26	7	4										
1983 TOR A	15	.265	.353	34	9	1	1	0	0.0	5	2	2	2	0	2	1	16	17	0	6	2.2	1.000	SS-13, DH-1
1984	88	.270	.356	233	63	5	3	3	1.3	29	19	17	15	5	6	1	119	195	9	41	3.7	.972	SS-73, 3B-10, DH-1
1985	161	.289	.390	564	163	31	10	2	0.4	71	51	43	41	13	3	1	283	478	30	109	4.9	.962	SS-160
1986	163	.310	.428	**687**	213	33	9	10	1.5	91	65	27	52	25	1	1	294	445	13	103	4.6	.983	SS-163
1987	146	.322	.426	578	186	29	8	5	0.9	90	67	51	48	32	1	0	270	396	14	88	4.7	.979	SS-146
1988	154	.287	.386	648	186	41	4	5	0.8	76	70	45	65	15	0	0	247	470	14	106	4.7	.981	SS-154
1989	140	.257	.389	573	147	25	9	11	1.9	64	64	29	51	22	0	0	260	475	6	93	5.3	.992	SS-140
1990	161	.276	.391	635	175	27	**17**	4	0.6	84	66	71	70	26	0	0	297	480	9	93	4.9	.989	SS-161
8 yrs.	1028	.289	.399	3952	1142	192	61	40	1.0	510	404	285	344	138	13	4	1786	2956	95	639	4.7	.980	SS-1010, 3B-10, DH-2
LEAGUE CHAMPIONSHIP SERIES																							
1985 TOR A	7	.333	.417	24	8	2	0	0	0.0	2	2	1	2	0	0	0	11	14	2	2	3.9	.926	SS-7
1989	5	.350	.500	20	7	3	0	0	0.0	6	1	1	2	5	0	0	9	15	0	3	4.8	1.000	SS-5
2 yrs.	12	.341	.455	44	15	5	0	0	0.0	8	3	2	4	5	0	0	20	29	2	5	4.3	.961	SS-12

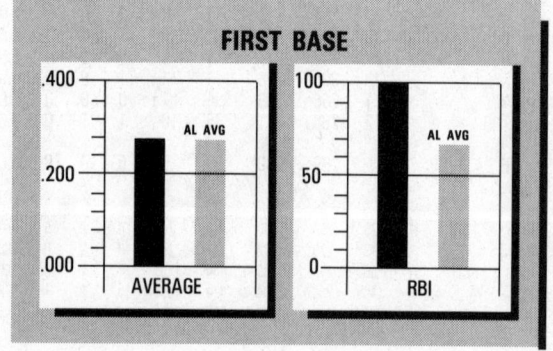

Cecil Fielder

FIELDER, CECIL GRANT
B. Sept. 21, 1963, Los Angeles, Calif.
BR TR 6' 3" 230 lbs.

Split	Games	BA	SA	AB	H	2B	3B	HR	HR%	R	RBI	BB	SO	SB
April	20	.243	.557	70	17	1	0	7	10.0	11	19	8	19	0
May	28	.369	.786	103	38	10	0	11	10.7	21	23	15	31	0
June	28	.263	.515	99	26	1	0	8	8.1	17	23	16	33	0
July	27	.255	.520	98	25	5	0	7	7.1	18	21	19	36	0
Aug	26	.298	.681	94	28	7	1	9	9.6	20	25	21	31	0
Sept/Oct	30	.229	.486	109	25	1	0	9	8.3	17	21	11	32	0
Day	44	.213	.497	155	33	2	0	14	9.0	20	37	25	53	0
Night	115	.301	.627	418	126	23	1	37	8.9	84	95	65	129	0
vs. Left		.371	.854	178	66	11	0	25	14.0	41	54	37	47	0
vs. Right		.235	.473	395	93	14	1	26	6.6	63	78	53	135	0

Year	Team	Games	BA	SA	AB	H	2B	3B	HR	HR%	R	RBI	BB	SO	SB	PINCH HIT AB	PINCH HIT H	PO	A	E	DP	TC/G	FA	G by Pos

Cecil Fielder *Continued*

Year	Team	Games	BA	SA	AB	H	2B	3B	HR	HR%	R	RBI	BB	SO	SB	AB	H	PO	A	E	DP	TC/G	FA	G by Pos
On Grass		136	.271	.581	484	131	21	0	43	8.9	88	107	77	152	0									
On Turf		23	.315	.652	89	28	4	1	8	9.0	16	25	13	30	0									
Home		80	.280	.605	271	76	13	0	25	9.2	47	60	52	81	0									
Road		79	.275	.579	302	83	12	1	26	8.6	57	72	38	101	0									
Division Rivals																								
vs. BAL		13	.214	.476	42	9	2	0	3	7.1	6	7	3	8	0									
vs. BOS		11	.216	.378	37	8	0	0	2	5.4	5	5	11	14	0									
vs. CLE		13	.438	1.000	48	21	3	0	8	16.7	13	18	6	10	0									
vs. MIL		13	.311	.822	45	14	2	0	7	15.6	8	14	7	8	0									
vs. NY		13	.255	.627	51	13	1	0	6	11.8	12	14	5	22	0									
vs. TOR		12	.383	.915	47	18	4	0	7	14.9	9	14	5	11	0									
On 3B < 2 Out			.314	.543	35	11	0	1	2	5.7	2	28	12	14										
1985	TOR A	30	.311	.527	74	23	4	0	4	5.4	6	16	6	16	0	4	1	171	17	4	21	6.4	.979	1B-25
1986		34	.157	.325	83	13	2	0	4	4.8	7	13	6	27	0	9	1	37	4	1	3	1.2	.976	DH-22, 1B-7, 3B-2, OF-1
1987		82	.269	.560	175	47	7	1	14	8.0	30	32	20	48	0	19	4	98	6	0	12	1.3	1.000	DH-55, 1B-16, 3B-2
1988		74	.230	.431	174	40	6	1	9	5.2	24	23	14	53	0	21	5	101	12	1	10	1.5	.991	1B-17, 3B-3, 2B-2
1990	DET A	159	.277	**.592**	573	159	25	1	**51**	**8.9**	104	**132**	90	**182**	0	3	0	1190	111	14	137	9.2	.989	1B-143, DH-15
5 yrs.		379	.261	.536	1079	282	44	3	82	7.6	171	216	136	326	0	56	11	1597	150	20	183	4.7	.989	1B-208, DH-92, 3B-7, 2B-2, OF-1

LEAGUE CHAMPIONSHIP SERIES

Year	Team	Games	BA	SA	AB	H	2B	3B	HR	HR%	R	RBI	BB	SO	SB	AB	H	PO	A	E	DP	TC/G	FA	G by Pos
1985	TOR A	3	.333	.667	3	1	1	0	0	0.0	0	0	0	1	0	3	1	0	0	0	0	0.0	—	

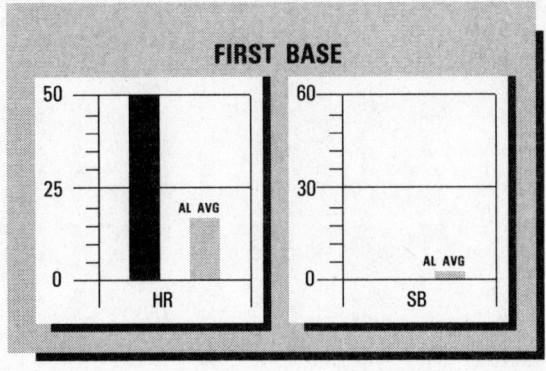

Steve Finley

FINLEY, STEVEN ALLEN
B. May 12, 1965, Union City, Tenn.
BL TL 6' 2" 175 lbs.

Period	Games	BA	SA	AB	H	2B	3B	HR	HR%	R	RBI	BB	SO	SB
April	17	.293	.397	58	17	2	2	0	0.0	8	5	7	7	3
May	21	.187	.253	75	14	3	1	0	0.0	8	4	6	9	1
June	26	.247	.309	81	20	5	0	0	0.0	9	4	4	7	6
July	22	.280	.360	50	14	1	0	1	2.0	7	4	4	9	1
Aug	25	.308	.346	78	24	3	0	0	0.0	7	6	5	5	8
Sept/Oct	31	.246	.328	122	30	2	1	2	1.6	7	14	6	16	3
Day	36	.208	.242	120	25	4	0	0	0.0	10	5	9	8	10
Night	106	.273	.358	344	94	12	4	3	0.9	36	32	23	45	12
vs. Left		.193	.237	114	22	2	0	1	0.9	5	9	2	15	3
vs. Right		.277	.357	350	97	14	4	2	0.6	41	28	30	38	19
On Grass	124	.257	.321	405	104	15	4	1	0.2	40	29	29	46	21
On Turf	18	.254	.373	59	15	1	0	2	3.4	6	8	3	7	1
Home	75	.231	.304	247	57	9	3	1	0.4	24	14	15	31	11
Road	67	.286	.355	217	62	7	1	2	0.9	22	23	17	22	11
Division Rivals														
vs. BOS	13	.196	.217	46	9	1	0	0	0.0	6	1	5	4	3
vs. CLE	13	.250	.273	44	11	1	0	0	0.0	5	3	1	2	3
vs. DET	12	.333	.513	39	13	0	2	1	2.6	6	4	4	4	3
vs. MIL	12	.179	.179	39	7	0	0	0	0.0	2	1	1	6	1
vs. NY	12	.342	.421	38	13	3	0	0	0.0	2	4	1	5	4
vs. TOR	10	.242	.394	33	8	0	1	1	3.0	3	7	2	4	0
On 3B < 2 Out		.316	.316	19	6	0	0	0	0.0	0	15	1	6	

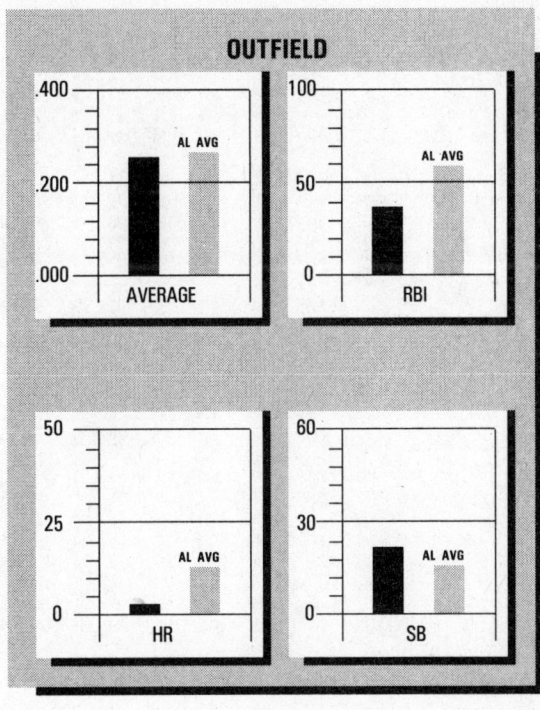

Year	Team	Games	BA	SA	AB	H	2B	3B	HR	HR%	R	RBI	BB	SO	SB	AB	H	PO	A	E	DP	TC/G	FA	G by Pos
1989	BAL A	81	.249	.318	217	54	5	2	2	0.9	35	25	15	30	17	5	1	144	1	2	0	1.8	.986	OF-76, DH-3
1990		142	.256	.328	464	119	16	4	3	0.6	46	37	32	53	22	12	0	298	4	7	1	2.3	.977	OF-133, DH-2
2 yrs.		223	.254	.325	681	173	21	6	5	0.7	81	62	47	83	39	17	1	442	5	9	1	2.0	.980	OF-209, DH-5

Carlton Fisk

FISK, CARLTON ERNEST (Pudge)
B. Dec. 26, 1947, Bellows Falls, Vt.
BR TR 6′ 3″ 200 lbs.

Year	Team	Games	BA	SA	AB	H	2B	3B	HR	HR%	R	RBI	BB	SO	SB	AB	H	PO	A	E	DP	TC/G	FA	G by Pos
April		15	.309	.382	55	17	4	0	0	0.0	5	5	4	10	1									
May		25	.250	.369	84	21	1	0	3	3.6	8	13	13	15	3									
June		18	.278	.463	54	15	1	0	3	5.6	9	6	11	5	0									
July		23	.300	.500	70	21	5	0	3	4.3	13	10	11	6	3									
Aug		27	.247	.447	85	21	5	0	4	4.7	13	13	10	19	0									
Sept/Oct		29	.327	.519	104	34	5	0	5	4.8	17	18	12	18	0									
Day		26	.263	.382	76	20	3	0	2	2.6	7	3	7	11	1									
Night		111	.290	.465	376	109	18	0	16	4.3	58	62	54	62	6									
vs. Left			.315	.539	165	52	10	0	9	5.5	25	30	21	23	3									
vs. Right			.268	.401	287	77	11	0	9	3.1	40	35	40	50	4									
On Grass		116	.296	.458	378	112	19	0	14	3.7	57	57	51	60	6									
On Turf		21	.230	.419	74	17	2	0	4	5.4	8	8	10	13	1									
Home		69	.288	.416	219	63	13	0	5	2.3	28	37	33	30	2									
Road		68	.283	.485	233	66	8	0	13	5.6	37	28	28	43	5									
Division Rivals																								
vs. CAL		10	.294	.529	34	10	2	0	2	5.9	2	5	4	7	0									
vs. KC		12	.293	.512	41	12	3	0	2	4.9	6	4	4	3	1									
vs. MIN		9	.171	.257	35	6	0	0	1	2.9	4	3	1	10	0									
vs. OAK		11	.364	.394	33	12	1	0	0	0.0	8	5	5	1	0									
vs. SEA		11	.229	.429	35	8	1	0	2	5.7	6	7	6	7	0									
vs. TEX		10	.200	.333	30	6	1	0	1	3.3	2	3	4	6	0									
On 3B < 2 Out			.278	.333	18	5	1	0	0	0.0	0	16	5	3										
1969	BOS A	2	.000	.000	5	0	0	0	0	0.0	0	0	0	2	0	1	0	2	0	0	1	1.0	1.000	C-1
1971		14	.313	.521	48	15	2	1	2	4.2	7	6	1	10	0	0	0	72	6	2	1	5.7	.975	C-14
1972		131	.293	.538	457	134	28	9	22	4.8	74	61	52	83	5	0	0	846	72	15	10	7.1	.984	C-131
1973		135	.246	.441	508	125	21	0	26	5.1	65	71	37	99	7	1	1	739	50	14	8	5.9	.983	C-131, DH-3
1974		52	.299	.551	187	56	12	1	11	5.9	36	26	24	23	5	0	0	267	26	6	2	5.8	.980	C-50, DH-2
1975		79	.331	.529	263	87	14	4	10	3.8	47	52	27	32	4	2	0	347	30	8	2	4.9	.979	C-71, DH-6
1976		134	.255	.415	487	124	17	5	17	3.5	76	58	56	71	12	1	0	649	73	12	9	5.5	.984	C-133, DH-1
1977		152	.315	.521	536	169	26	3	26	4.9	106	102	75	85	7	2	0	779	69	11	7	5.7	.987	C-151
1978		157	.284	.475	571	162	39	5	20	3.5	94	88	71	83	7	2	1	734	90	17	13	5.4	.980	C-154, DH-1, OF-1
1979		91	.272	.450	320	87	23	2	10	3.1	49	42	10	38	3	13	3	155	8	3	1	1.8	.982	DH-42, C-39, OF-1
1980		131	.289	.467	478	138	25	3	18	3.8	73	62	36	62	11	0	0	543	56	11	8	4.7	.982	C-115, DH-5, OF-5, 1B-3, 3B-3
1981	CHI A	96	.263	.361	338	89	12	0	7	2.1	44	45	38	37	3	0	0	479	46	6	14	5.5	.989	C-95, 1B-1, 3B-1, OF-1
1982		135	.267	.403	476	127	17	3	14	2.9	66	65	46	60	17	3	1	648	63	5	8	5.3	.993	C-133, 1B-2
1983		138	.289	.518	488	141	26	4	26	5.3	85	86	46	88	9	6	1	709	46	7	5	5.5	.991	C-133, DH-2
1984		102	.231	.468	359	83	20	1	21	5.8	54	43	26	60	6	11	1	421	38	6	4	4.6	.987	C-90, DH-5
1985		153	.238	.488	543	129	23	1	37	6.8	85	107	52	81	17	1	0	801	60	10	13	5.7	.989	C-130, DH-28
1986		125	.221	.337	457	101	11	0	14	3.1	42	63	22	92	2	8	1	455	44	8	3	4.1	.984	C-71, OF-31, DH-22
1987		135	.256	.460	454	116	22	1	23	5.1	68	71	39	72	1	12	3	597	66	7	22	5.0	.990	C-122, 1B-9, OF-2
1988		76	.277	.542	253	70	8	1	19	7.5	37	50	37	40	0	6	0	338	36	2	7	4.9	.995	C-74
1989		103	.293	.475	375	110	25	2	13	3.5	47	68	36	60	1	3	0	419	37	3	1	4.5	.993	C-90, DH-13
1990		137	.285	.451	452	129	21	0	18	3.9	65	65	61	73	7	9	2	660	63	4	14	6.3	.995	C-116, DH-14
21 yrs.		2278	.272	.464	8055	2192	392	46	354	4.4	1220	1231	792	1251	124	81	14	10660	979	157	153	0.8	.913	C-2044, DH-144, OF-41, 1B-15, 3B-4

LEAGUE CHAMPIONSHIP SERIES

Year	Team	Games	BA	SA	AB	H	2B	3B	HR	HR%	R	RBI	BB	SO	SB	AB	H	PO	A	E	DP	TC/G	FA	G by Pos
1975	BOS A	3	.417	.500	12	5	1	0	0	0.0	4	2	0	2	1	0	0	15	0	0	0	5.0	1.000	C-3
1983	CHI A	4	.176	.235	17	3	1	0	0	0.0	0	0	1	3	0	0	0	27	3	0	0	7.5	1.000	C-4
2 yrs.		7	.276	.345	29	8	2	0	0	0.0	4	2	1	5	1	0	0	42	3	0	0	6.4	.000	C-7

WORLD SERIES

Year	Team	Games	BA	SA	AB	H	2B	3B	HR	HR%	R	RBI	BB	SO	SB	AB	H	PO	A	E	DP	TC/G	FA	G by Pos
1975	BOS A	7	.240	.480	25	6	0	0	2	8.0	5	4	7	7	0	0	0	37	3	2	1	6.0	.952	C-7

CATCHER

(Bar charts: AVERAGE, RBI, HR, SB — each showing player value vs. AL AVG)

Year	Team	Games	BA	SA	AB	H	2B	3B	HR	HR%	R	RBI	BB	SO	SB	PINCH HIT AB	H	PO	A	E	DP	TC/G	FA	G by Pos

Mike Fitzgerald

FITZGERALD, MICHAEL ROY (Fitz)
B. July 13, 1960, Long Beach, Calif.
BR TR 6′ 185 lbs.

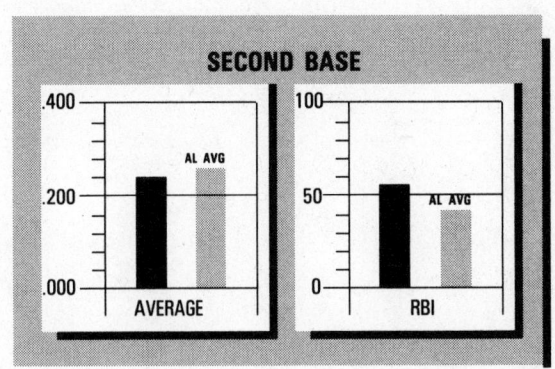

CATCHER

Year	Team	Games	BA	SA	AB	H	2B	3B	HR	HR%	R	RBI	BB	SO	SB	PINCH HIT AB	H	PO	A	E	DP	TC/G	FA	G by Pos
April		10	.200	.400	20	4	1	0	1	5.0	4	2	10	1	2									
May		20	.267	.450	60	16	8	0	1	1.7	5	6	4	15	0									
June		23	.242	.409	66	16	3	1	2	3.0	10	9	14	14	2									
July		20	.210	.371	62	13	1	0	3	4.8	9	9	11	14	3									
Aug		16	.156	.222	45	7	0	0	1	2.2	2	5	12	4	1									
Sept/Oct		22	.333	.467	60	20	5	0	1	1.7	6	10	9	12	0									
Day		32	.313	.573	96	30	10	0	5	5.2	15	18	20	20	1									
Night		79	.212	.313	217	46	8	1	4	1.8	21	23	40	40	7									
vs. Left			.225	.362	138	31	4	0	5	3.6	15	20	30	21	4									
vs. Right			.257	.417	175	45	14	1	4	2.3	21	21	30	39	4									
On Grass		29	.253	.440	91	23	5	0	4	4.4	15	17	17	18	2									
On Turf		82	.239	.374	222	53	13	1	5	2.3	21	24	43	42	6									
Home		54	.246	.366	134	33	10	0	2	1.5	12	14	27	23	4									
Road		57	.240	.413	179	43	8	1	7	3.9	24	27	33	37	4									
Division Rivals																								
vs. CHI		12	.281	.313	32	9	1	0	0	0.0	9	3	9	6	0									
vs. NY		13	.216	.324	37	8	1	0	1	2.7	3	5	6	7	1									
vs. PHI		11	.167	.267	30	5	0	0	1	3.3	2	4	7	5	1									
vs. PIT		17	.222	.333	45	10	2	0	1	2.2	4	3	8	7	1									
vs. STL		9	.296	.593	27	8	3	1	1	3.7	3	5	2	6	0									
On 3B < 2 Out			.250	.313	16	4	1	0	0	0.0	0	7	4	7										
1983	NY N	8	.100	.250	20	2	0	0	1	5.0	1	2	3	6	0	0	0	37	8	2	2	5.9	.957	C-8
1984		112	.242	.306	360	87	15	1	2	0.6	20	33	24	71	1	7	1	715	47	4	6	6.8	.995	C-107
1985	MON N	108	.207	.288	295	61	7	1	5	1.7	25	34	38	55	5	3	1	542	46	8	7	5.5	.987	C-108
1986		73	.282	.440	209	59	13	1	6	2.9	20	37	27	34	3	3	0	415	35	3	5	6.2	.993	C-71
1987		107	.240	.310	287	69	11	0	3	1.0	32	36	42	54	3	5	2	603	27	12	2	6.0	.981	C-104, 1B-1, 2B-1
1988		63	.271	.419	155	42	6	1	5	3.2	17	23	19	22	2	15	4	262	21	6	2	4.6	.979	C-47, OF-4
1989		100	.238	.386	290	69	18	2	7	2.4	33	42	35	61	3	10	3	465	44	8	5	5.2	.985	C-77, 3B-8, OF-6
1990		111	.243	.393	313	76	18	1	9	2.8	36	41	60	60	8	11	4	565	42	6	10	6.0	.990	C-98, OF-6
8 yrs.		682	.241	.353	1929	465	88	7	38	2.0	184	248	248	363	25	54	15	3604	270	49	39	5.8	.988	C-620, OF-16, 3B-8, 1B-1, 2B-1

Darrin Fletcher

FLETCHER, DARRIN GLEN
B. Oct. 3, 1966, Elmhurst, Ill.
BL TR 6′ 2″ 195 lbs.

Year	Team	Games	BA	SA	AB	H	2B	3B	HR	HR%	R	RBI	BB	SO	SB	PINCH HIT AB	H	PO	A	E	DP	TC/G	FA	G by Pos
1989	LA N	5	.500	.875	8	4	0	0	1	12.5	1	2	1	0	0	2	1	16	1	0	0	3.4	1.000	C-5
1990	2 teams	LA N (2G — .000)		PHI N (9G — .136)																				
''	total	11	.130	.174	23	3	1	0	0	0.0	3	1	1	6	0	4	0	30	3	0	0	4.7	1.000	C-7
2 yrs.		16	.226	.355	31	7	1	0	1	3.2	4	3	2	6	0	6	1	46	4	0	0	3.1	.000	C-12

Scott Fletcher

FLETCHER, SCOTT BRIAN
B. July 30, 1958, Fort Walton Beach, Fla.
BR TR 5′ 11″ 168 lbs.

SECOND BASE

Year	Team	Games	BA	SA	AB	H	2B	3B	HR	HR%	R	RBI	BB	SO	SB	PINCH HIT AB	H	PO	A	E	DP	TC/G	FA	G by Pos
April		16	.173	.192	52	9	1	0	0	0.0	7	3	10	12	0									
May		27	.230	.356	87	20	4	2	1	1.1	9	7	10	11	0									
June		27	.275	.374	91	25	4	1	1	1.1	12	7	5	6	0									
July		24	.317	.390	82	26	3	0	1	1.2	11	13	7	9	1									
Aug		25	.220	.220	91	20	0	0	0	0.0	6	11	4	10	0									
Sept/Oct		32	.217	.302	106	23	6	0	1	0.9	9	15	9	15	0									
Day		37	.264	.328	125	33	6	1	0	0.0	13	16	17	12	1									
Night		114	.234	.307	384	90	12	2	4	1.0	41	40	28	51	0									
vs. Left			.283	.324	173	49	4	0	1	0.6	25	13	21	16	1									
vs. Right			.220	.307	336	74	14	3	3	0.9	29	43	24	47	0									

Year	Team	Games	BA	SA	AB	H	2B	3B	HR	HR%	R	RBI	BB	SO	SB	PINCH HIT AB	H	PO	A	E	DP	TC/G	FA	G by Pos

Scott Fletcher *Continued*

On Grass		124	.242	.311	421	102	15	1	4	1.0	45	48	38	54	1									
On Turf		27	.239	.318	88	21	3	2	0	0.0	9	8	7	9	0									
Home		77	.242	.294	265	64	9	1	1	0.4	31	29	20	32	1									
Road		74	.242	.332	244	59	9	2	3	1.2	23	27	25	31	0									
Division Rivals																								
vs. CAL		13	.255	.298	47	12	2	0	0	0.0	6	7	2	5	0									
vs. KC		13	.227	.295	44	10	3	0	0	0.0	6	4	7	4	0									
vs. MIN		13	.209	.233	43	9	1	0	0	0.0	2	1	0	2	0									
vs. OAK		13	.250	.417	48	12	2	0	2	4.2	6	5	2	6	0									
vs. SEA		13	.310	.429	42	13	3	1	0	0.0	7	7	5	4	0									
vs. TEX		12	.227	.273	44	10	1	0	0	0.0	2	4	3	10	0									
On 3B < 2 Out			.308	.385	26	8	2	0	0	0.0	0	22	1	3										
1981	CHI N	19	.217	.304	46	10	4	0	0	0.0	6	1	2	4	0	0	0	34	44	3	10	4.3	.963	2B-13, SS-4, 3B-1
1982		11	.167	.167	24	4	0	0	0	0.0	4	1	4	5	1	0	0	11	23	0	3	3.1	1.000	SS-11
1983		114	.237	.370	262	62	16	5	3	1.1	42	31	29	22	5	0	0	126	308	16	64	3.9	.964	SS-100, 2B-12, 3B-7, DH-1
1984		149	.250	.311	456	114	13	3	3	0.7	46	35	46	46	10	0	0	234	439	19	89	4.6	.973	SS-134, 2B-28, 3B-3
1985		119	.256	.309	301	77	8	1	2	0.7	38	31	35	47	5	12	3	123	208	8	36	2.8	.976	3B-55, SS-44, 2B-37, DH-2
1986	TEX A	147	.300	.400	530	159	34	5	3	0.6	82	50	47	59	12	0	0	216	388	16	93	4.2	.974	SS-136, 3B-12, 2B-11, DH-1
1987		156	.287	.374	588	169	28	4	5	0.9	82	63	61	66	13	3	1	249	413	23	98	4.4	.966	SS-155
1988		140	.276	.328	515	142	19	4	0	0.0	59	47	62	34	8	2	0	215	414	11	90	4.6	.983	SS-139
1989	2 teams	TEX A	(83G — .239)		CHI A	(59G — .272)																		
"	total	142	.253	.311	546	138	25	2	1	0.2	77	43	64	60	2	1	0	241	362	15	88	4.4	.976	SS-89, 2B-53, DH-1
1990	CHI A	151	.242	.312	509	123	18	3	4	0.7	54	56	45	63	1	0	0	305	436	9	115	5.0	.988	2B-151
10 yrs.		1148	.264	.339	3777	998	165	27	21	0.6	490	358	395	406	57	18	4	1754	3035	120	686	4.3	.976	SS-812, 2B-305, 3B-78, DH-5
LEAGUE CHAMPIONSHIP SERIES																								
1983	CHI A	3	.000	.000	7	0	0	0	0	0.0	0	0	1	0	0	0	0	3	8	0	1	3.7	1.000	SS-3

Tom Foley

FOLEY, THOMAS MICHAEL
B. Sept. 9, 1959, Fort Benning, Ga.
BL TR 6' 1" 160 lbs.

1983	CIN N	68	.204	.265	98	20	4	1	0	0.0	7	9	13	17	1	20	4	54	76	2	16	1.9	.985	SS-37, 2B-5
1984		106	.253	.357	277	70	8	3	5	1.8	26	27	24	36	3	13	5	119	228	11	36	3.4	.969	SS-83, 2B-10, 3B-1
1985	2 teams	CIN N	(43G — .196)		PHI N	(46G — .266)																		
"	total	89	.240	.336	250	60	13	1	3	1.2	24	23	19	34	2	12	1	127	202	7	47	3.8	.979	SS-60, 2B-18, 3B-1
1986	2 teams	PHI N	(39G — .295)		MON N	(64G — .257)																		
"		103	.266	.357	263	70	15	3	1	0.4	26	23	30	37	10	22	5	117	190	6	29	3.0	.981	SS-53, 2B-26, 3B-16
1987	MON N	106	.293	.432	280	82	18	3	5	1.8	35	28	11	40	6	24	5	134	190	9	43	3.1	.973	SS-49, 2B-39, 3B-9
1988		127	.265	.377	377	100	21	3	5	1.3	33	43	30	49	2	14	1	204	324	15	61	4.3	.972	2B-89, SS-32, 3B-9
1989		122	.229	.347	375	86	19	2	7	1.9	34	39	45	53	2	12	2	203	317	8	58	4.3	.985	2B-108, 3B-16, SS-14, P-1
1990		73	.213	.238	164	35	2	1	0	0.0	11	12	12	22	0	10	1	80	123	5	26	3.0	.976	SS-45, 2B-20, 3B-7, 1B-1
8 yrs.		794	.251	.353	2084	523	100	17	26	1.2	196	204	184	288	26	127	24	1038	1650	63	316	3.5	.977	SS-373, 2B-315, 3B-59, P-1, 1B-1

Curt Ford

FORD, CURTIS GLENN
B. Oct. 11, 1960, Jackson, Miss.
BL TR 5' 10" 150 lbs.

1985	STL N	11	.500	.667	12	6	2	0	0	0.0	2	3	4	1	1	4	2	3	0	1	0	0.4	.750	OF-4
1986		85	.248	.364	214	53	15	2	2	0.9	30	29	23	29	13	25	5	109	7	3	5	1.4	.975	OF-64
1987		89	.285	.408	228	65	9	5	3	1.3	32	26	14	32	11	18	7	157	2	3	0	1.8	.981	OF-75
1988		91	.195	.266	128	25	6	0	1	0.8	11	18	8	26	6	40	9	95	6	2	5	1.1	.981	OF-40, 1B-7
1989	PHI N	108	.218	.289	142	31	5	1	1	0.7	13	13	16	33	5	62	11	46	5	0	0	0.5	1.000	OF-52, 1B-1, 2B-1
1990		22	.111	.111	18	2	0	0	0	0.0	0	0	1	5	0	17	2	2	0	0	0	0.7	1.000	OF-3
6 yrs.		406	.245	.345	742	182	37	8	7	0.9	88	89	66	126	36	166	36	412	20	9	10	1.1	.980	OF-238, 1B-8, 2B-1
LEAGUE CHAMPIONSHIP SERIES																								
1987	STL N	4	.333	.333	9	3	0	0	0	0.0	2	0	1	1	0	1	1	6	0	0	0	1.5	1.000	OF-4

Year	Team		Games	BA	SA	AB	H	2B	3B	HR	HR%	R	RBI	BB	SO	SB	PINCH HIT AB	H	PO	A	E	DP	TC/G	FA	G by Pos

Curt Ford *Continued*

WORLD SERIES

Year	Team		Games	BA	SA	AB	H	2B	3B	HR	HR%	R	RBI	BB	SO	SB	PH AB	PH H	PO	A	E	DP	TC/G	FA	G by Pos
1987	STL	N	5	.308	.308	13	4	0	0	0	0.0	1	2	1	1	0	1	0	5	0	0	0	1.0	1.000	OF-4

Julio Franco

FRANCO, JULIO CESAR
Born Julio Cesar Robles y Franco.
B. Aug. 23, 1958, Hato Mayor, Dominican Republic
BB TR 6′ 160 lbs.

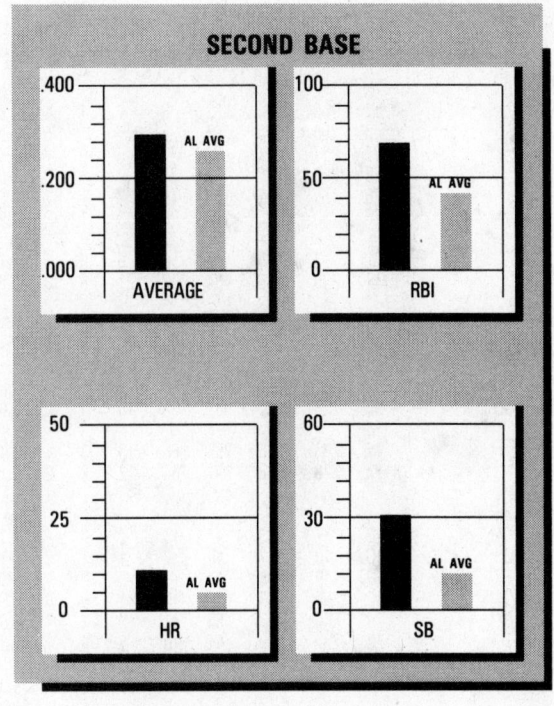

SECOND BASE

	Games	BA	SA	AB	H	2B	3B	HR	HR%	R	RBI	BB	SO	SB	PH AB	PH H	PO	A	E	DP	TC/G	FA	G by Pos
April	20	.247	.333	81	20	4	0	1	1.2	14	10	7	14	2									
May	27	.340	.505	97	33	7	0	3	3.1	15	12	13	17	7									
June	29	.289	.386	114	33	3	1	2	1.8	13	17	12	13	4									
July	23	.314	.419	86	27	6	0	1	1.2	19	9	14	12	5									
Aug	28	.309	.340	97	30	3	0	0	0.0	14	10	17	11	8									
Sept/Oct	30	.271	.421	107	29	4	0	4	3.7	21	11	19	16	5									
Day	27	.266	.426	94	25	4	1	3	3.2	18	15	23	17	7									
Night	130	.301	.398	488	147	23	0	8	1.6	78	54	59	66	24									
vs. Left		.296	.397	179	53	9	0	3	1.7	31	19	31	25	11									
vs. Right		.295	.404	403	119	18	1	8	2.0	65	50	51	58	20									
On Grass	132	.299	.402	485	145	23	0	9	1.9	81	53	68	70	26									
On Turf	25	.278	.402	97	27	4	1	2	2.1	15	16	14	13	5									
Home	81	.317	.409	303	96	16	0	4	1.3	52	27	41	37	17									
Road	76	.272	.394	279	76	11	1	7	2.5	44	42	41	46	14									
Division Rivals																							
vs. CAL	13	.378	.422	45	17	2	0	0	0.0	5	3	7	6	1									
vs. CHI	13	.208	.264	53	11	3	0	0	0.0	6	3	4	11	3									
vs. KC	12	.364	.614	44	16	2	0	3	6.8	14	10	9	7	3									
vs. MIN	13	.255	.314	51	13	3	0	0	0.0	4	9	4	6	3									
vs. OAK	13	.217	.413	46	10	3	0	2	4.3	8	5	10	5	3									
vs. SEA	13	.286	.375	56	16	0	1	1	1.8	8	5	4	8	3									
On 3B < 2 Out		.320	.440	25	8	0	0	1	4.0	1	21	4	2										

Year	Team		Games	BA	SA	AB	H	2B	3B	HR	HR%	R	RBI	BB	SO	SB	PH AB	PH H	PO	A	E	DP	TC/G	FA	G by Pos
1982	PHI	N	16	.276	.310	29	8	1	0	0	0.0	3	3	2	4	0	0	0	8	25	0	2	2.1	1.000	SS-11, 3B-2
1983	CLE	A	149	.273	.388	560	153	24	8	8	1.4	68	80	27	50	32	0	0	247	438	28	92	4.8	.961	SS-149
1984			160	.286	.348	658	188	22	5	3	0.5	82	79	43	68	19	0	0	280	481	36	116	5.0	.955	SS-159, DH-1
1985			160	.288	.381	636	183	33	4	6	0.9	97	90	54	74	13	2	0	252	437	36	99	4.5	.950	SS-151, 2B-8, DH-1
1986			149	.306	.422	599	183	30	5	10	1.7	80	74	32	66	10	1	0	248	413	19	90	4.6	.972	SS-134, 2B-13, DH-3
1987			128	.319	.428	495	158	24	3	8	1.6	86	52	57	56	32	1	1	175	313	18	56	4.0	.964	SS-111, 2B-9, DH-8
1988			152	.303	.409	613	186	23	6	10	1.6	88	54	56	72	25	0	0	310	434	14	87	5.0	.982	2B-151, DH-1
1989	TEX	A	150	.316	.462	548	173	31	5	13	2.4	80	92	66	69	21	1	1	256	386	13	70	4.4	.980	2B-140, DH-10
1990			157	.296	.402	582	172	27	1	11	1.8	96	69	82	83	31	1	1	310	444	19	101	5.1	.975	2B-152, DH-3
9 yrs.			1221	.297	.403	4720	1404	215	37	69	1.5	680	593	419	542	183	6	3	2086	3371	183	713	4.6	.968	SS-715, 2B-473, DH-27, 3B-2

Terry Francona

FRANCONA, TERRY JON
Son of Tito Francona.
B. Apr. 22, 1959, Aberdeen, S. D.
BL TL 6′ 1″ 190 lbs.

Year	Team		Games	BA	SA	AB	H	2B	3B	HR	HR%	R	RBI	BB	SO	SB	PH AB	PH H	PO	A	E	DP	TC/G	FA	G by Pos
1981	MON	N	34	.274	.326	95	26	0	1	1	1.1	11	8	5	6	1	10	5	41	5	0	0	1.4	1.000	OF-26, 1B-1
1982			46	.321	.344	131	42	3	0	0	0.0	14	9	8	11	2	7	2	65	0	3	2	1.5	.956	OF-33, 1B-16
1983			120	.257	.352	230	59	11	1	3	1.3	21	22	6	20	1	38	8	172	10	3	10	1.5	.984	OF-51, 1B-47
1984			58	.346	.467	214	74	19	2	1	0.5	18	18	5	12	0	3	0	431	50	3	43	8.3	.994	1B-50, OF-6
1985			107	.267	.349	281	75	15	1	2	0.7	19	31	12	12	5	31	6	431	40	6	32	4.5	.987	1B-57, OF-28, 3B-1
1986	CHI	N	86	.250	.323	124	31	3	0	2	1.6	13	8	6	8	0	42	8	123	7	0	9	1.5	1.000	OF-30, 1B-23
1987	CIN	N	102	.227	.295	207	47	5	0	3	1.4	16	12	10	12	2	43	11	377	45	2	38	4.2	.995	1B-57, OF-8
1988	CLE	A	62	.311	.363	212	66	8	0	1	0.5	24	12	5	18	0	15	5	47	5	1	3	0.9	.981	DH-38, 1B-5, OF-5
1989	MIL	A	90	.232	.322	233	54	10	1	3	1.3	26	23	8	20	2	8	1	339	26	4	32	4.1	.989	1B-46, DH-28, OF-16, P-1
1990			3	.000	.000	4	0	0	0	0	0.0	1	0	0	0	0	0	0	6	0	0	1	3.0	1.000	1B-2, DH-1
10 yrs.			708	.274	.351	1731	474	74	6	16	0.9	163	143	65	119	12	197	46	2032	188	22	170	3.2	.990	1B-304, OF-203, DH-67, P-1, 3B-1

DIVISIONAL PLAYOFF SERIES

Year	Team		Games	BA	SA	AB	H	2B	3B	HR	HR%	R	RBI	BB	SO	SB	PH AB	PH H	PO	A	E	DP	TC/G	FA	G by Pos
1981	MON	N	5	.333	.333	12	4	0	0	0	0.0	0	0	2	2	2	0	0	0	0	0	0	0.0	—	OF-5

LEAGUE CHAMPIONSHIP SERIES

Year	Team		Games	BA	SA	AB	H	2B	3B	HR	HR%	R	RBI	BB	SO	SB	PH AB	PH H	PO	A	E	DP	TC/G	FA	G by Pos
1981	MON	N	2	.000	.000	1	0	0	0	0	0.0	0	0	1	0	0	0	0	0	0	0	0	0.0	—	OF-1

Year	Team		Games	BA	SA	AB	H	2B	3B	HR	HR%	R	RBI	BB	SO	SB	PINCH HIT AB	H	PO	A	E	DP	TC/G	FA	G by Pos

Travis Fryman

FRYMAN, DAVID TRAVIS
B. Mar. 25, 1969, Lexington, Ky.
BR TR 6′ 1″ 180 lbs.

| 1990 | DET | A | 66 | .297 | .470 | 232 | 69 | 11 | 1 | 9 | 3.8 | 32 | 27 | 17 | 51 | 3 | 1 | 0 | 47 | 145 | 14 | 21 | 3.2 | .932 | 3B-48, SS-17, DH-1 |

Gary Gaetti

GAETTI, GARY JOSEPH
B. Aug. 19, 1958, Centralia, Ill.
BR TR 6′ 180 lbs.

Year/Split			Games	BA	SA	AB	H	2B	3B	HR	HR%	R	RBI	BB	SO	SB	PH AB	H	PO	A	E	DP	TC/G	FA	G by Pos
April			17	.258	.371	62	16	2	1	1	1.6	5	5	7	13	0									
May			28	.258	.505	97	25	7	1	5	5.2	16	26	7	17	3									
June			27	.227	.371	97	22	5	0	3	3.1	10	11	4	19	0									
July			28	.250	.426	108	27	8	1	3	2.8	12	19	12	15	0									
Aug			26	.158	.257	101	16	2	1	2	2.0	10	8	3	20	1									
Sept/Oct			28	.232	.330	112	26	3	1	2	1.8	8	16	3	17	2									
Day			37	.210	.315	143	30	6	0	3	2.1	17	21	10	28	2									
Night			117	.235	.396	434	102	21	5	13	3.0	44	64	26	73	4									
vs. Left				.223	.361	166	37	8	0	5	3.0	21	18	14	28	3									
vs. Right				.231	.382	411	95	19	5	11	2.7	40	67	22	73	3									
On Grass			58	.231	.366	216	50	9	1	6	2.8	13	33	18	42	4									
On Turf			96	.227	.382	361	82	18	4	10	2.8	48	52	18	59	2									
Home			77	.238	.385	286	68	15	3	7	2.4	38	43	16	40	1									
Road			77	.220	.368	291	64	12	2	9	3.1	23	42	20	61	5									
Division Rivals																									
vs. CAL			12	.277	.383	47	13	2	0	1	2.1	4	7	3	9	0									
vs. CHI			13	.143	.327	49	7	1	1	2	4.1	6	5	2	12	0									
vs. KC			13	.149	.255	47	7	2	0	1	2.1	2	3	3	9	1									
vs. OAK			13	.250	.269	52	13	1	0	0	0.0	3	5	3	5	0									
vs. SEA			13	.200	.382	55	11	2	1	2	3.6	9	6	2	12	0									
vs. TEX			12	.227	.318	44	10	1	0	1	2.3	5	7	2	8	0									
On 3B < 2 Out				.188	.438	32	6	2	0	2	6.3	2	31	2	7										
1981	MIN	A	9	.192	.423	26	5	0	0	2	7.7	4	3	0	6	0	0	0	5	17	0	1	2.4	1.000	3B-8, DH-1
1982			145	.230	.443	508	117	25	4	25	4.9	59	84	37	107	0	1	0	106	291	17	36	2.9	.959	3B-142, SS-2
1983			157	.245	.414	584	143	30	3	21	3.6	81	78	54	121	7	2	1	131	361	17	46	3.2	.967	3B-154, SS-3, DH-1
1984			162	.262	.350	588	154	29	4	5	0.9	55	65	44	81	11	0	0	163	335	21	27	3.2	.960	3B-154, OF-8, SS-2
1985			160	.246	.409	560	138	31	0	20	3.6	71	63	37	89	13	1	0	162	316	18	31	3.1	.964	3B-156, OF-4, DH-1, 1B-1
1986			157	.287	.518	596	171	34	1	34	5.7	91	108	52	108	14	1	0	120	335	21	36	3.0	.956	3B-156, SS-2, 2B-1, OF-1
1987			154	.257	.485	584	150	36	2	31	5.3	95	109	37	92	10	3	2	134	261	11	28	2.6	.973	3B-150, DH-2
1988			133	.301	.551	468	141	29	2	28	6.0	66	88	36	85	7	14	4	105	191	7	24	2.3	.977	3B-115, DH-5, SS-2
1989			130	.251	.404	498	125	11	4	19	3.8	63	75	25	87	6	3	1	115	253	10	24	2.9	.974	3B-125, DH-3, 1B-2
1990			154	.229	.376	577	132	27	5	16	2.7	61	85	36	101	6	2	0	125	319	18	36	3.0	.961	3B-151, 1B-2, SS-2
10 yrs.			1361	.256	.437	4989	1276	252	25	201	4.0	646	758	358	877	74	27	8	1166	2679	140	289	2.9	.965	3B-1311, DH-13, SS-13, OF-13, 1B-5, 2B-1

LEAGUE CHAMPIONSHIP SERIES

| 1987 | MIN | A | 5 | .300 | .650 | 20 | 6 | 1 | 0 | 2 | 10.0 | 5 | 5 | 1 | 3 | 0 | 0 | 0 | 8 | 7 | 0 | 1 | 3.0 | 1.000 | 3B-5 |

WORLD SERIES

| 1987 | MIN | A | 7 | .259 | .519 | 27 | 7 | 2 | 1 | 1 | 3.7 | 4 | 4 | 2 | 5 | 2 | 0 | 0 | 6 | 15 | 0 | 1 | 3.0 | 1.000 | 3B-7 |

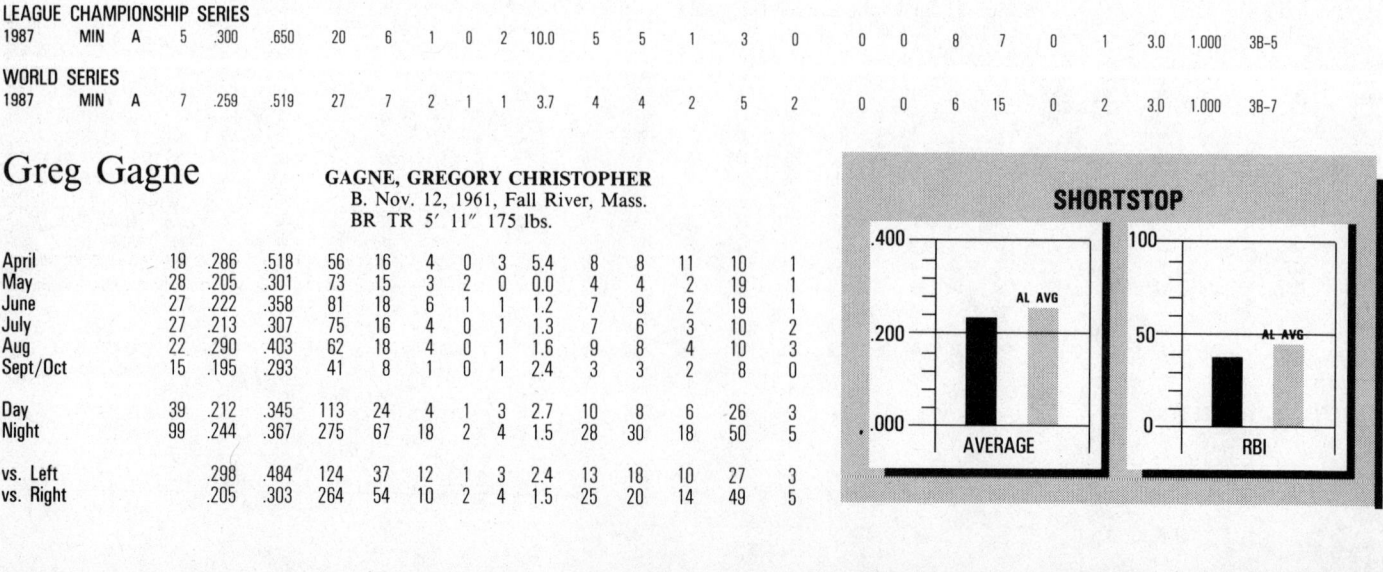

Greg Gagne

GAGNE, GREGORY CHRISTOPHER
B. Nov. 12, 1961, Fall River, Mass.
BR TR 5′ 11″ 175 lbs.

Split	Games	BA	SA	AB	H	2B	3B	HR	HR%	R	RBI	BB	SO	SB
April	19	.286	.518	56	16	4	0	3	5.4	8	8	11	10	1
May	28	.205	.301	73	15	3	2	0	0.0	4	4	2	19	1
June	27	.222	.358	81	18	6	1	1	1.2	7	9	2	19	1
July	27	.213	.307	75	16	4	0	1	1.3	7	6	3	10	2
Aug	22	.290	.403	62	18	4	0	1	1.6	9	8	4	10	3
Sept/Oct	15	.195	.293	41	8	1	0	1	2.4	3	3	2	8	0
Day	39	.212	.345	113	24	4	1	3	2.7	10	8	6	26	3
Night	99	.244	.367	275	67	18	2	4	1.5	28	30	18	50	5
vs. Left		.298	.484	124	37	12	1	3	2.4	13	18	10	27	3
vs. Right		.205	.303	264	54	10	2	4	1.5	25	20	14	49	5

Year	Team	Games	BA	SA	AB	H	2B	3B	HR	HR%	R	RBI	BB	SO	SB	PINCH HIT AB	PINCH HIT H	PO	A	E	DP	TC/G	FA	G by Pos

Greg Gagne *Continued*

Year	Team	Games	BA	SA	AB	H	2B	3B	HR	HR%	R	RBI	BB	SO	SB	PH AB	PH H	PO	A	E	DP	TC/G	FA	G by Pos
On Grass		54	.239	.344	163	39	9	1	2	1.2	14	13	8	26	0									
On Turf		84	.231	.373	225	52	13	2	5	2.2	24	25	16	50	8									
Home		69	.247	.390	182	45	13	2	3	1.6	20	20	13	37	7									
Road		69	.223	.335	206	46	9	1	4	1.9	18	18	11	39	1									
Division Rivals																								
vs. CAL		10	.440	.480	25	11	1	0	0	0.0	3	4	7	3	1									
vs. CHI		12	.314	.543	35	11	3	1	1	2.9	5	5	1	4	3									
vs. KC		10	.250	.292	24	6	1	0	0	0.0	1	3	2	5	1									
vs. OAK		11	.184	.316	38	7	2	0	1	2.6	2	5	0	6	0									
vs. SEA		9	.192	.346	26	5	1	0	1	3.8	3	1	2	9	1									
vs. TEX		12	.237	.368	38	9	5	0	0	0.0	4	3	0	9	0									
On 3B < 2 Out			.375	.438	16	6	1	0	0	0.0	0	15	2	2										
1983	MIN A	10	.111	.148	27	3	1	0	0	0.0	2	3	0	6	0	0	0	10	14	2	2	2.6	.923	SS-10
1984		2	.000	.000	1	0	0	0	0	0.0	0	0	0	0	0	1	0	0	0	0	0	0.0	—	
1985		114	.225	.317	293	66	15	3	2	0.7	37	23	20	57	10	4	1	149	269	14	48	3.8	.968	SS-106, DH-5
1986		156	.250	.398	472	118	22	6	12	2.5	63	54	30	108	12	0	0	228	381	26	96	4.1	.959	SS-155, 2B-4
1987		137	.265	.430	437	116	28	7	10	2.3	68	40	25	84	6	0	0	196	391	18	75	4.4	.970	SS-136, OF-4, 2B-1
1988		149	.236	.397	461	109	20	6	14	3.0	70	48	27	110	15	1	0	202	373	18	79	4.0	.970	SS-146, OF-2, 2B-1, 3B-1
1989		149	.272	.424	460	125	29	7	9	2.0	69	48	17	80	11	5	0	218	389	18	66	4.2	.971	SS-146, OF-1
1990		138	.235	.361	388	91	22	3	7	1.8	38	38	24	76	8	2	0	184	377	14	62	4.2	.976	SS-135, DH-2, OF-1
8 yrs.		855	.247	.390	2539	628	137	32	54	2.1	347	254	143	521	62	13	1	1187	2194	110	428	4.1	.968	SS-834, OF-8, DH-7, 2B-6, 3B-1
LEAGUE CHAMPIONSHIP SERIES																								
1987	MIN A	5	.278	.778	18	5	3	0	2	11.1	5	3	3	4	0	0	0	9	13	2	2	4.8	.917	SS-5
WORLD SERIES																								
1987	MIN A	7	.200	.333	30	6	1	0	1	3.3	5	3	1	6	0	0	0	6	20	2	2	4.0	.929	SS-7

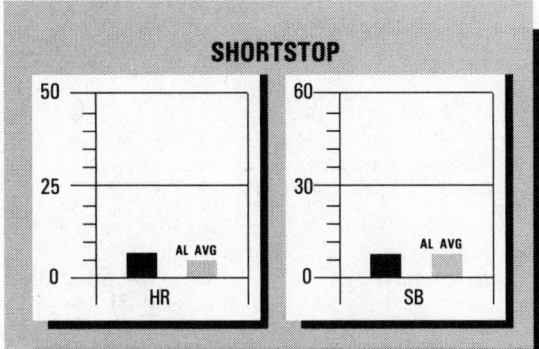

SHORTSTOP — HR (AL AVG), SB (AL AVG)

Andres Galarraga

GALARRAGA, ANDRES JOSE (Big Cat)
Born Andres Jose Padovani y Galarraga.
B. June 18, 1961, Caracas, Venezuela
BR TR 6' 3" 235 lbs.

Year	Team	Games	BA	SA	AB	H	2B	3B	HR	HR%	R	RBI	BB	SO	SB	PH AB	PH H	PO	A	E	DP	TC/G	FA	G by Pos
April		19	.227	.318	66	15	3	0	1	1.5	6	6	11	20	1									
May		26	.286	.459	98	28	5	0	4	4.1	13	19	6	27	2									
June		28	.250	.337	104	26	6	0	1	1.0	10	10	5	28	0									
July		26	.265	.520	98	26	7	0	6	6.1	13	21	5	28	1									
Aug		25	.204	.344	93	19	4	0	4	4.3	11	10	5	32	1									
Sept/Oct		31	.283	.442	120	34	7	0	4	3.3	12	21	8	34	5									
Day		46	.207	.366	164	34	5	0	7	4.3	17	23	15	56	4									
Night		109	.275	.427	415	114	24	0	13	3.1	48	64	25	113	6									
vs. Left			.226	.392	217	49	9	0	9	4.1	23	35	11	62	0									
vs. Right			.273	.420	362	99	20	0	11	3.0	42	52	29	107	10									
On Grass		40	.218	.374	147	32	2	0	7	4.8	20	25	9	44	3									
On Turf		115	.269	.421	432	116	27	0	13	3.0	45	62	31	125	7									
Home		78	.266	.399	286	76	20	0	6	2.1	31	42	21	82	6									
Road		77	.246	.420	293	72	9	0	14	4.8	34	45	19	87	4									
Division Rivals																								
vs. CHI		17	.180	.246	61	11	1	0	1	1.6	5	6	3	16	0									
vs. NY		17	.239	.388	67	16	1	0	3	4.5	7	9	3	20	4									
vs. PHI		16	.311	.443	61	19	5	0	1	1.6	3	10	6	16	1									
vs. PIT		18	.274	.397	73	20	3	0	2	2.7	10	7	4	27	0									
vs. STL		18	.258	.318	66	17	4	0	0	0.0	9	10	5	15	1									
On 3B < 2 Out			.323	.419	31	10	0	0	1	3.2	1	26	2	7										
1985	MON N	24	.187	.280	75	14	1	0	2	2.7	9	4	3	18	1	2	1	173	22	1	14	8.2	.995	1B-23
1986		105	.271	.405	321	87	13	0	10	3.1	39	42	30	79	6	7	1	805	40	4	59	8.1	.995	1B-102
1987		147	.305	.459	551	168	40	3	13	2.4	72	90	41	127	7	1	0	1300	103	10	96	9.6	.993	1B-146
1988		157	.302	.540	609	**184**	**42**	8	29	4.8	99	92	39	**153**	13	2	1	1464	103	15	124	10.1	.991	1B-156
1989		152	.257	.434	572	147	30	1	23	4.0	76	85	48	**158**	12	6	1	1335	91	11	97	9.5	.992	1B-147
1990		155	.256	.409	579	148	29	0	20	3.4	65	87	40	**169**	10	7	0	1300	94	10	93	9.1	.993	1B-154
6 yrs.		740	.276	.450	2707	748	155	12	97	3.6	360	400	201	704	49	25	4	6377	453	51	483	9.3	.993	1B-728

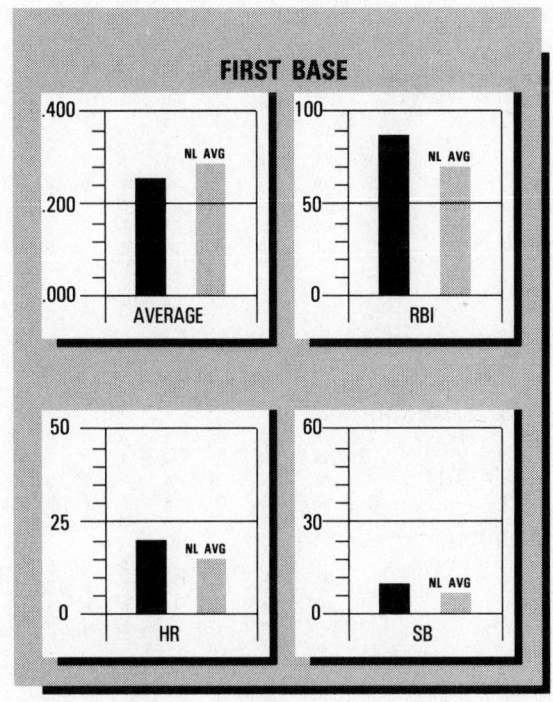

FIRST BASE — AVERAGE (NL AVG), RBI (NL AVG), HR (NL AVG), SB (NL AVG)

Year	Team		Games	BA	SA	AB	H	2B	3B	HR	HR%	R	RBI	BB	SO	SB	PINCH HIT AB	H	PO	A	E	DP	TC/G	FA	G by Pos

Dave Gallagher

GALLAGHER, DAVID THOMAS
B. Sept. 20, 1960, Trenton, N. J.
BR TR 6′ 180 lbs.

1987	CLE	A	15	.111	.194	36	4	1	1	0	0.0	2	1	2	5	2	0	0	34	1	1	1	2.4	.972	OF–14
1988	CHI	A	101	.303	.406	347	105	15	3	5	1.4	59	31	29	40	5	11	2	228	5	0	2	2.3	1.000	OF–95, DH–2
1989			161	.266	.314	601	160	22	2	1	0.2	74	46	46	79	5	2	0	390	8	3	4	2.5	.993	OF–160, DH–1
1990	2 teams					CHI A (45G — .280)			BAL A (23G — .216)																	
"	total		68	.254	.302	126	32	4	1	0	0.0	12	7	7	12	1	10	2	96	3	2	2	1.8	.980	OF–57, DH–6
4 yrs.			345	.271	.338	1110	301	42	7	6	0.5	147	85	84	136	13	23	4	748	17	6	9	2.2	.992	OF–326, DH–9

Mike Gallego

GALLEGO, MICHAEL ANTHONY
B. Oct. 31, 1960, Whittier, Calif.
BR TR 5′ 8″ 160 lbs.

April			18	.091	.182	44	4	1	0	1	2.3	3	4	5	4	0
May			22	.281	.421	57	16	4	2	0	0.0	5	8	6	10	1
June			21	.246	.281	57	14	2	0	0	0.0	6	5	4	9	0
July			30	.204	.290	93	19	5	0	1	1.1	8	9	5	8	1
Aug			22	.212	.258	66	14	0	0	1	1.5	6	7	9	3	2
Sept/Oct			27	.181	.194	72	13	1	0	0	0.0	8	1	6	16	1
Day			56	.201	.242	149	30	4	1	0	0.0	14	13	17	19	2
Night			84	.208	.292	240	50	9	1	3	1.3	22	21	18	31	3
vs. Left				.180	.242	128	23	5	0	1	0.8	8	9	9	19	2
vs. Right				.218	.287	261	57	8	2	2	0.8	28	25	26	31	3
On Grass			117	.216	.275	324	70	9	2	2	0.6	30	27	31	36	5
On Turf			23	.154	.262	65	10	4	0	1	1.5	6	7	4	14	0
Home			69	.214	.262	187	40	4	1	1	0.5	14	14	24	20	4
Road			71	.198	.282	202	40	9	1	2	1.0	22	20	11	30	1
Division Rivals																
vs. CAL			12	.275	.400	40	11	2	0	1	2.5	4	4	1	4	0
vs. CHI			9	.296	.407	27	8	0	0	1	3.7	3	2	2	2	0
vs. KC			12	.188	.188	32	6	0	0	0	0.0	0	3	3	5	1
vs. MIN			11	.118	.176	34	4	2	0	0	0.0	2	2	3	7	0
vs. SEA			13	.111	.222	36	4	1	0	1	2.8	3	3	6	4	0
vs. TEX			11	.206	.206	34	7	0	0	0	0.0	6	0	4	7	1
On 3B < 2 Out				.278	.333	18	5	1	0	0	0.0	0	14	2	1

SECOND BASE — AVERAGE / RBI / HR / SB (with AL AVG)

1985	OAK	A	76	.208	.338	77	16	5	1	1	1.3	13	9	12	14	1	2	0	57	94	1	25	2.0	.993	2B–42, SS–21, 3B–12
1986			20	.270	.324	37	10	2	0	0	0.0	2	4	1	6	0	0	0	24	51	1	6	3.8	.987	2B–19, 3B–2, SS–1
1987			72	.250	.347	124	31	6	0	2	1.6	18	14	12	21	0	4	1	75	122	8	29	2.8	.961	2B–31, 3B–24, SS–17
1988			129	.209	.260	277	58	8	0	2	0.7	38	20	34	53	2	3	0	155	254	8	49	3.2	.981	2B–83, SS–42, 3B–16
1989			133	.252	.328	357	90	14	2	3	0.8	45	30	35	43	7	2	0	211	363	19	86	4.5	.968	SS–94, 2B–41, 3B–3, DH–1
1990			140	.206	.272	389	80	13	2	3	0.7	36	34	35	50	5	2	1	207	379	13	78	4.3	.978	2B–83, SS–38, 3B–27, DH–1, OF–1
6 yrs.			570	.226	.298	1261	285	48	5	11	0.9	152	111	129	187	15	13	2	729	1263	50	273	3.6	.976	2B–299, SS–213, 3B–84, DH–2, OF–1

LEAGUE CHAMPIONSHIP SERIES

1988	OAK	A	4	.083	.083	12	1	0	0	0	0.0	1	0	0	3	0	0	0	7	6	0	4	3.3	1.000	2B–4
1989			4	.273	.364	11	3	1	0	0	0.0	3	1	0	2	0	0	0	6	14	0	2	5.0	1.000	2B–2, SS–2
1990			4	.400	.500	10	4	1	0	0	0.0	1	2	1	1	0	0	0	8	10	0	2	4.5	1.000	SS–3, 2B–2
3 yrs.			12	.242	.303	33	8	2	0	0	0.0	5	3	1	6	0	0	0	21	30	0	8	4.3	.000	2B–8, SS–5

WORLD SERIES

1988	OAK	A	1	—	—	0	0	0	0	0	—	0	0	0	0	0	0	0	0	0	0	0	0.0	—	2B–1
1989			2	.000	.000	1	0	0	0	0	0.0	0	0	0	0	0	1	0	0	0	0	0	0.0	—	2B–1, 3B–1
1990			4	.091	.091	11	1	0	0	0	0.0	0	1	1	3	1	0	0	7	10	1	3	4.5	.944	SS–4
3 yrs.			7	.083	.083	12	1	0	0	0	0.0	0	1	1	3	1	1	0	7	10	1	3	2.6	.944	SS–4, 2B–2, 3B–1

Year	Team	Games	BA	SA	AB	H	2B	3B	HR	HR%	R	RBI	BB	SO	SB	PINCH HIT AB	PINCH HIT H	PO	A	E	DP	TC/G	FA	G by Pos

Ron Gant

GANT, RONALD EDWIN
B. Mar. 2, 1965, Victoria, Tex.
BR TR 6′ 172 lbs.

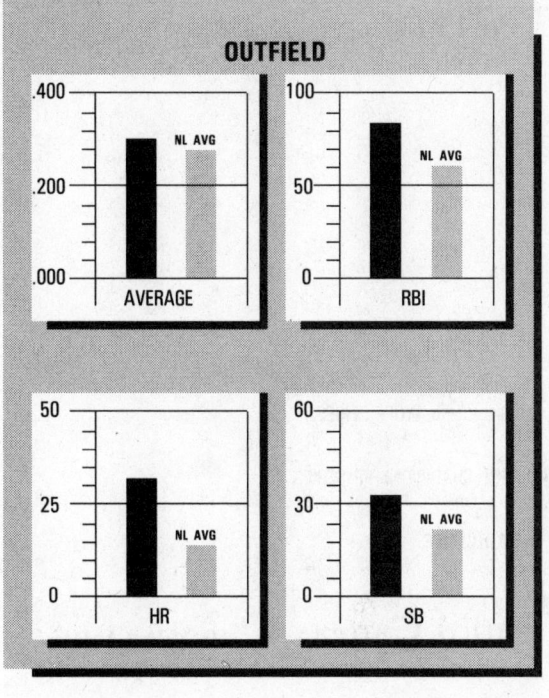

OUTFIELD
AVERAGE — NL AVG
RBI — NL AVG
HR — NL AVG
SB — NL AVG

Split	Games	BA	SA	AB	H	2B	3B	HR	HR%	R	RBI	BB	SO	SB	PO	A	E	DP
April	12	.200	.280	25	5	2	0	0	0.0	4	1	2	3	1				
May	24	.355	.645	93	33	6	0	7	7.5	22	14	6	14	6				
June	27	.306	.611	108	33	7	1	8	7.4	18	18	11	13	1				
July	29	.250	.431	116	29	6	0	5	4.3	21	17	8	20	6				
Aug	30	.316	.553	114	36	8	2	5	4.4	20	13	11	14	9				
Sept/Oct	30	.319	.538	119	38	5	0	7	5.9	22	21	12	22	10				
Day	36	.299	.530	134	40	5	1	8	6.0	27	23	13	23	8				
Night	116	.304	.542	441	134	29	2	24	5.4	80	61	37	63	25				
vs. Left		.299	.520	204	61	15	0	10	4.9	43	32	21	20	10				
vs. Right		.305	.550	371	113	19	3	22	5.9	64	52	29	66	23				
On Grass	115	.305	.538	429	131	20	1	26	6.1	84	68	40	65	22				
On Turf	37	.295	.541	146	43	14	2	6	4.1	23	16	10	21	11				
Home	77	.313	.559	288	90	15	1	18	6.3	57	47	22	37	13				
Road	75	.293	.519	287	84	19	2	14	4.9	50	37	28	49	20				
Division Rivals																		
vs. CIN	18	.295	.656	61	18	5	1	5	8.2	12	13	5	9	2				
vs. HOU	14	.286	.411	56	16	5	1	0	0.0	6	7	4	6	6				
vs. LA	18	.265	.426	68	18	2	0	3	4.4	10	6	3	12	3				
vs. SD	18	.300	.543	70	21	5	0	4	5.7	13	9	12	13	3				
vs. SF	18	.313	.531	64	20	2	0	4	6.3	13	12	8	9	6				
On 3B < 2 Out		.357	.429	28	10	2	0	0	0.0	0	19	3	7					

Year	Team	Games	BA	SA	AB	H	2B	3B	HR	HR%	R	RBI	BB	SO	SB	PH AB	PH H	PO	A	E	DP	TC/G	FA	G by Pos
1987	ATL N	21	.265	.386	83	22	4	0	2	2.4	9	9	1	11	4	1	0	45	59	3	17	5.1	.972	2B-20
1988		146	.259	.439	563	146	28	8	19	3.4	85	60	46	118	19	2	0	316	417	31	88	5.2	.959	2B-122, 3B-22
1989		75	.177	.335	260	46	8	3	9	3.5	26	25	20	63	9	8	1	70	103	17	8	2.5	.911	3B-53, OF-14
1990		152	.303	.539	575	174	34	3	32	5.5	107	84	50	86	33	10	2	357	7	8	2	2.5	.978	OF-146
4 yrs.		394	.262	.456	1481	388	74	14	62	4.2	227	178	117	278	65	21	3	788	586	59	115	3.6	.959	OF-160, 2B-142, 3B-75

Jim Gantner

GANTNER, JAMES ELMER
B. Jan. 5, 1953, Fond du Lac, Wis.
BL TR 6′ 180 lbs.

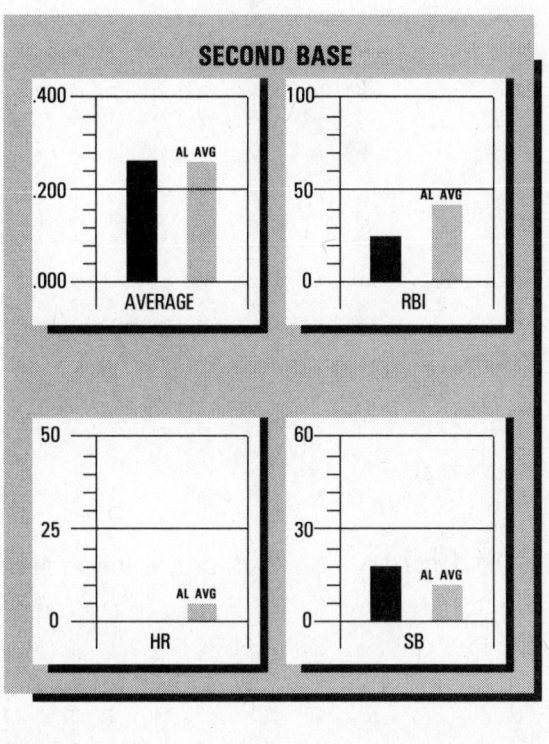

SECOND BASE
AVERAGE — AL AVG
RBI — AL AVG
HR — AL AVG
SB — AL AVG

Split	Games	BA	SA	AB	H	2B	3B	HR	HR%	R	RBI	BB	SO	SB	PO	A	E	DP
April				0	0	0	0	0		0	0	0	0	0				
May				0	0	0	0	0		0	0	0	0	0				
June	10	.273	.303	33	9	1	0	0	0.0	5	2	5	2	2				
July	25	.229	.240	96	22	1	0	0	0.0	11	10	12	7	5				
Aug	24	.292	.371	89	26	1	3	0	0.0	6	9	3	5	5				
Sept/Oct	29	.267	.352	105	28	5	2	0	0.0	14	4	9	5	6				
Day	22	.250	.275	80	20	2	0	0	0.0	6	10	6	3	1				
Night	66	.267	.333	243	65	6	5	0	0.0	30	15	23	16	17				
vs. Left		.307	.330	88	27	1	0	0	0.0	12	9	12	6	8				
vs. Right		.247	.315	235	58	6	5	0	0.0	24	16	17	13	10				
On Grass	77	.272	.323	279	76	8	3	0	0.0	34	19	27	16	18				
On Turf	11	.205	.295	44	9	0	2	0	0.0	2	6	2	3	0				
Home	44	.278	.310	158	44	5	0	0	0.0	22	12	17	9	12				
Road	44	.248	.327	165	41	3	5	0	0.0	14	13	12	10	6				
Division Rivals																		
vs. BAL	6	.182	.227	22	4	1	0	0	0.0	2	0	1	1	0				
vs. BOS	6	.182	.273	22	4	0	1	0	0.0	2	1	0	0	1				
vs. CLE	9	.375	.438	32	12	1	0	0	0.0	6	2	4	3	4				
vs. DET	6	.368	.368	19	7	0	0	0	0.0	1	1	1	0	3				
vs. NY	10	.306	.389	36	11	1	1	0	0.0	3	2	3	1	3				
vs. TOR	6	.208	.250	24	5	1	0	0	0.0	4	1	2	0	1				
On 3B < 2 Out		.211	.263	19	4	1	0	0	0.0	0	10	2	2					

Year	Team	Games	BA	SA	AB	H	2B	3B	HR	HR%	R	RBI	BB	SO	SB	PH AB	PH H	PO	A	E	DP	TC/G	FA	G by Pos
1976	MIL A	26	.246	.261	69	17	1	0	0	0.0	6	7	6	11	1	1	0	17	37	1	3	2.1	.982	3B-24, DH-2
1977		14	.298	.383	47	14	1	0	1	2.1	4	2	2	5	2	1	1	8	29	4	3	2.9	.902	3B-14
1978		43	.216	.258	97	21	1	0	1	1.0	14	8	6	10	2	4	1	46	82	5	13	3.1	.962	2B-21, 3B-15, 1B-1, SS-1
1979		70	.284	.389	208	59	10	3	2	1.0	29	22	16	17	3	0	0	80	161	7	26	3.5	.972	3B-42, 2B-22, SS-3, P-1
1980		132	.282	.376	415	117	21	3	4	1.0	47	40	30	29	11	2	0	159	335	15	70	3.9	.971	3B-69, 2B-66, SS-1

Year	Team	Games	BA	SA	AB	H	2B	3B	HR	HR%	R	RBI	BB	SO	SB	PINCH HIT AB	H	PO	A	E	DP	TC/G	FA	G by Pos

Jim Gantner *Continued*

Year	Team	Games	BA	SA	AB	H	2B	3B	HR	HR%	R	RBI	BB	SO	SB	PH AB	PH H	PO	A	E	DP	TC/G	FA	G by Pos
1981		107	.267	.330	352	94	14	1	2	0.6	35	33	29	29	3	3	0	251	352	10	95	5.7	.984	2B-107
1982		132	.295	.369	447	132	17	2	4	0.9	48	43	26	36	6	4	1	307	398	13	104	5.4	.982	2B-131
1983		161	.282	.401	603	170	23	8	11	1.8	85	74	38	46	5	3	0	374	512	14	128	5.6	.984	2B-158
1984		153	.282	.344	613	173	27	1	3	0.5	61	56	30	51	6	2	1	362	469	13	111	5.5	.985	2B-153
1985		143	.254	.327	523	133	15	4	5	1.0	63	44	33	42	11	1	1	278	436	11	94	5.1	.985	2B-124, 3B-24, SS-1
1986		139	.274	.370	497	136	25	1	7	1.4	58	38	26	50	13	2	0	309	353	10	87	4.8	.985	2B-135, 3B-3, DH-1, SS-1
1987		81	.272	.370	265	72	14	0	4	1.5	37	30	19	22	6	3	1	119	193	6	44	3.9	.981	2B-57, 3B-38, DH-1
1988		155	.276	.336	539	149	28	2	0	0.0	67	47	34	50	20	2	1	325	430	11	92	4.9	.986	2B-154, 3B-1
1989		116	.274	.333	409	112	18	3	0	0.0	51	34	21	33	20	1	0	241	362	8	88	5.3	.987	2B-114, DH-2
1990		88	.263	.319	323	85	8	5	0	0.0	36	25	29	19	18	0	0	167	240	9	56	4.7	.978	2B-80, 3B-9
15 yrs.		1560	.274	.352	5407	1484	223	33	44	0.8	641	503	344	450	127	29	7	3043	4389	137	1014	4.9	.982	2B-1322, 3B-239, SS-7, DH-6, P-1, 1B-1

DIVISIONAL PLAYOFF SERIES

Year	Team	Games	BA	SA	AB	H	2B	3B	HR	HR%	R	RBI	BB	SO	SB	PH AB	PH H	PO	A	E	DP	TC/G	FA	G by Pos
1981	MIL A	4	.143	.214	14	2	1	0	0	0.0	1	0	0	2	0	0	0	3	15	2	0	5.0	.900	2B-4

LEAGUE CHAMPIONSHIP SERIES

Year	Team	Games	BA	SA	AB	H	2B	3B	HR	HR%	R	RBI	BB	SO	SB	PH AB	PH H	PO	A	E	DP	TC/G	FA	G by Pos
1982	MIL A	5	.188	.188	16	3	0	0	0	0.0	1	2	1	1	0	0	0	12	8	0	4	4.0	1.000	2B-5

WORLD SERIES

Year	Team	Games	BA	SA	AB	H	2B	3B	HR	HR%	R	RBI	BB	SO	SB	PH AB	PH H	PO	A	E	DP	TC/G	FA	G by Pos
1982	MIL A	7	.333	.583	24	8	4	1	0	0.0	5	4	1	1	0	0	0	9	33	5	2	6.7	.894	2B-7

Carlos Garcia

GARCIA, CARLOS JESUS
B. Oct. 15, 1967, Tachira, Venezuela
BR TR 6' 1" 185 lbs.

Year	Team	Games	BA	SA	AB	H	2B	3B	HR	HR%	R	RBI	BB	SO	SB	PH AB	PH H	PO	A	E	DP	TC/G	FA	G by Pos
1990	PIT N	4	.500	.500	4	2	0	0	0	0.0	1	0	0	2	0	1	1	0	4	0	1	1.3	1.000	SS-3

Rich Gedman

GEDMAN, RICHARD LEO
B. Sept. 26, 1959, Worcester, Mass.
BL TR 6' 210 lbs.

Year	Team	Games	BA	SA	AB	H	2B	3B	HR	HR%	R	RBI	BB	SO	SB	PH AB	PH H	PO	A	E	DP	TC/G	FA	G by Pos
1980	BOS A	9	.208	.208	24	5	0	0	0	0.0	2	1	0	5	0	5	0	13	0	2	0	1.7	.867	DH-4, C-2
1981		62	.288	.434	205	59	15	0	5	2.4	22	26	9	31	0	3	1	275	30	3	1	5.0	.990	C-59
1982		92	.249	.363	289	72	17	2	4	1.4	30	26	10	37	0	9	2	397	29	10	5	4.7	.977	C-86
1983		81	.294	.412	204	60	16	1	2	1.0	21	18	15	37	0	19	5	274	26	6	5	3.8	.980	C-69
1984		133	.269	.506	449	121	26	4	24	5.3	54	72	29	72	0	15	5	693	58	18	5	5.8	.977	C-125
1985		144	.295	.484	498	147	30	5	18	3.6	66	80	50	79	2	9	4	768	78	15	13	6.0	.983	C-139
1986		135	.258	.424	462	119	29	0	16	3.5	49	65	37	61	1	9	4	866	65	6	10	6.9	.994	C-134
1987		52	.205	.278	151	31	8	0	1	0.7	11	13	10	24	0	4	1	306	14	8	1	6.3	.976	C-51
1988		95	.231	.368	299	69	14	0	9	3.0	33	39	18	49	0	2	0	570	40	5	4	6.5	.992	C-93, DH-1
1989		93	.212	.292	260	55	9	0	4	1.5	24	16	23	47	0	5	1	486	36	10	6	5.7	.981	C-91
1990	2 teams		BOS A	(10G — .200)			HOU N	(40G — .202)																
"	total	50	.202	.286	119	24	7	0	1	0.8	7	10	20	30	0	4	1	207	30	1	6	5.0	.996	C-48
11 yrs.		946	.257	.408	2960	762	171	12	84	2.8	319	366	221	472	3	84	24	4855	406	84	56	5.7	.984	C-897, DH-5

LEAGUE CHAMPIONSHIP SERIES

Year	Team	Games	BA	SA	AB	H	2B	3B	HR	HR%	R	RBI	BB	SO	SB	PH AB	PH H	PO	A	E	DP	TC/G	FA	G by Pos
1986	BOS A	7	.357	.500	28	10	1	0	1	3.6	4	6	1	4	0	0	0	45	4	0	0	7.0	1.000	C-7
1988		4	.357	.571	14	5	0	0	1	7.1	1	1	2	1	0	0	0	34	5	0	1	9.8	1.000	C-4
2 yrs.		11	.357	.524	42	15	1	0	2	4.8	5	7	2	5	0	0	0	79	9	0	1	8.0	.000	C-11

WORLD SERIES

Year	Team	Games	BA	SA	AB	H	2B	3B	HR	HR%	R	RBI	BB	SO	SB	PH AB	PH H	PO	A	E	DP	TC/G	FA	G by Pos
1986	BOS A	7	.200	.333	30	6	1	0	1	3.3	1	1	0	10	0	0	0	46	3	2	2	7.3	.961	C-7

Bob Geren

GEREN, ROBERT PETER
B. Sept. 22, 1961, San Diego, Calif.
BR TR 6' 3" 205 lbs.

Split	Games	BA	SA	AB	H	2B	3B	HR	HR%	R	RBI	BB	SO	SB
April	8	.346	.462	26	9	3	0	0	0.0	3	2	1	5	0
May	21	.169	.310	71	12	1	0	3	4.2	7	6	4	21	0
June	16	.244	.356	45	11	2	0	1	2.2	2	5	1	12	0
July	25	.226	.371	62	14	0	0	3	4.8	4	11	2	17	0
Aug	21	.256	.349	43	11	1	0	1	2.3	2	6	2	7	0
Sept/Oct	19	.067	.067	30	2	0	0	0	0.0	3	1	3	11	0
Day	29	.268	.380	71	19	2	0	2	2.8	6	10	3	18	0
Night	81	.194	.306	206	40	5	0	6	2.9	15	21	10	55	0
vs. Left		.254	.395	114	29	4	0	4	3.5	11	10	7	25	0
vs. Right		.184	.276	163	30	3	0	4	2.5	10	21	6	48	0

CATCHER

Bar chart (AVERAGE): player ~.210, AL AVG ~.260
Bar chart (RBI): player ~30, AL AVG ~50

Year	Team	Games	BA	SA	AB	H	2B	3B	HR	HR%	R	RBI	BB	SO	SB	PINCH HIT AB	H	PO	A	E	DP	TC/G	FA	G by Pos

Bob Geren *Continued*

On Grass		91	.211	.309	223	47	7	0	5	2.2	17	20	11	63	0									
On Turf		19	.222	.389	54	12	0	0	3	5.6	4	11	2	10	0									
Home		57	.217	.336	143	31	5	0	4	2.8	10	15	5	41	0									
Road		53	.209	.313	134	28	2	0	4	3.0	11	16	8	32	0									
Division Rivals																								
vs. BAL		5	.091	.091	11	1	0	0	0	0.0	0	0	1	2	0									
vs. BOS		7	.143	.286	7	1	1	0	0	0.0	0	1	1	3	0									
vs. CLE		10	.261	.348	23	6	2	0	0	0.0	2	3	1	4	0									
vs. DET		8	.211	.211	19	4	0	0	0	0.0	1	1	0	9	0									
vs. MIL		9	.217	.261	23	5	1	0	0	0.0	2	1	2	5	0									
vs. TOR		10	.286	.429	21	6	0	0	1	4.8	1	3	1	5	0									
On 3B < 2 Out			.222	.222	9	2	0	0	0	0.0	0	5	2	3										
1988	NY A	10	.100	.100	10	1	0	0	0	0.0	0	0	2	3	0	0	0	18	3	0	0	2.1	1.000	C-10
1989		65	.288	.454	205	59	5	1	9	4.4	26	27	12	44	0	7	1	308	24	3	4	5.2	.991	C-60, DH-2
1990		110	.213	.325	277	59	7	0	8	2.8	21	31	13	73	0	7	1	487	55	4	5	5.1	.993	C-107, DH-1
3 yrs.		185	.242	.374	492	119	12	1	17	3.5	47	58	27	120	0	14	2	813	82	7	9	4.9	.992	C-177, DH-3

Kirk Gibson

GIBSON, KIRK HAROLD
B. May 28, 1957, Pontiac, Mich.
BL TL 6' 3" 215 lbs.

April					0	0	0	0	0		0	0	0	0	0									
May					0	0	0	0	0		0	0	0	0	0									
June		18	.200	.383	60	12	2	0	3	5.0	6	10	7	14	4									
July		23	.337	.478	92	31	10	0	1	1.1	20	11	8	9	5									
Aug		27	.298	.468	94	28	4	0	4	4.3	22	13	13	25	12									
Sept/Oct		21	.159	.217	69	11	4	0	0	0.0	11	4	11	17	5									
Day		20	.224	.421	76	17	6	0	3	3.9	15	13	10	18	5									
Night		69	.272	.393	239	65	14	0	5	2.1	44	25	29	47	21									
vs. Left			.255	.412	102	26	7	0	3	2.9	19	15	12	30	5									
vs. Right			.263	.394	213	56	13	0	5	2.3	40	23	27	35	21									
On Grass		67	.243	.368	239	58	12	0	6	2.5	44	31	30	51	21									
On Turf		22	.316	.500	76	24	8	0	2	2.6	15	7	9	14	5									
Home		43	.248	.338	157	39	8	0	2	1.3	24	19	20	29	16									
Road		46	.272	.462	158	43	12	0	6	3.8	35	19	19	36	10									
Division Rivals																								
vs. ATL		13	.205	.364	44	9	4	0	1	2.3	9	4	7	8	3									
vs. CIN		11	.194	.389	36	7	1	0	2	5.6	4	4	3	8	1									
vs. HOU		9	.333	.556	27	9	3	0	1	3.7	3	1	5	4	2									
vs. SD		9	.152	.333	33	5	0	0	2	6.1	6	7	4	12	2									
vs. SF		11	.300	.500	40	12	2	0	2	5.0	14	7	8	5	5									
On 3B < 2 Out			.333	.667	12	4	1	0	1	8.3	1	10	2	6										
1979	DET A	12	.237	.395	38	9	3	0	1	2.6	3	4	1	3	3	2	0	15	0	0	0	1.3	1.000	OF-10
1980		51	.263	.440	175	46	2	1	9	5.1	23	16	10	45	4	5	1	122	1	1	0	2.4	.992	OF-49, DH-1
1981		83	.328	.479	290	95	11	3	9	3.1	41	40	18	64	17	8	1	142	1	4	0	1.8	.973	OF-67, DH-9
1982		69	.278	.444	266	74	16	2	8	3.0	34	35	25	41	9	1	0	167	4	1	3	2.5	.994	OF-64, DH-4
1983		128	.227	.414	401	91	12	9	15	3.7	60	51	53	96	14	20	5	116	2	3	0	0.9	.975	DH-66, OF-54
1984		149	.282	.516	531	150	23	10	27	5.1	92	91	63	103	29	11	1	245	4	12	2	1.8	.954	OF-139, DH-6
1985		154	.287	.518	581	167	37	5	29	5.0	96	97	71	137	30	3	2	286	1	11	0	1.9	.963	OF-144, DH-8
1986		119	.268	.492	441	118	11	2	28	6.3	84	86	68	107	34	2	1	190	2	2	1	1.6	.990	OF-114, DH-4
1987		128	.277	.489	487	135	25	3	24	4.9	95	79	71	117	26	3	0	253	6	7	0	2.1	.974	OF-121, DH-4
1988	LA N	150	.290	.483	542	157	28	1	25	4.6	106	76	73	120	31	3	0	311	6	12	3	2.2	.964	OF-148
1989		71	.213	.368	253	54	8	2	9	3.6	35	28	35	55	12	2	1	146	3	3	2	2.1	.980	OF-70
1990		89	.260	.400	315	82	20	0	8	2.5	59	38	39	65	26	6	1	191	4	1	1	2.4	.995	OF-81
12 yrs.		1203	.273	.469	4320	1178	196	38	192	4.4	728	641	527	953	235	66	13	2184	34	57	12	1.9	.975	OF-1061, DH-102
LEAGUE CHAMPIONSHIP SERIES																								
1984	DET A	3	.417	.750	12	5	1	0	1	8.3	2	2	2	1	1	0	0	7	0	0	0	2.3	1.000	OF-3
1987		5	.286	.476	21	6	1	0	1	4.8	4	4	3	8	3	0	0	10	1	0	0	2.2	1.000	OF-5
1988	LA N	7	.154	.385	26	4	0	0	2	7.7	2	6	3	6	2	0	0	17	1	0	0	2.6	1.000	OF-7
3 yrs.		15	.254	.492	59	15	2	0	4	6.8	8	12	8	15	6	0	0	34	2	0	0	2.4	.000	OF-15

CATCHER

HR — AL AVG

SB — AL AVG

OUTFIELD

AVERAGE — NL AVG

RBI — NL AVG

HR — NL AVG

SB — NL AVG

Year	Team		Games	BA	SA	AB	H	2B	3B	HR	HR%	R	RBI	BB	SO	SB	PINCH HIT AB	H	PO	A	E	DP	TC/G	FA	G by Pos

Kirk Gibson *Continued*

WORLD SERIES

Year	Team		Games	BA	SA	AB	H	2B	3B	HR	HR%	R	RBI	BB	SO	SB	AB	H	PO	A	E	DP	TC/G	FA	G by Pos
1984	DET	A	5	.333	.667	18	6	0	0	2	11.1	4	7	4	4	3	0	0	5	1	2	0	1.6	.750	OF–5
1988	LA	N	1	1.000	4.000	1	1	0	0	1	100.0	1	2	0	0	0	1	1	0	0	0	0	0.0	—	
2 yrs.			6	.368	.842	19	7	0	0	3	15.8	5	9	4	4	3	1	1	5	1	2	0	1.3	.750	OF–5

Brian Giles

GILES, BRIAN JEFFREY
B. Apr. 27, 1960, Manhattan, Kans.
BR TR 6′ 1″ 165 lbs.

Year	Team		Games	BA	SA	AB	H	2B	3B	HR	HR%	R	RBI	BB	SO	SB	AB	H	PO	A	E	DP	TC/G	FA	G by Pos
1981	NY	N	9	.000	.000	7	0	0	0	0	0.0	0	0	0	3	0	2	0	5	8	0	2	1.4	1.000	2B–2, SS–2
1982			45	.210	.312	138	29	5	0	3	2.2	14	10	12	29	6	0	0	122	133	2	28	5.7	.992	2B–45, SS–2
1983			145	.245	.298	400	98	15	0	2	0.5	39	27	36	77	17	5	0	309	390	14	90	4.9	.980	2B–140, SS–12
1985	MIL	A	34	.172	.241	58	10	1	0	1	1.7	6	1	7	16	2	0	0	48	58	2	10	3.2	.981	SS–20, 2B–13, DH–2
1986	CHI	A	9	.273	.273	11	3	0	0	0	0.0	0	1	0	2	0	1	0	15	11	0	6	2.9	1.000	2B–7, SS–1
1990	SEA	A	45	.232	.421	95	22	6	0	4	4.2	15	11	15	24	2	5	1	57	88	3	28	3.8	.980	SS–37, 2B–2, DH–1, 3B–1
6 yrs.			287	.228	.309	709	162	27	0	10	1.4	74	50	70	151	27	13	1	556	688	21	164	4.4	.983	2B–209, SS–74, DH–3, 3B–1

Bernard Gilkey

GILKEY, OTIS BERNARD
B. Sept. 24, 1966, St. Louis, Mo.
BR TR 6′ 170 lbs.

Year	Team		Games	BA	SA	AB	H	2B	3B	HR	HR%	R	RBI	BB	SO	SB	AB	H	PO	A	E	DP	TC/G	FA	G by Pos
1990	STL	N	18	.297	.484	64	19	5	2	1	1.5	11	3	8	5	6	0	0	47	2	2	0	2.8	.961	OF–18

Joe Girardi

GIRARDI, JOSEPH ELLIOTT
B. Oct. 14, 1964, Peoria, Ill.
BR TR 5′ 11″ 195 lbs.

	Games	BA	SA	AB	H	2B	3B	HR	HR%	R	RBI	BB	SO	SB
April	17	.333	.356	45	15	1	0	0	0.0	5	1	0	5	4
May	24	.228	.329	79	18	6	1	0	0.0	9	11	5	10	1
June	26	.289	.434	76	22	6	1	1	1.3	8	7	2	11	0
July	23	.342	.397	73	25	4	0	0	0.0	5	9	3	3	0
Aug	24	.259	.318	85	22	5	0	0	0.0	7	5	5	11	1
Sept/Oct	19	.180	.213	61	11	2	0	0	0.0	2	5	2	10	2
Day	66	.260	.338	204	53	11	1	1	0.5	21	24	9	22	5
Night	67	.279	.349	215	60	13	1	0	0.0	15	14	8	28	3
vs. Left		.326	.468	141	46	15	1	1	0.7	15	16	3	11	1
vs. Right		.241	.281	278	67	9	1	0	0.0	21	22	14	39	7
On Grass	91	.285	.356	284	81	15	1	1	0.4	27	30	12	30	7
On Turf	42	.237	.319	135	32	9	1	0	0.0	9	8	5	20	1
Home	66	.272	.351	202	55	11	1	1	0.5	21	25	7	26	2
Road	67	.267	.336	217	58	13	1	0	0.0	15	13	10	24	6
Division Rivals														
vs. MON	15	.179	.231	39	7	2	0	0	0.0	3	3	2	5	1
vs. NY	13	.205	.205	44	9	0	0	0	0.0	4	4	0	5	3
vs. PHI	13	.361	.556	36	13	4	0	1	2.8	5	5	1	5	0
vs. PIT	13	.243	.297	37	9	2	0	0	0.0	2	4	0	5	0
vs. STL	16	.200	.255	55	11	1	1	0	0.0	5	1	2	9	0
On 3B < 2 Out		.250	.250	20	5	0	0	0	0.0	0	12	1	5	

CATCHER

Year	Team		Games	BA	SA	AB	H	2B	3B	HR	HR%	R	RBI	BB	SO	SB	AB	H	PO	A	E	DP	TC/G	FA	G by Pos
1989	CHI	N	59	.248	.331	157	39	10	0	1	0.6	15	14	11	26	2	0	0	332	28	7	1	6.2	.981	C–59
1990			133	.270	.344	419	113	24	2	1	0.2	36	38	17	50	8	0	0	653	61	11	5	5.5	.985	C–133
2 yrs.			192	.264	.340	576	152	34	2	2	0.3	51	52	28	76	10	0	0	985	89	18	6	5.7	.984	C–192

LEAGUE CHAMPIONSHIP SERIES

Year	Team		Games	BA	SA	AB	H	2B	3B	HR	HR%	R	RBI	BB	SO	SB	AB	H	PO	A	E	DP	TC/G	FA	G by Pos
1989	CHI	N	4	.100	.100	10	1	0	0	0	0.0	1	0	1	2	0	0	0	20	0	0	0	5.0	1.000	C–4

Year	Team		Games	BA	SA	AB	H	2B	3B	HR	HR%	R	RBI	BB	SO	SB	PINCH HIT AB	H	PO	A	E	DP	TC/G	FA	G by Pos

Dan Gladden

GLADDEN, CLINTON DANIEL III
B. July 7, 1957, San Jose, Calif.
BR TR 5' 11" 175 lbs.

Split			Games	BA	SA	AB	H	2B	3B	HR	HR%	R	RBI	BB	SO	SB
April			17	.328	.478	67	22	7	0	1	1.5	12	7	3	4	2
May			28	.313	.452	115	36	5	1	3	2.6	19	10	6	17	7
June			26	.248	.297	101	25	3	1	0	0.0	7	5	4	17	2
July			21	.253	.313	83	21	3	1	0	0.0	4	5	5	9	7
Aug			23	.226	.333	93	21	5	1	1	1.1	11	7	4	11	4
Sept/Oct			21	.293	.400	75	22	4	2	0	0.0	11	6	4	9	3
Day			34	.323	.433	127	41	7	2	1	0.8	19	9	8	18	10
Night			102	.260	.359	407	106	20	4	4	1.0	45	31	18	49	15
vs. Left				.270	.356	163	44	8	0	2	1.2	18	16	5	18	5
vs. Right				.278	.385	371	103	19	6	3	0.8	46	24	21	49	20
On Grass			52	.240	.319	204	49	8	1	2	1.0	21	18	9	33	11
On Turf			84	.297	.412	330	98	19	5	3	0.9	43	22	17	34	14
Home			69	.300	.418	263	79	15	5	2	0.8	36	17	14	27	11
Road			67	.251	.336	271	68	12	1	3	1.1	28	23	12	40	14
Division Rivals																
vs. CAL			9	.250	.344	32	8	3	0	0	0.0	4	3	1	1	1
vs. CHI			12	.240	.260	50	12	1	0	0	0.0	4	3	3	7	3
vs. KC			12	.275	.471	51	14	3	2	1	2.0	7	6	2	6	1
vs. OAK			12	.347	.469	49	17	1	1	1	2.0	6	4	2	5	3
vs. SEA			10	.311	.378	45	14	3	0	0	0.0	3	3	1	4	0
vs. TEX			12	.273	.341	44	12	3	0	0	0.0	7	3	1	6	2
On 3B < 2 Out				.292	.333	24	7	1	0	0	0.0	0	11	2	3	

OUTFIELD — AVERAGE, RBI, HR, SB (vs AL AVG)

Year	Team		Games	BA	SA	AB	H	2B	3B	HR	HR%	R	RBI	BB	SO	SB	AB	H	PO	A	E	DP	TC/G	FA	G by Pos
1983	SF	N	18	.222	.302	63	14	2	0	1	1.6	6	9	5	11	4	1	0	53	0	0	0	2.9	1.000	OF-18
1984			86	.351	.447	342	120	17	2	4	1.2	71	31	33	37	31	2	0	232	8	3	1	2.8	.988	OF-85
1985			142	.243	.347	502	122	15	8	7	1.4	64	41	40	78	32	19	8	273	3	7	0	2.0	.975	OF-124
1986			102	.276	.362	351	97	16	1	4	1.1	55	29	39	59	27	9	1	226	7	3	2	2.3	.987	OF-89
1987	MIN	A	121	.249	.361	438	109	21	2	8	1.8	69	38	38	72	25	9	2	223	9	3	2	1.9	.987	OF-111, DH-4
1988			141	.269	.403	576	155	32	6	11	1.9	91	62	46	74	28	4	1	319	12	3	5	2.4	.991	OF-141, P-1, 3B-1
1989			121	.295	.410	461	136	23	3	8	1.7	69	46	23	53	23	1	1	245	8	9	3	2.2	.966	OF-117, DH-2, P-1
1990			136	.275	.376	534	147	27	6	5	0.9	64	40	26	67	25	5	1	286	12	6	3	2.3	.980	OF-133, DH-2
8 yrs.			867	.275	.384	3267	900	153	28	48	1.5	489	296	250	451	195	50	14	1857	59	34	16	2.2	.983	OF-818, DH-8, P-2, 3B-1

LEAGUE CHAMPIONSHIP SERIES

| 1987 | MIN | A | 5 | .350 | .450 | 20 | 7 | 2 | 0 | 0 | 0.0 | 5 | 5 | 2 | 1 | 0 | 0 | 0 | 12 | 0 | 0 | 0 | 2.4 | 1.000 | OF-5 |

WORLD SERIES

| 1987 | MIN | A | 7 | .290 | .516 | 31 | 9 | 2 | 1 | 1 | 3.2 | 3 | 7 | 3 | 4 | 2 | 0 | 0 | 12 | 0 | 0 | 0 | 1.7 | 1.000 | OF-7 |

Jerry Goff

GOFF, JERRY LEROY
B. Apr. 12, 1964, San Rafael, Calif.
BL TR 6' 3" 205 lbs.

| 1990 | MON | N | 52 | .227 | .311 | 119 | 27 | 1 | 0 | 3 | 2.5 | 14 | 7 | 21 | 36 | 0 | 6 | 3 | 216 | 17 | 9 | 3 | 5.6 | .963 | C-38, 1B-3, 3B-3 |

Leo Gomez

GOMEZ, LEONARDO
B. Mar. 2, 1967, Canovanas, Puerto Rico
BR TR 6' 180 lbs.

| 1990 | BAL | A | 12 | .231 | .231 | 39 | 9 | 0 | 0 | 0 | 0.0 | 3 | 1 | 8 | 7 | 0 | 0 | 0 | 11 | 20 | 4 | 2 | 2.9 | .886 | 3B-12 |

Rene Gonzales

GONZALES, RENE ADRIAN
B. Sept. 23, 1960, Austin, Tex.
BR TR 6' 3" 180 lbs.

1984	MON	N	29	.233	.267	30	7	1	0	0	0.0	5	2	2	5	0	0	0	17	28	2	5	1.6	.957	SS-27
1986			11	.115	.115	26	3	0	0	0	0.0	1	0	2	7	0	0	0	7	19	0	3	2.4	1.000	SS-6, 3B-5
1987	BAL	A	37	.267	.383	60	16	2	1	1	1.7	14	7	3	11	1	0	0	22	43	2	5	1.8	.970	3B-29, 2B-6, SS-1
1988			92	.215	.266	237	51	6	0	2	0.8	13	15	13	32	2	0	0	66	185	8	26	2.8	.969	3B 80, 2B-14, SS-2, 1B-1, OF-1
1989			71	.217	.259	166	36	4	0	1	0.6	16	11	12	30	5	2	0	103	146	7	37	3.6	.973	2B-54, 3B-17, SS-1

Year	Team		Games	BA	SA	AB	H	2B	3B	HR	HR%	R	RBI	BB	SO	SB	PINCH HIT AB	H	PO	A	E	DP	TC/G	FA	G by Pos

Rene Gonzales *Continued*

Year	Team		Games	BA	SA	AB	H	2B	3B	HR	HR%	R	RBI	BB	SO	SB	PH AB	H	PO	A	E	DP	TC/G	FA	G by Pos
1990			67	.214	.291	103	22	3	1	1	0.9	13	12	12	14	1	0	0	68	114	2	23	2.9	.989	2B-43, 3B-16, SS-9, OF-1
6 yrs.			307	.217	.273	622	135	16	2	5	0.8	62	47	44	99	9	2	0	283	535	21	99	2.7	.975	3B-147, 2B-117, SS-46, OF-2, 1B-1

Jose Gonzalez

GONZALEZ, JOSE RAFAEL
Born Jose Rafael Gonzalez y Gutierrez.
B. Nov. 23, 1964, Puerto Plata, Dominican Republic
BR TR 6′ 3″ 197 lbs.

Year	Team		Games	BA	SA	AB	H	2B	3B	HR	HR%	R	RBI	BB	SO	SB	PH AB	H	PO	A	E	DP	TC/G	FA	G by Pos
1985	LA	N	23	.273	.455	11	3	2	0	0	0.0	6	0	1	3	1	1	0	10	0	0	0	0.4	1.000	OF-18
1986			57	.215	.355	93	20	5	1	2	2.2	15	6	7	29	4	5	1	73	0	6	0	1.4	.924	OF-57
1987			19	.188	.313	16	3	2	0	0	0.0	2	1	1	2	5	2	0	19	1	0	0	1.1	1.000	OF-16
1988			37	.083	.125	24	2	1	0	0	0.0	7	0	2	10	3	9	2	15	0	1	0	0.4	.938	OF-24
1989			95	.268	.360	261	70	11	2	3	1.1	31	18	23	53	9	14	5	171	8	6	2	1.9	.968	OF-87
1990			106	.232	.404	99	23	5	3	2	2.0	15	8	6	27	3	21	3	62	1	0	0	0.8	1.000	OF-81
6 yrs.			337	.240	.357	504	121	26	6	7	1.4	76	33	40	124	25	52	11	350	10	13	2	1.1	.965	OF-283

LEAGUE CHAMPIONSHIP SERIES

Year	Team		Games	BA	SA	AB	H	2B	3B	HR	HR%	R	RBI	BB	SO	SB	PH AB	H	PO	A	E	DP	TC/G	FA	G by Pos
1988	LA	N	5	—	—	0	0	0	0	0	—	2	0	0	0	0	0	0	3	0	0	0	0.6	1.000	OF-4

WORLD SERIES

Year	Team		Games	BA	SA	AB	H	2B	3B	HR	HR%	R	RBI	BB	SO	SB	PH AB	H	PO	A	E	DP	TC/G	FA	G by Pos
1988	LA	N	4	.000	.000	2	0	0	0	0	0.0	0	0	0	2	0	2	0	2	0	0	0	0.5	1.000	OF-3

Juan Gonzalez

GONZALEZ, JUAN ALBERTO
Born Juan Alberto Gonzalez y Vazquez.
B. Oct. 20, 1969, Arecibo, Puerto Rico
BR TR 6′ 3″ 175 lbs.

Year	Team		Games	BA	SA	AB	H	2B	3B	HR	HR%	R	RBI	BB	SO	SB	PH AB	H	PO	A	E	DP	TC/G	FA	G by Pos
1989	TEX	A	24	.150	.250	60	9	3	0	1	1.7	6	7	6	17	0	1	0	53	0	2	0	2.3	.964	OF-24
1990			25	.289	.522	90	26	7	1	4	4.4	11	12	2	18	0	3	1	33	0	0	0	2.1	1.000	OF-16, DH-9
2 yrs.			49	.233	.413	150	35	10	1	5	3.3	17	19	8	35	0	4	1	86	0	2	0	1.8	.000	OF-40, DH-9

Luis Gonzalez

GONZALEZ, LUIS EMILIO
B. Sept. 3, 1967, Tampa, Fla.
BL TR 6′ 2″ 180 lbs.

Year	Team		Games	BA	SA	AB	H	2B	3B	HR	HR%	R	RBI	BB	SO	SB	PH AB	H	PO	A	E	DP	TC/G	FA	G by Pos
1990	HOU	N	12	.190	.286	21	4	2	0	0	0.0	1	0	2	5	0	5	1	22	10	0	1	5.3	1.000	3B-4, 1B-2

Mark Grace

GRACE, MARK EUGENE
B. June 28, 1964, Winston-Salem, N. C.
BL TL 6′ 2″ 190 lbs.

	Games	BA	SA	AB	H	2B	3B	HR	HR%	R	RBI	BB	SO	SB
April	19	.262	.292	65	17	2	0	0	0.0	7	4	12	8	5
May	26	.257	.327	113	29	5	0	1	0.9	16	9	3	11	2
June	30	.320	.437	103	33	7	1	1	1.0	11	17	14	7	2
July	25	.287	.368	87	25	4	0	1	1.1	7	6	5	9	1
Aug	27	.398	.583	108	43	8	0	4	3.7	14	26	10	11	3
Sept/Oct	30	.310	.416	113	35	6	0	2	1.8	17	20	15	8	2
Day	81	.320	.450	309	99	20	1	6	1.9	46	46	36	28	8
Night	76	.296	.371	280	83	12	0	3	1.1	26	36	23	26	7
vs. Left		.308	.422	185	57	12	0	3	1.6	22	33	20	21	4
vs. Right		.309	.408	404	125	20	1	6	1.5	50	49	39	33	11
On Grass	112	.311	.407	428	133	23	0	6	1.4	56	60	42	41	10
On Turf	45	.304	.429	161	49	9	1	3	1.9	16	22	17	13	5
Home	79	.331	.429	308	102	18	0	4	1.3	38	46	29	24	4
Road	78	.285	.395	281	80	14	1	5	1.8	34	36	30	30	11
Division Rivals														
vs. MON	18	.314	.414	70	22	7	0	0	0.0	11	12	9	9	2
vs. NY	18	.274	.411	73	20	4	0	2	2.7	11	12	8	11	6
vs. PHI	17	.345	.414	58	20	4	0	0	0.0	8	12	11	1	0
vs. PIT	17	.373	.441	59	22	1	0	1	1.7	7	4	5	6	1
vs. STL	17	.393	.518	56	22	2	1	1	1.8	5	10	8	4	2
On 3B < 2 Out		.371	.429	35	13	2	0	0	0.0	0	34	9		2

FIRST BASE

AVERAGE — .400 / .200 / .000 — NL AVG

RBI — 100 / 50 / 0 — NL AVG

HR — 50 / 25 / 0 — NL AVG

SB — 60 / 30 / 0 — NL AVG

Year	Team		Games	BA	SA	AB	H	2B	3B	HR	HR%	R	RBI	BB	SO	SB	PINCH HIT AB	H	PO	A	E	DP	TC/G	FA	G by Pos

Mark Grace *Continued*

Year	Team		Games	BA	SA	AB	H	2B	3B	HR	HR%	R	RBI	BB	SO	SB	AB	H	PO	A	E	DP	TC/G	FA	G by Pos
1988	CHI	N	134	.296	.403	486	144	23	4	7	1.4	65	57	60	43	3	7	3	1182	87	17	91	9.6	.987	1B-133
1989			142	.314	.457	510	160	28	3	13	2.5	74	79	80	42	14	1	1	1230	126	6	93	9.6	.996	1B-142
1990			157	.309	.413	589	182	32	1	9	1.5	72	82	59	54	15	7	2	1324	180	12	116	9.9	.992	1B-153
3 yrs.			433	.307	.424	1585	486	83	8	29	1.8	211	218	199	139	32	15	6	3736	393	35	300	9.6	.992	1B-428

LEAGUE CHAMPIONSHIP SERIES

Year	Team		Games	BA	SA	AB	H	2B	3B	HR	HR%	R	RBI	BB	SO	SB	AB	H	PO	A	E	DP	TC/G	FA	G by Pos
1989	CHI	N	5	.647	1.118	17	11	3	1	1	5.9	3	8	4	1	1	0	0	44	3	0	1	9.4	1.000	1B-5

Craig Grebeck

GREBECK, CRAIG ALLEN
B. Dec. 29, 1964, Johnstown, Pa.
BR TR 5' 8" 160 lbs.

Year	Team		Games	BA	SA	AB	H	2B	3B	HR	HR%	R	RBI	BB	SO	SB	AB	H	PO	A	E	DP	TC/G	FA	G by Pos
1990	CHI	A	59	.168	.235	119	20	3	1	1	0.8	7	9	8	24	0	4	1	36	98	3	10	2.4	.978	3B-35, SS-16, 2B-6, DH-1

Gary Green

GREEN, GARY ALLAN
Son of Freddie Green.
B. Jan. 14, 1962, Pittsburgh, Pa.
BR TR 6' 3" 175 lbs.

Year	Team		Games	BA	SA	AB	H	2B	3B	HR	HR%	R	RBI	BB	SO	SB	AB	H	PO	A	E	DP	TC/G	FA	G by Pos
1986	SD	N	13	.212	.242	33	7	1	0	0	0.0	2	2	1	11	0	0	0	16	35	0	9	3.9	1.000	SS-13
1989			15	.259	.370	27	7	3	0	0	0.0	4	0	1	1	0	0	0	6	29	3	7	2.5	.921	SS-11, 3B-1
1990	TEX	A	62	.216	.250	88	19	3	0	0	0.0	10	8	6	18	1	0	0	61	112	5	27	3.1	.972	SS-58
3 yrs.			90	.223	.270	148	33	7	0	0	0.0	16	10	8	30	1	0	0	83	176	8	43	3.0	.970	SS-82, 3B-1

Mike Greenwell

GREENWELL, MICHAEL LEWIS
B. July 18, 1963, Louisville, Ky.
BL TR 6' 170 lbs.

	Games	BA	SA	AB	H	2B	3B	HR	HR%	R	RBI	BB	SO	SB
April	18	.221	.324	68	15	1	0	2	2.9	5	4	9	8	0
May	25	.250	.271	96	24	2	0	0	0.0	9	3	13	7	1
June	29	.313	.375	112	35	5	1	0	0.0	9	17	13	7	1
July	29	.299	.458	107	32	6	1	3	2.8	11	10	11	7	2
Aug	27	.306	.472	108	33	4	1	4	3.7	19	17	9	5	4
Sept/Oct	31	.353	.630	119	42	12	3	5	4.2	18	22	10	9	0
Day	47	.343	.486	181	62	15	1	3	1.7	21	21	18	14	2
Night	112	.277	.413	429	119	15	5	11	2.6	50	52	47	29	6
vs. Left		.257	.361	202	52	8	2	3	1.5	18	22	17	19	2
vs. Right		.316	.471	408	129	22	4	11	2.7	53	51	48	24	6
On Grass	136	.307	.444	525	161	29	5	11	2.1	65	66	56	37	8
On Turf	23	.235	.376	85	20	1	1	3	3.5	6	7	9	6	0
Home	81	.310	.451	306	95	21	2	6	2.0	39	41	34	24	2
Road	78	.283	.418	304	86	9	4	8	2.6	32	32	31	19	6
Division Rivals														
vs. BAL	13	.250	.411	56	14	3	0	2	3.6	6	3	3	3	0
vs. CLE	13	.333	.481	54	18	3	1	1	1.9	8	12	4	3	1
vs. DET	13	.327	.469	49	16	4	0	1	2.0	7	6	6	3	1
vs. MIL	12	.213	.234	47	10	1	0	0	0.0	2	2	4	4	1
vs. NY	13	.479	.813	48	23	4	3	2	4.2	8	14	7	3	1
vs. TOR	12	.356	.511	45	16	4	0	1	2.2	7	8	4	4	1
On 3B < 2 Out		.256	.385	39	10	2	0	1	2.6	1	27	7	6	

OUTFIELD

AVERAGE · AL AVG
RBI · AL AVG
HR · AL AVG
SB · AL AVG

Year	Team		Games	BA	SA	AB	H	2B	3B	HR	HR%	R	RBI	BB	SO	SB	AB	H	PO	A	E	DP	TC/G	FA	G by Pos
1985	BOS	A	17	.323	.742	31	10	1	0	4	12.9	7	8	3	4	1	1	0	14	0	0	0	0.8	1.000	OF-17
1986			31	.314	.371	35	11	2	0	0	0.0	4	4	5	7	0	12	2	18	1	0	1	0.6	1.000	OF-15, DH-3
1987			125	.328	.570	412	135	31	6	19	4.6	71	89	35	40	5	17	5	165	8	6	0	1.4	.966	OF-91, DH-15, C-1
1988			158	.325	.531	590	192	39	8	22	3.7	86	119	87	38	16	0	0	302	6	6	2	2.0	.981	OF-147, DH-11
1989			145	.308	.443	578	178	36	0	14	2.4	87	95	56	44	13	1	1	220	11	8	1	1.6	.967	OF-139, DH-5
1990			159	.297	.434	610	181	30	6	14	2.2	71	73	65	43	8	1	0	287	13	7	1	1.9	.977	OF-159
6 yrs.			635	.313	.490	2256	707	139	20	73	3.2	326	388	251	176	43	32	8	1006	39	27	5	1.7	.975	OF-568, DH-34, C-1

LEAGUE CHAMPIONSHIP SERIES

Year	Team		Games	BA	SA	AB	H	2B	3B	HR	HR%	R	RBI	BB	SO	SB	AB	H	PO	A	E	DP	TC/G	FA	G by Pos
1986	BOS	A	2	.500	.500	2	1	0	0	0	0.0	0	0	0	0	0	2	1	0	0	0	0	0.0	—	
1988			4	.214	.500	14	3	1	0	1	7.1	2	3	3	0	0	0	0	4	0	0	0	1.0	1.000	OF-4
1990			4	.000	.000	14	0	0	0	0	0.0	1	0	2	2	0	0	0	3	0	1	0	1.0	.750	OF-4
3 yrs.			10	.133	.267	30	4	1	0	1	3.3	3	3	5	2	0	2	1	7	0	1	0	0.8	.000	OF-8

Year	Team		Games	BA	SA	AB	H	2B	3B	HR	HR%	R	RBI	BB	SO	SB	PINCH HIT AB	PINCH HIT H	PO	A	E	DP	TC/G	FA	G by Pos

Mike Greenwell *Continued*

WORLD SERIES

Year	Team		Games	BA	SA	AB	H	2B	3B	HR	HR%	R	RBI	BB	SO	SB	PH AB	PH H	PO	A	E	DP	TC/G	FA	G by Pos
1986	BOS	A	4	.000	.000	3	0	0	0	0	0.0	0	0	1	2	0	3	0	0	0	0	0	0.0	—	

Tommy Gregg

GREGG, WILLIAM THOMAS
B. July 29, 1963, Boone, N. C.
BL TL 6′ 1″ 190 lbs.

Year	Team		Games	BA	SA	AB	H	2B	3B	HR	HR%	R	RBI	BB	SO	SB	PH AB	PH H	PO	A	E	DP	TC/G	FA	G by Pos
1987	PIT	N	10	.250	.375	8	2	1	0	0	0.0	3	0	0	2	0	7	2	1	0	0	0	0.1	1.000	OF-4
1988	2 teams			PIT N (14G — .200)			ATL N (11G — .345)																		
''	total		25	.295	.455	44	13	4	0	1	2.3	5	7	3	6	0	12	2	26	1	0	1	1.1	1.000	OF-13
1989	ATL	N	102	.243	.337	276	67	8	0	6	2.2	24	23	18	45	3	28	6	321	17	2	18	3.3	.994	OF-48, 1B-37
1990			124	.264	.389	239	63	13	1	5	2.0	18	32	20	39	4	51	**18**	356	34	6	31	5.7	.985	1B-50, OF-20
4 yrs.			261	.256	.369	567	145	26	1	12	2.1	50	62	41	92	7	98	28	704	52	8	50	2.9	.990	1B-87, OF-85

Ken Griffey

GRIFFEY, GEORGE KENNETH, JR.
Son of Ken Griffey.
B. Nov. 21, 1969, Donora, Pa.
BL TL 6′ 3″ 195 lbs.

	Games	BA	SA	AB	H	2B	3B	HR	HR%	R	RBI	BB	SO	SB
April	20	.388	.625	80	31	2	1	5	6.3	10	17	5	14	1
May	29	.315	.514	111	35	5	1	5	4.5	23	14	13	9	6
June	28	.308	.442	104	32	8	0	2	1.9	15	7	16	11	4
July	26	.279	.442	104	29	8	0	3	2.9	18	11	10	16	1
Aug	28	.259	.426	108	28	5	2	3	2.8	11	14	12	17	.3
Sept/Oct	24	.267	.467	90	24	0	3	4	4.4	14	17	7	14	1
Day	39	.349	.624	149	52	4	2	11	7.4	29	24	12	20	3
Night	116	.283	.433	448	127	24	5	11	2.5	62	56	51	61	13
vs. Left		.306	.447	219	67	14	1	5	2.3	34	22	17	45	6
vs. Right		.296	.500	378	112	14	6	17	4.5	57	58	46	36	10
On Grass	59	.323	.539	232	75	10	2	12	5.2	38	32	22	35	4
On Turf	96	.285	.444	365	104	18	5	10	2.7	53	48	41	46	12
Home	80	.292	.452	305	89	17	4	8	2.6	45	45	34	33	11
Road	75	.308	.510	292	90	11	3	14	4.8	46	35	29	48	5
Division Rivals														
vs. CAL	12	.311	.600	45	14	4	0	3	6.7	7	9	3	8	0
vs. CHI	11	.231	.359	39	9	1	2	0	0.0	5	5	3	5	0
vs. KC	13	.222	.333	45	10	0	1	1	2.2	5	2	7	9	2
vs. MIN	10	.325	.500	40	13	1	0	2	5.0	8	7	4	7	1
vs. OAK	13	.314	.529	51	16	2	0	3	5.9	5	11	4	6	0
vs. TEX	13	.275	.510	51	14	1	1	3	5.9	9	11	7	8	2
On 3B < 2 Out		.524	.762	21	11	2	0	1	4.8	1	22	2	1	

OUTFIELD
AVERAGE / RBI / HR / SB (AL AVG comparisons)

Year	Team		Games	BA	SA	AB	H	2B	3B	HR	HR%	R	RBI	BB	SO	SB	PH AB	PH H	PO	A	E	DP	TC/G	FA	G by Pos
1989	SEA	A	127	.264	.420	455	120	23	0	16	3.5	61	61	44	83	16	3	1	302	12	10	6	2.6	.969	OF-127
1990			155	.300	.481	597	179	28	7	22	3.6	91	80	63	81	16	3	1	330	8	7	1	2.3	.980	OF-151, DH-2
2 yrs.			282	.284	.454	1052	299	51	7	38	3.6	152	141	107	164	32	6	2	632	20	17	7	2.4	.975	OF-278, DH-2

Ken Griffey

GRIFFEY, GEORGE KENNETH, SR.
Father of Ken Griffey.
B. Apr. 10, 1950, Donora, Pa.
BL TL 5′ 11″ 190 lbs.

Year	Team		Games	BA	SA	AB	H	2B	3B	HR	HR%	R	RBI	BB	SO	SB	PH AB	PH H	PO	A	E	DP	TC/G	FA	G by Pos
1973	CIN	N	25	.384	.570	86	33	5	1	3	3.5	19	14	6	10	4	3	2	25	1	0	0	1.0	1.000	OF-21
1974			88	.251	.361	227	57	9	5	2	0.9	24	19	27	43	9	15	4	115	5	0	1	1.4	1.000	OF-70
1975			132	.305	.402	463	141	15	9	4	0.9	95	46	67	67	16	10	2	202	6	7	0	1.6	.967	OF-119
1976			148	.336	.450	562	189	28	9	6	1.1	111	74	62	65	34	10	3	270	10	6	2	1.9	.979	OF-144
1977			154	.318	.467	585	186	35	8	12	2.1	117	57	69	84	17	4	1	298	10	3	3	2.0	.990	OF-147
1978			158	.288	.417	614	177	33	8	10	1.6	90	63	54	70	23	6	3	296	13	10	2	2.0	.969	OF-154
1979			95	.316	.471	380	120	27	4	8	2.1	62	32	36	39	12	1	1	175	8	3	1	2.0	.984	OF-93
1980			146	.294	.454	544	160	28	10	13	2.4	89	85	62	77	23	7	4	266	5	6	3	1.9	.978	OF-138
1981			101	.311	.409	396	123	21	6	2	0.5	65	34	39	42	12	1	0	268	8	3	1	2.8	.989	OF-99
1982	NY	A	127	.277	.407	484	134	23	2	12	2.5	70	54	39	58	10	7	1	282	8	5	2	2.3	.983	OF-125
1983			118	.306	.437	458	140	21	3	11	2.4	60	46	34	45	6	5	1	870	57	8	82	7.9	.991	1B-101, OF-14, DH-2
1984			120	.273	.381	399	109	20	1	7	1.8	44	56	29	32	2	18	2	422	22	16	23	3.8	.965	OF-82, 1B-27, DH-2
1985			127	.274	.425	438	120	28	4	10	2.3	68	69	41	51	7	18	2	227	8	7	3	1.9	.971	OF-110, DH-7, 1B-1
1986	2 teams			NY A (59G — .303)			ATL N (80G — .308)																		
''	total		139	.306	.492	490	150	22	3	21	4.3	69	58	35	67	14	19	8	232	7	5	2	1.8	.980	OF-128, DH-2, 1B-1

Year	Team		Games	BA	SA	AB	H	2B	3B	HR	HR%	R	RBI	BB	SO	SB	PINCH HIT AB	H	PO	A	E	DP	TC/G	FA	G by Pos

Ken Griffey   *Continued*

Year	Team		Games	BA	SA	AB	H	2B	3B	HR	HR%	R	RBI	BB	SO	SB	AB	H	PO	A	E	DP	TC/G	FA	G by Pos
1987	ATL	N	122	.286	.456	399	114	24	1	14	3.5	65	64	46	54	4	18	11	205	8	2	3	1.8	.991	OF-107, 1B-3
1988	2 teams					ATL N	(69G — .249)			CIN N	(25G — .280)														
"	total		94	.255	.329	243	62	6	0	4	1.6	26	23	19	31	1	31	5	193	16	4	9	2.3	.981	OF-42, 1B-21
1989	CIN	N	106	.263	.424	236	62	8	3	8	3.4	26	30	29	42	4	42	8	122	2	2	4	1.2	.984	OF-58, 1B-9
1990	2 teams					CIN N	(46G — .206)			SEA A	(21G — .377)														
"	total		67	.300	.414	140	42	4	0	4	2.8	19	26	12	8	2	32	6	79	5	2	2	2.5	.977	OF-26, 1B-9
18 yrs.			2067	.297	.432	7144	2119	357	77	151	2.1	1119	850	706	885	200	247	67	4547	199	89	143	2.3	.982	OF-1677, 1B-172, DH-13

LEAGUE CHAMPIONSHIP SERIES

Year	Team		Games	BA	SA	AB	H	2B	3B	HR	HR%	R	RBI	BB	SO	SB	AB	H	PO	A	E	DP	TC/G	FA	G by Pos
1973	CIN	N	3	.143	.286	7	1	1	0	0	0.0	0	0	0	1	0	1	0	2	0	0	0	0.7	1.000	OF-2
1974			3	.333	.417	12	4	1	0	0	0.0	4	4	0	3	3	0	0	4	1	0	0	1.7	1.000	OF-3
1976			3	.385	.538	13	5	0	1	0	0.0	2	2	2	1	2	0	0	11	0	0	0	3.7	1.000	OF-3
3 yrs.			9	.313	.438	32	10	2	1	0	0.0	6	6	2	5	5	1	0	17	1	0	0	2.0	.000	OF-8

WORLD SERIES

Year	Team		Games	BA	SA	AB	H	2B	3B	HR	HR%	R	RBI	BB	SO	SB	AB	H	PO	A	E	DP	TC/G	FA	G by Pos
1975	CIN	N	7	.269	.462	26	7	3	1	0	0.0	4	4	4	2	2	0	0	10	1	0	0	1.6	1.000	OF-7
1976			4	.059	.059	17	1	0	0	0	0.0	2	1	0	1	1	0	0	5	0	0	0	1.3	1.000	OF-4
2 yrs.			11	.186	.302	43	8	3	1	0	0.0	6	5	4	3	3	0	0	15	1	0	0	1.5	.000	OF-11

Alfredo Griffin

GRIFFIN, ALFREDO CLAUDINO
Born Alfredo Claudino Baptist y Griffin.
B. Oct. 6, 1957, Santo Domingo, Dominican Republic
BB TR 5′ 11″ 160 lbs.

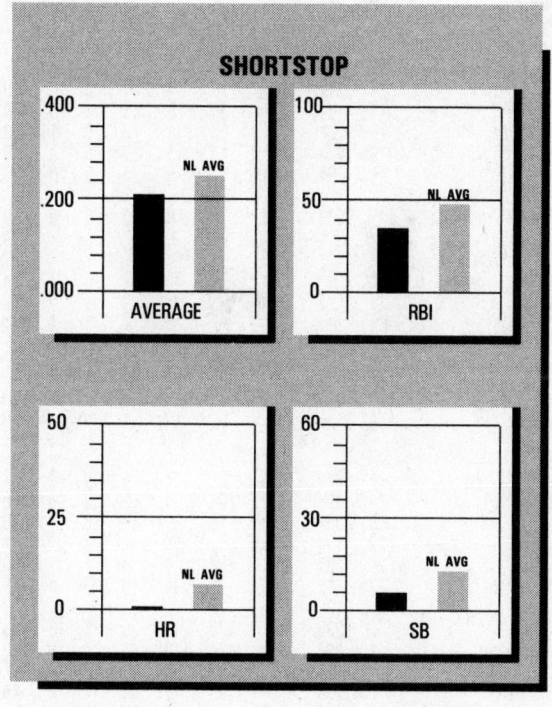

SHORTSTOP

	Games	BA	SA	AB	H	2B	3B	HR	HR%	R	RBI	BB	SO	SB
April	21	.329	.429	70	23	5	1	0	0.0	11	5	8	5	1
May	27	.258	.290	93	24	3	0	0	0.0	11	8	6	14	2
June	26	.174	.228	92	16	0	1	1	1.1	4	10	4	18	2
July	20	.182	.197	66	12	1	0	0	0.0	3	3	3	9	0
Aug	26	.160	.173	81	13	1	0	0	0.0	6	3	5	12	0
Sept/Oct	21	.153	.203	59	9	1	1	0	0.0	3	6	3	7	1
Day	35	.179	.205	117	21	3	0	0	0.0	13	9	9	18	1
Night	106	.221	.270	344	76	8	3	1	0.3	25	26	20	47	5
vs. Left		.207	.237	169	35	2	0	1	0.6	20	12	11	30	1
vs. Right		.212	.264	292	62	9	3	0	0.0	18	23	18	35	5
On Grass	102	.203	.233	330	67	8	1	0	0.0	26	24	22	54	4
On Turf	39	.229	.305	131	30	3	2	1	0.8	12	11	7	11	2
Home	68	.220	.248	218	48	4	1	0	0.0	17	22	14	36	3
Road	73	.202	.259	243	49	7	2	1	0.4	21	13	15	29	3
Division Rivals														
vs. ATL	14	.156	.156	45	7	0	0	0	0.0	4	0	2	8	2
vs. CIN	18	.270	.349	63	17	0	1	1	1.6	4	8	2	7	0
vs. HOU	18	.236	.291	55	13	1	1	0	0.0	6	2	3	4	0
vs. SD	13	.200	.250	40	8	0	1	0	0.0	3	5	3	12	1
vs. SF	13	.196	.261	46	9	3	0	0	0.0	2	4	3	6	0
On 3B < 2 Out		.174	.217	23	4	1	0	0	0.0	0	17	3	4	

Year	Team		Games	BA	SA	AB	H	2B	3B	HR	HR%	R	RBI	BB	SO	SB	AB	H	PO	A	E	DP	TC/G	FA	G by Pos
1976	CLE	A	12	.250	.250	4	1	0	0	0	0.0	0	0	0	2	0	0	0	1	2	1	0	0.3	.750	SS-6, DH-4
1977			14	.146	.171	41	6	1	0	0	0.0	5	3	3	5	2	0	0	17	30	3	6	3.6	.940	SS-13, DH-1
1978			5	.500	.750	4	2	1	0	0	0.0	1	0	2	1	0	0	0	4	7	1	5	2.4	.917	SS-2
1979	TOR	A	153	.287	.364	624	179	22	10	2	0.3	81	31	40	59	21	0	0	272	501	36	124	5.3	.956	SS-153
1980			155	.254	.349	653	166	26	**15**	2	0.3	63	41	24	58	18	0	0	295	489	37	126	5.3	.955	SS-155
1981			101	.209	.289	388	81	19	6	0	0.0	30	21	17	38	8	1	0	191	279	31	66	5.0	.938	SS-97, 3B-4, 2B-1
1982			162	.241	.314	539	130	20	8	1	0.2	57	48	22	48	10	0	0	319	479	26	92	5.1	.968	SS-162
1983			162	.250	.348	528	132	22	9	4	0.8	62	47	27	44	8	0	0	287	422	25	86	4.5	.966	SS-157, 2B-5, DH-1
1984			140	.241	.298	419	101	8	2	4	1.0	53	30	4	33	11	0	0	230	320	21	72	4.1	.963	SS-115, 2B-21, DH-5
1985	OAK	A	162	.270	.332	614	166	18	7	2	0.3	75	64	20	50	24	0	0	278	440	30	87	4.6	.960	SS-162
1986			162	.285	.364	594	169	23	6	4	0.7	74	51	35	52	33	0	0	282	421	25	85	4.5	.966	SS-162
1987			144	.263	.348	494	130	23	5	3	0.6	69	60	28	41	26	0	0	250	389	24	73	4.6	.964	SS-137, 2B-1
1988	LA	N	95	.199	.253	316	63	8	3	1	0.3	39	27	24	30	7	0	0	145	264	15	44	4.5	.965	SS-93
1989			136	.247	.308	506	125	27	2	0	0.0	49	29	29	57	10	5	1	208	333	14	69	4.1	.975	SS-131
1990			141	.210	.254	461	97	11	3	1	0.2	38	35	29	65	6	1	0	221	382	26	63	4.5	.959	SS-139
15 yrs.			1744	.250	.324	6185	1548	229	76	24	0.4	696	487	304	583	184	7	1	3000	4758	315	998	4.6	.961	SS-1684, 2B-28, DH-11, 3B-4

LEAGUE CHAMPIONSHIP SERIES

Year	Team		Games	BA	SA	AB	H	2B	3B	HR	HR%	R	RBI	BB	SO	SB	AB	H	PO	A	E	DP	TC/G	FA	G by Pos
1988	LA	N	7	.160	.200	25	4	1	0	0	0.0	1	3	0	5	0	0	0	17	13	0	7	4.3	1.000	SS-7

Year	Team	Games	BA	SA	AB	H	2B	3B	HR	HR%	R	RBI	BB	SO	SB	PINCH HIT AB	H	PO	A	E	DP	TC/G	FA	G by Pos

Alfredo Griffin *Continued*

WORLD SERIES

Year	Team	Games	BA	SA	AB	H	2B	3B	HR	HR%	R	RBI	BB	SO	SB	AB	H	PO	A	E	DP	TC/G	FA	G by Pos
1988	LA N	5	.188	.188	16	3	0	0	0	0.0	2	0	2	4	0	0	0	7	13	1	2	4.2	.952	SS-5

Marquis Grissom

GRISSOM, MARQUIS DEON
B. Apr. 17, 1967, Atlanta, Ga.
BR TR 5′ 11″ 190 lbs.

	Games	BA	SA	AB	H	2B	3B	HR	HR%	R	RBI	BB	SO	SB	AB	H	PO	A	E	DP	TC/G	FA	G by Pos
April	19	.230	.338	74	17	8	0	0	0.0	8	5	7	12	7									
May	23	.263	.289	76	20	2	0	0	0.0	13	4	5	8	5									
June	1	.500	.750	4	2	1	0	0	0.0	2	1	1	1	0									
July	19	.281	.421	57	16	1	2	1	1.8	10	6	6	9	1									
Aug	16	.216	.324	37	8	1	0	1	2.7	4	6	2	3	3									
Sept/Oct	20	.275	.375	40	11	1	0	1	2.5	5	7	6	7	6									
Day	30	.235	.318	85	20	4	0	1	1.2	14	6	11	15	7									
Night	68	.266	.365	203	54	10	2	2	1.0	28	23	16	25	15									
vs. Left		.243	.359	181	44	11	2	2	1.1	24	16	20	20	12									
vs. Right		.280	.336	107	30	3	0	1	0.9	18	13	7	20	10									
On Grass	25	.225	.239	71	16	1	0	0	0.0	11	1	7	10	5									
On Turf	73	.267	.387	217	58	13	2	3	1.4	31	28	20	30	17									
Home	52	.247	.349	146	36	5	2	2	1.4	20	17	16	22	12									
Road	46	.268	.352	142	38	9	0	1	0.7	22	12	11	18	10									
Division Rivals																								
vs. CHI	8	.211	.263	19	4	1	0	0	0.0	1	2	2	3	0									
vs. NY	13	.139	.222	36	5	1	1	0	0.0	2	2	4	5	4									
vs. PHI	13	.222	.361	36	8	2	0	1	2.8	4	6	3	8	4									
vs. PIT	9	.423	.692	26	11	1	0	2	7.7	8	8	2	2	3									
vs. STL	5	.294	.529	17	5	4	0	0	0.0	3	2	2	1	1									
On 3B < 2 Out		.333	.333	18	6	0	0	0	0.0	0	11	0	4										
1989 MON N	26	.257	.324	74	19	2	0	1	1.4	16	2	12	21	1	3	0	32	1	2	0	1.3	.943	OF-23
1990	98	.257	.351	288	74	14	2	3	1.0	42	29	27	40	22	21	6	165	5	2	0	2.0	.988	OF-87
2 yrs.	124	.257	.345	362	93	16	2	4	1.1	58	31	39	61	23	24	6	197	6	4	0	1.7	.981	OF-110

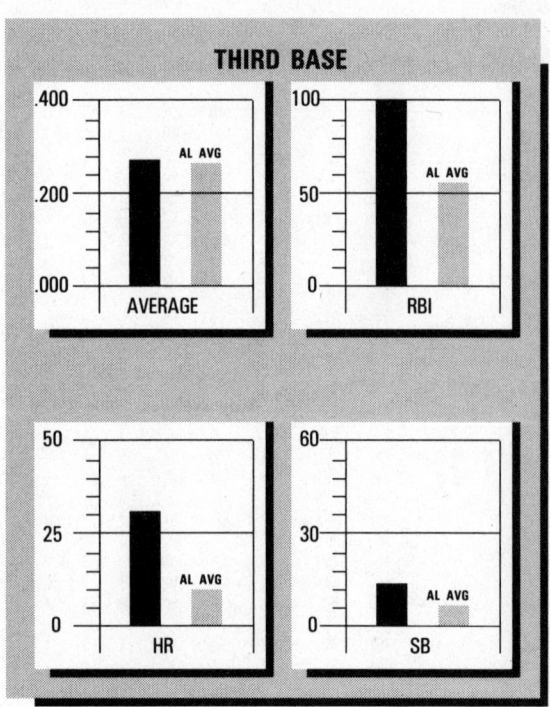

OUTFIELD

Kelly Gruber

GRUBER, KELLY WAYNE
B. Feb. 26, 1962, Houston, Tex.
BR TR 6′ 175 lbs.

	Games	BA	SA	AB	H	2B	3B	HR	HR%	R	RBI	BB	SO	SB	AB	H	PO	A	E	DP	TC/G	FA	G by Pos
April	21	.325	.639	83	27	5	0	7	8.4	11	20	4	15	1									
May	26	.300	.570	100	30	9	0	6	6.0	18	20	12	20	2									
June	28	.302	.578	116	35	7	2	7	6.0	28	24	10	14	1									
July	22	.169	.258	89	15	2	0	2	2.2	8	11	5	15	3									
Aug	26	.206	.294	102	21	4	1	1	1.0	6	12	4	18	4									
Sept/Oct	27	.333	.716	102	34	9	3	8	7.8	21	31	13	12	3									
Day	46	.236	.511	178	42	6	2	13	7.3	30	37	14	35	3									
Night	104	.290	.512	414	120	30	4	18	4.3	62	81	34	59	11									
vs. Left		.295	.554	166	49	11	4	8	4.8	31	34	16	27	3									
vs. Right		.265	.495	426	113	25	2	23	5.4	61	84	32	67	11									
On Grass	59	.240	.438	233	56	21	2	7	3.0	34	43	22	37	5									
On Turf	91	.295	.560	359	106	15	4	24	6.7	58	75	26	57	9									
Home	77	.292	.587	305	89	13	2	23	7.5	48	62	17	47	5									
Road	73	.254	.432	287	73	23	2	8	2.8	44	56	31	47	9									
Division Rivals																								
vs. BAL	13	.352	.685	54	19	6	0	4	7.4	8	16	2	4	0									
vs. BOS	13	.164	.436	55	9	3	0	4	7.3	10	13	3	13	0									
vs. CLE	13	.434	1.000	53	23	5	2	7	13.2	11	17	6	14	2									
vs. DET	10	.257	.486	35	9	2	0	2	5.7	7	10	2	5	1									
vs. MIL	12	.250	.396	48	12	1	0	2	4.2	8	7	5	4	1									
vs. NY	12	.286	.490	49	14	4	3	0	0.0	9	6	3	5	1									
On 3B < 2 Out		.355	.645	31	11	1	1	2	6.5	2	37	7	4										

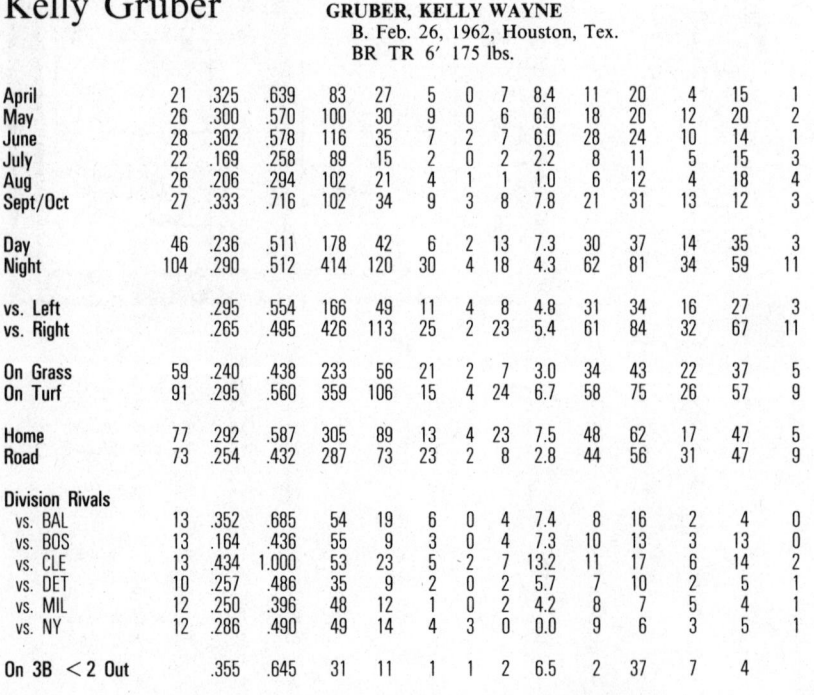

THIRD BASE

Year	Team		Games	BA	SA	AB	H	2B	3B	HR	HR%	R	RBI	BB	SO	SB	PINCH HIT AB	H	PO	A	E	DP	TC/G	FA	G by Pos

Kelly Gruber *Continued*

Year	Team		Games	BA	SA	AB	H	2B	3B	HR	HR%	R	RBI	BB	SO	SB	PH AB	PH H	PO	A	E	DP	TC/G	FA	G by Pos
1984	TOR	A	15	.063	.250	16	1	0	0	1	6.3	1	2	0	5	0	4	1	6	12	2	0	1.3	.900	3B-12, OF-2, SS-1
1985			5	.231	.231	13	3	0	0	0	0.0	0	1	0	3	0	1	1	2	6	0	0	1.6	1.000	3B-5, 2B-1
1986			87	.196	.343	143	28	4	1	5	3.5	20	15	5	27	2	9	2	43	77	7	8	1.5	.945	3B-42, DH-14, 2B-14, OF-9, SS-5
1987			138	.235	.399	341	80	14	3	12	3.5	50	36	17	70	12	16	2	76	200	13	19	2.1	.955	3B-119, SS-21, 2B-7, OF-2
1988			158	.278	.438	569	158	33	5	16	2.8	75	81	38	92	23	3	0	121	365	16	35	3.2	.968	3B-156, 2B-7, OF-2, SS-1
1989			135	.290	.448	545	158	24	4	18	3.3	83	73	30	60	10	1	1	121	295	22	16	3.2	.950	3B-119, OF-16, DH-1, SS-1
1990			150	.274	.512	592	162	36	6	31	5.2	92	118	48	94	14	2	1	129	280	19	21	2.9	.956	3B-145, OF-6, DH-1
7 yrs.			688	.266	.445	2219	590	111	19	83	3.7	321	326	138	351	61	36	8	498	1235	79	99	2.6	.956	3B-598, OF-37, 2B-29, SS-29, DH-16

LEAGUE CHAMPIONSHIP SERIES

Year	Team		Games	BA	SA	AB	H	2B	3B	HR	HR%	R	RBI	BB	SO	SB	PH AB	PH H	PO	A	E	DP	TC/G	FA	G by Pos
1989	TOR	A	5	.294	.353	17	5	1	0	0	0.0	2	1	3	2	1	0	0	4	8	0	1	2.4	1.000	3B-5

Pedro Guerrero

GUERRERO, PEDRO (Pete)
B. June 29, 1956, San Pedro de Macoris, Dominican Republic
BR TR 5′ 11″ 176 lbs.

FIRST BASE

	Games	BA	SA	AB	H	2B	3B	HR	HR%	R	RBI	BB	SO	SB
April	20	.295	.513	78	23	2	0	5	6.4	11	20	7	10	1
May	25	.276	.414	87	24	9	0	1	1.1	4	13	11	14	0
June	28	.303	.450	109	33	8	1	2	1.8	11	15	9	18	0
July	25	.269	.441	93	25	7	0	3	3.2	8	17	5	12	0
Aug	14	.235	.314	51	12	1	0	1	2.0	3	4	7	8	0
Sept/Oct	24	.288	.375	80	23	4	0	1	1.3	5	11	5	8	0
Day	39	.321	.450	140	45	7	1	3	2.1	16	23	12	19	0
Night	97	.265	.416	358	95	24	0	10	2.8	26	57	32	51	1
vs. Left		.274	.446	168	46	17	0	4	2.4	15	30	13	28	0
vs. Right		.285	.415	330	94	14	1	9	2.7	27	50	31	42	1
On Grass	36	.288	.453	139	40	6	1	5	3.6	15	19	13	15	1
On Turf	100	.279	.415	359	100	25	0	8	2.2	27	61	31	55	0
Home	72	.276	.437	261	72	18	0	8	3.1	22	50	26	42	0
Road	64	.287	.414	237	68	13	1	5	2.1	20	30	18	28	1
Division Rivals														
vs. CHI	18	.377	.580	69	26	6	1	2	2.9	10	10	9	10	0
vs. MON	15	.408	.551	49	20	4	0	1	2.0	8	10	5	8	0
vs. NY	15	.291	.382	55	16	2	0	1	1.8	4	9	3	8	0
vs. PHI	16	.143	.238	63	9	3	0	1	1.6	2	10	2	4	0
vs. PIT	16	.246	.443	61	15	3	0	3	4.9	5	8	5	12	0
On 3B < 2 Out		.258	.484	31	8	4	0	1	3.2	1	32	5	4	

Year	Team		Games	BA	SA	AB	H	2B	3B	HR	HR%	R	RBI	BB	SO	SB	PH AB	PH H	PO	A	E	DP	TC/G	FA	G by Pos
1978	LA	N	5	.625	.875	8	5	0	1	0	0.0	3	1	0	0	0	1	1	25	1	0	0	5.2	1.000	1B-4
1979			25	.242	.371	62	15	2	0	2	3.2	7	9	1	14	2	7	3	53	4	1	1	2.3	.983	OF-12, 1B-8, 3B-3
1980			75	.322	.497	183	59	9	1	7	3.8	27	31	12	31	2	17	11	103	37	3	5	1.9	.979	OF-40, 2B-12, 3B-3, 1B-2
1981			98	.300	.464	347	104	17	2	12	3.5	46	48	34	57	5	4	1	165	55	11	5	2.4	.952	OF-75, 3B-21, 1B-1
1982			150	.304	.536	575	175	27	5	32	5.6	87	100	65	89	22	0	0	282	53	12	9	2.3	.965	OF-137, 3B-24
1983			160	.298	.531	584	174	28	6	32	5.5	87	103	72	110	23	1	1	130	308	31	22	2.9	.934	3B-157, 1B-2
1984			144	.303	.462	535	162	29	4	16	3.0	85	72	49	105	9	7	1	271	151	22	24	3.1	.950	3B-76, OF-58, 1B-16
1985			137	.320	**.577**	487	156	22	2	33	**6.8**	99	87	83	68	12	3	0	251	123	13	18	2.8	.966	OF-81, 3B-44, 1B-12
1986			31	.246	.541	61	15	3	0	5	8.2	7	10	2	19	0	17	3	39	1	0	4	1.3	1.000	OF-10, 1B-4
1987			152	.338	.539	545	184	25	2	27	5.0	89	89	74	85	9	4	0	482	44	12	30	3.5	.978	OF-109, 1B-40
1988	2 teams		LA N (59G — .298)			STL N (44G — .268)																			
"	total		103	.286	.418	364	104	14	2	10	2.7	40	65	46	59	4	1	0	466	99	12	26	5.6	.979	1B-52, 3B-45, OF-9
1989	STL	N	162	.311	.477	570	177	42	1	17	3.0	60	117	79	84	2	1	1	1445	72	15	99	9.5	.990	1B-160
1990			136	.281	.426	498	140	31	1	13	2.6	42	80	44	70	1	3	1	1083	73	13	74	8.9	.989	1B-132
13 yrs.			1378	.305	.496	4819	1470	249	27	206	4.3	679	812	561	791	91	66	23	4795	1021	145	317	4.3	.976	OF-531, 1B-433, 3B-373, 2B-12

DIVISIONAL PLAYOFF SERIES

Year	Team		Games	BA	SA	AB	H	2B	3B	HR	HR%	R	RBI	BB	SO	SB	PH AB	PH H	PO	A	E	DP	TC/G	FA	G by Pos
1981	LA	N	5	.176	.412	17	3	1	0	1	5.9	1	1	2	4	1	0	0	3	15	0	0	3.6	1.000	3B-5

Year	Team		Games	BA	SA	AB	H	2B	3B	HR	HR%	R	RBI	BB	SO	SB	PINCH HIT AB	PINCH HIT H	PO	A	E	DP	TC/G	FA	G by Pos

Pedro Guerrero *Continued*

LEAGUE CHAMPIONSHIP SERIES

Year	Team		Games	BA	SA	AB	H	2B	3B	HR	HR%	R	RBI	BB	SO	SB	PH AB	PH H	PO	A	E	DP	TC/G	FA	G by Pos
1981	LA	N	5	.105	.263	19	2	0	0	1	5.3	1	2	1	4	0	0	0	0	9	2	1	2.2	1.000	OF-5
1983			4	.250	.500	12	3	1	1	0	0.0	1	2	3	3	0	0	0	0	9	0	1	2.3	1.000	3B-4
1985			6	.250	.300	20	5	1	0	0	0.0	2	4	5	2	2	0	0	11	0	0	0	1.8	1.000	OF-6
3 yrs.			15	.196	.333	51	10	2	1	1	2.0	4	8	9	9	2	0	0	11	18	2	2	2.1	.935	OF-11, 3B-4

WORLD SERIES

Year	Team		Games	BA	SA	AB	H	2B	3B	HR	HR%	R	RBI	BB	SO	SB	PH AB	PH H	PO	A	E	DP	TC/G	FA	G by Pos
1981	LA	N	6	.333	.762	21	7	1	1	2	9.5	2	7	2	6	0	0	0	17	1	0	0	3.0	1.000	OF-6

Ozzie Guillen

GUILLEN, OSWALDO JOSE
Born Oswaldo Jose Guillen y Barrios.
B. Jan. 20, 1964, Oculare del Tuy, Venezuela
BL TR 5' 11" 160 lbs.

	Games	BA	SA	AB	H	2B	3B	HR	HR%	R	RBI	BB	SO	SB
April	16	.296	.407	54	16	2	2	0	0.0	9	5	2	3	5
May	28	.383	.457	94	36	3	2	0	0.0	10	8	5	4	5
June	26	.268	.305	82	22	3	0	0	0.0	9	10	1	6	1
July	27	.277	.298	94	26	2	0	0	0.0	14	10	7	7	0
Aug	32	.228	.317	101	23	6	0	1	1.0	9	13	4	5	0
Sept/Oct	31	.231	.286	91	21	5	0	0	0.0	10	12	7	12	2
Day	40	.291	.386	127	37	8	2	0	0.0	18	19	8	11	2
Night	120	.275	.326	389	107	13	2	1	0.3	43	39	18	26	11
vs. Left		.267	.316	206	55	8	1	0	0.0	20	28	6	19	4
vs. Right		.287	.358	310	89	13	3	1	0.3	41	30	20	18	9
On Grass	133	.273	.331	429	117	16	3	1	0.2	47	43	22	33	12
On Turf	27	.310	.391	87	27	5	1	0	0.0	14	15	4	4	1
Home	79	.279	.356	247	69	10	3	1	0.4	29	25	14	19	8
Road	81	.279	.327	269	75	11	1	0	0.0	32	33	12	18	5
Division Rivals														
vs. CAL	13	.353	.441	34	12	3	0	0	0.0	2	7	2	2	1
vs. KC	13	.395	.512	43	17	3	1	0	0.0	8	6	4	1	1
vs. MIN	12	.275	.325	40	11	2	0	0	0.0	3	4	0	2	1
vs. OAK	13	.209	.256	43	9	2	0	0	0.0	4	5	0	1	0
vs. SEA	13	.250	.313	32	8	2	0	0	0.0	5	7	1	5	1
vs. TEX	13	.170	.319	47	8	2	1	1	2.1	3	6	2	3	2
On 3B < 2 Out		.400	.480	25	10	2	0	0	0.0	0	25	4	1	

SHORTSTOP — AVERAGE / RBI / HR / SB (with AL AVG)

Year	Team		Games	BA	SA	AB	H	2B	3B	HR	HR%	R	RBI	BB	SO	SB	PH AB	PH H	PO	A	E	DP	TC/G	FA	G by Pos
1985	CHI	A	150	.273	.358	491	134	21	9	1	0.2	71	33	12	36	7	13	1	220	382	12	80	4.1	.980	SS-150
1986			159	.250	.311	547	137	19	4	2	0.4	58	47	12	52	8	2	0	261	459	22	93	4.7	.970	SS-157, DH-1
1987			149	.279	.354	560	156	22	7	2	0.4	64	51	22	52	25	2	1	266	475	19	105	5.1	.975	SS-149
1988			156	.261	.314	566	148	16	7	0	0.0	58	39	25	40	25	0	0	273	570	20	115	5.5	.977	SS-156
1989			155	.253	.318	597	151	20	8	1	0.2	63	54	15	48	36	0	0	272	512	22	106	5.2	.973	SS-155
1990			160	.279	.341	516	144	21	4	1	0.1	61	58	26	37	13	2	0	252	474	17	100	4.7	.977	SS-159
6 yrs.			929	.265	.332	3277	870	119	39	7	0.2	375	282	112	265	114	19	2	1544	2872	112	599	4.9	.975	SS-926, DH-1

Chris Gwynn

GWYNN, CHRISTOPHER KARLTON
Brother of Tony Gwynn.
B. Oct. 13, 1964, Los Angeles, Calif.
BL TL 6' 200 lbs.

Year	Team		Games	BA	SA	AB	H	2B	3B	HR	HR%	R	RBI	BB	SO	SB	PH AB	PH H	PO	A	E	DP	TC/G	FA	G by Pos
1987	LA	N	17	.219	.250	32	7	1	0	0	0.0	2	2	1	7	0	6	0	12	0	0	0	0.7	1.000	OF-10
1988			12	.182	.182	11	2	0	0	0	0.0	1	0	1	2	0	9	2	0	0	0	0	0.0	—	OF-4
1989			32	.235	.324	68	16	4	1	0	0.0	8	7	2	9	1	14	3	26	1	0	1	0.8	1.000	OF-19
1990			101	.284	.418	141	40	2	1	5	3.5	19	22	7	28	0	56	13	39	1	0	0	0.9	1.000	OF-44
4 yrs.			162	.258	.361	252	65	7	2	5	2.0	30	31	11	46	1	85	18	77	2	0	1	0.5	.000	OF-77

Year	Team		Games	BA	SA	AB	H	2B	3B	HR	HR%	R	RBI	BB	SO	SB	PINCH HIT AB	H	PO	A	E	DP	TC/G	FA	G by Pos

Tony Gwynn

GWYNN, ANTHONY KEITH
Brother of Chris Gwynn.
B. May 9, 1960, Los Angeles, Calif.
BL TL 5' 11" 185 lbs.

Split	Games	BA	SA	AB	H	2B	3B	HR	HR%	R	RBI	BB	SO	SB
April	19	.303	.447	76	23	6	1	1	1.3	14	5	5	2	1
May	27	.327	.442	104	34	7	1	1	1.0	15	11	8	4	3
June	26	.315	.407	108	34	4	3	0	0.0	14	15	12	8	5
July	28	.299	.444	117	35	7	2	2	1.7	12	15	5	4	4
Aug	26	.321	.349	109	35	3	0	0	0.0	14	14	9	4	3
Sept/Oct	15	.271	.407	59	16	2	3	0	0.0	10	12	5	1	1
Day	41	.255	.358	165	42	10	2	1	0.6	19	14	13	10	4
Night	100	.331	.439	408	135	19	8	3	0.7	60	58	31	13	13
vs. Left		.281	.373	228	64	8	2	3	1.3	21	28	8	10	3
vs. Right		.328	.443	345	113	21	8	1	0.3	58	44	36	13	14
On Grass	105	.306	.417	422	129	23	9	2	0.5	60	54	34	17	13
On Turf	36	.318	.411	151	48	6	1	2	1.3	19	18	10	6	4
Home	76	.310	.422	306	95	16	6	2	0.7	43	42	22	10	10
Road	65	.307	.408	267	82	13	4	2	0.7	36	30	22	13	7
Division Rivals														
vs. ATL	16	.300	.429	70	21	3	3	0	0.0	12	15	6	5	2
vs. CIN	11	.362	.468	47	17	5	0	0	0.0	6	7	3	2	3
vs. HOU	16	.359	.469	64	23	3	2	0	0.0	12	10	4	2	3
vs. LA	13	.245	.367	49	12	1	1	1	2.0	10	7	8	2	1
vs. SF	15	.328	.459	61	20	4	2	0	0.0	8	6	5	2	1
On 3B < 2 Out		.500	.600	30	15	3	0	0	0.0	0	27	4	1	

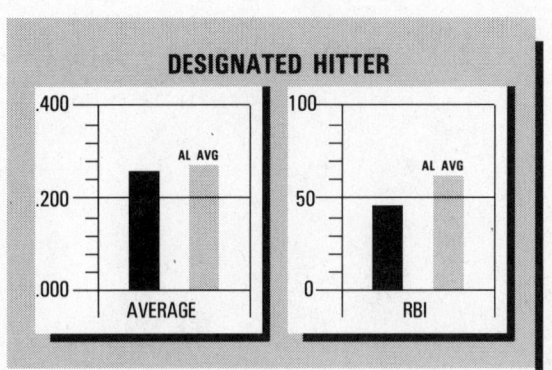

OUTFIELD — AVERAGE / RBI (NL AVG) / HR (NL AVG) / SB (NL AVG)

Year	Team		Games	BA	SA	AB	H	2B	3B	HR	HR%	R	RBI	BB	SO	SB	AB	H	PO	A	E	DP	TC/G	FA	G by Pos
1982	SD	N	54	.289	.389	190	55	12	2	1	0.5	33	17	14	16	8	4	1	110	1	1	0	2.1	.991	OF-52
1983			86	.309	.372	304	94	12	2	1	0.3	34	37	23	21	7	6	1	163	9	1	1	2.0	.994	OF-81
1984			158	**.351**	.444	606	**213**	21	10	5	0.8	88	71	59	23	33	2	1	345	11	4	4	2.3	.989	OF-156
1985			154	.317	.408	622	197	29	5	6	1.0	90	46	45	33	14	2	0	337	14	4	2	2.3	.989	OF-152
1986			160	.329	.467	**642**	**211**	33	7	14	2.2	**107**	59	52	35	37	1	0	337	19	4	3	2.3	.989	OF-160
1987			157	**.370**	.511	589	**218**	36	13	7	1.2	119	54	82	35	56	2	1	298	13	6	1	2.0	.981	OF-156
1988			133	**.313**	.415	521	163	22	5	7	1.3	64	70	51	40	26	0	0	264	8	5	1	2.1	.982	OF-133
1989			158	**.336**	.424	604	**203**	27	7	4	0.7	82	62	56	30	40	0	0	353	13	6	1	2.4	.984	OF-157
1990			141	.309	.415	573	177	29	10	4	0.6	79	72	44	23	17	0	0	327	11	5	2	2.4	.985	OF-141
9 yrs.			1201	.329	.435	4651	1531	221	61	49	1.1	696	488	426	256	238	17	4	2534	99	36	15	2.2	.987	OF-1188

LEAGUE CHAMPIONSHIP SERIES

Year	Team		Games	BA	SA	AB	H	2B	3B	HR	HR%	R	RBI	BB	SO	SB	AB	H	PO	A	E	DP	TC/G	FA	G by Pos
1984	SD	N	5	.368	.526	19	7	3	0	0	0.0	6	3	1	2	0	0	0	9	0	0	0	1.8	1.000	OF-5

WORLD SERIES

Year	Team		Games	BA	SA	AB	H	2B	3B	HR	HR%	R	RBI	BB	SO	SB	AB	H	PO	A	E	DP	TC/G	FA	G by Pos
1984	SD	N	5	.263	.263	19	5	0	0	0	0.0	1	0	3	2	1	0	0	12	1	1	1	2.8	.929	OF-5

Chip Hale

HALE, WALTER WILLIAM
B. Dec. 2, 1964, Santa Clara, Calif.
BL TR 5' 11" 180 lbs.

Year	Team		Games	BA	SA	AB	H	2B	3B	HR	HR%	R	RBI	BB	SO	SB	AB	H	PO	A	E	DP	TC/G	FA	G by Pos
1989	MIN	A	28	.209	.254	67	14	3	0	0	0.0	6	4	1	6	0	8	0	15	40	1	8	2.0	.982	2B-16, 3B-9, DH-2
1990			1	.000	.000	2	0	0	0	0	0.0	0	2	0	1	0	0	0	2	6	0	2	8.0	1.000	2B-1
2 yrs.			29	.203	.246	69	14	3	0	0	0.0	6	6	1	7	0	8	0	17	46	1	10	2.2	.984	2B-17, 3B-9, DH-2

Mel Hall

HALL, MELVIN, JR.
B. Sept. 16, 1960, Lyons, N. Y.
BL TL 6' 185 lbs.

Split	Games	BA	SA	AB	H	2B	3B	HR	HR%	R	RBI	BB	SO	SB
April	13	.273	.500	44	12	2	1	2	4.5	4	7	1	6	0
May	25	.222	.395	81	18	8	0	2	2.5	10	7	0	6	0
June	26	.286	.516	91	26	6	0	5	5.5	12	15	3	10	0
July	11	.325	.425	40	13	4	0	0	0.0	4	6	1	6	0
Aug	26	.211	.329	76	16	3	0	2	2.6	6	7	1	14	0
Sept/Oct	12	.286	.464	28	8	0	1	1	3.6	5	4	5	4	0
Day	33	.216	.314	102	22	7	0	1	1.0	8	9	3	13	0
Night	80	.275	.481	258	71	16	2	11	4.3	33	37	3	33	0
vs. Left		.207	.310	58	12	3	0	1	1.7	5	5	0	11	0
vs. Right		.268	.457	302	81	20	2	11	3.6	36	41	6	35	0

DESIGNATED HITTER — AVERAGE (AL AVG) / RBI (AL AVG)

Year	Team		Games	BA	SA	AB	H	2B	3B	HR	HR%	R	RBI	BB	SO	SB	PINCH HIT AB	PINCH HIT H	PO	A	E	DP	TC/G	FA	G by Pos

Mel Hall *Continued*

Year	Team		Games	BA	SA	AB	H	2B	3B	HR	HR%	R	RBI	BB	SO	SB	PH AB	PH H	PO	A	E	DP	TC/G	FA	G by Pos
On Grass			95	.244	.403	303	74	17	2	9	3.0	30	38	6	38	0									
On Turf			18	.333	.596	57	19	6	0	3	5.3	11	8	0	8	0									
Home			60	.273	.412	187	51	13	2	3	1.6	16	25	3	27	0									
Road			53	.243	.457	173	42	10	0	9	5.2	25	21	3	19	0									
Division Rivals																									
vs. BAL			8	.185	.259	27	5	2	0	0	0.0	2	1	2	5	0									
vs. BOS			10	.200	.480	25	5	1	0	2	8.0	3	6	1	2	0									
vs. CLE			7	.235	.412	17	4	0	0	1	5.9	2	5	0	2	0									
vs. DET			5	.286	.429	21	6	0	0	1	4.8	3	1	0	2	0									
vs. MIL			10	.281	.438	32	9	2	0	1	3.1	2	4	1	4	0									
vs. TOR			11	.344	.594	32	11	2	0	2	6.3	6	4	0	4	0									
On 3B < 2 Out				.000	.000	12	0	0	0	0	0.0	0	8	1	2										
1981	CHI	N	10	.091	.364	11	1	0	0	1	9.1	1	2	1	4	0	7	1	0	0	0	0	0.0	—	OF-3
1982			24	.263	.350	80	21	3	2	0	0.0	6	4	5	17	0	1	0	42	4	3	1	2.0	.939	OF-22
1983			112	.283	.488	410	116	23	5	17	4.1	60	56	42	101	6	2	1	239	8	3	2	2.2	.988	OF-112
1984	2 teams		CHI N	(48G — .280)					CLE A	(83G — .257)															
"	total		131	.265	.425	407	108	24	4	11	2.7	68	52	47	78	3	14	3	212	8	4	2	1.7	.982	OF-115, DH-9
1985	CLE	A	23	.318	.409	66	21	6	0	0	0.0	7	12	8	12	0	6	2	18	0	0	0	0.8	1.000	OF-15, DH-5
1986			140	.296	.493	442	131	29	2	18	4.1	68	77	33	65	6	19	6	233	7	7	1	1.8	.972	OF-126, DH-7
1987			142	.280	.439	485	136	21	1	18	3.7	57	76	20	68	5	17	2	264	3	3	2	1.9	.989	OF-122, DH-14
1988			150	.280	.392	515	144	32	4	6	1.2	69	71	28	50	7	11	4	288	3	10	1	2.0	.967	OF-141, DH-6
1989	NY	A	113	.260	.427	361	94	9	0	17	4.7	54	58	21	37	0	16	4	141	3	1	2	1.3	.993	OF-75, DH-34
1990			113	.258	.433	360	93	23	2	12	3.3	41	46	6	46	0	15	3	70	2	2	0	1.5	.973	DH-54, OF-50
10 yrs.			958	.276	.438	3137	865	170	20	100	3.2	431	454	211	478	27	108	26	1507	38	33	11	1.6	.979	OF-781, DH-129

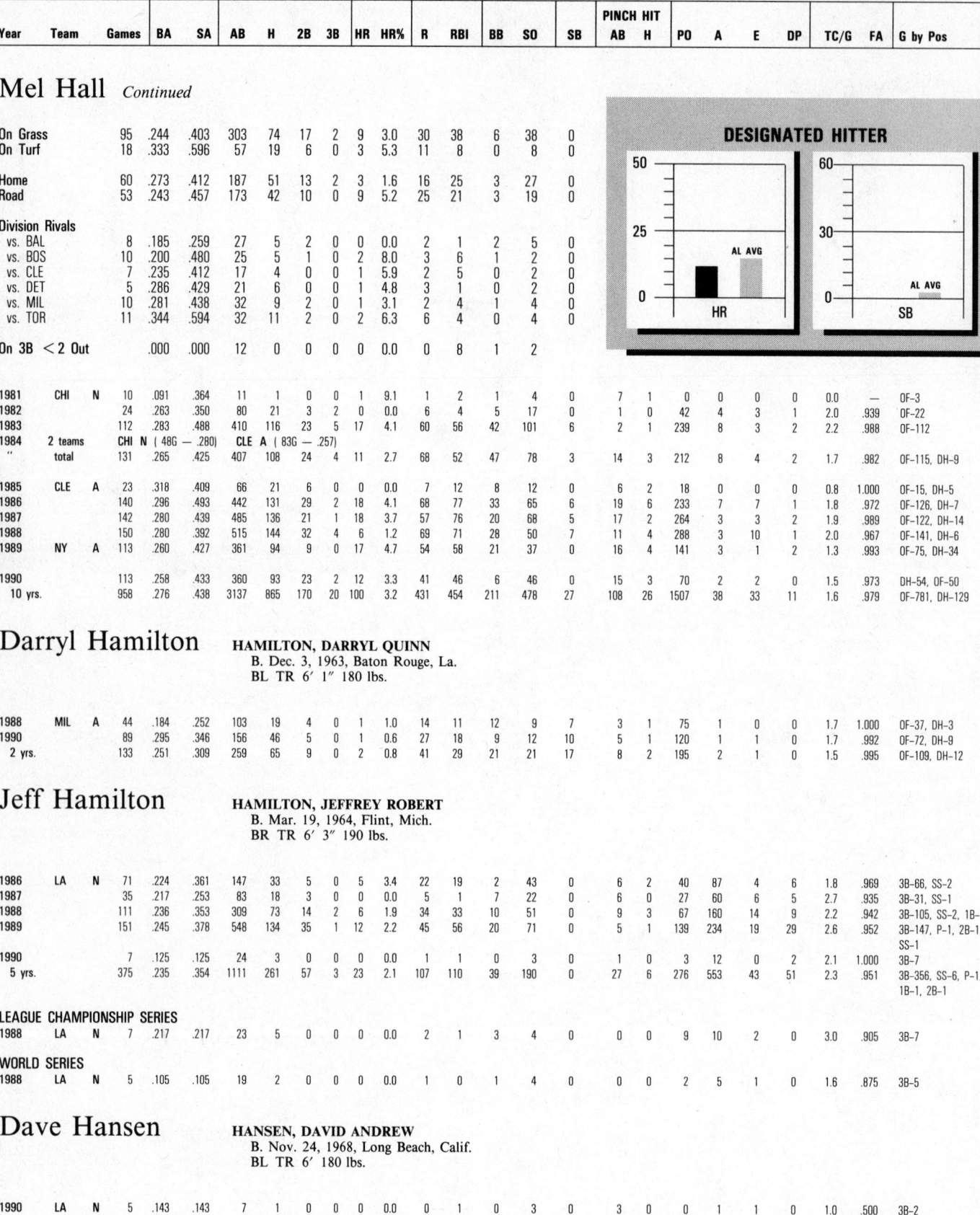

DESIGNATED HITTER

Darryl Hamilton

HAMILTON, DARRYL QUINN
B. Dec. 3, 1963, Baton Rouge, La.
BL TR 6′ 1″ 180 lbs.

Year	Team		Games	BA	SA	AB	H	2B	3B	HR	HR%	R	RBI	BB	SO	SB	PH AB	PH H	PO	A	E	DP	TC/G	FA	G by Pos
1988	MIL	A	44	.184	.252	103	19	4	0	1	1.0	14	11	12	9	7	3	1	75	1	0	0	1.7	1.000	OF-37, DH-3
1990			89	.295	.346	156	46	5	0	1	0.6	27	18	9	12	10	5	1	120	1	1	0	1.7	.992	OF-72, DH-9
2 yrs.			133	.251	.309	259	65	9	0	2	0.8	41	29	21	21	17	8	2	195	2	1	0	1.5	.995	OF-109, DH-12

Jeff Hamilton

HAMILTON, JEFFREY ROBERT
B. Mar. 19, 1964, Flint, Mich.
BR TR 6′ 3″ 190 lbs.

Year	Team		Games	BA	SA	AB	H	2B	3B	HR	HR%	R	RBI	BB	SO	SB	PH AB	PH H	PO	A	E	DP	TC/G	FA	G by Pos
1986	LA	N	71	.224	.361	147	33	5	0	5	3.4	22	19	2	43	0	6	2	40	87	4	6	1.8	.969	3B-66, SS-2
1987			35	.217	.253	83	18	3	0	0	0.0	5	1	7	22	0	6	0	27	60	6	5	2.7	.935	3B-31, SS-1
1988			111	.236	.353	309	73	14	2	6	1.9	34	33	10	51	0	9	3	67	160	14	9	2.2	.942	3B-105, SS-2, 1B-1
1989			151	.245	.378	548	134	35	1	12	2.2	45	56	20	71	0	5	1	139	234	19	29	2.6	.952	3B-147, P-1, 2B-1, SS-1
1990			7	.125	.125	24	3	0	0	0	0.0	1	1	0	3	0	1	0	3	12	0	2	2.1	1.000	3B-7
5 yrs.			375	.235	.354	1111	261	57	3	23	2.1	107	110	39	190	0	27	6	276	553	43	51	2.3	.951	3B-356, SS-6, P-1, 1B-1, 2B-1

LEAGUE CHAMPIONSHIP SERIES

Year	Team		Games	BA	SA	AB	H	2B	3B	HR	HR%	R	RBI	BB	SO	SB	PH AB	PH H	PO	A	E	DP	TC/G	FA	G by Pos
1988	LA	N	7	.217	.217	23	5	0	0	0	0.0	2	1	3	4	0	0	0	9	10	2	0	3.0	.905	3B-7

WORLD SERIES

Year	Team		Games	BA	SA	AB	H	2B	3B	HR	HR%	R	RBI	BB	SO	SB	PH AB	PH H	PO	A	E	DP	TC/G	FA	G by Pos
1988	LA	N	5	.105	.105	19	2	0	0	0	0.0	1	0	1	4	0	0	0	2	5	1	0	1.6	.875	3B-5

Dave Hansen

HANSEN, DAVID ANDREW
B. Nov. 24, 1968, Long Beach, Calif.
BL TR 6′ 180 lbs.

Year	Team		Games	BA	SA	AB	H	2B	3B	HR	HR%	R	RBI	BB	SO	SB	PH AB	PH H	PO	A	E	DP	TC/G	FA	G by Pos
1990	LA	N	5	.143	.143	7	1	0	0	0	0.0	0	1	0	3	0	3	0	0	1	1	0	1.0	.500	3B-2

Year	Team		Games	BA	SA	AB	H	2B	3B	HR	HR%	R	RBI	BB	SO	SB	PINCH HIT AB	PINCH HIT H	PO	A	E	DP	TC/G	FA	G by Pos

Brian Harper

HARPER, BRIAN DAVID
B. Oct. 16, 1959, Los Angeles, Calif.
BR TR 6′ 2″ 195 lbs.

Split			Games	BA	SA	AB	H	2B	3B	HR	HR%	R	RBI	BB	SO	SB	PH AB	PH H	PO	A	E	DP	TC/G	FA	G by Pos
April			16	.278	.426	54	15	5	0	1	1.9	8	6	2	2	0									
May			25	.337	.542	83	28	8	0	3	3.6	15	15	3	7	0									
June			23	.286	.351	77	22	3	1	0	0.0	5	9	4	4	0									
July			25	.378	.520	98	37	11	0	1	1.0	12	13	5	4	2									
Aug			23	.230	.391	87	20	9	1	1	1.1	13	8	1	4	0									
Sept/Oct			22	.238	.338	80	19	6	1	0	0.0	8	3	4	6	1									
Day			30	.306	.491	108	33	11	0	3	2.8	19	17	5	8	1									
Night			104	.291	.415	371	108	31	3	3	0.8	42	37	14	19	2									
vs. Left				.315	.541	146	46	19	1	4	2.7	30	20	8	10	1									
vs. Right				.285	.384	333	95	23	2	2	0.6	31	34	11	17	2									
On Grass			52	.297	.453	192	57	18	0	4	2.1	21	21	5	10	1									
On Turf			82	.293	.418	287	84	24	3	2	0.7	40	33	14	17	2									
Home			66	.283	.391	230	65	18	2	1	0.4	29	24	12	15	2									
Road			68	.305	.470	249	76	24	1	5	2.0	32	30	7	12	1									
Division Rivals																									
vs. CAL			12	.333	.513	39	13	4	0	1	2.6	5	5	2	2	0									
vs. CHI			12	.163	.209	43	7	2	0	0	0.0	1	2	2	3	0									
vs. KC			9	.250	.313	32	8	2	0	0	0.0	2	3	1	0	0									
vs. OAK			11	.341	.409	44	15	3	0	0	0.0	7	7	3	2	3									
vs. SEA			11	.289	.500	38	11	5	0	1	2.6	6	5	3	3	0									
vs. TEX			12	.300	.375	40	12	3	0	0	0.0	5	3	3	2	0									
On 3B < 2 Out				.407	.667	27	11	4	0	1	3.7	1	21	1	2										
1979	CAL	A	1	.000	.000	2	0	0	0	0	0.0	0	0	0	1	0	1	0	0	0	0	0	0.0	—	DH-1
1981			4	.273	.273	11	3	0	0	0	0.0	1	1	0	0	1	1	0	5	0	1	0	1.5	.833	OF-2, DH-1
1982	PIT	N	20	.276	.517	29	8	1	0	2	6.9	4	4	1	4	0	12	5	10	0	0	0	0.5	1.000	OF-8
1983			61	.221	.427	131	29	4	1	7	5.3	16	20	2	15	0	27	6	40	0	0	0	0.7	1.000	OF-35, 1B-1
1984			48	.259	.348	112	29	4	0	2	1.8	4	11	5	11	0	11	2	57	3	1	0	1.3	.984	OF-37, C-2
1985	STL	N	43	.250	.327	52	13	4	0	0	0.0	5	8	2	3	0	26	7	15	5	0	0	0.5	1.000	OF-13, 3B-6, C-2, 1B-1
1986	DET	A	19	.139	.167	36	5	1	0	0	0.0	2	3	3	3	0	4	2	25	2	1	2	1.5	.964	OF-11, DH-6, C-2, 1B-2
1987	OAK	A	11	.235	.294	17	4	1	0	0	0.0	1	3	0	4	0	4	1	0	0	0	0	0.0	—	DH-7, OF-1
1988	MIN	A	60	.295	.428	166	49	11	1	3	1.8	15	20	10	12	0	7	1	208	15	2	0	3.8	.991	C-48, DH-5, 3B-2
1989			126	.325	.449	385	125	24	0	8	2.1	43	57	13	16	2	7	1	462	36	11	7	4.0	.978	C-101, DH-19, OF-3, 1B-2, 3B-2
1990			134	.294	.432	479	141	42	3	6	1.2	61	54	19	27	3	1	0	686	58	11	5	6.1	.985	C-120, DH-11, 3B-3, 1B-2
11 yrs.			527	.286	.417	1420	406	92	5	28	2.0	152	181	55	96	6	101	25	1508	119	27	14	3.1	.984	C-275, OF-110, DH-50, 3B-13, 1B-8

LEAGUE CHAMPIONSHIP SERIES

Year	Team		Games	BA	SA	AB	H	2B	3B	HR	HR%	R	RBI	BB	SO	SB	PH AB	PH H	PO	A	E	DP	TC/G	FA	G by Pos
1985	STL	N	1	.000	.000	1	0	0	0	0	0.0	0	0	0	0	0	1	0	0	0	0	0	0.0	—	

WORLD SERIES

Year	Team		Games	BA	SA	AB	H	2B	3B	HR	HR%	R	RBI	BB	SO	SB	PH AB	PH H	PO	A	E	DP	TC/G	FA	G by Pos
1985	STL	N	4	.250	.250	4	1	0	0	0	0.0	0	1	0	1	0	4	1	0	0	0	0	0.0	—	

Lenny Harris

HARRIS, LEONARD ANTHONY
B. Oct. 28, 1964, Miami, Fla.
BL TR 5′ 10″ 195 lbs.

Split	Games	BA	SA	AB	H	2B	3B	HR	HR%	R	RBI	BB	SO	SB
April	16	.225	.275	40	9	0	1	0	0.0	1	5	3	1	3
May	23	.368	.474	76	28	4	2	0	0.0	12	9	3	6	3
June	21	.280	.360	75	21	3	0	1	1.3	12	1	4	6	1
July	23	.295	.359	78	23	3	1	0	0.0	13	3	7	4	3
Aug	28	.259	.272	81	21	1	0	0	0.0	9	7	4	6	3
Sept/Oct	26	.358	.457	81	29	5	0	1	1.2	14	4	8	8	2
Day	34	.300	.390	100	30	1	1	2	2.0	18	11	6	6	1
Night	103	.305	.369	331	101	15	3	0	0.0	43	18	23	25	14
vs. Left		.238	.286	42	10	0	1	0	0.0	8	6	3	5	0
vs. Right		.311	.383	389	121	16	3	2	0.5	53	23	26	26	15

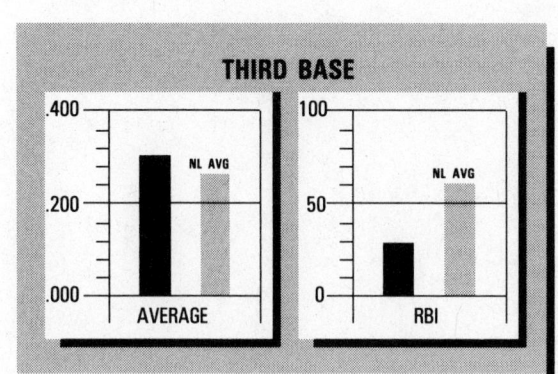

Year	Team	Games	BA	SA	AB	H	2B	3B	HR	HR%	R	RBI	BB	SO	SB	PINCH HIT AB	PINCH HIT H	PO	A	E	DP	TC/G	FA	G by Pos

Lenny Harris *Continued*

Year	Team	Games	BA	SA	AB	H	2B	3B	HR	HR%	R	RBI	BB	SO	SB	PINCH HIT AB	PINCH HIT H	PO	A	E	DP	TC/G	FA	G by Pos
On Grass		101	.311	.374	318	99	11	3	1	0.3	44	22	22	23	14									
On Turf		36	.283	.372	113	32	5	1	1	0.9	17	7	7	8	1									
Home		69	.276	.332	217	60	8	2	0	0.0	27	9	15	15	10									
Road		68	.332	.416	214	71	8	2	2	0.9	34	20	14	16	5									
Division Rivals																								
vs. ATL		15	.256	.302	43	11	2	0	0	0.0	4	0	4	3	3									
vs. CIN		14	.257	.286	35	9	1	0	0	0.0	7	0	4	7	1									
vs. HOU		15	.315	.389	54	17	2	1	0	0.0	4	4	4	5	3									
vs. SD		11	.361	.472	36	13	1	0	1	2.8	6	1	3	1	0									
vs. SF		17	.281	.368	57	16	3	1	0	0.0	9	4	4	5	1									
On 3B < 2 Out			.389	.500	18	7	0	1	0	0.0	0	15	3	2										
1988	CIN N	16	.372	.395	43	16	1	0	0	0.0	7	8	5	4	4	0	0	14	33	1	2	3.0	.979	3B-10, 2B-6
1989	2 teams		CIN N	(61G — .223)			LA N	(54G — .252)																
''	total	115	.236	.299	335	79	10	1	3	0.9	36	26	20	33	14	20	8	147	168	15	32	2.9	.955	2B-46, 3B-24, OF-21, SS-18
1990	LA N	137	.304	.374	431	131	16	4	2	0.4	61	29	29	31	15	23	3	140	205	11	24	2.8	.969	3B-94, 2B-44, OF-2, SS-1
3 yrs.		268	.279	.344	809	226	27	5	5	0.6	104	63	54	68	33	43	11	301	406	27	58	2.7	.963	3B-128, 2B-96, OF-23, SS-19

Bill Haselman

HASELMAN, WILLIAM JOSEPH
B. May 25, 1966, Long Branch, N. J.
BR TR 6′ 3″ 205 lbs.

Year	Team	Games	BA	SA	AB	H	2B	3B	HR	HR%	R	RBI	BB	SO	SB	PINCH HIT AB	PINCH HIT H	PO	A	E	DP	TC/G	FA	G by Pos
1990	TEX A	7	.154	.154	13	2	0	0	0	0.0	0	3	1	5	0	3	1	8	0	0	0	8.0	1.000	DH-3, C-1

Ron Hassey

HASSEY, RONALD WILLIAM
B. Feb. 27, 1953, Tucson, Ariz.
BL TR 6′ 2″ 200 lbs.

Year	Team	Games	BA	SA	AB	H	2B	3B	HR	HR%	R	RBI	BB	SO	SB	PINCH HIT AB	PINCH HIT H	PO	A	E	DP	TC/G	FA	G by Pos
1978	CLE A	25	.203	.284	74	15	0	0	2	2.7	5	9	5	7	2	1	0	130	15	1	1	5.8	.993	C-24
1979		75	.287	.404	223	64	14	0	4	1.8	20	32	19	19	1	7	2	368	29	3	5	5.3	.993	C-68, 1B-2, DH-1
1980		130	.318	.446	390	124	18	4	8	2.1	43	65	49	51	0	18	6	564	52	4	9	4.8	.994	C-113, DH-7, 1B-3
1981		61	.232	.268	190	44	4	0	1	0.5	8	25	17	11	0	4	2	327	44	3	7	6.1	.992	C-56, 1B-5, DH-1
1982		113	.251	.353	323	81	18	0	5	1.5	33	34	53	32	3	10	3	566	38	4	6	5.4	.993	C-105, DH-2, 1B-2
1983		117	.270	.384	341	92	21	0	6	1.8	48	42	38	35	2	9	3	514	43	3	4	4.8	.995	C-113, DH-1
1984	2 teams	CLE A	(48G — .255)			CHI N	(19G — .333)																	
''	total	67	.269	.341	182	49	5	1	2	1.1	16	24	19	32	1	9	2	263	18	2	3	4.2	.993	C-50, 1B-5, DH-1
1985	NY A	92	.296	.509	267	79	16	1	13	4.9	31	42	28	21	0	20	5	420	20	7	4	4.9	.984	C-69, DH-2, 1B-2
1986	2 teams	NY A	(64G — .298)			CHI A	(49G — .353)																	
''	total	113	.323	.481	341	110	25	1	9	2.6	45	49	46	27	1	18	10	318	14	4	4	3.0	.988	C-62, DH-37
1987	CHI A	49	.214	.338	145	31	9	0	3	2.1	15	12	17	11	0	6	0	114	12	0	4	2.6	1.000	C-24, DH-18
1988	OAK A	107	.257	.368	323	83	15	0	7	2.2	32	45	30	42	2	14	2	465	31	3	7	4.7	.994	C-91, DH-9
1989		97	.228	.328	268	61	12	0	5	1.9	29	23	24	45	1	16	3	425	25	4	4	4.7	.991	C-78, DH-2, 1B-1
1990		94	.213	.299	254	54	7	0	5	1.9	18	22	27	29	0	20	6	312	18	1	3	5.3	.997	C-59, DH-15, 1B-3
13 yrs.		1140	.267	.384	3321	887	164	7	70	2.1	343	424	372	362	13	152	44	4786	359	39	61	4.5	.992	C-912, DH-96, 1B-23
LEAGUE CHAMPIONSHIP SERIES																								
1988	OAK A	4	.500	1.000	8	4	1	0	1	12.5	2	3	1	1	0	0	0	13	0	0	0	3.3	1.000	C-4
1989		2	.167	.167	6	1	0	0	0	0.0	0	1	1	2	0	0	0	10	0	0	0	5.0	1.000	C-2
1990		2	.333	.333	3	1	0	0	0	0.0	0	0	2	0	0	0	0	6	0	0	0	6.0	1.000	DH-1, C-1
3 yrs.		8	.353	.588	17	6	1	0	1	5.9	2	4	4	3	0	0	0	29	0	0	0	3.6	.000	C-7, DH-1
WORLD SERIES																								
1988	OAK A	5	.250	.250	8	2	0	0	0	0.0	0	1	3	3	0	1	1	28	1	0	0	5.8	1.000	C-4
1990		3	.333	.333	6	2	0	0	0	0.0	0	1	0	0	0	2	0	2	0	1	0	3.0	.667	C-1
2 yrs.		8	.286	.286	14	4	0	0	0	0.0	0	2	3	3	0	3	1	30	1	1	0	4.0	.969	C-5

THIRD BASE

HR   NL AVG

SB   NL AVG

Year	Team	Games	BA	SA	AB	H	2B	3B	HR	HR%	R	RBI	BB	SO	SB	PINCH HIT AB	H	PO	A	E	DP	TC/G	FA	G by Pos

Billy Hatcher

HATCHER, WILLIAM AUGUSTUS
B. Oct. 4, 1960, Williams, Ariz.
BR TR 5' 9" 175 lbs.

OUTFIELD

Split		Games	BA	SA	AB	H	2B	3B	HR	HR%	R	RBI	BB	SO	SB	AB	H	PO	A	E	DP	TC/G	FA	G by Pos
April		15	.333	.476	63	21	2	2	1	1.6	12	4	4	6	6									
May		25	.313	.384	99	31	5	1	0	0.0	11	3	3	11	5									
June		28	.291	.379	103	30	5	2	0	0.0	11	5	10	10	8									
July		22	.231	.321	78	18	4	0	1	1.3	8	2	3	7	5									
Aug		25	.247	.482	85	21	11	0	3	3.5	14	6	3	5	1									
Sept/Oct		24	.237	.250	76	18	1	0	0	0.0	12	5	10	3	5									
Day		36	.235	.361	119	28	6	0	3	2.5	10	8	10	6	8									
Night		103	.288	.387	385	111	22	5	2	0.5	58	17	23	36	22									
vs. Left			.246	.319	207	51	10	1	1	0.5	21	8	16	16	12									
vs. Right			.296	.424	297	88	18	4	4	1.3	47	17	17	26	18									
On Grass		40	.267	.360	150	40	4	2	2	1.3	23	8	15	11	10									
On Turf		99	.280	.390	354	99	24	3	3	0.8	45	17	18	31	20									
Home		73	.264	.378	246	65	16	3	2	0.8	32	11	16	18	15									
Road		66	.287	.384	258	74	12	2	3	1.2	36	14	17	24	15									
Division Rivals																								
vs. ATL		18	.268	.380	71	19	3	1	1	1.4	8	7	7	6	4									
vs. HOU		16	.207	.241	58	12	2	0	0	0.0	6	1	1	10	1									
vs. LA		15	.241	.296	54	13	3	0	0	0.0	8	2	5	5	5									
vs. SD		15	.327	.473	55	18	2	0	2	3.6	14	4	8	2	7									
vs. SF		15	.237	.263	38	9	1	0	0	0.0	6	0	5	0	2									
On 3B < 2 Out			.353	.471	17	6	2	0	0	0.0	0	9	2	3										

Year	Team	Games	BA	SA	AB	H	2B	3B	HR	HR%	R	RBI	BB	SO	SB	AB	H	PO	A	E	DP	TC/G	FA	G by Pos
1984	CHI N	8	.111	.111	9	1	0	0	0	0.0	1	0	1	0	2	3	0	2	1	0	0	0.4	1.000	OF-4
1985		53	.245	.368	163	40	12	1	2	1.2	24	10	8	12	2	9	1	77	2	1	0	1.5	.988	OF-44
1986	HOU N	127	.258	.356	419	108	15	4	6	1.4	55	36	22	52	38	4	0	226	7	4	0	1.9	.983	OF-121
1987		141	.296	.415	564	167	28	3	11	2.0	96	63	42	70	53	1	1	276	16	4	6	2.1	.986	OF-140
1988		145	.268	.370	530	142	25	4	7	1.3	79	52	37	56	32	5	1	280	7	5	2	2.0	.983	OF-142
1989	2 teams					HOU N (108G — .228)				PIT N (27G — .244)														
"	total	135	.231	.308	481	111	19	3	4	0.8	59	51	30	62	24	15	5	250	1	2	1	1.9	.992	OF-124
1990	CIN N	139	.276	.381	504	139	28	5	5	0.9	68	25	33	42	30	13	3	308	10	1	2	2.4	.997	OF-131
7 yrs.		748	.265	.367	2670	708	127	20	35	1.3	382	237	173	294	181	50	11	1419	44	17	11	2.0	.989	OF-706

LEAGUE CHAMPIONSHIP SERIES

Year	Team	Games	BA	SA	AB	H	2B	3B	HR	HR%	R	RBI	BB	SO	SB	AB	H	PO	A	E	DP	TC/G	FA	G by Pos
1986	HOU N	6	.280	.400	25	7	0	0	1	4.0	4	2	3	2	3	0	0	11	0	1	0	2.0	.917	OF-6
1990	CIN N	4	.333	.600	15	5	1	0	1	6.6	2	2	0	2	0	0	0	5	1	0	0	1.5	1.000	OF-4
2 yrs.		10	.300	.475	40	12	1	0	2	5.0	6	4	3	4	3	0	0	16	1	1	0	1.8	.944	OF-10

WORLD SERIES

Year	Team	Games	BA	SA	AB	H	2B	3B	HR	HR%	R	RBI	BB	SO	SB	AB	H	PO	A	E	DP	TC/G	FA	G by Pos
1990	CIN N	4	.750	1.250	12	9	4	1	0	0.0	6	2	2	0	0	0	0	11	0	0	0	2.8	1.000	OF-4

Mickey Hatcher

HATCHER, MICHAEL VAUGHN, JR.
B. Mar. 15, 1955, Cleveland, Ohio
BR TR 6' 2" 200 lbs.

Year	Team	Games	BA	SA	AB	H	2B	3B	HR	HR%	R	RBI	BB	SO	SB	AB	H	PO	A	E	DP	TC/G	FA	G by Pos
1979	LA N	33	.269	.366	93	25	4	1	1	1.1	9	5	7	12	1	6	1	47	24	5	0	2.3	.934	OF-19, 3B-17
1980		57	.226	.286	84	19	2	0	1	1.2	4	5	2	12	0	21	4	31	23	3	2	1.0	.947	OF-25, 3B-18
1981	MIN A	99	.255	.350	377	96	23	2	3	0.8	36	37	15	29	3	2	1	296	11	3	5	3.1	.990	OF-91, 1B-7, 3B-2, DH-1
1982		84	.249	.343	277	69	13	2	3	1.1	23	26	8	27	0	9	3	81	17	1	1	1.2	.990	OF-47, DH-29, 3B-5
1983		105	.317	.445	375	119	15	3	9	2.4	50	47	14	19	2	15	6	199	11	3	9	2.0	.986	OF-56, DH-39, 1B-7, 3B-1
1984		152	.302	.406	576	174	35	5	5	0.9	61	69	37	34	0	2	0	364	20	9	10	2.6	.977	OF-100, DH-37, 1B-17, 3B-1
1985		116	.282	.365	444	125	28	0	3	0.7	46	49	16	23	0	6	2	246	7	3	4	2.2	.988	OF-97, DH-11, 1B-4
1986		115	.278	.366	317	88	13	3	3	0.9	40	32	19	26	2	38	6	220	16	4	16	2.1	.983	OF-46, DH-28, 1B-22, 3B-3
1987	LA N	101	.282	.429	287	81	19	1	7	2.4	27	42	20	19	2	16	1	277	105	11	36	3.9	.972	3B-49, 1B-37, OF-7
1988		88	.293	.351	191	56	8	0	1	0.5	22	25	7	7	0	38	12	189	19	3	4	2.4	.986	OF-29, 1B-25, 3B-3
1989		94	.295	.379	224	66	9	2	2	0.9	18	25	13	16	1	34	6	89	21	4	7	1.2	.965	OF-48, 3B-16, 1B-5, P-1
1990		85	.212	.250	132	28	3	1	0	0.0	12	13	6	22	0	47	14	86	17	3	9	2.5	.972	1B-25, 3B-10, OF-10
12 yrs.		1129	.280	.377	3377	946	172	20	38	1.1	348	375	164	246	11	234	56	2125	291	52	106	2.2	.979	OF-575, 1B-149, DH-145, 3B-125, P-1

LEAGUE CHAMPIONSHIP SERIES

Year	Team	Games	BA	SA	AB	H	2B	3B	HR	HR%	R	RBI	BB	SO	SB	AB	H	PO	A	E	DP	TC/G	FA	G by Pos
1988	LA N	6	.238	.333	21	5	2	0	0	0.0	4	3	3	0	0	0	0	34	1	2	6	6.2	.946	1B-6, OF-1

Year	Team	Games	BA	SA	AB	H	2B	3B	HR	HR%	R	RBI	BB	SO	SB	PINCH HIT AB	H	PO	A	E	DP	TC/G	FA	G by Pos

Mickey Hatcher *Continued*

WORLD SERIES

Year	Team	Games	BA	SA	AB	H	2B	3B	HR	HR%	R	RBI	BB	SO	SB	PINCH HIT AB	H	PO	A	E	DP	TC/G	FA	G by Pos
1988	LA N	5	.368	.737	19	7	1	0	2	10.5	5	5	1	3	0	0	0	8	0	0	0	1.6	1.000	OF-5

Charlie Hayes

HAYES, CHARLES DEWAYNE
B. May 29, 1965, Hattiesburg, Miss.
BR TR 6′ 190 lbs.

	Games	BA	SA	AB	H	2B	3B	HR	HR%	R	RBI	BB	SO	SB	AB	H	PO	A	E	DP	TC/G	FA	G by Pos
April	17	.231	.262	65	15	2	0	0	0.0	3	5	4	10	1									
May	23	.314	.453	86	27	3	0	3	3.5	11	9	7	16	0									
June	28	.303	.404	109	33	5	0	2	1.8	11	13	2	13	0									
July	26	.253	.400	95	24	2	0	4	4.2	14	16	5	14	1									
Aug	28	.213	.269	108	23	6	0	0	0.0	9	4	4	17	1									
Sept/Oct	30	.235	.286	98	23	2	0	1	1.0	8	10	6	21	1									
Day	37	.204	.310	142	29	6	0	3	2.1	9	9	4	27	0									
Night	115	.277	.360	419	116	14	0	7	1.7	47	48	24	64	4									
vs. Left		.295	.425	193	57	10	0	5	2.6	28	22	8	26	2									
vs. Right		.239	.307	368	88	10	0	5	1.4	28	35	20	65	2									
On Grass	39	.295	.418	146	43	9	0	3	2.1	12	13	8	22	0									
On Turf	113	.246	.323	415	102	11	0	7	1.7	44	44	20	69	4									
Home	77	.245	.309	282	69	9	0	3	1.1	29	26	12	47	2									
Road	75	.272	.387	279	76	11	0	7	2.5	27	31	16	44	2									
Division Rivals																							
vs. CHI	16	.259	.414	58	15	3	0	2	3.4	7	10	4	7	0									
vs. MON	17	.172	.172	64	11	0	0	0	0.0	2	4	2	11	3									
vs. NY	17	.222	.286	63	14	1	0	1	1.6	10	6	2	17	0									
vs. PIT	17	.311	.508	61	19	3	0	3	4.9	7	7	3	7	0									
vs. STL	17	.313	.344	64	20	2	0	0	0.0	9	8	3	5	0									
On 3B < 2 Out		.286	.286	35	10	0	0	0	0.0		20	2	8										
1988	SF N	7	.091	.091	11	1	0	0	0	0.0	0	0	0	3	0	2	0	5	0	0	0	0.7	1.000	OF-4, 3B-3
1989	2 teams		SF N	(3G — .200)		PHI N	(84G — .258)																	
"	total	87	.257	.391	304	78	15	1	8	2.6	26	43	11	50	3	5	2	51	174	22	15	2.8	.911	3B-85
1990	PHI N	152	.258	.348	561	145	20	0	10	1.7	56	57	28	91	4	6	2	151	329	20	31	3.4	.960	3B-146, 1B-4, 2B-1
3 yrs.		246	.256	.360	876	224	35	1	18	2.1	82	100	39	144	7	13	4	207	503	42	46	3.1	.944	3B-234, 1B-4, OF-4, 2B-1

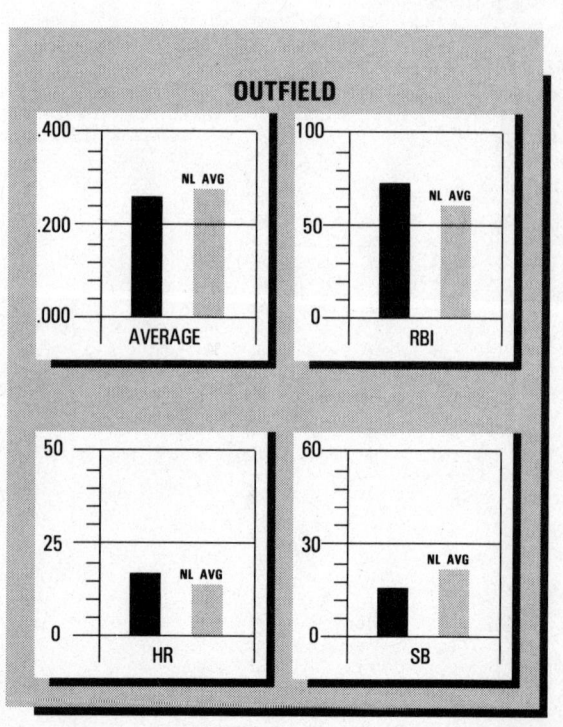

Von Hayes

HAYES, VON FRANCIS
B. Aug. 31, 1958, Stockton, Calif.
BL TR 6′ 5″ 185 lbs.

	Games	BA	SA	AB	H	2B	3B	HR	HR%	R	RBI	BB	SO	SB
April	19	.297	.406	64	19	1	0	2	3.1	13	7	17	9	1
May	25	.290	.581	93	27	5	2	6	6.5	16	23	15	12	3
June	15	.192	.269	52	10	1	0	1	1.9	9	7	14	12	3
July	16	.262	.311	61	16	0	0	1	1.6	5	7	9	13	2
Aug	30	.248	.453	117	29	4	1	6	5.1	17	18	19	17	4
Sept/Oct	24	.263	.338	80	21	3	0	1	1.3	10	11	13	18	3
Day	35	.292	.513	113	33	4	0	7	6.2	22	26	32	16	8
Night	94	.251	.381	354	89	10	3	10	2.8	48	47	55	65	8
vs. Left		.274	.419	179	49	6	1	6	3.4	24	28	24	36	2
vs. Right		.253	.410	288	73	8	2	11	3.8	46	45	63	45	14
On Grass	39	.241	.333	141	34	4	0	3	2.1	12	22	27	25	4
On Turf	90	.270	.448	326	88	10	3	14	4.3	58	51	60	56	12
Home	58	.276	.478	203	56	5	3	10	4.9	37	36	40	33	8
Road	71	.250	.364	264	66	9	0	7	2.7	33	37	47	48	8
Division Rivals														
vs. CHI	8	.182	.182	22	4	0	0	0	0.0	2	2	10	5	1
vs. MON	10	.300	.400	40	12	1	0	1	2.5	7	3	7	8	2
vs. NY	18	.262	.431	65	17	2	0	3	4.6	7	12	9	17	2
vs. PIT	18	.206	.381	63	13	2	0	3	4.8	10	7	12	13	3
vs. STL	16	.230	.361	61	14	2	0	2	3.3	11	8	9	10	1
On 3B < 2 Out		.320	.360	25	8	1	0	0	0.0	0	25	7	3	

Year	Team		Games	BA	SA	AB	H	2B	3B	HR	HR%	R	RBI	BB	SO	SB	PINCH HIT AB	H	PO	A	E	DP	TC/G	FA	G by Pos

Von Hayes *Continued*

Year	Team		Games	BA	SA	AB	H	2B	3B	HR	HR%	R	RBI	BB	SO	SB	AB	H	PO	A	E	DP	TC/G	FA	G by Pos
1981	CLE	A	43	.257	.394	109	28	8	2	1	0.9	21	17	14	10	8	9	4	30	4	3	1	0.9	.919	DH-21, OF-13, 3B-5
1982			150	.250	.389	527	132	25	3	14	2.7	65	82	42	63	32	11	2	323	17	6	6	2.3	.983	OF-139, 3B-5, 1B-4
1983	PHI	N	124	.265	.370	351	93	9	5	6	1.7	45	32	36	55	20	21	5	165	7	5	0	1.4	.972	OF-103
1984			152	.292	.447	561	164	27	6	16	2.9	85	67	59	84	48	12	2	341	2	4	1	2.3	.988	OF-148
1985			152	.263	.398	570	150	30	4	13	2.3	76	70	61	99	21	6	4	368	9	6	1	2.5	.984	OF-146
1986			158	.305	.480	610	186	**46**	2	19	3.1	**107**	98	74	77	24	2	0	1247	100	13	106	8.6	.990	1B-134, OF-31
1987			158	.277	.473	556	154	36	5	21	3.8	84	84	121	77	16	4	0	1216	80	13	100	8.3	.990	1B-144, OF-32
1988			104	.272	.409	367	100	28	2	6	1.6	43	45	49	59	20	5	1	756	58	9	66	7.9	.989	1B-85, OF-16, 3B-3
1989			154	.259	.461	540	140	27	2	26	4.8	93	78	101	103	28	4	0	426	47	9	24	3.1	.981	OF-128, 1B-30, 3B-10
1990			129	.261	.413	467	122	14	3	17	3.6	70	73	87	81	16	3	1	272	8	6	0	2.3	.979	OF-127
10 yrs.			1324	.272	.430	4658	1269	250	34	139	3.0	689	646	644	708	233	77	19	5144	332	74	305	4.2	.987	OF-883, 1B-397, 3B-23, DH-21

LEAGUE CHAMPIONSHIP SERIES

| 1983 | PHI | N | 2 | .000 | .000 | 2 | 0 | 0 | 0 | 0 | 0.0 | 0 | 0 | 0 | 0 | 0 | 1 | 0 | 0 | 0 | 0 | 0 | 0.0 | — | OF-1 |

WORLD SERIES

| 1983 | PHI | N | 4 | .000 | .000 | 3 | 0 | 0 | 0 | 0 | 0.0 | 0 | 0 | 0 | 1 | 0 | 3 | 0 | 1 | 0 | 0 | 0 | 0.3 | 1.000 | OF-1 |

Mike Heath

HEATH, MICHAEL THOMAS
B. Feb. 5, 1955, Tampa, Fla.
BR TR 5' 11" 180 lbs.

	Games	BA	SA	AB	H	2B	3B	HR	HR%	R	RBI	BB	SO	SB
April	14	.444	.611	36	16	2	1	0	0.0	3	2	1	3	1
May	27	.318	.424	85	27	6	0	1	1.2	13	9	4	14	1
June	19	.304	.393	56	17	2	0	1	1.8	6	3	4	9	2
July	21	.181	.319	72	13	1	0	3	4.2	7	12	2	22	1
Aug	18	.211	.316	57	12	3	0	1	1.8	9	5	6	11	1
Sept/Oct	23	.234	.344	64	15	4	0	1	1.6	8	7	2	12	1
Day	34	.257	.436	101	26	4	1	4	4.0	11	12	4	18	2
Night	88	.275	.368	269	74	14	1	3	1.1	35	26	15	53	5
vs. Left		.228	.329	149	34	6	0	3	2.0	11	15	8	28	4
vs. Right		.299	.425	221	66	12	2	4	1.8	35	23	11	43	3
On Grass	105	.268	.403	313	84	17	2	7	2.2	38	36	18	60	7
On Turf	17	.281	.298	57	16	1	0	0	0.0	8	2	1	11	0
Home	58	.272	.402	169	46	9	2	3	1.8	21	15	10	35	4
Road	64	.269	.373	201	54	9	0	4	2.0	25	23	9	36	3
Division Rivals														
vs. BAL	9	.320	.320	25	8	0	0	0	0.0	1	3	1	5	0
vs. BOS	7	.217	.304	23	5	0	1	0	0.0	2	3	0	5	0
vs. CLE	7	.238	.333	21	5	2	0	0	0.0	3	2	4	6	1
vs. MIL	10	.484	.806	31	15	5	1	1	3.2	5	3	1	3	1
vs. NY	10	.258	.452	31	8	3	0	1	3.2	3	4	1	5	0
vs. TOR	10	.294	.324	34	10	1	0	0	0.0	3	1	0	4	1
On 3B < 2 Out		.292	.458	24	7	1	0	1	4.2	1	16	1	4	

CATCHER

Year	Team		Games	BA	SA	AB	H	2B	3B	HR	HR%	R	RBI	BB	SO	SB	AB	H	PO	A	E	DP	TC/G	FA	G by Pos
1978	NY	A	33	.228	.283	92	21	3	1	0	0.0	6	8	4	9	0	0	0	151	11	5	4	5.1	.970	C-33
1979	OAK	A	74	.256	.322	258	66	8	0	3	1.2	19	27	17	18	1	5	3	167	32	5	2	2.8	.975	OF-46, C-22, 3B-7, DH-3
1980			92	.243	.298	305	74	10	2	1	0.3	27	33	16	28	3	6	1	292	20	4	5	3.4	.987	C-47, DH-31, OF-8
1981			84	.236	.346	301	71	7	1	8	2.7	26	30	13	36	3	4	2	399	45	10	6	5.4	.978	C-78, OF-6
1982			101	.242	.352	318	77	18	4	3	0.9	43	39	27	36	8	2	1	368	54	12	8	4.3	.972	C-90, OF-10, 3B-5
1983			96	.281	.383	345	97	17	0	6	1.7	45	33	18	59	3	3	1	362	47	11	6	4.4	.974	C-80, OF-24, DH-2, 3B-2
1984			139	.248	.396	475	118	21	5	13	2.7	49	64	26	72	7	10	1	495	56	8	4	4.0	.986	C-108, OF-45, 3B-2, SS-1
1985			138	.250	.408	436	109	18	6	13	3.0	71	55	41	63	7	6	3	539	67	12	10	4.5	.981	C-112, OF-35, 3B-13
1986	2 teams		STL N (65G — .205)			DET A (30G — .265)																			
"	total		95	.226	.354	288	65	11	1	8	2.8	30	36	27	53	6	4	0	405	39	13	5	4.8	.972	C-92, OF-2, 3B-1

Year	Team		Games	BA	SA	AB	H	2B	3B	HR	HR%	R	RBI	BB	SO	SB	PINCH HIT AB	H	PO	A	E	DP	TC/G	FA	G by Pos

Mike Heath *Continued*

Year	Team		Games	BA	SA	AB	H	2B	3B	HR	HR%	R	RBI	BB	SO	SB	AB	H	PO	A	E	DP	TC/G	FA	G by Pos
1987	DET	A	93	.281	.430	270	76	16	0	8	3.0	34	33	21	42	1	12	3	384	43	5	8	4.6	.988	C-67, OF-24, 1B-4, 3B-4, SS-2, DH-1, 2B-1
1988			86	.247	.365	219	54	7	2	5	2.3	24	18	18	32	1	6	0	361	24	6	3	4.5	.985	C-75, OF-9
1989			122	.263	.389	396	104	16	2	10	2.5	38	43	24	71	7	11	3	584	68	10	10	5.4	.985	C-117, 3B-4, OF-3, DH-1
1990			122	.270	.386	370	100	18	2	7	1.8	46	38	19	71	7	8	3	588	54	13	7	5.6	.980	C-117, OF-3, DH-2, SS-1
13 yrs.			1275	.253	.370	4073	1032	170	26	85	2.1	458	457	271	590	54	77	21	5095	560	114	79	4.5	.980	C-1038, OF-215, DH-40, 3B-38, 1B-4, SS-4, 2B-1

DIVISIONAL PLAYOFF SERIES

Year	Team		Games	BA	SA	AB	H	2B	3B	HR	HR%	R	RBI	BB	SO	SB	AB	H	PO	A	E	DP	TC/G	FA	G by Pos
1981	OAK	A	2	.000	.000	8	0	0	0	0	0.0	0	0	0	1	0	0	0	9	1	0	0	5.0	1.000	C-2

LEAGUE CHAMPIONSHIP SERIES

Year	Team		Games	BA	SA	AB	H	2B	3B	HR	HR%	R	RBI	BB	SO	SB	AB	H	PO	A	E	DP	TC/G	FA	G by Pos
1981	OAK	A	3	.333	.333	6	2	0	0	0	0.0	1	0	0	1	0	0	0	3	1	0	0	0.0	1.000	C-2, OF-1
1987	DET	A	3	.286	.714	7	2	0	0	1	14.3	1	2	0	0	0	0	0	14	0	0	0	4.7	1.000	C-3
2 yrs.			6	.308	.538	13	4	0	0	1	7.7	2	2	0	1	0	0	0	17	1	0	0	3.0	.000	C-5, OF-1

WORLD SERIES

Year	Team		Games	BA	SA	AB	H	2B	3B	HR	HR%	R	RBI	BB	SO	SB	AB	H	PO	A	E	DP	TC/G	FA	G by Pos
1978	NY	A	1	—	—	0	0	0	0	0	—	0	0	0	0	0	0	0	0	0	0	0	0.0	—	C-1

Danny Heep

HEEP, DANIEL WILLIAM
B. July 3, 1957, San Antonio, Tex.
BL TL 5' 11" 185 lbs.

Year	Team		Games	BA	SA	AB	H	2B	3B	HR	HR%	R	RBI	BB	SO	SB	AB	H	PO	A	E	DP	TC/G	FA	G by Pos
1979	HOU	N	14	.143	.143	14	2	0	0	0	0.0	0	2	1	4	0	10	1	7	0	0	0	0.5	1.000	OF-2
1980			33	.276	.368	87	24	8	0	0	0.0	6	6	8	9	0	8	2	188	8	2	8	6.0	.990	1B-22
1981			33	.250	.281	96	24	3	0	0	0.0	6	11	10	11	0	9	4	198	9	2	12	6.3	.990	1B-22, OF-1
1982			85	.237	.379	198	47	14	1	4	2.0	16	22	21	31	0	23	6	192	6	1	10	2.3	.995	OF-39, 1B-16
1983	NY	N	115	.253	.395	253	64	12	0	8	3.2	30	21	29	40	3	40	11	159	11	0	12	1.5	1.000	OF-61, 1B-14
1984			99	.231	.312	199	46	9	2	1	0.5	36	12	27	22	3	38	8	137	7	4	4	1.5	.973	OF-48, 1B-10
1985			95	.280	.421	271	76	17	0	7	2.6	26	42	27	27	2	13	1	154	5	4	3	1.7	.975	OF-78, 1B-4
1986			86	.282	.421	195	55	8	2	5	2.6	24	33	30	31	1	30	9	83	2	1	1	1.0	.988	OF-56
1987	LA	N	60	.163	.204	98	16	4	0	0	0.0	7	9	8	10	1	35	5	52	6	1	3	1.0	.983	OF-22, 1B-6
1988			95	.242	.255	149	36	2	0	0	0.0	14	11	22	13	2	44	4	129	10	3	5	1.5	.979	OF-32, 1B-12, P-1
1989	BOS	A	113	.300	.400	320	96	17	0	5	1.6	36	49	29	26	0	20	4	216	14	3	18	2.1	.987	OF-75, 1B-19, DH-9
1990			41	.174	.217	69	12	1	1	0	0.0	3	8	7	14	0	18	2	42	4	1	2	2.5	.979	OF-14, DH-6, 1B-5, P-1
12 yrs.			869	.256	.357	1949	498	95	6	30	1.5	204	226	219	238	12	288	57	1557	82	22	78	1.9	.987	OF-428, 1B-130, DH-15, P-2

LEAGUE CHAMPIONSHIP SERIES

Year	Team		Games	BA	SA	AB	H	2B	3B	HR	HR%	R	RBI	BB	SO	SB	AB	H	PO	A	E	DP	TC/G	FA	G by Pos
1980	HOU	N	1	.000	.000	1	0	0	0	0	0.0	0	0	0	0	0	1	0	0	0	0	0	0.0	—	
1986	NY	N	5	.250	.250	4	1	0	0	0	0.0	0	1	0	2	0	3	1	0	0	0	0	0.0	—	OF-1
1988	LA	N	3	.000	.000	1	0	0	0	0	0.0	0	0	1	1	0	1	0	0	0	0	0	0.0	—	
1990	BOS	A	2	.000	.000	2	0	0	0	0	0.0	0	0	0	0	0	2	0	0	0	0	0	0.0	1.000	
4 yrs.			11	.125	.125	8	1	0	0	0	0.0	0	1	1	3	0	7	1	0	0	0	0	0.0	.000	OF-1

WORLD SERIES

Year	Team		Games	BA	SA	AB	H	2B	3B	HR	HR%	R	RBI	BB	SO	SB	AB	H	PO	A	E	DP	TC/G	FA	G by Pos
1986	NY	N	5	.091	.091	11	1	0	0	0	0.0	0	2	1	1	0	2	0	1	0	0	0	0.2	1.000	DH-2, OF-1
1988	LA	N	3	.250	.375	8	2	1	0	0	0.0	0	0	0	2	0	2	0	0	0	0	0	0.0	—	DH-1, OF-1
2 yrs.			8	.158	.211	19	3	1	0	0	0.0	0	2	1	3	0	4	0	1	0	0	0	0.1	.000	DH-3, OF-2

Scott Hemond

HEMOND, SCOTT MATHEW
B. Nov. 18, 1965, Taunton, Mass.
BR TR 6' 205 lbs.

Year	Team		Games	BA	SA	AB	H	2B	3B	HR	HR%	R	RBI	BB	SO	SB	AB	H	PO	A	E	DP	TC/G	FA	G by Pos
1989	OAK	A	4	—	—	0	0	0	0	0	—	2	0	0	0	0	0	0	0	0	0	0	0.0	—	DH-3
1990			7	.154	.154	13	2	0	0	0	0.0	0	1	0	5	0	0	0	2	5	0	0	1.0	1.000	3B-7, 2B-1
2 yrs.			11	.154	.154	13	2	0	0	0	0.0	2	1	0	5	0	0	0	2	5	0	0	0.6	.000	3B-7, DH-3, 2B-1

Year	Team	Games	BA	SA	AB	H	2B	3B	HR	HR%	R	RBI	BB	SO	SB	PINCH HIT AB	PINCH HIT H	PO	A	E	DP	TC/G	FA	G by Pos

Dave Henderson
HENDERSON, DAVID LEE (Hendu)
B. July 21, 1958, Merced, Calif.
BR TR 6′ 2″ 210 lbs.

Split		Games	BA	SA	AB	H	2B	3B	HR	HR%	R	RBI	BB	SO	SB
April		17	.200	.369	65	13	2	0	3	4.6	9	7	10	15	0
May		24	.284	.477	88	25	8	0	3	3.4	10	13	6	17	0
June		26	.263	.576	99	26	7	0	8	8.1	16	5	28	1	
July		31	.306	.444	108	33	6	0	3	2.8	17	7	12	20	2
Aug		17	.284	.448	67	19	5	0	2	3.0	8	11	4	16	0
Sept/Oct		12	.261	.391	23	6	0	0	1	4.3	5	4	3	9	0
Day		50	.263	.441	179	47	14	0	6	3.4	23	26	16	45	2
Night		77	.277	.483	271	75	14	0	14	5.2	42	37	24	60	1
vs. Left			.353	.654	133	47	7	0	11	8.3	31	23	10	22	3
vs. Right			.237	.388	317	75	21	0	9	2.8	34	40	30	83	0
On Grass		106	.279	.479	384	107	23	0	18	4.7	60	55	33	81	2
On Turf		21	.227	.394	66	15	5	0	2	3.0	5	8	7	24	1
Home		62	.302	.514	222	67	14	0	11	5.0	34	36	18	46	1
Road		65	.241	.421	228	55	14	0	9	3.9	31	27	22	59	2
Division Rivals															
vs. CAL		12	.333	.563	48	16	2	0	3	6.3	12	9	2	5	1
vs. CHI		8	.367	.767	30	11	3	0	3	10.0	7	9	3	6	0
vs. KC		9	.174	.217	23	4	1	0	0	0.0	1	0	1	7	1
vs. MIN		9	.333	.467	30	10	1	0	1	3.3	4	3	4	13	0
vs. SEA		8	.258	.452	31	8	0	0	2	6.5	5	5	4	7	0
vs. TEX		10	.129	.355	31	4	1	0	2	6.5	4	3	2	12	0
On 3B < 2 Out			.333	.417	24	8	2	0	0	0.0	0	12	5	7	

Year	Team		Games	BA	SA	AB	H	2B	3B	HR	HR%	R	RBI	BB	SO	SB	PH AB	PH H	PO	A	E	DP	TC/G	FA	G by Pos
1981	SEA	A	59	.167	.333	126	21	3	0	6	4.8	17	13	16	24	2	6	1	105	4	0	1	1.8	1.000	OF-58
1982			104	.253	.441	324	82	17	1	14	4.3	47	48	36	67	2	4	0	249	11	4	4	2.5	.985	OF-101
1983			137	.269	.444	484	130	24	5	17	3.5	50	55	28	93	9	4	1	304	17	6	4	2.4	.982	OF-133, DH-3
1984			112	.280	.466	350	98	23	0	14	4.0	42	43	19	56	5	5	1	242	11	3	5	2.3	.988	OF-97, DH-10
1985			139	.241	.388	502	121	28	2	14	2.8	70	68	48	104	6	2	1	335	8	5	3	2.5	.986	OF-138
1986	2 teams		SEA A (103G — .276)			BOS A (36G — .196)																			
"	total		139	.265	.459	388	103	22	4	15	3.9	59	47	39	110	2	8	2	193	9	4	1	1.5	.981	OF-112, DH-22
1987	2 teams		BOS A (75G — .234)			SF N (15G — .238)																			
"			90	.234	.410	205	48	12	0	8	3.9	32	26	30	53	3	15	3	124	1	5	0	1.4	.962	OF-73
1988	OAK	A	146	.304	.525	507	154	38	1	24	4.7	100	94	47	92	2	6	3	382	5	7	2	2.7	.982	OF-143
1989			152	.250	.380	579	145	24	3	15	2.6	77	80	54	131	8	4	0	385	6	9	1	2.6	.977	OF-149, DH-2
1990			127	.271	.467	450	122	28	0	20	4.4	65	63	40	105	3	7	1	319	5	4	1	2.8	.988	OF-116, DH-6
10 yrs.			1205	.262	.438	3915	1024	219	16	147	3.8	559	537	357	835	42	61	13	2638	76	47	22	2.3	.983	OF-1120, DH-43
LEAGUE CHAMPIONSHIP SERIES																									
1986	BOS	A	5	.111	.444	9	1	0	0	1	11.1	3	4	2	2	0	0	0	11	0	0	0	2.2	1.000	OF-5
1988	OAK	A	4	.375	.625	16	6	1	0	1	6.3	2	4	1	7	0	0	0	11	0	2	0	3.3	.846	OF-4
1989			5	.263	.579	19	5	3	0	1	5.3	4	1	2	5	0	0	0	22	0	0	0	4.4	1.000	OF-5
1990			2	.167	.167	6	1	0	0	0	0.0	0	1	0	2	1	0	0	7	0	0	0	3.5	1.000	OF-2
4 yrs.			16	.260	.520	50	13	4	0	3	6.0	9	10	5	16	1	0	0	51	0	2	0	3.3	.000	OF-16
WORLD SERIES																									
1986	BOS	A	7	.400	.760	25	10	1	1	2	8.0	6	5	2	6	0	0	0	22	0	0	0	3.1	1.000	OF-7
1988	OAK	A	5	.300	.400	20	6	2	0	0	0.0	1	1	2	7	0	0	0	12	0	0	0	2.4	1.000	OF-5
1989			4	.308	.923	13	4	2	0	2	15.4	6	4	4	3	0	0	0	13	0	0	0	3.3	1.000	OF-4
1990			4	.231	.308	13	3	1	0	0	0.0	2	0	1	3	0	1	0	7	0	0	0	2.3	1.000	OF-3
4 yrs.			20	.324	.606	71	23	6	1	4	5.6	15	10	9	19	0	1	0	54	0	0	0	2.7	.000	OF-19

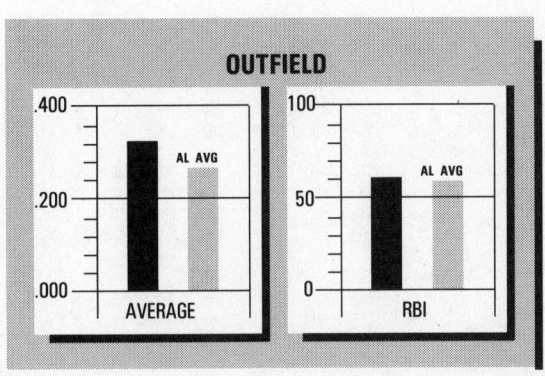

Rickey Henderson
HENDERSON, RICKEY HENLEY
B. Dec. 25, 1957, Chicago, Ill.
BR TL 5′ 10″ 180 lbs.

Split	Games	BA	SA	AB	H	2B	3B	HR	HR%	R	RBI	BB	SO	SB
April	17	.338	.585	65	22	7	0	3	4.6	16	7	11	9	11
May	26	.330	.585	94	31	7	1	5	5.3	22	10	19	5	12
June	25	.341	.600	85	29	5	1	5	5.9	20	11	20	10	15
July	23	.352	.659	88	31	4	1	7	8.0	22	15	12	9	9
Aug	19	.273	.470	66	18	4	0	3	4.5	15	7	16	12	5
Sept/Oct	26	.308	.538	91	28	6	0	5	5.5	24	11	19	15	13
Day	47	.293	.512	164	48	9	0	9	5.5	40	21	32	19	19
Night	89	.342	.609	325	111	24	3	19	5.8	79	40	65	41	46
vs. Left		.313	.604	134	42	12	0	9	6.7	33	17	24	22	18
vs. Right		.330	.566	355	117	21	3	19	5.4	86	44	73	38	47

Year	Team		Games	BA	SA	AB	H	2B	3B	HR	HR%	R	RBI	BB	SO	SB	PINCH HIT AB	H	PO	A	E	DP	TC/G	FA	G by Pos

Rickey Henderson *Continued*

Year	Team		Games	BA	SA	AB	H	2B	3B	HR	HR%	R	RBI	BB	SO	SB	AB	H	PO	A	E	DP	TC/G	FA	G by Pos
On Grass			114	.304	.532	408	124	23	2	22	5.4	94	44	84	55	53									
On Turf			22	.432	.802	81	35	10	1	6	7.4	25	17	13	5	12									
Home			64	.305	.486	220	67	12	2	8	3.6	47	22	44	26	34									
Road			72	.342	.651	269	92	21	1	20	7.4	72	39	53	34	31									
Division Rivals																									
vs. CAL			13	.302	.472	53	16	3	0	2	3.8	14	3	11	11	8									
vs. CHI			12	.244	.366	41	10	2	0	1	2.4	8	1	11	6	4									
vs. KC			11	.488	.744	43	21	5	0	2	4.7	8	6	5	2	3									
vs. MIN			12	.333	.619	42	14	4	1	2	4.8	9	5	6	2	6									
vs. SEA			10	.410	.615	39	16	5	0	1	2.6	11	7	7	8	9									
vs. TEX			11	.308	.487	39	12	4	0	1	2.6	8	3	7	5	7									
On 3B < 2 Out				.421	.579	19	8	0	0	1	5.3	1	14	3	3										
1979	OAK	A	89	.274	.336	351	96	13	3	1	0.3	49	26	34	39	33	0	0	215	5	6	0	2.5	.973	OF-88
1980			158	.303	.399	591	179	22	4	9	1.5	111	53	117	54	100	0	0	407	15	7	1	2.7	.984	OF-157, DH-1
1981			108	.319	.437	423	**135**	18	7	6	1.4	**89**	35	64	68	56	1	0	327	7	7	0	3.2	.979	OF-107
1982			149	.267	.382	536	143	24	4	10	1.9	119	51	**116**	94	130[1]	0	0	379	2	9	0	2.6	.977	OF-144, DH-4
1983			145	.292	.421	513	150	25	7	9	1.8	105	48	**103**	80	108	6	1	349	9	3	1	2.5	.992	OF-142, DH-1
1984			142	.293	.458	502	147	27	4	16	3.2	113	58	86	81	66	2	0	341	7	11	1	2.5	.969	OF-140
1985	NY	A	143	.314	.516	547	172	28	5	24	4.4	**146**	72	99	65	80	1	0	439	7	9	3	3.2	.980	OF-141, DH-1
1986			153	.263	.469	608	160	31	5	28	4.6	**130**	74	89	81	87	3	0	426	4	6	0	2.8	.986	OF-146, DH-5
1987			95	.291	.497	358	104	17	3	17	4.7	78	37	80	52	41	2	0	189	3	4	1	2.1	.980	OF-69, DH-24
1988			140	.305	.399	554	169	30	2	6	1.1	118	50	82	54	93	0	0	320	7	12	5	2.4	.965	OF-136, DH-3
1989	2 teams					NY A (65G — .247)				OAK A (85G — .294)															
"	total		150	.274	.399	541	148	26	3	12	2.2	**113**	57	**126**	68	77	2	2	335	6	4	1	2.3	.988	OF-147, DH-3
1990	OAK	A	136	.325	.577	489	159	33	3	28	5.7	**119**	61	97	60	65	1	0	289	5	5	0	2.5	.983	OF-118, DH-15
12 yrs.			1608	.293	.441	6013	1762	294	50	166	2.8	1290	622	1093	796	936	18	3	4016	77	83	13	2.6	.980	OF-1535, DH-57

DIVISIONAL PLAYOFF SERIES

Year	Team		Games	BA	SA	AB	H	2B	3B	HR	HR%	R	RBI	BB	SO	SB	AB	H	PO	A	E	DP	TC/G	FA	G by Pos
1981	OAK	A	3	.182	.182	11	2	0	0	0	0.0	3	0	2	0	2	0	0	0	0	0	0	0.0	—	OF-3

LEAGUE CHAMPIONSHIP SERIES

Year	Team		Games	BA	SA	AB	H	2B	3B	HR	HR%	R	RBI	BB	SO	SB	AB	H	PO	A	E	DP	TC/G	FA	G by Pos
1981	OAK	A	3	.364	.727	11	4	2	1	0	0.0	0	1	1	2	2	0	0	6	0	1	0	2.3	.857	OF-3
1989			5	.400	1.000	15	6	1	1	2	13.3	8	5	7	0	8	0	0	13	0	1	0	2.8	.929	OF-5
1990			4	.294	.294	17	5	0	0	0	0.0	1	3	1	2	2	0	0	10	0	0	0	2.5	1.000	OF-4
3 yrs.			12	.349	.651	43	15	3	2	2	4.7	9	9	9	4	12	0	0	29	0	2	0	2.6	.000	OF-12

WORLD SERIES

Year	Team		Games	BA	SA	AB	H	2B	3B	HR	HR%	R	RBI	BB	SO	SB	AB	H	PO	A	E	DP	TC/G	FA	G by Pos
1989	OAK	A	4	.474	.895	19	9	1	2	1	5.3	4	3	2	2	3	0	0	9	0	0	0	2.3	1.000	OF-4
1990			4	.333	.667	15	5	2	0	1	6.6	2	1	3	4	3	0	0	12	1	0	0	3.3	1.000	OF-4
2 yrs.			8	.412	.794	34	14	3	2	2	5.9	6	4	5	6	6	0	0	21	1	0	0	2.8	.000	OF-8

Carlos Hernandez   HERNANDEZ, CARLOS ALBERTO
B. May 24, 1967, San Felix, Bolivar, Venezuela
BR TR 5′ 11″ 185 lbs.

Year	Team		Games	BA	SA	AB	H	2B	3B	HR	HR%	R	RBI	BB	SO	SB	AB	H	PO	A	E	DP	TC/G	FA	G by Pos
1990	LA	N	10	.200	.250	20	4	1	0	0	0.0	2	1	0	2	0	0	0	37	2	0	0	3.9	1.000	C-10

Keith Hernandez   HERNANDEZ, KEITH (Mex)
B. Oct. 20, 1953, San Francisco, Calif.
BL TL 6′ 180 lbs.

Year	Team		Games	BA	SA	AB	H	2B	3B	HR	HR%	R	RBI	BB	SO	SB	AB	H	PO	A	E	DP	TC/G	FA	G by Pos
1974	STL	N	14	.294	.441	34	10	1	2	0	0.0	3	2	7	8	0	3	1	70	1	2	8	5.2	.973	1B-9
1975			64	.250	.362	188	47	8	2	3	1.6	20	20	17	26	0	9	3	469	36	2	34	7.9	.996	1B-56
1976			129	.289	.428	374	108	21	5	7	1.9	54	46	49	53	4	17	4	862	107	10	87	7.6	.990	1B-110
1977			161	.291	.459	560	163	41	4	15	2.7	90	91	79	88	7	6	1	1453	106	12	146	9.8	.992	1B-158
1978			159	.255	.389	542	138	32	4	11	2.0	90	64	82	68	13	5	1	1436	96	10	124	9.7	.994	1B-158
1979			161	**.344**	.513	610	210	**48**	11	11	1.8	**116**	105	80	78	11	2	2	1489	146	8	145	10.2	.995	1B-160
1980			159	.321	.494	595	191	39	8	16	2.7	**111**	99	86	73	14	2	0	1572	115	9	146	10.7	.995	1B-157
1981			103	.306	.463	376	115	27	4	8	2.1	65	48	61	45	12	2	0	1056	86	3	99	11.1	.997	1B-98, OF-3
1982			160	.299	.413	579	173	33	6	7	1.2	79	94	100	67	19	1	1	1591	135	11	140	10.9	.994	1B-158, OF-4
1983	2 teams					STL N (55G — .284)				NY N (95G — .306)															
"	total		150	.297	.433	538	160	23	7	12	2.2	77	63	88	72	9	5	1	1418	147	13	147	10.5	.992	1B-144
1984	NY	N	154	.311	.449	550	171	31	0	15	2.7	83	94	97	89	2	1	0	1214	142	8	127	8.9	.994	1B-153
1985			158	.309	.430	593	183	34	4	10	1.7	87	91	77	59	3	3	1	1310	139	4	113	9.2	.997	1B-157
1986			149	.310	.446	551	171	34	1	13	2.4	94	83	**94**	69	2	0	0	1199	149	5	115	9.1	.996	1B-149

Year	Team	Games	BA	SA	AB	H	2B	3B	HR	HR%	R	RBI	BB	SO	SB	PINCH HIT AB	PINCH HIT H	PO	A	E	DP	TC/G	FA	G by Pos

Keith Hernandez   *Continued*

Year	Team		Games	BA	SA	AB	H	2B	3B	HR	HR%	R	RBI	BB	SO	SB	AB	H	PO	A	E	DP	TC/G	FA	G by Pos
1987			154	.290	.436	587	170	28	2	18	3.1	87	89	81	104	0	1	0	1298	149	10	110	9.5	.993	1B–154
1988			95	.276	.417	348	96	16	0	11	3.2	43	55	31	57	2	1	0	734	77	2	63	8.6	.998	1B–93
1989			75	.233	.326	215	50	8	0	4	1.9	18	19	27	39	0	17	2	405	31	4	22	5.9	.991	1B–58
1990	CLE	A	43	.200	.238	130	26	2	0	1	0.7	7	8	14	17	0	1	0	340	20	2	28	8.6	.994	1B–42
17 yrs.			2088	.296	.436	7370	2182	426	60	162	2.2	1124	1071	1070	1012	98	76	17	17916	1682	115	1654	4.7	.988	1B–2014, OF–7

LEAGUE CHAMPIONSHIP SERIES

Year	Team		Games	BA	SA	AB	H	2B	3B	HR	HR%	R	RBI	BB	SO	SB	AB	H	PO	A	E	DP	TC/G	FA	G by Pos
1982	STL	N	3	.333	.333	12	4	0	0	0	0.0	3	1	2	3	0	0	0	35	1	0	3	12.0	1.000	1B–3
1986	NY	N	6	.269	.385	26	7	1	1	0	0.0	3	3	3	6	0	0	0	66	11	0	5	12.8	1.000	1B–6
1988			7	.269	.385	26	7	0	0	1	3.8	2	5	6	7	1	0	0	57	4	1	2	8.9	.984	1B–7
3 yrs.			16	.281	.375	64	18	1	1	1	1.6	8	9	11	16	1	0	0	158	16	1	10	10.9	.994	1B–16

WORLD SERIES

Year	Team		Games	BA	SA	AB	H	2B	3B	HR	HR%	R	RBI	BB	SO	SB	AB	H	PO	A	E	DP	TC/G	FA	G by Pos
1982	STL	N	7	.259	.444	27	7	2	0	1	3.7	4	8	4	2	0	0	0	62	7	2	10	10.1	.972	1B–7
1986	NY	N	7	.231	.231	26	6	0	0	0	0.0	1	4	5	1	0	0	0	48	4	1	4	7.6	.981	1B–7
2 yrs.			14	.245	.340	53	13	2	0	1	1.9	5	12	9	3	0	0	0	110	11	3	14	8.9	.976	1B–14

Tommy Herr

HERR, THOMAS MITCHELL
B. Apr. 4, 1956, Lancaster, Pa.
BB TR 6′ 175 lbs.

	Games	BA	SA	AB	H	2B	3B	HR	HR%	R	RBI	BB	SO	SB
April	18	.304	.464	69	21	5	0	2	2.9	7	5	6	4	1
May	22	.274	.333	84	23	5	0	0	0.0	9	14	9	12	1
June	25	.216	.294	102	22	3	1	1	1.0	6	10	6	10	2
July	26	.290	.410	100	29	5	2	1	1.0	13	14	8	14	2
Aug	28	.250	.283	92	23	3	0	0	0.0	4	7	7	7	1
Sept/Oct	27	.250	.330	100	25	5	0	1	1.0	9	10	14	11	0
Day	40	.245	.309	139	34	4	1	1	0.7	9	12	9	21	0
Night	106	.267	.360	408	109	22	2	4	1.0	39	48	41	37	7
vs. Left		.264	.327	208	55	8	1	1	0.5	12	20	20	19	3
vs. Right		.260	.360	339	88	18	2	4	1.2	36	40	30	39	4
On Grass	52	.270	.335	185	50	6	0	2	1.1	17	14	17	19	2
On Turf	94	.257	.354	362	93	20	3	3	0.8	31	46	33	39	5
Home	70	.272	.389	265	72	15	2	4	1.5	28	38	27	31	2
Road	76	.252	.309	282	71	11	1	1	0.4	20	22	23	27	5
Division Rivals														
vs. CHI	13	.196	.216	51	10	1	0	0	0.0	2	1	3	5	0
vs. MON	16	.283	.367	60	17	2	0	1	1.7	3	7	6	5	2
vs. PHI	5	.235	.294	17	4	1	0	0	0.0	3	2	5	3	0
vs. PIT	18	.211	.282	71	15	1	2	0	0.0	5	7	3	8	0
vs. STL	16	.290	.435	62	18	6	0	1	1.6	5	8	7	5	1
On 3B < 2 Out		.323	.355	31	10	1	0	0	0.0	0	20	2	3	

SECOND BASE

Year	Team		Games	BA	SA	AB	H	2B	3B	HR	HR%	R	RBI	BB	SO	SB	AB	H	PO	A	E	DP	TC/G	FA	G by Pos
1979	STL	N	14	.200	.200	10	2	0	0	0	0.0	4	1	2	2	1	1	0	12	11	0	3	1.6	1.000	2B–6
1980			76	.248	.347	222	55	12	5	0	0.0	29	15	16	21	9	9	2	124	184	7	47	4.1	.978	2B–58, SS–14
1981			103	.268	.345	411	110	14	9	0	0.0	50	46	39	30	23	0	0	211	374	5	74	5.7	.992	2B–103
1982			135	.266	.320	493	131	19	4	0	0.0	83	36	57	56	25	5	2	263	427	9	97	5.2	.987	2B–128
1983			89	.323	.412	313	101	14	4	2	0.6	43	31	43	27	6	5	2	178	245	6	60	4.8	.986	2B–86
1984			145	.276	.346	558	154	23	2	4	0.7	67	49	49	56	13	1	1	328	452	6	106	5.4	.992	2B–144
1985			159	.302	.416	596	180	38	3	8	1.3	97	110	80	55	31	1	1	337	448	12	120	5.0	.985	2B–158
1986			152	.252	.331	559	141	30	4	2	0.4	48	61	73	75	22	0	0	352	414	9	121	5.1	.988	2B–152
1987			141	.263	.331	510	134	29	0	2	0.4	73	83	68	62	19	2	1	306	350	7	103	4.7	.989	2B–137
1988	2 teams			STL N (15G — .260)				MIN A (86G — .263)																	
"	total		101	.263	.325	354	93	16	0	2	0.6	46	24	51	51	13	10	3	168	230	5	63	4.0	.988	2B–88, DH–3, SS–2
1989	PHI	N	151	.287	.364	561	161	25	6	2	0.4	65	37	54	63	10	8	3	281	415	7	80	4.7	.990	2B–144
1990	2 teams			PHI N (119G — .264)				NY N (27G — .250)																	
"	total		146	.261	.347	547	143	26	3	5	0.9	48	60	50	58	7	7	2	275	349	7	94	4.5	.989	2B–140
12 yrs.			1412	.274	.353	5134	1405	246	40	27	0.5	653	553	582	556	179	49	17	2835	3899	80	968	4.8	.988	2B–1344, SS–16, DH–3

LEAGUE CHAMPIONSHIP SERIES

Year	Team		Games	BA	SA	AB	H	2B	3B	HR	HR%	R	RBI	BB	SO	SB	AB	H	PO	A	E	DP	TC/G	FA	G by Pos
1982	STL	N	3	.231	.308	13	3	1	0	0	0.0	1	0	1	2	0	0	0	6	10	0	3	5.3	1.000	2B–3
1985			6	.333	.667	21	7	4	0	1	4.8	2	6	5	2	1	0	0	13	10	0	3	3.8	1.000	2B–6
1987			7	.222	.222	27	6	0	0	0	0.0	0	3	0	1	1	0	0	12	11	1	3	3.4	.958	2B–7
3 yrs.			16	.262	.393	61	16	5	0	1	1.6	3	9	6	5	2	0	0	31	31	1	9	3.9	.984	2B–16

WORLD SERIES

Year	Team		Games	BA	SA	AB	H	2B	3B	HR	HR%	R	RBI	BB	SO	SB	AB	H	PO	A	E	DP	TC/G	FA	G by Pos
1982	STL	N	7	.160	.240	25	4	2	0	0	0.0	2	5	3	3	0	0	0	11	19	1	6	4.4	.968	2B–7
1985			7	.154	.231	26	4	2	0	0	0.0	2	0	2	2	0	0	0	11	13	0	8	3.4	1.000	2B–7
1987			7	.250	.357	28	7	0	0	1	3.6	2	1	2	2	0	0	0	23	17	0	1	5.7	1.000	2B–7
3 yrs.			21	.190	.278	79	15	4	0	1	1.3	6	6	7	7	0	0	0	45	49	1	15	4.5	.989	2B–21

Year	Team	Games	BA	SA	AB	H	2B	3B	HR	HR%	R	RBI	BB	SO	SB	PINCH HIT AB	H	PO	A	E	DP	TC/G	FA	G by Pos

Donnie Hill

HILL, DONALD EARL
B. Nov. 12, 1960, Pomona, Calif.
BB TR 5' 10" 165 lbs.

Year	Team	Games	BA	SA	AB	H	2B	3B	HR	HR%	R	RBI	BB	SO	SB	PH AB	H	PO	A	E	DP	TC/G	FA	G by Pos
1983	OAK A	53	.266	.348	158	42	7	0	2	1.3	20	15	4	21	1	1	0	87	136	9	24	4.4	.961	SS-53
1984		73	.230	.299	174	40	6	0	2	1.1	21	16	5	12	1	5	0	102	128	12	28	3.3	.950	SS-66, 2B-4, DH-2, 3B-2
1985		123	.285	.351	393	112	13	2	3	0.8	45	48	23	33	8	2	0	228	320	15	56	4.6	.973	2B-122
1986		108	.283	.378	339	96	16	2	4	1.2	37	29	23	38	5	15	4	104	213	9	31	3.0	.972	2B-68, 3B-33, DH-3, SS-2
1987	CHI A	111	.239	.368	410	98	14	6	9	2.2	57	46	30	35	1	3	1	167	278	14	55	4.1	.969	2B-84, 3B-32, DH-1
1988		83	.217	.281	221	48	6	1	2	0.9	17	20	26	32	3	12	3	118	152	6	38	3.3	.971	2B-59, 3B-12, DH-5
1990	CAL A	103	.264	.352	352	93	18	2	3	0.8	36	32	29	27	1	9	2	194	255	11	64	4.8	.976	2B-60, SS-24, 3B-21, 1B-3, DH-1, P-1
7 yrs.		654	.258	.347	2047	529	80	13	25	1.2	233	206	140	198	20	47	10	1000	1482	78	296	3.9	.970	2B-397, SS-145, 3B-100, DH-12, 1B-3, P-1

Glenallen Hill

HILL, GLENALLEN
B. Mar. 22, 1965, Santa Cruz, Calif.
BR TR 6' 3" 210 lbs.

	Games	BA	SA	AB	H	2B	3B	HR	HR%	R	RBI	BB	SO	SB
April	12	.310	.524	42	13	3	0	2	4.8	10	4	3	5	2
May	17	.161	.357	56	9	2	0	3	5.4	8	8	4	14	2
June	14	.222	.333	36	8	1	0	1	2.8	5	6	3	6	0
July	9	.265	.559	34	9	1	0	3	8.8	8	5	1	7	1
Aug	22	.239	.507	71	17	4	3	3	4.2	13	9	6	23	2
Sept/Oct	10	.190	.190	21	4	0	0	0	0.0	3	0	1	7	1
Day	27	.195	.322	87	17	5	0	2	2.3	11	9	5	23	2
Night	57	.249	.491	173	43	6	3	10	5.8	36	23	13	39	6
vs. Left		.224	.406	143	32	5	3	5	3.5	28	12	10	36	2
vs. Right		.239	.470	117	28	6	0	7	6.0	19	20	8	26	6
On Grass	29	.232	.414	99	23	2	2	4	4.0	18	13	5	31	7
On Turf	55	.230	.447	161	37	9	1	8	5.0	29	19	13	31	1
Home	48	.236	.443	140	33	8	0	7	5.0	25	17	11	29	1
Road	36	.225	.425	120	27	3	3	5	4.2	22	15	7	33	7
Division Rivals														
vs. BAL	5	.294	.471	17	5	0	0	1	5.9	4	2	0	5	1
vs. BOS	4	.167	.333	6	1	1	0	0	0.0	2	0	1	4	0
vs. CLE	9	.258	.645	31	8	1	1	3	9.7	9	5	4	8	2
vs. DET	10	.156	.313	32	5	2	0	1	3.1	4	4	2	9	1
vs. MIL	7	.167	.167	18	3	0	0	0	0.0	1	2	0	6	0
vs. NY	10	.219	.250	32	7	1	0	0	0.0	2	3	2	7	0
On 3B < 2 Out		.250	.250	12	3	0	0	0	0.0	0	6	2	3	

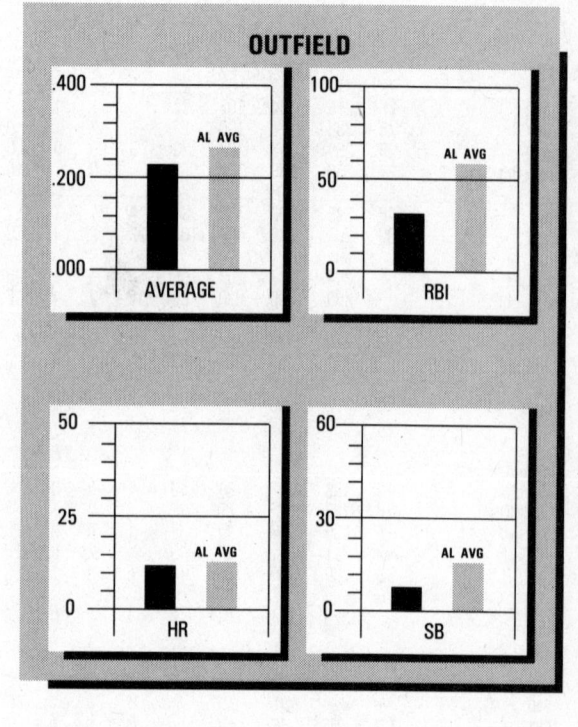

OUTFIELD

AVERAGE — AL AVG
RBI — AL AVG
HR — AL AVG
SB — AL AVG

Year	Team	Games	BA	SA	AB	H	2B	3B	HR	HR%	R	RBI	BB	SO	SB	PH AB	H	PO	A	E	DP	TC/G	FA	G by Pos
1989	TOR A	19	.288	.346	52	15	0	0	1	1.9	4	7	3	12	2	0	0	27	0	1	0	1.5	.964	OF-16, DH-3
1990		84	.231	.435	260	60	11	3	12	4.6	47	32	18	62	8	7	2	115	4	2	0	2.0	.983	OF-60, DH-20
2 yrs.		103	.240	.420	312	75	11	3	13	4.2	51	39	21	74	10	7	2	142	4	3	0	1.4	.980	OF-76, DH-23

Chris Hoiles

HOILES, CHRISTOPHER ALLEN
B. Mar. 20, 1965, Bowling Green, Ohio
BR TR 6' 195 lbs.

Year	Team	Games	BA	SA	AB	H	2B	3B	HR	HR%	R	RBI	BB	SO	SB	PH AB	H	PO	A	E	DP	TC/G	FA	G by Pos
1989	BAL A	6	.111	.222	9	1	1	0	0	0.0	0	1	1	3	0	2	0	11	0	0	0	1.8	1.000	DH-3, C-3
1990		23	.190	.286	63	12	3	0	1	1.5	7	6	5	12	0	3	0	62	6	0	6	5.2	1.000	DH-7, C-7, 1B-6
2 yrs.		29	.181	.278	72	13	4	0	1	1.4	7	7	6	15	0	5	0	73	6	0	6	2.7	.000	DH-10, C-10, 1B-6

Dave Hollins

HOLLINS, DAVID MICHAEL
B. May 25, 1966, Buffalo, N. Y.
BB TR 6' 1" 195 lbs.

Year	Team	Games	BA	SA	AB	H	2B	3B	HR	HR%	R	RBI	BB	SO	SB	PH AB	H	PO	A	E	DP	TC/G	FA	G by Pos
1990	PHI N	72	.184	.316	114	21	0	0	5	4.3	14	15	10	28	0	37	8	27	37	4	0	2.2	.941	3B-30, 1B-1

Year	Team		Games	BA	SA	AB	H	2B	3B	HR	HR%	R	RBI	BB	SO	SB	PINCH HIT AB	H	PO	A	E	DP	TC/G	FA	G by Pos

Sam Horn

HORN, SAMUEL LEE
B. Nov. 2, 1963, Dallas, Tex.
BL TL 6′ 5″ 215 lbs.

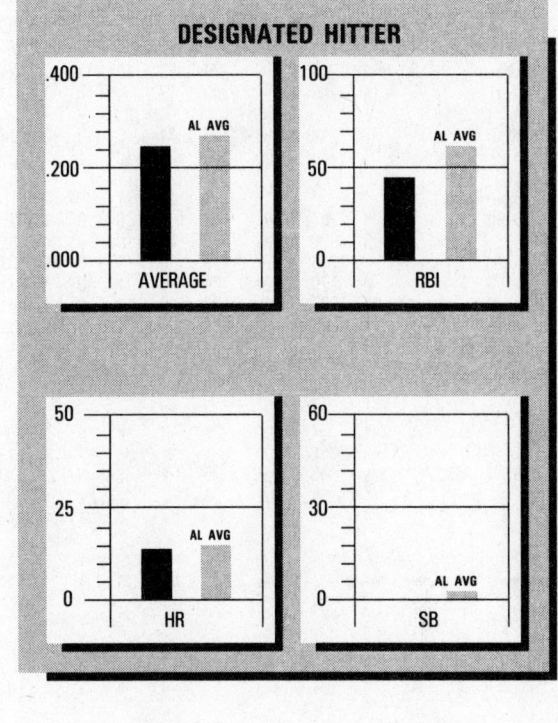

DESIGNATED HITTER

	Games	BA	SA	AB	H	2B	3B	HR	HR%	R	RBI	BB	SO	SB	PH AB	PH H	PO	A	E	DP	TC/G	FA	G by Pos
April	16	.286	.429	56	16	2	0	2	3.6	5	10	8	16	0									
May	5	.158	.368	19	3	1	0	1	5.3	2	2	0	3	0									
June	2	.250	.250	4	1	0	0	0	0.0	0	0	1	1	0									
July	16	.267	.644	45	12	2	0	5	11.1	8	9	7	12	0									
Aug	18	.214	.357	56	12	2	0	2	3.6	8	5	11	10	0									
Sept/Oct	22	.258	.530	66	17	6	0	4	6.1	7	19	5	20	0									
Day	22	.264	.486	72	19	4	0	4	5.6	7	13	6	15	0									
Night	57	.241	.466	174	42	9	0	10	5.7	23	32	26	47	0									
vs. Left		.059	.059	17	1	0	0	0	0.0	2	0	0	7										
vs. Right		.262	.502	229	60	13	0	14	6.1	28	45	32	55										
On Grass	66	.227	.411	207	47	11	0	9	4.3	23	31	29	60										
On Turf	13	.359	.795	39	14	2	0	5	12.8	7	14	3	2										
Home	40	.250	.500	120	30	6	0	8	6.7	18	21	22	38										
Road	39	.246	.444	126	31	7	0	6	4.8	12	24	10	24										
Division Rivals																							
vs. BOS	6	.211	.474	19	4	2	0	1	5.3	3	6	1	5	0									
vs. CLE	5	.056	.056	18	1	0	0	0	0.0	1	2	2	4	0									
vs. DET	9	.121	.182	33	4	2	0	0	0.0	1	1	6	11	0									
vs. MIL	4	.273	.273	11	3	0	0	0	0.0	1	2	1	4	0									
vs. NY	7	.200	.267	15	3	1	0	0	0.0	0	0	5	5	0									
vs. TOR	10	.273	.636	22	6	2	0	2	9.1	5	5	3	6	0									
On 3B < 2 Out		.353	.765	17	6	1	0	2	11.8	2	16	2	5										
1987 BOS A	46	.278	.589	158	44	7	0	14	8.9	31	34	17	55	0	6	1	0	0	0	0	0.0	—	DH-40
1988	24	.148	.246	61	9	0	0	2	3.3	4	8	11	20	0	4	0	0	0	0	0	0.0	—	DH-16
1989	33	.148	.185	54	8	2	0	0	0.0	1	4	8	16	0	17	4	5	0	0	0	0.2	1.000	DH-14, 1B-2
1990 BAL A	79	.248	.472	246	61	13	0	14	5.6	30	45	32	62	0	9	4	58	6	2	7	6.6	.970	DH-63, 1B-10
4 yrs.	182	.235	.451	519	122	22	0	30	5.8	66	91	68	153	0	36	9	63	6	2	7	0.4	.972	DH-133, 1B-12

Steve Howard

HOWARD, STEVEN BERNARD
B. Dec. 7, 1963, Oakland, Calif.
BR TR 6′ 2″ 205 lbs.

Year	Team		Games	BA	SA	AB	H	2B	3B	HR	HR%	R	RBI	BB	SO	SB	PH AB	PH H	PO	A	E	DP	TC/G	FA	G by Pos
1990	OAK	A	21	.231	.308	52	12	4	0	0	0.0	5	1	4	17	0	3	1	14	0	1	0	1.1	.933	OF-14, DH-7

Thomas Howard

HOWARD, THOMAS SYLVESTER
B. Dec. 11, 1964, Middletown, Ohio
BB TR 6′ 200 lbs.

Year	Team		Games	BA	SA	AB	H	2B	3B	HR	HR%	R	RBI	BB	SO	SB	PH AB	PH H	PO	A	E	DP	TC/G	FA	G by Pos
1990	SD	N	20	.273	.318	44	12	2	0	0	0.0	4	0	0	11	0	8	1	19	0	1	0	1.5	.950	OF-13

Jack Howell

HOWELL, JACK ROBERT
B. Aug. 18, 1961, Tucson, Ariz.
BL TR 6′ 185 lbs.

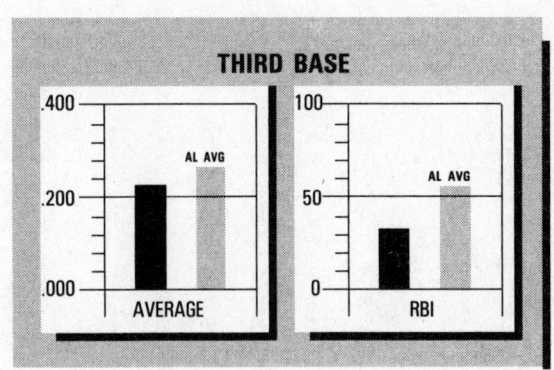

THIRD BASE

	Games	BA	SA	AB	H	2B	3B	HR	HR%	R	RBI	BB	SO	SB
April	15	.280	.460	50	14	6	0	1	2.0	6	5	9	6	0
May	19	.220	.441	59	13	5	1	2	3.4	6	7	3	11	1
June	19	.122	.204	49	6	1	0	1	2.0	1	4	6	11	0
July	21	.214	.357	56	12	2	0	2	3.6	6	3	14	13	2
Aug	4	.357	.357	14	5	0	0	0	0.0	4	2	1	1	0
Sept/Oct	27	.250	.375	88	22	5	0	2	2.3	12	12	13	19	0
Day	26	.292	.458	72	21	6	0	2	2.8	9	7	9	14	1
Night	79	.209	.344	244	51	13	1	6	2.5	26	26	37	47	2
vs. Left		.177	.210	62	11	2	0	0	0.0	6	5	9	16	1
vs. Right		.240	.409	254	61	17	1	8	3.1	29	28	37	45	2

Year	Team	Games	BA	SA	AB	H	2B	3B	HR	HR%	R	RBI	BB	SO	SB	PINCH HIT AB	H	PO	A	E	DP	TC/G	FA	G by Pos

Jack Howell *Continued*

Year	Team	Games	BA	SA	AB	H	2B	3B	HR	HR%	R	RBI	BB	SO	SB	PH AB	PH H	PO	A	E	DP	TC/G	FA	G by Pos
On Grass		91	.218	.358	271	59	15	1	7	2.6	32	30	43	55	3									
On Turf		14	.289	.444	45	13	4	0	1	2.2	3	3	3	6	0									
Home		53	.218	.333	156	34	9	0	3	1.9	16	17	20	31	0									
Road		52	.238	.406	160	38	10	1	5	3.1	19	16	26	30	3									
Division Rivals																								
vs. CHI		9	.267	.367	30	8	0	0	1	3.3	4	2	2	8	0									
vs. KC		9	.290	.290	31	9	0	0	0	0.0	1	0	0	8	0									
vs. MIN		8	.276	.379	29	8	3	0	0	0.0	3	4	3	7	0									
vs. OAK		8	.179	.321	28	5	1	0	1	3.6	1	3	4	4	1									
vs. SEA		8	.227	.545	22	5	4	0	1	4.5	2	3	3	3	0									
vs. TEX		7	.200	.250	20	4	1	0	0	0.0	4	3	2	2	0									
On 3B < 2 Out			.167	.500	12	2	1	0	1	8.3	1	10	3	2										
1985	CAL A	43	.197	.336	137	27	4	0	5	3.6	19	18	16	33	1	2	1	33	75	8	10	2.7	.931	3B-42
1986		63	.272	.470	151	41	14	2	4	2.6	26	21	19	28	2	16	4	38	57	2	5	1.5	.979	3B-39, OF-8, DH-2
1987		138	.245	.461	449	110	18	5	23	5.1	64	64	57	118	4	18	6	185	95	7	15	2.1	.976	OF-89, 3B-48, 2B-13
1988		154	.254	.422	500	127	32	2	16	3.2	59	63	46	130	2	4	1	97	249	17	19	2.4	.953	3B-152, OF-2
1989		144	.228	.411	474	108	19	4	20	4.2	56	52	52	125	0	3	1	97	322	11	27	3.0	.974	3B-142, OF-4
1990		105	.228	.370	316	72	19	1	8	2.5	35	33	46	61	3	6	2	76	196	18	18	2.8	.938	3B-102, 1B-1, SS-1
6 yrs.		647	.239	.418	2027	485	106	14	76	3.7	259	251	236	495	12	49	15	526	994	63	94	2.4	.960	3B-525, OF-103, 2B-13, DH-2, 1B-1, SS-1

LEAGUE CHAMPIONSHIP SERIES

Year	Team	Games	BA	SA	AB	H	2B	3B	HR	HR%	R	RBI	BB	SO	SB	PH AB	PH H	PO	A	E	DP	TC/G	FA	G by Pos
1986	CAL A	2	.000	.000	1	0	0	0	0	0.0	0	0	1	1	0	1	0	0	0	0	0	0.0	—	

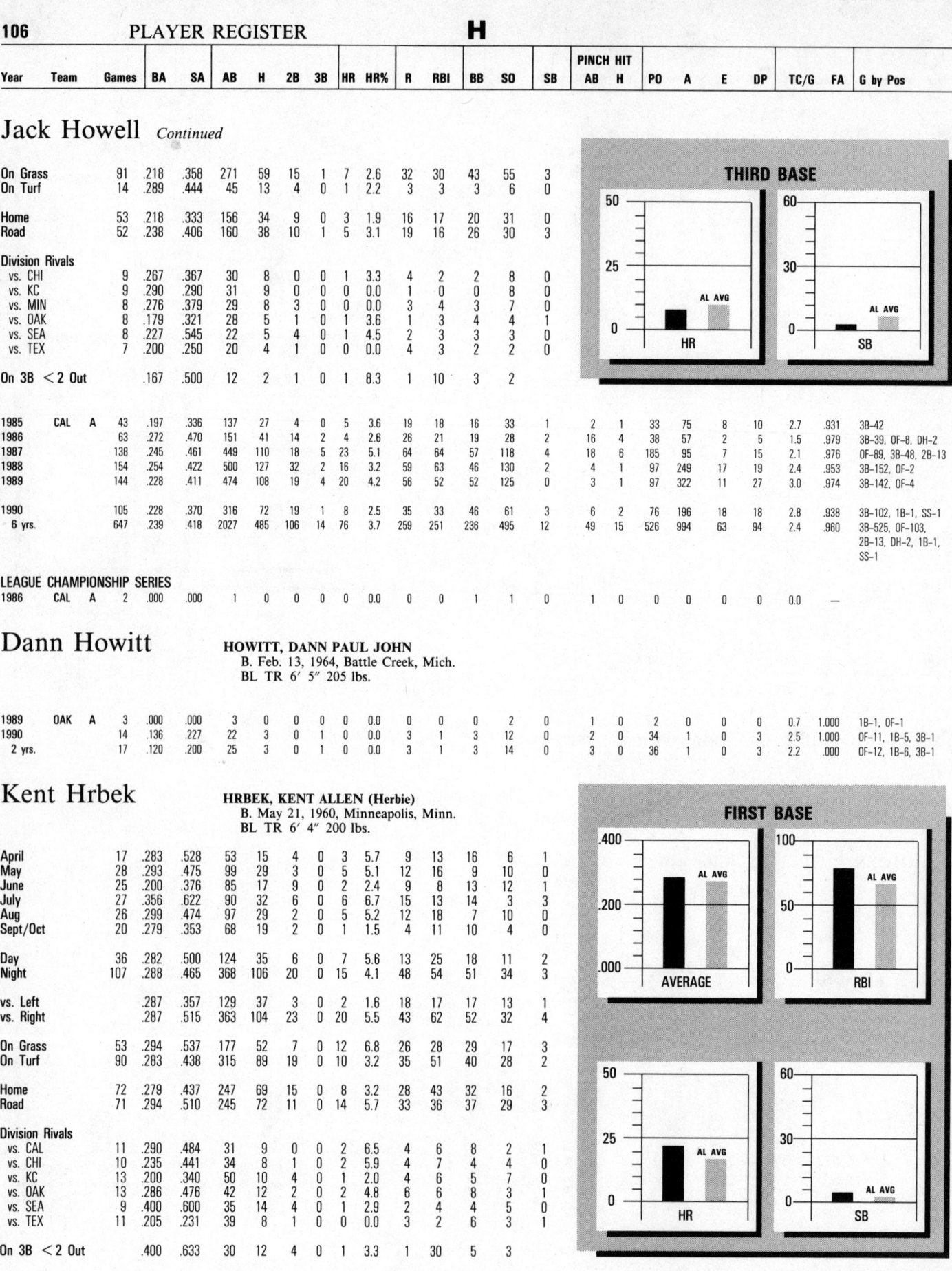

THIRD BASE

HR — AL AVG

SB — AL AVG

Dann Howitt

HOWITT, DANN PAUL JOHN
B. Feb. 13, 1964, Battle Creek, Mich.
BL TR 6′ 5″ 205 lbs.

Year	Team	Games	BA	SA	AB	H	2B	3B	HR	HR%	R	RBI	BB	SO	SB	PH AB	PH H	PO	A	E	DP	TC/G	FA	G by Pos
1989	OAK A	3	.000	.000	3	0	0	0	0	0.0	0	0	0	2	0	1	0	2	0	0	0	0.7	1.000	1B-1, OF-1
1990		14	.136	.227	22	3	0	1	0	0.0	3	1	3	12	0	2	0	34	1	0	3	2.5	1.000	OF-11, 1B-5, 3B-1
2 yrs.		17	.120	.200	25	3	0	1	0	0.0	3	1	3	14	0	3	0	36	1	0	3	2.2	.000	OF-12, 1B-6, 3B-1

Kent Hrbek

HRBEK, KENT ALLEN (Herbie)
B. May 21, 1960, Minneapolis, Minn.
BL TR 6′ 4″ 200 lbs.

Year	Team	Games	BA	SA	AB	H	2B	3B	HR	HR%	R	RBI	BB	SO	SB
April		17	.283	.528	53	15	4	0	3	5.7	9	13	16	6	1
May		28	.293	.475	99	29	3	0	5	5.1	12	16	9	10	0
June		25	.200	.376	85	17	9	0	2	2.4	9	8	13	12	1
July		27	.356	.622	90	32	6	0	6	6.7	15	13	14	3	3
Aug		26	.299	.474	97	29	2	0	5	5.2	12	18	7	10	0
Sept/Oct		20	.279	.353	68	19	2	0	1	1.5	4	11	10	4	0
Day		36	.282	.500	124	35	6	0	7	5.6	13	25	18	11	2
Night		107	.288	.465	368	106	20	0	15	4.1	48	54	51	34	3
vs. Left			.287	.357	129	37	3	0	2	1.6	18	17	17	13	1
vs. Right			.287	.515	363	104	23	0	20	5.5	43	62	52	32	4
On Grass		53	.294	.537	177	52	7	0	12	6.8	26	28	29	17	3
On Turf		90	.283	.438	315	89	19	0	10	3.2	35	51	40	28	2
Home		72	.279	.437	247	69	15	0	8	3.2	28	43	32	16	2
Road		71	.294	.510	245	72	11	0	14	5.7	33	36	37	29	3
Division Rivals															
vs. CAL		11	.290	.484	31	9	0	0	2	6.5	4	6	8	2	1
vs. CHI		10	.235	.441	34	8	1	0	2	5.9	4	7	4	4	0
vs. KC		13	.200	.340	50	10	4	0	1	2.0	4	6	5	7	0
vs. OAK		13	.286	.476	42	12	2	0	2	4.8	6	6	8	3	1
vs. SEA		9	.400	.600	35	14	4	0	1	2.9	2	4	4	5	0
vs. TEX		11	.205	.231	39	8	1	0	0	0.0	3	2	6	3	1
On 3B < 2 Out			.400	.633	30	12	4	0	1	3.3	1	30	5	3	

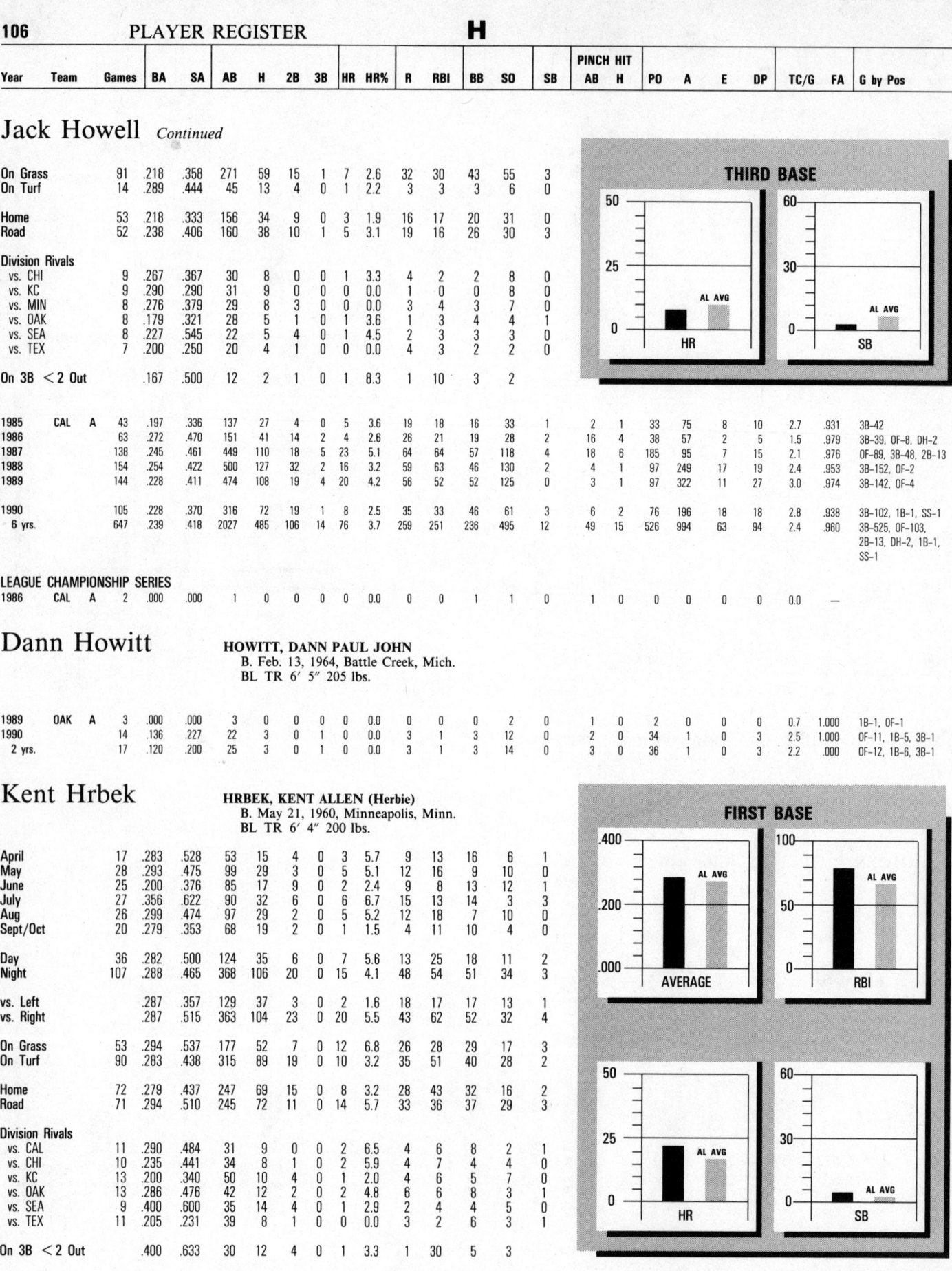

FIRST BASE

AVERAGE — AL AVG

RBI — AL AVG

HR — AL AVG

SB — AL AVG

Year	Team	Games	BA	SA	AB	H	2B	3B	HR	HR%	R	RBI	BB	SO	SB	PINCH HIT AB	H	PO	A	E	DP	TC/G	FA	G by Pos

Kent Hrbek *Continued*

Year	Team	Games	BA	SA	AB	H	2B	3B	HR	HR%	R	RBI	BB	SO	SB	AB	H	PO	A	E	DP	TC/G	FA	G by Pos
1981	MIN A	24	.239	.358	67	16	5	0	1	1.5	5	7	5	9	0	5	2	124	4	0	14	5.3	1.000	1B-13, DH-8
1982		140	.301	.485	532	160	21	4	23	4.3	82	92	54	80	3	1	0	1174	88	9	125	9.1	.993	1B-138, DH-2
1983		141	.297	.489	515	153	41	5	16	3.1	75	84	57	71	4	3	0	1151	89	13	125	8.9	.990	1B-137, DH-2
1984		149	.311	.522	559	174	31	3	27	4.8	80	107	65	87	1	1	1	1320	99	14	113	9.6	.990	1B-148, DH-1
1985		158	.278	.444	593	165	31	2	21	3.5	78	93	67	87	1	5	2	1339	114	8	114	9.2	.995	1B-156, DH-2
1986		149	.267	.478	550	147	27	1	29	5.3	85	91	71	81	2	3	0	1218	104	10	137	8.9	.992	1B-147, DH-1
1987		143	.285	.545	477	136	20	1	34	7.1	85	90	84	60	5	5	1	1179	68	5	112	8.8	.996	1B-137, DH-1
1988		143	.312	.520	510	159	31	0	25	4.9	75	76	67	54	0	2	1	842	57	3	92	6.3	.997	1B-105, DH-37
1989		109	.272	.517	375	102	17	0	25	6.7	59	84	53	35	3	4	1	723	60	4	66	7.2	.995	1B-89, DH-18
1990		143	.287	.474	492	141	26	0	22	4.4	61	79	69	45	5	4	2	1057	83	3	100	9.5	.997	1B-120, DH-20, 3B-1
10 yrs.		1299	.290	.493	4670	1353	250	16	223	4.8	685	803	592	609	24	33	10	10127	766	69	998	0.7	.928	1B-1190, DH-92, 3B-1

LEAGUE CHAMPIONSHIP SERIES

1987	MIN A	5	.150	.300	20	3	0	0	1	5.0	4	1	3	0	0	0	0	40	3	0	3	8.6	1.000	1B-5

WORLD SERIES

1987	MIN A	7	.208	.333	24	5	0	0	1	4.2	4	6	5	3	0	0	0	68	2	0	3	10.0	1.000	1B-7

Rex Hudler

HUDLER, REX ALLEN
B. Sept. 2, 1960, Tempe, Ariz.
BR TR 6' 1" 180 lbs.

Year	Team	Games	BA	SA	AB	H	2B	3B	HR	HR%	R	RBI	BB	SO	SB	AB	H	PO	A	E	DP	TC/G	FA	G by Pos
1984	NY A	9	.143	.286	7	1	1	0	0	0.0	2	0	1	5	0	0	0	4	7	0	1	1.2	1.000	2B-9
1985		20	.157	.196	51	8	0	1	0	0.0	4	1	1	9	0	0	0	42	51	2	14	4.8	.979	2B-16, 1B-1, SS-1
1986	BAL A	14	.000	.000	1	0	0	0	0	0.0	1	0	0	0	1	0	0	2	3	1	0	0.4	.833	2B-13, 3B-1
1988	MON N	77	.273	.412	216	59	14	2	4	1.9	38	14	10	34	29	3	0	116	168	10	30	3.8	.966	2B-41, SS-27, OF-4
1989		92	.245	.406	155	38	7	0	6	3.9	21	13	6	23	15	27	4	59	59	7	13	1.4	.944	2B-38, OF-23, SS-18
1990	2 teams	MON N (4G — .333)			STL N (89G — .281)																			
"	total	93	.282	.445	220	62	11	2	7	3.1	31	22	12	32	18	21	4	158	42	5	9	3.1	.976	OF-45, 2B-10, 1B-6, 3B-6, SS-1
6 yrs.		305	.258	.403	650	168	33	5	17	2.6	97	50	30	103	63	51	8	381	330	25	67	2.4	.966	2B-127, OF-72, SS-47, 1B-7, 3B-7

Keith Hughes

HUGHES, KEITH WILLS
B. Sept. 12, 1963, Bryn Mawr, Pa.
BL TL 6' 3" 210 lbs.

Year	Team	Games	BA	SA	AB	H	2B	3B	HR	HR%	R	RBI	BB	SO	SB	AB	H	PO	A	E	DP	TC/G	FA	G by Pos
1987	2 teams	NY A (4G — .000)			PHI N (37G — .263)																			
"	total	41	.250	.275	80	20	2	0	0	0.0	8	10	7	13	0	23	8	26	0	1	0	0.7	.963	OF-23
1988	BAL A	41	.194	.324	108	21	4	2	2	1.9	10	14	16	27	1	8	0	59	4	2	2	1.6	.969	OF-31
1990	NY N	8	.000	.000	9	0	0	0	0	0.0	0	0	0	4	0	6	0	5	0	0	0	1.0	1.000	OF-5
3 yrs.		90	.208	.289	197	41	6	2	2	1.0	18	24	23	44	1	37	8	90	4	3	2	1.1	.969	OF-59

Tim Hulett

HULETT, TIMOTHY CRAIG
B. Jan. 20, 1960, Springfield, Ill.
BR TR 6' 185 lbs.

Year	Team	Games	BA	SA	AB	H	2B	3B	HR	HR%	R	RBI	BB	SO	SB	AB	H	PO	A	E	DP	TC/G	FA	G by Pos
1983	CHI A	6	.200	.200	5	1	0	0	0	0.0	0	0	0	0	1	0	0	8	6	2	1	2.7	.875	2B-6
1984		8	.000	.000	7	0	0	0	0	0.0	1	0	1	4	1	1	0	4	15	0	2	2.4	1.000	3B-4, 2B-3
1985		141	.268	.375	395	106	19	4	5	1.3	52	36	30	81	6	2	1	117	256	24	41	2.8	.940	3B-115, 2B-28, OF-1
1986		150	.231	.379	520	120	16	5	17	3.3	53	44	21	91	4	5	1	179	331	15	54	3.5	.971	3B-89, 2B-66
1987		68	.217	.346	240	52	10	0	7	2.9	20	28	10	41	0	0	0	55	142	9	19	3.0	.956	3B-61, 2B-8
1989	BAL A	33	.278	.423	97	27	5	0	3	3.1	12	18	10	17	0	1	0	70	71	4	13	4.4	.972	2B-23, 3B-11
1990		53	.255	.373	153	39	7	1	3	1.9	16	16	15	41	0	9	1	44	101	4	15	3.7	.973	3B-24, 2B-16, DH-8
7 yrs.		459	.243	.372	1417	345	57	10	35	2.5	154	142	87	275	13	18	3	477	922	58	145	3.2	.960	3B-304, 2B-150, DH-8, OF-1

Todd Hundley

HUNDLEY, TODD RANDOLPH
Son of Randy Hundley.
B. May 27, 1969, Martinsville, Va.
BB TR 5' 11" 170 lbs.

Year	Team	Games	BA	SA	AB	H	2B	3B	HR	HR%	R	RBI	BB	SO	SB	AB	H	PO	A	E	DP	TC/G	FA	G by Pos
1990	NY N	36	.209	.299	67	14	6	0	0	0.0	8	2	6	18	0	3	0	162	8	2	2	4.8	.988	C-36

Year	Team	Games	BA	SA	AB	H	2B	3B	HR	HR%	R	RBI	BB	SO	SB	PINCH HIT AB	PINCH HIT H	PO	A	E	DP	TC/G	FA	G by Pos

Jeff Huson

HUSON, JEFFREY KENT (Huey)
B. Aug. 15, 1964, Scottsdale, Ariz.
BL TR 6′ 3″ 180 lbs.

Year	Team	Games	BA	SA	AB	H	2B	3B	HR	HR%	R	RBI	BB	SO	SB	PINCH HIT AB	PINCH HIT H	PO	A	E	DP	TC/G	FA	G by Pos
April		17	.278	.306	36	10	1	0	0	0.0	5	5	8	6	1									
May		25	.295	.385	78	23	7	0	0	0.0	11	3	6	8	2									
June		27	.269	.321	78	21	2	1	0	0.0	13	4	10	9	2									
July		24	.234	.286	77	18	2	1	0	0.0	12	7	7	9	2									
Aug		25	.167	.167	66	11	0	0	0	0.0	7	4	10	12	0									
Sept/Oct		27	.197	.197	61	12	0	0	0	0.0	9	5	5	10	5									
Day		27	.254	.282	71	18	2	0	0	0.0	14	7	10	10	3									
Night		118	.237	.280	325	77	10	2	0	0.0	43	21	36	44	9									
vs. Left			.261	.283	46	12	1	0	0	0.0	9	3	4	1										
vs. Right			.237	.280	350	83	11	2	0	0.0	48	25	42	45	11									
On Grass		121	.239	.281	327	78	10	2	0	0.0	53	24	37	48	9									
On Turf		24	.246	.275	69	17	2	0	0	0.0	4	4	9	6	3									
Home		74	.220	.272	191	42	8	1	0	0.0	28	11	18	33	5									
Road		71	.259	.288	205	53	4	1	0	0.0	29	17	28	21	7									
Division Rivals																								
vs. CAL		12	.161	.226	31	5	0	1	0	0.0	2	3	4	6	0									
vs. CHI		12	.308	.385	26	8	2	0	0	0.0	5	4	9	3	1									
vs. KC		13	.250	.318	44	11	3	0	0	0.0	6	3	5	7	1									
vs. MIN		11	.276	.345	29	8	2	0	0	0.0	4	1	3	2	3									
vs. OAK		11	.207	.207	29	6	0	0	0	0.0	3	0	1	4	0									
vs. SEA		12	.200	.200	30	6	0	0	0	0.0	4	0	5	6	1									
On 3B < 2 Out			.333	.333	12	4	0	0	0	0.0	0	12	2	0										
1988	MON N	20	.310	.357	42	13	2	0	0	0.0	7	3	4	3	2	2	2	18	41	4	5	3.2	.937	SS-15, 2B-2, 3B-1, OF-1
1989		32	.162	.230	74	12	5	0	0	0.0	1	2	6	6	3	4	1	40	65	8	11	3.5	.929	SS-20, 2B-9, 3B-1
1990	TEX A	145	.240	.280	396	95	12	2	0	0.0	57	28	46	54	12	18	3	183	304	19	76	3.7	.962	SS-119, 3B-36, 2B-12
3 yrs.		197	.234	.279	512	120	19	2	0	0.0	65	33	56	63	17	24	6	241	410	31	92	3.5	.955	SS-154, 3B-38, 2B-23, OF-1

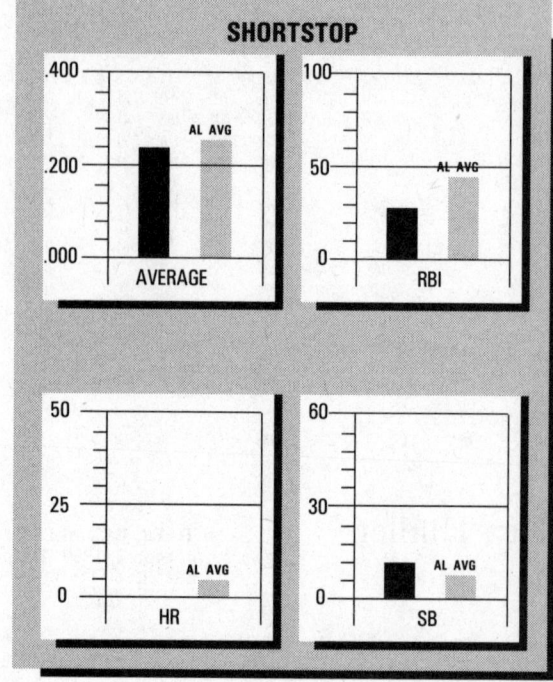

SHORTSTOP

AVERAGE · RBI · HR · SB (AL AVG)

Pete Incaviglia

INCAVIGLIA, PETER JOSEPH (Inky)
B. Apr. 2, 1964, Pebble Beach, Calif.
BR TR 6′ 1″ 225 lbs.

Year	Team	Games	BA	SA	AB	H	2B	3B	HR	HR%	R	RBI	BB	SO	SB	PINCH HIT AB	PINCH HIT H	PO	A	E	DP	TC/G	FA	G by Pos
April		19	.243	.486	70	17	5	0	4	5.7	7	15	6	24	1									
May		25	.197	.368	76	15	4	0	3	3.9	7	10	6	25	0									
June		29	.283	.472	106	30	5	0	5	4.7	15	16	9	22	0									
July		26	.263	.495	95	25	7	0	5	5.3	11	19	10	25	1									
Aug		26	.179	.262	84	15	1	0	2	2.4	9	9	4	26	1									
Sept/Oct		28	.214	.418	98	21	5	0	5	5.1	10	16	10	24	0									
Day		27	.161	.218	87	14	5	0	0	0.0	3	6	12	26	0									
Night		126	.247	.459	442	109	22	0	24	5.4	56	79	33	120	3									
vs. Left			.249	.444	169	42	4	0	8	4.7	21	30	21	36	2									
vs. Right			.225	.408	360	81	18	0	16	4.4	38	55	24	110	1									
On Grass		127	.228	.416	435	99	22	0	20	4.6	48	64	37	128	3									
On Turf		26	.255	.436	94	24	5	0	4	4.3	11	21	8	18	0									
Home		76	.247	.482	247	61	13	0	15	6.1	33	45	28	73	3									
Road		77	.220	.365	282	62	14	0	9	3.2	26	40	17	73	0									
Division Rivals																								
vs. CAL		13	.298	.553	47	14	3	0	3	6.4	6	5	4	11	0									
vs. CHI		12	.186	.349	43	8	1	0	2	4.7	3	5	3	13	0									
vs. KC		13	.186	.395	43	8	0	0	3	7.0	3	10	3	14	0									
vs. MIN		12	.211	.421	38	8	2	0	2	5.3	6	6	2	13	0									
vs. OAK		13	.224	.367	49	11	1	0	2	4.1	4	4	4	13	0									
vs. SEA		13	.341	.545	44	15	3	0	2	4.5	9	12	4	10	0									
On 3B < 2 Out			.286	.514	35	10	2	0	2	5.7	2	25	2	11										
1986	TEX A	153	.250	.463	540	135	21	2	30	5.6	82	88	55	**185**	3	4	0	157	6	14	1	1.2	.921	OF-114, DH-36
1987		139	.271	.497	509	138	26	4	27	5.3	85	80	48	168	9	3	0	216	8	13	0	1.7	.945	OF-132, DH-6
1988		116	.249	.467	418	104	19	3	22	5.3	59	54	39	**153**	6	0	0	172	12	2	1	1.6	.989	OF-93, DH-21
1989		133	.236	.453	453	107	27	4	21	4.6	48	81	32	136	5	5	2	213	7	6	2	1.7	.973	OF-125, DH-5
1990		153	.233	.420	529	123	27	0	24	4.5	59	85	45	146	3	13	2	290	12	8	2	2.1	.974	OF-145, DH-2
5 yrs.		694	.248	.459	2449	607	120	13	124	5.1	333	388	219	788	26	25	4	1048	45	43	6	1.6	.962	OF-609, DH-70

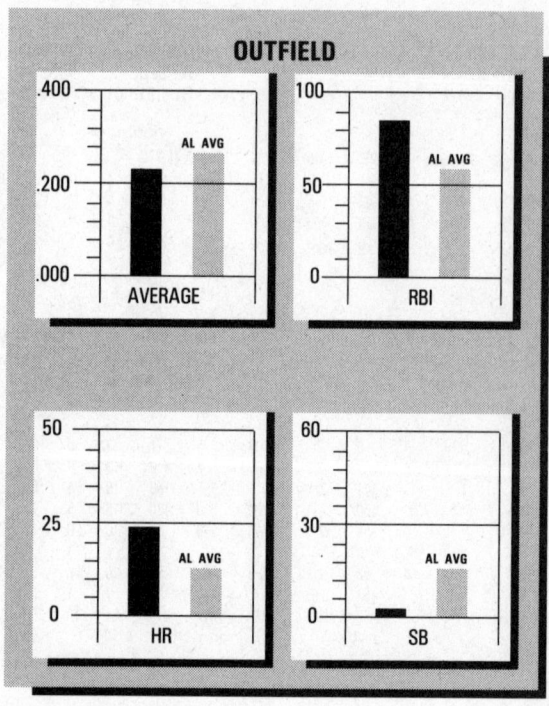

OUTFIELD

AVERAGE · RBI · HR · SB (AL AVG)

Year	Team		Games	BA	SA	AB	H	2B	3B	HR	HR%	R	RBI	BB	SO	SB	PINCH HIT AB	H	PO	A	E	DP	TC/G	FA	G by Pos

Alexis Infante

INFANTE, FERMIN ALEXIS
Born Fermin Alexis Infante y Carpio.
B. Dec. 4, 1961, Barquisimeto, Venezuela
BR TR 5' 10" 175 lbs.

Year	Team		Games	BA	SA	AB	H	2B	3B	HR	HR%	R	RBI	BB	SO	SB	PH AB	PH H	PO	A	E	DP	TC/G	FA	G by Pos
1987	TOR	A	1	—	—	0	0	0	0	0	—	0	0	0	0	0	0	0	0	0	0	0	0.0	—	SS-1
1988			19	.200	.200	15	3	0	0	0	0.0	7	0	2	4	0	0	0	4	6	1	0	0.6	.909	3B-9, SS-2
1989			20	.167	.167	12	2	0	0	0	0.0	1	0	0	1	1	0	0	6	13	0	3	1.0	1.000	SS-9, DH-4, 3B-4, 2B-1
1990	ATL	N	20	.036	.071	28	1	1	0	0	0.0	3	0	0	7	0	3	0	22	24	2	4	3.2	.958	2B-10, 3B-4, SS-3
4 yrs.			60	.109	.127	55	6	1	0	0	0.0	11	0	2	12	1	3	0	32	43	3	7	1.3	.962	3B-17, SS-15, 2B-11, DH-4

Bo Jackson

JACKSON, VINCENT EDWARD
B. Nov. 30, 1962, Bessemer, Ala.
BR TR 6' 1" 222 lbs.

	Games	BA	SA	AB	H	2B	3B	HR	HR%	R	RBI	BB	SO	SB
April	14	.340	.453	53	18	3	0	1	1.9	11	5	6	20	2
May	27	.264	.443	106	28	4	0	5	4.7	21	14	12	34	5
June	26	.237	.464	97	23	4	0	6	6.2	14	15	12	36	3
July	12	.273	.818	44	12	1	1	7	15.9	9	23	5	10	0
Aug	5	.500	1.125	16	8	1	0	3	18.8	6	7	3	0	2
Sept/Oct	27	.236	.472	89	21	3	0	6	6.7	13	14	6	28	3
Day	28	.276	.571	105	29	4	0	9	8.6	22	17	9	37	5
Night	83	.270	.507	300	81	12	1	19	6.3	52	61	35	91	10
vs. Left		.273	.510	143	39	4	0	10	7.0	28	24	16	46	6
vs. Right		.271	.531	262	71	12	1	18	6.9	46	54	28	82	9
On Grass	44	.244	.474	156	38	1	1	11	7.1	24	30	18	48	9
On Turf	67	.289	.554	249	72	15	0	17	6.8	50	48	26	80	6
Home	52	.307	.573	192	59	15	0	12	6.3	41	37	21	58	3
Road	59	.239	.479	213	51	1	1	16	7.5	33	41	23	70	12
Division Rivals														
vs. CAL	12	.178	.356	45	8	2	0	2	4.4	6	4	3	18	1
vs. CHI	9	.194	.306	36	7	1	0	1	2.8	4	2	0	12	2
vs. MIN	10	.220	.390	41	9	1	0	2	4.9	5	7	3	14	0
vs. OAK	11	.316	.684	38	12	2	0	4	10.5	8	9	6	9	3
vs. SEA	9	.300	.833	30	9	1	0	5	16.7	7	9	4	8	2
vs. TEX	8	.280	.520	25	7	0	0	2	8.0	6	6	8	7	2
On 3B < 2 Out		.250	.600	20	5	1	0	2	10.0	2	18	4	10	

OUTFIELD

AVERAGE — AL AVG
RBI — AL AVG
HR — AL AVG
SB — AL AVG

Year	Team		Games	BA	SA	AB	H	2B	3B	HR	HR%	R	RBI	BB	SO	SB	PH AB	PH H	PO	A	E	DP	TC/G	FA	G by Pos
1986	KC	A	25	.207	.329	82	17	2	1	2	2.4	9	9	7	34	3	0	0	29	2	4	0	1.4	.886	OF-23, DH-1
1987			116	.235	.455	396	93	17	2	22	5.6	46	53	30	158	10	2	0	180	9	9	1	1.7	.955	OF-113, DH-1
1988			124	.246	.472	439	108	16	4	25	5.7	63	68	25	146	27	1	0	246	11	7	2	2.1	.973	OF-121, DH-2
1989			135	.256	.495	515	132	15	6	32	6.2	86	105	39	**172**	26	1	0	224	11	8	2	1.8	.967	OF-110, DH-24
1990			111	.272	.523	405	110	16	1	28	6.9	74	78	44	128	15	4	1	230	8	12	2	2.6	.952	OF-97, DH-10
5 yrs.			511	.250	.480	1837	460	66	14	109	5.9	278	313	145	638	81	8	1	909	41	40	7	1.9	.960	OF-464, DH-38

Darrin Jackson

JACKSON, DARRIN JAY
B. Aug. 22, 1963, Los Angeles, Calif.
BR TR 6' 185 lbs.

Year	Team		Games	BA	SA	AB	H	2B	3B	HR	HR%	R	RBI	BB	SO	SB	PH AB	PH H	PO	A	E	DP	TC/G	FA	G by Pos
1985	CHI	N	5	.091	.091	11	1	0	0	0	0.0	0	0	0	3	0	1	0	7	0	0	0	1.4	1.000	OF-4
1987			7	.800	1.000	5	4	1	0	0	0.0	2	0	0	0	0	4	3	1	0	0	0	0.1	1.000	OF-5
1988			100	.266	.452	188	50	11	3	6	3.2	29	20	5	28	4	21	5	116	1	2	0	1.2	.983	OF-74
1989	2 teams		CHI N (45G — .229)			SD N (25G — .207)																			
"	total		70	.218	.329	170	37	7	0	4	2.4	17	20	13	34	1	14	1	121	5	5	4	1.9	.962	OF-63
1990	SD	N	58	.257	.363	113	29	3	0	3	2.6	10	9	5	24	3	18	4	63	1	1	1	1.7	.985	OF-39
5 yrs.			240	.248	.386	487	121	22	3	13	2.7	58	49	23	89	8	58	13	308	7	8	5	1.3	.975	OF-185

Year	Team		Games	BA	SA	AB	H	2B	3B	HR	HR%	R	RBI	BB	SO	SB	PINCH HIT AB	H	PO	A	E	DP	TC/G	FA	G by Pos

Brook Jacoby

JACOBY, BROOK WALLACE
B. Nov. 23, 1959, Philadelphia, Pa.
BR TR 5′ 11″ 175 lbs.

Split			Games	BA	SA	AB	H	2B	3B	HR	HR%	R	RBI	BB	SO	SB	PH AB	PH H	PO	A	E	DP	TC/G	FA	G by Pos
April			15	.333	.500	54	18	2	2	1	1.9	10	4	6	3	0									
May			26	.226	.376	93	21	3	1	3	3.2	13	9	8	16	0									
June			28	.394	.625	104	41	4	1	6	5.8	17	21	11	8	1									
July			30	.252	.320	103	26	1	0	2	1.9	7	13	14	10	0									
Aug			27	.223	.298	94	21	4	0	1	1.1	16	12	14	8	0									
Sept/Oct			29	.333	.457	105	35	10	0	1	1.0	14	16	10	13	0									
Day			41	.269	.365	156	42	4	1	3	1.9	19	19	11	16	1									
Night			114	.302	.451	397	120	20	3	11	2.8	58	56	52	42	0									
vs. Left				.316	.411	158	50	4	1	3	1.9	19	18	16	13	0									
vs. Right				.284	.433	395	112	20	3	11	2.8	58	57	47	45	1									
On Grass			132	.301	.447	468	141	20	3	14	3.0	62	69	52	50	1									
On Turf			23	.247	.318	85	21	4	1	0	0.0	15	6	11	8	0									
Home			78	.287	.464	261	75	10	3	10	3.8	33	41	36	21	1									
Road			77	.298	.394	292	87	14	1	4	1.4	44	34	27	37	0									
Division Rivals																									
vs. BAL			13	.267	.422	45	12	1	0	2	4.4	7	8	7	2	0									
vs. BOS			13	.327	.429	49	16	2	0	1	2.0	5	6	5	6	1									
vs. DET			13	.310	.548	42	13	4	0	2	4.8	9	5	8	1	0									
vs. MIL			12	.400	.620	50	20	0	1	3	6.0	10	13	4	5	0									
vs. NY			13	.354	.521	48	17	5	0	1	2.1	9	8	2	7	0									
vs. TOR			13	.326	.478	46	15	2	1	1	2.2	8	4	3	3	0									
On 3B < 2 Out				.276	.310	29	8	1	0	0	0.0	0	19	8	3										
1981	ATL	N	11	.200	.200	10	2	0	0	0	0.0	0	1	0	3	0	8	2	3	4	0	1	0.6	1.000	3B-3
1983			4	.000	.000	8	0	0	0	0	0.0	0	0	0	1	0	2	0	0	2	0	0	0.5	1.000	3B-2
1984	CLE	A	126	.264	.369	439	116	19	3	7	1.6	64	40	32	73	3	0	0	86	188	14	17	2.3	.951	3B-126, SS-1
1985			161	.274	.426	606	166	26	3	20	3.3	72	87	48	120	2	1	0	114	319	19	26	2.8	.958	3B-161, 2B-1
1986			158	.288	.441	583	168	30	4	17	2.9	83	80	56	137	2	0	0	109	292	25	24	2.7	.941	3B-158
1987			155	.300	.541	540	162	26	4	32	5.9	73	69	75	73	2	2	1	192	261	22	24	3.1	.954	3B-144, 1B-7, DH-4
1988			152	.241	.335	552	133	25	0	9	1.6	59	49	48	101	2	1	0	99	298	10	23	2.7	.975	3B-151
1989			147	.272	.416	519	141	26	5	13	2.5	49	64	62	90	2	0	0	92	268	17	15	2.6	.955	3B-144, DH-3
1990			155	.293	.427	553	162	24	4	14	2.5	77	75	63	58	1	3	2	628	186	6	75	5.4	.993	3B-99, 1B-78
9 yrs.			1069	.276	.422	3810	1050	176	23	112	2.9	477	465	384	656	14	17	5	1323	1818	113	205	3.0	.965	3B-988, 1B-85, DH-7, 2B-1, SS-1

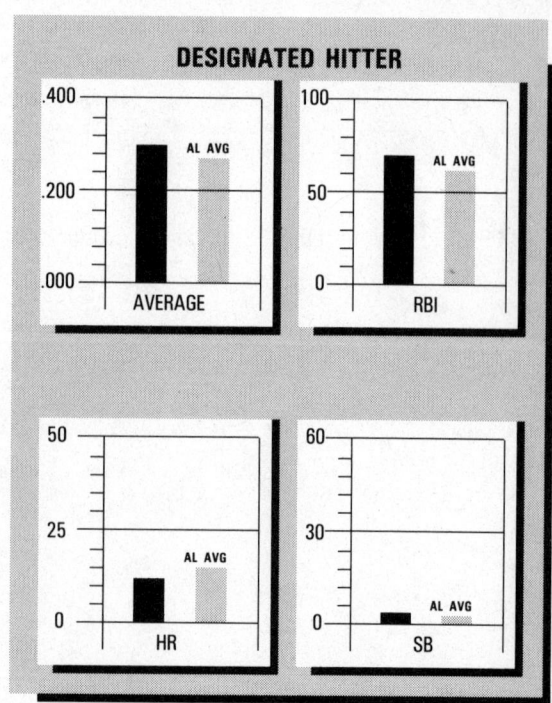

THIRD BASE — AVERAGE (AL AVG), RBI (AL AVG), HR (AL AVG), SB (AL AVG)

Chris James

JAMES, DONALD CHRIS
B. Oct. 4, 1962, Rusk, Tex.
BR TR 6′ 1″ 190 lbs.

Split	Games	BA	SA	AB	H	2B	3B	HR	HR%	R	RBI	BB	SO	SB
April	13	.122	.195	41	5	0	0	1	2.4	2	3	0	7	0
May	22	.321	.432	81	26	6	0	1	1.2	9	11	5	10	1
June	26	.317	.462	104	33	5	2	2	1.9	10	17	6	16	2
July	28	.286	.439	98	28	7	1	2	2.0	13	8	9	15	0
Aug	28	.357	.554	112	40	8	1	4	3.6	18	17	7	12	0
Sept/Oct	23	.283	.413	92	26	6	0	2	2.2	10	14	4	11	1
Day	39	.324	.525	139	45	14	1	4	2.9	18	25	5	17	2
Night	101	.290	.414	389	113	18	3	8	2.1	44	45	26	54	2
vs. Left		.302	.432	162	49	7	1	4	2.5	20	22	15	25	3
vs. Right		.298	.448	366	109	25	3	8	2.2	42	48	16	46	1
On Grass	121	.307	.441	449	138	27	3	9	2.0	52	58	28	59	3
On Turf	19	.253	.456	79	20	5	1	3	3.8	10	12	3	12	1
Home	67	.286	.427	234	67	13	1	6	2.6	27	33	15	33	1
Road	73	.310	.456	294	91	19	3	6	2.0	35	37	16	38	3
Division Rivals														
vs. BAL	9	.256	.333	39	10	3	0	0	0.0	4	2	2	4	1
vs. BOS	13	.269	.423	52	14	1	2	1	1.9	3	5	2	9	1
vs. DET	13	.277	.596	47	13	3	0	4	8.5	8	8	6	7	0
vs. MIL	12	.417	.479	48	20	3	0	0	0.0	7	11	3	3	0
vs. NY	11	.275	.475	40	11	5	0	1	2.5	6	3	4	9	0
vs. TOR	11	.171	.268	41	7	1	0	1	2.4	5	3	0	8	0
On 3B < 2 Out		.313	.406	32	10	3	0	0	0.0	0	23	5	7	

DESIGNATED HITTER — AVERAGE (AL AVG), RBI (AL AVG), HR (AL AVG), SB (AL AVG)

Year	Team		Games	BA	SA	AB	H	2B	3B	HR	HR%	R	RBI	BB	SO	SB	PINCH HIT AB	H	PO	A	E	DP	TC/G	FA	G by Pos

Chris James *Continued*

Year	Team		Games	BA	SA	AB	H	2B	3B	HR	HR%	R	RBI	BB	SO	SB	AB	H	PO	A	E	DP	TC/G	FA	G by Pos
1986	PHI	N	16	.283	.413	46	13	3	0	1	2.2	5	5	1	13	0	6	2	19	0	0	0	1.2	1.000	OF-11
1987			115	.293	.525	358	105	20	6	17	4.7	48	54	27	67	3	9	5	198	5	2	1	1.8	.990	OF-108
1988			150	.242	.389	566	137	24	1	19	3.4	57	66	31	73	7	4	1	282	51	9	6	2.3	.974	OF-116, 3B-31
1989	2 teams			PHI N	(45G — .207)	SD N	(87G — .264)																		
"	total		132	.243	.367	482	117	17	2	13	2.7	55	65	26	68	5	8	2	215	27	7	4	1.9	.972	OF-116, 3B-17
1990	CLE	A	140	.299	.443	528	158	32	4	12	2.2	62	70	31	71	4	6	2	25	1	0	0	1.9	1.000	DH-124, OF-14
5 yrs.			553	.268	.423	1980	530	96	13	62	3.1	227	260	116	292	19	33	12	739	84	18	11	1.5	.979	OF-365, DH-124, 3B-48

Dion James

JAMES, DION
B. Nov. 9, 1962, Philadelphia, Pa.
BL TL 6' 1" 170 lbs.

	Games	BA	SA	AB	H	2B	3B	HR	HR%	R	RBI	BB	SO	SB
April	14	.242	.273	33	8	1	0	0	0.0	2	2	4	3	0
May	19	.255	.309	55	14	3	0	0	0.0	5	3	5	7	2
June	15	.286	.408	49	14	4	1	0	0.0	7	3	6	3	2
July	11	.294	.441	34	10	3	1	0	0.0	5	5	5	2	1
Aug	18	.286	.393	56	16	3	0	1	1.8	9	7	4	5	0
Sept/Oct	10	.286	.333	21	6	1	0	0	0.0	0	2	3	3	0
Day	27	.254	.338	71	18	2	2	0	0.0	11	7	7	6	3
Night	60	.282	.373	177	50	13	0	1	0.6	17	15	20	17	2
vs. Left		.111	.222	9	1	1	0	0	0.0	1	1	1	0	0
vs. Right		.280	.368	239	67	14	2	1	0.4	27	21	26	23	5
On Grass	74	.278	.375	216	60	14	2	1	0.5	27	20	25	20	5
On Turf	13	.250	.281	32	8	1	0	0	0.0	1	2	2	3	0
Home	41	.325	.439	123	40	12	1	0	0.0	14	10	15	12	4
Road	46	.224	.288	125	28	3	1	1	0.8	14	12	12	11	1
Division Rivals														
vs. BAL	4	.182	.182	11	2	0	0	0	0.0	0	1	1	3	0
vs. BOS	9	.273	.394	33	9	2	1	0	0.0	4	0	3	0	1
vs. DET	9	.259	.296	27	7	1	0	0	0.0	4	3	5	2	1
vs. MIL	4	.308	.385	13	4	1	0	0	0.0	3	2	1	2	0
vs. NY	9	.278	.500	18	5	1	0	1	5.6	5	2	3	0	1
vs. TOR	8	.381	.429	21	8	1	0	0	0.0	0	1	3	3	0
On 3B < 2 Out		.500	.750	12	6	1	1	0	0.0	0	12	3	2	

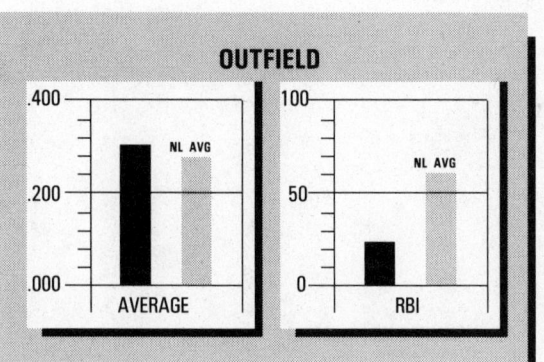

FIRST BASE

AVERAGE — AL AVG
RBI — AL AVG
HR — AL AVG
SB — AL AVG

Year	Team		Games	BA	SA	AB	H	2B	3B	HR	HR%	R	RBI	BB	SO	SB	AB	H	PO	A	E	DP	TC/G	FA	G by Pos
1983	MIL	A	11	.100	.100	20	2	0	0	0	0.0	1	1	2	2	1	0	0	12	1	0	0	1.2	1.000	OF-9, DH-2
1984			128	.295	.377	387	114	19	5	1	0.3	52	30	32	41	10	17	3	252	7	3	1	2.0	.989	OF-118
1985			18	.224	.245	49	11	1	0	0	0.0	5	3	6	6	0	4	0	20	0	0	0	1.1	1.000	OF-11, DH-3
1987	ATL	N	134	.312	.472	494	154	37	6	10	2.0	80	61	70	63	10	11	1	262	4	1	1	2.0	.996	OF-126
1988			132	.256	.350	386	99	17	5	3	0.8	46	30	58	59	9	15	3	222	5	3	0	1.7	.987	OF-120
1989	2 teams			ATL N	(63G — .259)	CLE A	(71G — .306)																		
"	total		134	.287	.366	415	119	18	0	5	1.2	41	40	49	49	2	28	5	211	8	3	5	1.7	.986	OF-83, DH-27, 1B-10
1990	CLE	A	87	.274	.363	248	68	15	2	1	0.4	28	22	27	23	5	14	3	282	17	4	21	4.7	.987	1B-35, OF-33, DH-10
7 yrs.			644	.284	.385	1999	567	107	18	20	1.0	253	187	244	243	37	89	15	1261	42	14	28	2.0	.989	OF-500, 1B-45, DH-42

Stan Javier

JAVIER, STANLEY JULIAN
Born Stanley Julian Javier y DeJavier.
Son of Julian Javier.
B. Sept. 1, 1965, San Francisco De Macoris,
Dominican Republic
BB TR 6' 180 lbs.

	Games	BA	SA	AB	H	2B	3B	HR	HR%	R	RBI	BB	SO	SB
April	13	.231	.385	26	6	0	2	0	0.0	3	3	0	6	0
May	20	.255	.353	51	13	1	2	0	0.0	9	7	11	7	3
June	20	.400	.538	65	26	4	1	1	1.5	16	6	5	10	4
July	19	.270	.270	37	10	0	0	0	0.0	8	4	5	7	1
Aug	22	.173	.250	52	9	2	1	0	0.0	9	3	10	13	4
Sept/Oct	29	.359	.462	78	28	2	0	2	2.6	15	4	9	7	3
Day	33	.293	.370	92	27	2	1	1	1.1	15	10	12	18	4
Night	90	.300	.406	217	65	7	5	2	0.9	45	17	28	32	11
vs. Left		.315	.403	124	39	2	3	1	0.8	28	10	18	14	5
vs. Right		.286	.389	185	53	7	3	2	1.1	32	17	22	36	10

OUTFIELD

AVERAGE — NL AVG
RBI — NL AVG

Year	Team	Games	BA	SA	AB	H	2B	3B	HR	HR%	R	RBI	BB	SO	SB	PINCH HIT AB	H	PO	A	E	DP	TC/G	FA	G by Pos

Stan Javier *Continued*

Year	Team	Games	BA	SA	AB	H	2B	3B	HR	HR%	R	RBI	BB	SO	SB	AB	H	PO	A	E	DP	TC/G	FA	G by Pos
On Grass		96	.249	.294	245	61	4	2	1	0.4	39	20	36	40	9									
On Turf		27	.484	.781	64	31	5	4	2	3.1	21	7	4	10	6									
Home		64	.286	.348	161	46	3	2	1	0.6	25	16	21	24	6									
Road		59	.311	.446	148	46	6	4	2	1.4	35	11	19	26	9									
Division Rivals																								
vs. ATL		15	.211	.211	38	8	0	0	0	0.0	9	3	6	7	3									
vs. CIN		12	.483	.793	29	14	4	1	1	3.4	10	2	5	5	3									
vs. HOU		9	.375	.500	24	9	0	0	1	4.2	8	2	1	2	1									
vs. SD		13	.357	.452	42	15	1	0	1	2.4	7	3	6	3	2									
vs. SF		10	.370	.407	27	10	1	0	0	0.0	5	2	5	5	1									
On 3B < 2 Out			.200	.400	10	2	0	1	0	0.0	0	8	4	1										
1984	NY A	7	.143	.143	7	1	0	0	0	0.0	1	0	0	1	0	0	0	3	0	0	0	0.4	1.000	OF-5
1986	OAK A	59	.202	.272	114	23	8	0	0	0.0	13	8	16	27	8	0	0	118	1	0	1	2.0	1.000	OF-51, DH-2
1987		81	.185	.258	151	28	3	1	2	1.3	22	9	19	33	3	7	0	149	5	3	4	1.9	.981	OF-71, 1B-6, DH-1
1988		125	.257	.320	397	102	13	3	2	0.5	49	35	32	63	20	9	2	274	7	5	5	2.3	.983	OF-115, 1B-4, DH-2
1989		112	.248	.316	310	77	12	3	1	0.3	42	28	31	45	12	7	0	221	8	2	2	2.1	.991	OF-107, 1B-1, 2B-1
1990	2 teams		OAK A (19G — .242)							LA N (104G — .304)														
"	total	123	.298	.395	309	92	9	6	3	0.9	60	27	40	50	15	31	8	223	2	0	1	2.3	1.000	OF-100, DH-2
6 yrs.		507	.251	.325	1288	323	45	13	8	0.6	187	107	138	219	58	54	10	988	23	10	13	2.0	.990	OF-449, 1B-11, DH-7, 2B-1
LEAGUE CHAMPIONSHIP SERIES																								
1988	OAK A	2	.500	.500	4	2	0	0	0	0.0	0	1	1	0	0	0	0	5	0	0	0	2.5	1.000	OF-2
1989		1	.000	.000	2	0	0	0	0	0.0	0	0	0	1	0	0	0	1	0	0	0	1.0	1.000	OF-1
2 yrs.		3	.333	.333	6	2	0	0	0	0.0	0	1	1	1	0	0	0	6	0	0	0	2.0	1.000	OF-3
WORLD SERIES																								
1988	OAK A	3	.500	.500	4	2	0	0	0	0.0	0	2	0	1	0	0	0	1	0	0	0	0.3	1.000	OF-2
1989		1	—	—	0	0	0	0	0	—	0	0	0	0	0	0	0	0	0	0	0	0.0	—	OF-1
2 yrs.		4	.500	.500	4	2	0	0	0	0.0	0	2	0	1	0	0	0	1	0	0	0	0.3	.000	OF-3

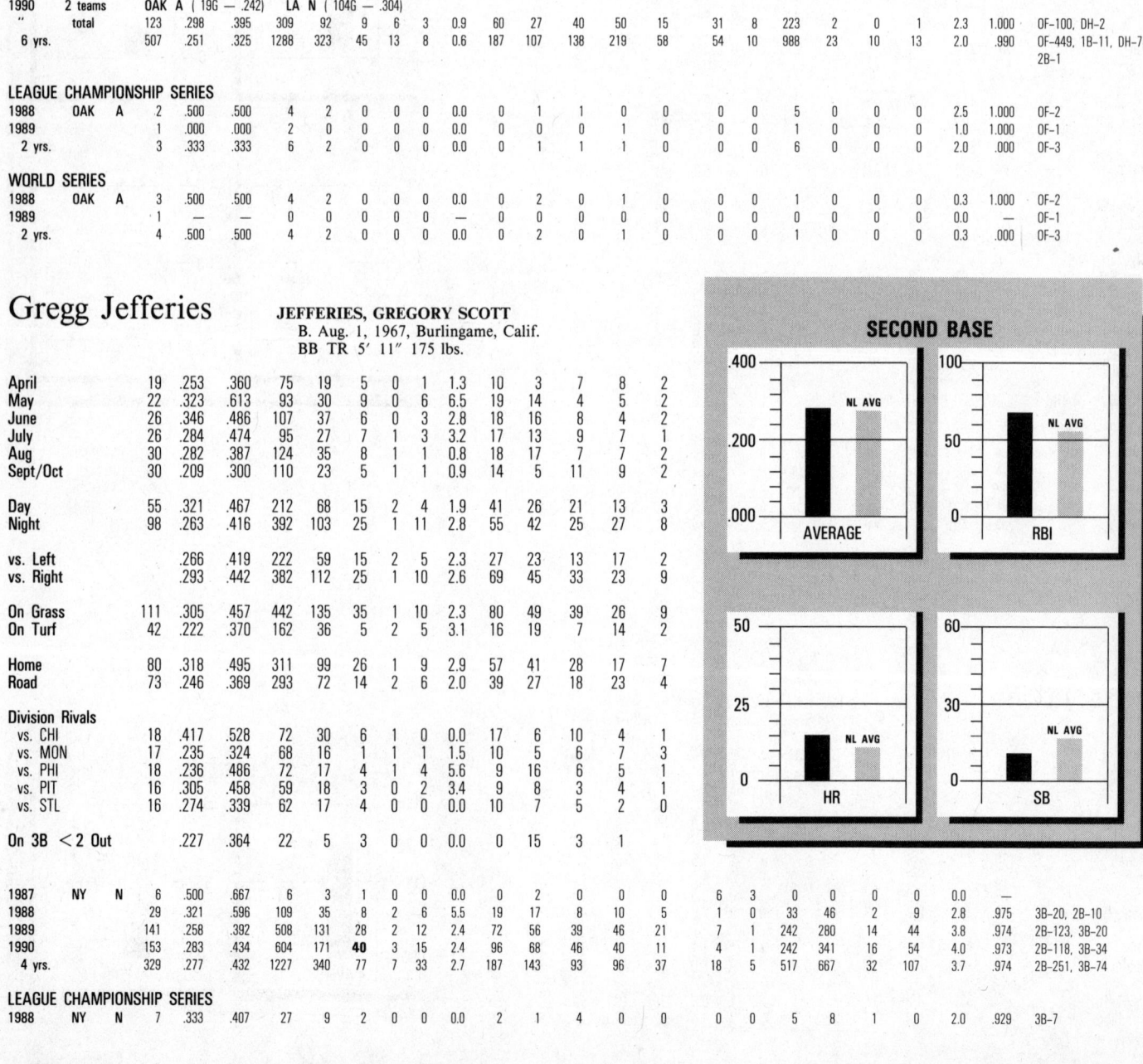

OUTFIELD / SECOND BASE

Gregg Jefferies

JEFFERIES, GREGORY SCOTT
B. Aug. 1, 1967, Burlingame, Calif.
BB TR 5′ 11″ 175 lbs.

Period		Games	BA	SA	AB	H	2B	3B	HR	HR%	R	RBI	BB	SO	SB	AB	H	PO	A	E	DP	TC/G	FA	G by Pos
April		19	.253	.360	75	19	5	0	1	1.3	10	3	7	8	2									
May		22	.323	.613	93	30	9	0	6	6.5	19	14	4	5	2									
June		26	.346	.486	107	37	6	0	3	2.8	18	16	8	4	2									
July		26	.284	.474	95	27	7	1	3	3.2	17	13	9	7	1									
Aug		30	.282	.387	124	35	8	1	1	0.8	18	17	7	7	2									
Sept/Oct		30	.209	.300	110	23	5	1	1	0.9	14	5	11	9	2									
Day		55	.321	.467	212	68	15	2	4	1.9	41	26	21	13	3									
Night		98	.263	.416	392	103	25	1	11	2.8	55	42	25	27	8									
vs. Left			.266	.419	222	59	15	2	5	2.3	27	23	13	17	2									
vs. Right			.293	.442	382	112	25	1	10	2.6	69	45	33	23	9									
On Grass		111	.305	.457	442	135	35	1	10	2.3	80	49	39	26	9									
On Turf		42	.222	.370	162	36	5	2	5	3.1	16	19	7	14	2									
Home		80	.318	.495	311	99	26	1	9	2.9	57	41	28	17	7									
Road		73	.246	.369	293	72	14	2	6	2.0	39	27	18	23	4									
Division Rivals																								
vs. CHI		18	.417	.528	72	30	6	1	0	0.0	17	6	10	4	1									
vs. MON		17	.235	.324	68	16	1	1	1	1.5	10	5	6	7	3									
vs. PHI		18	.236	.486	72	17	4	1	4	5.6	9	16	6	5	1									
vs. PIT		16	.305	.458	59	18	3	0	2	3.4	9	8	3	4	1									
vs. STL		16	.274	.339	62	17	4	0	0	0.0	10	7	5	2	0									
On 3B < 2 Out			.227	.364	22	5	3	0	0	0.0	0	15	3	1										
1987	NY N	6	.500	.667	6	3	1	0	0	0.0	0	2	0	0	0	6	3	0	0	0	0	0.0	—	
1988		29	.321	.596	109	35	8	2	6	5.5	19	17	8	10	5	1	0	33	46	2	9	2.8	.975	3B-20, 2B-10
1989		141	.258	.392	508	131	28	2	12	2.4	72	56	39	46	21	7	1	242	280	14	44	3.8	.974	2B-123, 3B-20
1990		153	.283	.434	604	171	**40**	3	15	2.4	96	68	46	40	11	4	1	242	341	16	54	4.0	.973	2B-118, 3B-34
4 yrs.		329	.277	.432	1227	340	77	7	33	2.7	187	143	93	96	37	18	5	517	667	32	107	3.7	.974	2B-251, 3B-74
LEAGUE CHAMPIONSHIP SERIES																								
1988	NY N	7	.333	.407	27	9	2	0	0	0.0	2	1	4	0	0	0	0	5	8	1	0	2.0	.929	3B-7

Year	Team		Games	BA	SA	AB	H	2B	3B	HR	HR%	R	RBI	BB	SO	SB	PINCH HIT AB	PINCH HIT H	PO	A	E	DP	TC/G	FA	G by Pos

Stan Jefferson

JEFFERSON, STANLEY
B. Dec. 4, 1962, New York, N. Y.
BB TR 5′ 11″ 175 lbs.

Year	Team		Games	BA	SA	AB	H	2B	3B	HR	HR%	R	RBI	BB	SO	SB	AB	H	PO	A	E	DP	TC/G	FA	G by Pos
1986	NY	N	14	.208	.375	24	5	1	0	1	4.2	6	3	2	8	0	5	0	13	0	0	0	0.9	1.000	OF-7
1987	SD	N	116	.230	.339	422	97	8	7	8	1.9	59	29	39	92	34	9	0	232	3	3	1	2.1	.987	OF-107
1988			49	.144	.216	111	16	1	2	1	0.9	16	4	9	22	5	3	0	62	0	0	0	1.3	1.000	OF-38
1989	2 teams		NY A (10G — .083)			BAL A (35G — .260)																			
"	total		45	.245	.381	139	34	7	0	4	2.9	20	21	4	26	10	6	1	82	3	1	1	1.9	.988	OF-39, DH-3
1990	2 teams		BAL A (10G — .000)			CLE A (49G — .276)																			
"			59	.231	.350	117	27	8	0	2	1.7	22	10	10	26	9	5	0	70	4	1	1	1.9	.987	OF-39, DH-6
5 yrs.			283	.220	.332	813	179	25	9	16	2.0	123	67	64	174	58	28	1	459	10	5	3	1.7	.989	OF-230, DH-9

Chris Jelic

JELIC, CHRISTOPHER JOHN, JR.
B. Dec. 16, 1963, Bethlehem, Pa.
BR TR 5′ 11″ 180 lbs.

Year	Team		Games	BA	SA	AB	H	2B	3B	HR	HR%	R	RBI	BB	SO	SB	AB	H	PO	A	E	DP	TC/G	FA	G by Pos
1990	NY	N	4	.091	.364	11	1	0	0	1	9.0	2	1	0	3	0	1	0	1	0	0	0	0.3	1.000	OF-4

Steve Jeltz

JELTZ, LARRY STEVEN
B. May 28, 1959, Paris, France
BB TR 5′ 11″ 180 lbs.

Year	Team		Games	BA	SA	AB	H	2B	3B	HR	HR%	R	RBI	BB	SO	SB	AB	H	PO	A	E	DP	TC/G	FA	G by Pos
1983	PHI	N	13	.125	.375	8	1	0	1	0	0.0	0	1	1	2	0	3	0	4	5	0	1	0.7	1.000	2B-4, 3B-2, SS-2
1984			28	.206	.279	68	14	0	1	1	1.5	7	7	7	11	2	0	0	37	93	1	8	4.7	.992	SS-27, 3B-1
1985			89	.189	.219	196	37	4	1	0	0.0	17	12	26	55	1	0	0	106	215	14	38	3.8	.958	SS-86
1986			145	.219	.262	439	96	11	4	0	0.0	44	36	65	97	6	5	2	229	406	22	81	4.5	.967	SS-141
1987			114	.232	.304	293	68	9	6	0	0.0	37	12	39	54	1	1	1	192	271	14	55	4.2	.971	SS-114, OF-1
1988			148	.187	.237	379	71	11	4	0	0.0	39	27	59	58	3	3	0	195	368	14	73	3.9	.976	SS-148
1989			116	.243	.338	263	64	7	3	4	1.5	28	25	45	44	4	13	2	111	205	6	33	2.8	.981	SS-63, 3B-30, 2B-23, OF-1
1990	KC	A	74	.155	.194	103	16	4	0	0	0.0	11	10	6	21	1	1	0	58	98	4	21	2.4	.975	2B-34, SS-23, OF-13, DH-3, 3B-3
8 yrs.			727	.210	.268	1749	367	46	20	5	0.3	183	130	248	342	18	26	5	932	1661	75	310	3.7	.972	SS-604, 2B-61, 3B-36, OF-15, DH-3

Doug Jennings

JENNINGS, JAMES DOUGLAS
B. Sept. 30, 1964, Atlanta, Ga.
BL TL 5′ 10″ 175 lbs.

Year	Team		Games	BA	SA	AB	H	2B	3B	HR	HR%	R	RBI	BB	SO	SB	AB	H	PO	A	E	DP	TC/G	FA	G by Pos
1988	OAK	A	71	.208	.297	101	21	6	0	1	1.0	9	15	21	28	0	27	5	85	5	1	8	1.3	.989	OF-23, 1B-14, DH-2
1989			4	.000	.000	4	0	0	0	0	0.0	0	0	0	2	0	1	0	2	0	0	0	0.5	1.000	OF-3
1990			64	.192	.301	156	30	7	2	2	1.2	19	14	17	48	0	14	2	90	1	1	5	1.9	.989	OF-45, DH-8, 1B-4
3 yrs.			139	.195	.295	261	51	13	2	3	1.1	28	29	38	78	0	42	7	177	6	2	13	1.3	.989	OF-71, 1B-18, DH-10

LEAGUE CHAMPIONSHIP SERIES

Year	Team		Games	BA	SA	AB	H	2B	3B	HR	HR%	R	RBI	BB	SO	SB	AB	H	PO	A	E	DP	TC/G	FA	G by Pos
1990	OAK	A	1	.000	.000	1	0	0	0	0	0.0	0	0	0	0	0	0	0	0	0	0	0	0.0	1.000	OF-1

WORLD SERIES

Year	Team		Games	BA	SA	AB	H	2B	3B	HR	HR%	R	RBI	BB	SO	SB	AB	H	PO	A	E	DP	TC/G	FA	G by Pos
1990	OAK	A	1	1.000	1.000	1	1	0	0	0	0.0	0	0	0	0	0	1	1	0	0	0	0	0.0	1.000	

Howard Johnson

JOHNSON, HOWARD MICHAEL (Hojo)
B. Nov. 29, 1960, Clearwater, Fla.
BB TR 5′ 11″ 175 lbs.

Split	Games	BA	SA	AB	H	2B	3B	HR	HR%	R	RBI	BB	SO	SB
April	18	.250	.472	72	18	4	0	4	5.6	10	12	6	11	3
May	23	.253	.407	91	23	2	0	4	4.4	12	11	11	19	6
June	26	.213	.463	108	23	11	2	4	3.7	19	18	7	15	5
July	27	.267	.436	101	27	6	1	3	3.0	14	16	15	21	10
Aug	30	.254	.456	114	29	8	0	5	4.4	15	19	15	16	4
Sept/Oct	30	.231	.375	104	24	6	0	3	2.9	19	14	15	18	6
Day	55	.264	.464	220	58	17	0	9	4.1	35	39	17	34	11
Night	99	.232	.416	370	86	20	3	14	3.8	54	51	52	66	23
vs. Left		.208	.344	221	46	12	0	6	2.7	26	23	29	50	9
vs. Right		.266	.488	369	98	25	3	17	4.6	63	67	40	50	25

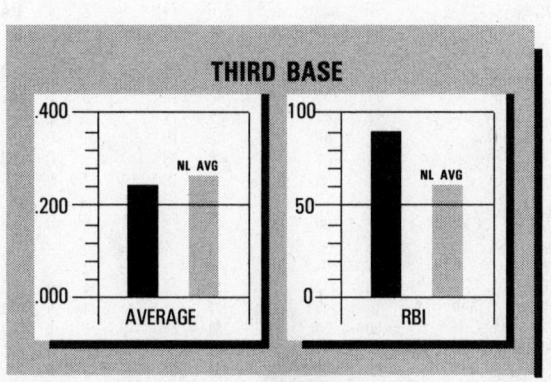

THIRD BASE — AVERAGE / RBI (NL AVG)

Year	Team		Games	BA	SA	AB	H	2B	3B	HR	HR%	R	RBI	BB	SO	SB	PINCH HIT AB	PINCH HIT H	PO	A	E	DP	TC/G	FA	G by Pos

Howard Johnson *Continued*

Year	Team		Games	BA	SA	AB	H	2B	3B	HR	HR%	R	RBI	BB	SO	SB	AB	H	PO	A	E	DP	TC/G	FA	G by Pos
On Grass			110	.249	.442	425	106	23	1	19	4.5	65	69	44	71	20									
On Turf			44	.230	.412	165	38	14	2	4	2.4	24	21	25	29	14									
Home			77	.234	.416	291	68	12	1	13	4.5	43	45	27	49	17									
Road			77	.254	.452	299	76	25	2	10	3.3	46	45	42	51	17									
Division Rivals																									
vs. CHI			18	.205	.466	73	15	7	0	4	5.5	15	18	11	16	3									
vs. MON			17	.271	.443	70	19	4	1	2	2.9	9	4	6	12	8									
vs. PHI			18	.222	.460	63	14	5	2	2	3.2	15	7	13	8	2									
vs. PIT			13	.120	.220	50	6	2	0	1	2.0	4	4	0	6	0									
vs. STL			17	.258	.409	66	17	4	0	2	3.0	10	9	6	18	5									
On 3B < 2 Out				.391	.783	23	9	3	0	2	8.7	2	28	6	5										
1982	DET	A	54	.316	.426	155	49	5	0	4	2.6	23	14	16	30	7	7	1	36	40	7	6	1.5	.916	3B-33, DH-10, OF-9
1983			27	.212	.348	66	14	0	0	3	4.5	11	5	7	10	0	6	2	10	30	7	2	1.7	.851	3B-21, DH-2
1984			116	.248	.394	355	88	14	1	12	3.4	43	50	40	67	10	7	2	63	150	14	21	2.0	.938	3B-108, SS-9, DH-4, 1B-1, OF-1
1985	NY	N	126	.242	.393	389	94	18	4	11	2.8	38	46	34	78	6	12	4	78	190	18	27	2.3	.937	3B-113, SS-7, OF-1
1986			88	.245	.445	220	54	14	0	10	4.5	30	39	31	64	8	17	2	52	136	20	24	2.4	.904	3B-45, SS-34, OF-1
1987			157	.265	.504	554	147	22	1	36	6.5	93	99	83	113	32	2	1	118	305	26	27	2.9	.942	3B-140, SS-38, OF-2
1988			148	.230	.422	495	114	21	1	24	4.8	85	68	86	104	23	3	1	110	274	18	37	2.7	.955	3B-131, SS-52
1989			153	.287	.559	571	164	41	3	36	6.3	**104**	101	77	126	41	0	0	97	217	24	22	2.2	.929	3B-143, SS-31
1990			154	.244	.434	590	144	37	3	23	3.8	89	90	69	100	34	1	0	150	335	28	39	3.4	.945	3B-92, SS-73
9 yrs.			1023	.256	.454	3395	868	172	13	159	4.7	516	512	443	692	161	55	13	714	1677	162	205	2.5	.937	3B-826, SS-244, DH-16, OF-14, 1B-1
LEAGUE CHAMPIONSHIP SERIES																									
1986	NY	N	2	.000	.000	2	0	0	0	0	0.0	0	0	0	0	0	2	0	0	0	0	0	0.0	—	
1988			6	.056	.056	18	1	0	0	0	0.0	3	0	1	6	1	2	0	6	9	1	0	2.7	.938	SS-5, 3B-1
2 yrs.			8	.050	.050	20	1	0	0	0	0.0	3	0	1	6	1	4	0	6	9	1	0	2.0	.938	SS-5, 3B-1
WORLD SERIES																									
1984	DET	A	1	.000	.000	1	0	0	0	0	0.0	0	0	0	0	0	1	0	0	0	0	0	0.0	—	
1986	NY	N	2	.000	.000	5	0	0	0	0	0.0	0	0	0	2	0	1	0	1	0	0	0	0.5	1.000	3B-1, SS-1
2 yrs.			3	.000	.000	6	0	0	0	0	0.0	0	0	0	2	0	2	0	1	0	0	0	0.3	.000	3B-1, SS-1

THIRD BASE

Lance Johnson

JOHNSON, KENNETH LANCE
B. July 6, 1963, Cincinnati, Ohio
BL TL 5' 10" 160 lbs.

Year	Team		Games	BA	SA	AB	H	2B	3B	HR	HR%	R	RBI	BB	SO	SB	AB	H	PO	A	E	DP	TC/G	FA	G by Pos
April			16	.276	.310	58	16	2	0	0	0.0	5	8	3	7	3									
May			25	.287	.327	101	29	4	0	0	0.0	15	8	10	6	6									
June			25	.277	.373	83	23	4	2	0	0.0	13	10	4	9	4									
July			26	.247	.320	97	24	2	1	1	1.0	17	10	6	7	5									
Aug			27	.235	.353	85	20	2	4	0	0.0	10	8	4	7	8									
Sept/Oct			32	.359	.427	117	42	4	2	0	0.0	16	7	6	9	10									
Day			39	.299	.372	137	41	6	2	0	0.0	23	17	12	11	11									
Night			112	.280	.351	404	113	12	7	1	0.2	53	34	21	34	25									
vs. Left				.321	.378	156	50	3	3	0	0.0	15	19	9	18	12									
vs. Right				.270	.348	385	104	15	6	1	0.3	61	32	24	27	24									
On Grass			126	.284	.365	458	130	16	9	1	0.2	69	43	26	42	32									
On Turf			25	.289	.313	83	24	2	0	0	0.0	7	8	7	3	4									
Home			75	.302	.381	265	80	9	6	0	0.0	42	25	15	20	24									
Road			76	.268	.333	276	74	9	3	1	0.4	34	26	18	25	12									
Division Rivals																									
vs. CAL			10	.435	.565	23	10	1	1	0	0.0	4	2	1	0	5									
vs. KC			12	.255	.298	47	12	2	0	0	0.0	8	5	5	3	6									
vs. MIN			12	.282	.359	39	11	1	1	0	0.0	4	5	0	2	3									
vs. OAK			13	.189	.245	53	10	1	1	0	0.0	9	3	3	5	3									
vs. SEA			13	.400	.475	40	16	1	1	0	0.0	5	5	4	6	1									
vs. TEX			10	.205	.333	39	8	1	2	0	0.0	4	3	1	8	1									
On 3B < 2 Out				.296	.333	27	8	1	0	0	0.0	0	17	1	2										
1987	STL	N	33	.220	.288	59	13	2	1	0	0.0	4	7	4	6	6	8	2	27	0	2	0	0.9	.931	OF-25
1988	CHI	A	33	.185	.234	124	23	4	1	0	0.0	11	6	6	11	6	3	0	63	1	2	0	2.0	.970	OF-31, DH-1
1989			50	.300	.367	180	54	8	2	0	0.0	28	16	17	24	16	3	1	113	0	2	0	2.3	.983	OF-45, DH-1
1990			151	.285	.357	541	154	18	9	1	0.1	76	51	33	45	36	17	4	353	5	10	3	2.5	.973	OF-148, DH-1
4 yrs.			267	.270	.337	904	244	32	13	1	0.1	119	80	60	86	64	31	7	556	6	16	3	2.2	.972	OF-249, DH-3

OUTFIELD

Year	Team		Games	BA	SA	AB	H	2B	3B	HR	HR%	R	RBI	BB	SO	SB	PINCH HIT AB	H	PO	A	E	DP	TC/G	FA	G by Pos

Lance Johnson *Continued*

LEAGUE CHAMPIONSHIP SERIES

Year	Team		Games	BA	SA	AB	H	2B	3B	HR	HR%	R	RBI	BB	SO	SB	PH AB	PH H	PO	A	E	DP	TC/G	FA	G by Pos
1987	STL	N	1	—	—	0	0	0	0	0	—	1	0	0	0	1	0	0	0	0	0	0	0	0.0	—	

WORLD SERIES

Year	Team		Games	BA	SA	AB	H	2B	3B	HR	HR%	R	RBI	BB	SO	SB	PH AB	PH H	PO	A	E	DP	TC/G	FA	G by Pos
1987	STL	N	1	—	—	0	0	0	0	0	—	0	0	0	0	1	0	0	0	0	0	0	0	0.0	—	

Wallace Johnson

JOHNSON, WALLACE DARNELL
B. Dec. 25, 1956, Gary, Ind.
BB TR 6′ 173 lbs.

Year	Team		Games	BA	SA	AB	H	2B	3B	HR	HR%	R	RBI	BB	SO	SB	PH AB	PH H	PO	A	E	DP	TC/G	FA	G by Pos
1981	MON	N	11	.222	.444	9	2	0	1	0	0.0	1	3	1	1	1	7	2	1	2	0	1	0.3	1.000	2B-1
1982			36	.193	.263	57	11	0	2	0	0.0	5	2	5	5	4	21	4	22	18	2	4	1.2	.952	2B-13
1983	2 teams		MON N (3G — .500)			SF N (7G — .125)																				
''	total		10	.200	.200	10	2	0	0	0	0.0	1	1	1	0	0	7	1	3	2	0	1	0.5	1.000	2B-1
1984	MON	N	17	.208	.208	24	5	0	0	0	0.0	3	4	5	4	0	10	3	27	3	1	3	1.8	.968	1B-4
1986			61	.283	.346	127	36	3	1	1	0.8	13	10	7	9	6	37	11	204	17	2	15	3.7	.991	1B-27
1987			75	.247	.341	85	21	5	0	1	1.2	7	14	7	6	5	61	**17**	68	2	2	4	1.0	.972	1B-9
1988			86	.309	.383	94	29	5	1	0	0.0	7	3	12	15	0	**64**	**22**	80	9	1	3	1.0	.989	1B-13, 2B-1
1989			85	.272	.368	114	31	3	1	2	1.8	9	17	7	12	1	59	14	130	7	4	8	1.7	.972	1B-18
1990			47	.163	.245	49	8	1	0	1	2.0	6	5	7	6	1	34	4	39	0	0	7	5.6	1.000	1B-7
9 yrs.			428	.255	.332	569	145	17	6	5	0.9	52	59	52	58	19	300	78	574	60	12	46	1.5	.981	1B-78, 2B-16

DIVISIONAL PLAYOFF SERIES

Year	Team		Games	BA	SA	AB	H	2B	3B	HR	HR%	R	RBI	BB	SO	SB	PH AB	PH H	PO	A	E	DP	TC/G	FA	G by Pos
1981	MON	N	2	.500	.500	2	1	0	0	0	0.0	0	1	0	0	0	2	1	0	0	0	0	0.0	—	

Ron Jones

JONES, RONALD GLEN
B. June 11, 1964, Sequin, Tex.
BL TR 5′ 10″ 195 lbs.

Year	Team		Games	BA	SA	AB	H	2B	3B	HR	HR%	R	RBI	BB	SO	SB	PH AB	PH H	PO	A	E	DP	TC/G	FA	G by Pos
1988	PHI	N	33	.290	.548	124	36	6	1	8	6.5	15	26	2	14	0	1	0	70	1	0	0	2.2	1.000	OF-32
1989			12	.290	.484	31	9	0	0	2	6.5	7	4	9	1	1	0	0	27	1	0	1	2.3	1.000	OF-12
1990			24	.276	.466	58	16	2	0	3	5.1	5	7	9	9	0	8	2	25	1	0	0	1.6	1.000	OF-16
3 yrs.			69	.286	.516	213	61	8	1	13	6.1	27	37	20	24	1	9	2	122	3	0	1	1.8	.000	OF-60

Tim Jones

JONES, WILLIAM TIMOTHY
B. Dec. 1, 1962, Sumter, S. C.
BL TR 5′ 10″ 172 lbs.

Year	Team		Games	BA	SA	AB	H	2B	3B	HR	HR%	R	RBI	BB	SO	SB	PH AB	PH H	PO	A	E	DP	TC/G	FA	G by Pos
1988	STL	N	31	.269	.269	52	14	0	0	0	0.0	2	3	4	10	4	9	1	26	40	1	7	2.2	.985	SS-9, 2B-8, 3B-1
1989			42	.293	.373	75	22	6	0	0	0.0	11	7	7	8	1	10	2	33	48	2	4	2.0	.976	2B-12, SS-12, 3B-5, C-1, OF-1
1990			67	.219	.313	128	28	7	1	1	0.7	9	12	12	20	3	14	4	43	105	7	15	3.0	.955	SS-29, 2B-19, 3B-6, P-1
3 yrs.			140	.251	.322	255	64	13	1	1	0.4	22	22	23	38	8	33	7	102	193	10	26	2.2	.967	SS-50, 2B-39, 3B-12, P-1, C-1, OF-1

Tracy Jones

JONES, TRACY DONALD
B. Mar. 31, 1961, Hawthorne, Calif.
BR TR 6′ 3″ 180 lbs.

Year	Team		Games	BA	SA	AB	H	2B	3B	HR	HR%	R	RBI	BB	SO	SB	PH AB	PH H	PO	A	E	DP	TC/G	FA	G by Pos
1986	CIN	N	46	.349	.453	86	30	3	0	2	2.3	16	10	9	5	7	12	2	46	1	0	0	1.0	1.000	OF-24, 1B-2
1987			117	.290	.437	359	104	17	3	10	2.8	53	44	23	40	31	25	6	189	2	2	0	1.6	.990	OF-95
1988	2 teams		CIN N (37G — .229)			MON N (53G — .333)																				
''	total		90	.295	.371	224	66	6	1	3	1.3	29	24	20	18	18	23	6	96	2	2	0	1.1	.980	OF-68
1989	2 teams		SF N (40G — .186)			DET A (46G — .259)																				
''			86	.231	.322	255	59	14	0	3	1.2	22	38	21	30	3	16	3	107	0	1	0	1.3	.991	OF-66, DH-8
1990	2 teams		DET A (50G — .229)			SEA A (25G — .302)																				
''			75	.260	.397	204	53	8	1	6	2.9	23	24	9	25	1	16	3	68	3	2	0	1.6	.973	OF-45, DH-25
5 yrs.			414	.277	.392	1128	312	48	5	24	2.1	143	140	82	118	60	92	20	506	8	7	0	1.3	.987	OF-298, DH-33, 1B-2

Year	Team	Games	BA	SA	AB	H	2B	3B	HR	HR%	R	RBI	BB	SO	SB	PINCH HIT AB	PINCH HIT H	PO	A	E	DP	TC/G	FA	G by Pos

Ricky Jordan

JORDAN, PAUL SCOTT
B. May 26, 1965, Richmond, Calif.
BR TR 6′ 5″ 210 lbs.

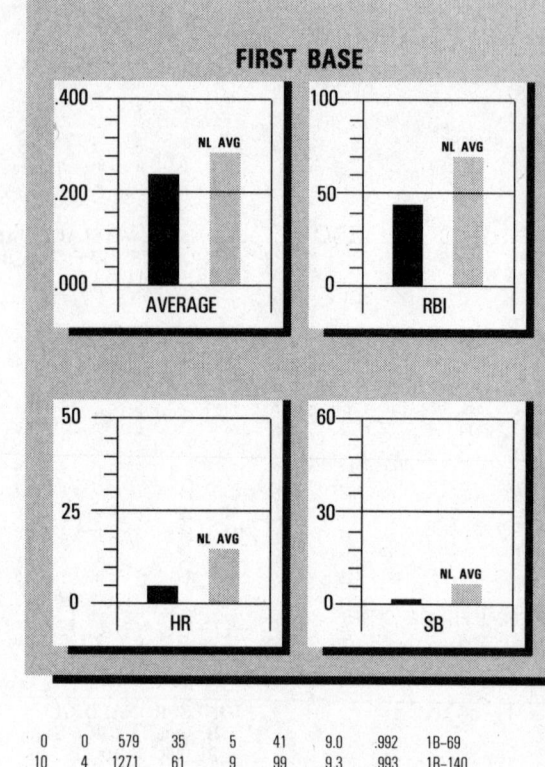

FIRST BASE

Split	Games	BA	SA	AB	H	2B	3B	HR	HR%	R	RBI	BB	SO	SB	PH AB	PH H	PO	A	E	DP	TC/G	FA	G by Pos
April	16	.267	.333	60	16	4	0	0	0.0	3	9	5	6	0									
May	21	.264	.414	87	23	4	0	3	3.4	11	13	0	11	0									
June	12	.205	.385	39	8	4	0	1	2.6	6	5	5	6	2									
July	17	.186	.254	59	11	4	0	0	0.0	5	8	2	10	0									
Aug	7	.176	.294	17	3	2	0	0	0.0	2	2	0	1	0									
Sept/Oct	19	.274	.371	62	17	3	0	1	1.6	5	7	1	5	0									
Day	25	.258	.438	89	23	7	0	3	3.4	8	18	2	7	0									
Night	67	.234	.319	235	55	14	0	2	0.9	24	26	11	32	2									
vs. Left		.246	.373	118	29	9	0	2	1.7	14	12	10	9	1									
vs. Right		.238	.340	206	49	12	0	3	1.5	18	32	3	30	1									
On Grass	23	.267	.456	90	24	8	0	3	3.3	11	17	1	6	0									
On Turf	69	.231	.312	234	54	13	0	2	0.9	21	27	12	33	2									
Home	44	.234	.317	145	34	6	0	2	1.4	14	18	2	26	1									
Road	48	.246	.380	179	44	15	0	3	1.7	18	26	11	13	1									
Division Rivals																							
vs. CHI	14	.327	.510	49	16	3	0	2	4.1	5	10	0	3	0									
vs. MON	10	.212	.303	33	7	3	0	0	0.0	2	2	2	7	0									
vs. NY	9	.242	.364	33	8	4	0	0	0.0	5	5	1	6	1									
vs. PIT	7	.063	.063	16	1	0	0	0	0.0	0	0	0	2	0									
vs. STL	14	.244	.311	45	11	3	0	0	0.0	3	5	6	2	1									
On 3B < 2 Out		.238	.476	21	5	2	0	1	4.8	1	17	2	6										
1988 PHI N	69	.308	.491	273	84	15	1	11	4.0	41	43	7	39	1	0	0	579	35	5	41	9.0	.992	1B-69
1989	144	.285	.407	523	149	22	3	12	2.3	63	75	23	62	4	10	4	1271	61	9	99	9.3	.993	1B-140
1990	92	.241	.352	324	78	21	0	5	1.5	32	44	13	39	2	8	2	743	37	4	65	9.3	.995	1B-84
3 yrs.	305	.278	.412	1120	311	58	4	28	2.5	136	162	43	140	7	18	6	2593	133	18	205	9.0	.993	1B-293

Felix Jose

JOSE, DOMINGO FELIX ANDUJAR
Born Domingo Felix Andujar y Jose.
B. May 2, 1965, Santo Domingo, Dominican Republic
BB TR 6′ 1″ 190 lbs.

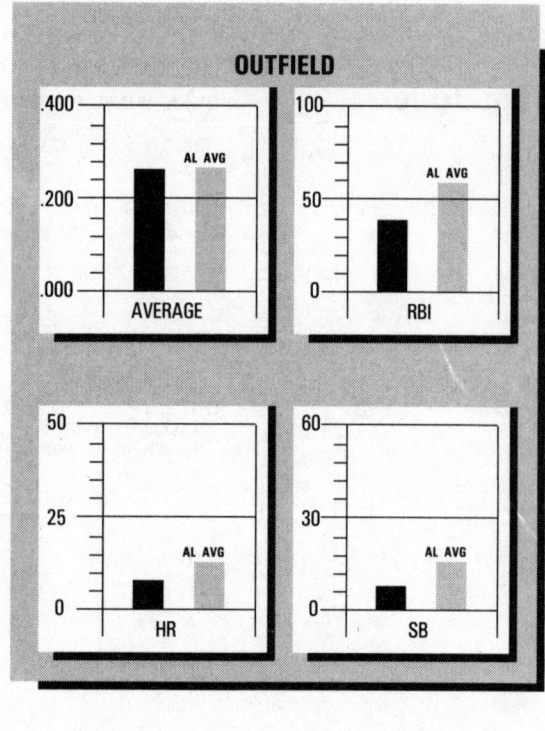

OUTFIELD

Split	Games	BA	SA	AB	H	2B	3B	HR	HR%	R	RBI	BB	SO	SB	PH AB	PH H	PO	A	E	DP	TC/G	FA	G by Pos
April	12	.375	.625	32	12	2	0	2	6.3	6	6	2	5	1									
May	19	.206	.294	68	14	0	0	2	2.9	6	9	3	12	1									
June	21	.214	.286	70	15	5	0	0	0.0	9	4	2	13	1									
July	26	.302	.477	86	26	3	0	4	4.7	14	14	6	20	4									
Aug	24	.281	.303	89	25	2	0	0	0.0	7	6	3	16	2									
Sept/Oct	24	.259	.444	81	21	4	1	3	3.7	12	13	8	15	3									
Day	51	.237	.349	169	40	7	0	4	2.4	22	18	10	31	4									
Night	75	.284	.409	257	73	9	1	7	2.7	32	34	14	50	8									
vs. Left		.301	.427	103	31	5	1	2	1.9	11	16	7	21	3									
vs. Right		.254	.372	323	82	11	0	9	2.8	43	36	17	60	9									
On Grass	94	.270	.361	319	86	11	0	6	1.9	38	33	17	59	8									
On Turf	32	.252	.458	107	27	5	1	5	4.7	16	19	7	22	4									
Home	65	.233	.348	210	49	7	1	5	2.4	26	27	16	44	5									
Road	61	.296	.421	216	64	9	0	6	2.8	28	25	8	37	7									
Division Rivals																							
vs. CHI	3	.222	.556	9	2	0	0	1	11.1	2	2	1	3	1									
vs. MON	5	.214	.429	14	3	0	0	1	7.1	2	2	2	2	1									
vs. NY	4	.214	.286	14	3	1	0	0	0.0	2	0	2	5	0									
vs. PHI	6	.333	.625	24	8	2	1	1	4.2	4	7	2	3	1									
vs. PIT	4	.417	.500	12	5	1	0	0	0.0	2	2	1	1	0									
On 3B < 2 Out		.533	.533	15	8	0	0	0	0.0	0	11	0	0										
1988 OAK A	8	.333	.500	6	2	1	0	0	0.0	2	1	0	1	1	2	0	8	0	0	0	1.0	1.000	OF-6
1989	20	.193	.228	57	11	2	0	0	0.0	3	5	4	13	0	3	1	35	2	1	0	1.9	.974	OF-19
1990 2 teams		OAK A (101G — .264)		STL N (25G — .271)																			
" total	126	.265	.385	426	113	16	1	11	2.5	54	52	24	81	12	13	2	254	5	5	1	2.3	.981	OF-115, DH-7
3 yrs.	154	.258	.368	489	126	19	1	11	2.2	59	58	28	95	13	18	3	297	7	6	1	2.0	.981	OF-140, DH-7

Year	Team	Games	BA	SA	AB	H	2B	3B	HR	HR%	R	RBI	BB	SO	SB	PINCH HIT AB	PINCH HIT H	PO	A	E	DP	TC/G	FA	G by Pos

Wally Joyner

JOYNER, WALLACE KEITH (Wally World)
B. June 16, 1962, Atlanta, Ga.
BL TL 6′ 2″ 185 lbs.

Year	Team	Games	BA	SA	AB	H	2B	3B	HR	HR%	R	RBI	BB	SO	SB	PINCH HIT AB	PINCH HIT H	PO	A	E	DP	TC/G	FA	G by Pos
April		19	.243	.392	74	18	5	0	2	2.7	6	7	9	8	0									
May		29	.337	.515	101	34	3	0	5	5.0	16	22	18	9	1									
June		26	.234	.298	94	22	3	0	1	1.1	11	9	12	13	1									
July		9	.220	.317	41	9	4	0	0	0.0	2	3	2	4	0									
Aug					0	0	0	0	0		0	0	0	0	0									
Sept/Oct					0	0	0	0	0		0	0	0	0	0									
Day		19	.265	.412	68	18	4	0	2	2.9	10	13	8	13	0									
Night		64	.269	.388	242	65	11	0	6	2.5	25	28	33	21	2									
vs. Left			.226	.302	106	24	2	0	2	1.9	6	17	10	15	0									
vs. Right			.289	.441	204	59	13	0	6	2.9	29	24	31	19	2									
On Grass		68	.251	.380	255	64	12	0	7	2.7	30	36	36	26	2									
On Turf		15	.345	.455	55	19	3	0	1	1.8	5	5	5	8	0									
Home		37	.274	.422	135	37	5	0	5	3.7	19	21	21	13	0									
Road		46	.263	.371	175	46	10	0	3	1.7	16	20	20	21	2									
Division Rivals																								
vs. CHI		6	.083	.208	24	2	0	0	1	4.2	3	1	3	3	0									
vs. KC		5	.308	.385	13	4	1	0	0	0.0	2	1	2	3	0									
vs. MIN		7	.107	.214	28	3	0	0	1	3.6	1	1	2	5	0									
vs. OAK		2	.250	.250	8	2	0	0	0	0.0	1	1	1	0	0									
vs. SEA		6	.381	.429	21	8	1	0	0	0.0	1	3	4	5	0									
vs. TEX		6	.320	.320	25	8	0	0	0	0.0	2	3	2	3	1									
On 3B < 2 Out			.333	.333	15	5	0	0	0	0.0	0	12	2	4										
1986	CAL A	154	.290	.457	593	172	27	3	22	3.7	82	100	57	58	5	4	1	1222	139	15	128	8.9	.989	1B-152
1987		149	.285	.528	564	161	33	1	34	6.0	100	117	72	64	8	2	0	1276	92	10	133	9.2	.993	1B-149
1988		158	.295	.419	597	176	31	2	13	2.2	81	85	55	51	8	4	2	1369	143	8	148	9.6	.995	1B-156
1989		159	.282	.420	593	167	30	2	16	2.7	78	79	46	58	3	2	1	1487	99	4	146	10.0	.997	1B-159
1990		83	.268	.394	310	83	15	0	8	2.5	35	41	41	34	2	1	0	727	62	4	78	9.6	.995	1B-83
5 yrs.		703	.286	.448	2657	759	136	8	93	3.5	376	422	271	265	26	13	4	6081	535	41	633	9.5	.994	1B-699

LEAGUE CHAMPIONSHIP SERIES

Year	Team	Games	BA	SA	AB	H	2B	3B	HR	HR%	R	RBI	BB	SO	SB	PINCH HIT AB	PINCH HIT H	PO	A	E	DP	TC/G	FA	G by Pos
1986	CAL A	3	.455	.909	11	5	2	0	1	9.1	3	2	2	0	0	0	0	26	1	0	2	9.0	1.000	1B-3

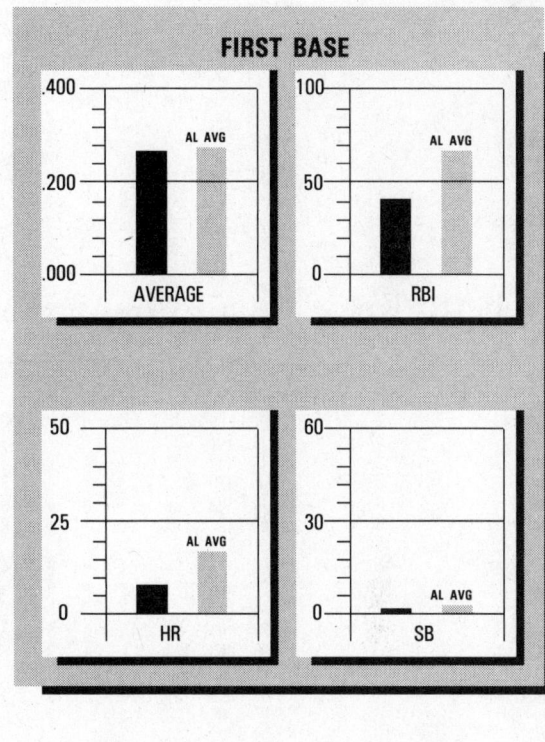

FIRST BASE

Dave Justice

JUSTICE, DAVID CHRISTOPHER
B. Apr. 14, 1966, Cincinnati, Ohio
BL TL 6′ 3″ 195 lbs.

Year	Team	Games	BA	SA	AB	H	2B	3B	HR	HR%	R	RBI	BB	SO	SB	PINCH HIT AB	PINCH HIT H	PO	A	E	DP	TC/G	FA	G by Pos
April					0	0	0	0	0		0	0	0	0	0									
May		14	.352	.574	54	19	6	0	2	3.7	3	10	5	10	1									
June		26	.220	.341	91	20	3	1	2	2.2	18	9	14	19	2									
July		26	.213	.400	75	16	2	0	4	5.3	11	9	10	21	2									
Aug		30	.301	.655	113	34	7	0	11	9.7	20	29	9	24	2									
Sept/Oct		31	.330	.651	106	35	5	1	9	8.5	24	21	26	18	4									
Day		26	.237	.454	97	23	3	0	6	6.2	12	16	13	14	2									
Night		101	.295	.558	342	101	20	2	22	6.4	64	62	51	78	9									
vs. Left			.366	.656	131	48	8	0	10	7.6	29	32	18	22	4									
vs. Right			.247	.484	308	76	15	2	18	5.8	47	46	46	70	7									
On Grass		96	.292	.563	336	98	21	2	22	6.5	60	60	46	74	8									
On Turf		31	.252	.447	103	26	2	0	6	5.8	16	18	18	18	3									
Home		64	.320	.662	225	72	18	1	19	8.4	42	48	32	49	5									
Road		63	.243	.402	214	52	5	1	9	4.2	34	30	32	43	6									
Division Rivals																								
vs. CIN		12	.349	.698	43	15	3	0	4	9.3	14	9	10	9	3									
vs. HOU		15	.170	.319	47	8	1	0	2	4.3	4	7	11	13	0									
vs. LA		18	.291	.600	55	16	3	1	4	7.3	8	13	9	16	1									
vs. SD		17	.299	.582	67	20	1	0	6	9.0	14	12	5	14	1									
vs. SF		15	.231	.423	52	12	2	1	2	3.8	9	5	11	6	2									
On 3B < 2 Out			.500	1.063	16	8	3	0	2	12.5	2	20	5	2										
1989	ATL N	16	.235	.353	51	12	3	0	1	2.0	7	3	3	9	2	0	0	24	0	0	0	1.5	1.000	OF-16
1990		127	.282	.535	439	124	23	2	28	6.3	76	78	64	92	11	5	2	604	42	14	44	5.2	.979	1B-69, OF-61
2 yrs.		143	.278	.516	490	136	26	2	29	5.9	83	81	67	101	13	5	2	628	42	14	44	4.8	.980	OF-77, 1B-69

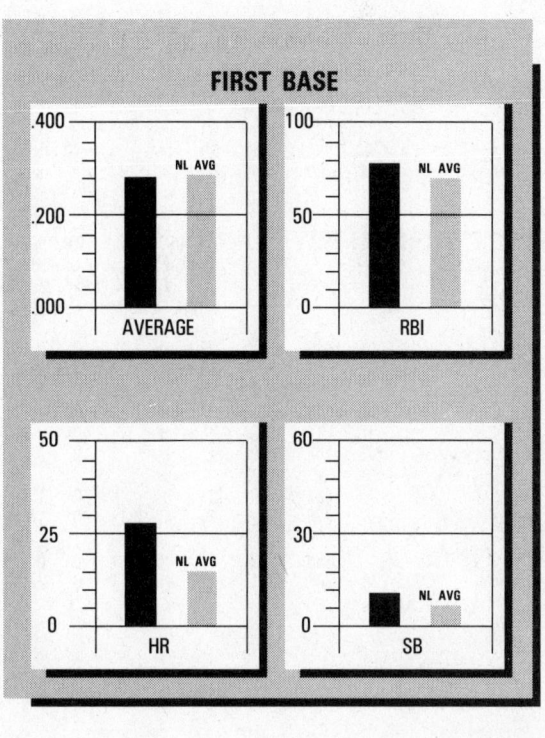

FIRST BASE

Year	Team	Games	BA	SA	AB	H	2B	3B	HR	HR%	R	RBI	BB	SO	SB	PINCH HIT AB	H	PO	A	E	DP	TC/G	FA	G by Pos

Ron Karkovice

KARKOVICE, RONALD JOSEPH
B. Aug. 8, 1963, Union, N. J.
BR TR 6' 1" 210 lbs.

Year	Team	Games	BA	SA	AB	H	2B	3B	HR	HR%	R	RBI	BB	SO	SB	AB	H	PO	A	E	DP	TC/G	FA	G by Pos
1986	CHI A	37	.247	.443	97	24	7	0	4	4.1	13	13	9	37	1	0	0	227	19	1	4	6.7	.996	C–37
1987		39	.071	.141	85	6	0	0	2	2.4	7	7	7	40	3	0	0	147	20	3	3	4.4	.982	C–37
1988		46	.174	.287	115	20	4	0	3	2.6	10	9	7	30	4	0	0	190	24	1	4	4.7	.995	C–46
1989		71	.264	.385	182	48	9	2	3	1.6	21	24	10	56	0	0	0	299	47	5	6	4.9	.986	C–68, DH–2
1990		68	.246	.399	183	45	10	0	6	3.2	30	20	16	52	2	4	2	296	31	2	4	5.1	.994	C–64, DH–1
5 yrs.		261	.216	.349	662	143	30	2	18	2.7	81	73	49	215	10	4	2	1159	141	12	21	5.0	.991	C–252, DH–3

Roberto Kelly

KELLY, ROBERTO CONRADO
Born Roberto Conrado Kelly y Gray.
B. Oct. 1, 1964, Panama City, Panama
BR TR 6' 2" 180 lbs.

	Games	BA	SA	AB	H	2B	3B	HR	HR%	R	RBI	BB	SO	SB
April	17	.317	.350	60	19	2	0	0	0.0	7	4	1	10	4
May	27	.280	.411	107	30	6	1	2	1.9	14	15	8	32	4
June	28	.282	.391	110	31	4	1	2	1.8	17	3	7	33	8
July	29	.275	.450	120	33	7	1	4	3.3	18	18	3	24	7
Aug	30	.320	.541	122	39	9	0	6	4.9	17	11	7	27	10
Sept/Oct	31	.254	.328	122	31	4	1	1	0.8	12	10	7	22	9
Day	45	.309	.469	175	54	10	0	6	3.4	27	22	8	36	10
Night	117	.277	.399	466	129	22	4	9	1.9	58	39	25	112	32
vs. Left		.304	.442	181	55	10	0	5	2.8	29	17	12	46	16
vs. Right		.278	.409	460	128	22	4	10	2.2	56	44	21	102	26
On Grass	137	.284	.419	542	154	28	3	13	2.4	70	48	26	120	40
On Turf	25	.293	.414	99	29	4	1	2	2.0	15	13	7	28	2
Home	81	.305	.435	315	96	22	2	5	1.6	44	25	14	57	24
Road	81	.267	.402	326	87	10	2	10	3.1	41	36	19	91	18
Division Rivals														
vs. BAL	13	.163	.286	49	8	0	0	2	4.1	5	2	2	19	4
vs. BOS	13	.327	.449	49	16	1	1	1	2.0	6	2	0	9	5
vs. CLE	13	.288	.596	52	15	1	0	5	9.6	10	12	1	8	1
vs. DET	13	.339	.446	56	19	2	2	0	0.0	8	6	3	13	6
vs. MIL	13	.263	.404	57	15	2	0	2	3.5	10	5	1	14	6
vs. TOR	13	.400	.564	55	22	6	0	1	1.8	9	6	4	9	3
On 3B < 2 Out		.217	.304	23	5	0	1	0	0.0	0	15	1	9	

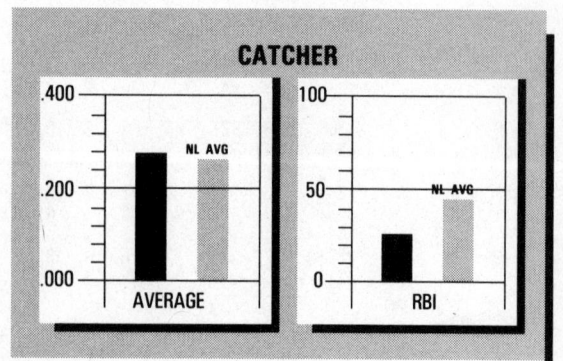

OUTFIELD

Year	Team	Games	BA	SA	AB	H	2B	3B	HR	HR%	R	RBI	BB	SO	SB	AB	H	PO	A	E	DP	TC/G	FA	G by Pos
1987	NY A	23	.269	.385	52	14	3	0	1	1.9	12	7	5	15	9	0	0	42	0	2	0	1.9	.955	OF–17
1988		38	.247	.364	77	19	4	1	1	1.3	9	7	3	15	5	1	1	70	1	1	0	1.9	.986	OF–30
1989		137	.302	.417	441	133	18	3	9	2.0	65	48	41	89	35	2	2	353	9	6	2	2.7	.984	OF–137
1990		162	.285	.418	641	183	32	4	15	2.3	85	61	33	148	42	4	1	420	5	5	0	2.7	.988	OF–160, DH–1
4 yrs.		360	.288	.413	1211	349	57	8	26	2.1	171	123	82	267	91	7	4	885	15	14	2	2.5	.985	OF–344, DH–1

Terry Kennedy

KENNEDY, TERRENCE EDWARD
Son of Bob Kennedy.
B. June 4, 1956, Euclid, Ohio
BL TR 6' 3" 220 lbs.

	Games	BA	SA	AB	H	2B	3B	HR	HR%	R	RBI	BB	SO	SB
April	14	.410	.564	39	16	6	0	0	0.0	5	3	3	2	0
May	22	.291	.382	55	16	2	0	1	1.8	3	6	10	8	1
June	18	.179	.232	56	10	3	0	0	0.0	6	5	5	8	0
July	20	.250	.383	60	15	5	0	1	1.7	4	4	5	8	0
Aug	18	.314	.373	51	16	3	0	0	0.0	4	3	3	5	0
Sept/Oct	15	.262	.333	42	11	3	0	0	0.0	3	5	5	7	0
Day	43	.287	.380	129	37	9	0	1	0.8	9	9	10	16	0
Night	64	.270	.362	174	47	13	0	1	0.6	16	17	21	22	1
vs. Left		.188	.219	32	6	1	0	0	0.0	4	1	3	4	1
vs. Right		.288	.387	271	78	21	0	2	0.7	21	25	28	34	0

CATCHER

Year	Team	Games	BA	SA	AB	H	2B	3B	HR	HR%	R	RBI	BB	SO	SB	PINCH HIT AB	H	PO	A	E	DP	TC/G	FA	G by Pos

Terry Kennedy *Continued*

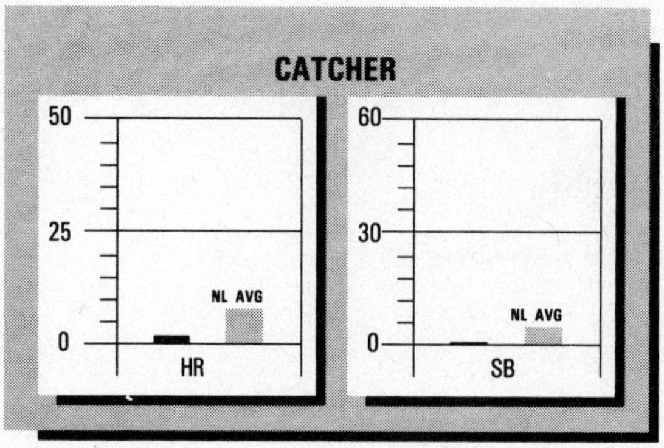

Year	Team	Games	BA	SA	AB	H	2B	3B	HR	HR%	R	RBI	BB	SO	SB	AB	H	PO	A	E	DP	TC/G	FA	G by Pos
On Grass		79	.305	.414	220	67	18	0	2	0.9	22	24	25	25	0									
On Turf		28	.205	.253	83	17	4	0	0	0.0	3	2	6	13	1									
Home		55	.291	.399	148	43	10	0	2	1.4	15	18	19	14	0									
Road		52	.265	.342	155	41	12	0	0	0.0	10	8	12	24	1									
Division Rivals																								
vs. ATL		11	.320	.400	25	8	2	0	0	0.0	6	3	6	5	0									
vs. CIN		8	.192	.308	26	5	0	0	1	3.8	2	5	1	1	0									
vs. HOU		13	.214	.262	42	9	2	0	0	0.0	3	0	3	6	0									
vs. LA		9	.333	.433	30	10	3	0	0	0.0	2	4	1	2	0									
vs. SD		12	.212	.303	33	7	3	0	0	0.0	3	1	3	3	0									
On 3B < 2 Out			.385	.769	13	5	2	0	1	7.7	1	13	3	2										
1978	STL N	10	.172	.172	29	5	0	0	0	0.0	0	2	4	3	0	1	0	46	4	1	1	5.1	.980	C-10
1979		33	.284	.404	109	31	7	0	2	1.8	11	17	6	20	0	5	1	135	7	1	1	4.3	.993	C-32
1980		84	.254	.375	248	63	12	3	4	1.6	28	34	28	34	0	12	2	231	22	7	3	3.1	.973	C-41, OF-28
1981	SD N	101	.301	.385	382	115	24	1	2	0.5	32	41	22	53	0	3	0	465	63	20	12	5.4	.964	C-100
1982		153	.295	.486	562	166	42	1	21	3.7	75	97	26	91	1	5	2	777	66	9	18	5.6	.989	C-139, 1B-12
1983		149	.284	.434	549	156	27	2	17	3.1	47	98	51	89	1	4	2	807	82	12	12	6.0	.987	C-143, 1B-4
1984		148	.240	.353	530	127	16	1	14	2.6	54	57	33	99	1	5	0	708	54	14	6	5.2	.982	C-147
1985		143	.261	.372	532	139	27	1	10	1.9	54	74	31	102	0	5	2	662	68	10	12	5.2	.986	C-140, 1B-5
1986		141	.264	.403	432	114	22	1	12	2.8	46	57	37	74	0	23	11	692	70	8	13	5.5	.990	C-123
1987	BAL A	143	.250	.385	512	128	13	1	18	3.5	51	62	35	112	1	5	0	750	58	6	11	5.7	.993	C-142
1988		85	.226	.298	265	60	10	0	3	1.1	20	16	15	53	0	8	1	332	23	2	3	4.2	.994	C-79
1989	SF N	125	.239	.324	355	85	15	0	5	1.4	19	34	35	56	1	11	3	519	47	8	6	4.6	.986	C-121, 1B-2
1990		107	.277	.370	303	84	22	0	2	0.6	25	26	31	38	1	12	4	390	38	4	3	4.2	.991	C-103
13 yrs.		1422	.265	.387	4808	1273	237	11	110	2.3	462	615	354	824	6	99	28	6514	602	102	101	5.1	.986	C-1320, OF-28, 1B-23

LEAGUE CHAMPIONSHIP SERIES

Year	Team	Games	BA	SA	AB	H	2B	3B	HR	HR%	R	RBI	BB	SO	SB	AB	H	PO	A	E	DP	TC/G	FA	G by Pos
1984	SD N	5	.222	.222	18	4	0	0	0	0.0	2	1	1	3	0	0	0	28	4	0	1	6.4	1.000	C-5
1989	SF N	5	.188	.250	16	3	1	0	0	0.0	0	0	1	4	0	0	0	26	1	0	2	5.4	1.000	C-5
2 yrs.		10	.206	.235	34	7	1	0	0	0.0	2	1	2	7	0	0	0	54	5	0	3	5.9	.000	C-10

WORLD SERIES

Year	Team	Games	BA	SA	AB	H	2B	3B	HR	HR%	R	RBI	BB	SO	SB	AB	H	PO	A	E	DP	TC/G	FA	G by Pos
1984	SD N	5	.211	.421	19	4	1	0	1	5.3	2	3	1	1	0	0	0	30	2	0	1	6.4	1.000	C-5
1989	SF N	4	.167	.167	12	2	0	0	0	0.0	1	2	1	3	0	0	0	23	1	1	1	6.3	.960	C-4
2 yrs.		9	.194	.323	31	6	1	0	1	3.2	3	5	2	4	0	0	0	53	3	1	2	6.3	.982	C-9

Jeff King

KING, JEFFREY WAYNE
B. Dec. 26, 1964, Marion, Ind.
BR TR 6' 1" 175 lbs.

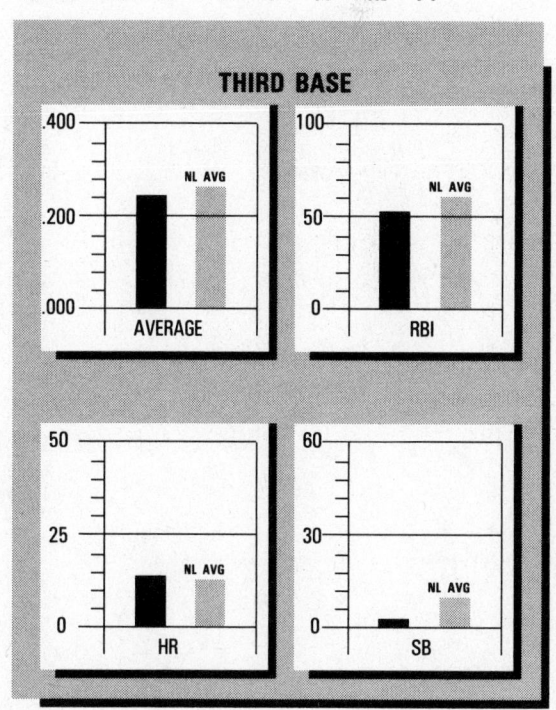

	Games	BA	SA	AB	H	2B	3B	HR	HR%	R	RBI	BB	SO	SB
April	13	.103	.205	39	4	1	0	1	2.6	3	4	3	8	0
May	18	.260	.400	50	13	4	0	1	2.0	7	4	4	4	0
June	20	.255	.275	51	13	1	0	0	0.0	7	4	2	7	0
July	17	.308	.481	52	16	3	0	2	3.8	10	11	3	4	1
Aug	28	.256	.500	86	22	4	1	5	5.8	9	16	2	15	1
Sept/Oct	31	.247	.452	93	23	4	0	5	5.4	10	14	7	12	1
Day	36	.259	.422	116	30	4	0	5	4.3	10	17	4	19	0
Night	91	.239	.404	255	61	13	1	9	3.5	36	36	17	31	3
vs. Left		.264	.446	231	61	13	1	9	3.9	29	36	14	24	3
vs. Right		.214	.350	140	30	4	0	5	3.6	17	17	7	26	0
On Grass	30	.209	.308	91	19	3	0	2	2.2	7	10	4	17	0
On Turf	97	.257	.443	280	72	14	1	12	4.3	39	43	17	33	3
Home	63	.274	.475	179	49	9	0	9	5.0	26	30	9	23	1
Road	64	.219	.349	192	42	8	1	5	2.6	20	23	12	27	2
Division Rivals														
vs. CHI	12	.256	.436	39	10	1	0	2	5.1	4	3	0	10	0
vs. MON	13	.216	.324	37	8	1	0	1	2.7	3	6	3	3	1
vs. NY	16	.313	.458	48	15	1	0	2	4.2	6	6	2	7	0
vs. PHI	17	.226	.321	53	12	3	1	0	0.0	7	4	5	4	0
vs. STL	16	.209	.326	43	9	5	0	0	0.0	6	4	3	5	1
On 3B < 2 Out		.217	.217	23	5	0	0	0	0.0	0	13	3	6	

Year	Team		Games	BA	SA	AB	H	2B	3B	HR	HR%	R	RBI	BB	SO	SB	PINCH HIT AB	H	PO	A	E	DP	TC/G	FA	G by Pos

Jeff King *Continued*

Year	Team		Games	BA	SA	AB	H	2B	3B	HR	HR%	R	RBI	BB	SO	SB	AB	H	PO	A	E	DP	TC/G	FA	G by Pos
1989	PIT	N	75	.195	.353	215	42	13	3	5	2.3	31	19	20	34	4	15	3	403	59	4	36	6.2	.991	1B-46, 3B-13, 2B-7, SS-1
1990			127	.245	.410	371	91	17	1	14	3.7	46	53	21	50	3	19	5	61	215	18	15	2.6	.939	3B-115, 1B-1
2 yrs.			202	.227	.389	586	133	30	4	19	3.2	77	72	41	84	7	34	8	464	274	22	51	3.8	.971	3B-128, 1B-47, 2B-7, SS-1

LEAGUE CHAMPIONSHIP SERIES

| 1990 | PIT | N | 5 | .100 | .100 | 10 | 1 | 0 | 0 | 0 | 0.0 | 0 | 0 | 1 | 5 | 0 | 2 | 0 | 1 | 4 | 0 | 0 | 1.3 | 1.000 | 3B-4 |

Mike Kingery

KINGERY, MICHAEL SCOTT
B. Mar. 29, 1961, St. James, Minn.
BL TL 6′ 180 lbs.

Year	Team		Games	BA	SA	AB	H	2B	3B	HR	HR%	R	RBI	BB	SO	SB	AB	H	PO	A	E	DP	TC/G	FA	G by Pos
1986	KC	A	62	.258	.388	209	54	8	5	3	1.4	25	14	12	30	7	5	2	102	6	3	2	1.8	.973	OF-59
1987	SEA	A	120	.280	.449	354	99	25	4	9	2.5	38	52	27	43	7	9	3	226	15	2	3	2.0	.992	OF-114, DH-4
1988			57	.203	.276	123	25	6	0	1	0.8	21	9	19	23	3	5	0	102	6	2	1	1.9	.982	OF-44, 1B-10
1989			31	.224	.342	76	17	3	0	2	2.6	14	6	7	14	1	6	0	70	0	0	0	2.3	1.000	OF-23
1990	SF	N	105	.295	.338	207	61	7	1	0	0.0	24	24	12	19	6	17	7	126	7	3	2	1.4	.978	OF-95
5 yrs.			375	.264	.382	969	256	49	10	15	1.5	122	105	77	129	24	42	12	626	34	10	8	1.8	.985	OF-335, 1B-10, DH-4

Ron Kittle

KITTLE, RONALD DALE (Kitty)
B. Jan. 5, 1958, Gary, Ind.
BR TR 6′ 4″ 200 lbs.

Split	Games	BA	SA	AB	H	2B	3B	HR	HR%	R	RBI	BB	SO	SB	AB	H	PO	A	E	DP	TC/G	FA	G by Pos
April	16	.283	.453	53	15	3	0	2	3.8	6	8	5	12	0									
May	24	.300	.614	70	21	4	0	6	8.6	9	21	8	24	0									
June	24	.174	.419	86	15	3	0	6	7.0	7	7	4	26	0									
July	21	.243	.392	74	18	5	0	2	2.7	7	7	7	16	0									
Aug	15	.143	.257	35	5	1	0	1	2.9	3	2	2	11	0									
Sept/Oct	5	.200	.350	20	4	0	0	1	5.0	1	1	0	2	0									
Day	29	.236	.415	106	25	7	0	4	3.8	12	11	4	28	0									
Night	76	.228	.448	232	53	9	0	14	6.0	21	35	22	63	0									
vs. Left		.225	.523	151	34	6	0	13	8.6	21	25	13	38	0									
vs. Right		.235	.369	187	44	10	0	5	2.7	12	21	13	53	0									
On Grass	91	.235	.433	293	69	16	0	14	4.8	29	39	24	75	0									
On Turf	14	.200	.467	45	9	0	0	4	8.9	4	7	2	16	0									
Home	57	.227	.427	185	42	13	0	8	4.3	17	20	14	53	0									
Road	48	.235	.451	153	36	3	0	10	6.5	16	26	12	38	0									
Division Rivals																							
vs. BOS	5	.625	1.125	8	5	1	0	1	12.5	1	3	2	1	0									
vs. CLE	9	.206	.353	34	7	2	0	1	2.9	4	3	3	5	0									
vs. DET	12	.341	.659	44	15	2	0	4	9.1	6	9	6	12	0									
vs. MIL	6	.273	.500	22	6	2	0	1	4.5	3	1	0	4	0									
vs. NY	13	.194	.419	31	6	4	0	1	3.2	4	7	4	9	0									
vs. TOR	9	.161	.387	31	5	1	0	2	6.5	3	4	0	11	0									
On 3B < 2 Out		.231	.308	13	3	1	0	0	0.0	0	8	1	7										

DESIGNATED HITTER
(bar charts: AVERAGE, RBI, HR, SB — each showing player value vs. AL AVG)

Year	Team		Games	BA	SA	AB	H	2B	3B	HR	HR%	R	RBI	BB	SO	SB	AB	H	PO	A	E	DP	TC/G	FA	G by Pos
1982	CHI	A	20	.241	.414	29	7	0	0	1	3.4	3	7	3	12	0	13	2	3	0	0	0	0.2	1.000	OF-5, DH-3
1983			145	.254	.504	520	132	19	3	35	**6.7**	75	100	39	**150**	8	6	0	234	7	9	0	1.7	.964	OF-139, DH-2
1984			139	.215	.453	466	100	15	0	32	**6.9**	67	74	49	137	3	13	4	226	14	7	2	1.8	.972	OF-124, DH-7
1985			116	.230	.467	379	87	12	0	26	6.9	51	58	31	92	1	9	0	88	2	1	1	0.8	.989	DH-57, OF-57
1986	2 teams			CHI A (86G — .213)			NY A (30G — .238)																		
"	total		116	.218	.420	376	82	13	0	21	5.6	42	60	35	110	4	12	2	39	3	0	0	0.4	1.000	DH-86, OF-21
1987	NY	A	59	.277	.535	159	44	5	0	12	7.5	21	28	10	36	0	13	1	4	1	0	0	0.1	1.000	DH-49, OF-2
1988	CLE	A	75	.258	.533	225	58	8	0	18	8.0	31	43	16	65	0	13	5	0	0	0	0	0.0	—	DH-63
1989	CHI	A	51	.302	.556	169	51	10	0	11	6.5	26	37	22	42	0	3	1	216	12	4	28	4.5	.983	1B-27, DH-17, OF-5
1990	2 teams			CHI A (83G — .245)			BAL A (22G — .164)																		
"	total		105	.231	.438	338	78	16	0	18	5.3	33	46	26	91	0	14	4	176	6	2	19	6.1	.989	DH-67, 1B-30
9 yrs.			826	.240	.476	2661	639	100	3	174	6.5	349	453	231	735	16	96	19	986	45	23	50	1.3	.978	OF-353, DH-351, 1B-57

LEAGUE CHAMPIONSHIP SERIES

| 1983 | CHI | A | 3 | .286 | .429 | 7 | 2 | 1 | 0 | 0 | 0.0 | 1 | 0 | 1 | 2 | 0 | 0 | 0 | 3 | 0 | 0 | 0 | 0.8 | 1.000 | OF-3 |

Year	Team		Games	BA	SA	AB	H	2B	3B	HR	HR%	R	RBI	BB	SO	SB	PINCH HIT		PO	A	E	DP	TC/G	FA	G by Pos
																	AB	H							

Brad Komminsk

KOMMINSK, BRAD LYNN
B. Apr. 4, 1961, Lima, Ohio
BR TR 6′ 2″ 202 lbs.

Year	Team		Games	BA	SA	AB	H	2B	3B	HR	HR%	R	RBI	BB	SO	SB	AB	H	PO	A	E	DP	TC/G	FA	G by Pos
1983	ATL	N	19	.222	.278	36	8	2	0	0	0.0	2	4	5	7	0	7	2	16	1	1	0	0.9	.944	OF-13
1984			90	.203	.316	301	61	10	0	8	2.7	37	36	29	77	18	10	4	135	2	1	0	1.5	.993	OF-80
1985			106	.227	.327	300	68	12	3	4	1.3	52	21	38	71	10	15	0	161	2	7	0	1.6	.959	OF-92
1986			5	.400	.400	5	2	0	0	0	0.0	1	1	0	1	0	1	0	1	2	0	0	0.6	1.000	3B-2, OF-2
1987	MIL	A	7	.067	.067	15	1	0	0	0	0.0	0	0	1	7	1	1	0	10	0	0	0	1.4	1.000	OF-5, DH-1
1989	CLE	A	71	.237	.419	198	47	8	2	8	4.0	27	33	24	55	8	5	1	181	3	1	1	2.6	.995	OF-68
1990	2 teams		SF N	(8G — .200)	BAL A	(46G — .238)																			
"	total		54	.236	.358	106	25	4	0	3	2.8	20	8	15	31	1	11	2	70	2	0	0	1.5	1.000	OF-47, DH-2
7 yrs.			352	.221	.340	961	212	36	5	23	2.4	139	103	112	249	38	50	9	574	12	10	1	1.7	.983	OF-307, DH-3, 3B-2

Jim Kremers

KREMERS, JAMES EDWARD
B. Oct. 8, 1965, Little Rock, Ark.
BL TR 6′ 3″ 205 lbs.

Year	Team		Games	BA	SA	AB	H	2B	3B	HR	HR%	R	RBI	BB	SO	SB	AB	H	PO	A	E	DP	TC/G	FA	G by Pos
1990	ATL	N	29	.110	.192	73	8	1	1	1	1.3	7	2	6	27	0	5	0	107	10	1	2	4.4	.992	C-27

Chad Kreuter

KREUTER, CHAD MICHAEL
B. Aug. 26, 1964, Greenbrae, Calif.
BB TR 6′ 2″ 190 lbs.

Year	Team		Games	BA	SA	AB	H	2B	3B	HR	HR%	R	RBI	BB	SO	SB	AB	H	PO	A	E	DP	TC/G	FA	G by Pos
1988	TEX	A	16	.275	.412	51	14	2	1	1	2.0	3	5	7	13	0	0	0	93	8	1	0	6.4	.990	C-16
1989			87	.152	.266	158	24	3	0	5	3.2	16	9	27	40	0	1	0	453	26	4	4	5.6	.992	C-85
1990			22	.045	.091	22	1	1	0	0	0.0	2	2	8	9	0	0	0	39	4	1	0	2.2	.977	C-20, DH-1
3 yrs.			125	.169	.281	231	39	6	1	6	2.6	21	16	42	62	0	1	0	585	38	6	4	5.0	.990	C-121, DH-1

John Kruk

KRUK, JOHN MARTIN
B. Feb. 9, 1961, Charleston, W. Va.
BL TL 5′ 10″ 170 lbs.

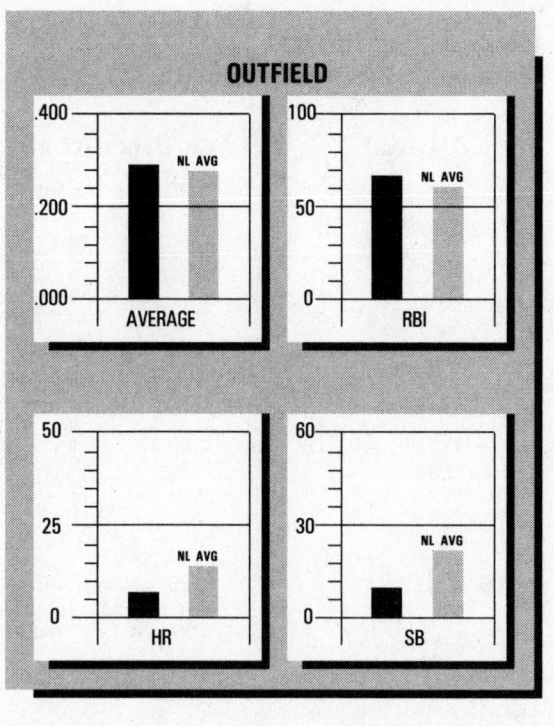

OUTFIELD

	Games	BA	SA	AB	H	2B	3B	HR	HR%	R	RBI	BB	SO	SB
April	18	.241	.362	58	14	2	1	1	1.7	5	13	5	9	1
May	24	.291	.468	79	23	5	3	1	1.3	15	9	10	11	1
June	24	.267	.320	75	20	4	0	0	0.0	5	7	16	12	2
July	21	.296	.352	54	16	3	0	0	0.0	8	5	16	9	4
Aug	26	.308	.440	91	28	4	1	2	2.2	7	18	13	12	1
Sept/Oct	29	.326	.581	86	28	7	3	3	3.5	12	15	9	17	1
Day	36	.296	.472	108	32	9	2	2	1.9	11	15	20	19	1
Night	106	.290	.418	335	97	16	6	5	1.5	41	52	49	51	9
vs. Left		.222	.325	117	26	2	2	2	1.7	11	15	14	20	2
vs. Right		.316	.469	326	103	23	6	5	1.5	41	52	55	50	8
On Grass	39	.280	.432	118	33	6	3	2	1.7	14	17	19	22	1
On Turf	103	.295	.431	325	96	19	5	5	1.5	38	50	50	48	9
Home	70	.318	.450	220	70	15	4	2	0.9	22	37	31	29	3
Road	72	.265	.413	223	59	10	4	5	2.2	30	30	38	41	7
Division Rivals														
vs. CHI	16	.289	.467	45	13	6	1	0	0.0	6	8	10	7	0
vs. MON	14	.267	.400	45	12	1	1	1	2.2	3	4	6	6	1
vs. NY	14	.324	.486	37	12	2	2	0	0.0	2	5	4	8	1
vs. PIT	15	.250	.350	40	10	1	0	1	2.5	3	6	12	6	1
vs. STL	17	.304	.393	56	17	2	0	1	1.8	9	13	5	8	1
On 3B < 2 Out		.389	.667	18	7	0	1	1	5.6	1	16	13	3	

Year	Team		Games	BA	SA	AB	H	2B	3B	HR	HR%	R	RBI	BB	SO	SB	AB	H	PO	A	E	DP	TC/G	FA	G by Pos
1986	SD	N	122	.309	.424	278	86	16	2	4	1.4	33	38	45	58	2	32	8	139	6	3	3	1.2	.980	OF-74, 1B-9
1987			138	.313	.488	447	140	14	2	20	4.5	72	91	73	93	18	12	6	911	78	5	74	7.2	.995	1B-101, OF-29
1988			120	.241	.362	378	91	17	1	9	2.4	54	44	80	68	5	7	2	634	37	3	45	5.6	.996	1B-63, OF-55
1989	2 teams		SD N	(31G — .184)	PHI N	(81G — .331)																			
"	total		112	.300	.437	357	107	13	6	8	2.2	53	44	44	53	3	8	1	212	9	4	4	2.0	.982	OF-99, 1B-7
1990	PHI	N	142	.291	.431	443	129	25	8	7	1.5	52	67	69	70	10	13	5	543	45	4	34	4.4	.993	OF-87, 1B-61
5 yrs.			634	.291	.431	1903	553	85	19	48	2.5	264	284	311	342	38	72	22	2439	175	19	160	4.2	.993	OF-344, 1B-241

Year	Team		Games	BA	SA	AB	H	2B	3B	HR	HR%	R	RBI	BB	SO	SB	PINCH HIT AB	H	PO	A	E	DP	TC/G	FA	G by Pos

Jeff Kunkel

KUNKEL, JEFFREY WILLIAM
Son of Bill Kunkel.
B. Mar. 25, 1962, West Palm Beach, Fla.
BR TR 6′ 2″ 175 lbs.

Year	Team		Games	BA	SA	AB	H	2B	3B	HR	HR%	R	RBI	BB	SO	SB	AB	H	PO	A	E	DP	TC/G	FA	G by Pos
1984	TEX	A	50	.204	.324	142	29	2	3	3	2.1	13	7	2	35	4	0	0	81	120	17	22	4.4	.922	SS–48, DH–1
1985			2	.250	.250	4	1	0	0	0	0.0	1	0	0	3	0	0	0	2	5	0	1	3.5	1.000	SS–2
1986			8	.231	.462	13	3	0	0	1	7.7	3	2	0	2	0	1	0	4	6	3	0	1.6	.769	SS–5, DH–1
1987			15	.219	.313	32	7	0	0	1	3.1	1	2	0	10	0	1	0	19	27	3	8	3.3	.939	2B–10, 3B–3, OF–3, DH–1, 1B–1, SS–1
1988			55	.227	.357	154	35	8	3	2	1.3	14	15	4	35	0	3	0	78	119	8	23	3.7	.961	2B–28, SS–19, 3B–10, OF–6, DH–3, P–1
1989			108	.270	.437	293	79	21	2	8	2.7	39	29	20	75	3	6	1	143	168	22	27	3.1	.934	SS–59, OF–30, 2B–8, DH–5, 3B–4, P–1
1990			99	.170	.280	200	34	11	1	3	1.5	17	17	11	66	2	6	1	101	172	11	34	3.0	.961	SS–67, 3B–15, 2B–13, OF–5, DH–1
7 yrs.			337	.224	.360	838	188	42	9	18	2.1	88	72	37	226	9	17	2	428	617	64	115	3.3	.942	SS–201, 2B–59, OF–44, 3B–32, DH–12, P–2, 1B–1

Randy Kutcher

KUTCHER, RANDY SCOTT
B. Apr. 30, 1960, Anchorage, Alaska
BR TR 5′ 11″ 170 lbs.

Year	Team		Games	BA	SA	AB	H	2B	3B	HR	HR%	R	RBI	BB	SO	SB	AB	H	PO	A	E	DP	TC/G	FA	G by Pos
1986	SF	N	71	.237	.409	186	44	9	1	7	3.8	28	16	11	41	6	13	1	111	11	1	3	1.7	.992	OF–51, SS–13, 3B–4, 2B–3
1987			14	.188	.375	16	3	1	1	0	0.0	7	1	1	5	1	2	0	14	5	0	1	1.4	1.000	OF–6, 2B–2, 3B–2, SS–1
1988	BOS	A	19	.167	.250	12	2	1	0	0	0.0	2	0	0	2	0	0	0	6	5	1	0	0.6	.917	OF–7, 3B–2
1989			77	.225	.363	160	36	10	3	2	1.3	28	18	11	46	3	5	2	112	8	3	0	1.6	.976	OF–57, DH–6, 3B–6, C–1
1990			63	.230	.351	74	17	4	1	1	1.3	18	5	13	18	3	1	0	55	26	0	2	1.6	1.000	OF–34, 3B–11, DH–5, 2B–5
5 yrs.			244	.228	.377	448	102	25	6	10	2.2	83	40	36	112	13	21	3	298	55	5	6	1.5	.986	OF–155, 3B–25, SS–14, DH–11, 2B–10, C–1

LEAGUE CHAMPIONSHIP SERIES

Year	Team		Games	BA	SA	AB	H	2B	3B	HR	HR%	R	RBI	BB	SO	SB	AB	H	PO	A	E	DP	TC/G	FA	G by Pos
1990	BOS	A	2	.000	.000	0	0	0	0	0	0.0	0	0	0	0	0	0	0	0	0	0	0	0.0	1.000	

Mike Laga

LAGA, MICHAEL RUSSELL
B. June 14, 1960, Ridgewood, N. J.
BL TL 6′ 2″ 210 lbs.

Year	Team		Games	BA	SA	AB	H	2B	3B	HR	HR%	R	RBI	BB	SO	SB	AB	H	PO	A	E	DP	TC/G	FA	G by Pos
1982	DET	A	27	.261	.466	88	23	9	0	3	3.4	6	11	4	23	1	4	1	163	4	1	18	6.2	.994	1B–19, DH–8
1983			12	.190	.190	21	4	0	0	0	0.0	2	2	1	9	0	3	1	9	1	0	2	0.8	1.000	DH–6, 1B–5
1984			9	.545	.545	11	6	0	0	0	0.0	1	1	1	2	0	3	3	12	1	0	1	1.4	1.000	DH–4, 1B–4
1985			9	.167	.361	36	6	1	0	2	5.6	3	6	0	9	0	0	0	33	5	1	4	4.3	.974	DH–5, 1B–4
1986	2 teams		DET A	(15G —	.200)		STL N	(18G —	.217)																
"	total		33	.209	.462	91	19	5	0	6	6.6	13	16	10	31	0	5	0	207	21	0	19	6.9	1.000	1B–28, DH–3
1987	STL	N	17	.138	.276	29	4	1	0	1	3.4	4	4	2	7	0	5	1	66	7	2	10	4.4	.973	1B–12
1988			41	.130	.160	100	13	0	0	1	1.0	5	4	2	21	0	5	0	293	17	0	26	7.6	1.000	1B–37
1989	SF	N	17	.200	.400	20	4	1	0	1	5.0	1	7	1	6	0	11	2	16	1	0	0	1.0	1.000	1B–4
1990			23	.185	.444	27	5	1	0	2	7.4	4	4	1	7	0	11	2	33	5	0	4	3.8	1.000	1B–10
9 yrs.			188	.199	.355	423	84	18	0	16	3.8	39	55	22	115	1	47	10	832	62	4	84	4.8	.996	1B–123, DH–26

Steve Lake

LAKE, STEVEN MICHAEL
B. Mar. 14, 1957, Inglewood, Calif.
BR TR 6′ 1″ 180 lbs.

Year	Team		Games	BA	SA	AB	H	2B	3B	HR	HR%	R	RBI	BB	SO	SB	AB	H	PO	A	E	DP	TC/G	FA	G by Pos
1983	CHI	N	38	.259	.365	85	22	4	1	1	1.2	9	7	2	6	0	5	0	115	22	0	3	3.6	1.000	C–32
1984			25	.222	.407	54	12	4	0	2	3.7	4	7	0	7	0	1	0	72	13	4	0	3.6	.955	C–24
1985			58	.151	.193	119	18	2	0	1	0.8	5	11	3	21	1	4	1	182	25	1	1	3.6	.995	C–55
1986	2 teams		CHI N	(10G —	.421)		STL N	(26G —	.245)																
"	total		36	.294	.412	68	20	2	0	2	2.9	8	14	3	7	0	0	0	105	9	2	3	3.2	.983	C–36
1987	STL	N	74	.251	.346	179	45	7	2	2	1.1	19	19	10	18	0	14	4	253	21	1	2	3.7	.996	C–59
1988			36	.278	.389	54	15	3	0	1	1.9	5	4	3	15	0	17	5	51	8	1	1	1.7	.983	C–19
1989	PHI	N	58	.252	.335	155	39	5	1	2	1.3	9	14	12	20	0	7	3	262	33	3	3	5.1	.990	C–55
1990			29	.250	.275	80	20	2	0	0	0.0	4	6	3	12	0	1	0	115	19	1	1	4.8	.993	C–28
8 yrs.			354	.241	.329	794	191	29	4	11	1.4	63	82	36	106	1	49	13	1155	150	13	14	3.7	.990	C–308

Year	Team		Games	BA	SA	AB	H	2B	3B	HR	HR%	R	RBI	BB	SO	SB	PINCH HIT AB	PINCH HIT H	PO	A	E	DP	TC/G	FA	G by Pos

Steve Lake   *Continued*

LEAGUE CHAMPIONSHIP SERIES

Year	Team		Games	BA	SA	AB	H	2B	3B	HR	HR%	R	RBI	BB	SO	SB	PH AB	PH H	PO	A	E	DP	TC/G	FA	G by Pos
1984	CHI	N	1	1.000	2.000	1	1	1	0	0	0.0	0	0	0	0	0	0	0	0	0	0	0	0.0	—	C-1

WORLD SERIES

| 1987 | STL | N | 3 | .333 | .333 | 3 | 1 | 0 | 0 | 0 | 0.0 | 0 | 1 | 0 | 0 | 0 | 0 | 0 | 8 | 1 | 0 | 0 | 3.0 | 1.000 | C-3 |

Tom Lampkin

LAMPKIN, THOMAS MICHAEL
B. Mar. 4, 1964, Cincinnati, Ohio
BL TR 5′ 11″ 180 lbs.

Year	Team		Games	BA	SA	AB	H	2B	3B	HR	HR%	R	RBI	BB	SO	SB	PH AB	PH H	PO	A	E	DP	TC/G	FA	G by Pos
1988	CLE	A	4	.000	.000	4	0	0	0	0	0.0	0	0	1	0	0	1	0	3	0	0	0	0.8	1.000	C-3
1990	SD	N	26	.222	.302	63	14	0	1	1	1.5	4	4	4	9	0	6	1	91	10	3	1	5.2	.971	C-20
2 yrs.			30	.209	.284	67	14	0	1	1	1.5	4	4	5	9	0	7	1	94	10	3	1	3.6	.972	C-23

Rick Lancellotti

LANCELLOTTI, RICHARD ANTHONY
B. July 5, 1956, Providence, R. I.
BL TL 6′ 3″ 195 lbs.

Year	Team		Games	BA	SA	AB	H	2B	3B	HR	HR%	R	RBI	BB	SO	SB	PH AB	PH H	PO	A	E	DP	TC/G	FA	G by Pos
1982	SD	N	17	.179	.231	39	7	2	0	0	0.0	2	4	2	8	0	8	1	63	2	1	7	3.9	.985	1B-7, OF-3
1986	SF	N	15	.222	.556	18	4	0	0	2	11.1	2	6	0	7	0	13	4	7	0	0	0	0.5	1.000	1B-1, OF-1
1990	BOS	A	4	.000	.000	8	0	0	0	0	0.0	0	1	0	3	0	1	0	20	2	0	3	11.0	1.000	1B-2
3 yrs.			36	.169	.292	65	11	2	0	2	3.1	4	11	2	18	0	22	5	90	4	1	10	2.6	.989	1B-10, OF-4

Ray Lankford

LANKFORD, RAYMOND LEWIS
B. June 5, 1967, Modesto, Calif.
BL TL 5′ 11″ 180 lbs.

Year	Team		Games	BA	SA	AB	H	2B	3B	HR	HR%	R	RBI	BB	SO	SB	PH AB	PH H	PO	A	E	DP	TC/G	FA	G by Pos
1990	STL	N	39	.286	.452	126	36	10	1	3	2.3	12	12	13	27	8	7	3	92	1	1	0	2.7	.989	OF-35

Carney Lansford

LANSFORD, CARNEY RAY
Brother of Joe Lansford.
B. Feb. 7, 1957, San Jose, Calif.
BR TR 6′ 2″ 195 lbs.

	Games	BA	SA	AB	H	2B	3B	HR	HR%	R	RBI	BB	SO	SB
April	18	.296	.395	81	24	5	0	1	1.2	9	9	3	4	4
May	26	.313	.343	99	31	3	0	0	0.0	14	14	10	7	4
June	24	.226	.280	93	21	2	0	1	1.1	9	7	7	12	2
July	15	.250	.304	56	14	0	0	1	1.8	4	4	5	5	2
Aug	27	.296	.333	108	32	4	0	0	0.0	15	13	7	10	2
Sept/Oct	24	.200	.243	70	14	1	1	0	0.0	7	3	13	12	2
Day	47	.260	.284	169	44	4	0	0	0.0	14	15	21	16	7
Night	87	.272	.337	338	92	11	1	3	0.9	44	35	24	34	9
vs. Left		.345	.429	119	41	5	1	1	0.8	24	11	19	13	8
vs. Right		.245	.286	388	95	10	0	2	0.5	34	39	26	37	8
On Grass	115	.263	.311	437	115	12	0	3	0.7	48	44	40	44	12
On Turf	19	.300	.371	70	21	3	1	0	0.0	10	6	5	6	4
Home	59	.298	.335	215	64	5	0	1	0.5	20	19	23	22	10
Road	75	.247	.308	292	72	10	1	2	0.7	38	31	22	28	6
Division Rivals														
vs. CAL	9	.242	.364	33	8	1	0	1	3.0	5	6	2	2	0
vs. CHI	12	.255	.277	47	12	1	0	0	0.0	4	1	4	5	0
vs. KC	8	.179	.179	28	5	0	0	0	0.0	3	2	1	5	0
vs. MIN	12	.205	.250	44	9	2	0	0	0.0	4	2	5	5	2
vs. SEA	10	.357	.452	42	15	2	1	0	0.0	4	4	2	4	5
vs. TEX	13	.286	.286	42	12	0	0	0	0.0	3	6	8	10	1
On 3B < 2 Out		.435	.478	23	10	1	0	0	0.0	0	24	3	4	

THIRD BASE — AVERAGE / RBI / HR / SB (with AL AVG comparison)

Year	Team		Games	BA	SA	AB	H	2B	3B	HR	HR%	R	RBI	BB	SO	SB	PH AB	PH H	PO	A	E	DP	TC/G	FA	G by Pos
1978	CAL	A	121	.294	.406	453	133	23	2	8	1.8	63	52	31	67	20	2	0	94	186	18	18	2.5	.940	3B-117, SS-2, DH-1
1979			157	.287	.436	654	188	30	5	19	2.9	114	79	39	115	20	0	0	135	263	7	29	2.6	.983	3B-157
1980			151	.261	.390	602	157	27	3	15	2.5	87	80	50	93	14	1	1	151	250	19	29	2.8	.955	3B-150
1981	BOS	A	102	.336	.439	399	134	23	3	4	1.0	61	52	34	28	15	1	0	70	180	13	17	2.6	.951	3B-86, DH-16
1982			128	.301	.444	482	145	28	4	11	2.3	65	63	46	48	9	1	0	83	216	10	19	2.4	.968	3B-114, DH-13

Year	Team		Games	BA	SA	AB	H	2B	3B	HR	HR%	R	RBI	BB	SO	SB	PINCH HIT AB	H	PO	A	E	DP	TC/G	FA	G by Pos

Carney Lansford *Continued*

Year	Team		Games	BA	SA	AB	H	2B	3B	HR	HR%	R	RBI	BB	SO	SB	AB	H	PO	A	E	DP	TC/G	FA	G by Pos
1983	OAK	A	80	.308	.475	299	92	16	2	10	3.3	43	45	22	33	3	3	1	60	163	10	19	2.9	.957	3B-78, SS-1
1984			151	.300	.439	597	179	31	5	14	2.3	70	74	40	62	9	0	0	137	268	18	27	2.8	.957	3B-151
1985			98	.277	.429	401	111	18	2	13	3.2	51	46	18	27	2	1	0	85	119	5	11	2.1	.976	3B-97
1986			151	.284	.421	591	168	16	4	19	3.2	80	72	39	51	16	1	0	480	170	6	37	4.3	.991	3B-100, 1B-60, DH-2, 2B-1
1987			151	.289	.455	554	160	27	4	19	3.4	89	76	60	44	27	2	1	156	258	7	20	2.8	.983	3B-142, 1B-17, DH-4
1988			150	.279	.360	556	155	20	2	7	1.3	80	57	35	35	29	4	0	125	221	7	18	2.4	.980	3B-143, 1B-9, 2B-1
1989			148	.336	.405	551	185	28	2	2	0.4	81	52	51	25	37	0	0	195	188	13	20	2.7	.967	3B-136, 1B-15, DH-3
1990			134	.268	.320	507	136	15	1	3	0.5	58	50	45	50	16	2	0	128	195	9	24	2.6	.973	3B-126, DH-5, 1B-5
13 yrs.			1722	.292	.415	6646	1943	302	39	144	2.2	942	798	510	678	217	18	3	1899	2677	142	288	2.7	.970	3B-1597, 1B-106, DH-44, SS-3, 2B-2

LEAGUE CHAMPIONSHIP SERIES

Year	Team		Games	BA	SA	AB	H	2B	3B	HR	HR%	R	RBI	BB	SO	SB	AB	H	PO	A	E	DP	TC/G	FA	G by Pos
1979	CAL	A	4	.294	.294	17	5	0	0	0	0.0	2	3	1	2	1	0	0	4	8	0	3	3.0	1.000	3B-4
1988	OAK	A	4	.294	.529	17	5	1	0	1	5.9	4	2	0	2	0	0	0	7	8	0	2	3.8	1.000	3B-4
1989			3	.455	.455	11	5	0	0	0	0.0	2	4	2	1	2	0	0	1	2	0	0	1.0	1.000	3B-3
1990			4	.438	.500	16	7	1	0	0	0.0	2	2	0	1	0	0	0	3	11	0	1	3.5	1.000	3B-4
4 yrs.			15	.361	.443	61	22	2	0	1	1.6	10	11	3	6	3	0	0	15	29	0	6	2.9	.000	3B-15

WORLD SERIES

Year	Team		Games	BA	SA	AB	H	2B	3B	HR	HR%	R	RBI	BB	SO	SB	AB	H	PO	A	E	DP	TC/G	FA	G by Pos
1988	OAK	A	5	.167	.167	18	3	0	0	0	0.0	2	1	2	2	0	0	0	8	7	0	1	3.0	1.000	3B-5
1989			4	.438	.688	16	7	1	0	1	6.3	5	4	3	1	0	0	0	5	5	0	0	2.5	1.000	3B-4
1990			4	.267	.267	15	4	0	0	0	0.0	0	1	1	0	1	0	0	1	14	0	0	3.8	1.000	3B-4
3 yrs.			13	.286	.367	49	14	1	0	1	2.0	7	6	6	3	1	0	0	14	26	0	1	3.1	.000	3B-13

Barry Larkin

LARKIN, BARRY LOUIS
B. Apr. 28, 1964, Cincinnati, Ohio
BR TR 6′ 185 lbs.

	Games	BA	SA	AB	H	2B	3B	HR	HR%	R	RBI	BB	SO	SB
April	16	.385	.446	65	25	2	1	0	0.0	12	12	8	5	4
May	26	.323	.365	96	31	2	1	0	0.0	13	14	10	7	9
June	30	.275	.358	120	33	4	0	2	1.7	15	10	3	13	7
July	28	.321	.532	109	35	12	1	3	2.8	16	10	7	6	3
Aug	29	.246	.307	114	28	3	2	0	0.0	10	10	10	12	2
Sept/Oct	29	.300	.391	110	33	2	1	2	1.8	19	11	11	6	5
Day	43	.292	.323	161	47	3	1	0	0.0	25	18	14	15	8
Night	115	.305	.422	453	138	22	5	7	1.5	60	49	35	34	22
vs. Left		.266	.404	203	54	10	3	4	2.0	34	21	23	10	9
vs. Right		.319	.392	411	131	15	3	3	0.7	51	46	26	39	21
On Grass	47	.330	.435	191	63	13	2	1	0.5	30	22	8	16	10
On Turf	111	.288	.378	423	122	12	4	6	1.4	55	45	41	33	20
Home	78	.273	.357	286	78	8	2	4	1.4	36	26	29	21	11
Road	80	.326	.430	328	107	17	4	3	0.9	49	41	20	28	19
Division Rivals														
vs. ATL	18	.333	.440	75	25	5	0	1	1.3	12	9	8	2	3
vs. HOU	17	.323	.452	62	20	0	1	2	3.2	9	7	4	7	4
vs. LA	18	.246	.319	69	17	3	1	0	0.0	11	6	4	7	0
vs. SD	17	.397	.529	68	27	6	0	1	1.5	11	11	5	7	5
vs. SF	16	.226	.258	62	14	2	0	0	0.0	4	4	2	8	2
On 3B < 2 Out		.360	.440	25	9	2	0	0	0.0	0	16	5	2	

SHORTSTOP

AVERAGE (.400 / .200 / .000) — NL AVG
RBI (100 / 50 / 0) — NL AVG
HR (50 / 25 / 0) — NL AVG
SB (60 / 30 / 0) — NL AVG

Year	Team		Games	BA	SA	AB	H	2B	3B	HR	HR%	R	RBI	BB	SO	SB	AB	H	PO	A	E	DP	TC/G	FA	G by Pos
1986	CIN	N	41	.283	.403	159	45	4	3	3	1.9	27	19	9	21	8	4	0	51	125	4	22	4.4	.978	SS-36, 2B-3
1987			125	.244	.371	439	107	16	2	12	2.7	64	43	36	52	21	4	1	168	358	19	72	4.4	.965	SS-119
1988			151	.296	.429	588	174	32	5	12	2.0	91	56	41	24	40	2	0	231	470	29	67	4.8	.960	SS-148
1989			97	.342	.446	325	111	14	4	4	1.2	47	36	20	23	10	10	4	142	267	10	31	4.3	.976	SS-82
1990			158	.301	.396	614	185	25	6	7	1.1	85	67	49	49	30	3	1	254	469	17	86	4.7	.977	SS-156
5 yrs.			572	.293	.408	2125	622	91	20	38	1.8	314	221	155	169	109	23	6	846	1689	79	278	4.6	.970	SS-541, 2B-3

LEAGUE CHAMPIONSHIP SERIES

Year	Team		Games	BA	SA	AB	H	2B	3B	HR	HR%	R	RBI	BB	SO	SB	AB	H	PO	A	E	DP	TC/G	FA	G by Pos
1990	CIN	N	6	.261	.348	23	6	2	0	0	0.0	5	1	3	1	3	0	0	21	15	1	2	6.2	.973	SS-6

WORLD SERIES

Year	Team		Games	BA	SA	AB	H	2B	3B	HR	HR%	R	RBI	BB	SO	SB	AB	H	PO	A	E	DP	TC/G	FA	G by Pos
1990	CIN	N	4	.353	.529	17	6	1	1	0	0.0	3	1	2	0	0	0	0	1	14	0	2	3.8	1.000	SS-4

Year	Team	Games	BA	SA	AB	H	2B	3B	HR	HR%	R	RBI	BB	SO	SB	PINCH HIT AB	H	PO	A	E	DP	TC/G	FA	G by Pos

Gene Larkin

LARKIN, EUGENE THOMAS
B. Oct. 24, 1962, Flushing, N. Y.
BB TR 6′ 3″ 195 lbs.

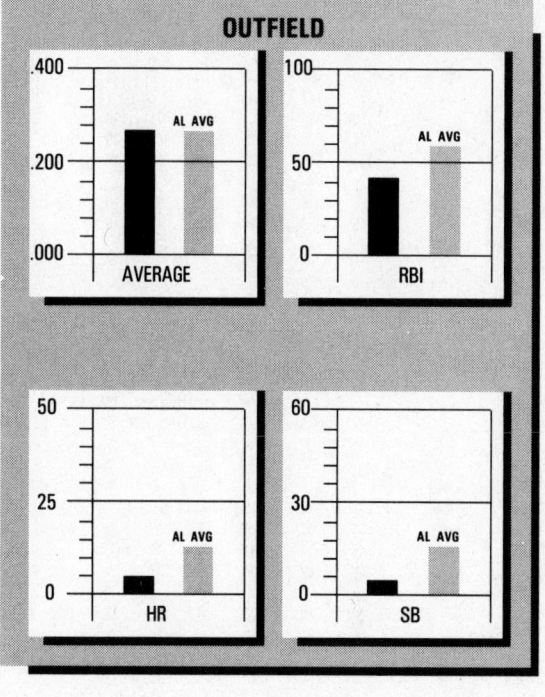

OUTFIELD

Period	G	BA	SA	AB	H	2B	3B	HR	HR%	R	RBI	BB	SO	SB
April	17	.344	.469	64	22	6	1	0	0.0	10	9	5	8	0
May	26	.310	.512	84	26	8	0	3	3.6	15	16	12	13	2
June	26	.190	.298	84	16	4	1	1	1.2	5	4	9	16	1
July	11	.286	.381	42	12	2	1	0	0.0	7	3	4	4	0
Aug	24	.280	.390	82	23	4	1	1	1.2	5	10	8	10	1
Sept/Oct	15	.200	.244	45	9	2	0	0	0.0	4	0	4	4	1
Day	33	.232	.339	112	26	7	1	1	0.9	15	5	17	10	2
Night	86	.284	.412	289	82	19	3	4	1.4	31	37	25	45	3
vs. Left		.248	.331	121	30	6	2	0	0.0	15	12	10	14	2
vs. Right		.279	.418	280	78	20	2	5	1.8	31	30	32	41	3
On Grass	44	.248	.324	145	36	7	2	0	0.0	13	13	17	18	4
On Turf	75	.281	.430	256	72	19	2	5	2.0	33	29	25	37	1
Home	58	.286	.462	199	57	16	2	5	2.5	30	26	20	25	1
Road	61	.252	.322	202	51	10	2	0	0.0	16	16	22	30	4
Division Rivals														
vs. CAL	12	.289	.333	45	13	2	0	0	0.0	5	4	2	4	0
vs. CHI	12	.225	.375	40	9	1	1	1	2.5	5	4	5	6	1
vs. KC	11	.171	.229	35	6	2	0	0	0.0	0	0	2	9	0
vs. OAK	5	.294	.294	17	5	0	0	0	0.0	3	0	2	3	1
vs. SEA	8	.222	.259	27	6	1	0	0	0.0	3	2	4	5	0
vs. TEX	11	.286	.429	35	10	3	1	0	0.0	3	5	5	6	1
On 3B < 2 Out		.400	.467	15	6	1	0	0	0.0	0	12	4	2	

Year	Team		Games	BA	SA	AB	H	2B	3B	HR	HR%	R	RBI	BB	SO	SB	PH AB	PH H	PO	A	E	DP	TC/G	FA	G by Pos
1987	MIN	A	85	.266	.382	233	62	11	2	4	1.7	23	28	25	31	1	17	5	165	10	2	12	2.1	.989	DH-40, 1B-26
1988			149	.267	.382	505	135	30	2	8	1.6	56	70	68	55	3	4	0	466	28	3	46	3.3	.994	DH-86, 1B-60
1989			136	.267	.368	446	119	25	1	6	1.3	61	46	54	57	5	11	3	524	28	4	45	4.1	.993	1B-67, DH-41, OF-32
1990			119	.269	.392	401	108	26	4	5	1.2	46	42	42	55	5	5	0	299	18	2	29	4.5	.994	OF-47, DH-43, 1B-28
4 yrs.			489	.268	.380	1585	424	92	9	23	1.5	186	186	189	198	14	37	8	1454	84	11	132	3.2	.993	DH-210, 1B-181, OF-79

LEAGUE CHAMPIONSHIP SERIES

| 1987 | MIN | A | 1 | 1.000 | 2.000 | 1 | 1 | 1 | 0 | 0 | 0.0 | 0 | 1 | 0 | 0 | 0 | 1 | 1 | 0 | 0 | 0 | 0 | 0.0 | — | |

WORLD SERIES

| 1987 | MIN | A | 5 | .000 | .000 | 3 | 0 | 0 | 0 | 0 | 0.0 | 1 | 0 | 1 | 0 | 0 | 3 | 0 | 1 | 0 | 0 | 0 | 0.2 | 1.000 | DH-1, 1B-1 |

Mike LaValliere

LaVALLIERE, MICHAEL EUGENE (Spanky)
B. Aug. 18, 1960, Charlotte, N. C.
BL TR 5′ 10″ 180 lbs.

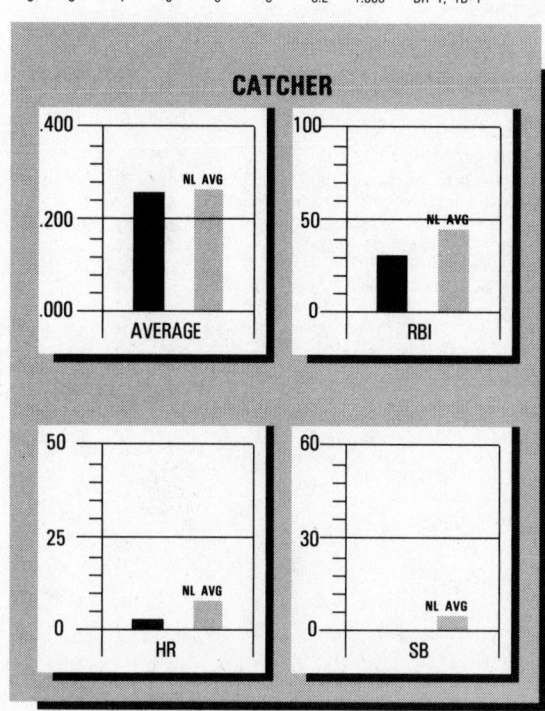

CATCHER

Period	G	BA	SA	AB	H	2B	3B	HR	HR%	R	RBI	BB	SO	SB
April	13	.200	.229	35	7	1	0	0	0.0	5	2	7	0	0
May	13	.405	.524	42	17	2	0	1	2.4	6	7	8	4	0
June	12	.206	.235	34	7	1	0	0	0.0	3	3	5	1	0
July	16	.163	.204	49	8	2	0	0	0.0	3	3	9	5	0
Aug	18	.264	.472	53	14	5	0	2	3.8	3	12	8	6	0
Sept/Oct	24	.288	.348	66	19	4	0	0	0.0	7	4	7	4	0
Day	27	.276	.355	76	21	3	0	1	1.3	8	6	11	5	0
Night	69	.251	.340	203	51	12	0	2	1.0	19	25	33	15	0
vs. Left		.375	.536	56	21	3	0	2	3.6	7	11	9	6	0
vs. Right		.229	.296	223	51	12	0	1	0.4	20	20	35	14	0
On Grass	27	.230	.264	87	20	3	0	0	0.0	9	4	16	11	0
On Turf	69	.271	.380	192	52	12	0	3	1.6	18	27	28	9	0
Home	46	.276	.378	127	35	7	0	2	1.6	12	15	18	6	0
Road	50	.243	.316	152	37	8	0	1	0.7	15	16	26	14	0
Division Rivals														
vs. CHI	13	.200	.200	40	8	0	0	0	0.0	2	4	4	3	0
vs. MON	12	.281	.375	32	9	3	0	0	0.0	3	2	4	0	0
vs. NY	10	.269	.308	26	7	1	0	0	0.0	3	1	6	2	0
vs. PHI	9	.190	.429	21	4	2	0	1	4.8	3	6	6	0	0
vs. STL	12	.212	.242	33	7	1	0	0	0.0	3	3	0	1	0
On 3B < 2 Out		.467	.733	15	7	1	0	1	6.7	1	13	2	0	

Year	Team		Games	BA	SA	AB	H	2B	3B	HR	HR%	R	RBI	BB	SO	SB	PINCH HIT AB	H	PO	A	E	DP	TC/G	FA	G by Pos

Mike LaValliere   *Continued*

Year	Team		Games	BA	SA	AB	H	2B	3B	HR	HR%	R	RBI	BB	SO	SB	AB	H	PO	A	E	DP	TC/G	FA	G by Pos
1984	PHI	N	6	.000	.000	7	0	0	0	0	0.0	0	0	2	2	0	0	0	20	2	0	0	3.7	1.000	C-6
1985	STL	N	12	.147	.176	34	5	1	0	0	0.0	2	6	7	3	0	0	0	48	5	0	3	4.4	1.000	C-12
1986			110	.234	.310	303	71	10	2	3	1.0	18	30	36	37	0	4	0	468	47	6	8	4.7	.988	C-108
1987	PIT	N	121	.300	.365	340	102	19	0	1	0.3	33	36	43	32	0	14	5	584	70	5	11	5.4	.992	C-112
1988			120	.261	.330	352	92	18	0	2	0.6	24	47	50	34	3	10	1	565	55	8	6	5.2	.987	C-114
1989			68	.316	.400	190	60	10	0	2	1.1	15	23	29	24	0	3	0	306	24	3	3	4.9	.991	C-65
1990			96	.258	.344	279	72	15	0	3	1.0	27	31	44	20	0	2	1	478	36	5	6	5.5	.990	C-95
7 yrs.			533	.267	.340	1505	402	73	2	11	0.7	119	173	211	152	3	33	7	2469	239	27	37	5.1	.990	C-512

LEAGUE CHAMPIONSHIP SERIES

Year	Team		Games	BA	SA	AB	H	2B	3B	HR	HR%	R	RBI	BB	SO	SB	AB	H	PO	A	E	DP	TC/G	FA	G by Pos
1990	PIT	N	3	.000	.000	6	0	0	0	0	0.0	1	0	3	1	0	0	0	17	2	0	0	6.3	1.000	C-3

Tom Lawless

LAWLESS, THOMAS JAMES
B. Dec. 19, 1956, Erie, Pa.
BR TR 5′ 11″ 170 lbs.

Year	Team		Games	BA	SA	AB	H	2B	3B	HR	HR%	R	RBI	BB	SO	SB	AB	H	PO	A	E	DP	TC/G	FA	G by Pos
1982	CIN	N	49	.212	.248	165	35	6	0	0	0.0	19	4	9	30	16	1	0	87	136	5	35	4.7	.978	2B-47
1984	2 teams			CIN N	(43G — .250)		MON N	(11G — .176)																	
"	total		54	.237	.299	97	23	3	0	1	1.0	11	2	8	16	7	5	1	50	52	1	8	1.9	.990	2B-32, 3B-6
1985	STL	N	47	.207	.293	58	12	3	1	0	0.0	8	8	5	4	2	9	2	19	44	1	4	1.4	.984	3B-13, 2B-11
1986			46	.282	.308	39	11	1	0	0	0.0	5	3	2	8	8	12	2	11	15	2	1	0.6	.929	3B-12, 2B-7, OF-1
1987			19	.080	.120	25	2	1	0	0	0.0	5	0	3	5	2	5	0	5	15	0	3	1.1	1.000	2B-7, 3B-3, OF-1
1988			54	.154	.262	65	10	2	1	1	1.5	9	3	7	9	6	10	1	23	29	0	3	1.0	1.000	3B-24, OF-6, 2B-5, 1B-1
1989	TOR	A	59	.229	.243	70	16	1	0	0	0.0	20	3	7	12	12	7	3	39	26	3	6	1.2	.956	OF-16, DH-12, 3B-12, 2B-7, C-1
1990			15	.083	.083	12	1	0	0	0	0.0	1	1	0	1	0	0	0	11	4	1	1	2.3	.938	DH-5, 3B-4, OF-2, 2B-1
8 yrs.			343	.207	.258	531	110	17	2	2	0.4	78	24	41	85	53	49	9	245	321	13	61	1.7	.978	2B-117, 3B-74, OF-26, DH-17, C-1, 1B-1

LEAGUE CHAMPIONSHIP SERIES

Year	Team		Games	BA	SA	AB	H	2B	3B	HR	HR%	R	RBI	BB	SO	SB	AB	H	PO	A	E	DP	TC/G	FA	G by Pos
1987	STL	N	3	.333	.333	6	2	0	0	0	0.0	0	0	1	1	0	2	1	1	4	0	0	1.7	1.000	3B-2, OF-1

WORLD SERIES

Year	Team		Games	BA	SA	AB	H	2B	3B	HR	HR%	R	RBI	BB	SO	SB	AB	H	PO	A	E	DP	TC/G	FA	G by Pos
1985	STL	N	1	—	—	0	0	0	0	0	—	0	0	0	0	0	0	0	0	0	0	0	0.0	—	
1987			3	.100	.400	10	1	0	0	1	10.0	1	3	0	4	0	0	0	3	6	1	1	3.3	.900	3B-3
2 yrs.			4	.100	.400	10	1	0	0	1	10.0	1	3	0	4	0	0	0	3	6	1	1	2.5	.900	3B-3

Rick Leach

LEACH, RICHARD MAX
B. May 4, 1957, Ann Arbor, Mich.
BL TL 6′ 1″ 180 lbs.

Year	Team		Games	BA	SA	AB	H	2B	3B	HR	HR%	R	RBI	BB	SO	SB	AB	H	PO	A	E	DP	TC/G	FA	G by Pos
1981	DET	A	54	.193	.289	83	16	3	1	1	1.2	9	11	16	15	0	10	2	149	14	0	15	3.0	1.000	1B-32, OF-15, DH-2
1982			82	.239	.330	218	52	7	2	3	1.4	23	12	21	29	4	14	2	430	29	2	36	5.6	.996	1B-56, OF-14, DH-4
1983			99	.248	.355	242	60	17	0	3	1.2	22	26	19	21	2	18	4	465	45	4	37	5.2	.992	1B-73, OF-13, DH-3
1984	TOR	A	65	.261	.375	88	23	6	2	0	0.0	11	7	8	14	0	22	8	92	14	0	9	1.6	1.000	OF-23, 1B-15, DH-6, P-1
1985			16	.200	.257	35	7	0	1	0	0.0	2	1	3	9	0	4	1	78	6	0	8	5.3	.988	1B-10, OF-4
1986			110	.309	.435	246	76	14	1	5	2.0	35	39	13	24	0	31	10	107	5	3	11	1.0	.974	DH-42, OF-39, 1B-7
1987			98	.282	.405	195	55	13	1	3	1.5	26	25	25	25	0	28	7	57	1	1	0	0.6	.983	OF-43, DH-42, 1B-5
1988			87	.276	.352	199	55	13	1	0	0.0	21	23	18	27	0	19	1	93	5	0	1	1.1	1.000	OF-49, DH-25, 1B-4
1989	TEX	A	110	.272	.351	239	65	14	1	1	0.4	32	23	32	33	2	30	6	74	2	3	2	0.7	.962	DH-44, OF-41, 1B-4
1990	SF	N	78	.293	.402	174	51	13	0	2	1.1	24	16	21	20	0	20	7	123	5	1	4	2.2	.992	OF-52, 1B-7
10 yrs.			799	.268	.369	1719	460	100	10	18	1.0	205	183	176	217	8	196	48	1668	126	15	123	2.3	.992	OF-293, 1B-213, DH-168, P-1

Year	Team		Games	BA	SA	AB	H	2B	3B	HR	HR%	R	RBI	BB	SO	SB	PINCH HIT AB	H	PO	A	E	DP	TC/G	FA	G by Pos

Manny Lee

LEE, MANUEL
Born Manuel Lora y Lee.
B. June 17, 1965, San Pedro de Macoris,
Dominican Republic
BB TR 5′ 9″ 150 lbs.

	Games	BA	SA	AB	H	2B	3B	HR	HR%	R	RBI	BB	SO	SB
April	11	.306	.306	36	11	0	0	0	0.0	4	3	2	8	0
May	14	.271	.667	48	13	0	2	5	10.4	6	8	3	13	1
June	18	.274	.387	62	17	4	0	1	1.6	10	6	4	17	0
July	19	.159	.203	69	11	1	1	0	0.0	4	6	1	13	2
Aug	28	.221	.253	95	21	3	0	0	0.0	11	11	8	21	0
Sept/Oct	27	.272	.346	81	22	4	1	0	0.0	10	7	8	18	0
Day	36	.272	.432	125	34	4	2	4	3.2	13	17	6	26	2
Night	81	.229	.297	266	61	8	2	2	0.8	32	24	20	64	1
vs. Left		.242	.410	178	43	8	2	6	3.4	22	20	6	41	1
vs. Right		.244	.282	213	52	4	2	0	0.0	23	21	20	49	2
On Grass	48	.211	.317	161	34	4	2	3	1.9	13	19	11	32	0
On Turf	69	.265	.357	230	61	8	2	3	1.3	32	22	15	58	3
Home	58	.263	.337	190	50	4	2	2	1.1	21	19	11	45	3
Road	59	.224	.343	201	45	8	2	4	2.0	24	22	15	45	0
Division Rivals														
vs. BAL	8	.167	.167	24	4	0	0	0	0.0	2	2	1	4	0
vs. BOS	10	.207	.241	29	6	1	0	0	0.0	3	0	2	5	0
vs. CLE	9	.194	.222	36	7	1	0	0	0.0	3	2	0	9	0
vs. DET	9	.161	.355	31	5	0	0	2	6.5	4	4	5	8	1
vs. MIL	10	.333	.455	33	11	2	1	0	0.0	5	8	3	9	0
vs. NY	11	.306	.444	36	11	2	0	1	2.8	3	7	2	6	0
On 3B < 2 Out		.227	.273	22	5	1	0	0	0.0	0	15	1	4	

SECOND BASE

(Bar charts: AVERAGE, RBI, HR, SB — each with AL AVG comparison)

Year	Team		Games	BA	SA	AB	H	2B	3B	HR	HR%	R	RBI	BB	SO	SB	AB	H	PO	A	E	DP	TC/G	FA	G by Pos
1985	TOR	A	64	.200	.200	40	8	0	0	0	0.0	9	0	2	9	1	3	1	34	56	3	11	1.5	.968	2B-38, DH-8, SS-8, 3B-5
1986			35	.205	.269	78	16	0	1	1	1.3	8	7	4	10	0	0	0	36	76	2	11	3.3	.982	2B-29, SS-5, 3B-2
1987			56	.256	.347	121	31	2	3	1	0.8	14	11	6	13	2	3	2	77	110	5	26	3.4	.974	2B-27, SS-26
1988			116	.291	.365	381	111	16	3	2	0.5	38	38	26	64	3	2	0	250	308	12	71	4.9	.979	2B-98, SS-23, 3B-8
1989			99	.260	.333	300	78	9	2	3	1.0	27	34	20	60	4	13	1	152	201	11	51	3.7	.970	2B-40, SS-28, 3B-17, DH-13, OF-1
1990			117	.243	.340	391	95	12	4	6	1.5	45	41	26	90	3	3	0	265	301	4	66	4.9	.993	2B-112, SS-9
6 yrs.			487	.259	.338	1311	339	39	13	13	1.0	141	131	84	246	13	24	4	814	1052	37	236	3.9	.981	2B-344, SS-99, 3B-32, DH-21, OF-1

LEAGUE CHAMPIONSHIP SERIES

Year	Team		Games	BA	SA	AB	H	2B	3B	HR	HR%	R	RBI	BB	SO	SB	AB	H	PO	A	E	DP	TC/G	FA	G by Pos
1985	TOR	A	1	—	—	0	0	0	0	0	—	0	0	0	0	0	0	0	0	0	0	0	0.0	—	2B-1
1989			2	.250	.250	8	2	0	0	0	0.0	2	0	0	1	0	0	0	4	1	0	1	2.5	1.000	2B-2
2 yrs.			3	.250	.250	8	2	0	0	0	0.0	2	0	0	1	0	0	0	4	1	0	1	1.7	.000	2B-3

Terry Lee

LEE, TERRY JAMES
B. Mar. 13, 1962, San Francisco, Calif.
BR TR 6′ 5″ 215 lbs.

Year	Team		Games	BA	SA	AB	H	2B	3B	HR	HR%	R	RBI	BB	SO	SB	AB	H	PO	A	E	DP	TC/G	FA	G by Pos
1990	CIN	N	12	.211	.263	19	4	1	0	0	0.0	1	3	2	2	0	6	2	28	3	0	1	5.2	1.000	1B-6

Scott Leius

LEIUS, SCOTT THOMAS
B. Sept. 24, 1965, Yonkers, N. Y.
BR TR 6′ 3″ 180 lbs.

Year	Team		Games	BA	SA	AB	H	2B	3B	HR	HR%	R	RBI	BB	SO	SB	AB	H	PO	A	E	DP	TC/G	FA	G by Pos
1990	MIN	A	14	.240	.400	25	6	1	0	1	4.0	4	4	2	2	0	0	0	20	25	0	10	3.5	1.000	SS-12, 3B-1

Year	Team	Games	BA	SA	AB	H	2B	3B	HR	HR%	R	RBI	BB	SO	SB	PINCH HIT AB	PINCH HIT H	PO	A	E	DP	TC/G	FA	G by Pos

Mark Lemke

LEMKE, MARK ALAN
B. Aug. 13, 1965, Utica, N. Y.
BB TR 5′ 10″ 167 lbs.

April		14	.167	.233	30	5	2	0	0	0.0	2	4	2	5	0									
May		21	.174	.217	46	8	2	0	0	0.0	7	2	11	5	0									
June			.000	.000	0	0	0	0	0	0.0	0	0	0	0	0									
July		13	.290	.355	31	9	2	0	0	0.0	2	6	4	0	0									
Aug		26	.217	.233	60	13	1	0	0	0.0	4	5	2	8	0									
Sept/Oct		28	.264	.347	72	19	6	0	0	0.0	7	4	2	4	0									
Day		25	.234	.313	64	15	5	0	0	0.0	2	8	3	3	0									
Night		77	.223	.269	175	39	8	0	0	0.0	20	13	18	19	0									
vs. Left			.268	.351	97	26	8	0	0	0.0	12	11	9	6	0									
vs. Right			.197	.232	142	28	5	0	0	0.0	10	10	12	16	0									
On Grass		76	.246	.304	171	42	10	0	0	0.0	19	17	14	13	0									
On Turf		26	.176	.221	68	12	3	0	0	0.0	3	4	7	9	0									
Home		50	.211	.275	109	23	7	0	0	0.0	9	10	8	9	0									
Road		52	.238	.285	130	31	6	0	0	0.0	13	11	13	13	0									
Division Rivals																								
vs. CIN		8	.375	.563	16	6	3	0	0	0.0	1	2	1	0	0									
vs. HOU		13	.206	.265	34	7	2	0	0	0.0	1	3	3	3	0									
vs. LA		9	.231	.308	13	3	1	0	0	0.0	2	2	2	1	0									
vs. SD		11	.333	.400	30	10	2	0	0	0.0	4	5	1	3	0									
vs. SF		10	.121	.152	33	4	1	0	0	0.0	3	3	0	2	0									
On 3B < 2 Out			.444	.556	9	4	1	0	0	0.0	0	7	1	0										
1988	ATL N	16	.224	.293	58	13	4	0	0	0.0	8	2	4	5	0	0	0	47	51	3	11	6.3	.970	2B-16
1989		14	.182	.364	55	10	2	1	2	3.6	4	10	5	7	0	1	1	25	40	0	7	4.6	1.000	2B-14
1990		102	.226	.280	239	54	13	0	0	0.0	22	21	21	22	0	15	2	90	193	4	29	3.3	.986	3B-45, 2B-44, SS-1
3 yrs.		132	.219	.295	352	77	19	1	2	0.6	34	33	30	34	0	16	3	162	284	7	47	3.4	.985	2B-74, 3B-45, SS-1

Chet Lemon

LEMON, CHESTER EARL
B. Feb. 12, 1955, Jackson, Miss.
BR TR 6′ 185 lbs.

April		15	.205	.318	44	9	2	0	1	2.3	5	6	4	7	0									
May		13	.333	.667	42	14	3	1	3	7.1	7	7	4	5	1									
June		9	.250	.286	28	7	1	0	0	0.0	4	3	6	3	1									
July		20	.306	.403	62	19	4	1	0	0.0	9	3	13	10	0									
Aug		24	.200	.307	75	15	4	2	0	0.0	6	8	12	22	0									
Sept/Oct		23	.268	.338	71	19	2	0	1	1.4	8	5	9	14	1									
Day		31	.281	.406	96	27	4	1	2	2.1	14	9	9	18	1									
Night		73	.248	.367	226	56	12	3	3	1.3	25	23	39	43	2									
vs. Left			.283	.420	138	39	4	3	3	2.2	17	12	21	22	0									
vs. Right			.239	.348	184	44	12	1	2	1.1	22	20	27	39	3									
On Grass		86	.241	.349	261	63	13	3	3	1.1	34	26	42	51	2									
On Turf		18	.328	.508	61	20	3	1	2	3.3	5	6	6	10	1									
Home		47	.256	.361	133	34	6	1	2	1.5	17	17	25	27	0									
Road		57	.259	.392	189	49	10	3	3	1.6	22	15	23	34	3									
Division Rivals																								
vs. BAL		9	.278	.278	18	5	0	0	0	0.0	3	3	4	4	0									
vs. BOS		11	.237	.316	38	9	3	0	0	0.0	6	4	5	9	0									
vs. CLE		9	.143	.179	28	4	1	0	0	0.0	3	0	6	5	1									
vs. MIL		7	.261	.565	23	6	1	0	2	8.7	5	7	2	0	1									
vs. NY		11	.195	.293	41	8	2	1	0	0.0	3	2	6	10	0									
vs. TOR		10	.343	.600	35	12	1	1	2	5.7	4	5	4	6	1									
On 3B < 2 Out			.471	.647	17	8	3	0	0	0.0	0	17	3	2										
1975	CHI A	9	.257	.314	35	9	2	0	0	0.0	2	1	2	6	1	1	0	5	7	1	0	1.4	.923	3B-6, DH-2, OF-1
1976		132	.246	.328	451	111	15	5	4	0.9	46	38	28	65	13	1	0	353	12	3	1	2.8	.992	OF-131
1977		150	.273	.459	553	151	38	4	19	3.4	99	67	52	88	8	0	0	512	12	12	2	3.6	.978	OF-149
1978		105	.300	.510	357	107	24	6	13	3.6	51	55	39	46	5	1	0	284	8	5	2	2.8	.983	OF-95, DH-10
1979		148	.318	.496	556	177	**44**	2	17	3.1	79	86	56	68	7	0	0	411	10	10	2	2.9	.977	OF-147, DH-1

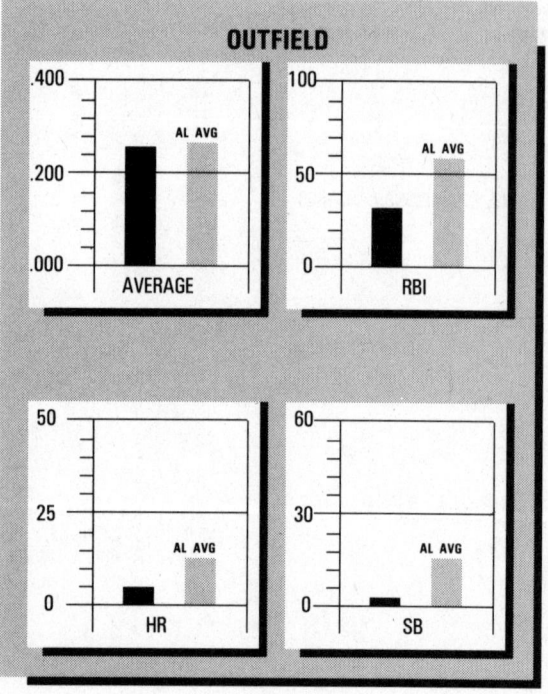

THIRD BASE

OUTFIELD

Year	Team		Games	BA	SA	AB	H	2B	3B	HR	HR%	R	RBI	BB	SO	SB	PINCH HIT AB	H	PO	A	E	DP	TC/G	FA	G by Pos

Chet Lemon *Continued*

Year	Team		Games	BA	SA	AB	H	2B	3B	HR	HR%	R	RBI	BB	SO	SB	PH AB	H	PO	A	E	DP	TC/G	FA	G by Pos
1980			147	.292	.442	514	150	32	6	11	2.1	76	51	71	56	6	1	0	347	11	7	2	2.5	.981	OF-139, DH-6, 2B-1
1981			94	.302	.491	328	99	23	6	9	2.7	50	50	33	48	5	0	0	240	2	4	1	2.6	.984	OF-93
1982	DET	A	125	.266	.447	436	116	20	1	19	4.4	75	52	56	69	1	2	1	242	11	4	2	2.1	.984	OF-121, DH-1
1983			145	.255	.464	491	125	21	5	24	4.9	78	69	54	70	0	2	1	406	6	5	3	2.9	.988	OF-145
1984			141	.287	.495	509	146	34	6	20	3.9	77	76	51	83	5	3	1	427	6	2	1	3.1	.995	OF-140, DH-1
1985			145	.265	.439	517	137	28	4	18	3.5	69	68	45	93	0	1	0	411	6	4	3	2.9	.990	OF-144
1986			126	.251	.407	403	101	21	3	12	3.0	45	53	39	53	2	8	2	316	6	5	1	2.6	.985	OF-124
1987			146	.277	.481	470	130	30	3	20	4.3	75	70	70	82	0	11	5	350	4	3	1	2.4	.992	OF-145
1988			144	.264	.436	512	135	29	4	17	3.3	67	64	59	65	1	2	0	296	8	8	3	2.2	.974	OF-144
1989			127	.237	.343	414	98	19	2	7	1.7	45	47	46	71	1	13	4	189	6	3	0	1.6	.985	OF-111, DH-13
1990			104	.258	.379	322	83	16	4	5	1.5	39	32	48	61	3	9	2	209	7	6	0	2.3	.973	OF-96, DH-6
16 yrs.			1988	.273	.442	6868	1875	396	61	215	3.1	973	884	749	1024	58	55	16	4998	122	82	25	2.6	.984	OF-1925, DH-40, 3B-6, 2B-1

LEAGUE CHAMPIONSHIP SERIES

Year	Team		Games	BA	SA	AB	H	2B	3B	HR	HR%	R	RBI	BB	SO	SB	PH AB	H	PO	A	E	DP	TC/G	FA	G by Pos
1984	DET	A	3	.000	.000	13	0	0	0	0	0.0	1	0	0	1	0	0	0	9	0	0	0	3.0	1.000	OF-3
1987			5	.278	.611	18	5	0	0	2	11.1	4	4	1	4	0	0	0	13	0	0	0	2.6	1.000	OF-5
2 yrs.			8	.161	.355	31	5	0	0	2	6.5	5	4	1	5	0	0	0	22	0	0	0	2.8	.000	OF-8

WORLD SERIES

Year	Team		Games	BA	SA	AB	H	2B	3B	HR	HR%	R	RBI	BB	SO	SB	PH AB	H	PO	A	E	DP	TC/G	FA	G by Pos
1984	DET	A	5	.294	.294	17	5	0	0	0	0.0	1	1	2	2	2	0	0	15	0	0	0	3.0	1.000	OF-5

Jeffrey Leonard

LEONARD, JEFFREY (Hac-Man)
B. Sept. 22, 1955, Philadelphia, Pa.
BR TR 6' 2" 200 lbs.

OUTFIELD

		Games	BA	SA	AB	H	2B	3B	HR	HR%	R	RBI	BB	SO	SB
April		20	.275	.425	80	22	3	0	3	3.8	6	13	3	8	1
May		29	.233	.371	116	27	4	0	4	3.4	8	21	3	19	3
June		28	.226	.321	106	24	4	0	2	1.9	10	15	8	29	0
July		24	.227	.295	88	20	3	0	1	1.1	9	14	5	21	0
Aug		21	.197	.262	61	12	4	0	0	0.0	2	2	11	15	0
Sept/Oct		12	.556	.630	27	15	2	0	0	0.0	4	10	7	5	0
Day		33	.252	.328	119	30	6	0	1	0.8	12	17	14	22	1
Night		101	.251	.365	359	90	14	0	9	2.5	27	58	23	75	3
vs. Left			.309	.463	175	54	9	0	6	3.4	18	40	15	28	1
vs. Right			.218	.294	303	66	11	0	4	1.3	21	35	22	69	3
On Grass		53	.285	.337	193	55	7	0	1	0.5	13	26	15	32	3
On Turf		81	.228	.368	285	65	13	0	9	3.2	26	49	22	65	1
Home		66	.222	.363	234	52	12	0	7	3.0	20	37	21	50	1
Road		68	.279	.348	244	68	8	0	3	1.2	19	38	16	47	3
Division Rivals															
vs. CAL		11	.359	.564	39	14	2	0	2	5.1	6	11	5	7	0
vs. CHI		7	.385	.423	26	10	1	0	0	0.0	3	2	2	6	0
vs. KC		7	.136	.136	22	3	0	0	0	0.0	0	0	2	10	0
vs. MIN		11	.333	.462	39	13	2	0	1	2.6	5	8	3	8	0
vs. OAK		10	.175	.300	40	7	2	0	1	2.5	3	7	4	2	1
vs. TEX		10	.176	.206	34	6	1	0	0	0.0	3	5	5	9	0
On 3B < 2 Out			.406	.531	32	13	1	0	1	3.1	1	29	3	5	

Year	Team		Games	BA	SA	AB	H	2B	3B	HR	HR%	R	RBI	BB	SO	SB	PH AB	H	PO	A	E	DP	TC/G	FA	G by Pos
1977	LA	N	11	.300	.500	10	3	0	1	0	0.0	1	2	1	4	0	3	0	7	0	0	0	0.6	1.000	OF-10
1978	HOU	N	8	.385	.462	26	10	2	0	0	0.0	2	4	1	2	0	1	0	16	1	0	1	2.1	1.000	OF-8
1979			134	.290	.350	411	119	15	5	0	0.0	47	47	46	68	23	11	2	227	6	10	1	1.8	.959	OF-123
1980			88	.213	.333	216	46	7	5	3	1.4	29	20	19	46	4	24	6	161	9	3	7	2.0	.983	OF-56, 1B-11
1981	2 teams			HOU N (7G — .167)		SF N (37G — .307)																			
"	total		44	.290	.510	145	42	12	4	4	2.8	21	29	12	25	5	6	1	152	5	1	5	3.6	.994	1B-30, OF-7
1982	SF	N	80	.259	.421	278	72	16	1	9	3.2	32	49	19	65	18	2	1	137	2	9	0	1.9	.939	OF-74, 1B-1
1983			139	.279	.461	516	144	17	7	21	4.1	74	87	35	116	26	4	2	253	17	7	2	2.0	.975	OF-136
1984			136	.302	.484	514	155	27	2	21	4.1	76	86	47	123	17	4	0	247	14	8	4	2.0	.970	OF-131
1985			133	.241	.393	507	122	20	3	17	3.4	49	62	21	107	11	7	1	203	10	5	0	1.6	.977	OF-126
1986			89	.279	.381	341	95	11	3	6	1.8	48	42	20	62	16	4	2	158	4	5	1	1.9	.970	OF-87
1987			131	.280	.467	503	141	29	4	19	3.8	70	63	21	68	16	11	6	193	7	7	2	1.6	.966	OF-127
1988	2 teams			SF N (44G — .256)		MIL A (94G — .235)																			
"	total		138	.242	.352	534	129	27	1	10	1.9	57	64	25	92	17	3	0	265	4	4	1	2.0	.985	OF-134, DH-2
1989	SEA	A	150	.254	.420	566	144	20	1	24	4.2	69	93	38	125	6	2	0	54	2	1	0	0.4	.982	DH-123, OF-26
1990			134	.251	.356	478	120	20	0	10	2.0	39	75	37	97	4	9	2	118	0	2	0	1.5	.983	OF-79, DH-48
14 yrs.			1415	.266	.411	5045	1342	223	37	144	2.9	614	723	342	1000	163	91	23	2191	81	62	24	1.6	.973	OF-1124, DH-173, 1B-42

Year	Team		Games	BA	SA	AB	H	2B	3B	HR	HR%	R	RBI	BB	SO	SB	PINCH HIT AB	H	PO	A	E	DP	TC/G	FA	G by Pos

Jeffrey Leonard *Continued*

LEAGUE CHAMPIONSHIP SERIES

Year	Team		Games	BA	SA	AB	H	2B	3B	HR	HR%	R	RBI	BB	SO	SB	AB	H	PO	A	E	DP	TC/G	FA	G by Pos
1980	HOU	N	3	.000	.000	3	0	0	0	0	0.0	0	0	0	2	0	2	0	2	1	0	1	1.0	1.000	OF-1
1987	SF	N	7	.417	.917	24	10	0	0	4	16.7	5	5	3	4	0	0	0	14	1	0	0	2.1	1.000	OF-7
2 yrs.			10	.370	.815	27	10	0	0	4	14.8	5	5	3	6	0	2	0	16	2	0	1	1.8	.000	OF-8

Mark Leonard

LEONARD, MARK DAVID
B. Aug. 14, 1964, Mountain View, Calif.
BL TR 6' 1" 195 lbs.

Year	Team		Games	BA	SA	AB	H	2B	3B	HR	HR%	R	RBI	BB	SO	SB	AB	H	PO	A	E	DP	TC/G	FA	G by Pos
1990	SF	N	11	.176	.412	17	3	1	0	1	5.8	3	2	3	8	0	4	0	10	0	0	0	1.4	1.000	OF-7

Darren Lewis

LEWIS, DARREN JOEL
B. Aug. 28, 1967, Berkeley, Calif.
BR TR 6' 180 lbs.

Year	Team		Games	BA	SA	AB	H	2B	3B	HR	HR%	R	RBI	BB	SO	SB	AB	H	PO	A	E	DP	TC/G	FA	G by Pos
1990	OAK	A	25	.229	.229	35	8	0	0	0	0.0	4	1	7	4	2	4	0	33	0	0	0	1.4	1.000	OF-23, DH-2

Jim Leyritz

LEYRITZ, JAMES JOSEPH
B. Dec. 27, 1963, Lakewood, Ohio
BR TR 6' 190 lbs.

	Games	BA	SA	AB	H	2B	3B	HR	HR%	R	RBI	BB	SO	SB
April		.000	.000	0	0	0	0	0	0.0	0	0	0	0	0
May		.000	.000	0	0	0	0	0	0.0	0	0	0	0	0
June	20	.343	.478	67	23	3	0	2	3.0	6	7	2	8	0
July	26	.227	.273	88	20	1	0	1	1.1	11	4	15	16	1
Aug	25	.262	.369	84	22	4	1	1	1.2	5	4	6	16	0
Sept/Oct	21	.203	.328	64	13	5	0	1	1.6	6	10	4	11	1
Day	26	.271	.318	85	23	2	1	0	0.0	9	3	12	16	0
Night	66	.252	.372	218	55	11	0	5	2.3	19	22	15	35	2
vs. Left		.291	.437	103	30	7	1	2	1.9	10	7	15	15	2
vs. Right		.240	.315	200	48	6	0	3	1.5	18	18	12	36	0
On Grass	78	.253	.354	257	65	12	1	4	1.6	24	21	23	46	2
On Turf	14	.283	.370	46	13	1	0	1	2.2	4	4	4	5	0
Home	49	.265	.361	166	44	11	1	1	0.6	15	13	15	25	1
Road	43	.248	.350	137	34	2	0	4	2.9	13	12	12	26	1
Division Rivals														
vs. BAL	6	.400	.533	15	6	2	0	0	0.0	2	3	0	3	0
vs. BOS	6	.167	.167	12	2	0	0	0	0.0	0	1	1	2	0
vs. CLE	9	.214	.250	28	6	1	0	0	0.0	6	2	4	8	0
vs. DET	9	.242	.364	33	8	1	0	1	3.0	4	2	5	5	1
vs. MIL	10	.351	.432	37	13	3	0	0	0.0	1	1	2	4	0
vs. TOR	12	.279	.395	43	12	2	0	1	2.3	4	5	1	4	0
On 3B < 2 Out		.250	.250	8	2	0	0	0	0.0	0	5	2	2	

Year	Team		Games	BA	SA	AB	H	2B	3B	HR	HR%	R	RBI	BB	SO	SB	AB	H	PO	A	E	DP	TC/G	FA	G by Pos
1990	NY	A	92	.257	.356	303	78	13	1	5	1.6	28	25	27	51	2	4	2	117	107	13	5	2.7	.945	3B-69, OF-14, C-11

THIRD BASE

(Bar charts: AVERAGE, RBI, HR, SB — each compared with AL AVG)

Dave Liddell

LIDDELL, DAVID ALEXANDER
B. June 15, 1966, Los Angeles, Calif.
BR TR 6' 190 lbs.

Year	Team		Games	BA	SA	AB	H	2B	3B	HR	HR%	R	RBI	BB	SO	SB	AB	H	PO	A	E	DP	TC/G	FA	G by Pos
1990	NY	N	1	1.000	1.000	1	1	0	0	0	0.0	1	0	0	0	0	1	1	1	0	0	0	1.0	1.000	C-1

Year	Team		Games	BA	SA	AB	H	2B	3B	HR	HR%	R	RBI	BB	SO	SB	PINCH HIT AB	H	PO	A	E	DP	TC/G	FA	G by Pos

Jose Lind

LIND, JOSE (Chico)
Born Jose Lind y Salgado.
B. May 1, 1964, Toabaja, Puerto Rico
BR TR 5′ 11″ 155 lbs.

Year	Team		Games	BA	SA	AB	H	2B	3B	HR	HR%	R	RBI	BB	SO	SB	AB	H	PO	A	E	DP	TC/G	FA	G by Pos
April			20	.286	.329	70	20	3	0	0	0.0	6	6	7	7	0									
May			25	.333	.444	90	30	8	1	0	0.0	9	13	4	6	2									
June			26	.295	.398	88	26	7	1	0	0.0	9	9	5	9	2									
July			23	.275	.375	80	22	3	1	1	1.3	9	9	5	7	2									
Aug			29	.176	.216	102	18	4	0	0	0.0	5	6	5	12	1									
Sept/Oct			29	.214	.298	84	18	3	2	0	0.0	8	5	9	11	1									
Day			39	.307	.386	127	39	6	2	0	0.0	15	11	9	14	3									
Night			113	.245	.326	387	95	22	3	1	0.3	31	37	26	38	5									
vs. Left				.231	.329	216	50	12	3	1	0.5	16	19	18	21	1									
vs. Right				.282	.349	298	84	16	2	0	0.0	30	29	17	31	7									
On Grass			40	.224	.266	143	32	4	1	0	0.0	15	13	10	15	1									
On Turf			112	.275	.369	371	102	24	4	1	0.3	31	35	25	37	7									
Home			75	.261	.347	245	64	14	2	1	0.4	17	30	13	26	6									
Road			77	.260	.335	269	70	14	3	0	0.0	29	18	22	26	2									
Division Rivals																									
vs. CHI			18	.222	.270	63	14	1	1	0	0.0	2	4	3	8	0									
vs. MON			15	.345	.418	55	19	4	0	0	0.0	4	4	2	6	2									
vs. NY			18	.216	.255	51	11	2	0	0	0.0	4	7	3	6	1									
vs. PHI			18	.286	.393	56	16	4	1	0	0.0	7	5	6	6	0									
vs. STL			17	.276	.379	58	16	6	0	0	0.0	5	3	6	5	1									
On 3B < 2 Out				.300	.400	20	6	0	1	0	0.0	0	19	1	4										
1987	PIT	N	35	.322	.434	143	46	8	4	0	0.0	21	11	8	12	2	0	0	53	139	1	12	5.5	.995	2B-35
1988			154	.262	.324	611	160	24	4	2	0.3	82	49	42	75	15	4	2	333	473	11	73	5.3	.987	2B-153
1989			153	.232	.289	578	134	21	3	2	0.3	52	48	39	64	15	5	2	309	438	18	81	5.0	.976	2B-151
1990			152	.261	.340	514	134	28	5	1	0.1	46	48	35	52	8	0	0	330	449	7	74	5.2	.991	2B-152
4 yrs.			494	.257	.326	1846	474	81	16	5	0.3	201	156	124	203	40	9	4	1025	1499	37	240	5.2	.986	2B-491

LEAGUE CHAMPIONSHIP SERIES

| 1990 | PIT | N | 6 | .238 | .524 | 21 | 5 | 1 | 1 | 1 | 4.7 | 1 | 2 | 1 | 4 | 0 | 0 | 0 | 19 | 19 | 0 | 4 | 6.3 | 1.000 | 2B-6 |

SECOND BASE

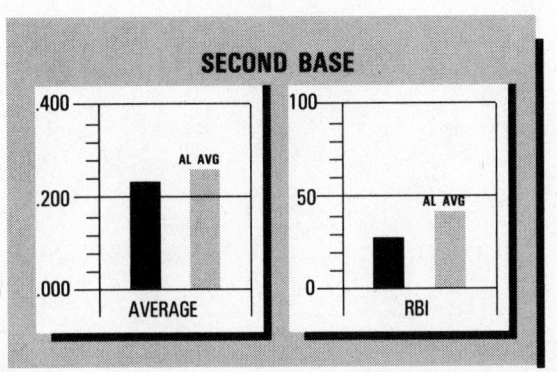

Jim Lindeman

LINDEMAN, JAMES WILLIAM
B. Jan. 10, 1962, Evanston, Ill.
BR TR 6′ 1″ 200 lbs.

Year	Team		Games	BA	SA	AB	H	2B	3B	HR	HR%	R	RBI	BB	SO	SB	AB	H	PO	A	E	DP	TC/G	FA	G by Pos
1986	STL	N	19	.255	.327	55	14	1	0	1	1.8	7	6	2	10	1	2	1	118	10	1	8	6.8	.992	1B-17, 3B-1, OF-1
1987			75	.208	.386	207	43	13	0	8	3.9	20	28	11	56	3	13	2	196	14	3	13	2.8	.986	OF-49, 1B-20
1988			17	.209	.372	43	9	1	0	2	4.7	3	7	2	9	0	4	2	36	2	1	2	2.3	.974	OF-12, 1B-3
1989			73	.111	.133	45	5	1	0	0	0.0	8	2	3	18	0	26	2	93	6	1	7	1.4	.990	1B-42, OF-5
1990	DET	A	12	.219	.438	32	7	1	0	2	6.2	5	8	2	13	0	5	0	5	0	0	0	2.5	1.000	DH-10, 1B-1, OF-1
5 yrs.			196	.204	.351	382	78	17	0	13	3.4	43	51	20	106	4	50	7	448	32	6	30	2.5	.988	1B-83, OF-68, DH-10, 3B-1

LEAGUE CHAMPIONSHIP SERIES

| 1987 | STL | N | 5 | .308 | .538 | 13 | 4 | 0 | 0 | 1 | 7.7 | 1 | 3 | 0 | 3 | 0 | 1 | 0 | 33 | 2 | 0 | 3 | 7.0 | 1.000 | 1B-5 |

WORLD SERIES

| 1987 | STL | N | 6 | .333 | .400 | 15 | 5 | 1 | 0 | 0 | 0.0 | 3 | 2 | 0 | 3 | 0 | 1 | 0 | 28 | 2 | 3 | 2 | 5.5 | .909 | 1B-6, OF-1 |

Nelson Liriano

LIRIANO, NELSON ARTURO
Born Nelson Arturo Liriano y Bonilla.
B. June 3, 1964, Santo Domingo, Dominican Republic
BB TR 5′ 10″ 165 lbs.

Year	Team		Games	BA	SA	AB	H	2B	3B	HR	HR%	R	RBI	BB	SO	SB	AB	H	PO	A	E	DP	TC/G	FA	G by Pos
April			13	.184	.342	38	7	1	1	1	2.6	6	3	8	5	1									
May			16	.204	.296	54	11	3	1	0	0.0	4	8	2	6	1									
June			14	.245	.286	49	12	2	0	0	0.0	5	2	3	5	1									
July			10	.184	.211	38	7	1	0	0	0.0	3	2	5	4	0									
Aug			27	.287	.386	101	29	4	3	0	0.0	14	8	8	13	2									
Sept/Oct			23	.227	.347	75	17	1	4	0	0.0	14	5	12	11	3									
Day			29	.253	.319	91	23	2	2	0	0.0	13	9	13	9	2									
Night			74	.227	.330	264	60	10	7	1	0.4	33	19	25	35	6									
vs. Left				.194	.299	67	13	1	3	0	0.0	8	6	11	12	1									
vs. Right				.243	.333	288	70	11	6	1	0.3	38	22	27	32	7									

SECOND BASE

Year	Team	Games	BA	SA	AB	H	2B	3B	HR	HR%	R	RBI	BB	SO	SB	PINCH HIT AB	H	PO	A	E	DP	TC/G	FA	G by Pos

Nelson Liriano *Continued*

		Games	BA	SA	AB	H	2B	3B	HR	HR%	R	RBI	BB	SO	SB	AB	H	PO	A	E	DP	TC/G	FA	G by Pos
On Grass		34	.227	.309	110	25	3	3	0	0.0	10	2	9	10	1									
On Turf		69	.237	.335	245	58	9	6	1	0.4	36	26	29	34	7									
Home		52	.253	.371	178	45	6	6	1	0.6	30	22	21	23	6									
Road		51	.215	.282	177	38	6	3	0	0.0	16	6	17	21	2									
Division Rivals																								
vs. CAL		8	.200	.367	30	6	1	2	0	0.0	7	6	4	4	0									
vs. CHI		10	.345	.448	29	10	1	1	0	0.0	5	6	3	3	3									
vs. KC		10	.238	.429	42	10	1	2	1	2.4	5	6	3	8	0									
vs. OAK		8	.136	.136	22	3	0	0	0	0.0	0	0	1	1	0									
vs. SEA		13	.143	.184	49	7	2	0	0	0.0	3	3	5	8	1									
vs. TEX		8	.125	.125	24	3	0	0	0	0.0	1	0	3	4	1									
On 3B < 2 Out			.500	.833	12	6	2	1	0	0.0	0	11	0	2										
1987	TOR A	37	.241	.342	158	38	6	2	2	1.3	29	10	16	22	13	1	1	83	107	1	28	5.2	.995	2B-37
1988		99	.264	.333	276	73	6	2	3	1.1	36	23	11	40	12	16	4	121	177	12	48	3.1	.961	2B-80, DH-11, 3B-1
1989		132	.263	.376	418	110	26	3	5	1.2	51	53	43	51	16	7	4	267	330	12	76	4.6	.980	2B-122, DH-5
1990	2 teams	TOR A	(50G — .212)		MIN A	(53G — .254)																		
"	total	103	.234	.327	355	83	12	9	1	0.2	46	28	38	44	8	5	2	176	260	11	53	4.5	.975	2B-99, DH-2, SS-1
4 yrs.		371	.252	.347	1207	304	50	16	11	0.9	162	114	108	157	49	29	11	647	874	36	205	4.2	.977	2B-338, DH-18, 3B-1, SS-1

LEAGUE CHAMPIONSHIP SERIES

1989	TOR A	3	.429	.429	7	3	0	0	0	0.0	1	1	2	0	3	0	0	4	3	1	1	2.7	.875	2B-3

Greg Litton

LITTON, JON GREGORY
B. July 13, 1964, New Orleans, La.
BR TR 6' 175 lbs.

Year	Team	Games	BA	SA	AB	H	2B	3B	HR	HR%	R	RBI	BB	SO	SB	AB	H	PO	A	E	DP	TC/G	FA	G by Pos
1989	SF N	71	.252	.413	143	36	5	3	4	2.8	12	17	7	29	0	27	9	44	66	3	5	1.6	.973	3B-34, 2B-15, SS-9, OF-6, C-2
1990		93	.245	.314	204	50	9	1	1	0.4	17	24	11	45	0	35	5	90	43	1	10	1.7	.993	OF-56, 2B-18, SS-7, 3B-5
2 yrs.		164	.248	.354	347	86	14	4	5	1.4	29	41	18	74	1	62	14	134	109	4	15	1.5	.984	OF-62, 3B-39, 2B-33, SS-16, C-2

LEAGUE CHAMPIONSHIP SERIES

1989	SF N	1	1.000	1.000	1	1	0	0	0	0.0	0	0	0	0	0	1	1	0	0	0	0	0.0	—	

WORLD SERIES

1989	SF N	2	.500	1.167	6	3	1	0	1	16.7	1	3	0	0	0	1	1	2	3	0	0	2.5	1.000	2B-2, 3B-1

Steve Lombardozzi

LOMBARDOZZI, STEPHEN PAUL (Lombo)
B. Apr. 26, 1960, Malden, Mass.
BR TR 6' 175 lbs.

Year	Team	Games	BA	SA	AB	H	2B	3B	HR	HR%	R	RBI	BB	SO	SB	AB	H	PO	A	E	DP	TC/G	FA	G by Pos
1985	MIN A	28	.370	.481	54	20	4	1	0	0.0	10	6	6	6	3	1	0	31	80	2	16	4.0	.982	2B-26
1986		156	.227	.347	453	103	20	5	8	1.8	53	33	52	76	3	0	0	289	407	6	102	4.5	.991	2B-155
1987		136	.238	.352	432	103	19	3	8	1.9	51	38	33	66	5	0	0	245	356	14	77	4.5	.977	2B-133
1988		103	.209	.307	287	60	15	2	3	1.0	34	27	35	48	2	1	1	152	237	5	54	3.8	.987	2B-90, SS-12, 3B-5
1989	HOU N	21	.216	.432	37	8	3	1	1	2.7	5	3	4	9	0	2	0	20	28	4	5	2.5	.923	2B-18, 3B-1
1990		2	.000	.000	1	0	0	0	0	0.0	0	0	1	1	0	1	0	0	0	0	0	0.0	.958	
6 yrs.		446	.233	.347	1264	294	61	12	20	1.6	153	107	131	206	13	5	1	737	1108	31	254	4.2	.983	2B-422, SS-12, 3B-6

LEAGUE CHAMPIONSHIP SERIES

1987	MIN A	5	.267	.267	15	4	0	0	0	0.0	1	1	2	2	0	0	0	8	9	1	3	3.6	.944	2B-5

WORLD SERIES

1987	MIN A	6	.412	.647	17	7	1	0	1	5.9	3	4	2	2	0	0	0	9	24	0	3	5.5	1.000	2B-6

Luis Lopez

LOPEZ, LUIS ANTONIO
B. Sept. 1, 1964, Brooklyn, N. Y.
BR TR 6' 1" 190 lbs.

Year	Team	Games	BA	SA	AB	H	2B	3B	HR	HR%	R	RBI	BB	SO	SB	AB	H	PO	A	E	DP	TC/G	FA	G by Pos
1990	LA N	6	.000	.000	6	0	0	0	0	0.0	0	0	0	2	0	5	0	4	0	0	1	4.0	1.000	1B-1

SECOND BASE

(Bar charts showing HR and SB compared to AL AVG)

Year	Team		Games	BA	SA	AB	H	2B	3B	HR	HR%	R	RBI	BB	SO	SB	PINCH HIT AB	H	PO	A	E	DP	TC/G	FA	G by Pos

Scott Lusader

LUSADER, SCOTT EDWARD
B. Sept. 30, 1964, Chicago, Ill.
BL TL 5' 10" 165 lbs.

Year	Team		Games	BA	SA	AB	H	2B	3B	HR	HR%	R	RBI	BB	SO	SB	AB	H	PO	A	E	DP	TC/G	FA	G by Pos
1987	DET	A	23	.319	.489	47	15	3	1	1	2.1	8	8	5	7	1	0	0	29	0	1	0	1.3	.967	OF-22, DH-1
1988			16	.063	.250	16	1	0	0	1	6.3	3	3	1	4	0	5	0	7	0	0	0	0.4	1.000	DH-6, OF-4
1989			40	.252	.320	103	26	4	0	1	1.0	15	8	9	21	3	8	1	56	0	4	0	1.5	.933	OF-33, DH-1
1990			45	.241	.333	87	21	2	0	2	2.2	13	16	12	8	0	1	0	53	1	1	0	1.3	.982	OF-42, DH-2
4 yrs.			124	.249	.352	253	63	9	1	5	2.0	39	35	27	40	4	14	1	145	1	6	0	1.2	.961	OF-101, DH-10

Fred Lynn

LYNN, FREDRIC MICHAEL
B. Feb. 3, 1952, Chicago, Ill.
BL TL 6' 1" 185 lbs.

Year	Team		Games	BA	SA	AB	H	2B	3B	HR	HR%	R	RBI	BB	SO	SB	AB	H	PO	A	E	DP	TC/G	FA	G by Pos
1974	BOS	A	15	.419	.698	43	18	2	2	2	4.7	5	10	6	6	0	2	0	18	2	0	0	1.3	1.000	OF-15, DH-1
1975			145	.331	**.566**	528	175	**47**	7	21	4.0	**103**	105	62	90	10	2	1	404	11	7	1	2.9	.983	OF-144
1976			132	.314	.467	507	159	32	8	10	2.0	76	65	48	67	14	1	0	367	13	6	4	2.9	.984	OF-128, DH-5
1977			129	.260	.447	497	129	29	5	18	3.6	81	76	51	63	2	3	0	333	7	2	1	2.7	.994	OF-125, DH-1
1978			150	.298	.492	541	161	33	3	22	4.1	75	82	75	50	3	0	0	408	11	7	2	2.8	.984	OF-149
1979			147	**.333**	**.637**	531	177	42	1	39	7.3	116	122	82	79	2	4	1	381	10	5	4	2.7	.987	OF-143, DH-1
1980			110	.301	.480	415	125	32	3	12	2.9	67	61	58	39	12	0	0	302	11	2	4	2.9	.994	OF-110
1981	CAL	A	76	.219	.316	256	56	8	1	5	2.0	28	31	38	42	1	9	1	176	4	4	1	2.4	.978	OF-69
1982			138	.299	.517	472	141	38	1	21	4.4	89	86	58	72	7	10	5	317	6	3	3	2.4	.991	OF-133
1983			117	.272	.483	437	119	20	3	22	5.0	56	74	55	83	2	3	0	274	8	2	4	2.4	.993	OF-113, DH-2
1984			142	.271	.474	517	140	28	4	23	4.4	84	79	77	98	2	5	2	321	12	6	5	2.4	.982	OF-140
1985	BAL	A	124	.263	.449	448	118	12	1	23	5.1	59	68	53	100	7	1	0	314	6	2	2	2.6	.994	OF-123
1986			112	.287	.499	397	114	13	1	23	5.8	67	67	53	59	2	7	3	244	2	4	1	2.2	.984	OF-107, DH-1
1987			111	.253	.487	396	100	24	0	23	5.8	49	60	39	72	3	4	1	229	2	2	1	2.1	.991	OF-101, DH-8
1988	2 teams					BAL A (87G — .252)					DET A (27G — .222)														
"	total		114	.246	.478	391	96	14	1	25	6.4	46	56	33	82	2	7	2	257	3	2	0	2.3	.992	OF-105, DH-5
1989	DET	A	117	.241	.371	353	85	11	1	11	3.1	44	46	47	71	1	17	3	119	5	1	0	1.1	.992	OF-68, DH-46
1990	SD	N	90	.240	.357	196	47	3	1	6	3.0	18	23	22	44	2	32	1	92	1	0	0	1.7	1.000	OF-55
17 yrs.			1969	.283	.484	6925	1960	388	43	306	4.4	1063	1111	857	1117	72	107	30	4556	114	55	33	2.4	.988	OF-1828, DH-70

LEAGUE CHAMPIONSHIP SERIES

Year	Team		Games	BA	SA	AB	H	2B	3B	HR	HR%	R	RBI	BB	SO	SB	AB	H	PO	A	E	DP	TC/G	FA	G by Pos
1975	BOS	A	3	.364	.455	11	4	1	0	0	0.0	1	3	0	0	0	0	0	12	1	1	1	4.7	.929	OF-3
1982	CAL	A	5	.611	.889	18	11	2	0	1	5.6	4	5	2	3	0	0	0	16	0	1	0	3.4	.941	OF-5
2 yrs.			8	.517	.724	29	15	3	0	1	3.4	5	8	2	3	0	0	0	28	1	2	1	3.9	.935	OF-8

WORLD SERIES

Year	Team		Games	BA	SA	AB	H	2B	3B	HR	HR%	R	RBI	BB	SO	SB	AB	H	PO	A	E	DP	TC/G	FA	G by Pos
1975	BOS	A	7	.280	.440	25	7	1	0	1	4.0	3	5	3	5	0	0	0	23	1	0	0	3.4	1.000	OF-7

Barry Lyons

LYONS, BARRY STEPHEN
B. June 3, 1960, Biloxi, Miss.
BR TR 6' 1" 205 lbs.

Year	Team		Games	BA	SA	AB	H	2B	3B	HR	HR%	R	RBI	BB	SO	SB	AB	H	PO	A	E	DP	TC/G	FA	G by Pos
1986	NY	N	6	.000	.000	9	0	0	0	0	0.0	1	2	1	2	0	2	0	16	0	1	0	2.8	.941	C-3
1987			53	.254	.392	130	33	4	1	4	3.1	15	24	8	24	0	4	1	223	17	4	0	4.6	.984	C-49
1988			50	.231	.330	91	21	7	1	0	0.0	5	11	3	12	0	18	3	130	9	3	0	2.8	.979	C-32, 1B-1
1989			79	.247	.340	235	58	13	0	3	1.3	15	27	11	28	0	8	2	463	29	10	4	6.4	.980	C-76
1990	2 teams					NY N (24G — .238)					LA N (3G — .200)														
"	total		27	.235	.341	85	20	0	0	3	3.5	9	9	2	10	0	4	1	183	12	4	1	8.0	.980	C-25
5 yrs.			215	.240	.345	550	132	24	2	10	1.8	45	73	25	76	0	36	7	1015	67	22	5	5.1	.980	C-185, 1B-1

Steve Lyons

LYONS, STEPHEN JOHN (Psycho)
B. June 3, 1960, Tacoma, Wash.
BL TR 6' 3" 190 lbs.

Year	Team		Games	BA	SA	AB	H	2B	3B	HR	HR%	R	RBI	BB	SO	SB	AB	H	PO	A	E	DP	TC/G	FA	G by Pos
1985	BOS	A	133	.264	.358	371	98	14	3	5	1.3	52	30	32	64	12	13	2	253	6	7	0	2.0	.974	OF-114, DH-5, 3B-1, SS-1
1986	2 teams					BOS A (59G — .250)					CHI A (42G — .203)														
"	total		101	.227	.300	247	56	9	3	1	0.4	30	20	19	47	4	7	1	175	11	4	1	1.9	.979	OF-90, 3B-3, DH-1, 1B-1
1987	CHI	A	76	.280	.363	193	54	11	1	1	0.5	26	19	12	37	3	4	0	69	101	4	12	2.3	.977	3B-51, OF-15, 2B-1
1988			146	.269	.373	472	127	28	3	5	1.1	59	45	32	59	1	3	1	128	243	29	38	2.7	.928	3B-128, OF-14, 2B-4, C-2, 1B-1

Year	Team	Games	BA	SA	AB	H	2B	3B	HR	HR%	R	RBI	BB	SO	SB	PINCH HIT AB	H	PO	A	E	DP	TC/G	FA	G by Pos

Steve Lyons   *Continued*

1989		140	.264	.339	443	117	21	3	2	0.5	51	50	35	68	9	14	5	414	245	15	73	4.8	.978	2B-70, 1B-40, 3B-28, OF-20, SS-3, DH-1, C-1
1990		94	.192	.267	146	28	6	1	1	0.6	22	11	10	41	1	21	3	244	54	5	33	3.7	.984	1B-61, 2B-15, OF-7, 3B-5, DH-3, P-1, SS-1
6 yrs.		690	.256	.343	1872	480	89	14	15	0.8	240	175	140	316	30	62	12	1283	660	64	157	2.9	.968	OF-260, 3B-216, 1B-103, 2B-90, DH-10, SS-5, C-3, P-1

Kevin Maas

MAAS, KEVIN CHRISTIAN
B. Jan. 20, 1965, Castro Valley, Calif.
BL TL 6′ 3″ 195 lbs.

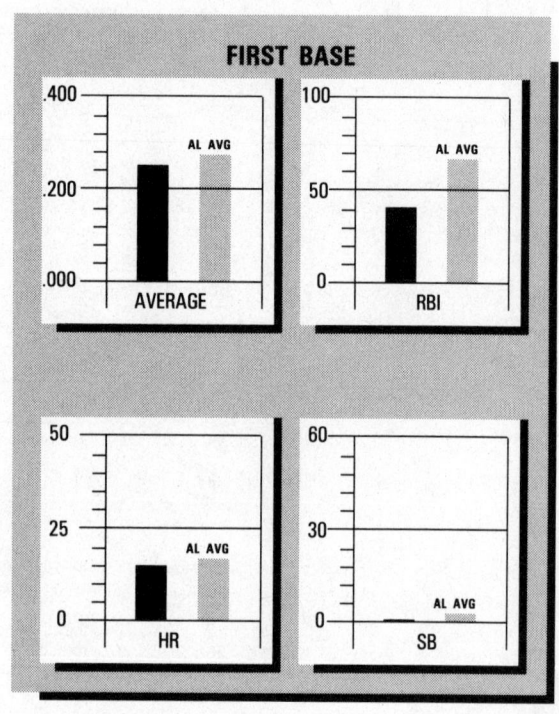

FIRST BASE

	Games	BA	SA	AB	H	2B	3B	HR	HR%	R	RBI	BB	SO	SB
April				0	0	0	0	0		0	0	0	0	0
May				0	0	0	0	0		0	0	0	0	0
June	2	.333	.333	6	2	0	0	0	0.0	0	1	1	1	0
July	21	.270	.667	63	17	1	0	8	12.7	14	14	13	21	0
Aug	30	.260	.548	104	27	6	0	8	7.7	17	15	12	31	1
Sept/Oct	26	.222	.432	81	18	2	0	5	6.2	11	11	17	23	0
Day	22	.254	.537	67	17	1	0	6	9.0	9	14	10	19	1
Night	57	.251	.535	187	47	8	0	15	8.0	33	27	33	57	0
vs. Left		.164	.313	67	11	1	0	3	4.5	4	8	10	28	0
vs. Right		.283	.615	187	53	8	0	18	9.6	38	33	33	48	1
On Grass	68	.263	.553	217	57	9	0	18	8.3	36	38	36	63	1
On Turf	11	.189	.432	37	7	0	0	3	8.1	6	3	7	13	0
Home	43	.281	.593	135	38	6	0	12	8.9	26	27	23	38	1
Road	36	.218	.471	119	26	3	0	9	7.6	16	14	20	38	0
Division Rivals														
vs. BAL	7	.448	.759	29	13	3	0	2	6.9	7	5	2	5	0
vs. BOS	6	.143	.143	14	2	0	0	0	0.0	0	1	2	5	0
vs. CLE	8	.179	.321	28	5	1	0	1	3.6	2	3	5	7	0
vs. DET	7	.400	1.000	25	10	0	0	5	20.0	8	7	7	3	0
vs. MIL	6	.150	.200	20	3	1	0	0	0.0	2	0	2	7	1
vs. TOR	6	.250	.550	20	5	0	0	2	10.0	4	3	5	6	0
On 3B < 2 Out		.444	.778	9	4	0	0	1	11.1	1	8	4	2	

Year	Team		Games	BA	SA	AB	H	2B	3B	HR	HR%	R	RBI	BB	SO	SB	AB	H	PO	A	E	DP	TC/G	FA	G by Pos
1990	NY	A	79	.252	.535	254	64	9	0	21	8.2	42	41	43	76	1	5	0	486	35	9	45	9.3	.983	1B-57, DH-18

Mike Macfarlane

MACFARLANE, MICHAEL ANDREW (Mac)
B. Apr. 12, 1964, Stockton, Calif.
BR TR 6′ 1″ 200 lbs.

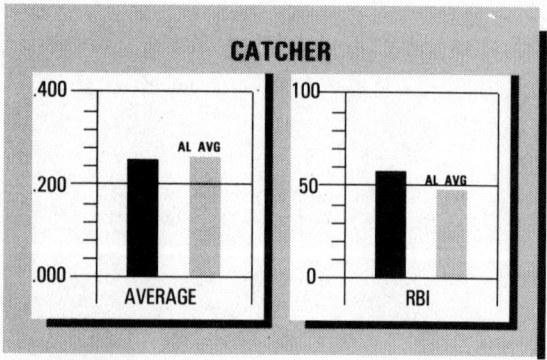

CATCHER

	Games	BA	SA	AB	H	2B	3B	HR	HR%	R	RBI	BB	SO	SB
April	8	.346	.500	26	9	4	0	0	0.0	0	3	0	4	0
May	20	.271	.443	70	19	5	2	1	1.4	5	11	4	15	0
June	25	.220	.268	82	18	2	1	0	0.0	6	9	3	8	1
July	25	.333	.506	81	27	8	0	2	2.5	15	16	7	14	0
Aug	25	.200	.347	75	15	2	0	3	4.0	5	16	6	16	0
Sept/Oct	21	.212	.288	66	14	3	1	0	0.0	6	3	5	12	0
Day	25	.273	.424	66	18	5	1	1	1.5	8	10	5	11	0
Night	99	.251	.371	334	84	19	3	5	1.5	29	48	20	58	1
vs. Left		.245	.381	147	36	8	3	2	1.4	15	12	9	26	1
vs. Right		.261	.379	253	66	16	1	4	1.6	22	46	16	43	0

Year	Team	Games	BA	SA	AB	H	2B	3B	HR	HR%	R	RBI	BB	SO	SB	PINCH HIT AB	H	PO	A	E	DP	TC/G	FA	G by Pos

Mike Macfarlane *Continued*

Year	Team	Games	BA	SA	AB	H	2B	3B	HR	HR%	R	RBI	BB	SO	SB	AB	H	PO	A	E	DP	TC/G	FA	G by Pos
On Grass		49	.256	.378	156	40	8	1	3	1.9	17	22	10	27	0									
On Turf		75	.254	.381	244	62	16	3	3	1.2	20	36	15	42	1									
Home		61	.257	.372	191	49	13	3	1	0.5	17	30	13	32	0									
Road		63	.254	.388	209	53	11	1	5	2.4	20	28	12	37	1									
Division Rivals																								
vs. CAL		11	.278	.389	36	10	2	1	0	0.0	6	3	2	5	0									
vs. CHI		7	.217	.261	23	5	1	0	0	0.0	1	3	4	1	0									
vs. MIN		9	.265	.412	34	9	2	0	1	2.9	2	7	1	7	0									
vs. OAK		13	.139	.194	36	5	0	1	0	0.0	2	4	1	7	0									
vs. SEA		12	.216	.270	37	8	2	0	0	0.0	2	3	1	7	1									
vs. TEX		11	.194	.226	31	6	1	0	0	0.0	1	4	4	8	0									
On 3B < 2 Out			.350	.500	20	7	0	0	1	5.0	1	18	1	5										
1987	KC A	8	.211	.263	19	4	1	0	0	0.0	0	3	2	2	0	0	0	29	2	0	0	3.9	1.000	C-8
1988		70	.265	.393	211	56	15	0	4	1.9	25	26	21	37	0	4	0	309	18	2	3	4.7	.994	C-68
1989		69	.223	.299	157	35	6	0	2	1.3	13	19	7	27	0	12	2	249	17	1	4	3.9	.996	C-59, DH-4
1990		124	.255	.380	400	102	24	4	6	1.5	37	58	25	69	1	13	3	660	23	6	9	6.2	.991	C-112, DH-5
4 yrs.		271	.250	.365	787	197	46	4	12	1.5	75	106	55	135	1	29	5	1247	60	9	16	4.9	.993	C-247, DH-9

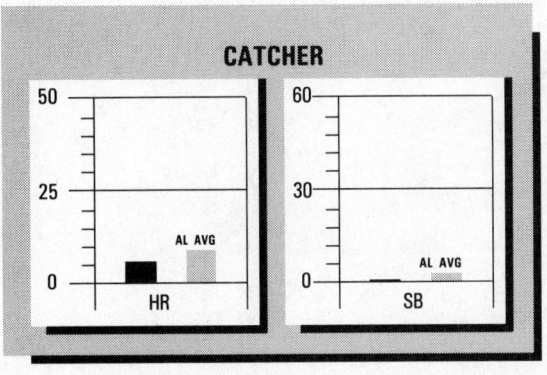

CATCHER

Shane Mack

MACK, SHANE LEE
B. Dec. 7, 1963, Los Angeles, Calif.
BR TR 6′ 185 lbs.

Year	Team	Games	BA	SA	AB	H	2B	3B	HR	HR%	R	RBI	BB	SO	SB	AB	H	PO	A	E	DP	TC/G	FA	G by Pos
April		12	.333	.611	18	6	2	0	1	5.6	5	2	3	1	0									
May		18	.424	.576	33	14	1	2	0	0.0	8	5	3	6	1									
June		17	.231	.385	39	9	0	0	2	5.1	6	5	3	12	1									
July		25	.306	.431	72	22	1	1	2	2.8	13	6	8	18	3									
Aug		25	.206	.286	63	13	2	0	1	1.6	5	9	5	15	2									
Sept/Oct		28	.432	.568	88	38	4	1	2	2.3	13	17	7	17	6									
Day		35	.371	.485	97	36	6	1	1	1.0	16	20	7	20	3									
Night		90	.306	.449	216	66	4	3	7	3.2	34	24	22	49	10									
vs. Left			.370	.548	146	54	9	1	5	3.4	20	27	15	26	4									
vs. Right			.287	.383	167	48	1	3	3	1.8	30	17	14	43	9									
On Grass		52	.307	.365	137	42	3	1	1	0.7	15	13	13	23	9									
On Turf		73	.341	.534	176	60	7	3	7	4.0	35	31	16	46	4									
Home		59	.369	.560	141	52	6	3	5	3.5	31	21	14	33	3									
Road		66	.291	.378	172	50	4	1	3	1.7	19	23	15	36	10									
Division Rivals																								
vs. CAL		12	.467	.667	30	14	3	0	1	3.3	6	4	6	6	1									
vs. CHI		9	.238	.286	21	5	1	0	0	0.0	2	2	2	6	3									
vs. KC		9	.250	.250	16	4	0	0	0	0.0	2	2	2	5	1									
vs. OAK		12	.192	.192	26	5	0	0	0	0.0	4	1	2	8	0									
vs. SEA		10	.321	.393	28	9	2	0	0	0.0	3	3	3	10	0									
vs. TEX		11	.217	.348	23	5	0	0	1	4.3	3	2	1	5	0									
On 3B < 2 Out			.400	.467	15	6	1	0	0	0.0	0	11	6	4										
1987	SD N	105	.239	.361	238	57	11	3	4	1.7	28	25	18	47	4	20	3	159	1	3	0	1.6	.982	OF-91
1988		56	.244	.269	119	29	3	0	0	0.0	13	12	14	21	5	0	0	110	4	2	1	2.1	.983	OF-55
1990	MIN A	125	.326	.460	313	102	10	4	8	2.5	50	44	29	69	13	16	7	230	8	3	1	2.2	.988	OF-109, DH-4
3 yrs.		286	.281	.391	670	188	24	7	12	1.8	91	81	61	137	22	36	10	499	13	8	2	1.8	.985	OF-255, DH-4

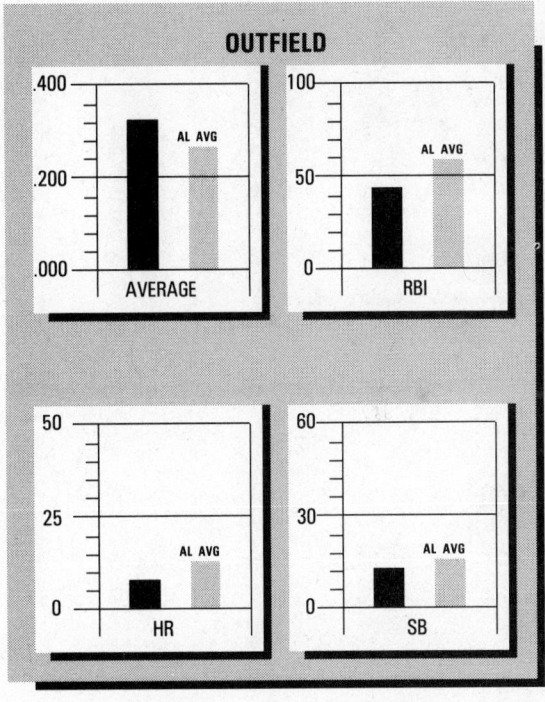

OUTFIELD

Year	Team	Games	BA	SA	AB	H	2B	3B	HR	HR%	R	RBI	BB	SO	SB	PINCH HIT AB	H	PO	A	E	DP	TC/G	FA	G by Pos

Dave Magadan

MAGADAN, DAVID JOSEPH
B. Sept. 30, 1962, Tampa, Fla.
BL TR 6′ 3″ 190 lbs.

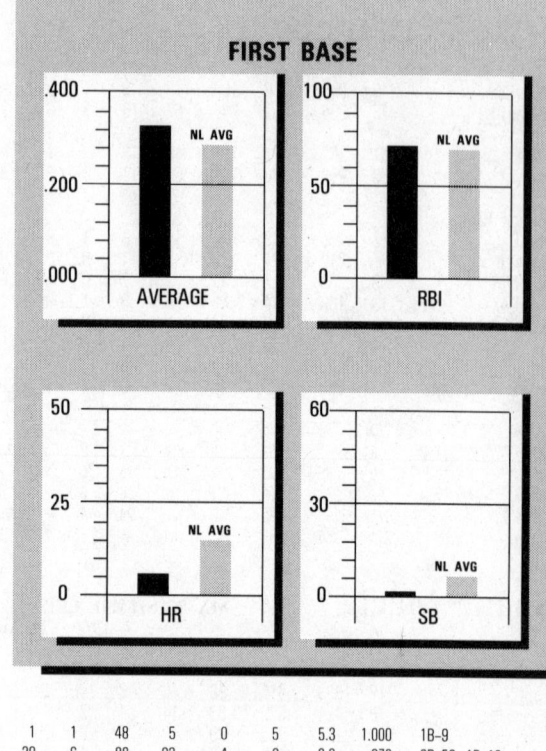

FIRST BASE

Year	Team	Games	BA	SA	AB	H	2B	3B	HR	HR%	R	RBI	BB	SO	SB	PH AB	H	PO	A	E	DP	TC/G	FA	G by Pos
April		15	.231	.269	26	6	1	0	0	0.0	1	1	4	5	0									
May		15	.353	.353	34	12	0	0	0	0.0	2	2	5	6	0									
June		27	.402	.598	87	35	5	3	2	2.3	23	17	14	9	0									
July		28	.333	.490	102	34	8	1	2	2.0	19	17	13	8	0									
Aug		29	.284	.324	102	29	4	0	0	0.0	14	13	23	12	2									
Sept/Oct		30	.320	.520	100	32	10	2	2	2.0	15	22	15	15	0									
Day		47	.310	.483	145	45	9	2	4	2.8	31	25	25	19	0									
Night		97	.337	.444	306	103	19	4	2	0.7	43	47	49	36	2									
vs. Left			.256	.351	168	43	6	2	2	1.2	24	27	20	22	1									
vs. Right			.371	.519	283	105	22	4	4	1.4	50	45	54	33	1									
On Grass		102	.308	.410	305	94	13	3	4	1.3	55	54	59	41	2									
On Turf		42	.370	.555	146	54	15	3	2	1.4	19	18	15	14	0									
Home		73	.278	.373	212	59	10	2	2	0.9	40	34	42	26	1									
Road		71	.372	.531	239	89	18	4	4	1.7	34	38	32	29	1									
Division Rivals																								
vs. CHI		16	.364	.582	55	20	4	1	2	3.6	9	18	10	12	0									
vs. MON		17	.311	.444	45	14	6	0	0	0.0	6	4	6	6	0									
vs. PHI		17	.263	.509	57	15	2	3	2	3.5	17	9	10	6	0									
vs. PIT		16	.391	.587	46	18	6	0	1	2.2	8	7	7	3	0									
vs. STL		16	.344	.453	64	22	3	2	0	0.0	10	11	7	7	0									
On 3B < 2 Out			.350	.500	20	7	0	0	1	5.0	1	25	2	2										
1986	NY N	10	.444	.444	18	8	0	0	0	0.0	3	3	3	1	0	1	1	48	5	0	5	5.3	1.000	1B-9
1987		85	.318	.443	192	61	13	1	3	1.6	21	24	22	22	0	30	6	88	92	4	9	2.2	.978	3B-50, 1B-13
1988		112	.277	.334	314	87	15	0	1	0.3	39	35	60	39	0	12	1	459	99	10	42	5.1	.982	1B-71, 3B-48
1989		127	.286	.393	374	107	22	3	4	1.1	47	41	49	37	1	23	5	587	89	7	54	5.4	.990	1B-87, 3B-28
1990		144	.328	.457	451	148	28	6	6	1.3	74	72	74	55	2	22	9	837	99	3	53	7.4	.997	1B-113, 3B-19
5 yrs.		478	.305	.408	1349	411	78	10	14	1.0	184	175	208	154	3	88	22	2019	384	24	163	5.1	.990	1B-293, 3B-145

LEAGUE CHAMPIONSHIP SERIES

Year	Team	Games	BA	SA	AB	H	2B	3B	HR	HR%	R	RBI	BB	SO	SB	PH AB	H	PO	A	E	DP	TC/G	FA	G by Pos
1988	NY N	3	.000	.000	3	0	0	0	0	0.0	0	0	0	2	0	3	0	0	0	0	0	0.0	—	

Candy Maldonado

MALDONADO, CANDIDO
Born Candido Maldonado y Guadarrama.
B. Sept. 5, 1960, Humacao, Puerto Rico
BR TR 6′ 185 lbs.

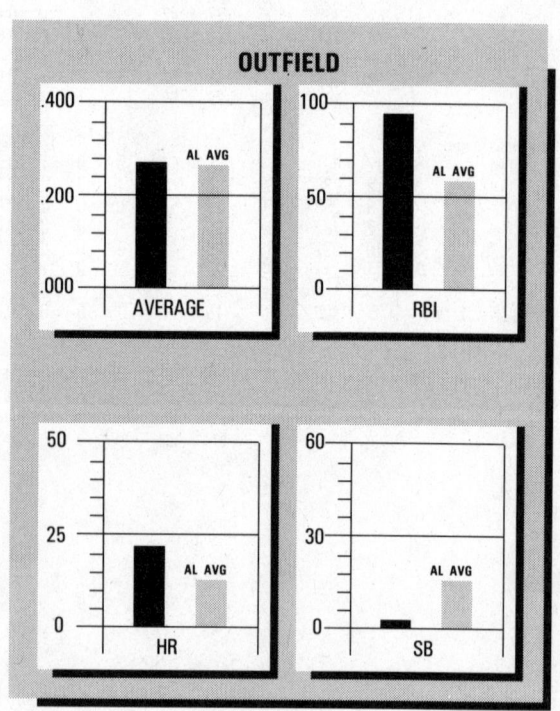

OUTFIELD

Year	Team	Games	BA	SA	AB	H	2B	3B	HR	HR%	R	RBI	BB	SO	SB
April		18	.319	.551	69	22	4	0	4	5.8	9	12	3	16	1
May		25	.300	.567	90	27	6	0	6	6.7	16	20	10	24	0
June		26	.204	.367	98	20	7	0	3	3.1	13	12	12	20	0
July		30	.268	.366	112	30	5	0	2	1.8	12	13	12	30	2
Aug		27	.284	.413	109	31	5	0	3	2.8	13	19	7	21	0
Sept/Oct		29	.277	.464	112	31	5	2	4	3.6	13	19	5	23	0
Day		43	.343	.590	166	57	8	0	11	6.6	28	38	10	33	1
Night		112	.245	.389	424	104	24	2	11	2.6	48	57	39	101	2
vs. Left			.331	.543	175	58	7	0	10	5.7	27	34	16	32	2
vs. Right			.248	.405	415	103	25	2	12	2.9	49	61	33	102	1
On Grass		132	.272	.434	500	136	25	1	18	3.6	61	81	40	112	2
On Turf		23	.278	.511	90	25	7	1	4	4.4	15	14	9	22	1
Home		78	.268	.426	298	80	11	0	12	4.0	35	48	19	73	1
Road		77	.277	.466	292	81	21	2	10	3.4	41	47	30	61	2
Division Rivals															
vs. BAL		12	.250	.333	48	12	1	0	1	2.1	3	7	5	4	0
vs. BOS		13	.236	.309	55	13	4	0	0	0.0	6	5	3	18	0
vs. DET		13	.213	.383	47	10	2	0	2	4.3	3	9	7	12	0
vs. MIL		12	.302	.512	43	13	3	0	2	4.7	7	7	4	7	0
vs. NY		13	.220	.300	50	11	1	0	1	2.0	6	11	6	10	0
vs. TOR		12	.200	.489	45	9	1	0	4	8.9	5	7	0	10	0
On 3B < 2 Out			.289	.342	38	11	2	0	0	0.0	0	31	9	11	

Year	Team		Games	BA	SA	AB	H	2B	3B	HR	HR%	R	RBI	BB	SO	SB	PINCH HIT AB	H	PO	A	E	DP	TC/G	FA	G by Pos

Candy Maldonado *Continued*

Year	Team		Games	BA	SA	AB	H	2B	3B	HR	HR%	R	RBI	BB	SO	SB	PH AB	H	PO	A	E	DP	TC/G	FA	G by Pos
1981	LA	N	11	.083	.083	12	1	0	0	0	0.0	0	0	0	5	0	4	0	8	0	0	0	0.7	1.000	OF-9
1982			6	.000	.000	4	0	0	0	0	0.0	0	0	1	2	0	2	0	5	0	0	0	0.8	1.000	OF-3
1983			42	.194	.290	62	12	1	1	1	1.6	5	6	5	14	0	9	2	26	0	0	0	0.6	1.000	OF-33
1984			116	.268	.382	254	68	14	0	5	2.0	25	28	19	29	0	31	9	124	5	8	0	1.2	.942	OF-102, 3B-4
1985			121	.225	.338	213	48	7	1	5	2.3	20	19	19	40	1	31	7	121	6	2	0	1.1	.984	OF-113
1986	SF	N	133	.252	.477	405	102	31	3	18	4.4	49	85	20	77	4	40	17	161	11	3	0	1.3	.983	OF-101, 3B-1
1987			118	.292	.509	442	129	28	4	20	4.5	69	85	34	78	8	4	1	176	7	5	0	1.6	.973	OF-116
1988			142	.255	.377	499	127	23	1	12	2.4	53	68	37	89	6	5	0	251	5	10	1	1.9	.962	OF-139
1989			129	.217	.362	345	75	23	0	9	2.6	39	41	37	69	4	30	7	181	6	5	1	1.5	.974	OF-116
1990	CLE	A	155	.273	.446	590	161	32	2	22	3.7	76	95	49	134	3	1	0	293	9	2	1	2.3	.993	OF-134, DH-20
10 yrs.			973	.256	.418	2826	723	159	12	92	3.3	336	427	221	537	26	157	43	1346	49	35	3	1.5	.976	OF-866, DH-20, 3B-5

LEAGUE CHAMPIONSHIP SERIES

Year	Team		Games	BA	SA	AB	H	2B	3B	HR	HR%	R	RBI	BB	SO	SB	PH AB	H	PO	A	E	DP	TC/G	FA	G by Pos
1983	LA	N	2	.000	.000	2	0	0	0	0	0.0	0	0	0	1	0	2	0	0	0	0	0	0.0	—	OF-3
1985			4	.143	.143	7	1	0	0	0	0.0	0	1	0	3	0	1	0	4	0	1	0	1.3	.800	OF-3
1987	SF	N	5	.211	.263	19	4	1	0	0	0.0	2	2	0	3	0	0	0	7	0	0	0	1.4	1.000	OF-5
1989			3	.000	.000	3	0	0	0	0	0.0	1	1	2	0	0	1	0	2	0	0	0	0.7	1.000	OF-3
4 yrs.			14	.161	.194	31	5	1	0	0	0.0	3	4	2	7	0	4	0	13	0	1	0	1.0	.000	OF-11

WORLD SERIES

Year	Team		Games	BA	SA	AB	H	2B	3B	HR	HR%	R	RBI	BB	SO	SB	PH AB	H	PO	A	E	DP	TC/G	FA	G by Pos
1989	SF	N	4	.091	.273	11	1	0	1	0	0.0	1	0	0	4	0	1	1	5	0	0	0	1.3	1.000	OF-3

Kelly Mann

MANN, KELLY JOHN
B. Aug. 17, 1967, Santa Monica, Calif.
BR TR 6′ 3″ 215 lbs.

Year	Team		Games	BA	SA	AB	H	2B	3B	HR	HR%	R	RBI	BB	SO	SB	PH AB	H	PO	A	E	DP	TC/G	FA	G by Pos
1989	ATL	N	7	.208	.292	24	5	2	0	0	0.0	1	1	0	6	0	0	0	48	5	0	0	7.6	1.000	C-7
1990			11	.143	.286	28	4	1	0	1	3.5	2	2	0	6	0	1	0	40	3	0	1	4.3	1.000	C-10
2 yrs.			18	.173	.288	52	9	3	0	1	1.9	3	3	0	12	0	1	0	88	8	0	1	5.3	.000	C-17

Fred Manrique

MANRIQUE, FRED ELOY
Born Fred Eloy Manrique y Reyes.
B. May 11, 1961, Edo Bolivar, Venezuela
BR TR 6′ 1″ 175 lbs.

Year	Team		Games	BA	SA	AB	H	2B	3B	HR	HR%	R	RBI	BB	SO	SB	PH AB	H	PO	A	E	DP	TC/G	FA	G by Pos
1981	TOR	A	14	.143	.143	28	4	0	0	0	0.0	1	1	0	12	0	2	1	10	27	3	7	2.9	.925	SS-11, 3B-2, DH-1
1984			10	.333	.333	9	3	0	0	0	0.0	0	1	0	1	0	1	0	5	10	1	3	1.6	.938	2B-9, DH-1
1985	MON	N	9	.308	.769	13	4	1	1	1	7.7	5	1	1	3	0	4	2	5	10	0	1	1.7	1.000	2B-2, SS-2, 3B-1
1986	STL	N	13	.176	.353	17	3	0	0	1	5.9	2	1	1	1	1	7	1	1	3	0	0	0.3	1.000	3B-4, 2B-1
1987	CHI	A	115	.258	.362	298	77	13	3	4	1.3	30	29	19	69	5	1	0	176	286	7	64	4.1	.985	2B-92, SS-23
1988			140	.235	.342	345	81	10	6	5	1.4	43	37	21	54	6	5	1	241	343	13	83	4.3	.978	2B-129, SS-12
1989	2 teams		CHI A (65G — .299)			TEX A (54G — .288)																			
"	total		119	.294	.397	378	111	25	1	4	1.1	46	52	17	63	4	8	3	177	250	21	61	3.8	.953	2B-74, SS-39, 3B-7, DH-1
1990	MIN	A	69	.237	.346	228	54	10	0	5	2.1	22	29	4	35	2	5	1	104	155	7	40	4.0	.974	2B-67, DH-1
8 yrs.			489	.256	.363	1316	337	59	11	20	1.5	149	151	63	238	18	33	9	719	1084	52	259	3.8	.972	2B-374, SS-87, 3B-14, DH-4

Jeff Manto

MANTO, JEFFERY PAUL
B. Aug. 23, 1964, Bristol, Pa.
BR TR 6′ 3″ 210 lbs.

Year	Team		Games	BA	SA	AB	H	2B	3B	HR	HR%	R	RBI	BB	SO	SB	PH AB	H	PO	A	E	DP	TC/G	FA	G by Pos
1990	CLE	A	30	.224	.395	76	17	5	1	2	2.6	12	14	21	18	0	1	0	185	24	2	18	7.3	.991	1B-25, 3B-5

Kirt Manwaring

MANWARING, KIRT DEAN
B. July 15, 1965, Elmira, N. Y.
BR TR 6′ 1″ 195 lbs.

Year	Team		Games	BA	SA	AB	H	2B	3B	HR	HR%	R	RBI	BB	SO	SB	PH AB	H	PO	A	E	DP	TC/G	FA	G by Pos
1987	SF	N	6	.143	.143	7	1	0	0	0	0.0	0	0	0	1	0	0	0	9	1	1	0	1.8	.909	C-6
1988			40	.250	.336	116	29	7	0	1	0.9	12	15	2	21	0	0	0	162	24	4	2	4.8	.979	C-40
1989			85	.210	.250	200	42	4	2	0	0.0	14	18	11	28	2	9	2	289	32	6	3	3.8	.982	C-81
1990			8	.154	.308	13	2	0	1	0	0.0	0	1	0	3	0	0	0	22	3	0	1	3.1	1.000	C-8
4 yrs.			139	.220	.280	336	74	11	3	1	0.3	26	34	13	53	2	9	2	482	60	11	6	4.0	.980	C-135

LEAGUE CHAMPIONSHIP SERIES

Year	Team		Games	BA	SA	AB	H	2B	3B	HR	HR%	R	RBI	BB	SO	SB	PH AB	H	PO	A	E	DP	TC/G	FA	G by Pos
1989	SF	N	3	.000	.000	2	0	0	0	0	0.0	0	0	0	0	0	1	0	5	0	0	0	1.7	1.000	C-3

Year	Team		Games	BA	SA	AB	H	2B	3B	HR	HR%	R	RBI	BB	SO	SB	PINCH HIT AB	PINCH HIT H	PO	A	E	DP	TC/G	FA	G by Pos

Kirt Manwaring   *Continued*

WORLD SERIES

Year	Team		Games	BA	SA	AB	H	2B	3B	HR	HR%	R	RBI	BB	SO	SB	PH AB	PH H	PO	A	E	DP	TC/G	FA	G by Pos
1989	SF	N	1	1.000	2.000	1	1	1	0	0	0.0	1	0	0	0	0	0	0	0	0	0	0	0.0	—	C-1

Mike Marshall

MARSHALL, MICHAEL ALLEN (Moose)
B. Jan. 12, 1960, Libertyville, Ill.
BR TR 6′ 5″ 215 lbs.
See Player Register Supplement for complete graphic analysis.

Year	Team		Games	BA	SA	AB	H	2B	3B	HR	HR%	R	RBI	BB	SO	SB	PH AB	PH H	PO	A	E	DP	TC/G	FA	G by Pos
1981	LA	N	14	.200	.320	25	5	3	0	0	0.0	2	1	1	4	0	7	3	14	2	0	2	1.1	1.000	1B-3, 3B-3, OF-2
1982			49	.242	.432	95	23	3	0	5	5.3	10	9	13	23	2	20	3	122	5	2	6	2.6	.984	OF-19, 1B-13
1983			140	.284	.434	465	132	17	1	17	3.7	47	65	43	127	7	6	1	395	21	6	16	3.0	.986	OF-109, 1B-33
1984			134	.257	.438	495	127	27	0	21	4.2	69	65	40	93	4	7	2	331	17	5	12	2.6	.986	OF-118, 1B-15
1985			135	.293	.515	518	152	27	2	28	5.4	72	95	37	137	3	3	0	265	12	4	9	2.1	.986	OF-125, 1B-7
1986			103	.233	.439	330	77	11	0	19	5.8	47	53	27	90	4	1	0	149	8	6	1	1.6	.963	OF-97
1987			104	.294	.460	402	118	19	0	16	4.0	45	72	18	79	0	2	1	147	4	2	0	1.5	.987	OF-102
1988			144	.277	.445	542	150	27	2	20	3.7	63	82	24	93	4	4	0	605	49	7	31	4.6	.989	OF-143
1989			105	.260	.408	377	98	21	1	11	2.9	41	42	33	78	2	5	2	179	2	4	0	1.8	.978	OF-102
1990	2 teams		NY N	(53G — .239)		BOS A	(30G — .286)																		
"	total		83	.258	.433	275	71	14	2	10	3.6	34	39	11	66	0	9	1	332	31	3	24	6.2	.992	1B-50, DH-14, OF-9
	10 yrs.		1011	.270	.448	3524	953	169	8	147	4.2	430	523	247	790	26	64	13	2539	151	39	101	2.7	.986	OF-826, 1B-121, DH-14, 3B-3

DIVISIONAL PLAYOFF SERIES

Year	Team		Games	BA	SA	AB	H	2B	3B	HR	HR%	R	RBI	BB	SO	SB	PH AB	PH H	PO	A	E	DP	TC/G	FA	G by Pos
1981	LA	N	1	.000	.000	1	0	0	0	0	0.0	0	0	0	1	0	1	0	0	0	0	0	0.0	—	

LEAGUE CHAMPIONSHIP SERIES

Year	Team		Games	BA	SA	AB	H	2B	3B	HR	HR%	R	RBI	BB	SO	SB	PH AB	PH H	PO	A	E	DP	TC/G	FA	G by Pos
1983	LA	N	4	.133	.400	15	2	1	0	1	6.7	1	2	1	6	0	0	0	18	2	0	0	5.0	1.000	1B-3, OF-2
1985			6	.217	.435	23	5	2	0	1	4.3	1	3	1	3	0	0	0	8	0	0	0	1.3	1.000	OF-6
1988			7	.233	.333	30	7	1	1	0	0.0	3	5	2	9	0	0	0	14	0	0	0	2.0	1.000	OF-7
1990	BOS	A	3	.333	.333	3	1	0	0	0	0.0	0	0	0	0	0	3	1	0	0	0	0	0.0	1.000	
	4 yrs.		20	.211	.380	71	15	4	1	2	2.8	5	10	4	18	0	3	1	40	2	0	0	2.1	1.000	OF-15, 1B-3

WORLD SERIES

Year	Team		Games	BA	SA	AB	H	2B	3B	HR	HR%	R	RBI	BB	SO	SB	PH AB	PH H	PO	A	E	DP	TC/G	FA	G by Pos
1988	LA	N	5	.231	.615	13	3	0	1	1	7.7	2	3	0	5	0	0	0	6	0	0	0	1.2	1.000	OF-5

Carlos Martinez

MARTINEZ, CARLOS ALBERTO
Born Carlos Alberto Escobar y Martinez.
B. Aug. 11, 1964, LaGuaira, Venezuela
BR TR 6′ 5″ 175 lbs.

	Games	BA	SA	AB	H	2B	3B	HR	HR%	R	RBI	BB	SO	SB
April	15	.241	.426	54	13	2	1	2	3.7	9	10	2	7	0
May	23	.145	.237	76	11	2	1	1	1.3	3	8	4	13	0
June	18	.294	.314	51	15	1	0	0	0.0	2	2	2	9	0
July	12	.270	.405	37	10	1	2	0	0.0	2	1	1	3	0
Aug	19	.190	.310	42	8	0	1	1	2.4	2	1	1	3	0
Sept/Oct	5	.333	.333	12	4	0	0	0	0.0	0	2	0	5	0
Day	23	.152	.242	66	10	0	0	2	3.0	5	8	4	10	0
Night	69	.248	.354	206	51	6	5	2	1.0	13	16	6	30	0
vs. Left		.221	.307	140	31	2	2	2	1.4	9	7	5	20	0
vs. Right		.227	.348	132	30	4	3	2	1.5	9	17	5	20	0
On Grass	79	.230	.339	230	53	6	5	3	1.3	16	23	9	36	0
On Turf	13	.190	.262	42	8	0	0	1	2.4	2	1	1	4	0
Home	51	.224	.340	147	33	5	3	2	1.4	10	16	6	24	0
Road	41	.224	.312	125	28	1	2	2	1.6	8	8	4	16	0
Division Rivals														
vs. CAL	10	.185	.185	27	5	0	0	0	0.0	0	1	1	5	0
vs. KC	7	.136	.273	22	3	1	1	0	0.0	0	3	1	3	0
vs. MIN	8	.318	.500	22	7	1	0	1	4.5	1	3	1	4	0
vs. OAK	2	.000	.000	0	0	0	0	0	0.0	0	0	1	0	0
vs. SEA	6	.333	.333	18	6	0	0	0	0.0	2	0	0	3	0
vs. TEX	11	.355	.452	31	11	1	1	0	0.0	4	3	1	4	0
On 3B < 2 Out		.286	.571	7	2	0	1	0	0.0	0	3	3	3	

FIRST BASE

AVERAGE · RBI · HR · SB (bar charts with AL AVG comparisons)

Year	Team		Games	BA	SA	AB	H	2B	3B	HR	HR%	R	RBI	BB	SO	SB	PINCH HIT AB	PINCH HIT H	PO	A	E	DP	TC/G	FA	G by Pos

Carlos Martinez *Continued*

Year	Team		Games	BA	SA	AB	H	2B	3B	HR	HR%	R	RBI	BB	SO	SB	PH AB	PH H	PO	A	E	DP	TC/G	FA	G by Pos
1988	CHI	A	17	.164	.182	55	9	1	0	0	0.0	5	0	0	12	1	0	0	7	33	4	1	2.6	.909	3B-15
1989			109	.300	.406	350	105	22	0	5	1.4	44	32	21	57	4	5	2	283	134	20	25	4.0	.954	3B-68, 1B-34, OF-10, DH-1
1990			92	.224	.327	272	61	6	5	4	1.4	18	24	10	40	0	10	3	632	38	8	50	8.3	.988	1B-82, DH-3, OF-1
3 yrs.			218	.258	.356	677	175	29	5	9	1.3	67	56	31	109	5	15	5	922	205	32	76	5.3	.972	1B-116, 3B-83, OF-11, DH-4

Carmelo Martinez

MARTINEZ, CARMELO
Born Carmelo Martinez y Salgado.
B. July 28, 1960, Dorado, Puerto Rico
BR TR 6′ 2″ 185 lbs.

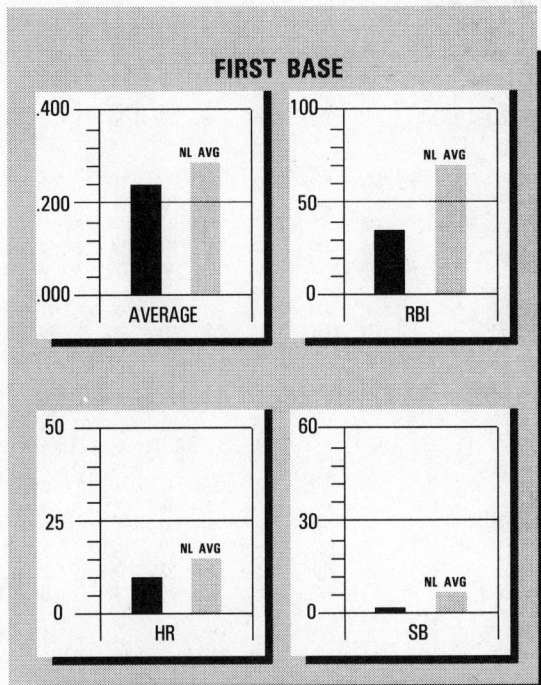

FIRST BASE
AVERAGE · RBI · HR · SB (NL AVG)

Split	Games	BA	SA	AB	H	2B	3B	HR	HR%	R	RBI	BB	SO	SB	PH AB	PH H	PO	A	E	DP	TC/G	FA	G by Pos
April	13	.222	.444	27	6	0	0	2	7.4	4	6	6	4	0									
May	10	.300	.600	30	9	3	0	2	6.7	4	7	3	6	1									
June	10	.267	.400	30	8	1	0	1	3.3	2	7	1	6	0									
July	22	.232	.391	69	16	2	0	3	4.3	10	8	14	13	0									
Aug	17	.209	.256	43	9	2	0	0	0.0	3	3	5	8	1									
Sept/Oct	11	.222	.611	18	4	1	0	2	11.1	3	4	1	5	0									
Day	19	.255	.400	55	14	2	0	2	3.6	4	12	5	9	2									
Night	64	.235	.426	162	38	7	0	8	4.9	22	23	25	33	0									
vs. Left		.233	.456	90	21	5	0	5	5.6	14	16	15	15	0									
vs. Right		.244	.394	127	31	4	0	5	3.9	12	19	15	27	2									
On Grass	18	.280	.580	50	14	3	0	4	8.0	10	12	9	11	0									
On Turf	65	.228	.371	167	38	6	0	6	3.6	16	23	21	31	2									
Home	46	.230	.418	122	28	5	0	6	4.9	13	17	12	25	1									
Road	37	.253	.421	95	24	4	0	4	4.2	13	18	18	17	1									
Division Rivals																							
vs. CHI	6	.235	.235	17	4	0	0	0	0.0	2	3	5	3	0									
vs. MON	10	.111	.111	18	2	0	0	0	0.0	0	0	0	4	0									
vs. NY	10	.333	.704	27	9	1	0	3	11.1	4	8	3	7	0									
vs. PHI	1	.500	1.500	4	2	1	0	1	25.0	2	2	0	2	0									
vs. STL	6	.059	.059	17	1	0	0	0	0.0	1	0	3	2	0									
On 3B < 2 Out		.400	.900	10	4	2	0	1	10.0	1	8	1	1										

Year	Team		Games	BA	SA	AB	H	2B	3B	HR	HR%	R	RBI	BB	SO	SB	PH AB	PH H	PO	A	E	DP	TC/G	FA	G by Pos
1983	CHI	N	29	.258	.494	89	23	3	0	6	6.7	8	16	4	19	0	4	1	233	17	2	18	8.7	.992	1B-26, 3B-1, OF-1
1984	SD	N	149	.250	.395	488	122	28	2	13	2.7	64	66	68	82	1	4	0	317	15	8	4	2.3	.976	OF-142, 1B-2
1985			150	.253	.434	514	130	28	1	21	4.1	64	72	87	82	0	0	0	302	14	7	5	2.2	.978	OF-150, 1B-3
1986			113	.238	.389	244	58	10	0	9	3.7	28	25	35	46	1	36	8	142	14	2	4	1.4	.987	OF-60, 1B-26, 3B-1
1987			139	.273	.430	447	122	21	2	15	3.4	59	70	70	82	5	7	1	591	42	9	41	4.6	.986	OF-78, 1B-65
1988			121	.236	.416	365	86	12	0	18	4.9	48	65	35	57	1	28	8	430	32	4	31	3.9	.991	OF-64, 1B-41
1989			111	.221	.348	267	59	12	2	6	2.2	23	39	32	54	0	32	7	225	18	2	11	2.2	.992	OF-65, 1B-32
1990	2 teams			PHI N (71G — .242)			PIT N (12G — .211)																		
"	total		83	.240	.419	217	52	9	0	10	4.6	26	35	30	42	2	17	4	374	29	2	35	6.2	.995	1B-48, OF-22
8 yrs.			895	.248	.412	2631	652	123	7	98	3.7	320	388	361	464	10	128	29	2614	181	36	149	3.2	.987	OF-582, 1B-243, 3B-2

LEAGUE CHAMPIONSHIP SERIES

Year	Team		Games	BA	SA	AB	H	2B	3B	HR	HR%	R	RBI	BB	SO	SB	PH AB	PH H	PO	A	E	DP	TC/G	FA	G by Pos
1984	SD	N	5	.176	.176	17	3	0	0	0	0.0	1	0	2	4	0	0	0	6	0	0	0	1.2	1.000	OF-5
1990	PIT	N	2	.250	.500	8	2	2	0	0	0.0	0	2	0	1	0	0	0	14	1	0	1	7.5	1.000	1B-2
2 yrs.			7	.200	.280	25	5	2	0	0	0.0	1	2	2	5	0	0	0	20	1	0	1	3.0	.000	OF-5, 1B-2

WORLD SERIES

Year	Team		Games	BA	SA	AB	H	2B	3B	HR	HR%	R	RBI	BB	SO	SB	PH AB	PH H	PO	A	E	DP	TC/G	FA	G by Pos
1984	SD	N	5	.176	.176	17	3	0	0	0	0.0	0	0	1	9	0	0	0	7	0	1	0	1.6	.875	OF-5

Dave Martinez

MARTINEZ, DAVID
B. Sept. 26, 1964, New York, N. Y.
BL TL 5′ 10″ 150 lbs.

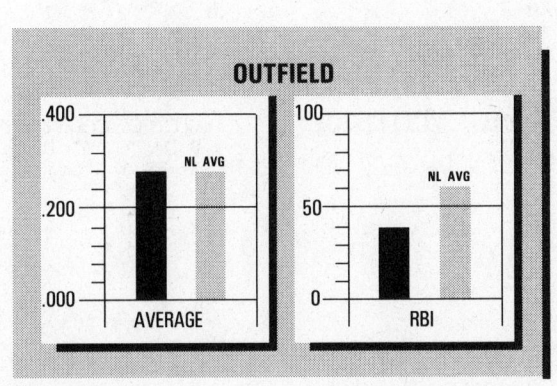

OUTFIELD
AVERAGE · RBI (NL AVG)

Split	Games	BA	SA	AB	H	2B	3B	HR	HR%	R	RBI	BB	SO	SB
April	5	.143	.143	7	1	0	0	0	0.0	2	0	0	3	0
May	16	.277	.383	47	13	2	0	1	2.1	4	5	2	7	2
June	30	.304	.500	112	34	4	3	4	3.6	17	14	10	17	3
July	21	.333	.530	66	22	1	0	4	6.1	16	5	4	6	3
Aug	23	.277	.410	83	23	3	1	2	2.4	12	12	3	7	4
Sept/Oct	23	.211	.276	76	16	3	1	0	0.0	9	3	5	8	1
Day	32	.243	.408	103	25	3	1	4	3.9	16	11	8	19	5
Night	86	.292	.427	288	84	10	4	7	2.4	44	28	16	29	8
vs. Left		.244	.308	78	19	0	1	1	1.3	10	11	11	15	3
vs. Right		.288	.450	313	90	13	4	10	3.2	50	28	13	33	10

Year	Team		Games	BA	SA	AB	H	2B	3B	HR	HR%	R	RBI	BB	SO	SB	PINCH HIT AB	H	PO	A	E	DP	TC/G	FA	G by Pos

Dave Martinez *Continued*

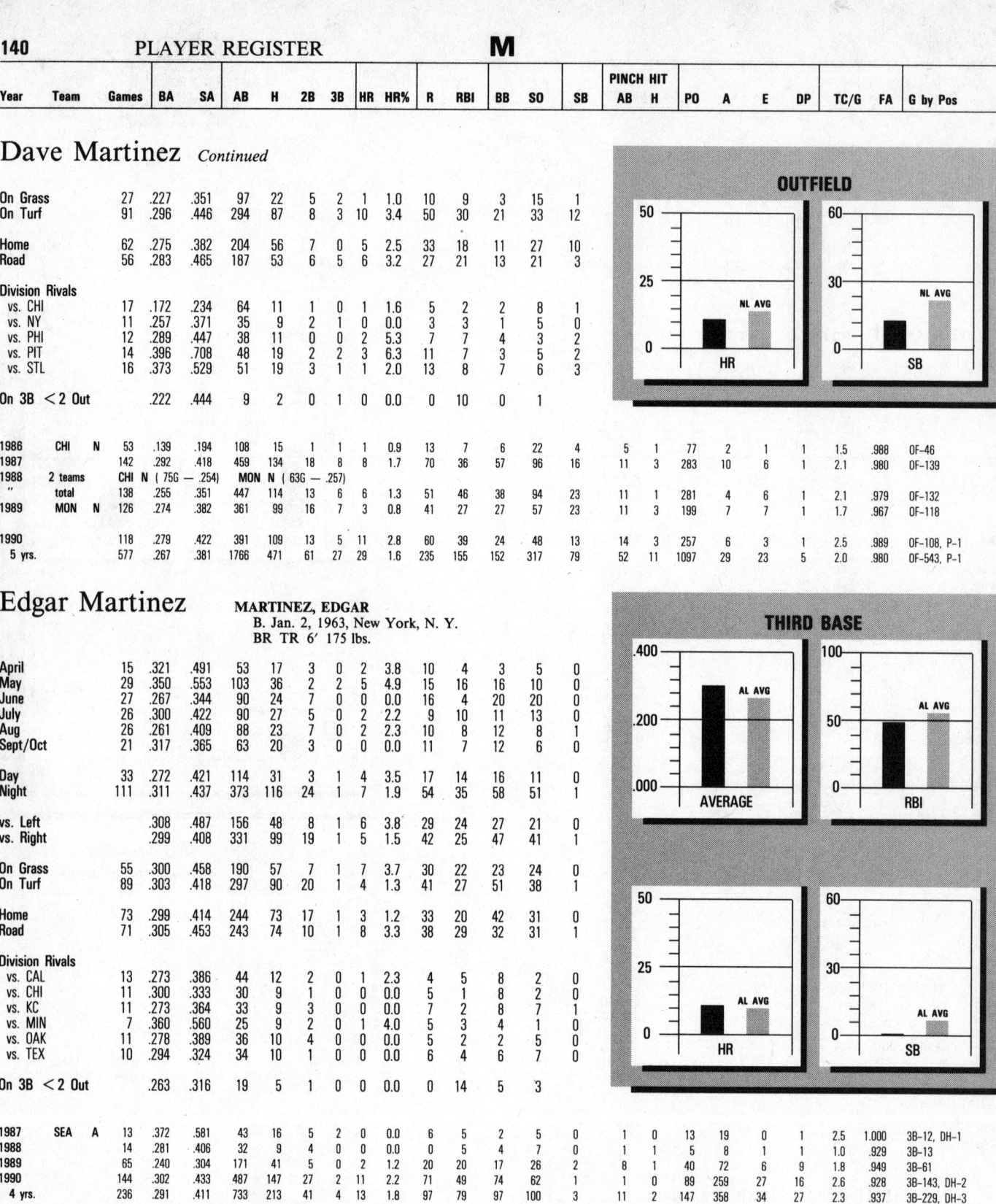

Year	Team		Games	BA	SA	AB	H	2B	3B	HR	HR%	R	RBI	BB	SO	SB	AB	H	PO	A	E	DP	TC/G	FA	G by Pos
On Grass			27	.227	.351	97	22	5	2	1	1.0	10	9	3	15	1									
On Turf			91	.296	.446	294	87	8	3	10	3.4	50	30	21	33	12									
Home			62	.275	.382	204	56	7	0	5	2.5	33	18	11	27	10									
Road			56	.283	.465	187	53	6	5	6	3.2	27	21	13	21	3									
Division Rivals																									
vs. CHI			17	.172	.234	64	11	1	0	1	1.6	5	2	2	8	1									
vs. NY			11	.257	.371	35	9	2	1	0	0.0	3	3	1	5	0									
vs. PHI			12	.289	.447	38	11	0	0	2	5.3	7	7	4	3	2									
vs. PIT			14	.396	.708	48	19	2	2	3	6.3	11	7	3	5	2									
vs. STL			16	.373	.529	51	19	3	1	1	2.0	13	8	7	5	3									
On 3B < 2 Out				.222	.444	9	2	0	1	0	0.0	0	10	0	1										
1986	CHI	N	53	.139	.194	108	15	1	1	1	0.9	13	7	6	22	4	5	1	77	2	1	1	1.5	.988	OF-46
1987			142	.292	.418	459	134	18	8	8	1.7	70	36	57	96	16	11	3	283	10	6	1	2.1	.980	OF-139
1988	2 teams	CHI N (75G — .254)						MON N (63G — .257)																	
"	total		138	.255	.351	447	114	13	6	6	1.3	51	46	38	94	23	11	1	281	4	6	1	2.1	.979	OF-132
1989	MON	N	126	.274	.382	361	99	16	7	3	0.8	41	27	27	57	23	11	3	199	7	7	1	1.7	.967	OF-118
1990			118	.279	.422	391	109	13	5	11	2.8	60	39	24	48	13	14	3	257	6	3	1	2.5	.989	OF-108, P-1
5 yrs.			577	.267	.381	1766	471	61	27	29	1.6	235	155	152	317	79	52	11	1097	29	23	5	2.0	.980	OF-543, P-1

Edgar Martinez

MARTINEZ, EDGAR
B. Jan. 2, 1963, New York, N. Y.
BR TR 6′ 175 lbs.

Year	Team		Games	BA	SA	AB	H	2B	3B	HR	HR%	R	RBI	BB	SO	SB	AB	H	PO	A	E	DP	TC/G	FA	G by Pos
April			15	.321	.491	53	17	3	0	2	3.8	10	4	3	5	0									
May			29	.350	.553	103	36	2	2	5	4.9	15	16	16	10	0									
June			27	.267	.344	90	24	7	0	0	0.0	16	4	20	20	0									
July			26	.300	.422	90	27	5	0	2	2.2	9	10	11	13	0									
Aug			26	.261	.409	88	23	7	0	2	2.3	10	8	12	8	1									
Sept/Oct			21	.317	.365	63	20	3	0	0	0.0	11	7	12	6	0									
Day			33	.272	.421	114	31	3	1	4	3.5	17	14	16	11	0									
Night			111	.311	.437	373	116	24	1	7	1.9	54	35	58	51	1									
vs. Left				.308	.487	156	48	8	1	6	3.8	29	24	27	21	0									
vs. Right				.299	.408	331	99	19	1	5	1.5	42	25	47	41	1									
On Grass			55	.300	.458	190	57	7	1	7	3.7	30	22	23	24	0									
On Turf			89	.303	.418	297	90	20	1	4	1.3	41	27	51	38	1									
Home			73	.299	.414	244	73	17	1	3	1.2	33	20	42	31	0									
Road			71	.305	.453	243	74	10	1	8	3.3	38	29	32	31	1									
Division Rivals																									
vs. CAL			13	.273	.386	44	12	2	0	1	2.3	4	5	8	2	0									
vs. CHI			11	.300	.333	30	9	1	0	0	0.0	5	1	8	2	0									
vs. KC			11	.273	.364	33	9	3	0	0	0.0	7	2	8	7	1									
vs. MIN			7	.360	.560	25	9	2	0	1	4.0	5	3	4	1	0									
vs. OAK			11	.278	.389	36	10	4	0	0	0.0	5	2	2	5	0									
vs. TEX			10	.294	.324	34	10	1	0	0	0.0	6	4	6	7	0									
On 3B < 2 Out				.263	.316	19	5	1	0	0	0.0	0	14	5	3										
1987	SEA	A	13	.372	.581	43	16	5	0	0	0.0	6	5	2	5	0	1	0	13	19	0	1	2.5	1.000	3B-12, DH-1
1988			14	.281	.406	32	9	4	0	0	0.0	0	5	4	7	0	1	1	5	8	1	1	1.0	.929	3B-13
1989			65	.240	.304	171	41	5	0	2	1.2	20	20	17	26	2	8	1	40	72	6	9	1.8	.949	3B-61
1990			144	.302	.433	487	147	27	2	11	2.2	71	49	74	62	1	1	0	89	259	27	16	2.6	.928	3B-143, DH-2
4 yrs.			236	.291	.411	733	213	41	4	13	1.8	97	79	97	100	3	11	2	147	358	34	27	2.3	.937	3B-229, DH-3

Tino Martinez

MARTINEZ, CONSTANTINO
B. Dec. 7, 1967, Tampa, Fla.
BL TR 6′ 2″ 205 lbs.

Year	Team		Games	BA	SA	AB	H	2B	3B	HR	HR%	R	RBI	BB	SO	SB	AB	H	PO	A	E	DP	TC/G	FA	G by Pos
1990	SEA	A	24	.221	.279	68	15	4	0	0	0.0	4	5	9	9	0	2	0	155	12	0	25	7.3	1.000	1B-23

Year	Team		Games	BA	SA	AB	H	2B	3B	HR	HR%	R	RBI	BB	SO	SB	PINCH HIT AB	PINCH HIT H	PO	A	E	DP	TC/G	FA	G by Pos

John Marzano

MARZANO, JOHN ROBERT
B. Feb. 14, 1963, Philadelphia, Pa.
BR TR 5′ 11″ 185 lbs.

Year	Team		Games	BA	SA	AB	H	2B	3B	HR	HR%	R	RBI	BB	SO	SB	PH AB	PH H	PO	A	E	DP	TC/G	FA	G by Pos
1987	BOS	A	52	.244	.399	168	41	11	0	5	3.0	20	24	7	41	0	1	0	337	24	5	7	7.0	.986	C–52
1988			10	.138	.172	29	4	1	0	0	0.0	3	1	1	3	0	0	0	77	4	0	0	8.1	1.000	C–10
1989			7	.444	.778	18	8	3	0	1	5.6	5	3	0	2	0	1	1	29	4	0	0	4.7	1.000	C–7
1990			32	.241	.289	83	20	4	0	0	0.0	8	6	5	10	0	0	0	153	14	0	3	5.2	1.000	C–32
4 yrs.			101	.245	.369	298	73	19	0	6	2.0	36	34	13	56	0	2	1	596	46	5	10	6.4	.992	C–101

Don Mattingly

MATTINGLY, DONALD ARTHUR
B. Apr. 20, 1961, Evansville, Ind.
BL TL 6′ 185 lbs.

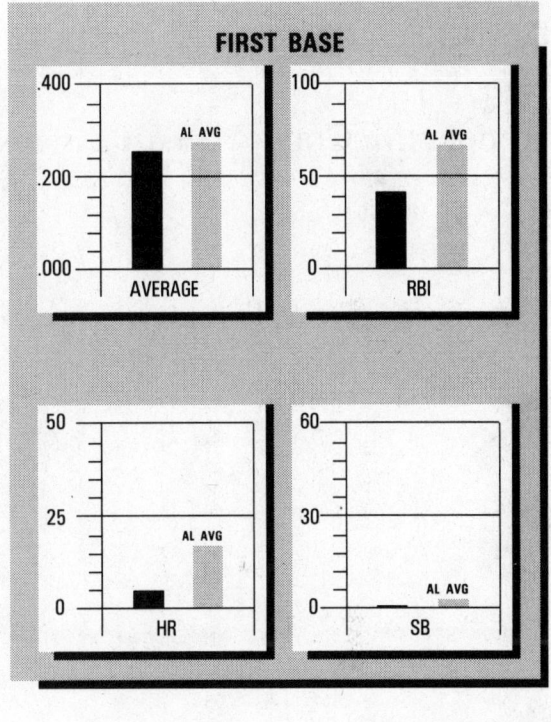

FIRST BASE — AVERAGE, RBI, HR, SB (AL AVG)

	Games	BA	SA	AB	H	2B	3B	HR	HR%	R	RBI	BB	SO	SB	PH AB	PH H	PO	A	E	DP	TC/G	FA	G by Pos
April	17	.313	.469	64	20	4	0	2	3.1	8	6	5	3	0									
May	27	.269	.398	108	29	5	0	3	2.8	14	18	6	11	0									
June	28	.216	.241	116	25	3	0	0	0.0	9	9	6	4	1									
July	14	.182	.200	55	10	1	0	0	0.0	3	2	5	2	0									
Aug				0	0	0	0	0		0	0	0	0	0									
Sept/Oct	16	.333	.392	51	17	3	0	0	0.0	6	7	6	0	0									
Day	29	.316	.386	114	36	5	0	1	0.9	10	15	13	3	1									
Night	73	.232	.314	280	65	11	0	4	1.4	30	27	15	17	0									
vs. Left		.262	.310	126	33	6	0	0	0.0	11	17	7	8	0									
vs. Right		.254	.347	268	68	10	0	5	1.9	29	25	21	12	1									
On Grass	83	.257	.343	315	81	12	0	5	1.6	32	34	24	15	1									
On Turf	19	.253	.304	79	20	4	0	0	0.0	8	8	4	5	0									
Home	48	.246	.333	183	45	4	0	4	2.2	14	20	16	11	0									
Road	54	.265	.336	211	56	12	0	1	0.5	26	22	12	9	0									
Division Rivals																								
vs. BAL	8	.313	.344	32	10	1	0	0	0.0	4	3	2	1	1									
vs. BOS	10	.162	.162	37	6	0	0	0	0.0	2	0	4	1	0									
vs. CLE	3	.333	.417	12	4	1	0	0	0.0	0	1	1	0	0									
vs. DET	7	.368	.421	19	7	1	0	0	0.0	1	2	0	0	0									
vs. MIL	9	.343	.400	35	12	2	0	0	0.0	5	9	4	0	0									
vs. TOR	10	.233	.279	43	10	2	0	0	0.0	2	3	2	2	0									
On 3B < 2 Out		.417	.458	24	10	1	0	0	0.0	0	16	2	4										

Year	Team		Games	BA	SA	AB	H	2B	3B	HR	HR%	R	RBI	BB	SO	SB	PH AB	PH H	PO	A	E	DP	TC/G	FA	G by Pos
1982	NY	A	7	.167	.167	12	2	0	0	0	0.0	0	1	0	1	0	1	0	15	1	0	0	2.3	1.000	OF–6, 1B–1
1983			91	.283	.409	279	79	15	4	4	1.4	34	32	21	31	0	8	1	350	15	3	31	4.0	.992	OF–48, 1B–42, 2B–1
1984			153	**.343**	.537	603	**207**	**44**	2	23	3.8	91	110	41	33	1	3	1	1143	126	6	136	8.3	.995	1B–133, OF–19
1985			159	.324	.567	652	211	**48**	3	35	5.4	107	**145**	56	41	2	0	0	1318	87	7	154	8.9	.995	1B–159
1986			162	.352	**.573**	677	**238**	**53**	2	31	4.6	117	113	53	35	0	0	0	1378	111	7	134	9.2	.995	1B–160, 3B–3, DH–1
1987			141	.327	.559	569	186	38	2	30	5.3	93	115	51	38	1	1	0	1239	91	5	122	9.5	.996	1B–140, DH–1
1988			144	.311	.462	599	186	37	0	18	3.0	94	88	41	29	1	1	0	1250	99	9	131	9.4	.993	1B–143, DH–1, OF–1
1989			158	.303	.477	631	191	37	2	23	3.6	79	113	51	30	3	0	0	1276	87	7	143	8.7	.995	1B–145, DH–17, OF–1
1990			102	.256	.335	394	101	16	0	5	1.2	40	42	28	20	1	4	2	800	78	3	81	9.9	.997	1B–89, DH–13, OF–1
9 yrs.			1117	.317	.504	4416	1401	288	15	169	3.8	655	759	342	258	9	18	4	8769	695	47	932	8.5	.995	1B–1012, OF–76, DH–33, 3B–3, 2B–1

Derrick May

MAY, DERRICK BRANT
Son of Dave May.
B. July 14, 1968, Rochester, N. Y.
BL TR 6′ 4″ 210 lbs.

Year	Team		Games	BA	SA	AB	H	2B	3B	HR	HR%	R	RBI	BB	SO	SB	PH AB	PH H	PO	A	E	DP	TC/G	FA	G by Pos
1990	CHI	N	17	.246	.344	61	15	3	0	1	1.6	8	11	2	7	1	0	0	34	1	1	0	2.1	.972	OF–17

Brent Mayne

MAYNE, BRENT DANEN
B. Apr. 19, 1968, Loma Linda, Calif.
BL TR 6′ 1″ 195 lbs.

Year	Team		Games	BA	SA	AB	H	2B	3B	HR	HR%	R	RBI	BB	SO	SB	PH AB	PH H	PO	A	E	DP	TC/G	FA	G by Pos
1990	KC	A	5	.231	.231	13	3	0	0	0	0.0	2	1	3	3	0	1	0	29	3	1	0	6.6	.970	C–5

Year	Team		Games	BA	SA	AB	H	2B	3B	HR	HR%	R	RBI	BB	SO	SB	PINCH HIT AB	PINCH HIT H	PO	A	E	DP	TC/G	FA	G by Pos

Lloyd McClendon   McCLENDON, LLOYD GLENN
B. Jan. 11, 1959, Gary, Ind.
BR TR 5′ 10″ 190 lbs.

Year	Team		Games	BA	SA	AB	H	2B	3B	HR	HR%	R	RBI	BB	SO	SB	AB	H	PO	A	E	DP	TC/G	FA	G by Pos
1987	CIN	N	45	.208	.361	72	15	5	0	2	2.8	8	13	4	15	1	24	6	80	5	2	3	1.9	.977	C-12, 1B-5, 3B-1, OF-1
1988			72	.219	.314	137	30	4	0	3	2.2	9	14	15	22	4	24	6	197	13	4	11	3.0	.981	C-23, OF-17, 1B-12, 3B-2
1989	CHI	N	92	.286	.479	259	74	12	1	12	4.6	47	40	37	31	6	16	5	310	18	6	21	3.6	.982	OF-45, 1B-28, 3B-6, C-5
1990	2 teams		CHI N (49G — .159)		PIT N (4G — .333)																				
''	total		53	.164	.245	110	18	3	0	2	1.8	6	12	14	22	1	16	2	120	9	1	5	3.4	.992	OF-24, C-8, 1B-8
4 yrs.			262	.237	.381	578	137	24	1	19	3.3	70	79	70	90	12	80	19	707	45	13	40	2.9	.983	OF-87, 1B-53, C-48, 3B-9

LEAGUE CHAMPIONSHIP SERIES
| 1989 | CHI | N | 3 | .667 | .667 | 3 | 2 | 0 | 0 | 0 | 0.0 | 0 | 0 | 1 | 0 | 0 | 2 | 1 | 3 | 0 | 0 | 0 | 1.0 | 1.000 | C-2, OF-1 |

Rodney McCray   McCRAY, RODNEY DUNCAN
B. Sept. 13, 1963, Detroit, Mich.
BR TR 5′ 10″ 175 lbs.

Year	Team		Games	BA	SA	AB	H	2B	3B	HR	HR%	R	RBI	BB	SO	SB	AB	H	PO	A	E	DP	TC/G	FA	G by Pos
1990	CHI	A	32	.000	.000	6	0	0	0	0	0.0	8	0	1	4	6	2	0	8	0	0	0	0.6	1.000	OF-13, DH-7

Oddibe McDowell   McDOWELL, ODDIBE, JR.
B. Aug. 25, 1962, Hollywood, Fla.
BL TL 5′ 9″ 165 lbs.

		Games	BA	SA	AB	H	2B	3B	HR	HR%	R	RBI	BB	SO	SB									
April		13	.200	.360	50	10	2	0	2	4.0	8	8	4	10	1									
May		23	.246	.354	65	16	4	0	1	1.5	8	5	5	10	5									
June		23	.324	.446	74	24	3	0	2	2.7	11	10	2	11	2									
July		17	.190	.310	42	8	2	0	1	2.4	8	1	4	8	3									
Aug		21	.222	.289	45	10	3	0	0	0.0	7	0	5	3	1									
Sept/Oct		16	.207	.310	29	6	0	0	1	3.4	5	1	1	11	1									
Day		25	.214	.304	56	12	2	0	1	1.8	7	6	2	10	1									
Night		88	.249	.369	249	62	12	0	6	2.4	40	19	19	43	12									
vs. Left			.103	.103	39	4	0	0	0	0.0	4	1	5	8	0									
vs. Right			.263	.395	266	70	14	0	7	2.6	43	24	16	45	13									
On Grass		87	.248	.378	230	57	9	0	7	3.0	38	23	16	38	12									
On Turf		26	.227	.293	75	17	5	0	0	0.0	9	2	5	15	1									
Home		58	.273	.400	150	41	7	0	4	2.7	26	14	10	21	10									
Road		55	.213	.316	155	33	7	0	3	1.9	21	11	11	32	3									
Division Rivals																								
vs. CIN		10	.214	.393	28	6	2	0	1	3.6	5	4	2	7	0									
vs. HOU		13	.235	.294	34	8	2	0	0	0.0	6	0	2	10	2									
vs. LA		15	.222	.289	45	10	0	0	1	2.2	6	2	1	8	1									
vs. SD		14	.286	.543	35	10	3	0	2	5.7	8	4	4	5	1									
vs. SF		9	.360	.480	25	9	0	0	1	4.0	3	6	1	1	0									
On 3B < 2 Out			.375	.375	8	3	0	0	0	0.0	0	6	1	2										

OUTFIELD — AVERAGE, RBI, HR, SB (with NL AVG comparison bars)

Year	Team		Games	BA	SA	AB	H	2B	3B	HR	HR%	R	RBI	BB	SO	SB	AB	H	PO	A	E	DP	TC/G	FA	G by Pos
1985	TEX	A	111	.239	.431	406	97	14	5	18	4.4	63	42	36	85	25	8	2	282	9	2	2	2.6	.993	OF-103, DH-4
1986			154	.266	.427	572	152	24	7	18	3.1	105	49	65	112	33	8	2	325	13	3	3	2.2	.991	OF-148, DH-1
1987			128	.241	.428	407	98	26	4	14	3.4	65	52	51	99	24	11	1	263	5	3	1	2.1	.989	OF-125
1988			120	.247	.355	437	108	19	5	6	1.4	55	37	41	89	33	9	2	267	2	3	1	2.3	.989	OF-113, DH-3
1989	2 teams		CLE A (69G — .222)		ATL N (76G — .304)																				
''	total		145	.266	.391	519	138	23	6	10	1.9	89	46	52	73	27	9	3	303	7	5	1	2.2	.984	OF-132, DH-2
1990	ATL	N	113	.243	.357	305	74	14	0	7	2.2	47	25	21	53	13	34	7	134	2	4	0	1.9	.971	OF-72
6 yrs.			771	.252	.401	2646	667	120	27	73	2.8	424	251	266	511	155	79	17	1574	38	20	8	2.1	.988	OF-693, DH-10

Willie McGee

McGEE, WILLIE DEAN
B. Nov. 2, 1958, San Francisco, Calif.
BB TR 6' 1" 176 lbs.

Year	Team	Games	BA	SA	AB	H	2B	3B	HR	HR%	R	RBI	BB	SO	SB	PINCH HIT AB	H	PO	A	E	DP	TC/G	FA	G by Pos
April		20	.361	.482	83	30	8	1	0	0.0	15	12	7	18	5									
May		27	.271	.346	107	29	3	1	1	0.9	18	7	6	11	4									
June		28	.321	.411	112	36	6	2	0	0.0	17	15	14	22	12									
July		25	.392	.495	97	38	7	0	1	1.0	12	15	5	19	4									
Aug		26	.330	.453	106	35	8	1	1	0.9	15	14	6	16	3									
Sept/Oct		28	.284	.349	109	31	3	2	0	0.0	22	14	10	18	3									
Day		44	.373	.470	166	62	7	3	1	0.6	32	20	17	29	10									
Night		110	.306	.400	448	137	28	4	2	0.4	67	57	31	75	21									
vs. Left			.324	.427	225	73	11	3	2	0.9	29	27	10	43	7									
vs. Right			.324	.414	389	126	24	4	1	0.3	70	50	38	61	24									
On Grass		56	.307	.381	218	67	7	3	1	0.5	35	26	21	43	7									
On Turf		98	.333	.439	396	132	28	4	2	0.5	64	51	27	61	24									
Home		82	.335	.424	328	110	18	4	1	0.3	53	47	24	45	20									
Road		72	.311	.413	286	89	17	3	2	0.7	46	30	24	59	11									
Division Rivals																								
vs. CAL		2	.333	.333	6	2	0	0	0	0.0	1	0	0	1	0									
vs. CHI		3	.300	.300	10	3	0	0	0	0.0	2	0	1	1	1									
vs. KC		1	.200	.200	5	1	0	0	0	0.0	2	0	0	1	0									
vs. MIN		4	.389	.500	18	7	0	1	0	0.0	3	4	1	1	0									
vs. SEA		3	.267	.400	15	4	2	0	0	0.0	2	2	0	4	0									
vs. TEX		7	.174	.217	23	4	1	0	0	0.0	3	2	2	3	1									
On 3B < 2 Out			.419	.548	31	13	4	0	0	0.0	0	24		4	7									
1982	STL N	123	.296	.391	422	125	12	8	4	0.9	43	56	12	58	24	15	6	245	3	11	0	2.1	.958	OF-117
1983		147	.286	.374	601	172	22	8	5	0.8	75	75	26	98	39	3	2	385	7	5	1	2.7	.987	OF-145
1984		145	.291	.394	571	166	19	11	6	1.1	82	50	29	80	43	5	0	374	10	6	4	2.7	.985	OF-141
1985		152	**.353**	.503	612	**216**	26	**18**	10	1.6	114	82	34	86	56	4	2	382	11	9	2	2.6	.978	OF-149
1986		124	.256	.370	497	127	22	7	7	1.4	65	48	37	82	19	2	0	325	9	3	0	2.7	.991	OF-121
1987		153	.285	.434	620	177	37	11	11	1.8	76	105	24	90	16	2	1	354	10	7	1	2.4	.981	OF-152, SS-1
1988		137	.292	.372	562	164	24	6	3	0.5	73	50	32	84	41	2	1	348	9	9	0	2.7	.975	OF-135
1989		58	.236	.352	199	47	10	2	3	1.5	23	17	10	34	8	10	2	118	2	3	0	2.1	.976	OF-47
1990	2 teams	STL N (125G — .335)		OAK A (29G — .274)																				
"	total	154	.324	.419	614	199	35	7	3	0.4	99	77	48	104	31	2	0	413	14	17	0	2.9	.962	OF-152, DH-1
9 yrs.		1193	.297	.407	4698	1393	207	78	52	1.1	650	560	252	716	277	45	14	2944	75	70	13	2.6	.977	OF-1159, DH-1, SS-1

LEAGUE CHAMPIONSHIP SERIES

Year	Team	Games	BA	SA	AB	H	2B	3B	HR	HR%	R	RBI	BB	SO	SB	PINCH HIT AB	H	PO	A	E	DP	TC/G	FA	G by Pos
1982	STL N	3	.308	.846	13	4	0	2	1	7.7	4	5	0	5	0	0	0	12	0	1	0	4.3	.923	OF-3
1985		6	.269	.308	26	7	1	0	0	0.0	6	3	3	6	2	0	0	17	0	0	0	2.8	1.000	OF-6
1987		7	.308	.423	26	8	1	1	0	0.0	2	2	0	5	0	0	0	16	0	0	0	2.3	1.000	OF-7
1990	OAK A	3	.222	.333	9	2	1	0	0	0.0	3	0	1	2	2	0	0	2	0	0	0	1.0	1.000	OF-2, DH-1
4 yrs.		19	.284	.446	74	21	3	3	1	1.4	15	10	4	18	4	0	0	47	0	1	0	2.5	.000	OF-18, DH-1

WORLD SERIES

Year	Team	Games	BA	SA	AB	H	2B	3B	HR	HR%	R	RBI	BB	SO	SB	PINCH HIT AB	H	PO	A	E	DP	TC/G	FA	G by Pos
1982	STL N	6	.240	.480	25	6	0	0	2	8.0	6	5	1	3	2	0	0	24	0	0	0	4.0	1.000	OF-6
1985		7	.259	.444	27	7	2	0	1	3.7	2	2	1	3	1	0	0	15	0	0	0	2.1	1.000	OF-7
1987		7	.370	.444	27	10	2	0	0	0.0	2	4	0	9	0	0	0	21	1	1	0	3.3	.957	OF-7
1990	OAK A	4	.200	.300	10	2	1	0	0	0.0	1	0	0	2	1	1	0	5	0	0	0	1.7	1.000	OF-3
4 yrs.		24	.281	.438	89	25	5	0	3	3.4	11	11	2	17	4	1	0	65	1	1	0	2.8	.985	OF-23

OUTFIELD (charts: AVERAGE, RBI, HR, SB with NL AVG comparison)

Fred McGriff

McGRIFF, FREDERICK STANLEY
B. Oct. 31, 1963, Tampa, Fla.
BL TL 6' 3" 200 lbs.

Year	Team	Games	BA	SA	AB	H	2B	3B	HR	HR%	R	RBI	BB	SO	SB
April		20	.283	.483	60	17	0	0	4	6.7	10	7	22	17	1
May		22	.198	.346	81	16	3	0	3	3.7	11	12	11	18	0
June		26	.319	.638	94	30	3	0	9	9.6	21	23	17	15	0
July		26	.299	.557	97	29	4	0	7	7.2	20	16	14	21	0
Aug		29	.371	.610	105	39	8	1	5	4.8	15	15	18	22	3
Sept/Oct		30	.300	.500	120	36	3	0	7	5.8	14	15	12	15	1
Day		48	.294	.537	177	52	7	0	12	6.8	27	34	23	29	1
Night		105	.303	.526	380	115	14	1	23	6.1	64	54	71	79	4
vs. Left			.257	.411	202	52	5	1	8	4.0	26	30	21	48	0
vs. Right			.324	.597	355	115	16	0	27	7.6	65	58	73	60	5

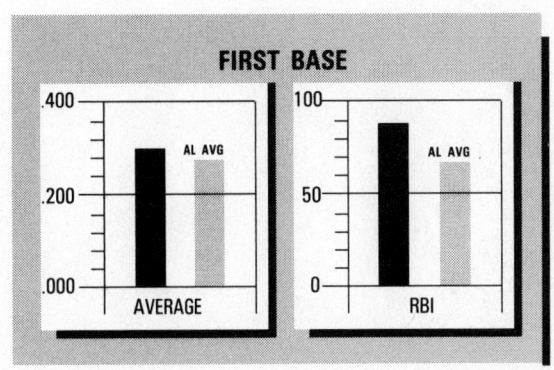

FIRST BASE (charts: AVERAGE, RBI with AL AVG comparison)

Year	Team		Games	BA	SA	AB	H	2B	3B	HR	HR%	R	RBI	BB	SO	SB	PINCH HIT AB	H	PO	A	E	DP	TC/G	FA	G by Pos

Fred McGriff *Continued*

On Grass			59	.330	.562	233	77	10	1	14	6.0	39	34	28	56	4									
On Turf			94	.278	.506	324	90	11	0	21	6.5	52	54	66	52	1									
Home			77	.277	.473	264	73	10	0	14	5.3	42	38	55	37	1									
Road			76	.321	.580	293	94	11	1	21	7.2	49	50	39	71	4									
Division Rivals																									
vs. BAL			13	.283	.457	46	13	2	0	2	4.3	8	5	9	7	0									
vs. BOS			13	.396	.563	48	19	2	0	2	4.2	8	8	7	7	1									
vs. CLE			10	.474	.842	38	18	2	0	4	10.5	5	8	7	5	1									
vs. DET			10	.400	.800	40	16	4	0	4	10.0	9	11	6	10	0									
vs. MIL			13	.184	.265	49	9	1	0	1	2.0	7	6	9	5	0									
vs. NY			11	.300	.475	40	12	1	0	2	5.0	5	5	6	11	0									
On 3B < 2 Out				.261	.391	23	6	0	0	1	4.3	1	18	5	5										
1986	TOR	A	3	.200	.200	5	1	0	0	0	0.0	1	0	0	2	0	0	0	3	0	0	0	1.0	1.000	DH-2, 1B-1
1987			107	.247	.505	295	73	16	0	20	6.8	58	43	60	104	3	14	1	108	7	2	5	1.1	.983	DH-90, 1B-14
1988			154	.282	.552	536	151	35	4	34	6.3	100	82	79	149	6	5	2	1344	93	5	143	9.4	.997	1B-153
1989			161	.269	.525	551	148	27	3	**36**	6.5	98	92	119	132	7	1	0	1460	115	17	148	9.9	.989	1B-159, DH-2
1990			153	.300	.530	557	167	21	1	35	6.2	91	88	94	108	5	0	0	1246	126	6	119	9.4	.996	1B-147, DH-6
5 yrs.			578	.278	.530	1944	540	99	8	125	6.4	348	305	352	495	21	20	3	4161	341	30	415	7.8	.993	1B-474, DH-100

LEAGUE CHAMPIONSHIP SERIES

1989	TOR	A	5	.143	.143	21	3	0	0	0	0.0	1	3	0	4	0	0	0	35	2	1	3	7.6	.974	1B-5

Terry McGriff

McGRIFF, TERENCE ROY
B. Sept. 23, 1963, Fort Pierce, Fla.
BR TR 6′ 2″ 190 lbs.

1987	CIN	N	34	.225	.326	89	20	3	0	2	2.2	6	11	8	17	0	0	0	160	14	3	1	5.2	.983	C-33
1988			35	.198	.260	96	19	3	0	1	1.0	9	4	12	31	1	1	0	177	14	2	1	5.5	.990	C-32
1989			6	.273	.273	11	3	0	0	0	0.0	1	2	2	3	0	0	0	23	3	2	0	4.7	.929	C-6
1990	2 teams		CIN N (2G — .000)			HOU N (4G — .000)																			
"	total		6	.000	.000	9	0	0	0	0	0.0	0	0	0	1	0	1	0	13	2	1	1	3.2	.938	C-5
4 yrs.			81	.205	.278	205	42	6	0	3	1.5	16	17	22	52	1	2	0	373	33	8	3	5.1	.981	C-76

Mark McGwire

McGWIRE, MARK DAVID
B. Oct. 1, 1963, Pomona, Calif.
BR TR 6′ 5″ 215 lbs.

April			18	.246	.590	61	15	0	0	7	11.5	12	18	15	10	0									
May			26	.193	.410	83	16	3	0	5	6.0	12	14	23	15	0									
June			25	.250	.545	88	22	2	0	8	9.1	14	18	12	21	1									
July			31	.202	.413	109	22	2	0	7	6.4	14	16	15	24	1									
Aug			26	.225	.461	89	20	3	0	6	6.7	14	21	20	21	0									
Sept/Oct			30	.301	.559	93	28	6	0	6	6.5	21	21	25	25	0									
Day			60	.221	.462	199	44	6	0	14	7.0	31	36	36	46	0									
Night			96	.244	.506	324	79	10	0	25	7.7	56	72	74	70	2									
vs. Left				.258	.530	132	34	3	0	11	8.3	26	38	29	19	0									
vs. Right				.228	.476	391	89	13	0	28	7.2	61	70	81	97	2									
On Grass			131	.232	.495	436	101	13	0	34	7.8	72	91	96	96	1									
On Turf			25	.253	.460	87	22	3	0	5	5.7	15	17	14	20	1									
Home			76	.224	.429	245	55	8	0	14	5.7	34	37	54	61	1									
Road			80	.245	.543	278	68	8	0	25	9.0	53	71	56	55	1									
Division Rivals																									
vs. CAL			13	.244	.488	41	10	1	0	3	7.3	8	8	17	7	0									
vs. CHI			13	.250	.458	48	12	1	0	3	6.3	5	6	11	11	0									
vs. KC			13	.340	.553	47	16	4	0	2	4.3	6	12	6	12	0									
vs. MIN			13	.304	.543	46	14	2	0	3	6.5	11	8	10	8	1									
vs. SEA			12	.158	.316	38	6	0	0	2	5.3	6	5	9	11	0									
vs. TEX			10	.296	.556	27	8	1	0	2	7.4	5	5	9	9	0									
On 3B < 2 Out				.321	.571	28	9	1	0	2	7.1	2	27	4	10										

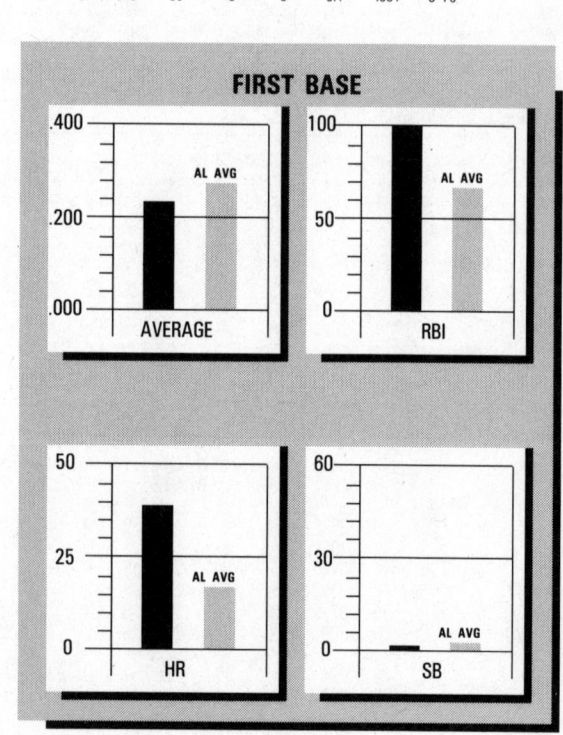

FIRST BASE

Year	Team		Games	BA	SA	AB	H	2B	3B	HR	HR%	R	RBI	BB	SO	SB	PINCH HIT AB	H	PO	A	E	DP	TC/G	FA	G by Pos

Mark McGwire *Continued*

Year	Team		Games	BA	SA	AB	H	2B	3B	HR	HR%	R	RBI	BB	SO	SB	PH AB	PH H	PO	A	E	DP	TC/G	FA	G by Pos
1986	OAK	A	18	.189	.377	53	10	1	0	3	5.7	10	9	4	18	0	3	1	10	20	6	1	2.0	.833	3B-16
1987			151	.289	**.618**	557	161	28	4	**49**	8.8	97	118	71	131	1	2	1	1176	101	13	91	8.5	.990	1B-145, 3B-8, OF-3
1988			155	.260	.478	550	143	22	1	32	5.8	87	99	76	117	0	4	2	1228	88	9	118	8.5	.993	1B-154, OF-1
1989			143	.231	.467	490	113	17	0	33	**6.7**	74	95	83	94	1	1	0	1170	114	6	122	9.0	.995	1B-141, DH-2
1990			156	.235	.489	523	123	16	0	39	7.4	87	108	**110**	116	2	1	0	1329	95	5	126	9.3	.997	1B-154, DH-2
5 yrs.			623	.253	.512	2173	550	84	5	156	7.2	355	429	344	476	4	11	4	4913	418	39	458	8.6	.993	1B-594, 3B-24, DH-4, OF-4

LEAGUE CHAMPIONSHIP SERIES

Year	Team		Games	BA	SA	AB	H	2B	3B	HR	HR%	R	RBI	BB	SO	SB	PH AB	PH H	PO	A	E	DP	TC/G	FA	G by Pos
1988	OAK	A	4	.333	.533	15	5	0	0	1	6.7	4	3	1	5	0	0	0	24	2	0	4	6.5	1.000	1B-4
1989			5	.389	.611	18	7	1	0	1	5.6	3	3	1	4	0	0	0	46	1	1	4	9.6	.979	1B-5
1990			4	.154	.154	13	2	0	0	0	0.0	2	2	3	3	0	0	0	40	0	0	3	10.0	1.000	1B-4
3 yrs.			13	.304	.457	46	14	1	0	2	4.3	9	8	5	12	0	0	0	110	3	1	11	8.8	.991	1B-13

WORLD SERIES

Year	Team		Games	BA	SA	AB	H	2B	3B	HR	HR%	R	RBI	BB	SO	SB	PH AB	PH H	PO	A	E	DP	TC/G	FA	G by Pos
1988	OAK	A	5	.059	.235	17	1	0	0	1	5.9	1	1	3	4	0	0	0	40	3	0	2	8.6	1.000	1B-5
1989			4	.294	.353	17	5	1	0	0	0.0	0	1	1	3	0	0	0	28	2	0	1	7.5	1.000	1B-4
1990			4	.214	.214	14	3	0	0	0	0.0	1	0	2	4	0	0	0	42	1	2	5	11.3	.956	1B-4
3 yrs.			13	.188	.271	48	9	1	0	1	2.1	2	2	6	11	0	0	0	110	6	2	8	9.1	.983	1B-13

Tim McIntosh

McINTOSH, TIMOTHY ALLEN
B. Mar. 21, 1965, Minneapolis, Minn.
BR TR 5' 11" 195 lbs.

Year	Team		Games	BA	SA	AB	H	2B	3B	HR	HR%	R	RBI	BB	SO	SB	PH AB	PH H	PO	A	E	DP	TC/G	FA	G by Pos
1990	MIL	A	5	.200	.800	5	1	0	0	1	20.0	1	1	0	2	0	1	0	6	1	1	0	2.0	.875	C-4

Jeff McKnight

McKNIGHT, JEFFERSON ALAN
Son of Jim McKnight.
B. Feb. 18, 1963, Conway, Ark.
BB TR 6' 170 lbs.

Year	Team		Games	BA	SA	AB	H	2B	3B	HR	HR%	R	RBI	BB	SO	SB	PH AB	PH H	PO	A	E	DP	TC/G	FA	G by Pos
1989	NY	N	6	.250	.250	12	3	0	0	0	0.0	2	0	2	1	0	3	1	4	5	1	1	1.7	.900	2B-4, 1B-1, 3B-1, SS-1
1990	BAL	A	29	.200	.267	75	15	2	0	1	1.3	11	4	5	17	0	2	0	106	20	0	11	4.7	1.000	1B-15, OF-8, 2B-5, DH-1, SS-1
2 yrs.			35	.207	.264	87	18	2	0	1	1.1	13	4	7	18	0	5	1	110	25	1	12	3.9	.993	1B-16, 2B-9, OF-8, SS-2, DH-1, 3B-1

Mark McLemore

McLEMORE, MARK TREMELL
B. Oct. 4, 1964, San Diego, Calif.
BB TR 5' 11" 175 lbs.

Year	Team		Games	BA	SA	AB	H	2B	3B	HR	HR%	R	RBI	BB	SO	SB	PH AB	PH H	PO	A	E	DP	TC/G	FA	G by Pos
1986	CAL	A	5	.000	.000	4	0	0	0	0	0.0	0	0	1	2	0	0	0	3	10	0	1	2.6	1.000	2B-2
1987			138	.236	.300	433	102	13	3	3	0.7	61	41	48	72	25	1	0	293	363	17	98	4.9	.975	2B-132, SS-6, DH-3
1988			77	.240	.330	233	56	11	2	2	0.9	38	16	25	28	13	9	3	108	178	6	53	3.8	.979	2B-63, 3B-5, DH-1
1989			32	.243	.291	103	25	3	1	0	0.0	12	14	7	19	6	1	0	55	88	5	24	4.6	.966	2B-27, DH-1
1990	2 teams		CAL A (20G — .146)			CLE A (8G — .167)																			
"	total		28	.150	.183	60	9	2	0	0	0.0	6	2	4	15	1	2	0	37	39	4	10	3.5	.950	2B-11, SS-8, 3B-4, DH-2
5 yrs.			280	.230	.298	833	192	29	6	5	0.6	117	73	85	136	45	13	3	496	678	32	186	4.3	.973	2B-235, SS-14, 3B-9, DH-7

Brian McRae

McRAE, BRIAN WESLEY
Son of Hal McRae.
B. Aug. 27, 1967, Bradenton, Fla.
BB TR 6' 175 lbs.

Year	Team		Games	BA	SA	AB	H	2B	3B	HR	HR%	R	RBI	BB	SO	SB	PH AB	PH H	PO	A	E	DP	TC/G	FA	G by Pos
1990	KC	A	46	.286	.405	168	48	8	3	2	1.1	21	23	9	29	4	1	1	120	1	0	0	2.7	1.000	OF-45

Year	Team	Games	BA	SA	AB	H	2B	3B	HR	HR%	R	RBI	BB	SO	SB	PINCH HIT AB	H	PO	A	E	DP	TC/G	FA	G by Pos

Kevin McReynolds

McREYNOLDS, WALTER KEVIN (Big Mac)
B. Oct. 16, 1959, Little Rock, Ark.
BR TR 6' 1" 205 lbs.

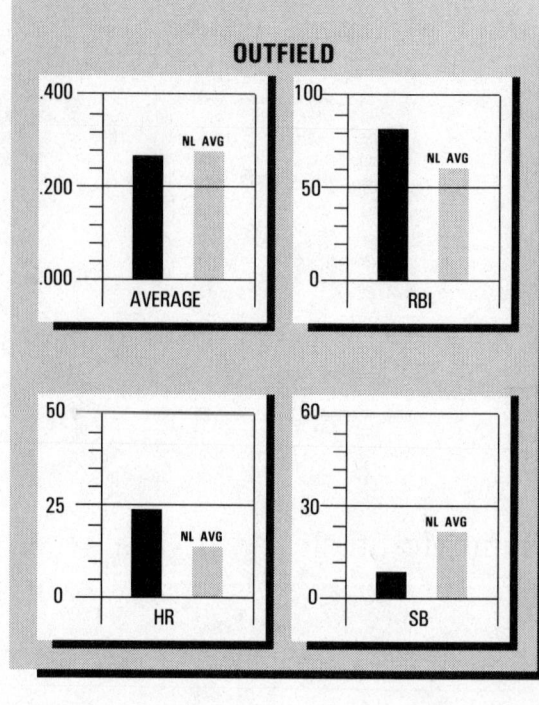

OUTFIELD — AVERAGE (NL AVG), RBI (NL AVG), HR (NL AVG), SB (NL AVG)

Year	Team	Games	BA	SA	AB	H	2B	3B	HR	HR%	R	RBI	BB	SO	SB	AB	H	PO	A	E	DP	TC/G	FA	G by Pos
April		16	.288	.365	52	15	1	0	1	1.9	4	8	7	3	2									
May		23	.253	.470	83	21	3	0	5	6.0	13	15	12	9	1									
June		27	.231	.505	91	21	7	0	6	6.6	14	16	20	9	1									
July		28	.278	.392	97	27	6	1	1	1.0	18	12	20	10	2									
Aug		26	.250	.404	104	26	1	0	5	4.8	10	15	6	17	1									
Sept/Oct		27	.319	.564	94	30	5	0	6	6.4	16	16	6	13	2									
Day		50	.303	.560	175	53	9	0	12	6.9	27	31	24	22	1									
Night		97	.251	.402	346	87	14	1	12	3.5	48	51	47	39	8									
vs. Left			.232	.351	194	45	11	0	4	2.1	23	15	38	20	2									
vs. Right			.291	.517	327	95	12	1	20	6.1	52	67	33	41	7									
On Grass		103	.276	.496	359	99	16	0	21	5.8	60	64	46	38	5									
On Turf		44	.253	.364	162	41	/	1	3	1.9	15	18	25	23	4									
Home		72	.258	.426	244	63	8	0	11	4.5	37	39	31	25	4									
Road		75	.278	.480	277	77	15	1	13	4.7	38	43	40	36	5									
Division Rivals																								
vs. CHI		10	.567	1.167	30	17	6	0	4	13.3	12	10	3	2	0									
vs. MON		17	.317	.413	63	20	0	0	2	3.2	4	10	6	8	2									
vs. PHI		18	.179	.299	67	12	3	1	1	1.5	6	8	7	13	1									
vs. PIT		15	.160	.300	50	8	1	0	2	4.0	3	2	8	4	1									
vs. STL		18	.295	.574	61	18	5	0	4	6.6	10	12	13	4	2									
On 3B < 2 Out			.412	.941	17	7	0	0	3	17.6	3	24	9	1										
1983	SD N	39	.221	.343	140	31	3	1	4	2.9	15	14	12	29	2	2	1	87	4	1	1	2.4	.989	OF-38
1984		147	.278	.465	525	146	26	6	20	3.8	68	75	34	69	3	5	1	422	10	4	1	3.0	.991	OF-143
1985		152	.234	.371	564	132	24	4	15	2.7	61	75	43	81	4	2	0	430	12	3	3	2.9	.993	OF-150
1986		158	.288	.504	560	161	31	6	26	4.6	89	96	66	83	8	4	1	332	9	8	4	2.2	.977	OF-154
1987	NY N	151	.276	.495	590	163	32	5	29	4.9	86	95	39	70	14	3	2	286	8	4	0	2.0	.987	OF-150
1988		147	.288	.496	552	159	30	2	27	4.9	82	99	38	56	21	3	1	252	18	4	5	1.9	.985	OF-147
1989		148	.272	.450	545	148	25	3	22	4.0	74	85	46	74	15	3	1	307	10	10	3	2.2	.969	OF-145
1990		147	.269	.455	521	140	23	1	24	4.6	75	82	71	61	9	2	1	237	14	3	2	1.8	.988	OF-144
8 yrs.		1089	.270	.458	3997	1080	194	28	167	4.2	550	621	349	523	76	24	8	2353	85	37	19	2.3	.985	OF-1071
LEAGUE CHAMPIONSHIP SERIES																								
1984	SD N	4	.300	.600	10	3	0	0	1	10.0	2	4	3	1	0	0	0	10	0	0	0	2.5	1.000	OF-4
1988	NY N	7	.250	.536	28	7	2	0	2	7.1	4	4	3	5	2	0	0	19	0	0	0	2.7	1.000	OF-7
2 yrs.		11	.263	.553	38	10	2	0	3	7.9	6	8	6	6	2	0	0	29	0	0	0	2.6	1.000	OF-11

Louie Meadows

MEADOWS, MICHAEL RAY
B. Apr. 29, 1961, Maysville, N. C.
BL TL 5' 11" 190 lbs.

Year	Team	Games	BA	SA	AB	H	2B	3B	HR	HR%	R	RBI	BB	SO	SB	AB	H	PO	A	E	DP	TC/G	FA	G by Pos
1986	HOU N	6	.333	.333	6	2	0	0	0	0.0	1	0	0	0	1	6	2	0	0	0	0	0.0	—	OF-1
1988		35	.190	.381	42	8	0	1	2	4.8	5	3	6	8	4	18	3	18	1	0	0	0.5	1.000	OF-10
1989		31	.176	.353	51	9	0	0	3	5.9	5	10	1	14	1	20	2	13	0	0	0	0.4	1.000	OF-14, 1B-1
1990	2 teams		HOU N (15G — .143)			PHI N (15G — .107)																		
"	total	30	.107	.107	28	3	0	0	0	0.0	4	0	3	6	0	16	0	8	0	0	0	0.6	1.000	OF-13
4 yrs.		102	.173	.307	127	22	0	1	5	3.9	15	13	10	28	6	60	7	39	1	0	0	0.4	.000	OF-38, 1B-1

Bob Melvin

MELVIN, ROBERT PAUL
B. Oct. 28, 1961, Palo Alto, Calif.
BR TR 6' 4" 205 lbs.

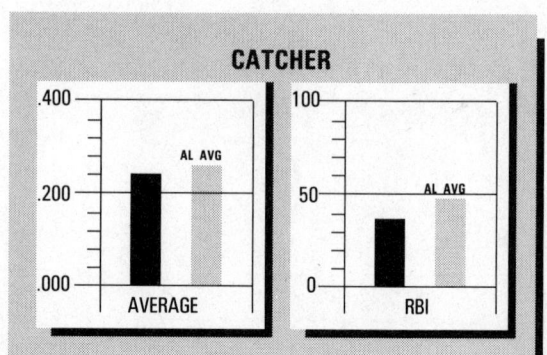

CATCHER — AVERAGE (AL AVG), RBI (AL AVG)

Year	Team	Games	BA	SA	AB	H	2B	3B	HR	HR%	R	RBI	BB	SO	SB	AB	H	PO	A	E	DP	TC/G	FA	G by Pos
April		12	.162	.297	37	6	0	0	1	2.7	4	5	2	7	0									
May		16	.321	.464	56	18	5	0	1	1.8	6	10	2	8	0									
June		17	.191	.255	47	9	3	0	0	0.0	4	4	2	13	0									
July		16	.167	.204	54	9	0	1	0	0.0	2	5	1	13	0									
Aug		15	.264	.396	53	14	1	0	2	3.8	6	8	7	13	0									
Sept/Oct		17	.315	.426	54	17	3	0	1	1.9	8	6	3	9	0									
Day		28	.356	.471	87	31	5	1	1	1.1	12	13	5	13	0									
Night		65	.196	.294	214	42	9	0	4	1.9	18	24	6	40	0									
vs. Left			.276	.408	152	42	11	0	3	2.0	16	16	6	18	0									
vs. Right			.208	.282	149	31	3	1	2	1.3	14	21	5	35	0									

Year	Team		Games	BA	SA	AB	H	2B	3B	HR	HR%	R	RBI	BB	SO	SB	PINCH HIT AB	PINCH HIT H	PO	A	E	DP	TC/G	FA	G by Pos

Bob Melvin *Continued*

Year	Team		Games	BA	SA	AB	H	2B	3B	HR	HR%	R	RBI	BB	SO	SB	PINCH HIT AB	PINCH HIT H	PO	A	E	DP	TC/G	FA	G by Pos
On Grass			77	.235	.350	243	57	11	1	5	2.1	25	32	8	43	0									
On Turf			16	.276	.328	58	16	3	0	0	0.0	5	5	3	10	0									
Home			40	.174	.289	121	21	3	1	3	2.5	9	13	3	28	0									
Road			53	.289	.383	180	52	11	0	2	1.1	21	24	8	25	0									

Division Rivals

Year	Team		Games	BA	SA	AB	H	2B	3B	HR	HR%	R	RBI	BB	SO	SB
vs. BOS			3	.250	.375	8	2	1	0	0	0.0	0	0	1	2	0
vs. CLE			8	.200	.250	20	4	1	0	0	0.0	1	0	1	3	0
vs. DET			8	.207	.379	29	6	2	0	1	3.4	4	5	1	3	0
vs. MIL			9	.214	.214	28	6	0	0	0	0.0	2	3	1	5	0
vs. NY			7	.190	.333	21	4	3	0	0	0.0	3	0	0	5	0
vs. TOR			8	.258	.290	31	8	1	0	0	0.0	2	2	1	5	0
On 3B < 2 Out				.200	.200	20	4	0	0	0	0.0	0	10	1	7	

Year	Team		Games	BA	SA	AB	H	2B	3B	HR	HR%	R	RBI	BB	SO	SB	AB	H	PO	A	E	DP	TC/G	FA	G by Pos
1985	DET	A	41	.220	.293	82	18	4	1	0	0.0	10	4	3	21	0	0	0	175	13	2	1	4.6	.989	C-41
1986	SF	N	89	.224	.347	268	60	14	2	5	1.9	24	25	15	69	3	6	1	443	60	6	7	5.7	.988	C-84, 3B-1
1987			84	.199	.366	246	49	8	0	11	4.5	31	31	17	44	0	8	1	414	44	1	8	5.5	.998	C-78, 1B-1
1988			92	.234	.377	273	64	13	1	8	2.9	23	27	13	46	0	4	1	406	31	7	4	4.8	.984	C-89, 1B-1
1989	BAL	A	85	.241	.295	278	67	10	1	1	0.4	22	32	15	53	1	5	0	303	20	3	1	3.8	.991	C-75, DH-9
1990			93	.243	.346	301	73	14	1	5	1.6	30	37	11	53	0	11	2	365	26	1	2	5.1	.997	C-76, DH-10, 1B-1
6 yrs.			484	.229	.343	1448	331	63	6	30	2.1	140	156	74	286	4	34	5	2106	194	20	23	4.8	.991	C-443, DH-19, 1B-3, 3B-1

LEAGUE CHAMPIONSHIP SERIES

Year	Team		Games	BA	SA	AB	H	2B	3B	HR	HR%	R	RBI	BB	SO	SB	AB	H	PO	A	E	DP	TC/G	FA	G by Pos
1987	SF	N	3	.429	.429	7	3	0	0	0	0.0	0	0	1	1	0	1	0	14	1	0	0	5.0	1.000	C-2

Orlando Mercado

MERCADO, ORLANDO
Born Orlando Mercado y Rodriguez.
B. Nov. 7, 1961, Arecibo, Puerto Rico
BR TR 6′ 180 lbs.

Year	Team		Games	BA	SA	AB	H	2B	3B	HR	HR%	R	RBI	BB	SO	SB	AB	H	PO	A	E	DP	TC/G	FA	G by Pos
1982	SEA	A	9	.118	.294	17	2	0	0	1	5.9	1	6	0	5	0	0	0	31	1	0	0	3.6	1.000	C-8, DH-1
1983			66	.197	.298	178	35	11	2	1	0.6	10	16	14	27	2	2	0	342	27	2	2	5.6	.995	C-65
1984			30	.218	.282	78	17	3	1	0	0.0	5	5	4	12	1	3	1	118	10	1	0	4.3	.992	C-29
1986	TEX	A	46	.235	.294	102	24	1	1	1	1.0	7	7	6	13	0	1	0	240	25	1	5	5.8	.996	C-45
1987	2 teams		DET A (10G — .136)			LA N (7G — .600)																			
''	total		17	.222	.259	27	6	1	0	0	0.0	3	2	3	1	0	0	0	53	8	1	1	3.6	.984	C-17
1988	OAK	A	16	.125	.250	24	3	0	0	1	4.2	3	1	3	8	0	0	0	45	2	2	0	3.1	.959	C-16
1989	MIN	A	19	.105	.105	38	4	0	0	0	0.0	1	1	4	4	1	0	0	73	9	0	2	4.3	1.000	C-19
1990	2 teams		NY N (42G — .211)			MON N (8G — .250)																			
''	total		50	.214	.316	98	21	1	0	3	3.0	10	7	8	12	0	4	0	239	9	2	2	5.2	.992	C-48
8 yrs.			253	.199	.281	562	112	17	4	7	1.2	40	45	42	82	4	10	1	1141	91	9	12	4.9	.993	C-247, DH-1

Orlando Merced

MERCED, ORLANDO LUIS
Born Orlando Luis Merced y Villanueva.
B. Nov. 2, 1966, San Juan, Puerto Rico
BB TR 5′ 11″ 170 lbs.

Year	Team		Games	BA	SA	AB	H	2B	3B	HR	HR%	R	RBI	BB	SO	SB	AB	H	PO	A	E	DP	TC/G	FA	G by Pos
1990	PIT	N	25	.208	.250	24	5	1	0	0	0.0	3	0	1	9	0	24	5	0	0	0	0	0.0	1.000	C-1, OF-1

Hensley Meulens

MEULENS, HENSLEY FILEMON ACASIO (Bam-Bam)
B. June 23, 1967, Curacao, Netherlands, Ant.
BR TR 6′ 4″ 200 lbs.

Year	Team		Games	BA	SA	AB	H	2B	3B	HR	HR%	R	RBI	BB	SO	SB	AB	H	PO	A	E	DP	TC/G	FA	G by Pos
1989	NY	A	8	.179	.179	28	5	0	0	0	0.0	2	1	2	8	0	0	0	5	23	4	1	4.0	.875	3B-8
1990			23	.241	.434	83	20	7	0	3	3.6	12	10	9	25	1	0	0	49	3	2	1	2.3	.963	OF-23
2 yrs.			31	.225	.369	111	25	7	0	3	2.7	14	11	11	33	1	0	0	54	26	6	2	2.8	.930	OF-23, 3B-8

Year	Team	Games	BA	SA	AB	H	2B	3B	HR	HR%	R	RBI	BB	SO	SB	PINCH HIT AB	PINCH HIT H	PO	A	E	DP	TC/G	FA	G by Pos

Keith Miller

MILLER, KEITH ALAN
B. June 12, 1963, Midland, Mich.
BR TR 5' 11" 175 lbs.

Year	Team	Games	BA	SA	AB	H	2B	3B	HR	HR%	R	RBI	BB	SO	SB	PINCH HIT AB	PINCH HIT H	PO	A	E	DP	TC/G	FA	G by Pos
April		14	.250	.404	52	13	5	0	1	1.9	12	3	8	9	6									
May		7	.280	.280	25	7	0	0	0	0.0	3	0	0	4	2									
June		19	.295	.318	44	13	1	0	0	0.0	6	4	3	7	3									
July		17	.357	.357	28	10	0	0	0	0.0	4	1	0	6	2									
Aug		11	.242	.242	33	8	0	0	0	0.0	8	3	3	9	1									
Sept/Oct		20	.176	.216	51	9	2	0	0	0.0	9	1	9	11	2									
Day		34	.283	.374	99	28	6	0	1	1.0	20	5	11	14	7									
Night		54	.239	.254	134	32	2	0	0	0.0	22	7	12	32	9									
vs. Left			.289	.336	149	43	7	0	0	0.0	21	8	12	27	9									
vs. Right			.202	.250	84	17	1	0	1	1.2	21	4	11	19	7									
On Grass		53	.241	.290	145	35	4	0	1	0.7	24	10	20	28	9									
On Turf		35	.284	.330	88	25	4	0	0	0.0	18	2	3	18	7									
Home		39	.234	.290	107	25	3	0	1	0.9	18	9	19	19	7									
Road		49	.278	.317	126	35	5	0	0	0.0	24	3	4	27	9									
Division Rivals																								
vs. CHI		14	.179	.205	39	7	1	0	0	0.0	6	4	9	13	1									
vs. MON		15	.267	.422	45	12	4	0	1	2.2	12	3	4	6	6									
vs. PHI		14	.229	.286	35	8	2	0	0	0.0	7	1	5	9	1									
vs. PIT		11	.344	.375	32	11	1	0	0	0.0	3	1	2	1	3									
vs. STL		9	.250	.250	20	5	0	0	0	0.0	6	1	1	5	0									
On 3B < 2 Out			.167	.167	6	1	0	0	0	0.0	0	7	1	1										
1987	NY N	25	.373	.490	51	19	2	2	0	0.0	14	1	2	6	8	0	0	21	38	2	6	2.4	.967	2B-16
1988		40	.214	.300	70	15	1	1	1	1.4	9	5	6	10	0	9	2	34	24	5	3	1.6	.921	2B-16, SS-8, 3B-6, OF-1
1989		57	.231	.301	143	33	7	0	1	0.7	15	7	5	27	6	7	2	90	52	5	8	2.6	.966	2B-23, OF-14, SS-8, 3B-2
1990		88	.258	.305	233	60	8	0	1	0.4	42	12	23	46	16	16	4	168	21	4	8	2.6	.979	OF-61, 2B-11, SS-4
4 yrs.		210	.256	.322	497	127	18	3	3	0.6	80	25	36	89	30	32	8	313	135	16	25	2.2	.966	OF-76, 2B-66, SS-20, 3B-8

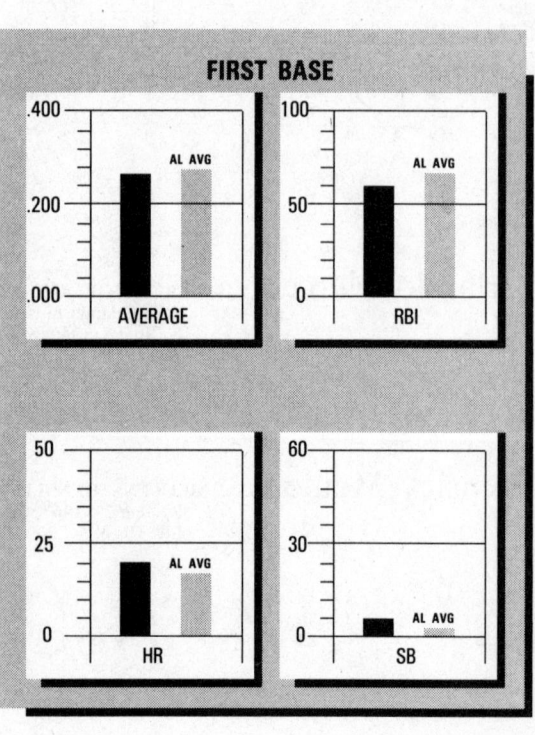

Randy Milligan

MILLIGAN, RANDY ANDRE
B. Nov. 27, 1961, San Diego, Calif.
BR TR 6' 2" 200 lbs.

Year	Team	Games	BA	SA	AB	H	2B	3B	HR	HR%	R	RBI	BB	SO	SB	PINCH HIT AB	PINCH HIT H	PO	A	E	DP	TC/G	FA	G by Pos
April		20	.259	.379	58	15	1	0	2	3.4	12	9	17	14	0									
May		25	.205	.397	78	16	6	0	3	3.8	15	10	27	17	4									
June		28	.327	.644	101	33	8	0	8	7.9	16	24	21	17	1									
July		28	.248	.505	101	25	5	0	7	6.9	17	15	20	14	1									
Aug		5	.214	.357	14	3	0	1	0	0.0	3	0	3	4	0									
Sept/Oct		3	.400	.400	10	4	0	0	0	0.0	1	2	0	2	0									
Day		29	.293	.478	92	27	5	0	4	4.3	16	16	22	15	2									
Night		80	.256	.496	270	69	15	1	16	5.9	48	44	66	53	4									
vs. Left			.330	.680	100	33	9	1	8	8.0	19	22	28	14	0									
vs. Right			.240	.420	262	63	11	0	12	4.6	45	38	60	54	6									
On Grass		91	.267	.493	300	80	18	1	16	5.3	53	50	75	58	6									
On Turf		18	.258	.484	62	16	2	0	4	6.5	11	10	13	10	0									
Home		53	.265	.536	166	44	10	1	11	6.6	32	31	45	33	4									
Road		56	.265	.454	196	52	10	0	9	4.6	32	29	43	35	2									
Division Rivals																								
vs. BOS		7	.261	.304	23	6	1	0	0	0.0	3	5	7	7	0									
vs. CLE		7	.435	.913	23	10	2	0	3	13.0	4	5	8	3	0									
vs. DET		10	.185	.259	27	5	2	0	0	0.0	5	3	9	6	0									
vs. MIL		7	.345	.586	29	10	4	0	1	3.4	2	6	2	1	1									
vs. NY		6	.409	1.000	22	9	1	0	4	18.2	6	9	3	5	0									
vs. TOR		8	.318	.455	22	7	0	0	1	4.5	7	3	7	4	0									
On 3B < 2 Out			.308	.538	13	4	0	0	1	7.7	1	12	8	3										
1987	NY N	3	.000	.000	1	0	0	0	0	0.0	0	0	1	1	0	1	0	0	0	0	0	0.0	—	
1988	PIT N	40	.220	.390	82	18	5	0	3	3.7	10	8	20	24	1	13	3	213	15	3	19	5.8	.987	1B-25, OF-1
1989	BAL A	124	.268	.458	365	98	23	5	12	3.3	56	45	74	75	9	11	2	914	83	5	92	8.1	.995	1B-117, DH-1
1990		109	.265	.492	362	96	20	1	20	5.5	64	60	88	68	6	0	0	846	87	9	94	9.6	.990	1B-98, DH-9
4 yrs.		276	.262	.465	810	212	48	6	35	4.3	130	113	183	168	16	25	5	1973	185	17	205	7.9	.992	1B-240, DH-10, OF-1

Year	Team	Games	BA	SA	AB	H	2B	3B	HR	HR%	R	RBI	BB	SO	SB	PINCH HIT AB	H	PO	A	E	DP	TC/G	FA	G by Pos

Kevin Mitchell

MITCHELL, KEVIN DARNELL (Mitch, World)
B. Jan. 13, 1962, San Diego, Calif.
BR TR 5′ 10″ 185 lbs.

Year	Team	Games	BA	SA	AB	H	2B	3B	HR	HR%	R	RBI	BB	SO	SB	PINCH HIT AB	H	PO	A	E	DP	TC/G	FA	G by Pos
April		19	.310	.535	71	22	4	0	4	5.6	14	9	8	15	0									
May		25	.313	.615	96	30	3	1	8	8.3	17	15	11	15	0									
June		24	.308	.604	91	28	6	0	7	7.7	20	21	10	11	2									
July		21	.325	.597	77	25	3	0	6	7.8	11	17	9	16	0									
Aug		28	.269	.481	104	28	4	0	6	5.8	16	18	11	15	2									
Sept/Oct		23	.224	.435	85	19	4	1	4	4.7	12	13	9	15	0									
Day		54	.300	.505	200	60	11	0	10	5.0	29	32	22	33	2									
Night		86	.284	.568	324	92	13	2	25	7.7	61	61	36	54	2									
vs. Left			.306	.547	170	52	11	0	10	5.9	25	29	27	24	1									
vs. Right			.282	.542	354	100	13	2	25	7.1	65	64	31	63	3									
On Grass		102	.290	.517	383	111	19	1	22	5.7	71	63	43	64	3									
On Turf		38	.291	.617	141	41	5	1	13	9.2	19	30	15	23	1									
Home		66	.278	.515	241	67	10	1	15	6.2	46	39	31	36	2									
Road		74	.300	.569	283	85	14	1	20	7.1	44	54	27	51	2									
Division Rivals																								
vs. ATL		14	.345	.618	55	19	4	1	3	5.5	13	10	6	9	1									
vs. CIN		15	.246	.509	57	14	3	0	4	7.0	9	10	5	12	0									
vs. HOU		16	.190	.349	63	12	1	0	3	4.8	5	11	3	9	1									
vs. LA		13	.292	.583	48	14	2	0	4	8.3	9	7	6	6	0									
vs. SD		17	.284	.507	67	19	6	0	3	4.5	11	11	4	10	0									
On 3B < 2 Out			.258	.323	31	8	2	0	0	0.0	0	23	3	4										
1984	NY N	7	.214	.214	14	3	0	0	0	0.0	0	1	0	3	0	4	1	1	4	1	2	0.9	.833	3B-5
1986		108	.277	.466	328	91	22	2	12	3.7	51	43	33	61	3	20	3	158	69	10	10	2.2	.958	OF-68, SS-24, 3B-7, 1B-2
1987	2 teams	SD N (62G — .245)			SF N (69G — .306)																			
''	total	131	.280	.474	464	130	20	2	22	4.7	68	70	48	88	9	9	2	76	240	15	19	2.5	.955	3B-119, OF-6, SS-1
1988	SF N	148	.251	.442	505	127	25	7	19	3.8	60	80	48	85	5	10	2	118	205	22	18	2.3	.936	3B-102, OF-40
1989		154	.291	.635	543	158	34	6	47	8.7	100	125	87	115	3	3	1	305	10	7	0	2.1	.978	OF-147, 3B-2
1990		140	.290	.544	524	152	24	2	35	6.6	90	93	58	87	4	2	1	295	9	9	3	2.3	.971	OF-138
6 yrs.		688	.278	.517	2378	661	125	19	135	5.7	369	412	274	439	24	48	10	953	537	64	52	2.3	.959	OF-399, 3B-235, SS-25, 1B-2

LEAGUE CHAMPIONSHIP SERIES

Year	Team	Games	BA	SA	AB	H	2B	3B	HR	HR%	R	RBI	BB	SO	SB	PINCH HIT AB	H	PO	A	E	DP	TC/G	FA	G by Pos
1986	NY N	2	.250	.250	8	2	0	0	0	0.0	1	0	0	1	0	0	0	3	0	0	0	1.5	1.000	OF-2
1987	SF N	7	.267	.400	30	8	1	0	1	3.3	2	2	0	3	1	0	0	4	10	1	1	2.1	.933	3B-7
1989		5	.353	.706	17	6	0	0	2	11.8	5	7	3	3	0	0	0	15	1	1	1	3.4	.941	OF-5
3 yrs.		14	.291	.473	55	16	1	0	3	5.5	8	9	3	7	1	0	0	22	11	2	2	2.5	.943	3B-7, OF-7

WORLD SERIES

Year	Team	Games	BA	SA	AB	H	2B	3B	HR	HR%	R	RBI	BB	SO	SB	PINCH HIT AB	H	PO	A	E	DP	TC/G	FA	G by Pos
1986	NY N	5	.250	.250	8	2	0	0	0	0.0	1	0	0	3	0	2	1	0	2	0	0	0.4	1.000	OF-2, DH-1
1989	SF N	4	.294	.471	17	5	0	0	1	5.9	2	2	0	3	0	0	0	10	0	1	0	2.8	.909	OF-4
2 yrs.		9	.280	.400	25	7	0	0	1	4.0	3	2	0	6	0	2	1	10	2	1	0	1.4	.923	OF-6, DH-1

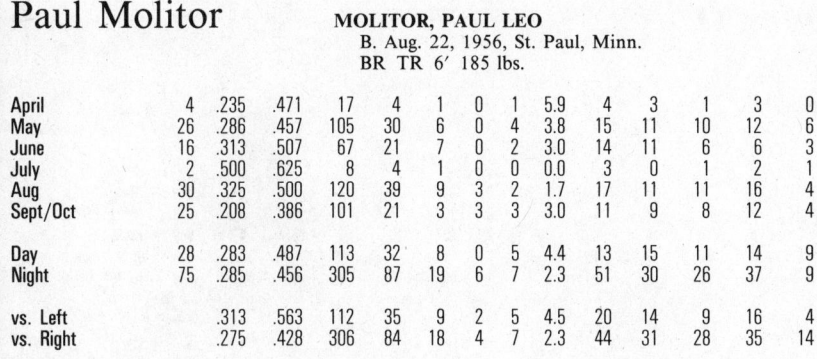

Paul Molitor

MOLITOR, PAUL LEO
B. Aug. 22, 1956, St. Paul, Minn.
BR TR 6′ 185 lbs.

Year	Team	Games	BA	SA	AB	H	2B	3B	HR	HR%	R	RBI	BB	SO	SB	PINCH HIT AB	H	PO	A	E	DP	TC/G	FA	G by Pos
April		4	.235	.471	17	4	1	0	1	5.9	4	3	1	3	0									
May		26	.286	.457	105	30	6	0	4	3.8	15	11	10	12	6									
June		16	.313	.507	67	21	7	0	2	3.0	14	11	6	6	3									
July		2	.500	.625	8	4	1	0	0	0.0	3	0	1	2	1									
Aug		30	.325	.500	120	39	9	3	2	1.7	17	11	11	16	4									
Sept/Oct		25	.208	.386	101	21	3	3	3	3.0	11	9	8	12	4									
Day		28	.283	.487	113	32	8	0	5	4.4	13	15	11	14	9									
Night		75	.285	.456	305	87	19	6	7	2.3	51	30	26	37	9									
vs. Left			.313	.563	112	35	9	2	5	4.5	20	14	9	16	4									
vs. Right			.275	.428	306	84	18	4	7	2.3	44	31	28	35	14									

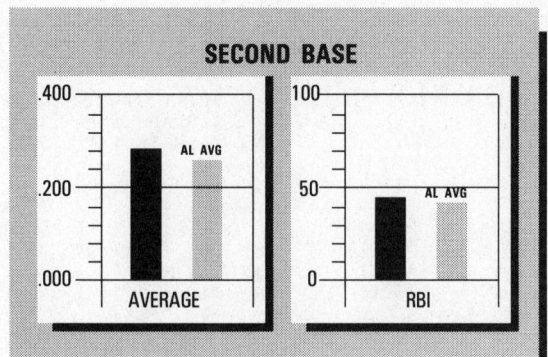

Year	Team		Games	BA	SA	AB	H	2B	3B	HR	HR%	R	RBI	BB	SO	SB	PINCH HIT AB	H	PO	A	E	DP	TC/G	FA	G by Pos

Paul Molitor *Continued*

On Grass			82	.268	.428	325	87	21	5	7	2.2	48	28	33	43	13									
On Turf			21	.344	.591	93	32	6	1	5	5.4	16	17	4	8	5									
Home			48	.286	.470	185	53	14	1	6	3.2	27	19	17	20	10									
Road			55	.283	.459	233	66	13	5	6	2.6	37	26	20	31	8									
Division Rivals																									
vs. BAL			13	.231	.442	52	12	5	0	2	3.8	7	4	6	6	2									
vs. BOS			4	.056	.167	18	1	0	1	0	0.0	1	0	0	5	0									
vs. CLE			8	.394	.606	33	13	5	1	0	0.0	8	2	2	3	1									
vs. DET			13	.313	.521	48	15	2	1	2	4.2	10	6	9	4	3									
vs. NY			4	.278	.278	18	5	0	0	0	0.0	1	1	1	4	0									
vs. TOR			13	.273	.491	55	15	1	1	3	5.5	10	10	2	5	4									
On 3B < 2 Out				.333	.444	9	3	1	0	0	0.0	0	5	5	1									
1978	MIL	A	125	.273	.372	521	142	26	4	6	1.2	73	45	19	54	30	3	0	253	401	22	74	5.4	.967	2B-91, SS-31, DH-2, 3B-1
1979			140	.322	.469	584	188	27	16	9	1.5	88	62	48	48	33	2	0	309	440	16	84	5.5	.979	2B-122, SS-10, DH-8
1980			111	.304	.438	450	137	29	2	9	2.0	81	37	48	48	34	2	1	260	336	20	90	5.5	.968	2B-91, SS-12, DH-7, 3B-1
1981			64	.267	.335	251	67	11	0	2	0.8	45	19	25	29	10	1	0	119	4	3	1	2.0	.976	OF-46, DH-16
1982			160	.302	.450	**666**	201	26	8	19	2.9	**136**	71	69	93	41	0	0	134	350	32	48	3.2	.938	3B-150, DH-6, SS-4
1983			152	.270	.410	608	164	28	6	15	2.5	95	47	59	74	41	2	0	105	343	16	37	3.1	.966	3B-146, DH-2
1984			13	.217	.239	46	10	1	0	0	0.0	3	6	2	8	1	2	0	7	21	2	3	2.3	.933	3B-7, DH-4
1985			140	.297	.408	576	171	28	3	10	1.7	93	48	54	80	21	1	0	126	263	19	30	2.9	.953	3B-135, DH-4
1986			105	.281	.426	437	123	24	6	9	2.1	62	55	40	81	20	0	0	86	171	15	25	2.6	.945	3B-91, DH-10, OF-4
1987			118	.353	.566	465	164	**41**	5	16	3.4	**114**	75	69	67	45	1	0	60	113	5	24	1.5	.972	DH-58, 3B-41, 2B-19
1988			154	.312	.452	609	190	34	6	13	2.1	115	60	71	54	41	0	0	87	188	17	15	1.9	.942	3B-105, DH-49, 2B-1
1989			155	.315	.439	615	194	35	4	11	1.8	84	56	64	67	27	0	0	106	287	18	27	2.7	.956	3B-112, DH-28, 2B-16
1990			103	.285	.464	418	119	27	6	12	2.8	64	45	37	51	18	1	0	463	222	10	65	7.1	.986	2B-60, 1B-37, DH-4, 3B-2
13 yrs.			1540	.299	.437	6246	1870	337	66	131	2.1	1053	626	605	754	362	15	1	2115	3139	195	523	3.5	.964	3B-791, 2B-400, DH-198, SS-57, OF-50, 1B-37

DIVISIONAL PLAYOFF SERIES

Year	Team		Games	BA	SA	AB	H	2B	3B	HR	HR%	R	RBI	BB	SO	SB	AB	H	PO	A	E	DP	TC/G	FA	G by Pos
1981	MIL	A	5	.250	.400	20	5	0	0	1	5.0	2	1	2	5	0	0	0	12	0	0	0	2.4	1.000	OF-5

LEAGUE CHAMPIONSHIP SERIES

Year	Team		Games	BA	SA	AB	H	2B	3B	HR	HR%	R	RBI	BB	SO	SB	AB	H	PO	A	E	DP	TC/G	FA	G by Pos
1982	MIL	A	5	.316	.684	19	6	1	0	2	10.5	4	5	2	3	1	0	0	4	11	2	2	3.0	.882	3B-5

WORLD SERIES

Year	Team		Games	BA	SA	AB	H	2B	3B	HR	HR%	R	RBI	BB	SO	SB	AB	H	PO	A	E	DP	TC/G	FA	G by Pos
1982	MIL	A	7	.355	.355	31	11	0	0	0	0.0	5	2	2	4	1	0	0	4	9	0	1	1.9	1.000	3B-7

Mickey Morandini   MORANDINI, MICHAEL ROBERT
B. Apr. 22, 1966, Kittanning, Pa.
BL TR 5′ 11″ 170 lbs.

Year	Team		Games	BA	SA	AB	H	2B	3B	HR	HR%	R	RBI	BB	SO	SB	AB	H	PO	A	E	DP	TC/G	FA	G by Pos
1990	PHI	N	25	.241	.329	79	19	4	0	1	1.2	9	3	6	19	3	1	0	37	61	1	10	4.0	.990	2B-25

Russ Morman   MORMAN, RUSSELL LEE
B. Apr. 28, 1962, Independence, Mo.
BR TR 6′ 4″ 215 lbs.

Year	Team		Games	BA	SA	AB	H	2B	3B	HR	HR%	R	RBI	BB	SO	SB	AB	H	PO	A	E	DP	TC/G	FA	G by Pos
1986	CHI	A	49	.252	.358	159	40	5	0	4	2.5	18	17	16	36	1	1	0	342	26	4	31	7.6	.989	1B-47
1988			40	.240	.267	75	18	2	0	0	0.0	8	3	3	17	0	5	2	114	5	2	8	3.0	.983	1B-22, OF-10, DH-2
1989			37	.224	.259	58	13	2	0	0	0.0	5	8	6	16	1	2	2	157	13	2	21	4.6	.988	1B-35, DH-1
1990	KC	A	12	.270	.568	37	10	4	2	1	2.7	5	3	3	3	0	1	0	27	4	0	1	3.1	1.000	OF-8, 1B-3, DH-1
4 yrs.			138	.246	.343	329	81	13	2	5	1.5	36	31	28	72	2	9	4	640	48	8	61	5.0	.989	1B-107, OF-18, DH-5

Year	Team		Games	BA	SA	AB	H	2B	3B	HR	HR%	R	RBI	BB	SO	SB	PINCH HIT AB	PINCH HIT H	PO	A	E	DP	TC/G	FA	G by Pos

Hal Morris

MORRIS, WILLIAM HAROLD
B. Apr. 9, 1965, Fort Rucker, Ala.
BL TL 6′ 3″ 200 lbs.

Year	Team		Games	BA	SA	AB	H	2B	3B	HR	HR%	R	RBI	BB	SO	SB	PH AB	PH H	PO	A	E	DP	TC/G	FA	G by Pos
April			7	.167	.167	12	2	0	0	0	0.0	2	0	1	4	0									
May			11	.267	.333	15	4	1	0	0	0.0	2	1	1	1	1									
June			10	.444	.556	18	8	2	0	0	0.0	2	3	1	2	1									
July			24	.427	.640	75	32	3	2	3	4.0	17	13	3	6	3									
Aug			26	.301	.484	93	28	8	0	3	3.2	12	8	4	9	2									
Sept/Oct			29	.323	.458	96	31	8	1	1	1.0	15	11	11	10	2									
Day			33	.313	.505	99	31	10	0	3	3.0	19	12	6	12	3									
Night			74	.352	.495	210	74	12	3	4	1.9	31	24	15	20	6									
vs. Left				.224	.224	76	17	0	0	0	0.0	10	5	6	13	1									
vs. Right				.378	.588	233	88	22	3	7	3.0	40	31	15	19	8									
On Grass			33	.303	.431	109	33	7	2	1	0.9	19	8	7	14	2									
On Turf			74	.360	.535	200	72	15	1	6	3.0	31	28	14	18	7									
Home			57	.338	.493	148	50	12	1	3	2.0	19	20	12	13	3									
Road			50	.342	.503	161	55	10	2	4	2.5	31	16	9	19	6									
Division Rivals																									
vs. ATL			9	.467	.533	15	7	1	0	0	0.0	4	1	4	4	1									
vs. HOU			8	.280	.360	25	7	0	1	0	0.0	2	2	4	2	1									
vs. LA			13	.317	.439	41	13	3	1	0	0.0	8	3	2	3	1									
vs. SD			17	.302	.415	53	16	1	1	1	1.9	7	6	3	6	0									
vs. SF			13	.465	.837	43	20	7	0	3	7.0	10	9	4	3	2									
On 3B < 2 Out				.348	.391	23	8	1	0	0	0.0	0	11	3	4										
1988	NY	A	15	.100	.100	20	2	0	0	0	0.0	1	0	0	9	0	10	2	7	0	0	0	0.5	1.000	OF-4, DH-1
1989			15	.278	.278	18	5	0	0	0	0.0	2	4	1	4	0	9	1	12	0	0	2	0.8	1.000	OF-5, 1B-2, DH-1
1990	CIN	N	107	.340	.498	309	105	22	3	7	2.2	50	36	21	32	9	21	7	595	53	4	50	7.6	.994	1B-80, OF-6
3 yrs.			137	.323	.464	347	112	22	3	7	2.0	53	40	22	45	9	40	10	614	53	4	52	4.9	.994	1B-82, OF-15, DH-2

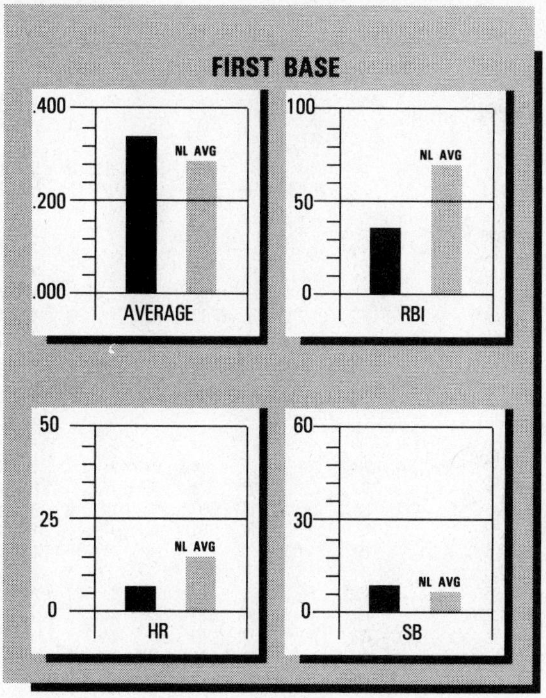

LEAGUE CHAMPIONSHIP SERIES

Year	Team		Games	BA	SA	AB	H	2B	3B	HR	HR%	R	RBI	BB	SO	SB	PH AB	PH H	PO	A	E	DP	TC/G	FA	G by Pos
1990	CIN	N	5	.417	.500	12	5	1	0	0	0.0	3	1	1	0	0	1	1	20	2	0	2	5.5	1.000	1B-4

WORLD SERIES

Year	Team		Games	BA	SA	AB	H	2B	3B	HR	HR%	R	RBI	BB	SO	SB	PH AB	PH H	PO	A	E	DP	TC/G	FA	G by Pos
1990	CIN	N	4	.071	.071	14	1	0	0	0	0.0	0	2	1	1	0	0	0	18	1	0	1	9.5	1.000	DH-2, 1B-2

FIRST BASE

AVERAGE — NL AVG
RBI — NL AVG
HR — NL AVG
SB — NL AVG

John Morris

MORRIS, JOHN DANIEL
B. Feb. 23, 1961, Freeport, N. Y.
BL TL 6′ 1″ 185 lbs.

Year	Team		Games	BA	SA	AB	H	2B	3B	HR	HR%	R	RBI	BB	SO	SB	PH AB	PH H	PO	A	E	DP	TC/G	FA	G by Pos
1986	STL	N	39	.240	.290	100	24	0	1	1	1.0	8	14	7	15	6	11	3	68	0	1	0	1.8	.986	OF-31
1987			101	.261	.408	157	41	6	4	3	1.9	22	23	11	22	5	30	10	86	0	1	0	0.9	.989	OF-74
1988			20	.289	.395	38	11	2	1	0	0.0	3	3	1	7	0	6	2	12	0	2	0	0.7	.857	OF-16
1989			96	.239	.342	117	28	4	1	2	1.7	8	14	4	22	1	41	9	45	0	0	0	0.5	1.000	OF-51
1990			18	.111	.111	18	2	0	0	0	0.0	0	0	3	6	0	9	1	4	0	0	0	0.7	1.000	OF-6
5 yrs.			274	.247	.349	430	106	12	7	6	1.4	41	54	26	72	12	97	25	215	0	4	0	0.8	.000	OF-178

LEAGUE CHAMPIONSHIP SERIES

Year	Team		Games	BA	SA	AB	H	2B	3B	HR	HR%	R	RBI	BB	SO	SB	PH AB	PH H	PO	A	E	DP	TC/G	FA	G by Pos
1987	STL	N	2	.000	.000	3	0	0	0	0	0.0	0	0	0	0	0	0	0	1	0	0	0	0.5	1.000	OF-2

WORLD SERIES

Year	Team		Games	BA	SA	AB	H	2B	3B	HR	HR%	R	RBI	BB	SO	SB	PH AB	PH H	PO	A	E	DP	TC/G	FA	G by Pos
1987	STL	N	1	.000	.000	2	0	0	0	0	0.0	0	0	0	0	0	0	0	2	0	0	0	2.0	1.000	OF-1

Lloyd Moseby

MOSEBY, LLOYD ANTHONY
B. Nov. 5, 1959, Portland, Ark.
BL TR 6′ 3″ 200 lbs.

Year	Team		Games	BA	SA	AB	H	2B	3B	HR	HR%	R	RBI	BB	SO	SB	PH AB	PH H	PO	A	E	DP	TC/G	FA	G by Pos
April			18	.333	.424	66	22	4	1	0	0.0	10	4	7	12	4									
May			27	.200	.421	95	19	1	1	6	6.3	14	11	9	21	2									
June			20	.250	.324	68	17	2	0	1	1.5	9	6	7	10	4									
July			15	.304	.565	46	14	1	1	3	6.5	10	10	11	8	4									
Aug			20	.228	.418	79	18	4	1	3	3.8	13	17	8	16	1									
Sept/Oct			22	.221	.338	77	17	4	1	1	1.3	8	3	6	10	2									
Day			37	.209	.313	115	24	4	1	2	1.7	13	5	14	19	4									
Night			85	.263	.440	316	83	12	4	12	3.8	51	46	34	58	13									
vs. Left				.182	.242	132	24	2	0	2	1.5	12	9	10	26	3									
vs. Right				.278	.478	299	83	14	5	12	4.0	52	42	38	51	14									

OUTFIELD

AVERAGE — AL AVG
RBI — AL AVG

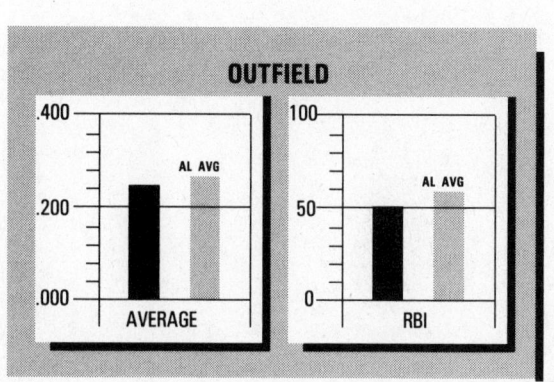

Year	Team	Games	BA	SA	AB	H	2B	3B	HR	HR%	R	RBI	BB	SO	SB	PINCH HIT AB	H	PO	A	E	DP	TC/G	FA	G by Pos

Lloyd Moseby *Continued*

Year	Team	Games	BA	SA	AB	H	2B	3B	HR	HR%	R	RBI	BB	SO	SB	AB	H	PO	A	E	DP	TC/G	FA	G by Pos
On Grass		109	.241	.386	381	92	11	4	12	3.1	57	42	44	69	14									
On Turf		13	.300	.560	50	15	5	1	2	4.0	7	9	4	8	3									
Home		65	.240	.394	221	53	4	3	8	3.6	38	25	31	39	11									
Road		57	.257	.419	210	54	12	2	6	2.9	26	26	17	38	6									
Division Rivals																								
vs. BAL		12	.300	.450	40	12	3	0	1	2.5	7	5	7	5	2									
vs. BOS		12	.271	.375	48	13	2	0	1	2.1	9	4	4	7	2									
vs. CLE		10	.200	.314	35	7	1	0	1	2.9	3	4	3	4	3									
vs. MIL		12	.263	.342	38	10	0	0	1	2.6	7	2	5	7	2									
vs. NY		7	.241	.552	29	7	1	1	2	6.9	4	8	2	4	0									
vs. TOR		10	.171	.371	35	6	1	0	2	5.7	4	4	6	6	0									
On 3B < 2 Out			.269	.462	26	7	0	1	1	3.8	-	1	18	2	3									
1980	TOR A	114	.229	.365	389	89	24	1	9	2.3	44	46	25	85	4	2	0	208	12	4	1	2.0	.982	OF-104, DH-6
1981		100	.233	.357	378	88	16	2	9	2.4	36	43	24	86	11	2	0	259	4	3	0	2.7	.989	OF-100
1982		147	.236	.370	487	115	20	9	9	1.8	51	52	33	106	11	7	3	361	4	3	0	2.5	.992	OF-145
1983		151	.315	.499	539	170	31	7	18	3.3	104	81	51	85	27	9	4	399	10	7	1	2.8	.983	OF-147
1984		158	.280	.470	592	166	28	**15**	18	3.0	97	92	78	122	39	3	1	473	8	5	2	3.1	.990	OF-156
1985		152	.259	.426	584	151	30	7	18	3.1	92	71	76	91	37	1	0	394	7	8	1	2.7	.980	OF-152
1986		152	.253	.418	589	149	24	5	21	3.6	89	86	64	122	32	4	0	371	6	6	1	2.5	.984	OF-147, DH-3
1987		155	.282	.473	592	167	27	4	26	4.4	106	96	70	124	39	0	0	294	7	6	1	2.0	.980	OF-153, DH-2
1988		128	.239	.369	472	113	17	7	10	2.1	77	42	70	93	31	3	0	304	2	5	1	2.4	.984	OF-125, DH-1
1989		135	.221	.349	502	111	25	3	11	2.2	72	43	56	101	24	4	1	288	3	4	1	2.2	.986	OF-120, DH-14
1990	DET A	122	.248	.406	431	107	16	5	14	3.2	64	51	48	77	17	7	0	288	9	5	5	2.6	.983	OF-116, DH-4
11 yrs.		1514	.257	.415	5555	1426	258	65	163	2.9	832	703	595	1092	272	42	9	3639	72	56	14	2.5	.985	OF-1465, DH-30
LEAGUE CHAMPIONSHIP SERIES																								
1985	TOR A	7	.226	.258	31	7	1	0	0	0.0	5	4	2	3	1	0	0	10	0	0	0	1.4	1.000	OF-7
1989		5	.313	.500	16	5	0	0	1	6.3	4	2	5	2	1	0	0	15	0	0	0	3.0	1.000	OF-5
2 yrs.		12	.255	.340	47	12	1	0	1	2.1	9	6	7	5	2	0	0	25	0	0	0	2.1	.000	OF-12

OUTFIELD (graphs: HR — player vs AL AVG; SB — player vs AL AVG)

John Moses

MOSES, JOHN WILLIAM
B. Aug. 9, 1957, Los Angeles, Calif.
BB TL 5' 10" 165 lbs.

Year	Team	Games	BA	SA	AB	H	2B	3B	HR	HR%	R	RBI	BB	SO	SB	AB	H	PO	A	E	DP	TC/G	FA	G by Pos
1982	SEA A	22	.318	.545	44	14	5	1	1	2.3	7	3	4	5	5	2	1	16	2	1	0	0.9	.947	OF-19
1983		93	.208	.254	130	27	4	1	0	0.0	19	6	12	20	11	4	1	87	8	2	1	1.0	.979	OF-71, DH-10
1984		19	.343	.429	35	12	1	1	0	0.0	3	2	2	5	1	0	0	26	1	0	0	1.4	1.000	OF-22
1985		33	.194	.194	62	12	0	0	0	0.0	4	3	2	8	5	0	0	35	1	0	0	1.1	1.000	OF-29
1986		103	.256	.333	399	102	16	3	3	0.8	56	34	34	65	25	2	0	249	11	5	4	2.6	.981	OF-93, 1B-7, DH-4
1987		116	.246	.331	390	96	16	4	3	0.8	58	38	29	49	23	3	1	271	7	4	3	2.4	.986	OF-100, 1B-16, DH-5
1988	MIN A	105	.316	.422	206	65	10	3	2	1.0	33	12	15	21	11	21	6	123	1	0	0	1.2	1.000	OF-82, DH-2
1989		129	.281	.368	242	68	12	3	1	0.4	33	31	19	23	14	30	8	168	3	2	0	1.3	.988	OF-108, DH-3, 1B-2, P-1
1990		115	.221	.267	172	38	3	1	1	0.5	26	14	19	19	2	25	7	108	2	0	0	1.2	1.000	OF-85, DH-10, 1B-6, P-2
9 yrs.		735	.258	.338	1680	434	67	17	11	0.7	239	143	136	215	97	87	24	1083	36	14	8	1.5	.988	OF-606, DH-35, 1B-31, P-3

Rance Mulliniks

MULLINIKS, STEVEN RANCE
B. Jan. 15, 1956, Tulare, Calif.
BL TR 5' 11" 162 lbs.

Year	Team	Games	BA	SA	AB	H	2B	3B	HR	HR%	R	RBI	BB	SO	SB	AB	H	PO	A	E	DP	TC/G	FA	G by Pos
1977	CAL A	78	.269	.365	271	73	13	2	3	1.1	36	21	23	36	1	1	0	112	229	13	37	4.5	.963	SS-77
1978		50	.185	.252	119	22	3	1	1	0.8	6	6	8	23	2	1	0	68	93	8	22	3.4	.953	SS-47, DH-2
1979		22	.147	.191	68	10	0	0	1	1.5	7	8	4	14	0	0	0	46	43	4	13	4.2	.957	SS-22
1980	KC A	36	.259	.315	54	14	3	0	0	0.0	8	6	7	10	0	0	0	30	53	1	9	2.3	.988	SS-18, 2B-14
1981		24	.227	.295	44	10	3	0	0	0.0	6	5	2	7	0	0	0	25	39	5	9	2.9	.928	2B-10, SS-7, 3B-5
1982	TOR A	112	.244	.363	311	76	25	0	4	1.3	32	35	37	49	3	22	3	69	154	14	16	2.1	.941	3B-102, SS-16
1983		129	.275	.467	364	100	34	3	10	2.7	54	49	57	43	0	23	10	77	185	7	19	2.1	.974	3B-116, SS-15, 2B-2
1984		125	.324	.440	343	111	21	5	3	0.9	41	42	33	44	2	18	6	67	152	8	10	1.8	.965	3B-119, SS-3, 2B-1
1985		129	.295	.454	366	108	26	1	10	2.7	55	56	55	54	2	16	9	75	162	7	16	1.9	.971	3B-119
1986		117	.259	.417	348	90	22	0	11	3.2	50	45	43	60	1	16	2	60	176	6	13	2.1	.975	3B-110, DH-5, 2B-1

Year	Team	Games	BA	SA	AB	H	2B	3B	HR	HR%	R	RBI	BB	SO	SB	PINCH HIT AB	H	PO	A	E	DP	TC/G	FA	G by Pos

Rance Mulliniks *Continued*

Year	Team	Games	BA	SA	AB	H	2B	3B	HR	HR%	R	RBI	BB	SO	SB	AB	H	PO	A	E	DP	TC/G	FA	G by Pos
1987		124	.310	.500	332	103	28	1	11	3.3	37	44	34	55	1	24	8	29	137	13	14	1.4	.927	3B-96, DH-22, SS-1
1988		119	.300	.475	337	101	21	1	12	3.6	49	48	56	57	1	17	6	3	5	0	0	0.1	1.000	DH-108, 3B-7
1989		103	.238	.326	273	65	11	2	3	1.1	25	29	34	40	0	18	3	15	50	1	9	0.6	.985	DH-73, 3B-29
1990		57	.289	.392	97	28	4	0	2	2.0	11	16	22	19	2	22	8	23	25	2	5	2.1	.960	3B-22, DH-10, 1B-3
14 yrs.		1225	.274	.412	3327	911	214	16	71	2.1	417	410	415	511	15	181	55	699	1503	89	192	1.9	.961	3B-725, DH-220, SS-206, 2B-28, 1B-3

LEAGUE CHAMPIONSHIP SERIES

Year	Team	Games	BA	SA	AB	H	2B	3B	HR	HR%	R	RBI	BB	SO	SB	AB	H	PO	A	E	DP	TC/G	FA	G by Pos
1985	TOR A	5	.364	.727	11	4	1	0	1	9.1	1	3	2	2	0	2	2	1	4	0	0	1.0	1.000	3B-5
1989		1	.000	.000	1	0	0	0	0	0.0	0	0	0	1	0	1	0	0	0	0	0	0.0	—	
2 yrs.		6	.333	.667	12	4	1	0	1	8.3	1	3	2	3	0	3	2	1	4	0	0	0.8	.000	3B-5

Pedro Munoz

MUNOZ, PEDRO JAVIER
B. Sept. 19, 1968, Ponce, Puerto Rico
BR TR 5' 11" 170 lbs.

Year	Team	Games	BA	SA	AB	H	2B	3B	HR	HR%	R	RBI	BB	SO	SB	AB	H	PO	A	E	DP	TC/G	FA	G by Pos
1990	MIN A	22	.271	.341	85	23	4	1	0	0.0	13	5	2	16	3	0	0	34	1	1	1	1.7	.972	OF-21, DH-1

Dale Murphy

MURPHY, DALE BRYAN
B. Mar. 12, 1956, Portland, Ore.
BR TR 6' 4" 210 lbs.

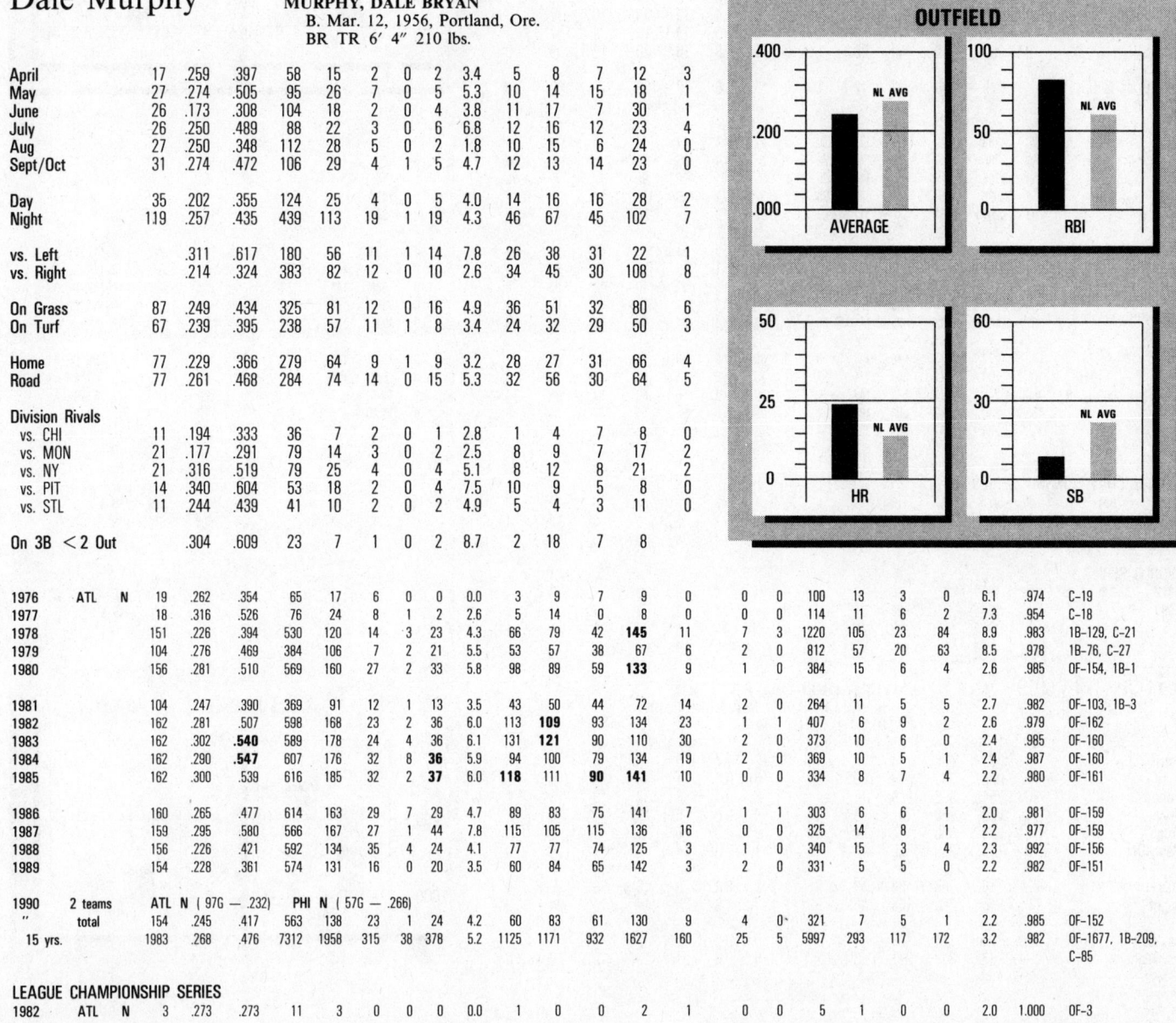

OUTFIELD

	Games	BA	SA	AB	H	2B	3B	HR	HR%	R	RBI	BB	SO	SB
April	17	.259	.397	58	15	2	0	2	3.4	5	8	7	12	3
May	27	.274	.505	95	26	7	0	5	5.3	10	14	15	18	1
June	26	.173	.308	104	18	2	0	4	3.8	11	17	7	30	1
July	26	.250	.489	88	22	3	0	6	6.8	12	16	12	23	4
Aug	27	.250	.348	112	28	5	0	2	1.8	10	15	6	24	0
Sept/Oct	31	.274	.472	106	29	4	1	5	4.7	12	13	14	23	0
Day	35	.202	.355	124	25	4	0	5	4.0	14	16	16	28	2
Night	119	.257	.435	439	113	19	1	19	4.3	46	67	45	102	7
vs. Left		.311	.617	180	56	11	1	14	7.8	26	38	31	22	1
vs. Right		.214	.324	383	82	12	0	10	2.6	34	45	30	108	8
On Grass	87	.249	.434	325	81	12	0	16	4.9	36	51	32	80	6
On Turf	67	.239	.395	238	57	11	1	8	3.4	24	32	29	50	3
Home	77	.229	.366	279	64	9	1	9	3.2	28	27	31	66	4
Road	77	.261	.468	284	74	14	0	15	5.3	32	56	30	64	5
Division Rivals														
vs. CHI	11	.194	.333	36	7	2	0	1	2.8	1	4	7	8	0
vs. MON	21	.177	.291	79	14	3	0	2	2.5	8	9	7	17	2
vs. NY	21	.316	.519	79	25	4	0	4	5.1	8	12	8	21	2
vs. PIT	14	.340	.604	53	18	2	0	4	7.5	10	9	5	8	0
vs. STL	11	.244	.439	41	10	2	0	2	4.9	5	4	3	11	0
On 3B < 2 Out		.304	.609	23	7	1	0	2	8.7	2	18	7	8	

Year	Team	Games	BA	SA	AB	H	2B	3B	HR	HR%	R	RBI	BB	SO	SB	AB	H	PO	A	E	DP	TC/G	FA	G by Pos
1976	ATL N	19	.262	.354	65	17	6	0	0	0.0	3	9	7	9	0	0	0	100	13	3	0	6.1	.974	C-19
1977		18	.316	.526	76	24	8	1	2	2.6	5	14	0	8	0	0	0	114	11	6	2	7.3	.954	C-18
1978		151	.226	.394	530	120	14	3	23	4.3	66	79	42	**145**	11	7	3	1220	105	23	84	8.9	.983	1B-129, C-21
1979		104	.276	.469	384	106	7	2	21	5.5	53	57	38	67	6	2	0	812	57	20	63	8.5	.978	1B-76, C-27
1980		156	.281	.510	569	160	27	2	33	5.8	98	89	59	**133**	9	1	0	384	15	6	4	2.6	.985	OF-154, 1B-1
1981		104	.247	.390	369	91	12	1	13	3.5	43	50	44	72	14	2	0	264	11	5	5	2.7	.982	OF-103, 1B-3
1982		162	.281	.507	598	168	23	2	36	6.0	113	**109**	93	134	23	1	1	407	6	9	2	2.6	.979	OF-162
1983		162	.302	**.540**	589	178	24	4	36	6.1	131	**121**	90	110	30	2	0	373	10	6	0	2.4	.985	OF-160
1984		162	.290	**.547**	607	176	32	8	**36**	5.9	94	100	79	134	19	2	0	369	10	5	1	2.4	.987	OF-160
1985		162	.300	.539	616	185	32	2	**37**	6.0	**118**	111	**90**	**141**	10	0	0	334	8	7	4	2.2	.980	OF-161
1986		160	.265	.477	614	163	29	7	29	4.7	89	83	75	141	7	1	1	303	6	6	1	2.0	.981	OF-159
1987		159	.295	.580	566	167	27	1	44	7.8	115	105	115	136	16	0	0	325	14	8	1	2.2	.977	OF-159
1988		156	.226	.421	592	134	35	4	24	4.1	77	77	74	125	3	1	0	340	15	3	4	2.3	.992	OF-156
1989		154	.228	.361	574	131	16	0	20	3.5	60	84	65	142	3	2	0	331	5	5	0	2.2	.982	OF-151
1990	2 teams	ATL N (97G — .232)			PHI N (57G — .266)																			
"	total	154	.245	.417	563	138	23	1	24	4.2	60	83	61	130	9	4	0*	321	7	5	1	2.2	.985	OF-152
15 yrs.		1983	.268	.476	7312	1958	315	38	378	5.2	1125	1171	932	1627	160	25	5	5997	293	117	172	3.2	.982	OF-1677, 1B-209, C-85

LEAGUE CHAMPIONSHIP SERIES

Year	Team	Games	BA	SA	AB	H	2B	3B	HR	HR%	R	RBI	BB	SO	SB	AB	H	PO	A	E	DP	TC/G	FA	G by Pos
1982	ATL N	3	.273	.273	11	3	0	0	0	0.0	1	0	0	2	1	0	0	5	1	0	0	2.0	1.000	OF-3

Year	Team		Games	BA	SA	AB	H	2B	3B	HR	HR%	R	RBI	BB	SO	SB	PINCH HIT AB	H	PO	A	E	DP	TC/G	FA	G by Pos

Eddie Murray

MURRAY, EDDIE CLARENCE
Brother of Rich Murray.
B. Feb. 24, 1956, Los Angeles, Calif.
BB TR 6' 2" 190 lbs.

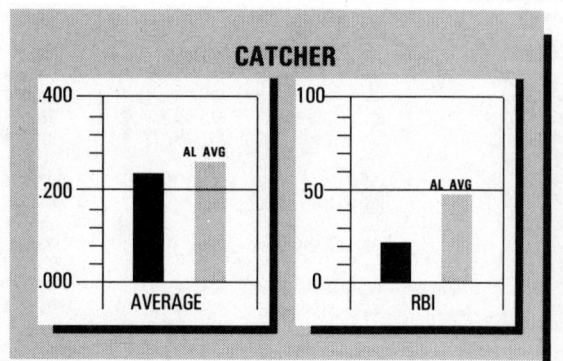

			Games	BA	SA	AB	H	2B	3B	HR	HR%	R	RBI	BB	SO	SB	AB	H	PO	A	E	DP	TC/G	FA	G by Pos
April			21	.282	.436	78	22	3	0	3	3.8	9	11	11	11	0									
May			23	.310	.479	71	22	4	1	2	2.8	10	11	11	7	1									
June			24	.280	.476	82	23	2	1	4	4.9	12	14	12	9	2									
July			27	.357	.622	98	35	5	0	7	7.1	24	18	17	16	2									
Aug			30	.308	.444	117	36	2	1	4	3.4	19	24	12	11	0									
Sept/Oct			30	.411	.625	112	46	6	0	6	5.4	22	17	19	10	3									
Day			36	.295	.455	132	39	3	0	6	4.5	21	20	16	12	1									
Night			119	.340	.540	426	145	19	3	20	4.7	75	75	66	52	7									
vs. Left				.316	.466	206	65	7	0	8	3.9	28	36	25	22	5									
vs. Right				.338	.551	352	119	15	3	18	5.1	68	59	57	42	3									
On Grass			115	.330	.537	410	139	16	1	21	5.1	73	73	64	44	8									
On Turf			40	.304	.473	148	45	6	2	5	3.4	23	22	18	20	0									
Home			79	.343	.524	271	93	11	1	12	4.4	47	43	49	28	7									
Road			76	.317	.516	287	91	11	2	14	4.9	49	52	33	36	1									
Division Rivals																									
vs. ATL			17	.403	.612	67	27	5	0	3	4.5	11	16	10	5	3									
vs. CIN			17	.269	.385	52	14	1	1	1	1.9	6	7	8	6	0									
vs. HOU			18	.294	.500	68	20	3	1	3	4.4	10	10	10	11	0									
vs. SD			17	.358	.612	67	24	2	0	5	7.5	13	10	8	7	2									
vs. SF			18	.382	.662	68	26	1	0	6	8.8	16	20	12	4	0									
On 3B < 2 Out				.375	.406	32	12	1	0	0	0.0	0	26	12	2										
1977	BAL	A	160	.283	.470	611	173	29	2	27	4.4	81	88	48	104	0	4	0	375	17	3	34	2.5	.992	DH-111, 1B-42, OF-3
1978			161	.285	.480	610	174	32	3	27	4.4	85	95	70	97	6	0	0	1507	112	6	144	10.1	.996	1B-157, 3B-3, DH-1
1979			159	.295	.475	606	179	30	2	25	4.1	90	99	72	78	10	0	0	1456	107	10	135	9.9	.994	1B-157, DH-2
1980			158	.300	.519	621	186	36	2	32	5.2	100	116	54	71	7	3	1	1369	77	9	158	9.2	.994	1B-154, DH-1
1981			99	.294	.534	378	111	21	2	**22**	5.8	57	**78**	40	43	2	0	0	899	91	1	98	10.0	.999	1B-99
1982			151	.316	.549	550	174	30	1	32	5.8	87	110	70	82	7	0	0	1269	97	4	106	9.1	.997	1B-149, DH-2
1983			156	.306	.538	582	178	30	3	33	5.7	115	111	86	90	5	2	0	1393	114	10	136	9.7	.993	1B-153, DH-2
1984			162	.306	.509	588	180	26	3	29	4.9	97	110	**107**	87	10	0	0	1538	143	13	152	10.5	.992	1B-159, DH-3
1985			156	.297	.523	583	173	37	1	31	5.3	111	124	84	68	5	0	0	1338	152	19	154	9.7	.987	1B-154, DH-2
1986			137	.305	.463	495	151	25	1	17	3.4	61	84	78	49	3	2	0	1045	88	13	100	8.4	.989	1B-119, DH-16
1987			160	.277	.477	618	171	28	3	30	4.9	89	91	73	80	1	0	0	1371	145	10	146	9.5	.993	1B-156, DH-4
1988			161	.284	.474	603	171	27	2	28	4.6	75	84	75	78	5	0	0	867	106	11	101	6.1	.989	1B-103, DH-58
1989	LA	N	160	.247	.401	594	147	29	1	20	3.4	66	88	87	85	7	1	1	1316	137	6	122	9.1	.996	1B-159, 3B-2
1990			155	.330	.520	558	184	22	3	26	4.6	96	95	82	64	8	4	0	1180	113	10	88	8.7	.992	1B-150
14 yrs.			2135	.294	.494	7997	2352	402	29	379	4.7	1210	1373	1026	1076	76	16	2	16923	1499	125	1674	4.0	.985	1B-1911, DH-202, 3B-5, OF-3

LEAGUE CHAMPIONSHIP SERIES

Year	Team		Games	BA	SA	AB	H	2B	3B	HR	HR%	R	RBI	BB	SO	SB	AB	H	PO	A	E	DP	TC/G	FA	G by Pos
1979	BAL	A	4	.417	.667	12	5	0	0	1	8.3	3	5	5	2	0	0	0	44	3	2	4	12.3	.959	1B-4
1983			4	.267	.467	15	4	0	0	1	6.7	5	3	3	3	1	0	0	36	2	1	2	9.8	.974	1B-4
2 yrs.			8	.333	.556	27	9	0	0	2	7.4	8	8	8	5	1	0	0	80	5	3	6	11.0	.966	1B-8

WORLD SERIES

Year	Team		Games	BA	SA	AB	H	2B	3B	HR	HR%	R	RBI	BB	SO	SB	AB	H	PO	A	E	DP	TC/G	FA	G by Pos
1979	BAL	A	7	.154	.308	26	4	1	0	1	3.8	3	2	4	4	1	0	0	60	7	0	5	9.6	1.000	1B-7
1983			5	.250	.550	20	5	0	0	2	10.0	2	3	1	4	0	0	0	46	1	1	5	9.6	.979	1B-5
2 yrs.			12	.196	.413	46	9	1	0	3	6.5	5	5	5	8	1	0	0	106	8	1	10	9.6	.991	1B-12

Greg Myers

MYERS, GREGORY RICHARD
B. Apr. 14, 1966, Riverside, Calif.
BL TR 6' 1" 200 lbs.

			Games	BA	SA	AB	H	2B	3B	HR	HR%	R	RBI	BB	SO	SB
April			16	.302	.465	43	13	1	0	2	4.7	10	8	6	2	0
May			5	.000	.000	14	0	0	0	0	0.0	1	0	2	3	0
June			20	.254	.390	59	15	2	0	2	3.4	8	8	3	11	0
July			13	.220	.268	41	9	0	1	0	0.0	5	8	2	6	0
Aug			14	.326	.395	43	14	3	0	0	0.0	5	1	2	7	0
Sept/Oct			19	.160	.240	50	8	1	0	1	2.0	4	2	7	4	0
Day			22	.210	.306	62	13	0	0	2	3.2	8	5	8	9	0
Night			65	.245	.340	188	46	7	1	3	1.6	25	17	14	24	0
vs. Left				.174	.174	23	4	0	0	0	0.0	2	2	3	4	0
vs. Right				.242	.348	227	55	7	1	5	2.2	31	20	19	29	0

Year	Team		Games	BA	SA	AB	H	2B	3B	HR	HR%	R	RBI	BB	SO	SB	PINCH HIT AB	H	PO	A	E	DP	TC/G	FA	G by Pos

Greg Myers *Continued*

Year	Team		Games	BA	SA	AB	H	2B	3B	HR	HR%	R	RBI	BB	SO	SB	AB	H	PO	A	E	DP	TC/G	FA	G by Pos
On Grass			34	.250	.375	96	24	4	1	2	2.1	15	7	9	9	0									
On Turf			53	.227	.305	154	35	3	0	3	1.9	18	15	13	24	0									
Home			43	.238	.328	122	29	2	0	3	2.5	15	13	13	19	0									
Road			44	.234	.336	128	30	5	1	2	1.6	18	9	9	14	0									
Division Rivals																									
vs. BAL			7	.167	.167	18	3	0	0	0	0.0	1	3	1	0	0									
vs. BOS			12	.222	.259	27	6	1	0	0	0.0	1	0	3	4	0									
vs. CLE			6	.222	.389	18	4	0	0	1	5.6	3	3	3	1	0									
vs. DET			5	.182	.182	11	2	0	0	0	0.0	0	0	1	1	0									
vs. MIL			8	.276	.448	29	8	2	0	1	3.4	6	2	2	3	0									
vs. NY			7	.211	.421	19	4	1	0	1	5.3	4	2	2	3	0									
On 3B < 2 Out				.143	.143	7	1	0	0	0	0.0	0	6	0	0										
1987	TOR	A	7	.111	.111	9	1	0	0	0	0.0	1	0	0	3	0	0	0	24	1	0	0	3.6	1.000	C-7
1989			17	.114	.159	44	5	2	0	0	0.0	0	1	2	9	0	1	0	46	6	0	1	3.1	1.000	C-11, DH-6
1990			87	.236	.332	250	59	7	1	5	2.0	33	22	22	33	0	7	2	411	30	3	4	5.1	.993	C-87
3 yrs.			111	.215	.300	303	65	9	1	5	1.7	34	23	24	45	0	8	2	481	37	3	5	4.7	.994	C-105, DH-6

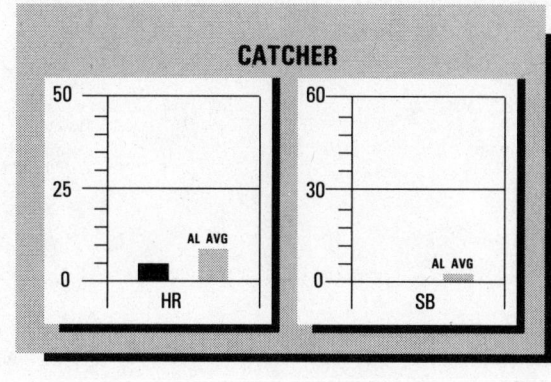

Tim Naehring

NAEHRING, TIMOTHY JAMES
B. Feb. 1, 1967, Cincinnati, Ohio
BR TR 6' 2" 190 lbs.

Year	Team		Games	BA	SA	AB	H	2B	3B	HR	HR%	R	RBI	BB	SO	SB	AB	H	PO	A	E	DP	TC/G	FA	G by Pos
1990	BOS	A	24	.271	.412	85	23	6	0	2	2.3	10	12	8	15	0	0	0	36	66	9	13	4.6	.919	SS-19, 3B-5, 2B-1

Rob Nelson

NELSON, ROBERT AUGUSTUS
B. May 17, 1964, Pasadena, Calif.
BL TL 6' 4" 215 lbs.

Year	Team		Games	BA	SA	AB	H	2B	3B	HR	HR%	R	RBI	BB	SO	SB	AB	H	PO	A	E	DP	TC/G	FA	G by Pos
1986	OAK	A	5	.222	.333	9	2	1	0	0	0.0	1	0	1	4	0	2	1	3	1	1	1	1.0	.800	1B-2, DH-1
1987	2 teams		OAK A (7G — .167)			SD N (10G — .091)																			
"	total		17	.143	.171	35	5	0	0	0	0.0	1	1	9	20	0	7	1	63	11	2	7	4.5	.974	1B-9
1988	SD	N	7	.190	.333	21	4	0	0	1	4.8	4	3	2	9	0	2	0	48	5	1	5	7.7	.981	1B-5
1989			42	.195	.329	82	16	0	1	3	3.7	6	7	20	29	1	11	1	201	23	2	17	5.4	.991	1B-31
1990			5	.000	.000	5	0	0	0	0	0.0	0	0	0	4	0	5	0	0	0	0	0	0.0	1.000	
5 yrs.			76	.178	.283	152	27	2	1	4	2.6	12	11	24	66	1	27	3	315	40	6	30	4.8	.983	1B-47, DH-1

Al Newman

NEWMAN, ALBERT DWAYNE
B. June 30, 1960, Kansas City, Mo.
BB TR 5' 9" 175 lbs.

Year	Team		Games	BA	SA	AB	H	2B	3B	HR	HR%	R	RBI	BB	SO	SB	AB	H	PO	A	E	DP	TC/G	FA	G by Pos
April			18	.209	.279	43	9	3	0	0	0.0	8	3	4	5	3									
May			27	.265	.294	68	18	2	0	0	0.0	8	7	2	4	2									
June			23	.222	.259	54	12	2	0	0	0.0	2	5	4	4	0									
July			29	.277	.340	94	26	6	0	0	0.0	13	7	10	7	5									
Aug			21	.241	.241	58	14	0	0	0	0.0	5	2	3	3	0									
Sept/Oct			26	.211	.225	71	15	1	0	0	0.0	7	6	10	11	3									
Day			41	.297	.356	118	35	7	0	0	0.0	19	11	10	6	6									
Night			103	.219	.244	270	59	7	0	0	0.0	24	19	23	28	7									
vs. Left				.252	.301	123	31	6	0	0	0.0	15	6	15	14	2									
vs. Right				.238	.268	265	63	8	0	0	0.0	28	24	18	20	11									
On Grass			58	.243	.276	152	37	5	0	0	0.0	14	8	8	18	3									
On Turf			86	.242	.280	236	57	9	0	0	0.0	29	22	25	16	10									
Home			72	.261	.302	199	52	8	0	0	0.0	27	19	23	13	8									
Road			72	.222	.254	189	42	6	0	0	0.0	16	11	10	21	5									
Division Rivals																									
vs. CAL			13	.233	.267	30	7	1	0	0	0.0	8	2	6	2	1									
vs. CHI			9	.273	.273	22	6	0	0	0	0.0	1	2	3	3	0									
vs. KC			10	.158	.158	19	3	0	0	0	0.0	1	2	2	1	1									
vs. OAK			13	.250	.333	36	9	3	0	0	0.0	4	3	2	3	1									
vs. SEA			12	.212	.273	33	7	2	0	0	0.0	7	5	5	3	3									
vs. TEX			12	.222	.259	27	6	1	0	0	0.0	2	3	4	4	0									
On 3B < 2 Out				.400	.500	20	8	2	0	0	0.0	0	18	5	1										

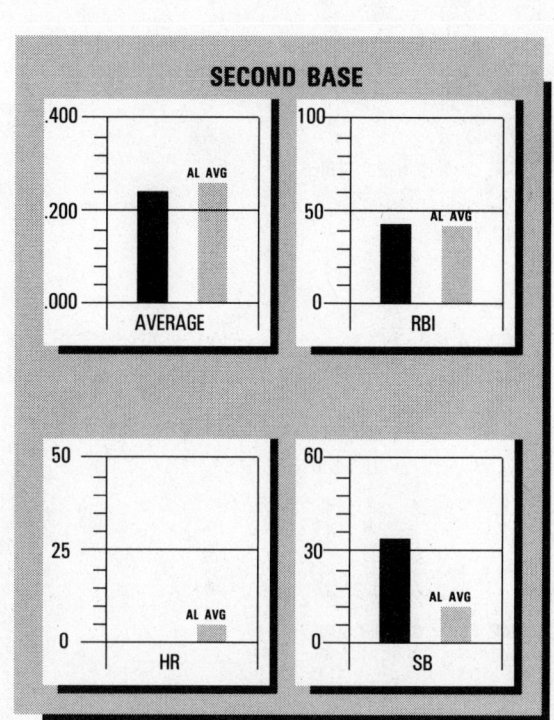

Year	Team		Games	BA	SA	AB	H	2B	3B	HR	HR%	R	RBI	BB	SO	SB	PINCH HIT AB	H	PO	A	E	DP	TC/G	FA	G by Pos

Al Newman *Continued*

Year	Team		Games	BA	SA	AB	H	2B	3B	HR	HR%	R	RBI	BB	SO	SB	AB	H	PO	A	E	DP	TC/G	FA	G by Pos
1985	MON	N	25	.172	.207	29	5	1	0	0	0.0	7	1	3	4	2	2	0	19	36	0	7	2.2	1.000	2B-15, SS-2
1986			95	.200	.232	185	37	3	0	1	0.5	23	8	21	20	11	14	2	98	161	11	35	2.8	.959	2B-59, SS-22
1987	MIN	A	110	.221	.303	307	68	15	5	0	0.0	44	29	34	27	15	6	0	120	225	5	44	3.2	.986	SS-55, 2B-47, 3B-12, DH-5, OF-2
1988			105	.223	.250	260	58	7	0	0	0.0	35	19	29	34	12	3	0	97	155	6	33	2.5	.977	3B-60, SS-28, 2B-23
1989			141	.253	.303	446	113	18	2	0	0.0	62	38	59	46	25	9	2	191	282	16	58	3.5	.967	2B-84, 3B-37, SS-31, OF-4, DH-2
1990			144	.242	.278	388	94	14	0	0	0.0	43	30	33	34	13	12	2	190	304	13	81	3.6	.974	2B-89, SS-48, 3B-28, OF-3
6 yrs.			620	.232	.279	1615	375	58	7	1	0.1	214	125	179	165	78	46	6	715	1163	51	258	3.1	.974	2B-317, SS-186, 3B-137, OF-9, DH-7

LEAGUE CHAMPIONSHIP SERIES

| 1987 | MIN | A | 1 | .000 | .000 | 2 | 0 | 0 | 0 | 0 | 0.0 | 0 | 0 | 0 | 0 | 0 | 0 | 0 | 0 | 1 | 0 | 0 | 1.0 | 1.000 | 2B-1 |

WORLD SERIES

| 1987 | MIN | A | 4 | .200 | .200 | 5 | 1 | 0 | 0 | 0 | 0.0 | 0 | 0 | 1 | 1 | 0 | 1 | 0 | 1 | 2 | 0 | 0 | 0.8 | 1.000 | 2B-3 |

Carl Nichols

NICHOLS, CARL EDWARD
B. Oct. 14, 1962, Los Angeles, Calif.
BR TR 6′ 184 lbs.

Year	Team		Games	BA	SA	AB	H	2B	3B	HR	HR%	R	RBI	BB	SO	SB	AB	H	PO	A	E	DP	TC/G	FA	G by Pos
1986	BAL	A	5	.000	.000	5	0	0	0	0	0.0	0	0	1	4	0	0	0	11	0	0	0	2.2	1.000	C-5
1987			13	.381	.429	21	8	1	0	0	0.0	4	3	1	4	0	0	0	39	3	0	1	3.2	1.000	C-13
1988			18	.191	.213	47	9	1	0	0	0.0	2	1	3	10	0	1	0	71	13	1	2	4.7	.988	C-13, OF-3
1989	HOU	N	8	.077	.077	13	1	0	0	0	0.0	0	2	0	3	0	4	0	16	1	0	0	2.1	1.000	C-6
1990			32	.204	.265	49	10	3	0	0	0.0	7	11	8	11	0	11	3	86	10	3	4	5.2	.970	C-15, 1B-3, OF-1
5 yrs.			76	.207	.244	135	28	5	0	0	0.0	13	17	13	32	0	16	3	223	27	4	7	3.3	.984	C-52, OF-4, 1B-3

Tom Nieto

NIETO, THOMAS ANDREW
B. Oct. 27, 1960, Downey, Calif.
BR TR 6′ 1″ 205 lbs.

Year	Team		Games	BA	SA	AB	H	2B	3B	HR	HR%	R	RBI	BB	SO	SB	AB	H	PO	A	E	DP	TC/G	FA	G by Pos
1984	STL	N	33	.279	.430	86	24	4	0	3	3.5	7	12	5	18	0	2	0	135	18	1	0	4.7	.994	C-32
1985			95	.225	.281	253	57	10	2	0	0.0	15	34	26	37	0	1	0	384	28	4	3	4.4	.990	C-95
1986	MON	N	30	.200	.323	65	13	3	1	1	1.5	5	7	6	21	0	1	1	123	11	3	1	4.6	.978	C-30
1987	MIN	A	41	.200	.314	105	21	7	1	1	1.0	7	12	8	24	0	1	1	210	17	1	5	5.6	.996	C-40, DH-1
1988			24	.067	.067	60	4	0	0	0	0.0	1	0	1	17	0	0	0	108	6	1	1	4.8	.991	C-24
1989	PHI	N	11	.150	.150	20	3	0	0	0	0.0	1	0	6	7	0	0	0	63	2	0	0	5.9	1.000	C-11
1990			17	.167	.167	30	5	0	0	0	0.0	1	4	3	11	0	1	0	57	5	1	1	3.7	.984	C-17
7 yrs.			251	.205	.281	619	127	24	4	5	0.8	37	69	55	135	0	6	2	1080	87	11	11	4.7	.991	C-249, DH-1

LEAGUE CHAMPIONSHIP SERIES

| 1985 | STL | N | 1 | .000 | .000 | 3 | 0 | 0 | 0 | 0 | 0.0 | 1 | 0 | 1 | 2 | 0 | 0 | 0 | 0 | 0 | 0 | 0 | 0.0 | — | C-1 |

WORLD SERIES

| 1985 | STL | N | 2 | .000 | .000 | 5 | 0 | 0 | 0 | 0 | 0.0 | 0 | 1 | 1 | 2 | 0 | 0 | 0 | 23 | 1 | 0 | 0 | 12.0 | 1.000 | C-2 |

Donell Nixon

NIXON, ROBERT DONELL
Brother of Otis Nixon.
B. Dec. 31, 1961, Evergreen, N. C.
BR TR 6′ 1″ 185 lbs.

Year	Team		Games	BA	SA	AB	H	2B	3B	HR	HR%	R	RBI	BB	SO	SB	AB	H	PO	A	E	DP	TC/G	FA	G by Pos
1987	SEA	A	46	.250	.348	132	33	4	0	3	2.3	17	12	13	28	21	0	0	76	1	0	0	1.7	1.000	OF-32, DH-6
1988	SF	N	59	.346	.385	78	27	3	0	0	0.0	15	6	10	12	11	5	1	59	0	1	0	1.0	.983	OF-46
1989			95	.265	.295	166	44	2	0	1	0.6	23	15	11	30	10	25	5	87	0	3	0	0.9	.967	OF-64
1990	BAL	A	8	.250	.350	20	5	2	0	0	0.0	1	2	1	7	5	0	0	5	0	0	0	1.3	1.000	OF-4, DH-3
4 yrs.			208	.275	.333	396	109	11	0	4	1.0	56	35	35	77	47	30	6	227	1	4	0	1.1	.983	OF-146, DH-9

LEAGUE CHAMPIONSHIP SERIES

| 1989 | SF | N | 3 | .000 | .000 | 3 | 0 | 0 | 0 | 0 | 0.0 | 0 | 0 | 0 | 1 | 1 | 0 | 0 | 2 | 0 | 1 | 0 | 1.0 | .667 | OF-2 |

WORLD SERIES

| 1989 | SF | N | 2 | .200 | .200 | 5 | 1 | 0 | 0 | 0 | 0.0 | 1 | 0 | 1 | 1 | 0 | 1 | 0 | 2 | 0 | 0 | 0 | 1.0 | 1.000 | OF-2 |

Year	Team		Games	BA	SA	AB	H	2B	3B	HR	HR%	R	RBI	BB	SO	SB	PINCH HIT AB	H	PO	A	E	DP	TC/G	FA	G by Pos

Otis Nixon

NIXON, OTIS JUNIOR
Brother of Donell Nixon.
B. Jan. 9, 1959, Evergreen, N. C.
BB TR 6′ 2″ 175 lbs.

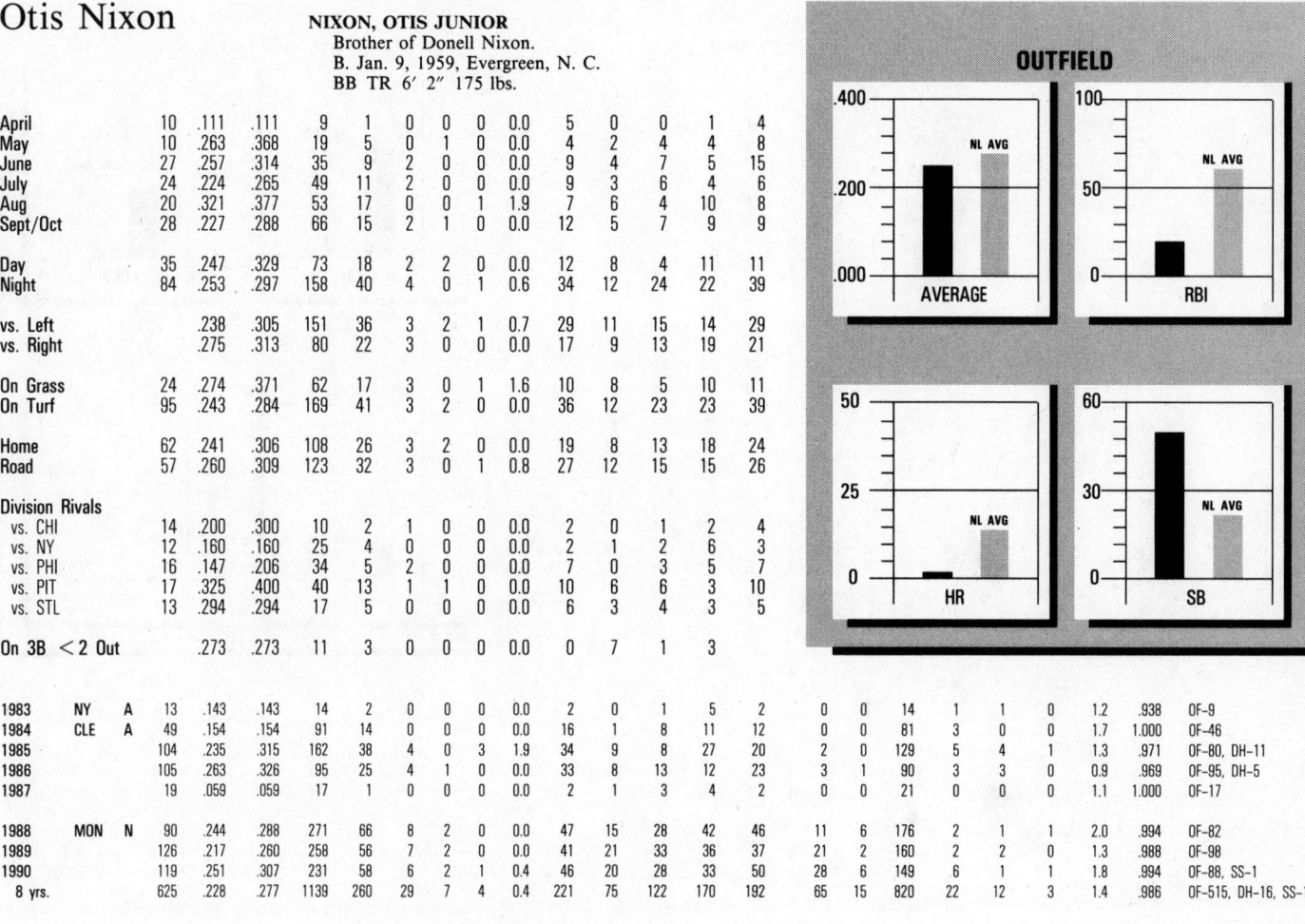

OUTFIELD

	Games	BA	SA	AB	H	2B	3B	HR	HR%	R	RBI	BB	SO	SB	AB	H	PO	A	E	DP	TC/G	FA	G by Pos
April	10	.111	.111	9	1	0	0	0	0.0	5	0	0	1	4									
May	10	.263	.368	19	5	0	1	0	0.0	4	2	4	4	8									
June	27	.257	.314	35	9	2	0	0	0.0	9	4	7	5	15									
July	24	.224	.265	49	11	2	0	0	0.0	9	3	6	4	6									
Aug	20	.321	.377	53	17	0	0	1	1.9	7	6	4	10	8									
Sept/Oct	28	.227	.288	66	15	2	1	0	0.0	12	5	7	9	9									
Day	35	.247	.329	73	18	2	2	0	0.0	12	8	4	11	11									
Night	84	.253	.297	158	40	4	0	1	0.6	34	12	24	22	39									
vs. Left		.238	.305	151	36	3	2	1	0.7	29	11	15	14	29									
vs. Right		.275	.313	80	22	3	0	0	0.0	17	9	13	19	21									
On Grass	24	.274	.371	62	17	3	0	1	1.6	10	8	5	10	11									
On Turf	95	.243	.284	169	41	3	2	0	0.0	36	12	23	23	39									
Home	62	.241	.306	108	26	3	2	0	0.0	19	8	13	18	24									
Road	57	.260	.309	123	32	3	0	1	0.8	27	12	15	15	26									
Division Rivals																							
vs. CHI	14	.200	.300	10	2	1	0	0	0.0	2	0	1	2	4									
vs. NY	12	.160	.160	25	4	0	0	0	0.0	2	1	2	6	3									
vs. PHI	16	.147	.206	34	5	2	0	0	0.0	7	0	3	5	7									
vs. PIT	17	.325	.400	40	13	1	1	0	0.0	10	6	6	3	10									
vs. STL	13	.294	.294	17	5	0	0	0	0.0	6	3	4	3	5									
On 3B < 2 Out		.273	.273	11	3	0	0	0	0.0	0	7	1	3										
1983	NY	A	13	.143	.143	14	2	0	0	0	0.0	2	0	1	5	2	0	0	14	1	1	0	1.2	.938	OF-9
1984	CLE	A	49	.154	.154	91	14	0	0	0	0.0	16	1	8	11	12	0	0	81	3	0	0	1.7	1.000	OF-46
1985			104	.235	.315	162	38	4	0	3	1.9	34	9	8	27	20	2	0	129	5	4	1	1.3	.971	OF-80, DH-11
1986			105	.263	.326	95	25	4	1	0	0.0	33	8	13	12	23	3	1	90	3	3	0	0.9	.969	OF-95, DH-5
1987			19	.059	.059	17	1	0	0	0	0.0	2	1	3	4	2	0	0	21	0	0	0	1.1	1.000	OF-17
1988	MON	N	90	.244	.288	271	66	8	2	0	0.0	47	15	28	42	46	11	6	176	2	1	1	2.0	.994	OF-82
1989			126	.217	.260	258	56	7	2	0	0.0	41	21	33	36	37	21	2	160	2	2	0	1.3	.988	OF-98
1990			119	.251	.307	231	58	6	2	1	0.4	46	20	28	33	50	28	6	149	6	1	1	1.8	.994	OF-88, SS-1
8 yrs.			625	.228	.277	1139	260	29	7	4	0.4	221	75	122	170	192	65	15	820	22	12	3	1.4	.986	OF-515, DH-16, SS-1

Junior Noboa

NOBOA, MILCIADES ARTURO
Born Milciades Arturo Noboa y Diaz.
B. Nov. 10, 1964, Azua, Dominican Republic
BR TR 5′ 10″ 155 lbs.

Year	Team		Games	BA	SA	AB	H	2B	3B	HR	HR%	R	RBI	BB	SO	SB	AB	H	PO	A	E	DP	TC/G	FA	G by Pos
1984	CLE	A	23	.364	.364	11	4	0	0	0	0.0	3	0	0	2	1	0	0	7	13	0	4	0.9	1.000	2B-19, DH-1
1987			39	.225	.275	80	18	2	1	0	0.0	7	7	3	6	1	2	0	28	66	3	8	2.5	.969	2B-21, SS-8, 3B-5
1988	CAL	A	21	.063	.063	16	1	0	0	0	0.0	4	0	0	1	0	0	0	8	24	1	7	1.6	.970	2B-9, SS-3, 3B-3
1989	MON	N	21	.227	.227	44	10	0	0	0	0.0	3	1	1	3	0	5	3	17	45	0	5	3.0	1.000	2B-13, SS-4, 3B-1
1990			81	.266	.335	158	42	7	2	0	0.0	15	14	7	14	4	35	10	47	52	2	10	2.0	.980	2B-31, OF-9, 3B-8, SS-7, P-1
5 yrs.			185	.243	.291	309	75	9	3	0	0.0	32	22	11	26	6	42	13	107	200	6	36	1.7	.981	2B-93, SS-22, 3B-16, OF-9, DH-1, P-1

Paul Noce

NOCE, PAUL DAVID
B. Dec. 16, 1959, San Francisco, Calif.
BR TR 5′ 10″ 175 lbs.

Year	Team		Games	BA	SA	AB	H	2B	3B	HR	HR%	R	RBI	BB	SO	SB	AB	H	PO	A	E	DP	TC/G	FA	G by Pos
1987	CHI	N	70	.228	.350	180	41	9	2	3	1.7	17	14	6	49	5	2	0	117	157	5	39	4.0	.982	2B-36, SS-35, 3B-2
1990	CIN	N	1	1.000	1.000	1	1	0	0	0	0.0	0	0	0	0	0	1	1	0	0	0	0	0.0		
2 yrs.			71	.232	.354	181	42	9	2	3	1.7	17	14	6	49	5	3	1	117	157	5	39	3.9	.982	2B-36, SS-35, 3B-2

Year	Team	Games	BA	SA	AB	H	2B	3B	HR	HR%	R	RBI	BB	SO	SB	PINCH HIT AB	PINCH HIT H	PO	A	E	DP	TC/G	FA	G by Pos

Matt Nokes

NOKES, MATTHEW DODGE
B. Oct. 31, 1963, San Diego, Calif.
BL TR 6′ 1″ 180 lbs.

CATCHER

	Games	BA	SA	AB	H	2B	3B	HR	HR%	R	RBI	BB	SO	SB	AB	H	PO	A	E	DP	TC/G	FA	G by Pos
April	17	.294	.353	51	15	3	0	0	0.0	5	2	3	4	0									
May	25	.273	.509	55	15	2	1	3	5.5	7	6	1	8	0									
June	24	.246	.446	65	16	1	0	4	6.2	5	16	2	8	0									
July	25	.250	.353	68	17	1	0	2	2.9	6	5	7	12	1									
Aug	24	.250	.367	60	15	1	0	2	3.3	8	6	9	7	0									
Sept/Oct	21	.173	.192	52	9	1	0	0	0.0	2	5	2	8	1									
Day	44	.272	.377	114	31	3	0	3	2.6	10	15	9	16	0									
Night	92	.236	.371	237	56	6	1	8	3.4	23	25	15	31	2									
vs. Left		.143	.143	14	2	0	0	0	0.0	1	2	0	5	0									
vs. Right		.252	.383	337	85	9	1	11	3.3	32	38	24	42	2									
On Grass	112	.233	.329	283	66	6	0	7	2.5	23	28	21	32	2									
On Turf	24	.309	.559	68	21	3	1	4	5.9	10	12	3	15	0									
Home	64	.255	.350	157	40	3	0	4	2.5	13	20	12	13	1									
Road	72	.242	.392	194	47	6	1	7	3.6	20	20	12	34	1									
Division Rivals																								
vs. BAL	15	.286	.469	49	14	3	0	2	4.1	8	7	4	5	0									
vs. BOS	14	.139	.167	36	5	1	0	0	0.0	0	2	4	5	0									
vs. CLE	8	.150	.150	20	3	0	0	0	0.0	1	0	3	4	0									
vs. DET	6	.067	.067	15	1	0	0	0	0.0	0	0	0	1	1									
vs. MIL	17	.289	.444	45	13	1	0	2	4.4	3	7	1	3	0									
vs. TOR	18	.293	.561	41	12	2	0	3	7.3	5	10	1	6	0									
On 3B < 2 Out		.308	.769	13	4	0	0	2	15.4	2	12	1	2										
1985	SF N	19	.208	.358	53	11	2	0	2	3.8	3	5	1	9	0	5	0	84	2	2	0	4.6	.977	C-14
1986	DET A	7	.333	.500	24	8	1	0	1	4.2	2	2	1	1	0	0	0	43	2	0	2	6.4	1.000	C-7
1987		135	.289	.536	461	133	14	2	32	6.9	69	87	35	70	2	19	4	600	32	5	2	4.7	.992	C-109, OF-3, 3B-2
1988		122	.251	.424	382	96	18	0	16	4.2	53	53	34	58	0	16	3	574	45	7	8	5.1	.989	C-110, DH-4
1989		87	.250	.388	268	67	10	0	9	3.4	15	39	17	37	1	11	1	235	26	6	3	3.1	.978	C-51, DH-33
1990	2 teams				DET A (44G — .270)				NY A (92G — .238)															
"	total	136	.248	.373	351	87	9	1	11	3.1	33	40	24	47	2	34	8	237	34	2	6	4.1	.993	C-65, DH-54, OF-2
6 yrs.		506	.261	.439	1539	402	54	3	71	4.6	175	226	112	222	5	85	16	1773	141	22	21	3.8	.989	C-356, DH-91, OF-5, 3B-2

LEAGUE CHAMPIONSHIP SERIES

Year	Team	Games	BA	SA	AB	H	2B	3B	HR	HR%	R	RBI	BB	SO	SB	AB	H	PO	A	E	DP	TC/G	FA	G by Pos
1987	DET A	5	.143	.357	14	2	0	0	1	7.1	2	2	1	4	0	2	0	11	2	0	0	2.6	1.000	C-3, DH-2

Ken Oberkfell

OBERKFELL, KENNETH RAY (Obie)
B. May 4, 1956, Highland, Ill.
BL TR 6′ 175 lbs.

Year	Team	Games	BA	SA	AB	H	2B	3B	HR	HR%	R	RBI	BB	SO	SB	AB	H	PO	A	E	DP	TC/G	FA	G by Pos
1977	STL N	9	.111	.111	9	1	0	0	0	0.0	0	1	0	3	0	3	0	3	4	0	1	0.8	1.000	2B-6
1978		24	.120	.140	50	6	1	0	0	0.0	7	0	3	1	0	3	0	30	48	1	8	3.3	.987	2B-17, 3B-4
1979		135	.301	.388	369	111	19	5	1	0.3	53	35	57	35	4	13	3	223	343	9	67	4.3	.984	2B-117, 3B-17, SS-2
1980		116	.303	.417	422	128	27	6	3	0.7	58	46	51	23	4	1	0	227	340	7	64	4.9	.988	2B-101, 3B-16
1981		102	.293	.372	376	110	12	6	2	0.5	43	45	37	28	13	1	0	77	247	15	23	3.3	.956	3B-102, SS-1
1982		137	.289	.370	470	136	22	5	2	0.4	55	34	40	31	11	3	1	80	305	11	23	2.9	.972	3B-135, 2B-1
1983		151	.293	.385	488	143	26	5	3	0.6	62	38	61	27	12	8	3	132	303	18	44	3.0	.960	3B-127, 2B-32, SS-1
1984	2 teams				STL N (50G — .309)				ATL N (50G — .233)															
"	total	100	.269	.349	324	87	19	4	1	0.3	38	21	31	27	2	6	1	64	173	8	15	2.5	.967	3B-91, 2B-6, SS-1
1985	ATL N	134	.272	.359	412	112	19	4	3	0.7	30	35	51	38	1	10	2	88	257	12	26	2.7	.966	3B-117, 2B-16
1986		151	.270	.360	503	136	24	3	5	1.0	62	48	83	40	7	4	1	116	335	11	39	3.1	.976	3B-130, 2B-41
1987		135	.280	.362	508	142	29	2	3	0.6	59	48	48	29	3	5	0	89	265	7	23	2.7	.981	3B-126, 2B-11
1988	2 teams				ATL N (120G — .277)				PIT N (20G — .222)															
"	total	140	.271	.353	476	129	22	4	3	0.6	49	42	37	34	4	15	2	107	237	15	24	2.6	.958	3B-115, 2B-12, SS-3, 1B-1
1989	2 teams				PIT N (14G — .125)				SF N (83G — .319)															
"		97	.269	.282	156	42	6	1	2	1.3	19	17	10	10	0	50	**18**	131	47	4	11	1.9	.978	3B-38, 1B-16, 2B-10
1990	HOU N	77	.207	.280	150	31	6	1	1	0.6	10	12	15	17	1	30	4	93	52	4	16	3.5	.973	3B-24, 1B-11, 2B-11
14 yrs.		1508	.279	.365	4713	1314	232	44	29	0.6	545	422	524	343	62	152	35	1460	2956	122	384	3.0	.973	3B-1042, 2B-381, 1B-28, SS-8

LEAGUE CHAMPIONSHIP SERIES

Year	Team	Games	BA	SA	AB	H	2B	3B	HR	HR%	R	RBI	BB	SO	SB	AB	H	PO	A	E	DP	TC/G	FA	G by Pos
1982	STL N	3	.200	.200	15	3	0	0	0	0.0	1	2	0	0	0	0	0	2	4	1	1	1.7	.857	3B-3
1989	SF N	3	.000	.000	4	0	0	0	0	0.0	0	0	0	0	0	0	0	0	1	0	0	0.3	1.000	3B-1
2 yrs.		6	.158	.158	19	3	0	0	0	0.0	1	2	0	0	0	3	0	2	5	1	1	1.3	.875	3B-4

Year	Team		Games	BA	SA	AB	H	2B	3B	HR	HR%	R	RBI	BB	SO	SB	PINCH HIT AB	PINCH HIT H	PO	A	E	DP	TC/G	FA	G by Pos

Ken Oberkfell *Continued*

WORLD SERIES

1982	STL	N	7	.292	.333	24	7	1	0	0	0.0	4	1	2	1	2	0	0	3	21	1	2	3.6	.960	3B-7
1989	SF	N	4	.333	.333	6	2	0	0	0	0.0	1	0	3	0	0	1	1	0	5	1	1	1.5	.833	3B-4
2 yrs.			11	.300	.333	30	9	1	0	0	0.0	5	1	5	1	2	1	1	3	26	2	3	2.8	.935	3B-11

Charlie O'Brien

O'BRIEN, CHARLES HUGH
B. May 1, 1960, Tulsa, Okla.
BR TR 6' 2" 195 lbs.

1985	OAK	A	16	.273	.364	11	3	1	0	0	0.0	3	1	3	3	0	0	0	23	0	1	0	1.5	.958	C-16
1987	MIL	A	10	.200	.343	35	7	3	1	0	0.0	2	0	4	4	0	0	0	78	11	0	0	8.9	1.000	C-10
1988			40	.220	.322	118	26	6	0	2	1.7	12	9	5	16	0	0	0	210	20	2	4	5.8	.991	C-40
1989			62	.234	.383	188	44	10	0	6	3.2	22	35	21	11	0	0	0	314	36	5	5	5.7	.986	C-62
1990	2 teams		MIL A (46G — .186)		NY N (28G — .162)																				
"	total		74	.178	.244	213	38	10	2	0	0.0	17	20	21	34	0	0	0	408	45	5	6	6.2	.989	C-74
5 yrs.			202	.209	.315	565	118	30	3	8	1.4	56	65	54	68	0	0	0	1033	112	13	15	5.7	.989	C-202

Pete O'Brien

O'BRIEN, PETER MICHAEL
B. Feb. 9, 1958, Santa Monica, Calif.
BL TL 6' 180 lbs.

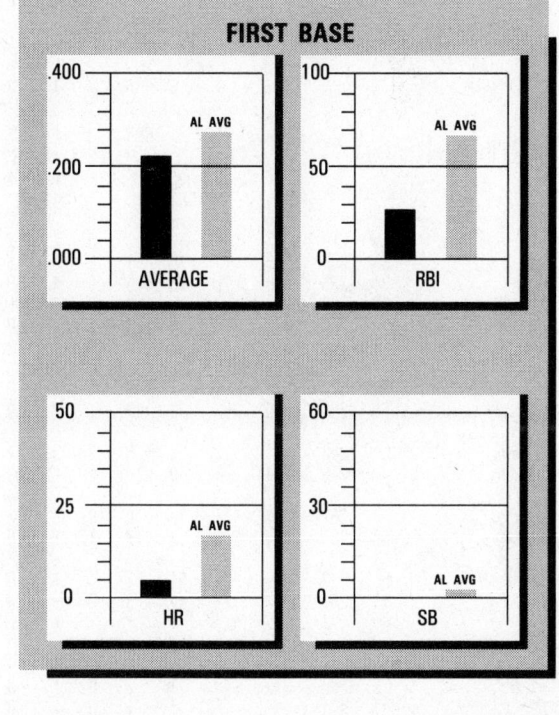

FIRST BASE

April	20	.151	.205	73	11	1	0	1	1.4	7	7	6	6	0
May	3	.308	.615	13	4	1	0	1	7.7	3	2	1	3	0
June	10	.216	.270	37	8	2	0	0	0.0	4	1	5	5	0
July	27	.207	.283	92	19	4	0	1	1.1	8	8	14	5	0
Aug	22	.273	.403	77	21	4	0	2	2.6	5	5	7	8	0
Sept/Oct	26	.257	.338	74	19	6	0	0	0.0	5	4	11	6	0
Day	26	.185	.259	81	15	3	0	1	1.2	3	6	10	9	0
Night	82	.235	.330	285	67	15	0	4	1.4	29	21	34	24	0
vs. Left		.200	.238	130	26	2	0	1	0.8	10	12	16	13	0
vs. Right		.237	.356	236	56	16	0	4	1.7	22	15	28	20	0
On Grass	42	.185	.238	151	28	5	0	1	0.7	12	10	15	15	0
On Turf	66	.251	.367	215	54	13	0	4	1.9	20	17	29	18	0
Home	52	.262	.372	172	45	10	0	3	1.7	17	14	26	13	0
Road	56	.191	.263	194	37	8	0	2	1.0	15	13	18	20	0
Division Rivals														
vs. CAL	12	.190	.238	42	8	2	0	0	0.0	5	0	5	4	0
vs. CHI	6	.091	.091	11	1	0	0	0	0.0	0	1	2	0	0
vs. KC	12	.229	.343	35	8	1	0	1	2.9	5	1	9	5	0
vs. MIN	11	.194	.194	31	6	0	0	0	0.0	2	5	2	3	0
vs. OAK	13	.217	.304	46	10	1	0	1	2.2	4	4	5	4	0
vs. TEX	6	.208	.292	24	5	2	0	0	0.0	3	1	3	2	0
On 3B < 2 Out		.240	.320	25	6	2	0	0	0.0	0	16	0	3	

1982	TEX	A	20	.239	.507	67	16	4	1	4	6.0	13	13	6	8	1	0	0	39	3	0	5	2.1	1.000	OF-11, DH-4, 1B-3
1983			154	.237	.347	524	124	24	5	8	1.5	53	53	58	62	5	6	2	1191	121	11	105	8.6	.992	1B-133, OF-27, DH-1
1984			142	.287	.448	520	149	26	2	18	3.5	57	80	53	50	3	2	1	1271	105	11	103	9.8	.992	1B-141, OF-1
1985			159	.267	.452	573	153	34	3	22	3.8	69	92	69	53	5	3	0	1457	98	8	125	9.8	.995	1B-159
1986			156	.290	.468	551	160	23	3	23	4.2	86	90	87	66	4	3	1	1224	115	11	123	8.7	.992	1B-155
1987			159	.286	.457	569	163	26	1	23	4.0	84	88	59	61	0	3	0	1233	146	11	118	8.7	.992	1B-158, OF-2
1988			156	.272	.408	547	149	24	1	16	2.9	57	71	72	73	1	5	1	1346	140	8	124	9.6	.995	1B-155, DH-1
1989	CLE	A	155	.260	.372	554	144	24	1	12	2.2	75	55	83	48	3	4	0	1359	114	9	111	9.6	.994	1B-154, DH-1
1990	SEA	A	108	.224	.314	366	82	18	0	5	1.3	32	27	44	33	0	6	0	852	76	5	68	9.4	.995	1B-97, DH-6, OF-6
9 yrs.			1209	.267	.414	4271	1140	203	17	131	3.1	526	569	531	454	22	32	5	9972	918	74	882	0.8	.923	1B-1155, OF-47, DH-13

Ron Oester

OESTER, RONALD JOHN
B. May 5, 1956, Cincinnati, Ohio
BB TR 6' 2" 185 lbs.

1978	CIN	N	6	.375	.375	8	3	0	0	0	0.0	1	1	0	2	0	0	0	3	9	0	2	2.0	1.000	SS-6
1979			6	.000	.000	3	0	0	0	0	0.0	0	0	0	1	0	1	0	1	2	0	0	0.5	1.000	SS-2
1980			100	.277	.363	303	84	16	2	2	0.7	40	20	26	44	6	10	3	161	224	10	46	4.0	.975	2B-79, SS-17, 3B-3
1981			105	.271	.398	354	96	16	7	5	1.4	45	42	42	49	2	6	1	213	341	11	64	5.4	.981	2B-103, SS-9
1982			151	.260	.359	549	143	19	4	9	1.6	63	47	35	82	5	6	1	304	403	22	87	4.8	.970	2B-118, SS-29, 3B-13

Year	Team	Games	BA	SA	AB	H	2B	3B	HR	HR%	R	RBI	BB	SO	SB	PINCH HIT AB	PINCH HIT H	PO	A	E	DP	TC/G	FA	G by Pos

Ron Oester *Continued*

Year	Team	Games	BA	SA	AB	H	2B	3B	HR	HR%	R	RBI	BB	SO	SB	PH AB	PH H	PO	A	E	DP	TC/G	FA	G by Pos
1983		157	.264	.384	549	145	23	5	11	2.0	63	58	49	106	2	5	2	315	413	17	80	4.7	.977	2B-154
1984		150	.242	.316	553	134	26	3	3	0.5	54	38	41	97	7	6	2	357	388	15	75	5.1	.980	2B-147, SS-1
1985		152	.295	.361	526	155	26	3	1	0.2	59	34	51	65	5	2	0	366	457	9	100	5.5	.989	2B-149
1986		153	.258	.356	523	135	23	2	8	1.5	52	44	52	84	9	4	0	367	475	19	100	5.6	.978	2B-151
1987		69	.253	.367	237	60	9	6	2	0.8	28	23	22	51	2	0	0	183	186	10	37	5.5	.974	2B-69
1988		54	.280	.327	150	42	7	0	0	0.0	20	10	9	24	0	3	1	110	113	1	26	4.1	.996	2B-49, SS-5
1989		109	.246	.305	305	75	15	0	1	0.3	23	14	32	47	1	8	3	215	249	7	44	4.3	.985	2B-102, SS-2
1990		64	.299	.377	154	46	10	1	0	0.0	10	13	10	29	1	13	1	80	90	4	14	3.3	.977	2B-50, 3B-3
13 yrs.		1276	.265	.356	4214	1118	190	33	42	1.0	458	344	369	681	40	58	13	2675	3350	125	675	4.8	.980	2B-1171, SS-71, 3B-19

LEAGUE CHAMPIONSHIP SERIES

Year	Team		Games	BA	SA	AB	H	2B	3B	HR	HR%	R	RBI	BB	SO	SB	PH AB	PH H	PO	A	E	DP	TC/G	FA	G by Pos
1990	CIN	N	4	.333	.333	3	1	0	0	0	0.0	1	0	0	1	0	2	0	0	1	0	0	0.5	1.000	2B-2

WORLD SERIES

Year	Team		Games	BA	SA	AB	H	2B	3B	HR	HR%	R	RBI	BB	SO	SB	PH AB	PH H	PO	A	E	DP	TC/G	FA	G by Pos
1990	CIN	N	1	1.000	1.000	1	1	0	0	0	0.0	0	1	0	0	0	1	1	0	0	0	0	0.0	1.000	

Jose Offerman

OFFERMAN, JOSE ANTONIO
Born Jose Antonio Oferman y Dono.
B. Nov. 8, 1968, San Pedro de Macoris, Dominican Republic
BB TR 6′ 160 lbs.

Year	Team		Games	BA	SA	AB	H	2B	3B	HR	HR%	R	RBI	BB	SO	SB	PH AB	PH H	PO	A	E	DP	TC/G	FA	G by Pos
1990	LA	N	29	.155	.207	58	9	0	0	1	1.7	7	7	4	14	1	1	0	30	40	4	5	2.7	.946	SS-27

John Olerud

OLERUD, JOHN GARRETT
B. Aug. 5, 1968, Bellevue, Wash.
BL TL 6′ 5″ 205 lbs.

	Games	BA	SA	AB	H	2B	3B	HR	HR%	R	RBI	BB	SO	SB
April	15	.250	.417	48	12	2	0	2	4.2	7	5	8	7	0
May	23	.239	.366	71	17	1	1	2	2.8	9	10	16	19	0
June	21	.333	.560	75	25	5	0	4	5.3	10	15	8	16	0
July	19	.284	.463	67	19	3	0	3	4.5	7	7	8	11	0
Aug	20	.212	.364	66	14	4	0	2	3.0	8	7	8	14	0
Sept/Oct	13	.258	.355	31	8	0	0	1	3.2	2	4	9	8	0
Day	33	.177	.240	96	17	3	0	1	1.0	4	7	15	29	0
Night	78	.298	.500	262	78	12	1	13	5.0	39	41	42	46	0
vs. Left		.342	.534	73	25	5	0	3	4.1	10	15	15	18	0
vs. Right		.246	.404	285	70	10	1	11	3.9	33	33	42	57	0
On Grass	43	.281	.407	135	38	8	0	3	2.2	16	19	24	26	0
On Turf	68	.256	.444	223	57	7	1	11	4.9	27	29	33	49	0
Home	58	.273	.497	187	51	7	1	11	5.9	25	26	29	43	0
Road	53	.257	.357	171	44	8	0	3	1.8	18	22	28	32	0
Division Rivals														
vs. BAL	10	.367	.667	30	11	0	0	3	10.0	6	7	3	7	0
vs. BOS	13	.256	.372	43	11	2	0	1	2.3	2	6	7	11	0
vs. CLE	7	.444	.667	18	8	1	0	1	5.6	3	3	6	2	0
vs. DET	11	.257	.429	35	9	0	0	2	5.7	6	7	8	8	0
vs. MIL	8	.367	.433	30	11	2	0	0	0.0	5	3	0	5	0
vs. NY	6	.455	1.000	22	10	3	0	3	13.6	5	7	4	3	0
On 3B < 2 Out		.500	.900	10	5	1	0	1	10.0	1	12	1	4	

DESIGNATED HITTER

AVERAGE — AL AVG
RBI — AL AVG
HR — AL AVG
SB — AL AVG

Year	Team		Games	BA	SA	AB	H	2B	3B	HR	HR%	R	RBI	BB	SO	SB	PH AB	PH H	PO	A	E	DP	TC/G	FA	G by Pos
1989	TOR	A	6	.375	.375	8	3	0	0	0	0.0	2	0	0	1	0	1	0	19	2	0	0	3.5	1.000	1B-5, DH-1
1990			111	.265	.430	358	95	15	1	14	3.9	43	48	57	75	0	7	1	133	10	2	10	8.1	.986	DH-90, 1B-18
2 yrs.			117	.268	.429	366	98	15	1	14	3.8	45	48	57	76	0	8	1	152	12	2	10	1.4	.988	DH-91, 1B-23

Year	Team	Games	BA	SA	AB	H	2B	3B	HR	HR%	R	RBI	BB	SO	SB	PINCH HIT AB	H	PO	A	E	DP	TC/G	FA	G by Pos

Joe Oliver

OLIVER, JOSEPH MELTON
B. July 24, 1965, Memphis, Tenn.
BR TR 6′ 3″ 215 lbs.

Split	Games	BA	SA	AB	H	2B	3B	HR	HR%	R	RBI	BB	SO	SB	PH AB	PH H	PO	A	E	DP	TC/G	FA	G by Pos
April	15	.250	.308	52	13	3	0	0	0.0	8	2	7	10	1									
May	24	.263	.500	76	20	3	0	5	6.6	10	16	11	10	0									
June	24	.205	.247	73	15	3	0	0	0.0	4	9	9	18	0									
July	23	.214	.329	70	15	5	0	1	1.4	6	12	6	19	0									
Aug	18	.245	.449	49	12	4	0	2	4.1	4	8	1	8	0									
Sept/Oct	17	.205	.318	44	9	5	0	0	0.0	2	5	3	10	0									
Day	28	.329	.529	85	28	8	0	3	3.5	11	16	8	14	0									
Night	93	.201	.308	279	56	15	0	5	1.8	23	36	29	61	1									
vs. Left		.283	.439	180	51	13	0	5	2.8	18	28	18	34	0									
vs. Right		.179	.283	184	33	10	0	3	1.6	16	24	19	41	1									
On Grass	34	.210	.343	105	22	8	0	2	1.9	7	14	6	26	0									
On Turf	87	.239	.367	259	62	15	0	6	2.3	27	38	31	49	1									
Home	60	.221	.349	172	38	13	0	3	1.7	18	25	20	38	0									
Road	61	.240	.370	192	46	10	0	5	2.6	16	27	17	37	1									
Division Rivals																							
vs. ATL	16	.250	.333	48	12	4	0	0	0.0	6	2	2	9	0									
vs. HOU	12	.219	.281	32	7	2	0	0	0.0	2	0	9	7	0									
vs. LA	14	.174	.217	46	8	2	0	0	0.0	2	8	2	9	0									
vs. SD	13	.146	.195	41	6	2	0	0	0.0	1	4	3	10	0									
vs. SF	10	.100	.133	30	3	1	0	0	0.0	2	3	3	9	0									
On 3B < 2 Out		.353	.412	17	6	1	0	0	0.0	0	11	4	6										

Year	Team	Lg	Games	BA	SA	AB	H	2B	3B	HR	HR%	R	RBI	BB	SO	SB	PH AB	PH H	PO	A	E	DP	TC/G	FA	G by Pos
1989	CIN	N	49	.272	.384	151	41	8	0	3	2.0	13	23	6	28	0	7	2	260	21	4	1	5.8	.986	C-47
1990			121	.231	.360	364	84	23	0	8	2.1	34	52	37	75	1	8	4	686	59	6	8	6.4	.992	C-118
2 yrs.			170	.243	.367	515	125	31	0	11	2.1	47	75	43	103	1	15	6	946	80	10	9	6.1	.990	C-165

LEAGUE CHAMPIONSHIP SERIES

1990	CIN	N	5	.143	.143	14	2	0	0	0	0.0	1	0	0	2	0	0	0	27	1	0	0	5.6	1.000	C-5

WORLD SERIES

1990	CIN	N	4	.333	.500	18	6	3	0	0	0.0	2	2	0	1	0	0	0	27	1	3	0	7.8	.903	C-4

CATCHER — AVERAGE (NL AVG), RBI (NL AVG), HR (NL AVG), SB (NL AVG)

Greg Olson

OLSON, GREGORY WILLIAM
B. Sept. 6, 1960, Marshall, Minn.
BR TR 6′ 200 lbs.

Split	Games	BA	SA	AB	H	2B	3B	HR	HR%	R	RBI	BB	SO	SB	PH AB	PH H	PO	A	E	DP	TC/G	FA	G by Pos
April	5	.273	.364	11	3	1	0	0	0.0	0	1	2	3	0									
May	21	.293	.534	58	17	2	0	4	6.9	10	11	6	12	0									
June	24	.308	.410	78	24	2	0	2	2.6	10	12	10	8	0									
July	21	.167	.182	66	11	1	0	0	0.0	3	2	6	12	1									
Aug	17	.377	.585	53	20	6	1	1	1.9	10	9	3	10	0									
Sept/Oct	12	.094	.094	32	3	0	0	0	0.0	3	1	3	6	0									
Day	23	.279	.368	68	19	3	0	1	1.5	5	7	12	11	0									
Night	77	.257	.383	230	59	9	1	6	2.6	31	29	18	40	1									
vs. Left		.312	.481	154	48	9	1	5	3.2	21	25	15	26	1									
vs. Right		.208	.271	144	30	3	0	2	1.4	15	11	15	25	0									
On Grass	73	.257	.372	218	56	8	1	5	2.3	24	25	21	32	1									
On Turf	27	.275	.400	80	22	4	0	2	2.5	12	11	9	19	0									
Home	50	.285	.417	151	43	6	1	4	2.6	17	21	12	20	1									
Road	50	.238	.340	147	35	6	0	3	2.0	19	15	18	31	0									
Division Rivals																							
vs. CIN	8	.310	.414	29	9	0	0	1	3.4	2	7	4	6	0									
vs. HOU	7	.238	.238	21	5	0	0	0	0.0	1	0	1	4	1									
vs. LA	11	.167	.333	30	5	0	1	1	3.3	5	3	3	3	0									
vs. SD	13	.209	.233	43	9	1	0	0	0.0	6	2	3	6	0									
vs. SF	8	.393	.464	28	11	2	0	0	0.0	2	3	2	3	0									
On 3B < 2 Out		.462	.923	13	6	0	0	2	15.4	2	16	0	1										

Year	Team	Lg	Games	BA	SA	AB	H	2B	3B	HR	HR%	R	RBI	BB	SO	SB	PH AB	PH H	PO	A	E	DP	TC/G	FA	G by Pos
1989	MIN	A	3	.500	.500	2	1	0	0	0	0.0	0	0	0	0	0	0	0	4	0	0	0	1.3	1.000	C-3
1990	ATL	N	100	.262	.379	298	78	12	1	7	2.3	36	36	30	51	1	9	1	501	43	7	3	5.7	.987	C-97, 3B-1
2 yrs.			103	.263	.380	300	79	12	1	7	2.3	36	36	30	51	1	9	1	505	43	7	3	5.4	.987	C-100, 3B-1

CATCHER — AVERAGE (NL AVG), RBI (NL AVG), HR (NL AVG), SB (NL AVG)

Year	Team		Games	BA	SA	AB	H	2B	3B	HR	HR%	R	RBI	BB	SO	SB	PINCH HIT AB	H	PO	A	E	DP	TC/G	FA	G by Pos

Tom O'Malley

O'MALLEY, THOMAS PATRICK
B. Dec. 25, 1960, Orange, N. J.
BL TR 6′ 170 lbs.

Year	Team		Games	BA	SA	AB	H	2B	3B	HR	HR%	R	RBI	BB	SO	SB	PH AB	PH H	PO	A	E	DP	TC/G	FA	G by Pos
1982	SF	N	92	.275	.364	291	80	12	4	2	0.7	26	27	33	39	0	9	3	60	161	8	10	2.5	.965	3B-83, 2B-1, SS-1
1983			135	.259	.339	410	106	16	1	5	1.2	40	45	52	47	2	17	5	70	213	18	12	2.2	.940	3B-117
1984	2 teams		SF N	(13G — .120)		CHI A	(12G — .125)																		
"	total		25	.122	.122	41	5	0	0	0	0.0	2	3	2	7	0	13	2	7	9	0	1	0.6	1.000	3B-13
1985	BAL	A	8	.071	.286	14	1	0	0	1	7.1	1	2	0	2	0	5	0	2	3	1	0	0.8	.833	3B-3
1986			56	.254	.320	181	46	9	0	1	0.6	19	18	17	21	0	4	0	37	98	9	8	2.6	.938	3B-55
1987	TEX	A	45	.274	.368	117	32	8	0	1	0.9	10	12	15	9	0	8	2	21	56	3	3	1.8	.963	3B-40, 2B-1
1988	MON	N	14	.259	.259	27	7	0	0	0	0.0	3	2	3	4	0	5	1	4	15	2	0	1.5	.905	3B-7
1989	NY	N	9	.545	.727	11	6	2	0	0	0.0	2	8	0	2	0	7	4	2	1	0	0	0.3	1.000	3B-3
1990			82	.223	.355	121	27	7	0	3	2.4	14	14	11	20	0	40	7	41	33	2	4	1.9	.974	3B-38, 1B-3
9 yrs.			466	.256	.340	1213	310	54	5	13	1.1	117	131	133	151	2	108	24	244	589	43	38	1.9	.951	3B-359, 1B-3, 2B-2, SS-1

Paul O'Neill

O'NEILL, PAUL ANDREW
B. Feb. 25, 1963, Columbus, Ohio
BL TL 6′ 4″ 200 lbs.

	Games	BA	SA	AB	H	2B	3B	HR	HR%	R	RBI	BB	SO	SB
April	16	.283	.433	60	17	3	0	2	3.3	10	15	8	13	4
May	26	.281	.406	96	27	6	0	2	2.1	11	12	6	26	1
June	27	.287	.540	87	25	4	0	6	6.9	15	15	13	13	3
July	23	.222	.333	81	18	3	0	2	2.5	8	9	7	18	1
Aug	27	.337	.533	92	31	9	0	3	3.3	11	14	10	17	4
Sept/Oct	26	.207	.276	87	18	3	0	1	1.1	4	13	9	16	0
Day	41	.250	.410	144	36	8	0	5	3.5	14	23	14	30	5
Night	104	.279	.426	359	100	20	0	11	3.1	45	55	39	73	8
vs. Left		.259	.406	143	37	12	0	3	2.1	14	25	11	45	0
vs. Right		.275	.428	360	99	16	0	13	3.6	45	53	42	58	13
On Grass	45	.257	.401	152	39	7	0	5	3.3	13	21	14	29	4
On Turf	100	.276	.430	351	97	21	0	11	3.1	46	57	39	74	9
Home	70	.290	.456	241	70	10	0	10	4.1	33	36	25	48	4
Road	75	.252	.389	262	66	18	0	6	2.3	26	42	28	55	9
Division Rivals														
vs. ATL	14	.175	.175	40	7	0	0	0	0.0	3	6	6	17	1
vs. HOU	18	.233	.317	60	14	2	0	1	1.7	6	11	10	8	3
vs. LA	16	.269	.442	52	14	0	0	3	5.8	8	6	8	9	2
vs. SD	14	.381	.476	42	16	1	0	1	2.4	3	6	3	7	4
vs. SF	18	.239	.552	67	16	3	0	6	9.0	10	16	8	6	1
On 3B < 2 Out		.371	.600	35	13	2	0	2	5.7	2	27	7	9	

OUTFIELD (bar charts: AVERAGE, RBI, HR, SB — with NL AVG comparison)

Year	Team		Games	BA	SA	AB	H	2B	3B	HR	HR%	R	RBI	BB	SO	SB	PH AB	PH H	PO	A	E	DP	TC/G	FA	G by Pos
1985	CIN	N	5	.333	.417	12	4	1	0	0	0.0	1	1	0	2	0	3	1	3	1	0	0	0.8	1.000	OF-2
1986			3	.000	.000	2	0	0	0	0	0.0	0	0	1	1	0	2	0	0	0	0	0	0.0	—	
1987			84	.256	.488	160	41	14	1	7	4.4	24	28	18	29	2	37	11	90	2	4	2	1.1	.958	OF-42, 1B-2, P-1
1988			145	.252	.414	485	122	25	3	16	3.3	58	73	38	65	8	11	0	410	13	6	14	3.0	.986	OF-139
1989			117	.276	.446	428	118	24	2	15	3.5	49	74	46	64	20	3	3	223	7	4	1	2.0	.983	OF-115
1990			145	.270	.421	503	136	28	0	16	3.1	59	78	53	103	13	8	2	271	12	2	0	2.0	.993	OF-141
6 yrs.			499	.265	.432	1590	421	92	6	54	3.4	191	254	156	264	43	64	17	997	35	16	17	2.1	.985	OF-439, 1B-2, P-1

LEAGUE CHAMPIONSHIP SERIES

Year	Team		Games	BA	SA	AB	H	2B	3B	HR	HR%	R	RBI	BB	SO	SB	PH AB	PH H	PO	A	E	DP	TC/G	FA	G by Pos
1990	CIN	N	5	.471	.824	17	8	3	0	1	5.8	1	4	1	1	1	0	0	9	2	0	1	2.2	1.000	OF-5

WORLD SERIES

Year	Team		Games	BA	SA	AB	H	2B	3B	HR	HR%	R	RBI	BB	SO	SB	PH AB	PH H	PO	A	E	DP	TC/G	FA	G by Pos
1990	CIN	N	4	.083	.083	12	1	0	0	0	0.0	2	1	5	2	1	0	0	11	0	0	0	2.8	1.000	OF-4

Year	Team		Games	BA	SA	AB	H	2B	3B	HR	HR%	R	RBI	BB	SO	SB	PINCH HIT AB	H	PO	A	E	DP	TC/G	FA	G by Pos

Jose Oquendo

OQUENDO, JOSE MANUEL
Born Jose Manuel Oquendo y Contreras.
B. July 4, 1963, Rio Peidras, Puerto Rico
BB TR 5′ 10″ 160 lbs.
BR 1984

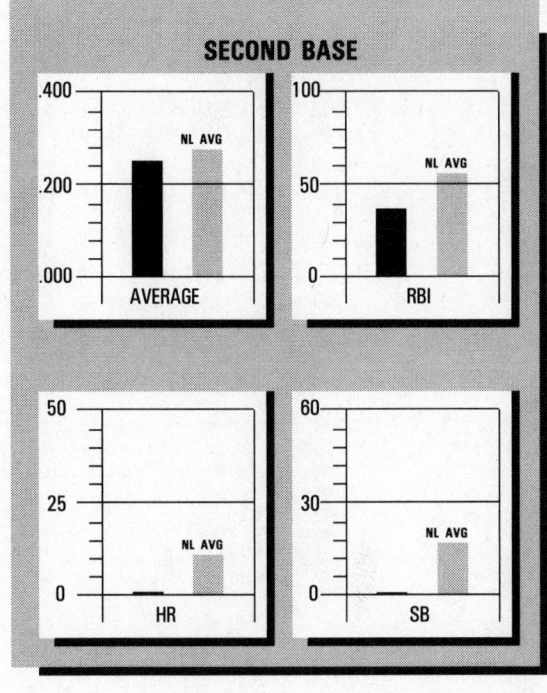

SECOND BASE

Split			Games	BA	SA	AB	H	2B	3B	HR	HR%	R	RBI	BB	SO	SB	AB	H	PO	A	E	DP	TC/G	FA	G by Pos
April			20	.281	.344	64	18	2	1	0	0.0	5	6	12	7	0									
May			27	.159	.183	82	13	2	0	0	0.0	3	2	15	13	0									
June			28	.303	.404	89	27	4	1	1	1.1	12	15	13	4	0									
July			27	.225	.292	89	20	4	1	0	0.0	8	2	13	12	1									
Aug			27	.298	.357	84	25	5	0	0	0.0	6	7	15	5	0									
Sept/Oct			27	.246	.311	61	15	0	2	0	0.0	4	5	6	5	0									
Day			44	.201	.278	144	29	5	3	0	0.0	11	14	17	12	0									
Night			112	.274	.332	325	89	12	2	1	0.3	27	23	57	34	1									
vs. Left				.220	.287	164	36	4	2	1	0.6	9	7	24	13	0									
vs. Right				.269	.331	305	82	13	3	0	0.0	29	30	50	33	1									
On Grass			40	.307	.394	137	42	6	3	0	0.0	11	12	18	16	0									
On Turf			116	.229	.283	332	76	11	2	1	0.3	27	25	56	30	1									
Home			79	.239	.294	238	57	8	1	1	0.4	20	17	33	21	1									
Road			77	.264	.338	231	61	9	4	0	0.0	18	20	41	25	0									
Division Rivals																									
vs. CHI			16	.292	.417	48	14	2	2	0	0.0	5	10	8	0	0									
vs. MON			16	.260	.300	50	13	2	0	0	0.0	5	5	5	5	0									
vs. NY			18	.268	.411	56	15	3	1	1	1.8	3	6	5	7	0									
vs. PHI			18	.216	.270	37	8	0	1	0	0.0	3	2	14	4	0									
vs. PIT			18	.267	.317	60	16	3	0	0	0.0	6	5	5	3	0									
On 3B < 2 Out				.389	.556	18	7	1	1	0	0.0	0	16	5	2										
1983	NY	N	120	.213	.244	328	70	7	0	0	0.3	29	17	19	60	8	1	0	182	326	21	65	4.4	.960	SS-116
1984			81	.222	.249	189	42	5	0	0	0.0	23	10	15	26	10	3	2	95	152	7	33	3.1	.972	SS-67
1986	STL	N	76	.297	.341	138	41	4	1	0	0.0	20	13	15	20	2	27	6	52	94	8	23	2.0	.948	SS-29, 2B-21, 3B-1, OF-1
1987			116	.286	.335	248	71	9	0	1	0.4	43	24	54	29	4	26	10	149	133	4	31	2.5	.986	OF-46, 2B-32, SS-23, 3B-8, 1B-3, P-1
1988			148	.277	.350	451	125	10	1	7	1.6	36	46	52	40	4	10	2	268	315	11	61	4.0	.981	2B-69, 3B-47, SS-17, 1B-16, OF-15, P-1, C-1
1989			163	.291	.372	556	162	28	7	1	0.2	59	48	79	59	3	1	1	356	523	6	108	5.4	.993	2B-156, SS-7, 1B-1
1990			156	.252	.316	469	118	17	5	1	0.2	38	37	74	46	1	3	0	294	403	4	67	4.6	.994	2B-150, SS-4
7 yrs.			860	.264	.324	2379	629	80	14	11	0.5	248	195	308	280	32	71	21	1396	1946	61	388	4.0	.982	2B-428, SS-263, OF-62, 3B-56, 1B-20, P-2, C-1

LEAGUE CHAMPIONSHIP SERIES

Year	Team		Games	BA	SA	AB	H	2B	3B	HR	HR%	R	RBI	BB	SO	SB	AB	H	PO	A	E	DP	TC/G	FA	G by Pos
1987	STL	N	5	.167	.417	12	2	0	0	1	8.3	3	4	3	2		1	0	7	0	0	0	1.4	1.000	OF-5, 3B-1

WORLD SERIES

Year	Team		Games	BA	SA	AB	H	2B	3B	HR	HR%	R	RBI	BB	SO	SB	AB	H	PO	A	E	DP	TC/G	FA	G by Pos
1987	STL	N	7	.250	.250	24	6	0	0	0	0.0	2	2	1	4	0	0	0	8	10	0	0	2.6	1.000	3B-4, OF-3

Joe Orsulak

ORSULAK, JOSEPH MICHAEL
B. May 31, 1962, Glen Ridge, N. J.
BL TL 6′ 1″ 185 lbs.

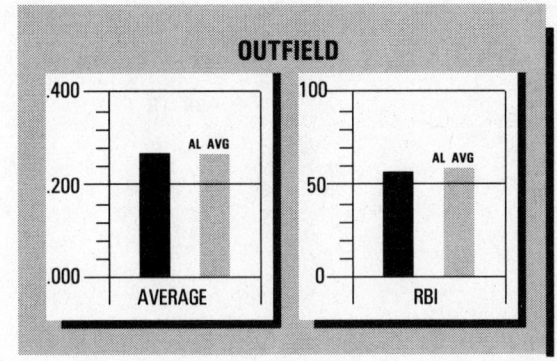

OUTFIELD

Split			Games	BA	SA	AB	H	2B	3B	HR	HR%	R	RBI	BB	SO	SB
April			18	.293	.414	58	17	2	1	1	1.7	6	6	6	8	0
May			22	.333	.641	78	26	5	2	5	6.4	16	23	11	7	1
June			26	.247	.270	89	22	2	0	0	0.0	10	6	8	4	2
July			24	.308	.451	91	28	4	0	3	3.3	10	12	7	8	1
Aug			21	.184	.276	76	14	1	0	2	2.6	6	10	8	16	1
Sept/Oct			13	.190	.190	21	4	0	0	0	0.0	1	0	6	5	1
Day			31	.243	.379	103	25	3	1	3	2.9	13	14	13	10	1
Night			93	.277	.403	310	86	11	2	8	2.6	36	43	33	38	5
vs. Left				.250	.278	72	18	0	1	0	0.0	6	7	8	8	0
vs. Right				.273	.422	341	93	14	2	11	3.2	43	50	38	40	6

Year	Team	Games	BA	SA	AB	H	2B	3B	HR	HR%	R	RBI	BB	SO	SB	PINCH HIT AB	H	PO	A	E	DP	TC/G	FA	G by Pos

Joe Orsulak *Continued*

On Grass		104	.270	.396	356	96	10	1	11	3.1	44	53	38	42	6									
On Turf		20	.263	.404	57	15	4	2	0	0.0	5	4	8	6	0									
Home		63	.272	.441	202	55	5	1	9	4.5	26	34	23	28	3									
Road		61	.265	.355	211	56	9	2	2	0.9	23	23	23	20	3									
Division Rivals																								
vs. BOS		10	.324	.324	34	11	0	0	0	0.0	3	4	5	3	2									
vs. CLE		8	.174	.174	23	4	0	0	0	0.0	2	3	5	3	0									
vs. DET		9	.250	.344	32	8	0	0	1	3.1	4	4	5	3	0									
vs. MIL		10	.152	.152	33	5	0	0	0	0.0	3	2	2	3	2									
vs. NY		11	.167	.190	42	7	1	0	0	0.0	3	0	2	5	0									
vs. TOR		6	.250	.333	12	3	1	0	0	0.0	0	3	2	1	0									
On 3B < 2 Out			.368	.474	19	7	2	0	0	0.0	0	13	6	3										

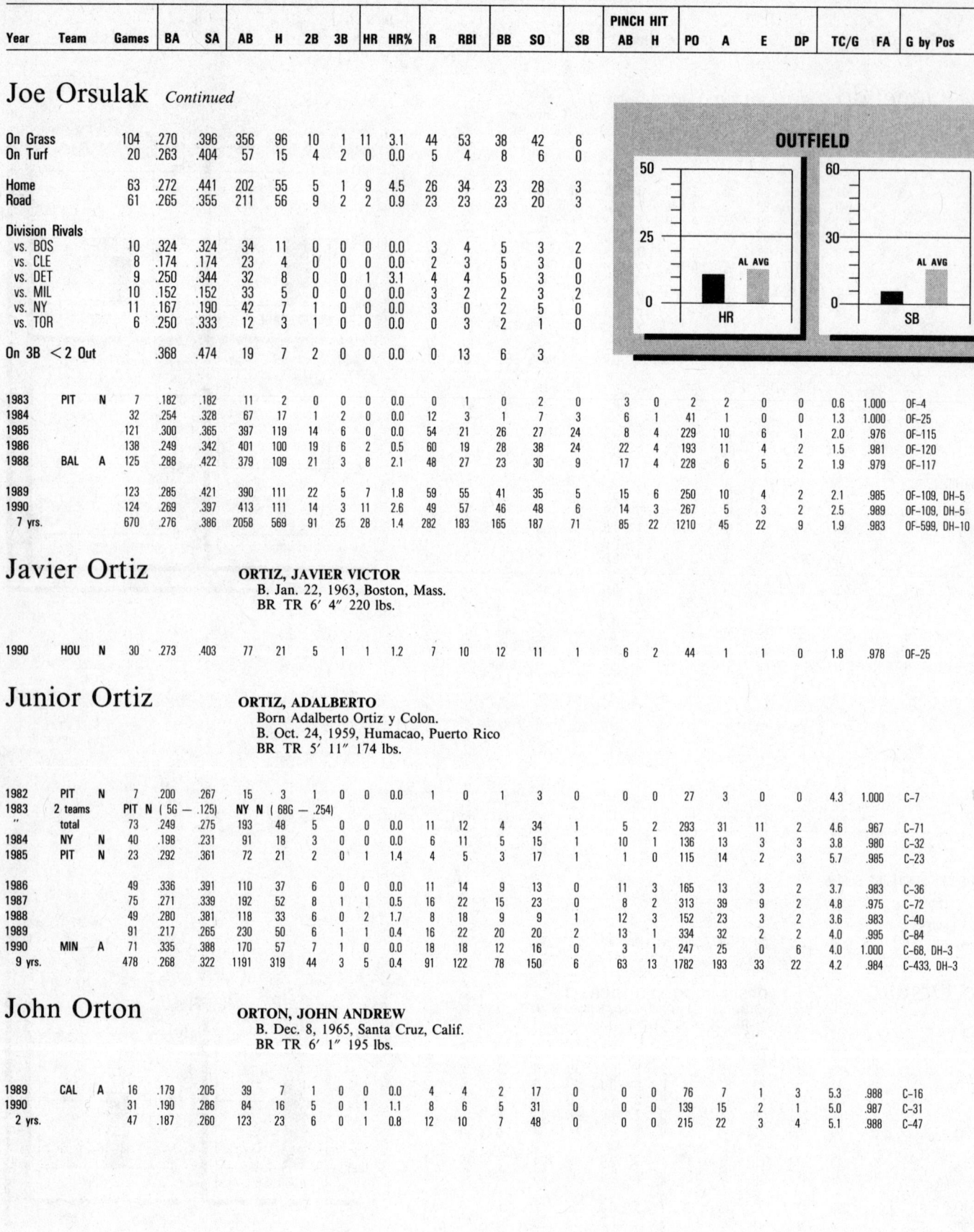

OUTFIELD

1983	PIT	N	7	.182	.182	11	2	0	0	0	0.0	0	1	0	2	0	3	0	2	2	0	0	0.6	1.000	OF-4
1984		32	.254	.328	67	17	1	2	0	0.0	12	3	1	7	3	6	1	41	1	0	0	1.3	1.000	OF-25
1985		121	.300	.365	397	119	14	6	0	0.0	54	21	26	27	24	8	4	229	10	6	1	2.0	.976	OF-115
1986		138	.249	.342	401	100	19	6	2	0.5	60	19	28	38	24	22	4	193	11	4	2	1.5	.981	OF-120
1988	BAL	A	125	.288	.422	379	109	21	3	8	2.1	48	27	23	30	9	17	4	228	6	5	2	1.9	.979	OF-117
1989		123	.285	.421	390	111	22	5	7	1.8	59	55	41	35	5	15	6	250	10	4	2	2.1	.985	OF-109, DH-5
1990		124	.269	.397	413	111	14	3	11	2.6	49	57	46	48	6	14	3	267	5	3	2	2.5	.989	OF-109, DH-5
7 yrs.		670	.276	.386	2058	569	91	25	28	1.4	282	183	165	187	71	85	22	1210	45	22	9	1.9	.983	OF-599, DH-10

Javier Ortiz

ORTIZ, JAVIER VICTOR
B. Jan. 22, 1963, Boston, Mass.
BR TR 6′ 4″ 220 lbs.

1990	HOU	N	30	.273	.403	77	21	5	1	1	1.2	7	10	12	11	1	6	2	44	1	1	0	1.8	.978	OF-25

Junior Ortiz

ORTIZ, ADALBERTO
Born Adalberto Ortiz y Colon.
B. Oct. 24, 1959, Humacao, Puerto Rico
BR TR 5′ 11″ 174 lbs.

1982	PIT	N	7	.200	.267	15	3	1	0	0	0.0	1	0	1	3	0	0	0	27	3	0	0	4.3	1.000	C-7
1983	2 teams	PIT N	(5G — .125)		NY N	(68G — .254)																		
"	total	73	.249	.275	193	48	5	0	0	0.0	11	12	4	34	1	5	2	293	31	11	2	4.6	.967	C-71
1984	NY	N	40	.198	.231	91	18	3	0	0	0.0	6	11	5	15	1	10	1	136	13	3	3	3.8	.980	C-32
1985	PIT	N	23	.292	.361	72	21	2	0	1	1.4	4	5	3	17	1	1	0	115	14	2	3	5.7	.985	C-23
1986		49	.336	.391	110	37	6	0	0	0.0	11	14	9	13	0	11	3	165	13	3	2	3.7	.983	C-36
1987		75	.271	.339	192	52	8	1	1	0.5	16	22	15	23	0	8	2	313	39	9	2	4.8	.975	C-72
1988		49	.280	.381	118	33	6	0	2	1.7	8	18	9	9	1	12	3	152	23	3	2	3.6	.983	C-40
1989		91	.217	.265	230	50	6	1	0	0.4	16	22	20	20	2	13	1	334	32	2	2	4.0	.995	C-84
1990	MIN	A	71	.335	.388	170	57	7	1	0	0.0	18	18	12	16	0	3	1	247	25	0	6	4.0	1.000	C-68, DH-3
9 yrs.		478	.268	.322	1191	319	44	3	5	0.4	91	122	78	150	6	63	13	1782	193	33	22	4.2	.984	C-433, DH-3

John Orton

ORTON, JOHN ANDREW
B. Dec. 8, 1965, Santa Cruz, Calif.
BR TR 6′ 1″ 195 lbs.

1989	CAL	A	16	.179	.205	39	7	1	0	0	0.0	4	4	2	17	0	0	0	76	7	1	3	5.3	.988	C-16
1990		31	.190	.286	84	16	5	0	1	1.1	8	6	5	31	0	0	0	139	15	2	1	5.0	.987	C-31
2 yrs.		47	.187	.260	123	23	6	0	1	0.8	12	10	7	48	0	0	0	215	22	3	4	5.1	.988	C-47

Year	Team	Games	BA	SA	AB	H	2B	3B	HR	HR%	R	RBI	BB	SO	SB	PINCH HIT AB	H	PO	A	E	DP	TC/G	FA	G by Pos

Spike Owen

OWEN, SPIKE DEE
Brother of Dave Owen.
B. Apr. 19, 1961, Cleburne, Tex.
BB TR 5′ 9″ 160 lbs.

Year	Team	Games	BA	SA	AB	H	2B	3B	HR	HR%	R	RBI	BB	SO	SB	PINCH HIT AB	H	PO	A	E	DP	TC/G	FA	G by Pos
April		19	.359	.578	64	23	7	2	1	1.6	6	7	5	5	2									
May		24	.230	.284	74	17	1	0	1	1.4	6	6	15	13	1									
June		28	.179	.284	95	17	4	0	2	2.1	13	10	18	14	2									
July		26	.203	.319	69	14	3	1	1	1.4	9	3	15	11	2									
Aug		24	.240	.293	75	18	4	0	0	0.0	11	5	7	10	0									
Sept/Oct		28	.224	.342	76	17	5	2	0	0.0	10	4	10	7	1									
Day		43	.242	.406	128	31	7	4	2	1.6	20	13	20	23	1									
Night		106	.231	.317	325	75	17	1	3	0.9	35	22	50	37	7									
vs. Left			.259	.403	201	52	16	2	3	1.5	26	17	23	25	3									
vs. Right			.214	.294	252	54	8	3	2	0.8	29	18	47	35	5									
On Grass		39	.228	.333	123	28	5	1	2	1.6	18	12	22	25	1									
On Turf		110	.236	.345	330	78	19	4	3	0.9	37	23	48	35	7									
Home		74	.228	.335	215	49	11	3	2	0.9	24	16	34	25	4									
Road		75	.239	.349	238	57	13	2	3	1.3	31	19	36	35	4									
Division Rivals																								
vs. CHI		17	.140	.200	50	7	0	0	1	2.0	5	3	8	10	1									
vs. NY		18	.240	.440	50	12	4	3	0	0.0	7	5	8	6	1									
vs. PHI		17	.208	.375	48	10	5	0	1	2.1	6	4	10	6	1									
vs. PIT		17	.260	.340	50	13	4	0	0	0.0	6	4	6	3	0									
vs. STL		15	.246	.368	57	14	2	1	1	1.8	8	6	3	5	1									
On 3B < 2 Out			.304	.391	23	7	0	1	0	0.0	0	17	6	6										
1983	SEA A	80	.196	.271	306	60	11	3	2	0.7	36	21	24	44	10	1	0	122	233	11	45	4.6	.970	SS-80
1984		152	.245	.326	530	130	18	8	3	0.6	67	43	46	63	16	1	1	245	463	17	86	4.8	.977	SS-151
1985		118	.259	.372	352	91	10	6	6	1.7	41	37	34	27	11	0	0	196	361	14	76	4.8	.975	SS-117
1986	2 teams	SEA A (112G — .246)			BOS A	(42G — .183)																		
"	total	154	.231	.309	528	122	24	7	1	0.2	67	45	51	51	4	0	0	221	393	22	101	4.1	.965	SS-154
1987	BOS A	132	.259	.343	437	113	17	7	2	0.5	50	48	53	43	11	1	0	176	336	13	69	4.0	.975	SS-130
1988		89	.249	.370	257	64	14	1	5	1.9	40	18	27	27	0	6	1	102	192	10	34	3.4	.967	SS-76, DH-7
1989	MON N	142	.233	.332	437	102	17	4	6	1.4	52	41	76	44	3	1	0	232	388	13	65	4.5	.979	SS-142
1990		149	.234	.342	453	106	24	5	5	1.1	55	35	70	60	8	5	0	216	340	6	52	3.8	.989	SS-148
8 yrs.		1016	.239	.332	3300	788	135	41	30	0.9	408	288	381	359	63	15	2	1510	2706	106	528	4.3	.975	SS-998, DH-7
LEAGUE CHAMPIONSHIP SERIES																								
1986	BOS A	7	.429	.524	21	9	0	1	0	0.0	5	3	2	2	1	0	0	12	21	5	2	5.4	.868	SS-7
1988		1	—	—	0	0	0	0	0	—	0	0	1	0	0	0	0	0	0	0	0	0.0	—	
2 yrs.		8	.429	.524	21	9	0	1	0	0.0	5	3	3	2	1	0	0	12	21	5	2	4.8	.868	SS-7
WORLD SERIES																								
1986	BOS A	7	.300	.300	20	6	0	0	0	0.0	2	2	5	6	0	0	0	10	13	0	3	3.3	1.000	SS-7

Mike Pagliarulo

PAGLIARULO, MICHAEL TIMOTHY (Pags)
B. Mar. 15, 1960, Medford, Mass.
BL TR 6′ 2″ 195 lbs.

Year	Team	Games	BA	SA	AB	H	2B	3B	HR	HR%	R	RBI	BB	SO	SB	PINCH HIT AB	H	PO	A	E	DP	TC/G	FA	G by Pos
April		12	.091	.091	11	1	0	0	0	0.0	0	1	3	6	0									
May		23	.316	.461	76	24	8	0	1	1.3	10	8	12	6	0									
June		20	.238	.375	80	19	3	1	2	2.5	4	6	5	16	1									
July		22	.277	.385	65	18	5	1	0	0.0	2	8	9	16	0									
Aug		25	.179	.190	84	15	1	0	0	0.0	2	5	6	15	0									
Sept/Oct		26	.293	.512	82	24	6	0	4	4.9	11	10	4	7	0									
Day		38	.237	.351	114	27	8	1	1	0.9	9	5	11	23	1									
Night		90	.261	.384	284	74	15	1	6	2.1	20	33	28	43	0									
vs. Left			.248	.396	101	25	3	0	4	4.0	10	13	15	21	0									
vs. Right			.256	.367	297	76	20	2	3	1.0	19	25	24	45	1									

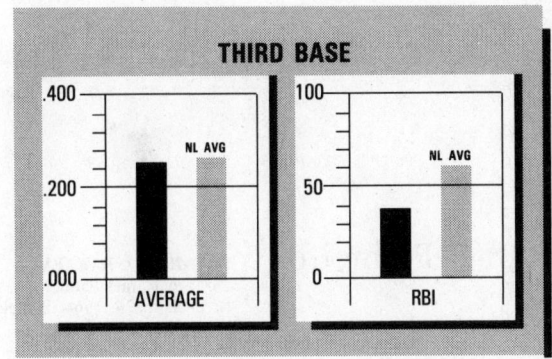

Year	Team		Games	BA	SA	AB	H	2B	3B	HR	HR%	R	RBI	BB	SO	SB	PINCH HIT AB	H	PO	A	E	DP	TC/G	FA	G by Pos

Mike Pagliarulo *Continued*

Year	Team		Games	BA	SA	AB	H	2B	3B	HR	HR%	R	RBI	BB	SO	SB	AB	H	PO	A	E	DP	TC/G	FA	G by Pos
On Grass			94	.270	.400	285	77	18	2	5	1.8	25	29	29	46	1									
On Turf			34	.212	.310	113	24	5	0	2	1.8	4	9	10	20	0									
Home			60	.272	.361	169	46	10	1	1	0.6	13	14	19	31	1									
Road			68	.240	.384	229	55	13	1	6	2.6	16	24	20	35	0									
Division Rivals																									
vs. ATL			12	.263	.395	38	10	2	0	1	2.6	1	6	2	9	0									
vs. CIN			15	.250	.417	48	12	3	1	1	2.1	2	7	3	7	0									
vs. HOU			13	.220	.300	50	11	4	0	0	0.0	1	5	3	9	1									
vs. LA			16	.340	.623	53	18	3	0	4	7.5	9	7	2	7	0									
vs. SF			13	.194	.278	36	7	1	1	0	0.0	2	2	1	5	0									
On 3B < 2 Out				.500	.667	12	6	0	1	0	0.0	0	14	3	2										
1984	NY	A	67	.239	.448	201	48	15	3	7	3.5	24	34	15	46	0	0	0	44	106	7	16	2.3	.955	3B-67
1985			138	.239	.442	380	91	16	2	19	5.0	55	62	45	86	0	19	6	67	187	13	15	1.9	.951	3B-134
1986			149	.238	.464	504	120	24	3	28	5.6	71	71	54	120	4	9	1	104	283	19	25	2.7	.953	3B-143, SS-2
1987			150	.234	.479	522	122	26	3	32	6.1	76	87	53	111	1	8	0	97	297	17	35	2.7	.959	3B-147, 1B-1
1988			125	.216	.367	444	96	20	1	15	3.4	46	67	37	104	1	9	0	82	232	19	16	2.7	.943	3B-124
1989	2 teams			NY A (74G — .197)		SD N (50G — .196)																			
"	total		124	.197	.299	371	73	17	0	7	1.9	31	30	37	82	3	10	1	44	205	17	9	2.1	.936	3B-118, DH-1
1990	SD	N	128	.254	.374	398	101	23	2	7	1.7	29	38	39	66	1	15	3	79	200	13	16	2.5	.955	3B-116
7 yrs.			881	.231	.413	2820	651	141	14	115	4.1	332	389	280	615	10	70	11	517	1510	105	132	2.4	.951	3B-849, SS-2, DH-1, 1B-1

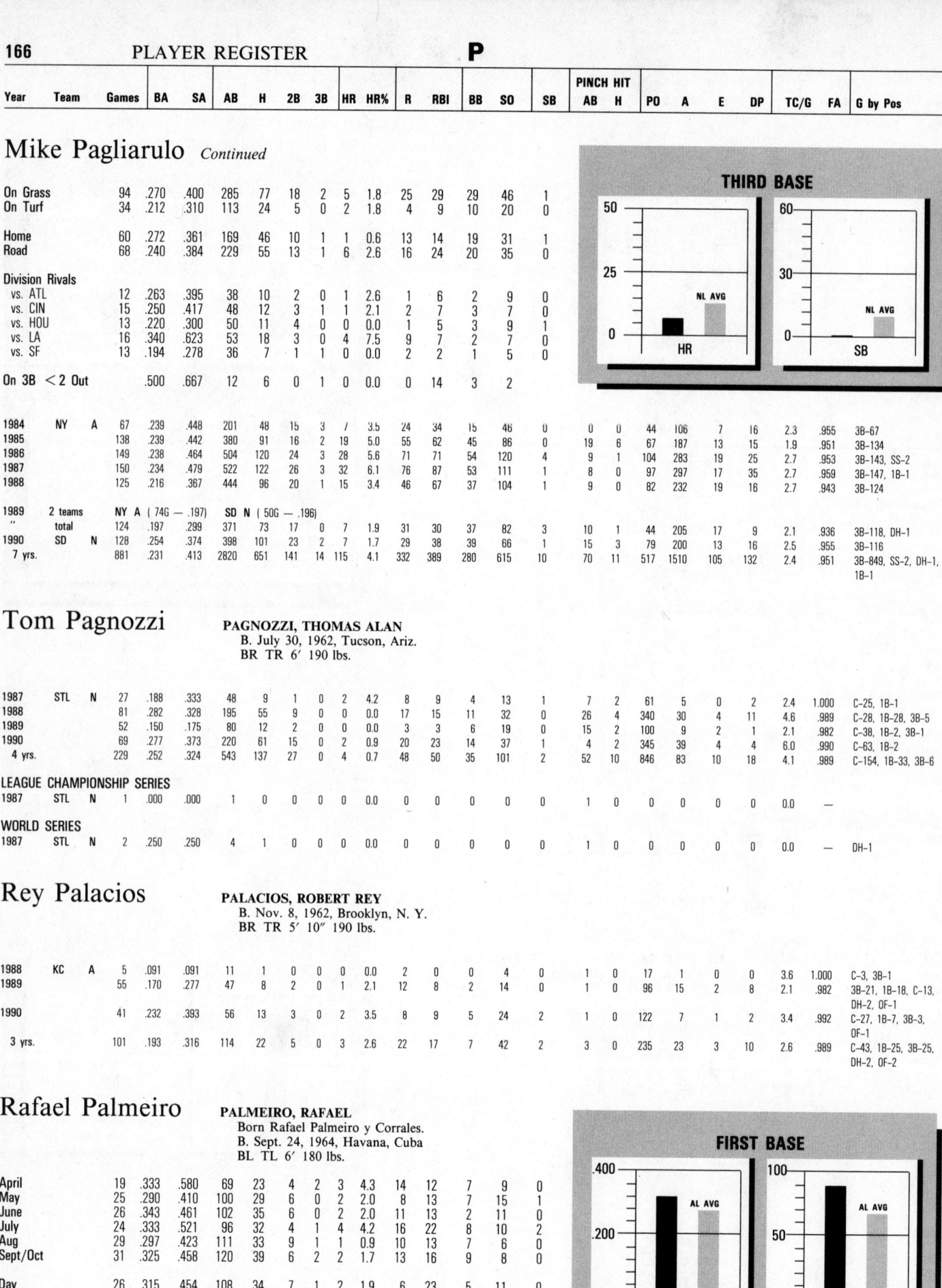

Tom Pagnozzi

PAGNOZZI, THOMAS ALAN
B. July 30, 1962, Tucson, Ariz.
BR TR 6′ 190 lbs.

Year	Team		Games	BA	SA	AB	H	2B	3B	HR	HR%	R	RBI	BB	SO	SB	AB	H	PO	A	E	DP	TC/G	FA	G by Pos
1987	STL	N	27	.188	.333	48	9	1	0	2	4.2	8	9	4	13	1	7	2	61	5	0	2	2.4	1.000	C-25, 1B-1
1988			81	.282	.328	195	55	9	0	0	0.0	17	15	11	32	0	26	4	340	30	4	11	4.6	.989	C-28, 1B-28, 3B-5
1989			52	.150	.175	80	12	2	0	0	0.0	3	3	6	19	0	15	2	100	9	2	1	2.1	.982	C-38, 1B-2, 3B-1
1990			69	.277	.373	220	61	15	0	2	0.9	20	23	14	37	1	4	2	345	39	4	4	6.0	.990	C-63, 1B-2
4 yrs.			229	.252	.324	543	137	27	0	4	0.7	48	50	35	101	2	52	10	846	83	10	18	4.1	.989	C-154, 1B-33, 3B-6
LEAGUE CHAMPIONSHIP SERIES																									
1987	STL	N	1	.000	.000	1	0	0	0	0	0.0	0	0	0	0	0	1	0	0	0	0	0	0.0	—	
WORLD SERIES																									
1987	STL	N	2	.250	.250	4	1	0	0	0	0.0	0	0	0	0	0	1	0	0	0	0	0	0.0	—	DH-1

Rey Palacios

PALACIOS, ROBERT REY
B. Nov. 8, 1962, Brooklyn, N. Y.
BR TR 5′ 10″ 190 lbs.

Year	Team		Games	BA	SA	AB	H	2B	3B	HR	HR%	R	RBI	BB	SO	SB	AB	H	PO	A	E	DP	TC/G	FA	G by Pos
1988	KC	A	5	.091	.091	11	1	0	0	0	0.0	2	0	0	4	0	1	0	17	1	0	0	3.6	1.000	C-3, 3B-1
1989			55	.170	.277	47	8	2	0	1	2.1	12	8	2	14	0	1	0	96	15	2	8	2.1	.982	3B-21, 1B-18, C-13, DH-2, OF-1
1990			41	.232	.393	56	13	3	0	2	3.5	8	9	5	24	2	1	0	122	7	1	2	3.4	.992	C-27, 1B-7, 3B-3, OF-1
3 yrs.			101	.193	.316	114	22	5	0	3	2.6	22	17	7	42	2	3	0	235	23	3	10	2.6	.989	C-43, 1B-25, 3B-25, DH-2, OF-2

Rafael Palmeiro

PALMEIRO, RAFAEL
Born Rafael Palmeiro y Corrales.
B. Sept. 24, 1964, Havana, Cuba
BL TL 6′ 180 lbs.

Year	Team		Games	BA	SA	AB	H	2B	3B	HR	HR%	R	RBI	BB	SO	SB	AB	H	PO	A	E	DP	TC/G	FA	G by Pos
April			19	.333	.580	69	23	4	2	3	4.3	14	12	7	9	0									
May			25	.290	.410	100	29	6	0	2	2.0	8	13	7	15	1									
June			26	.343	.461	102	35	6	0	2	2.0	11	13	2	11	0									
July			24	.333	.521	96	32	4	1	4	4.2	16	22	8	10	2									
Aug			29	.297	.423	111	33	9	1	1	0.9	10	13	7	6	0									
Sept/Oct			31	.325	.458	120	39	6	2	2	1.7	13	16	9	8	0									
Day			26	.315	.454	108	34	7	1	2	1.9	6	23	5	11	0									
Night			128	.320	.471	490	157	28	5	12	2.4	66	66	35	48	3									
vs. Left				.339	.476	189	64	9	1	5	2.6	26	32	8	17	1									
vs. Right				.311	.465	409	127	26	5	9	2.2	46	57	32	42	2									

Year	Team		Games	BA	SA	AB	H	2B	3B	HR	HR%	R	RBI	BB	SO	SB	PINCH HIT AB	PINCH HIT H	PO	A	E	DP	TC/G	FA	G by Pos

Rafael Palmeiro *Continued*

Year	Team		Games	BA	SA	AB	H	2B	3B	HR	HR%	R	RBI	BB	SO	SB	AB	H	PO	A	E	DP	TC/G	FA	G by Pos
On Grass			130	.318	.480	510	162	29	6	14	2.7	62	84	37	50	3									
On Turf			24	.330	.398	88	29	6	0	0	0.0	10	5	3	9	0									
Home			78	.288	.478	295	85	19	5	9	3.1	38	46	30	31	1									
Road			76	.350	.459	303	106	16	1	5	1.7	34	43	10	28	2									
Division Rivals																									
vs. CAL			12	.333	.548	42	14	1	1	2	4.8	6	8	1	3	0									
vs. CHI			12	.213	.319	47	10	2	0	1	2.1	3	5	5	4	0									
vs. KC			12	.277	.426	47	13	7	0	0	0.0	6	6	6	7	0									
vs. MIN			12	.318	.364	44	14	2	0	0	0.0	4	4	3	2	0									
vs. OAK			13	.296	.444	54	16	3	1	1	1.9	5	5	3	4	0									
vs. SEA			12	.308	.333	39	12	1	0	0	0.0	5	4	1	4	0									
On 3B < 2 Out				.364	.409	22	8	1	0	0	0.0	0	21	9	2										
1986	CHI	N	22	.247	.425	73	18	4	0	3	4.1	9	12	4	6	1	2	0	34	2	4	1	1.8	.900	OF-20
1987			84	.276	.543	221	61	15	1	14	6.3	32	30	20	26	2	27	5	176	9	1	16	2.2	.995	OF-45, 1B-18
1988			152	.307	.436	580	178	41	5	8	1.4	75	53	38	34	12	5	0	322	11	5	2	2.2	.985	OF-152
1989	TEX	A	156	.275	.374	559	154	23	4	8	1.4	76	64	63	48	4	3	1	1167	119	12	106	8.3	.991	1B-147, DH-6
1990			154	.319	.468	598	**191**	35	6	14	2.3	72	89	40	59	3	4	0	1215	91	7	123	9.0	.995	1B-146, DH-6
5 yrs.			568	.296	.440	2031	602	118	16	47	2.3	264	248	165	173	22	41	6	2914	232	29	248	5.6	.991	1B-311, OF-217, DH-12

Jim Pankovits

PANKOVITS, JAMES FRANKLIN
B. Aug. 6, 1955, Pennington Gap, Va.
BR TR 5' 10" 170 lbs.

Year	Team		Games	BA	SA	AB	H	2B	3B	HR	HR%	R	RBI	BB	SO	SB	AB	H	PO	A	E	DP	TC/G	FA	G by Pos
1984	HOU	N	53	.284	.407	81	23	7	0	1	1.2	6	14	2	20	2	40	9	22	22	3	7	0.9	.936	2B-15, SS-4, OF-3
1985			75	.244	.331	172	42	3	0	4	2.3	24	14	17	29	1	23	5	81	38	2	8	1.6	.983	OF-33, 2B-21, 3B-1, SS-1
1986			70	.283	.381	113	32	6	1	1	0.9	12	7	11	25	1	38	11	42	58	4	10	1.5	.962	2B-26, OF-5, C-1
1987			50	.230	.311	61	14	2	0	1	1.6	7	8	6	13	2	32	7	19	15	0	3	0.7	1.000	2B-9, OF-6, 3B-4
1988			68	.221	.329	140	31	7	1	2	1.4	13	12	8	28	2	27	2	48	80	11	20	2.0	.921	2B-31, 3B-11, 1B-2
1990	BOS	A	2	.000	.000	0	0	0	0	0	0.0	0	0	0	0	0	0	0	0	0	0	0	0.0	—	2B-2
6 yrs.			318	.250	.349	567	142	25	2	9	1.6	62	55	44	115	8	160	34	212	213	20	48	1.4	.955	2B-104, OF-47, 3B-16, SS-5, 1B-2, C-1

LEAGUE CHAMPIONSHIP SERIES

Year	Team		Games	BA	SA	AB	H	2B	3B	HR	HR%	R	RBI	BB	SO	SB	AB	H	PO	A	E	DP	TC/G	FA	G by Pos
1986	HOU	N	2	.000	.000	2	0	0	0	0	0.0	0	0	0	1	0	2	0	0	0	0	0	0.0	—	

Johnny Paredes

PAREDES, JHONNY ALFONSO
Born Jhonny Alfonso Paredes y Isambert.
B. Sept. 2, 1962, Maracaibo, Venezuela
BR TR 5' 11" 165 lbs.

Year	Team		Games	BA	SA	AB	H	2B	3B	HR	HR%	R	RBI	BB	SO	SB	AB	H	PO	A	E	DP	TC/G	FA	G by Pos
1988	MON	N	35	.187	.242	91	17	2	0	1	1.1	6	10	9	17	5	2	2	46	77	3	18	3.6	.976	2B-28, OF-1
1990	2 teams		DET A (6G — .125)			MON N (3G — .333)																			
"	total		9	.214	.286	14	3	1	0	0	0.0	2	1	2	0	0	1	0	5	14	2	4	3.5	.905	2B-6
2 yrs.			44	.190	.248	105	20	3	0	1	1.0	8	11	11	17	5	3	2	51	91	5	22	3.3	.966	2B-34, OF-1

Mark Parent

PARENT, MARK ALAN
B. Sept. 16, 1961, Ashland, Ore.
BR TR 6' 5" 215 lbs.

Year	Team		Games	BA	SA	AB	H	2B	3B	HR	HR%	R	RBI	BB	SO	SB	AB	H	PO	A	E	DP	TC/G	FA	G by Pos
1986	SD	N	8	.143	.143	14	2	0	0	0	0.0	1	0	1	3	0	4	0	16	0	2	0	2.3	.889	C-3
1987			12	.080	.080	25	2	0	0	0	0.0	0	2	0	9	0	2	0	36	3	0	0	3.3	1.000	C-10
1988			41	.195	.373	118	23	3	0	6	5.1	9	15	6	23	0	3	1	203	15	3	3	5.4	.986	C-36
1989			52	.191	.369	141	27	4	0	7	5.0	12	21	8	34	1	9	2	246	17	0	2	5.1	1.000	C-41, 1B-1
1990			65	.222	.328	189	42	11	0	3	1.5	13	16	16	29	1	5	1	324	31	3	6	6.0	.992	C-60
5 yrs.			178	.197	.333	487	96	18	0	16	3.3	35	54	31	98	2	23	4	825	66	8	11	5.1	.991	C-150, 1B-1

Year	Team		Games	BA	SA	AB	H	2B	3B	HR	HR%	R	RBI	BB	SO	SB	PINCH HIT AB	PINCH HIT H	PO	A	E	DP	TC/G	FA	G by Pos

Dave Parker

PARKER, DAVID GENE (The Cobra)
B. June 9, 1951, Calhoun, Miss.
BL TR 6′ 5″ 230 lbs.

Split	Games	BA	SA	AB	H	2B	3B	HR	HR%	R	RBI	BB	SO	SB
April	17	.308	.492	65	20	7	1	1	1.5	9	11	5	12	1
May	24	.356	.478	90	32	4	2	1	1.1	8	17	5	19	1
June	29	.302	.534	116	35	6	0	7	6.0	17	22	9	18	1
July	27	.260	.452	104	27	5	0	5	4.8	12	16	12	13	0
Aug	30	.319	.513	119	38	5	0	6	5.0	15	19	5	15	0
Sept/Oct	30	.207	.259	116	24	3	0	1	0.9	10	7	5	25	1
Day	52	.279	.401	197	55	9	0	5	2.5	17	22	12	36	1
Night	105	.293	.475	413	121	21	3	16	3.9	54	70	29	66	3
vs. Left		.259	.389	185	48	6	0	6	3.2	17	24	5	35	1
vs. Right		.301	.478	425	128	24	3	15	3.5	54	68	36	67	3
On Grass	133	.278	.434	514	143	28	2	16	3.1	59	83	33	88	3
On Turf	24	.344	.542	96	33	2	1	5	5.2	12	9	8	14	1
Home	77	.273	.427	293	80	16	1	9	3.1	33	46	20	58	1
Road	80	.303	.473	317	96	14	2	12	3.8	38	46	21	44	3
Division Rivals														
vs. BAL	13	.280	.400	50	14	0	0	2	4.0	7	6	4	13	2
vs. BOS	13	.388	.551	49	19	5	0	1	2.0	9	7	5	8	0
vs. CLE	13	.370	.685	54	20	5	0	4	7.4	9	15	2	5	0
vs. DET	11	.239	.304	46	11	3	0	0	0.0	5	3	2	7	0
vs. NY	13	.260	.440	50	13	0	0	3	6.0	7	10	2	8	0
vs. TOR	13	.302	.585	53	16	3	0	4	7.5	9	7	4	10	0
On 3B < 2 Out		.387	.581	31	12	0	0	2	6.5	2	34	3	6	

DESIGNATED HITTER

Year	Team		Games	BA	SA	AB	H	2B	3B	HR	HR%	R	RBI	BB	SO	SB	PH AB	PH H	PO	A	E	DP	TC/G	FA	G by Pos
1973	PIT	N	54	.288	.453	139	40	9	1	4	2.9	17	14	2	27	1	15	4	77	3	3	1	1.5	.964	OF-39
1974			73	.282	.409	220	62	10	3	4	1.8	27	29	10	53	3	21	4	154	8	4	10	2.3	.976	OF-49, 1B-6
1975			148	.308	.541	558	172	35	10	25	4.5	75	101	38	89	8	7	4	311	7	9	2	2.2	.972	OF-141
1976			138	.313	.475	537	168	28	10	13	2.4	82	90	30	80	19	4	2	294	12	14	0	2.3	.956	OF-134
1977			159	.338	.531	637	215	44	8	21	3.3	107	88	58	107	17	0	0	389	26	15	0	2.7	.965	OF-158, 2B-1
1978			148	.334	.585	581	194	32	12	30	5.2	102	117	57	92	20	0	0	302	12	13	3	2.2	.960	OF-147
1979			158	.310	.526	622	193	45	7	25	4.0	109	94	67	101	20	0	0	341	15	15	1	2.3	.960	OF-158
1980			139	.295	.458	518	153	31	1	17	3.3	71	79	25	69	10	7	2	235	14	9	0	1.9	.965	OF-130
1981			67	.258	.454	240	62	14	3	9	3.8	29	48	9	25	6	6	3	110	1	7	0	1.8	.941	OF-60
1982			73	.270	.447	244	66	19	3	6	2.5	41	29	22	45	7	7	2	108	2	5	1	1.6	.957	OF-63
1983			144	.279	.411	552	154	29	4	12	2.2	68	69	28	89	12	2	0	282	3	8	2	2.0	.973	OF-142
1984	CIN	N	156	.285	.410	607	173	28	0	16	2.6	73	94	41	89	11	6	0	296	6	8	1	2.0	.974	OF-151
1985			160	.312	.551	635	198	42	4	34	5.4	88	125	52	80	5	2	1	329	12	10	1	2.2	.972	OF-159
1986			162	.273	.477	637	174	31	3	31	4.9	89	116	56	126	1	3	1	278	9	9	2	1.8	.970	OF-159
1987			153	.253	.433	589	149	28	0	26	4.4	77	97	44	104	7	3	0	354	17	11	10	2.5	.971	OF-142, 1B-9
1988	OAK	A	101	.257	.406	377	97	18	1	12	3.2	43	55	32	70	0	9	4	63	5	3	0	0.7	.958	DH-61, OF-34, 1B-1
1989			144	.264	.432	553	146	27	0	22	4.0	56	97	38	91	0	7	0	2	0	0	0	0.0	1.000	DH-140, OF-1
1990	MIL	A	157	.289	.451	610	176	30	3	21	3.4	71	92	41	102	4	1	1	24	0	1	4	8.3	.960	DH-153, 1B-3
18 yrs.			2334	.293	.477	8856	2592	500	73	328	3.7	1225	1434	650	1439	151	100	28	3949	152	144	38	1.8	.966	OF-1867, DH-354, 1B-19, 2B-1

LEAGUE CHAMPIONSHIP SERIES

Year	Team		Games	BA	SA	AB	H	2B	3B	HR	HR%	R	RBI	BB	SO	SB	PH AB	PH H	PO	A	E	DP	TC/G	FA	G by Pos
1974	PIT	N	3	.125	.125	8	1	0	0	0	0.0	0	0	0	1	0	1	0	4	1	0	0	1.7	1.000	OF-2
1975			3	.000	.000	10	0	0	0	0	0.0	2	0	1	3	0	0	0	13	1	0	1	4.7	1.000	OF-3
1979			3	.333	.333	12	4	0	0	0	0.0	2	2	2	3	1	0	0	9	0	0	0	3.0	1.000	OF-3
1988	OAK	A	3	.250	.333	12	3	1	0	0	0.0	1	0	0	4	0	0	0	1	0	1	0	0.7	.500	DH-2, OF-1
1989			4	.188	.563	16	3	0	0	2	12.5	2	3	0	0	0	0	0	0	0	0	0	0.0	—	DH-4
5 yrs.			16	.190	.310	58	11	1	0	2	3.4	7	5	3	11	1	1	0	27	2	1	1	1.9	.967	OF-9, DH-6

WORLD SERIES

Year	Team		Games	BA	SA	AB	H	2B	3B	HR	HR%	R	RBI	BB	SO	SB	PH AB	PH H	PO	A	E	DP	TC/G	FA	G by Pos
1979	PIT	N	7	.345	.448	29	10	3	0	0	0.0	2	4	2	7	0	0	0	13	1	1	1	2.1	.933	OF-7
1988	OAK	A	4	.200	.200	15	3	0	0	0	0.0	0	0	2	4	0	0	0	4	0	0	0	1.0	1.000	DH-2, OF-2
1989			3	.222	.667	9	2	1	0	1	11.1	2	2	0	2	0	1	0	0	0	0	0	0.0	—	DH-2
3 yrs.			14	.283	.415	53	15	4	0	1	1.9	4	6	4	13	0	1	0	17	1	1	1	1.4	.947	OF-9, DH-4

Rick Parker

PARKER, RICHARD ALAN
B. Mar. 20, 1963, Kansas City, Mo.
BR TR 6′ 185 lbs.

Year	Team		Games	BA	SA	AB	H	2B	3B	HR	HR%	R	RBI	BB	SO	SB	PH AB	PH H	PO	A	E	DP	TC/G	FA	G by Pos
1990	SF	N	54	.243	.346	107	26	5	0	2	1.8	19	14	10	15	6	19	4	45	3	2	0	1.4	.960	OF-35, 2B-2, 3B-1, SS-1

Year	Team		Games	BA	SA	AB	H	2B	3B	HR	HR%	R	RBI	BB	SO	SB	PINCH HIT AB	H	PO	A	E	DP	TC/G	FA	G by Pos

Lance Parrish

PARRISH, LANCE MICHAEL
B. June 15, 1956, Clairton, Pa.
BR TR 6′ 3″ 210 lbs.

	Games	BA	SA	AB	H	2B	3B	HR	HR%	R	RBI	BB	SO	SB	AB	H	PO	A	E	DP	TC/G	FA
April	15	.188	.333	48	9	1	0	2	4.2	3	4	4	12	0								
May	22	.320	.573	75	24	4	0	5	6.7	8	17	7	12	1								
June	27	.326	.587	92	30	3	0	7	7.6	13	17	13	18	0								
July	22	.291	.430	79	23	2	0	3	3.8	9	12	8	20	0								
Aug	23	.195	.341	82	16	0	0	4	4.9	10	11	9	29	0								
Sept/Oct	24	.255	.394	94	24	4	0	3	3.2	11	9	5	16	1								
Day	23	.208	.444	72	15	2	0	5	6.9	8	16	6	15	0								
Night	110	.279	.452	398	111	12	0	19	4.8	46	54	40	92	2								
vs. Left		.304	.488	125	38	2	0	7	5.6	20	17	13	27	1								
vs. Right		.255	.438	345	88	12	0	17	4.9	34	53	33	80	1								
On Grass	114	.277	.474	401	111	13	0	22	5.5	48	65	40	88	2								
On Turf	19	.217	.319	69	15	1	0	2	2.9	6	5	6	19	0								
Home	66	.277	.485	235	65	7	0	14	6.0	26	39	23	55	0								
Road	67	.260	.417	235	61	7	0	10	4.3	28	31	23	52	2								
Division Rivals																						
vs. CHI	12	.222	.389	36	8	0	0	2	5.6	5	4	7	10	0								
vs. KC	11	.357	.690	42	15	2	0	4	9.5	7	7	4	6	0								
vs. MIN	9	.222	.389	36	8	0	0	2	5.6	4	5	1	6	0								
vs. OAK	10	.171	.220	41	7	2	0	0	0.0	3	2	3	16	0								
vs. SEA	11	.184	.211	38	7	1	0	0	0.0	1	0	4	13	0								
vs. TEX	13	.333	.556	45	15	1	0	3	6.7	8	9	5	8	1								
On 3B < 2 Out		.294	.529	17	5	1	0	1	5.9	1	12	3	6									

CATCHER — AVERAGE / RBI / HR / SB (with AL AVG comparisons)

Year	Team		Games	BA	SA	AB	H	2B	3B	HR	HR%	R	RBI	BB	SO	SB	AB	H	PO	A	E	DP	TC/G	FA	G by Pos
1977	DET	A	12	.196	.435	46	9	2	0	3	6.5	10	7	5	12	0	0	0	76	6	0	0	6.8	1.000	C-12
1978			85	.219	.424	288	63	11	3	14	4.9	37	41	11	71	0	6	1	353	39	5	5	4.7	.987	C-79
1979			143	.276	.456	493	136	26	3	19	3.9	65	65	49	105	6	3	1	707	79	9	10	5.6	.989	C-142
1980			144	.286	.499	553	158	34	6	24	4.3	79	82	31	109	6	4	1	607	67	7	15	4.7	.990	C-121, DH-16, 1B-5, OF-5
1981			96	.244	.394	348	85	18	2	10	2.9	39	46	34	52	2	0	0	407	40	3	6	4.7	.993	C-90, DH-5
1982			133	.284	.529	486	138	19	2	32	6.6	75	87	40	99	3	2	1	627	76	8	8	5.3	.989	C-132, OF-1
1983			155	.269	.483	605	163	42	3	27	4.5	80	114	44	106	1	2	0	695	73	4	8	5.0	.995	C-131, DH-27
1984			147	.237	.443	578	137	16	2	33	5.7	75	98	41	120	2	3	1	720	67	7	11	5.4	.991	C-127, DH-22
1985			140	.273	.479	549	150	27	1	28	5.1	64	98	41	90	2	1	1	695	53	5	9	5.4	.993	C-120, DH-22
1986			91	.257	.483	327	84	6	1	22	6.7	53	62	38	83	0	4	0	483	48	6	5	5.9	.989	C-85, DH-6
1987	PHI	N	130	.245	.399	466	114	21	0	17	3.6	42	67	47	104	0	4	0	724	66	9	1	6.1	.989	C-127
1988			123	.215	.370	424	91	17	2	15	3.5	44	60	47	93	0	3	2	640	73	9	12	5.9	.988	C-117, 1B-1
1989	CAL	A	124	.238	.388	433	103	12	1	17	3.9	48	50	42	104	1	2	0	638	63	5	7	5.7	.993	C-122, DH-2
1990			133	.268	.451	470	126	14	0	24	5.1	54	70	46	107	2	1	0	794	90	6	21	6.7	.993	C-131, 1B-4, DH-1
14 yrs.			1656	.257	.450	6066	1557	265	26	285	4.7	765	947	516	1255	25	35	8	8166	840	83	118	5.5	.991	C-1536, DH-101, 1B-10, OF-6

LEAGUE CHAMPIONSHIP SERIES

Year	Team		Games	BA	SA	AB	H	2B	3B	HR	HR%	R	RBI	BB	SO	SB	AB	H	PO	A	E	DP	TC/G	FA	G by Pos
1984	DET	A	3	.250	.583	12	3	1	0	1	8.3	1	3	0	3	0	0	0	21	2	0	0	7.7	1.000	C-3

WORLD SERIES

Year	Team		Games	BA	SA	AB	H	2B	3B	HR	HR%	R	RBI	BB	SO	SB	AB	H	PO	A	E	DP	TC/G	FA	G by Pos
1984	DET	A	5	.278	.500	18	5	1	0	1	5.6	3	2	3	2	1	0	0	30	3	1	1	6.8	.971	C-5

Dan Pasqua

PASQUA, DANIEL ANTHONY
B. Oct. 17, 1961, Yonkers, N. Y.
BL TL 6′ 205 lbs.
See Player Register Supplement for complete graphic analysis.

Year	Team		Games	BA	SA	AB	H	2B	3B	HR	HR%	R	RBI	BB	SO	SB	AB	H	PO	A	E	DP	TC/G	FA	G by Pos
1985	NY	A	60	.209	.426	148	31	3	1	9	6.1	17	25	16	38	0	15	2	72	2	0	0	1.2	1.000	OF-37, DH-14
1986			102	.293	.525	280	82	17	0	16	5.7	44	45	47	78	2	22	7	172	4	2	6	1.7	.989	OF-81, 1B-5, DH-3
1987			113	.233	.421	318	74	7	1	17	5.3	42	42	40	99	0	22	3	214	10	2	2	2.0	.991	OF-74, DH-20, 1B-12
1988	CHI	A	129	.227	.417	422	96	16	2	20	4.7	48	50	46	100	1	15	1	316	14	2	13	2.6	.994	OF-119, DH-2
1989			73	.248	.427	246	61	9	1	11	4.5	26	47	25	58	1	3	1	149	3	1	2	2.1	.993	OF-66, DH-5
1990			112	.274	.495	325	89	27	3	13	4.0	43	58	37	66	1	18	4	71	5	3	1	1.8	.962	DH-57, OF-43
6 yrs.			589	.249	.452	1739	433	79	8	86	4.9	220	267	211	439	5	95	19	994	38	10	24	1.8	.990	OF-420, DH-101, 1B-17

Year	Team	Games	BA	SA	AB	H	2B	3B	HR	HR%	R	RBI	BB	SO	SB	PINCH HIT AB	PINCH HIT H	PO	A	E	DP	TC/G	FA	G by Pos

Bill Pecota

PECOTA, WILLIAM JOSEPH
B. Feb. 16, 1960, Redwood City, Calif.
BR TR 6′ 2″ 195 lbs.
See Player Register Supplement for complete graphic analysis.

Year	Team	Games	BA	SA	AB	H	2B	3B	HR	HR%	R	RBI	BB	SO	SB	PH AB	PH H	PO	A	E	DP	TC/G	FA	G by Pos
1986	KC	A	12	.207	.276	29	6	2	0	0	0.0	3	2	3	3	0	0	0	7	31	1	1	3.3	.974	3B–12, SS–2
1987			66	.276	.378	156	43	5	1	3	1.9	22	14	15	25	5	7	0	67	135	6	28	3.2	.971	SS–36, 3B–17, 2B–15
1988			90	.208	.275	178	37	3	3	1	0.6	25	15	18	34	7	1	1	98	145	6	25	2.8	.976	SS–41, 3B–21, 1B–11, OF–9, DH–4, 2B–3, C–1
1989			65	.205	.410	83	17	4	2	3	3.6	21	5	7	9	5	0	0	50	79	2	14	2.0	.985	SS–29, OF–15, 2B–12, 3B–7, 1B–4, DH–1
1990			87	.242	.383	240	58	15	2	5	2.0	43	20	33	39	8	2	0	160	195	5	44	4.4	.986	2B–50, SS–21, 3B–11, OF–6, 1B–4, DH–2
5 yrs.			320	.235	.353	686	161	29	8	12	1.7	114	56	76	110	25	10	1	382	585	20	112	3.1	.980	SS–129, 2B–80, 3B–68, OF–30, 1B–19, DH–7, C–1

Geronimo Pena

PENA, GERONIMO
B. Mar. 29, 1967, Distrito Nacional, Dominican Republic
BR TR 6′ 1″ 170 lbs.

Year	Team	Games	BA	SA	AB	H	2B	3B	HR	HR%	R	RBI	BB	SO	SB	PH AB	PH H	PO	A	E	DP	TC/G	FA	G by Pos
1990	STL	N	18	.244	.289	45	11	2	0	0	0.0	5	2	4	14	1	6	3	24	30	1	7	5.0	.982	2B–11

Tony Pena

PENA, ANTONIO FRANCESCO
Born Antonio Francesco Pena y Padilla.
Brother of Ramon Pena.
B. June 4, 1957, Monte Cristi, Dominican Republic
BR TR 6′ 175 lbs.

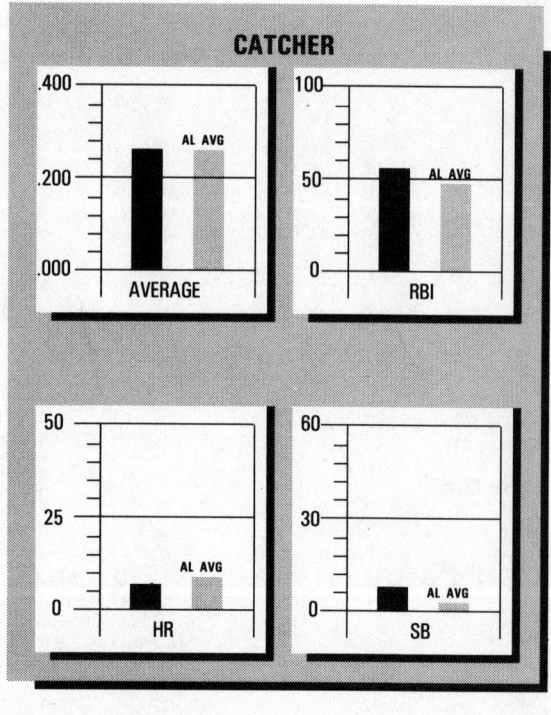

	Games	BA	SA	AB	H	2B	3B	HR	HR%	R	RBI	BB	SO	SB
April	19	.403	.556	72	29	5	0	2	2.8	8	13	0	9	0
May	26	.209	.297	91	19	2	0	2	2.2	11	8	5	16	0
June	20	.243	.300	70	17	2	1	0	0.0	6	8	10	8	0
July	26	.174	.186	86	15	1	0	0	0.0	5	5	3	15	0
Aug	23	.266	.367	79	21	2	0	2	2.5	15	9	14	14	3
Sept/Oct	29	.301	.409	93	28	7	0	1	1.1	17	13	11	9	5
Day	39	.246	.306	134	33	5	0	1	0.7	16	10	8	25	3
Night	104	.269	.364	357	96	14	1	6	1.7	46	46	35	46	5
vs. Left		.290	.413	155	45	4	0	5	3.2	21	22	12	14	2
vs. Right		.250	.318	336	84	15	1	2	0.6	41	34	31	57	6
On Grass	121	.273	.364	418	114	18	1	6	1.4	56	51	39	60	7
On Turf	22	.205	.260	73	15	1	0	1	1.4	6	5	4	11	1
Home	74	.275	.348	247	68	9	0	3	1.2	33	30	27	41	5
Road	69	.250	.348	244	61	10	1	4	1.6	29	26	16	30	3
Division Rivals														
vs. BAL	10	.231	.308	26	6	2	0	0	0.0	7	5	12	3	3
vs. CLE	10	.275	.425	40	11	1	1	1	2.5	5	7	2	5	1
vs. DET	11	.209	.372	43	9	1	0	2	4.7	4	8	1	4	0
vs. MIL	12	.294	.324	34	10	1	0	0	0.0	4	1	4	6	1
vs. NY	9	.344	.406	32	11	2	0	0	0.0	3	3	2	2	1
vs. TOR	13	.279	.349	43	12	3	0	0	0.0	5	4	5	7	1
On 3B < 2 Out		.345	.414	29	10	2	0	0	0.0	0	19	1	1	

Year	Team	Games	BA	SA	AB	H	2B	3B	HR	HR%	R	RBI	BB	SO	SB	PH AB	PH H	PO	A	E	DP	TC/G	FA	G by Pos
1980	PIT	N	8	.429	.571	21	9	1	1	0	0.0	1	1	0	4	0	2	1	38	2	2	0	5.3	.952	C–6
1981			66	.300	.381	210	63	9	1	2	1.0	16	17	8	23	1	2	1	286	41	5	10	5.0	.985	C–64
1982			138	.296	.435	497	147	28	4	11	2.2	53	63	17	57	2	0	0	763	89	16	6	6.3	.982	C–137
1983			151	.301	.435	542	163	22	3	15	2.8	51	70	31	73	6	2	1	976	90	9	9	7.1	.992	C–149
1984			147	.286	.425	546	156	27	2	15	2.7	77	78	36	79	12	1	1	895	95	9	15	6.8	.991	C–146
1985			147	.249	.361	546	136	27	2	10	1.8	53	59	29	67	12	0	0	925	102	12	9	7.1	.988	C–146, 1B–1
1986			144	.288	.406	510	147	26	2	10	2.0	56	52	53	69	9	7	1	824	99	18	13	6.5	.981	C–139, 1B–4
1987	STL	N	116	.214	.307	384	82	13	4	5	1.3	40	44	36	54	6	4	1	624	51	8	8	5.9	.988	C–112, 1B–4, OF–2
1988			149	.263	.372	505	133	23	1	10	2.0	55	51	33	60	6	8	1	796	72	6	9	5.9	.993	C–142, 1B–3
1989			141	.259	.337	424	110	17	2	4	0.9	36	37	35	33	5	7	1	675	70	7	13	5.3	.997	C–134, OF–1
1990	BOS	A	143	.263	.348	491	129	19	1	7	1.4	62	56	43	71	8	5	2	866	74	5	13	6.6	.995	C–142, 1B–1
11 yrs.			1350	.273	.385	4676	1275	212	23	89	1.9	500	528	321	590	67	38	10	7668	785	92	105	6.3	.989	C–1317, 1B–13, OF–3

Year	Team		Games	BA	SA	AB	H	2B	3B	HR	HR%	R	RBI	BB	SO	SB	PINCH HIT AB	H	PO	A	E	DP	TC/G	FA	G by Pos

Tony Pena *Continued*

LEAGUE CHAMPIONSHIP SERIES

Year	Team		Games	BA	SA	AB	H	2B	3B	HR	HR%	R	RBI	BB	SO	SB	AB	H	PO	A	E	DP	TC/G	FA	G by Pos
1987	STL	N	7	.381	.476	21	8	0	1	0	0.0	5	0	3	4	1	0	0	55	5	0	0	8.6	1.000	C-7
1990	BOS	A	4	.214	.214	14	3	0	0	0	0.0	0	0	0	0	0	0	0	22	4	1	1	6.8	.963	C-4
2 yrs.			11	.314	.371	35	11	0	1	0	0.0	5	0	3	4	1	0	0	77	9	1	1	7.9	.989	C-11

WORLD SERIES

Year	Team		Games	BA	SA	AB	H	2B	3B	HR	HR%	R	RBI	BB	SO	SB	AB	H	PO	A	E	DP	TC/G	FA	G by Pos
1987	STL	N	7	.409	.455	22	9	1	0	0	0.0	2	4	3	2	1	0	0	32	1	1	0	4.9	.971	C-6, DH-1

Terry Pendleton

PENDLETON, TERRY LEE
B. July 16, 1960, Los Angeles, Calif.
BB TR 5′ 9″ 180 lbs.

			Games	BA	SA	AB	H	2B	3B	HR	HR%	R	RBI	BB	SO	SB
April			14	.231	.308	52	12	4	0	0	0.0	6	8	4	4	1
May			21	.231	.333	78	18	2	0	2	2.6	8	13	6	8	0
June			28	.299	.486	107	32	7	2	3	2.8	19	23	10	19	0
July			27	.127	.167	102	13	1	0	1	1.0	2	6	3	15	1
Aug			23	.241	.287	87	21	4	0	0	0.0	9	7	7	11	4
Sept/Oct			8	.333	.429	21	7	2	0	0	0.0	2	1	0	1	1
Day			33	.273	.394	132	36	8	1	2	1.5	15	20	7	14	1
Night			88	.213	.295	315	67	12	1	4	1.3	31	38	23	44	6
vs. Left				.209	.361	158	33	12	0	4	2.5	12	23	6	15	2
vs. Right				.242	.304	289	70	8	2	2	0.7	34	35	24	43	5
On Grass			29	.219	.267	105	23	3	1	0	0.0	6	16	7	10	0
On Turf			92	.234	.342	342	80	17	1	6	1.8	40	42	23	48	7
Home			67	.243	.375	251	61	13	1	6	2.4	32	32	17	31	2
Road			54	.214	.260	196	42	7	1	0	0.0	14	26	13	27	5
Division Rivals																
vs. CHI			12	.255	.340	47	12	2	1	0	0.0	5	13	3	5	0
vs. MON			12	.282	.436	39	11	3	0	1	2.6	5	6	6	6	0
vs. NY			16	.283	.417	60	17	6	1	0	0.0	6	8	0	7	1
vs. PHI			12	.196	.373	51	10	3	0	2	3.9	8	7	4	9	2
vs. PIT			12	.243	.324	37	9	3	0	0	0.0	7	5	5	9	2
On 3B < 2 Out				.348	.478	23	8	3	0	0	0.0	0	23	4	4	

THIRD BASE

Year	Team		Games	BA	SA	AB	H	2B	3B	HR	HR%	R	RBI	BB	SO	SB	PINCH HIT AB	H	PO	A	E	DP	TC/G	FA	G by Pos
1984	STL	N	67	.324	.420	262	85	16	3	1	0.4	37	33	16	32	20	1	0	59	155	13	10	3.4	.943	3B-66
1985			149	.240	.306	559	134	16	3	5	0.9	56	69	37	75	17	2	1	129	361	18	26	3.4	.965	3B-149
1986			159	.239	.306	578	138	26	5	1	0.2	56	59	34	59	24	3	0	133	371	20	36	3.3	.962	3B-156, OF-1
1987			159	.286	.412	583	167	29	4	12	2.1	82	96	70	74	19	1	1	117	369	26	27	3.2	.949	3B-158
1988			110	.253	.361	391	99	20	2	6	1.5	44	53	21	51	3	11	4	75	239	12	13	3.0	.963	3B-101
1989			162	.264	.390	613	162	28	5	13	2.1	83	74	44	81	9	3	0	113	392	15	25	3.2	.971	3B-161
1990			121	.230	.324	447	103	20	2	6	1.3	46	58	30	58	7	5	3	91	248	19	18	3.1	.947	3B-117
7 yrs.			927	.259	.356	3433	888	155	24	44	1.3	404	442	252	430	99	26	9	717	2135	123	155	3.2	.959	3B-908, OF-1

LEAGUE CHAMPIONSHIP SERIES

Year	Team		Games	BA	SA	AB	H	2B	3B	HR	HR%	R	RBI	BB	SO	SB	AB	H	PO	A	E	DP	TC/G	FA	G by Pos
1985	STL	N	6	.208	.250	24	5	1	0	0	0.0	2	4	1	2	0	0	0	6	18	1	2	4.2	.960	3B-6
1987			6	.211	.316	19	4	0	1	0	0.0	3	1	0	6	0	0	0	3	11	0	1	2.3	1.000	3B-6
2 yrs.			12	.209	.279	43	9	1	1	0	0.0	5	5	1	8	0	0	0	9	29	1	3	3.3	.974	3B-12

WORLD SERIES

Year	Team		Games	BA	SA	AB	H	2B	3B	HR	HR%	R	RBI	BB	SO	SB	AB	H	PO	A	E	DP	TC/G	FA	G by Pos
1985	STL	N	7	.261	.391	23	6	1	1	0	0.0	3	3	3	2	0	0	0	6	14	1	3	3.0	.952	3B-7
1987			3	.429	.429	7	3	0	0	0	0.0	2	1	1	1	2	0	0	0	0	0	0	0.0	—	DH-2
2 yrs.			10	.300	.400	30	9	1	1	0	0.0	5	4	4	3	2	0	0	6	14	1	3	2.1	.952	3B-7, DH-2

Tony Perezchica

PEREZCHICA, ANTONIO LLAMAS
Born Antonio Llamas Perezchica y Gonzalez.
B. Apr. 20, 1966, Mexicali, Mexico
BR TR 5′ 11″ 165 lbs.

Year	Team		Games	BA	SA	AB	H	2B	3B	HR	HR%	R	RBI	BB	SO	SB	PINCH HIT AB	H	PO	A	E	DP	TC/G	FA	G by Pos
1988	SF	N	7	.125	.125	8	1	0	0	0	0.0	1	1	2	1	0	0	0	5	5	0	0	1.4	1.000	2B-6
1990			4	.333	.333	3	1	0	0	0	0.0	1	0	1	2	0	1	0	2	0	0	0	0.5	1.000	2B-2, SS-2
2 yrs.			11	.182	.182	11	2	0	0	0	0.0	2	1	3	3	0	1	0	7	5	0	0	1.1	1.000	2B-8, SS-2

Year	Team		Games	BA	SA	AB	H	2B	3B	HR	HR%	R	RBI	BB	SO	SB	PINCH HIT AB	H	PO	A	E	DP	TC/G	FA	G by Pos

Gerald Perry

PERRY, GERALD JUNE
B. Oct. 30, 1960, Savannah, Ga.
BL TR 5′ 11″ 172 lbs.

Split	Games	BA	SA	AB	H	2B	3B	HR	HR%	R	RBI	BB	SO	SB	PH AB	PH H	PO	A	E	DP	TC/G	FA	G by Pos
April	16	.270	.333	63	17	1	0	1	1.6	6	4	8	8	1									
May	28	.275	.440	109	30	7	1	3	2.8	14	20	5	13	0									
June	22	.203	.253	79	16	4	0	0	0.0	9	8	7	10	3									
July	26	.281	.438	96	27	6	0	3	3.1	15	13	12	11	7									
Aug	21	.313	.388	67	21	3	1	0	0.0	9	10	3	8	4									
Sept/Oct	20	.137	.216	51	7	1	0	1	2.0	4	2	4	6	2									
Day	32	.308	.470	117	36	5	1	4	3.4	18	13	10	12	4									
Night	101	.236	.325	348	82	17	1	4	1.1	39	44	29	44	13									
vs. Left		.209	.269	134	28	5	0	1	0.7	12	14	7	19	7									
vs. Right		.272	.399	331	90	17	2	7	2.1	45	43	32	37	10									
On Grass	52	.227	.346	185	42	5	1	5	2.7	21	24	17	21	10									
On Turf	81	.271	.371	280	76	17	1	3	1.1	36	33	22	35	7									
Home	68	.286	.395	238	68	15	1	3	1.3	29	30	17	28	5									
Road	65	.220	.326	227	50	7	1	5	2.2	28	27	22	28	12									

Division Rivals

Split	Games	BA	SA	AB	H	2B	3B	HR	HR%	R	RBI	BB	SO	SB
vs. CAL	8	.120	.240	25	3	0	0	1	4.0	2	2	2	3	1
vs. CHI	11	.270	.405	37	10	2	0	1	2.7	2	9	4	6	1
vs. MIN	7	.240	.400	25	6	4	0	0	0.0	5	1	1	4	1
vs. OAK	11	.262	.333	42	11	1	1	0	0.0	5	4	2	3	1
vs. SEA	10	.071	.107	28	2	1	0	0	0.0	0	2	4	2	2
vs. TEX	10	.375	.563	32	12	3	0	1	3.1	7	8	2	3	2
On 3B < 2 Out		.318	.636	22	7	4	0	1	4.5	1	23	2	1	

Year	Team		Games	BA	SA	AB	H	2B	3B	HR	HR%	R	RBI	BB	SO	SB	PH AB	PH H	PO	A	E	DP	TC/G	FA	G by Pos
1983	ATL	N	27	.359	.487	39	14	2	0	1	2.6	5	6	5	4	0	16	7	55	0	1	5	2.1	.982	1B-7, OF-1
1984			122	.265	.372	347	92	12	2	7	2.0	52	47	61	38	15	16	8	550	28	12	41	4.8	.980	1B-64, OF-53
1985			110	.214	.273	238	51	5	0	3	1.3	22	13	23	28	9	44	6	541	37	9	48	5.3	.985	1B-55, OF-1
1986			29	.271	.386	70	19	2	0	2	2.9	6	11	8	4	0	11	3	24	1	2	2	0.9	.926	OF-21, 1B-1
1987			142	.270	.411	533	144	35	2	12	2.3	77	74	48	63	42	5	1	1297	72	14	118	9.7	.990	1B-136, OF-7
1988			141	.300	.400	547	164	29	1	8	1.5	61	74	36	49	29	0	0	1282	106	17	102	10.0	.988	1B-141
1989			72	.252	.338	266	67	11	0	4	1.5	24	21	32	28	10	0	0	618	51	9	49	9.4	.987	1B-72
1990	KC	A	133	.254	.361	465	118	22	2	8	1.7	57	57	39	56	17	12	0	394	40	6	41	8.6	.986	DH-68, 1B-51
8 yrs.			776	.267	.374	2505	669	118	7	45	1.8	304	303	252	270	122	104	25	4761	335	70	406	6.7	.986	1B-527, OF-83, DH-68

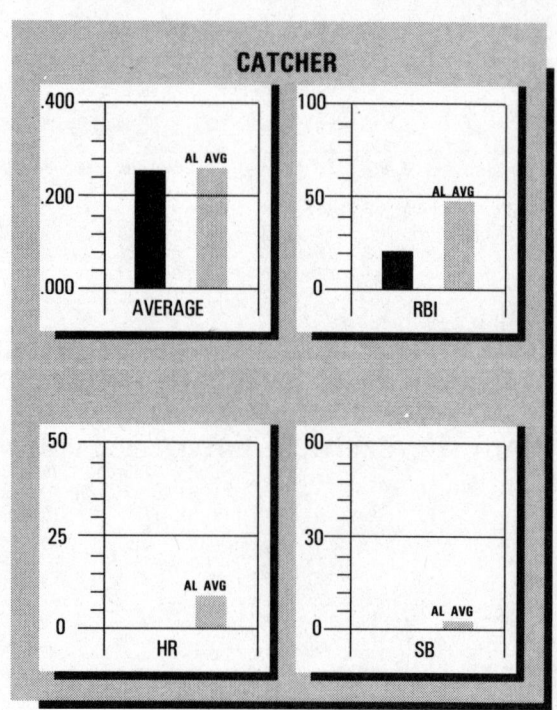

Geno Petralli

PETRALLI, EUGENE JAMES
B. Sept. 25, 1959, Sacramento, Calif.
BB TR 6′ 2″ 185 lbs.

Split	Games	BA	SA	AB	H	2B	3B	HR	HR%	R	RBI	BB	SO	SB
April	17	.289	.356	45	13	3	0	0	0.0	7	3	10	7	0
May	22	.213	.279	61	13	2	1	0	0.0	4	5	7	9	0
June	18	.216	.243	37	8	1	0	0	0.0	0	4	2	4	0
July	21	.196	.216	51	10	1	0	0	0.0	5	3	10	7	0
Aug	26	.344	.375	64	22	2	0	0	0.0	7	5	8	11	0
Sept/Oct	29	.254	.313	67	17	4	0	0	0.0	5	1	13	11	0
Day	23	.293	.362	58	17	4	0	0	0.0	9	5	11	7	0
Night	110	.247	.288	267	66	9	1	0	0.0	19	16	39	42	0
vs. Left		.300	.300	20	6	0	0	0	0.0	4	3	8	1	0
vs. Right		.252	.302	305	77	13	1	0	0.0	24	18	42	48	0
On Grass	112	.252	.298	282	71	11	1	0	0.0	25	20	39	44	0
On Turf	21	.279	.326	43	12	2	0	0	0.0	3	1	11	5	0
Home	69	.265	.306	170	45	7	0	0	0.0	16	11	28	31	0
Road	64	.245	.297	155	38	6	1	0	0.0	12	10	22	18	0

Division Rivals

Split	Games	BA	SA	AB	H	2B	3B	HR	HR%	R	RBI	BB	SO	SB
vs. CAL	9	.368	.368	19	7	0	0	0	0.0	1	0	1	4	0
vs. CHI	12	.257	.343	35	9	1	1	0	0.0	5	4	5	7	0
vs. KC	10	.429	.571	28	12	4	0	0	0.0	4	2	8	6	0
vs. MIN	7	.267	.333	15	4	1	0	0	0.0	1	2	2	3	0
vs. OAK	12	.250	.286	28	7	1	0	0	0.0	0	2	5	4	0
vs. SEA	12	.174	.174	23	4	0	0	0	0.0	0	2	1	3	0
On 3B < 2 Out		.250	.250	8	2	0	0	0	0.0	0	7	3	0	

Year	Team		Games	BA	SA	AB	H	2B	3B	HR	HR%	R	RBI	BB	SO	SB	PINCH HIT AB	H	PO	A	E	DP	TC/G	FA	G by Pos

Geno Petralli *Continued*

Year	Team		Games	BA	SA	AB	H	2B	3B	HR	HR%	R	RBI	BB	SO	SB	AB	H	PO	A	E	DP	TC/G	FA	G by Pos
1982	TOR	A	16	.364	.409	44	16	2	0	0	0.0	3	1	4	6	0	3	1	51	4	1	0	3.5	.982	C-12, 3B-3
1983			6	.000	.000	4	0	0	0	0	0.0	0	0	1	1	1	1	0	7	0	0	0	1.2	1.000	C-5, DH-1
1984			3	.000	.000	3	0	0	0	0	0.0	0	0	0	0	0	2	0	1	1	0	0	0.7	1.000	DH-1, C-1
1985	TEX	A	42	.270	.290	100	27	2	0	0	0.0	7	11	8	12	1	3	1	179	16	2	6	4.7	.990	C-41
1986			69	.255	.409	137	35	9	3	2	1.5	17	18	5	14	3	22	4	163	14	4	2	2.6	.978	C-41, 3B-15, DH-2, 2B-2
1987			101	.302	.480	202	61	11	2	7	3.5	28	31	27	29	0	26	5	370	34	5	4	4.0	.988	C-63, 3B-17, 1B-5, 2B-4, OF-3, DH-2
1988			129	.282	.393	351	99	14	2	7	2.0	35	36	41	52	0	23	6	421	54	10	8	3.8	.979	C-85, DH-23, 3B-9, 1B-2, 2B-2
1989			70	.304	.408	184	56	7	0	4	2.2	18	23	17	24	0	15	4	258	15	3	3	3.9	.989	C-49, DH-16
1990			133	.255	.302	325	83	13	1	0	0.0	28	21	50	49	0	24	5	602	46	6	7	5.4	.991	C-118, 3B-7, 2B-3
9 yrs.			569	.279	.379	1350	377	58	8	20	1.5	136	141	153	187	5	119	25	2052	184	31	30	4.0	.986	C-415, 3B-51, DH-45, 2B-11, 1B-7, OF-3

Gary Pettis

PETTIS, GARY GEORGE
B. Apr. 3, 1958, Oakland, Calif.
BB TR 6' 1" 165 lbs.

OUTFIELD

	Games	BA	SA	AB	H	2B	3B	HR	HR%	R	RBI	BB	SO	SB
April	19	.219	.297	64	14	3	1	0	0.0	12	3	9	19	4
May	26	.224	.329	76	17	2	0	2	2.6	6	8	10	18	8
June	21	.274	.425	73	20	4	2	1	1.4	14	10	8	17	10
July	19	.222	.315	54	12	3	1	0	0.0	9	2	5	17	3
Aug	27	.242	.326	95	23	2	3	0	0.0	15	4	17	26	4
Sept/Oct	24	.246	.311	61	15	2	1	0	0.0	10	4	8	21	9
Day	23	.300	.425	80	24	8	1	0	0.0	19	7	15	23	9
Night	113	.224	.315	343	77	8	7	3	0.9	47	24	42	95	29
vs. Left		.217	.296	152	33	6	3	0	0.0	25	7	23	38	15
vs. Right		.251	.358	271	68	10	5	3	1.1	41	24	34	80	23
On Grass	116	.236	.327	352	83	13	5	3	0.9	55	27	49	98	31
On Turf	20	.254	.380	71	18	3	3	0	0.0	11	4	8	20	7
Home	71	.253	.362	221	56	7	4	3	1.4	34	21	30	59	19
Road	65	.223	.307	202	45	9	4	0	0.0	32	10	27	59	19
Division Rivals														
vs. CAL	11	.257	.371	35	9	2	1	0	0.0	8	3	5	11	7
vs. CHI	12	.158	.237	38	6	1	1	0	0.0	7	1	8	12	4
vs. KC	11	.243	.324	37	9	1	1	0	0.0	5	4	4	9	3
vs. MIN	9	.182	.318	22	4	0	0	1	4.5	4	4	8	6	3
vs. OAK	12	.295	.455	44	13	3	2	0	0.0	4	5	3	14	4
vs. SEA	11	.244	.268	41	10	1	0	0	0.0	7	1	5	7	3
On 3B < 2 Out		.250	.313	16	4	1	0	0	0.0	0	12	3	5	

Year	Team		Games	BA	SA	AB	H	2B	3B	HR	HR%	R	RBI	BB	SO	SB	AB	H	PO	A	E	DP	TC/G	FA	G by Pos
1982	CAL	A	10	.200	.800	5	1	0	0	1	20.0	5	1	0	2	0	0	0	5	1	0	0	0.6	1.000	OF-8
1983			22	.294	.494	85	25	2	3	3	3.5	19	6	7	15	8	0	0	49	5	1	2	2.5	.982	OF-21
1984			140	.227	.300	397	90	11	6	2	0.5	63	29	60	115	48	2	0	337	11	6	4	2.5	.983	OF-134
1985			125	.257	.323	443	114	10	8	1	0.2	67	32	62	125	56	0	0	368	13	4	5	3.1	.990	OF-122
1986			154	.258	.343	539	139	23	4	5	0.9	93	58	69	132	50	0	0	462	9	7	3	3.1	.985	OF-153, DH-1
1987			133	.208	.259	394	82	13	2	1	0.3	49	17	52	124	24	0	0	344	2	7	2	2.7	.980	OF-131
1988	DET	A	129	.210	.277	458	96	14	4	3	0.7	65	36	47	85	44	2	0	361	5	5	0	2.9	.987	OF-126, DH-2
1989			119	.257	.309	444	114	8	6	1	0.2	77	18	84	106	43	1	0	325	1	4	0	2.8	.988	OF-119
1990	TEX	A	136	.239	.336	423	101	16	8	3	0.7	66	31	57	118	38	5	1	285	10	2	4	2.3	.993	OF-128, DH-2
9 yrs.			968	.239	.314	3188	762	97	41	20	0.6	504	228	438	822	311	10	1	2536	57	36	20	2.7	.986	OF-942, DH-5

LEAGUE CHAMPIONSHIP SERIES

Year	Team		Games	BA	SA	AB	H	2B	3B	HR	HR%	R	RBI	BB	SO	SB	AB	H	PO	A	E	DP	TC/G	FA	G by Pos
1986	CAL	A	7	.346	.500	26	9	1	0	1	3.8	4	4	3	5	0	0	0	24	0	1	0	3.6	.960	OF-7

Ken Phelps

PHELPS, KENNETH ALLEN
B. Aug. 6, 1954, Seattle, Wash.
BL TL 6' 1" 209 lbs.

Year	Team		Games	BA	SA	AB	H	2B	3B	HR	HR%	R	RBI	BB	SO	SB	AB	H	PO	A	E	DP	TC/G	FA	G by Pos
1980	KC	A	3	.000	.000	4	0	0	0	0	0.0	0	0	0	2	0	1	0	14	0	0	2	4.7	1.000	1B-2
1981			21	.136	.227	22	3	0	1	0	0.0	1	1	1	13	0	15	2	4	1	0	0	0.2	1.000	DH-4, 1B-2
1982	MON	N	10	.250	.250	8	2	0	0	0	0.0	0	0	0	3	0	8	2	0	0	0	0	0.0	—	
1983	SEA	A	50	.236	.449	127	30	4	1	7	5.5	10	16	13	25	0	11	3	164	16	0	11	3.6	1.000	1B-22, DH-19
1984			101	.241	.521	290	70	4	1	24	8.3	52	51	61	73	3	15	2	72	4	1	7	0.8	.987	DH-84, 1B-9

Year	Team	Games	BA	SA	AB	H	2B	3B	HR	HR%	R	RBI	BB	SO	SB	PINCH HIT		PO	A	E	DP	TC/G	FA	G by Pos
																AB	H							

Ken Phelps *Continued*

Year	Team	Games	BA	SA	AB	H	2B	3B	HR	HR%	R	RBI	BB	SO	SB	AB	H	PO	A	E	DP	TC/G	FA	G by Pos
1985		61	.207	.466	116	24	3	0	9	7.8	18	24	24	33	2	25	5	31	2	0	5	0.5	1.000	DH–25, 1B–8
1986		125	.247	.526	344	85	16	4	24	7.0	69	64	88	96	2	16	3	487	34	9	58	4.2	.983	1B–55, DH–52
1987		120	.259	.548	332	86	13	1	27	8.1	68	68	80	75	1	12	2	8	0	0	0	0.1	1.000	DH–114, 1B–1
1988	2 teams				SEA A (72G — .284)				NY A (45G — .224)															
"	total	117	.263	.549	297	78	13	0	24	8.1	54	54	70	61	1	17	2	18	2	1	2	0.2	.952	DH–92, 1B–4
1989	2 teams				NY A (86G — .249)				OAK A (11G — .111)															
"		97	.242	.371	194	47	4	0	7	3.6	26	29	31	47	0	38	11	56	2	1	5	0.6	.983	DH–56, 1B–9
1990	2 teams				OAK A (32G — .186)				CLE A (24G — .115)															
"		56	.150	.192	120	18	2	0	1	0.8	10	6	22	21	1	17	4	111	10	1	7	6.4	.992	DH–21, 1B–19
	11 yrs.	761	.239	.480	1854	443	64	7	123	6.6	308	313	390	449	10	175	36	965	71	13	97	1.4	.988	DH–467, 1B–131

LEAGUE CHAMPIONSHIP SERIES

Year	Team	Games	BA	SA	AB	H	2B	3B	HR	HR%	R	RBI	BB	SO	SB	AB	H	PO	A	E	DP	TC/G	FA	G by Pos
1989	OAK A	1	1.000	2.000	1	1	1	0	0	0.0	0	0	0	0	0	1	1	0	0	0	0	0.0	—	

WORLD SERIES

Year	Team	Games	BA	SA	AB	H	2B	3B	HR	HR%	R	RBI	BB	SO	SB	AB	H	PO	A	E	DP	TC/G	FA	G by Pos
1989	OAK A	1	.000	.000	1	0	0	0	0	0.0	0	0	0	0	0	1	0	0	0	0	0	0.0	—	

Tony Phillips

PHILLIPS, KEITH ANTHONY
B. Apr. 25, 1959, Atlanta, Ga.
BB TR 5′ 9″ 155 lbs.

	Games	BA	SA	AB	H	2B	3B	HR	HR%	R	RBI	BB	SO	SB
April	20	.202	.258	89	18	1	2	0	0.0	10	8	5	11	4
May	29	.257	.398	113	29	6	2	2	1.8	16	14	19	15	6
June	25	.207	.354	82	17	3	0	3	3.7	16	9	17	13	2
July	27	.216	.268	97	21	3	1	0	0.0	14	5	23	14	3
Aug	23	.333	.419	93	31	5	0	1	1.1	21	9	16	14	1
Sept/Oct	28	.283	.394	99	28	5	0	2	2.0	20	10	19	18	3
Day	41	.236	.286	161	38	5	0	1	0.6	25	13	18	27	5
Night	111	.257	.376	412	106	18	5	7	1.7	72	42	81	58	14
vs. Left		.248	.351	202	50	11	2	2	1.0	28	19	27	22	3
vs. Right		.253	.350	371	94	12	3	6	1.6	69	36	72	63	16
On Grass	128	.247	.331	478	118	17	4	5	1.0	77	43	83	73	15
On Turf	24	.274	.453	95	26	6	1	3	3.2	20	12	16	12	4
Home	79	.241	.322	286	69	7	2	4	1.4	46	23	50	53	7
Road	73	.261	.380	287	75	16	3	4	1.4	51	32	49	32	12
Division Rivals														
vs. BAL	13	.192	.231	52	10	2	0	0	0.0	8	2	7	7	2
vs. BOS	9	.235	.235	34	8	0	0	0	0.0	5	5	4	3	1
vs. CLE	12	.238	.286	42	10	2	0	0	0.0	6	5	8	9	0
vs. MIL	12	.260	.360	50	13	0	1	1	2.0	4	4	3	6	1
vs. NY	13	.196	.216	51	10	1	0	0	0.0	9	3	9	5	0
vs. TOR	13	.259	.407	54	14	5	0	1	1.9	7	4	6	12	2
On 3B < 2 Out		.417	.708	24	10	0	2	1	4.2	1	22	4	3	

THIRD BASE — AVERAGE · RBI · HR · SB (AL AVG)

Year	Team	Games	BA	SA	AB	H	2B	3B	HR	HR%	R	RBI	BB	SO	SB	AB	H	PO	A	E	DP	TC/G	FA	G by Pos
1982	OAK A	40	.210	.284	81	17	2	2	0	0.0	11	8	12	26	2	0	0	46	95	7	17	3.7	.953	SS–39
1983		148	.248	.320	412	102	12	3	4	1.0	54	35	48	70	16	1	1	218	383	30	85	4.3	.952	SS–101, 2B–63, 3B–4, DH–1
1984		154	.266	.359	451	120	24	3	4	0.9	62	37	42	86	10	2	0	255	391	28	90	4.4	.958	SS–91, 2B–90, OF–1
1985		42	.280	.453	161	45	12	2	4	2.5	23	17	13	34	3	1	0	54	103	3	13	3.8	.981	3B–31, 2B–24
1986		118	.256	.345	441	113	14	5	5	1.1	76	52	76	82	15	0	0	191	326	13	43	4.5	.975	2B–88, 3B–30, OF–4, DH–2, SS–1
1987		111	.240	.372	379	91	20	0	10	2.6	48	46	57	76	7	6	1	179	299	14	47	4.4	.972	2B–87, 3B–11, SS–9, OF–2
1988		79	.203	.307	212	43	8	4	2	0.9	32	17	36	50	0	5	1	84	80	10	18	2.2	.943	3B–32, OF–31, 2B–27, SS–10, 1B–3
1989		143	.262	.348	451	118	15	6	4	0.9	48	47	58	66	3	10	3	184	321	15	54	3.6	.971	2B–84, 3B–49, SS–17, OF–16, 1B–1
1990	DET A	152	.251	.351	573	144	23	5	8	1.3	97	55	99	85	19	1	0	180	368	23	62	3.8	.960	3B–104, 2B–47, SS–11, OF–8, DH–4
	9 yrs.	987	.251	.350	3161	793	130	30	41	1.3	451	314	441	575	75	26	6	1391	2366	143	429	4.0	.963	2B–510, SS–279, 3B–261, OF–62, DH–7, 1B–4

LEAGUE CHAMPIONSHIP SERIES

Year	Team	Games	BA	SA	AB	H	2B	3B	HR	HR%	R	RBI	BB	SO	SB	AB	H	PO	A	E	DP	TC/G	FA	G by Pos
1988	OAK A	2	.286	.429	7	2	1	0	0	0.0	0	0	1	3	0	0	0	10	0	0	1	5.0	1.000	OF–2, 2B–1
1989		5	.167	.222	18	3	1	0	0	0.0	1	1	2	4	2	0	0	4	14	0	2	3.6	1.000	2B–3, 3B–3
	2 yrs.	7	.200	.280	25	5	2	0	0	0.0	1	1	3	7	2	0	0	14	14	0	3	4.0	.000	2B–4, 3B–3, OF–2

Year	Team	Games	BA	SA	AB	H	2B	3B	HR	HR%	R	RBI	BB	SO	SB	PINCH HIT AB	H	PO	A	E	DP	TC/G	FA	G by Pos

Tony Phillips *Continued*

WORLD SERIES

Year	Team	Games	BA	SA	AB	H	2B	3B	HR	HR%	R	RBI	BB	SO	SB	PINCH HIT AB	H	PO	A	E	DP	TC/G	FA	G by Pos
1988	OAK A	2	.250	.250	4	1	0	0	0	0.0	1	0	1	2	0	0	0	3	5	0	1	4.0	1.000	2B-1, OF-1
1989		4	.235	.471	17	4	1	0	1	5.9	2	3	0	3	0	0	0	8	15	0	1	5.8	1.000	2B-4, 3B-2, OF-1
2 yrs.		6	.238	.429	21	5	1	0	1	4.8	3	3	1	5	0	0	0	11	20	0	2	5.2	.000	2B-5, 3B-2, OF-2

Phil Plantier

PLANTIER, PHILLIP ALAN
B. Jan. 27, 1969, Manchester, N. H.
BL TR 6′ 175 lbs.

Year	Team	Games	BA	SA	AB	H	2B	3B	HR	HR%	R	RBI	BB	SO	SB	PINCH HIT AB	H	PO	A	E	DP	TC/G	FA	G by Pos
1990	BOS A	14	.133	.200	15	2	1	0	0	0.0	1	3	4	6	0	6	1	0	0	0	0	0.0	.949	DH-4, OF-1

Gus Polidor

POLIDOR, GUSTAVO ADOLFO
Born Gustavo Adolfo Polidor y Gonzalez.
B. Oct. 26, 1961, Caracas, Venezuela
BR TR 6′ 170 lbs.

Year	Team	Games	BA	SA	AB	H	2B	3B	HR	HR%	R	RBI	BB	SO	SB	PINCH HIT AB	H	PO	A	E	DP	TC/G	FA	G by Pos
1985	CAL A	2	1.000	1.000	1	1	0	0	0	0.0	1	0	0	0	0	0	0	0	2	0	0	1.0	1.000	SS-1, OF-1
1986		6	.263	.316	19	5	1	0	0	0.0	1	1	1	0	0	0	0	10	13	0	2	3.8	1.000	2B-4, 3B-1, SS-1
1987		63	.263	.328	137	36	3	0	2	1.5	12	15	2	15	0	3	1	46	92	2	14	2.2	.986	SS-46, 3B-11, 2B-3
1988		54	.148	.185	81	12	3	0	0	0.0	4	4	3	11	0	8	2	31	54	1	9	1.6	.988	SS-25, 3B-22, 2B-3
1989	MIL A	79	.194	.234	175	34	7	0	0	0.0	15	14	6	18	3	3	0	78	123	12	20	2.7	.944	3B-30, 2B-29, SS-21, DH-2
1990		18	.067	.067	15	1	0	0	0	0.0	0	1	0	1	0	0	0	2	13	0	0	0.8	1.000	3B-14, 2B-2, SS-2
6 yrs.		222	.208	.255	428	89	14	0	2	0.5	33	35	12	45	3	14	3	167	297	15	45	2.2	.969	SS-96, 3B-78, 2B-41, DH-2, OF-1

Luis Polonia

POLONIA, LUIS ANDREW
Born Luis Andrew Polonia y Almonte.
B. Dec. 10, 1964, Santiago, Dominican Republic
BL TL 5′ 8″ 155 lbs.

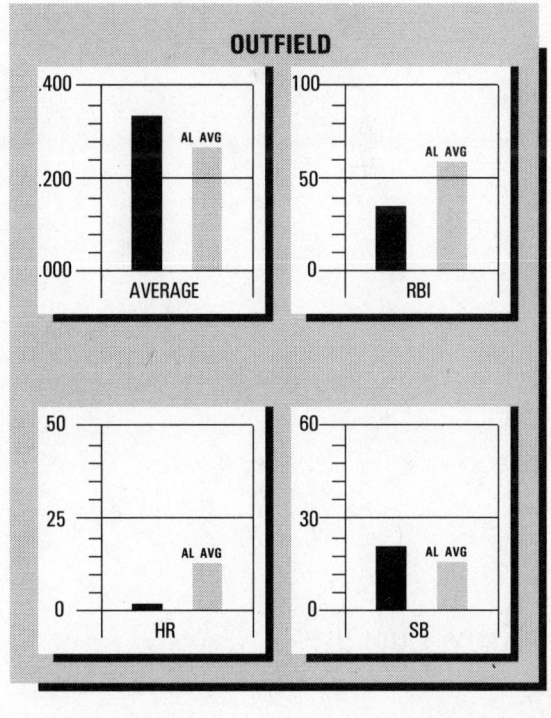

OUTFIELD

	Games	BA	SA	AB	H	2B	3B	HR	HR%	R	RBI	BB	SO	SB
April	11	.318	.318	22	7	0	0	0	0.0	2	3	0	1	1
May	18	.284	.358	67	19	0	1	1	1.5	9	3	2	9	5
June	19	.322	.390	59	19	2	1	0	0.0	6	5	8	5	5
July	24	.292	.371	89	26	1	3	0	0.0	10	3	2	10	2
Aug	19	.348	.449	69	24	2	1	1	1.4	8	14	1	8	1
Sept/Oct	29	.412	.495	97	40	2	3	0	0.0	17	7	12	10	7
Day	29	.343	.394	99	34	1	2	0	0.0	13	7	8	10	6
Night	91	.332	.418	304	101	6	7	2	0.7	39	28	17	33	15
vs. Left		.294	.373	51	15	0	2	0	0.0	11	3	4	11	3
vs. Right		.341	.418	352	120	7	7	2	0.6	41	32	21	32	18
On Grass	102	.339	.420	336	114	5	8	2	0.6	43	29	21	34	18
On Turf	18	.313	.373	67	21	2	1	0	0.0	9	6	4	9	3
Home	60	.353	.430	207	73	2	4	2	1.0	23	23	8	23	5
Road	60	.316	.393	196	62	5	5	0	0.0	29	12	17	20	16
Division Rivals														
vs. CHI	11	.355	.355	31	11	0	0	0	0.0	3	3	5	1	2
vs. KC	10	.341	.463	41	14	1	2	0	0.0	5	5	3	7	0
vs. MIN	5	.389	.389	18	7	0	0	0	0.0	3	2	1	2	1
vs. OAK	11	.419	.558	43	18	0	3	0	0.0	9	5	4	3	4
vs. SEA	11	.344	.344	32	11	0	0	0	0.0	4	0	3	4	4
vs. TEX	12	.300	.400	40	12	2	1	0	0.0	5	4	2	5	0
On 3B < 2 Out		.313	.438	16	5	0	1	0	0.0	0	13	2	0	

Year	Team	Games	BA	SA	AB	H	2B	3B	HR	HR%	R	RBI	BB	SO	SB	PINCH HIT AB	H	PO	A	E	DP	TC/G	FA	G by Pos
1987	OAK A	125	.287	.398	435	125	16	10	4	0.9	78	49	32	64	29	8	3	235	2	5	1	1.9	.979	OF-104, DH-18
1988		84	.292	.378	288	84	11	4	2	0.7	51	27	21	40	24	9	2	155	3	2	1	1.9	.988	OF-76, DH-2
1989	2 teams	OAK A (59G — .286)			NY A (66G — .313)																			
"	total	125	.300	.388	433	130	17	6	3	0.7	70	46	25	44	22	14	6	231	9	4	2	2.0	.984	OF-108, DH-9
1990	2 teams	NY A (11G — .318)			CAL A (109G — .336)																			
"		120	.335	.412	403	135	7	9	2	0.4	52	35	25	43	21	19	6	142	3	3	2	1.7	.980	OF-85, DH-15
4 yrs.		454	.304	.395	1559	474	51	29	11	0.7	251	157	103	191	96	50	17	763	17	14	6	1.7	.982	OF-373, DH-44

LEAGUE CHAMPIONSHIP SERIES

Year	Team	Games	BA	SA	AB	H	2B	3B	HR	HR%	R	RBI	BB	SO	SB	PINCH HIT AB	H	PO	A	E	DP	TC/G	FA	G by Pos
1988	OAK A	3	.400	.400	5	2	0	0	0	0.0	0	0	1	2	0	0	0	2	0	0	0	0.7	1.000	OF-1

Year	Team	Games	BA	SA	AB	H	2B	3B	HR	HR%	R	RBI	BB	SO	SB	PINCH HIT AB	H	PO	A	E	DP	TC/G	FA	G by Pos

Luis Polonia *Continued*

WORLD SERIES

Year	Team	Games	BA	SA	AB	H	2B	3B	HR	HR%	R	RBI	BB	SO	SB	AB	H	PO	A	E	DP	TC/G	FA	G by Pos
1988	OAK	A	3	.111	.111	9	1	0	0	0	0.0	1	0	0	2	0	2	0	2	0	0	0	0.7	1.000	OF-2

Jim Presley

PRESLEY, JAMES ARTHUR
B. Oct. 23, 1961, Pensacola, Fla.
BR TR 6′ 1″ 176 lbs.

Split	Games	BA	SA	AB	H	2B	3B	HR	HR%	R	RBI	BB	SO	SB
April	17	.303	.439	66	20	6	0	1	1.5	6	7	1	11	0
May	23	.297	.516	91	27	11	0	3	3.3	17	16	8	24	0
June	26	.236	.387	106	25	4	0	4	3.8	9	14	5	25	0
July	29	.236	.527	110	26	5	0	9	8.2	15	18	9	31	0
Aug	25	.177	.250	96	17	2	1	1	1.0	8	8	4	24	1
Sept/Oct	20	.222	.347	72	16	6	0	1	1.4	4	9	2	15	0
Day	28	.239	.419	117	28	4	1	5	4.3	14	19	1	19	0
Night	112	.243	.413	424	103	30	0	14	3.3	45	53	28	111	1
vs. Left		.267	.450	180	48	15	0	6	3.3	20	28	17	38	0
vs. Right		.230	.396	361	83	19	1	13	3.6	39	44	12	92	1
On Grass	108	.246	.417	415	102	27	1	14	3.4	46	54	21	98	1
On Turf	32	.230	.405	126	29	7	0	5	4.0	13	18	8	32	0
Home	75	.260	.427	288	75	18	0	10	3.5	33	38	16	64	1
Road	65	.221	.399	253	56	16	1	9	3.6	26	34	13	66	0
Division Rivals														
vs: CIN	16	.328	.500	64	21	5	0	2	3.1	5	6	3	11	0
vs: HOU	14	.170	.255	47	8	1	0	1	2.1	4	3	3	16	1
vs: LA	16	.150	.217	60	9	1	0	1	1.7	2	7	5	17	0
vs: SD	18	.213	.333	75	16	6	0	1	1.3	7	11	4	15	0
vs: SF	14	.208	.340	53	11	1	0	2	3.8	5	4	2	14	0
On 3B < 2 Out		.333	.458	24	8	3	0	0	0.0	0	18	4	8	

Year	Team	Games	BA	SA	AB	H	2B	3B	HR	HR%	R	RBI	BB	SO	SB	AB	H	PO	A	E	DP	TC/G	FA	G by Pos
1984	SEA	A	70	.227	.402	251	57	12	1	10	4.0	27	36	6	63	1	1	0	48	113	7	12	2.4	.958	3B-69, DH-1
1985			155	.275	.484	570	157	33	1	28	4.9	71	84	44	100	2	1	0	82	335	17	24	2.8	.961	3B-154
1986			155	.265	.463	616	163	33	4	27	4.4	83	107	32	172	0	0	0	110	308	15	31	2.8	.965	3B-155
1987			152	.247	.433	575	142	23	6	24	4.2	78	88	38	157	2	1	1	113	315	21	29	3.0	.953	3B-148, SS-4, DH-1
1988			150	.230	.355	544	125	26	0	14	2.6	50	62	36	114	3	0	0	112	234	22	25	2.5	.940	3B-146, DH-4
1989			117	.236	.385	390	92	20	1	12	3.1	42	41	21	107	0	6	1	222	169	18	29	3.5	.956	3B-90, 1B-30, DH-1
1990	ATL	N	140	.242	.414	541	131	34	1	19	3.5	59	72	29	130	1	1	0	178	242	26	29	3.2	.942	3B-133, 1B-17
7 yrs.			939	.249	.424	3487	867	181	14	134	3.8	410	490	206	843	9	10	2	865	1716	126	179	2.9	.953	3B-895, 1B-47, DH-7, SS-4

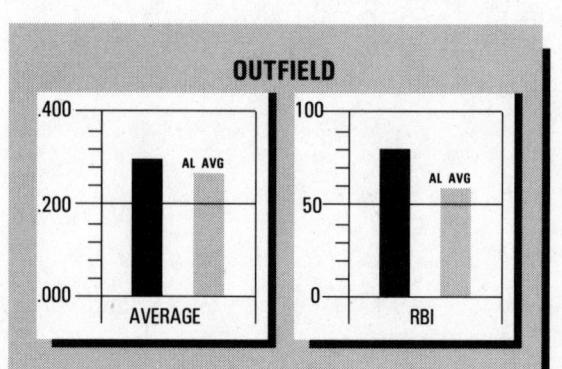

Tom Prince

PRINCE, THOMAS ALBERT
B. Aug. 13, 1964, Kankakee, Ill.
BR TR 5′ 11″ 185 lbs.

Year	Team	Games	BA	SA	AB	H	2B	3B	HR	HR%	R	RBI	BB	SO	SB	AB	H	PO	A	E	DP	TC/G	FA	G by Pos
1987	PIT	N	4	.222	.667	9	2	1	0	1	11.1	1	2	0	2	0	0	0	14	3	0	0	4.3	1.000	C-4
1988			29	.176	.203	74	13	2	0	0	0.0	3	6	4	15	0	2	0	108	8	2	1	4.1	.983	C-28
1989			21	.135	.212	52	7	4	0	0	0.0	1	5	6	12	1	0	0	85	11	4	1	4.8	.960	C-21
1990			4	.100	.100	10	1	0	0	0	0.0	1	0	1	2	0	0	0	16	1	0	0	5.7	1.000	C-3
4 yrs.			58	.159	.228	145	23	7	0	1	0.7	6	13	11	31	1	3	0	223	23	6	2	4.3	.976	C-56

Kirby Puckett

PUCKETT, KIRBY
B. Mar. 14, 1961, Chicago, Ill.
BR TR 5′ 8″ 178 lbs.

Split	Games	BA	SA	AB	H	2B	3B	HR	HR%	R	RBI	BB	SO	SB
April	19	.270	.432	74	20	4	1	2	2.7	13	11	10	9	2
May	28	.382	.706	102	39	13	1	6	5.9	23	21	13	9	0
June	27	.242	.374	99	24	5	1	2	2.0	11	11	8	16	0
July	27	.311	.443	106	33	8	0	2	1.9	20	19	13	17	0
Aug	20	.284	.351	74	21	5	0	0	0.0	7	7	6	17	2
Sept/Oct	25	.281	.333	96	27	5	0	0	0.0	8	11	7	5	1
Day	41	.358	.556	151	54	18	0	4	2.6	24	27	23	16	1
Night	105	.275	.405	400	110	22	3	8	2.0	58	53	34	57	4
vs. Left		.299	.451	164	49	11	1	4	2.4	19	22	22	21	2
vs. Right		.297	.444	387	115	29	2	8	2.1	63	58	35	52	3

Year	Team	Games	BA	SA	AB	H	2B	3B	HR	HR%	R	RBI	BB	SO	SB	PINCH HIT AB	H	PO	A	E	DP	TC/G	FA	G by Pos

Kirby Puckett *Continued*

Year	Team	Games	BA	SA	AB	H	2B	3B	HR	HR%	R	RBI	BB	SO	SB	AB	H	PO	A	E	DP	TC/G	FA	G by Pos
On Grass		55	.245	.396	212	52	10	2	6	2.8	28	27	25	24	2									
On Turf		91	.330	.478	339	112	30	1	6	1.8	54	53	32	49	3									
Home		73	.344	.505	273	94	24	1	6	2.2	44	47	27	40	2									
Road		73	.252	.388	278	70	16	2	6	2.2	38	33	30	33	3									
Division Rivals																								
vs. CAL		12	.298	.447	47	14	2	1	1	2.1	6	9	6	8	1									
vs. CHI		9	.176	.294	34	6	1	0	1	2.9	2	4	3	3	0									
vs. KC		12	.267	.378	45	12	5	0	0	0.0	6	4	3	8	1									
vs. OAK		13	.314	.392	51	16	4	0	0	0.0	8	5	7	5	1									
vs. SEA		12	.273	.341	44	12	3	0	0	0.0	5	5	5	5	1									
vs. TEX		10	.289	.447	38	11	1	1	1	2.6	5	6	2	6	0									
On 3B < 2 Out			.485	.727	33	16	5	0	1	3.0	1	31	8	4										
1984	MIN A	128	.296	.336	557	165	12	5	0	0.0	63	31	16	69	14	0	0	438	16	3	4	3.6	.993	OF-128
1985		161	.288	.385	**691**	199	29	13	4	0.6	80	74	41	87	21	1	0	465	19	8	5	3.1	.984	OF-161
1986		161	.328	.537	680	223	37	6	31	4.6	119	96	34	99	20	4	1	429	8	6	3	2.8	.986	OF-160
1987		157	.332	.534	624	**207**	32	5	28	4.5	96	99	32	91	12	2	0	341	8	5	2	2.3	.986	OF-147, DH-8
1988		158	.356	.545	**657**	**234**	42	5	24	3.7	109	121	23	83	6	1	0	450	12	3	4	2.9	.994	OF-158
1989		159	**.339**	.465	635	**215**	45	4	9	1.4	75	85	41	59	11	2	1	438	13	4	4	2.9	.991	OF-157, DH-2
1990		146	.298	.446	551	164	40	3	12	2.1	82	80	57	73	5	1	1	354	9	4	4	2.6	.989	OF-141, DH-4, 2B-1, 3B-1, SS-1
7 yrs.		1070	.320	.466	4395	1407	237	41	108	2.5	624	586	244	561	89	11	3	2915	85	33	24	2.8	.989	OF-1052, DH-14, 2B-1, 3B-1, SS-1

LEAGUE CHAMPIONSHIP SERIES

Year	Team	Games	BA	SA	AB	H	2B	3B	HR	HR%	R	RBI	BB	SO	SB	AB	H	PO	A	E	DP	TC/G	FA	G by Pos
1987	MIN A	5	.208	.375	24	5	1	0	1	4.2	3	3	0	5	1	0	0	7	0	0	0	1.4	1.000	OF-5

WORLD SERIES

Year	Team	Games	BA	SA	AB	H	2B	3B	HR	HR%	R	RBI	BB	SO	SB	AB	H	PO	A	E	DP	TC/G	FA	G by Pos
1987	MIN A	7	.357	.464	28	10	1	1	0	0.0	5	3	2	1	1	0	0	15	1	1	0	2.4	.941	OF-7

Terry Puhl

PUHL, TERRY STEPHEN
B. July 8, 1956, Melville, Sask., Canada
BL TR 6′ 2″ 195 lbs.

Year	Team	Games	BA	SA	AB	H	2B	3B	HR	HR%	R	RBI	BB	SO	SB	AB	H	PO	A	E	DP	TC/G	FA	G by Pos
1977	HOU N	60	.301	.402	229	69	13	5	0	0.0	40	10	30	31	10	0	0	119	3	1	0	2.1	.992	OF-59
1978		149	.289	.368	585	169	25	6	3	0.5	87	35	48	46	32	1	1	386	6	3	2	2.7	.992	OF-148
1979		157	.287	.377	600	172	22	4	8	1.3	87	49	58	46	30	5	1	352	7	0	3	2.3	1.000	OF-152
1980		141	.282	.419	535	151	24	5	13	2.4	75	55	60	52	27	6	0	311	14	3	3	2.3	.991	OF-135
1981		96	.251	.354	350	88	19	4	3	0.9	43	28	31	49	22	8	1	185	5	0	1	2.0	1.000	OF-88
1982		145	.262	.379	507	133	17	9	8	1.6	64	50	51	49	17	7	3	257	4	3	3	1.8	.989	OF-138
1983		137	.292	.428	465	136	25	7	8	1.7	66	44	36	48	24	15	4	220	4	2	1	1.6	.991	OF-124
1984		132	.301	.434	449	135	19	7	9	2.0	66	55	59	45	13	5	2	213	6	3	4	1.7	.986	OF-126
1985		57	.284	.418	194	55	14	3	2	1.0	34	23	18	23	6	3	1	92	3	0	1	1.7	1.000	OF-53
1986		81	.244	.355	172	42	10	0	3	1.7	17	14	15	24	3	28	8	65	0	0	0	0.8	1.000	OF-47
1987		90	.230	.320	122	28	5	0	2	1.6	9	15	11	16	1	52	15	48	0	1	0	0.5	.980	OF-40
1988		113	.303	.389	234	71	7	2	3	1.3	42	19	35	30	22	36	11	116	2	2	0	1.1	.983	OF-78
1989		121	.271	.364	354	96	25	4	0	0.0	41	27	45	39	9	15	4	212	3	0	1	1.8	1.000	OF-103, 1B-3
1990		37	.293	.317	41	12	1	0	0	0.0	5	8	5	7	1	20	8	9	0	0	0	1.0	1.000	OF-8, 1B-1
14 yrs.		1516	.281	.389	4837	1357	226	56	62	1.3	676	432	502	505	217	201	59	2585	57	18	19	1.8	.993	OF-1299, 1B-4

DIVISIONAL PLAYOFF SERIES

Year	Team	Games	BA	SA	AB	H	2B	3B	HR	HR%	R	RBI	BB	SO	SB	AB	H	PO	A	E	DP	TC/G	FA	G by Pos
1981	HOU N	5	.190	.238	21	4	1	0	0	0.0	2	0	0	1	1	0	0	7	1	0	0	1.6	1.000	OF-5

LEAGUE CHAMPIONSHIP SERIES

Year	Team	Games	BA	SA	AB	H	2B	3B	HR	HR%	R	RBI	BB	SO	SB	AB	H	PO	A	E	DP	TC/G	FA	G by Pos
1980	HOU N	5	.526	.632	19	10	2	0	0	0.0	4	3	3	2	2	1	0	13	0	0	0	2.6	1.000	OF-4
1986		3	.667	.667	3	2	0	0	0	0.0	0	0	0	0	1	3	2	0	0	0	0	0.0	—	
2 yrs.		8	.545	.636	22	12	2	0	0	0.0	4	3	3	2	3	4	2	13	0	0	0	1.6	.000	OF-4

Tom Quinlan

QUINLAN, THOMAS RAYMOND
B. Mar. 27, 1968, St. Paul, Minn.
BR TR 6′ 3″ 200 lbs.

Year	Team	Games	BA	SA	AB	H	2B	3B	HR	HR%	R	RBI	BB	SO	SB	AB	H	PO	A	E	DP	TC/G	FA	G by Pos
1990	TOR A	1	.500	.500	2	1	0	0	0	0.0	0	0	0	1	0	0	0	0	1	0	0	1.0	1.000	3B-1

OUTFIELD charts showing HR and SB vs AL AVG.

Year	Team		Games	BA	SA	AB	H	2B	3B	HR	HR%	R	RBI	BB	SO	SB	PINCH HIT AB	H	PO	A	E	DP	TC/G	FA	G by Pos

Luis Quinones

QUINONES, LUIS RAUL
Born Luis Raul Quinones y Torruellas.
B. Apr. 28, 1962, Ponce, Puerto Rico
BB TR 5′ 11″ 165 lbs.

Year	Team		Games	BA	SA	AB	H	2B	3B	HR	HR%	R	RBI	BB	SO	SB	AB	H	PO	A	E	DP	TC/G	FA	G by Pos
1983	OAK	A	19	.190	.286	42	8	2	1	0	0.0	5	4	1	4	1	1	1	22	24	1	7	2.5	.979	2B-6, DH-4, 3B-4, OF-4, SS-3
1986	SF	N	71	.179	.245	106	19	1	3	0	0.0	13	11	3	17	3	7	0	28	66	8	10	1.4	.922	SS-33, 3B-31, 2B-8
1987	CHI	N	49	.218	.277	101	22	6	0	0	0.0	12	8	10	16	0	23	4	35	58	3	10	2.0	.969	SS-28, 2B-4, 3B-1
1988	CIN	N	23	.231	.346	52	12	3	0	1	1.9	4	11	2	11	1	6	1	15	37	2	5	2.3	.963	SS-10, 2B-4, 3B-4
1989			97	.244	.412	340	83	13	4	12	3.5	43	34	25	46	2	5	1	112	213	10	25	3.5	.970	2B-53, 3B-50, SS-5
1990			83	.241	.331	145	35	7	0	2	1.3	10	17	13	29	1	36	13	44	85	6	15	3.1	.956	3B-22, 2B-13, SS-9, 1B-1
6 yrs.			342	.228	.346	786	179	32	8	15	1.9	87	85	54	123	8	78	20	256	483	30	72	2.2	.961	3B-112, 2B-88, SS-88, DH-4, OF-4, 1B-1

LEAGUE CHAMPIONSHIP SERIES

Year	Team		Games	BA	SA	AB	H	2B	3B	HR	HR%	R	RBI	BB	SO	SB	AB	H	PO	A	E	DP	TC/G	FA	G by Pos
1990	CIN	N	3	.500	.500	2	1	0	0	0	0.0	1	2	0	0	1	2	1	0	0	0	0	0.0	.900	

Carlos Quintana

QUINTANA, CARLOS NARCIS
Born Carlos Narcis Quintana y Hernandez.
B. Aug. 26, 1965, Estado, Mirana, Venezuela
BR TR 6′ 175 lbs.

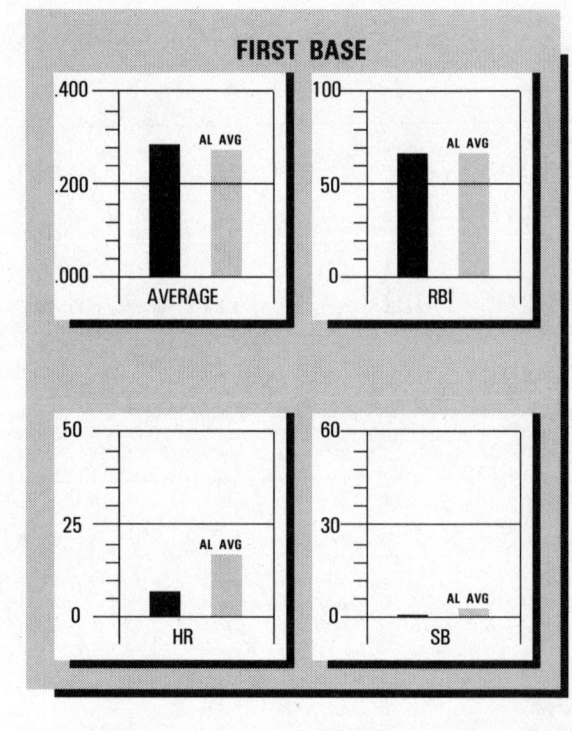

FIRST BASE

		Games	BA	SA	AB	H	2B	3B	HR	HR%	R	RBI	BB	SO	SB
April		14	.364	.455	22	8	2	0	0	0.0	4	0	5	4	0
May		23	.307	.427	75	23	6	0	1	1.3	6	14	4	5	0
June		29	.297	.386	101	30	3	0	2	2.0	11	12	4	18	0
July		29	.330	.528	106	35	9	0	4	3.8	14	20	17	15	0
Aug		28	.240	.280	100	24	4	0	0	0.0	12	11	17	17	1
Sept/Oct		26	.250	.287	108	27	4	0	0	0.0	9	10	5	15	0
Day		47	.296	.454	152	45	15	0	3	2.0	19	29	22	21	0
Night		102	.283	.353	360	102	13	0	4	1.1	37	38	30	53	1
vs. Left			.352	.467	182	64	12	0	3	1.6	25	27	16	24	0
vs. Right			.252	.336	330	83	16	0	4	1.2	31	40	36	50	1
On Grass		125	.313	.412	432	135	25	0	6	1.4	52	59	49	56	0
On Turf		24	.150	.225	80	12	3	0	1	1.3	4	8	3	18	1
Home		74	.299	.378	251	75	11	0	3	1.2	30	31	26	36	0
Road		75	.276	.387	261	72	17	0	4	1.5	26	36	26	38	1
Division Rivals															
vs. BAL		12	.263	.395	38	10	2	0	1	2.6	5	6	6	3	0
vs. CLE		13	.339	.375	56	19	2	0	0	0.0	7	5	5	9	0
vs. DET		11	.400	.543	35	14	5	0	0	0.0	6	4	8	4	0
vs. MIL		12	.405	.595	37	15	4	0	1	2.7	2	4	3	2	0
vs. NY		13	.167	.167	48	8	0	0	0	0.0	5	4	4	11	0
vs. TOR		13	.244	.366	41	10	2	0	1	2.4	5	4	1	10	0
On 3B < 2 Out			.160	.280	25	4	0	0	1	4.0	1	15	3	5	

Year	Team		Games	BA	SA	AB	H	2B	3B	HR	HR%	R	RBI	BB	SO	SB	AB	H	PO	A	E	DP	TC/G	FA	G by Pos
1988	BOS	A	5	.333	.333	6	2	0	0	0	0.0	1	2	2	3	0	0	0	4	0	0	0	0.8	1.000	OF-3, DH-1
1989			34	.208	.273	77	16	5	0	0	0.0	6	6	7	12	0	7	2	31	0	2	0	1.0	.939	OF-21, DH-7, 1B-1
1990			149	.287	.383	512	147	28	0	7	1.3	56	67	52	74	1	7	3	1190	137	17	116	9.1	.987	1B-148, OF-3
3 yrs.			188	.277	.368	595	165	33	0	7	1.2	63	75	61	89	1	14	5	1225	137	19	116	7.3	.986	1B-149, OF-27, DH-8

LEAGUE CHAMPIONSHIP SERIES

Year	Team		Games	BA	SA	AB	H	2B	3B	HR	HR%	R	RBI	BB	SO	SB	AB	H	PO	A	E	DP	TC/G	FA	G by Pos
1990	BOS	A	4	.000	.000	13	0	0	0	0	0.0	0	1	1	0	0	0	0	29	2	0	5	7.8	1.000	1B-4

Jamie Quirk

QUIRK, JAMES PATRICK
B. Oct. 22, 1954, Whittier, Calif.
BL TR 6′ 4″ 190 lbs.

Year	Team		Games	BA	SA	AB	H	2B	3B	HR	HR%	R	RBI	BB	SO	SB	AB	H	PO	A	E	DP	TC/G	FA	G by Pos
1975	KC	A	14	.256	.333	39	10	0	0	1	2.6	2	5	2	7	0	1	1	19	3	2	0	1.7	.917	OF-10, 3B-2, DH-1
1976			64	.246	.325	114	28	6	0	1	0.9	11	15	7	22	0	32	7	9	14	2	2	0.4	.920	DH-19, SS-12, 3B-11, 1B-2
1977	MIL	A	93	.217	.330	221	48	14	1	3	1.4	16	13	8	47	0	29	5	19	4	2	2	0.3	.920	DH-53, OF-10, 3B-8
1978	KC	A	17	.207	.276	29	6	2	0	0	0.0	3	2	5	4	0	4	2	11	16	2	1	1.7	.931	3B-10, SS-2, DH-1
1979			51	.304	.443	79	24	6	1	1	1.3	8	11	5	13	0	30	8	16	9	1	0	0.5	.962	DH-9, C-9, SS-5, 3B-3

Year	Team		Games	BA	SA	AB	H	2B	3B	HR	HR%	R	RBI	BB	SO	SB	PINCH HIT AB	H	PO	A	E	DP	TC/G	FA	G by Pos

Jamie Quirk *Continued*

Year	Team		Games	BA	SA	AB	H	2B	3B	HR	HR%	R	RBI	BB	SO	SB	PINCH HIT AB	H	PO	A	E	DP	TC/G	FA	G by Pos
1980			62	.276	.399	163	45	5	0	5	3.1	13	21	7	24	3	12	1	72	66	8	3	2.4	.945	3B-28, C-15, 1B-1
1981			46	.250	.320	100	25	7	0	0	0.0	8	10	6	17	0	18	4	63	23	4	2	2.0	.956	C-22, 3B-8, DH-1, 2B-1
1982			36	.231	.308	78	18	3	0	1	1.3	8	5	3	15	0	7	1	110	12	0	1	3.4	1.000	C-29, 1B-6, 3B-1, OF-1
1983	STL	N	48	.209	.326	86	18	2	1	2	2.3	3	11	6	27	0	17	1	68	13	6	1	1.8	.931	C-22, 3B-7, SS-1
1984	2 teams			CHI A	(3G — .000)		CLE A	(1G — 1.000)																	
''	total		4	.333	1.333	3	1	0	0	1	33.3	1	2	0	2	0	2	0	1	0	0	0	0.3	1.000	C-1, 3B-1
1985	KC	A	19	.281	.368	57	16	3	1	0	0.0	3	4	2	9	0	4	0	66	8	1	1	3.9	.987	C-17, 1B-1
1986			80	.215	.370	219	47	10	0	8	3.7	24	26	17	41	0	20	4	303	64	4	13	4.6	.989	C-41, SS-24, 1B-6, OF-1
1987			109	.236	.345	296	70	17	0	5	1.7	24	33	28	56	1	5	2	532	40	8	3	5.3	.986	C-108, SS-1
1988			84	.240	.408	196	47	7	1	8	4.1	22	25	28	41	1	7	0	412	34	8	5	5.4	.982	C-79, 1B-1, 3B-1
1989	3 teams			NY A	(13G — .083)		OAK A	(9G — .200)		BAL A	(25G — .216)														
''	total		47	.176	.235	85	15	2	0	1	1.2	6	10	12	20	0	11	1	129	15	1	3	3.1	.993	C-32, 3B-3, DH-1, 1B-1, SS-1, OF-1
1990	OAK	A	56	.281	.413	121	34	5	1	3	2.4	12	26	14	34	0	11	4	168	18	5	4	3.8	.974	C-37, 1B-8, 3B-8, DH-1, OF-1
16 yrs.			830	.240	.357	1886	452	89	6	40	2.1	164	219	145	379	5	210	41	1998	339	54	41	2.9	.977	C-412, 3B-91, DH-86, SS-46, 1B-26, OF-24, 2B-1

LEAGUE CHAMPIONSHIP SERIES

Year	Team		Games	BA	SA	AB	H	2B	3B	HR	HR%	R	RBI	BB	SO	SB	PINCH HIT AB	H	PO	A	E	DP	TC/G	FA	G by Pos
1976	KC	A	4	.143	.429	7	1	0	1	0	0.0	1	2	0	2	0	1	0	0	0	0	0	0.0	—	DH-2
1985			1	.000	.000	1	0	0	0	0	0.0	0	0	0	0	0	1	0	0	0	0	0	0.0	—	
1990	OAK	A	1	1.000	1.000	1	1	0	0	0	0.0	0	0	0	0	0	1	1	0	0	0	0	0.00	1.000	
3 yrs.			6	.222	.444	9	2	0	1	0	0.0	1	2	0	2	0	3	1	0	0	0	0	0.0	.000	DH-2

WORLD SERIES

Year	Team		Games	BA	SA	AB	H	2B	3B	HR	HR%	R	RBI	BB	SO	SB	PINCH HIT AB	H	PO	A	E	DP	TC/G	FA	G by Pos
1990	OAK	A	1	.000	.000	3	0	0	0	0	0.0	0	0	0	2	0	0	0	2	2	0	0	4.0	1.000	C-1

Tim Raines

RAINES, TIMOTHY (Rock)
B. Sept. 16, 1959, Sanford, Fla.
BB TR 5' 8" 160 lbs.

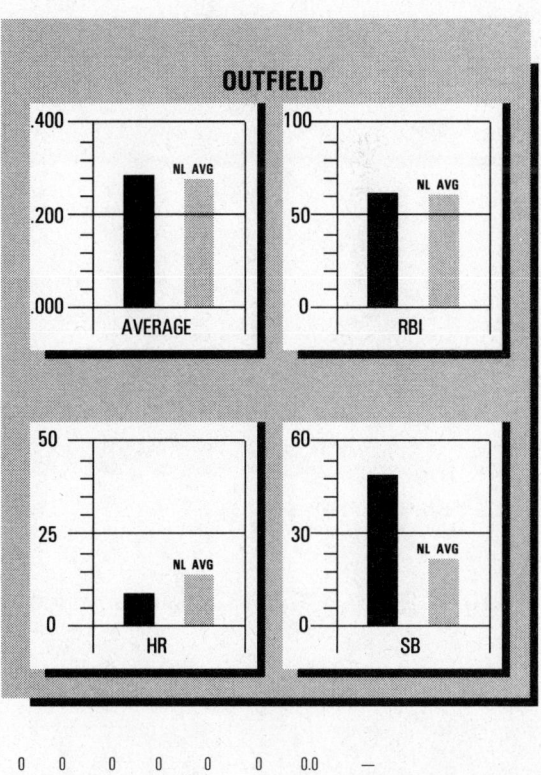

OUTFIELD

	Games	BA	SA	AB	H	2B	3B	HR	HR%	R	RBI	BB	SO	SB
April	19	.236	.264	72	17	0	1	0	0.0	7	10	8	8	8
May	25	.300	.411	90	27	0	2	2	2.2	17	12	19	10	9
June	16	.327	.388	49	16	3	0	0	0.0	7	3	8	3	7
July	19	.297	.406	64	19	2	1	1	1.6	6	12	6	6	9
Aug	26	.277	.447	94	26	4	0	4	4.3	13	14	15	10	6
Sept/Oct	25	.295	.409	88	26	2	1	2	2.3	15	11	14	6	10
Day	37	.273	.394	132	36	1	3	3	2.3	19	15	21	15	14
Night	93	.292	.391	325	95	10	2	6	1.8	46	47	49	28	35
vs. Left		.289	.361	180	52	0	2	3	1.7	24	27	21	13	18
vs. Right		.285	.412	277	79	11	3	6	2.2	41	35	49	30	31
On Grass	37	.289	.373	142	41	1	1	3	2.1	23	19	23	15	12
On Turf	93	.286	.400	315	90	10	4	6	1.9	42	43	47	28	37
Home	59	.307	.446	202	62	6	2	6	3.0	32	28	28	18	30
Road	71	.271	.349	255	69	5	3	3	1.2	33	34	42	25	19
Division Rivals														
vs. CHI	13	.214	.357	42	9	3	0	1	2.4	2	4	3	1	2
vs. NY	17	.308	.385	65	20	2	0	1	1.5	9	5	9	8	11
vs. PHI	14	.250	.313	48	12	0	0	1	2.1	6	4	8	2	5
vs. PIT	13	.268	.366	41	11	2	1	0	0.0	6	5	5	3	5
vs. STL	15	.373	.529	51	19	3	1	1	2.0	10	13	11	3	7
On 3B < 2 Out		.364	.545	22	8	1	0	1	4.5	1	29	8	1	

Year	Team		Games	BA	SA	AB	H	2B	3B	HR	HR%	R	RBI	BB	SO	SB	PINCH HIT AB	H	PO	A	E	DP	TC/G	FA	G by Pos
1979	MON	N	6	—	—	0	0	0	0	0	—	3	0	0	0	2	0	0	0	0	0	0	0.0	—	
1980			15	.050	.050	20	1	0	0	0	0.0	5	0	6	3	5	0	0	15	16	0	2	2.1	1.000	2B-7, OF-1
1981			88	.304	.438	313	95	13	7	5	1.6	61	37	45	31	71	0	0	162	8	4	0	2.0	.977	OF-81, 2B-1
1982			156	.277	.369	647	179	32	8	4	0.6	90	43	75	83	78	0	0	293	126	8	12	2.7	.981	OF-120, 2B-36
1983			156	.298	.429	615	183	32	8	11	1.8	133	71	97	70	90	1	1	314	23	4	3	2.2	.988	OF-154, 2B-7
1984			160	.309	.437	622	192	38	9	8	1.3	106	60	87	69	75	0	0	420	8	6	1	2.7	.986	OF-160, 2B-2
1985			150	.320	.475	575	184	30	13	11	1.9	115	41	81	60	70	7	2	284	8	2	4	2.0	.993	OF-145
1986			151	.334	.476	580	194	35	10	9	1.6	91	62	78	60	70	4	1	270	13	6	1	1.9	.979	OF-147
1987			139	.330	.526	530	175	34	8	18	3.4	123	68	90	52	50	1	0	297	9	4	1	2.2	.987	OF-139
1988			109	.270	.431	429	116	19	7	12	2.8	66	48	53	44	33	1	0	235	5	3	1	2.2	.988	OF-108

Year	Team		Games	BA	SA	AB	H	2B	3B	HR	HR%	R	RBI	BB	SO	SB	PINCH HIT		PO	A	E	DP	TC/G	FA	G by Pos
																	AB	H							

Tim Raines *Continued*

Year	Team		Games	BA	SA	AB	H	2B	3B	HR	HR%	R	RBI	BB	SO	SB	AB	H	PO	A	E	DP	TC/G	FA	G by Pos
1989			145	.286	.418	517	148	29	6	9	1.7	76	60	93	48	41	4	3	253	7	1	0	1.8	.996	OF-139
1990			130	.287	.392	457	131	11	5	9	1.9	65	62	70	43	49	8	2	239	3	6	1	2.0	.976	OF-123
12 yrs.			1405	.301	.438	5305	1598	273	81	96	1.8	934	552	775	563	634	25	7	2782	226	44	26	2.2	.986	OF-1317, 2B-53

LEAGUE CHAMPIONSHIP SERIES

| 1981 | MON | N | 5 | .238 | .333 | 21 | 5 | 2 | 0 | 0 | 0.0 | 1 | 1 | 0 | 3 | 0 | 0 | 0 | 9 | 0 | 0 | 0 | 1.8 | 1.000 | OF-5 |

Rafael Ramirez

RAMIREZ, RAFAEL EMILIO (Raffy)
Born Rafael Emilio Ramirez y Peguero.
B. Feb. 18, 1958, San Pedro de Macoris,
Dominican Republic
BR TR 6' 170 lbs.

SHORTSTOP

	Games	BA	SA	AB	H	2B	3B	HR	HR%	R	RBI	BB	SO	SB	AB	H	PO	A	E	DP	TC/G	FA	G by Pos
April	19	.270	.317	63	17	1	1	0	0.0	6	6	1	9	1									
May	24	.221	.279	86	19	2	0	1	1.2	11	7	4	7	2									
June	26	.306	.388	85	26	5	1	0	0.0	7	5	6	7	6									
July	11	.282	.333	39	11	2	0	0	0.0	4	2	2	6	0									
Aug	26	.233	.337	86	20	6	0	1	1.2	9	10	6	9	1									
Sept/Oct	26	.267	.326	86	23	3	1	0	0.0	7	7	5	8	0									
Day	34	.254	.404	114	29	5	3	2	1.8	16	17	6	9	3									
Night	98	.263	.305	331	87	14	0	0	0.0	28	20	18	37	7									
vs. Left		.260	.333	192	50	9	1	1	0.5	22	15	13	17	4									
vs. Right		.261	.328	253	66	10	2	1	0.4	22	22	11	29	6									
On Grass	39	.279	.321	140	39	6	0	0	0.0	15	10	4	14	2									
On Turf	93	.252	.334	305	77	13	3	2	0.7	29	27	20	32	8									
Home	64	.267	.350	206	55	8	3	1	0.5	19	20	16	21	7									
Road	68	.255	.314	239	61	11	0	1	0.4	25	17	8	25	3									
Division Rivals																							
vs. ATL	13	.318	.409	44	14	4	0	0	0.0	7	7	1	4	0									
vs. CIN	17	.269	.327	52	14	1	1	0	0.0	5	1	3	5	2									
vs. LA	15	.327	.382	55	18	3	0	0	0.0	6	5	2	5	0									
vs. SD	17	.305	.322	59	18	1	0	0	0.0	3	3	3	9	4									
vs. SF	16	.176	.275	51	9	2	0	1	2.0	4	5	3	4	2									
On 3B < 2 Out		.500	.833	12	6	2	1	0	0.0	0	14	3	0										

Year	Team		Games	BA	SA	AB	H	2B	3B	HR	HR%	R	RBI	BB	SO	SB	AB	H	PO	A	E	DP	TC/G	FA	G by Pos
1980	ATL	N	50	.267	.352	165	44	6	1	2	1.2	17	11	2	33	2	0	0	63	140	11	25	4.3	.949	SS-46
1981			95	.218	.303	307	67	16	2	2	0.7	30	20	24	47	7	0	0	181	306	30	55	5.4	.942	SS-95
1982			157	.278	.379	609	169	24	4	10	1.6	74	52	36	49	27	0	0	300	528	38	130	5.5	.956	SS-157
1983			152	.297	.368	622	185	13	5	7	1.1	82	58	36	48	16	0	0	232	490	39	116	5.0	.949	SS-152
1984			145	.266	.327	591	157	22	4	2	0.3	51	48	26	70	14	0	0	251	443	30	94	5.0	.959	SS-145
1985			138	.248	.333	568	141	25	4	5	0.9	54	58	20	63	2	3	2	214	451	32	115	5.1	.954	SS-133
1986			134	.240	.335	496	119	21	1	8	1.6	57	33	21	60	19	5	1	156	371	29	68	4.1	.948	SS-86, 3B-57, OF-3
1987			56	.263	.346	179	47	12	0	1	0.6	22	21	8	16	6	8	2	66	110	10	33	3.3	.946	SS-38, 3B-12
1988	HOU	N	155	.276	.378	566	156	30	5	6	1.1	51	59	18	61	3	4	3	232	408	23	68	4.3	.965	SS-155
1989			151	.246	.324	537	132	20	2	6	1.1	46	54	29	64	3	5	1	189	326	30	60	3.6	.945	SS-149
1990			132	.261	.330	445	116	19	3	2	0.4	44	37	24	46	10	5	0	190	321	25	57	4.2	.953	SS-129
11 yrs.			1365	.262	.345	5085	1333	208	31	51	1.0	528	451	244	557	109	31	9	2074	3894	297	821	4.6	.953	SS-1284, 3B-69, OF-3

LEAGUE CHAMPIONSHIP SERIES

| 1982 | ATL | N | 3 | .182 | .182 | 11 | 2 | 0 | 0 | 0 | 0.0 | 1 | 1 | 1 | 1 | 0 | 0 | 0 | 5 | 11 | 1 | 0 | 5.7 | .941 | SS-3 |

Domingo Ramos

RAMOS, DOMINGO ANTONIO
Born Domingo Antonio Ramos y DeRamos.
B. Mar. 29, 1958, Santiago, Dominican Republic
BR TR 5' 10" 154 lbs.

Year	Team		Games	BA	SA	AB	H	2B	3B	HR	HR%	R	RBI	BB	SO	SB	AB	H	PO	A	E	DP	TC/G	FA	G by Pos
1978	NY	A	1	—	—	0	0	0	0	0	—	0	0	0	0	0	0	0	0	0	0	0	0.0	—	SS-1
1980	TOR	A	5	.125	.125	16	2	0	0	0	0.0	0	0	2	5	0	0	0	5	10	0	3	3.0	1.000	2B-2, SS-2, DH-1
1982	SEA	A	8	.154	.231	26	4	2	0	0	0.0	3	1	3	2	0	0	0	9	14	2	0	3.1	.920	SS-8
1983			53	.283	.362	127	36	4	0	2	1.6	14	10	7	12	3	9	1	51	109	8	22	3.2	.952	2B-8, 3B-8, DH-2
1984			59	.185	.210	81	15	2	0	0	0.0	6	2	5	12	2	2	0	51	49	5	10	1.8	.952	3B-38, SS-13, 1B-5, 2B-3

Year	Team		Games	BA	SA	AB	H	2B	3B	HR	HR%	R	RBI	BB	SO	SB	PINCH HIT AB	H	PO	A	E	DP	TC/G	FA	G by Pos

Domingo Ramos *Continued*

1985			75	.196	.250	168	33	6	0	1	0.6	19	15	17	23	0	2	0	87	119	10	26	2.9	.954	SS-36, 2B-20, 1B-14, 3B-7
1986			49	.182	.202	99	18	2	0	0	0.0	8	5	8	13	0	0	0	55	93	6	16	3.1	.961	SS-21, 2B-16, 3B-8, DH-2
1987			42	.311	.427	103	32	6	0	2	1.9	9	11	3	12	0	1	0	47	88	5	19	3.3	.964	SS-25, 3B-7, 2B-6
1988	2 teams		32	CLE A (22G — .261)	CAL A (10G — .133)																				
"	total		32	.230	.246	61	14	1	0	0	0.0	10	5	3	7	0	4	1	37	43	1	8	2.5	.988	2B-11, 3B-10, 1B-5, SS-4, OF-1
1989	CHI	N	85	.263	.335	179	47	6	2	1	0.6	18	19	17	23	1	14	6	49	142	11	20	2.4	.946	SS-42, 3B-30
1990			98	.265	.314	226	60	5	0	2	0.8	22	17	27	29	0	18	2	62	100	10	19	2.0	.942	3B-66, SS-21, 2B-1
11 yrs.			507	.240	.297	1086	261	34	2	8	0.7	109	85	92	138	6	50	10	453	767	58	143	2.5	.955	3B-174, SS-173, 2B-67, 1B-24, DH-5, OF-1

LEAGUE CHAMPIONSHIP SERIES

| 1989 | CHI | N | 1 | .000 | .000 | 1 | 0 | 0 | 0 | 0 | 0.0 | 0 | 0 | 0 | 0 | 0 | 1 | 0 | 0 | 0 | 0 | 0 | 0.0 | — | |

Willie Randolph

RANDOLPH, WILLIE LARRY
B. July 6, 1954, Holly Hill, S. C.
BR TR 5′ 11″ 165 lbs.

			Games	BA	SA	AB	H	2B	3B	HR	HR%	R	RBI	BB	SO	SB
April			17	.273	.318	66	18	0	0	1	1.5	10	7	7	7	0
May			22	.237	.329	76	18	4	0	1	1.3	13	3	10	4	1
June			22	.217	.275	69	15	4	0	0	0.0	5	7	7	8	2
July			12	.289	.421	38	11	3	1	0	0.0	5	3	3	2	1
Aug			20	.254	.286	63	16	0	1	0	0.0	9	2	3	5	1
Sept/Oct			26	.303	.355	76	23	2	1	0	0.0	10	8	15	8	2
Day			47	.259	.340	147	38	4	1	2	1.4	23	14	18	12	5
Night			72	.261	.315	241	63	9	2	0	0.0	29	16	27	22	2
vs. Left				.353	.440	116	41	8	1	0	0.0	21	12	10	5	1
vs. Right				.221	.276	272	60	5	2	2	0.7	31	18	35	29	6
On Grass			97	.259	.318	305	79	9	3	1	0.3	41	19	36	31	7
On Turf			22	.265	.349	83	22	4	0	1	1.2	11	11	9	3	0
Home			54	.250	.311	164	41	5	1	1	0.6	23	11	18	12	6
Road			65	.268	.335	224	60	8	2	1	0.4	29	19	27	22	1
Division Rivals																
vs. CAL			5	.231	.231	13	3	0	0	0	0.0	1	0	0	2	0
vs. CHI			10	.231	.346	26	6	1	1	0	0.0	1	3	2	2	0
vs. KC			11	.262	.310	42	11	2	0	0	0.0	5	6	3	1	1
vs. MIN			4	.308	.308	13	4	0	0	0	0.0	2	1	2	1	1
vs. SEA			2	.500	.500	8	4	0	0	0	0.0	2	1	1	1	0
vs. TEX			11	.182	.273	33	6	1	1	0	0.0	6	3	8	6	2
On 3B < 2 Out				.294	.294	17	5	0	0	0	0.0	0	9	4	2	

SECOND BASE

Year	Team		Games	BA	SA	AB	H	2B	3B	HR	HR%	R	RBI	BB	SO	SB	PINCH HIT AB	H	PO	A	E	DP	TC/G	FA	G by Pos
1975	PIT	N	30	.164	.180	61	10	1	0	0	0.0	9	3	7	6	1	8	2	34	45	6	8	2.8	.929	2B-14, 3B-1
1976	NY	A	125	.267	.328	430	115	15	4	1	0.2	59	40	58	39	37	1	0	307	415	19	87	5.9	.974	2B-124
1977			147	.274	.387	551	151	28	11	4	0.7	91	40	64	53	13	0	0	350	454	16	108	5.6	.980	2B-147
1978			134	.279	.357	499	139	18	6	3	0.6	87	42	82	51	36	0	0	296	400	16	80	5.3	.978	2B-134
1979			153	.270	.368	574	155	15	13	5	0.9	98	61	95	39	33	0	0	355	478	13	128	5.5	.985	2B-153
1980			138	.294	.407	513	151	23	7	7	1.4	99	46	**119**	45	30	0	0	361	401	19	97	5.7	.976	2B-138
1981			93	.232	.305	357	83	14	3	2	0.6	59	24	57	24	14	0	0	205	268	11	74	5.2	.977	2B-93
1982			144	.280	.349	553	155	21	4	3	0.5	85	36	75	35	16	0	0	352	380	14	100	5.2	.981	2B-142, DH-1
1983			104	.279	.348	420	117	21	1	2	0.5	73	38	53	32	12	0	0	265	298	12	77	5.5	.979	2B-104
1984			142	.287	.348	564	162	24	2	2	0.4	86	31	86	42	10	0	0	334	419	13	112	5.4	.983	2B-142
1985			143	.276	.356	497	137	21	2	5	1.0	75	40	85	39	16	0	0	303	425	11	104	5.2	.985	2B-143
1986			141	.276	.346	492	136	15	2	5	1.0	76	50	94	49	15	2	1	313	381	20	94	5.1	.972	2B-139, DH-1
1987			120	.305	.414	449	137	24	2	7	1.6	96	67	82	25	11	0	0	286	338	12	89	5.3	.981	2B-119, DH-1
1988			110	.230	.300	404	93	20	1	2	0.5	43	34	55	39	8	0	0	254	339	7	83	5.5	.988	2B-110
1989	LA	N	145	.282	.326	549	155	18	0	2	0.4	62	36	71	51	7	3	0	260	412	9	85	4.7	.987	2B-140
1990	2 teams			LA N (26G — .271)	OAK A (93G — .257)																				
"	total		119	.260	.325	388	101	13	3	2	0.5	52	30	45	34	7	2	1	198	313	11	72	4.7	.979	2B-110, DH-6
16 yrs.			1988	.274	.351	7301	1997	291	61	52	0.7	1150	618	1128	603	266	16	4	4473	5766	209	1398	0.2	.533	2B-1952, DH-9, 3B-1

DIVISIONAL PLAYOFF SERIES

| 1981 | NY | A | 5 | .200 | .200 | 20 | 4 | 0 | 0 | 0 | 0.0 | 0 | 1 | 1 | 4 | 0 | 0 | 0 | 7 | 10 | 0 | 0 | 3.4 | 1.000 | 2B-5 |

Year	Team		Games	BA	SA	AB	H	2B	3B	HR	HR%	R	RBI	BB	SO	SB	PINCH HIT AB	H	PO	A	E	DP	TC/G	FA	G by Pos

Willie Randolph *Continued*

LEAGUE CHAMPIONSHIP SERIES

1975	PIT	N	2	.000	.000	2	0	0	0	0	0.0	1	0	0	1	0	1	0	0	1	0	0	0.5	1.000	2B-1
1976	NY	A	5	.118	.118	17	2	0	0	0	0.0	0	1	3	1	1	0	0	8	14	0	2	4.4	1.000	2B-5
1977			5	.278	.333	18	5	1	0	0	0.0	4	2	1	0	0	0	0	13	9	0	2	4.4	1.000	2B-5
1980			3	.385	.538	13	5	2	0	0	0.0	0	1	1	3	0	0	0	2	9	0	2	3.7	1.000	2B-3
1981			3	.333	.583	12	4	0	0	1	8.3	2	2	0	1	0	0	0	12	12	0	4	0.0	1.000	2B-3
1990	OAK	A	4	.375	.375	8	3	0	0	0	0.0	1	3	1	0	0	0	0	5	9	0	1	3.5	1.000	2B-4
6 yrs.			22	.271	.357	70	19	3	0	1	1.4	8	9	6	6	1	1	0	40	54	0	11	4.3	.000	2B-21

WORLD SERIES

1976	NY	A	4	.071	.071	14	1	0	0	0	0.0	1	0	1	3	0	0	0	13	8	0	5	5.3	1.000	2B-4
1977			6	.160	.360	25	4	2	0	1	4.0	5	1	2	2	0	0	0	13	14	0	1	4.5	1.000	2B-6
1981			6	.222	.722	18	4	1	1	2	11.1	5	3	9	0	1	0	0	13	11	0	2	4.0	1.000	2B-6
1990	OAK	A	4	.267	.267	15	4	0	0	0	0.0	0	0	1	0	1	0	0	14	12	0	5	6.5	1.000	2B-4
4 yrs.			20	.181	.375	72	13	3	1	3	4.2	11	4	13	5	2	0	0	53	45	0	13	4.9	.000	2B-20

Johnny Ray

RAY, JOHNNY CORNELIUS
B. Mar. 1, 1957, Chouteau, Okla.
BB TR 5′ 11″ 170 lbs.

			Games	BA	SA	AB	H	2B	3B	HR	HR%	R	RBI	BB	SO	SB	PINCH HIT AB	H	PO	A	E	DP	TC/G	FA	G by Pos
April			15	.218	.291	55	12	1	0	1	1.8	7	6	6	6	1									
May			20	.289	.408	76	22	6	0	1	1.3	12	10	6	7	1									
June			6	.111	.148	27	3	1	0	0	0.0	0	0	0	6	0									
July			20	.333	.414	87	29	4	0	1	1.1	9	5	2	9	0									
Aug			19	.295	.361	61	18	4	0	0	0.0	7	6	2	6	0									
Sept/Oct			25	.286	.418	98	28	7	0	2	2.0	12	16	3	10	0									
Day			25	.311	.422	90	28	4	0	2	2.2	7	8	3	10	0									
Night			80	.268	.357	314	84	19	0	3	1.0	40	35	16	34	2									
vs. Left				.300	.342	120	36	5	0	0	0.0	9	15	3	14	0									
vs. Right				.268	.384	284	76	18	0	5	1.8	38	28	16	30	2									
On Grass			93	.281	.374	356	100	18	0	5	1.4	40	41	17	37	2									
On Turf			12	.250	.354	48	12	5	0	0	0.0	7	2	2	7	0									
Home			57	.271	.386	210	57	9	0	5	2.4	27	21	10	19	0									
Road			48	.284	.356	194	55	14	0	0	0.0	20	22	9	25	2									
Division Rivals																									
vs. CHI			5	.368	.421	19	7	1	0	0	0.0	1	1	0	3	0									
vs. KC			8	.219	.375	32	7	2	0	1	3.1	4	5	0	5	0									
vs. MIN			9	.211	.342	38	8	2	0	1	2.6	5	2	1	1	0									
vs. OAK			9	.278	.333	36	10	2	0	0	0.0	3	3	2	4	0									
vs. SEA			10	.263	.447	38	10	4	0	1	2.6	8	5	4	4	0									
vs. TEX			8	.188	.250	32	6	2	0	0	0.0	2	1	1	3	0									
On 3B < 2 Out				.381	.476	21	8	2	0	0	0.0	0	18	1	3										

SECOND BASE

1981	PIT	N	31	.245	.353	102	25	11	0	0	0.0	10	6	6	9	0	2	1	52	96	2	22	4.8	.987	2B-31
1982			162	.281	.382	647	182	30	7	7	1.1	79	63	36	34	16	0	0	381	512	21	89	5.6	.977	2B-162
1983			151	.283	.399	576	163	**38**	7	5	0.9	68	53	35	26	18	5	1	320	452	13	102	5.2	.983	2B-151, 3B-1
1984			155	.312	.434	555	173	**38**	6	6	1.1	75	67	37	31	11	9	3	331	400	12	90	4.8	.984	2B-149
1985			154	.274	.375	594	163	33	3	7	1.2	67	70	46	24	13	4	1	305	423	18	89	4.8	.976	2B-151
1986			155	.301	.394	579	174	33	0	7	1.2	67	78	58	47	6	8	2	280	479	5	89	4.9	.993	2B-151
1987	2 teams	PIT N (123G — .273)		CAL A (30G — .346)																					
''	total		153	.289	.374	599	173	30	3	5	0.8	64	69	44	46	4	6	1	300	448	14	103	5.0	.982	2B-148, DH-1
1988	CAL	A	153	.306	.429	602	184	42	7	6	1.0	75	83	36	38	4	4	2	269	328	20	64	4.0	.968	2B-104, OF-40, DH-6
1989			134	.289	.358	530	153	16	3	5	0.9	52	62	36	30	6	4	2	279	403	11	98	5.2	.984	2B-130
1990			105	.277	.371	404	112	23	0	5	1.2	47	43	19	44	2	5	0	241	295	7	82	5.4	.987	2B-100, DH-1
10 yrs.			1353	.290	.391	5188	1502	294	36	53	1.0	604	594	353	329	80	47	13	2758	3836	123	828	5.0	.982	2B-1277, OF-40, DH-8, 3B-1

Year	Team		Games	BA	SA	AB	H	2B	3B	HR	HR%	R	RBI	BB	SO	SB	PINCH HIT AB	H	PO	A	E	DP	TC/G	FA	G by Pos

Randy Ready

READY, RANDY MAX
B. Jan. 8, 1960, San Mateo, Calif.
BR TR 5′ 11″ 175 lbs.

Year	Team		Games	BA	SA	AB	H	2B	3B	HR	HR%	R	RBI	BB	SO	SB	AB	H	PO	A	E	DP	TC/G	FA	G by Pos
1983	MIL	A	12	.405	.676	37	15	3	2	1	2.7	8	6	6	3	0	1	0	5	8	0	1	1.1	1.000	DH-6, 3B-4
1984			37	.187	.325	123	23	6	1	3	2.4	13	13	14	18	0	1	0	29	76	6	4	3.0	.946	3B-36
1985			48	.265	.387	181	48	9	5	1	0.6	29	21	14	23	0	2	0	93	14	1	1	2.3	.991	OF-37, 3B-7, 2B-3, DH-2
1986	2 teams		MIL A (23G — .190)		SD N (1G — .000)																				
"	total		24	.183	.268	82	15	4	0	1	1.2	8	4	9	10	2	2	0	35	23	4	4	2.6	.935	OF-11, 2B-7, 3B-4, DH-1
1987	SD	N	124	.309	.520	350	108	26	6	12	3.4	69	54	67	44	7	25	6	124	220	15	35	2.9	.958	3B-52, 2B-51, OF-16
1988			114	.266	.390	331	88	16	2	7	2.1	43	39	39	38	6	24	5	112	153	11	22	2.4	.960	3B-57, 2B-26, OF-16
1989	2 teams		SD N (28G — .254)		PHI N (72G — .267)																				
"	total		100	.264	.425	254	67	13	2	8	3.1	37	26	42	37	4	28	6	80	72	9	13	1.6	.944	OF-37, 3B-32, 2B-9
1990	PHI	N	101	.244	.309	217	53	9	1	1	0.4	26	26	29	35	3	45	12	78	86	2	18	2.9	.988	OF-30, 2B-28
8 yrs.			560	.265	.408	1575	417	86	19	34	2.2	233	189	220	208	22	128	29	556	652	48	98	2.2	.962	3B-192, OF-147, 2B-124, DH-9

Gary Redus

REDUS, GARY EUGENE
B. Nov. 1, 1956, Tanner, Ala.
BR TR 6′ 1″ 180 lbs.

		Games	BA	SA	AB	H	2B	3B	HR	HR%	R	RBI	BB	SO	SB
April		13	.200	.400	35	7	0	2	1	2.9	3	5	3	3	2
May		15	.200	.267	30	6	2	0	0	0.0	3	3	3	5	1
June		14	.357	.452	42	15	4	0	0	0.0	3	2	6	8	2
July		14	.100	.267	30	3	2	0	1	3.3	2	5	5	8	0
Aug		24	.304	.518	56	17	4	1	2	3.6	17	4	10	9	4
Sept/Oct		16	.235	.500	34	8	3	0	2	5.9	4	4	6	5	2
Day		29	.190	.365	63	12	3	1	2	3.2	9	10	11	11	3
Night		67	.268	.439	164	44	12	2	4	2.4	23	13	22	27	8
vs. Left			.262	.455	202	53	15	3	6	3.0	26	23	27	29	9
vs. Right			.120	.120	25	3	0	0	0	0.0	6	0	6	9	2
On Grass		20	.278	.426	54	15	3	1	1	1.9	3	4	7	13	3
On Turf		76	.237	.416	173	41	12	2	5	2.9	29	19	26	25	8
Home		54	.204	.343	108	22	7	1	2	1.9	20	12	21	15	6
Road		42	.286	.487	119	34	8	2	4	3.4	12	11	12	23	5
Division Rivals															
vs. CHI		8	.200	.250	20	4	1	0	0	0.0	1	1	3	1	0
vs. MON		13	.192	.346	26	5	1	0	1	3.8	3	1	3	4	1
vs. NY		10	.281	.438	32	9	2	0	1	3.1	3	3	3	8	2
vs. PHI		13	.294	.588	34	10	4	0	2	5.9	7	2	4	7	1
vs. STL		11	.269	.385	26	7	1	1	0	0.0	2	4	5	1	3
On 3B < 2 Out			.400	1.400	5	2	0	1	1	20.0	1	9	1	0	

FIRST BASE

AVERAGE / RBI / HR / SB (with NL AVG)

Year	Team		Games	BA	SA	AB	H	2B	3B	HR	HR%	R	RBI	BB	SO	SB	AB	H	PO	A	E	DP	TC/G	FA	G by Pos
1982	CIN	N	20	.217	.337	83	18	3	2	1	1.2	12	7	5	21	11	0	0	29	3	1	0	1.7	.970	OF-20
1983			125	.247	.444	453	112	20	9	17	3.8	90	51	71	111	39	4	2	235	11	7	0	2.0	.972	OF-120
1984			123	.254	.376	394	100	21	3	7	1.8	69	22	52	71	48	10	3	200	6	7	3	1.7	.967	OF-114
1985			101	.252	.415	246	62	14	4	6	2.4	51	28	44	52	48	17	6	140	3	2	0	1.4	.986	OF-85
1986	PHI	N	90	.247	.432	340	84	22	4	11	3.2	62	33	47	78	25	2	0	185	8	4	2	2.2	.980	OF-89
1987	CHI	A	130	.236	.392	475	112	26	6	12	2.5	78	48	69	90	52	0	0	262	13	6	4	2.2	.979	OF-123, DH-4
1988	2 teams		CHI A (77G — .263)		PIT N (30G — .197)																				
"	total		107	.249	.381	333	83	12	4	8	2.4	54	38	48	71	31	16	4	182	9	4	1	1.8	.979	OF-87, DH-2
1989	PIT	N	98	.283	.462	279	79	18	7	6	2.2	42	33	40	51	25	12	3	583	55	9	43	6.6	.986	1B-72, OF-16
1990			96	.247	.419	227	56	15	3	6	2.6	32	23	33	38	11	19	3	461	36	8	29	6.5	.984	1B-72, OF-7
9 yrs.			890	.249	.411	2830	706	151	42	74	2.6	490	283	409	583	290	80	21	2277	144	48	82	2.8	.981	OF-661, 1B-144, DH-6

LEAGUE CHAMPIONSHIP SERIES

Year	Team		Games	BA	SA	AB	H	2B	3B	HR	HR%	R	RBI	BB	SO	SB	AB	H	PO	A	E	DP	TC/G	FA	G by Pos
1990	PIT	N	5	.250	.250	8	2	0	0	0	0.0	1	0	1	3	1	3	1	16	0	0	0	8.0	1.000	1B-2

Darren Reed

REED, DARREN DOUGLAS
B. Oct. 16, 1965, Ventura, Calif.
BR TR 6′ 1″ 190 lbs.

Year	Team		Games	BA	SA	AB	H	2B	3B	HR	HR%	R	RBI	BB	SO	SB	AB	H	PO	A	E	DP	TC/G	FA	G by Pos
1990	NY	N	26	.205	.436	39	8	4	1	1	2.5	5	2	3	11	1	8	0	20	1	1	0	1.6	.955	OF-14

Year	Team		Games	BA	SA	AB	H	2B	3B	HR	HR%	R	RBI	BB	SO	SB	PINCH HIT AB	PINCH HIT H	PO	A	E	DP	TC/G	FA	G by Pos

Jeff Reed

REED, JEFFREY SCOTT
B. Nov. 12, 1962, Joliet, Ill.
BL TR 6' 2" 190 lbs.

Year	Team		Games	BA	SA	AB	H	2B	3B	HR	HR%	R	RBI	BB	SO	SB	PH AB	PH H	PO	A	E	DP	TC/G	FA	G by Pos
1984	MIN	A	18	.143	.286	21	3	3	0	0	0.0	3	1	2	6	0	0	0	41	2	1	1	2.4	.977	C-18
1985			7	.200	.200	10	2	0	0	0	0.0	2	0	0	3	0	1	0	9	3	0	0	1.7	1.000	C-7
1986			68	.236	.321	165	39	6	1	2	1.2	13	9	16	19	1	7	3	332	19	2	5	5.2	.994	C-64
1987	MON	N	75	.213	.280	207	44	11	0	1	0.5	15	21	12	20	0	5	1	357	36	12	6	5.4	.970	C-74
1988	2 teams		MON N (43G — .220)			CIN N (49G — .232)																			
"	total		92	.226	.287	265	60	9	2	1	0.4	20	16	28	41	1	6	1	468	38	3	3	5.5	.994	C-88
1989	CIN	N	102	.223	.293	287	64	11	0	3	1.0	16	23	34	46	0	5	0	504	50	7	2	5.5	.988	C-99
1990			72	.251	.360	175	44	8	1	3	1.7	12	16	24	26	0	3	0	358	26	5	1	5.6	.987	C-70
7 yrs.			434	.227	.303	1130	256	48	4	10	0.9	81	86	116	161	2	27	5	2069	174	30	18	5.2	.987	C-420

LEAGUE CHAMPIONSHIP SERIES

Year	Team		Games	BA	SA	AB	H	2B	3B	HR	HR%	R	RBI	BB	SO	SB	PH AB	PH H	PO	A	E	DP	TC/G	FA	G by Pos
1990	CIN	N	4	.000	.000	7	0	0	0	0	0.0	0	0	0	2	0	0	0	24	1	0	0	6.3	1.000	C-4

Jody Reed

REED, JODY ERIC
B. July 26, 1962, Tampa, Fla.
BR TR 5' 9" 170 lbs.

	Games	BA	SA	AB	H	2B	3B	HR	HR%	R	RBI	BB	SO	SB
April	18	.333	.492	63	21	4	0	2	3.2	8	12	8	5	0
May	26	.250	.320	100	25	7	0	0	0.0	7	4	11	15	0
June	27	.308	.452	104	32	12	0	1	1.0	18	11	9	9	1
July	28	.368	.528	106	39	14	0	1	0.9	16	6	14	13	1
Aug	25	.275	.339	109	30	4	0	1	0.9	9	13	10	10	0
Sept/Oct	31	.224	.259	116	26	4	0	0	0.0	12	5	23	13	2
Day	48	.328	.441	177	58	17	0	1	0.6	22	24	27	17	0
Night	107	.273	.368	421	115	28	0	4	1.0	48	27	48	48	4
vs. Left		.299	.386	184	55	16	0	0	0.0	29	14	23	17	1
vs. Right		.285	.391	414	118	29	0	5	1.2	41	37	52	48	3
On Grass	133	.289	.391	512	148	37	0	5	1.0	64	47	71	53	4
On Turf	22	.291	.384	86	25	8	0	0	0.0	6	4	4	12	0
Home	80	.293	.405	311	91	26	0	3	1.0	40	31	34	39	1
Road	75	.286	.373	287	82	19	0	2	0.7	30	20	41	26	3
Division Rivals														
vs. BAL	13	.283	.396	53	15	6	0	0	0.0	8	7	6	2	0
vs. CLE	10	.256	.372	43	11	2	0	1	2.3	4	5	3	6	0
vs. DET	13	.306	.449	49	15	4	0	1	2.0	8	6	6	6	1
vs. MIL	12	.216	.270	37	8	2	0	0	0.0	3	3	10	2	0
vs. NY	13	.298	.383	47	14	4	0	0	0.0	8	6	10	5	1
vs. TOR	13	.327	.491	55	18	6	0	1	1.8	7	3	2	5	0
On 3B < 2 Out		.389	.500	18	7	2	0	0	0.0	0	20	4	2	

SECOND BASE — AVERAGE / RBI / HR / SB (vs AL AVG)

Year	Team		Games	BA	SA	AB	H	2B	3B	HR	HR%	R	RBI	BB	SO	SB	PH AB	PH H	PO	A	E	DP	TC/G	FA	G by Pos
1987	BOS	A	9	.300	.400	30	9	1	1	0	0.0	4	8	4	0	1	0	0	11	26	0	9	4.1	1.000	SS-6, 2B-2, 3B-1
1988			109	.293	.376	338	99	23	1	1	0.3	60	28	45	21	1	0	0	147	282	11	57	4.0	.975	SS-94, 2B-11, 3B-4
1989			146	.288	.393	524	151	42	2	3	0.6	76	40	73	44	4	3	1	255	423	19	88	4.8	.973	SS-77, 2B-70, 3B-4, DH-1, OF-1
1990			155	.289	.390	598	173	**45**	0	5	0.8	70	51	75	65	4	1	0	278	478	16	103	5.0	.979	2B-119, SS-50, DH-1
4 yrs.			419	.290	.388	1490	432	111	4	9	0.6	210	127	197	130	10	4	1	691	1209	46	257	4.6	.976	SS-227, 2B-202, 3B-9, DH-2, OF-1

LEAGUE CHAMPIONSHIP SERIES

Year	Team		Games	BA	SA	AB	H	2B	3B	HR	HR%	R	RBI	BB	SO	SB	PH AB	PH H	PO	A	E	DP	TC/G	FA	G by Pos
1988	BOS	A	4	.273	.364	11	3	1	0	0	0.0	0	0	2	1	0	0	0	3	10	0	2	3.3	1.000	SS-4
1990			4	.133	.133	15	2	0	0	0	0.0	0	1	0	2	0	0	0	11	11	0	4	5.5	1.000	2B-4, SS-3
2 yrs.			8	.192	.231	26	5	1	0	0	0.0	0	1	2	3	0	0	0	14	21	0	6	4.4	.000	SS-7, 2B-4

Kevin Reimer

REIMER, KEVIN MICHAEL
B. June 28, 1964, Macon, Ga.
BL TR 6' 2" 215 lbs.

Year	Team		Games	BA	SA	AB	H	2B	3B	HR	HR%	R	RBI	BB	SO	SB	PH AB	PH H	PO	A	E	DP	TC/G	FA	G by Pos
1988	TEX	A	12	.120	.240	25	3	0	0	1	4.0	2	2	0	6	0	5	0	0	0	0	0	0.0	—	DH-7, OF-1
1989			3	.000	.000	5	0	0	0	0	0.0	0	0	0	1	0	2	0	0	0	0	0	0.0	—	DH-1
1990			64	.260	.430	100	26	9	1	2	2.0	5	15	10	22	0	40	**12**	12	0	2	0	1.6	.857	DH-21, OF-9
3 yrs.			79	.223	.377	130	29	9	1	3	2.3	7	17	10	29	0	47	12	12	0	2	0	0.2	.000	DH-29, OF-10

Year	Team		Games	BA	SA	AB	H	2B	3B	HR	HR%	R	RBI	BB	SO	SB	PINCH HIT AB	H	PO	A	E	DP	TC/G	FA	G by Pos

Harold Reynolds

REYNOLDS, HAROLD CRAIG
Brother of Don Reynolds.
B. Nov. 26, 1960, Eugene, Ore.
BB TR 5' 11" 165 lbs.

	Games	BA	SA	AB	H	2B	3B	HR	HR%	R	RBI	BB	SO	SB
April	20	.193	.277	83	16	2	1	1	1.2	14	6	7	5	3
May	29	.254	.356	118	30	10	1	0	0.0	13	13	15	13	4
June	26	.258	.340	97	25	4	2	0	0.0	17	9	20	7	9
July	27	.295	.390	105	31	5	1	1	1.0	17	10	16	4	6
Aug	28	.211	.281	114	24	8	0	0	0.0	12	2	12	10	5
Sept/Oct	30	.288	.416	125	36	7	0	3	2.4	27	15	11	13	4
Day	39	.234	.342	158	37	8	3	1	0.6	20	15	16	10	3
Night	121	.258	.349	484	125	28	2	4	0.8	80	40	65	42	28
vs. Left		.285	.391	207	59	15	2	1	0.5	45	22	17	7	10
vs. Right		.237	.326	435	103	21	3	4	0.9	55	33	64	45	21
On Grass	62	.257	.388	268	69	17	3	4	1.5	48	30	23	25	8
On Turf	98	.249	.318	374	93	19	2	1	0.3	52	25	58	27	23
Home	79	.253	.310	297	75	15	1	0	0.0	42	21	46	18	19
Road	81	.252	.380	345	87	21	4	5	1.4	58	34	35	34	12
Division Rivals														
vs. CAL	13	.200	.236	55	11	2	0	0	0.0	10	0	6	4	3
vs. CHI	11	.256	.279	43	11	1	0	0	0.0	8	2	5	6	1
vs. KC	13	.288	.385	52	15	3	1	0	0.0	4	3	8	5	2
vs. MIN	13	.189	.321	53	10	2	1	1	1.9	11	2	6	2	5
vs. OAK	13	.286	.429	49	14	2	1	1	2.0	12	5	7	3	1
vs. TEX	13	.286	.375	56	16	3	1	0	0.0	9	6	3	6	5
On 3B < 2 Out		.250	.450	20	5	1	0	1	5.0	1	19	2	3	

SECOND BASE (graphs: AVERAGE, RBI, HR, SB — with AL AVG comparisons)

Year	Team		Games	BA	SA	AB	H	2B	3B	HR	HR%	R	RBI	BB	SO	SB	PH AB	H	PO	A	E	DP	TC/G	FA	G by Pos
1983	SEA	A	20	.203	.305	59	12	4	1	0	0.0	8	1	2	9	0	0	0	30	48	2	14	4.0	.975	2B-18
1984			10	.300	.300	10	3	0	0	0	0.0	3	0	0	1	1	0	0	8	12	0	3	2.0	1.000	2B-6
1985			66	.144	.192	104	15	3	1	0	0.0	15	6	17	14	3	2	0	69	123	8	22	3.0	.960	2B-61
1986			126	.222	.290	445	99	19	4	1	0.2	46	24	29	42	30	0	0	278	415	16	111	5.6	.977	2B-126
1987			160	.275	.370	530	146	31	8	1	0.2	73	35	39	34	**60**	0	0	347	507	20	111	5.5	.977	2B-160
1988			158	.283	.383	598	169	26	**11**	4	0.7	61	41	51	51	35	0	0	303	471	18	111	5.0	.977	2B-158
1989			153	.300	.369	613	184	24	9	0	0.0	87	43	55	45	25	2	0	311	506	17	109	5.5	.980	2B-151, DH-1
1990			160	.252	.347	**642**	162	36	5	5	0.7	100	55	81	52	31	0	0	330	499	19	110	5.3	.978	2B-160
8 yrs.			853	.263	.348	3001	790	143	39	11	0.4	393	205	274	248	185	4	0	1676	2581	100	591	5.1	.977	2B-840, DH-1

R. J. Reynolds

REYNOLDS, ROBERT JAMES
B. Apr. 19, 1959, Sacramento, Calif.
BB TR 6' 180 lbs.

Year	Team		Games	BA	SA	AB	H	2B	3B	HR	HR%	R	RBI	BB	SO	SB	PH AB	H	PO	A	E	DP	TC/G	FA	G by Pos
1983	LA	N	24	.236	.345	55	13	0	0	2	3.6	5	11	3	11	5	7	2	25	2	2	1	1.2	.931	OF-18
1984			73	.258	.350	240	62	12	2	2	0.8	23	24	14	38	7	13	5	104	4	3	1	1.5	.973	OF-63
1985	2 teams					LA N (73G — .266)			PIT N (31G — .308)																	
"	total		104	.282	.395	337	95	15	7	3	0.9	44	42	22	49	18	19	3	159	6	6	0	1.6	.965	OF-85
1986	PIT	N	118	.269	.420	402	108	30	2	9	2.2	63	48	40	78	16	11	2	190	2	9	0	1.7	.955	OF-112
1987			117	.260	.400	335	87	24	1	7	2.1	47	51	34	80	14	23	6	134	7	1	2	1.2	.993	OF-99
1988			130	.248	.359	323	80	14	2	6	1.9	35	51	20	62	15	42	9	142	7	4	2	1.2	.974	OF-95
1989			125	.270	.375	363	98	16	2	6	1.7	45	48	34	66	22	31	9	200	6	2	3	1.7	.990	OF-98
1990			95	.288	.344	215	62	10	1	0	0.0	25	19	23	35	12	38	8	102	3	3	0	1.8	.972	OF-59
8 yrs.			786	.267	.381	2270	605	121	17	35	1.5	287	294	190	419	109	184	44	1056	37	30	9	1.4	.973	OF-629

LEAGUE CHAMPIONSHIP SERIES

Year	Team		Games	BA	SA	AB	H	2B	3B	HR	HR%	R	RBI	BB	SO	SB	PH AB	H	PO	A	E	DP	TC/G	FA	G by Pos
1990	PIT	N	6	.200	.200	10	2	0	0	0	0.0	0	0	2	2	1	3	0	2	0	1	0	1.0	.667	OF-3

Ronn Reynolds

REYNOLDS, RONN DWAYNE
B. Sept. 28, 1958, Wichita, Kans.
BR TR 6' 200 lbs.

Year	Team		Games	BA	SA	AB	H	2B	3B	HR	HR%	R	RBI	BB	SO	SB	PH AB	H	PO	A	E	DP	TC/G	FA	G by Pos
1982	NY	N	2	.000	.000	4	0	0	0	0	0.0	0	0	1	1	0	0	0	3	0	0	0	1.5	1.000	C-2
1983			24	.197	.212	66	13	1	0	0	0.0	4	2	8	12	0	0	0	99	14	7	2	5.0	.942	C-24
1985			28	.209	.256	43	9	2	0	0	0.0	4	1	0	18	0	2	0	86	9	1	2	3.4	.990	C-25
1986	PHI	N	43	.214	.317	126	27	4	0	3	2.4	8	10	5	30	0	1	1	198	16	2	3	5.0	.991	C-42
1987	HOU	N	38	.167	.235	102	17	4	0	1	1.0	5	7	3	29	0	0	0	216	16	6	1	6.3	.975	C-38
1990	SD	N	8	.067	.133	15	1	1	0	0	0.0	1	1	1	6	0	0	0	26	2	0	0	3.5	1.000	C-8
6 yrs.			143	.188	.256	356	67	12	0	4	1.1	22	21	18	96	0	3	1	628	57	16	8	4.9	.977	C-139

Year	Team	Games	BA	SA	AB	H	2B	3B	HR	HП%	R	RBI	BB	SO	SB	PINCH HIT AB	H	PO	A	E	DP	TC/G	FA	G by Pos

Karl Rhodes

RHODES, KARL DERRICK
B. Aug. 21, 1968, Cincinnati, Ohio
BL TL 6' 175 lbs.

Year	Team	Games	BA	SA	AB	H	2B	3B	HR	HП%	R	RBI	BB	SO	SB	AB	H	PO	A	E	DP	TC/G	FA	G by Pos
1990	HOU	N	38	.244	.372	86	21	6	1	1	1.1	12	3	13	12	4	6	3	61	2	3	0	2.2	.955	OF-30

Ernest Riles

RILES, ERNEST
B. Oct. 2, 1960, Cairo, Ga.
BL TR 6' 1" 180 lbs.

Year	Team	Games	BA	SA	AB	H	2B	3B	HR	HП%	R	RBI	BB	SO	SB	AB	H	PO	A	E	DP	TC/G	FA	G by Pos
1985	MIL	A	116	.286	.377	448	128	12	7	5	1.1	54	45	36	54	2	1	0	183	310	22	62	4.4	.957	SS-115, DH-1
1986			145	.252	.357	524	132	24	2	9	1.7	69	47	54	80	7	4	0	212	327	20	76	3.9	.964	SS-142
1987			83	.261	.351	276	72	11	1	4	1.4	38	38	30	47	3	4	0	76	152	13	25	2.9	.946	3B-65, SS-21
1988	2 teams	MIL A	(41G — .252)		SF N	(79G — .294)																			
"	total		120	.277	.376	314	87	13	3	4	1.3	33	37	17	59	3	26	6	82	197	7	25	2.4	.976	3B-58, SS-25, 2B-17, DH-5
1989	SF	N	122	.278	.404	302	84	13	2	7	2.3	43	40	28	50	0	38	9	69	144	9	16	1.8	.959	3B-83, 2B-18, SS-7, OF-5
1990			92	.200	.381	155	31	2	1	8	5.1	22	21	26	26	0	42	12	53	105	3	14	2.8	.981	SS-26, 2B-24, 3B-10
6 yrs.			678	.264	.372	2019	534	75	16	37	1.8	259	228	191	316	15	115	27	675	1235	74	218	2.9	.963	SS-336, 3B-216, 2B-59, DH-6, OF-5

LEAGUE CHAMPIONSHIP SERIES
Year	Team	Games	BA	SA	AB	H	2B	3B	HR	HП%	R	RBI	BB	SO	SB	AB	H	PO	A	E	DP	TC/G	FA	G by Pos
1989	SF	N	1	.000	.000	1	0	0	0	0	0.0	0	0	0	0	1	0	0	0	0	0	0	0.0	—	—

WORLD SERIES
Year	Team	Games	BA	SA	AB	H	2B	3B	HR	HП%	R	RBI	BB	SO	SB	AB	H	PO	A	E	DP	TC/G	FA	G by Pos
1989	SF	N	4	.000	.000	8	0	0	0	0	0.0	0	0	0	1	0	1	0	0	0	0	0	0.0	—	DH-2

Billy Ripken

RIPKEN, WILLIAM OLIVER
Son of Cal Ripken. Brother of Cal Ripken.
B. Dec. 16, 1964, Havre de Grace, Md.
BR TR 6' 1" 180 lbs.

SECOND BASE

	Games	BA	SA	AB	H	2B	3B	HR	HП%	R	RBI	BB	SO	SB
April	15	.209	.279	43	9	3	0	0	0.0	4	1	5	2	1
May	21	.269	.343	67	18	3	1	0	0.0	6	7	2	10	1
June	24	.278	.356	90	25	4	0	1	1.1	7	8	1	6	1
July	26	.329	.395	76	25	5	0	0	0.0	11	4	7	4	1
Aug	14	.351	.459	37	13	4	0	0	0.0	5	3	6	5	0
Sept/Oct	29	.301	.462	93	28	9	0	2	2.2	15	15	7	16	1
Day	32	.344	.417	96	33	4	0	1	1.0	10	8	11	8	3
Night	97	.274	.377	310	85	24	1	2	0.6	38	30	17	35	2
vs. Left		.314	.421	140	44	9	0	2	1.4	13	11	12	16	1
vs. Right		.278	.368	266	74	19	1	1	0.4	35	27	16	27	4
On Grass	111	.276	.361	352	97	24	0	2	0.6	38	33	24	38	5
On Turf	18	.389	.556	54	21	4	1	1	1.9	10	5	4	5	0
Home	65	.278	.394	198	55	17	0	2	1.0	25	20	13	16	2
Road	64	.303	.380	208	63	11	1	1	0.5	23	18	15	27	3
Division Rivals														
vs. BOS	11	.265	.353	34	9	3	0	0	0.0	6	2	3	4	0
vs. CLE	10	.381	.500	42	16	5	0	0	0.0	3	5	1	5	0
vs. DET	12	.237	.342	38	9	4	0	0	0.0	5	1	4	5	1
vs. MIL	12	.231	.333	39	9	4	0	0	0.0	6	1	2	4	2
vs. NY	12	.300	.400	40	12	1	0	1	2.5	3	8	3	7	0
vs. TOR	13	.316	.447	38	12	2	0	1	2.6	5	2	3	4	0
On 3B < 2 Out		.333	.389	18	6	1	0	0	0.0	0	11	1	4	

Year	Team	Games	BA	SA	AB	H	2B	3B	HR	HП%	R	RBI	BB	SO	SB	AB	H	PO	A	E	DP	TC/G	FA	G by Pos
1987	BAL	A	58	.308	.372	234	72	9	0	2	0.9	27	20	21	23	4	0	0	133	162	3	53	5.1	.990	2B-58
1988			150	.207	.258	512	106	18	1	2	0.4	52	34	33	63	8	0	0	310	440	12	110	5.1	.984	2B-149, 3B-2
1989			115	.239	.305	318	76	11	2	2	0.6	31	26	22	53	1	0	0	255	335	9	81	5.2	.985	2B-114, DH-1
1990			129	.291	.387	406	118	28	1	3	0.7	48	38	28	43	5	1	1	250	366	8	84	4.9	.987	2B-127
4 yrs.			452	.253	.322	1470	372	66	4	9	0.6	158	118	104	182	18	1	1	948	1303	32	328	5.1	.986	2B-448, 3B-2, DH-1

Year	Team	Games	BA	SA	AB	H	2B	3B	HR	HR%	R	RBI	BB	SO	SB	PINCH HIT AB	H	PO	A	E	DP	TC/G	FA	G by Pos

Cal Ripken

RIPKEN, CALVIN EDWIN, JR.
Son of Cal Ripken. Brother of Billy Ripken.
B. Aug. 24, 1960, Havre de Grace, Md.
BR TR 6′ 4″ 200 lbs.

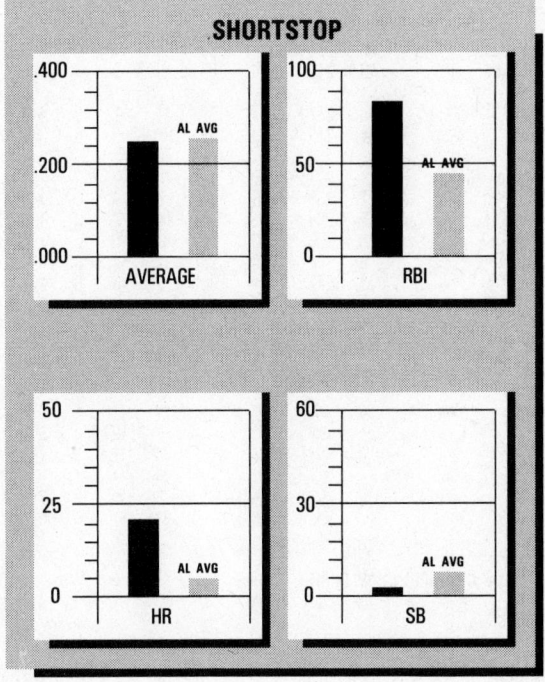

SHORTSTOP

	Games	BA	SA	AB	H	2B	3B	HR	HR%	R	RBI	BB	SO	SB	AB	H	PO	A	E	DP	TC/G	FA	G by Pos
April	20	.224	.342	76	17	1	1	2	2.6	11	11	15	10	0									
May	27	.206	.423	97	20	4	1	5	5.2	15	15	18	8	0									
June	28	.309	.409	110	34	8	0	1	0.9	13	11	11	8	1									
July	28	.277	.436	94	26	6	0	3	3.2	12	16	18	11	0									
Aug	27	.265	.529	102	27	5	2	6	5.9	14	21	11	15	0									
Sept/Oct	31	.215	.347	121	26	4	0	4	3.3	13	10	9	14	2									
Day	42	.275	.497	153	42	7	0	9	5.9	20	20	25	18	1									
Night	119	.242	.387	447	108	21	4	12	2.7	58	64	57	48	2									
vs. Left		.264	.473	182	48	9	1	9	4.9	25	24	30	17	1									
vs. Right		.244	.390	418	102	19	3	12	2.9	53	60	52	49	2									
On Grass	136	.241	.401	511	123	23	4	17	3.3	62	68	66	59	3									
On Turf	25	.303	.494	89	27	5	0	4	4.5	16	16	16	7	0									
Home	80	.213	.350	300	64	13	2	8	2.7	30	42	35	33	0									
Road	81	.287	.480	300	86	15	2	13	4.3	48	42	47	33	3									
Division Rivals																							
vs. BOS	13	.423	.538	52	22	3	0	1	1.9	6	4	4	5	0									
vs. CLE	13	.292	.458	48	14	2	0	2	4.2	6	6	10	4	1									
vs. DET	13	.283	.435	46	13	2	1	1	2.2	5	10	10	8	0									
vs. MIL	13	.220	.300	50	11	4	0	0	0.0	5	5	5	4	0									
vs. NY	13	.196	.412	51	10	3	1	2	3.9	5	8	2	6	2									
vs. TOR	13	.288	.500	52	15	2	0	3	5.8	9	9	3	4	0									
On 3B < 2 Out		.333	.528	36	12	5	1	0	0.0	0	34	11	3										

Year	Team	Games	BA	SA	AB	H	2B	3B	HR	HR%	R	RBI	BB	SO	SB	AB	H	PO	A	E	DP	TC/G	FA	G by Pos
1981	BAL A	23	.128	.128	39	5	0	0	0	0.0	1	0	1	8	0	4	0	13	30	3	6	2.0	.935	SS-12, 3B-6
1982		160	.264	.475	598	158	32	5	28	4.7	90	93	46	95	3	0	0	221	440	19	64	4.3	.972	SS-94, 3B-71
1983		162	.318	.517	663	211	47	2	27	4.1	121	102	58	97	0	0	0	272	534	25	113	5.1	.970	SS-162
1984		162	.304	.510	641	195	37	7	27	4.2	103	86	71	89	2	0	0	297	583	26	122	5.6	.971	SS-162
1985		161	.282	.469	642	181	32	5	26	4.0	116	110	67	68	2	0	0	286	474	26	123	4.9	.967	SS-161
1986		162	.282	.461	627	177	35	1	25	4.0	98	81	70	60	4	0	0	240	482	13	105	4.5	.982	SS-162
1987		162	.252	.436	624	157	28	3	27	4.3	97	98	81	77	3	0	0	240	480	20	103	4.6	.973	SS-162
1988		161	.264	.431	575	152	25	1	23	4.0	87	81	102	69	2	0	0	284	480	21	119	4.9	.973	SS-161
1989		162	.257	.401	646	166	30	0	21	3.3	80	93	57	72	3	0	0	276	531	8	119	5.0	.990	SS-162
1990		161	.250	.415	600	150	28	4	21	3.5	78	84	82	66	3	0	0	242	435	3	94	4.2	.996	SS-161
10 yrs.		1476	.274	.456	5655	1552	294	28	225	4.0	871	828	635	701	22	4	0	2371	4469	164	968	4.7	.977	SS-1399, 3B-77

LEAGUE CHAMPIONSHIP SERIES

Year	Team	Games	BA	SA	AB	H	2B	3B	HR	HR%	R	RBI	BB	SO	SB	AB	H	PO	A	E	DP	TC/G	FA	G by Pos
1983	BAL A	4	.400	.533	15	6	2	0	0	0.0	5	1	2	3	0	0	0	7	11	0	2	4.5	1.000	SS-4

WORLD SERIES

Year	Team	Games	BA	SA	AB	H	2B	3B	HR	HR%	R	RBI	BB	SO	SB	AB	H	PO	A	E	DP	TC/G	FA	G by Pos
1983	BAL A	5	.167	.167	18	3	0	0	0	0.0	2	1	3	4	0	0	0	6	14	0	3	4.0	1.000	SS-5

Luis Rivera

RIVERA, LUIS ANTONIO
Born Luis Antonio Rivera y Pedraza.
B. Jan. 3, 1964, Cidra, Puerto Rico
BR TR 5′ 11″ 165 lbs.

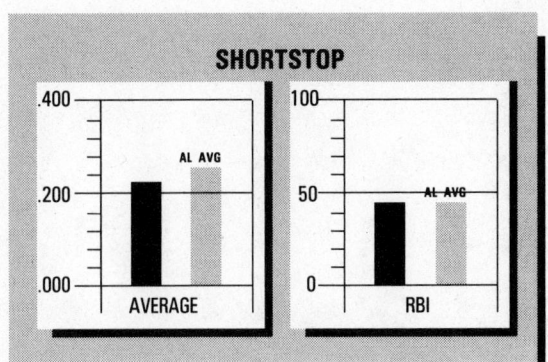

SHORTSTOP

	Games	BA	SA	AB	H	2B	3B	HR	HR%	R	RBI	BB	SO	SB
April	8	.000	.000	8	0	0	0	0	0.0	2	1	2	1	0
May	21	.333	.417	72	24	3	0	1	1.4	7	9	4	11	1
June	25	.167	.238	84	14	3	0	1	1.2	10	6	6	15	0
July	17	.156	.378	45	7	4	0	2	4.4	5	6	1	9	0
Aug	22	.234	.422	64	15	3	0	3	4.7	10	14	5	8	2
Sept/Oct	25	.247	.342	73	18	7	0	0	0.0	4	9	7	14	1
Day	37	.212	.384	99	21	8	0	3	3.0	14	12	11	15	1
Night	81	.231	.328	247	57	12	0	4	1.6	24	33	14	43	3
vs. Left		.172	.267	116	20	5	0	2	1.7	10	15	8	24	0
vs. Right		.252	.383	230	58	15	0	5	2.2	28	30	17	34	4

Year	Team	Games	BA	SA	AB	H	2B	3B	HR	HR%	R	RBI	BB	SO	SB	PINCH HIT AB	PINCH HIT H	PO	A	E	DP	TC/G	FA	G by Pos

Luis Rivera *Continued*

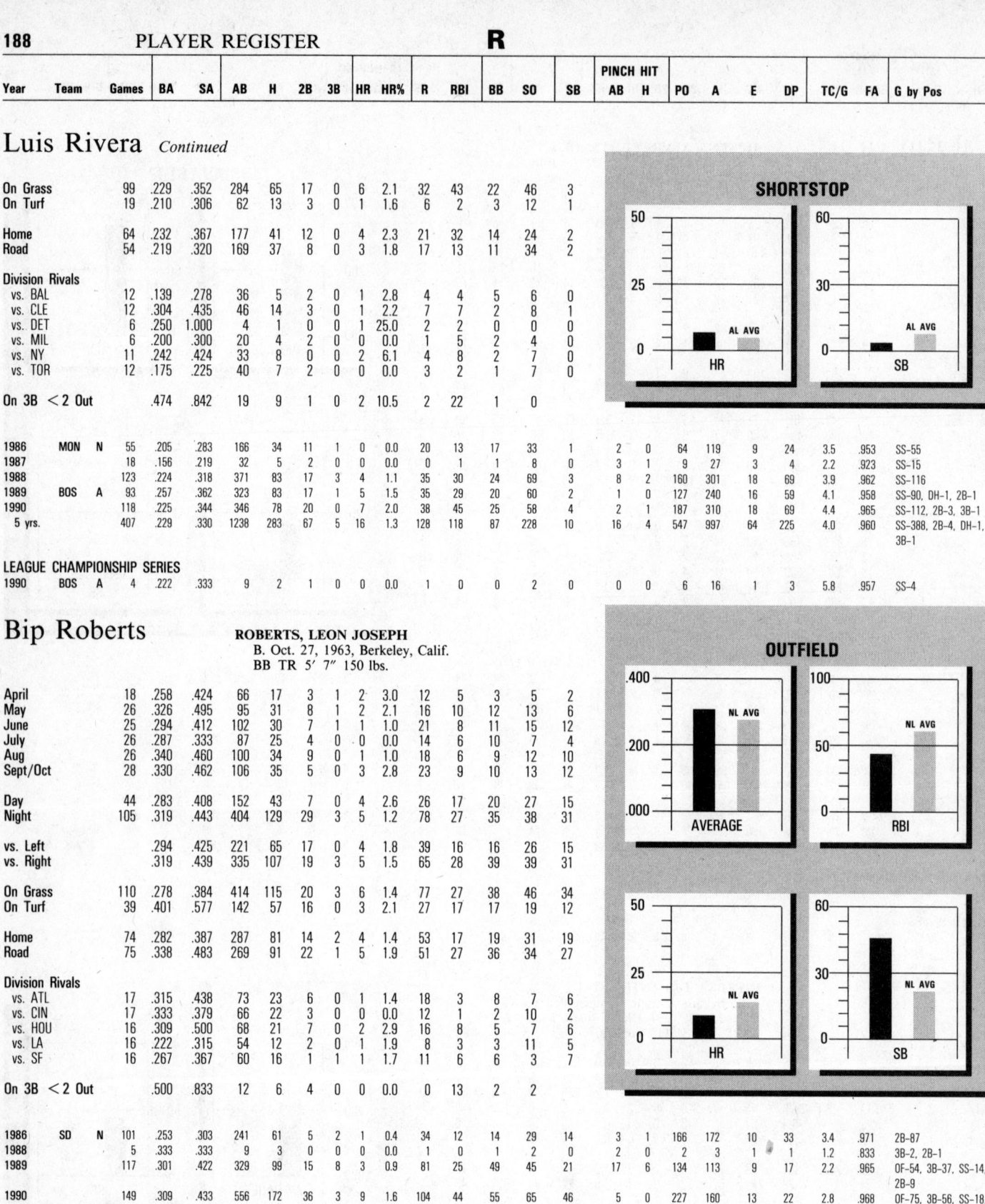

On Grass		99	.229	.352	284	65	17	0	6	2.1	32	43	22	46	3									
On Turf		19	.210	.306	62	13	3	0	1	1.6	6	2	3	12	1									
Home		64	.232	.367	177	41	12	0	4	2.3	21	32	14	24	2									
Road		54	.219	.320	169	37	8	0	3	1.8	17	13	11	34	2									

Division Rivals

vs. BAL		12	.139	.278	36	5	2	0	1	2.8	4	4	5	6	0									
vs. CLE		12	.304	.435	46	14	3	0	1	2.2	7	7	2	8	1									
vs. DET		6	.250	1.000	4	1	0	0	1	25.0	2	2	0	0	0									
vs. MIL		6	.200	.300	20	4	2	0	0	0.0	1	5	2	4	0									
vs. NY		11	.242	.424	33	8	0	0	2	6.1	4	8	2	7	0									
vs. TOR		12	.175	.225	40	7	2	0	0	0.0	3	2	1	7	0									
On 3B < 2 Out			.474	.842	19	9	1	0	2	10.5	2	22	1	0										

1986	MON N	55	.205	.283	166	34	11	1	0	0.0	20	13	17	33	1	2	0	64	119	9	24	3.5	.953	SS-55
1987		18	.156	.219	32	5	2	0	0	0.0	0	1	1	8	0	3	1	9	27	3	4	2.2	.923	SS-15
1988		123	.224	.318	371	83	17	3	4	1.1	35	30	24	69	3	8	2	160	301	18	69	3.9	.962	SS-116
1989	BOS A	93	.257	.362	323	83	17	1	5	1.5	35	29	20	60	2	1	0	127	240	16	59	4.1	.958	SS-90, DH-1, 2B-1
1990		118	.225	.344	346	78	20	0	7	2.0	38	45	25	58	4	2	1	187	310	18	69	4.4	.965	SS-112, 2B-3, 3B-1
5 yrs.		407	.229	.330	1238	283	67	5	16	1.3	128	118	87	228	10	16	4	547	997	64	225	4.0	.960	SS-388, 2B-4, DH-1, 3B-1

LEAGUE CHAMPIONSHIP SERIES

1990	BOS A	4	.222	.333	9	2	1	0	0	0.0	1	0	0	2	0	0	0	6	16	1	3	5.8	.957	SS-4

Bip Roberts

ROBERTS, LEON JOSEPH
B. Oct. 27, 1963, Berkeley, Calif.
BB TR 5' 7" 150 lbs.

April		18	.258	.424	66	17	3	1	2	3.0	12	5	3	5	2									
May		26	.326	.495	95	31	8	1	2	2.1	16	10	12	13	6									
June		25	.294	.412	102	30	7	1	1	1.0	21	8	11	15	12									
July		26	.287	.333	87	25	4	0	0	0.0	14	6	10	7	4									
Aug		26	.340	.460	100	34	9	0	1	1.0	18	6	9	12	10									
Sept/Oct		28	.330	.462	106	35	5	0	3	2.8	23	9	10	13	12									
Day		44	.283	.408	152	43	7	0	4	2.6	26	17	20	27	15									
Night		105	.319	.443	404	129	29	3	5	1.2	78	27	35	38	31									
vs. Left			.294	.425	221	65	17	0	4	1.8	39	16	16	26	15									
vs. Right			.319	.439	335	107	19	3	5	1.5	65	28	39	39	31									
On Grass		110	.278	.384	414	115	20	3	6	1.4	77	27	38	46	34									
On Turf		39	.401	.577	142	57	16	0	3	2.1	27	17	17	19	12									
Home		74	.282	.387	287	81	14	2	4	1.4	53	17	19	31	19									
Road		75	.338	.483	269	91	22	1	5	1.9	51	27	36	34	27									

Division Rivals

vs. ATL		17	.315	.438	73	23	6	0	1	1.4	18	3	8	7	6									
vs. CIN		17	.333	.379	66	22	3	0	0	0.0	12	1	2	10	2									
vs. HOU		16	.309	.500	68	21	7	0	2	2.9	16	8	5	7	6									
vs. LA		16	.222	.315	54	12	2	0	1	1.9	8	3	3	11	5									
vs. SF		16	.267	.367	60	16	1	1	1	1.7	11	6	6	3	7									
On 3B < 2 Out			.500	.833	12	6	4	0	0	0.0	0	13	2	2										

1986	SD N	101	.253	.303	241	61	5	2	1	0.4	34	12	14	29	14	3	1	166	172	10	33	3.4	.971	2B-87
1988		5	.333	.333	9	3	0	0	0	0.0	1	0	1	2	0	2	0	2	3	1	1	1.2	.833	3B-2, 2B-1
1989		117	.301	.422	329	99	15	8	3	0.9	81	25	49	45	21	17	6	134	113	9	17	2.2	.965	OF-54, 3B-37, SS-14, 2B-9
1990		149	.309	.433	556	172	36	3	9	1.6	104	44	55	65	46	5	0	227	160	13	22	2.8	.968	OF-75, 3B-56, SS-18, 2B-8
4 yrs.		372	.295	.402	1135	335	56	13	13	1.1	220	81	119	141	81	27	7	529	448	33	73	2.7	.967	OF-129, 2B-105, 3B-95, SS-32

Year	Team	Games	BA	SA	AB	H	2B	3B	HR	HR%	R	RBI	BB	SO	SB	PINCH HIT AB	H	PO	A	E	DP	TC/G	FA	G by Pos

Billy Jo Robidoux

ROBIDOUX, WILLIAM JOSEPH
B. Jan. 13, 1964, Ware, Mass.
BL TR 6′ 1″ 200 lbs.

Year	Team	Games	BA	SA	AB	H	2B	3B	HR	HR%	R	RBI	BB	SO	SB	AB	H	PO	A	E	DP	TC/G	FA	G by Pos
1985	MIL	A	18	.176	.392	51	9	2	0	3	5.9	5	8	12	16	0	4	0	64	6	0	6	3.9	1.000	OF–11, 1B–6, DH–1
1986			56	.227	.287	181	41	8	0	1	0.6	15	21	33	36	0	2	0	326	29	5	35	6.4	.986	1B–43, DH–10
1987			23	.194	.194	62	12	0	0	0	0.0	9	4	8	17	0	4	0	53	4	1	9	2.5	.983	DH–10, 1B–10
1988			33	.253	.308	91	23	5	0	0	0.0	9	5	8	14	1	3	1	212	25	4	21	7.3	.983	1B–30, DH–1
1989	CHI	A	16	.128	.179	39	5	2	0	0	0.0	2	1	4	9	0	1	0	93	7	1	17	6.3	.990	1B–15, OF–1
1990	BOS	A	27	.182	.341	44	8	4	0	1	2.2	3	4	6	14	0	11	1	49	4	1	4	4.9	.981	1B–11, DH–4
6 yrs.			173	.209	.286	468	98	21	0	5	1.1	43	43	71	106	1	25	2	797	75	12	92	5.1	.986	1B–115, DH–26, OF–12

Dave Rohde

ROHDE, DAVID GRANT
B. May 8, 1964, Los Altos, Calif.
BB TR 6′ 2″ 180 lbs.

Year	Team	Games	BA	SA	AB	H	2B	3B	HR	HR%	R	RBI	BB	SO	SB	AB	H	PO	A	E	DP	TC/G	FA	G by Pos
1990	HOU	N	59	.184	.224	98	18	4	0	0	0.0	8	5	9	20	0	22	3	28	70	0	11	2.6	1.000	2B–32, 3B–4, SS–2

Ed Romero

ROMERO, EDGARDO RALPH
Born Edgardo Ralph Romero y Rivera.
B. Dec. 9, 1957, Santurce, Puerto Rico
BR TR 5′ 11″ 160 lbs.

Year	Team	Games	BA	SA	AB	H	2B	3B	HR	HR%	R	RBI	BB	SO	SB	AB	H	PO	A	E	DP	TC/G	FA	G by Pos
1977	MIL	A	10	.280	.320	25	7	1	0	0	0.0	4	2	4	3	0	0	0	9	24	1	3	3.4	.971	SS–10
1980			42	.260	.356	104	27	7	0	1	1.0	20	10	9	11	2	1	0	60	102	12	20	4.1	.931	SS–22, 2B–15, 3B–3
1981			44	.198	.264	91	18	3	0	1	1.1	6	10	4	9	0	0	0	61	102	6	29	3.8	.964	SS–22, 2B–18, 3B–3
1982			52	.250	.326	144	36	8	0	1	0.7	18	7	8	16	0	2	1	103	113	7	34	4.3	.969	2B–39, SS–10, 3B–2, OF–1
1983			59	.317	.386	145	46	7	0	1	0.7	17	18	8	8	1	14	6	59	58	5	14	2.1	.959	SS–22, OF–15, DH–5, 3B–5, 2B–3
1984			116	.252	.294	357	90	12	0	1	0.3	36	31	29	25	3	1	0	141	256	18	35	3.6	.957	3B–59, SS–39, 2B–11, 1B–4, DH–2, OF–1
1985			88	.251	.303	251	63	11	1	0	0.0	24	21	26	20	1	0	0	157	219	8	53	4.4	.979	SS–43, 2B–31, OF–14, 3B–1
1986	BOS	A	100	.210	.283	233	49	11	0	2	0.9	41	23	18	16	2	0	0	111	159	12	32	2.8	.957	SS–75, 3B–18, 2B–4, OF–1
1987			88	.272	.294	235	64	5	0	0	0.0	23	14	18	22	0	6	1	122	151	6	28	3.2	.978	2B–29, 3B–24, SS–24, 1B–8
1988			31	.240	.280	75	18	3	0	0	0.0	3	5	3	8	0	2	0	21	42	0	5	2.0	1.000	3B–15, SS–8, 2B–5, DH–1, 1B–1
1989	3 teams	BOS A (46G — .212)			ATL N (7G — .263)				MIL A (15G — .200)															
"	total	68	.214	.275	182	39	8	0	1	0.5	18	10	7	17	0	2	0	89	152	5	32	3.6	.980	2B–37, 3B–19, SS–13, DH–2
1990	DET	A	32	.229	.271	70	16	3	0	0	0.0	8	4	6	4	0	5	1	15	41	1	9	2.1	.982	3B–27, DH–3
12 yrs.			730	.247	.302	1912	473	79	1	8	0.4	218	155	140	159	9	33	9	948	1419	81	294	3.4	.967	SS–288, 2B–192, 3B–176, OF–32, DH–13, 1B–13

DIVISIONAL PLAYOFF SERIES

Year	Team	Games	BA	SA	AB	H	2B	3B	HR	HR%	R	RBI	BB	SO	SB	AB	H	PO	A	E	DP	TC/G	FA	G by Pos
1981	MIL	A	1	.500	.500	2	1	0	0	0	0.0	0	0	0	1	0	0	0	2	2	0	0	4.0	1.000	2B–1

LEAGUE CHAMPIONSHIP SERIES

Year	Team	Games	BA	SA	AB	H	2B	3B	HR	HR%	R	RBI	BB	SO	SB	AB	H	PO	A	E	DP	TC/G	FA	G by Pos
1986	BOS	A	1	.000	.000	2	0	0	0	0	0.0	0	0	0	0	0	0	0	0	0	0	0	0.0	—	SS–1
1988			1	—	—	0	0	0	0	0	—	0	0	0	0	0	0	0	0	0	0	0	0.0	—	
2 yrs.			2	.000	.000	2	0	0	0	0	0.0	0	0	0	0	0	0	0	0	0	0	0	0.0	.000	SS–1

WORLD SERIES

Year	Team	Games	BA	SA	AB	H	2B	3B	HR	HR%	R	RBI	BB	SO	SB	AB	H	PO	A	E	DP	TC/G	FA	G by Pos
1986	BOS	A	3	.000	.000	1	0	0	0	0	0.0	0	0	0	0	0	0	0	0	1	0	0	0.3	1.000	SS–3

Kevin Romine

ROMINE, KEVIN ANDREW
B. May 23, 1961, Exeter, N. H.
BR TR 5′ 11″ 185 lbs.

Year	Team	Games	BA	SA	AB	H	2B	3B	HR	HR%	R	RBI	BB	SO	SB	AB	H	PO	A	E	DP	TC/G	FA	G by Pos
1985	BOS	A	24	.214	.286	28	6	2	0	0	0.0	3	1	1	4	1	1	1	20	1	0	0	0.9	1.000	OF–23, DH–1
1986			35	.257	.314	35	9	2	0	0	0.0	6	2	3	9	2	1	0	45	1	0	1	1.3	1.000	OF–33
1987			9	.292	.375	24	7	2	0	0	0.0	5	2	2	6	0	1	0	10	1	0	1	1.2	1.000	OF–7, DH–2
1988			57	.192	.282	78	15	2	1	1	1.3	17	6	7	15	2	3	0	44	0	2	0	0.8	.957	OF–45, DH–5
1989			92	.274	.332	274	75	13	0	1	0.4	30	23	21	53	1	8	3	157	9	3	4	1.8	.982	OF–89, DH–2
1990			70	.272	.368	136	37	7	0	2	1.4	21	14	12	27	4	5	2	81	0	2	0	1.3	.976	OF–64, DH–1
6 yrs.			287	.259	.332	575	149	28	1	4	0.7	82	48	46	114	10	19	6	357	12	7	6	1.3	.981	OF–261, DH–11

Year	Team		Games	BA	SA	AB	H	2B	3B	HR	HR%	R	RBI	BB	SO	SB	PINCH HIT AB	H	PO	A	E	DP	TC/G	FA	G by Pos

Kevin Romine *Continued*

LEAGUE CHAMPIONSHIP SERIES

Year	Team		Games	BA	SA	AB	H	2B	3B	HR	HR%	R	RBI	BB	SO	SB	PH AB	H	PO	A	E	DP	TC/G	FA	G by Pos
1988	BOS	A	2	—	—	0	0	0	0	0	—	1	0	0	0	0	0	0	0	0	0	0	0.0	—	

Rolando Roomes

ROOMES, ROLANDO AUDLEY
B. Feb 15, 1962, Kingston, Jamaica
BR TR 6′ 3″ 180 lbs.

Year	Team		Games	BA	SA	AB	H	2B	3B	HR	HR%	R	RBI	BB	SO	SB	PH AB	H	PO	A	E	DP	TC/G	FA	G by Pos
1988	CHI	N	17	.188	.188	16	3	0	0	0	0.0	3	0	0	4	0	4	0	5	0	1	0	0.4	.833	OF-5
1989	CIN	N	107	.263	.419	315	83	18	5	7	2.2	36	34	13	100	12	11	4	201	4	4	0	2.0	.981	OF-100
1990	2 teams			CIN N	(30G —	.213)		MON N	(16G —	.286)																
"	total		46	.227	.333	75	17	0	1	2	2.6	6	8	1	26	0	14	4	39	1	0	0	1.6	1.000	OF-25
3 yrs.			170	.254	.394	406	103	18	6	9	2.2	45	42	14	130	12	29	8	245	5	5	0	1.5	.980	OF-130

Victor Rosario

ROSARIO, VICTOR MANUEL
Born Victor Manuel Rosario y Paredes.
B. Aug. 26, 1966 Hato Mayor Del Ray, Dominican Republic
BR TR 5′ 11″ 155 lbs.

Year	Team		Games	BA	SA	AB	H	2B	3B	HR	HR%	R	RBI	BB	SO	SB	PH AB	H	PO	A	E	DP	TC/G	FA	G by Pos
1990	ATL	N	9	.143	.143	7	1	0	0	0	0.0	3	0	1	1	0	1	0	3	4	0	0	1.8	1.000	SS-3, 2B-1

Bobby Rose

ROSE, ROBERT RICHARD
B. Mar. 15, 1967, Covina, Calif.
BR TR 5′ 11″ 170 lbs.

Year	Team		Games	BA	SA	AB	H	2B	3B	HR	HR%	R	RBI	BB	SO	SB	PH AB	H	PO	A	E	DP	TC/G	FA	G by Pos
1989	CAL	A	14	.211	.421	38	8	1	2	1	2.6	4	3	2	10	0	1	0	10	21	2	1	2.4	.939	3B-10, 2B-3
1990			7	.385	.615	13	5	0	0	1	7.6	5	2	2	1	0	2	1	3	7	0	1	1.4	1.000	2B-4, 3B-3
2 yrs.			21	.255	.471	51	13	1	2	2	3.9	9	5	4	11	0	3	1	13	28	2	2	2.0	.953	3B-13, 2B-7

Richard Rowland

ROWLAND, RICHARD GARNET
B. Feb. 25, 1967, Cloverdale, Calif.
BR TR 6′ 1″ 210 lbs.

Year	Team		Games	BA	SA	AB	H	2B	3B	HR	HR%	R	RBI	BB	SO	SB	PH AB	H	PO	A	E	DP	TC/G	FA	G by Pos
1990	DET	A	7	.158	.211	19	3	1	0	0	0.0	3	0	2	4	0	1	0	29	0	1	0	6.0	.967	C-5, DH-2

John Russell

RUSSELL, JOHN WILLIAM
B. Jan. 5, 1961, Oklahoma City, Okla.
BR TR 6′ 195 lbs.

Year	Team		Games	BA	SA	AB	H	2B	3B	HR	HR%	R	RBI	BB	SO	SB	PH AB	H	PO	A	E	DP	TC/G	FA	G by Pos
1984	PHI	N	39	.283	.444	99	28	8	1	2	2.0	11	11	12	33	0	9	4	51	1	0	0	1.3	1.000	OF-29, C-2
1985			81	.218	.398	216	47	12	0	9	4.2	22	23	18	72	2	15	4	170	9	4	7	2.3	.978	OF-49, 1B-18
1986			93	.241	.444	315	76	21	2	13	4.1	35	60	25	103	0	4	1	498	39	13	10	5.9	.976	C-89
1987			24	.145	.306	62	9	1	0	3	4.8	5	8	3	17	0	6	2	48	1	1	0	2.1	.980	OF-10, C-7
1988			22	.245	.388	49	12	1	0	2	4.1	5	4	3	15	0	7	0	77	9	5	3	4.1	.945	C-15
1989	ATL	N	74	.182	.233	159	29	2	0	2	1.3	14	9	8	53	0	17	1	196	28	4	1	3.1	.982	C-45, OF-14, 1B-2, 3B-2, P-1
1990	TEX	A	68	.273	.352	128	35	4	0	2	1.5	16	8	11	41	1	17	4	148	11	3	0	4.0	.981	C-31, DH-19, OF-6, 1B-3, 3B-1
7 yrs.			401	.230	.379	1028	236	49	3	33	3.2	108	123	80	334	3	75	16	1188	98	30	21	3.3	.977	C-158, OF-102, P-28, 1B-20, 3B-2

Mark Ryal

RYAL, MARK DWAYNE
B. Apr. 28, 1960, Henryetta, Okla.
BL TL 6′ 1″ 180 lbs.

Year	Team		Games	BA	SA	AB	H	2B	3B	HR	HR%	R	RBI	BB	SO	SB	PH AB	H	PO	A	E	DP	TC/G	FA	G by Pos
1982	KC	A	6	.077	.077	13	1	0	0	0	0.0	0	0	1	3	0	1	0	9	0	1	0	1.7	.900	OF-5
1985	CHI	A	12	.152	.242	33	5	3	0	0	0.0	4	3	3	3	0	0	0	21	0	0	0	1.8	1.000	OF-12
1986	CAL	A	13	.375	.563	32	12	0	0	2	6.3	6	5	2	4	1	5	2	32	2	1	1	2.7	.971	OF-6, 1B-4, DH-2
1987			58	.200	.410	100	20	6	0	5	5.0	7	18	5	15	0	31	10	50	1	3	1	0.9	.944	OF-21, DH-5, 1B-4
1989	PHI	N	29	.242	.303	33	8	2	0	0	0.0	2	5	1	9	0	19	4	17	0	0	0	0.6	1.000	1B-4, OF-4
1990	PIT	N	9	.083	.083	12	1	0	0	0	0.0	0	0	0	3	0	7	0	4	0	0	0	1.0	1.000	OF-4
6 yrs.			127	.211	.354	223	47	11	0	7	3.1	19	31	10	34	1	63	16	133	3	5	2	1.1	.965	OF-52, 1B-12, DH-7

Year	Team	Games	BA	SA	AB	H	2B	3B	HR	HR%	R	RBI	BB	SO	SB	PINCH HIT AB	H	PO	A	E	DP	TC/G	FA	G by Pos

Chris Sabo

SABO, CHRISTOPHER ANDREW (Spuds)
B. Jan. 19, 1962, Detroit, Mich.
BR TR 5′ 11″ 185 lbs.

Year	Team	Games	BA	SA	AB	H	2B	3B	HR	HR%	R	RBI	BB	SO	SB	AB	H	PO	A	E	DP	TC/G	FA	G by Pos
April		15	.391	.719	64	25	6	0	5	7.8	16	12	12	7	4									
May		25	.277	.485	101	28	6	0	5	5.0	19	15	9	7	9									
June		28	.301	.549	113	34	8	1	6	5.3	24	15	12	15	8									
July		26	.173	.296	98	17	6	0	2	2.0	12	7	11	9	2									
Aug		28	.255	.471	102	26	5	1	5	4.9	15	12	8	8	2									
Sept/Oct		26	.258	.404	89	23	7	0	2	2.2	9	10	9	12	0									
Day		36	.231	.440	134	31	7	0	7	5.2	18	20	15	15	6									
Night		112	.282	.487	433	122	31	2	18	4.2	77	51	46	43	19									
vs. Left			.327	.589	214	70	12	1	14	6.5	46	33	27	12	14									
vs. Right			.235	.408	353	83	26	1	11	3.1	49	38	34	46	11									
On Grass		43	.260	.458	177	46	14	0	7	4.0	25	18	14	16	5									
On Turf		105	.274	.485	390	107	24	2	18	4.6	70	53	47	42	20									
Home		76	.280	.509	275	77	18	0	15	5.5	49	45	33	28	15									
Road		72	.260	.445	292	76	20	2	10	3.4	46	26	28	30	10									
Division Rivals																								
vs. ATL		18	.386	.700	70	27	7	0	5	7.1	16	12	11	8	7									
vs. HOU		18	.262	.410	61	16	1	1	2	3.3	10	5	10	11	4									
vs. LA		16	.153	.441	59	9	2	0	5	8.5	9	15	5	6	1									
vs. SD		16	.246	.551	69	17	6	0	5	7.2	11	8	3	7	0									
vs. SF		15	.317	.467	60	19	9	0	0	0.0	6	6	4	5	1									
On 3B < 2 Out			.280	.480	25	7	2	0	1	4.0	1	16	4	3										
1988	CIN N	137	.271	.414	538	146	40	2	11	2.0	74	44	29	52	46	2	0	75	318	14	31	3.0	.966	3B-135, SS-2
1989		82	.260	.395	304	79	21	1	6	2.0	40	29	25	33	14	5	0	36	145	11	12	2.3	.943	3B-76
1990		148	.270	.476	567	153	38	2	25	4.4	95	71	61	58	25	1	0	70	273	12	17	2.4	.966	3B-146
3 yrs.		367	.268	.435	1409	378	99	5	42	3.0	209	144	115	143	85	8	0	181	736	37	60	2.6	.961	3B-357, SS-2

LEAGUE CHAMPIONSHIP SERIES

1990	CIN N	6	.227	.364	22	5	0	0	1	4.5	1	3	1	4	0	0	0	7	7	0	1	2.3	1.000	3B-6

WORLD SERIES

1990	CIN N	4	.563	1.000	16	9	1	0	2	12.5	2	5	2	2	0	0	0	3	14	0	0	4.3	1.000	3B-4

THIRD BASE — AVERAGE · RBI · HR · SB (NL AVG)

Mark Salas

SALAS, MARK BRUCE
B. Mar. 8, 1961, Montebello, Calif.
BL TR 6′ 180 lbs.

Year	Team	Games	BA	SA	AB	H	2B	3B	HR	HR%	R	RBI	BB	SO	SB	AB	H	PO	A	E	DP	TC/G	FA	G by Pos
1984	STL N	14	.100	.150	20	2	1	0	0	0.0	1	1	0	3	0	8	1	13	2	0	0	1.1	1.000	C-4, OF-3
1985	MIN A	120	.300	.458	360	108	20	5	9	2.5	51	41	18	37	0	12	1	529	39	5	10	4.8	.991	C-115, DH-3
1986		91	.233	.384	258	60	7	4	8	3.1	28	33	18	32	3	25	5	358	32	8	5	4.4	.980	C-69, DH-8
1987	2 teams	MIN A (22G — .378)		NY A (50G — .200)																				
"	total	72	.250	.400	160	40	6	0	6	3.8	21	21	15	23	0	19	4	258	16	1	0	3.8	.996	C-55, DH-4, OF-1
1988	CHI A	75	.250	.332	196	49	7	0	3	1.5	17	9	12	17	0	7	1	251	35	6	5	3.9	.979	C-69, DH-1
1989	CLE A	30	.221	.377	77	17	4	1	2	2.6	4	7	5	13	0	11	0	3	1	0	0	0.1	1.000	DH-20, C-5
1990	DET A	74	.232	.415	164	38	3	0	9	5.4	18	24	21	28	0	17	2	227	23	3	3	4.4	.988	C-57, DH-3, 3B-1
7 yrs.		476	.254	.399	1235	314	48	10	37	3.0	140	136	89	153	3	99	14	1639	148	23	23	3.8	.987	C-374, DH-39, OF-4, 3B-1

Luis Salazar

SALAZAR, LUIS ERNESTO
Born Luis Ernesto Salazar y Garacia.
B. May 19, 1956, Barcelona, Venezuela
BR TR 5′ 9″ 180 lbs.

Year	Team	Games	BA	SA	AB	H	2B	3B	HR	HR%	R	RBI	BB	SO	SB	AB	H	PO	A	E	DP	TC/G	FA	G by Pos
April		15	.245	.283	53	13	2	0	0	0.0	1	3	2	5	0									
May		14	.156	.289	45	7	0	0	2	4.4	5	7	7	8	1									
June		15	.438	.688	48	21	4	1	2	4.2	11	10	3	6	1									
July		25	.237	.376	93	22	2	1	3	3.2	11	12	3	12	0									
Aug		24	.236	.404	89	21	3	0	4	4.5	11	8	3	15	1									
Sept/Oct		22	.244	.329	82	20	2	1	1	1.2	5	7	1	13	0									
Day		61	.263	.401	217	57	5	2	7	3.2	28	26	9	30	2									
Night		54	.244	.373	193	47	8	1	5	2.6	16	21	10	29	1									
vs. Left			.293	.465	157	46	7	1	6	3.8	19	22	6	18	1									
vs. Right			.229	.340	253	58	6	2	6	2.4	25	25	13	41	2									

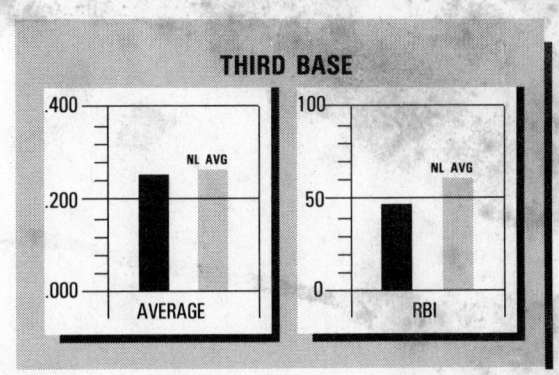

THIRD BASE — AVERAGE · RBI (NL AVG)

Year	Team	Games	BA	SA	AB	H	2B	3B	HR	HR%	R	RBI	BB	SO	SB	PINCH HIT AB	PINCH HIT H	PO	A	E	DP	TC/G	FA	G by Pos

Luis Salazar *Continued*

Year	Team	Games	BA	SA	AB	H	2B	3B	HR	HR%	R	RBI	BB	SO	SB	PH AB	PH H	PO	A	E	DP	TC/G	FA	G by Pos
On Grass		90	.267	.428	318	85	9	3	12	3.8	37	39	16	44	2									
On Turf		25	.207	.250	92	19	4	0	0	0.0	7	8	3	15	1									
Home		61	.294	.440	218	64	7	2	7	3.2	26	20	11	29	2									
Road		54	.208	.328	192	40	6	1	5	2.6	18	27	8	30	1									
Division Rivals																								
vs. MON		10	.333	.583	36	12	1	1	2	5.6	6	5	1	5	1									
vs. NY		16	.259	.407	54	14	2	0	2	3.7	7	6	1	6	0									
vs. PHI		9	.333	.364	33	11	1	0	0	0.0	4	3	2	3	0									
vs. PIT		15	.263	.368	57	15	3	0	1	1.8	5	7	0	10	0									
vs. STL		11	.283	.391	46	13	2	0	1	2.2	6	4	1	9	1									
On 3B < 2 Out			.364	.455	22	8	0	1	0	0.0	0	14	1	3										
1980	SD N	44	.337	.462	169	57	4	7	1	0.6	28	25	9	25	11	0	0	39	88	7	7	3.0	.948	3B-42, OF-4
1981		109	.303	.403	400	121	19	6	3	0.8	37	38	16	72	11	2	0	108	191	14	17	2.9	.955	3B-94, OF-23
1982		145	.242	.336	524	127	15	5	8	1.5	55	62	23	80	32	2	0	133	326	29	32	3.4	.941	3B-129, SS-18, OF-1
1983		134	.258	.387	481	124	16	2	14	2.9	52	45	17	80	24	6	2	122	274	21	22	3.1	.950	3B-118, SS-19
1984		93	.241	.329	228	55	7	2	3	1.3	20	17	6	38	11	14	4	87	97	6	5	2.0	.968	3B-58, OF-24, SS-4
1985	CHI A	122	.245	.404	327	80	18	2	10	3.1	39	45	12	60	14	15	6	180	57	10	13	2.0	.960	OF-84, 3B-39, DH-8, 1B-6
1986		4	.143	.143	7	1	0	0	0	0.0	1	0	1	3	0	2	0	0	0	0	0	0.0	—	DH-2
1987	SD N	84	.254	.328	189	48	5	0	3	1.6	13	17	14	30	3	18	3	56	95	9	11	1.9	.944	3B-38, SS-22, OF-10, P-2, 1B-1
1988	DET A	130	.270	.385	452	122	14	1	12	2.7	61	62	21	70	6	9	5	199	151	10	22	2.8	.972	OF-68, SS-37, 3B-31, 2B-5, 1B-4
1989	2 teams		SD N	(95G — .268)		CHI N	(26G — .325)																	
"	total	121	.282	.414	326	92	12	2	9	2.8	34	34	15	57	1	15	6	74	131	8	18	1.8	.962	3B-97, OF-16, SS-9, 1B-2
1990	CHI N	115	.254	.388	410	104	13	3	12	2.9	44	47	19	59	3	5	1	96	137	12	12	2.2	.951	3B-91, OF-28
11 yrs.		1101	.265	.381	3513	931	123	30	75	2.1	384	392	153	574	116	88	27	1094	1547	126	159	2.5	.954	3B-737, OF-258, SS-109, 1B-13, DH-10, 2B-5, P-2

LEAGUE CHAMPIONSHIP SERIES

Year	Team	Games	BA	SA	AB	H	2B	3B	HR	HR%	R	RBI	BB	SO	SB	PH AB	PH H	PO	A	E	DP	TC/G	FA	G by Pos
1984	SD N	3	.200	.600	5	1	0	1	0	0.0	0	0	0	1	0	1	0	0	3	0	0	1.0	1.000	OF-2, 3B-1
1989	CHI N	5	.368	.632	19	7	0	1	1	5.3	2	2	0	0	0	0	0	4	5	1	0	2.0	.900	3B-5
2 yrs.		8	.333	.625	24	8	0	2	1	4.2	2	2	0	1	0	1	0	4	8	1	0	1.6	.923	3B-6, OF-2

WORLD SERIES

Year	Team	Games	BA	SA	AB	H	2B	3B	HR	HR%	R	RBI	BB	SO	SB	PH AB	PH H	PO	A	E	DP	TC/G	FA	G by Pos
1984	SD N	4	.333	.333	3	1	0	0	0	0.0	0	0	0	0	0	1	1	1	0	0	0	0.3	1.000	OF-2, 3B-1

Juan Samuel

SAMUEL, JUAN MILTON ROMERO (Sammy)
Born Juan Milton Romero y Samuel.
B. Dec. 9, 1960, San Pedro de Macoris,
Dominican Republic
BR TR 5′ 11″ 170 lbs.

	Games	BA	SA	AB	H	2B	3B	HR	HR%	R	RBI	BB	SO	SB
April	21	.207	.317	82	17	4	1	1	1.2	10	4	11	29	11
May	25	.235	.333	102	24	4	0	2	2.0	12	7	4	27	9
June	21	.184	.329	76	14	5	0	2	2.6	7	7	8	23	6
July	27	.250	.380	92	23	3	0	3	3.3	14	13	12	18	7
Aug	23	.164	.200	55	9	0	1	0	0.0	3	3	9	17	2
Sept/Oct	26	.376	.671	85	32	8	1	5	5.9	16	18	7	12	3
Day	33	.248	.336	113	28	7	0	1	0.9	14	6	16	26	12
Night	110	.240	.396	379	91	17	3	12	3.2	48	46	35	100	26
vs. Left		.289	.524	187	54	10	2	10	5.3	28	25	17	43	10
vs. Right		.213	.295	305	65	14	1	3	1.0	34	27	34	83	28
On Grass	104	.252	.404	349	88	17	3	10	2.9	44	35	39	86	25
On Turf	39	.217	.329	143	31	7	0	3	2.1	18	17	12	40	13
Home	69	.246	.388	224	55	8	3	6	2.7	31	26	25	60	14
Road	74	.239	.377	268	64	16	0	7	2.6	31	26	26	66	24
Division Rivals														
vs. ATL	16	.283	.396	53	15	3	0	1	1.9	9	5	15	11	4
vs. CIN	17	.321	.554	56	18	8	1	1	1.8	5	11	2	11	2
vs. HOU	15	.125	.208	48	6	2	1	0	0.0	6	3	8	20	8
vs. SD	15	.276	.500	58	16	1	0	4	6.9	8	7	3	12	3
vs. SF	13	.313	.521	48	15	4	0	2	4.2	9	8	8	11	3
On 3B < 2 Out		.296	.481	27	8	2	0	1	3.7	1	19	0	9	

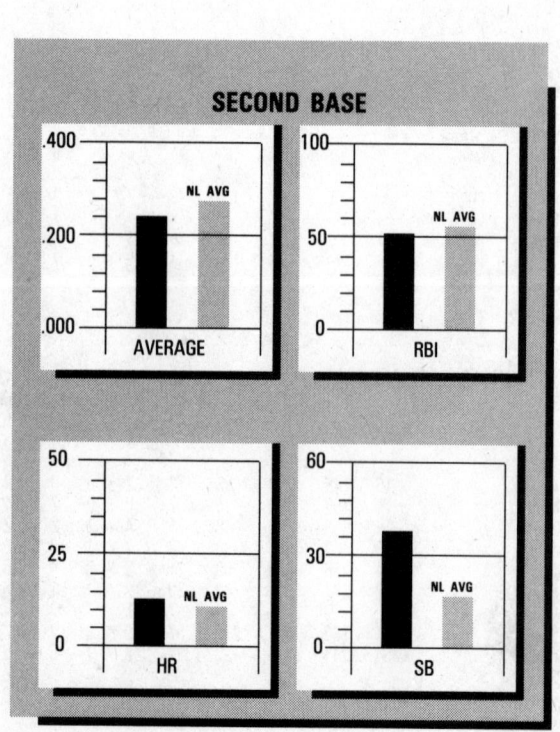

Year	Team		Games	BA	SA	AB	H	2B	3B	HR	HR%	R	RBI	BB	SO	SB	PINCH HIT AB	H	PO	A	E	DP	TC/G	FA	G by Pos

Juan Samuel *Continued*

Year	Team		Games	BA	SA	AB	H	2B	3B	HR	HR%	R	RBI	BB	SO	SB	AB	H	PO	A	E	DP	TC/G	FA	G by Pos
1983	PHI	N	18	.277	.446	65	18	1	2	2	3.1	14	5	4	16	3	0	0	44	54	9	9	5.9	.916	2B-18
1984			160	.272	.442	701	191	36	19	15	2.1	105	69	28	168	72	2	1	388	438	33	77	5.4	.962	2B-160
1985			161	.264	.436	663	175	31	13	19	2.9	101	74	33	141	53	1	0	389	463	15	88	5.4	.983	2B-159
1986			145	.266	.448	591	157	36	12	16	2.7	90	78	26	142	42	2	2	290	440	25	83	5.2	.967	2B-143
1987			160	.272	.502	655	178	37	15	28	4.3	113	100	60	162	35	0	0	374	434	18	99	5.2	.978	2B-160
1988			157	.243	.380	629	153	32	9	12	1.9	68	67	39	151	33	1	1	351	387	16	92	4.8	.979	2B-152, OF-3, 3B-1
1989	2 teams	PHI N (51G — .246)					NY N (86G — .228)																		
"	total		137	.235	.335	532	125	16	2	11	2.1	69	48	42	120	42	2	1	339	6	4	3	2.5	.989	OF-134
1990	LA	N	143	.242	.382	492	119	24	3	13	2.6	62	52	51	126	38	6	1	273	262	16	47	4.0	.971	2B-108, OF-31
8 yrs.			1081	.258	.422	4328	1116	213	75	116	2.7	622	493	283	1026	318	14	6	2448	2484	136	498	4.7	.973	2B-900, OF-168, 3B-1

LEAGUE CHAMPIONSHIP SERIES

Year	Team		Games	BA	SA	AB	H	2B	3B	HR	HR%	R	RBI	BB	SO	SB	AB	H	PO	A	E	DP	TC/G	FA
1983	PHI	N	1	—	—	0	0	0	0	0	—	0	0	0	0	0	0	0	0	0	0	0	0.0	—

WORLD SERIES

Year	Team		Games	BA	SA	AB	H	2B	3B	HR	HR%	R	RBI	BB	SO	SB	AB	H	PO	A	E	DP	TC/G	FA
1983	PHI	N	3	.000	.000	1	0	0	0	0	0.0	0	0	0	0	0	1	0	0	0	0	0	0.0	—

Ryne Sandberg

SANDBERG, RYNE DEE (Ryno)
B. Sept. 18, 1959, Spokane, Wash.
BR TR 6' 1" 175 lbs.

SECOND BASE — AVERAGE, RBI, HR, SB (player vs. NL AVG)

	Games	BA	SA	AB	H	2B	3B	HR	HR%	R	RBI	BB	SO	SB
April	19	.250	.329	76	19	3	0	1	1.3	8	7	2	11	3
May	28	.373	.686	118	44	10	0	9	7.6	22	21	12	13	6
June	29	.377	.789	114	43	3	1	14	12.3	32	25	13	16	6
July	25	.204	.296	98	20	4	1	1	1.0	14	10	6	15	1
Aug	26	.280	.514	107	30	5	1	6	5.6	19	16	8	16	6
Sept/Oct	28	.314	.627	102	32	5	0	9	8.8	21	21	9	13	3
Day	79	.320	.585	316	101	16	1	22	7.0	65	56	28	44	13
Night	76	.291	.532	299	87	14	2	18	6.0	51	44	22	40	12
vs. Left		.252	.453	214	54	13	0	10	4.7	38	23	21	34	7
vs. Right		.334	.616	401	134	17	3	30	7.5	78	77	29	50	18
On Grass	109	.329	.600	435	143	25	3	29	6.7	84	76	36	64	18
On Turf	46	.250	.461	180	45	5	0	11	6.1	32	24	14	20	7
Home	78	.357	.679	305	109	21	1	25	8.2	67	62	27	44	12
Road	77	.255	.442	310	79	9	2	15	4.8	49	38	23	40	13
Division Rivals														
vs. MON	17	.308	.569	65	20	2	0	5	7.7	18	8	5	8	3
vs. NY	18	.342	.671	76	26	2	1	7	9.2	13	22	7	15	3
vs. PHI	15	.356	.627	59	21	4	0	4	6.8	13	7	2	8	1
vs. PIT	18	.275	.464	69	19	4	0	3	4.3	11	8	1	6	5
vs. STL	17	.328	.672	67	22	2	0	7	10.4	16	13	11	4	3
On 3B < 2 Out		.286	.619	21	6	1	0	2	9.5	2	24	2	4	

Year	Team		Games	BA	SA	AB	H	2B	3B	HR	HR%	R	RBI	BB	SO	SB	AB	H	PO	A	E	DP	TC/G	FA	G by Pos
1981	PHI	N	13	.167	.167	6	1	0	0	0	0.0	2	0	0	1	0	0	0	7	7	0	1	1.1	1.000	SS-5, 2B-1
1982	CHI	N	156	.271	.372	635	172	33	5	7	1.1	103	54	36	90	32	1	0	136	373	12	28	3.3	.977	3B-133, 2B-24
1983			158	.261	.351	633	165	25	4	8	1.3	94	48	51	79	37	4	2	330	571	13	126	5.8	.986	2B-157, SS-1
1984			156	.314	.520	636	200	36	19	19	3.0	114	84	52	101	32	0	0	314	550	6	102	5.6	.993	2B-156
1985			153	.305	.504	609	186	31	6	26	4.3	113	83	57	97	54	1	0	353	501	12	99	5.7	.986	2B-153, SS-1
1986			154	.284	.411	627	178	28	5	14	2.2	68	76	46	79	34	1	1	309	492	5	86	5.2	.994	2B-153
1987			132	.294	.442	523	154	25	2	16	3.1	81	59	59	79	21	2	1	294	375	10	84	5.1	.985	2B-131
1988			155	.264	.419	618	163	23	8	19	3.1	77	69	54	91	25	2	0	291	522	11	79	5.3	.987	2B-153
1989			157	.290	.497	606	176	25	5	30	5.0	104	76	59	85	15	2	0	294	466	6	80	4.9	.992	2B-155
1990			155	.306	.559	615	188	30	3	40	6.5	116	100	50	84	25	2	0	278	469	8	81	4.9	.989	2B-154
10 yrs.			1389	.287	.452	5508	1583	256	57	179	4.6	872	649	464	786	275	15	4	2606	4326	83	766	5.1	.988	2B-1237, 3B-133, SS-7

LEAGUE CHAMPIONSHIP SERIES

Year	Team		Games	BA	SA	AB	H	2B	3B	HR	HR%	R	RBI	BB	SO	SB	AB	H	PO	A	E	DP	TC/G	FA	G by Pos
1984	CHI	N	5	.368	.474	19	7	2	0	0	0.0	3	2	3	2	3	0	0	12	18	1	6	6.2	.968	2B-5
1989			5	.400	.800	20	8	3	1	1	5.0	6	4	3	4	0	0	0	7	11	0	1	3.6	1.000	2B-5
2 yrs.			10	.385	.641	39	15	5	1	1	2.6	9	6	6	6	3	0	0	19	29	1	7	4.9	.980	2B-10

Year	Team	Games	BA	SA	AB	H	2B	3B	HR	HR%	R	RBI	BB	SO	SB	PINCH HIT AB	PINCH HIT H	PO	A	E	DP	TC/G	FA	G by Pos

Deion Sanders

SANDERS, DEION LUWYNN (Neon, Prime Time)
B. Aug. 9, 1967, Fort Myers, Fla.
BL TL 6′ 1″ 195 lbs.

Year	Team	Games	BA	SA	AB	H	2B	3B	HR	HR%	R	RBI	BB	SO	SB	PH AB	PH H	PO	A	E	DP	TC/G	FA	G by Pos
1989	NY A	14	.234	.404	47	11	2	0	2	4.3	7	7	3	8	1	1	0	30	1	1	0	2.3	.969	OF-14
1990		57	.158	.271	133	21	2	2	3	2.2	24	9	13	27	8	4	0	69	2	2	1	1.7	.973	OF-42, DH-4
2 yrs.		71	.178	.306	180	32	4	2	5	2.8	31	16	16	35	9	5	0	99	3	3	1	1.5	.971	OF-56, DH-4

Andres Santana

SANTANA, ANDRES CONFESOR
Born Andres Confesor Santana y Belonis.
B. Mar. 19, 1968, San Pedro de Macoris, Dominican Republic
BB TR 5′ 11″ 160 lbs.

Year	Team	Games	BA	SA	AB	H	2B	3B	HR	HR%	R	RBI	BB	SO	SB	PH AB	PH H	PO	A	E	DP	TC/G	FA	G by Pos
1990	SF N	6	.000	.000	2	0	0	0	0	0.0	0	1	0	0	0	0	0	2	1	0	1	1.0	1.000	SS-3

Rafael Santana

SANTANA, RAFAEL FRANCISCO (Ralph)
Born Rafael Francisco Santana y de la Cruz.
B. Jan. 31, 1958, La Romana, Dominican Republic
BR TR 6′ 1″ 156 lbs.

Year	Team	Games	BA	SA	AB	H	2B	3B	HR	HR%	R	RBI	BB	SO	SB	PH AB	PH H	PO	A	E	DP	TC/G	FA	G by Pos
1983	STL N	30	.214	.214	14	3	0	0	0	0.0	1	2	2	2	0	4	0	3	3	4	3	0.5	.733	2B-9, SS-6, 3B-4
1984	NY N	51	.276	.382	152	42	11	1	1	0.7	14	12	9	17	0	1	0	92	104	6	34	4.0	.970	SS-50
1985		154	.257	.302	529	136	19	1	1	0.2	41	29	29	54	1	1	0	301	396	25	81	4.7	.965	SS-153
1986		139	.218	.254	394	86	11	0	1	0.3	38	28	36	43	0	2	0	203	369	16	68	4.2	.973	SS-137, 2B-1
1987		139	.255	.346	439	112	21	2	5	1.1	41	44	29	57	1	1	0	213	396	17	82	4.5	.973	SS-138
1988		148	.240	.294	480	115	12	1	4	0.8	50	38	33	61	1	0	0	202	421	22	96	4.4	.966	SS-148
1990	CLE A	7	.231	.462	13	3	0	0	1	7.6	3	3	0	0	0	0	0	2	9	0	2	1.6	1.000	SS-7
7 yrs.		668	.246	.307	2021	497	74	5	13	0.6	188	156	138	234	3	9	0	1016	1703	90	366	4.2	.968	SS-639, 2B-10, 3B-4

LEAGUE CHAMPIONSHIP SERIES

Year	Team	Games	BA	SA	AB	H	2B	3B	HR	HR%	R	RBI	BB	SO	SB	PH AB	PH H	PO	A	E	DP	TC/G	FA	G by Pos
1986	NY N	6	.176	.176	17	3	0	0	0	0.0	0	0	0	3	0	0	0	13	18	0	5	5.2	1.000	SS-6

WORLD SERIES

Year	Team	Games	BA	SA	AB	H	2B	3B	HR	HR%	R	RBI	BB	SO	SB	PH AB	PH H	PO	A	E	DP	TC/G	FA	G by Pos
1986	NY N	7	.250	.250	20	5	0	0	0	0.0	3	2	2	5	0	0	0	11	17	1	4	4.1	.966	SS-7

Benito Santiago

SANTIAGO, BENITO
Born Benito Santiago y Rivera.
B. Mar. 9, 1965, Ponce, Puerto Rico
BR TR 6′ 1″ 180 lbs.

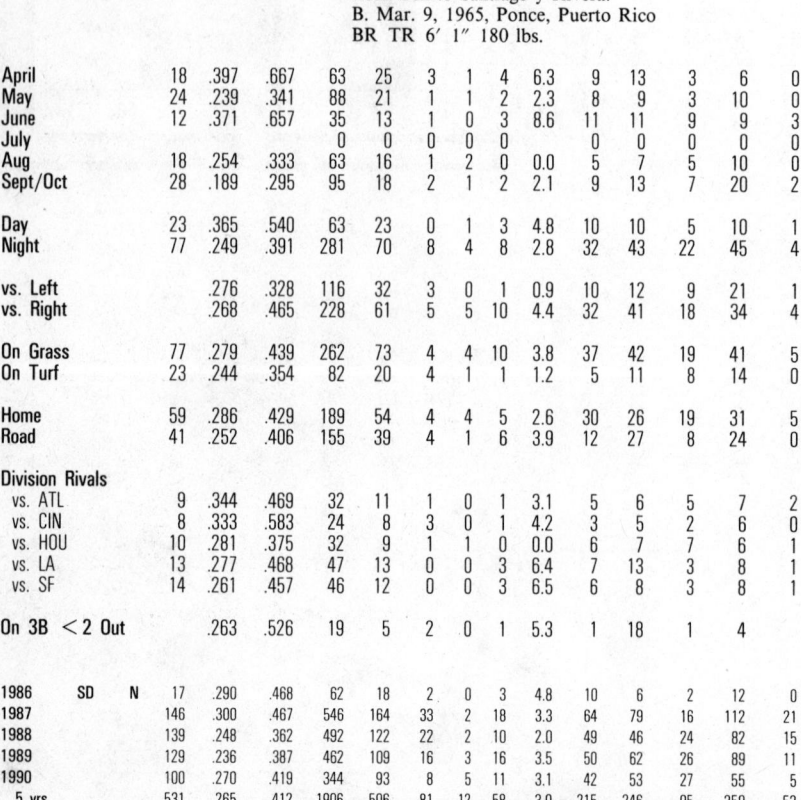

Split	Games	BA	SA	AB	H	2B	3B	HR	HR%	R	RBI	BB	SO	SB
April	18	.397	.667	63	25	3	1	4	6.3	9	13	3	6	0
May	24	.239	.341	88	21	1	1	2	2.3	8	9	3	10	0
June	12	.371	.657	35	13	1	0	3	8.6	11	11	9	9	3
July				0	0	0	0	0		0	0	0	0	0
Aug	18	.254	.333	63	16	1	2	0	0.0	5	7	5	10	0
Sept/Oct	28	.189	.295	95	18	2	1	2	2.1	9	13	7	20	2
Day	23	.365	.540	63	23	0	1	3	4.8	10	10	5	10	1
Night	77	.249	.391	281	70	8	4	8	2.8	32	43	22	45	4
vs. Left		.276	.328	116	32	3	0	1	0.9	10	12	9	21	1
vs. Right		.268	.465	228	61	5	5	10	4.4	32	41	18	34	4
On Grass	77	.279	.439	262	73	4	4	10	3.8	37	42	19	41	5
On Turf	23	.244	.354	82	20	4	1	1	1.2	5	11	8	14	0
Home	59	.286	.429	189	54	4	4	5	2.6	30	26	19	31	5
Road	41	.252	.406	155	39	4	1	6	3.9	12	27	8	24	0
Division Rivals														
vs. ATL	9	.344	.469	32	11	1	0	1	3.1	5	6	5	7	2
vs. CIN	8	.333	.583	24	8	3	0	1	4.2	3	5	2	6	0
vs. HOU	10	.281	.375	32	9	1	1	0	0.0	6	7	7	6	1
vs. LA	13	.277	.468	47	13	0	0	3	6.4	7	13	3	8	1
vs. SF	14	.261	.457	46	12	0	0	3	6.5	6	8	3	8	1
On 3B < 2 Out		.263	.526	19	5	2	0	1	5.3	1	18	1	4	

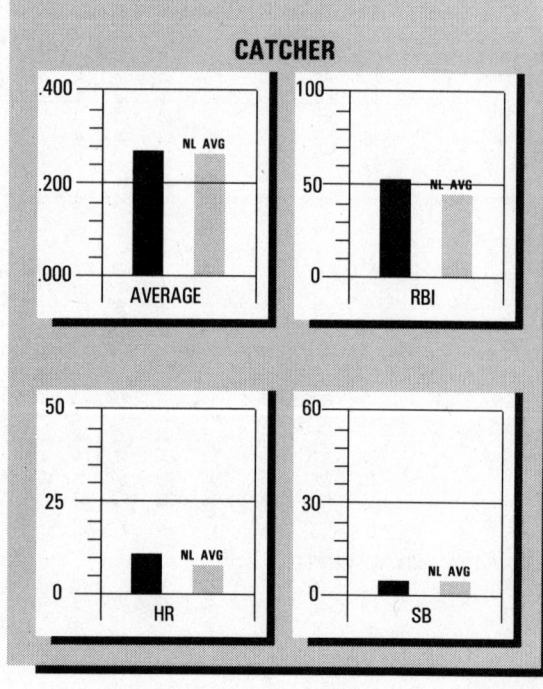

CATCHER

AVERAGE — NL AVG
RBI — NL AVG
HR — NL AVG
SB — NL AVG

Year	Team	Games	BA	SA	AB	H	2B	3B	HR	HR%	R	RBI	BB	SO	SB	PH AB	PH H	PO	A	E	DP	TC/G	FA	G by Pos
1986	SD N	17	.290	.468	62	18	2	0	3	4.8	10	6	2	12	0	0	0	80	7	5	2	5.4	.946	C-17
1987		146	.300	.467	546	164	33	2	18	3.3	64	79	16	112	21	0	0	817	80	22	12	6.3	.976	C-146
1988		139	.248	.362	492	122	22	2	10	2.0	49	46	24	82	15	7	2	725	75	12	11	5.8	.985	C-136
1989		129	.236	.387	462	109	16	3	16	3.5	50	62	26	89	11	2	0	685	81	20	10	6.1	.975	C-127
1990		100	.270	.419	344	93	8	5	11	3.1	42	53	27	55	5	2	0	538	51	12	6	6.1	.980	C-98
5 yrs.		531	.265	.412	1906	506	81	12	58	3.0	215	246	95	350	52	13	3	2845	294	71	41	6.0	.978	C-524

Year	Team		Games	BA	SA	AB	H	2B	3B	HR	HR%	R	RBI	BB	SO	SB	PINCH HIT AB	H	PO	A	E	DP	TC/G	FA	G by Pos

Nelson Santovenia SANTOVENIA, NELSON GIL
Born Nelson Gil Santovenia y Mayol.
B. July 27, 1961, Pinar del Rio, Cuba
BR TR 6′ 3″ 195 lbs.

Year	Team		Games	BA	SA	AB	H	2B	3B	HR	HR%	R	RBI	BB	SO	SB	AB	H	PO	A	E	DP	TC/G	FA	G by Pos
1987	MON	N	2	.000	.000	1	0	0	0	0	0.0	0	0	0	0	0	1	0	1	0	0	0	0.5	1.000	C-1
1988			92	.236	.392	309	73	20	2	8	2.6	26	41	24	77	2	1	1	465	63	9	7	5.8	.983	C-86, 1B-1
1989			97	.250	.352	304	76	14	1	5	1.6	30	31	24	37	2	7	1	564	66	12	8	6.6	.981	C-89, 1B-1
1990			59	.190	.331	163	31	3	1	6	3.6	13	28	8	31	0	10	4	264	24	6	7	5.8	.980	C-51
4 yrs.			250	.232	.363	777	180	37	4	19	2.4	69	100	56	145	4	19	6	1294	153	27	22	5.9	.982	C-227, 1B-2

Mackey Sasser SASSER, MACK DANIEL
B. Aug. 3, 1962, Fort Gaines, Ga.
BL TR 6′ 1″ 190 lbs.

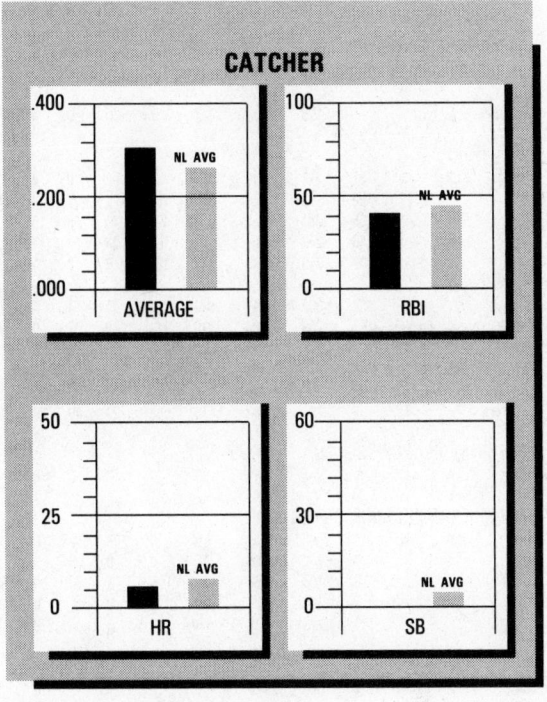

	Games	BA	SA	AB	H	2B	3B	HR	HR%	R	RBI	BB	SO	SB
April	8	.053	.053	19	1	0	0	0	0.0	1	0	1	2	0
May	14	.382	.500	34	13	1	0	1	2.9	6	6	5	2	0
June	22	.352	.465	71	25	5	0	1	1.4	10	8	5	3	0
July	18	.407	.704	54	22	4	0	4	7.4	10	20	0	3	0
Aug	25	.246	.308	65	16	4	0	0	0.0	3	3	3	7	0
Sept/Oct	13	.222	.222	27	6	0	0	0	0.0	1	4	1	2	0
Day	31	.352	.420	88	31	3	0	1	1.1	8	9	2	7	0
Night	69	.286	.429	182	52	11	0	5	2.7	23	32	13	12	0
vs. Left		.208	.321	53	11	3	0	1	1.9	5	7	3	10	0
vs. Right		.332	.452	217	72	11	0	5	2.3	26	34	12	9	0
On Grass	75	.275	.382	204	56	10	0	4	2.0	25	32	11	16	0
On Turf	25	.409	.561	66	27	4	0	2	3.0	6	9	4	3	0
Home	55	.245	.371	143	35	9	0	3	2.1	19	21	10	10	0
Road	45	.378	.488	127	48	5	0	3	2.4	12	20	5	9	0
Division Rivals														
vs. CHI	10	.226	.226	31	7	0	0	0	0.0	4	2	1	6	0
vs. MON	10	.276	.345	29	8	2	0	0	0.0	1	0	2	0	0
vs. PHI	11	.371	.629	35	13	3	0	2	5.7	3	6	2	2	0
vs. PIT	8	.286	.381	21	6	2	0	0	0.0	2	3	2	1	0
vs. STL	14	.333	.444	36	12	1	0	1	2.8	4	9	1	2	0
On 3B < 2 Out		.250	.750	12	3	0	0	2	16.7	2	9	2	2	

Year	Team		Games	BA	SA	AB	H	2B	3B	HR	HR%	R	RBI	BB	SO	SB	AB	H	PO	A	E	DP	TC/G	FA	G by Pos
1987	2 teams	SF N (2G — .000)				PIT N (12G — .217)																			
"	total		14	.185	.185	27	5	0	0	0	0.0	2	2	0	2	0	9	4	29	0	0	0	2.1	1.000	C-6
1988	NY	N	60	.285	.407	123	35	10	1	1	0.8	9	17	6	9	0	19	3	235	17	6	2	4.3	.977	C-42, 3B-1, OF-1
1989			72	.291	.407	182	53	14	2	1	0.5	17	22	7	15	0	17	5	335	19	3	3	5.0	.992	C-62, 3B-1
1990			100	.307	.426	270	83	14	0	6	2.2	31	41	15	19	0	25	6	501	43	14	4	6.4	.975	C-87, 1B-1
4 yrs.			246	.292	.405	602	176	38	3	8	1.3	59	82	28	45	0	70	18	1100	79	23	9	4.9	.981	C-197, 3B-2, 1B-1, OF-1

LEAGUE CHAMPIONSHIP SERIES
Year	Team		Games	BA	SA	AB	H	2B	3B	HR	HR%	R	RBI	BB	SO	SB	AB	H	PO	A	E	DP	TC/G	FA	G by Pos
1988	NY	N	4	.200	.200	5	1	0	0	0	0.0	0	0	0	1	0	2	0	2	0	0	0	0.5	1.000	C-2

Steve Sax SAX, STEPHEN LOUIS
Brother of Dave Sax.
B. Jan. 29, 1960, Sacramento, Calif.
BR TR 5′ 11″ 185 lbs.

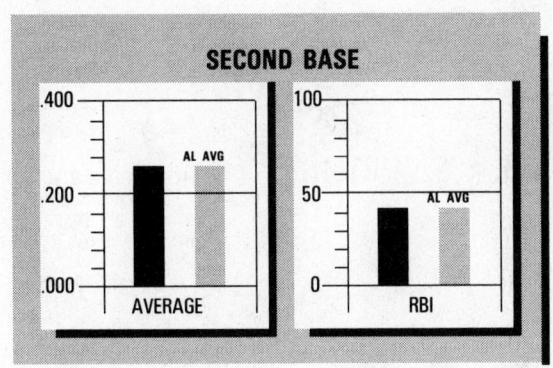

	Games	BA	SA	AB	H	2B	3B	HR	HR%	R	RBI	BB	SO	SB
April	17	.294	.353	68	20	1	0	1	1.5	7	5	7	3	3
May	25	.257	.297	101	26	4	0	0	0.0	15	5	9	5	9
June	27	.294	.358	109	32	5	1	0	0.0	14	8	6	12	6
July	28	.246	.351	114	28	6	0	2	1.8	10	13	9	11	10
Aug	29	.196	.223	112	22	3	0	0	0.0	7	4	7	11	5
Sept/Oct	29	.288	.378	111	32	5	1	1	0.9	17	7	11	4	10
Day	44	.322	.412	177	57	11	1	1	0.6	26	19	17	12	13
Night	111	.235	.290	438	103	13	1	3	0.7	44	23	32	34	30
vs. Left		.249	.299	177	44	7	1	0	0.0	19	11	20	10	17
vs. Right		.265	.336	438	116	17	1	4	0.9	51	31	29	36	26

Year	Team		Games	BA	SA	AB	H	2B	3B	HR	HR%	R	RBI	BB	SO	SB	PINCH HIT AB	H	PO	A	E	DP	TC/G	FA	G by Pos

Steve Sax *Continued*

On Grass			130	.255	.327	505	129	20	2	4	0.8	58	36	44	37	38									
On Turf			25	.282	.318	110	31	4	0	0	0.0	12	6	5	9	5									
Home			77	.259	.347	294	76	13	2	3	1.0	36	27	30	22	23									
Road			78	.262	.305	321	84	11	0	1	0.3	34	15	19	24	20									
Division Rivals																									
vs. BAL			12	.348	.413	46	16	3	0	0	0.0	9	3	3	4	5									
vs. BOS			13	.235	.392	51	12	3	1	1	2.0	6	4	1	6	3									
vs. CLE			12	.200	.244	45	9	2	0	0	0.0	5	4	6	3	5									
vs. DET			11	.238	.262	42	10	1	0	0	0.0	6	2	4	3	6									
vs. MIL			13	.367	.429	49	18	3	0	0	0.0	7	4	4	3	4									
vs. TOR			12	.264	.340	53	14	2	1	0	0.0	3	4	4	5	1									
On 3B < 2 Out				.318	.455	22	7	0	0	1	4.5	1	20	2	3										
1981	LA	N	31	.277	.345	119	33	2	0	2	1.7	15	9	7	14	5	2	1	64	93	4	22	5.2	.975	2B-29
1982			150	.282	.359	638	180	23	7	4	0.6	88	47	49	53	49	1	1	347	452	19	83	5.5	.977	2B-149
1983			155	.281	.350	623	175	18	5	5	0.8	94	41	58	73	56	4	1	331	399	30	74	4.9	.961	2B-152
1984			145	.243	.304	569	138	24	4	1	0.2	70	35	47	53	34	3	0	318	450	21	99	5.4	.973	2B-141
1985			136	.279	.318	488	136	8	4	1	0.2	62	42	54	43	27	1	0	330	358	22	84	5.2	.969	2B-135, 3B-1
1986			157	.332	.441	633	210	43	4	6	0.9	91	56	59	58	40	3	1	367	432	16	71	5.2	.980	2B-154
1987			157	.280	.369	610	171	22	7	6	1.0	84	46	44	61	37	5	0	343	420	14	92	4.9	.982	2B-152, 3B-1, OF-1
1988			160	.277	.343	**632**	175	19	4	5	0.8	70	57	45	51	42	2	2	276	429	14	69	4.5	.981	2B-158
1989	NY	A	158	.315	.387	**651**	205	26	3	5	0.8	88	63	52	44	43	0	0	312	460	10	117	4.9	.987	2B-158
1990			155	.260	.325	615	160	24	2	4	0.6	70	42	49	46	43	0	0	292	457	10	102	4.9	.987	2B-154
10 yrs.			1404	.284	.357	5578	1583	209	40	39	0.7	732	438	464	496	376	21	6	2980	3950	160	813	5.0	.977	2B-1382, 3B-2, OF-1
DIVISIONAL PLAYOFF SERIES																									
1981	LA	N	1	—	—	0	0	0	0	0	—	0	0	0	0	0	0	0	0	0	0	0	0.0	—	2B-1
LEAGUE CHAMPIONSHIP SERIES																									
1981	LA	N	1	—	—	0	0	0	0	0	—	0	0	0	0	0	0	0	0	1	0	0	1.0	1.000	2B-1
1983			4	.250	.250	16	4	0	0	0	0.0	0	0	1	0	1	0	0	11	12	0	3	5.8	1.000	2B-4
1985			6	.300	.450	20	6	3	0	0	0.0	1	1	1	5	0	0	0	12	20	0	6	5.3	1.000	2B-6
1988			7	.267	.267	30	8	0	0	0	0.0	7	3	3	3	5	0	0	12	23	0	6	4.9	1.000	2B-7
4 yrs.			18	.273	.318	66	18	3	0	0	0.0	8	4	5	8	6	0	0	35	55	0	9	5.0	.000	2B-18
WORLD SERIES																									
1981	LA	N	2	.000	.000	1	0	0	0	0	0.0	0	0	0	0	0	1	0	0	0	0	0	0.0	—	2B-1
1988			5	.300	.300	20	6	0	0	0	0.0	3	0	1	1	1	0	0	11	11	0	2	4.4	1.000	2B-5
2 yrs.			7	.286	.286	21	6	0	0	0	0.0	3	0	1	1	1	1	0	11	11	0	2	3.1	.000	2B-6

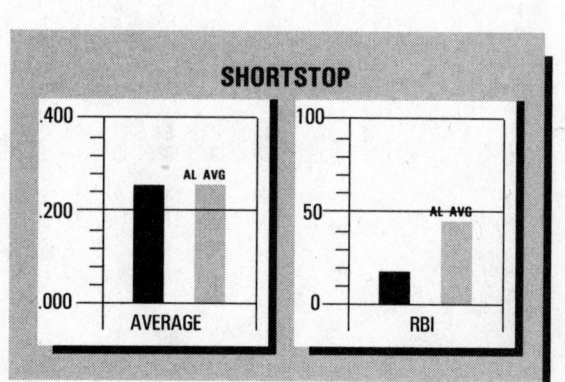

SECOND BASE
HR / AL AVG
SB / AL AVG

Jeff Schaefer

SCHAEFER, JEFFREY SCOTT
B. May 31, 1960, Patchogue, N.Y.
BR TR 5′ 10″ 170 lbs.

Year	Team		Games	BA	SA	AB	H	2B	3B	HR	HR%	R	RBI	BB	SO	SB	PINCH HIT AB	H	PO	A	E	DP	TC/G	FA	G by Pos
1989	CHI	A	15	.100	.100	10	1	0	0	0	0.0	2	0	0	2	1	0	0	5	7	2	4	0.9	.857	SS-5, 2B-4, 3B-4, DH-1
1990	SEA	A	55	.206	.234	107	22	3	0	0	0.0	11	6	3	11	4	2	1	52	87	5	20	2.8	.965	3B-26, SS-24, 2B-3
2 yrs.			70	.197	.222	117	23	3	0	0	0.0	13	6	3	13	5	2	1	57	94	7	24	2.3	.956	3B-30, SS-29, 2B-7, DH-1

Dick Schofield

SCHOFIELD, RICHARD CRAIG
Son of Dick Schofield.
B. Nov. 21, 1962, Springfield, Ill.
BR TR 5′ 10″ 175 lbs.

			Games	BA	SA	AB	H	2B	3B	HR	HR%	R	RBI	BB	SO	SB
April						0	0	0	0	0		0	0	0	0	0
May						0	0	0	0	0		0	0	0	0	0
June			22	.197	.242	66	13	0	0	1	1.5	7	1	13	13	0
July			22	.176	.176	74	13	0	0	0	0.0	4	2	8	20	0
Aug			28	.313	.350	80	25	3	0	0	0.0	19	7	19	15	2
Sept/Oct			27	.311	.389	90	28	5	1	0	0.0	11	8	12	13	1
Day			27	.208	.260	77	16	2	1	0	0.0	9	6	12	9	0
Night			72	.270	.309	233	63	6	0	1	0.4	32	12	40	52	3
vs. Left				.281	.337	89	25	2	0	1	1.1	18	6	18	14	1
vs. Right				.244	.281	221	54	6	1	0	0.0	23	12	34	47	2

SHORTSTOP
AVERAGE / AL AVG
RBI / AL AVG

Year	Team		Games	BA	SA	AB	H	2B	3B	HR	HR%	R	RBI	BB	SO	SB	PINCH HIT AB	PINCH HIT H	PO	A	E	DP	TC/G	FA	G by Pos

Dick Schofield *Continued*

Year	Team		Games	BA	SA	AB	H	2B	3B	HR	HR%	R	RBI	BB	SO	SB	PH AB	PH H	PO	A	E	DP	TC/G	FA	G by Pos
On Grass			86	.260	.302	265	69	6	1	1	0.4	39	15	47	51	3									
On Turf			13	.222	.267	45	10	2	0	0	0.0	2	3	5	10	0									
Home			54	.272	.329	158	43	4	1	1	0.6	24	12	30	26	2									
Road			45	.237	.263	152	36	4	0	0	0.0	17	6	22	35	1									
Division Rivals																									
vs. CHI			13	.268	.317	41	11	0	1	0	0.0	3	1	10	8	0									
vs. KC			11	.273	.333	33	9	2	0	0	0.0	2	1	5	9	0									
vs. MIN			5	.450	.550	20	9	2	0	0	0.0	4	3	2	1	0									
vs. OAK			6	.316	.421	19	6	2	0	0	0.0	5	1	3	2	1									
vs. SEA			7	.217	.217	23	5	0	0	0	0.0	2	4	3	3	0									
vs. TEX			9	.172	.276	29	5	0	0	1	3.4	6	3	6	8	0									
On 3B < 2 Out				.455	.455	11	5	0	0	0	0.0	0	8	3	2										
1983	CAL	A	21	.204	.407	54	11	2	0	3	5.6	4	4	6	8	0	0	0	24	67	7	10	4.7	.929	SS–21
1984			140	.193	.263	400	77	10	3	4	1.0	39	21	33	79	4	0	0	218	420	12	95	4.6	.982	SS–140
1985			147	.219	.331	438	96	19	3	8	1.8	50	41	35	70	11	1	0	261	397	25	108	4.6	.963	SS–147
1986			139	.249	.397	458	114	17	6	13	2.8	67	57	48	55	23	0	0	246	389	18	103	4.7	.972	SS–137
1987			134	.251	.355	479	120	17	3	9	1.9	52	46	37	63	19	0	0	205	351	9	76	4.2	.984	SS–131, 2B–2, DH–1
1988			155	.239	.317	527	126	11	6	6	1.1	61	34	40	57	20	0	0	278	492	13	125	5.1	.983	SS–155
1989			91	.228	.318	302	69	11	2	4	1.3	42	26	28	47	9	1	1	118	276	7	56	4.4	.983	SS–90
1990			99	.255	.297	310	79	8	1	1	0.3	41	18	52	61	3	0	0	170	318	17	77	5.1	.966	SS–99
8 yrs.			926	.233	.330	2968	692	95	24	48	1.6	356	247	279	440	89	2	1	1520	2710	108	650	4.7	.975	SS–920, 2B–2, DH–1

LEAGUE CHAMPIONSHIP SERIES

Year	Team		Games	BA	SA	AB	H	2B	3B	HR	HR%	R	RBI	BB	SO	SB	PH AB	PH H	PO	A	E	DP	TC/G	FA	G by Pos
1986	CAL	A	7	.300	.433	30	9	1	0	1	3.3	4	2	1	5	1	0	0	12	23	2	3	5.3	.946	SS–7

Bill Schroeder

SCHROEDER, ALFRED WILLIAM III
B. Sept. 7, 1958, Baltimore, Md.
BR TR 6' 2" 210 lbs.

Year	Team		Games	BA	SA	AB	H	2B	3B	HR	HR%	R	RBI	BB	SO	SB	PH AB	PH H	PO	A	E	DP	TC/G	FA	G by Pos
1983	MIL	A	23	.178	.356	73	13	2	1	3	4.1	7	7	3	23	0	0	0	92	5	2	1	4.3	.980	C–23
1984			61	.257	.486	210	54	6	0	14	6.7	29	25	8	54	0	1	0	277	24	4	2	5.0	.987	C–58, DH–3, 1B–1
1985			53	.242	.407	194	47	8	0	8	4.1	18	25	12	61	0	0	0	216	23	3	5	4.6	.988	C–48, DH–4, 1B–1
1986			64	.212	.373	217	46	14	0	7	3.2	32	19	9	59	1	0	0	307	25	1	13	5.2	.997	C–35, 1B–19, DH–10
1987			75	.332	.548	250	83	12	0	14	5.6	35	42	16	56	5	4	0	373	27	2	8	5.4	.995	C–67, 1B–4, DH–2
1988			41	.156	.295	122	19	2	0	5	4.1	9	10	6	36	0	0	0	197	21	0	3	5.3	1.000	C–30, 1B–10, DH–1
1989	CAL	A	41	.203	.348	138	28	2	0	6	4.3	16	15	3	44	0	0	0	252	32	3	10	7.0	.990	C–33, 1B–8
1990			18	.224	.483	58	13	3	0	4	6.8	7	9	1	10	0	0	0	100	10	0	2	6.1	1.000	C–15, 1B–3
8 yrs.			376	.240	.426	1262	303	49	1	61	4.8	153	152	58	343	6	5	0	1814	167	15	44	5.3	.992	C–309, 1B–46, DH–20

Rick Schu

SCHU, RICHARD SPENCER
B. Jan. 26, 1962, Philadelphia, Pa.
BR TR 6' 170 lbs.

Year	Team		Games	BA	SA	AB	H	2B	3B	HR	HR%	R	RBI	BB	SO	SB	PH AB	PH H	PO	A	E	DP	TC/G	FA	G by Pos
1984	PHI	N	17	.276	.621	29	8	2	1	2	6.9	12	5	6	6	0	2	0	7	13	1	3	1.2	.952	3B–15
1985			112	.252	.373	416	105	21	4	7	1.7	54	24	38	78	8	1	0	86	191	20	19	2.7	.933	3B–111
1986			92	.274	.447	208	57	10	1	8	3.8	32	25	18	44	2	29	7	42	94	13	6	1.6	.913	3B–58
1987			92	.235	.403	196	46	6	3	7	3.6	24	23	20	36	0	24	2	193	71	10	11	3.0	.964	3B–45, 1B–28
1988	BAL	A	89	.256	.363	270	69	9	4	4	1.5	22	20	21	49	6	5	1	94	110	11	8	2.4	.949	3B–72, DH–9, 1B–4
1989	2 teams		BAL A (1G — .000)					DET A (98G — .214)																	
"	total		99	.214	.335	266	57	11	0	7	2.6	25	21	24	37	1	10	2	59	126	12	14	2.0	.939	3B–83, DH–9, 2B–6, 1B–3, SS–3
1990	CAL	A	61	.268	.433	157	42	8	0	6	3.8	19	14	11	25	0	11	2	104	81	11	16	3.5	.944	3B–38, 1B–15, OF–4, 2B–1
7 yrs.			562	.249	.389	1542	384	67	13	41	2.7	188	132	138	275	17	82	14	585	686	78	77	2.4	.942	3B–422, 1B–50, DH–18, 2B–7, OF–4, SS–3

Jeff Schulz

SCHULZ, JEFFREY ALAN
B. June 2, 1961, Evansville, Ind.
BL TR 6' 1" 190 lbs.

Year	Team		Games	BA	SA	AB	H	2B	3B	HR	HR%	R	RBI	BB	SO	SB	PH AB	PH H	PO	A	E	DP	TC/G	FA	G by Pos
1989	KC	A	7	.222	.222	9	2	0	0	0	0.0	0	1	0	2	0	2	2	6	0	0	0	0.9	1.000	OF–5
1990			30	.258	.364	66	17	5	1	0	0.0	5	6	6	13	0	10	1	33	0	2	0	1.6	.943	OF–22, DH–1
2 yrs.			37	.253	.347	75	19	5	1	0	0.0	5	7	6	15	0	12	3	39	0	2	0	1.1	.000	OF–27, DH–1

SHORTSTOP

HR — AL AVG

SB — AL AVG

Year	Team		Games	BA	SA	AB	H	2B	3B	HR	HR%	R	RBI	BB	SO	SB	PINCH HIT AB	PINCH HIT H	PO	A	E	DP	TC/G	FA	G by Pos

Mike Scioscia

SCIOSCIA, MICHAEL LORRI
B. Nov. 27, 1958, Upper Darby, Pa.
BL TR 6′ 2″ 200 lbs.

April			20	.294	.456	68	20	2	0	3	4.4	10	8	3	3	0									
May			24	.276	.447	76	21	4	0	3	3.9	8	14	8	5	1									
June			24	.208	.312	77	16	2	0	2	2.6	8	9	7	8	0									
July			20	.269	.418	67	18	7	0	1	1.5	3	14	11	2	1									
Aug			24	.310	.465	71	22	5	0	2	2.8	7	13	15	8	2									
Sept/Oct			23	.237	.342	76	18	5	0	1	1.3	10	8	11	5	0									
Day			31	.297	.475	101	30	6	0	4	4.0	8	14	10	7	2									
Night			104	.254	.383	334	85	19	0	8	2.4	38	52	45	24	2									
vs. Left				.235	.328	119	28	5	0	2	1.7	13	18	10	11	2									
vs. Right				.275	.434	316	87	20	0	10	3.2	33	48	45	20	2									
On Grass			98	.275	.396	313	86	17	0	7	2.2	34	46	40	18	4									
On Turf			37	.238	.426	122	29	8	0	5	4.1	12	20	15	13	0									
Home			67	.279	.409	208	58	12	0	5	2.4	26	32	29	12	3									
Road			68	.251	.401	227	57	13	0	7	3.1	20	34	26	19	1									
Division Rivals																									
vs. ATL			16	.216	.294	51	11	1	0	1	2.0	5	6	9	3	0									
vs. CIN			13	.256	.359	39	10	4	0	0	0.0	5	3	6	7	0									
vs. HOU			18	.226	.435	62	14	1	0	4	6.5	7	9	3	2	0									
vs. SD			12	.154	.256	39	6	1	0	1	2.6	1	3	2	4	0									
vs. SF			16	.328	.517	58	19	5	0	2	3.4	10	9	6	3	1									
On 3B < 2 Out				.357	.393	28	10	1	0	0	0.0	0	23	3	2										
1980	LA	N	54	.254	.328	134	34	5	1	1	0.7	8	8	12	9	1	1	0	226	26	2	5	4.7	.992	C-54
1981			93	.276	.331	290	80	10	0	2	0.7	27	29	36	18	0	2	1	493	48	7	4	5.9	.987	C-91
1982			129	.219	.296	365	80	11	1	5	1.4	31	38	44	31	2	8	0	631	57	10	10	5.4	.986	C-123
1983			12	.314	.486	35	11	3	0	1	2.9	3	7	5	2	0	1	0	55	4	0	0	4.9	1.000	C-11
1984			114	.273	.370	341	93	18	0	5	1.5	29	38	52	26	2	7	0	701	64	12	8	6.8	.985	C-112
1985			141	.296	.420	429	127	26	3	7	1.6	47	53	77	21	3	7	1	818	66	13	8	6.4	.986	C-139
1986			122	.251	.345	374	94	18	1	5	1.3	36	26	62	23	3	10	1	756	64	15	4	6.8	.982	C-119
1987			142	.265	.364	461	122	26	1	6	1.3	44	38	55	23	7	11	4	925	80	11	11	7.2	.989	C-138
1988			130	.257	.324	408	105	18	0	3	0.7	29	35	38	31	0	7	1	748	63	7	10	6.3	.991	C-123
1989			133	.250	.363	408	102	16	0	10	2.5	40	44	52	29	0	6	2	822	82	11	12	6.9	.988	C-130
1990			135	.264	.405	435	115	25	0	12	2.7	46	66	55	31	4	5	0	842	58	10	9	6.9	.989	C-132
11 yrs.			1205	.262	.360	3680	963	176	7	57	1.5	340	382	488	244	22	65	10	7017	612	98	81	6.4	.987	C-1172

DIVISIONAL PLAYOFF SERIES

Year	Team		Games	BA	SA	AB	H	2B	3B	HR	HR%	R	RBI	BB	SO	SB	PINCH HIT AB	PINCH HIT H	PO	A	E	DP	TC/G	FA	G by Pos
1981	LA	N	4	.154	.154	13	2	0	0	0	0.0	0	1	1	2	0	0	0	21	3	0	0	6.0	1.000	C-4

LEAGUE CHAMPIONSHIP SERIES

1981	LA	N	5	.133	.333	15	2	0	0	1	6.7	1	1	2	1	0	0	0	27	1	0	0	5.6	1.000	C-5
1985			6	.250	.250	16	4	0	0	0	0.0	2	1	4	0	0	0	0	31	4	1	0	6.0	.972	C-6
1988			7	.364	.545	22	8	1	0	1	4.5	3	2	1	2	0	0	0	37	4	0	1	5.9	1.000	C-7
3 yrs.			18	.264	.396	53	14	1	0	2	3.8	6	4	7	3	0	0	0	95	9	1	1	5.8	.990	C-18

WORLD SERIES

1981	LA	N	3	.250	.250	4	1	0	0	0	0.0	1	0	1	0	0	1	0	7	1	0	0	2.7	1.000	C-3
1988			4	.214	.214	14	3	0	0	0	0.0	0	1	0	2	0	0	0	28	0	1	0	7.3	.966	C-4
2 yrs.			7	.222	.222	18	4	0	0	0	0.0	1	1	1	2	0	1	0	35	1	1	0	5.3	.973	C-7

David Segui

SEGUI, DAVID VINCENT
Son of Diego Segui.
B. July 19, 1966, Kansas City, Kans.
BB TL 6′ 1″ 170 lbs.

1990	BAL	A	40	.244	.350	123	30	7	0	2	1.6	14	15	11	15	0	0	0	283	26	3	24	8.7	.990	1B-36, DH-4

Year	Team	Games	BA	SA	AB	H	2B	3B	HR	HR%	R	RBI	BB	SO	SB	PINCH HIT AB	PINCH HIT H	PO	A	E	DP	TC/G	FA	G by Pos

Kevin Seitzer

SEITZER, KEVIN LEE
B. Mar. 26, 1962, Springfield, Ill.
BR TR 5′ 11″ 180 lbs.

Period	Games	BA	SA	AB	H	2B	3B	HR	HR%	R	RBI	BB	SO	SB
April	18	.231	.256	78	18	2	0	0	0.0	5	2	2	7	1
May	27	.324	.426	108	35	6	1	1	0.9	16	6	14	12	0
June	27	.330	.486	109	36	9	1	2	1.8	15	9	9	7	1
July	28	.250	.336	116	29	3	2	1	0.9	20	8	13	13	3
Aug	29	.257	.330	109	28	6	1	0	0.0	21	7	14	12	2
Sept/Oct	29	.245	.353	102	25	5	0	2	2.0	14	6	15	15	0
Day	38	.245	.350	143	35	7	1	2	1.4	23	6	16	15	1
Night	120	.284	.376	479	136	24	4	4	0.8	68	32	51	51	6
vs. Left		.278	.455	209	58	17	4	4	1.9	29	23	22	22	0
vs. Right		.274	.327	413	113	14	1	2	0.5	62	15	45	44	7
On Grass	59	.232	.270	233	54	5	2	0	0.0	27	8	26	24	2
On Turf	99	.301	.429	389	117	26	3	6	1.5	64	30	41	42	5
Home	80	.312	.451	308	96	22	3	5	1.6	56	26	35	32	4
Road	78	.239	.290	314	75	9	2	1	0.3	35	12	32	34	3
Division Rivals														
vs. CAL	12	.318	.341	44	14	1	0	0	0.0	7	1	8	4	0
vs. CHI	13	.333	.467	45	15	4	1	0	0.0	9	3	7	2	0
vs. MIN	13	.314	.490	51	16	3	0	2	3.9	10	5	6	4	2
vs. OAK	13	.231	.365	52	12	4	0	1	1.9	6	3	4	5	0
vs. SEA	13	.292	.396	48	14	3	1	0	0.0	7	3	7	7	0
vs. TEX	13	.245	.265	49	12	1	0	0	0.0	7	1	6	7	1
On 3B < 2 Out		.250	.500	16	4	0	2	0	0.0	0	9	4	3	

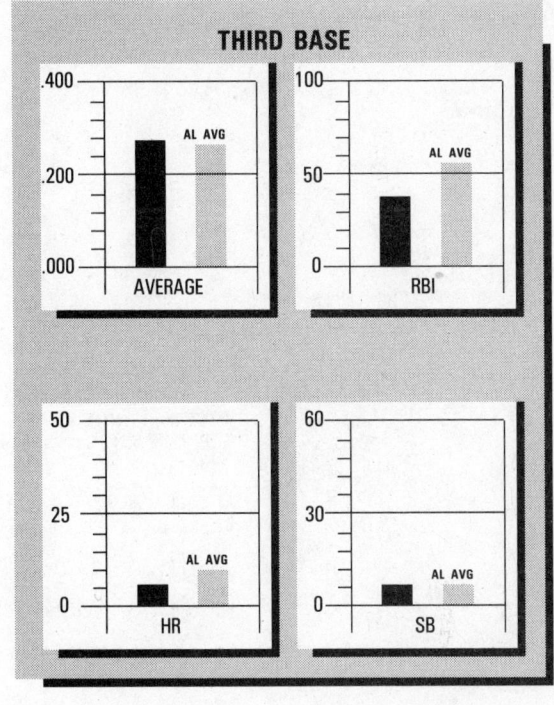

THIRD BASE — AVERAGE (AL AVG), RBI (AL AVG), HR (AL AVG), SB (AL AVG)

Year	Team		Games	BA	SA	AB	H	2B	3B	HR	HR%	R	RBI	BB	SO	SB	AB	H	PO	A	E	DP	TC/G	FA	G by Pos
1986	KC	A	28	.323	.448	96	31	4	1	2	2.1	16	11	19	14	0	1	1	224	19	3	17	8.8	.988	1B-22, OF-5, 3B-3
1987			161	.323	.470	641	**207**	33	8	15	2.3	105	83	80	85	12	0	0	290	315	24	51	3.9	.962	3B-141, 1B-25, OF-3
1988			149	.304	.406	559	170	32	5	5	0.9	90	60	72	64	10	1	0	93	297	26	33	2.8	.938	3B-147, DH-1, OF-1
1989			160	.281	.337	597	168	17	2	4	0.7	78	48	102	76	17	0	0	118	277	20	30	2.6	.952	3B-159, SS-6, OF-3, 1B-2
1990			158	.275	.370	622	171	31	5	6	0.9	91	38	67	66	7	5	3	118	281	19	36	2.7	.955	3B-152, 2B-10
5 yrs.			656	.297	.398	2515	747	117	21	32	1.3	380	240	340	305	46	7	4	843	1189	92	167	3.2	.957	3B-602, 1B-49, OF-12, 2B-10, SS-6, DH-1

Mike Sharperson

SHARPERSON, MICHAEL TYRONE
B. Oct. 4, 1961, Orangeburg, S. C.
BR TR 6′ 1″ 175 lbs.

Period	Games	BA	SA	AB	H	2B	3B	HR	HR%	R	RBI	BB	SO	SB
April	13	.276	.345	29	8	2	0	0	0.0	3	3	2	1	0
May	23	.306	.355	62	19	3	0	0	0.0	8	5	7	10	5
June	20	.339	.393	56	19	1	1	0	0.0	5	9	9	6	2
July	18	.348	.413	46	16	3	0	0	0.0	5	4	7	5	1
Aug	26	.282	.365	85	24	1	0	2	2.4	9	6	12	10	6
Sept/Oct	29	.253	.367	79	20	4	1	1	1.3	12	9	9	7	1
Day	32	.351	.464	97	34	5	0	2	2.1	13	18	10	12	8
Night	97	.277	.338	260	72	9	2	1	0.4	29	18	36	27	7
vs. Left		.322	.385	208	67	8	1	1	0.5	29	17	25	23	10
vs. Right		.262	.356	149	39	6	1	2	1.3	13	19	21	16	5
On Grass	99	.318	.379	280	89	9	1	2	0.7	32	27	35	29	13
On Turf	30	.221	.351	77	17	5	1	1	1.3	10	9	11	10	2
Home	69	.308	.369	195	60	7	1	1	0.5	22	19	21	18	7
Road	60	.284	.377	162	46	7	1	2	1.2	20	17	25	21	8
Division Rivals														
vs. ATL	13	.400	.489	45	18	4	0	0	0.0	5	6	7	4	3
vs. CIN	16	.280	.360	50	14	2	1	0	0.0	8	3	2	3	1
vs. HOU	12	.250	.393	28	7	2	1	0	0.0	2	2	9	3	2
vs. SD	14	.229	.229	35	8	0	0	0	0.0	3	6	3	3	0
vs. SF	15	.250	.250	40	10	0	0	0	0.0	5	5	7	8	1
On 3B < 2 Out		.353	.353	17	6	0	0	0	0.0	0	14	3	1	

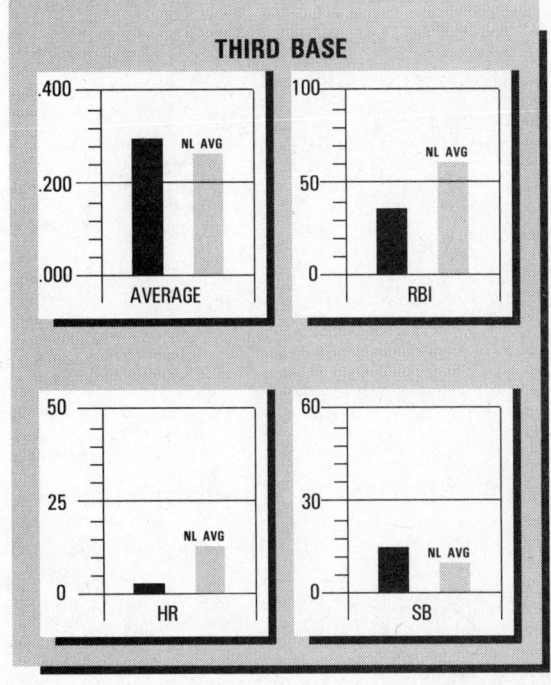

THIRD BASE — AVERAGE (NL AVG), RBI (NL AVG), HR (NL AVG), SB (NL AVG)

Year	Team	Games	BA	SA	AB	H	2B	3B	HR	HR%	R	RBI	BB	SO	SB	PINCH HIT AB	H	PO	A	E	DP	TC/G	FA	G by Pos

Mike Sharperson *Continued*

Year	Team	Games	BA	SA	AB	H	2B	3B	HR	HR%	R	RBI	BB	SO	SB	AB	H	PO	A	E	DP	TC/G	FA	G by Pos
1987	2 teams		TOR A	(32G — .208)		LA N	(10G — .273)																	
"	total	42	.225	.287	129	29	6	1	0	0.0	11	10	11	20	2	0	0	68	97	5	18	4.0	.971	2B-38, 3B-7
1988	LA N	46	.271	.288	59	16	1	0	0	0.0	8	4	1	12	0	22	3	19	31	2	5	1.1	.962	2B-20, 3B-6, SS-4
1989		27	.250	.357	28	7	3	0	0	0.0	2	5	4	7	0	15	3	11	8	0	2	0.7	1.000	2B-4, 1B-2, 3B-2, SS-1
1990		129	.297	.373	357	106	14	2	3	0.8	42	36	46	39	15	19	7	152	193	15	23	3.0	.958	3B-106, SS-15, 2B-9, 1B-6
4 yrs.		244	.276	.344	573	158	24	3	3	0.5	63	55	62	78	17	56	13	250	329	22	48	2.5	.963	3B-121, 2B-71, SS-20, 1B-8

LEAGUE CHAMPIONSHIP SERIES

Year	Team	Games	BA	SA	AB	H	2B	3B	HR	HR%	R	RBI	BB	SO	SB	AB	H	PO	A	E	DP	TC/G	FA	G by Pos
1988	LA N	2	.000	.000	1	0	0	0	0	0.0	0	1	1	0	0	1	0	1	0	0	0	0.5	1.000	3B-1, SS-1

Larry Sheets

SHEETS, LARRY KENT
B. Dec. 6, 1959, Staunton, Va.
BL TR 6' 4" 210 lbs.

	Games	BA	SA	AB	H	2B	3B	HR	HR%	R	RBI	BB	SO	SB
April	16	.295	.386	44	13	4	0	0	0.0	6	5	5	5	0
May	25	.328	.508	61	20	2	0	3	4.9	10	7	2	2	0
June	20	.214	.357	56	12	3	1	1	1.8	5	6	5	7	0
July	21	.264	.458	72	19	3	1	3	4.2	8	17	5	11	1
Aug	25	.306	.431	72	22	3	0	2	2.8	7	12	4	7	0
Sept/Oct	24	.145	.236	55	8	2	0	1	1.8	4	5	3	10	0
Day	36	.245	.383	94	23	5	1	2	2.1	13	11	11	10	0
Night	95	.267	.410	266	71	12	1	8	3.0	27	41	13	32	1
vs. Left		.235	.235	17	4	0	0	0	0.0	3	1	1	3	0
vs. Right		.262	.411	343	90	17	2	10	2.9	37	51	23	39	1
On Grass	112	.260	.412	308	80	16	2	9	2.9	37	39	20	38	1
On Turf	19	.269	.346	52	14	1	0	1	1.9	3	13	4	4	0
Home	67	.246	.419	179	44	8	1	7	3.9	17	30	11	27	1
Road	64	.276	.387	181	50	9	1	3	1.7	23	22	13	15	0
Division Rivals														
vs. BAL	12	.237	.447	38	9	2	0	2	5.3	5	5	2	6	0
vs. BOS	10	.343	.629	35	12	5	1	1	2.9	7	9	3	5	0
vs. CLE	10	.303	.333	33	10	1	0	0	0.0	1	4	1	2	0
vs. MIL	12	.233	.300	30	7	2	0	0	0.0	3	1	0	2	0
vs. NY	9	.222	.333	27	6	0	0	1	3.7	2	4	1	5	0
vs. TOR	11	.240	.520	25	6	1	0	2	8.0	4	6	0	2	0
On 3B < 2 Out		.368	.684	19	7	1	1	1	5.3	1	18	1	4	

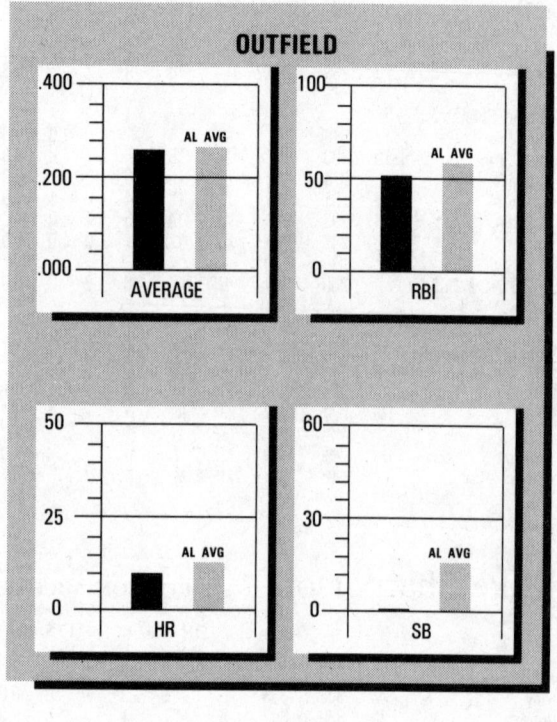

OUTFIELD
AVERAGE · RBI · HR · SB (AL AVG)

Year	Team	Games	BA	SA	AB	H	2B	3B	HR	HR%	R	RBI	BB	SO	SB	AB	H	PO	A	E	DP	TC/G	FA	G by Pos
1984	BAL A	8	.438	.688	16	7	1	0	1	6.3	3	2	1	3	0	1	0	12	1	0	0	1.6	1.000	OF-7
1985		113	.262	.442	328	86	8	0	17	5.2	43	50	28	52	0	16	4	12	1	1	1	0.1	.929	DH-93, OF-9, 1B-1
1986		112	.272	.488	338	92	17	1	18	5.3	42	60	21	56	2	13	2	90	8	3	4	0.9	.970	DH-58, OF-32, C-6, 1B-4, 3B-2
1987		135	.316	.563	469	148	23	0	31	6.6	74	94	31	67	1	6	3	243	7	7	3	1.9	.973	OF-124, DH-7, 1B-3
1988		136	.230	.343	452	104	19	1	10	2.2	38	47	42	72	1	12	5	159	12	4	3	1.3	.977	OF-76, DH-50, 1B-3
1989		102	.243	.359	304	74	12	1	7	2.3	33	33	26	58	1	18	6	0	0	0	0	0.0	—	DH-88
1990	DET A	131	.261	.403	360	94	17	2	10	2.7	40	52	24	42	1	21	4	98	7	2	1	1.4	.981	OF-79, DH-44
7 yrs.		737	.267	.438	2267	605	97	5	94	4.1	273	338	173	350	6	87	24	614	36	17	12	0.9	.975	DH-340, OF-327, 1B-11, C-6, 3B-2

Gary Sheffield

SHEFFIELD, GARY ANTONIAN
B. Nov. 18, 1968, Tampa, Fla.
BR TR 5' 11" 190 lbs.

	Games	BA	SA	AB	H	2B	3B	HR	HR%	R	RBI	BB	SO	SB
April	16	.267	.350	60	16	5	0	0	0.0	6	10	5	4	2
May	18	.362	.507	69	25	7	0	1	1.4	15	3	6	6	7
June	25	.276	.449	98	27	8	0	3	3.1	14	18	9	15	4
July	27	.368	.521	117	43	7	1	3	2.6	14	21	6	4	5
Aug	28	.221	.298	104	23	2	0	2	1.9	12	12	12	10	5
Sept/Oct	11	.231	.333	39	9	1	0	1	2.6	6	3	6	2	2
Day	41	.277	.403	159	44	8	0	4	2.5	20	23	13	12	11
Night	84	.302	.430	328	99	22	1	6	1.8	47	44	31	29	14
vs. Left		.274	.444	135	37	12	1	3	2.2	22	18	14	15	9
vs. Right		.301	.412	352	106	18	0	7	2.0	45	49	30	26	16

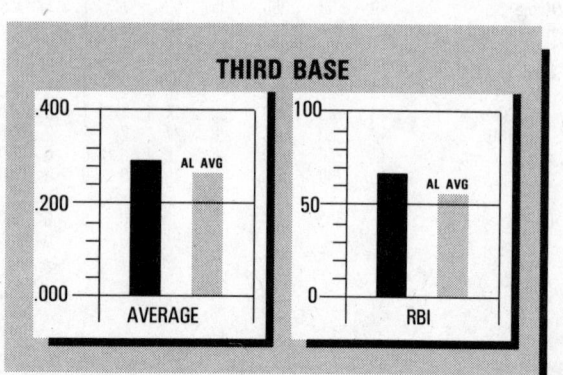

THIRD BASE
AVERAGE · RBI (AL AVG)

Year	Team	Games	BA	SA	AB	H	2B	3B	HR	HR%	R	RBI	BB	SO	SB	PINCH HIT AB	PINCH HIT H	PO	A	E	DP	TC/G	FA	G by Pos

Gary Sheffield *Continued*

Year	Team	Games	BA	SA	AB	H	2B	3B	HR	HR%	R	RBI	BB	SO	SB	AB	H	PO	A	E	DP	TC/G	FA	G by Pos
On Grass		108	.301	.438	418	126	28	1	9	2.2	60	55	40	37	22									
On Turf		17	.246	.319	69	17	2	0	1	1.4	7	12	4	4	3									
Home		63	.272	.381	239	65	15	1	3	1.3	32	28	24	22	13									
Road		62	.315	.460	248	78	15	0	7	2.8	35	39	20	19	12									
Division Rivals																								
vs. BAL		7	.296	.370	27	8	2	0	0	0.0	3	5	4	6	1									
vs. BOS		12	.340	.540	50	17	4	0	2	4.0	5	8	3	4	2									
vs. CLE		9	.143	.371	35	5	2	0	2	5.7	5	8	2	8	2									
vs. DET		10	.306	.444	36	11	2	0	1	2.8	7	4	6	4	1									
vs. NY		10	.333	.472	36	12	2	0	1	2.8	6	3	8	3	3									
vs. TOR		7	.214	.286	28	6	2	0	0	0.0	4	1	2	4	1									
On 3B < 2 Out			.409	.500	22	9	2	0	0	0.0	0	24	4	3										
1988	MIL A	24	.238	.400	80	19	1	0	4	5.0	12	12	7	7	3	0	0	39	48	3	9	3.8	.967	SS–24
1989		95	.247	.337	368	91	18	0	5	1.4	34	32	27	33	10	0	0	100	238	16	44	3.7	.955	SS–70, 3B–21, DH–4
1990		125	.294	.421	487	143	30	1	10	2.0	67	67	44	41	25	0	0	98	254	25	16	3.0	.934	3B–125
3 yrs.		244	.271	.386	935	253	49	1	19	2.0	113	111	78	81	38	0	0	237	540	44	69	3.4	.946	3B–146, SS–94, DH–4

THIRD BASE

John Shelby

SHELBY, JOHN T. (T-Bone)
B. Feb. 23, 1958, Lexington, Ky.
BB TR 6′ 1″ 175 lbs.

Year	Team	Games	BA	SA	AB	H	2B	3B	HR	HR%	R	RBI	BB	SO	SB	AB	H	PO	A	E	DP	TC/G	FA	G by Pos
April		8	.167	.167	6	1	0	0	0	0.0	0	0	0	2	0									
May		16	.357	.429	14	5	1	0	0	0.0	2	2	0	4	1									
June		13	.255	.353	51	13	2	0	1	2.0	4	5	0	9	0									
July		21	.217	.333	60	13	2	1	1	1.7	7	5	5	17	1									
Aug		23	.298	.544	57	17	4	2	2	3.5	7	8	2	13	1									
Sept/Oct		22	.207	.224	58	12	1	0	0	0.0	4	2	3	13	1									
Day		26	.273	.491	55	15	1	1	3	5.5	7	11	4	13	0									
Night		77	.241	.325	191	46	9	2	1	0.5	17	11	6	45	4									
vs. Left			.179	.308	78	14	2	1	2	2.6	10	6	3	21	1									
vs. Right			.280	.387	168	47	8	2	2	1.2	14	16	7	37	3									
On Grass		84	.241	.362	199	48	8	2	4	2.0	22	19	9	44	3									
On Turf		19	.277	.362	47	13	2	1	0	0.0	2	3	1	14	1									
Home		51	.254	.404	114	29	6	1	3	2.6	14	11	6	27	1									
Road		52	.242	.326	132	32	4	2	1	0.8	10	11	4	31	3									
Division Rivals																								
vs. BAL		4	.250	.250	12	3	0	0	0	0.0	1	0	0	3	0									
vs. BOS		7	.067	.267	15	1	0	0	1	6.7	1	3	1	3	0									
vs. CLE		4	.333	.333	9	3	0	0	0	0.0	0	0	0	1	0									
vs. MIL		4	.200	.200	10	2	0	0	0	0.0	1	0	1	2	0									
vs. NY		9	.095	.095	21	2	0	0	0	0.0	1	0	1	4	0									
vs. TOR		5	.231	.308	13	3	1	0	0	0.0	1	0	1	5	1									
On 3B < 2 Out			.125	.125	8	1	0	0	0	0.0	0	1	0	3										
1981	BAL A	7	.000	.000	2	0	0	0	0	0.0	2	0	0	1	2	0	0	1	0	0	0	0.1	1.000	OF–4
1982		26	.314	.486	35	11	3	0	1	2.9	8	2	0	5	0	3	1	20	1	0	1	0.8	1.000	OF–24
1983		126	.258	.363	325	84	15	2	5	1.5	52	27	18	64	15	27	7	200	9	4	3	1.7	.981	OF–115, DH–1
1984		128	.209	.313	383	80	12	5	6	1.6	44	30	20	71	12	12	4	261	9	2	1	2.1	.993	OF–124
1985		69	.283	.434	205	58	6	2	7	3.4	28	27	7	44	5	12	3	148	4	3	0	2.2	.981	OF–59, DH–3, 2B–1
1986		135	.228	.364	404	92	14	4	11	2.7	54	49	18	75	18	19	6	222	5	5	2	1.7	.978	OF–121, DH–2
1987	2 teams	BAL A	(21G — .188)		LA N	(120G — .277)																		
"	total	141	.272	.453	508	138	26	0	22	4.3	65	72	32	110	16	3	1	294	9	8	2	2.2	.974	OF–136, DH–1
1988	LA N	140	.263	.395	494	130	23	6	10	2.0	65	64	44	128	16	0	0	329	7	6	1	2.4	.982	OF–140
1989		108	.183	.229	345	63	11	1	1	0.3	28	12	25	92	10	11	0	220	3	2	1	2.1	.991	OF–98
1990	2 teams	LA N	(25G — .250)		DET A	(78G — .248)																		
"	total	103	.248	.362	246	61	10	3	4	1.6	24	22	10	58	4	27	7	146	5	4	3	1.9	.974	OF–80, DH–5
10 yrs.		983	.243	.368	2947	717	120	23	67	2.3	370	305	174	648	98	114	29	1841	52	34	15	2.0	.982	OF–901, DH–12, 2B–1
LEAGUE CHAMPIONSHIP SERIES																								
1983	BAL A	3	.222	.222	9	2	0	0	0	0.0	1	0	1	3	1	0	0	3	0	0	0	1.0	1.000	OF–2
1988	LA N	7	.167	.167	24	4	0	0	0	0.0	3	3	5	12	2	0	0	19	0	0	0	2.7	1.000	OF–7
2 yrs.		10	.182	.182	33	6	0	0	0	0.0	4	3	6	15	3	0	0	22	0	0	0	2.2	.000	OF–9

OUTFIELD

Year	Team		Games	BA	SA	AB	H	2B	3B	HR	HR%	R	RBI	BB	SO	SB	PINCH HIT AB	PINCH HIT H	PO	A	E	DP	TC/G	FA	G by Pos

John Shelby *Continued*

WORLD SERIES

Year	Team		Games	BA	SA	AB	H	2B	3B	HR	HR%	R	RBI	BB	SO	SB	AB	H	PO	A	E	DP	TC/G	FA	G by Pos
1983	BAL	A	5	.444	.444	9	4	0	0	0	0.0	1	1	0	4	0	3	0	10	0	0	0	2.0	1.000	OF-5
1988	LA	N	5	.222	.278	18	4	1	0	0	0.0	0	1	2	7	1	0	0	14	0	0	0	2.8	1.000	OF-5
2 yrs.			10	.296	.333	27	8	1	0	0	0.0	1	2	2	11	1	3	0	24	0	0	0	2.4	.000	OF-10

Terry Shumpert

SHUMPERT, TERRANCE DARNELL
B. Aug. 16, 1966, Paducah, Ky.
BR TR 6′ 1″ 190 lbs.

Year	Team		Games	BA	SA	AB	H	2B	3B	HR	HR%	R	RBI	BB	SO	SB	AB	H	PO	A	E	DP	TC/G	FA	G by Pos
1990	KC	A	32	.275	.363	91	25	6	1	0	0.0	7	8	2	17	3	0	0	56	74	3	15	4.9	.977	2B-27, DH-3

Ruben Sierra

SIERRA, RUBEN ANGEL
Born Ruben Angel Sierra y Garcia.
B. Oct. 6, 1965, Rio Piedras, Puerto Rico
BB TR 6′ 1″ 175 lbs.

			Games	BA	SA	AB	H	2B	3B	HR	HR%	R	RBI	BB	SO	SB
April			20	.313	.525	80	25	5	0	4	5.0	10	16	7	15	2
May			25	.184	.299	87	16	4	0	2	2.3	9	7	10	15	1
June			29	.313	.435	115	36	6	1	2	1.7	13	16	9	14	3
July			25	.274	.474	95	26	7	0	4	4.2	15	23	7	9	0
Aug			29	.316	.518	114	36	12	1	3	2.6	15	17	7	16	1
Sept/Oct			31	.265	.316	117	31	3	0	1	0.9	8	17	9	17	2
Day			28	.259	.366	112	29	6	0	2	1.8	6	18	11	10	2
Night			131	.284	.440	496	141	31	2	14	2.8	64	78	38	76	7
vs. Left				.324	.440	216	70	16	0	3	1.4	24	31	14	25	6
vs. Right				.255	.418	392	100	21	2	13	3.3	46	65	35	61	3
On Grass			133	.259	.412	502	130	30	1	15	3.0	60	80	42	73	9
On Turf			26	.377	.491	106	40	7	1	1	0.9	10	16	7	13	0
Home			80	.266	.429	301	80	17	1	10	3.3	38	46	23	51	5
Road			79	.293	.423	307	90	20	1	6	2.0	32	50	26	35	4
Division Rivals																
vs. CAL			13	.271	.375	48	13	2	0	1	2.1	6	8	3	6	1
vs. CHI			13	.283	.491	53	15	5	0	2	3.8	6	9	3	9	2
vs. KC			13	.306	.510	49	15	4	0	2	4.1	8	12	6	7	0
vs. MIN			13	.265	.347	49	13	2	1	0	0.0	3	1	3	9	1
vs. OAK			13	.235	.333	51	12	2	0	1	2.0	3	7	4	8	2
vs. SEA			13	.404	.500	52	21	2	0	1	1.9	6	8	5	6	0
On 3B < 2 Out				.278	.500	36	10	2	0	2	5.6	2	33	6	6	

Year	Team		Games	BA	SA	AB	H	2B	3B	HR	HR%	R	RBI	BB	SO	SB	AB	H	PO	A	E	DP	TC/G	FA	G by Pos
1986	TEX	A	113	.264	.476	382	101	13	10	16	4.2	50	55	22	65	7	6	1	200	7	6	1	1.9	.972	OF-107, DH-3
1987			158	.263	.470	**643**	169	35	4	30	4.7	97	109	39	114	16	2	0	272	17	11	6	1.9	.963	OF-157
1988			156	.254	.424	615	156	32	2	23	3.7	77	91	44	91	18	3	1	310	11	7	3	2.1	.979	OF-153, DH-1
1989			162	.306	**.543**	634	194	35	**14**	29	4.6	101	**119**	43	82	8	0	0	313	13	9	2	2.1	.973	OF-162
1990			159	.280	.426	608	170	37	2	16	2.6	70	96	49	86	9	2	1	283	7	10	1	2.0	.967	OF-151, DH-7
5 yrs.			748	.274	.468	2882	790	152	32	114	4.0	395	470	197	438	58	13	3	1378	55	43	13	2.0	.971	OF-730, DH-11

Mike Simms

SIMMS, MICHAEL HOWARD
B. Jan. 12, 1967, Orange, Calif.
BR TR 6′ 4″ 185 lbs.

Year	Team		Games	BA	SA	AB	H	2B	3B	HR	HR%	R	RBI	BB	SO	SB	AB	H	PO	A	E	DP	TC/G	FA	G by Pos
1990	HOU	N	12	.308	.615	13	4	1	0	1	7.6	3	2	0	4	0	5	0	20	1	0	2	3.5	1.000	1B-6

Matt Sinatro

SINATRO, MATTHEW STEPHEN
B. Mar. 22, 1960, Hartford, Conn.
BR TR 5′ 9″ 174 lbs.

Year	Team		Games	BA	SA	AB	H	2B	3B	HR	HR%	R	RBI	BB	SO	SB	AB	H	PO	A	E	DP	TC/G	FA	G by Pos
1981	ATL	N	12	.281	.375	32	9	1	1	0	0.0	4	4	5	4	1	0	0	56	10	0	1	5.5	1.000	C-12
1982			37	.136	.198	81	11	2	0	1	1.2	10	4	4	9	0	0	0	112	25	0	1	3.7	1.000	C-35
1983			7	.167	.167	12	2	0	0	0	0.0	0	2	2	1	0	0	0	24	5	1	1	4.3	.967	C-7
1984			2	.000	.000	4	0	0	0	0	0.0	0	0	0	0	0	0	0	4	0	0	0	2.0	1.000	C-2
1987	OAK	A	6	.000	.000	3	0	0	0	0	0.0	0	0	0	1	0	2	0	4	0	0	0	0.7	1.000	C-6

OUTFIELD — AVERAGE, RBI, HR, SB (with AL AVG comparison bars)

Year	Team	Games	BA	SA	AB	H	2B	3B	HR	HR%	R	RBI	BB	SO	SB	PINCH HIT AB	H	PO	A	E	DP	TC/G	FA	G by Pos

Matt Sinatro   *Continued*

Year	Team	Games	BA	SA	AB	H	2B	3B	HR	HR%	R	RBI	BB	SO	SB	PINCH HIT AB	H	PO	A	E	DP	TC/G	FA	G by Pos
1988		10	.333	.556	9	3	2	0	0	0.0	1	5	0	1	0	0	0	21	2	0	1	2.3	1.000	C-9
1989	DET A	13	.120	.120	25	3	0	0	0	0.0	2	1	1	3	0	0	0	42	2	0	0	3.4	1.000	C-13
1990	SEA A	30	.300	.320	50	15	1	0	0	0.0	2	4	4	10	1	2	0	112	16	1	1	4.6	.992	C-28
8 yrs.		117	.199	.250	216	43	6	1	1	0.5	19	20	16	29	2	4	0	375	60	2	5	3.7	.995	C-112

Joel Skinner

SKINNER, JOEL PATRICK
Son of Bob Skinner.
B. Feb. 21, 1961, La Jolla, Calif.
BR TR 6′ 4″ 195 lbs.

Year	Team	Games	BA	SA	AB	H	2B	3B	HR	HR%	R	RBI	BB	SO	SB	PINCH HIT AB	H	PO	A	E	DP	TC/G	FA	G by Pos
1983	CHI A	6	.273	.273	11	3	0	0	0	0.0	2	1	0	1	0	0	0	20	4	1	1	4.2	.960	C-6
1984		43	.213	.238	80	17	2	0	0	0.0	4	3	7	19	1	0	0	171	11	2	1	4.3	.989	C-43
1985		22	.341	.545	44	15	4	1	1	2.3	9	5	5	13	0	2	0	94	8	3	0	4.8	.971	C-21
1986	2 teams	CHI A (60G — .201)		NY A (54G — .259)																				
"	total	114	.232	.314	315	73	9	1	5	1.6	23	37	16	83	1	0	0	507	37	9	9	4.9	.984	C-114
1987	NY A	64	.137	.230	139	19	4	0	3	2.2	9	14	8	46	0	1	0	232	18	4	2	4.0	.984	C-64
1988		88	.227	.335	251	57	15	0	4	1.6	23	23	14	72	0	0	0	396	16	4	5	4.7	.990	C-85, OF-2, 1B-1
1989	CLE A	79	.230	.303	178	41	10	0	1	0.6	10	13	9	42	1	0	0	280	22	3	1	3.9	.990	C-79
1990		49	.252	.338	139	35	4	1	2	1.4	16	16	7	44	0	0	0	222	16	1	3	4.9	.996	C-49
8 yrs.		465	.225	.313	1157	260	48	3	16	1.4	96	112	66	320	3	3	0	1922	132	27	22	4.5	.987	C-461, OF-2, 1B-1

Don Slaught

SLAUGHT, DONALD MARTIN (Sluggo)
B. Sept. 11, 1958, Long Beach, Calif.
BR TR 6′ 1″ 190 lbs.

	Games	BA	SA	AB	H	2B	3B	HR	HR%	R	RBI	BB	SO	SB
April	11	.484	.774	31	15	3	0	2	6.5	5	5	1	0	0
May	18	.333	.588	51	17	3	2	2	3.9	10	7	7	6	0
June	16	.366	.463	41	15	4	0	0	0.0	3	8	3	5	0
July	7	.143	.190	21	3	1	0	0	0.0	5	1	3	2	0
Aug	18	.228	.333	57	13	4	1	0	0.0	3	5	5	6	0
Sept/Oct	14	.207	.310	29	6	3	0	0	0.0	1	3	8	8	0
Day	23	.260	.480	50	13	3	1	2	4.0	10	10	13	7	0
Night	61	.311	.450	180	56	15	2	2	1.1	17	19	14	20	0
vs. Left		.317	.457	164	52	13	2	2	1.2	17	17	22	20	0
vs. Right		.258	.455	66	17	5	1	2	3.0	10	12	5	7	0
On Grass	17	.383	.553	47	18	2	0	2	4.3	4	9	1	5	0
On Turf	67	.279	.432	183	51	16	3	2	1.1	23	20	26	22	0
Home	43	.274	.425	113	31	10	2	1	0.9	19	12	19	14	0
Road	41	.325	.487	117	38	8	1	3	2.6	8	17	8	13	0
Division Rivals														
vs. CHI	6	.286	.500	14	4	0	0	1	7.1	2	3	1	2	0
vs. MON	12	.174	.217	23	4	1	0	0	0.0	2	2	6	2	0
vs. NY	9	.350	.450	20	7	2	0	0	0.0	1	3	1	2	0
vs. PHI	11	.278	.389	36	10	4	0	0	0.0	3	4	4	5	0
vs. STL	9	.452	.613	31	14	5	0	0	0.0	3	4	1	3	0
On 3B < 2 Out		.833	1.000	6	5	1	0	0	0.0	0	12	1	1	

CATCHER

.400 / .200 / .000 — AVERAGE — NL AVG
100 / 50 / 0 — RBI — NL AVG
50 / 25 / 0 — HR — NL AVG
60 / 30 / 0 — SB — NL AVG

Year	Team	Games	BA	SA	AB	H	2B	3B	HR	HR%	R	RBI	BB	SO	SB	PINCH HIT AB	H	PO	A	E	DP	TC/G	FA	G by Pos
1982	KC A	43	.278	.409	115	32	6	0	3	2.6	14	8	9	12	0	0	0	156	7	1	1	3.8	.994	C-43
1983		83	.312	.388	276	86	13	4	0	0.0	21	28	11	27	3	5	2	299	18	12	7	4.0	.964	C-79, DH-1
1984		124	.264	.379	409	108	27	4	4	1.0	48	42	20	55	0	5	2	547	44	11	8	4.9	.982	C-123, DH-1
1985	TEX A	102	.280	.423	343	96	17	4	8	2.3	34	35	20	41	5	1	0	550	33	6	4	5.8	.990	C-102
1986		95	.264	.449	314	83	17	1	13	4.1	39	46	16	59	3	3	3	533	40	4	1	6.1	.993	C-91, DH-2
1987		95	.224	.405	237	53	15	2	8	3.4	25	16	24	51	0	22	5	429	39	7	5	5.0	.985	C-85, DH-5
1988	NY A	97	.283	.450	322	91	25	1	9	2.8	33	43	24	54	1	6	2	496	24	11	4	5.5	.979	C-94, DH-1
1989		117	.251	.371	350	88	21	3	5	1.4	34	38	30	57	1	12	3	493	44	5	8	4.6	.991	C-105, DH-3
1990	PIT N	84	.300	.457	230	69	18	3	4	1.7	27	29	27	27	0	16	5	345	36	8	4	5.0	.979	C-78
9 yrs.		840	.272	.413	2596	706	159	22	54	2.1	275	285	181	383	13	70	22	3848	285	65	42	5.0	.985	C-800, DH-13

LEAGUE CHAMPIONSHIP SERIES

Year	Team	Games	BA	SA	AB	H	2B	3B	HR	HR%	R	RBI	BB	SO	SB	PINCH HIT AB	H	PO	A	E	DP	TC/G	FA	G by Pos
1984	KC A	3	.364	.364	11	4	0	0	0	0.0	0	0	0	0	0	0	0	17	0	3	0	6.7	.850	C-3
1990	PIT N	4	.091	.182	11	1	1	0	0	0.0	0	1	2	3	0	0	0	23	1	1	0	6.3	.960	C-4
2 yrs.		7	.227	.273	22	5	1	0	0	0.0	0	1	2	3	0	0	0	40	1	4	0	6.4	.911	C-7

Year	Team	Games	BA	SA	AB	H	2B	3B	HR	HR%	R	RBI	BB	SO	SB	PINCH HIT AB	H	PO	A	E	DP	TC/G	FA	G by Pos

Dwight Smith

SMITH, JOHN DWIGHT
B. Nov. 8, 1963, Tallahassee, Fla.
BL TR 5' 11" 175 lbs.

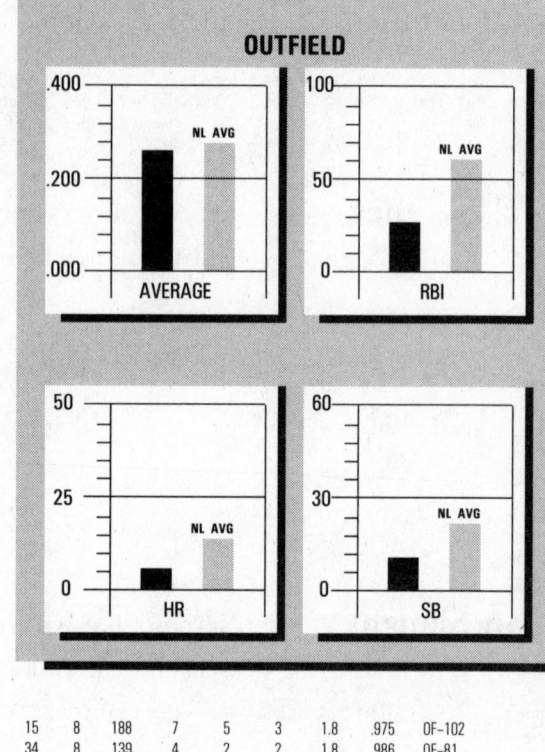

OUTFIELD

Year	Team	Games	BA	SA	AB	H	2B	3B	HR	HR%	R	RBI	BB	SO	SB	PINCH HIT AB	H	PO	A	E	DP	TC/G	FA	G by Pos
April		17	.244	.366	41	10	2	0	1	2.4	4	4	6	4	1									
May		25	.324	.473	74	24	5	0	2	2.7	11	6	7	12	6									
June		24	.239	.380	71	17	4	0	2	2.8	9	5	6	12	1									
July		14	.189	.189	37	7	0	0	0	0.0	3	0	3	6	3									
Aug		14	.296	.333	27	8	1	0	0	0.0	3	3	1	5	0									
Sept/Oct		23	.250	.400	40	10	3	0	1	2.5	4	9	5	7	0									
Day		59	.263	.362	152	40	9	0	2	1.3	17	15	14	25	7									
Night		58	.261	.391	138	36	6	0	4	2.9	17	12	14	21	4									
vs. Left			.222	.361	36	8	2	0	1	2.8	4	3	1	11	0									
vs. Right			.268	.378	254	68	13	0	5	2.0	30	24	27	35	11									
On Grass		81	.284	.421	197	56	12	0	5	2.5	27	18	20	31	7									
On Turf		36	.215	.280	93	20	3	0	1	1.1	7	9	8	15	4									
Home		58	.252	.382	131	33	8	0	3	2.3	16	12	13	25	2									
Road		59	.270	.371	159	43	7	0	3	1.9	18	15	15	21	9									
Division Rivals																								
vs. MON		13	.296	.556	27	8	1	0	2	7.4	6	6	3	3	1									
vs. NY		14	.273	.318	22	6	1	0	0	0.0	3	3	5	5	1									
vs. PHI		13	.143	.286	28	4	1	0	1	3.6	2	2	5	5	0									
vs. PIT		11	.259	.333	27	7	2	0	0	0.0	1	2	1	2	0									
vs. STL		15	.213	.255	47	10	2	0	0	0.0	4	4	4	11	1									
On 3B < 2 Out			.333	.333	15	5	0	0	0	0.0	0	11	4	2										
1989	CHI N	109	.324	.493	343	111	19	6	9	2.6	52	52	31	51	9	15	8	188	7	5	3	1.8	.975	OF-102
1990		117	.262	.376	290	76	15	0	6	2.0	34	27	28	46	11	34	8	139	4	2	2	1.8	.986	OF-81
2 yrs.		226	.295	.439	633	187	34	6	15	2.4	86	79	59	97	20	49	16	327	11	7	5	1.5	.980	OF-183
LEAGUE CHAMPIONSHIP SERIES																								
1989	CHI N	4	.200	.267	15	3	1	0	0	0.0	2	0	2	2	1	0	0	10	0	0	0	2.5	1.000	OF-4

Greg Smith

SMITH, GREGORY ALAN
B. Apr. 5, 1967, Baltimore, Md.
BB TR 5' 11" 170 lbs.

Year	Team	Games	BA	SA	AB	H	2B	3B	HR	HR%	R	RBI	BB	SO	SB	PINCH HIT AB	H	PO	A	E	DP	TC/G	FA	G by Pos
1989	CHI N	4	.400	.400	5	2	0	0	0	0.0	1	2	0	0	0	1	0	4	3	2	1	2.3	.778	2B-2
1990		18	.205	.295	44	9	2	1	0	0.0	4	5	2	5	1	2	1	20	38	3	8	4.4	.951	2B-7, SS-7
2 yrs.		22	.224	.306	49	11	2	1	0	0.0	5	7	2	5	1	3	1	24	41	5	9	3.2	.929	2B-9, SS-7

Lonnie Smith

SMITH, LONNIE
B. Dec. 22, 1955, Chicago, Ill.
BR TR 5' 9" 170 lbs.

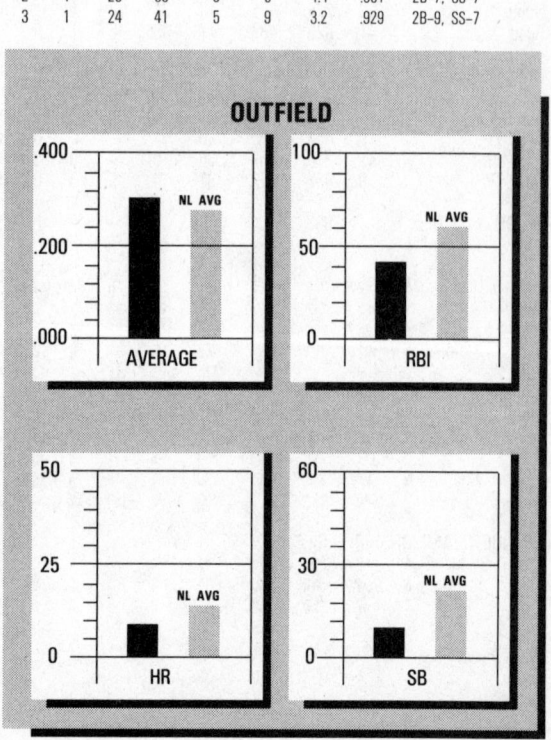

OUTFIELD

Year	Team	Games	BA	SA	AB	H	2B	3B	HR	HR%	R	RBI	BB	SO	SB	PINCH HIT AB	H	PO	A	E	DP	TC/G	FA	G by Pos
April		16	.218	.345	55	12	2	1	1	1.8	8	6	8	13	2									
May		20	.224	.313	67	15	4	1	0	0.0	8	6	6	15	3									
June		23	.364	.667	66	24	4	2	4	6.1	10	7	8	9	0									
July		24	.337	.453	86	29	4	3	0	0.0	14	4	14	11	1									
Aug		25	.318	.420	88	28	7	1	0	0.0	12	9	7	6	1									
Sept/Oct		27	.327	.519	104	34	6	1	4	3.8	20	10	15	15	3									
Day		32	.325	.439	114	37	5	1	2	1.8	24	6	20	16	2									
Night		103	.298	.466	352	105	22	8	7	2.0	48	36	38	53	8									
vs. Left			.294	.487	197	58	14	3	6	3.0	33	18	21	22	2									
vs. Right			.312	.439	269	84	13	6	3	1.1	39	24	37	47	8									
On Grass		98	.315	.470	336	106	22	6	6	1.8	54	30	44	51	9									
On Turf		37	.277	.431	130	36	5	3	3	2.3	18	12	14	18	1									
Home		67	.312	.442	231	72	16	4	2	0.9	35	16	27	34	9									
Road		68	.298	.477	235	70	11	5	7	3.0	37	26	31	35	1									
Division Rivals																								
vs. CIN		17	.279	.492	61	17	3	2	2	3.3	9	5	8	9	1									
vs. HOU		16	.279	.393	61	17	5	1	0	0.0	10	3	4	3	1									
vs. LA		13	.311	.467	45	14	5	1	0	0.0	7	4	6	6	0									
vs. SD		17	.388	.653	49	19	4	0	3	6.1	9	11	8	5	0									
vs. SF		16	.271	.441	59	16	2	1	2	3.4	9	2	9	14	0									
On 3B < 2 Out			.429	.429	14	6	0	0	0	0.0	0	17	5	1										

Lonnie Smith *Continued*

Year	Team		Games	BA	SA	AB	H	2B	3B	HR	HR%	R	RBI	BB	SO	SB	PINCH HIT AB	H	PO	A	E	DP	TC/G	FA	G by Pos
1978	PHI	N	17	.000	.000	4	0	0	0	0	0.0	6	0	4	3	4	1	0	5	1	0	0	0.4	1.000	OF-11
1979			17	.167	.233	30	5	2	0	0	0.0	4	3	1	7	2	4	0	19	1	0	0	1.2	1.000	OF-11
1980			100	.339	.443	298	101	14	4	3	1.0	69	20	26	48	33	8	2	121	2	4	0	1.3	.969	OF-82
1981			62	.324	.472	176	57	14	3	2	1.1	40	11	18	14	21	5	3	89	10	3	2	1.6	.971	OF-51
1982	STL	N	156	.307	.434	592	182	35	8	8	1.4	**120**	69	64	74	68	9	1	303	16	10	3	2.1	.970	OF-149
1983			130	.321	.453	492	158	31	5	8	1.6	83	45	41	55	43	5	1	225	14	15	4	2.0	.941	OF-126
1984			145	.250	.341	504	126	20	4	6	1.2	77	49	70	90	50	3	1	184	18	11	0	1.5	.948	OF-140
1985	2 teams		STL N	(28G	—	.260)	KC	A	(120G	—	.257)															
"	total		148	.257	.358	544	140	25	6	6	1.1	92	48	56	89	52	2	0	51	4	1	1	0.4	.982	OF-147
1986	KC	A	134	.287	.411	508	146	25	7	8	1.6	80	44	46	78	26	4	2	245	5	9	1	1.9	.965	OF-118, DH-10
1987			48	.251	.359	167	42	7	1	3	1.8	26	8	24	31	9	1	0	52	2	5	0	1.2	.915	OF-32, DH-15
1988	ATL	N	43	.237	.342	114	27	3	0	3	2.6	14	9	10	25	4	14	3	59	2	2	0	1.5	.968	OF-35
1989			134	.315	.533	482	152	34	4	21	4.4	89	79	76	95	25	3	0	289	3	2	0	2.2	.993	OF-132
1990			135	.305	.459	466	142	27	9	9	1.9	72	42	58	69	10	19	5	254	6	12	2	2.2	.956	OF-122
13 yrs.			1269	.292	.422	4377	1278	237	51	77	1.8	772	427	494	678	347	78	18	1896	84	74	13	1.6	.964	OF-1156, DH-25

DIVISIONAL PLAYOFF SERIES

Year	Team		Games	BA	SA	AB	H	2B	3B	HR	HR%	R	RBI	BB	SO	SB	PINCH HIT AB	H	PO	A	E	DP	TC/G	FA	G by Pos
1981	PHI	N	5	.263	.316	19	5	1	0	0	0.0	1	0	0	4	0	0	0	0	0	0	0	0.0	—	OF-5

LEAGUE CHAMPIONSHIP SERIES

Year	Team		Games	BA	SA	AB	H	2B	3B	HR	HR%	R	RBI	BB	SO	SB	PINCH HIT AB	H	PO	A	E	DP	TC/G	FA	G by Pos
1980	PHI	N	3	.600	.600	5	3	0	0	0	0.0	2	0	0	0	1	0	0	2	1	0	1	1.0	1.000	OF-2
1982	STL	N	3	.273	.273	11	3	0	0	0	0.0	1	1	0	1	0	0	0	2	0	0	0	0.7	1.000	OF-3
1985	KC	A	7	.250	.321	28	7	2	0	0	0.0	2	1	3	6	1	0	0	8	3	1	0	1.7	.917	OF-7
3 yrs.			13	.295	.341	44	13	2	0	0	0.0	5	2	3	7	2	0	0	12	4	1	1	1.3	.941	OF-12

WORLD SERIES

Year	Team		Games	BA	SA	AB	H	2B	3B	HR	HR%	R	RBI	BB	SO	SB	PINCH HIT AB	H	PO	A	E	DP	TC/G	FA	G by Pos
1980	PHI	N	6	.263	.316	19	5	1	0	0	0.0	2	1	1	1	0	0	0	4	1	0	0	0.8	1.000	OF-4, DH-1
1982	STL	N	7	.321	.536	28	9	4	1	0	0.0	6	1	1	5	2	0	0	11	0	0	0	1.6	1.000	OF-6, DH-1
1985	KC	A	7	.333	.444	27	9	3	0	0	0.0	4	4	3	8	2	0	0	7	2	0	0	1.3	1.000	OF-7
3 yrs.			20	.311	.446	74	23	8	1	0	0.0	12	6	5	14	4	0	0	22	3	0	0	1.3	.000	OF-17, DH-2

Ozzie Smith

SMITH, OSBORNE EARL (The Wizard)
B. Dec. 26, 1954, Mobile, Ala.
BB TR 5' 11" 150 lbs.

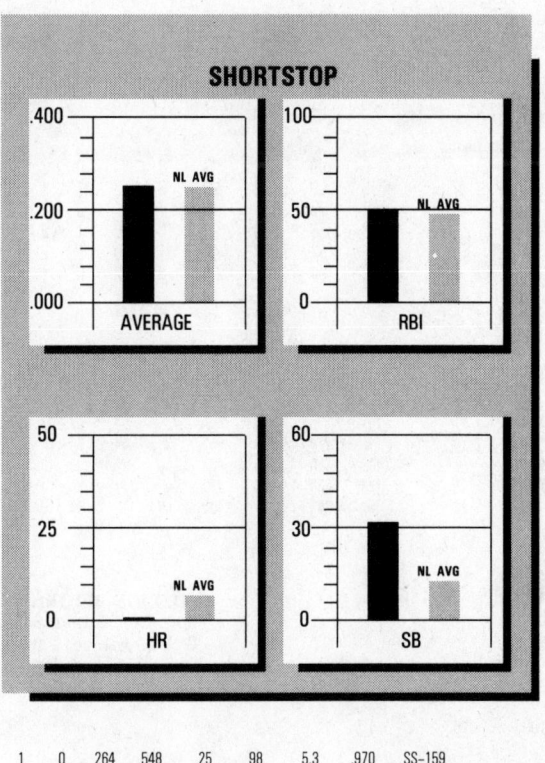

SHORTSTOP

	Games	BA	SA	AB	H	2B	3B	HR	HR%	R	RBI	BB	SO	SB
April	15	.218	.236	55	12	1	0	0	0.0	8	5	7	3	1
May	27	.240	.302	96	23	6	0	0	0.0	13	7	9	7	7
June	27	.198	.220	91	18	2	0	0	0.0	10	11	19	8	8
July	26	.338	.413	80	27	6	0	0	0.0	10	10	9	3	3
Aug	24	.260	.333	96	25	2	1	1	1.0	13	13	12	7	7
Sept/Oct	24	.266	.309	94	25	4	0	0	0.0	7	4	5	5	6
Day	43	.236	.293	157	37	7	1	0	0.0	19	12	12	9	11
Night	100	.262	.310	355	93	14	0	1	0.3	42	38	49	24	21
vs. Left		.289	.373	201	58	12	1	1	0.5	27	23	21	11	12
vs. Right		.232	.260	311	72	9	0	0	0.0	34	27	40	22	20
On Grass	39	.252	.293	147	37	6	0	0	0.0	16	13	14	12	3
On Turf	104	.255	.310	365	93	15	1	1	0.3	45	37	47	21	29
Home	73	.266	.332	256	68	15	1	0	0.0	35	25	35	17	21
Road	70	.242	.277	256	62	6	0	1	0.4	26	25	26	16	11
Division Rivals														
vs. CHI	17	.219	.250	64	14	2	0	0	0.0	10	5	13	6	4
vs. MON	13	.205	.205	44	9	0	0	0	0.0	5	5	3	1	4
vs. NY	17	.222	.222	54	12	0	0	0	0.0	5	6	7	5	1
vs. PHI	15	.216	.255	51	11	2	0	0	0.0	5	6	12	4	1
vs. PIT	14	.298	.368	57	17	4	0	0	0.0	7	3	2	4	7
On 3B < 2 Out		.433	.467	30	13	1	0	0	0.0	0	29	4	0	

Year	Team		Games	BA	SA	AB	H	2B	3B	HR	HR%	R	RBI	BB	SO	SB	PINCH HIT AB	H	PO	A	E	DP	TC/G	FA	G by Pos
1978	SD	N	159	.258	.312	590	152	17	6	1	0.2	69	46	47	43	40	1	0	264	548	25	98	5.3	.970	SS-159
1979			156	.211	.262	587	124	18	6	0	0.0	77	27	37	37	28	0	0	256	555	20	86	5.3	.976	SS-155
1980			158	.230	.276	609	140	18	5	0	0.0	67	35	71	49	57	0	0	288	621	24	113	5.9	.974	SS-158
1981			110	.222	.256	**450**	100	11	2	0	0.0	53	21	41	37	22	0	0	220	422	16	72	6.0	.976	SS-110
1982	STL	N	140	.248	.314	488	121	24	1	2	0.4	58	43	68	32	25	1	0	279	535	13	101	5.9	.984	SS-139
1983			159	.243	.335	552	134	30	6	3	0.5	69	50	64	36	34	2	0	304	519	21	100	5.3	.975	SS-158
1984			124	.257	.337	412	106	20	5	1	0.2	53	44	56	17	35	0	0	233	437	12	94	5.5	.982	SS-124
1985			158	.276	.361	537	148	22	3	6	1.1	70	54	65	27	31	0	0	264	549	14	111	5.2	.983	SS-158
1986			153	.280	.333	514	144	19	4	0	0.0	67	54	79	27	31	8	2	229	453	15	96	4.6	.978	SS-144
1987			158	.303	.383	600	182	40	4	0	0.0	104	75	89	36	43	2	1	245	516	10	111	4.9	.987	SS-158

Year	Team	Games	BA	SA	AB	H	2B	3B	HR	HR%	R	RBI	BB	SO	SB	PINCH HIT AB	H	PO	A	E	DP	TC/G	FA	G by Pos

Ozzie Smith *Continued*

Year	Team	Games	BA	SA	AB	H	2B	3B	HR	HR%	R	RBI	BB	SO	SB	AB	H	PO	A	E	DP	TC/G	FA	G by Pos
1988		153	.270	.336	575	155	27	1	3	0.5	80	51	74	43	57	2	0	234	519	22	79	5.1	.972	SS-150
1989		155	.273	.361	593	162	30	8	2	0.3	82	50	55	37	29	2	1	209	483	17	73	4.6	.976	SS-153
1990		143	.254	.305	512	130	21	1	1	0.1	61	50	61	33	32	2	0	212	378	12	66	4.3	.980	SS-140
13 yrs.		1926	.256	.321	7019	1798	297	52	19	0.3	910	600	807	454	464	20	4	3237	6535	221	1200	5.2	.978	SS-1906

LEAGUE CHAMPIONSHIP SERIES

Year	Team	Games	BA	SA	AB	H	2B	3B	HR	HR%	R	RBI	BB	SO	SB	AB	H	PO	A	E	DP	TC/G	FA	G by Pos
1982	STL N	3	.556	.556	9	5	0	0	0	0.0	0	3	3	0	1	0	0	4	11	0	1	5.0	1.000	SS-3
1985		6	.435	.696	23	10	1	1	1	4.3	4	3	3	1	1	0	0	6	16	0	2	3.7	1.000	SS-6
1987		7	.200	.280	25	5	0	1	0	0.0	2	1	3	4	0	0	0	10	19	1	4	4.3	.967	SS-7
3 yrs.		16	.351	.491	57	20	1	2	1	1.8	6	7	9	5	2	0	0	20	46	1	7	4.2	.985	SS-16

WORLD SERIES

Year	Team	Games	BA	SA	AB	H	2B	3B	HR	HR%	R	RBI	BB	SO	SB	AB	H	PO	A	E	DP	TC/G	FA	G by Pos
1982	STL N	7	.208	.208	24	5	0	0	0	0.0	3	1	3	0	1	0	0	22	17	0	5	5.6	1.000	SS-7
1985		7	.087	.087	23	2	0	0	0	0.0	1	0	4	0	1	0	0	10	16	1	5	3.9	.963	SS-7
1987		7	.214	.214	28	6	0	0	0	0.0	3	2	2	3	2	0	0	7	19	0	1	3.7	1.000	SS-7
3 yrs.		21	.173	.173	75	13	0	0	0	0.0	7	3	9	3	4	0	0	39	52	1	11	4.4	.989	SS-21

Cory Snyder

SNYDER, JAMES CORY
B. Nov. 11, 1962, Inglewood, Calif.
BR TR 6′ 4″ 175 lbs.

	Games	BA	SA	AB	H	2B	3B	HR	HR%	R	RBI	BB	SO	SB
April	18	.329	.543	70	23	6	0	3	4.3	10	13	2	16	0
May	26	.182	.318	88	16	6	0	2	2.3	10	8	3	32	1
June	26	.290	.590	100	29	8	2	6	6.0	14	19	6	17	0
July	26	.191	.303	89	17	5	1	1	1.1	4	7	6	27	0
Aug	21	.203	.270	74	15	2	0	1	1.4	6	6	2	19	0
Sept/Oct	6	.118	.294	17	2	0	0	1	5.9	2	2	2	7	0
Day	35	.271	.489	133	36	5	0	8	6.0	16	21	2	30	0
Night	88	.216	.367	305	66	22	3	6	2.0	30	34	19	88	1
vs. Left		.222	.370	135	30	6	1	4	3.0	16	14	12	36	1
vs. Right		.238	.419	303	72	21	2	10	3.3	30	41	9	82	0
On Grass	106	.228	.385	377	86	20	3	11	2.9	38	45	17	101	1
On Turf	17	.262	.525	61	16	7	0	3	4.9	8	10	4	17	0
Home	59	.235	.357	196	46	13	1	3	1.5	18	17	14	55	0
Road	64	.231	.442	242	56	14	2	11	4.5	28	38	7	63	1
Division Rivals														
vs. BAL	7	.296	.667	27	8	4	0	2	7.4	5	4	0	8	0
vs. BOS	6	.300	.650	20	6	2	1	1	5.0	3	5	2	2	0
vs. DET	11	.175	.300	40	7	2	0	1	2.5	2	2	2	10	0
vs. MIL	9	.278	.500	36	10	0	1	2	5.6	4	7	1	5	0
vs. NY	11	.262	.452	42	11	0	1	2	4.8	4	6	0	10	0
vs. TOR	10	.184	.342	38	7	3	0	1	2.6	4	5	2	14	0
On 3B < 2 Out		.207	.345	29	6	1	0	1	3.4	1	17	2	9	

OUTFIELD

AVERAGE / RBI / HR / SB (AL AVG)

Year	Team	Games	BA	SA	AB	H	2B	3B	HR	HR%	R	RBI	BB	SO	SB	AB	H	PO	A	E	DP	TC/G	FA	G by Pos
1986	CLE A	103	.272	.500	416	113	21	1	24	5.8	58	69	16	123	2	0	0	213	84	10	22	3.0	.967	OF-74, SS-34, 3B-11, DH-1
1987		157	.236	.456	577	136	24	2	33	5.7	74	82	31	166	5	7	2	313	53	15	9	2.4	.961	OF-139, SS-18
1988		142	.272	.483	511	139	24	3	26	5.1	71	75	42	101	5	1	0	314	16	5	0	2.4	.985	OF-141
1989		132	.215	.360	489	105	17	0	18	3.7	49	59	23	134	6	8	0	297	32	1	7	2.5	.997	OF-125, SS-7, DH-2
1990		123	.233	.404	438	102	27	3	14	3.1	46	55	21	118	1	4	1	229	18	7	4	2.1	.972	OF-120, SS-5
5 yrs.		657	.245	.441	2431	595	113	9	115	4.7	298	340	133	642	19	20	3	1366	203	38	42	2.4	.976	OF-599, SS-64, 3B-11, DH-3

Luis Sojo

SOJO, LUIS BELTRAN
Born Luis Beltran Sojo y Sojo.
B. Jan. 3, 1966, Caracas, Venezuela
BR TR 5′ 11″ 174 lbs.

Year	Team	Games	BA	SA	AB	H	2B	3B	HR	HR%	R	RBI	BB	SO	SB	AB	H	PO	A	E	DP	TC/G	FA	G by Pos
1990	TOR A	33	.225	.300	80	18	3	0	1	1.2	14	9	5	5	1	4	0	34	31	5	7	2.4	.929	2B-15, SS-5, OF-5, 3B-4, DH-3

Paul Sorrento

SORRENTO, PAUL ANTHONY
B. Nov. 17, 1965, Somerville, Mass.
BL TR 6′ 2″ 195 lbs.

Year	Team	Games	BA	SA	AB	H	2B	3B	HR	HR%	R	RBI	BB	SO	SB	AB	H	PO	A	E	DP	TC/G	FA	G by Pos
1989	MIN A	14	.238	.238	21	5	0	0	0	0.0	2	1	5	4	0	3	0	13	0	0	1	0.9	1.000	DH-5, 1B-5
1990		41	.207	.380	121	25	4	1	5	4.1	11	13	12	31	1	6	2	118	7	1	14	8.4	.992	DH-23, 1B-15
2 yrs.		55	.211	.359	142	30	4	1	5	3.5	13	14	17	35	1	9	2	131	7	1	15	2.5	.993	DH-28, 1B-20

Sammy Sosa

SOSA, SAMUEL PERALTA
B. Nov. 10, 1968, San Pedro de Macoris, Dominican Republic
BR TR 6′ 165 lbs.

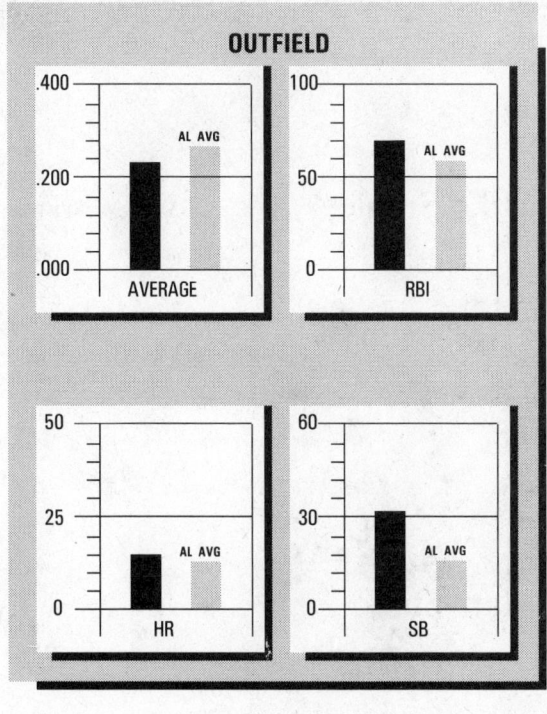

OUTFIELD

Year	Team	Games	BA	SA	AB	H	2B	3B	HR	HR%	R	RBI	BB	SO	SB	PINCH HIT AB	H	PO	A	E	DP	TC/G	FA	G by Pos
April		16	.298	.509	57	17	2	2	2	3.5	11	9	4	16	2									
May		27	.213	.319	94	20	4	0	2	2.1	10	6	4	28	6									
June		27	.313	.573	96	30	6	5	3	3.1	14	13	4	25	5									
July		26	.190	.360	100	19	7	2	2	2.0	13	16	6	29	5									
Aug		28	.184	.306	98	18	3	0	3	3.1	11	13	9	24	5									
Sept/Oct		29	.230	.402	87	20	4	1	3	3.4	13	13	6	28	9									
Day		38	.186	.326	129	24	5	2	3	2.3	15	18	6	43	6									
Night		115	.248	.429	403	100	21	8	12	3.0	57	52	27	107	26									
vs. Left			.262	.502	233	61	14	3	12	5.2	36	37	20	59	17									
vs. Right			.211	.328	299	63	12	7	3	1.0	36	33	13	91	15									
On Grass		131	.229	.416	454	104	23	10	14	3.1	59	58	30	125	23									
On Turf		22	.256	.333	78	20	3	0	1	1.3	13	12	3	25	9									
Home		77	.256	.477	266	68	15	7	10	3.8	40	36	19	72	17									
Road		76	.211	.331	266	56	11	3	5	1.9	32	34	14	78	15									
Division Rivals																								
vs. CAL		12	.362	.638	47	17	3	2	2	4.3	6	6	3	13	2									
vs. KC		12	.167	.200	30	5	1	0	0	0.0	7	3	1	13	5									
vs. MIN		12	.205	.333	39	8	3	1	0	0.0	5	2	3	10	4									
vs. OAK		13	.304	.565	46	14	2	2	2	4.3	5	9	2	11	1									
vs. SEA		12	.250	.350	40	10	1	0	1	2.5	8	7	3	13	4									
vs. TEX		12	.222	.244	45	10	1	0	0	0.0	5	2	5	10	1									
On 3B < 2 Out			.174	.174	23	4	0	0	0	0.0	0	16	4	8										
1989	2 teams	TEX A (25G — .238)					CHI A (33G — .273)																	
"	total	58	.257	.366	183	47	8	0	4	2.2	27	13	11	47	7	4	0	94	2	4	0	1.7	.960	OF-52, DH-6
1990	CHI A	153	.233	.404	532	124	26	10	15	2.8	72	70	33	150	32	0	0	315	14	13	1	2.3	.962	OF-152
2 yrs.		211	.239	.394	715	171	34	10	19	2.7	99	83	44	197	39	4	0	409	16	17	1	2.1	.962	OF-204, DH-6

Bill Spiers

SPIERS, WILLIAM JAMES
B. June 5, 1966, Orangeburg, S. C.
BL TR 6′ 2″ 190 lbs.

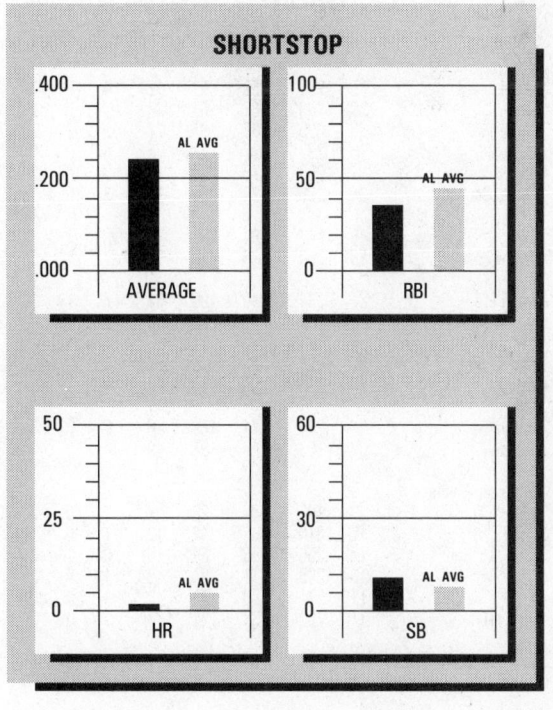

SHORTSTOP

Year	Team	Games	BA	SA	AB	H	2B	3B	HR	HR%	R	RBI	BB	SO	SB	PINCH HIT AB	H	PO	A	E	DP	TC/G	FA	G by Pos
April					0	0	0	0	0	.0	0	0	0	0	0									
May		13	.128	.154	39	5	1	0	0	0.0	2	4	2	6	1									
June		25	.315	.461	89	28	8	1	1	1.1	18	9	5	10	3									
July		24	.250	.325	80	20	3	0	1	1.3	10	10	4	14	1									
Aug		24	.179	.224	67	12	1	1	0	0.0	7	3	3	4	3									
Sept/Oct		26	.261	.307	88	23	2	1	0	0.0	7	10	2	11	3									
Day		34	.231	.317	104	24	4	1	1	1.0	16	13	8	19	4									
Night		78	.247	.317	259	64	11	2	1	0.4	28	23	8	26	7									
vs. Left			.235	.296	81	19	3	1	0	0.0	7	7	5	13	0									
vs. Right			.245	.323	282	69	12	2	2	0.7	37	29	11	32	11									
On Grass		96	.247	.327	312	77	13	3	2	0.6	34	32	12	41	9									
On Turf		16	.216	.255	51	11	2	0	0	0.0	10	4	4	4	2									
Home		56	.267	.375	176	47	7	3	2	1.1	22	22	9	19	5									
Road		56	.219	.262	187	41	8	0	0	0.0	22	14	7	26	6									
Division Rivals																								
vs. BAL		13	.364	.523	44	16	5	1	0	0.0	7	5	3	3	2									
vs. BOS		7	.333	.417	24	8	2	0	0	0.0	1	6	1	4	0									
vs. CLE		8	.207	.379	29	6	2	0	1	3.4	5	4	0	2	1									
vs. DET		6	.313	.313	16	5	0	0	0	0.0	1	3	0	2	0									
vs. NY		10	.281	.344	32	9	0	1	0	0.0	3	4	0	6	1									
vs. TOR		10	.294	.353	34	10	2	0	0	0.0	8	3	3	1	1									
On 3B < 2 Out			.318	.455	22	7	1	1	0	0.0	0	20	2	2										
1989	MIL A	114	.255	.333	345	88	9	3	4	1.2	44	33	21	63	10	4	3	164	295	21	62	4.2	.956	SS-89, 3B-12, DH-4, 2B-4, 1B-2
1990		112	.242	.317	363	88	15	3	2	0.5	44	36	16	45	11	2	1	159	326	12	72	4.5	.976	SS-111
2 yrs.		226	.249	.325	708	176	24	6	6	0.8	88	69	37	108	21	6	4	323	621	33	134	4.3	.966	SS-200, 3B-12, DH-4, 2B-4, 1B-2

Year	Team		Games	BA	SA	AB	H	2B	3B	HR	HR%	R	RBI	BB	SO	SB	PINCH HIT AB	H	PO	A	E	DP	TC/G	FA	G by Pos

Steve Springer

SPRINGER, STEVEN MICHAEL
B. Feb. 11, 1961, Long Beach, Calif.
BR TR 6′ 190 lbs.

Year	Team		Games	BA	SA	AB	H	2B	3B	HR	HR%	R	RBI	BB	SO	SB	AB	H	PO	A	E	DP	TC/G	FA	G by Pos
1990	CLE	A	4	.167	.167	12	2	0	0	0	0.0	1	1	0	6	0	1	0	2	3	0	0	1.7	1.000	3B-3, DH-1

Mike Stanley

STANLEY, ROBERT MICHAEL
B. June 25, 1963, Fort Lauderdale, Fla.
BR TR 6′ 1″ 185 lbs.

Year	Team		Games	BA	SA	AB	H	2B	3B	HR	HR%	R	RBI	BB	SO	SB	AB	H	PO	A	E	DP	TC/G	FA	G by Pos
1986	TEX	A	15	.333	.533	30	10	3	0	1	3.3	4	1	3	7	1	5	2	14	8	1	2	1.5	.957	3B-7, C-4, DH-3, OF-1
1987			78	.273	.403	216	59	8	1	6	2.8	34	37	31	48	3	6	4	389	26	7	7	5.4	.983	C-61, 1B-12, OF-1
1988			94	.229	.297	249	57	8	0	3	1.2	21	27	37	62	0	15	3	342	17	4	4	3.9	.989	C-64, 1B-7, 3B-2
1989			67	.246	.311	122	30	3	1	1	0.8	9	11	12	29	1	23	6	117	8	3	3	1.9	.977	C-25, DH-21, 1B-7, 3B-3
1990			103	.249	.333	189	47	8	1	2	1.0	21	19	30	25	1	27	7	261	25	4	2	3.9	.986	C-63, DH-14, 3B-8, 1B-6
5 yrs.			357	.252	.345	806	203	30	3	13	1.6	89	95	113	171	6	76	22	1123	84	19	18	3.4	.985	C-217, DH-38, 1B-32, 3B-20, OF-2

Matt Stark

STARK, MATTHEW SCOTT
B. Jan. 21, 1965, Whittier, Calif.
BR TR 6′ 4″ 225 lbs.

Year	Team		Games	BA	SA	AB	H	2B	3B	HR	HR%	R	RBI	BB	SO	SB	AB	H	PO	A	E	DP	TC/G	FA	G by Pos
1987	TOR	A	5	.083	.083	12	1	0	0	0	0.0	0	0	0	0	0	2	0	25	1	0	0	5.2	1.000	C-5
1990	CHI	A	8	.250	.313	16	4	1	0	0	0.0	0	3	1	6	0	2	0	0	0	0	0	0.0	.987	DH-6
2 yrs.			13	.179	.214	28	5	1	0	0	0.0	0	3	1	6	0	4	0	25	1	0	0	2.0	.000	DH-6, C-5

Terry Steinbach

STEINBACH, TERRY LEE
B. Mar. 2, 1962, New Ulm, Minn.
BR TR 6′ 1″ 195 lbs.

	Games	BA	SA	AB	H	2B	3B	HR	HR%	R	RBI	BB	SO	SB
April	15	.226	.358	53	12	4	0	1	1.9	2	5	4	7	0
May	23	.169	.265	83	14	2	0	2	2.4	6	7	4	15	0
June	25	.325	.482	83	27	3	2	2	2.4	8	14	3	18	0
July	6	.227	.227	22	5	0	0	0	0.0	2	3	2	5	0
Aug	21	.253	.373	75	19	3	0	2	2.7	7	7	2	13	0
Sept/Oct	24	.286	.429	63	18	3	0	2	3.2	7	21	4	8	0
Day	46	.247	.364	162	40	8	1	3	1.9	15	22	9	31	0
Night	68	.253	.378	217	55	7	1	6	2.8	17	35	10	35	0
vs. Left		.284	.440	109	31	6	1	3	2.8	14	16	8	15	0
vs. Right		.237	.344	270	64	9	1	6	2.2	18	41	11	51	0
On Grass	95	.254	.375	315	80	11	0	9	2.9	30	50	17	49	0
On Turf	19	.234	.359	64	15	4	2	0	0.0	2	7	2	17	0
Home	57	.249	.324	185	46	5	0	3	1.6	18	28	12	33	0
Road	57	.253	.418	194	49	10	2	6	3.1	14	29	7	33	0
Division Rivals														
vs. CAL	8	.192	.269	26	5	2	0	0	0.0	1	0	1	2	0
vs. CHI	12	.310	.405	42	13	1	0	1	2.4	3	7	1	9	0
vs. KC	12	.256	.308	39	10	0	1	0	0.0	4	4	2	13	0
vs. MIN	10	.265	.471	34	9	1	0	2	5.9	4	8	3	5	0
vs. SEA	11	.211	.289	38	8	3	0	0	0.0	2	9	2	7	0
vs. TEX	11	.292	.333	24	7	1	0	0	0.0	1	4	2	1	0
On 3B < 2 Out		.524	.762	21	11	2	0	1	4.8	1	23	0	4	

CATCHER — AVERAGE, RBI, HR, SB (AL AVG)

Year	Team		Games	BA	SA	AB	H	2B	3B	HR	HR%	R	RBI	BB	SO	SB	AB	H	PO	A	E	DP	TC/G	FA	G by Pos
1986	OAK	A	6	.333	.733	15	5	0	0	2	13.3	3	4	1	0	0	2	1	21	4	1	1	4.3	.962	C-5
1987			122	.284	.463	391	111	16	3	16	4.1	66	56	32	66	1	7	4	642	44	10	6	5.7	.986	C-107, 3B-10, 1B-1
1988			104	.265	.402	351	93	19	1	9	2.6	42	51	33	47	3	4	2	536	58	9	10	5.8	.985	C-84, 3B-9, 1B-8, DH-7, OF-1
1989			130	.273	.352	454	124	13	1	7	1.5	37	42	30	66	1	8	2	612	47	11	14	5.2	.984	C-103, OF-14, 1B-10, DH-4, 3B-3
1990			114	.251	.372	379	95	15	2	9	2.3	32	57	19	66	0	14	4	401	31	5	1	5.1	.989	C-83, DH-25, 1B-3
5 yrs.			476	.269	.399	1590	428	63	7	43	2.7	180	210	115	245	5	35	13	2212	184	36	32	5.1	.985	C-382, DH-36, 1B-22, 3B-22, OF-15

Year	Team		Games	BA	SA	AB	H	2B	3B	HR	HR%	R	RBI	BB	SO	SB	PH AB	PH H	PO	A	E	DP	TC/G	FA	G by Pos

Terry Steinbach *Continued*

LEAGUE CHAMPIONSHIP SERIES

Year	Team		Games	BA	SA	AB	H	2B	3B	HR	HR%	R	RBI	BB	SO	SB	PH AB	PH H	PO	A	E	DP	TC/G	FA	G by Pos
1988	OAK	A	2	.250	.250	4	1	0	0	0	0.0	0	0	2	0	0	0	0	12	0	0	0	6.0	1.000	C-2
1989			4	.200	.200	15	3	0	0	0	0.0	0	1	1	5	0	0	0	17	0	0	0	4.3	1.000	C-3, DH-1
1990			3	.455	.455	11	5	0	0	0	0.0	2	1	1	2	0	0	0	11	0	0	0	3.7	1.000	C-3
3 yrs.			9	.300	.300	30	9	0	0	0	0.0	2	2	4	7	0	0	0	40	0	0	0	4.4	.000	C-8, DH-1

WORLD SERIES

Year	Team		Games	BA	SA	AB	H	2B	3B	HR	HR%	R	RBI	BB	SO	SB	PH AB	PH H	PO	A	E	DP	TC/G	FA	G by Pos
1988	OAK	A	3	.364	.455	11	4	1	0	0	0.0	0	0	0	2	0	0	0	11	3	0	0	4.7	1.000	C-2, DH-1
1989			4	.250	.563	16	4	0	1	1	6.3	3	7	2	1	0	0	0	27	2	0	0	7.3	1.000	C-4
1990			3	.125	.125	8	1	0	0	0	0.0	0	0	0	1	0	0	0	8	1	0	0	3.0	1.000	C-3
3 yrs.			10	.257	.429	35	9	1	1	1	2.9	3	7	2	4	0	0	0	46	6	0	0	5.2	.000	C-9, DH-1

Ray Stephens

STEPHENS, CARL RAY
B. Sept. 22, 1962, Houston, Tex.
BR TR 6' 190 lbs.

Year	Team		Games	BA	SA	AB	H	2B	3B	HR	HR%	R	RBI	BB	SO	SB	PH AB	PH H	PO	A	E	DP	TC/G	FA	G by Pos
1990	STL	N	5	.133	.400	15	2	1	0	1	6.6	2	1	0	3	0	0	0	31	2	0	0	6.6	1.000	C-5

Phil Stephenson

STEPHENSON, PHILLIP RAYMOND
B. Sept. 19, 1960, Guthrie, Okla.
BL TL 6' 1" 195 lbs.

Year	Team		Games	BA	SA	AB	H	2B	3B	HR	HR%	R	RBI	BB	SO	SB	PH AB	PH H	PO	A	E	DP	TC/G	FA	G by Pos
1989	2 teams		CHI N (17G — .143)			SD N (10G — .353)																			
"	total		27	.237	.395	38	9	0	0	2	5.3	4	2	5	5	1	14	2	42	4	1	3	1.7	.979	1B-8, OF-3
1990	SD	N	103	.209	.335	182	38	9	1	4	2.1	26	19	30	43	2	35	7	345	36	1	33	6.4	.997	1B-60
2 yrs.			130	.214	.345	220	47	9	1	6	2.7	30	21	35	48	3	49	9	387	40	2	36	3.3	.995	1B-68, OF-3

Lee Stevens

STEVENS, DeWAIN LEE
B. July 10, 1967, Kansas City, Mo.
BL TL 6' 4" 205 lbs.

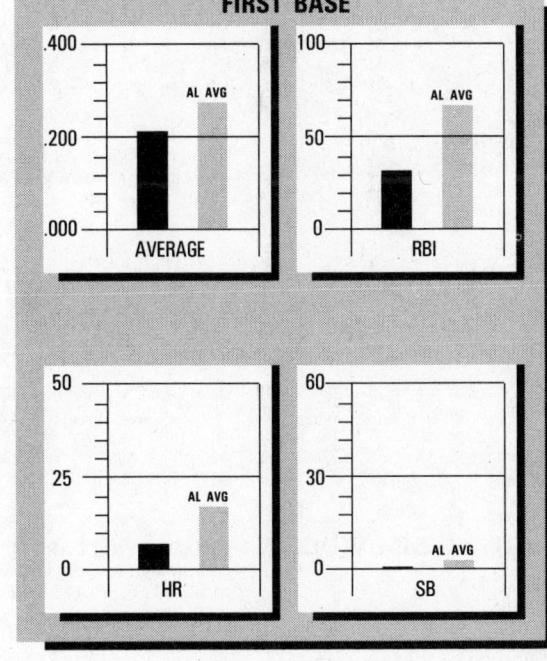

FIRST BASE

	Games	BA	SA	AB	H	2B	3B	HR	HR%	R	RBI	BB	SO	SB
April				0	0	0	0	0		0	0	0	0	0
May				0	0	0	0	0		0	0	0	0	0
June				0	0	0	0	0		0	0	0	0	0
July	15	.232	.411	56	13	4	0	2	3.6	6	8	4	16	0
Aug	27	.233	.330	103	24	1	0	3	2.9	14	13	11	29	0
Sept/Oct	25	.180	.303	89	16	5	0	2	2.2	8	11	7	30	1
Day	18	.130	.159	69	9	2	0	0	0.0	3	4	2	27	0
Night	49	.246	.408	179	44	8	0	7	3.9	25	28	20	48	1
vs. Left		.204	.278	54	11	1	0	1	1.9	4	9	5	19	0
vs. Right		.216	.356	194	42	9	0	6	3.1	24	23	17	56	1
On Grass	58	.213	.333	216	46	8	0	6	2.8	24	28	20	67	1
On Turf	9	.219	.375	32	7	2	0	1	3.1	4	4	2	8	0
Home	36	.256	.391	133	34	6	0	4	3.0	18	20	12	38	0
Road	31	.165	.278	115	19	4	0	3	2.6	10	12	10	37	1
Division Rivals														
vs. CHI	7	.154	.308	26	4	1	0	1	3.8	1	5	2	6	0
vs. KC	7	.214	.357	28	6	4	0	0	0.0	2	1	1	9	0
vs. MIN	6	.400	.600	20	8	1	0	1	5.0	4	5	3	5	0
vs. OAK	10	.268	.463	41	11	2	0	2	4.9	6	4	3	14	0
vs. SEA	6	.118	.118	17	2	0	0	0	0.0	2	2	2	4	0
vs. TEX	5	.294	.294	17	5	0	0	0	0.0	3	1	2	5	1
On 3B < 2 Out		.200	.200	15	3	0	0	0	0.0	0	10	1	6	

Year	Team		Games	BA	SA	AB	H	2B	3B	HR	HR%	R	RBI	BB	SO	SB	PH AB	PH H	PO	A	E	DP	TC/G	FA	G by Pos
1990	CAL	A	67	.214	.339	248	53	10	0	7	2.8	28	32	22	75	1	3	0	597	36	4	62	9.5	.994	1B-67

																PINCH HIT								
Year	Team	Games	BA	SA	AB	H	2B	3B	HR	HR%	R	RBI	BB	SO	SB	AB	H	PO	A	E	DP	TC/G	FA	G by Pos

Kurt Stillwell

STILLWELL, KURT ANDREW
Son of Ron Stillwell.
B. June 4, 1965, Glendale, Calif.
BB TR 5′ 11″ 165 lbs.

Year	Team	Games	BA	SA	AB	H	2B	3B	HR	HR%	R	RBI	BB	SO	SB	AB	H	PO	A	E	DP	TC/G	FA	G by Pos
April		17	.386	.596	57	22	7	1	1	1.8	10	9	5	11	0									
May		27	.273	.333	99	27	4	1	0	0.0	14	7	15	11	0									
June		24	.264	.402	87	23	8	2	0	0.0	10	12	5	9	0									
July		25	.182	.253	99	18	4	0	1	1.0	9	10	4	13	0									
Aug		25	.230	.276	87	20	4	0	0	0.0	9	6	3	10	0									
Sept/Oct		26	.208	.351	77	16	8	0	1	1.3	8	7	7	6	0									
Day		35	.306	.425	134	41	13	0	1	0.7	16	13	12	13	0									
Night		109	.228	.325	372	85	22	4	2	0.5	44	38	27	47	0									
vs. Left			.211	.313	128	27	9	2	0	0.0	21	20	17	15	0									
vs. Right			.262	.365	378	99	26	2	3	0.8	39	31	22	45	0									
On Grass		56	.223	.280	211	47	12	0	0	0.0	18	13	15	21	0									
On Turf		88	.268	.403	295	79	23	4	3	1.0	42	38	24	39	0									
Home		73	.268	.413	254	68	20	4	3	1.2	37	34	20	32	0									
Road		71	.230	.290	252	58	15	0	0	0.0	23	17	19	28	0									
Division Rivals																								
vs. CAL		12	.244	.366	41	10	3	1	0	0.0	2	5	3	6	0									
vs. CHI		11	.268	.268	41	11	0	0	0	0.0	3	2	4	4	0									
vs. MIN		12	.184	.184	38	7	0	0	0	0.0	5	3	1	4	0									
vs. OAK		11	.171	.366	41	7	5	0	1	2.4	6	8	2	2	0									
vs. SEA		10	.385	.654	26	10	5	1	0	0.0	7	3	5	3	0									
vs. TEX		13	.224	.347	49	11	3	0	1	2.0	6	5	3	9	0									
On 3B < 2 Out			.389	.667	18	7	2	0	1	5.6	1	23	2	1										
1986	CIN N	104	.229	.258	279	64	6	1	0	0.0	31	26	30	47	6	20	6	107	205	16	40	3.2	.951	SS-80
1987		131	.258	.375	395	102	20	7	4	1.0	54	33	32	50	4	29	8	144	247	23	38	3.2	.944	SS-51, 2B-37, 3B-20
1988	KC A	128	.251	.399	459	115	28	5	10	2.2	63	53	47	76	6	4	0	170	349	13	60	4.2	.976	SS-124
1989		130	.261	.380	463	121	20	7	7	1.5	52	54	42	64	9	4	1	179	334	16	65	4.1	.970	SS-130
1990		144	.249	.352	506	126	35	4	3	0.5	60	51	39	60	0	9	2	181	350	24	79	3.9	.957	SS-141
5 yrs.		637	.251	.360	2102	528	109	24	24	1.1	260	217	190	297	25	66	17	781	1485	92	282	3.7	.961	SS-526, 2B-37, 3B-20

Jeff Stone

STONE, JEFFREY GLEN
B. Dec. 26, 1960, Kennett, Mo.
BL TR 6′ 175 lbs.

Year	Team	Games	BA	SA	AB	H	2B	3B	HR	HR%	R	RBI	BB	SO	SB	AB	H	PO	A	E	DP	TC/G	FA	G by Pos
1983	PHI N	9	.750	1.750	4	3	0	2	0	0.0	2	3	0	1	4	1	1	0	0	0	0	0.0	—	OF-1
1984		51	.362	.465	185	67	4	6	1	0.5	27	15	9	26	27	5	0	75	1	7	0	1.6	.916	OF-46
1985		88	.265	.337	264	70	4	3	3	1.1	36	11	15	50	15	18	5	82	4	3	0	1.0	.966	OF-69
1986		82	.277	.406	249	69	6	4	6	2.4	32	19	20	52	19	21	7	103	8	2	1	1.4	.982	OF-58
1987		66	.256	.352	125	32	7	1	1	0.8	19	16	8	38	3	37	9	32	3	0	1	0.5	1.000	OF-25
1988	BAL A	26	.164	.180	61	10	1	0	0	0.0	4	1	4	11	4	7	2	23	3	1	1	1.0	.963	OF-21, DH-1
1989	2 teams		TEX A	(22G — .167)				BOS A	(18G — .200)															
"	total	40	.176	.275	51	9	1	2	0	0.0	8	6	4	7	3	12	1	8	0	0	0	0.2	1.000	DH-18, OF-14
1990	BOS A	10	.500	.500	2	1	0	0	0	0.0	1	1	0	1	0	1	0	0	0	0	0	0.0	1.000	DH-2
8 yrs.		372	.277	.375	941	261	23	18	11	1.2	129	72	60	186	75	102	25	323	19	13	3	1.0	.963	OF-234, DH-21

Darryl Strawberry

STRAWBERRY, DARRYL EUGENE (The Straw Man)
B. Mar. 12, 1962, Los Angeles, Calif.
BL TL 6′ 6″ 190 lbs.

Year	Team	Games	BA	SA	AB	H	2B	3B	HR	HR%	R	RBI	BB	SO	SB	AB	H	PO	A	E	DP	TC/G	FA	G by Pos
April		19	.288	.424	66	19	1	1	2	3.0	9	9	13	17	3									
May		24	.214	.405	84	18	1	0	5	6.0	11	10	9	19	2									
June		26	.376	.731	93	35	3	0	10	10.8	22	27	17	12	3									
July		28	.247	.536	97	24	4	0	8	8.2	19	21	12	21	5									
Aug		29	.265	.422	102	27	4	0	4	3.9	14	18	13	20	2									
Sept/Oct		26	.270	.560	100	27	5	0	8	8.0	17	23	6	21	0									
Day		51	.301	.503	183	55	8	1	9	4.9	29	38	23	37	3									
Night		101	.265	.526	359	95	10	0	28	7.8	63	70	47	73	12									
vs. Left			.244	.406	217	53	8	0	9	4.1	23	29	17	51	5									
vs. Right			.298	.594	325	97	10	1	28	8.6	69	79	53	59	10									

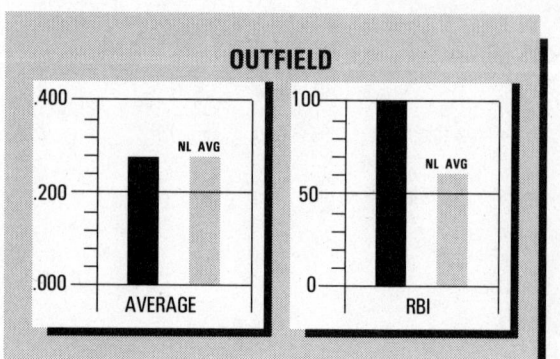

Year	Team	Games	BA	SA	AB	H	2B	3B	HR	HR%	R	RBI	BB	SO	SB	PINCH HIT AB	H	PO	A	E	DP	TC/G	FA	G by Pos

Darryl Strawberry *Continued*

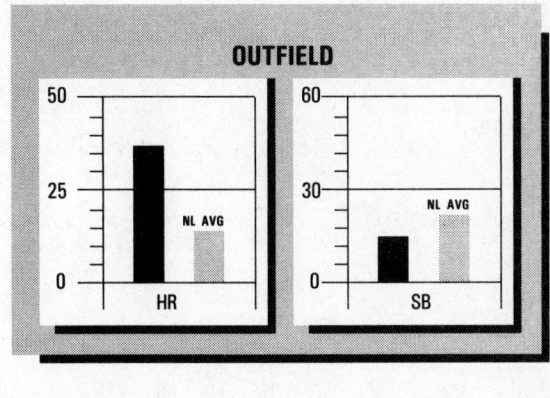

On Grass		109	.268	.520	396	106	11	1	29	7.3	72	82	45	76	8									
On Turf		43	.301	.514	146	44	7	0	8	5.5	20	26	25	34	7									
Home		77	.254	.549	268	68	5	1	24	9.0	49	67	31	52	5									
Road		75	.299	.489	274	82	13	0	13	4.7	43	41	39	58	10									
Division Rivals																								
vs. CHI		14	.283	.509	53	15	3	0	3	5.7	14	8	10	12	0									
vs. MON		17	.333	.533	60	20	1	1	3	5.0	7	14	6	11	2									
vs. PHI		18	.328	.517	58	19	2	0	3	5.2	8	13	11	8	1									
vs. PIT		14	.239	.761	46	11	0	0	8	17.4	9	18	7	12	1									
vs. STL		18	.338	.515	68	23	6	0	2	2.9	9	14	8	17	1									
On 3B < 2 Out			.346	.500	26	9	1	0	1	3.8	1	19	4	6										
1983	NY N	122	.257	.512	420	108	15	7	26	6.2	63	74	47	128	19	4	0	232	8	4	0	2.0	.984	OF-117
1984		147	.251	.467	522	131	27	4	26	5.0	75	97	75	131	27	4	2	276	11	6	3	2.0	.980	OF-146
1985		111	.277	.557	393	109	15	4	29	7.4	78	79	73	96	26	2	0	211	5	2	2	2.0	.991	OF-110
1986		136	.259	.507	475	123	27	5	27	5.7	76	93	72	141	28	8	0	226	10	6	3	1.8	.975	OF-131
1987		154	.284	.583	532	151	32	5	39	7.3	108	104	97	122	36	3	1	272	6	8	3	1.9	.972	OF-151
1988		153	.269	**.545**	543	146	27	3	**39**	7.2	101	101	85	127	29	2	0	297	4	9	3	2.0	.971	OF-150
1989		134	.225	.466	476	107	26	1	29	6.1	69	77	61	105	11	6	1	272	4	8	2	2.1	.972	OF-131
1990		152	.277	.518	542	150	18	1	37	**6.8**	92	108	70	110	15	5	0	268	10	3	4	1.9	.989	OF-149
8 yrs.		1109	.263	.520	3903	1025	187	30	252	6.4	662	733	580	960	191	34	4	2054	58	46	20	1.9	.979	OF-1085

LEAGUE CHAMPIONSHIP SERIES

Year	Team	Games	BA	SA	AB	H	2B	3B	HR	HR%	R	RBI	BB	SO	SB	AB	H	PO	A	E	DP	TC/G	FA	G by Pos
1986	NY N	6	.227	.545	22	5	1	0	2	9.1	4	5	3	12	1	0	0	9	0	0	0	1.5	1.000	OF-6
1988		7	.300	.467	30	9	2	0	1	3.3	5	6	2	5	0	0	0	11	0	0	0	1.6	1.000	OF-7
2 yrs.		13	.269	.500	52	14	3	0	3	5.8	9	11	5	17	1	0	0	20	0	0	0	1.5	.000	OF-13

WORLD SERIES

Year	Team	Games	BA	SA	AB	H	2B	3B	HR	HR%	R	RBI	BB	SO	SB	AB	H	PO	A	E	DP	TC/G	FA	G by Pos
1986	NY N	7	.208	.375	24	5	1	0	1	4.2	4	1	4	6	3	0	0	19	0	0	0	2.7	1.000	OF-7

Franklin Stubbs

STUBBS, FRANKLIN LEE
B. Oct. 21, 1960, Richland, N. C.
BL TL 6' 2" 205 lbs.

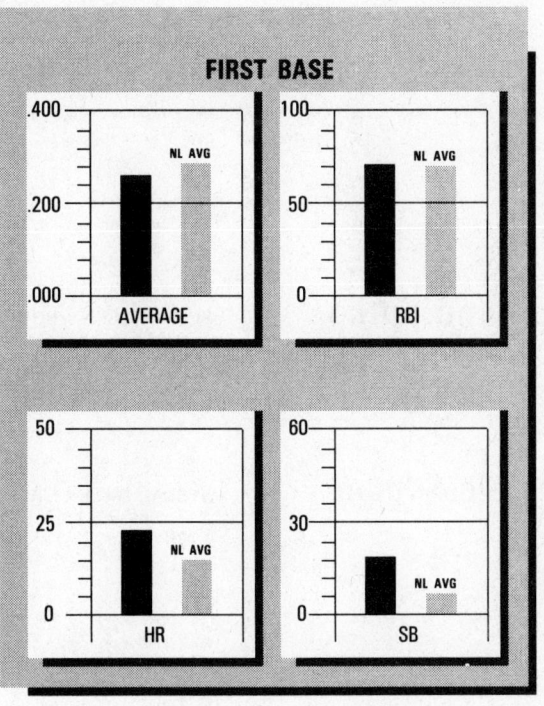

April		15	.250	.500	36	9	3	0	2	5.6	3	5	2	10	1									
May		24	.245	.510	49	12	2	1	3	6.1	7	6	8	11	1									
June		26	.269	.513	78	21	4	0	5	6.4	7	14	6	23	3									
July		29	.204	.352	108	22	4	0	4	3.7	15	13	7	33	3									
Aug		25	.304	.544	79	24	0	0	5	6.3	14	16	14	18	5									
Sept/Oct		27	.296	.500	98	29	6	1	4	4.1	13	17	11	19	6									
Day		39	.227	.378	119	27	6	0	4	3.4	13	17	7	35	5									
Night		107	.274	.511	329	90	17	2	19	5.8	46	54	41	79	14									
vs. Left			.258	.465	159	41	10	1	7	4.4	19	23	10	41	4									
vs. Right			.263	.481	289	76	13	1	16	5.5	40	48	38	73	15									
On Grass		43	.229	.412	131	30	3	0	7	5.3	20	18	14	35	1									
On Turf		103	.274	.502	317	87	20	2	16	5.0	39	53	34	79	18									
Home		74	.253	.445	229	58	15	1	9	3.9	27	39	25	57	12									
Road		72	.269	.507	219	59	8	1	14	6.4	32	32	23	57	7									
Division Rivals																								
vs. ATL		14	.271	.458	48	13	3	0	2	4.2	7	6	6	8	1									
vs. CIN		15	.286	.469	49	14	1	1	2	4.1	3	6	4	14	5									
vs. LA		17	.245	.642	53	13	3	0	6	11.3	11	13	6	17	1									
vs. SD		17	.169	.271	59	10	3	0	1	1.7	3	3	6	18	2									
vs. SF		17	.250	.364	44	11	2	0	1	2.3	6	8	5	9	1									
On 3B < 2 Out			.227	.455	22	5	2	0	1	4.5	1	15	3	8										
1984	LA N	87	.194	.341	217	42	2	3	8	3.7	22	17	24	63	2	22	4	417	37	4	31	5.3	.991	1B-51, OF-20
1985		10	.222	.222	9	2	0	0	0	0.0	0	2	0	3	0	7	2	11	0	0	1	1.1	1.000	1B-4
1986		132	.226	.421	420	95	11	1	23	5.5	55	58	37	107	7	12	0	244	14	7	3	2.0	.974	OF-124, 1B-13
1987		129	.233	.415	386	90	16	1	16	4.1	48	52	31	85	8	11	3	830	79	5	65	7.1	.995	1B-111, OF-18
1988		115	.223	.376	242	54	13	0	8	3.3	30	34	23	61	11	26	8	530	57	13	41	5.2	.978	1B-84, OF-13
1989		69	.291	.466	103	30	6	0	4	3.9	11	15	16	27	3	26	6	70	5	3	5	1.1	.962	OF-28, 1B-7
1990	HOU N	146	.261	.475	448	117	23	2	23	5.1	59	71	48	114	19	11	3	609	43	6	42	4.8	.991	1B-72, OF-71
7 yrs.		688	.236	.419	1825	430	71	9	82	4.5	225	249	179	460	50	115	26	2711	235	38	188	4.3	.987	1B-342, OF-274

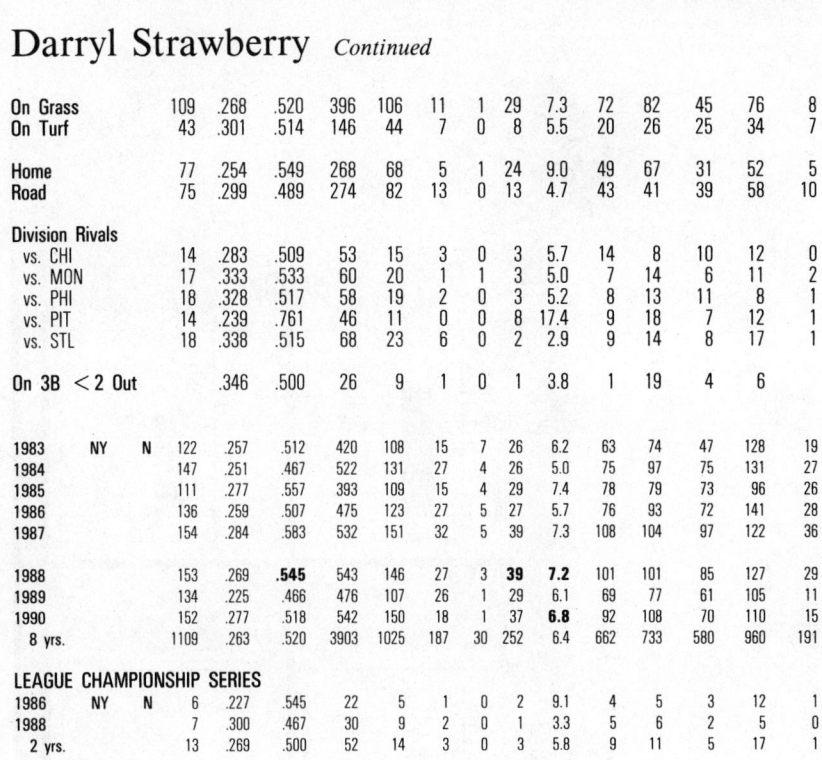

Year	Team	Games	BA	SA	AB	H	2B	3B	HR	HR%	R	RBI	BB	SO	SB	PINCH HIT AB	PINCH HIT H	PO	A	E	DP	TC/G	FA	G by Pos

Franklin Stubbs *Continued*

LEAGUE CHAMPIONSHIP SERIES

Year	Team	Games	BA	SA	AB	H	2B	3B	HR	HR%	R	RBI	BB	SO	SB	PH AB	PH H	PO	A	E	DP	TC/G	FA	G by Pos
1988	LA	N	4	.250	.250	8	2	0	0	0	0.0	0	0	0	4	0	2	0	16	2	0	2	4.5	1.000	1B-3

WORLD SERIES

1988	LA	N	5	.294	.412	17	5	2	0	0	0.0	3	2	1	3	0	0	0	34	0	0	3	6.8	1.000	1B-5

B. J. Surhoff

SURHOFF, WILLIAM JAMES
Brother of Rick Surhoff.
B. Aug. 4, 1964, Bronx, N. Y.
BL TR 6′ 1″ 185 lbs.

	Games	BA	SA	AB	H	2B	3B	HR	HR%	R	RBI	BB	SO	SB
April	14	.255	.447	47	12	4	1	1	2.1	10	9	5	6	2
May	23	.253	.360	75	19	2	0	2	2.7	9	9	7	6	3
June	26	.320	.470	100	32	7	1	2	2.0	9	6	2	8	4
July	20	.257	.286	70	18	2	0	0	0.0	10	8	9	7	5
Aug	21	.297	.351	74	22	2	1	0	0.0	8	10	6	4	2
Sept/Oct	31	.259	.343	108	28	4	1	1	0.9	9	17	12	6	2
Day	43	.253	.347	150	38	7	2	1	0.7	21	17	12	15	5
Night	92	.287	.389	324	93	14	2	5	1.5	34	42	29	22	13
vs. Left		.317	.433	104	33	4	1	2	1.9	8	17	8	9	5
vs. Right		.265	.359	370	98	17	3	4	1.1	47	42	33	28	13
On Grass	114	.271	.374	406	110	18	3	6	1.5	48	52	35	31	15
On Turf	21	.309	.382	68	21	3	1	0	0.0	7	7	6	6	3
Home	69	.306	.417	235	72	10	2	4	1.7	32	35	22	18	10
Road	66	.247	.335	239	59	11	2	2	0.8	23	24	19	19	8
Division Rivals														
vs. BAL	13	.346	.500	52	18	2	0	2	3.8	6	4	2	4	3
vs. BOS	13	.179	.256	39	7	1	1	0	0.0	7	6	4	2	3
vs. CLE	10	.179	.205	39	7	1	0	0	0.0	0	1	3	4	2
vs. DET	11	.250	.425	40	10	1	0	2	5.0	5	10	5	2	1
vs. NY	8	.241	.310	29	7	2	0	0	0.0	2	2	2	1	0
vs. TOR	13	.422	.622	45	19	5	2	0	0.0	7	11	2	3	0
On 3B < 2 Out		.478	.826	23	11	1	2	1	4.3	1	28	1	3	

Year	Team		Games	BA	SA	AB	H	2B	3B	HR	HR%	R	RBI	BB	SO	SB	PH AB	PH H	PO	A	E	DP	TC/G	FA	G by Pos
1987	MIL	A	115	.299	.423	395	118	22	3	7	1.8	50	68	36	30	11	10	3	648	56	11	12	6.2	.985	C-98, 3B-10, 1B-1
1988			139	.245	.318	493	121	21	0	5	1.0	47	38	31	49	21	9	2	550	94	8	3	4.7	.988	C-106, 3B-31, 1B-2, SS-1, OF-1
1989			126	.248	.339	436	108	17	4	5	1.1	42	55	25	29	14	5	0	530	58	10	7	4.7	.983	C-106, DH-12, 3B-6
1990			135	.276	.376	474	131	21	4	6	1.2	55	59	41	37	18	8	2	619	62	12	11	5.3	.983	C-125, 3B-11
4 yrs.			515	.266	.362	1798	478	81	11	23	1.3	194	220	133	145	64	32	7	2347	270	41	33	5.2	.985	C-435, 3B-58, DH-12, 1B-3, SS-1, OF-1

Glenn Sutko

SUTKO, GLENN EDWARD
B. May 9, 1968, Atlanta, Ga.
BR TR 6′ 3″ 225 lbs.

Year	Team		Games	BA	SA	AB	H	2B	3B	HR	HR%	R	RBI	BB	SO	SB	PH AB	PH H	PO	A	E	DP	TC/G	FA	G by Pos
1990	CIN	N	1	.000	.000	1	0	0	0	0	0.0	0	0	0	1	0	0	0	3	0	0	0	3.0	1.000	C-1

Dale Sveum

SVEUM, DALE CURTIS
B. Nov. 23, 1963, Richmond, Calif.
BB TR 6′ 2″ 185 lbs.

Year	Team		Games	BA	SA	AB	H	2B	3B	HR	HR%	R	RBI	BB	SO	SB	PH AB	PH H	PO	A	E	DP	TC/G	FA	G by Pos
1986	MIL	A	91	.246	.366	317	78	13	2	7	2.2	35	35	32	63	4	2	0	92	179	30	19	3.3	.900	3B-65, 2B-13, SS-13
1987			153	.252	.454	535	135	27	3	25	4.7	86	95	40	133	2	1	1	242	396	23	89	4.3	.965	SS-142, 2B-13
1988			129	.242	.347	467	113	14	4	9	1.9	41	51	21	122	1	0	0	209	375	27	94	4.7	.956	SS-127, DH-1, 2B-1
1990			48	.197	.282	117	23	7	0	1	0.8	15	12	12	30	0	6	0	59	63	6	10	2.8	.953	3B-22, 2B-16, 1B-5, SS-5
4 yrs.			421	.243	.386	1436	349	61	9	42	2.9	177	193	105	348	7	9	1	602	1013	86	212	4.0	.949	SS-287, 3B-87, 2B-43, 1B-5, DH-1

Year	Team		Games	BA	SA	AB	H	2B	3B	HR	HR%	R	RBI	BB	SO	SB	PINCH HIT AB	PINCH HIT H	PO	A	E	DP	TC/G	FA	G by Pos

Pat Tabler

TABLER, PATRICK SEAN
B. Feb. 2, 1958, Hamilton, Ohio
BR TR 6' 3" 175 lbs.

Split			Games	BA	SA	AB	H	2B	3B	HR	HR%	R	RBI	BB	SO	SB
April			12	.233	.267	30	7	1	0	0	0.0	1	1	3	2	0
May			12	.231	.269	26	6	1	0	0	0.0	2	3	2	5	0
June			12	.229	.343	35	8	4	0	0	0.0	2	1	5	8	0
July			23	.313	.448	67	21	6	0	1	1.5	6	13	8	3	0
Aug			16	.297	.351	37	11	2	0	0	0.0	1	1	2	3	0
Sept/Oct			17	.279	.419	43	12	1	1	1	2.3	6	10	3	8	0
Day			27	.197	.239	71	14	3	0	0	0.0	2	9	11	8	0
Night			65	.305	.425	167	51	12	1	2	1.2	16	20	12	21	0
vs. Left				.333	.448	105	35	7	1	1	1.0	8	14	11	13	0
vs. Right				.226	.308	133	30	8	0	1	0.8	10	15	12	16	0
On Grass			36	.310	.414	87	27	3	0	2	2.3	7	18	10	9	0
On Turf			56	.252	.344	151	38	12	1	0	0.0	11	11	13	20	0
Home			48	.246	.342	114	28	8	0	1	0.9	7	13	14	14	0
Road			44	.298	.395	124	37	7	1	1	0.8	11	16	9	15	0
Division Rivals																
vs. CHI			5	.133	.333	15	2	0	0	1	6.7	1	3	3	3	0
vs. MON			4	.200	.400	10	2	0	1	0	0.0	1	0	0	3	0
vs. PHI			1	1.000	1.000	2	2	0	0	0	0.0	0	2	0	0	0
vs. PIT			5	.333	.400	15	5	1	0	0	0.0	3	3	0	2	0
vs. STL			2	1.000	1.000	1	1	0	0	0	0.0	1	2	0	0	0
On 3B < 2 Out				.462	.462	13	6	0	0	0	0.0	0	12	3	1	

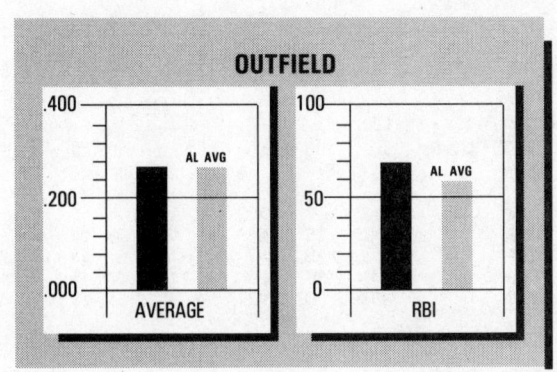

OUTFIELD

Year	Team		Games	BA	SA	AB	H	2B	3B	HR	HR%	R	RBI	BB	SO	SB	PINCH HIT AB	H	PO	A	E	DP	TC/G	FA	G by Pos
1981	CHI	N	35	.188	.267	101	19	3	1	1	1.0	11	5	13	26	0	0	0	70	93	3	17	4.7	.982	2B-35
1982			25	.235	.365	85	20	4	2	1	1.2	9	7	6	20	0	0	0	23	33	3	3	2.4	.949	3B-25
1983	CLE	A	124	.291	.409	430	125	23	5	6	1.4	56	65	56	63	2	5	2	197	55	11	6	2.1	.958	OF-80, 3B-25, DH-6, 2B-2
1984			144	.290	.410	473	137	21	3	10	2.1	66	68	47	62	3	6	1	532	89	7	54	4.4	.989	1B-67, OF-43, 3B-36, DH-1, 2B-1
1985			117	.275	.371	404	111	18	3	5	1.2	47	59	27	55	0	8	4	744	77	14	78	7.1	.983	1B-92, DH-18, 3B-4, 2B-1
1986			130	.326	.433	473	154	29	6	6	1.3	61	48	29	75	3	9	1	846	84	9	87	7.2	.990	1B-107, DH-18
1987			151	.307	.439	553	170	34	3	11	2.0	66	86	51	84	5	7	2	650	75	12	49	4.9	.984	1B-82, DH-66
1988	2 teams		CLE A (41G — .224)			KC A (89G — .309)																			
"	total		130	.282	.358	444	125	22	3	2	0.5	53	66	46	68	3	8	2	182	10	5	11	1.5	.975	OF-37, DH-29, 1B-17, 3B-1
1989	KC	A	123	.259	.308	390	101	11	1	2	0.5	36	42	37	42	0	13	2	217	25	4	11	2.0	.984	OF-55, DH-39, 1B-20, 2B-3, 3B-1
1990	2 teams		KC A (75G — .272)			NY N (17G — .279)																			
"	total		92	.273	.370	238	65	15	1	2	0.8	18	29	23	29	0	18	4	121	11	2	8	2.2	.985	OF-52, DH-15, 3B-6, 1B-5
10 yrs.			1071	.286	.388	3591	1027	180	24	46	1.3	423	475	335	524	16	74	18	3582	552	70	324	3.9	.983	1B-390, OF-267, DH-192, 3B-98, 2B-42

Danny Tartabull

TARTABULL, DANILO
Born Danilo Tartabull y Mora. Son of Jose Tartabull.
B. Oct. 30, 1962, San Juan, Puerto Rico
BR TR 6' 1" 185 lbs.

Split			Games	BA	SA	AB	H	2B	3B	HR	HR%	R	RBI	BB	SO	SB
April			1	.400	1.000	5	2	0	0	1	20.0	2	2	0	1	0
May			12	.119	.190	42	5	0	0	1	2.4	1	4	3	13	0
June			24	.303	.573	89	27	6	0	6	6.7	15	19	9	28	0
July			8	.222	.333	27	6	3	0	0	0.0	3	6	4	7	1
Aug			28	.290	.500	100	29	3	0	6	6.0	14	16	14	31	0
Sept/Oct			15	.300	.500	50	15	7	0	1	2.0	6	13	6	13	0
Day			18	.296	.634	71	21	3	0	7	9.9	13	21	3	26	0
Night			70	.260	.426	242	63	16	0	8	3.3	28	39	33	67	1
vs. Left				.321	.509	106	34	5	0	5	4.7	15	17	21	28	0
vs. Right				.242	.454	207	50	14	0	10	4.8	26	43	15	65	1

OUTFIELD

Year	Team		Games	BA	SA	AB	H	2B	3B	HR	HR%	R	RBI	BB	SO	SB	PINCH HIT AB	H	PO	A	E	DP	TC/G	FA	G by Pos

Danny Tartabull *Continued*

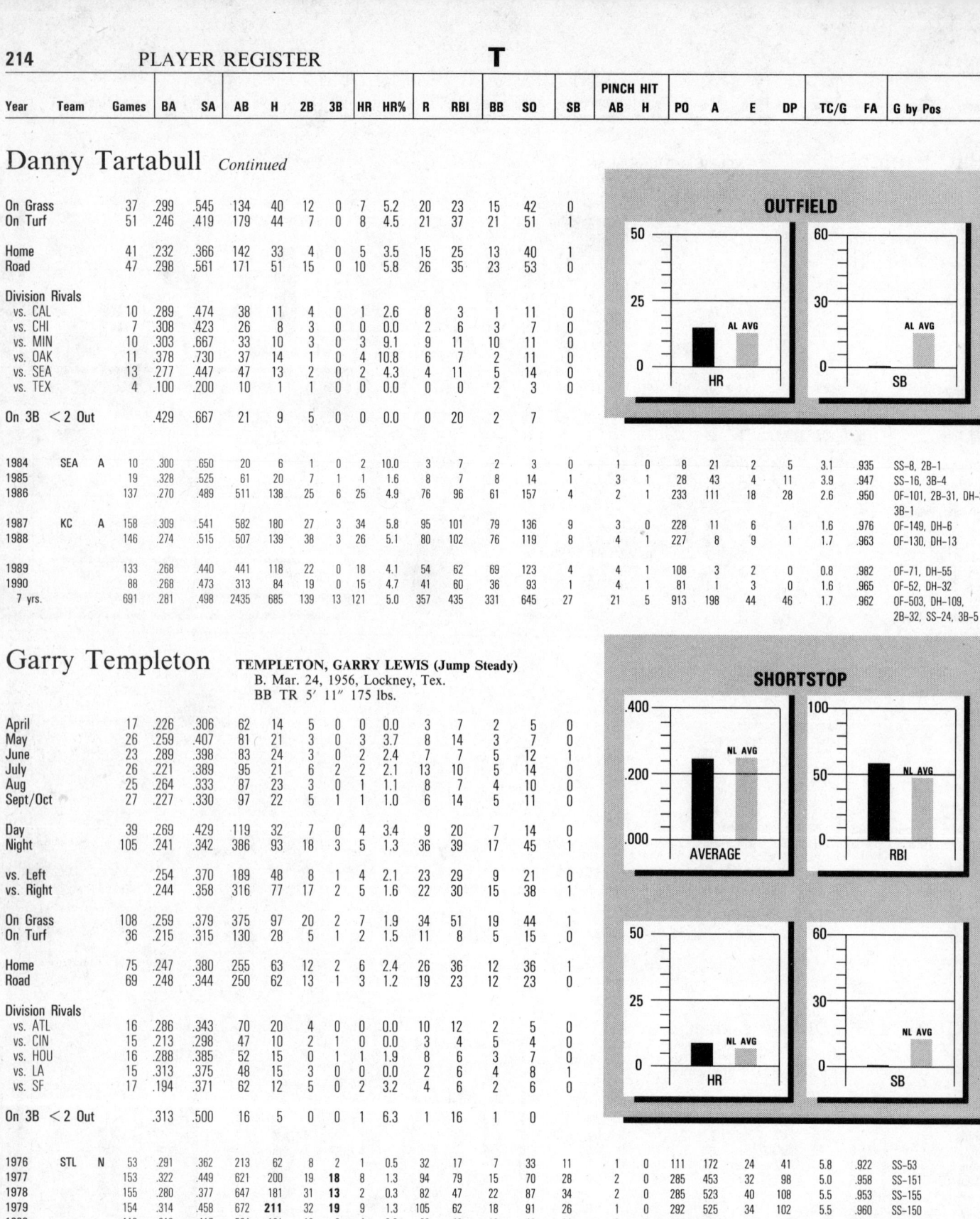

On Grass			37	.299	.545	134	40	12	0	7	5.2	20	23	15	42	0									
On Turf			51	.246	.419	179	44	7	0	8	4.5	21	37	21	51	1									
Home			41	.232	.366	142	33	4	0	5	3.5	15	25	13	40	1									
Road			47	.298	.561	171	51	15	0	10	5.8	26	35	23	53	0									
Division Rivals																									
vs. CAL			10	.289	.474	38	11	4	0	1	2.6	8	3	1	11	0									
vs. CHI			7	.308	.423	26	8	3	0	0	0.0	2	6	3	7	0									
vs. MIN			10	.303	.667	33	10	3	0	3	9.1	9	11	10	11	0									
vs. OAK			11	.378	.730	37	14	1	0	4	10.8	6	7	2	11	0									
vs. SEA			13	.277	.447	47	13	2	0	2	4.3	4	11	5	14	0									
vs. TEX			4	.100	.200	10	1	1	0	0	0.0	0	0	2	3	0									
On 3B < 2 Out				.429	.667	21	9	5	0	0	0.0	0	20	2	7										
1984	SEA	A	10	.300	.650	20	6	1	0	2	10.0	3	7	2	3	0	1	0	8	21	2	5	3.1	.935	SS-8, 2B-1
1985			19	.328	.525	61	20	7	1	1	1.6	8	7	8	14	1	3	1	28	43	4	11	3.9	.947	SS-16, 3B-4
1986			137	.270	.489	511	138	25	6	25	4.9	76	96	61	157	4	2	1	233	111	18	28	2.6	.950	OF-101, 2B-31, DH-3, 3B-1
1987	KC	A	158	.309	.541	582	180	27	3	34	5.8	95	101	79	136	9	3	0	228	11	6	1	1.6	.976	OF-149, DH-6
1988			146	.274	.515	507	139	38	3	26	5.1	80	102	76	119	8	4	1	227	8	9	1	1.7	.963	OF-130, DH-13
1989			133	.268	.440	441	118	22	0	18	4.1	54	62	69	123	4	4	1	108	3	2	0	0.8	.982	OF-71, DH-55
1990			88	.268	.473	313	84	19	0	15	4.7	41	60	36	93	1	4	1	81	1	3	0	1.6	.965	OF-52, DH-32
7 yrs.			691	.281	.498	2435	685	139	13	121	5.0	357	435	331	645	27	21	5	913	198	44	46	1.7	.962	OF-503, DH-109, 2B-32, SS-24, 3B-5

Garry Templeton

TEMPLETON, GARRY LEWIS (Jump Steady)
B. Mar. 24, 1956, Lockney, Tex.
BB TR 5' 11" 175 lbs.

April			17	.226	.306	62	14	5	0	0	0.0	3	7	2	5	0									
May			26	.259	.407	81	21	3	0	3	3.7	8	14	3	7	0									
June			23	.289	.398	83	24	3	0	2	2.4	7	7	5	12	1									
July			26	.221	.389	95	21	6	2	2	2.1	13	10	5	14	0									
Aug			25	.264	.333	87	23	3	0	1	1.1	8	7	4	10	0									
Sept/Oct			27	.227	.330	97	22	5	1	1	1.0	6	14	5	11	0									
Day			39	.269	.429	119	32	7	0	4	3.4	9	20	7	14	0									
Night			105	.241	.342	386	93	18	3	5	1.3	36	39	17	45	1									
vs. Left				.254	.370	189	48	8	1	4	2.1	23	29	9	21	0									
vs. Right				.244	.358	316	77	17	2	5	1.6	22	30	15	38	1									
On Grass			108	.259	.379	375	97	20	2	7	1.9	34	51	19	44	1									
On Turf			36	.215	.315	130	28	5	1	2	1.5	11	8	5	15	0									
Home			75	.247	.380	255	63	12	2	6	2.4	26	36	12	36	1									
Road			69	.248	.344	250	62	13	1	3	1.2	19	23	12	23	0									
Division Rivals																									
vs. ATL			16	.286	.343	70	20	4	0	0	0.0	10	12	2	5	0									
vs. CIN			15	.213	.298	47	10	2	1	0	0.0	3	4	5	4	0									
vs. HOU			16	.288	.385	52	15	0	1	1	1.9	8	6	3	7	0									
vs. LA			15	.313	.375	48	15	3	0	0	0.0	2	6	4	8	1									
vs. SF			17	.194	.371	62	12	5	0	2	3.2	4	6	2	6	0									
On 3B < 2 Out				.313	.500	16	5	0	0	1	6.3	1	16	1	0										
1976	STL	N	53	.291	.362	213	62	8	2	1	0.5	32	17	7	33	11	1	0	111	172	24	41	5.8	.922	SS-53
1977			153	.322	.449	621	200	19	**18**	8	1.3	94	79	15	70	28	2	0	285	453	32	98	5.0	.958	SS-151
1978			155	.280	.377	647	181	31	**13**	2	0.3	82	47	22	87	34	2	0	285	523	40	108	5.5	.953	SS-155
1979			154	.314	.458	672	**211**	32	**19**	9	1.3	105	62	18	91	26	1	0	292	525	34	102	5.5	.960	SS-150
1980			118	.319	.417	504	161	19	9	4	0.8	83	43	18	43	31	1	0	223	451	29	85	6.0	.959	SS-115
1981			80	.288	.393	333	96	16	8	1	0.3	47	33	14	55	8	4	0	160	272	18	54	5.6	.960	SS-76
1982	SD	N	141	.247	.352	563	139	25	8	6	1.1	76	64	26	82	27	6	1	220	422	26	70	4.7	.961	SS-136
1983			126	.263	.335	460	121	20	2	3	0.7	39	40	21	57	16	3	0	219	355	24	66	4.7	.960	SS-123
1984			148	.258	.320	493	127	19	3	2	0.4	40	35	39	81	8	2	0	225	407	26	79	4.4	.960	SS-146
1985			148	.282	.377	546	154	30	2	6	1.1	63	55	41	88	16	0	0	245	460	23	96	4.9	.968	SS-148

Year	Team		Games	BA	SA	AB	H	2B	3B	HR	HR%	R	RBI	BB	SO	SB	PINCH HIT AB	H	PO	A	E	DP	TC/G	FA	G by Pos

Garry Templeton *Continued*

Year	Team		Games	BA	SA	AB	H	2B	3B	HR	HR%	R	RBI	BB	SO	SB	AB	H	PO	A	E	DP	TC/G	FA	G by Pos
1986			147	.247	.308	510	126	21	2	2	0.4	42	44	35	86	10	9	4	207	358	20	60	4.0	.966	SS-144
1987			148	.222	.296	510	113	13	5	5	1.0	42	48	42	92	14	1	0	253	447	20	77	4.9	.972	SS-146
1988			110	.249	.354	362	90	15	7	3	0.8	35	36	20	50	8	5	0	170	316	16	62	4.6	.968	SS-105, 3B-2
1989			142	.255	.354	506	129	26	3	6	1.2	43	40	23	80	1	3	0	232	409	20	74	4.7	.970	SS-140
1990			144	.248	.362	505	125	25	3	9	1.7	45	59	24	59	1	9	2	214	367	26	74	4.5	.957	SS-135
15 yrs.			1967	.273	.371	7445	2035	319	104	67	0.9	868	702	365	1054	239	50	7	3341	5937	378	1146	4.9	.961	SS-1923, 3B-2

LEAGUE CHAMPIONSHIP SERIES
Year	Team		Games	BA	SA	AB	H	2B	3B	HR	HR%	R	RBI	BB	SO	SB	AB	H	PO	A	E	DP	TC/G	FA	G by Pos
1984	SD	N	5	.333	.400	15	5	1	0	0	0.0	2	2	2	0	1			19	11	1	3	6.2	.968	SS-5

WORLD SERIES
Year	Team		Games	BA	SA	AB	H	2B	3B	HR	HR%	R	RBI	BB	SO	SB	AB	H	PO	A	E	DP	TC/G	FA	G by Pos
1984	SD	N	5	.316	.368	19	6	1	0	0	0.0	1	0	0	3	0	0	0	8	11	0	1	3.8	1.000	SS-5

Mickey Tettleton

TETTLETON, MICKEY LEE
B. Sept. 16, 1960, Oklahoma City, Okla.
BB TR 6' 2" 190 lbs.

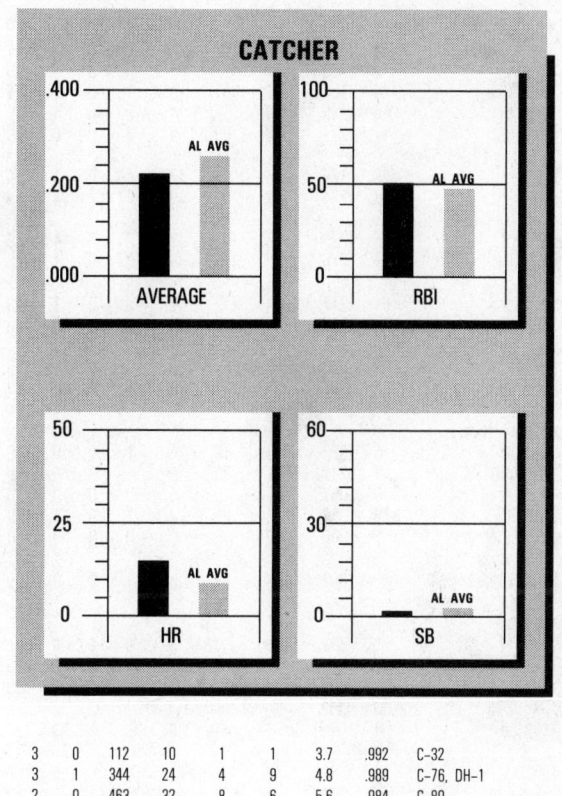

CATCHER

	Games	BA	SA	AB	H	2B	3B	HR	HR%	R	RBI	BB	SO	SB
April	17	.211	.281	57	12	4	0	0	0.0	5	6	14	26	0
May	23	.253	.506	79	20	5	0	5	6.3	17	15	15	28	1
June	28	.279	.547	86	24	1	2	6	7.0	21	16	30	29	0
July	25	.145	.217	83	12	3	0	1	1.2	7	5	19	31	0
Aug	24	.205	.244	78	16	3	0	0	0.0	8	2	15	23	1
Sept/Oct	18	.246	.475	61	15	5	0	3	4.9	10	7	13	23	0
Day	36	.213	.378	127	27	7	1	4	3.1	17	11	17	46	0
Night	99	.227	.382	317	72	14	1	11	3.5	51	40	89	114	2
vs. Left		.234	.414	128	30	8	0	5	3.9	16	18	24	50	1
vs. Right		.218	.367	316	69	13	2	10	3.2	52	33	82	110	1
On Grass	111	.230	.414	365	84	18	2	15	4.1	59	48	86	131	2
On Turf	24	.190	.228	79	15	3	0	0	0.0	9	3	20	29	0
Home	66	.237	.419	215	51	11	2	8	3.7	31	27	56	79	2
Road	69	.210	.345	229	48	10	0	7	3.1	37	24	50	81	0
Division Rivals														
vs. BOS	10	.263	.474	38	10	3	1	1	2.6	5	4	5	11	0
vs. CLE	11	.296	.556	27	8	1	0	2	7.4	10	3	16	10	0
vs. DET	9	.194	.258	31	6	2	0	0	0.0	4	1	9	16	0
vs. MIL	11	.243	.486	37	9	0	0	3	8.1	8	8	10	10	0
vs. NY	12	.175	.425	40	7	2	1	2	5.0	6	6	10	16	1
vs. TOR	9	.233	.400	30	7	2	0	1	3.3	4	4	6	8	0
On 3B < 2 Out		.263	.421	19	5	0	0	1	5.3	1	19	12	7	

Year	Team		Games	BA	SA	AB	H	2B	3B	HR	HR%	R	RBI	BB	SO	SB	AB	H	PO	A	E	DP	TC/G	FA	G by Pos
1984	OAK	A	33	.263	.355	76	20	2	1	1	1.3	10	5	11	21	0	3	0	112	10	1	1	3.7	.992	C-32
1985			78	.251	.351	211	53	12	0	3	1.4	23	15	28	59	2	3	1	344	24	4	9	4.8	.989	C-76, DH-1
1986			90	.204	.389	211	43	9	0	10	4.7	26	35	39	51	7	2	0	463	32	8	6	5.6	.984	C-89
1987			82	.194	.322	211	41	3	0	8	3.8	19	26	30	65	1	2	0	435	29	6	1	5.7	.987	C-80, DH-1, 1B-1
1988	BAL	A	86	.261	.424	283	74	11	1	11	3.9	31	37	28	70	0	9	0	361	31	3	1	4.6	.992	C-80
1989			117	.258	.509	411	106	21	2	26	6.3	72	65	73	117	3	3	1	297	42	2	1	2.9	.994	C-75, DH-43
1990			135	.223	.381	444	99	21	2	15	3.3	68	51	106	160	2	2	1	458	39	5	4	5.3	.990	C-90, DH-40, 1B-5, OF-1
7 yrs.			621	.236	.406	1847	436	79	6	74	4.0	249	234	315	543	15	24	3	2470	207	29	23	4.4	.989	C-522, DH-85, 1B-6, OF-1

Tim Teufel

TEUFEL, TIMOTHY SHAWN (Tuff)
B. July 7, 1958, Greenwich, Conn.
BR TR 6' 175 lbs.

Year	Team		Games	BA	SA	AB	H	2B	3B	HR	HR%	R	RBI	BB	SO	SB	AB	H	PO	A	E	DP	TC/G	FA	G by Pos
1983	MIN	A	21	.308	.538	78	24	7	1	3	3.8	11	6	2	8	0	2	0	47	58	1	14	5.0	.991	2B-18, DH-1, SS-1
1984			157	.262	.400	568	149	30	3	14	2.5	76	61	76	73	1	0	0	315	485	13	81	5.2	.984	2B-157
1985			138	.260	.399	434	113	24	3	10	2.3	58	50	48	70	4	6	1	237	352	12	67	4.4	.980	2B-137, DH-1
1986	NY	N	93	.247	.369	279	69	20	1	4	1.4	35	31	32	42	1	16	3	143	174	9	28	3.5	.972	2B-84, 1B-3, 3B-1
1987			97	.308	.545	299	92	29	0	14	4.7	55	61	44	53	3	18	8	139	214	11	44	3.8	.970	2B-92, 1B-1
1988			90	.234	.352	273	64	20	0	4	1.5	35	31	29	41	0	14	4	175	213	7	49	4.4	.982	2B-84, 1B-3
1989			83	.256	.333	219	56	7	2	2	0.9	27	15	32	50	1	12	3	261	112	10	30	4.6	.974	2B-40, 1B-33
1990			80	.246	.480	175	43	11	0	10	5.7	28	24	15	33	0	29	8	141	58	4	16	3.8	.980	1B-24, 2B-24, 3B-10
8 yrs.			759	.262	.413	2325	610	148	10	61	2.6	325	279	278	370	10	97	27	1458	1666	67	329	4.2	.979	2B-636, 1B-64, 3B-11, DH-2, SS-1

Year	Team	Games	BA	SA	AB	H	2B	3B	HR	HR%	R	RBI	BB	SO	SB	PINCH HIT AB	PINCH HIT H	PO	A	E	DP	TC/G	FA	G by Pos

Tim Teufel   *Continued*

LEAGUE CHAMPIONSHIP SERIES

1986	NY	N	2	.167	.167	6	1	0	0	0	0.0	0	0	0	0	0	0	0	2	8	0	1	5.0	1.000	2B-2
1988			1	.000	.000	3	0	0	0	0	0.0	0	0	0	1	0	0	0	1	3	0	0	4.0	1.000	2B-1
2 yrs.			3	.111	.111	9	1	0	0	0	0.0	0	0	0	1	0	0	0	3	11	0	1	4.7	.000	2B-3

WORLD SERIES

| 1986 | NY | N | 3 | .444 | .889 | 9 | 4 | 1 | 0 | 1 | 11.1 | 1 | 1 | 0 | 2 | 0 | 0 | 0 | 3 | 3 | 1 | 1 | 2.3 | .857 | 2B-3 |

Andres Thomas

THOMAS, ANDRES PEREZ
Born Andres Perez y Thomas.
B. Nov. 10, 1963, Boca Chica, Dominican Republic
BR TR 6' 1" 170 lbs.

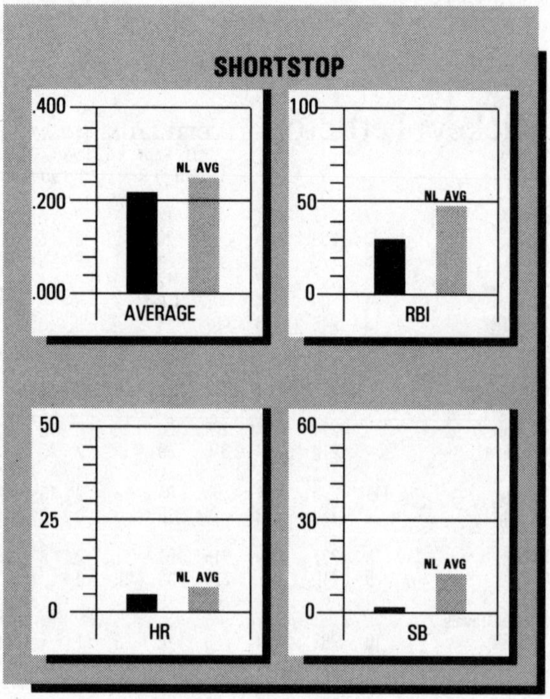

	Games	BA	SA	AB	H	2B	3B	HR	HR%	R	RBI	BB	SO	SB
April	8	.091	.091	22	2	0	0	0	0.0	1	1	1	5	0
May	19	.271	.356	59	16	2	0	1	1.7	7	6	5	13	0
June	7	.238	.381	21	5	0	0	1	4.8	3	1	0	4	0
July	24	.185	.272	81	15	1	0	2	2.5	7	5	2	11	2
Aug	15	.246	.333	57	14	2	0	1	1.8	3	10	1	8	0
Sept/Oct	11	.237	.316	38	9	3	0	0	0.0	5	7	2	2	0
Day	22	.174	.275	69	12	4	0	1	1.4	7	6	2	16	0
Night	62	.234	.311	209	49	4	0	4	1.9	19	24	9	27	2
vs. Left		.225	.363	102	23	2	0	4	3.9	14	15	5	15	0
vs. Right		.216	.267	176	38	6	0	1	0.6	12	15	6	28	2
On Grass	64	.217	.274	212	46	6	0	2	0.9	18	20	8	32	1
On Turf	20	.227	.394	66	15	2	0	3	4.5	8	10	3	11	1
Home	46	.229	.274	157	36	4	0	1	0.6	13	12	7	24	1
Road	38	.207	.339	121	25	4	0	4	3.3	13	18	4	19	1
Division Rivals														
vs. CIN	5	.333	.417	12	4	1	0	0	0.0	4	2	1	1	0
vs. HOU	7	.217	.261	23	5	1	0	0	0.0	1	3	0	5	0
vs. LA	6	.067	.067	15	1	0	0	0	0.0	0	0	0	2	0
vs. SD	6	.286	.524	21	6	2	0	1	4.8	3	5	1	3	0
vs. SF	2	.000	.000	5	0	0	0	0	0.0	1	0	1	1	0
On 3B < 2 Out		.357	.429	14	5	1	0	0	0.0	0	8	1	2	

Year	Team		Games	BA	SA	AB	H	2B	3B	HR	HR%	R	RBI	BB	SO	SB	AB	H	PO	A	E	DP	TC/G	FA	G by Pos
1985	ATL	N	15	.278	.278	18	5	0	0	0	0.0	6	2	0	2	0	1	1	6	17	2	2	1.7	.920	SS-10
1986			102	.251	.372	323	81	17	2	6	1.9	26	32	8	49	4	6	3	143	290	19	62	4.4	.958	SS-97
1987			82	.231	.312	324	75	11	0	5	1.5	29	39	14	50	6	1	0	128	276	20	56	5.2	.953	SS-81
1988			153	.252	.360	606	153	22	2	13	2.1	54	68	14	95	7	3	1	230	456	29	90	4.7	.959	SS-150
1989			141	.213	.316	554	118	18	0	13	2.3	41	57	12	62	3	2	0	231	400	29	81	4.7	.956	SS-138
1990			84	.219	.302	278	61	8	0	5	1.7	26	30	11	43	2	10	4	104	200	10	43	4.1	.968	SS-72, 3B-5
6 yrs.			577	.234	.334	2103	493	76	4	42	2.0	182	228	59	301	22	23	9	842	1639	109	334	4.5	.958	SS-548, 3B-5

Frank Thomas

THOMAS, FRANK EDWARD
B. May 27, 1968, Columbus, Ga.
BR TR 6' 5" 240 lbs.

Year	Team		Games	BA	SA	AB	H	2B	3B	HR	HR%	R	RBI	BB	SO	SB	AB	H	PO	A	E	DP	TC/G	FA	G by Pos
1990	CHI	A	60	.330	.529	191	63	11	3	7	3.6	39	31	44	54	0	1	1	428	26	5	53	9.0	.989	1B-51, DH-8

Milt Thompson

THOMPSON, MILTON BERNARD
B. Jan. 5, 1959, Washington, D. C.
BL TR 5' 11" 170 lbs.

	Games	BA	SA	AB	H	2B	3B	HR	HR%	R	RBI	BB	SO	SB
April	13	.143	.257	35	5	1	0	1	2.9	5	4	5	3	0
May	24	.200	.288	80	16	2	1	1	1.3	6	4	8	11	7
June	25	.253	.429	91	23	2	4	2	2.2	12	11	8	11	7
July	26	.165	.228	79	13	1	2	0	0.0	7	2	8	14	3
Aug	23	.284	.358	67	19	5	0	0	0.0	7	5	5	16	5
Sept/Oct	24	.227	.364	66	15	3	0	2	3.0	5	4	5	5	3
Day	43	.232	.355	138	32	7	2	2	1.4	15	8	12	16	9
Night	92	.211	.314	280	59	7	5	4	1.4	27	22	27	44	16
vs. Left		.175	.233	120	21	3	2	0	0.0	11	4	5	26	3
vs. Right		.235	.366	298	70	11	5	6	2.0	31	26	34	34	22

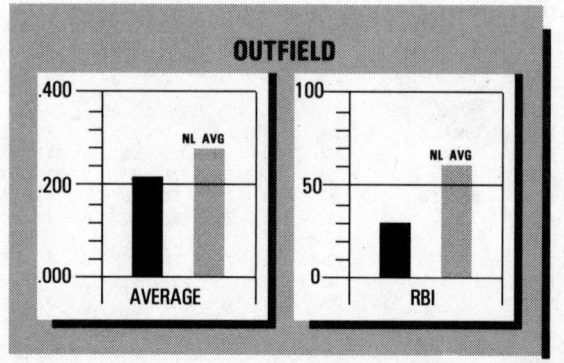

Year	Team		Games	BA	SA	AB	H	2B	3B	HR	HR%	R	RBI	BB	SO	SB	PINCH HIT AB	H	PO	A	E	DP	TC/G	FA	G by Pos

Milt Thompson *Continued*

Year	Team		Games	BA	SA	AB	H	2B	3B	HR	HR%	R	RBI	BB	SO	SB	PH AB	PH H	PO	A	E	DP	TC/G	FA	G by Pos
On Grass			35	.198	.333	111	22	6	3	1	0.9	14	2	11	18	3									
On Turf			100	.225	.326	307	69	8	4	5	1.6	28	28	28	42	22									
Home			73	.213	.312	221	47	5	4	3	1.4	23	20	21	27	17									
Road			62	.223	.345	197	44	9	3	3	1.5	19	10	18	33	8									
Division Rivals																									
vs. CHI			16	.148	.278	54	8	2	1	1	1.9	6	4	6	6	2									
vs. MON			16	.200	.309	55	11	0	0	2	3.6	6	6	5	8	4									
vs. NY			16	.250	.375	56	14	3	2	0	0.0	5	0	3	15	4									
vs. PHI			13	.286	.371	35	10	1	1	0	0.0	3	7	3	5	0									
vs. PIT			14	.295	.409	44	13	2	0	1	2.3	4	4	5	4	2									
On 3B < 2 Out				.091	.182	11	1	1	0	0	0.0	0	5	4	3										
1984	ATL	N	25	.303	.374	99	30	1	0	2	2.0	16	4	11	11	14	2	2	37	6	2	1	1.8	.956	OF–25
1985			73	.302	.363	182	55	7	2	0	0.0	17	6	7	36	9	30	13	78	2	3	0	1.1	.964	OF–49
1986	PHI	N	96	.251	.341	299	75	7	1	6	2.0	38	23	26	62	19	10	1	212	6	1	2	2.2	.991	OF–89
1987			150	.302	.425	527	159	26	9	7	1.3	86	43	42	87	46	15	5	354	4	4	1	2.4	.989	OF–146
1988			122	.288	.357	378	109	16	2	2	0.5	53	33	39	59	17	16	4	278	5	5	1	2.4	.983	OF–112
1989	STL	N	155	.290	.393	545	158	28	8	4	0.7	60	68	39	91	27	10	1	348	5	8	1	2.3	.978	OF–147
1990			135	.218	.328	418	91	14	7	6	1.4	42	30	39	60	25	21	4	232	4	7	0	2.1	.971	OF–116
7 yrs.			756	.277	.374	2448	677	99	29	27	1.1	312	207	203	406	157	104	30	1539	27	31	5	2.1	.981	OF–684

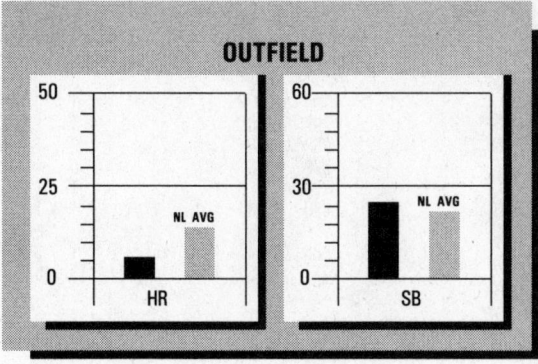

OUTFIELD — HR (NL AVG), SB (NL AVG)

Robby Thompson   THOMPSON, ROBERT RANDALL
B. May 10, 1962, West Palm Beach, Fla.
BR TR 5′ 11″ 165 lbs.

Split			Games	BA	SA	AB	H	2B	3B	HR	HR%	R	RBI	BB	SO	SB	PH AB	PH H	PO	A	E	DP	TC/G	FA	G by Pos
April			20	.230	.324	74	17	2	1	1	1.4	10	7	6	18	4									
May			26	.202	.333	99	20	4	0	3	3.0	10	10	4	15	1									
June			27	.286	.451	91	26	1	1	4	4.4	18	16	6	15	2									
July			22	.243	.351	74	18	5	0	1	1.4	6	5	6	13	1									
Aug			26	.279	.500	86	24	5	1	4	4.7	14	11	7	22	4									
Sept/Oct			23	.230	.378	74	17	5	0	2	2.7	9	7	5	13	2									
Day			57	.250	.402	204	51	6	2	7	3.4	25	26	14	35	6									
Night			87	.241	.384	294	71	16	1	8	2.7	42	30	20	61	8									
vs. Left				.273	.475	183	50	11	1	8	4.4	33	27	13	34	5									
vs. Right				.229	.343	315	72	11	2	7	2.2	34	29	21	62	9									
On Grass			106	.263	.403	357	94	16	2	10	2.8	52	43	33	67	10									
On Turf			38	.199	.362	141	28	6	1	5	3.5	15	13	1	29	4									
Home			76	.266	.435	248	66	14	2	8	3.2	35	37	24	47	7									
Road			68	.224	.348	250	56	8	1	7	2.8	32	19	10	49	7									
Division Rivals																									
vs. ATL			17	.353	.588	51	18	3	0	3	5.9	15	9	5	12	0									
vs. CIN			17	.226	.403	62	14	3	1	2	3.2	8	7	2	14	2									
vs. HOU			17	.246	.415	65	16	2	0	3	4.6	8	7	2	12	2									
vs. LA			13	.286	.551	49	14	2	1	3	6.1	9	9	3	11	3									
vs. SD			16	.204	.259	54	11	3	0	0	0.0	3	3	5	10	1									
On 3B < 2 Out				.360	.720	25	9	1	1	2	8.0	2	22	2	6										
1986	SF	N	149	.271	.370	549	149	27	3	7	1.3	73	47	42	112	12	1	0	255	451	17	97	4.9	.976	2B–149, SS–1
1987			132	.262	.419	420	110	26	5	10	2.4	62	44	40	91	16	4	2	246	341	17	99	4.6	.972	2B–126
1988			138	.264	.384	477	126	24	6	7	1.5	66	48	40	111	14	5	1	255	365	14	88	4.6	.978	2B–134
1989			148	.241	.400	547	132	26	11	13	2.4	91	50	51	133	12	0	0	307	425	8	88	5.0	.989	2B–148
1990			144	.245	.392	498	122	22	3	15	3.0	67	56	34	96	14	3	1	287	441	8	94	5.2	.989	2B–142
5 yrs.			711	.257	.392	2491	639	125	28	52	2.1	359	245	207	543	68	13	4	1350	2023	64	466	4.8	.981	2B–699, SS–1
LEAGUE CHAMPIONSHIP SERIES																									
1987	SF	N	7	.100	.350	20	2	0	1	1	5.0	4	2	5	7	2	1	0	11	19	1	6	4.4	.968	2B–6
1989			5	.278	.611	18	5	0	0	2	11.1	5	3	3	2	0	0	0	10	13	0	4	4.6	1.000	2B–5
2 yrs.			12	.184	.474	38	7	0	1	3	7.9	9	5	8	9	2	1	0	21	32	1	10	4.5	.981	2B–11
WORLD SERIES																									
1989	SF	N	4	.091	.091	11	1	0	0	0	0.0	0	0	0	4	0	1	1	4	10	0	2	3.5	1.000	2B–4

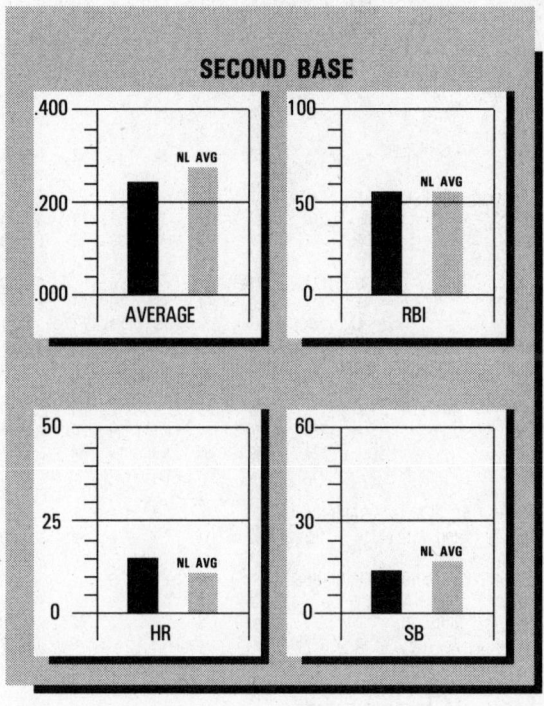

SECOND BASE — AVERAGE (NL AVG), RBI (NL AVG), HR (NL AVG), SB (NL AVG)

Year	Team		Games	BA	SA	AB	H	2B	3B	HR	HR%	R	RBI	BB	SO	SB	PINCH HIT AB	H	PO	A	E	DP	TC/G	FA	G by Pos

Dickie Thon

THON, RICHARD WILLIAM
B. June 20, 1958, South Bend, Ind.
BR TR 5′ 11″ 160 lbs.

Year	Team		Games	BA	SA	AB	H	2B	3B	HR	HR%	R	RBI	BB	SO	SB	AB	H	PO	A	E	DP	TC/G	FA	G by Pos
April			17	.194	.242	62	12	1	1	0	0.0	2	3	5	6	0									
May			25	.297	.385	91	27	3	1	1	1.1	12	13	9	15	2									
June			25	.253	.326	95	24	4	0	1	1.1	10	5	5	13	2									
July			24	.299	.443	97	29	2	0	4	4.1	13	17	3	12	3									
Aug			30	.262	.355	107	28	5	1	1	0.9	10	8	11	16	2									
Sept/Oct			28	.210	.310	100	21	5	1	1	1.0	7	2	4	15	3									
Day			38	.185	.304	135	25	8	1	2	1.5	12	6	10	13	2									
Night			111	.278	.365	417	116	12	3	6	1.4	42	42	27	64	10									
vs. Left				.262	.391	202	53	9	1	5	2.5	21	21	14	25	2									
vs. Right				.251	.326	350	88	11	3	3	0.9	33	27	23	52	10									
On Grass			40	.261	.340	153	40	7	1	1	0.7	16	8	8	24	1									
On Turf			109	.253	.353	399	101	13	3	7	1.8	38	40	29	53	11									
Home			73	.248	.311	254	63	7	0	3	1.2	22	28	25	37	8									
Road			76	.262	.383	298	78	13	4	5	1.7	32	20	12	40	4									
Division Rivals																									
vs. CHI			16	.186	.220	59	11	2	0	0	0.0	3	2	3	7	0									
vs. MON			17	.274	.355	62	17	2	0	1	1.6	4	2	3	7	2									
vs. NY			16	.161	.242	62	10	2	0	1	1.6	7	6	3	13	2									
vs. PIT			17	.313	.469	64	20	4	0	2	3.1	7	7	3	9	1									
vs. STL			16	.262	.344	61	16	1	2	0	0.0	5	4	3	6	3									
On 3B < 2 Out				.259	.370	27	7	0	0	1	3.7	1	16	1	0										
1979	CAL	A	35	.339	.393	56	19	3	0	0	0.0	6	8	5	10	0	0	0	38	46	8	13	2.6	.913	2B-24, SS-8, DH-1, 3B-1
1980			80	.255	.315	267	68	12	2	0	0.0	32	15	10	28	7	13	2	70	128	10	28	2.6	.952	SS-22, 2B-21, DH-15, 3B-10, 1B-1
1981	HOU	N	49	.274	.337	95	26	6	0	0	0.0	13	3	9	13	6	2	0	53	63	6	13	2.5	.951	2B-28, SS-13, 3B-5
1982			136	.276	.397	496	137	31	**10**	3	0.6	73	36	37	48	37	9	4	183	412	17	82	4.5	.972	SS-119, 3B-8, 2B-1
1983			154	.286	.457	619	177	28	9	20	3.2	81	79	54	73	34	0	0	258	533	28	114	5.3	.966	SS-154
1984			5	.353	.471	17	6	0	1	0	0.0	3	1	0	4	0	0	0	8	13	0	1	4.2	1.000	SS-5
1985			84	.251	.355	251	63	6	1	6	2.4	26	29	18	50	8	6	1	106	218	11	48	4.0	.967	SS-79
1986			106	.248	.335	278	69	13	1	3	1.1	24	21	29	49	6	20	5	142	210	10	39	3.4	.972	SS-104
1987			32	.212	.273	66	14	1	0	1	1.5	6	3	16	13	3	9	3	21	53	6	7	2.5	.925	SS-31
1988	SD	N	95	.264	.337	258	68	12	2	1	0.4	36	18	33	49	19	19	3	84	171	12	29	2.8	.955	SS-70, 2B-2, 3B-1
1989	PHI	N	136	.271	.434	435	118	18	4	15	3.4	45	60	33	81	6	7	3	174	380	16	65	4.2	.972	SS-129
1990			149	.255	.350	552	141	20	4	8	1.4	54	48	37	77	12	6	1	222	439	25	86	4.6	.964	SS-148
12 yrs.			1061	.267	.382	3390	906	150	34	57	1.7	399	321	281	495	138	91	22	1359	2666	149	525	3.9	.964	SS-882, 2B-76, 3B-25, DH-16, 1B-1

DIVISIONAL PLAYOFF SERIES

| 1981 | HOU | N | 4 | .182 | .182 | 11 | 2 | 0 | 0 | 0 | 0.0 | 0 | 0 | 1 | 0 | 0 | 1 | 0 | 0 | 0 | 1 | 0 | 0.3 | — | SS-4 |

LEAGUE CHAMPIONSHIP SERIES

1979	CAL	A	1	—	—	0	0	0	0	0	—	1	0	0	0	0	0	0	0	0	0	0	0.0	—	SS-1
1986	HOU	N	6	.250	.500	12	3	0	0	1	8.3	1	1	0	1	0	1	0	6	9	0	2	2.5	1.000	SS-6
2 yrs.			7	.250	.500	12	3	0	0	1	8.3	2	1	0	1	0	1	0	6	9	0	2	2.1	.000	SS-7

Lou Thornton

THORNTON, LOUIS, JR.
B. Apr. 26, 1963, Montgomery, Ala.
BL TR 6′ 170 lbs.

1985	TOR	A	56	.236	.319	72	17	1	1	1	1.4	18	8	2	24	1	3	1	44	0	2	0	0.8	.957	OF-35, DH-16
1987			12	.500	.500	2	1	0	0	0	0.0	5	0	1	0	0	0	0	0	0	0	0	0.0	—	OF-4
1988			11	.000	.000	2	0	0	0	0	0.0	1	0	0	0	0	0	0	1	0	0	0	0.1	1.000	OF-10
1989	NY	N	13	.308	.385	13	4	1	0	0	0.0	5	1	0	1	2	1	0	9	0	0	0	0.7	1.000	OF-6
1990			3	.000	.000	0	0	0	0	0	0.0	0	0	0	0	0	0	0	1	0	0	0	0.5	1.000	OF-2
5 yrs.			95	.247	.326	89	22	2	1	1	1.1	29	9	3	25	3	4	1	55	0	2	0	0.6	.000	OF-57, DH-16

LEAGUE CHAMPIONSHIP SERIES

| 1985 | TOR | A | 2 | — | — | 0 | 0 | 0 | 0 | 0 | — | 1 | 0 | 0 | 0 | 0 | 0 | 0 | 0 | 0 | 0 | 0 | 0.0 | — | |

Year	Team		Games	BA	SA	AB	H	2B	3B	HR	HR%	R	RBI	BB	SO	SB	PINCH HIT AB	PINCH HIT H	PO	A	E	DP	TC/G	FA	G by Pos

Gary Thurman

THURMAN, GARY MONTEZ
B. Nov. 12, 1964, Indianapolis, Ind.
BR TR 5′ 10″ 170 lbs.

Year	Team		Games	BA	SA	AB	H	2B	3B	HR	HR%	R	RBI	BB	SO	SB	PH AB	PH H	PO	A	E	DP	TC/G	FA	G by Pos
1987	KC	A	27	.296	.321	81	24	2	0	0	0.0	12	5	8	20	7	0	0	61	5	2	1	2.5	.971	OF-27
1988			35	.167	.182	66	11	1	0	0	0.0	6	2	4	20	5	1	0	36	1	2	0	1.1	.949	OF-32, DH-1
1989			72	.195	.241	87	17	2	1	0	0.0	24	5	15	26	16	1	0	54	2	3	0	0.8	.949	OF-60, DH-4
1990			23	.233	.283	60	14	3	0	0	0.0	5	3	2	12	1	0	0	32	0	0	0	1.5	1.000	OF-21
4 yrs.			157	.224	.259	294	66	8	1	0	0.0	47	15	29	78	29	2	0	183	8	7	1	1.3	.965	OF-140, DH-5

Ron Tingley

TINGLEY, RONALD IRVIN
B. May 27, 1959, Presque Isle, Me.
BR TR 6′ 2″ 160 lbs.

Year	Team		Games	BA	SA	AB	H	2B	3B	HR	HR%	R	RBI	BB	SO	SB	PH AB	PH H	PO	A	E	DP	TC/G	FA	G by Pos
1982	SD	N	8	.100	.100	20	2	0	0	0	0.0	0	0	0	7	0	0	0	40	4	2	1	5.8	.957	C-8
1988	CLE	A	9	.167	.292	24	4	0	0	1	4.2	1	2	2	8	0	1	1	48	6	0	1	6.0	1.000	C-9
1989	CAL	A	4	.333	.333	3	1	0	0	0	0.0	0	0	1	0	0	0	0	7	1	1	0	2.3	.889	C-4
1990			5	.000	.000	3	0	0	0	0	0.0	0	0	1	1	0	0	0	12	0	0	0	2.4	1.000	C-5
4 yrs.			26	.140	.200	50	7	0	0	1	2.0	1	2	4	16	0	1	1	107	11	3	2	4.7	.975	C-26

Wayne Tolleson

TOLLESON, JIMMY WAYNE
B. Nov. 22, 1955, Spartanburg, S. C.
BB TR 5′ 9″ 160 lbs.

Year	Team		Games	BA	SA	AB	H	2B	3B	HR	HR%	R	RBI	BB	SO	SB	PH AB	PH H	PO	A	E	DP	TC/G	FA	G by Pos
1981	TEX	A	14	.167	.167	24	4	0	0	0	0.0	6	1	1	5	2	1	0	5	8	0	0	0.9	1.000	3B-6, SS-2
1982			38	.114	.129	70	8	1	0	0	0.0	6	2	5	14	1	0	0	47	70	5	20	3.2	.959	SS-26, 3B-4, 2B-1
1983			134	.260	.315	470	122	13	2	3	0.6	64	20	40	68	33	0	0	268	372	17	81	4.9	.974	2B-112, SS-26, DH-1
1984			118	.213	.251	338	72	9	2	0	0.0	35	9	27	47	22	0	0	195	287	10	62	4.2	.980	2B-109, SS-7, 3B-5, DH-1, OF-1
1985			123	.313	.381	323	101	9	5	1	0.3	45	18	21	46	21	5	1	149	255	14	48	3.4	.967	SS-81, 2B-29, 3B-12, DH-6
1986	2 teams	CHI A (81G — .250)		NY A (60G — .284)																					
''	total		141	.265	.339	475	126	16	5	3	0.6	61	43	52	76	17	3	0	147	327	14	50	3.5	.971	SS-74, 3B-72, 2B-3, DH-2, OF-2
1987	NY	A	121	.221	.241	349	77	4	0	1	0.3	48	22	43	72	5	0	0	162	326	15	66	4.2	.970	SS-119, 3B-3
1988			21	.254	.288	59	15	2	0	0	0.0	8	5	8	12	1	1	0	28	54	3	9	4.0	.965	2B-12, 3B-10, SS-1
1989			80	.164	.250	140	23	5	2	1	0.7	16	9	16	23	5	10	0	45	107	7	20	2.0	.956	3B-28, SS-28, 2B-12, DH-10
1990			73	.149	.189	74	11	1	1	0	0.0	12	4	6	21	1	5	1	57	86	2	26	2.4	.986	SS-45, 2B-13, DH-5, 3B-3
10 yrs.			863	.241	.293	2322	559	60	17	9	0.4	301	133	219	384	108	25	2	1103	1892	87	382	3.6	.972	SS-409, 2B-291, 3B-143, DH-25, OF-3

Kelvin Torve

TORVE, KELVIN CURTIS
B. Jan. 10, 1960, Rapid City, S. D.
BL TR 6′ 3″ 205 lbs.

Year	Team		Games	BA	SA	AB	H	2B	3B	HR	HR%	R	RBI	BB	SO	SB	PH AB	PH H	PO	A	E	DP	TC/G	FA	G by Pos
1988	MIN	A	12	.188	.375	16	3	0	0	1	6.3	1	2	1	2	0	6	1	14	1	0	1	1.3	1.000	1B-4
1990	NY	N	20	.289	.395	38	11	4	0	0	0.0	0	2	4	9	0	9	3	65	0	0	6	6.5	1.000	1B-9, OF-1
2 yrs.			32	.259	.389	54	14	4	0	1	1.9	1	4	5	11	0	15	4	79	1	0	7	2.5	.000	1B-13, OF-1

Alan Trammell

TRAMMELL, ALAN STUART
B. Feb. 21, 1958, Garden Grove, Calif.
BR TR 6′ 165 lbs.

	Games	BA	SA	AB	H	2B	3B	HR	HR%	R	RBI	BB	SO	SB
April	20	.325	.475	80	26	7	1	1	1.3	12	11	11	9	0
May	26	.290	.390	100	29	4	0	2	2.0	7	17	14	12	6
June	28	.296	.398	108	32	2	0	3	2.8	14	18	12	12	2
July	26	.323	.441	93	30	8	0	1	1.1	13	10	19	7	2
Aug	25	.350	.650	103	36	13	0	6	5.8	19	21	7	7	0
Sept/Oct	21	.227	.307	75	17	3	0	1	1.3	6	12	5	8	2
Day	42	.333	.448	165	55	10	0	3	1.8	21	28	21	20	3
Night	104	.292	.449	394	115	27	1	11	2.8	50	61	47	35	9
vs. Left		.289	.486	173	50	11	1	7	4.0	23	27	23	14	2
vs. Right		.311	.433	386	120	26	0	7	1.8	48	62	45	41	10

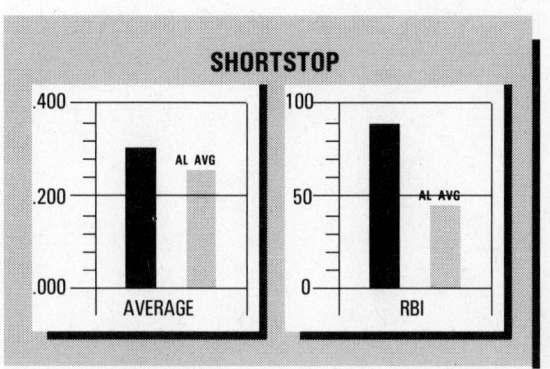

SHORTSTOP

AVERAGE — AL AVG

RBI — AL AVG

Year	Team		Games	BA	SA	AB	H	2B	3B	HR	HR%	R	RBI	BB	SO	SB	PINCH HIT AB	H	PO	A	E	DP	TC/G	FA	G by Pos

Alan Trammell *Continued*

Year	Team		Games	BA	SA	AB	H	2B	3B	HR	HR%	R	RBI	BB	SO	SB	PINCH HIT AB	H	PO	A	E	DP	TC/G	FA	G by Pos
On Grass			124	.309	.451	470	145	32	1	11	2.3	59	83	61	44	11									
On Turf			22	.281	.438	89	25	5	0	3	3.4	12	6	7	11	1									
Home			74	.339	.513	271	92	18	1	9	3.3	41	59	36	24	6									
Road			72	.271	.389	288	78	19	0	5	1.7	30	30	32	31	6									
Division Rivals																									
vs. BAL			11	.308	.462	39	12	6	0	0	0.0	4	6	4	4	0									
vs. BOS			13	.340	.440	50	17	5	0	0	0.0	7	10	6	5	1									
vs. CLE			13	.385	.577	52	20	4	0	2	3.8	10	9	2	1	0									
vs. MIL			11	.341	.488	41	14	1	1	1	2.4	5	5	7	3	0									
vs. NY			7	.364	.409	22	8	1	0	0	0.0	5	4	4	1	1									
vs. TOR			13	.380	.660	50	19	5	0	3	6.0	9	10	6	10	2									
On 3B < 2 Out				.529	.824	34	18	4	0	2	5.9	2	34	4	4										
1977	DET	A	19	.186	.186	43	8	0	0	0	0.0	6	0	4	12	0	0	0	15	34	2	5	2.7	.961	SS-19
1978			139	.268	.339	448	120	14	6	2	0.4	49	34	45	56	3	0	0	239	421	14	95	4.8	.979	SS-139
1979			142	.276	.357	460	127	11	4	6	1.3	68	50	43	55	17	0	0	245	388	26	99	4.6	.961	SS-142
1980			146	.300	.404	560	168	21	5	9	1.6	107	65	59	63	12	2	0	225	412	13	89	4.5	.980	SS-144
1981			105	.258	.327	392	101	15	3	2	0.5	52	31	49	31	10	1	1	181	347	9	65	5.1	.983	SS-105
1982			157	.258	.395	489	126	34	3	9	1.8	66	57	52	47	19	0	0	259	459	16	97	4.7	.978	SS-157
1983			142	.319	.471	505	161	31	2	14	2.8	83	66	57	64	30	0	0	236	367	13	71	4.3	.979	SS-140
1984			139	.314	.468	555	174	34	5	14	2.5	85	69	60	63	19	3	1	180	314	10	71	3.6	.980	SS-114, DH-22
1985			149	.258	.380	605	156	21	7	13	2.1	79	57	50	71	14	0	0	225	400	15	89	4.3	.977	SS-149
1986			151	.277	.469	574	159	33	7	21	3.7	107	75	59	57	25	1	0	238	445	22	99	4.7	.969	SS-149, DH-2
1987			151	.343	.551	597	205	34	3	28	4.7	109	105	60	47	21	3	0	222	421	19	94	4.4	.971	SS-149
1988			128	.311	.464	466	145	24	1	15	3.2	73	69	46	46	7	2	2	195	355	11	67	4.4	.980	SS-125
1989			121	.243	.334	449	109	20	3	5	1.1	54	43	45	45	10	2	1	188	396	9	71	4.9	.985	SS-117, DH-2
1990			146	.304	.449	559	170	37	1	14	2.5	71	89	68	55	12	2	0	232	409	14	102	4.6	.979	SS-142, DH-3
14 yrs.			1835	.288	.420	6702	1929	329	50	152	2.3	1009	810	707	712	199	16	5	2880	5168	193	1114	4.5	.977	SS-1791, DH-29

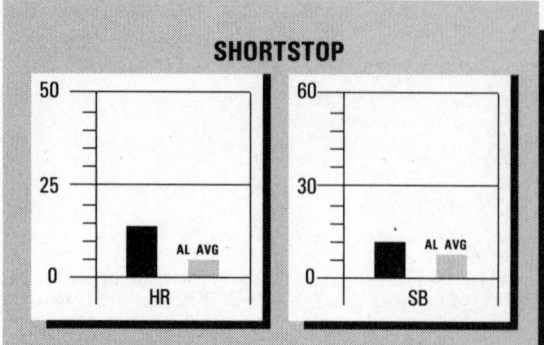

SHORTSTOP

LEAGUE CHAMPIONSHIP SERIES

Year	Team		Games	BA	SA	AB	H	2B	3B	HR	HR%	R	RBI	BB	SO	SB	PINCH HIT AB	H	PO	A	E	DP	TC/G	FA	G by Pos
1984	DET	A	3	.364	.818	11	4	0	1	1	9.1	2	3	3	1	0	0	0	1	8	0	0	3.0	1.000	SS-3
1987			5	.200	.250	20	4	1	0	0	0.0	3	2	1	2	0	0	0	6	9	1	1	3.2	.938	SS-5
2 yrs.			8	.258	.452	31	8	1	1	1	3.2	5	5	4	3	0	0	0	7	17	1	1	3.1	.960	SS-8

WORLD SERIES

Year	Team		Games	BA	SA	AB	H	2B	3B	HR	HR%	R	RBI	BB	SO	SB	PINCH HIT AB	H	PO	A	E	DP	TC/G	FA	G by Pos
1984	DET	A	5	.450	.800	20	9	1	0	2	10.0	5	6	2	2	1	0	0	8	9	1	0	3.6	.944	SS-5

Brian Traxler

TRAXLER, BRIAN LEE
B. Sept. 26, 1967, Waukegan, Ill.
BL TL 5' 10" 200 lbs.

Year	Team		Games	BA	SA	AB	H	2B	3B	HR	HR%	R	RBI	BB	SO	SB	PINCH HIT AB	H	PO	A	E	DP	TC/G	FA	G by Pos
1990	LA	N	9	.091	.182	11	1	1	0	0	0.0	0	0	0	4	0	8	1	6	2	0	0	2.7	1.000	1B-3

Jeff Treadway

TREADWAY, HUGH JEFFERY
B. Jan. 22, 1963, Columbus, Ga.
BL TR 5' 10" 170 lbs.

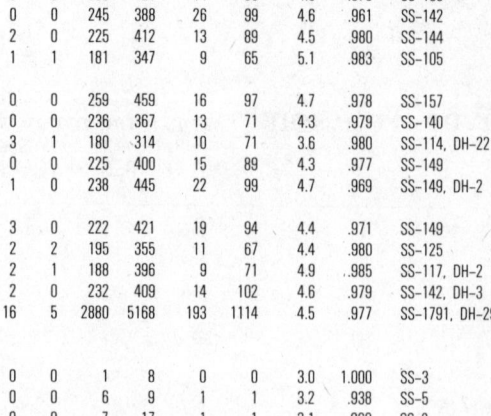

SECOND BASE

	Team		Games	BA	SA	AB	H	2B	3B	HR	HR%	R	RBI	BB	SO	SB	PINCH HIT AB	H	PO	A	E	DP	TC/G	FA	G by Pos
April			13	.300	.380	50	15	1	0	1	2.0	5	3	0	2	0									
May			24	.315	.517	89	28	4	1	4	4.5	11	17	4	4	0									
June			28	.297	.414	111	33	7	0	2	1.8	15	16	6	14	1									
July			19	.254	.388	67	17	0	0	3	4.5	8	9	4	9	0									
Aug			22	.247	.306	85	21	2	0	1	1.2	6	5	3	8	0									
Sept/Oct			22	.278	.389	72	20	6	1	0	0.0	11	9	8	5	2									
Day			30	.283	.387	106	30	3	1	2	1.9	13	13	5	11	0									
Night			98	.283	.408	368	104	17	1	9	2.4	43	46	20	31	3									
vs. Left				.303	.445	119	36	5	0	4	3.4	14	20	10	10	1									
vs. Right				.276	.389	355	98	15	2	7	2.0	42	39	15	32	2									

Year	Team	Games	BA	SA	AB	H	2B	3B	HR	HR%	R	RBI	BB	SO	SB	PINCH HIT AB	H	PO	A	E	DP	TC/G	FA	G by Pos

Jeff Treadway *Continued*

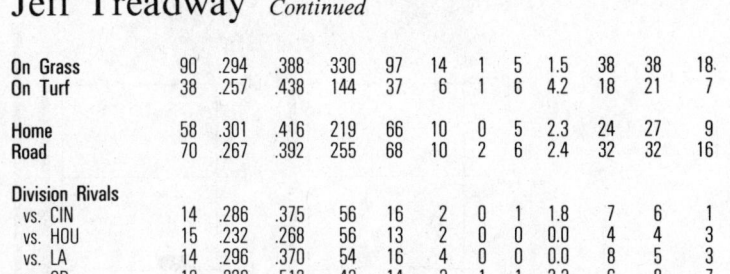

On Grass		90	.294	.388	330	97	14	1	5	1.5	38	38	18	35	2									
On Turf		38	.257	.438	144	37	6	1	6	4.2	18	21	7	7	1									
Home		58	.301	.416	219	66	10	0	5	2.3	24	27	9	20	1									
Road		70	.267	.392	255	68	10	2	6	2.4	32	32	16	22	2									
Division Rivals																								
vs. CIN		14	.286	.375	56	16	2	0	1	1.8	7	6	1	5	1									
vs. HOU		15	.232	.268	56	13	2	0	0	0.0	4	4	3	2	1									
vs. LA		14	.296	.370	54	16	4	0	0	0.0	8	5	3	11	0									
vs. SD		13	.326	.512	43	14	3	1	1	2.3	6	8	7	2	0									
vs. SF		17	.254	.333	63	16	2	0	1	1.6	6	8	4	7	1									
On 3B < 2 Out			.421	.737	19	8	1	1	1	5.3	1	17	2	2										
1987	CIN N	23	.333	.452	84	28	4	0	2	2.4	9	4	2	6	1	2	1	44	48	4	14	4.2	.958	2B-21
1988		103	.252	.362	301	76	19	4	2	0.7	30	23	27	30	2	7	4	189	253	8	50	4.4	.982	2B-97, 3B-2
1989	ATL N	134	.277	.378	473	131	18	3	8	1.7	58	40	30	38	3	11	3	273	341	12	80	4.7	.981	2B-123, 3B-6
1990		128	.283	.403	474	134	20	2	11	2.3	56	59	25	42	3	6	2	241	360	15	72	5.0	.976	2B-122
4 yrs.		388	.277	.388	1332	369	61	9	23	1.7	153	126	84	116	9	26	10	747	1002	39	216	4.6	.978	2B-363, 3B-8

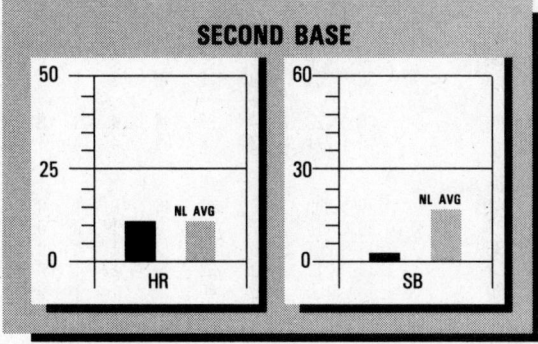

Alex Trevino

TREVINO, ALEJANDRO
Born Alejandro Trevino y Castro. Brother of Bobby Trevino.
B. Aug. 26, 1957, Monterrey, Mexico
BR TR 5′ 10″ 165 lbs.

Year	Team	Games	BA	SA	AB	H	2B	3B	HR	HR%	R	RBI	BB	SO	SB	PINCH HIT AB	H	PO	A	E	DP	TC/G	FA	G by Pos
1978	NY N	6	.250	.250	12	3	0	0	0	0.0	3	0	1	2	0	1	0	12	4	0	0	2.7	1.000	C-5, 3B-1
1979		79	.271	.333	207	56	11	1	0	0.0	24	20	20	27	2	16	5	229	71	9	14	3.9	.971	C-36, 3B-27, 2B-8
1980		106	.256	.299	355	91	11	2	0	0.0	26	37	13	41	0	12	3	450	76	16	7	5.1	.970	C-86, 3B-14, 2B-1
1981		56	.262	.275	149	39	2	0	0	0.0	17	10	13	19	3	10	3	215	25	9	1	4.4	.964	C-45, 2B-4, OF-2, 3B-1
1982	CIN N	120	.251	.304	355	89	10	3	1	0.3	24	33	34	34	3	7	1	725	61	17	7	6.7	.979	C-116, 3B-2
1983		74	.216	.293	167	36	8	1	1	0.6	14	13	17	20	0	7	2	359	32	5	2	5.4	.987	C-63, 3B-4, 2B-1
1984	2 teams	CIN N (6G — .167)			ATL N (79G — .244)																			
"	total	85	.243	.335	272	66	16	0	3	1.1	36	28	16	29	5	7	1	403	61	5	5	5.5	.989	C-83
1985	SF N	57	.217	.408	157	34	10	1	6	3.8	17	19	20	24	0	2	0	299	19	7	1	5.7	.978	C-55, 3B-1
1986	LA N	89	.262	.386	202	53	13	0	4	2.0	31	26	27	35	0	31	7	304	46	11	4	4.1	.970	C-63, 1B-1
1987		72	.222	.347	144	32	7	1	3	2.1	16	16	6	28	1	33	7	206	22	3	3	3.2	.987	C-45, OF-2, 3B-1
1988	HOU N	78	.249	.368	193	48	17	0	2	1.0	19	13	24	29	5	5	1	360	24	9	5	5.0	.977	C-74, OF-1
1989		59	.290	.405	131	38	7	1	2	1.5	15	16	7	18	0	21	1	173	12	2	2	3.2	.989	C-32, 1B-2, 3B-2
1990	3 teams	HOU N (42G — .188)			NY N (9G — .300)				CIN N (7G — .429)															
"	total	58	.221	.314	86	19	5	0	1	1.1	3	13	7	11	0	22	7	172	9	4	0	4.6	.978	C-39, 1B-1
13 yrs.		939	.249	.333	2430	604	117	10	23	0.9	245	244	205	317	19	174	38	3907	463	97	51	4.8	.978	C-742, 3B-53, 2B-14, OF-5, 1B-4

Jose Uribe

URIBE, JOSE ALTAGRACIA
Born Jose Altagracia Gonzalez y Uribe.
Played as Jose Gonzalez in 1984.
B. Jan. 21, 1952, San Cristobal, Dominican Republic
BB TR 5′ 10″ 156 lbs.

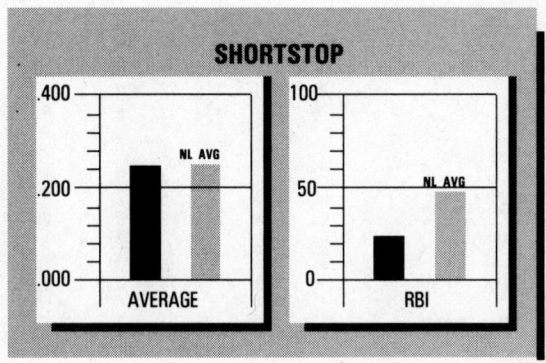

April		18	.308	.404	52	16	1	2	0	0.0	6	7	2	5	1									
May		28	.293	.370	92	27	2	1	1	1.1	9	5	7	8	1									
June		27	.270	.290	100	27	0	1	0	0.0	6	6	2	8	1									
July		24	.184	.224	76	14	1	1	0	0.0	7	2	4	8	1									
Aug		20	.250	.339	56	14	3	1	0	0.0	3	4	9	13	1									
Sept/Oct		21	.128	.154	39	5	1	0	0	0.0	4	0	5	7	0									
Day		53	.196	.252	163	32	3	3	0	0.0	11	4	8	21	1									
Night		85	.282	.337	252	71	5	3	1	0.4	24	20	21	28	4									
vs. Left			.282	.324	142	40	4	1	0	0.0	13	7	9	13	0									
vs. Right			.231	.293	273	63	4	5	1	0.4	22	17	20	36	5									

Year	Team		Games	BA	SA	AB	H	2B	3B	HR	HR%	R	RBI	BB	SO	SB	PINCH HIT AB	H	PO	A	E	DP	TC/G	FA	G by Pos

Jose Uribe *Continued*

On Grass			100	.246	.290	297	73	5	4	0	0.0	24	16	22	38	4									
On Turf			38	.254	.339	118	30	3	2	1	0.8	11	8	7	11	1									
Home			68	.223	.264	197	44	4	2	0	0.0	12	8	17	27	2									
Road			70	.271	.339	218	59	4	4	1	0.5	23	16	12	22	3									
Division Rivals																									
vs. ATL			16	.390	.439	41	16	0	1	0	0.0	9	7	1	2	2									
vs. CIN			16	.118	.137	51	6	1	0	0	0.0	2	0	5	7	0									
vs. HOU			14	.261	.326	46	12	1	1	0	0.0	2	1	3	3	0									
vs. LA			13	.211	.289	38	8	1	1	0	0.0	4	1	1	11	1									
vs. SD			13	.150	.225	40	6	1	1	0	0.0	1	3	2	2	0									
On 3B < 2 Out				.278	.278	18	5	0	0	0	0.0	0	8	4	1										
1984	STL	N	8	.211	.211	19	4	0	0	0	0.0	4	3	0	2	1	0	0	7	15	1	4	2.9	.957	SS-5, 2B-1
1985	SF	N	147	.237	.315	476	113	20	4	3	0.6	46	26	30	57	8	2	0	209	438	26	77	4.6	.961	SS-145, 2B-1
1986			157	.223	.280	453	101	15	1	3	0.7	46	43	61	76	22	2	1	249	444	16	95	4.5	.977	SS-156
1987			95	.291	.424	309	90	16	5	5	1.6	44	30	24	35	12	3	1	145	286	13	62	4.7	.971	SS-95
1988			141	.252	.318	493	124	10	7	3	0.6	47	35	36	69	14	0	0	212	404	19	77	4.5	.970	SS-140
1989			151	.221	.280	453	100	12	6	1	0.2	34	30	34	74	6	0	0	225	436	18	85	4.5	.973	SS-150
1990			138	.248	.304	415	103	8	6	1	0.2	35	24	29	49	5	4	1	182	373	20	73	4.3	.965	SS-134
7 yrs.			837	.243	.314	2618	635	81	29	16	0.6	256	191	214	362	68	11	3	1229	2396	113	473	4.5	.970	SS-825, 2B-2

LEAGUE CHAMPIONSHIP SERIES

1987	SF	N	7	.269	.308	26	7	1	0	0	0.0	1	2	0	4	1	0	0	11	21	1	7	4.7	.970	SS-7
1989			5	.235	.294	17	4	1	0	0	0.0	2	1	1	5	1	0	0	6	9	2	2	3.4	.882	SS-5
2 yrs.			12	.256	.302	43	11	2	0	0	0.0	3	3	1	9	2	0	0	17	30	3	9	4.2	.940	SS-12

WORLD SERIES

| 1989 | SF | N | 3 | .200 | .200 | 5 | 1 | 0 | 0 | 0 | 0.0 | 1 | 0 | 0 | 0 | 0 | 0 | 0 | 1 | 3 | 0 | 0 | 1.3 | 1.000 | SS-3 |

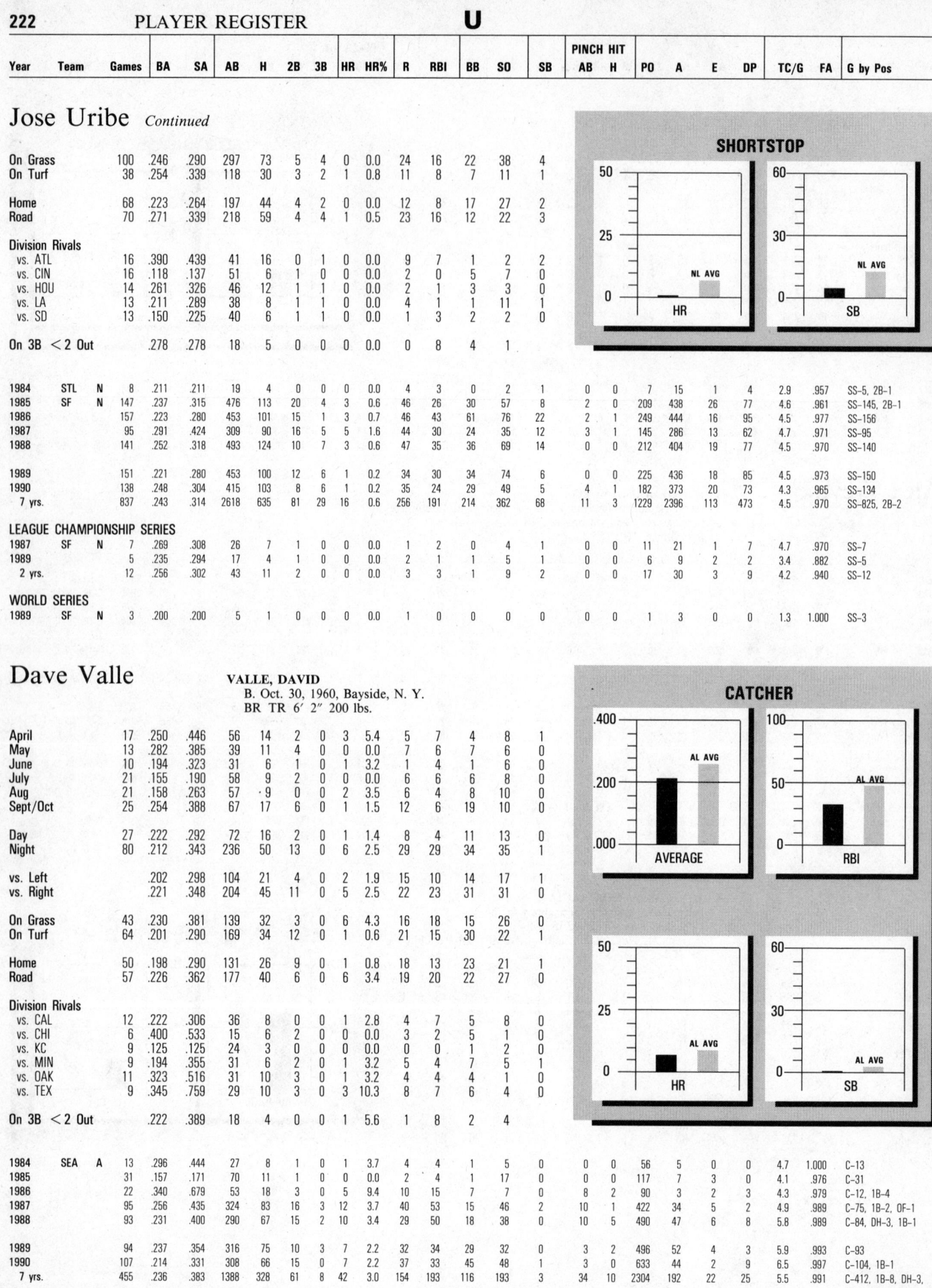

SHORTSTOP

Dave Valle

VALLE, DAVID
B. Oct. 30, 1960, Bayside, N.Y.
BR TR 6' 2" 200 lbs.

April			17	.250	.446	56	14	2	0	3	5.4	5	7	4	8	1									
May			13	.282	.385	39	11	4	0	0	0.0	7	6	7	6	0									
June			10	.194	.323	31	6	1	0	1	3.2	1	4	1	6	0									
July			21	.155	.190	58	9	2	0	0	0.0	6	6	6	8	0									
Aug			21	.158	.263	57	9	0	0	2	3.5	6	4	8	10	0									
Sept/Oct			25	.254	.388	67	17	6	0	1	1.5	12	6	19	10	0									
Day			27	.222	.292	72	16	2	0	1	1.4	8	4	11	13	0									
Night			80	.212	.343	236	50	13	0	6	2.5	29	29	34	35	1									
vs. Left				.202	.298	104	21	4	0	1	1.9	15	10	14	17	1									
vs. Right				.221	.348	204	45	11	0	5	2.5	22	23	31	31	0									
On Grass			43	.230	.381	139	32	3	0	6	4.3	16	18	15	26	0									
On Turf			64	.201	.290	169	34	12	0	1	0.6	21	15	30	22	1									
Home			50	.198	.290	131	26	9	0	1	0.8	18	13	23	21	1									
Road			57	.226	.362	177	40	6	0	6	3.4	19	20	22	27	0									
Division Rivals																									
vs. CAL			12	.222	.306	36	8	0	0	1	2.8	4	7	5	8	0									
vs. CHI			6	.400	.533	15	6	2	0	0	0.0	3	2	5	1	0									
vs. KC			9	.125	.125	24	3	0	0	0	0.0	0	0	1	2	0									
vs. MIN			9	.194	.355	31	6	2	0	1	3.2	5	4	7	5	1									
vs. OAK			11	.323	.516	31	10	3	0	1	3.2	4	4	4	1	0									
vs. TEX			9	.345	.759	29	10	3	0	3	10.3	8	7	6	4	0									
On 3B < 2 Out				.222	.389	18	4	0	0	1	5.6	1	8	2	4										
1984	SEA	A	13	.296	.444	27	8	1	0	1	3.7	4	4	1	5	0	0	0	56	5	0	0	4.7	1.000	C-13
1985			31	.157	.171	70	11	1	0	0	0.0	2	4	1	17	0	0	0	117	7	3	0	4.1	.976	C-31
1986			22	.340	.679	53	18	3	0	5	9.4	10	15	7	7	0	8	2	90	3	2	3	4.3	.979	C-12, 1B-4
1987			95	.256	.435	324	83	16	3	12	3.7	40	53	15	46	2	10	1	422	34	5	2	4.9	.989	C-75, 1B-2, OF-1
1988			93	.231	.400	290	67	15	2	10	3.4	29	50	18	38	0	10	5	490	47	6	8	5.8	.989	C-84, DH-3, 1B-1
1989			94	.237	.354	316	75	10	3	7	2.2	32	34	29	32	0	3	2	496	52	4	3	5.9	.993	C-93
1990			107	.214	.331	308	66	15	0	7	2.2	37	33	45	48	1	3	0	633	44	2	9	6.5	.997	C-104, 1B-1
7 yrs.			455	.236	.383	1388	328	61	8	42	3.0	154	193	116	193	3	34	10	2304	192	22	25	5.5	.991	C-412, 1B-8, DH-3, OF-1

CATCHER

Year	Team	Games	BA	SA	AB	H	2B	3B	HR	HR%	R	RBI	BB	SO	SB	PINCH HIT AB	PINCH HIT H	PO	A	E	DP	TC/G	FA	G by Pos

Andy Van Slyke

VAN SLYKE, ANDREW JAMES (Slick)
B. Dec. 21, 1960, Utica, N. Y.
BL TR 6' 1" 190 lbs.

OUTFIELD

AVERAGE — RBI — HR — SB

Split	Games	BA	SA	AB	H	2B	3B	HR	HR%	R	RBI	BB	SO	SB	AB	H	PO	A	E	DP	TC/G	FA	G by Pos
April	19	.290	.536	69	20	3	1	4	5.8	12	11	8	11	1									
May	23	.361	.458	83	30	2	0	2	2.4	11	15	14	12	6									
June	23	.253	.398	83	21	5	2	1	1.2	7	11	10	18	1									
July	22	.226	.393	84	19	5	0	3	3.6	11	6	9	12	1									
Aug	20	.309	.500	68	21	2	1	3	4.4	11	12	13	12	4									
Sept/Oct	29	.274	.509	106	29	9	2	4	3.8	15	22	12	24	1									
Day	39	.277	.527	148	41	12	2	7	4.7	22	23	14	36	4									
Night	97	.287	.438	345	99	14	4	10	2.9	45	54	52	53	10									
vs. Left		.261	.378	188	49	3	2	5	2.7	21	28	26	35	2									
vs. Right		.298	.518	305	91	23	4	12	3.9	46	49	40	54	12									
On Grass	39	.327	.567	150	49	6	3	8	5.3	28	26	24	28	5									
On Turf	97	.265	.420	343	91	20	3	9	2.6	39	51	42	61	9									
Home	64	.288	.447	219	63	15	1	6	2.7	27	35	31	40	5									
Road	72	.281	.478	274	77	11	5	11	4.0	40	42	35	49	9									

Division Rivals

Split	Games	BA	SA	AB	H	2B	3B	HR	HR%	R	RBI	BB	SO	SB									
vs. CHI	18	.410	.770	61	25	4	3	4	6.6	15	20	13	12	1									
vs. MON	12	.256	.512	43	11	5	0	2	4.7	3	8	4	11	0									
vs. NY	15	.245	.434	53	13	4	0	2	3.8	7	6	4	12	0									
vs. PHI	14	.235	.392	51	12	2	0	2	3.9	7	8	6	8	2									
vs. STL	16	.214	.393	56	12	3	2	1	1.8	6	6	5	7	0									
On 3B < 2 Out		.259	.444	27	7	0	1	1	3.7	1	24	7	8										

Year	Team		Games	BA	SA	AB	H	2B	3B	HR	HR%	R	RBI	BB	SO	SB	AB	H	PO	A	E	DP	TC/G	FA	G by Pos
1983	STL	N	101	.262	.421	309	81	15	5	8	2.6	51	38	46	64	21	5	1	203	59	6	16	2.7	.978	OF-69, 3B-30, 1B-9
1984			137	.244	.368	361	88	16	4	7	1.9	45	50	63	71	28	11	4	357	82	8	40	3.3	.982	OF-81, 3B-32, 1B-30
1985			146	.259	.439	424	110	25	6	13	3.1	61	55	47	54	34	19	4	237	13	1	6	1.7	.996	OF-142, 1B-2
1986			137	.270	.452	418	113	23	7	13	3.1	48	61	47	85	21	10	2	415	34	8	25	3.3	.982	OF-110, 1B-38
1987	PIT	N	157	.293	.507	564	165	36	11	21	3.7	93	82	56	122	34	7	1	338	10	4	9	2.2	.989	OF-150, 1B-1
1988			154	.288	.506	587	169	23	**15**	25	4.3	101	100	57	126	30	5	0	406	12	4	2	2.7	.991	OF-152
1989			130	.237	.370	476	113	18	9	9	1.9	64	53	47	100	16	10	1	344	9	4	6	2.7	.989	OF-123, 1B-2
1990			136	.284	.465	493	140	26	6	17	3.4	67	77	66	89	14	4	0	326	6	8	0	2.6	.976	OF-133
8 yrs.			1098	.270	.448	3632	979	182	63	113	3.1	530	516	429	711	198	71	13	2626	225	43	104	2.6	.985	OF-960, 1B-82, 3B-62

LEAGUE CHAMPIONSHIP SERIES

Year	Team		Games	BA	SA	AB	H	2B	3B	HR	HR%	R	RBI	BB	SO	SB	AB	H	PO	A	E	DP	TC/G	FA	G by Pos
1985	STL	N	5	.091	.091	11	1	0	0	0	0.0	1	1	2	1	0	0	0	7	0	0	0	1.4	1.000	OF-5
1990	PIT	N	6	.208	.333	24	5	1	1	0	0.0	3	3	1	7	1	0	0	13	1	0	0	2.3	.989	OF-6
2 yrs.			11	.171	.257	35	6	1	1	0	0.0	4	4	3	8	1	0	0	20	1	0	0	1.9	.000	OF-11

WORLD SERIES

Year	Team		Games	BA	SA	AB	H	2B	3B	HR	HR%	R	RBI	BB	SO	SB	AB	H	PO	A	E	DP	TC/G	FA	G by Pos
1985	STL	N	6	.091	.091	11	1	0	0	0	0.0	0	0	0	5	0	0	0	8	0	0	0	1.3	1.000	OF-6

Gary Varsho

VARSHO, GARY ANDREW
B. June 20, 1961, Marshfield, Wis.
BL TR 5' 11" 190 lbs.

Year	Team		Games	BA	SA	AB	H	2B	3B	HR	HR%	R	RBI	BB	SO	SB	AB	H	PO	A	E	DP	TC/G	FA	G by Pos
1988	CHI	N	46	.274	.315	73	20	3	0	0	0.0	6	5	1	6	5	28	11	29	0	3	0	0.7	.906	OF-18
1989			61	.184	.276	87	16	4	2	0	0.0	10	6	4	13	3	36	5	25	1	2	0	0.5	.929	OF-21
1990			46	.250	.333	48	12	4	0	0	0.0	10	1	1	6	2	43	11	2	0	0	0	0.7	1.000	OF-3
3 yrs.			153	.231	.303	208	48	11	2	0	0.0	26	12	6	25	10	107	27	56	1	5	0	0.4	.919	OF-42

Jim Vatcher

VATCHER, JAMES ERNEST
B. May 27, 1966, Santa Monica, Calif.
BR TR 5' 9" 165 lbs.

Year	Team		Games	BA	SA	AB	H	2B	3B	HR	HR%	R	RBI	BB	SO	SB	AB	H	PO	A	E	DP	TC/G	FA	G by Pos
1990	2 teams		PHI N (36G — .261)			ATL N (21G — .259)																			
"	total		57	.260	.356	73	19	2	1	1	1.3	7	7	5	15	0	32	10	27	0	0	0	0.9	1.000	OF-30

Year	Team		Games	BA	SA	AB	H	2B	3B	HR	HR%	R	RBI	BB	SO	SB	PINCH HIT AB	H	PO	A	E	DP	TC/G	FA	G by Pos

Greg Vaughn

VAUGHN, GREGORY LAMONT
B. July 3, 1965, Sacramento, Calif.
BR TR 6′ 195 lbs.

	Games	BA	SA	AB	H	2B	3B	HR	HR%	R	RBI	BB	SO	SB	AB	H	PO	A	E	DP	TC/G	FA	G by Pos
April	16	.275	.451	51	14	6	0	1	2.0	7	9	5	13	1									
May	14	.190	.452	42	8	2	0	3	7.1	8	11	9	9	0									
June	20	.258	.424	66	17	6	1	1	1.5	10	6	3	15	2									
July	27	.207	.435	92	19	4	1	5	5.4	12	18	8	27	2									
Aug	14	.111	.222	36	4	1	0	1	2.8	3	2	0	10	1									
Sept/Oct	29	.232	.495	95	22	7	0	6	6.3	11	15	8	17	1									
Day	32	.202	.383	94	19	5	0	4	4.3	9	14	8	20	1									
Night	88	.226	.448	288	65	21	2	13	4.5	42	47	25	71	6									
vs. Left		.197	.386	127	25	10	1	4	3.1	14	12	10	29	1									
vs. Right		.231	.455	255	59	16	1	13	5.1	37	49	23	62	6									
On Grass	106	.222	.440	343	76	23	2	16	4.7	47	56	32	79	6									
On Turf	14	.205	.359	39	8	3	0	1	2.6	4	5	1	12	1									
Home	61	.218	.435	193	42	13	1	9	4.7	31	32	17	42	3									
Road	59	.222	.429	189	42	13	1	8	4.2	20	29	16	49	4									
Division Rivals																							
vs. BAL	9	.258	.484	31	8	1	0	2	6.5	3	4	1	3	0									
vs. BOS	13	.304	.478	46	14	5	0	1	2.2	5	12	2	16	1									
vs. CLE	11	.275	.450	40	11	4	0	1	2.5	4	3	1	12	0									
vs. DET	10	.121	.242	33	4	1	0	1	3.0	6	3	4	3	1									
vs. NY	9	.240	.560	25	6	3	1	1	4.0	5	2	0	4	1									
vs. TOR	7	.381	.571	21	8	4	0	0	0.0	4	4	4	4	2									
On 3B < 2 Out		.400	.680	25	10	4	0	1	4.0	1	20	3	8										
1989	MIL	A	38	.265	.425	113	30	3	0	5	4.4	18	23	13	23	4	1	0	32	1	2	0	0.9	.943	OF–24, DH–13
1990			120	.220	.432	382	84	26	2	17	4.4	51	61	33	91	7	5	0	195	8	7	1	2.0	.967	OF–106, DH–8
2 yrs.			158	.230	.430	495	114	29	2	22	4.4	69	84	46	114	11	6	0	227	9	9	1	1.6	.963	OF–130, DH–21

Randy Velarde

VELARDE, RANDY LEE
B. Nov. 24, 1962, Midland, Tex.
BR TR 6′ 185 lbs.

	Games	BA	SA	AB	H	2B	3B	HR	HR%	R	RBI	BB	SO	SB	AB	H	PO	A	E	DP	TC/G	FA	G by Pos
April	10	.125	.188	16	2	1	0	0	0.0	2	0	3	4	0									
May	15	.191	.234	47	9	0	1	0	0.0	5	1	5	10	0									
June	17	.224	.347	49	11	1	1	1	2.0	3	4	1	8	0									
July	13	.143	.190	21	3	1	0	0	0.0	2	0	3	8	0									
Aug	16	.250	.500	28	7	1	0	2	7.1	3	6	2	7	0									
Sept/Oct	24	.235	.353	68	16	2	0	2	2.9	6	8	6	16	0									
Day	29	.288	.318	66	19	2	0	0	0.0	6	1	3	12	0									
Night	66	.178	.319	163	29	4	2	5	3.1	15	18	17	41	0									
vs. Left		.277	.385	65	18	2	1	1	1.5	5	2	4	15	0									
vs. Right		.183	.293	164	30	4	1	4	2.4	16	17	16	38	0									
On Grass	80	.229	.351	188	43	6	1	5	2.7	16	19	17	42	0									
On Turf	15	.122	.171	41	5	0	1	0	0.0	5	0	3	11	0									
Home	47	.210	.276	105	22	4	0	1	1.0	10	9	14	23	0									
Road	48	.210	.355	124	26	2	2	4	3.2	11	10	6	30	0									
Division Rivals																							
vs. BAL	13	.200	.400	45	9	1	1	2	4.4	4	9	3	11	0									
vs. BOS	13	.324	.541	37	12	2	0	2	5.4	3	5	1	7	0									
vs. CLE	8	.125	.125	8	1	0	0	0	0.0	1	0	0	1	0									
vs. DET	5	.143	.143	14	2	0	0	0	0.0	1	0	2	3	0									
vs. MIL	6	.313	.500	16	5	0	0	1	6.3	1	1	1	4	0									
vs. TOR	7	.125	.125	8	1	0	0	0	0.0	1	0	0	1	0									
On 3B < 2 Out		.500	.667	6	3	1	0	0	0.0	0	5	1	2										
1987	NY	A	8	.182	.182	22	4	0	0	0	0.0	1	1	0	6	0	0	0	8	20	2	3	3.8	.933	SS–8
1988			48	.174	.357	115	20	6	0	5	4.3	18	12	8	24	1	0	0	72	98	8	26	3.7	.955	2B–24, SS–14, 3B–11
1989			33	.340	.480	100	34	4	2	2	2.0	12	11	7	14	0	2	1	26	61	4	16	2.8	.956	3B–27, SS–9
1990			95	.210	.319	229	48	6	4	5	2.1	21	19	20	53	0	7	1	70	159	12	18	2.7	.950	3B–74, SS–15, OF–5, DH–3, 2B–3
4 yrs.			184	.227	.356	466	106	16	4	12	2.6	52	43	35	97	1	9	2	176	338	26	63	2.9	.952	3B–112, SS–46, 2B–27, OF–5, DH–3

OUTFIELD

AVERAGE · RBI · HR · SB (AL AVG)

THIRD BASE

AVERAGE · RBI · HR · SB (AL AVG)

Year	Team		Games	BA	SA	AB	H	2B	3B	HR	HR%	R	RBI	BB	SO	SB	PINCH HIT AB	H	PO	A	E	DP	TC/G	FA	G by Pos

Max Venable

VENABLE, WILLIAM McKINLEY, JR.
B. June 6, 1957, Phoenix, Ariz.
BL TR 5′ 10″ 185 lbs.

Year	Team		Games	BA	SA	AB	H	2B	3B	HR	HR%	R	RBI	BB	SO	SB	AB	H	PO	A	E	DP	TC/G	FA	G by Pos
1979	SF	N	55	.165	.200	85	14	1	1	0	0.0	12	3	10	18	3	17	5	30	2	3	0	0.6	.914	OF-25
1980			64	.268	.304	138	37	5	0	0	0.0	13	10	15	22	8	26	9	61	0	0	0	1.0	1.000	OF-40
1981			18	.188	.313	32	6	0	2	0	0.0	2	1	4	3	3	12	1	12	0	0	0	0.7	1.000	OF-5
1982			71	.224	.280	125	28	2	1	1	0.8	17	7	7	16	9	17	3	66	6	1	2	1.0	.986	OF-53
1983			94	.219	.364	228	50	7	4	6	2.6	28	27	22	34	15	22	6	141	5	1	0	1.6	.993	OF-66
1984	MON	N	38	.239	.352	71	17	2	0	2	2.8	7	7	3	7	1	13	4	33	0	0	0	0.9	1.000	OF-27
1985	CIN	N	77	.289	.422	135	39	12	3	0	0.0	21	10	6	17	11	35	13	60	3	0	0	0.8	1.000	OF-39
1986			108	.211	.313	147	31	7	1	2	1.4	17	15	17	24	7	51	8	63	0	2	0	0.6	.969	OF-57
1987			7	.143	.143	7	1	0	0	0	0.0	2	2	0	0	0	2	1	3	0	0	0	0.4	1.000	OF-4
1989	CAL	A	20	.358	.434	53	19	4	0	0	0.0	7	4	1	16	0	6	1	21	0	0	0	1.1	1.000	OF-13
1990			93	.259	.402	189	49	9	3	4	2.1	26	21	24	31	5	16	3	112	3	3	1	1.5	.975	OF-77, DH-1
11 yrs.			645	.240	.343	1210	291	49	15	15	1.2	152	107	109	188	62	217	54	602	19	10	3	1.0	.984	OF-406, DH-1

Robin Ventura

VENTURA, ROBIN MARK
B. July 14, 1967, Santa Maria, Calif.
BL TR 6′ 1″ 185 lbs.

		Games	BA	SA	AB	H	2B	3B	HR	HR%	R	RBI	BB	SO	SB	AB	H	PO	A	E	DP	TC/G	FA	G by Pos
April		15	.167	.310	42	7	1	1	1	2.4	4	3	8	10	0									
May		25	.181	.278	72	13	1	0	2	2.8	8	7	11	8	0									
June		25	.298	.351	94	28	5	0	0	0.0	10	11	10	15	1									
July		27	.262	.318	107	28	3	0	1	0.9	11	11	6	7	1									
Aug		28	.173	.200	75	13	2	0	0	0.0	5	7	10	8	0									
Sept/Oct		30	.330	.408	103	34	5	0	1	1.0	10	15	10	5	0									
Day		36	.238	.317	126	30	8	1	0	0.0	15	14	14	14	1									
Night		114	.253	.319	367	93	9	0	5	1.4	33	40	41	39	0									
vs. Left			.221	.247	154	34	2	1	0	0.0	14	12	22	26	0									
vs. Right			.263	.351	339	89	15	0	5	1.5	34	42	33	27	1									
On Grass		128	.253	.319	427	108	14	1	4	0.9	43	46	45	46	1									
On Turf		22	.227	.318	66	15	3	0	1	1.5	5	8	10	7	0									
Home		75	.273	.324	238	65	4	1	2	0.8	21	25	27	24	0									
Road		75	.227	.314	255	58	13	0	3	1.2	27	29	28	29	1									
Division Rivals																								
vs. CAL		12	.200	.229	35	7	1	0	0	0.0	6	2	9	6	1									
vs. KC		13	.231	.333	39	9	1	0	1	2.6	4	6	6	6	0									
vs. MIN		11	.257	.286	35	9	1	0	0	0.0	1	5	3	5	0									
vs. OAK		13	.333	.444	45	15	5	0	0	0.0	4	5	4	4	0									
vs. SEA		11	.366	.488	41	15	2	0	1	2.4	6	8	6	6	0									
vs. TEX		11	.111	.148	27	3	1	0	0	0.0	2	2	4	5	0									
On 3B < 2 Out			.320	.400	25	8	2	0	0	0.0	0	21	4	4										

Year	Team		Games	BA	SA	AB	H	2B	3B	HR	HR%	R	RBI	BB	SO	SB	AB	H	PO	A	E	DP	TC/G	FA	G by Pos
1989	CHI	A	16	.178	.244	45	8	3	0	0	0.0	5	7	8	6	0	1	0	17	33	2	2	3.3	.962	3B-16
1990			150	.249	.318	493	123	17	1	5	1.0	48	54	55	53	1	7	2	116	268	25	32	2.8	.939	3B-147, 1B-1
2 yrs.			166	.243	.312	538	131	20	1	5	0.9	53	61	63	59	1	8	2	133	301	27	34	2.8	.941	3B-163, 1B-1

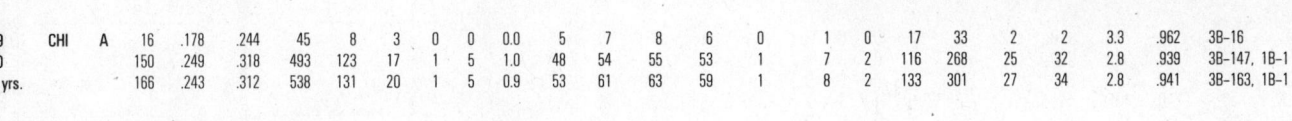

THIRD BASE — AVERAGE / RBI / HR / SB (AL AVG)

Hector Villanueva

VILLANUEVA, HECTOR
B. Oct. 2, 1964, San Juan, Puerto Rico
BR TR 6′ 1″ 220 lbs.

Year	Team		Games	BA	SA	AB	H	2B	3B	HR	HR%	R	RBI	BB	SO	SB	AB	H	PO	A	E	DP	TC/G	FA	G by Pos
1990	CHI	N	52	.272	.509	114	31	4	1	7	6.1	14	18	4	27	1	18	3	170	10	2	6	5.1	.989	C-23, 1B-14

Ozzie Virgil

VIRGIL, OSVALDO JOSE
Born Osvaldo Jose Virgil y Lopez. Son of Ozzie Virgil.
B. Dec. 7, 1956, Mayaguez, Puerto Rico
BR TR 6′ 1″ 205 lbs.

Year	Team		Games	BA	SA	AB	H	2B	3B	HR	HR%	R	RBI	BB	SO	SB	AB	H	PO	A	E	DP	TC/G	FA	G by Pos
1980	PHI	N	1	.200	.400	5	1	1	0	0	0.0	1	0	0	1	0	0	0	4	0	0	0	4.0	1.000	C-1
1981			6	.000	.000	6	0	0	0	0	0.0	0	0	0	2	0	5	0	2	0	0	0	0.3	1.000	C-1
1982			49	.238	.386	101	24	6	0	3	3.0	11	8	10	26	0	14	3	173	14	7	3	4.0	.964	C-35
1983			55	.214	.393	140	30	7	0	6	4.3	11	23	8	34	0	8	2	228	24	9	2	4.7	.966	C-51
1984			141	.261	.434	456	119	21	2	18	3.9	61	68	45	91	1	8	2	722	58	6	6	5.6	.992	C-137

Year	Team		Games	BA	SA	AB	H	2B	3B	HR	HR%	R	RBI	BB	SO	SB	PINCH HIT AB	H	PO	A	E	DP	TC/G	FA	G by Pos

Ozzie Virgil *Continued*

Year	Team		Games	BA	SA	AB	H	2B	3B	HR	HR%	R	RBI	BB	SO	SB	AB	H	PO	A	E	DP	TC/G	FA	G by Pos
1985			131	.246	.432	426	105	16	3	19	4.5	47	55	49	85	0	12	4	667	52	4	11	5.5	.994	C-120
1986	ATL	N	114	.223	.373	359	80	9	0	15	4.2	45	48	63	73	1	5	0	682	93	13	9	6.9	.984	C-111
1987			123	.247	.471	429	106	13	1	27	6.3	57	72	47	81	0	3	0	654	74	8	12	6.0	.989	C-122
1988			107	.256	.372	320	82	10	0	9	2.8	23	31	22	54	2	15	7	448	45	5	3	4.7	.990	C-96
1989	TOR	A	9	.182	.545	11	2	1	0	1	9.1	2	2	4	3	0	2	1	1	0	0	0	0.1	1.000	DH-6, C-1
1990			3	.000	.000	5	0	0	0	0	0.0	0	0	0	3	0	0	0	1	0	0	0	0.5	1.000	C-2, DH-1
11 yrs.			739	.243	.416	2258	549	84	6	98	4.3	258	307	248	453	4	72	19	3582	360	52	46	5.4	.987	C-677, DH-7

LEAGUE CHAMPIONSHIP SERIES

Year	Team		Games	BA	SA	AB	H	2B	3B	HR	HR%	R	RBI	BB	SO	SB	AB	H	PO	A	E	DP	TC/G	FA	G by Pos
1983	PHI	N	1	.000	.000	1	0	0	0	0	0.0	0	0	0	1	0	1	0	0	0	0	0	0.0	—	

WORLD SERIES

Year	Team		Games	BA	SA	AB	H	2B	3B	HR	HR%	R	RBI	BB	SO	SB	AB	H	PO	A	E	DP	TC/G	FA	G by Pos
1983	PHI	N	3	.500	.500	2	1	0	0	0	0.0	0	1	0	0	0	2	1	1	0	0	0	0.3	1.000	C-1

Jose Vizcaino

VIZCAINO, JOSE LUIS
Born Jose Luis Vizcaino y Pimental.
B. Mar. 26, 1968, San Cristobal, Dominican Republic
BB TR 6′ 1″ 150 lbs.

Year	Team		Games	BA	SA	AB	H	2B	3B	HR	HR%	R	RBI	BB	SO	SB	AB	H	PO	A	E	DP	TC/G	FA	G by Pos
1989	LA	N	7	.200	.200	10	2	0	0	0	0.0	2	0	0	1	0	1	1	6	9	2	2	2.4	.882	SS-5
1990			37	.275	.333	51	14	1	1	0	0.0	3	2	4	8	1	15	2	23	27	2	6	3.1	.962	SS-11, 2B-6
2 yrs.			44	.262	.311	61	16	1	1	0	0.0	5	2	4	9	1	16	3	29	36	4	8	1.6	.942	SS-16, 2B-6

Omar Vizquel

VIZQUEL, OMAR ENRIQUE
Born Omar Enrique Vizquel y Gonzalez.
B. Apr. 24, 1967, Caracas, Venezuela
BB TR 5′ 9″ 155 lbs.

	Games	BA	SA	AB	H	2B	3B	HR	HR%	R	RBI	BB	SO	SB
April				0	0	0	0			0	0	0	0	0
May				0	0	0	0			0	0	0	0	0
June				0	0	0	0			0	0	0	0	0
July	23	.282	.380	71	20	1	0	2	2.8	6	8	1	6	1
Aug	28	.204	.237	93	19	1	1	0	0.0	3	6	5	10	2
Sept/Oct	30	.264	.297	91	24	1	1	0	0.0	10	4	12	6	1
Day	22	.265	.279	68	18	1	0	0	0.0	3	1	2	4	1
Night	59	.241	.305	187	45	2	2	2	1.1	16	17	16	18	3
vs. Left		.235	.296	81	19	2	0	1	1.2	6	6	5	8	0
vs. Right		.253	.299	174	44	1	2	1	0.6	13	10	13	14	4
On Grass	29	.260	.320	100	26	1	1	1	1.0	9	7	6	7	0
On Turf	52	.239	.284	155	37	2	1	1	0.6	10	11	12	15	4
Home	39	.237	.254	114	27	2	0	0	0.0	7	6	11	14	1
Road	42	.255	.333	141	36	1	2	2	1.4	12	12	7	8	3
Division Rivals														
vs. CAL	8	.273	.318	22	6	1	0	0	0.0	1	1	1	6	0
vs. CHI	7	.350	.350	20	7	0	0	0	0.0	5	0	4	1	0
vs. KC	7	.200	.200	20	4	0	0	0	0.0	1	0	4	0	3
vs. MIN	10	.265	.441	34	9	1	1	1	2.9	1	6	2	3	0
vs. OAK	6	.158	.158	19	3	0	0	0	0.0	0	1	0	1	0
vs. TEX	6	.150	.250	20	3	0	1	0	0.0	1	2	1	2	0
On 3B < 2 Out		.231	.231	13	3	0	0	0	0.0	0	6	0	1	

SHORTSTOP

- AVERAGE — .400 / .200 / .000 (AL AVG)
- RBI — 100 / 50 / 0 (AL AVG)
- HR — 50 / 25 / 0 (AL AVG)
- SB — 60 / 30 / 0 (AL AVG)

Year	Team		Games	BA	SA	AB	H	2B	3B	HR	HR%	R	RBI	BB	SO	SB	AB	H	PO	A	E	DP	TC/G	FA	G by Pos
1989	SEA	A	143	.220	.261	387	85	7	3	1	0.3	45	20	28	40	1	2	0	208	388	18	102	4.3	.971	SS-143
1990			81	.247	.298	255	63	3	2	2	0.7	19	18	18	22	4	0	0	103	239	7	48	4.3	.980	SS-81
2 yrs.			224	.231	.276	642	148	10	5	3	0.5	64	38	46	62	5	2	0	311	627	25	150	4.3	.974	SS-224

Jim Walewander

WALEWANDER, JAMES
B. May 2, 1962, Chicago, Ill.
BB TR 5′ 10″ 160 lbs.

Year	Team		Games	BA	SA	AB	H	2B	3B	HR	HR%	R	RBI	BB	SO	SB	AB	H	PO	A	E	DP	TC/G	FA	G by Pos
1987	DET	A	53	.241	.389	54	13	3	1	1	1.9	24	4	7	6	2	2	0	26	58	1	12	1.6	.988	2B-24, 3B-17, SS-3
1988			88	.211	.240	175	37	5	0	0	0.0	23	6	12	26	11	2	0	125	154	6	38	3.2	.979	2B-61, SS-8, 3B-3
1990	NY	A	9	.200	.400	5	1	1	0	0	0.0	1	1	0	0	1	1	0	4	5	0	0	2.3	1.000	DH-2, 2B-2, 3B-2, SS-1
3 yrs.			150	.218	.278	234	51	9	1	1	0.4	48	11	19	32	14	5	0	155	217	7	50	2.5	.982	2B-87, 3B-22, SS-12, DH-2

Year	Team		Games	BA	SA	AB	H	2B	3B	HR	HR%	R	RBI	BB	SO	SB	PINCH HIT AB	H	PO	A	E	DP	TC/G	FA	G by Pos

Greg Walker

WALKER, GREGORY LEE
B. Oct. 6, 1959, Douglas, Ga.
BL TR 6′ 3″ 205 lbs.

Year	Team		Games	BA	SA	AB	H	2B	3B	HR	HR%	R	RBI	BB	SO	SB	AB	H	PO	A	E	DP	TC/G	FA	G by Pos
1982	CHI	A	11	.412	1.000	17	7	2	1	2	11.8	3	7	2	3	0	4	2	0	0	0	0	0.0	—	DH-4
1983			118	.270	.440	307	83	16	3	10	3.3	32	55	28	57	2	35	13	426	19	7	40	3.8	.985	1B-59, DH-21
1984			136	.294	.532	442	130	29	2	24	5.4	62	75	35	66	8	16	3	791	51	4	66	6.2	.995	1B-101, DH-21
1985			163	.258	.454	601	155	38	4	24	4.0	77	92	44	100	5	9	3	1217	97	8	116	8.1	.994	1B-151, DH-7
1986			78	.277	.493	282	78	10	6	13	4.6	37	51	29	44	1	3	1	670	57	5	57	9.4	.993	1B-77, DH-1
1987			157	.256	.465	566	145	33	2	27	4.8	85	94	75	112	2	4	0	1402	80	9	135	9.5	.994	1B-154, DH-3
1988			99	.247	.374	377	93	22	1	8	2.1	45	42	29	77	0	1	0	935	41	7	93	9.9	.993	1B-98
1989			77	.210	.335	233	49	14	0	5	2.1	25	26	23	50	0	9	0	373	17	5	38	5.1	.987	1B-48, DH-23
1990	2 teams		CHI A (2G — .200)			BAL A (14G — .147)																			
"	total		16	.154	.154	39	6	0	0	0	0.0	2	2	3	11	1	3	0	14	1	U	2	15.0	1.000	DH-12, 1B-1
9 yrs.			855	.260	.449	2864	746	164	19	113	3.9	368	444	268	520	19	84	22	5828	363	45	547	7.3	.993	1B-689, DH-92

LEAGUE CHAMPIONSHIP SERIES

1983	CHI	A	2	.333	.333	3	1	0	0	0	0.0	0	0	1	2	0	1	0	8	0	0	2	4.0	1.000	1B-1

Larry Walker

WALKER, LARRY KENNETH ROBERT
B. Dec. 1, 1966, Maple Ridge B. C., Canada
BL TR 6′ 2″ 185 lbs.

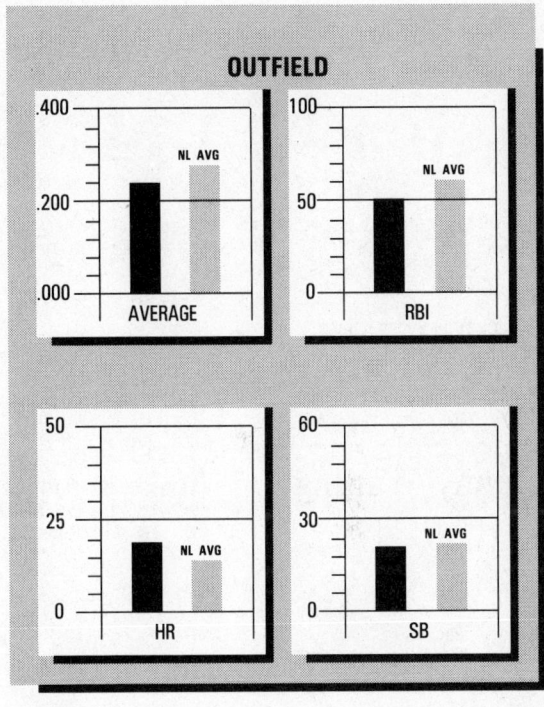

OUTFIELD

	Games	BA	SA	AB	H	2B	3B	HR	HR%	R	RBI	BB	SO	SB
April	17	.245	.415	53	13	6	0	1	1.9	8	5	7	20	5
May	22	.277	.446	65	18	3	1	2	3.1	7	6	6	13	4
June	27	.260	.534	73	19	5	0	5	6.8	14	12	11	14	0
July	21	.145	.263	76	11	0	0	3	3.9	8	6	3	29	2
Aug	20	.268	.493	71	19	1	0	5	7.0	10	13	5	17	7
Sept/Oct	26	.259	.457	81	21	3	2	3	3.7	12	9	17	19	3
Day	36	.216	.440	116	25	6	1	6	5.2	18	17	17	31	6
Night	97	.251	.432	303	76	12	2	13	4.3	41	34	32	81	15
vs. Left		.207	.414	116	24	6	0	6	5.2	16	18	8	30	5
vs. Right		.254	.442	303	77	12	3	13	4.3	43	33	41	82	16
On Grass	33	.286	.543	105	30	4	1	7	6.7	15	17	16	29	7
On Turf	100	.226	.398	314	71	14	2	12	3.8	44	34	33	83	14
Home	64	.255	.454	196	50	8	2	9	4.6	32	27	22	50	9
Road	69	.229	.417	223	51	10	1	10	4.5	27	24	27	62	12
Division Rivals														
vs. CHI	15	.318	.636	44	14	3	1	3	6.8	7	10	14	7	2
vs. NY	12	.219	.375	32	7	2	0	1	3.1	3	2	6	17	2
vs. PHI	14	.234	.362	47	11	3	0	1	2.1	3	3	5	14	3
vs. PIT	14	.178	.356	45	8	2	0	2	4.4	6	7	2	11	2
vs. STL	17	.217	.370	46	10	1	0	2	4.3	10	6	10	8	1
On 3B < 2 Out		.130	.174	23	3	1	0	0	0.0	0	10	5	7	

Year	Team		Games	BA	SA	AB	H	2B	3B	HR	HR%	R	RBI	BB	SO	SB	AB	H	PO	A	E	DP	TC/G	FA	G by Pos
1989	MON	N	20	.170	.170	47	8	0	0	0	0.0	4	4	5	13	1	7	0	19	2	0	1	1.1	1.000	OF-15
1990			133	.241	.434	419	101	18	3	19	4.5	59	51	49	112	21	11	1	249	12	4	5	2.1	.985	OF-124
2 yrs.			153	.234	.408	466	109	18	3	19	4.1	63	55	54	125	22	18	1	268	14	4	6	1.9	.986	OF-139

Tim Wallach

WALLACH, TIMOTHY CHARLES
B. Sept. 14, 1957, Huntington Park, Calif.
BR TR 6′ 3″ 220 lbs.

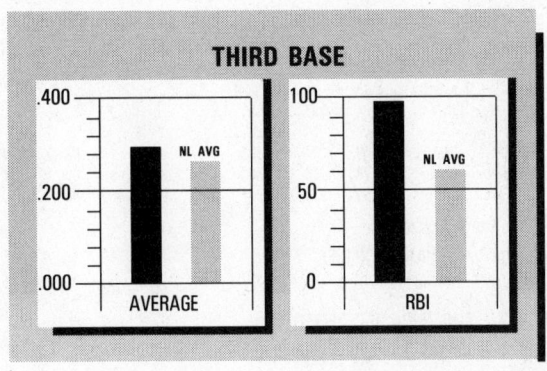

THIRD BASE

	Games	BA	SA	AB	H	2B	3B	HR	HR%	R	RBI	BB	SO	SB
April	19	.319	.486	72	23	6	0	2	2.8	6	9	6	13	0
May	27	.324	.695	105	34	10	1	9	8.6	17	25	7	12	1
June	29	.273	.391	110	30	8	1	1	0.9	9	15	10	15	1
July	27	.267	.495	101	27	4	2	5	5.0	15	15	10	15	1
Aug	27	.355	.400	110	39	5	0	0	0.0	6	10	3	8	3
Sept/Oct	32	.250	.391	128	32	4	1	4	3.1	16	20	6	17	0
Day	46	.335	.559	179	60	10	3	8	4.5	21	33	14	20	3
Night	115	.280	.436	447	125	27	2	13	2.9	48	65	28	60	3
vs. Left		.289	.456	204	59	12	2	6	2.9	22	29	21	23	2
vs. Right		.299	.479	422	126	25	3	15	3.6	47	69	21	57	4

Year	Team	Games	BA	SA	AB	H	2B	3B	HR	HR%	R	RBI	BB	SO	SB	PINCH HIT AB	PINCH HIT H	PO	A	E	DP	TC/G	FA	G by Pos

Tim Wallach *Continued*

Year	Team	Games	BA	SA	AB	H	2B	3B	HR	HR%	R	RBI	BB	SO	SB	AB	H	PO	A	E	DP	TC/G	FA	G by Pos
On Grass		42	.341	.555	173	59	13	0	8	4.6	25	33	7	15	1									
On Turf		119	.278	.439	453	126	24	5	13	2.9	44	65	35	65	5									
Home		81	.276	.452	301	83	16	5	9	3.0	34	46	24	43	4									
Road		80	.314	.489	325	102	21	0	12	3.7	35	52	18	37	2									
Division Rivals																								
vs. CHI		18	.236	.333	72	17	3	2	0	0.0	5	4	3	6	0									
vs. NY		18	.319	.417	72	23	4	0	1	1.4	7	3	3	12	1									
vs. PHI		18	.271	.357	70	19	3	0	1	1.4	5	7	7	9	1									
vs. PIT		18	.235	.324	68	16	3	0	1	1.5	6	12	5	9	0									
vs. STL		17	.288	.455	66	19	6	1	1	1.5	8	12	3	7	1									
On 3B < 2 Out			.387	.806	31	12	3	2	2	6.5	2	29	7	6										
1980	MON N	5	.182	.455	11	2	0	0	1	9.1	1	2	1	5	0	2	0	12	0	0	0	2.4	1.000	OF-3, 1B-1
1981		71	.236	.344	212	50	9	1	4	1.9	19	13	15	37	0	6	1	207	31	1	9	3.4	.996	OF-35, 1B-16, 3B-15
1982		158	.268	.471	596	160	31	3	28	4.7	89	97	36	81	6	3	1	132	287	23	23	2.8	.948	3B-156, OF-2, 1B-1
1983		156	.269	.434	581	156	33	3	19	3.3	54	70	55	97	0	0	0	151	265	19	25	2.8	.956	3B-156
1984		160	.246	.395	582	143	25	4	18	3.1	55	72	50	101	3	0	0	162	332	21	29	3.2	.959	3B-160, SS-1
1985		155	.260	.450	569	148	36	3	22	3.9	70	81	38	79	9	2	0	148	383	18	34	3.5	.967	3B-154
1986		134	.233	.396	480	112	22	1	18	3.8	50	71	44	72	8	1	0	94	270	16	26	2.8	.958	3B-132
1987		153	.298	.514	593	177	**42**	4	26	4.4	89	123	37	98	9	3	0	128	292	21	21	2.9	.952	3B-150, P-1
1988		159	.257	.389	592	152	32	5	12	2.0	52	69	38	88	2	8	2	124	329	18	32	3.0	.962	3B-153, 2B-1
1989		154	.277	.419	573	159	**42**	0	13	2.3	76	77	58	81	3	1	1	113	302	18	20	2.8	.958	3B-153, P-1
1990		161	.296	.471	626	185	37	5	21	3.3	69	98	42	80	6	0	0	128	309	21	23	2.8	.954	3B-161
11 yrs.		1466	.267	.435	5415	1444	309	29	182	3.4	624	773	414	819	46	26	5	1399	2800	176	242	3.0	.960	3B-1390, OF-40, 1B-18, P-2, 2B-1, SS-1

DIVISIONAL PLAYOFF SERIES

Year	Team	Games	BA	SA	AB	H	2B	3B	HR	HR%	R	RBI	BB	SO	SB	AB	H	PO	A	E	DP	TC/G	FA	G by Pos
1981	MON N	4	.250	.500	4	1	1	0	0	0.0	1	0	4	0	0	0	0	4	0	0	0	1.0	1.000	OF-3

LEAGUE CHAMPIONSHIP SERIES

Year	Team	Games	BA	SA	AB	H	2B	3B	HR	HR%	R	RBI	BB	SO	SB	AB	H	PO	A	E	DP	TC/G	FA	G by Pos
1981	MON N	1	.000	.000	1	0	0	0	0	0.0	0	0	0	0	0	1	0	0	0	0	0	0.0	—	

Denny Walling

WALLING, DENNIS MARTIN
B. Apr. 17, 1954, Neptune, N. J.
BL TR 6′ 180 lbs.

Year	Team	Games	BA	SA	AB	H	2B	3B	HR	HR%	R	RBI	BB	SO	SB	AB	H	PO	A	E	DP	TC/G	FA	G by Pos
1975	OAK A	6	.125	.250	8	1	1	0	0	0.0	0	2	0	4	0	4	1	3	0	0	0	0.5	1.000	OF-3
1976		3	.273	.273	11	3	0	0	0	0.0	1	0	0	3	0	0	0	8	0	1	0	3.0	.889	OF-3
1977	HOU N	6	.286	.381	21	6	0	1	0	0.0	1	6	2	4	0	1	1	14	0	0	0	2.3	1.000	OF-5
1978		120	.251	.356	247	62	11	3	3	1.2	30	36	30	24	9	39	10	140	4	3	2	1.2	.980	OF-78
1979		82	.327	.497	147	48	8	4	3	2.0	21	31	17	21	3	37	14	65	2	1	0	0.8	.985	OF-42
1980		100	.299	.387	284	85	6	5	3	1.1	30	29	35	26	4	21	4	525	31	6	46	5.6	.989	1B-63, OF-19
1981		65	.234	.367	158	37	6	0	5	3.2	23	23	28	17	2	18	6	226	9	2	18	3.6	.992	1B-27, OF-27
1982		85	.205	.267	146	30	4	1	1	0.7	22	14	23	19	4	30	6	167	11	1	8	2.1	.994	OF-32, 1B-20
1983		100	.296	.444	135	40	5	3	3	2.2	24	19	15	16	2	37	8	134	29	6	13	1.7	.964	1B-42, 3B-13, OF-13
1984		87	.281	.402	249	70	11	5	3	1.2	37	31	16	28	7	26	7	116	102	7	21	2.6	.969	3B-52, 1B-16, OF-6
1985		119	.270	.394	345	93	20	1	7	2.0	44	45	25	26	5	23	2	326	124	12	31	3.9	.974	3B-51, 1B-46, OF-13
1986		130	.312	.479	382	119	23	1	13	3.4	54	58	36	31	1	31	12	108	161	9	8	2.1	.968	3B-102, OF-11, 1B-4
1987		110	.283	.418	325	92	21	4	5	1.5	45	33	39	37	5	15	8	175	119	10	21	2.8	.967	3B-79, 1B-16, OF-7
1988	2 teams	HOU N (65G — .244)		STL N (19G — .224)																				
"	total	84	.239	.325	234	56	13	2	1	0.4	22	21	17	25	2	20	3	73	112	9	17	2.3	.954	3B-56, OF-12, 1B-4
1989	STL N	69	.304	.430	79	24	7	0	1	1.3	9	11	14	12	0	32	11	67	9	4	4	1.2	.950	1B-20, 3B-9, OF-6
1990		78	.220	.283	127	28	5	0	1	0.7	7	19	8	15	0	46	11	103	26	0	5	4.0	1.000	1B-15, 3B-11, OF-8
16 yrs.		1244	.274	.394	2898	794	141	30	49	1.7	370	378	305	308	44	380	104	2250	739	71	194	2.5	.977	3B-373, OF-285, 1B-273

DIVISIONAL PLAYOFF SERIES

Year	Team	Games	BA	SA	AB	H	2B	3B	HR	HR%	R	RBI	BB	SO	SB	AB	H	PO	A	E	DP	TC/G	FA	G by Pos
1981	HOU N	3	.333	.333	6	2	0	0	0	0.0	0	1	0	1	0	1	1	6	1	1	0	2.7	.875	1B-1, OF-1

LEAGUE CHAMPIONSHIP SERIES

Year	Team	Games	BA	SA	AB	H	2B	3B	HR	HR%	R	RBI	BB	SO	SB	AB	H	PO	A	E	DP	TC/G	FA	G by Pos
1980	HOU N	3	.111	.111	9	1	0	0	0	0.0	2	2	1	0	0	1	0	6	0	0	0	2.0	1.000	OF-2, 1B-1
1986		5	.158	.211	19	3	1	0	0	0.0	1	2	0	4	0	2	1	3	6	0	0	1.8	1.000	3B-5
2 yrs.		8	.143	.179	28	4	1	0	0	0.0	3	4	1	4	0	3	1	9	6	0	0	1.9	1.000	3B-5, OF-2, 1B-1

THIRD BASE
HR — NL AVG
SB — NL AVG

Year	Team	Games	BA	SA	AB	H	2B	3B	HR	HR%	R	RBI	BB	SO	SB	PINCH HIT AB	H	PO	A	E	DP	TC/G	FA	G by Pos

Jerome Walton

WALTON, JEROME O'TERRELL
B. July 8, 1965, Newman, Ga.
BR TR 6' 1" 175 lbs.

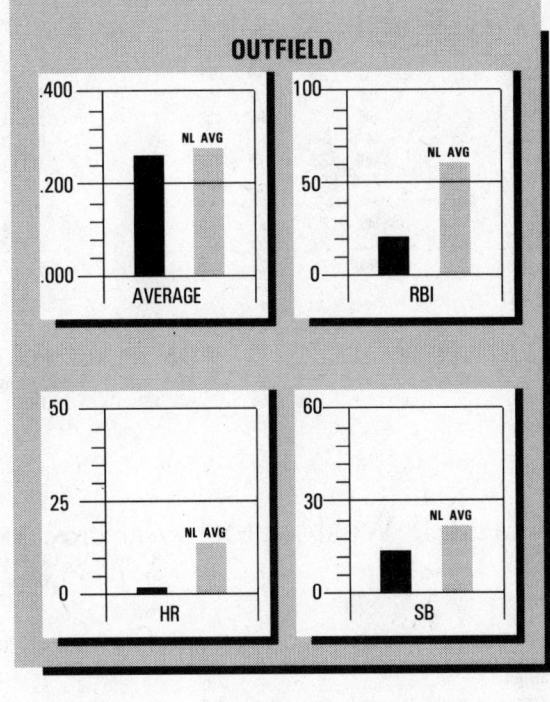

Year	Team	Games	BA	SA	AB	H	2B	3B	HR	HR%	R	RBI	BB	SO	SB	PINCH HIT AB	H	PO	A	E	DP	TC/G	FA	G by Pos
April		18	.286	.314	70	20	2	0	0	0.0	10	2	8	13	4									
May		21	.305	.378	82	25	4	1	0	0.0	12	5	10	14	5									
June		18	.206	.270	63	13	4	0	0	0.0	9	6	11	12	1									
July			.000	.000	0	0	0	0	0	0.0	0	0	0	0	0									
Aug		20	.269	.333	78	21	2	0	1	1.3	15	4	11	16	2									
Sept/Oct		24	.242	.333	99	24	4	1	1	1.0	17	4	10	15	2									
Day		52	.271	.345	203	55	8	2	1	0.5	35	13	26	38	8									
Night		49	.254	.312	189	48	8	0	1	0.5	28	8	24	32	6									
vs. Left			.288	.370	146	42	7	1	1	0.7	20	12	19	20	6									
vs. Right			.248	.305	246	61	9	1	1	0.4	43	9	31	50	8									
On Grass		70	.287	.354	268	77	8	2	2	0.7	52	12	35	43	11									
On Turf		31	.210	.274	124	26	0	0	0	0.0	11	9	15	27	3									
Home		52	.290	.365	200	58	5	2	2	1.0	43	8	24	32	7									
Road		49	.234	.292	192	45	11	0	0	0.0	20	13	26	38	7									
Division Rivals																								
vs. MON		6	.320	.360	25	8	1	0	0	0.0	7	0	4	6	1									
vs. NY		15	.356	.356	59	21	0	0	0	0.0	14	3	9	11	5									
vs. PHI		15	.231	.308	52	12	4	0	0	0.0	7	7	10	7	1									
vs. PIT		15	.220	.305	59	13	2	0	1	1.7	6	1	4	10	0									
vs. STL		12	.196	.314	51	10	3	0	1	2.0	11	3	6	8	1									
On 3B < 2 Out			.188	.188	16	3	0	0	0	0.0	0	9	4	4										
1989	CHI N	116	.293	.385	475	139	23	3	5	1.1	64	46	27	77	24	0	0	289	2	3	1	2.5	.990	OF-115
1990		101	.263	.329	392	103	16	2	2	0.5	63	21	50	70	14	0	0	247	3	6	0	2.6	.977	OF-98
2 yrs.		217	.279	.360	867	242	39	5	7	0.8	127	67	77	147	38	0	0	536	5	9	1	2.5	.984	OF-213
LEAGUE CHAMPIONSHIP SERIES																								
1989	CHI N	5	.364	.364	22	8	0	0	0	0.0	4	2	2	2	0	0	0	11	0	0	0	2.2	1.000	OF-5

Gary Ward

WARD, GARY LAMELL
B. Dec. 6, 1953, Los Angeles, Calif.
BR TR 6' 2" 195 lbs.

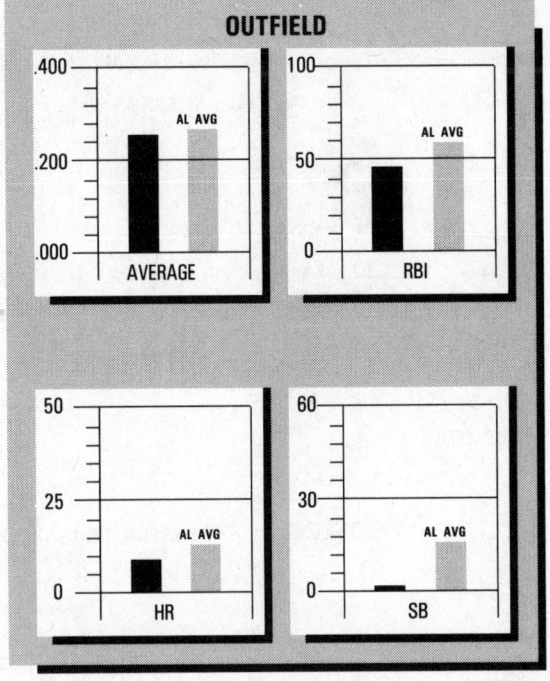

Year	Team	Games	BA	SA	AB	H	2B	3B	HR	HR%	R	RBI	BB	SO	SB	PINCH HIT AB	H	PO	A	E	DP	TC/G	FA	G by Pos
April		16	.298	.421	57	17	1	0	2	3.5	7	9	7	6	0									
May		25	.235	.321	81	19	4	0	1	1.2	6	7	5	7	1									
June		12	.143	.229	35	5	0	0	1	2.9	1	3	3	8	0									
July		14	.333	.519	27	9	2	0	1	3.7	2	8	4	5	0									
Aug		19	.250	.406	64	16	2	1	2	3.1	7	10	3	13	0									
Sept/Oct		20	.289	.511	45	13	2	1	2	4.4	9	9	8	11	1									
Day		32	.287	.347	101	29	6	0	0	0.0	8	9	10	14	1									
Night		74	.240	.413	208	50	5	2	9	4.3	24	37	20	36	1									
vs. Left			.257	.421	152	39	6	2	5	3.3	16	20	14	22	1									
vs. Right			.255	.363	157	40	5	0	4	2.5	16	26	16	28	1									
On Grass		89	.248	.370	254	63	9	2	6	2.4	26	38	24	44	2									
On Turf		17	.291	.491	55	16	2	0	3	5.5	6	8	6	6	0									
Home		47	.260	.389	131	34	7	2	2	1.5	14	17	14	24	0									
Road		59	.253	.393	178	45	4	0	7	3.9	18	29	16	26	2									
Division Rivals																								
vs. BAL		8	.321	.464	28	9	1	0	1	3.6	3	6	5	1	0									
vs. BOS		8	.200	.200	30	6	0	0	0	0.0	3	2	1	7	0									
vs. CLE		6	.235	.412	17	4	0	0	1	5.9	1	3	2	5	0									
vs. MIL		10	.226	.258	31	7	1	0	0	0.0	3	3	2	5	1									
vs. NY		10	.367	.700	30	11	1	0	3	10.0	4	9	3	5	0									
vs. TOR		9	.250	.500	28	7	2	1	1	3.6	3	1	3	4	0									
On 3B < 2 Out			.500	.833	12	6	1	0	1	8.3	1	16	3	1										
1979	MIN A	10	.286	.286	14	4	0	0	0	0.0	2	1	3	3	0	1	0	8	0	0	0	0.8	1.000	OF-5, DH-3
1980		13	.463	.780	41	19	6	2	1	2.4	11	10	3	6	0	2	0	14	0	0	0	1.1	1.000	OF-12
1981		85	.264	.359	295	78	7	6	3	1.0	42	29	28	48	5	5	1	185	8	5	4	2.3	.975	OF-80, DH-2
1982		152	.289	.519	570	165	33	7	28	4.9	85	91	37	105	13	5	2	343	13	4	3	2.4	.989	OF-150, DH-2
1983		157	.278	.440	623	173	34	5	19	3.0	76	88	44	98	8	4	0	374	24	9	6	2.6	.978	OF-152, DH-2

Year	Team	Games	BA	SA	AB	H	2B	3B	HR	HR%	R	RBI	BB	SO	SB	PINCH HIT AB	H	PO	A	E	DP	TC/G	FA	G by Pos

Gary Ward *Continued*

Year	Team	Games	BA	SA	AB	H	2B	3B	HR	HR%	R	RBI	BB	SO	SB	AB	H	PO	A	E	DP	TC/G	FA	G by Pos
1984	TEX A	153	.284	.447	602	171	21	7	21	3.5	97	79	55	95	7	4	0	376	11	5	1	2.6	.987	OF-148, DH-5
1985		154	.287	.433	593	170	28	7	15	2.5	77	70	39	97	26	1	1	304	11	10	2	2.1	.969	OF-153, DH-1
1986		105	.316	.405	380	120	15	2	5	1.3	54	51	31	72	12	0	0	237	8	1	3	2.3	.996	OF-104, DH-1
1987	NY A	146	.248	.384	529	131	22	1	16	3.0	65	78	33	101	9	12	8	318	10	3	11	2.3	.991	OF-94, DH-36, 1B-15
1988		91	.225	.312	231	52	8	0	4	1.7	26	24	24	41	0	17	5	220	5	2	9	2.5	.991	OF-54, 1B-11, 3B-2
1989	2 teams	NY A (8G — .294)		DET A (105G — .251)																				
"	total	113	.253	.397	292	74	11	2	9	3.1	27	30	24	59	1	32	6	234	16	3	15	2.2	.988	OF-57, DH-27, 1B-26
1990	DET A	106	.256	.392	309	79	11	2	9	2.9	32	46	30	50	2	14	5	164	2	2	1	2.0	.988	OF-85, DH-13, 1B-2
12 yrs.		1285	.276	.425	4479	1236	196	41	130	2.9	594	597	351	775	83	97	28	2777	108	44	55	2.3	.985	OF-1094, DH-92, 1B-54, 3B-2

Turner Ward

WARD, TURNER MAX
B. Apr. 11, 1965, Orlando, Fla.
BB TR 6' 2" 200 lbs.

Year	Team	Games	BA	SA	AB	H	2B	3B	HR	HR%	R	RBI	BB	SO	SB	AB	H	PO	A	E	DP	TC/G	FA	G by Pos
1990	CLE A	14	.348	.500	46	16	2	1	1	2.1	10	10	3	8	3	0	0	20	2	1	0	1.8	.957	OF-13, DH-1

Claudell Washington

WASHINGTON, CLAUDELL
B. Aug. 31, 1954, Los Angeles, Calif.
BL TL 6' 190 lbs.

Year	Team	Games	BA	SA	AB	H	2B	3B	HR	HR%	R	RBI	BB	SO	SB	AB	H	PO	A	E	DP	TC/G	FA	G by Pos
1974	OAK A	73	.285	.376	221	63	10	5	0	0.0	16	19	13	44	7	8	3	63	2	1	0	0.9	.985	DH-38, OF-32
1975		148	.308	.424	590	182	24	7	10	1.7	86	77	32	80	40	2	1	305	8	7	1	2.2	.978	OF-148
1976		134	.257	.353	490	126	20	6	5	1.0	65	53	30	90	37	3	2	276	10	11	2	2.2	.963	OF-126, DH-6
1977	TEX A	129	.284	.420	521	148	31	2	12	2.3	63	68	25	112	21	2	0	255	11	6	3	2.1	.978	OF-127, DH-1
1978	2 teams	TEX A (12G — .167)		CHI A (86G — .264)																				
"	total	98	.253	.376	356	90	16	5	6	1.7	34	33	13	69	5	6	2	170	6	8	0	1.9	.957	OF-89, DH-5
1979	CHI A	131	.280	.454	471	132	33	5	13	2.8	79	66	28	93	19	13	4	256	7	7	3	2.1	.974	OF-122, DH-3
1980	2 teams	CHI A (32G — .289)		NY N (79G — .275)																				
"	total	111	.278	.452	374	104	20	6	11	2.9	53	54	25	82	21	17	1	164	13	6	2	1.6	.967	OF-93, DH-2
1981	ATL N	85	.291	.425	320	93	22	3	5	1.6	37	37	15	47	12	5	3	145	5	1	0	1.8	.993	OF-79
1982		150	.266	.416	563	150	24	6	16	2.8	94	80	50	107	33	7	0	221	9	12	3	1.6	.950	OF-139
1983		134	.278	.413	496	138	24	8	9	1.8	75	44	35	103	31	7	2	218	8	6	3	1.7	.974	OF-128
1984		120	.286	.469	416	119	21	2	17	4.1	62	61	59	77	21	12	2	170	4	6	0	1.5	.967	OF-107
1985		122	.276	.455	398	110	14	6	15	3.8	62	43	40	66	14	26	2	122	3	5	1	1.1	.962	OF-99
1986	2 teams	ATL N (40G — .270)		NY A (54G — .237)																				
"	total	94	.254	.434	272	69	16	0	11	4.0	36	30	21	59	10	28	5	110	1	3	0	1.2	.974	OF-76
1987	NY A	102	.279	.420	312	87	17	0	9	2.9	42	44	27	54	10	21	4	166	3	2	1	1.7	.988	OF-72, DH-13
1988		126	.308	.442	455	140	22	3	11	2.4	62	64	24	74	15	19	4	309	5	5	1	2.5	.984	OF-117
1989	CAL A	110	.273	.428	418	114	18	4	13	3.1	53	42	27	84	13	6	2	187	6	5	2	1.8	.975	OF-100, DH-7
1990	2 teams	CAL A (12G — .176)		NY A (33G — .163)																				
"	total	45	.167	.228	114	19	2	1	1	0.8	7	9	4	25	4	11	3	61	3	0	0	2.1	1.000	OF-30, DH-2
17 yrs.		1912	.278	.420	6787	1884	334	69	164	2.4	926	824	468	1266	313	193	44	3198	104	91	22	1.8	.973	OF-1684, DH-77

LEAGUE CHAMPIONSHIP SERIES

Year	Team	Games	BA	SA	AB	H	2B	3B	HR	HR%	R	RBI	BB	SO	SB	AB	H	PO	A	E	DP	TC/G	FA	G by Pos
1974	OAK A	4	.273	.364	11	3	1	0	0	0.0	1	0	0	0	0	1	1	11	0	0	0	2.8	1.000	OF-3
1975		3	.250	.333	12	3	1	0	0	0.0	1	1	0	2	0	0	0	1	0	2	0	1.0	.333	OF-2, DH-1
1982	ATL N	3	.333	.333	9	3	0	0	0	0.0	0	0	2	2	0	0	0	5	1	0	0	2.0	1.000	OF-3
3 yrs.		10	.281	.344	32	9	2	0	0	0.0	2	1	2	4	0	1	1	17	1	2	0	2.0	.900	OF-8, DH-1

WORLD SERIES

Year	Team	Games	BA	SA	AB	H	2B	3B	HR	HR%	R	RBI	BB	SO	SB	AB	H	PO	A	E	DP	TC/G	FA	G by Pos
1974	OAK A	5	.571	.571	7	4	0	0	0	0.0	1	0	1	1	0	1	1	3	0	0	0	0.6	1.000	OF-5

Lenny Webster

WEBSTER, LEONARD IRELL
B. Feb. 10, 1965, New Orleans, La.
BR TR 5' 9" 185 lbs.

Year	Team	Games	BA	SA	AB	H	2B	3B	HR	HR%	R	RBI	BB	SO	SB	AB	H	PO	A	E	DP	TC/G	FA	G by Pos
1989	MIN A	14	.300	.400	20	6	2	0	0	0.0	3	1	3	2	0	1	1	32	0	0	0	2.3	1.000	C-14
1990		2	.333	.500	6	2	1	0	0	0.0	1	0	1	1	0	0	0	9	0	0	0	4.5	1.000	C-2
2 yrs.		16	.308	.423	26	8	3	0	0	0.0	4	1	4	3	0	1	1	41	0	0	0	2.6	.000	C-16

Year	Team		Games	BA	SA	AB	H	2B	3B	HR	HR%	R	RBI	BB	SO	SB	PINCH HIT AB	H	PO	A	E	DP	TC/G	FA	G by Pos

Mitch Webster

WEBSTER, MITCHELL DEAN
B. May 16, 1959, Larned, Kans.
BB TL 6′ 1/2″ 170 lbs.

	Games	BA	SA	AB	H	2B	3B	HR	HR%	R	RBI	BB	SO	SB
April	14	.375	.625	48	18	4	1	2	4.2	9	8	1	5	1
May	25	.192	.343	99	19	2	2	3	3.0	11	12	6	19	4
June	24	.250	.321	84	21	2	2	0	0.0	7	6	2	18	5
July	26	.300	.450	100	30	7	1	2	2.0	13	10	4	7	6
Aug	21	.224	.483	58	13	3	0	4	6.9	12	14	2	8	4
Sept/Oct	18	.188	.292	48	9	2	0	1	2.1	6	5	5	4	2
Day	35	.224	.312	125	28	7	2	0	0.0	16	14	7	22	8
Night	93	.263	.446	312	82	13	4	12	3.8	42	41	13	39	14
vs. Left		.292	.495	192	56	11	2	8	4.2	26	33	7	14	8
vs. Right		.220	.339	245	54	9	4	4	1.6	32	22	13	47	14
On Grass	110	.247	.388	369	91	13	6	9	2.4	47	45	17	53	19
On Turf	18	.279	.515	68	19	7	0	3	4.4	11	10	3	8	3
Home	66	.247	.372	231	57	7	2	6	2.6	29	35	12	32	12
Road	62	.257	.447	206	53	13	4	6	2.9	29	20	8	29	10
Division Rivals														
vs. BAL	11	.162	.216	37	6	2	0	0	0.0	4	0	2	8	1
vs. BOS	9	.143	.238	21	3	0	1	0	0.0	0	1	1	9	0
vs. DET	11	.242	.545	33	8	1	0	3	9.1	5	11	2	5	3
vs. MIL	11	.324	.378	37	12	0	1	0	0.0	7	4	2	2	5
vs. NY	9	.208	.250	24	5	1	0	0	0.0	2	2	1	3	2
vs. TOR	9	.241	.483	29	7	1	0	2	6.9	5	5	3	1	0
On 3B < 2 Out		.267	.467	15	4	0	0	1	6.7	1	15	4	2	

Year	Team		Games	BA	SA	AB	H	2B	3B	HR	HR%	R	RBI	BB	SO	SB	PH AB	PH H	PO	A	E	DP	TC/G	FA	G by Pos
1983	TOR	A	11	.182	.182	11	2	0	0	0	0.0	2	0	1	1	0	1	0	5	0	0	0	0.5	1.000	OF-7, DH-2
1984			26	.227	.409	22	5	2	1	0	0.0	9	4	1	7	0	7	1	16	0	2	1	0.7	.889	OF-10, DH-9, 1B-1
1985	2 teams				TOR A (4G — .000)				MON N (74G — .274)																
"	total		78	.272	.484	213	58	8	2	11	5.2	32	30	20	33	15	9	1	133	3	1	0	1.8	.993	OF-66, DH-2
1986	MON	N	151	.290	.431	576	167	31	13	8	1.4	89	49	57	78	36	4	1	325	12	8	3	2.3	.977	OF-146
1987			156	.281	.435	588	165	30	8	15	2.6	101	63	70	95	33	7	4	266	8	5	0	1.8	.982	OF-153
1988	2 teams				MON N (81G — .255)				CHI N (70G — .265)																
"	total		151	.260	.356	523	136	16	8	6	1.1	69	39	55	87	22	17	3	322	3	6	0	2.2	.982	OF-136
1989	CHI	N	98	.257	.364	272	70	12	4	3	1.1	40	19	30	55	14	30	4	161	3	6	0	1.7	.965	OF-74
1990	CLE	A	128	.252	.407	437	110	20	6	12	2.7	58	55	20	61	22	12	4	345	3	5	2	2.9	.986	OF-118, DH-3, 1B-3
8 yrs.			799	.270	.409	2642	713	119	42	55	2.1	400	259	254	417	142	87	18	1573	32	33	6	2.1	.980	OF-710, DH-16, 1B-4

LEAGUE CHAMPIONSHIP SERIES

Year	Team		Games	BA	SA	AB	H	2B	3B	HR	HR%	R	RBI	BB	SO	SB	PH AB	PH H	PO	A	E	DP	TC/G	FA	G by Pos
1989	CHI	N	3	.333	.333	3	1	0	0	0	0.0	0	0	0	0	0	1	0	0	0	0	0	0.0	—	OF-2

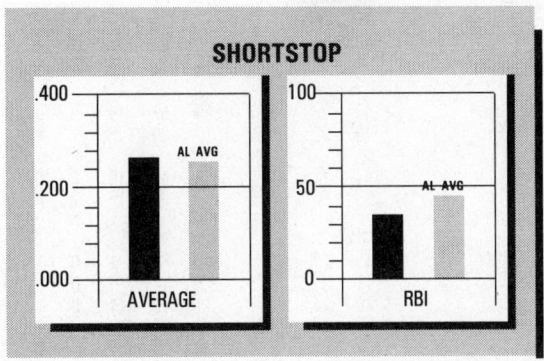

Walt Weiss

WEISS, WALTER WILLIAM
B. Nov. 28, 1963, Tuxedo, N. Y.
BB TR 6′ 175 lbs.

	Games	BA	SA	AB	H	2B	3B	HR	HR%	R	RBI	BB	SO	SB
April	19	.300	.443	70	21	4	0	2	2.9	10	6	2	7	1
May	27	.274	.310	84	23	3	0	0	0.0	11	3	9	7	2
June	26	.277	.361	83	23	5	1	0	0.0	10	5	8	14	2
July	28	.232	.263	95	22	3	0	0	0.0	9	9	9	9	2
Aug	17	.291	.327	55	16	2	0	0	0.0	5	8	6	9	2
Sept/Oct	21	.224	.224	58	13	0	0	0	0.0	5	4	12	7	0
Day	57	.276	.324	185	51	6	0	1	0.5	20	16	20	20	3
Night	81	.258	.319	260	67	11	1	1	0.4	30	19	26	33	6
vs. Left		.261	.304	115	30	5	0	0	0.0	11	12	8	10	2
vs. Right		.267	.327	330	88	12	1	2	0.6	39	23	38	43	7

Year	Team	Games	BA	SA	AB	H	2B	3B	HR	HR%	R	RBI	BB	SO	SB	PINCH HIT AB	H	PO	A	E	DP	TC/G	FA	G by Pos

Walt Weiss *Continued*

Year	Team	Games	BA	SA	AB	H	2B	3B	HR	HR%	R	RBI	BB	SO	SB	AB	H	PO	A	E	DP	TC/G	FA	G by Pos
On Grass		114	.264	.322	367	97	13	1	2	0.5	40	26	36	47	7									
On Turf		24	.269	.321	78	21	4	0	0	0.0	10	9	10	6	2									
Home		74	.247	.281	235	58	5	0	1	0.4	24	16	22	33	4									
Road		64	.286	.367	210	60	12	1	1	0.5	26	19	24	20	5									
Division Rivals																								
vs. CAL		11	.214	.214	42	9	0	0	0	0.0	4	4	6	10	0									
vs. CHI		11	.286	.286	35	10	0	0	0	0.0	3	1	3	3	0									
vs. KC		10	.242	.273	33	8	1	0	0	0.0	4	1	5	4	0									
vs. MIN		13	.333	.361	36	12	1	0	0	0.0	3	2	4	0	0									
vs. SEA		12	.268	.366	41	11	1	0	1	2.4	6	6	2	8	1									
vs. TEX		8	.250	.357	28	7	1	1	0	0.0	1	2	2	4	2									
On 3B < 2 Out			.333	.400	15	5	1	0	0	0.0	0	13	3	2										
1987	OAK A	16	.462	.615	26	12	4	0	0	0.0	3	1	2	2	1	1	0	8	30	1	4	2.4	.974	SS–11
1988		147	.250	.321	452	113	17	3	3	0.7	44	39	35	56	4	1	0	254	431	15	83	4.8	.979	SS–147
1989		84	.233	.318	236	55	11	0	3	1.3	30	21	21	39	6	0	0	106	195	15	44	3.8	.953	SS–84
1990		138	.265	.321	445	118	17	1	2	0.4	50	35	46	53	9	3	1	194	373	12	77	4.2	.979	SS–137
4 yrs.		385	.257	.327	1159	298	49	4	8	0.7	127	96	104	150	20	5	1	562	1029	43	208	4.2	.974	SS–379
LEAGUE CHAMPIONSHIP SERIES																								
1988	OAK A	4	.333	.467	15	5	2	0	0	0.0	2	2	0	4	0	0	0	7	10	0	3	4.3	1.000	SS–4
1989		4	.111	.222	9	1	1	0	0	0.0	2	0	1	1	1	0	0	5	9	0	2	3.5	1.000	SS–4
1990		2	.000	.000	7	0	0	0	0	0.0	2	0	2	2	0	0	0	2	7	1	1	5.0	.900	SS–2
3 yrs.		10	.194	.290	31	6	3	0	0	0.0	6	2	3	7	1	0	0	14	26	1	6	4.1	.976	SS–10
WORLD SERIES																								
1988	OAK A	5	.063	.063	16	1	0	0	0	0.0	1	0	0	2	1	0	0	5	11	1	1	3.4	.941	SS–5
1989		4	.133	.333	15	2	0	0	1	6.7	3	1	2	2	0	0	0	7	8	0	1	3.8	1.000	SS–4
2 yrs.		9	.097	.194	31	3	0	0	1	3.2	4	1	2	4	1	0	0	12	19	1	2	3.6	.969	SS–9

Lou Whitaker

WHITAKER, LOUIS RODMAN (Sweet Lou)
B. May 12, 1957, Brooklyn, N. Y.
BL TR 5′ 11″ 160 lbs.

Year	Team	Games	BA	SA	AB	H	2B	3B	HR	HR%	R	RBI	BB	SO	SB	AB	H	PO	A	E	DP	TC/G	FA	G by Pos
April		19	.188	.297	64	12	1	0	2	3.1	5	8	11	9	0									
May		26	.195	.345	87	17	1	0	4	4.6	9	11	13	20	1									
June		26	.228	.424	92	21	6	0	4	4.3	19	19	12	13	0									
July		24	.299	.515	97	29	8	2	3	3.1	20	14	12	14	4									
Aug		20	.329	.521	73	24	5	0	3	4.1	19	11	19	7	3									
Sept/Oct		17	.153	.271	59	9	1	0	2	3.4	3	6	7	8	0									
Day		39	.221	.366	131	29	7	0	4	3.1	20	10	18	12	1									
Night		93	.243	.422	341	83	15	2	14	4.1	55	50	56	59	7									
vs. Left			.162	.253	99	16	1	1	2	2.0	10	7	16	19	0									
vs. Right			.257	.448	373	96	21	1	16	4.3	65	53	58	52	8									
On Grass		113	.233	.397	395	92	19	2	14	3.5	59	49	61	63	8									
On Turf		19	.260	.455	77	20	3	0	4	5.2	16	11	13	8	0									
Home		64	.215	.370	219	47	10	0	8	3.7	34	27	34	36	6									
Road		68	.257	.439	253	65	12	2	10	4.0	41	33	40	35	2									
Division Rivals																								
vs. BAL		13	.205	.295	44	9	1	0	1	2.3	3	5	6	6	0									
vs. BOS		11	.333	.595	42	14	5	0	2	4.8	10	8	9	5	2									
vs. CLE		10	.147	.265	34	5	1	0	1	2.9	5	4	3	2	1									
vs. MIL		13	.231	.327	52	12	2	0	1	1.9	5	2	4	7	2									
vs. NY		7	.207	.207	29	6	0	0	0	0.0	6	1	7	2	0									
vs. TOR		10	.133	.133	30	4	0	0	0	0.0	3	2	5	4	1									
On 3B < 2 Out			.115	.154	26	3	1	0	0	0.0	0	11	7	7										
1977	DET A	11	.250	.281	32	8	1	0	0	0.0	5	2	4	6	2	0	0	17	18	0	2	3.2	1.000	2B–9
1978		139	.285	.357	484	138	12	7	3	0.6	71	58	61	65	7	6	3	301	458	17	95	5.6	.978	2B–136, DH–2
1979		127	.286	.378	423	121	14	8	3	0.7	75	42	78	66	20	5	0	280	369	9	103	5.2	.986	2B–126
1980		145	.233	.283	477	111	19	1	1	0.2	68	45	73	79	8	8	2	340	428	12	93	5.4	.985	2B–143
1981		109	.263	.373	335	88	14	4	5	1.5	48	36	40	42	5	2	1	227	354	9	77	5.4	.985	2B–108
1982		152	.286	.434	560	160	22	8	15	2.7	76	65	48	58	11	4	1	331	470	10	120	5.3	.988	2B–149, DH–1
1983		161	.320	.457	643	206	40	6	12	1.9	94	72	67	70	17	7	3	299	447	13	92	4.7	.983	2B–160
1984		143	.289	.407	558	161	25	1	13	2.3	90	56	62	63	6	6	1	290	405	15	83	5.0	.979	2B–142
1985		152	.280	.457	608	170	29	8	21	3.5	102	73	80	56	6	6	0	314	414	11	101	4.9	.985	2B–150
1986		144	.269	.437	584	157	26	6	20	3.4	95	73	63	70	13	6	4	276	421	11	98	4.9	.984	2B–141

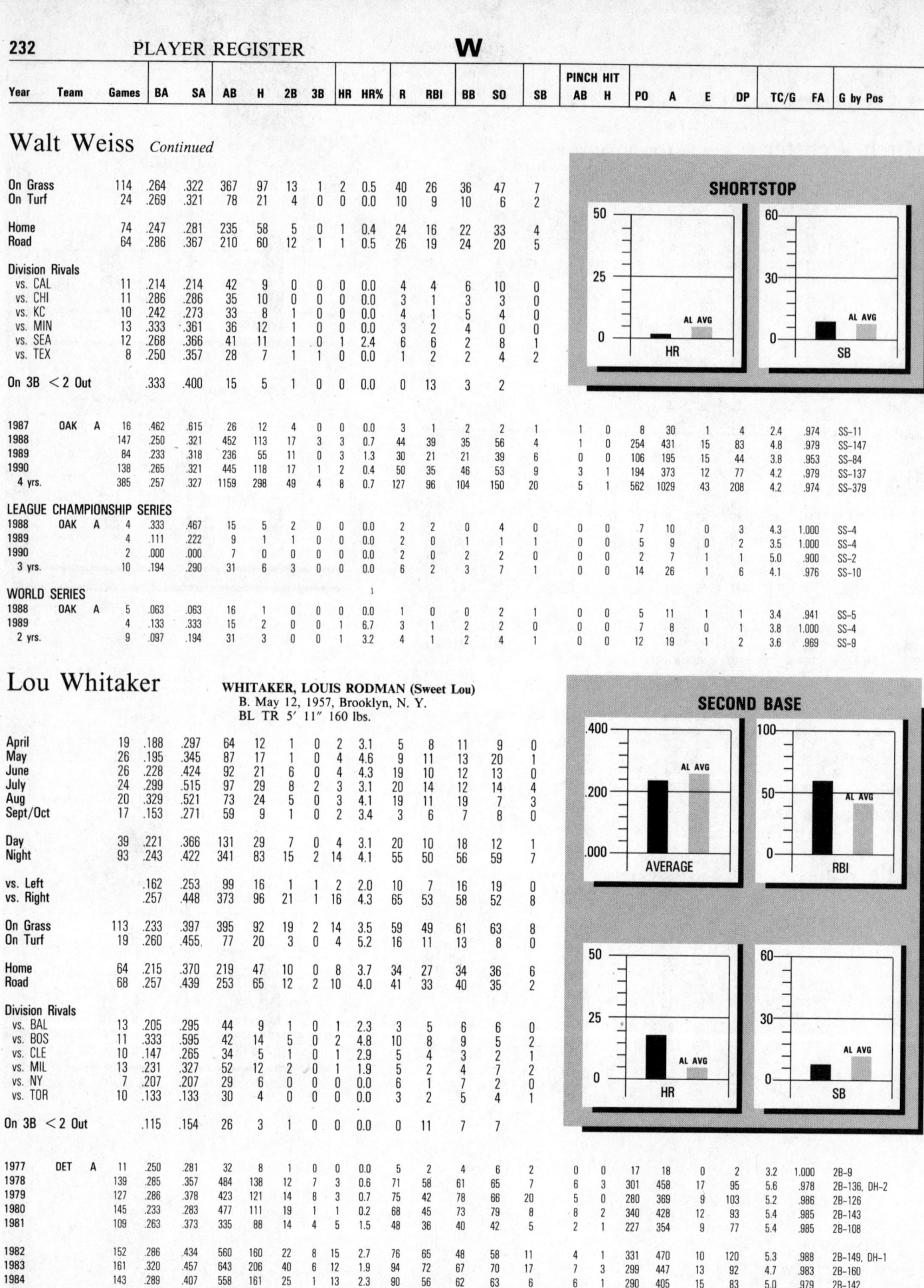

SHORTSTOP

HR — AL AVG

SB — AL AVG

SECOND BASE

AVERAGE — AL AVG

RBI — AL AVG

HR — AL AVG

SB — AL AVG

Year	Team	Games	BA	SA	AB	H	2B	3B	HR	HR%	R	RBI	BB	SO	SB	PINCH HIT AB	H	PO	A	E	DP	TC/G	FA	G by Pos

Lou Whitaker *Continued*

Year	Team	Games	BA	SA	AB	H	2B	3B	HR	HR%	R	RBI	BB	SO	SB	AB	H	PO	A	E	DP	TC/G	FA	G by Pos
1987		149	.265	.427	604	160	38	6	16	2.6	110	59	71	108	13	3	1	275	416	17	99	4.8	.976	2B-148
1988		115	.275	.419	403	111	18	2	12	3.0	54	55	66	61	2	9	3	218	284	8	53	4.4	.984	2B-110
1989		148	.251	.462	509	128	21	1	28	5.5	77	85	89	59	6	6	0	327	393	11	99	4.9	.985	2B-146, DH-2
1990		132	.237	.407	472	112	22	2	18	3.8	75	60	74	71	8	11	1	286	372	6	98	5.1	.991	2B-130, DH-1
14 yrs.		1827	.274	.411	6692	1831	301	60	167	2.5	1040	781	876	874	124	77	20	3781	5249	149	1213	5.0	.984	2B-1798, DH-6

LEAGUE CHAMPIONSHIP SERIES

Year	Team	Games	BA	SA	AB	H	2B	3B	HR	HR%	R	RBI	BB	SO	SB	AB	H	PO	A	E	DP	TC/G	FA	G by Pos
1984	DET A	3	.143	.143	14	2	0	0	0	0.0	3	0	0	3	0	0	0	5	6	0	0	3.7	1.000	2B-3
1987		5	.176	.353	17	3	0	0	1	5.9	4	1	7	3	1	0	0	11	14	0	1	5.0	1.000	2B-5
2 yrs.		8	.161	.258	31	5	0	0	1	3.2	7	1	7	6	1	0	0	16	20	0	1	4.5	.000	2B-8

WORLD SERIES

Year	Team	Games	BA	SA	AB	H	2B	3B	HR	HR%	R	RBI	BB	SO	SB	AB	H	PO	A	E	DP	TC/G	FA	G by Pos
1984	DET A	5	.278	.389	18	5	2	0	0	0.0	6	0	4	0	0	0	0	15	18	0	2	6.6	1.000	2B-5

Devon White

WHITE, DEVON MARKES
B. Dec. 29, 1962, Kingston, Jamaica
BB TR 6' 1" 170 lbs.

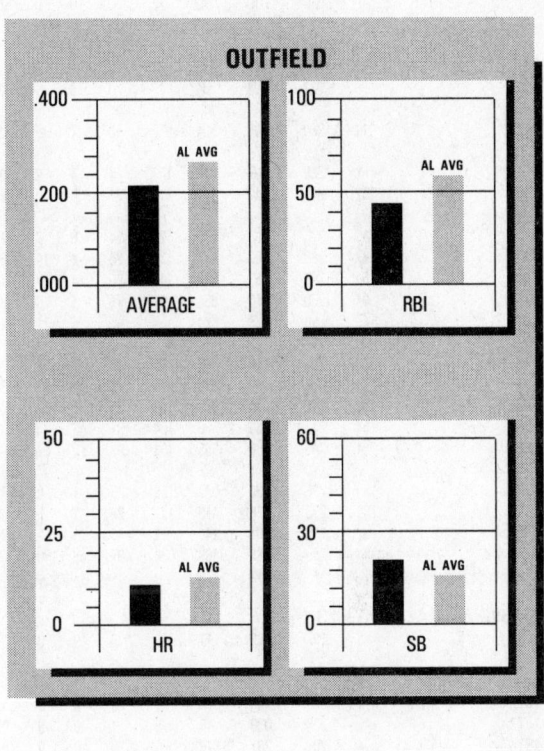

	Games	BA	SA	AB	H	2B	3B	HR	HR%	R	RBI	BB	SO	SB
April	17	.182	.273	66	12	3	0	1	1.5	5	2	4	19	2
May	28	.231	.407	108	25	8	1	3	2.8	20	10	11	21	6
June	23	.217	.377	69	15	2	0	3	4.3	8	9	9	23	3
July	9	.243	.297	37	9	2	0	0	0.0	3	2	4	12	2
Aug	24	.198	.363	91	18	2	2	3	3.3	12	12	9	19	4
Sept/Oct	24	.236	.278	72	17	0	0	1	1.4	9	9	7	22	4
Day	28	.230	.368	87	20	2	2	2	2.3	11	8	9	22	4
Night	97	.213	.337	356	76	15	1	9	2.5	46	36	35	94	17
vs. Left		.246	.354	130	32	5	0	3	2.3	18	10	12	22	3
vs. Right		.204	.339	313	64	12	3	8	2.6	39	34	32	94	18
On Grass	105	.223	.363	372	83	16	3	10	2.7	47	38	34	94	18
On Turf	20	.183	.239	71	13	1	0	1	1.4	10	6	10	22	3
Home	61	.215	.352	219	47	9	3	5	2.3	26	20	19	55	8
Road	64	.219	.335	224	49	8	0	6	2.7	31	24	25	61	13
Division Rivals														
vs. CHI	9	.167	.233	30	5	2	0	0	0.0	2	3	1	8	0
vs. KC	13	.184	.184	38	7	0	0	0	0.0	3	3	3	14	2
vs. MIN	12	.302	.419	43	13	2	0	1	2.3	6	5	3	10	3
vs. OAK	6	.214	.500	28	6	1	2	1	3.6	3	4	1	8	0
vs. SEA	10	.205	.231	39	8	1	0	0	0.0	4	2	5	11	2
vs. TEX	10	.200	.300	30	6	0	0	1	3.3	4	3	6	8	1
On 3B < 2 Out		.261	.435	23	6	1	0	1	4.3	1	14	6	7	

Year	Team	Games	BA	SA	AB	H	2B	3B	HR	HR%	R	RBI	BB	SO	SB	AB	H	PO	A	E	DP	TC/G	FA	G by Pos
1985	CAL A	21	.143	.143	7	1	0	0	0	0.0	7	0	1	3	3	0	0	10	1	0	0	0.5	1.000	OF-16
1986		28	.235	.353	51	12	1	1	1	2.0	8	3	6	8	6	0	0	49	0	2	0	1.8	.961	OF-28
1987		159	.263	.443	639	168	33	5	24	3.8	103	87	39	135	32	0	0	424	16	9	3	2.8	.980	OF-159
1988		122	.259	.389	455	118	22	2	11	2.4	76	51	23	84	17	5	2	364	7	9	2	3.1	.976	OF-116
1989		156	.245	.371	636	156	18	13	12	1.9	86	66	31	129	44	1	0	430	10	5	3	2.9	.989	OF-154, DH-1
1990		125	.217	.343	443	96	17	3	11	2.4	57	44	44	116	21	3	0	302	11	9	4	2.6	.972	OF-122
6 yrs.		611	.247	.389	2231	551	91	24	59	2.6	337	251	144	475	123	9	2	1579	45	34	12	2.7	.979	OF-595, DH-1

LEAGUE CHAMPIONSHIP SERIES

Year	Team	Games	BA	SA	AB	H	2B	3B	HR	HR%	R	RBI	BB	SO	SB	AB	H	PO	A	E	DP	TC/G	FA	G by Pos
1986	CAL A	3	.500	.500	2	1	0	0	0	0.0	2	0	0	1	0	0	0	2	0	0	0	0.7	1.000	OF-3

Frank White

WHITE, FRANK JR.
B. Sept. 4, 1950, Greenville, Miss.
BR TR 5' 11" 165 lbs.

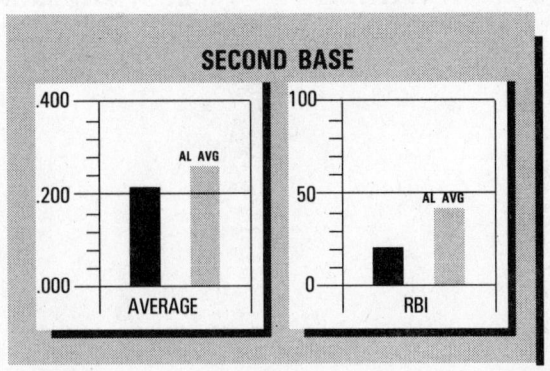

	Games	BA	SA	AB	H	2B	3B	HR	HR%	R	RBI	BB	SO	SB
April	14	.143	.262	42	6	2	0	1	2.4	3	7	1	5	0
May	7	.313	.375	16	5	1	0	0	0.0	2	1	0	3	0
June	18	.218	.291	55	12	4	0	0	0.0	7	2	3	10	0
July	12	.324	.486	37	12	1	1	1	2.7	4	5	3	4	0
Aug	16	.170	.208	53	9	2	0	0	0.0	2	4	2	8	0
Sept/Oct	15	.211	.316	38	8	4	0	0	0.0	2	2	1	2	1
Day	12	.222	.361	36	8	2	0	1	2.8	2	4	1	7	0
Night	70	.215	.298	205	44	12	1	1	0.5	18	17	9	25	1
vs. Left		.194	.280	93	18	5	0	1	1.1	8	6	6	15	0
vs. Right		.230	.324	148	34	9	1	1	0.7	12	15	4	17	1

Frank White *Continued*

Year	Team		Games	BA	SA	AB	H	2B	3B	HR	HR%	R	RBI	BB	SO	SB	PH AB	PH H	PO	A	E	DP	TC/G	FA	G by Pos
On Grass			26	.206	.279	68	14	5	0	0	0.0	4	5	0	10	0									
On Turf			56	.220	.318	173	38	9	1	2	1.2	16	16	10	22	1									
Home			46	.248	.366	145	36	9	1	2	1.4	15	15	6	20	1									
Road			36	.167	.219	96	16	5	0	0	0.0	5	6	4	12	0									
Division Rivals																									
vs. CAL			8	.118	.235	17	2	2	0	0	0.0	1	1	0	5	0									
vs. CHI			6	.118	.118	17	2	0	0	0	0.0	1	1	1	3	0									
vs. MIN			7	.250	.333	24	6	2	0	0	0.0	2	2	0	2	0									
vs. OAK			9	.308	.423	26	8	3	0	0	0.0	3	0	1	3	1									
vs. SEA			10	.161	.161	31	5	0	0	0	0.0	2	1	3	6	0									
vs. TEX			3	.111	.222	9	1	1	0	0	0.0	1	0	0	0	0									
On 3B <2 Out				.100	.100	10	1	0	0	0	0.0	0	5	1	4										
1973	KC	A	51	.223	.281	139	31	6	1	0	0.0	20	5	8	23	3	1	0	71	121	12	36	4.0	.941	SS-37, 2B-11
1974			99	.221	.294	204	45	6	3	1	0.5	19	18	5	33	3	3	0	119	189	12	40	3.2	.963	2B-50, SS-29, 3B-16, DH-3
1975			111	.250	.365	304	76	10	2	7	2.3	43	36	20	39	11	0	0	180	272	11	56	4.2	.976	2B-67, SS-42, 3B-4, DH-2
1976			152	.229	.307	446	102	17	6	2	0.4	39	46	19	42	20	0	0	296	479	23	89	5.3	.971	2B-130, SS-37
1977			152	.245	.342	474	116	21	5	5	1.1	59	50	25	67	23	0	0	310	437	8	86	5.0	.989	2B-152, SS-4
1978			143	.275	.399	461	127	24	6	7	1.5	66	50	26	59	13	3	0	325	385	16	96	5.1	.978	2B-140
1979			127	.266	.403	467	124	26	4	10	2.1	73	48	25	54	28	1	0	317	332	12	78	5.2	.982	2B-125
1980			154	.264	.357	560	148	23	4	7	1.3	70	60	19	69	19	3	0	395	448	10	103	5.5	.988	2B-153
1981			94	.250	.376	364	91	17	1	9	2.5	35	38	19	50	4	1	1	226	263	6	70	5.3	.988	2B-93
1982			145	.298	.469	524	156	45	6	11	2.1	71	56	16	65	10	1	0	361	389	17	99	5.3	.978	2B-144
1983			146	.260	.406	549	143	35	6	11	2.0	52	77	20	51	13	3	2	390	442	8	123	5.8	.990	2B-145
1984			129	.271	.445	479	130	22	5	17	3.5	58	56	27	72	5	1	0	299	425	11	97	5.7	.985	2B-129
1985			149	.249	.414	563	140	25	1	22	3.9	62	69	28	86	10	0	0	342	490	17	101	5.7	.980	2B-149
1986			151	.272	.465	566	154	37	3	22	3.9	76	84	43	88	4	6	1	317	441	10	92	5.1	.987	2B-151, 3B-1, SS-1
1987			154	.245	.400	563	138	32	2	17	3.0	67	78	51	86	1	1	0	320	458	10	89	5.1	.987	2B-152, DH-1
1988			150	.235	.330	537	126	25	1	8	1.5	48	58	21	67	7	6	2	293	426	4	88	4.8	.994	2B-148, DH-3
1989			135	.256	.328	418	107	22	1	2	0.5	34	36	30	52	3	4	0	238	407	10	64	4.9	.985	2B-132, OF-1
1990			82	.216	.307	241	52	14	1	2	0.8	20	21	10	32	1	2	0	142	218	8	51	4.6	.978	2B-79, OF-1
18 yrs.			2324	.255	.383	7859	2006	407	58	160	2.0	912	886	412	1035	178	36	6	4941	6622	205	1458	0.8	.884	2B-2150, SS-150, 3B-21, DH-9, OF-2

DIVISIONAL PLAYOFF SERIES

| 1981 | KC | A | 3 | .182 | .182 | 11 | 2 | 0 | 0 | 0 | 0.0 | 1 | 0 | 1 | 1 | 0 | 0 | 0 | 5 | 6 | 1 | 0 | 4.0 | .917 | 2B-3 |

LEAGUE CHAMPIONSHIP SERIES

1976	KC	A	4	.125	.125	8	1	0	0	0	0.0	2	0	0	1	0	0	0	6	11	0	3	4.3	1.000	2B-4
1977			5	.278	.333	18	5	1	0	0	0.0	1	2	0	4	1	0	0	13	16	0	1	5.8	1.000	2B-5
1978			4	.231	.231	13	3	0	0	0	0.0	1	2	0	4	0	0	0	9	12	0	3	5.3	1.000	2B-4
1980			3	.545	.909	11	6	1	0	1	9.1	3	3	0	0	1	0	0	9	10	1	3	6.7	.950	2B-3
1984			3	.083	.083	12	1	0	0	0	0.0	1	0	0	3	0	0	0	7	3	0	2	3.3	1.000	2B-3
1985			7	.200	.200	25	5	0	0	0	0.0	1	3	1	2	0	0	0	9	28	0	4	5.3	1.000	2B-7
6 yrs.			26	.241	.299	87	21	2	0	1	1.1	9	10	1	10	2	0	0	53	80	1	16	5.2	.993	2B-26

WORLD SERIES

1980	KC	A	6	.080	.080	25	2	0	0	0	0.0	0	0	1	5	1	0	0	13	21	2	6	6.0	.944	2B-6
1985			7	.250	.464	28	7	3	0	1	3.6	4	6	3	4	1	0	0	10	20	0	2	4.3	1.000	2B-7
2 yrs.			13	.170	.283	53	9	3	0	1	1.9	4	6	4	9	2	0	0	23	41	2	8	5.1	.970	2B-13

Mark Whiten

WHITEN, MARK ANTHONY
B. Nov. 25, 1966, Pensacola, Fla.
BR TR 6' 3" 210 lbs.

| 1990 | TOR | A | 33 | .273 | .375 | 88 | 24 | 1 | 1 | 2 | 2.2 | 12 | 7 | 7 | 14 | 2 | 3 | 0 | 60 | 3 | 0 | 0 | 2.1 | 1.000 | OF-30, DH-2 |

Year	Team		Games	BA	SA	AB	H	2B	3B	HR	HR%	R	RBI	BB	SO	SB	PINCH HIT AB	H	PO	A	E	DP	TC/G	FA	G by Pos

Ernie Whitt

WHITT, LEO ERNEST
B. June 13, 1952, Detroit, Mich.
BL TR 6′ 2″ 200 lbs.

Year	Team		Games	BA	SA	AB	H	2B	3B	HR	HR%	R	RBI	BB	SO	SB	AB	H	PO	A	E	DP	TC/G	FA	G by Pos
1976	BOS	A	8	.222	.500	18	4	2	0	1	5.6	4	3	2	2	0	1	0	24	0	0	0	3.0	1.000	C-8
1977	TOR	A	23	.171	.244	41	7	3	0	0	0.0	4	6	2	12	0	9	1	62	4	0	0	2.9	1.000	C-14
1978			2	.000	.000	4	0	0	0	0	0.0	0	0	1	1	0	1	0	7	1	0	0	4.0	1.000	C-1
1980			106	.237	.353	295	70	12	2	6	2.0	23	34	22	30	1	1	0	436	56	7	11	4.7	.986	C-105
1981			74	.236	.297	195	46	9	0	1	0.5	16	16	20	30	5	4	0	297	46	3	5	4.7	.991	C-72
1982			105	.261	.440	284	74	14	2	11	3.9	28	42	26	34	3	21	7	406	30	8	0	4.2	.982	C-98, DH-1
1983			123	.256	.459	344	88	15	2	17	4.9	53	56	50	55	1	17	5	554	50	5	4	5.0	.992	C-119
1984			124	.238	.425	315	75	12	1	15	4.8	35	46	43	49	0	16	5	583	40	8	8	5.1	.994	C-118
1985			139	.245	.444	412	101	21	2	19	4.6	55	64	47	59	3	16	2	649	38	8	6	5.0	.988	C-134
1986			131	.268	.448	395	106	19	2	16	4.1	48	56	35	39	0	11	3	709	41	7	7	5.8	.991	C-129
1987			135	.269	.455	446	120	24	1	19	4.3	57	75	44	50	0	12	1	803	55	5	10	6.4	.994	C-131
1988			127	.251	.410	398	100	11	2	16	4.0	63	70	61	38	4	11	0	643	43	4	10	5.4	.994	C-123
1989			129	.262	.416	385	101	24	1	11	2.9	42	53	52	53	5	16	3	550	43	5	5	4.6	.992	C-115, DH-8
1990	ATL	N	67	.172	.250	180	31	8	0	2	1.1	14	10	23	27	0	9	3	296	42	3	1	5.8	.991	C-59
14 yrs.			1293	.249	.412	3712	923	174	15	134	3.6	442	531	428	479	22	145	30	6019	489	59	67	5.1	.991	C-1226, DH-9

LEAGUE CHAMPIONSHIP SERIES

Year	Team		Games	BA	SA	AB	H	2B	3B	HR	HR%	R	RBI	BB	SO	SB	AB	H	PO	A	E	DP	TC/G	FA	G by Pos
1985	TOR	A	7	.190	.238	21	4	1	0	0	0.0	1	2	2	4	0	0	0	50	3	0	1	7.6	1.000	C-7
1989			5	.125	.313	16	2	0	0	1	6.3	1	3	2	3	0	0	0	32	2	0	0	6.8	1.000	C-5
2 yrs.			12	.162	.270	37	6	1	0	1	2.7	2	5	4	7	0	0	0	82	5	0	1	7.3	.000	C-12

Curtis Wilkerson

WILKERSON, CURTIS VERNON
B. Apr. 26, 1961, Petersburg, Va.
BB TR 5′ 9″ 158 lbs.

Year	Team		Games	BA	SA	AB	H	2B	3B	HR	HR%	R	RBI	BB	SO	SB	AB	H	PO	A	E	DP	TC/G	FA	G by Pos
1983	TEX	A	16	.171	.229	35	6	0	1	0	0.0	7	1	2	5	3	1	0	18	31	1	5	3.1	.980	SS-9, 2B-2, 3B-2
1984			153	.248	.279	484	120	12	0	1	0.2	47	26	22	72	12	0	0	227	391	30	73	4.2	.954	SS-116, 2B-47
1985			129	.244	.308	360	88	11	6	0	0.0	35	22	22	63	14	2	1	165	328	21	65	4.0	.959	SS-110, 2B-19, DH-2
1986			110	.237	.305	236	56	10	3	0	0.0	27	15	11	42	9	3	0	125	199	13	56	3.1	.961	2B-60, SS-56, DH-2
1987			85	.268	.391	138	37	5	3	2	1.4	28	14	6	16	6	3	1	79	98	6	18	2.2	.967	SS-33, 2B-28, 3B-18
1988			117	.293	.358	338	99	12	5	0	0.0	41	28	26	43	9	6	0	186	299	15	58	4.3	.970	2B-87, SS-24, 3B-11
1989	CHI	N	77	.244	.313	160	39	4	2	1	0.6	18	10	8	33	4	28	11	42	91	8	10	1.8	.943	3B-26, 2B-15, SS-7, OF-1
1990			77	.220	.258	186	41	5	1	0	0.0	21	16	7	36	2	13	5	49	93	14	7	2.4	.910	3B-52, 2B-14, SS-1, OF-1
8 yrs.			764	.251	.309	1937	486	59	21	4	0.2	224	132	104	310	59	56	18	891	1530	108	292	3.3	.957	SS-356, 2B-272, 3B-109, DH-4, OF-2

LEAGUE CHAMPIONSHIP SERIES

Year	Team		Games	BA	SA	AB	H	2B	3B	HR	HR%	R	RBI	BB	SO	SB	AB	H	PO	A	E	DP	TC/G	FA	G by Pos
1989	CHI	N	3	.500	.500	2	1	0	0	0	0.0	1	0	0	0	0	2	1	0	0	0	0	0.0	—	3B-1

Jerry Willard

WILLARD, GERALD DUANE, JR.
B. Mar. 14, 1960, Oxnard, Calif.
BL TR 6′ 2″ 200 lbs.

Year	Team		Games	BA	SA	AB	H	2B	3B	HR	HR%	R	RBI	BB	SO	SB	AB	H	PO	A	E	DP	TC/G	FA	G by Pos
1984	CLE	A	87	.224	.386	246	55	8	1	10	4.1	21	37	26	55	1	12	1	335	35	7	7	4.3	.981	C-76, DH-1
1985			104	.270	.383	300	81	13	0	7	2.3	39	36	28	59	0	10	2	427	52	5	11	4.7	.990	C-96, DH-1
1986	OAK	A	75	.267	.385	161	43	7	0	4	2.5	17	26	22	28	0	7	4	300	12	2	1	4.2	.994	C-71, DH-7
1987			7	.167	.167	6	1	0	0	0	0.0	1	0	2	1	0	1	0	1	0	0	1	0.1	1.000	DH-3, 1B-1, 3B-1
1990	CHI	A	3	.000	.000	3	0	0	0	0	0.0	0	0	0	2	0	2	0	0	0	0	0	0.0	.976	C-1
5 yrs.			276	.251	.381	716	180	28	1	21	2.9	78	99	78	145	1	32	7	1063	99	14	20	4.3	.988	C-244, DH-12, 1B-1, 3B-1

Eddie Williams

WILLIAMS, EDWARD LAQUAN
B. Nov. 1, 1964, Shreveport, La.
BR TR 6′ 175 lbs.

Year	Team		Games	BA	SA	AB	H	2B	3B	HR	HR%	R	RBI	BB	SO	SB	AB	H	PO	A	E	DP	TC/G	FA	G by Pos
1986	CLE	A	5	.143	.143	7	1	0	0	0	0.0	2	1	0	3	0	2	0	0	0	0	0	0.0	—	OF-4
1987			22	.172	.281	64	11	4	0	1	1.6	9	4	9	19	0	0	0	17	37	1	6	2.5	.982	3B-22
1988			10	.190	.190	21	4	0	0	0	0.0	3	1	0	3	0	0	0	3	18	0	0	2.1	1.000	3B-10
1989	CHI	A	66	.274	.358	201	55	8	0	3	1.5	25	10	18	31	1	1	0	37	123	16	21	2.7	.909	3B-65
1990	SD	N	14	.286	.571	42	12	3	0	3	7.1	5	4	5	6	0	2	0	5	21	3	2	2.2	.897	3B-13
5 yrs.			117	.248	.355	335	83	15	0	7	2.1	44	20	32	62	1	5	0	62	199	20	29	2.4	.929	3B-110, OF-4

Year	Team		Games	BA	SA	AB	H	2B	3B	HR	HR%	R	RBI	BB	SO	SB	PINCH HIT AB	H	PO	A	E	DP	TC/G	FA	G by Pos

Ken Williams

WILLIAMS, KENNETH ROYAL
B. Apr. 6, 1964, Berkeley, Calif.
BR TR 6' 2" 187 lbs.

Year	Team		Games	BA	SA	AB	H	2B	3B	HR	HR%	R	RBI	BB	SO	SB	PINCH HIT AB	H	PO	A	E	DP	TC/G	FA	G by Pos
1986	CHI	A	15	.129	.226	31	4	0	0	1	3.2	2	1	1	11	1	0	0	18	1	0	1	1.3	1.000	OF-10, DH-1
1987			116	.281	.422	391	110	18	2	11	2.8	48	50	10	83	21	1	0	303	5	6	2	2.7	.981	OF-115
1988			73	.159	.305	220	35	4	2	8	3.6	18	28	10	64	6	2	1	87	69	17	4	2.4	.902	OF-38, 3B-32, DH-3
1989	DET	A	94	.205	.302	258	53	5	1	6	2.3	29	23	18	63	9	10	1	180	11	4	3	2.1	.979	OF-87, DH-1, 1B-1
1990	2 teams		DET A (57G — .133)			TOR A	(49G — .194)																		
"	total		106	.161	.226	155	25	8	1	0	0.0	23	13	10	42	9	18	2	103	5	0	2	1.4	1.000	OF-77, DH-15
	5 yrs.		404	.215	.334	1055	227	35	6	26	2.5	120	115	49	263	46	31	4	691	91	27	12	2.0	.967	OF-327, 3B-32, DH-20, 1B-1

Matt Williams

WILLIAMS, MATTHEW DERRICK
B. Nov. 28, 1965, Bishop, Calif.
BR TR 6' 2" 205 lbs.

	Games	BA	SA	AB	H	2B	3B	HR	HR%	R	RBI	BB	SO	SB
April	20	.299	.416	77	23	3	0	2	2.6	8	15	4	16	0
May	27	.267	.505	105	28	4	0	7	6.7	14	18	6	22	2
June	27	.336	.582	110	37	6	0	7	6.4	19	29	4	27	0
July	27	.245	.443	106	26	5	2	4	3.8	13	21	5	26	1
Aug	27	.221	.452	104	23	3	0	7	6.7	13	15	6	23	2
Sept/Oct	31	.296	.504	115	34	6	0	6	5.2	20	24	8	24	2
Day	62	.287	.546	251	72	12	1	17	6.8	38	55	7	50	3
Night	97	.270	.448	366	99	15	1	16	4.4	49	67	26	88	4
vs. Left		.284	.500	208	59	9	0	12	5.8	29	48	13	40	6
vs. Right		.274	.482	409	112	18	2	21	5.1	58	74	20	98	1
On Grass	118	.298	.535	460	137	23	1	28	6.1	74	101	22	94	3
On Turf	41	.217	.350	157	34	4	1	5	3.2	13	21	11	44	4
Home	79	.271	.521	303	82	14	1	20	6.6	51	63	15	66	3
Road	80	.283	.455	314	89	13	1	13	4.1	36	59	18	72	4
Division Rivals														
vs. ATL	18	.391	.609	69	27	3	0	4	5.8	10	21	2	16	1
vs. CIN	18	.212	.333	66	14	2	0	2	3.0	7	13	6	20	1
vs. HOU	18	.162	.265	68	11	1	0	2	2.9	5	5	4	17	1
vs. LA	18	.211	.394	71	15	4	0	3	4.2	11	14	6	9	1
vs. SD	18	.352	.634	71	25	5	0	5	7.0	10	15	2	15	0
On 3B < 2 Out		.400	.533	30	12	1	0	1	3.3	1	31	4	3	

THIRD BASE — AVERAGE, RBI, HR, SB (vs. NL AVG)

Year	Team		Games	BA	SA	AB	H	2B	3B	HR	HR%	R	RBI	BB	SO	SB	PINCH HIT AB	H	PO	A	E	DP	TC/G	FA	G by Pos
1987	SF	N	84	.188	.339	245	46	9	2	8	3.3	28	21	16	68	4	3	2	110	234	9	52	4.2	.975	SS-70, 3B-17
1988			52	.205	.410	156	32	6	1	8	5.1	17	19	8	41	0	2	0	48	108	7	9	3.1	.957	3B-43, SS-14
1989			84	.202	.455	292	59	18	1	18	6.2	31	50	14	72	1	3	0	90	168	10	15	3.2	.963	3B-73, SS-30
1990			159	.277	.488	617	171	27	2	33	5.3	87	122	33	138	7	1	1	140	306	19	33	2.9	.959	3B-159
	4 yrs.		379	.235	.444	1310	308	60	6	67	5.1	163	212	71	319	12	9	3	388	816	45	109	3.3	.964	3B-292, SS-114

LEAGUE CHAMPIONSHIP SERIES

Year	Team		Games	BA	SA	AB	H	2B	3B	HR	HR%	R	RBI	BB	SO	SB	PINCH HIT AB	H	PO	A	E	DP	TC/G	FA	G by Pos
1989	SF	N	5	.300	.650	20	6	1	0	2	10.0	2	9	0	2	0	0	0	5	12	0	2	3.4	1.000	3B-5, SS-1

WORLD SERIES

Year	Team		Games	BA	SA	AB	H	2B	3B	HR	HR%	R	RBI	BB	SO	SB	PINCH HIT AB	H	PO	A	E	DP	TC/G	FA	G by Pos
1989	SF	N	4	.125	.313	16	2	0	0	1	6.3	1	1	0	6	0	0	0	4	12	0	2	4.0	1.000	SS-4, 3B-3

Craig Wilson

WILSON, CRAIG
B. Nov. 28, 1964, Annapolis, Md.
BR TR 5' 11" 175 lbs.

Year	Team		Games	BA	SA	AB	H	2B	3B	HR	HR%	R	RBI	BB	SO	SB	PINCH HIT AB	H	PO	A	E	DP	TC/G	FA	G by Pos
1989	STL	N	6	.250	.250	4	1	0	0	0	0.0	1	1	1	2	0	4	1	1	0	1	0	0.3	.500	3B-2
1990			55	.248	.264	121	30	2	0	0	0.0	13	7	8	14	0	23	9	45	30	1	5	2.2	.987	3B-13, OF-13, 2B-9, 1B-1
	2 yrs.		61	.248	.264	125	31	2	0	0	0.0	14	8	9	16	0	27	10	46	30	2	5	1.3	.974	3B-15, OF-13, 2B-9, 1B-1

Glenn Wilson

WILSON, GLENN DWIGHT
B. Dec. 22, 1958, Baytown, Tex.
BR TR 6′ 1″ 190 lbs.

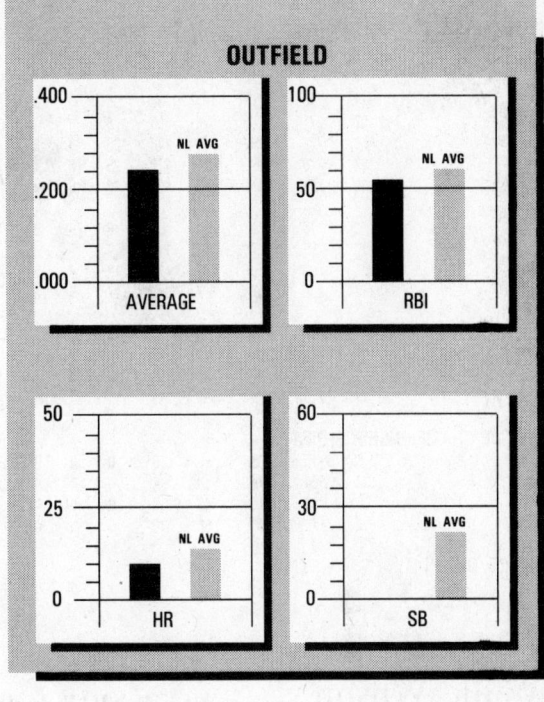

OUTFIELD

Year	Team		Games	BA	SA	AB	H	2B	3B	HR	HR%	R	RBI	BB	SO	SB	PINCH HIT AB	H	PO	A	E	DP	TC/G	FA	G by Pos
April			17	.219	.328	64	14	1	0	2	3.1	10	5	4	8	0									
May			26	.250	.324	68	17	2	0	1	1.5	7	9	3	8	0									
June			24	.256	.427	82	21	2	0	4	4.9	10	17	6	18	0									
July			24	.206	.309	68	14	4	0	1	1.5	4	10	10	17	0									
Aug			25	.282	.412	85	24	5	0	2	2.4	11	13	3	13	0									
Sept/Oct			2	.000	.000	1	0	0	0	0	0.0	0	1	0	0	0									
Day			29	.295	.443	88	26	7	0	2	2.3	19	14	8	14	0									
Night			89	.229	.339	280	64	7	0	8	2.9	23	41	18	50	0									
vs. Left				.262	.360	164	43	10	0	2	1.2	17	25	13	27	0									
vs. Right				.230	.368	204	47	4	0	8	3.9	25	30	13	37	0									
On Grass			34	.208	.321	106	22	0	0	4	3.8	13	13	8	22	0									
On Turf			84	.260	.382	262	68	14	0	6	2.3	29	42	18	42	0									
Home			58	.259	.402	174	45	10	0	5	2.9	23	33	13	28	0									
Road			60	.232	.330	194	45	4	0	5	2.6	19	22	13	36	0									
Division Rivals																									
vs. ATL			12	.229	.375	48	11	1	0	2	4.2	7	10	1	11	0									
vs. CIN			8	.222	.370	27	6	1	0	1	3.7	2	6	0	8	0									
vs. LA			12	.279	.558	43	12	0	0	4	9.3	8	8	3	9	0									
vs. SD			11	.158	.263	38	6	1	0	1	2.6	3	5	2	8	0									
vs. SF			12	.289	.342	38	11	2	0	0	0.0	7	3	4	4	0									
On 3B < 2 Out				.316	.368	19	6	1	0	0	0.0	0	16	2	5										
1982	DET	A	84	.292	.457	322	94	15	1	12	3.7	39	34	15	51	2	2	0	215	8	3	1	2.7	.987	OF-80, DH-4
1983			144	.268	.408	503	135	25	6	11	2.2	55	65	25	79	1	7	3	225	12	3	2	1.7	.988	OF-143
1984	PHI	N	132	.240	.372	341	82	21	3	6	1.8	28	31	17	56	7	19	2	153	7	7	0	1.3	.958	OF-109, 3B-4
1985			161	.275	.424	608	167	39	5	14	2.3	73	102	35	117	7	5	2	343	18	12	4	2.3	.968	OF-158
1986			155	.271	.413	584	158	30	4	15	2.6	70	84	42	91	5	3	0	331	20	4	5	2.3	.989	OF-154
1987			154	.264	.381	569	150	21	2	14	2.5	55	54	38	82	3	2	1	315	19	11	2	2.2	.968	OF-154, P-1
1988	2 teams		SEA A (78G — .250)			PIT N (37G — .270)																			
"	total		115	.256	.341	410	105	18	1	5	1.2	39	32	18	70	1	3	1	206	5	4	2	1.9	.981	OF-110, DH-2
1989	2 teams		PIT N (100G — .282)			HOU N (28G — .216)																			
"			128	.266	.421	432	115	26	4	11	2.5	50	64	37	53	1	15	4	249	13	6	2	2.1	.978	OF-110, 1B-10
1990	HOU	N	118	.245	.364	368	90	14	0	10	2.7	42	55	26	64	0	15	3	227	12	6	6	2.3	.976	OF-108, 1B-1
9 yrs.			1191	.265	.399	4137	1096	209	26	98	2.4	451	521	253	663	27	71	16	2264	114	56	24	2.0	.977	OF-1126, 1B-11, DH-6, 3B-4, P-1

Mookie Wilson

WILSON, WILLIAM HAYWARD
B. Feb. 9, 1956, Bamberg, S. C.
BR TR 5′ 10″ 170 lbs.

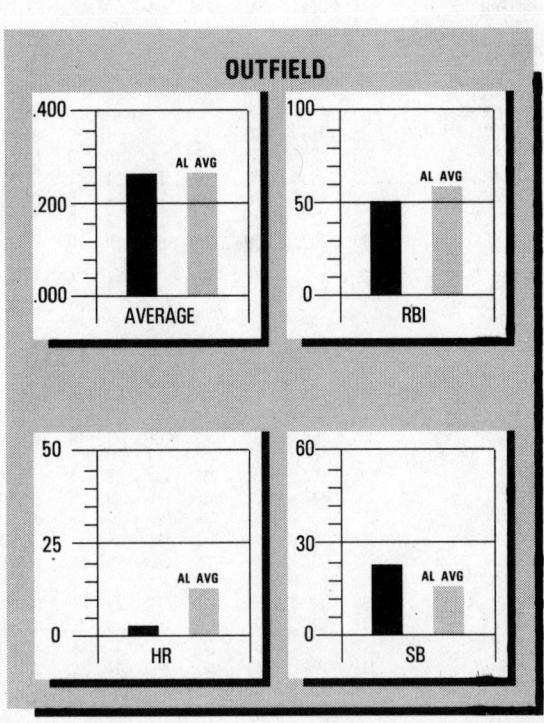

OUTFIELD

Year	Team	Games	BA	SA	AB	H	2B	3B	HR	HR%	R	RBI	BB	SO	SB
April		19	.205	.244	78	16	3	0	0	0.0	9	2	6	13	3
May		22	.253	.363	91	23	7	0	1	1.1	15	8	9	12	6
June		27	.250	.313	96	24	6	0	0	0.0	13	11	7	26	5
July		26	.269	.355	93	25	6	1	0	0.0	10	3	3	20	4
Aug		24	.333	.485	99	33	8	2	1	1.0	16	16	3	13	4
Sept/Oct		29	.267	.351	131	35	6	1	1	0.8	18	11	3	18	1
Day		43	.231	.314	169	39	12	1	0	0.0	20	17	6	31	8
Night		104	.279	.372	419	117	24	3	3	0.7	61	34	25	71	15
vs. Left			.245	.351	188	46	10	2	2	1.1	22	21	14	36	3
vs. Right			.275	.358	400	110	26	2	1	0.3	59	30	17	66	20
On Grass		60	.273	.384	245	67	16	1	3	1.2	35	22	14	37	12
On Turf		87	.259	.335	343	89	20	3	0	0.0	46	29	17	65	11
Home		69	.247	.321	271	67	16	2	0	0.0	31	20	12	50	10
Road		78	.281	.385	317	89	20	2	3	0.9	50	31	19	52	13
Division Rivals															
vs. BAL		13	.356	.424	59	21	4	0	0	0.0	12	1	1	7	3
vs. BOS		13	.275	.314	51	14	2	0	0	0.0	8	5	2	7	2
vs. CLE		11	.241	.259	54	13	1	0	0	0.0	7	4	2	11	1
vs. DET		9	.270	.568	37	10	5	0	2	5.4	7	5	5	7	4
vs. MIL		13	.204	.265	49	10	3	0	0	0.0	6	6	3	4	2
vs. NY		12	.186	.256	43	8	1	1	0	0.0	2	6	3	13	1
On 3B < 2 Out			.357	.536	28	10	5	0	0	0.0	0	23	0	3	

Mookie Wilson *Continued*

Year	Team	Games	BA	SA	AB	H	2B	3B	HR	HR%	R	RBI	BB	SO	SB	PH AB	PH H	PO	A	E	DP	TC/G	FA	G by Pos
1980	NY N	27	.248	.352	105	26	5	3	0	0.0	16	4	12	19	7	0	0	72	1	2	0	2.8	.973	OF-26
1981		92	.271	.372	328	89	8	8	3	0.9	49	14	20	59	24	10	1	226	3	4	2	2.5	.983	OF-80
1982		159	.279	.369	639	178	25	9	5	0.8	90	55	32	102	58	7	2	415	12	5	4	2.7	.988	OF-156
1983		152	.276	.367	**638**	176	25	6	7	1.1	91	51	18	103	54	7	0	422	5	7	1	2.9	.984	OF-148
1984		154	.276	.409	587	162	28	10	10	1.7	88	54	26	90	46	8	5	396	8	4	6	2.6	.990	OF-146
1985		93	.276	.424	337	93	16	8	6	1.8	56	26	28	52	24	8	1	216	0	8	0	2.4	.964	OF-83
1986		123	.289	.430	381	110	17	5	9	2.4	61	45	32	72	25	20	7	228	7	5	2	2.0	.979	OF-114
1987		124	.299	.455	385	115	19	7	9	2.3	58	34	35	85	21	32	10	205	3	8	2	1.7	.963	OF-109
1988		112	.296	.431	378	112	17	5	8	2.1	61	41	27	63	15	22	7	200	4	5	1	1.9	.976	OF-104
1989	2 teams	NY N (80G — .205)					TOR A (54G — .298)																	
"	total	134	.251	.329	487	122	19	2	5	1.0	54	35	13	84	19	22	4	162	2	2	1	1.3	.976	OF-125
1990	TOR A	147	.265	.355	588	156	36	4	3	0.5	81	51	31	102	23	0	0	370	5	3	2	2.7	.992	OF-141, DH-6
11 yrs.		1317	.276	.388	4853	1339	215	67	65	1.3	705	410	274	831	316	136	37	2912	50	55	20	2.3	.982	OF-1232, DH-6

LEAGUE CHAMPIONSHIP SERIES

Year	Team	Games	BA	SA	AB	H	2B	3B	HR	HR%	R	RBI	BB	SO	SB	PH AB	PH H	PO	A	E	DP	TC/G	FA	G by Pos
1986	NY N	6	.115	.115	26	3	0	0	0	0.0	2	1	1	7	1	0	0	16	1	0	1	2.8	1.000	OF-6
1988		4	.154	.154	13	2	0	0	0	0.0	2	1	2	2	0	1	0	6	0	0	0	1.5	1.000	OF-3
1989	TOR A	5	.263	.263	19	5	0	0	0	0.0	2	2	2	2	1	0	0	10	0	0	0	2.0	1.000	OF-5
3 yrs.		15	.172	.172	58	10	0	0	0	0.0	6	4	5	11	2	1	0	32	1	0	1	2.2	.000	OF-14

WORLD SERIES

Year	Team	Games	BA	SA	AB	H	2B	3B	HR	HR%	R	RBI	BB	SO	SB	PH AB	PH H	PO	A	E	DP	TC/G	FA	G by Pos
1986	NY N	7	.269	.308	26	7	1	0	0	0.0	3	0	1	6	3	0	0	15	2	0	0	2.4	1.000	OF-7

Willie Wilson

WILSON, WILLIE JAMES
B. July 9, 1955, Montgomery, Ala.
BB TR 6' 3" 190 lbs.

	Games	BA	SA	AB	H	2B	3B	HR	HR%	R	RBI	BB	SO	SB
April	16	.345	.509	55	19	4	1	1	1.8	9	10	6	5	7
May	20	.163	.186	43	7	1	0	0	0.0	9	4	5	11	3
June	22	.313	.358	67	21	1	1	0	0.0	8	9	4	13	6
July	22	.300	.400	50	15	3	1	0	0.0	11	11	5	11	5
Aug	23	.274	.371	62	17	3	0	1	1.6	8	7	5	13	2
Sept/Oct	12	.333	.367	30	10	1	0	0	0.0	4	1	5	4	1
Day	24	.246	.277	65	16	2	0	0	0.0	7	7	3	10	6
Night	91	.302	.397	242	73	11	3	2	0.8	42	35	27	47	18
vs. Left		.272	.350	103	28	6	1	0	0.0	13	17	5	19	10
vs. Right		.299	.382	204	61	7	2	2	1.0	36	25	25	38	14
On Grass	44	.243	.311	103	25	4	0	1	1.0	18	16	14	21	7
On Turf	71	.314	.402	204	64	9	3	1	0.5	31	26	16	36	17
Home	59	.331	.422	166	55	8	2	1	0.6	26	22	13	27	14
Road	56	.241	.312	141	34	5	1	1	0.7	23	20	17	30	10
Division Rivals														
vs. CAL	9	.414	.448	29	12	1	0	0	0.0	5	5	3	3	2
vs. CHI	9	.222	.222	18	4	0	0	0	0.0	0	0	1	3	0
vs. MIN	8	.385	.500	26	10	1	1	0	0.0	4	6	2	5	4
vs. OAK	9	.429	.476	21	9	1	0	0	0.0	4	2	2	1	0
vs. SEA	9	.125	.250	24	3	0	0	1	4.2	3	1	0	9	1
vs. TEX	10	.200	.200	25	5	0	0	0	0.0	1	3	4	5	2
On 3B < 2 Out		.238	.286	21	5	1	0	0	0.0	0	15	1	5	

OUTFIELD

AVERAGE / AL AVG · RBI / AL AVG · HR / AL AVG · SB / AL AVG

Year	Team	Games	BA	SA	AB	H	2B	3B	HR	HR%	R	RBI	BB	SO	SB	PH AB	PH H	PO	A	E	DP	TC/G	FA	G by Pos
1976	KC A	12	.167	.167	6	1	0	0	0	0.0	0	0	0	2	2	0	0	6	1	1	0	0.7	.875	OF-6
1977		13	.324	.382	34	11	2	0	0	0.0	10	1	1	8	6	0	0	24	0	1	0	1.9	.960	OF-9, DH-2
1978		127	.217	.278	198	43	8	2	0	0.0	43	16	16	33	46	0	0	171	6	4	2	1.4	.978	OF-112, DH-6
1979		154	.315	.420	588	185	18	13	6	1.0	113	49	28	92	**83**	0	0	384	13	6	0	2.6	.985	OF-152, DH-2
1980		161	.326	.421	**705¹**	230	28	15	3	0.4	**133**	49	28	81	79	3	0	482	9	6	1	3.1	.988	OF-159
1981		102	.303	.364	439	133	10	7	1	0.2	54	32	18	42	34	0	0	299	14	4	3	3.1	.987	OF-101
1982		136	**.332**	.431	585	194	19	15	3	0.5	87	46	26	81	37	1	0	376	4	5	0	2.8	.987	OF-135
1983		137	.276	.352	576	159	22	8	2	0.3	90	33	33	75	59	3	1	354	3	9	0	2.7	.975	OF-136
1984		128	.301	.390	541	163	24	9	2	0.4	81	44	39	56	47	0	0	383	6	4	2	3.1	.990	OF-128
1985		141	.278	.408	605	168	25	21	4	0.7	87	43	29	94	43	0	0	378	4	2	1	2.7	.995	OF-140
1986		156	.269	.366	631	170	20	7	9	1.4	77	44	31	97	34	6	0	408	4	3	2	2.7	.993	OF-155
1987		146	.279	.377	610	170	18	15	4	0.7	97	30	32	88	59	1	0	342	3	1	1	2.4	.997	OF-143, DH-2
1988		147	.262	.333	591	155	17	11	1	0.2	81	37	22	106	35	4	1	365	1	4	0	2.5	.989	OF-142
1989		112	.253	.358	383	97	17	7	3	0.8	58	43	27	78	24	2	2	252	2	6	0	2.3	.977	OF-108, DH-1
1990		115	.290	.371	307	89	13	3	2	0.6	49	42	30	57	24	2	0	187	2	0	1	1.8	1.000	OF-106, DH-1
15 yrs.		1787	.289	.382	6799	1968	241	133	40	0.6	1060	509	360	990	612	29	4	4411	72	56	13	2.5	.988	OF-1732, DH-14

Year	Team		Games	BA	SA	AB	H	2B	3B	HR	HR%	R	RBI	BB	SO	SB	PINCH HIT AB	H	PO	A	E	DP	TC/G	FA	G by Pos

Willie Wilson *Continued*

DIVISIONAL PLAYOFF SERIES

Year	Team		Games	BA	SA	AB	H	2B	3B	HR	HR%	R	RBI	BB	SO	SB	AB	H	PO	A	E	DP	TC/G	FA	G by Pos
1981	KC	A	3	.308	.308	13	4	0	0	0	0.0	0	1	0	0	0	0	0	6	0	0	0	2.0	1.000	OF-3

LEAGUE CHAMPIONSHIP SERIES

Year	Team		Games	BA	SA	AB	H	2B	3B	HR	HR%	R	RBI	BB	SO	SB	AB	H	PO	A	E	DP	TC/G	FA	G by Pos
1978	KC	A	3	.250	.250	4	1	0	0	0	0.0	0	0	0	2	0	0	0	2	0	0	0	0.7	1.000	OF-3
1980			3	.308	.615	13	4	2	1	0	0.0	2	4	1	2	0	0	0	6	1	0	0	2.3	1.000	OF-3
1984			3	.154	.154	13	2	0	0	0	0.0	0	0	1	2	0	0	0	10	0	0	0	3.3	1.000	OF-3
1985			7	.310	.414	29	9	0	0	1	3.4	5	2	1	5	1	0	0	12	0	0	0	1.7	1.000	OF-7
4 yrs.			16	.271	.390	59	16	2	1	1	1.7	7	6	3	11	1	0	0	30	1	0	0	1.9	.000	OF-16

WORLD SERIES

Year	Team		Games	BA	SA	AB	H	2B	3B	HR	HR%	R	RBI	BB	SO	SB	AB	H	PO	A	E	DP	TC/G	FA	G by Pos
1980	KC	A	6	.154	.192	26	4	1	0	0	0.0	3	0	4	12	2	0	0	15	0	0	0	2.7	1.000	OF-6
1985			7	.367	.433	30	11	0	1	0	0.0	2	3	1	4	3	0	0	19	1	0	0	2.9	1.000	OF-7
2 yrs.			13	.268	.321	56	15	1	1	0	0.0	5	3	5	16	5	0	0	34	2	0	0	2.8	.000	OF-13

Dave Winfield

WINFIELD, DAVID MARK (Winny)
B. Oct. 3, 1951, St. Paul, Minn.
BR TR 6′ 6″ 220 lbs.

	Games	BA	SA	AB	H	2B	3B	HR	HR%	R	RBI	BB	SO	SB
April	14	.191	.362	47	9	0	0	2	4.3	5	5	3	11	0
May	18	.226	.339	62	14	1	0	2	3.2	7	4	3	11	0
June	23	.259	.531	81	21	5	1	5	6.2	15	15	11	11	0
July	26	.260	.410	100	26	3	0	4	4.0	15	16	8	15	0
Aug	23	.333	.488	84	28	7	0	2	2.4	13	13	17	19	0
Sept/Oct	28	.287	.515	101	29	3	1	6	5.9	15	15	10	14	0
Day	37	.233	.333	129	30	4	0	3	2.3	16	16	13	24	0
Night	95	.280	.497	346	97	17	2	18	5.2	54	62	39	57	0
vs. Left		.288	.468	156	45	9	2	5	3.2	26	32	20	22	0
vs. Right		.257	.445	319	82	12	0	16	5.0	44	46	32	59	0
On Grass	116	.258	.447	407	105	19	2	18	4.4	62	65	49	67	0
On Turf	16	.324	.485	68	22	2	0	3	4.4	8	13	3	14	0
Home	69	.261	.483	238	62	12	1	13	5.5	40	41	27	44	0
Road	63	.274	.422	237	65	9	1	8	3.4	30	37	25	37	0
Division Rivals														
vs. CHI	12	.250	.350	40	10	4	0	0	0.0	4	4	5	4	0
vs. KC	10	.351	.730	37	13	2	0	4	10.8	7	11	2	9	0
vs. MIN	6	.583	.708	24	14	0	0	1	4.2	6	6	1	2	0
vs. OAK	14	.304	.500	46	14	3	0	2	4.3	7	7	5	5	0
vs. SEA	10	.098	.317	41	4	0	0	3	7.3	4	9	1	11	0
vs. TEX	16	.327	.635	52	17	4	0	4	7.7	10	12	9	10	0
On 3B < 2 Out		.314	.400	35	11	0	0	1	2.9	1	29	7	6	

OUTFIELD — AVERAGE (AL AVG), RBI (AL AVG), HR (AL AVG), SB (AL AVG)

Year	Team		Games	BA	SA	AB	H	2B	3B	HR	HR%	R	RBI	BB	SO	SB	AB	H	PO	A	E	DP	TC/G	FA	G by Pos
1973	SD	N	56	.277	.383	141	39	4	1	3	2.1	9	12	12	19	0	17	8	65	1	3	0	1.2	.957	OF-36, 1B-1
1974			145	.265	.438	498	132	18	4	20	4.0	57	75	40	96	9	15	4	276	11	12	2	2.1	.960	OF-131
1975			143	.267	.403	509	136	20	2	15	2.9	74	76	69	82	23	2	0	302	9	9	1	2.2	.972	OF-138
1976			137	.283	.431	492	139	26	4	13	2.6	81	69	65	78	26	2	1	304	15	6	4	2.4	.982	OF-134
1977			157	.275	.467	615	169	29	7	25	4.1	104	92	58	75	16	2	1	368	15	11	3	2.5	.972	OF-156
1978			158	.308	.499	587	181	30	5	24	4.1	88	97	55	81	21	5	1	328	8	7	1	2.2	.980	OF-154, 1B-2
1979			159	.308	.558	597	184	27	10	34	5.7	97	**118**	85	71	15	2	0	344	14	5	3	2.3	.986	OF-157
1980			162	.276	.450	558	154	25	6	20	3.6	89	87	79	83	23	9	3	273	20	4	4	1.8	.987	OF-159
1981	NY	A	105	.294	.464	388	114	25	1	13	3.4	52	68	43	41	11	4	3	196	1	3	0	1.9	.985	OF-102, DH-1
1982			140	.280	.560	539	151	24	8	37	6.9	84	106	45	64	5	1	0	279	17	8	2	2.2	.974	OF-135, DH-4
1983			152	.283	.513	598	169	26	8	32	5.4	99	116	58	77	15	3	2	313	5	7	2	2.1	.978	OF-151
1984			141	.340	.515	567	193	34	4	19	3.4	106	100	53	71	6	0	0	306	3	2	1	2.2	.994	OF-140
1985			155	.275	.471	633	174	34	6	26	4.1	105	114	52	96	19	1	1	316	13	3	3	2.1	.991	OF-152, DH-2
1986			154	.262	.462	565	148	31	5	24	4.2	90	104	77	106	6	7	1	292	9	5	5	2.0	.984	OF-145, DH-6, 3B-2
1987			156	.275	.457	575	158	22	1	27	4.7	83	97	76	96	5	4	2	253	6	3	1	1.7	.989	OF-145, DH-8
1988			149	.322	.530	559	180	37	2	25	4.5	96	107	69	88	9	4	0	276	3	3	1	1.9	.989	OF-141, DH-4
1990	2 teams		NY A	(20G — .213)		CAL A	(112G — .275)																		
"	total		132	.267	.453	475	127	21	2	21	4.4	70	78	52	81	0	1	1	177	7	2	1	1.6	.989	OF-120, DH-10
17 yrs.			2401	.286	.480	8896	2548	433	76	378	4.2	1384	1516	988	1305	209	85	28	4668	157	93	34	2.0	.981	OF-2296, DH-35, 1B-3, 3B-2

DIVISIONAL PLAYOFF SERIES

Year	Team		Games	BA	SA	AB	H	2B	3B	HR	HR%	R	RBI	BB	SO	SB	AB	H	PO	A	E	DP	TC/G	FA	G by Pos
1981	NY	A	5	.350	.500	20	7	3	0	0	0.0	2	0	1	5	0	0	0	10	1	0	0	2.2	1.000	OF-5

LEAGUE CHAMPIONSHIP SERIES

Year	Team		Games	BA	SA	AB	H	2B	3B	HR	HR%	R	RBI	BB	SO	SB	AB	H	PO	A	E	DP	TC/G	FA	G by Pos
1981	NY	A	3	.154	.231	13	2	1	0	0	0.0	2	2	2	2	1	0	0	6	0	0	0	2.0	1.000	OF-3

Year	Team		Games	BA	SA	AB	H	2B	3B	HR	HR%	R	RBI	BB	SO	SB	PINCH HIT AB	H	PO	A	E	DP	TC/G	FA	G by Pos

Dave Winfield *Continued*

WORLD SERIES

Year	Team		Games	BA	SA	AB	H	2B	3B	HR	HR%	R	RBI	BB	SO	SB	AB	H	PO	A	E	DP	TC/G	FA	G by Pos
1981	NY	A	6	.045	.045	22	1	0	0	0	0.0	0	1	5	4	1	0	0	13	1	0	0	2.3	1.000	OF-6

Herm Winningham   WINNINGHAM, HERMAN SON
B. Dec. 1, 1961, Orangeburg, S. C.
BL TR 6′ 1″ 170 lbs.

Year	Team		Games	BA	SA	AB	H	2B	3B	HR	HR%	R	RBI	BB	SO	SB	AB	H	PO	A	E	DP	TC/G	FA	G by Pos
1984	NY	N	14	.407	.519	27	11	1	1	0	0.0	5	5	1	7	2	4	1	7	0	0	0	0.5	1.000	OF-10
1985	MON	N	125	.237	.317	312	74	6	5	3	1.0	30	21	28	72	20	13	6	229	6	4	2	1.9	.983	OF-116
1986			90	.216	.346	185	40	6	3	4	2.2	23	11	18	51	12	23	3	97	2	2	1	1.1	.980	OF-66, SS-1
1987			137	.239	.349	347	83	20	3	4	1.2	34	41	34	68	29	20	5	225	5	6	1	1.7	.975	OF-131
1988	2 teams		100	MON N (47G — .233)		CIN N (53G — .230)																			
''	total		100	.232	.286	203	47	3	4	0	0.0	16	21	17	45	12	21	4	128	1	1	0	1.3	.992	OF-72
1989	CIN	N	115	.251	.355	251	63	11	3	3	1.2	40	13	24	50	14	29	7	146	3	3	0	1.3	.980	OF-85
1990			84	.256	.425	160	41	8	5	3	1.8	20	17	14	31	6	20	5	89	3	0	0	1.4	1.000	OF-64
7 yrs.			665	.242	.345	1485	359	55	24	17	1.1	168	129	136	324	95	130	31	921	20	16	4	1.4	.983	OF-544, SS-1

LEAGUE CHAMPIONSHIP SERIES

Year	Team		Games	BA	SA	AB	H	2B	3B	HR	HR%	R	RBI	BB	SO	SB	AB	H	PO	A	E	DP	TC/G	FA	G by Pos
1990	CIN	N	3	.286	.429	7	2	1	0	0	0.0	1	1	1	1	1	1	0	7	0	0	0	3.5	1.000	OF-2

WORLD SERIES

Year	Team		Games	BA	SA	AB	H	2B	3B	HR	HR%	R	RBI	BB	SO	SB	AB	H	PO	A	E	DP	TC/G	FA	G by Pos
1990	CIN	N	2	.500	.500	4	2	0	0	0	0.0	1	0	0	0	0	1	0	3	0	0	0	3.0	1.000	OF-1

Craig Worthington   WORTHINGTON, CRAIG RICHARD
B. Apr. 17, 1965, Los Angeles, Calif.
BR TR 6′ 160 lbs.

Split		Games	BA	SA	AB	H	2B	3B	HR	HR%	R	RBI	BB	SO	SB
April		20	.260	.411	73	19	5	0	2	2.7	8	10	10	20	0
May		24	.186	.256	86	16	3	0	1	1.2	8	6	8	22	1
June		23	.241	.405	79	19	1	0	4	5.1	10	12	11	15	0
July		25	.169	.225	71	12	1	0	1	1.4	10	9	14	14	0
Aug		19	.241	.278	54	13	2	0	0	0.0	6	3	9	9	0
Sept/Oct		22	.274	.355	62	17	5	0	0	0.0	4	4	11	16	0
Day		36	.232	.375	112	26	4	0	4	3.6	13	13	24	25	1
Night		97	.224	.304	313	70	13	0	4	1.3	33	31	39	71	0
vs. Left			.254	.357	126	32	7	0	2	1.6	18	12	27	21	0
vs. Right			.214	.308	299	64	10	0	6	2.0	28	32	36	75	1
On Grass		110	.233	.320	347	81	15	0	5	1.4	38	34	54	77	1
On Turf		23	.192	.333	78	15	2	0	3	3.8	8	10	9	19	0
Home		67	.234	.325	209	49	10	0	3	1.4	19	20	29	49	0
Road		66	.218	.319	216	47	7	0	5	2.3	27	24	34	47	1
Division Rivals															
vs. BOS		9	.154	.385	26	4	0	0	2	7.7	2	3	5	5	0
vs. CLE		6	.211	.211	19	4	0	0	0	0.0	2	1	4	4	0
vs. DET		13	.235	.382	34	8	2	0	1	2.9	6	5	11	12	0
vs. MIL		11	.351	.568	37	13	2	0	2	5.4	7	6	4	5	0
vs. NY		9	.229	.286	35	8	2	0	0	0.0	4	1	2	8	0
vs. TOR		13	.256	.372	43	11	2	0	1	2.3	2	7	4	9	0
On 3B < 2 Out			.167	.167	18	3	0	0	0	0.0	0	12	2	5	

THIRD BASE

Year	Team		Games	BA	SA	AB	H	2B	3B	HR	HR%	R	RBI	BB	SO	SB	AB	H	PO	A	E	DP	TC/G	FA	G by Pos
1988	BAL	A	26	.185	.284	81	15	2	0	2	2.5	5	4	9	24	1	0	0	20	53	3	4	2.9	.961	3B-26
1989			145	.247	.384	497	123	23	0	15	3.0	57	70	61	114	1	0	0	113	277	20	22	2.8	.951	3B-145
1990			133	.226	.322	425	96	17	0	8	1.8	46	44	63	96	1	0	0	90	218	18	28	2.5	.945	3B-131, DH-2
3 yrs.			304	.233	.350	1003	234	42	0	25	2.5	108	118	133	234	3	0	0	223	548	41	54	2.7	.950	3B-302, DH-2

Rick Wrona   WRONA, RICHARD JAMES
B. Dec. 10, 1963, Tulsa, Okla.
BR TR 6′ 1″ 185 lbs.

Year	Team		Games	BA	SA	AB	H	2B	3B	HR	HR%	R	RBI	BB	SO	SB	AB	H	PO	A	E	DP	TC/G	FA	G by Pos
1988	CHI	N	4	.000	.000	6	0	0	0	0	0.0	0	0	0	1	0	1	0	11	1	0	0	3.0	1.000	C-2
1989			38	.283	.391	92	26	2	1	2	2.2	11	14	2	21	0	3	2	158	15	3	1	4.6	.983	C-37
1990			16	.172	.172	29	5	0	0	0	0.0	3	0	2	11	1	0	0	55	9	2	2	4.1	.970	C-16
3 yrs.			58	.244	.323	127	31	2	1	2	1.6	14	14	4	33	1	4	2	224	25	5	3	4.4	.980	C-55

LEAGUE CHAMPIONSHIP SERIES

Year	Team		Games	BA	SA	AB	H	2B	3B	HR	HR%	R	RBI	BB	SO	SB	AB	H	PO	A	E	DP	TC/G	FA	G by Pos
1989	CHI	N	2	.000	.000	5	0	0	0	0	0.0	0	0	0	3	0	0	0	9	1	0	0	5.0	1.000	C-2

Year	Team		Games	BA	SA	AB	H	2B	3B	HR	HR%	R	RBI	BB	SO	SB	PINCH HIT AB	PINCH HIT H	PO	A	E	DP	TC/G	FA	G by Pos

Marvell Wynne

WYNNE, MARVELL
B. Dec. 17, 1959, Chicago, Ill.
BL TL 5' 11" 176 lbs.

Year	Team		Games	BA	SA	AB	H	2B	3B	HR	HR%	R	RBI	BB	SO	SB	AB	H	PO	A	E	DP	TC/G	FA	G by Pos
1983	PIT	N	103	.243	.355	366	89	16	2	7	1.9	66	26	38	52	12	1	0	223	3	4	2	2.2	.983	OF-102
1984			154	.266	.337	653	174	24	11	0	0.0	77	39	42	81	24	0	0	373	8	4	1	2.5	.990	OF-154
1985			103	.205	.258	337	69	6	3	2	0.6	21	18	18	48	10	3	0	229	7	3	1	2.3	.987	OF-99
1986	SD	N	137	.264	.417	288	76	19	2	7	2.4	34	37	15	45	11	12	3	203	3	3	2	1.5	.986	OF-125
1987			98	.250	.346	188	47	8	2	2	1.1	17	24	20	37	11	30	6	100	2	2	0	1.1	.981	OF-71
1988			128	.264	.426	333	88	13	4	11	3.3	37	42	31	62	3	23	2	216	5	3	2	1.8	.987	OF-113
1989	2 teams		SD N (105G — .252)			CHI N (20G — .188)																			
"	total		125	.243	.354	342	83	13	2	7	2.0	27	39	13	48	6	17	2	163	7	5	2	1.4	.971	OF-109
1990	CHI	N	92	.204	.333	186	38	8	2	4	2.1	21	19	14	25	3	26	4	108	3	1	2	1.7	.991	OF-66
8 yrs.			940	.247	.352	2693	664	107	28	40	1.5	300	244	191	398	80	112	17	1615	38	25	12	1.8	.985	OF-839

LEAGUE CHAMPIONSHIP SERIES

Year	Team		Games	BA	SA	AB	H	2B	3B	HR	HR%	R	RBI	BB	SO	SB	AB	H	PO	A	E	DP	TC/G	FA	G by Pos
1989	CHI	N	4	.167	.167	6	1	0	0	0	0.0	0	0	0	0	0	2	0	3	0	0	0	0.8	1.000	OF-2

Eric Yelding

YELDING, ERIC GIRARD
B. Feb. 22, 1965, Montrose, Ala.
BR TR 6' 1" 170 lbs.

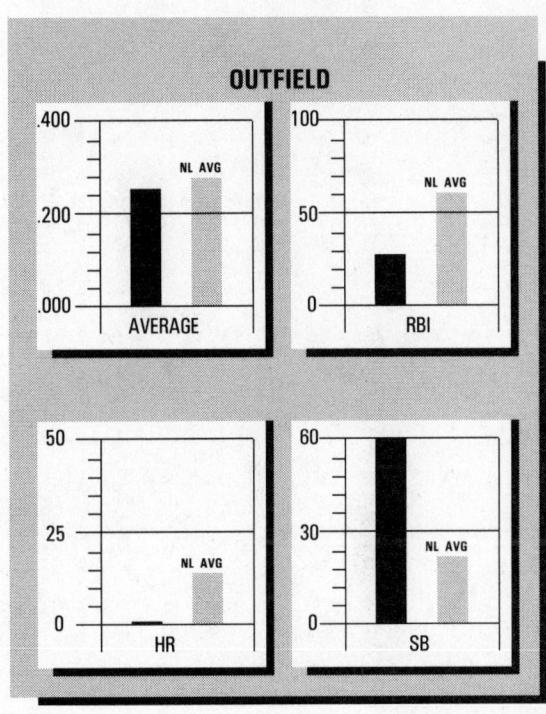

OUTFIELD

		Games	BA	SA	AB	H	2B	3B	HR	HR%	R	RBI	BB	SO	SB
April		11	.278	.333	36	10	0	1	0	0.0	6	6	1	5	7
May		27	.307	.330	88	27	0	1	0	0.0	16	6	6	13	11
June		25	.215	.241	79	17	0	1	0	0.0	11	1	10	14	12
July		29	.304	.348	112	34	3	1	0	0.0	14	8	8	19	12
Aug		23	.181	.213	94	17	3	0	0	0.0	7	3	4	14	8
Sept/Oct		27	.245	.324	102	25	3	1	1	1.0	15	4	10	22	14
Day		35	.255	.285	137	35	2	1	0	0.0	22	8	15	23	20
Night		107	.254	.302	374	95	7	4	1	0.3	47	20	24	64	44
vs. Left			.281	.332	235	66	6	3	0	0.0	27	16	16	31	29
vs. Right			.232	.268	276	64	3	2	1	0.4	42	12	23	56	35
On Grass		44	.289	.343	166	48	7	1	0	0.0	26	11	15	26	19
On Turf		98	.238	.275	345	82	2	4	1	0.3	43	17	24	61	45
Home		69	.253	.290	245	62	1	4	0	0.0	35	13	23	38	41
Road		73	.256	.305	266	68	8	1	1	0.4	34	15	16	49	23
Division Rivals																
vs. ATL		15	.288	.339	59	17	3	0	0	0.0	13	6	6	9	10
vs. CIN		14	.225	.300	40	9	0	0	1	2.5	6	2	2	9	4
vs. LA		13	.171	.171	41	7	0	0	0	0.0	4	2	1	7	7
vs. SD		16	.250	.300	60	15	1	1	0	0.0	8	3	3	10	9
vs. SF		18	.258	.303	66	17	1	1	0	0.0	9	2	13	11	11
On 3B < 2 Out			.462	.692	13	6	1	1	0	0.0	0	13	2	0	

Year	Team		Games	BA	SA	AB	H	2B	3B	HR	HR%	R	RBI	BB	SO	SB	AB	H	PO	A	E	DP	TC/G	FA	G by Pos
1989	HOU	N	70	.233	.256	90	21	2	0	0	0.0	19	9	7	19	11	16	4	37	57	3	9	1.4	.969	SS-15, 2B-13, OF-8
1990			142	.254	.297	511	130	9	5	1	0.1	69	28	39	87	64	2	0	315	124	17	21	3.4	.963	OF-94, SS-40, 2B-10, 3B-3
2 yrs.			212	.251	.291	601	151	11	5	1	0.2	88	37	46	106	75	18	4	352	181	20	30	2.6	.964	OF-102, SS-55, 2B-23, 3B-3

Gerald Young

YOUNG, GERALD ANTHONY
B. Oct. 22, 1964, Tele, Honduras
BB TR 6' 2" 185 lbs.

Year	Team		Games	BA	SA	AB	H	2B	3B	HR	HR%	R	RBI	BB	SO	SB	AB	H	PO	A	E	DP	TC/G	FA	G by Pos
1987	HOU	N	71	.321	.380	274	88	9	2	1	0.4	44	15	26	27	26	2	1	143	5	3	1	2.1	.980	OF-67
1988			149	.257	.325	576	148	21	9	0	0.0	79	37	66	66	65	5	2	357	10	3	1	2.5	.992	OF-145
1989			146	.233	.276	533	124	17	3	0	0.0	71	38	74	60	34	2	1	412	15	1	5	2.9	.998	OF-143
1990			57	.175	.234	154	27	4	1	1	0.6	15	4	20	23	6	5	0	99	4	1	1	2.1	.990	OF-50
4 yrs.			423	.252	.308	1537	387	51	15	2	0.1	209	94	186	176	131	14	4	1011	34	8	8	2.5	.992	OF-405

Year	Team	Games	BA	SA	AB	H	2B	3B	HR	HR%	R	RBI	BB	SO	SB	PINCH HIT AB	PINCH HIT H	PO	A	E	DP	TC/G	FA	G by Pos

Robin Yount

YOUNT, ROBIN R.
Brother of Larry Yount.
B. Sept. 16, 1955, Danville, Ill.
BR TR 6' 165 lbs.

	Games	BA	SA	AB	H	2B	3B	HR	HR%	R	RBI	BB	SO	SB
April	18	.271	.414	70	19	2	1	2	2.9	13	11	8	8	1
May	26	.237	.309	97	23	2	1	1	1.0	19	11	10	16	2
June	29	.245	.377	106	26	2	0	4	3.8	12	13	17	14	2
July	27	.243	.417	103	25	3	3	3	2.9	20	13	18	17	6
Aug	30	.173	.273	110	19	2	0	3	2.7	18	10	13	20	3
Sept/Oct	28	.327	.505	101	33	6	0	4	4.0	16	19	12	14	1
Day	50	.201	.293	184	37	2	0	5	2.7	23	17	24	31	2
Night	108	.268	.419	403	108	15	5	12	3.0	75	60	54	58	13
vs. Left		.269	.410	156	42	5	1	5	3.2	27	20	23	27	4
vs. Right		.239	.369	431	103	12	4	12	2.8	71	57	55	62	11
On Grass	134	.248	.390	495	123	15	5	15	3.0	82	67	65	73	13
On Turf	24	.239	.326	92	22	2	0	2	2.2	16	10	13	16	2
Home	80	.222	.365	293	65	10	4	8	2.7	42	35	36	42	8
Road	78	.272	.395	294	80	7	1	9	3.1	56	42	42	47	7
Division Rivals														
vs. BAL	10	.262	.357	42	11	1	0	1	2.4	4	7	2	5	1
vs. BOS	13	.300	.500	50	15	2	1	2	4.0	12	6	5	8	1
vs. CLE	13	.261	.478	46	12	1	0	3	6.5	9	7	8	5	0
vs. DET	13	.288	.577	52	15	3	0	4	7.7	10	11	4	5	0
vs. NY	12	.100	.100	40	4	0	0	0	0.0	3	1	9	7	0
vs. TOR	13	.234	.319	47	11	1	0	1	2.1	5	7	8	9	2
On 3B < 2 Out		.393	.464	28	11	2	0	0	0.0	0	26	1	6	

OUTFIELD

Year	Team		Games	BA	SA	AB	H	2B	3B	HR	HR%	R	RBI	BB	SO	SB	PINCH HIT AB	PINCH HIT H	PO	A	E	DP	TC/G	FA	G by Pos
1974	MIL	A	107	.250	.346	344	86	14	5	3	0.9	48	26	12	46	7	0	0	148	327	19	55	4.6	.962	SS-107
1975			147	.267	.367	558	149	28	2	8	1.4	67	52	33	69	12	2	0	273	402	44	80	4.9	.939	SS-145
1976			161	.252	.301	638	161	19	3	2	0.3	59	54	38	69	16	0	0	290	510	31	104	5.2	.963	SS-161, OF-1
1977			154	.288	.377	605	174	34	4	4	0.7	66	49	41	80	16	3	1	256	449	26	94	4.7	.964	SS-153
1978			127	.293	.428	502	147	23	9	9	1.8	66	71	24	43	16	2	1	246	453	30	78	5.7	.959	SS-125
1979			149	.267	.371	577	154	26	5	8	1.4	72	51	35	52	11	0	0	267	517	25	97	5.4	.969	SS-149
1980			143	.293	.519	611	179	**49**	10	23	3.8	121	87	26	67	20	2	0	239	455	28	89	5.0	.961	SS-133, DH-9
1981			96	.273	.419	377	103	15	5	10	2.7	50	49	22	37	4	1	1	161	370	8	83	5.6	.985	SS-93, DH-3
1982			156	.331	**.578**	635	**210**	**46**	12	29	4.6	129	114	54	63	14	2	1	253	489	24	95	4.9	.969	SS-154, DH-1
1983			149	.308	.503	578	178	42	**10**	17	2.9	102	80	72	58	12	2	2	256	420	19	86	4.7	.973	SS-139, DH-8
1984			160	.298	.441	624	186	27	7	16	2.6	105	80	67	67	14	0	0	199	402	18	80	3.9	.971	SS-120, DH-39
1985			122	.277	.442	466	129	26	3	15	3.2	76	68	49	56	10	0	0	267	5	8	2	2.3	.971	OF-108, DH-12, 1B-3
1986			140	.312	.450	522	163	31	7	9	1.7	82	46	62	73	14	1	0	365	9	2	5	2.7	.995	OF-131, DH-6, 1B-3
1987			158	.312	.479	635	198	25	9	21	3.3	99	103	76	94	19	0	0	380	5	5	2	2.5	.987	OF-150, DH-8
1988			162	.306	.465	621	190	38	**11**	13	2.1	92	91	63	63	22	0	0	444	12	2	2	2.8	.996	OF-158, DH-4
1989			160	.318	.511	614	195	38	9	21	3.4	101	103	63	71	19	0	0	361	8	7	2	2.4	.981	OF-143, DH-17
1990			158	.247	.380	587	145	17	5	17	2.8	98	77	78	89	15	0	0	422	3	4	0	2.7	.991	OF-157, DH-1
17 yrs.			2449	.289	.437	9494	2747	498	116	225	2.4	1433	1201	815	1097	241	15	6	4827	4836	300	954	4.1	.970	SS-1479, OF-848, DH-108, 1B-6

DIVISIONAL PLAYOFF SERIES

Year	Team		Games	BA	SA	AB	H	2B	3B	HR	HR%	R	RBI	BB	SO	SB	AB	H	PO	A	E	DP	TC/G	FA	G by Pos
1981	MIL	A	5	.316	.421	19	6	0	1	0	0.0	4	1	2	2	1	0	0	6	16	1	0	4.6	.957	SS-5

LEAGUE CHAMPIONSHIP SERIES

Year	Team		Games	BA	SA	AB	H	2B	3B	HR	HR%	R	RBI	BB	SO	SB	AB	H	PO	A	E	DP	TC/G	FA	G by Pos
1982	MIL	A	5	.250	.250	16	4	0	0	0	0.0	1	0	5	0	0	0	0	11	12	1	4	4.8	.958	SS-5

WORLD SERIES

Year	Team		Games	BA	SA	AB	H	2B	3B	HR	HR%	R	RBI	BB	SO	SB	AB	H	PO	A	E	DP	TC/G	FA	G by Pos
1982	MIL	A	7	.414	.621	29	12	3	0	1	3.4	6	6	2	2	0	0	0	20	19	3	1	6.0	.929	SS-7

Year	Team	Games	BA	SA	AB	H	2B	3B	HR	HR%	R	RBI	BB	SO	SB	PINCH HIT AB	H	PO	A	E	DP	TC/G	FA	G by Pos

Todd Zeile

ZEILE, TODD EDWARD
B. Sept. 9, 1965, Van Nuys, Calif.
BR TR 6′ 1″ 190 lbs.

		Games	BA	SA	AB	H	2B	3B	HR	HR%	R	RBI	BB	SO	SB	AB	H	PO	A	E	DP	TC/G	FA	G by Pos
April		18	.258	.439	66	17	4	1	2	3.0	10	8	9	12	0									
May		25	.187	.320	75	14	4	0	2	2.7	5	10	10	15	0									
June		25	.239	.413	92	22	2	1	4	4.3	17	10	14	13	0									
July		23	.222	.375	72	16	2	0	3	4.2	5	7	6	10	2									
Aug		25	.324	.431	102	33	3	1	2	2.0	14	11	8	14	0									
Sept/Oct		28	.216	.398	88	19	10	0	2	2.3	11	11	20	13	0									
Day		34	.255	.434	106	27	7	0	4	3.8	14	16	14	19	1									
Night		110	.242	.388	389	94	18	3	11	2.8	48	41	53	58	1									
vs. Left			.266	.451	173	46	12	1	6	3.5	21	22	21	21	1									
vs. Right			.233	.370	322	75	13	2	9	2.8	41	35	46	56	1									
On Grass		39	.203	.331	133	27	8	0	3	2.3	15	12	15	31	1									
On Turf		105	.260	.423	362	94	17	3	12	3.3	47	45	52	46	1									
Home		70	.262	.429	233	61	11	2	8	3.4	33	26	34	31	1									
Road		74	.229	.370	262	60	14	1	7	2.7	29	31	33	46	1									
Division Rivals																								
vs. CHI		13	.245	.367	49	12	1	1	1	2.0	8	2	11	9	0									
vs. MON		16	.212	.385	52	11	4	1	1	1.9	7	5	10	11	0									
vs. NY		15	.200	.360	50	10	2	0	2	4.0	9	4	5	6	0									
vs. PHI		15	.362	.621	58	21	6	0	3	5.2	11	12	10	7	0									
vs. PIT		17	.266	.453	64	17	4	1	2	3.1	9	10	9	5	0									
On 3B < 2 Out			.176	.294	17	3	2	0	0	0.0	0	15	7	7										
1989	STL N	28	.256	.354	82	21	3	1	1	1.2	7	8	9	14	0	5	0	125	10	4	1	5.0	.971	C–23
1990		144	.244	.398	495	121	25	3	15	3.0	62	57	67	77	2	3	0	648	106	15	12	5.5	.980	C–105, 3B–24, 1B–11, OF–1

CATCHER

Pitcher Register

The Pitcher Register is an alphabetical listing of every man who pitched in the major leagues in 1990. Also included are those players who played in 1990 and had pitched (however briefly) in previous seasons.

As in the Player Register, boldface print indicates a league leader for the season. A superscript "1" means that the figure is the all-time single season record (since 1893, when the mound was fixed at a distance of 60 feet 6 inches), and figures underneath a player's career and World Series career totals provide his rank in the top ten all-time.

Partial innings pitched are indicated by adding ".1" or ".2" to the figure in the IP column; "55.2" would mean that the pitcher had pitched fifty-five and two-third innings. Meaningless averages are indicated with a dash; these would include the winning percentage of a pitcher with an 0-0 record, or the batting average of a pitcher with no at bats. Any time the infinity symbol "∞" is shown for a pitcher's earned run average, it means that he allowed at least one run in that season without retiring a batter.

An asterisk (*) shown in the lifetime batting totals means that that pitcher's complete batting record is included in the Player Register.

Additional statistical and graphic analyses are provided for each starting pitcher who faced at least 300 batters in 1990 and for each relief pitcher who made at least 20 relief appearances during the year. See the Introduction for more information about these features.

Year	Team	W	L	%	ERA	G	GS	CG	IP	H	BB	SO	ShO	RELIEF PITCHING W	L	SV	BATTING AB	H	HR	BA	PO	A	E	DP	TC/G	FA

Don Aase

AASE, DONALD WILLIAM
B. Sept. 8, 1954, Orange, Calif.
BR TR 6′ 3″ 190 lbs.

	W	L	%	ERA	G	GS	CG	IP	H	BB	SO	ShO	W	L	SV	AB	H	HR	BA	PO	A	E	DP	TC/G	FA
April	1	1	.500	3.27	8	0	0	11	8	6	9	0	1	1	1										
May	1	0	1.000	3.60	9	0	0	10	8	4	5	0	1	0	2										
June	0	0	—	4.26	6	0	0	6.1	4	3	3	0	0	0	0										
July	—	—	—	0	0	—	—	0	0	0	0	—	0	0	0										
Aug	1	0	1.000	4.76	3	0	0	5.2	5	0	2	0	1	0	0										
Sept/Oct	0	0	—	12.60	6	0	0	5	8	6	5	0	0	0	0										
Day	1	1	.500	3.68	7	0	0	7.1	6	3	5	0	1	1	2										
Night	2	0	1.000	5.28	25	0	0	30.2	27	16	19	0	2	0	1										
vs. Left	—	—	—	—	—	—	—	—	14	9	14		—	—	—										
vs. Right	—	—	—	—	—	—	—	—	19	10	10		—	—	—										
On Grass	3	1	.750	4.28	25	0	0	27.1	24	13	16	0	3	1	3										
On Turf	0	0	—	6.75	7	0	0	10.2	9	6	8	0	0	0	0										
Home	2	0	1.000	3.27	19	0	0	22	21	11	9	0	2	0	2										
Road	1	1	.500	7.31	13	0	0	16	12	8	15	0	1	1	1										
Division Rivals																									
vs. ATL	0	0	—	0.00	1	0	0	0.1	0	0	0	0	0	0	0										
vs. CIN	1	0	1.000	4.50	2	0	0	4	3	3	0	0	1	0	0										
vs. HOU	0	0	—	2.89	6	0	0	9.1	5	4	5	0	0	0	0										
vs. SD	0	1	.000	11.57	6	0	0	4.2	6	6	5	0	0	1	1										
vs. SF	1	0	1.000	2.70	3	0	0	3.1	3	1	5	0	1	0	0										
1977	BOS A	6	2	.750	3.12	13	13	4	92.1	85	19	49	2	0	0	0	0	0	0	—	5	13	1	0	1.5	.947
1978	CAL A	11	8	.579	4.03	29	29	6	178.2	185	80	93	1	0	0	0	0	0	0	—	16	26	3	2	1.6	.933
1979		9	10	.474	4.82	37	28	7	185	200	77	96	1	1	1	2	0	0	0	—	8	17	2	3	0.7	.926
1980		8	13	.381	4.06	40	21	5	175	193	66	74	1	3	0	2	0	0	0	—	10	22	4	2	0.9	.889
1981		4	4	.500	2.35	39	0	0	65	56	24	38	0	4	4	11	0	0	0	—	2	10	1	1	0.3	.923
1982		3	3	.500	3.46	24	0	0	52	45	23	40	0	3	3	4	0	0	0	—	3	5	0	0	0.3	1.000
1984		4	1	.800	1.62	23	0	0	39	30	19	28	0	4	1	8	0	0	0	—	1	5	1	0	0.3	.857
1985	BAL A	10	6	.625	3.78	54	0	0	88	83	35	67	0	10	6	14	0	0	0	—	8	10	0	0	0.3	1.000
1986		6	7	.462	2.98	66	0	0	81.2	71	28	67	0	6	7	34	0	0	0	—	5	12	1	1	0.3	.944
1987		1	0	1.000	2.25	7	0	0	8	8	4	3	0	1	0	2	0	0	0	—	0	1	0	0	0.1	1.000
1988		0	0	—	4.05	35	0	0	46.2	40	37	28	0	0	0	0	0	0	0	—	2	3	0	1	0.1	1.000
1989	NY N	1	5	.167	3.94	49	0	0	59.1	56	26	34	0	1	5	2	5	0	0	.000	6	8	0	0	0.3	1.000
1990	LA N	3	1	.750	4.97	32	0	0	38	33	19	24	0	3	1	3	0	0	0	—	1	3	0	0	0.1	1.000
13 yrs.		66	60	.524	3.80	448	91	22	1108.2	1085	457	641	5	36	28	82	5	0	0	.000	67	135	13	10	0.5	.940

LEAGUE CHAMPIONSHIP SERIES

Year	Team	W	L	%	ERA	G	GS	CG	IP	H	BB	SO	ShO	W	L	SV	AB	H	HR	BA	PO	A	E	DP	TC/G	FA
1979	CAL A	1	0	1.000	1.80	2	0	0	5	4	2	6	0	1	0	0	0	0	0	—	0	1	0	0	0.5	1.000

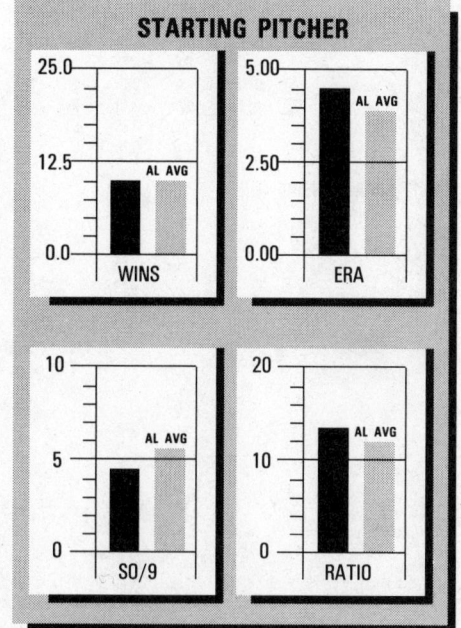

RELIEF PITCHER
WINS — NL AVG
ERA — NL AVG
SAVES — NL AVG
RATIO — NL AVG

Jim Abbott

ABBOTT, JAMES ANTHONY
B. Sept. 19, 1967, Flint, Mich.
BL TL 6′ 3″ 200 lbs.

	W	L	%	ERA	G	GS	CG	IP	H	BB	SO	ShO	W	L	SV	AB	H	HR	BA	PO	A	E	DP	TC/G	FA
April	0	1	.000	6.06	3	3	0	16.1	21	9	5	0	0	0	0										
May	2	3	.400	5.01	7	7	0	41.1	47	18	22	0	0	0	0										
June	3	2	.600	4.35	6	6	1	39.1	40	14	20	0	0	0	0										
July	2	3	.400	2.63	5	5	2	37.2	37	8	16	1	0	0	0										
Aug	2	3	.400	6.08	6	6	0	37	51	12	20	0	0	0	0										
Sept/Oct	1	2	.333	3.83	6	6	1	40	50	11	22	0	0	0	0										
Day	1	4	.200	3.00	5	5	2	39	38	8	19	0	0	0	0										
Night	9	10	.474	4.85	28	28	2	172.2	208	64	86	1	0	0	0										
vs. Left	—	—	—	—	—	—	—	—	35	15	20		—	—	—										
vs. Right	—	—	—	—	—	—	—	—	211	57	85		—	—	—										
On Grass	8	11	.421	4.54	28	28	3	178.1	209	60	89	1	0	0	0										
On Turf	2	3	.400	4.32	5	5	1	33.1	37	12	16	0	0	0	0										
Home	4	7	.364	4.75	17	17	2	110	138	31	46	1	0	0	0										
Road	6	7	.462	4.25	16	16	2	101.2	108	41	59	0	0	0	0										
Division Rivals																									
vs. CHI	1	1	.500	3.14	2	2	0	14.1	14	6	7	0	0	0	0										
vs. KC	0	2	.000	5.85	3	3	1	20	26	4	9	0	0	0	0										
vs. MIN	1	1	.500	4.76	3	3	0	17	23	9	3	0	0	0	0										
vs. OAK	0	1	.000	6.48	3	3	0	16.2	24	7	7	0	0	0	0										
vs. SEA	1	1	.500	5.11	2	2	0	12.1	19	7	5	0	0	0	0										
vs. TEX	2	0	1.000	3.26	3	3	0	19.1	21	8	16	0	0	0	0										

STARTING PITCHER
WINS — AL AVG
ERA — AL AVG
SO/9 — AL AVG
RATIO — AL AVG

Year	Team	W	L	%	ERA	G	GS	CG	IP	H	BB	SO	ShO	RELIEF PITCHING W	L	SV	BATTING AB	H	HR	BA	PO	A	E	DP	TC/G	FA

Jim Abbott *Continued*

Year	Team	W	L	%	ERA	G	GS	CG	IP	H	BB	SO	ShO	W	L	SV	AB	H	HR	BA	PO	A	E	DP	TC/G	FA
1989	CAL A	12	12	.500	3.92	29	29	4	181.1	190	74	115	2	0	0	0	0	0	0	—	6	26	3	1	1.2	.914
1990		10	14	.417	4.51	33	33	4	211.2	246	72	105	1	0	0	0	0	0	0	—	8	36	1	4	1.4	.978
2 yrs.		22	26	.458	4.24	62	62	8	393	436	146	220	3	0	0	0	0	0	0	—	14	62	4	5	1.3	.950

Paul Abbott

ABBOTT, PAUL DAVID
B. Sept. 15, 1967, Van Nuys, Calif.
BR TR 6′ 3″ 185 lbs.

Year	Team	W	L	%	ERA	G	GS	CG	IP	H	BB	SO	ShO	W	L	SV	AB	H	HR	BA	PO	A	E	DP	TC/G	FA
1990	MIN A	0	5	.000	5.97	7	7	0	34.2	37	28	25	0	0	0	0	0	0	0	—	2	2	1	1	0.7	.800

Jim Acker

ACKER, JAMES JUSTIN
B. Sept. 24, 1958, Freer, Tex.
BR TR 6′ 2″ 210 lbs.

Year	Team	W	L	%	ERA	G	GS	CG	IP	H	BB	SO	ShO	W	L	SV	AB	H	HR	BA	PO	A	E	DP	TC/G	FA
April		0	0	—	3.45	9	0	0	15.2	16	5	13	0	0	0	0										
May		1	1	.500	0.45	11	0	0	20	14	5	9	0	1	1	0										
June		0	1	.000	7.62	8	0	0	13	16	10	4	0	0	1	1										
July		1	0	1.000	3.38	9	0	0	16	21	5	11	0	1	0	0										
Aug		1	2	.333	5.19	11	0	0	17.1	21	4	10	0	1	2	0										
Sept/Oct		1	0	1.000	4.66	11	0	0	9.2	15	1	7	0	1	0	0										
Day		2	0	1.000	3.67	20	0	0	34.1	39	14	17	0	2	0	1										
Night		2	4	.333	3.92	39	0	0	57.1	64	16	37	0	2	4	0										
vs. Left		—	—	—	—	—	—	—	—	43	14	13	—	—	—	—										
vs. Right		—	—	—	—	—	—	—	—	60	16	41	—	—	—	—										
On Grass		1	1	.500	3.66	21	0	0	32	30	6	26	0	1	1	0										
On Turf		3	3	.500	3.92	38	0	0	59.2	73	24	28	0	3	3	1										
Home		2	3	.400	3.76	32	0	0	52.2	63	20	27	0	2	3	1										
Road		2	1	.667	3.92	27	0	0	39	40	10	27	0	2	1	0										
Division Rivals																										
vs. BAL		0	0	—	1.42	6	0	0	6.1	7	2	4	0	0	0	0										
vs. BOS		0	0	—	0.00	3	0	0	3.1	3	1	2	0	0	0	0										
vs. CLE		2	0	1.000	6.52	5	0	0	9.2	10	1	6	0	2	0	0										
vs. DET		0	0	—	1.86	7	0	0	9.2	6	0	7	0	0	0	0										
vs. MIL		0	1	.000	5.14	4	0	0	7	8	7	5	0	0	1	0										
vs. NY		0	2	.000	4.00	5	0	0	9	11	3	2	0	0	2	1										
1983	TOR A	5	1	.833	4.33	38	5	0	97.2	103	38	44	0	2	1	1	0	0	0	—	12	15	0	4	0.7	1.000
1984		3	5	.375	4.38	32	3	0	72	79	25	33	0	3	4	1	0	0	0	—	7	8	1	0	0.5	.938
1985		7	2	.778	3.23	61	0	0	86.1	86	43	42	0	7	2	10	0	0	0	—	10	16	0	1	0.4	1.000
1986	2 teams	TOR A	(23G 2 – 4)		ATL N	(21G 3 – 8)																				
''	total	5	12	.294	4.01	44	19	0	155	163	48	69	0	2	2	0	28	3	0	.107	16	28	0	4	1.0	1.000
1987	ATL N	4	9	.308	4.16	68	0	0	114.2	109	51	68	0	4	9	14	14	3	0	.214	6	23	0	2	0.4	1.000
1988		0	4	.000	4.71	21	1	0	42	45	14	25	0	0	3	0	5	2	0	.400	3	7	0	0	0.5	1.000
1989	2 teams	ATL N	(59G 0 – 6)		TOR A	(14G 2 – 1)																				
''	total	2	7	.222	2.43	73	0	0	126	108	32	92	0	2	7	2	7	1	0	.143	13	15	0	0	0.4	1.000
1990	TOR A	4	4	.500	3.83	59	0	0	91.2	103	30	54	0	4	4	1	0	0	0	—	5	19	0	0	0.4	1.000
8 yrs.		30	44	.405	3.78	396	28	0	785.1	796	281	427	0	24	32	29	54	9	0	.167	72	131	1	11	0.5	.995

LEAGUE CHAMPIONSHIP SERIES

Year	Team	W	L	%	ERA	G	GS	CG	IP	H	BB	SO	ShO	W	L	SV	AB	H	HR	BA	PO	A	E	DP	TC/G	FA
1985	TOR A	0	0	—	0.00	2	0	0	6	2	0	5	0	0	0	0	0	0	0	—	0	1	0	0	0.5	1.000
1989		0	0	—	1.42	5	0	0	6.1	4	1	4	0	0	0	0	0	0	0	—	1	1	0	0	0.4	1.000
2 yrs.		0	0	—	0.73	7	0	0	12.1	6	1	9	0	0	0	0	0	0	0	—	1	2	0	0	0.4	1.000

Steve Adkins

ADKINS, STEVEN THOMAS
B. Oct. 26, 1964, Chicago, Ill.
BR TL 6′ 6″ 210 lbs.

Year	Team	W	L	%	ERA	G	GS	CG	IP	H	BB	SO	ShO	W	L	SV	AB	H	HR	BA	PO	A	E	DP	TC/G	FA
1990	NY A	1	2	.333	6.38	5	5	0	24	19	29	14	0	0	0	0	0	0	0	—	0	3	0	0	0.6	1.000

RELIEF PITCHER

WINS | AL AVG
ERA | AL AVG
SAVES | AL AVG
RATIO | AL AVG

Year	Team	W	L	%	ERA	G	GS	CG	IP	H	BB	SO	ShO	RELIEF PITCHING W	L	SV	BATTING AB	H	HR	BA	PO	A	E	DP	TC/G	FA

Juan Agosto

AGOSTO, JUAN ROBERTO
Born Juan Roberto Agosto y Gonzalez.
B. Feb. 23, 1958, Rio Pedras, Puerto Rico
BL TL 6' 175 lbs.

Year	Team	W	L	%	ERA	G	GS	CG	IP	H	BB	SO	ShO	W	L	SV	AB	H	HR	BA	PO	A	E	DP	TC/G	FA
April		1	1	.500	0.82	10	0	0	11	7	6	10	0	1	1	0										
May		3	0	1.000	1.59	17	0	0	22.2	14	4	8	0	3	0	0										
June		0	0	—	4.70	16	0	0	15.1	20	9	9	0	0	0	1										
July		1	5	.167	7.52	17	0	0	20.1	24	8	10	0	1	5	0										
Aug		1	1	.500	5.59	9	0	0	9.2	13	4	6	0	1	1	1										
Sept/Oct		3	1	.750	5.40	13	0	0	13.1	13	8	7	0	3	1	2										
Day		2	2	.500	3.92	18	0	0	20.2	23	7	12	0	2	2	0										
Night		7	6	.538	4.40	64	0	0	71.2	68	32	38	0	7	6	4										
vs. Left		—	—	—	—	—	—	—		25	7	24	—	—	—	—										
vs. Right		—	—	—	—	—	—	—		66	32	26	—	—	—	—										
On Grass		2	3	.400	7.66	23	0	0	24.2	37	10	8	0	2	3	0										
On Turf		7	5	.583	3.06	59	0	0	67.2	54	29	42	0	7	5	4										
Home		6	4	.600	2.47	40	0	0	43.2	27	22	30	0	6	4	3										
Road		3	4	.429	5.92	42	0	0	48.2	64	17	20	0	3	4	1										
Division Rivals																										
vs. ATL		1	1	.500	7.71	6	0	0	7	8	3	5	0	1	1	0										
vs. CIN		1	1	.500	3.00	12	0	0	12	12	4	9	0	1	1	1										
vs. LA		1	1	.500	4.09	11	0	0	11	9	10	6	0	1	1	0										
vs. SD		0	0	—	13.50	7	0	0	5.1	6	5	3	0	0	0	0										
vs. SF		1	2	.333	5.87	9	0	0	7.2	14	2	1	0	1	2	1										
1981	CHI A	0	0	—	4.50	2	0	0	6	5	0	3	0	0	0	0	0	0	0	—	0	1	0	0	0.5	1.000
1982		0	0	—	18.00	1	0	0	2	7	0	1	0	0	0	0	0	0	0	—	0	1	0	0	1.0	1.000
1983		2	2	.500	4.10	39	0	0	41.2	41	11	29	0	2	2	7	0	0	0	—	2	8	2	1	0.3	.833
1984		2	1	.667	3.09	49	0	0	55.1	54	34	26	0	2	1	7	0	0	0	—	7	16	1	5	0.5	.958
1985		4	3	.571	3.58	54	0	0	60.1	45	23	39	0	4	3	1	0	0	0	—	10	15	1	0	0.5	.962
1986	2 teams	CHI A (9G 0 – 2)			MIN A (17G 1 – 2)																					
"	total	1	4	.200	8.64	26	1	0	25	49	18	12	0	1	3	1	0	0	0	—	3	4	2	0	0.3	.778
1987	HOU N	1	1	.500	2.63	27	0	0	27.1	26	10	6	0	1	1	2	1	0	0	.000	3	10	1	1	0.5	.929
1988		10	2	.833	2.26	75	0	0	91.2	74	30	33	0	10	2	4	5	0	0	.000	12	34	2	0	0.6	.958
1989		4	5	.444	2.93	71	0	0	83	81	32	46	0	4	5	5	1	0		.200	4	19	3	2	0.4	.885
1990		9	8	.529	4.29	**82**	0	0	92.1	91	39	50	0	9	8	4	2	0	0	.000	11	18	0	1	0.4	1.000
10 yrs.		33	26	.559	3.62	426	1	0	484.2	473	197	245	0	33	25	27	13	1	0	.077	52	126	12	10	0.4	.937

LEAGUE CHAMPIONSHIP SERIES

Year	Team	W	L	%	ERA	G	GS	CG	IP	H	BB	SO	ShO	W	L	SV	AB	H	HR	BA	PO	A	E	DP	TC/G	FA
1983	CHI A	0	0	—	0.00	1	0	0	0.1	0	0	0	0	0	0	0	0	0	0	—	0	0	0	0	0.0	

RELIEF PITCHER — WINS / ERA / SAVES / RATIO (NL AVG)

Rick Aguilera

AGUILERA, RICHARD WARREN (Aggie)
B. Dec. 31, 1961, San Gabriel, Calif.
BR TR 6' 4" 195 lbs.

Year	Team	W	L	%	ERA	G	GS	CG	IP	H	BB	SO	ShO	W	L	SV	AB	H	HR	BA	PO	A	E	DP	TC/G	FA
April		0	1	.000	3.52	7	0	0	7.2	4	2	7	0	0	1	4										
May		1	0	1.000	1.17	11	0	0	15.1	11	1	16	0	1	0	10										
June		0	0	—	1.64	11	0	0	11	9	2	8	0	0	0	4										
July		2	2	.500	4.26	11	0	0	12.2	11	5	16	0	2	2	5										
Aug		1	0	1.000	1.93	7	0	0	9.1	9	4	8	0	1	0	3										
Sept/Oct		1	0	1.000	4.82	9	0	0	9.1	11	5	6	0	1	0	6										
Day		3	2	.600	2.92	22	0	0	24.2	29	11	20	0	3	2	11										
Night		2	1	.667	2.66	34	0	0	40.2	26	8	41	0	2	1	21										
vs. Left		—	—	—	—	—	—	—		25	12	29	—	—	—	—										
vs. Right		—	—	—	—	—	—	—		30	7	32	—	—	—	—										
On Grass		1	1	.500	3.00	19	0	0	21	16	4	23	0	1	1	13										
On Turf		4	2	.667	2.64	37	0	0	44.1	39	15	38	0	4	2	19										
Home		3	2	.600	3.44	30	0	0	34	34	13	32	0	3	2	16										
Road		2	1	.667	2.01	26	0	0	31.1	21	6	29	0	2	1	16										
Division Rivals																										
vs. CAL		0	1	.000	22.50	3	0	0	2	5	2	2	0	0	1	1										
vs. CHI		0	0	—	0.00	6	0	0	7	2	1	6	0	0	0	3										
vs. KC		0	0	—	1.80	5	0	0	5	6	1	4	0	0	0	2										
vs. OAK		1	0	1.000	2.08	3	0	0	4.1	2	1	7	0	1	0	1										
vs. SEA		1	0	1.000	0.00	4	0	0	7.1	3	1	5	0	1	0	3										
vs. TEX		0	0	—	0.00	4	0	0	3.2	1	1	6	0	0	0	3										

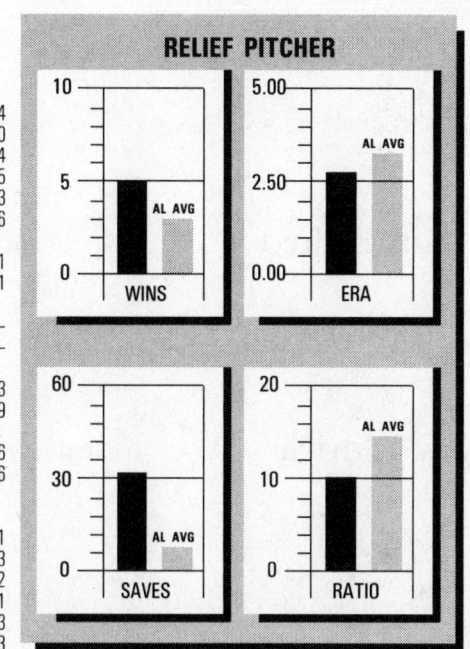

RELIEF PITCHER — WINS / ERA / SAVES / RATIO (AL AVG)

Year	Team	W	L	%	ERA	G	GS	CG	IP	H	BB	SO	ShO	RELIEF PITCHING W	L	SV	BATTING AB	H	HR	BA	PO	A	E	DP	TC/G	FA

Rick Aguilera *Continued*

Year	Team	W	L	%	ERA	G	GS	CG	IP	H	BB	SO	ShO	W	L	SV	AB	H	HR	BA	PO	A	E	DP	TC/G	FA
1985	NY N	10	7	.588	3.24	21	19	2	122.1	118	37	74	0	1	0	0	36	10	0	.278	8	16	0	1	1.1	1.000
1986		10	7	.588	3.88	28	20	2	141.2	145	36	104	0	1	1	0	51	8	2	.157	13	26	0	1	1.4	1.000
1987		11	3	.786	3.60	18	17	1	115	124	33	77	0	0	0	0	40	9	1	.225	7	29	2	1	2.1	.947
1988		0	4	.000	6.93	11	3	0	24.2	29	10	16	0	0	2	0	4	1	0	.250	3	5	0	0	0.7	1.000
1989	2 teams				NY N (36G 6 – 6)			MIN A (11G 3 – 5)																		
"	total	9	11	.450	2.79	47	11	3	145	130	38	137	0	6	6	7	7	0	0	.000	6	21	1	2	0.6	.964
1990	MIN A	5	3	.625	2.76	56	0	0	65.1	55	19	61	0	5	3	32	0	0	0	—	2	4	0	0	0.1	1.000
6 yrs.		45	35	.563	3.44	181	70	8	614	601	173	469	0	13	12	39	138	28	3	.203	39	101	3	5	0.8	.979

LEAGUE CHAMPIONSHIP SERIES

Year	Team	W	L	%	ERA	G	GS	CG	IP	H	BB	SO	ShO	W	L	SV	AB	H	HR	BA	PO	A	E	DP	TC/G	FA
1986	NY N	0	0	—	0.00	2	0	0	5	2	2	2	0	0	0	0	0	0	0	—	1	1	0	0	1.0	1.000
1988		0	0	—	1.29	3	0	0	7	3	2	4	0	0	0	0	1	0	0	.000	0	1	0	0	0.3	1.000
2 yrs.		0	0	—	0.75	5	0	0	12	5	4	6	0	0	0	0	1	0	0	.000	1	2	0	0	0.6	1.000

WORLD SERIES

Year	Team	W	L	%	ERA	G	GS	CG	IP	H	BB	SO	ShO	W	L	SV	AB	H	HR	BA	PO	A	E	DP	TC/G	FA
1986	NY N	1	0	1.000	12.00	2	0	0	3	8	1	4	0	1	0	0	0	0	0	—	0	0	0	0	0.0	—

Darrel Akerfelds

AKERFELDS, DARREL WAYNE
B. June 12, 1962, Denver, Colo.
BR TR 6' 2" 210 lbs.

	W	L	%	ERA	G	GS	CG	IP	H	BB	SO	ShO	W	L	SV	AB	H	HR	BA	PO	A	E	DP	TC/G	FA
April	0	0	—	0.00	6	0	0	5.2	1	5	1	0	0	0	0										
May	0	0	—	3.00	13	0	0	15	8	9	9	0	0	0	0										
June	2	0	1.000	2.75	14	0	0	19.2	8	14	6	0	2	0	0										
July	2	0	1.000	2.86	13	0	0	22	17	9	12	0	2	0	3										
Aug	0	1	.000	6.41	16	0	0	19.2	21	11	8	0	0	1	0										
Sept/Oct	1	1	.500	5.73	9	0	0	11	10	7	6	0	1	1	0										
Day	1	0	1.000	3.68	14	0	0	14.2	10	8	5	0	1	0	0										
Night	4	2	.667	3.79	57	0	0	78.1	55	46	37	0	4	2	3										
vs. Left	—	—	—	—	—	—	—	—	31	25	19	—	—	—	—										
vs. Right	—	—	—	—	—	—	—	—	34	29	23	—	—	—	—										
On Grass	0	1	.000	5.40	18	0	0	23.1	18	13	10	0	0	1	1										
On Turf	5	1	.833	3.23	53	0	0	69.2	47	41	32	0	5	1	2										
Home	5	0	1.000	2.88	37	0	0	50	33	32	22	0	5	0	1										
Road	0	2	.000	4.81	34	0	0	43	32	22	20	0	0	2	2										
Division Rivals																									
vs. CHI	2	0	1.000	1.69	7	0	0	10.2	6	7	3	0	2	0	0										
vs. MON	0	0	—	2.70	8	0	0	6.2	8	6	5	0	0	0	0										
vs. NY	1	1	.500	5.91	5	0	0	10.2	7	7	5	0	1	1	0										
vs. PIT	0	1	.000	3.97	6	0	0	11.1	7	5	1	0	0	1	0										
vs. STL	0	0	—	3.12	7	0	0	8.2	4	7	3	0	0	0	0										

RELIEF PITCHER

WINS — NL AVG · ERA — NL AVG · SAVES — NL AVG · RATIO — NL AVG

Year	Team	W	L	%	ERA	G	GS	CG	IP	H	BB	SO	ShO	W	L	SV	AB	H	HR	BA	PO	A	E	DP	TC/G	FA
1986	OAK A	0	0	—	6.75	2	0	0	5.1	7	3	5	0	0	0	0	0	0	0	—	1	1	0	0	1.0	1.000
1987	CLE A	2	6	.250	6.75	16	13	1	74.2	84	38	42	0	0	0	0	0	0	0	—	0	11	1	1	0.8	.917
1989	TEX A	0	1	.000	3.27	6	0	0	11	11	5	9	0	0	1	0	0	0	0	—	0	2	0	0	0.3	1.000
1990	PHI N	5	2	.714	3.77	71	0	0	93	65	54	42	0	5	2	3	6	1	0	.167	2	14	1	0	0.2	.941
4 yrs.		7	9	.438	5.04	95	13	1	184	167	100	98	0	5	3	3	6	1	0	.167	3	28	2	1	0.3	.939

Scott Aldred

ALDRED, SCOTT PHILLIP
B. June 12, 1968, Flint, Mich.
BL TL 6' 4" 195 lbs.

Year	Team	W	L	%	ERA	G	GS	CG	IP	H	BB	SO	ShO	W	L	SV	AB	H	HR	BA	PO	A	E	DP	TC/G	FA
1990	DET A	1	2	.333	3.77	4	3	0	14.1	13	10	7	0	0	0	0	0	0	0	—	0	2	0	0	0.5	1.000

Jay Aldrich

ALDRICH, JAY ROBERT
B. Apr. 14, 1961, Alexandria, La.
BR TR 6' 3" 210 lbs.

Year	Team	W	L	%	ERA	G	GS	CG	IP	H	BB	SO	ShO	W	L	SV	AB	H	HR	BA	PO	A	E	DP	TC/G	FA
1987	MIL A	3	1	.750	4.94	31	0	0	58.1	71	13	22	0	0	0	0	0	0	0	—	6	5	1	0	0.4	.917
1989	2 teams				MIL A (16G 1 – 0)			ATL N (8G 1 – 2)																		
"	total	2	2	.500	3.29	24	0	0	38.1	31	19	19	0	2	2	1	1	0	0	.000	4	5	1	1	0.4	.900
1990	BAL A	1	2	.333	8.25	7	0	0	12	17	7	5	0	1	2	1	1	0	0	—	2	1	0	0	0.4	1.000
3 yrs.		6	5	.545	4.72	62	0	0	108.2	119	39	46	0	3	4	2	1	0	0	.000	12	11	2	1	0.4	.920

Year	Team	W	L	%	ERA	G	GS	CG	IP	H	BB	SO	ShO	RELIEF PITCHING W	L	SV	BATTING AB	H	HR	BA	PO	A	E	DP	TC/G	FA

Gerald Alexander

ALEXANDER, GERALD PAUL
B. Mar. 26, 1968, Baton Rouge, La.
BR TR 5′ 11″ 190 lbs.

Year	Team	W	L	%	ERA	G	GS	CG	IP	H	BB	SO	ShO	W	L	SV	AB	H	HR	BA	PO	A	E	DP	TC/G	FA
1990	TEX A	0	0	—	7.71	3	2	0	7	14	5	8	0	0	0	0	0	0	0	—	1	0	0	1	0.3	1.000

Larry Andersen

ANDERSEN, LARRY EUGENE
B. May 6, 1953, Portland, Ore.
BR TR 6′ 3″ 200 lbs.

	W	L	%	ERA	G	GS	CG	IP	H	BB	SO	ShO	W	L	SV
April	2	0	1.000	0.82	8	0	0	11	10	3	8	0	2	0	0
May	0	1	.000	2.00	11	0	0	18	12	9	12	0	0	1	2
June	2	0	1.000	1.29	11	0	0	14	12	3	14	0	2	0	0
July	1	1	.500	5.40	10	0	0	13.1	12	4	16	0	1	1	2
Aug	0	0	—	0.52	10	0	0	17.1	15	5	18	0	0	0	2
Sept/Oct	0	0	—	1.23	15	0	0	22	18	3	25	0	0	0	1
Day	2	1	.667	4.35	14	0	0	20.2	23	7	18	0	2	1	2
Night	3	1	.750	1.08	51	0	0	75	56	20	75	0	3	1	5
vs. Left	—	—	—	—	—	—	—	—	46	17	26	—	—	—	—
vs. Right	—	—	—	—	—	—	—	—	33	10	67	—	—	—	—
On Grass	0	0	—	1.70	28	0	0	42.1	36	7	38	0	0	0	4
On Turf	5	2	.714	1.86	37	0	0	53.1	43	20	55	0	5	2	3
Home	4	0	1.000	0.68	37	0	0	53.1	41	10	57	0	4	0	3
Road	1	2	.333	3.19	28	0	0	42.1	38	17	36	0	1	2	4
Division Rivals															
vs. BAL	0	0	—	0.00	1	0	0	2	0	1	4	0	0	0	0
vs. CLE	0	0	—	3.86	2	0	0	2.1	6	0	1	0	0	0	0
vs. DET	—	—	—	—	0	—	—	0	0	0	0	—	0	0	0
vs. MIL	0	0	—	0.00	1	0	0	1	0	1	1	0	0	0	0
vs. NY	0	0	—	0.00	3	0	0	3.2	1	0	2	0	0	0	1
vs. TOR	0	0	—	0.00	1	0	0	0.2	2	0	0	0	0	0	0

RELIEF PITCHER

WINS · ERA · SAVES · RATIO (NL AVG)

Year	Team	W	L	%	ERA	G	GS	CG	IP	H	BB	SO	ShO	W	L	SV	AB	H	HR	BA	PO	A	E	DP	TC/G	FA
1975	CLE A	0	0	—	4.76	3	0	0	5.2	4	2	4	0	0	0	0	0	0	0	—	1	1	0	0	0.7	1.000
1977		0	1	.000	3.21	11	0	0	14	10	9	8	0	0	1	0	0	0	0	—	3	6	2	4	1.0	.818
1979		0	0	—	7.41	8	0	0	17	25	4	7	0	0	0	0	0	0	0	—	0	4	0	1	0.5	1.000
1981	SEA A	3	3	.500	2.65	41	0	0	68	57	18	40	0	3	3	5	0	0	0	—	5	9	0	1	0.3	1.000
1982		0	0	—	5.99	40	1	0	79.2	100	23	32	0	0	0	1	0	0	0	—	8	14	0	2	0.6	1.000
1983	PHI N	1	0	1.000	2.39	17	0	0	26.1	19	9	14	0	1	0	0	2	0	0	.000	2	6	0	0	0.5	1.000
1984		3	7	.300	2.38	64	0	0	90.2	85	25	54	0	3	7	4	4	0	0	.000	5	16	4	4	0.4	.840
1985		3	3	.500	4.32	57	0	0	73	78	26	50	0	3	3	3	4	0	0	.000	5	21	2	2	0.5	.929
1986	2 teams			PHI N (10G 0 – 0)				HOU N (38G 2 – 1)																		
"	total	2	1	.667	3.03	48	0	0	77.1	83	26	42	0	2	1	1	6	0	0	.000	2	2	1	1	0.1	.800
1987	HOU N	9	5	.643	3.45	67	0	0	101.2	95	41	94	0	9	5	5	6	1	0	.167	12	10	3	0	0.4	.880
1988		2	4	.333	2.94	53	0	0	82.2	82	20	66	0	2	4	5	6	2	0	.333	9	9	2	1	0.4	.900
1989		4	4	.500	1.54	60	0	0	87.2	63	24	85	0	4	4	3	3	1	0	.333	10	13	4	0	0.5	.852
1990	2 teams			HOU N (50G 5 – 2)				BOS A (15G 0 – 0)																		
"	total	5	2	.714	1.79	65	0	0	95.2	79	27	93	0	5	2	7	3	0	0	.000	13	12	2	1	0.4	.926
	13 yrs.	32	30	.516	3.15	534	1	0	819.1	780	254	589	0	32	30	34	34	4	0	.118	75	123	20	14	0.4	.908

LEAGUE CHAMPIONSHIP SERIES

Year	Team	W	L	%	ERA	G	GS	CG	IP	H	BB	SO	ShO	W	L	SV	AB	H	HR	BA	PO	A	E	DP	TC/G	FA
1986	HOU N	0	0	—	0.00	2	0	0	5	1	2	3	0	0	0	0	0	0	0	—	0	0	0	0	0.0	—
1990	BOS A	0	1	.000	6.00	3	0	0	3	3	3	3	0	0	1	0	0	0	0	—	1	0	0	0	0.3	1.000
	2 yrs.	0	1	.000	2.25	5	0	0	8	4	5	6	0	0	1	0	0	0	0	—	1	0	0	0	0.2	1.000

WORLD SERIES

Year	Team	W	L	%	ERA	G	GS	CG	IP	H	BB	SO	ShO	W	L	SV	AB	H	HR	BA	PO	A	E	DP	TC/G	FA
1983	PHI N	0	0	—	2.25	2	0	0	4	4	0	1	0	0	0	0	0	0	0	—	1	1	0	1	1.0	1.000

Year	Team	W	L	%	ERA	G	GS	CG	IP	H	BB	SO	ShO	RELIEF PITCHING W	L	SV	BATTING AB	H	HR	BA	PO	A	E	DP	TC/G	FA

Allan Anderson

ANDERSON, ALLAN LEE
B. Jan. 7, 1964, Lancaster, Ohio
BL TL 5' 11" 178 lbs.

Year	Team	W	L	%	ERA	G	GS	CG	IP	H	BB	SO	ShO	W	L	SV	AB	H	HR	BA	PO	A	E	DP	TC/G	FA
April		1	3	.250	5.47	5	5	0	26.1	36	8	10	0	0	0	0										
May		1	3	.250	4.86	6	6	1	33.1	34	10	12	0	0	0	0										
June		0	5	.000	6.55	6	6	0	33	52	8	16	0	0	0	0										
July		2	3	.400	3.95	6	6	1	41	43	4	19	0	0	0	0										
Aug		2	2	.500	2.73	4	4	3	33	28	6	19	1	0	0	0										
Sept/Oct		1	2	.333	3.68	4	4	0	22	21	3	6	0	0	0	0										
Day		2	5	.286	5.70	8	8	1	47.1	61	4	17	0	0	0	0										
Night		5	13	.278	4.14	23	23	4	141.1	153	35	65	1	0	0	0										
vs. Left		—	—	—	—	—	—	—	—	28	7	11	—	—	—	—										
vs. Right		—	—	—	—	—	—	—	—	186	32	71	—	—	—	—										
On Grass		2	5	.286	3.94	10	10	0	59.1	73	11	20	0	0	0	0										
On Turf		5	13	.278	4.80	21	21	5	129.1	141	28	62	1	0	0	0										
Home		4	12	.250	4.77	18	18	4	111.1	119	25	51	1	0	0	0										
Road		3	6	.333	4.19	13	13	1	77.1	95	14	31	0	0	0	0										
Division Rivals																										
vs. CAL		1	2	.333	4.67	3	3	0	17.1	23	4	6	0	0	0	0										
vs. CHI		1	2	.333	3.32	3	3	1	21.2	23	5	10	1	0	0	0										
vs. KC		0	1	.000	31.50	1	1	0	2	10	0	2	0	0	0	0										
vs. OAK		1	2	.333	6.88	3	3	1	17	22	8	8	0	0	0	0										
vs. SEA		0	2	.000	6.61	3	3	0	16.1	20	4	11	0	0	0	0										
vs. TEX		0	0	—	0.84	2	2	0	10.2	11	1	5	0	0	0	0										
1986	MIN A	3	6	.333	5.55	21	10	1	84.1	106	30	51	0	1	1	1	0	0	0	—	4	14	1	1	0.9	.947
1987		1	0	1.000	10.95	4	2	0	12.1	20	10	3	0	0	0	0	0	0	0	—	1	0	0	0	0.3	1.000
1988		16	9	.640	**2.45**	30	30	3	202.1	199	37	83	1	0	0	0	0	0	0	—	9	34	2	3	1.5	.956
1989		17	10	.630	3.80	33	33	4	196.2	214	53	69	1	0	0	0	1	0	0	.000	12	27	1	5	1.2	.975
1990		7	18	.280	4.53	31	31	5	188.2	214	39	82	1	0	0	0	0	0	0	—	7	37	0	2	1.4	1.000
5 yrs.		44	43	.506	3.95	119	106	13	684.1	753	169	288	3	1	1	1	1	0	0	.000	33	112	4	11	1.3	.973

Scott Anderson

ANDERSON, SCOTT RICHARD
B. Aug. 1, 1962, Corvallis, Ore.
BR TR 6' 6" 186 lbs.

Year	Team	W	L	%	ERA	G	GS	CG	IP	H	BB	SO	ShO	W	L	SV	AB	H	HR	BA	PO	A	E	DP	TC/G	FA
1987	TEX A	0	1	.000	9.53	8	0	0	11.1	17	8	6	0	0	1	0	0	0	0	—	2	3	0	1	0.6	1.000
1990	MON N	0	1	.000	3.00	4	3	0	18	12	5	16	0	0	0	0	4	0	0	.000	0	2	0	0	0.5	1.000
2 yrs.		0	2	.000	5.52	12	3	0	29.1	29	13	22	0	0	1	0	4	0	0	.000	2	5	0	1	0.6	1.000

Kevin Appier

APPIER, ROBERT KEVIN
B. Dec. 6, 1967, Lancaster, Calif.
BR TR 6' 2" 180 lbs.

Year	Team	W	L	%	ERA	G	GS	CG	IP	H	BB	SO	ShO	W	L	SV	AB	H	HR	BA	PO	A	E	DP	TC/G	FA
April		0	0	—	0.00	2	1	0	2.1	2	2	4	0	0	0	0										
May		1	0	1.000	3.75	7	2	0	24	33	8	12	0	0	0	0										
June		1	3	.250	3.00	6	5	0	36	32	13	24	0	0	0	0										
July		4	1	.800	3.02	6	6	2	44.2	38	12	36	2	0	0	0										
Aug		5	0	1.000	1.85	5	5	1	34	29	7	20	1	0	0	0										
Sept/Oct		1	4	.200	2.62	6	6	0	44.2	45	12	31	0	0	0	0										
Day		3	1	.750	1.91	6	4	0	28.1	29	14	18	0	0	0	0										
Night		9	7	.563	2.92	26	20	3	157.1	150	40	109	3	0	0	0										
vs. Left		—	—	—	—	—	—	—	—	81	35	50	—	—	—	—										
vs. Right		—	—	—	—	—	—	—	—	98	19	77	—	—	—	—										
On Grass		5	3	.625	2.79	14	10	2	80.2	79	30	54	2	0	0	0										
On Turf		7	5	.583	2.74	18	14	1	105	100	24	73	1	0	0	0										
Home		7	4	.636	2.77	15	11	1	84.1	83	18	59	1	0	0	0										
Road		5	4	.556	2.75	17	13	2	101.1	96	36	68	2	0	0	0										
Division Rivals																										
vs. CAL		1	0	1.000	1.74	2	1	0	10.1	12	5	10	0	0	0	0										
vs. CHI		1	1	.500	3.44	4	2	0	18.1	24	4	11	0	0	0	0										
vs. MIN		1	0	1.000	0.53	2	2	0	17	9	3	11	0	0	0	0										
vs. OAK		1	3	.250	3.10	4	4	1	29	26	9	19	1	0	0	0										
vs. SEA		1	1	.500	1.83	3	3	0	19.2	17	8	14	0	0	0	0										
vs. TEX		1	1	.500	2.60	4	3	0	17.1	12	5	16	0	0	0	0										

Year	Team		W	L	%	ERA	G	GS	CG	IP	H	BB	SO	ShO	RELIEF PITCHING W	L	SV	BATTING AB	H	HR	BA	PO	A	E	DP	TC/G	FA

Kevin Appier *Continued*

Year	Team		W	L	%	ERA	G	GS	CG	IP	H	BB	SO	ShO	W	L	SV	AB	H	HR	BA	PO	A	E	DP	TC/G	FA
1989	KC	A	1	4	.200	9.14	6	5	0	21.2	34	12	10	0	0	0	0	0	0	0	—	1	0	0	0	0.2	1.000
1990			12	8	.600	2.76	32	24	3	185.2	179	54	127	3	0	0	0	0	0	0	—	15	21	3	3	1.2	.923
2 yrs.			13	12	.520	3.43	38	29	3	207.1	213	66	137	3	0	0	0	0	0	0	—	16	21	3	3	1.1	.925

Luis Aquino

AQUINO, LUIS ANTONIO
Born Luis Antonio Aquino y Colon.
B. May 19, 1964, Santurce, Puerto Rico
BR TR 6' 155 lbs.

Year	Team		W	L	%	ERA	G	GS	CG	IP	H	BB	SO	ShO	W	L	SV	AB	H	HR	BA	PO	A	E	DP	TC/G	FA
1986	TOR	A	1	1	.500	6.35	7	0	0	11.1	14	3	5	0	1	1	0	0	0	0	—	1	1	0	0	0.3	1.000
1988	KC	A	1	0	1.000	2.79	7	5	1	29	33	17	11	1	0	0	0	0	0	0	—	2	2	1	1	0.7	.800
1989			6	8	.429	3.50	34	16	2	141.1	148	35	68	1	2	0	0	0	0	0	—	11	23	0	3	1.0	1.000
1990			4	1	.800	3.16	20	3	1	68.1	59	27	28	0	2	0	0	0	0	0	—	4	10	0	2	0.7	1.000
4 yrs.			12	10	.545	3.46	68	24	4	250	254	82	112	2	5	1	0	0	0	0	—	18	36	1	6	0.8	.982

Jack Armstrong

ARMSTRONG, JACK WILLIAM
B. Mar. 7, 1965, Englewood, N. J.
BR TR 6' 5" 220 lbs.

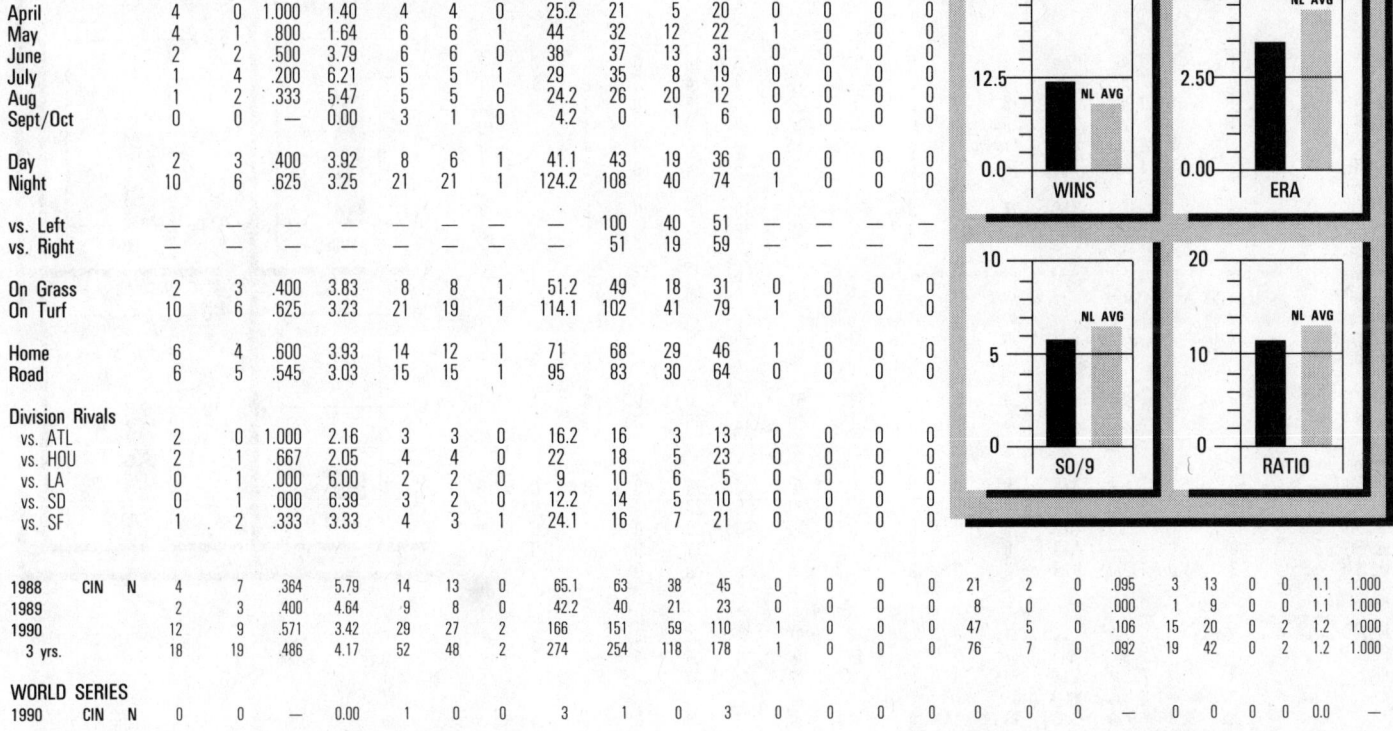

STARTING PITCHER

	W	L	%	ERA	G	GS	CG	IP	H	BB	SO	ShO	W	L	SV
April	4	0	1.000	1.40	4	4	0	25.2	21	5	20	0	0	0	0
May	4	1	.800	1.64	6	6	1	44	32	12	22	1	0	0	0
June	2	2	.500	3.79	6	6	0	38	37	13	31	0	0	0	0
July	1	4	.200	6.21	5	5	1	29	35	8	19	0	0	0	0
Aug	1	2	.333	5.47	5	5	0	24.2	26	20	12	0	0	0	0
Sept/Oct	0	0	—	0.00	3	1	0	4.2	0	1	6	0	0	0	0
Day	2	3	.400	3.92	8	6	1	41.1	43	19	36	0	0	0	0
Night	10	6	.625	3.25	21	21	1	124.2	108	40	74	1	0	0	0
vs. Left	—	—	—	—	—	—	—	—	100	40	51	—	—	—	—
vs. Right	—	—	—	—	—	—	—	—	51	19	59	—	—	—	—
On Grass	2	3	.400	3.83	8	8	1	51.2	49	18	31	0	0	0	0
On Turf	10	6	.625	3.23	21	19	1	114.1	102	41	79	1	0	0	0
Home	6	4	.600	3.93	14	12	1	71	68	29	46	1	0	0	0
Road	6	5	.545	3.03	15	15	1	95	83	30	64	0	0	0	0
Division Rivals															
vs. ATL	2	0	1.000	2.16	3	3	0	16.2	16	3	13	0	0	0	0
vs. HOU	2	1	.667	2.05	4	4	0	22	18	5	23	0	0	0	0
vs. LA	0	1	.000	6.00	2	2	0	9	10	6	5	0	0	0	0
vs. SD	0	1	.000	6.39	3	2	0	12.2	14	5	10	0	0	0	0
vs. SF	1	2	.333	3.33	4	3	1	24.1	16	7	21	0	0	0	0

Year	Team		W	L	%	ERA	G	GS	CG	IP	H	BB	SO	ShO	W	L	SV	AB	H	HR	BA	PO	A	E	DP	TC/G	FA
1988	CIN	N	4	7	.364	5.79	14	13	0	65.1	63	38	45	0	0	0	0	21	2	0	.095	3	13	0	0	1.1	1.000
1989			2	3	.400	4.64	9	8	0	42.2	40	21	23	0	0	0	0	8	0	0	.000	1	9	0	0	1.1	1.000
1990			12	9	.571	3.42	29	27	2	166	151	59	110	1	0	0	0	47	5	0	.106	15	20	0	2	1.2	1.000
3 yrs.			18	19	.486	4.17	52	48	2	274	254	118	178	1	0	0	0	76	7	0	.092	19	42	0	2	1.2	1.000

WORLD SERIES

Year	Team		W	L	%	ERA	G	GS	CG	IP	H	BB	SO	ShO	W	L	SV	AB	H	HR	BA	PO	A	E	DP	TC/G	FA
1990	CIN	N	0	0	—	0.00	1	0	0	3	1	0	3	0	0	0	0	0	0	0	—	0	0	0	0	0.0	—

Brad Arnsberg

ARNSBERG, BRADLEY JAMES
B. Aug. 20, 1963, Seattle, Wash.
BR TR 6' 4" 205 lbs.

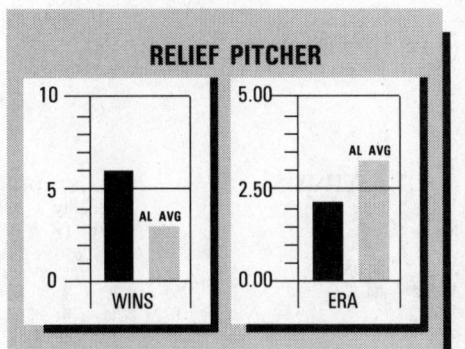

RELIEF PITCHER

	W	L	%	ERA	G	GS	CG	IP	H	BB	SO	ShO	W	L	SV
April	—	—	—	—	0	0	0	0	0	0	0	—	0	0	0
May	0	0	—	2.25	2	0	0	4	3	2	5	0	0	0	0
June	2	1	.667	1.06	12	0	0	17	12	6	11	0	2	1	0
July	2	0	1.000	1.29	12	0	0	14	10	11	12	0	2	0	3
Aug	1	0	1.000	3.38	11	0	0	16	17	5	6	0	1	0	2
Sept/Oct	1	0	1.000	3.09	16	0	0	11.2	14	9	10	0	1	0	0
Day	3	1	.750	0.77	10	0	0	11.2	8	7	9	0	3	1	0
Night	3	0	1.000	2.47	43	0	0	51	48	26	35	0	3	0	5
vs. Left	—	—	—	—	—	—	—	—	20	10	12	—	—	—	—
vs. Right	—	—	—	—	—	—	—	—	36	23	32	—	—	—	—

Year	Team	W	L	%	ERA	G	GS	CG	IP	H	BB	SO	ShO	W	L	SV	AB	H	HR	BA	PO	A	E	DP	TC/G	FA

(Header spans: RELIEF PITCHING = W, L, SV; BATTING = AB, H, HR)

Brad Arnsberg *Continued*

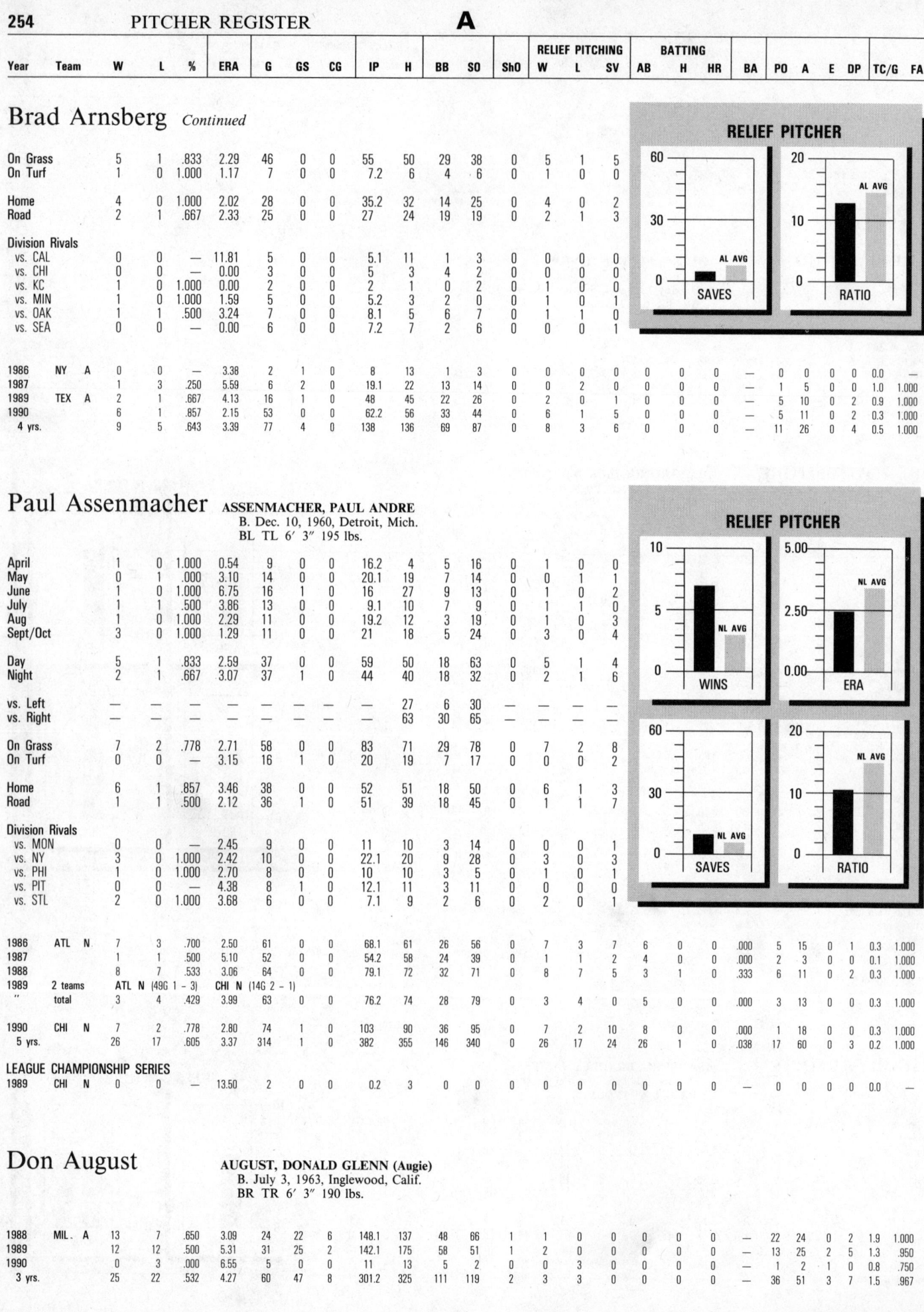

Year	Team	W	L	%	ERA	G	GS	CG	IP	H	BB	SO	ShO	W	L	SV	AB	H	HR	BA	PO	A	E	DP	TC/G	FA
On Grass		5	1	.833	2.29	46	0	0	55	50	29	38	0	5	1	5										
On Turf		1	0	1.000	1.17	7	0	0	7.2	6	4	6	0	1	0	0										
Home		4	0	1.000	2.02	28	0	0	35.2	32	14	25	0	4	0	2										
Road		2	1	.667	2.33	25	0	0	27	24	19	19	0	2	1	3										
Division Rivals																										
vs. CAL		0	0	—	11.81	5	0	0	5.1	11	1	3	0	0	0	0										
vs. CHI		0	0	—	0.00	3	0	0	5	3	4	2	0	0	0	0										
vs. KC		1	0	1.000	0.00	2	0	0	2	1	0	2	0	1	0	0										
vs. MIN		1	0	1.000	1.59	5	0	0	5.2	3	2	0	0	1	0	1										
vs. OAK		1	1	.500	3.24	7	0	0	8.1	5	6	7	0	1	1	0										
vs. SEA		0	0	—	0.00	6	0	0	7.2	7	2	6	0	0	0	1										
1986	NY A	0	0		3.38	2	1	0	8	13	1	3	0	0	0	0	0	0	0	—	0	0	0	0	0.0	—
1987		1	3	.250	5.59	6	2	0	19.1	22	13	14	0	0	2	0	0	0	0	—	1	5	0	0	1.0	1.000
1989	TEX A	2	1	.667	4.13	16	1	0	48	45	22	26	0	2	0	1	0	0	0	—	5	10	0	0	0.9	1.000
1990		6	1	.857	2.15	53	0	0	62.2	56	33	44	0	6	1	5	0	0	0	—	5	11	0	2	0.3	1.000
4 yrs.		9	5	.643	3.39	77	4	0	138	136	69	87	0	8	3	6	0	0	0	—	11	26	0	4	0.5	1.000

Paul Assenmacher ASSENMACHER, PAUL ANDRE
B. Dec. 10, 1960, Detroit, Mich.
BL TL 6′ 3″ 195 lbs.

Year	Team	W	L	%	ERA	G	GS	CG	IP	H	BB	SO	ShO	W	L	SV	AB	H	HR	BA	PO	A	E	DP	TC/G	FA
April		1	0	1.000	0.54	9	0	0	16.2	4	5	16	0	1	0	0										
May		0	1	.000	3.10	14	0	0	20.1	19	7	14	0	0	1	1										
June		1	0	1.000	6.75	16	1	0	16	27	9	13	0	1	0	2										
July		1	1	.500	3.86	13	0	0	9.1	10	7	9	0	1	1	0										
Aug		1	0	1.000	2.29	11	0	0	19.2	12	3	19	0	1	0	3										
Sept/Oct		3	0	1.000	1.29	11	0	0	21	18	5	24	0	3	0	4										
Day		5	1	.833	2.59	37	0	0	59	50	18	63	0	5	1	4										
Night		2	1	.667	3.07	37	1	0	44	40	18	32	0	2	1	6										
vs. Left		—		—	—	—				27	6	30	—	—	—	—										
vs. Right		—		—	—	—				63	30	65	—	—	—	—										
On Grass		7	2	.778	2.71	58	0	0	83	71	29	78	0	7	2	8										
On Turf		0	0	—	3.15	16	1	0	20	19	7	17	0	0	0	2										
Home		6	1	.857	3.46	38	0	0	52	51	18	50	0	6	1	3										
Road		1	1	.500	2.12	36	1	0	51	39	18	45	0	1	1	7										
Division Rivals																										
vs. MON		0	0	—	2.45	9	0	0	11	10	3	14	0	0	0	1										
vs. NY		3	0	1.000	2.42	10	0	0	22.1	20	9	28	0	3	0	3										
vs. PHI		1	0	1.000	2.70	8	0	0	10	10	3	5	0	1	0	1										
vs. PIT		0	0	—	4.38	8	1	0	12.1	11	3	11	0	0	0	1										
vs. STL		2	0	1.000	3.68	7	0	0	7.1	9	2	6	0	2	0	1										
1986	ATL N	7	3	.700	2.50	61	0	0	68.1	61	26	56	0	7	3	7	6	0	0	.000	5	15	0	1	0.3	1.000
1987		1	1	.500	5.10	52	0	0	54.2	58	24	39	0	1	1	2	4	0	0	.000	2	3	0	1	0.1	1.000
1988		8	7	.533	3.06	64	0	0	79.1	72	32	71	0	8	7	5	3	1	0	.333	6	11	0	2	0.3	1.000
1989	2 teams	ATL N	(49G 1 - 3)			CHI N	(14G 2 - 1)																			
"	total	3	4	.429	3.99	63	0	0	76.2	74	28	79	0	3	4	0	5	0	0	.000	3	13	0	0	0.3	1.000
1990	CHI N	7	2	.778	2.80	74	1	0	103	90	36	95	0	7	2	10	8	0	0	.000	1	18	0	0	0.3	1.000
5 yrs.		26	17	.605	3.37	314	1	0	382	355	146	340	0	26	17	24	26	1	0	.038	17	60	0	3	0.2	1.000

LEAGUE CHAMPIONSHIP SERIES

Year	Team	W	L	%	ERA	G	GS	CG	IP	H	BB	SO	ShO	W	L	SV	AB	H	HR	BA	PO	A	E	DP	TC/G	FA
1989	CHI N	0	0	—	13.50	2	0	0	0.2	3	0	0	0	0	0	0	0	0	0	—	0	0	0	0	0.0	—

Don August AUGUST, DONALD GLENN (Augie)
B. July 3, 1963, Inglewood, Calif.
BR TR 6′ 3″ 190 lbs.

Year	Team	W	L	%	ERA	G	GS	CG	IP	H	BB	SO	ShO	W	L	SV	AB	H	HR	BA	PO	A	E	DP	TC/G	FA
1988	MIL. A	13	7	.650	3.09	24	22	6	148.1	137	48	66	1	1	0	0	0	0	0	—	22	24	0	2	1.9	1.000
1989		12	12	.500	5.31	31	25	2	142.1	175	58	51	1	2	0	0	0	0	0	—	13	25	2	5	1.3	.950
1990		0	3	.000	6.55	5	0	0	11	13	5	2	0	0	0	0	0	0	0	—	1	2	1	0	0.8	.750
3 yrs.		25	22	.532	4.27	60	47	8	301.2	325	111	119	2	3	0	0	0	0	0	—	36	51	3	7	1.5	.967

Year	Team	W	L	%	ERA	G	GS	CG	IP	H	BB	SO	ShO	RELIEF PITCHING W	L	SV	BATTING AB	H	HR	BA	PO	A	E	DP	TC/G	FA

Steve Avery

AVERY, STEVEN THOMAS
B. Apr. 14, 1970, Trenton, Mich.
BL TL 6' 4" 180 lbs.

Split	W	L	%	ERA	G	GS	CG	IP	H	BB	SO	ShO	W	L	SV	AB	H	HR	BA	PO	A	E	DP	TC/G	FA
April	—	—	—	—	0	—	—	0	0	0	0	—	0	0	0										
May	—	—	—	—	0	3	—	0	0	0	0	—	0	0	0										
June	1	1	.500	6.43	3	3	0	14	18	10	10	0	0	0	0										
July	0	4	.000	4.63	6	6	0	35	38	16	18	0	0	0	0										
Aug	2	3	.400	4.36	6	6	1	33	34	13	33	1	0	0	0										
Sept/Oct	0	3	.000	9.53	6	5	0	17	31	6	14	0	0	1	0										
Day	0	4	.000	8.26	7	6	0	28.1	42	9	22	0	0	1	0										
Night	3	7	.300	4.58	14	14	1	70.2	79	36	53	1	0	0	0										
vs. Left	—	—	—	—	—	—	—	—	16	5	19	—	—	—	—										
vs. Right	—	—	—	—	—	—	—	—	105	40	56	—	—	—	—										
On Grass	3	6	.333	4.63	16	15	1	79.2	92	32	56	1	0	1	0										
On Turf	0	5	.000	9.78	5	5	0	19.1	29	13	19	0	0	0	0										
Home	3	4	.429	4.25	11	11	1	59.1	65	27	43	1	0	0	0										
Road	0	7	.000	7.71	10	9	0	39.2	56	18	32	0	0	1	0										
Division Rivals																									
vs. CIN	0	2	.000	10.20	4	4	0	15	26	8	14	0	0	0	0										
vs. HOU	0	2	.000	6.35	3	3	0	11.1	19	6	11	0	0	0	0										
vs. LA	2	0	1.000	1.29	2	2	0	14	11	7	9	0	0	0	0										
vs. SD	0	1	.000	7.84	3	3	0	10.1	18	3	5	0	0	0	0										
vs. SF	0	1	.000	13.50	1	0	0	2	5	0	0	0	0	1	0										
1990 ATL N	3	11	.214	5.64	21	20	1	99	121	45	75	1	0	1	0	30	4	0	.133	4	22	2	0	1.3	.929

STARTING PITCHER (chart)

Scott Bailes

BAILES, SCOTT ALAN
B. Dec. 18, 1961, Chillicothe, Ohio
BL TL 6' 2" 170 lbs.

Split	W	L	%	ERA	G	GS	CG	IP	H	BB	SO	ShO	W	L	SV	AB	H	HR	BA	PO	A	E	DP	TC/G	FA
April	0	0	—	2.45	5	0	0	7.1	5	7	2	0	0	0	0										
May	1	0	1.000	3.14	9	0	0	14.1	12	9	6	0	1	0	0										
June	1	0	1.000	8.10	8	0	0	10	15	1	6	0	1	0	0										
July	0	0	—	22.09	5	0	0	3.2	14	3	2	0	0	0	0										
Aug	—	—	—	—	0	0	—	0	0	0	0	—	0	0	0										
Sept/Oct	—	—	—	—	0	0	—	0	0	0	0	—	0	0	0										
Day	0	0	—	9.00	4	0	0	5	8	2	2	0	0	0	0										
Night	2	0	1.000	5.93	23	0	0	30.1	38	18	14	0	2	0	0										
vs. Left	—	—	—	—	—	—	—	—	14	5	6	—	—	—	—										
vs. Right	—	—	—	—	—	—	—	—	32	15	10	—	—	—	—										
On Grass	2	0	1.000	5.74	23	0	0	26.2	35	12	13	0	2	0	0										
On Turf	0	0	—	8.31	4	0	0	8.2	11	8	3	0	0	0	0										
Home	2	0	1.000	8.03	13	0	0	12.1	20	5	7	0	2	0	0										
Road	0	0	—	5.48	14	0	0	23	26	15	9	0	0	0	0										
Division Rivals																									
vs. CHI	0	0	—	0.00	1	0	0	0	1	0	0	0	0	0	0										
vs. KC	0	0	—	54.00	1	0	0	0.2	5	1	2	0	0	0	0										
vs. MIN	0	0	—	4.91	2	0	0	3.2	3	5	1	0	0	0	0										
vs. OAK	0	0	—	81.00	1	0	0	0.1	3	0	0	0	0	0	0										
vs. SEA	0	0	—	3.60	2	0	0	5	5	3	1	0	0	0	0										
vs. TEX	0	0	—	6.75	3	0	0	4	5	0	3	0	0	0	0										
1986 CLE A	10	10	.500	4.95	62	10	0	112.2	123	43	60	0	8	7	7	0	0	0	—	4	13	1	0	0.3	.944
1987	7	8	.467	4.64	39	17	0	120.1	145	47	65	0	2	1	6	0	0	0	—	6	19	2	0	0.7	.926
1988	9	14	.391	4.90	37	21	5	145	149	46	53	2	2	3	0	0	0	0	—	14	19	1	0	0.9	.971
1989	5	9	.357	4.28	34	11	0	113.2	116	29	47	0	2	3	0	0	0	0	—	4	20	2	2	0.8	.923
1990 CAL A	2	0	1.000	6.37	27	0	0	35.1	46	20	16	0	2	0	0	0	0	0	—	2	10	1	0	0.5	.923
5 yrs.	33	41	.446	4.82	199	59	5	527	579	185	241	2	16	14	13	0	0	0	—	30	81	7	2	0.6	.941

RELIEF PITCHER (chart)

Year	Team	W	L	%	ERA	G	GS	CG	IP	H	BB	SO	ShO	W	L	SV	AB	H	HR	BA	PO	A	E	DP	TC/G	FA

Doug Bair

BAIR, CHARLES DOUGLAS
B. Aug. 22, 1949, Defiance, Ohio
BR TR 6′ 180 lbs.

RELIEF PITCHER

Period	W	L	%	ERA	G	GS	CG	IP	H	BB	SO	ShO	W	L	SV	AB	H	HR	BA	PO	A	E	DP	TC/G	FA
April	0	0	—	2.16	8	0	0	8.1	6	5	6	0	0	0	0										
May	0	0	—	27.00	1	0	0	0.2	3	0	0	0	0	0	0										
June	0	0	—	6.75	4	0	0	4	6	5	2	0	0	0	0										
July	—	—	—	—	0	—	—	0	0	0	0	—	0	0	0										
Aug	0	0	—	1.35	4	0	0	6.2	8	0	6	0	0	0	0										
Sept/Oct	0	0	—	9.64	5	0	0	4.2	7	1	5	0	0	0	0										
Day	0	0	—	4.97	10	0	0	12.2	11	5	8	0	0	0	0										
Night	0	0	—	4.63	12	0	0	11.2	19	6	11	0	0	0	0										
vs. Left	—	—						—	16	5	7	—	—	—	—										
vs. Right	—	—						—	14	6	12	—	—	—	—										
On Grass	0	0	—	7.11	9	0	0	6.1	8	5	4	0	0	0	0										
On Turf	0	0	—	4.00	13	0	0	18	22	6	15	0	0	0	0										
Home	0	0	—	2.70	10	0	0	16.2	17	3	15	0	0	0	0										
Road	0	0	—	9.39	12	0	0	7.2	13	8	4	0	0	0	0										
Division Rivals																									
vs. CHI	0	0	—	0.00	3	0	0	3.1	2	0	3	0	0	0	0										
vs. MON	0	0	—	6.75	3	0	0	1.1	3	1	2	0	0	0	0										
vs. NY	0	0	—	5.63	6	0	0	8	7	6	5	0	0	0	0										
vs. PHI	0	0	—	0.00	1	0	0	0	2	2	0	0	0	0	0										
vs. STL	0	0	—	2.08	2	0	0	4.1	7	1	4	0	0	0	0										
1976	PIT N	0	0	—	5.68	4	0	0	6.1	4	5	4	0	0	0	0	0	0	0	—	1	0	0	0	0.3	1.000
1977	OAK A	4	6	.400	3.47	45	0	0	83	78	57	68	0	4	6	8	0	0	0	—	7	14	1	1	0.5	.955
1978	CIN N	7	6	.538	1.98	70	0	0	100	87	38	91	0	7	6	28	14	2	0	.143	11	7	1	1	0.3	.947
1979		11	7	.611	4.31	65	0	0	94	93	51	86	0	11	7	16	8	0	0	.000	5	9	1	1	0.2	.933
1980		3	6	.333	4.24	61	0	0	85	91	39	62	0	3	6	6	2	0	0	.000	3	21	0	1	0.4	1.000
1981	2 teams	CIN N	(24G 2 – 2)		STL N	(11G 2 – 0)																				
"	total	4	2	.667	5.10	35	0	0	54.2	55	19	30	0	4	2	1	6	1	1	.167	2	6	1	0	0.3	.889
1982	STL N	5	3	.625	2.55	63	0	0	91.2	69	36	68	0	5	3	8	13	1	0	.077	9	13	1	1	0.4	.957
1983	2 teams	STL N	(26G 1 – 1)		DET A	(27G 7 – 3)																				
"	total	8	4	.667	3.59	53	1	0	85.1	75	32	60	0	7	4	5	2	0	0	.000	3	10	1	0	0.3	.929
1984	DET A	5	3	.625	3.75	47	1	0	93.2	82	36	57	0	5	2	4	0	0	0	—	12	11	0	2	0.5	1.000
1985	2 teams	DET A	(21G 2 – 0)		STL N	(2G 0 – 0)																				
"	total	2	0	1.000	5.96	23	3	0	51.1	55	27	30	0	1	0	0	0	0	0	—	4	9	0	0	0.6	1.000
1986	OAK A	2	3	.400	3.00	31	0	0	45	37	18	40	0	2	3	4	0	0	0	—	2	7	0	1	0.3	1.000
1987	PHI N	2	0	1.000	5.93	11	0	0	13.2	17	5	10	0	2	0	0	1	0	0	.000	1	2	1	0	0.4	.750
1988	TOR A	0	0	—	4.05	10	0	0	13.1	14	3	8	0	0	0	0	0	0	0	—	2	1	0	0	0.3	1.000
1989	PIT N	2	3	.400	2.27	44	0	0	67.1	52	28	56	0	2	3	1	5	1	0	.200	8	10	1	0	0.4	.947
1990		0	0	—	4.81	22	0	0	24.1	30	11	19	0	0	0	0	1	0	0	.000	2	4	1	1	0.3	.857
15 yrs.		55	43	.561	3.63	584	5	0	908.2	839	405	689	0	53	42	81	52	5	1	.096	72	124	9	9	0.4	.956
LEAGUE CHAMPIONSHIP SERIES																										
1979	CIN N	0	1	.000	9.00	1	0	0	1	2	1	0	0	0	1	0	0	0	0	—	0	1	0	0	1.0	1.000
1982	STL N	0	0	—	0.00	1	0	0	1	2	3	0	0	0	0	0	0	0	0	—	0	1	0	0	1.0	1.000
2 yrs.		0	1	.000	4.50	2	0	0	2	4	4	0	0	0	1	0	0	0	0	—	0	2	0	0	1.0	1.000
WORLD SERIES																										
1982	STL N	0	1	.000	9.00	3	0	0	2	2	2	3	0	0	1	0	0	0	0	—	0	0	0	0	0.0	—
1984	DET A	0	0	—	0.00	1	0	0	0.2	0	0	1	0	0	0	0	0	0	0	—	0	0	0	0	0.0	—
2 yrs.		0	1	.000	6.75	4	0	0	2.2	2	2	4	0	0	1	0	0	0	0	—	0	0	0	0	0.0	—

Jeff Ballard

BALLARD, JEFFREY SCOTT
B. Aug. 13, 1963, Billings, Mont.
BL TL 6′ 3″ 210 lbs.

STARTING PITCHER

Period	W	L	%	ERA	G	GS	CG	IP	H	BB	SO	ShO	W	L	SV	AB	H	HR	BA	PO	A	E	DP	TC/G	FA
April	0	3	.000	3.91	4	4	0	25.1	23	3	7	0	0	0	0										
May	1	2	.333	3.95	5	5	0	27.1	33	13	7	0	0	0	0										
June	0	4	.000	7.34	6	6	0	34.1	49	11	16	0	0	0	0										
July	0	0	—	2.08	10	1	0	13	8	3	5	0	0	0	0										
Aug	0	1	.000	6.52	10	0	0	19.1	25	9	8	0	0	0	0										
Sept/Oct	1	1	.500	3.21	9	1	0	14	14	3	7	0	0	1	0										
Day	2	2	.500	6.00	11	4	0	33	36	10	12	0	0	1	0										
Night	0	9	.000	4.57	33	13	0	100.1	116	32	38	0	0	1	0										
vs. Left	—	—	—	—	—	—	—	—	39	9	23	—	—	—	—										
vs. Right	—	—	—	—	—	—	—	—	113	33	27	—	—	—	—										

Year	Team		W	L	%	ERA	G	GS	CG	IP	H	BB	SO	ShO	RELIEF PITCHING W	L	SV	BATTING AB	H	HR	BA	PO	A	E	DP	TC/G	FA

Jeff Ballard *Continued*

On Grass			2	9	.182	4.94	37	15	0	116.2	133	36	46	0	1	1	0										
On Turf			0	2	.000	4.86	7	2	0	16.2	19	6	4	0	0	0	0										
Home			1	5	.167	4.52	20	8	0	67.2	71	17	29	0	1	1	0										
Road			1	6	.143	5.35	24	9	0	65.2	81	25	21	0	0	0	0										
Division Rivals																											
vs. BOS			0	2	.000	9.64	4	2	0	14	26	8	8	0	0	0	0										
vs. CLE			0	1	.000	9.39	3	1	0	7.2	13	2	3	0	0	0	0										
vs. DET			0	0	—	1.93	3	1	0	9.1	6	2	2	0	0	0	0										
vs. MIL			1	0	1.000	5.63	5	2	0	16	20	3	9	0	0	1	0										
vs. NY			0	2	.000	4.05	3	2	0	13.1	14	3	6	0	0	0	0										
vs. TOR			0	2	.000	6.52	5	1	0	9.2	10	2	3	0	0	1	0										
1987	BAL	A	2	8	.200	6.59	14	14	0	69.2	100	35	27	0	0	0	0	0	0	0	—	5	10	0	1	1.1	1.000
1988			8	12	.400	4.40	25	25	6	153.1	167	42	41	1	0	0	0	0	0	0	—	9	13	0	3	0.9	1.000
1989			18	8	.692	3.43	35	35	4	215.1	240	57	62	1	0	0	0	0	0	0	—	13	55	2	6	2.0	.971
1990			2	11	.154	4.93	44	17	0	133.1	152	42	50	0	1	1	0	0	0	0	—	11	20	1	0	0.7	.969
4 yrs.			30	39	.435	4.42	118	91	10	571.2	659	176	180	2	1	1	0	0	0	0	—	38	98	3	10	1.2	.978

Jay Baller

BALLER, JAY SCOTT
B. Oct. 6, 1960, Stayton, Ore.
BR TR 6' 6" 215 lbs.

1982	PHI	N	0	0	—	3.38	4	1	0	8	7	2	7	0	0	0	0	0	0	0	—	0	1	0	0	0.3	1.000
1985	CHI	N	2	3	.400	3.46	20	4	0	52	52	17	31	0	2	0	1	8	0	0	.000	4	6	0	0	0.5	1.000
1986			2	4	.333	5.37	36	0	0	53.2	58	28	42	0	2	4	5	5	0	0	.000	2	4	0	0	0.2	1.000
1987			0	1	.000	6.75	23	0	0	29.1	38	20	27	0	0	1	0	1	1	0	1.000	0	3	1	0	0.2	.750
1990	KC	A	0	1	.000	15.43	3	0	0	2.1	4	2	1	0	0	1	0	0	0	0	—	0	0	0	0	0.0	—
5 yrs.			4	9	.308	5.02	86	5	0	145.1	159	69	108	0	4	6	6	14	1	0	.071	6	14	1	0	0.2	.952

Scott Bankhead

BANKHEAD, MICHAEL SCOTT
B. July 31, 1963, Raleigh, N.C.
BR TR 5' 10" 175 lbs.

1986	KC	A	8	9	.471	4.61	24	17	0	121	121	37	94	0	2	1	0	0	0	0	—	11	12	1	0	1.0	.958
1987	SEA	A	9	8	.529	5.42	27	25	2	149.1	168	37	95	0	0	0	0	0	0	0	—	9	9	0	1	0.7	1.000
1988			7	9	.438	3.07	21	21	2	135	115	38	102	1	0	0	0	0	0	0	—	7	11	0	0	1.0	1.000
1989			14	6	.700	3.34	33	33	3	210.1	187	63	140	2	0	0	0	0	0	0	—	14	19	0	2	1.0	1.000
1990			0	2	.000	11.08	4	4	0	13	18	7	10	0	0	0	0	0	0	0	—	0	0	0	0	0.0	—
5 yrs.			38	34	.528	4.18	109	100	7	628.2	609	182	441	3	2	1	0	0	0	0	—	41	51	1	3	0.9	.989

John Barfield

BARFIELD, JOHN DAVID
B. Oct. 15, 1964, Pine Bluff, Ark.
BL TL 6' 1" 185 lbs.

April			—	—	—	—	0	—	—	0	0	0	0		0	0	0										
May			—	—	—	—	0	—	—	0	0	0	0		0	0	0										
June			1	0	1.000	4.91	3	0	0	7.1	12	1	4	0	1	0	0										
July			0	0	—	3.38	9	0	0	8	5	4	4	0	0	0	1										
Aug			2	2	.500	4.91	11	0	0	22	19	7	8	0	2	2	0										
Sept/Oct			1	1	.500	5.14	10	0	0	7	6	1	1	0	1	1	0										
Day			0	0	—	1.69	6	0	0	5.1	6	2	2	0	0	0	1										
Night			4	3	.571	5.08	27	0	0	39	36	11	15	0	4	3	0										
vs. Left			—	—	—	—	—	—	—	—	15	4	4	—	—	—	—										
vs. Right			—	—	—	—	—	—	—	—	27	9	13	—	—	—	—										
On Grass			3	3	.500	5.94	27	0	0	33.1	37	12	14	0	3	3	0										
On Turf			1	0	1.000	0.82	6	0	0	11	5	1	3	0	1	0	1										
Home			2	0	1.000	4.82	14	0	0	18.2	19	6	4	0	2	0	0										
Road			2	3	.400	4.56	19	0	0	25.2	23	7	13	0	2	3	1										
Division Rivals																											
vs. CAL			0	2	.000	18.90	4	0	0	3.1	7	3	1	0	0	2	0										
vs. CHI			1	0	1.000	1.13	3	0	0	8	1	2	4	0	1	0	0										
vs. KC			0	0	—	1.50	1	0	0	6	4	1	2	0	0	0	0										
vs. MIN			1	0	1.000	3.86	3	0	0	4.2	6	0	1	0	1	0	0										
vs. OAK			0	0	—	0.00	2	0	0	0.1	1	0	0	0	0	0	0										
vs. SEA			1	0	1.000	4.32	4	0	0	8.1	10	2	1	0	1	0	0										

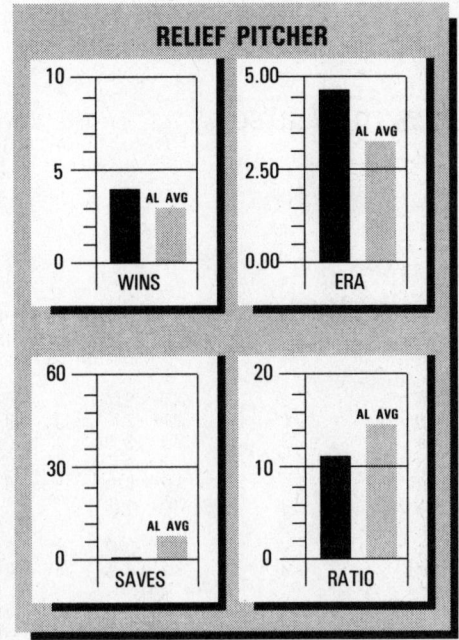

STARTING PITCHER

SO/9 — AL AVG

RATIO — AL AVG

RELIEF PITCHER

WINS — AL AVG

ERA — AL AVG

SAVES — AL AVG

RATIO — AL AVG

Year	Team	W	L	%	ERA	G	GS	CG	IP	H	BB	SO	ShO	RELIEF PITCHING W	L	SV	BATTING AB	H	HR	BA	PO	A	E	DP	TC/G	FA

John Barfield *Continued*

Year	Team	W	L	%	ERA	G	GS	CG	IP	H	BB	SO	ShO	W	L	SV	AB	H	HR	BA	PO	A	E	DP	TC/G	FA
1989	TEX A	0	1	.000	6.17	4	2	0	11.2	15	4	9	0	0	0	0	0	0	0	—	1	1	0	0	0.5	1.000
1990		4	3	.571	4.67	33	0	0	44.1	42	13	17	0	4	3	1	0	0	0	—	4	7	0	0	0.3	1.000
2 yrs.		4	4	.500	4.98	37	2	0	56	57	17	26	0	4	3	1	0	0	0	—	5	8	0	0	0.4	1.000

Brian Barnes

BARNES, BRIAN KEITH
B. Mar. 25, 1967, Roanoke Rapids, N. C.
BL TL 5′ 9″ 170 lbs.

Year	Team	W	L	%	ERA	G	GS	CG	IP	H	BB	SO	ShO	W	L	SV	AB	H	HR	BA	PO	A	E	DP	TC/G	FA
1990	MON N	1	1	.500	2.89	4	4	1	28	25	7	23	0	0	0	0	9	0	0	.000	4	3	1	0	2.0	.875

Jose Bautista

BAUTISTA, JOSE JOAQUIN
Born Jose Joaquin Bautista y Arias.
B. July 25, 1964, Bani, Dominican Republic
BR TR 6′ 1″ 177 lbs.

Period	Team	W	L	%	ERA	G	GS	CG	IP	H	BB	SO	ShO	W	L	SV	AB	H	HR	BA	PO	A	E	DP	TC/G	FA
April		0	0	—	2.08	4	0	0	4.1	5	1	3	0	0	0	0										
May		—	—	—	—	0	—	—	0	0	0	0	—	0	0	0										
June		0	0	—	3.38	3	0	0	5.1	7	3	7	0	0	0	0										
July		—	—	—	—	0	—	—	0	0	0	0	—	0	0	0										
Aug		0	0	—	4.76	5	0	0	11.1	9	1	3	0	0	0	0										
Sept/Oct		1	0	1.000	4.76	10	0	0	5.2	7	2	2	0	1	0	0										
Day		0	0	—	5.56	8	0	0	11.1	11	1	7	0	0	0	0										
Night		1	0	1.000	2.93	14	0	0	15.1	17	6	8	0	1	0	0										
vs. Left		—	—	—	—				—	15	3	1	—	—	—	—										
vs. Right		—	—	—	—				—	13	4	14	—	—	—	—										
On Grass		1	0	1.000	4.44	20	0	0	24.1	25	6	14	0	1	0	0										
On Turf		0	0	—	0.00	2	0	0	2.1	3	1	1	0	0	0	0										
Home		0	0	—	3.18	13	0	0	17	19	3	10	0	0	0	0										
Road		1	0	1.000	5.59	9	0	0	9.2	9	4	5	0	1	0	0										
Division Rivals																										
vs. BOS		0	0	—	3.86	2	0	0	4.2	4	1	2	0	0	0	0										
vs. CLE		0	0	—	7.04	3	0	0	7.2	8	0	0	0	0	0	0										
vs. DET		0	0	—	3.86	3	0	0	2.1	3	0	2	0	0	0	0										
vs. MIL		0	0	—	4.15	4	0	0	4.1	7	2	4	0	0	0	0										
vs. NY		1	0	1.000	2.25	5	0	0	4	1	3	4	0	1	0	0										
vs. TOR		0	0	—	0.00	1	0	0	0.1	1	0	0	0	0	0	0										

RELIEF PITCHER
(WINS, ERA, SAVES, RATIO charts with AL AVG)

Year	Team	W	L	%	ERA	G	GS	CG	IP	H	BB	SO	ShO	W	L	SV	AB	H	HR	BA	PO	A	E	DP	TC/G	FA
1988	BAL A	6	15	.286	4.30	33	25	3	171.2	171	45	76	0	0	1	0	0	0	0	—	27	11	1	3	1.2	.974
1989		3	4	.429	5.31	15	10	0	78	84	15	30	0	0	0	0	0	0	0	—	3	10	1	0	0.9	.929
1990		1	0	1.000	4.05	22	0	0	26.2	28	7	15	0	1	0	0	0	0	0	—	1	2	0	0	0.1	1.000
3 yrs.		10	19	.345	4.56	70	35	3	276.1	283	67	121	0	1	1	0	0	0	0	—	31	23	2	3	0.8	.964

Kevin Bearse

BEARSE, KEVIN GERARD
B. Nov. 7, 1965, Jersey City, N. J.
BL TL 6′ 2″ 195 lbs.

Year	Team	W	L	%	ERA	G	GS	CG	IP	H	BB	SO	ShO	W	L	SV	AB	H	HR	BA	PO	A	E	DP	TC/G	FA
1990	CLE A	0	2	.000	12.91	3	3	0	7.2	16	5	2	0	0	0	0	0	0	0	—	0	1	0	0	0.3	1.000

Steve Bedrosian

BEDROSIAN, STEPHEN WAYNE (Bedrock)
B. Dec. 6, 1957, Methuen, Mass.
BR TR 6′ 3″ 200 lbs.

Period	Team	W	L	%	ERA	G	GS	CG	IP	H	BB	SO	ShO	W	L	SV	AB	H	HR	BA	PO	A	E	DP	TC/G	FA
April		0	2	.000	9.00	6	0	0	8	10	5	4	0	0	2	3										
May		0	1	.000	2.77	13	0	0	13	9	8	5	0	0	1	4										
June		3	2	.600	3.50	14	0	0	18	16	6	16	0	3	2	0										
July		2	1	.667	4.15	11	0	0	13	12	11	7	0	2	1	0										
Aug		1	2	.333	6.00	13	0	0	15	18	9	4	0	1	2	3										
Sept/Oct		3	1	.750	1.46	11	0	0	12.1	7	5	7	0	3	1	7										
Day		6	3	.667	3.92	33	0	0	39	40	15	24	0	6	3	6										
Night		3	6	.333	4.46	35	0	0	40.1	32	29	19	0	3	6	11										
vs. Left		—	—	—	—	—	—	—	—	44	26	23	—	—	—	—										
vs. Right		—	—	—	—	—	—	—	—	28	18	20	—	—	—	—										

RELIEF PITCHER
(WINS, ERA charts with NL AVG)

Year	Team	W	L	%	ERA	G	GS	CG	IP	H	BB	SO	ShO	RELIEF PITCHING W	L	SV	BATTING AB	H	HR	BA	PO	A	E	DP	TC/G	FA

Steve Bedrosian *Continued*

Year	Team	W	L	%	ERA	G	GS	CG	IP	H	BB	SO	ShO	W	L	SV	AB	H	HR	BA	PO	A	E	DP	TC/G	FA
On Grass		8	5	.615	3.13	49	0	0	60.1	48	23	35	0	8	5	15										
On Turf		1	4	.200	7.58	19	0	0	19	24	21	8	0	1	4	2										
Home		8	4	.667	3.54	37	0	0	48.1	40	19	28	0	8	4	11										
Road		1	5	.167	5.23	31	0	0	31	32	25	15	0	1	5	6										
Division Rivals																										
vs. ATL		3	0	1.000	0.00	6	0	0	8.1	5	1	6	0	3	0	1										
vs. CIN		1	0	1.000	2.31	9	0	0	11.2	7	3	8	0	1	0	2										
vs. HOU		3	3	.500	12.00	9	0	0	9	12	14	4	0	3	3	0										
vs. LA		0	0	—	7.11	4	0	0	6.1	9	1	3	0	0	0	1										
vs. SD		0	2	.000	3.00	9	0	0	9	9	1	6	0	0	2	5										
1981	ATL N	1	2	.333	4.50	15	1	0	24	15	15	9	0	1	1	0	2	0	0	.000	1	2	0	1	0.2	1.000
1982		8	6	.571	2.42	64	3	0	137.2	102	57	123	0	7	4	11	26	1	0	.038	12	14	1	2	0.4	.963
1983		9	10	.474	3.60	70	1	0	120	100	51	114	0	9	10	19	19	2	0	.105	4	16	0	2	0.3	1.000
1984		9	6	.600	2.37	40	4	0	83.2	65	33	81	0	6	5	11	17	2	0	.118	1	8	1	0	0.3	.900
1985		7	15	.318	3.83	37	37	0	206.2	198	111	134	0	0	0	0	64	5	0	.078	13	23	4	3	1.1	.900
1986	PHI N	8	6	.571	3.39	68	0	0	90.1	79	34	82	0	8	6	29	5	1	0	.200	2	10	0	1	0.2	1.000
1987		5	3	.625	2.83	65	0	0	89	79	28	74	0	5	3	**40**	4	0	0	.000	3	7	0	0	0.2	1.000
1988		6	6	.500	3.75	57	0	0	74.1	75	27	61	0	6	6	28	2	0	0	.000	5	9	0	0	0.2	1.000
1989	2 teams	PHI N (28G 2–3)				SF N (40G 1–4)																				
"	total	3	7	.300	2.87	68	0	0	84.2	56	39	58	0	3	7	23	6	1	0	.167	2	5	1	1	0.1	.875
1990	SF N	9	9	.500	4.20	68	0	0	79.1	72	44	43	0	9	**9**	17	4	2	0	.500	9	11	1	1	0.3	.952
10 yrs.		65	70	.481	3.31	552	46	0	989.2	841	439	779	0	54	51	178	149	14	0	.094	52	105	8	11	0.3	.952

LEAGUE CHAMPIONSHIP SERIES

Year	Team	W	L	%	ERA	G	GS	CG	IP	H	BB	SO	ShO	W	L	SV	AB	H	HR	BA	PO	A	E	DP	TC/G	FA
1982	ATL N	0	0	—	18.00	2	0	0	1	3	1	2	0	0	0	0	0	0	0	—	0	0	0	0	0.0	—
1989	SF N	0	0	—	2.70	4	0	0	3.1	4	2	2	0	0	0	3	0	0	0	—	0	0	0	0	0.0	—
2 yrs.		0	0	—	6.23	6	0	0	4.1	7	3	4	0	0	0	3	0	0	0	—	0	0	0	0	0.0	—

WORLD SERIES

Year	Team	W	L	%	ERA	G	GS	CG	IP	H	BB	SO	ShO	W	L	SV	AB	H	HR	BA	PO	A	E	DP	TC/G	FA
1989	SF N	0	0	—	0.00	2	0	0	2.2	0	2	2	0	0	0	0	0	0	0	—	0	0	0	0	0.0	—

Tim Belcher

BELCHER, TIMOTHY WAYNE
B. Oct. 19, 1961, Mount Gilead, Ohio
BR TR 6′ 3″ 210 lbs.

Year	Team	W	L	%	ERA	G	GS	CG	IP	H	BB	SO	ShO	W	L	SV	AB	H	HR	BA	PO	A	E	DP	TC/G	FA
April		1	2	.333	4.45	4	4	1	28.1	26	5	20	1	0	0	0										
May		3	1	.750	2.50	5	5	1	36	27	9	27	0	0	0	0										
June		1	3	.250	6.12	6	6	0	32.1	39	12	23	0	0	0	0										
July		4	2	.667	2.05	6	6	3	44	28	16	21	1	0	0	0										
Aug		0	1	.000	8.76	3	3	0	12.1	16	6	11	0	0	0	0										
Sept/Oct		—	—	—	—	0	—	—	0	0	0	0	0	0	0	0										
Day		1	2	.333	5.17	6	6	0	31.1	35	10	23	0	0	0	0										
Night		8	7	.533	3.70	18	18	5	121.2	101	38	79	2	0	0	0										
vs. Left		—	—	—	—	—	—	—	—	68	31	55	—	—	—	—										
vs. Right		—	—	—	—	—	—	—	—	68	17	47	—	—	—	—										
On Grass		8	6	.571	3.62	18	18	4	117	111	36	70	1	0	0	0										
On Turf		1	3	.250	5.25	6	6	1	36	25	12	32	1	0	0	0										
Home		6	3	.667	2.77	10	10	3	74.2	62	22	45	0	0	0	0										
Road		3	6	.333	5.17	14	14	2	78.1	74	26	57	2	0	0	0										
Division Rivals																										
vs. ATL		1	1	.500	3.71	3	3	0	17	13	11	12	0	0	0	0										
vs. CIN		0	2	.000	5.82	3	3	0	17	16	5	11	0	0	0	0										
vs. HOU		1	2	.333	4.97	4	4	0	25.1	24	7	23	0	0	0	0										
vs. SD		1	0	1.000	3.21	2	2	1	14	13	1	5	1	0	0	0										
vs. SF		0	0	—	36.00	1	1	0	1	4	3	1	0	0	0	0										
1987	LA N	4	2	.667	2.38	6	5	0	34	30	7	23	0	1	0	0	10	2	0	.200	1	5	0	0	1.0	1.000
1988		12	6	.667	2.91	36	27	4	179.2	143	51	152	1	1	0	4	56	4	1	.071	14	19	0	2	0.9	1.000
1989		15	12	.556	2.82	39	30	**10**	230	182	80	200	8	1	2	1	70	7	0	.100	21	18	3	3	1.1	.929
1990		9	9	.500	4.00	24	24	5	153	136	48	102	2	0	0	0	43	7	0	.163	11	11	0	1	0.9	1.000
4 yrs.		40	29	.580	3.12	105	86	19	596.2	491	186	477	11	3	2	5	179	20	1	.112	47	53	3	6	1.0	.971

LEAGUE CHAMPIONSHIP SERIES

Year	Team	W	L	%	ERA	G	GS	CG	IP	H	BB	SO	ShO	W	L	SV	AB	H	HR	BA	PO	A	E	DP	TC/G	FA
1988	LA N	2	0	1.000	4.11	2	2	0	15.1	12	4	16	0	0	0	0	8	1	0	.125	1	0	0	0	0.5	1.000

WORLD SERIES

Year	Team	W	L	%	ERA	G	GS	CG	IP	H	BB	SO	ShO	W	L	SV	AB	H	HR	BA	PO	A	E	DP	TC/G	FA
1988	LA N	1	0	1.000	6.23	2	2	0	8.2	10	6	10	0	0	0	0	0	0	0	—	0	0	0	0	0.0	—

Year	Team	W	L	%	ERA	G	GS	CG	IP	H	BB	SO	ShO	W	L	SV	AB	H	HR	BA	PO	A	E	DP	TC/G	FA
														RELIEF PITCHING			**BATTING**									

Stan Belinda

BELINDA, STANLEY PETER
B. Aug. 6, 1966, Huntingdon, Pa.
BR TR 6′ 3″ 185 lbs.

Year	Team	W	L	%	ERA	G	GS	CG	IP	H	BB	SO	ShO	W	L	SV	AB	H	HR	BA	PO	A	E	DP	TC/G	FA
April		—	—	—	—	0	—	—	0	0	0	0	—	0	0	0										
May		0	0	—	3.38	5	0	0	5.1	2	1	5	0	0	0	0										
June		2	2	.500	2.70	13	0	0	13.1	10	10	12	0	2	2	3										
July		0	1	.000	3.38	13	0	0	13.1	10	6	12	0	0	1	2										
Aug		0	1	.000	5.50	16	0	0	18	21	7	17	0	0	1	2										
Sept/Oct		1	0	1.000	1.08	8	0	0	8.1	5	5	9	0	1	0	1										
Day		0	1	.000	5.28	14	0	0	15.1	15	11	12	0	0	1	3										
Night		3	3	.500	2.93	41	0	0	43	33	18	43	0	3	3	5										
vs. Left		—	—	—	—	—	—	—	—	16	13	22	—	—	—	—										
vs. Right		—	—	—	—	—	—	—	—	32	16	33	—	—	—	—										
On Grass		0	0	—	0.64	11	0	0	14	3	6	12	0	0	0	1										
On Turf		3	4	.429	4.47	44	0	0	44.1	45	23	43	0	3	4	7										
Home		1	2	.333	4.97	26	0	0	25.1	30	18	21	0	1	2	2										
Road		2	2	.500	2.45	29	0	0	33	18	11	34	0	2	2	6										
Division Rivals																										
vs. CHI		1	0	1.000	1.35	4	0	0	6.2	3	3	7	0	1	0	0										
vs. MON		0	3	.000	7.00	10	0	0	9	8	6	11	0	0	3	2										
vs. NY		0	0	—	2.45	4	0	0	3.2	2	4	1	0	0	0	0										
vs. PHI		1	0	1.000	1.69	6	0	0	5.1	3	3	8	0	1	0	1										
vs. STL		1	0	1.000	1.80	6	0	0	5	6	6	5	0	1	0	1										
1989	PIT N	0	1	.000	6.10	8	0	0	10.1	13	2	10	0	0	1	0	0	0	0	—	0	0	0	0	0.0	—
1990		3	4	.429	3.55	55	0	0	58.1	48	29	55	0	3	4	8	5	0	0	.000	2	4	0	0	0.1	1.000
2 yrs.		3	5	.375	3.93	63	0	0	68.2	61	31	65	0	3	5	8	5	0	0	.000	2	4	0	0	0.1	1.000

LEAGUE CHAMPIONSHIP SERIES

Year	Team	W	L	%	ERA	G	GS	CG	IP	H	BB	SO	ShO	W	L	SV	AB	H	HR	BA	PO	A	E	DP	TC/G	FA
1990	PIT N	0	0	—	2.45	3	0	0	3.2	3	0	4	0	0	0	0	0	0	0	—	0	0	0	0	0.0	—

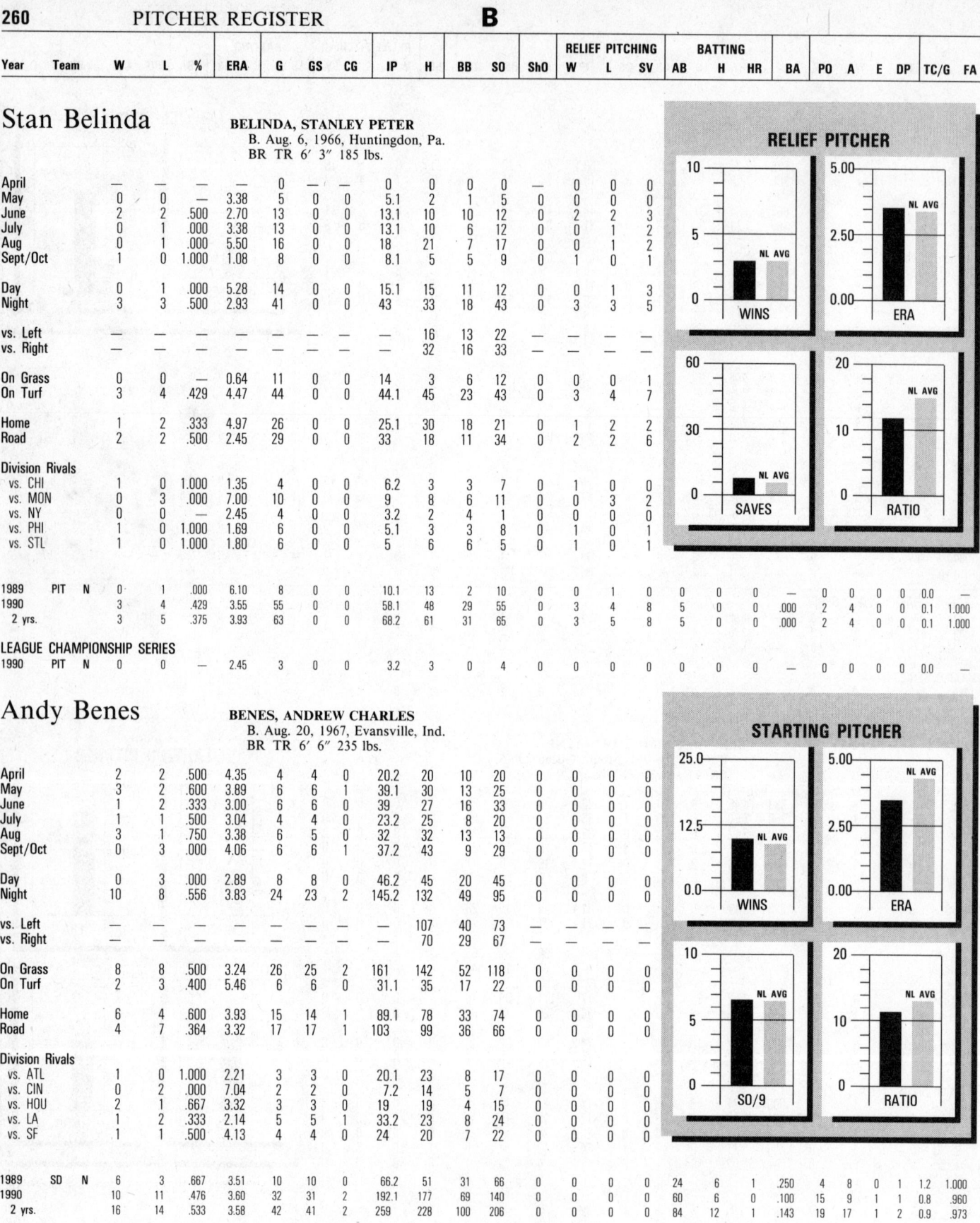

RELIEF PITCHER

Andy Benes

BENES, ANDREW CHARLES
B. Aug. 20, 1967, Evansville, Ind.
BR TR 6′ 6″ 235 lbs.

Year	Team	W	L	%	ERA	G	GS	CG	IP	H	BB	SO	ShO	W	L	SV	AB	H	HR	BA	PO	A	E	DP	TC/G	FA
April		2	2	.500	4.35	4	4	0	20.2	20	10	20	0	0	0	0										
May		3	2	.600	3.89	6	6	1	39.1	30	13	25	0	0	0	0										
June		1	2	.333	3.00	6	6	0	39	27	16	33	0	0	0	0										
July		1	1	.500	3.04	4	4	0	23.2	25	8	20	0	0	0	0										
Aug		3	1	.750	3.38	6	5	0	32	32	13	13	0	0	0	0										
Sept/Oct		0	3	.000	4.06	6	6	1	37.2	43	9	29	0	0	0	0										
Day		0	3	.000	2.89	8	8	0	46.2	45	20	45	0	0	0	0										
Night		10	8	.556	3.83	24	23	2	145.2	132	49	95	0	0	0	0										
vs. Left		—	—	—	—	—	—	—	—	107	40	73	—	—	—	—										
vs. Right		—	—	—	—	—	—	—	—	70	29	67	—	—	—	—										
On Grass		8	8	.500	3.24	26	25	2	161	142	52	118	0	0	0	0										
On Turf		2	3	.400	5.46	6	6	0	31.1	35	17	22	0	0	0	0										
Home		6	4	.600	3.93	15	14	1	89.1	78	33	74	0	0	0	0										
Road		4	7	.364	3.32	17	17	1	103	99	36	66	0	0	0	0										
Division Rivals																										
vs. ATL		1	0	1.000	2.21	3	3	0	20.1	23	8	17	0	0	0	0										
vs. CIN		0	2	.000	7.04	2	2	0	7.2	14	5	7	0	0	0	0										
vs. HOU		2	1	.667	3.32	3	3	0	19	19	4	15	0	0	0	0										
vs. LA		1	2	.333	2.14	5	5	1	33.2	18	8	24	0	0	0	0										
vs. SF		1	1	.500	4.13	4	4	0	24	20	7	22	0	0	0	0										
1989	SD N	6	3	.667	3.51	10	10	0	66.2	51	31	66	0	0	0	0	24	6	1	.250	4	8	0	1	1.2	1.000
1990		10	11	.476	3.60	32	31	2	192.1	177	69	140	0	0	0	0	60	6	0	.100	15	9	1	1	0.8	.960
2 yrs.		16	14	.533	3.58	42	41	2	259	228	100	206	0	0	0	0	84	12	1	.143	19	17	1	2	0.9	.973

STARTING PITCHER

Year	Team	W	L	%	ERA	G	GS	CG	IP	H	BB	SO	ShO	RELIEF PITCHING W	L	SV	BATTING AB	H	HR	BA	PO	A	E	DP	TC/G	FA

Juan Berenguer

BERENGUER, JUAN BAUTISTA
B. Nov. 30, 1954, Aguadulce, Panama
BR TR 5' 11" 186 lbs.

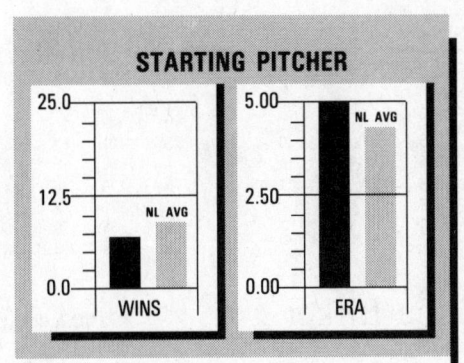

RELIEF PITCHER

April		1	0	1.000	6.10	5	0	0	10.1	9	10	8	0	1	0	0										
May		3	0	1.000	3.57	9	0	0	17.2	16	8	12	0	3	0	0										
June		1	1	.500	3.79	10	0	0	19	18	15	15	0	1	1	0										
July		2	2	.500	2.60	10	0	0	17.1	18	7	16	0	2	2	0										
Aug		0	0	—	1.96	9	0	0	18.1	12	9	8	0	0	0	0										
Sept/Oct		1	2	.333	3.57	8	0	0	17.2	12	9	18	0	1	2	0										
Day		2	1	.667	2.30	15	0	0	31.1	24	22	24	0	2	1	0										
Night		6	4	.600	3.91	36	0	0	69	61	36	53	0	6	4	0										
vs. Left		—	—	—	—	—	—	—	—	42	23	34	—	—	—	—										
vs. Right		—	—	—	—	—	—	—	—	43	35	43	—	—	—	—										
On Grass		3	3	.500	4.42	21	0	0	38.2	33	21	30	0	3	3	0										
On Turf		5	2	.714	2.77	30	0	0	61.2	52	37	47	0	5	2	0										
Home		4	2	.667	3.54	24	0	0	48.1	46	34	37	0	4	2	0										
Road		4	3	.571	3.29	27	0	0	52	39	24	40	0	4	3	0										
Division Rivals																										
vs. CAL		0	0	—	3.38	4	0	0	8	6	7	6	0	0	0	0										
vs. CHI		0	1	.000	1.08	6	0	0	8.1	2	1	7	0	0	1	0										
vs. KC		0	0	—	2.08	3	0	0	8.2	5	4	8	0	0	0	0										
vs. OAK		1	1	.500	3.27	5	0	0	11	6	8	14	0	1	1	0										
vs. SEA		1	0	1.000	1.29	4	0	0	7	4	2	4	0	1	0	0										
vs. TEX		1	1	.500	2.84	5	0	0	12.2	12	8	6	0	1	1	0										
1978	NY N	0	2	.000	8.31	5	3	0	13	17	11	8	0	0	0	0	3	0	0	.000	0	2	0	0	0.4	1.000
1979		1	1	.500	2.90	5	5	0	31	28	12	25	0	0	0	0	7	1	0	.143	0	1	1	0	0.4	.500
1980		0	1	.000	6.00	6	0	0	9	9	10	7	0	0	1	0	0	0	0	—	0	2	0	0	0.3	1.000
1981	2 teams	KC A (8G 0 - 4)							TOR A (12G 2 - 9)																	
"	total	2	13	.133	5.24	20	14	1	91	84	51	49	0	0	2	0	0	0	0	—	1	9	0	0	0.5	1.000
1982	DET A	0	0	—	6.75	2	1	0	6.2	5	9	8	0	0	0	0	0	0	0	—	0	0	0	0	0.0	—
1983		9	5	.643	3.14	37	19	2	157.2	110	71	129	1	2	0	1	0	0	0	—	10	11	3	1	0.6	.875
1984		11	10	.524	3.48	31	27	2	168.1	146	79	118	1	0	0	0	0	0	0	—	11	15	2	0	0.9	.929
1985		5	6	.455	5.59	31	13	0	95	96	48	82	0	1	1	0	0	0	0	—	11	12	2	1	0.8	.920
1986	SF N	2	3	.400	2.70	46	4	0	73.1	64	44	72	0	2	2	4	7	1	0	.143	2	7	1	0	0.2	.900
1987	MIN A	8	1	.889	3.94	47	6	0	112	100	47	110	0	6	1	4	0	0	0	—	5	7	1	0	0.3	.923
1988		8	4	.667	3.96	57	1	0	100	74	61	99	0	8	4	2	0	0	0	—	7	10	0	1	0.3	1.000
1989		9	3	.750	3.48	56	0	0	106	96	47	93	0	9	3	3	0	0	0	—	2	11	0	1	0.2	1.000
1990		8	5	.615	3.41	51	0	0	100.1	85	58	77	0	8	5	0	0	0	0	—	3	5	0	0	0.2	1.000
13 yrs.		63	54	.538	3.88	394	93	5	1063.1	914	548	877	2	36	19	14	17	2	0	.118	52	92	10	4	0.4	.935

LEAGUE CHAMPIONSHIP SERIES

Year	Team	W	L	%	ERA	G	GS	CG	IP	H	BB	SO	ShO	W	L	SV	AB	H	HR	BA	PO	A	E	DP	TC/G	FA
1987	MIN A	0	0	—	1.50	4	0	0	6	1	3	6	0	0	0	1	0	0	0	—	0	0	0	0	0.0	—

WORLD SERIES

Year	Team	W	L	%	ERA	G	GS	CG	IP	H	BB	SO	ShO	W	L	SV	AB	H	HR	BA	PO	A	E	DP	TC/G	FA
1987	MIN A	0	1	.000	10.38	3	0	0	4.1	10	0	1	0	0	1	0	0	0	0	—	0	0	0	0	0.0	—

Mike Bielecki

BIELECKI, MICHAEL JOSEPH
B. July 31, 1959, Baltimore, Md.
BR TR 6' 3" 195 lbs.

STARTING PITCHER

April		0	2	.000	4.09	4	4	0	22	22	9	10	0	0	0	0										
May		3	1	.750	3.44	6	6	0	36.2	42	15	22	0	0	0	0										
June		0	4	.000	8.07	6	6	0	29	38	16	21	0	0	0	0										
July		1	1	.500	8.14	7	3	0	21	29	5	10	0	1	0	0										
Aug		2	1	.667	4.76	6	6	0	28.1	27	12	20	0	0	0	0										
Sept/Oct		2	2	.500	2.32	7	4	0	31	30	13	20	0	0	0	1										
Day		2	5	.286	5.04	16	11	0	69.2	73	26	52	0	1	0	1										
Night		6	6	.500	4.85	20	18	0	98.1	115	44	51	0	0	0	0										
vs. Left		—	—	—	—	—	—	—	—	109	45	62	—	—	—	—										
vs. Right		—	—	—	—	—	—	—	—	79	25	41	—	—	—	—										

Mike Bielecki *Continued*

Year	Team	W	L	%	ERA	G	GS	CG	IP	H	BB	SO	ShO	W	L	SV	AB	H	HR	BA	PO	A	E	DP	TC/G	FA
On Grass		4	9	.308	5.33	24	19	0	103	115	47	68	0	1	0	0										
On Turf		4	2	.667	4.29	12	10	0	65	73	23	35	0	0	0	1										
Home		2	7	.222	4.88	18	13	0	75.2	77	31	54	0	1	0	0										
Road		6	4	.600	4.97	18	16	0	92.1	111	39	49	0	0	0	1										
Division Rivals																										
vs. MON		1	0	1.000	2.45	4	3	0	18.1	16	8	15	0	0	0	0										
vs. NY		0	1	.000	37.80	2	2	0	1.2	8	4	2	0	0	0	0										
vs. PHI		1	2	.333	3.91	4	4	0	25.1	24	12	11	0	0	0	0										
vs. PIT		0	2	.000	4.95	5	3	0	20	22	6	14	0	0	0	0										
vs. STL		0	2	.000	7.15	6	4	0	22.2	30	11	12	0	0	0	1										
1984	PIT N	0	0	—	0.00	4	0	0	4.1	4	0	1	0	0	0	0	0	0	0	—	0	1	0	0	0.3	1.000
1985		2	3	.400	4.53	12	7	0	45.2	45	31	22	0	0	0	0	10	0	0	.000	5	11	0	1	1.3	1.000
1986		6	11	.353	4.66	31	27	0	148.2	149	83	83	0	0	0	0	48	3	0	.063	17	16	1	1	1.3	.971
1987		2	3	.400	4.73	8	8	2	45.2	43	12	25	0	0	0	0	16	1	0	.063	6	5	1	0	1.1	.917
1988	CHI N	2	2	.500	3.35	19	5	0	48.1	55	16	33	0	1	0	0	10	1	0	.100	4	5	0	0	0.5	1.000
1989		18	7	.720	3.14	33	33	4	212.1	187	81	147	3	0	0	0	70	3	0	.043	18	21	1	0	1.2	.975
1990		8	11	.421	4.93	36	29	0	168	188	70	103	0	1	0	1	43	7	0	.163	17	33	3	2	1.5	.943
7 yrs.		38	37	.507	4.12	143	109	6	673	671	293	414	3	2	0	1	197	15	0	.076	67	92	6	3	1.2	.964
LEAGUE CHAMPIONSHIP SERIES																										
1989	CHI N	0	1	.000	3.65	2	2	0	12.1	7	6	11	0	0	0	0	5	1	0	.200	1	2	0	0	1.5	1.000

STARTING PITCHER — SO/9, RATIO (NL AVG)

Tim Birtsas

BIRTSAS, TIMOTHY DEAN
B. Sept. 5, 1960, Pontiac, Mich.
BL TL 6' 7" 240 lbs.

Year	Team	W	L	%	ERA	G	GS	CG	IP	H	BB	SO	ShO	W	L	SV	AB	H	HR	BA	PO	A	E	DP	TC/G	FA
April		1	0	1.000	0.00	4	0	0	6	5	4	4	0	1	0	0										
May		0	2	.000	4.41	9	0	0	16.1	25	6	11	0	0	2	0										
June		0	0	—	4.35	6	0	0	10.1	11	4	12	0	0	0	0										
July		0	0	—	5.14	6	0	0	14	21	8	10	0	0	0	0										
Aug		—	—		0	0	0		0	0	0	0	0	0	0	0										
Sept/Oct		0	1	.000	1.93	4	0	0	4.2	7	2	4	0	1	0	1										
Day		1	3	.250	3.07	10	0	0	14.2	15	7	11	0	1	3	0										
Night		0	0	—	4.17	19	0	0	36.2	54	17	30	0	0	0	0										
vs. Left		—	—	—					—	22	6	19	—	—	—	—										
vs. Right		—	—	—					—	47	18	22	—	—	—	—										
On Grass		1	0	1.000	4.91	9	0	0	14.2	21	10	15	0	1	0	0										
On Turf		0	3	.000	3.44	20	0	0	36.2	48	14	26	0	0	3	0										
Home		0	2	.000	3.76	14	0	0	26.1	34	11	20	0	0	2	0										
Road		1	1	.500	3.96	15	0	0	25	35	13	21	0	1	1	0										
Division Rivals																										
vs. ATL		1	0	1.000	5.14	4	0	0	7	9	3	7	0	1	0	0										
vs. HOU		0	1	.000	6.75	2	0	0	1.1	1	1	1	0	0	1	0										
vs. LA		0	0	—	0.00	1	0	0	2	3	1	1	0	0	0	0										
vs. SD		0	0	—	6.43	3	0	0	7	13	5	6	0	0	0	0										
vs. SF		0	0	—	2.08	3	0	0	4.1	4	1	7	0	0	0	0										
1985	OAK A	10	6	.625	4.01	29	25	2	141.1	124	91	94	0	0	0	0	0	0	0	—	0	11	1	1	0.4	.917
1986		0	0	—	22.50	2	0	0	2	2	4	1	0	0	0	0	0	0	0	—	0	0	0	0	0.0	—
1988	CIN N	1	3	.250	4.20	36	4	0	64.1	61	24	38	0	0	0	0	10	0	0	.000	2	8	0	0	0.3	.833
1989		2	2	.500	3.75	42	1	0	69.2	68	27	57	0	2	1	1	4	1	1	.250	0	9	1	0	0.2	.900
1990		1	3	.250	3.86	29	0	0	51.1	69	24	41	0	1	3	0	4	0	0	.000	3	8	0	1	0.4	1.000
5 yrs.		14	14	.500	4.08	138	30	2	328.2	324	170	231	0	4	4	1	18	1	1	.056	5	36	4	1	0.3	.911

RELIEF PITCHER — WINS, ERA, SAVES, RATIO (NL AVG)

Joe Bitker

BITKER, JOSEPH ANTHONY
B. Feb. 12, 1964, Glendale, Calif.
BR TR 6' 1" 175 lbs.

Year	Team	W	L	%	ERA	G	GS	CG	IP	H	BB	SO	ShO	W	L	SV	AB	H	HR	BA	PO	A	E	DP	TC/G	FA
1990	2 teams	OAK A (1G 0-0)			TEX A (5G 0-0)																					
"	total	0	0	—	2.25	6	0	0	12	8	4	8	0	0	0	0	0	0	0	—	1	2	0	1	0.5	1.000

Year	Team	W	L	%	ERA	G	GS	CG	IP	H	BB	SO	ShO	W	L	SV	AB	H	HR	BA	PO	A	E	DP	TC/G	FA
														RELIEF PITCHING			BATTING									

Bud Black

BLACK, HARRY RALSTON
B. June 30, 1957, San Mateo, Calif.
BL TL 6′ 2″ 180 lbs.

Year	Team	W	L	%	ERA	G	GS	CG	IP	H	BB	SO	ShO	W	L	SV	AB	H	HR	BA	PO	A	E	DP	TC/G	FA
April		2	0	1.000	2.73	4	4	0	26.1	21	6	11	0	0	0	0										
May		2	2	.500	1.50	6	6	1	48	36	11	23	1	0	0	0										
June		2	2	.500	6.88	6	6	0	34	38	21	15	0	0	0	0										
July		3	2	.600	2.83	6	6	2	41.1	29	11	22	1	0	0	0										
Aug		1	2	.333	6.52	4	4	0	19.1	28	8	17	0	0	0	0										
Sept/Oct		3	3	.500	3.11	6	5	1	37.2	29	4	18	0	1	0	0										
Day		3	2	.600	2.33	7	7	1	46.1	36	13	26	0	0	0	0										
Night		10	9	.526	3.93	25	24	4	160.1	145	48	80	2	1	0	0										
vs. Left		—	—	—	—	—	—	—	—	39	11	12	—	—	—	—										
vs. Right		—	—	—	—	—	—	—	—	142	50	94	—	—	—	—										
On Grass		11	9	.550	3.73	27	27	4	176.1	161	52	97	2	0	0	0										
On Turf		2	2	.500	2.67	5	4	1	30.1	20	9	9	0	1	0	0										
Home		8	5	.615	3.13	16	15	2	103.2	94	27	53	2	1	0	0										
Road		5	6	.455	4.02	16	16	3	103	87	34	53	0	0	0	0										
Division Rivals																										
vs. BAL		1	0	1.000	2.45	2	2	0	14.2	8	8	8	0	0	0	0										
vs. BOS		0	0	—	16.88	1	1	0	2.2	7	4	2	0	0	0	0										
vs. CLE		—	—	—	—	0	—	0	—	0	0	0	—	0	0	0										
vs. DET		1	1	.500	4.50	2	2	1	16	15	7	4	0	0	0	0										
vs. MIL		1	2	.333	9.37	4	4	0	16.1	19	4	7	0	0	0	0										
vs. NY		2	1	.667	5.71	4	3	0	17.1	18	6	7	0	1	0	0										
1981	SEA A	0	0	—	0.00	2	0	0	1	2	3	0	0	0	0	0	0	0	0	—	0	1	0	0	0.5	1.000
1982	KC A	4	6	.400	4.58	22	14	0	88.1	92	34	40	0	0	0	0	0	0	0	—	6	12	1	1	0.9	.947
1983		10	7	.588	3.79	24	24	3	161.1	159	43	58	0	0	0	0	0	0	0	—	7	32	1	5	1.7	.975
1984		17	12	.586	3.12	35	35	8	257	226	64	140	1	0	0	0	0	0	0	—	13	51	2	2	1.9	.970
1985		10	15	.400	4.33	33	33	5	205.2	216	59	122	2	0	0	0	0	0	0	—	6	30	4	0	1.2	.900
1986		5	10	.333	3.20	56	4	0	121	100	43	68	0	4	7	9	0	0	0	—	3	21	0	1	0.4	1.000
1987		8	6	.571	3.60	29	18	0	122.1	126	35	61	0	1	1	1	0	0	0	—	4	19	0	0	0.8	1.000
1988	2 teams	KC A (17G 2 – 1)					CLE A (16G 2 – 3)																			
"	total	4	4	.500	5.00	33	7	0	81	82	34	63	0	3	2	0	0	0	0	—	5	12	0	0	0.5	1.000
1989	CLE A	12	11	.522	3.36	33	32	6	222.1	213	52	88	3	1	0	0	0	0	0	—	13	33	2	3	1.5	.958
1990	2 teams	CLE A (29G 11 – 10)					TOR A (3G 2 – 1)																			
"	total	13	11	.542	3.57	32	31	5	206.2	181	61	106	2	1	0	0	0	0	0	—	7	33	1	2	1.3	.976
10 yrs.		83	82	.503	3.70	299	198	27	1466.2	1397	428	746	8	10	10	11	0	0	0	—	64	244	11	14	1.1	.966

LEAGUE CHAMPIONSHIP SERIES

Year	Team	W	L	%	ERA	G	GS	CG	IP	H	BB	SO	ShO	W	L	SV	AB	H	HR	BA	PO	A	E	DP	TC/G	FA
1984	KC A	0	1	.000	7.20	1	1	0	5	7	1	3	0	0	0	0	0	0	0	—	1	1	0	0	2.0	1.000
1985		0	0	—	1.69	3	1	0	10.2	11	4	8	0	0	0	0	0	0	0	—	1	2	0	1	1.0	1.000
2 yrs.		0	1	.000	3.45	4	2	0	15.2	18	5	11	0	0	0	0	0	0	0	—	2	3	0	1	1.3	1.000

WORLD SERIES

Year	Team	W	L	%	ERA	G	GS	CG	IP	H	BB	SO	ShO	W	L	SV	AB	H	HR	BA	PO	A	E	DP	TC/G	FA
1985	KC A	0	1	.000	5.06	2	1	0	5.1	4	5	4	0	0	0	0	1	0	0	.000	1	2	1	1	2.0	.750

Willie Blair

BLAIR, WILLIAM ALLEN
B. Dec. 18, 1965, Paintsville, Ky.
BR TR 6′ 1″ 185 lbs.

Year	Team	W	L	%	ERA	G	GS	CG	IP	H	BB	SO	ShO	W	L	SV	AB	H	HR	BA	PO	A	E	DP	TC/G	FA
April		0	0	—	1.17	5	0	0	7.2	5	4	5	0	0	0	0										
May		0	1	.000	3.80	5	3	0	21.1	19	8	16	0	0	0	0										
June		0	4	.000	4.85	6	3	0	26	31	10	15	0	0	0	2										
July		1	0	1.000	6.10	6	0	0	10.1	11	6	4	0	1	0	0										
Aug		0	0	—	0.00	2	0	0	1.2	0	0	2	0	0	0	0										
Sept/Oct		2	0	1.000	0.00	3	0	0	1.2	0	0	1	0	2	0	0										
Day		2	2	.500	6.26	12	3	0	27.1	30	9	18	0	2	0	0										
Night		1	3	.250	2.61	15	3	0	41.1	36	19	25	0	1	0	2										
vs. Left		—	—	—	—	—	—	—	—	31	14	18	—	—	—	—										
vs. Right		—	—	—	—	—	—	—	—	35	14	25	—	—	—	—										

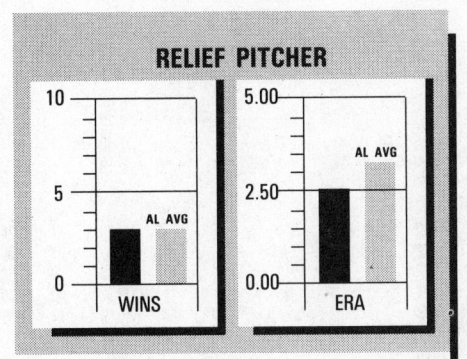

STARTING PITCHER

RELIEF PITCHER

Year	Team	W	L	%	ERA	G	GS	CG	IP	H	BB	SO	ShO	W	L	SV	AB	H	HR	BA	PO	A	E	DP	TC/G	FA

Willie Blair *Continued*

RELIEF PITCHER

Year	Team	W	L	%	ERA	G	GS	CG	IP	H	BB	SO	ShO	W	L	SV	AB	H	HR	BA	PO	A	E	DP	TC/G	FA
On Grass		0	3	.000	4.61	7	3	0	27.1	30	8	18	0	0	1	0										
On Turf		3	2	.600	3.70	20	3	0	41.1	36	20	25	0	3	1	0										
Home		3	2	.600	3.90	18	2	0	32.1	25	15	21	0	3	1	0										
Road		0	3	.000	4.21	9	4	0	36.1	41	13	22	0	0	1	0										
Division Rivals																										
vs. BAL		2	0	1.000	0.00	3	0	0	2	2	2	1	0	2	0	0										
vs. BOS		0	1	.000	3.18	1	0	0	5.2	7	1	2	0	0	1	0										
vs. CLE		0	0	—	0.00	2	0	0	2	0	0	1	0	0	0	0										
vs. DET		0	0	—	1.93	2	0	0	4.2	2	0	3	0	0	0	0										
vs. MIL		0	1	.000	9.82	1	1	0	3.2	6	3	3	0	0	0	0										
vs. NY		0	1	.000	0.79	2	1	0	11.1	9	4	6	0	0	1	0										
1990	TOR A	3	5	.375	4.06	27	6	0	68.2	66	28	43	0	3	2	0	0	0	0	—	3	6	0	0	0.3	1.000

Kevin Blankenship BLANKENSHIP, KEVIN DeWAYNE
B. Jan. 26, 1963, Anaheim, Calif.
BR TR 6′ 180 lbs.

Year	Team	W	L	%	ERA	G	GS	CG	IP	H	BB	SO	ShO	W	L	SV	AB	H	HR	BA	PO	A	E	DP	TC/G	FA
1988	2 teams	ATL N (2G 0 – 1)			CHI N (1G 1 – 0)																					
''	total	1	1	.500	4.60	3	3	0	15.2	14	8	9	0	0	0	0	6	0	0	.000	1	0	0	0	0.3	1.000
1989	CHI N	0	0	—	1.69	2	0	0	5.1	4	2	2	0	0	0	0	1	0	0	.000	1	0	0	0	0.5	1.000
1990		0	2	.000	5.84	3	2	0	12.1	13	6	5	0	0	0	0	4	0	0	.000	1	2	1	0	1.3	.750
3 yrs.		1	3	.250	4.59	8	5	0	33.1	31	16	16	0	0	0	0	11	0	0	.000	3	2	1	0	0.8	.833

Bert Blyleven BLYLEVEN, RIK AALBERT
B. Apr. 6, 1951, Zeist, Netherlands
BR TR 6′ 3″ 200 lbs.

STARTING PITCHER

Year	Team	W	L	%	ERA	G	GS	CG	IP	H	BB	SO	ShO	W	L	SV	AB	H	HR	BA	PO	A	E	DP	TC/G	FA
April		0	2	.000	9.00	4	4	0	19	31	0	8	0	0	0	0										
May		3	1	.750	2.50	6	6	1	39.2	37	7	29	0	0	0	0										
June		4	1	.800	4.39	6	6	1	41	46	9	19	0	0	0	0										
July		1	3	.250	8.58	6	6	0	28.1	45	8	10	0	0	0	0										
Aug		0	0	—	1.50	1	1	0	6	4	1	3	0	0	0	0										
Sept/Oct		—	—	—		0			0		0	0	0	—	0	0										
Day		0	3	.000	11.05	5	5	0	22	36	7	11	0	0	0	0										
Night		8	4	.667	4.10	18	18	2	112	127	18	58	0	0	0	0										
vs. Left		—	—	—		—			—		84	14	27	—	0	0	0									
vs. Right		—	—	—		—			—		79	11	42	—	0	0	0									
On Grass		7	4	.636	4.75	19	19	2	110	133	20	58	0	0	0	0										
On Turf		1	3	.250	7.50	4	4	0	24	30	5	11	0	0	0	0										
Home		4	2	.667	3.82	11	11	2	70.2	78	10	30	0	0	0	0										
Road		4	5	.444	6.82	12	12	0	63.1	85	15	39	0	0	0	0										
Division Rivals																										
vs. CHI		0	0	—	11.12	1	1	0	5.2	12	1	6	0	0	0	0										
vs. KC		2	0	1.000	2.04	2	2	1	17.2	14	5	9	0	0	0	0										
vs. MIN		0	2	.000	8.64	3	3	0	16.2	23	2	4	0	0	0	0										
vs. OAK		0	1	.000	14.73	1	1	0	3.2	8	2	2	0	0	0	0										
vs. SEA		0	1	.000	9.00	1	1	0	5	7	2	2	0	0	0	0										
vs. TEX		1	0	1.000	3.18	1	1	0	5.2	7	1	2	0	0	0	0										
1970	MIN A	10	9	.526	3.18	27	25	5	164	143	47	135	1	0	1	0	50	7	0	.140	5	16	1	1	0.8	.955
1971		16	15	.516	2.82	38	38	17	278	267	59	224	5	0	0	0	91	12	0	.132	19	38	2	0	1.6	.966
1972		17	17	.500	2.73	39	38	11	287	247	69	228	3	0	1	0	94	15	0	.160	18	45	3	4	1.7	.955
1973		20	17	.541	2.52	40	40	25	325	296	67	258	9	0	0	0	0	0	0	—	21	34	1	0	1.4	.982
1974		17	17	.500	2.66	37	37	19	281	244	77	249	3	0	0	0	0	0	0	—	19	34	3	2	1.5	.946
1975		15	10	.600	3.00	35	35	20	275.2	219	84	233	3	0	0	0	0	0	0	—	16	48	6	5	2.0	.914
1976	2 teams	MIN A (12G 4 – 5)			TEX A (24G 9 – 11)																					
''	total	13	16	.448	2.87	36	36	18	297.2	283	81	219	6	0	0	0	0	0	0	—	22	44	0	4	1.8	1.000
1977	TEX A	14	12	.538	2.72	30	30	15	235	181	69	182	5	0	0	0	0	0	0	—	10	35	1	4	1.5	.978
1978	PIT N	14	10	.583	3.02	34	34	11	244	217	66	182	4	0	0	0	85	11	0	.129	11	41	1	4	1.6	.981
1979		12	5	.706	3.61	37	37	4	237	238	92	172	0	0	0	0	70	9	0	.129	14	20	0	0	0.9	1.000
1980		8	13	.381	3.82	34	32	5	217	219	59	168	2	0	0	0	61	5	0	.082	10	30	2	2	1.2	.952
1981	CLE A	11	7	.611	2.89	20	20	9	159	145	40	107	1	0	0	0	0	0	0	—	9	16	1	2	1.3	.962
1982		2	2	.500	4.87	4	4	0	20.1	16	11	19	0	0	0	0	0	0	0	—	2	2	0	0	1.0	1.000
1983		· 7	10	.412	3.91	24	24	5	156.1	160	44	123	0	0	0	0	0	0	0	—	7	26	1	3	1.4	.971

Year	Team	W	L	%	ERA	G	GS	CG	IP	H	BB	SO	ShO	W	L	SV	AB	H	HR	BA	PO	A	E	DP	TC/G	FA
														RELIEF PITCHING			BATTING									

Bert Blyleven *Continued*

Year	Team	W	L	%	ERA	G	GS	CG	IP	H	BB	SO	ShO	W	L	SV	AB	H	HR	BA	PO	A	E	DP	TC/G	FA
1984		19	7	.731	2.87	33	32	12	245	204	74	170	4	0	0	0	0	0	0	—	21	30	2	2	1.6	.962
1985	2 teams	CLE A	(23G 9 - 11)		MIN A	(14G 8 - 5)																				
''	total	17	16	.515	3.16	37	37	24	293.2	264	75	206	5	0	0	0	0	0	0	—	17	32	0	2	1.3	1.000
1986	MIN A	17	14	.548	4.01	36	36	16	271.2	262	58	215	3	0	0	0	0	0	0	—	15	31	0	0	1.3	1.000
1987		15	12	.556	4.01	37	37	8	267	249	101	196	1	0	0	0	0	0	0	—	17	43	4	3	1.7	.938
1988		10	17	.370	5.43	33	33	7	207.1	240	51	145	0	0	0	0	0	0	0	—	12	22	1	3	1.1	.971
1989	CAL A	17	5	.773	2.73	33	33	8	241	225	44	131	5	0	0	0	0	0	0	—	14	38	0	6	1.6	1.000
1990		8	7	.533	5.24	23	23	2	134	163	25	69	0	0	0	0	0	0	0	—	3	24	1	0	1.2	.964
21 yrs.		279	238	.540	3.27	667	661	241	4836.2	4482	1293	3631	60	0	2	0	451	59	0	.131	282	649	30	47	1.4	.969
													4th			8th										

LEAGUE CHAMPIONSHIP SERIES

Year	Team	W	L	%	ERA	G	GS	CG	IP	H	BB	SO	ShO	W	L	SV	AB	H	HR	BA	PO	A	E	DP	TC/G	FA
1970	MIN A	0	0	—	0.00	1	0	0	2	2	0	2	0	0	0	0	0	0	0	—	1	0	0	0	1.0	1.000
1979	PIT N	1	0	1.000	1.00	1	1	1	9	8	0	9	0	0	0	0	3	1	0	.333	1	1	0	0	2.0	1.000
1987	MIN A	2	0	1.000	4.05	2	2	0	13.1	12	3	9	0	0	0	0	0	0	0	—	0	1	0	0	0.5	1.000
3 yrs.		3	0	1.000	2.59	4	3	1	24.1	22	3	20	0	0	0	0	3	1	0	.333	2	2	0	0	1.0	1.000

WORLD SERIES

Year	Team	W	L	%	ERA	G	GS	CG	IP	H	BB	SO	ShO	W	L	SV	AB	H	HR	BA	PO	A	E	DP	TC/G	FA
1979	PIT N	1	0	1.000	1.80	2	1	0	10	8	3	4	0	1	0	0	3	0	0	.000	0	1	0	1	0.5	1.000
1987	MIN A	1	1	.500	2.77	2	2	0	13	13	2	12	0	0	0	0	1	0	0	.000	0	1	0	0	0.5	1.000
2 yrs.		2	1	.667	2.35	4	3	0	23	21	5	16	0	0	0	0	4	0	0	.000	0	2	0	1	0.5	1.000

Mike Boddicker

BODDICKER, MICHAEL JAMES
B. Aug. 23, 1957, Cedar Rapids, Iowa
BR TR 5′ 11″ 172 lbs.

	W	L	%	ERA	G	GS	CG	IP	H	BB	SO	ShO	W	L	SV
April	2	3	.400	4.85	5	5	0	26	29	5	14	0	0	0	0
May	4	0	1.000	2.63	5	5	0	37.2	28	12	26	0	0	0	0
June	4	0	1.000	2.87	6	6	1	47	43	11	27	0	0	0	0
July	1	3	.250	7.34	6	6	1	30.2	49	11	24	0	0	0	0
Aug	2	2	.500	1.11	5	5	1	40.2	33	12	25	0	0	0	0
Sept/Oct	4	0	1.000	2.93	7	7	0	46	43	18	27	0	0	0	0
Day	6	2	.750	3.19	10	10	1	59.1	58	24	46	0	0	0	0
Night	11	6	.647	3.42	24	24	3	168.2	167	45	97	0	0	0	0
vs. Left	—	—	—	—	—	—	—	—	121	33	51	—	—	—	—
vs. Right	—	—	—	—	—	—	—	—	104	36	92	—	—	—	—
On Grass	16	8	.667	3.44	31	31	4	204.1	205	63	129	0	0	0	0
On Turf	1	0	1.000	2.66	3	3	0	23.2	20	6	14	0	0	0	0
Home	11	5	.688	2.97	20	20	4	136.1	138	36	83	0	0	0	0
Road	6	3	.667	3.93	14	14	0	91.2	87	33	60	0	0	0	0
Division Rivals															
vs. BAL	4	0	1.000	3.30	4	4	0	30	30	12	23	0	0	0	0
vs. CLE	1	0	1.000	2.78	3	3	0	22.2	21	5	9	0	0	0	0
vs. DET	1	1	.500	3.38	3	3	0	13.1	14	5	9	0	0	0	0
vs. MIL	1	3	.250	7.06	4	4	1	21.2	26	5	11	0	0	0	0
vs. NY	2	0	1.000	1.29	3	3	1	21	10	7	15	0	0	0	0
vs. TOR	1	0	1.000	4.73	2	2	0	13.1	13	3	9	0	0	0	0

STARTING PITCHER

Year	Team	W	L	%	ERA	G	GS	CG	IP	H	BB	SO	ShO	W	L	SV	AB	H	HR	BA	PO	A	E	DP	TC/G	FA
1980	BAL A	0	1	.000	6.43	1	1	0	7	6	5	4	0	0	0	0	0	0	0	—	0	0	1	0	1.0	—
1981		0	0	—	4.50	2	0	0	6	6	2	2	0	0	0	0	0	0	0	—	1	0	1	0	1.0	.500
1982		1	0	1.000	3.51	7	0	0	25.2	25	12	20	0	1	0	0	0	0	0	—	5	3	1	0	1.3	.889
1983		16	8	.667	2.77	27	26	10	179	141	52	120	5	0	0	0	0	0	0	—	24	32	3	4	2.2	.949
1984		20	11	.645	2.79	34	34	16	261.1	218	81	128	4	0	0	0	0	0	0	—	49	49	7	6	3.1	.933
1985		12	17	.414	4.07	32	32	9	203.1	227	89	135	2	0	0	0	0	0	0	—	26	46	2	6	2.3	.973
1986		14	12	.538	4.70	33	33	7	218.1	214	74	175	0	0	0	0	0	0	0	—	28	36	3	4	2.0	.955
1987		10	12	.455	4.18	33	33	7	226	212	78	152	2	0	0	0	0	0	0	—	18	46	2	5	2.0	.970
1988	2 teams	BAL A	(21G 6 - 12)		BOS A	(15G 7 - 3)																				
''	total	13	15	.464	3.39	36	35	5	236	234	77	156	1	0	0	0	0	0	0	—	22	33	2	1	1.6	.965
1989	BOS A	15	11	.577	4.00	34	34	3	211.2	217	71	145	2	0	0	0	0	0	0	—	14	36	3	2	1.6	.943
1990		17	8	.680	3.36	34	34	4	228	225	69	143	0	0	0	0	0	0	0	—	29	27	2	6	1.7	.966
11 yrs.		118	95	.554	3.66	273	262	61	1802.1	1725	610	1180	16	1	0	0	0	0	0	—	216	308	27	34	2.0	.951

LEAGUE CHAMPIONSHIP SERIES

Year	Team	W	L	%	ERA	G	GS	CG	IP	H	BB	SO	ShO	W	L	SV	AB	H	HR	BA	PO	A	E	DP	TC/G	FA
1983	BAL A	1	0	1.000	0.00	1	1	1	9	5	3	14	0	0	0	0	0	0	0	—	0	1	0	0	1.0	1.000
1988	BOS A	0	1	.000	20.25	1	1	0	2.2	8	1	2	0	0	0	0	0	0	0	—	0	0	0	0	0.0	—
1990		0	1	.000	2.25	1	1	1	8	6	3	7	0	0	0	0	0	0	0	—	0	2	1	0	3.0	.667
3 yrs.		1	2	.333	3.66	3	3	2	19.2	19	7	23	0	0	0	0	0	0	0	—	0	3	1	0	1.3	.750

WORLD SERIES

Year	Team	W	L	%	ERA	G	GS	CG	IP	H	BB	SO	ShO	W	L	SV	AB	H	HR	BA	PO	A	E	DP	TC/G	FA
1983	BAL A	1	0	1.000	0.00	1	1	1	9	3	0	6	0	0	0	0	3	0	0	.000	1	2	0	0	3.0	1.000

Year	Team	W	L	%	ERA	G	GS	CG	IP	H	BB	SO	ShO	W	L	SV	AB	H	HR	BA	PO	A	E	DP	TC/G	FA

Joe Boever

BOEVER, JOSEPH MARTIN
B. Oct. 4, 1960, St. Louis, Mo.
BR TR 6' 1" 200 lbs.

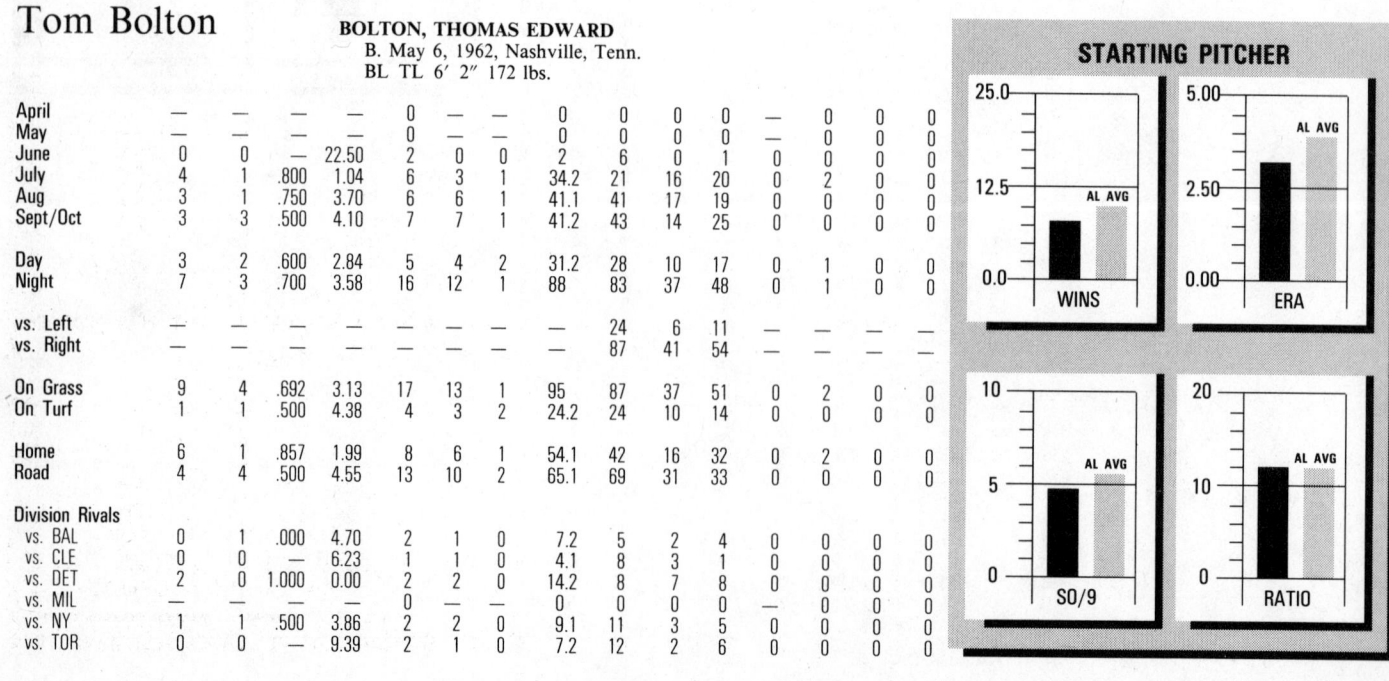

RELIEF PITCHER

April		0	1	.000	3.38	6	0	0	10.2	8	7	8	0	0	1	1										
May		1	1	.500	2.70	10	0	0	10	9	8	10	0	1	1	4										
June		0	1	.000	6.46	11	0	0	15.1	15	15	16	0	0	1	1										
July		0	0	—	4.50	10	0	0	10	11	6	3	0	0	0	4										
Aug		1	2	.333	3.15	15	0	0	20	20	9	17	0	1	2	1										
Sept/Oct		1	1	.500	1.21	15	0	0	22.1	14	6	21	0	1	1	3										
Day		1	0	1.000	4.24	15	0	0	23.1	21	11	21	0	1	0	4										
Night		2	6	.250	3.05	52	0	0	65	56	40	54	0	2	6	10										
vs. Left		—	—	—	—	—	—	—	—	32	34	41	—	—	—	—										
vs. Right		—	—	—	—	—	—	—	—	45	17	34	—	—	—	—										
On Grass		2	2	.500	5.12	32	0	0	38.2	42	27	31	0	2	2	4										
On Turf		1	4	.200	1.99	35	0	0	49.2	35	24	44	0	1	4	10										
Home		2	3	.400	4.10	39	0	0	52.2	51	32	45	0	2	3	5										
Road		1	3	.250	2.27	28	0	0	35.2	26	19	30	0	1	3	9										
Division Rivals																										
vs. CHI		0	0	—	2.35	6	0	0	7.2	8	3	7	0	0	0	1										
vs. MON		0	0	—	2.51	9	0	0	14.1	14	9	14	0	0	0	2										
vs. NY		0	0	—	2.00	8	0	0	9	9	2	7	0	0	0	2										
vs. PIT		0	1	.000	0.96	10	0	0	9.1	7	4	8	0	0	1	4										
vs. STL		1	1	.500	4.91	6	0	0	7.1	7	7	5	0	1	1	1										
1985	STL N	0	0	—	4.41	13	0	0	16.1	17	4	20	0	0	0	0	0	0	0	—	0	0	0	0	0.0	—
1986		0	1	.000	1.66	11	0	0	21.2	19	11	8	0	0	0	0	2	1	0	.500	1	2	0	0	0.3	1.000
1987	ATL N	1	0	1.000	7.36	14	0	0	18.1	29	12	18	0	1	0	0	0	0	0	—	0	2	0	0	0.1	1.000
1988		0	2	.000	1.77	16	0	0	20.1	12	1	7	0	0	2	1	0	0	0	—	2	3	0	1	0.3	1.000
1989		4	11	.267	3.94	66	0	0	82.1	78	34	68	0	4	11	21	1	0	0	.000	7	15	0	0	0.3	1.000
1990	2 teams	ATL N	(33G 1 – 3)		PHI N	(34G 2 – 3)																				
"	total	3	6	.333	3.36	67	0	0	88.1	77	51	75	0	3	6	14	3	0	0	.000	6	7	2	1	0.2	.867
6 yrs.		8	20	.286	3.64	187	0	0	247.1	232	113	196	0	8	20	36	6	1	0	.167	16	29	2	2	0.3	.957

Brian Bohanon

BOHANON, BRIAN EDWARD
B. Aug. 1, 1968, Denton, Tex.
BL TL 6' 2" 210 lbs.

Year	Team	W	L	%	ERA	G	GS	CG	IP	H	BB	SO	ShO	W	L	SV	AB	H	HR	BA	PO	A	E	DP	TC/G	FA
1990	TEX A	0	3	.000	6.62	11	6	0	34	40	18	15	0	0	0	0	0	0	0	—	1	10	0	2	1.0	1.000

Tom Bolton

BOLTON, THOMAS EDWARD
B. May 6, 1962, Nashville, Tenn.
BL TL 6' 2" 172 lbs.

STARTING PITCHER

April		—	—	—	—	0	—	0	0	0	0	0	—	0	0	0										
May		—	—	—	—	0	—	0	0	0	0	0	—	0	0	0										
June		0	0	—	22.50	2	0	0	2	6	0	1	0	0	0	0										
July		4	1	.800	1.04	6	3	1	34.2	21	16	20	0	2	0	0										
Aug		3	1	.750	3.70	6	6	1	41.1	41	17	19	0	0	0	0										
Sept/Oct		3	3	.500	4.10	7	7	1	41.2	43	14	25	0	0	0	0										
Day		3	2	.600	2.84	5	4	2	31.2	28	10	17	0	1	0	0										
Night		7	3	.700	3.58	16	12	1	88	83	37	48	0	1	0	0										
vs. Left		—	—	—	—	—	—	—	—	24	6	11	—	—	—	—										
vs. Right		—	—	—	—	—	—	—	—	87	41	54	—	—	—	—										
On Grass		9	4	.692	3.13	17	13	1	95	87	37	51	0	2	0	0										
On Turf		1	1	.500	4.38	4	3	2	24.2	24	10	14	0	0	0	0										
Home		6	1	.857	1.99	8	6	1	54.1	42	16	32	0	2	0	0										
Road		4	4	.500	4.55	13	10	2	65.1	69	31	33	0	0	0	0										
Division Rivals																										
vs. BAL		0	1	.000	4.70	2	1	0	7.2	5	2	4	0	0	0	0										
vs. CLE		0	0	—	6.23	1	1	0	4.1	8	3	1	0	0	0	0										
vs. DET		2	0	1.000	0.00	2	2	0	14.2	8	7	8	0	0	0	0										
vs. MIL		—	—	—	—	0	—	0	0	0	0	0	—	0	0	0										
vs. NY		1	1	.500	3.86	2	2	0	9.1	11	3	5	0	0	0	0										
vs. TOR		0	0	—	9.39	2	1	0	7.2	12	2	6	0	0	0	0										

Year	Team	W	L	%	ERA	G	GS	CG	IP	H	BB	SO	ShO	RELIEF PITCHING			BATTING				PO	A	E	DP	TC/G	FA
														W	L	SV	AB	H	HR	BA						

Tom Bolton *Continued*

Year	Team	W	L	%	ERA	G	GS	CG	IP	H	BB	SO	ShO	W	L	SV	AB	H	HR	BA	PO	A	E	DP	TC/G	FA
1987	BOS A	1	0	1.000	4.38	29	0	0	61.2	83	27	49	0	1	0	0	0	0	0	—	3	9	0	1	0.4	1.000
1988		1	3	.250	4.75	28	0	0	30.1	35	14	21	0	1	3	1	0	0	0	—	1	10	0	0	0.4	1.000
1989		0	4	.000	8.31	4	4	0	17.1	21	10	9	0	0	0	0	0	0	0	—	1	2	0	0	0.8	1.000
1990		10	5	.667	3.38	21	16	3	119.2	111	47	65	0	2	0	0	0	0	0	—	4	21	1	1	1.2	.962
4 yrs.		12	12	.500	4.21	82	20	3	229	250	98	144	0	4	3	1	0	0	0	—	9	42	1	2	0.6	.981

LEAGUE CHAMPIONSHIP SERIES

Year	Team	W	L	%	ERA	G	GS	CG	IP	H	BB	SO	ShO	W	L	SV	AB	H	HR	BA	PO	A	E	DP	TC/G	FA
1990	BOS A	0	0	—	0.00	2	0	0	3	2	2	3	0	0	0	0	0	0	0	—	0	0	0	0	0.0	—

Greg Booker

BOOKER, GREGORY SCOTT
B. June 22, 1960, Lynchburg, Va.
BR TR 6′ 6″ 230 lbs.

Year	Team	W	L	%	ERA	G	GS	CG	IP	H	BB	SO	ShO	W	L	SV	AB	H	HR	BA	PO	A	E	DP	TC/G	FA
1983	SD N	0	1	.000	7.71	6	1	0	11.2	18	9	5	0	0	0	0	1	0	0	.000	0	3	0	0	0.5	1.000
1984		1	1	.500	3.30	32	1	0	57.1	67	27	28	0	1	1	0	7	2	0	.286	9	7	1	1	0.5	.941
1985		0	1	.000	6.85	17	0	0	22.1	20	17	7	0	0	1	0	1	0	0	.000	1	3	1	0	0.3	.800
1986		1	0	1.000	1.64	9	0	0	11	10	4	7	0	1	0	0	0	0	0	—	1	1	1	0	0.3	.667
1987		1	1	.500	3.16	44	0	0	68.1	62	30	17	0	1	1	1	6	0	0	.000	8	8	1	1	0.4	.941
1988		2	2	.500	3.39	34	2	0	63.2	68	19	43	0	1	2	0	8	2	0	.250	6	12	0	0	0.5	1.000
1989	2 teams	SD N	(11G 0 - 1)		MIN A	(6G 0 - 0)																				
"	total	0	1	.000	4.23	17	0	0	27.2	26	12	11	0	0	1	0	0	0	0	—	3	7	0	1	0.6	1.000
1990	SF N	0	0	—	13.50	2	0	0	2	7	0	1	0	0	0	0	0	0	0	—	0	0	0	0	0.0	—
8 yrs.		5	7	.417	3.89	161	4	0	264	278	118	119	0	4	6	1	23	4	0	.174	28	41	4	3	0.5	.945

LEAGUE CHAMPIONSHIP SERIES

Year	Team	W	L	%	ERA	G	GS	CG	IP	H	BB	SO	ShO	W	L	SV	AB	H	HR	BA	PO	A	E	DP	TC/G	FA
1984	SD N	0	0	—	0.00	1	0	0	2	2	1	2	0	0	0	0	0	0	0	—	0	0	0	0	0.0	—

WORLD SERIES

Year	Team	W	L	%	ERA	G	GS	CG	IP	H	BB	SO	ShO	W	L	SV	AB	H	HR	BA	PO	A	E	DP	TC/G	FA
1984	SD N	0	0	—	9.00	1	0	0	1	0	4	0	0	0	0	0	0	0	0	—	0	1	0	0	1.0	1.000

Danny Boone

BOONE, DANIEL HUGH
B. Jan. 14, 1954, Long Beach, Calif.
BL TL 5′ 8″ 150 lbs.

Year	Team	W	L	%	ERA	G	GS	CG	IP	H	BB	SO	ShO	W	L	SV	AB	H	HR	BA	PO	A	E	DP	TC/G	FA
1981	SD N	1	0	1.000	2.86	37	0	0	63	63	21	43	0	1	0	2	4	2	0	.500	7	14	1	1	0.6	.950
1982	2 teams	SD N	(10G 1 - 0)		HOU N	(10G 0 - 1)																				
"	total	1	1	.500	4.71	20	0	0	28.2	28	7	12	0	1	1	2	6	1	0	.167	0	7	1	0	0.4	.870
1990	BAL A	0	0	—	2.79	4	1	0	9.2	12	3	2	0	0	0	0	0	0	0	—	0	2	0	0	0.5	1.000
3 yrs.		2	1	.667	3.38	61	1	0	101.1	103	31	57	0	2	1	4	10	3	0	.300	7	23	2	1	0.5	.938

Chris Bosio

BOSIO, CHRISTOPHER LOUIS
B. Apr. 3, 1963, Carmichael, Calif.
BR TR 6′ 3″ 220 lbs.

	W	L	%	ERA	G	GS	CG	IP	H	BB	SO	ShO	W	L	SV
April	3	0	1.000	1.39	5	5	1	32.1	22	8	17	1	0	0	0
May	1	3	.250	3.19	6	6	3	48	45	6	28	0	0	0	0
June	0	3	.000	8.07	5	5	0	29	43	12	17	0	0	0	0
July	0	3	.000	4.24	4	4	0	23.1	21	12	14	0	0	0	0
Aug	—	—	—	—	0			0	0	0	0	—	0	0	0
Sept/Oct	—	—	—	—	0			0	0	0	0	—	0	0	0
Day	2	3	.400	1.92	8	8	2	51.2	38	16	29	0	0	0	0
Night	2	6	.250	5.33	12	12	2	81	93	22	47	1	0	0	0
vs. Left	—	—	—	—				—	78	19	25	—	—	—	—
vs. Right	—	—	—	—				—	53	19	51	—	—	—	—
On Grass	4	8	.333	4.11	19	19	3	124.2	120	38	71	1	0	0	0
On Turf	0	1	.000	2.25	1	1	1	8	11	0	5	0	0	0	0
Home	2	7	.222	5.11	12	12	2	81	87	25	46	0	0	0	0
Road	2	2	.500	2.26	8	8	2	51.2	44	13	30	1	0	0	0
Division Rivals															
vs. BAL	0	0	—	12.15	2	2	0	6.2	14	5	5	0	0	0	0
vs. BOS	0	1	.000	1.50	2	2	0	12	8	8	8	0	0	0	0
vs. CLE	0	1	.000	10.80	1	1	0	6.2	9	2	4	0	0	0	0
vs. DET	1	1	.500	1.88	2	2	1	14.1	11	2	7	0	0	0	0
vs. NY	0	1	.000	4.50	1	1	0	8	9	2	6	0	0	0	0
vs. TOR	0	1	.000	5.87	1	1	0	7.2	11	3	2	0	0	0	0

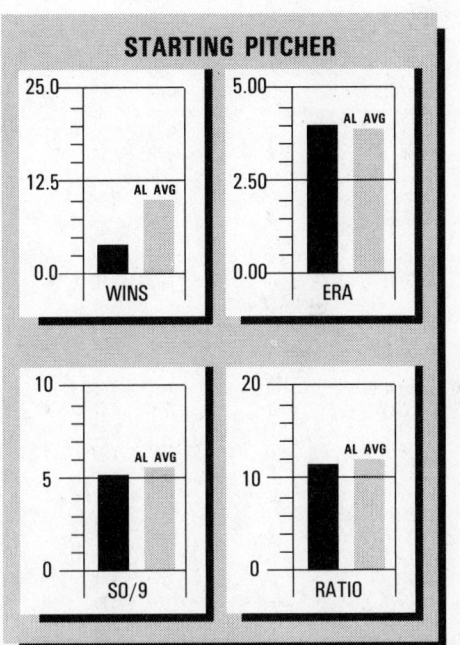

STARTING PITCHER

WINS · ERA · SO/9 · RATIO (AL AVG)

Year	Team	W	L	%	ERA	G	GS	CG	IP	H	BB	SO	ShO	W	L	SV	AB	H	HR	BA	PO	A	E	DP	TC/G	FA
														RELIEF PITCHING			BATTING									

Chris Bosio *Continued*

Year	Team	W	L	%	ERA	G	GS	CG	IP	H	BB	SO	ShO	W	L	SV	AB	H	HR	BA	PO	A	E	DP	TC/G	FA
1986	MIL A	0	4	.000	7.01	10	4	0	34.2	41	13	29	0	0	1	0	0	0	0	—	4	5	1	1	1.0	.900
1987		11	8	.579	5.24	46	19	2	170	187	50	150	1	3	1	2	0	0	0	—	14	24	4	5	0.9	.905
1988		7	15	.318	3.36	38	22	9	182	190	38	84	1	1	3	6	0	0	0	—	22	33	3	7	1.5	.948
1989		15	10	.600	2.95	33	33	8	234.2	225	48	173	2	0	0	0	0	0	0	—	16	35	2	2	1.6	.962
1990		4	9	.308	4.00	20	20	4	132.2	131	38	76	1	0	0	0	0	0	0	—	12	24	1	2	1.9	.973
5 yrs.		37	46	.446	3.94	147	98	23	754	774	187	512	5	4	5	8	0	0	0	—	68	121	11	17	1.4	.945

Shawn Boskie

BOSKIE, SHAWN KEALOHA
B. Mar. 28, 1967, Hawthorne, Nev.
BR TR 6′ 3″ 205 lbs.

	W	L	%	ERA	G	GS	CG	IP	H	BB	SO	ShO	W	L	SV	AB	H	HR	BA	PO	A	E	DP	TC/G	FA
April	—	—	—	—	0			0	0	0	0	—	0	0	0										
May	1	2	.333	3.38	3	3	1	24	23	5	11	0	0	0	0										
June	1	2	.333	4.82	5	5	0	28	29	13	21	0	0	0	0										
July	2	2	.500	3.40	6	6	0	39.2	40	12	16	0	0	0	0										
Aug	1	0	1.000	1.50	1	1	0	6	7	1	1	0	0	0	0										
Sept/Oct	—	—	—	—	0			0	0	0	0	—	0	0	0										
Day	2	3	.400	3.00	7	7	1	54	52	10	27	0	0	0	0										
Night	3	3	.500	4.53	8	8	0	43.2	47	21	22	0	0	0	0										
vs. Left	—	—	—	—				—	59	28	23	—	—	—	—										
vs. Right	—	—	—	—				—	40	3	26	—	—	—	—										
On Grass	3	5	.375	4.10	11	11	0	68	74	26	31	0	0	0	0										
On Turf	2	1	.667	2.73	4	4	1	29.2	25	5	18	0	0	0	0										
Home	2	5	.286	4.07	9	9	0	59.2	64	16	27	0	0	0	0										
Road	3	1	.750	3.08	6	6	1	38	35	15	22	0	0	0	0										
Division Rivals																									
vs. MON	2	1	.667	2.33	4	4	0	27	22	9	13	0	0	0	0										
vs. NY	—	—	—	—	0			0	0	0	0	0	0	0	0										
vs. PHI	0	0	—	2.57	1	1	0	7	5	2	8	0	0	0	0										
vs. PIT	0	2	.000	11.88	2	2	0	8.1	15	2	5	0	0	0	0										
vs. STL	—	—	—	—	0			0	0	0	0	0	0	0	0										
1990	CHI N	5	6	.455	3.69	15	15	1	97.2	99	31	49	0	0	0	0	36	8	0	.222	12	12	0	2	1.6	1.000

STARTING PITCHER

Oil Can Boyd

BOYD, DENNIS RAY
B. Oct. 6, 1959, Meridian, Miss.
BR TR 6′ 1″ 155 lbs.

	W	L	%	ERA	G	GS	CG	IP	H	BB	SO	ShO	W	L	SV	AB	H	HR	BA	PO	A	E	DP	TC/G	FA
April	1	2	.333	7.06	4	4	0	21.2	27	5	13	0	0	0	0										
May	2	0	1.000	0.55	5	5	2	33	26	9	24	2	0	0	0										
June	0	1	.000	4.03	5	5	0	29	28	5	17	0	0	0	0										
July	3	0	1.000	2.08	6	6	0	39	27	10	20	0	0	0	0										
Aug	1	2	.333	4.03	5	5	0	29	30	9	12	0	0	0	0										
Sept/Oct	3	1	.750	1.85	6	6	1	39	26	14	27	1	0	0	0										
Day	3	4	.429	3.29	11	11	1	65.2	61	15	35	1	0	0	0										
Night	7	2	.778	2.74	20	20	2	125	103	37	78	2	0	0	0										
vs. Left	—	—	—	—				—	96	35	67	—	—	—	—										
vs. Right	—	—	—	—				—	68	17	46	—	—	—	—										
On Grass	2	2	.500	2.60	11	11	1	65.2	62	18	31	1	0	0	0										
On Turf	8	4	.667	3.10	20	20	2	125	102	34	82	2	0	0	0										
Home	6	3	.667	2.91	14	14	2	89.2	77	19	61	2	0	0	0										
Road	4	3	.571	2.94	17	17	1	101	87	33	52	1	0	0	0										
Division Rivals																									
vs. CHI	0	1	.000	3.12	4	4	0	26	24	4	18	0	0	0	0										
vs. NY	1	1	.500	3.38	4	4	0	24	25	6	14	0	0	0	0										
vs. PHI	1	1	.500	4.22	4	4	0	21.1	22	7	15	0	0	0	0										
vs. PIT	1	0	1.000	1.35	1	1	0	6.2	3	4	6	0	0	0	0										
vs. STL	2	1	.667	4.32	4	4	0	25	19	6	11	0	0	0	0										
1982	BOS A	0	1	.000	5.40	3	1	0	8.1	11	2	2	0	0	0	0	0	0	0	—	0	1	0	0	0.3	1.000
1983		4	8	.333	3.28	15	13	5	98.2	103	23	43	0	0	0	0	0	0	0	—	5	10	1	1	1.1	.938
1984		12	12	.500	4.37	29	26	10	197.2	207	53	134	3	0	0	0	0	0	0	—	20	31	2	3	1.8	.962
1985		15	13	.536	3.70	35	35	13	272.1	**273**	67	154	3	0	0	0	0	0	0	—	42	41	1	2	2.4	.988
1986		16	10	.615	3.78	30	30	10	214.1	222	45	129	0	0	0	0	0	0	0	—	24	27	2	4	1.8	.962

STARTING PITCHER

Year	Team	W	L	%	ERA	G	GS	CG	IP	H	BB	SO	ShO	RELIEF PITCHING			BATTING			BA	PO	A	E	DP	TC/G	FA
														W	L	SV	AB	H	HR							

Oil Can Boyd *Continued*

Year	Team	W	L	%	ERA	G	GS	CG	IP	H	BB	SO	ShO	W	L	SV	AB	H	HR	BA	PO	A	E	DP	TC/G	FA
1987		1	3	.250	5.89	7	7	0	36.2	47	9	12	0	0	0	0	0	0	0	—	4	11	0	0	2.1	1.000
1988		9	7	.563	5.34	23	23	1	129.2	147	41	71	0	0	0	0	0	0	0	—	8	15	2	0	1.1	.920
1989		3	2	.600	4.42	10	10	0	59	57	19	26	0	0	0	0	0	0	0	—	7	10	0	1	1.7	1.000
1990	MON N	10	6	.625	2.93	31	31	3	190.2	164	52	113	3	0	0	0	59	3	0	.051	7	24	3	0	1.1	.912
9 yrs.		70	62	.530	3.96	183	176	42	1207.1	1231	311	684	9	0	1	0	59	3	0	.051	117	170	11	12	1.6	.963

LEAGUE CHAMPIONSHIP SERIES

| 1986 | BOS A | 1 | 1 | .500 | 4.61 | 2 | 2 | 0 | 13.2 | 17 | 3 | 8 | 0 | 0 | 0 | 0 | 0 | 0 | 0 | — | 2 | 3 | 0 | 0 | 2.5 | 1.000 |

WORLD SERIES

| 1986 | BOS A | 0 | 1 | .000 | 7.71 | 1 | 1 | 0 | 7 | 9 | 1 | 3 | 0 | 0 | 0 | 0 | 0 | 0 | 0 | — | 1 | 0 | 0 | 0 | 1.0 | 1.000 |

Jeff Brantley

BRANTLEY, JEFFREY HOKE
B. Sept. 5, 1963, Florence, Ala.
BR TR 5′ 11″ 180 lbs.

	Team	W	L	%	ERA	G	GS	CG	IP	H	BB	SO	ShO	W	L	SV	AB	H	HR	BA	PO	A	E	DP	TC/G	FA
April		0	1	.000	2.76	10	0	0	16.1	14	7	14	0	0	1	1										
May		1	0	1.000	0.00	12	0	0	19	15	5	9	0	1	0	4										
June		1	0	1.000	1.82	14	0	0	24.2	21	5	14	0	1	0	5										
July		2	2	.500	1.88	11	0	0	14.1	12	5	13	0	2	2	6										
Aug		1	0	1.000	0.93	6	0	0	9.2	11	9	9	0	1	0	2										
Sept/Oct		0	0	—	3.38	2	0	0	2.2	4	2	2	0	0	0	1										
Day		4	3	.571	2.10	22	0	0	34.1	31	12	27	0	4	3	5										
Night		1	0	1.000	1.20	33	0	0	52.1	46	21	34	0	1	0	14										
vs. Left		—	—	—	—	—	—	—		51	20	27	—	—	—	—										
vs. Right		—	—	—	—	—	—	—		26	13	34	—	—	—	—										
On Grass		4	3	.571	2.01	40	0	0	62.2	61	25	43	0	4	3	12										
On Turf		1	0	1.000	0.38	15	0	0	24	16	8	18	0	1	0	7										
Home		4	1	.800	1.77	26	0	0	40.2	35	17	31	0	4	1	9										
Road		1	2	.333	1.37	29	0	0	46	42	16	30	0	1	2	10										

Division Rivals

	Team	W	L	%	ERA	G	GS	CG	IP	H	BB	SO	ShO	W	L	SV	AB	H	HR	BA	PO	A	E	DP	TC/G	FA
vs. ATL		0	0	—	2.00	5	0	0	9	4	2	6	0	0	0	1										
vs. CIN		1	0	1.000	0.90	5	0	0	10	10	4	5	0	1	0	3										
vs. HOU		1	0	1.000	1.17	5	0	0	7.2	5	3	10	0	1	0	2										
vs. LA		0	0	—	7.71	2	0	0	2.1	4	1	2	0	0	0	0										
vs. SD		0	1	.000	2.70	7	0	0	13.1	15	4	6	0	0	1	2										

Year	Team	W	L	%	ERA	G	GS	CG	IP	H	BB	SO	ShO	W	L	SV	AB	H	HR	BA	PO	A	E	DP	TC/G	FA
1988	SF N	0	1	.000	5.66	9	1	0	20.2	22	6	11	0	0	0	1	2	1	0	.500	0	7	0	0	0.8	1.000
1989		7	1	.875	4.07	59	1	0	97.1	101	37	69	0	7	0	0	12	1	0	.083	3	16	0	0	0.3	1.000
1990		5	3	.625	1.56	55	0	0	86.2	77	33	61	0	5	3	19	7	2	0	.286	6	11	1	1	0.3	.944
3 yrs.		12	5	.706	3.17	123	2	0	204.2	200	76	141	0	12	3	20	21	4	0	.190	9	34	1	1	0.4	.977

LEAGUE CHAMPIONSHIP SERIES

| 1989 | SF N | 0 | 0 | — | 0.00 | 3 | 0 | 0 | 5 | 1 | 2 | 3 | 0 | 0 | 0 | 0 | 0 | 0 | 0 | — | 0 | 0 | 0 | 0 | 0.0 | — |

WORLD SERIES

| 1989 | SF N | 0 | 0 | — | 4.15 | 3 | 0 | 0 | 4.1 | 5 | 3 | 1 | 0 | 0 | 0 | 0 | 0 | 0 | 0 | — | 1 | 0 | 0 | 0 | 0.3 | 1.000 |

RELIEF PITCHER

WINS — ERA — SAVES — RATIO (NL AVG)

Keith Brown

BROWN, KEITH EDWARD
B. Feb. 14, 1964, Flagstaff, Ariz.
BB TR 6′ 4″ 215 lbs.

Year	Team	W	L	%	ERA	G	GS	CG	IP	H	BB	SO	ShO	W	L	SV	AB	H	HR	BA	PO	A	E	DP	TC/G	FA
1988	CIN N	2	1	.667	2.76	4	3	0	16.1	14	4	6	0	0	0	0	4	0	0	.000	0	3	0	1	0.8	1.000
1990		0	0	—	4.76	8	0	0	11.1	12	3	8	0	0	0	0	0	0	0	—	1	2	0	0	0.4	1.000
2 yrs.		2	1	.667	3.58	12	3	0	27.2	26	7	14	0	0	0	0	4	0	0	.000	1	5	0	1	0.5	1.000

Kevin Brown

BROWN, JAMES KEVIN
B. Mar. 14, 1965, Milledgeville, Ga.
BR TR 6′ 4″ 195 lbs.

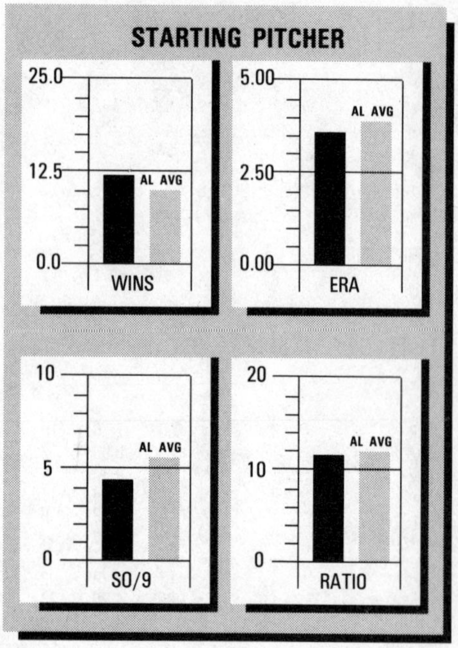
STARTING PITCHER
25.0
12.5
0.0
AL AVG
WINS
5.00
2.50
0.00
AL AVG
ERA
10
5
0
AL AVG
SO/9
20
10
0
AL AVG
RATIO

	W	L	%	ERA	G	GS	CG	IP	H	BB	SO	ShO	Relief W	Relief L	Relief SV
April	4	0	1.000	3.58	4	4	0	27.2	30	9	15	0	0	0	0
May	1	4	.200	4.29	6	6	0	42	39	20	14	0	0	0	0
June	4	1	.800	1.50	5	5	4	42	27	5	19	1	0	0	0
July	3	2	.600	3.67	6	6	2	41.2	39	17	23	1	0	0	0
Aug	0	2	.000	5.40	4	4	0	21.2	31	8	13	0	0	0	0
Sept/Oct	0	1	.000	7.20	1	1	0	5	9	1	4	0	0	0	0
Day	4	2	.667	4.66	7	7	1	48.1	53	16	22	0	0	0	0
Night	8	8	.500	3.21	19	19	5	131.2	122	44	66	2	0	0	0
vs. Left	—	—	—	—	—	—	—	—	84	30	47	—	—	—	—
vs. Right	—	—	—	—	—	—	—	—	91	30	41	—	—	—	—
On Grass	9	8	.529	3.46	20	20	4	140.1	135	51	67	2	0	0	0
On Turf	3	2	.600	4.08	6	6	2	39.2	40	9	21	0	0	0	0
Home	6	4	.600	2.58	12	12	3	87.1	78	28	44	2	0	0	0
Road	6	6	.500	4.56	14	14	3	92.2	97	32	44	0	0	0	0
Division Rivals															
vs. CAL	2	0	1.000	1.23	3	3	1	22	14	4	11	0	0	0	0
vs. CHI	—	—	—	—	0	—	—	0	0	0	0	—	0	0	0
vs. KC	1	2	.333	5.17	3	3	0	15.2	21	4	3	0	0	0	0
vs. MIN	1	1	.500	1.59	2	2	2	17	10	1	8	1	0	0	0
vs. OAK	—	—	—	—	0	—	—	0	0	0	0	—	0	0	0
vs. SEA	1	0	1.000	3.00	1	1	1	9	7	3	2	0	0	0	0

Year	Team		W	L	%	ERA	G	GS	CG	IP	H	BB	SO	ShO	Relief W	Relief L	Relief SV	AB	H	HR	BA	PO	A	E	DP	TC/G	FA
1986	TEX	A	1	0	1.000	3.60	1	1	0	5	6	0	4	0	0	0	0	0	0	0	—	0	1	0	0	1.0	1.000
1988			1	1	.500	4.24	4	4	1	23.1	33	8	12	0	0	0	0	0	0	0	—	1	2	0	0	0.8	1.000
1989			12	9	.571	3.35	28	28	7	191	167	70	104	0	0	0	0	0	0	0	—	15	41	2	6	2.1	.966
1990			12	10	.545	3.60	26	26	6	180	175	60	88	2	0	0	0	1	0	0	.000	15	24	3	0	1.6	.929
4 yrs.			26	20	.565	3.52	59	59	14	399.1	381	138	208	2	0	0	0	1	0	0	.000	31	68	5	6	1.8	.952

Kevin Brown

BROWN, KEVIN DEWAYNE
B. Mar. 5, 1966, Oroville, Calif.
BL TL 6′ 1″ 185 lbs.

Year	Team		W	L	%	ERA	G	GS	CG	IP	H	BB	SO	ShO	Relief W	Relief L	Relief SV	AB	H	HR	BA	PO	A	E	DP	TC/G	FA
1990	2 teams	NY N (2G 0 – 0) MIL A (5G 1 – 1)																									
"	total		1	1	.500	2.35	7	3	0	23	16	8	12	0	0	0	0	0	0	0	—	2	6	0	0	1.1	1.000

Tom Browning

BROWNING, THOMAS LEO
B. Apr. 28, 1960, Casper, Wyo.
BL TL 6′ 1″ 190 lbs.

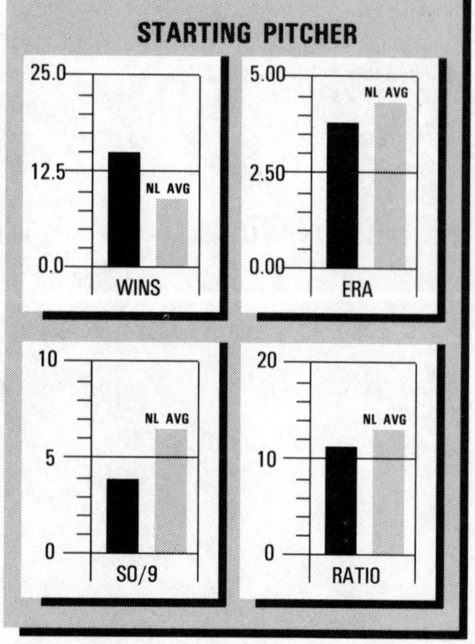
STARTING PITCHER
25.0
12.5
0.0
NL AVG
WINS
5.00
2.50
0.00
NL AVG
ERA
10
5
0
NL AVG
SO/9
20
10
0
NL AVG
RATIO

	W	L	%	ERA	G	GS	CG	IP	H	BB	SO	ShO	Relief W	Relief L	Relief SV
April	2	1	.667	3.34	5	5	0	29.2	32	6	17	0	0	0	0
May	2	3	.400	1.97	6	6	1	45.2	31	10	16	1	0	0	0
June	3	1	.750	3.73	6	6	1	41	47	9	18	0	0	0	0
July	3	0	1.000	2.28	6	6	0	43.1	38	6	20	0	0	0	0
Aug	2	2	.500	5.52	5	5	0	31	37	9	11	0	0	0	0
Sept/Oct	3	2	.600	6.81	7	7	0	37	50	12	17	0	0	0	0
Day	3	3	.500	4.03	10	10	0	60.1	68	19	26	0	0	0	0
Night	12	6	.667	3.71	25	25	2	167.1	167	33	73	1	0	0	0
vs. Left	—	—	—	—	—	—	—	—	41	13	30	—	—	—	—
vs. Right	—	—	—	—	—	—	—	—	194	39	69	—	—	—	—
On Grass	5	1	.833	3.22	10	10	0	64.1	71	12	29	0	0	0	0
On Turf	10	8	.556	4.02	25	25	2	163.1	164	40	70	1	0	0	0
Home	8	8	.500	4.64	20	20	1	128	141	30	52	0	0	0	0
Road	7	1	.875	2.71	15	15	1	99.2	94	22	47	1	0	0	0
Division Rivals															
vs. ATL	3	1	.750	4.50	6	6	1	38	48	9	14	0	0	0	0
vs. HOU	0	0	—	3.50	3	3	0	18	18	6	11	0	0	0	0
vs. LA	4	1	.800	4.55	5	5	0	31.2	35	9	15	0	0	0	0
vs. SD	3	1	.750	5.40	4	4	0	20	30	3	8	0	0	0	0
vs. SF	1	2	.333	5.18	4	4	0	24.1	30	7	11	0	0	0	0

Year	Team	W	L	%	ERA	G	GS	CG	IP	H	BB	SO	ShO	RELIEF PITCHING			BATTING			BA	PO	A	E	DP	TC/G	FA
														W	L	SV	AB	H	HR							

Tom Browning *Continued*

Year	Team	W	L	%	ERA	G	GS	CG	IP	H	BB	SO	ShO	W	L	SV	AB	H	HR	BA	PO	A	E	DP	TC/G	FA
1984	CIN N	1	0	1.000	1.54	3	3	0	23.1	27	5	14	0	0	0	0	7	1	0	.143	1	3	0	0	1.3	1.000
1985		20	9	.690	3.55	38	38	6	261.1	242	73	155	4	0	0	0	88	17	0	.193	12	34	2	1	1.3	.958
1986		14	13	.519	3.81	39	**39**	4	243.1	225	70	147	2	0	0	0	86	14	0	.163	11	26	3	5	1.0	.925
1987		10	13	.435	5.02	32	31	2	183	201	61	117	0	0	0	0	52	8	0	.154	5	23	3	1	1.0	.903
1988		18	5	.783	3.41	36	**36**	5	250.2	205	64	124	2	0	0	0	83	12	0	.145	8	30	3	3	1.1	.927
1989		15	12	.556	3.39	37	**37**	9	249.2	241	64	118	2	0	0	0	78	7	0	.090	8	35	0	3	1.2	1.000
1990		15	9	.625	3.80	35	**35**	2	227.2	235	52	99	1	0	0	0	75	7	0	.093	8	27	3	1	1.1	.921
7 yrs.		93	61	.604	3.73	220	219	28	1439	1376	389	774	11	0	0	0	469	66	0	.141	53	178	14	14	1.1	.943

LEAGUE CHAMPIONSHIP SERIES

Year	Team	W	L	%	ERA	G	GS	CG	IP	H	BB	SO	ShO	W	L	SV	AB	H	HR	BA	PO	A	E	DP	TC/G	FA
1990	CIN N	1	1	.500	3.27	2	2	0	11	9	6	5	0	0	0	0	3	0	0	.000	1	1	0	0	1.0	1.000

WORLD SERIES

Year	Team	W	L	%	ERA	G	GS	CG	IP	H	BB	SO	ShO	W	L	SV	AB	H	HR	BA	PO	A	E	DP	TC/G	FA
1990	CIN N	1	0	1.000	4.50	1	1	0	6	6	2	2	0	0	0	0	0	0	0	—	0	0	0	0	0.0	—

Dave Burba

BURBA, DAVID ALLEN
B. July 7, 1966, Dayton, Ohio
BR TR 6′ 4″ 220 lbs.

Year	Team	W	L	%	ERA	G	GS	CG	IP	H	BB	SO	ShO	W	L	SV	AB	H	HR	BA	PO	A	E	DP	TC/G	FA
1990	SEA A	0	0	—	4.50	6	0	0	8	8	2	4	0	0	0	0	0	0	0	—	1	2	1	0	0.7	.750

Tim Burke

BURKE, TIMOTHY PHILIP
B. Feb. 19, 1959, Omaha, Neb.
BR TR 6′ 3″ 205 lbs.

	W	L	%	ERA	G	GS	CG	IP	H	BB	SO	ShO	W	L	SV
April	0	0	—	5.06	10	0	0	10.2	16	3	6	0	0	0	6
May	0	1	.000	3.65	12	0	0	12.1	13	5	9	0	0	1	5
June	—	—	—	—	0	—	—	0	0	0	0	—	0	0	0
July	1	1	.500	2.13	9	0	0	12.2	15	5	7	0	1	1	2
Aug	0	1	.000	3.31	12	0	0	16.1	18	4	11	0	0	1	2
Sept/Oct	2	0	1.000	0.39	15	0	0	23	9	4	14	0	2	0	5
Day	0	2	.000	1.82	19	0	0	29.2	21	6	20	0	0	2	7
Night	3	1	.750	2.98	39	0	0	45.1	50	15	27	0	3	1	13
vs. Left	—	—	—	—	—	—	—	—	41	10	19	—	—	—	—
vs. Right	—	—	—	—	—	—	—	—	30	11	28	—	—	—	—
On Grass	1	1	.500	1.93	15	0	0	18.2	18	4	16	0	1	1	5
On Turf	2	2	.500	2.72	43	0	0	56.1	53	17	31	0	2	2	15
Home	2	2	.500	2.87	27	0	0	31.1	31	11	19	0	2	2	8
Road	1	1	.500	2.27	31	0	0	43.2	40	10	28	0	1	1	12
Division Rivals															
vs. CHI	1	1	.500	0.00	5	0	0	7.2	6	2	1	0	1	1	1
vs. NY	1	0	1.000	2.89	8	0	0	9.1	7	1	5	0	1	0	4
vs. PHI	0	0	—	1.86	6	0	0	9.2	3	3	8	0	0	0	1
vs. PIT	0	0	—	0.00	7	0	0	9.1	6	3	4	0	0	0	2
vs. STL	1	0	1.000	4.15	5	0	0	8.2	12	4	6	0	1	0	2

RELIEF PITCHER

Year	Team	W	L	%	ERA	G	GS	CG	IP	H	BB	SO	ShO	W	L	SV	AB	H	HR	BA	PO	A	E	DP	TC/G	FA
1985	MON N	9	4	.692	2.39	**78**	0	0	120.1	86	44	87	0	9	4	8	10	1	0	.100	5	21	1	2	0.3	.963
1986		9	7	.563	2.93	68	2	0	101.1	103	46	82	0	8	7	4	7	0	0	.000	4	22	1	1	0.4	.963
1987		7	0	1.000	1.19	55	0	0	91	64	17	58	0	7	0	18	10	0	0	.000	6	17	0	0	0.4	1.000
1988		3	5	.375	3.40	61	0	0	82	84	25	42	0	3	5	18	2	0	0	.000	8	14	0	0	0.4	1.000
1989		9	3	.750	2.55	68	0	0	84.2	68	22	54	0	9	3	28	3	0	0	.000	4	16	0	0	0.3	1.000
1990		3	3	.500	2.52	58	0	0	75	71	21	47	0	3	3	20	6	1	0	.167	3	20	0	1	0.4	1.000
6 yrs.		40	22	.645	2.48	388	2	0	554.1	476	175	370	0	39	22	96	38	2	0	.053	30	110	2	4	0.4	.986

Year	Team	W	L	%	ERA	G	GS	CG	IP	H	BB	SO	ShO	W	L	SV	AB	H	HR	BA	PO	A	E	DP	TC/G	FA

John Burkett

BURKETT, JOHN DAVID
B. Nov. 28, 1964, New Brighton, Pa.
BR TR 6′ 2″ 175 lbs.

Year	Team	W	L	%	ERA	G	GS	CG	IP	H	BB	SO	ShO	W	L	SV	AB	H	HR	BA	PO	A	E	DP	TC/G	FA
April		1	0	1.000	2.57	1	1	0	7	7	1	3	0	0	0	0										
May		3	1	.750	4.86	6	6	0	33.1	37	16	14	0	0	0	0										
June		3	1	.750	2.68	6	6	1	43.2	34	12	31	0	0	0	0										
July		2	1	.667	3.65	6	6	0	37	39	8	23	0	0	0	0										
Aug		2	2	.500	3.96	6	6	0	36.1	34	11	19	0	0	0	0										
Sept/Oct		3	2	.600	4.24	8	7	1	46.2	50	13	28	0	0	0	1										
Day		8	2	.800	3.25	16	16	1	105.1	99	30	60	0	0	0	0										
Night		6	5	.545	4.38	17	16	1	98.2	102	31	58	0	0	0	1										
vs. Left		—	—	—	—	—	—	—	—	117	36	63	—	—	—	—										
vs. Right		—	—	—	—	—	—	—	—	84	25	55	—	—	—	—										
On Grass		10	4	.714	3.54	24	23	2	152.1	145	47	92	0	0	0	1										
On Turf		4	3	.571	4.53	9	9	0	51.2	56	14	26	0	0	0	0										
Home		6	2	.750	3.98	16	16	1	104	102	33	67	0	0	0	0										
Road		8	5	.615	3.60	17	16	1	100	99	28	51	0	0	0	1										
Division Rivals																										
vs. ATL		3	0	1.000	3.77	4	4	0	28.2	27	7	23	0	0	0	0										
vs. CIN		3	1	.750	3.18	5	5	1	34	29	7	21	0	0	0	0										
vs. HOU		0	2	.000	1.80	2	2	0	15	11	2	8	0	0	0	0										
vs. LA		3	1	.750	3.41	5	5	1	31.2	32	12	20	0	0	0	0										
vs. SD		0	0	—	2.79	2	1	0	9.2	6	4	6	0	0	0	1										
1987	SF N	0	0	—	4.50	3	0	0	6	7	3	5	0	0	0	0	1	0	0	.000	0	1	0	1	0.3	1.000
1990		14	7	.667	3.79	33	32	2	204	201	61	118	0	0	0	1	63	3	0	.048	11	25	1	4	1.1	.973
2 yrs.		14	7	.667	3.81	36	32	2	210	208	64	123	0	0	0	1	64	3	0	.047	11	26	1	5	1.1	.974

Todd Burns

BURNS, TODD EDWARD
B. July 6, 1963, Maywood, Calif.
BR TR 6′ 2″ 186 lbs.

Year	Team	W	L	%	ERA	G	GS	CG	IP	H	BB	SO	ShO	W	L	SV	AB	H	HR	BA	PO	A	E	DP	TC/G	FA
April		0	0	—	6.75	6	0	0	5.1	8	4	4	0	0	0	0										
May		1	0	1.000	0.00	8	0	0	13.1	10	0	9	0	1	0	1										
June		1	1	.500	3.86	7	0	0	9.1	10	6	4	0	1	1	1										
July		0	1	.000	2.77	8	0	0	13	15	8	7	0	0	1	1										
Aug		0	1	.000	6.75	6	0	0	8	10	5	8	0	0	1	0										
Sept/Oct		1	0	1.000	2.43	8	2	0	29.2	25	9	11	0	0	0	1										
Day		2	2	.500	2.37	17	0	0	30.1	25	15	23	0	2	2	1										
Night		1	1	.500	3.35	26	2	0	48.1	53	17	20	0	0	1	2										
vs. Left		—	—	—	—	—	—	—	—	34	17	11	—	—	—	—										
vs. Right		—	—	—	—	—	—	—	—	44	15	32	—	—	—	—										
On Grass		3	2	.600	3.09	37	2	0	70	62	29	38	0	2	2	3										
On Turf		0	1	.000	2.08	6	0	0	8.2	16	3	5	0	0	1	0										
Home		2	1	.667	2.85	22	1	0	41	39	14	20	0	2	1	2										
Road		1	2	.333	3.11	21	1	0	37.2	39	18	23	0	0	2	1										
Division Rivals																										
vs. CAL		0	1	.000	5.91	5	0	0	10.2	11	4	6	0	0	1	1										
vs. CHI		0	0	—	10.13	2	0	0	2.2	4	1	1	0	0	0	0										
vs. KC		0	0	—	4.91	3	0	0	3.2	8	1	3	0	0	0	0										
vs. MIN		0	0	—	0.60	5	1	0	15	13	4	3	0	0	0	0										
vs. SEA		0	0	—	10.80	3	0	0	1.2	5	1	0	0	0	0	0										
vs. TEX		2	0	1.000	1.17	4	1	0	15.1	12	4	8	0	1	0	0										
1988	OAK A	8	2	.800	3.16	17	14	2	102.2	93	34	57	0	1	0	1	0	0	0	—	3	11	0	1	0.8	1.000
1989		6	5	.545	2.24	50	2	0	96.1	66	28	49	0	5	5	8	0	0	0	—	9	9	3	1	0.4	.857
1990		3	3	.500	2.97	43	2	0	78.2	78	32	43	0	2	3	3	0	0	0	—	2	7	0	1	0.2	1.000
3 yrs.		17	10	.630	2.79	110	18	2	277.2	237	94	149	0	8	8	12	0	0	0	—	14	27	3	3	0.4	.932
WORLD SERIES																										
1988	OAK A	0	0	—	0.00	1	0	0	0.1	0	0	0	0	0	0	0	0	0	0	—	0	0	0	0	0.0	—
1989		0	0	—	0.00	2	0	0	1.2	1	1	0	0	0	0	0	0	0	0	—	0	0	0	0	0.0	—
1990		0	0	—	16.20	2	0	0	1.2	5	2	0	0	0	0	0	0	0	0	—	0	0	0	0	0.0	—
3 yrs.		0	0	—	7.36	5	0	0	3.2	6	3	0	0	0	0	0	0	0	0	—	0	0	0	0	0.0	—

Year	Team	W	L	%	ERA	G	GS	CG	IP	H	BB	SO	ShO	RELIEF PITCHING W	L	SV	BATTING AB	H	HR	BA	PO	A	E	DP	TC/G	FA

Greg Cadaret

CADARET, GREGORY JAMES
B. Feb. 27, 1962, Detroit, Mich.
BL TL 6′ 3″ 200 lbs.

Year	Team	W	L	%	ERA	G	GS	CG	IP	H	BB	SO	ShO	W	L	SV	AB	H	HR	BA	PO	A	E	DP	TC/G	FA
April		1	1	.500	7.90	5	3	0	13.2	18	7	9	0	0	0	0										
May		0	3	.000	4.24	8	3	0	23.1	22	9	13	0	0	1	0										
June		1	0	1.000	3.20	10	0	0	25.1	30	11	15	0	1	0	0										
July		1	0	1.000	1.93	13	0	0	23.1	20	10	9	0	1	0	2										
Aug		2	0	1.000	3.22	8	0	0	22.1	19	15	22	0	2	0	0										
Sept/Oct		0	0	—	7.43	10	0	0	13.1	11	12	12	0	0	0	1										
Day		3	2	.600	4.50	22	5	0	64	60	33	40	0	2	0	3										
Night		2	2	.500	3.77	32	1	0	57.1	60	31	40	0	2	1	0										
vs. Left		—	—	—	—	—	—	—	—	30	15	17	—	—	—	—										
vs. Right		—	—	—	—	—	—	—	—	90	49	63	—	—	—	—										
On Grass		3	2	.600	4.09	44	5	0	99	94	56	70	0	2	0	3										
On Turf		2	2	.500	4.43	10	1	0	22.1	26	8	10	0	2	1	0										
Home		3	0	1.000	2.78	25	3	0	58.1	47	31	41	0	2	0	0										
Road		2	4	.333	5.43	29	3	0	63	73	33	39	0	2	1	3										
Division Rivals																										
vs. BAL		0	0	—	5.87	3	0	0	7.2	10	2	8	0	0	0	0										
vs. BOS		0	0	—	5.79	4	0	0	9.1	13	8	5	0	0	0	0										
vs. CLE		1	0	1.000	4.50	6	1	0	10	6	3	9	0	1	0	2										
vs. DET		0	0	—	0.00	3	0	0	6.2	4	4	4	0	0	0	0										
vs. MIL		0	0	—	0.00	3	0	0	10.1	5	4	7	0	0	0	1										
vs. TOR		2	0	1.000	1.69	5	0	0	16	11	6	10	0	2	0	0										
1987	OAK A	6	2	.750	4.54	29	0	0	39.2	37	24	30	0	6	2	0	0	0	0	—	6	6	0	1	0.4	1.000
1988		5	2	.714	2.89	58	0	0	71.2	60	36	64	0	5	2	3	0	0	0	—	3	9	0	1	0.2	1.000
1989	2 teams	OAK A	(26G 0 - 0)		NY A	(20G 5 - 5)																				
''	total	5	5	.500	4.05	46	13	3	120	130	57	80	1	1	0	0	0	0	0	—	9	21	2	2	0.7	.938
1990	NY A	5	4	.556	4.15	54	6	0	121.1	120	64	80	0	4	1	3	0	0	0	—	7	27	1	1	0.6	.971
4 yrs.		21	13	.618	3.90	187	19	3	352.2	347	181	254	1	16	5	6	0	0	0	—	25	63	3	5	0.5	.967

LEAGUE CHAMPIONSHIP SERIES

Year	Team	W	L	%	ERA	G	GS	CG	IP	H	BB	SO	ShO	W	L	SV	AB	H	HR	BA	PO	A	E	DP	TC/G	FA
1988	OAK A	0	0	—	27.00	1	0	0	0.1	1	0	0	0	0	0	0	0	0	0	—	0	0	0	0	0.0	—

WORLD SERIES

Year	Team	W	L	%	ERA	G	GS	CG	IP	H	BB	SO	ShO	W	L	SV	AB	H	HR	BA	PO	A	E	DP	TC/G	FA
1988	OAK A	0	0	—	0.00	3	0	0	2	2	0	3	0	0	0	0	0	0	0	—	0	0	0	0	0.0	—

Ernie Camacho

CAMACHO, ERNEST CARLOS
B. Feb. 1, 1955, Salinas, Calif.
BR TR 6′ 1″ 180 lbs.

Year	Team	W	L	%	ERA	G	GS	CG	IP	H	BB	SO	ShO	W	L	SV	AB	H	HR	BA	PO	A	E	DP	TC/G	FA
1980	OAK A	0	0	—	6.75	5	0	0	12	20	5	9	0	0	0	0	0	0	0	—	0	0	0	0	0.0	—
1981	PIT N	0	1	.000	4.91	7	3	0	22	23	15	11	0	0	0	0	4	0	0	.000	0	3	0	1	0.4	1.000
1983	CLE A	0	1	.000	5.06	4	0	0	5.1	5	2	2	0	0	1	0	0	0	0	—	0	0	0	0	0.0	—
1984		5	9	.357	2.43	69	0	0	100	83	37	48	0	5	9	23	0	0	0	—	1	15	0	0	0.2	1.000
1985		0	1	.000	8.10	2	0	0	3.1	4	1	2	0	0	1	0	0	0	0	—	0	1	0	0	0.5	1.000
1986		2	4	.333	4.08	51	0	0	57.1	60	31	36	0	2	4	20	0	0	0	—	5	11	1	0	0.3	.941
1987		0	1	.000	9.22	15	0	0	13.2	21	5	9	0	0	1	1	0	0	0	—	1	5	0	0	0.4	1.000
1988	HOU N	0	3	.000	7.64	13	0	0	17.2	25	12	13	0	0	3	1	1	0	0	.000	1	3	0	0	0.3	1.000
1989	SF N	3	0	1.000	2.76	13	0	0	16.1	10	11	14	0	3	0	1	1	0	0	.000	2	5	0	0	0.5	1.000
1990	2 teams	SF N	(8G 0 - 0)		STL N	(6G 0 - 0)																				
''	total	0	0	—	5.17	14	0	0	15.2	17	9	15	0	0	0	0	0	0	0	—	0	1	0	0	0.1	1.000
10 yrs.		10	20	.333	4.20	193	3	0	263.1	268	128	159	0	10	19	45	6	0	0	.000	10	44	1	1	0.3	.982

Jim Campbell

CAMPBELL, JAMES MARCUS
B. May 19, 1966, Santa Maria, Calif.
BL TL 5′ 11″ 175 lbs.

Year	Team	W	L	%	ERA	G	GS	CG	IP	H	BB	SO	ShO	W	L	SV	AB	H	HR	BA	PO	A	E	DP	TC/G	FA
1990	KC A	1	0	1.000	8.38	2	2	0	9.2	15	1	2	0	0	0	0	0	0	0	—	1	0	0	0	0.5	1.000

Year	Team	W	L	%	ERA	G	GS	CG	IP	H	BB	SO	ShO	W	L	SV	AB	H	HR	BA	PO	A	E	DP	TC/G	FA

John Candelaria

CANDELARIA, JOHN ROBERT (The Candy Man)
B. Nov. 6, 1953, New York, N. Y.
BL TL 6' 7" 205 lbs.

Year	Team	W	L	%	ERA	G	GS	CG	IP	H	BB	SO	ShO	W	L	SV	AB	H	HR	BA	PO	A	E	DP	TC/G	FA
April		1	0	1.000	3.00	7	0	0	15	13	1	11	0	1	0	1										
May		4	1	.800	5.49	9	1	0	19.2	23	2	14	0	4	0	1										
June		2	2	.500	1.76	9	0	0	15.1	14	3	13	0	2	2	1										
July		0	0	—	2.25	11	0	0	12	11	3	11	0	0	0	2										
Aug		0	3	.000	6.75	6	2	0	12	19	7	7	0	0	1	0										
Sept/Oct		0	0	—	4.76	5	0	0	5.2	7	4	7	0	0	0	0										
Day		2	0	1.000	1.71	14	0	0	21	20	3	16	0	2	0	3										
Night		5	6	.455	4.76	33	3	0	58.2	67	17	47	0	5	3	2										
vs. Left		—	—	—	—	—	—	—	—	20	3	21	—	—	—	—										
vs. Right		—	—	—	—	—	—	—	—	67	17	42	—	—	—	—										
On Grass		4	4	.500	4.46	21	2	0	34.1	39	14	31	0	4	2	0										
On Turf		3	2	.600	3.57	26	1	0	45.1	48	6	32	0	3	1	5										
Home		2	2	.500	3.66	21	1	0	39.1	42	4	28	0	2	1	5										
Road		5	4	.556	4.24	26	2	0	40.1	45	16	35	0	5	2	0										
Division Rivals																										
vs. BAL		0	0	—	4.50	4	0	0	4	6	1	2	0	0	0	1										
vs. BOS		2	0	1.000	0.00	7	0	0	9	7	2	4	0	2	0	0										
vs. CLE		0	1	.000	5.00	3	1	0	9	11	1	6	0	0	0	0										
vs. DET		2	0	1.000	2.19	4	0	0	12.1	10	2	8	0	2	0	0										
vs. MIL		1	0	1.000	13.50	3	0	0	3.1	6	2	3	0	1	0	0										
vs. NY		0	1	.000	9.35	5	1	0	8.2	14	1	9	0	0	0	0										
1975	PIT N	8	6	.571	2.75	18	18	4	121	95	36	95	1	0	0	0	43	6	0	.140	3	13	4	0	1.1	.800
1976		16	7	.696	3.15	32	31	11	220	173	60	138	4	0	0	1	76	14	0	.184	3	31	0	2	1.1	1.000
1977		20	5	**.800**	**2.34**	33	33	6	231	197	50	133	1	0	0	0	80	18	0	.225	6	30	1	3	1.1	.973
1978		12	11	.522	3.24	30	29	3	189	191	49	94	1	0	0	1	52	9	0	.173	4	25	0	0	1.0	1.000
1979		14	9	.609	3.22	33	30	8	207	201	41	101	0	0	0	1	68	9	0	.132	2	36	0	3	1.2	1.000
1980		11	14	.440	4.02	35	34	7	233	246	50	97	0	0	0	1	77	15	0	.195	8	38	2	3	1.4	.958
1981		2	2	.500	3.51	6	6	0	41	42	11	14	0	0	0	0	13	3	0	.231	1	7	0	1	1.3	1.000
1982		12	7	.632	2.94	31	30	1	174.2	166	37	133	1	0	0	0	54	12	0	.222	1	23	1	1	0.8	.960
1983		15	8	.652	3.23	33	32	2	197.2	191	45	157	0	0	0	0	65	9	0	.138	5	20	0	1	0.8	1.000
1984		12	11	.522	2.72	33	28	3	185.1	179	34	133	1	0	1	2	62	8	1	.129	3	21	0	1	0.7	1.000
1985	2 teams	PIT N	(37G 2 – 4)			CAL A	(13G 7 – 3)																			
"	total	9	7	.563	3.73	50	13	1	125.1	127	38	100	1	2	4	9	1	0	0	.000	3	16	2	0	0.4	.905
1986	CAL A	10	2	.833	2.55	16	16	1	91.2	68	26	81	1	0	0	0	0	0	0	—	3	10	0	0	0.8	1.000
1987	2 teams	CAL A	(20G 8 – 6)			NY N	(3G 2 – 0)																			
"	total	10	6	.625	4.81	23	23	0	129	144	23	84	0	0	0	0	5	1	0	.200	6	24	0	1	1.3	1.000
1988	NY A	13	7	.650	3.38	25	24	6	157	150	23	121	2	0	0	1	0	0	0	—	4	22	0	0	1.0	1.000
1989	2 teams	NY A	(10G 3 – 3)			MON N	(12G 0 – 2)																			
"	total	3	5	.375	4.68	22	6	1	65.1	66	16	51	0	0	0	3	0	0	0	—	2	7	1	0	0.5	.900
1990	2 teams	MIN A	(34G 7 – 3)			TOR A	(13G 0 – 3)																			
"		7	6	.538	3.95	47	3	0	79.2	87	20	63	0	7	3	5	0	0	0	—	4	9	0	0	0.3	1.000
16 yrs.		174	113	.606	3.29	467	356	54	2447.2	2323	559	1595	13	9	12	21	596	104	1	.174	58	332	11	16	0.9	.973

LEAGUE CHAMPIONSHIP SERIES

Year	Team	W	L	%	ERA	G	GS	CG	IP	H	BB	SO	ShO	W	L	SV	AB	H	HR	BA	PO	A	E	DP	TC/G	FA
1975	PIT N	0	0	—	3.52	1	1	0	7.2	3	2	14	0	0	0	0	3	0	0	.000	0	0	0	0	0.0	—
1979		0	0	—	2.57	1	1	0	7	5	1	4	0	0	0	0	3	0	0	.000	0	0	0	0	0.0	—
1986	CAL A	1	1	.500	0.84	2	2	0	10.2	11	6	7	0	0	0	0	0	1	0	—	0	1	0	0	0.5	1.000
3 yrs.		1	1	.500	2.13	4	4	0	25.1	19	9	25	0	0	0	0	6	0	0	.000	0	1	0	0	0.3	1.000

WORLD SERIES

Year	Team	W	L	%	ERA	G	GS	CG	IP	H	BB	SO	ShO	W	L	SV	AB	H	HR	BA	PO	A	E	DP	TC/G	FA
1979	PIT N	1	1	.500	5.00	2	2	0	9	14	2	4	0	0	0	0	3	1	0	.333	0	1	0	0	0.5	1.000

RELIEF PITCHER

WINS — AL AVG
ERA — AL AVG
SAVES — AL AVG
RATIO — AL AVG

Year	Team	W	L	%	ERA	G	GS	CG	IP	H	BB	SO	ShO	W	L	SV	AB	H	HR	BA	PO	A	E	DP	TC/G	FA

(Header groups: RELIEF PITCHING = W, L, SV; BATTING = AB, H, HR)

Tom Candiotti

CANDIOTTI, THOMAS CAESAR
B. Aug. 31, 1957, Walnut Creek, Calif.
BR TR 6′ 3″ 205 lbs.

Year	Team	W	L	%	ERA	G	GS	CG	IP	H	BB	SO	ShO	W	L	SV	AB	H	HR	BA	PO	A	E	DP	TC/G	FA
April		3	0	1.000	4.91	3	3	0	18.1	17	4	14	0	0	0	0										
May		2	2	.500	3.38	4	4	0	26.2	26	10	15	0	0	0	0										
June		4	1	.800	3.00	6	6	0	42	42	14	19	0	0	0	0										
July		2	3	.400	2.82	7	5	1	44.2	42	13	28	0	0	0	0										
Aug		2	3	.400	4.39	6	6	1	41	44	9	36	0	0	0	0										
Sept/Oct		2	2	.500	4.30	5	5	1	29.1	36	5	16	1	0	0	0										
Day		6	1	.857	3.55	7	7	0	50.2	49	12	35	0	0	0	0										
Night		9	10	.474	3.69	24	22	3	151.1	158	43	93	1	0	0	0										
vs. Left		—	—	—	—	—	—	—	—	103	32	52	—	—	—	—										
vs. Right		—	—	—	—	—	—	—	—	104	23	76	—	—	—	—										
On Grass		12	11	.522	3.68	28	26	3	183.2	189	49	110	1	0	0	0										
On Turf		3	0	1.000	3.44	3	3	0	18.1	18	6	18	0	0	0	0										
Home		7	6	.538	4.10	18	16	0	112	112	38	74	0	0	0	0										
Road		8	5	.615	3.10	13	13	3	90	95	17	54	1	0	0	0										
Division Rivals																										
vs. BAL		0	0	—	0.00	1	1	0	6.1	8	5	2	0	0	0	0										
vs. BOS		1	2	.333	6.88	3	3	0	17	23	4	11	0	0	0	0										
vs. DET		2	2	.500	4.81	4	4	2	24.1	32	7	17	1	0	0	0										
vs. MIL		3	0	1.000	3.80	3	3	0	23.2	25	4	14	0	0	0	0										
vs. NY		1	1	.500	0.57	2	2	0	15.2	5	6	12	0	0	0	0										
vs. TOR		1	2	.333	5.75	3	3	0	20.1	20	9	14	0	0	0	0										
1983	MIL A	4	4	.500	3.23	10	8	2	55.2	62	16	21	1	0	0	0	0	0	0	—	4	5	0	1	0.9	1.000
1984		2	2	.500	5.29	8	6	0	32.1	38	10	23	0	0	0	0	0	0	0	—	3	1	0	0	0.5	1.000
1986	CLE A	16	12	.571	3.57	36	34	17	252.1	234	106	167	3	0	0	0	0	0	0	—	27	41	3	7	2.0	.958
1987		7	18	.280	4.78	32	32	7	201.2	193	93	111	0	0	0	0	0	0	0	—	17	29	1	1	1.5	.979
1988		14	8	.636	3.28	31	31	11	216.2	225	53	137	1	0	0	0	0	0	0	—	17	36	1	2	1.7	.981
1989		13	10	.565	3.10	31	31	4	206	188	55	124	0	0	0	0	0	0	0	—	28	41	1	1	2.3	.986
1990		15	11	.577	3.65	31	29	3	202	207	55	128	1	0	0	0	0	0	0	—	22	37	2	1	2.0	.967
7 yrs.		71	65	.522	3.69	179	171	44	1166.2	1147	388	711	8	0	0	0	0	0	0	—	118	190	8	13	1.8	.975

STARTING PITCHER (charts: WINS, ERA, SO/9, RATIO with AL AVG)

John Cangelosi

CANGELOSI, JOHN ANTHONY
B. Mar. 10, 1963, Brooklyn, N. Y.
BB TL 5′ 8″ 150 lbs.

Year	Team	W	L	%	ERA	G	GS	CG	IP	H	BB	SO	ShO	W	L	SV	AB	H	HR	BA	PO	A	E	DP	TC/G	FA
1988	PIT N	0	0	—	0.00	1	0	0	2	1	0	0	0	0	0	0	*				0	0	0	0	0.0	—

Mike Capel

CAPEL, MICHAEL LEE
B. Oct. 13, 1961, Marshall, Tex.
BR TR 6′ 1″ 175 lbs.

Year	Team	W	L	%	ERA	G	GS	CG	IP	H	BB	SO	ShO	W	L	SV	AB	H	HR	BA	PO	A	E	DP	TC/G	FA
1988	CHI N	2	1	.667	4.91	22	0	0	29.1	34	13	19	0	2	1	0	2	0	0	.000	4	3	1	0	0.4	.875
1990	MIL A	0	0	—	135.00	2	0	0	0.1	6	1	1	0	0	0	0	0	0	0	—	0	0	0	0	0.0	—
2 yrs.		2	1	.667	6.37	24	0	0	29.2	40	14	20	0	2	1	0	2	0	0	.000	4	3	1	0	0.3	.875

Don Carman

CARMAN, DONALD WAYNE
B. Aug. 14, 1959, Oklahoma City, Okla.
BL TL 6′ 3″ 195 lbs.

Year	Team	W	L	%	ERA	G	GS	CG	IP	H	BB	SO	ShO	W	L	SV	AB	H	HR	BA	PO	A	E	DP	TC/G	FA
April		0	0	—	1.08	7	0	0	8.1	4	2	7	0	0	0	0										
May		2	0	1.000	4.95	12	0	0	20	16	10	13	0	2	0	0										
June		2	0	1.000	2.45	10	0	0	18.1	8	5	10	0	2	0	0										
July		0	0	—	4.05	10	0	0	13.1	9	4	12	0	0	0	0										
Aug		1	2	.333	7.53	11	1	0	14.1	21	8	10	0	1	1	1										
Sept/Oct		1	0	1.000	3.65	9	0	0	12.1	11	9	6	0	1	0	0										
Day		3	1	.750	4.45	17	1	0	28.1	30	23	15	0	3	0	0										
Night		3	1	.750	4.01	42	0	0	58.1	39	15	43	0	3	1	1										
vs. Left		—	—	—	—	—	—	—	—	18	10	19	—	—	—	—										
vs. Right		—	—	—	—	—	—	—	—	51	28	39	—	—	—	—										

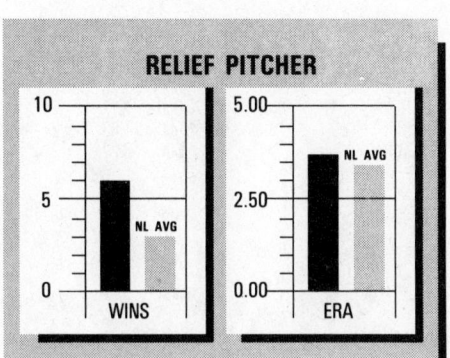

RELIEF PITCHER (charts: WINS, ERA with NL AVG)

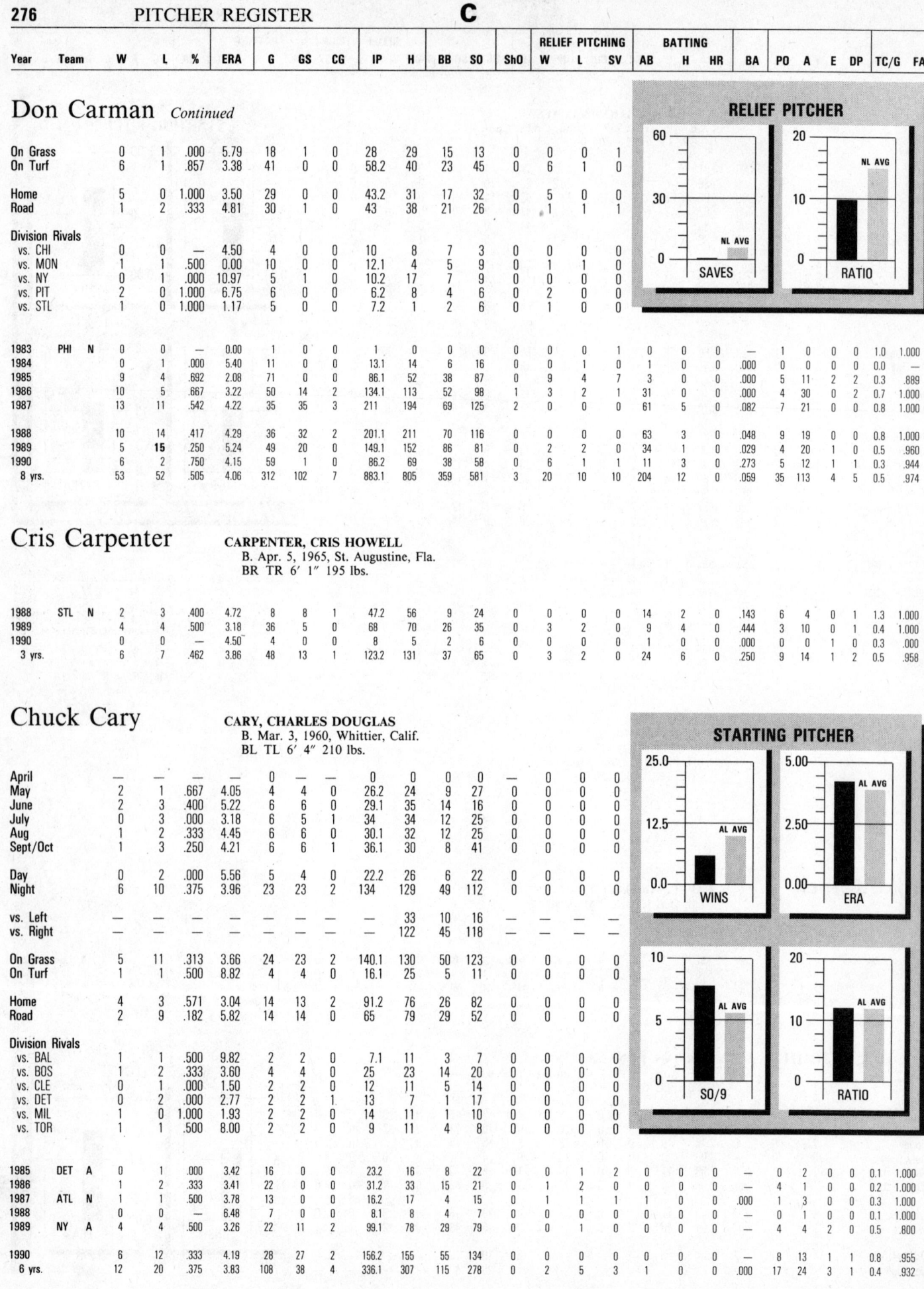

Year	Team	W	L	%	ERA	G	GS	CG	IP	H	BB	SO	ShO	W	L	SV	AB	H	HR	BA	PO	A	E	DP	TC/G	FA

Don Carman *Continued*

Split	W	L	%	ERA	G	GS	CG	IP	H	BB	SO	ShO	W	L	SV	AB	H	HR	BA	PO	A	E	DP	TC/G	FA
On Grass	0	1	.000	5.79	18	1	0	28	29	15	13	0	0	0	1										
On Turf	6	1	.857	3.38	41	0	0	58.2	40	23	45	0	6	1	0										
Home	5	0	1.000	3.50	29	0	0	43.2	31	17	32	0	5	0	0										
Road	1	2	.333	4.81	30	1	0	43	38	21	26	0	1	1	1										
Division Rivals																									
vs. CHI	0	0	—	4.50	4	0	0	10	8	7	3	0	0	0	0										
vs. MON	1	1	.500	0.00	10	0	0	12.1	4	5	9	0	1	1	0										
vs. NY	0	1	.000	10.97	5	1	0	10.2	17	7	9	0	0	0	0										
vs. PIT	2	0	1.000	6.75	6	0	0	6.2	8	4	6	0	2	0	0										
vs. STL	1	0	1.000	1.17	5	0	0	7.2	1	2	6	0	1	0	0										
1983 PHI N	0	0	—	0.00	1	0	0	1	0	0	0	0	0	0	1	0	0	0	—	1	0	0	0	1.0	1.000
1984	0	1	.000	5.40	11	0	0	13.1	14	6	16	0	0	1	0	1	0	0	.000	0	0	0	0	0.0	—
1985	9	4	.692	2.08	71	0	0	86.1	52	38	87	0	9	4	7	3	0	0	.000	5	11	2	2	0.3	.889
1986	10	5	.667	3.22	50	14	2	134.1	113	52	98	1	3	2	1	31	0	0	.000	4	30	0	0	0.7	1.000
1987	13	11	.542	4.22	35	35	3	211	194	69	125	2	0	0	0	61	5	0	.082	7	21	0	0	0.8	1.000
1988	10	14	.417	4.29	36	32	2	201.1	211	70	116	0	0	0	0	63	3	0	.048	9	19	0	0	0.8	1.000
1989	5	**15**	.250	5.24	49	20	0	149.1	152	86	81	0	2	2	0	34	1	0	.029	4	20	0	0	0.5	.960
1990	6	2	.750	4.15	59	1	0	86.2	69	38	58	0	6	1	1	11	3	0	.273	5	12	1	1	0.3	.944
8 yrs.	53	52	.505	4.06	312	102	7	883.1	805	359	581	3	20	10	10	204	12	0	.059	35	113	4	5	0.5	.974

Cris Carpenter

CARPENTER, CRIS HOWELL
B. Apr. 5, 1965, St. Augustine, Fla.
BR TR 6′ 1″ 195 lbs.

Year	Team	W	L	%	ERA	G	GS	CG	IP	H	BB	SO	ShO	W	L	SV	AB	H	HR	BA	PO	A	E	DP	TC/G	FA
1988 STL N	2	3	.400	4.72	8	8	1	47.2	56	9	24	0	0	0	0	14	2	0	.143	6	4	0	1	1.3	1.000
1989	4	4	.500	3.18	36	5	0	68	70	26	35	0	3	2	0	9	4	0	.444	3	10	0	1	0.4	1.000
1990	0	0	—	4.50	4	0	0	8	5	2	6	0	0	0	0	1	0	0	.000	0	0	1	0	0.3	.000
3 yrs.	6	7	.462	3.86	48	13	1	123.2	131	37	65	0	3	2	0	24	6	0	.250	9	14	1	2	0.5	.958

Chuck Cary

CARY, CHARLES DOUGLAS
B. Mar. 3, 1960, Whittier, Calif.
BL TL 6′ 4″ 210 lbs.

Split	W	L	%	ERA	G	GS	CG	IP	H	BB	SO	ShO	W	L	SV	AB	H	HR	BA	PO	A	E	DP	TC/G	FA
April	—			—	0			0	0	0	0	—	0	0	0										
May	2	1	.667	4.05	4	4	0	26.2	24	9	27	0	0	0	0										
June	2	3	.400	5.22	6	6	0	29.1	35	14	16	0	0	0	0										
July	0	3	.000	3.18	6	5	1	34	34	12	25	0	0	0	0										
Aug	1	2	.333	4.45	6	6	0	30.1	32	12	25	0	0	0	0										
Sept/Oct	1	3	.250	4.21	6	6	1	36.1	30	8	41	0	0	0	0										
Day	0	2	.000	5.56	5	4	0	22.2	26	6	22	0	0	0	0										
Night	6	10	.375	3.96	23	23	2	134	129	49	112	0	0	0	0										
vs. Left	—	—	—	—	—	—	—	—	33	10	16	—	—	—	—										
vs. Right	—	—	—	—	—	—	—	—	122	45	118	—	—	—	—										
On Grass	5	11	.313	3.66	24	23	2	140.1	130	50	123	0	0	0	0										
On Turf	1	1	.500	8.82	4	4	0	16.1	25	5	11	0	0	0	0										
Home	4	3	.571	3.04	14	13	2	91.1	76	26	82	0	0	0	0										
Road	2	9	.182	5.82	14	14	0	65	79	29	52	0	0	0	0										
Division Rivals																									
vs. BAL	1	1	.500	9.82	2	2	0	7.1	11	3	7	0	0	0	0										
vs. BOS	1	2	.333	3.60	4	4	0	25	23	14	20	0	0	0	0										
vs. CLE	0	1	.000	1.50	2	2	0	12	11	5	14	0	0	0	0										
vs. DET	0	2	.000	2.77	2	2	1	13	7	1	17	0	0	0	0										
vs. MIL	1	0	1.000	1.93	2	2	0	14	11	1	10	0	0	0	0										
vs. TOR	1	1	.500	8.00	2	2	0	9	11	4	9	0	0	0	0										
1985 DET A	0	1	.000	3.42	16	0	0	23.2	16	8	22	0	0	1	2	0	0	0	—	0	2	0	0	0.1	1.000
1986	1	2	.333	3.41	22	0	0	31.2	33	15	21	0	1	2	0	0	0	0	—	4	1	0	0	0.2	1.000
1987 ATL N	1	1	.500	3.78	13	0	0	16.2	17	4	15	0	1	1	1	1	0	0	.000	1	3	0	0	0.3	1.000
1988	0	0	—	6.48	7	0	0	8.1	8	4	7	0	0	0	0	0	0	0	—	1	0	0	0	0.1	1.000
1989 NY A	4	4	.500	3.26	22	11	2	99.1	78	29	79	0	0	1	0	0	0	0	—	4	4	2	0	0.5	.800
1990	6	12	.333	4.19	28	27	2	156.2	155	55	134	0	0	0	0	0	0	0	—	8	13	1	1	0.8	.955
6 yrs.	12	20	.375	3.83	108	38	4	336.1	307	115	278	0	2	5	3	1	0	0	.000	17	24	3	1	0.4	.932

Year	Team	W	L	%	ERA	G	GS	CG	IP	H	BB	SO	ShO	W	L	SV	AB	H	HR	BA	PO	A	E	DP	TC/G	FA

RELIEF PITCHING: W, L, SV — BATTING: AB, H, HR, BA

Larry Casian

CASIAN, LAWRENCE PAUL
B. Oct. 28, 1965, Lynwood, Calif.
BR TL 6′ 170 lbs.

Year	Team	W	L	%	ERA	G	GS	CG	IP	H	BB	SO	ShO	W	L	SV	AB	H	HR	BA	PO	A	E	DP	TC/G	FA
1990	MIN A	2	1	.667	3.22	5	3	0	22.1	26	4	11	0	1	0	0	0	0	0	—	0	3	0	1	0.6	1.000

Tony Castillo

CASTILLO, ANTONIO JOSE
B. Mar. 1, 1963, Quibor, Venezuela
BL TL 5′ 10″ 177 lbs.

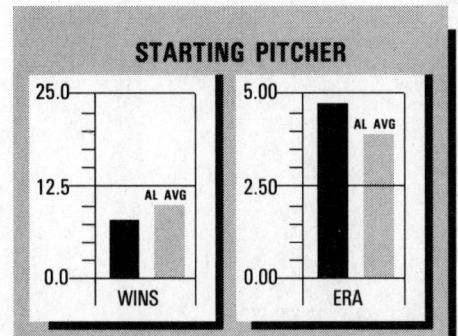

RELIEF PITCHER — WINS (NL AVG), ERA (NL AVG), SAVES (NL AVG), RATIO (NL AVG)

		W	L	%	ERA	G	GS	CG	IP	H	BB	SO	ShO	W	L	SV	AB	H	HR	BA	PO	A	E	DP	TC/G	FA
April		0	0	—	9.00	3	0	0	3	5	2	2	0	1	0	0										
May		1	0	1.000	3.50	11	0	0	18	18	2	17	0	1	0	0										
June		1	1	.500	4.76	11	0	0	17	23	5	16	0	1	1	0										
July		0	0	—	6.14	4	1	0	7.1	12	2	5	0	0	0	1										
Aug		2	0	1.000	3.32	10	2	0	19	17	4	14	0	0	0	0										
Sept/Oct		1	0	1.000	3.65	13	0	0	12.1	18	5	10	0	1	0	0										
Day		1	1	.500	5.91	11	0	0	10.2	14	2	8	0	1	1	0										
Night		4	0	1.000	3.95	41	3	0	66	79	18	56	0	2	0	1										
vs. Left		—	—	—	—	—	—	—	—	27	6	25	—	—	—	—										
vs. Right		—	—	—	—	—	—	—	—	66	14	39	—	—	—	—										
On Grass		2	1	.667	4.89	38	1	0	53.1	74	14	49	0	2	1	1										
On Turf		3	0	1.000	2.70	14	2	0	23.1	19	6	15	0	1	0	0										
Home		1	0	1.000	5.74	22	1	0	31.1	45	9	30	0	1	0	0										
Road		4	1	.800	3.18	30	2	0	45.1	48	11	34	0	2	1	1										
Division Rivals																										
vs. CIN		0	0	—	9.95	5	0	0	6.1	14	3	7	0	0	0	0										
vs. HOU		0	0	—	4.05	5	1	0	6.2	8	2	3	0	0	0	0										
vs. LA		0	0	—	2.45	7	0	0	11	12	2	9	0	0	0	0										
vs. SD		1	0	1.000	3.97	9	0	0	11.1	19	3	8	0	1	0	1										
vs. SF		0	1	.000	6.55	9	0	0	11	14	5	12	0	0	1	0										
1988	TOR A	1	0	1.000	3.00	14	0	0	15	10	2	14	0	1	0	0	0	0	0	—	0	3	0	0	0.2	1.000
1989	2 teams																									
	TOR A (17G 1 - 1)																									
	ATL N (12G 0 - 1)																									
"	total	1	2	.333	5.67	29	0	0	27	31	14	15	0	1	2	1	1	0	0	.000	2	3	0	0	0.2	1.000
1990	ATL N	5	1	.833	4.23	52	3	0	76.2	93	20	64	0	3	1	1	7	1	0	.143	5	13	0	1	0.3	1.000
3 yrs.		7	3	.700	4.40	95	3	0	118.2	134	36	93	0	5	3	2	8	1	0	.125	7	19	0	1	0.3	1.000

Rick Cerone

CERONE, RICHARD ALDO
B. May 19, 1954, Newark, N. J.
BR TR 5′ 11″ 192 lbs.

Year	Team	W	L	%	ERA	G	GS	CG	IP	H	BB	SO	ShO	W	L	SV	AB	H	HR	BA	PO	A	E	DP	TC/G	FA
1987	NY A	0	0	—	0.00	2	0	0	2	0	1	1	0	0	0	0	•				0	0	0	0	0.0	—

John Cerutti

CERUTTI, JOHN JOSEPH
B. Apr. 28, 1960, Albany, N. Y.
BL TL 6′ 2″ 190 lbs.

STARTING PITCHER — WINS (AL AVG), ERA (AL AVG)

		W	L	%	ERA	G	GS	CG	IP	H	BB	SO	ShO	W	L	SV	AB	H	HR	BA	PO	A	E	DP	TC/G	FA
April		1	3	.250	5.79	4	4	0	18.2	18	3	8	0	0	0	0										
May		1	2	.333	3.69	6	5	0	31.2	35	12	11	0	0	0	0										
June		2	1	.667	3.55	6	6	0	38	41	11	13	0	0	0	0										
July		3	1	.750	6.51	5	5	0	27.2	39	13	13	0	0	0	0										
Aug		1	2	.333	6.27	4	3	0	18.2	24	7	4	0	0	0	0										
Sept/Oct		1	0	1.000	1.69	5	0	0	5.1	5	3	0	0	1	0	0										
Day		2	1	.667	3.94	7	6	0	32	37	8	16	0	0	0	0										
Night		7	8	.467	5.00	23	17	0	108	125	41	33	0	1	0	0										
vs. Left		—	—	—	—	—	—	—	—	30	6	7	—	—	—	—										
vs. Right		—	—	—	—	—	—	—	—	132	43	42	—	—	—	—										

Year	Team	W	L	%	ERA	G	GS	CG	IP	H	BB	SO	ShO	W	L	SV	AB	H	HR	BA	PO	A	E	DP	TC/G	FA
														RELIEF PITCHING			BATTING									

John Cerutti *Continued*

Year	Team	W	L	%	ERA	G	GS	CG	IP	H	BB	SO	ShO	W	L	SV	AB	H	HR	BA	PO	A	E	DP	TC/G	FA
On Grass		2	4	.333	5.02	11	9	0	52	59	26	18	0	0	0	0										
On Turf		7	5	.583	4.60	19	14	0	88	103	23	31	0	1	0	0										
Home		5	5	.500	5.32	16	12	0	71	82	20	27	0	1	0	0										
Road		4	4	.500	4.17	14	11	0	69	80	29	22	0	0	0	0										
Division Rivals																										
vs. BAL		1	1	.500	5.40	3	2	0	10	11	4	6	0	0	0	0										
vs. BOS		0	0	—	2.25	1	1	0	8	8	1	0	0	0	0	0										
vs. CLE		0	1	.000	2.16	2	1	0	8.1	5	3	5	0	0	0	0										
vs. DET		0	0	—	2.08	1	1	0	4.1	6	3	1	0	0	0	0										
vs. MIL		0	0	—	4.15	4	2	0	13	13	7	9	0	0	0	0										
vs. NY		2	1	.667	5.91	3	2	0	10.2	13	7	2	0	1	0	0										
1985	TOR A	0	2	.000	5.40	4	1	0	6.2	10	4	5	0	0	1	0	0	0	0	—	0	1	0	0	0.3	1.000
1986		9	4	.692	4.15	34	20	2	145.1	150	47	89	1	2	0	1	0	0	0	—	8	21	0	2	0.9	1.000
1987		11	4	.733	4.40	44	21	2	151.1	144	59	92	0	2	0	0	0	0	0	—	5	15	1	1	0.5	.952
1988		6	7	.462	3.13	46	12	0	123.2	120	42	65	0	1	3	1	0	0	0	—	13	27	0	2	0.9	1.000
1989		11	11	.500	3.07	33	31	3	205.1	214	53	69	1	0	0	0	0	0	0	—	16	45	1	3	1.9	.984
1990		9	9	.500	4.76	30	23	0	140	162	49	49	0	1	0	0	0	0	0	—	11	18	0	2	1.0	1.000
6 yrs.		46	37	.554	3.87	191	108	7	772.1	800	254	369	2	6	4	2	0	0	0	—	53	127	2	10	1.0	.989

LEAGUE CHAMPIONSHIP SERIES

Year	Team	W	L	%	ERA	G	GS	CG	IP	H	BB	SO	ShO	W	L	SV	AB	H	HR	BA	PO	A	E	DP	TC/G	FA
1989	TOR A	0	0	—	0.00	2	0	0	2.2	0	3	1	0	0	0	0	0	0	0	—	0	2	0	0	1.0	1.000

Norm Charlton   CHARLTON, NORMAN WOOD
B. Jan. 6, 1963, Fort Polk, La.
BB TL 6′ 3″ 195 lbs.

Year	Team	W	L	%	ERA	G	GS	CG	IP	H	BB	SO	ShO	W	L	SV	AB	H	HR	BA	PO	A	E	DP	TC/G	FA
April		0	0	—	3.38	8	0	0	10.2	9	9	19	0	0	0	0										
May		3	1	.750	3.24	14	0	0	16.2	17	8	19	0	3	1	1										
June		3	0	1.000	2.65	13	0	0	17	17	4	13	0	3	0	1										
July		2	5	.286	2.37	8	4	0	30.1	25	10	19	0	0	3	0										
Aug		2	1	.667	1.22	6	6	1	44.1	30	18	25	1	0	0	0										
Sept/Oct		2	2	.500	4.58	7	6	0	35.1	33	21	22	0	0	0	0										
Day		2	3	.400	2.11	18	5	0	42.2	35	17	40	0	1	2	1										
Night		10	6	.625	2.98	38	11	1	111.2	96	53	77	1	5	2	1										
vs. Left		—	—	—	—	—	—	—	—	26	17	25	—	—	—	—										
vs. Right		—	—	—	—	—	—	—	—	105	53	92	—	—	—	—										
On Grass		4	4	.500	3.47	16	4	0	36.1	35	17	21	0	3	2	0										
On Turf		8	5	.615	2.52	40	12	1	118	96	53	96	1	3	2	2										
Home		6	4	.600	3.09	26	9	1	75.2	65	36	53	1	2	1	1										
Road		6	5	.545	2.40	30	7	0	78.2	66	34	64	0	4	3	1										
Division Rivals																										
vs. ATL		1	1	.500	7.36	8	1	0	11	13	6	7	0	1	0	0										
vs. HOU		1	0	1.000	2.05	7	2	0	22	14	8	19	0	0	0	0										
vs. LA		1	2	.333	4.91	6	2	0	14.2	21	12	10	0	1	1	1										
vs. SD		0	2	.000	2.45	4	3	0	22	22	13	15	0	0	0	0										
vs. SF		2	0	1.000	2.08	3	2	1	17.1	14	5	8	1	0	0	0										
1988	CIN N	4	5	.444	3.96	10	10	0	61.1	60	20	39	0	0	0	0	15	0	0	.000	1	9	0	0	1.0	1.000
1989		8	3	.727	2.93	69	0	0	95.1	67	40	98	0	8	3	0	5	0	0	.000	3	13	3	0	0.3	.842
1990		12	9	.571	2.74	56	16	0	154.1	131	70	117	1	6	4	2	37	5	0	.135	6	23	1	3	0.5	.967
3 yrs.		24	17	.585	3.04	135	26	1	311	258	130	254	1	14	7	2	57	5	0	.088	10	45	4	3	0.4	.932

LEAGUE CHAMPIONSHIP SERIES

Year	Team	W	L	%	ERA	G	GS	CG	IP	H	BB	SO	ShO	W	L	SV	AB	H	HR	BA	PO	A	E	DP	TC/G	FA
1990	CIN N	1	1	.500	1.80	4	0	0	5	4	3	3	0	1	1	0	0	0	0	—	1	0	0	1	0.3	1.000

WORLD SERIES

Year	Team	W	L	%	ERA	G	GS	CG	IP	H	BB	SO	ShO	W	L	SV	AB	H	HR	BA	PO	A	E	DP	TC/G	FA
1990	CIN N	0	0	—	0.00	1	0	0	1	1	0	0	0	0	0	0	0	0	0	—	0	0	0	0	0.0	—

Scott Chiamparino   CHIAMPARINO, SCOTT MICHAEL
B. Aug. 22, 1966, San Mateo, Calif.
BR TR 6′ 2″ 190 lbs.

Year	Team	W	L	%	ERA	G	GS	CG	IP	H	BB	SO	ShO	W	L	SV	AB	H	HR	BA	PO	A	E	DP	TC/G	FA
1990	TEX A	1	2	.333	2.63	6	6	0	37.2	36	12	19	0	0	0	0	0	0	0	—	3	1	0	0	0.7	1.000

Year	Team	W	L	%	ERA	G	GS	CG	IP	H	BB	SO	ShO	RELIEF PITCHING W	L	SV	BATTING AB	H	HR	BA	PO	A	E	DP	TC/G	FA

Steve Chitren

CHITREN, STEPHEN VINCENT
B. June 8, 1967, Tokyo, Japan
BR TR 6′ 180 lbs.

Year	Team	W	L	%	ERA	G	GS	CG	IP	H	BB	SO	ShO	W	L	SV	AB	H	HR	BA	PO	A	E	DP	TC/G	FA
1990	OAK A	1	0	1.000	1.02	8	0	0	17.2	7	4	19	0	1	0	0	0	0	0	—	1	2	0	0	0.4	1.000

Jim Clancy

CLANCY, JAMES
B. Dec. 18, 1955, Chicago, Ill.
BR TR 6′ 2″ 185 lbs.

Period	W	L	%	ERA	G	GS	CG	IP	H	BB	SO	ShO	W	L	SV	AB	H	HR	BA
April	1	0	1.000	1.76	5	2	0	15.1	9	3	8	0	0	0	0				
May	0	3	.000	7.16	6	3	0	16.1	29	7	7	0	0	0	0				
June	1	5	.167	6.38	6	5	0	24	34	14	15	0	0	1	0				
July	0	0	—	17.28	7	0	0	8.1	17	3	4	0	0	0	0				
Aug	—	—	—	—	0	0	0	0	0	0	0	—	0	0	0				
Sept/Oct	0	0	—	4.50	9	0	0	12	11	6	10	0	0	0	1				
Day	0	0	—	0.00	6	0	0	5.2	2	1	2	0	0	0	1				
Night	2	8	.200	7.04	27	10	0	70.1	98	32	42	0	0	1	0				
vs. Left	—	—	—	—	—	—	—	—	60	21	13	—	—	—	—				
vs. Right	—	—	—	—	—	—	—	—	40	12	31	—	—	—	—				
On Grass	1	4	.200	4.94	10	5	0	31	33	14	15	0	0	1	0				
On Turf	1	4	.200	7.60	23	5	0	45	67	19	29	0	0	0	1				
Home	1	2	.333	6.67	15	3	0	29.2	43	11	20	0	0	0	1				
Road	1	6	.143	6.41	18	7	0	46.1	57	22	24	0	0	1	0				
Division Rivals																			
vs. ATL	1	0	1.000	0.00	4	1	0	11	3	1	6	0	0	0	1				
vs. CIN	1	1	.500	6.19	6	2	0	16	20	9	14	0	0	0	0				
vs. LA	0	1	.000	4.91	4	2	0	11	12	5	8	0	0	0	0				
vs. SD	0	2	.000	6.35	4	2	0	11.1	16	6	5	0	0	0	0				
vs. SF	0	1	.000	4.50	2	0	0	2	3	2	0	0	0	1	0				

RELIEF PITCHER

(bar charts: WINS, ERA, SAVES, RATIO — with NL AVG markers)

Year	Team	W	L	%	ERA	G	GS	CG	IP	H	BB	SO	ShO	W	L	SV	AB	H	HR	BA	PO	A	E	DP	TC/G	FA
1977	TOR A	4	9	.308	5.03	13	13	4	77	80	47	44	1	0	0	0	0	0	0	—	6	14	3	4	1.8	.870
1978		10	12	.455	4.09	31	30	7	193.2	199	91	106	0	0	0	0	0	0	0	—	14	30	2	3	1.5	.957
1979		2	7	.222	5.48	12	11	2	64	65	31	33	0	0	0	0	0	0	0	—	1	11	0	0	1.0	1.000
1980		13	16	.448	3.30	34	34	15	251	217	**128**	152	2	0	0	0	0	0	0	—	14	35	2	2	1.5	.961
1981		6	12	.333	4.90	22	22	2	125	126	64	56	0	0	0	0	0	0	0	—	2	10	0	0	0.5	1.000
1982		16	14	.533	3.71	40	**40**	11	266.2	251	77	139	3	0	0	0	0	0	0	—	14	27	2	2	1.1	.953
1983		15	11	.577	3.91	34	34	11	223	238	61	99	1	0	0	0	0	0	0	—	23	17	1	1	1.2	.976
1984		13	15	.464	5.12	36	**36**	5	219.2	249	88	118	0	0	0	0	0	0	0	—	15	30	1	4	1.3	.978
1985		9	6	.600	3.78	23	23	1	128.2	117	37	66	0	0	0	0	0	0	0	—	6	15	1	1	1.0	.955
1986		14	14	.500	3.94	34	34	6	219.1	202	63	126	3	0	0	0	0	0	0	—	34	23	1	2	1.7	.983
1987		15	11	.577	3.54	37	37	5	241.1	234	80	180	1	0	0	0	0	0	0	—	25	36	2	4	1.7	.968
1988		11	13	.458	4.49	36	31	4	196.1	207	47	118	0	0	0	1	0	0	0	—	15	21	3	4	1.1	.923
1989	HOU N	7	14	.333	5.08	33	26	1	147	155	66	91	0	1	1	0	41	6	0	.146	9	10	7	2	0.8	.731
1990		2	8	.200	6.51	33	10	0	76	100	33	44	0	0	1	1	14	3	0	.214	4	13	0	1	0.5	1.000
14 yrs.		137	162	.458	4.24	418	381	74	2428.2	2440	913	1372	11	1	2	2	55	9	0	.164	182	292	25	30	1.2	.950

LEAGUE CHAMPIONSHIP SERIES

Year	Team	W	L	%	ERA	G	GS	CG	IP	H	BB	SO	ShO	W	L	SV	AB	H	HR	BA	PO	A	E	DP	TC/G	FA
1985	TOR A	0	1	.000	9.00	1	0	0	1	2	1	0	0	0	0	1	0	0	0	—	0	1	0	0	1.0	1.000

Bryan Clark

CLARK, BRYAN DONALD
B. July 12, 1956, Madera, Calif.
BL TL 6′ 2″ 185 lbs.

Year	Team	W	L	%	ERA	G	GS	CG	IP	H	BB	SO	ShO	W	L	SV	AB	H	HR	BA	PO	A	E	DP	TC/G	FA
1981	SEA A	2	5	.286	4.35	29	9	1	93	92	55	52	0	2	1	2	0	0	0	—	0	22	1	0	0.8	.957
1982		5	2	.714	2.75	37	5	1	114.2	104	58	70	1	2	1	0	0	0	0	—	7	20	0	3	0.7	1.000
1983		7	10	.412	3.94	41	17	2	162.1	160	72	76	0	4	2	0	0	0	0	—	8	38	3	4	1.2	.939
1984	TOR A	1	2	.333	5.91	20	3	0	45.2	66	22	21	0	1	1	0	0	0	0	—	1	13	0	0	0.7	1.000
1985	CLE A	3	4	.429	6.32	31	3	0	62.2	78	34	24	0	3	2	2	0	0	0	—	7	13	1	2	0.7	.952
1986	CHI A	0	0	—	4.50	5	0	0	8	8	2	5	0	0	0	0	0	0	0	—	2	0	0	0	0.4	1.000
1987		0	0	—	2.41	11	0	0	18.2	19	8	8	0	0	0	0	0	0	0	—	0	1	0	0	0.1	1.000
1990	SEA A	2	0	1.000	3.27	12	0	0	11	9	10	3	0	2	0	0	0	0	0	—	1	3	0	1	0.3	1.000
8 yrs.		20	23	.465	4.15	186	37	4	516	536	261	259	1	14	7	4	0	0	0	—	26	110	5	10	0.8	.965

Year	Team		W	L	%	ERA	G	GS	CG	IP	H	BB	SO	ShO	RELIEF PITCHING			BATTING			BA	PO	A	E	DP	TC/G	FA
															W	L	SV	AB	H	HR							

Terry Clark

CLARK, TERRY LEE
B. Oct. 18, 1960, Los Angeles, Calif.
BR TR 6′ 2″ 190 lbs.

Year	Team		W	L	%	ERA	G	GS	CG	IP	H	BB	SO	ShO	W	L	SV	AB	H	HR	BA	PO	A	E	DP	TC/G	FA
1988	CAL	A	6	6	.500	5.07	15	15	2	94	120	31	39	1	0	0	0	0	0	0	—	8	13	0	0	1.4	1.000
1989			0	2	.000	4.91	4	2	0	11	13	3	7	0	0	0	0	0	0	0	—	0	2	0	0	0.5	1.000
1990	HOU	N	0	0	—	13.50	1	1	0	4	9	3	2	0	0	0	0	2	1	0	.500	0	0	0	0	0.0	—
3 yrs.			6	8	.429	5.37	20	18	2	109	142	37	48	1	0	0	0	2	1	0	.500	8	15	0	0	1.2	1.000

Stan Clarke

CLARKE, STANLEY MARTEN
B. Aug. 9, 1960, Toledo, Ohio
BR TL 6′ 1″ 180 lbs.

Year	Team		W	L	%	ERA	G	GS	CG	IP	H	BB	SO	ShO	W	L	SV	AB	H	HR	BA	PO	A	E	DP	TC/G	FA
1983	TOR	A	1	1	.500	3.27	10	0	0	11	10	5	7	0	1	1	0	0	0	0	—	0	2	0	0	0.2	1.000
1985			0	0	—	4.50	4	0	0	4	3	2	2	0	0	0	0	0	0	0	—	0	1	0	0	0.3	1.000
1986			0	1	.000	9.24	10	0	0	12.2	18	10	9	0	0	1	0	0	0	0	—	0	3	0	0	0.3	1.000
1987	SEA	A	2	2	.500	5.48	22	0	0	23	31	10	13	0	2	2	0	0	0	0	—	1	2	0	0	0.1	1.000
1989	KC	A	0	2	.000	15.43	2	2	0	7	14	4	2	0	0	0	0	0	0	0	—	0	1	0	0	0.5	1.000
1990	STL	N	0	0	—	2.70	2	0	0	3.1	2	0	3	0	0	0	0	0	0	0	—	0	0	0	0	0.0	—
6 yrs.			3	6	.333	6.78	50	2	0	61	78	31	36	0	3	4	0	0	0	0	—	1	9	0	0	0.2	1.000

Marty Clary

CLARY, MARTIN KEITH
B. Apr. 3, 1962, Detroit, Mich.
BR TR 6′ 4″ 190 lbs.

	W	L	%	ERA	G	GS	CG	IP	H	BB	SO	ShO	W	L	SV
April	0	1	.000	3.65	2	2	0	12.1	11	7	10	0	0	0	0
May	1	2	.333	6.08	6	5	0	23.2	34	10	8	0	0	0	0
June	0	0	—	3.86	9	0	0	14	26	1	6	0	0	0	0
July	0	5	.000	5.45	6	6	0	34.2	35	12	13	0	0	0	0
Aug	0	2	.000	12.60	7	1	0	10	19	7	5	0	0	0	0
Sept/Oct	0	0	—	2.57	3	0	0	7	3	2	2	0	0	0	0
Day	0	2	.000	3.67	9	3	0	27	29	10	9	0	0	0	0
Night	1	8	.111	6.39	24	11	0	74.2	99	29	35	0	0	1	0
vs. Left	—	—	—	—	—	—	—	—	77	22	19	—	—	—	—
vs. Right	—	—	—	—	—	—	—	—	51	17	25	—	—	—	—
On Grass	0	7	.000	6.29	23	9	0	68.2	92	22	34	0	0	1	0
On Turf	1	3	.250	4.36	10	5	0	33	36	17	10	0	0	0	0
Home	0	5	.000	5.01	17	5	0	46.2	65	13	19	0	0	1	0
Road	1	5	.167	6.22	16	9	0	55	63	26	25	0	0	0	0
Division Rivals															
vs. CIN	0	1	.000	3.86	5	1	0	11.2	16	7	4	0	0	0	0
vs. HOU	0	0	—	7.50	3	0	0	6	6	3	2	0	0	0	0
vs. LA	0	2	.000	8.59	3	1	0	7.1	9	2	4	0	0	1	0
vs. SD	0	1	.000	7.00	6	2	0	18	24	8	8	0	0	0	0
vs. SF	0	0	—	9.00	2	0	0	3	7	0	2	0	0	0	0

STARTING PITCHER

WINS — NL AVG

ERA — NL AVG

SO/9 — NL AVG

RATIO — NL AVG

Year	Team		W	L	%	ERA	G	GS	CG	IP	H	BB	SO	ShO	W	L	SV	AB	H	HR	BA	PO	A	E	DP	TC/G	FA
1987	ATL	N	0	1	.000	6.14	7	1	0	14.2	20	4	7	0	0	0	0	1	0	0	.000	0	2	0	0	0.3	1.000
1989			4	3	.571	3.15	18	17	2	108.2	103	31	30	1	0	0	0	31	5	0	.161	10	18	0	1	1.6	1.000
1990			1	10	.091	5.67	33	14	0	101.2	128	39	44	0	0	1	0	28	0	0	.000	6	20	1	0	0.8	.963
3 yrs.			5	14	.263	4.48	58	32	2	225	251	74	81	1	0	1	0	60	5	0	.083	16	40	1	1	1.0	.982

Mark Clear

CLEAR, MARK ALAN
B. May 27, 1956, Los Angeles, Calif.
BR TR 6′ 4″ 200 lbs.

Year	Team		W	L	%	ERA	G	GS	CG	IP	H	BB	SO	ShO	W	L	SV	AB	H	HR	BA	PO	A	E	DP	TC/G	FA
1979	CAL	A	11	5	.688	3.63	52	0	0	109	87	68	98	0	11	5	14	0	0	0	—	4	10	2	0	0.3	.875
1980			11	11	.500	3.31	58	0	0	106	82	65	105	0	11	11	9	0	0	0	—	3	10	0	0	0.2	1.000
1981	BOS	A	8	3	.727	4.09	34	0	0	77	69	51	82	0	8	3	9	0	0	0	—	5	4	0	0	0.3	1.000
1982			14	9	.609	3.00	55	0	0	105	92	61	109	0	14	9	14	0	0	0	—	7	11	3	0	0.4	.857
1983			4	5	.444	6.28	48	0	0	96	101	68	81	0	4	5	4	0	0	0	—	8	5	1	0	0.3	.929
1984			8	3	.727	4.03	47	0	0	67	47	70	76	0	8	3	8	0	0	0	—	4	8	0	0	0.3	1.000
1985			1	3	.250	3.72	41	0	0	55.2	45	50	55	0	1	3	3	0	0	0	—	4	12	2	0	0.4	.889
1986	MIL	A	5	5	.500	2.20	59	0	0	73.2	53	36	85	0	5	5	16	0	0	0	—	4	6	1	0	0.2	.909
1987			8	5	.615	4.48	58	1	0	78.1	70	55	81	0	8	4	6	0	0	0	—	8	12	1	0	0.4	.952
1988			1	0	1.000	2.79	25	0	0	29	23	21	26	0	1	0	0	0	0	0	—	2	1	0	0	0.1	1.000
1990	CAL	A	0	0	—	5.87	4	0	0	7.2	5	9	6	0	0	0	0	0	0	0	—	0	0	0	0	0.0	—
11 yrs.			71	49	.592	3.85	481	1	0	804.1	674	554	804	0	71	48	83	0	0	0	—	49	79	10	0	0.3	.928

Year	Team	W	L	%	ERA	G	GS	CG	IP	H	BB	SO	ShO	W	L	SV	AB	H	HR	BA	PO	A	E	DP	TC/G	FA
														RELIEF PITCHING			**BATTING**									

Mark Clear *Continued*

LEAGUE CHAMPIONSHIP SERIES

Year	Team	W	L	%	ERA	G	GS	CG	IP	H	BB	SO	ShO	W	L	SV	AB	H	HR	BA	PO	A	E	DP	TC/G	FA
1979	CAL A	0	0	—	4.76	1	0	0	5.2	4	2	3	0	0	0	0	0	0	0	—	0	0	0	0	0.0	—

Roger Clemens

CLEMENS, WILLIAM ROGER (Rocket Man)
B. Aug. 4, 1962, Dayton, Ohio
BR TR 6′ 4″ 205 lbs.

Split		W	L	%	ERA	G	GS	CG	IP	H	BB	SO	ShO	W	L	SV	AB	H	HR	BA	PO	A	E	DP	TC/G	FA
April		4	1	.800	3.09	5	5	0	35	26	9	34	0	0	0	0										
May		4	1	.800	2.54	6	6	2	46	34	11	35	0	0	0	0										
June		4	1	.800	2.38	6	6	0	41.2	43	12	43	0	0	0	0										
July		2	2	.500	1.00	6	6	2	45	38	9	38	2	0	0	0										
Aug		6	0	1.000	1.09	6	6	3	49.1	43	5	48	2	0	0	0										
Sept/Oct		1	1	.500	1.59	2	2	0	11.1	9	8	11	0	0	0	0										
Day		9	1	.900	1.09	12	12	2	91	70	23	75	2	0	0	0										
Night		12	5	.706	2.49	19	19	5	137.1	123	31	134	2	0	0	0										
vs. Left		—	—	—	—	—	—	—	—	107	27	97	—	—	—	—										
vs. Right		—	—	—	—	—	—	—	—	86	27	112	—	—	—	—										
On Grass		19	4	.826	2.00	26	26	5	189.1	164	44	183	3	0	0	0										
On Turf		2	2	.500	1.62	5	5	2	39	29	10	26	1	0	0	0										
Home		11	2	.846	1.53	15	15	2	111.2	95	31	95	1	0	0	0										
Road		10	4	.714	2.31	16	16	5	116.2	98	23	114	3	0	0	0										
Division Rivals																										
vs. BAL		0	1	.000	2.53	2	2	0	10.2	13	7	7	0	0	0	0										
vs. CLE		3	0	1.000	2.25	3	3	1	24	24	4	28	0	0	0	0										
vs. DET		2	0	1.000	1.76	2	2	0	15.1	12	4	13	0	0	0	0										
vs. MIL		2	0	1.000	1.72	2	2	1	15.2	11	2	19	1	0	0	0										
vs. NY		1	0	1.000	1.13	1	1	0	8	6	0	8	0	0	0	0										
vs. TOR		3	0	1.000	1.17	3	3	1	23	17	5	20	1	0	0	0										
1984	BOS A	9	4	.692	4.32	21	20	5	133.1	146	29	126	1	0	0	0	0	0	0	—	11	14	0	0	1.2	1.000
1985		7	5	.583	3.29	15	15	3	98.1	83	37	74	1	0	0	0	0	0	0	—	12	9	0	1	1.4	1.000
1986		**24**	4	**.857**	**2.48**	33	33	10	254	179	67	238	1	0	0	0	0	0	0	—	27	21	4	0	1.6	.923
1987		**20**	9	**.690**	2.97	36	36	**18**	281.2	248	83	256	7	0	0	0	0	0	0	—	15	25	0	1	1.1	1.000
1988		18	12	.600	2.93	35	35	**14**	264	217	62	**291**	8	0	0	0	0	0	0	—	17	17	1	1	1.0	.971
1989		17	11	.607	3.13	35	35	8	253.1	215	93	230	3	0	0	0	0	0	0	—	17	27	0	1	1.3	1.000
1990		21	6	.778	**1.93**	31	31	7	228.1	193	54	209	**4**	0	0	0	0	0	0	—	23	26	2	1	1.6	.961
7 yrs.		116	51	.695	2.89	206	205	65	1513	1281	425	1424	25	0	0	0	0	0	0	—	122	139	7	5	1.3	.974

LEAGUE CHAMPIONSHIP SERIES

Year	Team	W	L	%	ERA	G	GS	CG	IP	H	BB	SO	ShO	W	L	SV	AB	H	HR	BA	PO	A	E	DP	TC/G	FA
1986	BOS A	1	1	.500	4.37	3	3	0	22.2	22	7	17	0	0	0	0	0	0	0	—	1	2	0	0	1.0	1.000
1988		0	0	—	3.86	1	1	0	7	6	0	8	0	0	0	0	0	0	0	—	0	0	1	0	1.0	—
1990		0	1	.000	3.52	2	2	0	7.2	7	5	4	0	0	0	0	0	0	0	—	0	1	0	0	0.5	1.000
3 yrs.		1	2	.333	4.12	6	6	0	37.1	35	12	29	0	0	0	0	0	0	0	—	1	3	1	0	0.8	.800

WORLD SERIES

Year	Team	W	L	%	ERA	G	GS	CG	IP	H	BB	SO	ShO	W	L	SV	AB	H	HR	BA	PO	A	E	DP	TC/G	FA
1986	BOS A	0	0	—	3.18	2	2	0	11.1	9	6	11	0	0	0	0	4	0	0	.000	1	2	0	0	1.5	1.000

Pat Clements

CLEMENTS, PATRICK BRIAN
B. Feb. 2, 1962, McCloud, Calif.
BR TL 6′ 175 lbs.

Year	Team	W	L	%	ERA	G	GS	CG	IP	H	BB	SO	ShO	W	L	SV	AB	H	HR	BA	PO	A	E	DP	TC/G	FA
1985	2 teams	CAL A	(41G 5 – 0)		PIT N	(27G 0 – 2)																				
"	total	5	2	.714	3.46	68	0	0	96.1	86	40	36	0	5	2	3	3	1	0	.333	2	18	1	2	0.3	.952
1986	PIT N	0	4	.000	2.80	65	0	0	61	53	32	31	0	0	4	2	6	0	0	.000	7	11	0	1	0.3	1.000
1987	NY A	3	3	.500	4.95	55	0	0	80	91	30	36	0	3	3	7	0	0	0	—	5	15	0	2	0.4	1.000
1988		0	0	—	6.48	6	1	0	8.1	12	4	3	0	0	0	0	0	0	0	—	1	1	0	0	0.3	1.000
1989	SD N	4	1	.800	3.92	23	1	0	39	39	15	18	0	4	0	0	6	0	0	.000	1	8	0	1	0.4	1.000
1990		0	0	—	4.15	9	0	0	13	20	7	6	0	0	0	0	0	0	0	—	3	2	0	0	0.6	1.000
6 yrs.		12	10	.545	3.90	226	2	0	297.2	301	128	130	0	12	9	12	15	1	0	.067	19	55	1	6	0.3	.987

STARTING PITCHER

Year	Team		W	L	%	ERA	G	GS	CG	IP	H	BB	SO	ShO	RELIEF PITCHING			BATTING			BA	PO	A	E	DP	TC/G	FA
															W	L	SV	AB	H	HR							

Chris Codiroli

CODIROLI, CHRISTOPHER ALLEN
B. Mar. 26, 1958, Oxnard, Calif.
BR TR 6' 1" 160 lbs.

Year	Team		W	L	%	ERA	G	GS	CG	IP	H	BB	SO	ShO	W	L	SV	AB	H	HR	BA	PO	A	E	DP	TC/G	FA
1982	OAK	A	1	2	.333	4.32	3	3	0	16.2	16	4	5	0	0	0	0	0	0	0	—	3	3	0	0	2.0	1.000
1983			12	12	.500	4.46	37	31	7	205.2	208	72	85	2	1	1	1	0	0	0	—	14	21	4	1	1.1	.897
1984			6	4	.600	5.84	28	14	1	89.1	111	34	44	0	1	1	1	0	0	0	—	5	11	1	1	0.6	.941
1985			14	14	.500	4.46	37	**37**	4	226	228	78	111	0	0	0	0	0	0	0	—	18	27	4	1	1.3	.918
1986			5	8	.385	4.03	16	16	1	91.2	91	38	43	0	0	0	0	0	0	0	—	13	15	5	2	2.1	.848
1987			0	2	.000	8.74	3	3	0	11.1	12	8	4	0	0	0	0	0	0	0	—	1	1	0	0	0.7	1.000
1988	CLE	A	0	4	.000	9.31	14	2	0	19.1	32	10	12	0	0	2	1	0	0	0	—	3	2	0	1	0.4	1.000
1990	KC	A	0	1	.000	9.58	6	2	0	10.1	13	17	8	0	0	0	0	0	0	0	—	1	0	0	0	0.2	1.000
8 yrs.			38	47	.447	4.94	144	108	13	670.1	711	261	312	2	1	3	3	0	0	0	—	58	80	14	6	1.1	.908

Kevin Coffman

COFFMAN, KEVIN REESE
B. Jan. 19, 1965, Austin, Tex.
BR TR 6' 2" 175 lbs.

Year	Team		W	L	%	ERA	G	GS	CG	IP	H	BB	SO	ShO	W	L	SV	AB	H	HR	BA	PO	A	E	DP	TC/G	FA
1987	ATL	N	2	3	.400	4.62	5	5	0	25.1	31	22	14	0	0	0	0	10	1	0	.100	1	9	0	1	2.0	1.000
1988			2	6	.250	5.78	18	11	0	67	62	54	24	0	0	0	0	22	5	0	.227	9	12	2	1	1.3	.913
1990	CHI	N	0	2	.000	11.29	8	2	0	18.1	26	19	9	0	0	0	0	5	1	0	.200	3	4	0	0	0.9	1.000
3 yrs.			4	11	.267	6.42	31	18	0	110.2	119	95	47	0	0	0	0	37	7	0	.189	13	25	2	2	1.3	.950

Pat Combs

COMBS, PATRICK DENNIS
B. Oct. 29, 1966, Newport, R. I.
BL TL 6' 3" 200 lbs.

	W	L	%	ERA	G	GS	CG	IP	H	BB	SO	ShO	W	L	SV
April	1	2	.333	4.29	4	4	0	21	19	9	13	0	0	0	0
May	1	3	.250	4.81	5	5	0	24.1	36	13	17	0	0	0	0
June	2	1	.667	3.28	6	5	1	35.2	29	20	20	1	0	0	0
July	2	2	.500	4.45	5	5	0	32.1	34	15	22	0	0	0	0
Aug	0	1	.000	4.40	6	6	0	28.2	29	15	17	0	0	0	0
Sept/Oct	4	1	.800	3.70	6	6	2	41.1	32	14	19	1	0	0	0
Day	3	4	.429	3.66	8	8	0	46.2	39	23	26	0	0	0	0
Night	7	6	.538	4.21	24	23	3	136.2	140	63	82	2	0	0	0
vs. Left	—	—	—	—	—	—	—	—	35	17	26	—	—	—	—
vs. Right	—	—	—	—	—	—	—	—	144	69	82	—	—	—	—
On Grass	1	6	.143	5.40	9	9	1	43.1	48	25	22	0	0	0	0
On Turf	9	4	.692	3.66	23	22	2	140	131	61	86	2	0	0	0
Home	4	2	.667	3.05	13	13	2	82.2	72	33	47	2	0	0	0
Road	6	8	.429	4.92	19	18	1	100.2	107	53	61	0	0	0	0
Division Rivals															
vs. CHI	0	1	.000	8.10	2	2	0	10	18	4	4	0	0	0	0
vs. MON	1	1	.500	2.33	4	4	1	27	19	12	18	1	0	0	0
vs. NY	3	1	.750	2.56	6	6	1	38.2	23	18	14	0	0	0	0
vs. PIT	0	1	.000	4.42	3	3	0	18.1	15	10	13	0	0	0	0
vs. STL	2	0	1.000	4.73	3	2	0	13.1	11	8	6	0	0	0	0

Year	Team		W	L	%	ERA	G	GS	CG	IP	H	BB	SO	ShO	W	L	SV	AB	H	HR	BA	PO	A	E	DP	TC/G	FA
1989	PHI	N	4	0	1.000	2.09	6	6	1	38.2	36	6	30	1	0	0	0	12	2	0	.167	1	3	0	0	0.7	1.000
1990			10	10	.500	4.07	32	31	3	183.1	179	86	108	2	0	0	0	60	9	0	.150	10	25	0	1	1.1	1.000
2 yrs.			14	10	.583	3.73	38	37	4	222	215	92	138	3	0	0	0	72	11	0	.153	11	28	0	1	1.0	1.000

STARTING PITCHER

Keith Comstock

COMSTOCK, KEITH MARTIN
B. Dec. 23, 1955, San Francisco, Calif.
BL TL 6' 174 lbs.

	W	L	%	ERA	G	GS	CG	IP	H	BB	SO	ShO	W	L	SV
April	0	1	.000	1.29	7	0	0	7	4	4	11	0	0	1	0
May	1	0	1.000	1.69	13	0	0	10.2	9	3	7	0	1	0	0
June	2	1	.667	3.68	7	0	0	7.1	5	5	4	0	2	1	0
July	2	0	1.000	1.46	13	0	0	12.1	9	3	12	0	2	0	0
Aug	1	1	.500	2.92	12	0	0	12.1	8	6	11	0	1	1	1
Sept/Oct	1	1	.500	8.53	8	0	0	6.1	5	5	5	0	1	1	1
Day	2	0	1.000	4.15	13	0	0	8.2	10	4	7	0	2	0	0
Night	5	4	.556	2.66	47	0	0	47.1	30	22	43	0	5	4	2
vs. Left	—	—	—	—	—	—	—	—	17	8	13	—	—	—	—
vs. Right	—	—	—	—	—	—	—	—	23	18	37	—	—	—	—

RELIEF PITCHER

Year	Team	W	L	%	ERA	G	GS	CG	IP	H	BB	SO	ShO	W	L	SV	AB	H	HR	BA	PO	A	E	DP	TC/G	FA
														RELIEF PITCHING			BATTING									

Keith Comstock *Continued*

Year	Team	W	L	%	ERA	G	GS	CG	IP	H	BB	SO	ShO	W	L	SV	AB	H	HR	BA	PO	A	E	DP	TC/G	FA
On Grass		2	2	.500	3.86	24	0	0	21	17	17	23	0	2	2	0										
On Turf		5	2	.714	2.31	36	0	0	35	23	9	27	0	5	2	2										
Home		4	2	.667	2.40	29	0	0	30	21	9	22	0	4	2	2										
Road		3	2	.600	3.46	31	0	0	26	19	17	28	0	3	2	0										
Division Rivals																										
vs. CAL		0	1	.000	5.40	6	0	0	5	2	3	5	0	0	1	0										
vs. CHI		0	0	—	0.00	2	0	0	4.1	1	3	1	0	0	0	0										
vs. KC		1	0	1.000	12.00	4	0	0	3	4	1	2	0	1	0	0										
vs. MIN		0	1	.000	1.29	4	0	0	7	5	2	5	0	0	1	1										
vs. OAK		0	0	—	4.50	5	0	0	4	4	2	6	0	0	0	1										
vs. TEX		1	0	1.000	1.69	5	0	0	5.1	4	3	4	0	1	0	0										
1984	MIN A	0	0	—	8.53	4	0	0	6.1	6	4	2	0	0	0	0	0	0	0	—	1	2	0	0	0.8	1.000
1987	2 teams	SF N (15G 2 - 0)							SD N (26G 0 - 1)																	
"	total	2	1	.667	4.61	41	0	0	56.2	52	31	59	0	2	1	1	2	0	0	.000	2	4	0	1	0.1	1.000
1988	SD N	0	0	—	6.75	7	0	0	8	8	3	9	0	0	0	0	0	0	0	—	1	1	0	0	0.3	1.000
1989	SEA A	1	2	.333	2.81	31	0	0	25.2	26	10	22	0	1	2	0	0	0	0	—	0	4	1	0	0.2	.800
1990		7	4	.636	2.89	60	0	0	56	40	26	50	0	7	4	2	0	0	0		2	11	1	0	0.2	.929
5 yrs.		10	7	.588	3.95	143	0	0	152.2	132	74	142	0	10	7	3	2	0	0	.000	6	22	2	1	0.2	.933

RELIEF PITCHER

David Cone

CONE, DAVID BRIAN
B. Jan. 2, 1963, Kansas City, Mo.
BL TR 6′ 1″ 180 lbs.

Year	Team	W	L	%	ERA	G	GS	CG	IP	H	BB	SO	ShO	W	L	SV	AB	H	HR	BA	PO	A	E	DP	TC/G	FA
April		0	2	.000	6.65	4	4	0	21.2	27	12	29	0	0	0	0										
May		1	1	.500	5.59	4	3	0	19.1	17	2	16	0	0	0	0										
June		3	1	.750	2.63	5	5	1	37.2	33	8	41	1	0	0	0										
July		3	1	.750	2.70	5	5	0	36.2	26	11	46	0	0	0	0										
Aug		3	2	.600	2.27	6	6	3	47.2	36	12	47	1	0	0	0										
Sept/Oct		4	3	.571	2.59	7	7	2	48.2	38	20	54	0	0	0	0										
Day		3	3	.500	3.25	9	9	1	61	57	15	68	0	0	0	0										
Night		11	7	.611	3.23	22	21	5	150.2	120	50	165	2	0	0	0										
vs. Left		—	—	—	—	—	—	—	—	100	38	124	—	—	—	—										
vs. Right		—	—	—	—	—	—	—	—	77	27	109	—	—	—	—										
On Grass		10	9	.526	3.77	22	22	5	152.2	139	46	165	2	0	0	0										
On Turf		4	1	.800	1.83	9	8	1	59	38	19	68	0	0	0	0										
Home		7	6	.538	3.85	16	16	3	107.2	98	35	114	2	0	0	0										
Road		7	4	.636	2.60	15	14	3	104	79	30	119	0	0	0	0										
Division Rivals																										
vs. CHI		0	2	.000	5.40	2	2	0	13.1	17	6	16	0	0	0	0										
vs. MON		1	1	.500	2.53	3	3	0	21.1	18	8	27	0	0	0	0										
vs. PHI		1	2	.333	5.63	4	4	0	24	22	8	27	0	0	0	0										
vs. PIT		3	0	1.000	1.07	3	3	2	25.1	12	8	29	0	0	0	0										
vs. STL		2	1	.667	1.16	4	4	1	31	18	6	27	1	0	0	0										
1986	KC A	0	0	—	5.56	11	0	0	22.2	29	13	21	0	0	0	0	0	0	0	—	4	0	0	0	0.4	1.000
1987	NY N	5	6	.455	3.71	21	13	1	99.1	87	44	68	0	1	1	1	31	2	0	.065	12	10	1	0	1.1	.957
1988		20	3	**.870**	2.22	35	28	8	231.1	178	80	213	4	2	0	0	80	12	0	.150	17	23	1	0	1.2	.976
1989		14	8	.636	3.52	34	33	7	219.2	183	74	190	2	0	0	0	77	18	0	.234	21	14	1	0	1.1	.972
1990		14	10	.583	3.23	31	30	6	211.2	177	65	**233**	2	0	0	0	70	14	0	.200	17	20	3	1	1.3	.925
5 yrs.		53	27	.663	3.14	132	104	22	784.2	654	276	725	8	3	1	1	258	46	0	.178	71	67	6	1	1.1	.958

LEAGUE CHAMPIONSHIP SERIES

Year	Team	W	L	%	ERA	G	GS	CG	IP	H	BB	SO	ShO	W	L	SV	AB	H	HR	BA	PO	A	E	DP	TC/G	FA
1988	NY N	1	1	.500	4.50	3	2	1	12	10	5	9	0	0	0	0	4	0	0	.000	1	0	0	0	0.3	1.000

STARTING PITCHER

Year	Team	W	L	%	ERA	G	GS	CG	IP	H	BB	SO	ShO	RELIEF PITCHING W	L	SV	BATTING AB	H	HR	BA	PO	A	E	DP	TC/G	FA

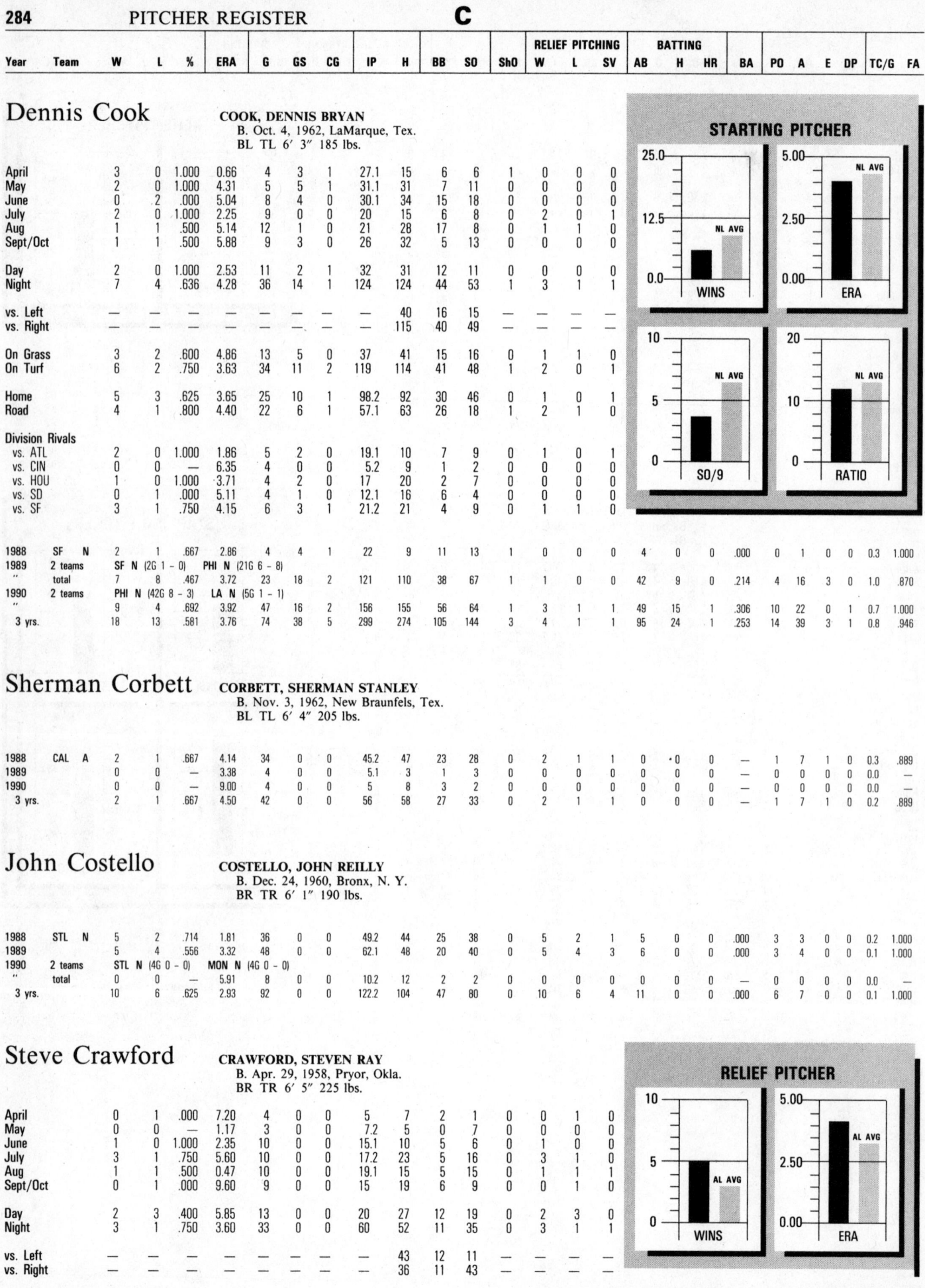

Dennis Cook

COOK, DENNIS BRYAN
B. Oct. 4, 1962, LaMarque, Tex.
BL TL 6′ 3″ 185 lbs.

STARTING PITCHER

	W	L	%	ERA	G	GS	CG	IP	H	BB	SO	ShO	W	L	SV	AB	H	HR	BA	PO	A	E	DP	TC/G	FA
April	3	0	1.000	0.66	4	3	1	27.1	15	6	6	1	0	0	0										
May	2	0	1.000	4.31	5	5	1	31.1	31	7	11	0	0	0	0										
June	0	2	.000	5.04	8	4	0	30.1	34	15	18	0	0	0	0										
July	2	0	1.000	2.25	9	0	0	20	15	6	8	0	2	0	1										
Aug	1	1	.500	5.14	12	1	0	21	28	17	8	0	1	1	0										
Sept/Oct	1	1	.500	5.88	9	3	0	26	32	5	13	0	0	0	0										
Day	2	0	1.000	2.53	11	2	1	32	31	12	11	0	0	0	0										
Night	7	4	.636	4.28	36	14	1	124	124	44	53	1	3	1	1										
vs. Left	—	—	—	—	—	—	—	—	40	16	15	—	—	—	—										
vs. Right	—	—	—	—	—	—	—	—	115	40	49	—	—	—	—										
On Grass	3	2	.600	4.86	13	5	0	37	41	15	16	0	1	1	0										
On Turf	6	2	.750	3.63	34	11	2	119	114	41	48	1	2	0	1										
Home	5	3	.625	3.65	25	10	1	98.2	92	30	46	0	1	0	1										
Road	4	1	.800	4.40	22	6	1	57.1	63	26	18	1	2	1	0										
Division Rivals																									
vs. ATL	2	0	1.000	1.86	5	2	0	19.1	10	7	9	0	1	0	1										
vs. CIN	0	0	—	6.35	4	0	0	5.2	9	1	2	0	0	0	0										
vs. HOU	1	0	1.000	3.71	4	2	0	17	20	2	7	0	0	0	0										
vs. SD	0	1	.000	5.11	4	1	0	12.1	16	6	4	0	0	0	0										
vs. SF	3	1	.750	4.15	6	3	1	21.2	21	4	9	0	1	1	0										
1988	SF N	2	1	.667	2.86	4	4	1	22	9	11	13	1	0	0	0	4	0	0	.000	0	1	0	0	0.3	1.000
1989	2 teams	SF N (2G 1 - 0)			PHI N (21G 6 - 8)																					
"	total	7	8	.467	3.72	23	18	2	121	110	38	67	1	1	0	0	42	9	0	.214	4	16	3	0	1.0	.870
1990	2 teams	PHI N (42G 8 - 3)			LA N (5G 1 - 1)																					
"		9	4	.692	3.92	47	16	2	156	155	56	64	1	3	1	1	49	15	1	.306	10	22	0	1	0.7	1.000
3 yrs.		18	13	.581	3.76	74	38	5	299	274	105	144	3	4	1	1	95	24	1	.253	14	39	3	1	0.8	.946

Sherman Corbett

CORBETT, SHERMAN STANLEY
B. Nov. 3, 1962, New Braunfels, Tex.
BL TL 6′ 4″ 205 lbs.

Year	Team	W	L	%	ERA	G	GS	CG	IP	H	BB	SO	ShO	W	L	SV	AB	H	HR	BA	PO	A	E	DP	TC/G	FA
1988	CAL A	2	1	.667	4.14	34	0	0	45.2	47	23	28	0	2	1	1	0	•0	0	—	1	7	1	0	0.3	.889
1989		0	0	—	3.38	4	0	0	5.1	3	1	3	0	0	0	0	0	0	0	—	0	0	0	0	0.0	—
1990		0	0	—	9.00	4	0	0	5	8	3	2	0	0	0	0	0	0	0	—	0	0	0	0	0.0	—
3 yrs.		2	1	.667	4.50	42	0	0	56	58	27	33	0	2	1	1	0	0	0	—	1	7	1	0	0.2	.889

John Costello

COSTELLO, JOHN REILLY
B. Dec. 24, 1960, Bronx, N. Y.
BR TR 6′ 1″ 190 lbs.

Year	Team	W	L	%	ERA	G	GS	CG	IP	H	BB	SO	ShO	W	L	SV	AB	H	HR	BA	PO	A	E	DP	TC/G	FA
1988	STL N	5	2	.714	1.81	36	0	0	49.2	44	25	38	0	5	2	1	5	0	0	.000	3	3	0	0	0.2	1.000
1989		5	4	.556	3.32	48	0	0	62.1	48	20	40	0	5	4	3	6	0	0	.000	3	4	0	0	0.1	1.000
1990	2 teams	STL N (4G 0 - 0)			MON N (4G 0 - 0)																					
"	total	0	0	—	5.91	8	0	0	10.2	12	2	2	0	0	0	0	0	0	0	—	0	0	0	0	0.0	—
3 yrs.		10	6	.625	2.93	92	0	0	122.2	104	47	80	0	10	6	4	11	0	0	.000	6	7	0	0	0.1	1.000

Steve Crawford

CRAWFORD, STEVEN RAY
B. Apr. 29, 1958, Pryor, Okla.
BR TR 6′ 5″ 225 lbs.

RELIEF PITCHER

	W	L	%	ERA	G	GS	CG	IP	H	BB	SO	ShO	W	L	SV	AB	H	HR	BA	PO	A	E	DP	TC/G	FA
April	0	1	.000	7.20	4	0	0	5	7	2	1	0	0	1	0										
May	0	0	—	1.17	3	0	0	7.2	5	0	7	0	0	0	0										
June	1	0	1.000	2.35	10	0	0	15.1	10	5	6	0	1	0	0										
July	3	1	.750	5.60	10	0	0	17.2	23	5	16	0	3	1	0										
Aug	1	1	.500	0.47	10	0	0	19.1	15	5	15	0	1	1	1										
Sept/Oct	0	1	.000	9.60	9	0	0	15	19	6	9	0	0	0	0										
Day	2	3	.400	5.85	13	0	0	20	27	12	19	0	2	3	0										
Night	3	1	.750	3.60	33	0	0	60	52	11	35	0	3	1	1										
vs. Left	—	—	—	—	—	—	—	—	43	12	11	—	—	—	—										
vs. Right	—	—	—	—	—	—	—	—	36	11	43	—	—	—	—										

Year	Team	W	L	%	ERA	G	GS	CG	IP	H	BB	SO	ShO	W	L	SV	AB	H	HR	BA	PO	A	E	DP	TC/G	FA

Steve Crawford *Continued*

Year	Team	W	L	%	ERA	G	GS	CG	IP	H	BB	SO	ShO	W	L	SV	AB	H	HR	BA	PO	A	E	DP	TC/G	FA
On Grass		1	2	.333	3.22	13	0	0	22.1	26	8	19	0	1	2	0										
On Turf		4	2	.667	4.53	33	0	0	57.2	53	15	35	0	4	2	1										
Home		4	1	.800	4.09	27	0	0	50.2	44	12	33	0	4	1	1										
Road		1	3	.250	4.30	19	0	0	29.1	35	11	21	0	1	3	0										
Division Rivals																										
vs. CAL		0	0	—	10.80	2	0	0	3.1	3	2	2	0	0	0	0										
vs. CHI		0	0	—	0.00	2	0	0	5	3	1	3	0	0	0	0										
vs. MIN		1	0	1.000	2.45	5	0	0	7.1	6	2	1	0	1	0	0										
vs. OAK		0	1	.000	3.86	4	0	0	9.1	11	4	4	0	0	1	0										
vs. SEA		0	1	.000	3.86	6	0	0	7	6	1	3	0	0	1	0										
vs. TEX		0	0	—	2.57	3	0	0	7	7	2	8	0	0	0	0										
1980	BOS A	2	0	1.000	3.66	6	4	2	32	41	8	10	0	0	0	0	0	0	0	—	4	2	0	0	1.0	1.000
1981		0	5	.000	4.97	14	11	0	58	69	18	29	0	0	0	0	0	0	0	—	8	8	0	1	1.1	1.000
1982		1	0	1.000	2.00	5	0	0	9	14	0	2	0	1	0	0	0	0	0	—	0	1	0	0	0.2	1.000
1984		5	0	1.000	3.34	35	0	0	62	69	21	21	0	5	0	1	0	0	0	—	4	8	0	1	0.3	1.000
1985		6	5	.545	3.76	44	1	0	91	103	28	58	0	5	5	12	0	0	0	—	7	15	3	2	0.6	.880
1986		0	2	.000	3.92	40	0	0	57.1	69	19	32	0	0	2	4	0	0	0	—	4	7	1	2	0.3	.917
1987		5	4	.556	5.33	29	0	0	72.2	91	32	43	0	5	4	0	0	0	0	—	8	10	0	2	0.6	1.000
1989	KC A	3	1	.750	2.83	25	0	0	54	48	19	33	0	3	1	0	0	0	0	—	7	13	0	1	0.8	1.000
1990		5	4	.556	4.16	46	0	0	80	79	23	54	0	5	4	1	0	0	0	—	8	13	0	0	0.5	.969
9 yrs.		27	21	.563	4.01	244	16	2	516	583	168	282	0	24	16	18	0	0	0	—	50	77	4	9	0.5	.969

LEAGUE CHAMPIONSHIP SERIES

Year	Team	W	L	%	ERA	G	GS	CG	IP	H	BB	SO	ShO	W	L	SV	AB	H	HR	BA	PO	A	E	DP	TC/G	FA
1986	BOS A	1	0	1.000	0.00	1	0	0	1.2	1	2	1	0	1	0	0	0	0	0	—	1	0	0	0	1.0	1.000

WORLD SERIES

Year	Team	W	L	%	ERA	G	GS	CG	IP	H	BB	SO	ShO	W	L	SV	AB	H	HR	BA	PO	A	E	DP	TC/G	FA
1986	BOS A	1	0	1.000	6.23	3	0	0	4.1	5	0	4	0	1	0	0	1	0	0	.000	0	0	0	0	0.0	—

Tim Crews

CREWS, STANLEY TIMOTHY
B. Apr. 3, 1961, Tampa, Fla.
BR TR 6′ 180 lbs.

Year	Team	W	L	%	ERA	G	GS	CG	IP	H	BB	SO	ShO	W	L	SV	AB	H	HR	BA	PO	A	E	DP	TC/G	FA
April		0	0	—	2.25	7	0	0	12	15	2	9	0	0	0	1										
May		1	1	.500	4.91	9	1	0	18.1	26	9	17	0	1	0	1										
June		0	1	.000	1.80	12	0	0	15	10	3	8	0	0	1	1										
July		0	1	.000	1.69	11	0	0	21.1	16	4	16	0	0	1	1										
Aug		0	1	.000	2.60	14	0	0	17.1	12	2	12	0	0	1	1										
Sept/Oct		3	1	.750	3.09	13	1	0	23.1	19	4	14	0	2	1	0										
Day		2	2	.500	1.65	17	1	0	32.2	35	9	28	0	2	1	2										
Night		2	3	.400	3.25	49	1	0	74.2	63	15	48	0	1	3	3										
vs. Left		—	—	—	—	—	—	—	—	57	11	32	—	—	—	—										
vs. Right		—	—	—	—	—	—	—	—	41	13	44	—	—	—	—										
On Grass		2	5	.286	2.62	50	2	0	79	79	17	52	0	1	4	3										
On Turf		2	0	1.000	3.18	16	0	0	28.1	19	7	24	0	2	0	2										
Home		0	4	.000	3.04	31	1	0	50.1	55	7	40	0	0	3	2										
Road		4	1	.800	2.53	35	1	0	57	43	17	36	0	3	1	3										
Division Rivals																										
vs. ATL		1	0	1.000	2.04	8	1	0	17.2	10	3	9	0	0	0	1										
vs. CIN		0	1	.000	2.70	6	0	0	6.2	3	1	5	0	0	1	1										
vs. HOU		0	0	—	1.64	9	0	0	11	5	1	7	0	0	0	0										
vs. SD		1	1	.500	4.50	6	0	0	8	8	4	3	0	1	1	0										
vs. SF		0	0	—	1.80	10	0	0	15	18	5	9	0	0	0	1										
1987	LA N	1	1	.500	2.48	20	0	0	29	30	8	20	0	1	1	3	2	0	0	.000	2	5	0	0	0.4	1.000
1988		4	0	1.000	3.14	42	0	0	71.2	77	16	45	0	4	0	0	5	1	0	.200	6	4	1	1	0.3	.909
1989		0	1	.000	3.21	44	0	0	61.2	69	23	56	0	0	1	1	0	0	0	—	3	7	0	0	0.2	1.000
1990		4	5	.444	2.77	66	2	0	107.1	98	24	76	0	3	4	5	7	0	0	.000	8	7	1	0	0.2	.938
4 yrs.		9	7	.563	2.94	172	2	0	269.2	274	71	197	0	8	6	9	14	1	0	.071	19	23	2	1	0.3	.955

Year	Team	W	L	%	ERA	G	GS	CG	IP	H	BB	SO	ShO	RELIEF PITCHING W	L	SV	BATTING AB	H	HR	BA	PO	A	E	DP	TC/G	FA

Chuck Crim

CRIM, CHARLES ROBERT
B. July 23, 1961, Van Nuys, Calif.
BR TR 6' 175 lbs.

Year	Team	W	L	%	ERA	G	GS	CG	IP	H	BB	SO	ShO	W	L	SV	AB	H	HR	BA	PO	A	E	DP	TC/G	FA
April		1	0	1.000	2.57	10	0	0	14	15	3	4	0	1	0	2										
May		1	1	.500	5.06	12	0	0	10.2	12	3	6	0	1	1	0										
June		0	3	.000	6.41	15	0	0	19.2	26	9	9	0	0	3	4										
July		0	0	—	0.00	7	0	0	11.1	6	2	9	0	0	0	0										
Aug		1	0	1.000	1.32	9	0	0	13.2	11	2	4	0	1	0	2										
Sept/Oct		0	1	.000	3.86	14	0	0	16.1	18	4	7	0	0	1	3										
Day		0	2	.000	2.66	19	0	0	23.2	18	5	10	0	0	2	2										
Night		3	3	.500	3.77	48	0	0	62	70	18	29	0	3	3	9										
vs. Left		—	—	—	—	—	—	—	—	33	7	16	—	—	—	—										
vs. Right		—	—	—	—	—	—	—	—	55	16	23	—	—	—	—										
On Grass		2	4	.333	3.25	57	0	0	74.2	77	20	32	0	2	4	10										
On Turf		1	1	.500	4.91	10	0	0	11	11	3	7	0	1	1	1										
Home		0	3	.000	3.10	33	0	0	40.2	45	7	20	0	0	3	6										
Road		3	2	.600	3.80	34	0	0	45	43	16	19	0	3	2	5										
Division Rivals																										
vs. BAL		0	0	—	1.29	6	0	0	7	9	2	3	0	0	0	2										
vs. BOS		1	0	1.000	0.87	4	0	0	10.1	8	2	2	0	1	0	2										
vs. CLE		0	0	—	4.70	6	0	0	7.2	9	4	3	0	0	0	1										
vs. DET		1	0	1.000	0.00	8	0	0	11	5	2	2	0	1	0	2										
vs. NY		0	1	.000	6.75	9	0	0	9.1	15	3	3	0	0	1	3										
vs. TOR		0	1	.000	7.94	4	0	0	5.2	7	2	3	0	0	1	1										
1987	MIL A	6	8	.429	3.67	53	5	0	130	133	39	56	0	5	4	12	0	0	0	—	14	17	4	3	0.7	.886
1988		7	6	.538	2.91	70	0	0	105	95	28	58	0	7	6	9	0	0	0	—	12	13	3	1	0.4	.893
1989		9	7	.563	2.83	76	0	0	117.2	114	36	59	0	9	7	7	0	0	0	—	5	13	1	2	0.3	.947
1990		3	5	.375	3.47	67	0	0	85.2	88	23	39	0	3	5	11	0	0	0	—	10	12	1	1	0.3	.957
4 yrs.		25	26	.490	3.22	266	5	0	438.1	430	126	212	0	24	22	39	0	0	0	—	41	55	9	7	0.4	.914

Steve Cummings

CUMMINGS, STEVEN BRENT
B. July 15, 1964, Houston, Tex.
BB TR 6' 2" 200 lbs.

Year	Team	W	L	%	ERA	G	GS	CG	IP	H	BB	SO	ShO	W	L	SV	AB	H	HR	BA	PO	A	E	DP	TC/G	FA
1989	TOR A	2	0	1.000	3.00	5	2	0	21	18	11	8	0	1	0	0	0	0	0	—	0	4	1	0	1.0	.800
1990		0	0	—	5.11	6	2	0	12.1	22	5	4	0	0	0	0	0	0	0	—	1	1	0	0	0.3	1.000
2 yrs.		2	0	1.000	3.78	11	4	0	33.1	40	16	12	0	1	0	0	0	0	0	—	1	5	1	0	0.6	.857

Ron Darling

DARLING, RONALD MAURICE JR.
B. Aug. 19, 1960, Honolulu, Hawaii
BR TR 6' 3" 205 lbs.

Year	Team	W	L	%	ERA	G	GS	CG	IP	H	BB	SO	ShO	W	L	SV	AB	H	HR	BA	PO	A	E	DP	TC/G	FA
April		1	2	.333	3.00	3	2	0	12	12	4	17	0	1	0	0										
May		0	2	.000	8.35	5	3	0	18.1	19	10	13	0	0	1	0										
June		1	0	1.000	2.79	5	2	0	19.1	21	7	12	0	0	0	0										
July		2	1	.667	2.51	6	4	1	28.2	26	6	26	0	0	0	0										
Aug		1	4	.200	6.51	6	5	0	27.2	38	9	21	0	0	1	0										
Sept/Oct		2	0	1.000	3.60	8	2	0	20	19	8	10	0	0	0	0										
Day		3	2	.600	4.76	12	5	0	39.2	45	16	25	0	0	2	0										
Night		4	7	.364	4.38	21	13	1	86.1	90	28	74	0	1	0	0										
vs. Left		—	—	—	—	—	—	—	—	73	30	56	—	—	—	—										
vs. Right		—	—	—	—	—	—	—	—	62	14	43	—	—	—	—										
On Grass		6	6	.500	4.78	22	12	1	84.2	86	29	70	0	1	2	0										
On Turf		1	3	.250	3.92	11	6	0	41.1	49	15	29	0	0	0	0										
Home		4	2	.667	3.52	14	7	1	53.2	49	19	41	0	1	0	0										
Road		3	7	.300	5.23	19	11	0	72.1	86	25	58	0	0	2	0										
Division Rivals																										
vs. CHI		2	1	.667	5.27	3	3	0	13.2	18	4	7	0	0	0	0										
vs. MON		1	2	.333	3.12	5	4	0	26	26	9	22	0	0	0	0										
vs. PHI		0	0	—	9.53	3	0	0	5.2	9	2	4	0	0	0	0										
vs. PIT		0	0	—	0.00	2	0	0	3.2	1	0	2	0	0	0	0										
vs. STL		1	1	.500	3.27	4	3	1	22	21	11	12	0	0	0	0										

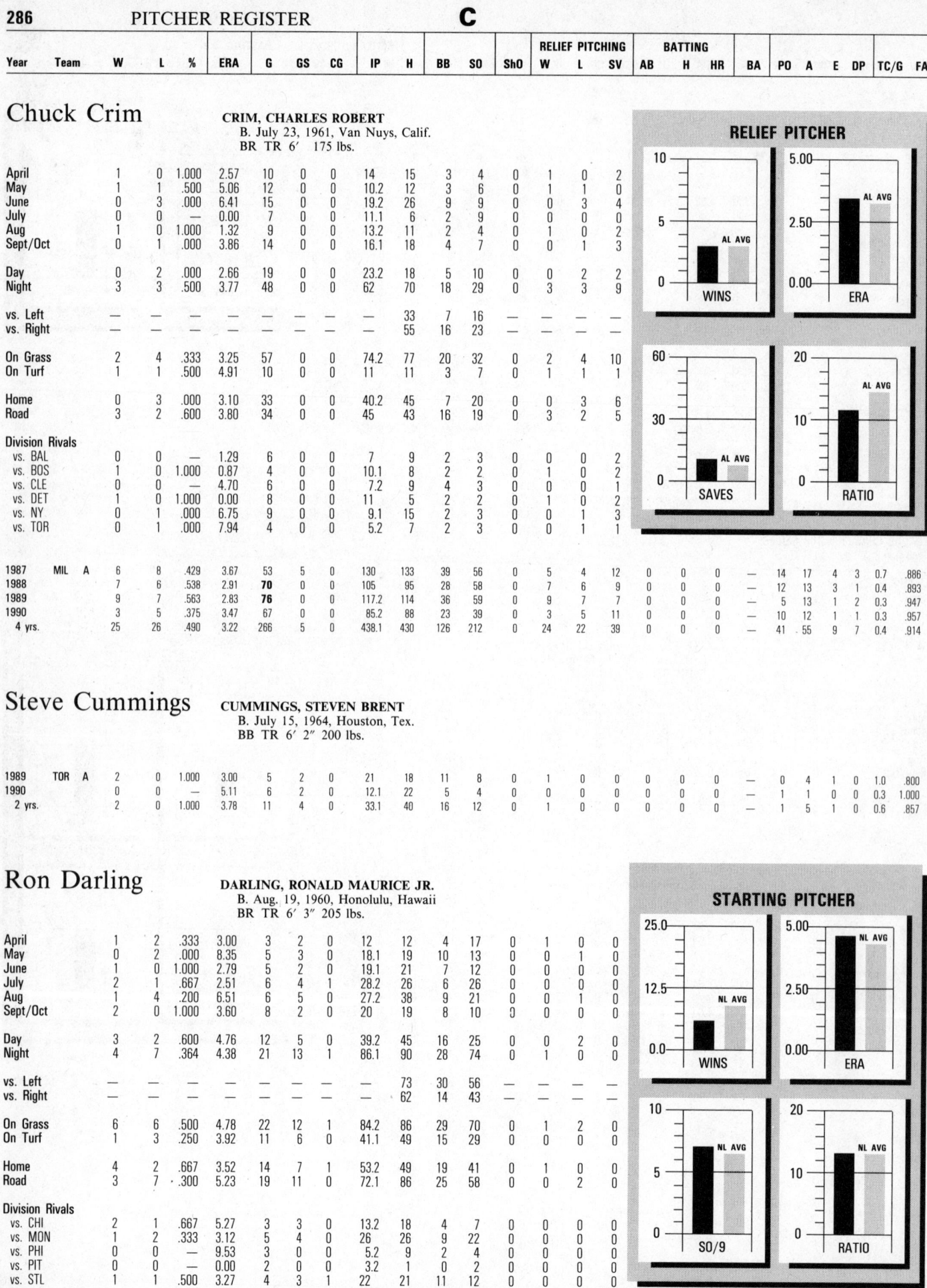

RELIEF PITCHER (Chuck Crim charts: WINS, ERA, SAVES, RATIO with AL AVG)

STARTING PITCHER (Ron Darling charts: WINS, ERA, SO/9, RATIO with NL AVG)

Year	Team	W	L	%	ERA	G	GS	CG	IP	H	BB	SO	ShO	W	L	SV	AB	H	HR	BA	PO	A	E	DP	TC/G	FA

Ron Darling *Continued*

Year	Team	W	L	%	ERA	G	GS	CG	IP	H	BB	SO	ShO	W	L	SV	AB	H	HR	BA	PO	A	E	DP	TC/G	FA
1983	NY N	1	3	.250	2.80	5	5	1	35.1	31	17	23	0	0	0	0	10	1	0	.100	2	6	0	1	1.6	1.000
1984		12	9	.571	3.81	33	33	2	205.2	179	104	136	2	0	0	0	67	10	0	.149	17	38	3	3	1.8	.948
1985		16	6	.727	2.90	36	35	4	248	214	**114**	167	2	0	0	0	76	13	0	.171	24	47	2	5	2.0	.973
1986		15	6	.714	2.81	34	34	4	237	203	81	184	2	0	0	0	81	8	0	.099	24	47	7	7	2.3	.910
1987		12	8	.600	4.29	32	32	2	207.2	183	96	167	0	0	0	0	65	8	0	.123	17	43	3	5	2.0	.952
1988		17	9	.654	3.25	34	34	7	240.2	218	60	161	4	0	0	0	82	18	0	.220	17	35	3	4	1.6	.945
1989		14	14	.500	3.52	33	33	4	217.1	214	70	153	0	0	0	2	73	9	2	.123	15	37	4	5	1.7	.929
1990		7	9	.438	4.50	33	18	1	126	135	44	99	0	1	2	0	31	4	0	.129	7	22	2	0	0.9	.935
8 yrs.		94	64	.595	3.48	240	224	25	1517.2	1377	586	1090	10	1	2	0	485	71	2	.146	123	275	24	30	1.8	.943

LEAGUE CHAMPIONSHIP SERIES

Year	Team	W	L	%	ERA	G	GS	CG	IP	H	BB	SO	ShO	W	L	SV	AB	H	HR	BA	PO	A	E	DP	TC/G	FA
1986	NY N	0	0	—	7.20	1	1	0	5	6	2	5	0	0	0	0	1	0	0	.000	1	2	0	0	3.0	1.000
1988		0	1	.000	7.71	2	2	0	7	11	4	7	0	0	0	0	3	0	0	.000	1	3	0	0	2.0	1.000
2 yrs.		0	1	.000	7.50	3	3	0	12	17	6	12	0	0	0	0	4	0	0	.000	2	5	0	0	2.3	1.000

WORLD SERIES

Year	Team	W	L	%	ERA	G	GS	CG	IP	H	BB	SO	ShO	W	L	SV	AB	H	HR	BA	PO	A	E	DP	TC/G	FA
1986	NY N	1	1	.500	1.53	3	3	0	17.2	13	10	12	0	0	0	0	3	0	0	.000	0	4	0	0	1.3	1.000

Danny Darwin

DARWIN, DANIEL WAYNE
B. Oct. 25, 1955, Bonham, Tex.
BR TR 6′ 3″ 185 lbs.

	W	L	%	ERA	G	GS	CG	IP	H	BB	SO	ShO	W	L	SV
April	1	0	1.000	1.80	7	0	0	10	7	1	9	0	1	0	0
May	0	0	—	0.95	13	0	0	19	14	3	14	0	0	0	1
June	1	1	.500	4.50	11	0	0	16	17	4	12	0	1	1	1
July	4	0	1.000	1.04	6	6	1	43.1	28	7	28	0	0	0	0
Aug	4	0	1.000	2.25	5	5	2	36	31	7	21	0	0	0	0
Sept/Oct	1	3	.250	3.29	6	6	0	38.1	39	9	25	0	0	0	0
Day	5	2	.714	2.81	14	5	1	48	49	9	34	0	2	1	0
Night	6	2	.750	1.96	34	12	2	114.2	87	22	75	0	0	0	2
vs. Left	—	—	—	—	—	—	—	—	96	23	68	—	—	—	—
vs. Right	—	—	—	—	—	—	—	—	40	8	41	—	—	—	—
On Grass	3	2	.600	2.82	14	4	1	44.2	39	10	32	0	0	1	1
On Turf	8	2	.800	1.98	34	13	2	118	97	21	77	0	2	0	1
Home	6	2	.750	2.42	24	8	1	78	72	16	59	0	2	0	1
Road	5	2	.714	2.02	24	9	2	84.2	64	15	50	0	0	1	1
Division Rivals															
vs. ATL	2	1	.667	1.93	5	4	1	28	21	7	25	0	0	0	0
vs. CIN	1	0	1.000	0.66	5	1	0	13.2	7	1	9	0	1	0	0
vs. LA	0	0	—	1.93	6	0	0	9.1	10	1	9	0	0	0	1
vs. SD	0	1	.000	7.80	5	2	0	15	24	5	10	0	0	0	0
vs. SF	2	1	.667	2.18	5	2	0	20.2	16	5	10	0	0	1	1

STARTING PITCHER

WINS (NL AVG) · ERA (NL AVG) · SO/9 (NL AVG) · RATIO (NL AVG)

Year	Team	W	L	%	ERA	G	GS	CG	IP	H	BB	SO	ShO	W	L	SV	AB	H	HR	BA	PO	A	E	DP	TC/G	FA
1978	TEX A	1	0	1.000	4.15	3	1	0	8.2	11	1	8	0	1	0	0	0	0	0	—	0	0	0	0	0.0	—
1979		4	4	.500	4.04	20	6	1	78	50	30	58	0	1	3	0	0	0	0	—	2	6	0	0	0.4	1.000
1980		13	4	.765	2.62	53	2	0	110	98	50	104	0	12	3	8	0	0	0	—	7	11	0	1	0.3	1.000
1981		9	9	.500	3.64	22	22	6	146	115	57	98	2	0	0	0	0	0	0	—	8	16	2	3	1.2	.923
1982		10	8	.556	3.44	56	1	0	89	95	37	61	0	10	7	7	0	0	0	—	5	19	0	0	0.4	1.000
1983		8	13	.381	3.49	28	26	9	183	175	62	92	2	0	0	0	0	0	0	—	20	18	3	1	1.5	.927
1984		8	12	.400	3.94	35	32	5	223.2	249	54	123	1	0	0	0	0	0	0	—	13	21	3	2	1.1	.919
1985	MIL A	8	18	.308	3.80	39	29	11	217.2	212	65	125	1	1	2	2	0	0	0	—	15	16	2	1	0.8	.939
1986	2 teams	MIL A	(27G 6 - 8)		HOU N	(12G 5 - 2)																				
"	total	11	10	.524	3.17	39	22	6	184.2	170	44	120	1	3	1	0	16	1	0	.063	10	27	3	2	1.0	.925
1987	HOU N	9	10	.474	3.59	33	30	3	195.2	184	69	134	1	0	0	0	66	12	0	.182	10	22	2	0	1.0	.941
1988		8	13	.381	3.84	44	20	3	192	189	48	129	0	4	3	3	56	4	1	.071	14	37	1	2	1.2	.981
1989		11	4	.733	2.36	68	0	0	122	92	33	104	0	11	4	7	17	2	0	.118	2	12	2	2	0.2	.875
1990		11	4	.733	**2.21**	48	17	3	162.2	136	31	109	0	2	1	2	38	5	0	.132	11	15	1	1	0.6	.963
13 yrs.		111	109	.505	3.39	488	208	47	1913	1776	581	1265	8	45	24	29	193	24 .	1	.124	117	220	19	15	0.7	.947

Doug Dascenzo

DASCENZO, DOUGLAS CRAIG
B. June 30, 1964, Cleveland, Ohio
BB TL 5′ 7″ 150 lbs.

Year	Team	W	L	%	ERA	G	GS	CG	IP	H	BB	SO	ShO	W	L	SV	AB	H	HR	BA	PO	A	E	DP	TC/G	FA
1990	CHI N	0	0	—	0.00	1	0	0	1	1	0	0	0	0	0	0	*				0	0	0	0	0.0	—

Year	Team	W	L	%	ERA	G	GS	CG	IP	H	BB	SO	ShO	RELIEF PITCHING W	L	SV	BATTING AB	H	HR	BA	PO	A	E	DP	TC/G	FA

John Davis

DAVIS, JOHN KIRK
B. Jan. 5, 1963, Chicago, Ill.
BR TR 6' 7" 215 lbs.

Year	Team		W	L	%	ERA	G	GS	CG	IP	H	BB	SO	ShO	W	L	SV	AB	H	HR	BA	PO	A	E	DP	TC/G	FA
1987	KC	A	5	2	.714	2.27	27	0	0	43.2	29	26	24	0	5	2	2	0	0	0	—	5	7	1	1	0.5	.923
1988	CHI	A	2	5	.286	6.64	34	1	0	63.2	77	50	37	0	2	4	1	0	0	0	—	5	7	1	1	0.4	.923
1989			0	1	.000	4.50	4	0	0	6	5	2	5	0	0	1	1	0	0	0	—	0	1	0	0	0.3	1.000
1990	SD	N	0	1	.000	5.79	6	0	0	9.1	9	4	7	0	0	1	0	1	0	0	.000	0	1	0	0	0.2	1.000
4 yrs.			7	9	.438	4.92	71	1	0	122.2	120	82	73	0	7	8	4	1	0	0	.000	10	16	2	2	0.4	.929

Mark Davis

DAVIS, MARK WILLIAM
B. Oct. 19, 1960, Livermore, Calif.
BL TL 6' 3" 180 lbs.

RELIEF PITCHER

	W	L	%	ERA	G	GS	CG	IP	H	BB	SO	ShO	W	L	SV	AB	H	HR	BA	PO	A	E	DP	TC/G	FA
April	0	1	.000	6.48	9	0	0	8.1	11	6	12	0	0	1	4										
May	1	1	.500	6.23	13	0	0	13	18	10	15	0	1	1	1										
June	0	3	.000	3.72	11	0	0	9.2	9	6	13	0	0	3	0										
July	0	1	.000	8.03	7	2	0	12.1	14	16	7	0	0	0	0										
Aug	0	1	.000	7.71	1	1	0	4.2	5	2	3	0	0	0	0										
Sept/Oct	1	0	1.000	2.18	12	0	0	20.2	14	12	23	0	1	0	1										
Day	1	2	.333	6.66	19	2	0	24.1	23	27	25	0	0	1	2										
Night	1	5	.167	4.26	34	1	0	44.1	48	25	48	0	1	4	4										
vs. Left	—	—	—	—	—	—	—	—	10	11	19	—	—	—	—										
vs. Right	—	—	—	—	—	—	—	—	61	41	54	—	—	—	—										
On Grass	0	4	.000	5.70	17	2	0	23.2	29	16	21	0	0	2	1										
On Turf	2	3	.400	4.80	36	1	0	45	42	36	52	0	2	3	5										
Home	2	1	.667	4.46	30	1	0	38.1	35	29	43	0	2	1	5										
Road	0	6	.000	5.93	23	2	0	30.1	36	23	30	0	0	4	1										

Division Rivals

	W	L	%	ERA	G	GS	CG	IP	H	BB	SO	ShO	W	L	SV	AB	H	HR	BA	PO	A	E	DP	TC/G	FA
vs. CAL	1	1	.500	5.59	7	0	0	9.2	12	5	13	0	1	1	0										
vs. CHI	0	1	.000	11.57	3	0	0	2.1	6	2	4	0	0	1	0										
vs. MIN	0	0	—	0.00	2	0	0	2	0	1	3	0	0	0	0										
vs. OAK	0	0	—	0.00	4	0	0	5	3	4	2	0	0	0	0										
vs. SEA	0	2	.000	11.57	4	0	0	2.1	4	3	4	0	0	2	0										
vs. TEX	0	1	.000	9.64	5	0	0	4.2	8	5	7	0	0	1	1										

Year	Team		W	L	%	ERA	G	GS	CG	IP	H	BB	SO	ShO	W	L	SV	AB	H	HR	BA	PO	A	E	DP	TC/G	FA
1980	PHI	N	0	0	—	2.57	2	1	0	7	4	5	5	0	0	0	0	2	1	0	.500	0	0	0	0	0.0	—
1981			1	4	.200	7.74	9	9	0	43	49	24	29	0	0	0	0	11	1	0	.091	0	6	0	0	0.7	1.000
1983	SF	N	6	4	.600	3.49	20	20	2	111	93	50	83	2	0	0	0	30	4	0	.133	4	13	0	0	0.9	1.000
1984			5	17	.227	5.36	46	27	1	174.2	201	54	124	0	3	4	0	46	6	0	.130	1	22	3	1	0.6	.885
1985			5	12	.294	3.54	77	1	0	114.1	89	41	131	0	5	11	7	12	3	0	.250	2	12	0	0	0.2	1.000
1986			5	7	.417	2.99	67	2	0	84.1	63	34	90	0	5	6	4	8	1	0	.125	3	11	3	1	0.3	.824
1987	2 teams		SF N (20G 4 - 5)				SD N (43G 5 - 3)																				
"	total		9	8	.529	3.99	63	11	1	133	123	59	98	0	5	3	2	30	7	0	.233	4	20	2	3	0.4	.923
1988	SD	N	5	10	.333	2.01	62	0	0	98.1	70	42	102	0	5	10	28	10	2	1	.200	4	21	1	2	0.4	.962
1989			4	3	.571	1.85	70	0	0	92.2	66	31	92	0	4	3	44	13	0	0	.000	1	11	3	0	0.2	.800
1990	KC	A	2	7	.222	5.11	53	3	0	68.2	71	52	73	0	2	5	6	0	0	0	—	1	6	1	0	0.2	.875
10 yrs.			42	72	.368	3.86	469	74	4	927	829	392	827	2	29	42	91	162	25	1	.154	20	122	13	7	0.3	.916

Storm Davis

DAVIS, GEORGE EARL
B. Dec. 26, 1961, Dallas, Tex.
BR TR 6' 4" 210 lbs.

STARTING PITCHER

	W	L	%	ERA	G	GS	CG	IP	H	BB	SO	ShO
April	1	3	.250	4.57	4	4	0	21.2	27	6	15	0
May	0	2	.000	6.17	5	5	0	23.1	26	9	17	0
June	1	1	.500	4.91	2	2	0	11	13	3	5	0
July	2	1	.667	5.79	3	3	0	14	20	6	4	0
Aug	3	3	.500	3.32	6	6	0	38	37	11	17	0
Sept/Oct	0	0	—	6.75	1	0	0	4	6	0	4	0
Day	1	1	.500	4.35	2	2	0	10.1	12	4	3	0
Night	6	9	.400	4.78	19	18	0	101.2	117	31	59	0
vs. Left	—	—	—	—	—	—	—	—	69	22	32	—
vs. Right	—	—	—	—	—	—	—	—	60	13	30	—

Year	Team	W	L	%	ERA	G	GS	CG	IP	H	BB	SO	ShO	RELIEF PITCHING W	L	SV	BATTING AB	H	HR	BA	PO	A	E	DP	TC/G	FA

Storm Davis *Continued*

		W	L	%	ERA	G	GS	CG	IP	H	BB	SO	ShO	W	L	SV	AB	H	HR	BA	PO	A	E	DP	TC/G	FA
On Grass		1	2	.333	6.52	4	4	0	19.1	25	6	15	0	0	0	0										
On Turf		6	8	.429	4.37	17	16	0	92.2	104	29	47	0	0	0	0										
Home		5	7	.417	4.50	15	14	0	80	89	22	45	0	0	0	0										
Road		2	3	.400	5.34	6	6	0	32	40	13	17	0	0	0	0										

Division Rivals

		W	L	%	ERA	G	GS	CG	IP	H	BB	SO	ShO	W	L	SV	AB	H	HR	BA	PO	A	E	DP	TC/G	FA
vs. CAL		—	—	—	—	0			0	0	0	0	—	0	0	0										
vs. CHI		1	0	1.000	3.60	1	1	0	5	5	0	1	0	0	0	0										
vs. MIN		2	0	1.000	1.29	2	2	0	14	10	2	6	0	0	0	0										
vs. OAK		—	—	—	—	0			0	0	0	0	—	0	0	0										
vs. SEA		0	2	.000	6.23	2	2	0	13	16	9	5	0	0	0	0										
vs. TEX		0	3	.000	6.75	3	3	0	13.1	22	3	8	0	0	0	0										

Year	Team	W	L	%	ERA	G	GS	CG	IP	H	BB	SO	ShO	W	L	SV	AB	H	HR	BA	PO	A	E	DP	TC/G	FA
1982	BAL A	8	4	.667	3.49	29	8	1	100.2	96	28	67	0	3	2	0	0	0	0	—	6	12	1	0	0.7	.947
1983		13	7	.650	3.59	34	29	6	200.1	180	64	125	1	0	0	0	0	0	0	—	14	19	3	1	1.1	.917
1984		14	9	.609	3.12	35	31	10	225	205	71	105	2	0	1	1	0	0	0	—	15	18	2	1	1.0	.943
1985		10	8	.556	4.53	31	28	8	175	172	70	93	1	0	0	0	0	0	0	—	15	20	0	0	1.1	1.000
1986		9	12	.429	3.62	25	25	2	154	166	49	96	0	0	0	0	0	0	0	—	22	21	1	3	1.8	.977
1987	2 teams	SD N (21G 2 – 7)			OAK A (5G 1 – 1)																					
"	total	3	8	.273	5.23	26	15	0	93	98	47	65	0	0	1	0	16	1	0	.063	8	9	1	0	0.7	.944
1988	OAK A	16	7	.696	3.70	33	33	1	201.2	211	91	127	0	0	0	0	0	0	0	—	6	21	1	2	0.8	.964
1989		19	7	.731	4.36	31	31	1	169.1	187	68	91	0	0	0	0	0	0	0	—	12	17	2	0	1.0	.935
1990	KC A	7	10	.412	4.74	21	20	0	112	129	35	62	0	0	0	0	0	0	0	—	4	10	1	3	0.7	.933
9 yrs.		99	72	.579	3.93	265	220	29	1431	1444	523	831	4	3	4	1	16	1	0	.063	102	147	12	10	1.0	.954

LEAGUE CHAMPIONSHIP SERIES

Year	Team	W	L	%	ERA	G	GS	CG	IP	H	BB	SO	ShO	W	L	SV	AB	H	HR	BA	PO	A	E	DP	TC/G	FA
1983	BAL A	0	0	—	0.00	1	1	0	6	5	2	2	0	0	0	0	0	0	0		0	0	0	0	0.0	—
1988	OAK A	0	0	—	0.00	1	1	0	6.1	2	5	4	0	0	0	0	0	0	0		0	2	0	0	2.0	1.000
1989		0	1	.000	7.11	1	1	0	6.1	5	2	3	0	0	0	0	0	0	0		0	0	0	0	0.0	—
3 yrs.		0	1	.000	2.41	3	3	0	18.2	12	9	9	0	0	0	0	0	0	0		0	2	0	0	0.7	1.000

WORLD SERIES

Year	Team	W	L	%	ERA	G	GS	CG	IP	H	BB	SO	ShO	W	L	SV	AB	H	HR	BA	PO	A	E	DP	TC/G	FA
1983	BAL A	1	0	1.000	5.40	1	1	0	5	6	1	3	0	0	0	0	2	0	0	.000	0	1	0	0	1.0	1.000
1988	OAK A	0	2	.000	11.25	2	2	0	8	14	1	7	0	0	0	0	1	0	0	.000	2	1	0	0	1.5	1.000
2 yrs.		1	2	.333	9.00	3	3	0	13	20	2	10	0	0	0	0	3	0	0	.000	2	2	0	0	1.3	1.000

Ken Dayley

DAYLEY, KENNETH GRANT
B. Feb. 25, 1959, Jerome, Ida.
BL TL 6′ 178 lbs.

		W	L	%	ERA	G	GS	CG	IP	H	BB	SO	ShO	W	L	SV	AB	H	HR	BA	PO	A	E	DP	TC/G	FA
April		1	0	1.000	0.00	7	0	0	8	6	0	1	0	1	0	1										
May		0	1	.000	2.57	8	0	0	7	7	.2	12	0	0	1	0										
June		0	1	.000	5.14	12	0	0	14	16	7	11	0	0	1	0										
July		1	0	1.000	7.71	7	0	0	7	11	6	3	0	1	0	0										
Aug		1	0	1.000	1.42	11	0	0	19	8	6	13	0	1	0	0										
Sept/Oct		1	2	.333	4.91	13	0	0	18.1	15	9	11	0	1	2	1										
Day		2	1	.667	2.93	20	0	0	27.2	24	11	26	0	2	1	0										
Night		2	3	.400	3.94	38	0	0	45.2	39	19	25	0	2	3	2										
vs. Left		—	—	—	—					30	8	22	—	—	—	—										
vs. Right		—	—	—	—					33	22	29	—	—	—	—										
On Grass		0	1	.000	3.31	16	0	0	16.1	15	7	12	0	0	1	0										
On Turf		4	3	.571	3.63	42	0	0	57	48	23	39	0	4	3	2										
Home		3	1	.750	3.23	27	0	0	39	36	16	24	0	3	1	0										
Road		1	3	.250	3.93	31	0	0	34.1	27	14	27	0	1	3	2										

Division Rivals

		W	L	%	ERA	G	GS	CG	IP	H	BB	SO	ShO	W	L	SV	AB	H	HR	BA	PO	A	E	DP	TC/G	FA
vs. CHI		0	1	.000	4.70	6	0	0	7.2	8	5	2	0	0	1	0										
vs. MON		2	1	.667	6.75	6	0	0	8	7	6	6	0	2	1	0										
vs. NY		0	1	.000	3.09	7	0	0	11.2	10	4	6	0	0	1	0										
vs. PHI		0	0	—	4.91	7	0	0	7.1	9	4	4	0	0	0	1										
vs. PIT		1	0	1.000	0.00	9	0	0	13.1	5	2	7	0	1	0	1										

Year	Team	W	L	%	ERA	G	GS	CG	IP	H	BB	SO	ShO	W	L	SV	AB	H	HR	BA	PO	A	E	DP	TC/G	FA
1982	ATL N	5	6	.455	4.54	20	11	0	71.1	79	25	34	0	2	0	0	20	5	0	.250	3	5	0	0	0.4	1.000
1983		5	8	.385	4.30	24	16	0	104.2	100	39	70	0	1	2	0	32	7	0	.219	0	7	0	0	0.3	1.000
1984	2 teams	ATL N (4G 0 – 3)			STL N (3G 0 – 2)																					
"	total	0	5	.000	7.99	7	6	0	23.2	44	11	10	0	0	0	0	4	2	0	.500	1	4	0	0	0.7	1.000
1985	STL N	4	4	.500	2.76	57	0	0	65.1	65	18	62	0	4	4	11	5	2	0	.400	5	15	0	0	0.4	1.000

Year	Team	W	L	%	ERA	G	GS	CG	IP	H	BB	SO	ShO	RELIEF PITCHING W	L	SV	BATTING AB	H	HR	BA	PO	A	E	DP	TC/G	FA

Ken Dayley *Continued*

Year	Team	W	L	%	ERA	G	GS	CG	IP	H	BB	SO	ShO	W	L	SV	AB	H	HR	BA	PO	A	E	DP	TC/G	FA
1986		0	3	.000	3.26	31	0	0	38.2	42	11	33	0	0	3	5	5	1	0	.200	1	7	0	0	0.3	1.000
1987		9	5	.643	2.66	53	0	0	61	52	33	63	0	9	5	4	0	0	0	—	3	4	0	1	0.1	1.000
1988		2	7	.222	2.77	54	0	0	55.1	48	19	38	0	2	7	5	4	0	0	.000	2	7	0	0	0.2	1.000
1989		4	3	.571	2.87	71	0	0	75.1	63	30	40	0	4	3	12	5	0	0	.000	2	5	1	0	0.1	.875
1990		4	4	.500	3.56	58	0	0	73.1	63	30	51	0	4	4	2	6	0	0	.000	5	8	1	1	0.2	.929
9 yrs.		33	45	.423	3.62	375	33	0	568.2	556	216	401	0	26	28	39	81	17	0	.210	22	62	2	2	0.2	.977

LEAGUE CHAMPIONSHIP SERIES

Year	Team	W	L	%	ERA	G	GS	CG	IP	H	BB	SO	ShO	W	L	SV	AB	H	HR	BA	PO	A	E	DP	TC/G	FA
1985	STL N	0	0	—	0.00	5	0	0	6	2	1	3	0	0	0	2	2	1	0	.500	0	1	0	0	0.2	1.000
1987		0	0	—	0.00	3	0	0	4	1	2	4	0	0	0	2	0	0	0	—	0	0	0	0	0.0	—
2 yrs.		0	0	—	0.00	8	0	0	10	3	3	7	0	0	0	4	2	1	0	.500	0	1	0	0	0.1	1.000

WORLD SERIES

Year	Team	W	L	%	ERA	G	GS	CG	IP	H	BB	SO	ShO	W	L	SV	AB	H	HR	BA	PO	A	E	DP	TC/G	FA
1985	STL N	1	0	1.000	0.00	4	0	0	6	1	3	5	0	1	0	0	0	0	0	—	0	0	0	0	0.0	—
1987		0	0	—	1.93	4	0	0	4.2	2	0	3	0	0	0	1	1	0	0	.000	0	0	0	0	0.0	—
2 yrs.		1	0	1.000	0.84	8	0	0	10.2	3	3	8	0	1	0	1	1	0	0	.000	0	0	0	0	0.0	—

Jose DeJesus

DeJESUS, JOSE LUIS
B. Jan. 6, 1965, Brooklyn, N. Y.
BR TR 6′ 5″ 175 lbs.

	W	L	%	ERA	G	GS	CG	IP	H	BB	SO	ShO	W	L	SV	AB	H	HR	BA	PO	A	E	DP	TC/G	FA
April	—	—	—	—	0	—	—	0	0	0	0	—	0	0	0										
May	—	—	—	—	0	0	—	0	0	0	0	—	0	0	0										
June	0	1	.000	2.65	3	3	0	17	13	14	8	0	0	0	0										
July	2	1	.667	3.94	6	6	0	32	29	17	25	0	0	0	0										
Aug	2	3	.400	3.07	6	6	2	41	25	16	29	1	0	0	0										
Sept/Oct	3	3	.500	4.73	7	7	1	40	30	26	25	0	0	0	0										
Day	2	3	.400	6.04	6	6	0	28.1	28	22	27	0	0	0	0										
Night	5	5	.500	3.10	16	16	3	101.2	69	51	60	1	0	0	0										
vs. Left	—	—	—	—	—	—	—	—	57	53	57	—	—	—	—										
vs. Right	—	—	—	—	—	—	—	—	40	20	30	—	—	—	—										
On Grass	3	1	.750	2.87	6	6	2	37.2	23	19	23	1	0	0	0										
On Turf	4	7	.364	4.09	16	16	1	92.1	74	54	64	0	0	0	0										
Home	2	5	.286	3.68	11	11	1	71	57	34	49	0	0	0	0										
Road	5	3	.625	3.81	11	11	2	59	40	39	38	1	0	0	0										

Division Rivals

	W	L	%	ERA	G	GS	CG	IP	H	BB	SO	ShO													
vs. CHI	1	1	.500	10.80	2	2	0	6.2	8	6	3	0	0	0	0										
vs. MON	0	1	.000	5.63	3	3	0	16	13	13	11	0	0	0	0										
vs. NY	3	0	1.000	1.07	3	3	2	25.1	9	10	13	1	0	0	0										
vs. PIT	0	1	.000	3.75	3	3	0	12	10	11	6	0	0	0	0										
vs. STL	0	2	.000	6.10	2	2	0	10.1	9	8	7	0	0	0	0										

Year	Team	W	L	%	ERA	G	GS	CG	IP	H	BB	SO	ShO	W	L	SV	AB	H	HR	BA	PO	A	E	DP	TC/G	FA
1988	KC A	0	1	.000	27.00	2	1	0	2.2	6	5	2	0	0	0	0	0	0	0	—	0	0	0	0	0.0	—
1989		0	0	—	4.50	3	1	0	8	7	8	2	0	0	0	0	0	0	0	—	0	1	0	0	0.3	1.000
1990	PHI N	7	8	.467	3.74	22	22	3	130	97	73	87	1	0	0	0	38	3	0	.079	9	14	2	1	1.1	.920
3 yrs.		7	9	.438	4.22	27	24	3	140.2	110	86	91	1	0	0	0	38	3	0	.079	9	15	2	1	1.0	.923

Jose DeLeon

DeLEON, JOSE
Born Jose Deleon y Chestaro.
B. Dec. 20, 1960, La Vega, Dominican Republic
BR TR 6′ 3″ 195 lbs.

	W	L	%	ERA	G	GS	CG	IP	H	BB	SO	ShO	W	L	SV
April	2	0	1.000	2.95	4	4	0	18.1	17	6	16	0	0	0	0
May	2	3	.400	4.50	6	6	0	36	35	11	36	0	0	0	0
June	2	3	.400	3.49	6	6	0	38.2	34	24	37	0	0	0	0
July	0	5	.000	4.85	5	5	0	29.2	26	15	22	0	0	0	0
Aug	1	3	.250	4.58	6	6	0	35.1	27	15	37	0	0	0	0
Sept/Oct	0	5	.000	6.20	5	5	0	24.2	29	15	16	0	0	0	0
Day	2	3	.400	4.21	8	8	0	47	46	19	54	0	0	0	0
Night	5	16	.238	4.51	24	24	0	135.2	122	67	110	0	0	0	0
vs. Left	—	—	—	—	—	—	—	—	115	58	69	—	—	—	—
vs. Right	—	—	—	—	—	—	—	—	53	28	95	—	—	—	—

Year	Team	W	L	%	ERA	G	GS	CG	IP	H	BB	SO	ShO	W	L	SV	AB	H	HR	BA	PO	A	E	DP	TC/G	FA

Jose DeLeon *Continued*

Year	Team	W	L	%	ERA	G	GS	CG	IP	H	BB	SO	ShO	W	L	SV	AB	H	HR	BA	PO	A	E	DP	TC/G	FA
On Grass		2	6	.250	3.70	10	10	0	65.2	60	22	65	0	0	0	0										
On Turf		5	13	.278	4.85	22	22	0	117	108	64	99	0	0	0	0										
Home		3	9	.250	5.55	16	16	0	84.1	87	43	74	0	0	0	0										
Road		4	10	.286	3.48	16	16	0	98.1	81	43	90	0	0	0	0										
Division Rivals																										
vs. CHI		1	2	.333	2.38	5	5	0	34	25	14	33	0	0	0	0										
vs. MON		1	2	.333	4.81	4	4	0	24.1	22	14	24	0	0	0	0										
vs. NY		0	2	.000	6.88	3	3	0	17	19	11	7	0	0	0	0										
vs. PHI		0	1	.000	3.38	2	2	0	2.2	4	3	1	0	0	0	0										
vs. PIT		1	2	.333	4.30	3	3	0	14.2	13	10	9	0	0	0	0										
1983	PIT N	7	3	.700	2.83	15	15	3	108	75	47	118	2	0	0	0	34	2	0	.059	6	9	1	0	1.1	.938
1984		7	13	.350	3.74	30	28	5	192.1	147	92	153	1	1	0	0	59	5	0	.085	6	16	2	1	0.8	.917
1985		2	**19**	.095	4.70	31	25	1	162.2	138	89	149	0	0	1	3	36	2	0	.056	9	16	1	1	0.8	.962
1986	2 teams	PIT N	(9G 1 - 3)		CHI A	(13G 4 - 5)																				
"	total	5	8	.385	3.87	22	14	1	95.1	66	59	79	0	1	2	1	1	0	0	.000	6	14	1	2	1.0	.952
1987	CHI A	11	12	.478	4.02	33	31	2	206	177	97	153	0	0	0	0	0	0	0	—	10	14	3	0	0.8	.889
1988	STL N	13	10	.565	3.67	34	34	3	225.1	198	86	208	1	0	0	0	72	10	0	.139	10	21	0	0	0.9	1.000
1989		16	12	.571	3.05	36	36	5	244.2	173	80	**201**	3	0	0	0	83	8	0	.096	9	16	5	0	0.8	.833
1990		7	**19**	.269	4.43	32	32	0	182.2	168	86	164	0	0	0	0	56	6	0	.107	8	15	2	0	0.8	.920
8 yrs.		68	96	.415	3.79	233	215	20	1417	1142	636	1225	7	2	3	4	341	33	0	.097	64	121	15	4	0.9	.925

Rich DeLucia

DeLUCIA, RICHARD ANTHONY
B. Oct. 7, 1964, Reading, Pa.
BR TR 6′ 185 lbs.

Year	Team	W	L	%	ERA	G	GS	CG	IP	H	BB	SO	ShO	W	L	SV	AB	H	HR	BA	PO	A	E	DP	TC/G	FA
1990	SEA A	1	2	.333	2.00	5	5	1	36	30	9	20	0	0	0	0	0	0	0	—	3	2	1	0	1.2	.833

Jim Deshaies

DESHAIES, JAMES JOSEPH
B. June 23, 1960, Massena, N. Y.
BL TL 6′ 4″ 222 lbs.

Year	Team	W	L	%	ERA	G	GS	CG	IP	H	BB	SO	ShO	W	L	SV	AB	H	HR	BA	PO	A	E	DP	TC/G	FA
April		1	0	1.000	1.99	5	5	0	31.2	22	13	14	0	0	0	0										
May		2	2	.500	4.63	6	6	0	35	31	13	15	0	0	0	0										
June		1	3	.250	6.75	5	5	0	24	31	11	10	0	0	0	0										
July		0	4	.000	4.59	6	6	0	33.1	33	18	21	0	0	0	0										
Aug		2	2	.500	4.50	5	5	1	34	33	8	22	0	0	0	0										
Sept/Oct		1	1	.500	1.93	7	7	1	51.1	36	21	37	0	0	0	0										
Day		1	1	.500	4.40	8	8	0	47	45	14	25	0	0	0	0										
Night		6	11	.353	3.60	26	26	2	162.1	141	70	94	0	0	0	0										
vs. Left		—	—	—	—	—	—	—	—	35	23	20	—	—	—	—										
vs. Right		—	—	—	—	—	—	—	—	151	61	99	—	—	—	—										
On Grass		3	2	.600	3.84	10	10	0	61	58	21	36	0	0	0	0										
On Turf		4	10	.286	3.76	24	24	2	148.1	128	63	83	0	0	0	0										
Home		4	3	.571	2.75	15	15	2	98.1	79	32	51	0	0	0	0										
Road		3	9	.250	4.70	19	19	0	111	107	52	68	0	0	0	0										
Division Rivals																										
vs. ATL		1	1	.500	3.38	3	3	1	21.1	18	6	10	0	0	0	0										
vs. CIN		0	2	.000	4.34	5	5	0	29	26	20	16	0	0	0	0										
vs. LA		2	0	1.000	2.05	3	3	1	22	14	5	17	0	0	0	0										
vs. SD		1	2	.333	3.31	5	5	0	32.2	29	10	19	0	0	0	0										
vs. SF		1	1	.500	3.77	3	3	0	14.1	14	6	10	0	0	0	0										
1984	NY A	0	1	.000	11.57	2	2	0	7	14	7	5	0	0	0	0	0	0	0	—	0	1	0	0	0.5	1.000
1985	HOU N	0	0	—	0.00	2	0	0	3	1	0	2	0	0	0	0	0	0	0	—	0	0	0	0	0.0	—
1986		12	5	.706	3.25	26	26	1	144	124	59	128	1	0	0	0	43	2	0	.047	9	13	2	0	0.9	.917
1987		11	6	.647	4.62	26	25	1	152	149	57	104	0	0	0	0	53	5	0	.094	5	22	1	0	1.1	.964
1988		11	14	.440	3.00	31	31	3	207	164	72	127	2	0	0	0	63	3	0	.048	7	25	2	1	1.1	.941
1989		15	10	.600	2.91	34	34	6	225.2	180	79	153	3	0	0	0	75	9	0	.120	8	31	3	2	1.2	.929
1990		7	12	.368	3.78	34	34	2	209.1	186	84	119	0	0	0	0	63	4	0	.063	3	32	2	1	1.1	.946
7 yrs.		56	48	.538	3.50	155	152	13	948	818	358	638	6	0	0	0	297	23	0	.077	32	124	10	4	1.1	.940

Year	Team	W	L	%	ERA	G	GS	CG	IP	H	BB	SO	ShO	RELIEF PITCHING W	L	SV	BATTING AB	H	HR	BA	PO	A	E	DP	TC/G	FA

Mark Dewey

DEWEY, MARK ALAN
B. Jan. 3, 1965, Grand Rapids, Mich.
BR TR 6' 185 lbs.

Year	Team		W	L	%	ERA	G	GS	CG	IP	H	BB	SO	ShO	W	L	SV	AB	H	HR	BA	PO	A	E	DP	TC/G	FA
1990	SF	N	1	1	.500	2.78	14	0	0	22.2	22	5	11	0	1	1	0	1	0	0	.000	2	2	0	1	0.3	1.000

Rob Dibble

DIBBLE, ROBERT KEITH
B. Jan. 24, 1964, Bridgeport, Conn.
BL TR 6' 4" 230 lbs.

Split	W	L	%	ERA	G	GS	CG	IP	H	BB	SO	ShO	W	L	SV
April	1	0	1.000	0.00	10	0	0	13.2	9	5	23	0	1	0	3
May	2	0	1.000	2.92	11	0	0	12.1	12	7	19	0	2	0	2
June	1	2	.333	2.00	12	0	0	18	8	5	27	0	1	2	2
July	0	0	—	2.70	11	0	0	16.2	8	10	19	0	0	0	1
Aug	2	1	.667	1.83	11	0	0	19.2	13	4	24	0	2	1	2
Sept/Oct	2	0	1.000	1.02	13	0	0	17.2	12	3	24	0	2	0	1
Day	3	1	.750	3.08	17	0	0	26.1	16	12	37	0	3	1	1
Night	5	2	.714	1.26	51	0	0	71.2	46	22	99	0	5	2	10
vs. Left	—	—	—	—	—	—	—	—	32	24	69	—	—	—	—
vs. Right	—	—	—	—	—	—	—	—	30	10	67	—	—	—	—
On Grass	1	2	.333	1.47	21	0	0	30.2	18	6	45	0	1	2	3
On Turf	7	1	.875	1.87	47	0	0	67.1	44	28	91	0	7	1	8
Home	4	1	.800	2.15	32	0	0	46	32	20	61	0	4	1	6
Road	4	2	.667	1.38	36	0	0	52	30	14	75	0	4	2	5
Division Rivals															
vs. ATL	1	1	.500	1.93	10	0	0	14	6	3	25	0	1	1	2
vs. HOU	1	0	1.000	0.00	11	0	0	15	10	4	21	0	1	0	1
vs. LA	0	0	—	1.50	5	0	0	6	4	2	11	0	0	0	1
vs. SD	1	1	.500	1.59	6	0	0	11.1	8	2	13	0	1	1	1
vs. SF	0	1	.000	2.38	7	0	0	11.1	7	3	14	0	0	1	1

Year	Team		W	L	%	ERA	G	GS	CG	IP	H	BB	SO	ShO	W	L	SV	AB	H	HR	BA	PO	A	E	DP	TC/G	FA
1988	CIN	N	1	1	.500	1.82	37	0	0	59.1	43	21	59	0	1	1	0	2	0	0	.000	1	3	0	0	0.1	1.000
1989			10	5	.667	2.09	74	0	0	99	62	39	141	0	10	5	2	2	0	0	.000	3	5	1	0	0.1	.889
1990			8	3	.727	1.74	68	0	0	98	62	34	136	0	8	3	11	7	0	0	.000	5	8	0	0	0.2	1.000
3 yrs.			19	9	.679	1.90	179	0	0	256.1	167	94	336	0	19	9	13	17	0	0	.000	9	16	1	0	0.1	.962

LEAGUE CHAMPIONSHIP SERIES

Year	Team		W	L	%	ERA	G	GS	CG	IP	H	BB	SO	ShO	W	L	SV	AB	H	HR	BA	PO	A	E	DP	TC/G	FA
1990	CIN	N	0	0	—	0.00	4	0	0	5	0	1	10	0	0	0	1	2	0	0	.000	0	0	0	0	0.0	—

WORLD SERIES

Year	Team		W	L	%	ERA	G	GS	CG	IP	H	BB	SO	ShO	W	L	SV	AB	H	HR	BA	PO	A	E	DP	TC/G	FA
1990	CIN	N	1	0	1.000	0.00	3	0	0	4.2	3	1	4	0	1	0	0	0	0	0	—	0	0	0	0	0.0	—

Lance Dickson

DICKSON, LANCE MICHAEL
B. Oct. 19, 1969, Fullerton, Calif.
BR TL 6' 185 lbs.

Year	Team		W	L	%	ERA	G	GS	CG	IP	H	BB	SO	ShO	W	L	SV	AB	H	HR	BA	PO	A	E	DP	TC/G	FA
1990	CHI	N	0	3	.000	7.24	3	3	0	13.2	20	4	4	0	0	0	0	3	0	0	.000	1	6	0	1	2.3	1.000

Frank DiPino

DiPINO, FRANK MICHAEL
B. Oct. 22, 1956, Syracuse, N. Y.
BL TL 5' 10" 175 lbs.

Split	W	L	%	ERA	G	GS	CG	IP	H	BB	SO	ShO	W	L	SV
April	0	0	—	1.80	8	0	0	10	14	1	0	0	0	0	0
May	1	0	1.000	7.71	9	0	0	7	16	2	7	0	1	0	0
June	2	1	.667	6.75	11	0	0	16	19	10	12	0	2	1	0
July	1	0	1.000	2.50	11	0	0	18	15	5	12	0	1	0	2
Aug	1	1	.500	4.60	12	0	0	15.2	16	6	6	0	1	1	0
Sept/Oct	0	0	—	5.02	11	0	0	14.1	12	7	12	0	0	0	0
Day	2	0	1.000	4.66	17	0	0	19.1	27	6	12	0	2	0	1
Night	3	2	.600	4.52	45	0	0	61.2	65	25	37	0	3	2	2
vs. Left	—	—	—	—	—	—	—	—	39	12	18	—	—	—	—
vs. Right	—	—	—	—	—	—	—	—	53	19	31	—	—	—	—

Year	Team	W	L	%	ERA	G	GS	CG	IP	H	BB	SO	ShO	RELIEF PITCHING W	L	SV	BATTING AB	H	HR	BA	PO	A	E	DP	TC/G	FA

Frank DiPino *Continued*

		W	L	%	ERA	G	GS	CG	IP	H	BB	SO	ShO	W	L	SV	AB	H	HR	BA	PO	A	E	DP	TC/G	FA
On Grass		2	0	1.000	5.16	18	0	0	22.2	32	9	11	0	2	0	0										
On Turf		3	2	.600	4.32	44	0	0	58.1	60	22	38	0	3	2	3										
Home		3	2	.600	3.92	33	0	0	41.1	46	15	26	0	3	2	3										
Road		2	0	1.000	5.22	29	0	0	39.2	46	16	23	0	2	0	0										
Division Rivals																										
vs. CHI		0	0	—	0.00	3	0	0	3.2	1	1	0	0	0	0	0										
vs. MON		0	0	—	9.00	7	0	0	9	10	3	7	0	0	0	0										
vs. NY		0	0	—	6.75	11	0	0	13.1	18	7	11	0	0	0	1										
vs. PHI		2	0	1.000	4.05	7	0	0	13.1	13	6	6	0	2	0	0										
vs. PIT		0	1	.000	2.38	8	0	0	11.1	11	5	5	0	0	0	0										

RELIEF PITCHER

1981	MIL A	0	0	—	0.00	2	0	0	2	0	3	3	0	0	0	0	0	0	0	—	0	0	0	0	0.0	—
1982	HOU N	2	2	.500	6.04	6	6	0	28.1	32	11	25	0	0	0	0	8	0	0	.000	0	2	0	0	0.3	1.000
1983		3	4	.429	2.65	53	0	0	71.1	52	20	67	0	3	4	20	6	1	0	.167	5	11	0	1	0.3	1.000
1984		4	9	.308	3.35	57	0	0	75.1	74	36	65	0	4	9	14	10	0	0	.000	3	12	0	0	0.3	1.000
1985		3	7	.300	4.03	54	0	0	76	69	43	49	0	3	7	6	12	2	0	.167	3	5	1	0	0.2	.889
1986	2 teams	HOU N (31G 1 – 3)			CHI N (30G 2 – 4)																					
"	total	3	7	.300	4.37	61	0	0	80.1	74	30	70	0	3	7	3	6	1	0	.167	8	17	1	1	0.4	.962
1987	CHI N	3	3	.500	3.15	69	0	0	80	75	34	61	0	3	3	4	2	1	0	.500	2	16	1	2	0.3	.947
1988		2	3	.400	4.98	69	0	0	90.1	102	32	69	0	2	3	6	10	1	0	.100	3	12	0	0	0.2	1.000
1989	STL N	9	0	1.000	2.45	67	0	0	88.1	73	20	44	0	9	0	0	13	1	0	.077	6	13	0	0	0.3	1.000
1990		5	2	.714	4.56	62	0	0	81	92	31	49	0	5	2	3	4	1	0	.250	2	15	0	1	0.3	1.000
10 yrs.		34	37	.479	3.80	494	6	0	673	643	260	502	0	32	35	56	71	8	0	.113	32	103	3	5	0.3	.978

John Dopson

DOPSON, JOHN ROBERT JR.
B. July 14, 1963, Baltimore, Md.
BL TR 6′ 4″ 205 lbs.

1985	MON N	0	2	.000	11.08	4	3	0	13	25	4	4	0	0	0	0	4	0	0	.000	0	2	0	0	0.5	1.000
1988		3	11	.214	3.04	26	26	1	168.2	150	58	101	0	0	0	0	51	3	0	.059	10	15	2	1	1.0	.926
1989	BOS A	12	8	.600	3.99	29	28	2	169.1	166	69	95	0	1	0	0	0	0	0	—	20	34	1	1	1.9	.982
1990		0	0	—	2.04	4	4	0	17.2	13	9	9	0	0	0	0	0	0	0	—	1	5	0	0	1.5	1.000
4 yrs.		15	21	.417	3.71	63	61	3	368.2	354	140	209	0	1	0	0	55	3	0	.055	31	56	3	2	1.4	.967

Richard Dotson

DOTSON, RICHARD ELLIOTT
B. Jan. 10, 1959, Cincinnati, Ohio
BR TR 6′ 1″ 190 lbs.

1979	CHI A	2	0	1.000	3.75	5	5	1	24	28	6	13	1	0	0	0	0	0	0	—	1	4	0	0	1.0	1.000
1980		12	10	.545	4.27	33	32	8	198	185	87	109	0	0	0	0	0	0	0	—	13	33	1	0	1.4	.979
1981		9	8	.529	3.77	24	24	5	141	145	49	73	4	0	0	0	0	0	0	—	7	20	0	4	1.1	1.000
1982		11	15	.423	3.84	34	31	3	196.2	219	73	109	1	0	0	0	0	0	0	—	13	24	1	1	1.1	.974
1983		22	7	.759	3.23	35	35	8	240	209	106	137	1	0	0	0	0	0	0	—	20	48	1	8	2.0	.986
1984		14	15	.483	3.59	32	32	14	245.2	216	103	120	1	0	0	0	0	0	0	—	8	36	1	3	1.4	.978
1985		3	4	.429	4.47	9	9	0	52.1	53	17	33	0	0	0	0	0	0	0	—	3	5	0	0	0.9	1.000
1986		10	17	.370	5.48	34	34	3	197	226	69	110	1	0	0	0	0	0	0	—	13	23	3	0	1.1	.923
1987		11	12	.478	4.17	31	31	7	211.1	201	86	114	2	0	0	0	0	0	0	—	14	38	2	4	1.7	.963
1988	NY A	12	9	.571	5.00	32	29	4	171	178	72	77	0	0	0	0	0	0	0	—	17	14	0	1	1.0	1.000
1989	2 teams	NY A (11G 2 – 5)			CHI A (17G 3 – 7)																					
"	total	5	12	.294	4.46	28	26	2	151.1	181	58	69	0	0	0	0	0	0	0	—	5	21	2	3	1.0	.929
1990	KC A	0	4	.000	8.48	8	7	0	28.2	43	14	9	0	0	0	0	0	0	0	—	2	3	0	1	0.6	1.000
12 yrs.		111	113	.496	4.23	305	295	55	1857	1884	740	973	11	0	0	0	0	0	0	—	116	269	11	25	1.3	.972

LEAGUE CHAMPIONSHIP SERIES

| 1983 | CHI A | 0 | 1 | .000 | 10.80 | 1 | 1 | 0 | 5 | 6 | 3 | 3 | 0 | 0 | 0 | 0 | 0 | 0 | 0 | — | 1 | 1 | 0 | 0 | 2.0 | 1.000 |

Year	Team		W	L	%	ERA	G	GS	CG	IP	H	BB	SO	ShO	RELIEF PITCHING W	L	SV	BATTING AB	H	HR	BA	PO	A	E	DP	TC/G	FA

Kelly Downs

DOWNS, KELLY ROBERT
Brother of Dave Downs.
B. Oct. 25, 1960, Ogden, Utah
BR TR 6' 4" 195 lbs.

Year	Team	Lg	W	L	%	ERA	G	GS	CG	IP	H	BB	SO	ShO	W	L	SV	AB	H	HR	BA	PO	A	E	DP	TC/G	FA
1986	SF	N	4	4	.500	2.75	14	14	1	88.1	78	30	64	0	0	0	0	29	5	0	.172	6	13	1	0	1.4	.950
1987			12	9	.571	3.63	41	28	4	186	185	67	137	3	1	1	1	56	8	0	.143	11	10	3	0	0.6	.875
1988			13	9	.591	3.32	27	26	6	168	140	47	118	3	0	0	0	54	9	0	.167	15	22	1	2	1.4	.974
1989			4	8	.333	4.79	18	15	0	82.2	82	26	49	0	0	0	0	22	2	0	.091	7	8	1	1	0.9	.938
1990			3	2	.600	3.43	13	9	0	63	56	20	31	0	0	0	0	13	0	0	.000	6	12	1	1	1.5	.947
5 yrs.			36	32	.529	3.55	113	92	11	588	541	190	399	6	1	1	1	174	24	0	.138	45	65	7	3	1.0	.940

LEAGUE CHAMPIONSHIP SERIES

Year	Team	Lg	W	L	%	ERA	G	GS	CG	IP	H	BB	SO	ShO	W	L	SV	AB	H	HR	BA	PO	A	E	DP	TC/G	FA
1987	SF	N	0	0	—	0.00	1	0	0	1.1	1	0	0	0	0	0	0	—	0	0	0	0	0.0	—
1989			1	0	1.000	3.12	2	0	0	8.2	8	6	6	0	1	0	0	3	0	0	.000	0	1	0	1	0.5	1.000
2 yrs.			1	0	1.000	2.70	3	0	0	10	9	6	6	0	1	0	0	3	0	0	.000	0	1	0	1	0.3	1.000

WORLD SERIES

Year	Team	Lg	W	L	%	ERA	G	GS	CG	IP	H	BB	SO	ShO	W	L	SV	AB	H	HR	BA	PO	A	E	DP	TC/G	FA
1989	SF	N	0	0	—	7.71	3	0	0	4.2	3	2	4	0	0	0	0		0	0	0	—	0	0	0	0	0.0	—

Doug Drabek

DRABEK, DOUGLAS DEAN
B. July 25, 1962, Victoria, Tex.
BR TR 6' 1" 185 lbs.

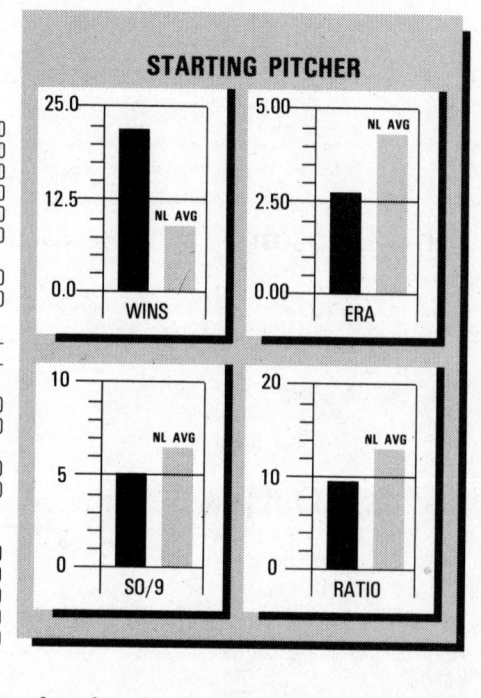

STARTING PITCHER — WINS, ERA, SO/9, RATIO (with NL AVG)

Split		W	L	%	ERA	G	GS	CG	IP	H	BB	SO	ShO	W	L	SV
April		4	1	.800	2.37	5	5	0	30.1	26	9	16	0	0	0	0
May		3	0	1.000	2.93	4	4	1	30.2	22	7	16	0	0	0	0
June		1	3	.250	4.29	6	6	1	35.2	44	13	16	0	0	0	0
July		5	0	1.000	2.23	6	6	1	44.1	33	13	29	0	0	0	0
Aug		4	1	.800	2.23	6	6	3	44.1	34	6	30	2	0	0	0
Sept/Oct		5	1	.833	2.74	6	6	3	46	31	8	24	1	0	0	0
Day		9	1	.900	2.30	10	10	3	70.1	49	20	37	1	0	0	0
Night		13	5	.722	2.96	23	23	6	161	141	36	94	2	0	0	0
vs. Left		—	—	—	—	—	—	—	—	130	35	69	—	—	—	—
vs. Right		—	—	—	—	—	—	—	—	60	21	62	—	—	—	—
On Grass		6	1	.857	3.35	8	8	1	48.1	43	11	27	1	0	0	0
On Turf		16	5	.762	2.61	25	25	8	183	147	45	104	2	0	0	0
Home		11	3	.786	3.00	16	16	6	120	96	28	72	0	0	0	0
Road		11	3	.786	2.51	17	17	3	111.1	94	28	59	3	0	0	0
Division Rivals																
vs. CHI		3	1	.750	3.90	4	4	2	27.2	22	7	16	0	0	0	0
vs. MON		2	3	.400	3.38	5	5	0	34.2	36	9	20	0	0	0	0
vs. NY		1	1	.500	8.36	3	3	0	14	16	8	3	0	0	0	0
vs. PHI		3	0	1.000	0.67	3	3	3	27	7	8	19	1	0	0	0
vs. STL		2	1	.667	2.28	4	4	1	27.2	24	7	10	1	0	0	0

Year	Team	Lg	W	L	%	ERA	G	GS	CG	IP	H	BB	SO	ShO	W	L	SV	AB	H	HR	BA	PO	A	E	DP	TC/G	FA
1986	NY	A	7	8	.467	4.10	27	21	0	131.2	126	50	76	0	0	0	0	0	0	0	—	5	13	0	0	0.7	1.000
1987	PIT	N	11	12	.478	3.88	29	28	1	176.1	165	46	120	1	0	0	0	59	7	0	.119	24	23	2	0	1.7	.959
1988			15	7	.682	3.08	33	32	3	219.1	194	50	127	1	0	0	0	76	13	0	.171	29	21	6	6	1.7	.893
1989			14	12	.538	2.80	35	34	8	244.1	215	69	123	5	1	0	0	77	8	0	.104	24	34	2	0	1.7	.967
1990			**22**	6	**.786**	2.76	33	33	9	231.1	190	56	131	3	0	0	0	84	18	1	.214	25	36	1	1	1.9	.984
5 yrs.			69	45	.605	3.21	157	148	21	1003	890	271	577	10	1	0	0	296	46	1	.155	107	127	11	7	1.6	.955

LEAGUE CHAMPIONSHIP SERIES

Year	Team	Lg	W	L	%	ERA	G	GS	CG	IP	H	BB	SO	ShO	W	L	SV	AB	H	HR	BA	PO	A	E	DP	TC/G	FA
1990	PIT	N	1	1	.500	1.65	2	2	1	16.1	12	3	13	0	0	0	0	6	1	0	.167	1	6	1	0	4.0	.875

Tim Drummond

DRUMMOND, TIMOTHY DARNELL
B. Dec. 24, 1964, La Plata, Md.
BR TR 6' 3" 170 lbs.

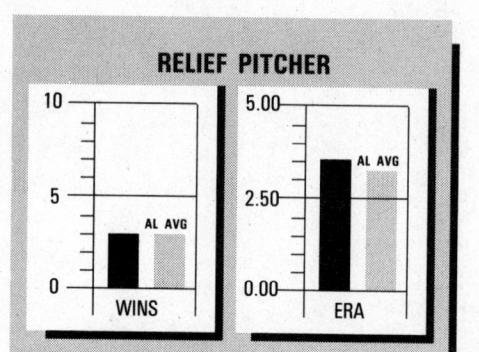

RELIEF PITCHER — WINS, ERA (with AL AVG)

Split		W	L	%	ERA	G	GS	CG	IP	H	BB	SO	ShO	W	L	SV
April		0	0	—	4.22	4	0	0	10.2	9	2	3	0	0	0	0
May		0	1	.000	3.50	6	2	0	18	21	9	14	0	0	0	0
June		0	2	.000	7.71	7	2	0	21	34	5	10	0	0	0	0
July		1	0	1.000	2.87	6	0	0	15.2	18	5	8	0	1	0	1
Aug		1	1	.500	3.21	7	0	0	14	12	9	6	0	1	1	0
Sept/Oct		1	1	.500	3.09	5	0	0	11.2	10	6	8	0	1	1	1
Day		1	0	1.000	2.11	9	0	0	21.1	21	7	10	0	1	0	1
Night		2	5	.286	5.04	26	4	0	69.2	83	29	39	0	2	2	0
vs. Left		—	—	—	—	—	—	—	45	14	15	—	—	—	—	—
vs. Right		—	—	—	—	—	—	—	59	22	34	—	—	—	—	—

Year	Team	W	L	%	ERA	G	GS	CG	IP	H	BB	SO	ShO	W	L	SV	AB	H	HR	BA	PO	A	E	DP	TC/G	FA

Tim Drummond *Continued*

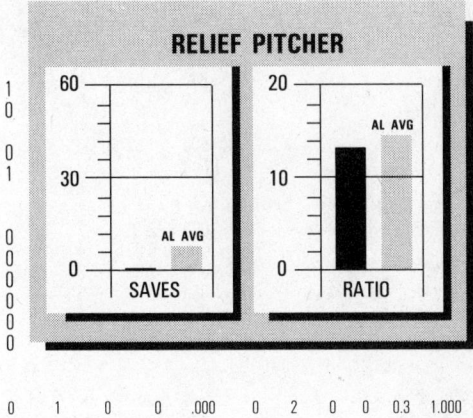

RELIEF PITCHER

SAVES / RATIO (AL AVG)

Year	Team	W	L	%	ERA	G	GS	CG	IP	H	BB	SO	ShO	W	L	SV	AB	H	HR	BA	PO	A	E	DP	TC/G	FA
On Grass		1	3	.250	4.19	13	2	0	34.1	34	16	22	0	1	2	1										
On Turf		2	2	.500	4.45	22	2	0	56.2	70	20	27	0	2	0	0										
Home		2	1	.667	4.46	17	1	0	40.1	52	16	24	0	2	0	0										
Road		1	4	.200	4.26	18	3	0	50.2	52	20	25	0	1	2	1										
Division Rivals																										
vs. CAL		0	1	.000	10.13	3	0	0	8	15	3	4	0	0	1	0										
vs. CHI		1	0	1.000	0.00	2	0	0	4.2	2	2	2	0	1	0	0										
vs. KC		0	1	.000	5.06	5	1	0	16	20	4	5	0	0	0	0										
vs. OAK		0	0	—	3.60	3	0	0	5	4	2	2	0	0	0	0										
vs. SEA		0	0	—	0.00	2	0	0	5.1	2	2	2	0	0	0	0										
vs. TEX		0	1	.000	10.50	3	1	0	6	11	2	5	0	0	0	0										
1987	PIT N	0	0	—	4.50	6	0	0	6	5	3	5	0	0	0	0	1	0	0	.000	0	2	0	0	0.3	1.000
1989	MIN A	0	0	—	3.86	8	0	0	16.1	16	8	9	0	0	0	1	0	0	0	—	0	1	0	0	0.1	1.000
1990		3	5	.375	4.35	35	4	0	91	104	36	49	0	3	2	1	0	0	0	—	6	7	1	1	0.4	.929
3 yrs.		3	5	.375	4.29	49	4	0	113.1	125	47	63	0	3	2	2	1	0	0	.000	6	10	1	1	0.3	.941

Brian DuBois

DuBOIS, BRIAN ANDREW
B. Apr. 18, 1967, Joliet, Ill.
BL TL 5′ 10″ 165 lbs.

Year	Team	W	L	%	ERA	G	GS	CG	IP	H	BB	SO	ShO	W	L	SV	AB	H	HR	BA	PO	A	E	DP	TC/G	FA
1989	DET A	0	4	.000	1.75	6	5	0	36	29	17	13	0	0	0	1	0	0	0	—	2	5	0	0	1.2	1.000
1990		3	5	.375	5.09	12	11	0	58.1	70	22	34	0	0	0	1	0	0	0	—	1	3	1	1	0.4	.800
2 yrs.		3	9	.250	3.82	18	16	0	94.1	99	39	47	0	0	0	1	0	0	0	—	3	8	1	1	0.7	.917

Mike Dunne

DUNNE, MICHAEL DENNIS
B. Oct. 27, 1962, South Bend, Ind.
BR TR 6′ 4″ 190 lbs.

Year	Team	W	L	%	ERA	G	GS	CG	IP	H	BB	SO	ShO	W	L	SV	AB	H	HR	BA	PO	A	E	DP	TC/G	FA
1987	PIT N	13	6	.684	3.03	23	23	5	163.1	143	68	72	1	0	0	0	53	5	0	.094	18	32	1	3	2.2	.980
1988		7	11	.389	3.92	30	28	1	170	163	88	70	0	0	0	0	46	5	0	.109	18	27	1	0	1.5	.978
1989	2 teams	PIT N (3G 1 - 1)			SEA A (15G 2 - 9)																					
"	total	3	10	.231	5.60	18	18	1	99.2	125	46	42	0	0	0	0	4	1	0	.250	7	17	1	2	1.4	.960
1990	SD N	0	3	.000	5.65	10	6	0	28.2	28	17	15	0	0	0	0	6	0	0	.000	4	5	0	0	0.9	1.000
4 yrs.		23	30	.434	4.07	81	75	7	461.2	459	219	199	1	0	0	0	109	11	0	.101	47	81	3	6	1.6	.977

Gary Eave

EAVE, GARY LOUIS
B. July 22, 1963, Monroe, La.
BR TR 6′ 4″ 200 lbs.

Year	Team	W	L	%	ERA	G	GS	CG	IP	H	BB	SO	ShO	W	L	SV	AB	H	HR	BA	PO	A	E	DP	TC/G	FA
1988	ATL N	0	0	—	9.00	5	0	0	5	7	3	0	0	0	0	0	0	0	0	—	0	0	0	0	0.0	—
1989		2	0	1.000	1.31	3	3	0	20.2	15	12	9	0	0	0	0	6	0	0	.000	1	0	0	0	0.3	1.000
1990	SEA A	0	3	.000	4.20	8	5	0	30	27	20	16	0	0	1	0	0	0	0	—	1	5	0	1	0.8	1.000
3 yrs.		2	3	.400	3.56	16	8	0	55.2	49	35	25	0	0	1	0	6	0	0	.000	2	5	0	1	0.4	1.000

Dennis Eckersley

ECKERSLEY, DENNIS LEE
B. Oct. 3, 1954, Oakland, Calif.
BR TR 6′ 2″ 190 lbs.

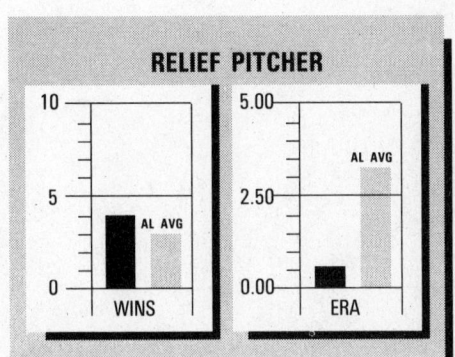

RELIEF PITCHER

WINS / ERA (AL AVG)

Year	Team	W	L	%	ERA	G	GS	CG	IP	H	BB	SO	ShO	W	L	SV	AB	H	HR	BA	PO	A	E	DP	TC/G	FA
April		1	0	1.000	0.00	8	0	0	10	5	0	9	0	1	0	7										
May		1	0	1.000	0.77	10	0	0	11.2	7	0	15	0	1	0	8										
June		0	1	.000	0.77	11	0	0	11.2	10	2	8	0	0	1	9										
July		0	1	.000	1.64	10	0	0	11	2	1	12	0	0	1	8										
Aug		1	0	1.000	0.64	11	0	0	14	8	0	13	0	1	0	8										
Sept/Oct		1	0	1.000	0.00	13	0	0	15	9	1	16	0	1	0	8										
Day		3	2	.600	0.88	26	0	0	30.2	16	4	34	0	3	2	17										
Night		1	0	1.000	0.42	37	0	0	42.2	25	0	39	0	1	0	31										
vs. Left		—	—	—	—	—	—	—	—	20	2	22	—													
vs. Right		—	—	—	—	—	—	—	—	21	2	51	—													

Year	Team	W	L	%	ERA	G	GS	CG	IP	H	BB	SO	ShO	W	L	SV	AB	H	HR	BA	PO	A	E	DP	TC/G	FA

Dennis Eckersley *Continued*

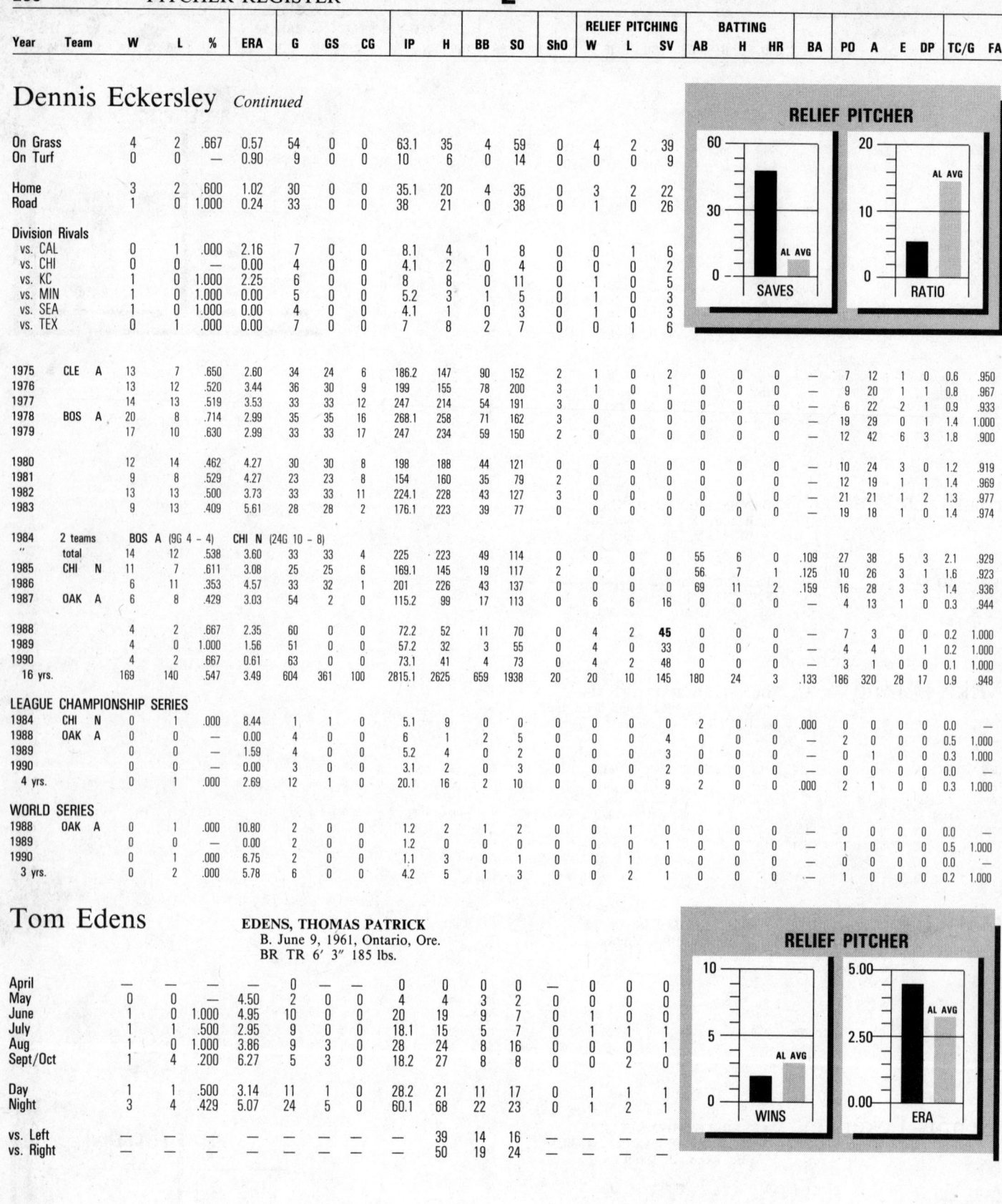

RELIEF PITCHER — SAVES (AL AVG) — RATIO (AL AVG)

Year	Team	W	L	%	ERA	G	GS	CG	IP	H	BB	SO	ShO	W	L	SV	AB	H	HR	BA	PO	A	E	DP	TC/G	FA
On Grass		4	2	.667	0.57	54	0	0	63.1	35	4	59	0	4	2	39					7	12	1	0	0.6	.950
On Turf		0	0	—	0.90	9	0	0	10	6	0	14	0	0	0	9										
Home		3	2	.600	1.02	30	0	0	35.1	20	4	35	0	3	2	22										
Road		1	0	1.000	0.24	33	0	0	38	21	0	38	0	1	0	26										
Division Rivals																										
vs. CAL		0	1	.000	2.16	7	0	0	8.1	4	1	8	0	0	1	6										
vs. CHI		0	0	—	0.00	4	0	0	4.1	2	0	4	0	0	0	2										
vs. KC		1	0	1.000	2.25	6	0	0	8	8	0	11	0	1	0	5										
vs. MIN		1	0	1.000	0.00	5	0	0	5.2	3	1	5	0	1	0	3										
vs. SEA		1	0	1.000	0.00	4	0	0	4.1	1	0	3	0	1	0	3										
vs. TEX		0	1	.000	0.00	7	0	0	7	8	2	7	0	0	1	6										
1975	CLE A	13	7	.650	2.60	34	24	6	186.2	147	90	152	2	1	0	2	0	0	0	—	7	12	1	0	0.6	.950
1976		13	12	.520	3.44	36	30	9	199	155	78	200	3	1	0	1	0	0	0	—	9	20	1	1	0.8	.967
1977		14	13	.519	3.53	33	33	12	247	214	54	191	3	0	0	0	0	0	0	—	6	22	2	1	0.9	.933
1978	BOS A	20	8	.714	2.99	35	35	16	268.1	258	71	162	3	0	0	0	0	0	0	—	19	29	0	1	1.4	1.000
1979		17	10	.630	2.99	33	33	17	247	234	59	150	2	0	0	0	0	0	0	—	12	42	6	3	1.8	.900
1980		12	14	.462	4.27	30	30	8	198	188	44	121	0	0	0	0	0	0	0	—	10	24	3	0	1.2	.919
1981		9	8	.529	4.27	23	23	8	154	160	35	79	2	0	0	0	0	0	0	—	12	19	1	1	1.4	.969
1982		13	13	.500	3.73	33	33	11	224.1	228	43	127	3	0	0	0	0	0	0	—	21	21	1	2	1.3	.977
1983		9	13	.409	5.61	28	28	2	176.1	223	39	77	0	0	0	0	0	0	0	—	19	18	1	0	1.4	.974
1984	2 teams		BOS A (9G 4 – 4)			CHI N (24G 10 – 8)																				
"	total	14	12	.538	3.60	33	33	4	225	223	49	114	0	0	0	0	55	6	0	.109	27	38	5	3	2.1	.929
1985	CHI N	11	7	.611	3.08	25	25	6	169.1	145	19	117	2	0	0	0	56	7	1	.125	10	26	3	1	1.6	.923
1986		6	11	.353	4.57	33	32	1	201	226	43	137	0	0	0	0	69	11	2	.159	16	28	3	3	1.4	.936
1987	OAK A	6	8	.429	3.03	54	2	0	115.2	99	17	113	0	6	6	16	0	0	0	—	4	13	1	0	0.3	.944
1988		4	2	.667	2.35	60	0	0	72.2	52	11	70	0	4	2	**45**	0	0	0	—	7	3	0	0	0.2	1.000
1989		4	0	1.000	1.56	51	0	0	57.2	32	3	55	0	4	0	33	0	0	0	—	4	4	0	1	0.2	1.000
1990		4	2	.667	0.61	63	0	0	73.1	41	4	73	0	4	2	48	0	0	0	—	3	1	0	0	0.1	1.000
16 yrs.		169	140	.547	3.49	604	361	100	2815.1	2625	659	1938	20	20	10	145	180	24	3	.133	186	320	28	17	0.9	.948

LEAGUE CHAMPIONSHIP SERIES

Year	Team	W	L	%	ERA	G	GS	CG	IP	H	BB	SO	ShO	W	L	SV	AB	H	HR	BA	PO	A	E	DP	TC/G	FA
1984	CHI N	0	1	.000	8.44	1	1	0	5.1	9	0	0	0	0	0	0	2	0	0	.000	0	0	0	0	0.0	—
1988	OAK A	0	0	—	0.00	4	0	0	6	1	2	5	0	0	0	4	0	0	0	—	2	0	0	0	0.5	1.000
1989		0	0	—	1.59	4	0	0	5.2	4	0	2	0	0	0	3	0	0	0	—	0	1	0	0	0.3	1.000
1990		0	0	—	0.00	3	0	0	3.1	2	0	3	0	0	0	2	0	0	0	—	0	0	0	0	0.0	—
4 yrs.		0	1	.000	2.69	12	1	0	20.1	16	2	10	0	0	0	9	2	0	0	.000	2	1	0	0	0.3	1.000

WORLD SERIES

Year	Team	W	L	%	ERA	G	GS	CG	IP	H	BB	SO	ShO	W	L	SV	AB	H	HR	BA	PO	A	E	DP	TC/G	FA
1988	OAK A	0	1	.000	10.80	2	0	0	1.2	2	1	2	0	0	1	0	0	0	0	—	0	0	0	0	0.0	—
1989		0	0	—	0.00	2	0	0	1.2	0	0	1	0	0	0	1	0	0	0	—	1	0	0	0	0.5	1.000
1990		0	1	.000	6.75	2	0	0	1.1	3	0	1	0	0	1	0	0	0	0	—	0	0	0	0	0.0	—
3 yrs.		0	2	.000	5.78	6	0	0	4.2	5	1	3	0	0	2	1	0	0	0	—	1	0	0	0	0.2	1.000

Tom Edens

EDENS, THOMAS PATRICK
B. June 9, 1961, Ontario, Ore.
BR TR 6′ 3″ 185 lbs.

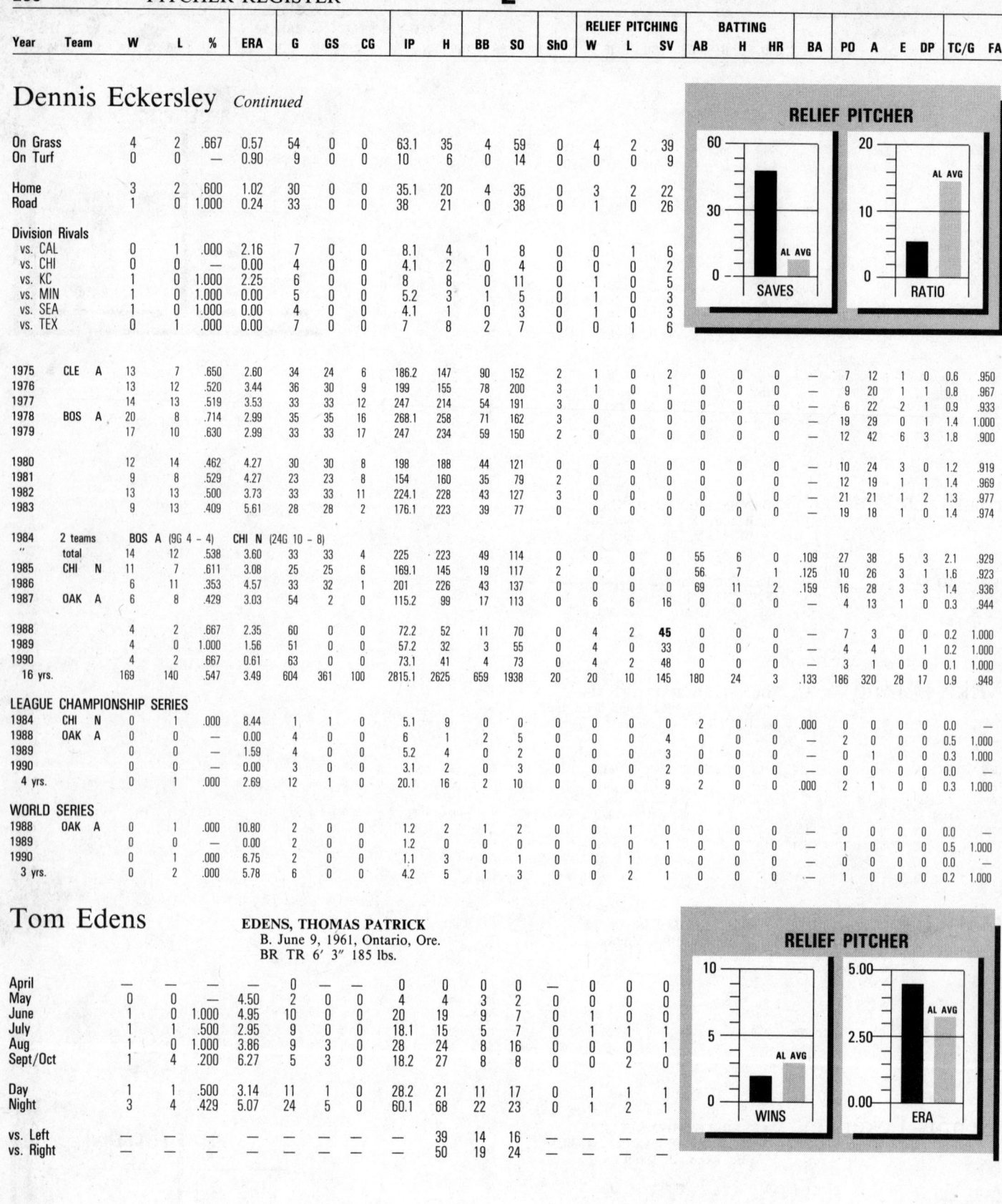

RELIEF PITCHER — WINS (AL AVG) — ERA (AL AVG)

Month	Team	W	L	%	ERA	G	GS	CG	IP	H	BB	SO	ShO	W	L	SV	AB	H	HR	BA	PO	A	E	DP	TC/G	FA
April		—		—		0	—	—	0	0	0	0	—	0	0	0										
May		0	0	—	4.50	2	0	0	4	4	3	2	0	0	0	0										
June		1	0	1.000	4.95	10	0	0	20	19	9	7	0	1	0	0										
July		1	1	.500	2.95	9	0	0	18.1	15	5	7	0	1	1	1										
Aug		1	0	1.000	3.86	9	3	0	28	24	8	16	0	0	0	1										
Sept/Oct		1	4	.200	6.27	5	3	0	18.2	27	8	8	0	0	2	0										
Day		1	1	.500	3.14	11	1	0	28.2	21	11	17	0	1	1	1										
Night		3	4	.429	5.07	24	5	0	60.1	68	22	23	0	1	2	1										
vs. Left		—	—	—	—	—	—	—	—	39	14	16	—	—	—	—										
vs. Right		—	—	—	—	—	—	—	—	50	19	24	—	—	—	—										

Year	Team	W	L	%	ERA	G	GS	CG	IP	H	BB	SO	ShO	RELIEF PITCHING W	L	SV	BATTING AB	H	HR	BA	PO	A	E	DP	TC/G	FA

Tom Edens *Continued*

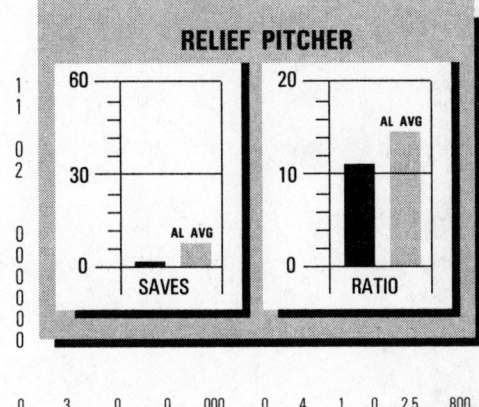

		W	L	%	ERA	G	GS	CG	IP	H	BB	SO	ShO	W	L	SV	AB	H	HR	BA	PO	A	E	DP	TC/G	FA
On Grass		4	5	.444	4.89	27	6	0	77.1	82	28	34	0	2	3	1										
On Turf		0	0	—	1.54	8	0	0	11.2	7	5	6	0	0	0	1										
Home		3	3	.500	5.90	16	2	0	39.2	49	12	12	0	2	2	0										
Road		1	2	.333	3.28	19	4	0	49.1	40	21	28	0	0	1	2										
Division Rivals																										
vs. BAL		0	0	—	12.00	2	0	0	3	4	2	1	0	0	0	0										
vs. BOS		1	0	1.000	1.50	1	1	0	6	5	3	4	0	0	0	0										
vs. CLE		2	0	1.000	3.31	5	1	0	16.1	15	4	4	0	1	0	0										
vs. DET		0	0	—	4.50	1	1	0	4	5	2	2	0	0	0	0										
vs. NY		0	1	.000	5.40	2	1	0	10	8	4	8	0	0	1	0										
vs. TOR		0	0	—	7.71	3	0	0	4.2	6	3	3	0	0	0	0										
1987	NY N	0	0	—	6.75	2	2	0	8	15	4	4	0	0	0	0	3	0	0	.000	0	4	1	0	2.5	.800
1990	MIL A	4	5	.444	4.45	35	6	0	89	89	33	40	0	2	3	2	0	0	0	—	7	10	3	0	0.6	.850
2 yrs.		4	5	.444	4.64	37	8	0	97	104	37	44	0	2	3	2	3	0	0	.000	7	14	4	0	0.7	.840

Wayne Edwards

EDWARDS, WAYNE MAURICE
B. Mar. 7, 1964, Burbank, Calif.
BL TL 6' 5" 185 lbs.

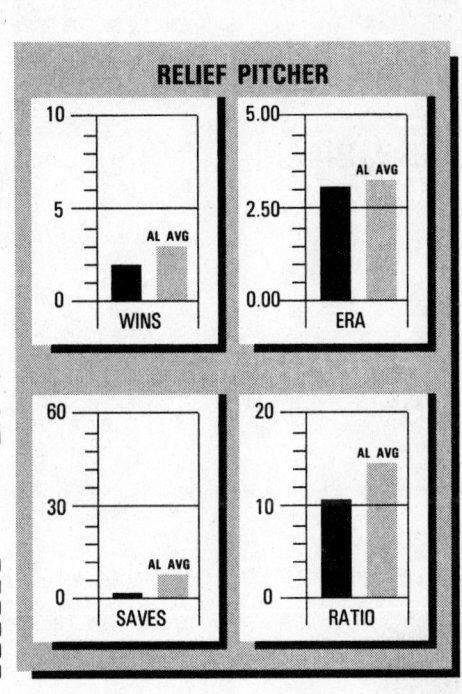

		W	L	%	ERA	G	GS	CG	IP	H	BB	SO	ShO	W	L	SV	AB	H	HR	BA	PO	A	E	DP	TC/G	FA
April		0	0	—	0.90	7	0	0	10	2	5	9	0	0	0	1										
May		0	2	.000	1.84	10	0	0	14.2	10	8	10	0	0	2	0										
June		0	0	—	4.15	8	0	0	13	12	6	9	0	0	0	0										
July		0	0	—	7.71	6	0	0	11.2	18	4	11	0	0	0	0										
Aug		3	1	.750	2.54	5	4	0	28.1	24	14	17	0	0	0	0										
Sept/Oct		2	0	1.000	3.12	6	1	0	17.1	15	4	7	0	2	0	1										
Day		0	1	.000	3.86	11	0	0	14	11	8	10	0	0	1	1										
Night		5	2	.714	3.11	31	5	0	81	70	33	53	0	2	1	1										
vs. Left		—	—	—	—	—	—	—	—	17	14	16	—	—	—	—										
vs. Right		—	—	—	—	—	—	—	—	64	27	47	—	—	—	—										
On Grass		5	1	.833	3.03	35	4	0	74.1	64	32	53	0	2	1	2										
On Turf		0	2	.000	3.92	7	1	0	20.2	17	9	10	0	0	1	0										
Home		4	1	.800	2.37	21	2	0	49.1	37	17	38	0	2	1	1										
Road		1	2	.333	4.14	21	3	0	45.2	44	24	25	0	0	1	1										
Division Rivals																										
vs. CAL		1	0	1.000	5.00	3	1	0	9	8	7	10	0	0	0	0										
vs. KC		1	0	1.000	0.00	4	0	0	11.2	4	4	7	0	1	0	0										
vs. MIN		0	1	.000	4.15	2	1	0	8.2	10	2	2	0	0	0	0										
vs. OAK		0	0	—	3.86	3	0	0	4.2	6	1	2	0	0	0	0										
vs. SEA		0	0	—	5.06	4	0	0	5.1	2	2	4	0	0	0	0										
vs. TEX		2	0	1.000	1.42	4	2	0	12.2	8	9	8	0	0	0	0										
1989	CHI A	0	0	—	3.68	7	0	0	7.1	7	3	9	0	0	0	0	0	0	0	—	0	1	0	1	0.1	1.000
1990		5	3	.625	3.22	42	5	0	95	81	41	63	0	2	2	2	0	0	0	—	6	14	1	1	0.5	.952
2 yrs.		5	3	.625	3.25	49	5	0	102.1	88	44	72	0	2	2	2	0	0	0	.000	6	15	1	2	0.4	.955

Mark Eichhorn

EICHHORN, MARK ANTHONY
B. Nov. 21, 1960, San Jose, Calif.
BR TR 6' 4" 200 lbs.

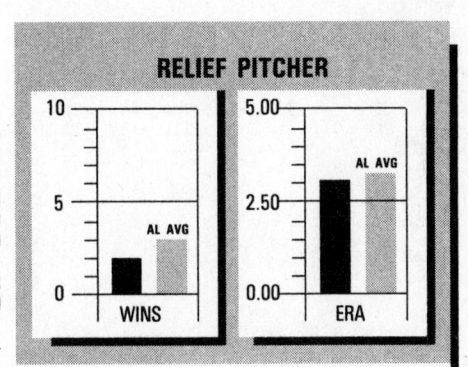

		W	L	%	ERA	G	GS	CG	IP	H	BB	SO	ShO	W	L	SV	AB	H	HR	BA	PO	A	E	DP	TC/G	FA
April		0	1	.000	1.04	9	0	0	17.1	11	3	16	0	0	1	4										
May		0	2	.000	1.83	13	0	0	19.2	17	5	15	0	0	2	5										
June		0	1	.000	2.00	14	0	0	18	24	2	17	0	0	1	4										
July		1	0	1.000	14.54	9	0	0	8.2	23	5	7	0	0	1	0										
Aug		1	0	1.000	1.46	8	0	0	12.1	12	6	10	0	0	1	0										
Sept/Oct		0	1	.000	3.12	7	0	0	8.2	11	2	4	0	0	1	0										
Day		0	0	—	4.13	18	0	0	24	31	10	27	0	0	0	3										
Night		2	5	.286	2.67	42	0	0	60.2	67	13	42	0	2	5	10										
vs. Left		—	—	—	—	—	—	—	—	45	10	29	—	—	—	—										
vs. Right		—	—	—	—	—	—	—	—	53	13	40	—	—	—	—										

Year	Team		W	L	%	ERA	G	GS	CG	IP	H	BB	SO	ShO	W	L	SV	AB	H	HR	BA	PO	A	E	DP	TC/G	FA

Mark Eichhorn *Continued*

On Grass			2	5	.286	3.44	50	0	0	70.2	85	16	58	0	2	5	8										
On Turf			0	0	—	1.29	10	0	0	14	13	7	11	0	0	0	5										
Home			2	4	.333	2.82	26	0	0	38.1	44	8	32	0	2	4	3										
Road			0	1	.000	3.30	34	0	0	46.1	54	15	37	0	0	1	10										
Division Rivals																											
vs. CHI			0	1	.000	3.86	4	0	0	4.2	6	1	3	0	0	1	1										
vs. KC			0	0	—	0.00	6	0	0	6.2	6	2	5	0	0	0	2										
vs. MIN			0	0	—	1.08	5	0	0	8.1	6	3	7	0	0	0	2										
vs. OAK			1	1	.500	8.68	6	0	0	9.1	17	4	7	0	1	1	0										
vs. SEA			0	0	—	2.45	2	0	0	3.2	4	1	2	0	0	0	1										
vs. TEX			0	0	—	1.50	4	0	0	6	5	0	6	0	0	0	1										
1982	TOR	A	0	3	.000	5.45	7	7	0	38	40	14	16	0	0	0	0	0	0	0	—	1	3	0	0	0.6	1.000
1986			14	6	.700	1.72	69	0	0	157	105	45	166	0	14	6	10	0	0	0	—	16	21	0	1	0.5	1.000
1987			10	6	.625	3.17	89	0	0	127.2	110	52	96	0	10	6	4	0	0	0	—	2	30	1	2	0.4	.970
1988			0	3	.000	4.19	37	0	0	66.2	79	27	28	0	0	3	1	0	0	0	—	5	13	0	1	0.5	1.000
1989	ATL	N	5	5	.500	4.35	45	0	0	68.1	70	19	49	0	5	5	0	2	0	0	.000	9	17	0	1	0.6	1.000
1990	CAL	A	2	5	.286	3.08	60	0	0	84.2	98	23	69	0	2	5	13	0	0	0	—	7	16	0	0	0.4	1.000
6 yrs.			31	28	.525	3.17	307	7	0	542.1	502	180	424	0	31	25	28	2	0	0	.000	40	100	1	5	0.5	.993

RELIEF PITCHER

SAVES — AL AVG

RATIO — AL AVG

Dave Eiland

EILAND, DAVID WILLIAM
B. July 5, 1966, Dade City, Fla.
BR TR 6′ 3″ 210 lbs.

Year	Team		W	L	%	ERA	G	GS	CG	IP	H	BB	SO	ShO	W	L	SV	AB	H	HR	BA	PO	A	E	DP	TC/G	FA
1988	NY	A	0	0	—	6.39	3	3	0	12.2	15	4	7	0	0	0	0	0	0	0	—	1	3	0	0	1.3	1.000
1989			1	3	.250	5.77	6	6	0	34.1	44	13	11	0	0	0	0	0	0	0	—	2	2	0	0	0.7	1.000
1990			2	1	.667	3.56	5	5	0	30.1	31	5	16	0	0	0	0	0	0	0	—	1	3	0	0	0.8	1.000
3 yrs.			3	4	.429	5.00	14	14	0	77.1	90	22	34	0	0	0	0	0	0	0	—	4	8	0	0	0.9	1.000

Narciso Elvira

ELVIRA, NARCISO DELGADO
B. Oct. 29, 1967, Vera Cruz, Mexico
BL TL 5′ 10″ 160 lbs.

Year	Team		W	L	%	ERA	G	GS	CG	IP	H	BB	SO	ShO	W	L	SV	AB	H	HR	BA	PO	A	E	DP	TC/G	FA
1990	MIL	A	0	0	—	5.40	4	0	0	5	6	5	6	0	0	0	0	0	0	0	—	0	1	0	0	0.3	1.000

Luis Encarnacion

ENCARNACION, LUIS MARTIN
B. Oct. 20, 1963, Santo Domingo, Dominican Republic
BR TR 5′ 10″ 180 lbs.

Year	Team		W	L	%	ERA	G	GS	CG	IP	H	BB	SO	ShO	W	L	SV	AB	H	HR	BA	PO	A	E	DP	TC/G	FA
1990	KC	A	0	0	—	7.84	4	0	0	10.1	14	4	8	0	0	0	0	0	0	0	—	1	0	0	0	0.3	1.000

Scott Erickson

ERICKSON, SCOTT GAVIN
B. Feb. 2, 1968, Long Beach, Calif.
BR TR 6′ 4″ 220 lbs.

			W	L	%	ERA	G	GS	CG	IP	H	BB	SO	ShO	W	L	SV
April			—	—	—	—	0	—	—	0	0	0	0	—	0	0	0
May			—	—	—	—	0	—	—	0	0	0	0	—	0	0	0
June			1	1	.500	2.92	2	2	0	12.1	9	8	9	0	0	0	0
July			1	1	.500	3.81	6	4	0	28.1	36	13	13	0	0	0	0
Aug			1	2	.333	4.56	5	5	0	25.2	36	9	10	0	0	0	0
Sept/Oct			5	0	1.000	1.35	6	6	1	46.2	27	21	21	0	0	0	0
Day			4	0	1.000	1.68	7	7	1	48.1	38	21	18	0	0	0	0
Night			4	4	.500	3.76	12	10	0	64.2	70	30	35	0	0	0	0
vs. Left			—	—	—	—	—	—	—	—	55	27	16	—	—	—	—
vs. Right			—	—	—	—	—	—	—	—	53	24	37	—	—	—	—

STARTING PITCHER

WINS — AL AVG

ERA — AL AVG

Year	Team	W	L	%	ERA	G	GS	CG	IP	H	BB	SO	ShO	RELIEF PITCHING W	L	SV	BATTING AB	H	HR	BA	PO	A	E	DP	TC/G	FA

Scott Erickson *Continued*

		W	L	%	ERA	G	GS	CG	IP	H	BB	SO	ShO	W	L	SV	AB	H	HR	BA	PO	A	E	DP	TC/G	FA
On Grass		1	1	.500	0.35	4	3	0	26	13	21	8	0	0	0	0										
On Turf		7	3	.700	3.62	15	14	1	87	95	30	45	0	0	0	0										
Home		7	2	.778	3.45	13	12	1	78.1	83	24	44	0	0	0	0										
Road		1	2	.333	1.56	6	5	0	34.2	25	27	9	0	0	0	0										
Division Rivals																										
vs. CAL		—	—	—	—	0	—	—	0	0	0	0	—	0	0	0										
vs. CHI		0	0	—	13.50	1	1	0	3.1	7	0	1	0	0	0	0										
vs. KC		1	1	.500	6.75	2	2	0	9.1	12	2	5	0	0	0	0										
vs. OAK		1	0	1.000	4.11	3	2	0	15.1	17	8	8	0	0	0	0										
vs. SEA		0	0	—	2.84	1	1	0	6.1	5	4	1	0	0	0	0										
vs. TEX		2	0	1.000	0.66	2	2	0	13.2	8	5	7	0	0	0	0										
1990	MIN A	8	4	.667	2.87	19	17	1	113	108	51	53	0	0	0	0	0	0	0	—	10	13	0	0	1.2	1.000

STARTING PITCHER

Howard Farmer

FARMER, HOWARD EARL
B. Jan. 18, 1966, Gary, Ind.
BR TR 6′ 3″ 185 lbs.

Year	Team	W	L	%	ERA	G	GS	CG	IP	H	BB	SO	ShO	W	L	SV	AB	H	HR	BA	PO	A	E	DP	TC/G	FA
1990	MON N	0	3	.000	7.04	6	4	0	23	26	10	14	0	0	1	0	5	2	0	.400	1	7	0	1	1.3	1.000

Steve Farr

FARR, STEVEN MICHAEL
B. Dec. 12, 1956, Cheverly, Md.
BR TR 5′ 10″ 190 lbs.

		W	L	%	ERA	G	GS	CG	IP	H	BB	SO	ShO	W	L	SV	AB	H	HR	BA	PO	A	E	DP	TC/G	FA
April		1	0	1.000	3.27	7	0	0	11	9	2	8	0	1	0	0										
May		3	2	.600	1.86	12	0	0	19.1	15	11	19	0	3	2	0										
June		1	1	.500	2.08	8	2	0	17.1	12	6	13	0	0	0	0										
July		3	2	.600	2.35	10	1	0	23	18	12	19	0	2	2	0										
Aug		2	0	1.000	1.35	11	0	0	26.2	21	3	17	0	2	0	1										
Sept/Oct		3	2	.600	1.82	9	3	1	29.2	24	14	18	1	0	2	0										
Day		2	4	.333	2.64	15	2	1	44.1	37	17	32	1	1	3	0										
Night		11	3	.786	1.63	42	4	0	82.2	62	31	62	0	7	3	1										
vs. Left		—	—	—	—	—	—	—		46	27	34	—	—	—	—										
vs. Right		—	—	—	—	—	—	—		53	21	60	—	—	—	—										
On Grass		2	5	.286	3.43	20	2	0	44.2	44	22	40	0	1	4	0										
On Turf		11	2	.846	1.20	37	4	1	82.1	55	26	54	1	7	2	1										
Home		9	2	.818	1.37	31	3	1	65.2	45	23	45	1	6	2	1										
Road		4	5	.444	2.64	26	3	0	61.1	54	25	49	0	2	4	0										
Division Rivals																										
vs. CAL		2	0	1.000	0.57	3	2	1	15.2	11	5	9	1	0	0	0										
vs. CHI		1	2	.333	4.22	6	0	0	10.2	9	7	9	0	1	2	1										
vs. MIN		1	0	1.000	0.00	3	1	0	9	5	0	6	0	0	0	0										
vs. OAK		0	1	.000	3.60	4	1	0	10	12	4	8	0	0	0	0										
vs. SEA		2	0	1.000	0.71	6	1	0	12.2	10	6	5	0	1	0	0										
vs. TEX		1	1	.500	2.00	5	0	0	9	8	4	11	0	1	1	0										
1984	CLE A	3	11	.214	4.58	31	16	0	116	106	46	83	0	1	2	1	0	0	0	—	7	18	2	1	0.9	.926
1985	KC A	2	1	.667	3.11	16	3	0	37.2	34	20	36	0	1	0	1	0	0	0	—	3	6	0	0	0.6	1.000
1986		8	4	.667	3.13	56	0	0	109.1	90	39	83	0	8	4	8	0	0	0	—	8	16	0	1	0.4	1.000
1987		4	3	.571	4.15	47	0	0	91	97	44	88	0	4	3	1	0	0	0	—	3	6	2	0	0.2	.818
1988		5	4	.556	2.50	62	1	0	82.2	74	30	72	0	4	4	20	0	0	0	—	3	7	0	0	0.2	1.000
1989		2	5	.286	4.12	51	2	0	63.1	75	22	56	0	1	5	18	0	0	0	—	7	4	0	0	0.2	1.000
1990		13	7	.650	1.98	57	6	1	127	99	48	94	1	8	6	1	0	0	0	—	7	18	2	1	0.5	.926
7 yrs.		37	35	.514	3.33	320	28	1	627	575	249	512	1	27	24	50	0	0	0	—	38	75	6	3	0.4	.950

RELIEF PITCHER

LEAGUE CHAMPIONSHIP SERIES

Year	Team	W	L	%	ERA	G	GS	CG	IP	H	BB	SO	ShO	W	L	SV	AB	H	HR	BA	PO	A	E	DP	TC/G	FA
1985	KC A	1	0	1.000	1.42	2	0	0	6.1	4	1	3	0	1	0	0	0	0	0	—	0	1	0	1	0.5	1.000

Year	Team	W	L	%	ERA	G	GS	CG	IP	H	BB	SO	ShO	RELIEF PITCHING W	L	SV	BATTING AB	H	HR	BA	PO	A	E	DP	TC/G	FA

John Farrell

FARRELL, JOHN EDWARD
B. Aug. 4, 1962, Monmouth Beach, N. J.
BR TR 6′ 4″ 210 lbs.

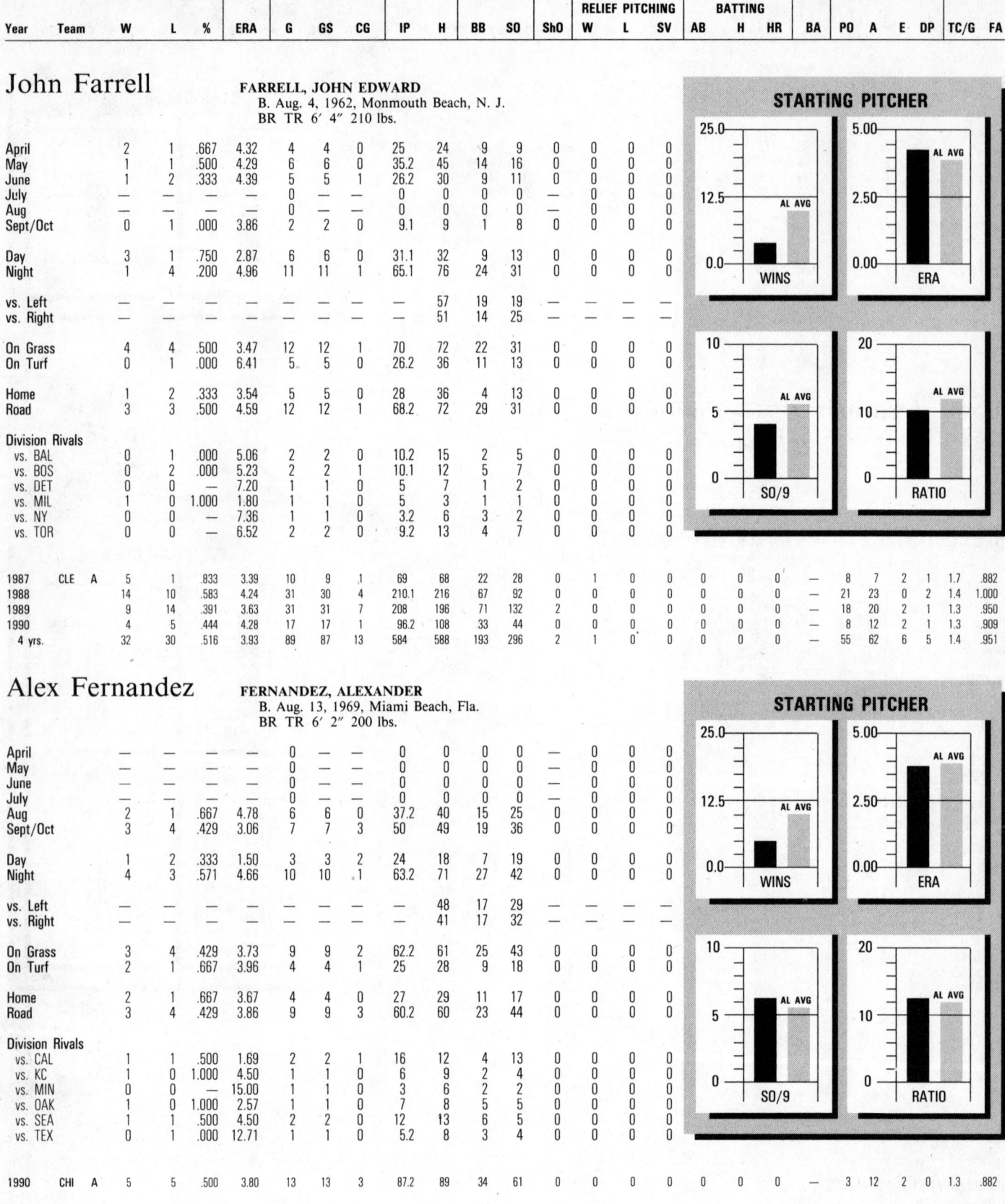

STARTING PITCHER
(WINS — AL AVG; ERA — AL AVG; SO/9 — AL AVG; RATIO — AL AVG)

		W	L	%	ERA	G	GS	CG	IP	H	BB	SO	ShO	W	L	SV	AB	H	HR	BA	PO	A	E	DP	TC/G	FA
April		2	1	.667	4.32	4	4	0	25	24	9	9	0	0	0	0										
May		1	1	.500	4.29	6	6	0	35.2	45	14	16	0	0	0	0										
June		1	2	.333	4.39	5	5	1	26.2	30	9	11	0	0	0	0										
July		—	—	—	—	0	—	—	0	0	0	0	—	0	0	0										
Aug		—	—	—	—	0	—	—	0	0	0	0	—	0	0	0										
Sept/Oct		0	1	.000	3.86	2	2	0	9.1	9	1	8	0	0	0	0										
Day		3	1	.750	2.87	6	6	0	31.1	32	9	13	0	0	0	0										
Night		1	4	.200	4.96	11	11	1	65.1	76	24	31	0	0	0	0										
vs. Left		—	—	—	—	—	—	—	—	57	19	19	—	—	—	—										
vs. Right		—	—	—	—	—	—	—	—	51	14	25	—	—	—	—										
On Grass		4	4	.500	3.47	12	12	1	70	72	22	31	0	0	0	0										
On Turf		0	1	.000	6.41	5	5	0	26.2	36	11	13	0	0	0	0										
Home		1	2	.333	3.54	5	5	0	28	36	4	13	0	0	0	0										
Road		3	3	.500	4.59	12	12	1	68.2	72	29	31	0	0	0	0										
Division Rivals																										
vs. BAL		0	1	.000	5.06	2	2	0	10.2	15	2	5	0	0	0	0										
vs. BOS		0	2	.000	5.23	2	2	1	10.1	12	5	7	0	0	0	0										
vs. DET		0	0	—	7.20	1	1	0	5	7	1	2	0	0	0	0										
vs. MIL		1	0	1.000	1.80	1	1	0	5	3	1	1	0	0	0	0										
vs. NY		0	0	—	7.36	1	1	0	3.2	6	3	2	0	0	0	0										
vs. TOR		0	0	—	6.52	2	2	0	9.2	13	4	7	0	0	0	0										
1987	CLE A	5	1	.833	3.39	10	9	1	69	68	22	28	0	1	0	0	0	0	0	—	8	7	2	1	1.7	.882
1988		14	10	.583	4.24	31	30	4	210.1	216	67	92	0	0	0	0	0	0	0	—	21	23	0	2	1.4	1.000
1989		9	14	.391	3.63	31	31	7	208	196	71	132	2	0	0	0	0	0	0	—	18	20	2	1	1.3	.950
1990		4	5	.444	4.28	17	17	1	96.2	108	33	44	0	0	0	0	0	0	0	—	8	12	2	1	1.3	.909
4 yrs.		32	30	.516	3.93	89	87	13	584	588	193	296	2	1	0	0	0	0	0	—	55	62	6	5	1.4	.951

Alex Fernandez

FERNANDEZ, ALEXANDER
B. Aug. 13, 1969, Miami Beach, Fla.
BR TR 6′ 2″ 200 lbs.

STARTING PITCHER
(WINS — AL AVG; ERA — AL AVG; SO/9 — AL AVG; RATIO — AL AVG)

		W	L	%	ERA	G	GS	CG	IP	H	BB	SO	ShO	W	L	SV	AB	H	HR	BA	PO	A	E	DP	TC/G	FA
April		—	—	—	—	0	—	—	0	0	0	0	—	0	0	0										
May		—	—	—	—	0	—	—	0	0	0	0	—	0	0	0										
June		—	—	—	—	0	—	—	0	0	0	0	—	0	0	0										
July		—	—	—	—	0	—	—	0	0	0	0	—	0	0	0										
Aug		2	1	.667	4.78	6	6	0	37.2	40	15	25	0	0	0	0										
Sept/Oct		3	4	.429	3.06	7	7	3	50	49	19	36	0	0	0	0										
Day		1	2	.333	1.50	3	3	2	24	18	7	19	0	0	0	0										
Night		4	3	.571	4.66	10	10	1	63.2	71	27	42	0	0	0	0										
vs. Left		—	—	—	—	—	—	—	—	48	17	29	—	—	—	—										
vs. Right		—	—	—	—	—	—	—	—	41	17	32	—	—	—	—										
On Grass		3	4	.429	3.73	9	9	2	62.2	61	25	43	0	0	0	0										
On Turf		2	1	.667	3.96	4	4	1	25	28	9	18	0	0	0	0										
Home		2	1	.667	3.67	4	4	0	27	29	11	17	0	0	0	0										
Road		3	4	.429	3.86	9	9	3	60.2	60	23	44	0	0	0	0										
Division Rivals																										
vs. CAL		1	1	.500	1.69	2	2	1	16	12	4	13	0	0	0	0										
vs. KC		1	0	1.000	4.50	1	1	0	6	9	2	4	0	0	0	0										
vs. MIN		0	0	—	15.00	1	1	0	3	6	2	2	0	0	0	0										
vs. OAK		1	0	1.000	2.57	1	1	0	7	8	5	5	0	0	0	0										
vs. SEA		1	1	.500	4.50	2	2	0	12	13	6	5	0	0	0	0										
vs. TEX		0	1	.000	12.71	1	1	0	5.2	8	3	4	0	0	0	0										
1990	CHI A	5	5	.500	3.80	13	13	3	87.2	89	34	61	0	0	0	0	0	0	0	—	3	12	2	0	1.3	.882

Year	Team	W	L	%	ERA	G	GS	CG	IP	H	BB	SO	ShO	W	L	SV	AB	H	HR	BA	PO	A	E	DP	TC/G	FA
														RELIEF PITCHING			BATTING									

Sid Fernandez

FERNANDEZ, CHARLES SIDNEY (El Sid)
B. Oct. 12, 1962, Honolulu, Hawaii
BL TL 6′ 1″ 220 lbs.

Year	Team	W	L	%	ERA	G	GS	CG	IP	H	BB	SO	ShO	W	L	SV	AB	H	HR	BA	PO	A	E	DP	TC/G	FA
April		1	2	.333	4.44	4	4	1	24.1	14	14	15	1	0	0	0										
May		2	2	.500	1.41	5	5	0	32	24	8	25	0	0	0	0										
June		2	1	.667	6.05	4	4	0	19.1	23	8	20	0	0	0	0										
July		2	2	.500	3.45	5	5	0	28.2	23	13	37	0	0	0	0										
Aug		2	3	.400	2.95	6	6	1	39.2	25	8	44	0	0	0	0										
Sept/Oct		0	4	.000	3.82	6	6	0	35.1	21	16	40	0	0	0	0										
Day		2	6	.250	4.41	12	12	1	67.1	62	26	59	1	0	0	0										
Night		7	8	.467	2.89	18	18	1	112	68	41	122	0	0	0	0										
vs. Left		—	—	—	—	—	—	—	—	28	16	44	—	—	—	—										
vs. Right		—	—	—	—	—	—	—	—	102	51	137	—	—	—	—										
On Grass		8	7	.533	2.83	21	21	2	136.2	81	44	136	1	0	0	0										
On Turf		1	7	.125	5.48	9	9	0	42.2	49	23	45	0	0	0	0										
Home		8	5	.615	2.41	15	15	2	104.2	55	34	99	1	0	0	0										
Road		1	9	.100	4.94	15	15	0	74.2	75	33	82	0	0	0	0										
Division Rivals																										
vs. CHI		1	0	1.000	5.09	4	4	1	23	15	10	15	0	0	0	0										
vs. MON		1	2	.333	3.60	4	4	1	20	11	7	16	1	0	0	0										
vs. PHI		1	3	.250	5.55	4	4	0	24.1	25	15	31	0	0	0	0										
vs. PIT		1	1	.500	4.15	2	2	0	13	6	5	12	0	0	0	0										
vs. STL		1	2	.333	2.65	3	3	0	17	19	4	20	0	0	0	0										
1983	LA N	0	1	.000	6.00	2	1	0	6	7	7	9	0	0	0	0	1	1	0	1.000	1	1	0	0	1.0	1.000
1984	NY N	6	6	.500	3.50	15	15	0	90	74	34	62	0	0	0	0	28	5	0	.179	0	6	0	0	0.4	1.000
1985		9	9	.500	2.80	26	26	3	170.1	108	80	180	0	0	0	0	52	11	0	.212	1	23	0	0	0.9	1.000
1986		16	6	.727	3.52	32	31	2	204.1	161	91	200	1	0	0	1	68	11	0	.162	3	18	1	1	0.7	.955
1987		12	8	.600	3.81	28	27	3	156	130	67	134	1	0	0	0	43	7	0	.163	4	12	1	0	0.6	.941
1988		12	10	.545	3.03	31	31	1	187	127	70	189	1	0	0	0	56	14	0	.250	2	13	0	0	0.5	1.000
1989		14	5	**.737**	2.83	35	32	6	219.1	157	75	198	2	0	0	0	71	15	1	.211	4	13	0	2	0.5	1.000
1990		9	14	.391	3.46	30	30	2	179.1	130	67	181	1	0	0	0	58	11	2	.190	1	16	2	0	0.6	.895
8 yrs.		78	59	.569	3.26	199	193	17	1212.1	894	491	1153	6	0	0	1	377	75	1	.199	16	102	4	3	0.6	.967

LEAGUE CHAMPIONSHIP SERIES

Year	Team	W	L	%	ERA	G	GS	CG	IP	H	BB	SO	ShO	W	L	SV	AB	H	HR	BA	PO	A	E	DP	TC/G	FA
1986	NY N	0	1	.000	4.50	1	1	0	6	3	1	5	0	0	0	0	1	0	0	.000	0	0	0	0	0.0	—
1988		0	1	.000	13.50	1	1	0	4	7	1	5	0	0	0	0	1	0	0	.000	0	0	0	0	0.0	—
2 yrs.		0	2	.000	8.10	2	2	0	10	10	2	10	0	0	0	0	2	0	0	.000	0	0	0	0	0.0	—

WORLD SERIES

Year	Team	W	L	%	ERA	G	GS	CG	IP	H	BB	SO	ShO	W	L	SV	AB	H	HR	BA	PO	A	E	DP	TC/G	FA
1986	NY N	0	0	—	1.35	3	0	0	6.2	6	1	10	0	0	0	0	0	0	0	—	0	0	0	0	0.0	—

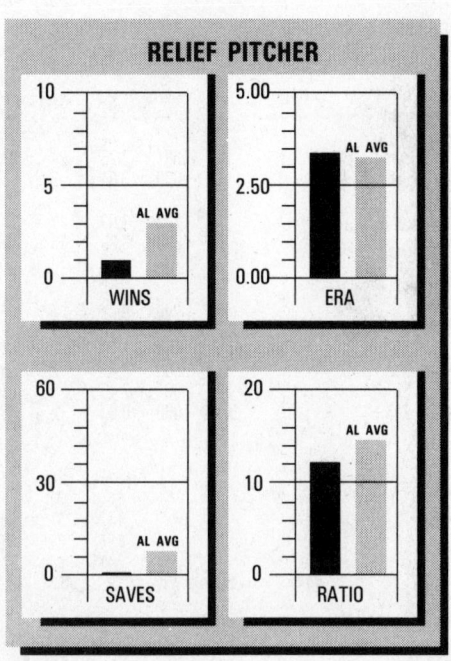

Mike Fetters

FETTERS, MICHAEL LEE
B. Dec. 19, 1964, Van Nuys, Calif.
BR TR 6′ 4″ 200 lbs.

Year	Team	W	L	%	ERA	G	GS	CG	IP	H	BB	SO	ShO	W	L	SV	AB	H	HR	BA	PO	A	E	DP	TC/G	FA
April		—	—	—		0			0	0	0	0		0	0	0										
May		0	0	—	8.10	2	1	0	6.2	8	3	3	0	0	0	0										
June		0	1	.000	3.45	6	0	0	15.2	16	4	5	0	0	1	0										
July		1	0	1.000	4.66	8	0	0	19.1	17	5	11	0	1	0	1										
Aug		0	0	—	3.86	4	0	0	11.2	18	3	6	0	0	0	0										
Sept/Oct		0	0	—	2.51	6	1	0	14.1	18	5	10	0	0	0	0										
Day		0	0	—	6.14	8	2	0	22	29	5	12	0	0	0	0										
Night		1	1	.500	3.15	18	0	0	45.2	48	15	23	0	1	1	1										
vs. Left		—	—	—	—	—	—	—	—	42	6	13	—	—	—	—										
vs. Right		—	—	—	—	—	—	—	—	35	14	22	—	—	—	—										
On Grass		1	1	.500	3.72	22	1	0	55.2	64	15	29	0	1	1	1										
On Turf		0	0	—	6.00	4	1	0	12	13	5	6	0	0	0	0										
Home		0	1	.000	3.03	12	0	0	32.2	38	9	13	0	0	1	1										
Road		1	0	1.000	5.14	14	2	0	35	39	11	22	0	1	0	0										
Division Rivals																										
vs. CHI		0	0	—	1.00	3	0	0	9	7	3	3	0	0	0	0										
vs. KC		0	0	—	2.70	2	0	0	3.1	5	2	0	0	0	0	0										
vs. MIN		—	—	—	—	0	—	—	0	0	0	0	—	0	0	0										
vs. OAK		0	0	—	4.63	3	1	0	11.2	18	3	8	0	0	0	0										
vs. SEA		0	0	—	3.18	2	0	0	5.2	5	4	3	0	0	0	0										
vs. TEX		0	1	.000	4.70	3	0	0	7.2	8	2	3	0	0	1	0										

Year	Team	W	L	%	ERA	G	GS	CG	IP	H	BB	SO	ShO	RELIEF PITCHING W	L	SV	BATTING AB	H	HR	BA	PO	A	E	DP	TC/G	FA

Mike Fetters *Continued*

Year	Team		W	L	%	ERA	G	GS	CG	IP	H	BB	SO	ShO	W	L	SV	AB	H	HR	BA	PO	A	E	DP	TC/G	FA
1989	CAL	A	0	0	—	8.10	1	0	0	3.1	5	1	4	0	0	0	0	0	0	0	—	0	1	0	0	1.0	1.000
1990			1	1	.500	4.12	26	2	0	67.2	77	20	35	0	1	1	1	0	0	0	—	9	11	1	0	0.8	.952
2 yrs.			1	1	.500	4.31	27	2	0	71	82	21	39	0	1	1	1	0	0	0	—	9	12	1	0	0.8	.955

Tom Filer

FILER, THOMAS CARSON
B. Dec. 1, 1956, Philadelphia, Pa.
BR TR 6′ 1″ 195 lbs.

Year	Team		W	L	%	ERA	G	GS	CG	IP	H	BB	SO	ShO	W	L	SV	AB	H	HR	BA	PO	A	E	DP	TC/G	FA
1982	CHI	N	1	2	.333	5.53	8	8	0	40.2	50	18	15	0	0	0	0	12	1	0	.083	13	10	0	2	2.9	1.000
1985	TOR	A	7	0	1.000	3.88	11	9	0	48.2	38	18	24	0	0	0	0	0	0	0	—	1	5	0	1	0.5	1.000
1988	MIL	A	5	8	.385	4.43	19	16	2	101.2	108	33	39	1	0	1	0	0	0	0	—	24	17	0	4	2.2	1.000
1989			7	3	.700	3.61	13	13	0	72.1	74	23	20	0	0	0	0	0	0	0	—	4	16	2	4	1.7	.909
1990			2	3	.400	6.14	7	4	0	22	26	9	8	0	0	1	0	0	0	0	—	1	1	0	0	0.3	1.000
5 yrs.			22	16	.579	4.42	58	50	2	285.1	296	101	106	1	0	2	0	12	1	0	.083	43	49	2	11	1.6	.979

Pete Filson

FILSON, WILLIAM PETER
B. Sept. 28, 1958, Darby, Pa.
BB TL 6′ 2″ 195 lbs.

Year	Team		W	L	%	ERA	G	GS	CG	IP	H	BB	SO	ShO	W	L	SV	AB	H	HR	BA	PO	A	E	DP	TC/G	FA
1982	MIN	A	0	2	.000	8.76	5	3	0	12.1	17	8	10	0	0	0	0	0	0	0	—	0	0	0	0	0.0	—
1983			4	1	.800	3.40	26	8	0	90	87	29	49	0	1	0	1	0	0	0	—	2	6	1	0	0.3	.889
1984			6	5	.545	4.10	55	7	0	118.2	106	54	59	0	4	3	1	0	0	0	—	2	13	1	0	0.3	.938
1985			4	5	.444	3.67	40	6	1	95.2	93	30	42	0	3	0	2	0	0	0	—	3	13	2	0	0.5	.889
1986	2 teams		MIN A	(4G 0 - 0)			CHI A	(3G 0 - 1)																			
''	total		0	1	.000	6.00	7	1	0	18	27	7	8	0	0	0	0	0	0	0	—	1	0	0	0	0.1	1.000
1987	NY	A	1	0	1.000	3.27	7	2	0	22	26	9	10	0	0	0	0	0	0	0	—	1	7	0	0	1.1	1.000
1990	KC	A	0	4	.000	5.91	8	7	0	35	42	13	9	0	0	0	0	0	0	0	—	2	3	0	0	0.6	1.000
7 yrs.			15	18	.455	4.18	148	34	1	391.2	398	150	187	0	8	3	4	0	0	0	—	11	42	4	0	0.4	.930

Chuck Finley

FINLEY, CHARLES EDWARD
B. Nov. 26, 1962, Monroe, La.
BL TL 6′ 6″ 220 lbs.

	W	L	%	ERA	G	GS	CG	IP	H	BB	SO	ShO	W	L	SV
April	3	1	.750	0.96	4	4	0	28	19	7	13	0	0	0	0
May	4	1	.800	3.41	5	5	1	34.1	30	10	24	1	0	0	0
June	3	2	.600	3.13	6	6	0	37.1	36	14	33	0	0	0	0
July	4	0	1.000	1.69	6	6	3	53.1	49	13	39	0	0	0	0
Aug	2	2	.500	3.53	5	5	1	35.2	33	15	24	1	0	0	0
Sept/Oct	2	3	.400	1.90	6	6	2	47.1	43	22	44	0	0	0	0
Day	8	5	.615	3.05	14	14	1	100.1	95	38	72	0	0	0	0
Night	10	4	.714	1.92	18	18	6	135.2	115	43	105	2	0	0	0
vs. Left	—	—	—	—	—	—	—	—	31	14	15	—	—	—	—
vs. Right	—	—	—	—	—	—	—	—	179	67	162	—	—	—	—
On Grass	15	7	.682	2.25	27	27	6	203.2	178	68	159	2	0	0	0
On Turf	3	2	.600	3.34	5	5	1	32.1	32	13	18	0	0	0	0
Home	11	4	.733	1.63	17	17	5	132.1	107	42	98	1	0	0	0
Road	7	5	.583	3.39	15	15	2	103.2	103	39	79	1	0	0	0
Division Rivals															
vs. CHI	1	1	.500	3.09	2	2	0	11.2	13	4	9	0	0	0	0
vs. KC	2	2	.500	1.50	4	4	0	30	22	16	27	0	0	0	0
vs. MIN	3	0	1.000	1.16	3	3	1	23.1	20	4	8	0	0	0	0
vs. OAK	0	1	.000	2.65	2	2	0	17	16	8	13	0	0	0	0
vs. SEA	2	1	.667	2.45	3	3	1	18.1	17	7	11	0	0	0	0
vs. TEX	0	1	.000	8.00	2	2	0	9	16	4	10	0	0	0	0

STARTING PITCHER

WINS · ERA · SO/9 · RATIO (AL AVG)

Year	Team		W	L	%	ERA	G	GS	CG	IP	H	BB	SO	ShO	W	L	SV	AB	H	HR	BA	PO	A	E	DP	TC/G	FA
1986	CAL	A	3	1	.750	3.30	25	0	0	46.1	40	23	37	0	3	1	0	0	0	0	—	8	8	0	1	0.6	1.000
1987			2	7	.222	4.67	35	3	0	90.2	102	43	63	0	2	6	0	0	0	0	—	6	11	1	1	0.5	.944
1988			9	15	.375	4.17	31	31	2	194.1	191	82	111	0	0	0	0	0	0	0	—	5	24	1	1	1.0	.967
1989			16	9	.640	2.57	29	29	9	199.2	171	82	156	0	0	0	0	0	0	0	—	4	16	2	0	0.8	.909
1990			18	9	.667	2.40	32	32	7	236	210	81	177	2	0	0	0	0	0	0	—	14	21	5	2	1.3	.875
5 yrs.			48	41	.539	3.22	152	95	18	767	714	311	544	3	5	7	0	0	0	0	—	37	80	9	5	0.8	.929

LEAGUE CHAMPIONSHIP SERIES

Year	Team		W	L	%	ERA	G	GS	CG	IP	H	BB	SO	ShO	W	L	SV	AB	H	HR	BA	PO	A	E	DP	TC/G	FA
1986	CAL	A	0	0	—	0.00	3	0	0	2	1	0	1	0	0	0	0	0	0	0	—	0	0	0	0	0.0	—

Year	Team		W	L	%	ERA	G	GS	CG	IP	H	BB	SO	ShO	RELIEF PITCHING			BATTING				PO	A	E	DP	TC/G	FA
															W	L	SV	AB	H	HR	BA						

Brian Fisher

FISHER, BRIAN KEVIN
B. Mar. 18, 1962, Honolulu, Hawaii
BR TR 6' 4" 210 lbs.

Year	Team		W	L	%	ERA	G	GS	CG	IP	H	BB	SO	ShO	W	L	SV	AB	H	HR	BA	PO	A	E	DP	TC/G	FA
1985	NY	A	4	4	.500	2.38	55	0	0	98.1	77	29	85	0	4	4	14	0	0	0	—	4	13	1	1	0.3	.944
1986			9	5	.643	4.93	62	0	0	96.2	105	37	67	0	9	5	6	0	0	0	—	3	7	1	1	0.2	.909
1987	PIT	N	11	9	.550	4.52	37	26	6	185.1	185	72	117	3	0	0	0	58	11	2	.190	13	20	1	1	0.9	.971
1988			8	10	.444	4.61	33	22	1	146.1	157	57	66	1	2	0	1	42	2	0	.048	6	17	3	2	0.8	.885
1989			0	3	.000	7.94	9	3	0	17	25	10	8	0	0	1	1	5	0	0	.000	2	1	0	0	0.3	1.000
1990	HOU	N	0	0	—	7.20	4	0	0	5	9	0	1	0	0	0	0	0	0	0	—	0	0	0	0	0.0	—
6 yrs.			32	31	.508	4.36	200	51	7	548.2	558	205	344	4	15	10	22	105	13	2	.124	28	58	6	5	0.5	.935

Mike Flanagan

FLANAGAN, MICHAEL KENDALL
B. Dec. 16, 1951, Manchester, N. H.
BL TL 6' 180 lbs.

Year	Team		W	L	%	ERA	G	GS	CG	IP	H	BB	SO	ShO	W	L	SV	AB	H	HR	BA	PO	A	E	DP	TC/G	FA
1975	BAL	A	0	1	.000	2.79	2	1	0	9.2	9	6	7	0	0	0	0	0	0	0	—	0	2	0	0	1.0	1.000
1976			3	5	.375	4.13	20	10	4	85	83	33	56	0	0	0	3	0	0	0	—	4	13	0	0	0.9	1.000
1977			15	10	.600	3.64	36	33	15	235	235	70	149	2	0	1	1	0	0	0	—	7	36	0	3	1.2	1.000
1978			19	15	.559	4.03	40	**40**	17	281.1	271	87	167	2	0	0	0	0	0	0	—	6	38	2	1	1.2	.957
1979			**23**	9	.719	3.08	39	38	16	266	245	70	190	5	0	0	0	0	0	0	—	4	41	2	1	1.2	.957
1980			16	13	.552	4.12	37	37	12	251	**278**	71	128	2	0	0	0	0	0	0	—	6	42	1	2	1.3	.980
1981			9	6	.600	4.19	20	20	3	116	108	37	72	2	0	0	0	0	0	0	—	4	24	1	1	1.5	.966
1982			15	11	.577	3.97	36	35	11	236	233	76	103	1	0	0	0	0	0	0	—	7	38	0	1	1.3	1.000
1983			12	4	.750	3.30	20	20	3	125.1	135	31	50	1	0	0	0	0	0	0	—	6	15	2	1	1.2	.913
1984			13	13	.500	3.53	34	34	10	226.2	213	81	115	2	0	0	0	0	0	0	—	3	33	0	2	1.1	1.000
1985			4	5	.444	5.13	15	15	1	86	101	28	42	0	0	0	0	0	0	0	—	4	11	0	1	1.0	1.000
1986			7	11	.389	4.24	29	28	2	172	179	66	96	0	0	0	0	0	0	0	—	4	17	0	1	0.7	1.000
1987	2 teams		BAL A (16G 3 - 6)							TOR A (7G 3 - 2)																	
''	total		6	8	.429	4.06	23	23	4	144	148	51	93	0	0	0	0	0	0	0	—	8	17	1	2	1.1	.962
1988	TOR	A	13	13	.500	4.18	34	34	2	211	220	80	99	1	0	0	0	0	0	0	—	6	35	0	2	1.2	1.000
1989			8	10	.444	3.93	30	30	1	171.2	186	47	47	1	0	0	0	0	0	0	—	8	33	0	4	1.4	1.000
1990			2	2	.500	5.31	5	5	0	20.1	28	8	9	0	0	0	0	0	0	0	—	0	6	1	0	1.4	.857
16 yrs.			165	136	.548	3.90	420	403	101	2637	2672	842	1419	19	0	4	1	0	0	0	—	77	401	10	22	1.2	.980

LEAGUE CHAMPIONSHIP SERIES

Year	Team		W	L	%	ERA	G	GS	CG	IP	H	BB	SO	ShO	W	L	SV	AB	H	HR	BA	PO	A	E	DP	TC/G	FA
1979	BAL	A	1	0	1.000	5.14	1	1	0	7	6	1	2	0	0	0	0	0	0	0	—	0	0	0	0	0.0	—
1983			1	0	1.000	1.80	1	1	0	5	5	0	1	0	0	0	0	0	0	0	—	0	0	0	0	0.0	—
1989	TOR	A	0	1	.000	10.38	1	1	0	4.1	7	1	3	0	0	0	0	0	0	0	—	2	3	0	2	5.0	1.000
3 yrs.			2	1	.667	5.51	3	3	0	16.1	18	2	6	0	0	0	0	0	0	0	—	2	3	0	2	1.7	1.000

WORLD SERIES

Year	Team		W	L	%	ERA	G	GS	CG	IP	H	BB	SO	ShO	W	L	SV	AB	H	HR	BA	PO	A	E	DP	TC/G	FA
1979	BAL	A	1	1	.500	3.00	3	2	1	15	18	2	13	0	0	0	0	5	0	0	.000	0	4	0	0	1.3	1.000
1983			0	0	—	4.50	1	1	0	4	6	1	1	0	0	0	0	1	0	0	.000	0	0	0	0	0.0	—
2 yrs.			1	1	.500	3.32	4	3	1	19	24	3	14	0	0	0	0	6	0	0	.000	0	4	0	0	1.0	1.000

Tom Foley

FOLEY, THOMAS MICHAEL
B. Sept. 9, 1959, Fort Benning, Ga.
BL TR 6' 1" 160 lbs.

Year	Team		W	L	%	ERA	G	GS	CG	IP	H	BB	SO	ShO	W	L	SV	AB	H	HR	BA	PO	A	E	DP	TC/G	FA
1989	MON	N	0	0	—	27.00	1	0	0	0.1	1	0	0	0	0	0	0	*				0	0	0	0	0.0	—

Tony Fossas

FOSSAS, EMILIO ANTONIO
Born Emilio Antonio Fossas y Morejon.
B. Sept. 23, 1957, Havana, Cuba
BL TL 6' 195 lbs.

		W	L	%	ERA	G	GS	CG	IP	H	BB	SO	ShO	W	L	SV
April		1	2	.333	6.94	10	0	0	11.2	17	5	8	0	1	2	0
May		0	1	.000	4.32	11	0	0	8.1	9	3	6	0	0	1	0
June		1	0	1.000	5.79	5	0	0	4.2	8	0	2	0	1	0	0
July		0	0	—	8.10	4	0	0	3.1	6	2	4	0	0	0	0
Aug		0	0	—	13.50	2	0	0	1.1	4	0	4	0	0	0	0
Sept/Oct		—	—	—	—	0	0	0	0	0	0	0	—	0	0	0
Day		1	1	.500	3.65	12	0	0	12.1	18	4	10	0	1	1	0
Night		1	2	.333	8.47	20	0	0	17	26	6	14	0	1	2	0
vs. Left		—	—	—	—	—	—	—	—	12	3	12	—	—	—	—
vs. Right		—	—	—	—	—	—	—	—	32	7	12	—	—	—	—

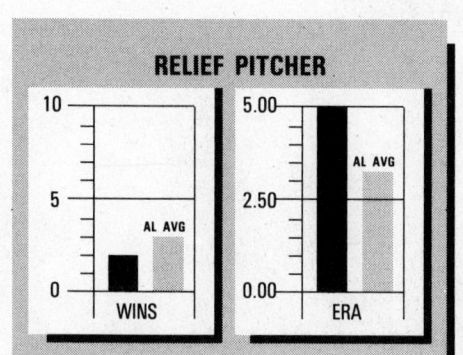

RELIEF PITCHER

(WINS: AL AVG; ERA: AL AVG)

Year	Team		W	L	%	ERA	G	GS	CG	IP	H	BB	SO	ShO	RELIEF PITCHING			BATTING			BA	PO	A	E	DP	TC/G	FA
															W	L	SV	AB	H	HR							

Tony Fossas *Continued*

		W	L	%	ERA	G	GS	CG	IP	H	BB	SO	ShO	W	L	SV	AB	H	HR	BA	PO	A	E	DP	TC/G	FA
On Grass		1	3	.250	7.09	29	0	0	26.2	43	10	23	0	1	3	0										
On Turf		1	0	1.000	0.00	3	0	0	2.2	1	0	1	0	1	0	0										
Home		0	0	—	4.50	18	0	0	16	20	3	13	0	0	0	0										
Road		2	3	.400	8.78	14	0	0	13.1	24	7	11	0	2	3	0										
Division Rivals																									
vs. BAL		0	0	—	16.20	3	0	0	1.2	6	0	0	0	0	0	0										
vs. BOS		0	0	—	0.00	6	0	0	4.1	4	2	5	0	0	0	0										
vs. CLE		—	—	—	—	0	—	—	0	0	0	0	—	0	0	0										
vs. DET		0	0	—	23.14	2	0	0	2.1	8	2	1	0	0	0	0										
vs. NY		—	—	—	—	0	0	0	0	0	0	0	—	0	0	0										
vs. TOR		1	0	1.000	0.00	2	0	0	3	2	0	2	0	1	0	0										
1988	TEX A	0	0	—	4.76	5	0	0	5.2	11	2	0	0	0	0	0	0	0	0	—	1	1	0	1	0.4	1.000
1989	MIL A	2	2	.500	3.54	51	0	0	61	57	22	42	0	2	2	1	0	0	0	—	1	12	2	0	0.3	.867
1990		2	3	.400	6.44	32	0	0	29.1	44	10	24	0	2	3	0	0	0	0	—	1	4	3	0	0.3	.625
3 yrs.		4	5	.444	4.50	88	0	0	96	112	34	66	0	4	5	1	0	0	0	—	3	17	5	1	0.3	.800

John Franco

FRANCO, JOHN ANTHONY
B. Sept. 17, 1960, Brooklyn, N. Y.
BL TL 5′ 10″ 175 lbs.

		W	L	%	ERA	G	GS	CG	IP	H	BB	SO	ShO	W	L	SV	AB	H	HR	BA	PO	A	E	DP	TC/G	FA
April		0	0	—	1.08	7	0	0	8.1	6	1	8	0	0	0	6										
May		1	0	1.000	5.14	6	0	0	7	7	4	6	0	1	0	2										
June		2	0	1.000	0.55	12	0	0	16.1	13	2	13	0	2	0	6										
July		1	0	1.000	2.51	11	0	0	14.1	11	4	14	0	1	0	9										
Aug		0	0	—	1.64	9	0	0	11	11	4	4	0	0	0	7										
Sept/Oct		1	3	.250	5.91	10	0	0	10.2	18	6	11	0	1	3	3										
Day		3	1	.750	2.67	22	0	0	27	29	14	27	0	3	1	11										
Night		2	2	.500	2.43	33	0	0	40.2	37	7	29	0	2	2	22										
vs. Left		—	—	—	—	—	—	—	—	13	8	16	—	—	—	—										
vs. Right		—	—	—	—	—	—	—	—	53	13	40	—	—	—	—										
On Grass		5	2	.714	2.85	40	0	0	47.1	51	18	45	0	5	2	23										
On Turf		0	1	.000	1.77	15	0	0	20.1	15	3	11	0	0	1	10										
Home		4	2	.667	2.82	31	0	0	38.1	45	13	38	0	4	2	17										
Road		1	1	.500	2.15	24	0	0	29.1	21	8	18	0	1	1	16										
Division Rivals																									
vs. CHI		1	1	.500	3.52	6	0	0	7.2	8	2	8	0	1	1	1										
vs. MON		1	1	.500	1.13	8	0	0	8	11	1	6	0	1	1	3										
vs. PHI		0	0	—	1.29	5	0	0	7	7	2	8	0	0	0	4										
vs. PIT		0	1	.000	1.17	6	0	0	7.2	5	2	7	0	0	1	4										
vs. STL		1	0	1.000	3.00	7	0	0	9	10	1	6	0	1	0	3										
1984	CIN N	6	2	.750	2.61	54	0	0	79.1	74	36	55	0	6	2	4	3	0	0	.000	5	15	0	0	0.4	1.000
1985		12	3	.800	2.18	67	0	0	99	83	40	61	0	**12**	3	12	6	2	0	.333	9	21	1	1	0.5	.968
1986		6	6	.500	2.94	74	0	0	101	90	44	84	0	6	6	29	4	0	0	.000	6	22	4	2	0.4	.875
1987		8	5	.615	2.52	68	0	0	82	76	27	61	0	8	5	32	2	0	0	.000	4	7	0	0	0.2	1.000
1988		6	6	.500	1.57	70	0	0	86	60	27	46	0	6	6	**39**	1	0	0	.000	3	18	1	1	0.3	.955
1989		4	8	.333	3.12	60	0	0	80.2	77	36	60	0	4	8	32	3	1	0	.333	2	19	1	1	0.4	.955
1990	NY N	5	3	.625	2.53	55	0	0	67.2	66	21	56	0	5	3	**33**	5	0	0	.000	4	13	1	0	0.3	.944
7 yrs.		47	33	.588	2.49	448	0	0	595.2	526	231	423	0	47	33	181	24	3	0	.125	33	115	8	5	0.3	.949

Terry Francona

FRANCONA, TERRY JON
Son of Tito Francona.
B. Apr. 22, 1959, Aberdeen, S. D.
BL TL 6′ 1″ 190 lbs.

		W	L	%	ERA	G	GS	CG	IP	H	BB	SO	ShO	W	L	SV	AB	H	HR	BA	PO	A	E	DP	TC/G	FA
1989	MIL A	0	0	—	0.00	1	0	0	1	0	0	1	0	0	0	0	*				0	0	0	0	0.0	—

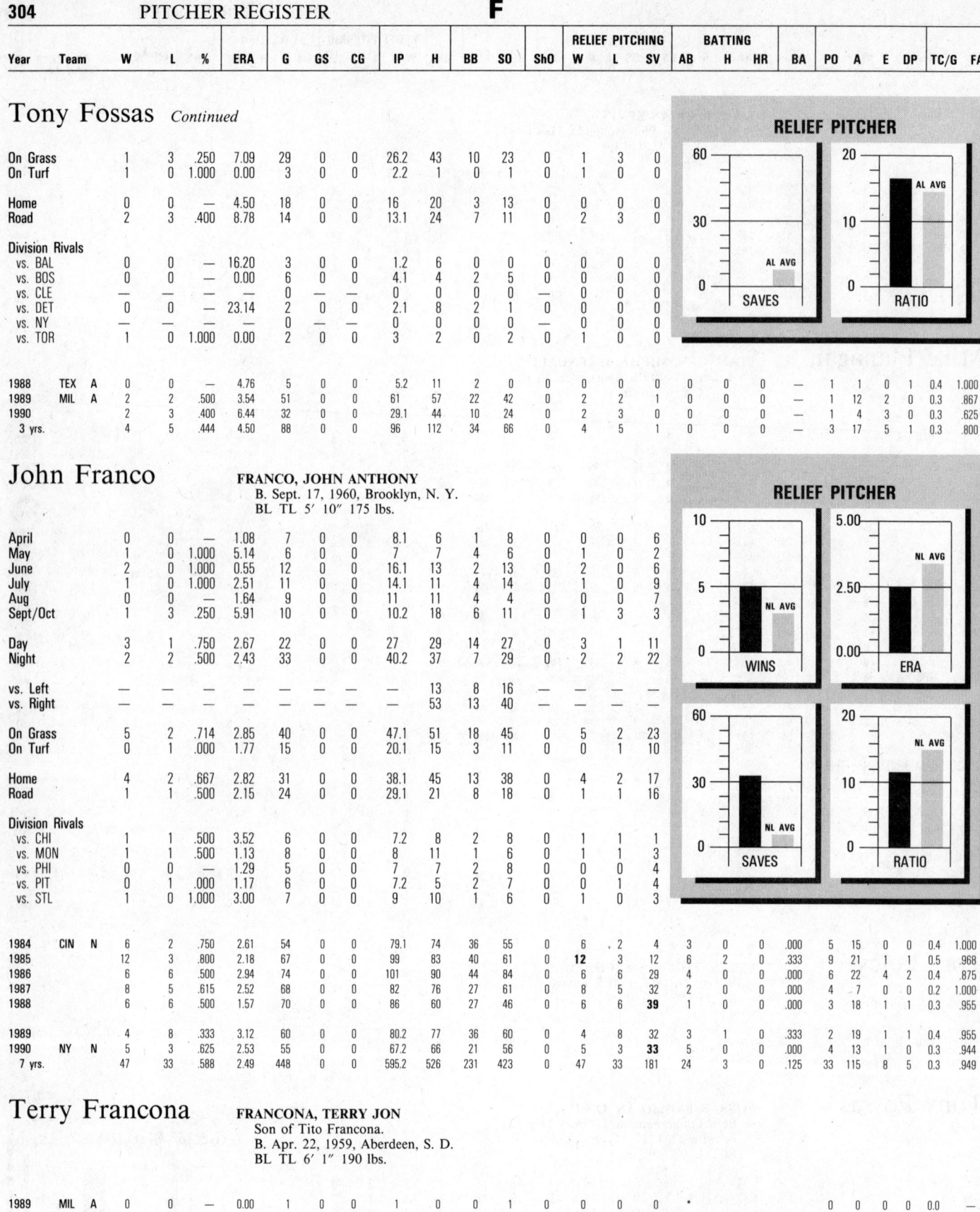

Year	Team	W	L	%	ERA	G	GS	CG	IP	H	BB	SO	ShO	RELIEF PITCHING W	L	SV	BATTING AB	H	HR	BA	PO	A	E	DP	TC/G	FA

Willie Fraser

FRASER, WILLIAM PATRICK
B. May 26, 1964, New York, N. Y.
BR TR 6′ 3″ 200 lbs.

	W	L	%	ERA	G	GS	CG	IP	H	BB	SO	ShO	W	L	SV	AB	H	HR	BA	PO	A	E	DP	TC/G	FA
April	0	1	.000	11.81	6	0	0	5.1	10	3	1	0	0	1	0										
May	2	1	.667	3.86	6	0	0	9.1	14	3	2	0	2	1	0										
June	0	0	—	4.82	6	0	0	9.1	11	5	7	0	0	0	0										
July	0	0	—	1.47	7	0	0	18.1	9	3	7	0	0	0	0										
Aug	3	1	.750	1.27	13	0	0	21.1	15	7	8	0	3	1	1										
Sept/Oct	0	1	.000	2.92	7	0	0	12.1	10	3	7	0	0	1	1										
Day	1	1	.500	3.00	10	0	0	15	17	4	6	0	1	1	1										
Night	4	3	.571	3.10	35	0	0	61	52	20	26	0	4	3	1										
vs. Left	—	—	—	—	—	—	—	—	25	14	16	—	—	—	—										
vs. Right	—	—	—	—	—	—	—	—	44	10	16	—	—	—	—										
On Grass	4	4	.500	2.71	40	0	0	69.2	62	20	31	0	4	4	2										
On Turf	1	0	1.000	7.11	5	0	0	6.1	7	4	1	0	1	0	0										
Home	4	1	.800	2.62	23	0	0	44.2	40	15	22	0	4	1	1										
Road	1	3	.250	3.73	22	0	0	31.1	29	9	10	0	1	3	1										

Division Rivals

	W	L	%	ERA	G	GS	CG	IP	H	BB	SO	ShO	W	L	SV	AB	H	HR	BA	PO	A	E	DP	TC/G	FA
vs. CHI	0	0	—	2.08	3	0	0	4.1	1	2	2	0	0	0	0										
vs. KC	0	0	—	0.00	2	0	0	2	2	0	1	0	0	0	0										
vs. MIN	0	0	—	7.20	4	0	0	5	7	5	2	0	0	0	0										
vs. OAK	0	2	.000	4.15	5	0	0	8.2	7	2	6	0	0	2	0										
vs. SEA	0	0	—	18.00	1	0	0	1	3	1	0	0	0	0	0										
vs. TEX	1	0	1.000	2.35	5	0	0	7.2	9	2	5	0	1	0	0										
1986	CAL A	0	0	—	8.31	1	1	0	4.1	6	1	2	0	0	0	0	0	0	0	—	0	0	0	0	0.0	—
1987		10	10	.500	3.92	36	23	5	176.2	160	63	106	1	3	1	1	0	0	0	—	6	15	1	0	0.6	.955
1988		12	13	.480	5.41	34	32	2	194.2	203	80	86	0	1	0	0	0	0	0	—	21	20	3	3	1.3	.932
1989		4	7	.364	3.24	44	0	0	91.2	80	23	46	0	4	7	2	0	0	0	—	6	14	0	1	0.5	1.000
1990		5	4	.556	3.08	45	0	0	76	69	24	32	0	5	4	2	0	0	0	—	2	6	0	0	0.2	1.000
5 yrs.		31	34	.477	4.26	160	56	7	543.1	518	191	272	1	13	12	5	0	0	0	—	35	55	4	4	0.6	.957

RELIEF PITCHER (graphs: WINS, ERA, SAVES, RATIO — AL AVG)

Marvin Freeman

FREEMAN, MARVIN (Starvin' Marvin)
B. Apr. 10, 1963, Chicago, Ill.
BR TR 6′ 7″ 200 lbs.

	W	L	%	ERA	G	GS	CG	IP	H	BB	SO	ShO	W	L	SV	AB	H	HR	BA	PO	A	E	DP	TC/G	FA
April	—	—	—		0	—	—	0	0	0	0	—	0	0	0										
May	0	0	—	3.27	6	0	0	11	9	4	8	0	0	0	1										
June	0	2	.000	6.91	4	3	0	14.1	17	6	10	0	0	1	0										
July	0	0	—	6.43	6	0	0	7	8	4	8	0	0	0	0										
Aug	—	—	—		0	—	—	0	0	0	0	—	0	0	0										
Sept/Oct	1	0	1.000	1.72	9	0	0	15.2	7	3	12	0	1	0	0										
Day	0	0	—	6.00	7	2	0	18	19	4	16	0	0	0	0										
Night	1	2	.333	3.30	18	1	0	30	22	13	22	0	1	1	1										
vs. Left	—	—	—	—	—	—	—	—	20	11	10	—	—	—	—										
vs. Right	—	—	—	—	—	—	—	—	21	6	28	—	—	—	—										
On Grass	1	0	1.000	3.03	13	2	0	29.2	19	7	25	0	1	0	0										
On Turf	0	2	.000	6.38	12	1	0	18.1	22	10	13	0	0	1	1										
Home	0	1	.000	3.86	10	1	0	18.2	17	8	11	0	0	0	1										
Road	1	1	.500	4.60	15	2	0	29.1	24	9	27	0	1	1	0										

Division Rivals

	W	L	%	ERA	G	GS	CG	IP	H	BB	SO	ShO	W	L	SV	AB	H	HR	BA	PO	A	E	DP	TC/G	FA
vs. CIN	0	0	—	0.00	4	0	0	7	4	1	5	0	0	0	0										
vs. HOU	0	1	.000	12.71	4	1	0	5.2	8	4	4	0	0	0	0										
vs. LA	0	0	—	0.00	4	0	0	5.1	3	1	5	0	0	0	0										
vs. SD	0	0	—	0.00	3	0	0	5.1	3	2	4	0	0	0	0										
vs. SF	1	0	1.000	1.42	3	0	0	6.1	3	0	7	0	1	0	0										
1986	PHI N	2	0	1.000	2.25	3	3	0	16	6	10	8	0	0	0	0	6	0	0	.000	0	1	0	0	0.3	1.000
1988		2	3	.400	6.10	11	11	0	51.2	55	43	37	0	0	0	0	14	3	0	.214	2	9	0	0	1.0	1.000
1989		0	0	—	6.00	1	1	0	3	2	5	0	0	0	0	0	2	0	0	.000	0	0	0	0	0.0	—
1990	2 teams	PHI N (9G 1 – 0)				ATL N (16G 0 – 2)																				
"	total	1	2	.333	4.31	25	3	0	48	41	17	38	0	1	1	1	7	0	0	.000	1	6	1	1	0.3	.875
4 yrs.		5	5	.500	4.85	40	18	0	118.2	104	75	83	0	1	1	1	29	3	0	.103	3	16	1	1	0.5	.950

RELIEF PITCHER (graphs: WINS, ERA, SAVES, RATIO — NL AVG)

Year	Team	W	L	%	ERA	G	GS	CG	IP	H	BB	SO	ShO	RELIEF PITCHING W	L	SV	BATTING AB	H	HR	BA	PO	A	E	DP	TC/G	FA

Steve Frey

FREY, STEVEN FRANCIS
B. July 29, 1963, Meadowbrook, Pa.
BR TL 5′ 9″ 170 lbs.

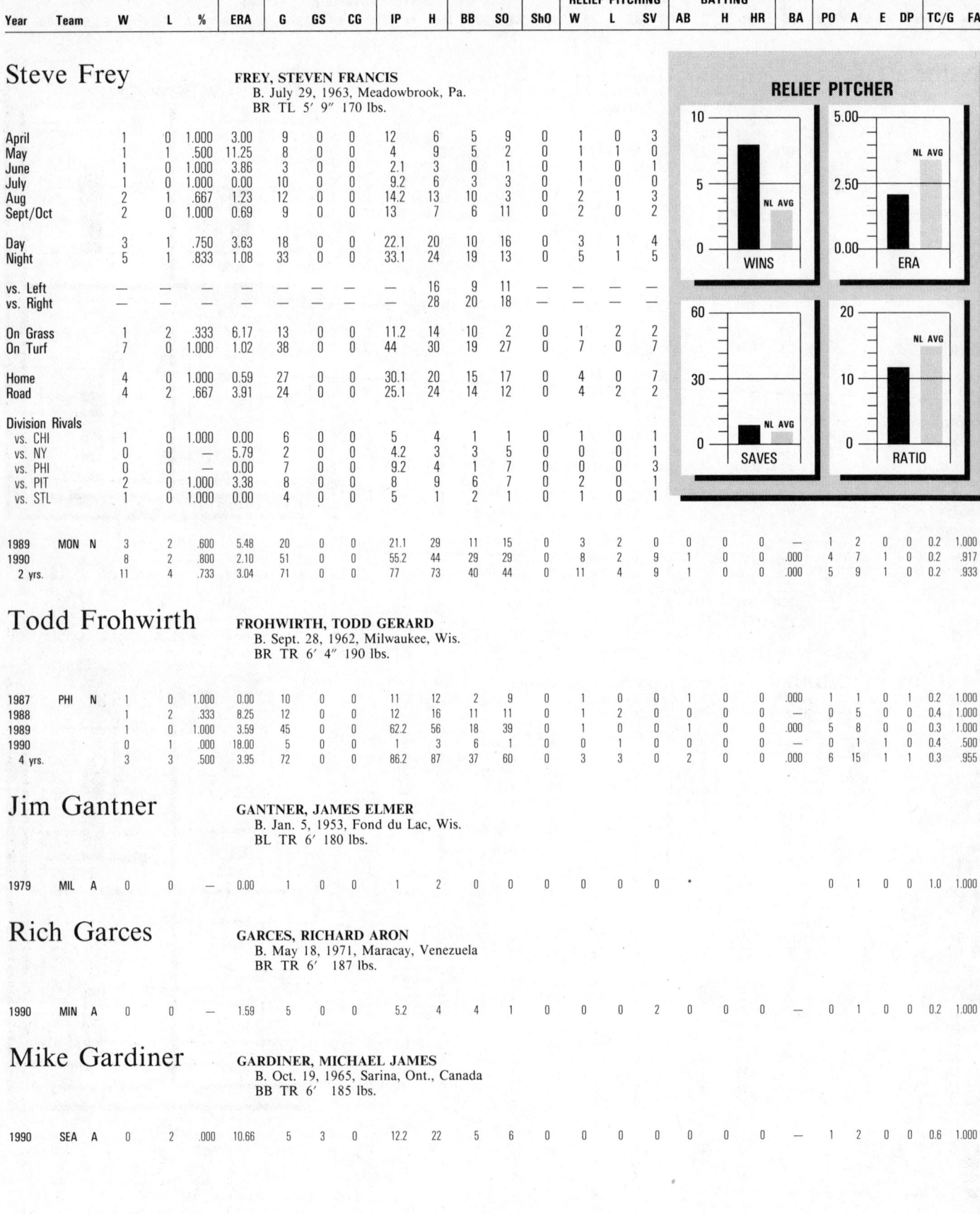

RELIEF PITCHER

April		1	0	1.000	3.00	9	0	0	12	6	5	9	0	1	0	3										
May		1	1	.500	11.25	8	0	0	4	9	5	2	0	1	1	0										
June		1	0	1.000	3.86	3	0	0	2.1	3	0	1	0	1	0	1										
July		1	0	1.000	0.00	10	0	0	9.2	6	3	3	0	1	0	0										
Aug		2	1	.667	1.23	12	0	0	14.2	13	10	3	0	2	1	3										
Sept/Oct		2	0	1.000	0.69	9	0	0	13	7	6	11	0	2	0	2										
Day		3	1	.750	3.63	18	0	0	22.1	20	10	16	0	3	1	4										
Night		5	1	.833	1.08	33	0	0	33.1	24	19	13	0	5	1	5										
vs. Left		—	—	—	—	—	—	—	—	16	9	11	—	—	—	—										
vs. Right		—	—	—	—	—	—	—	—	28	20	18	—	—	—	—										
On Grass		1	2	.333	6.17	13	0	0	11.2	14	10	2	0	1	2	2										
On Turf		7	0	1.000	1.02	38	0	0	44	30	19	27	0	7	0	7										
Home		4	0	1.000	0.59	27	0	0	30.1	20	15	17	0	4	0	7										
Road		4	2	.667	3.91	24	0	0	25.1	24	14	12	0	4	2	2										
Division Rivals																										
vs. CHI		1	0	1.000	0.00	6	0	0	5	4	1	1	0	1	0	1										
vs. NY		0	0	—	5.79	2	0	0	4.2	3	3	5	0	0	0	1										
vs. PHI		0	0	—	0.00	7	0	0	9.2	4	1	7	0	0	0	3										
vs. PIT		2	0	1.000	3.38	8	0	0	8	9	6	7	0	2	0	1										
vs. STL		1	0	1.000	0.00	4	0	0	5	1	2	1	0	1	0	1										
1989	MON N	3	2	.600	5.48	20	0	0	21.1	29	11	15	0	3	2	0	0	0	0	—	1	2	0	0	0.2	1.000
1990		8	2	.800	2.10	51	0	0	55.2	44	29	29	0	8	2	9	1	0	0	.000	4	7	1	0	0.2	.917
2 yrs.		11	4	.733	3.04	71	0	0	77	73	40	44	0	11	4	9	1	0	0	.000	5	9	1	0	0.2	.933

Todd Frohwirth

FROHWIRTH, TODD GERARD
B. Sept. 28, 1962, Milwaukee, Wis.
BR TR 6′ 4″ 190 lbs.

Year	Team	W	L	%	ERA	G	GS	CG	IP	H	BB	SO	ShO	W	L	SV	AB	H	HR	BA	PO	A	E	DP	TC/G	FA
1987	PHI N	1	0	1.000	0.00	10	0	0	11	12	2	9	0	1	0	0	1	0	0	.000	1	1	0	1	0.2	1.000
1988		1	2	.333	8.25	12	0	0	12	16	11	11	0	1	2	0	0	0	0	—	0	5	0	0	0.4	1.000
1989		1	0	1.000	3.59	45	0	0	62.2	56	18	39	0	1	0	0	1	0	0	.000	5	8	0	0	0.3	1.000
1990		0	1	.000	18.00	5	0	0	1	3	6	1	0	0	1	0	0	0	0	—	0	1	1	0	0.4	.500
4 yrs.		3	3	.500	3.95	72	0	0	86.2	87	37	60	0	3	3	0	2	0	0	.000	6	15	1	1	0.3	.955

Jim Gantner

GANTNER, JAMES ELMER
B. Jan. 5, 1953, Fond du Lac, Wis.
BL TR 6′ 180 lbs.

Year	Team	W	L	%	ERA	G	GS	CG	IP	H	BB	SO	ShO	W	L	SV	AB	H	HR	BA	PO	A	E	DP	TC/G	FA
1979	MIL A	0	0	—	0.00	1	0	0	1	2	0	0	0	0	0	0	*				0	1	0	0	1.0	1.000

Rich Garces

GARCES, RICHARD ARON
B. May 18, 1971, Maracay, Venezuela
BR TR 6′ 187 lbs.

Year	Team	W	L	%	ERA	G	GS	CG	IP	H	BB	SO	ShO	W	L	SV	AB	H	HR	BA	PO	A	E	DP	TC/G	FA
1990	MIN A	0	0	—	1.59	5	0	0	5.2	4	4	1	0	0	0	2	0	0	0	—	0	1	0	0	0.2	1.000

Mike Gardiner

GARDINER, MICHAEL JAMES
B. Oct. 19, 1965, Sarina, Ont., Canada
BB TR 6′ 185 lbs.

Year	Team	W	L	%	ERA	G	GS	CG	IP	H	BB	SO	ShO	W	L	SV	AB	H	HR	BA	PO	A	E	DP	TC/G	FA
1990	SEA A	0	2	.000	10.66	5	3	0	12.2	22	5	6	0	0	0	0	0	0	0	—	1	2	0	0	0.6	1.000

Year	Team	W	L	%	ERA	G	GS	CG	IP	H	BB	SO	ShO	RELIEF PITCHING W	L	SV	BATTING AB	H	HR	BA	PO	A	E	DP	TC/G	FA

Mark Gardner

GARDNER, MARK ALLAN
B. Mar. 1, 1962, Los Angeles, Calif.
BR TR 6′ 1″ 190 lbs.

		W	L	%	ERA	G	GS	CG	IP	H	BB	SO	ShO	W	L	SV	AB	H	HR	BA	PO	A	E	DP	TC/G	FA
April		0	2	.000	3.18	3	2	0	11.1	12	5	8	0	0	1	0										
May		2	0	1.000	2.03	6	6	1	40	31	13	36	1	0	0	0										
June		2	2	.500	3.57	6	6	0	35.1	29	16	23	0	0	0	0										
July		2	1	.667	1.35	5	5	2	40	19	11	40	2	0	0	0										
Aug		1	2	.333	6.85	5	5	0	22.1	29	12	25	0	0	0	0										
Sept/Oct		0	2	.000	19.64	2	2	0	3.2	9	4	3	0	0	0	0										
Day		1	4	.200	6.19	8	8	1	36.1	45	16	29	1	0	0	0										
Night		6	5	.545	2.55	19	18	2	116.1	84	45	106	2	0	1	0										
vs. Left		—	—	—	—					73	47	70	—	—	—	—										
vs. Right		—	—	—	—					56	14	65	—	—	—	—										
On Grass		2	3	.400	5.11	9	9	1	49.1	51	22	42	1	0	0	0										
On Turf		5	6	.455	2.61	18	17	2	103.1	78	39	93	2	0	1	0										
Home		5	3	.625	1.91	13	13	2	80	60	28	79	2	0	0	0										
Road		2	6	.250	5.08	14	13	1	72.2	69	33	56	1	0	1	0										
Division Rivals																										
vs. CHI		1	2	.333	4.70	4	4	0	23	19	5	22	0	0	0	0										
vs. NY		0	1	.000	4.50	2	2	0	10	10	7	6	0	0	0	0										
vs. PHI		0	0	—	0.90	2	2	0	10	8	4	9	0	0	0	0										
vs. PIT		—	—	—	—	0	—	—	0	0	0	0	—	0	0	0										
vs. STL		1	2	.333	3.79	4	3	0	19	16	8	10	0	0	1	0										
1989	MON N	0	3	.000	5.13	7	4	0	26.1	26	11	21	0	0	0	0	6	1	0	.167	1	3	0	0	0.6	1.000
1990		7	9	.438	3.42	27	26	3	152.2	129	61	135	3	0	1	0	44	5	0	.114	9	25	0	4	1.3	1.000
2 yrs.		7	12	.368	3.67	34	30	3	179	155	72	156	3	0	1	0	50	6	0	.120	10	28	0	4	1.1	1.000

Wes Gardner

GARDNER, WESLEY BRIAN
B. Apr. 29, 1961, Benton, Ark.
BR TR 6′ 4″ 195 lbs.

		W	L	%	ERA	G	GS	CG	IP	H	BB	SO	ShO	W	L	SV	AB	H	HR	BA	PO	A	E	DP	TC/G	FA
April		0	0	—	54.00	1	0	0	0.1	1	1	1	0	0	0	0										
May		0	2	.000	8.10	7	0	0	10	16	6	7	0	0	2	0										
June		2	2	.500	3.33	5	4	0	24.1	20	8	19	0	0	0	0										
July		0	2	.000	5.14	5	5	0	21	26	9	12	0	0	0	0										
Aug		1	0	1.000	0.00	3	0	0	2.1	0	0	1	0	1	0	0										
Sept/Oct		0	1	.000	4.66	13	0	0	19.1	14	11	18	0	0	1	0										
Day		0	1	.000	8.56	10	2	0	13.2	20	10	13	0	0	0	0										
Night		3	6	.333	4.10	24	7	0	63.2	57	25	45	0	1	3	0										
vs. Left		—	—	—	—					42	21	25	—	—	—	—										
vs. Right		—	—	—	—					35	14	33	—	—	—	—										
On Grass		3	5	.375	5.08	30	7	0	62	57	32	52	0	1	2	0										
On Turf		0	2	.000	4.11	4	2	0	15.1	20	3	6	0	0	1	0										
Home		1	2	.333	5.15	16	4	0	36.2	32	20	37	0	0	1	0										
Road		2	5	.286	4.65	18	5	0	40.2	45	15	21	0	1	2	0										
Division Rivals																										
vs. BAL		1	0	1.000	3.38	3	1	0	8	8	3	5	0	0	0	0										
vs. CLE		1	1	.500	3.24	4	1	0	8.1	4	4	8	0	1	0	0										
vs. DET		0	1	.000	22.50	2	1	0	2	3	4	1	0	0	0	0										
vs. MIL		0	1	.000	6.00	1	0	0	3	3	0	2	0	0	1	0										
vs. NY		0	0	—	3.60	3	0	0	5	4	1	5	0	0	0	0										
vs. TOR		1	1	.500	3.38	4	2	0	13.1	12	5	10	0	0	0	0										
1984	NY N	1	1	.500	6.39	21	0	0	25.1	34	8	19	0	1	1	1	1	0	0	.000	1	3	0	0	0.2	1.000
1985		0	2	.000	5.25	9	1	0	12	18	8	11	0	0	2	0	0	0	0	—	0	4	0	0	0.4	1.000
1986	BOS A	0	0	—	9.00	1	0	0	1	1	0	1	0	0	0	0	0	0	0	—	0	0	0	0	0.0	—
1987		3	6	.333	5.42	49	1	0	89.2	98	42	70	0	3	6	10	0	0	0	—	2	7	0	0	0.2	1.000
1988		8	6	.571	3.50	36	18	1	149	119	64	106	0	1	1	2	0	0	0	—	15	14	0	0	0.8	1.000
1989		3	7	.300	5.97	22	16	0	86	97	47	81	0	1	0	0	0	0	0	—	3	8	1	1	0.5	.917
1990		3	7	.300	4.89	34	9	0	77.1	77	35	58	0	1	3	0	0	0	0	—	8	7	1	1	0.5	.938
7 yrs.		18	29	.383	4.85	172	44	1	440.1	444	204	346	0	7	13	13	1	0	0	.000	29	43	2	2	0.4	.973

LEAGUE CHAMPIONSHIP SERIES

Year	Team	W	L	%	ERA	G	GS	CG	IP	H	BB	SO	ShO	W	L	SV	AB	H	HR	BA	PO	A	E	DP	TC/G	FA
1988	BOS A	0	0	—	5.79	1	0	0	4.2	6	2	8	0	0	0	0	0	0	0	—	0	0	0	0	0.0	—

Year	Team	W	L	%	ERA	G	GS	CG	IP	H	BB	SO	ShO	W	L	SV	AB	H	HR	BA	PO	A	E	DP	TC/G	FA

Scott Garrelts

GARRELTS, SCOTT WILLIAM
B. Oct. 30, 1961, Champaign, Ill.
BR TR 6′ 4″ 200 lbs.

Year	Team	W	L	%	ERA	G	GS	CG	IP	H	BB	SO	ShO	W	L	SV	AB	H	HR	BA	PO	A	E	DP	TC/G	FA
April		0	2	.000	4.29	4	4	0	21	22	11	5	0	0	0	0										
May		1	4	.200	8.54	7	7	0	32.2	54	16	11	0	0	0	0										
June		4	0	1.000	1.45	5	5	1	37.1	26	9	17	1	0	0	0										
July		4	1	.800	2.68	7	7	3	50.1	39	13	21	1	0	0	0										
Aug		1	3	.250	6.08	5	5	0	23.2	32	12	14	0	0	0	0										
Sept/Oct		2	1	.667	3.18	3	3	0	17	17	9	12	0	0	0	0										
Day		3	3	.500	3.59	10	10	2	62.2	60	16	33	2	0	0	0										
Night		9	8	.529	4.45	21	21	2	119.1	130	54	47	0	0	0	0										
vs. Left		—									115	41	33	—	—	—	—										
vs. Right		—									75	29	47	—	—	—	—										
On Grass		8	7	.533	3.70	21	21	2	124	127	47	60	2	0	0	0										
On Turf		4	4	.500	5.12	10	10	2	58	63	23	20	0	0	0	0										
Home		6	7	.462	3.83	18	18	2	103.1	106	42	54	2	0	0	0										
Road		6	4	.600	4.58	13	13	2	78.2	84	28	26	0	0	0	0										
Division Rivals																										
vs. ATL		3	0	1.000	1.16	3	3	1	23.1	12	10	13	1	0	0	0										
vs. CIN		3	2	.600	3.16	6	6	1	37	32	14	18	1	0	0	0										
vs. HOU		1	1	.500	3.38	2	2	0	13.1	14	5	5	0	0	0	0										
vs. LA		1	1	.500	6.94	3	3	0	11.2	18	7	3	0	0	0	0										
vs. SD		0	0	—	3.60	1	1	0	5	7	4	0	0	0	0	0										
1982	SF N	0	0	—	13.50	1	0	0	2	3	2	4	0	0	0	0	0	0	0	—	0	0	0	0	0.0	—
1983		2	2	.500	2.52	5	5	1	35.2	33	19	16	1	0	0	0	9	2	0	.222	1	7	0	1	1.6	1.000
1984		2	3	.400	5.65	21	3	0	43	45	34	32	0	2	3	0	10	1	0	.100	2	4	0	0	0.3	1.000
1985		9	6	.600	2.30	74	0	0	105.2	76	58	106	0	9	6	13	9	2	0	.222	7	22	2	0	0.4	.935
1986		13	9	.591	3.11	53	18	0	173.2	144	74	125	0	8	2	10	45	8	1	.178	9	37	2	2	0.9	.958
1987		11	7	.611	3.22	64	0	0	106.1	70	55	127	0	11	7	12	10	2	0	.200	5	10	1	1	0.3	.938
1988		5	9	.357	3.58	65	0	0	98	80	46	86	0	5	9	13	13	1	0	.077	5	12	2	0	0.3	.895
1989		14	5	**.737**	**2.28**	30	29	2	193.1	149	46	119	1	0	0	0	66	9	0	.136	18	24	1	0	1.4	.977
1990		12	11	.522	4.15	31	31	4	182	190	70	80	2	0	0	0	66	4	0	.061	5	26	3	0	1.1	.912
9 yrs.		68	52	.567	3.23	344	86	9	939.2	790	404	695	4	35	27	48	228	29	1	.127	52	142	11	4	0.6	.946

LEAGUE CHAMPIONSHIP SERIES

Year	Team	W	L	%	ERA	G	GS	CG	IP	H	BB	SO	ShO	W	L	SV	AB	H	HR	BA	PO	A	E	DP	TC/G	FA
1987	SF N	0	0	—	6.75	2	0	0	2.2	2	4	4	0	0	0	0	0	0	0	—	1	0	0	0	0.5	1.000
1989		1	0	1.000	5.40	2	2	0	11.2	16	2	8	0	0	0	0	4	0	0	.000	0	1	0	0	0.5	1.000
2 yrs.		1	0	1.000	5.65	4	2	0	14.1	18	6	12	0	0	0	0	4	0	0	.000	1	1	0	0	0.5	1.000

WORLD SERIES

Year	Team	W	L	%	ERA	G	GS	CG	IP	H	BB	SO	ShO	W	L	SV	AB	H	HR	BA	PO	A	E	DP	TC/G	FA
1989	SF N	0	2	.000	9.82	2	2	0	7.1	13	1	8	0	0	0	0	1	0	0	.000	0	2	0	0	1.0	1.000

Paul Gibson

GIBSON, PAUL MARSHALL
B. Jan. 4, 1960, Southampton, N. Y.
BR TL 6′ 165 lbs.

Year	Team	W	L	%	ERA	G	GS	CG	IP	H	BB	SO	ShO	W	L	SV	AB	H	HR	BA	PO	A	E	DP	TC/G	FA
April		0	0	—	5.40	7	0	0	10	15	8	4	0	0	0	0										
May		1	1	.500	1.14	13	0	0	23.2	18	13	13	0	1	1	1										
June		1	1	.500	1.46	10	0	0	12.1	15	5	9	0	1	1	0										
July		1	0	1.000	3.52	11	0	0	23	16	9	13	0	1	0	1										
Aug		0	2	.000	5.51	10	0	0	16.1	22	4	8	0	0	2	0										
Sept/Oct		2	0	1.000	2.25	10	0	0	12	13	5	9	0	2	0	1										
Day		1	0	1.000	1.77	13	0	0	20.1	18	10	10	0	1	0	2										
Night		4	4	.500	3.39	48	0	0	77	81	34	46	0	4	4	1										
vs. Left		—									31	11	11	—	—	—	—										
vs. Right		—									68	33	45	—	—	—	—										
On Grass		5	3	.625	2.90	50	0	0	80.2	81	36	49	0	5	3	2										
On Turf		0	1	.000	3.78	11	0	0	16.2	18	8	7	0	0	1	1										
Home		4	2	.667	2.58	31	0	0	52.1	48	26	35	0	4	2	2										
Road		1	2	.333	3.60	30	0	0	45	51	18	21	0	1	2	1										
Division Rivals																										
vs. BAL		1	0	1.000	4.76	3	0	0	5.2	7	4	3	0	1	0	0										
vs. BOS		1	0	1.000	4.22	5	0	0	10.2	12	3	3	0	1	0	0										
vs. CLE		0	0	—	0.00	2	0	0	1.1	2	1	1	0	0	0	0										
vs. MIL		0	0	—	2.79	4	0	0	9.2	8	1	2	0	0	0	0										
vs. NY		0	0	—	1.00	6	0	0	9	8	4	9	0	0	0	0										
vs. TOR		1	0	1.000	2.13	6	0	0	12.2	12	10	7	0	1	0	0										

Year	Team		W	L	%	ERA	G	GS	CG	IP	H	BB	SO	ShO	RELIEF PITCHING			BATTING				PO	A	E	DP	TC/G	FA
															W	L	SV	AB	H	HR	BA						

Paul Gibson *Continued*

Year	Team		W	L	%	ERA	G	GS	CG	IP	H	BB	SO	ShO	W	L	SV	AB	H	HR	BA	PO	A	E	DP	TC/G	FA
1988	DET	A	4	2	.667	2.93	40	1	0	92	83	34	50	0	3	2	0	0	0	0	—	7	11	0	2	0.5	1.000
1989			4	8	.333	4.64	45	13	0	132	129	57	77	0	3	3	0	0	0	0	—	6	20	2	0	0.6	.929
1990			5	4	.556	3.05	61	0	0	97.1	99	44	56	0	5	4	3	0	0	0	—	9	11	0	1	0.3	1.000
3 yrs.			13	14	.481	3.67	146	14	0	321.1	311	135	183	0	11	9	3	0	0	0	—	22	42	2	3	0.5	.970

Brett Gideon

GIDEON, BYRON BRETT
B. Aug. 8, 1963, Ozona, Tex.
BR TR 6′ 2″ 200 lbs.

Year	Team		W	L	%	ERA	G	GS	CG	IP	H	BB	SO	ShO	W	L	SV	AB	H	HR	BA	PO	A	E	DP	TC/G	FA
1987	PIT	N	1	5	.167	4.66	29	0	0	36.2	34	10	31	0	1	5	3	1	1	0	1.000	1	5	0	0	0.2	1.000
1989	MON	N	0	0	—	1.93	4	0	0	4.2	5	5	2	0	0	0	0	0	0	0	—	0	0	0	0	0.0	—
1990			0	0	—	9.00	1	0	0	1	2	4	0	0	0	0	0	0	0	0	—	0	1	0	0	1.0	1.000
3 yrs.			1	5	.167	4.46	34	0	0	42.1	41	19	33	0	1	5	3	1	1	0	1.000	1	6	0	0	0.2	1.000

Tom Gilles

GILLES, THOMAS BRADFORD
B. July 2, 1962, Peoria, Ill.
BR TR 6′ 1″ 185 lbs.

Year	Team		W	L	%	ERA	G	GS	CG	IP	H	BB	SO	ShO	W	L	SV	AB	H	HR	BA	PO	A	E	DP	TC/G	FA
1990	TOR	A	1	0	1.000	6.75	2	0	0	1.1	2	0	1	0	1	0	0	0	0	0	—	0	1	0	0	0.5	1.000

Dan Gladden

GLADDEN, CLINTON DANIEL III
B. July 7, 1957, San Jose, Calif.
BR TR 5′ 11″ 175 lbs.

Year	Team		W	L	%	ERA	G	GS	CG	IP	H	BB	SO	ShO	W	L	SV	AB	H	HR	BA	PO	A	E	DP	TC/G	FA
1988	MIN	A	0	0	—	0.00	1	0	0	1	0	0	0	0	0	0	0	576	155	11	.269	0	0	0	0	0.0	—
1989			0	0	—	9.00	1	0	0	1	2	1	0	0	0	0	0	461	136	8	.295	0	0	0	0	0.0	—
2 yrs.			0	0	—	4.50	2	0	0	2	2	1	0	0	0	0	0	*				0	0	0	0	0.0	—

Tom Glavine

GLAVINE, THOMAS MICHAEL
B. Mar. 25, 1966, Concord, Mass.
BL TL 6′ 175 lbs.

	W	L	%	ERA	G	GS	CG	IP	H	BB	SO	ShO	W	L	SV
April	1	2	.333	3.62	4	4	0	27.1	29	3	11	0	0	0	0
May	1	1	.500	2.72	6	6	0	39.2	32	18	33	0	0	0	0
June	2	2	.500	5.67	5	5	1	33.1	43	14	24	0	0	0	0
July	2	1	.667	4.32	5	5	0	33.1	34	12	13	0	0	0	0
Aug	0	5	.000	6.30	7	7	0	40	58	14	24	0	0	0	0
Sept/Oct	4	1	.800	3.10	6	6	0	40.2	36	17	24	0	0	0	0
Day	1	3	.250	5.02	9	9	0	57.1	71	23	35	0	0	0	0
Night	9	9	.500	4.01	24	24	1	157	161	55	94	0	0	0	0
vs. Left	—	—	—	—	—	—	—	—	34	20	34	—	—	—	—
vs. Right	—	—	—	—	—	—	—	—	198	58	95	—	—	—	—
On Grass	5	9	.357	4.94	22	22	0	140.1	166	51	93	0	0	0	0
On Turf	5	3	.625	3.04	11	11	1	74	66	27	36	0	0	0	0
Home	5	8	.385	4.86	16	16	0	103.2	115	31	65	0	0	0	0
Road	5	4	.556	3.74	17	17	1	110.2	117	47	64	0	0	0	0
Division Rivals															
vs. CIN	4	1	.800	3.05	5	5	1	38.1	34	11	27	0	0	0	0
vs. HOU	0	2	.000	5.11	2	2	0	12.1	14	1	4	0	0	0	0
vs. LA	0	2	.000	10.29	3	3	0	14	27	12	14	0	0	0	0
vs. SD	1	2	.333	4.50	4	4	0	24	29	13	12	0	0	0	0
vs. SF	1	1	.500	4.91	3	3	0	18.1	23	8	12	0	0	0	0

STARTING PITCHER

WINS — NL AVG

ERA — NL AVG

SO/9 — NL AVG

RATIO — NL AVG

Year	Team		W	L	%	ERA	G	GS	CG	IP	H	BB	SO	ShO	W	L	SV	AB	H	HR	BA	PO	A	E	DP	TC/G	FA
1987	ATL	N	2	4	.333	5.54	9	9	0	50.1	55	33	20	0	0	0	0	16	2	0	.125	1	13	1	0	1.7	.933
1988			7	17	.292	4.56	34	34	1	195.1	201	63	84	0	0	0	0	60	11	0	.183	12	41	4	3	1.7	.930
1989			14	8	.636	3.68	29	29	6	186	172	40	90	4	0	0	0	67	10	0	.149	7	37	4	4	1.7	.917
1990			10	12	.455	4.28	33	33	1	214.1	232	78	129	0	0	0	0	62	7	0	.113	19	33	1	1	1.6	.981
4 yrs.			33	41	.446	4.29	105	105	8	646	660	214	323	4	0	0	0	205	30	0	.146	39	124	10	8	1.6	.942

Year	Team	W	L	%	ERA	G	GS	CG	IP	H	BB	SO	ShO	W	L	SV	AB	H	HR	BA	PO	A	E	DP	TC/G	FA

Jerry Don Gleaton GLEATON, JERRY DON
B. Sept. 14, 1957, Brownwood, Tex.
BL TL 6′ 3″ 205 lbs.

Year	Team	W	L	%	ERA	G	GS	CG	IP	H	BB	SO	ShO	W	L	SV	AB	H	HR	BA	PO	A	E	DP	TC/G	FA
April		0	1	.000	5.14	8	0	0	7	6	2	2	0	0	1	0										
May		0	0	—	1.98	10	0	0	13.2	8	4	11	0	0	0	1										
June		1	0	1.000	2.84	10	0	0	19	12	6	16	0	1	0	0										
July		0	1	.000	3.63	11	0	0	17.1	11	6	7	0	0	1	3										
Aug		0	1	.000	3.38	10	0	0	16	17	4	11	0	0	1	5										
Sept/Oct		0	0	—	0.93	8	0	0	9.2	8	3	9	0	0	1	4										
Day		0	1	.000	4.26	20	0	0	25.1	20	5	18	0	0	1	4										
Night		1	2	.333	2.35	37	0	0	57.1	42	20	38	0	1	2	9										
vs. Left		—	—	—	—	—	—	—		22	3	13	—	—	—	—										
vs. Right		—	—	—	—	—	—	—		40	22	43	—	—	—	—										
On Grass		1	3	.250	2.86	48	0	0	72.1	52	22	51	0	1	3	11										
On Turf		0	0	—	3.48	9	0	0	10.1	10	3	5	0	0	0	2										
Home		1	2	.333	3.73	30	0	0	41	25	14	31	0	1	2	5										
Road		0	1	.000	2.16	27	0	0	41.2	37	11	25	0	0	1	8										
Division Rivals																										
vs. BAL		0	0	—	0.00	8	0	0	7.1	3	2	3	0	0	0	2										
vs. BOS		0	1	.000	5.40	4	0	0	5	7	1	3	0	0	1	2										
vs. CLE		0	0	—	3.86	2	0	0	4.2	4	0	3	0	0	0	1										
vs. MIL		0	1	.000	6.75	4	0	0	2.2	1	2	0	0	0	1	0										
vs. NY		0	0	—	2.84	3	0	0	6.1	6	3	3	0	0	0	1										
vs. TOR		0	0	—	2.45	6	0	0	7.1	5	2	8	0	0	0	1										
1979	TEX A	0	1	.000	6.30	5	2	0	10	15	2	2	0	0	0	0	0	0	0	—	0	4	0	0	0.8	1.000
1980		0	0	—	2.57	5	0	0	7	5	4	2	0	0	0	0	0	0	0	—	1	2	0	0	0.6	1.000
1981	SEA A	4	7	.364	4.76	20	13	1	85	88	38	31	0	0	0	0	0	0	0	—	5	12	1	0	0.9	.944
1982		0	0	—	13.50	3	0	0	4.2	7	2	1	0	0	0	0	0	0	0	—	1	0	0	0	0.3	1.000
1984	CHI A	1	2	.333	3.44	11	1	0	18.1	20	6	4	0	1	1	2	0	0	0	—	1	1	1	0	0.3	.667
1985		1	0	1.000	5.76	31	0	0	29.2	37	13	22	0	1	0	1	0	0	0	—	0	4	0	0	0.1	1.000
1987	KC A	4	4	.500	4.26	48	0	0	50.2	38	28	44	0	4	4	5	0	0	0	—	2	12	1	1	0.3	.933
1988		0	4	.000	3.55	42	0	0	38	33	17	29	0	0	4	3	0	0	0	—	3	3	0	0	0.1	1.000
1989		0	0	—	5.65	15	0	0	14.1	20	6	9	0	0	0	0	0	0	0	—	0	2	0	0	0.1	1.000
1990	DET A	1	3	.250	2.94	57	0	0	82.2	62	25	56	0	1	3	13	0	0	0	—	1	11	1	0	0.2	.923
10 yrs.		11	21	.344	4.28	237	16	1	340.1	325	141	200	0	7	12	24	0	0	0	—	14	51	4	1	0.3	.942

RELIEF PITCHER

WINS — AL AVG
ERA — AL AVG
SAVES — AL AVG
RATIO — AL AVG

Dwight Gooden GOODEN, DWIGHT EUGENE (Doc, Dr. K)
B. Nov. 16, 1964, Tampa, Fla.
BR TR 6′ 2″ 190 lbs.

Year	Team	W	L	%	ERA	G	GS	CG	IP	H	BB	SO	ShO	W	L	SV	AB	H	HR	BA	PO	A	E	DP	TC/G	FA
April		1	2	.333	3.82	5	5	0	30.2	27	10	32	0	0	0	0										
May		2	2	.500	4.59	5	5	0	33.1	32	12	38	0	0	0	0										
June		4	1	.800	4.15	6	6	1	43.1	46	13	33	1	0	0	0										
July		4	0	1.000	2.45	5	5	0	36.2	34	10	32	0	0	0	0										
Aug		3	1	.750	5.50	6	6	0	37.2	40	11	39	0	0	0	0										
Sept/Oct		5	1	.833	2.82	7	7	1	51	50	14	49	0	0	0	0										
Day		5	5	.500	4.40	13	13	0	86	89	26	80	0	0	0	0										
Night		14	2	.875	3.50	21	21	2	146.2	140	44	143	1	0	0	0										
vs. Left		—	—	—	—	—	—	—		135	44	132	—	—	—	—										
vs. Right		—	—	—	—	—	—	—		94	26	91	—	—	—	—										
On Grass		14	3	.824	3.70	24	24	1	167.2	155	51	160	1	0	0	0										
On Turf		5	4	.556	4.15	10	10	1	65	74	19	63	0	0	0	0										
Home		9	3	.750	3.56	18	18	1	126.1	117	31	119	1	0	0	0										
Road		10	4	.714	4.15	16	16	1	106.1	112	39	104	0	0	0	0										
Division Rivals																										
vs. CHI		4	0	1.000	2.70	4	4	0	30	27	8	31	0	0	0	0										
vs. MON		0	1	.000	7.20	2	2	0	10	15	5	7	0	0	0	0										
vs. PHI		2	1	.667	2.79	4	4	2	29	25	7	22	0	0	0	0										
vs. PIT		2	2	.500	6.16	5	5	0	30.2	40	10	29	0	0	0	0										
vs. STL		2	1	.667	2.25	3	3	0	20	19	3	16	0	0	0	0										
1984	NY N	17	9	.654	2.60	31	31	7	218	161	73	**276**	3	0	0	0	70	14	0	.200	21	22	2	0	1.5	.956
1985		**24**	4	.857	**1.53**	35	35	**16**	**276.2**	198	69	268	8	0	0	0	93	21	1	.226	25	38	2	6	1.9	.969
1986		17	6	.739	2.84	33	33	12	250	197	80	200	2	0	0	0	81	7	0	.086	36	36	2	5	2.2	.973
1987		15	7	.682	3.21	25	25	7	179.2	162	53	148	3	0	0	0	64	14	0	.219	15	22	3	3	1.6	.925
1988		18	9	.667	3.19	34	34	10	248.1	242	57	175	3	0	0	0	90	16	1	.178	27	56	5	3	2.6	.943

STARTING PITCHER

WINS — NL AVG
ERA — NL AVG
SO/9 — NL AVG
RATIO — NL AVG

Year	Team	W	L	%	ERA	G	GS	CG	IP	H	BB	SO	ShO	RELIEF PITCHING W	L	SV	BATTING AB	H	HR	BA	PO	A	E	DP	TC/G	FA

Dwight Gooden *Continued*

Year	Team	W	L	%	ERA	G	GS	CG	IP	H	BB	SO	ShO	W	L	SV	AB	H	HR	BA	PO	A	E	DP	TC/G	FA
1989		9	4	.692	2.89	19	17	0	118.1	93	47	101	0	0	0	1	40	8	0	.200	8	16	3	0	1.4	.889
1990		19	7	.731	3.83	34	34	2	232.2	229	70	223	1	0	0	0	75	14	1	.187	15	35	4	5	1.6	.926
7 yrs.		119	46	.721	2.82	211	209	54	1523.2	1282	449	1391	20	0	0	1	513	94	3	.183	147	225	21	22	1.9	.947

LEAGUE CHAMPIONSHIP SERIES

Year	Team	W	L	%	ERA	G	GS	CG	IP	H	BB	SO	ShO	W	L	SV	AB	H	HR	BA	PO	A	E	DP	TC/G	FA
1986	NY N	0	1	.000	1.06	2	2	0	17	16	5	9	0	0	0	0	5	0	0	.000	3	2	0	0	2.5	1.000
1988		0	0	—	2.95	3	2	0	18.1	10	8	20	0	0	0	0	5	1	0	.200	1	3	0	0	1.3	1.000
2 yrs.		0	1	.000	2.04	5	4	0	35.1	26	13	29	0	0	0	0	10	1	0	.100	4	5	0	0	1.8	1.000

WORLD SERIES

Year	Team	W	L	%	ERA	G	GS	CG	IP	H	BB	SO	ShO	W	L	SV	AB	H	HR	BA	PO	A	E	DP	TC/G	FA
1986	NY N	0	2	.000	8.00	2	2	0	9	17	4	9	0	0	0	0	2	1	0	.500	1	2	0	0	1.5	1.000

Tom Gordon

GORDON, THOMAS (Flash)
B. Nov. 18, 1967, Sebring, Fla.
BR TR 5′ 9″ 160 lbs.

		W	L	%	ERA	G	GS	CG	IP	H	BB	SO	ShO	W	L	SV	AB	H	HR	BA	PO	A	E	DP	TC/G	FA
April		1	0	1.000	1.59	3	3	0	17	15	6	25	0	0	0	0										
May		1	3	.250	4.41	6	6	1	32.2	29	25	30	0	0	0	0										
June		3	1	.750	2.78	5	5	0	32.1	27	12	32	0	0	0	0										
July		1	3	.250	4.96	6	6	0	32.2	45	22	24	0	0	0	0										
Aug		3	2	.600	3.00	6	6	4	45	40	15	37	0	0	0	0										
Sept/Oct		3	2	.600	4.79	6	6	1	35.2	36	19	27	1	0	0	0										
Day		3	2	.600	2.57	7	7	2	42	42	16	34	1	0	0	0										
Night		9	9	.500	4.05	25	25	4	153.1	150	83	141	0	0	0	0										
vs. Left		—	—	—	—	—	—	—	—	92	55	75	—	—	—	—										
vs. Right		—	—	—	—	—	—	—	—	100	44	100	—	—	—	—										
On Grass		1	5	.167	5.25	11	11	1	60	75	32	51	0	0	0	0										
On Turf		11	6	.647	3.06	21	21	5	135.1	117	67	124	1	0	0	0										
Home		7	5	.583	3.10	15	15	4	93	83	45	90	0	0	0	0										
Road		5	6	.455	4.31	17	17	2	102.1	109	54	85	1	0	0	0										
Division Rivals																										
vs. CAL		0	1	.000	2.16	3	3	0	16.2	15	4	17	0	0	0	0										
vs. CHI		1	0	1.000	1.20	2	2	1	15	9	6	14	0	0	0	0										
vs. MIN		3	1	.750	4.62	4	4	1	25.1	25	13	24	0	0	0	0										
vs. OAK		1	1	.500	3.86	3	3	0	18.2	21	14	18	0	0	0	0										
vs. SEA		2	0	1.000	0.53	2	2	1	17	9	8	10	1	0	0	0										
vs. TEX		0	1	.000	5.63	3	3	0	16	20	10	17	0	0	0	0										
1988	KC A	0	2	.000	5.17	5	2	0	15.2	16	7	18	0	0	0	0	0	0	0	—	2	2	0	0	0.8	1.000
1989		17	9	.654	3.64	49	16	1	163	122	86	153	1	10	2	1	0	0	0	—	15	26	0	7	0.8	1.000
1990		12	11	.522	3.73	32	32	6	195.1	192	99	175	1	0	0	0	0	0	0	—	17	24	1	1	1.3	.976
3 yrs.		29	22	.569	3.75	86	50	7	374	330	192	346	2	10	2	1	0	0	0	—	34	52	1	8	1.0	.989

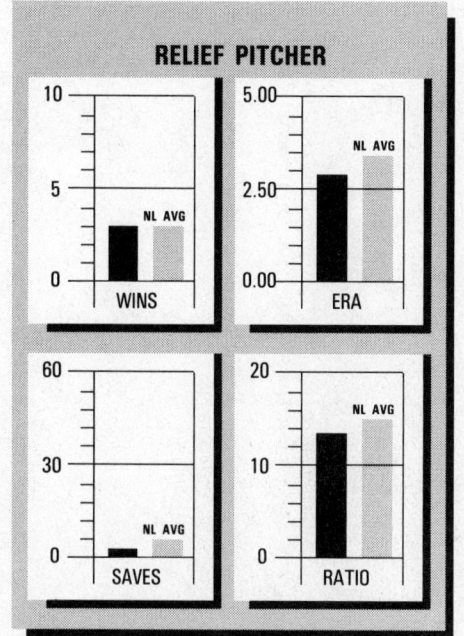

STARTING PITCHER — WINS (AL AVG), ERA (AL AVG), SO/9 (AL AVG), RATIO (AL AVG)

Jim Gott

GOTT, JAMES WILLIAM
B. Aug. 3, 1959, Hollywood, Calif.
BR TR 6′ 4″ 200 lbs.

		W	L	%	ERA	G	GS	CG	IP	H	BB	SO	ShO	W	L	SV	AB	H	HR	BA	PO	A	E	DP	TC/G	FA
April		—	—	—	—	0	0	—	0	0	0	0	—	0	0	0										
May		0	0	—	10.80	2	0	0	1.2	3	4	0	0	0	0	0										
June		0	2	.000	5.68	11	0	0	12.2	18	7	12	0	0	2	0										
July		0	0	—	0.73	11	0	0	12.1	9	9	4	0	0	0	0										
Aug		2	1	.667	0.49	13	0	0	18.1	9	6	13	0	2	1	3										
Sept/Oct		1	2	.333	4.24	13	0	0	17	20	12	15	0	1	2	0										
Day		0	0	—	1.69	10	0	0	10.2	7	5	12	0	0	0	1										
Night		3	5	.375	3.16	40	0	0	51.1	52	29	32	0	3	5	2										
vs. Left		—	—	—	—	—	—	—	—	38	20	22	—	—	—	—										
vs. Right		—	—	—	—	—	—	—	—	21	14	22	—	—	—	—										
On Grass		2	5	.286	2.88	38	0	0	50	47	30	35	0	2	5	3										
On Turf		1	0	1.000	3.00	12	0	0	12	12	4	9	0	1	0	0										
Home		2	3	.400	2.88	26	0	0	34.1	26	21	25	0	2	3	1										
Road		1	2	.333	2.93	24	0	0	27.2	33	13	19	0	1	2	2										
Division Rivals																										
vs. ATL		0	0	—	2.92	9	0	0	12.1	14	6	9	0	0	0	2										
vs. CIN		0	0	—	8.53	4	0	0	6.1	12	1	5	0	0	0	0										
vs. HOU		1	1	.500	2.45	7	0	0	7.1	4	4	8	0	1	1	0										
vs. SD		0	1	.000	4.15	4	0	0	4.1	5	4	1	0	0	1	0										
vs. SF		0	1	.000	1.42	5	0	0	6.1	4	6	5	0	0	1	0										

RELIEF PITCHER — WINS (NL AVG), ERA (NL AVG), SAVES (NL AVG), RATIO (NL AVG)

Year	Team	W	L	%	ERA	G	GS	CG	IP	H	BB	SO	ShO	RELIEF PITCHING			BATTING				PO	A	E	DP	TC/G	FA
														W	L	SV	AB	H	HR	BA						

Jim Gott *Continued*

Year	Team	W	L	%	ERA	G	GS	CG	IP	H	BB	SO	ShO	W	L	SV	AB	H	HR	BA	PO	A	E	DP	TC/G	FA
1982	TOR A	5	10	.333	4.43	30	23	1	136	134	66	82	1	0	0	0	0	0	0	—	6	18	1	2	0.8	.960
1983		9	14	.391	4.74	34	30	6	176.2	195	68	121	1	0	1	0	0	0	0	—	9	20	1	2	0.9	.967
1984		7	6	.538	4.02	35	12	1	109.2	93	49	73	1	2	1	2	0	0	0	—	6	9	1	0	0.5	.938
1985	SF N	7	10	.412	3.88	26	26	2	148.1	144	51	78	0	0	0	0	51	10	3	.196	9	28	0	0	1.4	1.000
1986		0	0	—	7.62	9	2	0	13	16	13	9	0	0	0	1	3	0	0	.000	0	2	0	0	0.2	1.000
1987	2 teams				SF N (30G 1-0)			PIT N (25G 0-2)																		
"	total	1	2	.333	3.41	55	3	0	87	81	40	90	0	1	2	13	11	1	1	.091	5	10	1	0	0.3	.938
1988	PIT N	6	6	.500	3.49	67	0	0	77.1	68	22	76	0	6	6	34	1	0	0	.000	4	8	0	0	0.2	1.000
1989		0	0	—	0.00	1	0	0	0.2	1	1	1	0	0	0	0	0	0	0	—	0	0	0	0	0.0	—
1990	LA N	3	5	.375	2.90	50	0	0	62	59	34	44	0	3	5	3	1	0	0	.000	6	5	0	0	0.2	1.000
9 yrs.		38	53	.418	4.07	307	96	10	810.2	791	344	574	3	12	15	53	67	11	4	.164	45	100	4	4	0.5	.973

Mauro Gozzo

GOZZO, MAURO PAUL (Goose)
B. Mar. 7, 1966, New Britain, Conn.
BR TR 6′ 2″ 210 lbs.

Year	Team	W	L	%	ERA	G	GS	CG	IP	H	BB	SO	ShO	W	L	SV	AB	H	HR	BA	PO	A	E	DP	TC/G	FA
1989	TOR A	4	1	.800	4.83	9	3	0	31.2	35	9	10	0	1	1	0	0	0	0	—	3	3	0	0	0.7	1.000
1990	CLE A	0	0	—	0.00	2	0	0	3	2	2	2	0	0	0	0	0	0	0	—	0	0	0	0	0.0	—
2 yrs.		4	1	.800	4.41	11	3	0	34.2	37	11	12	0	1	1	0	0	0	0	—	3	3	0	0	0.5	1.000

Joe Grahe

GRAHE, JOSEPH MILTON
B. Aug. 14, 1967, West Palm Beach, Fla.
BR TR 6′ 195 lbs.

Year	Team	W	L	%	ERA	G	GS	CG	IP	H	BB	SO	ShO	W	L	SV	AB	H	HR	BA	PO	A	E	DP	TC/G	FA
1990	CAL A	3	4	.429	4.98	8	8	0	43.1	51	23	25	0	0	0	0	0	0	0	—	2	11	0	2	1.6	1.000

Mark Grant

GRANT, MARK ANDREW
B. Oct. 24, 1963, Aurora, Ill.
BR TR 6′ 2″ 205 lbs.

	W	L	%	ERA	G	GS	CG	IP	H	BB	SO	ShO	W	L	SV	AB	H	HR	BA	PO	A	E	DP	TC/G	FA
April	0	0	—	8.76	8	0	0	12.1	17	8	9	0	0	0	0										
May	1	0	1.000	2.61	7	0	0	10.1	13	2	4	0	1	0	0										
June	0	1	.000	3.09	7	0	0	11.2	14	4	11	0	0	1	0										
July	0	1	.000	9.00	13	0	0	15	27	11	15	0	0	1	0										
Aug	0	0	—	5.17	11	1	0	15.2	18	9	11	0	0	1	0										
Sept/Oct	1	1	.500	1.71	13	0	0	26.1	19	3	19	0	0	1	3										
Day	1	1	.500	6.12	15	0	0	25	27	13	23	0	1	1	0										
Night	1	2	.333	4.21	44	1	0	66.1	81	24	46	0	1	2	3										
vs. Left	—	—	—	—	—	—	—	—	60	21	42		—	—	—										
vs. Right	—	—	—	—	—	—	—	—	48	16	27		—	—	—										
On Grass	1	2	.333	5.40	45	1	0	68.1	81	30	57	0	1	2	3										
On Turf	1	1	.500	2.74	14	0	0	23	27	7	12	0	1	1	0										
Home	1	0	1.000	5.70	31	1	0	47.1	54	24	41	0	1	0	2										
Road	1	3	.250	3.68	28	0	0	44	54	13	28	0	1	3	1										
Division Rivals																									
vs. CIN	1	0	1.000	1.50	5	0	0	12	9	2	9	0	1	0	0										
vs. HOU	0	1	.000	4.66	7	0	0	9.2	11	5	7	0	0	1	0										
vs. LA	0	1	.000	6.43	9	1	0	14	16	10	9	0	0	1	0										
vs. SD	0	0	—	3.38	4	0	0	8	7	2	4	0	0	0	1										
vs. SF	0	1	.000	4.50	8	0	0	14	16	4	12	0	0	1	2										

RELIEF PITCHER

(Bar charts: WINS, ERA, SAVES, RATIO — each compared to NL AVG)

Year	Team	W	L	%	ERA	G	GS	CG	IP	H	BB	SO	ShO	W	L	SV	AB	H	HR	BA	PO	A	E	DP	TC/G	FA
1984	SF N	1	4	.200	6.37	11	10	0	53.2	56	19	32	0	0	0	1	17	0	0	.000	6	6	1	0	1.2	.923
1986		0	1	.000	3.60	4	1	0	10	6	5	5	0	0	0	0	1	0	0	.000	0	1	0	1	0.3	1.000
1987	2 teams				SF N (16G 1-2)			SD N (17G 6-7)																		
"	total	7	9	.438	4.24	33	25	2	163.1	170	73	90	1	1	1	0	44	4	0	.091	10	21	4	0	1.1	.886
1988	SD N	2	8	.200	3.69	33	11	0	97.2	97	36	61	0	1	3	0	16	0	0	.000	4	16	0	1	0.6	1.000
1989		8	2	.800	3.33	50	0	0	116.1	105	32	69	0	8	2	2	20	1	0	.050	9	14	1	1	0.5	.958
1990	2 teams				SD N (26G 1-1)			ATL N (33G 1-2)																		
"	total	2	3	.400	4.73	59	1	0	91.1	108	37	69	0	2	3	2	6	2	0	.333	6	14	1	1	0.4	.952
6 yrs.		20	27	.426	4.23	190	48	2	532.1	542	202	326	1	12	9	7	104	7	0	.067	35	72	7	4	0.6	.939

Year	Team	W	L	%	ERA	G	GS	CG	IP	H	BB	SO	ShO	W	L	SV	AB	H	HR	BA	PO	A	E	DP	TC/G	FA

Jeff Gray

GRAY, JEFFREY EDWARD
B. Apr. 10, 1963, Richmond, Va.
BR TR 6′ 1″ 175 lbs.

Year	Team	W	L	%	ERA	G	GS	CG	IP	H	BB	SO	ShO	W	L	SV	AB	H	HR	BA	PO	A	E	DP	TC/G	FA
April		—	—	—	—	0	—	—	0	0	0	0	—	0	0	0										
May		—	—	—	—	0	—	—	0	0	0	0	—	0	0	0										
June		1	1	.500	3.65	9	0	0	12.1	9	2	11	0	1	1	2										
July		0	2	.000	7.94	9	0	0	11.1	21	4	7	0	0	2	0										
Aug		0	0	—	0.60	12	0	0	15	6	4	17	0	0	0	6										
Sept/Oct		1	1	.500	6.75	11	0	0	12	17	5	15	0	1	1	1										
Day		1	1	.500	2.95	15	0	0	18.1	14	6	19	0	1	1	3										
Night		1	3	.250	5.29	26	0	0	32.1	39	9	31	0	1	3	6										
vs. Left		—	—	—	—	—	—	—		27	8	26	—	—	—	—										
vs. Right		—	—	—	—	—	—	—		26	7	24	—	—	—	—										
On Grass		2	4	.333	3.64	33	0	0	42	45	11	37	0	2	4	7										
On Turf		0	0	—	8.31	8	0	0	8.2	8	4	13	0	0	0	2										
Home		2	2	.500	4.01	20	0	0	24.2	26	4	20	0	2	2	6										
Road		0	2	.000	4.85	21	0	0	26	27	11	30	0	0	2	3										
Division Rivals																										
vs. BAL		1	0	1.000	0.00	5	0	0	5.1	3	1	8	0	1	0	2										
vs. CLE		0	0	—	3.00	3	0	0	3	1	3	5	0	0	0	1										
vs. DET		0	0	—	3.00	3	0	0	3	5	0	0	0	0	0	0										
vs. MIL		0	0	—	6.75	2	0	0	4	7	1	1	0	0	0	1										
vs. NY		0	1	.000	10.13	3	0	0	2.2	3	3	6	0	0	1	1										
vs. TOR		0	0	—	5.63	8	0	0	8	9	1	6	0	0	0	3										
1988	CIN N	0	0	—	3.86	5	0	0	9.1	12	4	5	0	0	0	0	1	0	0	.000	1	3	0	0	0.8	1.000
1990	BOS A	2	4	.333	4.44	41	0	0	50.2	53	15	50	0	2	4	9	0	0	0	—	2	5	0	1	0.2	1.000
2 yrs.		2	4	.333	4.35	46	0	0	60	65	19	55	0	2	4	9	1	0	0	.000	3	8	0	1	0.2	1.000

LEAGUE CHAMPIONSHIP SERIES

Year	Team	W	L	%	ERA	G	GS	CG	IP	H	BB	SO	ShO	W	L	SV	AB	H	HR	BA	PO	A	E	DP	TC/G	FA
1990	BOS A	0	0	—	2.70	2	0	0	3.1	4	1	2	0	0	0	0	0	0	0	—	0	0	1	0	0.5	.000

Tommy Greene

GREENE, IRA THOMAS
B. Apr. 6, 1967, Lumberton, N. C.
BR TR 6′ 5″ 225 lbs.

Year	Team	W	L	%	ERA	G	GS	CG	IP	H	BB	SO	ShO	W	L	SV	AB	H	HR	BA	PO	A	E	DP	TC/G	FA
1989	ATL N	1	2	.333	4.10	4	4	1	26.1	22	6	17	1	0	0	0	10	1	0	.100	2	2	0	0	1.0	1.000
1990	2 teams	ATL N	(5G 1 - 0)		PHI N	(10G 2 - 3)																				
"	total	3	3	.500	5.08	15	9	0	51.1	50	26	21	0	0	0	0	12	2	0	.167	3	6	1	0	0.7	.900
2 yrs.		4	5	.444	4.75	19	13	1	77.2	72	32	38	1	0	0	0	22	3	0	.136	5	8	1	0	0.7	.929

Jason Grimsley

GRIMSLEY, JASON ALAN
B. Aug. 7, 1967, Cleveland, Tex.
BR TR 6′ 3″ 180 lbs.

Year	Team	W	L	%	ERA	G	GS	CG	IP	H	BB	SO	ShO	W	L	SV	AB	H	HR	BA	PO	A	E	DP	TC/G	FA
1989	PHI N	1	3	.250	5.89	4	4	0	18.1	19	19	7	0	0	0	0	5	0	0	.000	1	4	1	1	1.5	.833
1990		3	2	.600	3.30	11	11	0	57.1	47	43	41	0	0	0	0	16	3	0	.188	13	8	1	2	2.0	.955
2 yrs.		4	5	.444	3.92	15	15	0	75.2	66	62	48	0	0	0	0	21	3	0	.143	14	12	2	3	1.9	.929

Kevin Gross

GROSS, KEVIN FRANK
B. June 8, 1961, Downey, Calif.
BR TR 6′ 5″ 200 lbs.

Year	Team	W	L	%	ERA	G	GS	CG	IP	H	BB	SO	ShO	W	L	SV	AB	H	HR	BA	PO	A	E	DP	TC/G	FA
April		2	1	.667	2.84	4	4	0	25.1	23	17	13	0	0	0	0										
May		4	2	.667	4.74	6	5	0	38	36	10	25	0	1	0	0										
June		2	2	.500	3.07	6	6	2	41	39	12	34	1	0	0	0										
July		0	3	.000	6.17	3	3	0	11.2	9	9	6	0	0	0	0										
Aug		0	2	.000	7.56	5	5	0	25	41	10	18	0	0	0	0										
Sept/Oct		1	2	.333	4.84	7	3	0	22.1	23	7	15	0	0	0	0										
Day		3	3	.500	3.52	11	7	0	53.2	53	16	34	0	1	0	0										
Night		6	9	.400	5.09	20	19	2	109.2	118	49	77	1	0	0	0										
vs. Left		—	—	—	—	—	—	—		109	48	73	—	—	—	—										
vs. Right		—	—	—	—	—	—	—		62	17	38	—	—	—	—										

Year	Team	W	L	%	ERA	G	GS	CG	IP	H	BB	SO	ShO	W	L	SV	AB	H	HR	BA	PO	A	E	DP	TC/G	FA

Kevin Gross *Continued*

Year	Team	W	L	%	ERA	G	GS	CG	IP	H	BB	SO	ShO	W	L	SV	AB	H	HR	BA	PO	A	E	DP	TC/G	FA
On Grass		2	6	.250	6.57	9	8	1	49.1	61	19	32	0	1	0	0										
On Turf		7	6	.538	3.71	22	18	1	114	110	46	79	1	0	0	0										
Home		3	5	.375	4.43	13	11	0	69	72	27	40	0	0	0	0										
Road		6	7	.462	4.67	18	15	2	94.1	99	38	71	1	1	0	0										
Division Rivals																										
vs. CHI		0	4	.000	11.12	4	4	0	17	28	10	7	0	0	0	0										
vs. NY		0	2	.000	4.35	3	3	1	20.2	19	8	11	0	0	0	0										
vs. PHI		1	1	.500	2.12	3	2	1	17	10	12	15	1	0	0	0										
vs. PIT		1	1	.500	4.71	4	4	0	21	25	7	19	0	0	0	0										
vs. STL		1	0	1.000	1.84	4	2	0	14.2	15	2	11	0	0	0	0										
1983	PHI N	4	6	.400	3.56	17	17	1	96	100	35	66	1	0	0	0	33	3	0	.091	11	13	0	0	1.4	1.000
1984		8	5	.615	4.12	44	14	1	129	140	44	84	0	4	0	1	30	2	0	.067	9	22	2	3	0.8	.939
1985		15	13	.536	3.41	38	31	6	205.2	194	81	151	2	1	0	2	65	9	1	.138	18	34	3	0	1.4	.945
1986		12	12	.500	4.02	37	36	7	241.2	240	94	154	2	0	0	0	80	15	1	.188	25	28	2	2	1.5	.964
1987		9	16	.360	4.35	34	33	3	200.2	205	87	110	1	1	0	0	63	12	1	.190	13	23	3	1	1.1	.923
1988		12	14	.462	3.69	33	33	5	231.2	209	**89**	162	1	0	0	0	75	13	0	.173	13	34	2	2	1.5	.959
1989	MON N	11	12	.478	4.38	31	31	4	201.1	188	88	158	3	0	0	0	64	9	0	.141	15	25	2	1	1.4	.952
1990		9	12	.429	4.57	31	26	2	163.1	171	65	111	1	1	0	0	50	10	1	.200	6	13	1	0	0.6	.950
8 yrs.		80	90	.471	4.02	265	221	29	1469.1	1447	583	996	11	7	2	1	460	73	4	.159	110	192	15	9	1.2	.953

Kip Gross

GROSS, KIP LEE
B. Aug. 24, 1964, Scottsbluff, Neb.
BR TR 6′ 2″ 195 lbs.

Year	Team	W	L	%	ERA	G	GS	CG	IP	H	BB	SO	ShO	W	L	SV	AB	H	HR	BA	PO	A	E	DP	TC/G	FA
1990	CIN N	0	0	—	4.26	5	0	0	6.1	6	2	3	0	0	0	0	0	0	0	—	0	0	0	0	0.0	—

Cecilio Guante

GUANTE, CECILIO
Born Cecilio Guante y Magallane.
B. Feb. 1, 1960, Villa Mella, Dominican Republic
BR TR 6′ 3″ 200 lbs.

Year	Team	W	L	%	ERA	G	GS	CG	IP	H	BB	SO	ShO	W	L	SV	AB	H	HR	BA	PO	A	E	DP	TC/G	FA
April		0	0	—	1.93	7	0	0	9.1	4	1	10	0	0	0	0										
May		2	2	.500	4.63	8	0	0	11.2	7	6	6	0	2	2	0										
June		0	0	—	4.02	7	0	0	15.2	16	7	9	0	0	0	0										
July		0	1	.000	9.90	4	1	0	10	11	4	5	0	0	0	0										
Aug		—	—	—	—	0	—	—	0	0	0	0	—	0	0	0										
Sept/Oct		—	—	—	—	0	—	—	0	0	0	0	—	0	0	0										
Day		1	2	.333	4.66	9	1	0	19.1	11	6	13	0	1	1	0										
Night		1	1	.500	5.27	17	0	0	27.1	27	12	17	0	1	1	0										
vs. Left		—	—	—	—	—	—	—	—	13	8	7	—	—	—	—										
vs. Right		—	—	—	—	—	—	—	—	25	10	23	—	—	—	—										
On Grass		2	3	.400	5.26	23	1	0	39.1	34	16	24	0	2	2	0										
On Turf		0	0	—	3.68	3	0	0	7.1	4	2	6	0	0	0	0										
Home		1	3	.250	5.70	17	1	0	30	25	13	15	0	1	2	0										
Road		1	0	1.000	3.78	9	0	0	16.2	13	5	15	0	1	0	0										
Division Rivals																										
vs. BAL		0	0	—	0.00	1	0	0	0.2	2	0	0	0	0	0	0										
vs. BOS		0	0	—	7.20	2	0	0	5	5	3	2	0	0	0	0										
vs. DET		0	0	—	0.00	1	0	0	4	0	2	2	0	0	0	0										
vs. MIL		0	0	—	4.91	2	0	0	3.2	8	2	4	0	0	0	0										
vs. NY		0	1	.000	6.35	3	1	0	5.2	6	1	3	0	0	0	0										
vs. TOR		0	0	—	6.00	2	0	0	3	3	2	3	0	0	0	0										
1982	PIT N	0	0	—	3.33	10	0	0	27	28	5	26	0	0	0	0	5	0	0	.000	1	2	0	0	0.3	1.000
1983		2	6	.250	3.32	49	0	0	100.1	90	46	82	0	2	6	9	22	2	0	.091	5	9	2	0	0.3	.875
1984		2	3	.400	2.61	27	0	0	41.1	32	16	30	0	2	3	2	4	0	0	.000	2	3	0	0	0.2	1.000
1985		4	6	.400	2.72	63	0	0	109	84	40	92	0	4	6	5	17	1	0	.059	6	13	1	0	0.3	.950
1986		5	2	.714	3.35	52	0	0	78	65	29	63	0	5	2	4	1	0	0	.000	1	5	1	0	0.1	.857
1987	NY A	3	2	.600	5.73	23	0	0	44	42	20	46	0	3	2	1	0	0	0	—	1	2	1	0	0.2	.750
1988	2 teams	NY A	(56G 5 – 6)			TEX A	(7G 0 – 0)																			
"	total	5	6	.455	2.82	63	0	0	79.2	67	26	65	0	5	6	12	0	0	0	—	2	3	1	0	0.1	.833
1989	TEX A	6	6	.500	3.91	50	0	0	69	66	36	69	0	6	6	2	0	0	0	—	4	5	0	0	0.2	1.000
1990	CLE A	2	3	.400	5.01	26	1	0	46.2	38	18	30	0	2	2	0	0	0	0	—	3	5	0	2	0.3	1.000
9 yrs.		29	34	.460	3.48	363	1	0	595	512	236	503	0	29	33	35	49	3	0	.061	25	47	6	2	0.2	.923

Year	Team	W	L	%	ERA	G	GS	CG	IP	H	BB	SO	ShO	RELIEF PITCHING W	L	SV	BATTING AB	H	HR	BA	PO	A	E	DP	TC/G	FA

Mark Gubicza

GUBICZA, MARK STEVEN
B. Aug. 14, 1962, Philadelphia, Pa.
BR TR 6' 6" 215 lbs.

Period	W	L	%	ERA	G	GS	CG	IP	H	BB	SO	ShO	RW	RL	SV	AB	H	HR	BA	PO	A	E	DP	TC/G	FA
April	1	3	.250	6.38	4	4	1	18.1	22	13	17	0	0	0	0										
May	1	2	.333	4.76	6	6	1	39.2	43	16	24	0	0	0	0										
June	2	2	.500	3.25	6	6	0	36	36	9	30	0	0	0	0										
July	—	—	—	—	0	—	—	0	0	0	0	—	0	0	0										
Aug	—	—	—	—	0	—	—	0	0	0	0	—	0	0	0										
Sept/Oct	—	—	—	—	0	—	—	0	0	0	0	—	0	0	0										
Day	1	2	.333	2.94	5	5	1	33.2	28	11	29	0	0	0	0										
Night	3	5	.375	5.37	11	11	1	60.1	73	27	42	0	0	0	0										
vs. Left	—	—	—	—	—	—	—	—	42	24	30	—	—	—	—										
vs. Right	—	—	—	—	—	—	—	—	59	14	41	—	—	—	—										
On Grass	1	3	.250	3.40	7	7	2	45	44	16	34	0	0	0	0										
On Turf	3	4	.429	5.51	9	9	0	49	57	22	37	0	0	0	0										
Home	3	2	.600	5.45	7	7	0	38	45	16	28	0	0	0	0										
Road	1	5	.167	3.86	9	9	2	56	56	22	43	0	0	0	0										

Division Rivals

vs.	W	L	%	ERA	G	GS	CG	IP	H	BB	SO	ShO	RW	RL	SV
vs. CAL	0	0	—	0.00	1	1	0	1	2	1	1	0	0	0	0
vs. CHI	0	0	—	1.29	1	1	0	7	3	4	5	0	0	0	0
vs. MIN	0	1	.000	5.14	1	1	0	7	7	2	7	0	0	0	0
vs. OAK	1	1	.500	2.93	2	2	0	15.1	14	0	11	0	0	0	0
vs. SEA	1	0	1.000	2.70	1	1	0	6.2	5	4	9	0	0	0	0
vs. TEX	1	0	1.000	5.14	1	1	0	7	4	3	7	0	0	0	0

Year	Team	W	L	%	ERA	G	GS	CG	IP	H	BB	SO	ShO	RW	RL	SV	AB	H	HR	BA	PO	A	E	DP	TC/G	FA
1984	KC A	10	14	.417	4.05	29	29	4	189	172	75	111	2	0	0	0	0	0	0	—	19	31	2	1	1.8	.962
1985		14	10	.583	4.06	29	28	0	177.1	160	77	99	0	1	0	0	0	0	0	—	23	26	0	4	1.7	1.000
1986		12	6	.667	3.64	35	24	3	180.2	155	84	118	2	1	1	0	0	0	0	—	17	32	0	3	1.4	1.000
1987		13	18	.419	3.98	35	35	10	241.2	231	120	166	2	0	0	0	0	0	0	—	32	40	2	7	2.1	.973
1988		20	8	.714	2.70	35	35	8	269.2	237	83	183	4	0	0	0	0	0	0	—	29	44	1	3	2.1	.986
1989		15	11	.577	3.04	36	**36**	8	255	252	63	173	2	0	0	0	0	0	0	—	18	49	5	0	2.0	.931
1990		4	7	.364	4.50	16	16	2	94	101	38	71	0	0	0	0	0	0	0	—	9	10	1	3	1.3	.950
7 yrs.		88	74	.543	3.57	215	203	35	1407.1	1308	540	921	12	2	1	0	0	0	0	—	147	232	11	21	1.8	.972

LEAGUE CHAMPIONSHIP SERIES

Year	Team	W	L	%	ERA	G	GS	CG	IP	H	BB	SO	ShO	RW	RL	SV	AB	H	HR	BA	PO	A	E	DP	TC/G	FA
1985	KC A	1	0	1.000	3.24	2	1	0	8.1	4	4	4	0	0	0	0	0	0	0	—	0	1	0	0	0.5	1.000

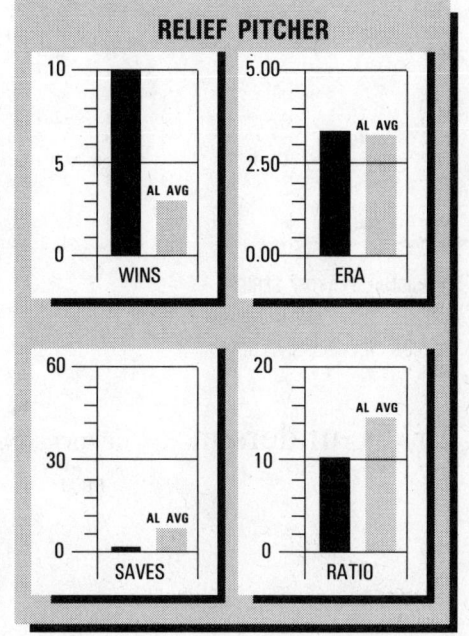

Lee Guetterman

GUETTERMAN, ARTHUR LEE
B. Nov. 22, 1958, Chattanooga, Tenn.
BL TL 6' 8" 225 lbs.

Period	W	L	%	ERA	G	GS	CG	IP	H	BB	SO	ShO	RW	RL	SV
April	1	1	.500	4.15	7	0	0	13	11	2	13	0	1	1	0
May	1	1	.500	0.63	11	0	0	14.1	11	4	7	0	1	1	0
June	3	0	1.000	1.88	17	0	0	24	16	7	10	0	3	0	0
July	1	2	.333	5.91	8	0	0	10.2	13	4	3	0	1	2	0
Aug	3	0	1.000	2.60	12	0	0	17.1	13	3	9	0	3	0	2
Sept/Oct	2	3	.400	7.24	9	0	0	13.2	16	6	6	0	2	3	0
Day	3	1	.750	1.90	18	0	0	23.2	14	7	12	0	3	1	0
Night	8	6	.571	3.89	46	0	0	69.1	66	19	36	0	8	6	2
vs. Left	—	—	—	—	—	—	—	—	24	9	21	—	—	—	—
vs. Right	—	—	—	—	—	—	—	—	56	17	27	—	—	—	—
On Grass	10	5	.667	2.94	57	0	0	79.2	64	22	42	0	10	5	1
On Turf	1	2	.333	6.08	7	0	0	13.1	16	4	6	0	1	2	1
Home	9	4	.692	2.64	36	0	0	58	44	15	31	0	9	4	1
Road	2	3	.400	4.63	28	0	0	35	36	11	17	0	2	3	1

Division Rivals

vs.	W	L	%	ERA	G	GS	CG	IP	H	BB	SO	ShO	RW	RL	SV
vs. BAL	0	0	—	0.00	7	0	0	11	2	1	6	0	0	0	0
vs. BOS	1	0	1.000	0.00	6	0	0	4.2	6	3	1	0	1	0	0
vs. CLE	1	0	1.000	5.79	3	0	0	4.2	7	3	3	0	1	0	0
vs. DET	1	0	1.000	27.00	2	0	0	1	1	1	0	0	1	0	0
vs. MIL	3	0	1.000	0.87	6	0	0	10.1	5	2	6	0	3	0	0
vs. TOR	0	1	.000	3.86	4	0	0	9.1	8	2	4	0	0	1	1

Year	Team	W	L	%	ERA	G	GS	CG	IP	H	BB	SO	ShO	RELIEF PITCHING W	L	SV	BATTING AB	H	HR	BA	PO	A	E	DP	TC/G	FA

Lee Guetterman Continued

Year	Team	W	L	%	ERA	G	GS	CG	IP	H	BB	SO	ShO	W	L	SV	AB	H	HR	BA	PO	A	E	DP	TC/G	FA
1984	SEA A	0	0	—	4.15	3	0	0	4.1	9	2	2	0	0	0	0	0	0	0	—	0	1	0	1	0.3	1.000
1986		0	4	.000	7.34	41	4	1	76	108	30	38	0	0	2	0	0	0	0	—	5	12	2	1	0.5	.895
1987		11	4	.733	3.81	25	17	2	113.1	117	35	42	1	1	0	0	0	0	0	—	7	22	0	3	1.2	1.000
1988	NY A	1	2	.333	4.65	20	2	0	40.2	49	14	15	0	1	0	0	0	0	0	—	2	5	0	0	0.4	1.000
1989		5	5	.500	2.45	70	0	0	103	98	26	51	0	5	5	13	0	0	0	—	6	24	3	4	0.5	.909
1990		11	7	.611	3.39	64	0	0	93	80	26	48	0	11	7	2	0	0	0	—	6	19	2	1	0.4	.926
6 yrs.		28	22	.560	4.10	223	23	3	430.1	461	133	196	1	18	14	15	0	0	0	—	26	83	7	10	0.5	.940

Bill Gullickson

GULLICKSON, WILLIAM LEE
B. Feb. 20, 1959, Marshall, Minn.
BR TR 6′ 3″ 200 lbs.

		W	L	%	ERA	G	GS	CG	IP	H	BB	SO	ShO	W	L	SV	AB	H	HR	BA	PO	A	E	DP	TC/G	FA
April		1	1	.500	4.97	3	3	0	12.2	16	3	8	0	0	0	0										
May		2	2	.500	3.63	6	6	0	34.2	40	15	16	0	0	0	0										
June		2	3	.400	2.42	6	6	0	44.2	46	12	23	0	0	0	0										
July		1	2	.333	6.26	5	5	0	27.1	40	8	6	0	0	0	0										
Aug		2	4	.333	4.00	6	6	1	36	37	10	11	0	0	0	0										
Sept/Oct		2	2	.500	3.32	6	6	1	38	42	13	9	1	0	0	0										
Day		3	1	.750	1.58	7	7	1	51.1	50	18	22	1	0	0	0										
Night		7	13	.350	4.63	25	25	1	142	171	43	51	0	0	0	0										
vs. Left		—	—	—	—	—	—	—	—	146	43	29	—	—	—	—										
vs. Right		—	—	—	—	—	—	—	—	75	18	44	—	—	—	—										
On Grass		1	3	.250	3.48	7	7	0	44	52	14	17	0	0	0	0										
On Turf		9	11	.450	3.92	25	25	2	149.1	169	47	56	1	0	0	0										
Home		8	7	.533	3.94	19	19	2	114.1	127	31	45	1	0	0	0										
Road		2	7	.222	3.65	13	13	0	79	94	30	28	0	0	0	0										
Division Rivals																										
vs. ATL		2	1	.667	3.28	4	4	1	24.2	27	5	5	1	0	0	0										
vs. CIN		0	1	.000	4.26	2	2	0	12.2	15	3	3	0	0	0	0										
vs. LA		2	2	.500	2.92	4	4	0	24.2	26	5	9	0	0	0	0										
vs. SD		0	3	.000	7.71	3	3	0	16.1	19	8	3	0	0	0	0										
vs. SF		2	0	1.000	1.10	4	4	1	32.2	29	10	19	0	0	0	0										
1979	MON N	0	0	—	0.00	1	0	0	1	2	0	0	0	0	0	0	0	0	0	—	0	0	0	0	0.0	—
1980		10	5	.667	3.00	24	19	5	141	127	50	120	2	0	1	0	40	7	0	.175	4	21	1	2	1.1	.962
1981		7	9	.438	2.81	22	22	3	157	142	34	115	2	0	0	0	46	7	0	.152	12	16	1	2	1.3	.966
1982		12	14	.462	3.57	34	34	6	236.2	231	61	155	0	0	0	0	82	10	0	.122	16	18	3	1	1.1	.919
1983		17	12	.586	3.75	34	34	10	242.1	230	59	120	1	0	0	0	82	11	1	.134	27	25	1	3	1.6	.981
1984		12	9	.571	3.61	32	32	3	226.2	230	37	100	0	0	0	0	73	8	0	.110	14	19	4	2	1.2	.892
1985		14	12	.538	3.52	29	29	4	181.1	187	47	68	1	0	0	0	64	12	0	.188	10	26	1	0	1.3	.973
1986	CIN N	15	12	.556	3.38	37	37	6	244.2	245	60	121	2	0	0	0	79	6	0	.076	14	32	3	3	1.3	.939
1987	2 teams	CIN N	(27G 10 – 11)		NY A	(8G 4 – 2)																				
"	total	14	13	.519	4.86	35	35	4	213	218	50	117	1	0	0	0	53	11	1	.208	16	21	0	0	1.1	1.000
1990	HOU N	10	14	.417	3.82	32	32	2	193.1	221	61	73	1	0	0	0	57	9	1	.158	11	13	0	1	0.8	1.000
10 yrs.		111	100	.526	3.64	280	274	43	1837	1833	459	989	10	0	1	0	576	81	3	.141	124	191	14	14	1.2	.957

DIVISIONAL PLAYOFF SERIES

Year	Team	W	L	%	ERA	G	GS	CG	IP	H	BB	SO	ShO	W	L	SV	AB	H	HR	BA	PO	A	E	DP	TC/G	FA
1981	MON N	1	0	1.000	1.17	1	1	0	7.2	6	1	3	0	0	0	0	3	0	0	.000	0	0	0	0	0.0	—

LEAGUE CHAMPIONSHIP SERIES

Year	Team	W	L	%	ERA	G	GS	CG	IP	H	BB	SO	ShO	W	L	SV	AB	H	HR	BA	PO	A	E	DP	TC/G	FA
1981	MON N	0	2	.000	2.51	2	2	0	14.1	12	6	12	0	0	0	0	3	0	0	.000	0	2	0	0	1.0	1.000

Eric Gunderson

GUNDERSON, ERIC ANDREW
B. Mar. 29, 1966, Portland, Ore.
BR TL 6′ 175 lbs.

Year	Team	W	L	%	ERA	G	GS	CG	IP	H	BB	SO	ShO	W	L	SV	AB	H	HR	BA	PO	A	E	DP	TC/G	FA
1990	SF N	1	2	.333	5.49	7	4	0	19.2	24	11	14	0	0	0	0	6	0	0	.000	0	4	0	0	0.6	1.000

STARTING PITCHER

WINS · ERA · SO/9 · RATIO (charts showing NL AVG comparisons)

Year	Team	W	L	%	ERA	G	GS	CG	IP	H	BB	SO	ShO	RELIEF PITCHING W	L	SV	BATTING AB	H	HR	BA	PO	A	E	DP	TC/G	FA

Mark Guthrie

GUTHRIE, MARK ANDREW
B. Sept. 22, 1965, Buffalo, N. Y.
BB TR 5′ 11″ 192 lbs.

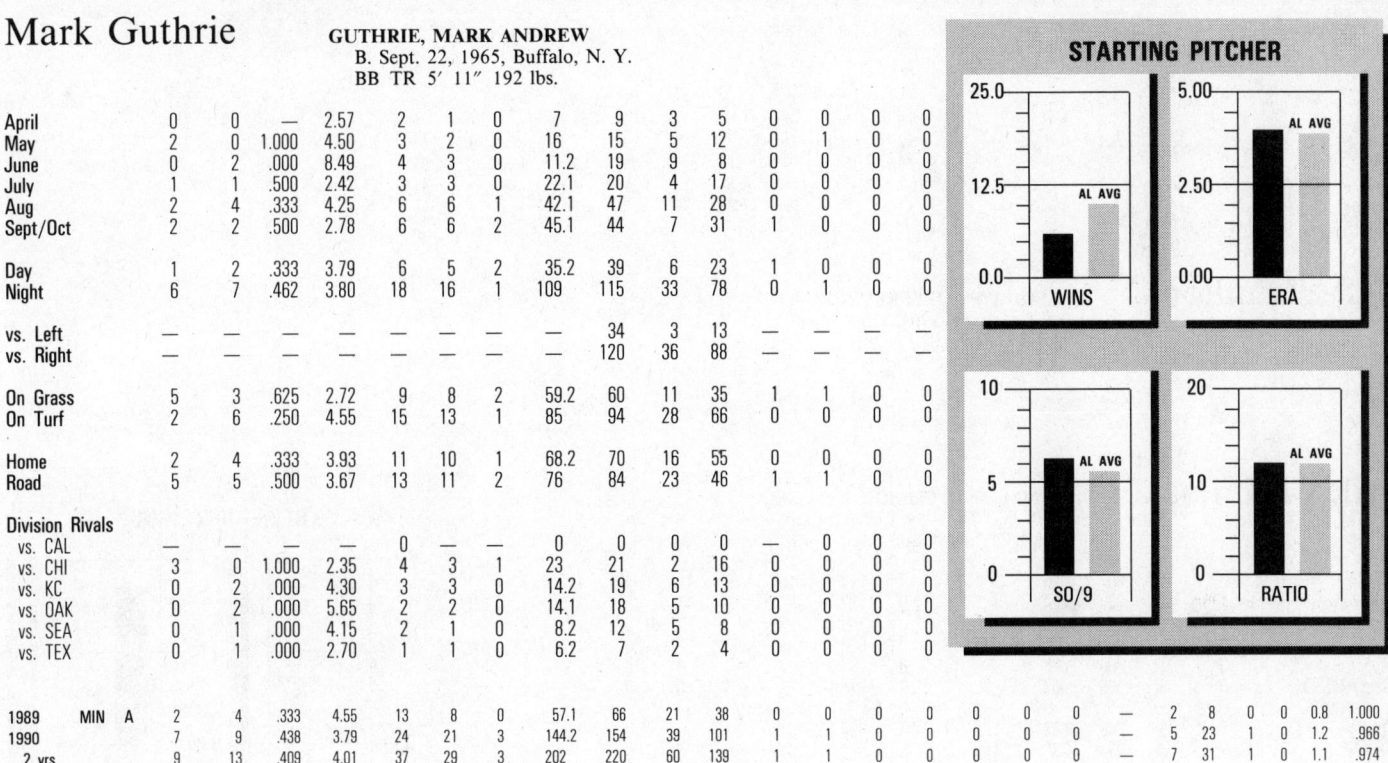

Year	Team	W	L	%	ERA	G	GS	CG	IP	H	BB	SO	ShO	W	L	SV	AB	H	HR	BA	PO	A	E	DP	TC/G	FA
April		0	0	—	2.57	2	1	0	7	9	3	5	0	0	0	0										
May		2	0	1.000	4.50	3	2	0	16	15	5	12	0	1	0	0										
June		0	2	.000	8.49	4	3	0	11.2	19	9	8	0	0	0	0										
July		1	1	.500	2.42	3	3	0	22.1	20	4	17	0	0	0	0										
Aug		2	4	.333	4.25	6	6	1	42.1	47	11	28	0	0	0	0										
Sept/Oct		2	2	.500	2.78	6	6	2	45.1	44	7	31	1	0	0	0										
Day		1	2	.333	3.79	6	5	2	35.2	39	6	23	1	0	0	0										
Night		6	7	.462	3.80	18	16	1	109	115	33	78	0	1	0	0										
vs. Left		—	—	—	—	—	—	—	—	34	3	13	—	—	—	0										
vs. Right		—	—	—	—	—	—	—	—	120	36	88	—	—	—	0										
On Grass		5	3	.625	2.72	9	8	2	59.2	60	11	35	1	1	0	0										
On Turf		2	6	.250	4.55	15	13	1	85	94	28	66	0	0	0	0										
Home		2	4	.333	3.93	11	10	1	68.2	70	16	55	0	0	0	0										
Road		5	5	.500	3.67	13	11	2	76	84	23	46	1	1	0	0										
Division Rivals																										
vs. CAL		—	—	—	—	0	—	—	0	0	0	0	—	0	0	0										
vs. CHI		3	0	1.000	2.35	4	3	1	23	21	2	16	0	0	0	0										
vs. KC		0	2	.000	4.30	3	3	0	14.2	19	6	13	0	0	0	0										
vs. OAK		0	2	.000	5.65	2	2	0	14.1	18	5	10	0	0	0	0										
vs. SEA		0	1	.000	4.15	2	1	0	8.2	12	5	8	0	0	0	0										
vs. TEX		0	1	.000	2.70	1	1	0	6.2	7	2	4	0	0	0	0										
1989	MIN A	2	4	.333	4.55	13	8	0	57.1	66	21	38	0	0	0	0	0	0	0	—	2	8	0	0	0.8	1.000
1990		7	9	.438	3.79	24	21	3	144.2	154	39	101	1	1	0	0	0	0	0	—	5	23	1	0	1.2	.966
2 yrs.		9	13	.409	4.01	37	29	3	202	220	60	139	1	1	0	0	0	0	0	—	7	31	1	0	1.1	.974

John Habyan

HABYAN, JOHN GABRIEL
B. Jan. 29, 1963, Bay Shore, N. Y.
BR TR 6′ 1″ 195 lbs.

Year	Team	W	L	%	ERA	G	GS	CG	IP	H	BB	SO	ShO	W	L	SV	AB	H	HR	BA	PO	A	E	DP	TC/G	FA
1985	BAL A	1	0	1.000	0.00	2	0	0	2.2	3	0	2	0	1	0	0	0	0	0	—	1	0	0	0	0.5	1.000
1986		1	3	.250	4.44	6	5	0	26.1	24	18	14	0	0	0	0	0	0	0	—	1	3	0	0	0.7	1.000
1987		6	7	.462	4.80	27	13	0	116.1	110	40	64	0	4	0	1	0	0	0	—	15	17	2	2	1.2	1.000
1988		1	0	1.000	4.30	7	0	0	14.2	22	4	4	0	1	0	0	0	0	0	—	5	1	0	0	0.9	1.000
1990	NY A	0	0	—	2.08	6	0	0	8.2	10	2	4	0	0	0	0	0	0	0	—	2	0	0	0	0.3	1.000
5 yrs.		9	10	.474	4.48	48	18	0	168.2	169	64	88	0	6	0	1	0	0	0	—	24	21	0	2	0.9	1.000

Drew Hall

HALL, ANDREW CLARK
B. Mar. 27, 1963, Louisville, Ky.
BL TL 6′ 4″ 220 lbs.

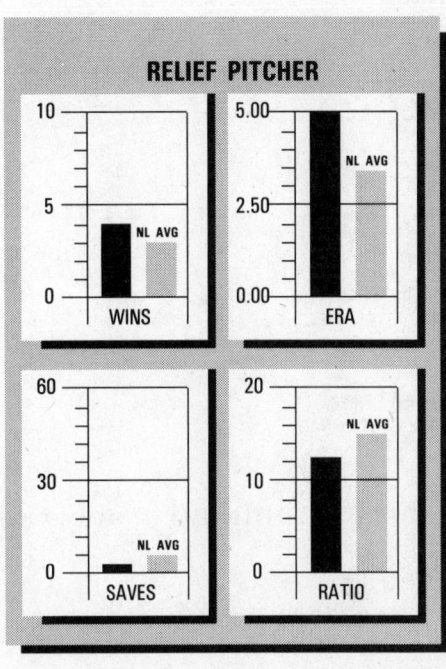

Year	Team	W	L	%	ERA	G	GS	CG	IP	H	BB	SO	ShO	W	L	SV	AB	H	HR	BA	PO	A	E	DP	TC/G	FA
April		1	2	.333	3.65	10	0	0	12.1	8	7	8	0	1	2	0										
May		2	3	.400	2.45	10	0	0	18.1	14	7	11	0	2	3	2										
June		1	2	.333	5.00	14	0	0	18	14	9	16	0	1	2	1										
July		0	0	—	21.21	4	0	0	4.2	11	4	5	0	0	0	0										
Aug		—	—	—	—	0	—	0	0	0	0	0	0	0	0	0										
Sept/Oct		0	0	—	3.60	4	0	0	5	5	2	0	0	0	0	0										
Day		1	1	.500	4.30	11	0	0	14.2	13	7	9	0	1	1	0										
Night		3	6	.333	5.36	31	0	0	43.2	39	22	31	0	3	6	3										
vs. Left		—	—	—	—	—	—	—	—	17	9	13	—	—	—	—										
vs. Right		—	—	—	—	—	—	—	—	35	20	27	—	—	—	—										
On Grass		0	2	.000	6.57	9	0	0	12.1	14	7	8	0	0	2	1										
On Turf		4	5	.444	4.70	33	0	0	46	38	22	32	0	4	5	2										
Home		3	2	.600	2.37	19	0	0	30.1	22	7	23	0	3	2	1										
Road		1	5	.167	8.04	23	0	0	28	30	22	17	0	1	5	2										
Division Rivals																										
vs. CHI		0	0	—	2.25	2	0	0	4	1	2	2	0	0	0	0										
vs. NY		0	1	.000	5.40	4	0	0	6.2	7	1	7	0	0	1	0										
vs. PHI		2	0	1.000	1.42	5	0	0	6.1	3	2	4	0	2	0	1										
vs. PIT		0	1	.000	4.91	6	0	0	7.1	8	4	5	0	0	1	0										
vs. STL		0	1	.000	6.23	6	0	0	4.1	5	3	3	0	0	1	0										

Year	Team		W	L	%	ERA	G	GS	CG	IP	H	BB	SO	ShO	RELIEF PITCHING W	L	SV	BATTING AB	H	HR	BA	PO	A	E	DP	TC/G	FA

Drew Hall *Continued*

Year	Team		W	L	%	ERA	G	GS	CG	IP	H	BB	SO	ShO	W	L	SV	AB	H	HR	BA	PO	A	E	DP	TC/G	FA
1986	CHI	N	1	2	.333	4.56	5	4	1	23.2	24	10	21	0	0	0	1	7	1	0	.143	0	2	0	0	0.4	1.000
1987			1	1	.500	6.89	21	0	0	32.2	40	14	20	0	1	1	0	4	0	0	.000	3	3	0	0	0.3	1.000
1988			1	1	.500	7.66	19	0	0	22.1	26	9	22	0	1	1	1	1	0	0	.000	0	4	0	0	0.2	1.000
1989	TEX	A	2	1	.667	3.70	38	0	0	58.1	42	33	45	0	2	1	0	0	0	0	—	2	8	0	1	0.3	1.000
1990	MON	N	4	7	.364	5.09	42	0	0	58.1	52	29	40	0	4	7	3	4	0	0	.000	2	11	1	1	0.3	.929
5 yrs.			9	12	.429	5.21	125	4	1	195.1	184	95	148	0	8	10	5	16	1	0	.063	7	28	1	2	0.3	.972

Jeff Hamilton

HAMILTON, JEFFREY ROBERT
B. Mar. 19, 1964, Flint, Mich.
BR TR 6′ 3″ 190 lbs.

Year	Team		W	L	%	ERA	G	GS	CG	IP	H	BB	SO	ShO	W	L	SV	AB	H	HR	BA	PO	A	E	DP	TC/G	FA
1989	LA	N	0	1	.000	5.40	1	0	0	1.2	2	1	2	0	0	1	0	*				0	1	0	0	1.0	1.000

Atlee Hammaker

HAMMAKER, CHARLTON ATLEE
B. Jan. 24, 1958, Carmel, Calif.
BB TL 6′ 3″ 200 lbs.

Year	Team		W	L	%	ERA	G	GS	CG	IP	H	BB	SO	ShO	W	L	SV	AB	H	HR	BA	PO	A	E	DP	TC/G	FA
April			2	1	.667	2.25	6	2	0	24	15	5	10	0	0	1	0										
May			1	2	.333	5.24	9	2	0	22.1	31	8	11	0	1	1	0										
June			1	1	.500	6.75	2	2	0	9.1	12	3	2	0	0	0	0										
July			0	1	.000	3.00	5	0	0	6	5	2	2	0	0	1	0										
Aug			0	1	.000	5.06	5	0	0	10.2	7	4	9	0	0	1	0										
Sept/Oct			0	3	.000	5.02	7	1	0	14.1	15	5	10	0	0	2	0										
Day			1	3	.250	3.62	14	2	0	32.1	31	12	14	0	0	2	0										
Night			3	6	.333	4.80	20	5	0	54.1	54	15	30	0	1	4	0										
vs. Left			—	—	—	—	—	—	—	—	13	7	13	—	—	—	—										
vs. Right			—	—	—	—	—	—	—	—	72	20	31	—	—	—	—										
On Grass			4	7	.364	4.01	27	6	0	74	73	19	38	0	1	5	0										
On Turf			0	2	.000	6.39	7	1	0	12.2	12	8	6	0	0	1	0										
Home			3	5	.375	4.81	17	4	0	48.2	54	12	27	0	1	4	0										
Road			1	4	.200	3.79	17	3	0	38	31	15	17	0	0	2	0										
Division Rivals																											
vs. ATL			0	1	.000	4.32	4	1	0	8.1	9	2	6	0	0	0	0										
vs. CIN			0	1	.000	3.86	2	1	0	7	7	2	6	0	0	0	0										
vs. HOU			1	0	1.000	4.50	2	1	0	6	4	3	1	0	0	0	0										
vs. LA			0	2	.000	8.00	5	0	0	9	10	3	6	0	0	2	0										
vs. SF			0	1	.000	4.50	2	0	0	4	6	1	2	0	0	1	0										

RELIEF PITCHER — WINS / ERA / SAVES / RATIO (NL AVG comparison charts)

Year	Team		W	L	%	ERA	G	GS	CG	IP	H	BB	SO	ShO	W	L	SV	AB	H	HR	BA	PO	A	E	DP	TC/G	FA
1981	KC	A	1	3	.250	5.54	10	6	0	39	44	12	11	0	0	0	0	0	0	0	—	1	4	0	1	0.5	1.000
1982	SF	N	12	8	.600	4.11	29	27	4	175	189	28	102	1	0	0	0	59	4	0	.068	5	35	1	0	1.4	.976
1983			10	9	.526	**2.25**	23	23	8	172.1	147	32	127	3	0	0	0	59	6	0	.102	3	31	3	2	1.6	.919
1984			2	0	1.000	2.18	6	6	0	33	32	9	24	0	0	0	0	11	2	0	.182	0	6	0	0	1.0	1.000
1985			5	12	.294	3.74	29	29	1	170.2	161	47	100	1	0	0	0	47	4	0	.085	6	32	1	1	1.3	.974
1987			10	10	.500	3.58	31	27	2	168.1	159	57	107	0	1	0	0	57	7	0	.123	7	23	0	1	1.0	1.000
1988			9	9	.500	3.73	43	17	3	144.2	136	41	65	1	4	2	5	33	4	0	.121	7	33	0	3	0.9	1.000
1989			6	6	.500	3.76	28	9	0	76.2	78	23	30	0	3	3	0	19	7	0	.368	3	9	1	0	0.5	.923
1990	2 teams		SF N (25G 4 – 5)				SD N (9G 0 – 4)																				
"	total		4	9	.308	4.36	34	7	0	86.2	85	27	44	0	1	6	0	19	2	0	.105	6	7	0	2	0.4	1.000
9 yrs.			59	66	.472	3.60	233	151	18	1066.1	1031	276	610	6	9	11	5	304	36	0	.118	38	180	6	10	1.0	.973

LEAGUE CHAMPIONSHIP SERIES

Year	Team		W	L	%	ERA	G	GS	CG	IP	H	BB	SO	ShO	W	L	SV	AB	H	HR	BA	PO	A	E	DP	TC/G	FA
1987	SF	N	0	1	.000	7.88	2	2	0	8	12	0	7	0	0	0	0	3	0	0	.000	0	1	0	0	0.5	1.000
1989			0	0	—	0.00	1	0	0	1	1	0	0	0	0	0	0	0	0	0	—	0	0	0	0	0.0	—
2 yrs.			0	1	.000	7.00	3	2	0	9	13	0	7	0	0	0	0	3	0	0	.000	0	1	0	0	0.3	1.000

WORLD SERIES

Year	Team		W	L	%	ERA	G	GS	CG	IP	H	BB	SO	ShO	W	L	SV	AB	H	HR	BA	PO	A	E	DP	TC/G	FA
1989	SF	N	0	0	—	15.43	2	0	0	2.1	8	0	2	0	0	0	0	0	0	0	—	0	1	0	0	0.5	1.000

Chris Hammond

HAMMOND, CHRISTOPHER ANDREW
B. Jan. 21, 1966, Atlanta, Ga.
Brother of Steve Hammond.
BL TL 6′ 1″ 190 lbs.

Year	Team		W	L	%	ERA	G	GS	CG	IP	H	BB	SO	ShO	W	L	SV	AB	H	HR	BA	PO	A	E	DP	TC/G	FA
1990	CIN	N	0	2	.000	6.35	3	3	0	11.1	13	12	4	0	0	0	0	3	0	0	.000	0	3	2	0	1.7	.600

Erik Hanson

HANSON, ERIK BRIAN
B. May 18, 1965, Kinnelon, N. J.
BR TR 6′ 6″ 210 lbs.

Year	Team	W	L	%	ERA	G	GS	CG	IP	H	BB	SO	ShO	RELIEF PITCHING W	L	SV	BATTING AB	H	HR	BA	PO	A	E	DP	TC/G	FA
April		2	0	1.000	3.13	4	4	0	23	22	9	25	0	0	0	0										
May		3	3	.500	3.92	6	6	0	39	43	12	35	0	0	0	0										
June		3	3	.500	5.05	6	6	1	41	41	15	38	0	0	0	0										
July		3	2	.600	3.28	5	5	0	35.2	25	15	30	0	0	0	0										
Aug		1	1	.500	2.28	6	6	1	47.1	37	9	40	0	0	0	0										
Sept/Oct		6	0	1.000	2.16	6	6	3	50	37	8	43	1	0	0	0										
Day		1	2	.333	2.88	5	5	0	34.1	28	12	34	0	0	0	0										
Night		17	7	.708	3.30	28	28	5	201.2	177	56	177	1	0	0	0										
vs. Left		—	—	—	—	—	—	—		103	41	114	—	—	—	—										
vs. Right		—	—	—	—	—	—	—		102	27	97	—	—	—	—										
On Grass		9	2	.818	2.82	14	14	1	102	76	33	99	0	0	0	0										
On Turf		9	7	.563	3.56	19	19	4	134	129	35	112	1	0	0	0										
Home		7	6	.538	3.56	16	16	3	111.1	103	32	94	0	0	0	0										
Road		11	3	.786	2.96	17	17	2	124.2	102	36	117	1	0	0	0										
Division Rivals																										
vs. CAL		3	0	1.000	0.92	4	4	1	29.1	19	10	25	0	0	0	0										
vs. CHI		1	1	.500	6.39	2	2	1	12.2	15	4	7	0	0	0	0										
vs. KC		1	1	.500	5.93	2	2	0	13.2	19	3	11	0	0	0	0										
vs. MIN		1	0	1.000	3.65	2	2	1	12.1	15	1	11	1	0	0	0										
vs. OAK		2	0	1.000	1.07	3	3	0	25.1	14	3	28	0	0	0	0										
vs. TEX		1	0	1.000	5.27	2	2	0	13.2	16	5	11	0	0	0	0										
1988	SEA A	2	3	.400	3.24	6	6	0	41.2	35	12	36	0	0	0	0	0	0	0	—	0	4	0	1	0.7	1.000
1989		9	5	.643	3.18	17	17	1	113.1	103	32	75	0	0	0	0	0	0	0	—	8	16	0	0	1.4	1.000
1990		18	9	.667	3.24	33	33	5	236	205	68	211	1	0	0	0	0	0	0	—	30	20	4	0	1.6	.926
3 yrs.		29	17	.630	3.22	56	56	6	391	343	112	322	1	0	0	0	0	0	0	—	38	40	4	1	1.5	.951

Mike Harkey

HARKEY, MICHAEL ANTHONY
B. Oct. 25, 1966, San Diego, Calif.
BR TR 6′ 5″ 220 lbs.

Year	Team	W	L	%	ERA	G	GS	CG	IP	H	BB	SO	ShO	RELIEF PITCHING W	L	SV	BATTING AB	H	HR	BA	PO	A	E	DP	TC/G	FA
April		2	1	.667	2.60	3	3	0	17.1	9	7	11	0	0	0	0										
May		3	0	1.000	5.35	6	6	0	33.2	43	13	20	0	0	0	0										
June		0	2	.000	2.79	4	4	0	29	23	9	14	0	0	0	0										
July		4	2	.667	3.82	6	6	1	35.1	39	10	17	0	0	0	0										
Aug		3	1	.750	2.42	7	7	1	52	38	16	28	1	0	0	0										
Sept/Oct		0	0	—	0.00	1	1	0	6.1	1	4	4	0	0	0	0										
Day		9	2	.818	2.79	17	17	2	116	95	32	65	1	0	0	0										
Night		3	4	.429	4.21	10	10	0	57.2	58	27	29	0	0	0	0										
vs. Left		—	—	—	—	—	—	—		96	37	56	—	—	—	—										
vs. Right		—	—	—	—	—	—	—		57	22	38	—	—	—	—										
On Grass		9	3	.750	2.62	19	19	2	130.2	109	39	73	1	0	0	0										
On Turf		3	3	.500	5.23	8	8	0	43	44	20	21	0	0	0	0										
Home		5	2	.714	2.43	12	12	2	85.1	79	28	46	1	0	0	0										
Road		7	4	.636	4.08	15	15	0	88.1	74	31	48	0	0	0	0										
Division Rivals																										
vs. MON		2	1	.667	4.05	3	3	0	20	14	5	10	0	0	0	0										
vs. NY		1	2	.333	2.95	3	3	0	18.1	15	5	10	0	0	0	0										
vs. PHI		0	0	—	0.00	1	1	0	6.1	1	4	4	0	0	0	0										
vs. PIT		1	0	1.000	1.50	1	1	0	6	5	1	2	0	0	0	0										
vs. STL		0	1	.000	4.42	3	3	0	18.1	20	14	9	0	0	0	0										
1988	CHI N	0	3	.000	2.60	5	5	0	34.2	33	15	18	0	0	0	0	11	1	0	.091	2	3	2	0	1.4	.714
1990		12	6	.667	3.26	27	27	2	173.2	153	59	94	1	0	0	0	56	14	0	.250	19	16	1	0	1.3	.972
2 yrs.		12	9	.571	3.15	32	32	2	208.1	186	74	112	1	0	0	0	67	15	0	.224	21	19	3	0	1.3	.930

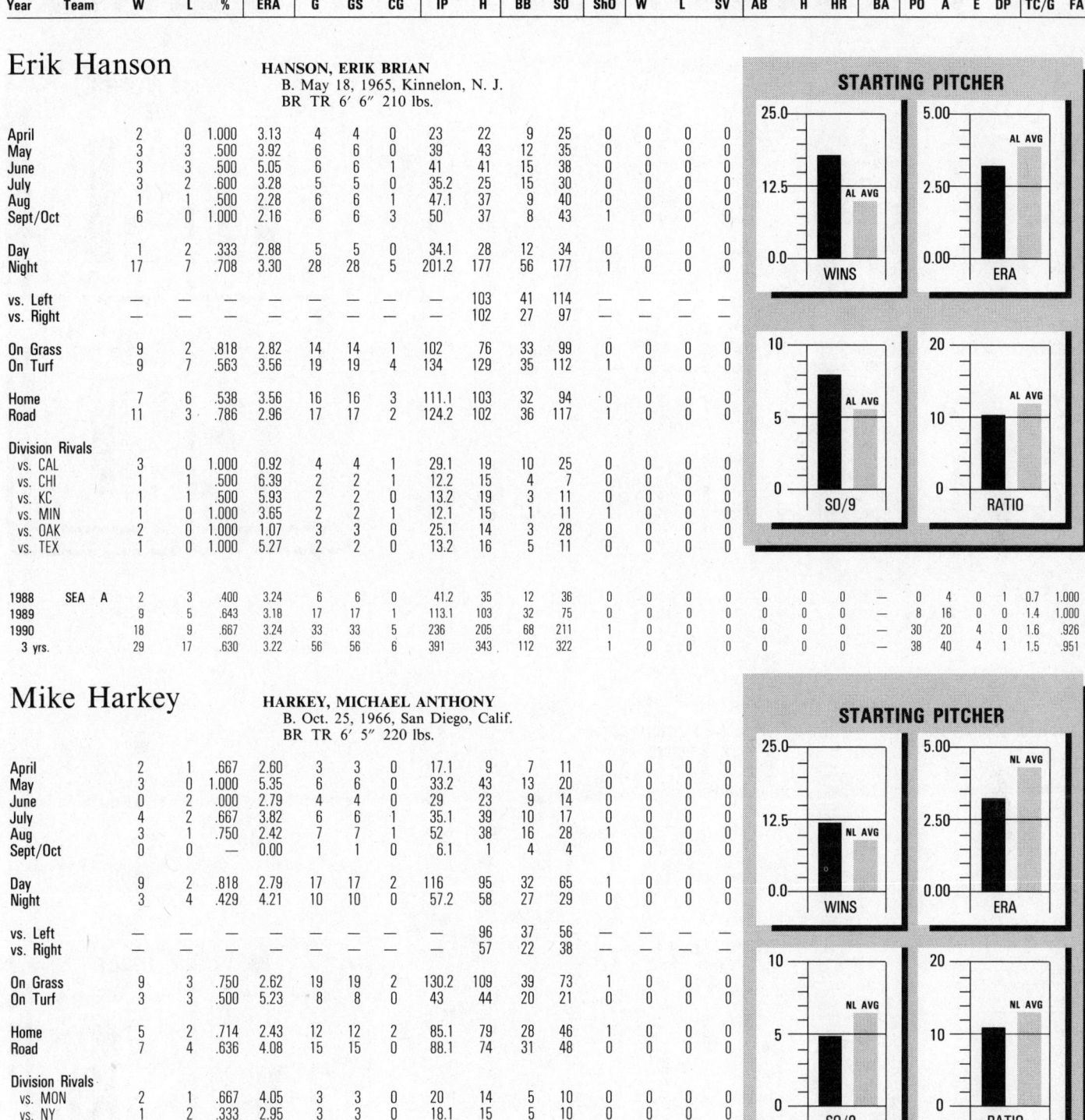

Year	Team	W	L	%	ERA	G	GS	CG	IP	H	BB	SO	ShO	RELIEF PITCHING W	L	SV	BATTING AB	H	HR	BA	PO	A	E	DP	TC/G	FA

Pete Harnisch

HARNISCH, PETER THOMAS
B. Sept. 23, 1966, Commack, N. Y.
BB TR 6′ 1″ 195 lbs.

Period	W	L	%	ERA	G	GS	CG	IP	H	BB	SO	ShO	W	L	SV	AB	H	HR	BA	PO	A	E	DP	TC/G	FA
April	2	0	1.000	4.43	4	4	0	22.1	23	10	12	0	0	0	0										
May	3	2	.600	3.57	6	6	2	40.1	37	16	20	0	0	0	0										
June	2	2	.500	3.86	5	5	0	30.1	27	15	26	0	0	0	0										
July	2	1	.667	5.45	6	6	0	36.1	39	13	26	0	0	0	0										
Aug	1	4	.200	3.82	6	6	1	33	35	24	25	0	0	0	0										
Sept/Oct	1	2	.333	5.13	4	4	0	26.1	28	8	13	0	0	0	0										
Day	2	0	1.000	3.60	4	4	0	25	19	11	13	0	0	0	0										
Night	9	11	.450	4.45	27	27	3	163.2	170	75	109	0	0	0	0										
vs. Left	—	—	—	—	—	—	—	—	125	49	59	—	—	—	—										
vs. Right	—	—	—	—	—	—	—	—	64	37	63	—	—	—	—										
On Grass	10	9	.526	3.93	24	24	3	149	139	66	105	0	0	0	0										
On Turf	1	2	.333	5.90	7	7	0	39.2	50	20	17	0	0	0	0										
Home	7	6	.538	4.63	15	15	1	89.1	85	33	67	0	0	0	0										
Road	4	5	.444	4.08	16	16	2	99.1	104	53	55	0	0	0	0										
Division Rivals																									
vs. BOS	0	2	.000	5.19	2	2	0	8.2	9	11	6	0	0	0	0										
vs. CLE	1	2	.333	5.03	3	3	0	19.2	20	7	12	0	0	0	0										
vs. DET	0	1	.000	8.00	2	2	0	9	14	5	5	0	0	0	0										
vs. MIL	1	0	1.000	3.18	2	2	0	11.1	11	9	9	0	0	0	0										
vs. NY	2	0	1.000	1.06	2	2	1	17	9	3	19	0	0	0	0										
vs. TOR	1	0	1.000	3.86	2	2	0	14	13	1	7	0	0	0	0										
1988 BAL A	0	2	.000	5.54	2	2	0	13	13	9	10	0	0	0	0	0	0	0	—	2	2	0	0	2.0	1.000
1989	5	9	.357	4.62	18	17	2	103.1	97	64	70	0	0	0	0	0	0	0	—	7	9	0	2	0.9	1.000
1990	11	11	.500	4.34	31	31	3	188.2	189	86	122	0	0	0	0	0	0	0	—	12	14	1	0	0.9	.963
3 yrs.	16	22	.421	4.49	51	50	5	305	299	159	202	0	0	0	0	0	0	0	—	21	25	1	2	0.9	.979

STARTING PITCHER — WINS / ERA / SO/9 / RATIO (AL AVG)

Gene Harris

HARRIS, TYRONE EUGENE
B. Dec. 5, 1964, Sebring, Fla.
BR TR 5′ 11″ 190 lbs.

Year	Team	W	L	%	ERA	G	GS	CG	IP	H	BB	SO	ShO	W	L	SV	AB	H	HR	BA	PO	A	E	DP	TC/G	FA
1989 2 teams	MON N (11G 1 – 1)												SEA A (10G 1 – 4)													
″ total	2	5	.286	5.91	21	6	0	53.1	63	25	25	0	1	2	1	1	0	0	.000	2	13	0	0	0.7	1.000
1990 SEA A	1	2	.333	4.74	25	0	0	38	31	30	43	0	1	2	0	0	0	0	—	4	2	0	1	2	1.000
2 yrs.	3	7	.300	5.42	46	6	0	91.1	94	55	68	0	2	4	1	1	0	0	.000	6	15	0	1	0.5	1.000

Greg Harris

HARRIS, GREG ALLEN
B. Nov. 2, 1955, Lynwood, Calif.
BB TR 6′ 165 lbs.

Period	W	L	%	ERA	G	GS	CG	IP	H	BB	SO	ShO	W	L	SV	AB	H	HR	BA	PO	A	E	DP	TC/G	FA
April	2	0	1.000	0.90	5	5	0	10	7	5	6	0	1	0	0										
May	2	3	.400	4.24	6	6	0	34	38	11	19	0	0	0	0										
June	3	0	1.000	2.63	6	6	0	37.2	28	10	23	0	0	0	0										
July	1	1	.500	3.03	5	5	1	32.2	35	16	15	0	0	0	0										
Aug	4	1	.800	3.43	6	6	0	42	34	19	33	0	0	0	0										
Sept/Oct	1	4	.200	8.68	6	6	0	28	44	16	21	0	0	0	0										
Day	6	0	1.000	2.36	10	7	0	45.2	35	22	30	0	1	0	0										
Night	7	9	.438	4.54	24	23	1	138.2	151	55	87	0	0	0	0										
vs. Left	—	—	—	—	—	—	—	—	84	37	52	—	—	—	—										
vs. Right	—	—	—	—	—	—	—	—	102	40	65	—	—	—	—										
On Grass	11	9	.550	4.25	31	27	1	165	169	68	103	0	1	0	0										
On Turf	2	0	1.000	1.86	3	3	0	19.1	17	9	14	0	0	0	0										
Home	8	5	.615	4.45	17	15	0	89	91	37	66	0	1	0	0										
Road	5	4	.556	3.59	17	15	1	95.1	95	40	51	0	0	0	0										
Division Rivals																									
vs. BAL	3	1	.750	3.33	4	4	0	27	21	15	18	0	0	0	0										
vs. CLE	0	1	.000	7.00	2	2	0	9	12	3	5	0	0	0	0										
vs. DET	3	1	.750	2.55	5	3	1	24.2	26	9	14	0	1	0	0										
vs. MIL	1	0	1.000	2.30	4	2	0	15.2	15	7	9	0	0	0	0										
vs. NY	2	0	1.000	2.74	3	3	0	23	12	1	14	0	0	0	0										
vs. TOR	1	0	1.000	3.86	2	2	0	9.1	7	4	10	0	0	0	0										

STARTING PITCHER — WINS / ERA / SO/9 / RATIO (AL AVG)

Year	Team	W	L	%	ERA	G	GS	CG	IP	H	BB	SO	ShO	RELIEF PITCHING W	L	SV	BATTING AB	H	HR	BA	PO	A	E	DP	TC/G	FA

Greg Harris *Continued*

Year	Team	W	L	%	ERA	G	GS	CG	IP	H	BB	SO	ShO	W	L	SV	AB	H	HR	BA	PO	A	E	DP	TC/G	FA
1981	NY N	3	5	.375	4.43	16	14	0	69	65	28	54	0	0	0	1	22	4	0	.182	3	7	1	2	0.7	.909
1982	CIN N	2	6	.250	4.83	34	10	1	91.1	96	37	67	0	0	1	1	18	3	0	.167	8	13	2	2	0.7	.913
1983		0	0	—	27.00	1	0	0	1	2	3	1	0	0	0	0	1	0	0	.000	0	1	0	0	1.0	1.000
1984	2 teams	MON N (15G 0 – 1)							SD N (19G 2 – 1)																	
"	total	2	2	.500	2.48	34	1	0	54.1	38	25	45	0	1	2	3	9	3	0	.333	3	7	1	0	0.3	.909
1985	TEX A	5	4	.556	2.47	58	0	0	113	74	43	111	0	5	4	11	0	0	0	—	8	16	1	4	0.4	.960
1986		10	8	.556	2.83	73	0	0	111.1	103	42	95	0	10	8	20	0	0	0	—	7	18	2	2	0.4	.926
1987		5	10	.333	4.86	42	19	0	140.2	157	56	106	0	1	4	0	0	0	0	—	14	20	5	1	0.9	.872
1988	PHI N	4	6	.400	2.36	66	1	0	107	80	52	71	0	4	5	1	9	3	0	.333	5	17	3	0	0.4	.880
1989	2 teams	PHI N (44G 2 – 2)							BOS A (15G 2 – 2)																	
"	total	4	4	.500	3.31	59	0	0	103.1	85	58	76	0	4	4	1	6	1	0	.167	4	20	3	0	0.5	.889
1990	BOS A	13	9	.591	4.00	34	30	1	184.1	186	77	117	0	1	0	0	0	0	0	—	23	36	4	1	1.9	.937
10 yrs.		48	54	.471	3.61	417	75	2	975.1	886	421	743	0	26	28	38	65	14	0	.215	75	155	22	12	0.6	.913

LEAGUE CHAMPIONSHIP SERIES

Year	Team	W	L	%	ERA	G	GS	CG	IP	H	BB	SO	ShO	W	L	SV	AB	H	HR	BA	PO	A	E	DP	TC/G	FA
1984	SD N	0	0	—	31.50	1	0	0	2	9	3	2	0	0	0	0	0	0	0	—	0	0	0	0	0.0	—
1990	BOS A	0	1	.000	27.00	1	0	0	0.1	3	0	0	0	0	1	0	0	0	0	—	0	0	0	0	0.0	—
2 yrs.		0	1	.000	30.90	2	0	0	2.1	12	3	2	0	0	1	0	0	0	0	—	0	0	0	0	0.0	—

WORLD SERIES

Year	Team	W	L	%	ERA	G	GS	CG	IP	H	BB	SO	ShO	W	L	SV	AB	H	HR	BA	PO	A	E	DP	TC/G	FA
1984	SD N	0	0	—	0.00	1	0	0	5.1	3	3	5	0	0	0	0	0	0	0	—	0	0	0	0	0.0	—

Greg Harris

HARRIS, GREGORY WADE
B. Dec. 1, 1963, Greensboro, N. C.
BR TR 6′ 3″ 190 lbs.

	W	L	%	ERA	G	GS	CG	IP	H	BB	SO	ShO	W	L	SV
April	2	0	1.000	1.20	8	0	0	15	9	3	13	0	2	0	0
May	1	0	1.000	2.05	13	0	0	22	16	12	22	0	1	0	3
June	1	2	.333	2.84	14	0	0	19	16	12	14	0	1	2	1
July	1	3	.250	4.43	14	0	0	22.1	18	8	11	0	1	3	1
Aug	2	1	.667	1.62	12	0	0	16.2	13	9	16	0	2	1	1
Sept/Oct	1	2	.333	1.21	12	0	0	22.1	20	5	21	0	1	2	3
Day	4	4	.500	4.89	22	0	0	35	30	18	19	0	4	4	3
Night	4	4	.500	1.20	51	0	0	82.1	62	31	78	0	4	4	6
vs. Left	—	—	—	—	—	—	—	—	61	27	36	—	—	—	—
vs. Right	—	—	—	—	—	—	—	—	31	22	61	—	—	—	—
On Grass	6	5	.545	1.89	54	0	0	85.2	71	31	73	0	6	5	7
On Turf	2	3	.400	3.41	19	0	0	31.2	21	18	24	0	2	3	2
Home	4	4	.500	2.10	37	0	0	55.2	49	21	52	0	4	4	3
Road	4	4	.500	2.48	36	0	0	61.2	43	28	45	0	4	4	6
Division Rivals															
vs. ATL	0	1	.000	2.45	9	0	0	14.2	10	4	17	0	0	1	2
vs. CIN	2	1	.667	1.42	7	0	0	12.2	10	5	10	0	2	1	1
vs. HOU	2	0	1.000	0.75	7	0	0	12	7	6	4	0	2	0	0
vs. LA	1	0	1.000	1.17	9	0	0	15.1	12	2	16	0	1	0	2
vs. SF	2	0	1.000	0.00	8	0	0	13.1	4	5	8	0	2	0	1

Year	Team	W	L	%	ERA	G	GS	CG	IP	H	BB	SO	ShO	W	L	SV	AB	H	HR	BA	PO	A	E	DP	TC/G	FA
1988	SD N	2	0	1.000	1.50	3	1	1	18	13	3	15	0	1	0	0	7	0	0	.000	0	2	0	1	0.7	1.000
1989		8	9	.471	2.60	56	8	0	135	106	52	106	0	5	5	6	19	1	0	.053	12	21	0	2	0.6	1.000
1990		8	8	.500	2.30	73	0	0	117.1	92	49	97	0	8	8	9	12	1	0	.083	4	17	0	1	0.3	1.000
3 yrs.		18	17	.514	2.40	132	9	1	270.1	211	104	218	0	14	13	15	38	2	0	.053	16	40	0	4	0.4	1.000

Reggie Harris

HARRIS, REGINALD ALLEN
B. Aug. 12, 1968, Waynesboro, Va.
BR TR 6′ 1″ 180 lbs.

Year	Team	W	L	%	ERA	G	GS	CG	IP	H	BB	SO	ShO	W	L	SV	AB	H	HR	BA	PO	A	E	DP	TC/G	FA
1990	OAK A	1	0	1.000	3.48	16	1	0	41.1	25	21	31	0	1	0	0	0	0	0	—	2	3	0	1	0.3	1.000

RELIEF PITCHER

(Bar charts: WINS, ERA, SAVES, RATIO — each compared to NL AVG)

Year	Team	W	L	%	ERA	G	GS	CG	IP	H	BB	SO	ShO	RELIEF PITCHING W	L	SV	BATTING AB	H	HR	BA	PO	A	E	DP	TC/G	FA

Mike Hartley

HARTLEY, MICHAEL EDWARD
B. Aug. 31, 1961, Hawthorne, Calif.
BR TR 6′ 1″ 192 lbs.

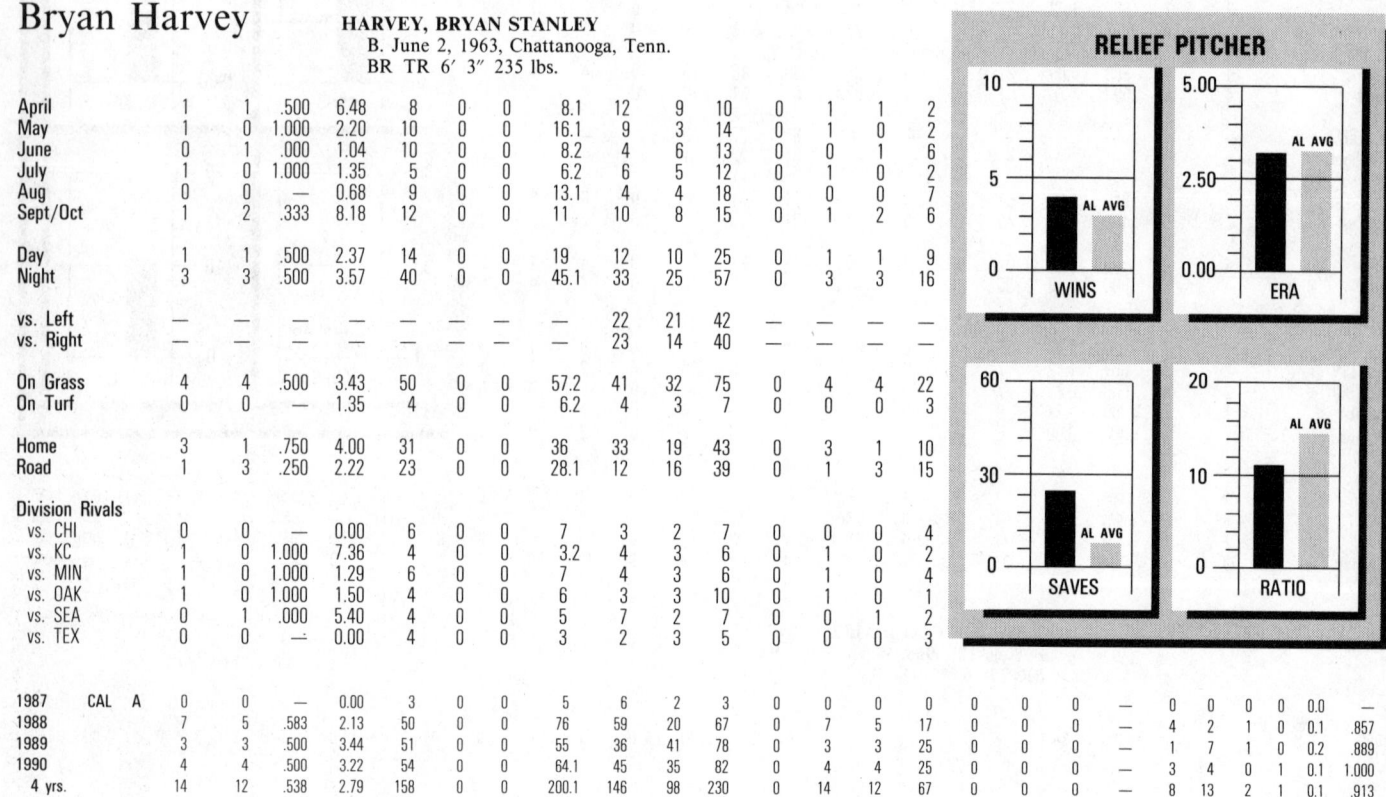

RELIEF PITCHER

Year	Team	W	L	%	ERA	G	GS	CG	IP	H	BB	SO	ShO	W	L	SV	AB	H	HR	BA	PO	A	E	DP	TC/G	FA
April		0	0	—	3.60	3	0	0	5	2	1	6	0	0	0	0										
May		0	0	—	3.29	11	0	0	13.2	16	9	16	0	0	0	1										
June		0	1	.000	7.36	4	0	0	7.1	8	4	9	0	0	1	0										
July		2	0	1.000	2.13	7	0	0	12.2	8	4	18	0	2	0	0										
Aug		3	0	1.000	0.78	4	3	0	23	10	8	15	0	1	0	0										
Sept/Oct		1	2	.333	4.08	3	3	1	17.2	14	4	12	1	0	0	0										
Day		2	0	1.000	2.61	11	1	0	20.2	20	10	18	0	1	0	1										
Night		4	3	.571	3.07	21	5	1	58.2	38	20	58	1	2	1	0										
vs. Left		—	—	—	—					33	24	40	—	—	—	—										
vs. Right		—	—	—	—					25	6	36	—	—	—	—										
On Grass		6	2	.750	2.13	23	5	1	63.1	36	22	59	1	3	1	1										
On Turf		0	1	.000	6.19	9	1	0	16	22	8	17	0	0	0	0										
Home		4	1	.800	1.45	15	3	1	43.1	22	12	43	1	2	1	1										
Road		2	2	.500	4.75	17	3	0	36	36	18	33	0	1	0	0										
Division Rivals																										
vs. ATL		2	0	1.000	0.00	3	1	1	12.2	4	1	11	1	1	0	0										
vs. CIN		0	0	—	9.00	2	0	0	4	4	3	4	0	0	0	0										
vs. HOU		0	0	—	0.00	1	0	0	2.1	3	0	3	0	0	0	0										
vs. SD		0	2	.000	12.71	3	1	0	5.2	7	4	6	0	0	1	0										
vs. SF		1	0	1.000	0.90	3	0	0	10	5	0	15	0	1	0	0										
1989	LA N	0	1	.000	1.50	5	0	0	6	2	0	4	0	0	1	0	1	0	0	.000	2	0	0	0	0.4	1.000
1990		6	3	.667	2.95	32	6	1	79.1	58	30	76	1	3	1	1	13	1	0	.077	3	8	1	1	0.4	.917
2 yrs.		6	4	.600	2.85	37	6	1	85.1	60	30	80	1	3	2	1	14	1	0	.071	5	8	1	1	0.4	.929

Bryan Harvey

HARVEY, BRYAN STANLEY
B. June 2, 1963, Chattanooga, Tenn.
BR TR 6′ 3″ 235 lbs.

RELIEF PITCHER

Year	Team	W	L	%	ERA	G	GS	CG	IP	H	BB	SO	ShO	W	L	SV	AB	H	HR	BA	PO	A	E	DP	TC/G	FA
April		1	1	.500	6.48	8	0	0	8.1	12	9	10	0	1	1	2										
May		1	0	1.000	2.20	10	0	0	16.1	9	3	14	0	1	0	2										
June		0	1	.000	1.04	10	0	0	8.2	4	6	13	0	0	1	6										
July		1	0	1.000	1.35	5	0	0	6.2	6	5	12	0	1	0	2										
Aug		0	0	—	0.68	9	0	0	13.1	4	4	18	0	0	0	7										
Sept/Oct		1	2	.333	8.18	12	0	0	11	10	8	15	0	1	2	6										
Day		1	1	.500	2.37	14	0	0	19	12	10	25	0	1	1	9										
Night		3	3	.500	3.57	40	0	0	45.1	33	25	57	0	3	3	16										
vs. Left		—	—	—	—					22	21	42	—	—	—	—										
vs. Right		—	—	—	—					23	14	40	—	—	—	—										
On Grass		4	4	.500	3.43	50	0	0	57.2	41	32	75	0	4	4	22										
On Turf		0	0	—	1.35	4	0	0	6.2	4	3	7	0	0	0	3										
Home		3	1	.750	4.00	31	0	0	36	33	19	43	0	3	1	10										
Road		1	3	.250	2.22	23	0	0	28.1	12	16	39	0	1	3	15										
Division Rivals																										
vs. CHI		0	0	—	0.00	6	0	0	7	3	2	7	0	0	0	4										
vs. KC		1	0	1.000	7.36	4	0	0	3.2	4	3	6	0	1	0	2										
vs. MIN		1	0	1.000	1.29	6	0	0	7	4	3	6	0	1	0	4										
vs. OAK		1	0	1.000	1.50	6	0	0	6	3	3	10	0	1	0	1										
vs. SEA		0	1	.000	5.40	4	0	0	5	7	2	7	0	0	1	2										
vs. TEX		0	0	—	0.00	4	0	0	3	2	3	5	0	0	0	3										
1987	CAL A	0	0	—	0.00	3	0	0	5	6	2	3	0	0	0	0	0	0	0	—	0	0	0	0	0.0	—
1988		7	5	.583	2.13	50	0	0	76	59	20	67	0	7	5	17	0	0	0	—	4	2	1	0	0.1	.857
1989		3	3	.500	3.44	51	0	0	55	36	41	78	0	3	3	25	0	0	0	—	1	7	1	0	0.2	.889
1990		4	4	.500	3.22	54	0	0	64.1	45	35	82	0	4	4	25	0	0	0	—	3	4	0	1	0.1	1.000
4 yrs.		14	12	.538	2.79	158	0	0	200.1	146	98	230	0	14	12	67	0	0	0	—	8	13	2	1	0.1	.913

Mickey Hatcher

HATCHER, MICHAEL VAUGHN, JR.
B. Mar. 15, 1955, Cleveland, Ohio
BR TR 6′ 2″ 200 lbs.

Year	Team	W	L	%	ERA	G	GS	CG	IP	H	BB	SO	ShO	W	L	SV	AB	H	HR	BA	PO	A	E	DP	TC/G	FA
1989	LA N	0	0	—	9.00	1	0	0	1	0	3	0	0	0	0	0	*				0	0	0	0	0.0	—

Year	Team	W	L	%	ERA	G	GS	CG	IP	H	BB	SO	ShO	W	L	SV	AB	H	HR	BA	PO	A	E	DP	TC/G	FA

(RELIEF PITCHING: W L SV; BATTING: AB H HR BA)

Andy Hawkins

HAWKINS, MELTON ANDREW
B. Jan. 21, 1960, Waco, Tex.
BR TR 6' 4" 200 lbs.

Year	Team	W	L	%	ERA	G	GS	CG	IP	H	BB	SO	ShO	W	L	SV	AB	H	HR	BA	PO	A	E	DP	TC/G	FA
April		0	2	.000	7.88	3	3	0	16	21	10	8	0	0	0	0										
May		1	2	.333	7.30	5	5	0	24.2	34	12	9	0	0	0	0										
June		0	0	—	4.94	5	4	0	27.1	27	15	17	0	0	0	0										
July		1	4	.200	4.40	6	6	2	43	29	18	22	1	0	0	0										
Aug		3	2	.600	3.18	6	6	0	39.2	34	20	14	0	0	0	0										
Sept/Oct		0	2	.000	12.86	3	2	0	7	11	7	4	0	0	0	0										
Day		1	4	.200	5.74	6	6	1	31.1	34	15	14	0	0	0	0										
Night		4	8	.333	5.27	22	20	1	126.1	122	67	60	1	0	0	0										
vs. Left		—	—	—	—	—	—	—	—	92	55	31	—	—	—	—										
vs. Right		—	—	—	—	—	—	—	—	64	27	43	—	—	—	—										
On Grass		5	11	.313	5.03	24	22	2	139.2	128	70	68	1	0	0	0										
On Turf		0	1	.000	8.00	4	4	0	18	28	12	6	0	0	0	0										
Home		2	8	.200	5.44	15	14	0	89.1	87	49	41	0	0	0	0										
Road		3	4	.429	5.27	13	12	2	68.1	69	33	33	1	0	0	0										
Division Rivals																										
vs. BAL		1	0	1.000	2.25	2	1	0	16	10	6	9	0	0	0	0										
vs. BOS		0	1	.000	135.00	2	2	0	0.2	8	3	0	0	0	0	0										
vs. CLE		2	0	1.000	0.53	2	2	1	17	10	2	8	1	0	0	0										
vs. DET		0	1	.000	13.50	1	1	0	2.2	5	3	3	0	0	0	0										
vs. MIL		0	0	—	2.70	1	1	0	6.2	8	2	4	0	0	0	0										
vs. TOR		1	0	1.000	2.53	3	3	0	21.1	17	12	8	0	0	0	0										
1982	SD N	2	5	.286	4.10	15	10	1	63.2	66	27	25	0	0	0	0	15	0	0	.000	6	6	1	0	0.9	.923
1983		5	7	.417	2.93	21	19	4	119.2	106	48	59	1	0	0	0	31	2	0	.065	13	18	1	2	1.5	.969
1984		8	9	.471	4.68	36	22	2	146	143	72	77	1	2	1	0	41	8	0	.195	10	16	2	1	0.8	.929
1985		18	8	.692	3.15	33	33	5	228.2	229	65	69	2	0	0	0	77	6	0	.078	21	30	1	3	1.6	.981
1986		10	8	.556	4.30	37	35	3	209.1	218	75	117	1	1	0	0	67	10	0	.149	7	28	0	0	0.9	1.000
1987		3	10	.231	5.05	24	20	0	117.2	131	49	51	0	0	0	0	32	5	0	.156	8	18	0	3	1.1	1.000
1988		14	11	.560	3.35	33	33	4	217.2	196	76	91	2	0	0	0	62	7	0	.113	14	23	2	4	1.2	.949
1989	NY A	15	15	.500	4.80	34	34	5	208.1	238	76	98	2	0	0	0	0	0	0	—	8	20	2	1	0.9	.933
1990		5	12	.294	5.37	28	26	2	157.2	156	82	74	1	0	0	0	0	0	0	—	12	9	0	3	0.8	1.000
9 yrs.		80	85	.485	4.14	261	232	26	1468.2	1483	570	661	10	3	1	0	325	38	0	.117	99	168	9	17	1.1	.967

LEAGUE CHAMPIONSHIP SERIES

Year	Team	W	L	%	ERA	G	GS	CG	IP	H	BB	SO	ShO	W	L	SV	AB	H	HR	BA	PO	A	E	DP	TC/G	FA
1984	SD N	0	0	—	0.00	3	0	0	3.2	0	2	1	0	0	0	0	0	0	0	—	0	1	0	1	0.3	1.000

WORLD SERIES

Year	Team	W	L	%	ERA	G	GS	CG	IP	H	BB	SO	ShO	W	L	SV	AB	H	HR	BA	PO	A	E	DP	TC/G	FA
1984	SD N	1	1	.500	0.75	3	0	0	12	4	6	4	0	1	1	0	0	0	0	—	0	1	0	0	0.3	1.000

Neal Heaton

HEATON, NEAL
B. Mar. 3, 1960, Jamaica, N. Y.
BL TL 6' 2" 197 lbs.

Year	Team	W	L	%	ERA	G	GS	CG	IP	H	BB	SO	ShO	W	L	SV	AB	H	HR	BA	PO	A	E	DP	TC/G	FA
April		4	0	1.000	2.59	4	4	0	24.1	22	4	14	0	0	0	0										
May		4	1	.800	3.16	5	5	0	31.1	28	10	14	0	0	0	0										
June		2	2	.500	4.01	6	6	0	33.2	36	7	10	0	0	0	0										
July		0	4	.000	6.75	4	4	0	18.2	21	6	12	0	0	0	0										
Aug		1	1	.500	1.73	6	4	0	26	24	10	11	0	0	0	0										
Sept/Oct		1	1	.500	3.00	5	1	0	12	12	1	7	0	0	0	1										
Day		5	2	.714	2.84	9	7	0	44.1	41	13	23	0	0	0	0										
Night		7	7	.500	3.72	21	17	0	101.2	102	25	45	0	0	0	1										
vs. Left		—	—	—	—	—	—	—	—	28	10	13	—	—	—	—										
vs. Right		—	—	—	—	—	—	—	—	115	28	55	—	—	—	—										
On Grass		3	3	.500	4.34	8	7	0	37.1	47	6	18	0	0	0	0										
On Turf		9	6	.600	3.15	22	17	0	108.2	96	32	50	0	0	0	1										
Home		6	5	.545	3.02	16	13	0	80.1	73	27	40	0	0	0	0										
Road		6	4	.600	3.97	14	11	0	65.2	70	11	28	0	0	0	1										
Division Rivals																										
vs. CHI		1	0	1.000	3.00	1	1	0	6	5	0	2	0	0	0	0										
vs. MON		1	1	.500	2.78	5	3	0	22.2	23	9	8	0	0	0	1										
vs. NY		2	1	.667	1.96	5	4	0	23	22	4	9	0	0	0	0										
vs. PHI		0	1	.000	5.19	3	2	0	8.2	10	2	5	0	0	0	0										
vs. STL		2	0	1.000	3.07	2	2	0	14.2	12	2	6	0	0	0	0										

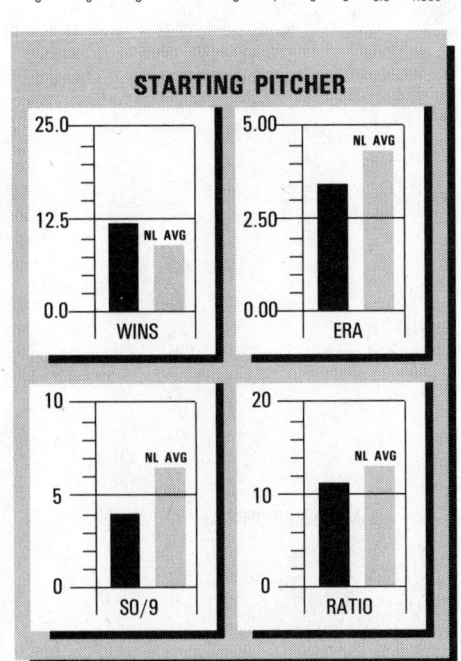

STARTING PITCHER

Year	Team	W	L	%	ERA	G	GS	CG	IP	H	BB	SO	ShO	W	L	SV	AB	H	HR	BA	PO	A	E	DP	TC/G	FA

(Header groupings: RELIEF PITCHING = W, L, SV; BATTING = AB, H, HR)

Neal Heaton *Continued*

Year	Team		W	L	%	ERA	G	GS	CG	IP	H	BB	SO	ShO	W	L	SV	AB	H	HR	BA	PO	A	E	DP	TC/G	FA
1982	CLE	A	0	2	.000	5.23	8	4	0	31	32	16	14	0	0	0	0	0	0	0	—	2	3	0	0	0.6	1.000
1983			11	7	.611	4.16	39	16	4	149.1	157	44	75	3	4	2	7	0	0	0	—	7	14	0	0	0.5	1.000
1984			12	15	.444	5.21	38	34	4	198.2	231	75	75	1	0	1	0	0	0	0	—	9	19	2	0	0.8	.933
1985			9	17	.346	4.90	36	33	5	207.2	244	80	82	1	0	1	0	0	0	0	—	8	21	1	1	0.8	.967
1986	2 teams	CLE A (12G 3 – 6)								MIN A (21G 4 – 9)																	
''	total		7	15	.318	4.08	33	29	0	198.2	201	81	90	0	0	0	1	0	0	0	—	13	24	1	1	1.2	.974
1987	MON	N	13	10	.565	4.52	32	32	3	193.1	207	37	105	1	0	0	0	67	14	0	.209	5	28	3	1	1.1	.917
1988			3	10	.231	4.99	32	11	0	97.1	98	43	43	0	1	4	2	21	3	0	.143	6	14	1	2	0.7	.952
1989	PIT	N	6	7	.462	3.05	42	18	1	147.1	127	55	67	0	2	0	0	42	9	0	.214	6	28	1	1	0.8	.971
1990			12	9	.571	3.45	30	24	0	146	143	38	68	0	0	1	0	43	2	0	.047	5	22	2	1	1.0	.931
9 yrs.			73	92	.442	4.35	290	201	22	1369.1	1440	469	619	6	7	9	10	173	28	0	.162	61	173	11	7	0.8	.955

Danny Heep

HEEP, DANIEL WILLIAM
B. July 3, 1957, San Antonio, Tex.
BL TL 5' 11" 185 lbs.

Year	Team		W	L	%	ERA	G	GS	CG	IP	H	BB	SO	ShO	W	L	SV	AB	H	HR	BA	PO	A	E	DP	TC/G	FA
1988	LA	N	0	0	—	9.00	1	0	0	2	2	0	0	0	0	0	0	149	36	0	.242	0	0	0	0	0.0	—
1990	BOS	A	0	0	—	9.00	1	0	0	1	4	0	0	0	0	0	0	69	12	0	.174	0	0	0	0	0.0	—
2 yrs.			0	0	—	9.00	2	0	0	3	6	0	0	0	0	0	0	*			—	0	0	0	0	0.0	—

Tom Henke

HENKE, THOMAS ANTHONY (The Terminator)
B. Dec. 21, 1957, Kansas City, Mo.
BR TR 6' 5" 215 lbs.

RELIEF PITCHER — WINS (AL AVG), ERA (AL AVG), SAVES (AL AVG), RATIO (AL AVG)

	W	L	%	ERA	G	GS	CG	IP	H	BB	SO	ShO	W	L	SV
April	0	0	—	2.89	9	0	0	9.1	11	2	8	0	0	0	1
May	0	1	.000	1.76	12	0	0	15.1	9	3	19	0	0	1	5
June	0	0	—	0.73	8	0	0	12.1	4	1	13	0	0	0	6
July	0	1	.000	3.38	12	0	0	13.1	12	6	12	0	0	1	9
Aug	1	0	1.000	0.75	9	0	0	12	12	1	12	0	1	0	5
Sept/Oct	1	2	.333	3.65	11	0	0	12.1	10	6	12	0	1	2	6
Day	0	1	.000	0.93	15	0	0	19.1	13	9	23	0	0	1	8
Night	2	3	.400	2.60	46	0	0	55.1	45	10	52	0	2	3	24
vs. Left	—	—	—	—	—	—	—	—	29	11	42	—	—	—	—
vs. Right	—	—	—	—	—	—	—	—	29	8	33	—	—	—	—
On Grass	0	4	.000	2.32	25	0	0	31	24	8	29	0	0	4	12
On Turf	2	0	1.000	2.06	36	0	0	43.2	34	11	46	0	2	0	20
Home	2	0	1.000	2.39	31	0	0	37.2	31	11	40	0	2	0	16
Road	0	4	.000	1.95	30	0	0	37	27	8	35	0	0	4	16
Division Rivals															
vs. BAL	1	1	.500	4.15	6	0	0	8.2	4	2	4	0	1	1	3
vs. BOS	1	1	.500	5.79	4	0	0	4.2	6	4	7	0	1	1	1
vs. CLE	0	0	—	5.40	5	0	0	5	7	0	4	0	0	0	1
vs. DET	0	0	—	1.42	5	0	0	6.1	5	0	6	0	0	0	1
vs. MIL	0	0	—	0.00	5	0	0	7.2	6	1	5	0	0	0	3
vs. NY	0	0	—	1.93	4	0	0	4.2	3	1	8	0	0	0	4

Year	Team		W	L	%	ERA	G	GS	CG	IP	H	BB	SO	ShO	W	L	SV	AB	H	HR	BA	PO	A	E	DP	TC/G	FA
1982	TEX	A	1	0	1.000	1.15	8	0	0	15.2	14	8	9	0	1	0	0	0	0	0	—	2	2	0	0	0.5	1.000
1983			1	0	1.000	3.38	8	0	0	16	16	4	17	0	1	0	1	0	0	0	—	0	3	1	0	0.5	.750
1984			1	1	.500	6.35	25	0	0	28.1	36	20	25	0	1	1	2	0	0	0	—	1	2	0	0	0.1	1.000
1985	TOR	A	3	3	.500	2.03	28	0	0	40	29	8	42	0	3	3	13	0	0	0	—	3	3	0	0	0.2	1.000
1986			9	5	.643	3.35	63	0	0	91.1	63	32	118	0	9	5	27	0	0	0	—	2	2	0	1	0.1	1.000
1987			0	6	.000	2.49	72	0	0	94	62	25	128	0	0	6	34	0	0	0	—	9	12	0	1	0.3	1.000
1988			4	4	.500	2.91	52	0	0	68	60	24	66	0	4	4	25	0	0	0	—	1	9	0	1	0.2	1.000
1989			8	3	.727	1.92	64	0	0	89	66	25	116	0	8	3	20	0	0	0	—	3	10	1	0	0.2	.929
1990			2	4	.333	2.17	61	0	0	74.2	58	19	75	0	2	4	32	0	0	0	—	6	5	0	0	0.2	1.000
9 yrs.			29	26	.527	2.72	381	0	0	517	404	165	596	0	29	26	154	0	0	0	—	27	48	2	3	0.2	.974

LEAGUE CHAMPIONSHIP SERIES

Year	Team		W	L	%	ERA	G	GS	CG	IP	H	BB	SO	ShO	W	L	SV	AB	H	HR	BA	PO	A	E	DP	TC/G	FA
1985	TOR	A	2	0	1.000	4.26	3	0	0	6.1	5	4	4	0	2	0	0	0	0	0	—	1	0	0	0	0.3	1.000
1989			0	0	—	0.00	3	0	0	2.2	0	0	3	0	0	0	0	0	0	0	—	0	1	0	0	0.3	1.000
2 yrs.			2	0	1.000	3.00	6	0	0	9	5	4	7	0	2	0	0	0	0	0	—	1	1	0	0	0.3	1.000

Year	Team	W	L	%	ERA	G	GS	CG	IP	H	BB	SO	ShO	RELIEF PITCHING W	L	SV	BATTING AB	H	HR	BA	PO	A	E	DP	TC/G	FA

Mike Henneman

HENNEMAN, MICHAEL ALAN
B. Dec. 11, 1961, St. Charles, Mo.
BR TR 6' 4" 205 lbs.

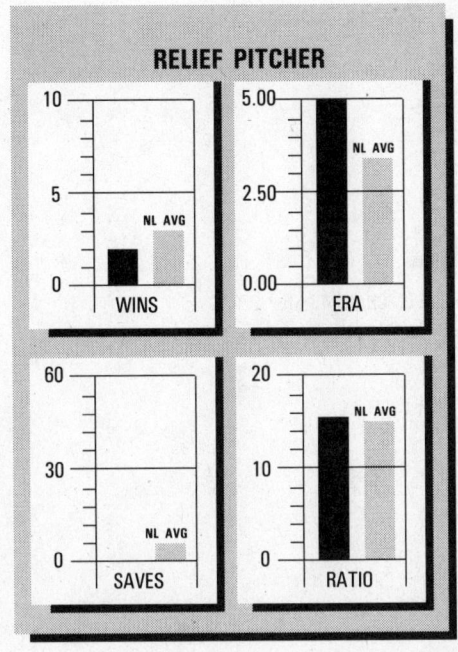

RELIEF PITCHER

Year	Team	W	L	%	ERA	G	GS	CG	IP	H	BB	SO	ShO	RP W	L	SV	AB	H	HR	BA	PO	A	E	DP	TC/G	FA
April		0	1	.000	1.46	10	0	0	12.1	13	4	4	0	0	1	5										
May		1	3	.250	4.96	12	0	0	16.1	14	7	6	0	1	3	6										
June		3	0	1.000	1.02	13	0	0	17.2	13	7	13	0	3	0	6										
July		2	2	.500	8.59	12	0	0	14.2	22	8	7	0	2	2	1										
Aug		1	0	1.000	1.50	10	0	0	18	16	4	8	0	1	0	1										
Sept/Oct		1	0	1.000	1.17	12	0	0	15.1	12	3	12	0	1	0	4										
Day		2	3	.400	4.75	20	0	0	30.1	41	12	14	0	2	3	8										
Night		6	3	.667	2.25	49	0	0	64	49	21	36	0	6	3	14										
vs. Left		—	—	—	—	—	—	—	—	40	18	14	—	—	—	—										
vs. Right		—	—	—	—	—	—	—	—	50	15	36	—	—	—	—										
On Grass		7	5	.583	3.17	59	0	0	82.1	83	28	44	0	7	5	15										
On Turf		1	1	.500	2.25	10	0	0	12	7	5	6	0	1	1	7										
Home		5	3	.625	3.72	35	0	0	48.1	43	12	26	0	5	3	8										
Road		3	3	.500	2.35	34	0	0	46	47	21	24	0	3	3	14										
Division Rivals																										
vs. BAL		1	1	.500	6.75	8	0	0	9.1	15	4	4	0	1	1	2										
vs. BOS		0	0	—	5.14	6	0	0	7	10	2	2	0	0	0	0										
vs. CLE		1	0	1.000	0.87	5	0	0	10.1	10	1	8	0	1	0	1										
vs. MIL		0	0	—	2.70	3	0	0	3.1	3	0	0	0	0	0	1										
vs. NY		0	0	—	1.50	4	0	0	6	4	1	8	0	0	0	1										
vs. TOR		0	1	.000	5.14	5	0	0	7	7	2	3	0	0	1	2										
1987	DET A	11	3	.786	2.98	55	0	0	96.2	86	30	75	0	11	3	7	1	0	0	.000	8	11	0	2	0.3	1.000
1988		9	6	.600	1.87	65	0	0	91.1	72	24	58	0	9	6	22	0	0	0	—	4	8	1	0	0.2	.923
1989		11	4	.733	3.70	60	0	0	90	84	51	69	0	11	4	8	0	0	0	—	5	12	0	2	0.3	1.000
1990		8	6	.571	3.05	69	0	0	94.1	90	33	50	0	8	6	22	0	0	0	—	7	16	3	2	0.4	.885
4 yrs.		39	19	.672	2.90	249	0	0	372.1	332	138	252	0	39	19	59	1	0	0	.000	24	47	4	6	0.3	.947

LEAGUE CHAMPIONSHIP SERIES

Year	Team	W	L	%	ERA	G	GS	CG	IP	H	BB	SO	ShO	RP W	L	SV	AB	H	HR	BA	PO	A	E	DP	TC/G	FA
1987	DET A	1	0	1.000	10.80	3	0	0	5	6	6	3	0	1	0	0	0	0	0	—	0	2	0	0	0.7	1.000

Randy Hennis

HENNIS, RANDALL PHILIP
B. Dec. 16, 1965, Clearlake, Calif.
BR TR 6' 6" 220 lbs.

Year	Team	W	L	%	ERA	G	GS	CG	IP	H	BB	SO	ShO	RP W	L	SV	AB	H	HR	BA	PO	A	E	DP	TC/G	FA
1990	HOU N	0	0	—	0.00	3	1	0	9.2	1	3	4	0	0	0	0	2	0	0	.000	2	0	0	0	0.7	1.000

Dwayne Henry

HENRY, DWAYNE ALLEN
B. Feb. 16, 1962, Elkton, Md.
BR TR 6' 3" 210 lbs.

RELIEF PITCHER

Year	Team	W	L	%	ERA	G	GS	CG	IP	H	BB	SO	ShO	RP W	L	SV	AB	H	HR	BA	PO	A	E	DP	TC/G	FA
April		0	0	—	5.68	7	0	0	6.1	8	3	4	0	0	0	0										
May		1	1	.500	6.14	8	0	0	7.1	10	5	8	0	1	1	0										
June		0	0	—	23.14	3	0	0	2.1	7	2	1	0	0	0	0										
July		1	0	1.000	1.35	5	0	0	6.2	4	4	11	0	1	0	0										
Aug		0	1	.000	3.38	7	0	0	10.2	10	8	5	0	0	1	0										
Sept/Oct		0	0	—	7.20	4	0	0	5	2	3	5	0	0	0	0										
Day		0	1	.000	6.30	10	0	0	10	12	8	9	0	0	1	0										
Night		2	1	.667	5.40	24	0	0	28.1	29	17	25	0	2	1	0										
vs. Left		—	—	—	—	—	—	—	—	19	14	15	—	—	—	—										
vs. Right		—	—	—	—	—	—	—	—	22	11	19	—	—	—	—										
On Grass		2	2	.500	5.87	27	0	0	30.2	34	19	26	0	2	2	0										
On Turf		0	0	—	4.70	7	0	0	7.2	7	6	8	0	0	0	0										
Home		1	1	.500	6.65	18	0	0	21.2	25	12	17	0	1	1	0										
Road		1	1	.500	4.32	16	0	0	16.2	16	13	17	0	1	1	0										
Division Rivals																										
vs. CIN		0	0	—	9.00	2	0	0	1	2	0	0	0	0	0	0										
vs. HOU		0	0	—	3.72	7	0	0	9.2	7	6	11	0	0	0	0										
vs. LA		0	0	—	0.90	6	0	0	10	6	6	9	0	0	0	0										
vs. SD		1	0	1.000	4.91	4	0	0	3.2	1	4	4	0	1	0	0										
vs. SF		0	0	—	22.09	3	0	0	3.2	11	3	2	0	0	0	0										

Year	Team		W	L	%	ERA	G	GS	CG	IP	H	BB	SO	ShO	RELIEF PITCHING			BATTING				PO	A	E	DP	TC/G	FA
															W	L	SV	AB	H	HR	BA						

Dwayne Henry *Continued*

Year	Team		W	L	%	ERA	G	GS	CG	IP	H	BB	SO	ShO	W	L	SV	AB	H	HR	BA	PO	A	E	DP	TC/G	FA
1984	TEX	A	0	1	.000	8.31	3	0	0	4.1	5	7	2	0	0	1	0	0	0	0	—	0	0	0	0	0.0	—
1985			2	2	.500	2.57	16	0	0	21	16	7	20	0	2	2	3	0	0	0	—	1	2	1	1	0.3	.750
1986			1	0	1.000	4.66	19	0	0	19.1	14	22	17	0	1	0	0	0	0	0	—	0	4	0	0	0.2	1.000
1987			0	0	—	9.00	5	0	0	10	12	9	7	0	0	0	0	0	0	0	—	2	1	0	0	0.6	1.000
1988			0	1	.000	8.71	11	0	0	10.1	15	9	10	0	0	1	0	0	0	0	—	1	0	0	0	0.1	1.000
1989	ATL	N	0	2	.000	4.26	12	0	0	12.2	12	5	16	0	0	2	1	0	0	0	—	1	0	1	0	0.2	.500
1990			2	2	.500	5.63	34	0	0	38.1	41	25	34	0	2	2	0	0	0	0	—	4	1	0	0	0.1	1.000
7 yrs.			5	8	.385	5.43	100	0	0	116	115	84	106	0	5	8	5	0	0	0	—	9	8	2	1	0.2	.895

Xavier Hernandez   HERNANDEZ, FRANCIS XAVIER
B. Aug. 16, 1965, Port Arthur, Tex.
BL TR 6′ 2″ 185 lbs.

	W	L	%	ERA	G	GS	CG	IP	H	BB	SO	ShO	W	L	SV	AB	H	HR	BA	PO	A	E	DP	TC/G	FA
April	0	0	—	0.00	5	0	0	5.1	2	2	2	0	0	0	0										
May	0	0	—	11.08	7	0	0	13	19	2	6	0	0	0	0										
June	0	0	—	2.84	6	0	0	12.2	13	7	3	0	0	0	0										
July	0	0	—	7.15	5	0	0	11.1	13	7	7	0	0	0	0										
Aug	0	0	—	0.00	4	0	0	8	6	0	3	0	0	0	0										
Sept/Oct	2	1	.667	2.25	7	1	0	12	7	6	3	0	0	2	0										
Day	0	0	—	6.00	5	0	0	9	11	2	2	0	0	0	0										
Night	2	1	.667	4.39	29	1	0	53.1	49	22	22	0	2	0	0										
vs. Left	—	—	—	—	—	—	—	—	33	18	6		—	—	—	—										
vs. Right									27	6	18															
On Grass	0	0	—	6.11	11	0	0	17.2	23	6	7	0	0	0	0										
On Turf	2	1	.667	4.03	23	1	0	44.2	37	18	17	0	2	0	0										
Home	2	0	1.000	0.64	16	0	0	28	16	7	13	0	2	0	0										
Road	0	1	.000	7.86	18	1	0	34.1	44	17	11	0	0	0	0										
Division Rivals																									
vs. ATL	0	0	—	0.00	3	0	0	2.1	1	0	1	0	0	0	0										
vs. CIN	1	1	.500	4.35	5	1	0	10.1	8	7	3	0	1	0	0										
vs. LA	0	0	—	0.00	5	0	0	5.2	5	1	2	0	0	0	0										
vs. SD	0	0	—	5.87	5	0	0	7.2	9	3	1	0	0	0	0										
vs. SF	1	0	1.000	0.00	3	0	0	8.1	5	4	3	0	1	0	0										

RELIEF PITCHER

WINS (NL AVG) — 10 / 5 / 0
ERA (NL AVG) — 5.00 / 2.50 / 0.00
SAVES (NL AVG) — 60 / 30 / 0
RATIO (NL AVG) — 20 / 10 / 0

Year	Team		W	L	%	ERA	G	GS	CG	IP	H	BB	SO	ShO	W	L	SV	AB	H	HR	BA	PO	A	E	DP	TC/G	FA
1989	TOR	A	1	0	1.000	4.76	7	0	0	22.2	25	8	7	0	1	0	0	0	0	0	—	1	2	1	0	0.6	.750
1990	HOU	N	2	1	.667	4.62	34	1	0	62.1	60	24	24	0	2	0	0	3	1	0	.333	3	5	0	0	0.2	1.000
2 yrs.			3	1	.750	4.66	41	1	0	85	85	32	31	0	3	0	0	3	1	0	.333	4	7	1	0	0.3	.917

Orel Hershiser   HERSHISER, OREL LEONARD QUINTON IV (Bulldog)
B. Sept. 16, 1958, Buffalo, N. Y.
BR TR 6′ 3″ 190 lbs.

Year	Team		W	L	%	ERA	G	GS	CG	IP	H	BB	SO	ShO	W	L	SV	AB	H	HR	BA	PO	A	E	DP	TC/G	FA
1983	LA	N	0	0	—	3.38	8	0	0	8	7	6	5	0	0	0	1	0	0	0	—	0	2	0	1	0.3	1.000
1984			11	8	.579	2.66	45	20	8	189.2	160	50	150	4	3	0	2	50	10	0	.200	17	28	5	2	1.1	.900
1985			19	3	**.864**	2.03	36	34	9	239.2	179	68	157	5	1	0	0	76	15	0	.197	20	45	7	4	2.0	.903
1986			14	14	.500	3.85	35	35	8	231.1	213	86	153	1	0	0	0	71	17	0	.239	22	36	3	6	1.7	.951
1987			16	16	.500	3.06	37	35	10	**264.2**	247	74	190	1	0	1	1	90	19	0	.211	37	34	5	6	2.1	.934
1988			**23**	8	.742	2.26	35	34	**15**	267	208	73	178	**8**	0	0	1	85	11	0	.129	32	60	6	6	2.8	.939
1989			15	**15**	.500	2.31	35	33	8	**256.2**	226	77	178	4	0	0	0	77	14	0	.182	24	51	4	2	2.3	.949
1990			1	1	.500	4.26	4	4	0	25.1	26	4	16	0	0	0	0	7	0	0	.000	1	3	0	0	1.0	1.000
8 yrs.			99	65	.604	2.71	235	195	58	1482.1	1266	438	1027	23	4	1	5	456	86	0	.189	153	259	30	27	1.9	.932

LEAGUE CHAMPIONSHIP SERIES

Year	Team		W	L	%	ERA	G	GS	CG	IP	H	BB	SO	ShO	W	L	SV	AB	H	HR	BA	PO	A	E	DP	TC/G	FA
1985	LA	N	1	0	1.000	3.52	2	2	1	15.1	17	6	5	0	0	0	0	7	2	0	.286	2	0	1	0	2.0	1.000
1988			1	0	1.000	1.09	4	3	1	24.2	18	7	15	1	0	0	1	9	0	0	.000	3	3	0	1	1.5	1.000
2 yrs.			2	0	1.000	2.03	6	5	2	40	35	13	20	1	0	0	1	16	2	0	.125	5	5	0	1	1.7	1.000

WORLD SERIES

Year	Team		W	L	%	ERA	G	GS	CG	IP	H	BB	SO	ShO	W	L	SV	AB	H	HR	BA	PO	A	E	DP	TC/G	FA
1988	LA	N	2	0	1.000	1.00	2	2	2	18	7	6	17	1	0	0	0	3	3	0	1.000	1	1	0	0	1.0	1.000

Year	Team	W	L	%	ERA	G	GS	CG	IP	H	BB	SO	ShO	RELIEF PITCHING W	L	SV	BATTING AB	H	HR	BA	PO	A	E	DP	TC/G	FA

Joe Hesketh

HESKETH, JOSEPH THOMAS
B. Feb. 15, 1959, Lackawanna, N. Y.
BL TL 6′ 2″ 165 lbs.

Period	W	L	%	ERA	G	GS	CG	IP	H	BB	SO	ShO	W	L	SV
April	1	0	1.000	0.00	2	0	0	3	2	2	3	0	1	0	0
May	0	1	.000	3.38	10	0	0	13.1	12	2	12	0	0	1	2
June	0	0	—	9.00	14	0	0	12	13	7	7	0	0	0	3
July	0	1	.000	4.76	7	0	0	5.2	5	3	2	0	0	1	0
Aug	0	1	.000	3.12	6	0	0	8.2	13	4	10	0	0	1	0
Sept/Oct	0	3	.000	3.71	6	2	0	17	24	7	16	0	0	1	0
Day	0	2	.000	3.78	10	1	0	16.2	20	7	11	0	0	1	0
Night	1	4	.200	4.81	35	1	0	43	49	18	39	0	1	3	5
vs. Left	—	—	—	—	—	—	—	—	19	9	19	—	—	—	—
vs. Right	—	—	—	—	—	—	—	—	50	16	31	—	—	—	—
On Grass	0	4	.000	5.21	35	2	0	48.1	61	21	41	0	0	2	3
On Turf	1	2	.333	1.59	10	0	0	11.1	8	4	9	0	1	2	2
Home	1	3	.250	4.08	26	1	0	35.1	41	14	30	0	1	2	3
Road	0	3	.000	5.18	19	1	0	24.1	28	11	20	0	0	2	2

Division Rivals

Opp	W	L	%	ERA	G	GS	CG	IP	H	BB	SO	ShO	W	L	SV
vs. BAL	0	0	—	0.00	2	0	0	4	4	2	6	0	0	0	0
vs. CLE	—	—	—	—	0	—	—	0	0	0	0	—	0	0	0
vs. DET	0	0	—	13.50	2	0	0	1.1	2	1	0	0	0	0	0
vs. MIL	—	—	—	—	0	—	—	0	0	0	0	—	0	0	0
vs. NY	0	0	—	0.00	1	0	0	2	1	0	0	0	0	0	0
vs. TOR	0	2	.000	7.36	2	0	0	3.2	9	3	2	0	0	2	0

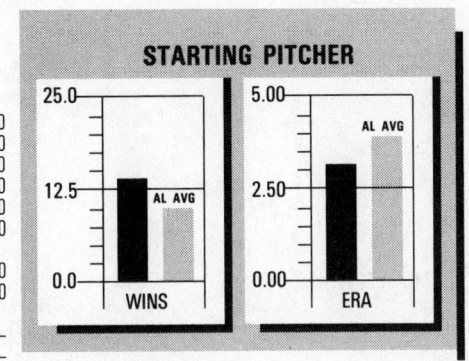

RELIEF PITCHER — WINS / ERA / SAVES / RATIO (NL AVG)

Year	Team	W	L	%	ERA	G	GS	CG	IP	H	BB	SO	ShO	W	L	SV	AB	H	HR	BA	PO	A	E	DP	TC/G	FA
1984	MON N	2	2	.500	1.80	11	5	1	45	38	15	32	1	0	1	1	10	1	0	.100	2	6	1	1	0.8	.889
1985		10	5	.667	2.49	25	25	2	155.1	125	45	113	1	0	0	0	44	4	0	.091	3	22	0	0	1.0	1.000
1986		6	5	.545	5.01	15	15	0	82.2	92	31	67	0	0	0	0	23	0	0	.000	2	8	1	0	0.7	.909
1987		0	0	—	3.14	18	0	0	28.2	23	15	31	0	0	0	1	4	0	0	.000	1	1	1	0	0.2	.667
1988		4	3	.571	2.85	60	0	0	72.2	63	35	64	0	4	3	9	2	0	0	.000	6	14	0	2	0.3	1.000
1989		6	4	.600	5.77	43	0	0	48.1	54	26	44	0	6	4	3	2	1	0	.500	3	9	1	3	0.3	.923
1990	3 teams	MON N (2G 1 - 0)			ATL N (31G 0 - 2)				BOS A (12G 0 - 4)																	
"	total	1	6	.143	4.53	45	2	0	59.2	69	25	50	0	1	4	5	1	0	0	.000	4	6	2	0	0.3	.833
7 yrs.		29	25	.537	3.51	217	47	3	492.1	464	192	401	2	11	12	19	86	6	0	.070	21	66	6	6	0.4	.935

Eric Hetzel

HETZEL, ERIC PAUL
B. Sept. 25, 1963, Crowley, La.
BR TR 6′ 3″ 175 lbs.

Year	Team	W	L	%	ERA	G	GS	CG	IP	H	BB	SO	ShO	W	L	SV	AB	H	HR	BA	PO	A	E	DP	TC/G	FA
1989	BOS A	2	3	.400	6.26	12	11	0	50.1	61	28	33	0	0	1	0	0	0	0	—	3	1	0	1	0.3	1.000
1990		1	4	.200	5.91	9	8	0	35	39	21	20	0	0	0	0	0	0	0	—	2	3	0	0	0.6	1.000
2 yrs.		3	7	.300	6.12	21	19	0	85.1	100	49	53	0	0	1	0	0	0	0	—	5	4	0	1	0.4	1.000

Greg Hibbard

HIBBARD, JAMES GREGORY
B. Sept. 13, 1964, New Orleans, La.
BL TL 6′ 180 lbs.

Period	W	L	%	ERA	G	GS	CG	IP	H	BB	SO	ShO	W	L	SV
April	2	1	.667	2.89	3	3	0	18.2	17	4	10	0	0	0	0
May	2	2	.500	2.21	6	6	1	40.2	33	10	18	0	0	0	0
June	2	1	.667	2.90	5	5	0	31	29	11	16	0	0	0	0
July	2	1	.667	3.68	6	6	0	36.2	42	4	14	0	0	0	0
Aug	3	3	.500	3.68	7	7	1	44	46	13	15	0	0	0	0
Sept/Oct	3	1	.750	3.38	6	6	0	40	35	13	19	1	0	0	0
Day	2	2	.500	2.74	7	7	0	46	45	8	26	0	0	0	0
Night	12	7	.632	3.27	26	26	3	165	157	47	66	1	0	0	0
vs. Left	—	—	—	—	—	—	—	—	19	8	10	—	—	—	—
vs. Right	—	—	—	—	—	—	—	—	183	47	82	—	—	—	—

STARTING PITCHER — WINS / ERA (AL AVG)

Year	Team	W	L	%	ERA	G	GS	CG	IP	H	BB	SO	ShO	W	L	SV	AB	H	HR	BA	PO	A	E	DP	TC/G	FA

Greg Hibbard *Continued*

		W	L	%	ERA	G	GS	CG	IP	H	BB	SO	ShO	W	L	SV	AB	H	HR	BA	PO	A	E	DP	TC/G	FA
On Grass		12	7	.632	2.89	29	29	3	189.2	174	46	76	1	0	0	0										
On Turf		2	2	.500	5.48	4	4	0	21.1	28	9	16	0	0	0	0										
Home		8	5	.615	2.98	19	19	1	120.2	104	33	51	1	0	0	0										
Road		6	4	.600	3.39	14	14	2	90.1	98	22	41	0	0	0	0										
Division Rivals																										
vs. CAL		2	1	.667	2.60	4	4	0	27.2	28	7	8	0	0	0	0										
vs. KC		1	1	.500	3.97	2	2	1	11.1	13	6	7	1	0	0	0										
vs. MIN		2	0	1.000	1.20	2	2	0	15	9	3	9	0	0	0	0										
vs. OAK		1	0	1.000	1.93	2	2	0	14	13	2	5	0	0	0	0										
vs. SEA		0	2	.000	11.00	2	2	0	9	11	8	5	0	0	0	0										
vs. TEX		0	1	.000	2.70	2	2	0	13.1	8	5	8	0	0	0	0										
1989	CHI A	6	7	.462	3.21	23	23	2	137.1	142	41	55	0	0	0	0	0	0	0	—	5	27	0	4	1.4	1.000
1990		14	9	.609	3.16	33	33	3	211	202	55	92	1	0	0	0	0	0	0	—	7	29	0	2	1.1	1.000
2 yrs.		20	16	.556	3.18	56	56	5	348.1	344	96	147	1	0	0	0	0	0	0	—	12	56	0	6	1.2	1.000

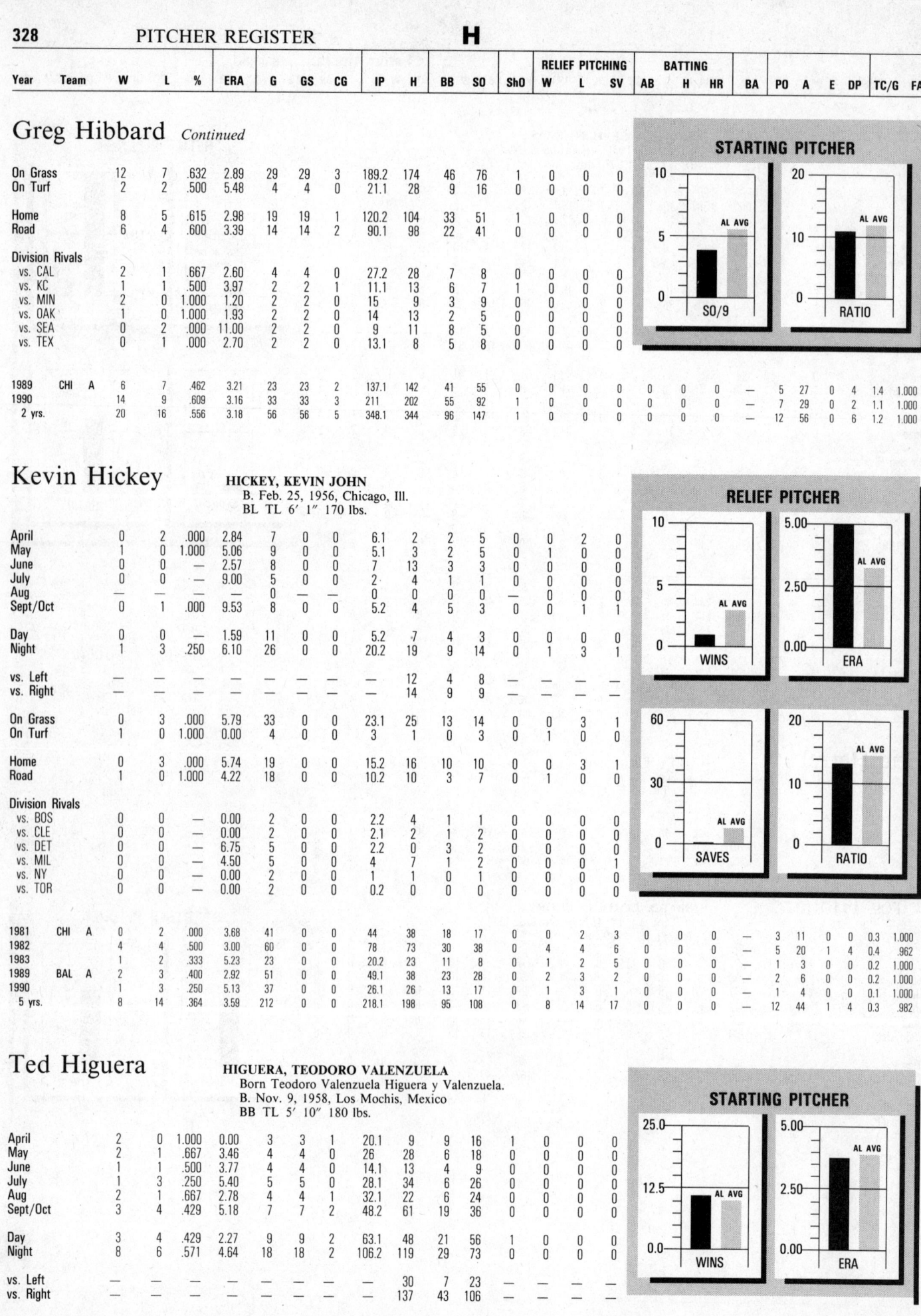

Kevin Hickey

HICKEY, KEVIN JOHN
B. Feb. 25, 1956, Chicago, Ill.
BL TL 6' 1" 170 lbs.

		W	L	%	ERA	G	GS	CG	IP	H	BB	SO	ShO	W	L	SV	AB	H	HR	BA	PO	A	E	DP	TC/G	FA
April		0	2	.000	2.84	7	0	0	6.1	2	2	5	0	0	2	0										
May		1	0	1.000	5.06	9	0	0	5.1	3	2	5	0	1	0	0										
June		0	0	—	2.57	8	0	0	7	13	3	3	0	0	0	0										
July		0	0	—	9.00	5	0	0	2	4	1	1	0	0	0	0										
Aug		—	—	—	—	0	—	—	0	0	0	0	0	0	0	0										
Sept/Oct		0	1	.000	9.53	8	0	0	5.2	4	5	3	0	0	1	1										
Day		0	0	—	1.59	11	0	0	5.2	7	4	3	0	0	0	0										
Night		1	3	.250	6.10	26	0	0	20.2	19	9	14	0	1	3	1										
vs. Left		—	—	—	—	—	—	—	—	12	4	8	—	—	—	—										
vs. Right		—	—	—	—	—	—	—	—	14	9	9	—	—	—	—										
On Grass		0	3	.000	5.79	33	0	0	23.1	25	13	14	0	0	3	1										
On Turf		1	0	1.000	0.00	4	0	0	3	1	0	3	0	1	0	0										
Home		0	3	.000	5.74	19	0	0	15.2	16	10	10	0	0	3	1										
Road		1	0	1.000	4.22	18	0	0	10.2	10	3	7	0	1	0	0										
Division Rivals																										
vs. BOS		0	0	—	0.00	2	0	0	2.2	4	1	1	0	0	0	0										
vs. CLE		0	0	—	0.00	2	0	0	2.1	2	1	2	0	0	0	0										
vs. DET		0	0	—	6.75	5	0	0	2.2	2	3	2	0	0	0	0										
vs. MIL		0	0	—	4.50	5	0	0	4	7	1	2	0	0	0	1										
vs. NY		0	0	—	0.00	2	0	0	1	1	0	1	0	0	0	0										
vs. TOR		0	0	—	0.00	2	0	0	0.2	0	0	0	0	0	0	0										
1981	CHI A	0	2	.000	3.68	41	0	0	44	38	18	17	0	0	2	3	0	0	0	—	3	11	0	0	0.3	1.000
1982		4	4	.500	3.00	60	0	0	78	73	30	38	0	4	4	6	0	0	0	—	5	20	1	4	0.4	.962
1983		1	2	.333	5.23	23	0	0	20.2	23	11	8	0	1	2	5	0	0	0	—	1	3	0	0	0.2	1.000
1989	BAL A	2	3	.400	2.92	51	0	0	49.1	38	23	28	0	2	3	2	0	0	0	—	2	6	0	0	0.2	1.000
1990		1	3	.250	5.13	37	0	0	26.1	26	13	17	0	1	3	1	0	0	0	—	1	4	0	0	0.1	1.000
5 yrs.		8	14	.364	3.59	212	0	0	218.1	198	95	108	0	8	14	17	0	0	0	—	12	44	1	4	0.3	.982

Ted Higuera

HIGUERA, TEODORO VALENZUELA
Born Teodoro Valenzuela Higuera y Valenzuela.
B. Nov. 9, 1958, Los Mochis, Mexico
BB TL 5' 10" 180 lbs.

		W	L	%	ERA	G	GS	CG	IP	H	BB	SO	ShO	W	L	SV	AB	H	HR	BA	PO	A	E	DP	TC/G	FA
April		2	0	1.000	0.00	3	3	1	20.1	9	9	16	1	0	0	0										
May		2	1	.667	3.46	4	4	0	26	28	6	18	0	0	0	0										
June		1	1	.500	3.77	4	4	0	14.1	13	4	9	0	0	0	0										
July		1	3	.250	5.40	5	5	0	28.1	34	6	26	0	0	0	0										
Aug		2	1	.667	2.78	4	4	1	32.1	22	6	24	0	0	0	0										
Sept/Oct		3	4	.429	5.18	7	7	2	48.2	61	19	36	0	0	0	0										
Day		3	4	.429	2.27	9	9	2	63.1	48	21	56	1	0	0	0										
Night		8	6	.571	4.64	18	18	2	106.2	119	29	73	0	0	0	0										
vs. Left		—	—	—	—	—	—	—	—	30	7	23	—	—	—	—										
vs. Right		—	—	—	—	—	—	—	—	137	43	106	—	—	—	—										

Year	Team	W	L	%	ERA	G	GS	CG	IP	H	BB	SO	ShO	RELIEF PITCHING W	L	SV	BATTING AB	H	HR	BA	PO	A	E	DP	TC/G	FA

Ted Higuera *Continued*

STARTING PITCHER

		W	L	%	ERA	G	GS	CG	IP	H	BB	SO	ShO	W	L	SV	AB	H	HR	BA	PO	A	E	DP	TC/G	FA
On Grass		8	9	.471	3.78	23	23	3	143	143	42	106	1	0	0	0										
On Turf		3	1	.750	3.67	4	4	1	27	24	8	23	0	0	0	0										
Home		7	4	.636	3.36	15	15	1	96.1	89	24	79	1	0	0	0										
Road		4	6	.400	4.28	12	12	3	73.2	78	26	50	0	0	0	0										
Division Rivals																										
vs. BAL		1	1	.500	2.18	4	4	1	20.2	19	7	11	0	0	0	0										
vs. BOS		2	1	.667	2.11	3	3	1	21.1	18	8	14	1	0	0	0										
vs. CLE		0	2	.000	4.41	2	2	1	16.1	16	5	8	0	0	0	0										
vs. DET		1	0	1.000	6.75	1	1	0	6.2	7	3	6	0	0	0	0										
vs. NY		0	1	.000	14.73	1	1	0	3.2	9	0	6	0	0	0	0										
vs. TOR		2	0	1.000	1.80	2	2	1	9	5	4	16	0	0	0	0										
1985	MIL A	15	8	.652	3.90	32	30	7	212.1	186	63	127	2	0	0	0	0	0	0	—	8	18	1	2	0.8	.963
1986		20	11	.645	2.79	34	34	15	248.1	226	74	207	4	0	0	0	0	0	0	—	9	26	0	1	1.0	1.000
1987		18	10	.643	3.85	35	35	14	261.2	236	87	240	3	0	0	0	0	0	0	—	9	23	2	3	1.0	.941
1988		16	9	.640	2.45	31	31	8	227.1	168	59	192	1	0	0	0	0	0	0	—	12	33	0	1	1.5	1.000
1989		9	6	.600	3.46	22	22	2	135.1	125	48	91	1	0	0	0	0	0	0	—	5	10	1	0	0.7	.938
1990		11	10	.524	3.76	27	27	4	170	167	50	129	1	0	0	0	0	0	0	—	7	18	2	2	1.0	.926
6 yrs.		89	54	.622	3.34	181	179	50	1255	1108	381	986	12	0	0	0	0	0	0	—	50	128	6	9	1.0	.967

Donnie Hill

HILL, DONALD EARL
B. Nov. 12, 1960, Pomona, Calif.
BB TR 5′ 10″ 165 lbs.

Year	Team	W	L	%	ERA	G	GS	CG	IP	H	BB	SO	ShO	W	L	SV	AB	H	HR	BA	PO	A	E	DP	TC/G	FA
1990	CAL A	0	0	—	0.00	1	0	0	1	0	1	1	0	0	0	0				*	0	0	0	0	0.0	—

Ken Hill

HILL, KENNETH WADE (Thrill)
B. Dec. 14, 1965, Lynn, Mass.
BR TR 6′ 4″ 200 lbs.

STARTING PITCHER

		W	L	%	ERA	G	GS	CG	IP	H	BB	SO	ShO	W	L	SV	AB	H	HR	BA	PO	A	E	DP	TC/G	FA
April		0	0	—	17.18	3	0	0	3.2	8	3	2	0	0	0	0										
May		—	—	—	—	0	—	—	0	0	0	0	—	0	0	0										
June		—	—	—	—	0	—	—	0	0	0	0	—	0	0	0										
July		1	0	1.000	1.17	1	1	0	7.2	3	3	9	0	0	0	0										
Aug		3	2	.600	3.86	6	6	1	32.2	27	13	24	0	0	0	0										
Sept/Oct		1	4	.200	6.75	7	7	0	34.2	41	14	23	0	0	0	0										
Day		3	3	.500	4.17	8	8	0	41	42	15	32	0	0	0	0										
Night		2	3	.400	6.93	9	6	1	37.2	37	18	26	0	0	0	0										
vs. Left		—	—	—	—	—	—	—	—	48	25	31	—	—	—	—										
vs. Right		—	—	—	—	—	—	—	—	31	8	27	—	—	—	—										
On Grass		2	1	.667	4.15	5	4	0	30.1	25	8	23	0	0	0	0										
On Turf		3	5	.375	6.33	12	10	1	48.1	54	25	35	0	0	0	0										
Home		2	2	.500	6.75	7	6	1	28	36	10	15	0	0	0	0										
Road		3	4	.429	4.80	10	8	0	50.2	43	23	43	0	0	0	0										
Division Rivals																										
vs. CHI		1	1	.500	5.06	2	2	0	10.2	12	2	5	0	0	0	0										
vs. MON		0	1	.000	8.64	3	2	0	8.1	11	4	7	0	0	0	0										
vs. NY		2	0	1.000	4.26	3	3	0	19	18	4	16	0	0	0	0										
vs. PHI		0	1	.000	135.00	1	1	0	0.1	2	4	0	0	0	0	0										
vs. PIT		1	1	.500	5.68	3	2	0	12.2	12	8	9	0	0	0	0										
1988	STL N	0	1	.000	5.14	4	1	0	14	16	6	6	0	0	0	0	3	0	0	.000	0	3	0	0	0.8	1.000
1989		7	15	.318	3.80	33	33	2	196.2	186	99	112	1	0	0	0	59	9	0	.153	12	31	1	1	1.3	.977
1990		5	6	.455	5.49	17	14	1	78.2	79	33	58	0	0	0	0	19	4	0	.211	7	10	1	1	1.1	.944
3 yrs.		12	22	.353	4.32	54	48	3	289.1	281	138	176	1	0	0	0	81	13	0	.160	19	44	2	2	1.2	.969

Year	Team	W	L	%	ERA	G	GS	CG	IP	H	BB	SO	ShO	W	L	SV	AB	H	HR	BA	PO	A	E	DP	TC/G	FA

Header groups: RELIEF PITCHING (W, L, SV) · BATTING (AB, H, HR)

Shawn Hillegas

HILLEGAS, SHAWN PATRICK
B. Aug. 21, 1964, Dos Palos, Calif.
BR TR 6′ 3″ 205 lbs.

Year	Team	W	L	%	ERA	G	GS	CG	IP	H	BB	SO	ShO	W	L	SV	AB	H	HR	BA	PO	A	E	DP	TC/G	FA
1987	LA N	4	3	.571	3.57	12	10	0	58	52	31	51	0	0	0	0	14	0	0	.000	4	2	1	0	0.6	.857
1988	2 teams			LA N	(11G 3 – 4)				CHI A	(6G 3 – 2)																
"	total	6	6	.500	3.72	17	16	0	96.2	84	35	56	0	0	0	0	15	2	0	.133	10	8	1	0	1.1	.947
1989	CHI A	7	11	.389	4.74	50	13	0	119.2	132	51	76	0	5	4	3	0	0	0	—	5	13	3	1	0.4	.857
1990		0	0	—	0.79	7	0	0	11.1	4	5	5	0	0	0	0	0	0	0	—	2	2	0	0	0.6	1.000
4 yrs.		17	20	.459	4.00	86	39	0	285.2	272	122	188	0	5	4	3	29	2	0	.069	21	25	5	1	0.6	.902

Howard Hilton

HILTON, HOWARD JAMES
B. Jan. 3, 1964, Oxnard, Calif.
BR TR 6′ 3″ 230 lbs.

Year	Team	W	L	%	ERA	G	GS	CG	IP	H	BB	SO	ShO	W	L	SV	AB	H	HR	BA	PO	A	E	DP	TC/G	FA
1990	STL N	0	0	—	0.00	2	0	0	3	2	3	2	0	0	0	0	0	0	0	—	0	0	0	0	0.0	—

Brian Holman

HOLMAN, BRIAN SCOTT
B. Jan. 25, 1965, Denver, Colo.
BR TR 6′ 4″ 185 lbs.

	W	L	%	ERA	G	GS	CG	IP	H	BB	SO	ShO	W	L	SV
April	3	2	.600	3.86	5	5	1	30.1	25	10	23	0	0	0	0
May	3	1	.750	4.04	5	5	0	35.2	38	14	20	0	0	0	0
June	2	3	.400	4.68	5	5	0	32.2	41	9	22	0	0	0	0
July	2	1	.667	3.12	6	6	0	40.1	37	13	20	0	0	0	0
Aug	1	3	.250	4.23	6	6	2	44.2	40	16	34	0	0	0	0
Sept/Oct	0	1	.000	6.00	1	1	0	6	7	4	2	0	0	0	0
Day	1	4	.200	4.89	6	6	0	38.2	36	15	22	0	0	0	0
Night	10	7	.588	3.81	22	22	3	151	152	51	99	0	0	0	0
vs. Left	—	—	—	—	—	—	—	—	106	38	49	—	—	—	—
vs. Right	—	—	—	—	—	—	—	—	82	28	72	—	—	—	—
On Grass	5	3	.625	4.75	9	9	1	55	50	16	39	0	0	0	0
On Turf	6	8	.429	3.74	19	19	2	134.2	138	50	82	0	0	0	0
Home	4	6	.400	4.04	15	15	1	104.2	114	44	59	0	0	0	0
Road	7	5	.583	4.02	13	13	2	85	74	22	62	0	0	0	0
Division Rivals															
vs. CAL	3	0	1.000	2.29	3	3	0	19.2	20	7	13	0	0	0	0
vs. CHI	1	0	1.000	7.20	1	1	0	5	9	1	4	0	0	0	0
vs. KC	1	3	.250	3.90	4	4	1	30	30	8	16	0	0	0	0
vs. MIN	1	0	1.000	2.25	1	1	0	8	7	1	5	0	0	0	0
vs. OAK	1	1	.500	2.25	2	2	1	16	7	4	12	0	0	0	0
vs. TEX	0	1	.000	6.35	1	1	0	5.2	9	3	2	0	0	0	0

Year	Team	W	L	%	ERA	G	GS	CG	IP	H	BB	SO	ShO	W	L	SV	AB	H	HR	BA	PO	A	E	DP	TC/G	FA
1988	MON N	4	8	.333	3.23	18	16	1	100.1	101	34	58	1	0	0	0	28	3	0	.107	4	11	1	0	0.9	.938
1989	2 teams			MON N	(10G 1 – 2)				SEA A	(23G 8 – 10)																
"	total	9	12	.429	3.67	33	25	6	191.1	194	77	105	2	0	1	0	8	1	0	.125	11	31	2	3	1.3	.955
1990	SEA A	11	11	.500	4.03	28	28	3	189.2	188	66	121	0	0	0	0	1	0	0	.000	16	17	1	0	1.2	.971
3 yrs.		24	31	.436	3.72	79	69	10	481.1	483	177	284	3	0	1	0	37	4	0	.108	31	59	4	3	1.2	.957

STARTING PITCHER — WINS · ERA · SO/9 · RATIO (AL AVG)

Darren Holmes

HOLMES, DARREN LEE
B. Apr. 25, 1966, Asheville, N. C.
BR TR 6′ 199 lbs.

Year	Team	W	L	%	ERA	G	GS	CG	IP	H	BB	SO	ShO	W	L	SV	AB	H	HR	BA	PO	A	E	DP	TC/G	FA
1990	LA N	0	1	.000	5.19	14	0	0	17.1	15	11	19	0	0	1	0	0	0	0	—	1	1	0	0	0.1	1.000

Year	Team	W	L	%	ERA	G	GS	CG	IP	H	BB	SO	ShO	W	L	SV	AB	H	HR	BA	PO	A	E	DP	TC/G	FA

Brian Holton

HOLTON, BRIAN JOHN
B. Nov. 29, 1959, McKeesport, Pa.
BR TR 6′ 3″ 190 lbs.

Year	Team	W	L	%	ERA	G	GS	CG	IP	H	BB	SO	ShO	W	L	SV	AB	H	HR	BA	PO	A	E	DP	TC/G	FA
April		1	0	1.000	8.22	7	0	0	7.2	10	5	5	0	1	0	0										
May		0	1	.000	3.71	10	0	0	17	18	2	8	0	0	1	0										
June		1	2	.333	1.88	11	0	0	24	21	10	9	0	1	2	0										
July		0	0	—	9.64	5	0	0	9.1	19	4	5	0	0	0	0										
Aug		—	—	—	—	0	—	—	0	0	0	0	—	0	0	0										
Sept/Oct		—	—	—	—	0	—	—	0	0	0	0	—	0	0	0										
Day		0	0	—	3.79	10	0	0	19	22	6	5	0	0	0	0										
Night		2	3	.400	4.85	23	0	0	39	46	15	22	0	2	3	0										
vs. Left		—	—	—	—	—	—	—	—	25	10	13	—	—	—	—										
vs. Right		—	—	—	—	—	—	—	—	43	11	14	—	—	—	—										
On Grass		2	3	.400	3.88	29	0	0	51	58	16	26	0	2	3	0										
On Turf		0	0	—	9.00	4	0	0	7	10	5	1	0	0	0	0										
Home		2	1	.667	3.51	15	0	0	33.1	35	8	13	0	2	1	0										
Road		0	2	.000	5.84	18	0	0	24.2	33	13	14	0	0	2	0										
Division Rivals																										
vs. BOS		0	0	—	0.00	4	0	0	5.1	3	4	2	0	0	0	0										
vs. CLE		0	1	.000	3.60	2	0	0	5	7	2	0	0	0	1	0										
vs. DET		0	0	—	8.31	4	0	0	4.1	6	1	4	0	0	0	0										
vs. MIL		0	1	.000	3.60	2	0	0	5	4	2	3	0	0	1	0										
vs. NY		1	0	1.000	1.04	3	0	0	8.2	7	2	4	0	1	0	0										
vs. TOR		0	0	—	12.71	2	0	0	5.2	12	4	4	0	0	0	0										
1985	LA N	1	1	.500	9.00	3	0	0	4	9	1	1	0	1	1	0	0	0	0	—	0	1	0	0	0.3	1.000
1986		2	3	.400	4.44	12	3	0	24.1	28	6	24	0	2	1	0	5	0	0	.000	3	3	0	0	0.5	1.000
1987		3	2	.600	3.89	53	1	0	83.1	87	32	58	0	3	2	2	5	1	0	.200	8	14	0	2	0.4	1.000
1988		7	3	.700	1.70	45	0	0	84.2	69	26	49	0	7	3	1	10	0	0	.000	8	11	0	0	0.4	1.000
1989	BAL A	5	7	.417	4.02	39	12	0	116.1	140	39	51	0	2	4	0	0	0	0	—	22	9	1	1	0.8	.969
1990		2	3	.400	4.50	33	0	0	58	68	21	27	0	2	3	0	0	0	0	—	6	10	1	0	0.5	.941
6 yrs.		20	19	.513	3.62	185	16	0	370.2	401	125	210	0	17	14	3	20	1	0	.050	47	48	2	3	0.5	.979

LEAGUE CHAMPIONSHIP SERIES

Year	Team	W	L	%	ERA	G	GS	CG	IP	H	BB	SO	ShO	W	L	SV	AB	H	HR	BA	PO	A	E	DP	TC/G	FA
1988	LA N	0	0	—	2.25	3	0	0	4	2	1	2	0	0	0	1	1	1	0	1.000	0	1	0	0	0.3	1.000

WORLD SERIES

Year	Team	W	L	%	ERA	G	GS	CG	IP	H	BB	SO	ShO	W	L	SV	AB	H	HR	BA	PO	A	E	DP	TC/G	FA
1988	LA N	0	0	—	0.00	1	0	0	2	0	1	0	0	0	0	0	0	0	0	—	0	1	0	0	1.0	1.000

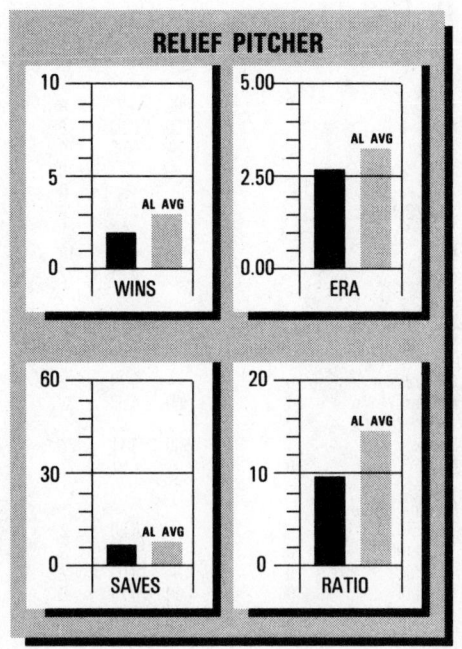

Rick Honeycutt

HONEYCUTT, FREDERICK WAYNE
B. June 29, 1952, Chattanooga, Tenn.
BL TL 6′ 1″ 185 lbs.

Year	Team	W	L	%	ERA	G	GS	CG	IP	H	BB	SO	ShO	W	L	SV	AB	H	HR	BA	PO	A	E	DP	TC/G	FA
April		0	0	—	1.74	6	0	0	10.1	5	4	8	0	0	0	1										
May		1	1	.500	1.04	10	0	0	8.2	5	3	4	0	1	1	1										
June		0	0	—	2.84	10	0	0	12.2	12	0	8	0	0	0	0										
July		1	1	.500	5.11	14	0	0	12.1	13	7	5	0	1	1	2										
Aug		0	0	—	1.23	10	0	0	7.1	4	4	4	0	0	0	2										
Sept/Oct		0	0	—	3.00	13	0	0	12	7	4	9	0	0	0	1										
Day		1	1	.500	1.55	25	0	0	29	19	10	19	0	1	1	4										
Night		1	1	.500	3.67	38	0	0	34.1	27	12	19	0	1	1	3										
vs. Left		—	—	—	—	—	—	—	—	14	5	17	—	—	—	—										
vs. Right		—	—	—	—	—	—	—	—	32	17	21	—	—	—	—										
On Grass		2	1	.667	2.15	52	0	0	54.1	36	18	35	0	2	1	7										
On Turf		0	1	.000	6.00	11	0	0	9	10	4	3	0	0	1	0										
Home		2	0	1.000	1.80	28	0	0	30	19	10	17	0	2	0	6										
Road		0	2	.000	3.51	35	0	0	33.1	27	12	21	0	0	2	1										
Division Rivals																										
vs. CAL		0	0	—	0.00	7	0	0	8	3	1	3	0	0	0	0										
vs. CHI		0	0	—	1.59	5	0	0	5.2	3	2	2	0	0	0	0										
vs. KC		0	0	—	3.00	3	0	0	3	3	0	0	0	0	0	0										
vs. MIN		0	1	.000	8.10	5	0	0	6.2	9	4	5	0	0	1	1										
vs. SEA		1	0	1.000	1.93	5	0	0	4.2	3	4	3	0	1	0	0										
vs. TEX		0	0	—	1.04	8	0	0	8.2	7	1	8	0	0	0	0										

Year	Team	W	L	%	ERA	G	GS	CG	IP	H	BB	SO	ShO	RELIEF PITCHING W	L	SV	BATTING AB	H	HR	BA	PO	A	E	DP	TC/G	FA

Rick Honeycutt *Continued*

Year	Team	W	L	%	ERA	G	GS	CG	IP	H	BB	SO	ShO	W	L	SV	AB	H	HR	BA	PO	A	E	DP	TC/G	FA
1977	SEA A	0	1	.000	4.34	10	3	0	29	26	11	17	0	0	0	0	0	0	0	—	0	2	0	0	0.2	1.000
1978		5	11	.313	4.89	26	24	4	134.1	150	49	50	1	0	0	0	0	0	0	—	9	28	2	1	1.5	.949
1979		11	12	.478	4.04	33	28	8	194	201	67	83	1	1	3	0	0	0	0	—	6	28	5	2	1.2	.872
1980		10	17	.370	3.95	30	30	9	203	221	60	79	1	0	0	0	0	0	0	—	9	32	2	1	1.4	.953
1981	TEX A	11	6	.647	3.30	20	20	8	128	120	17	40	2	0	0	0	0	0	0	—	3	30	3	1	1.8	.917
1982		5	17	.227	5.27	30	26	4	164	201	54	64	1	0	0	0	0	0	0	—	3	35	2	0	1.3	.950
1983	2 teams	TEX A	(25G	14 – 8)	LA N	(9G	2 – 3)																			
"	total	16	11	.593	3.03	34	32	6	213.2	214	50	74	2	0	0	0	12	1	0	.083	13	55	1	5	2.0	.986
1984	LA N	10	9	.526	2.84	29	28	6	183.2	180	51	75	2	0	0	0	56	8	0	.143	10	42	3	2	1.9	.945
1985		8	12	.400	3.42	31	25	1	142	141	49	67	0	0	1	1	38	5	0	.132	9	37	2	1	1.5	.958
1986		11	9	.550	3.32	32	28	0	171	164	45	100	0	1	0	0	43	3	0	.070	9	35	1	2	1.4	.978
1987	2 teams	LA N	(27G	2 – 12)	OAK A	(7G	1 – 4)																			
"	total	3	16	.158	4.72	34	24	1	139.1	158	54	102	1	0	1	0	30	7	0	.233	5	20	2	0	0.8	.926
1988	OAK A	3	2	.600	3.50	55	0	0	79.2	74	25	47	0	3	2	7	0	0	0	—	3	18	2	3	0.4	.913
1989		2	2	.500	2.35	64	0	0	76.2	56	26	52	0	2	2	12	0	0	0	—	4	16	1	1	0.3	.952
1990		2	2	.500	2.70	63	0	0	63.1	46	22	38	0	2	2	7	2	0	0	.000	0	15	1	0	0.3	.938
14 yrs.		97	127	.433	3.73	491	268	47	1921.2	1952	580	888	11	9	11	27	181	24	0	.133	83	393	27	19	1.0	.946

LEAGUE CHAMPIONSHIP SERIES

Year	Team	W	L	%	ERA	G	GS	CG	IP	H	BB	SO	ShO	W	L	SV	AB	H	HR	BA	PO	A	E	DP	TC/G	FA
1983	LA N	0	0	—	21.60	2	0	0	1.2	4	0	2	0	0	0	0	0	0	0	—	1	0	0	0	0.5	1.000
1985		0	0	—	13.50	2	0	0	1.1	4	2	1	0	0	0	0	0	0	0	—	0	1	0	0	0.5	1.000
1988	OAK A	1	0	1.000	0.00	3	0	0	2	0	0	2	0	1	0	0	0	0	0	—	0	0	0	0	0.0	—
1989		0	0	—	32.40	3	0	0	1.2	6	5	1	0	0	0	0	0	0	0	—	0	0	0	0	0.0	—
1990		0	0	—	0.00	3	0	0	1.2	0	2	0	0	0	0	1	0	0	0	—	0	0	0	0	0.0	—
5 yrs.		1	0	1.000	12.97	13	0	0	8.1	14	9	4	0	1	0	1	0	0	0	—	1	1	0	0	0.2	1.000

WORLD SERIES

Year	Team	W	L	%	ERA	G	GS	CG	IP	H	BB	SO	ShO	W	L	SV	AB	H	HR	BA	PO	A	E	DP	TC/G	FA
1988	OAK A	1	0	1.000	0.00	3	0	0	3.1	0	0	5	0	1	0	0	0	0	0	—	0	0	0	0	0.0	—
1989		0	0	—	6.75	3	0	0	2.2	4	0	2	0	0	0	0	0	0	0	—	0	0	0	0	0.0	—
1990		0	0	—	0.00	1	0	0	1.2	2	1	0	0	0	0	0	0	0	0	—	0	0	0	0	0.0	—
3 yrs.		1	0	1.000	2.35	7	0	0	7.2	6	1	7	0	1	0	0	0	0	0	—	0	0	0	0	0.0	—

John Hoover

HOOVER, JOHN NICKLAUS
B. Dec. 22, 1962, Fresno, Calif.
BR TR 6′ 2″ 190 lbs.

Year	Team	W	L	%	ERA	G	GS	CG	IP	H	BB	SO	ShO	W	L	SV	AB	H	HR	BA	PO	A	E	DP	TC/G	FA
1990	TEX A	0	0	—	11.57	2	0	0	4.2	8	3	0	0	0	0	0	0	0	0	—	0	0	0	0	0.0	—

Ricky Horton

HORTON, RICKY NEAL
B. July 30, 1959, Poughkeepsie, N. Y.
BL TL 6′ 2″ 197 lbs.

	W	L	%	ERA	G	GS	CG	IP	H	BB	SO	ShO	W	L	SV
April	0	1	.000	4.32	8	0	0	8.1	8	5	5	0	0	1	1
May	1	0	1.000	0.00	6	0	0	9.2	8	2	2	0	1	0	0
June	0	0	—	10.38	10	0	0	13	27	7	5	0	0	0	0
July	0	0	—	3.27	8	0	0	11	9	8	6	0	0	0	0
Aug	—	—	—		0	—	—	0	0	0	0	—	0	0	0
Sept/Oct	—	—	—		0	—	—	0	0	0	0	—	0	0	0
Day	0	1	.000	5.40	10	0	0	8.1	9	6	6	0	0	1	0
Night	1	0	1.000	4.81	22	0	0	33.2	43	16	13	0	1	0	1
vs. Left	—	—	—		—	—	—		19	9	10	—	—	—	—
vs. Right	—	—	—		—	—	—		33	13	8	—	—	—	—
On Grass	0	0	—	5.79	9	0	0	9.1	12	5	9	0	0	0	0
On Turf	1	1	.500	4.68	23	0	0	32.2	40	17	9	0	1	1	1
Home	1	1	.500	3.41	20	0	0	29	31	14	9	0	1	1	0
Road	0	0	—	8.31	12	0	0	13	21	8	9	0	0	0	1
Division Rivals															
vs. CHI	0	0	—	6.00	2	0	0	3	4	0	2	0	0	0	0
vs. MON	0	0	—	23.14	3	0	0	2.1	8	2	0	0	0	0	0
vs. NY	0	0	—	9.00	2	0	0	2	4	2	1	0	0	0	0
vs. PHI	0	1	.000	6.75	6	0	0	8	12	2	4	0	0	1	0
vs. PIT	0	0	—	1.80	3	0	0	5	4	4	0	0	0	0	1

RELIEF PITCHER

WINS — NL AVG

ERA — NL AVG

SAVES — NL AVG

RATIO — NL AVG

Year	Team	W	L	%	ERA	G	GS	CG	IP	H	BB	SO	ShO	W	L	SV	AB	H	HR	BA	PO	A	E	DP	TC/G	FA
1984	STL N	9	4	.692	3.44	37	18	1	125.2	140	39	76	1	1	0	1	31	2	0	.065	5	35	3	3	1.2	.930
1985		3	2	.600	2.91	49	3	0	89.2	84	34	59	0	2	2	1	16	1	0	.063	9	21	2	0	0.7	.938
1986		4	3	.571	2.24	42	9	1	100.1	77	26	49	0	1	0	3	18	1	0	.056	4	24	0	3	0.7	1.000
1987		8	3	.727	3.82	67	6	0	125	127	42	55	0	6	2	7	29	5	0	.172	12	31	2	2	0.7	.956

Year	Team	W	L	%	ERA	G	GS	CG	IP	H	BB	SO	ShO	RELIEF PITCHING			BATTING			BA	PO	A	E	DP	TC/G	FA
														W	L	SV	AB	H	HR							

Ricky Horton *Continued*

Year	Team	W	L	%	ERA	G	GS	CG	IP	H	BB	SO	ShO	W	L	SV	AB	H	HR	BA	PO	A	E	DP	TC/G	FA
1988	2 teams	CHI A	(52G 6 - 10)		LA N	(12G 1 - 1)																				
''	total	7	11	.389	4.87	64	9	1	118.1	131	38	36	0	4	5	2	0	0	0	—	5	27	2	4	0.5	.941
1989	2 teams	LA N	(23G 0 - 0)		STL N	(11G 0 - 3)																				
''		0	3	.000	4.85	34	8	0	72.1	85	21	26	0	0	0	0	12	3	0	.250	2	13	0	2	0.4	1.000
1990	STL N	1	1	.500	4.93	32	0	0	42	52	22	18	0	1	1	1	4	0	0	.000	2	14	0	2	0.5	1.000
7 yrs.		32	27	.542	3.76	325	53	3	673.1	696	222	319	1	15	10	15	110	12	0	.109	39	165	9	16	0.7	.958

LEAGUE CHAMPIONSHIP SERIES

Year	Team	W	L	%	ERA	G	GS	CG	IP	H	BB	SO	ShO	W	L	SV	AB	H	HR	BA	PO	A	E	DP	TC/G	FA
1985	STL N	0	0	—	9.00	3	0	0	3	4	2	1	0	0	0	0	0	0	0	—	1	2	0	0	1.0	1.000
1987		0	0	—	0.00	1	0	0	3	2	0	2	0	0	0	0	0	0	0	—	0	0	0	0	0.0	—
1988	LA N	0	0	—	0.00	4	0	0	4.1	4	2	3	0	0	0	0	0	0	0	—	0	1	0	1	0.3	1.000
3 yrs.		0	0	—	2.61	8	0	0	10.1	10	4	6	0	0	0	0	0	0	0	—	1	3	0	1	0.5	1.000

WORLD SERIES

Year	Team	W	L	%	ERA	G	GS	CG	IP	H	BB	SO	ShO	W	L	SV	AB	H	HR	BA	PO	A	E	DP	TC/G	FA
1985	STL N	0	0	—	6.75	3	0	0	4	4	5	5	0	0	0	0	1	0	0	.000	2	0	0	0	0.7	1.000
1987		0	0	—	6.00	2	0	0	3	5	0	1	0	0	0	0	0	0	0	—	0	1	0	0	0.5	1.000
2 yrs.		0	0	—	6.43	5	0	0	7	9	5	6	0	0	0	0	1	0	0	.000	2	1	0	0	0.6	1.000

Charlie Hough

HOUGH, CHARLES OLIVER
B. Jan. 5, 1948, Honolulu, Hawaii
BR TR 6′ 2″ 190 lbs.

STARTING PITCHER

	W	L	%	ERA	G	GS	CG	IP	H	BB	SO	ShO	W	L	SV	AB	H	HR	BA	PO	A	E	DP	TC/G	FA
April	1	1	.500	4.44	4	4	0	24.1	21	14	15	0	0	0	0										
May	4	2	.667	3.20	6	6	2	45	34	23	19	0	0	0	0										
June	2	2	.500	5.26	6	6	1	37.2	31	20	25	0	0	0	0										
July	0	2	.000	3.95	4	4	0	27.1	30	15	13	0	0	0	0										
Aug	3	2	.600	3.46	6	6	1	41.2	35	27	25	0	0	0	0										
Sept/Oct	2	3	.400	4.43	6	6	1	42.2	39	20	17	0	0	0	0										
Day	2	2	.500	3.09	6	6	1	43.2	35	22	28	0	0	0	0										
Night	10	10	.500	4.32	26	26	4	175	155	97	86	0	0	0	0										
vs. Left	—	—	—	—	—	—	—	—	84	56	47	—	—	—	—										
vs. Right	—	—	—	—	—	—	—	—	106	63	67	—	—	—	—										
On Grass	12	9	.571	4.04	27	27	5	187.1	160	0	92	0	0	0	0										
On Turf	0	3	.000	4.31	5	5	0	31.1	30	19	22	0	0	0	0										
Home	5	8	.385	4.47	14	14	3	96.2	91	53	48	0	0	0	0										
Road	7	4	.636	3.76	18	18	2	122	99	66	66	0	0	0	0										
Division Rivals																									
vs. CAL	1	1	.500	6.27	3	3	0	18.2	13	18	8	0	0	0	0										
vs. CHI	2	1	.667	4.01	3	3	2	24.2	27	6	11	0	0	0	0										
vs. KC	2	0	1.000	4.95	3	3	0	20	17	14	10	0	0	0	0										
vs. MIN	1	1	.500	3.00	2	2	1	15	12	7	13	0	0	0	0										
vs. OAK	0	2	.000	2.92	3	3	1	24.2	19	11	10	0	0	0	0										
vs. SEA	0	2	.000	7.36	3	3	0	14.2	16	10	8	0	0	0	0										

Year	Team	W	L	%	ERA	G	GS	CG	IP	H	BB	SO	ShO	W	L	SV	AB	H	HR	BA	PO	A	E	DP	TC/G	FA
1970	LA N	0	0	—	5.29	8	0	0	17	18	11	8	0	0	0	2	3	1	0	.333	1	3	0	0	0.5	1.000
1971		0	0	—	4.50	4	0	0	4	3	3	4	0	0	0	0	0	0	0	—	0	1	0	0	0.3	1.000
1972		0	0	—	3.38	2	0	0	2.2	2	2	4	0	0	0	0	0	0	0	—	0	1	0	0	0.5	1.000
1973		4	2	.667	2.76	37	0	0	71.2	52	45	70	0	4	2	5	14	3	0	.214	4	11	1	1	0.4	.938
1974		9	4	.692	3.75	49	0	0	96	65	40	63	0	9	4	1	12	0	0	.000	3	14	1	1	0.4	.944
1975		3	7	.300	2.95	38	0	0	61	43	34	34	0	3	7	4	6	2	0	.333	4	7	2	0	0.3	.846
1976		12	8	.600	2.21	77	0	0	142.2	102	77	81	0	12	8	18	21	6	0	.286	3	22	1	0	0.3	.962
1977		6	12	.333	3.33	70	1	0	127	98	70	105	0	5	12	22	22	4	1	.182	6	15	1	1	0.3	.955
1978		5	5	.500	3.29	55	0	0	93	69	48	66	0	5	5	7	12	4	0	.333	5	11	0	2	0.3	1.000
1979		7	5	.583	4.77	42	14	0	151	152	66	76	0	1	2	0	38	6	0	.158	5	26	1	0	0.8	.969
1980	2 teams	LA N	(19G 1 - 3)		TEX A	(16G 2 - 2)																				
''	total	3	5	.375	4.55	35	3	2	93	91	58	72	1	2	3	2	0	0	0	.500	2	10	1	0	0.4	.923
1981	TEX A	4	1	.800	2.96	21	5	2	82	61	31	69	0	0	0	1	0	0	0	—	2	8	0	1	0.5	1.000
1982		16	13	.552	3.95	34	34	12	228	217	72	128	2	0	0	0	0	0	0	—	14	35	1	4	1.5	.980
1983		15	13	.536	3.18	34	33	11	252	219	95	152	3	1	0	0	0	0	0	—	25	46	2	4	2.1	.973
1984		16	14	.533	3.76	36	**36**	**17**	266	**260**	94	165	1	0	0	0	0	0	0	—	12	51	1	2	1.8	.984
1985		14	16	.467	3.31	34	34	14	250.1	198	83	141	1	0	0	0	0	0	0	—	18	35	2	5	1.6	.964
1986		17	10	.630	3.79	33	33	7	230.1	188	89	146	2	0	0	0	0	0	0	—	20	32	1	2	1.6	.981
1987		18	13	.581	3.79	40	**40**	13	**285.1**	238	124	223	0	0	0	0	0	0	0	—	30	46	1	3	1.9	.987
1988		15	16	.484	3.32	34	34	10	252	202	**126**	174	0	0	0	0	0	0	0	—	27	43	1	4	2.1	.986
1989		10	13	.435	4.35	30	30	5	182	168	95	94	1	0	0	0	0	0	0	—	13	18	1	3	1.1	.969
1990		12	12	.500	4.07	32	32	5	218.2	190	119	114	0	0	0	0	0	0	0	—	11	31	2	2	1.4	.955
21 yrs.		186	169	.524	3.63	745	329	98	3105.2	2636	1382	1989	11	42	43	61	130	27	1	.208	205	466	20	35	0.9	.971

Year	Team	W	L	%	ERA	G	GS	CG	IP	H	BB	SO	ShO	RELIEF PITCHING W	L	SV	BATTING AB	H	HR	BA	PO	A	E	DP	TC/G	FA

Charlie Hough *Continued*

LEAGUE CHAMPIONSHIP SERIES

Year	Team	W	L	%	ERA	G	GS	CG	IP	H	BB	SO	ShO	W	L	SV	AB	H	HR	BA	PO	A	E	DP	TC/G	FA
1974	LA N	0	0	—	7.71	1	0	0	2.1	4	0	2	0	0	0	0	0	0	0	—	0	0	1	0	1.0	—
1977		0	0	—	4.50	1	0	0	2	2	0	3	0	0	0	0	0	0	0	—	0	1	0	0	1.0	1.000
1978		0	0	—	4.50	1	0	0	2	1	0	1	0	0	0	0	0	0	0	—	1	1	0	0	2.0	1.000
3 yrs.		0	0	—	5.68	3	0	0	6.1	7	0	6	0	0	0	0	0	0	0	—	1	2	1	0	1.3	.750

WORLD SERIES

Year	Team	W	L	%	ERA	G	GS	CG	IP	H	BB	SO	ShO	W	L	SV	AB	H	HR	BA	PO	A	E	DP	TC/G	FA
1974	LA N	0	0	—	0.00	1	0	0	2	0	1	4	0	0	0	0	0	0	0	—	0	0	0	0	0.0	—
1977		0	0	—	1.80	2	0	0	5	3	0	5	0	0	0	0	0	0	0	—	0	0	0	0	0.0	—
1978		0	0	—	8.44	2	0	0	5.1	10	2	5	0	0	0	0	0	0	0	—	1	0	0	0	0.5	1.000
3 yrs.		0	0	—	4.38	5	0	0	12.1	13	3	14	0	0	0	0	0	0	0	—	1	0	0	0	0.2	1.000

Jay Howell

HOWELL, JAY CANFIELD
B. Nov. 26, 1955, Miami, Fla.
BR TR 6′ 3″ 200 lbs.

Split	W	L	%	ERA	G	GS	CG	IP	H	BB	SO	ShO	W	L	SV
April	1	1	.500	4.50	3	0	0	4	4	2	2	0	1	1	0
May	0	2	.000	4.05	5	0	0	6.2	12	2	4	0	0	2	1
June	2	1	.667	2.65	11	0	0	17	15	7	17	0	2	1	3
July	0	0	—	0.82	6	0	0	11	5	2	11	0	0	0	4
Aug	1	1	.500	1.10	12	0	0	16.1	12	4	13	0	1	1	5
Sept/Oct	1	0	1.000	2.45	8	0	0	11	11	3	12	0	1	0	3
Day	1	2	.333	0.77	11	0	0	11.2	6	4	9	0	1	2	3
Night	4	3	.571	2.48	34	0	0	54.1	53	16	50	0	4	3	13
vs. Left	—	—	—	—	—	—	—	—	36	10	41	—	—	—	—
vs. Right	—	—	—	—	—	—	—	—	23	10	18	—	—	—	—
On Grass	2	4	.333	2.57	34	0	0	49	43	13	42	0	2	4	14
On Turf	3	1	.750	1.06	11	0	0	17	16	7	17	0	3	1	2
Home	1	3	.250	2.91	23	0	0	34	29	9	29	0	1	3	8
Road	4	2	.667	1.41	22	0	0	32	30	11	30	0	4	2	8
Division Rivals															
vs. ATL	2	0	1.000	3.52	4	0	0	7.2	7	3	10	0	2	0	1
vs. CIN	1	0	1.000	2.25	5	0	0	8	6	2	7	0	1	0	1
vs. HOU	2	1	.667	2.00	6	0	0	9	6	4	8	0	2	1	2
vs. SD	0	1	.000	3.24	6	0	0	8.1	8	5	7	0	0	1	2
vs. SF	0	1	.000	6.00	3	0	0	3	3	0	5	0	0	1	

RELIEF PITCHER

WINS — 10 / 5 / 0 — NL AVG
ERA — 5.00 / 2.50 / 0.00 — NL AVG
SAVES — 60 / 30 / 0 — NL AVG
RATIO — 20 / 10 / 0 — NL AVG

Year	Team	W	L	%	ERA	G	GS	CG	IP	H	BB	SO	ShO	W	L	SV	AB	H	HR	BA	PO	A	E	DP	TC/G	FA
1980	CIN N	0	0	—	15.00	5	0	0	3	8	0	1	0	0	0	0	0	0	0	—	0	0	0	0	0.0	—
1981	CHI N	2	0	1.000	4.91	10	2	0	22	23	10	10	0	0	0	0	2	0	0	.000	2	9	0	1	1.1	1.000
1982	NY A	2	3	.400	7.71	6	6	0	28	42	13	21	0	0	0	0	0	0	0	—	2	2	0	0	0.7	1.000
1983		1	5	.167	5.38	19	12	2	82	89	35	61	0	0	0	0	0	0	0	—	7	10	1	0	0.9	.944
1984		9	4	.692	2.69	61	1	0	103.2	86	34	109	0	8	4	7	0	0	0	—	11	16	1	3	0.5	.964
1985	OAK A	9	8	.529	2.85	63	0	0	98	98	31	68	0	9	8	29	0	0	0	—	1	15	0	1	0.3	1.000
1986		3	6	.333	3.38	38	0	0	53.1	53	23	42	0	3	6	16	0	0	0	—	2	6	0	0	0.2	1.000
1987		3	4	.429	5.89	36	0	0	44.1	48	21	35	0	3	4	16	0	0	0	—	3	4	1	0	0.2	.875
1988	LA N	5	3	.625	2.08	50	0	0	65	44	21	70	0	5	3	21	2	0	0	.000	7	6	1	0	0.3	.929
1989		5	3	.625	1.58	56	0	0	79.2	60	22	55	0	5	3	28	3	0	0	.000	5	10	1	2	0.3	.938
1990		5	5	.500	2.18	45	0	0	66	59	20	59	0	5	5	16	2	0	0	.000	3	8	0	0	0.2	1.000
11 yrs.		44	41	.518	3.43	389	21	2	645	610	230	531	0	38	33	133	9	0	0	.000	43	86	5	7	0.3	.963

LEAGUE CHAMPIONSHIP SERIES

Year	Team	W	L	%	ERA	G	GS	CG	IP	H	BB	SO	ShO	W	L	SV	AB	H	HR	BA	PO	A	E	DP	TC/G	FA
1988	LA N	0	1	.000	27.00	2	0	0	0.2	1	2	1	0	0	1	0	0	0	0	—	0	0	0	0	0.0	—

WORLD SERIES

Year	Team	W	L	%	ERA	G	GS	CG	IP	H	BB	SO	ShO	W	L	SV	AB	H	HR	BA	PO	A	E	DP	TC/G	FA
1988	LA N	0	1	.000	3.38	2	0	0	2.2	3	1	2	0	0	1	1	0	0	0	—	0	0	0	0	0.0	—

Year	Team	W	L	%	ERA	G	GS	CG	IP	H	BB	SO	ShO	RELIEF PITCHING W	L	SV	BATTING AB	H	HR	BA	PO	A	E	DP	TC/G	FA

Ken Howell

HOWELL, KENNETH
B. Nov. 28, 1960, Detroit, Mich.
BR TR 6′ 3″ 195 lbs.

Year	Team	W	L	%	ERA	G	GS	CG	IP	H	BB	SO	ShO	W	L	SV	AB	H	HR	BA	PO	A	E	DP	TC/G	FA
April		2	2	.500	3.28	4	4	0	24.2	22	14	18	0	0	0	0										
May		3	1	.750	4.31	5	5	0	31.1	25	13	18	0	0	0	0										
June		3	2	.600	3.98	6	6	2	40.2	42	13	27	0	0	0	0										
July		0	2	.000	13.50	2	2	0	6	11	5	4	0	0	0	0										
Aug		0	0	—	9.00	1	1	0	4	6	4	3	0	0	0	0										
Sept/Oct		—	—	—	—	0	—	—	0	0	0	0	—	0	0	0										
Day		2	0	1.000	3.57	3	3	0	17.2	12	10	14	0	0	0	0										
Night		6	7	.462	4.85	15	15	2	89	94	39	56	0	0	0	0										
vs. Left		—	—	—	—	—	—	—	—	76	36	33	—	—	—	—										
vs. Right		—	—	—	—	—	—	—	—	30	13	37	—	—	—	—										
On Grass		3	1	.750	3.33	4	4	1	24.1	18	10	19	0	0	0	0										
On Turf		5	6	.455	5.03	14	14	1	82.1	88	39	51	0	0	0	0										
Home		4	4	.500	5.43	11	11	0	61.1	69	29	32	0	0	0	0										
Road		4	3	.571	3.57	7	7	2	45.1	37	20	38	0	0	0	0										
Division Rivals																										
vs. CHI		1	0	1.000	1.69	2	2	1	16	13	4	9	0	0	0	0										
vs. MON		2	0	1.000	3.00	2	2	0	15	16	8	10	0	0	0	0										
vs. NY		1	1	.500	8.31	2	2	0	8.2	14	4	7	0	0	0	0										
vs. PIT		0	1	.000	6.75	2	2	1	12	14	6	11	0	0	0	0										
vs. STL		0	2	.000	6.52	2	2	0	9.2	10	7	6	0	0	0	0										
1984	LA N	5	5	.500	3.33	32	1	0	51.1	51	9	54	0	5	5	6	5	0	0	.000	6	6	0	0	0.4	1.000
1985		4	7	.364	3.77	56	0	0	86	66	35	85	0	4	7	12	4	0	0	.000	7	11	1	0	0.3	.947
1986		6	12	.333	3.87	62	0	0	97.2	86	63	104	0	6	**12**	12	5	0	0	.000	5	7	1	0	0.2	.923
1987		3	4	.429	4.91	40	2	0	55	54	29	60	0	2	3	1	4	1	0	.250	5	5	0	0	0.3	1.000
1988		0	1	.000	6.39	4	1	0	12.2	16	4	12	0	0	0	0	1	0	0	.000	0	1	0	0	0.3	1.000
1989	PHI N	12	12	.500	3.44	33	32	1	204	155	86	164	1	0	0	0	65	6	0	.092	13	19	0	2	1.0	1.000
1990		8	7	.533	4.64	18	18	2	106.2	106	49	70	0	0	0	0	30	2	0	.067	6	11	2	0	1.1	.895
7 yrs.		38	48	.442	3.95	245	54	3	613.1	534	275	549	1	17	27	31	114	9	0	.079	42	60	4	2	0.4	.962
LEAGUE CHAMPIONSHIP SERIES																										
1985	LA N	0	0	—	0.00	1	0	0	2	0	0	2	0	0	0	0	0	0	0	—	0	1	0	0	1.0	1.000

Mark Huismann

HUISMANN, MARK LAWRENCE
B. May 11, 1958, Lincoln, Neb.
BR TR 6′ 3″ 195 lbs.

Year	Team	W	L	%	ERA	G	GS	CG	IP	H	BB	SO	ShO	W	L	SV	AB	H	HR	BA	PO	A	E	DP	TC/G	FA
1983	KC A	2	1	.667	5.58	13	0	0	30.2	29	17	20	0	2	1	0	0	0	0	—	1	2	0	0	0.2	1.000
1984		3	3	.500	4.08	38	0	0	75	83	21	54	0	3	3	3	0	0	0	—	7	10	3	0	0.5	.850
1985		1	0	1.000	1.93	9	0	0	18.2	14	3	9	0	1	0	0	0	0	0	—	1	3	0	0	0.4	1.000
1986	2 teams	KC A (10G 0 - 1)							SEA A (36G 3 - 3)																	
"	total	3	4	.429	3.79	46	1	0	97.1	98	25	72	0	3	3	5	0	0	0	—	12	12	3	1	0.6	.889
1987	2 teams	SEA A (6G 0 - 0)							CLE A (20G 2 - 3)																	
"		2	3	.400	5.04	26	0	0	50	48	12	38	0	2	3	2	0	0	0	—	4	8	3	0	0.6	.800
1988	DET A	1	0	1.000	5.06	5	0	0	5.1	6	2	6	0	1	0	0	0	0	0	—	0	2	0	1	0.4	1.000
1989	BAL A	0	0	—	6.35	8	0	0	11.1	13	0	13	0	0	0	1	0	0	0	—	3	3	0	0	0.8	1.000
1990	PIT N	1	0	1.000	9.00	2	0	0	3	6	1	2	0	1	0	0	0	0	0	—	0	0	0	0	0.0	—
8 yrs.		13	11	.542	4.36	147	1	0	291.1	297	81	214	0	13	10	11	0	0	0	—	28	40	9	2	0.5	.883
LEAGUE CHAMPIONSHIP SERIES																										
1984	KC A	0	0	—	10.13	1	0	0	2.2	6	1	2	0	0	0	0	0	0	0	—	0	0	0	0	0.0	—

STARTING PITCHER

WINS (NL AVG) — scale 0.0 to 25.0
ERA (NL AVG) — scale 0.00 to 5.00
SO/9 (NL AVG) — scale 0 to 10
RATIO (NL AVG) — scale 0 to 20

Year	Team	W	L	%	ERA	G	GS	CG	IP	H	BB	SO	ShO	RELIEF PITCHING W	L	SV	BATTING AB	H	HR	BA	PO	A	E	DP	TC/G	FA

Bruce Hurst

HURST, BRUCE VEE
B. Mar. 24, 1958, St. George, Utah
BL TL 6′ 4″ 200 lbs.

Year	Team	W	L	%	ERA	G	GS	CG	IP	H	BB	SO	ShO	W	L	SV	AB	H	HR	BA	PO	A	E	DP	TC/G	FA
April		0	3	.000	4.55	4	4	1	27.2	22	8	14	0	0	0	0										
May		3	2	.600	3.63	6	6	1	39.2	39	10	35	0	0	0	0										
June		1	2	.333	6.21	6	6	0	29	33	13	24	0	0	0	0										
July		2	1	.667	2.79	6	6	2	42	29	10	27	1	0	0	0										
Aug		2	1	.667	1.89	5	5	2	38	30	14	29	1	0	0	0										
Sept/Oct		3	0	1.000	1.33	6	6	3	47.1	35	8	33	2	0	0	0										
Day		1	4	.200	4.27	10	10	2	65.1	61	20	49	0	0	0	0										
Night		10	5	.667	2.67	23	23	7	158.1	127	43	113	4	0	0	0										
vs. Left		—	—	—	—	—	—	—	—	38	17	43	—	—	—	—										
vs. Right		—	—	—	—	—	—	—	—	150	46	119	—	—	—	—										
On Grass		9	4	.692	2.96	22	22	6	152	119	45	115	3	0	0	0										
On Turf		2	5	.286	3.52	11	11	3	71.2	69	18	47	1	0	0	0										
Home		7	3	.700	2.66	17	17	4	122	94	33	97	2	0	0	0										
Road		4	6	.400	3.72	16	16	5	101.2	94	30	65	2	0	0	0										
Division Rivals																										
vs. ATL		1	0	1.000	3.50	3	3	1	18	17	4	13	1	0	0	0										
vs. CIN		2	0	1.000	1.72	4	4	2	31.1	20	6	20	1	0	0	0										
vs. HOU		1	1	.500	1.93	4	4	1	28	20	6	23	1	0	0	0										
vs. LA		1	1	.500	3.27	3	3	2	22	14	5	14	1	0	0	0										
vs. SF		1	2	.333	5.09	4	4	0	23	24	11	15	0	0	0	0										
1980	BOS A	2	2	.500	9.00	12	7	0	31	39	16	16	0	0	0	0	0	0	0	—	1	4	0	0	0.4	1.000
1981		2	0	1.000	4.30	5	5	0	23	23	12	11	0	0	0	0	0	0	0	—	0	2	0	0	0.4	1.000
1982		3	7	.300	5.77	28	19	0	117	161	40	53	0	0	0	1	0	0	0	—	6	22	1	1	1.0	.966
1983		12	12	.500	4.09	33	32	6	211.1	241	62	115	2	0	0	0	0	0	0	—	12	34	2	2	1.5	.958
1984		12	12	.500	3.92	33	33	4	218	232	88	136	2	0	0	0	0	0	0	—	10	30	0	1	1.2	1.000
1985		11	13	.458	4.51	35	31	6	229.1	243	70	189	1	0	0	2	0	0	0	—	11	32	3	0	1.3	.935
1986		13	8	.619	2.99	25	25	11	174.1	169	50	167	4	0	0	0	0	0	0	—	7	18	2	2	1.1	.926
1987		15	13	.536	4.41	33	33	15	238.2	239	76	190	3	0	0	0	0	0	0	—	12	34	3	2	1.5	.939
1988		18	6	.750	3.66	33	32	7	216.2	222	65	166	1	0	0	0	0	0	0	—	7	31	0	0	1.2	1.000
1989	SD N	15	11	.577	2.69	33	33	**10**	244.2	214	66	179	2	0	0	0	70	5	0	.071	8	42	0	2	1.5	1.000
1990		11	9	.550	3.14	33	33	9	223.2	188	63	162	**4**	0	0	0	67	6	0	.090	7	34	1	3	1.3	.976
11 yrs.		114	93	.551	3.91	303	283	73	1927.2	1971	608	1384	19	0	3	0	137	11	0	.080	81	283	12	13	1.2	.968

LEAGUE CHAMPIONSHIP SERIES

Year	Team	W	L	%	ERA	G	GS	CG	IP	H	BB	SO	ShO	W	L	SV	AB	H	HR	BA	PO	A	E	DP	TC/G	FA
1986	BOS A	1	0	1.000	2.40	2	2	1	15	18	1	8	0	0	0	0	0	0	0	—	1	2	0	0	1.5	1.000
1988		0	2	.000	2.77	2	2	1	13	10	5	12	0	0	0	0	0	0	0	—	0	4	0	0	2.0	1.000
2 yrs.		1	2	.333	2.57	4	4	2	28	28	6	20	0	0	0	0	0	0	0	—	1	6	0	0	1.8	1.000

WORLD SERIES

Year	Team	W	L	%	ERA	G	GS	CG	IP	H	BB	SO	ShO	W	L	SV	AB	H	HR	BA	PO	A	E	DP	TC/G	FA
1986	BOS A	2	0	1.000	1.96	3	3	1	23	18	6	17	0	0	0	0	3	0	0	.000	1	3	0	0	1.3	1.000

Jeff Innis

INNIS, JEFFREY DAVID
B. July 5, 1962, Decatur, Ill.
BR TR 6′ 1″ 170 lbs.

Year	Team	W	L	%	ERA	G	GS	CG	IP	H	BB	SO	ShO	W	L	SV	AB	H	HR	BA	PO	A	E	DP	TC/G	FA
1987	NY N	0	1	.000	3.16	17	1	0	25.2	29	4	28	0	0	1	0	3	0	0	.000	3	2	0	0	0.3	1.000
1988		1	1	.500	1.89	12	0	0	19	19	2	14	0	1	1	0	0	0	0	—	0	0	0	0	0.0	—
1989		0	1	.000	3.18	29	0	0	39.2	38	8	16	0	0	1	0	2	0	0	.000	7	8	1	0	0.6	.938
1990		1	3	.250	2.39	18	0	0	26.1	19	10	12	0	1	3	1	0	0	0	—	4	3	0	0	0.4	1.000
4 yrs.		2	6	.250	2.76	76	1	0	110.2	105	24	70	0	2	6	1	5	0	0	.000	14	13	1	0	0.4	.964

Daryl Irvine

IRVINE, DARYL KEITH
B. Nov. 15, 1964, Harrisonburg, Va.
BR TR 6′ 3″ 195 lbs.

Year	Team	W	L	%	ERA	G	GS	CG	IP	H	BB	SO	ShO	W	L	SV	AB	H	HR	BA	PO	A	E	DP	TC/G	FA
1990	BOS A	1	1	.500	4.67	11	0	0	17.1	15	10	9	0	1	1	0	0	0	0	—	1	3	0	0	0.4	1.000

STARTING PITCHER

Bar charts: WINS, ERA, SO/9, RATIO (each compared to NL AVG)

Year	Team	W	L	%	ERA	G	GS	CG	IP	H	BB	SO	ShO	W	L	SV	AB	H	HR	BA	PO	A	E	DP	TC/G	FA

Danny Jackson

JACKSON, DANNY LYNN
B. Jan. 5, 1962, San Antonio, Tex.
BR TL 6' 205 lbs.

Period		W	L	%	ERA	G	GS	CG	IP	H	BB	SO	ShO	W	L	SV	AB	H	HR	BA	PO	A	E	DP	TC/G	FA
April		0	0	—	10.80	2	2	0	3.1	7	1	2	0	0	0	0										
May		0	1	.000	2.13	2	2	0	12.2	13	4	2	0	0	0	0										
June		2	1	.667	3.60	6	6	0	35	33	16	19	0	0	0	0										
July		2	0	1.000	1.33	3	3	0	20.1	14	9	15	0	0	0	0										
Aug		1	0	1.000	5.14	2	1	0	7	9	1	5	0	0	0	0										
Sept/Oct		1	4	.200	4.38	7	7	0	39	43	9	33	0	0	0	0										
Day		1	2	.333	2.25	8	8	0	44	40	15	22	0	0	0	0										
Night		5	4	.556	4.42	14	13	0	73.1	79	25	54	0	0	0	0										
vs. Left		—	—	—	—	—	—	—	—	20	11	16	—	—	—	—										
vs. Right		—	—	—	—	—	—	—	—	99	29	60	—	—	—	—										
On Grass		3	2	.600	3.61	8	8	0	47.1	50	15	33	0	0	0	0										
On Turf		3	4	.429	3.60	14	13	0	70	69	25	43	0	0	0	0										
Home		2	3	.400	3.83	11	10	0	54	50	17	36	0	0	0	0										
Road		4	3	.571	3.41	11	11	0	63.1	69	23	40	0	0	0	0										

Division Rivals

		W	L	%	ERA	G	GS	CG	IP	H	BB	SO	ShO	W	L	SV	AB	H	HR	BA	PO	A	E	DP	TC/G	FA
vs. ATL		0	2	.000	9.00	3	3	0	12	21	6	7	0	0	0	0										
vs. HOU		1	1	.500	4.61	3	3	0	13.2	20	7	8	0	0	0	0										
vs. LA		1	2	.333	3.48	4	3	0	20.2	21	4	15	0	0	0	0										
vs. SD		1	0	1.000	3.50	3	3	0	18	15	4	17	0	0	0	0										
vs. SF		0	0	—	1.84	2	2	0	14.2	6	6	8	0	0	0	0										
1983	KC A	1	1	.500	5.21	4	3	0	19	26	6	9	0	1	0	0	—				2	3	0	0	1.3	1.000
1984		2	6	.250	4.26	15	11	1	76	84	35	40	0	1	0	0	0	0	0	—	6	7	1	2	0.9	.929
1985		14	12	.538	3.42	32	32	4	208	209	76	114	3	0	0	0	0	0	0	—	8	27	3	2	1.2	.921
1986		11	12	.478	3.20	32	27	4	185.2	177	79	115	1	0	0	1	0	0	0	—	14	21	2	1	1.2	.946
1987		9	18	.333	4.02	36	34	11	224	219	109	152	2	0	0	0	0	0	0	—	13	23	2	2	1.1	.947
1988	CIN N	**23**	8	.742	2.73	35	35	**15**	260.2	206	71	161	6	0	0	0	90	13	0	.144	10	52	3	2	1.9	.954
1989		6	11	.353	5.60	20	20	1	115.2	122	57	70	0	0	0	0	36	8	0	.222	5	15	0	1	1.0	1.000
1990		6	6	.500	3.61	22	21	0	117.1	119	40	76	0	0	0	0	37	2	0	.054	4	13	1	0	0.8	.944
8 yrs.		72	74	.493	3.66	196	183	36	1206.1	1162	473	737	12	2	0	1	163	23	0	.141	62	161	12	9	1.2	.949

LEAGUE CHAMPIONSHIP SERIES

Year	Team	W	L	%	ERA	G	GS	CG	IP	H	BB	SO	ShO	W	L	SV	AB	H	HR	BA	PO	A	E	DP	TC/G	FA
1985	KC A	1	0	1.000	0.00	2	1	1	10	10	1	7	1	0	0	0	0	0	0	—	0	0	0	0	0.0	—
1990	CIN N	1	0	1.000	2.38	2	2	0	11.1	8	7	8	0	0	0	0	3	0	0	.000	0	2	0	0	1.0	1.000
2 yrs.		2	0	1.000	1.27	4	3	1	21.1	18	8	15	1	0	0	0	3	0	0	.000	0	2	0	0	0.5	1.000

WORLD SERIES

Year	Team	W	L	%	ERA	G	GS	CG	IP	H	BB	SO	ShO	W	L	SV	AB	H	HR	BA	PO	A	E	DP	TC/G	FA
1985	KC A	1	1	.500	1.69	2	2	1	16	9	5	12	0	0	0	0	6	0	0	.000	0	4	1	0	2.5	.800
1990	CIN N	0	0	—	10.13	1	1	0	2.2	6	2	0	0	0	0	0	1	0	0	.000	0	1	1	0	2.0	.500
2 yrs.		1	1	.500	2.89	3	3	1	18.2	15	7	12	0	0	0	0	7	0	0	.000	0	5	2	0	2.3	.714

Mike Jackson

JACKSON, MICHAEL RAY
B. Dec. 22, 1964, Houston, Tex.
BR TR 6' 1" 185 lbs.

Period		W	L	%	ERA	G	GS	CG	IP	H	BB	SO	ShO	W	L	SV	AB	H	HR	BA	PO	A	E	DP	TC/G	FA
April		1	1	.500	3.09	7	0	0	11.2	10	1	12	0	1	1	1										
May		0	2	.000	4.86	12	0	0	16.2	12	9	17	0	0	2	0										
June		2	0	1.000	1.35	10	0	0	13.1	6	4	13	0	2	0	1										
July		1	0	1.000	9.00	12	0	0	12	11	9	8	0	1	0	0										
Aug		1	3	.250	5.40	12	0	0	13.1	13	11	7	0	1	3	0										
Sept/Oct		0	1	.000	3.48	10	0	0	10.1	12	10	12	0	0	1	1										
Day		0	2	.000	3.18	18	0	0	22.2	12	11	18	0	0	2	2										
Night		5	5	.500	5.10	45	0	0	54.2	52	33	51	0	5	5	1										
vs. Left		—	—	—	—	—	—	—	—	27	21	9	—	—	—	—										
vs. Right		—	—	—	—	—	—	—	—	37	23	60	—	—	—	—										

Year	Team	W	L	%	ERA	G	GS	CG	IP	H	BB	SO	ShO	RELIEF PITCHING W	L	SV	BATTING AB	H	HR	BA	PO	A	E	DP	TC/G	FA

Mike Jackson *Continued*

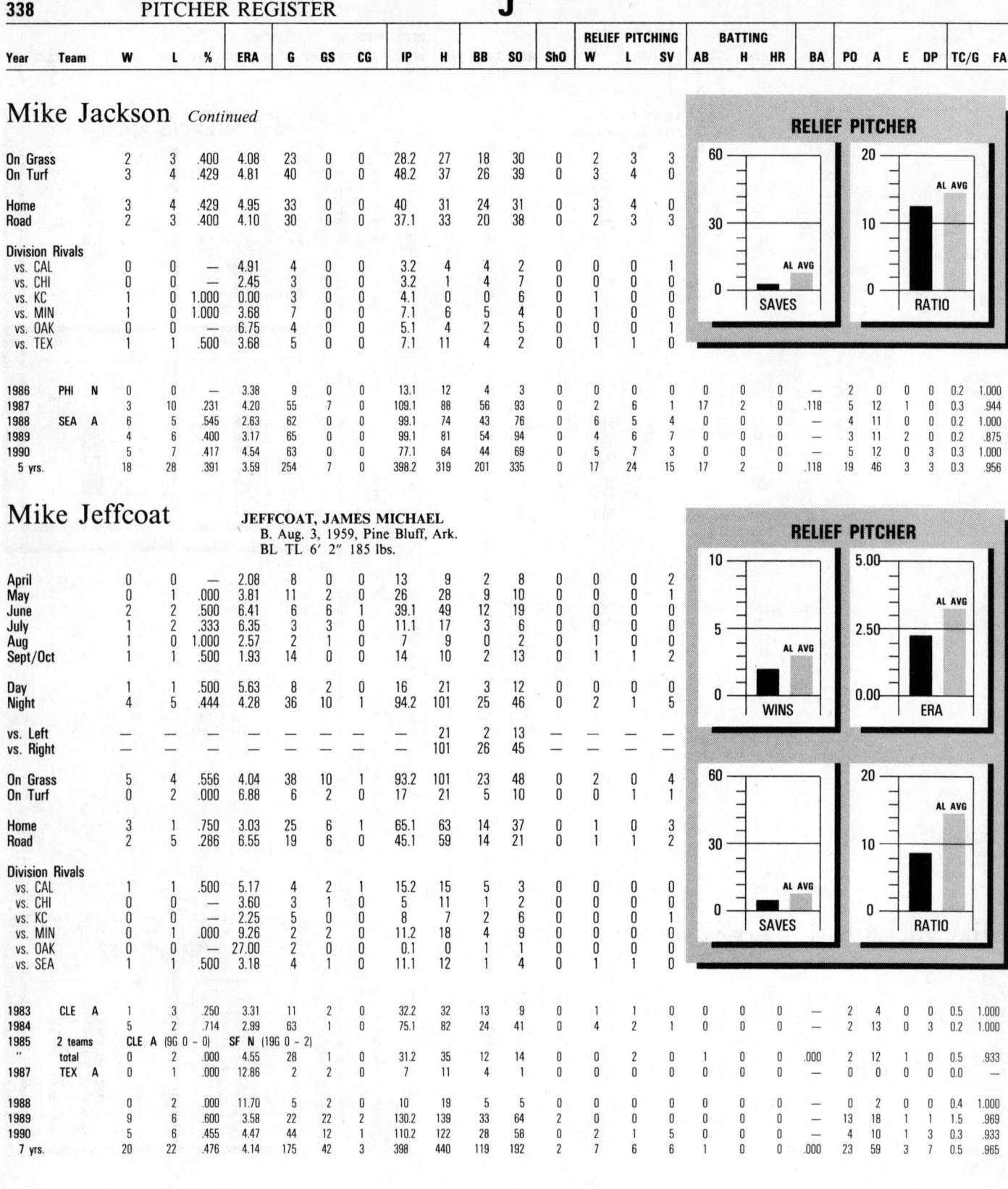

Year	Team	W	L	%	ERA	G	GS	CG	IP	H	BB	SO	ShO	W	L	SV	AB	H	HR	BA	PO	A	E	DP	TC/G	FA
On Grass		2	3	.400	4.08	23	0	0	28.2	27	18	30	0	2	3	3										
On Turf		3	4	.429	4.81	40	0	0	48.2	37	26	39	0	3	4	0										
Home		3	4	.429	4.95	33	0	0	40	31	24	31	0	3	4	0										
Road		2	3	.400	4.10	30	0	0	37.1	33	20	38	0	2	3	3										
Division Rivals																										
vs. CAL		0	0	—	4.91	4	0	0	3.2	4	4	2	0	0	0	1										
vs. CHI		0	0	—	2.45	3	0	0	3.2	1	4	7	0	0	0	0										
vs. KC		1	0	1.000	0.00	3	0	0	4.1	0	0	6	0	1	0	0										
vs. MIN		1	0	1.000	3.68	7	0	0	7.1	6	5	4	0	1	0	0										
vs. OAK		0	0	—	6.75	4	0	0	5.1	4	2	5	0	0	0	1										
vs. TEX		1	1	.500	3.68	5	0	0	7.1	11	4	2	0	1	1	0										
1986	PHI N	0	0	—	3.38	9	0	0	13.1	12	4	3	0	0	0	0	0	0	0	—	2	0	0	0	0.2	1.000
1987		3	10	.231	4.20	55	7	0	109.1	88	56	93	0	2	6	1	17	2	0	.118	5	12	1	0	0.3	.944
1988	SEA A	6	5	.545	2.63	62	0	0	99.1	74	43	76	0	6	5	4	0	0	0	—	4	11	0	0	0.2	1.000
1989		4	6	.400	3.17	65	0	0	99.1	81	54	94	0	4	6	7	0	0	0	—	3	11	2	0	0.2	.875
1990		5	7	.417	4.54	63	0	0	77.1	64	44	69	0	5	7	3	0	0	0	—	5	12	0	3	0.3	1.000
5 yrs.		18	28	.391	3.59	254	7	0	398.2	319	201	335	0	17	24	15	17	2	0	.118	19	46	3	3	0.3	.956

Mike Jeffcoat

JEFFCOAT, JAMES MICHAEL
B. Aug. 3, 1959, Pine Bluff, Ark.
BL TL 6' 2" 185 lbs.

Year	Team	W	L	%	ERA	G	GS	CG	IP	H	BB	SO	ShO	W	L	SV	AB	H	HR	BA	PO	A	E	DP	TC/G	FA
April		0	0	—	2.08	8	0	0	13	9	2	8	0	0	0	2										
May		0	1	.000	3.81	11	2	0	26	28	9	10	0	0	0	1										
June		2	2	.500	6.41	6	6	0	39.1	49	12	19	0	0	0	0										
July		1	2	.333	6.35	3	3	0	11.1	17	3	6	0	0	0	0										
Aug		1	0	1.000	2.57	2	1	0	7	9	0	2	0	1	0	0										
Sept/Oct		1	1	.500	1.93	14	0	0	14	10	2	13	0	1	1	2										
Day		1	1	.500	5.63	8	2	0	16	21	3	12	0	0	0	0										
Night		4	5	.444	4.28	36	10	1	94.2	101	25	46	0	2	1	5										
vs. Left		—	—	—	—	—	—	—	—	21	2	13	—	—	—	—										
vs. Right		—	—	—	—	—	—	—	—	101	26	45	—	—	—	—										
On Grass		5	4	.556	4.04	38	10	1	93.2	101	23	48	0	2	0	4										
On Turf		0	2	.000	6.88	6	2	0	17	21	5	10	0	0	1	1										
Home		3	1	.750	3.03	25	6	1	65.1	63	14	37	0	1	0	3										
Road		2	5	.286	6.55	19	6	0	45.1	59	14	21	0	1	1	2										
Division Rivals																										
vs. CAL		1	1	.500	5.17	4	2	1	15.2	15	5	3	0	0	0	0										
vs. CHI		0	0	—	3.60	3	1	0	5	11	1	2	0	0	0	0										
vs. KC		0	0	—	2.25	5	0	0	8	7	2	6	0	0	0	1										
vs. MIN		0	1	.000	9.26	2	2	0	11.2	18	4	9	0	0	0	0										
vs. OAK		0	0	—	27.00	2	0	0	0.1	0	1	1	0	0	0	0										
vs. SEA		1	1	.500	3.18	4	1	0	11.1	12	1	4	0	1	1	0										
1983	CLE A	1	3	.250	3.31	11	2	0	32.2	32	13	9	0	1	1	0	0	0	0	—	2	4	0	0	0.5	1.000
1984		5	2	.714	2.99	63	1	0	75.1	82	24	41	0	4	2	1	0	0	0	—	2	13	0	3	0.2	1.000
1985	2 teams	CLE A (9G 0 – 0)			SF N (19G 0 – 2)																					
"	total	0	2	.000	4.55	28	1	0	31.2	35	12	14	0	0	2	1	0	0	0	.000	2	12	1	0	0.5	.933
1987	TEX A	0	1	.000	12.86	2	2	0	7	11	4	1	0	0	0	0	0	0	0	—	0	0	0	0	0.0	—
1988		0	2	.000	11.70	5	2	0	10	19	5	5	0	0	0	0	0	0	0	—	0	2	0	0	0.4	1.000
1989		9	6	.600	3.58	22	22	2	130.2	139	33	64	2	0	0	0	0	0	0	—	13	18	1	1	1.5	.969
1990		5	6	.455	4.47	44	12	1	110.2	122	28	58	0	2	1	5	0	0	0	—	4	10	1	3	0.3	.933
7 yrs.		20	22	.476	4.14	175	42	3	398	440	119	192	2	7	6	6	1	0	0	.000	23	59	3	7	0.5	.965

Year	Team	W	L	%	ERA	G	GS	CG	IP	H	BB	SO	ShO	RELIEF PITCHING W	L	SV	BATTING AB	H	HR	BA	PO	A	E	DP	TC/G	FA

Dave Johnson

JOHNSON, DAVID WAYNE
B. Oct. 24, 1959, Baltimore, Md.
BR TR 5' 10" 180 lbs.

Year	Team	W	L	%	ERA	G	GS	CG	IP	H	BB	SO	ShO	W	L	SV	AB	H	HR	BA	PO	A	E	DP	TC/G	FA
April		2	1	.667	4.50	4	4	0	24	29	10	8	0	0	0	0										
May		1	2	.333	4.18	5	5	1	32.1	40	5	16	0	0	0	0										
June		4	1	.800	3.23	6	6	1	39	43	8	5	0	0	0	0										
July		3	2	.600	5.20	6	6	1	36.1	33	7	20	0	0	0	0										
Aug		1	2	.333	5.79	3	3	0	14	14	3	7	0	0	0	0										
Sept/Oct		2	1	.667	2.88	6	5	0	34.1	37	10	12	0	0	0	0										
Day		4	1	.800	3.63	10	10	0	62	65	16	19	0	0	0	0										
Night		9	8	.529	4.35	20	19	3	118	131	27	49	0	0	0	0										
vs. Left		—	—	—	—	—	—	—	—	103	24	24	—	—	—	—										
vs. Right		—	—	—	—	—	—	—	—	93	19	44	—	—	—	—										
On Grass		11	7	.611	3.81	24	23	3	149	157	38	58	0	0	0	0										
On Turf		2	2	.500	5.52	6	6	0	31	39	5	10	0	0	0	0										
Home		5	6	.455	3.72	14	13	3	87	88	25	30	0	0	0	0										
Road		8	3	.727	4.45	16	16	0	93	108	18	38	0	0	0	0										

Division Rivals

		W	L	%	ERA	G	GS	CG	IP	H	BB	SO	ShO	W	L	SV										
vs. BOS		1	0	1.000	2.16	2	2	1	16.2	16	4	0	0	0	0	0										
vs. CLE		1	0	1.000	2.25	1	1	0	8	8	2	3	0	0	0	0										
vs. DET		3	0	1.000	1.80	4	4	0	25	28	7	13	0	0	0	0										
vs. MIL		2	1	.667	4.32	3	3	0	16.2	19	5	4	0.	0	0	0										
vs. NY		1	0	1.000	3.60	1	1	0	5	8	0	0	0	0	0	0										
vs. TOR		0	1	.000	4.73	2	2	0	13.1	14	3	4	0	0	0	0										

Year	Team		W	L	%	ERA	G	GS	CG	IP	H	BB	SO	ShO	W	L	SV	AB	H	HR	BA	PO	A	E	DP	TC/G	FA
1987	PIT	N	0	0	—	9.95	5	0	0	6.1	13	2	4	0	0	0	0	0	0	0	—	1	1	0	1	0.4	1.000
1989	BAL	A	4	7	.364	4.23	14	14	4	89.1	90	28	26	0	0	0	0	0	0	0	—	6	5	0	0	0.8	1.000
1990			13	9	.591	4.10	30	29	3	180	196	43	68	0	0	0	0	0	0	0	—	13	10	2	1	0.8	.920
3 yrs.			17	16	.515	4.28	49	43	7	275.2	299	73	98	0	0	0	0	0	0	0	—	20	16	2	2	0.8	.947

STARTING PITCHER

Charts: WINS (25.0 / 12.5 / 0.0, AL AVG), ERA (5.00 / 2.50 / 0.00, AL AVG), SO/9 (10 / 5 / 0, AL AVG), RATIO (20 / 10 / 0, AL AVG)

Randy Johnson

JOHNSON, RANDALL DAVID
B. Sept. 10, 1963, Walnut Creek, Calif.
BL TL 6' 10" 225 lbs.

Year	Team	W	L	%	ERA	G	GS	CG	IP	H	BB	SO	ShO	W	L	SV	AB	H	HR	BA	PO	A	E	DP	TC/G	FA
April		2	1	.667	4.07	4	4	0	24.1	18	11	19	0	0	0	0										
May		1	2	.333	5.19	6	6	0	34.2	29	22	32	0	0	0	0										
June		5	0	1.000	2.40	6	6	2	45	30	23	38	1	0	0	0										
July		1	4	.200	3.34	5	5	1	35	29	20	34	0	0	0	0										
Aug		4	1	.800	2.74	6	6	1	46	29	22	41	1	0	0	0										
Sept/Oct		1	3	.250	4.93	6	6	1	34.2	39	22	30	0	0	0	0										
Day		4	2	.667	3.51	10	10	1	66.2	54	37	57	0	0	0	0										
Night		10	9	.526	3.71	23	23	4	153	120	83	137	2	0	0	0										
vs. Left		—	—	—	—	—	—	—	—	16	7	23	—	—	—	—										
vs. Right		—	—	—	—	—	—	—	—	158	13	171	—	—	—	—										
On Grass		5	4	.556	3.88	14	14	3	92.2	79	46	83	0	0	0	0										
On Turf		9	7	.563	3.47	19	19	2	127	95	74	111	2	0	0	0										
Home		8	4	.667	2.90	15	15	2	102.1	71	60	84	2	0	0	0										
Road		6	7	.462	4.30	18	18	3	117.1	103	60	110	0	0	0	0										

Division Rivals

		W	L	%	ERA	G	GS	CG	IP	H	BB	SO	ShO	W	L	SV										
vs. CAL		0	1	.000	3.75	2	2	0	12	12	4	7	0	0	0	0										
vs. CHI		3	1	.750	2.81	4	4	2	25.2	21	10	26	0	0	0	0										
vs. KC		1	1	.500	4.61	2	2	0	13.2	10	7	12	0	0	0	0										
vs. MIN		1	2	.333	4.78	4	4	0	26.1	22	16	23	0	0	0	0										
vs. OAK		0	2	.000	4.58	3	3	0	19.2	16	14	22	0	0	0	0										
vs. TEX		2	0	1.000	4.35	3	3	0	20.2	23	11	18	0	0	0	0										

Year	Team		W	L	%	ERA	G	GS	CG	IP	H	BB	SO	ShO	W	L	SV	AB	H	HR	BA	PO	A	E	DP	TC/G	FA
1988	MON	N	3	0	1.000	2.42	4	4	1	26	23	7	25	0	0	0	0	9	1	0	.111	0	0	1	0	0.3	—
1989	2 teams		MON N (7G 0 - 4)			SEA A (22G 7 - 9)																					
"	total		7	13	.350	4.82	29	28	2	160.2	147	96	130	0	0	0	0	7	1	0	.143	8	26	7	1	1.4	.829
1990	SEA	A	14	11	.560	3.65	33	33	5	219.2	174	120	194	2	0	0	0	0	0	0	—	6	24	5	2	1.1	.857
3 yrs.			24	24	.500	4.03	66	65	8	406.1	344	223	349	2	0	0	0	16	2	0	.125	14	50	13	3	1.2	.831

STARTING PITCHER

Charts: WINS (25.0 / 12.5 / 0.0, AL AVG), ERA (5.00 / 2.50 / 0.00, AL AVG), SO/9 (10 / 5 / 0, AL AVG), RATIO (20 / 10 / 0, AL AVG)

Year	Team	W	L	%	ERA	G	GS	CG	IP	H	BB	SO	ShO	RELIEF PITCHING W	L	SV	BATTING AB	H	HR	BA	PO	A	E	DP	TC/G	FA

Barry Jones

JONES, BARRY LOUIS
B. Feb. 15, 1963, Centerville, Ind.
BR TR 6′ 2″ 215 lbs.

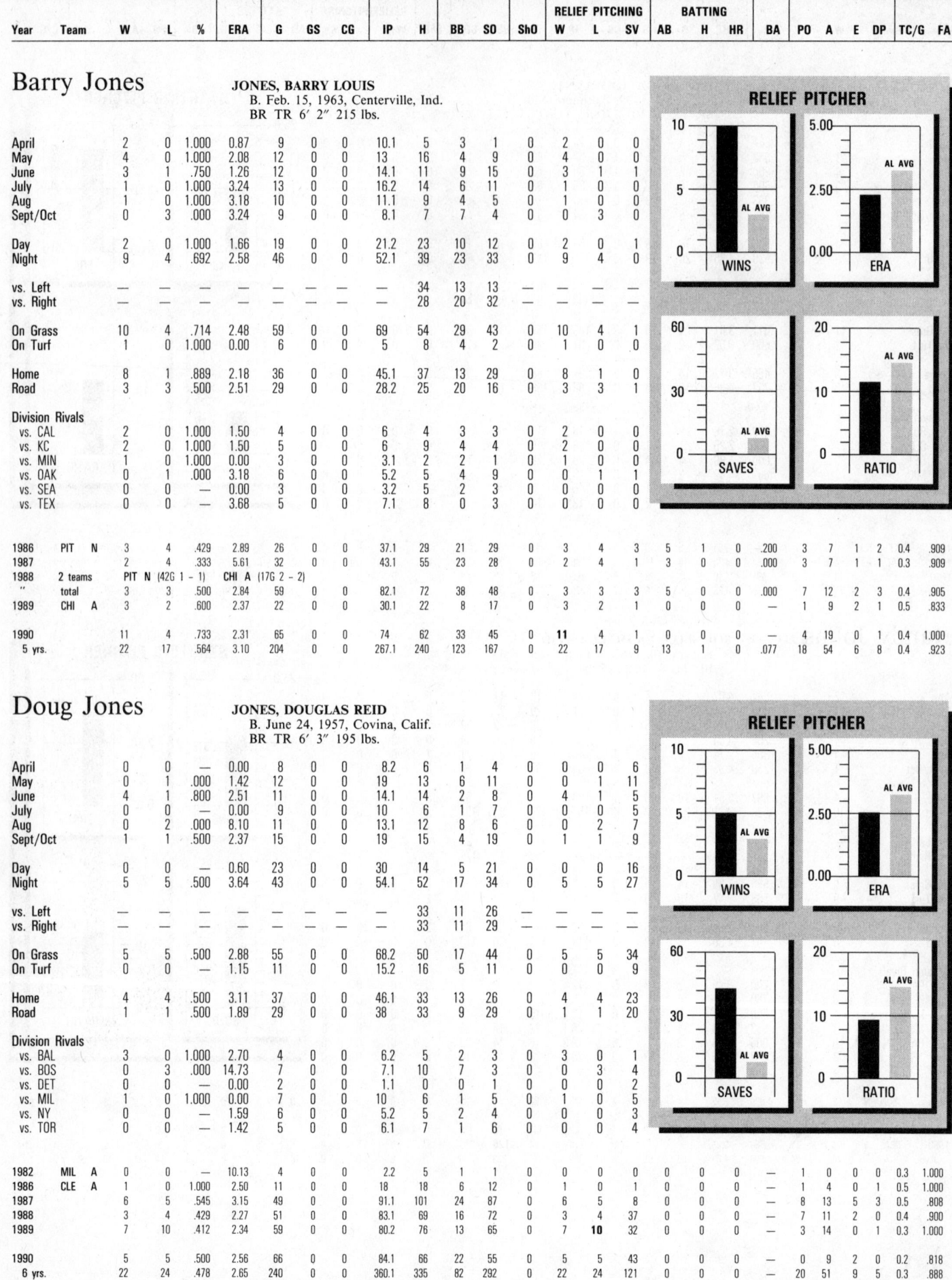

RELIEF PITCHER

Year	Team	W	L	%	ERA	G	GS	CG	IP	H	BB	SO	ShO	W	L	SV	AB	H	HR	BA	PO	A	E	DP	TC/G	FA
April		2	0	1.000	0.87	9	0	0	10.1	5	3	1	0	2	0	0										
May		4	0	1.000	2.08	12	0	0	13	16	4	9	0	4	0	0										
June		3	1	.750	1.26	12	0	0	14.1	11	9	15	0	3	1	1										
July		1	0	1.000	3.24	13	0	0	16.2	14	6	11	0	1	0	0										
Aug		1	0	1.000	3.18	10	0	0	11.1	9	4	5	0	1	0	0										
Sept/Oct		0	3	.000	3.24	9	0	0	8.1	7	7	4	0	0	3	0										
Day		2	0	1.000	1.66	19	0	0	21.2	23	10	12	0	2	0	1										
Night		9	4	.692	2.58	46	0	0	52.1	39	23	33	0	9	4	0										
vs. Left		—	—	—	—	—	—	—	—	34	13	13	—	—	—	—										
vs. Right		—	—	—	—	—	—	—	—	28	20	32	—	—	—	—										
On Grass		10	4	.714	2.48	59	0	0	69	54	29	43	0	10	4	1										
On Turf		1	0	1.000	0.00	6	0	0	5	8	4	2	0	1	0	0										
Home		8	1	.889	2.18	36	0	0	45.1	37	13	29	0	8	1	0										
Road		3	3	.500	2.51	29	0	0	28.2	25	20	16	0	3	3	1										
Division Rivals																										
vs. CAL		2	0	1.000	1.50	4	0	0	6	4	3	3	0	2	0	0										
vs. KC		2	0	1.000	1.50	5	0	0	6	9	4	4	0	2	0	0										
vs. MIN		1	0	1.000	0.00	3	0	0	3.1	2	2	1	0	1	0	0										
vs. OAK		0	1	.000	3.18	6	0	0	5.2	5	4	9	0	0	1	1										
vs. SEA		0	0	—	0.00	3	0	0	3.2	5	2	3	0	0	0	0										
vs. TEX		0	0	—	3.68	5	0	0	7.1	8	0	3	0	0	0	0										
1986	PIT N	3	4	.429	2.89	26	0	0	37.1	29	21	29	0	3	4	3	5	1	0	.200	3	7	1	2	0.4	.909
1987		2	4	.333	5.61	32	0	0	43.1	55	23	28	0	2	4	1	3	0	0	.000	3	7	1	1	0.3	.909
1988	2 teams	PIT N	(42G 1 - 1)		CHI A	(17G 2 - 2)																				
"	total	3	3	.500	2.84	59	0	0	82.1	72	38	48	0	3	3	3	5	0	0	.000	7	12	2	3	0.4	.905
1989	CHI A	3	2	.600	2.37	22	0	0	30.1	22	8	17	0	3	2	1	0	0	0	—	1	9	2	1	0.5	.833
1990		11	4	.733	2.31	65	0	0	74	62	33	45	0	11	4	1	0	0	0	—	4	19	0	1	0.4	1.000
5 yrs.		22	17	.564	3.10	204	0	0	267.1	240	123	167	0	22	17	9	13	1	0	.077	18	54	6	8	0.4	.923

Doug Jones

JONES, DOUGLAS REID
B. June 24, 1957, Covina, Calif.
BR TR 6′ 3″ 195 lbs.

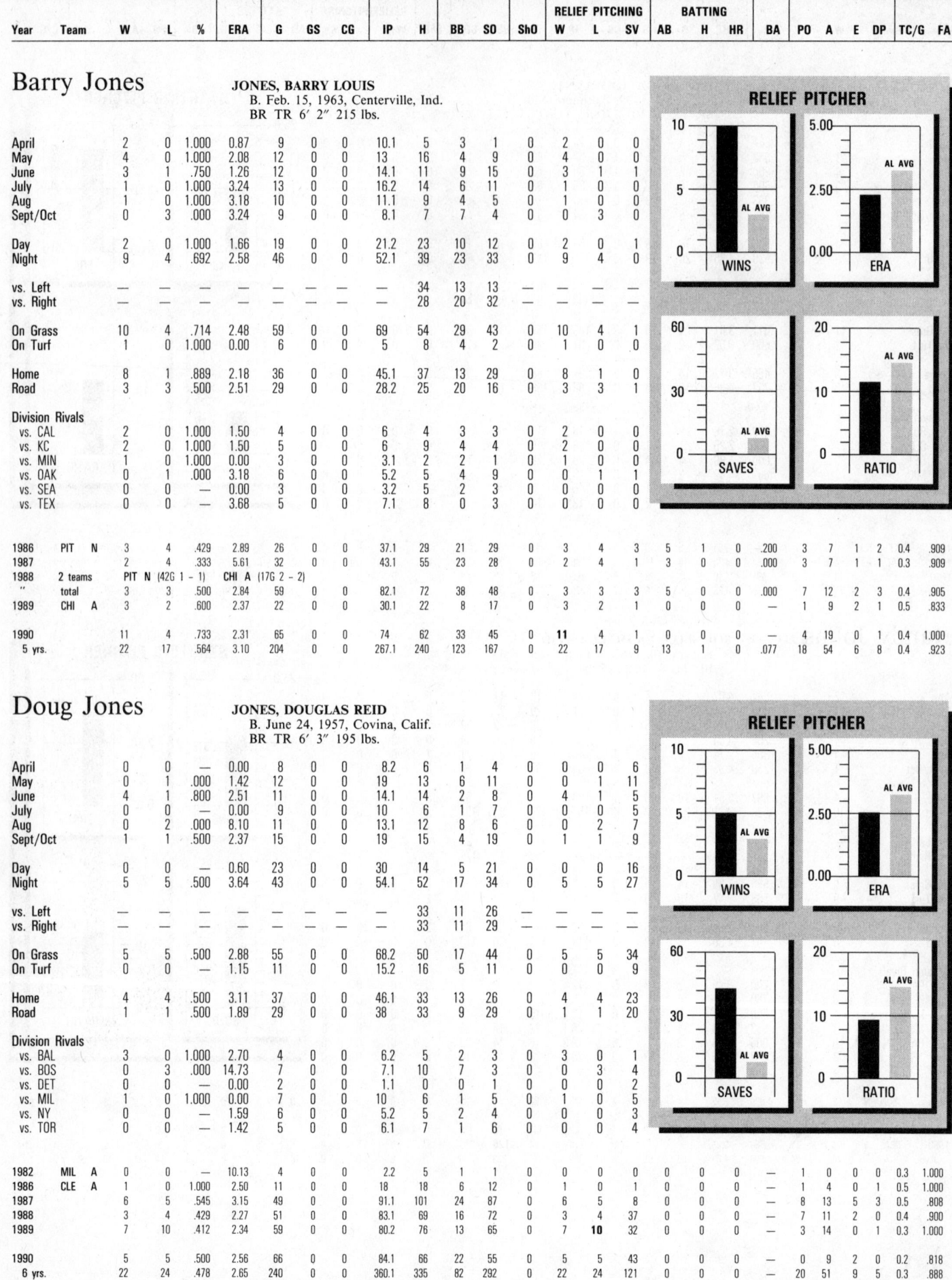

RELIEF PITCHER

Year	Team	W	L	%	ERA	G	GS	CG	IP	H	BB	SO	ShO	W	L	SV	AB	H	HR	BA	PO	A	E	DP	TC/G	FA
April		0	0	—	0.00	8	0	0	8.2	6	1	4	0	0	0	6										
May		0	1	.000	1.42	12	0	0	19	13	6	11	0	0	1	11										
June		4	1	.800	2.51	11	0	0	14.1	14	2	8	0	4	1	5										
July		0	0	—	0.00	9	0	0	10	6	1	7	0	0	0	5										
Aug		0	2	.000	8.10	11	0	0	13.1	12	8	6	0	0	2	7										
Sept/Oct		1	1	.500	2.37	15	0	0	19	15	4	19	0	1	1	9										
Day		0	0	—	0.60	23	0	0	30	14	5	21	0	0	0	16										
Night		5	5	.500	3.64	43	0	0	54.1	52	17	34	0	5	5	27										
vs. Left		—	—	—	—	—	—	—	—	33	11	26	—	—	—	—										
vs. Right		—	—	—	—	—	—	—	—	33	11	29	—	—	—	—										
On Grass		5	5	.500	2.88	55	0	0	68.2	50	17	44	0	5	5	34										
On Turf		0	0	—	1.15	11	0	0	15.2	16	5	11	0	0	0	9										
Home		4	4	.500	3.11	37	0	0	46.1	33	13	26	0	4	4	23										
Road		1	1	.500	1.89	29	0	0	38	33	9	29	0	1	1	20										
Division Rivals																										
vs. BAL		3	0	1.000	2.70	4	0	0	6.2	5	2	3	0	3	0	1										
vs. BOS		0	3	.000	14.73	7	0	0	7.1	10	7	3	0	0	3	4										
vs. DET		0	0	—	0.00	2	0	0	1.1	0	0	1	0	0	0	2										
vs. MIL		1	0	1.000	0.00	7	0	0	10	6	1	6	0	1	0	5										
vs. NY		0	0	—	1.59	6	0	0	5.2	5	2	4	0	0	0	3										
vs. TOR		0	0	—	1.42	5	0	0	6.1	7	1	6	0	0	0	4										
1982	MIL A	0	0	—	10.13	4	0	0	2.2	5	1	1	0	0	0	0	0	0	0	—	1	0	0	0	0.3	1.000
1986	CLE A	1	0	1.000	2.50	11	0	0	18	18	6	12	0	1	0	1	0	0	0	—	1	4	0	1	0.5	1.000
1987		6	5	.545	3.15	49	0	0	91.1	101	24	87	0	6	5	8	0	0	0	—	8	13	5	3	0.5	.808
1988		3	4	.429	2.27	51	0	0	83.1	69	16	72	0	3	4	37	0	0	0	—	7	11	2	0	0.4	.900
1989		7	10	.412	2.34	59	0	0	80.2	76	13	65	0	7	10	32	0	0	0	—	3	14	0	1	0.3	1.000
1990		5	5	.500	2.56	66	0	0	84.1	66	22	55	0	5	5	43	0	0	0	—	0	9	2	0	0.2	.818
6 yrs.		22	24	.478	2.65	240	0	0	360.1	335	82	292	0	22	24	121	0	0	0	—	20	51	9	5	0.3	.888

Year	Team		W	L	%	ERA	G	GS	CG	IP	H	BB	SO	ShO	RELIEF PITCHING W	L	SV	BATTING AB	H	HR	BA	PO	A	E	DP	TC/G	FA

Jimmy Jones

JONES, JAMES CONDIA
B. Apr. 20, 1964, Dallas, Tex.
BR TR 6' 2" 175 lbs.

Year	Team		W	L	%	ERA	G	GS	CG	IP	H	BB	SO	ShO	W	L	SV	AB	H	HR	BA	PO	A	E	DP	TC/G	FA
1986	SD	N	2	0	1.000	2.50	3	3	1	18	10	3	15	1	0	0	0	6	1	0	.167	1	2	0	0	1.0	1.000
1987			9	7	.563	4.14	30	22	2	145.2	154	54	51	1	2	0	0	49	8	1	.163	15	28	0	1	1.4	1.000
1988			9	14	.391	4.12	29	29	3	179	192	44	82	0	0	0	0	55	9	1	.164	17	32	0	3	1.7	1.000
1989	NY	A	2	1	.667	5.25	11	6	0	48	56	16	25	0	0	0	0	0	0	0	—	2	14	0	1	1.5	1.000
1990			1	2	.333	6.30	17	7	0	50	72	23	25	0	0	0	0	0	0	0	—	1	5	1	1	0.4	.857
5 yrs.			23	24	.489	4.43	90	67	6	440.2	484	140	198	2	2	0	0	110	18	2	.164	36	81	1	6	1.3	.992

Tim Jones

JONES, WILLIAM TIMOTHY
B. Dec. 1, 1962, Sumter, S. C.
BL TR 5' 10" 172 lbs.

Year	Team		W	L	%	ERA	G	GS	CG	IP	H	BB	SO	ShO	W	L	SV	AB	H	HR	BA	PO	A	E	DP	TC/G	FA
1990	STL	N	0	0	—	6.75	1	0	0	1.1	1	2	0	0	0	0	0				*	0	0	0	0	0.0	—

Jeff Kaiser

KAISER, JEFFREY PATRICK
B. July 24, 1960, Wyandotte, Mich.
BR TL 6' 3" 195 lbs.

Year	Team		W	L	%	ERA	G	GS	CG	IP	H	BB	SO	ShO	W	L	SV	AB	H	HR	BA	PO	A	E	DP	TC/G	FA
1985	OAK	A	0	0	—	14.58	15	0	0	16.2	25	20	10	0	0	0	0				—	4	3	0	1	0.5	1.000
1987	CLE	A	0	0	—	16.20	2	0	0	3.1	4	3	2	0	0	0	0				—	1	0	0	0	0.5	1.000
1988			0	0	—	0.00	3	0	0	2.2	2	1	0	0	0	0	0				—	0	2	0	0	0.7	1.000
1989			0	1	.000	7.36	6	0	0	3.2	5	5	4	0	0	1	0				—	0	0	0	0	0.0	—
1990			0	0	—	3.55	5	0	0	12.2	16	7	9	0	0	0	0				—	3	1	0	0	0.8	1.000
5 yrs.			0	1	.000	9.46	31	0	0	39	52	36	25	0	0	1	0				—	8	6	0	1	0.5	1.000

Charley Kerfeld

KERFELD, CHARLES PATRICK
B. Sept. 28, 1963, Knob Noster, Mo.
BR TR 6' 6" 225 lbs.

	W	L	%	ERA	G	GS	CG	IP	H	BB	SO	ShO	W	L	SV	
April	0	2	.000	16.20	5	0	0	3.1	9	6	4	0	0	2	0	
May	2	0	1.000	3.21	12	0	0	14	12	10	14	0	2	0	2	
June	1	1	.500	10.38	7	0	0	8.2	11	7	7	0	1	1	0	
July	0	0	—	4.50	6	0	0	8	8	6	6	0	0	0	0	
Aug	—	—	—	—	0	—		0	0	0	0	0	—	0	0	0
Sept/Oct	—	—	—	—	0	—	—	0	0	0	0	—	0	0	0	
Day	1	1	.500	0.90	7	0	0	10	6	7	10	0	1	1	0	
Night	2	2	.500	9.00	23	0	0	24	34	22	21	0	2	2	2	
vs. Left	—	—	—	—	—	—		—	17	17	15	—	—	—	—	
vs. Right	—	—	—	—	—	—		—	23	12	16	—	—	—	—	
On Grass	2	1	.667	6.48	19	0	0	25	25	15	22	0	2	1	2	
On Turf	1	2	.333	7.00	11	0	0	9	15	14	9	0	1	2	0	
Home	0	2	.000	8.50	16	0	0	18	30	12	19	0	0	2	2	
Road	3	1	.750	4.50	14	0	0	16	10	17	12	0	3	1	0	
Division Rivals																
vs. CIN	0	1	.000	45.00	2	0	0	1	6	4	2	0	0	1	0	
vs. HOU	—	—	—	—	0	—	—	0	0	0	0	—	0	0	0	
vs. LA	0	2	.000	9.00	5	0	0	5	6	6	4	0	0	2	0	
vs. SD	1	0	1.000	3.18	4	0	0	5.2	2	3	4	0	1	0	0	
vs. SF	0	0	—	36.00	1	0	0	1	5	0	1	0	0	0	0	

RELIEF PITCHER (WINS, ERA, SAVES, RATIO bar charts with NL AVG)

Year	Team		W	L	%	ERA	G	GS	CG	IP	H	BB	SO	ShO	W	L	SV	AB	H	HR	BA	PO	A	E	DP	TC/G	FA
1985	HOU	N	4	2	.667	4.06	11	6	0	44.1	44	25	30	0	0	2	0	14	0	0	.000	5	2	1	1	0.7	.875
1986			11	2	.846	2.59	61	0	0	93.2	71	42	77	0	11	2	7	9	1	0	.111	7	9	0	1	0.3	1.000
1987			0	2	.000	6.67	21	0	0	29.2	34	21	17	0	0	2	0	3	0	0	.000	5	3	1	0	0.4	.889
1990	2 teams		HOU N (5G 0 - 2)			ATL N (25G 3 - 1)																					
"	total		3	3	.500	6.62	30	0	0	34	40	29	31	0	3	3	2	0	0	0	—	2	2	3	0	0.2	.571
4 yrs.			18	9	.667	4.19	123	6	0	201.2	189	117	155	0	16	7	9	26	1	0	.038	19	16	5	2	0.3	.875

LEAGUE CHAMPIONSHIP SERIES

Year	Team		W	L	%	ERA	G	GS	CG	IP	H	BB	SO	ShO	W	L	SV	AB	H	HR	BA	PO	A	E	DP	TC/G	FA
1986	HOU	N	0	1	.000	2.25	3	0	0	4	2	1	4	0	0	1	0	0	0	0	—	0	0	1	0	0.3	—

Year	Team	W	L	%	ERA	G	GS	CG	IP	H	BB	SO	ShO	RELIEF PITCHING W	L	SV	BATTING AB	H	HR	BA	PO	A	E	DP	TC/G	FA

Jimmy Key

KEY, JAMES EDWARD
B. Apr. 22, 1961, Huntsville, Ala.
BR TL 6' 1" 180 lbs.

Year	Team	W	L	%	ERA	G	GS	CG	IP	H	BB	SO	ShO	W	L	SV	AB	H	HR	BA	PO	A	E	DP	TC/G	FA
April		2	1	.667	5.21	4	4	0	19	25	0	10	0	0	0	0										
May		2	1	.667	8.10	4	4	0	16.2	21	5	7	0	0	0	0										
June		0	1	.000	7.84	2	2	0	10.1	19	2	5	0	0	0	0										
July		2	2	.500	2.12	5	5	0	34	27	7	14	0	0	0	0										
Aug		3	1	.750	3.38	6	6	0	37.1	41	1	24	0	0	0	0										
Sept/Oct		4	1	.800	3.86	6	6	0	37.1	36	7	28	0	0	0	0										
Day		5	6	.455	5.58	13	13	0	69.1	89	13	42	0	0	0	0										
Night		8	1	.889	3.16	14	14	0	85.1	80	9	46	0	0	0	0										
vs. Left		—	—	—	—	—	—	—	—	16	4	14	—	—	—	—										
vs. Right		—	—	—	—	—	—	—	—	153	18	74	—	—	—	—										
On Grass		3	4	.429	5.48	8	8	0	46	60	8	24	0	0	0	0										
On Turf		10	3	.769	3.73	19	19	0	108.2	109	14	64	0	0	0	0										
Home		7	3	.700	4.47	16	16	0	88.2	97	13	52	0	0	0	0										
Road		6	4	.600	3.95	11	11	0	66	72	9	36	0	0	0	0										
Division Rivals																										
vs. BAL		0	0	—	3.60	2	2	0	10	7	1	5	0	0	0	0										
vs. BOS		1	1	.500	5.00	3	3	0	18	24	2	12	0	0	0	0										
vs. CLE		1	0	1.000	1.80	1	1	0	5	5	0	3	0	0	0	0										
vs. DET		3	1	.750	4.62	4	4	0	25.1	31	3	13	0	0	0	0										
vs. MIL		2	0	1.000	3.46	2	2	0	13	11	2	11	0	0	0	0										
vs. NY		1	0	1.000	6.17	2	2	0	11.2	15	2	8	0	0	0	0										
1984	TOR A	4	5	.444	4.65	63	0	0	62	70	32	44	0	4	5	10	0	0	0	—	9	11	1	0	0.3	.952
1985		14	6	.700	3.00	35	32	3	212.2	188	50	85	0	1	0	0	0	0	0	—	15	52	3	3	2.0	.957
1986		14	11	.560	3.57	36	35	4	232	222	74	141	2	0	0	0	0	0	0	—	18	42	0	4	1.7	1.000
1987		17	8	.680	**2.76**	36	36	8	261	210	66	161	1	0	0	0	0	0	0	—	17	44	3	5	1.8	.953
1988		12	5	.706	3.29	21	21	2	131.1	127	30	65	2	0	0	0	0	0	0	—	5	19	0	1	1.1	1.000
1989		13	14	.481	3.88	33	33	5	216	226	27	118	1	0	0	0	0	0	0	—	11	44	2	2	1.7	.965
1990		13	7	.650	4.25	27	27	0	154.2	169	22	88	0	0	0	0	0	0	0	—	8	22	1	3	1.1	.968
7 yrs.		87	56	.608	3.47	251	184	22	1269.2	1212	301	702	6	5	5	10	0	0	0	—	83	234	10	18	1.3	.969

LEAGUE CHAMPIONSHIP SERIES

Year	Team	W	L	%	ERA	G	GS	CG	IP	H	BB	SO	ShO	W	L	SV	AB	H	HR	BA	PO	A	E	DP	TC/G	FA
1985	TOR A	0	1	.000	5.19	2	2	0	8.2	15	2	5	0	0	0	0	0	0	0	—	0	3	0	0	1.5	1.000
1989		1	0	1.000	4.50	1	1	0	6	7	2	2	0	0	0	0	0	0	0	—	0	0	0	0	0.0	—
2 yrs.		1	1	.500	4.91	3	3	0	14.2	22	4	7	0	0	0	0	0	0	0	—	0	3	0	0	1.0	1.000

Dana Kiecker

KIECKER, DANA ERVIN
B. Feb. 25, 1961, Sleepy Eye, Minn.
BR TR 6' 3" 180 lbs.

Year	Team	W	L	%	ERA	G	GS	CG	IP	H	BB	SO	ShO	W	L	SV	AB	H	HR	BA	PO	A	E	DP	TC/G	FA
April		0	0	—	8.38	3	1	0	9.2	11	6	6	0	0	0	0										
May		0	2	.000	3.60	5	3	0	20	24	6	10	0	0	0	0										
June		2	1	.667	3.69	6	6	0	31.2	31	5	24	0	0	0	0										
July		2	1	.667	4.08	6	4	0	28.2	27	12	21	0	0	0	0										
Aug		2	2	.500	2.86	6	5	0	28.1	25	12	20	0	0	0	0										
Sept/Oct		2	3	.400	4.01	6	6	0	33.2	27	13	12	0	0	0	0										
Day		1	3	.250	5.19	11	7	0	50.1	56	19	37	0	0	0	0										
Night		7	6	.538	3.36	21	18	0	101.2	89	35	56	0	0	0	0										
vs. Left		—	—	—	—	—	—	—	—	95	29	21	—	—	—	—										
vs. Right		—	—	—	—	—	—	—	—	50	25	72	—	—	—	—										
On Grass		5	7	.417	5.23	25	18	0	103.1	107	36	64	0	0	0	0										
On Turf		3	2	.600	1.29	7	7	0	48.2	38	18	29	0	0	0	0										
Home		3	5	.375	6.50	17	13	0	63.2	79	24	30	0	0	0	0										
Road		5	4	.556	2.14	15	12	0	88.1	66	30	63	0	0	0	0										
Division Rivals																										
vs. BAL		0	1	.000	0.00	1	1	0	0	3	2	0	0	0	0	0										
vs. CLE		3	0	1.000	0.95	3	3	0	19	8	9	15	0	0	0	0										
vs. DET		0	0	—	7.00	4	0	0	9	10	7	11	0	0	0	0										
vs. MIL		0	1	.000	6.75	2	1	0	9.1	9	1	3	0	0	0	0										
vs. NY		1	1	.500	2.00	3	3	0	18	10	3	12	0	0	0	0										
vs. TOR		2	1	1.000	2.60	3	3	0	17.1	14	6	10	0	0	0	0										
1990	BOS A	8	9	.471	3.97	32	25	0	152	145	54	93	0	0	0	0	0	0	0	—	18	27	2	1	1.5	.957

Year	Team	W	L	%	ERA	G	GS	CG	IP	H	BB	SO	ShO	RELIEF PITCHING W	L	SV	BATTING AB	H	HR	BA	PO	A	E	DP	TC/G	FA

Dana Kiecker *Continued*

LEAGUE CHAMPIONSHIP SERIES

Year	Team	W	L	%	ERA	G	GS	CG	IP	H	BB	SO	ShO	W	L	SV	AB	H	HR	BA	PO	A	E	DP	TC/G	FA
1990	BOS A	0	0	—	1.59	1	1	0	5.2	6	1	2	0	0	0	0	0	0	0	—	0	0	0	0	0.0	—

Paul Kilgus

KILGUS, PAUL NELSON
B. Feb. 2, 1962, Bowling Green, Ky.
BL TL 6′ 1″ 175 lbs.

Year	Team	W	L	%	ERA	G	GS	CG	IP	H	BB	SO	ShO	W	L	SV	AB	H	HR	BA	PO	A	E	DP	TC/G	FA
1987	TEX A	2	7	.222	4.13	25	12	0	89.1	95	31	42	0	0	0	2	0	0	0	—	7	9	4	2	0.8	.800
1988		12	15	.444	4.16	32	32	5	203.1	190	71	88	3	0	0	0	0	0	0	—	11	34	2	4	1.5	.957
1989	CHI N	6	10	.375	4.39	35	23	0	145.2	164	49	61	0	0	0	2	41	3	0	.073	10	25	2	0	1.1	.946
1990	TOR A	0	0	—	6.06	11	0	0	16.1	19	7	7	0	0	0	0	0	0	0	—	1	3	0	0	0.4	1.000
4 yrs.		20	32	.385	4.30	103	67	5	454.2	468	158	198	3	0	2	2	41	3	0	.073	29	71	8	6	1.0	.926

LEAGUE CHAMPIONSHIP SERIES

Year	Team	W	L	%	ERA	G	GS	CG	IP	H	BB	SO	ShO	W	L	SV	AB	H	HR	BA	PO	A	E	DP	TC/G	FA
1989	CHI N	0	0	—	0.00	1	0	0	3	4	1	1	0	0	0	0	0	0	0	—	0	0	0	0	0.0	—

Eric King

KING, ERIC STEVEN
B. Apr. 10, 1964, Oxnard, Calif.
BR TR 6′ 2″ 180 lbs.

	W	L	%	ERA	G	GS	CG	IP	H	BB	SO	ShO	W	L	SV	AB	H	HR	BA	PO	A	E	DP	TC/G	FA
April	1	0	1.000	3.15	4	4	0	20	18	7	14	0	0	0	0										
May	3	0	1.000	2.31	5	5	1	35	24	8	12	1	0	0	0										
June	4	1	.800	1.50	5	5	1	36	30	7	24	1	0	0	0										
July	0	3	.000	6.97	6	6	0	31	41	8	14	0	0	0	0										
Aug	—	—	—	—	0	0	0	0	0	0	0	—	0	0	0										
Sept/Oct	4	0	1.000	2.79	5	5	0	29	22	10	6	0	0	0	0										
Day	3	1	.750	4.99	7	7	0	39.2	43	12	12	0	0	0	0										
Night	9	3	.750	2.67	18	18	2	111.1	92	28	58	2	0	0	0										
vs. Left	—	—	—	—	—	—	—	—	58	25	30	—	—	—	—										
vs. Right	—	—	—	—	—	—	—	—	77	15	40	—	—	—	—										
On Grass	9	4	.692	3.51	22	22	1	130.2	120	35	63	1	0	0	0										
On Turf	3	0	1.000	1.77	3	3	1	20.1	15	5	7	1	0	0	0										
Home	5	3	.625	3.93	13	13	0	75.2	74	18	26	0	0	0	0										
Road	7	1	.875	2.63	12	12	2	75.1	61	22	44	2	0	0	0										
Division Rivals																									
vs. CAL	1	0	1.000	2.45	1	1	0	7.1	4	5	4	0	0	0	0										
vs. KC	1	0	1.000	1.89	3	3	1	19	19	3	8	1	0	0	0										
vs. MIN	1	1	.500	1.93	2	2	0	14	10	1	8	0	0	0	0										
vs. OAK	2	0	1.000	0.61	2	2	1	14.2	16	1	12	1	0	0	0										
vs. SEA	2	0	1.000	3.00	2	2	0	12	7	5	3	0	0	0	0										
vs. TEX	0	0	—	0.00	1	1	0	7	2	1	7	0	0	0	0										

STARTING PITCHER — WINS (AL AVG), ERA (AL AVG), SO/9 (AL AVG), RATIO (AL AVG)

Year	Team	W	L	%	ERA	G	GS	CG	IP	H	BB	SO	ShO	W	L	SV	AB	H	HR	BA	PO	A	E	DP	TC/G	FA
1986	DET A	11	4	.733	3.51	33	16	3	138.1	108	63	79	1	3	0	3	0	0	0	—	19	15	1	0	1.1	.971
1987		6	9	.400	4.89	55	4	0	116	111	60	89	0	6	7	9	0	0	0	—	15	22	1	3	0.7	.974
1988		4	1	.800	3.41	23	5	0	68.2	60	34	45	0	1	0	3	0	0	0	—	3	8	2	0	0.6	.846
1989	CHI A	9	10	.474	3.39	25	25	1	159.1	144	64	72	0	0	0	0	0	0	0	—	15	20	3	2	1.5	.921
1990		12	4	.750	3.28	25	25	2	151	135	40	70	2	0	0	0	0	0	0	—	8	15	0	1	0.9	1.000
5 yrs.		42	28	.600	3.67	161	75	6	633.1	558	261	355	4	10	7	15	0	0	0	—	60	80	7	6	0.9	.952

LEAGUE CHAMPIONSHIP SERIES

Year	Team	W	L	%	ERA	G	GS	CG	IP	H	BB	SO	ShO	W	L	SV	AB	H	HR	BA	PO	A	E	DP	TC/G	FA
1987	DET A	0	0	—	1.69	2	0	0	5.1	3	2	4	0	0	0	0	0	0	0	—	1	1	0	0	1.0	1.000

Matt Kinzer

KINZER, MATTHEW ROY
B. June 17, 1963, Indianapolis, Ind.
BR TR 6′ 2″ 210 lbs.

Year	Team	W	L	%	ERA	G	GS	CG	IP	H	BB	SO	ShO	W	L	SV	AB	H	HR	BA	PO	A	E	DP	TC/G	FA
1989	STL N	0	2	.000	12.83	8	1	0	13.1	25	4	8	0	0	1	0	1	0	0	.000	0	0	0	0	0.0	—
1990	DET A	0	0	—	16.20	1	0	0	1.2	3	3	1	0	0	0	0	0	0	0	—	0	0	0	0	0.0	—
2 yrs.		0	2	.000	13.20	9	1	0	15	28	7	9	0	0	1	0	1	0	0	.000	0	0	0	0	0.0	—

Year	Team	W	L	%	ERA	G	GS	CG	IP	H	BB	SO	ShO	RELIEF PITCHING W	L	SV	BATTING AB	H	HR	BA	PO	A	E	DP	TC/G	FA

Bob Kipper

KIPPER, ROBERT WAYNE
B. July 8, 1964, Aurora, Ill.
BR TL 6' 2" 190 lbs.

Year	Team	W	L	%	ERA	G	GS	CG	IP	H	BB	SO	ShO	W	L	SV	AB	H	HR	BA	PO	A	E	DP	TC/G	FA
April		—	—	—		0		—	0	0	0	0	—	0	0	0										
May		0	1	.000	9.31	6	1	0	9.2	10	5	9	0	0	0	0										
June		3	0	1.000	1.62	11	0	0	16.2	10	7	9	0	3	0	1										
July		1	0	1.000	1.23	8	0	0	14.2	5	6	7	0	1	0	0										
Aug		1	1	.500	4.26	9	0	0	12.2	14	5	4	0	1	1	1										
Sept/Oct		0	0	—	0.00	7	0	0	9	5	3	6	0	0	0	1										
Day		3	0	1.000	0.56	13	0	0	16	5	8	12	0	3	0	2										
Night		2	2	.500	3.86	28	1	0	46.2	39	18	23	0	2	1	1										
vs. Left		—	—	—	—	—	—	—	—	18	9	12	—	—	—	—										
vs. Right		—	—	—	—	—	—	—	—	26	17	23	—	—	—	—										
On Grass		1	1	.500	5.00	11	1	0	18	9	7	8	0	1	0	1										
On Turf		4	1	.800	2.22	30	0	0	44.2	35	19	27	0	4	1	2										
Home		4	1	.800	2.70	18	0	0	30	24	12	19	0	4	1	0										
Road		1	1	.500	3.31	23	1	0	32.2	20	14	16	0	1	0	3										
Division Rivals																										
vs. CHI		0	0	—	0.00	1	0	0	1.2	0	0	0	0	0	0	0										
vs. MON		0	0	—	0.00	7	0	0	6.2	2	3	5	0	0	0	0										
vs. NY		1	0	1.000	0.68	7	0	0	13.1	7	3	8	0	1	0	1										
vs. PHI		1	0	1.000		5	0	0	10	7	6	5	0	1	0	0										
vs. STL		0	0	—	15.00	2	0	0	3	7	2	1	0	0	0	0										
1985	2 teams	CAL A		(2G 0 - 1)		PIT N		(5G 1 - 2)																		
"	total	1	3	.250	7.07	7	5	0	28	28	10	13	0	0	0	0	8	2	0	.250	1	5	1	0	1.0	.857
1986	PIT N	6	8	.429	4.03	20	19	0	114	123	34	81	0	0	0	0	33	1	0	.030	1	15	1	2	0.9	.941
1987		5	9	.357	5.94	24	20	1	110.2	117	52	83	1	0	0	0	33	8	0	.242	3	16	0	1	0.8	1.000
1988		2	6	.250	3.74	50	0	0	65	54	26	39	0	2	6	0	4	0	0	.000	4	16	0	1	0.4	1.000
1989		3	4	.429	2.93	52	0	0	83	55	33	58	0	3	4	4	9	1	0	.111	3	10	2	1	0.3	.867
1990		5	2	.714	3.02	41	1	0	62.2	44	26	35	0	5	1	3	7	1	0	.143	5	8	0	0	0.3	1.000
6 yrs.		22	32	.407	4.29	194	45	1	463.1	421	181	309	1	10	11	7	94	13	0	.138	17	70	4	5	0.5	.956

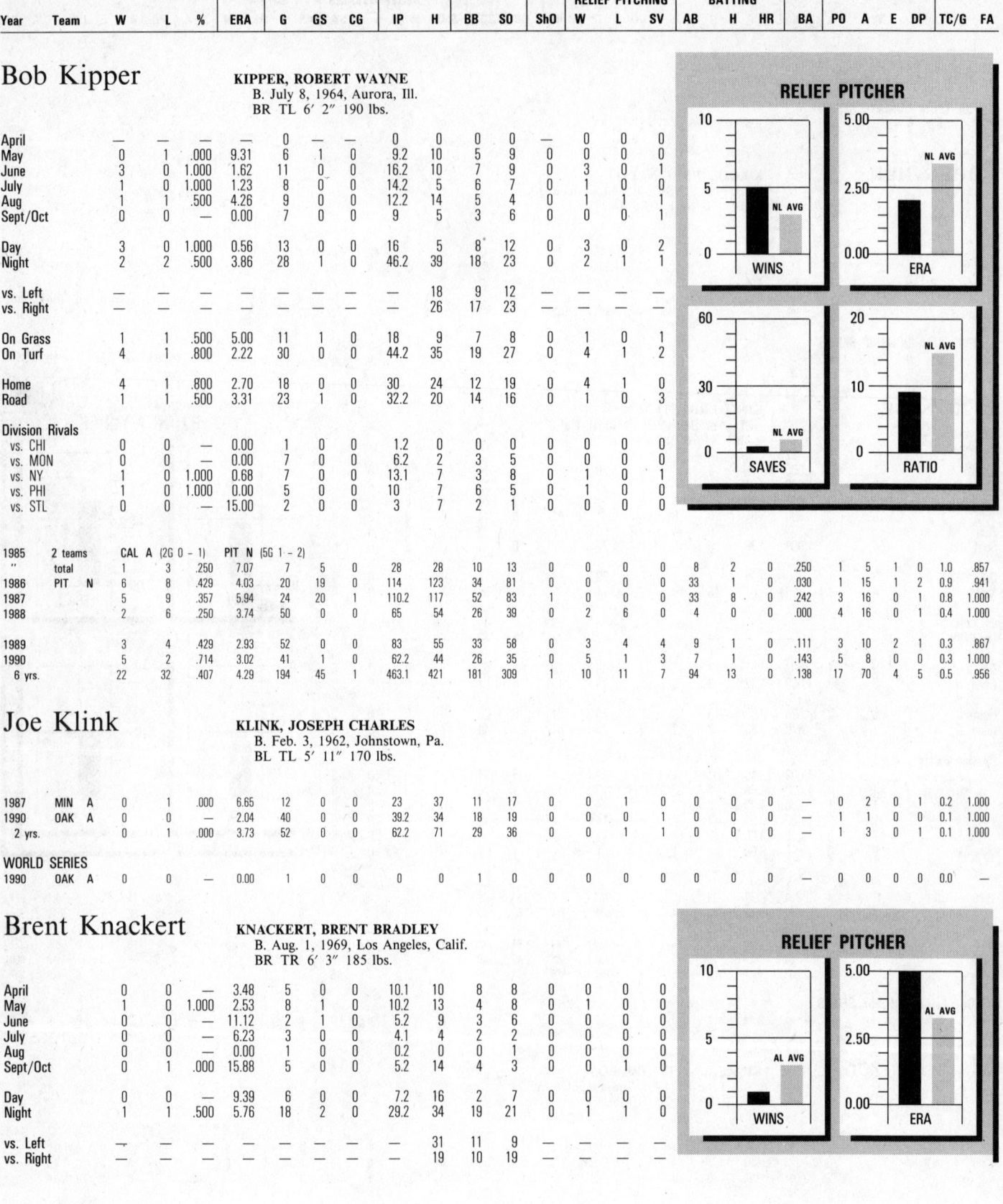

RELIEF PITCHER — WINS, ERA (NL AVG), SAVES, RATIO (NL AVG)

Joe Klink

KLINK, JOSEPH CHARLES
B. Feb. 3, 1962, Johnstown, Pa.
BL TL 5' 11" 170 lbs.

Year	Team	W	L	%	ERA	G	GS	CG	IP	H	BB	SO	ShO	W	L	SV	AB	H	HR	BA	PO	A	E	DP	TC/G	FA
1987	MIN A	0	1	.000	6.65	12	0	0	23	37	11	17	0	0	1	0	0	0	0	—	0	2	0	1	0.2	1.000
1990	OAK A	0	0	—	2.04	40	0	0	39.2	34	18	19	0	0	0	1	0	0	0	—	1	1	0	0	0.1	1.000
2 yrs.		0	1	.000	3.73	52	0	0	62.2	71	29	36	0	0	1	1	0	0	0	—	1	3	0	1	0.1	1.000

WORLD SERIES

Year	Team	W	L	%	ERA	G	GS	CG	IP	H	BB	SO	ShO	W	L	SV	AB	H	HR	BA	PO	A	E	DP	TC/G	FA
1990	OAK A	0	0	—	0.00	1	0	0	0	1	0	0	0	0	0	0	0	0	0	—	0	0	0	0	0.0	—

Brent Knackert

KNACKERT, BRENT BRADLEY
B. Aug. 1, 1969, Los Angeles, Calif.
BR TR 6' 3" 185 lbs.

Year	Team	W	L	%	ERA	G	GS	CG	IP	H	BB	SO	ShO	W	L	SV
April		0	0	—	3.48	5	0	0	10.1	10	8	8	0	0	0	0
May		1	0	1.000	2.53	8	1	0	10.2	13	4	8	0	1	0	0
June		0	0	—	11.12	2	1	0	5.2	9	3	6	0	0	0	0
July		0	0	—	6.23	3	0	0	4.1	4	2	2	0	0	0	0
Aug		0	0	—	0.00	1	0	0	0.2	0	2	0	0	0	0	0
Sept/Oct		0	1	.000	15.88	5	0	0	5.2	14	4	3	0	0	1	0
Day		0	0	—	9.39	6	0	0	7.2	16	2	7	0	0	0	0
Night		1	1	.500	5.76	18	2	0	29.2	34	19	21	0	1	1	0
vs. Left		—	—	—	—	—	—	—	—	31	11	9	—	—	—	—
vs. Right		—	—	—	—	—	—	—	—	19	10	19	—	—	—	—

RELIEF PITCHER — WINS (AL AVG), ERA (AL AVG)

Year	Team	W	L	%	ERA	G	GS	CG	IP	H	BB	SO	ShO	RELIEF PITCHING W	L	SV	BATTING AB	H	HR	BA	PO	A	E	DP	TC/G	FA

Brent Knackert *Continued*

Year	Team	W	L	%	ERA	G	GS	CG	IP	H	BB	SO	ShO	W	L	SV	AB	H	HR	BA	PO	A	E	DP	TC/G	FA
On Grass		0	0	—	5.60	9	1	0	17.2	17	12	12	0	0	0	0										
On Turf		1	1	.500	7.32	15	1	0	19.2	33	9	16	0	1	1	0										
Home		1	1	.500	7.23	14	1	0	18.2	31	9	16	0	1	1	0										
Road		0	0	—	5.79	10	1	0	18.2	19	12	12	0	0	0	0										
Division Rivals																										
vs. CAL		1	0	1.000	6.00	2	0	0	3	4	4	2	0	1	0	0										
vs. CHI		0	1	.000	14.54	2	0	0	4.1	11	3	4	0	0	1	0										
vs. KC		0	0	—	9.00	1	0	0	1	1	1	0	0	0	0	0										
vs. MIN		—	—	—	—	0	—	—	0	0	0	0	—	0	0	0										
vs. OAK		0	0	—	3.18	4	0	0	5.2	3	2	6	0	0	0	0										
vs. TEX		0	0	—	27.00	1	0	0	1.1	5	1	2	0	0	0	0										
1990	SEA A	1	1	.500	6.51	24	2	0	37.1	50	21	28	0	1	1	0	0	0	0	—	4	4	2	0	0.4	.800

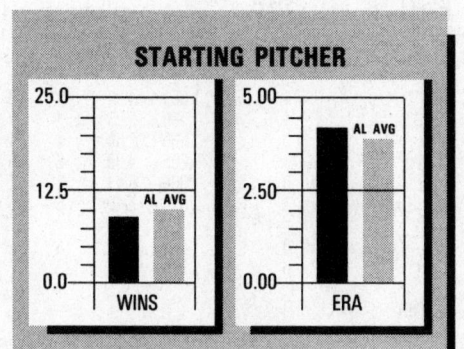

RELIEF PITCHER — SAVES — RATIO (AL AVG)

Bob Knepper

KNEPPER, ROBERT WESLEY
B. May 25, 1954, Akron, Ohio
BL TL 6' 3" 195 lbs.

Year	Team	W	L	%	ERA	G	GS	CG	IP	H	BB	SO	ShO	W	L	SV	AB	H	HR	BA	PO	A	E	DP	TC/G	FA
1976	SF N	1	2	.333	3.24	4	4	0	25	26	7	11	0	0	0	0	9	1	0	.111	1	4	0	1	1.3	1.000
1977		11	9	.550	3.36	27	27	6	166	151	72	100	2	0	0	0	55	10	0	.182	10	21	1	1	1.2	.969
1978		17	11	.607	2.63	36	35	16	260	218	85	147	6	0	0	0	79	5	0	.063	4	33	0	3	1.0	1.000
1979		9	12	.429	4.65	34	34	6	207	241	77	123	2	0	0	0	66	12	1	.182	8	26	5	1	1.1	.872
1980		9	16	.360	4.10	35	33	8	215	242	61	103	1	0	0	0	66	10	0	.152	7	45	3	3	1.6	.945
1981	HOU N	9	5	.643	2.18	22	22	6	157	128	38	75	5	0	0	0	47	7	1	.149	6	26	3	1	1.6	.914
1982		5	15	.250	4.45	33	29	4	180	193	60	108	0	0	0	1	52	3	0	.058	8	32	1	3	1.2	.976
1983		6	13	.316	3.19	35	29	4	203	202	71	125	3	1	1	0	66	12	1	.182	2	40	3	4	1.3	.933
1984		15	10	.600	3.20	35	34	11	233.2	223	55	140	3	0	0	0	76	13	1	.171	7	32	2	2	1.2	.951
1985		15	13	.536	3.55	37	37	4	241	253	54	131	0	0	0	0	78	11	1	.141	5	30	3	1	1.0	.921
1986		17	12	.586	3.14	40	38	8	258	232	62	143	5	1	0	0	91	9	0	.099	23	47	3	6	1.8	.959
1987		8	17	.320	5.27	33	31	1	177.2	226	54	76	0	0	0	0	51	5	0	.098	7	39	2	2	1.5	.958
1988		14	5	.737	3.14	27	27	3	175	156	67	103	2	0	0	0	48	6	0	.125	6	39	2	3	1.7	.957
1989	2 teams	HOU N (22G 4 - 10)			SF N (13G 3 - 2)																					
"	total	7	12	.368	5.13	35	26	1	165	190	75	64	1	1	0	0	43	8	1	.186	8	29	2	1	1.1	.949
1990	SF N	3	3	.500	5.68	12	7	0	44.1	56	19	24	0	0	1	0	13	3	0	.231	1	8	0	0	0.8	1.000
15 yrs.		146	155	.485	3.68	445	413	78	2707.2	2737	857	1473	30	3	2	1	840	115	6	.137	103	451	30	32	1.3	.949

DIVISIONAL PLAYOFF SERIES

Year	Team	W	L	%	ERA	G	GS	CG	IP	H	BB	SO	ShO	W	L	SV	AB	H	HR	BA	PO	A	E	DP	TC/G	FA
1981	HOU N	0	1	.000	5.40	1	1	0	5	6	2	4	0	0	0	0	1	0	0	.000	0	0	0	0	0.0	—

LEAGUE CHAMPIONSHIP SERIES

Year	Team	W	L	%	ERA	G	GS	CG	IP	H	BB	SO	ShO	W	L	SV	AB	H	HR	BA	PO	A	E	DP	TC/G	FA
1986	HOU N	0	0	—	3.52	2	2	0	15.1	13	1	9	0	0	0	0	5	0	0	.000	0	0	0	0	0.0	—

Mark Knudson

KNUDSON, MARK RICHARD
B. Oct. 28, 1960, Denver, Colo.
BR TR 6' 5" 215 lbs.

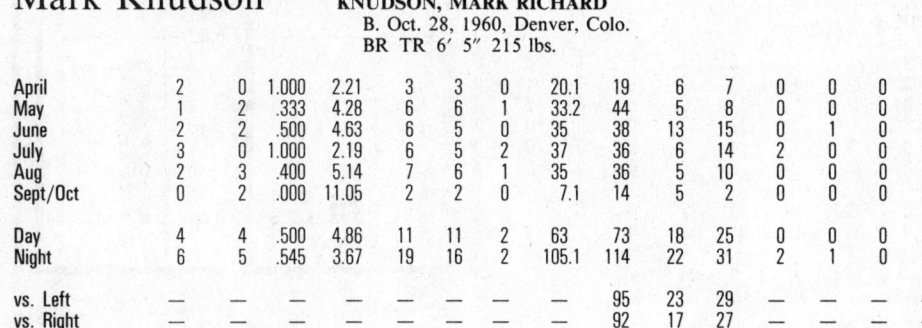

Period	W	L	%	ERA	G	GS	CG	IP	H	BB	SO	ShO	W	L	SV
April	2	0	1.000	2.21	3	3	0	20.1	19	6	7	0	0	0	0
May	1	2	.333	4.28	6	6	1	33.2	44	5	8	0	0	0	0
June	2	2	.500	4.63	6	5	0	35	38	13	15	0	1	0	0
July	3	0	1.000	2.19	6	5	2	37	36	6	14	2	0	0	0
Aug	2	3	.400	5.14	7	6	1	35	36	5	10	0	0	0	0
Sept/Oct	0	2	.000	11.05	2	2	0	7.1	14	5	2	0	0	0	0
Day	4	4	.500	4.86	11	11	2	63	73	18	25	0	0	0	0
Night	6	5	.545	3.67	19	16	2	105.1	114	22	31	2	1	0	0
vs. Left	—	—	—	—	—	—	—	—	95	23	29	—	—	—	—
vs. Right	—	—	—	—	—	—	—	—	92	17	27	—	—	—	—

STARTING PITCHER — WINS — ERA (AL AVG)

Year	Team	W	L	%	ERA	G	GS	CG	IP	H	BB	SO	ShO	W	L	SV	AB	H	HR	BA	PO	A	E	DP	TC/G	FA

Mark Knudson *Continued*

Split	W	L	%	ERA	G	GS	CG	IP	H	BB	SO	ShO	W	L	SV	AB	H	HR	BA	PO	A	E	DP	TC/G	FA
On Grass	10	5	.667	3.74	25	22	4	142	144	35	52	2	1	0	0										
On Turf	0	4	.000	6.15	5	5	0	26.1	43	5	4	0	0	0	0										
Home	5	3	.625	3.55	13	12	3	78.2	75	19	29	1	0	0	0										
Road	5	6	.455	4.62	17	15	1	89.2	112	21	27	1	1	0	0										
Division Rivals																									
vs. BAL	1	0	1.000	1.35	1	0	0	6.2	5	3	3	0	1	0	0										
vs. BOS	1	1	.500	3.55	2	2	1	12.2	14	1	4	0	0	0	0										
vs. CLE	0	1	.000	27.00	1	1	0	1.2	4	3	2	0	0	0	0										
vs. DET	1	0	1.000	6.14	4	3	0	14.2	18	5	4	0	0	0	0										
vs. NY	2	0	1.000	1.23	3	3	0	22	19	3	6	0	0	0	0										
vs. TOR	0	2	.000	8.80	3	3	0	15.1	24	4	7	0	0	0	0										

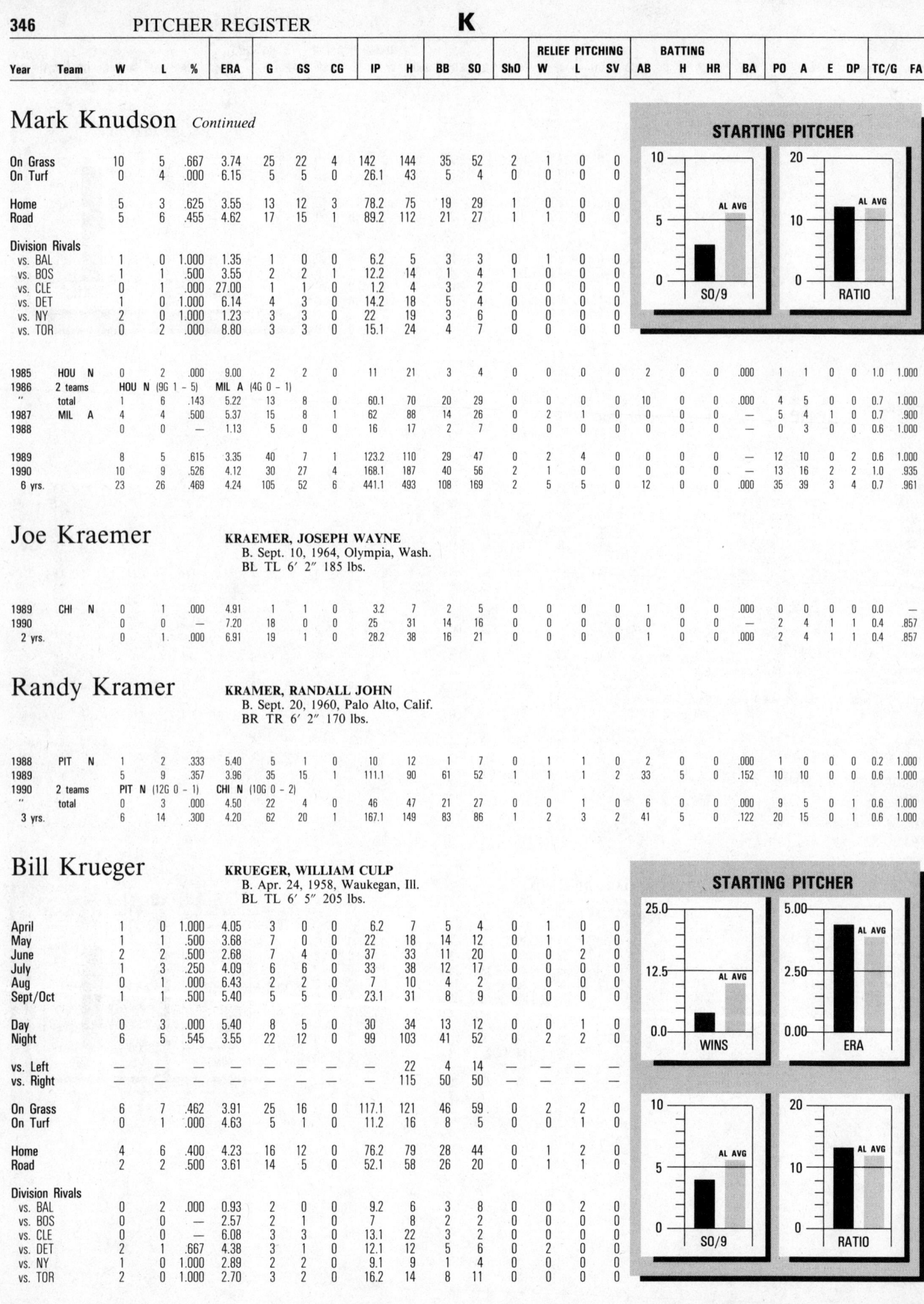

STARTING PITCHER — SO/9 (AL AVG), RATIO (AL AVG)

Year	Team	W	L	%	ERA	G	GS	CG	IP	H	BB	SO	ShO	W	L	SV	AB	H	HR	BA	PO	A	E	DP	TC/G	FA
1985	HOU N	0	2	.000	9.00	2	2	0	11	21	3	4	0	0	0	0	2	0	0	.000	1	1	0	0	1.0	1.000
1986	2 teams							HOU N (9G 1 – 5)				MIL A (4G 0 – 1)													
"	total	1	6	.143	5.22	13	8	0	60.1	70	20	29	0	0	0	0	10	0	0	.000	4	5	0	0	0.7	1.000
1987	MIL A	4	4	.500	5.37	15	8	1	62	88	14	26	0	2	1	0	0	0	0	—	5	4	1	0	0.7	.900
1988		0	0	—	1.13	5	0	0	16	17	2	7	0	0	0	0	0	0	0	—	0	3	0	0	0.6	1.000
1989		8	5	.615	3.35	40	7	1	123.2	110	29	47	0	2	4	0	0	0	0	—	12	10	0	2	0.6	1.000
1990		10	9	.526	4.12	30	27	4	168.1	187	40	56	2	1	0	0	0	0	0	—	13	16	2	2	1.0	.935
6 yrs.		23	26	.469	4.24	105	52	6	441.1	493	108	169	2	5	5	5	12	0	0	.000	35	39	3	4	0.7	.961

Joe Kraemer

KRAEMER, JOSEPH WAYNE
B. Sept. 10, 1964, Olympia, Wash.
BL TL 6' 2" 185 lbs.

Year	Team	W	L	%	ERA	G	GS	CG	IP	H	BB	SO	ShO	W	L	SV	AB	H	HR	BA	PO	A	E	DP	TC/G	FA
1989	CHI N	0	1	.000	4.91	1	1	0	3.2	7	2	5	0	0	0	0	1	0	0	.000	0	0	0	0	0.0	—
1990		0	0	—	7.20	18	0	0	25	31	14	16	0	0	0	0	0	0	0	—	2	4	1	1	0.4	.857
2 yrs.		0	1	.000	6.91	19	1	0	28.2	38	16	21	0	0	0	0	1	0	0	.000	2	4	1	1	0.4	.857

Randy Kramer

KRAMER, RANDALL JOHN
B. Sept. 20, 1960, Palo Alto, Calif.
BR TR 6' 2" 170 lbs.

Year	Team	W	L	%	ERA	G	GS	CG	IP	H	BB	SO	ShO	W	L	SV	AB	H	HR	BA	PO	A	E	DP	TC/G	FA
1988	PIT N	1	2	.333	5.40	5	1	0	10	12	1	7	0	1	1	0	2	0	0	.000	1	0	0	0	0.2	1.000
1989		5	9	.357	3.96	35	15	1	111.1	90	61	52	1	1	1	1	33	5	0	.152	10	10	0	0	0.6	1.000
1990	2 teams							PIT N (12G 0 – 1)				CHI N (10G 0 – 2)													
"	total	0	3	.000	4.50	22	4	0	46	47	21	27	0	0	1	2	6	0	0	.000	9	5	0	1	0.6	1.000
3 yrs.		6	14	.300	4.20	62	20	1	167.1	149	83	86	1	2	3	2	41	5	0	.122	20	15	0	1	0.6	1.000

Bill Krueger

KRUEGER, WILLIAM CULP
B. Apr. 24, 1958, Waukegan, Ill.
BL TL 6' 5" 205 lbs.

Split	W	L	%	ERA	G	GS	CG	IP	H	BB	SO	ShO	W	L	SV	AB	H	HR	BA	PO	A	E	DP	TC/G	FA
April	1	0	1.000	4.05	3	0	0	6.2	7	5	4	0	1	0	0										
May	1	1	.500	3.68	7	0	0	22	18	14	12	0	1	1	0										
June	2	2	.500	2.68	7	4	0	37	33	11	20	0	0	2	0										
July	1	3	.250	4.09	6	6	0	33	38	12	17	0	0	0	0										
Aug	0	1	.000	6.43	2	2	0	7	10	4	2	0	0	0	0										
Sept/Oct	1	1	.500	5.40	5	5	0	23.1	31	8	9	0	1	0	0										
Day	0	3	.000	5.40	8	5	0	30	34	13	12	0	0	1	0										
Night	6	5	.545	3.55	22	12	0	99	103	41	52	0	2	2	0										
vs. Left	—	—	—	—	—	—	—		22	4	14	—	—	—	—										
vs. Right	—	—	—	—	—	—	—		115	50	50	—	—	—	—										
On Grass	6	7	.462	3.91	25	16	0	117.1	121	46	59	0	2	2	0										
On Turf	0	1	.000	4.63	5	1	0	11.2	16	8	5	0	0	1	0										
Home	4	6	.400	4.23	16	12	0	76.2	79	28	44	0	1	2	0										
Road	2	2	.500	3.61	14	5	0	52.1	58	26	20	0	1	1	0										
Division Rivals																									
vs. BAL	0	2	.000	0.93	2	0	0	9.2	6	3	8	0	0	2	0										
vs. BOS	0	0	—	2.57	2	1	0	7	8	2	2	0	0	0	0										
vs. CLE	0	0	—	6.08	3	3	0	13.1	22	3	6	0	0	0	0										
vs. DET	2	1	.667	4.38	3	1	0	12.1	12	5	6	0	2	0	0										
vs. NY	1	0	1.000	2.89	2	2	0	9.1	9	1	4	0	0	0	0										
vs. TOR	2	0	1.000	2.70	3	2	0	16.2	14	8	11	0	0	0	0										

STARTING PITCHER — WINS (AL AVG), ERA (AL AVG), SO/9 (AL AVG), RATIO (AL AVG)

Year	Team	W	L	%	ERA	G	GS	CG	IP	H	BB	SO	ShO	RELIEF PITCHING W	L	SV	BATTING AB	H	HR	BA	PO	A	E	DP	TC/G	FA

Bill Krueger *Continued*

Year	Team	W	L	%	ERA	G	GS	CG	IP	H	BB	SO	ShO	W	L	SV	AB	H	HR	BA	PO	A	E	DP	TC/G	FA
1983	OAK A	7	6	.538	3.61	17	16	2	109.2	104	53	58	0	1	0	0	0	0	0	—	3	7	1	0	0.6	.909
1984		10	10	.500	4.75	26	24	1	142	156	85	61	0	0	0	0	0	0	0	—	6	12	0	1	0.7	1.000
1985		9	10	.474	4.52	32	23	2	151.1	165	69	56	0	1	0	0	0	0	0	—	3	23	2	0	0.9	.929
1986		1	2	.333	6.03	11	3	0	34.1	40	13	10	0	0	1	1	0	0	0	—	2	8	1	1	1.0	.909
1987	2 teams	OAK A	(9G 0 – 3)		LA N	(2G 0 – 0)																				
''	total	0	3	.000	6.75	11	0	0	8	12	9	4	0	0	3	0	0	0	0	—	0	0	0	0	0.0	—
1988	LA N	0	0	—	11.57	1	1	0	2.1	4	2	1	0	0	0	0	0	0	0	—	0	2	0	0	2.0	1.000
1989	MIL A	3	2	.600	3.84	34	5	0	93.2	96	33	72	0	1	0	3	0	0	0	—	5	11	0	0	0.5	1.000
1990		6	8	.429	3.98	30	17	0	129	137	54	64	0	2	3	0	0	0	0	—	2	17	0	2	0.6	1.000
8 yrs.		36	41	.468	4.35	162	89	5	670.1	714	318	326	0	5	7	4	0	0	0	—	21	80	4	4	0.6	.962

Jeff Kunkel

KUNKEL, JEFFREY WILLIAM
Son of Bill Kunkel.
B. Mar. 25, 1962, West Palm Beach, Fla.
BR TR 6′ 2″ 175 lbs.

Year	Team	W	L	%	ERA	G	GS	CG	IP	H	BB	SO	ShO	W	L	SV	AB	H	HR	BA	PO	A	E	DP	TC/G	FA
1988	TEX A	0	0	—	0.00	1	0	0	1	0	0	1	0	0	0	0	154	35	2	.227	0	0	0	0	0.0	—
1989		0	0	—	21.60	1	0	0	1.2	4	3	0	0	0	0	0	293	79	8	.270	1	0	0	0	1.0	1.000
2 yrs.		0	0	—	13.50	2	0	0	2.2	4	3	1	0	0	0	0	*				1	0	0	0	0.5	1.000

Jerry Kutzler

KUTZLER, JERRY SCOTT
B. Mar. 25, 1965, Waukegan, Ill.
BL TR 6′ 1″ 175 lbs.

Year	Team	W	L	%	ERA	G	GS	CG	IP	H	BB	SO	ShO	W	L	SV	AB	H	HR	BA	PO	A	E	DP	TC/G	FA
1990	CHI A	2	1	.667	6.03	7	7	0	31.1	38	14	21	0	0	0	0	0	0	0	—	2	2	0	0	0.6	1.000

Mike LaCoss

LaCOSS, MICHAEL JAMES
B. May 30, 1956, Glendale, Calif.
BR TR 6′ 5″ 185 lbs.

	W	L	%	ERA	G	GS	CG	IP	H	BB	SO	ShO	W	L	SV	AB	H	HR	BA
April	3	1	.750	2.28	4	4	1	27.2	20	11	19	0	0	0	0				
May	—	—	—	—	0	—	—	0	0	0	0	—	0	0	0				
June	—	—	—	—	0	—	—	0	0	0	0	—	0	0	0				
July	—	—	—	—	0	—	—	0	0	0	0	—	0	0	0				
Aug	1	2	.333	6.29	5	4	0	24.1	30	15	7	0	0	0	0				
Sept/Oct	2	1	.667	3.51	4	4	0	25.2	25	13	13	0	0	0	0				
Day	1	1	.500	1.72	2	2	0	15.2	14	6	14	0	0	0	0				
Night	5	3	.625	4.50	11	10	1	62	61	33	25	0	0	0	0				
vs. Left	—	—	—	—	—	—	—	—	43	28	21	—	—	—	—				
vs. Right	—	—	—	—	—	—	—	—	32	11	18	—	—	—	—				
On Grass	6	4	.600	4.41	10	10	1	63.1	65	31	34	0	0	0	0				
On Turf	0	0	—	1.88	3	2	0	14.1	10	8	5	0	0	0	0				
Home	2	2	.500	3.67	4	4	0	27	32	12	18	0	0	0	0				
Road	4	2	.667	4.09	9	8	1	50.2	43	27	21	0	0	0	0				
Division Rivals																			
vs. ATL	1	0	1.000	1.80	1	1	0	5	5	4	4	0	0	0	0				
vs. CIN	0	0	—	0.00	1	0	0	2	1	2	1	0	0	0	0				
vs. HOU	1	0	1.000	1.29	2	2	0	14	12	7	8	0	0	0	0				
vs. LA	1	1	.500	3.68	2	2	1	14.2	11	8	5	0	0	0	0				
vs. SD	2	0	1.000	4.50	2	2	0	12	10	4	7	0	0	0	0				

STARTING PITCHER

WINS (25.0 / 12.5 / 0.0) — NL AVG
ERA (5.00 / 2.50 / 0.00) — NL AVG
SO/9 (10 / 5 / 0) — NL AVG
RATIO (20 / 10 / 0) — NL AVG

Year	Team	W	L	%	ERA	G	GS	CG	IP	H	BB	SO	ShO	W	L	SV	AB	H	HR	BA	PO	A	E	DP	TC/G	FA
1978	CIN N	4	8	.333	4.50	16	15	2	96	104	46	31	1	0	0	0	30	2	0	.067	8	13	0	0	1.3	1.000
1979		14	8	.636	3.50	35	32	6	206	202	79	73	1	0	0	0	70	9	0	.129	15	34	2	4	1.5	.961
1980		10	12	.455	4.63	34	29	4	169	207	68	59	2	2	0	0	55	5	0	.091	9	34	3	4	1.4	.935
1981		4	7	.364	6.12	20	13	1	78	102	30	22	1	2	0	1	19	0	0	.000	6	14	1	0	1.1	.952
1982	HOU N	6	6	.500	2.90	41	8	0	115	107	54	51	0	3	3	0	24	6	0	.250	7	16	3	3	0.6	.885
1983		5	7	.417	4.43	38	17	2	138	142	56	53	0	0	1	1	35	3	0	.086	6	27	0	1	0.9	1.000
1984		7	5	.583	4.02	39	18	2	132	132	55	86	1	1	0	3	31	4	0	.129	9	20	2	2	0.8	.935
1985	KC A	1	1	.500	5.09	21	0	0	40.2	49	29	26	0	1	1	0	0	0	0	—	1	8	0	1	0.4	1.000
1986	SF N	10	13	.435	3.57	37	31	4	204.1	179	70	86	1	0	0	0	61	14	2	.230	19	34	1	2	1.5	.981
1987		13	10	.565	3.68	39	26	2	171	184	63	79	1	1	0	0	50	3	0	.060	15	43	2	4	1.5	.967
1988		7	7	.500	3.62	19	19	1	114.1	99	47	70	1	0	0	0	33	8	0	.242	10	32	0	1	2.2	1.000
1989		10	10	.500	3.17	45	18	1	150.1	143	65	78	0	3	5	4	41	3	0	.073	12	20	4	1	0.8	.889
1990		6	4	.600	3.94	13	12	1	77.2	75	39	39	0	0	0	0	23	1	0	.043	5	8	1	1	1.1	.929
13 yrs.		97	98	.497	3.93	397	238	26	1692.1	1725	701	753	9	13	10	12	472	58	2	.123	122	303	19	24	1.1	.957

Year	Team		W	L	%	ERA	G	GS	CG	IP	H	BB	SO	ShO	RELIEF PITCHING			BATTING			BA	PO	A	E	DP	TC/G	FA
															W	L	SV	AB	H	HR							

Mike LaCoss *Continued*

LEAGUE CHAMPIONSHIP SERIES

Year	Team		W	L	%	ERA	G	GS	CG	IP	H	BB	SO	ShO	W	L	SV	AB	H	HR	BA	PO	A	E	DP	TC/G	FA
1979	CIN	N	0	1	.000	10.80	1	1	0	1.2	1	4	0	0	0	0	0	0	0	0	—	0	1	0	0	1.0	1.000
1987	SF	N	0	0	—	0.00	2	0	0	3.1	1	3	2	0	0	0	0	0	0	0	—	0	2	0	0	1.0	1.000
1989			0	0	—	9.00	1	1	0	3	7	0	2	0	0	0	0	1	0	0	.000	0	0	1	0	1.0	—
3 yrs.			0	1	.000	5.63	4	2	0	8	9	7	4	0	0	0	0	1	0	0	.000	0	3	1	0	1.0	.750

WORLD SERIES

Year	Team		W	L	%	ERA	G	GS	CG	IP	H	BB	SO	ShO	W	L	SV	AB	H	HR	BA	PO	A	E	DP	TC/G	FA
1989	SF	N	0	0	—	6.23	2	0	0	4.1	4	3	2	0	0	0	0	1	0	0	.000	1	0	0	0	0.5	1.000

Dennis Lamp

LAMP, DENNIS PATRICK
B. Sept. 23, 1952, Los Angeles, Calif.
BR TR 6′ 4″ 200 lbs.

			W	L	%	ERA	G	GS	CG	IP	H	BB	SO	ShO	W	L	SV	AB	H	HR	BA	PO	A	E	DP	TC/G	FA
April			0	0	—	3.24	7	0	0	16.2	16	3	7	0	0	0	0										
May			0	1	.000	1.83	9	0	0	19.2	19	3	8	0	0	0	1										
June			1	1	.500	3.12	9	0	0	17.1	22	7	10	0	1	1	0										
July			2	1	.667	7.20	9	0	0	20	22	8	7	0	2	1	0										
Aug			0	1	.000	7.15	5	0	0	11.1	15	3	6	0	0	1	0										
Sept/Oct			0	1	.000	6.10	8	1	0	20.2	20	6	11	0	0	1	0										
Day			1	2	.333	5.92	18	0	0	38	47	12	14	0	1	2	0										
Night			2	3	.400	3.99	29	1	0	67.2	67	18	35	0	2	3	0										
vs. Left			—	—	—	—	—	—	—	—	58	17	24	—	—	—	—										
vs. Right			—	—	—	—	—	—	—	—	56	13	25	—	—	—	—										
On Grass			2	5	.286	4.71	44	1	0	101.1	109	30	48	0	2	5	0										
On Turf			1	0	1.000	4.15	3	0	0	4.1	5	0	1	0	1	0	0										
Home			2	2	.500	4.40	26	1	0	57.1	65	17	28	0	2	2	0										
Road			1	3	.250	5.03	21	0	0	48.1	49	13	21	0	1	3	0										
Division Rivals																											
vs. BAL			0	0	—	11.81	4	0	0	5.1	10	3	1	0	0	0	0										
vs. CLE			0	1	.000	3.60	4	0	0	10	13	3	6	0	0	1	0										
vs. DET			0	1	.000	8.10	6	0	0	10	13	3	4	0	0	1	0										
vs. MIL			0	0	—	5.94	5	1	0	16.2	19	9	7	0	0	0	0										
vs. NY			0	0	—	1.69	2	0	0	5.1	5	0	3	0	0	0	0										
vs. TOR			1	0	1.000	7.88	2	0	0	8	9	2	6	0	1	0	0										
1977	CHI	N	0	2	.000	6.30	11	3	0	30	43	8	12	0	0	0	1	0	8	3	0	.375	1	8	1	0	0.9	.900
1978			7	15	.318	3.29	37	36	6	224	221	56	73	3	0	0	0	0	73	15	0	.205	18	51	1	1	1.9	.986
1979			11	10	.524	3.51	38	32	6	200	223	46	86	1	0	0	0	0	58	9	0	.155	17	45	3	3	1.7	.954
1980			10	14	.417	5.19	41	37	2	203	259	82	83	1	1	2	0	0	61	6	0	.098	8	47	2	3	1.4	.965
1981			7	6	.538	2.41	27	10	3	127	103	43	71	0	3	1	0	0	0	0	0	—	5	23	1	4	1.1	.966
1982			11	8	.579	3.99	44	27	3	189.2	206	59	78	2	1	1	5	0	0	0	0	—	9	39	5	1	1.2	.906
1983			7	7	.500	3.71	49	5	1	116.1	123	29	44	0	4	5	15	0	0	0	0	—	9	16	0	2	0.5	1.000
1984	TOR	A	8	8	.500	4.55	56	4	0	85	97	38	45	0	5	7	9	0	0	0	0	—	9	15	2	3	0.5	.923
1985			11	0	1.000	3.32	53	1	0	105.2	96	27	68	0	11	0	2	0	0	0	0	—	11	21	0	3	0.6	1.000
1986			2	6	.250	5.05	40	2	0	73	93	23	30	0	2	4	2	0	0	0	0	—	5	11	1	2	0.4	.941
1987	OAK	A	1	3	.250	5.08	36	5	0	56.2	76	22	36	0	0	0	0	0	0	0	0	—	1	9	0	0	0.3	1.000
1988	BOS	A	7	6	.538	3.48	46	0	0	82.2	92	19	49	0	7	6	0	0	0	0	0	—	5	18	1	0	0.5	.958
1989			4	2	.667	2.32	42	0	0	112.1	96	27	61	0	4	2	2	0	0	0	0	—	12	20	0	3	0.8	1.000
1990			3	5	.375	4.68	47	1	0	105.2	114	30	49	0	3	5	0	0	0	0	0	—	12	14	0	0	0.6	1.000
14 yrs.			89	92	.492	3.87	567	163	21	1711	1842	509	785	7	41	34	35	200	33	0		.165	122	337	17	25	0.8	.964

LEAGUE CHAMPIONSHIP SERIES

Year	Team		W	L	%	ERA	G	GS	CG	IP	H	BB	SO	ShO	W	L	SV	AB	H	HR	BA	PO	A	E	DP	TC/G	FA
1983	CHI	A	0	0	—	0.00	3	0	0	2	0	2	1	0	0	0	0	0	0	0	—	0	0	0	0	0.0	—
1985	TOR	A	0	0	—	0.00	3	0	0	9.1	2	1	10	0	0	0	0	0	0	0	—	0	0	0	0	0.0	—
1990	BOS	A	0	0	—	108.00	1	0	0	0.1	2	2	0	0	0	0	0	0	0	0	—	0	0	0	0	0.0	—
3 yrs.			0	0	—	3.08	7	0	0	11.2	4	5	11	0	0	0	0	0	0	0	—	0	0	0	0	0.0	—

RELIEF PITCHER

WINS — AL AVG

ERA — AL AVG

SAVES — AL AVG

RATIO — AL AVG

Year	Team		W	L	%	ERA	G	GS	CG	IP	H	BB	SO	ShO	W	L	SV	AB	H	HR	BA	PO	A	E	DP	TC/G	FA
															RELIEF PITCHING W L SV			**BATTING** AB H HR									

Les Lancaster

LANCASTER, LESTER WAYNE
B. Apr. 21, 1962, Dallas, Tex.
BR TR 6' 2" 200 lbs.

Year	Team		W	L	%	ERA	G	GS	CG	IP	H	BB	SO	ShO	W	L	SV	AB	H	HR	BA	PO	A	E	DP	TC/G	FA
April			1	1	.500	2.13	8	0	0	12.2	12	5	7	0	1	1	0										
May			2	1	.667	4.91	8	4	1	29.1	39	11	16	1	0	0	1										
June			3	2	.600	6.75	15	0	0	24	31	14	17	0	3	2	3										
July			1	1	.500	6.75	10	0	0	17.1	21	6	10	0	1	1	1										
Aug			0	0	—	2.45	4	0	0	3.2	6	0	3	0	0	0	0										
Sept/Oct			2	0	1.000	2.05	10	2	0	22	12	4	12	0	1	0	1										
Day			6	5	.545	5.98	28	4	1	55.2	64	20	37	1	4	4	3										
Night			3	0	1.000	3.21	27	2	0	53.1	57	20	28	0	2	0	3										
vs. Left			—	—	—	—	—	—	—	—	65	30	30	—	—	—	—										
vs. Right			—	—	—	—	—	—	—	—	56	10	35	—	—	—	—										
On Grass			6	4	.600	4.92	42	5	1	82.1	92	29	51	1	4	3	4										
On Turf			3	1	.750	3.71	13	1	0	26.2	29	11	14	0	2	1	2										
Home			4	3	.571	5.37	30	3	1	57	65	19	36	1	3	2	3										
Road			5	2	.714	3.81	25	3	0	52	56	21	29	0	3	2	3										
Division Rivals																											
vs. MON			1	1	.500	9.95	6	0	0	6.1	13	5	5	0	1	1	1										
vs. NY			1	1	.500	7.56	4	2	0	16.2	20	2	10	0	0	1	0										
vs. PHI			2	0	1.000	1.06	11	0	0	17	11	7	11	0	2	0	3										
vs. PIT			0	1	.000	3.52	4	0	0	7.2	9	1	7	0	0	1	0										
vs. STL			2	0	1.000	2.12	9	0	0	17	13	5	7	0	2	0	0										
1987	CHI	N	8	3	.727	4.90	27	18	0	132.1	138	51	78	0	1	0	0	49	4	0	.082	12	14	0	0	1.0	1.000
1988			4	6	.400	3.78	44	3	1	85.2	89	34	36	0	3	6	5	20	1	0	.050	6	17	0	0	0.5	1.000
1989			4	2	.667	1.36	42	0	0	72.2	60	15	56	0	4	2	8	11	2	0	.182	8	5	0	1	0.3	1.000
1990			9	5	.643	4.62	55	6	1	109	121	40	65	1	6	4	6	20	1	0	.050	9	19	0	1	0.5	1.000
4 yrs.			25	16	.610	3.94	168	27	2	399.2	408	140	235	1	14	12	19	100	8	0	.080	35	55	0	2	0.5	1.000

LEAGUE CHAMPIONSHIP SERIES

Year	Team		W	L	%	ERA	G	GS	CG	IP	H	BB	SO	ShO	W	L	SV	AB	H	HR	BA	PO	A	E	DP	TC/G	FA
1989	CHI	N	1	1	.500	6.00	3	0	0	6	6	1	3	0	1	1	0	1	0	0	.000	0	1	0	0	0.3	1.000

Bill Landrum

LANDRUM, THOMAS WILLIAM
Son of Joe Landrum.
B. Aug. 17, 1957, Columbia. S. C.
BR TR 6' 2" 185 lbs.

Year	Team		W	L	%	ERA	G	GS	CG	IP	H	BB	SO	ShO	W	L	SV	AB	H	HR	BA	PO	A	E	DP	TC/G	FA
April			0	0	—	0.87	7	0	0	10.1	7	1	9	0	0	0	3										
May			1	0	1.000	1.20	11	0	0	15	11	2	5	0	1	0	4										
June			1	1	.500	3.09	9	0	0	11.2	14	7	8	0	1	1	4										
July			1	1	.500	2.35	11	0	0	15.1	16	4	9	0	1	1	1										
Aug			1	1	.500	5.40	10	0	0	10	16	5	4	0	1	1	1										
Sept/Oct			3	0	1.000	0.00	6	0	0	9.1	5	2	4	0	3	0	0										
Day			1	0	1.000	2.70	11	0	0	13.1	15	5	13	0	1	0	1										
Night			6	3	.667	2.01	43	0	0	58.1	54	16	26	0	6	3	12										
vs. Left			—	—	—	—	—	—	—	—	37	13	16	—	—	—	—										
vs. Right			—	—	—	—	—	—	—	—	32	8	23	—	—	—	—										
On Grass			1	0	1.000	2.20	13	0	0	16.1	13	4	10	0	1	0	4										
On Turf			6	3	.667	2.11	41	0	0	55.1	56	17	29	0	6	3	9										
Home			4	2	.667	1.93	28	0	0	37.1	37	9	20	0	4	2	7										
Road			3	1	.750	2.36	26	0	0	34.1	32	12	19	0	3	1	6										
Division Rivals																											
vs. CHI			0	0	—	2.70	6	0	0	6.2	8	0	4	0	0	0	2										
vs. MON			1	1	.500	4.26	5	0	0	6.1	6	4	5	0	1	1	0										
vs. NY			1	0	1.000	0.00	4	0	0	4.2	2	2	3	0	1	0	1										
vs. PHI			2	2	.500	1.64	7	0	0	11	14	5	6	0	2	2	1										
vs. STL			1	0	1.000	0.96	6	0	0	9.1	6	2	4	0	1	0	2										
1986	CIN	N	0	0	—	6.75	10	0	0	13.1	23	4	14	0	0	0	0	2	0	0	.000	0	1	0	0	0.1	1.000
1987			3	2	.600	4.71	44	2	0	65	68	34	42	0	3	1	2	5	1	0	.200	3	12	0	4	0.3	1.000
1988	CHI	N	1	0	1.000	5.84	7	0	0	12.1	19	3	6	0	1	0	0	2	0	0	.000	2	0	0	0	0.3	1.000
1989	PIT	N	2	3	.400	1.67	56	0	0	81	60	28	51	0	2	3	26	3	0	0	.000	8	10	0	0	0.3	1.000
1990			7	3	.700	2.13	54	0	0	71.2	69	21	39	0	7	3	13	9	1	0	.111	11	6	0	0	0.3	1.000
5 yrs.			13	8	.619	3.11	171	2	0	243.1	239	90	152	0	13	7	41	21	2	0	.095	24	29	0	4	0.3	1.000

LEAGUE CHAMPIONSHIP SERIES

Year	Team		W	L	%	ERA	G	GS	CG	IP	H	BB	SO	ShO	W	L	SV	AB	H	HR	BA	PO	A	E	DP	TC/G	FA
1990	PIT	N	0	0	—	0.00	2	0	0	2	0	0	1	0	0	0	0	0	0	0	—	0	0	0	0	0.0	—

Year	Team	W	L	%	ERA	G	GS	CG	IP	H	BB	SO	ShO	RELIEF PITCHING W	L	SV	BATTING AB	H	HR	BA	PO	A	E	DP	TC/G	FA

Mark Langston

LANGSTON, MARK EDWARD
B. Aug. 20, 1960, San Diego, Calif.
BB TL 6′ 2″ 175 lbs.

Year	Team	W	L	%	ERA	G	GS	CG	IP	H	BB	SO	ShO	W	L	SV	AB	H	HR	BA	PO	A	E	DP	TC/G	FA
April		2	1	.667	2.16	4	4	0	25	18	12	19	0	0	0	0										
May		1	4	.200	4.36	6	6	0	43.1	35	22	40	0	0	0	0										
June		1	3	.250	2.37	5	5	1	38	36	14	41	0	0	0	0										
July		0	5	.000	7.46	6	6	0	35	45	19	23	0	0	0	0										
Aug		4	3	.571	5.76	7	7	1	45.1	51	22	41	0	0	0	0										
Sept/Oct		2	1	.667	3.47	5	5	1	36.1	30	15	31	1	0	0	0										
Day		2	5	.286	6.55	8	8	0	45.1	54	22	43	0	0	0	0										
Night		8	12	.400	3.85	25	25	5	177.2	161	82	152	1	0	0	0										
vs. Left		—	—	—	—	—	—	—	—	34	15	27	—	—	—	—										
vs. Right		—	—	—	—	—	—	—	—	181	89	168	—	—	—	—										
On Grass		8	14	.364	4.14	28	28	4	193.1	177	92	174	1	0	0	0										
On Turf		2	3	.400	6.07	5	5	1	29.2	38	12	21	0	0	0	0										
Home		3	11	.214	4.55	17	17	3	118.2	108	52	104	1	0	0	0										
Road		7	6	.538	4.23	16	16	2	104.1	107	52	91	0	0	0	0										
Division Rivals																										
vs. CHI		1	3	.250	3.52	4	4	1	30.2	35	11	28	0	0	0	0										
vs. KC		1	1	.500	6.75	2	2	0	13.1	21	5	9	0	0	0	0										
vs. MIN		2	0	1.000	2.40	2	2	1	15	14	3	9	1	0	0	0										
vs. OAK		0	0	—	6.00	1	1	0	6	7	2	6	0	0	0	0										
vs. SEA		1	2	.333	3.51	4	4	1	25.2	18	13	18	0	0	0	0										
vs. TEX		1	1	.500	2.20	2	2	0	16.1	8	10	20	0	0	0	0										
1984	SEA A	17	10	.630	3.40	35	33	5	225	188	118	204	2	1	0	0	0	0	0	—	15	30	2	2	1.3	.957
1985		7	14	.333	5.47	24	24	2	126.2	122	91	72	0	0	0	0	0	0	0	—	9	26	2	4	1.5	.946
1986		12	14	.462	4.85	37	36	9	239.1	234	123	245	0	0	0	0	0	0	0	—	7	27	6	3	1.1	.850
1987		19	13	.594	3.84	35	35	14	272	242	114	262	3	0	0	0	0	0	0	—	8	41	2	3	1.5	.961
1988		15	11	.577	3.34	35	35	9	261.1	222	110	235	3	0	0	0	0	0	0	—	11	45	4	6	1.7	.933
1989	2 teams	SEA A (10G 4 – 5)			MON N (24G 12 – 9)																					
"	total	16	14	.533	2.74	34	34	8	250	198	112	235	5	0	0	0	64	11	0	.172	15	28	2	2	1.3	.956
1990	CAL A	10	17	.370	4.40	33	33	5	223	215	104	195	1	0	0	0	0	0	0	—	7	42	3	0	1.6	.942
7 yrs.		96	93	.508	3.88	233	230	52	1597.1	1421	772	1448	14	1	0	0	64	11	0	.172	72	239	21	20	1.4	.937

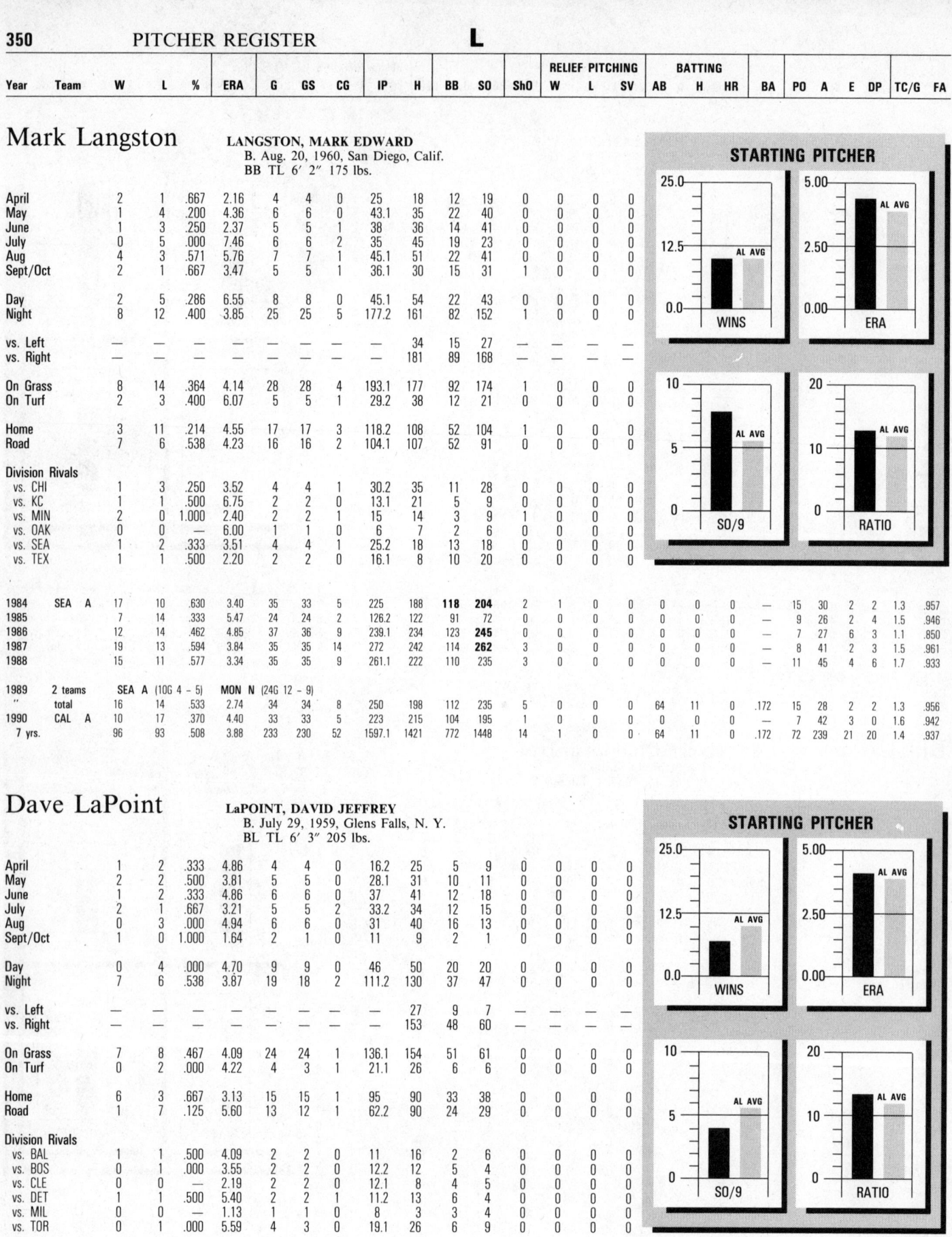

Dave LaPoint

LaPOINT, DAVID JEFFREY
B. July 29, 1959, Glens Falls, N. Y.
BL TL 6′ 3″ 205 lbs.

Year	Team	W	L	%	ERA	G	GS	CG	IP	H	BB	SO	ShO	W	L	SV	AB	H	HR	BA	PO	A	E	DP	TC/G	FA
April		1	2	.333	4.86	4	4	0	16.2	25	5	9	0	0	0	0										
May		2	2	.500	3.81	5	5	0	28.1	31	10	11	0	0	0	0										
June		1	2	.333	4.86	6	6	0	37	41	12	18	0	0	0	0										
July		2	1	.667	3.21	5	5	2	33.2	34	12	15	0	0	0	0										
Aug		0	3	.000	4.94	6	6	0	31	40	16	13	0	0	0	0										
Sept/Oct		1	0	1.000	1.64	2	1	0	11	9	2	1	0	0	0	0										
Day		0	4	.000	4.70	9	9	0	46	50	20	20	0	0	0	0										
Night		7	6	.538	3.87	19	18	2	111.2	130	37	47	0	0	0	0										
vs. Left		—	—	—	—	—	—	—	—	27	9	7	—	—	—	—										
vs. Right		—	—	—	—	—	—	—	—	153	48	60	—	—	—	—										
On Grass		7	8	.467	4.09	24	24	1	136.1	154	51	61	0	0	0	0										
On Turf		0	2	.000	4.22	4	3	1	21.1	26	6	6	0	0	0	0										
Home		6	3	.667	3.13	15	15	1	95	90	33	38	0	0	0	0										
Road		1	7	.125	5.60	13	12	1	62.2	90	24	29	0	0	0	0										
Division Rivals																										
vs. BAL		1	1	.500	4.09	2	2	0	11	16	2	6	0	0	0	0										
vs. BOS		0	1	.000	3.55	2	2	0	12.2	12	5	4	0	0	0	0										
vs. CLE		0	0	—	2.19	2	2	0	12.1	8	4	5	0	0	0	0										
vs. DET		1	1	.500	5.40	2	2	1	11.2	13	6	4	0	0	0	0										
vs. MIL		0	0	—	1.13	1	1	0	8	3	3	4	0	0	0	0										
vs. TOR		0	1	.000	5.59	4	3	0	19.1	26	6	9	0	0	0	0										
1980	MIL A	1	0	1.000	6.00	5	3	0	15	17	13	5	0	0	0	1	0	0	0	—	0	0	0	0	0.0	—
1981	STL N	1	0	1.000	4.09	3	2	0	11	12	2	4	0	0	0	0	5	0	0	.000	1	2	0	0	1.0	1.000
1982		9	3	.750	3.42	42	21	0	152.2	170	52	81	0	1	0	0	38	2	0	.053	2	13	1	0	0.4	.938
1983		12	9	.571	3.95	37	29	1	191.1	191	84	113	0	2	0	0	59	9	0	.153	11	24	0	1	0.9	1.000
1984		12	10	.545	3.96	33	33	2	193	205	77	130	1	0	0	0	59	4	0	.068	2	23	1	4	0.8	.962

Year	Team	W	L	%	ERA	G	GS	CG	IP	H	BB	SO	ShO	RELIEF PITCHING W	L	SV	BATTING AB	H	HR	BA	PO	A	E	DP	TC/G	FA

Dave LaPoint *Continued*

Year	Team	W	L	%	ERA	G	GS	CG	IP	H	BB	SO	ShO	W	L	SV	AB	H	HR	BA	PO	A	E	DP	TC/G	FA
1985	SF N	7	17	.292	3.57	31	31	2	206.2	215	74	122	1	0	0	0	60	10	0	.167	8	23	1	1	1.0	.969
1986	2 teams	DET A	(16G 3 - 6)	SD N	(24G 1 - 4)																					
"	total	4	10	.286	5.02	40	12	0	129	152	56	77	0	0	0	3	8	0	0	.000	5	16	1	2	0.6	.955
1987	2 teams	STL N	(6G 1 - 1)	CHI A	(14G 6 - 3)																					
"		7	4	.636	3.56	20	14	2	98.2	95	36	51	1	1	1	0	4	0	0	.000	2	26	1	0	1.5	.966
1988	2 teams	CHI A	(25G 10 - 11)	PIT N	(8G 4 - 2)																					
"		14	13	.519	3.25	33	33	2	213.1	205	57	98	1	0	0	0	16	1	0	.063	7	24	1	1	1.0	.969
1989	NY A	6	9	.400	5.62	20	20	0	113.2	146	45	51	0	0	0	0	0	0	0	—	2	10	0	1	0.6	1.000
1990		7	10	.412	4.11	28	27	2	157.2	180	57	67	0	0	0	0	0	0	0	—	6	23	2	3	1.1	.935
11 yrs.		80	85	.485	3.98	292	225	11	1482	1588	553	799	4	5	5	1	249	26	0	.104	46	184	8	13	0.8	.966

WORLD SERIES

Year	Team	W	L	%	ERA	G	GS	CG	IP	H	BB	SO	ShO	W	L	SV	AB	H	HR	BA	PO	A	E	DP	TC/G	FA
1982	STL N	0	0	—	3.24	2	1	0	8.1	10	2	3	0	0	0	0	0	0	0	—	0	2	1	0	1.5	.667

Tim Layana

LAYANA, TIMOTHY JOSEPH
B. Mar. 2, 1964, Inglewood, Calif.
BR TR 6' 2" 195 lbs.

	W	L	%	ERA	G	GS	CG	IP	H	BB	SO	ShO	W	L	SV	AB	H	HR	BA	PO	A	E	DP	TC/G	FA
April	2	0	1.000	4.50	8	0	0	10	9	10	4	0	2	0	0										
May	1	0	1.000	1.42	7	0	0	6.1	9	4	5	0	1	0	0										
June	0	0	—	1.56	9	0	0	17.1	14	4	13	0	0	0	1										
July	1	0	1.000	2.51	8	0	0	14.1	12	6	7	0	1	0	0										
Aug	1	1	.500	4.02	10	0	0	15.2	10	8	11	0	1	1	1										
Sept/Oct	0	2	.000	6.06	13	0	0	16.1	17	12	13	0	0	2	0										
Day	0	1	.000	3.26	16	0	0	19.1	17	14	11	0	0	1	1										
Night	5	2	.714	3.56	39	0	0	60.2	54	30	42	0	5	2	1										
vs. Left	—	—	—	—	—	—	—	—	34	25	22	—	—	—											
vs. Right	—	—	—	—	—	—	—	—	37	19	31	—	—	—											
On Grass	0	1	.000	2.89	16	0	0	18.2	20	14	15	0	0	1	0										
On Turf	5	2	.714	3.67	39	0	0	61.1	51	30	38	0	5	2	2										
Home	4	2	.667	3.77	28	0	0	45.1	36	21	25	0	4	2	1										
Road	1	1	.500	3.12	27	0	0	34.2	35	23	28	0	1	1	1										
Division Rivals																								
vs. ATL	0	1	.000	4.38	9	0	0	12.1	12	7	8	0	0	1	0										
vs. HOU	1	1	.500	1.93	7	0	0	9.1	5	7	10	0	1	1	0										
vs. LA	0	0	—	4.70	5	0	0	7.2	6	1	5	0	0	0	1										
vs. SD	1	0	1.000	2.45	7	0	0	11	8	6	9	0	1	0	0										
vs. SF	1	0	1.000	3.52	5	0	0	7.2	7	4	5	0	1	0	0										
1990 CIN N	5	3	.625	3.49	55	0	0	80	71	44	53	0	5	3	2	5	0	0	.000	10	9	0	1	0.3	1.000

RELIEF PITCHER

Rick Leach

LEACH, RICHARD MAX
B. May 4, 1957, Ann Arbor, Mich.
BL TL 6' 1" 180 lbs.

Year	Team	W	L	%	ERA	G	GS	CG	IP	H	BB	SO	ShO	W	L	SV	AB	H	HR	BA	PO	A	E	DP	TC/G	FA
1984	TOR A	0	0	—	27.00	1	0	0	1	2	2	0	0	0	0	0	*				0	0	0	0	0.0	—

Terry Leach

LEACH, TERRY HESTER
B. Mar. 13, 1954, Selma, Ala.
BR TR 6' 215 lbs.

	W	L	%	ERA	G	GS	CG	IP	H	BB	SO	ShO	W	L	SV
April	1	0	1.000	0.00	8	0	0	12.1	5	2	8	0	1	0	0
May	1	0	1.000	3.50	12	0	0	18	15	5	7	0	1	0	0
June	0	1	.000	4.02	10	0	0	15.2	21	2	10	0	0	1	0
July	0	2	.000	1.98	7	0	0	13.2	11	4	6	0	0	2	2
Aug	0	2	.000	4.76	9	0	0	11.1	17	1	5	0	0	2	2
Sept/Oct	0	0	—	5.06	9	0	0	10.2	15	7	10	0	0	0	0
Day	1	2	.333	5.01	20	0	0	23.1	24	9	9	0	1	2	0
Night	1	3	.250	2.47	35	0	0	58.1	60	12	37	0	1	3	2
vs. Left	—	—	—	—	—	—	—	—	34	11	9	—	—	—	
vs. Right	—	—	—	—	—	—	—	—	50	10	37	—	—	—	

RELIEF PITCHER

Year	Team	W	L	%	ERA	G	GS	CG	IP	H	BB	SO	ShO	RELIEF PITCHING W	L	SV	BATTING AB	H	HR	BA	PO	A	E	DP	TC/G	FA

Terry Leach *Continued*

		W	L	%	ERA	G	GS	CG	IP	H	BB	SO	ShO	W	L	SV	AB	H	HR	BA	PO	A	E	DP	TC/G	FA
On Grass		1	4	.200	2.20	22	0	0	28.2	28	8	15	0	1	4	1										
On Turf		1	1	.500	3.74	33	0	0	53	56	13	31	0	1	1	1										
Home		0	0	—	3.53	27	0	0	43.1	45	13	27	0	0	0	1										
Road		2	5	.286	2.82	28	0	0	38.1	39	8	19	0	2	5	1										
Division Rivals																										
vs. CAL		0	0	—	0.00	5	0	0	8.2	6	2	6	0	0	0	1										
vs. CHI		0	1	.000	6.75	2	0	0	2.2	4	0	2	0	0	1	0										
vs. KC		0	0	—	4.26	4	0	0	6.1	7	0	5	0	0	0	0										
vs. OAK		0	0	—	2.84	5	0	0	6.1	7	2	4	0	0	0	0										
vs. SEA		1	0	1.000	2.00	5	0	0	9	8	1	4	0	1	0	0										
vs. TEX		0	1	.000	4.50	6	0	0	6	8	3	4	0	0	1	0										
1981	NY N	1	1	.500	2.57	21	1	0	35	26	12	16	0	1	1	0	1	0	0	.000	4	7	0	0	0.5	1.000
1982		2	1	.667	4.17	21	1	1	45.1	46	18	30	1	1	1	3	8	1	0	.125	0	8	1	0	0.4	.889
1985		3	4	.429	2.91	22	4	1	55.2	48	14	30	1	0	3	1	12	2	0	.167	5	14	0	0	0.9	1.000
1986		0	0	—	2.70	6	0	0	6.2	6	3	4	0	0	0	0	0	0	0	—	0	2	0	0	0.3	1.000
1987		11	1	.917	3.22	44	12	1	131.1	132	29	61	1	4	0	0	33	2	0	.061	18	21	2	3	0.9	.951
1988		7	2	.778	2.54	52	0	0	92	95	24	51	0	7	2	3	14	2	0	.143	10	22	0	0	0.6	1.000
1989	2 teams	NY N	(10G 0 - 0)		KC A	(30G 5 - 6)																				
''	total	5	6	.455	4.17	40	3	0	95	97	40	36	0	4	4	0	4	0	0	.000	7	25	4	0	0.9	.889
1990	MIN A	2	5	.286	3.20	55	0	0	81.2	84	21	46	0	2	5	2	0	0	0	—	12	11	1	0	0.4	.958
8 yrs.		31	20	.608	3.27	261	21	3	542.2	534	161	274	3	19	15	9	72	7	0	.097	56	110	8	3	0.7	.954
LEAGUE CHAMPIONSHIP SERIES																										
1988	NY N	0	0	—	0.00	3	0	0	5	4	1	4	0	0	0	0	0	0	0	—	1	0	0	0	0.3	1.000

Tim Leary

LEARY, TIMOTHY JAMES
B. Mar. 21, 1958, Santa Monica, Calif.
BR TR 6' 3" 205 lbs.

		W	L	%	ERA	G	GS	CG	IP	H	BB	SO	ShO	W	L	SV	AB	H	HR	BA	PO	A	E	DP	TC/G	FA
April		1	1	.500	2.75	3	3	0	19.2	19	8	19	0	0	0	0										
May		2	4	.333	2.44	6	6	4	48	40	11	36	1	0	0	0										
June		0	5	.000	4.75	6	6	1	41.2	51	10	18	0	0	0	0										
July		2	3	.400	6.75	6	6	0	32	43	15	16	0	0	0	0										
Aug		3	3	.500	3.43	6	6	1	42	29	20	32	0	0	0	0										
Sept/Oct		1	3	.250	5.11	4	4	0	24.2	20	14	17	0	0	0	0										
Day		2	5	.286	5.53	9	9	0	53.2	55	26	38	0	0	0	0										
Night		7	14	.333	3.62	22	22	6	154.1	147	52	100	1	0	0	0										
vs. Left		—	—	—	—	—	—	—	—	106	46	61	—	—	—	—										
vs. Right		—	—	—	—	—	—	—	—	96	32	77	—	—	—	—										
On Grass		5	16	.238	4.25	24	24	4	158.2	159	64	99	0	0	0	0										
On Turf		4	3	.571	3.65	7	7	2	49.1	43	14	39	1	0	0	0										
Home		1	9	.100	4.73	13	13	2	83.2	89	34	59	0	0	0	0										
Road		8	10	.444	3.69	18	18	4	124.1	113	44	79	1	0	0	0										
Division Rivals																										
vs. BAL		1	1	.500	3.00	2	2	0	12	13	5	6	0	0	0	0										
vs. BOS		0	2	.000	3.52	2	2	0	15.1	18	2	6	0	0	0	0										
vs. CLE		1	1	.500	7.11	2	2	0	12.2	13	6	7	0	0	0	0										
vs. DET		2	0	1.000	1.29	2	2	0	14	9	6	9	0	0	0	0										
vs. MIL		0	2	.000	2.25	3	3	2	24	19	8	11	0	0	0	0										
vs. TOR		0	2	.000	11.32	2	2	0	10.1	16	3	7	0	0	0	0										
1981	NY N	0	0	—	0.00	1	1	0	2	0	1	3	0	0	0	0	1	0	0	.000	0	0	0	0	0.0	—
1983		1	1	.500	3.38	2	2	1	10.2	15	4	9	0	0	0	0	3	1	0	.333	1	3	0	0	2.0	1.000
1984		3	3	.500	4.02	20	7	0	53.2	61	18	29	0	3	0	0	10	3	1	.300	3	4	1	0	0.4	.875
1985	MIL A	1	4	.200	4.05	5	5	0	33.1	40	8	29	0	0	0	0	0	0	0	—	1	7	0	0	1.6	1.000
1986		12	12	.500	4.21	33	30	3	188.1	216	53	110	2	0	0	0	0	0	0	—	22	26	1	1	1.5	.980
1987	LA N	3	11	.214	4.76	39	12	0	107.2	121	36	61	0	1	4	1	23	7	0	.304	9	18	0	2	0.7	1.000
1988		17	11	.607	2.91	35	34	9	228.2	201	56	180	6	0	0	0	67	18	0	.269	24	34	1	4	1.7	.983
1989	2 teams	LA N	(19G 6 - 7)		CIN N	(14G 2 - 7)																				
''	total	8	14	.364	3.52	33	31	2	207	205	68	123	0	1	1	0	59	7	0	.119	20	31	2	2	1.6	.962
1990	NY A	9	**19**	.321	4.11	31	31	6	208	202	78	138	1	0	0	0	0	0	0	—	14	36	4	4	1.7	.926
9 yrs.		54	75	.419	3.79	199	153	21	1039.1	1061	322	682	9	5	5	1	163	36	1	.221	94	159	9	13	1.3	.966
LEAGUE CHAMPIONSHIP SERIES																										
1988	LA N	0	1	.000	6.23	2	1	0	4.1	8	3	3	0	0	0	0	1	0	0	.000	0	1	0	0	0.5	1.000

Year	Team	W	L	%	ERA	G	GS	CG	IP	H	BB	SO	ShO	W	L	SV	AB	H	HR	BA	PO	A	E	DP	TC/G	FA
														RELIEF PITCHING			BATTING									

Tim Leary *Continued*

WORLD SERIES

Year	Team	W	L	%	ERA	G	GS	CG	IP	H	BB	SO	ShO	W	L	SV	AB	H	HR	BA	PO	A	E	DP	TC/G	FA
1988	LA N	0	0	—	1.35	2	0	0	6.2	6	2	4	0	0	0	0	0	0	0	—	1	3	0	1	2.0	1.000

Mark Lee

LEE, MARK OWEN
B. July 20, 1964, Williston, N. D.
BL TL 6′ 3″ 198 lbs.

Year	Team	W	L	%	ERA	G	GS	CG	IP	H	BB	SO	ShO	W	L	SV	AB	H	HR	BA	PO	A	E	DP	TC/G	FA
1988	KC A	0	0	—	3.60	4	0	0	5	6	1	0	0	0	0	0	0	0	0	—	0	1	0	1	0.3	1.000
1990	MIL A	1	0	1.000	2.11	11	0	0	21.1	20	4	14	0	1	0	0	0	0	0	—	1	1	0	0	0.2	1.000
2 yrs.		1	0	1.000	2.39	15	0	0	26.1	26	5	14	0	1	0	0	0	0	0	—	1	2	0	1	0.2	1.000

Craig Lefferts

LEFFERTS, CRAIG LINDSAY
B. Sept. 29, 1957, Munich, West Germany
BL TL 6′ 1″ 180 lbs.

	W	L	%	ERA	G	GS	CG	IP	H	BB	SO	ShO	W	L	SV	AB	H	HR	BA	PO	A	E	DP	TC/G	FA
April	1	0	1.000	1.17	6	0	0	7.2	4	0	8	0	1	0	2										
May	1	1	.500	1.84	9	0	0	14.2	6	5	11	0	1	1	6										
June	3	1	.750	3.09	14	0	0	23.1	19	9	17	0	3	1	3										
July	1	2	.333	4.15	8	0	0	13	16	3	11	0	1	2	3										
Aug	0	0	—	1.46	12	0	0	12.1	12	2	4	0	0	0	8										
Sept/Oct	1	1	.500	2.35	7	0	0	7.2	11	3	9	0	1	1	1										
Day	3	3	.500	3.95	19	0	0	27.1	24	6	20	0	3	3	6										
Night	4	2	.667	1.75	37	0	0	51.1	44	16	40	0	4	2	17										
vs. Left	—	—	—	—	—	—	—	—	18	8	18	—	—	—	—										
vs. Right	—	—	—	—	—	—	—	—	50	14	42	—	—	—	—										
On Grass	7	5	.583	3.02	43	0	0	62.2	57	19	49	0	7	5	17										
On Turf	0	0	—	0.56	13	0	0	16	11	3	11	0	0	0	6										
Home	4	2	.667	2.39	28	0	0	37.2	32	8	33	0	4	2	11										
Road	3	3	.500	2.63	28	0	0	41	36	14	27	0	3	3	12										
Division Rivals																									
vs. ATL	2	1	.667	6.30	7	0	0	10	12	5	6	0	2	1	2										
vs. CIN	0	0	—	1.42	5	0	0	6.1	6	1	3	0	0	0	2										
vs. HOU	1	0	1.000	1.04	8	0	0	8.2	10	2	9	0	1	0	5										
vs. LA	1	1	.500	0.77	8	0	0	11.2	8	3	13	0	1	1	2										
vs. SF	2	0	1.000	1.17	4	0	0	7.2	5	1	3	0	2	0	1										

RELIEF PITCHER

WINS — ERA — SAVES — RATIO (with NL AVG comparison bars)

Year	Team	W	L	%	ERA	G	GS	CG	IP	H	BB	SO	ShO	W	L	SV	AB	H	HR	BA	PO	A	E	DP	TC/G	FA
1983	CHI N	3	4	.429	3.13	56	5	0	89	80	29	60	0	2	3	1	18	2	0	.111	8	13	1	0	0.4	.955
1984	SD N	3	4	.429	2.13	62	0	0	105.2	88	24	56	0	3	4	10	17	5	0	.294	5	10	1	2	0.3	.938
1985		7	6	.538	3.35	60	0	0	83.1	75	30	48	0	7	6	2	4	1	0	.250	4	11	0	1	0.3	1.000
1986		9	8	.529	3.09	**83**	0	0	107.2	98	44	72	0	9	8	4	8	1	1	.125	3	24	0	3	0.3	1.000
1987	2 teams	SD N	(33G 2 – 2)		SF N	(44G 3 – 3)																				
""	total	5	5	.500	3.83	77	0	0	98.2	92	33	57	0	5	5	6	7	2	0	.286	5	11	2	1	0.2	.889
1988	SF N	3	8	.273	2.92	64	0	0	92.1	74	23	58	0	3	8	11	9	0	0	.000	2	11	0	0	0.2	1.000
1989		2	4	.333	2.69	70	0	0	107	93	22	71	0	2	4	20	7	0	0	.000	5	9	0	2	0.2	1.000
1990	SD N	7	5	.583	2.52	56	0	0	78.2	68	22	60	0	7	5	23	4	1	0	.250	6	10	0	2	0.3	1.000
8 yrs.		39	44	.470	2.95	528	5	0	762.1	668	227	482	0	38	43	77	74	12	1	.162	38	99	4	11	0.3	.972

LEAGUE CHAMPIONSHIP SERIES

Year	Team	W	L	%	ERA	G	GS	CG	IP	H	BB	SO	ShO	W	L	SV	AB	H	HR	BA	PO	A	E	DP	TC/G	FA
1984	SD N	2	0	1.000	0.00	3	0	0	4	1	1	1	0	2	0	0	0	0	0	—	0	0	0	0	0.0	—
1987	SF N	0	0	—	0.00	3	0	0	2	3	1	0	0	0	0	0	0	0	0	—	0	2	0	1	0.7	1.000
1989		0	0	—	9.00	2	0	0	1	1	2	1	0	0	0	0	0	0	0	—	0	0	0	0	0.0	—
3 yrs.		2	0	1.000	1.29	8	0	0	7	5	4	2	0	2	0	0	0	0	0	—	0	2	0	1	0.3	1.000

WORLD SERIES

Year	Team	W	L	%	ERA	G	GS	CG	IP	H	BB	SO	ShO	W	L	SV	AB	H	HR	BA	PO	A	E	DP	TC/G	FA
1984	SD N	0	0	—	0.00	3	0	0	6	2	1	7	0	0	0	1	0	0	0	—	0	0	0	0	0.0	—
1989	SF N	0	0	—	3.38	3	0	0	2.2	2	2	1	0	0	0	0	0	0	0	—	0	1	1	0	0.7	.500
2 yrs.		0	0	—	1.04	6	0	0	8.2	4	3	8	0	0	0	1	0	0	0	—	0	1	1	0	0.3	.500

Year	Team	W	L	%	ERA	G	GS	CG	IP	H	BB	SO	ShO	W	L	SV	AB	H	HR	BA	PO	A	E	DP	TC/G	FA
														RELIEF PITCHING			**BATTING**									

Charlie Leibrandt — LEIBRANDT, CHARLES LOUIS, JR.
B. Oct. 4, 1956, Chicago, Ill.
BR TL 6′ 3″ 195 lbs.

Year	Team	W	L	%	ERA	G	GS	CG	IP	H	BB	SO	ShO	W	L	SV	AB	H	HR	BA	PO	A	E	DP	TC/G	FA
April		—	—	—	—	0	0	0	0	0	0	0	—	0	0	0										
May		—	—	—	—	0	0	0	0	0	0	0	—	0	0	0										
June		3	1	.750	2.72	6	6	2	46.1	48	6	16	1	0	0	0										
July		1	3	.250	5.13	5	5	0	33.1	34	12	26	0	0	0	0										
Aug		2	4	.333	3.60	6	6	0	35	38	7	13	0	0	0	0										
Sept/Oct		3	3	.500	1.89	7	7	3	47.2	44	10	21	1	0	0	0										
Day		2	3	.400	2.93	7	7	1	43	45	7	23	1	0	0	0										
Night		7	8	.467	3.24	17	17	4	119.1	119	28	53	1	0	0	0										
vs. Left		—	—	—	—	—	—	—	—	22	6	14	—	—	—	—										
vs. Right		—	—	—	—	—	—	—	—	142	29	62	—	—	—	—										
On Grass		8	8	.500	2.66	19	19	5	132	126	27	61	2	0	0	0										
On Turf		1	3	.250	5.34	5	5	0	30.1	38	8	15	0	0	0	0										
Home		6	5	.545	2.59	12	12	4	87	90	17	33	2	0	0	0										
Road		3	6	.333	3.82	12	12	1	75.1	74	18	43	0	0	0	0										
Division Rivals																										
vs. CIN		1	0	1.000	1.69	2	2	1	16	13	2	5	1	0	0	0										
vs. HOU		2	3	.400	4.06	5	5	1	31	35	6	19	0	0	0	0										
vs. LA		0	3	.000	4.98	3	3	0	21.2	27	8	11	0	0	0	0										
vs. SD		1	1	.500	0.86	3	3	1	21	16	5	10	0	0	0	0										
vs. SF		1	1	.500	2.37	3	3	1	19	18	0	12	0	0	0	0										
1979	CIN N	0	0	—	0.00	3	0	0	4	2	2	1	0	0	0	0	0	0	0	—	1	0	0	1	0.3	1.000
1980		10	9	.526	4.24	36	27	5	174	200	54	62	2	0	0	0	56	11	0	.196	10	35	3	3	1.3	.938
1981		1	1	.500	3.60	7	4	1	30	28	15	9	1	0	0	0	8	0	0	.000	0	7	0	0	1.0	1.000
1982		5	7	.417	5.10	36	11	0	107.2	130	48	34	0	2	1	2	25	2	0	.080	5	18	1	0	0.7	.958
1984	KC A	11	7	.611	3.63	23	23	0	143.2	158	38	53	0	0	0	0	0	0	0	—	9	15	3	1	1.2	.889
1985		17	9	.654	2.69	33	33	8	237.2	223	68	108	3	0	0	0	0	0	0	—	19	53	1	2	2.2	.986
1986		14	11	.560	4.09	35	34	8	231.1	238	63	108	1	0	0	0	0	0	0	—	14	43	1	3	1.7	.983
1987		16	11	.593	3.41	35	35	8	240.1	235	74	151	3	0	0	0	0	0	0	—	15	55	4	4	2.1	.946
1988		13	12	.520	3.19	35	35	7	243	244	62	125	2	0	0	0	0	0	0	—	19	43	3	2	1.9	.954
1989		5	11	.313	5.14	33	27	3	161	196	54	73	1	0	0	0	0	0	0	—	6	26	2	0	1.0	.941
1990	ATL N	9	11	.450	3.16	24	24	5	162.1	164	35	76	2	0	0	0	50	9	0	.180	10	28	0	2	1.6	1.000
11 yrs.		101	89	.532	3.71	300	253	45	1735	1818	513	800	15	2	1	2	139	22	0	.158	108	323	18	18	1.5	.960

LEAGUE CHAMPIONSHIP SERIES

Year	Team	W	L	%	ERA	G	GS	CG	IP	H	BB	SO	ShO	W	L	SV	AB	H	HR	BA	PO	A	E	DP	TC/G	FA
1979	CIN N	0	0	—	0.00	1	0	0	0.1	0	0	0	0	0	0	0	0	0	0	—	0	0	0	0	0.0	—
1984	KC A	0	1	.000	1.13	1	1	1	8	3	4	6	0	0	0	0	0	0	0	—	1	2	0	0	3.0	1.000
1985		1	2	.333	5.28	3	2	0	15.1	17	4	6	0	0	0	0	0	0	0	—	3	7	0	0	3.3	1.000
3 yrs.		1	3	.250	3.80	5	3	1	23.2	20	8	12	0	1	0	0	0	0	0	—	4	9	0	0	2.6	1.000

WORLD SERIES

Year	Team	W	L	%	ERA	G	GS	CG	IP	H	BB	SO	ShO	W	L	SV	AB	H	HR	BA	PO	A	E	DP	TC/G	FA
1985	KC A	0	1	.000	2.76	2	2	0	16.1	10	4	10	0	0	0	0	4	0	0	.000	1	2	0	0	1.5	1.000

John Leister — LEISTER, JOHN WILLIAM
B. Jan. 3, 1961, San Antonio, Tex.
BR TR 6′ 2″ 200 lbs.

Year	Team	W	L	%	ERA	G	GS	CG	IP	H	BB	SO	ShO	W	L	SV	AB	H	HR	BA	PO	A	E	DP	TC/G	FA
1987	BOS A	0	2	.000	9.20	8	6	0	30.1	49	12	16	0	0	0	0	0	0	0	—	2	2	0	0	0.5	1.000
1990		0	0	—	4.76	2	1	0	5.2	7	4	3	0	0	0	0	0	0	0	—	0	0	0	0	0.0	—
2 yrs.		0	2	.000	8.50	10	7	0	36	56	16	19	0	0	0	0	0	0	0	—	2	2	0	0	0.4	1.000

Al Leiter — LEITER, ALOIS TERRY
Brother of Mark Leiter.
B. Oct. 23, 1965, Toms River, N. J.
BL TL 6′ 2″ 200 lbs.

Year	Team	W	L	%	ERA	G	GS	CG	IP	H	BB	SO	ShO	W	L	SV	AB	H	HR	BA	PO	A	E	DP	TC/G	FA
1987	NY A	2	2	.500	6.35	4	4	0	22.2	24	15	28	0	0	0	0	0	0	0	—	0	2	0	0	0.5	1.000
1988		4	4	.500	3.92	14	14	0	57.1	49	33	60	0	0	0	0	0	0	0	—	0	11	1	0	0.9	.917
1989	2 teams	NY A	(4G 1 - 2)		TOR A	(1G 0 - 0)																				
"	total	1	2	.333	5.67	5	5	0	33.1	32	23	26	0	0	0	0	0	0	0	—	1	2	0	0	0.6	1.000
1990	TOR A	0	0	—	0.00	4	0	0	6.1	1	2	5	0	0	0	0	0	0	0	—	1	1	0	0	0.5	1.000
4 yrs.		7	8	.467	4.66	27	23	0	119.2	106	73	119	0	0	0	0	0	0	0	—	2	16	1	0	0.7	.947

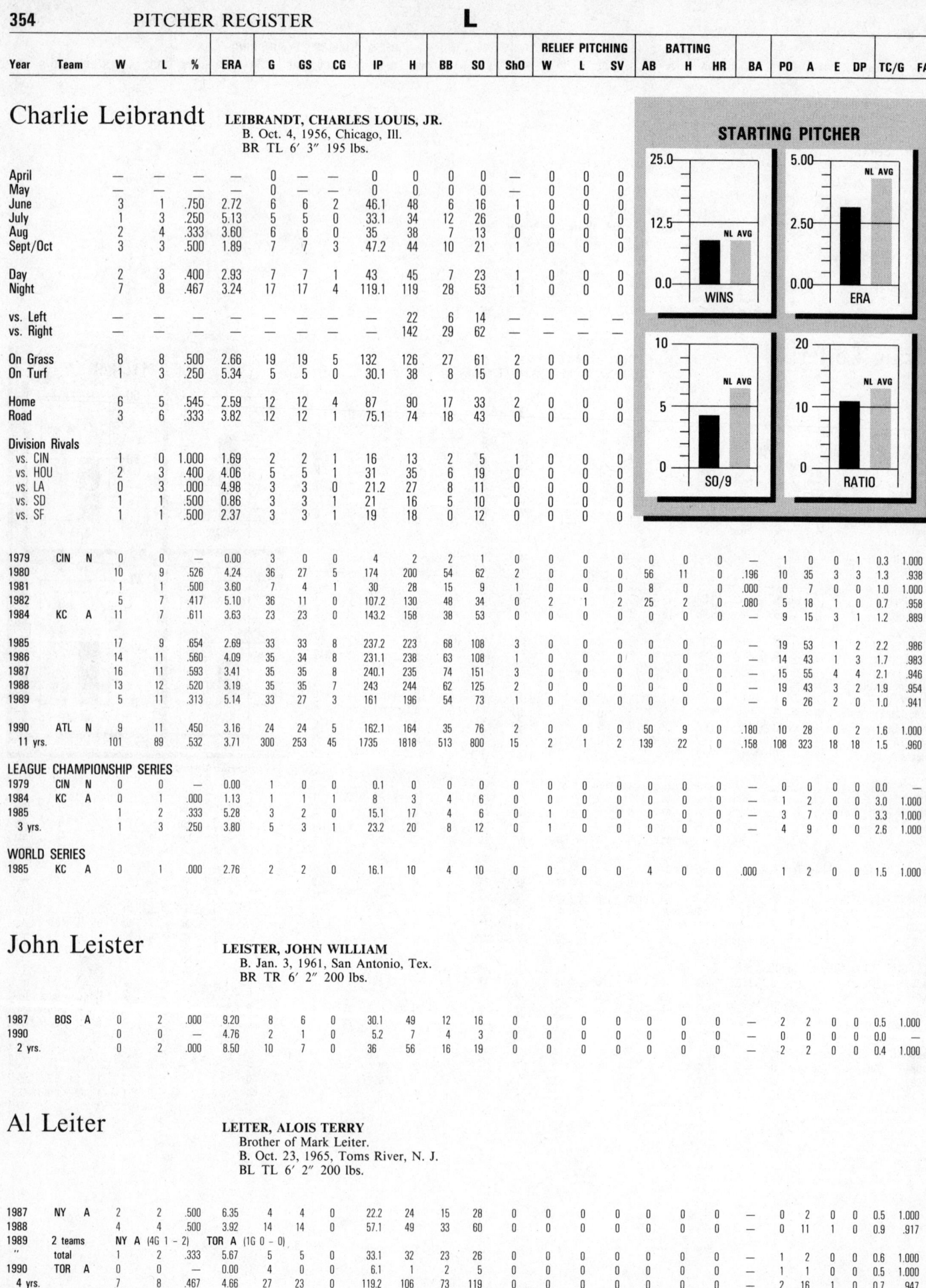

STARTING PITCHER

WINS — NL AVG
ERA — NL AVG
SO/9 — NL AVG
RATIO — NL AVG

Year	Team	W	L	%	ERA	G	GS	CG	IP	H	BB	SO	ShO	RELIEF PITCHING W	L	SV	BATTING AB	H	HR	BA	PO	A	E	DP	TC/G	FA

Mark Leiter

LEITER, MARK EDWARD
Brother of Al Leiter.
B. Apr. 13, 1963, Joliet, Ill.
BR TR 6′ 3″ 200 lbs.

Year	Team	W	L	%	ERA	G	GS	CG	IP	H	BB	SO	ShO	W	L	SV	AB	H	HR	BA	PO	A	E	DP	TC/G	FA
1990	NY A	1	1	.500	6.84	8	3	0	26.1	33	9	21	0	0	1	0	0	0	0	—	0	8	0	1	1.0	1.000

Scott Lewis

LEWIS, SCOTT ALLEN
B. Dec. 5, 1965, Grant's Pass, Ore.
BR TR 6′ 3″ 190 lbs.

Year	Team	W	L	%	ERA	G	GS	CG	IP	H	BB	SO	ShO	W	L	SV	AB	H	HR	BA	PO	A	E	DP	TC/G	FA
1990	CAL A	1	1	.500	2.20	2	2	1	16.1	10	2	9	0	0	0	0	0	0	0	—	0	1	0	0	0.5	1.000

Derek Lilliquist

LILLIQUIST, DEREK JANSEN
B. Feb. 20, 1966, Winter Park, Fla.
BL TL 6′ 200 lbs.

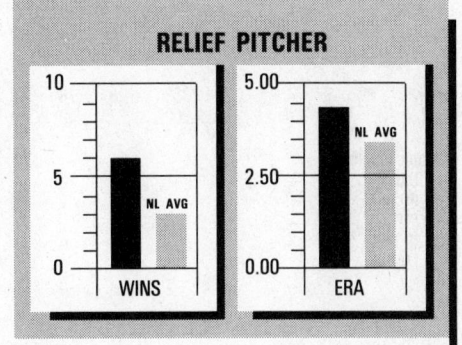

STARTING PITCHER

	W	L	%	ERA	G	GS	CG	IP	H	BB	SO	ShO	W	L	SV	AB	H	HR	BA	PO	A	E	DP	TC/G	FA
April	0	3	.000	7.98	3	3	0	14.2	22	4	11	0	0	0	0										
May	2	3	.400	3.66	6	6	0	39.1	34	11	19	0	0	0	0										
June	0	2	.000	16.43	3	2	0	7.2	19	4	4	0	0	0	0										
July	0	0	—	5.84	5	1	0	12.1	15	5	4	0	0	0	0										
Aug	1	0	1.000	2.95	5	1	1	18.1	15	8	7	1	0	0	0										
Sept/Oct	2	3	.400	4.55	6	5	0	29.2	31	10	18	0	0	0	1										
Day	1	2	.333	3.60	7	4	0	30	31	12	15	0	0	0	0										
Night	4	9	.308	5.87	21	14	1	92	105	30	48	1	0	1	0										
vs. Left	—	—	—	—	—	—	—	—	30	9	23	—	—	—	—										
vs. Right	—	—	—	—	—	—	—	—	106	33	40	—	—	—	—										
On Grass	3	9	.250	6.08	20	11	0	80	94	28	47	0	0	1	0										
On Turf	2	2	.500	3.86	8	7	1	42	42	14	16	1	0	0	0										
Home	2	6	.250	4.71	14	7	0	57.1	58	18	38	0	0	1	0										
Road	3	5	.375	5.85	14	11	1	64.2	78	24	25	1	0	0	0										

Division Rivals

	W	L	%	ERA	G	GS	CG	IP	H	BB	SO	ShO	W	L	SV	AB	H	HR	BA	PO	A	E	DP	TC/G	FA
vs. ATL	0	2	.000	14.00	4	1	0	9	15	8	5	0	0	1	0										
vs. CIN	1	1	.500	3.78	4	2	0	16.2	18	5	10	0	0	0	0										
vs. HOU	1	2	.333	5.19	3	3	1	17.1	18	4	10	0	0	0	0										
vs. LA	1	0	1.000	6.00	1	1	0	6	7	2	2	0	0	0	0										
vs. SF	0	2	.000	7.84	3	2	0	10.1	16	2	6	0	0	0	0										
1989	ATL N	8	10	.444	3.97	32	30	0	165.2	202	34	79	0	0	0	0	63	12	0	.190	9	20	2	1	1.0	.935
1990	2 teams	ATL N (12G 2 - 8)						SD N (16G 3 - 3)																		
"	total	5	11	.313	5.31	28	18	1	122	136	42	63	1	0	1	0	43	11	2	.256	4	7	0	0	0.4	1.000
2 yrs.		13	21	.382	4.54	60	48	1	287.2	338	76	142	1	0	1	0	106	23	2	.217	13	27	2	1	0.7	.952

Bill Long

LONG, WILLIAM DOUGLAS
B. Feb. 29, 1960, Cincinnati, Ohio
BR TR 6′ 185 lbs.

RELIEF PITCHER

	W	L	%	ERA	G	GS	CG	IP	H	BB	SO	ShO	W	L	SV	AB	H	HR	BA	PO	A	E	DP	TC/G	FA
April	0	1	.000	6.35	4	0	0	5.2	6	2	2	0	0	1	0										
May	2	0	1.000	4.00	14	0	0	18	23	5	13	0	2	0	0										
June	1	0	1.000	2.53	4	0	0	10.2	9	4	4	0	1	0	0										
July	1	0	1.000	2.89	8	0	0	9.1	8	4	7	0	1	0	3										
Aug	2	0	1.000	3.00	7	0	0	6	6	1	6	0	2	0	2										
Sept/Oct	0	1	.000	8.49	9	0	0	11.2	20	7	8	0	0	1	0										
Day	4	1	.800	6.83	21	0	0	29	44	8	20	0	4	1	2										
Night	2	1	.667	2.51	25	0	0	32.1	28	15	14	0	2	1	3										
vs. Left	—	—	—	—	—	—	—	—	40	14	17	—	—	—	—										
vs. Right	—	—	—	—	—	—	—	—	32	9	17	—	—	—	—										

Year	Team	W	L	%	ERA	G	GS	CG	IP	H	BB	SO	ShO	W	L	SV	AB	H	HR	BA	PO	A	E	DP	TC/G	FA

Bill Long *Continued*

On Grass		5	2	.714	6.00	34	0	0	39	58	14	21	0	5	2	3										
On Turf		1	0	1.000	2.01	12	0	0	22.1	14	9	13	0	1	0	2										
Home		4	2	.667	6.41	22	0	0	26.2	40	12	10	0	4	2	1										
Road		2	0	1.000	3.12	24	0	0	34.2	32	11	24	0	2	0	4										
Division Rivals																										
vs. MON		1	1	.500	4.50	5	0	0	8	8	6	2	0	1	1	1										
vs. NY		0	0	—	13.50	2	0	0	2	5	1	2	0	0	0	0										
vs. PHI		0	0	—	0.00	1	0	0	0.2	0	0	0	0	0	0	0										
vs. PIT		0	0	—	6.48	4	0	0	8.1	12	5	4	0	0	0	0										
vs. STL		1	0	1.000	1.86	5	0	0	9.2	9	3	6	0	1	0	0										
1985	CHI A	0	1	.000	10.29	4	3	0	14	25	5	13	0	0	0	0	0	0	0	—	2	3	0	0	1.3	1.000
1987		8	8	.500	4.37	29	23	5	169	179	28	72	2	1	1	1	0	0	0	—	14	25	3	2	1.4	.929
1988		8	11	.421	4.03	47	18	3	174	187	43	77	0	2	2	2	0	0	0	—	7	25	0	0	0.7	1.000
1989		5	5	.500	3.92	30	8	0	98.2	101	37	51	0	2	0	1	0	0	0	—	9	15	0	0	0.8	1.000
1990	2 teams	CHI A	(4G 0 - 1)			CHI N	(42G 6 - 1)																			
"	total	6	2	.750	4.55	46	0	0	61.1	72	23	34	0	6	2	5	5	0	0	.000	6	11	1	0	0.4	.944
5 yrs.		27	27	.500	4.35	156	52	8	517	564	136	247	2	11	5	9	5	0	0	.000	38	79	4	2	0.8	.967

Vance Lovelace

LOVELACE, VANCE ODELL
B. Aug. 9, 1963, Tampa, Fla.
BL TL 6′ 5″ 205 lbs.

Year	Team	W	L	%	ERA	G	GS	CG	IP	H	BB	SO	ShO	W	L	SV	AB	H	HR	BA	PO	A	E	DP	TC/G	FA
1988	CAL A	0	0	—	13.50	3	0	0	1.1	2	3	0	0	0	0	0	0	0	0	—	0	0	0	0	0.0	—
1989		0	0	—	0.00	1	0	0	1	0	1	1	0	0	0	0	0	0	0	—	0	0	0	0	0.0	—
1990	SEA A	0	0	—	3.86	5	0	0	2.1	3	6	1	0	0	0	0	0	0	0	—	0	0	0	0	0.0	—
3 yrs.		0	0	—	5.79	9	0	0	4.2	5	10	2	0	0	0	0	0	0	0	—	0	0	0	0	0.0	—

Rick Luecken

LUECKEN, RICHARD FRED
B. Nov. 15, 1960, McAllen, Tex.
BR TR 6′ 6″ 210 lbs.

April		0	0	—	7.45	7	0	0	9.2	15	6	3	0	0	0	0										
May		0	0	—	9.00	3	0	0	3	5	3	2	0	0	0	0										
June		1	2	.333	3.86	9	0	0	14	14	5	9	0	1	2	1										
July		0	2	.000	7.71	8	0	0	9.1	18	6	7	0	0	2	0										
Aug		0	0	—	5.40	8	0	0	15	19	9	12	0	0	0	0										
Sept/Oct		0	0	—	3.00	2	0	0	3	4	2	2	0	0	0	0										
Day		1	0	1.000	7.43	10	0	0	13.1	17	9	10	0	1	0	0										
Night		0	4	.000	5.31	27	0	0	40.2	58	22	25	0	0	4	1										
vs. Left		—	—							39	15	16		—	—	—										
vs. Right		—	—							36	16	19		—	—	—										
On Grass		1	4	.200	6.75	28	0	0	37.1	56	25	23	0	1	4	0										
On Turf		0	0	—	3.78	9	0	0	16.2	19	6	12	0	0	0	1										
Home		1	2	.333	8.28	18	0	0	25	36	18	16	0	1	2	0										
Road		0	2	.000	3.72	19	0	0	29	39	13	19	0	0	2	1										
Division Rivals																										
vs. BAL		—	—		0	—	—	—	0	0	0	0	0	0	0	0										
vs. BOS		0	0	—	9.00	1	0	0	1	2	1	0	0	0	0	0										
vs. CLE		—	—		0	—	—	—	0	0	0	0	0	0	0	0										
vs. DET		—	—		0	—	—	—	0	0	0	0	0	0	0	0										
vs. MIL		—	—		0	—	—	—	0	0	0	0	0	0	0	0										
vs. NY		—	—		0	—	—	—	0	0	0	0	0	0	0	0										
1989	KC A	2	1	.667	3.42	19	0	0	23.2	23	13	16	0	2	1	1	0	0	0	—	2	2	0	0	0.2	1.000
1990	2 teams	ATL N	(36G 1 - 4)			TOR A	(1G 0 - 0)																			
"	total	1	4	.200	5.83	37	0	0	54	75	31	35	0	1	4	1	3	1	0	.333	5	6	0	0	0.3	1.000
2 yrs.		3	5	.375	5.10	56	0	0	77.2	98	44	51	0	3	5	2	3	1	0	.333	7	8	0	0	0.3	1.000

Year	Team	W	L	%	ERA	G	GS	CG	IP	H	BB	SO	ShO	RELIEF PITCHING W	L	SV	BATTING AB	H	HR	BA	PO	A	E	DP	TC/G	FA

Urbano Lugo

LUGO, URBANO RAFAEL
Born Urbano Rafael Lugo y Colina.
B. Aug. 12, 1962, Punto Fijo, Venezuela
BR TR 6′ 185 lbs.

Year	Team		W	L	%	ERA	G	GS	CG	IP	H	BB	SO	ShO	W	L	SV	AB	H	HR	BA	PO	A	E	DP	TC/G	FA
1985	CAL	A	3	4	.429	3.69	20	10	1	83	86	29	42	0	0	0	0	0	0	0	—	4	13	2	2	1.0	.895
1986			1	1	.500	3.80	6	3	0	21.1	21	6	9	0	0	0	0	0	0	0	—	2	2	0	0	0.7	1.000
1987			0	2	.000	9.32	7	5	0	28	42	18	24	0	0	0	0	0	0	0	—	2	2	0	0	0.6	1.000
1988			0	0	—	9.00	1	0	0	2	2	1	1	0	0	0	0	0	0	0	—	0	0	0	0	0.0	—
1989	MON	N	0	0	—	6.75	3	0	0	4	4	0	3	0	0	0	0	0	0	0	—	1	0	0	0	0.3	1.000
1990	DET	A	2	0	1.000	7.03	13	1	0	24.1	30	13	12	0	2	0	0	0	0	0	—	0	7	0	0	0.5	1.000
6 yrs.			6	7	.462	5.31	50	19	1	162.2	185	67	91	0	2	0	0	0	0	0	—	9	24	2	2	0.7	.943

Steve Lyons

LYONS, STEPHEN JOHN (Psycho)
B. June 3, 1960, Tacoma, Wash.
BL TR 6′ 3″ 190 lbs.

Year	Team		W	L	%	ERA	G	GS	CG	IP	H	BB	SO	ShO	W	L	SV	AB	H	HR	BA	PO	A	E	DP	TC/G	FA
1990	CHI	A	0	0	—	4.50	1	0	0	2	2	4	1	0	0	0	0	*				0	0	0	0	0.0	—

Bob MacDonald

MacDONALD, ROBERT JOSEPH
B. Apr. 27, 1965, East Orange, N. J.
BL TL 6′ 3″ 200 lbs.

Year	Team		W	L	%	ERA	G	GS	CG	IP	H	BB	SO	ShO	W	L	SV	AB	H	HR	BA	PO	A	E	DP	TC/G	FA
1990	TOR	A	0	0	—	0.00	4	0	0	2.1	0	2	0	0	0	0	0	0	0	0	—	0	0	0	0	0.0	

Julio Machado

MACHADO, JULIO SEGUNDO (Iguana Man)
B. Dec. 1, 1965, Zulia, Venezuela
BR TR 6′ 175 lbs.

	W	L	%	ERA	G	GS	CG	IP	H	BB	SO	ShO	W	L	SV
April	2	1	.667	1.86	8	0	0	9.2	8	3	11	0	2	1	0
May	0	0	—	2.25	5	0	0	4	3	0	2	0	0	0	0
June	0	0	—	5.14	5	0	0	7	8	3	5	0	0	0	0
July	1	0	1.000	9.00	3	0	0	3	4	2	3	0	1	0	0
Aug	1	0	1.000	1.69	6	0	0	10.2	9	9	6	0	1	0	0
Sept/Oct	0	0	—	0.69	10	0	0	13	9	8	12	0	0	0	3
Day	1	1	.500	2.84	10	0	0	12.2	12	6	6	0	1	1	1
Night	3	0	1.000	2.34	27	0	0	34.2	29	19	33	0	3	0	2
vs. Left	—	—	—	—	—	—	—	—	15	13	19	—	—	—	—
vs. Right	—	—	—	—	—	—	—	—	26	12	20	—	—	—	—
On Grass	1	0	1.000	1.49	28	0	0	36.1	30	17	32	0	1	0	3
On Turf	3	1	.750	5.73	9	0	0	11	11	8	7	0	3	1	0
Home	1	0	1.000	0.86	16	0	0	21	15	9	24	0	1	0	2
Road	3	1	.750	3.76	21	0	0	26.1	26	16	15	0	3	1	1
Division Rivals															
vs. BAL	0	0	—	0.00	1	0	0	0.1	1	2	0	0	0	0	0
vs. BOS	0	0	—	0.00	1	0	0	1.1	2	1	1	0	0	0	0
vs. CLE	0	0	—	0.00	1	0	0	0.2	1	0	1	0	0	0	0
vs. DET	0	0	—	0.00	1	0	0	0.1	0	0	0	0	0	0	1
vs. NY	0	0	—	0.00	1	0	0	1.1	1	2	2	0	0	0	0
vs. TOR	0	0	—	0.00	1	0	0	0.2	1	0	0	0	0	0	0

RELIEF PITCHER (charts: WINS, ERA, SAVES, RATIO with NL AVG)

Year	Team		W	L	%	ERA	G	GS	CG	IP	H	BB	SO	ShO	W	L	SV	AB	H	HR	BA	PO	A	E	DP	TC/G	FA
1989	NY	N	0	1	.000	3.27	10	0	0	11	9	3	14	0	0	1	0	0	0	0	—	2	0	0	0	0.2	1.000
1990	2 teams		NY N (27G 4 - 1)			MIL A (10G 0 - 0)																					
"	total		4	1	.800	2.47	37	0	0	47.1	41	25	39	0	4	1	3	0	0	0	—	2	4	0	0	0.2	1.000
2 yrs.			4	2	.667	2.62	47	0	0	58.1	50	28	53	0	4	2	3	0	0	0	—	4	4	0	0	0.2	1.000

Year	Team	W	L	%	ERA	G	GS	CG	IP	H	BB	SO	ShO	W	L	SV	AB	H	HR	BA	PO	A	E	DP	TC/G	FA

Greg Maddux

MADDUX, GREGORY ALAN
Brother of Mike Maddux.
B. Apr. 14, 1966, San Angelo, Tex.
BR TR 6′ 170 lbs.

Year	Team	W	L	%	ERA	G	GS	CG	IP	H	BB	SO	ShO	W	L	SV	AB	H	HR	BA	PO	A	E	DP	TC/G	FA
April		3	1	.750	1.95	4	4	1	27.2	20	5	13	1	0	0	0										
May		1	3	.250	5.12	5	5	1	31.2	37	6	18	0	0	0	0										
June		0	4	.000	5.03	6	6	1	34	40	11	22	0	0	0	0										
July		3	1	.750	3.86	6	6	0	39.2	38	14	23	0	0	0	0										
Aug		5	2	.714	1.91	7	7	4	56.2	50	18	36	1	0	0	0										
Sept/Oct		3	4	.429	3.61	7	7	1	47.1	57	17	32	0	0	0	0										
Day		7	5	.583	4.04	15	15	3	100.1	120	38	61	1	0	0	0										
Night		8	10	.444	3.03	20	20	5	136.2	122	33	83	1	0	0	0										
vs. Left		—	—	—	—	—	—	—	—	164	53	81	—	—	—	—										
vs. Right		—	—	—	—	—	—	—	—	78	18	63	—	—	—	—										
On Grass		10	11	.476	3.96	25	25	6	166	182	59	96	2	0	0	0										
On Turf		5	4	.556	2.28	10	10	2	71	60	12	48	0	0	0	0										
Home		8	6	.571	3.58	16	16	4	115.2	127	40	66	1	0	0	0										
Road		7	9	.438	3.34	19	19	4	121.1	115	31	78	1	0	0	0										
Division Rivals																										
vs. MON		2	1	.667	1.74	4	4	1	31	20	12	21	0	0	0	0										
vs. NY		1	3	.250	5.58	5	5	0	30.2	38	12	20	0	0	0	0										
vs. PHI		2	1	.667	1.17	3	3	1	23	20	2	17	0	0	0	0										
vs. PIT		3	1	.750	2.39	4	4	2	26.1	18	10	16	1	0	0	0										
vs. STL		1	2	.333	2.91	3	3	0	21.2	26	5	13	0	0	0	0										
1986	CHI N	2	4	.333	5.52	6	5	1	31	44	11	20	0	0	1	0	12	4	0	.333	1	6	1	0	1.3	.875
1987		6	14	.300	5.61	30	27	1	155.2	181	74	101	1	0	0	0	42	5	0	.119	16	50	4	7	2.3	.943
1988		18	8	.692	3.18	34	34	9	249	230	81	140	3	0	0	0	96	19	0	.198	28	45	3	3	2.2	.961
1989		19	12	.613	2.95	35	35	7	238.1	222	82	135	1	0	0	0	81	17	0	.210	35	41	3	4	2.3	.962
1990		15	15	.500	3.46	**35**	35	8	237	**242**	71	144	2	0	0	0	83	12	0	.145	39	55	0	6	2.7	1.000
5 yrs.		60	53	.531	3.68	140	136	26	911	919	319	540	7	0	1	0	314	57	0	.182	119	197	11	20	2.3	.966

LEAGUE CHAMPIONSHIP SERIES

Year	Team	W	L	%	ERA	G	GS	CG	IP	H	BB	SO	ShO	W	L	SV	AB	H	HR	BA	PO	A	E	DP	TC/G	FA
1989	CHI N	0	1	.000	13.50	2	2	0	7.1	13	4	5	0	0	0	0	3	0	0	.000	0	0	1	0	0.5	—

Mike Maddux

MADDUX, MICHAEL AUSLEY
Brother of Greg Maddux.
B. Aug. 27, 1961, Dayton, Ohio
BL TR 6′ 2″ 180 lbs.

Year	Team	W	L	%	ERA	G	GS	CG	IP	H	BB	SO	ShO	W	L	SV	AB	H	HR	BA	PO	A	E	DP	TC/G	FA
1986	PHI N	3	7	.300	5.42	16	16	0	78	88	34	44	0	0	0	0	22	1	0	.045	5	10	2	0	1.1	.882
1987		2	0	1.000	2.65	7	2	0	17	17	5	15	0	1	0	0	3	0	0	.000	1	1	1	0	0.4	.667
1988		4	3	.571	3.76	25	11	0	88.2	91	34	59	0	2	0	0	23	3	0	.130	8	18	4	1	1.2	.867
1989		1	3	.250	5.15	16	4	2	43.2	52	14	26	0	0	1	1	10	0	0	.000	7	12	0	1	1.2	1.000
1990	LA N	0	1	.000	6.53	11	2	0	20.2	24	4	11	0	0	0	0	2	0	0	.000	0	2	0	0	0.2	1.000
5 yrs.		10	14	.417	4.68	75	35	2	248	272	91	155	1	3	1	1	60	4	0	.067	21	43	7	2	0.9	.901

Joe Magrane

MAGRANE, JOSEPH DAVID
B. July 2, 1964, Des Moines, Iowa
BR TL 6′ 6″ 225 lbs.

Year	Team	W	L	%	ERA	G	GS	CG	IP	H	BB	SO	ShO	W	L	SV	AB	H	HR	BA	PO	A	E	DP	TC/G	FA
April		0	4	.000	5.54	5	5	0	26	31	9	13	0	0	0	0										
May		2	4	.333	3.35	6	6	1	43	42	8	17	1	0	0	0										
June		2	2	.500	4.06	5	5	1	37.2	39	14	23	1	0	0	0										
July		2	2	.500	3.28	6	6	0	35.2	39	8	22	0	0	0	0										
Aug		2	3	.400	2.65	5	5	1	37.1	31	11	14	0	0	0	0										
Sept/Oct		2	2	.500	3.04	4	4	0	23.2	22	9	11	0	0	0	0										
Day		4	3	.571	3.64	7	7	1	47	42	14	35	1	0	0	0										
Night		6	14	.300	3.57	24	24	2	156.1	162	45	65	1	0	0	0										
vs. Left		—	—	—	—	—	—	—	—	43	16	26	—	—	—	—										
vs. Right		—	—	—	—	—	—	—	—	161	43	74	—	—	—	—										

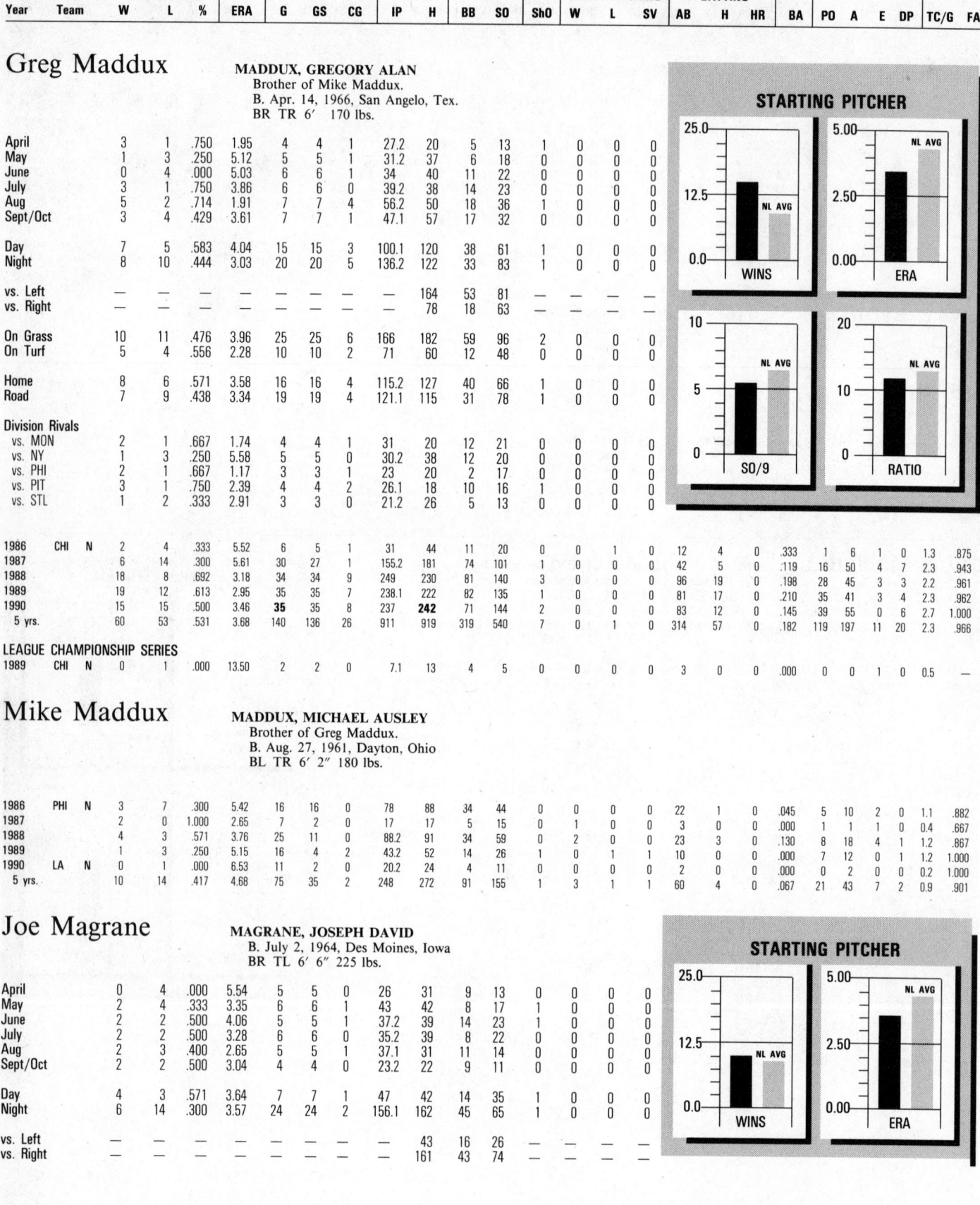

Year	Team	W	L	%	ERA	G	GS	CG	IP	H	BB	SO	ShO	W	L	SV	AB	H	HR	BA	PO	A	E	DP	TC/G	FA

(Header spanning groups: RELIEF PITCHING — W L SV; BATTING — AB H HR BA)

Joe Magrane *Continued*

Year	Team	W	L	%	ERA	G	GS	CG	IP	H	BB	SO	ShO	W	L	SV	AB	H	HR	BA	PO	A	E	DP	TC/G	FA
On Grass		2	4	.333	3.44	6	6	1	36.2	35	14	27	1	0	0	0										
On Turf		8	13	.381	3.62	25	25	2	166.2	169	45	73	1	0	0	0										
Home		4	10	.286	4.27	18	18	1	116	122	28	49	1	0	0	0										
Road		6	7	.462	2.68	13	13	2	87.1	82	31	51	1	0	0	0										
Division Rivals																										
vs. CHI		1	0	1.000	3.27	2	2	1	11	10	3	11	1	0	0	0										
vs. MON		1	1	.500	4.43	3	3	0	20.1	22	7	9	0	0	0	0										
vs. NY		3	1	.750	1.65	4	4	0	27.1	22	9	14	0	0	0	0										
vs. PHI		1	2	.333	4.56	4	4	0	23.2	27	9	10	0	0	0	0										
vs. PIT		1	2	.333	2.63	3	3	0	24	20	7	8	0	0	0	0										
1987	STL N	9	7	.563	3.54	27	26	4	170.1	157	60	101	2	0	0	0	52	7	1	.135	10	26	3	3	1.4	.923
1988		5	9	.357	2.18	24	24	4	165.1	133	51	100	3	0	0	0	48	8	1	.167	16	37	5	0	2.4	.914
1989		18	9	.667	2.91	34	33	9	234.2	219	72	127	3	0	0	0	80	11	1	.138	11	31	2	1	1.3	.955
1990		10	17	.370	3.59	31	31	3	203.1	204	59	100	2	0	0	0	55	7	0	.127	8	38	1	1	1.5	.979
4 yrs.		42	42	.500	3.07	116	114	20	773.2	713	242	428	10	0	0	0	235	33	3	.140	45	132	11	5	1.6	.941
LEAGUE CHAMPIONSHIP SERIES																										
1987	STL N	0	0	—	9.00	1	1	0	4	4	2	3	0	0	0	0	1	0	0	.000	0	1	0	0	1.0	1.000
WORLD SERIES																										
1987	STL N	0	1	.000	8.59	2	2	0	7.1	9	5	5	0	0	0	0				—	1	1	0	0	1.0	1.000

Rick Mahler

MAHLER, RICHARD KEITH
Brother of Mickey Mahler.
B. Aug. 5, 1953, Austin, Tex.
BR TR 6' 1" 195 lbs.

Month/Split	Team	W	L	%	ERA	G	GS	CG	IP	H	BB	SO	ShO	W	L	SV	AB	H	HR	BA	PO	A	E	DP	TC/G	FA
April		1	0	1.000	5.68	3	2	0	12.2	11	3	4	0	0	0	1										
May		0	0	—	5.14	4	1	0	7	7	3	3	0	0	0	0										
June		1	3	.250	4.30	6	5	0	29.1	33	12	17	0	0	0	0										
July		2	1	.667	3.58	7	3	1	27.2	29	7	15	1	1	0	1										
Aug		2	1	.667	4.50	8	2	0	30	30	9	16	0	0	1	1										
Sept/Oct		1	1	.500	3.86	7	3	1	28	24	5	13	0	0	0	1										
Day		2	1	.667	3.46	10	5	1	39	29	7	19	0	0	0	1										
Night		5	5	.500	4.61	25	11	1	95.2	105	32	49	1	1	1	3										
vs. Left		—	—	—	—	—	—	—	—	82	22	37	—	—	—	—										
vs. Right		—	—	—	—	—	—	—	—	52	17	31	—	—	—	—										
On Grass		1	4	.200	5.04	9	6	1	44.2	47	9	20	0	0	0	1										
On Turf		6	2	.750	3.90	26	10	1	90	87	30	48	1	1	1	3										
Home		3	1	.750	4.45	18	6	0	56.2	58	18	33	0	1	1	1										
Road		4	5	.444	4.15	17	10	2	78	76	21	35	1	0	0	3										
Division Rivals																										
vs. ATL		0	1	.000	3.12	3	3	0	17.1	19	5	10	0	0	0	0										
vs. HOU		0	1	.000	5.91	4	2	0	10.2	15	6	8	0	0	0	1										
vs. LA		1	0	1.000	5.87	3	1	0	15.1	18	1	12	0	0	0	0										
vs. SD		0	2	.000	9.64	5	1	0	14	19	4	6	0	0	1	1										
vs. SF		0	1	.000	4.50	2	1	0	8	8	4	3	0	0	0	0										
1979	ATL N	0	0	—	6.14	15	0	0	22	28	11	12	0	0	0	0	2	1	0	.500	1	3	1	0	0.3	.800
1980		0	0	—	2.25	2	0	0	4	2	0	1	0	0	0	0	0	0	0	—	0	1	0	0	0.5	1.000
1981		8	6	.571	2.81	34	14	1	112	109	43	54	0	2	0	2	27	4	0	.148	14	19	2	0	1.0	.943
1982		9	10	.474	4.21	39	33	5	205.1	213	62	105	2	0	0	0	58	11	1	.190	19	36	1	5	1.4	.982
1983		0	0	—	5.02	10	0	0	14.1	16	9	7	0	0	0	0	2	0	0	.000	1	1	1	1	0.3	.667
1984		13	10	.565	3.12	38	29	9	222	209	62	106	1	0	0	0	71	21	0	.296	20	42	2	5	1.7	.969
1985		17	15	.531	3.48	39	39	6	266.2	272	79	107	1	0	0	0	90	14	0	.156	21	45	4	9	1.8	.943
1986		14	18	.438	4.88	39	39	7	237.2	283	95	137	1	0	0	0	83	16	0	.193	23	41	3	2	1.7	.955
1987		8	13	.381	4.98	39	28	3	197	212	85	95	1	2	1	0	65	11	0	.169	13	42	1	2	1.4	.982
1988		9	16	.360	3.69	39	34	5	249	279	42	131	0	2	0	0	72	9	0	.125	22	43	3	4	1.7	.956
1989	CIN N	9	13	.409	3.83	40	31	5	220.2	242	51	102	2	0	0	0	62	11	0	.177	8	35	1	2	1.1	.977
1990		7	6	.538	4.28	35	16	2	134.2	134	39	68	1	1	1	4	35	4	0	.114	11	17	1	1	0.8	.966
12 yrs.		94	107	.468	3.98	369	263	43	1885.1	1999	578	925	9	7	2	6	567	102	1	.180	153	325	20	31	1.3	.960
LEAGUE CHAMPIONSHIP SERIES																										
1982	ATL N	0	0	—	0.00	1	0	0	1.2	3	2	0	0	0	0	0	0	0	0	—	0	1	0	0	1.0	1.000
1990	CIN N	0	0	—	0.00	1	0	0	1.2	2	0	2	0	0	0	0	0	0	0	—	0	0	0	0	0.0	—
2 yrs.		0	0	—	0.00	2	0	0	3.1	5	2	2	0	0	0	0	0	0	0	—	0	1	0	0	0.5	1.000

STARTING PITCHER charts (Joe Magrane): SO/9, RATIO — with NL AVG.

STARTING PITCHER charts (Rick Mahler): WINS, ERA, SO/9, RATIO — with NL AVG.

Year	Team	W	L	%	ERA	G	GS	CG	IP	H	BB	SO	ShO	RELIEF PITCHING W	L	SV	BATTING AB	H	HR	BA	PO	A	E	DP	TC/G	FA

Carlos Maldonado

MALDONADO, CARLOS CESAR
B. Oct. 18, 1966, Chepo, Panama
BB TR 6' 1" 210 lbs.

| 1990 | KC A | 0 | 0 | — | 9.00 | 4 | 0 | 0 | 6 | 9 | 4 | 9 | 0 | 0 | 0 | 0 | 0 | 0 | 0 | — | 0 | 0 | 0 | 0 | 0.0 | — |

Bob Malloy

MALLOY, ROBERT WILLIAM
B. Nov. 24, 1964, Arlington, Va.
BR TR 6' 5" 200 lbs.

1987	TEX A	0	0	—	6.55	2	2	0	11	13	3	8	0	0	0	0	0	0	0	—	0	1	0	0	0.5	1.000
1990	MON N	0	0	—	0.00	1	0	0	2	1	1	1	0	0	0	0	0	0	0	—	0	0	0	0	0.0	—
2 yrs.		0	0	—	5.54	3	2	0	13	14	4	9	0	0	0	0	0	0	0	—	0	1	0	0	0.3	1.000

Chuck Malone

MALONE, CHARLES RAY, JR.
B. July 8, 1965, Harrisburg, Ark.
BR TR 6' 7" 250 lbs.

| 1990 | PHI N | 1 | 0 | 1.000 | 3.68 | 7 | 0 | 0 | 7.1 | 3 | 11 | 7 | 0 | 1 | 0 | 0 | 0 | 0 | 0 | — | 0 | 0 | 0 | 0 | 0.0 | — |

Ramon Manon

MANON, RAMON
Born Ramon Manon y Reyes.
B. Jan. 20, 1968, Santo Domingo, Dominican Republic
BR TR 6' 170 lbs.

| 1990 | TEX A | 0 | 0 | — | 13.50 | 1 | 0 | 0 | 2 | 3 | 3 | 0 | 0 | 0 | 0 | 0 | 0 | 0 | 0 | — | 2 | 0 | 0 | 0 | 2.0 | 1.000 |

Paul Marak

MARAK, PAUL PATRICK
B. Aug. 2, 1965, Lakenheath, England
BR TR 6' 2" 175 lbs.

| 1990 | ATL N | 1 | 2 | .333 | 3.69 | 7 | 7 | 0 | 39 | 39 | 19 | 15 | 1 | 0 | 0 | 0 | 11 | 1 | 0 | .091 | 6 | 9 | 0 | 1 | 2.1 | 1.000 |

Dave Martinez

MARTINEZ, DAVID
B. Sept. 26, 1964, New York, N. Y.
BL TL 5' 10" 150 lbs.

| 1990 | MON N | 0 | 0 | — | 5.40 | 1 | 0 | 0 | 0.1 | 2 | 2 | 0 | 0 | 0 | 0 | 0 | * | | | | 0 | 0 | 0 | 0 | 0.0 | — |

Dennis Martinez

MARTINEZ, JOSE DENNIS
Born Jose Dennis Martinez y Emilia.
B. May 14, 1955, Granada, Nicaragua
BR TR 6' 1" 175 lbs.

	W	L	%	ERA	G	GS	CG	IP	H	BB	SO	ShO	W	L	SV
April	2	1	.667	2.31	5	5	1	35	30	12	21	1	0	0	0
May	1	3	.250	2.84	5	5	1	38	33	8	30	0	0	0	0
June	2	2	.500	2.79	6	6	1	42	32	11	25	0	0	0	0
July	2	1	.667	3.70	6	6	1	41.1	38	6	33	1	0	0	0
Aug	3	2	.600	2.85	6	6	2	47.1	39	6	33	0	0	0	0
Sept/Oct	0	2	.000	3.22	4	4	1	22.1	19	6	14	0	0	0	0
Day	3	4	.429	3.24	10	10	1	66.2	67	11	45	0	0	0	0
Night	7	7	.500	2.82	22	22	6	159.1	124	38	111	2	0	0	0
vs. Left	—	—	—	—	—	—	—	—	113	28	95	—	—	—	—
vs. Right	—	—	—	—	—	—	—	—	78	21	61	—	—	—	—
On Grass	2	1	.667	2.00	5	5	1	36	32	10	33	0	0	0	0
On Turf	8	10	.444	3.13	27	27	6	190	159	39	123	2	0	0	0
Home	6	10	.375	3.41	18	18	4	134.2	117	26	84	1	0	0	0
Road	4	1	.800	2.27	14	14	3	91.1	74	23	72	1	0	0	0
Division Rivals															
vs. CHI	1	1	.500	3.86	3	3	2	23.1	17	2	9	0	0	0	0
vs. NY	1	2	.333	4.43	3	3	0	20.1	27	5	11	0	0	0	0
vs. PHI	1	0	1.000	1.71	3	3	1	21	13	5	15	1	0	0	0
vs. PIT	2	1	.667	1.67	5	5	2	32.1	22	5	21	1	0	0	0
vs. STL	1	0	1.000	4.09	2	2	0	11	13	5	7	0	0	0	0

STARTING PITCHER

WINS — ERA — SO/9 — RATIO (with NL AVG comparisons)

Year	Team	W	L	%	ERA	G	GS	CG	IP	H	BB	SO	ShO	W	L	SV	AB	H	HR	BA	PO	A	E	DP	TC/G	FA

Dennis Martinez *Continued*

Year	Team	W	L	%	ERA	G	GS	CG	IP	H	BB	SO	ShO	W	L	SV	AB	H	HR	BA	PO	A	E	DP	TC/G	FA
1976	BAL A	1	2	.333	2.57	4	2	1	28	23	8	18	0	1	0	0	0	0	0	—	3	4	0	0	1.8	1.000
1977		14	7	.667	4.10	42	13	5	167	157	64	107	0	8	4	4	0	0	0	—	9	26	1	2	0.9	.972
1978		16	11	.593	3.52	40	38	15	276.1	257	93	142	2	0	0	0	0	0	0	—	27	51	1	6	2.0	.987
1979		15	16	.484	3.67	40	39	18	292	279	78	132	3	0	0	0	0	0	0	—	26	59	5	3	2.3	.944
1980		6	4	.600	3.96	25	12	2	100	103	44	42	0	0	1	1	0	0	0	—	5	16	0	1	0.8	1.000
1981		14	5	.737	3.32	25	24	9	179	173	62	88	2	0	0	0	0	0	0	—	20	44	2	4	2.6	.970
1982		16	12	.571	4.21	40	39	10	252	262	87	111	2	0	0	0	0	0	0	—	13	38	1	2	1.3	.981
1983		7	16	.304	5.53	32	25	4	153	209	45	71	0	1	0	0	0	0	0	—	16	42	1	0	1.8	.983
1984		6	9	.400	5.02	34	20	2	141.2	145	37	77	0	1	0	2	0	0	0	—	17	19	2	4	1.1	.947
1985		13	11	.542	5.15	33	31	3	180	203	63	68	1	1	0	0	0	0	0	—	17	26	1	0	1.3	.977
1986	2 teams	BAL A	(4G	0 – 0)					MON N	(19G	3 – 6)															
"	total	3	6	.333	4.73	23	15	1	104.2	114	30	65	1	0	0	0	30	3	0	.100	4	25	1	0	1.3	.967
1987	MON N	11	4	.733	3.30	22	22	2	144.2	133	40	84	1	0	0	0	46	3	0	.065	10	23	1	3	1.5	.971
1988		15	13	.536	2.72	34	34	9	235.1	215	55	120	2	0	0	0	78	15	0	.192	19	39	6	3	1.9	.906
1989		16	7	.696	3.18	34	33	5	232	227	49	142	2	0	0	1	72	9	0	.125	11	50	2	6	1.9	.968
1990		10	11	.476	2.95	32	32	7	226	191	49	156	2	0	0	0	68	7	0	.103	16	35	1	2	1.6	.981
15 yrs.		163	134	.549	3.82	460	379	93	2711.2	2691	804	1423	18	12	8	5	294	37	0	.126	213	497	25	36	1.6	.966

LEAGUE CHAMPIONSHIP SERIES

Year	Team	W	L	%	ERA	G	GS	CG	IP	H	BB	SO	ShO	W	L	SV	AB	H	HR	BA	PO	A	E	DP	TC/G	FA
1979	BAL A	0	0	—	3.24	1	1	0	8.1	8	0	4	0	0	0	0	0	0	0	—	2	0	0	0	2.0	1.000

WORLD SERIES

Year	Team	W	L	%	ERA	G	GS	CG	IP	H	BB	SO	ShO	W	L	SV	AB	H	HR	BA	PO	A	E	DP	TC/G	FA
1979	BAL A	0	0	—	18.00	2	1	0	2	6	0	0	0	0	0	0	0	0	0	—	0	1	0	1	0.5	1.000

Ramon Martinez

MARTINEZ, RAMON JAIME
Born Ramon Jaime y Martinez.
B. Mar. 22, 1968, Santo Domingo, Dominican Republic
BR TR 6′ 4″ 165 lbs.

	W	L	%	ERA	G	GS	CG	IP	H	BB	SO	ShO	W	L	SV	AB	H	HR	BA	PO	A	E	DP	TC/G	FA
April	2	0	1.000	2.25	4	4	2	28	20	5	28	1	0	0	0										
May	3	3	.500	4.76	6	6	1	34	34	13	41	0	0	0	0										
June	4	0	1.000	1.76	6	6	3	46	36	15	56	1	0	0	0										
July	4	1	.800	2.72	5	5	1	36.1	26	8	34	0	0	0	0										
Aug	3	2	.600	3.71	6	6	1	43.2	40	15	31	0	0	0	0										
Sept/Oct	4	0	1.000	2.53	6	6	4	46.1	35	11	33	1	0	0	0										
Day	6	2	.750	2.89	10	10	3	74.2	54	24	72	1	0	0	0										
Night	14	4	.778	2.93	23	23	9	159.2	137	43	151	2	0	0	0										
vs. Left	—	—	—	—	—	—	—	—	125	53	118	—	—	—	—										
vs. Right	—	—	—	—	—	—	—	—	66	14	105	—	—	—	—										
On Grass	15	3	.833	2.84	24	24	10	177.1	137	51	169	2	0	0	0										
On Turf	5	3	.625	3.16	9	9	2	57	54	16	54	1	0	0	0										
Home	12	2	.857	2.71	17	17	8	129.2	96	39	134	2	0	0	0										
Road	8	4	.667	3.18	16	16	4	104.2	95	28	89	1	0	0	0										
Division Rivals																										
vs. ATL	3	0	1.000	1.38	3	3	2	26	16	2	36	1	0	0	0										
vs. CIN	3	0	1.000	2.42	3	3	2	26	20	5	25	1	0	0	0										
vs. HOU	2	0	1.000	2.77	4	4	1	26	19	7	25	1	0	0	0										
vs. SD	3	0	1.000	1.60	5	5	3	39.1	25	10	33	0	0	0	0										
vs. SF	2	0	1.000	1.57	3	3	2	23	15	7	16	0	0	0	0										
1988	LA N	1	3	.250	3.79	9	6	0	35.2	27	22	23	0	0	0	0	7	0	0	.000	1	5	0	0	0.7	1.000
1989		6	4	.600	3.19	15	15	2	98.2	79	41	89	2	0	0	0	37	6	0	.162	11	14	0	1	1.7	1.000
1990		20	6	.769	2.92	33	33	12	234.1	191	67	223	3	0	0	0	80	10	0	.125	16	27	1	0	1.3	.977
3 yrs.		27	13	.675	3.08	57	54	14	368.2	297	130	335	5	0	0	0	124	16	0	.129	28	46	1	1	1.3	.987

STARTING PITCHER — WINS / ERA / SO/9 / RATIO (with NL AVG comparison bars)

Greg Mathews

MATHEWS, GREGORY INMAN
B. May 17, 1962, Harbor City, Calif.
BB TL 6′ 2″ 180 lbs.

Year	Team	W	L	%	ERA	G	GS	CG	IP	H	BB	SO	ShO	W	L	SV	AB	H	HR	BA	PO	A	E	DP	TC/G	FA
1986	STL N	11	8	.579	3.65	23	22	1	145.1	139	44	67	0	0	0	0	43	2	0	.047	3	17	0	1	0.9	1.000
1987		11	11	.500	3.73	32	32	2	197.2	184	71	108	1	0	0	0	68	13	0	.191	3	31	4	2	1.2	.895
1988		4	6	.400	4.24	13	13	0	68	61	33	31	0	0	0	0	23	4	0	.174	3	13	2	0	1.4	.889
1990		0	5	.000	5.33	11	10	0	50.2	53	30	18	0	0	0	1	14	3	0	.214	2	15	1	1	1.6	.944
4 yrs.		26	30	.464	3.96	79	77	4	461.2	437	178	224	1	0	0	1	148	22	0	.149	11	76	7	4	1.2	.926

LEAGUE CHAMPIONSHIP SERIES

Year	Team	W	L	%	ERA	G	GS	CG	IP	H	BB	SO	ShO	W	L	SV	AB	H	HR	BA	PO	A	E	DP	TC/G	FA
1987	STL N	1	0	1.000	3.48	2	2	0	10.1	6	3	10	0	0	0	0	2	2	0	1.000	0	0	0	0	0.0	—

Year	Team	W	L	%	ERA	G	GS	CG	IP	H	BB	SO	ShO	W	L	SV	AB	H	HR	BA	PO	A	E	DP	TC/G	FA

Column group headers: RELIEF PITCHING (W, L, SV); BATTING (AB, H, HR)

Greg Mathews *Continued*

WORLD SERIES

Year	Team	W	L	%	ERA	G	GS	CG	IP	H	BB	SO	ShO	W	L	SV	AB	H	HR	BA	PO	A	E	DP	TC/G	FA
1987	STL N	0	0	—	2.45	1	1	0	3.2	2	2	3	0	0	0	0	1	0	0	.000	0	1	0	0	1.0	1.000

Randy McCament   McCAMENT, LARRY RANDALL
B. July 29, 1962, Albuquerque, N. M.
BR TR 6′ 3″ 195 lbs.

Year	Team	W	L	%	ERA	G	GS	CG	IP	H	BB	SO	ShO	W	L	SV	AB	H	HR	BA	PO	A	E	DP	TC/G	FA
1989	SF N	1	1	.500	3.93	25	0	0	36.2	32	23	12	0	1	1	0	3	1	0	.333	3	8	1	1	0.5	.917
1990		0	0	—	3.00	3	0	0	6	8	5	5	0	0	0	0	1	0	0	.000	1	0	0	0	0.3	1.000
2 yrs.		1	1	.500	3.80	28	0	0	42.2	40	28	17	0	1	1	0	4	1	0	.250	4	8	1	1	0.5	.923

Kirk McCaskill   McCASKILL, KIRK EDWARD
B. Apr. 29, 1961, Kapuskasing, Ont., Canada
BR TR 6′ 1″ 185 lbs.

	W	L	%	ERA	G	GS	CG	IP	H	BB	SO	ShO	W	L	SV
April	2	0	1.000	1.07	4	4	0	25.1	22	13	13	0	0	0	0
May	1	2	.333	5.03	4	4	0	19.2	25	8	11	0	0	0	0
June	3	2	.600	1.78	5	5	0	30.1	24	13	9	0	0	0	0
July	1	3	.250	3.41	5	5	0	29	22	16	10	0	0	0	0
Aug	3	2	.600	3.76	6	6	1	38.1	38	14	19	1	0	0	0
Sept/Oct	2	2	.500	4.55	5	5	1	31.2	30	8	16	0	0	0	0
Day	3	1	.750	1.65	4	4	1	27.1	19	7	10	0	0	0	0
Night	9	10	.474	3.55	25	25	1	147	142	65	68	1	0	0	0
vs. Left	—	—	—	—	—	—	—	—	84	34	30	—	—	—	—
vs. Right	—	—	—	—	—	—	—	—	77	38	48	—	—	—	—
On Grass	11	8	.579	2.91	25	25	2	148.1	134	59	67	1	0	0	0
On Turf	1	3	.250	5.19	4	4	0	26	27	13	11	0	0	0	0
Home	7	3	.700	2.77	14	14	1	81.1	74	31	37	1	0	0	0
Road	5	8	.385	3.68	15	15	1	93	87	41	41	0	0	0	0
Division Rivals															
vs. CHI	1	1	.500	5.91	2	2	0	10.2	11	5	2	0	0	0	0
vs. KC	1	0	1.000	5.87	1	1	0	7.2	9	0	5	0	0	0	0
vs. MIN	1	0	1.000	1.50	1	1	0	6	3	5	1	0	0	0	0
vs. OAK	0	1	.000	4.02	3	3	0	15.2	13	13	9	0	0	0	0
vs. SEA	0	2	.000	4.19	3	3	0	19.1	16	11	9	0	0	0	0
vs. TEX	2	2	.500	2.52	4	4	1	25	19	8	13	1	0	0	0

STARTING PITCHER

Year	Team	W	L	%	ERA	G	GS	CG	IP	H	BB	SO	ShO	W	L	SV	AB	H	HR	BA	PO	A	E	DP	TC/G	FA
1985	CAL A	12	12	.500	4.70	30	29	6	189.2	189	64	102	1	0	0	0	0	0	0	—	11	27	3	1	1.4	.927
1986		17	10	.630	3.36	34	33	10	246.1	207	92	202	2	0	0	0	0	0	0	—	24	26	1	0	1.5	.980
1987		4	6	.400	5.67	14	13	1	74.2	84	34	56	1	0	0	0	0	0	0	—	8	12	1	1	1.5	.952
1988		8	6	.571	4.31	23	23	4	146.1	155	61	98	2	0	0	0	0	0	0	—	12	18	3	2	1.4	.909
1989		15	10	.600	2.93	32	32	6	212	202	59	107	4	0	0	0	0	0	0	—	16	42	3	5	1.9	.951
1990		12	11	.522	3.25	29	29	2	174.1	161	72	78	1	0	0	0	0	0	0	—	19	29	3	2	1.8	.941
6 yrs.		68	55	.553	3.80	162	159	29	1043.1	998	382	643	11	0	0	0	0	0	0	—	90	154	14	11	1.6	.946

LEAGUE CHAMPIONSHIP SERIES

Year	Team	W	L	%	ERA	G	GS	CG	IP	H	BB	SO	ShO	W	L	SV	AB	H	HR	BA	PO	A	E	DP	TC/G	FA
1986	CAL A	0	2	.000	7.71	2	2	0	9.1	16	5	7	0	0	0	0	0	0	0	—	0	0	0	0	0.0	—

Paul McClellan   McCLELLAN, PAUL WILLIAM
B. Feb. 8, 1966, San Mateo, Calif.
BB TR 6′ 2″ 180 lbs.

Year	Team	W	L	%	ERA	G	GS	CG	IP	H	BB	SO	ShO	W	L	SV	AB	H	HR	BA	PO	A	E	DP	TC/G	FA
1990	SF N	0	1	.000	11.74	4	1	0	7.2	14	6	2	0	0	0	0	2	1	0	.500	1	2	0	1	0.8	1.000

Bob McClure   McCLURE, ROBERT CRAIG
B. Apr. 29, 1952, Oakland, Calif.
BB TL 5′ 11″ 170 lbs.

Year	Team	W	L	%	ERA	G	GS	CG	IP	H	BB	SO	ShO	W	L	SV	AB	H	HR	BA	PO	A	E	DP	TC/G	FA
1975	KC A	1	0	1.000	0.00	12	0	0	15.1	4	14	15	0	1	0	1	0	0	0	—	0	0	0	0	0.0	—
1976		0	0	—	9.00	8	0	0	4	3	8	3	0	0	0	0	0	0	0	—	0	0	0	0	0.0	—
1977	MIL A	2	1	.667	2.54	68	0	0	71	64	34	57	0	2	1	6	0	0	0	—	2	19	2	2	0.3	.913
1978		2	6	.250	3.74	44	0	0	65	53	30	47	0	2	6	9	0	0	0	—	1	8	1	0	0.2	.900
1979		5	2	.714	3.88	36	0	0	51	53	24	37	0	5	2	5	0	0	0	—	1	7	3	1	0.3	.727

Year	Team	W	L	%	ERA	G	GS	CG	IP	H	BB	SO	ShO	RELIEF PITCHING W	L	SV	BATTING AB	H	HR	BA	PO	A	E	DP	TC/G	FA

Bob McClure *Continued*

Year	Team	W	L	%	ERA	G	GS	CG	IP	H	BB	SO	ShO	W	L	SV	AB	H	HR	BA	PO	A	E	DP	TC/G	FA
1980		5	8	.385	3.07	52	5	2	91	83	37	47	1	1	7	10	0	0	0	—	3	9	0	0	0.2	1.000
1981		0	0	—	3.38	4	0	0	8	7	4	6	0	0	0	0	0	0	0	—	1	0	0	0	0.3	1.000
1982		12	7	.632	4.22	34	26	5	172.2	160	74	99	0	2	0	0	0	0	0	—	4	23	3	3	0.9	.900
1983		9	9	.500	4.50	24	23	4	142	152	68	68	0	0	0	0	0	0	0	—	4	19	1	1	1.0	.958
1984		4	8	.333	4.38	39	18	1	139.2	154	52	68	0	0	2	1	0	0	0	—	4	21	2	2	0.7	.926
1985		4	1	.800	4.31	38	1	0	85.2	91	30	57	0	4	1	3	0	0	0	—	3	11	0	0	0.4	1.000
1986	2 teams	MIL A	(13G 2 – 1)		MON N	(52G 2 – 5)																				
''	total	4	6	.400	3.19	65	0	0	79	71	33	53	0	4	6	6	4	1	0	.250	2	12	1	1	0.2	.933
1987	MON N	6	1	.857	3.44	52	0	0	52.1	47	20	33	0	6	1	5	2	0	0	.000	3	8	0	0	0.2	1.000
1988	2 teams	MON N	(19G 1 – 3)		NY N	(14G 1 – 0)																				
''	total	2	3	.400	5.40	33	0	0	30	35	8	19	0	2	3	3	2	0	0	.000	0	5	0	0	0.2	1.000
1989	CAL A	6	1	.857	1.55	48	0	0	52.1	39	15	36	0	6	1	3	0	0	0	—	2	4	0	0	0.1	1.000
1990		2	0	1.000	6.43	11	0	0	7	7	3	6	0	2	0	0	0	0	0	—	0	1	0	0	0.1	1.000
16 yrs.		64	53	.547	3.78	568	73	12	1066	1023	454	651	1	37	30	52	8	1	0	.125	30	147	13	12	0.3	.932

DIVISIONAL PLAYOFF SERIES
Year	Team	W	L	%	ERA	G	GS	CG	IP	H	BB	SO	ShO	W	L	SV	AB	H	HR	BA	PO	A	E	DP	TC/G	FA
1981	MIL A	0	0	—	0.00	3	0	0	3.1	4	0	2	0	0	0	0	0	0	0	—	0	0	0	0	0.0	—

LEAGUE CHAMPIONSHIP SERIES
Year	Team	W	L	%	ERA	G	GS	CG	IP	H	BB	SO	ShO	W	L	SV	AB	H	HR	BA	PO	A	E	DP	TC/G	FA
1982	MIL A	1	0	1.000	0.00	1	0	0	1.2	2	0	0	0	0	0	0	0	0	0	—	0	0	0	0	0.0	—

WORLD SERIES
Year	Team	W	L	%	ERA	G	GS	CG	IP	H	BB	SO	ShO	W	L	SV	AB	H	HR	BA	PO	A	E	DP	TC/G	FA
1982	MIL A	0	2	.000	4.15	5	0	0	4.1	5	3	5	0	0	2	2	0	0	0	—	0	0	0	0	0.0	—
														2nd												

Lance McCullers

McCULLERS, LANCE GRAYE
B. Mar. 8, 1964, Tampa, Fla.
BB TR 6′ 1″ 185 lbs.

Year	Team	W	L	%	ERA	G	GS	CG	IP	H	BB	SO	ShO	W	L	SV	AB	H	HR	BA	PO	A	E	DP	TC/G	FA
1985	SD N	0	2	.000	2.31	21	0	0	35	23	16	27	0	0	2	5	4	0	0	.000	2	6	2	0	0.5	.800
1986		10	10	.500	2.78	70	7	0	136	103	58	92	0	9	6	5	22	2	0	.091	6	16	2	1	0.3	.917
1987		8	10	.444	3.72	78	0	0	123.1	115	59	126	0	8	**10**	16	14	1	0	.071	9	17	2	1	0.4	.929
1988		3	6	.333	2.49	60	0	0	97.2	70	55	81	0	3	6	10	8	2	0	.250	6	14	2	1	0.4	.909
1989	NY A	4	3	.571	4.57	52	1	0	84.2	83	37	82	0	4	2	3	0	0	0	—	5	10	2	0	0.3	.882
1990	2 teams	NY A	(11G 1 – 0)		DET A	(9G 1 – 0)																				
''	total	2	0	1.000	3.02	20	1	0	44.2	32	19	31	0	2	0	0	0	0	0	—	4	2	0	0	0.3	1.000
6 yrs.		27	31	.466	3.23	301	9	0	521.1	426	244	439	0	26	26	39	48	5	0	104	32	65	10	3	0.4	.907

Ben McDonald

McDONALD, LARRY BENARD
B. Nov. 14, 1967, Baton Rouge, La.
BR TR 6′ 7″ 212 lbs.

	W	L	%	ERA	G	GS	CG	IP	H	BB	SO	ShO	W	L	SV
April	—	—	—	—	0	—	—	0	0	0	0	—	0	0	0
May	—	—	—	—	0	—	—	0	0	0	0	—	0	0	0
June	—	—	—	—	0	—	—	0	0	0	0	—	0	0	0
July	3	0	1.000	1.39	9	3	1	32.1	25	6	19	1	0	0	0
Aug	2	3	.400	4.22	5	5	0	32	28	11	15	0	0	0	0
Sept/Oct	3	2	.600	1.99	7	7	2	54.1	35	18	31	1	0	0	0
Day	1	1	.500	3.05	5	3	0	20.2	16	8	5	0	0	0	0
Night	7	4	.636	2.30	16	12	3	98	72	27	60	2	0	0	0
vs. Left	—	—	—	—	—	—	—	—	39	17	38	—	—	—	—
vs. Right	—	—	—	—	—	—	—	—	49	18	27	—	—	—	—
On Grass	6	5	.545	2.44	19	13	3	103.1	78	28	55	2	0	0	0
On Turf	2	0	1.000	2.35	2	2	0	15.1	10	7	10	0	0	0	0
Home	4	3	.571	2.41	13	9	2	74.2	59	18	43	1	0	0	0
Road	4	2	.667	2.45	8	6	1	44	29	17	22	1	0	0	0
Division Rivals															
vs. BOS	0	2	.000	11.05	2	2	0	7.1	8	9	4	0	0	0	0
vs. CLE	1	0	1.000	0.00	1	1	1	9	4	1	4	1	0	0	0
vs. DET	1	0	1.000	1.00	1	1	1	9	3	3	7	0	0	0	0
vs. MIL	0	1	.000	1.69	2	2	0	16	10	5	2	0	0	0	0
vs. NY	0	1	.000	4.91	1	1	0	7.1	9	0	5	0	0	0	0
vs. TOR	1	0	1.000	2.30	2	2	0	15.2	17	3	11	0	0	0	0

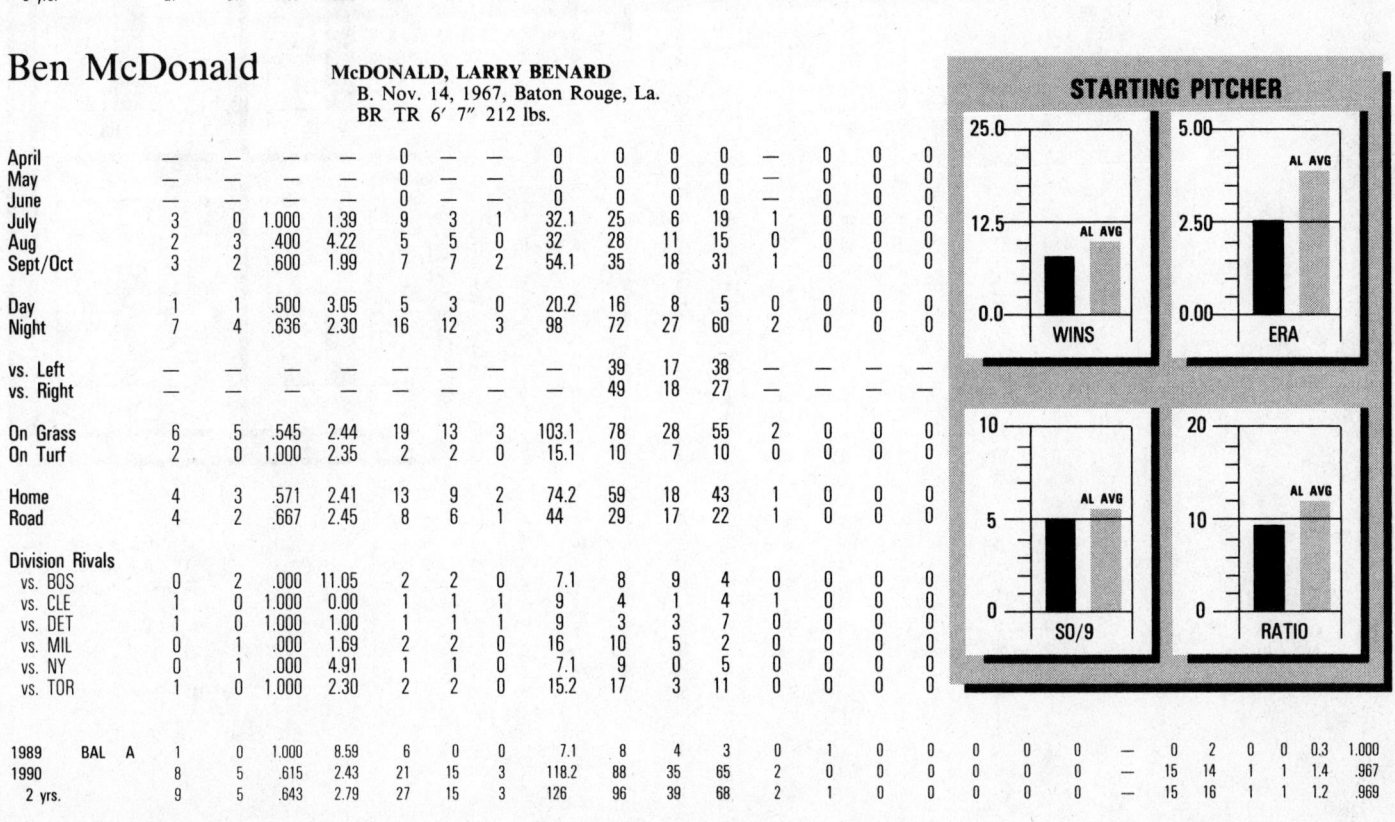

STARTING PITCHER

WINS — AL AVG

ERA — AL AVG

SO/9 — AL AVG

RATIO — AL AVG

Year	Team	W	L	%	ERA	G	GS	CG	IP	H	BB	SO	ShO	W	L	SV	AB	H	HR	BA	PO	A	E	DP	TC/G	FA
1989	BAL A	1	0	1.000	8.59	6	0	0	7.1	8	4	3	0	1	0	0	0	0	0	—	0	2	0	0	0.3	1.000
1990		8	5	.615	2.43	21	15	3	118.2	88	35	65	2	0	0	0	0	0	0	—	15	14	1	1	1.4	.967
2 yrs.		9	5	.643	2.79	27	15	3	126	96	39	68	2	1	0	0	0	0	0	—	15	16	1	1	1.2	.969

Year	Team	W	L	%	ERA	G	GS	CG	IP	H	BB	SO	ShO	RELIEF PITCHING W	L	SV	BATTING AB	H	HR	BA	PO	A	E	DP	TC/G	FA

Jack McDowell

McDOWELL, JACK BURNS
B. Jan. 16, 1966, Van Nuys, Calif.
BR TR 6′ 5″ 180 lbs.

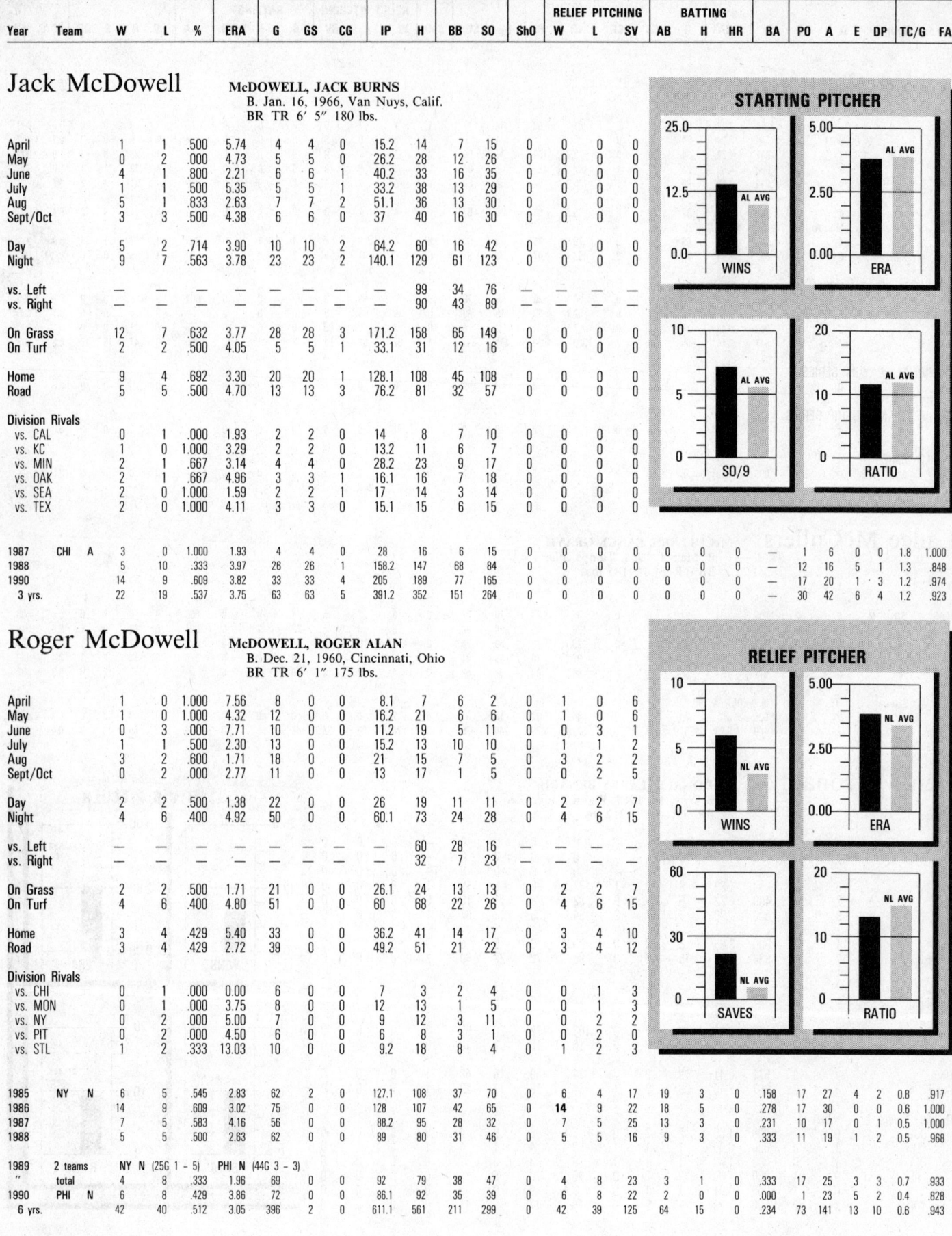

STARTING PITCHER

Period	W	L	%	ERA	G	GS	CG	IP	H	BB	SO	ShO	W	L	SV	AB	H	HR	BA	PO	A	E	DP	TC/G	FA
April	1	1	.500	5.74	4	4	0	15.2	14	7	15	0	0	0	0										
May	0	2	.000	4.73	5	5	0	26.2	28	12	26	0	0	0	0										
June	4	1	.800	2.21	6	6	1	40.2	33	16	35	0	0	0	0										
July	1	1	.500	5.35	5	5	1	33.2	38	13	29	0	0	0	0										
Aug	5	1	.833	2.63	7	7	2	51.1	36	13	30	0	0	0	0										
Sept/Oct	3	3	.500	4.38	6	6	0	37	40	16	30	0	0	0	0										
Day	5	2	.714	3.90	10	10	2	64.2	60	16	42	0	0	0	0										
Night	9	7	.563	3.78	23	23	2	140.1	129	61	123	0	0	0	0										
vs. Left	—	—	—	—	—	—	—	—	99	34	76	—	—	—	—										
vs. Right	—	—	—	—	—	—	—	—	90	43	89	—	—	—	—										
On Grass	12	7	.632	3.77	28	28	3	171.2	158	65	149	0	0	0	0										
On Turf	2	2	.500	4.05	5	5	1	33.1	31	12	16	0	0	0	0										
Home	9	4	.692	3.30	20	20	1	128.1	108	45	108	0	0	0	0										
Road	5	5	.500	4.70	13	13	3	76.2	81	32	57	0	0	0	0										
Division Rivals																									
vs. CAL	0	1	.000	1.93	2	2	0	14	8	7	10	0	0	0	0										
vs. KC	1	0	1.000	3.29	2	2	0	13.2	11	6	7	0	0	0	0										
vs. MIN	2	1	.667	3.14	4	4	0	28.2	23	9	17	0	0	0	0										
vs. OAK	2	1	.667	4.96	3	3	1	16.1	16	7	18	0	0	0	0										
vs. SEA	2	0	1.000	1.59	2	2	1	17	14	3	14	0	0	0	0										
vs. TEX	2	0	1.000	4.11	3	3	0	15.1	15	6	15	0	0	0	0										
1987 CHI A	3	0	1.000	1.93	4	4	0	28	16	6	15	0	0	0	0	0	0	0	—	1	6	0	0	1.8	1.000
1988	5	10	.333	3.97	26	26	1	158.2	147	68	84	0	0	0	0	0	0	0	—	12	16	5	1	1.3	.848
1990	14	9	.609	3.82	33	33	4	205	189	77	165	0	0	0	0	0	0	0	—	17	20	1	3	1.2	.974
3 yrs.	22	19	.537	3.75	63	63	5	391.2	352	151	264	0	0	0	0	0	0	0	—	30	42	6	4	1.2	.923

Roger McDowell

McDOWELL, ROGER ALAN
B. Dec. 21, 1960, Cincinnati, Ohio
BR TR 6′ 1″ 175 lbs.

RELIEF PITCHER

Period	W	L	%	ERA	G	GS	CG	IP	H	BB	SO	ShO	W	L	SV	AB	H	HR	BA	PO	A	E	DP	TC/G	FA
April	1	0	1.000	7.56	8	0	0	8.1	7	6	2	0	1	0	6										
May	1	0	1.000	4.32	12	0	0	16.2	21	6	6	0	1	0	6										
June	0	3	.000	7.71	10	0	0	11.2	19	5	11	0	0	3	1										
July	1	1	.500	2.30	13	0	0	15.2	13	10	10	0	1	1	2										
Aug	3	2	.600	1.71	18	0	0	21	15	7	5	0	3	2	2										
Sept/Oct	0	2	.000	2.77	11	0	0	13	17	1	5	0	0	2	5										
Day	2	2	.500	1.38	22	0	0	26	19	11	11	0	2	2	7										
Night	4	6	.400	4.92	50	0	0	60.1	73	24	28	0	4	6	15										
vs. Left	—	—	—	—	—	—	—	—	60	28	16	—	—	—	—										
vs. Right	—	—	—	—	—	—	—	—	32	7	23	—	—	—	—										
On Grass	2	2	.500	1.71	21	0	0	26.1	24	13	13	0	2	2	7										
On Turf	4	6	.400	4.80	51	0	0	60	68	22	26	0	4	6	15										
Home	3	4	.429	5.40	33	0	0	36.2	41	14	17	0	3	4	10										
Road	3	4	.429	2.72	39	0	0	49.2	51	21	22	0	3	4	12										
Division Rivals																									
vs. CHI	0	1	.000	0.00	6	0	0	7	3	2	4	0	0	1	3										
vs. MON	0	1	.000	3.75	8	0	0	12	13	1	5	0	0	1	3										
vs. NY	0	2	.000	5.00	7	0	0	9	12	3	11	0	0	2	2										
vs. PIT	0	2	.000	4.50	6	0	0	6	8	3	1	0	0	2	3										
vs. STL	1	2	.333	13.03	10	0	0	9.2	18	8	4	0	1	2	3										
1985 NY N	6	5	.545	2.83	62	2	0	127.1	108	37	70	0	6	4	17	19	3	0	.158	17	27	4	2	0.8	.917
1986	14	9	.609	3.02	75	0	0	128	107	42	65	0	**14**	9	22	18	5	0	.278	17	30	0	0	0.6	1.000
1987	7	5	.583	4.16	56	0	0	88.2	95	28	32	0	7	5	25	13	3	0	.231	10	17	0	1	0.5	1.000
1988	5	5	.500	2.63	62	0	0	89	80	31	46	0	5	5	16	9	3	0	.333	11	19	1	2	0.5	.968
1989 2 teams	NY N (25G 1 - 5)			PHI N (44G 3 - 3)																					
" total	4	8	.333	1.96	69	0	0	92	79	38	47	0	4	8	23	3	1	0	.333	17	25	3	3	0.7	.933
1990 PHI N	6	8	.429	3.86	72	0	0	86.1	92	35	39	0	6	8	22	2	0	0	.000	1	23	5	2	0.4	.828
6 yrs.	42	40	.512	3.05	396	2	0	611.1	561	211	299	0	42	39	125	64	15	0	.234	73	141	13	10	0.6	.943

Year	Team	W	L	%	ERA	G	GS	CG	IP	H	BB	SO	ShO	W	L	SV	AB	H	HR	BA	PO	A	E	DP	TC/G	FA

Roger McDowell *Continued*

LEAGUE CHAMPIONSHIP SERIES

Year	Team	W	L	%	ERA	G	GS	CG	IP	H	BB	SO	ShO	W	L	SV	AB	H	HR	BA	PO	A	E	DP	TC/G	FA
1986	NY N	0	0	—	0.00	2	0	0	7	1	0	3	0	0	0	0	1	0	0	.000	3	1	0	0	2.0	1.000
1988		0	1	.000	4.50	4	0	0	6	6	2	5	0	0	1	0	0	0	0	—	0	3	1	0	1.0	.750
2 yrs.		0	1	.000	2.08	6	0	0	13	7	2	8	0	0	1	0	1	0	0	.000	3	4	1	0	1.3	.875

WORLD SERIES

Year	Team	W	L	%	ERA	G	GS	CG	IP	H	BB	SO	ShO	W	L	SV	AB	H	HR	BA	PO	A	E	DP	TC/G	FA
1986	NY N	1	0	1.000	4.91	5	0	0	7.1	10	6	2	0	1	0	0	0	0	0	—	1	4	0	0	1.0	1.000

Chuck McElroy   **McELROY, CHARLES DWAYNE**
B. Oct. 1, 1967, Galveston, Tex.
BL TL 6′ 160 lbs.

Year	Team	W	L	%	ERA	G	GS	CG	IP	H	BB	SO	ShO	W	L	SV	AB	H	HR	BA	PO	A	E	DP	TC/G	FA
1989	PHI N	0	0	—	1.74	11	0	0	10.1	12	4	8	0	0	0	0	0	0	0	—	1	0	0	0	0.1	1.000
1990		0	1	.000	7.71	16	0	0	14	24	10	16	0	0	1	0	0	0	0	—	1	0	1	0	0.1	.500
2 yrs.		0	1	.000	5.18	27	0	0	24.1	36	14	24	0	0	1	0	0	0	0	—	2	0	1	0	0.1	.667

Andy McGaffigan   **McGAFFIGAN, ANDREW JOSEPH**
B. Oct. 25, 1956, West Palm Beach, Fla.
BR TR 6′ 3″ 185 lbs.

Year	Team	W	L	%	ERA	G	GS	CG	IP	H	BB	SO	ShO	W	L	SV	AB	H	HR	BA	PO	A	E	DP	TC/G	FA
1981	NY A	0	0	—	2.57	2	0	0	7	5	3	2	0	0	0	0	0	0	0	—	0	0	0	0	0.0	—
1982	SF N	1	0	1.000	0.00	4	0	0	8	5	1	4	0	1	0	0	1	0	0	.000	0	0	0	0	0.0	—
1983		3	9	.250	4.29	43	16	0	134.1	131	39	93	0	1	0	2	30	2	0	.067	8	4	2	0	0.3	.857
1984	2 teams	MON N	(21G 3 - 4)			CIN N	(9G 0 - 2)																			
"	total	3	6	.333	3.52	30	6	0	69	60	23	57	0	1	3	0	10	0	0	.000	3	6	1	1	0.3	.900
1985	CIN N	3	3	.500	3.72	15	15	2	94.1	88	30	83	0	0	0	0	29	1	0	.034	8	12	1	2	1.4	.952
1986	MON N	10	5	.667	2.65	48	14	1	142.2	114	55	104	1	5	1	2	33	2	0	.061	6	17	5	1	0.6	.821
1987		5	2	.714	2.39	69	0	0	120.1	105	42	100	0	5	2	12	17	0	0	.000	5	17	4	2	0.4	.846
1988		6	0	.000	2.76	63	0	0	91.1	81	37	71	0	6	0	4	5	0	0	.000	7	8	1	0	0.3	.938
1989		3	5	.375	4.68	57	0	0	75	85	30	40	0	3	5	2	1	1	0	1.000	3	8	2	0	0.2	.846
1990	2 teams	SF N	(4G 0 - 0)			KC A	(24G 4 - 3)																			
"	total	4	3	.571	3.89	28	11	0	83.1	85	32	53	0	1	0	1	0	0	0	—	5	6	1	0	0.4	.917
10 yrs.		38	33	.535	3.37	359	62	3	825.1	759	292	607	1	23	11	24	126	6	0	.048	45	78	17	6	0.4	.879

Craig McMurtry   **McMURTRY, JOE CRAIG**
B. Nov. 5, 1959, Temple, Tex.
BR TR 6′ 5″ 195 lbs.

	W	L	%	ERA	G	GS	CG	IP	H	BB	SO	ShO	W	L	SV
April	0	0	—	11.57	2	0	0	2.1	4	2	0	0	0	0	0
May	—	—	—	—	0	—	—	0	0	0	0	0	0	0	0
June	0	0	—	2.92	8	0	0	12.1	12	9	5	0	0	0	0
July	0	1	.000	4.32	7	0	0	8.1	10	7	2	0	0	1	0
Aug	0	1	.000	2.57	3	2	0	14	9	9	3	0	0	0	0
Sept/Oct	0	1	.000	9.64	3	1	0	4.2	8	3	4	0	0	0	0
Day	0	1	.000	7.11	3	0	0	6.1	8	5	4	0	0	1	0
Night	0	2	.000	3.82	20	3	0	35.1	35	25	10	0	0	0	0
vs. Left	—	—	—	—	—	—	—	—	15	12	7	—	—	—	—
vs. Right	—	—	—	—	—	—	—	—	28	18	7	—	—	—	—
On Grass	0	2	.000	3.48	20	3	0	41.1	37	29	14	0	0	0	0
On Turf	0	1	.000	108.00	3	0	0	0.1	6	1	0	0	0	1	0
Home	0	1	.000	4.43	13	2	0	22.1	23	14	9	0	0	0	0
Road	0	2	.000	4.19	10	1	0	19.1	20	16	5	0	0	1	0
Division Rivals															
vs. CAL	0	0	—	2.45	2	0	0	3.2	2	4	1	0	0	0	0
vs. CHI	0	1	.000	7.71	1	1	0	4.2	5	4	2	0	0	0	0
vs. KC	0	0	—	6.75	1	1	0	2.2	2	0	3	0	0	0	0
vs. MIN	0	0	—	0.00	1	1	0	5	2	3	1	0	0	0	0
vs. OAK	0	1	.000	3.60	3	1	0	10	10	6	2	0	0	0	0
vs. SEA	0	0	—	6.00	4	0	0	3	5	3	3	0	0	0	0

RELIEF PITCHER — WINS / ERA / SAVES / RATIO (AL AVG)

Year	Team	W	L	%	ERA	G	GS	CG	IP	H	BB	SO	ShO	W	L	SV	AB	H	HR	BA	PO	A	E	DP	TC/G	FA
1983	ATL N	15	9	.625	3.08	36	35	6	224.2	204	88	105	3	0	0	0	70	6	0	.086	15	51	3	3	1.9	.957
1984		9	17	.346	4.32	37	30	0	183.1	184	102	99	0	0	2	0	52	6	0	.115	10	48	1	2	1.6	.983
1985		0	3	.000	6.60	17	6	0	45	56	27	28	0	0	0	0	14	1	0	.071	2	12	2	0	0.9	.875
1986		1	6	.143	4.74	37	5	0	79.2	82	43	50	0	1	3	0	16	2	0	.125	6	11	0	1	0.5	1.000
1988	TEX A	3	3	.500	2.25	32	0	0	60	37	24	35	0	3	3	3	0	0	0	—	8	10	2	3	0.6	.900

Year	Team		W	L	%	ERA	G	GS	CG	IP	H	BB	SO	ShO	RELIEF PITCHING			BATTING			BA	PO	A	E	DP	TC/G	FA
															W	L	SV	AB	H	HR							

Craig McMurtry *Continued*

Year	Team		W	L	%	ERA	G	GS	CG	IP	H	BB	SO	ShO	W	L	SV	AB	H	HR	BA	PO	A	E	DP	TC/G	FA
1989			0	0	—	7.43	19	0	0	23	29	13	14	0	0	0	0	0	0	0	—	1	5	1	0	0.4	.857
1990			0	3	.000	4.32	23	3	0	41.2	43	30	14	0	0	1	0	0	0	0	—	1	8	0	3	0.4	1.000
7 yrs.			28	41	.406	4.03	201	79	6	657.1	635	327	345	3	4	9	4	152	15	0	.099	43	145	9	12	1.0	.954

Larry McWilliams

McWILLIAMS, LARRY DEAN
B. Feb. 10, 1954, Wichita, Kans.
BL TL 6′ 5″ 180 lbs.

Year	Team		W	L	%	ERA	G	GS	CG	IP	H	BB	SO	ShO	W	L	SV	AB	H	HR	BA	PO	A	E	DP	TC/G	FA
1978	ATL	N	9	3	.750	2.82	15	15	3	99	84	35	42	1	0	0	0	32	2	0	.063	10	19	0	1	1.9	1.000
1979			3	2	.600	5.59	13	13	1	66	69	22	32	0	0	0	0	24	5	0	.208	2	17	1	2	1.5	.950
1980			9	14	.391	4.94	30	30	4	164	188	39	77	1	0	0	0	51	8	0	.157	11	24	3	1	1.3	.921
1981			2	1	.667	3.08	6	5	2	38	31	8	23	1	0	0	0	10	1	0	.100	4	9	0	2	2.2	1.000
1982	2 teams		ATL N (27G 2 – 3)				PIT N (19G 6 – 5)																				
"	total		8	8	.500	3.84	46	20	2	159.1	158	44	118	2	2	2	1	38	7	0	.184	9	40	0	2	1.1	1.000
1983	PIT	N	15	8	.652	3.25	35	35	8	238	205	87	199	4	0	0	0	79	9	0	.114	10	40	5	5	1.6	.909
1984			12	11	.522	2.93	34	32	7	227.1	226	78	149	2	0	0	1	74	9	0	.122	15	32	0	4	1.4	1.000
1985			7	9	.438	4.70	30	19	2	126.1	139	62	52	0	1	1	0	40	5	0	.125	4	21	0	0	0.8	1.000
1986			3	11	.214	5.15	49	15	0	122.1	129	49	80	0	2	3	0	29	4	0	.138	7	17	0	2	0.5	1.000
1987	ATL	N	0	1	.000	5.75	9	2	0	20.1	25	7	13	0	0	0	0	5	1	0	.200	1	3	0	1	0.4	1.000
1988	STL	N	6	9	.400	3.90	42	17	2	136	130	45	70	1	1	3	1	37	6	0	.162	5	24	2	0	0.7	.935
1989	2 teams		PHI N (40G 2 – 11)				KC A (8G 2 – 2)																				
"	total		4	13	.235	4.11	48	21	3	153.1	154	57	78	1	0	1	0	27	3	0	.111	7	26	2	2	0.7	.943
1990	KC	A	0	0	—	9.72	13	0	0	8.1	10	9	7	0	0	0	0	0	0	0	—	0	3	0	0	0.2	1.000
13 yrs.			78	90	.464	3.99	370	224	34	1558.1	1548	542	940	13	6	10	3	446	60	0	.135	85	275	13	22	1.0	.965

Scott Medvin

MEDVIN, SCOTT HOWARD
B. Sept. 16, 1961, North Olmsted, Ohio
BR TR 6′ 1″ 195 lbs.

Year	Team		W	L	%	ERA	G	GS	CG	IP	H	BB	SO	ShO	W	L	SV	AB	H	HR	BA	PO	A	E	DP	TC/G	FA
1988	PIT	N	3	0	1.000	4.88	17	0	0	27.2	23	9	16	0	3	0	0	3	0	0	.000	0	6	0	0	0.4	1.000
1989			0	1	.000	5.68	6	0	0	6.1	6	5	4	0	0	1	0	0	0	0	—	1	2	0	0	0.5	1.000
1990	SEA	A	0	1	.000	6.23	5	0	0	4.1	7	2	1	0	0	1	0	0	0	0	—	1	2	1	0	0.8	.750
3 yrs.			3	2	.600	5.17	28	0	0	38.1	36	16	21	0	3	2	0	3	0	0	.000	2	10	1	0	0.5	.923

Jose Melendez

MELENDEZ, JOSE LUIS
Born Jose Luis Melendez y Garcia.
B. Sept. 2, 1965, Naguabo, Puerto Rico
BR TR 6′ 2″ 175 lbs.

Year	Team		W	L	%	ERA	G	GS	CG	IP	H	BB	SO	ShO	W	L	SV	AB	H	HR	BA	PO	A	E	DP	TC/G	FA
1990	SEA	A	0	0	—	11.81	3	0	0	5.1	8	3	7	0	0	0	0	0	0	0	—	0	0	0	0	0.0	—

Kent Mercker

MERCKER, KENT FRANKLIN
B. Feb. 1, 1968, Indianapolis, Ind.
BL TL 6′ 1″ 175 lbs.

	W	L	%	ERA	G	GS	CG	IP	H	BB	SO	ShO	W	L	SV
April	—	—	—	—	0	—	—	0	0	0	0	—	0	0	0
May	—	—	—	—	0	—	—	0	0	0	0	—	0	0	0
June	0	0	—	0.00	1	0	0	0	1	0	0	0	0	0	0
July	4	1	.800	1.77	12	0	0	20.1	16	12	19	0	4	1	1
Aug	0	2	.000	2.93	11	0	0	15.1	12	3	17	0	0	2	3
Sept/Oct	0	4	.000	5.68	12	0	0	12.2	14	9	3	0	0	4	3
Day	1	4	.200	5.19	7	0	0	8.2	10	3	7	0	1	4	0
Night	3	3	.500	2.72	29	0	0	39.2	33	21	32	0	3	3	7
vs. Left	—	—	—	—	—				12	8	11	—	—	—	—
vs. Right	—	—	—	—	—				31	16	28	—	—	—	—

RELIEF PITCHER

WINS — NL AVG

ERA — NL AVG

Year	Team	W	L	%	ERA	G	GS	CG	IP	H	BB	SO	ShO	W	L	SV	AB	H	HR	BA	PO	A	E	DP	TC/G	FA

Kent Mercker *Continued*

RELIEF PITCHER

Year	Team	W	L	%	ERA	G	GS	CG	IP	H	BB	SO	ShO	W	L	SV	AB	H	HR	BA	PO	A	E	DP	TC/G	FA
On Grass		4	5	.444	2.97	26	0	0	36.1	32	20	24	0	4	5	6										
On Turf		0	2	.000	3.75	10	0	0	12	11	4	15	0	0	2	1										
Home		3	2	.600	2.53	16	0	0	21.1	20	8	16	0	3	2	5										
Road		1	5	.167	3.67	20	0	0	27	23	16	23	0	1	5	2										
Division Rivals																										
vs. CIN		0	0	—	0.00	2	0	0	2	3	2	1	0	0	0	1										
vs. HOU		1	2	.333	7.71	4	0	0	4.2	5	2	5	0	1	2	0										
vs. LA		0	0	—	2.57	5	0	0	7	5	7	8	0	0	0	1										
vs. SD		0	1	.000	2.70	4	0	0	6.2	3	4	4	0	0	1	0										
vs. SF		0	1	.000	4.91	3	0	0	3.2	6	3	1	0	0	1	1										
1989	ATL N	0	0	—	12.46	2	1	0	4.1	8	6	4	0	0	0	0	1	0	0	.000	0	0	0	0	0.0	—
1990		4	7	.364	3.17	36	0	0	48.1	43	24	39	0	4	7	7	3	0	0	.000	2	1	1	0	0.1	.750
2 yrs.		4	7	.364	3.93	38	1	0	52.2	51	30	43	0	4	7	7	4	0	0	.000	2	1	1	0	0.1	.750

Jose Mesa

MESA, JOSE RAMON
B. May 22, 1966, Pueblo Viejo, Dominican Republic
BR TR 6′ 3″ 170 lbs.

Year	Team	W	L	%	ERA	G	GS	CG	IP	H	BB	SO	ShO	W	L	SV	AB	H	HR	BA	PO	A	E	DP	TC/G	FA
1987	BAL A	1	3	.250	6.03	6	5	0	31.1	38	15	17	0	0	0	0	0	0	0	—	1	1	0	0	0.3	1.000
1990		3	2	.600	3.86	7	7	0	46.2	37	27	24	0	0	0	0	0	0	0	—	3	5	1	1	1.3	.889
2 yrs.		4	5	.444	4.73	13	12	0	78	75	42	41	0	0	0	0	0	0	0	—	4	6	1	1	0.8	.909

Brian Meyer

MEYER, BRIAN SCOTT
B. Jan. 29, 1963, Camden, N. J.
BR TR 6′ 1″ 190 lbs.

Year	Team	W	L	%	ERA	G	GS	CG	IP	H	BB	SO	ShO	W	L	SV	AB	H	HR	BA	PO	A	E	DP	TC/G	FA
1988	HOU N	0	0	—	1.46	8	0	0	12.1	9	4	10	0	0	0	0	0	0	0	—	0	5	0	0	0.6	1.000
1989		0	1	.000	4.50	12	0	0	18	16	13	13	0	0	1	1	0	0	0	—	2	2	0	0	0.3	1.000
1990		0	4	.000	2.21	14	0	0	20.1	16	6	6	0	0	4	1	1	0	0	0	.000	2	7	0	0	0.6	1.000
3 yrs.		0	5	.000	2.84	34	0	0	50.2	41	23	29	0	0	5	2	1	0	0	0	.000	4	14	0	0	0.5	1.000

Gary Mielke

MIELKE, GARY ROGER
B. Jan. 28, 1963, St. James, Minn.
BR TR 6′ 3″ 185 lbs.

RELIEF PITCHER

Year	Team	W	L	%	ERA	G	GS	CG	IP	H	BB	SO	ShO	W	L	SV	AB	H	HR	BA	PO	A	E	DP	TC/G	FA
April		0	0	—	3.00	9	0	0	9	8	1	5	0	0	0	0										
May		0	1	.000	9.72	10	0	0	8.1	15	8	2	0	0	1	0										
June		—	—	—		0	—	—	0	0	0	0	—	0	0	0										
July		0	0	—	2.08	1	0	0	4.1	4	1	0	0	0	0	0										
Aug		0	2	.000	3.00	6	0	0	9	6	1	2	0	0	2	0										
Sept/Oct		0	0	—	0.87	7	0	0	10.1	9	4	4	0	0	0	0										
Day		0	0	—	4.35	7	0	0	10.1	15	5	2	0	0	0	0										
Night		0	3	.000	3.52	26	0	0	30.2	27	10	11	0	0	3	0										
vs. Left		—	—	—	—	—	—	—	—	14	6	3	—	—	—	—										
vs. Right		—	—	—	—	—	—	—	—	28	9	10	—	—	—	—										
On Grass		0	2	.000	4.02	26	0	0	31.1	33	13	11	0	0	2	0										
On Turf		0	1	.000	2.79	7	0	0	9.2	9	2	2	0	0	1	0										
Home		0	1	.000	6.06	17	0	0	16.1	21	10	10	0	0	1	0										
Road		0	2	.000	2.19	16	0	0	24.2	21	5	3	0	0	2	0										
Division Rivals																										
vs. CAL		0	0	—	0.00	1	0	0	0	2	1	0	0	0	0	0										
vs. CHI		0	0	—	1.35	3	0	0	6.2	4	0	1	0	0	0	0										
vs. KC		0	1	.000	7.36	5	0	0	3.2	3	1	3	0	0	1	0										
vs. MIN		0	1	.000	6.75	2	0	0	1.1	3	0	1	0	0	1	0										
vs. OAK		0	0	—	0.00	2	0	0	2.2	2	2	2	0	0	0	0										
vs. SEA		—	—	—	—	0			0	0	0	0	0													
1987	TEX A	0	0	—	6.00	3	0	0	3	3	1	3	0	0	0	0	0	0	0	—	0	0	0	0	0.0	—
1989		1	0	1.000	3.26	43	0	0	49.2	52	25	26	0	1	0	1	0	0	0	—	3	6	1	0	0.2	.900
1990		0	3	.000	3.73	33	0	0	41	42	15	13	0	0	3	0	0	0	0	—	2	7	0	0	0.3	1.000
3 yrs.		1	3	.250	3.56	79	0	0	93.2	97	41	42	0	1	3	1	0	0	0	—	5	13	1	0	0.2	.947

Year	Team	W	L	%	ERA	G	GS	CG	IP	H	BB	SO	ShO	RELIEF PITCHING W	L	SV	BATTING AB	H	HR	BA	PO	A	E	DP	TC/G	FA

Bob Milacki

MILACKI, ROBERT
B. July 28, 1964, Trenton, N. J.
BR TR 6′ 4″ 220 lbs.

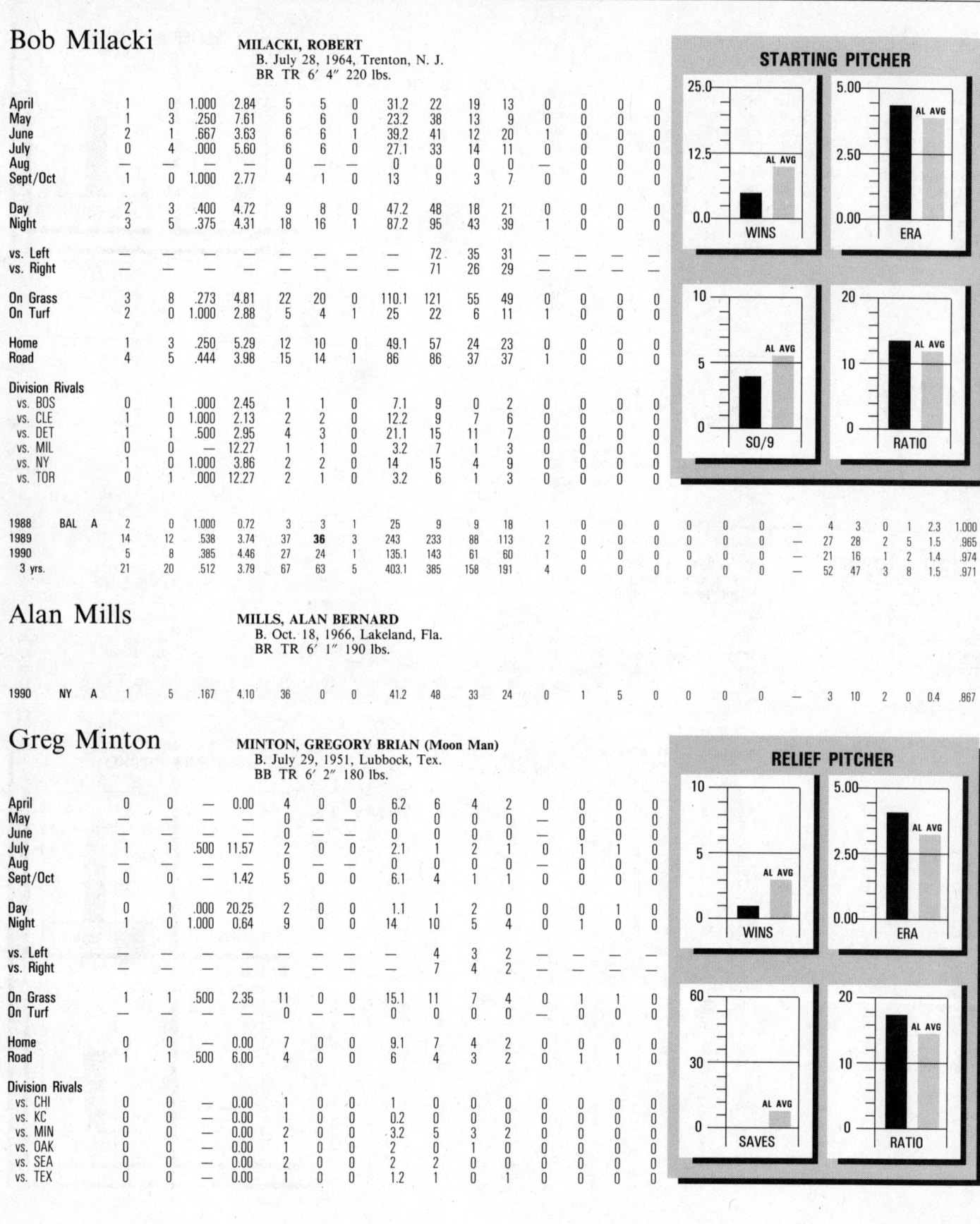

STARTING PITCHER

		W	L	%	ERA	G	GS	CG	IP	H	BB	SO	ShO	W	L	SV	AB	H	HR	BA	PO	A	E	DP	TC/G	FA
April		1	0	1.000	2.84	5	5	0	31.2	22	19	13	0	0	0	0										
May		1	3	.250	7.61	6	6	0	23.2	38	13	9	0	0	0	0										
June		2	1	.667	3.63	6	6	1	39.2	41	12	20	1	0	0	0										
July		0	4	.000	5.60	6	6	0	27.1	33	14	11	0	0	0	0										
Aug		—	—	—	—	0	—	—	0	0	0	0	—	0	0	0										
Sept/Oct		1	0	1.000	2.77	4	1	0	13	9	3	7	0	0	0	0										
Day		2	3	.400	4.72	9	8	0	47.2	48	18	21	0	0	0	0										
Night		3	5	.375	4.31	18	16	1	87.2	95	43	39	1	0	0	0										
vs. Left		—	—	—	—					72	35	31														
vs. Right		—	—	—	—					71	26	29														
On Grass		3	8	.273	4.81	22	20	0	110.1	121	55	49	0	0	0	0										
On Turf		2	0	1.000	2.88	5	4	1	25	22	6	11	0	0	0	0										
Home		1	3	.250	5.29	12	10	0	49.1	57	24	23	0	0	0	0										
Road		4	5	.444	3.98	15	14	1	86	86	37	37	1	0	0	0										
Division Rivals																										
vs. BOS		0	1	.000	2.45	1	1	0	7.1	9	0	2	0	0	0	0										
vs. CLE		1	0	1.000	2.13	2	2	0	12.2	9	7	6	0	0	0	0										
vs. DET		1	1	.500	2.95	4	3	0	21.1	15	11	7	0	0	0	0										
vs. MIL		0	0	—	12.27	1	1	0	3.2	7	1	3	0	0	0	0										
vs. NY		1	0	1.000	3.86	2	2	0	14	15	4	9	0	0	0	0										
vs. TOR		0	1	.000	12.27	2	1	0	3.2	6	1	3	0	0	0	0										
1988	BAL A	2	0	1.000	0.72	3	3	1	25	9	9	18	1	0	0	0	0	0	0	—	4	3	0	1	2.3	1.000
1989		14	12	.538	3.74	37	**36**	3	243	233	88	113	2	0	0	0	0	0	0	—	27	28	2	5	1.5	.965
1990		5	8	.385	4.46	27	24	1	135.1	143	61	60	1	0	0	0	0	0	0	—	21	16	1	2	1.4	.974
3 yrs.		21	20	.512	3.79	67	63	5	403.1	385	158	191	4	0	0	0	0	0	0	—	52	47	3	8	1.5	.971

Alan Mills

MILLS, ALAN BERNARD
B. Oct. 18, 1966, Lakeland, Fla.
BR TR 6′ 1″ 190 lbs.

Year	Team	W	L	%	ERA	G	GS	CG	IP	H	BB	SO	ShO	W	L	SV	AB	H	HR	BA	PO	A	E	DP	TC/G	FA
1990	NY A	1	5	.167	4.10	36	0	0	41.2	48	33	24	0	1	5	0	0	0	0	—	3	10	2	0	0.4	.867

Greg Minton

MINTON, GREGORY BRIAN (Moon Man)
B. July 29, 1951, Lubbock, Tex.
BB TR 6′ 2″ 180 lbs.

RELIEF PITCHER

		W	L	%	ERA	G	GS	CG	IP	H	BB	SO	ShO	W	L	SV	AB	H	HR	BA	PO	A	E	DP	TC/G	FA
April		0	0	—	0.00	4	0	0	6.2	6	4	2	0	0	0	0										
May		—	—	—	—	0	—	—	0	0	0	0	—	0	0	0										
June		—	—	—	—	0	—	—	0	0	0	0	—	0	0	0										
July		1	1	.500	11.57	2	0	0	2.1	1	2	1	0	1	1	0										
Aug		—	—	—	—	0	—	—	0	0	0	0	—	0	0	0										
Sept/Oct		0	0	—	1.42	5	0	0	6.1	4	1	1	0	0	0	0										
Day		0	1	.000	20.25	2	0	0	1.1	1	2	0	0	0	1	0										
Night		1	0	1.000	0.64	14	0	0	14	10	5	4	0	1	0	0										
vs. Left		—	—	—	—	—	—	—	—	4	3	2														
vs. Right		—	—	—	—	—	—	—	—	7	4	2														
On Grass		1	1	.500	2.35	11	0	0	15.1	11	7	4	0	1	1	0										
On Turf		—	—	—	—	0	—	—	0	0	0	0	—	0	0	0										
Home		0	0	—	0.00	7	0	0	9.1	7	4	2	0	0	0	0										
Road		1	1	.500	6.00	4	0	0	6	4	3	2	0	1	1	0										
Division Rivals																										
vs. CHI		0	0	—	0.00	1	0	0	1	0	0	0	0	0	0	0										
vs. KC		0	0	—	0.00	1	0	0	0.2	0	0	0	0	0	0	0										
vs. MIN		0	0	—	0.00	2	0	0	3.2	5	3	2	0	0	0	0										
vs. OAK		0	0	—	0.00	1	0	0	2	0	1	0	0	0	0	0										
vs. SEA		0	0	—	0.00	2	0	0	2	2	0	0	0	0	0	0										
vs. TEX		0	0	—	0.00	1	0	0	1.2	1	0	1	0	0	0	0										

Year	Team		W	L	%	ERA	G	GS	CG	IP	H	BB	SO	ShO	RELIEF PITCHING			BATTING			BA	PO	A	E	DP	TC/G	FA
															W	L	SV	AB	H	HR							

Greg Minton *Continued*

Year	Team		W	L	%	ERA	G	GS	CG	IP	H	BB	SO	ShO	W	L	SV	AB	H	HR	BA	PO	A	E	DP	TC/G	FA
1975	SF	N	1	1	.500	6.88	4	2	0	17	19	11	6	0	0	0	0	6	0	0	.000	2	4	0	1	1.5	1.000
1976			0	3	.000	4.91	10	2	0	25.2	32	12	7	0	0	2	0	5	1	0	.200	3	4	2	0	0.9	.778
1977			1	1	.500	4.50	2	2	0	14	14	4	5	0	0	0	0	3	1	0	.333	2	4	0	0	3.0	1.000
1978			0	1	.000	7.88	11	0	0	16	22	8	6	0	0	1	0	1	0	0	.000	2	2	0	1	0.4	1.000
1979			4	3	.571	1.80	46	0	0	80	59	27	33	0	4	3	4	4	0	0	.000	3	23	1	2	0.6	.963
1980			4	6	.400	2.47	68	0	0	91	81	34	42	0	4	6	19	8	1	0	.125	8	21	1	2	0.4	.967
1981			4	5	.444	2.89	55	0	0	84	84	36	29	0	4	5	21	12	0	0	.000	11	25	0	1	0.7	1.000
1982			10	4	.714	1.83	78	0	0	123	108	42	58	0	10	4	30	17	3	0	.176	11	22	3	2	0.5	.917
1983			7	11	.389	3.54	73	0	0	106.2	117	47	38	0	7	**11**	22	11	6	1	.545	5	18	1	0	0.3	.958
1984			4	9	.308	3.76	74	1	0	124.1	130	57	48	0	3	9	19	21	1	0	.048	8	31	2	1	0.6	.951
1985			5	4	.556	3.54	68	0	0	96.2	98	54	37	0	5	4	4	8	0	0	.000	7	27	1	1	0.5	.971
1986			4	4	.500	3.93	48	0	0	68.2	63	34	34	0	4	4	5	5	2	0	.400	7	19	2	1	0.6	.929
1987	2 teams		SF N (15G 1 - 0)			CAL A (41G 5 - 4)																					
"	total		6	4	.600	3.17	56	0	0	99.1	101	39	44	0	6	4	11	2	0	0	.000	7	23	0	2	0.5	1.000
1988	CAL	A	4	5	.444	2.85	44	0	0	79	67	34	46	0	4	5	7	0	0	0	—	11	15	0	3	0.6	1.000
1989			4	3	.571	2.20	62	0	0	90	76	37	42	0	4	3	8	0	0	0	—	8	20	0	0	0.5	1.000
1990			1	1	.500	2.35	11	0	0	15.1	11	7	4	0	1	1	0	0	0	0	—	0	3	0	0	0.3	1.000
16 yrs.			59	65	.476	3.10	710	7	0	1130.2	1082	483	479	0	56	62	150	103	15	1	.146	95	261	13	17	0.5	.965

Gino Minutelli

MINUTELLI, GINO MICHAEL
B. May 23, 1964, Wilmington, Del.
BL TL 6'   180 lbs.

Year	Team		W	L	%	ERA	G	GS	CG	IP	H	BB	SO	ShO	W	L	SV	AB	H	HR	BA	PO	A	E	DP	TC/G	FA
1990	CIN	N	0	0	—	9.00	2	0	0	1	0	2	0	0	0	0	0	0	0	0	—	0	0	0	0	0.0	—

Paul Mirabella

MIRABELLA, PAUL THOMAS
B. Mar. 20, 1954, Belleville, N. J.
BL TL 6' 1" 190 lbs.

	W	L	%	ERA	G	GS	CG	IP	H	BB	SO	ShO	W	L	SV
April	0	0	—	6.14	3	1	0	7.1	10	4	6	0	0	0	0
May	2	0	1.000	1.35	7	0	0	13.1	13	5	4	0	2	0	0
June	0	1	.000	6.55	10	1	0	11	13	5	5	0	0	0	0
July	1	1	.500	2.08	11	0	0	13	11	5	7	0	1	1	0
Aug	1	0	1.000	3.12	8	0	0	8.2	10	4	4	0	1	0	0
Sept/Oct	0	0	—	7.94	5	0	0	5.2	9	4	2	0	0	0	0
Day	2	2	.500	4.26	17	1	0	25.1	28	13	7	0	2	1	0
Night	2	0	1.000	3.74	27	1	0	33.2	38	14	21	0	2	0	0
vs. Left	—	—	—	—				—	16	10	13	—	—	—	—
vs. Right	—	—	—	—				—	50	17	15	—	—	—	—
On Grass	4	1	.800	3.99	35	2	0	47.1	55	20	24	0	4	0	0
On Turf	0	1	.000	3.86	9	0	0	11.2	11	7	4	0	0	1	0
Home	2	1	.667	3.72	22	1	0	29	31	15	11	0	2	0	0
Road	2	1	.667	4.20	22	1	0	30	35	12	17	0	2	1	0
Division Rivals															
vs. BAL	0	1	.000	6.23	1	1	0	4.1	4	2	1	0	0	0	0
vs. BOS	—	—	—	—	0	—	—	0	0	0	0	0	0	0	0
vs. CLE	0	0	—	20.25	3	0	0	1.1	4	1	1	0	0	0	0
vs. DET	2	0	1.000	3.86	4	1	0	11.2	13	2	8	0	2	0	0
vs. NY	0	0	—	0.00	4	0	0	1	1	1	0	0	0	0	0
vs. TOR	0	0	—	3.72	4	0	0	9.2	10	2	4	0	0	0	0

RELIEF PITCHER

WINS (AL AVG) — ERA (AL AVG) — SAVES (AL AVG) — RATIO (AL AVG)

Year	Team		W	L	%	ERA	G	GS	CG	IP	H	BB	SO	ShO	W	L	SV	AB	H	HR	BA	PO	A	E	DP	TC/G	FA
1978	TEX	A	3	2	.600	5.79	10	4	0	28	30	17	23	0	1	1	1	0	0	0	—	0	3	0	0	0.3	1.000
1979	NY	A	0	4	.000	9.00	10	1	0	14	16	10	4	0	0	3	0	0	0	0	—	0	2	0	0	0.2	1.000
1980	TOR	A	5	12	.294	4.33	33	22	3	131	151	66	53	1	0	0	0	0	0	0	—	9	20	1	1	0.9	.967
1981			0	0	—	7.20	8	1	0	15	20	7	9	0	0	0	0	0	0	0	—	1	0	0	0	0.1	1.000
1982	TEX	A	1	1	.500	4.80	40	0	0	50.2	46	22	29	0	1	1	3	0	0	0	—	2	6	1	2	0.2	.889
1983	BAL	A	0	0	—	5.59	3	2	0	9.2	9	7	4	0	0	0	0	0	0	0	—	1	1	0	0	0.7	.500
1984	SEA	A	2	5	.286	4.37	52	1	0	68	74	32	41	0	2	4	3	0	0	0	—	4	11	0	1	0.3	1.000
1985			0	0	—	1.32	10	0	0	13.2	9	4	8	0	0	0	0	0	0	0	—	0	1	0	0	0.1	1.000
1986			0	0	—	8.53	8	0	0	6.1	13	3	6	0	0	0	0	0	0	0	—	0	1	0	0	0.1	1.000
1987	MIL	A	2	1	.667	4.91	29	0	0	29.1	30	16	14	0	2	1	2	0	0	0	—	7	5	1	1	0.4	.923
1988			2	2	.500	1.65	38	0	0	60	44	21	33	0	2	2	4	0	0	0	—	6	10	0	1	0.4	1.000
1989			0	0	—	7.63	13	0	0	15.1	18	7	6	0	0	0	0	0	0	0	—	0	6	2	0	0.6	.750
1990			4	2	.667	3.97	44	2	0	59	66	27	28	0	4	1	0	0	0	0	—	4	7	1	1	0.3	.917
13 yrs.			19	29	.396	4.45	298	33	3	500	526	239	258	1	12	13	13	0	0	0	—	33	73	7	7	0.4	.938

Year	Team	W	L	%	ERA	G	GS	CG	IP	H	BB	SO	ShO	RELIEF PITCHING W	L	SV	BATTING AB	H	HR	BA	PO	A	E	DP	TC/G	FA

John Mitchell

MITCHELL, JOHN KYLE
Brother of Charlie Mitchell.
B. Aug. 11, 1965, Dickson, Tenn.
BR TR 6′ 2″ 165 lbs.

Split	W	L	%	ERA	G	GS	CG	IP	H	BB	SO	ShO	W	L	SV
April	0	0	—	3.00	3	0	0	9	8	4	2	0	0	0	0
May	—	—	—	—		0	—	—	0	0	0	0	—	0	0	0
June	0	1	.000	5.03	3	3	0	19.2	20	7	7	0	0	0	0
July	3	2	.600	3.89	6	6	0	37	33	16	17	0	0	0	0
Aug	3	3	.500	5.35	7	7	0	37	53	15	13	0	0	0	0
Sept/Oct	0	0	—	5.40	5	1	0	11.2	19	6	4	0	0	0	0
Day	2	1	.667	4.74	6	4	0	24.2	29	13	8	0	0	0	0
Night	4	5	.444	4.62	18	13	0	89.2	104	35	35	0	0	0	0
vs. Left	—	—	—	—	—	—	—	—	64	29	16	—	—	—	—
vs. Right	—	—	—	—	—	—	—	—	69	19	27	—	—	—	—
On Grass	5	6	.455	5.04	21	16	0	103.2	126	46	39	0	0	0	0
On Turf	1	0	1.000	0.84	3	1	0	10.2	7	2	4	0	0	0	0
Home	2	2	.500	4.47	10	8	0	50.1	62	26	17	0	0	0	0
Road	4	4	.500	4.78	14	9	0	64	71	22	26	0	0	0	0
Division Rivals															
vs. BOS	1	1	.500	6.43	3	2	0	14	24	4	4	0	0	0	0
vs. CLE	0	0	—	4.58	4	3	0	17.2	20	8	9	0	0	0	0
vs. DET	0	1	.000	9.39	2	1	0	7.2	10	5	7	0	0	0	0
vs. MIL	0	1	.000	3.38	1	1	0	5.1	9	1	1	0	0	0	0
vs. NY	0	0	—	4.50	1	0	0	2	1	1	1	0	0	0	0
vs. TOR	0	0	—	0.00	2	0	0	3.1	3	1	0	0	0	0	0

Year	Team	W	L	%	ERA	G	GS	CG	IP	H	BB	SO	ShO	W	L	SV	AB	H	HR	BA	PO	A	E	DP	TC/G	FA
1986	NY N	0	1	.000	3.60	4	1	0	10	10	4	2	0	0	0	0	2	0	0	.000	3	1	0	0	1.0	1.000
1987		3	6	.333	4.11	20	19	1	111.2	124	36	57	0	0	0	0	35	4	0	.114	16	21	6	3	2.2	.860
1988		0	0	—	0.00	1	0	0	1	2	1	1	0	0	0	0	1	0	0	.000	0	0	0	0	0.0	—
1989		0	1	.000	6.00	2	0	0	3	3	4	4	0	0	0	1	0	0	0	—	0	0	0	0	0.0	—
1990	BAL A	6	6	.500	4.64	24	17	0	114.1	133	48	43	0	0	0	0	0	0	0	—	7	19	2	3	1.2	.929
5 yrs.		9	14	.391	4.35	51	37	1	240	272	93	107	0	0	0	1	38	4	0	.105	26	41	8	6	1.5	.893

Dale Mohorcic

MOHORCIC, DALE ROBERT
B. Jan. 25, 1956, Cleveland, Ohio
BR TR 6′ 3″ 220 lbs.

Split	W	L	%	ERA	G	GS	CG	IP	H	BB	SO	ShO	W	L	SV
April	—	—	—	—	—	0	0	0	0	0	0	0	0	0	0
May	0	0	—	0.00	1	0	0	0.1	0	1	0	0	0	0	0
June	1	1	.500	2.13	10	0	0	12.2	9	7	4	0	1	1	1
July	0	0	—	4.91	8	0	0	11	16	1	9	0	0	0	1
Aug	0	1	.000	1.38	6	0	0	13	15	4	8	0	0	1	0
Sept/Oct	0	0	—	4.50	9	0	0	16	16	5	2	0	0	0	0
Day	0	0	—	9.26	9	0	0	11.2	22	5	6	0	0	0	0
Night	1	2	.333	1.52	25	0	0	41.1	34	13	23	0	1	2	2
vs. Left	—	—	—	—	—	—	—	—	31	7	14	—	—	—	—
vs. Right	—	—	—	—	—	—	—	—	25	11	15	—	—	—	—
On Grass	0	1	.000	3.72	10	0	0	19.1	26	7	15	0	0	1	0
On Turf	1	1	.500	2.94	24	0	0	33.2	30	11	14	0	1	1	1
Home	1	0	1.000	2.95	13	0	0	21.1	22	4	10	0	1	0	0
Road	0	2	.000	3.41	21	0	0	31.2	34	14	19	0	0	2	2
Division Rivals															
vs. CHI	1	0	1.000	0.00	6	0	0	11.2	10	3	7	0	1	0	0
vs. NY	0	1	.000	1.50	3	0	0	6	6	3	1	0	0	1	0
vs. PHI	0	0	—	1.35	5	0	0	6.2	3	5	3	0	0	0	0
vs. PIT	0	1	.000	3.86	5	0	0	4.2	4	3	1	0	0	1	1
vs. STL	0	0	—	5.40	4	0	0	6.2	9	2	3	0	0	0	0

Year	Team	W	L	%	ERA	G	GS	CG	IP	H	BB	SO	ShO	W	L	SV	AB	H	HR	BA	PO	A	E	DP	TC/G	FA
1986	TEX A	2	4	.333	2.51	58	0	0	79	86	15	29	0	2	4	7	0	0	0	—	5	12	0	3	0.3	1.000
1987		7	6	.538	2.99	74	0	0	99.1	88	19	48	0	7	6	16	0	0	0	—	9	23	2	3	0.5	.941
1988	2 teams	TEX A (43G 2-6)			NY A (13G 2-2)																					
"	total	4	8	.333	4.22	56	0	0	74.2	83	29	44	0	4	**8**	6	0	0	0	—	7	9	1	0	0.3	.941
1989	NY A	2	1	.667	4.99	32	0	0	57.2	65	18	24	0	2	1	2	0	0	0	—	5	10	0	2	0.5	1.000
1990	MON N	1	2	.333	3.23	34	0	0	53	56	18	29	0	1	2	2	8	1	0	.125	2	9	0	3	0.3	1.000
5 yrs.		16	21	.432	3.49	254	0	0	363.2	378	99	174	0	16	21	33	8	1	0	.125	28	63	3	10	0.4	.968

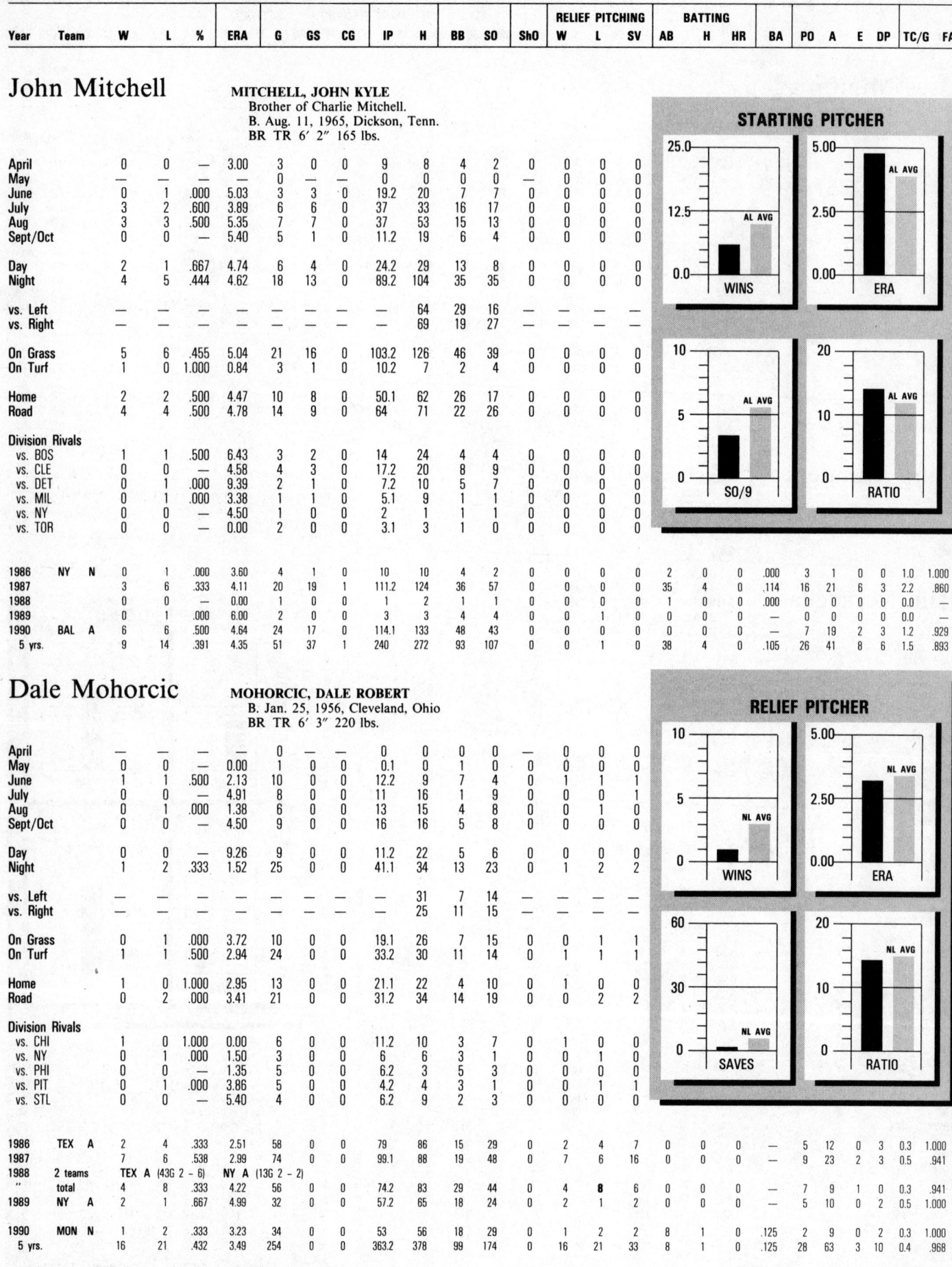

STARTING PITCHER (John Mitchell) — WINS, ERA, SO/9, RATIO (AL AVG)

RELIEF PITCHER (Dale Mohorcic) — WINS, ERA, SAVES, RATIO (NL AVG)

Year	Team	W	L	%	ERA	G	GS	CG	IP	H	BB	SO	ShO	RELIEF PITCHING W	L	SV	BATTING AB	H	HR	BA	PO	A	E	DP	TC/G	FA

Rich Monteleone

MONTELEONE, RICHARD
B. Mar. 22, 1963, Tampa, Fla.
BR TR 6′ 2″ 205 lbs.

Year	Team	W	L	%	ERA	G	GS	CG	IP	H	BB	SO	ShO	W	L	SV	AB	H	HR	BA	PO	A	E	DP	TC/G	FA
1987	SEA A	0	0	—	6.43	3	0	0	7	10	4	2	0	0	0	0	0	0	0	—	0	3	0	0	1.0	1.000
1988	CAL A	0	0	—	0.00	3	0	0	4.1	4	1	3	0	0	0	0	0	0	0	—	0	1	0	0	0.3	1.000
1989		2	2	.500	3.18	24	0	0	39.2	39	13	27	0	2	2	0	0	0	0	—	1	9	1	1	0.5	.909
1990	NY A	0	1	.000	6.14	5	0	0	7.1	8	2	8	0	0	1	0	0	0	0	—	1	1	0	0	0.4	1.000
4 yrs.		2	3	.400	3.70	35	0	0	58.1	61	20	40	0	2	3	0	0	0	0	—	2	14	1	1	0.5	.941

Jeff Montgomery

MONTGOMERY, JEFFREY THOMAS
B. Jan. 7, 1962, Wellston, Ohio
BR TR 5′ 11″ 170 lbs.

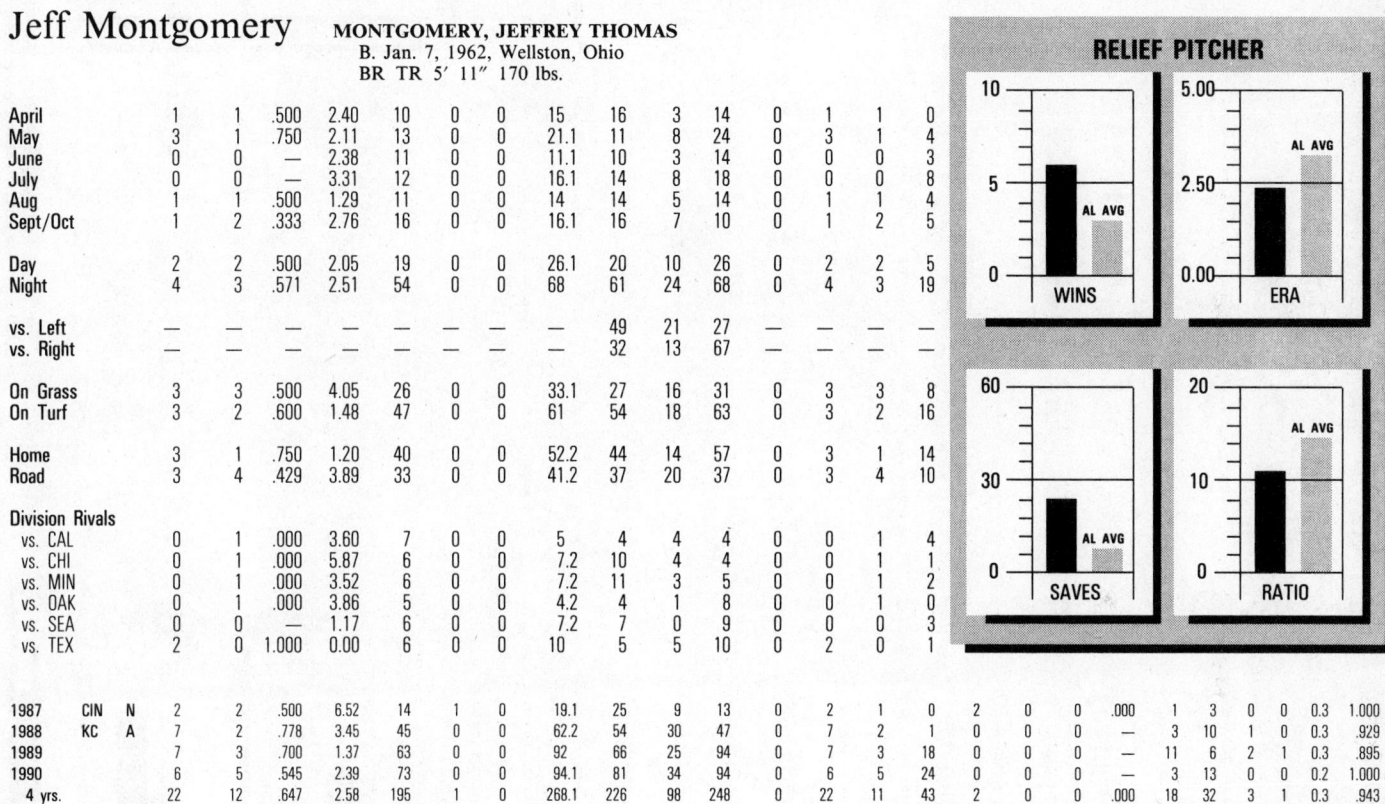

RELIEF PITCHER

	W	L	%	ERA	G	GS	CG	IP	H	BB	SO	ShO	W	L	SV	AB	H	HR	BA	PO	A	E	DP	TC/G	FA
April	1	1	.500	2.40	10	0	0	15	16	3	14	0	1	1	0										
May	3	1	.750	2.11	13	0	0	21.1	11	8	24	0	3	1	4										
June	0	0	—	2.38	11	0	0	11.1	10	3	14	0	0	0	3										
July	0	0	—	3.31	12	0	0	16.1	14	8	18	0	0	0	8										
Aug	1	1	.500	1.29	11	0	0	14	14	5	14	0	1	1	4										
Sept/Oct	1	2	.333	2.76	16	0	0	16.1	16	7	10	0	1	2	5										
Day	2	2	.500	2.05	19	0	0	26.1	20	10	26	0	2	2	5										
Night	4	3	.571	2.51	54	0	0	68	61	24	68	0	4	3	19										
vs. Left	—	—	—	—	—	—	—	—	49	21	27	—	—	—	—										
vs. Right	—	—	—	—	—	—	—	—	32	13	67	—	—	—	—										
On Grass	3	3	.500	4.05	26	0	0	33.1	27	16	31	0	3	3	8										
On Turf	3	2	.600	1.48	47	0	0	61	54	18	63	0	3	2	16										
Home	3	1	.750	1.20	40	0	0	52.2	44	14	57	0	3	1	14										
Road	3	4	.429	3.89	33	0	0	41.2	37	20	37	0	3	4	10										
Division Rivals																									
vs. CAL	0	1	.000	3.60	7	0	0	5	4	4	4	0	0	1	4										
vs. CHI	0	1	.000	5.87	6	0	0	7.2	10	4	4	0	0	1	1										
vs. MIN	0	1	.000	3.52	6	0	0	7.2	11	3	5	0	0	1	2										
vs. OAK	0	1	.000	3.86	5	0	0	4.2	4	1	8	0	0	1	0										
vs. SEA	0	0	—	1.17	6	0	0	7.2	7	0	9	0	0	0	3										
vs. TEX	2	0	1.000	0.00	6	0	0	10	5	5	10	0	2	0	1										
1987	CIN N	2	2	.500	6.52	14	1	0	19.1	25	9	13	0	2	1	0	2	0	0	.000	1	3	0	0	0.3	1.000
1988	KC A	7	2	.778	3.45	45	0	0	62.2	54	30	47	0	7	2	1	0	0	0	—	3	10	1	0	0.3	.929
1989		7	3	.700	1.37	63	0	0	92	66	25	94	0	7	3	18	0	0	0	—	11	6	2	1	0.3	.895
1990		6	5	.545	2.39	73	0	0	94.1	81	34	94	0	6	5	24	0	0	0	—	3	13	0	0	0.2	1.000
4 yrs.		22	12	.647	2.58	195	1	0	268.1	226	98	248	0	22	11	43	2	0	0	.000	18	32	3	1	0.3	.943

Brad Moore

MOORE, BRADLEY ALAN
B. June 21, 1964, Loveland, Colo.
BR TR 6′ 1″ 185 lbs.

Year	Team	W	L	%	ERA	G	GS	CG	IP	H	BB	SO	ShO	W	L	SV	AB	H	HR	BA	PO	A	E	DP	TC/G	FA
1988	PHI N	0	0	—	0.00	5	0	0	5.2	4	4	2	0	0	0	0	0	0	0	—	2	1	0	0	0.6	1.000
1990		0	0	—	3.38	3	0	0	2.2	4	2	1	0	0	0	0	0	0	0	—	0	1	0	0	0.3	1.000
2 yrs.		0	0	—	1.08	8	0	0	8.1	8	6	3	0	0	0	0	0	0	0	—	2	2	0	0	0.5	1.000

Mike Moore

MOORE, MICHAEL WAYNE
B. Nov. 26, 1959, Carnegie, Okla.
BR TR 6′ 4″ 205 lbs.

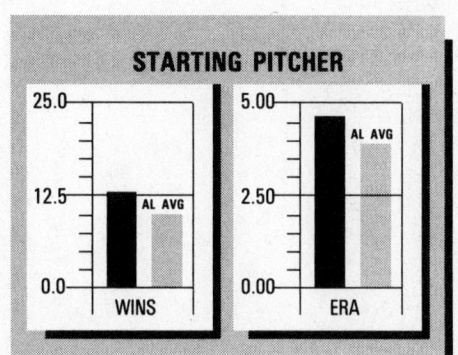

STARTING PITCHER

	W	L	%	ERA	G	GS	CG	IP	H	BB	SO	ShO
April	1	1	.500	6.08	4	4	0	23.2	22	12	6	0
May	3	3	.500	3.24	6	6	1	41.2	33	10	12	0
June	1	3	.250	4.81	6	6	1	33.2	44	11	15	0
July	4	3	.571	3.69	7	7	0	46.1	44	25	14	0
Aug	2	2	.500	4.20	5	5	1	30	27	14	13	0
Sept/Oct	2	3	.400	7.88	5	5	0	24	34	12	13	0
Day	5	6	.455	4.73	14	14	0	83.2	90	35	32	0
Night	8	9	.471	4.59	19	19	3	115.2	114	49	41	0
vs. Left	—	—	—	—	—	—	—	—	105	47	34	—
vs. Right	—	—	—	—	—	—	—	—	99	37	39	—

Year	Team	W	L	%	ERA	G	GS	CG	IP	H	BB	SO	ShO	RELIEF PITCHING W	L	SV	BATTING AB	H	HR	BA	PO	A	E	DP	TC/G	FA

Mike Moore *Continued*

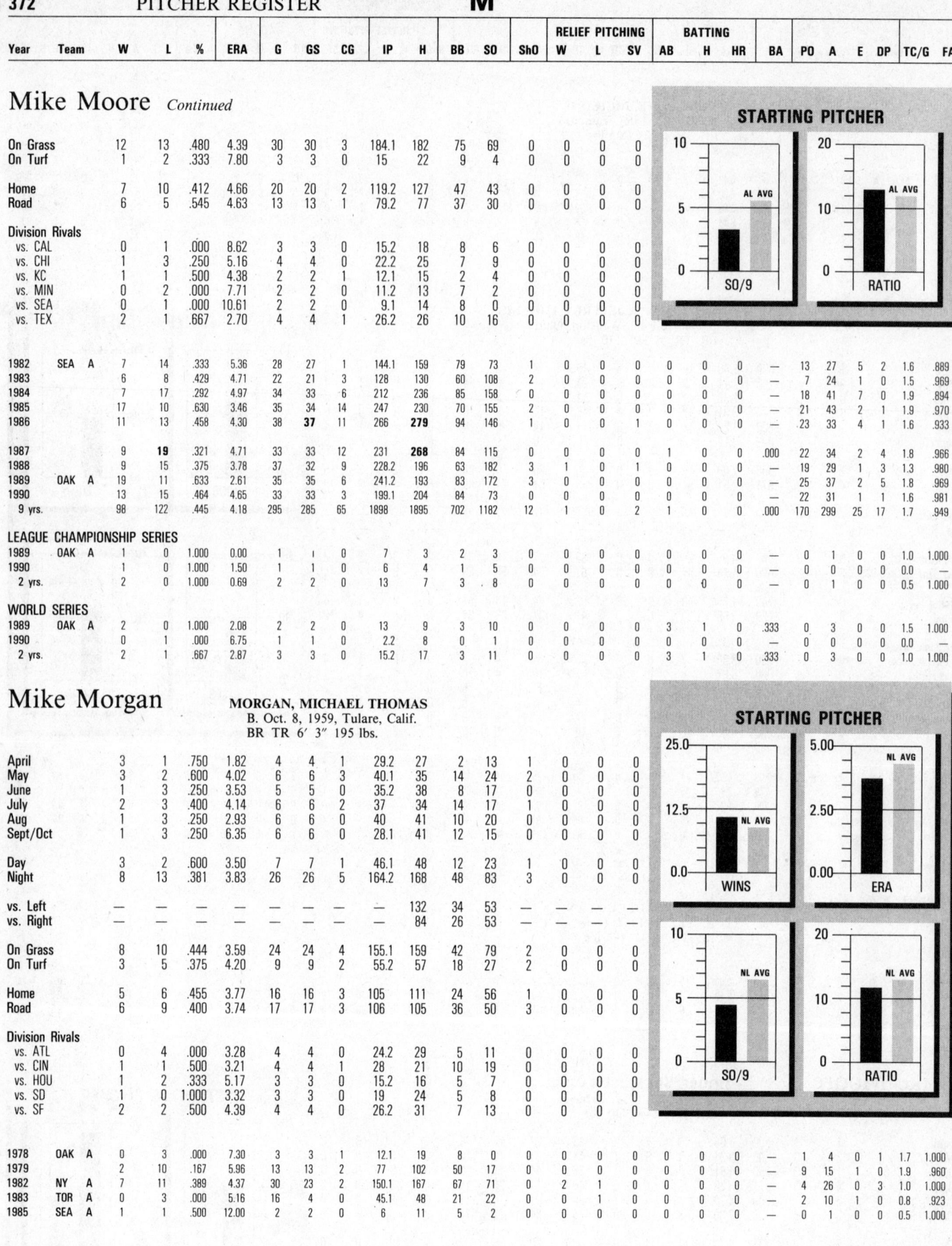

STARTING PITCHER

Year	Team	W	L	%	ERA	G	GS	CG	IP	H	BB	SO	ShO	W	L	SV	AB	H	HR	BA	PO	A	E	DP	TC/G	FA
On Grass		12	13	.480	4.39	30	30	3	184.1	182	75	69	0	0	0	0										
On Turf		1	2	.333	7.80	3	3	0	15	22	9	4	0	0	0	0										
Home		7	10	.412	4.66	20	20	2	119.2	127	47	43	0	0	0	0										
Road		6	5	.545	4.63	13	13	1	79.2	77	37	30	0	0	0	0										
Division Rivals																										
vs. CAL		0	1	.000	8.62	3	3	0	15.2	18	8	6	0	0	0	0										
vs. CHI		1	3	.250	5.16	4	4	0	22.2	25	7	9	0	0	0	0										
vs. KC		1	1	.500	4.38	2	2	1	12.1	15	2	4	0	0	0	0										
vs. MIN		0	2	.000	7.71	2	2	0	11.2	13	7	2	0	0	0	0										
vs. SEA		0	1	.000	10.61	2	2	0	9.1	14	8	0	0	0	0	0										
vs. TEX		2	1	.667	2.70	4	4	1	26.2	26	10	16	0	0	0	0										
1982	SEA A	7	14	.333	5.36	28	27	1	144.1	159	79	73	1	0	0	0	0	0	0	—	13	27	5	2	1.6	.889
1983		6	8	.429	4.71	22	21	3	128	130	60	108	2	0	0	0	0	0	0	—	7	24	1	0	1.5	.969
1984		7	17	.292	4.97	34	33	6	212	236	85	158	0	0	0	0	0	0	0	—	18	41	7	0	1.9	.894
1985		17	10	.630	3.46	35	34	14	247	230	70	155	2	0	0	0	0	0	0	—	21	43	2	1	1.9	.970
1986		11	13	.458	4.30	38	**37**	11	266	**279**	94	146	1	0	0	1	0	0	0	.23	23	33	4	1	1.6	.933
1987		9	**19**	.321	4.71	33	33	12	231	**268**	84	115	0	0	0	0	1	0	0	.000	22	34	2	4	1.8	.966
1988		9	15	.375	3.78	37	32	9	228.2	196	63	182	3	1	0	1	0	0	0	—	19	29	1	3	1.3	.980
1989	OAK A	19	11	.633	2.61	35	35	6	241.2	193	83	172	3	0	0	0	0	0	0	—	25	37	2	5	1.8	.969
1990		13	15	.464	4.65	33	33	3	199.1	204	84	73	0	0	0	0	0	0	0	—	22	31	1	1	1.6	.981
9 yrs.		98	122	.445	4.18	295	285	65	1898	1895	702	1182	12	1	0	2	1	0	0	.000	170	299	25	17	1.7	.949

LEAGUE CHAMPIONSHIP SERIES

Year	Team	W	L	%	ERA	G	GS	CG	IP	H	BB	SO	ShO	W	L	SV	AB	H	HR	BA	PO	A	E	DP	TC/G	FA
1989	OAK A	1	0	1.000	0.00	1	1	0	7	3	2	3	0	0	0	0	0	0	0	—	0	1	0	0	1.0	1.000
1990		1	0	1.000	1.50	1	1	0	6	4	1	5	0	0	0	0	0	0	0	—	0	0	0	0	0.0	—
2 yrs.		2	0	1.000	0.69	2	2	0	13	7	3	8	0	0	0	0	0	0	0	—	0	1	0	0	0.5	1.000

WORLD SERIES

Year	Team	W	L	%	ERA	G	GS	CG	IP	H	BB	SO	ShO	W	L	SV	AB	H	HR	BA	PO	A	E	DP	TC/G	FA
1989	OAK A	2	0	1.000	2.08	2	2	0	13	9	3	10	0	0	0	0	3	1	0	.333	0	3	0	0	1.5	1.000
1990		0	1	.000	6.75	1	1	0	2.2	8	0	1	0	0	0	0	0	0	0	—	0	0	0	0	0.0	—
2 yrs.		2	1	.667	2.87	3	3	0	15.2	17	3	11	0	0	0	0	3	1	0	.333	0	3	0	0	1.0	1.000

Mike Morgan

MORGAN, MICHAEL THOMAS
B. Oct. 8, 1959, Tulare, Calif.
BR TR 6′ 3″ 195 lbs.

STARTING PITCHER

Year	Team	W	L	%	ERA	G	GS	CG	IP	H	BB	SO	ShO	W	L	SV	AB	H	HR	BA	PO	A	E	DP	TC/G	FA
April		3	1	.750	1.82	4	4	1	29.2	27	2	13	1	0	0	0										
May		3	2	.600	4.02	6	6	3	40.1	35	14	24	2	0	0	0										
June		1	3	.250	3.53	5	5	0	35.2	38	8	17	0	0	0	0										
July		2	3	.400	4.14	6	6	2	37	34	14	17	1	0	0	0										
Aug		1	3	.250	2.93	6	6	0	40	41	10	20	0	0	0	0										
Sept/Oct		1	3	.250	6.35	6	6	0	28.1	41	12	15	0	0	0	0										
Day		3	2	.600	3.50	7	7	1	46.1	48	12	23	1	0	0	0										
Night		8	13	.381	3.83	26	26	5	164.2	168	48	83	3	0	0	0										
vs. Left		—	—	—	—	—	—	—	—	132	34	53	—	—	—	—										
vs. Right		—	—	—	—	—	—	—	—	84	26	53	—	—	—	—										
On Grass		8	10	.444	3.59	24	24	4	155.1	159	42	79	2	0	0	0										
On Turf		3	5	.375	4.20	9	9	2	55.2	57	18	27	2	0	0	0										
Home		5	6	.455	3.77	16	16	3	105	111	24	56	1	0	0	0										
Road		6	9	.400	3.74	17	17	3	106	105	36	50	3	0	0	0										
Division Rivals																										
vs. ATL		0	4	.000	3.28	4	4	0	24.2	29	5	11	0	0	0	0										
vs. CIN		1	1	.500	3.21	4	4	1	28	21	10	19	0	0	0	0										
vs. HOU		1	2	.333	5.17	3	3	0	15.2	16	5	7	0	0	0	0										
vs. SD		1	0	1.000	3.32	3	3	0	19	24	5	8	0	0	0	0										
vs. SF		2	2	.500	4.39	4	4	0	26.2	31	7	13	0	0	0	0										
1978	OAK A	0	3	.000	7.30	3	3	1	12.1	19	8	0	0	0	0	0	0	0	0	—	1	4	0	1	1.7	1.000
1979		2	10	.167	5.96	13	13	2	77	102	50	17	0	0	0	0	0	0	0	—	9	15	1	0	1.9	.960
1982	NY A	7	11	.389	4.37	30	23	2	150.1	167	67	71	0	2	1	0	0	0	0	—	4	26	0	3	1.0	1.000
1983	TOR A	0	3	.000	5.16	16	4	0	45.1	48	21	22	0	0	1	0	0	0	0	—	2	10	1	0	0.8	.923
1985	SEA A	1	1	.500	12.00	2	2	0	6	11	5	2	0	0	0	0	0	0	0	—	0	1	0	0	0.5	1.000

Year	Team		W	L	%	ERA	G	GS	CG	IP	H	BB	SO	ShO	RELIEF PITCHING			BATTING			BA	PO	A	E	DP	TC/G	FA
															W	L	SV	AB	H	HR							

Mike Morgan *Continued*

Year	Team		W	L	%	ERA	G	GS	CG	IP	H	BB	SO	ShO	W	L	SV	AB	H	HR	BA	PO	A	E	DP	TC/G	FA
1986			11	**17**	.393	4.53	37	33	9	216.1	243	86	116	1	0	0	1	0	0	0	—	14	27	2	5	1.2	.953
1987			12	17	.414	4.65	34	31	8	207	245	53	85	2	0	0	0	0	0	0	—	18	35	2	5	1.6	.964
1988	BAL	A	1	6	.143	5.43	22	10	2	71.1	70	23	29	0	1	0	1	0	0	0	—	9	9	0	1	0.8	1.000
1989	LA	N	8	11	.421	2.53	40	19	0	152.2	130	33	72	0	2	0	0	36	3	0	.083	20	41	2	2	1.6	.968
1990			11	15	.423	3.75	33	33	6	211	216	60	106	**4**	0	0	0	71	8	0	.113	25	39	1	3	2.0	.985
10 yrs.			53	94	.361	4.37	230	171	30	1149.1	1251	406	520	7	5	2	2	107	11	0	.103	102	207	9	20	1.4	.972

Jack Morris

MORRIS, JOHN SCOTT
B. May 16, 1955, St. Paul, Minn.
BR TR 6′ 3″ 195 lbs.

			W	L	%	ERA	G	GS	CG	IP	H	BB	SO	ShO	W	L	SV	AB	H	HR	BA	PO	A	E	DP	TC/G	FA
April			2	2	.500	5.34	5	5	0	30.1	36	12	23	0	0	0	0										
May			0	5	.000	5.20	6	6	1	45	41	21	23	0	0	0	0										
June			4	2	.667	5.86	6	6	1	35.1	45	12	27	0	0	0	0										
July			2	4	.333	3.20	6	6	3	45	33	13	32	1	0	0	0										
Aug			3	2	.600	5.79	6	6	1	37.1	37	19	17	1	0	0	0										
Sept/Oct			4	3	.571	2.86	7	7	5	56.2	39	20	40	1	0	0	0										
Day			6	5	.545	3.95	12	12	2	82	77	32	50	1	0	0	0										
Night			9	13	.409	4.78	24	24	9	167.2	154	65	112	2	0	0	0										
vs. Left			—	—	—	—	—	—	—	—	125	58	70	—	—	—	—										
vs. Right			—	—	—	—	—	—	—	—	106	39	92	—	—	—	—										
On Grass			13	16	.448	4.14	31	31	10	219.2	198	86	144	3	0	0	0										
On Turf			2	2	.500	7.20	5	5	1	30	33	11	18	0	0	0	0										
Home			8	8	.500	4.06	16	16	3	113	109	30	71	2	0	0	0										
Road			7	10	.412	4.87	20	20	8	136.2	122	67	91	1	0	0	0										
Division Rivals																											
vs. BAL			1	1	.500	3.80	3	3	1	21.1	16	13	22	0	0	0	0										
vs. BOS			0	2	.000	1.15	2	2	1	15.2	11	5	8	0	0	0	0										
vs. CLE			2	1	.667	5.31	3	3	1	20.1	21	12	16	1	0	0	0										
vs. MIL			0	3	.000	7.59	3	3	2	21.1	20	11	6	0	0	0	0										
vs. NY			3	0	1.000	3.00	3	3	1	21	21	2	12	0	0	0	0										
vs. TOR			0	2	.000	9.26	2	2	0	11.2	17	6	5	0	0	0	0										
1977	DET	A	1	1	.500	3.72	7	6	1	46	38	23	28	0	0	0	0	0	0	0	—	2	8	0	0	1.4	1.000
1978			3	5	.375	4.33	28	7	0	106	107	49	48	0	3	3	0	0	0	0	—	5	15	2	3	0.8	.909
1979			17	7	.708	3.27	27	27	9	198	179	59	113	1	0	0	0	0	0	0	—	14	23	2	1	1.4	.949
1980			16	15	.516	4.18	36	36	11	250	252	87	112	2	0	0	0	0	0	0	—	31	43	2	2	2.1	.974
1981			**14**	7	.667	3.05	25	25	15	198	153	**78**	97	1	0	0	0	0	0	0	—	16	28	0	2	1.8	1.000
1982			17	16	.515	4.06	37	37	17	266.1	247	96	135	3	0	0	0	0	0	0	—	26	31	1	2	1.6	.983
1983			20	13	.606	3.34	37	37	20	**293.2**	257	83	**232**	1	0	0	0	0	0	0	—	29	26	2	2	1.5	.965
1984			19	11	.633	3.65	35	35	9	241.1	224	87	149	1	0	0	0	0	0	0	—	29	32	3	4	1.8	.953
1985			16	11	.593	3.33	35	35	13	257	212	110	191	4	0	0	0	0	0	0	—	25	25	4	2	1.5	.926
1986			21	8	.724	3.27	35	35	15	267	229	82	223	**6**	0	0	0	0	0	0	—	27	27	2	4	1.6	.964
1987			18	11	.621	3.38	34	34	13	266	227	93	208	0	0	0	0	1	0	0	.000	31	18	0	1	1.4	1.000
1988			15	13	.536	3.94	34	34	10	235	225	83	168	2	0	0	0	0	0	0	—	31	21	1	1	1.6	.981
1989			6	14	.300	4.86	24	24	10	170.1	189	59	115	0	0	0	0	0	0	0	—	17	22	1	3	1.7	.975
1990			15	18	.455	4.51	36	**36**	**11**	249.2	231	97	162	3	0	0	0	0	0	0	—	38	14	2	2	1.5	.963
14 yrs.			198	150	.569	3.73	430	408	154	3044.1	2770	1086	1981	24	3	3	0	1	0	0	.000	321	333	22	31	1.6	.967

LEAGUE CHAMPIONSHIP SERIES

Year	Team		W	L	%	ERA	G	GS	CG	IP	H	BB	SO	ShO	W	L	SV	AB	H	HR	BA	PO	A	E	DP	TC/G	FA
1984	DET	A	1	0	1.000	1.29	1	1	0	7	5	1	4	0	0	0	0	0	0	0	—	1	1	0	0	2.0	1.000
1987			0	1	.000	6.75	1	1	1	8	6	3	7	0	0	0	0	0	0	0	—	0	0	0	0	0.0	—
2 yrs.			1	1	.500	4.20	2	2	1	15	11	4	11	0	0	0	0	0	0	0	—	1	1	0	0	1.0	1.000

WORLD SERIES

Year	Team		W	L	%	ERA	G	GS	CG	IP	H	BB	SO	ShO	W	L	SV	AB	H	HR	BA	PO	A	E	DP	TC/G	FA
1984	DET	A	2	0	1.000	2.00	2	2	2	18	13	3	13	0	0	0	0	0	0	0	—	5	1	0	0	3.0	1.000

John Moses

MOSES, JOHN WILLIAM
B. Aug. 9, 1957, Los Angeles, Calif.
BB TL 5′ 10″ 165 lbs.

Year	Team		W	L	%	ERA	G	GS	CG	IP	H	BB	SO	ShO	W	L	SV	AB	H	HR	BA	PO	A	E	DP	TC/G	FA
1989	MIN	A	0	0	—	0.00	1	0	0	1	0	1	0	0	0	0	0	242	68	1	.281	0	0	0	0	0.0	—
1990			0	0	—	13.50	2	0	0	2	5	2	0	0	0	0	0	172	38	1	.221	0	0	0	0	0.0	—
2 yrs.			0	0	—	9.00	3	0	0	3	5	3	0	0	0	0	0	*				0	0	0	0	0.0	—

STARTING PITCHER
WINS — AL AVG
ERA — AL AVG
SO/9 — AL AVG
RATIO — AL AVG

Year	Team	W	L	%	ERA	G	GS	CG	IP	H	BB	SO	ShO	RELIEF PITCHING W	L	SV	BATTING AB	H	HR	BA	PO	A	E	DP	TC/G	FA

Jamie Moyer

MOYER, JAMIE
B. Nov. 11, 1962, Sellersville, Pa.
BL TL 6′ 170 lbs.

Period	W	L	%	ERA	G	GS	CG	IP	H	BB	SO	ShO	W	L	SV	AB	H	HR	BA	PO	A	E	DP	TC/G	FA
April	0	3	.000	4.08	5	3	0	17.2	21	6	5	0	0	0	1	0									
May	0	0	—	3.55	6	0	0	12.2	10	6	11	0	0	0	0	0									
June	0	0	—	5.11	8	0	0	12.1	19	2	10	0	0	0	0	0									
July	0	0	—	6.63	6	1	0	19	22	10	14	0	0	0	0	0									
Aug	1	3	.250	4.00	6	6	1	36	35	13	14	0	0	0	0	0									
Sept/Oct	1	0	1.000	5.79	2	0	0	4.2	8	2	4	0	0	1	0										
Day	0	0	—	13.97	4	1	0	9.2	17	8	7	0	0	0	0	0									
Night	2	6	.250	3.69	29	9	1	92.2	98	31	51	0	0	1	1	0									
vs. Left	—	—	—	—	—	—	—	—	18	4	9	—	—	—	—										
vs. Right	—	—	—	—	—	—	—	—	97	35	49	—	—	—	—										
On Grass	2	5	.286	4.30	26	7	1	81.2	88	29	50	0	0	1	1	0									
On Turf	0	1	.000	6.10	7	3	0	20.2	27	10	8	0	0	0	0	0									
Home	2	2	.500	3.77	17	5	1	59.2	61	22	44	0	0	1	0	0									
Road	0	4	.000	5.91	16	5	0	42.2	54	17	14	0	0	0	1	0									
Division Rivals																									
vs. CAL	0	0	—	2.70	2	0	0	3.1	6	1	3	0	0	0	0										
vs. CHI	0	2	.000	1.80	4	2	0	15	16	3	7	0	0	0	1										
vs. KC	0	0	—	2.03	3	1	0	13.1	10	6	9	0	0	0	0										
vs. MIN	0	0	—	9.00	3	1	0	9	16	1	4	0	0	0	0										
vs. OAK	0	1	.000	8.59	4	1	0	7.1	12	3	5	0	0	0	0										
vs. SEA	0	0	—	2.45	2	0	0	3.2	3	1	5	0	0	0	0										
1986	CHI N	7	4	.636	5.05	16	16	1	87.1	107	42	45	1	0	0	0	22	2	0	.091	2	22	0	1.5	1.000
1987		12	15	.444	5.10	35	33	1	201	210	97	147	0	1	0	0	61	14	0	.230	15	37	4	3	1.6	.929
1988		9	15	.375	3.48	34	30	3	202	212	55	121	1	1	0	0	60	5	0	.083	11	45	1	3	1.7	.982
1989	TEX A	4	9	.308	4.86	15	15	1	76	84	33	44	0	0	0	0	0	0	0	—	5	14	0	2	1.3	1.000
1990		2	6	.250	4.66	33	10	1	102.1	115	39	58	0	1	1	0	0	0	0	—	6	14	0	2	0.6	1.000
5 yrs.		34	49	.410	4.51	133	104	7	668.2	728	266	415	2	3	1	0	143	21	0	.147	39	132	5	10	1.3	.972

Terry Mulholland

MULHOLLAND, TERENCE JOHN
B. Mar. 9, 1963, Uniontown, Pa.
BR TL 6′ 3″ 200 lbs.

Period	W	L	%	ERA	G	GS	CG	IP	H	BB	SO	ShO	W	L	SV	AB	H	HR	BA	PO	A	E	DP	TC/G	FA
April	1	0	1.000	4.66	4	4	0	19.1	24	6	5	0	0	0	0										
May	2	2	.500	2.77	6	4	0	26	27	8	7	0	0	0	0										
June	0	1	.000	10.24	4	2	0	9.2	14	4	3	0	0	0	0										
July	2	1	.667	2.05	6	3	2	30.2	29	4	11	0	0	0	0										
Aug	2	4	.333	3.75	7	7	2	48	48	11	31	1	0	0	0										
Sept/Oct	2	2	.500	2.11	6	6	2	47	30	9	18	0	0	0	0										
Day	2	5	.286	4.22	8	7	1	42.2	43	12	20	0	0	0	0										
Night	7	5	.583	3.07	25	19	5	138	129	30	55	1	0	0	0										
vs. Left	—	—	—	—	—	—	—	—	28	3	13	—	—	—	—										
vs. Right	—	—	—	—	—	—	—	—	144	39	62	—	—	—	—										
On Grass	4	4	.500	3.72	10	9	2	55.2	59	17	24	0	0	0	0										
On Turf	5	6	.455	3.17	23	17	4	125	113	25	51	1	0	0	0										
Home	3	4	.429	2.66	12	9	2	71	59	13	33	1	0	0	0										
Road	6	6	.500	3.78	21	17	4	109.2	113	29	42	0	0	0	0										
Division Rivals																									
vs. CHI	2	1	.667	6.06	3	3	0	16.1	18	3	9	0	0	0	0										
vs. MON	1	1	.500	3.38	3	3	1	21.1	19	5	5	0	0	0	0										
vs. NY	0	1	.000	4.50	1	1	0	6	6	5	2	0	0	0	0										
vs. PIT	1	1	.500	4.91	3	3	1	22	28	4	4	0	0	0	0										
vs. STL	1	1	.500	4.35	6	5	1	31	28	4	15	0	0	0	0										
1986	SF N	1	7	.125	4.94	15	10	0	54.2	51	35	27	0	0	0	0	19	1	0	.053	1	9	3	0	0.9	.769
1988		2	1	.667	3.72	9	6	2	46	50	7	18	1	0	0	0	14	0	0	.000	7	7	0	0	1.6	1.000
1989	2 teams				SF N (5G 0 - 0)				PHI N (20G 4 - 7)																	
"	total	4	7	.364	4.92	25	18	2	115.1	137	36	66	1	0	0	0	36	2	0	.056	2	25	4	1	1.2	.871
1990	PHI N	9	10	.474	3.34	33	26	6	180.2	172	42	75	1	0	0	0	62	6	0	.097	8	17	3	0	0.8	.893
4 yrs.		16	25	.390	4.06	82	60	10	396.2	410	120	186	3	0	0	0	131	9	0	.069	18	58	10	1	1.0	.884

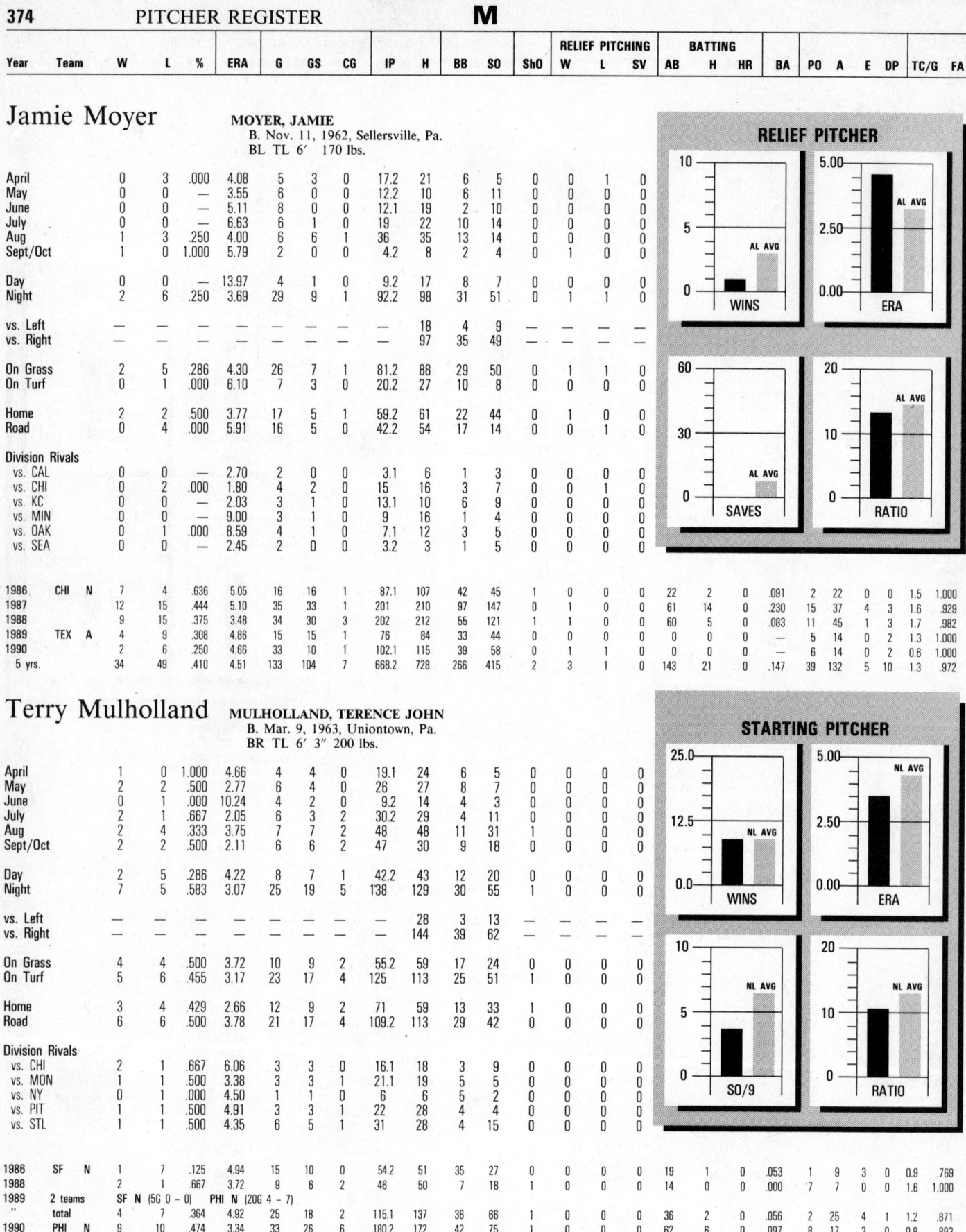

Year	Team	W	L	%	ERA	G	GS	CG	IP	H	BB	SO	ShO	W	L	SV	AB	H	HR	BA	PO	A	E	DP	TC/G	FA

Mike Munoz

MUNOZ, MICHAEL ANTHONY
B. July 12, 1965, Baldwin Park, Calif.
BL TL 6' 2" 190 lbs.

Year	Team	W	L	%	ERA	G	GS	CG	IP	H	BB	SO	ShO	W	L	SV	AB	H	HR	BA	PO	A	E	DP	TC/G	FA
1989	LA N	0	0	—	16.88	3	0	0	2.2	5	2	3	0	0	0	0	0	0	0	—	1	1	0	0	0.7	1.000
1990		0	1	.000	3.18	8	0	0	5.2	6	3	2	0	0	1	0	1	0	0	.000	0	0	0	0	0.0	—
2 yrs.		0	1	.000	7.56	11	0	0	8.1	11	5	5	0	0	1	0	1	0	0	.000	1	1	0	0	0.2	1.000

Rob Murphy

MURPHY, ROBERT ALBERT, JR.
B. May 26, 1960, Miami, Fla.
BL TL 6' 2" 200 lbs.

RELIEF PITCHER

		W	L	%	ERA	G	GS	CG	IP	H	BB	SO	ShO	W	L	SV	AB	H	HR	BA	PO	A	E	DP	TC/G	FA
April		0	1	.000	3.86	11	0	0	16.1	18	5	19	0	0	1	0										
May		0	1	.000	6.55	13	0	0	11	16	6	7	0	0	1	1										
June		0	2	.000	6.75	16	0	0	10.2	16	4	14	0	0	2	3										
July		0	2	.000	9.95	10	0	0	6.1	14	5	6	0	0	2	1										
Aug		0	0	—	7.36	9	0	0	7.1	12	9	6	0	0	0	2										
Sept/Oct		0	0	—	6.75	9	0	0	5.1	9	3	2	0	0	0	0										
Day		0	2	.000	4.30	17	0	0	14.2	18	8	12	0	0	2	2										
Night		0	4	.000	7.02	51	0	0	42.1	67	24	42	0	0	4	5										
vs. Left		—	—	—	—	—	—	—	—	20	12	19	—	—	—	—										
vs. Right		—	—	—	—	—	—	—	—	65	20	35	—	—	—	—										
On Grass		0	4	.000	6.26	58	0	0	46	72	26	47	0	0	4	5										
On Turf		0	2	.000	6.55	10	0	0	11	13	6	7	0	0	2	2										
Home		0	2	.000	5.10	33	0	0	30	41	11	33	0	0	2	2										
Road		0	4	.000	7.67	35	0	0	27	44	21	21	0	0	4	5										
Division Rivals																										
vs. BAL		0	0	—	1.93	6	0	0	4.2	5	3	4	0	0	0	2										
vs. CLE		0	1	.000	12.00	4	0	0	3	9	3	3	0	0	1	0										
vs. DET		0	0	—	0.00	5	0	0	5	2	4	4	0	0	0	2										
vs. MIL		0	1	.000	18.00	5	0	0	3	9	2	3	0	0	1	0										
vs. NY		0	1	.000	13.50	5	0	0	3.1	7	2	3	0	0	1	0										
vs. TOR		0	0	—	0.00	4	0	0	3.1	2	1	6	0	0	0	1										
1985	CIN N	0	0	—	6.00	2	0	0	3	2	2	1	0	0	0	0	0	0	0	—	0	0	0	0	0.0	—
1986		6	0	1.000	0.72	34	0	0	50.1	26	21	36	0	6	0	1	3	0	0	.000	1	9	0	0	0.3	1.000
1987		8	5	.615	3.04	87	0	0	100.2	91	32	99	0	8	5	3	5	1	0	.200	7	14	0	0	0.2	1.000
1988		0	6	.000	3.08	**76**	0	0	84.2	69	38	74	0	0	6	3	0	0	0	—	4	14	0	2	0.2	1.000
1989	BOS A	5	7	.417	2.74	74	0	0	105	97	41	107	0	5	7	9	0	0	0	—	7	15	0	1	0.3	1.000
1990		0	6	.000	6.32	68	0	0	57	85	32	54	0	0	6	7	0	0	0	—	4	7	1	2	0.2	.917
6 yrs.		19	24	.442	3.17	341	0	0	400.2	370	166	371	0	19	24	23	8	1	0	.125	23	59	1	5	0.2	.988

LEAGUE CHAMPIONSHIP SERIES

Year	Team	W	L	%	ERA	G	GS	CG	IP	H	BB	SO	ShO	W	L	SV	AB	H	HR	BA	PO	A	E	DP	TC/G	FA
1990	BOS A	0	0	—	13.50	1	0	0	0.2	2	1	0	0	0	0	0	0	0	0	—	0	0	0	0	0.0	—

Jeff Musselman

MUSSELMAN, JEFFREY JOSEPH
B. June 21, 1963, Doylestown, Pa.
BL TL 6' 180 lbs.

RELIEF PITCHER

		W	L	%	ERA	G	GS	CG	IP	H	BB	SO	ShO	W	L	SV	AB	H	HR	BA	PO	A	E	DP	TC/G	FA
April		0	0	—	2.16	7	0	0	8.1	6	2	2	0	0	0	0										
May		0	0	—	3.48	9	0	0	10.1	13	3	7	0	0	0	0										
June		0	2	.000	9.53	10	0	0	11.1	17	5	4	0	0	2	0										
July		—	—	—	—	0	0	0	0	0	0	0	—	0	0	0										
Aug		—	—	—	—	0	0	0	0	0	0	0	—	0	0	0										
Sept/Oct		0	0	—	9.00	2	0	0	2	4	1	1	0	0	0	0										
Day		0	1	.000	8.31	11	0	0	13	18	7	4	0	0	1	0										
Night		0	1	.000	3.79	17	0	0	19	22	4	10	0	0	1	0										
vs. Left		—	—	—	—	—	—	—	—	11	4	5	—	—	—	—										
vs. Right		—	—	—	—	—	—	—	—	29	7	9	—	—	—	—										

Year	Team	W	L	%	ERA	G	GS	CG	IP	H	BB	SO	ShO	W	L	SV	AB	H	HR	BA	PO	A	E	DP	TC/G	FA
														RELIEF PITCHING			BATTING									

Jeff Musselman *Continued*

Year	Team	W	L	%	ERA	G	GS	CG	IP	H	BB	SO	ShO	W	L	SV	AB	H	HR	BA	PO	A	E	DP	TC/G	FA
On Grass		0	2	.000	5.40	20	0	0	23.1	28	10	10	0	0	2	0					1	1	0		0.3	1.000
On Turf		0	0	—	6.23	8	0	0	8.2	12	1	4	0	0	0	0										
Home		0	2	.000	5.06	14	0	0	16	18	8	7	0	0	2	0										
Road		0	0	—	6.19	14	0	0	16	22	3	7	0	0	0	0										
Division Rivals																										
vs. CHI		0	0	—	19.29	2	0	0	2.1	7	1	1	0	0	0	0										
vs. MON		0	0	—	0.00	4	0	0	3	1	1	1	0	0	0	0										
vs. PHI		0	0	—	4.50	3	0	0	4	4	1	1	0	0	0	0										
vs. PIT		0	1	.000	5.63	6	0	0	8	10	4	3	0	0	1	0										
vs. STL		0	0	—	0.00	1	0	0	0.2	1	0	1	0	0	0	0										
1986	TOR A	0	0	—	10.13	6	0	0	5.1	8	5	4	0	0	0	0	0	0	0	—	1	1	0	0	0.3	1.000
1987		12	5	.706	4.15	68	1	0	89	75	54	54	0	**12**	5	3	0	0	0	—	9	15	0	2	0.4	1.000
1988		8	5	.615	3.18	15	15	0	85	80	30	39	0	0	0	0	0	0	0	—	3	8	1	0	0.8	.917
1989	2 teams				TOR A (5G 0 – 1)				NY N (20G 3 – 2)																	
"	total	3	3	.500	5.30	25	3	0	37.1	46	23	14	0	3	2	0	0	0	0	—	6	12	2	0	0.8	.900
1990	NY N	0	2	.000	5.63	28	0	0	32	40	11	14	0	0	2	0	1	0	0	.000	5	5	0	0	0.4	1.000
5 yrs.		23	15	.605	4.31	142	19	0	248.2	249	123	125	0	15	9	3	1	0	0	.000	24	41	3	3	0.5	.956

Randy Myers

MYERS, RANDALL KIRK
B. Sept. 19, 1962, Vancouver, Wash.
BL TL 6′ 1″ 190 lbs.

Year	Team	W	L	%	ERA	G	GS	CG	IP	H	BB	SO	ShO	W	L	SV	AB	H	HR	BA	PO	A	E	DP	TC/G	FA
April		1	0	1.000	4.66	8	0	0	9.2	10	7	14	0	1	0	4										
May		0	0	—	0.64	12	0	0	14	5	2	20	0	0	0	6										
June		2	2	.500	2.33	12	0	0	19.1	12	11	18	0	2	2	5										
July		0	1	.000	0.66	12	0	0	13.2	9	4	14	0	0	1	6										
Aug		0	1	.000	2.35	11	0	0	15.1	14	4	12	0	0	1	6										
Sept/Oct		1	2	.333	2.45	11	0	0	14.2	9	10	20	0	1	2	4										
Day		0	2	.000	2.59	19	0	0	24.1	20	8	28	0	0	2	7										
Night		4	4	.500	1.88	47	0	0	62.1	39	30	70	0	4	4	24										
vs. Left		—	—	—	—	—	—	—	—	13	12	32	—	—	—	—										
vs. Right		—	—	—	—	—	—	—	—	46	26	66	—	—	—	—										
On Grass		1	2	.333	2.96	20	0	0	27.1	21	12	37	0	1	2	10										
On Turf		3	4	.429	1.67	46	0	0	59.1	38	26	61	0	3	4	21										
Home		2	2	.500	0.62	33	0	0	43.1	30	17	43	0	2	2	15										
Road		2	4	.333	3.53	33	0	0	43.1	29	21	55	0	2	4	16										
Division Rivals																										
vs. ATL		1	0	1.000	2.79	8	0	0	9.2	8	7	10	0	1	0	2										
vs. HOU		2	2	.500	4.22	9	0	0	10.2	5	7	14	0	2	2	4										
vs. LA		0	1	.000	0.71	7	0	0	12.2	4	4	17	0	0	1	4										
vs. SD		0	1	.000	1.35	5	0	0	6.2	6	4	6	0	0	1	2										
vs. SF		1	1	.500	2.89	8	0	0	9.1	10	3	11	0	1	1	3										
1985	NY N	0	0	—	0.00	1	0	0	2	0	1	2	0	0	0	0	0	0	0	—	0	1	0	0	1.0	1.000
1986		0	0	—	4.22	10	0	0	10.2	11	9	13	0	0	0	0	0	0	0	—	0	2	0	0	0.2	1.000
1987		3	6	.333	3.96	54	0	0	75	61	30	92	0	3	6	6	7	2	0	.286	5	9	1	0	0.3	.933
1988		7	3	.700	1.72	55	0	0	68	45	17	69	0	7	3	26	4	1	0	.250	4	3	0	1	0.1	1.000
1989		7	4	.636	2.35	65	0	0	84.1	62	40	88	0	7	4	24	5	0	0	.000	3	11	0	0	0.2	1.000
1990	CIN N	4	6	.400	2.08	66	0	0	86.2	59	38	98	0	4	6	31	4	1	0	.250	1	12	0	0	0.2	1.000
6 yrs.		21	19	.525	2.56	251	0	0	326.2	238	135	362	0	21	19	87	20	4	0	.200	13	38	1	1	0.2	.981

LEAGUE CHAMPIONSHIP SERIES

Year	Team	W	L	%	ERA	G	GS	CG	IP	H	BB	SO	ShO	W	L	SV	AB	H	HR	BA	PO	A	E	DP	TC/G	FA
1988	NY N	2	0	1.000	0.00	3	0	0	4.2	1	2	0	0	2	0	0	0	0	0	—	0	1	0	0	0.3	1.000
1990	CIN N	0	0	—	0.00	4	0	0	5.2	2	3	7	0	0	0	3	0	0	0	—	0	0	0	0	0.0	—
2 yrs.		2	0	1.000	0.00	7	0	0	10.1	3	5	7	0	2	0	3	0	0	0	—	0	1	0	0	0.1	1.000

WORLD SERIES

Year	Team	W	L	%	ERA	G	GS	CG	IP	H	BB	SO	ShO	W	L	SV	AB	H	HR	BA	PO	A	E	DP	TC/G	FA
1990	CIN N	0	0	—	0.00	3	0	0	3	2	0	3	0	0	0	1	0	0	0	—	0	0	0	0	0.0	—

Chris Nabholz

NABHOLZ, CHRISTOPHER WILLIAM
B. Jan. 5, 1967, Harrisburg, Pa.
BL TL 6′ 5″ 210 lbs.

Year	Team	W	L	%	ERA	G	GS	CG	IP	H	BB	SO	ShO	W	L	SV	AB	H	HR	BA	PO	A	E	DP	TC/G	FA
1990	MON N	6	2	.750	2.83	11	11	1	70	43	32	53	1	0	0	0	21	0	0	.000	3	10	1	0	1.3	.929

Year	Team		W	L	%	ERA	G	GS	CG	IP	H	BB	SO	ShO	RELIEF PITCHING			BATTING			BA	PO	A	E	DP	TC/G	FA
															W	L	SV	AB	H	HR							

Charles Nagy

NAGY, CHARLES HARRISON
B. May 5, 1967, Bridgeport, Conn.
BL TR 6' 3" 200 lbs.

Year	Team		W	L	%	ERA	G	GS	CG	IP	H	BB	SO	ShO	W	L	SV	AB	H	HR	BA	PO	A	E	DP	TC/G	FA
1990	CLE	A	2	4	.333	5.91	9	8	0	45.2	58	21	26	0	0	0	0	0	0	0	—	3	8	1	2	1.3	.917

Jaime Navarro

NAVARRO, JAIME
Born Jaime Navarro y Cintron.
Son of Julio Navarro.
B. Mar. 27, 1967, Bayamon, Puerto Rico
BR TR 6' 4" 210 lbs.

	W	L	%	ERA	G	GS	CG	IP	H	BB	SO	ShO	W	L	SV	AB	H	HR	BA	PO	A	E	DP	TC/G	FA
April	0	0	—	5.21	4	4	0	19	27	8	8	0	0	0	0										
May	1	1	.500	8.82	4	4	0	16.1	30	4	6	0	0	0	0										
June	1	1	.500	5.79	2	2	0	9.1	8	9	4	0	0	0	0										
July	0	0	—	1.59	9	0	0	22.2	17	4	14	0	0	0	1										
Aug	3	3	.500	5.06	7	6	0	37.1	45	8	26	0	0	0	0										
Sept/Oct	3	2	.600	3.22	6	6	1	44.2	49	8	17	0	0	0	0										
Day	2	2	.500	4.09	12	6	1	44	50	14	26	0	0	0	0										
Night	6	5	.545	4.61	20	16	2	105.1	126	27	49	0	0	0	1										
vs. Left	—	—	—	—	—	—	—	—	96	25	37	—	—	—	—										
vs. Right	—	—	—	—	—	—	—	—	80	16	38	—	—	—	—										
On Grass	5	5	.500	4.00	26	16	2	117	132	34	53	0	0	0	1										
On Turf	3	2	.600	6.12	6	6	1	32.1	44	7	22	0	0	0	0										
Home	4	4	.500	4.09	16	10	1	72.2	79	26	33	0	0	0	1										
Road	4	3	.571	4.81	16	12	2	76.2	97	15	42	0	0	0	0										
Division Rivals																									
vs. BAL	2	0	1.000	1.88	2	2	0	14.1	10	6	7	0	0	0	0										
vs. BOS	0	0	—	2.63	3	2	0	13.2	12	7	6	0	0	0	0										
vs. CLE	0	1	.000	6.75	2	1	0	6.2	11	2	2	0	0	0	0										
vs. DET	1	0	1.000	6.61	3	3	0	16.1	24	3	2	0	0	0	0										
vs. NY	2	0	1.000	1.00	2	2	2	18	16	1	8	0	0	0	0										
vs. TOR	1	2	.333	6.35	3	3	1	17	21	7	11	0	0	0	0										

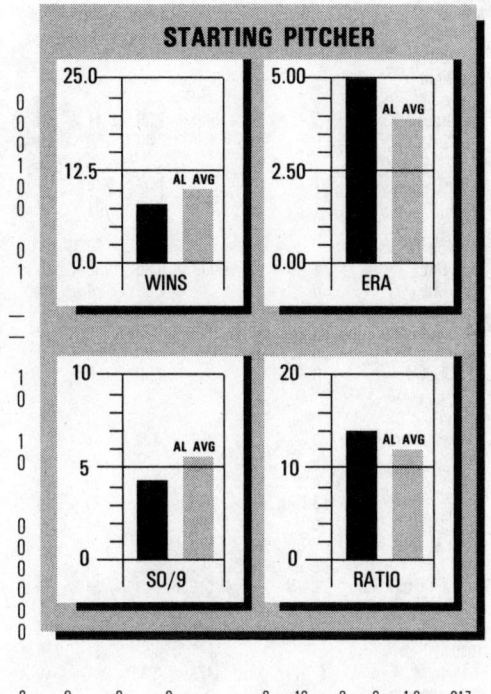

STARTING PITCHER — WINS (AL AVG), ERA (AL AVG), SO/9 (AL AVG), RATIO (AL AVG)

Year	Team		W	L	%	ERA	G	GS	CG	IP	H	BB	SO	ShO	W	L	SV	AB	H	HR	BA	PO	A	E	DP	TC/G	FA
1989	MIL	A	7	8	.467	3.12	19	17	1	109.2	119	32	56	0	1	0	0	0	0	0	—	6	16	2	0	1.3	.917
1990			8	7	.533	4.46	32	22	3	149.1	176	41	75	0	0	0	1	0	0	0	—	10	19	1	2	0.9	.967
2 yrs.			15	15	.500	3.89	51	39	4	259	295	73	131	0	1	0	1	0	0	0	—	16	35	3	2	1.1	.944

Jim Neidlinger

NEIDLINGER, JAMES LLEWELLYN
B. Sept. 24, 1964, Vallejo, Calif.
BB TR 6' 4" 180 lbs.

	W	L	%	ERA	G	GS	CG	IP	H	BB	SO	ShO	W	L	SV	AB	H	HR	BA	PO	A	E	DP	TC/G	FA
April	—	—	—	—	0	—	—	0	0	0	0	—	0	0	0										
May	—	—	—	—	0	—	—	0	0	0	0	—	0	0	0										
June	—	—	—	—	0	—	—	0	0	0	0	—	0	0	0										
July	—	—	—	—	0	—	—	0	0	0	0	—	0	0	0										
Aug	3	1	.750	2.45	6	6	0	40.1	36	8	30	0	0	0	0										
Sept/Oct	2	2	.500	4.28	6	6	0	33.2	31	7	16	0	0	0	0										
Day	1	2	.333	6.63	4	4	0	19	23	5	9	0	0	0	0										
Night	4	1	.800	2.13	8	8	0	55	44	10	37	0	0	0	0										
vs. Left	—	—	—	—	—	—	—	—	47	11	21	—	—	—	—										
vs. Right	—	—	—	—	—	—	—	—	20	4	25	—	—	—	—										
On Grass	4	2	.667	3.46	9	9	0	54.2	53	8	35	0	0	0	0										
On Turf	1	1	.500	2.79	3	3	0	19.1	14	7	11	0	0	0	0										
Home	2	1	.667	3.34	5	5	0	29.2	30	5	20	0	0	0	0										
Road	3	2	.600	3.25	7	7	0	44.1	37	10	26	0	0	0	0										
Division Rivals																									
vs. ATL	2	0	1.000	1.93	2	2	0	14	11	0	5	0	0	0	0										
vs. CIN	1	1	.500	0.00	2	2	0	15.2	6	2	9	0	0	0	0										
vs. HOU	—	—	—	—	0	0	0	0	0	0	0	—	0	0	0										
vs. SD	0	0	—	4.05	1	1	0	6.2	7	2	7	0	0	0	0										
vs. SF	0	2	.000	5.40	3	3	0	13.1	17	3	7	0	0	0	0										

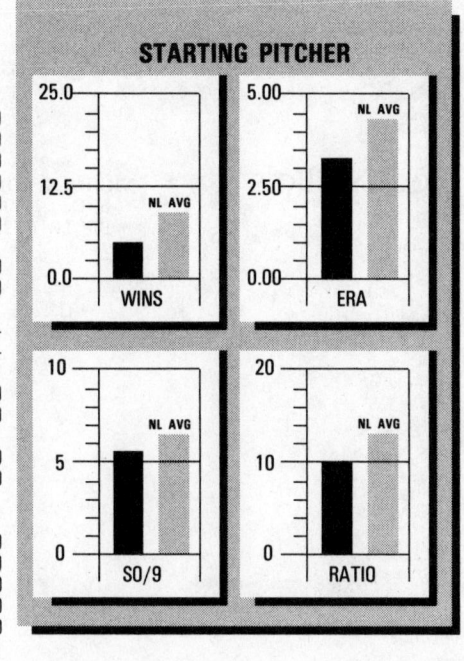

STARTING PITCHER — WINS (NL AVG), ERA (NL AVG), SO/9 (NL AVG), RATIO (NL AVG)

Year	Team		W	L	%	ERA	G	GS	CG	IP	H	BB	SO	ShO	W	L	SV	AB	H	HR	BA	PO	A	E	DP	TC/G	FA
1990	LA	N	5	3	.625	3.28	12	12	0	74	67	15	46	0	0	0	0	25	3	0	.120	8	5	0	0	1.1	1.000

Year	Team	W	L	%	ERA	G	GS	CG	IP	H	BB	SO	ShO	RELIEF PITCHING W	L	SV	BATTING AB	H	HR	BA	PO	A	E	DP	TC/G	FA

Gene Nelson

NELSON, WAYLAND EUGENE
B. Dec. 3, 1960, Tampa, Fla.
BR TR 6′ 172 lbs.

Year	Team	W	L	%	ERA	G	GS	CG	IP	H	BB	SO	ShO	W	L	SV	AB	H	HR	BA	PO	A	E	DP	TC/G	FA
April		1	1	.500	0.87	7	0	0	10.1	9	2	5	0	1	1	1										
May		0	1	.000	1.98	8	0	0	13.2	6	3	9	0	0	1	2										
June		0	0	—	1.04	7	0	0	8.2	6	2	4	0	0	0	0										
July		1	0	1.000	1.84	9	0	0	14.2	16	3	6	0	1	0	1										
Aug		1	0	1.000	1.17	9	0	0	15.1	8	2	9	0	1	0	1										
Sept/Oct		0	1	.000	2.25	11	0	0	12	10	5	5	0	0	1	0										
Day		0	1	.000	1.74	14	0	0	20.2	9	6	15	0	0	1	2										
Night		3	2	.600	1.50	37	0	0	54	46	11	23	0	3	2	3										
vs. Left		—	—	—	—	—	—	—	—	26	5	17	—	—	—	—										
vs. Right		—	—	—	—	—	—	—	—	29	12	21	—	—	—	—										
On Grass		3	3	.500	1.36	41	0	0	59.2	41	13	35	0	3	3	5										
On Turf		0	0	—	2.40	10	0	0	15	14	4	3	0	0	0	0										
Home		1	2	.333	1.91	20	0	0	28.1	18	8	17	0	1	2	3										
Road		2	1	.667	1.36	31	0	0	46.1	37	9	21	0	2	1	2										
Division Rivals																										
vs. CAL		1	0	1.000	0.96	6	0	0	9.1	10	1	4	0	1	0	1										
vs. CHI		0	0	—	1.59	4	0	0	5.2	3	2	3	0	0	0	0										
vs. KC		0	0	—	0.00	2	0	0	3.1	2	0	0	0	0	0	0										
vs. MIN		0	1	.000	4.50	4	0	0	8	10	4	2	0	0	1	0										
vs. SEA		0	0	—	1.80	5	0	0	5	5	0	0	0	0	0	0										
vs. TEX		0	0	—	0.00	6	0	0	7.1	4	1	4	0	0	0	0										
1981	NY A	3	1	.750	4.85	8	7	0	39	40	23	16	0	0	0	0	0	0	0	—	3	6	1	0	1.3	.900
1982	SEA A	6	9	.400	4.62	22	19	2	122.2	133	60	71	1	0	1	0	0	0	0	—	10	20	1	2	1.4	.968
1983		0	3	.000	7.88	10	5	1	32	38	21	11	0	0	0	0	0	0	0	—	5	6	1	0	1.2	.917
1984	CHI A	3	5	.375	4.46	20	9	2	74.2	72	17	36	0	2	0	1	0	0	0	—	11	8	0	1	1.0	1.000
1985		10	10	.500	4.26	46	18	1	145.2	144	67	101	0	4	3	2	1	0	0	.000	10	19	1	0	0.7	.967
1986		6	6	.500	3.85	54	1	0	114.2	118	41	70	0	6	5	6	0	0	0	—	8	17	0	3	0.5	1.000
1987	OAK A	6	5	.545	3.93	54	6	0	123.2	120	35	94	0	5	2	3	0	0	0	—	8	13	2	0	0.4	.913
1988		9	6	.600	3.06	54	1	0	111.2	93	38	67	0	**9**	5	3	0	0	0	—	4	11	0	1	0.3	1.000
1989		3	5	.375	3.26	50	0	0	80	60	30	70	0	3	5	3	0	0	0	—	6	3	0	0	0.2	1.000
1990		3	3	.500	1.57	51	0	0	74.2	55	17	38	0	3	3	5	0	0	0	—	4	8	1	0	0.3	.923
10 yrs.		49	53	.480	3.93	369	66	6	918.2	873	349	574	1	32	24	23	1	0	0	.000	69	111	7	7	0.5	.963

LEAGUE CHAMPIONSHIP SERIES

Year	Team	W	L	%	ERA	G	GS	CG	IP	H	BB	SO	ShO	W	L	SV	AB	H	HR	BA	PO	A	E	DP	TC/G	FA
1988	OAK A	2	0	1.000	0.00	2	0	0	4.2	5	1	0	0	2	0	0	0	0	0	—	0	0	0	0	0.0	—
1989		0	0	—	0.00	1	0	0	1.1	1	0	2	0	0	0	0	0	0	0	—	0	0	0	0	0.0	—
1990		0	0	—	0.00	1	0	0	1.2	3	0	0	0	0	0	0	0	0	0	—	0	0	0	0	0.0	—
3 yrs.		2	0	1.000	0.00	4	0	0	7.2	9	1	2	0	2	0	0	0	0	0	—	0	0	0	0	0.0	—

WORLD SERIES

Year	Team	W	L	%	ERA	G	GS	CG	IP	H	BB	SO	ShO	W	L	SV	AB	H	HR	BA	PO	A	E	DP	TC/G	FA
1988	OAK A	0	0	—	1.42	3	0	0	6.1	4	3	3	0	0	0	0	0	0	0	—	1	2	0	0	1.0	1.000
1989		0	0	—	54.00	2	0	0	1	4	2	1	0	0	0	0	0	0	0	—	0	0	0	0	0.0	—
1990		0	0	—	0.00	2	0	0	5	3	2	0	0	0	0	0	0	0	0	—	0	0	0	0	0.0	—
3 yrs.		0	0	—	5.11	7	0	0	12.1	11	7	4	0	0	0	0	0	0	0	—	1	2	0	0	0.4	1.000

Rod Nichols

NICHOLS, RODNEY LEA
B. Dec. 29, 1964, Burlington, Iowa
BR TR 6′ 2″ 190 lbs.

Year	Team	W	L	%	ERA	G	GS	CG	IP	H	BB	SO	ShO	W	L	SV	AB	H	HR	BA	PO	A	E	DP	TC/G	FA
1988	CLE A	1	7	.125	5.06	11	10	3	69.1	73	23	31	0	0	1	0	0	0	0	—	5	9	1	0	1.4	.933
1989		4	6	.400	4.40	15	11	0	71.2	81	24	42	0	0	2	0	0	0	0	—	4	8	0	2	0.8	1.000
1990		0	3	.000	7.88	4	2	0	16	24	6	3	0	0	1	0	0	0	0	—	0	4	0	0	1.0	1.000
3 yrs.		5	16	.238	5.04	30	23	3	157	178	53	76	0	0	4	0	0	0	0	—	9	21	1	2	1.0	.968

RELIEF PITCHER

WINS — AL AVG

ERA — AL AVG

SAVES — AL AVG

RATIO — AL AVG

Year	Team	W	L	%	ERA	G	GS	CG	IP	H	BB	SO	ShO	RELIEF PITCHING W	L	SV	BATTING AB	H	HR	BA	PO	A	E	DP	TC/G	FA

Tom Niedenfuer

NIEDENFUER, THOMAS EDWARD
B. Aug. 13, 1959, St. Louis Park, Minn.
BR TR 6′ 5″ 225 lbs.

Year	Team	W	L	%	ERA	G	GS	CG	IP	H	BB	SO	ShO	RP W	RP L	SV	AB	H	HR	BA	PO	A	E	DP	TC/G	FA
April		0	0	—	0.00	2	0	0	2	0	1	1	0	0	0	0										
May		0	0	—	2.70	13	0	0	16.2	15	6	10	0	0	0	0										
June		0	3	.000	3.18	14	0	0	17	13	6	9	0	0	3	1										
July		0	1	.000	2.08	11	0	0	13	14	5	6	0	0	1	0										
Aug		0	2	.000	5.68	8	0	0	12.2	21	5	3	0	0	2	1										
Sept/Oct		0	0	—	7.36	4	0	0	3.2	3	2	3	0	0	0	0										
Day		0	3	.000	5.47	17	0	0	24.2	28	7	13	0	0	3	0										
Night		0	3	.000	2.23	35	0	0	40.1	38	18	19	0	0	3	2										
vs. Left		—	—	—	—	—	—	—	—	34	18	8	—	—	—	—										
vs. Right		—	—	—	—	—	—	—	—	32	7	24	—	—	—	—										
On Grass		0	2	.000	2.81	14	0	0	16	15	6	8	0	0	2	1										
On Turf		0	4	.000	3.67	38	0	0	49	51	19	24	0	0	4	1										
Home		0	4	.000	3.92	32	0	0	41.1	46	17	20	0	0	4	1										
Road		0	2	.000	2.66	20	0	0	23.2	20	8	12	0	0	2	1										
Division Rivals																										
vs. CHI		0	2	.000	2.92	8	0	0	12.1	16	1	4	0	0	2	0										
vs. MON		0	1	.000	3.00	4	0	0	6	2	2	5	0	0	1	1										
vs. NY		0	0	—	6.75	6	0	0	6.2	8	3	2	0	0	0	0										
vs. PHI		0	0	—	3.86	4	0	0	2.1	2	3	2	0	0	0	0										
vs. PIT		0	1	.000	54.00	1	0	0	0.1	3	0	0	0	0	1	0										
1981	LA N	3	1	.750	3.81	17	0	0	26	25	6	12	0	3	1	2	0	0	0	—	4	2	0	0	0.4	1.000
1982		3	4	.429	2.71	55	0	0	69.2	71	25	60	0	3	4	9	3	0	0	.000	1	7	0	0	0.1	1.000
1983		8	3	.727	1.90	66	0	0	94.2	55	29	66	0	8	3	11	4	0	0	.000	8	8	1	0	0.3	.941
1984		2	5	.286	2.47	33	0	0	47.1	39	23	45	0	2	5	11	3	0	0	.000	1	5	1	0	0.2	.857
1985		7	9	.438	2.71	64	0	0	106.1	86	24	102	0	7	9	19	9	1	0	.111	8	7	0	0	0.2	1.000
1986		6	6	.500	3.71	60	0	0	80	86	29	55	0	6	6	11	4	2	0	.500	9	10	1	1	0.3	.950
1987	2 teams	LA N (15G 1 - 0)			BAL A (45G 3 - 5)																					
"	total	4	5	.444	4.46	60	0	0	68.2	68	31	47	0	4	5	14	0	0	0	—	7	6	1	2	0.2	.929
1988	BAL A	3	4	.429	3.51	52	0	0	59	59	19	40	0	3	4	18	0	0	0	—	3	5	1	1	0.2	.889
1989	SEA A	0	3	.000	6.69	25	0	0	36.1	46	15	15	0	0	3	0	0	0	0	—	6	5	2	0	0.5	.846
1990	STL N	0	6	.000	3.46	52	0	0	65	66	25	32	0	0	6	2	3	0	0	.000	3	7	2	0	0.2	.833
10 yrs.		36	46	.439	3.29	484	0	0	653	601	226	474	0	36	46	97	26	3	0	.115	50	62	9	4	0.3	.926

DIVISIONAL PLAYOFF SERIES

Year	Team	W	L	%	ERA	G	GS	CG	IP	H	BB	SO	ShO	RP W	RP L	SV	AB	H	HR	BA	PO	A	E	DP	TC/G	FA
1981	LA N	0	0	—	0.00	1	0	0	0.1	1	1	1	0	0	0	0	0	0	0	—	0	0	0	0	0.0	—

LEAGUE CHAMPIONSHIP SERIES

Year	Team	W	L	%	ERA	G	GS	CG	IP	H	BB	SO	ShO	RP W	RP L	SV	AB	H	HR	BA	PO	A	E	DP	TC/G	FA
1981	LA N	0	0	—	0.00	1	0	0	0.1	2	0	0	0	0	0	0	0	0	0	—	0	1	0	0	1.0	1.000
1983		0	0	—	0.00	2	0	0	2	0	1	3	0	0	0	1	0	0	0	—	0	1	0	0	0.5	1.000
1985		0	2	.000	6.35	3	0	0	5.2	5	2	5	0	0	2	1	1	0	0	.000	2	0	0	0	0.7	1.000
3 yrs.		0	2	.000	4.50	6	0	0	8	7	3	8	0	0	2	2	1	0	0	.000	2	2	0	0	0.7	1.000

WORLD SERIES

Year	Team	W	L	%	ERA	G	GS	CG	IP	H	BB	SO	ShO	RP W	RP L	SV	AB	H	HR	BA	PO	A	E	DP	TC/G	FA
1981	LA N	0	0	—	0.00	2	0	0	5	3	1	0	0	0	0	0	0	0	0	—	0	0	0	0	0.0	—

RELIEF PITCHER — WINS (NL AVG), ERA (NL AVG), SAVES (NL AVG), RATIO (NL AVG)

Al Nipper

NIPPER, ALBERT SAMUEL
B. Apr. 2, 1959, San Diego, Calif.
BR TR 6′ 188 lbs.

Year	Team	W	L	%	ERA	G	GS	CG	IP	H	BB	SO	ShO	RP W	RP L	SV	AB	H	HR	BA	PO	A	E	DP	TC/G	FA
1983	BOS A	1	1	.500	2.25	3	2	1	16	17	7	5	0	0	0	0	0	0	0	—	1	2	0	0	1.0	1.000
1984		11	6	.647	3.89	29	24	6	182.2	183	52	84	0	0	0	0	0	0	0	—	28	31	1	0	2.1	.983
1985		9	12	.429	4.06	25	25	5	162	157	82	85	0	0	0	0	0	0	0	—	24	28	5	4	2.3	.912
1986		10	12	.455	5.38	26	26	3	159	186	47	79	0	0	0	0	0	0	0	—	28	28	4	2	2.2	.982
1987		11	12	.478	5.43	30	30	6	174	196	62	89	0	0	0	0	0	0	0	—	20	27	2	2	1.6	.959
1988	CHI N	2	4	.333	3.04	22	12	0	80	72	34	27	0	0	1	1	23	2	0	.087	4	7	1	1	0.5	.917
1990	CLE A	2	3	.400	6.75	9	5	0	24	35	19	12	0	0	0	0	0	0	0	—	1	1	0	1	0.2	1.000
7 yrs.		46	50	.479	4.52	144	124	21	797.2	846	303	381	0	0	1	1	23	2	0	.087	106	124	10	12	1.7	.958

WORLD SERIES

Year	Team	W	L	%	ERA	G	GS	CG	IP	H	BB	SO	ShO	RP W	RP L	SV	AB	H	HR	BA	PO	A	E	DP	TC/G	FA
1986	BOS A	0	1	.000	7.11	2	1	0	6.1	10	2	2	0	0	0	0	0	0	0	—	1	2	0	0	1.5	1.000

Year	Team	W	L	%	ERA	G	GS	CG	IP	H	BB	SO	ShO	W	L	SV	AB	H	HR	BA	PO	A	E	DP	TC/G	FA
														RELIEF PITCHING			**BATTING**									

Junior Noboa

NOBOA, MILCIADES ARTURO
Born Milciades Arturo Noboa y Diaz.
B. Nov. 10, 1964, Azua, Dominican Republic

Year	Team	W	L	%	ERA	G	GS	CG	IP	H	BB	SO	ShO	W	L	SV	AB	H	HR	BA	PO	A	E	DP	TC/G	FA
1990	MON N	0	0	—	0.00	1	0	0	0.2	0	1	0	0	0	0	0	0	*			0	0	0	0	0.0	—

Dickie Noles

NOLES, DICKIE RAY
B. Nov. 19, 1956, Charlotte, N. C.
BR TR 6′ 2″ 160 lbs.

Year	Team	W	L	%	ERA	G	GS	CG	IP	H	BB	SO	ShO	W	L	SV	AB	H	HR	BA	PO	A	E	DP	TC/G	FA
1979	PHI N	3	4	.429	3.80	14	14	0	90	80	38	42	0	0	0	0	30	3	0	.100	4	17	1	1	1.6	.955
1980		1	4	.200	3.89	48	3	0	81	80	42	57	0	0	4	6	13	4	0	.308	8	10	2	0	0.4	.900
1981		2	2	.500	4.19	13	8	0	58	57	23	34	0	0	0	0	19	2	0	.105	1	5	2	0	0.6	.750
1982	CHI N	10	13	.435	4.42	31	30	2	171	180	61	85	2	0	0	0	56	6	0	.107	14	26	2	0	1.4	.952
1983		5	10	.333	4.72	24	18	1	116.1	133	37	59	1	0	1	0	38	9	0	.237	11	14	1	0	1.1	.962
1984	2 teams				CHI N	(21G 2 - 2)			TEX A	(18G 2 - 3)																
''	total	4	5	.444	5.15	39	7	0	108.1	120	46	53	0	4	3	0	10	0	0	.000	2	6	1	1	0.2	.889
1985	TEX A	4	8	.333	5.06	28	13	0	110.1	129	33	59	0	1	1	1	0	0	0	—	13	16	3	2	1.1	.906
1986	CLE A	3	2	.600	5.10	32	0	0	54.2	56	30	32	0	3	2	0	0	0	0	—	5	8	0	0	0.4	1.000
1987	2 teams				CHI N	(41G 4 - 2)			DET A	(4G 0 - 0)																
''	total	4	2	.667	3.53	45	1	0	66.1	61	28	33	0	4	1	4	11	0	0	.000	6	15	0	0	0.5	1.000
1988	BAL A	0	2	.000	24.30	2	2	0	3.1	11	0	1	0	0	0	0	0	0	0	—	0	0	0	0	0.0	—
1990	PHI N	0	1	.000	27.00	1	0	0	0.1	2	0	0	0	0	1	0	0	0	0	—	0	0	0	0	0.0	—
11 yrs.		36	53	.404	4.56	277	96	3	859.2	909	338	455	3	12	13	11	177	24	0	.136	64	117	12	4	0.7	.938

DIVISIONAL PLAYOFF SERIES

Year	Team	W	L	%	ERA	G	GS	CG	IP	H	BB	SO	ShO	W	L	SV	AB	H	HR	BA	PO	A	E	DP	TC/G	FA
1981	PHI N	0	0	—	4.50	1	1	0	4	4	2	5	0	0	0	0	0	0	0	—	0	0	0	0	0.0	—

LEAGUE CHAMPIONSHIP SERIES

Year	Team	W	L	%	ERA	G	GS	CG	IP	H	BB	SO	ShO	W	L	SV	AB	H	HR	BA	PO	A	E	DP	TC/G	FA
1980	PHI N	0	0	—	0.00	2	0	0	2.2	1	3	0	0	0	0	0	0	0	0	—	1	2	0	1	1.5	1.000

WORLD SERIES

Year	Team	W	L	%	ERA	G	GS	CG	IP	H	BB	SO	ShO	W	L	SV	AB	H	HR	BA	PO	A	E	DP	TC/G	FA
1980	PHI N	0	0	—	1.93	1	0	0	4.2	5	2	6	0	0	0	0	0	0	0	—	1	0	0	0	1.0	1.000

Mike Norris

NORRIS, MICHAEL KELVIN
B. Mar. 19, 1955, San Francisco, Calif.
BR TR 6′ 2″ 175 lbs.

Year	Team	W	L	%	ERA	G	GS	CG	IP	H	BB	SO	ShO	W	L	SV	AB	H	HR	BA	PO	A	E	DP	TC/G	FA
1975	OAK A	1	0	1.000	0.00	4	3	1	16.2	6	8	5	1	0	0	0	0	0	0	—	1	4	1	0	1.5	.833
1976		4	5	.444	4.78	24	19	1	96	91	56	44	1	0	0	0	0	0	0	—	11	29	2	1	1.8	.952
1977		2	7	.222	4.79	16	12	1	77	77	31	35	1	0	0	0	1	0	0	.000	8	17	2	1	1.7	.926
1978		0	5	.000	5.51	14	5	1	49	46	35	36	0	0	0	0	0	0	0	—	5	5	2	0	0.9	.833
1979		5	8	.385	4.81	29	18	3	146	146	94	96	0	0	0	0	0	0	0	—	6	17	1	0	0.8	.958
1980		22	9	.710	2.54	33	33	24	284	215	83	180	1	0	0	0	0	0	0	—	25	52	3	3	2.4	.963
1981		12	9	.571	3.75	23	23	12	173	145	63	78	2	0	0	0	0	0	0	—	16	25	1	0	1.8	.976
1982		7	11	.389	4.76	28	28	7	166.1	154	84	83	1	0	0	0	0	0	0	—	22	21	2	1	1.6	.956
1983		4	5	.444	3.76	16	16	2	88.2	68	36	63	0	0	0	0	0	0	0	—	3	4	1	1	0.5	.875
1990		1	0	1.000	3.00	14	0	0	27	24	9	16	0	1	0	0	0	0	0	—	3	3	0	0	0.4	1.000
10 yrs.		58	59	.496	3.89	201	157	52	1123.2	972	499	636	7	1	0	0	1	0	0	.000	100	177	15	7	1.5	.949

DIVISIONAL PLAYOFF SERIES

Year	Team	W	L	%	ERA	G	GS	CG	IP	H	BB	SO	ShO	W	L	SV	AB	H	HR	BA	PO	A	E	DP	TC/G	FA
1981	OAK A	1	0	1.000	0.00	1	1	1	9	4	3	2	1	0	0	0	0	0	0	—	0	1	0	0	1.0	—

LEAGUE CHAMPIONSHIP SERIES

Year	Team	W	L	%	ERA	G	GS	CG	IP	H	BB	SO	ShO	W	L	SV	AB	H	HR	BA	PO	A	E	DP	TC/G	FA
1981	OAK A	0	1	.000	3.68	1	1	0	7.1	6	2	4	0	0	0	0	0	0	0	—	1	2	0	0	3.0	1.000

Randy Nosek

NOSEK, RANDALL WILLIAM
B. Jan. 8, 1967, Omaha, Neb.
BR TR 6′ 4″ 215 lbs.

Year	Team	W	L	%	ERA	G	GS	CG	IP	H	BB	SO	ShO	W	L	SV	AB	H	HR	BA	PO	A	E	DP	TC/G	FA
1989	DET A	0	2	.000	13.50	2	2	0	5.1	7	10	4	0	0	0	0	0	0	0	—	0	0	0	0	0.0	—
1990		1	1	.500	7.71	3	2	0	7	7	9	3	0	0	0	0	0	0	0	—	0	0	0	0	0.0	—
2 yrs.		1	3	.250	10.22	5	4	0	12.1	14	19	7	0	0	0	0	0	0	0	—	0	0	0	0	0.0	—

Rafael Novoa

NOVOA, RAFAEL ANGEL
B. Oct. 26, 1967, New York, N. Y.
BL TL 6′ 180 lbs.

Year	Team	W	L	%	ERA	G	GS	CG	IP	H	BB	SO	ShO	W	L	SV	AB	H	HR	BA	PO	A	E	DP	TC/G	FA
1990	SF N	0	1	.000	6.75	7	2	0	18.2	21	13	14	0	0	0	1	5	1	0	.200	0	0	0	0	0.0	—

Year	Team	W	L	%	ERA	G	GS	CG	IP	H	BB	SO	ShO	RELIEF PITCHING W	L	SV	BATTING AB	H	HR	BA	PO	A	E	DP	TC/G	FA

Edwin Nunez

NUNEZ, EDWIN
Born Edwin Nunez y Martinez.
B. May 27, 1963, Humacao, Puerto Rico
BR TR 6′ 5″ 207 lbs.

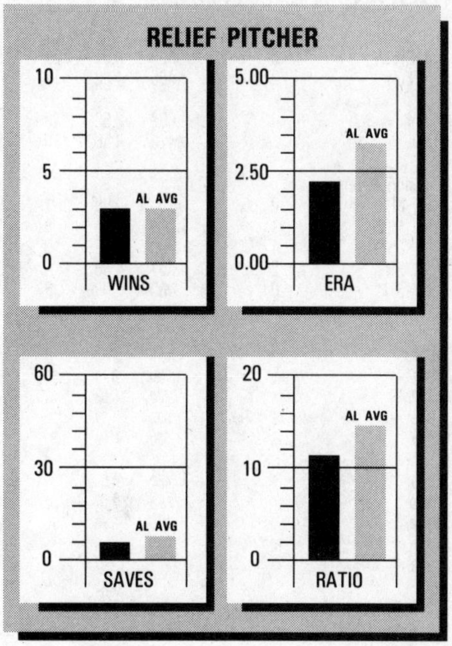

Split	W	L	%	ERA	G	GS	CG	IP	H	BB	SO	ShO	W	L	SV	AB	H	HR	BA	PO	A	E	DP	TC/G	FA
April	0	0	—	2.60	9	0	0	17.1	17	6	14	0	0	0	0										
May	1	0	1.000	2.25	7	0	0	12	6	4	7	0	1	0	0										
June	1	0	1.000	0.79	9	0	0	22.2	13	13	17	0	1	0	0										
July	1	0	1.000	2.25	3	0	0	4	3	0	2	0	1	0	0										
Aug	0	0	—	0.84	7	0	0	10.2	9	5	13	0	0	0	2										
Sept/Oct	0	1	.000	5.27	7	0	0	13.2	17	9	13	0	0	1	2										
Day	1	0	1.000	1.31	10	0	0	20.2	16	4	20	0	1	0	1										
Night	2	1	.667	2.56	32	0	0	59.2	49	33	46	0	2	1	5										
vs. Left	—	—	—	—	—	—	—	—	23	17	29	—	—	—	—										
vs. Right	—	—	—	—	—	—	—	—	42	20	37	—	—	—	—										
On Grass	2	1	.667	2.42	35	0	0	70.2	60	33	60	0	2	1	6										
On Turf	1	0	1.000	0.93	7	0	0	9.2	5	4	6	0	1	0	0										
Home	0	0	—	2.95	21	0	0	42.2	36	22	38	0	0	0	4										
Road	3	1	.750	1.43	21	0	0	37.2	29	15	28	0	3	1	2										
Division Rivals																									
vs. BAL	0	0	—	3.38	3	0	0	5.1	6	2	4	0	0	0	0										
vs. BOS	0	0	—	5.40	2	0	0	1.2	4	2	1	0	0	0	0										
vs. CLE	0	0	—	0.00	3	0	0	6.1	4	1	5	0	0	0	2										
vs. MIL	0	0	—	1.46	4	0	0	12.1	10	5	10	0	0	0	1										
vs. NY	0	1	.000	4.15	4	0	0	8.2	8	5	9	0	0	1	1										
vs. TOR	0	0	—	2.45	2	0	0	3.2	1	2	4	0	0	0	0										
1982 SEA A	1	2	.333	4.58	8	5	0	35.1	36	16	27	0	0	0	0	0	0	0	—	2	5	1	0	1.0	.875
1983	0	4	.000	4.38	14	5	0	37	40	22	35	0	0	0	0	0	0	0	—	0	6	0	1	0.4	1.000
1984	2	2	.500	3.18	37	0	0	68	55	21	57	0	2	2	7	0	0	0	—	4	6	1	0	0.3	.909
1985	7	3	.700	3.09	70	0	0	90.1	79	34	58	0	7	3	16	0	0	0	—	5	12	0	1	0.2	1.000
1986	1	2	.333	5.82	14	1	0	21.2	25	5	17	0	0	2	0	0	0	0	—	1	1	0	0	0.1	1.000
1987	3	4	.429	3.80	48	0	0	47.1	45	18	34	0	3	4	12	0	0	0	—	2	5	0	0	0.1	1.000
1988 2 teams			SEA A (14G 1 - 4)				NY N (10G 1 - 0)																		
" total	2	4	.333	6.85	24	3	0	43.1	66	17	27	0	2	1	0	0	0	0	—	6	8	2	1	0.7	.875
1989 DET A	3	4	.429	4.17	27	0	0	54	49	36	41	0	3	4	1	0	0	0	—	3	9	0	2	0.4	1.000
1990	3	1	.750	2.24	42	0	0	80.1	65	37	66	0	3	1	6	0	0	0	—	7	5	1	1	0.3	.923
9 yrs.	22	26	.458	3.83	284	14	0	477.1	460	206	362	0	20	17	42	0	0	0	—	30	57	5	6	0.3	.946

Jose Nunez

NUNEZ, JOSE
Born Jose Nunez y Jiminez.
B. Jan. 13, 1964, Jarabacoa, Dominican Republic
BR TR 6′ 3″ 175 lbs.

Year	Team	W	L	%	ERA	G	GS	CG	IP	H	BB	SO	ShO	W	L	SV	AB	H	HR	BA	PO	A	E	DP	TC/G	FA
1987 TOR A	5	2	.714	5.01	37	9	0	97	91	58	99	0	3	1	0	0	0	0	—	5	7	0	1	0.3	1.000
1988	0	1	.000	3.07	13	2	0	29.1	28	17	18	0	0	1	0	0	0	0	—	1	4	0	0	0.4	1.000
1989	0	0	—	2.53	6	1	0	10.2	8	2	14	0	0	0	0	0	0	0	—	1	1	0	1	0.3	.500
1990 CHI N	4	7	.364	6.53	21	10	0	60.2	61	34	40	0	1	2	0	11	0	0	.000	11	7	2	1	1.0	.900
4 yrs.	9	10	.474	5.05	77	22	0	197.2	188	111	171	0	4	4	0	11	0	0	.000	18	18	3	2	0.5	.923

Bob Ojeda

OJEDA, ROBERT MICHAEL (Bobby O.)
B. Dec. 17, 1957, Los Angeles, Calif.
BL TL 6′ 1″ 185 lbs.

Split	W	L	%	ERA	G	GS	CG	IP	H	BB	SO	ShO	W	L	SV	AB	H	HR	BA	PO	A	E	DP	TC/G	FA
April	0	0	—	1.64	5	0	0	11	7	4	9	0	0	0	0										
May	1	3	.250	2.60	6	3	0	27.2	18	5	15	0	0	1	0										
June	3	0	1.000	4.59	5	5	0	33.1	43	11	19	0	0	0	0										
July	0	2	.000	4.50	6	3	0	18	24	6	12	0	0	0	0										
Aug	3	0	1.000	2.89	11	0	0	18.2	15	8	5	0	3	0	0										
Sept/Oct	0	1	.000	5.79	5	1	0	9.1	16	6	2	0	0	0	0										
Day	2	0	1.000	2.51	11	3	0	32.1	27	10	13	0	0	0	0										
Night	5	6	.455	4.10	27	9	0	85.2	96	30	49	0	3	1	0										
vs. Left	—	—	—	—	—	—	—	—	19	7	20	—	—	—	—										
vs. Right	—	—	—	—	—	—	—	—	104	33	42	—	—	—	—										

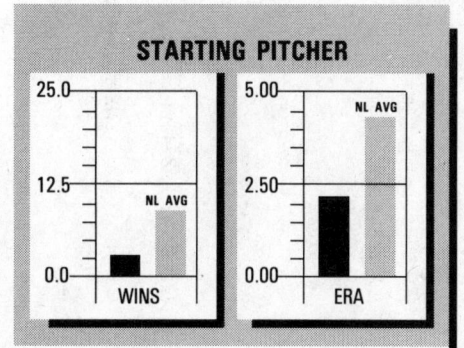

RELIEF PITCHER — WINS (AL AVG), ERA (AL AVG), SAVES (AL AVG), RATIO (AL AVG)

STARTING PITCHER — WINS (NL AVG), ERA (NL AVG)

Year	Team		W	L	%	ERA	G	GS	CG	IP	H	BB	SO	ShO	W	L	SV	AB	H	HR	BA	PO	A	E	DP	TC/G	FA
															RELIEF PITCHING			BATTING									

Bob Ojeda *Continued*

Year	Team		W	L	%	ERA	G	GS	CG	IP	H	BB	SO	ShO	W	L	SV	AB	H	HR	BA	PO	A	E	DP	TC/G	FA
On Grass			5	3	.625	3.51	27	8	0	82	84	25	46	0	2	1	0										
On Turf			2	3	.400	4.00	11	4	0	36	39	15	16	0	1	0	0										
Home			4	2	.667	3.50	20	6	0	64.1	67	20	38	0	2	0	0										
Road			3	4	.429	3.86	18	6	0	53.2	56	20	24	0	1	1	0										
Division Rivals																											
vs. CHI			0	0	—	0.00	1	0	0	2	1	1	0	0	0	0	0										
vs. MON			1	0	1.000	2.51	5	1	0	14.1	17	9	7	0	1	0	0										
vs. PHI			1	0	1.000	6.75	3	1	0	6.2	8	4	2	0	1	0	0										
vs. PIT			2	1	.667	4.50	4	3	0	20	25	6	6	0	0	0	0										
vs. STL			0	1	.000	6.08	5	1	0	13.1	19	5	9	0	0	0	0										
1980	BOS	A	1	1	.500	6.92	7	7	0	26	39	14	12	0	0	0	0	0	0	0	—	1	3	0	0	0.6	1.000
1981			6	2	.750	3.14	10	10	2	66	50	25	28	0	0	0	0	0	0	0	—	3	10	1	1	1.4	.929
1982			4	6	.400	5.63	22	14	0	78.1	95	29	52	0	1	0	0	0	0	0	—	2	7	1	0	0.5	.900
1983			12	7	.632	4.04	29	28	5	173.2	173	73	94	0	0	0	0	0	0	0	—	11	23	1	2	1.2	.971
1984			12	12	.500	3.99	33	32	8	216.2	211	96	137	**5**	0	0	0	0	0	0	—	10	32	2	3	1.3	.955
1985			9	11	.450	4.00	39	22	5	157.2	166	48	102	0	2	1	1	0	0	0	—	13	23	3	0	1.0	.923
1986	NY	N	18	5	**.783**	2.57	32	30	7	217.1	185	52	148	2	1	0	0	71	8	0	.113	9	37	1	3	1.5	.979
1987			3	5	.375	3.88	10	7	0	46.1	45	10	21	0	0	1	0	14	1	0	.071	5	6	0	2	1.1	1.000
1988			10	13	.435	2.88	29	29	5	190.1	158	33	133	5	0	0	0	61	10	0	.164	13	36	2	5	1.8	.961
1989			13	11	.542	3.47	31	31	5	192	179	78	95	2	0	0	0	66	7	0	.106	16	36	1	3	1.7	.981
1990			7	6	.538	3.66	38	12	0	118	123	40	62	0	3	1	0	30	4	0	.133	8	31	2	1	1.1	.951
11 yrs.			95	79	.546	3.65	280	222	37	1482.1	1424	498	884	14	7	3	1	242	30	0	.124	91	244	14	20	1.2	.960
LEAGUE CHAMPIONSHIP SERIES																											
1986	NY	N	1	0	1.000	2.57	2	2	1	14	15	4	6	0	0	0	0	5	0	0	.000	2	4	0	0	3.0	1.000
WORLD SERIES																											
1986	NY	N	1	0	1.000	2.08	2	2	0	13	13	5	9	0	0	0	0	2	0	0	.000	0	2	0	0	1.0	1.000

Steve Olin

OLIN, STEVEN ROBERT
B. Oct. 4, 1965, Portland, Ore.
BR TR 6′ 3″ 185 lbs.

Year	Team		W	L	%	ERA	G	GS	CG	IP	H	BB	SO	ShO	W	L	SV	AB	H	HR	BA	PO	A	E	DP	TC/G	FA
April			0	1	.000	2.25	5	0	0	8	10	1	9	0	0	1	0										
May			1	1	.500	3.94	10	0	0	16	15	3	7	0	1	1	0										
June			0	0	—	8.31	4	0	0	4.1	8	2	3	0	0	0	0										
July			0	0	—	3.55	7	0	0	12.2	12	4	10	0	0	0	0										
Aug			1	2	.333	4.37	11	0	0	22.2	25	8	16	0	1	2	0										
Sept/Oct			2	0	1.000	1.88	13	1	0	28.2	26	8	19	0	1	0	1										
Day			1	1	.500	6.00	16	0	0	27	40	8	30	0	1	1	0										
Night			3	3	.500	2.34	34	1	0	65.1	56	18	34	0	2	3	1										
vs. Left			—	—	—	—	—	—	—	—	42	11	19	—	—	—	—										
vs. Right			—	—	—	—	—	—	—	—	54	15	45	—	—	—	—										
On Grass			3	2	.600	3.51	41	1	0	74.1	76	22	55	0	2	2	0										
On Turf			1	2	.333	3.00	9	0	0	18	20	4	9	0	1	2	1										
Home			1	0	1.000	5.50	22	1	0	36	45	16	25	0	0	0	0										
Road			3	4	.429	2.08	28	0	0	56.1	51	10	39	0	3	4	1										
Division Rivals																											
vs. BAL			1	0	1.000	0.00	5	0	0	11.2	7	4	11	0	1	0	0										
vs. BOS			0	0	—	4.26	5	0	0	6.1	11	6	3	0	0	0	0										
vs. DET			0	0	—	7.36	3	0	0	3.2	4	1	5	0	0	0	0										
vs. MIL			1	1	.500	2.45	2	1	0	11	11	2	5	0	0	1	0										
vs. NY			0	1	.000	5.91	6	0	0	10.2	9	1	15	0	0	1	0										
vs. TOR			0	0	—	0.00	5	0	0	6.2	8	1	1	0	0	0	0										
1989	CLE	A	1	4	.200	3.75	25	0	0	36	35	14	24	0	1	4	1	0	0	0	—	2	5	0	0	0.3	1.000
1990			4	4	.500	3.41	50	1	0	92.1	96	26	64	0	3	4	1	0	0	0	—	3	24	3	1	0.6	.900
2 yrs.			5	8	.385	3.51	75	1	0	128.1	131	40	88	0	4	8	2	0	0	0	—	5	29	3	1	0.5	.919

STARTING PITCHER

SO/9 (NL AVG)

RATIO (NL AVG)

RELIEF PITCHER

WINS (AL AVG)

ERA (AL AVG)

SAVES (AL AVG)

RATIO (AL AVG)

Year	Team	W	L	%	ERA	G	GS	CG	IP	H	BB	SO	ShO	RELIEF PITCHING W	L	SV	BATTING AB	H	HR	BA	PO	A	E	DP	TC/G	FA

Omar Olivares

OLIVARES, OMAR
Born Omar Olivares y Palqu. Son of Ed Olivares.
B. July 6, 1967, Mayaguez, Puerto Rico
BR TR 6′ 185 lbs.

Year	Team	W	L	%	ERA	G	GS	CG	IP	H	BB	SO	ShO	W	L	SV	AB	H	HR	BA	PO	A	E	DP	TC/G	FA
1990	STL N	1	1	.500	2.92	9	6	0	49.1	45	17	20	0	0	0	0	17	3	1	.176	7	8	0	0	1.7	1.000

Francisco Oliveras

OLIVERAS, FRANCISCO JAVIER
Born Francisco Javier Oliveras y Noa.
B. Jan. 31, 1963, Santuree, Puerto Rico
BR TR 5′ 10″ 170 lbs.

	W	L	%	ERA	G	GS	CG	IP	H	BB	SO	ShO	W	L	SV	AB	H	HR	BA	PO	A	E	DP	TC/G	FA
April	—	—	—	—	0	—	—	0	0	0	0	—	0	0	0										
May	0	0	—	0.00	1	0	0	1.1	0	0	1	0	0	0	0										
June	0	1	.000	3.55	5	2	0	12.2	12	7	8	0	0	0	0										
July	0	1	.000	20.25	2	0	0	1.1	3	0	1	0	0	1	0										
Aug	1	0	1.000	2.53	13	0	0	21.1	22	6	17	0	1	0	0										
Sept/Oct	1	0	1.000	1.45	12	0	0	18.2	10	8	14	0	1	0	2										
Day	0	1	.000	5.14	12	1	0	21	21	10	17	0	0	1	2										
Night	2	1	.667	1.31	21	1	0	34.1	26	11	24	0	2	0	0										
vs. Left	—	—	—	—	—	—	—	—	26	14	19	—	—	—	—										
vs. Right	—	—	—	—	—	—	—	—	21	7	22	—	—	—	—										
On Grass	2	2	.500	3.35	26	2	0	43	39	17	29	0	2	1	2										
On Turf	0	0	—	0.73	7	0	0	12.1	8	4	12	0	0	0	0										
Home	2	2	.500	3.41	21	1	0	34.1	30	12	21	0	2	1	2										
Road	0	0	—	1.71	12	1	0	21	17	9	20	0	0	0	0										
Division Rivals																									
vs. ATL	0	0	—	2.00	5	0	0	9	6	2	8	0	0	0	2										
vs. CIN	0	0	—	1.59	3	0	0	5.2	3	2	5	0	0	0	0										
vs. HOU	0	0	—	0.00	6	0	0	6.1	2	4	5	0	0	0	0										
vs. LA	1	0	1.000	0.00	3	0	0	3.2	4	1	3	0	1	0	0										
vs. SD	0	1	.000	3.21	4	2	0	14	12	6	9	0	0	0	0										
1989	MIN A	3	4	.429	4.53	12	8	1	55.2	64	15	24	0	0	1	0	0	0	0	—	0	6	1	2	0.6	.857
1990	SF N	2	2	.500	2.77	33	2	0	55.1	47	21	41	0	2	1	2	5	0	0	.000	1	5	0	1	0.2	1.000
2 yrs.		5	6	.455	3.65	45	10	1	111	111	36	65	0	2	2	2	5	0	0	.000	1	11	1	3	0.3	.923

Gregg Olson

OLSON, GREGGORY WILLIAM
B. Oct. 11, 1966, Scribner, Neb.
BR TR 6′ 4″ 210 lbs.

	W	L	%	ERA	G	GS	CG	IP	H	BB	SO	ShO	W	L	SV	AB	H	HR	BA	PO	A	E	DP	TC/G	FA
April	1	0	1.000	0.00	7	0	0	12.1	5	3	7	0	1	0	4										
May	1	0	1.000	0.60	9	0	0	15	6	6	19	0	1	0	5										
June	2	2	.500	2.84	12	0	0	12.2	12	4	12	0	2	2	6										
July	1	1	.500	0.68	13	0	0	13.1	8	8	17	0	1	1	9										
Aug	0	1	.000	8.38	10	0	0	9.2	11	7	8	0	0	1	5										
Sept/Oct	1	1	.500	3.97	13	0	0	11.1	15	3	11	0	1	1	8										
Day	1	1	.500	1.57	17	0	0	23	10	5	16	0	1	1	15										
Night	5	4	.556	2.81	47	0	0	51.1	47	26	58	0	5	4	22										
vs. Left	—	—	—	—	—	—	—	—	29	19	34	—	—	—	—										
vs. Right	—	—	—	—	—	—	—	—	28	12	40	—	—	—	—										
On Grass	6	3	.667	2.37	52	0	0	60.2	43	25	65	0	6	3	30										
On Turf	0	2	.000	2.63	12	0	0	13.2	14	6	9	0	0	2	7										
Home	5	0	1.000	2.93	29	0	0	30.2	24	11	35	0	5	0	13										
Road	1	5	.167	2.06	35	0	0	43.2	33	20	39	0	1	5	24										
Division Rivals																									
vs. BOS	0	1	.000	5.40	4	0	0	3.1	3	1	2	0	0	1	2										
vs. CLE	1	1	.500	4.26	6	0	0	6.1	9	1	8	0	1	1	3										
vs. DET	1	0	1.000	0.00	5	0	0	7.1	3	4	4	0	1	0	2										
vs. MIL	1	0	1.000	2.08	5	0	0	4.1	3	2	4	0	1	0	4										
vs. NY	0	0	—	9.00	5	0	0	6	9	1	6	0	0	0	3										
vs. TOR	1	1	.500	3.68	7	0	0	7.1	9	4	7	0	1	1	4										
1988	BAL A	1	1	.500	3.27	10	0	0	11	10	10	9	0	1	1	0	0	0	0	—	1	2	0	0	0.3	1.000
1989		5	2	.714	1.69	64	0	0	85	57	46	90	0	5	2	27	0	0	0	—	5	12	1	0	0.3	.944
1990		6	5	.545	2.42	64	0	0	74.1	57	31	74	0	6	5	37	0	0	0	—	4	4	0	1	0.1	1.000
3 yrs.		12	8	.600	2.11	138	0	0	170.1	124	87	173	0	12	8	64	0	0	0	—	10	18	1	1	0.2	.966

Year	Team	W	L	%	ERA	G	GS	CG	IP	H	BB	SO	ShO	RELIEF PITCHING W	L	SV	BATTING AB	H	HR	BA	PO	A	E	DP	TC/G	FA

Randy O'Neal

O'NEAL, RANDALL JEFFREY
B. Aug. 30, 1960, Ashland, Ky.
BR TR 6′ 2″ 195 lbs.

Year	Team	W	L	%	ERA	G	GS	CG	IP	H	BB	SO	ShO	W	L	SV	AB	H	HR	BA	PO	A	E	DP	TC/G	FA
April		0	0	—	2.89	7	0	0	9.1	8	7	6	0	0	0	0										
May		0	0	—	12.00	3	0	0	3	6	0	2	0	0	0	0										
June		0	0	—	0.00	1	0	0	3.2	5	0	2	0	0	0	0										
July		0	0	—	1.69	5	0	0	10.2	10	1	7	0	0	0	0										
Aug		0	0	—	3.18	2	0	0	5.2	9	2	3	0	0	0	0										
Sept/Oct		1	0	1.000	5.52	8	0	0	14.2	20	8	10	0	0	1	0										
Day		1	0	1.000	3.60	9	0	0	15	18	4	8	0	0	1	0										
Night		0	0	—	3.94	17	0	0	32	40	14	22	0	0	0	0										
vs. Left		—	—	—	—					28	10	12	—	—	—	—										
vs. Right		—	—	—	—					30	8	18	—	—	—	—										
On Grass		1	0	1.000	4.37	20	0	0	35	42	16	22	0	0	1	0										
On Turf		0	0	—	2.25	6	0	0	12	16	2	8	0	0	0	0										
Home		1	0	1.000	4.76	15	0	0	22.2	30	11	14	0	0	1	0										
Road		0	0	—	2.96	11	0	0	24.1	28	7	16	0	0	0	0										
Division Rivals																										
vs. ATL		0	0	—	3.52	3	0	0	7.2	6	6	6	0	0	0	0										
vs. CIN		0	0	—	6.00	2	0	0	3	5	2	2	0	0	0	0										
vs. HOU		0	0	—	0.00	2	0	0	5.2	6	0	5	0	0	0	0										
vs. LA		0	0	—	6.94	5	0	0	11.2	20	4	5	0	0	1	0										
vs. SD		1	0	1.000	0.00	3	0	0	3	5	2	2	0	0	1	0										
1984	DET A	2	1	.667	3.38	4	3	0	18.2	16	6	12	0	0	0	0	0	0	0	—	2	1	1	0	1.0	.750
1985		5	5	.500	3.24	28	12	1	94.1	82	36	52	0	0	0	1	0	0	0	—	9	17	2	1	1.0	.929
1986		3	7	.300	4.33	37	11	1	122.2	121	44	68	0	0	0	3	2	0	0	—	15	19	2	0	1.0	.944
1987	2 teams	ATL N (16G 4 - 2)				STL N (1G 0 - 0)																				
''	total	4	2	.667	5.32	17	11	0	66	81	26	37	0	0	0	0	20	3	0	.150	4	17	0	1	1.2	1.000
1988	STL N	2	3	.400	4.58	10	8	0	53	57	10	20	0	0	0	1	0	19	0	0	.000	3	14	0	1	1.7	1.000
1989	PHI N	0	1	.000	6.23	20	1	0	39	46	9	29	0	0	0	1	0	5	0	0	.000	2	9	1	0	0.6	.917
1990	SF N	1	0	1.000	3.83	26	0	0	47	58	18	30	0	0	1	0	0	6	1	0	.167	1	8	0	1	0.3	1.000
7 yrs.		17	19	.472	4.35	142	46	2	440.2	461	149	248	0	1	5	3	50	4	0	.080	36	85	6	4	0.9	.953

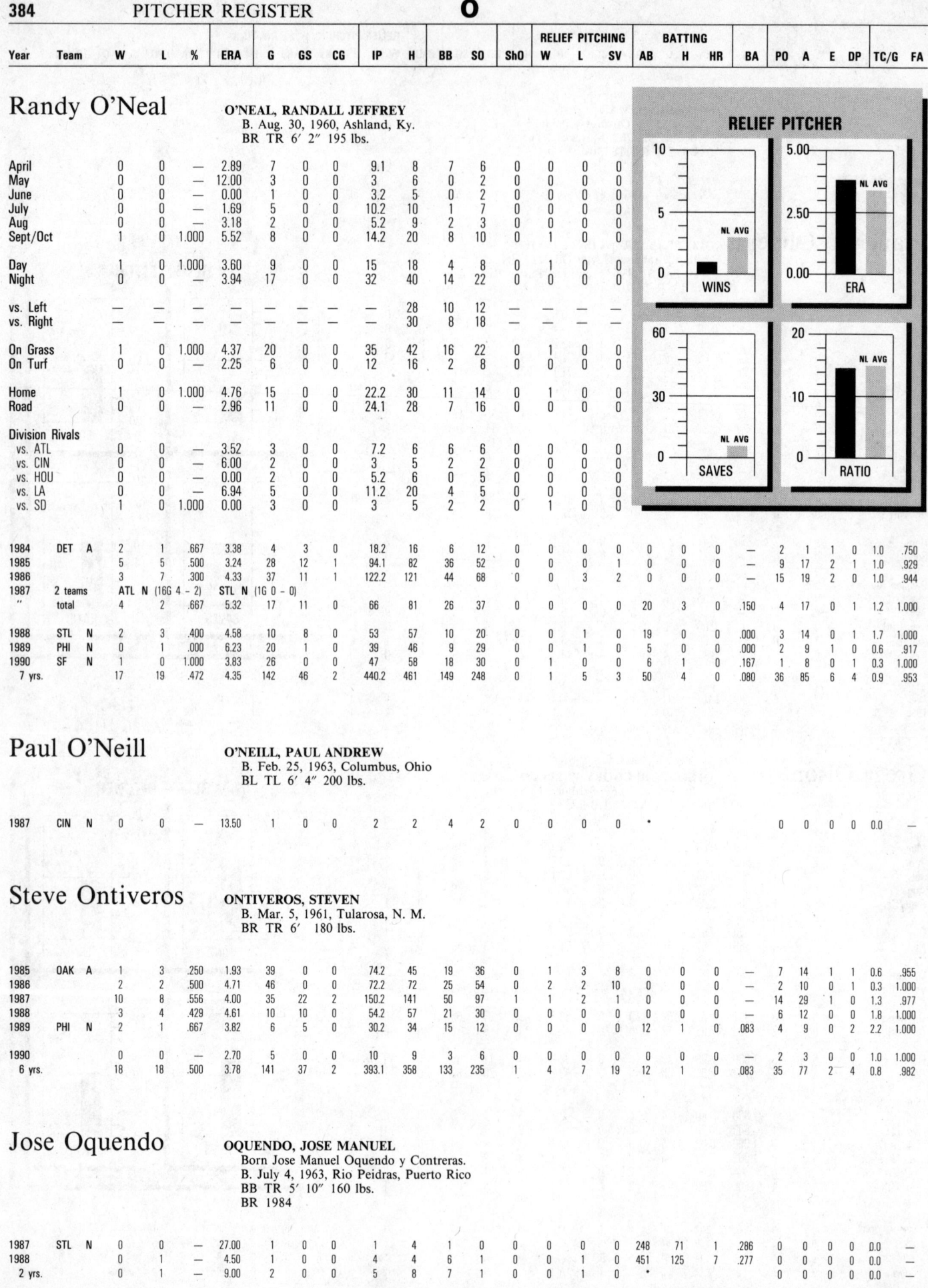

RELIEF PITCHER

WINS · ERA · SAVES · RATIO (with NL AVG comparisons)

Paul O'Neill

O'NEILL, PAUL ANDREW
B. Feb. 25, 1963, Columbus, Ohio
BL TL 6′ 4″ 200 lbs.

Year	Team	W	L	%	ERA	G	GS	CG	IP	H	BB	SO	ShO	W	L	SV	AB	H	HR	BA	PO	A	E	DP	TC/G	FA
1987	CIN N	0	0	—	13.50	1	0	0	2	2	4	2	0	0	0	0	*				0	0	0	0	0.0	—

Steve Ontiveros

ONTIVEROS, STEVEN
B. Mar. 5, 1961, Tularosa, N. M.
BR TR 6′ 180 lbs.

Year	Team	W	L	%	ERA	G	GS	CG	IP	H	BB	SO	ShO	W	L	SV	AB	H	HR	BA	PO	A	E	DP	TC/G	FA
1985	OAK A	1	3	.250	1.93	39	0	0	74.2	45	19	36	0	1	3	8	0	0	0	—	7	14	1	1	0.6	.955
1986		2	2	.500	4.71	46	0	0	72.2	72	25	54	0	2	2	10	0	0	0	—	2	10	0	1	0.3	1.000
1987		10	8	.556	4.00	35	22	2	150.2	141	50	97	1	1	2	1	0	0	0	—	14	29	1	0	1.3	.977
1988		3	4	.429	4.61	10	10	0	54.2	57	21	30	0	0	0	0	0	0	0	—	6	12	0	0	1.8	1.000
1989	PHI N	2	1	.667	3.82	6	5	0	30.2	34	15	12	0	0	0	0	12	1	0	.083	4	9	0	2	2.2	1.000
1990		0	0	—	2.70	5	0	0	10	9	3	6	0	0	0	0	0	0	0	—	2	3	0	0	1.0	1.000
6 yrs.		18	18	.500	3.78	141	37	2	393.1	358	133	235	1	4	7	19	12	1	0	.083	35	77	2	4	0.8	.982

Jose Oquendo

OQUENDO, JOSE MANUEL
Born Jose Manuel Oquendo y Contreras.
B. July 4, 1963, Rio Peidras, Puerto Rico
BB TR 5′ 10″ 160 lbs.
BR 1984

Year	Team	W	L	%	ERA	G	GS	CG	IP	H	BB	SO	ShO	W	L	SV	AB	H	HR	BA	PO	A	E	DP	TC/G	FA
1987	STL N	0	0	—	27.00	1	0	0	1	4	1	0	0	0	0	0	248	71	1	.286	0	0	0	0	0.0	—
1988		0	1	—	4.50	1	0	0	4	4	6	1	0	0	1	0	451	125	7	.277	0	0	0	0	0.0	—
2 yrs.		0	1	—	9.00	2	0	0	5	8	7	1	0	0	1	0	*				0	0	0	0	0.0	—

.Year	Team	W	L	%	ERA	G	GS	CG	IP	H	BB	SO	ShO	W	L	SV	AB	H	HR	BA	PO	A	E	DP	TC/G	FA

Jesse Orosco

OROSCO, JESSE RUSSELL
B. Apr. 21, 1957, Santa Barbara, Calif.
BR TL 6′ 2″ 174 lbs.

		W	L	%	ERA	G	GS	CG	IP	H	BB	SO	ShO	W	L	SV	AB	H	HR	BA	PO	A	E	DP	TC/G	FA
April		0	1	.000	1.59	7	0	0	5.2	2	6	4	0	0	1	1										
May		3	1	.750	5.79	10	0	0	9.1	10	4	4	0	3	1	1										
June		0	1	.000	5.52	10	0	0	14.2	12	7	13	0	0	1	0										
July		0	1	.000	2.51	11	0	0	14.1	12	13	13	0	0	1	0										
Aug		1	0	1.000	2.08	10	0	0	13	13	6	9	0	1	0	0										
Sept/Oct		1	0	1.000	5.87	7	0	0	7.2	9	2	12	0	1	0	0										
Day		2	2	.500	4.70	22	0	0	23	18	12	17	0	2	2	2										
Night		3	2	.600	3.46	33	0	0	41.2	40	26	38	0	3	2	0										
vs. Left		—	—	—	—	—	—	—	—	15	12	16	—	—	—	—										
vs. Right		—	—	—	—	—	—	—	—	43	26	39	—	—	—	—										
On Grass		4	4	.500	3.88	46	0	0	55.2	49	29	45	0	4	4	2										
On Turf		1	0	1.000	4.00	9	0	0	9	9	9	10	0	1	0	0										
Home		3	3	.500	3.00	29	0	0	39	34	17	35	0	3	3	2										
Road		2	1	.667	5.26	26	0	0	25.2	24	21	20	0	2	1	0										
Division Rivals																										
vs. BAL		0	1	.000	6.14	5	0	0	7.1	6	0	7	0	0	1	0										
vs. BOS		0	0	—	3.18	3	0	0	5.2	2	5	3	0	0	0	0										
vs. DET		0	0	—	0.00	3	0	0	3.2	3	2	5	0	0	0	0										
vs. MIL		0	0	—	6.23	5	0	0	4.1	5	2	3	0	0	0	0										
vs. NY		1	1	.500	1.23	6	0	0	7.1	6	4	7	0	1	1	0										
vs. TOR		0	0	—	2.79	7	0	0	9.2	7	5	13	0	0	0	0										
1979	NY N	1	2	.333	4.89	18	2	0	35	33	22	22	0	1	2	0	6	0	0	.000	2	9	0	1	0.6	1.000
1981		0	1	.000	1.59	8	0	0	17	13	6	18	0	0	1	1	2	0	0	.000	1	2	0	0	0.4	1.000
1982		4	10	.286	2.72	54	2	0	109.1	92	40	89	0	4	8	4	14	2	0	.143	4	16	0	1	0.4	1.000
1983		13	7	.650	1.47	62	0	0	110	76	38	84	0	13	7	17	12	4	0	.333	5	19	0	0	0.4	1.000
1984		10	6	.625	2.59	60	0	0	87	58	34	85	0	10	6	31	4	1	0	.250	2	11	1	1	0.2	.929
1985		8	6	.571	2.73	54	0	0	79	66	34	68	0	8	6	17	7	3	0	.429	3	8	1	2	0.2	.917
1986		8	6	.571	2.33	58	0	0	81	64	35	62	0	8	6	21	3	0	0	.000	4	8	0	0	0.2	1.000
1987		3	9	.250	4.44	58	0	0	77	78	31	78	0	3	9	16	8	0	0	.000	4	9	0	1	0.2	1.000
1988	LA N	3	2	.600	2.72	55	0	0	53	41	30	43	0	3	2	9	2	0	0	.000	1	10	0	1	0.2	1.000
1989	CLE A	3	4	.429	2.08	69	0	0	78	54	26	79	0	3	4	3	0	0	0	—	6	13	0	1	0.3	1.000
1990		5	4	.556	3.90	55	0	0	64.2	58	38	55	0	5	4	2	0	0	0	—	1	14	1	1	0.3	.938
11 yrs.		58	57	.504	2.76	551	4	0	791	633	334	683	0	58	55	121	58	10	0	.172	33	119	3	9	0.3	.981

LEAGUE CHAMPIONSHIP SERIES

1986	NY N	3	0	1.000	3.38	4	0	0	8	5	2	10	0	3	0	0	0	0	0	—	1	1	0	0	0.5	1.000
1988	LA N	0	0	—	7.71	4	0	0	2.1	4	3	0	0	0	0	0	0	0	0	—	1	0	0	0	0.3	1.000
2 yrs.		3	0	1.000	4.35	8	0	0	10.1	9	5	10	0	3	0	0	0	0	0	—	2	1	0	0	0.4	1.000

WORLD SERIES

| 1986 | NY N | 0 | 0 | — | 0.00 | 4 | 0 | 0 | 5.2 | 2 | 0 | 6 | 0 | 0 | 0 | 2 | 1 | 1 | 0 | 1.000 | 0 | 0 | 0 | 0 | 0.0 | — |

Al Osuna

OSUNA, ALFONSO, JR.
B. Aug. 10, 1965, Inglewood, Calif.
BR TL 6′ 3″ 200 lbs.

| 1990 | HOU N | 2 | 0 | 1.000 | 4.76 | 12 | 0 | 0 | 11.1 | 10 | 6 | 6 | 0 | 2 | 0 | 0 | 0 | 0 | 0 | — | 1 | 1 | 0 | 0 | 0.2 | 1.000 |

Dave Otto

OTTO, DAVID ALAN
B. Nov. 12, 1964, Chicago, Ill.
BL TL 6′ 7″ 210 lbs.

1987	OAK A	0	0	—	9.00	3	0	0	6	7	1	3	0	0	0	0	0	0	0	—	1	0	0	0	0.3	1.000
1988		0	0	—	1.80	3	2	0	10	9	6	7	0	0	0	0	0	0	0	—	1	1	0	0	0.7	1.000
1989		0	0	—	2.70	1	1	0	6.2	6	2	4	0	0	0	0	0	0	0	—	0	1	0	0	1.0	1.000
1990		0	0	—	7.71	2	0	0	2.1	3	3	2	0	0	0	0	0	0	0	—	0	2	0	1	1.0	1.000
4 yrs.		0	0	—	4.32	9	3	0	25	25	12	16	0	0	0	0	0	0	0	—	2	4	0	1	0.7	1.000

RELIEF PITCHER

(Bar charts: WINS, ERA, SAVES, RATIO — with AL AVG comparisons)

Year	Team		W	L	%	ERA	G	GS	CG	IP	H	BB	SO	ShO	RELIEF PITCHING W	L	SV	BATTING AB	H	HR	BA	PO	A	E	DP	TC/G	FA

Vicente Palacios

PALACIOS, VICENTE
Born Vicente Palacios y Hernandez.
B. July 19, 1963, Veracruz, Mexico
BR TR 6′ 3″ 165 lbs.

Year	Team		W	L	%	ERA	G	GS	CG	IP	H	BB	SO	ShO	W	L	SV	AB	H	HR	BA	PO	A	E	DP	TC/G	FA
1987	PIT	N	2	1	.667	4.30	6	4	0	29.1	27	9	13	0	0	0	0	9	1	0	.111	2	1	0	0	0.5	1.000
1988			1	2	.333	6.66	7	3	0	24.1	28	15	15	0	0	0	1	8	0	0	.000	3	5	0	0	1.1	1.000
1990			0	0	—	0.00	7	0	0	15	4	2	8	0	0	0	3	4	0	0	.000	2	0	0	0	0.3	1.000
3 yrs.			3	3	.500	4.19	20	7	0	68.2	59	26	36	0	0	1	3	21	1	0	.048	7	6	0	0	0.7	1.000

Donn Pall

PALL, DONN STEVEN
B. Jan. 11, 1962, Chicago, Ill.
BR TR 6′ 2″ 185 lbs.

	W	L	%	ERA	G	GS	CG	IP	H	BB	SO	ShO	W	L	SV
April	0	0	—	3.21	8	0	0	14	10	3	8	0	0	0	0
May	0	0	—	1.80	12	0	0	15	9	4	11	0	0	0	0
June	0	2	.000	2.84	11	0	0	12.2	13	4	2	0	0	2	0
July	2	2	.500	5.52	10	0	0	14.2	12	5	7	0	2	2	1
Aug	0	1	.000	2.08	7	0	0	8.2	9	3	6	0	0	1	0
Sept/Oct	1	0	1.000	4.09	8	0	0	11	10	5	5	0	1	0	1
Day	1	3	.250	4.81	18	0	0	24.1	23	7	7	0	1	3	0
Night	2	2	.500	2.61	38	0	0	51.2	40	17	32	0	2	2	2
vs. Left	—	—	—	—	—	—	—	—	32	12	17	—	—	—	—
vs. Right	—	—	—	—	—	—	—	—	31	12	22	—	—	—	—
On Grass	3	5	.375	3.75	48	0	0	62.1	53	22	33	0	3	5	1
On Turf	0	0	—	1.32	8	0	0	13.2	10	2	6	0	0	0	1
Home	0	3	.000	4.50	31	0	0	44	41	12	25	0	0	3	1
Road	3	2	.600	1.69	25	0	0	32	22	12	14	0	3	2	1

Division Rivals

	W	L	%	ERA	G	GS	CG	IP	H	BB	SO	ShO	W	L	SV
vs. CAL	0	0	—	4.91	5	0	0	3.2	6	1	2	0	0	0	0
vs. KC	0	0	—	2.08	2	0	0	4.1	4	0	1	0	0	0	0
vs. MIN	0	0	—	1.69	6	0	0	5.1	4	2	2	0	0	0	0
vs. OAK	0	1	.000	3.60	3	0	0	5	4	3	0	0	0	1	0
vs. SEA	0	1	.000	3.38	3	0	0	5.1	6	0	3	0	0	1	1
vs. TEX	0	1	.000	4.70	6	0	0	7.2	9	5	8	0	0	1	0

Year	Team		W	L	%	ERA	G	GS	CG	IP	H	BB	SO	ShO	W	L	SV	AB	H	HR	BA	PO	A	E	DP	TC/G	FA
1988	CHI	A	0	2	.000	3.45	17	0	0	28.2	39	8	16	0	0	0	2	0	0	0	—	4	6	0	1	0.6	1.000
1989			4	5	.444	3.31	53	0	0	87	90	19	58	0	4	5	6	0	0	0	—	5	7	2	0	0.3	.857
1990			3	5	.375	3.32	56	0	0	76	63	24	39	0	3	5	2	0	0	0	—	1	11	0	2	0.2	1.000
3 yrs.			7	12	.368	3.33	126	0	0	191.2	192	51	113	0	7	12	8	0	0	0	—	10	24	2	3	0.3	.944

RELIEF PITCHER — WINS / ERA / SAVES / RATIO (AL AVG)

Clay Parker

PARKER, JAMES CLAYTON
B. Dec. 19, 1962, Columbia, La.
BR TR 6′ 1″ 185 lbs.

	W	L	%	ERA	G	GS	CG	IP	H	BB	SO	ShO	W	L	SV
April	0	1	.000	5.14	4	1	0	14	13	5	14	0	0	0	0
May	1	0	1.000	3.38	1	1	0	8	6	2	6	0	0	0	0
June	—	—	—	—	0	—	—	0	0	0	0	0	0	0	0
July	0	0	—	3.79	6	0	0	19	17	12	11	0	0	0	0
Aug	2	0	1.000	2.84	9	0	0	19	22	6	6	0	2	0	0
Sept/Oct	0	2	.000	2.77	9	1	0	13	6	7	3	0	0	1	0
Day	0	0	—	3.48	5	0	0	10.1	9	8	7	0	0	0	0
Night	3	3	.500	3.59	24	3	0	62.2	55	24	33	0	2	1	0
vs. Left	—	—	—	—	—	—	—	—	20	17	12	—	—	—	—
vs. Right	—	—	—	—	—	—	—	—	44	15	28	—	—	—	—
On Grass	2	3	.400	3.84	27	3	0	68	58	32	39	0	1	1	0
On Turf	1	0	1.000	0.00	2	0	0	5	6	0	1	0	1	0	0
Home	0	2	.000	3.40	14	2	0	39.2	28	22	18	0	0	0	0
Road	3	1	.750	3.78	15	1	0	33.1	36	10	22	0	2	1	0

Division Rivals

	W	L	%	ERA	G	GS	CG	IP	H	BB	SO	ShO	W	L	SV
vs. BAL	0	0	—	1.69	1	0	0	5.1	2	3	4	0	0	0	0
vs. BOS	0	0	—	4.38	4	0	0	12.1	9	8	4	0	0	0	0
vs. CLE	0	0	—	0.00	2	0	0	2.2	4	0	2	0	0	0	0
vs. MIL	0	0	—	5.40	3	0	0	5	4	2	1	0	0	0	0
vs. NY	1	0	1.000	3.60	5	0	0	10	10	3	5	0	1	0	0
vs. TOR	0	1	.000	8.10	2	1	0	3.1	7	4	2	0	0	1	0

RELIEF PITCHER — WINS / ERA / SAVES / RATIO (AL AVG)

Year	Team	W	L	%	ERA	G	GS	CG	IP	H	BB	SO	ShO	W	L	SV	AB	H	HR	BA	PO	A	E	DP	TC/G	FA
														RELIEF PITCHING			BATTING									

Clay Parker *Continued*

Year	Team	W	L	%	ERA	G	GS	CG	IP	H	BB	SO	ShO	W	L	SV	AB	H	HR	BA	PO	A	E	DP	TC/G	FA
1987	SEA A	0	0	—	10.57	3	1	0	7.2	15	4	8	0	0	0	0	0	0	0	—	0	1	0	0	0.3	1.000
1989	NY A	4	5	.444	3.68	22	17	2	120	123	31	53	0	0	0	0	0	0	0	—	7	20	0	1	1.2	1.000
1990	2 teams				NY A	(5G	1 - 1)		DET A	(24G	2 - 2)															
"	total	3	3	.500	3.58	29	3	0	73	64	32	40	0	2	1	0	0	0	0	—	5	10	0	1	0.5	1.000
3 yrs.		7	8	.467	3.90	54	21	2	200.2	202	67	101	0	2	1	0	0	0	0	—	12	31	0	2	0.8	1.000

Jeff Parrett

PARRETT, JEFFREY DALE
B. Aug. 26, 1961, Indianapolis, Ind.
BR TR 6′ 4″ 185 lbs.

	W	L	%	ERA	G	GS	CG	IP	H	BB	SO	ShO	W	L	SV	AB	H	HR	BA	PO	A	E	DP	TC/G	FA
April	1	2	.333	4.50	12	0	0	18	24	5	13	0	1	2	1										
May	1	1	.500	7.02	14	0	0	16.2	18	12	14	0	1	1	0										
June	0	3	.000	4.80	13	0	0	15	14	5	13	0	0	3	0										
July	2	3	.400	4.50	6	5	0	28	30	13	21	0	1	0	0										
Aug	0	0	—	4.26	12	0	0	19	22	13	16	0	0	0	0										
Sept/Oct	1	1	.500	2.25	10	0	0	12	11	7	9	0	1	1	1										
Day	0	3	.000	5.53	19	2	0	27.2	35	13	21	0	0	2	1										
Night	5	7	.417	4.33	48	3	0	81	84	42	65	0	4	5	1										
vs. Left	—	—	—	—	—	—	—	—	57	39	36	—	—	—	—										
vs. Right	—	—	—	—	—	—	—	—	62	16	50	—	—	—	—										
On Grass	2	3	.400	4.76	29	0	0	34	41	23	23	0	2	3	1										
On Turf	3	7	.300	4.58	38	5	0	74.2	78	32	63	0	2	4	1										
Home	2	5	.286	5.06	30	3	0	58.2	62	32	44	0	1	4	2										
Road	3	5	.375	4.14	37	2	0	50	57	23	42	0	3	3	0										
Division Rivals																										
vs. CIN	0	1	.000	3.50	7	2	0	18	20	6	10	0	0	0	1										
vs. HOU	0	1	.000	9.90	5	1	0	10	13	4	12	0	0	0	0										
vs. LA	0	0	—	4.32	6	0	0	8.1	5	8	4	0	0	0	0										
vs. SD	1	2	.333	8.00	8	0	0	9	10	9	5	0	1	2	0										
vs. SF	0	0	—	0.00	5	0	0	6.2	6	3	5	0	0	0	0										

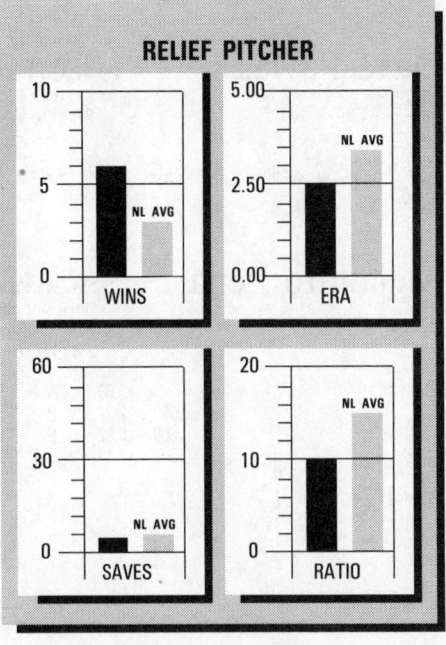

RELIEF PITCHER

Year	Team	W	L	%	ERA	G	GS	CG	IP	H	BB	SO	ShO	W	L	SV	AB	H	HR	BA	PO	A	E	DP	TC/G	FA
1986	MON N	0	1	.000	4.87	12	0	0	20.1	19	13	21	0	0	1	0	2	1	0	.500	1	2	0	1	0.3	1.000
1987		7	6	.538	4.21	45	0	0	62	53	30	56	0	7	6	6	5	0	0	.000	3	9	2	1	0.3	.857
1988		12	4	.750	2.65	61	0	0	91.2	66	45	62	0	**12**	4	6	0	0	0	—	7	9	1	0	0.3	.941
1989	PHI N	12	6	.667	2.98	72	0	0	105.2	90	44	98	0	**12**	6	6	5	0	0	.000	2	9	0	0	0.2	1.000
1990	2 teams				PHI N	(47G	4 - 9)		ATL N	(20G	1 - 1)															
"	total	5	10	.333	4.64	67	5	0	108.2	119	55	86	0	4	7	2	11	1	0	.091	1	18	4	1	0.3	.826
5 yrs.		36	27	.571	3.66	257	5	0	388.1	347	187	323	0	35	24	20	23	2	0	.087	14	47	7	3	0.3	.897

Bob Patterson

PATTERSON, ROBERT CHANDLER
B. May 16, 1959, Jacksonville, Fla.
BR TR 6′ 2″ 185 lbs.

	W	L	%	ERA	G	GS	CG	IP	H	BB	SO	ShO	W	L	SV	AB	H	HR	BA	PO	A	E	DP	TC/G	FA
April	2	0	1.000	0.84	10	0	0	10.2	8	3	12	0	2	0	0										
May	1	1	.500	4.41	9	1	0	16.1	17	2	15	0	0	1	1										
June	1	2	.333	4.05	4	4	0	20	21	6	9	0	0	0	0										
July	3	0	1.000	1.82	13	0	0	24.2	19	5	18	0	3	0	1										
Aug	1	2	.333	5.40	11	0	0	11.2	12	5	7	0	1	2	1										
Sept/Oct	0	0	—	0.79	8	0	0	11.1	11	0	9	0	0	0	2										
Day	1	1	.500	3.05	16	1	0	20.2	14	4	15	0	1	0	2										
Night	7	4	.636	2.92	39	4	0	74	74	17	55	0	5	3	3										
vs. Left	—	—	—	—	—	—	—	—	21	6	29	—	—	—	—										
vs. Right	—	—	—	—	—	—	—	—	67	15	41	—	—	—	—										
On Grass	3	1	.750	2.17	16	1	0	29	30	5	22	0	3	0	2										
On Turf	5	4	.556	3.29	39	4	0	65.2	58	16	48	0	3	3	3										
Home	4	1	.800	2.70	28	3	0	53.1	44	11	42	0	2	1	3										
Road	4	4	.500	3.27	27	2	0	41.1	44	10	28	0	4	2	2										
Division Rivals																										
vs. CHI	3	0	1.000	1.13	6	1	0	16	12	2	11	0	2	0	1										
vs. MON	0	0	—	3.86	6	0	0	4.2	6	1	5	0	0	0	0										
vs. NY	0	1	.000	4.32	5	1	0	8.1	13	2	7	0	0	0	0										
vs. PHI	1	1	.500	2.12	6	2	0	17	12	4	9	0	1	0	1										
vs. STL	0	0	—	4.91	3	0	0	3.2	5	2	2	0	0	0	0										

RELIEF PITCHER

Year	Team	W	L	%	ERA	G	GS	CG	IP	H	BB	SO	ShO	W	L	SV	AB	H	HR	BA	PO	A	E	DP	TC/G	FA

Bob Patterson *Continued*

Year	Team		W	L	%	ERA	G	GS	CG	IP	H	BB	SO	ShO	W	L	SV	AB	H	HR	BA	PO	A	E	DP	TC/G	FA
1985	SD	N	0	0	—	24.75	3	0	0	4	13	3	1	0	0	0	0	0	0	0	—	0	0	0	0	0.0	—
1986	PIT	N	2	3	.400	4.95	11	5	0	36.1	49	5	20	0	1	2	0	8	1	0	.125	1	9	0	1	0.9	1.000
1987			1	4	.200	6.70	15	7	0	43	49	22	27	0	0	0	0	12	1	0	.083	0	7	0	0	0.5	1.000
1989			4	3	.571	4.05	12	3	0	26.2	23	8	20	0	3	1	1	3	0	0	.000	1	2	0	0	0.3	1.000
1990			8	5	.615	2.95	55	5	0	94.2	88	21	70	0	6	3	5	19	1	0	.053	9	10	0	0	0.3	1.000
5 yrs.			15	15	.500	4.66	96	20	0	204.2	222	59	138	0	10	6	6	42	3	0	.071	11	28	0	1	0.4	1.000

LEAGUE CHAMPIONSHIP SERIES

Year	Team		W	L	%	ERA	G	GS	CG	IP	H	BB	SO	ShO	W	L	SV	AB	H	HR	BA	PO	A	E	DP	TC/G	FA
1990	PIT	N	0	0	—	0.00	2	0	0	1	1	2	0	0	0	0	1	0	0	0	—	0	1	0	0	0.5	1.000

Ken Patterson

PATTERSON, KENNETH BRIAN
B. July 8, 1964, Costa Mesa, Calif.
BL TL 6' 4" 210 lbs.

	W	L	%	ERA	G	GS	CG	IP	H	BB	SO	ShO	W	L	SV	AB	H	HR	BA	PO	A	E	DP	TC/G	FA
April	0	0	—	1.42	5	0	0	6.1	5	2	1	0	0	0	0										
May	1	0	1.000	1.96	5	0	0	18.1	8	9	13	0	1	0	0										
June	0	0	—	9.00	6	0	0	11	15	7	6	0	0	0	1										
July	1	1	.500	3.55	9	0	0	12.2	12	5	14	0	1	1	0										
Aug	0	0	—	3.18	9	0	0	11.1	14	4	4	0	0	0	0										
Sept/Oct	0	0	—	0.00	9	0	0	6.2	4	7	3	0	0	0	1										
Day	2	0	1.000	1.33	12	0	0	20.1	9	11	16	0	2	0	0										
Night	0	1	.000	4.30	31	0	0	46	49	23	24	0	0	1	2										
vs. Left	—	—	—	—	—	—	—	—	13	10	15		—	—	—	—										
vs. Right	—	—	—	—	—	—	—	—	45	24	25		—	—	—	—										
On Grass	2	1	.667	3.83	36	0	0	54	50	30	34	0	2	1	1										
On Turf	0	0	—	1.46	7	0	0	12.1	8	4	6	0	0	0	1										
Home	0	1	.000	4.79	22	0	0	35.2	35	17	22	0	0	1	1										
Road	2	0	1.000	1.76	21	0	0	30.2	23	17	18	0	2	0	1										
Division Rivals																										
vs. CAL	0	0	—	0.00	2	0	0	1.1	1	2	2	0	0	0	0										
vs. KC	0	0	—	1.29	3	0	0	7	4	2	4	0	0	0	0										
vs. MIN	0	0	—	0.00	2	0	0	4.2	3	2	3	0	0	0	0										
vs. OAK	0	0	—	5.68	2	0	0	6.1	8	3	4	0	0	0	0										
vs. SEA	0	0	—	7.36	4	0	0	7.1	8	5	2	0	0	0	1										
vs. TEX	0	0	—	0.00	5	0	0	7	6	3	5	0	0	0	0										

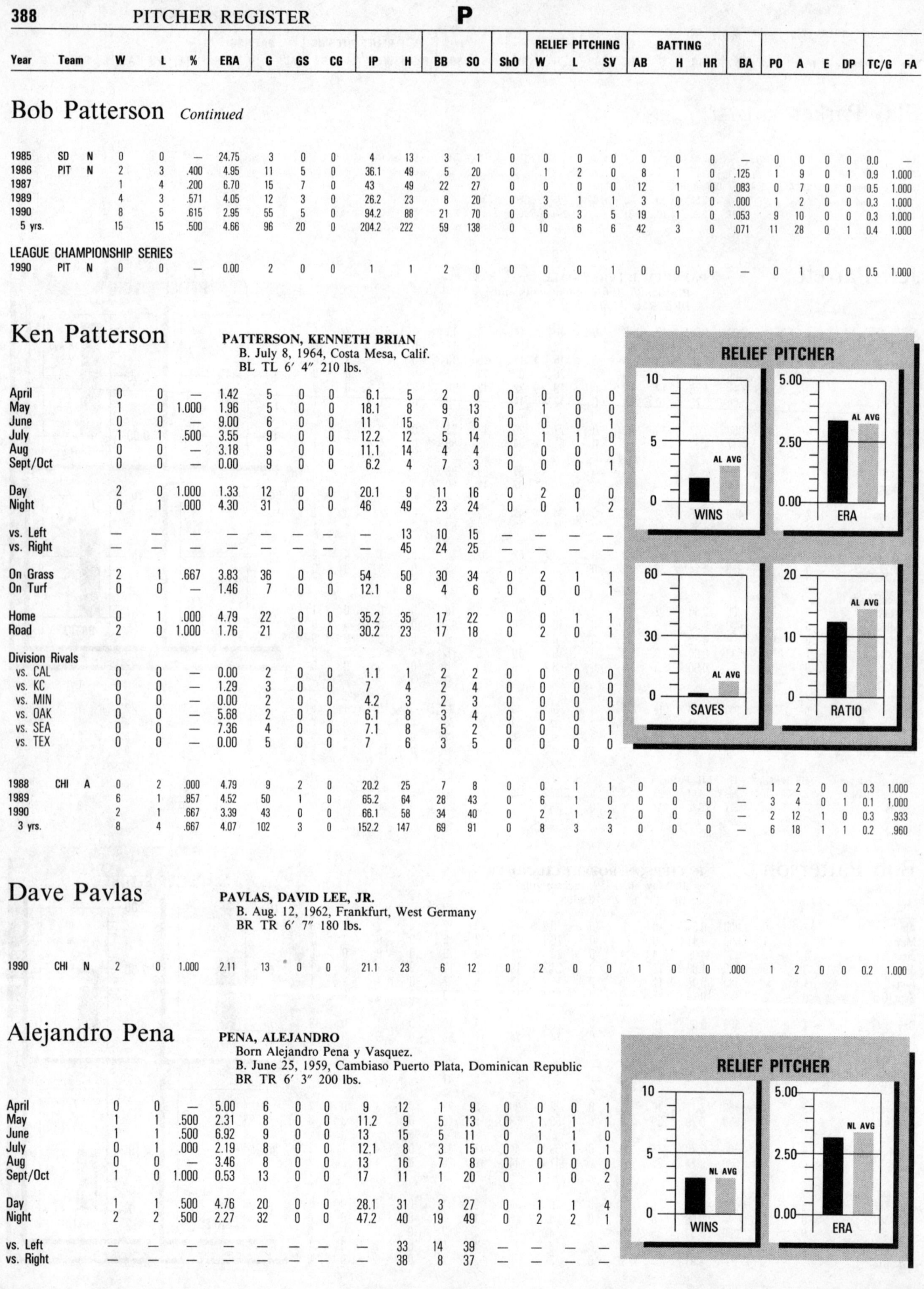

RELIEF PITCHER — WINS (AL AVG), ERA (AL AVG), SAVES (AL AVG), RATIO (AL AVG)

Year	Team		W	L	%	ERA	G	GS	CG	IP	H	BB	SO	ShO	W	L	SV	AB	H	HR	BA	PO	A	E	DP	TC/G	FA
1988	CHI	A	0	2	.000	4.79	9	2	0	20.2	25	7	8	0	0	1	1	0	0	0	—	1	2	0	0	0.3	1.000
1989			6	1	.857	4.52	50	1	0	65.2	64	28	43	0	6	1	0	0	0	0	—	3	4	0	1	0.1	1.000
1990			2	1	.667	3.39	43	0	0	66.1	58	34	40	0	2	1	2	0	0	0	—	2	12	1	0	0.3	.933
3 yrs.			8	4	.667	4.07	102	3	0	152.2	147	69	91	0	8	3	3	0	0	0	—	6	18	1	1	0.2	.960

Dave Pavlas

PAVLAS, DAVID LEE, JR.
B. Aug. 12, 1962, Frankfurt, West Germany
BR TR 6' 7" 180 lbs.

Year	Team		W	L	%	ERA	G	GS	CG	IP	H	BB	SO	ShO	W	L	SV	AB	H	HR	BA	PO	A	E	DP	TC/G	FA
1990	CHI	N	2	0	1.000	2.11	13	0	0	21.1	23	6	12	0	2	0	0	1	0	0	.000	1	2	0	0	0.2	1.000

Alejandro Pena

PENA, ALEJANDRO
Born Alejandro Pena y Vasquez.
B. June 25, 1959, Cambiaso Puerto Plata, Dominican Republic
BR TR 6' 3" 200 lbs.

	W	L	%	ERA	G	GS	CG	IP	H	BB	SO	ShO	W	L	SV	AB	H	HR	BA	PO	A	E	DP	TC/G	FA
April	0	0	—	5.00	6	0	0	9	12	1	9	0	0	0	1										
May	1	1	.500	2.31	8	0	0	11.2	9	5	13	0	1	1	1										
June	1	1	.500	6.92	9	0	0	13	15	5	11	0	1	1	0										
July	0	1	.000	2.19	8	0	0	12.1	8	3	15	0	0	1	1										
Aug	0	0	—	3.46	8	0	0	13	16	7	8	0	0	0	0										
Sept/Oct	1	0	1.000	0.53	13	0	0	17	11	1	20	0	1	0	2										
Day	1	1	.500	4.76	20	0	0	28.1	31	3	27	0	1	1	4										
Night	2	2	.500	2.27	32	0	0	47.2	40	19	49	0	2	2	1										
vs. Left	—	—	—	—	—	—	—	—	33	14	39		—	—	—	—										
vs. Right	—	—	—	—	—	—	—	—	38	8	37		—	—	—	—										

RELIEF PITCHER — WINS (NL AVG), ERA (NL AVG)

Year	Team	W	L	%	ERA	G	GS	CG	IP	H	BB	SO	ShO	RELIEF PITCHING W	L	SV	BATTING AB	H	HR	BA	PO	A	E	DP	TC/G	FA

Alejandro Pena *Continued*

Year	Team	W	L	%	ERA	G	GS	CG	IP	H	BB	SO	ShO	W	L	SV	AB	H	HR	BA	PO	A	E	DP	TC/G	FA
On Grass		1	2	.333	3.81	36	0	0	52	50	17	45	0	1	2	4										
On Turf		2	1	.667	1.88	16	0	0	24	21	5	31	0	2	1	1										
Home		1	0	1.000	3.19	23	0	0	31	25	13	27	0	1	0	2										
Road		2	3	.400	3.20	29	0	0	45	46	9	49	0	2	3	3										
Division Rivals																										
vs. CHI		0	1	.000	6.06	9	0	0	16.1	19	5	12	0	0	1	1										
vs. MON		1	0	1.000	0.69	8	0	0	13	4	3	15	0	1	0	0										
vs. PHI		0	0	—	5.40	6	0	0	6.2	12	4	6	0	0	0	0										
vs. PIT		0	0	—	9.00	4	0	0	4	8	1	7	0	0	0	1										
vs. STL		1	0	1.000	1.50	4	0	0	6	4	0	5	0	1	0	0										
1981	LA N	1	1	.500	2.88	14	0	0	25	18	11	14	0	1	1	2	6	0	0	.000	1	5	1	0	0.5	.857
1982		0	2	.000	4.79	29	0	0	35.2	37	21	20	0	0	2	0	0	0	0	—	3	11	2	1	0.6	.875
1983		12	9	.571	2.75	34	26	4	177	152	51	120	3	2	1	1	60	6	1	.100	13	32	4	4	1.4	.918
1984		12	6	.667	**2.48**	28	28	8	199.1	186	46	135	**4**	0	0	0	66	8	0	.121	17	21	4	1	1.5	.905
1985		0	1	.000	8.31	2	1	0	4.1	7	3	2	0	0	0	0	1	0	0	.000	0	1	1	0	1.0	.500
1986		1	2	.333	4.89	24	10	0	70	74	30	46	0	0	1	1	17	3	0	.176	1	8	0	0	0.4	1.000
1987		2	7	.222	3.50	37	7	0	87.1	82	37	76	0	2	2	11	13	1	0	.077	4	1	1	0	0.2	.833
1988		6	7	.462	1.91	60	0	0	94.1	75	27	83	0	6	7	12	6	0	0	.000	9	10	2	1	0.4	.905
1989		4	3	.571	2.13	53	0	0	76	62	18	75	0	4	3	5	1	1	0	1.000	1	5	1	0	0.1	1.000
1990	NY N	3	3	.500	3.20	52	0	0	76	71	22	76	0	3	3	5	6	1	0	.167	2	4	0	0	0.1	1.000
10 yrs.		41	41	.500	2.95	333	72	12	845	764	266	647	7	18	21	37	176	20	1	.114	51	98	16	7	0.5	.903

LEAGUE CHAMPIONSHIP SERIES

Year	Team	W	L	%	ERA	G	GS	CG	IP	H	BB	SO	ShO	W	L	SV	AB	H	HR	BA	PO	A	E	DP	TC/G	FA
1981	LA N	0	0	—	0.00	2	0	0	2.1	1	0	0	0	0	0	0	0	0	0	—	0	0	0	0	0.0	—
1983		0	0	—	6.75	1	0	0	2.2	4	1	3	0	0	0	0	1	1	0	1.000	0	0	0	0	0.0	—
1988		1	1	.500	4.15	3	0	0	4.1	1	5	1	0	1	1	1	0	0	0	—	0	0	0	0	0.0	—
3 yrs.		1	1	.500	3.86	6	0	0	9.1	6	6	4	0	1	1	1	1	1	0	1.000	0	0	0	0	0.0	—

WORLD SERIES

Year	Team	W	L	%	ERA	G	GS	CG	IP	H	BB	SO	ShO	W	L	SV	AB	H	HR	BA	PO	A	E	DP	TC/G	FA
1988	LA N	1	0	1.000	0.00	2	0	0	5	2	1	7	0	1	0	0	0	0	0	—	0	0	0	0	0.0	—

Melido Perez

PEREZ, MELIDO TURPEN
Born Melido Turpen Gross y Perez.
Brother of Pascual Perez.
B. Feb. 15, 1966, San Cristobal, Dominican Republic
BR TR 6′ 4″ 180 lbs.

Year	Team	W	L	%	ERA	G	GS	CG	IP	H	BB	SO	ShO	W	L	SV	AB	H	HR	BA	PO	A	E	DP	TC/G	FA
April		1	2	.333	4.50	4	4	0	22	18	7	20	0	0	0	0										
May		3	2	.600	4.28	6	6	0	33.2	22	18	35	0	0	0	0										
June		2	3	.400	3.66	7	7	1	39.1	35	12	22	1	0	0	0										
July		3	1	.750	3.29	5	5	1	27.1	18	11	24	1	0	0	0										
Aug		2	4	.333	6.57	6	6	0	37	46	18	28	0	0	0	0										
Sept/Oct		2	2	.500	5.02	7	7	1	37.2	38	20	32	1	0	0	0										
Day		2	3	.400	4.99	9	9	0	48.2	43	24	35	0	0	0	0										
Night		11	11	.500	4.49	26	26	3	148.1	134	62	126	3	0	0	0										
vs. Left		—	—	—	—	—	—	—	—	95	42	81	—	—	—	—										
vs. Right		—	—	—	—	—	—	—	—	82	44	80	—	—	—	—										
On Grass		12	11	.522	4.08	29	29	3	169.2	143	69	137	3	0	0	0										
On Turf		1	3	.250	7.90	6	6	0	27.1	34	17	24	0	0	0	0										
Home		5	6	.455	5.11	15	15	1	81	79	32	62	1	0	0	0										
Road		8	8	.500	4.27	20	20	2	116	98	54	99	2	0	0	0										
Division Rivals																										
vs. CAL		1	1	.500	4.50	2	2	0	12	12	9	12	0	0	0	0										
vs. KC		1	1	.500	5.93	3	3	0	13.2	16	6	10	0	0	0	0										
vs. MIN		0	1	.000	4.80	2	2	0	15	13	3	11	0	0	0	0										
vs. OAK		1	2	.333	3.52	4	4	1	23	23	7	18	1	0	0	0										
vs. SEA		2	0	1.000	2.60	3	3	1	17.1	13	6	12	1	0	0	0										
vs. TEX		2	2	.500	3.54	4	4	0	28	20	15	28	0	0	0	0										
1987	KC A	1	1	.500	7.84	3	3	0	10.1	18	5	5	0	0	0	0	0	0	0	—	0	0	1	0	0.3	—
1988	CHI A	12	10	.545	3.79	32	32	3	197	186	72	138	1	0	0	0	0	0	0	—	8	18	1	1	0.8	.963
1989		11	14	.440	5.01	31	31	2	183.1	187	90	141	0	0	0	0	0	0	0	—	9	19	1	3	0.9	.966
1990		13	14	.481	4.61	35	35	3	197	177	86	161	3	0	0	0	0	0	0	—	4	20	1	0	0.7	.960
4 yrs.		37	39	.487	4.52	101	101	8	587.2	568	253	445	4	0	0	0	0	0	0	—	21	57	4	4	0.8	.951

Year	Team	W	L	%	ERA	G	GS	CG	IP	H	BB	SO	ShO	RELIEF PITCHING			BATTING				PO	A	E	DP	TC/G	FA
														W	L	SV	AB	H	HR	BA						

Mike Perez

PEREZ, MICHAEL IRVIN
B. Oct. 19, 1964, Yauco, Puerto Rico
BR TR 6' 185 lbs.

Year	Team	W	L	%	ERA	G	GS	CG	IP	H	BB	SO	ShO	W	L	SV	AB	H	HR	BA	PO	A	E	DP	TC/G	FA
1990	STL N	1	0	1.000	3.95	13	0	0	13.2	12	3	5	0	1	0	1	1	0	0	.000	3	2	0	0	0.4	1.000

Pascual Perez

PEREZ, PASCUAL
Born Pascual Gross y Perez.
Brother of Melido Perez.
B. May 17, 1957, San Cristobal, Dominican Republic
BR TR 6' 2" 162 lbs.

Year	Team	W	L	%	ERA	G	GS	CG	IP	H	BB	SO	ShO	W	L	SV	AB	H	HR	BA	PO	A	E	DP	TC/G	FA
1980	PIT N	0	1	.000	3.75	2	2	0	12	15	2	7	0	0	0	0	4	1	0	.250	1	1	0	0	1.0	1.000
1981		2	7	.222	3.98	17	13	2	86	92	34	46	0	0	1	0	22	3	0	.136	7	13	1	0	1.2	.952
1982	ATL N	4	4	.500	3.06	16	11	0	79.1	85	17	29	0	2	0	0	18	3	0	.167	9	11	1	2	1.3	.952
1983		15	8	.652	3.43	33	33	7	215.1	213	51	144	1	0	0	0	75	12	0	.160	24	33	4	2	1.8	.934
1984		14	8	.636	3.74	30	30	4	211.2	208	51	145	1	0	0	0	66	5	0	.076	19	40	1	1	2.0	.983
1985		1	13	.071	6.14	22	22	0	95.1	115	57	57	0	0	0	0	25	3	0	.120	7	9	1	0	0.8	.941
1987	MON N	7	0	1.000	2.30	10	10	2	70.1	52	16	58	0	0	0	0	24	1	0	.042	6	17	3	0	2.6	.885
1988		12	8	.600	2.44	27	27	4	188	133	44	131	2	0	0	0	54	2	0	.037	13	38	0	2	1.9	1.000
1989		9	13	.409	3.31	33	28	2	198.1	178	45	152	0	1	1	0	54	11	0	.204	17	26	2	1	1.4	.956
1990	NY A	1	2	.333	1.29	3	3	0	14	8	3	12	0	0	0	0	0	0	0	—	0	0	0	0	0.0	—
10 yrs.		65	64	.504	3.45	193	179	21	1170.1	1099	320	781	4	3	2	0	342	41	0	.120	103	188	13	8	1.6	.957

LEAGUE CHAMPIONSHIP SERIES

Year	Team	W	L	%	ERA	G	GS	CG	IP	H	BB	SO	ShO	W	L	SV	AB	H	HR	BA	PO	A	E	DP	TC/G	FA
1982	ATL N	0	1	.000	5.19	2	1	0	8.2	10	2	4	0	0	0	0	3	0	0	.000	0	1	0	0	0.5	1.000

Pat Perry

PERRY, WILLIAM PATRICK (Atlas)
B. Feb. 4, 1959, Taylorville, Ill.
BL TL 6' 1" 190 lbs.

Year	Team	W	L	%	ERA	G	GS	CG	IP	H	BB	SO	ShO	W	L	SV	AB	H	HR	BA	PO	A	E	DP	TC/G	FA
1985	STL N	1	0	1.000	0.00	6	0	0	12.1	3	3	6	0	1	0	0	2	1	0	.500	0	1	0	0	0.2	1.000
1986		2	3	.400	3.80	46	0	0	68.2	59	34	29	0	2	3	2	8	0	0	.000	10	11	1	4	0.5	.955
1987	2 teams	STL N	(45G 4 – 2)						CIN N	(12G 1 – 0)																
"	total	5	2	.714	3.56	57	0	0	81	60	25	39	0	5	2	2	7	1	0	.143	12	12	1	2	0.4	.960
1988	2 teams	CIN N	(12G 2 – 2)						CHI N	(35G 2 – 2)																
"		4	4	.500	4.14	47	0	0	58.2	61	16	35	0	4	4	1	3	1	0	.333	4	7	0	0	0.2	1.000
1989	CHI N	0	1	.000	1.77	19	0	0	35.2	23	16	20	0	0	1	1	6	1	0	.167	2	3	1	0	0.3	.833
1990	LA N	0	0	—	8.10	7	0	0	6.2	9	5	2	0	0	1	0	0	1	0	.000	0	1	2	0	0.4	.333
6 yrs.		12	10	.545	3.46	182	0	0	263	215	99	131	0	12	10	6	27	4	1	.148	28	35	5	6	0.4	.926

Adam Peterson

PETERSON, ADAM CHARLES
B. Dec. 11, 1965, Long Beach, Calif.
BR TR 6' 3" 190 lbs.

Year	Team	W	L	%	ERA	G	GS	CG	IP	H	BB	SO	ShO	W	L	SV	AB	H	HR	BA	PO	A	E	DP	TC/G	FA
1987	CHI A	0	0	—	13.50	1	1	0	4	8	3	1	0	0	0	0	0	0	0	—	1	0	0	0	1.0	1.000
1988		0	1	.000	13.50	2	2	0	6	6	6	5	0	0	0	0	0	0	0	—	0	0	1	0	0.5	—
1989		0	1	.000	15.19	3	2	0	5.1	13	2	3	0	0	0	0	0	0	0	—	1	0	1	0	0.7	.500
1990		2	5	.286	4.55	20	11	2	85	90	26	29	0	0	1	0	0	0	0	—	4	7	1	0	0.6	.917
4 yrs.		2	7	.222	6.01	26	16	2	100.1	117	37	38	0	0	1	0	0	0	0	—	6	7	3	0	0.6	.813

Dan Petry

PETRY, DANIEL JOSEPH
B. Nov. 13, 1958, Palo Alto, Calif.
BR TR 6' 4" 185 lbs.

	W	L	%	ERA	G	GS	CG	IP	H	BB	SO	ShO	W	L	SV	
April	1	1	.500	3.20	7	2	0	19.2	18	13	11	0	1	0	0	
May	3	1	.750	2.48	6	6	1	40	33	17	26	0	0	0	0	
June	1	3	.250	5.16	6	6	0	29.2	31	21	12	0	0	0	0	
July	3	2	.600	5.40	6	5	0	31.2	31	12	12	0	1	0	0	
Aug	2	2	.500	6.38	4	4	0	24	30	10	11	0	0	0	0	
Sept/Oct	0	0	—	5.79				4.2	5	4	1	0	0	0	0	
Day	4	2	.667	3.80	11	6	0	45	46	19	31	0	2	0	0	
Night	6	7	.462	4.73	21	17	1	104.2	102	58	42	0	0	0	0	
vs. Left	—	—	—	—	—	—	—		61	37	32	—	—	—	—	
vs. Right	—	—	—	—	—	—	—		87	40	41	—	—	—	—	

STARTING PITCHER

WINS: 25.0 / 12.5 / 0.0 — AL AVG
ERA: 5.00 / 2.50 / 0.00 — AL AVG

Year	Team	W	L	%	ERA	G	GS	CG	IP	H	BB	SO	ShO	W	L	SV	AB	H	HR	BA	PO	A	E	DP	TC/G	FA

Dan Petry *Continued*

		W	L	%	ERA	G	GS	CG	IP	H	BB	SO	ShO	W	L	SV	AB	H	HR	BA	PO	A	E	DP	TC/G	FA
On Grass		9	8	.529	4.58	28	20	0	129.2	129	71	66	0	2	0	0										
On Turf		1	1	.500	3.60	4	3	1	20	19	6	7	0	0	0	0										
Home		4	5	.444	5.49	16	10	0	62.1	65	37	28	0	2	0	0										
Road		6	4	.600	3.71	16	13	1	87.1	83	40	45	0	0	0	0										
Division Rivals																										
vs. BAL		1	0	1.000	2.25	3	1	0	8	6	8	5	0	1	0	0										
vs. BOS		2	0	1.000	2.50	3	2	0	18	16	7	8	0	0	0	0										
vs. CLE		1	1	.500	6.35	2	2	0	11.1	14	8	5	0	0	0	0										
vs. MIL		1	2	.333	5.82	3	3	0	17	21	5	12	0	0	0	0										
vs. NY		0	1	.000	13.50	2	1	0	4	11	1	3	0	0	0	0										
vs. TOR		1	0	1.000	1.29	1	1	0	7	5	0	6	0	0	0	0										
1979	DET A	6	5	.545	3.95	15	15	2	98	90	33	43	0	0	0	0	0	0	0	—	9	11	2	0	1.5	.909
1980		10	9	.526	3.93	27	25	4	165	156	83	88	3	1	0	0	0	0	0	—	12	32	3	3	1.7	.936
1981		10	9	.526	3.00	23	22	7	141	115	57	79	2	0	0	0	0	0	0	.	14	26	1	6	1.8	.976
1982		15	9	.625	3.22	35	35	8	246	220	100	132	1	0	0	0	0	0	0	—	28	48	0	4	2.2	1.000
1983		19	11	.633	3.92	38	**38**	9	266.1	256	99	122	2	0	0	0	0	0	0	—	30	43	2	10	2.0	.973
1984		18	8	.692	3.24	35	35	7	233.1	231	66	144	2	0	0	0	0	0	0	—	38	34	1	4	2.1	.986
1985		15	13	.536	3.36	34	34	8	238.2	190	81	109	0	0	0	0	0	0	0	—	36	26	0	3	1.8	1.000
1986		5	10	.333	4.66	20	20	2	116	122	53	56	0	0	0	0	0	0	0	—	16	18	0	1	1.7	1.000
1987		9	7	.563	5.61	30	21	0	134.2	148	76	93	0	2	0	0	0	0	0	—	16	21	2	0	1.3	.949
1988	CAL A	3	9	.250	4.38	22	22	4	139.2	139	59	64	1	0	0	0	0	0	0	—	20	25	0	2	2.0	1.000
1989		3	2	.600	5.47	19	4	0	51	53	23	21	0	2	0	0	0	0	0	—	5	7	0	0	0.6	1.000
1990	DET A	10	9	.526	4.45	32	23	1	149.2	148	77	73	0	2	0	0	0	0	0	—	19	23	0	2	1.3	1.000
12 yrs.		123	101	.549	3.89	330	294	52	1979.1	1868	807	1024	11	7	0	0	0	0	0	—	243	314	11	35	1.7	.981

LEAGUE CHAMPIONSHIP SERIES

Year	Team	W	L	%	ERA	G	GS	CG	IP	H	BB	SO	ShO	W	L	SV	AB	H	HR	BA	PO	A	E	DP	TC/G	FA
1984	DET A	0	0	—	2.57	1	1	0	7	4	1	4	0	0	0	0	0	0	0	—	0	0	0	0	0.0	—
1987		0	0	—	0.00	1	0	0	3.1	1	0	1	0	0	0	0	0	0	0	—	0	1	0	0	1.0	1.000
2 yrs.		0	0	—	1.74	2	1	0	10.1	5	1	5	0	0	0	0	0	0	0	—	0	1	0	0	0.5	1.000

WORLD SERIES

Year	Team	W	L	%	ERA	G	GS	CG	IP	H	BB	SO	ShO	W	L	SV	AB	H	HR	BA	PO	A	E	DP	TC/G	FA
1984	DET A	0	1	.000	9.00	2	2	0	8	14	5	4	0	0	0	0	0	0	0	—	1	1	0	0	1.0	1.000

Jeff Pico

PICO, JEFFREY MARK
B. Feb. 12, 1966, Antioch, Calif.
BR TR 6' 1" 180 lbs.

		W	L	%	ERA	G	GS	CG	IP	H	BB	SO	ShO	W	L	SV	AB	H	HR	BA	PO	A	E	DP	TC/G	FA
April		0	0	—	10.13	5	1	0	8	14	8	3	0	0	0	0										
May		1	0	1.000	4.76	5	1	0	11.1	13	4	3	0	0	0	0										
June		3	0	1.000	3.66	6	4	0	32	35	11	16	0	0	0	0										
July		0	2	.000	3.32	7	2	0	21.2	28	5	7	0	0	0	2										
Aug		0	2	.000	6.88	7	1	0	17	29	7	6	0	0	1	0										
Sept/Oct		0	0	—	0.00	1	0	0	2	1	2	2	0	0	0	0										
Day		2	2	.500	5.40	18	4	0	55	75	24	21	0	0	1	2										
Night		2	2	.500	3.89	13	4	0	37	45	13	16	0	0	0	0										
vs. Left		—	—	—	—					74	25	13	—	—	—	—										
vs. Right		—	—	—	—					46	12	24	—	—	—	—										
On Grass		3	3	.500	5.06	26	6	0	74.2	102	33	29	0	0	1	2										
On Turf		1	1	.500	3.63	5	2	0	17.1	18	4	8	0	0	0	0										
Home		2	1	.667	5.37	21	3	0	53.2	76	22	22	0	0	1	2										
Road		2	3	.400	3.99	10	5	0	38.1	44	15	15	0	0	0	0										
Division Rivals																										
vs. MON		1	0	1.000	2.89	2	1	0	9.1	10	1	5	0	0	0	0										
vs. NY		0	0	—	11.88	3	1	0	8.1	15	6	4	0	0	0	0										
vs. PHI		2	0	1.000	1.65	3	2	0	16.1	15	8	6	0	0	0	0										
vs. PIT		0	0	—	3.52	3	0	0	7.2	7	3	4	0	0	0	0										
vs. STL		0	0	—	2.53	4	0	0	10.2	10	5	5	0	0	0	0										
1988	CHI N	6	7	.462	4.15	29	13	3	112.2	108	37	57	2	2	1	1	34	5	0	.147	5	18	1	3	0.8	.958
1989		3	1	.750	3.77	53	5	0	90.2	99	31	38	0	2	0	2	10	1	0	.100	4	22	3	2	0.5	.897
1990		4	4	.500	4.79	31	8	0	92	120	37	37	0	0	1	2	22	6	0	.273	13	16	1	2	1.0	.967
3 yrs.		13	12	.520	4.24	113	26	3	295.1	327	105	132	2	4	2	5	66	12	0	.182	22	56	5	7	0.7	.940

Year	Team	W	L	%	ERA	G	GS	CG	IP	H	BB	SO	ShO	RELIEF PITCHING W	L	SV	BATTING AB	H	HR	BA	PO	A	E	DP	TC/G	FA

Dan Plesac

PLESAC, DANIEL THOMAS
B. Feb. 4, 1962, Gary, Ind.
BL TL 6′ 5″ 205 lbs.

Split	W	L	%	ERA	G	GS	CG	IP	H	BB	SO	ShO	RW	RL	SV	AB	H	HR	BA	PO	A	E	DP	TC/G	FA
April	0	1	.000	2.00	7	0	0	9	6	3	6	0	0	1	2										
May	0	1	.000	7.84	10	0	0	10.1	16	3	12	0	0	1	7										
June	0	1	.000	7.59	15	0	0	10.2	13	8	8	0	0	1	4										
July	2	1	.667	2.25	11	0	0	16	13	6	18	0	2	1	3										
Aug	1	2	.333	3.21	14	0	0	14	7	7	14	0	1	2	5										
Sept/Oct	0	1	.000	5.00	9	0	0	9	12	4	7	0	0	1	3										
Day	1	4	.200	4.13	24	0	0	28.1	28	11	32	0	1	4	5										
Night	2	3	.400	4.65	42	0	0	40.2	39	20	33	0	2	3	19										
vs. Left	—	—	—	—	—	—	—	—	10	6	18	—	—	—	—										
vs. Right	—	—	—	—	—	—	—	—	57	25	47	—	—	—	—										
On Grass	3	6	.333	5.08	55	0	0	56.2	59	25	55	0	3	6	19										
On Turf	0	1	.000	1.46	11	0	0	12.1	8	6	10	0	0	1	5										
Home	2	3	.400	6.03	32	0	0	31.1	33	15	28	0	2	3	11										
Road	1	4	.200	3.11	34	0	0	37.2	34	16	37	0	1	4	13										
Division Rivals																									
vs. BAL	0	1	.000	4.50	4	0	0	4	2	2	3	0	0	1	2										
vs. BOS	1	1	.500	5.14	4	0	0	7	10	1	7	0	1	1	1										
vs. CLE	1	0	1.000	6.23	6	0	0	4.1	5	2	1	0	1	0	1										
vs. DET	0	0	—	0.00	6	0	0	4.2	5	0	4	0	0	0	5										
vs. NY	0	1	.000	4.91	6	0	0	7.1	7	6	11	0	0	1	1										
vs. TOR	0	0	—	4.15	5	0	0	4.1	2	4	4	0	0	0	2										
1986 MIL A	10	7	.588	2.97	51	0	0	91	81	29	75	0	10	7	14	0	0	0	—	1	11	0	0	0.2	1.000
1987	5	6	.455	2.61	57	0	0	79.1	63	23	89	0	5	6	23	0	0	0	—	0	12	2	1	0.2	.857
1988	1	2	.333	2.41	50	0	0	52.1	46	12	52	0	1	2	30	0	0	0	—	0	6	0	0	0.1	1.000
1989	3	4	.429	2.35	52	0	0	61.1	47	17	52	0	3	4	33	0	0	0	—	2	8	0	0	0.2	1.000
1990	3	7	.300	4.43	66	0	0	69	67	31	65	0	3	7	24	0	0	0	—	1	7	0	1	0.1	1.000
5 yrs.	22	26	.458	2.98	276	0	0	353	304	112	333	0	22	26	124	0	0	0	—	4	44	2	2	0.2	.960

Eric Plunk

PLUNK, ERIC VAUGHN
B. Sept. 3, 1963, Wilmington, Calif.
BR TR 6′ 5″ 210 lbs.

Split	W	L	%	ERA	G	GS	CG	IP	H	BB	SO	ShO	RW	RL	SV	AB	H	HR	BA	PO	A	E	DP	TC/G	FA
April	2	0	1.000	2.00	7	0	0	9	10	5	3	0	2	0	0										
May	0	1	.000	3.65	8	0	0	12.1	16	9	10	0	0	1	0										
June	0	1	.000	2.79	7	0	0	9.2	6	8	9	0	0	1	0										
July	2	0	1.000	1.80	6	0	0	10	6	7	6	0	2	0	0										
Aug	1	0	1.000	3.60	8	0	0	15	7	10	19	0	1	0	0										
Sept/Oct	1	1	.500	2.16	11	0	0	16.2	13	4	20	0	1	1	0										
Day	5	1	.833	1.33	16	0	0	20.1	20	14	15	0	5	1	0										
Night	1	2	.333	3.27	31	0	0	52.1	38	29	52	0	1	2	0										
vs. Left	—	—	—	—	—	—	—	—	26	17	25	—	—	—	—										
vs. Right	—	—	—	—	—	—	—	—	32	26	42	—	—	—	—										
On Grass	5	2	.714	2.44	40	0	0	55.1	45	33	50	0	5	2	0										
On Turf	1	1	.500	3.63	7	0	0	17.1	13	10	17	0	1	1	0										
Home	4	0	1.000	3.71	19	0	0	26.2	29	15	24	0	4	0	0										
Road	2	3	.400	2.15	28	0	0	46	29	28	43	0	2	3	0										
Division Rivals																									
vs. BAL	0	0	—	0.00	3	0	0	5.2	2	4	4	0	0	0	0										
vs. BOS	1	1	.500	4.91	8	0	0	7.1	6	4	9	0	1	1	0										
vs. CLE	2	0	1.000	1.08	5	0	0	8.1	9	4	3	0	2	0	0										
vs. DET	0	0	—	15.00	3	0	0	3	5	3	5	0	0	0	0										
vs. MIL	0	0	—	0.00	1	0	0	1	0	1	1	0	0	0	0										
vs. TOR	0	1	.000	2.35	4	0	0	7.2	6	3	8	0	0	1	0										
1986 OAK A	4	7	.364	5.31	26	15	0	120.1	91	102	98	0	0	1	0	0	0	0	—	3	6	1	0	0.4	.900
1987	4	6	.400	4.74	32	11	0	95	91	62	90	0	3	2	2	0	0	0	—	1	9	0	0	0.3	1.000
1988	7	2	.778	3.00	49	0	0	78	62	39	79	0	7	2	5	0	0	0	—	2	5	1	0	0.2	.875
1989 2 teams	OAK A (23G 1 – 1)			NY A	(27G 7 – 5)																				
" total	8	6	.571	3.28	50	7	0	104.1	82	64	85	0	4	3	1	0	0	0	—	2	7	1	0	0.2	.900
1990 NY A	6	3	.667	2.72	47	0	0	72.2	58	43	67	0	6	3	0	0	0	0	—	3	18	2	2	0.5	.913
5 yrs.	29	24	.547	3.96	204	33	0	470.1	384	310	419	0	20	11	8	0	0	0	—	11	45	5	2	0.3	.918

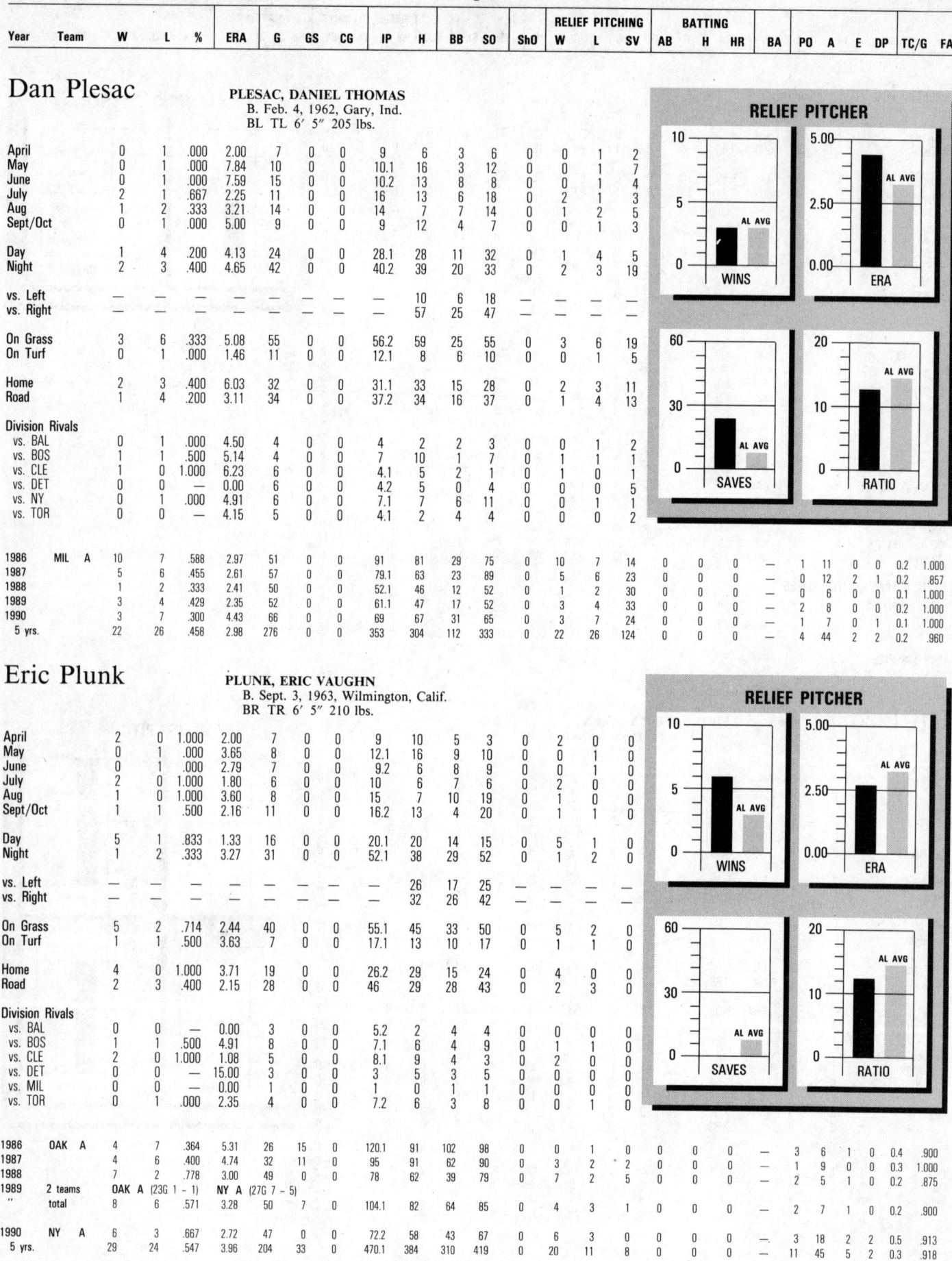

Year	Team	W	L	%	ERA	G	GS	CG	IP	H	BB	SO	ShO	RELIEF PITCHING W	L	SV	BATTING AB	H	HR	BA	PO	A	E	DP	TC/G	FA

Eric Plunk *Continued*

LEAGUE CHAMPIONSHIP SERIES

Year	Team	W	L	%	ERA	G	GS	CG	IP	H	BB	SO	ShO	W	L	SV	AB	H	HR	BA	PO	A	E	DP	TC/G	FA
1988	OAK A	0	0	—	0.00	1	0	0	0.1	1	0	1	0	0	0	0	0	0	0	—	0	0	0	0	0.0	—

WORLD SERIES

Year	Team	W	L	%	ERA	G	GS	CG	IP	H	BB	SO	ShO	W	L	SV	AB	H	HR	BA	PO	A	E	DP	TC/G	FA
1988	OAK A	0	0	—	0.00	2	0	0	1.2	0	0	3	0	0	0	0	0	0	0	—	0	0	0	0	0.0	—

Jim Poole

POOLE, JAMES RICHARD
B. Apr. 28, 1966, Rochester, N. Y.
BL TL 6′ 2″ 190 lbs.

Year	Team	W	L	%	ERA	G	GS	CG	IP	H	BB	SO	ShO	W	L	SV	AB	H	HR	BA	PO	A	E	DP	TC/G	FA
1990	LA N	0	0	—	4.22	16	0	0	10.2	7	8	6	0	0	0	0	0	0	0	—	0	1	0	0	0.1	1.000

Mark Portugal

PORTUGAL, MARK STEVEN
B. Oct. 30, 1962, Los Angeles, Calif.
BR TR 6′ 170 lbs.

	W	L	%	ERA	G	GS	CG	IP	H	BB	SO	ShO	W	L	SV										
April	1	3	.250	3.68	4	4	0	22	27	4	14	0	0	0	0										
May	0	2	.000	5.02	5	5	0	28.2	32	11	14	0	0	0	0										
June	1	2	.333	3.40	6	6	0	39.2	30	12	28	0	0	0	0										
July	2	2	.500	4.24	6	6	0	34	36	12	27	0	0	0	0										
Aug	4	0	1.000	1.27	5	5	1	35.1	33	12	29	0	0	0	0										
Sept/Oct	3	1	.750	4.38	6	6	0	37	29	16	24	0	0	0	0										
Day	3	5	.375	4.28	11	11	0	67.1	69	21	45	0	0	0	0										
Night	8	5	.615	3.27	21	21	1	129.1	118	46	91	0	0	0	0										
vs. Left	—	—	—	—	—	—	—	—	97	44	90	—	—	—	—										
vs. Right	—	—	—	—	—	—	—	—	90	23	46	—	—	—	—										
On Grass	2	6	.250	6.31	12	12	1	67	85	18	42	0	0	0	0										
On Turf	9	4	.692	2.22	20	20	0	129.2	102	49	94	0	0	0	0										
Home	8	2	.800	1.78	15	15	0	101.1	78	31	74	0	0	0	0										
Road	3	8	.273	5.57	17	17	1	95.1	109	36	62	0	0	0	0										
Division Rivals																									
vs. ATL	3	0	1.000	2.89	3	3	0	18.2	16	10	14	0	0	0	0										
vs. CIN	1	2	.333	6.75	3	3	0	14.2	16	6	9	0	0	0	0										
vs. LA	0	1	.000	6.64	4	4	0	20.1	27	7	15	0	0	0	0										
vs. SD	0	2	.000	3.92	3	3	0	20.2	18	7	12	0	0	0	0										
vs. SF	3	1	.750	1.99	6	6	0	40.2	31	9	33	0	0	0	0										

STARTING PITCHER

Year	Team	W	L	%	ERA	G	GS	CG	IP	H	BB	SO	ShO	W	L	SV	AB	H	HR	BA	PO	A	E	DP	TC/G	FA
1985	MIN A	1	3	.250	5.55	6	4	0	24.1	24	14	12	0	0	0	0	0	0	0	—	4	7	1	1	2.0	.917
1986		6	10	.375	4.31	27	15	3	112.2	112	50	67	0	2	4	1	0	0	0	—	5	14	1	3	0.7	.950
1987		1	3	.250	7.77	13	7	0	44	58	24	28	0	0	1	0	0	0	0	—	1	6	0	2	0.5	1.000
1988		3	3	.500	4.53	26	0	0	57.2	60	17	31	0	3	3	3	0	0	0	—	2	1	1	0	0.2	.750
1989	HOU N	7	1	.875	2.75	20	15	2	108	91	37	86	1	0	0	0	34	7	1	.206	11	15	2	0	1.4	.929
1990		11	10	.524	3.62	32	32	1	196.2	187	67	136	0	0	0	0	66	9	0	.136	23	19	1	2	1.3	.977
6 yrs.		29	30	.492	4.11	124	73	6	543.1	532	209	360	1	5	8	4	100	16	1	.160	46	62	6	8	0.9	.947

Dennis Powell

POWELL, DENNIS CLAY
B. Aug. 13, 1963, Moultrie, Ga.
BR TL 6′ 3″ 175 lbs.

Year	Team	W	L	%	ERA	G	GS	CG	IP	H	BB	SO	ShO	W	L	SV	AB	H	HR	BA	PO	A	E	DP	TC/G	FA
1985	LA N	1	1	.500	5.22	16	2	0	29.1	30	13	19	0	1	0	1	3	0	0	.000	0	6	0	2	0.4	1.000
1986		2	7	.222	4.27	27	6	0	65.1	65	25	31	0	1	2	0	14	3	0	.214	7	6	1	1	0.5	.929
1987	SEA A	1	3	.250	3.15	16	3	0	34.1	32	15	17	0	1	2	0	0	0	0	—	2	6	0	0	0.5	1.000
1988		1	3	.250	8.68	12	2	0	18.2	29	11	15	0	1	2	0	0	0	0	—	1	3	0	0	0.3	1.000
1989		2	2	.500	5.00	43	1	0	45	49	21	27	0	2	1	2	0	0	0	—	2	11	0	0	0.3	1.000
1990	2 teams	SEA A	(2G 0 - 0)		MIL A	(9G 0 - 4)																				
"	total	0	4	.000	7.02	11	7	0	42.1	64	21	23	0	0	0	0	0	0	0	—	2	9	0	0	1.0	1.000
6 yrs.		7	20	.259	5.21	125	21	0	235	269	106	132	0	6	7	3	17	3	0	.176	14	41	1	3	0.4	.982

Year	Team	W	L	%	ERA	G	GS	CG	IP	H	BB	SO	ShO	RELIEF PITCHING W	L	SV	BATTING AB	H	HR	BA	PO	A	E	DP	TC/G	FA

Ted Power

POWER, TED HENRY
B. Jan. 31, 1955, Guthrie, Okla.
BR TR 6′ 4″ 220 lbs.

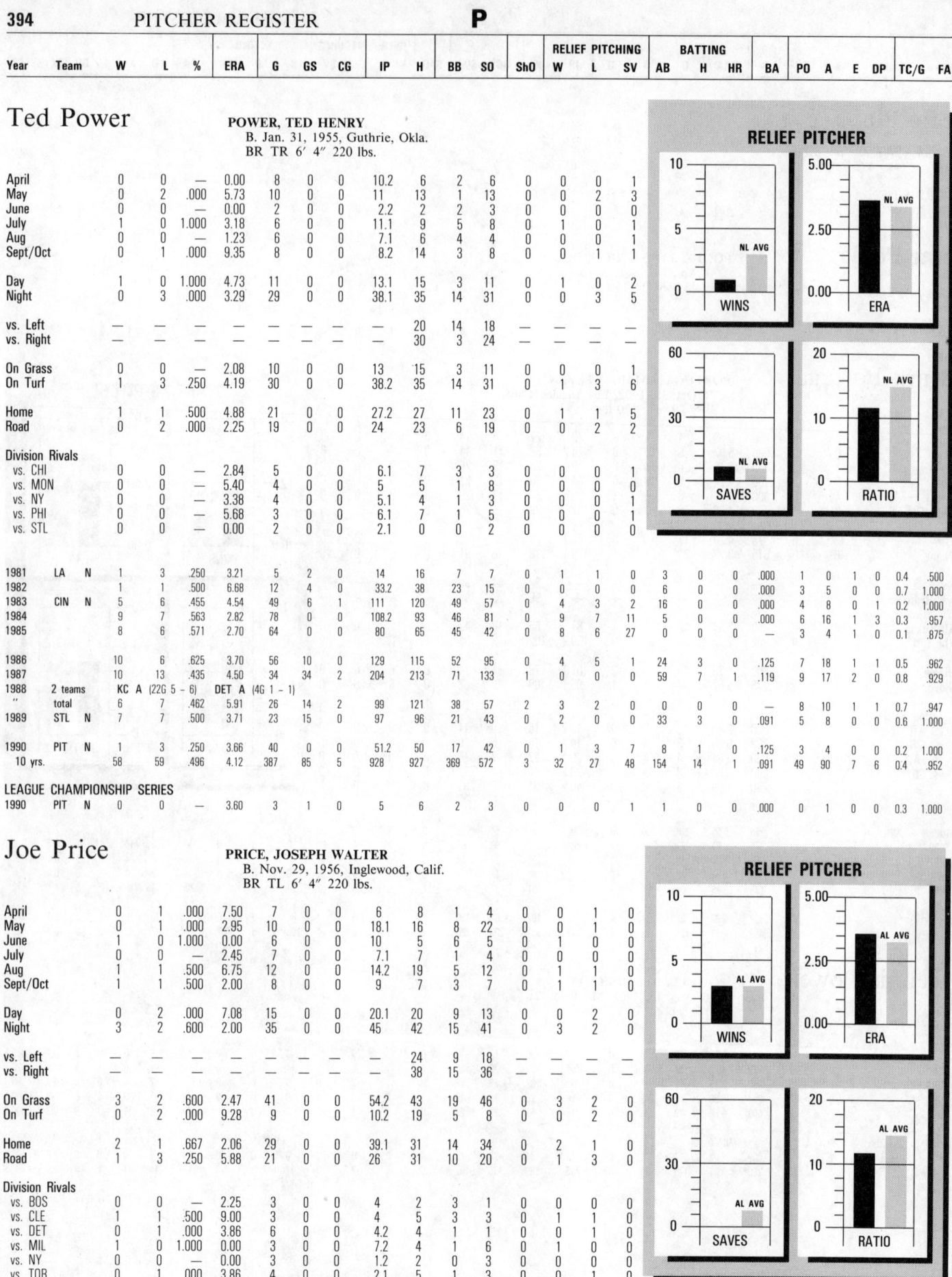

RELIEF PITCHER — WINS / ERA / SAVES / RATIO (NL AVG)

Period	W	L	%	ERA	G	GS	CG	IP	H	BB	SO	ShO	W	L	SV	AB	H	HR	BA	PO	A	E	DP	TC/G	FA
April	0	0	—	0.00	8	0	0	10.2	6	2	6	0	0	0	1										
May	0	2	.000	5.73	10	0	0	11	13	1	13	0	0	2	3										
June	0	0	—	0.00	2	0	0	2.2	2	2	3	0	0	0	0										
July	1	0	1.000	3.18	6	0	0	11.1	9	5	8	0	1	0	1										
Aug	0	0	—	1.23	6	0	0	7.1	6	4	4	0	0	0	1										
Sept/Oct	0	1	.000	9.35	8	0	0	8.2	14	3	8	0	0	1	1										
Day	1	0	1.000	4.73	11	0	0	13.1	15	3	11	0	1	0	2										
Night	0	3	.000	3.29	29	0	0	38.1	35	14	31	0	0	3	5										
vs. Left	—	—	—	—	—	—	—	—	20	14	18	—	—	—	—										
vs. Right	—	—	—	—	—	—	—	—	30	3	24	—	—	—	—										
On Grass	0	0	—	2.08	10	0	0	13	15	3	11	0	0	0	1										
On Turf	1	3	.250	4.19	30	0	0	38.2	35	14	31	0	1	3	6										
Home	1	1	.500	4.88	21	0	0	27.2	27	11	23	0	1	1	5										
Road	0	2	.000	2.25	19	0	0	24	23	6	19	0	0	2	2										
Division Rivals																									
vs. CHI	0	0	—	2.84	5	0	0	6.1	7	3	3	0	0	0	1										
vs. MON	0	0	—	5.40	4	0	0	5	5	1	8	0	0	0	0										
vs. NY	0	0	—	3.38	4	0	0	5.1	4	1	3	0	0	0	1										
vs. PHI	0	0	—	5.68	3	0	0	6.1	7	1	5	0	0	0	1										
vs. STL	0	0	—	0.00	2	0	0	2.1	0	2	2	0	0	0	0										
1981	LA N	1	3	.250	3.21	5	2	0	14	16	7	7	0	1	1	0	3	0	0	.000	1	0	1	0	0.4	.500
1982		1	1	.500	6.68	12	4	0	33.2	38	23	15	0	0	0	0	6	0	0	.000	3	5	0	0	0.7	1.000
1983	CIN N	5	6	.455	4.54	49	6	1	111	120	49	57	0	4	3	2	16	0	0	.000	4	8	0	1	0.2	1.000
1984		9	7	.563	2.82	78	0	0	108.2	93	46	81	0	9	7	11	5	0	0	.000	6	16	1	3	0.3	.957
1985		8	6	.571	2.70	64	0	0	80	65	45	42	0	8	6	27	0	0	0	—	3	4	1	0	0.1	.875
1986		10	6	.625	3.70	56	10	0	129	115	52	95	0	4	5	1	24	3	0	.125	7	18	1	1	0.5	.962
1987		10	13	.435	4.50	34	34	2	204	213	71	133	1	0	0	0	59	7	1	.119	9	17	2	0	0.8	.929
1988	2 teams	KC A	(22G 5 – 6)		DET A	(4G 1 – 1)																				
"	total	6	7	.462	5.91	26	14	2	99	121	38	57	0	2	3	2	0	0	0	—	8	10	1	0	0.7	.947
1989	STL N	7	7	.500	3.71	23	15	0	97	96	21	43	0	2	0	0	33	3	0	.091	5	8	0	0	0.6	1.000
1990	PIT N	1	3	.250	3.66	40	0	0	51.2	50	17	42	0	1	3	7	8	1	0	.125	3	4	0	0	0.2	1.000
10 yrs.		58	59	.496	4.12	387	85	5	928	927	369	572	3	32	27	48	154	14	1	.091	49	90	7	6	0.4	.952

LEAGUE CHAMPIONSHIP SERIES

Year	Team	W	L	%	ERA	G	GS	CG	IP	H	BB	SO	ShO	W	L	SV	AB	H	HR	BA	PO	A	E	DP	TC/G	FA
1990	PIT N	0	0	—	3.60	3	1	0	5	6	2	3	0	0	0	1	1	0	0	.000	0	1	0	0	0.3	1.000

Joe Price

PRICE, JOSEPH WALTER
B. Nov. 29, 1956, Inglewood, Calif.
BR TL 6′ 4″ 220 lbs.

RELIEF PITCHER — WINS / ERA / SAVES / RATIO (AL AVG)

Period	W	L	%	ERA	G	GS	CG	IP	H	BB	SO	ShO	W	L	SV	AB	H	HR	BA	PO	A	E	DP	TC/G	FA
April	0	1	.000	7.50	7	0	0	6	8	1	4	0	0	1	0										
May	0	1	.000	2.95	10	0	0	18.1	16	8	22	0	0	1	0										
June	1	0	1.000	0.00	6	0	0	10	5	6	5	0	1	0	0										
July	0	0	—	2.45	7	0	0	7.1	7	1	4	0	0	0	0										
Aug	1	1	.500	6.75	12	0	0	14.2	19	5	12	0	1	1	0										
Sept/Oct	1	1	.500	2.00	8	0	0	9	7	3	7	0	1	1	0										
Day	0	2	.000	7.08	15	0	0	20.1	20	9	13	0	0	2	0										
Night	3	2	.600	2.00	35	0	0	45	42	15	41	0	3	2	0										
vs. Left	—	—	—	—	—	—	—	—	24	9	18	—	—	—	—										
vs. Right	—	—	—	—	—	—	—	—	38	15	36	—	—	—	—										
On Grass	3	2	.600	2.47	41	0	0	54.2	43	19	46	0	3	2	0										
On Turf	0	2	.000	9.28	9	0	0	10.2	19	5	8	0	0	2	0										
Home	2	1	.667	2.06	29	0	0	39.1	31	14	34	0	2	1	0										
Road	1	3	.250	5.88	21	0	0	26	31	10	20	0	1	3	0										
Division Rivals																									
vs. BOS	0	0	—	2.25	3	0	0	4	2	3	1	0	0	0	0										
vs. CLE	1	1	.500	9.00	3	0	0	4	5	3	3	0	1	1	0										
vs. DET	0	1	.000	3.86	6	0	0	4.2	4	1	1	0	0	1	0										
vs. MIL	1	0	1.000	0.00	3	0	0	7.2	4	1	6	0	1	0	0										
vs. NY	0	0	—	0.00	3	0	0	1.2	2	1	3	0	0	0	0										
vs. TOR	0	1	.000	3.86	4	0	0	2.1	5	1	3	0	0	1	0										

Year	Team	W	L	%	ERA	G	GS	CG	IP	H	BB	SO	ShO	RELIEF PITCHING W	L	SV	BATTING AB	H	HR	BA	PO	A	E	DP	TC/G	FA

Joe Price *Continued*

Year	Team	W	L	%	ERA	G	GS	CG	IP	H	BB	SO	ShO	W	L	SV	AB	H	HR	BA	PO	A	E	DP	TC/G	FA
1980	CIN N	7	3	.700	3.57	24	13	2	111	95	37	44	0	2	0	0	39	5	0	.128	3	16	2	0	0.9	.905
1981		6	1	.857	2.50	41	0	0	54	42	18	41	0	6	1	4	3	0	0	.000	1	13	2	0	0.4	.875
1982		3	4	.429	2.85	59	1	0	72.2	73	32	71	0	3	3	3	3	1	0	.333	1	8	2	0	0.2	.818
1983		10	6	.625	2.88	21	21	5	144	118	46	83	0	0	0	0	41	4	0	.098	8	21	4	3	1.6	.879
1984		7	13	.350	4.19	30	30	3	171.2	176	61	129	1	0	0	0	48	7	0	.146	4	14	0	0	0.6	1.000
1985		2	2	.500	3.90	26	8	0	64.2	59	23	52	0	0	0	1	14	0	0	.000	1	4	0	1	0.2	1.000
1986		1	2	.333	5.40	25	2	0	41.2	49	22	30	0	1	1	0	7	1	0	.143	2	2	0	0	0.2	1.000
1987	SF N	2	2	.500	2.57	20	0	0	35	19	13	42	0	2	2	1	6	1	0	.167	1	2	0	0	0.2	1.000
1988		1	6	.143	3.94	38	3	0	61.2	59	27	49	0	1	6	4	8	0	0	.000	3	8	0	0	0.3	1.000
1989	2 teams	SF N (7G 1 - 1)			BOS A (31G 2 - 5)																					
"	total	3	6	.333	4.59	38	6	0	84.1	87	34	62	0	1	3	0	2	0	0	.000	2	8	0	1	0.3	1.000
1990	BAL A	3	4	.429	3.58	50	0	0	65.1	62	24	54	0	3	4	0	0	0	0	—	1	8	2	0	0.2	.818
11 yrs.		45	49	.479	3.65	372	84	10	906	839	337	657	1	19	20	13	171	19	0	.111	27	104	12	5	0.4	.916

LEAGUE CHAMPIONSHIP SERIES

Year	Team	W	L	%	ERA	G	GS	CG	IP	H	BB	SO	ShO	W	L	SV	AB	H	HR	BA	PO	A	E	DP	TC/G	FA
1987	SF N	1	0	1.000	0.00	2	0	0	5.2	3	1	7	0	1	0	0	1	0	0	.000	0	0	0	0	0.0	—

Dan Quisenberry

QUISENBERRY, DANIEL RAYMOND (Quiz)
B. Feb. 7, 1953, Santa Monica, Calif.
BR TR 6′ 2″ 170 lbs.

Year	Team	W	L	%	ERA	G	GS	CG	IP	H	BB	SO	ShO	W	L	SV	AB	H	HR	BA	PO	A	E	DP	TC/G	FA
1979	KC A	3	2	.600	3.15	32	0	0	40	42	7	13	0	3	2	5	0	0	0	—	0	10	1	2	0.3	.909
1980		12	7	.632	3.09	75	0	0	128	129	27	37	0	12	7	33	0	0	0	—	17	29	2	4	0.6	.958
1981		1	4	.200	1.74	40	0	0	62	59	15	20	0	1	4	18	0	0	0	—	8	23	1	1	0.8	.969
1982		9	7	.563	2.57	72	0	0	136.2	126	12	46	0	9	7	35	0	0	0	—	18	46	2	3	0.9	.970
1983		5	3	.625	1.94	69	0	0	139	118	11	48	0	5	3	45	0	0	0	—	8	30	3	1	0.6	.927
1984		6	3	.667	2.64	72	0	0	129.1	121	12	41	0	6	3	44	0	0	0	—	15	29	0	1	0.6	1.000
1985		8	9	.471	2.37	84	0	0	129	142	16	54	0	8	9	37	0	0	0	—	8	24	2	2	0.4	.941
1986		3	7	.300	2.77	62	0	0	81.1	92	24	36	0	3	7	12	0	0	0	—	9	19	1	3	0.5	.966
1987		4	1	.800	2.76	47	0	0	49	58	10	17	0	4	1	8	0	0	0	—	6	13	0	3	0.4	1.000
1988	2 teams	KC A (20G 0 - 1)			STL N (33G 2 - 0)																					
"	total	2	1	.667	5.12	53	0	0	63.1	86	11	28	0	2	1	1	1	0	0	.000	1	18	1	1	0.4	.950
1989	STL N	3	1	.750	2.64	63	0	0	78.1	78	14	37	0	3	1	6	4	1	0	.250	7	22	0	1	0.5	1.000
1990	SF N	0	1	.000	13.50	5	0	0	6.2	13	3	2	0	0	1	0	1	0	0	.000	0	1	0	0	0.2	1.000
12 yrs.		56	46	.549	2.76	674	0	0	1042.2	1064	162	379	0	56	46	244 (6th)	6	1	0	.167	97	264	13	22	0.6	.965

DIVISIONAL PLAYOFF SERIES

Year	Team	W	L	%	ERA	G	GS	CG	IP	H	BB	SO	ShO	W	L	SV	AB	H	HR	BA	PO	A	E	DP	TC/G	FA
1981	KC A	0	0	—	0.00	1	0	0	1	1	0	0	0	0	0	0	0	0	0	—	0	0	0	0	0.0	—

LEAGUE CHAMPIONSHIP SERIES

Year	Team	W	L	%	ERA	G	GS	CG	IP	H	BB	SO	ShO	W	L	SV	AB	H	HR	BA	PO	A	E	DP	TC/G	FA
1980	KC A	1	0	1.000	0.00	2	0	0	4.2	4	2	1	0	1	0	1	0	0	0	—	1	0	0	0	0.5	1.000
1984		0	0	.000	3.00	1	0	0	3	2	1	1	0	0	0	0	0	0	0	—	1	1	0	0	2.0	1.000
1985		0	1	.000	3.86	4	0	0	4.2	7	0	3	0	0	1	1	0	0	0	—	1	1	0	0	0.5	1.000
3 yrs.		1	2	.333	2.19	7	0	0	12.1	13	3	5	0	1	2	2	0	0	0	—	3	2	0	0	0.7	1.000

WORLD SERIES

Year	Team	W	L	%	ERA	G	GS	CG	IP	H	BB	SO	ShO	W	L	SV	AB	H	HR	BA	PO	A	E	DP	TC/G	FA
1980	KC A	1	2	.333	5.23	6	0	0	10.1	10	3	1	0	1	2	1	0	0	0	—	1	1	0	0	0.3	1.000
1985		1	0	1.000	2.08	4	0	0	4.1	5	3	3	0	1	0	0	0	0	0	—	1	1	0	0	0.5	1.000
2 yrs.		2	2	.500	4.30	10	0	0	14.2	15	6	3	0	2 (2nd)	2 (2nd)	1	0	0	0	—	2	2	0	0	0.4	1.000

Scott Radinsky

RADINSKY, SCOTT DAVID
B. Mar. 3, 1968, Glendale, Calif.
BL TL 6′ 3″ 190 lbs.

Year	Team	W	L	%	ERA	G	GS	CG	IP	H	BB	SO	ShO	W	L	SV
April		1	0	1.000	1.50	8	0	0	6	4	4	4	0	1	0	0
May		3	0	1.000	2.08	14	0	0	13	4	6	14	0	3	0	2
June		1	0	1.000	2.61	12	0	0	10.1	10	6	7	0	1	0	0
July		1	1	.500	6.75	13	0	0	10.2	13	8	12	0	1	1	0
Aug		0	0	—	4.82	9	0	0	9.1	9	5	8	0	0	0	1
Sept/Oct		0	0	—	24.00	6	0	0	3	7	7	1	0	0	0	0
Day		3	1	.750	7.47	21	0	0	15.2	20	10	11	0	3	1	1
Night		3	0	1.000	3.68	41	0	0	36.2	27	26	35	0	3	0	3
vs. Left		—	—	—	—	—	—	—	—	11	7	20	—	—	—	—
vs. Right		—	—	—	—	—	—	—	—	36	29	26	—	—	—	—

RELIEF PITCHER

WINS — 10 / 5 / 0 scale; bar above AL AVG
ERA — 5.00 / 2.50 / 0.00 scale; bar above AL AVG

Year	Team	W	L	%	ERA	G	GS	CG	IP	H	BB	SO	ShO	RELIEF PITCHING W	L	SV	BATTING AB	H	HR	BA	PO	A	E	DP	TC/G	FA

Scott Radinsky *Continued*

On Grass	5	1	.833	4.71	50	0	0	42	35	29	40	0	5	1	4										
On Turf	1	0	1.000	5.23	12	0	0	10.1	12	7	6	0	1	0	0										
Home	2	1	.667	4.50	31	0	0	26	17	16	23	0	2	1	3										
Road	4	0	1.000	5.13	31	0	0	26.1	30	20	23	0	4	0	1										
Division Rivals																									
vs. CAL	0	0	—	8.10	4	0	0	3.1	5	2	2	0	0	0	1										
vs. KC	1	0	1.000	0.00	7	0	0	5.1	1	1	5	0	1	0	1										
vs. MIN	1	0	1.000	19.29	3	0	0	2.1	6	3	0	0	1	0	0										
vs. OAK	0	0	—	6.00	4	0	0	3	3	1	2	0	0	0	0										
vs. SEA	0	0	—	10.38	5	0	0	4.1	7	7	2	0	0	0	0										
vs. TEX	0	0	—	0.00	5	0	0	5.2	2	4	4	0	0	0	2										
1990 CHI A	6	1	.857	4.82	62	0	0	52.1	47	36	46	0	6	1	4	0	0	0	—	7	4	0	0	0.2	1.000

Dennis Rasmussen RASMUSSEN, DENNIS LEE

B. Apr. 18, 1959, Los Angeles, Calif.
BL TL 6′ 7″ 230 lbs.

April	1	1	.500	5.12	4	4	0	19.1	23	8	7	0	0	0	0										
May	4	1	.800	2.61	6	6	1	38	37	9	22	0	0	0	0										
June	2	2	.500	3.46	4	4	2	26	28	8	10	1	0	0	0										
July	0	5	.000	6.34	6	6	0	32.2	50	12	12	0	0	0	0										
Aug	1	4	.200	4.63	6	6	0	35	35	14	16	0	0	0	0										
Sept/Oct	3	2	.600	5.15	6	6	0	36.2	44	11	19	0	0	0	0										
Day	3	5	.375	4.83	11	11	1	59.2	68	21	30	0	0	0	0										
Night	8	10	.444	4.36	21	21	2	128	149	41	56	1	0	0	0										
vs. Left	—	—	—	—	—	—	—	—	36	7	13	—	—	—	—										
vs. Right	—	—	—	—	—	—	—	—	181	55	73	—	—	—	—										
On Grass	8	13	.381	4.81	25	25	1	144	172	42	65	0	0	0	0										
On Turf	3	2	.600	3.50	7	7	2	43.2	45	20	21	1	0	0	0										
Home	5	9	.357	4.37	17	17	1	101	119	31	45	0	0	0	0										
Road	6	6	.500	4.67	15	15	2	86.2	98	31	41	1	0	0	0										
Division Rivals																									
vs. ATL	2	1	.667	3.15	3	3	0	20	17	5	11	0	0	0	0										
vs. CIN	1	2	.333	8.59	4	4	0	14.2	25	8	5	0	0	0	0										
vs. HOU	3	1	.750	1.95	4	4	2	32.1	32	10	14	1	0	0	0										
vs. LA	1	1	.500	4.35	4	4	0	20.2	24	5	11	0	0	0	0										
vs. SF	0	2	.000	9.75	2	2	0	12	21	3	5	0	0	0	0										
1983 SD N	0	0	—	1.98	4	1	0	13.2	10	8	13	0	0	0	0	3	0	0	.000	0	4	0	1	1.0	1.000
1984 NY A	9	6	.600	4.57	24	24	1	147.2	127	60	110	0	0	0	0	0	0	0	—	7	14	2	1	1.0	.913
1985	3	5	.375	3.98	22	16	2	101.2	97	42	63	0	0	0	0	0	0	0	—	7	13	0	2	0.9	1.000
1986	18	6	.750	3.88	31	31	3	202	160	74	131	1	0	0	0	0	0	0	—	6	26	0	0	1.0	1.000
1987 2 teams	NY A (26G 9 – 7)			CIN N (7G 4 – 1)																					
" total	13	8	.619	4.56	33	32	2	191.1	184	67	128	0	0	0	0	15	1	0	.067	6	30	2	0	1.2	.947
1988 2 teams	CIN N (11G 2 – 6)			SD N (20G 14 – 4)																					
"	16	10	.615	3.43	31	31	7	204.2	199	58	112	1	0	0	0	70	14	0	.200	3	45	0	1	1.5	1.000
1989 SD N	10	10	.500	4.26	33	33	1	183.2	190	72	87	0	0	0	0	65	11	0	.169	6	27	0	3	1.0	1.000
1990	11	15	.423	4.51	32	32	3	187.2	217	62	86	1	0	0	0	62	18	0	.290	8	31	3	2	1.3	.929
8 yrs.	80	60	.571	4.13	210	200	19	1232.1	1184	443	730	3	0	0	0	215	44	0	.205	43	190	7	10	1.1	.971

RELIEF PITCHER — SAVES · RATIO (AL AVG)

STARTING PITCHER — WINS · ERA · SO/9 · RATIO (NL AVG)

Year	Team	W	L	%	ERA	G	GS	CG	IP	H	BB	SO	ShO	W	L	SV	AB	H	HR	BA	PO	A	E	DP	TC/G	FA
														RELIEF PITCHING			BATTING									

Jeff Reardon

REARDON, JEFFREY JAMES
B. Oct. 1, 1955, Pittsfield, Mass.
BR TR 6' 190 lbs.

Year	Team	W	L	%	ERA	G	GS	CG	IP	H	BB	SO	ShO	W	L	SV	AB	H	HR	BA	PO	A	E	DP	TC/G	FA
April		1	0	1.000	0.00	8	0	0	8.1	1	3	6	0	1	0	1										
May		0	1	.000	3.75	10	0	0	12	9	3	7	0	0	1	4										
June		2	1	.667	4.20	13	0	0	15	12	7	11	0	2	1	8										
July		0	1	.000	4.32	8	0	0	8.1	10	4	2	0	0	1	5										
Aug		—	—	—	—	0	—	—	0	0	0	0	—	0	0	0										
Sept/Oct		2	0	1.000	2.35	8	0	0	7.2	7	2	7	0	2	0	3										
Day		0	1	.000	3.38	10	0	0	10.2	9	1	5	0	0	1	2										
Night		5	2	.714	3.10	37	0	0	40.2	30	18	28	0	5	2	19										
vs. Left		—	—	—	—	—	—	—	—	13	12	12	—	—	—	—										
vs. Right		—	—	—	—	—	—	—	—	26	7	21	—	—	—	—										
On Grass		5	1	.833	1.93	42	0	0	46.2	28	15	32	0	5	1	19										
On Turf		0	2	.000	15.43	5	0	0	4.2	11	4	1	0	0	2	2										
Home		5	1	.833	2.03	26	0	0	26.2	17	8	19	0	5	1	12										
Road		0	2	.000	4.38	21	0	0	24.2	22	11	14	0	0	2	9										
Division Rivals																										
vs. BAL		0	0	—	4.50	2	0	0	2	2	2	0	0	0	0	1										
vs. CLE		0	0	—	1.50	4	0	0	6	3	3	8	0	0	0	2										
vs. DET		0	0	—	0.00	1	0	0	0.2	0	0	1	0	0	0	1										
vs. MIL		0	0	—	0.00	2	0	0	3	0	0	2	0	0	0	0										
vs. NY		2	0	1.000	1.93	4	0	0	4.2	2	1	3	0	2	0	2										
vs. TOR		1	0	1.000	2.08	5	0	0	4.1	2	2	2	0	1	0	4										
1979	NY N	1	2	.333	1.71	18	0	0	21	12	9	10	0	1	2	2	0	0	0	—	1	1	0	1	0.1	1.000
1980		8	7	.533	2.62	61	0	0	110	96	47	101	0	8	7	6	8	0	0	.000	1	7	4	0	0.2	.667
1981	2 teams	NY N (18G 1 – 0)			MON N (25G 2 – 0)																					
"	total	3	0	1.000	2.18	43	0	0	70.1	48	21	49	0	3	0	8	5	0	0	.000	0	2	0	0	0.0	1.000
1982	MON N	7	4	.636	2.06	75	0	0	109	87	36	86	0	7	4	26	10	1	0	.100	6	9	1	0	0.2	.938
1983		7	9	.438	3.03	66	0	0	92	87	44	78	0	7	9	21	8	1	0	.125	3	4	2	0	0.1	.778
1984		7	7	.500	2.90	68	0	0	87	70	37	79	0	7	7	23	9	0	0	.000	2	5	1	0	0.1	.875
1985		2	8	.200	3.18	63	0	0	87.2	68	26	67	0	2	8	41	7	2	0	.286	9	8	0	0	0.3	1.000
1986		7	9	.438	3.94	62	0	0	89	83	26	67	0	7	9	35	8	1	0	.125	8	10	0	1	0.3	1.000
1987	MIN A	8	8	.500	4.48	63	0	0	80.1	70	28	83	0	8	8	31	0	0	0	—	2	6	0	1	0.1	1.000
1988		2	4	.333	2.47	63	0	0	73	68	15	56	0	2	4	42	0	0	0	—	1	2	0	0	0.0	1.000
1989		5	4	.556	4.07	65	0	0	73	68	12	46	0	5	4	31	0	0	0	—	1	3	0	0	0.1	1.000
1990	BOS A	5	3	.625	3.16	47	0	0	51.1	39	19	33	0	5	3	21	0	0	0	—	1	4	1	0	0.1	.833
12 yrs.		62	65	.488	3.03	694	0	0	943.2	796	320	755	0	62	65	287 4th	55	5	0	.091	35	61	9	3	0.2	.914

DIVISIONAL PLAYOFF SERIES

Year	Team	W	L	%	ERA	G	GS	CG	IP	H	BB	SO	ShO	W	L	SV	AB	H	HR	BA	PO	A	E	DP	TC/G	FA
1981	MON N	0	1	.000	2.08	3	0	0	4.1	1	1	2	0	0	1	2	1	0	0	.000	0	0	0	0	0.0	—

LEAGUE CHAMPIONSHIP SERIES

Year	Team	W	L	%	ERA	G	GS	CG	IP	H	BB	SO	ShO	W	L	SV	AB	H	HR	BA	PO	A	E	DP	TC/G	FA
1981	MON N	0	0	—	27.00	1	0	0	1	3	0	0	0	0	0	0	0	0	0	—	0	0	0	0	0.0	—
1987	MIN A	1	1	.500	5.06	4	0	0	5.1	7	3	5	0	1	1	2	0	0	0	—	0	1	0	0	0.3	1.000
1990	BOS A	0	0	—	9.00	1	0	0	2	3	1	0	0	0	0	0	0	0	0	—	0	0	0	0	0.0	—
3 yrs.		1	1	.500	8.64	6	0	0	8.1	13	4	5	0	1	1	2	0	0	0	—	0	1	0	0	0.2	1.000

WORLD SERIES

Year	Team	W	L	%	ERA	G	GS	CG	IP	H	BB	SO	ShO	W	L	SV	AB	H	HR	BA	PO	A	E	DP	TC/G	FA
1987	MIN A	0	0	—	0.00	4	0	0	4.2	5	0	3	0	0	0	1	0	0	0	—	0	0	0	0	0.0	—

Jerry Reed

REED, JERRY MAXWELL
B. Oct. 8, 1955, Bryson City, N. C.
BR TR 6' 1" 190 lbs.

Year	Team	W	L	%	ERA	G	GS	CG	IP	H	BB	SO	ShO	W	L	SV	AB	H	HR	BA	PO	A	E	DP	TC/G	FA
April		0	1	.000	4.91	4	0	0	7.1	8	3	2	0	0	1	0										
May		1	0	1.000	4.50	8	0	0	14	15	6	6	0	1	0	0										
June		1	0	1.000	1.84	9	0	0	14.2	15	1	3	0	1	0	2										
July		0	1	.000	8.10	10	0	0	13.1	20	7	5	0	0	1	0										
Aug		0	0	—	6.00	2	0	0	3	5	2	3	0	0	0	0										
Sept/Oct		—	—	—	—	0	0	0	0	0	0	0	0	0	0	0										
Day		0	1	.000	5.74	10	0	0	15.2	20	6	3	0	0	1	1										
Night		2	1	.667	4.42	23	0	0	36.2	43	13	16	0	2	1	1										
vs. Left		—	—	—	—	—	—	—	—	27	12	5	—	—	—	—										
vs. Right		—	—	—	—	—	—	—	—	36	7	14	—	—	—	—										

RELIEF PITCHER (Jeff Reardon charts: WINS, ERA, SAVES, RATIO with AL AVG)

RELIEF PITCHER (Jerry Reed charts: WINS, ERA with AL AVG)

Year	Team	W	L	%	ERA	G	GS	CG	IP	H	BB	SO	ShO	RELIEF PITCHING W	L	SV	BATTING AB	H	HR	BA	PO	A	E	DP	TC/G	FA

Jerry Reed *Continued*

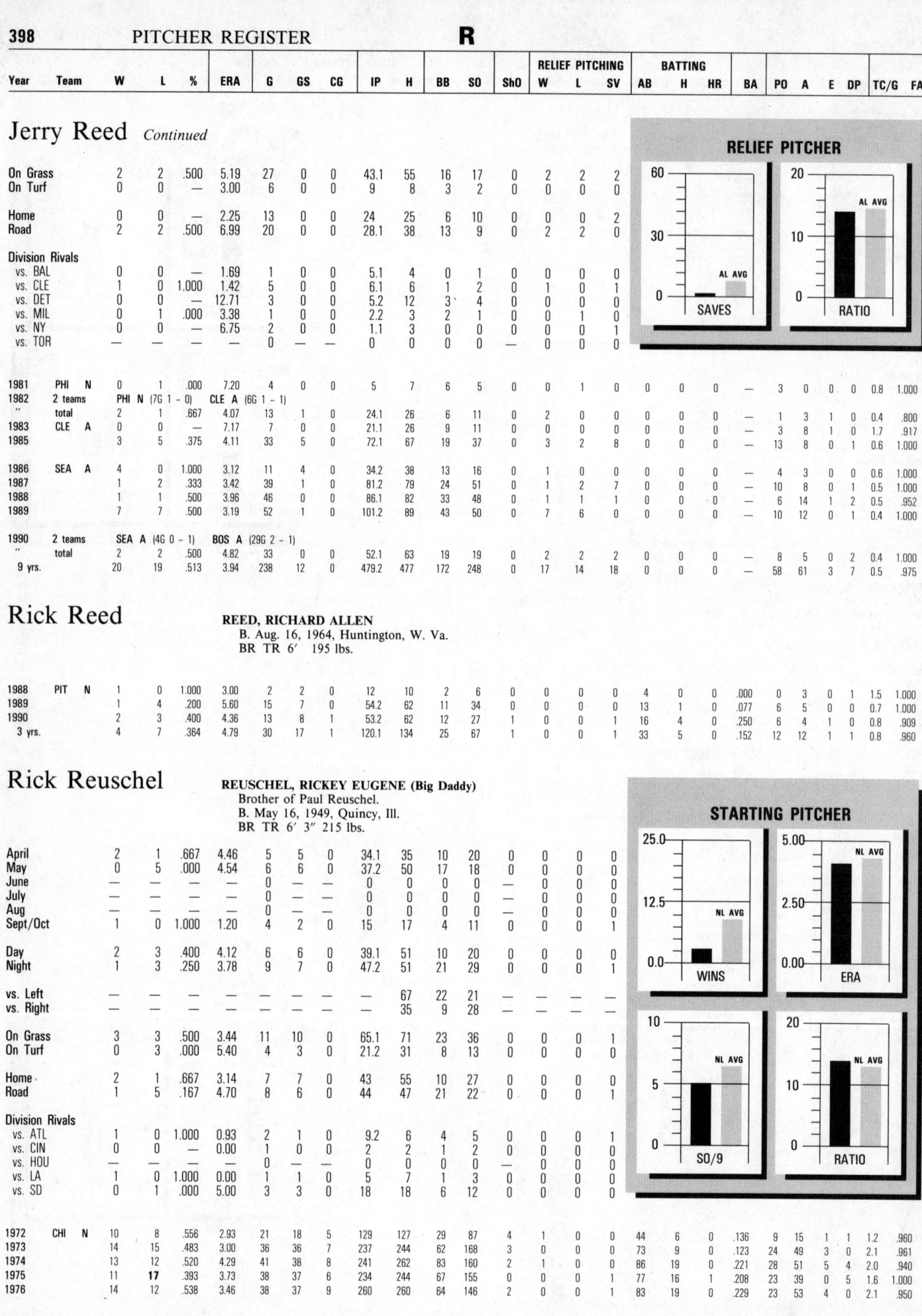

RELIEF PITCHER

Year	Team	W	L	%	ERA	G	GS	CG	IP	H	BB	SO	ShO	W	L	SV	AB	H	HR	BA	PO	A	E	DP	TC/G	FA
On Grass		2	2	.500	5.19	27	0	0	43.1	55	16	17	0	2	2	2										
On Turf		0	0	—	3.00	6	0	0	9	8	3	2	0	0	0	0										
Home		0	0	—	2.25	13	0	0	24	25	6	10	0	0	0	2										
Road		2	2	.500	6.99	20	0	0	28.1	38	13	9	0	2	2	0										
Division Rivals																										
vs. BAL		0	0	—	1.69	1	0	0	5.1	4	0	1	0	0	0	0										
vs. CLE		1	0	1.000	1.42	5	0	0	6.1	6	1	2	0	1	0	1										
vs. DET		0	0	—	12.71	3	0	0	5.2	12	3	4	0	0	0	0										
vs. MIL		0	1	.000	3.38	1	0	0	2.2	3	2	1	0	0	1	0										
vs. NY		0	0	—	6.75	2	0	0	1.1	3	0	0	0	0	0	1										
vs. TOR		—	—	—	—	0	—	—	0	0	0	0	0	0	0	0										
1981	PHI N	0	1	.000	7.20	4	0	0	5	7	6	5	0	0	1	0	0	0	0	—	3	0	0	0	0.8	1.000
1982	2 teams	PHI N	(7G 1 – 0)		CLE A	(6G 1 – 1)																				
"	total	2	1	.667	4.07	13	1	0	24.1	26	6	11	0	2	0	0	0	0	0	—	1	3	1	0	0.4	.800
1983	CLE A	0	0	—	7.17	7	0	0	21.1	26	9	11	0	0	0	0	0	0	0	—	3	8	1	0	1.7	.917
1985		3	5	.375	4.11	33	5	0	72.1	67	19	37	0	3	2	8	0	0	0	—	13	6	0	1	0.6	1.000
1986	SEA A	4	0	1.000	3.12	11	4	0	34.2	38	13	16	0	1	0	0	0	0	0	—	4	3	0	0	0.6	1.000
1987		1	2	.333	3.42	39	1	0	81.2	79	24	51	0	1	2	7	0	0	0	—	10	8	0	1	0.5	1.000
1988		1	1	.500	3.96	46	0	0	86.1	82	33	48	0	1	1	1	0	0	0	—	6	14	1	2	0.5	.952
1989		7	7	.500	3.19	52	1	0	101.2	89	43	50	0	7	6	0	0	0	0	—	10	12	0	1	0.4	1.000
1990	2 teams	SEA A	(4G 0 – 1)		BOS A	(29G 2 – 1)																				
"	total	2	2	.500	4.82	33	0	0	52.1	63	19	19	0	2	2	2	0	0	0	—	8	5	0	2	0.4	1.000
	9 yrs.	20	19	.513	3.94	238	12	0	479.2	477	172	248	0	17	14	18	0	0	0	—	58	61	3	7	0.5	.975

Rick Reed

REED, RICHARD ALLEN
B. Aug. 16, 1964, Huntington, W. Va.
BR TR 6′ 195 lbs.

Year	Team	W	L	%	ERA	G	GS	CG	IP	H	BB	SO	ShO	W	L	SV	AB	H	HR	BA	PO	A	E	DP	TC/G	FA
1988	PIT N	1	0	1.000	3.00	2	2	0	12	10	2	6	0	0	0	0	4	0	0	.000	0	3	0	1	1.5	1.000
1989		1	4	.200	5.60	15	7	0	54.2	62	11	34	0	0	0	0	13	1	0	.077	6	5	0	0	0.7	1.000
1990		2	3	.400	4.36	13	8	1	53.2	62	12	27	1	0	0	1	16	4	0	.250	6	4	1	0	0.8	.909
	3 yrs.	4	7	.364	4.79	30	17	1	120.1	134	25	67	1	0	0	1	33	5	0	.152	12	12	1	1	0.8	.960

Rick Reuschel

REUSCHEL, RICKEY EUGENE (Big Daddy)
Brother of Paul Reuschel.
B. May 16, 1949, Quincy, Ill.
BR TR 6′ 3″ 215 lbs.

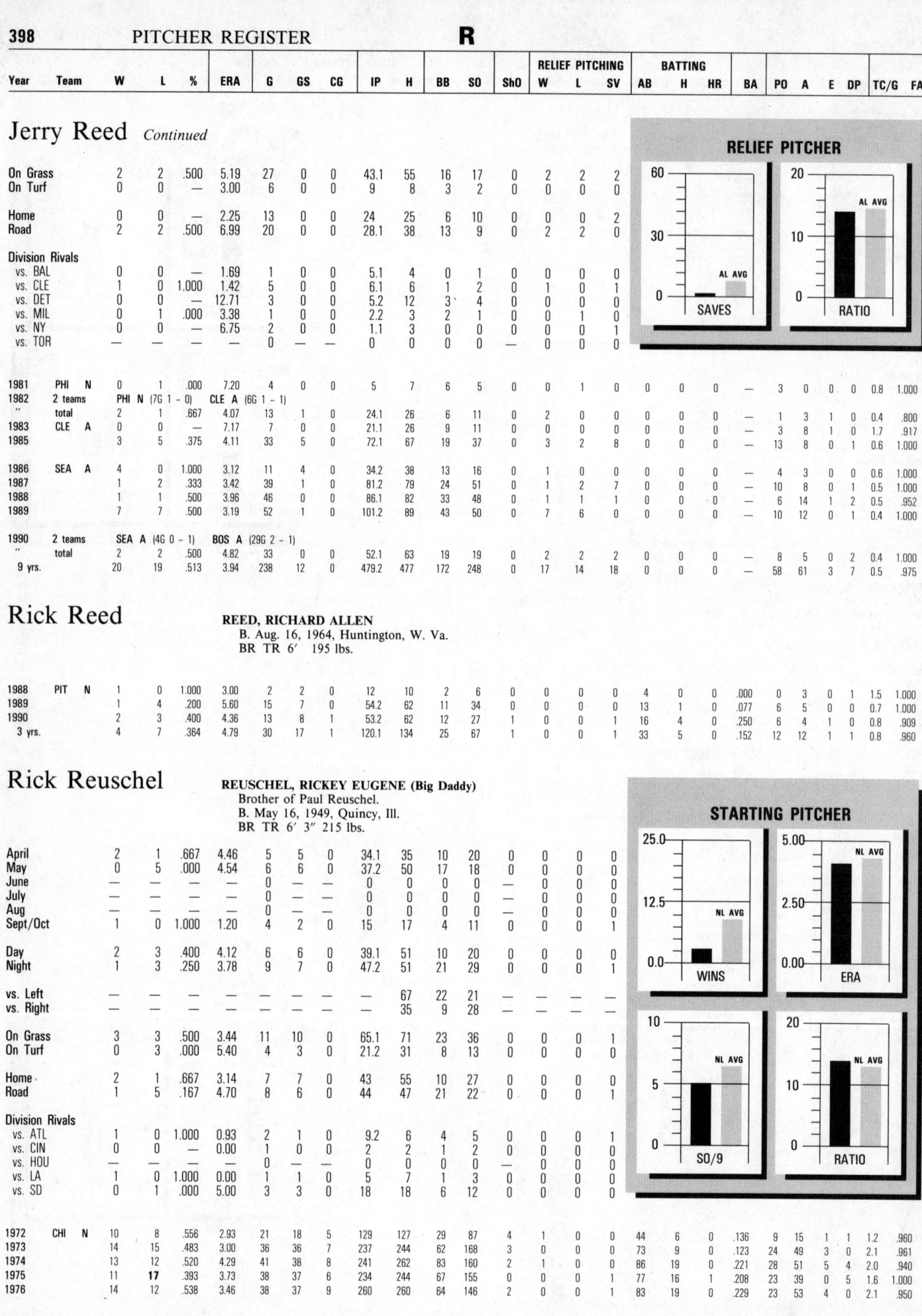

STARTING PITCHER

Year	Team	W	L	%	ERA	G	GS	CG	IP	H	BB	SO	ShO	W	L	SV	AB	H	HR	BA	PO	A	E	DP	TC/G	FA
April		2	1	.667	4.46	5	5	0	34.1	35	10	20	0	0	0	0										
May		0	5	.000	4.54	6	6	0	37.2	50	17	18	0	0	0	0										
June		—	—	—	—	0	—	—	0	0	0	0	0	0	0	0										
July		—	—	—	—	0	—	—	0	0	0	0	0	0	0	0										
Aug		—	—	—	—	0	—	—	0	0	0	0	0	0	0	0										
Sept/Oct		1	0	1.000	1.20	4	2	0	15	17	4	11	0	0	0	1										
Day		2	3	.400	4.12	6	6	0	39.1	51	10	20	0	0	0	0										
Night		1	3	.250	3.78	9	7	0	47.2	51	21	29	0	0	0	1										
vs. Left		—	—	—	—	—	—	—	—	67	22	21	—	—	—	—										
vs. Right		—	—	—	—	—	—	—	—	35	9	28	—	—	—	—										
On Grass		3	3	.500	3.44	11	10	0	65.1	71	23	36	0	0	0	1										
On Turf		0	3	.000	5.40	4	3	0	21.2	31	8	13	0	0	0	0										
Home		2	1	.667	3.14	7	7	0	43	55	10	27	0	0	0	0										
Road		1	5	.167	4.70	8	6	0	44	47	21	22	0	0	0	1										
Division Rivals																										
vs. ATL		1	0	1.000	0.93	2	1	0	9.2	6	4	5	0	0	0	1										
vs. CIN		0	0	—	0.00	1	0	0	2	2	1	2	0	0	0	0										
vs. HOU		—	—	—	—	0	—	—	0	0	0	0	—	0	0	0										
vs. LA		1	0	1.000	0.00	1	1	0	5	7	1	3	0	0	0	0										
vs. SD		0	1	.000	5.00	3	3	0	18	18	6	12	0	0	0	0										
1972	CHI N	10	8	.556	2.93	21	18	5	129	127	29	87	4	1	0	0	44	6	0	.136	9	15	1	1	1.2	.960
1973		14	15	.483	3.00	36	36	7	237	244	62	168	3	0	0	0	73	9	0	.123	24	49	3	0	2.1	.961
1974		13	12	.520	4.29	41	38	8	241	262	83	160	2	1	0	0	86	19	0	.221	28	51	5	4	2.0	.940
1975		11	17	.393	3.73	38	37	6	234	244	67	155	0	0	0	0	77	16	1	.208	23	39	0	5	1.6	1.000
1976		14	12	.538	3.46	38	37	9	260	260	64	146	2	0	0	1	83	19	0	.229	23	53	4	0	2.1	.950

Year	Team	W	L	%	ERA	G	GS	CG	IP	H	BB	SO	ShO	RELIEF PITCHING W	L	SV	BATTING AB	H	HR	BA	PO	A	E	DP	TC/G	FA

Rick Reuschel *Continued*

Year	Team	W	L	%	ERA	G	GS	CG	IP	H	BB	SO	ShO	W	L	SV	AB	H	HR	BA	PO	A	E	DP	TC/G	FA
1977		20	10	.667	2.79	39	37	8	252	233	74	166	4	1	0	1	87	18	1	.207	27	45	1	4	1.9	.986
1978		14	15	.483	3.41	35	35	9	243	235	54	115	1	0	0	0	73	10	0	.137	24	44	2	1	2.0	.971
1979		18	12	.600	3.62	36	36	5	239	251	75	125	1	0	0	0	79	13	0	.165	27	49	3	9	2.2	.962
1980		11	13	.458	3.40	38	**38**	6	257	**281**	76	140	0	0	0	0	82	13	0	.159	28	56	2	5	2.3	.977
1981	2 teams	CHI N (13G 4 – 7)					NY A (12G 4 – 4)																			
"	total	8	11	.421	3.10	25	24	4	157	162	33	75	0	0	0	0	25	2	0	.080	4	21	2	2	1.1	.926
1983	CHI N	1	1	.500	3.92	4	4	0	20.2	18	10	9	0	0	0	0	7	1	0	.143	4	7	0	0	2.8	1.000
1984		5	5	.500	5.17	19	14	0	92.1	123	23	43	0	1	0	0	29	7	0	.241	6	20	1	1	1.4	.963
1985	PIT N	14	8	.636	2.27	31	26	9	194	153	52	138	1	2	0	1	59	10	1	.169	24	40	0	2	2.1	1.000
1986		9	16	.360	3.96	35	34	4	215.2	232	57	125	2	0	0	0	70	11	0	.157	24	44	2	0	2.0	.971
1987	2 teams	PIT N (25G 8 – 6)					SF N (9G 5 – 3)																			
"	total	13	9	.591	3.09	34	33	**12**	227	207	42	107	**4**	0	1	0	79	11	1	.139	25	38	2	2	1.9	.969
1988	SF N	19	11	.633	3.12	36	**36**	7	245	242	42	92	2	0	0	0	73	8	0	.110	12	32	0	2	1.2	1.000
1989		17	8	.680	2.94	32	32	2	208.1	195	54	111	0	0	0	0	61	10	0	.164	8	33	0	0	1.3	1.000
1990		3	6	.333	3.93	15	13	0	87	102	31	49	0	0	0	1	26	4	0	.154	2	16	1	1	1.3	.947
18 yrs.		214	189	.531	3.37	553	528	102	3539	3571	928	2011	26	6	1	5	1113	187	4	.168	322	652	29	39	1.8	.971

DIVISIONAL PLAYOFF SERIES
Year	Team	W	L	%	ERA	G	GS	CG	IP	H	BB	SO	ShO	W	L	SV	AB	H	HR	BA	PO	A	E	DP	TC/G	FA
1981	NY A	0	1	.000	3.00	1	1	0	6	4	1	3	0	0	0	0	0	0	0	—	0	0	0	0	0.0	—

LEAGUE CHAMPIONSHIP SERIES
Year	Team	W	L	%	ERA	G	GS	CG	IP	H	BB	SO	ShO	W	L	SV	AB	H	HR	BA	PO	A	E	DP	TC/G	FA
1987	SF N	0	1	.000	6.30	2	2	0	10	15	2	2	0	0	0	0	2	0	0	.000	0	3	1	0	2.0	.750
1989		1	1	.500	5.19	2	2	0	8.2	12	2	5	0	0	0	0	2	0	0	.000	0	3	0	0	1.5	1.000
2 yrs.		1	2	.333	5.79	4	4	0	18.2	27	4	7	0	0	0	0	4	0	0	.000	0	6	1	0	1.8	.857

WORLD SERIES
Year	Team	W	L	%	ERA	G	GS	CG	IP	H	BB	SO	ShO	W	L	SV	AB	H	HR	BA	PO	A	E	DP	TC/G	FA
1981	NY A	0	0	—	4.91	2	1	0	3.2	7	3	2	0	0	0	0	2	0	0	.000	0	0	0	0	0.0	—
1989	SF N	0	1	.000	11.25	1	1	0	4	5	4	2	0	0	0	0	0	0	0	—	0	0	0	0	0.0	—
2 yrs.		0	1	.000	8.22	3	2	0	7.2	12	7	4	0	0	0	0	2	0	0	.000	0	0	0	0	0.0	—

Jerry Reuss

REUSS, JERRY
B. June 19, 1949, St. Louis, Mo.
BL TL 6′ 5″ 200 lbs.

Year	Team	W	L	%	ERA	G	GS	CG	IP	H	BB	SO	ShO	W	L	SV	AB	H	HR	BA	PO	A	E	DP	TC/G	FA
1969	STL N	1	0	1.000	0.00	1	1	0	7	2	3	3	0	0	0	0	3	1	0	.333	0	2	0	0	2.0	1.000
1970		7	8	.467	4.11	20	20	5	127	132	49	74	2	0	0	0	40	2	0	.050	8	18	1	0	1.4	.963
1971		14	14	.500	4.78	36	35	7	211	228	109	131	2	0	0	0	65	8	0	.123	6	26	2	0	0.9	.941
1972	HOU N	9	13	.409	4.17	33	30	4	192	177	83	174	1	0	0	1	66	7	0	.106	4	25	4	0	1.0	.879
1973		16	13	.552	3.74	41	**40**	12	279.1	271	117	177	3	1	0	0	95	13	0	.137	4	37	3	2	1.1	.932
1974	PIT N	16	11	.593	3.50	35	35	14	260	259	101	105	1	0	0	0	86	13	0	.151	11	37	5	1	1.5	.906
1975		18	11	.621	2.54	32	32	15	237	224	78	131	6	0	0	0	71	14	0	.197	6	48	0	1	1.7	1.000
1976		14	9	.609	3.53	31	29	11	209.1	209	51	108	3	0	0	2	66	16	0	.242	8	26	2	2	1.2	.944
1977		10	13	.435	4.11	33	33	8	208	225	71	116	2	1	0	0	70	12	0	.171	7	40	3	2	1.5	.940
1978		3	2	.600	4.88	23	12	3	83	97	23	42	1	0	0	0	27	5	0	.185	4	10	0	4	0.6	1.000
1979	LA N	7	14	.333	3.54	39	21	4	160	178	60	83	1	2	4	3	42	7	0	.167	2	35	3	1	1.0	.925
1980		18	6	.750	2.52	37	29	10	229	193	40	111	6	3	0	3	68	**6**	1	.088	18	40	5	5	1.7	.921
1981		10	4	.714	2.29	22	22	8	153	138	27	51	2	0	0	0	51	10	0	.196	10	38	1	4	2.2	.980
1982		18	11	.621	3.11	39	37	8	254.2	232	50	138	4	1	0	0	77	17	0	.221	21	46	3	4	1.8	.957
1983		12	11	.522	2.94	32	31	7	223.1	233	50	143	0	0	0	0	71	20	0	.282	17	52	4	4	2.3	.945
1984		5	7	.417	3.82	30	15	2	99	102	31	44	0	0	2	1	24	4	0	.167	4	16	1	0	0.7	.952
1985		14	10	.583	2.92	34	33	5	212.2	210	58	84	3	0	0	0	74	10	0	.135	12	27	3	0	1.2	.929
1986		2	6	.250	5.84	19	13	0	74	96	17	29	0	0	0	1	20	5	0	.250	5	16	0	1	1.1	1.000
1987	3 teams	LA N (1G 0 – 0)					CIN N (7G 0 – 5)			CAL A (17G 4 – 5)																	
"	total	4	10	.286	5.97	25	23	1	119	166	29	49	0	0	0	0	8	1	0	.125	8	21	1	4	1.2	.967
1988	CHI A	13	9	.591	3.44	32	29	2	183	183	43	73	0	0	0	0	0	0	0	—	10	27	1	2	1.2	.974
1989	2 teams	CHI A (23G 8 – 5)					MIL A (7G 1 – 4)																			
"	total	9	9	.500	5.13	30	26	1	140.1	171	34	40	0	0	0	0	0	0	0	—	4	14	0	1	0.6	1.000
1990	PIT N	0	0	—	3.52	4	1	0	7.2	8	3	1	0	0	0	0	0	0	0	—	1	2	0	0	0.8	1.000
22 yrs.		220	191	.535	3.64	628	547	127	3669.1	3734	1127	1907	39	7	6	11	1024	171	1	.167	170	603	42	38	1.3	.948

DIVISIONAL PLAYOFF SERIES
Year	Team	W	L	%	ERA	G	GS	CG	IP	H	BB	SO	ShO	W	L	SV	AB	H	HR	BA	PO	A	E	DP	TC/G	FA
1981	LA N	1	0	1.000	0.00	2	2	1	18	10	5	7	1	0	0	0	8	0	0	.000	0	0	0	0	0.0	—

LEAGUE CHAMPIONSHIP SERIES
Year	Team	W	L	%	ERA	G	GS	CG	IP	H	BB	SO	ShO	W	L	SV	AB	H	HR	BA	PO	A	E	DP	TC/G	FA
1974	PIT N	0	2	.000	3.72	2	2	0	9.2	7	8	3	0	0	0	0	2	0	0	.000	0	0	0	0	0.0	—
1975		0	1	.000	13.50	1	1	0	2.2	4	4	1	0	0	0	0	1	0	0	.000	0	1	0	0	1.0	1.000
1981	LA N	0	1	.000	5.14	1	1	0	7	7	1	2	0	0	0	0	1	0	0	.000	0	0	0	0	0.0	—
1983		0	2	.000	4.50	2	2	0	12	14	3	4	0	0	0	0	4	0	0	.000	0	1	0	0	0.5	1.000
1985		0	1	.000	10.80	1	1	0	1.2	5	1	0	0	0	0	0	0	0	0	—	0	0	1	0	1.0	—
5 yrs.		0	7	.000	5.45	7	7	0	33	37	17	10	0	0	0	0	8	0	0	.000	0	2	1	0	0.4	.667

Year	Team	W	L	%	ERA	G	GS	CG	IP	H	BB	SO	ShO	RELIEF PITCHING W	L	SV	BATTING AB	H	HR	BA	PO	A	E	DP	TC/G	FA

Jerry Reuss   *Continued*

WORLD SERIES

Year	Team	W	L	%	ERA	G	GS	CG	IP	H	BB	SO	ShO	W	L	SV	AB	H	HR	BA	PO	A	E	DP	TC/G	FA
1981	LA N	1	1	.500	3.86	2	2	1	11.2	10	3	8	0	0	0	0	3	0	0	.000	1	3	0	0	2.0	1.000

Rusty Richards

RICHARDS, RUSSELL EARL
B. Jan. 27, 1965, Houston, Tex.
BL TR 6′ 4″ 200 lbs.

Year	Team	W	L	%	ERA	G	GS	CG	IP	H	BB	SO	ShO	W	L	SV	AB	H	HR	BA	PO	A	E	DP	TC/G	FA
1989	ATL N	0	0	—	4.82	2	2	0	9.1	10	6	4	0	0	0	0	3	0	0	.000	1	3	0	0	2.0	1.000
1990		0	0	—	27.00	1	0	0	1	2	1	0	0	0	0	0	0	0	0	—	0	0	0	0	0.0	—
2 yrs.		0	0	—	6.97	3	2	0	10.1	12	7	4	0	0	0	0	3	0	0	.000	1	3	0	0	1.3	1.000

Jeff Richardson

RICHARDSON, JEFFREY SCOTT
B. Aug. 29, 1963, Wichita, Kans.
BR TR 6′ 3″ 185 lbs.

Year	Team	W	L	%	ERA	G	GS	CG	IP	H	BB	SO	ShO	W	L	SV	AB	H	HR	BA	PO	A	E	DP	TC/G	FA
1990	CAL A	0	0	—	0.00	1	0	0	0.1	1	0	0	0	0	0	0	0	0	0	—	0	1	0	0	1.0	1.000

Dave Righetti

RIGHETTI, DAVID ALLAN (Rags)
B. Nov. 28, 1958, San Jose, Calif.
BL TL 6′ 2″ 170 lbs.

RELIEF PITCHER (WINS, ERA, SAVES, RATIO vs AL AVG)

Split	W	L	%	ERA	G	GS	CG	IP	H	BB	SO	ShO	W	L	SV	AB	H	HR	BA	PO	A	E	DP	TC/G	FA
April	0	0	—	4.05	7	0	0	6.2	6	2	4	0	0	0	5										
May	0	0	—	4.50	7	0	0	6	8	4	6	0	0	0	4										
June	1	0	1.000	4.35	10	0	0	10.1	9	5	8	0	1	0	7										
July	0	0	—	3.86	10	0	0	11.2	11	6	9	0	0	0	5										
Aug	0	1	.000	4.22	11	0	0	10.2	12	5	12	0	0	1	8										
Sept/Oct	0	0	—	0.00	8	0	0	7.2	2	4	4	0	0	0	7										
Day	1	1	.500	7.24	16	0	0	13.2	16	9	15	0	1	1	8										
Night	0	0	—	2.29	37	0	0	39.1	32	17	28	0	0	0	28										
vs. Left	—	—	—	—	—	—	—	—	10	2	10	—	—	—	—										
vs. Right	—	—	—	—	—	—	—	—	38	24	33	—	—	—	—										
On Grass	1	1	.500	3.86	43	0	0	42	36	21	36	0	1	1	29										
On Turf	0	0	—	2.45	10	0	0	11	12	5	7	0	0	0	7										
Home	1	1	.500	2.60	29	0	0	27.2	23	13	26	0	1	1	21										
Road	0	0	—	4.62	24	0	0	25.1	25	13	17	0	0	0	15										
Division Rivals																									
vs. BAL	0	0	—	3.38	6	0	0	5.1	4	1	3	0	0	0	5										
vs. BOS	0	0	—	0.00	4	0	0	4	3	2	4	0	0	0	4										
vs. CLE	0	0	—	3.38	3	0	0	2.2	2	3	2	0	0	0	2										
vs. DET	0	0	—	0.00	4	0	0	5.1	2	4	4	0	0	0	4										
vs. MIL	1	1	.500	27.00	2	0	0	1.2	5	2	1	0	1	1	0										
vs. TOR	0	0	—	5.40	5	0	0	5	3	3	3	0	0	0	3										

Year	Team	W	L	%	ERA	G	GS	CG	IP	H	BB	SO	ShO	W	L	SV	AB	H	HR	BA	PO	A	E	DP	TC/G	FA
1979	NY A	0	1	.000	3.71	3	3	0	17	10	10	13	0	0	0	0	0	0	0	—	1	3	0	1	1.3	1.000
1981		8	4	.667	2.06	15	15	2	105	75	38	89	0	0	0	0	0	0	0	—	6	9	1	0	1.1	.938
1982		11	10	.524	3.79	33	27	4	183	155	**108**	163	0	0	0	1	0	0	0	—	5	18	3	1	0.8	.885
1983		14	8	.636	3.44	31	31	7	217	194	67	169	2	0	0	0	0	0	0	—	3	24	1	2	0.9	.964
1984		5	6	.455	2.34	64	0	0	96.1	79	37	90	0	5	6	31	0	0	0	—	2	13	2	0	0.3	.882
1985		12	7	.632	2.78	74	0	0	107	96	45	92	0	**12**	7	29	0	0	0	—	1	12	1	2	0.2	.929
1986		8	8	.500	2.45	74	0	0	106.2	88	35	83	0	8	8	**46**	0	0	0	—	1	10	0	2	0.1	1.000
1987		8	6	.571	3.51	60	0	0	95	95	44	77	0	8	6	31	0	0	0	—	3	12	1	0	0.3	.938
1988		5	4	.556	3.52	60	0	0	87	86	37	70	0	5	4	25	0	0	0	—	2	8	0	0	0.2	1.000
1989		2	6	.250	3.00	55	0	0	69	73	26	51	0	2	6	25	0	0	0	—	0	9	0	0	0.2	1.000
1990		1	1	.500	3.57	53	0	0	53	48	26	43	0	1	1	36	0	0	0	—	3	1	1	0	0.1	.800
11 yrs.		74	61	.548	3.11	522	76	13	1136	999	473	940	2	41	38	224	0	0	0	—	27	119	10	8	0.3	.936
																9th										

DIVISIONAL PLAYOFF SERIES

Year	Team	W	L	%	ERA	G	GS	CG	IP	H	BB	SO	ShO	W	L	SV	AB	H	HR	BA	PO	A	E	DP	TC/G	FA
1981	NY A	2	0	1.000	1.00	2	1	0	9	8	3	13	0	1	0	0	0	0	0	—	0	0	0	0	0.0	—

LEAGUE CHAMPIONSHIP SERIES

Year	Team	W	L	%	ERA	G	GS	CG	IP	H	BB	SO	ShO	W	L	SV	AB	H	HR	BA	PO	A	E	DP	TC/G	FA
1981	NY A	1	0	1.000	0.00	1	1	0	6	4	2	4	0	0	0	0	0	0	0	—	0	1	0	0	1.0	1.000

WORLD SERIES

Year	Team	W	L	%	ERA	G	GS	CG	IP	H	BB	SO	ShO	W	L	SV	AB	H	HR	BA	PO	A	E	DP	TC/G	FA
1981	NY A	0	0	—	13.50	1	1	0	2	5	2	1	0	0	0	0	1	0	0	.000	0	0	0	0	0.0	—

Jose Rijo

RIJO, JOSE ANTONIO
Born Jose Antonio Rijo y Abreu.
B. May 13, 1965, San Cristobal, Dominican Republic
BR TR 6′ 1″ 200 lbs.

Year	Team	W	L	%	ERA	G	GS	CG	IP	H	BB	SO	ShO	RELIEF PITCHING W	L	SV	BATTING AB	H	HR	BA	PO	A	E	DP	TC/G	FA
April		1	1	.500	3.94	3	3	0	16	17	6	14	0	0	0	0										
May		2	0	1.000	3.10	5	5	0	29	26	15	25	0	0	0	0										
June		2	2	.500	3.73	6	6	0	41	27	14	28	0	0	0	0										
July		2	1	.667	3.10	3	3	1	20.1	22	5	13	0	0	0	0										
Aug		3	2	.600	2.67	5	5	2	33.2	24	19	21	0	0	0	0										
Sept/Oct		4	2	.667	1.26	7	7	4	57	35	19	51	1	0	0	0										
Day		4	1	.800	2.21	6	6	2	40.2	32	14	30	0	0	0	0										
Night		10	7	.588	2.82	23	23	5	156.1	119	64	122	1	0	0	0										
vs. Left		—	—	—	—	—	—	—	—	89	58	83	—	—	—	—										
vs. Right		—	—	—	—	—	—	—	—	62	20	69	—	—	—	—										
On Grass		4	3	.571	3.00	8	8	3	57	49	20	33	0	0	0	0										
On Turf		10	5	.667	2.57	21	21	4	140	102	58	119	1	0	0	0										
Home		8	4	.667	2.24	15	15	4	108.1	71	45	93	1	0	0	0										
Road		6	4	.600	3.25	14	14	3	88.2	80	33	59	0	0	0	0										
Division Rivals																										
vs. ATL		1	1	.500	2.81	2	2	1	16	14	2	14	0	0	0	0										
vs. HOU		2	0	1.000	0.93	4	4	0	29	14	9	30	0	0	0	0										
vs. LA		1	1	.500	3.67	4	4	0	27	19	13	15	0	0	0	0										
vs. SD		2	1	.667	1.57	3	3	2	23	14	8	17	0	0	0	0										
vs. SF		1	2	.333	2.63	3	3	2	24	18	9	23	1	0	0	0										
1984	NY A	2	8	.200	4.76	24	5	0	62.1	74	33	47	0	2	4	2	0	0	0	—	2	12	1	0	0.6	.933
1985	OAK A	6	4	.600	3.53	12	9	0	63.2	57	28	65	0	2	1	0	0	0	0	—	2	5	0	0	0.6	1.000
1986		9	11	.450	4.65	39	26	4	193.2	172	108	176	0	0	4	1	0	0	0	—	13	18	3	0	0.9	.912
1987		2	7	.222	5.90	21	14	1	82.1	106	41	67	0	0	0	0	0	0	0	—	10	10	1	0	1.0	.952
1988	CIN N	13	8	.619	2.39	49	19	0	162	120	63	160	0	6	1	0	37	2	1	.054	7	23	1	1	0.6	.968
1989		7	6	.538	2.84	19	19	1	111	101	48	86	1	0	0	0	38	8	0	.211	6	14	0	0	1.1	1.000
1990		14	8	.636	2.70	29	29	7	197	151	78	152	1	0	0	0	62	10	0	.161	19	27	2	0	1.7	.958
7 yrs.		53	52	.505	3.60	193	121	13	872	781	399	753	2	10	10	3	137	20	1	.146	59	109	8	1	0.9	.955
LEAGUE CHAMPIONSHIP SERIES																										
1990	CIN N	1	0	1.000	4.38	2	2	0	12.1	10	7	15	0	0	0	0	5	0	0	.000	0	0	0	0	0.0	—
WORLD SERIES																										
1990	CIN N	2	0	1.000	0.59	2	2	0	15.1	9	5	14	0	0	0	0	3	1	0	.333	0	2	0	0	1.0	1.000

STARTING PITCHER

WINS · ERA · SO/9 · RATIO (NL AVG)

Kevin Ritz

RITZ, KEVIN D.
B. June 8, 1965, Eatontown, N. J.
BR TR 6′ 4″ 195 lbs.

Year	Team	W	L	%	ERA	G	GS	CG	IP	H	BB	SO	ShO	RELIEF PITCHING W	L	SV	BATTING AB	H	HR	BA	PO	A	E	DP	TC/G	FA
1989	DET A	4	6	.400	4.38	12	12	1	74	75	44	56	0	0	0	0	0	0	0	—	4	10	0	0	1.2	1.000
1990		0	4	.000	11.05	4	4	0	7.1	14	14	3	0	0	0	0	0	0	0	—	2	4	1	0	1.8	.857
2 yrs.		4	10	.286	4.98	16	16	1	81.1	89	58	59	0	0	0	0	0	0	0	—	6	14	1	0	1.3	.952

Don Robinson

ROBINSON, DON ALLEN
B. June 8, 1957, Ashland, Ky.
BR TR 6′ 4″ 225 lbs.

Year	Team	W	L	%	ERA	G	GS	CG	IP	H	BB	SO	ShO	RELIEF PITCHING W	L	SV	BATTING AB	H	HR	BA	PO	A	E	DP	TC/G	FA
April		—	—	—	—	0	0	0	0	0	0	0	—	0	0	0										
May		1	0	1.000	2.84	2	2	0	12.2	12	7	4	0	0	0	0										
June		2	1	.667	4.40	5	5	0	30.2	33	5	13	0	0	0	0										
July		4	0	1.000	3.33	6	6	1	46	41	9	23	0	0	0	0										
Aug		3	3	.500	3.80	7	7	2	47.1	44	11	27	0	0	0	0										
Sept/Oct		0	3	.000	10.29	6	5	1	21	43	9	11	0	0	0	0										
Day		2	2	.500	5.07	10	10	1	60.1	81	17	30	0	0	0	0										
Night		8	5	.615	4.25	16	15	3	97.1	92	24	48	0	0	0	0										
vs. Left		—	—	—	—	—	—	—	—	104	32	39	—	—	—	—										
vs. Right		—	—	—	—	—	—	—	—	69	9	39	—	—	—	—										

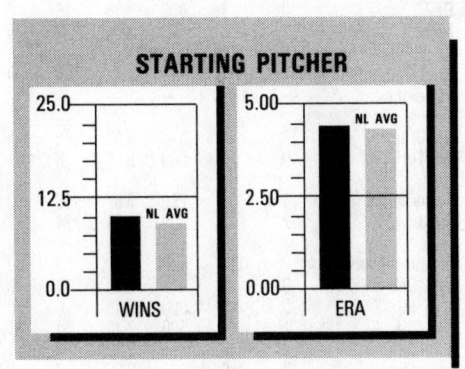

STARTING PITCHER

WINS · ERA (NL AVG)

Year	Team	W	L	%	ERA	G	GS	CG	IP	H	BB	SO	ShO	RELIEF PITCHING W	L	SV	BATTING AB	H	HR	BA	PO	A	E	DP	TC/G	FA

Don Robinson *Continued*

Year	Team	W	L	%	ERA	G	GS	CG	IP	H	BB	SO	ShO	W	L	SV	AB	H	HR	BA	PO	A	E	DP	TC/G	FA
On Grass		7	2	.778	4.54	17	16	3	101	117	18	55	0	0	0	0										
On Turf		3	5	.375	4.61	9	9	1	56.2	56	23	23	0	0	0	0										
Home		4	1	.800	5.04	11	10	2	60.2	77	10	37	0	0	0	0										
Road		6	6	.500	4.27	15	15	2	97	96	31	41	0	0	0	0										
Division Rivals																										
vs. ATL		0	0	—	15.88	3	2	0	5.2	15	3	2	0	0	0	0										
vs. CIN		2	2	.500	3.78	5	5	1	33.1	35	4	18	0	0	0	0										
vs. HOU		0	3	.000	5.59	3	3	1	19.1	23	8	10	0	0	0	0										
vs. LA		1	1	.500	6.75	2	2	1	12	13	3	7	0	0	0	0										
vs. SD		1	0	1.000	5.87	2	2	0	7.2	13	0	3	0	0	0	0										
1978	PIT N	14	6	.700	3.47	35	32	9	228	203	57	135	1	0	0	1	85	20	0	.235	10	32	1	1	1.2	.977
1979		8	8	.500	3.86	29	25	4	161	171	52	96	0	0	1	0	49	10	0	.204	7	10	2	1	0.7	.895
1980		7	10	.412	3.99	29	24	3	160	157	45	103	2	0	0	1	57	19	1	.333	13	23	2	2	1.3	.947
1981		0	3	.000	5.92	16	2	0	38	47	23	17	0	0	2	2	12	3	0	.250	7	8	0	1	0.9	1.000
1982		15	13	.536	4.28	38	30	6	227	213	103	165	0	2	0	0	85	24	2	.282	14	25	4	0	1.1	.907
1983		2	2	.500	4.46	9	6	0	36.1	43	21	28	0	1	0	0	13	2	1	.154	1	6	0	1	0.8	1.000
1984		5	6	.455	3.02	51	1	0	122/	99	49	110	0	5	5	10	31	9	1	.290	8	18	0	1	0.5	1.000
1985		5	11	.313	3.87	44	6	0	95.1	95	42	65	0	4	7	3	21	5	1	.238	7	11	0	2	0.4	1.000
1986		3	4	.429	3.38	50	0	0	69.1	61	27	53	0	3	4	14	6	4	0	.667	6	9	0	0	0.3	1.000
1987	2 teams	PIT N (42G 6 – 6)				SF N (25G 5 – 1)																				
"	total	11	7	.611	3.42	67	0	0	108	105	40	79	0	11	7	19	18	4	1	.222	8	12	0	0	0.3	1.000
1988	SF N	10	5	.667	2.45	51	19	3	176.2	152	49	122	2	2	1	6	52	9	1	.173	12	19	3	1	0.7	.912
1989		12	11	.522	3.43	34	32	5	197	184	37	96	1	0	1	0	81	15	3	.185	6	12	0	1	0.5	1.000
1990		10	7	.588	4.57	26	25	4	157.2	173	41	78	0	0	0	0	63	9	2	.143	4	18	0	1	0.8	1.000
13 yrs.		102	93	.523	3.70	479	202	34	1776.1	1703	586	1147	6	28	28	56	573	133	13	.232	103	203	12	10	0.7	.962
LEAGUE CHAMPIONSHIP SERIES																										
1979	PIT N	1	0	1.000	0.00	2	0	0	2	0	1	3	0	1	0	1	0	0	0	—	0	0	0	0	0.0	—
1987	SF N	0	1	.000	9.00	3	0	0	3	3	0	3	0	0	1	0	0	0	0	—	0	0	0	0	0.0	—
1989		1	0	1.000	0.00	1	0	0	1.2	3	0	0	0	1	0	0	0	0	0	—	0	0	0	0	0.0	—
3 yrs.		2	1	.667	4.05	6	0	0	6.2	6	1	6	0	2	1	1	0	0	0	—	0	0	0	0	0.0	—
WORLD SERIES																										
1979	PIT N	1	0	1.000	5.40	4	0	0	5	4	6	3	0	1	0	0	0	0	0	—	0	1	0	0	0.3	1.000
1989	SF N	0	1	.000	21.60	1	1	0	1.2	4	1	0	0	0	0	0	0	0	0	—	0	0	0	0	0.0	—
2 yrs.		1	1	.500	9.45	5	1	0	6.2	8	7	3	0	1	0	0	0	0	0	—	0	1	0	0	0.2	1.000

Jeff Robinson

ROBINSON, JEFFREY DANIEL
B. Dec. 13, 1960, Santa Ana, Calif.
BR TR 6′ 4″ 195 lbs.

Period	Team	W	L	%	ERA	G	GS	CG	IP	H	BB	SO	ShO	W	L	SV	AB	H	HR	BA	PO	A	E	DP	TC/G	FA
April		0	0	—	3.60	8	0	0	10	7	6	5	0	0	0	0										
May		0	3	.000	3.86	10	0	0	14	12	7	9	0	0	3	0										
June		1	2	.333	9.72	11	0	0	8.1	12	7	4	0	1	2	0										
July		2	1	.667	2.08	6	3	1	30.1	26	6	9	0	0	0	0										
Aug		0	0	—	3.86	10	1	0	18.2	19	5	10	0	0	0	0										
Sept/Oct		0	0	—	0.00	9	0	0	7.1	6	3	6	0	0	0	0										
Day		0	1	.000	3.15	15	0	0	20	13	10	15	0	0	1	0										
Night		3	5	.375	3.54	39	4	1	68.2	69	24	28	0	1	4	0										
vs. Left		—	—	—	—	—	—	—		31	10	14	—	—	—	—										
vs. Right		—	—	—	—	—	—	—		51	24	29	—	—	—	—										
On Grass		3	5	.375	3.43	48	3	0	76	68	31	39	0	1	5	0										
On Turf		0	1	.000	3.55	6	1	1	12.2	14	3	4	0	0	0	0										
Home		1	3	.250	3.02	30	2	0	44.2	37	21	27	0	0	3	0										
Road		2	3	.400	3.89	24	2	1	44	45	13	16	0	1	2	0										
Division Rivals																										
vs. BAL		0	0	—	3.00	4	0	0	3	4	1	3	0	0	0	0										
vs. BOS		0	1	.000	9.45	6	0	0	6.2	10	4	2	0	0	1	0										
vs. CLE		1	1	.500	2.70	4	1	0	10	12	3	3	0	0	1	0										
vs. DET		0	0	—	5.40	3	1	0	6.2	5	2	4	0	0	0	0										
vs. MIL		0	0	—	0.00	2	0	0	2	2	1	0	0	0	0	0										
vs. TOR		0	1	.000	27.00	4	0	0	1.1	3	2	3	0	0	1	0										

Year	Team	W	L	%	ERA	G	GS	CG	IP	H	BB	SO	ShO	W	L	SV	AB	H	HR	BA	PO	A	E	DP	TC/G	FA

Jeff Robinson *Continued*

Year	Team	W	L	%	ERA	G	GS	CG	IP	H	BB	SO	ShO	W	L	SV	AB	H	HR	BA	PO	A	E	DP	TC/G	FA
1984	SF N	7	15	.318	4.56	34	33	1	171.2	195	52	102	1	0	0	0	61	7	0	.115	14	24	1	1	1.1	.974
1985		0	0	—	5.11	8	0	0	12.1	16	10	8	0	0	0	0	0	0	0	—	0	0	0	0	0.0	—
1986		6	3	.667	3.36	64	1	0	104.1	92	32	90	0	6	3	8	15	1	0	.067	10	10	1	1	0.3	.952
1987	2 teams	SF N (63G 6 – 8)				PIT N (18G 2 – 1)																				
"	total	8	9	.471	2.85	81	0	0	123.1	89	54	101	0	8	9	14	22	3	1	.136	14	18	0	6	0.4	1.000
1988	PIT N	11	5	.688	3.03	75	0	0	124.2	113	39	87	0	11	5	9	16	3	0	.188	13	17	0	0	0.4	1.000
1989		7	13	.350	4.58	50	19	0	141.1	161	59	95	0	2	6	4	35	8	1	.229	13	26	5	2	0.9	.886
1990	NY A	3	6	.333	3.45	54	4	1	88.2	82	34	43	0	1	5	0	0	0	0	—	5	23	3	1	0.6	.903
7 yrs.		42	51	.452	3.76	366	57	2	766.1	748	280	526	1	28	28	35	149	22	2	.148	69	118	10	11	0.5	.949

Jeff Robinson

ROBINSON, JEFFREY MARK
B. Dec. 14, 1961, Ventura, Calif.
BR TR 6′ 6″ 210 lbs.

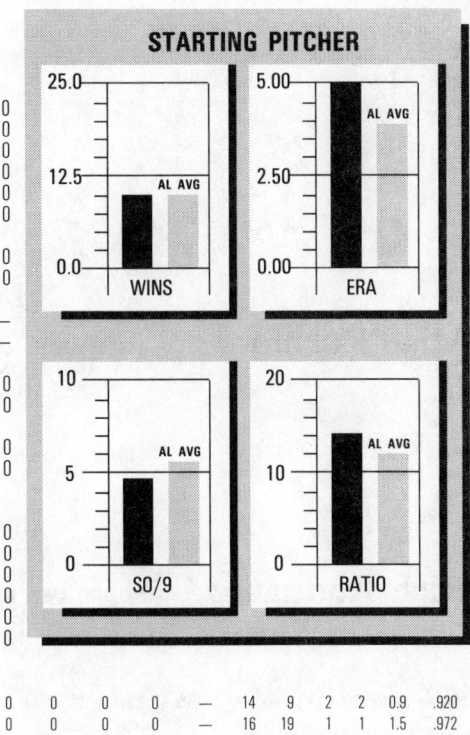

STARTING PITCHER

	W	L	%	ERA	G	GS	CG	IP	H	BB	SO	ShO	W	L	SV	AB	H	HR	BA	PO	A	E	DP	TC/G	FA
April	1	2	.333	5.83	5	5	0	29.1	33	12	15	0	0	0	0										
May	3	2	.600	6.35	5	5	1	28.1	30	16	21	1	0	0	0										
June	2	2	.500	3.72	6	6	0	36.1	29	26	13	0	0	0	0										
July	2	2	.500	5.68	5	5	0	25.1	22	20	17	0	0	0	0										
Aug	2	1	.667	9.12	6	6	0	25.2	27	14	10	0	0	0	0										
Sept/Oct	—	—	—	—	0	—	0	0	0	0	0	0	0	0	0										
Day	0	3	.000	7.83	5	5	0	23	31	11	15	0	0	0	0										
Night	10	6	.625	5.61	22	22	1	122	110	77	61	1	0	0	0										
vs. Left	—	—	—	—	—	—	—	62	39	35	—	—	—	—											
vs. Right	—	—	—	—	—	—	—	79	49	41	—	—	—	—											
On Grass	8	6	.571	5.89	21	21	1	113	112	69	63	1	0	0	0										
On Turf	2	3	.400	6.19	6	6	0	32	29	19	13	0	0	0	0										
Home	6	4	.600	5.63	15	15	0	86.1	80	54	45	0	0	0	0										
Road	4	5	.444	6.44	12	12	1	58.2	61	34	31	1	0	0	0										
Division Rivals																									
vs. BAL	1	1	.500	5.94	3	3	0	16.2	13	12	14	0	0	0	0										
vs. BOS	1	2	.333	6.75	4	4	0	17.1	20	10	10	0	0	0	0										
vs. CLE	0	0	—	8.31	1	1	0	4.1	4	5	0	0	0	0	0										
vs. MIL	0	1	.000	6.55	2	2	0	11	15	6	3	0	0	0	0										
vs. NY	—	—	—	—	0	—	—	0	0	0	0	—	0	0	0										
vs. TOR	2	1	.667	7.47	3	3	0	15.2	16	9	10	0	0	0	0										

Year	Team	W	L	%	ERA	G	GS	CG	IP	H	BB	SO	ShO	W	L	SV	AB	H	HR	BA	PO	A	E	DP	TC/G	FA
1987	DET A	9	6	.600	5.37	29	21	2	127.1	132	54	98	1	1	1	0	0	0	0	—	14	9	2	2	0.9	.920
1988		13	6	.684	2.98	24	23	6	172	121	72	114	2	0	0	0	0	0	0	—	16	19	1	1	1.5	.972
1989		4	5	.444	4.73	16	16	1	78	76	46	40	1	0	0	0	0	0	0	—	3	6	0	1	0.6	1.000
1990		10	9	.526	5.96	27	27	1	145	141	88	76	1	0	0	0	0	0	0	—	14	15	3	1	1.2	.906
4 yrs.		36	26	.581	4.65	96	87	10	522.1	470	260	328	5	1	1	0	0	0	0	—	47	49	6	5	1.1	.941

LEAGUE CHAMPIONSHIP SERIES

Year	Team	W	L	%	ERA	G	GS	CG	IP	H	BB	SO	ShO	W	L	SV	AB	H	HR	BA	PO	A	E	DP	TC/G	FA
1987	DET A	0	0	—	0.00	1	0	0	0.1	1	0	0	0	0	0	0	0	0	0	—	0	1	0	0	1.0	1.000

Ron Robinson

ROBINSON, RONALD DEAN
B. Mar. 24, 1962, Exeter, Calif.
BR TR 6′ 4″ 235 lbs.

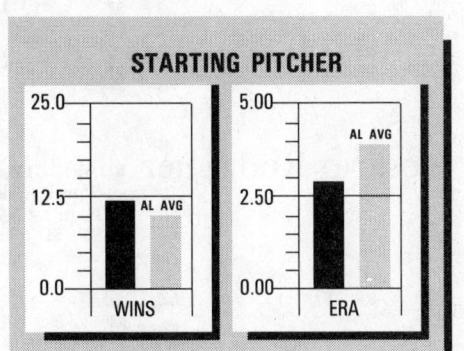

STARTING PITCHER

	W	L	%	ERA	G	GS	CG	IP	H	BB	SO	ShO	W	L	SV	AB	H	HR	BA	PO	A	E	DP	TC/G	FA
April	0	1	.000	3.86	1	0	0	4.2	3	3	1	0	0	0	1	0									
May	2	0	1.000	2.74	4	4	0	23	23	10	12	0	0	0	0										
June	1	2	.333	4.44	5	5	0	26.1	34	11	11	0	0	0	0										
July	3	1	.750	4.88	5	5	1	27.2	41	6	12	0	0	0	0										
Aug	4	1	.800	2.82	7	7	3	51	51	10	18	1	0	0	0										
Sept/Oct	4	2	.667	2.30	6	6	3	47	42	11	17	1	0	0	0										
Day	1	3	.250	7.16	7	6	0	32.2	48	12	18	0	0	0	1	0									
Night	13	4	.765	2.39	21	21	7	147	146	39	53	2	0	0	0										
vs. Left	—	—	—	—	—	—	—	98	30	30	—	—	—	—											
vs. Right	—	—	—	—	—	—	—	96	21	41	—	—	—	—											

Year	Team	W	L	%	ERA	G	GS	CG	IP	H	BB	SO	ShO	RELIEF PITCHING W	L	SV	BATTING AB	H	HR	BA	PO	A	E	DP	TC/G	FA

Ron Robinson *Continued*

		W	L	%	ERA	G	GS	CG	IP	H	BB	SO	ShO	W	L	SV	AB	H	HR	BA	PO	A	E	DP	TC/G	FA
On Grass		10	6	.625	3.67	20	20	5	127.2	147	29	50	1	0	0	0										
On Turf		4	1	.800	2.25	8	7	2	52	47	22	21	1	0	1	0										
Home		6	3	.667	2.40	12	11	4	86.1	85	21	33	1	0	1	0										
Road		8	4	.667	4.05	16	16	3	93.1	109	30	38	1	0	0	0										
Division Rivals																										
vs. BAL		1	1	.500	1.23	3	3	2	22	15	6	8	0	0	0	0										
vs. BOS		1	0	1.000	1.29	1	1	0	7	4	4	2	0	0	0	0										
vs. CLE		1	1	.500	3.26	3	3	0	19.1	20	2	8	0	0	0	0										
vs. DET		1	0	1.000	5.40	1	1	0	5	10	1	2	0	0	0	0										
vs. NY		0	0	—	1.42	1	1	0	6.1	6	1	2	0	0	0	0										
vs. TOR		1	0	1.000	0.00	1	1	1	9	7	1	1	1	0	0	0										
1984	CIN N	1	2	.333	2.72	12	5	1	39.2	35	13	24	0	0	0	0	8	0	0	.000	1	7	0	0	0.7	1.000
1985		7	7	.500	3.99	33	12	0	108.1	107	32	76	0	3	1	1	22	2	0	.091	9	17	2	4	0.8	.929
1986		10	3	.769	3.24	70	0	0	116.2	110	43	117	0	10	3	14	14	1	0	.071	8	20	0	2	0.4	1.000
1987		7	5	.583	3.68	48	18	0	154	148	43	99	0	1	2	4	36	7	0	.194	5	18	5	1	0.6	.821
1988		3	7	.300	4.12	17	16	0	78.2	88	26	38	0	0	0	0	25	5	0	.200	10	11	3	0	1.4	.875
1989		5	3	.625	3.35	15	15	0	83.1	80	28	36	0	0	0	0	28	6	0	.214	4	13	1	0	1.2	.944
1990	2 teams	CIN N (6G 2 - 2)				MIL A (22G 12 - 5)																				
"	total	14	7	.667	3.26	28	27	7	179.2	194	51	71	2	0	1	0	11	1	0	.091	19	21	0	1	1.4	1.000
7 yrs.		47	34	.580	3.52	223	93	8	760.1	762	236	461	2	14	7	19	144	22	0	.153	56	107	11	7	0.8	.937

Mike Rochford

ROCHFORD, MICHAEL JOSEPH
B. Mar. 14, 1963, Methuen, Mass.
BL TL 6' 4" 205 lbs.

Year	Team	W	L	%	ERA	G	GS	CG	IP	H	BB	SO	ShO	W	L	SV	AB	H	HR	BA	PO	A	E	DP	TC/G	FA
1988	BOS A	0	0	—	0.00	2	0	0	2.1	4	1	1	0	0	0	0	0	0	0	—	1	2	0	0	1.5	1.000
1989		0	0	—	6.75	4	0	0	4	4	4	1	0	0	0	0	0	0	0	—	0	0	0	0	0.0	—
1990		0	1	.000	18.00	2	1	0	4	10	4	0	0	0	0	0	0	0	0	—	0	0	0	0	0.0	—
3 yrs.		0	1	.000	9.58	8	1	0	10.1	18	9	2	0	0	0	0	0	0	0	—	1	2	0	0	0.4	1.000

Rich Rodriguez

RODRIGUEZ, RICHARD ANTHONY
B. Mar. 1, 1963, Los Angeles, Calif.
BL TL 5' 10" 185 lbs.

Year	Team	W	L	%	ERA	G	GS	CG	IP	H	BB	SO	ShO	W	L	SV	AB	H	HR	BA	PO	A	E	DP	TC/G	FA
1990	SD N	1	1	.500	2.83	32	0	0	47.2	52	16	22	0	1	1	1	3	0	0	.000	1	10	0	1	0.3	1.000

Rick Rodriguez

RODRIGUEZ, RICARDO
B. Sept. 21, 1960, Oakland, Calif.
BR TR 6' 3" 190 lbs.

Year	Team	W	L	%	ERA	G	GS	CG	IP	H	BB	SO	ShO	W	L	SV	AB	H	HR	BA	PO	A	E	DP	TC/G	FA
1986	OAK A	1	2	.333	6.61	3	3	0	16.1	17	7	2	0	0	0	0	0	0	0	—	1	4	0	0	1.7	1.000
1987		1	0	1.000	2.96	15	0	0	24.1	32	15	9	0	1	0	0	0	0	0	—	2	6	0	1	0.5	1.000
1988	CLE A	1	2	.333	7.09	10	5	0	33	43	17	9	0	0	0	0	0	0	0	—	4	8	0	1	1.2	1.000
1990	SF N	0	0	—	8.10	3	0	0	3.1	5	2	2	0	0	0	0	0	0	0	—	1	0	0	0	0.3	1.000
4 yrs.		3	4	.429	5.73	31	8	0	77	97	41	22	0	1	0	0	0	0	0	—	8	18	0	2	0.8	1.000

Rosario Rodriguez

RODRIGUEZ, ROSARIO ISABEL
Born Rosario Isabel Rodriguez y Echavarria.
B. July 8, 1969, Los Mochis, Mexico
BR TL 6' 185 lbs.

Year	Team	W	L	%	ERA	G	GS	CG	IP	H	BB	SO	ShO	W	L	SV	AB	H	HR	BA	PO	A	E	DP	TC/G	FA
1989	CIN N	1	1	.500	4.15	7	0	0	4.1	3	3	0	0	1	1	0	0	0	0	—	1	1	0	0	0.3	1.000
1990		0	0	—	6.10	9	0	0	10.1	15	2	8	0	0	0	0	0	0	0	—	0	3	0	0	0.3	1.000
2 yrs.		1	1	.500		16	0	0	14.2	18	5	8	0	1	1	0	0	0	0	—	1	4	0	0	0.3	1.000

Mike Roesler

ROESLER, MICHAEL JOSEPH
B. Sept. 12, 1963, Fort Wayne, Ind.
BR TR 6' 5" 195 lbs.

Year	Team	W	L	%	ERA	G	GS	CG	IP	H	BB	SO	ShO	W	L	SV	AB	H	HR	BA	PO	A	E	DP	TC/G	FA
1989	CIN N	0	1	.000	3.96	17	0	0	25	22	9	14	0	0	1	0	0	0	0	—	0	1	0	0	0.1	1.000
1990	PIT N	1	0	1.000	3.00	5	0	0	6	5	2	4	0	1	0	0	1	0	0	.000	0	0	0	0	0.0	—
2 yrs.		1	1	.500	3.77	22	0	0	31	27	11	18	0	1	1	0	1	0	0	.000	0	1	0	0	0.0	1.000

Year	Team	W	L	%	ERA	G	GS	CG	IP	H	BB	SO	ShO	RELIEF PITCHING W	L	SV	BATTING AB	H	HR	BA	PO	A	E	DP	TC/G	FA

Kenny Rogers

ROGERS, KENNETH SCOTT
B. Nov. 10, 1964, Savannah, Ga.
BL TL 6′ 1″ 200 lbs.

Year/Split	W	L	%	ERA	G	GS	CG	IP	H	BB	SO	ShO	W	L	SV	AB	H	HR	BA	PO	A	E	DP	TC/G	FA
April	1	1	.500	4.76	7	1	0	11.1	15	5	5	0	1	0	0										
May	1	0	1.000	5.40	13	0	0	20	19	5	12	0	1	0	0										
June	0	2	.000	2.70	14	0	0	16.2	19	9	16	0	0	2	5										
July	2	2	.500	2.03	12	0	0	13.1	9	7	17	0	2	2	5										
Aug	1	0	1.000	2.31	13	0	0	11.2	11	6	6	0	1	0	2										
Sept/Oct	5	1	.833	1.82	10	2	0	24.2	20	10	18	0	4	0	3										
Day	0	2	.000	5.06	12	1	0	16	17	7	13	0	0	1	4										
Night	10	4	.714	2.76	57	2	0	81.2	76	35	61	0	9	3	11										
vs. Left	—	—	—	—	—	—	—	—	21	6	19	—	—	—	—										
vs. Right	—	—	—	—	—	—	—	—	72	36	55	—	—	—	—										
On Grass	10	4	.714	2.41	58	2	0	82	74	33	62	0	9	3	14										
On Turf	0	2	.000	6.89	11	1	0	15.2	19	9	12	0	0	0	1										
Home	9	1	.900	2.01	36	1	0	53.2	50	18	37	0	8	1	8										
Road	1	5	.167	4.50	33	2	0	44	43	24	37	0	1	3	7										
Division Rivals																								
vs. CAL	1	0	1.000	0.00	4	1	0	10	5	3	10	0	0	0	1										
vs. CHI	2	0	1.000	1.50	5	0	0	6	4	0	3	0	2	0	1										
vs. KC	1	1	.500	5.40	4	1	0	6.2	9	3	2	0	1	0	0										
vs. MIN	0	0	—	3.86	4	0	0	4.2	5	3	4	0	0	0	1										
vs. OAK	0	0	—	0.00	6	0	0	6	5	4	6	0	0	0	3										
vs. SEA	0	2	.000	4.35	8	0	0	10.1	11	7	4	0	0	2	1										
1989 TEX A	3	4	.429	2.93	73	0	0	73.2	60	42	63	0	3	4	2	0	0	0	—	1	22	0	0	0.3	1.000
1990	10	6	.625	3.13	69	3	0	97.2	93	42	74	0	9	4	15	0	0	0	—	5	22	2	1	0.4	.931
2 yrs.	13	10	.565	3.05	142	3	0	171.1	153	84	137	0	12	8	17	0	0	0	—	6	44	2	1	0.4	.962

RELIEF PITCHER
WINS / ERA / SAVES / RATIO (AL AVG)

Mel Rojas

ROJAS, MELQUIADES
Born Melquiades Rojas y Medrano.
B. Dec. 10, 1966, Haina, Dominican Republic
BR TR 5′ 11″ 175 lbs.

Year	Team	W	L	%	ERA	G	GS	CG	IP	H	BB	SO	ShO	W	L	SV	AB	H	HR	BA	PO	A	E	DP	TC/G	FA
1990	MON N	3	1	.750	3.60	23	0	0	40	34	24	26	0	3	1	1	3	0	0	.000	2	4	1	0	0.3	.857

Steve Rosenberg

ROSENBERG, STEVEN ALLEN
B. Oct. 31, 1964, Brooklyn, N. Y.
BL TL 6′ 186 lbs.

Year/Split	W	L	%	ERA	G	GS	CG	IP	H	BB	SO	ShO	W	L	SV	AB	H	HR	BA	PO	A	E	DP	TC/G	FA
April	—	—	—	—	0	0	0	0	0	0	0	—	0	0	0										
May	—	—	—	—	0	0	—	0	0	0	0	—	0	0	0										
June	—	—	—	—	0	0	0	0	0	0	0	—	0	0	0										
July	—	—	—	—	0	0	0	0	0	0	0	—	0	0	0										
Aug	—	—	—	—	0	0	0	0	0	0	0	—	0	0	0										
Sept/Oct	1	0	1.000	5.40	6	0	0	10	10	5	4	0	1	0	0										
Day	0	0	—	0.00	2	0	0	2	0	1	0	0	0	0	0										
Night	1	0	1.000	6.75	4	0	0	8	10	5	3	0	1	0	0										
vs. Left	—	—	—	—	—	—	—	—	4	2	1	—	—	—	—										
vs. Right	—	—	—	—	—	—	—	—	6	3	3	—	—	—	—										
On Grass	0	0	—	19.29	3	0	0	2.1	5	4	1	0	0	0	0										
On Turf	1	0	1.000	1.17	3	0	0	7.2	5	1	3	0	1	0	0										
Home	0	0	—	0.00	1	0	0	0	2	0	0	0	0	0	0										
Road	1	0	1.000	4.50	5	0	0	10	9	3	4	0	1	0	0										
Division Rivals																								
vs. CAL	—	—	—	—	0	0	0	0	0	0	0	—	0	0	0										
vs. KC	—	—	—	—	0	0	0	0	0	0	0	—	0	0	0										
vs. MIN	—	—	—	—	0	0	0	0	0	0	0	—	0	0	0										
vs. OAK	0	0	—	0.00	1	0	0	1	0	0	0	0	0	0	0										
vs. SEA	1	0	1.000	2.70	3	0	0	6.2	6	3	2	0	1	0	0										
vs. TEX	—	—	—	—	0	0	0	0	0	0	0	—	0	0	0										
1988 CHI A	0	1	.000	4.30	33	0	0	46	53	19	28	0	0	1	0	0	0	0	—	0	6	0	0	0.2	1.000
1989	4	13	.235	4.94	38	21	2	142	148	58	77	0	1	2	0	0	0	0	—	8	20	3	5	0.8	.903
1990	1	0	1.000	5.40	6	0	0	10	10	5	4	0	1	0	0	0	0	0	—	1	2	0	0	0.5	1.000
3 yrs.	5	14	.263	4.82	77	21	2	198	211	82	109	0	2	3	1	0	0	0	—	9	28	3	5	0.5	.925

RELIEF PITCHER
WINS / ERA / SAVES / RATIO (NL AVG)

Year	Team		W	L	%	ERA	G	GS	CG	IP	H	BB	SO	ShO	RELIEF PITCHING			BATTING			BA	PO	A	E	DP	TC/G	FA
															W	L	SV	AB	H	HR							

Mark Ross

ROSS, MARK JOSEPH
B. Aug. 8, 1954, Galveston, Tex.
BR TR 6′ 195 lbs.

Year	Team		W	L	%	ERA	G	GS	CG	IP	H	BB	SO	ShO	W	L	SV	AB	H	HR	BA	PO	A	E	DP	TC/G	FA
1982	HOU	N	0	0	—	1.50	4	0	0	6	3	0	4	0	0	0	0	0	0	0	—	0	1	0	0	0.3	1.000
1984			1	0	1.000	0.00	2	0	0	2.1	1	0	1	0	1	0	0	0	0	0	—	0	0	0	0	0.0	—
1985			0	2	.000	4.85	8	0	0	13	12	2	3	0	0	2	1	1	0	0	.000	2	2	0	0	0.5	1.000
1987	PIT	N	0	0	—	9.00	1	0	0	1	1	0	0	0	0	0	0	0	0	0	—	0	1	0	0	1.0	1.000
1988	TOR	A	0	0	—	4.91	3	0	0	7.1	5	4	4	0	0	0	0	0	0	0	—	0	0	0	0	0.0	—
1990	PIT	N	1	0	1.000	3.55	9	0	0	12.2	11	4	5	0	1	0	0	1	0	0	.000	1	3	0	0	0.4	1.000
6 yrs.			2	2	.500	3.83	27	0	0	42.1	33	10	17	0	2	2	1	2	0	0	.000	3	7	0	0	0.4	1.000

Bruce Ruffin

RUFFIN, BRUCE WAYNE
B. Oct. 4, 1963, Lubbock, Tex.
BR TL 6′ 2″ 205 lbs.

		W	L	%	ERA	G	GS	CG	IP	H	BB	SO	ShO	W	L	SV	AB	H	HR	BA	PO	A	E	DP	TC/G	FA
April		1	2	.333	3.80	4	4	0	23.2	30	7	10	0	0	0	0										
May		2	3	.400	5.93	6	6	0	30.1	39	14	9	0	0	0	0										
June		2	2	.500	2.84	5	5	2	38	30	10	24	1	0	0	0										
July		1	3	.250	6.84	6	6	0	26.1	35	14	14	0	0	0	0										
Aug		0	1	.000	8.44	7	1	0	16	25	8	10	0	0	0	0										
Sept/Oct		0	2	.000	7.36	4	3	0	14.2	19	9	12	0	0	0	0										
Day		2	2	.500	5.13	9	7	0	47.1	52	14	23	0	0	0	0										
Night		4	11	.267	5.49	23	18	2	101.2	126	48	56	1	0	0	0										
vs. Left		—	—	—	—	—	—	—	—	35	12	19	—	—	—	—										
vs. Right		—	—	—	—	—	—	—	—	143	50	60	—	—	—	—										
On Grass		0	3	.000	7.64	9	5	0	33	49	8	16	0	0	0	0										
On Turf		6	10	.375	4.73	23	20	2	116	129	54	63	1	0	0	0										
Home		5	7	.417	5.40	16	14	1	78.1	91	40	41	1	0	0	0										
Road		1	6	.143	5.35	16	11	1	70.2	87	22	38	0	0	0	0										
Division Rivals																									
vs. CHI		1	1	.500	4.21	4	4	1	25.2	26	5	9	1	0	0	0										
vs. MON		0	1	.000	5.00	2	1	0	9	11	2	8	0	0	0	0										
vs. NY		0	1	.000	6.00	3	2	0	12	12	6	8	0	0	0	0										
vs. PIT		1	3	.250	4.55	6	5	1	31.2	33	12	16	0	0	0	0										
vs. STL		1	0	1.000	2.87	3	2	0	15.2	17	9	13	0	0	0	0										

Year	Team		W	L	%	ERA	G	GS	CG	IP	H	BB	SO	ShO	W	L	SV	AB	H	HR	BA	PO	A	E	DP	TC/G	FA
1986	PHI	N	9	4	.692	2.46	21	21	6	146.1	138	44	70	0	0	0	0	55	4	0	.073	8	20	1	0	1.4	.966
1987			11	14	.440	4.35	35	35	3	204.2	236	73	93	1	0	0	0	73	4	0	.055	7	32	2	3	1.2	.931
1988			6	10	.375	4.43	55	15	3	144.1	151	80	82	0	2	4	3	33	4	0	.121	11	25	2	2	0.7	.947
1989			6	10	.375	4.44	24	23	1	125.2	152	62	70	0	0	0	0	34	6	0	.176	3	34	4	0	1.7	.902
1990			6	13	.316	5.38	32	25	2	149	178	62	79	1	0	0	0	44	3	0	.068	5	23	0	2	0.9	1.000
5 yrs.			38	51	.427	4.22	167	119	15	770	855	321	394	2	2	4	3	239	21	0	.088	34	134	9	7	1.1	.949

STARTING PITCHER

WINS — ERA — SO/9 — RATIO (bar charts with NL AVG)

Scott Ruskin

RUSKIN, SCOTT DREW
B. June 6, 1963, Jacksonville, Fla.
BB TL 6′ 2″ 185 lbs.

		W	L	%	ERA	G	GS	CG	IP	H	BB	SO	ShO	W	L	SV	AB	H	HR	BA	PO	A	E	DP	TC/G	FA
April		0	0	—	2.08	10	0	0	8.2	7	4	6	0	0	0	0										
May		0	1	.000	3.29	10	0	0	13.2	12	9	12	0	0	1	2										
June		2	0	1.000	2.79	11	0	0	9.2	10	6	4	0	2	0	0										
July		0	0	—	3.18	10	0	0	11.1	14	6	10	0	0	0	0										
Aug		0	1	.000	2.30	14	0	0	15.2	19	6	8	0	0	0	0										
Sept/Oct		1	0	1.000	2.76	12	0	0	16.1	13	7	17	0	1	0	0										
Day		1	1	.500	2.14	19	0	0	21	16	9	11	0	1	1	1										
Night		2	1	.667	2.98	48	0	0	54.1	59	29	46	0	2	1	1										
vs. Left		—	—	—	—	—	—	—	—	32	13	26	—	—	—	—										
vs. Right		—	—	—	—	—	—	—	—	43	25	31	—	—	—	—										

RELIEF PITCHER

WINS — ERA (bar charts with NL AVG)

Year	Team	W	L	%	ERA	G	GS	CG	IP	H	BB	SO	ShO	RELIEF PITCHING W	L	SV	BATTING AB	H	HR	BA	PO	A	E	DP	TC/G	FA

Scott Ruskin *Continued*

		W	L	%	ERA	G	GS	CG	IP	H	BB	SO	ShO	W	L	SV	AB	H	HR	BA	PO	A	E	DP	TC/G	FA
On Grass		1	0	1.000	1.93	20	0	0	18.2	19	7	16	0	1	0	0										
On Turf		2	2	.500	3.02	47	0	0	56.2	56	31	41	0	2	2	2										
Home		2	0	1.000	1.31	32	0	0	41.1	35	22	30	0	2	0	2										
Road		1	2	.333	4.50	35	0	0	34	40	16	27	0	1	2	0										
Division Rivals																										
vs. CHI		0	0	—	2.70	5	0	0	3.1	5	1	1	0	0	0	0										
vs. NY		1	0	1.000	2.45	8	0	0	11	9	5	11	0	1	0	0										
vs. PHI		1	1	.500	4.76	7	0	0	11.1	16	4	5	0	1	1	0										
vs. PIT		1	0	1.000	5.40	5	0	0	5	5	2	7	0	1	0	0										
vs. STL		0	0	—	1.17	6	0	0	7.2	5	5	3	0	0	0	0										
1990	2 teams	PIT N (44G 2 – 2)			MON N (23G 1 – 0)																					
"	total	3	2	.600	2.75	67	0	0	75.1	75	38	57	0	3	2	2	8	2	0	.250	1	14	2	2	0.3	.882

RELIEF PITCHER — SAVES (NL AVG), RATIO (NL AVG)

Jeff Russell

RUSSELL, JEFFREY LEE
B. Sept. 2, 1961, Cincinnati, Ohio
BR TR 6′ 4″ 200 lbs.

		W	L	%	ERA	G	GS	CG	IP	H	BB	SO	ShO	W	L	SV	AB	H	HR	BA	PO	A	E	DP	TC/G	FA
April		1	1	.500	3.18	9	0	0	11.1	8	6	9	0	1	1	4										
May		0	4	.000	6.52	11	0	0	9.2	13	7	6	0	0	4	4										
June		—	—	—	—	0	—	—	0	0	0	0	—	0	0	0										
July		—	—	—	—	0	—	—	0	0	0	0	—	0	0	0										
Aug		—	—	—	—	0	—	—	0	0	0	0	—	0	0	0										
Sept/Oct		0	0	—	2.08	7	0	0	4.1	2	3	1	0	0	0	2										
Day		0	1	.000	1.80	6	0	0	5	3	0	2	0	0	1	1										
Night		1	4	.200	4.87	21	0	0	20.1	20	16	14	0	1	4	9										
vs. Left		—	—	—	—	—	—	—	—	5	4	7	—	—	—	—										
vs. Right		—	—	—	—	—	—	—	—	18	12	9	—	—	—	—										
On Grass		0	5	.000	3.91	24	0	0	23	21	15	15	0	0	5	10										
On Turf		1	0	1.000	7.71	3	0	0	2.1	2	1	1	0	1	0	0										
Home		0	4	.000	5.54	14	0	0	13	11	10	9	0	0	4	6										
Road		1	1	.500	2.92	13	0	0	12.1	12	6	7	0	1	1	4										
Division Rivals																										
vs. CAL		0	0	—	0.00	1	0	0	0.1	0	2	0	0	0	0	0										
vs. CHI		0	0	—	0.00	1	0	0	3	1	4	4	0	0	0	0										
vs. KC		1	0	1.000	6.75	1	0	0	1.1	2	0	1	0	1	0	0										
vs. MIN		0	0	—	0.00	1	0	0	1	0	0	0	0	0	0	0										
vs. OAK		0	0	—	0.00	1	0	0	0.1	0	0	1	0	0	0	1										
vs. SEA		0	0	—	0.00	1	0	0	0	0	0	1	0	0	0	0										
1983	CIN N	4	5	.444	3.03	10	10	2	68.1	58	22	40	0	0	0	0	21	3	1	.143	2	10	1	0	1.3	.923
1984		6	**18**	.250	4.26	33	30	4	181.2	186	65	101	2	0	0	0	57	8	0	.140	7	34	2	4	1.3	.953
1985	TEX A	3	6	.333	7.55	13	13	0	62	85	27	44	0	0	0	0	0	0	0	—	6	10	0	1	1.2	1.000
1986		5	2	.714	3.40	37	0	0	82	74	31	54	0	5	2	2	0	0	0	—	6	17	0	3	0.6	1.000
1987		5	4	.556	4.44	52	2	0	97.1	109	52	56	0	5	3	3	0	0	0	—	11	17	0	2	0.5	1.000
1988		10	9	.526	3.82	34	24	5	188.2	183	66	88	0	1	0	0	1	0	0	.000	12	37	5	3	1.6	.907
1989		6	4	.600	1.98	71	0	0	72.2	45	24	77	0	6	4	38	0	0	0	—	6	14	0	3	0.3	1.000
1990		1	5	.167	4.26	27	0	0	25.1	23	16	16	0	1	5	10	0	0	0	—	1	5	1	0	0.3	.857
8 yrs.		40	53	.430	4.03	277	79	11	778	763	303	476	2	18	14	53	79	11	1	.139	51	144	9	16	0.7	.956

RELIEF PITCHER — WINS (AL AVG), ERA (AL AVG), SAVES (AL AVG), RATIO (AL AVG)

John Russell

RUSSELL, JOHN WILLIAM
B. Jan. 5, 1961, Oklahoma City, Okla.
BR TL 6′ 195 lbs.

Year	Team	W	L	%	ERA	G	GS	CG	IP	H	BB	SO	ShO	W	L	SV	AB	H	HR	BA	PO	A	E	DP	TC/G	FA
1989	ATL N	0	0	—	0.00	1	0	0	0.1	0	0	0	0	0	0	0	*				0	0	0	0	0.0	—

Year	Team	W	L	%	ERA	G	GS	CG	IP	H	BB	SO	ShO	RELIEF PITCHING W	L	SV	BATTING AB	H	HR	BA	PO	A	E	DP	TC/G	FA

Nolan Ryan

RYAN, LYNN NOLAN (The Express)
B. Jan. 31, 1947, Refugio, Tex.
BR TR 6′ 2″ 170 lbs.

	W	L	%	ERA	G	GS	CG	IP	H	BB	SO	ShO	W	L	SV	AB	H	HR	BA	PO	A	E	DP	TC/G	FA
April	4	0	1.000	2.25	4	4	1	28	14	8	33	1	0	0	0										
May	0	2	.000	10.47	4	4	0	16.1	16	13	21	0	0	0	0										
June	3	2	.600	2.16	5	5	1	33.1	19	11	43	1	0	0	0										
July	4	0	1.000	3.61	6	6	0	42.1	34	19	46	0	0	0	0										
Aug	1	3	.250	3.23	5	5	2	39	29	7	38	0	0	0	0										
Sept/Oct	1	2	.333	2.60	6	6	1	45	25	16	51	0	0	0	0										
Day	1	1	.500	3.22	3	3	0	22.1	20	9	22	0	0	0	0										
Night	12	8	.600	3.47	27	27	5	181.2	117	65	210	2	0	0	0										
vs. Left	—	—	—	—	—	—	—	—	79	43	92	—	—	—	—										
vs. Right	—	—	—	—	—	—	—	—	58	31	140	—	—	—	—										
On Grass	12	8	.600	3.33	27	27	5	186.1	118	66	218	2	0	0	0										
On Turf	1	1	.500	4.58	3	3	0	17.2	19	8	14	0	0	0	0										
Home	8	5	.615	3.32	19	19	3	130	78	43	158	1	0	0	0										
Road	5	4	.556	3.65	11	11	2	74	59	31	74	1	0	0	0										

Division Rivals

	W	L	%	ERA	G	GS	CG	IP	H	BB	SO	ShO	W	L	SV	AB	H	HR	BA	PO	A	E	DP	TC/G	FA
vs. CAL	0	2	.000	2.12	2	2	2	17	7	3	22	0	0	0	0										
vs. CHI	1	2	.333	3.00	4	4	1	30	14	8	41	1	0	0	0										
vs. KC	0	1	.000	8.22	2	2	0	7.2	9	7	9	0	0	0	0										
vs. MIN	1	0	1.000	1.29	1	1	0	7	6	1	3	0	0	0	0										
vs. OAK	1	2	.333	1.69	3	3	1	21.1	7	9	33	1	0	0	0										
vs. SEA	2	1	.667	4.68	4	4	0	25	23	9	25	0	0	0	0										

Year	Team		W	L	%	ERA	G	GS	CG	IP	H	BB	SO	ShO	W	L	SV	AB	H	HR	BA	PO	A	E	DP	TC/G	FA
1966	NY	N	0	1	.000	15.00	2	1	0	3	5	3	6	0	0	0	0	0	0	0	—	1	0	0	0	0.5	1.000
1968			6	9	.400	3.09	21	18	3	134	93	75	133	0	0	0	0	44	5	0	.114	5	11	4	0	1.0	.800
1969			6	3	.667	3.53	25	10	2	89.1	60	53	92	0	3	0	1	29	3	0	.103	4	1	0	0	0.2	.800
1970			7	11	.389	3.41	27	19	5	132	86	97	125	2	0	0	1	45	8	0	.178	11	10	4	2	0.9	.840
1971			10	14	.417	3.97	30	26	3	152	125	116	137	0	1	0	0	47	6	0	.128	5	15	3	2	0.8	.870
1972	CAL	A	19	16	.543	2.28	39	39	20	284	166	**157**	**329**	**9**	0	0	0	96	13	0	.135	7	28	6	2	1.1	.854
1973			21	16	.568	2.87	41	39	26	326	238	**162**	**383**[1]	4	0	0	1	0	0	0	—	10	27	2	1	1.0	.949
1974			22	16	.579	2.89	42	41	26	333	221	**202**	**367**	3	1	0	0	0	0	0	—	12	48	6	1	1.6	.909
1975			14	12	.538	3.45	28	28	10	198	152	132	186	5	0	0	0	0	0	0	—	12	18	7	3	1.3	.811
1976			17	**18**	.486	3.36	39	39	21	284	193	**183**	**327**	7	0	0	0	0	0	0	—	14	34	7	1	1.4	.873
1977			19	16	.543	2.77	37	37	**22**	299	198	**204**	**341**	4	0	0	0	0	0	0	—	20	35	8	1	1.7	.873
1978			10	13	.435	3.71	31	31	14	235	183	**148**	**260**	3	0	0	0	0	0	0	—	13	33	8	3	1.7	.852
1979			16	14	.533	3.59	34	34	17	223	169	114	**223**	5	0	0	0	0	0	0	—	8	29	4	1	1.2	.902
1980	HOU	N	11	10	.524	3.35	35	35	4	234	205	**98**	200	2	0	0	0	70	6	1	.086	13	27	5	0	1.3	.889
1981			11	5	.688	**1.69**	21	21	5	149	99	68	140	3	0	0	0	51	11	0	.216	5	16	1	3	1.0	.955
1982			16	12	.571	3.16	35	35	10	250.1	196	**109**	245	3	0	0	0	83	10	0	.120	9	33	2	1	1.3	.955
1983			14	9	.609	2.98	29	29	5	196.1	134	101	183	2	0	0	0	69	5	0	.072	4	28	2	0	1.2	.941
1984			12	11	.522	3.04	30	30	5	183.2	143	69	197	2	0	0	0	61	6	0	.098	7	11	2	0	0.7	.900
1985			10	12	.455	3.80	35	35	4	232	205	95	209	0	0	0	0	63	7	0	.111	6	20	2	0	0.8	.929
1986			12	8	.600	3.34	30	30	1	178	119	82	194	0	0	0	0	59	6	0	.102	10	17	2	2	1.0	.931
1987			8	16	.333	**2.76**	34	34	0	211.2	154	87	**270**	0	0	0	0	65	4	1	.062	11	18	1	1	0.9	.967
1988			12	11	.522	3.52	33	33	4	220	186	87	**228**	1	0	0	0	70	4	0	.057	8	18	4	0	0.9	.867
1989	TEX	A	16	10	.615	3.20	32	32	6	239.1	162	98	**301**	2	0	0	0	0	0	0	—	11	19	3	0	1.0	.909
1990			13	9	.591	3.44	30	30	5	204	137	74	**232**	2	0	0	0	0	0	0	—	7	13	0	1	0.7	1.000
24 yrs.			302	272	.526	3.16	740	706	218	4990.2	3629	2614	5308	59	5	0	3	852	94	2	.110	209	512	84	25	1.1	.896
						6th						1st	1st	9th													

DIVISIONAL PLAYOFF SERIES

Year	Team		W	L	%	ERA	G	GS	CG	IP	H	BB	SO	ShO	W	L	SV	AB	H	HR	BA	PO	A	E	DP	TC/G	FA
1981	HOU	N	1	1	.500	1.80	2	2	1	15	6	3	14	0	0	0	0	4	1	0	.250	0	0	0	0	0.0	—

LEAGUE CHAMPIONSHIP SERIES

Year	Team		W	L	%	ERA	G	GS	CG	IP	H	BB	SO	ShO	W	L	SV	AB	H	HR	BA	PO	A	E	DP	TC/G	FA
1969	NY	N	1	0	1.000	2.57	1	0	0	7	3	2	7	0	1	0	0	4	2	0	.500	1	0	0	0	1.0	1.000
1979	CAL	A	0	0	—	1.29	1	1	0	7	4	3	8	0	0	0	0	0	0	0	—	0	0	0	0	0.0	—
1980	HOU	N	0	0	—	5.40	2	2	0	13.1	16	3	14	0	0	0	0	4	0	0	.000	1	3	0	0	2.0	1.000
1986			0	1	.000	3.86	2	2	0	14	9	1	17	0	0	0	0	4	0	0	.000	1	0	0	0	0.0	—
4 yrs.			1	1	.500	3.70	6	5	0	41.1	32	9	46	0	1	0	0	12	2	0	.167	2	3	0	0	0.8	1.000

WORLD SERIES

Year	Team		W	L	%	ERA	G	GS	CG	IP	H	BB	SO	ShO	W	L	SV	AB	H	HR	BA	PO	A	E	DP	TC/G	FA
1969	NY	N	0	0	—	0.00	1	0	0	2.1	1	2	3	0	0	0	1	0	0	0	—	0	0	0	0	0.0	—

STARTING PITCHER

WINS · ERA · SO/9 · RATIO (bar charts with AL AVG comparisons)

Year	Team	W	L	%	ERA	G	GS	CG	IP	H	BB	SO	ShO	W	L	SV	AB	H	HR	BA	PO	A	E	DP	TC/G	FA

Bret Saberhagen

SABERHAGEN, BRET WILLIAM
B. Apr. 11, 1964, Chicago Heights, Ill.
BR TR 6' 1" 160 lbs.

Year	Team	W	L	%	ERA	G	GS	CG	IP	H	BB	SO	ShO	W	L	SV	AB	H	HR	BA	PO	A	E	DP	TC/G	FA
April		1	2	.333	3.55	4	4	1	25.1	25	4	15	0	0	0	0										
May		3	1	.750	2.53	6	6	3	46.1	41	10	29	0	0	0	0										
June		1	4	.200	3.07	6	6	1	44	47	8	33	0	0	0	0										
July		0	0	—	4.82	2	2	0	9.1	19	3	0	0	0	0	0										
Aug		—	—	—	—	0	—	—	0	0	0	0	—	0	0	0										
Sept/Oct		0	2	.000	5.40	2	2	0	10	14	3	10	0	0	0	0										
Day		1	2	.333	3.26	7	7	1	47	46	10	35	0	0	0	0										
Night		4	7	.364	3.27	13	13	4	88	100	18	52	0	0	0	0										
vs. Left		—	—	—	—	—	—	—	—	61	16	42	—	—	—	—										
vs. Right		—	—	—	—	—	—	—	—	85	12	45	—	—	—	—										
On Grass		2	2	.500	2.06	6	6	3	43.2	36	8	26	0	0	0	0										
On Turf		3	7	.300	3.84	14	14	2	91.1	110	20	61	0	0	0	0										
Home		3	5	.375	3.42	11	11	2	73.2	88	14	52	0	0	0	0										
Road		2	4	.333	3.08	9	9	3	61.1	58	14	35	0	0	0	0										
Division Rivals																										
vs. CAL		0	3	.000	3.80	3	3	1	21.1	25	4	24	0	0	0	0										
vs. CHI		0	0	—	2.03	2	2	0	13.1	10	7	10	0	0	0	0										
vs. MIN		0	2	.000	3.86	2	2	0	14	16	0	4	0	0	0	0										
vs. OAK		1	1	.500	2.25	2	2	0	12	13	4	9	0	0	0	0										
vs. SEA		0	0	—	4.05	1	1	0	6.2	7	3	6	0	0	0	0										
vs. TEX		—	—	—	—	0	—	—	0	0	0	0	—	0	0	0										
1984	KC A	10	11	.476	3.48	38	18	2	157.2	138	36	73	1	4	1	1	0	0	0	—	15	22	1	1	1.0	.974
1985		20	6	.769	2.87	32	32	10	235.1	211	38	158	1	0	0	0	0	0	0	—	22	38	2	4	1.9	.968
1986		7	12	.368	4.15	30	25	4	156	165	29	112	2	1	0	0	0	0	0	—	14	26	2	0	1.4	.952
1987		18	10	.643	3.36	33	33	15	257	246	53	163	4	0	0	0	0	0	0	—	21	34	2	5	1.7	.965
1988		14	16	.467	3.80	35	35	9	260.2	**271**	59	171	0	0	0	0	0	0	0	—	15	34	3	3	1.5	.942
1989		**23**	6	**.793**	**2.16**	36	35	**12**	**262.1**	209	43	193	4	0	1	0	0	0	0	—	21	36	4	1	1.7	.934
1990		5	9	.357	3.27	20	20	5	135	146	28	87	0	0	0	0	0	0	0	—	16	28	1	2	2.3	.978
7 yrs.		97	70	.581	3.23	224	198	57	1464	1386	286	957	12	5	2	1	0	0	0	—	124	218	15	16	1.6	.958

LEAGUE CHAMPIONSHIP SERIES

Year	Team	W	L	%	ERA	G	GS	CG	IP	H	BB	SO	ShO	W	L	SV	AB	H	HR	BA	PO	A	E	DP	TC/G	FA
1984	KC A	0	0	—	2.25	1	1	0	8	6	1	5	0	0	0	0	0	0	0	—	1	1	1	0	3.0	.667
1985		0	0	—	6.14	2	2	0	7.1	12	2	6	0	0	0	0	0	0	0	—	2	1	0	0	1.5	1.000
2 yrs.		0	0	—	4.11	3	3	0	15.1	18	3	11	0	0	0	0	0	0	0	—	3	2	1	0	2.0	.833

WORLD SERIES

Year	Team	W	L	%	ERA	G	GS	CG	IP	H	BB	SO	ShO	W	L	SV	AB	H	HR	BA	PO	A	E	DP	TC/G	FA
1985	KC A	2	0	1.000	0.50	2	2	2	18	11	1	10	1	0	0	0	7	0	0	.000	0	0	0	0	0.0	—

Luis Salazar

SALAZAR, LUIS ERNESTO
Born Luis Ernesto Salazar y Garacia.
B. May 19, 1956, Barcelona, Venezuela
BR TR 5' 9" 180 lbs.

Year	Team	W	L	%	ERA	G	GS	CG	IP	H	BB	SO	ShO	W	L	SV	AB	H	HR	BA	PO	A	E	DP	TC/G	FA
1987	SD N	0	0	—	4.50	2	0	0	2	2	1	0	0	0	0	0	•				0	1	0	0	0.5	1.000

Bill Sampen

SAMPEN, WILLIAM ALBERT
B. Jan. 18, 1963, Lincoln, Ill.
BR TR 6' 1" 185 lbs.

Year	Team	W	L	%	ERA	G	GS	CG	IP	H	BB	SO	ShO	W	L	SV	AB	H	HR	BA	PO	A	E	DP	TC/G	FA
April		0	0	—	0.00	6	0	0	7.1	3	2	5	0	0	0	0										
May		2	0	1.000	2.89	10	2	0	18.2	19	3	18	0	1	0	0										
June		4	1	.800	1.89	12	0	0	19	17	8	16	0	4	1	1										
July		2	2	.500	5.71	11	1	0	17.1	25	13	13	0	2	2	0										
Aug		2	2	.500	2.57	10	0	0	14	11	5	12	0	2	1	1										
Sept/Oct		2	2	.500	3.21	10	1	0	14	19	2	5	0	2	1	0										
Day		3	1	.750	3.74	20	1	0	21.2	27	6	18	0	3	1	0										
Night		9	6	.600	2.75	39	3	0	68.2	67	27	51	0	8	5	2										
vs. Left		—	—	—	—	—	—	—	—	44	18	26	—	—	—	—										
vs. Right		—	—	—	—	—	—	—	—	50	15	43	—	—	—	—										

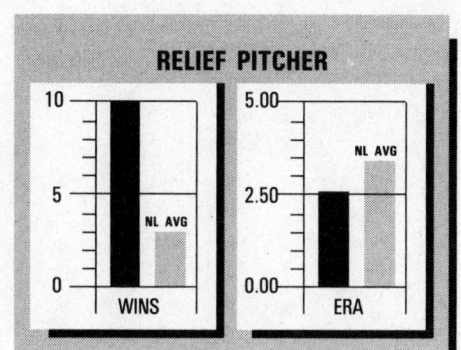

Year	Team	W	L	%	ERA	G	GS	CG	IP	H	BB	SO	ShO	W	L	SV	AB	H	HR	BA	PO	A	E	DP	TC/G	FA
														RELIEF PITCHING			BATTING									

Bill Sampen *Continued*

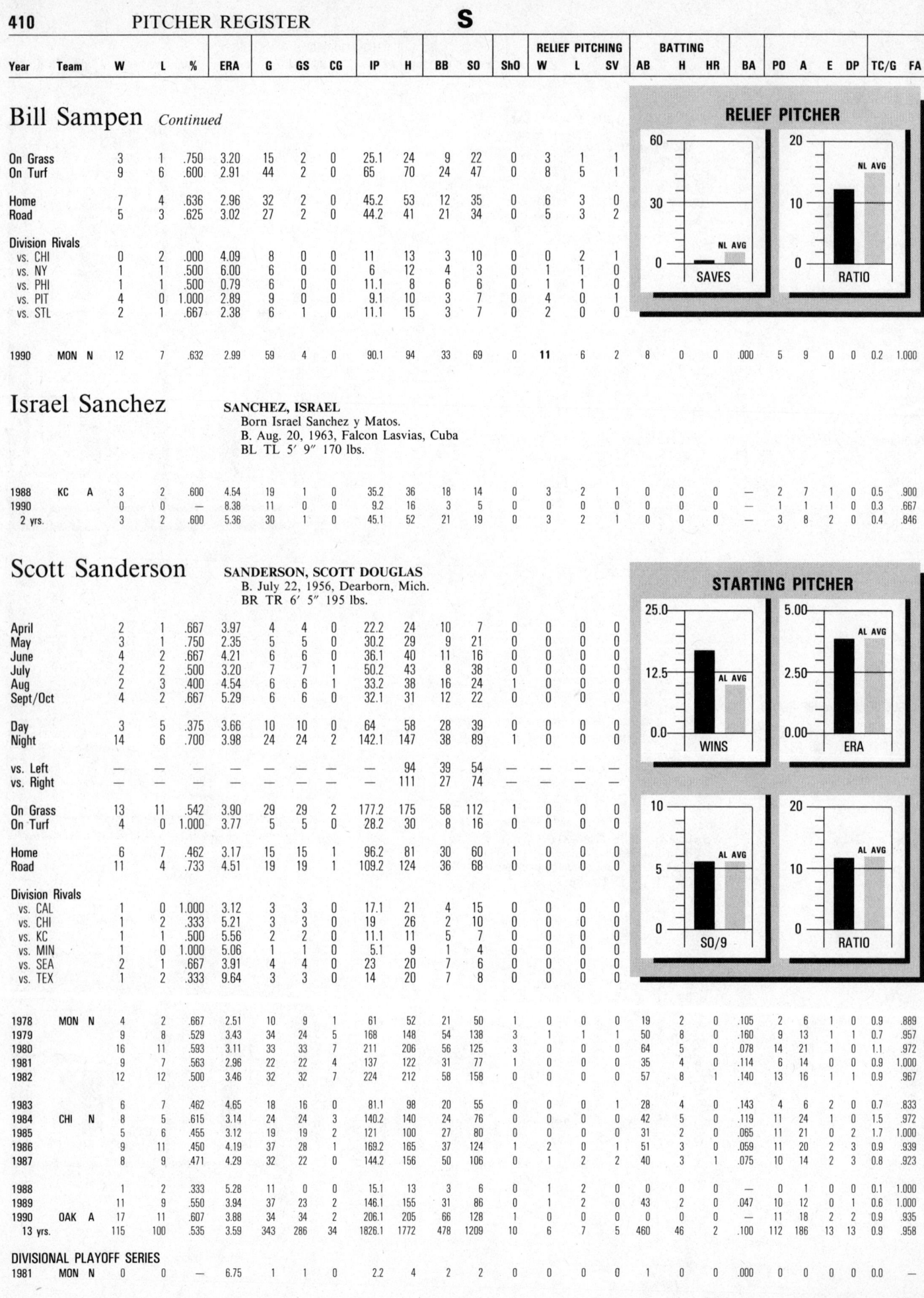

RELIEF PITCHER — SAVES (NL AVG) — RATIO (NL AVG)

Year	Team	W	L	%	ERA	G	GS	CG	IP	H	BB	SO	ShO	W	L	SV	AB	H	HR	BA	PO	A	E	DP	TC/G	FA
On Grass		3	1	.750	3.20	15	2	0	25.1	24	9	22	0	3	1	1										
On Turf		9	6	.600	2.91	44	2	0	65	70	24	47	0	8	5	1										
Home		7	4	.636	2.96	32	2	0	45.2	53	12	35	0	6	3	0										
Road		5	3	.625	3.02	27	2	0	44.2	41	21	34	0	5	3	2										
Division Rivals																										
vs. CHI		0	2	.000	4.09	8	0	0	11	13	3	10	0	0	2	1										
vs. NY		1	1	.500	6.00	6	0	0	6	12	4	3	0	1	1	0										
vs. PHI		1	1	.500	0.79	6	0	0	11.1	8	6	6	0	1	1	0										
vs. PIT		4	0	1.000	2.89	9	0	0	9.1	10	3	7	0	4	0	1										
vs. STL		2	1	.667	2.38	6	1	0	11.1	15	3	7	0	2	0	0										
1990	MON N	12	7	.632	2.99	59	4	0	90.1	94	33	69	0	11	6	2	8	0	0	.000	5	9	0	0	0.2	1.000

Israel Sanchez

SANCHEZ, ISRAEL
Born Israel Sanchez y Matos.
B. Aug. 20, 1963, Falcon Lasvias, Cuba
BL TL 5' 9" 170 lbs.

Year	Team	W	L	%	ERA	G	GS	CG	IP	H	BB	SO	ShO	W	L	SV	AB	H	HR	BA	PO	A	E	DP	TC/G	FA
1988	KC A	3	2	.600	4.54	19	1	0	35.2	36	18	14	0	3	2	1	0	0	0	—	2	7	1	0	0.5	.900
1990		0	0	—	8.38	11	0	0	9.2	16	3	5	0	0	0	0	0	0	0	—	1	1	1	0	0.3	.667
2 yrs.		3	2	.600	5.36	30	1	0	45.1	52	21	19	0	3	2	1	0	0	0	—	3	8	2	0	0.4	.846

Scott Sanderson

SANDERSON, SCOTT DOUGLAS
B. July 22, 1956, Dearborn, Mich.
BR TR 6' 5" 195 lbs.

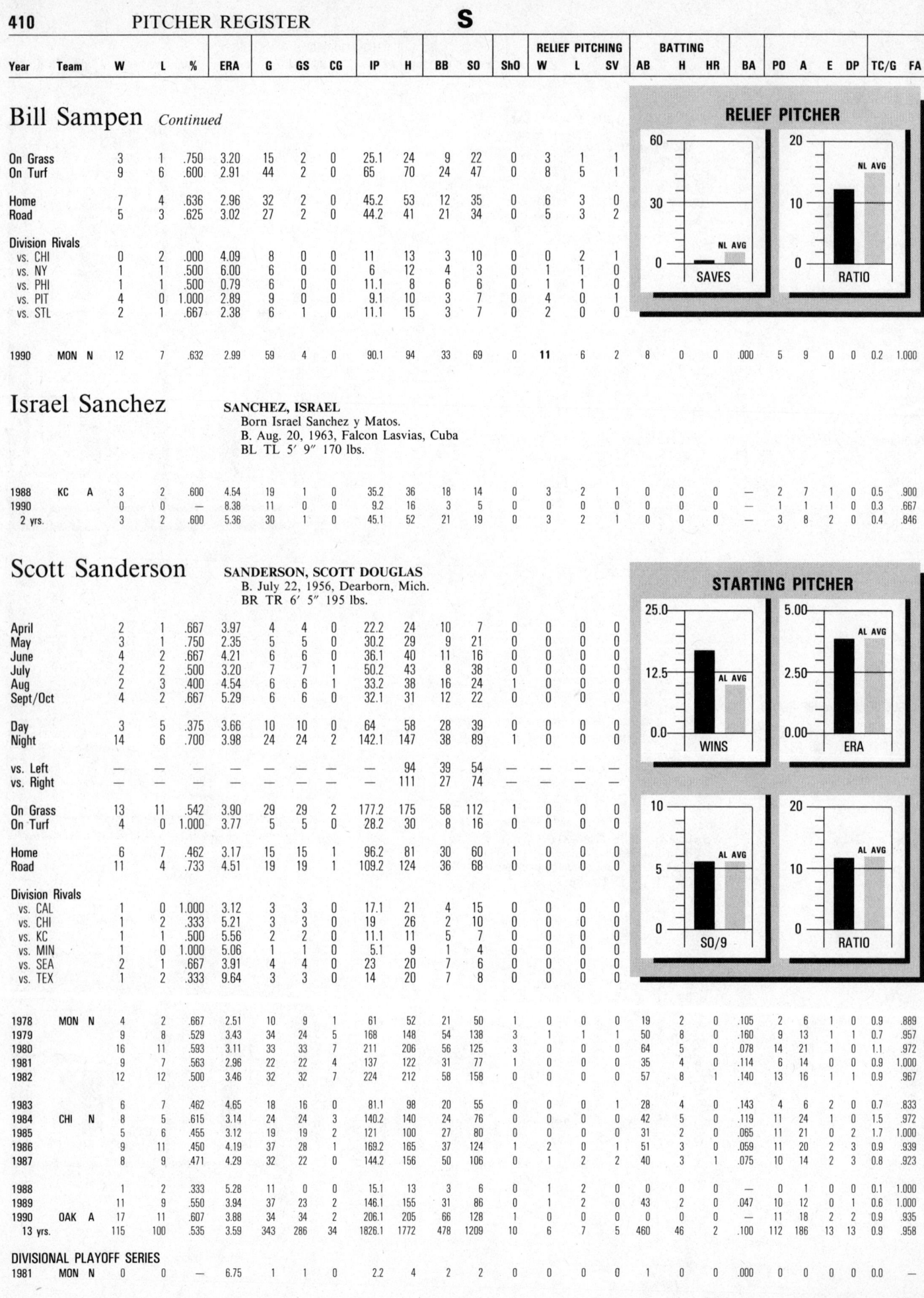

STARTING PITCHER — WINS (AL AVG) — ERA (AL AVG) — SO/9 (AL AVG) — RATIO (AL AVG)

Year	Team	W	L	%	ERA	G	GS	CG	IP	H	BB	SO	ShO	W	L	SV	AB	H	HR	BA	PO	A	E	DP	TC/G	FA
April		2	1	.667	3.97	4	4	0	22.2	24	10	7	0	0	0	0										
May		3	1	.750	2.35	5	5	0	30.2	29	9	21	0	0	0	0										
June		4	2	.667	4.21	6	6	0	36.1	40	11	16	0	0	0	0										
July		2	2	.500	3.20	7	7	1	50.2	43	8	38	0	0	0	0										
Aug		2	3	.400	4.54	6	6	0	33.2	38	16	24	1	0	0	0										
Sept/Oct		4	2	.667	5.29	6	6	0	32.1	31	12	22	0	0	0	0										
Day		3	5	.375	3.66	10	10	0	64	58	28	39	0	0	0	0										
Night		14	6	.700	3.98	24	24	2	142.1	147	38	89	1	0	0	0										
vs. Left		—	—	—	—				—	94	39	54	—	—	—	—										
vs. Right		—	—	—	—				—	111	27	74	—	—	—	—										
On Grass		13	11	.542	3.90	29	29	2	177.2	175	58	112	1	0	0	0										
On Turf		4	0	1.000	3.77	5	5	0	28.2	30	8	16	0	0	0	0										
Home		6	7	.462	3.17	15	15	0	96.2	81	30	60	1	0	0	0										
Road		11	4	.733	4.51	19	19	0	109.2	124	36	68	0	0	0	0										
Division Rivals																										
vs. CAL		1	0	1.000	3.12	3	3	0	17.1	21	4	15	0	0	0	0										
vs. CHI		1	2	.333	5.21	3	3	0	19	26	2	10	0	0	0	0										
vs. KC		1	1	.500	5.56	2	2	0	11.1	11	5	7	0	0	0	0										
vs. MIN		1	0	1.000	5.06	1	1	0	5.1	9	1	4	0	0	0	0										
vs. SEA		2	1	.667	3.91	4	4	0	23	20	7	6	0	0	0	0										
vs. TEX		1	2	.333	9.64	3	3	0	14	20	7	8	0	0	0	0										
1978	MON N	4	2	.667	2.51	10	9	1	61	52	21	50	1	0	0	0	19	2	0	.105	2	6	1	0	0.9	.889
1979		9	8	.529	3.43	34	24	5	168	148	54	138	3	1	1	1	50	8	0	.160	9	13	1	1	0.7	.957
1980		16	11	.593	3.11	33	33	7	211	206	56	125	3	0	0	0	64	5	0	.078	14	21	1	0	1.1	.972
1981		9	7	.563	2.96	22	22	4	137	122	31	77	1	0	0	0	35	4	0	.114	6	14	0	0	0.9	1.000
1982		12	12	.500	3.46	32	32	7	224	212	58	158	0	0	0	0	57	8	1	.140	13	16	1	1	0.9	.967
1983		6	7	.462	4.65	18	16	0	81.1	98	20	55	0	0	0	1	28	4	0	.143	4	6	2	0	0.7	.833
1984	CHI N	8	5	.615	3.14	24	24	3	140.2	140	24	76	0	0	0	0	42	5	0	.119	11	24	1	0	1.5	.972
1985		5	6	.455	3.12	19	19	2	121	100	27	80	0	0	0	0	31	2	0	.065	11	21	0	2	1.7	1.000
1986		9	11	.450	4.19	37	28	0	169.2	165	37	124	1	0	2	0	51	3	0	.059	11	20	2	3	0.9	.939
1987		8	9	.471	4.29	32	22	0	144.2	156	50	106	0	0	1	2	40	3	1	.075	10	14	2	3	0.8	.923
1988		1	2	.333	5.28	11	0	0	15.1	13	3	6	0	0	1	2	0	0	0	—	1	0	1	0	0.1	1.000
1989		11	9	.550	3.94	37	23	2	146.1	155	31	86	0	1	2	0	43	2	0	.047	10	12	0	1	0.6	1.000
1990	OAK A	17	11	.607	3.88	34	34	2	206.1	205	66	128	1	0	0	0	0	0	0	—	11	18	2	2	0.9	.935
13 yrs.		115	100	.535	3.59	343	286	34	1826.1	1772	478	1209	10	6	7	5	460	46	2	.100	112	186	13	13	0.9	.958

DIVISIONAL PLAYOFF SERIES

Year	Team	W	L	%	ERA	G	GS	CG	IP	H	BB	SO	ShO	W	L	SV	AB	H	HR	BA	PO	A	E	DP	TC/G	FA
1981	MON N	0	0	—	6.75	1	1	0	2.2	4	2	2	0	0	0	0	1	0	0	.000	0	0	0	0	0.0	—

Year	Team	W	L	%	ERA	G	GS	CG	IP	H	BB	SO	ShO	RELIEF PITCHING W	L	SV	BATTING AB	H	HR	BA	PO	A	E	DP	TC/G	FA

Scott Sanderson *Continued*

LEAGUE CHAMPIONSHIP SERIES

Year	Team	W	L	%	ERA	G	GS	CG	IP	H	BB	SO	ShO	W	L	SV	AB	H	HR	BA	PO	A	E	DP	TC/G	FA
1984	CHI N	0	0	—	5.79	1	1	0	4.2	6	1	2	0	0	0	0	2	0	0	.000	0	1	0	0	1.0	1.000
1989		0	0	—	0.00	1	0	0	2	2	0	1	0	0	0	0	0	0	0	—	0	0	0	0	0.0	—
2 yrs.		0	0	—	4.05	2	1	0	6.2	8	1	3	0	0	0	0	2	0	0	.000	0	1	0	0	0.5	1.000

WORLD SERIES

Year	Team	W	L	%	ERA	G	GS	CG	IP	H	BB	SO	ShO	W	L	SV	AB	H	HR	BA	PO	A	E	DP	TC/G	FA
1990	OAK A	0	0	—	10.80	2	0	0	1.2	4	1	0	0	0	0	0	0	0	0	—	0	0	0	0	0.0	—

Jack Savage

SAVAGE, JOHN JOSEPH
B. Apr. 22, 1964, Louisville, Ky.
BR TR 6′ 3″ 190 lbs.

Year	Team	W	L	%	ERA	G	GS	CG	IP	H	BB	SO	ShO	W	L	SV	AB	H	HR	BA	PO	A	E	DP	TC/G	FA
1987	LA N	0	0	—	2.70	3	0	0	3.1	4	0	0	0	0	0	0	0	0	0	—	0	0	0	0	0.0	—
1990	MIN A	0	2	.000	8.31	17	0	0	26	37	11	12	0	0	2	1	0	0	0	—	0	4	0	0	0.2	1.000
2 yrs.		0	2	.000	7.67	20	0	0	29.1	41	11	12	0	0	2	1	0	0	0	—	0	4	0	0	0.2	1.000

Dan Schatzeder

SCHATZEDER, DANIEL ERNEST
B. Dec. 1, 1954, Elmhurst, Ill.
BL TL 6′ 185 lbs.

Split		W	L	%	ERA	G	GS	CG	IP	H	BB	SO	ShO	W	L	SV	AB	H	HR	BA	PO	A	E	DP	TC/G	FA
April		1	0	1.000	1.54	8	0	0	11.2	9	2	7	0	1	0	0										
May		0	3	.000	3.93	10	2	0	18.1	20	9	7	0	0	1	0										
June		0	0	—	4.32	9	0	0	8.1	15	3	3	0	0	0	0										
July		0	0	—	0.71	9	0	0	12.2	11	5	12	0	0	0	0										
Aug		0	0	—	1.00	6	0	0	9	4	3	6	0	0	0	0										
Sept/Oct		0	0	—	0.93	9	0	0	9.2	7	1	4	0	0	0	0										
Day		0	1	.000	2.08	13	0	0	13	7	3	8	0	0	1	0										
Night		1	2	.333	2.22	38	2	0	56.2	59	20	31	0	1	0	0										
vs. Left		—	—	—	—	—	—	—	—	23	8	17	—	—	—	—										
vs. Right		—	—	—	—	—	—	—	—	43	15	22	—	—	—	—										
On Grass		0	1	.000	1.40	17	0	0	19.1	17	5	8	0	0	1	0										
On Turf		1	2	.333	2.50	34	2	0	50.1	49	18	31	0	1	0	0										
Home		1	2	.333	3.25	23	2	0	36	39	13	24	0	1	0	0										
Road		0	1	.000	1.07	28	0	0	33.2	27	10	15	0	0	1	0										
Division Rivals																										
vs. CHI		0	0	—	5.40	3	0	0	5	5	2	2	0	0	0	0										
vs. MON		0	0	—	1.59	5	0	0	5.2	5	2	2	0	0	0	0										
vs. PHI		0	0	—	1.00	8	0	0	9	11	3	6	0	0	0	0										
vs. PIT		0	1	.000	1.74	6	1	0	10.1	8	4	6	0	0	0	0										
vs. STL		0	1	.000	3.24	5	1	0	8.1	8	2	6	0	0	0	0										

RELIEF PITCHER (WINS, ERA, SAVES, RATIO charts with NL AVG comparisons)

Year	Team	W	L	%	ERA	G	GS	CG	IP	H	BB	SO	ShO	W	L	SV	AB	H	HR	BA	PO	A	E	DP	TC/G	FA
1977	MON N	2	1	.667	2.45	6	3	1	22	16	13	14	1	0	0	0	6	2	0	.333	1	3	0	0	0.7	1.000
1978		7	7	.500	3.06	29	18	2	144	108	68	69	0	2	0	0	45	10	1	.222	4	17	2	0	0.8	.913
1979		10	5	.667	2.83	32	21	3	162	136	59	106	0	1	1	1	51	11	1	.216	5	13	4	0	0.7	.818
1980	DET A	11	13	.458	4.01	32	26	9	193	178	58	94	2	2	0	0	0	0	0	—	7	21	3	3	1.0	.903
1981		6	8	.429	6.08	17	14	1	71	74	29	20	0	0	0	0	0	0	0	—	6	12	3	0	1.2	.857
1982	2 teams				SF N (13G 1 – 4)				MON N (26G 0 – 2)																	
"	total	1	6	.143	5.32	39	4	0	69.1	84	24	33	0	1	3	0	13	3	0	.231	3	11	1	2	0.4	.933
1983	MON N	5	2	.714	3.21	58	2	0	87	88	25	48	0	4	1	2	10	2	0	.200	9	8	1	0	0.3	.944
1984		7	7	.500	2.71	36	14	1	136	112	36	89	1	1	1	1	35	11	0	.314	9	8	5	0	0.6	.773
1985		3	5	.375	3.80	24	15	1	104.1	101	31	64	0	0	0	0	31	6	2	.194	3	20	4	1	1.1	.852
1986	2 teams				MON N (30G 3 – 2)				PHI N (25G 3 – 3)																	
"	total	6	5	.545	3.26	55	1	0	88.1	81	35	47	0	6	5	2	26	10	1	.385	3	9	0	0	0.2	1.000
1987	2 teams				PHI N (26G 3 – 1)				MIN A (30G 3 – 1)																	
"		6	2	.750	5.31	56	1	0	81.1	104	32	58	0	6	2	0	12	2	0	.167	3	3	1	0	0.1	.857
1988	2 teams				CLE A (15G 0 – 2)				MIN A (10G 0 – 1)																	
"		0	3	.000	6.49	25	0	0	26.1	34	7	17	0	0	3	3	0	0	0	—	3	1	0	0	0.2	1.000
1989	HOU N	4	1	.800	4.45	36	0	0	56.2	64	28	46	0	4	1	1	0	0	0	.000	2	9	2	1	0.4	.846
1990	2 teams				HOU N (45G 1 – 3)				NY N (6G 0 – 0)																	
"	total	1	3	.250	2.20	51	2	0	69.2	66	23	39	0	1	1	0	4	1	0	.250	1	10	1	0	0.2	.917
14 yrs.		69	68	.504	3.71	496	121	18	1311	1246	468	744	4	28	18	10	242	58	5	.240	59	145	27	7	0.5	.883

LEAGUE CHAMPIONSHIP SERIES

Year	Team	W	L	%	ERA	G	GS	CG	IP	H	BB	SO	ShO	W	L	SV	AB	H	HR	BA	PO	A	E	DP	TC/G	FA
1987	MIN A	0	0	—	0.00	2	0	0	4.1	2	0	5	0	0	0	0	0	0	0	—	1	1	0	0	1.0	1.000

WORLD SERIES

Year	Team	W	L	%	ERA	G	GS	CG	IP	H	BB	SO	ShO	W	L	SV	AB	H	HR	BA	PO	A	E	DP	TC/G	FA
1987	MIN A	1	0	1.000	6.23	3	0	0	4.1	4	3	3	0	1	0	0	0	0	0	—	0	0	0	0	0.0	—

Year	Team	W	L	%	ERA	G	GS	CG	IP	H	BB	SO	ShO	W	L	SV	AB	H	HR	BA	PO	A	E	DP	TC/G	FA
														RELIEF PITCHING			**BATTING**									

Curt Schilling

SCHILLING, CURTIS MONTAGUE
B. Nov. 14, 1966, Anchorage, Alaska
BR TR 6′ 5″ 205 lbs.

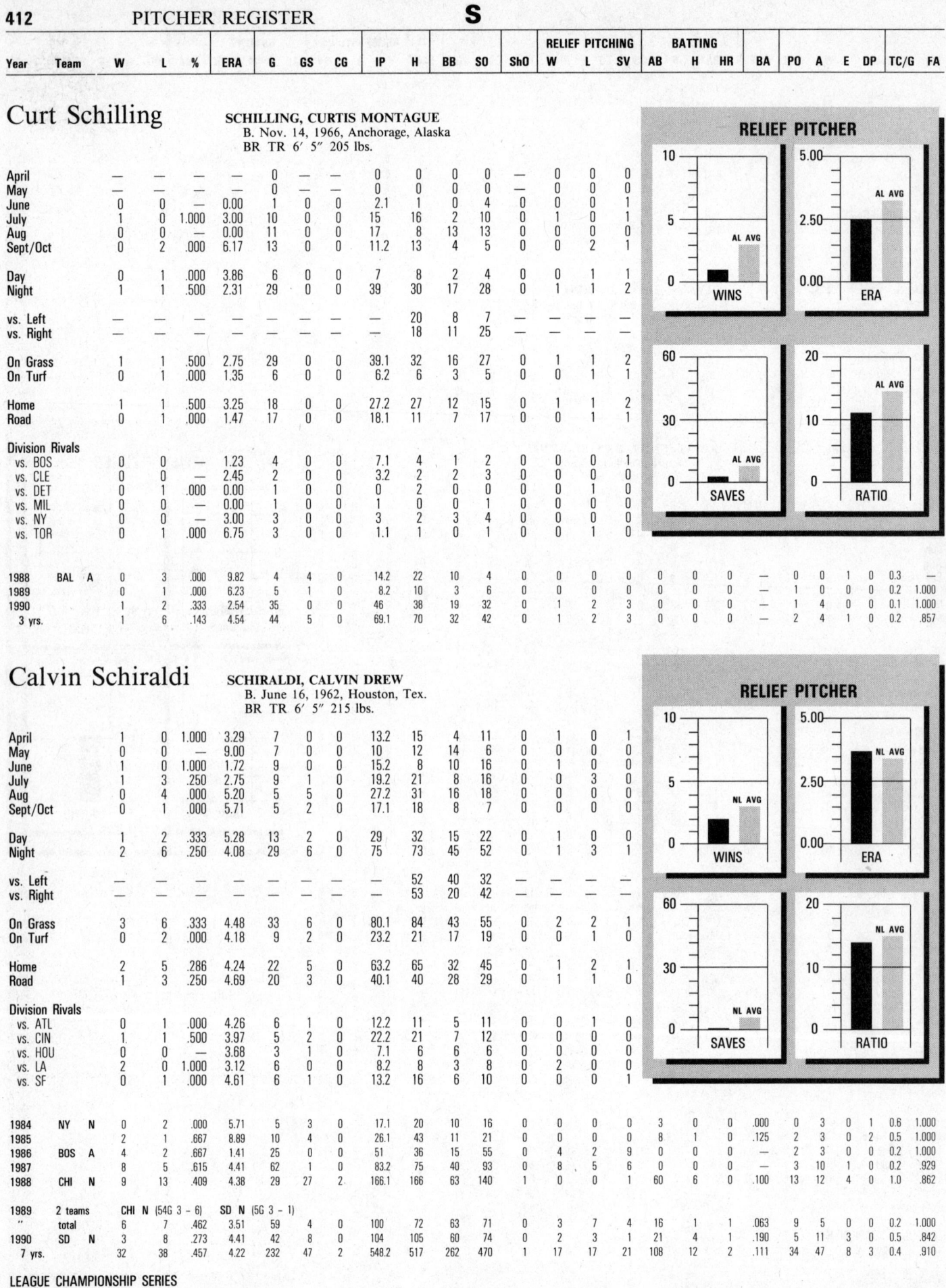

RELIEF PITCHER — WINS / ERA / SAVES / RATIO (AL AVG)

Year	Team	W	L	%	ERA	G	GS	CG	IP	H	BB	SO	ShO	W	L	SV	AB	H	HR	BA	PO	A	E	DP	TC/G	FA
April		—	—	—		0	—	—	0	0	0	0	—	0	0	0										
May		—	—	—		0	—	—	0	0	0	0	—	0	0	0										
June		0	0	—	0.00	1	0	0	2.1	1	0	4	0	0	0	1										
July		1	0	1.000	3.00	10	0	0	15	16	2	10	0	1	0	1										
Aug		0	0	—	0.00	11	0	0	17	8	13	13	0	0	0	0										
Sept/Oct		0	2	.000	6.17	13	0	0	11.2	13	4	5	0	0	2	1										
Day		0	1	.000	3.86	6	0	0	7	8	2	4	0	0	1	1										
Night		1	1	.500	2.31	29	0	0	39	30	17	28	0	1	1	2										
vs. Left		—	—	—	—	—	—	—	—	20	8	7	—	—	—	—										
vs. Right		—	—	—	—	—	—	—	—	18	11	25	—	—	—	—										
On Grass		1	1	.500	2.75	29	0	0	39.1	32	16	27	0	1	1	2										
On Turf		0	1	.000	1.35	6	0	0	6.2	6	3	5	0	0	1	0										
Home		1	1	.500	3.25	18	0	0	27.2	27	12	15	0	1	1	2										
Road		0	1	.000	1.47	17	0	0	18.1	11	7	17	0	0	1	1										
Division Rivals																										
vs. BOS		0	0	—	1.23	4	0	0	7.1	4	1	2	0	0	0	1										
vs. CLE		0	0	—	2.45	2	0	0	3.2	2	2	3	0	0	0	0										
vs. DET		0	1	.000	0.00	1	0	0	0	2	0	0	0	0	1	0										
vs. MIL		0	0	—	0.00	1	0	0	1	0	0	1	0	0	0	0										
vs. NY		0	0	—	3.00	3	0	0	3	2	3	4	0	0	0	0										
vs. TOR		0	1	.000	6.75	3	0	0	1.1	1	0	1	0	0	1	0										
1988	BAL A	0	3	.000	9.82	4	4	0	14.2	22	10	4	0	0	0	0	0	0	0	—	0	0	1	0	0.3	—
1989		0	1	.000	6.23	5	1	0	8.2	10	3	6	0	0	0	0	0	0	0	—	1	0	0	0	0.2	1.000
1990		1	2	.333	2.54	35	0	0	46	38	19	32	0	1	2	3	0	0	0	—	1	4	0	0	0.1	1.000
3 yrs.		1	6	.143	4.54	44	5	0	69.1	70	32	42	0	1	2	3	0	0	0	—	2	4	1	0	0.2	.857

Calvin Schiraldi

SCHIRALDI, CALVIN DREW
B. June 16, 1962, Houston, Tex.
BR TR 6′ 5″ 215 lbs.

RELIEF PITCHER — WINS / ERA / SAVES / RATIO (NL AVG)

Year	Team	W	L	%	ERA	G	GS	CG	IP	H	BB	SO	ShO	W	L	SV	AB	H	HR	BA	PO	A	E	DP	TC/G	FA
April		1	0	1.000	3.29	7	0	0	13.2	15	4	11	0	1	0	1										
May		0	0	—	9.00	7	0	0	10	12	14	6	0	0	0	0										
June		1	0	1.000	1.72	9	0	0	15.2	8	10	16	0	1	0	0										
July		1	3	.250	2.75	9	1	0	19.2	21	8	16	0	0	3	0										
Aug		0	4	.000	5.20	5	5	0	27.2	31	16	18	0	0	0	0										
Sept/Oct		0	1	.000	5.71	5	2	0	17.1	18	8	7	0	0	0	0										
Day		1	2	.333	5.28	13	2	0	29	32	15	22	0	1	0	1										
Night		2	6	.250	4.08	29	6	0	75	73	45	52	0	1	3	1										
vs. Left		—	—	—	—	—	—	—	—	52	40	32	—	—	—	—										
vs. Right		—	—	—	—	—	—	—	—	53	20	42	—	—	—	—										
On Grass		3	6	.333	4.48	33	6	0	80.1	84	43	55	0	2	2	1										
On Turf		0	2	.000	4.18	9	2	0	23.2	21	17	19	0	0	1	0										
Home		2	5	.286	4.24	22	5	0	63.2	65	32	45	0	1	2	1										
Road		1	3	.250	4.69	20	3	0	40.1	40	28	29	0	1	1	0										
Division Rivals																										
vs. ATL		0	1	.000	4.26	6	1	0	12.2	11	5	11	0	0	0	1										
vs. CIN		1	1	.500	3.97	5	2	0	22.2	21	7	12	0	0	0	0										
vs. HOU		0	0	—	3.68	3	1	0	7.1	6	6	6	0	0	0	0										
vs. LA		2	0	1.000	3.12	6	0	0	8.2	8	3	8	0	2	0	0										
vs. SF		0	1	.000	4.61	6	1	0	13.2	16	6	10	0	0	0	1										
1984	NY N	0	2	.000	5.71	5	3	0	17.1	20	10	16	0	0	0	0	3	0	0	.000	0	3	0	1	0.6	1.000
1985		2	1	.667	8.89	10	4	0	26.1	43	11	21	0	0	0	0	8	1	0	.125	2	3	0	2	0.5	1.000
1986	BOS A	4	2	.667	1.41	25	0	0	51	36	15	55	0	4	2	9				—	2	3	0	0	0.2	1.000
1987		8	5	.615	4.41	62	1	0	83.2	75	40	93	0	8	5	6				—	3	10	1	0	0.2	.929
1988	CHI N	9	13	.409	4.38	29	27	2	166.1	166	63	140	1	0	0	1	60	6	0	.100	13	12	4	0	1.0	.862
1989	2 teams	CHI N (54G 3 – 6)				SD N	(5G 3 – 1)																		
''	total	6	7	.462	3.51	59	4	0	100	72	63	71	0	3	7	4	16	1	1	.063	9	5	0	0	0.2	1.000
1990	SD N	3	8	.273	4.41	42	8	0	104	105	60	74	0	2	3	1	21	4	1	.190	5	11	3	0	0.5	.842
7 yrs.		32	38	.457	4.22	232	47	2	548.2	517	262	470	1	17	17	21	108	12	2	.111	34	47	8	3	0.4	.910

LEAGUE CHAMPIONSHIP SERIES

Year	Team	W	L	%	ERA	G	GS	CG	IP	H	BB	SO	ShO	W	L	SV	AB	H	HR	BA	PO	A	E	DP	TC/G	FA
1986	BOS A	0	1	.000	1.50	4	0	0	6	5	3	9	0	0	1	1	0	0	0	—	0	0	0	0	0.0	—

Year	Team	W	L	%	ERA	G	GS	CG	IP	H	BB	SO	ShO	W	L	SV	AB	H	HR	BA	PO	A	E	DP	TC/G	FA
														RELIEF PITCHING			BATTING									

Calvin Schiraldi *Continued*

WORLD SERIES

Year	Team	W	L	%	ERA	G	GS	CG	IP	H	BB	SO	ShO	W	L	SV	AB	H	HR	BA	PO	A	E	DP	TC/G	FA
1986	BOS A	0	2	.000	13.50	3	0	0	4	7	3	2	0	0	2	1	1	0	0	.000	0	1	0	0	0.3	1.000
													2nd													

Dave Schmidt

SCHMIDT, DAVID JOSEPH
B. Apr. 22, 1957, Niles, Mich.
BR TR 6' 1" 185 lbs.

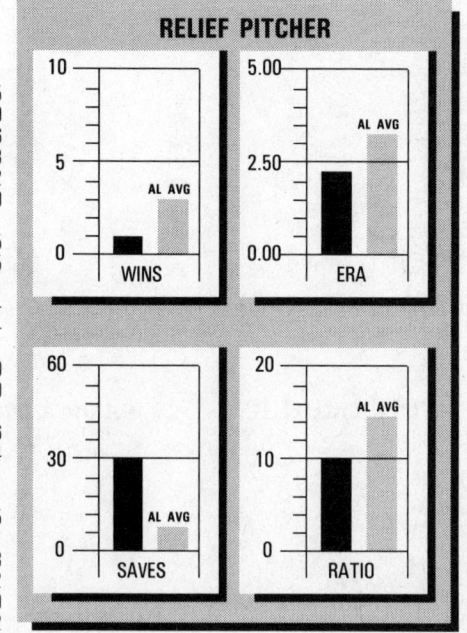

RELIEF PITCHER

Year	Team	W	L	%	ERA	G	GS	CG	IP	H	BB	SO	ShO	W	L	SV	AB	H	HR	BA	PO	A	E	DP	TC/G	FA
April		—	—	—	—	0	—	—	0	0	0	0	—	0	0	0										
May		1	0	1.000	4.50	12	0	0	16	19	7	13	0	1	0	0										
June		2	0	1.000	2.37	13	0	0	19	18	3	4	0	2	0	9										
July		0	3	.000	6.92	9	0	0	13	21	3	5	0	0	3	4										
Aug		—	—	—	—	0	—	—	0	0	0	0	—	0	0	0										
Sept/Oct		—	—	—	—	0	—	—	0	0	0	0	—	0	0	0										
Day		1	1	.500	5.63	6	0	0	8	11	1	3	0	1	1	2										
Night		2	2	.500	4.05	28	0	0	40	47	12	19	0	2	2	11										
vs. Left		—	—	—	—	—	—	—	—	33	9	10	—	—	—	—										
vs. Right		—	—	—	—	—	—	—	—	25	4	12	—	—	—	—										
On Grass		2	1	.667	6.59	10	0	0	13.2	18	3	6	0	2	1	2										
On Turf		1	2	.333	3.41	24	0	0	34.1	40	10	16	0	1	2	11										
Home		0	0	—	3.52	16	0	0	23	26	8	13	0	0	0	7										
Road		3	3	.500	5.04	18	0	0	25	32	5	9	0	3	3	6										
Division Rivals																										
vs. CHI		1	0	1.000	6.75	2	0	0	4	5	0	0	0	1	0	1										
vs. NY		0	0	—	0.00	1	0	0	2	1	0	0	0	0	0	1										
vs. PHI		1	0	1.000	2.70	2	0	0	3.1	3	1	1	0	1	0	1										
vs. PIT		0	0	—	6.75	4	0	0	5.1	6	2	1	0	0	0	2										
vs. STL		0	0	—	0.00	4	0	0	3.2	5	1	2	0	0	0	4										
1981	TEX A	0	1	.000	3.09	14	1	0	32	31	11	13	0	0	0	1	0	0	0	—	1	6	0	0	0.5	1.000
1982		4	6	.400	3.20	33	8	0	109.2	118	25	69	0	3	1	6	0	0	0	—	2	16	2	2	0.6	.900
1983		3	3	.500	3.88	31	0	0	46.1	42	14	29	0	3	3	2	0	0	0	—	6	4	0	1	0.3	1.000
1984		6	6	.500	2.56	43	0	0	70.1	69	20	46	0	6	6	12	0	0	0	—	6	13	1	2	0.5	.950
1985		7	6	.538	3.15	51	4	1	85.2	81	22	46	1	5	4	5	0	0	0	—	3	19	3	3	0.5	.880
1986	CHI A	3	6	.333	3.31	49	1	0	92.1	94	27	67	0	3	5	8	0	0	0	—	7	7	3	0	0.3	.824
1987	BAL A	10	5	.667	3.77	35	14	2	124	128	26	70	2	6	1	1	0	0	0	—	6	14	1	2	0.6	.952
1988		8	5	.615	3.40	41	9	0	129.2	129	38	67	0	3	3	2	0	0	0	—	18	20	1	2	1.0	.974
1989		10	13	.435	5.69	38	26	2	156.2	196	36	46	0	1	0	0	0	0	0	—	18	28	3	2	1.3	.939
1990	MON N	3	3	.500	4.31	34	0	0	48	58	13	22	0	3	3	13	3	0	0	.000	2	10	2	0	0.4	.857
10 yrs.		54	54	.500	3.79	369	63	5	894.2	946	232	475	3	33	26	50	3	0	0	.000	69	137	16	14	0.6	.928

Mike Schooler

SCHOOLER, MICHAEL RALPH
B. Aug. 10, 1962, Anaheim, Calif.
BR TR 6' 3" 220 lbs.

RELIEF PITCHER

Year	Team	W	L	%	ERA	G	GS	CG	IP	H	BB	SO	ShO	W	L	SV	AB	H	HR	BA	PO	A	E	DP	TC/G	FA
April		0	0	—	3.00	7	0	0	9	8	4	8	0	0	0	5										
May		1	0	1.000	0.57	14	0	0	15.2	8	5	14	0	1	0	9										
June		0	0	—	2.70	10	0	0	10	6	1	9	0	0	0	6										
July		0	1	.000	3.09	11	0	0	11.2	10	4	7	0	0	1	8										
Aug		0	3	.000	2.79	7	0	0	9.2	15	2	7	0	0	3	2										
Sept/Oct		—	—	—	—	0	—	—	0	0	0	0	—	0	0	0										
Day		1	2	.333	3.26	14	0	0	19.1	26	3	12	0	1	2	5										
Night		0	2	.000	1.72	35	0	0	36.2	21	13	33	0	0	2	25										
vs. Left		—	—	—	—	—	—	—	—	23	13	19	—	—	—	—										
vs. Right		—	—	—	—	—	—	—	—	24	3	26	—	—	—	—										
On Grass		1	1	.500	3.10	17	0	0	20.1	18	5	17	0	1	1	10										
On Turf		0	3	.000	1.77	32	0	0	35.2	29	11	28	0	0	3	20										
Home		0	3	.000	1.72	27	0	0	31.1	27	10	24	0	0	3	16										
Road		1	1	.500	2.92	22	0	0	24.2	20	6	21	0	1	1	14										
Division Rivals																										
vs. CAL		0	0	—	0.00	5	0	0	6	3	2	3	0	0	0	5										
vs. CHI		0	0	—	0.00	2	0	0	2	0	0	2	0	0	0	1										
vs. KC		0	0	—	0.00	4	0	0	3	0	0	4	0	0	0	3										
vs. MIN		0	1	.000	1.50	3	0	0	6	7	2	5	0	0	1	2										
vs. OAK		0	1	.000	8.10	3	0	0	3.1	8	1	1	0	0	1	0										
vs. TEX		0	0	—	2.45	3	0	0	3.2	4	1	2	0	0	0	2										

Year	Team	W	L	%	ERA	G	GS	CG	IP	H	BB	SO	ShO	RELIEF PITCHING W	L	SV	BATTING AB	H	HR	BA	PO	A	E	DP	TC/G	FA

Mike Schooler *Continued*

Year	Team	W	L	%	ERA	G	GS	CG	IP	H	BB	SO	ShO	W	L	SV	AB	H	HR	BA	PO	A	E	DP	TC/G	FA
1988	SEA A	5	8	.385	3.54	40	0	0	48.1	45	24	54	0	5	**8**	15	0	0	0	—	2	4	0	0	0.2	1.000
1989		1	7	.125	2.81	67	0	0	77	81	19	69	0	1	7	33	0	0	0	—	4	14	0	3	0.3	1.000
1990		1	4	.200	2.25	49	0	0	56	47	16	45	0	1	4	30	1	0	0	.000	3	9	1	0	0.3	.923
3 yrs.		7	19	.269	2.83	156	0	0	181.1	173	59	168	0	7	19	78	1	0	0	.000	9	27	1	3	0.2	.973

Mike Schwabe

SCHWABE, MICHAEL SCOTT
B. July 12, 1964, Fort Dodge, Iowa
BR TR 6′ 4″ 200 lbs.

Year	Team	W	L	%	ERA	G	GS	CG	IP	H	BB	SO	ShO	W	L	SV	AB	H	HR	BA	PO	A	E	DP	TC/G	FA
1989	DET A	2	4	.333	6.04	13	4	0	44.2	58	16	13	0	1	1	0	0	0	0	—	7	8	0	1	1.2	1.000
1990		0	0	—	2.45	1	0	0	3.2	5	0	1	0	0	0	0	0	0	0	—	0	3	0	0	3.0	1.000
2 yrs.		2	4	.333	5.77	14	4	0	48.1	63	16	14	0	1	1	0	0	0	0	—	7	11	0	1	1.3	1.000

Mike Scott

SCOTT, MICHAEL WARREN
B. Apr. 26, 1955, Santa Monica, Calif.
BR TR 6′ 2″ 210 lbs.

Year	Team	W	L	%	ERA	G	GS	CG	IP	H	BB	SO	ShO	W	L	SV	AB	H	HR	BA	PO	A	E	DP	TC/G	FA
April		0	2	.000	5.74	5	5	0	26.2	24	16	12	0	0	0	0										
May		2	3	.400	4.54	6	6	1	37.2	51	11	19	0	0	0	0										
June		4	2	.667	3.03	6	6	1	38.2	28	11	31	0	0	0	0										
July		2	3	.400	4.01	5	5	1	33.2	30	12	25	1	0	0	0										
Aug		1	2	.333	3.43	6	6	1	42	40	9	22	1	0	0	0										
Sept/Oct		0	1	.000	2.33	4	4	0	27	21	7	12	0	0	0	0										
Day		2	4	.333	4.91	9	9	1	55	66	19	25	0	0	0	0										
Night		7	9	.438	3.40	23	23	3	150.2	128	47	96	2	0	0	0										
vs. Left		—	—	—	—	—	—	—	—	106	43	54	—	—	—	—										
vs. Right		—	—	—	—	—	—	—	—	88	23	67	—	—	—	—										
On Grass		3	6	.333	5.30	9	9	1	56	63	18	26	0	0	0	0										
On Turf		6	7	.462	3.25	23	23	3	149.2	131	48	95	2	0	0	0										
Home		5	4	.556	2.42	19	19	3	130	100	38	81	0	0	0	0										
Road		4	9	.308	6.19	13	13	1	75.2	94	28	40	0	0	0	0										
Division Rivals																										
vs. ATL		1	1	.500	1.13	2	2	1	16	11	5	12	1	0	0	0										
vs. CIN		1	0	1.000	2.28	3	3	1	23.2	16	5	20	0	0	0	0										
vs. LA		1	2	.333	3.33	5	5	0	27	17	15	15	0	0	0	0										
vs. SD		2	1	.667	4.58	3	3	0	19.2	20	3	10	0	0	0	0										
vs. SF		0	1	.000	5.00	3	3	0	18	22	5	9	0	0	0	0										
1979	NY N	1	3	.250	5.37	18	9	0	52	59	20	21	0	0	0	0	12	0	0	.000	3	7	2	0	0.7	.833
1980		1	1	.500	4.34	6	6	1	29	40	8	13	1	0	0	0	9	1	0	.111	1	5	2	1	1.3	.750
1981		5	10	.333	3.90	23	23	1	136	130	34	54	0	0	0	0	41	3	0	.073	14	35	1	2	2.2	.980
1982		7	13	.350	5.14	37	22	1	147	185	60	63	0	1	3	3	48	7	0	.146	7	43	4	3	1.5	.926
1983	HOU N	10	6	.625	3.72	24	24	2	145	143	46	73	2	0	0	0	48	8	0	.167	20	20	2	0	1.8	.952
1984		5	11	.313	4.68	31	29	0	154	179	43	83	0	0	0	0	47	6	0	.128	10	23	1	1	1.1	.971
1985		18	8	.692	3.29	36	35	4	221.2	194	80	137	2	0	0	0	72	11	1	.153	21	22	2	1	1.3	.956
1986		18	10	.643	**2.22**	37	37	7	**275.1**	182	72	**306**	5	0	0	0	95	12	0	.126	24	39	2	2	1.8	.969
1987		16	13	.552	3.23	36	**36**	8	247.2	199	79	233	3	0	0	0	80	10	0	.125	17	32	2	2	1.4	.961
1988		14	8	.636	2.92	32	32	8	218.2	162	53	190	5	0	0	0	71	6	0	.085	14	27	0	0	1.3	1.000
1989		**20**	10	.667	3.10	33	32	9	229	180	62	172	2	1	0	1	75	10	0	.133	15	25	4	0	1.3	.909
1990		9	13	.409	3.81	32	32	4	205.2	194	66	121	2	0	0	0	54	7	0	.130	10	20	1	0	1.0	.968
12 yrs.		124	106	.539	3.51	345	317	45	2061	1847	623	1466	22	2	3	3	652	81	2	.124	156	298	23	12	1.4	.952

LEAGUE CHAMPIONSHIP SERIES

Year	Team	W	L	%	ERA	G	GS	CG	IP	H	BB	SO	ShO	W	L	SV	AB	H	HR	BA	PO	A	E	DP	TC/G	FA
1986	HOU N	2	0	1.000	0.50	2	2	2	18	8	1	19	1	0	0	0	6	0	0	.000	0	0	1	0	0.5	—

STARTING PITCHER

WINS · NL AVG
ERA · NL AVG
SO/9 · NL AVG
RATIO · NL AVG

Scott Scudder

SCUDDER, WILLIAM SCOTT
B. Feb. 14, 1968, Paris, Tex.
BR TR 6′ 2″ 180 lbs.

Year	Team	W	L	%	ERA	G	GS	CG	IP	H	BB	SO	ShO	W	L	SV	AB	H	HR	BA	PO	A	E	DP	TC/G	FA
1989	CIN N	4	9	.308	4.49	23	17	0	100.1	91	61	66	0	0	0	0	24	4	0	.167	5	9	1	0	0.7	.933
1990		5	5	.500	4.90	21	10	0	71.2	74	30	42	0	2	1	0	18	1	0	.056	5	6	1	0	0.6	.917
2 yrs.		9	14	.391	4.66	44	27	0	172	165	91	108	0	2	1	0	42	5	0	.119	10	15	2	0	0.6	.926

LEAGUE CHAMPIONSHIP SERIES

Year	Team	W	L	%	ERA	G	GS	CG	IP	H	BB	SO	ShO	W	L	SV	AB	H	HR	BA	PO	A	E	DP	TC/G	FA
1990	CIN N	0	0	—	0.00	1	0	0	1	1	0	1	0	0	0	0	0	0	0	—	0	0	0	0	0.0	—

Year	Team	W	L	%	ERA	G	GS	CG	IP	H	BB	SO	ShO	RELIEF PITCHING W	L	SV	BATTING AB	H	HR	BA	PO	A	E	DP	TC/G	FA

Scott Scudder *Continued*

WORLD SERIES

Year	Team	W	L	%	ERA	G	GS	CG	IP	H	BB	SO	ShO	W	L	SV	AB	H	HR	BA	PO	A	E	DP	TC/G	FA
1990	CIN N	0	0	—	0.00	1	0	0	1.1	0	2	2	0	0	0	0	0	0	0	—	0	0	0	0	0.0	—

Rudy Seanez

SEANEZ, RUDY CABALLERO
B. Oct. 20, 1968, Brawley, Calif.
BR TR 6′ 170 lbs.

	W	L	%	ERA	G	GS	CG	IP	H	BB	SO	ShO	W	L	SV	AB	H	HR	BA	PO	A	E	DP	TC/G	FA
April	—	—	—	—	0	—	—	0	0	0	0	—	0	0	0
May	0	0	—	10.80	2	0	0	1.2	4	2	1	0	0	0	0
June	1	1	.500	2.92	10	0	0	12.1	5	11	11	0	1	1	0
July	1	0	1.000	7.43	12	0	0	13.1	13	12	12	0	1	0	0
Aug	—	—	—	—	0	—	—	0	0	0	0	—	0	0	0
Sept/Oct	—	—	—	—	0	—	—	0	0	0	0	—	0	0	0
Day	0	0	—	2.16	7	0	0	8.1	5	7	7	0	0	0	0
Night	2	1	.667	7.11	17	0	0	19	17	18	17	0	2	1	0
vs. Left	—	—	—	—	—	—	—		13	11	3	—	—	—	—
vs. Right	—	—	—	—	—	—	—		9	14	21	—	—	—	—
On Grass	1	1	.500	6.29	21	0	0	24.1	19	24	22	0	1	1	0
On Turf	1	0	1.000	0.00	3	0	0	3	3	1	2	0	1	0	0
Home	0	0	—	8.10	8	0	0	10	8	11	8	0	0	0	0
Road	2	1	.667	4.15	16	0	0	17.1	14	14	16	0	2	1	0
Division Rivals															
vs. BAL	0	0	—	0.00	2	0	0	2.2	0	3	2	0	0	0	0
vs. BOS	1	0	1.000	4.91	3	0	0	3.2	2	4	4	0	1	0	0
vs. DET	0	1	.000	6.75	3	0	0	2.2	2	2	2	0	0	1	0
vs. MIL	0	0	—	0.00	2	0	0	3.1	1	2	3	0	0	0	0
vs. NY	0	0	—	0.00	1	0	0	1	0	1	0	0	0	0	0
vs. TOR	—	—	—	—	0	—	—	0	0	0	0	—	0	0	0
1989	CLE A	0	0	—	3.60	5	0	0	5	1	4	7	0	0	0	0	0	0	0	—	0	0	0	0	0.0	—
1990		2	1	.667	5.60	24	0	0	27.1	22	25	24	0	2	1	0	0	0	0	—	1	1	0	0	0.1	1.000
2 yrs.		2	1	.667	5.29	29	0	0	32.1	23	29	31	0	2	1	0	0	0	0	—	1	1	0	0	0.1	1.000

Ray Searage

SEARAGE, RAYMOND MARK
B. May 1, 1955, Freeport, N. Y.
BL TL 6′ 1″ 180 lbs.

	W	L	%	ERA	G	GS	CG	IP	H	BB	SO	ShO	W	L	SV	AB	H	HR	BA	PO	A	E	DP	TC/G	FA
April	0	0	—	2.57	7	0	0	7	4	3	7	0	0	0	0
May	0	0	—	10.13	3	0	0	2.2	6	0	2	0	0	0	0
June	—	—	—	—	0	—	—	0	0	0	0	—	0	0	0
July	1	0	1.000	1.93	10	0	0	14	11	5	5	0	1	0	0
Aug	0	0	—	2.70	7	0	0	6.2	9	2	4	0	0	0	0
Sept/Oct	0	0	—	0.00	2	0	0	2	0	1	1	0	0	0	0
Day	0	0	—	3.95	11	0	0	13.2	19	4	11	0	0	0	0
Night	1	0	1.000	1.93	18	0	0	18.2	11	6	8	0	1	0	0
vs. Left	—	—	—	—	—	—	—		12	4	9	—	—	—	—
vs. Right	—	—	—	—	—	—	—		18	6	10	—	—	—	—
On Grass	1	0	1.000	1.64	19	0	0	22	16	10	15	0	1	0	0
On Turf	0	0	—	5.23	10	0	0	10.1	14	0	4	0	0	0	0
Home	1	0	1.000	1.64	9	0	0	11	5	6	6	0	1	0	0
Road	0	0	—	3.38	20	0	0	21.1	25	4	13	0	0	0	0
Division Rivals															
vs. ATL	1	0	1.000	1.17	5	0	0	7.2	4	2	4	0	1	0	0
vs. CIN	0	0	—	0.00	1	0	0	0	0	0	0	0	0	0	0
vs. HOU	0	0	—	0.00	3	0	0	3	1	0	0	0	0	0	0
vs. SD	0	0	—	0.00	1	0	0	1.1	1	1	2	0	0	0	0
vs. SF	0	0	—	2.57	7	0	0	7	7	4	6	0	0	0	0
1981	NY N	1	0	1.000	3.65	26	0	0	37	34	17	16	0	1	0	1	1	1	0	1.000	2	5	0	0	0.3	1.000
1984	MIL A	2	1	.667	0.70	21	0	0	38.1	20	16	29	0	2	1	6	0	0	0	—	1	5	1	0	0.3	.857
1985		1	4	.200	5.92	33	0	0	38	54	24	36	0	1	4	0	0	0	0	—	1	2	1	0	0.1	.750
1986	2 teams	MIL A	(17G 0 - 1)		CHI A	(29G 1 - 0)																				
"	total	1	1	.500	3.35	46	0	0	51	44	28	36	0	1	1	0	0	0	0	—	3	8	0	0	0.2	1.000

Year	Team	W	L	%	ERA	G	GS	CG	IP	H	BB	SO	ShO	RELIEF PITCHING			BATTING				PO	A	E	DP	TC/G	FA
														W	L	SV	AB	H	HR	BA						

Ray Searage *Continued*

Year	Team	W	L	%	ERA	G	GS	CG	IP	H	BB	SO	ShO	W	L	SV	AB	H	HR	BA	PO	A	E	DP	TC/G	FA
1987	CHI A	2	3	.400	4.20	58	0	0	55.2	56	24	33	0	2	3	2	0	0	0	—	1	9	0	0	0.2	1.000
1989	LA N	3	4	.429	3.53	41	0	0	35.2	29	18	24	0	3	4	0	0	0	0	—	5	8	1	0	0.3	.929
1990		1	0	1.000	2.78	29	0	0	32.1	30	10	19	0	1	0	0	2	0	0	.000	2	8	0	0	0.3	1.000
7 yrs.		11	13	.458	3.50	254	0	0	288	267	137	193	0	11	13	11	3	1	0	.333	15	45	3	0	0.2	.952

Steve Searcy

SEARCY, WILLIAM STEVEN
B. June 4, 1964, Knoxville, Tenn.
BL TL 6′ 1″ 190 lbs.

Year	Team	W	L	%	ERA	G	GS	CG	IP	H	BB	SO	ShO	W	L	SV	AB	H	HR	BA	PO	A	E	DP	TC/G	FA
1988	DET A	0	2	.000	5.63	2	2	0	8	8	4	5	0	0	0	0	0	0	0	—	0	1	0	0	0.5	1.000
1989		1	1	.500	6.04	8	2	0	22.1	27	12	11	0	0	0	1	0	0	0	—	2	2	1	0	0.6	.800
1990		2	7	.222	4.66	16	12	1	75.1	76	51	66	0	0	0	0	0	0	0	—	3	7	0	0	0.6	1.000
3 yrs.		3	10	.231	5.03	26	16	1	105.2	111	67	82	0	0	0	1	0	0	0	—	5	10	1	0	0.6	.938

Bob Sebra

SEBRA, ROBERT BUSH
B. Dec. 11, 1961, Ridgewood, N. J.
BR TR 6′ 2″ 200 lbs.

Year	Team	W	L	%	ERA	G	GS	CG	IP	H	BB	SO	ShO	W	L	SV	AB	H	HR	BA	PO	A	E	DP	TC/G	FA
1985	TEX A	0	2	.000	7.52	7	4	0	20.1	26	14	13	0	0	0	0	0	0	0	—	1	1	0	1	0.3	1.000
1986	MON N	5	5	.500	3.55	17	13	3	91.1	82	25	66	1	1	1	0	29	6	0	.207	8	8	0	0	0.9	1.000
1987		6	15	.286	4.42	36	27	4	177.1	184	67	156	1	0	1	0	51	8	0	.157	11	21	2	0	0.9	.941
1988	PHI N	1	2	.333	7.94	3	3	0	11.1	15	10	7	0	0	0	0	5	0	0	.000	0	1	0	0	0.3	1.000
1989	2 teams	PHI N (6G 2–3)					CIN N (15G 0–0)																			
"	total	2	3	.400	5.20	21	5	0	55.1	65	28	35	0	0	1	1	11	0	0	.000	2	8	3	0	0.6	.769
1990	MIL A	1	2	.333	8.18	10	0	0	11	20	5	4	0	1	2	0	0	0	0	—	2	4	0	1	0.6	1.000
6 yrs.		15	29	.341	4.71	94	52	7	366.2	392	149	281	2	2	4	1	96	14	0	.146	24	43	5	4	0.8	.931

Jeff Shaw

SHAW, JEFFREY LEE
B. July 7, 1966, Washington Court House, Ohio
BR TR 6′ 2″ 185 lbs.

Year	Team	W	L	%	ERA	G	GS	CG	IP	H	BB	SO	ShO	W	L	SV	AB	H	HR	BA	PO	A	E	DP	TC/G	FA
1990	CLE A	3	4	.429	6.66	12	9	0	48.2	73	20	25	0	0	0	0	0	0	0	—	4	7	0	0	0.9	1.000

Tim Sherrill

SHERRILL, TIMOTHY SHAWN
B. Sept. 10, 1965, Harrison, Ark.
BL TL 5′ 11″ 170 lbs.

Year	Team	W	L	%	ERA	G	GS	CG	IP	H	BB	SO	ShO	W	L	SV	AB	H	HR	BA	PO	A	E	DP	TC/G	FA
1990	STL N	0	0	—	6.23	8	0	0	4.1	10	3	3	0	0	0	0	0	0	0	—	1	0	0	0	0.1	1.000

Eric Show

SHOW, ERIC VAUGHN
B. May 19, 1956, Riverside, Calif.
BR TR 6′ 1″ 185 lbs.

	W	L	%	ERA	G	GS	CG	IP	H	BB	SO	ShO	W	L	SV
April	0	3	.000	4.87	4	4	0	20.1	26	4	7	0	0	0	0
May	0	2	.000	14.09	4	2	0	7.2	17	4	9	0	0	0	0
June	0	1	.000	8.78	6	0	0	13.1	15	8	7	0	0	0	1
July	2	2	.500	3.77	5	4	0	28.2	36	12	12	0	1	0	0
Aug	2	0	1.000	3.29	7	1	0	13.2	12	5	8	0	1	0	0
Sept/Oct	2	0	1.000	5.96	13	1	0	22.2	25	8	12	0	1	0	1
Day	1	1	.500	5.59	7	2	0	19.1	19	6	12	0	1	0	0
Night	5	7	.417	5.79	32	10	0	87	112	35	43	0	2	1	1
vs. Left	—	—	—	—				—	72	31	25	—	—	—	
vs. Right	—	—	—	—				—	59	10	30	—	—	—	
On Grass	5	6	.455	5.58	31	10	0	88.2	107	32	46	0	2	1	1
On Turf	1	2	.333	6.62	8	2	0	17.2	24	9	9	0	1	0	0
Home	3	5	.375	6.22	19	6	0	50.2	64	22	28	0	2	1	0
Road	3	3	.500	5.34	20	6	0	55.2	67	19	27	0	1	0	1
Division Rivals															
vs. ATL	2	0	1.000	6.38	7	2	0	18.1	21	5	4	0	1	0	1
vs. CIN	0	0	—	21.00	3	0	0	3	7	3	1	0	0	0	0
vs. HOU	2	0	1.000	4.73	4	1	0	13.1	13	8	7	0	1	0	0
vs. LA	1	2	.333	6.11	6	2	0	17.2	24	7	10	0	1	0	0
vs. SF	0	1	.000	3.18	5	2	0	17	16	3	6	0	1	0	0

RELIEF PITCHER

WINS (NL AVG) — ERA (NL AVG) — SAVES (NL AVG) — RATIO (NL AVG)

Year	Team	W	L	%	ERA	G	GS	CG	IP	H	BB	SO	ShO	RELIEF PITCHING W	L	SV	BATTING AB	H	HR	BA	PO	A	E	DP	TC/G	FA

Eric Show *Continued*

Year	Team	W	L	%	ERA	G	GS	CG	IP	H	BB	SO	ShO	W	L	SV	AB	H	HR	BA	PO	A	E	DP	TC/G	FA
1981	SD N	1	3	.250	3.13	15	0	0	23	17	9	22	0	1	3	3	0	0	0	—	0	4	1	0	0.3	.800
1982		10	6	.625	2.64	47	14	2	150	117	48	88	2	6	3	3	41	6	0	.146	4	35	3	1	0.9	.929
1983		15	12	.556	4.17	35	33	4	200.2	201	74	120	2	0	0	0	64	11	0	.172	7	27	4	0	1.1	.895
1984		15	9	.625	3.40	32	32	3	206.2	175	88	104	1	0	0	0	69	17	3	.246	14	28	2	2	1.4	.955
1985		12	11	.522	3.09	35	35	5	233	212	87	141	2	0	0	0	79	10	1	.127	14	24	4	2	1.2	.905
1986		9	5	.643	2.97	24	22	2	136.1	109	69	94	0	1	0	0	43	7	0	.163	6	14	1	1	0.9	.952
1987		8	16	.333	3.84	34	34	5	206.1	188	85	117	3	0	0	0	70	5	0	.071	10	27	3	2	1.2	.925
1988		16	11	.593	3.26	32	32	13	234.2	201	53	144	1	0	0	0	81	12	0	.148	5	21	1	0	0.8	.963
1989		8	6	.571	4.23	16	16	1	106.1	113	39	66	0	0	0	0	34	8	0	.235	4	10	1	1	0.9	.933
1990		6	8	.429	5.76	39	12	0	106.1	131	41	55	0	3	1	1	25	5	0	.200	7	12	1	1	0.5	.950
10 yrs.		100	87	.535	3.59	309	230	35	1603.1	1464	593	951	11	11	7	7	506	81	4	.160	71	202	21	10	1.0	.929

LEAGUE CHAMPIONSHIP SERIES
Year	Team	W	L	%	ERA	G	GS	CG	IP	H	BB	SO	ShO	W	L	SV	AB	H	HR	BA	PO	A	E	DP	TC/G	FA
1984	SD N	0	1	.000	13.50	2	2	0	5.1	8	4	2	0	0	0	0	1	0	0	.000	0	0	0	0	0.0	—

WORLD SERIES
Year	Team	W	L	%	ERA	G	GS	CG	IP	H	BB	SO	ShO	W	L	SV	AB	H	HR	BA	PO	A	E	DP	TC/G	FA
1984	SD N	0	1	.000	10.13	1	1	0	2.2	4	1	2	0	0	0	0	0	0	0	—	0	0	0	0	0.0	—

Doug Sisk

SISK, DOUGLAS RANDALL
B. Sept. 26, 1957, Renton, Wash.
BR TR 6′ 2″ 210 lbs.

Year	Team	W	L	%	ERA	G	GS	CG	IP	H	BB	SO	ShO	W	L	SV	AB	H	HR	BA	PO	A	E	DP	TC/G	FA
1982	NY N	0	1	.000	1.04	8	0	0	8.2	5	4	4	0	0	1	1	0	0	0	—	0	2	0	0	0.3	1.000
1983		5	4	.556	2.24	67	0	0	104.1	88	59	33	0	5	4	11	6	3	0	.500	7	14	1	1	0.3	.955
1984		1	3	.250	2.09	50	0	0	77.2	57	54	32	0	1	3	15	11	1	0	.091	5	13	1	1	0.4	.947
1985		4	5	.444	5.30	42	0	0	73	86	40	26	0	4	5	2	12	0	0	.000	3	15	0	0	0.4	1.000
1986		4	2	.667	3.06	41	0	0	70.2	77	31	31	0	4	2	1	4	0	0	.000	10	6	0	0	0.4	1.000
1987		3	1	.750	3.46	55	0	0	78	83	22	37	0	3	1	3	5	0	0	.000	5	19	0	0	0.4	1.000
1988	BAL A	3	3	.500	3.72	52	0	0	94.1	109	45	26	0	3	3	0	0	0	0	—	9	16	3	1	0.5	.893
1990	ATL N	0	0	—	3.86	3	0	0	2.1	1	4	1	0	0	0	0	0	0	0	—	0	1	0	0	0.3	1.000
8 yrs.		20	19	.513	3.22	318	0	0	509	506	259	190	0	20	19	33	38	4	0	.105	39	86	5	3	0.4	.962

LEAGUE CHAMPIONSHIP SERIES
Year	Team	W	L	%	ERA	G	GS	CG	IP	H	BB	SO	ShO	W	L	SV	AB	H	HR	BA	PO	A	E	DP	TC/G	FA
1986	NY N	0	0	—	0.00	1	0	0	1	1	1	0	0	0	0	0	0	0	0	—	0	0	0	0	0.0	—

WORLD SERIES
Year	Team	W	L	%	ERA	G	GS	CG	IP	H	BB	SO	ShO	W	L	SV	AB	H	HR	BA	PO	A	E	DP	TC/G	FA
1986	NY N	0	0	—	0.00	1	0	0	0.2	0	1	1	0	0	0	0	0	0	0	—	0	0	0	0	0.0	—

John Smiley

SMILEY, JOHN PATRICK
B. Mar. 17, 1965, Phoenixville, Pa.
BL TL 6′ 4″ 180 lbs.

	W	L	%	ERA	G	GS	CG	IP	H	BB	SO	ShO	W	L	SV	
April	2	2	.500	3.33	4	4	1	27	21	4	18	0	0	0	0	
May	1	1	.500	3.38	3	3	0	18.2	20	1	11	0	0	0	0	
June	—	—	—	—	0	—	—	0	0	0	0	—	0	0	0	
July	1	2	.333	5.17	6	6	0	38.1	40	14	21	0	0	0	0	
Aug	3	2	.600	4.58	6	6	0	35.1	45	8	20	0	0	0	0	
Sept/Oct	2	3	.400	6.00	7	6	1	30	35	9	16	0	0	0	0	
Day	4	2	.667	4.54	7	7	1	39.2	45	7	20	0	0	0	0	
Night	5	8	.385	4.68	19	18	1	109.2	116	29	66	0	0	0	0	
vs. Left	—	—	—	—	—	—	—	—	28	7	9	—	—	—	—	
vs. Right	—	—	—	—	—	—	—	—	133	29	77	—	—	—	—	
On Grass	4	5	.444	4.76	10	10	2	56.2	65	8	29	0	0	0	0	
On Turf	5	5	.500	4.56	16	15	0	92.2	96	28	57	0	0	0	0	
Home	3	4	.429	3.80	11	10	0	64	63	20	43	0	0	0	0	
Road	6	6	.500	5.27	15	15	2	85.1	98	16	43	0	0	0	0	
Division Rivals																
vs. CHI	2	1	.667	7.82	3	3	0	12.2	21	2	11	0	0	0	0	
vs. MON	0	2	.000	3.60	3	3	0	20	22	5	15	0	0	0	0	
vs. NY	0	2	.000	2.57	3	2	1	14	12	3	4	0	0	0	0	
vs. PHI	0	0	—	3.86	1	1	0	7	5	2	3	0	0	0	0	
vs. STL	1	2	.333	6.62	4	4	0	17.2	25	8	7	0	0	0	0	

STARTING PITCHER

WINS — 25.0 / 12.5 / 0.0 (NL AVG)

ERA — 5.00 / 2.50 / 0.00 (NL AVG)

SO/9 — 10 / 5 / 0 (NL AVG)

RATIO — 20 / 10 / 0 (NL AVG)

Year	Team		W	L	%	ERA	G	GS	CG	IP	H	BB	SO	ShO	RELIEF PITCHING			BATTING				PO	A	E	DP	TC/G	FA
															W	L	SV	AB	H	HR	BA						

John Smiley *Continued*

Year	Team		W	L	%	ERA	G	GS	CG	IP	H	BB	SO	ShO	W	L	SV	AB	H	HR	BA	PO	A	E	DP	TC/G	FA
1986	PIT	N	1	0	1.000	3.86	12	0	0	11.2	4	4	9	0	1	0	0	0	0	0	—	1	2	0	0	0.3	1.000
1987			5	5	.500	5.76	63	0	0	75	69	50	58	0	5	5	4	7	1	0	.143	7	9	0	2	0.3	1.000
1988			13	11	.542	3.25	34	32	5	205	185	46	129	1	0	0	0	63	5	0	.079	14	27	0	3	1.2	1.000
1989			12	8	.600	2.81	28	28	8	205.1	174	49	123	1	0	0	0	65	9	0	.138	7	23	4	2	1.2	.882
1990			9	10	.474	4.64	26	25	2	149.1	161	36	86	0	0	0	0	49	6	0	.122	8	24	2	1	1.3	.941
5 yrs.			40	34	.541	3.73	163	85	15	646.1	593	185	405	2	6	5	4	184	21	0	.114	37	85	6	8	0.8	.953

LEAGUE CHAMPIONSHIP SERIES

Year	Team		W	L	%	ERA	G	GS	CG	IP	H	BB	SO	ShO	W	L	SV	AB	H	HR	BA	PO	A	E	DP	TC/G	FA
1990	PIT	N	0	0	—	0.00	1	0	0	2	2	0	0	0	0	0	0	0	0	0	—	0	0	0	0	0.0	—

Bryn Smith

SMITH, BRYN NELSON
B. Aug. 11, 1955, Marietta, Ga.
BR TR 6′ 2″ 200 lbs.

		W	L	%	ERA	G	GS	CG	IP	H	BB	SO	ShO	W	L	SV	AB	H	HR	BA	PO	A	E	DP	TC/G	FA
April		2	2	.500	2.67	4	4	0	27	30	4	8	0	0	0	0										
May		3	2	.600	3.72	6	6	0	38.2	38	9	26	0	0	0	0										
June		1	2	.333	7.04	6	5	0	23	30	7	18	0	0	0	0										
July		1	2	.333	5.33	5	5	0	25.1	32	5	14	0	0	0	0										
Aug		—	—	—	—	0	—	—	0	0	0	0	—	0	0	0										
Sept/Oct		2	0	1.000	3.29	5	5	0	27.1	30	5	12	0	0	0	0										
Day		2	3	.400	4.29	8	7	0	42	47	5	24	0	0	0	0										
Night		7	5	.583	4.26	18	18	0	99.1	113	25	54	0	0	0	0										
vs. Left		—	—	—	—	—	—	—	—	102	18	35		—	—	—										
vs. Right		—	—	—	—	—	—	—	—	58	12	43		—	—	—										
On Grass		2	2	.500	4.23	7	7	0	38.1	43	5	20	0	0	0	0										
On Turf		7	6	.538	4.28	19	18	0	103	117	25	58	0	0	0	0										
Home		6	4	.600	3.84	14	14	0	84.1	90	21	50	0	0	0	0										
Road		3	4	.429	4.89	12	11	0	57	70	9	28	0	0	0	0										
Division Rivals																										
vs. CHI		2	0	1.000	3.31	3	3	0	16.1	18	3	11	0	0	0	0										
vs. MON		1	1	.500	5.79	5	4	0	18.2	29	7	10	0	0	0	0										
vs. NY		0	2	.000	12.60	3	3	0	10	18	2	6	0	0	0	0										
vs. PHI		1	2	.333	3.76	4	4	0	26.1	26	3	10	0	0	0	0										
vs. PIT		—	—	—	—	0	0	0	0	0	0	0	—	0	0	0										

STARTING PITCHER (WINS, ERA, SO/9, RATIO bar charts with NL AVG)

Year	Team		W	L	%	ERA	G	GS	CG	IP	H	BB	SO	ShO	W	L	SV	AB	H	HR	BA	PO	A	E	DP	TC/G	FA
1981	MON	N	1	0	1.000	2.77	7	0	0	13	14	3	9	0	1	0	0	1	0	0	.000	0	1	1	0	0.3	.500
1982			2	4	.333	4.20	47	1	0	79.1	81	23	50	0	2	3	3	8	0	0	.000	2	15	1	0	0.4	.944
1983			6	11	.353	2.49	49	12	5	155.1	142	43	101	3	1	4	3	30	5	0	.167	10	22	0	3	0.7	1.000
1984			12	13	.480	3.32	28	28	4	179	178	51	101	2	0	0	0	53	7	0	.132	25	28	4	3	2.0	.930
1985			18	5	.783	2.91	32	32	4	222.1	193	41	127	2	0	0	0	72	14	1	.194	24	27	5	2	1.8	.911
1986			10	8	.556	3.94	30	30	1	187.1	182	63	105	0	0	0	0	58	8	1	.138	11	44	2	5	1.9	.965
1987			10	9	.526	4.37	26	26	2	150.1	164	31	94	0	0	0	0	44	6	0	.136	10	21	1	2	1.2	.969
1988			12	10	.545	3.00	32	32	1	198	179	32	122	0	0	0	0	55	6	0	.109	7	26	2	1	1.1	.943
1989			10	11	.476	2.84	33	32	3	215.2	177	54	129	1	0	0	0	62	4	0	.065	16	42	1	2	1.8	.983
1990	STL	N	9	8	.529	4.27	26	25	0	141.1	160	30	78	0	0	0	0	39	10	1	.256	10	16	2	2	1.1	.929
10 yrs.			90	79	.533	3.37	310	218	20	1541.2	1470	371	916	8	4	7	6	422	60	3	.142	115	242	19	20	1.2	.949

Daryl Smith

SMITH, DARYL CLINTON
B. July 29, 1960, Baltimore, Md.
BR TR 6′ 4″ 185 lbs.

Year	Team		W	L	%	ERA	G	GS	CG	IP	H	BB	SO	ShO	W	L	SV	AB	H	HR	BA	PO	A	E	DP	TC/G	FA
1990	KC	A	0	1	.000	4.05	2	1	0	6.2	5	4	6	0	0	0	0	0	0	0	—	0	0	0	0	0.0	—

Year	Team	W	L	%	ERA	G	GS	CG	IP	H	BB	SO	ShO	RELIEF PITCHING W	L	SV	BATTING AB	H	HR	BA	PO	A	E	DP	TC/G	FA

Dave Smith

SMITH, DAVID STANLEY
B. Jan. 21, 1955, Richmond, Calif.
BR TR 6′ 1″ 195 lbs.

Split	W	L	%	ERA	G	GS	CG	IP	H	BB	SO	ShO	RW	RL	SV	AB	H	HR	BA	PO	A	E	DP	TC/G	FA
April	0	1	.000	0.73	9	0	0	12.1	9	3	16	0	0	1	7										
May	2	1	.667	4.82	9	0	0	9.1	6	3	6	0	2	1	3										
June	0	0	—	3.12	8	0	0	8.2	7	2	7	0	0	1	5										
July	0	1	.000	2.00	8	0	0	9	7	2	10	0	0	1	3										
Aug	2	2	.500	2.31	8	0	0	11.2	11	5	3	0	2	2	2										
Sept/Oct	2	1	.667	1.93	7	0	0	9.1	5	5	8	0	2	1	3										
Day	2	2	.500	4.02	14	0	0	15.2	12	6	13	0	2	2	5										
Night	4	4	.500	1.81	35	0	0	44.2	33	14	37	0	4	4	18										
vs. Left	—	—	—	—	—	—	—	—	26	10	21	—	—	—											
vs. Right	—	—	—	—	—	—	—	—	19	10	29	—	—	—											
On Grass	1	2	.333	4.02	14	0	0	15.2	15	5	12	0	1	2	6										
On Turf	5	4	.556	1.81	35	0	0	44.2	30	15	38	0	5	4	17										
Home	3	4	.429	2.25	26	0	0	32	23	10	31	0	3	4	13										
Road	3	2	.600	2.54	23	0	0	28.1	22	10	19	0	3	2	10										

Division Rivals

	W	L	%	ERA	G	GS	CG	IP	H	BB	SO	ShO	RW	RL	SV
vs. ATL	0	0	—	0.00	5	0	0	7	5	1	6	0	0	0	2
vs. CIN	1	0	1.000	0.00	4	0	0	6.1	2	2	4	0	1	0	1
vs. LA	0	1	.000	2.00	4	0	0	9	8	4	8	0	0	1	7
vs. SD	0	2	.000	15.00	4	0	0	3	6	1	3	0	0	2	1
vs. SF	0	0	—	2.57	6	0	0	7	5	1	7	0	0	0	3

Year	Team	W	L	%	ERA	G	GS	CG	IP	H	BB	SO	ShO	RW	RL	SV	AB	H	HR	BA	PO	A	E	DP	TC/G	FA
1980	HOU N	7	5	.583	1.92	57	0	0	103	90	32	85	0	7	5	10	12	0	0	.000	3	11	1	0	0.3	.933
1981		5	3	.625	2.76	42	0	0	75	54	23	52	0	5	3	8	8	2	0	.250	3	11	1	0	0.4	.933
1982		5	4	.556	3.84	49	1	0	63.1	69	31	28	0	5	4	11	2	0	0	.000	3	7	2	2	0.2	.833
1983		3	1	.750	3.10	42	0	0	72.2	72	36	41	0	3	1	6	5	0	0	.000	3	4	2	0	0.2	.778
1984		5	4	.556	2.21	53	0	0	77.1	60	20	45	0	5	4	5	4	0	0	.000	5	9	1	1	0.3	.933
1985		9	5	.643	2.27	64	0	0	79.1	69	17	40	0	9	5	27	3	0	0	.000	4	7	3	1	0.2	.786
1986		4	7	.364	2.73	54	0	0	56	39	22	46	0	4	7	33	2	0	0	.000	7	6	0	0	0.2	1.000
1987		2	3	.400	1.65	50	0	0	60	39	21	73	0	2	3	24	2	1	0	.500	4	4	0	0	0.2	1.000
1988		4	5	.444	2.67	51	0	0	57.1	60	19	38	0	4	5	27	2	0	0	.000	3	8	0	0	0.3	1.000
1989		3	4	.429	2.64	52	0	0	58	49	19	31	0	3	4	25	1	0	0	.000	6	10	0	1	0.3	1.000
1990		6	6	.500	2.39	49	0	0	60.1	45	20	50	0	6	6	23	2	0	0	.000	1	3	1	1	0.1	.800
11 yrs.		53	47	.530	2.53	563	1	0	762.1	646	260	529	0	53	47	199	43	3	0	.070	42	80	11	6	0.2	.917

DIVISIONAL PLAYOFF SERIES

Year	Team	W	L	%	ERA	G	GS	CG	IP	H	BB	SO	ShO	RW	RL	SV	AB	H	HR	BA	PO	A	E	DP	TC/G	FA
1981	HOU N	0	0	—	3.86	2	0	0	2.1	2	0	4	0	0	0	0	0	0	0	—	0	0	0	0	0.0	—

LEAGUE CHAMPIONSHIP SERIES

Year	Team	W	L	%	ERA	G	GS	CG	IP	H	BB	SO	ShO	RW	RL	SV	AB	H	HR	BA	PO	A	E	DP	TC/G	FA
1980	HOU N	1	0	1.000	3.86	3	0	0	2.1	4	2	4	0	1	0	0	0	0	0	—	0	0	0	0	0.0	—
1986		0	1	.000	9.00	2	0	0	2	2	3	2	0	0	1	0	0	0	0	—	0	0	0	0	0.0	—
2 yrs.		1	1	.500	6.23	5	0	0	4.1	6	5	6	0	1	1	0	0	0	0	—	0	0	0	0	0.0	—

Lee Smith

SMITH, LEE ARTHUR JR.
B. Dec. 4, 1957, Jamestown, La.
BR TR 6′ 5″ 220 lbs.

Split	W	L	%	ERA	G	GS	CG	IP	H	BB	SO	ShO	RW	RL	SV
April	2	1	.667	2.03	10	0	0	13.1	13	9	16	0	2	1	4
May	1	0	1.000	2.04	13	0	0	17.2	10	2	18	0	1	0	4
June	0	2	.000	2.93	12	0	0	15.1	15	6	17	0	0	2	5
July	2	0	1.000	0.00	11	0	0	16.1	11	4	20	0	2	0	8
Aug	0	1	.000	3.65	10	0	0	12.1	16	2	10	0	0	1	5
Sept/Oct	0	1	.000	2.25	8	0	0	8	6	6	6	0	0	1	5
Day	2	0	1.000	0.76	25	0	0	35.2	25	10	39	0	2	0	12
Night	3	5	.375	3.04	39	0	0	47.1	46	19	48	0	3	5	19
vs. Left	—	—	—	—	—	—	—	—	41	24	54	—	—	—
vs. Right	—	—	—	—	—	—	—	—	30	5	33	—	—	—

Year	Team	W	L	%	ERA	G	GS	CG	IP	H	BB	SO	ShO	RELIEF PITCHING			BATTING				PO	A	E	DP	TC/G	FA
														W	L	SV	AB	H	HR	BA						

Lee Smith *Continued*

Year	Team	W	L	%	ERA	G	GS	CG	IP	H	BB	SO	ShO	W	L	SV	AB	H	HR	BA	PO	A	E	DP	TC/G	FA
On Grass		3	2	.600	2.08	25	0	0	30.1	24	16	32	0	3	2	13										
On Turf		2	3	.400	2.05	39	0	0	52.2	47	13	55	0	2	3	18										
Home		3	3	.500	2.49	36	0	0	47	47	16	48	0	3	3	12										
Road		2	2	.500	1.50	28	0	0	36	24	13	39	0	2	2	19										
Division Rivals																										
vs. CHI		0	1	.000	2.70	6	0	0	6.2	7	4	8	0	0	1	4										
vs. MON		0	0	—	0.00	4	0	0	5.1	2	0	6	0	0	0	3										
vs. NY		0	3	.000	5.19	7	0	0	8.2	10	3	10	0	0	3	4										
vs. PHI		0	0	—	3.38	5	0	0	8	8	4	4	0	0	0	2										
vs. PIT		0	0	—	2.08	6	0	0	4.1	4	2	5	0	0	0	3										
1980	CHI N	2	0	1.000	2.86	18	0	0	22	21	14	17	0	2	0	0	0	0	0	—	0	3	0	0	0.2	1.000
1981		3	6	.333	3.49	40	1	0	67	57	31	50	0	3	5	1	9	0	0	.000	3	9	0	0	0.3	1.000
1982		2	5	.286	2.69	72	5	0	117	105	37	99	0	2	1	17	16	1	1	.063	9	10	1	2	0.3	.950
1983		4	10	.286	1.65	66	0	0	103.1	70	41	91	0	4	10	**29**	9	1	0	.111	8	9	0	0	0.3	1.000
1984		9	7	.563	3.65	69	0	0	101	98	35	86	0	9	7	33	13	1	0	.077	6	13	0	2	0.3	1.000
1985		7	4	.636	3.04	65	0	0	97.2	87	32	112	0	7	4	33	6	0	0	.000	3	9	0	1	0.2	1.000
1986		9	9	.500	3.09	66	0	0	90.1	69	42	93	0	9	9	31	5	0	0	.000	1	12	0	2	0.2	1.000
1987		4	10	.286	3.12	62	0	0	83.2	84	32	96	0	4	**10**	36	2	0	0	.000	5	8	0	0	0.2	1.000
1988	BOS A	4	5	.444	2.80	64	0	0	83.2	72	37	96	0	4	5	29	0	0	0	—	5	4	1	0	0.2	.900
1989		6	1	.857	3.57	64	0	0	70.2	53	33	96	0	6	1	25	0	0	0	—	1	1	0	0	0.0	1.000
1990	2 teams	BOS A	(11G 2 – 1)		STL N	(53G 3 – 4)																				
"	total	5	5	.500	2.06	64	0	0	83	71	29	87	0	5	5	31	2	0	0	.000	2	3	0	0	0.1	1.000
11 yrs.		55	62	.470	2.88	650	6	0	919.1	787	363	923	0	55	57	265	62	3	1	.048	41	81	2	7	0.2	.984
																5th										

LEAGUE CHAMPIONSHIP SERIES

Year	Team	W	L	%	ERA	G	GS	CG	IP	H	BB	SO	ShO	W	L	SV	AB	H	HR	BA	PO	A	E	DP	TC/G	FA
1984	CHI N	0	1	.000	9.00	2	0	0	2	3	0	3	0	0	1	1	0	0	0	—	0	0	0	0	0.0	—
1988	BOS A	0	1	.000	8.10	2	0	0	3.1	6	1	4	0	0	1	0	0	0	0	—	0	0	0	0	0.0	—
2 yrs.		0	2	.000	8.44	4	0	0	5.1	9	1	7	0	0	2	1	0	0	0	—	0	0	0	0	0.0	—

RELIEF PITCHER

SAVES   RATIO
NL AVG   NL AVG
60 / 30 / 0   20 / 10 / 0

Mike Smith

SMITH, MICHAEL ANTHONY
B. Oct. 31, 1963, San Antonio, Tex.
BR TR 6′ 3″ 180 lbs.

Year	Team	W	L	%	ERA	G	GS	CG	IP	H	BB	SO	ShO	W	L	SV	AB	H	HR	BA	PO	A	E	DP	TC/G	FA
1989	BAL A	2	0	1.000	7.65	13	1	0	20	25	14	12	0	2	0	0	0	0	0	—	1	4	0	0	0.4	1.000
1990		0	0	—	12.00	2	0	0	3	4	1	2	0	0	0	0	0	0	0	—	0	0	0	0	0.0	—
2 yrs.		2	0	1.000	8.22	15	1	0	23	29	15	14	0	2	0	0	0	0	0	—	1	4	0	0	0.3	1.000

Pete Smith

SMITH, PETER JOHN
B. Feb. 27, 1966, Abington, Mass.
BR TR 6′ 2″ 185 lbs.

Year	Team	W	L	%	ERA	G	GS	CG	IP	H	BB	SO	ShO	W	L	SV	AB	H	HR	BA	PO	A	E	DP	TC/G	FA
April		2	1	.667	1.91	4	4	1	28.1	21	9	28	0	0	0	0										
May		2	3	.400	5.81	5	5	2	31	37	9	16	0	0	0	0										
June		1	2	.333	7.64	4	4	0	17.2	19	6	12	0	0	0	0										
July		—	—	—	—	0	—	—	0	0	0	0	0	0	0	0										
Aug		—	—	—	—	0	—	—	0	0	0	0	0	0	0	0										
Sept/Oct		—	—	—	—	0	—	—	0	0	0	0	0	0	0	0										
Day		1	2	.333	7.08	4	4	2	20.1	26	5	10	0	0	0	0										
Night		4	4	.500	3.97	9	9	1	56.2	51	19	46	0	0	0	0										
vs. Left		—	—	—	—				—	49	17	19	—	—	—	—										
vs. Right		—	—	—	—				—	28	7	37	—	—	—	—										
On Grass		4	6	.400	5.03	12	12	2	68	69	20	54	0	0	0	0										
On Turf		1	0	1.000	3.00	1	1	1	9	8	4	2	0	0	0	0										
Home		3	3	.500	6.35	7	7	1	39.2	49	14	33	0	0	0	0										
Road		2	3	.400	3.13	6	6	2	37.1	28	10	23	0	0	0	0										
Division Rivals																										
vs. CIN		0	1	.000	3.68	1	1	0	7.1	9	1	8	0	0	0	0										
vs. HOU		—	—	—	—	0	—	—	0	0	0	0	0	0	0	0										
vs. LA		1	0	1.000	0.00	1	1	0	7	1	3	5	0	0	0	0										
vs. SD		0	1	.000	4.09	2	2	0	11	14	1	3	0	0	0	0										
vs. SF		1	2	.333	9.26	3	3	0	11.2	15	7	11	0	0	0	0										

STARTING PITCHER

WINS   ERA
NL AVG   NL AVG
25.0 / 12.5 / 0.0   5.00 / 2.50 / 0.00

SO/9   RATIO
NL AVG   NL AVG
10 / 5 / 0   20 / 10 / 0

Year	Team	W	L	%	ERA	G	GS	CG	IP	H	BB	SO	ShO	RELIEF PITCHING W	L	SV	BATTING AB	H	HR	BA	PO	A	E	DP	TC/G	FA

Pete Smith *Continued*

Year	Team	W	L	%	ERA	G	GS	CG	IP	H	BB	SO	ShO	W	L	SV	AB	H	HR	BA	PO	A	E	DP	TC/G	FA
1987	ATL N	1	2	.333	4.83	6	6	0	31.2	39	14	11	0	0	0	0	11	1	0	.091	1	2	1	0	0.7	.750
1988		7	15	.318	3.69	32	32	5	195.1	183	88	124	3	0	0	0	53	6	0	.113	12	19	3	0	1.1	.912
1989		5	14	.263	4.75	28	27	1	142	144	57	115	0	0	0	0	41	4	0	.098	11	11	1	2	0.8	.957
1990		5	6	.455	4.79	13	13	3	77	77	24	56	0	0	0	0	23	2	0	.087	5	5	0	0	0.8	1.000
4 yrs.		18	37	.327	4.30	79	78	9	446	443	183	306	3	0	0	0	128	13	0	.102	29	37	5	2	0.9	.930

Roy Smith

SMITH, LEROY PURDY III
B. Sept. 6, 1961, Mt. Vernon, N. Y.
BR TR 6′ 3″ 205 lbs.

Year	Team	W	L	%	ERA	G	GS	CG	IP	H	BB	SO	ShO	W	L	SV	AB	H	HR	BA	PO	A	E	DP	TC/G	FA
April		0	3	.000	6.26	5	5	0	23	33	6	13	0	0	0	0										
May		4	1	.800	3.69	6	6	1	39	42	5	23	1	0	0	0										
June		0	2	.000	4.84	6	3	0	22.1	27	8	17	0	0	0	0										
July		1	2	.333	2.93	5	5	0	30.2	31	10	21	0	0	0	0										
Aug		0	2	.000	8.25	6	3	0	24	37	16	10	0	0	0	0										
Sept/Oct		0	0	—	3.77	4	1	0	14.1	21	2	3	0	0	0	0										
Day		1	3	.250	5.58	7	6	0	30.2	45	11	17	0	0	0	0										
Night		4	7	.364	4.62	25	17	1	122.2	146	36	70	1	0	0	0										
vs. Left		—	—	—	—	—	—	—	—	106	31	36	—	—	—	—										
vs. Right		—	—	—	—	—	—	—	—	85	16	51	—	—	—	—										
On Grass		1	4	.200	5.23	13	9	0	62	83	19	33	0	0	0	0										
On Turf		4	6	.400	4.53	19	14	1	91.1	108	28	54	1	0	0	0										
Home		4	5	.444	4.30	14	11	1	73.1	85	17	44	1	0	0	0										
Road		1	5	.167	5.29	18	12	0	80	106	30	43	0	0	0	0										
Division Rivals																										
vs. CAL		0	1	.000	12.10	3	2	0	9.2	20	2	5	0	0	0	0										
vs. CHI		0	1	.000	4.91	1	1	0	3.2	8	1	3	0	0	0	0										
vs. KC		0	0	—	1.93	3	0	0	4.2	4	3	2	0	0	0	0										
vs. OAK		1	1	.500	3.77	3	2	0	14.1	18	6	9	0	0	0	0										
vs. SEA		0	0	—	4.26	2	1	0	6.1	9	0	5	0	0	0	0										
vs. TEX		0	0	—	4.22	2	1	0	10.2	10	4	8	0	0	0	0										
1984	CLE A	5	5	.500	4.59	22	14	0	86.1	91	40	55	0	0	0	0	0	0	0	—	4	6	3	0	0.6	.769
1985		1	4	.200	5.34	12	11	1	62.1	84	17	28	0	0	0	0	0	0	0	—	6	3	0	0	0.8	1.000
1986	MIN A	0	2	.000	6.97	5	0	0	10.1	13	5	8	0	0	2	0	0	0	0	—	0	1	0	0	0.2	1.000
1987		1	0	1.000	4.96	7	1	0	16.1	20	6	8	0	0	0	0	0	0	0	—	0	2	0	0	0.3	1.000
1988		3	0	1.000	2.68	9	4	0	37	29	12	17	0	1	0	0	0	0	0	—	3	2	0	0	0.6	1.000
1989		10	6	.625	3.92	32	26	2	172.1	180	51	92	0	0	0	1	0	0	0	—	9	13	0	1	0.7	1.000
1990		5	10	.333	4.81	32	23	1	153.1	191	47	87	1	0	0	0	0	0	0	—	10	9	1	0	0.6	.950
7 yrs.		25	27	.481	4.45	119	79	4	538	608	178	295	1	1	2	1	0	0	0	—	32	36	4	1	0.6	.944

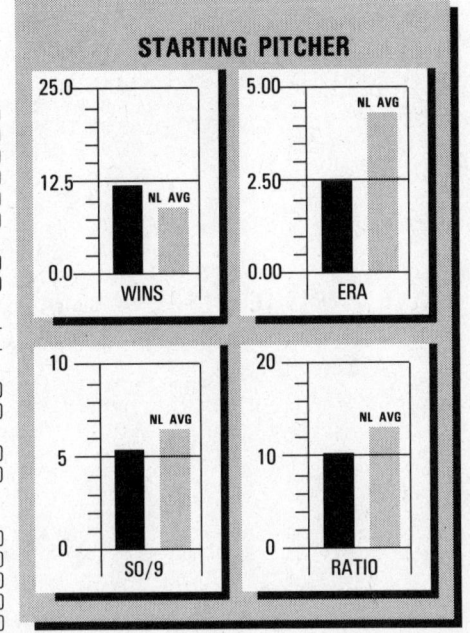

STARTING PITCHER (Roy Smith charts: WINS, ERA, SO/9, RATIO — AL AVG)

Zane Smith

SMITH, ZANE WILLIAM
B. Dec. 28, 1960, Madison, Wis.
BL TL 6′ 2″ 195 lbs.

Year	Team	W	L	%	ERA	G	GS	CG	IP	H	BB	SO	ShO	W	L	SV	AB	H	HR	BA	PO	A	E	DP	TC/G	FA
April		2	1	.667	1.61	4	4	0	28	22	6	18	0	0	0	0										
May		0	2	.000	4.94	4	4	0	23.2	34	13	9	0	0	0	0										
June		2	2	.500	3.44	6	6	0	36.2	35	12	20	0	0	0	0										
July		2	2	.500	3.08	6	5	1	38	38	10	25	0	0	0	0										
Aug		3	0	1.000	2.72	7	6	0	43	37	4	25	0	0	0	0										
Sept/Oct		3	2	.600	0.59	6	6	3	46	30	5	33	2	0	0	0										
Day		1	1	.500	2.52	5	4	0	25	24	8	10	0	0	0	0										
Night		11	8	.579	2.55	28	27	4	190.1	172	42	120	2	0	0	0										
vs. Left		—	—	—	—	—	—	—	—	19	10	28	—	—	—	—										
vs. Right		—	—	—	—	—	—	—	—	177	40	102	—	—	—	—										
On Grass		1	1	.500	2.70	3	3	0	20	14	7	8	0	0	0	0										
On Turf		11	8	.579	2.53	30	28	4	195.1	182	43	122	2	0	0	0										
Home		9	3	.750	2.05	18	16	4	118.1	105	27	83	2	0	0	0										
Road		3	6	.333	3.15	15	15	0	97	91	23	47	0	0	0	0										
Division Rivals																										
vs. CHI		1	0	1.000	1.08	3	2	1	16.2	11	3	8	0	0	0	0										
vs. MON		0	1	.000	1.29	1	1	0	7	7	3	3	0	0	0	0										
vs. NY		3	1	.750	0.97	5	5	1	37	22	4	25	1	0	0	0										
vs. PHI		0	1	.000	4.15	2	2	0	13	11	3	7	0	0	0	0										
vs. STL		2	2	.500	3.46	5	4	1	26	27	11	21	0	0	0	0										

STARTING PITCHER (Zane Smith charts: WINS, ERA, SO/9, RATIO — NL AVG)

Year	Team		W	L	%	ERA	G	GS	CG	IP	H	BB	SO	ShO	RELIEF PITCHING			BATTING			BA	PO	A	E	DP	TC/G	FA
															W	L	SV	AB	H	HR							

Zane Smith *Continued*

Year	Team		W	L	%	ERA	G	GS	CG	IP	H	BB	SO	ShO	W	L	SV	AB	H	HR	BA	PO	A	E	DP	TC/G	FA
1984	ATL	N	1	0	1.000	2.25	3	3	0	20	16	13	16	0	0	0	0	9	5	0	.556	2	3	1	1	2.0	.833
1985			9	10	.474	3.80	42	18	2	147	135	80	85	2	3	4	0	37	6	0	.162	7	35	3	2	1.1	.933
1986			8	16	.333	4.05	38	32	3	204.2	209	105	139	1	1	0	1	59	5	0	.085	7	45	1	4	1.4	.981
1987			15	10	.600	4.09	36	**36**	9	242	245	91	130	3	0	0	0	76	10	0	.132	15	43	0	4	1.6	1.000
1988			5	10	.333	4.30	23	22	3	140.1	159	44	59	0	0	0	0	42	7	0	.167	16	33	1	6	2.2	.980
1989	2 teams		ATL N (17G 1 – 12)				MON N (31G 0 – 1)																				
''	total		1	13	.071	3.49	48	17	0	147	141	52	93	0	0	1	2	32	6	0	.188	7	39	3	0	1.0	.939
1990	2 teams		MON N (22G 6 – 7)				PIT N (11G 6 – 2)																				
''			12	9	.571	2.55	33	31	4	215.1	196	50	130	2	0	0	0	68	11	0	.162	10	35	3	5	1.5	.938
7 yrs.			51	68	.429	3.66	223	159	21	1116.1	1101	435	652	8	4	5	3	323	50	0	.155	64	233	12	22	1.4	.961

LEAGUE CHAMPIONSHIP SERIES

Year	Team		W	L	%	ERA	G	GS	CG	IP	H	BB	SO	ShO	W	L	SV	AB	H	HR	BA	PO	A	E	DP	TC/G	FA
1990	PIT	N	0	2	.000	6.00	2	1	0	9	14	1	8	0	0	0	0	3	0	0	.000	0	1	0	0	0.5	1.000

John Smoltz

SMOLTZ, JOHN ANDREW
B. May 15, 1967, Detroit, Mich.
BR TR 6′ 3″ 210 lbs.

	W	L	%	ERA	G	GS	CG	IP	H	BB	SO	ShO	W	L	SV	AB	H	HR	BA	PO	A	E	DP	TC/G	FA
April	1	2	.333	7.40	4	4	0	20.2	27	9	15	0	0	0	0										
May	2	2	.500	3.15	5	5	2	34.1	24	12	29	1	0	0	0										
June	2	2	.500	5.17	6	6	2	38.1	44	12	31	1	0	0	0										
July	2	1	.667	2.93	6	6	1	46	29	20	34	0	0	0	0										
Aug	5	2	.714	2.03	7	7	1	53.1	44	16	39	0	0	0	0										
Sept/Oct	2	2	.500	4.89	6	6	0	38.2	38	21	22	0	0	0	0										
Day	2	3	.400	4.63	5	5	2	35	25	11	24	0	0	0	0										
Night	12	8	.600	3.71	29	29	4	196.1	181	79	146	2	0	0	0										
vs. Left	—	—	—	—	—	—	—	—	136	63	76	—	—	—	—										
vs. Right	—	—	—	—	—	—	—	—	70	27	94	—	—	—	—										
On Grass	11	6	.647	3.73	26	26	5	181	157	68	137	2	0	0	0										
On Turf	3	5	.375	4.29	8	8	1	50.1	49	22	33	0	0	0	0										
Home	9	4	.692	2.76	17	17	5	124	97	48	104	2	0	0	0										
Road	5	7	.417	5.11	17	17	1	107.1	109	42	66	0	0	0	0										
Division Rivals																									
vs. CIN	1	1	.500	4.85	2	2	1	13	13	10	10	0	0	0	0										
vs. HOU	1	2	.333	3.05	3	3	1	20.2	21	5	15	0	0	0	0										
vs. LA	3	0	1.000	2.37	5	5	1	38	35	10	22	1	0	0	0										
vs. SD	1	0	1.000	6.19	3	3	0	16	21	9	14	0	0	0	0										
vs. SF	1	4	.200	6.88	6	6	0	34	38	15	26	0	0	0	0										

STARTING PITCHER — WINS (NL AVG), ERA (NL AVG), SO/9 (NL AVG), RATIO (NL AVG)

Year	Team		W	L	%	ERA	G	GS	CG	IP	H	BB	SO	ShO	W	L	SV	AB	H	HR	BA	PO	A	E	DP	TC/G	FA
1988	ATL	N	2	7	.222	5.48	12	12	0	64	74	33	37	0	0	0	0	17	2	0	.118	4	6	0	1	0.8	1.000
1989			12	11	.522	2.94	29	29	5	208	160	72	168	0	0	0	0	62	7	1	.113	23	32	7	2	2.1	.887
1990			14	11	.560	3.85	34	34	6	231.1	206	**90**	170	2	0	0	0	74	12	0	.162	26	27	3	4	1.6	.946
3 yrs.			28	29	.491	3.68	75	75	11	503.1	440	195	375	2	0	0	0	153	21	1	.137	53	65	10	7	1.7	.922

Mike Stanton

STANTON, WILLIAM MICHAEL
B. June 2, 1967, Galena Park, Tex.
BL TL 6′ 1″ 190 lbs.

Year	Team		W	L	%	ERA	G	GS	CG	IP	H	BB	SO	ShO	W	L	SV	AB	H	HR	BA	PO	A	E	DP	TC/G	FA
1989	ATL	N	0	1	.000	1.50	20	0	0	24	17	8	27	0	0	1	7	0	0	0	—	1	2	1	0	0.2	.750
1990			0	3	.000	18.00	7	0	0	7	16	4	7	0	0	3	2	0	0	0	—	0	2	0	0	0.3	1.000
2 yrs.			0	4	.000	5.23	27	0	0	31	33	12	34	0	0	4	9	0	0	0	—	1	4	1	0	0.2	.833

Dave Stewart

STEWART, DAVID KEITH
B. Feb. 19, 1957, Oakland, Calif.
BR TR 6′ 2″ 200 lbs.

	W	L	%	ERA	G	GS	CG	IP	H	BB	SO	ShO	W	L	SV
April	5	0	1.000	1.32	5	5	0	34	26	12	14	0	0	0	0
May	3	2	.600	2.18	6	6	1	41.1	36	7	28	0	0	0	0
June	2	4	.333	3.72	6	6	4	48.1	37	18	37	2	0	0	0
July	3	2	.600	3.86	6	6	1	39.2	43	13	19	0	0	0	0
Aug	4	2	.667	2.63	7	7	2	54.2	43	17	40	1	0	0	0
Sept/Oct	5	1	.833	1.47	6	6	3	49	41	16	28	1	0	0	0
Day	9	3	.750	2.24	14	14	4	108.2	85	33	78	2	0	0	0
Night	13	8	.619	2.79	22	22	7	158.1	141	50	88	2	0	0	0
vs. Left	—	—	—	—	—	—	—	—	99	48	80				
vs. Right	—	—	—	—	—	—	—	—	127	35	86				

STARTING PITCHER — WINS (AL AVG), ERA (AL AVG)

Dave Stewart *Continued*

Year	Team	W	L	%	ERA	G	GS	CG	IP	H	BB	SO	ShO	W	L	SV	AB	H	HR	BA	PO	A	E	DP	TC/G	FA
On Grass		18	9	.667	2.45	30	30	8	224	196	68	140	2	0	0	0										
On Turf		4	2	.667	3.14	6	6	3	43	30	15	26	2	0	0	0										
Home		11	4	.733	1.74	18	18	7	145	111	39	86	2	0	0	0										
Road		11	7	.611	3.54	18	18	4	122	115	44	80	2	0	0	0										

Division Rivals

Year	Team	W	L	%	ERA	G	GS	CG	IP	H	BB	SO	ShO	W	L	SV	AB	H	HR	BA	PO	A	E	DP	TC/G	FA
vs. CAL		1	1	.500	2.57	3	3	1	21	26	5	13	0	0	0	0										
vs. CHI		1	3	.250	3.48	4	4	2	31	28	8	20	0	0	0	0										
vs. KC		2	1	.667	3.26	4	4	2	30.1	22	13	20	2	0	0	0										
vs. MIN		3	1	.750	3.25	4	4	2	27.2	28	6	13	0	0	0	0										
vs. SEA		3	0	1.000	0.73	3	3	1	24.2	12	7	7	1	0	0	0										
vs. TEX		—	—	—	—	0			0	0	0	0	0	0	0	0										

Year	Team	W	L	%	ERA	G	GS	CG	IP	H	BB	SO	ShO	W	L	SV	AB	H	HR	BA	PO	A	E	DP	TC/G	FA
1978	LA N	0	0	—	0.00	1	0	0	2	1	0	1	0	0	0	0	0	0	0	—	0	0	0	0	0.0	—
1981		4	3	.571	2.51	32	0	0	43	40	14	29	0	4	3	6	5	2	0	.400	4	7	0	0	0.3	1.000
1982		9	8	.529	3.81	45	14	0	146.1	137	49	80	0	6	3	1	39	7	0	.179	15	16	3	2	0.8	.912
1983	2 teams	LA N (46G 5 - 2)							TEX A (8G 5 - 2)																	
"	total	10	4	.714	2.60	54	9	2	135	117	50	78	0	5	2	0	7	1	0	.143	9	17	1	2	0.5	.963
1984	TEX A	7	14	.333	4.73	32	27	3	192.1	193	87	119	0	0	0	1	0	0	0	—	11	19	3	2	1.0	.909
1985	2 teams	TEX A (42G 0 - 6)							PHI N (4G 0 - 0)																	
"	total	0	6	.000	5.46	46	5	0	85.2	91	41	66	0	0	0	4	0	0	0	—	6	10	3	2	0.4	.842
1986	2 teams	PHI N (8G 0 - 0)							OAK A (29G 9 - 5)																	
"		9	5	.643	3.95	37	17	4	161.2	152	69	111	1	0	0	0	0	0	0	—	10	18	1	2	0.8	.966
1987	OAK A	**20**	13	.606	3.68	37	37	8	261.1	224	105	205	1	0	0	0	0	0	0	—	18	20	1	0	1.1	.974
1988		21	12	.636	3.23	37	**37**	14	**275.2**	240	110	192	2	0	0	0	0	0	0	—	26	16	5	2	1.3	.894
1989		21	9	.700	3.32	36	**36**	8	257.2	**260**	69	155	0	0	0	0	0	0	0	—	22	28	4	4	1.5	.926
1990		22	11	.667	2.56	36	**36**	11	**267**	226	83	166	**4**	0	0	0	0	0	0	—	25	23	0	2	1.3	1.000
11 yrs.		123	85	.591	3.52	393	218	50	1827.2	1681	677	1202	8	15	13	19	51	10	0	196	146	174	21	18	0.9	.938

DIVISIONAL PLAYOFF SERIES

Year	Team	W	L	%	ERA	G	GS	CG	IP	H	BB	SO	ShO	W	L	SV	AB	H	HR	BA	PO	A	E	DP	TC/G	FA
1981	LA N	0	2	.000	40.50	2	0	0	0.2	4	0	1	0	0	0	2	0	0	0	—	0	0	0	0	0.0	—

LEAGUE CHAMPIONSHIP SERIES

Year	Team	W	L	%	ERA	G	GS	CG	IP	H	BB	SO	ShO	W	L	SV	AB	H	HR	BA	PO	A	E	DP	TC/G	FA
1988	OAK A	1	0	1.000	1.35	2	2	0	13.1	9	6	11	0	0	0	0	0	0	0	—	0	2	0	0	1.0	1.000
1989		2	0	1.000	2.81	2	2	0	16	13	3	9	0	0	0	0	0	0	0	—	0	1	0	0	0.5	1.000
1990		2	0	1.000	1.13	2	2	0	16	8	2	4	0	0	0	0	0	0	0	—	0	3	0	0	1.5	1.000
3 yrs.		5	0	1.000	1.79	6	6	0	45.1	30	11	24	0	0	0	0	0	0	0	—	0	6	0	0	1.0	1.000

WORLD SERIES

Year	Team	W	L	%	ERA	G	GS	CG	IP	H	BB	SO	ShO	W	L	SV	AB	H	HR	BA	PO	A	E	DP	TC/G	FA
1981	LA N	0	0	—	0.00	2	0	0	1.2	1	2	1	0	0	0	0	0	0	0	—	0	1	0	1	0.5	—
1988	OAK A	0	1	.000	3.14	2	2	0	14.1	12	5	5	0	0	0	0	3	0	0	.000	0	1	0	0	0.5	1.000
1989		2	0	1.000	1.69	2	2	1	16	10	2	14	1	0	0	0	3	0	0	.000	3	0	1	0	2.0	.750
1990		0	2	.000	3.46	2	2	1	13	10	6	5	0	0	0	0	1	0	0	.000	2	1	1	0	2.0	.750
4 yrs.		2	3	.400	2.60	8	6	2	45	33	15	25	1	0	0	0	7	0	0	.000	5	2	3	0	1.3	.700

Dave Stieb

STIEB, DAVID ANDREW
B. July 22, 1957, Santa Ana, Calif.
BR TR 6' 185 lbs.

Year	Team	W	L	%	ERA	G	GS	CG	IP	H	BB	SO	ShO	W	L	SV	AB	H	HR	BA	PO	A	E	DP	TC/G	FA
April		3	1	.750	2.35	4	4	0	23	22	6	13	0	0	0	0										
May		3	1	.750	2.48	6	6	1	40	30	9	20	1	0	0	0										
June		4	1	.800	5.40	6	6	0	30	36	11	18	0	0	0	0										
July		3	0	1.000	0.94	4	4	0	28.2	16	13	17	0	0	0	0										
Aug		3	2	.600	3.86	6	6	0	39.2	34	11	22	0	0	0	0										
Sept/Oct		2	1	.667	2.47	7	7	1	47.1	41	14	35	1	0	0	0										
Day		7	2	.778	3.31	12	12	1	73.1	64	28	41	1	0	0	0										
Night		11	4	.733	2.73	21	21	1	135.1	115	36	84	1	0	0	0										
vs. Left		—	—	—	—	—	—	—	—	102	40	47	—	—	—	—										
vs. Right		—	—	—	—	—	—	—	—	77	24	78	—	—	—	—										
On Grass		6	1	.857	3.01	13	13	2	86.2	61	28	50	2	0	0	0										
On Turf		12	5	.706	2.88	20	20	0	122	118	36	75	0	0	0	0										
Home		9	5	.643	3.15	17	17	0	103	102	35	64	0	0	0	0										
Road		9	1	.900	2.73	16	16	2	105.2	77	29	61	2	0	0	0										

Division Rivals

Year	Team	W	L	%	ERA	G	GS	CG	IP	H	BB	SO	ShO	W	L	SV	AB	H	HR	BA	PO	A	E	DP	TC/G	FA
vs. BAL		1	1	.500	5.30	3	3	0	18.2	21	7	12	0	0	0	0										
vs. BOS		1	0	1.000	4.15	4	4	0	21.2	27	5	17	0	0	0	0										
vs. CLE		2	1	.667	2.81	4	4	0	25.2	16	8	17	1	0	0	0										
vs. DET		0	0	—	4.50	1	1	0	6	5	2	4	0	0	0	0										
vs. MIL		2	1	.667	3.86	3	3	0	21	23	6	9	0	0	0	0										
vs. NY		0	0	—	1.29	1	1	0	7	5	3	6	0	0	0	0										

Year	Team	W	L	%	ERA	G	GS	CG	IP	H	BB	SO	ShO	RELIEF PITCHING W	L	SV	BATTING AB	H	HR	BA	PO	A	E	DP	TC/G	FA

Dave Stieb *Continued*

Year	Team	W	L	%	ERA	G	GS	CG	IP	H	BB	SO	ShO	W	L	SV	AB	H	HR	BA	PO	A	E	DP	TC/G	FA
1979	TOR A	8	8	.500	4.33	18	18	7	129	139	48	52	1	0	0	0	0	0	0	—	12	31	1	1	2.4	.977
1980		12	15	.444	3.70	34	32	14	243	232	83	108	4	0	0	0	1	0	0	.000	20	58	1	8	2.3	.987
1981		11	10	.524	3.18	25	25	11	184	148	61	89	2	0	0	0	0	0	0	—	11	38	1	3	2.0	.980
1982		17	14	.548	3.25	38	38	**19**	**288.1**	**271**	75	141	**5**	0	0	0	0	0	0	—	27	53	2	6	2.2	.976
1983		17	12	.586	3.04	36	36	14	278	223	93	187	4	0	0	0	0	0	0	—	28	33	2	1	1.8	.968
1984		16	8	.667	2.83	35	35	11	267	215	88	198	2	0	0	0	0	0	0	—	22	34	1	4	1.6	.982
1985		14	13	.519	**2.48**	36	36	8	265	206	96	167	2	0	0	0	0	0	0	—	34	53	5	5	2.6	.946
1986		7	12	.368	4.74	37	34	1	205	239	87	127	1	0	0	1	0	0	0	—	15	33	1	4	1.3	.980
1987		13	9	.591	4.09	33	31	3	185	164	87	115	1	0	0	0	0	0	0	—	24	25	2	2	1.5	.961
1988		16	8	.667	3.04	32	31	8	207.1	157	79	147	4	0	0	0	0	0	0	—	19	26	0	3	1.4	1.000
1989		17	8	.680	3.35	33	33	3	206.2	164	76	101	2	0	0	0	0	0	0	—	18	29	0	1	1.4	1.000
1990		18	6	.750	2.93	33	33	2	208.2	179	64	125	2	0	0	0	0	0	0	—	24	40	4	3	2.1	.941
12 yrs.		166	123	.574	3.34	390	382	101	2667	2337	937	1557	30	0	0	1	1	0	0	.000	254	453	20	41	1.9	.972

LEAGUE CHAMPIONSHIP SERIES

Year	Team	W	L	%	ERA	G	GS	CG	IP	H	BB	SO	ShO	W	L	SV	AB	H	HR	BA	PO	A	E	DP	TC/G	FA
1985	TOR A	1	1	.500	3.10	3	3	0	20.1	11	10	18	0	0	0	0	0	0	0	—	1	3	0	0	1.3	1.000
1989		0	2	.000	6.35	2	2	0	11.1	12	6	10	0	0	0	0	0	0	0	—	0	1	0	0	0.5	1.000
2 yrs.		1	3	.250	4.26	5	5	0	31.2	23	16	28	0	0	0	0	0	0	0	—	1	4	0	0	1.0	1.000

Mel Stottlemyre

STOTTLEMYRE, MELVIN LEON, JR.
Son of Mel Stottlemyre. Brother of Todd Stottlemyre.
B. Dec. 28, 1963, Prosser, Wash.
BR TR 6′ 190 lbs.

Year	Team	W	L	%	ERA	G	GS	CG	IP	H	BB	SO	ShO	W	L	SV	AB	H	HR	BA	PO	A	E	DP	TC/G	FA
1990	KC A	0	1	.000	4.88	13	2	0	31.1	35	12	14	0	0	0	0	0	0	0	—	1	5	0	0	0.5	1.000

Todd Stottlemyre

STOTTLEMYRE, TODD VERNON
Son of Mel Stottlemyre. Brother of Mel Stottlemyre.
B. May 20, 1965, Sunnyside, Wash.
BL TR 6′ 3″ 195 lbs.

	W	L	%	ERA	G	GS	CG	IP	H	BB	SO	ShO	W	L	SV
April	3	2	.600	4.67	5	5	0	27	25	11	13	0	0	0	0
May	1	3	.250	5.04	5	5	1	30.1	31	13	17	0	0	0	0
June	4	2	.667	3.13	6	6	0	46	47	11	15	0	0	0	0
July	2	4	.333	5.86	6	6	1	27.2	39	11	20	0	0	0	0
Aug	1	3	.250	3.31	5	5	0	35.1	29	9	26	0	0	0	0
Sept/Oct	2	3	.400	4.91	6	6	0	36.2	43	14	24	0	0	0	0
Day	3	7	.300	4.35	10	10	2	62	65	19	35	0	0	0	0
Night	10	10	.500	4.34	23	23	2	141	149	50	80	0	0	0	0
vs. Left	—	—	—	—	—	—	—	—	118	37	42	—	—	—	—
vs. Right	—	—	—	—	—	—	—	—	96	32	73	—	—	—	—
On Grass	5	6	.455	3.67	12	12	3	76	70	20	44	0	0	0	0
On Turf	8	11	.421	4.75	21	21	1	127	144	49	71	0	0	0	0
Home	7	8	.467	4.28	16	16	1	103	112	35	62	0	0	0	0
Road	6	9	.400	4.41	17	17	3	100	102	34	53	0	0	0	0
Division Rivals															
vs. BAL	1	0	1.000	1.50	1	1	0	6	6	1	2	0	0	0	0
vs. BOS	0	3	.000	3.80	3	3	1	21.1	17	7	15	0	0	0	0
vs. CLE	3	1	.750	3.65	4	4	0	24.2	24	4	9	0	0	0	0
vs. DET	1	2	.333	5.40	3	3	1	16.2	21	6	11	0	0	0	0
vs. MIL	0	1	.000	3.38	1	1	0	8	9	3	3	0	0	0	0
vs. NY	2	0	1.000	3.94	4	4	1	29.2	32	9	14	0	0	0	0

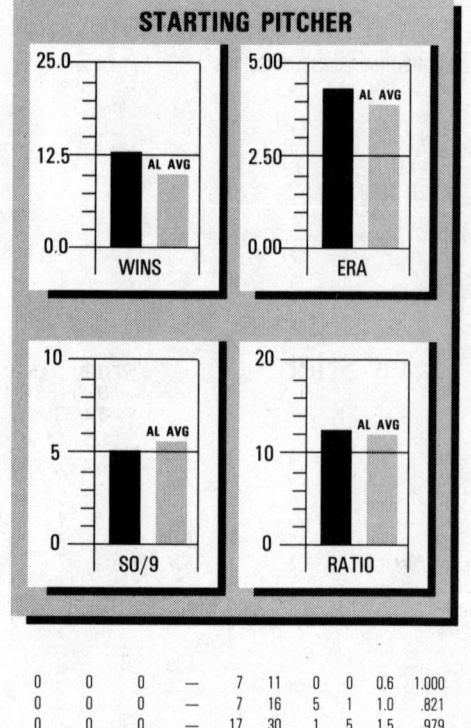

STARTING PITCHER

WINS — ERA — SO/9 — RATIO (AL AVG)

Year	Team	W	L	%	ERA	G	GS	CG	IP	H	BB	SO	ShO	W	L	SV	AB	H	HR	BA	PO	A	E	DP	TC/G	FA
1988	TOR A	4	8	.333	5.69	28	16	0	98	109	46	67	0	2	1	0	0	0	0	—	7	11	0	0	0.6	1.000
1989		7	7	.500	3.88	27	18	0	127.2	137	44	63	0	0	1	0	0	0	0	—	7	16	5	1	1.0	.821
1990		13	17	.433	4.34	33	33	4	203	214	69	115	0	0	0	0	0	0	0	—	17	30	1	5	1.5	.979
3 yrs.		24	32	.429	4.51	88	67	4	428.2	460	159	245	0	2	2	0	0	0	0	—	31	57	6	6	1.1	.936

LEAGUE CHAMPIONSHIP SERIES

Year	Team	W	L	%	ERA	G	GS	CG	IP	H	BB	SO	ShO	W	L	SV	AB	H	HR	BA	PO	A	E	DP	TC/G	FA
1989	TOR A	0	1	.000	7.20	1	1	0	5	7	2	3	0	0	0	0	0	0	0	—	0	0	0	0	0.0	—

Year	Team	W	L	%	ERA	G	GS	CG	IP	H	BB	SO	ShO	RELIEF PITCHING W	L	SV	BATTING AB	H	HR	BA	PO	A	E	DP	TC/G	FA

Rick Sutcliffe

SUTCLIFFE, RICHARD LEE
B. June 21, 1956, Independence, Mo.
BL TR 6′ 7″ 215 lbs.

Year	Team	W	L	%	ERA	G	GS	CG	IP	H	BB	SO	ShO	W	L	SV	AB	H	HR	BA	PO	A	E	DP	TC/G	FA
1976	LA N	0	0	—	0.00	1	1	0	5	2	1	3	0	0	0	0	1	0	0	.000	0	0	0	0	0.0	—
1978		0	0	—	0.00	2	0	0	2	2	1	0	0	0	0	0	0	0	0	—	0	1	0	1	0.5	1.000
1979		17	10	.630	3.46	39	30	5	242	217	97	117	1	1	2	0	85	21	1	.247	18	24	0	1	1.1	1.000
1980		3	9	.250	5.56	42	10	1	110	122	55	59	1	2	5	5	27	4	0	.148	6	13	0	0	0.5	1.000
1981		2	2	.500	4.02	14	6	0	47	41	20	16	0	0	0	0	11	2	0	.182	6	8	0	0	1.0	1.000
1982	CLE A	14	8	.636	**2.96**	34	27	6	216	174	98	142	1	2	1	1	0	0	0	—	14	32	1	1	1.4	.979
1983		17	11	.607	4.29	36	35	10	243.1	251	102	160	2	1	0	0	0	0	0	—	36	29	0	1	1.8	1.000
1984	2 teams	CLE A (15G 4 – 5)				CHI N (20G 16 – 1)																				
''	total	20	6	.769	3.64	35	35	9	244.2	234	85	213	3	0	0	0	56	14	0	.250	19	35	2	1	1.6	.964
1985	CHI N	8	8	.500	3.18	20	20	6	130	119	44	102	3	0	0	0	43	10	1	.233	12	23	1	0	1.8	.972
1986		5	14	.263	4.64	28	27	4	176.2	166	96	122	1	0	0	0	53	11	1	.208	8	30	1	4	1.4	.974
1987		**18**	10	.643	3.68	34	34	6	237.1	223	106	174	1	0	0	0	81	12	0	.148	12	54	4	4	2.1	.943
1988		13	14	.481	3.86	32	32	12	226	232	70	144	2	0	0	0	75	12	1	.160	21	37	3	2	1.9	.951
1989		16	11	.593	3.66	35	34	5	229	202	69	153	1	0	0	0	70	10	0	.143	22	31	1	3	1.5	.981
1990		0	2	.000	5.91	5	5	0	21.1	25	12	7	0	0	0	0	5	0	0	.000	2	5	0	0	1.4	1.000
14 yrs.		133	105	.559	3.83	357	296	64	2130.1	2010	856	1412	16	6	8	6	507	96	4	.189	176	322	13	18	1.4	.975

LEAGUE CHAMPIONSHIP SERIES

Year	Team	W	L	%	ERA	G	GS	CG	IP	H	BB	SO	ShO	W	L	SV	AB	H	HR	BA	PO	A	E	DP	TC/G	FA
1984	CHI N	1	1	.500	3.38	2	2	0	13.1	9	8	10	0	0	0	0	6	3	1	.500	0	0	0	0	0.0	—
1989		0	0	—	4.50	1	1	0	6	5	4	2	0	0	0	0	2	1	0	.500	0	2	0	0	2.0	1.000
2 yrs.		1	1	.500	3.72	3	3	0	19.1	14	12	12	0	0	0	0	8	4	1	.500	0	2	0	0	0.7	1.000

Russ Swan

SWAN, RUSSELL HOWARD
B. Jan. 3, 1964, Fremont, Calif.
BL TL 6′ 4″ 210 lbs.

Year	Team	W	L	%	ERA	G	GS	CG	IP	H	BB	SO	ShO	W	L	SV	AB	H	HR	BA	PO	A	E	DP	TC/G	FA
1989	SF N	0	2	.000	10.80	2	2	0	6.2	11	4	2	0	0	0	0	2	0	0	.000	1	1	0	0	1.0	1.000
1990	2 teams	SF N (2G 0 – 1)				SEA A (11G 2 – 3)																				
''	total	2	4	.333	3.65	13	9	0	49.1	48	22	16	0	0	0	0	1	0	0	.000	3	8	0	0	0.8	1.000
2 yrs.		2	6	.250	4.50	15	11	0	56	59	26	18	0	0	0	0	3	0	0	.000	4	9	0	0	0.9	1.000

Bill Swift

SWIFT, WILLIAM CHARLES
B. Oct. 27, 1961, Portland, Me.
BR TR 6′ 170 lbs.

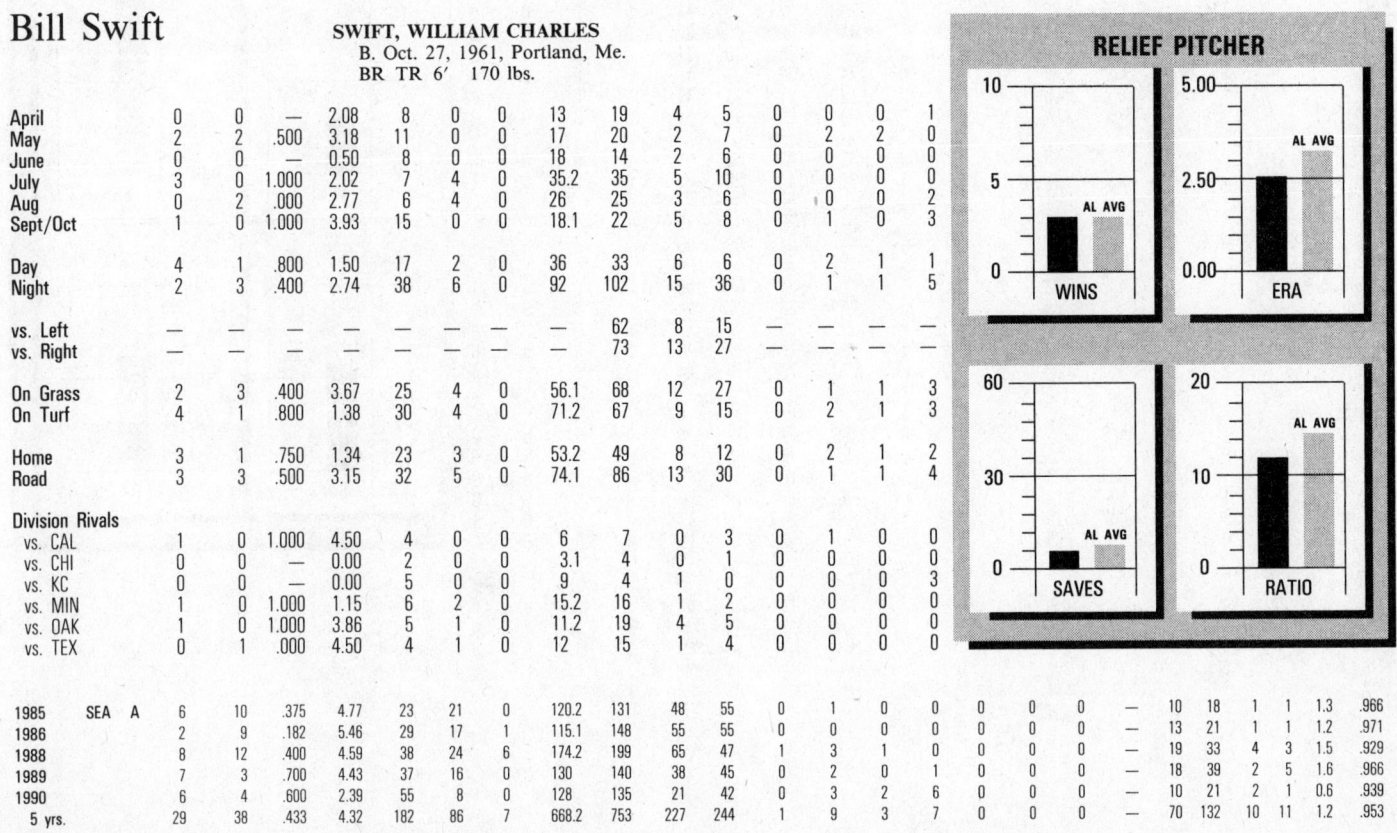

RELIEF PITCHER — WINS, ERA, SAVES, RATIO (AL AVG)

	W	L	%	ERA	G	GS	CG	IP	H	BB	SO	ShO	W	L	SV	AB	H	HR	BA	PO	A	E	DP	TC/G	FA
April	0	0	—	2.08	8	0	0	13	19	4	5	0	0	0	1										
May	2	2	.500	3.18	11	0	0	17	20	2	7	0	2	2	0										
June	0	0	—	0.50	8	0	0	18	14	2	6	0	0	0	0										
July	3	0	1.000	2.02	7	4	0	35.2	35	5	10	0	0	0	0										
Aug	0	2	.000	2.77	6	4	0	26	25	3	6	0	0	0	2										
Sept/Oct	1	0	1.000	3.93	15	0	0	18.1	22	5	8	0	1	0	3										
Day	4	1	.800	1.50	17	2	0	36	33	6	6	0	2	1	1										
Night	2	3	.400	2.74	38	6	0	92	102	15	36	0	1	1	5										
vs. Left	—	—	—	—	—	—	—	—	62	8	15	—	—	—	—										
vs. Right	—	—	—	—	—	—	—	—	73	13	27	—	—	—	—										
On Grass	2	3	.400	3.67	25	4	0	56.1	68	12	27	0	1	1	3										
On Turf	4	1	.800	1.38	30	4	0	71.2	67	9	15	0	2	1	3										
Home	3	1	.750	1.34	23	3	0	53.2	49	8	12	0	2	1	2										
Road	3	3	.500	3.15	32	5	0	74.1	86	13	30	0	1	1	4										
Division Rivals																									
vs. CAL	1	0	1.000	4.50	4	0	0	6	7	0	3	0	1	0	0										
vs. CHI	0	0	—	0.00	2	0	0	3.1	4	0	1	0	0	0	0										
vs. KC	0	0	—	0.00	5	0	0	9	4	1	0	0	0	0	3										
vs. MIN	1	0	1.000	1.15	6	2	0	15.2	16	1	2	0	0	0	0										
vs. OAK	1	0	1.000	3.86	5	1	0	11.2	19	4	5	0	0	0	0										
vs. TEX	0	1	.000	4.50	4	1	0	12	15	1	4	0	0	0	0										

Year	Team	W	L	%	ERA	G	GS	CG	IP	H	BB	SO	ShO	W	L	SV	AB	H	HR	BA	PO	A	E	DP	TC/G	FA
1985	SEA A	6	10	.375	4.77	23	21	0	120.2	131	48	55	0	1	0	0	0	0	0	—	10	18	1	1	1.3	.966
1986		2	9	.182	5.46	29	17	1	115.1	148	55	55	0	0	0	0	0	0	0	—	13	21	1	1	1.2	.971
1988		8	12	.400	4.59	38	24	6	174.2	199	65	47	0	3	1	0	0	0	0	—	19	33	4	3	1.5	.929
1989		7	3	.700	4.43	37	16	0	130	140	38	45	0	2	0	1	0	0	0	—	18	39	2	5	1.6	.966
1990		6	4	.600	2.39	55	8	0	128	135	21	42	0	3	2	6	0	0	0	—	10	21	2	1	0.6	.939
5 yrs.		29	38	.433	4.32	182	86	7	668.2	753	227	244	1	9	3	7	0	0	0	—	70	132	10	11	1.2	.953

Year	Team	W	L	%	ERA	G	GS	CG	IP	H	BB	SO	ShO	W	L	SV	AB	H	HR	BA	PO	A	E	DP	TC/G	FA

Greg Swindell

SWINDELL, FORREST GREGORY
B. Jan. 2, 1965, Houston, Tex.
BR TL 6' 2" 225 lbs.

Year	Team	W	L	%	ERA	G	GS	CG	IP	H	BB	SO	ShO	W	L	SV	AB	H	HR	BA	PO	A	E	DP	TC/G	FA
April		2	2	.500	4.79	4	4	0	20.2	21	7	12	0	0	0	0										
May		0	2	.000	6.18	5	5	1	27.2	36	8	10	0	0	0	0										
June		0	1	.000	4.54	6	6	0	35.2	40	11	31	0	0	0	0										
July		4	1	.800	2.49	6	6	1	47	39	8	27	0	0	0	0										
Aug		4	2	.667	4.37	7	7	1	47.1	61	9	36	0	0	0	0										
Sept/Oct		2	1	.667	5.20	6	6	0	36.1	48	4	19	0	0	0	0										
Day		5	2	.714	3.75	9	9	1	60	68	7	37	0	0	0	0										
Night		7	7	.500	4.66	25	25	2	154.2	177	40	98	0	0	0	0										
vs. Left		—	—	—	—	—	—	—	—	36	6	18	—	—	—	—										
vs. Right		—	—	—	—	—	—	—	—	209	41	117	—	—	—	—										
On Grass		11	7	.611	4.28	30	30	2	187.1	209	38	123	0	0	0	0										
On Turf		1	2	.333	5.27	4	4	1	27.1	36	9	12	0	0	0	0										
Home		7	4	.636	4.67	18	18	1	113.2	128	23	63	0	0	0	0										
Road		5	5	.500	4.10	16	16	2	101	117	24	72	0	0	0	0										
Division Rivals																										
vs. BAL		1	1	.500	3.96	4	4	0	25	34	7	17	0	0	0	0										
vs. BOS		1	0	1.000	1.77	3	3	0	20.1	19	2	16	0	0	0	0										
vs. DET		1	1	.500	6.17	2	2	0	11.2	13	4	6	0	0	0	0										
vs. MIL		0	0	—	7.43	2	2	0	13.1	14	2	12	0	0	0	0										
vs. NY		1	2	.333	4.18	4	4	1	23.2	23	4	18	0	0	0	0										
vs. TOR		0	2	.000	9.26	2	2	0	11.2	16	5	12	0	0	0	0										
1986	CLE A	5	2	.714	4.23	9	9	1	61.2	57	15	46	0	0	0	0	0	0	0	—	2	12	0	1	1.6	1.000
1987		3	8	.273	5.10	16	15	4	102.1	112	37	97	1	0	0	0	0	0	0	—	0	13	1	1	0.9	.929
1988		18	14	.563	3.20	33	33	12	242	234	45	180	4	0	0	0	0	0	0	—	8	29	1	0	1.2	.974
1989		13	6	.684	3.37	28	28	5	184.1	170	51	129	2	0	0	0	0	0	0	—	7	25	0	1	1.1	1.000
1990		12	9	.571	4.40	34	34	3	214.2	245	47	135	0	0	0	0	0	0	0	—	8	20	1	1	0.9	.966
5 yrs.		51	39	.567	3.88	120	119	25	805	818	195	587	7	0	0	0	0	0	0	—	25	99	3	4	1.1	.976

STARTING PITCHER

WINS (AL AVG) — ERA (AL AVG) — SO/9 (AL AVG) — RATIO (AL AVG)

Frank Tanana

TANANA, FRANK DARYL
B. July 3, 1953, Detroit, Mich.
BL TL 6' 2" 180 lbs.

Year	Team	W	L	%	ERA	G	GS	CG	IP	H	BB	SO	ShO	W	L	SV	AB	H	HR	BA	PO	A	E	DP	TC/G	FA
April		2	1	.667	6.29	4	4	0	24.1	32	5	11	0	0	0	0										
May		1	2	.333	4.17	6	6	1	41	39	10	22	0	0	0	0										
June		2	2	.500	6.75	5	5	0	28	35	10	21	0	0	0	0										
July		0	2	.000	9.38	7	6	0	24	34	14	18	0	0	0	0										
Aug		1	0	1.000	6.05	6	2	0	19.1	21	11	11	0	0	0	0										
Sept/Oct		3	1	.750	2.04	6	6	0	39.2	29	16	31	0	0	0	0										
Day		2	1	.667	5.95	7	7	0	39.1	43	13	27	0	0	0	0										
Night		7	7	.500	5.12	27	22	1	137	147	53	87	0	0	0	1										
vs. Left		—	—	—	—	—	—	—	—	26	7	15	—	—	—	—										
vs. Right		—	—	—	—	—	—	—	—	164	59	99	—	—	—	—										
On Grass		7	8	.467	6.02	29	25	1	142	164	54	100	0	0	0	1										
On Turf		2	0	1.000	2.36	5	4	0	34.1	26	12	14	0	0	0	0										
Home		4	6	.400	6.00	19	18	1	99	112	37	70	0	0	0	0										
Road		5	2	.714	4.42	15	11	0	77.1	78	29	44	0	0	0	1										
Division Rivals																										
vs. BAL		1	1	.500	5.59	2	2	0	9.2	7	3	8	0	0	0	0										
vs. BOS		0	0	—	18.00	2	2	0	5	13	2	3	0	0	0	0										
vs. CLE		1	0	1.000	9.82	2	1	0	7.1	10	4	9	0	0	0	0										
vs. MIL		1	1	.500	10.24	3	2	0	9.2	15	5	6	0	0	0	0										
vs. NY		2	1	.667	2.28	5	3	0	23.2	20	10	17	0	0	0	1										
vs. TOR		0	0	—	3.38	3	2	0	18.2	15	9	16	0	0	0	0										
1973	CAL A	2	2	.500	3.08	4	4	2	26.1	20	8	22	1	0	0	0	0	0	0	—	0	5	0	0	1.3	1.000
1974		14	19	.424	3.11	39	35	12	269	262	77	180	4	2	0	0	0	0	0	—	9	39	1	4	1.3	.980
1975		16	9	.640	2.62	34	33	16	257.1	211	73	**269**	5	0	0	0	0	0	0	—	9	44	2	5	1.6	.964
1976		19	10	.655	2.44	34	34	23	288	212	73	261	2	0	0	0	0	0	0	—	12	45	1	1	1.7	.983
1977		15	9	.625	**2.54**	31	31	20	241.1	201	61	205	**7**	0	0	0	0	0	0	—	15	37	1	2	1.7	.981

STARTING PITCHER

WINS (AL AVG) — ERA (AL AVG) — SO/9 (AL AVG) — RATIO (AL AVG)

Year	Team	W	L	%	ERA	G	GS	CG	IP	H	BB	SO	ShO	RELIEF PITCHING W	L	SV	BATTING AB	H	HR	BA	PO	A	E	DP	TC/G	FA

Frank Tanana *Continued*

Year	Team	W	L	%	ERA	G	GS	CG	IP	H	BB	SO	ShO	W	L	SV	AB	H	HR	BA	PO	A	E	DP	TC/G	FA
1978		18	12	.600	3.65	33	33	10	239	239	60	137	4	0	0	0	0	0	0	—	8	25	0	2	1.0	1.000
1979		7	5	.583	3.90	18	17	2	90	93	25	46	1	0	0	0	0	0	0	—	3	12	1	1	0.9	.938
1980		11	12	.478	4.15	32	31	7	204	223	45	113	0	0	0	0	0	0	0	—	12	24	0	1	1.1	1.000
1981	BOS A	4	10	.286	4.02	24	23	5	141	142	43	78	2	0	0	0	0	0	0	—	9	25	1	2	1.5	.971
1982	TEX A	7	**18**	.280	4.21	30	30	7	194.1	199	55	87	0	0	0	0	0	0	0	—	8	30	1	0	1.3	.974
1983		7	9	.438	3.16	29	22	3	159.1	144	49	108	0	1	0	0	0	0	0	—	9	37	2	0	1.7	.958
1984		15	15	.500	3.25	35	35	9	246.1	234	81	141	1	0	0	0	0	0	0	—	18	35	0	2	1.5	1.000
1985	2 teams	TEX A (13G 2 - 7)	DET A (20G 10 - 7)																							
"	total	12	14	.462	4.27	33	33	4	215	220	57	159	0	0	0	0	0	0	0	—	14	31	1	2	1.4	.978
1986	DET A	12	9	.571	4.16	32	31	3	188.1	196	65	119	1	0	0	0	0	0	0	—	19	26	2	5	1.5	.957
1987		15	10	.600	3.91	34	34	5	218.2	216	56	146	3	0	0	0	0	0	0	—	14	35	0	2	1.4	1.000
1988		14	11	.560	4.21	32	32	2	203	213	64	127	0	0	0	0	0	0	0	—	11	31	1	4	1.3	.977
1989		10	14	.417	3.58	33	33	6	223.2	227	74	147	1	0	0	0	0	0	0	—	16	41	0	2	1.7	1.000
1990		9	8	.529	5.31	34	29	1	176.1	190	66	114	0	0	0	1	0	0	0	—	9	27	0	0	1.1	1.000
18 yrs.		207	196	.514	3.58	541	520	137	3581	3442	1032	2459	32	3	0	1	0	0	0	—	195	549	14	35	1.4	.982

LEAGUE CHAMPIONSHIP SERIES

Year	Team	W	L	%	ERA	G	GS	CG	IP	H	BB	SO	ShO	W	L	SV	AB	H	HR	BA	PO	A	E	DP	TC/G	FA
1979	CAL A	0	0	—	3.60	1	1	0	5	6	2	3	0	0	0	0	0	0	0	—	0	0	0	0	0.0	—
1987	DET A	0	1	.000	5.06	1	1	0	5.1	6	4	1	0	0	0	0	0	0	0	—	0	1	0	0	1.0	1.000
2 yrs.		0	1	.000	4.35	2	2	0	10.1	12	6	4	0	0	0	0	0	0	0	—	0	1	0	0	0.5	1.000

Kevin Tapani

TAPANI, KEVIN RAY
B. Feb. 18, 1964, Des Moines, Iowa
BR TR 6′ 180 lbs.

Split	W	L	%	ERA	G	GS	CG	IP	H	BB	SO	ShO	W	L	SV
April	2	2	.500	2.86	4	4	0	22	20	5	15	0	0	0	0
May	4	1	.800	4.03	6	6	1	38	42	7	31	1	0	0	0
June	2	2	.500	4.82	6	6	0	37.1	40	5	24	0	0	0	0
July	3	0	1.000	3.10	5	5	0	29	27	3	17	0	0	0	0
Aug	0	1	.000	5.63	2	2	0	8	7	4	3	0	0	0	0
Sept/Oct	1	2	.333	4.68	5	5	0	25	28	5	11	0	0	0	0
Day	4	1	.800	2.38	7	7	1	45.1	37	7	34	1	0	0	0
Night	8	7	.533	4.74	21	21	0	114	127	22	67	0	0	0	0
vs. Left	—	—	—	—	—	—	—	—	90	21	53	—	—	—	—
vs. Right	—	—	—	—	—	—	—	—	74	8	48	—	—	—	—
On Grass	3	5	.375	4.66	13	13	1	67.2	69	11	48	1	0	0	0
On Turf	9	3	.750	3.63	15	15	0	91.2	95	18	53	0	0	0	0
Home	8	2	.800	3.38	12	12	0	74.2	78	16	44	0	0	0	0
Road	4	6	.400	4.68	16	16	1	84.2	86	13	57	1	0	0	0

Division Rivals

Split	W	L	%	ERA	G	GS	CG	IP	H	BB	SO	ShO	W	L	SV
vs. CAL	2	2	.500	2.78	4	4	0	22.2	18	3	17	0	0	0	0
vs. CHI	0	1	.000	1.80	2	2	0	15	13	0	7	0	0	0	0
vs. KC	2	0	1.000	1.20	2	2	0	15	10	1	11	0	0	0	0
vs. OAK	1	0	1.000	3.60	2	2	0	10	10	2	3	0	0	0	0
vs. SEA	2	0	1.000	2.33	3	3	0	19.1	17	5	8	0	0	0	0
vs. TEX	0	1	.000	8.31	2	2	0	8.2	12	1	5	0	0	0	0

STARTING PITCHER

WINS — 25.0 / 12.5 / 0.0 (AL AVG)
ERA — 5.00 / 2.50 / 0.00 (AL AVG)
SO/9 — 10 / 5 / 0 (AL AVG)
RATIO — 20 / 10 (AL AVG)

Year	Team	W	L	%	ERA	G	GS	CG	IP	H	BB	SO	ShO	W	L	SV	AB	H	HR	BA	PO	A	E	DP	TC/G	FA
1989	2 teams	NY N (3G 0 - 0)	MIN A (5G 2 - 2)																							
"	total	2	2	.500	3.83	8	5	0	40.	39	12	23	0	0	0	0	2	0	0	.000	4	4	0	1	1.0	1.000
1990	MIN A	12	8	.600	4.07	28	28	1	159.1	164	29	101	1	0	0	0	0	0	0	—	14	20	1	1	1.3	.971
2 yrs.		14	10	.583	4.02	36	33	1	199.1	203	41	124	1	0	0	0	2	0	0	.000	18	24	1	2	1.2	.977

Dorn Taylor

TAYLOR, DONALD CLYDE
B. Aug. 11, 1958, Abington, Pa.
BR TR 6′ 2″ 180 lbs.

Year	Team	W	L	%	ERA	G	GS	CG	IP	H	BB	SO	ShO	W	L	SV	AB	H	HR	BA	PO	A	E	DP	TC/G	FA
1987	PIT N	2	3	.400	5.74	14	8	0	53.1	48	28	37	0	1	0	0	18	3	0	.167	3	5	2	3	0.7	.800
1989		1	1	.500	5.06	9	0	0	10.2	14	5	3	0	1	1	0	1	0	0	.000	0	1	0	0	0.1	1.000
1990	BAL A	0	1	.000	2.45	4	0	0	3.2	4	2	4	0	0	1	0	0	0	0	—	0	0	0	0	0.0	—
3 yrs.		3	5	.375	5.45	27	8	0	67.2	66	35	44	0	2	2	0	19	3	0	.158	3	6	2	3	0.4	.818

Anthony Telford

TELFORD, ANTHONY CHARLES
B. Mar. 6, 1966, San Jose, Calif.
BR TR 6′ 175 lbs.

Year	Team	W	L	%	ERA	G	GS	CG	IP	H	BB	SO	ShO	W	L	SV	AB	H	HR	BA	PO	A	E	DP	TC/G	FA
1990	BAL A	3	3	.500	4.95	8	8	0	36.1	43	19	20	0	0	0	0	0	0	0	—	3	5	0	0	1.0	1.000

Year	Team	W	L	%	ERA	G	GS	CG	IP	H	BB	SO	ShO	RELIEF PITCHING W	L	SV	BATTING AB	H	HR	BA	PO	A	E	DP	TC/G	FA

Walt Terrell

TERRELL, CHARLES WALTER
B. May 11, 1958, Jeffersonville, Ind.
BL TR 6' 2" 205 lbs.

Split	W	L	%	ERA	G	GS	CG	IP	H	BB	SO	ShO	W	L	SV
April	0	0	—	4.08	3	3	0	17.2	18	6	5	0	0	0	0
May	2	4	.333	5.64	6	6	0	30.1	38	11	16	0	0	0	0
June	0	2	.000	6.59	5	5	0	27.1	32	13	11	0	0	0	0
July	0	1	.000	8.68	3	2	0	9.1	14	3	2	0	0	0	0
Aug	3	2	.600	5.71	6	6	0	34.2	44	12	14	0	0	0	0
Sept/Oct	3	2	.600	3.26	6	6	0	38.2	38	12	16	0	0	0	0
Day	2	1	.667	2.88	6	5	0	34.1	34	8	12	0	0	0	0
Night	6	10	.375	5.89	23	23	0	123.2	150	49	52	0	0	0	0
vs. Left	—	—	—	—				—	110	37	35	—	—	—	—
vs. Right	—	—	—	—				—	74	20	29	—	—	—	—
On Grass	5	7	.417	4.74	18	17	0	100.2	116	30	39	0	0	0	0
On Turf	3	4	.429	6.12	11	11	0	57.1	68	27	25	0	0	0	0
Home	5	4	.556	4.58	14	13	0	78.2	85	25	31	0	0	0	0
Road	3	7	.300	5.90	15	15	0	79.1	99	32	33	0	0	0	0
Division Rivals															
vs. BAL	—		—	—	0		—	0	0	0	0	0	0	0	0
vs. BOS	0	0	—	9.00	1	0	0	2	4	0	0	0	0	0	0
vs. CLE	2	0	1.000	3.68	2	2	0	14.2	16	1	5	0	0	0	0
vs. MIL	0	1	.000	6.75	1	1	0	6.2	11	3	2	0	0	0	0
vs. NY	0	1	.000	7.00	2	2	0	9	14	1	4	0	0	0	0
vs. TOR	1	1	.500	4.09	2	2	0	11	11	5	5	0	0	0	0

Year	Team	W	L	%	ERA	G	GS	CG	IP	H	BB	SO	ShO	W	L	SV	AB	H	HR	BA	PO	A	E	DP	TC/G	FA
1982	NY N	0	3	.000	3.43	3	3	0	21	22	14	8	0	0	0	0	5	2	0	.400	2	2	0	0	1.3	1.000
1983		8	8	.500	3.57	21	20	4	133.2	123	55	59	2	0	0	0	44	8	3	.182	16	15	0	2	1.5	1.000
1984		11	12	.478	3.52	33	33	3	215	232	80	114	1	0	0	0	75	6	0	.080	16	32	2	5	1.5	.960
1985	DET A	15	10	.600	3.85	34	34	5	229	221	95	130	3	0	0	0	0	0	0	—	21	43	2	8	1.9	.970
1986		15	12	.556	4.56	34	33	9	217.1	199	98	93	2	0	0	0	0	0	0	—	30	29	0	0	1.7	1.000
1987		17	10	.630	4.05	35	35	10	244.2	254	94	143	1	0	0	0	0	0	0	—	24	25	2	3	1.5	.961
1988		7	16	.304	3.97	29	29	11	206.1	199	78	84	1	0	0	0	0	0	0	—	22	29	2	3	1.8	.962
1989	2 teams	SD N (19G 5–13)			NY A (13G 6–5)																					
"	total	11	18	.379	4.49	32	32	5	206.1	236	50	93	2	0	0	0	40	4	0	.100	19	41	0	4	1.9	1.000
1990	2 teams	PIT N (16G 2–7)			DET A (13G 6–4)																					
"		8	11	.421	5.24	29	28	0	158	184	57	64	0	0	0	0	28	3	0	.107	13	21	1	2	1.2	.971
9 yrs.		92	100	.479	4.13	250	247	47	1631.1	1670	621	788	12	0	0	0	192	23	3	.120	163	237	9	27	1.6	.978

LEAGUE CHAMPIONSHIP SERIES

Year	Team	W	L	%	ERA	G	GS	CG	IP	H	BB	SO	ShO	W	L	SV	AB	H	HR	BA	PO	A	E	DP	TC/G	FA
1987	DET A	0	0	—	9.00	1	1	0	6	7	4	4	0	0	0	0	0	0	0	—	0	1	0	0	1.0	1.000

Scott Terry

TERRY, SCOTT RAY
B. Nov. 21, 1959, Hobbs, N. M.
BR TR 5' 11" 195 lbs.

Split	W	L	%	ERA	G	GS	CG	IP	H	BB	SO	ShO	W	L	SV
April	0	1	.000	9.82	4	0	0	3.2	5	4	2	0	0	1	1
May	0	2	.000	7.62	11	0	0	13	19	6	7	0	0	2	1
June	0	2	.000	5.84	8	1	0	12.1	18	5	4	0	0	1	0
July	1	0	1.000	3.18	6	1	0	11.1	12	1	6	0	1	0	0
Aug	1	1	.500	3.44	11	0	0	18.1	13	4	9	0	1	1	0
Sept/Oct	0	0	—	2.70	10	0	0	13.1	8	7	7	0	0	0	0
Day	0	1	.000	6.23	11	1	0	13	16	8	7	0	0	1	0
Night	2	5	.286	4.42	39	1	0	59	59	19	28	0	2	4	2
vs. Left	—	—	—	—				—	33	15	21	—	—	—	—
vs. Right	—	—	—	—				—	42	12	14	—	—	—	—
On Grass	0	2	.000	4.26	15	1	0	19	23	4	11	0	0	2	1
On Turf	2	4	.333	4.92	35	1	0	53	52	23	24	0	2	3	1
Home	1	3	.250	4.04	27	0	0	35.2	33	15	15	0	1	3	1
Road	1	3	.250	5.45	23	2	0	36.1	42	12	20	0	1	2	1
Division Rivals															
vs. CHI	1	1	.500	2.38	6	0	0	11.1	9	0	6	0	1	1	0
vs. MON	0	1	.000	5.00	5	1	0	9	11	6	3	0	0	1	1
vs. NY	0	0	—	0.00	5	0	0	6.2	4	2	3	0	0	0	0
vs. PHI	0	2	.000	9.00	4	0	0	7	10	2	4	0	0	2	0
vs. PIT	0	0	—	5.87	5	0	0	7.2	5	6	4	0	0	0	0

STARTING PITCHER

Charts: WINS (AL AVG), ERA (AL AVG), SO/9 (AL AVG), RATIO (AL AVG)

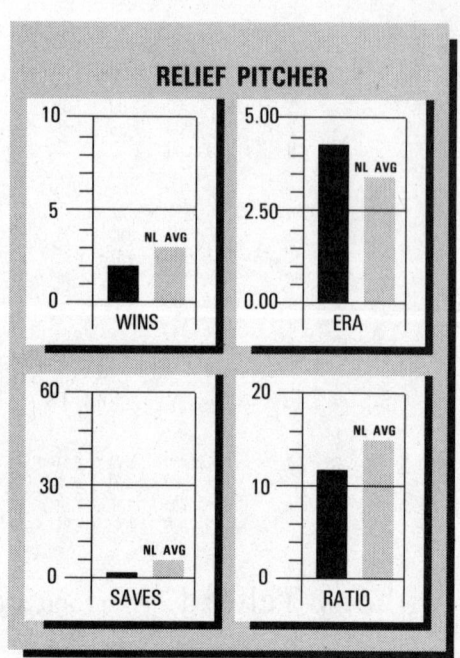

RELIEF PITCHER

Charts: WINS (NL AVG), ERA (NL AVG), SAVES (NL AVG), RATIO (NL AVG)

Year	Team		W	L	%	ERA	G	GS	CG	IP	H	BB	SO	ShO	W	L	SV	AB	H	HR	BA	PO	A	E	DP	TC/G	FA

Scott Terry *Continued*

Year	Team		W	L	%	ERA	G	GS	CG	IP	H	BB	SO	ShO	W	L	SV	AB	H	HR	BA	PO	A	E	DP	TC/G	FA
1986	CIN	N	1	2	.333	6.14	28	3	0	55.2	66	32	32	0	1	1	0	4	1	0	.250	2	9	1	2	0.4	.917
1987	STL	N	0	0	—	3.38	11	0	0	13.1	13	8	9	0	0	0	0	2	0	0	.000	0	4	0	0	0.4	1.000
1988			9	6	.600	2.92	51	11	1	129.1	119	34	65	0	2	3	3	28	7	0	.250	7	22	0	1	0.6	1.000
1989			8	10	.444	3.57	31	24	1	148.2	142	43	69	0	0	0	2	45	7	2	.156	6	33	2	2	1.3	.951
1990			2	6	.250	4.75	50	2	0	72	75	27	35	0	2	5	2	11	5	0	.455	3	14	1	0	0.4	.944
5 yrs.			20	24	.455	3.91	171	40	2	419	415	144	210	0	5	9	7	90	20	2	.222	18	82	4	5	0.6	.962

Bob Tewksbury

TEWKSBURY, ROBERT ALAN
B. Nov. 30, 1960, Concord, N. H.
BR TR 6′ 4″ 200 lbs.

	W	L	%	ERA	G	GS	CG	IP	H	BB	SO	ShO	W	L	SV	AB	H	HR	BA	PO	A	E	DP	TC/G	FA
April	0	0	—	6.35	6	6	0	11.1	19	4	2	0	0	0	0								1		
May	0	0	—	3.00	2	2	0	3	2	0	2	0	0	0	0								0		
June	3	0	1.000	2.91	3	3	0	21.2	18	2	7	0	0	0	0								0		
July	2	3	.400	2.25	5	5	0	32	33	5	13	0	0	0	0								0		
Aug	4	1	.800	1.60	6	6	3	45	38	2	12	2	0	0	0								0		
Sept/Oct	1	5	.167	6.68	6	6	0	32.1	41	2	14	0	0	0	0								0		
Day	4	3	.571	4.04	8	7	1	49	46	6	22	1	0	0	0								0		
Night	6	6	.500	3.18	20	13	2	96.1	105	9	28	0	0	0	0								1		
vs. Left	—	—	—	—	—	—	—		93	13	22	—	—	—	—										
vs. Right	—	—	—	—	—	—	—		58	2	28	—	—	—	—										
On Grass	3	2	.600	3.53	8	6	0	43.1	47	8	17	0	0	0	0										
On Turf	7	7	.500	3.44	20	14	3	102	104	7	33	2	0	0	1										
Home	4	5	.444	3.66	13	9	1	66.1	64	5	22	1	0	0	0										
Road	6	4	.600	3.30	15	11	2	79	87	10	28	1	0	0	1										
Division Rivals																									
vs. CHI	2	0	1.000	4.26	3	3	0	19	21	2	8	0	0	0	0										
vs. MON	1	1	.500	4.50	3	2	0	14	17	0	4	0	0	0	0										
vs. NY	0	2	.000	6.75	2	2	0	10.2	18	1	5	0	0	0	0										
vs. PHI	1	1	.500	8.10	4	2	0	13.1	24	2	3	0	0	0	1										
vs. PIT	2	2	.500	2.73	5	4	1	29.2	27	1	11	1	0	0	0										

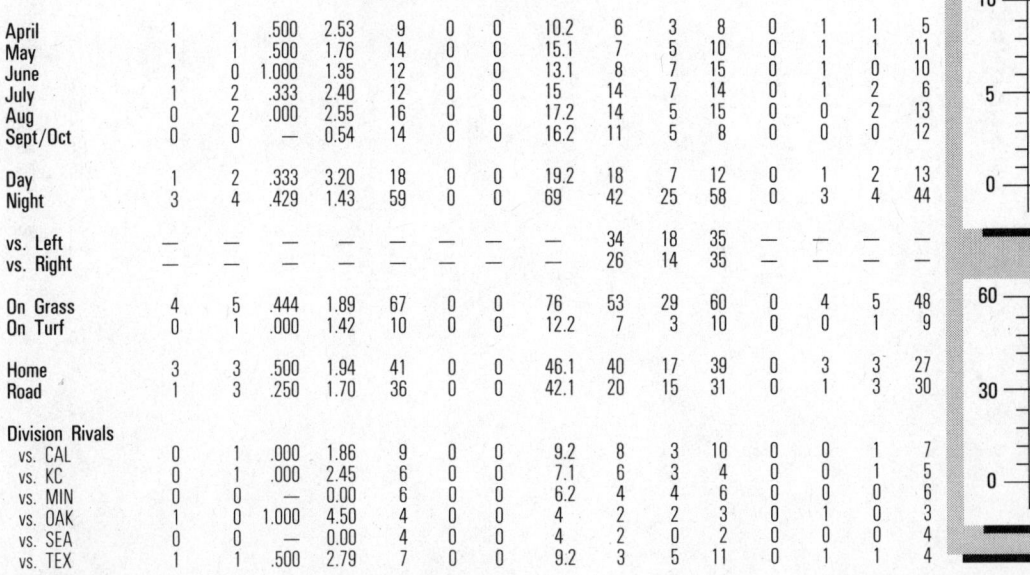

STARTING PITCHER

(bar charts: WINS NL AVG; ERA NL AVG; SO/9 NL AVG; RATIO NL AVG)

Year	Team		W	L	%	ERA	G	GS	CG	IP	H	BB	SO	ShO	W	L	SV	AB	H	HR	BA	PO	A	E	DP	TC/G	FA
1986	NY	A	9	5	.643	3.31	23	20	2	130.1	144	31	49	0	0	0	0	0	0	0	—	7	29	1	2	1.6	.973
1987	2 teams		NY A (8G 1 – 4)			CHI N (7G 0 – 4)																					
"	total		1	8	.111	6.66	15	9	0	51.1	79	20	22	0	0	0	1	0	5	0	0	.000	3	6	1	1	0.7	.900
1988	CHI	N	0	0	—	8.10	1	1	0	3.1	6	2	1	0	0	0	0	2	0	0	.000	0	1	0	0	1.0	1.000
1989	STL	N	1	0	1.000	3.30	7	4	1	30	25	10	17	1	0	0	0	9	1	0	.111	1	3	0	0	0.6	1.000
1990			10	9	.526	3.47	28	20	3	145.1	151	15	50	2	0	0	1	41	7	0	.171	6	20	1	2	1.0	.963
5 yrs.			21	22	.488	3.90	74	54	6	360.1	405	78	139	3	0	1	1	57	8	0	.140	17	59	3	5	1.1	.962

Bobby Thigpen

THIGPEN, ROBERT THOMAS
B. July 17, 1963, Tallahassee, Fla.
BR TR 6′ 3″ 195 lbs.

	W	L	%	ERA	G	GS	CG	IP	H	BB	SO	ShO	W	L	SV
April	1	1	.500	2.53	9	0	0	10.2	6	3	8	0	1	1	5
May	1	1	.500	1.76	14	0	0	15.1	7	5	10	0	1	1	11
June	1	0	1.000	1.35	12	0	0	13.1	8	7	15	0	1	0	10
July	1	2	.333	2.40	12	0	0	15	14	7	14	0	1	2	6
Aug	0	2	.000	2.55	16	0	0	17.2	14	5	15	0	0	2	13
Sept/Oct	0	0	—	0.54	14	0	0	16.2	11	5	8	0	0	0	12
Day	1	2	.333	3.20	18	0	0	19.2	18	7	12	0	1	2	13
Night	3	4	.429	1.43	59	0	0	69	42	25	58	0	3	4	44
vs. Left	—	—	—	—	—	—	—		34	18	35	—	—	—	
vs. Right	—	—	—	—	—	—	—		26	14	35	—	—	—	
On Grass	4	5	.444	1.89	67	0	0	76	53	29	60	0	4	5	48
On Turf	0	1	.000	1.42	10	0	0	12.2	7	3	10	0	0	1	9
Home	3	3	.500	1.94	41	0	0	46.1	40	17	39	0	3	3	27
Road	1	3	.250	1.70	36	0	0	42.1	20	15	31	0	1	3	30
Division Rivals															
vs. CAL	0	1	.000	1.86	9	0	0	9.2	8	3	10	0	0	1	7
vs. KC	0	1	.000	2.45	6	0	0	7.1	6	3	6	0	0	1	5
vs. MIN	0	0	—	0.00	6	0	0	6.2	4	4	6	0	0	0	6
vs. OAK	1	0	1.000	4.50	4	0	0	4	2	2	3	0	1	0	3
vs. SEA	0	0	—	0.00	4	0	0	4	2	0	2	0	0	0	4
vs. TEX	1	1	.500	2.79	7	0	0	9.2	3	5	11	0	1	1	4

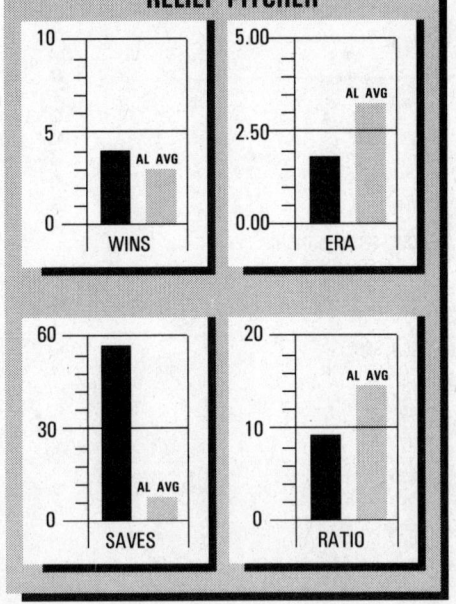

RELIEF PITCHER

(bar charts: WINS AL AVG; ERA AL AVG; SAVES AL AVG; RATIO AL AVG)

Year	Team	W	L	%	ERA	G	GS	CG	IP	H	BB	SO	ShO	RELIEF PITCHING W	L	SV	BATTING AB	H	HR	BA	PO	A	E	DP	TC/G	FA

Bobby Thigpen *Continued*

Year	Team	W	L	%	ERA	G	GS	CG	IP	H	BB	SO	ShO	W	L	SV	AB	H	HR	BA	PO	A	E	DP	TC/G	FA
1986	CHI A	2	0	1.000	1.77	20	0	0	35.2	26	12	20	0	2	0	7	0	0	0	—	2	4	0	1	0.3	1.000
1987		7	5	.583	2.73	51	0	0	89	86	24	52	0	7	5	16	0	0	0	—	8	14	2	1	0.5	.917
1988		5	8	.385	3.30	68	0	0	90	96	33	62	0	5	**8**	34	0	0	0	—	5	11	0	2	0.2	1.000
1989		2	6	.250	3.76	61	0	0	79	62	40	47	0	2	6	34	0	0	0	—	7	7	0	0	0.2	1.000
1990		4	6	.400	1.83	**77**	0	0	88.2	60	32	70	0	4	6	57[1]	0	0	0	—	10	8	1	2	0.2	.947
5 yrs.		20	25	.444	2.78	277	0	0	382.1	330	141	251	0	20	25	148	0	0	0	—	32	44	3	6	0.3	.962

Rich Thompson

THOMPSON, RICHARD NEIL
B. Nov. 1, 1958, New York, N. Y.
BB TR 6′ 3″ 225 lbs.

Year	Team	W	L	%	ERA	G	GS	CG	IP	H	BB	SO	ShO	W	L	SV	AB	H	HR	BA	PO	A	E	DP	TC/G	FA
1985	CLE A	3	8	.273	6.30	57	0	0	80	95	48	30	0	3	8	5	0	0	0	—	2	7	3	1	0.2	.750
1989	MON N	0	2	.000	2.18	19	1	0	33	27	11	15	0	0	1	0	2	0	0	.000	0	4	0	0	0.2	1.000
1990		0	0	—	0.00	1	0	0	1	1	0	0	0	0	0	0	0	0	0	.000	0	0	0	0	0.0	—
3 yrs.		3	10	.231	5.05	77	1	0	114	123	59	45	0	3	9	5	2	0	0	.000	2	11	3	1	0.2	.813

Mark Thurmond

THURMOND, MARK ANTHONY
B. Sept. 12, 1956, Houston, Tex.
BL TL 6′ 190 lbs.

RELIEF PITCHER

	W	L	%	ERA	G	GS	CG	IP	H	BB	SO	ShO	W	L	SV
April	—		—	—	0	0	0	0	0	0	0	—	0	0	0
May	1	0	1.000	2.55	12	0	0	17.2	14	3	9	0	1	0	0
June	0	2	.000	3.94	12	0	0	16	18	3	5	0	0	2	2
July	1	0	1.000	2.35	7	0	0	7.2	7	3	4	0	1	0	0
Aug	0	1	.000	3.86	11	0	0	14	10	8	6	0	0	1	2
Sept/Oct	0	0	—	6.75	1	0	0	1.1	4	1	0	0	0	0	0
Day	0	2	.000	3.43	17	0	0	21	21	7	11	0	0	2	1
Night	2	1	.667	3.28	26	0	0	35.2	32	11	13	0	2	1	3
vs. Left	—	—	—	—	—	—	—	—	14	6	8	—	—	—	—
vs. Right	—	—	—	—	—	—	—	—	39	12	16	—	—	—	—
On Grass	2	1	.667	3.72	28	0	0	38.2	39	11	15	0	2	1	3
On Turf	0	2	.000	2.50	15	0	0	18	14	7	9	0	0	2	1
Home	2	1	.667	3.00	23	0	0	27	22	7	10	0	2	1	1
Road	0	2	.000	3.64	20	0	0	29.2	31	11	14	0	0	2	3
Division Rivals															
vs. ATL	0	0	—	6.75	3	0	0	5.1	7	1	2	0	0	0	1
vs. CIN	1	1	.500	0.00	4	0	0	6	3	2	3	0	1	1	0
vs. HOU	0	0	—	1.13	7	0	0	8	8	5	4	0	0	0	0
vs. LA	0	0	—	6.75	2	0	0	2.2	4	1	1	0	0	0	1
vs. SD	0	0	—	0.00	3	0	0	5	2	0	1	0	0	0	1

Year	Team	W	L	%	ERA	G	GS	CG	IP	H	BB	SO	ShO	W	L	SV	AB	H	HR	BA	PO	A	E	DP	TC/G	FA
1983	SD N	7	3	.700	2.65	21	18	2	115.1	104	33	49	0	0	0	0	37	2	0	.054	7	22	0	0	1.4	1.000
1984		14	8	.636	2.97	32	29	1	178.2	174	55	57	1	0	0	1	58	11	0	.190	11	38	0	3	1.5	1.000
1985		7	11	.389	3.97	36	23	1	138.1	154	44	57	1	1	1	2	34	3	0	.088	8	27	1	2	1.0	.972
1986	2 teams	SD N (17G 3 - 7)					DET A (25G 4 - 1)																			
"	total	7	8	.467	4.56	42	19	2	122.1	140	44	49	1	2	0	3	24	6	0	.250	10	15	0	0	0.6	1.000
1987	DET A	0	1	.000	4.23	48	0	0	61.2	83	24	21	0	0	1	5	0	0	0	—	2	9	0	0	0.2	1.000
1988	BAL A	1	8	.111	4.58	43	6	0	74.2	80	27	29	0	1	2	3	0	0	0	—	3	8	1	0	0.3	.917
1989		2	4	.333	3.90	49	2	0	90	102	17	34	0	2	3	4	0	0	0	—	4	10	0	0	0.3	1.000
1990	SF N	2	3	.400	3.34	43	0	0	56.2	53	18	24	0	2	3	4	5	0	0	.000	4	15	1	2	0.5	.950
8 yrs.		40	46	.465	3.69	314	97	6	837.2	890	262	320	3	8	11	21	158	22	0	.139	49	144	3	7	0.6	.985

LEAGUE CHAMPIONSHIP SERIES

Year	Team	W	L	%	ERA	G	GS	CG	IP	H	BB	SO	ShO	W	L	SV	AB	H	HR	BA	PO	A	E	DP	TC/G	FA
1984	SD N	0	1	.000	9.82	1	1	0	3.2	7	2	1	0	0	0	0	1	1	0	1.000	0	1	0	0	1.0	1.000
1987	DET A	0	0	—	0.00	1	0	0	0.1	0	0	0	0	0	0	0	0	0	0	—	0	0	0	0	0.0	—
2 yrs.		0	1	.000	9.00	2	1	0	4	7	2	1	0	0	0	0	1	1	0	1.000	0	1	0	0	0.5	1.000

WORLD SERIES

Year	Team	W	L	%	ERA	G	GS	CG	IP	H	BB	SO	ShO	W	L	SV	AB	H	HR	BA	PO	A	E	DP	TC/G	FA
1984	SD N	0	1	.000	10.13	2	2	0	5.1	12	3	2	0	0	0	0	0	0	0	—	0	2	0	0	1.0	1.000

Year	Team	W	L	%	ERA	G	GS	CG	IP	H	BB	SO	ShO	RELIEF PITCHING W	L	SV	BATTING AB	H	HR	BA	PO	A	E	DP	TC/G	FA

Jay Tibbs

TIBBS, JAY LINDSEY
B. Jan. 4, 1962, Birmingham, Ala.
BR TR 6' 3" 185 lbs.

Year	Team	W	L	%	ERA	G	GS	CG	IP	H	BB	SO	ShO	W	L	SV	AB	H	HR	BA	PO	A	E	DP	TC/G	FA
1984	CIN N	6	2	.750	2.86	14	14	3	100.2	87	33	40	1	0	0	0	36	5	0	.139	6	10	1	1	1.2	.941
1985		10	16	.385	3.92	35	34	5	218	216	83	98	2	0	1	0	65	6	0	.092	15	40	3	4	1.7	.948
1986	MON N	7	9	.438	3.97	35	31	3	190.1	181	70	117	2	0	0	0	54	7	0	.130	14	24	0	2	1.1	1.000
1987		4	5	.444	4.99	19	12	0	83	95	34	54	0	0	0	0	25	3	0	.120	7	8	0	1	0.8	1.000
1988	BAL A	4	15	.211	5.39	30	24	1	158.2	184	63	82	0	0	0	0	0	0	0	—	17	18	0	0	1.2	1.000
1989		5	0	1.000	2.82	10	8	1	54.1	62	20	30	0	0	0	0	0	0	0	—	5	5	0	0	1.0	1.000
1990	2 teams	BAL A	(10G 2 - 7)		PIT N	(5G 1 - 0)																				
"	total	3	7	.300	5.31	15	10	0	57.2	62	16	27	0	1	0	0	0	0	0	—	7	9	0	0	1.1	1.000
7 yrs.		39	54	.419	4.20	158	133	13	862.2	887	319	448	5	1	2	180	21	0		.117	71	114	4	8	1.2	.979

Randy Tomlin

TOMLIN, RANDY LEON
B. June 14, 1966, Bainbridge, Md.
BL TL 5' 11" 179 lbs.

Year	Team	W	L	%	ERA	G	GS	CG	IP	H	BB	SO	ShO	W	L	SV	AB	H	HR	BA	PO	A	E	DP	TC/G	FA
1990	PIT N	4	4	.500	2.55	12	12	2	77.2	62	12	42	0	0	0	0	25	1	0	.040	1	19	0	0	1.7	1.000

John Tudor

TUDOR, JOHN THOMAS
B. Feb. 2, 1954, Schenectady, N. Y.
BL TL 6' 185 lbs.

	W	L	%	ERA	G	GS	CG	IP	H	BB	SO	ShO	W	L	SV	AB	H	HR	BA	PO	A	E	DP	TC/G	FA
April	4	0	1.000	0.96	4	4	0	28	19	7	8	0	0	0	0										
May	1	2	.333	4.67	5	5	0	27	30	4	10	0	0	0	0										
June	1	1	.500	3.19	5	5	0	31	36	7	14	0	0	0	0										
July	4	0	1.000	1.98	5	5	1	36.1	21	9	16	1	0	0	0										
Aug	1	0	1.000	0.00	2	2	0	10	5	1	10	0	0	0	0										
Sept/Oct	1	1	.500	1.93	4	3	0	14	9	2	5	0	1	0	0										
Day	2	1	.667	1.48	5	4	0	30.1	17	6	13	0	0	0	0										
Night	10	3	.769	2.64	20	18	1	116	103	24	50	1	1	0	0										
vs. Left	—	—	—	—	—	—	—	—	28	5	24	—	—	—	—										
vs. Right	—	—	—	—	—	—	—	—	92	25	39	—	—	—	—										
On Grass	4	2	.667	3.44	6	5	0	34	32	7	11	0	1	0	0										
On Turf	8	2	.800	2.08	19	17	1	112.1	88	23	52	1	0	0	0										
Home	4	1	.800	2.52	12	11	1	75	62	17	32	1	0	0	0										
Road	8	3	.727	2.27	13	11	0	71.1	58	13	31	0	1	0	0										
Division Rivals																										
vs. CHI	2	0	1.000	0.00	2	1	1	13	8	1	3	1	1	0	0										
vs. MON	0	0	—	0.00	2	0	0	4	2	0	1	0	0	0	0										
vs. NY	1	1	.500	2.25	3	3	0	20	19	4	9	0	0	0	0										
vs. PHI	2	0	1.000	0.90	3	3	0	20	13	6	10	0	0	0	0										
vs. PIT	2	0	1.000	1.93	4	4	0	23.1	17	6	14	0	0	0	0										

STARTING PITCHER

(Bar charts: WINS, ERA, SO/9, RATIO — each compared to NL AVG)

Year	Team	W	L	%	ERA	G	GS	CG	IP	H	BB	SO	ShO	W	L	SV	AB	H	HR	BA	PO	A	E	DP	TC/G	FA
1979	BOS A	1	2	.333	6.43	6	6	1	28	39	9	11	0	0	0	0	0	0	0	—	1	7	0	1	1.3	1.000
1980		8	5	.615	3.03	16	13	5	92	81	31	45	0	0	1	0	0	0	0	—	5	24	1	1	1.9	.967
1981		4	3	.571	4.56	18	11	2	79	74	28	44	0	1	1	1	0	0	0	—	2	17	0	1	1.1	1.000
1982		13	10	.565	3.63	32	30	6	195.2	215	59	146	1	0	0	0	0	0	0	—	5	39	2	4	1.4	.957
1983		13	12	.520	4.09	34	34	7	242	236	81	136	2	0	0	0	0	0	0	—	12	26	2	4	1.2	.950
1984	PIT N	12	11	.522	3.27	32	32	6	212	200	56	117	0	0	0	0	76	16	0	.211	11	31	0	0	1.3	1.000
1985	STL N	21	8	.724	1.93	36	36	14	275	209	49	169	10	0	0	0	94	13	0	.138	18	45	3	4	1.8	.955
1986		13	7	.650	2.92	30	30	3	219	197	53	107	0	0	0	0	72	11	0	.153	10	41	2	4	1.8	.962
1987		10	2	.833	3.84	16	16	0	96	100	32	54	0	0	0	0	35	7	0	.200	4	20	0	2	1.5	1.000
1988	2 teams	STL N	(21G 6 - 5)		LA N	(9G 4 - 3)																				
"	total	10	8	.556	2.32	30	30	5	197.2	189	41	87	1	0	0	0	59	5	0	.085	6	32	0	4	1.3	1.000
1989	LA N	0	0	—	3.14	6	3	0	14.1	17	6	9	0	0	0	0	2	0	0	.000	0	3	0	0	0.5	1.000
1990	STL N	12	4	.750	2.40	25	22	1	146.1	120	30	63	1	1	0	0	46	7	0	.152	10	29	1	2	1.6	.975
12 yrs.		117	72	.619	3.12	281	263	50	1797	1677	475	988	16	2	2	1	384	59	0	.154	84	314	11	27	1.5	.973

LEAGUE CHAMPIONSHIP SERIES

Year	Team	W	L	%	ERA	G	GS	CG	IP	H	BB	SO	ShO	W	L	SV	AB	H	HR	BA	PO	A	E	DP	TC/G	FA
1985	STL N	1	1	.500	2.84	2	2	0	12.2	10	3	8	0	0	0	0	4	0	0	.000	0	1	0	0	0.5	1.000
1987		1	1	.500	1.76	2	2	0	15.1	16	5	12	0	0	0	0	4	0	0	.000	0	4	0	0	2.0	1.000
1988	LA N	0	0	—	7.20	1	1	0	5	8	1	1	0	0	0	0	2	0	0	.000	1	2	0	0	3.0	1.000
3 yrs.		2	2	.500	3.00	5	5	0	33	34	9	21	0	0	0	0	10	0	0	.000	1	7	0	0	1.6	1.000

Year	Team	W	L	%	ERA	G	GS	CG	IP	H	BB	SO	ShO	RELIEF PITCHING W	L	SV	BATTING AB	H	HR	BA	PO	A	E	DP	TC/G	FA

John Tudor *Continued*

WORLD SERIES

Year	Team	W	L	%	ERA	G	GS	CG	IP	H	BB	SO	ShO	W	L	SV	AB	H	HR	BA	PO	A	E	DP	TC/G	FA
1985	STL N	2	1	.667	3.00	3	3	1	18	15	7	14	1	0	0	0	5	0	0	.000	0	3	0	0	1.0	1.000
1987		1	1	.500	5.73	2	2	0	11	15	3	8	0	0	0	0	2	0	0	.000	0	4	0	0	2.0	1.000
1988	LA N	0	0	—	0.00	1	1	0	1.1	0	0	0	1	0	0	0	0	0	0	—	0	0	0	0	0.0	—
3 yrs.		3	2	.600	3.86	6	6	1	30.1	30	10	23	1	0	0	0	7	0	0	.000	0	7	0	0	1.2	1.000

Efrain Valdez

VALDEZ, EFRAIN ANTONIO
B. June 11, 1966, Nizao Bani, Dominican Republic
BL TL 5′ 11″ 180 lbs.

Year	Team	W	L	%	ERA	G	GS	CG	IP	H	BB	SO	ShO	W	L	SV	AB	H	HR	BA	PO	A	E	DP	TC/G	FA
1990	CLE A	1	1	.500	3.04	13	0	0	23.2	20	14	13	0	1	1	0	0	0	0	—	2	3	1	0	0.5	.833

Rafael Valdez

VALDEZ, RAFAEL EMILIO
Born Rafael Emilio Valdez y Diaz.
B. Dec. 17, 1967, Nizao Bani, Puerto Rico
BR TR 5′ 11″ 165 lbs.

Year	Team	W	L	%	ERA	G	GS	CG	IP	H	BB	SO	ShO	W	L	SV	AB	H	HR	BA	PO	A	E	DP	TC/G	FA
1990	SD N	0	1	.000	11.12	3	0	0	5.2	11	2	3	0	0	1	0	1	0	0	.000	0	0	0	0	0.0	—

Sergio Valdez

VALDEZ, SERGIO
Born Sergio Sanchez y Valdez.
B. Sept. 7, 1964, Elias Pina, Dominican Republic
BR TR 6′ 165 lbs.

	W	L	%	ERA	G	GS	CG	IP	H	BB	SO	ShO	W	L	SV
April	0	0	—	6.75	6	0	0	5.1	6	3	3	0	0	0	0
May	1	1	.500	4.29	6	2	0	21	22	6	14	0	0	0	0
June	1	3	.250	6.91	9	2	0	28.2	30	12	21	0	1	1	0
July	0	1	.000	19.29	1	1	0	2.1	5	0	1	0	0	0	0
Aug	0	0	—	2.53	2	2	0	10.2	16	5	4	0	0	0	0
Sept/Oct	4	1	.800	3.18	6	6	0	39.2	36	12	23	0	0	0	0
Day	1	2	.333	7.30	9	4	0	24.2	32	8	17	0	0	0	0
Night	5	4	.556	4.12	21	9	0	83	83	30	49	0	1	1	0
vs. Left	—	—	—	—	—	—	—	40	21	29	—	—	—	—	
vs. Right	—	—	—	—	—	—	—	75	17	37	—	—	—	—	
On Grass	4	6	.400	5.26	24	10	0	87.1	94	30	57	0	1	1	0
On Turf	2	0	1.000	3.10	6	3	0	20.1	21	8	9	0	0	0	0
Home	3	2	.600	3.49	16	5	0	56.2	56	14	34	0	1	0	0
Road	3	4	.429	6.35	14	8	0	51	59	24	32	0	0	1	0
Division Rivals															
vs. BAL	0	2	.000	2.87	5	2	0	15.2	11	13	11	0	0	1	0
vs. BOS	1	1	.500	4.50	3	2	0	18	25	4	11	0	1	0	0
vs. DET	0	1	.000	5.23	2	1	0	10.1	8	4	4	0	0	0	0
vs. MIL	1	0	1.000	7.15	3	1	0	11.1	15	3	6	0	0	0	0
vs. NY	—	—	—	—	0	—	—	0	0	0	0	—	0	0	
vs. TOR	—	—	—	—	0	—	—	0	0	0	0	—	0	0	

STARTING PITCHER

Year	Team	W	L	%	ERA	G	GS	CG	IP	H	BB	SO	ShO	W	L	SV	AB	H	HR	BA	PO	A	E	DP	TC/G	FA
1986	MON N	0	4	.000	6.84	5	5	0	25	39	11	20	0	0	0	0	8	1	0	.125	3	1	1	1	1.0	.800
1989	ATL N	1	2	.333	6.06	19	1	0	32.2	31	17	26	0	1	1	0	1	1	0	1.000	2	2	0	0	0.2	1.000
1990	2 teams	ATL N (6G 0 – 0)			CLE A (24G 6 – 6)																					
"	total	6	6	.500	4.85	30	13	0	107.2	115	38	66	0	1	1	0	0	0	0	—	10	12	2	1	0.8	.917
3 yrs.		7	12	.368	5.39	54	19	0	165.1	185	66	112	0	2	2	0	9	2	0	.222	15	15	3	2	0.6	.909

Fernando Valenzuela

VALENZUELA, FERNANDO
Born Fernando Valenzuela y Anguamea.
B. Nov. 1, 1960, Navajoa, Mexico
BL TL 5′ 11″ 180 lbs.

Year	Team	W	L	%	ERA	G	GS	CG	IP	H	BB	SO	ShO	RELIEF PITCHING W	L	SV	BATTING AB	H	HR	BA	PO	A	E	DP	TC/G	FA
April		1	2	.333	3.12	4	4	1	26	23	7	17	1	0	0	0										
May		3	2	.600	4.79	6	6	1	35.2	39	16	17	0	0	0	0										
June		2	2	.500	3.21	6	6	1	42	35	17	31	1	0	0	0										
July		2	2	.500	4.73	5	5	0	32.1	39	9	17	0	0	0	0										
Aug		4	2	.667	3.79	6	6	1	38	39	14	21	0	0	0	0										
Sept/Oct		1	3	.250	8.40	6	6	1	30	48	14	12	0	0	0	0										
Day		1	2	.333	6.88	3	3	0	17	22	6	12	0	0	0	0										
Night		12	11	.522	4.38	30	30	5	187	201	71	103	2	0	0	0										
vs. Left		—	—	—	—	—	—	—	—	41	15	19	—	—	—	—										
vs. Right		—	—	—	—	—	—	—	—	182	62	96	—	—	—	—										
On Grass		10	9	.526	4.46	25	25	3	155.1	166	57	96	0	0	0	0										
On Turf		3	4	.429	4.99	8	8	2	48.2	57	20	19	0	0	0	0										
Home		8	5	.615	3.75	18	18	3	117.2	117	44	61	2	0	0	0										
Road		5	8	.385	5.73	15	15	2	86.1	106	33	54	0	0	0	0										
Division Rivals																										
vs. ATL		0	1	.000	12.19	2	2	0	10.1	20	4	8	0	0	0	0										
vs. CIN		2	3	.400	5.40	5	5	2	33.1	41	13	15	0	0	0	0										
vs. HOU		1	1	.500	5.64	4	4	0	22.1	28	10	13	0	0	0	0										
vs. SD		0	1	.000	3.47	4	4	0	23.1	27	9	19	0	0	0	0										
vs. SF		1	3	.250	5.32	4	4	0	22	23	8	18	0	0	0	0										
1980	LA N	2	0	1.000	0.00	10	0	0	18	8	5	16	0	2	0	1	1	0	0	.000	0	3	0	1	0.3	1.000
1981		13	7	.650	2.48	25	**25**	**11**	192	140	61	**180**	8	0	0	0	64	16	0	.250	12	33	3	2	1.9	.938
1982		19	13	.594	2.87	37	37	18	285	247	83	199	4	0	0	0	95	16	1	.168	20	64	2	4	2.3	.977
1983		15	10	.600	3.75	35	35	9	257	245	99	189	4	0	0	0	91	17	1	.187	20	54	2	5	2.2	.974
1984		12	17	.414	3.03	34	34	12	261	218	**106**	240	2	0	0	0	79	15	3	.190	21	48	2	4	2.1	.972
1985		17	10	.630	2.45	35	35	14	272.1	211	101	208	5	0	0	0	97	21	1	.216	18	45	0	1	1.8	1.000
1986		**21**	11	.656	3.14	34	34	**20**	269.1	226	85	242	3	0	0	0	109	24	0	.220	29	47	1	2	2.3	.987
1987		14	14	.500	3.98	34	34	**12**	251	**254**	**124**	190	1	0	0	0	92	13	1	.141	15	53	4	2	2.1	.944
1988		5	8	.385	4.24	23	22	3	142.1	142	76	64	0	0	0	1	44	8	0	.182	6	38	1	2	2.0	.978
1989		10	13	.435	3.43	31	31	3	196.2	185	98	116	0	0	0	0	66	12	0	.182	18	35	5	4	1.9	.914
1990		13	13	.500	4.59	33	33	5	204	223	77	115	2	0	0	0	69	21	1	.304	5	31	3	2	1.2	.923
11 yrs.		141	116	.549	3.31	331	320	107	2348.2	2099	915	1759	29	2	0	2	807	163	8	.202	164	451	23	28	1.9	.964
DIVISIONAL PLAYOFF SERIES																										
1981	LA N	1	0	1.000	1.06	2	2	1	17	10	3	10	0	0	0	0	4	0	0	.000	0	0	0	0	0.0	—
LEAGUE CHAMPIONSHIP SERIES																										
1981	LA N	1	1	.500	2.45	2	2	1	14.2	10	5	10	0	0	0	0	5	0	0	.000	0	2	0	0	1.0	1.000
1983		1	0	1.000	1.13	1	1	0	8	7	4	5	0	0	0	0	3	0	0	.000	1	0	0	0	1.0	1.000
1985		1	0	1.000	1.88	2	2	0	14.1	11	10	13	0	0	0	0	5	1	0	.200	1	3	1	0	2.5	.800
3 yrs.		3	1	.750	1.95	5	5	0	37	28	19	28	0	0	0	0	13	1	0	.077	2	5	1	0	1.6	.875
WORLD SERIES																										
1981	LA N	1	0	1.000	4.00	1	1	1	9	9	7	6	0	0	0	0	3	0	0	.000	0	1	0	0	1.0	1.000

Julio Valera

VALERA, JULIO ENRIQUE
B. Oct. 13, 1968, San Sebastian, Puerto Rico
BR TR 6′ 2″ 185 lbs.

Year	Team	W	L	%	ERA	G	GS	CG	IP	H	BB	SO	ShO	RELIEF PITCHING W	L	SV	BATTING AB	H	HR	BA	PO	A	E	DP	TC/G	FA
1990	NY N	1	1	.500	6.92	3	3	0	13	20	7	4	0	0	0	0	5	1	0	.200	1	0	1	0	0.7	.500

STARTING PITCHER

WINS (NL AVG) · ERA (NL AVG) · SO/9 (NL AVG) · RATIO (NL AVG)

Year	Team	W	L	%	ERA	G	GS	CG	IP	H	BB	SO	ShO	RELIEF W	PITCHING L	SV	BATTING AB	H	HR	BA	PO	A	E	DP	TC/G	FA

Randy Veres

VERES, RANDOLPH RUHLAND
B. Nov. 25, 1965, San Francisco, Calif.
BR TR 6′ 3″ 190 lbs.

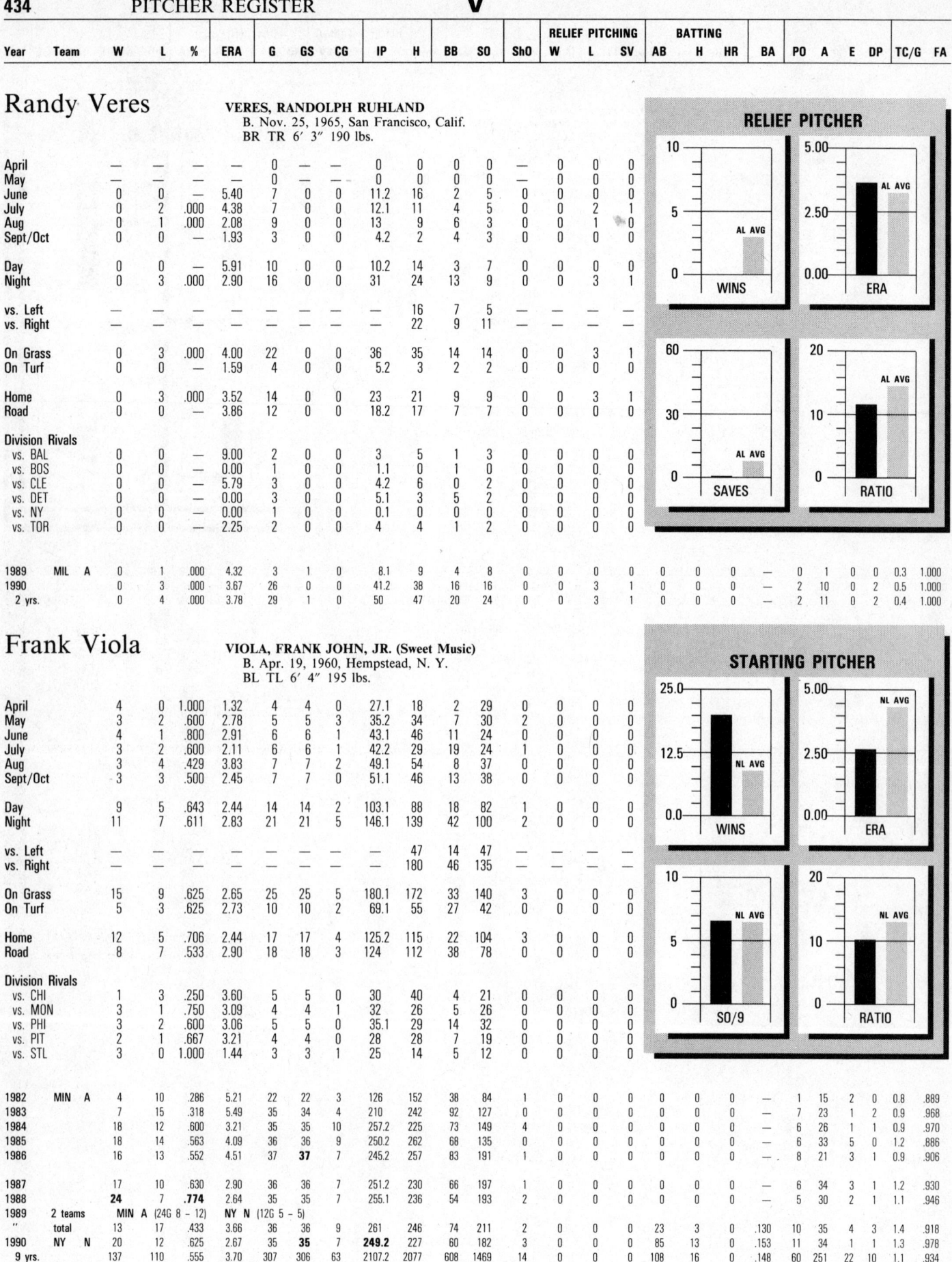

RELIEF PITCHER — WINS (AL AVG), ERA (AL AVG), SAVES (AL AVG), RATIO (AL AVG)

		W	L	%	ERA	G	GS	CG	IP	H	BB	SO	ShO	W	L	SV
April		—	—	—	—	0	—	—	0	0	0	0	—	0	0	0
May		—	—	—	—	0	—	—	0	0	0	0	—	0	0	0
June		0	0	—	5.40	7	0	0	11.2	16	2	5	0	0	0	0
July		0	2	.000	4.38	7	0	0	12.1	11	4	5	0	0	2	1
Aug		0	1	.000	2.08	9	0	0	13	9	6	3	0	0	1	0
Sept/Oct		0	0	—	1.93	3	0	0	4.2	2	4	3	0	0	0	0
Day		0	0	—	5.91	10	0	0	10.2	14	3	7	0	0	0	0
Night		0	3	.000	2.90	16	0	0	31	24	13	9	0	0	3	1
vs. Left		—	—	—	—	—	—	—	—	16	7	5	—	—	—	—
vs. Right		—	—	—	—	—	—	—	—	22	9	11	—	—	—	—
On Grass		0	3	.000	4.00	22	0	0	36	35	14	14	0	0	3	1
On Turf		0	0	—	1.59	4	0	0	5.2	3	2	2	0	0	0	0
Home		0	3	.000	3.52	14	0	0	23	21	9	9	0	0	3	1
Road		0	0	—	3.86	12	0	0	18.2	17	7	7	0	0	0	0
Division Rivals																
vs. BAL		0	0	—	9.00	2	0	0	3	5	1	3	0	0	0	0
vs. BOS		0	0	—	0.00	1	0	0	1.1	0	1	0	0	0	0	0
vs. CLE		0	0	—	5.79	4	0	0	4.2	6	0	2	0	0	0	0
vs. DET		0	0	—	0.00	3	0	0	5.1	3	5	2	0	0	0	0
vs. NY		0	0	—	0.00	1	0	0	0.1	0	1	0	0	0	0	0
vs. TOR		0	0	—	2.25	2	0	0	4	4	1	2	0	0	0	0

Year	Team	W	L	%	ERA	G	GS	CG	IP	H	BB	SO	ShO	W	L	SV	AB	H	HR	BA	PO	A	E	DP	TC/G	FA
1989	MIL A	0	1	.000	4.32	3	1	0	8.1	9	4	8	0	0	0	0	0	0	0	—	0	1	0	0	0.3	1.000
1990		0	3	.000	3.67	26	0	0	41.2	38	16	16	0	0	3	1	0	0	0	—	2	10	0	2	0.5	1.000
2 yrs.		0	4	.000	3.78	29	1	0	50	47	20	24	0	0	3	1	0	0	0	—	2	11	0	2	0.4	1.000

Frank Viola

VIOLA, FRANK JOHN, JR. (Sweet Music)
B. Apr. 19, 1960, Hempstead, N. Y.
BL TL 6′ 4″ 195 lbs.

STARTING PITCHER — WINS (NL AVG), ERA (NL AVG), SO/9 (NL AVG), RATIO (NL AVG)

		W	L	%	ERA	G	GS	CG	IP	H	BB	SO	ShO	W	L	SV
April		4	0	1.000	1.32	4	4	0	27.1	18	2	29	0	0	0	0
May		3	2	.600	2.78	5	5	3	35.2	34	7	30	2	0	0	0
June		4	1	.800	2.91	6	6	1	43.1	46	11	24	0	0	0	0
July		3	2	.600	2.11	6	6	1	42.2	29	19	24	1	0	0	0
Aug		3	4	.429	3.83	7	7	2	49.1	54	8	37	0	0	0	0
Sept/Oct		3	3	.500	2.45	7	7	0	51.1	46	13	38	0	0	0	0
Day		9	5	.643	2.44	14	14	2	103.1	88	18	82	1	0	0	0
Night		11	7	.611	2.83	21	21	5	146.1	139	42	100	2	0	0	0
vs. Left		—	—	—	—	—	—	—	—	47	14	47	—	—	—	—
vs. Right		—	—	—	—	—	—	—	—	180	46	135	—	—	—	—
On Grass		15	9	.625	2.65	25	25	5	180.1	172	33	140	3	0	0	0
On Turf		5	3	.625	2.73	10	10	2	69.1	55	27	42	0	0	0	0
Home		12	5	.706	2.44	17	17	4	125.2	115	22	104	3	0	0	0
Road		8	7	.533	2.90	18	18	3	124	112	38	78	0	0	0	0
Division Rivals																
vs. CHI		1	3	.250	3.60	5	5	0	30	40	4	21	0	0	0	0
vs. MON		3	1	.750	3.09	4	4	1	32	26	5	26	0	0	0	0
vs. PHI		3	2	.600	3.06	5	5	0	35.1	29	14	32	0	0	0	0
vs. PIT		2	1	.667	3.21	4	4	0	28	28	7	19	0	0	0	0
vs. STL		3	0	1.000	1.44	3	3	1	25	14	5	12	0	0	0	0

Year	Team	W	L	%	ERA	G	GS	CG	IP	H	BB	SO	ShO	W	L	SV	AB	H	HR	BA	PO	A	E	DP	TC/G	FA
1982	MIN A	4	10	.286	5.21	22	22	3	126	152	38	84	1	0	0	0	0	0	0	—	1	15	2	0	0.8	.889
1983		7	15	.318	5.49	35	34	4	210	242	92	127	0	0	0	0	0	0	0	—	7	23	1	2	0.9	.968
1984		18	12	.600	3.21	35	35	10	257.2	225	73	149	4	0	0	0	0	0	0	—	6	26	1	1	0.9	.970
1985		18	14	.563	4.09	36	36	9	250.2	262	68	135	0	0	0	0	0	0	0	—	6	33	5	0	1.2	.886
1986		16	13	.552	4.51	37	**37**	7	245.2	257	83	191	1	0	0	0	0	0	0	—	8	21	3	1	0.9	.906
1987		17	10	.630	2.90	36	36	7	251.2	230	66	197	1	0	0	0	0	0	0	—	6	34	3	1	1.2	.930
1988		**24**	7	**.774**	2.64	35	35	7	255.1	236	54	193	2	0	0	0	0	0	0	—	5	30	2	1	1.1	.946
1989	2 teams	MIN A (24G 8 - 12)		NY N (12G 5 - 5)																						
"	total	13	17	.433	3.66	36	36	9	261	246	74	211	2	0	0	0	23	3	0	.130	10	35	4	3	1.4	.918
1990	NY N	20	12	.625	2.67	35	**35**	7	**249.2**	227	60	182	3	0	0	0	85	13	0	.153	11	34	1	1	1.3	.978
9 yrs.		137	110	.555	3.70	307	306	63	2107.2	2077	608	1469	14	0	0	0	108	16	0	.148	60	251	22	10	1.1	.934

Year	Team		W	L	%	ERA	G	GS	CG	IP	H	BB	SO	ShO	W	L	SV	AB	H	HR	BA	PO	A	E	DP	TC/G	FA

Frank Viola *Continued*

LEAGUE CHAMPIONSHIP SERIES

Year	Team		W	L	%	ERA	G	GS	CG	IP	H	BB	SO	ShO	W	L	SV	AB	H	HR	BA	PO	A	E	DP	TC/G	FA
1987	MIN	A	1	0	1.000	5.25	2	2	0	12	14	5	9	0	0	0	0	0	0	0	—	0	1	0	0	0.5	1.000

WORLD SERIES

Year	Team		W	L	%	ERA	G	GS	CG	IP	H	BB	SO	ShO	W	L	SV	AB	H	HR	BA	PO	A	E	DP	TC/G	FA
1987	MIN	A	2	1	.667	3.72	3	3	0	19.1	17	3	16	0	0	0	0	1	0	0	.000	1	5	0	0	2.0	1.000

Ed Vosberg

VOSBERG, EDWARD JOHN
B. Sept. 28, 1961, Tucson, Ariz.
BL TL 6′ 1″ 190 lbs.

Year	Team		W	L	%	ERA	G	GS	CG	IP	H	BB	SO	ShO	W	L	SV	AB	H	HR	BA	PO	A	E	DP	TC/G	FA
1986	SD	N	0	1	.000	6.59	5	3	0	13.2	17	9	8	0	0	0	0	2	0	0	.000	0	1	1	0	0.4	.500
1990	SF	N	1	1	.500	5.55	18	0	0	24.1	21	12	12	0	1	1	0	0	0	0	—	1	5	0	0	0.3	1.000
2 yrs.			1	2	.333	5.92	23	3	0	38	38	21	20	0	1	1	0	2	0	0	.000	1	6	1	0	0.3	.875

Hector Wagner

WAGNER, HECTOR RAUL
B. Nov. 26, 1968, Santo Domingo, Dominican Republic
BR TR 6′ 3″ 185 lbs.

Year	Team		W	L	%	ERA	G	GS	CG	IP	H	BB	SO	ShO	W	L	SV	AB	H	HR	BA	PO	A	E	DP	TC/G	FA
1990	KC	A	0	2	.000	8.10	5	5	0	23.1	32	11	14	0	0	0	0	0	0	0	—	3	3	0	1	1.2	1.000

Bob Walk

WALK, ROBERT VERNON (Whirlybird)
B. Nov. 26, 1956, Van Nuys, Calif.
BR TR 6′ 3″ 185 lbs.

	W	L	%	ERA	G	GS	CG	IP	H	BB	SO	ShO	W	L	SV	AB	H	HR	BA	PO	A	E	DP	TC/G	FA
April	1	3	.250	3.92	4	4	0	20.2	27	6	11	0	0	0	0										
May	3	0	1.000	2.43	5	5	0	29.2	29	8	21	0	0	0	0										
June	0	1	.000	4.71	4	4	0	21	24	8	12	0	0	0	0										
July	1	0	1.000	4.34	4	4	0	18.2	17	5	7	0	0	0	0										
Aug	0	0	—	3.21	3	2	0	14	13	3	7	0	0	0	1										
Sept/Oct	2	1	.667	4.21	6	5	1	25.2	26	6	15	1	0	0	0										
Day	2	1	.667	4.73	8	7	1	40	42	11	19	1	0	0	1										
Night	5	4	.556	3.31	18	17	0	89.2	94	25	54	0	0	0	0										
vs. Left	—	—	—	—	—	—	—	—	78	26	36	—	—	—	—										
vs. Right	—	—	—	—	—	—	—	—	58	10	37	—	—	—	—										
On Grass	3	1	.750	3.12	6	5	0	26	26	6	15	0	0	0	1										
On Turf	4	4	.500	3.91	20	19	1	103.2	110	30	58	1	0	0	0										
Home	3	3	.500	3.90	11	11	0	60	63	17	31	0	0	0	0										
Road	4	2	.667	3.62	15	13	1	69.2	73	19	42	1	0	0	1										
Division Rivals																									
vs. CHI	1	1	.500	2.70	4	3	0	13.1	16	2	7	0	0	0	1										
vs. MON	0	1	.000	3.86	4	4	0	21	21	5	13	0	0	0	0										
vs. NY	0	1	.000	7.20	1	1	0	5	8	3	1	0	0	0	0										
vs. PHI	0	0	—	11.00	3	3	0	9	16	6	3	0	0	0	0										
vs. STL	1	2	.333	3.28	4	4	1	24.2	27	8	14	1	0	0	0										

STARTING PITCHER — WINS / ERA / SO/9 / RATIO (with NL AVG)

Year	Team		W	L	%	ERA	G	GS	CG	IP	H	BB	SO	ShO	W	L	SV	AB	H	HR	BA	PO	A	E	DP	TC/G	FA
1980	PHI	N	11	7	.611	4.56	27	27	2	152	163	71	94	0	0	0	0	50	7	0	.140	17	15	1	2	1.2	.970
1981	ATL	N	1	4	.200	4.60	12	8	0	43	41	23	16	0	0	0	0	7	1	0	.143	3	4	0	0	0.6	1.000
1982			11	9	.550	4.87	32	27	3	164.1	179	59	84	1	0	0	0	51	10	0	.196	12	17	6	2	1.1	.829
1983			0	0	—	7.36	1	1	0	3.2	7	2	4	0	0	0	0	1	0	0	.000	0	2	0	0	2.0	1.000
1984	PIT	N	1	1	.500	2.61	2	2	0	10.1	8	4	10	0	0	0	0	3	0	0	.000	0	0	0	0	0.0	—
1985			2	3	.400	3.68	9	9	1	58.2	60	18	40	1	0	0	0	17	0	0	.000	7	2	0	0	1.0	1.000
1986			7	8	.467	3.75	44	15	1	141.2	129	64	78	1	2	3	2	39	6	0	.154	21	28	3	4	1.2	.942
1987			8	2	.800	3.31	39	12	1	117	107	51	78	1	2	1	0	26	6	0	.231	9	22	2	2	0.8	.939
1988			12	10	.545	2.71	32	32	1	212.2	183	65	81	1	0	0	0	69	6	0	.087	23	34	3	3	1.9	.950
1989			13	10	.565	4.41	33	31	2	196	208	65	83	0	0	0	0	70	13	0	.186	19	31	3	3	1.6	.943
1990			7	5	.583	3.75	26	24	1	129.2	136	36	73	1	0	0	1	37	6	0	.162	12	11	3	0	1.0	.885
11 yrs.			73	59	.553	3.91	257	188	12	1229	1221	458	641	6	4	4	3	370	55	0	.149	123	166	21	16	1.2	.932

LEAGUE CHAMPIONSHIP SERIES

Year	Team		W	L	%	ERA	G	GS	CG	IP	H	BB	SO	ShO	W	L	SV	AB	H	HR	BA	PO	A	E	DP	TC/G	FA
1982	ATL	N	0	0	—	9.00	1	0	0	1	2	1	1	0	0	0	0	0	0	0	—	0	0	0	0	0.0	—
1990	PIT	N	1	1	.500	4.85	2	2	0	13	11	2	8	0	0	0	0	4	0	0	.000	2	1	0	0	1.5	1.000
2 yrs.			1	1	.500	5.14	3	2	0	14	13	3	9	0	0	0	0	4	0	0	.000	2	1	0	0	1.0	1.000

WORLD SERIES

Year	Team		W	L	%	ERA	G	GS	CG	IP	H	BB	SO	ShO	W	L	SV	AB	H	HR	BA	PO	A	E	DP	TC/G	FA
1980	PHI	N	1	0	1.000	7.71	1	1	0	7	8	3	3	0	0	0	0	0	0	0	—	2	0	0	0	2.0	1.000

Year	Team	W	L	%	ERA	G	GS	CG	IP	H	BB	SO	ShO	W	L	SV	AB	H	HR	BA	PO	A	E	DP	TC/G	FA
														RELIEF PITCHING			BATTING									

Mike Walker

WALKER, MICHAEL CHARLES
B. Oct. 4, 1966, Chicago, Ill.
BR TR 6' 1" 175 lbs.

Year	Team	W	L	%	ERA	G	GS	CG	IP	H	BB	SO	ShO	W	L	SV	AB	H	HR	BA	PO	A	E	DP	TC/G	FA
1988	CLE A	0	1	.000	7.27	3	1	0	8.2	8	10	7	0	0	0	0	0	0	0	—	0	3	0	0	1.0	1.000
1990		2	6	.250	4.88	18	11	0	75.2	82	42	34	0	1	0	0	0	0	0	—	4	9	0	1	0.7	1.000
2 yrs.		2	7	.222	5.12	21	12	0	84.1	90	52	41	0	1	0	0	0	0	0	—	4	12	0	1	0.8	1.000

Tim Wallach

WALLACH, TIMOTHY CHARLES
B. Sept. 14, 1957. Huntington Park, Calif.
BR TR 6' 3" 220 lbs.

Year	Team	W	L	%	ERA	G	GS	CG	IP	H	BB	SO	ShO	W	L	SV	AB	H	HR	BA	PO	A	E	DP	TC/G	FA
1987	MON N	0	0	—	0.00	1	0	0	1	1	0	0	0	0	0	0	593	177	26	.298	0	0	0	0	0.0	—
1989		0	0	—	9.00	1	0	0	1	2	0	0	0	0	0	0	573	159	13	.277	0	0	0	0	0.0	—
2 yrs.		0	0	—	4.50	2	0	0	2	3	0	0	0	0	0	0	*				0	0	0	0	0.0	—

Dave Walsh

WALSH, DAVID PETER
B. Sept. 25, 1960, Arlington, Mass.
BL TL 6' 1" 185 lbs.

	W	L	%	ERA	G	GS	CG	IP	H	BB	SO	ShO	W	L	SV
April	—	—	—	—	0	—	—	0	0	0	0	—	0	0	0
May	—	—	—	—	0	—	—	0	0	0	0	—	0	0	0
June	—	—	—	—	0	—	—	0	0	0	0	—	0	0	0
July	—	—	—	—	0	—	—	0	0	0	0	—	0	0	0
Aug	0	0	—	5.68	9	0	0	6.1	7	4	4	0	0	0	1
Sept/Oct	1	0	1.000	2.70	11	0	0	10	8	2	11	0	1	0	0
Day	0	0	—	0.00	4	0	0	4	3	1	3	0	0	0	0
Night	1	0	1.000	5.11	16	0	0	12.1	12	5	12	0	1	0	1
vs. Left	—	—	—	—	—	—	—	—	6	2	5	—	—	—	—
vs. Right	—	—	—	—	—	—	—	—	9	4	10	—	—	—	—
On Grass	1	0	1.000	4.38	15	0	0	12.1	12	5	13	0	1	0	0
On Turf	0	0	—	2.25	5	0	0	4	3	1	2	0	0	0	1
Home	1	0	1.000	5.79	6	0	0	4.2	4	3	8	0	1	0	0
Road	0	0	—	3.09	14	0	0	11.2	11	3	7	0	0	0	1
Division Rivals															
vs. ATL	0	0	—	9.00	1	0	0	2	3	2	3	0	0	0	0
vs. CIN	0	0	—	0.00	1	0	0	1.2	1	1	1	0	0	0	0
vs. HOU	0	0	—	8.10	3	0	0	3.1	3	1	7	0	0	0	0
vs. SD	1	0	1.000	0.00	4	0	0	3.1	3	0	2	0	1	0	0
vs. SF	0	0	—	0.00	2	0	0	0.2	1	0	1	0	0	0	0

RELIEF PITCHER (WINS, ERA, SAVES, RATIO vs NL AVG)

Year	Team	W	L	%	ERA	G	GS	CG	IP	H	BB	SO	ShO	W	L	SV	AB	H	HR	BA	PO	A	E	DP	TC/G	FA
1990	LA N	1	0	1.000	3.86	20	0	0	16.1	15	6	15	0	1	0	1	0	0	0	—	2	3	0	0	0.3	1.000

Steve Wapnick

WAPNICK, STEVEN LEE
B. Sept. 25, 1965, Panorama City, Calif.
BR TR 6' 2" 200 lbs.

Year	Team	W	L	%	ERA	G	GS	CG	IP	H	BB	SO	ShO	W	L	SV	AB	H	HR	BA	PO	A	E	DP	TC/G	FA
1990	DET A	0	0	—	6.43	4	0	0	7	8	10	6	0	0	0	0	0	0	0	—	0	1	0	0	0.3	.000

Colby Ward

WARD, ROBERT COLBY
B. Jan. 2, 1964, Lansing, Mich.
BR TR 6' 2" 185 lbs.

	W	L	%	ERA	G	GS	CG	IP	H	BB	SO	ShO	W	L	SV
April	—	—	—	—	0	—	—	0	0	0	0	—	0	0	0
May	—	—	—	—	0	—	—	0	0	0	0	—	0	0	0
June	—	—	—	—	0	—	—	0	0	0	0	—	0	0	0
July	0	0	—	2.08	3	0	0	8.2	5	6	5	0	0	0	0
Aug	1	2	.333	4.87	12	0	0	20.1	18	11	12	0	1	2	1
Sept/Oct	0	1	.000	5.14	7	0	0	7	8	4	6	0	0	1	0
Day	0	1	.000	1.13	5	0	0	8	4	6	5	0	0	1	0
Night	1	2	.333	5.14	17	0	0	28	27	15	18	0	1	2	1
vs. Left	—	—	—	—	—	—	—	—	12	12	7	—	—	—	—
vs. Right	—	—	—	—	—	—	—	—	19	9	16	—	—	—	—

RELIEF PITCHER (WINS, ERA vs AL AVG)

Year	Team	W	L	%	ERA	G	GS	CG	IP	H	BB	SO	ShO	W	L	SV	AB	H	HR	BA	PO	A	E	DP	TC/G	FA

Colby Ward *Continued*

		W	L	%	ERA	G	GS	CG	IP	H	BB	SO	ShO	W	L	SV	AB	H	HR	BA	PO	A	E	DP	TC/G	FA
On Grass		1	2	.333	4.65	18	0	0	31	28	17	19	0	1	2	1										
On Turf		0	1	.000	1.80	4	0	0	5	3	4	4	0	0	1	0										
Home		1	0	1.000	5.18	14	0	0	24.1	27	13	12	0	1	0	1										
Road		0	3	.000	2.31	8	0	0	11.2	4	8	11	0	0	3	0										
Division Rivals																										
vs. BAL		0	1	.000	5.40	2	0	0	3.1	2	4	3	0	0	1	0										
vs. BOS		0	0	—	3.86	2	0	0	4.2	5	2	1	0	0	0	0										
vs. DET		0	0	—	5.40	2	0	0	5	6	3	2	0	0	0	1										
vs. MIL		0	1	.000	3.00	2	0	0	3	1	0	5	0	0	1	0										
vs. NY		0	0	—	0.00	3	0	0	7	2	3	5	0	0	0	0										
vs. TOR		0	1	.000	13.50	3	0	0	2	2	5	2	0	0	1	0										
1990	CLE A	1	3	.250	4.25	22	0	0	36	31	21	23	0	1	3	1	0	0	0	—	3	3	0	0	0.3	1.000

Duane Ward

WARD, ROY DUANE
B. May 28, 1964, Park View, N. M.
BR TR 6' 4" 185 lbs.

		W	L	%	ERA	G	GS	CG	IP	H	BB	SO	ShO	W	L	SV	AB	H	HR	BA	PO	A	E	DP	TC/G	FA
April		0	0	—	1.08	10	0	0	16.2	10	4	18	0	0	0	3										
May		1	2	.333	4.57	13	0	0	21.2	21	14	22	0	1	2	1										
June		0	1	.000	5.09	14	0	0	23	27	9	15	0	0	1	2										
July		0	3	.000	3.15	10	0	0	20	15	4	16	0	0	3	2										
Aug		1	1	.500	1.52	13	0	0	23.2	14	2	22	0	1	1	2										
Sept/Oct		0	1	.000	4.76	13	0	0	22.2	14	9	19	0	0	1	1										
Day		1	1	.500	2.53	19	0	0	32	22	6	28	0	1	1	2										
Night		1	7	.125	3.76	54	0	0	95.2	79	36	84	0	1	7	9										
vs. Left		—	—	—	—	—	—	—	—	49	33	49	—	—	—	—										
vs. Right		—	—	—	—	—	—	—	—	52	9	63	—	—	—	—										
On Grass		2	3	.400	5.18	26	0	0	41.2	37	21	40	0	2	3	2										
On Turf		0	5	.000	2.62	47	0	0	86	64	21	72	0	0	5	9										
Home		0	4	.000	3.02	39	0	0	65.2	48	14	53	0	0	4	5										
Road		2	4	.333	3.92	34	0	0	62	53	28	59	0	2	4	6										
Division Rivals																										
vs. BAL		0	0	—	7.36	5	0	0	7.1	6	2	8	0	0	0	1										
vs. BOS		0	2	.000	6.55	7	0	0	11	10	7	6	0	0	2	0										
vs. CLE		0	0	—	0.00	6	0	0	13	6	1	13	0	0	0	2										
vs. DET		1	1	.500	4.50	7	0	0	10	6	10	12	0	1	1	0										
vs. MIL		0	0	—	9.72	6	0	0	8.1	12	4	3	0	0	0	1										
vs. NY		0	0	—	1.86	7	0	0	9.2	11	0	8	0	0	0	1										
1986	2 teams	ATL N	(10G 0 – 1)			TOR A	(2G 0 – 1)																			
"	total	0	2	.000	8.00	12	1	0	18	25	12	9	0	0	1	0	1	0	0	.000	1	6	0	0	0.6	1.000
1987	TOR A	1	0	1.000	6.94	12	1	0	11.2	14	12	10	0	1	0	0	0	0	0	—	2	2	0	0	0.3	1.000
1988		9	3	.750	3.30	64	0	0	111.2	101	60	91	0	9	3	15	0	0	0	—	6	12	1	0	0.3	.947
1989		4	10	.286	3.77	66	0	0	114.2	94	58	122	0	4	10	15	0	0	0	—	5	21	1	2	0.4	.963
1990		2	8	.200	3.45	73	0	0	127.2	101	42	112	0	2	8	11	0	0	0	—	9	18	1	0	0.4	.964
5 yrs.		16	23	.410	3.82	227	2	0	383.2	335	184	344	0	16	22	41	1	0	0	.000	23	59	3	2	0.4	.965

LEAGUE CHAMPIONSHIP SERIES

Year	Team	W	L	%	ERA	G	GS	CG	IP	H	BB	SO	ShO	W	L	SV	AB	H	HR	BA	PO	A	E	DP	TC/G	FA
1989	TOR A	0	0	—	7.36	2	0	0	3.2	6	3	5	0	0	0	0	0	0	0	—	1	0	0	0	0.5	1.000

Gary Wayne

WAYNE, GARY ANTHONY
B. Nov. 30, 1962, Dearborn, Mich.
BL TL 6' 3" 185 lbs.

		W	L	%	ERA	G	GS	CG	IP	H	BB	SO	ShO	W	L	SV	AB	H	HR	BA	PO	A	E	DP	TC/G	FA
April		0	0	—	0.00	6	0	0	4	4	0	3	0	0	0	0										
May		0	0	—	2.53	9	0	0	10.2	8	5	6	0	0	0	0										
June		0	0	—	9.64	8	0	0	9.1	15	3	6	0	0	0	0										
July		—	—	—	—	0	—	—	0	0	0	0	—	0	0	0										
Aug		0	0	—	3.52	4	0	0	7.2	5	1	5	0	0	0	1										
Sept/Oct		1	1	.500	2.57	11	0	0	7	6	4	8	0	1	1	0										
Day		0	0	—	4.32	10	0	0	8.1	9	3	6	0	0	0	0										
Night		1	1	.500	4.15	28	0	0	30.1	29	10	22	0	1	1	1										
vs. Left		—	—	—	—	—	—	—	—	8	5	8	—	—	—	—										
vs. Right		—	—	—	—	—	—	—	—	30	8	20	—	—	—	—										

Year	Team	W	L	%	ERA	G	GS	CG	IP	H	BB	SO	ShO	W	L	SV	AB	H	HR	BA	PO	A	E	DP	TC/G	FA
														RELIEF PITCHING			**BATTING**									

Gary Wayne *Continued*

		W	L	%	ERA	G	GS	CG	IP	H	BB	SO	ShO	W	L	SV	AB	H	HR	BA	PO	A	E	DP	TC/G	FA
On Grass		0	1	.000	2.41	18	0	0	18.2	13	7	15	0	0	1	0										
On Turf		1	0	1.000	5.85	20	0	0	20	25	6	13	0	1	0	1										
Home		1	0	1.000	5.63	17	0	0	16	18	6	12	0	1	0	1										
Road		0	1	.000	3.18	21	0	0	22.2	20	7	16	0	0	1	0										
Division Rivals																										
vs. CAL		0	0	—	0.00	6	0	0	4	4	1	4	0	0	0	0										
vs. CHI		0	0	—	2.25	3	0	0	4	2	0	3	0	0	0	1										
vs. KC		1	0	1.000	11.57	4	0	0	4.2	7	3	3	0	1	0	0										
vs. OAK		0	0	—	0.00	5	0	0	1.1	0	1	1	0	0	0	0										
vs. SEA		0	0	—	0.00	2	0	0	0.1	2	1	0	0	0	0	0										
vs. TEX		0	0	—	0.00	3	0	0	4.2	2	0	5	0	0	0	0										
1989	MIN A	3	4	.429	3.30	60	0	0	71	55	36	41	0	3	4	1	0	0	0	—	2	11	1	1	0.2	.929
1990		1	1	.500	4.19	38	0	0	38.2	38	13	28	0	1	1	1	0	0	0	—	1	4	0	1	0.1	1.000
2 yrs.		4	5	.444	3.61	98	0	0	109.2	93	49	69	0	4	5	2	0	0	0	—	3	15	1	2	0.2	.947

Bill Wegman

WEGMAN, WILLIAM EDWARD
B. Dec. 19, 1962, Cincinnati, Ohio
BR TR 6′ 5″ 200 lbs.

Year	Team	W	L	%	ERA	G	GS	CG	IP	H	BB	SO	ShO	W	L	SV	AB	H	HR	BA	PO	A	E	DP	TC/G	FA
1985	MIL A	2	0	1.000	3.57	3	3	0	17.2	17	3	6	0	0	0	0	0	0	0	—	3	0	0	0	1.0	1.000
1986		5	12	.294	5.13	35	32	2	198.1	217	43	82	0	0	0	0	0	0	0	—	20	19	1	4	1.1	.975
1987		12	11	.522	4.24	34	33	7	225	229	53	102	0	0	1	0	0	0	0	—	29	27	2	2	1.7	.966
1988		13	13	.500	4.12	32	31	4	199	207	50	84	1	0	0	0	0	0	0	—	14	24	3	3	1.3	.927
1989		2	6	.250	6.71	11	8	0	51	69	21	27	0	0	1	0	0	0	0	—	3	11	0	0	1.3	1.000
1990		2	2	.500	4.85	8	5	1	29.2	37	6	20	1	0	0	0	0	0	0	—	1	3	2	0	0.8	.667
6 yrs.		36	44	.450	4.63	123	112	14	720.2	776	176	321	2	0	2	0	0	0	0	—	70	84	8	9	1.3	.951

Bob Welch

WELCH, ROBERT LYNN
B. Nov. 3, 1956, Detroit, Mich.
BR TR 6′ 3″ 190 lbs.

		W	L	%	ERA	G	GS	CG	IP	H	BB	SO	ShO	W	L	SV	AB	H	HR	BA	PO	A	E	DP	TC/G	FA
April		3	1	.750	1.06	5	5	1	34	23	7	13	1	0	0	0										
May		4	1	.800	2.84	6	6	1	44.1	40	16	23	1	0	0	0										
June		6	0	1.000	3.83	6	6	0	42.1	41	15	21	0	0	0	0										
July		3	2	.600	4.78	5	5	0	26.1	31	14	20	0	0	0	0										
Aug		6	1	.857	3.47	7	7	0	46.2	43	16	31	0	0	0	0										
Sept/Oct		5	1	.833	2.03	6	6	0	44.1	36	9	19	0	0	0	0										
Day		10	2	.833	2.28	12	12	0	83	67	26	41	0	0	0	0										
Night		17	4	.810	3.31	23	23	2	155	147	51	86	2	0	0	0										
vs. Left		—	—	—	—	—	—	—	—	120	43	55	—	—	—	—										
vs. Right		—	—	—	—	—	—	—	—	94	34	72	—	—	—	—										
On Grass		22	4	.846	2.58	28	28	2	195.1	165	62	102	2	0	0	0										
On Turf		5	2	.714	4.64	7	7	0	42.2	49	15	25	0	0	0	0										
Home		14	2	.875	1.92	16	16	1	117	94	39	69	1	0	0	0										
Road		13	4	.765	3.94	19	19	1	121	120	38	58	1	0	0	0										
Division Rivals																										
vs. CAL		3	0	1.000	3.44	3	3	0	18.1	21	10	14	0	0	0	0										
vs. CHI		2	0	1.000	3.21	2	2	0	14	11	8	6	0	0	0	0										
vs. KC		3	0	1.000	3.00	3	3	0	21	24	7	9	0	0	0	0										
vs. MIN		2	1	.667	4.70	3	3	0	15.1	15	5	6	0	0	0	0										
vs. SEA		1	2	.333	3.15	3	3	0	20	17	7	8	0	0	0	0										
vs. TEX		2	0	1.000	3.14	2	2	0	14.1	13	1	13	0	0	0	0										
1978	LA N	7	4	.636	2.03	23	13	4	111	92	26	66	3	1	0	3	29	5	0	.172	6	12	0	0	0.8	.947
1979		5	6	.455	4.00	25	12	1	81	82	32	64	0	3	1	5	19	3	0	.158	2	8	3	3	0.5	.769
1980		14	9	.609	3.28	32	32	3	214	190	79	141	2	0	0	0	70	17	0	.243	15	26	1	3	1.3	.976
1981		9	5	.643	3.45	23	23	2	141	141	41	88	1	0	0	0	45	10	0	.222	4	18	0	1	1.0	1.000
1982		16	11	.593	3.36	36	36	9	235.2	199	81	176	3	0	0	0	85	12	0	.141	19	26	2	0	1.3	.957
1983		15	12	.556	2.65	31	31	4	204	164	72	156	3	0	0	0	73	7	1	.096	14	27	3	1	1.4	.932
1984		13	13	.500	3.78	31	29	3	178.2	191	58	126	1	0	0	0	51	4	0	.078	20	28	2	5	1.6	.960
1985		14	4	.778	2.31	23	23	8	167.1	141	35	96	3	0	0	0	50	9	0	.180	15	27	3	1	2.0	.933
1986		7	13	.350	3.28	33	33	7	235.2	227	55	183	3	0	0	0	76	8	1	.105	21	26	2	2	1.5	.959
1987		15	9	.625	3.22	35	35	6	251.2	204	86	196	4	0	0	0	83	13	0	.157	25	38	0	3	1.8	1.000

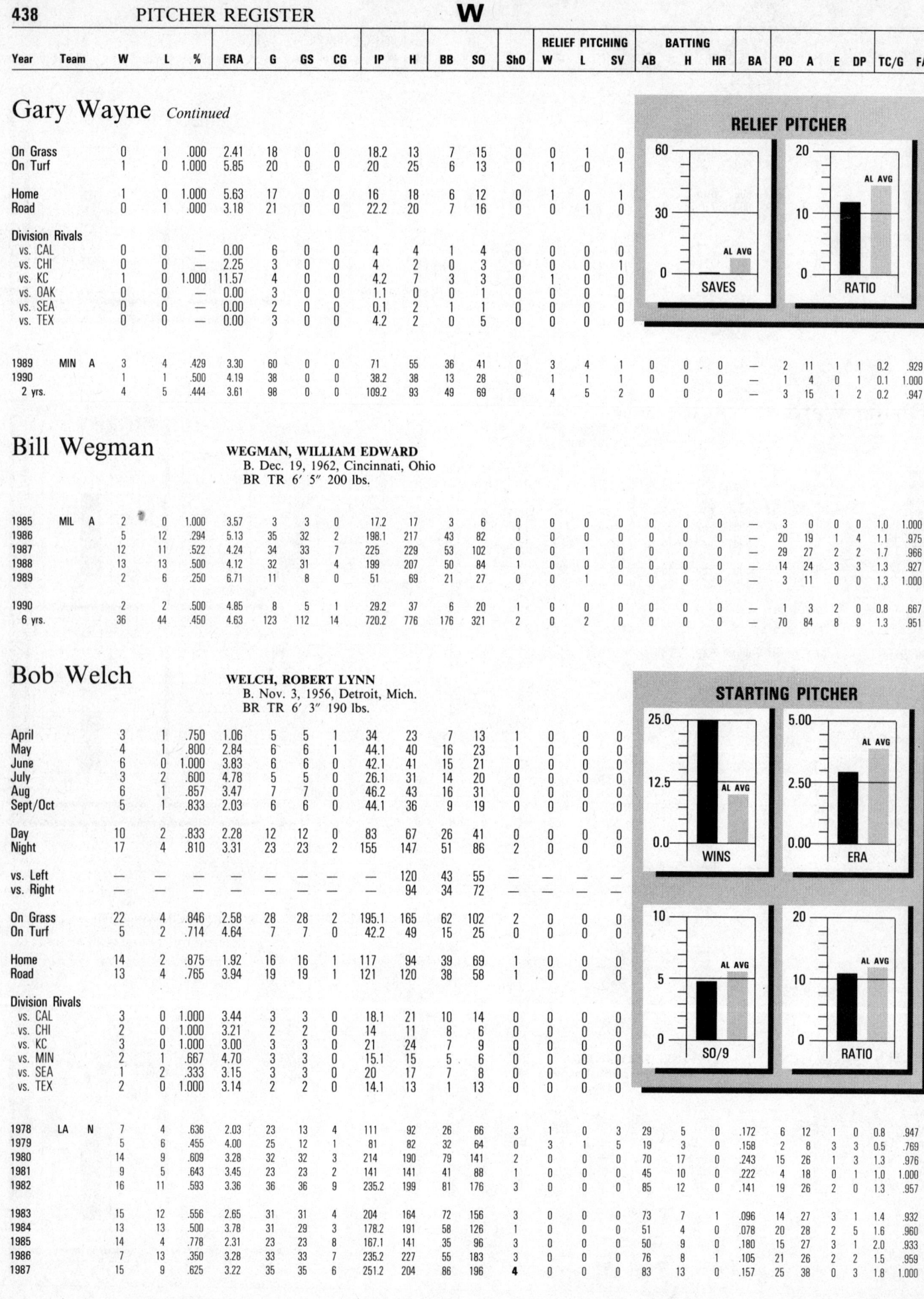

Year	Team	W	L	%	ERA	G	GS	CG	IP	H	BB	SO	ShO	W	L	SV	AB	H	HR	BA	PO	A	E	DP	TC/G	FA
														RELIEF PITCHING			BATTING									

Bob Welch *Continued*

Year	Team	W	L	%	ERA	G	GS	CG	IP	H	BB	SO	ShO	W	L	SV	AB	H	HR	BA	PO	A	E	DP	TC/G	FA
1988	OAK A	17	9	.654	3.64	36	36	4	244.2	237	81	158	2	0	0	0	0	0	0	—	16	32	1	2	1.4	.980
1989		17	8	.680	3.00	33	33	1	209.2	191	78	137	0	0	0	0	0	0	0	—	26	21	4	3	1.5	.922
1990		**27**	6	**.818**	2.95	35	35	2	238	214	77	127	2	0	0	0	0	0	0	—	20	31	0	2	1.5	1.000
13 yrs.		176	109	.618	3.16	396	371	54	2512.1	2273	801	1714	27	4	1	8	581	88	2	.151	203	320	22	26	1.4	.960

DIVISIONAL PLAYOFF SERIES
Year	Team	W	L	%	ERA	G	GS	CG	IP	H	BB	SO	ShO	W	L	SV	AB	H	HR	BA	PO	A	E	DP	TC/G	FA
1981	LA N	0	0	—	0.00	1	0	0	1	0	1	1	0	0	0	0	0	0	0	—	0	0	0	0	0.0	—

LEAGUE CHAMPIONSHIP SERIES
Year	Team	W	L	%	ERA	G	GS	CG	IP	H	BB	SO	ShO	W	L	SV	AB	H	HR	BA	PO	A	E	DP	TC/G	FA
1978	LA N	1	0	1.000	2.08	1	0	0	4.1	2	0	5	0	1	0	0	2	0	0	.000	0	1	0	0	1.0	1.000
1981		0	0	—	5.40	3	0	0	1.2	2	0	2	0	0	0	1	0	0	0	—	0	0	0	0	0.0	—
1983		0	1	.000	6.75	1	1	0	1.1	0	2	0	0	0	0	0	0	0	0	—	0	0	0	0	0.0	—
1985		0	1	.000	6.75	1	1	0	2.2	5	6	2	0	0	0	0	1	0	0	.000	0	1	0	1	1.0	—
1988	OAK A	0	0	—	27.00	1	1	0	1.2	6	2	0	0	0	0	0	0	0	0	—	1	0	0	0	1.0	1.000
1989		1	0	1.000	3.18	1	1	0	5.2	8	1	4	0	0	0	0	0	0	0	—	1	0	0	0	1.0	1.000
1990		1	0	1.000	1.23	1	1	0	7.1	6	3	4	0	0	0	0	0	0	0	—	0	3	0	0	3.0	1.000
7 yrs.		3	2	.600	4.74	9	5	0	24.2	29	14	17	0	1	0	1	3	0	0	.000	2	4	1	0	0.8	.857

WORLD SERIES
Year	Team	W	L	%	ERA	G	GS	CG	IP	H	BB	SO	ShO	W	L	SV	AB	H	HR	BA	PO	A	E	DP	TC/G	FA
1978	LA N	0	1	.000	6.23	3	0	0	4.1	4	2	6	0	0	1	1	0	0	0	—	0	0	0	0	0.0	—
1981		0	0	—		1	1	0	0	3	1	0	0	0	0	0	0	0	0	—	0	0	0	0	0.0	—
1988	OAK A	0	0	—	1.80	1	1	0	5	6	3	8	0	0	0	0	0	0	0	—	1	1	0	0	2.0	1.000
1990		0	0	—	4.91	1	1	0	7.1	9	2	2	0	0	0	0	3	0	0	.000	0	2	0	0	2.0	1.000
4 yrs.		0	1	.000	5.40	6	3	0	16.2	22	8	16	0	0	1	1	3	0	0	.000	1	3	0	0	0.7	1.000

David Wells

WELLS, DAVID LEE
B. May 20, 1963, Torrance, Calif.
BL TL 6′ 3″ 187 lbs.

Split	W	L	%	ERA	G	GS	CG	IP	H	BB	SO	ShO	W	L	SV	AB	H	HR	BA	PO	A	E	DP	TC/G	FA
April	0	0	—	0.93	8	0	0	9.2	3	1	8	0	0	0	3										
May	2	0	1.000	3.86	11	2	0	21	16	4	19	0	1	0	0										
June	3	2	.600	4.41	6	5	0	34.2	33	13	27	0	0	1	0										
July	2	0	1.000	1.82	6	6	0	39.2	34	7	20	0	0	0	0										
Aug	2	2	.500	3.89	6	6	0	39.1	41	13	16	0	0	0	0										
Sept/Oct	2	2	.500	2.82	6	6	0	44.2	38	7	25	0	0	0	0										
Day	2	2	.500	3.05	12	5	0	44.1	40	10	24	0	1	1	1										
Night	9	4	.692	3.17	31	20	0	144.2	125	35	91	0	0	0	2										
vs. Left	—	—	—	—	—	—	—	—	29	8	12	—	—	—	—										
vs. Right	—	—	—	—	—	—	—	—	136	37	103	—	—	—	—										
On Grass	6	4	.600	4.26	17	12	0	82.1	80	22	59	0	1	0	0										
On Turf	5	2	.714	2.28	26	13	0	106.2	85	23	56	0	0	1	3										
Home	3	2	.600	2.61	21	10	0	82.2	71	20	48	0	0	1	2										
Road	8	4	.667	3.55	22	15	0	106.1	94	25	67	0	1	0	1										

Division Rivals
Split	W	L	%	ERA	G	GS	CG	IP	H	BB	SO	ShO	W	L	SV
vs. BAL	0	1	.000	3.78	3	2	0	16.2	18	4	8	0	0	0	0
vs. BOS	0	2	.000	2.40	2	2	0	15	11	4	3	0	0	0	0
vs. CLE	0	0	—	3.14	4	2	0	14.1	13	3	6	0	0	0	1
vs. DET	3	0	1.000	5.82	5	2	0	17	20	5	13	0	1	0	0
vs. MIL	1	2	.333	4.61	3	2	0	13.2	16	3	10	0	0	1	0
vs. NY	1	0	1.000	3.86	2	2	0	14	15	3	12	0	0	0	0

STARTING PITCHER — WINS (AL AVG), ERA (AL AVG), SO/9 (AL AVG), RATIO (AL AVG)

Year	Team	W	L	%	ERA	G	GS	CG	IP	H	BB	SO	ShO	W	L	SV	AB	H	HR	BA	PO	A	E	DP	TC/G	FA
1987	TOR A	4	3	.571	3.99	18	2	0	29.1	37	12	32	0	4	1	1	0	0	0	—	2	4	0	1	0.3	1.000
1988		3	5	.375	4.62	41	0	0	64.1	65	31	56	0	3	5	4	0	0	0	—	5	5	0	1	0.2	1.000
1989		7	4	.636	2.40	54	0	0	86.1	66	28	78	0	7	4	2	0	0	0	—	9	11	1	0	0.4	.952
1990		11	6	.647	3.14	43	25	0	189	165	45	115	0	1	1	3	0	0	0	—	7	32	0	1	0.9	1.000
4 yrs.		25	18	.581	3.29	156	27	0	369	333	116	281	0	15	11	10	0	0	0	—	23	52	1	3	0.5	.987

LEAGUE CHAMPIONSHIP SERIES
Year	Team	W	L	%	ERA	G	GS	CG	IP	H	BB	SO	ShO	W	L	SV	AB	H	HR	BA	PO	A	E	DP	TC/G	FA
1989	TOR A	0	0	—	0.00	1	0	0	1	0	2	1	0	0	0	0	0	0	0	—	0	0	0	0	0.0	—

Terry Wells

WELLS, TERRY
B. Sept. 10, 1963, Kankakee, Ill.
BL TL 6′ 3″ 205 lbs.

Year	Team	W	L	%	ERA	G	GS	CG	IP	H	BB	SO	ShO	W	L	SV	AB	H	HR	BA	PO	A	E	DP	TC/G	FA
1990	LA N	1	2	.333	7.84	5	5	0	20.2	25	14	18	0	0	0	0	7	0	0	.000	1	0	2	0	0.6	.333

Year	Team	W	L	%	ERA	G	GS	CG	IP	H	BB	SO	ShO	W	L	SV	AB	H	HR	BA	PO	A	E	DP	TC/G	FA

(Column group headers: RELIEF PITCHING over W/L/SV; BATTING over AB/H/HR/BA)

David West

WEST, DAVID LEE
B. Sept. 1, 1964, Memphis, Tenn.
BL TL 6' 6" 205 lbs.

Year	Team	W	L	%	ERA	G	GS	CG	IP	H	BB	SO	ShO	W	L	SV	AB	H	HR	BA	PO	A	E	DP	TC/G	FA
April		1	3	.250	3.52	4	4	0	23	20	11	12	0	0	0	0										
May		1	0	1.000	6.56	5	5	1	23.1	21	16	12	0	0	0	0										
June		1	3	.250	4.88	6	6	0	31.1	35	12	29	0	0	0	0										
July		2	1	.667	5.93	6	6	0	30.1	37	18	19	0	0	0	0										
Aug		2	2	.500	5.00	7	5	1	36	29	19	20	0	0	0	0										
Sept/Oct		0	0	—	0.00	1	1	0	2.1	0	2	0	0	0	0	0										
Day		2	2	.500	6.38	9	8	0	36.2	37	25	27	0	0	0	0										
Night		5	7	.417	4.68	20	19	2	109.2	105	53	65	0	0	0	0										
vs. Left		—	—	—	—	—	—	—		22	12	14	—	—	—	—										
vs. Right		—	—	—	—	—	—	—		120	66	78	—	—	—	—										
On Grass		4	3	.571	4.35	12	12	1	62	63	35	37	0	0	0	0										
On Turf		3	6	.333	5.66	17	15	1	84.1	79	43	55	0	0	0	0										
Home		2	4	.333	6.03	13	12	0	62.2	62	33	46	0	0	0	0										
Road		5	5	.500	4.41	16	15	2	83.2	80	45	46	0	0	0	0										
Division Rivals																										
vs. CAL		1	1	.500	1.20	3	2	0	15	10	5	11	0	0	0	0										
vs. CHI		0	1	.000	3.26	3	3	0	19.1	17	8	19	0	0	0	0										
vs. KC		1	1	.500	3.46	2	2	0	13	10	7	10	0	0	0	0										
vs. OAK		0	0	—	13.50	1	1	0	2	3	2	2	0	0	0	0										
vs. SEA		0	2	.000	8.53	3	2	0	12.2	14	8	5	0	0	0	0										
vs. TEX		1	2	.333	15.00	3	3	0	9	20	6	4	0	0	0	0										
1988	NY N	1	0	1.000	3.00	2	1	0	6	6	3	3	0	0	0	0	2	2	0	1.000	1	0	0	0	0.5	1.000
1989	2 teams				NY N (11G 0 - 2)				MIN A (10G 3 - 2)																	
"	total	3	4	.429	6.79	21	7	0	63.2	73	33	50	0	0	0	0	5	1	0	.200	2	2	1	0	0.2	.800
1990	MIN A	7	9	.438	5.10	29	27	2	146.1	142	78	92	0	0	0	0	0	0	0	—	3	16	2	2	0.7	.905
3 yrs.		11	13	.458	5.54	52	35	2	216	221	114	145	0	0	0	0	7	3	0	.429	6	18	3	2	0.5	.889

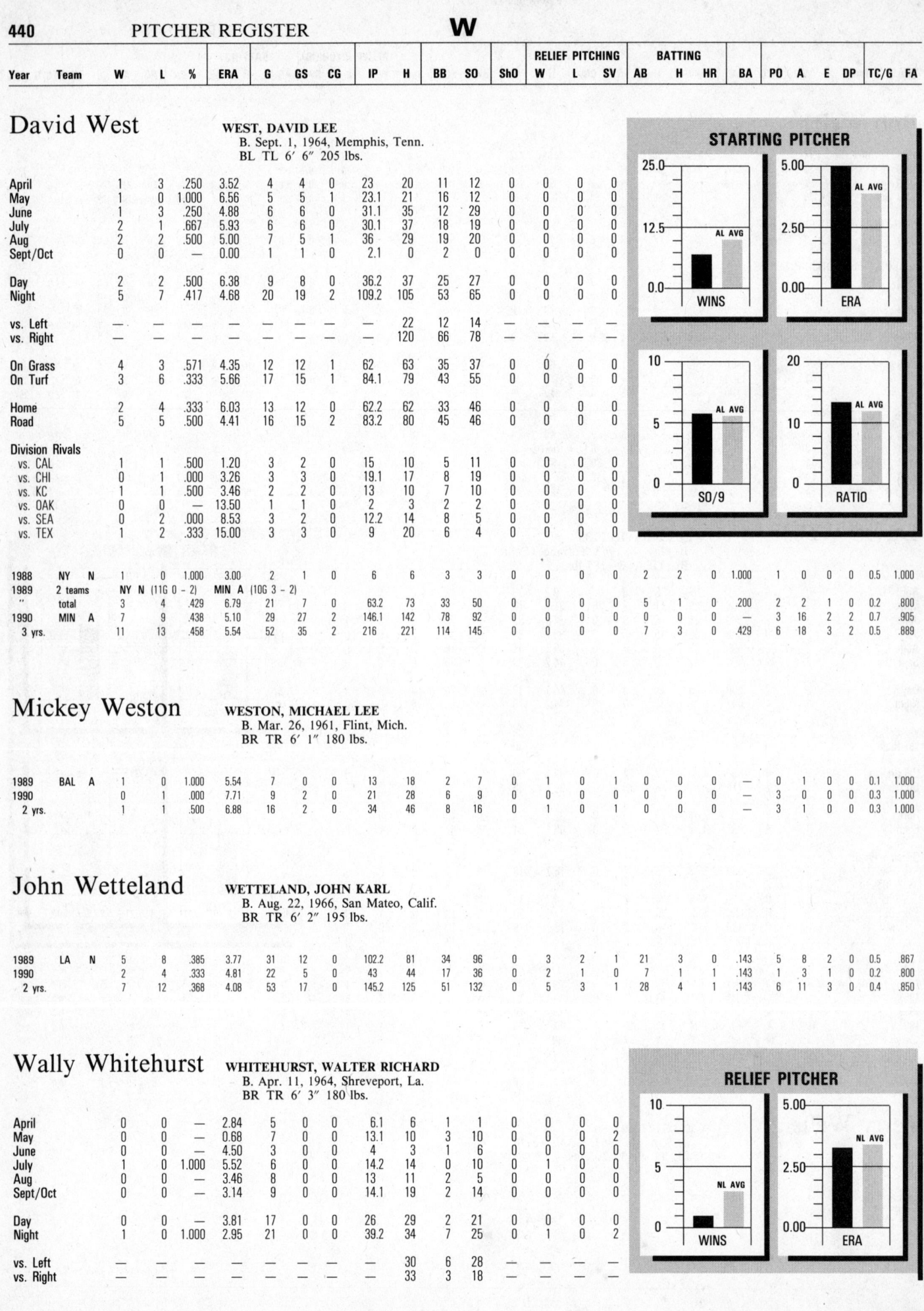

STARTING PITCHER — WINS (AL AVG), ERA (AL AVG), SO/9 (AL AVG), RATIO (AL AVG)

Mickey Weston

WESTON, MICHAEL LEE
B. Mar. 26, 1961, Flint, Mich.
BR TR 6' 1" 180 lbs.

Year	Team	W	L	%	ERA	G	GS	CG	IP	H	BB	SO	ShO	W	L	SV	AB	H	HR	BA	PO	A	E	DP	TC/G	FA
1989	BAL A	1	0	1.000	5.54	7	0	0	13	18	2	7	0	1	0	1	0	0	0	—	0	1	0	0	0.1	1.000
1990		0	1	.000	7.71	9	2	0	21	28	6	9	0	0	0	0	0	0	0	—	3	0	0	0	0.3	1.000
2 yrs.		1	1	.500	6.88	16	2	0	34	46	8	16	0	1	0	1	0	0	0	—	3	1	0	0	0.3	1.000

John Wetteland

WETTELAND, JOHN KARL
B. Aug. 22, 1966, San Mateo, Calif.
BR TR 6' 2" 195 lbs.

Year	Team	W	L	%	ERA	G	GS	CG	IP	H	BB	SO	ShO	W	L	SV	AB	H	HR	BA	PO	A	E	DP	TC/G	FA
1989	LA N	5	8	.385	3.77	31	12	0	102.2	81	34	96	0	3	2	1	21	3	0	.143	5	8	2	0	0.5	.867
1990		2	4	.333	4.81	22	5	0	43	44	17	36	0	2	1	0	7	1	1	.143	1	3	1	0	0.2	.800
2 yrs.		7	12	.368	4.08	53	17	0	145.2	125	51	132	0	5	3	1	28	4	1	.143	6	11	3	0	0.4	.850

Wally Whitehurst

WHITEHURST, WALTER RICHARD
B. Apr. 11, 1964, Shreveport, La.
BR TR 6' 3" 180 lbs.

Year	Team	W	L	%	ERA	G	GS	CG	IP	H	BB	SO	ShO	W	L	SV	AB	H	HR	BA	PO	A	E	DP	TC/G	FA
April		0	0	—	2.84	5	0	0	6.1	6	1	1	0	0	0	0										
May		0	0	—	0.68	7	0	0	13.1	10	3	10	0	0	0	2										
June		0	0	—	4.50	3	0	0	4	3	1	6	0	0	0	0										
July		1	0	1.000	5.52	6	0	0	14.2	14	0	10	0	1	0	0										
Aug		0	0	—	3.46	8	0	0	13	11	2	5	0	0	0	0										
Sept/Oct		0	0	—	3.14	9	0	0	14.1	19	2	14	0	0	0	0										
Day		0	0	—	3.81	17	0	0	26	29	2	21	0	0	0	0										
Night		1	0	1.000	2.95	21	0	0	39.2	34	7	25	0	1	0	2										
vs. Left		—	—	—	—	—	—	—		30	6	28	—	—	—	—										
vs. Right		—	—	—	—	—	—	—		33	3	18	—	—	—	—										

RELIEF PITCHER — WINS (NL AVG), ERA (NL AVG)

Year	Team	W	L	%	ERA	G	GS	CG	IP	H	BB	SO	ShO	RELIEF PITCHING W	L	SV	BATTING AB	H	HR	BA	PO	A	E	DP	TC/G	FA

Wally Whitehurst *Continued*

RELIEF PITCHER

On Grass		1	0	1.000	2.56	27	0	0	45.2	40	6	35	0	1	0	2										
On Turf		0	0	—	4.95	11	0	0	20	23	3	11	0	0	0	0										
Home		0	0	—	1.55	18	0	0	29	20	6	19	0	0	0	1										
Road		1	0	1.000	4.66	20	0	0	36.2	43	3	27	0	1	0	1										
Division Rivals																										
vs. CHI		0	0	—	3.65	6	0	0	12.1	10	1	10	0	0	0	0										
vs. MON		0	0	—	0.00	4	0	0	8	3	0	9	0	0	0	0										
vs. PHI		0	0	—	11.57	4	0	0	4.2	10	2	5	0	0	0	0										
vs. PIT		0	0	—	5.40	2	0	0	1.2	3	1	0	0	0	0	0										
vs. STL		0	0	—	7.50	3	0	0	6	9	1	3	0	0	0	0										
1989	NY N	0	1	.000	4.50	9	1	0	14	17	5	9	0	0	0	0	1	0	0	.000	1	1	0	0	0.2	1.000
1990		1	0	1.000	3.29	38	0	0	65.2	63	9	46	0	1	0	2	8	2	0	.250	4	9	0	1	0.3	1.000
2 yrs.		1	1	.500	3.50	47	1	0	79.2	80	14	55	0	1	0	2	9	2	0	.222	5	10	0	1	0.3	1.000

Ed Whitson

WHITSON, EDDIE LEE
B. May 19, 1955, Johnson City, Tenn.
BR TR 6′ 3″ 195 lbs.

STARTING PITCHER

April		2	0	1.000	1.50	3	3	2	24	22	3	9	1	0	0	0										
May		2	3	.400	3.95	6	6	1	41	38	10	25	0	0	0	0										
June		2	2	.500	2.61	6	6	1	41.1	33	10	25	1	0	0	0										
July		2	2	.500	2.49	6	6	0	43.1	38	4	21	0	0	0	0										
Aug		3	0	1.000	0.86	5	5	1	42	41	6	24	1	0	0	0										
Sept/Oct		3	2	.600	3.89	6	6	1	37	43	14	23	0	0	0	0										
Day		5	3	.625	3.13	10	10	2	69	67	17	36	0	0	0	0										
Night		9	6	.600	2.37	22	22	4	159.2	148	30	91	3	0	0	0										
vs. Left		—	—	—	—	—	—	—	—	141	30	72	—	—	—	—										
vs. Right		—	—	—	—	—	—	—	—	74	17	55	—	—	—	—										
On Grass		8	7	.533	2.74	22	22	5	160.2	143	26	93	3	0	0	0										
On Turf		6	2	.750	2.25	10	10	1	68	72	21	34	0	0	0	0										
Home		5	6	.455	2.65	17	17	4	125.2	110	21	77	3	0	0	0										
Road		9	3	.750	2.53	15	15	2	103	105	26	50	0	0	0	0										
Division Rivals																										
vs. ATL		2	1	.667	2.25	4	4	1	28	24	4	19	1	0	0	0										
vs. CIN		2	1	.667	4.07	4	4	1	24.1	32	6	17	0	0	0	0										
vs. HOU		2	0	1.000	0.84	3	3	0	21.1	18	11	12	0	0	0	0										
vs. LA		0	0	—	5.11	2	2	0	12.1	13	3	10	0	0	0	0										
vs. SF		1	2	.333	2.40	4	4	1	30	25	4	14	0	0	0	0										
1977	PIT N	1	0	1.000	3.38	5	2	0	16	11	9	10	0	1	0	0	4	0	0	.000	0	2	0	0	0.4	1.000
1978		5	6	.455	3.28	43	0	0	74	66	37	64	0	5	6	4	11	2	0	.182	3	8	1	0	0.3	.917
1979	2 teams	PIT N	(19G 2 – 3)			SF N	(18G 5 – 8)																			
"	total	7	11	.389	4.10	37	24	2	158	151	75	93	0	0	3	1	45	5	0	.111	4	21	2	2	0.7	.926
1980	SF N	11	13	.458	3.10	34	34	6	212	222	56	90	2	0	0	0	66	6	0	.091	8	27	3	0	1.1	.921
1981		6	9	.400	4.02	22	22	2	123	130	47	65	1	0	0	0	33	3	0	.091	10	11	3	1	1.1	.875
1982	CLE A	4	2	.667	3.26	40	9	1	107.2	91	58	61	1	2	1	2	0	0	0	—	4	8	0	0	0.3	1.000
1983	SD N	5	7	.417	4.30	31	21	2	144.1	143	50	81	0	0	0	0	44	8	0	.182	4	6	0	0	0.3	1.000
1984		14	8	.636	3.24	31	31	1	189	181	42	103	0	0	0	0	61	3	0	.049	11	35	0	1	1.5	1.000
1985	NY A	10	8	.556	4.88	30	30	2	158.2	201	43	89	2	0	0	0	0	0	0	—	8	16	3	3	0.9	.889
1986	2 teams	NY A	(14G 5 – 2)			SD N	(17G 1 – 7)																			
"	total	6	9	.400	6.23	31	16	0	112.2	139	60	73	0	4	0	0	18	3	0	.167	7	18	2	1	0.9	.926
1987	SD N	10	13	.435	4.73	36	34	3	205.2	197	64	135	1	0	0	0	65	8	0	.123	14	19	1	0	0.9	.971
1988		13	11	.542	3.77	34	33	3	205.1	202	45	118	1	1	0	0	66	11	0	.167	10	30	4	2	1.3	.909
1989		16	11	.593	2.66	33	33	5	227	198	48	117	1	0	0	0	72	10	0	.139	17	22	2	1	1.2	.951
1990		14	9	.609	2.60	32	32	6	228.2	215	47	127	3	0	0	0	67	10	1	.149	18	42	0	3	1.9	1.000
14 yrs.		122	117	.510	3.75	439	321	33	2162	2147	681	1226	12	13	10	8	552	69	1	.125	118	265	21	16	0.9	.948

LEAGUE CHAMPIONSHIP SERIES

Year	Team	W	L	%	ERA	G	GS	CG	IP	H	BB	SO	ShO	W	L	SV	AB	H	HR	BA	PO	A	E	DP	TC/G	FA
1984	SD N	1	0	1.000	1.13	1	1	0	8	5	2	6	0	0	0	0	3	0	0	.000	1	0	0	0	1.0	1.000

WORLD SERIES

Year	Team	W	L	%	ERA	G	GS	CG	IP	H	BB	SO	ShO	W	L	SV	AB	H	HR	BA	PO	A	E	DP	TC/G	FA
1984	SD N	0	0	—	40.50	1	1	0	0.2	5	0	0	0	0	0	0	0	0	0	—	0	0	0	0	0.0	—

Year	Team	W	L	%	ERA	G	GS	CG	IP	H	BB	SO	ShO	RELIEF PITCHING W	L	SV	BATTING AB	H	HR	BA	PO	A	E	DP	TC/G	FA

Kevin Wickander

WICKANDER, KEVIN DEAN
B. Jan. 4, 1965, Fort Dodge, Iowa
BL TL 6' 2" 202 lbs.

Year	Team	W	L	%	ERA	G	GS	CG	IP	H	BB	SO	ShO	W	L	SV	AB	H	HR	BA	PO	A	E	DP	TC/G	FA
1989	CLE A	0	0	—	3.38	2	0	0	2.2	6	2	0	0	0	0	0	0	0	0	—	0	0	0	0	0.0	—
1990		0	1	.000	3.65	10	0	0	12.1	14	4	10	0	0	1	0	0	0	0	—	0	1	0	0	0.1	1.000
2 yrs.		0	1	.000	3.60	12	0	0	15	20	6	10	0	0	1	0	0	0	0	—	0	1	0	0	0.1	1.000

Dean Wilkins

WILKINS, DEAN ALLAN
B. Aug. 24, 1966, Blue Island, Ill.
BR TR 6' 1" 170 lbs.

Year	Team	W	L	%	ERA	G	GS	CG	IP	H	BB	SO	ShO	W	L	SV	AB	H	HR	BA	PO	A	E	DP	TC/G	FA
1989	CHI N	1	0	1.000	5.17	11	0	0	15.2	13	9	14	0	1	0	0	1	0	0	.000	1	3	0	0	0.4	1.000
1990		0	0	—	9.82	7	0	0	7.1	11	7	3	0	0	0	1	0	0	0	—	0	0	0	0	0.0	—
2 yrs.		1	0	1.000	6.65	18	0	0	23	24	16	17	0	1	0	1	1	0	0	.000	1	3	0	0	0.2	1.000

Mitch Williams

WILLIAMS, MITCHELL STEVEN (Wild Thing)
B. Nov. 17, 1964, Santa Ana, Calif.
BL TL 6' 3" 180 lbs.

Year	Team	W	L	%	ERA	G	GS	CG	IP	H	BB	SO	ShO	W	L	SV	AB	H	HR	BA	PO	A	E	DP	TC/G	FA
April		0	1	.000	0.00	9	0	0	12	6	8	12	0	0	1	5										
May		0	3	.000	4.11	14	0	0	15.1	13	9	12	0	0	3	3										
June		1	1	.500	1.69	6	0	0	5.1	5	6	6	0	1	1	1										
July		0	1	.000	3.00	7	0	0	6	5	4	7	0	0	1	3										
Aug		0	1	.000	3.86	11	0	0	11.2	11	12	6	0	0	1	1										
Sept/Oct		0	1	.000	7.88	12	2	0	16	20	11	12	0	0	0	3										
Day		0	1	.000	3.38	29	0	0	29.1	28	22	23	0	0	1	6										
Night		1	7	.125	4.38	30	2	0	37	32	28	32	0	1	6	10										
vs. Left		—	—	—	—	—	—	—	—	15	16	18	—	—	—	—										
vs. Right		—	—	—	—	—	—	—	—	45	34	37	—	—	—	—										
On Grass		1	4	.200	3.77	39	1	0	43	43	32	35	0	1	4	7										
On Turf		0	4	.000	4.24	20	1	0	23.1	17	18	20	0	0	3	9										
Home		1	1	.500	3.78	30	1	0	33.1	32	25	25	0	1	1	4										
Road		0	7	.000	4.09	29	1	0	33	28	25	30	0	0	6	12										
Division Rivals																										
vs. MON		0	1	.000	4.91	4	1	0	7.1	7	4	5	0	0	1	1										
vs. NY		1	0	1.000	2.84	6	0	0	6.1	7	6	9	0	1	0	1										
vs. PHI		0	0	—	3.18	7	0	0	5.2	5	4	6	0	0	0	4										
vs. PIT		0	1	.000	3.18	10	0	0	11.1	8	9	9	0	0	1	2										
vs. STL		0	1	.000	5.68	5	1	0	6.1	7	4	5	0	0	0	3										
1986	TEX A	8	6	.571	3.58	**80**	0	0	98	69	79	90	0	8	6	8	0	0	0	—	1	10	2	1	0.2	.846
1987		8	6	.571	3.23	85	1	0	108.2	63	94	129	0	8	5	6	0	0	0	—	5	15	3	3	0.3	.870
1988		2	7	.222	4.63	67	0	0	68	48	47	61	0	2	7	18	0	0	0	—	3	10	1	0	0.2	.929
1989	CHI N	4	4	.500	2.64	**76**	0	0	81.2	71	52	67	0	4	4	36	5	1	1	.200	0	11	3	0	0.2	.786
1990		1	8	.111	3.93	59	2	0	66.1	60	50	55	0	1	7	16	5	0	0	.000	1	5	0	0	0.1	1.000
5 yrs.		23	31	.426	3.53	367	3	0	422.2	311	322	402	0	23	29	84	10	1	1	.100	10	51	9	4	0.2	.871

LEAGUE CHAMPIONSHIP SERIES

Year	Team	W	L	%	ERA	G	GS	CG	IP	H	BB	SO	ShO	W	L	SV	AB	H	HR	BA	PO	A	E	DP	TC/G	FA
1989	CHI N	0	0	—	0.00	2	0	0	1	1	0	2	0	0	0	0	0	0	0	—	0	0	0	0	0.0	—

Mark Williamson

WILLIAMSON, MARK ALAN
B. July 21, 1959, Corpus Christi, Tex.
BR TR 6' 155 lbs.

Year	Team	W	L	%	ERA	G	GS	CG	IP	H	BB	SO	ShO	W	L	SV	AB	H	HR	BA	PO	A	E	DP	TC/G	FA
April		1	0	1.000	0.00	5	0	0	7.1	3	5	6	0	1	0	0										
May		2	1	.667	2.49	13	0	0	21.2	15	8	8	0	2	1	0										
June		1	0	1.000	1.29	13	0	0	21	13	9	15	0	1	0	0										
July		4	1	.800	2.57	11	0	0	21	16	4	16	0	4	1	0										
Aug		0	0	—	3.77	7	0	0	14.1	18	2	15	0	0	0	1										
Sept/Oct		—	—	—	—	0	0	0	0	0	0	0	0	0	0	0										
Day		3	2	.600	2.86	15	0	0	22	19	10	16	0	3	2	1										
Night		5	0	1.000	1.99	34	0	0	63.1	46	18	44	0	5	0	0										
vs. Left		—	—	—	—	—	—	—	—	31	7	25	—	—	—	—										
vs. Right		—	—	—	—	—	—	—	—	34	21	35	—	—	—	—										

Year	Team		W	L	%	ERA	G	GS	CG	IP	H	BB	SO	ShO	RELIEF PITCHING W	L	SV	BATTING AB	H	HR	BA	PO	A	E	DP	TC/G	FA

Mark Williamson *Continued*

Year	Team		W	L	%	ERA	G	GS	CG	IP	H	BB	SO	ShO	W	L	SV	AB	H	HR	BA	PO	A	E	DP	TC/G	FA
On Grass			8	0	1.000	1.72	44	0	0	78.1	53	27	56	0	8	0	1										
On Turf			0	2	.000	7.71	5	0	0	7	12	1	4	0	0	2	0										
Home			5	0	1.000	1.35	23	0	0	46.2	28	12	30	0	5	0	0										
Road			3	2	.600	3.26	26	0	0	38.2	37	16	30	0	3	2	1										
Division Rivals																											
vs. BOS			0	0	—	1.69	3	0	0	5.1	1	2	2	0	0	0	0										
vs. CLE			0	0	—	0.00	3	0	0	3.2	1	2	4	0	0	0	0										
vs. DET			0	0	—	4.91	3	0	0	3.2	3	1	6	0	0	0	0										
vs. MIL			1	0	1.000	2.08	4	0	0	8.2	9	4	6	0	1	0	0										
vs. NY			0	0	—	0.00	3	0	0	3.1	2	1	3	0	0	0	0										
vs. TOR			0	0	—	6.23	2	0	0	4.1	5	0	6	0	0	0	0										
1987	BAL	A	8	9	.471	4.03	61	2	0	125	122	41	73	0	8	**8**	3	0	0	0	—	20	17	2	1	0.6	.949
1988			5	8	.385	4.90	37	10	2	117.2	125	40	69	0	4	2	2	0	0	0	—	9	14	1	0	0.6	.958
1989			10	5	.667	2.93	65	0	0	107.1	105	30	55	0	10	5	9	0	0	0	—	9	10	1	1	0.3	.931
1990			8	2	.800	2.21	49	0	0	85.1	65	28	60	0	8	2	1	0	0	0	—	14	13	2	2	0.6	.931
4 yrs.			31	24	.564	3.64	212	12	2	435.1	417	139	257	0	30	17	15	0	0	0	—	52	54	5	4	0.5	.955

RELIEF PITCHER — SAVES (60/30/0); RATIO (20/10/0, AL AVG)

Frank Wills

WILLS, FRANK LEE, JR.
B. Oct. 26, 1958, New Orleans, La.
BR TR 6′ 2″ 200 lbs.

Year	Team		W	L	%	ERA	G	GS	CG	IP	H	BB	SO	ShO	W	L	SV	AB	H	HR	BA	PO	A	E	DP	TC/G	FA
April			1	1	.500	8.74	9	0	0	11.1	17	4	11	0	1	1	0										
May			3	1	.750	5.59	9	0	0	19.1	20	10	10	0	3	1	0										
June			1	0	1.000	3.86	7	0	0	14	12	4	12	0	1	0	0										
July			0	1	.000	3.00	6	0	0	15	13	4	11	0	0	1	0										
Aug			0	0	—	2.37	6	1	0	19	14	6	11	0	0	0	0										
Sept/Oct			1	1	.500	5.75	7	3	0	20.1	25	10	17	0	0	1	0										
Day			1	2	.333	6.23	13	0	0	26	32	12	20	0	1	2	0										
Night			5	2	.714	4.19	31	4	0	73	69	26	52	0	4	2	0										
vs. Left			—	—	—	—	—	—	—	—	42	17	18	—	—	—	—										
vs. Right			—	—	—	—	—	—	—	—	59	21	54	—	—	—	—										
On Grass			1	0	1.000	5.34	16	1	0	28.2	30	20	28	0	1	0	0										
On Turf			5	4	.556	4.48	28	3	0	70.1	71	18	44	0	4	4	0										
Home			3	4	.429	4.50	26	2	0	62	60	16	40	0	3	4	0										
Road			3	0	1.000	5.11	18	2	0	37	41	22	32	0	2	0	0										
Division Rivals																											
vs. BAL			0	1	.000	5.40	5	1	0	11.2	15	6	11	0	0	1	0										
vs. BOS			0	0	—	0.00	1	0	0	0	3	1	0	0	0	0	0										
vs. CLE			1	1	.500	3.86	5	0	0	7	6	1	5	0	1	1	0										
vs. DET			0	0	—	1.35	2	1	0	6.2	1	8	7	0	0	0	0										
vs. MIL			0	0	—	6.75	4	1	0	6.2	7	3	2	0	0	0	0										
vs. NY			1	0	1.000	0.87	3	0	0	10.1	6	2	11	0	1	0	0										
1983	KC	A	2	1	.667	4.15	6	4	0	34.2	35	15	23	0	0	0	0	0	0	0	—	1	3	1	1	0.8	.800
1984			2	3	.400	5.11	10	5	0	37	39	13	21	0	1	0	0	0	0	0	—	3	2	2	0	0.7	.714
1985	SEA	A	5	11	.313	6.00	24	18	1	123	122	68	67	0	0	0	1	0	0	0	—	9	17	0	1	1.1	1.000
1986	CLE	A	4	4	.500	4.91	26	0	0	40.1	43	16	32	0	4	4	4	0	0	0	—	3	6	1	0	0.4	.900
1987			0	1	.000	5.06	6	0	0	5.1	3	7	4	0	0	1	1	0	0	0	—	0	2	0	0	0.3	1.000
1988	TOR	A	0	0	—	5.23	10	0	0	20.2	22	6	19	0	0	0	0	0	0	0	—	1	5	0	0	0.6	1.000
1989			3	1	.750	3.66	24	4	0	71.1	65	30	41	0	3	0	0	0	0	0	—	5	10	0	0	0.6	1.000
1990			6	4	.600	4.73	44	4	0	99	101	38	72	0	5	4	0	0	0	0	—	9	10	0	2	0.4	1.000
8 yrs.			22	25	.468	4.95	150	35	1	431.1	430	193	279	0	13	9	6	0	0	0	—	31	55	4	4	0.6	.956

RELIEF PITCHER — WINS (10/5/0, AL AVG); ERA (5.00/2.50/0.00, AL AVG); SAVES (60/30/0, AL AVG); RATIO (20/10/0, AL AVG)

Glenn Wilson

WILSON, GLENN DWIGHT
B. Dec. 22, 1958, Baytown, Tex.
BR TR 6′ 1″ 190 lbs.

Year	Team		W	L	%	ERA	G	GS	CG	IP	H	BB	SO	ShO	W	L	SV	AB	H	HR	BA	PO	A	E	DP	TC/G	FA
1987	PHI	N	0	0	—	0.00	1	0	0	1	0	0	1	0	0	0	0				*	0	1	0	0	1.0	1.000

Year	Team	W	L	%	ERA	G	GS	CG	IP	H	BB	SO	ShO	RELIEF PITCHING W	L	SV	BATTING AB	H	HR	BA	PO	A	E	DP	TC/G	FA

Steve Wilson

WILSON, STEPHEN DOUGLAS
B. Dec. 13, 1964, Victoria, B. C., Canada
BL TL 6′ 4″ 205 lbs.

STARTING PITCHER

Year	Team	W	L	%	ERA	G	GS	CG	IP	H	BB	SO	ShO	W	L	SV	AB	H	HR	BA	PO	A	E	DP	TC/G	FA
April		0	3	.000	5.85	4	4	0	20	27	7	8	0	0	0	0										
May		0	1	.000	7.36	6	1	0	14.2	19	6	8	0	0	1	0										
June		2	1	.667	2.91	9	3	0	34	25	12	18	0	1	0	1										
July		1	1	.500	3.96	8	3	1	25	23	7	23	0	0	0	0										
Aug		1	1	.500	4.35	9	1	0	20.2	20	2	18	0	1	0	0										
Sept/Oct		0	2	.000	6.20	9	3	0	24.2	26	9	20	0	0	1	0										
Day		2	5	.286	5.45	24	10	1	76	83	26	61	0	0	1	1										
Night		2	4	.333	4.00	21	5	0	63	57	17	34	0	2	1	0										
vs. Left		—	—	—	—	—	—	—	—	31	8	34	—	—	—											
vs. Right		—	—	—	—	—	—	—	—	109	35	61	—	—	—											
On Grass		4	5	.444	4.64	33	12	1	104.2	110	32	72	0	2	0	1										
On Turf		0	4	.000	5.24	12	3	0	34.1	30	11	23	0	0	2	0										
Home		2	5	.286	5.40	22	10	1	71.2	81	23	51	0	0	0	1										
Road		2	4	.333	4.14	23	5	0	67.1	59	20	44	0	2	2	0										
Division Rivals																										
vs. MON		0	0	—	1.23	5	0	0	7.1	2	2	5	0	0	0	1										
vs. NY		1	1	.500	4.07	4	3	0	24.1	20	3	20	0	1	0	0										
vs. PHI		1	2	.333	7.85	5	3	0	18.1	25	10	5	0	0	1	0										
vs. PIT		0	3	.000	5.60	4	3	0	17.2	20	5	14	0	0	0	0										
vs. STL		0	2	.000	6.28	6	2	0	14.1	14	7	12	0	0	0	0										
1988	TEX A	0	0	—	5.87	3	0	0	7.2	7	4	1	0	0	0	0	0	0	0	—	0	0	0	0	0.0	—
1989	CHI N	6	4	.600	4.20	53	8	0	85.2	83	31	65	0	3	2	2	16	1	0	.063	6	14	2	0	0.4	.909
1990		4	9	.308	4.79	45	15	1	139	140	43	95	0	2	2	1	37	6	0	.162	4	16	2	0	0.5	.909
3 yrs.		10	13	.435	4.61	101	23	1	232.1	230	78	161	0	5	4	3	53	7	0	.132	10	30	4	0	0.4	.909

LEAGUE CHAMPIONSHIP SERIES

Year	Team	W	L	%	ERA	G	GS	CG	IP	H	BB	SO	ShO	W	L	SV	AB	H	HR	BA	PO	A	E	DP	TC/G	FA
1989	CHI N	0	1	.000	4.91	2	0	0	3.2	3	1	4	0	0	1	0	0	0	0	—	0	1	0	0	0.5	1.000

Trevor Wilson

WILSON, TREVOR KIRK
B. June 7, 1966, Torrance, Calif.
BL TL 6′ 185 lbs.

Year	Team	W	L	%	ERA	G	GS	CG	IP	H	BB	SO	ShO	W	L	SV	AB	H	HR	BA	PO	A	E	DP	TC/G	FA
1988	SF N	0	2	.000	4.09	4	4	0	22	25	8	15	0	0	0	0	7	2	0	.286	1	1	0	0	0.5	1.000
1989		2	3	.400	4.35	14	4	0	39.1	28	24	22	0	1	1	0	8	2	0	.250	0	7	1	0	0.6	.875
1990		8	7	.533	4.00	27	17	3	110.1	87	49	66	2	1	1	0	29	4	0	.138	9	22	0	1	1.1	1.000
3 yrs.		10	12	.455	4.09	45	25	3	171.2	140	81	103	2	2	2	0	44	8	0	.182	10	30	1	1	0.9	.976

Bobby Witt

WITT, ROBERT ANDREW
B. May 11, 1964, Arlington, Mass.
BR TR 6′ 2″ 190 lbs.

STARTING PITCHER

Year	Team	W	L	%	ERA	G	GS	CG	IP	H	BB	SO	ShO	W	L	SV	AB	H	HR	BA	PO	A	E	DP	TC/G	FA
April		0	3	.000	5.12	4	3	0	19.1	21	12	16	0	0	0	0										
May		2	3	.400	4.96	5	5	0	32.2	32	17	31	0	0	0	0										
June		2	2	.500	4.23	6	6	0	38.1	42	20	40	0	0	0	0										
July		5	0	1.000	1.99	6	6	2	45.1	36	24	49	0	0	0	0										
Aug		4	0	1.000	2.31	5	5	3	39	29	11	35	1	0	0	0										
Sept/Oct		4	2	.667	3.04	7	7	2	47.1	37	26	50	0	0	0	0										
Day		2	3	.400	3.55	7	6	0	45.2	35	32	51	0	0	0	0										
Night		15	7	.682	3.32	26	26	7	176.1	162	78	170	1	0	0	0										
vs. Left		—	—	—	—	—	—	—	—	92	54	98	—	—	—											
vs. Right		—	—	—	—	—	—	—	—	105	56	123	—	—	—											
On Grass		13	9	.591	3.64	27	27	5	180.1	165	91	180	1	0	0	0										
On Turf		4	1	.800	2.16	6	5	2	41.2	32	19	41	0	0	0	0										
Home		7	5	.583	3.40	15	15	4	100.2	104	46	93	1	0	0	0										
Road		10	5	.667	3.34	18	17	3	121.1	93	64	128	0	0	0	0										
Division Rivals																										
vs. CAL		0	2	.000	7.71	2	2	0	11.2	21	6	12	0	0	0	0										
vs. CHI		0	1	.000	9.00	1	1	0	4	8	2	6	0	0	0	0										
vs. KC		2	0	1.000	0.44	3	2	1	20.2	10	10	24	0	0	0	0										
vs. MIN		3	0	1.000	0.72	3	3	2	25	14	9	20	1	0	0	0										
vs. OAK		2	0	1.000	2.53	3	3	0	21.1	13	19	29	0	0	0	0										
vs. SEA		1	1	.500	6.97	4	4	0	20.2	32	10	17	0	0	0	0										

Year	Team	W	L	%	ERA	G	GS	CG	IP	H	BB	SO	ShO	W	L	SV	AB	H	HR	BA	PO	A	E	DP	TC/G	FA

RELIEF PITCHING columns: W L SV — **BATTING** columns: AB H HR BA

Bobby Witt *Continued*

Year	Team	W	L	%	ERA	G	GS	CG	IP	H	BB	SO	ShO	W	L	SV	AB	H	HR	BA	PO	A	E	DP	TC/G	FA
1986	TEX A	11	9	.550	5.48	31	31	0	157.2	130	**143**	174	0	0	0	0	0	0	0	—	8	20	3	1	1.0	.903
1987		8	10	.444	4.91	26	25	1	143	114	**140**	160	0	0	0	0	1	0	0	.000	8	17	0	1	1.0	1.000
1988		8	10	.444	3.92	22	22	13	174.1	134	101	148	2	0	0	0	0	0	0	—	15	15	4	2	1.5	.882
1989		12	13	.480	5.14	31	31	5	194.1	182	**114**	166	1	0	0	0	0	0	0	—	13	22	1	1	1.2	.972
1990		17	10	.630	3.36	33	32	7	222	197	110	221	1	0	0	0	0	0	0	—	18	18	5	2	1.2	.878
5 yrs.		56	52	.519	4.48	143	141	26	891.1	757	608	869	4	0	0	0	1	0	0	.000	62	92	13	7	1.2	.922

Mike Witt

WITT, MICHAEL ATWATER
B. July 20, 1960, Fullerton, Calif.
BR TR 6′ 7″ 185 lbs.

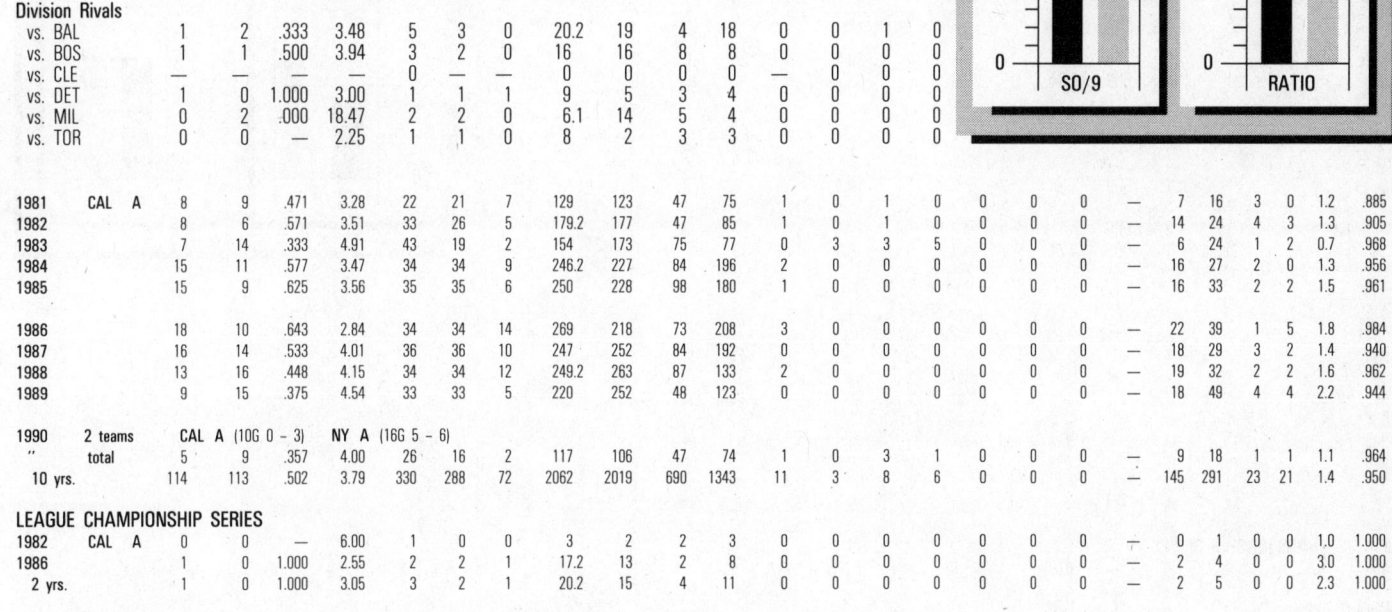

STARTING PITCHER — WINS / ERA / SO/9 / RATIO (AL AVG)

	W	L	%	ERA	G	GS	CG	IP	H	BB	SO	ShO	W	L	SV	AB	H	HR	BA	PO	A	E	DP	TC/G	FA
April	0	3	.000	3.00	6	0	0	12	11	8	8	0	0	3	1										
May	0	0	—	2.63	7	3	0	27.1	27	10	22	0	0	0	0										
June	0	1	.000	4.00	2	2	0	9	8	2	8	0	0	0	0										
July	—	—	—	—	0	—	—	0	0	0	0	—	0	0	0										
Aug	3	2	.600	4.66	5	5	1	29	27	11	15	1	0	0	0										
Sept/Oct	2	3	.400	4.76	6	6	1	39.2	33	16	21	0	0	0	0										
Day	2	3	.400	4.24	7	6	1	34	31	17	23	1	0	0	0										
Night	3	6	.333	3.90	19	10	1	83	75	30	51	0	0	3	1										
vs. Left	—	—	—	—	—	—	—	—	58	23	29	—	—	—	—										
vs. Right	—	—	—	—	—	—	—	—	48	24	45	—	—	—	—										
On Grass	4	9	.308	4.35	21	13	2	93	90	34	64	1	0	3	1										
On Turf	1	0	1.000	2.63	5	3	0	24	16	13	10	0	0	0	0										
Home	2	5	.286	3.29	11	6	1	52	46	15	34	1	0	2	1										
Road	3	4	.429	4.57	15	10	1	65	60	32	40	0	0	1	0										

Division Rivals

	W	L	%	ERA	G	GS	CG	IP	H	BB	SO	ShO	W	L	SV										
vs. BAL	1	2	.333	3.48	5	3	0	20.2	19	4	18	0	0	1	0										
vs. BOS	1	1	.500	3.94	3	2	0	16	16	8	8	0	0	0	0										
vs. CLE	—	—	—	—	0	—	—	0	0	0	0	—	0	0	0										
vs. DET	1	0	1.000	3.00	1	1	1	9	5	3	4	0	0	0	0										
vs. MIL	0	2	.000	18.47	2	2	0	6.1	14	5	4	0	0	0	0										
vs. TOR	0	0	—	2.25	1	1	0	8	2	3	3	0	0	0	0										

Year	Team	W	L	%	ERA	G	GS	CG	IP	H	BB	SO	ShO	W	L	SV	AB	H	HR	BA	PO	A	E	DP	TC/G	FA
1981	CAL A	8	9	.471	3.28	22	21	7	129	123	47	75	1	0	1	0	0	0	0	—	7	16	3	0	1.2	.885
1982		8	6	.571	3.51	33	26	5	179.2	177	47	85	1	0	1	0	0	0	0	—	14	24	4	3	1.3	.905
1983		7	14	.333	4.91	43	19	2	154	173	75	77	0	3	3	5	0	0	0	—	6	24	1	2	0.7	.968
1984		15	11	.577	3.47	34	34	9	246.2	227	84	196	2	0	0	0	0	0	0	—	16	27	2	0	1.3	.956
1985		15	9	.625	3.56	35	35	6	250	228	98	180	1	0	0	0	0	0	0	—	16	33	2	2	1.5	.961
1986		18	10	.643	2.84	34	34	14	269	218	73	208	3	0	0	0	0	0	0	—	22	39	1	5	1.8	.984
1987		16	14	.533	4.01	36	36	10	247	252	84	192	0	0	0	0	0	0	0	—	18	29	3	2	1.4	.940
1988		13	16	.448	4.15	34	34	12	249.2	263	87	133	2	0	0	0	0	0	0	—	19	32	2	2	1.6	.962
1989		9	15	.375	4.54	33	33	5	220	252	48	123	0	0	0	0	0	0	0	—	18	49	4	4	2.2	.944
1990	2 teams	CAL A (10G 0 – 3)				NY A (16G 5 – 6)																				
"	total	5	9	.357	4.00	26	16	2	117	106	47	74	1	0	3	1	0	0	0	—	9	18	1	1	1.1	.964
10 yrs.		114	113	.502	3.79	330	288	72	2062	2019	690	1343	11	3	8	6	0	0	0	—	145	291	23	21	1.4	.950

LEAGUE CHAMPIONSHIP SERIES

Year	Team	W	L	%	ERA	G	GS	CG	IP	H	BB	SO	ShO	W	L	SV	AB	H	HR	BA	PO	A	E	DP	TC/G	FA
1982	CAL A	0	0	—	6.00	1	0	0	3	2	2	3	0	0	0	0	0	0	0	—	0	1	0	0	1.0	1.000
1986		1	0	1.000	2.55	2	2	1	17.2	13	2	8	0	0	0	0	0	0	0	—	2	4	0	0	3.0	1.000
2 yrs.		1	0	1.000	3.05	3	2	1	20.2	15	4	11	0	0	0	0	0	0	0	—	2	5	0	0	2.3	1.000

Rich Yett

YETT, RICHARD MARTIN
B. Oct. 6, 1962, Pomona, Calif.
BR TR 6′ 2″ 187 lbs.

Year	Team	W	L	%	ERA	G	GS	CG	IP	H	BB	SO	ShO	W	L	SV	AB	H	HR	BA	PO	A	E	DP	TC/G	FA
1985	MIN A	0	0	—	27.00	1	1	0	0.1	1	2	0	0	0	0	0	0	0	0	—	0	0	0	0	0.0	—
1986	CLE A	5	3	.625	5.15	39	3	1	78.2	84	37	50	1	4	2	1	0	0	0	—	2	7	0	0	0.2	1.000
1987		3	9	.250	5.25	37	11	2	97.2	96	49	59	0	1	5	1	0	0	0	—	6	9	0	0	0.4	1.000
1988		9	6	.600	4.62	23	22	0	134.1	146	55	71	0	0	0	0	0	0	0	—	8	9	0	1	0.7	1.000
1989		5	6	.455	5.00	32	12	1	99	111	47	47	0	1	1	0	0	0	0	—	9	7	0	0	0.5	1.000
1990	MIN A	0	0	—	2.08	4	0	0	4.1	6	1	2	0	0	0	0	0	0	0	—	2	1	1	0	1.0	.750
6 yrs.		22	24	.478	4.95	136	49	4	414.1	444	191	229	1	6	8	2	0	0	0	—	27	33	1	2	0.4	.984

Year	Team	W	L	%	ERA	G	GS	CG	IP	H	BB	SO	ShO	RELIEF PITCHING W	L	SV	BATTING AB	H	HR	BA	PO	A	E	DP	TC/G	FA

Mike York

YORK, MICHAEL DAVID
B. Sept. 6, 1964, Oak Park, Ill.
BR TR 6′ 1″ 187 lbs.

Year	Team	W	L	%	ERA	G	GS	CG	IP	H	BB	SO	ShO	W	L	SV	AB	H	HR	BA	PO	A	E	DP	TC/G	FA
1990	PIT N	1	1	.500	2.84	4	1	0	12.2	13	5	4	0	0	1	0	3	1	0	.333	1	3	0	0	1.0	1.000

Cliff Young

YOUNG, CLIFFORD RAPHAEL
B. Aug. 2, 1964, Willis, Tex.
BL TL 6′ 4″ 200 lbs.

Year	Team	W	L	%	ERA	G	GS	CG	IP	H	BB	SO	ShO	W	L	SV	AB	H	HR	BA	PO	A	E	DP	TC/G	FA
1990	CAL A	1	1	.500	3.52	17	0	0	30.2	40	7	19	0	1	1	0	0	0	0	—	0	5	1	0	0.4	.833

Curt Young

YOUNG, CURTIS ALLEN
B. Apr. 16, 1960, Saginaw, Mich.
BR TL 6′ 175 lbs.

Year	Team	W	L	%	ERA	G	GS	CG	IP	H	BB	SO	ShO	W	L	SV	AB	H	HR	BA	PO	A	E	DP	TC/G	FA
April		0	1	.000	11.08	3	1	0	13	19	3	11	0	0	0	0										
May		2	0	1.000	3.60	4	4	0	25	20	10	11	0	0	0	0										
June		1	1	.500	2.45	4	3	0	18.1	9	11	12	0	0	0	0										
July		3	2	.600	3.97	6	6	0	34	38	10	19	0	0	0	0										
Aug		1	0	1.000	3.55	3	2	0	12.2	12	7	4	0	0	0	0										
Sept/Oct		2	2	.500	6.75	6	5	0	21.1	26	12	9	0	0	0	0										
Day		5	2	.714	4.77	16	12	0	77.1	75	35	37	0	0	0	0										
Night		4	4	.500	4.98	10	9	0	47	49	18	19	0	0	0	0										
vs. Left		—	—	—	—	—	—	—	—	25	6	13	—	—	—	—										
vs. Right		—	—	—	—	—	—	—	—	99	47	43	—	—	—	—										
On Grass		7	5	.583	4.05	21	17	0	102.1	94	49	51	0	0	0	0										
On Turf		2	1	.667	8.59	5	4	0	22	30	4	5	0	0	0	0										
Home		5	2	.714	3.18	14	11	0	70.2	56	36	40	0	0	0	0										
Road		4	4	.500	7.04	12	10	0	53.2	68	17	16	0	0	0	0										
Division Rivals																										
vs. CAL		1	0	1.000	4.32	2	1	0	8.1	6	3	8	0	0	0	0										
vs. CHI		—	—	—	—	0	0	—	0	0	0	0	0	0	0	0										
vs. KC		1	1	.500	5.23	2	2	0	10.1	9	3	3	0	0	0	0										
vs. MIN		0	0	—	13.50	2	2	0	6	17	1	1	0	0	0	0										
vs. SEA		1	0	1.000	5.11	3	1	0	12.1	12	2	3	0	0	0	0										
vs. TEX		0	1	.000	3.24	2	2	0	8.1	4	11	6	0	0	0	0										
1983	OAK A	0	1	.000	16.00	8	2	0	9	17	5	5	0	0	0	0	0	0	0	—	0	0	0	0	0.0	—
1984		9	4	.692	4.06	20	17	2	108.2	118	31	41	1	0	0	0	0	0	0	—	6	13	0	1	1.0	1.000
1985		0	4	.000	7.24	19	7	0	46	57	22	19	0	0	0	0	0	0	0	—	4	4	0	0	0.4	1.000
1986		13	9	.591	3.45	29	27	5	198	176	57	116	2	1	0	0	0	0	0	—	9	32	4	1	1.6	.911
1987		13	7	.650	4.08	31	31	6	203	194	44	124	0	0	0	0	1	0	0	.000	15	28	1	2	1.4	.977
1988		11	8	.579	4.14	26	26	1	156.1	162	50	69	0	0	0	0	0	0	0	—	11	16	0	0	1.0	1.000
1989		5	9	.357	3.73	25	20	1	111	117	47	55	0	0	0	0	0	0	0	—	2	14	0	0	0.6	1.000
1990		9	6	.600	4.85	26	21	0	124.1	124	53	56	0	0	0	0	0	0	0	—	6	25	1	3	1.2	.969
8 yrs.		60	48	.556	4.28	184	151	15	956.1	965	309	485	3	1	0	0	1	0	0	.000	53	132	6	7	1.0	.969

LEAGUE CHAMPIONSHIP SERIES

Year	Team	W	L	%	ERA	G	GS	CG	IP	H	BB	SO	ShO	W	L	SV	AB	H	HR	BA	PO	A	E	DP	TC/G	FA
1988	OAK A	0	0	—	0.00	1	0	0	1.1	1	0	2	0	0	0	0	0	0	0	—	0	0	0	0	0.0	—

WORLD SERIES

Year	Team	W	L	%	ERA	G	GS	CG	IP	H	BB	SO	ShO	W	L	SV	AB	H	HR	BA	PO	A	E	DP	TC/G	FA
1988	OAK A	0	0	—	0.00	1	0	0	1	1	0	0	0	0	0	0	0	0	0	—	0	1	0	0	1.0	1.000
1990		0	0	—	0.00	1	0	0	1	1	0	0	0	0	0	0	0	0	0	—	0	0	0	0	0.0	—
2 yrs.		0	0	—	0.00	2	0	0	2	2	0	0	0	0	0	0	0	0	0	—	0	1	0	0	0.5	1.000

STARTING PITCHER

WINS · ERA · SO/9 · RATIO (AL AVG comparison charts)

Matt Young

YOUNG, MATTHEW JOHN
B. Aug. 9, 1958, Pasadena, Calif.
BL TL 6′ 3″ 205 lbs.

Year	Team		W	L	%	ERA	G	GS	CG	IP	H	BB	SO	ShO	RELIEF PITCHING			BATTING			BA	PO	A	E	DP	TC/G	FA
															W	L	SV	AB	H	HR							
April			0	3	.000	5.03	4	4	0	19.2	19	13	11	0	0	0	0										
May			1	2	.333	4.68	6	6	0	32.2	34	15	25	0	0	0	0										
June			1	3	.250	2.84	6	5	2	38	30	14	39	1	0	0	0										
July			3	3	.500	3.27	6	6	2	44	30	26	28	0	0	0	0										
Aug			1	3	.250	2.47	6	6	2	47.1	39	16	33	0	0	0	0										
Sept/Oct			2	4	.333	3.92	6	6	1	43.2	46	23	40	0	0	0	0										
Day			5	4	.556	2.93	10	10	3	73.2	59	32	57	0	0	0	0										
Night			3	14	.176	3.80	24	23	4	151.2	139	75	119	1	0	0	0										
vs. Left			—	—	—	—	—	—	—	—	15	7	27	—	—	—	—										
vs. Right			—	—	—	—	—	—	—	—	183	—	149	—	—	—	—										
On Grass			2	8	.200	5.56	11	11	1	68	74	36	57	0	0	0	0										
On Turf			6	10	.375	2.63	23	22	6	157.1	124	71	119	1	0	0	0										
Home			4	10	.286	2.69	20	19	5	134	107	62	101	1	0	0	0										
Road			4	8	.333	4.73	14	14	2	91.1	91	45	75	0	0	0	0										
Division Rivals																											
vs. CAL			0	2	.000	7.16	3	3	0	16.1	19	10	15	0	0	0	0										
vs. CHI			0	4	.000	3.26	4	4	2	30.1	26	18	28	0	0	0	0										
vs. KC			0	0	—	2.03	2	2	0	13.1	12	4	14	0	0	0	0										
vs. MIN			1	1	.500	1.66	3	3	0	21.2	18	7	16	0	0	0	0										
vs. OAK			0	1	.000	5.40	1	1	0	5	5	3	1	0	0	0	0										
vs. TEX			1	2	.333	3.13	3	3	1	23	21	8	24	1	0	0	0										
1983	SEA	A	11	15	.423	3.27	33	32	5	203.2	178	79	130	2	0	0	0	0	0	0	—	9	39	3	0	1.5	.941
1984			6	8	.429	5.72	22	22	1	113.1	141	57	73	0	0	0	0	0	0	0	—	3	21	2	3	1.2	.923
1985			12	**19**	.387	4.91	37	35	5	218.1	242	76	136	2	0	0	1	0	0	0	—	6	24	1	1	0.8	.968
1986			8	6	.571	3.82	65	5	1	103.2	108	46	82	0	6	3	13	0	0	0	—	4	9	4	0	0.3	.765
1987	LA	N	5	8	.385	4.47	47	0	0	54.1	62	17	42	0	5	8	11	3	0	0	.000	3	1	2	0	0.1	.667
1989	OAK	A	1	4	.200	6.75	26	4	0	37.1	42	31	27	0	1	2	0	0	0	0	—	3	6	0	0	0.3	1.000
1990	SEA	A	8	18	.308	3.51	34	33	7	225.1	198	107	176	1	0	0	0	0	0	0	—	12	31	9	1	1.5	.827
7 yrs.			51	78	.395	4.26	264	131	19	956	971	413	666	5	12	13	25	3	0	0	.000	40	131	21	5	0.7	.891
LEAGUE CHAMPIONSHIP SERIES																											
1989	OAK	A	0	0	—	0.00	1	0	0	0.1	0	2	0	0	0	0	0	0	0	0	—	0	0	0	0	0.0	—

STARTING PITCHER

WINS — ERA — SO/9 — RATIO (with AL AVG comparisons)

Manager Register

The Manager Register is an alphabetical listing of every man who managed in the major leagues in 1990. Most of the information is self-explanatory. Column headings include G for games managed, W for wins, L for losses, T for ties, N for no-decision games, PCT for winning percentage, and Standing.

The figures in the Standing column show where the team stood at the end of the season and when there was a managerial change. There are four possible cases:

Only Manager for the Team That Year. Indicated by a single boldface figure that appears in the extreme left-hand column and shows the final standing of the team.

Manager Started Season, but Did Not Finish. Indicated by two figures: the first is boldface and shows the standing of the team when this manager left; the second shows the final standing of the team. (See Tony LaRussa, Chicago, 1986.)

Manager Finished Season, but Did Not Start. Indicated by two figures: the first shows the standing of the team when this manager started; the second is bold faced and shows the final standing of the team. (See Tony LaRussa, Oakland, 1986.)

Manager Did Not Start or Finish Season. Indicated by three figures: the first shows the standing of the team when this manager started; the second is boldface and shows the standing of the team when this manager left; the third shows the final standing of the team. (See Red Schoendienst, St. Louis, 1990.)

The managers' records for the 1981 split season are given separately for each half. "(1st)" or "(2nd)" will appear to the right of the standings to indicate which half.

	G	W	L	T	N	PCT	Standing

Sparky Anderson

ANDERSON, GEORGE LEE
B. Feb. 22, 1934, Bridgewater, S. D.

			G	W	L	T	N	PCT	Standing	
1970	CIN	N	162	102	60	0	0	.630	1	
1971			162	79	83	0	0	.488	4	
1972			154	95	59	0	0	.617	1	
1973			162	99	63	0	0	.611	1	
1974			163	98	64	1	0	.605	2	
1975			162	108	54	0	0	.667	1	
1976			162	102	60	0	0	.630	1	
1977			162	88	74	0	0	.543	2	
1978			161	92	69	0	0	.571	2	
1979	DET	A	106	56	50	0	0	.528	5	5
1980			163	84	78	1	0	.519	4	
1981			57	31	26	0	0	.544	4	(1st)
1981			52	29	23	0	0	.558	2	(2nd)
1982			162	83	79	0	0	.512	4	
1983			162	92	70	0	0	.568	2	
1984			162	104	58	0	0	.642	1	
1985			161	84	77	0	0	.522	3	
1986			162	87	75	0	0	.537	3	
1987			162	98	64	0	0	.605	1	
1988			162	88	74	0	0	.543	2	
1989			162	59	103	0	0	.364	7	
1990			162	79	83	0	0	.488	3	
21 yrs.			3285	1837	1446	2	0	.560		
									10th	

LEAGUE CHAMPIONSHIP SERIES

			G	W	L	T	N	PCT	Standing
1970	CIN	N	3	3	0	0	0	1.000	
1972			5	3	2	0	0	.600	
1973			5	2	3	0	0	.400	
1975			3	3	0	0	0	1.000	
1976			3	3	0	0	0	1.000	
1984	DET	A	3	3	0	0	0	1.000	
1987			5	1	4	0	0	.200	
7 yrs.			27	18	9	0	0	.667	
			3rd	1st	5th				3rd

WORLD SERIES

			G	W	L	T	N	PCT	Standing
1970	CIN	N	5	1	4	0	0	.200	
1972			7	3	4	0	0	.429	
1975			7	4	3	0	0	.571	
1976			4	4	0	0	0	1.000	
1984	DET	A	5	4	1	0	0	.800	
5 yrs.			28	16	12	0	0	.571	
			7th	7th	10th				3rd

Bobby Cox

COX, ROBERT JOE
B. May 21, 1941, Tulsa, Okla.

			G	W	L	T	N	PCT	Standing	
1978	ATL	N	162	69	93	0	0	.426	6	
1979			160	66	94	0	0	.413	6	
1980			161	81	80	0	0	.503	4	
1981			55	25	29	1	0	.463	4	(1st)
1981			52	25	27	0	0	.481	5	(2nd)
1982	TOR	A	162	78	84	0	0	.481	6	
1983			162	89	73	0	0	.549	4	
1984			163	89	73	1	0	.549	2	
1990	ATL	N	97	40	57	0	0	.412	6	6
9 yrs.			1335	661	672	0	0	.495		

LEAGUE CHAMPIONSHIP SERIES

			G	W	L	T	N	PCT	Standing
1985	TOR	A	7	3	4	0	0	.429	

Roger Craig

CRAIG, ROGER LEE
B. Feb. 17, 1930, Durham, N. C.

			G	W	L	T	N	PCT	Standing	
1978	SD	N	162	84	78	0	0	.519	4	
1979			161	68	93	0	0	.422	5	
1985	SF	N	18	6	12	0	0	.333	6	6
1986			162	83	79	0	0	.512	3	
1987			162	90	72	0	0	.556	1	
1988			162	83	79	0	0	.512	4	
1989			162	92	70	0	0	.568	1	
1990			162	85	77	0	0	.525	3	
8 yrs.			1151	591	560	0	0	.513		

LEAGUE CHAMPIONSHIP SERIES

			G	W	L	T	N	PCT	Standing
1987	SF	N	7	3	4	0	0	.429	
1989			5	4	1	0	0	.800	
2 yrs.			12	7	5	0	0	.583	
				8th					4th

WORLD SERIES

			G	W	L	T	N	PCT	Standing
1989	SF	N	4	0	4	0	0	.000	

Bucky Dent

DENT, RUSSELL EARL
Born Russell Earl O'Dey.
B. Nov. 25, 1951, Savannah, Ga.

			G	W	L	T	N	PCT	Standing	
1989	NY	A	40	18	22	0	0	.450	6	5
1990			49	18	31	0	0	.367	7	7
2 yrs.			89	36	53	0	0	.404		

Clarence Gaston

GASTON, CLARENCE EDWIN (Cito)
B. Mar. 17, 1944, San Antonio, Tex.

			G	W	L	T	N	PCT	Standing	
1989	TOR	A	126	77	49	0	0	.611	6	1
1990			162	86	76	0	0	.531	2	
2 yrs.			288	163	125	0	0	.566		

LEAGUE CHAMPIONSHIP SERIES

			G	W	L	T	N	PCT	Standing
1989	TOR	A	5	1	4	0	0	.200	

Bud Harrelson

HARRELSON, DERRELL McKINLEY
B. June 6, 1944, Niles, Calif.

			G	W	L	T	N	PCT	Standing	
1990	NY	N	120	71	49	0	0	.592	4	2

Whitey Herzog

HERZOG, DORREL NORMAN ELVERT
(The White Rat)
B. Nov. 9, 1931, New Athens, Ill.

			G	W	L	T	N	PCT	Standing	
1973	TEX	A	138	47	91	0	0	.341	6	6
1974	CAL	A	4	2	2	0	0	.500	6	6
1975	KC	A	66	41	25	0	0	.621	2	2
1976			162	90	72	0	0	.556	1	
1977			162	102	60	0	0	.630	1	
1978			162	92	70	0	0	.568	1	
1979			162	85	77	0	0	.525	2	
1980	STL	N	73	38	35	0	0	.521	6	5	4
1981			51	30	20	1	0	.600	2	(1st)
1981			52	29	23	0	0	.558	2	(2nd)

Whitey Herzog *continued*

			G	W	L	T	N	PCT	Standing	
1982			162	92	70	0	0	.568	1	
1983			162	79	83	0	0	.488	4	
1984			162	84	78	0	0	.519	3	
1985			162	101	61	0	0	.623	1	
1986			161	79	82	0	0	.491	3	
1987			162	95	67	0	0	.586	1	
1988			162	76	86	0	0	.469	5	
1989			162	86	76	0	0	.531	3	
1990			80	33	47	0	0	.413	6	6
18 yrs.			2407	1281	1125	1	0	.532		

LEAGUE CHAMPIONSHIP SERIES

			G	W	L	T	N	PCT	Standing
1976	KC	A	5	2	3	0	0	.400	
1977			5	2	3	0	0	.400	
1978			4	1	3	0	0	.250	
1982	STL	N	3	3	0	0	0	1.000	
1985			6	4	2	0	0	.667	
1987			7	4	3	0	0	.571	
6 yrs.			30	16	14	0	0	.533	
			1st	2nd	1st				6th

WORLD SERIES

			G	W	L	T	N	PCT	Standing
1982	STL	N	7	4	3	0	0	.571	
1985			7	3	4	0	0	.429	
1987			7	3	4	0	0	.429	
3 yrs.			21	10	11	0	0	.476	

Art Howe

HOWE, ARTHUR HENRY JR.
B. Dec. 15, 1946, Pittsburgh, Pa.

			G	W	L	T	N	PCT	Standing
1989	HOU	N	162	86	76	0	0	.531	3
1990			162	75	87	0	0	.463	4
2 yrs.			324	161	163	0	0	.497	

Davey Johnson

JOHNSON, DAVID ALLEN
B. Jan. 30, 1943, Orlando, Fla.

			G	W	L	T	N	PCT	Standing	
1984	NY	N	162	90	72	0	0	.556	2	
1985			162	98	64	0	0	.605	2	
1986			162	108	54	0	0	.667	1	
1987			162	92	70	0	0	.568	2	
1988			160	100	60	0	0	.625	1	
1989			162	87	75	0	0	.537	2	
1990			42	20	22	0	0	.476	4	2
7 yrs.			1012	595	417	0	0	.588		
									7th	

LEAGUE CHAMPIONSHIP SERIES

			G	W	L	T	N	PCT	Standing
1986	NY	N	6	4	2	0	0	.667	
1988			7	3	4	0	0	.429	
2 yrs.			13	7	6	0	0	.538	
			8th	8th					5th

WORLD SERIES

			G	W	L	T	N	PCT	Standing
1986	NY	N	7	4	3	0	0	.571	

Tom Kelly

KELLY, JAY THOMAS
B. Aug. 15, 1950, Graceville, Minn.

			G	W	L	T	N	PCT	Standing	
1986	MIN	A	23	12	11	0	0	.522	7	6
1987			162	85	77	0	0	.525	1	
1988			162	91	71	0	0	.562	2	
1989			162	80	82	0	0	.494	5	
1990			162	74	88	0	0	.457	7	
5 yrs.			671	342	329	0	0	.510		

LEAGUE CHAMPIONSHIP SERIES

			G	W	L	T	N	PCT	Standing
1987	MIN	A	5	4	1	0	0	.800	

WORLD SERIES

			G	W	L	T	N	PCT	Standing
1987	MIN	A	7	4	3	0	0	.571	

	G	W	L	T	N	PCT	Standing			G	W	L	T	N	PCT	Standing			G	W	L	T	N	PCT	Standing

Tony LaRussa

LaRUSSA, ANTHONY
B. Oct. 4, 1944, Tampa, Fla.

Year	Team	Lg	G	W	L	T	N	PCT	Standing	
1979	CHI	A	54	27	27	0	0	.500	5	5
1980			162	70	90	2	0	.438	5	
1981			53	31	22	0	0	.585	3	(1st)
1981			53	23	30	0	0	.434	6	(2nd)
1982			162	87	75	0	0	.537	3	
1983			162	99	63	0	0	.611	1	
1984			162	74	88	0	0	.457	5	
1985			163	85	77	1	0	.525	3	
1986			64	26	38	0	0	.406	6	5
1986	OAK	A	79	45	34	0	0	.570	7	3
1987			162	81	81	0	0	.500	3	
1988			162	104	58	0	0	.642	1	
1989			162	99	63	0	0	.611	1	
1990			162	103	59	0	0	.636	1	
12 yrs.			1762	954	805	3	0	.542		

LEAGUE CHAMPIONSHIP SERIES

Year	Team	Lg	G	W	L	T	N	PCT
1983	CHI	A	4	1	3	0	0	.250
1988	OAK	A	4	4	0	0	0	1.000
1989			5	4	1	0	0	.800
1990			4	4	0	0	0	1.000
4 yrs.			17	13	4	0	0	.765
			7th	5th				1st

WORLD SERIES

Year	Team	Lg	G	W	L	T	N	PCT
1988	OAK	A	5	1	4	0	0	.200
1989			4	4	0	0	0	1.000
1990			4	0	4	0	0	.000
3 yrs.			13	5	8	0	0	.385

Tom Lasorda

LASORDA, THOMAS CHARLES
B. Sept. 22, 1927, Norristown, Pa.

Year	Team	Lg	G	W	L	T	N	PCT	Standing	
1976	LA	N	4	2	2	0	0	.500	2	2
1977			162	98	64	0	0	.605	1	
1978			162	95	67	0	0	.586	1	
1979			162	79	83	0	0	.488	3	
1980			163	92	71	0	0	.564	2	
1981			57	36	21	0	0	.632	1	(1st)
1981			53	27	26	0	0	.509	4	(2nd)
1982			162	88	74	0	0	.543	2	
1983			163	91	71	1	0	.562	1	
1984			162	79	83	0	0	.488	4	
1985			162	95	67	0	0	.586	1	
1986			162	73	89	0	0	.451	5	
1987			162	73	89	0	0	.451	4	
1988			162	94	67	1	0	.584	1	
1989			160	77	83	0	0	.481	4	
1990			162	86	76	0	0	.531	2	
15 yrs.			2220	1185	1033	2	0	.534		

DIVISIONAL PLAYOFF SERIES

Year	Team	Lg	G	W	L	T	N	PCT
1981	LA	N	5	3	2	0	0	.600

LEAGUE CHAMPIONSHIP SERIES

Year	Team	Lg	G	W	L	T	N	PCT
1977	LA	N	4	3	1	0	0	.750
1978			4	3	1	0	0	.750
1981			5	3	2	0	0	.600
1983			4	1	3	0	0	.250
1985			6	2	4	0	0	.333
1988			7	4	3	0	0	.571
6 yrs.			30	16	14	0	0	.533
			1st	2nd	1st			6th

Tom Lasorda *continued*

WORLD SERIES

Year	Team	Lg	G	W	L	T	N	PCT
1977	LA	N	6	2	4	0	0	.333
1978			6	2	4	0	0	.333
1981			6	4	2	0	0	.667
1988			5	4	1	0	0	.800
4 yrs.			23	12	11	0	0	.522
			10th	8th				8th

Jim Lefebvre

LEFEBVRE, JAMES KENNETH (Frenchy)
B. Jan. 7, 1942, Inglewood, Calif.

Year	Team	Lg	G	W	L	T	N	PCT	Standing
1989	SEA	A	162	73	89	0	0	.451	6
1990			162	77	85	0	0	.475	5
			324	150	174	0	0	.463	

Jim Leyland

LEYLAND, JAMES RICHARD
B. Dec. 15, 1944, Toledo, Ohio

Year	Team	Lg	G	W	L	T	N	PCT	Standing
1986	PIT	N	162	64	98	0	0	.395	6
1987			162	80	82	0	0	.494	4
1988			160	85	75	0	0	.531	2
1989			162	74	88	0	0	.457	5
1990			162	95	67	0	0	.586	1
5 yrs.			808	398	410	0	0	.493	

LEAGUE CHAMPIONSHIP SERIES

Year	Team	Lg	G	W	L	T	N	PCT
1990	PIT	N	6	2	4	0	0	.333

Nick Leyva

LEYVA, NICHOLAS TOMAS
B. Aug. 16, 1953, Ontario, Calif.

Year	Team	Lg	G	W	L	T	N	PCT	Standing
1989	PHI	N	162	67	95	0	0	.414	6
1990			162	77	85	0	0	.475	4
2 yrs.			324	144	180	0	0	.444	

Jack McKeon

McKEON, JOHN ALOYSIUS
B. Nov. 23, 1930, South Amboy, N. J.

Year	Team	Lg	G	W	L	T	N	PCT	Standing	
1973	KC	A	162	88	74	0	0	.543	2	
1974			162	77	85	0	0	.475	5	
1975			96	50	46	0	0	.521	2	2
1977	OAK	A	53	26	27	0	0	.491	7	7
1978			123	45	78	0	0	.366	6	6
1988	SD	N	115	67	48	0	0	.583	5	3
1989			162	89	73	0	0	.549	2	
1990			80	37	43	0	0	.463	4	4
8 yrs.			953	479	474	0	0	.503		

John McNamara

McNAMARA, JOHN FRANCIS
B. June 4, 1932, Sacramento, Calif.

Year	Team	Lg	G	W	L	T	N	PCT	Standing	
1969	OAK	A	13	8	5	0	0	.615	2	2
1970			162	89	73	0	0	.549	2	
1974	SD	N	162	60	102	0	0	.370	6	
1975			162	71	91	0	0	.438	4	
1976			162	73	89	0	0	.451	5	
1977			48	20	28	0	0	.417	5	5
1979	CIN	N	161	90	71	0	0	.559	1	
1980			163	89	73	1	0	.549	3	
1981			56	35	21	0	0	.625	2	(1st)
1981			52	31	21	0	0	.596	2	(2nd)
1982			92	34	58	0	0	.370	6	6
1983	CAL	A	162	70	92	0	0	.432	5	
1984			162	81	81	0	0	.500	2	
1985	BOS	A	163	81	81	1	0	.500	5	
1986			161	95	66	0	0	.590	1	
1987			162	78	84	0	0	.481	5	
1988			85	43	42	0	0	.506	4	1
1990	CLE	A	162	77	85	0	0	.475	4	
17 yrs.			2290	1125	1163	0	0	.491		

LEAGUE CHAMPIONSHIP SERIES

Year	Team	Lg	G	W	L	T	N	PCT
1979	CIN	N	3	0	3	0	0	.000
1986	BOS	A	7	4	3	0	0	.571
2 yrs.			10	4	6	0	0	.400
								10th

WORLD SERIES

Year	Team	Lg	G	W	L	T	N	PCT
1986	BOS	A	7	3	4	0	0	.429

Stump Merrill

MERRILL, CARL HARRISON
B. Feb. 25, 1944, Brunswick, Me.

Year	Team	Lg	G	W	L	T	N	PCT	Standing	
1990	NY	A	113	49	64	0	0	.434	7	7

Joe Morgan

MORGAN, JOSEPH MICHAEL
B. Nov. 19, 1930, Walpole, Mass.

Year	Team	Lg	G	W	L	T	N	PCT	Standing	
1988	BOS	A	77	46	31	0	0	.597	4	1
1989			162	83	79	0	0	.512	3	
1990			162	88	74	0	0	.543	1	
3 yrs.			401	217	184	0	0	.541		

LEAGUE CHAMPIONSHIP SERIES

Year	Team	Lg	G	W	L	T	N	PCT
1988	BOS	A	4	0	4	0	0	.000
1990			4	0	4	0	0	.000
2 yrs.			8	0	8	0	0	.000
								9th

Russ Nixon

NIXON, RUSSELL EUGENE
B. Feb. 19, 1935, Cleves, Ohio

Year	Team	Lg	G	W	L	T	N	PCT	Standing	
1982	CIN	N	70	27	43	0	0	.386	6	6
1983			162	74	88	0	0	.457	6	
1988	ATL	N	121	42	79	0	0	.347	6	6
1989			160	63	97	0	0	.394	6	
1990			65	25	40	0	0	.385	6	6
5 yrs.			578	231	347	0	0	.400		

			G	W	L	T	N	PCT	Standing

Lou Piniella

PINIELLA, LOUIS VICTOR (Sweet Lou)
B. Aug. 28, 1943, Tampa, Fla.

			G	W	L	T	N	PCT	Standing	
1986	NY	A	162	90	72	0	0	.556	2	
1987			162	89	73	0	0	.549	4	
1988			93	45	48	0	0	.484	2	5
1990	CIN	N	162	91	71	0	0	.562	1	
4 yrs.			579	315	264	0	0	.544		

LEAGUE CHAMPIONSHIP SERIES
| 1990 | CIN | N | 6 | 4 | 2 | 0 | 0 | .667 | | |

WORLD SERIES
| 1990 | CIN | N | 4 | 4 | 0 | 0 | 0 | 1.000 | | |

Doug Rader

RADER, DOUGLAS LEE (Rojo, The Red Rooster)
B. July 30, 1944, Chicago, Ill.

			G	W	L	T	N	PCT	Standing	
1983	TEX	A	163	77	85	1	0	.475	3	
1984			161	69	92	0	0	.429	7	
1985			32	9	23	0	0	.281	7	7
1986	CHI	A	2	1	1	0	0	.500	6	5	5
1989	CAL	A	162	91	71	0	0	.562	3	
1990			162	80	82	0	0	.494	4	
6 yrs.			682	327	354	1	0	.480		

Greg Riddoch

RIDDOCH, GREGORY LEE
B. July 17, 1945, Greeley, Colo.

			G	W	L	T	N	PCT	Standing	
1990	SD	N	82	38	44	0	0	.463	4	4

Frank Robinson

ROBINSON, FRANK
B. Aug. 31, 1935, Beaumont, Tex.
Hall of Fame 1982.

			G	W	L	T	N	PCT	Standing	
1975	CLE	A	159	79	80	0	0	.497	4	
1976			159	81	78	0	0	.509	4	
1977			57	26	31	0	0	.456	6	5
1981	SF	N	59	27	32	0	0	.458	5		(1st)
1981			52	29	23	0	0	.558	3		(2nd)
1982			162	87	75	0	0	.537	3	
1983			162	79	83	0	0	.488	5	
1984			106	42	64	0	0	.396	6	6
1988	BAL	A	155	54	101	0	0	.348	6	7
1989			162	87	75	0	0	.537	2	
1990			161	76	85	0	0	.472	5	
10 yrs.			1394	667	727	0	0	.478		

Buck Rodgers

RODGERS, ROBERT LEROY
B. Aug. 16, 1938, Delaware, Ohio

			G	W	L	T	N	PCT	Standing	
1980	MIL	A	47	26	21	0	0	.553	2	3
1980			23	13	10	0	0	.565	4	3
1981			56	31	25	0	0	.554	3		(1st)
1981			53	31	22	0	0	.585	1		(2nd)
1982			47	23	24	0	0	.489	5	1

Buck Rodgers *continued*

			G	W	L	T	N	PCT	Standing	
1985	MON	N	161	84	77	0	0	.522	3	
1986			161	78	83	0	0	.484	4	
1987			162	91	71	0	0	.562	3	
1988			163	81	81	1	0	.500	3	
1989			162	81	81	0	0	.500	4	
1990			162	85	77	0	0	.525	3	
9 yrs.			1197	624	572	0	0	.521		

DIVISIONAL PLAYOFF SERIES
| 1981 | MIL | A | 5 | 2 | 3 | 0 | 0 | .400 | | |

Red Schoendienst

SCHOENDIENST, ALBERT FRED
B. Feb. 2, 1923, Germantown, Ill.
Hall of Fame 1989.

			G	W	L	T	N	PCT	Standing	
1965	STL	N	162	80	81	1	0	.497	7	
1966			162	83	79	0	0	.512	6	
1967			161	101	60	0	0	.627	1	
1968			162	97	65	0	0	.599	4	
1969			162	87	75	0	0	.537	4	
1970			162	76	86	0	0	.469	4	
1971			163	90	72	1	0	.556	2	
1972			156	75	81	0	0	.481	4	
1973			162	81	81	0	0	.500	2	
1974			161	86	75	0	0	.534	2	
1975			163	82	80	1	0	.506	3	
1976			162	72	90	0	0	.444	5	
1980			37	18	19	0	0	.486	5	4
1990			24	13	11	0	0	.542	6	6	6
14 yrs.			1999	1041	955	3	0	.522		

WORLD SERIES
1967	STL	N	7	4	3	0	0	.571		
1968			7	3	4	0	0	.429		
2 yrs.			14	7	7	0	0	.500		

Jeff Torborg

TORBORG, JEFFREY ALLEN
B. Nov. 26, 1941, Plainfield, N. J.

			G	W	L	T	N	PCT	Standing	
1977	CLE	A	104	45	59	0	0	.433	6	5
1978			159	69	90	0	0	.434	6	
1979			95	43	52	0	0	.453	6	6
1989	CHI	A	161	69	92	0	0	.429	7	
1990			162	94	68	0	0	.580	2	
5 yrs.			681	320	361	0	0	.470		

Joe Torre

TORRE, JOSEPH PAUL
Brother of Frank Torre.
B. July 18, 1940, Brooklyn, N. Y.

			G	W	L	T	N	PCT	Standing	
1977	NY	N	117	49	68	0	0	.419	6	6
1978			162	66	96	0	0	.407	6	
1979			163	63	99	1	0	.389	6	
1980			162	67	95	0	0	.414	5	
1981			52	17	34	1	0	.333	5		(1st)
1981			53	24	28	1	0	.462	4		(2nd)
1982	ATL	N	162	89	73	0	0	.549	1	
1983			162	88	74	0	0	.543	2	
1984			162	80	82	0	0	.494	2	
1990	STL	N	58	24	34	0	0	.414	6	6
9 yrs.			1253	567	683	3	0	.454		

LEAGUE CHAMPIONSHIP SERIES
| 1982 | ATL | N | 3 | 0 | 3 | 0 | 0 | .000 | | |

Tom Trebelhorn

TREBELHORN, THOMAS LYNN
B. Jan. 27, 1948, Portland, Ore.

			G	W	L	T	N	PCT	Standing	
1986	MIL	A	9	6	3	0	0	.667	6	6
1987			162	91	71	0	0	.562	3	
1988			162	87	75	0	0	.537	3	
1989			162	81	81	0	0	.500	4	
1990			162	74	88	0	0	.457	6	
5 yrs.			657	339	318	0	0	.516		

Bobby Valentine

VALENTINE, ROBERT JOHN
B. May 13, 1950, Stamford, Conn.

			G	W	L	T	N	PCT	Standing	
1985	TEX	A	129	53	76	0	0	.411	7	7
1986			162	87	75	0	0	.537	2	
1987			162	75	87	0	0	.463	6	
1988			161	70	91	0	0	.435	6	
1989			162	83	79	0	0	.512	4	
1990			162	83	79	0	0	.512	3	
6 yrs.			938	451	487	0	0	.481		

John Wathan

WATHAN, JOHN DAVID (Duke)
B. Oct. 4, 1949, Cedar Rapids, Iowa

			G	W	L	T	N	PCT	Standing	
1987	KC	A	36	21	15	0	0	.583	4	2
1988			161	84	77	0	0	.522	3	
1989			162	92	70	0	0	.568	2	
1990			161	75	86	0	0	.466	6	
4 yrs.			520	272	248	0	0	.523		

Don Zimmer

ZIMMER, DONALD WILLIAM
B. Jan. 17, 1931, Cincinnati, Ohio

			G	W	L	T	N	PCT	Standing	
1972	SD	N	142	54	88	0	0	.380	4	6
1973			162	60	102	0	0	.370	6	
1976	BOS	A	76	42	34	0	0	.553	3	3
1977			161	97	64	0	0	.602	2	
1978			163	99	64	0	0	.607	2	
1979			160	91	69	0	0	.569	3	
1980			155	82	73	0	0	.529	4	4
1981	TEX	A	56	33	22	1	0	.600	2		(1st)
1981			50	24	26	0	0	.480	3		(2nd)
1982			96	38	58	0	0	.396	6	6
1988	CHI	N	163	77	85	1	0	.475	4	
1989			162	93	69	0	0	.574	1	
1990			162	77	85	0	0	.475	4	
12 yrs.			1708	867	839	2	0	.508		

LEAGUE CHAMPIONSHIP SERIES
| 1989 | CHI | N | 5 | 1 | 4 | 0 | 0 | .200 | | |

World Series and League Championship Series

This section provides details of the National and American League Championship Series and World Series of 1990. Facts are provided about the individual games, including line scores and highlights.

Pitchers are listed in order of appearance. In parentheses following each pitcher's name is the number of innings he worked. "Doe (2.1)" indicates that Doe worked two and one-third innings; "(2.0)" means that he faced at least one batter in his third inning of work, but did not retire anyone. The winning and losing pitchers are listed in boldface print; a pitcher who is credited with a save has a bold "SV" after his innings pitched.

Home runs are listed in the order they were hit.

1990 NATIONAL LEAGUE CHAMPIONSHIP SERIES

LINE SCORES	PITCHERS (innings pitched)	HOME RUNS (men on)	HIGHLIGHTS

Cincinnati (West) defeats Pittsburgh (East) 4 games to 2

GAME 1 - OCTOBER 4

PIT E	001 200 100	4 7 1	Walk (6), Belinda (2), Patterson (0.1), Power (0.2) SV	Bream (1 on)
CIN W	300 000 000	3 5 0	Rijo (5.1), **Charlton** (2.2), Dibble (1)	

Leftfielder Davis misplayed Van Slyke's seventh-inning fly ball into a game-winning double as Pirates rallied from a 3-0 deficit. Bream's two-run homer tied the game in the fourth inning. Cincinnati put runners on first and third in the ninth with nobody out, but were turned back by Power.

GAME 2 - OCTOBER 5

PIT E	000 010 000	1 6 0	**Drabek** (8)	Lind
CIN W	100 010 00x	2 5 0	Browning (6), Dibble (1.1), Myers (1.2) SV	

O'Neill drove in both Cincinnati runs with a single and a double against Drabek, while Browning teamed with Dibble and Myers on a six-hitter that evened the series. Lind homered for Pittsburgh's only run.

GAME 3 - OCTOBER 8

CIN W	020 030 001	6 13 1	Jackson (5.1), Dibble (1.2), Charlton (1), Myers (1) SV	Hatcher (1 on) Duncan (2 on)
PIT E	000 200 010	3 8 0	**Smith** (5), Landrum (1), Smiley (2), Belinda (1)	

Duncan drove in four runs, three of them coming on a fifth-inning homer that put the Reds ahead to stay. Hatcher's two-run homer gave Cincinnati a 2-0 lead before the Pirates scored twice in the fourth inning.

GAME 4 - OCTOBER 9

CIN W	000 200 201	5 10 1	Rijo (7.0), Myers (1), Dibble (1) SV	O'Neill, Sabo (1 on)
PIT E	100 100 010	3 8 0	**Walk** (7), Power (2)	Bell

Two-run homer by Sabo broke a 2-2 tie in the seventh inning. Davis made the defensive play of the game for the Reds by throwing Bonilla out at third base in the eighth inning as he tried to stretch a double into a triple.

GAME 5 - OCTOBER 10

CIN W	100 000 010	2 7 0	**Browning** (5), Mahler (1.2), Charlton (0.1), Scudder (1)
PIT E	200 100 00x	3 6 1	**Drabek** (8.1), Patterson (0.2) SV

Drabek kept Pittsburgh's hopes alive with a strong performance before Patterson bailed him out of a ninth-inning jam. Reds scored a run in the top of the first, but Pirates scored twice in their half on Van Slyke's RBI triple and forceout.

GAME 6 - OCTOBER 12

PIT E	000 010 000	1 1 3	Power (2.1), **Smith** (4), Belinda (0.2), Landrum (1)
CIN W	100 000 10x	2 9 0	Jackson (6), **Charlton** (1), Myers (2) SV

Cincinnati nailed down first pennant since 1976 on the strength of a combined one-hitter by Jackson, Charlton, and Myers. Reds broke a 1-1 tie in the seventh inning as pinch-hitter Quinones singled home Oester. Martinez doubled for Pittsburgh's only hit and run, and was robbed of a possible two-run homer in the ninth on a brilliant catch by Braggs.

Team totals

	W	AB	H	2B	3B	HR	R	RBI	BA	BB	SO	ERA
CIN W	4	192	49	9	0	4	20	20	.255	10	37	2.38
PIT E	2	186	36	9	2	3	15	14	.194	27	49	3.29

Individual Batting

CINCINNATI (WEST)

	AB	H	2B	3B	HR	R	RBI	BA
B. Larkin, ss	23	6	2	0	0	5	1	.261
E. Davis, of	23	4	1	0	0	2	2	.174
C. Sabo, 3b	22	5	0	0	1	1	3	.227
M. Duncan, 2b	20	6	0	0	1	1	4	.300
P. O'Neill, of	17	8	3	0	1	1	4	.471
B. Hatcher, of	15	5	1	0	1	2	2	.333
J. Oliver, c	14	2	0	0	0	1	0	.143
H. Morris, 1b	12	5	1	0	0	3	1	.417
T. Benzinger, 1b	9	3	0	0	0	0	1	.333
H. Winningham, of	7	2	1	0	0	1	1	.286
J. Reed, c	7	0	0	0	0	0	0	.000
G. Braggs, of	5	1	0	0	0	0	0	.200
J. Rijo, p	5	0	0	0	0	0	0	.000
R. Oester, 2b	3	1	0	0	0	1	0	.333
T. Browning, p	3	0	0	0	0	0	0	.000
D. Jackson, p	3	0	0	0	0	0	0	.000
L. Quinones	2	1	0	0	0	1	2	.500
R. Dibble, p	2	0	0	0	0	0	0	.000
B. Bates	0	0	0	0	0	1	0	–

Errors: M. Duncan, B. Larkin.
Stolen Bases: B. Larkin (3), P. O'Neill, H. Winningham, L. Quinones.

PITTSBURGH (EAST)

	AB	H	2B	3B	HR	R	RBI	BA
A. Van Slyke, of	24	5	1	1	0	3	3	.208
J. Lind, 2b	21	5	1	1	1	1	2	.238
B. Bonilla, of, 3b	21	4	1	0	0	0	1	.190
J. Bell, ss	20	5	1	0	1	3	1	.250
B. Bonds, of	18	3	0	0	0	4	1	.167
D. Slaught, of	11	1	0	0	0	0	1	.091
R. Reynolds, of	10	2	0	0	0	0	0	.200
J. King, 3b	10	1	0	0	0	0	0	.100
S. Bream, 1b	8	4	1	0	1	1	3	.500
C. Martinez, 1b	8	2	2	0	0	2	0	.250
G. Redus, 1b	8	2	0	0	0	1	0	.250
W. Backman, 3b	7	1	1	0	0	1	0	.143
M. Lavalliere, c	6	0	0	0	0	0	0	.000
D. Drabek, p	6	1	0	0	0	0	0	.167
B. Walk, p	4	0	0	0	0	0	0	.000
Z. Smith, p	3	0	0	0	0	0	0	.000
T. Power, p	1	0	0	0	0	0	0	.000

Errors: J. Bell, B. Bonilla, D. Drabek, R. Reynolds, D. Slaught.
Stolen Bases: B. Bonds (2), G. Redus, W. Backman, A. Van Slyke, R. Reynolds.

Individual Pitching

CINCINNATI (WEST)

	W	L	ERA	IP	H	BB	SO	SV
J. Rijo	1	0	4.38	12.1	10	7	15	0
D. Jackson	1	0	2.38	11.1	8	7	8	0
R. Myers	0	0	0.00	5.2	2	3	7	3
N. Charlton	1	1	1.80	5	4	3	3	0
R. Dibble	0	0	0.00	5	0	1	10	1
R. Mahler	0	0	0.00	1.2	2	0	0	0
S. Scudder	0	0	0.00	1	0	0	0	0

PITTSBURGH (EAST)

	W	L	ERA	IP	H	BB	SO	SV
D. Drabek	1	1	1.65	16.1	12	3	13	0
B. Walk	1	1	4.85	13	11	2	8	0
Z. Smith	0	2	6.00	9	14	1	8	0
T. Power	0	0	3.60	5	6	2	3	1
S. Belinda	0	0	2.45	3.2	3	0	4	0
B. Landrum	0	0	0.00	2	0	1	0	0
J. Smiley	0	0	0.00	2	2	0	0	0
B. Patterson	0	0	0.00	1	1	2	0	1

1990 AMERICAN LEAGUE CHAMPIONSHIP SERIES

LINE SCORES	PITCHERS (innings pitched)	HOME RUNS (men on)	HIGHLIGHTS

Oakland (West) defeats Boston (East) 4 games to 0

GAME 1 - OCTOBER 6

OAK W	000 000 117	9 13 0	**Stewart** (8), Eckersley (1) **SV**	
BOS E	000 100 000	1 5 1	Clemens (6), **Andersen** (1.0), Bolton (0.1), Lamp (0.1), Murphy (0.2)	Boggs

Athletics broke open a 2-1 game with seven runs in the ninth inning. After Boggs homered in the fourth inning to give Boston a 1-0 lead, Oakland tied the score in the seventh on Rickey Henderson's sacrifice fly and gained the lead an inning later on an RBI single by Carney Lansford. Stewart pitched a four-hitter over eight innings to pick up the win.

GAME 2 - OCTOBER 7

OAK W	000 100 102	4 13 1	**Welch** (7.1), Honeycutt (0.1), Eckersley (1.1) **SV**
BOS E	001 000 000	1 6 0	Kiecker (5.2), **Harris** (0.1), Andersen (1.0), Reardon (2)

Baines drove in three runs to back Welch's strong pitching performance as Oakland took a 2-0 lead in the series. Baines singled home the Athletic's first run in the fourth to tie the game, drove in the go-ahead run with a grounder in the seventh, and doubled home an insurance run in the ninth.

GAME 3 - OCTOBER 9

BOS E	010 000 000	1 8 3	**Boddicker** (8)
OAK W	000 202 00x	4 6 0	**Moore** (6), Nelson (1.2), Honeycutt (0.1), Eckersley (1) **SV**

Randolph, filling in for the injured Weiss, hit two RBI singles to lift the Athletics to their third straight win. His first hit gave Oakland a 2-1 lead in the fourth inning, and he drove in their last run in the sixth.

GAME 4 - OCTOBER 10

BOS E	000 000 001	1 4 1	**Clemens** (1.2), Bolton (2.2), Gray (2.2), Andersen (1)
OAK W	030 000 00x	3 6 0	**Stewart** (8.0), Honeycutt (1) **SV**

Oakland became the first team to win three consecutive pennants since the Yankees of 1976-77-78 as Stewart and Honeycutt held Boston to four hits. With Oakland leading 1-0 in the second inning, Boston starter Roger Clemens was ejected by plate umpire Terry Cooney. Bolton replaced Clemens and gave up a two-run double to Mike Gallego. Athletics, who became first team to win a playoff series without hitting a homer, held Red Sox to just four runs in series.

Team totals

	W	AB	H	2B	3B	HR	R	RBI	BA	BB	SO	ERA
OAK W	4	127	38	4	0	0	20	18	.299	19	21	1.00
BOS E	0	126	23	5	0	1	4	4	.183	6	16	4.50

Individual Batting

OAKLAND (WEST)

	AB	H	2B	3B	HR	R	RBI	BA
R. Henderson, of	17	5	0	0	0	1	3	.294
C. Lansford, 3b	16	7	1	0	0	2	2	.438
H. Baines, dh	14	2	5	1	0	0	3	.357
M. McGwire, 1b	13	2	0	0	0	2	2	.154
T. Steinbach, c	11	5	0	0	0	2	1	.455
J. Canseco, of	11	2	0	0	0	3	1	.182
M. Gallego, 2b, ss	10	4	1	0	0	1	2	.400
W. McGee, of	9	2	1	0	0	3	0	.222
W. Randolph, 2b	8	3	0	0	0	1	3	.375
W. Weiss, ss	7	0	0	0	0	2	0	.000
D. Henderson, of	6	1	0	0	0	0	1	.167
R. Hassey, c	3	1	0	0	0	0	0	.333
J. Quirk	1	1	0	0	0	0	0	1.000
D. Jennings, of	1	0	0	0	0	0	0	.000
L. Blankenship	0	0	0	0	0	1	0	-

Errors: Weiss
Stolen Bases: J. Canseco (2), R. Henderson (2), W. McGee (2), H. Baines, D. Henderson, L. Blankenship

BOSTON (EAST)

	AB	H	2B	3B	HR	R	RBI	BA
W. Boggs, 3b	16	7	1	0	1	1	1	.438
E. Burks, of	15	4	2	0	0	1	0	.267
T. Pena, c	14	3	0	0	0	0	0	.214
M. Greenwell, of	14	0	0	0	0	1	0	.000
D. Evans, dh	13	3	1	0	0	0	0	.231
T. Brunansky, of	12	1	0	0	0	0	1	.083
L. Rivera, ss	9	2	1	0	0	1	0	.222
M. Marshall	3	1	0	0	0	0	0	.333
D. Heep	2	0	0	0	0	0	0	.000
M. Barrett, 2b	0	0	0	0	0	0	0	.000
R. Kutcher	0	0	0	0	0	0	0	.000

Errors: L. Rivera, T. Pena, M. Greenwell, M. Boddicker, J. Gray
Stolen Bases: E. Burks

Individual Pitching

OAKLAND (WEST)

	W	L	ERA	IP	H	BB	SO	SV
D. Stewart	2	0	1.13	16	8	2	4	0
B. Welch	1	0	1.23	7.1	6	3	4	0
M. Moore	1	0	1.50	6	4	1	5	0
D. Eckersley	0	0	0.00	3.1	2	0	3	2
R. Honeycutt	0	0	0.00	1.2	0	0	0	1
G. Nelson	0	0	0.00	1.2	3	0	0	0

BOSTON (EAST)

	W	L	ERA	IP	H	BB	SO	SV
M. Boddicker	0	1	2.25	8	6	3	7	0
R. Clemens	0	1	3.52	7.2	7	5	4	0
D. Kiecker	0	0	1.59	5.2	6	1	2	0
J. Gray	0	0	2.70	3.1	4	1	2	0
T. Bolton	0	0	0.00	3	2	2	3	0
L. Andersen	0	1	6.00	3	3	3	3	0
J. Reardon	0	0	9.00	2	3	1	0	0
R. Murphy	0	0	13.50	.2	2	1	0	0
G. Harris	0	1	27.00	.1	3	0	0	0
D. Lamp	0	0	108.00	.1	2	2	0	0

1990 WORLD SERIES

LINE SCORES	PITCHERS (innings pitched)	HOME RUNS (men on)	HIGHLIGHTS

Cincinnati (N.L.) defeats Oakland (A.L.) 4 games to 0

GAME 1 - OCTOBER 16

OAK A 000 000 000 0 9 1
CIN N 202 030 00x 7 10 0

Stewart (4), Burns (0.2), Nelson (1.1), Sanderson (1), Eckersley (1)
Rijo (7), Dibble (1), Myers (1)

Davis (1 on)

Cincinnati reached Stewart for four runs in the first three innings to win the Series opener. Two-run homer by Davis opened the scoring in the first inning, and the Reds went on to score twice more in the third and three times in the fifth. Rijo and two relievers kept Oakland off the scoreboard.

GAME 2 - OCTOBER 17

OAK A 103 000 000 0 4 10 2
CIN W 200 100 010 1 5 14 2

Welch (7.1), Honeycutt (1.2), Eckersley (0.1)
Jackson (2.2), Scudder (1.1), Armstrong (3.0), Charlton (1), **Dibble** (2)

Canseco

Oliver bounced a single down the leftfield line in the tenth inning to give the Reds a 2-0 lead in the Series. Oakland took a 4-2 lead with three runs in the third inning, but were held scoreless by the Cincinnati bullpen over the last seven frames. Reds' Hatcher went 4-for-4 to set a Series record with seven straight hits.

GAME 3 - OCTOBER 19

CIN N 017 000 000 8 14 1
OAK A 021 000 000 3 7 1

Browning (6.0), Dibble (1.2), Myers (1.1)
Moore (2.2), Sanderson (0.2), Klink (0), Nelson (3.2), Burns (1), Young (1)

Sabo, Sabo (1 on)
Baines (1 on), R. Henderson

Sabo cracked two home runs, including a two-run shot in Cincinnati's seven-run third inning. Sabo's first homer gave the Reds a 1-0 lead before Baines connected with a man on to give Oakland a 2-1 lead. Reds then erupted for seven runs against Moore and Sanderson to take an 8-2 lead.

GAME 4 - OCTOBER 20

CIN N 000 000 020 2 7 1
OAK A 100 000 000 1 2 1

Rijo (8.1), Myers (0.2) **SV**
Stewart (9)

Series MVP Rijo outpitched Stewart for the second time, leading Cincinnati to a sweep over the heavily favored Athletics. Trailing 1-0, the Reds loaded the bases in the eighth inning with nobody out. Braggs drove in the tying run with a ground ball, then a sacrifice fly by Morris plated the winning run. Rijo allowed Oakland's only run in the first inning, then retired 20 straight batters before Myers set down the final two. The championship was Cincinnati's first since 1976.

Team totals

	W	AB	H	2B	3B	HR	R	RBI	BA	BB	SO	ERA
CIN N	4	142	45	9	2	3	22	22	.317	15	9	1.70
OAK A	0	135	28	4	0	3	8	8	.207	12	28	3.82

Individual Batting

CINCINNATI (N.L.)

	AB	H	2B	3B	HR	R	RBI	BA
J. Oliver, c	18	6	3	0	0	2	1	.333
B. Larkin, ss	17	6	1	1	0	3	2	.353
C. Sabo, 3b	16	9	1	0	2	2	5	.563
E. Davis, of	14	4	0	0	1	3	5	.286
M. Duncan, 2b	14	2	0	0	0	1	1	.143
H. Morris, 1b	14	1	0	0	0	2	1	.071
B. Hatcher, of	12	9	4	1	0	6	2	.750
P. O'Neill, of	12	1	0	0	0	2	1	.083
T. Benzinger, 1b	11	2	0	0	1	0	0	.182
H. Winningham, of	4	2	0	0	0	1	0	.500
G. Braggs, of	4	0	0	0	0	0	2	.000
J. Rijo, p	3	1	0	0	0	0	0	.333
B. Bates	1	1	0	0	0	1	0	1.000
R. Oester, 2b	1	1	0	0	0	0	1	1.000
D. Jackson, p	1	0	0	0	0	0	0	.000

Errors: J. Oliver (3), D. Jackson
Stolen Bases: M. Duncan, P. O'Neill

OAKLAND (A.L.)

	AB	H	2B	3B	HR	R	RBI	BA
R. Henderson, of	15	5	2	0	1	2	1	.333
C. Lansford, 3b	15	4	0	0	0	0	1	.267
W. Randolph, 2b	15	4	0	0	0	1	3	.267
M. McGwire, 1b	14	3	0	0	0	1	0	.214
D. Henderson, of	13	3	1	0	0	2	0	.231
J. Canseco, of	12	1	0	0	1	1	2	.083
M. Gallego, ss	11	1	1	0	0	0	1	.091
W. McGee, of	10	2	1	0	0	1	0	.200
T. Steinbach, c	8	1	0	0	0	0	0	.125
H. Baines, dh	7	1	0	0	1	1	2	.143
R. Hassey, c	6	2	0	0	0	0	1	.333
J. Quirk, c	3	0	0	0	0	0	0	.000
B. Welch, p	3	0	0	0	0	0	0	.000
D. Jennings	1	1	0	0	0	0	0	1.000
L. Blankenship	1	0	0	0	0	0	0	.000
D. Stewart, p	1	0	0	0	0	0	0	.000
M. Bordick, ss	0	0	0	0	0	0	0	-

Errors: M. McGwire (2), R. Hassey, M. Gallego, D. Stewart
Stolen Bases: R. Henderson (2), W. McGee, C. Lansford, W. Randolph, M. Gallego

Individual Pitching

CINCINNATI (N.L.)

	W	L	ERA	IP	H	BB	SO	SV
J. Rijo	2	0	0.59	15.1	9	5	14	0
T. Browning	1	0	4.50	6	6	2	2	0
R. Dibble	1	0	0.00	4.2	3	1	4	0
R. Myers	0	0	0.00	3	2	0	3	1
J. Armstrong	0	0	0.00	3	1	0	3	0
D. Jackson	0	0	10.13	2.2	6	2	0	0
S. Scudder	0	0	0.00	1.1	0	2	2	0
N. Charlton	0	0	0.00	1	1	0	0	0

OAKLAND (WEST)

	W	L	ERA	IP	H	BB	SO	SV
D. Stewart	0	2	3.46	13	10	6	5	0
B. Welch	0	0	4.91	7.1	9	2	2	0
G. Nelson	0	0	0.00	5	3	2	0	0
M. Moore	0	1	6.75	2.2	8	0	1	0
S. Sanderson	0	0	10.80	1.2	4	1	0	0
R. Honeycutt	0	0	0.00	1.2	2	1	0	0
T. Burns	0	0	16.20	1.2	5	2	0	0
D. Eckersley	0	1	6.75	1.1	3	0	1	0
C. Young	0	0	0.00	1	1	0	0	0
J. Klink	0	0	-	0	0	1	0	0

Player
Register
Supplement

Year	Team	Games	BA	SA	AB	H	2B	3B	HR	HR%	R	RBI	BB	SO	SB	PINCH HIT AB	H	PO	A	E	DP	TC/G	FA	G by Pos

Carlos Baerga

BAERGA, CARLOS OBED
Born Carlos Obed Baerga y Ortiz.
B. Nov. 4, 1968, San Juan, Puerto Rico
BB TR 5′ 11″ 165 lbs.

Split	Games	BA	SA	AB	H	2B	3B	HR	HR%	R	RBI	BB	SO	SB	PH AB	PH H	PO	A	E	DP	TC/G	FA	G by Pos
April	12	.194	.333	36	7	0	1	1	2.8	5	5	2	4	0									
May	21	.232	.250	56	13	1	0	0	0.0	7	4	3	7	0									
June	20	.208	.438	48	10	5	0	2	4.2	6	10	4	12	0									
July	14	.179	.214	28	5	1	0	0	0.0	4	0	2	4	0									
Aug	16	.364	.545	55	20	4	0	2	3.6	9	11	1	8	0									
Sept/Oct	25	.292	.449	89	26	6	1	2	2.2	15	17	4	22	0									
Day	32	.248	.367	109	27	2	1	3	2.8	17	18	5	21	0									
Night	76	.266	.409	203	54	15	1	4	2.0	29	29	11	36	0									
vs. Left		.243	.340	103	25	4	0	2	1.9	15	16	1	22	0									
vs. Right		.268	.421	209	56	13	2	5	2.4	31	31	15	35	0									
On Grass	88	.271	.430	258	70	16	2	7	2.7	39	42	12	45	0									
On Turf	20	.204	.222	54	11	1	0	0	0.0	7	5	4	12	0									
Home	51	.300	.440	150	45	10	1	3	2.0	27	28	9	22	0									
Road	57	.222	.352	162	36	7	1	4	2.5	19	19	7	35	0									
Division Rivals																							
vs. BAL	12	.333	.641	39	13	3	0	3	7.7	7	11	4	9	0									
vs. BOS	12	.324	.412	34	11	3	0	0	0.0	5	3	2	8	0									
vs. DET	11	.267	.367	30	8	3	0	0	0.0	2	4	0	8	0									
vs. MIL	5	.167	.389	18	3	1	0	1	5.6	2	4	0	1	0									
vs. NY	2	.500	1.000	10	5	3	1	0	0.0	4	3	0	1	0									
vs. TOR	10	.143	.143	28	4	0	0	0	0.0	3	1	2	6	0									
On 3B < 2 Out		.583	.917	12	7	1	0	1	8.3	1	19	2	3										
1990	CLE A	108	.260	.394	312	81	17	2	7	2.2	46	47	16	57	0	31	11	79	164	17	27	2.6	.935	3B-50, SS-48, 2B-8

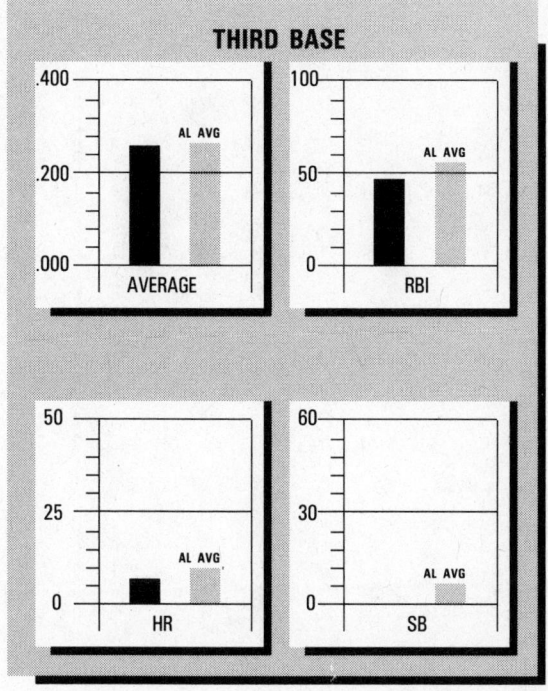

THIRD BASE
(AVERAGE — AL AVG; RBI — AL AVG; HR — AL AVG; SB — AL AVG)

Delino DeShields

DeSHIELDS, DELINO LAMONT
B. Jan. 15, 1969, Seaford, Del.
BL TR 6′ 1″ 170 lbs.

Split	Games	BA	SA	AB	H	2B	3B	HR	HR%	R	RBI	BB	SO	SB	PH AB	PH H	PO	A	E	DP	TC/G	FA	G by Pos
April	17	.329	.429	70	23	7	0	0	0.0	8	4	10	13	6									
May	25	.292	.448	96	28	5	2	2	2.1	18	8	16	19	8									
June	16	.293	.379	58	17	1	2	0	0.0	9	2	8	13	9									
July	17	.279	.361	61	17	5	0	0	0.0	8	8	8	6	6									
Aug	25	.269	.375	104	28	4	2	1	1.0	13	8	11	17	5									
Sept/Oct	29	.282	.364	110	31	6	0	1	0.9	13	15	13	28	8									
Day	35	.284	.366	134	38	11	0	0	0.0	15	14	14	30	10									
Night	94	.290	.403	365	106	17	6	4	1.1	54	31	52	66	32									
vs. Left		.264	.373	193	51	9	3	2	1.0	24	17	26	48	13									
vs. Right		.304	.405	306	93	19	3	2	0.7	45	28	40	48	29									
On Grass	35	.243	.329	140	34	5	2	1	0.7	16	6	12	32	8									
On Turf	94	.306	.418	359	110	23	4	3	0.8	53	39	54	64	34									
Home	59	.314	.438	226	71	15	2	3	1.3	36	27	32	41	24									
Road	70	.267	.355	273	73	13	4	1	0.4	33	18	34	55	18									
Division Rivals																							
vs. CHI	11	.356	.444	45	16	4	0	0	0.0	7	6	3	4	4									
vs. NY	17	.209	.254	67	14	3	0	0	0.0	5	4	4	20	7									
vs. PHI	16	.310	.362	58	18	1	1	0	0.0	10	4	15	11	4									
vs. PIT	13	.289	.422	45	13	4	1	0	0.0	6	6	5	9	4									
vs. STL	16	.368	.515	68	25	5	1	1	1.5	10	8	5	15	8									
On 3B < 2 Out		.455	.682	22	10	5	0	0	0.0	0	20	5	4										
1990	MON N	129	.289	.393	499	144	28	6	4	0.8	69	45	66	96	42	4	0	236	371	12	65	4.8	.981	2B-128

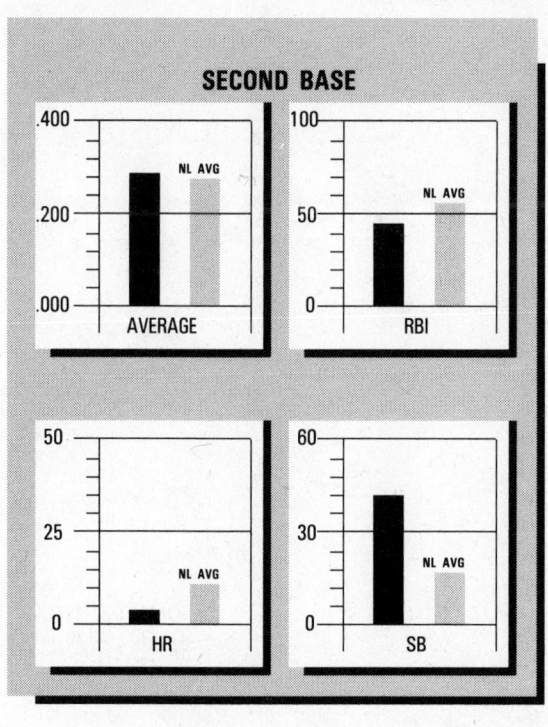

SECOND BASE
(AVERAGE — NL AVG; RBI — NL AVG; HR — NL AVG; SB — NL AVG)

Year	Team	Games	BA	SA	AB	H	2B	3B	HR	HR%	R	RBI	BB	SO	SB	PINCH HIT AB	H	PO	A	E	DP	TC/G	FA	G by Pos

Mike Marshall

MARSHALL, MICHAEL ALLEN (Moose)
B. Jan. 12, 1960, Libertyville, Ill.
BR TR 6′ 5″ 215 lbs.

Year	Team	Games	BA	SA	AB	H	2B	3B	HR	HR%	R	RBI	BB	SO	SB	PINCH HIT AB	H	PO	A	E	DP	TC/G	FA	G by Pos
April		15	.228	.404	57	13	2	1	2	3.5	7	9	1	13	0									
May		19	.226	.371	62	14	3	0	2	3.2	9	11	3	15	0									
June		14	.316	.553	38	12	3	0	2	5.3	8	6	3	8	0									
July		5	.000	.000	6	0	0	0	0	0.0	0	1	0	4	0									
Aug		11	.333	.513	39	13	1	0	2	5.1	3	7	1	6	0									
Sept/Oct		19	.260	.438	73	19	5	1	2	2.7	7	5	3	20	0									
Day		27	.261	.370	92	24	3	2	1	1.1	11	12	2	17	0									
Night		56	.257	.464	183	47	11	0	9	4.9	23	27	9	49	0									
vs. Left			.219	.406	96	21	6	0	4	4.2	9	9	5	27	0									
vs. Right			.279	.447	179	50	8	2	6	3.4	25	30	6	39	0									
On Grass		68	.256	.441	227	58	11	2	9	4.0	31	35	9	53	0									
On Turf		15	.271	.396	48	13	3	0	1	2.1	3	4	2	13	0									
Home		43	.253	.452	146	37	8	0	7	4.8	21	22	6	32	0									
Road		40	.264	.411	129	34	6	2	3	2.3	13	17	5	34	0									
Division Rivals																								
vs. BAL		5	.263	.474	19	5	1	0	1	5.3	3	2	1	4	0									
vs. CLE		5	.353	.588	17	6	1	0	1	5.9	1	3	0	1	0									
vs. DET			.000	.000	0	0	0	0	0	0.0	0	0	0	0	0									
vs. MIL		4	.267	.533	15	4	1	0	1	6.7	2	2	0	4	0									
vs. NY		4	.143	.143	14	2	0	0	0	0.0	1	0	2	4	0									
vs. TOR		3	.364	.364	11	4	0	0	0	0.0	0	2	0	3	0									
On 3B < 2 Out			.176	.235	17	3	1	0	0	0.0	0	9	0	5										
1981	LA N	14	.200	.320	25	5	3	0	0	0.0	2	1	1	4	0	7	3	14	2	0	2	1.1	1.000	1B-3, 3B-3, OF-2
1982		49	.242	.432	95	23	3	0	5	5.3	10	9	13	23	2	20	3	122	5	2	6	2.6	.984	OF-19, 1B-13
1983		140	.284	.434	465	132	17	1	17	3.7	47	65	43	127	7	6	1	395	21	6	16	3.0	.986	OF-109, 1B-33
1984		134	.257	.438	495	127	27	0	21	4.2	69	65	40	93	4	7	2	331	17	5	12	2.6	.986	OF-118, 1B-15
1985		135	.293	.515	518	152	27	2	28	5.4	72	95	37	137	3	3	0	265	12	4	9	2.1	.986	OF-125, 1B-7
1986		103	.233	.439	330	77	11	0	19	5.8	47	53	27	90	4	1	0	149	8	6	1	1.6	.963	OF-97
1987		104	.294	.460	402	118	19	0	16	4.0	45	72	18	79	0	2	1	147	4	2	0	1.5	.987	OF-102
1988		144	.277	.445	542	150	27	2	20	3.7	63	82	24	93	4	4	0	605	49	7	31	4.6	.989	OF-143
1989		105	.260	.408	377	98	21	1	11	2.9	41	42	33	78	2	5	2	179	2	4	0	1.8	.978	OF-102
1990	2 teams	NY N	(53G — .239)		BOS A	(30G — .206)																		
"	total	83	.258	.433	275	71	14	2	10	3.6	34	39	11	66	0	9	1	332	31	3	24	6.2	.992	1B-50, DH-14, OF-9
10 yrs.		1011	.270	.448	3524	953	169	8	147	4.2	430	523	247	790	26	64	13	2539	151	39	101	2.7	.986	OF-826, 1B-121, DH-14, 3B-3

DIVISIONAL PLAYOFF SERIES

Year	Team	Games	BA	SA	AB	H	2B	3B	HR	HR%	R	RBI	BB	SO	SB	AB	H	PO	A	E	DP	TC/G	FA	G by Pos
1981	LA N	1	.000	.000	1	0	0	0	0	0.0	0	0	0	1	0	1	0	0	0	0	0	0.0	—	

LEAGUE CHAMPIONSHIP SERIES

Year	Team	Games	BA	SA	AB	H	2B	3B	HR	HR%	R	RBI	BB	SO	SB	AB	H	PO	A	E	DP	TC/G	FA	G by Pos
1983	LA N	4	.133	.400	15	2	1	0	1	6.7	1	2	1	6	0	0	0	18	2	0	0	5.0	1.000	1B-3, OF-2
1985		6	.217	.435	23	5	2	0	1	4.3	1	3	1	3	0	0	0	8	0	0	0	1.3	1.000	OF-6
1988		7	.233	.333	30	7	1	1	0	0.0	3	5	2	9	0	0	0	14	0	0	0	2.0	1.000	OF-7
1990	BOS A	3	.333	.333	3	1	0	0	0	0.0	0	0	0	0	0	3	1	0	0	0	0	0.0	1.000	
4 yrs.		20	.211	.380	71	15	4	1	2	2.8	5	10	4	18	0	3	1	40	2	0	0	2.1	1.000	OF-15, 1B-3

WORLD SERIES

Year	Team	Games	BA	SA	AB	H	2B	3B	HR	HR%	R	RBI	BB	SO	SB	AB	H	PO	A	E	DP	TC/G	FA	G by Pos
1988	LA N	5	.231	.615	13	3	0	1	1	7.7	2	3	0	5	0	0	0	6	0	0	0	1.2	1.000	OF-5

Dan Pasqua

PASQUA, DANIEL ANTHONY
B. Oct. 17, 1961, Yonkers, N. Y.
BL TL 6′ 205 lbs.

Year	Team	Games	BA	SA	AB	H	2B	3B	HR	HR%	R	RBI	BB	SO	SB	AB	H	PO	A	E	DP	TC/G	FA	G by Pos
April		5	.143	.286	7	1	1	0	0	0.0	1	0	2	4	0									
May		21	.362	.672	58	21	4	1	4	6.9	10	13	13	12	1									
June		17	.268	.536	56	15	3	0	4	7.1	5	12	3	9	0									
July		23	.273	.519	77	21	8	1	3	3.9	12	16	4	17	0									
Aug		21	.254	.475	59	15	7	0	2	3.4	8	9	6	14	0									
Sept/Oct		25	.235	.324	68	16	4	1	0	0.0	7	8	9	10	0									
Day		29	.329	.600	85	28	9	1	4	4.7	14	16	7	17	1									
Night		83	.254	.458	240	61	18	2	9	3.8	29	42	30	49	0									
vs. Left			.194	.290	31	6	3	0	0	0.0	3	4	2	8	0									
vs. Right			.282	.517	294	83	24	3	13	4.4	40	54	35	58	1									

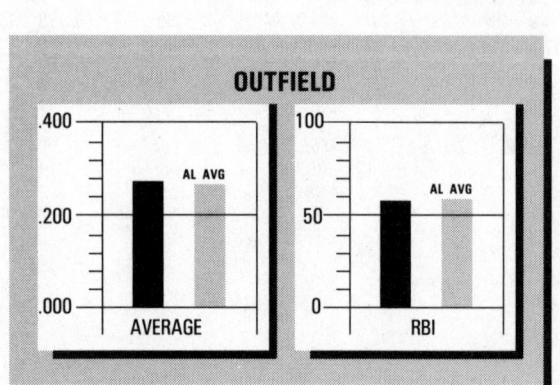

Year	Team		Games	BA	SA	AB	H	2B	3B	HR	HR%	R	RBI	BB	SO	SB	PINCH HIT AB	H	PO	A	E	DP	TC/G	FA	G by Pos

Dan Pasqua *Continued*

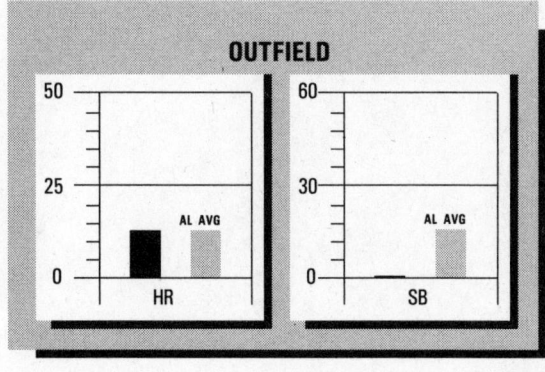

OUTFIELD

		Games	BA	SA	AB	H	2B	3B	HR	HR%	R	RBI	BB	SO	SB	PH AB	H	PO	A	E	DP	TC/G	FA	G by Pos
On Grass		94	.278	.491	273	76	22	3	10	3.7	39	48	33	57	1									
On Turf		18	.250	.519	52	13	5	0	3	5.8	4	10	4	9	0									
Home		54	.318	.529	157	50	15	3	4	2.5	24	29	19	28	1									
Road		58	.232	.464	168	39	12	0	9	5.4	19	29	18	38	0									
Division Rivals																								
vs. CAL		7	.278	.500	18	5	1	0	1	5.6	6	4	2	4	0									
vs. KC		10	.355	.548	31	11	3	0	1	3.2	4	9	5	7	1									
vs. MIN		9	.412	.824	17	7	4	0	1	5.9	1	4	1	4	0									
vs. OAK		13	.208	.417	48	10	4	0	2	4.2	5	7	3	7	0									
vs. SEA		6	.250	.500	20	5	0	1	1	5.0	1	4	2	3	0									
vs. TEX		9	.179	.286	28	5	0	0	1	3.6	3	5	2	9	0									
On 3B < 2 Out			.350	.750	20	7	2	0	2	10.0	2	19	4	8										
1985	NY A	60	.209	.426	148	31	3	1	9	6.1	17	25	16	38	0	15	2	72	2	0	0	1.2	1.000	OF-37, DH-14
1986		102	.293	.525	280	82	17	0	16	5.7	44	45	47	78	2	22	7	172	4	2	6	1.7	.989	OF-81, 1B-5, DH-3
1987		113	.233	.421	318	74	7	1	17	5.3	42	42	40	99	0	22	3	214	10	2	2	2.0	.991	OF-74, DH-20, 1B-12
1988	CHI A	129	.227	.417	422	96	16	2	20	4.7	48	50	46	100	1	15	1	316	14	2	13	2.6	.994	OF-119, DH-2
1989		73	.248	.427	246	61	9	1	11	4.5	26	47	25	58	1	3	2	149	3	1	2	2.1	.993	OF-66, DH-5
1990		112	.274	.495	325	89	27	3	13	4.0	43	58	37	66	1	18	4	71	5	3	1	1.8	.962	DH-57, OF-43
6 yrs.		589	.249	.452	1739	433	79	8	86	4.9	220	267	211	439	5	95	19	994	38	10	24	1.8	.990	OF-420, DH-101, 1B-17

Bill Pecota

PECOTA, WILLIAM JOSEPH
B. Feb. 16, 1960, Redwood City, Calif.
BR TR 6' 2" 195 lbs.

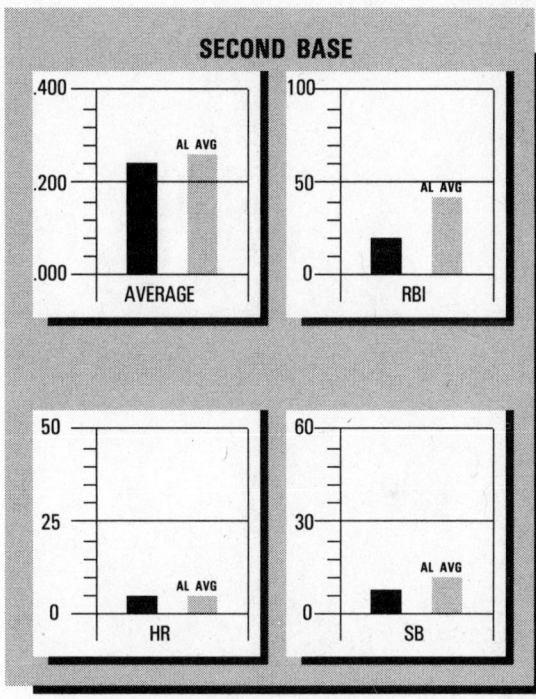

SECOND BASE

		Games	BA	SA	AB	H	2B	3B	HR	HR%	R	RBI	BB	SO	SB	PH AB	H	PO	A	E	DP	TC/G	FA	G by Pos
April		3	.000	.000	0	0	0	0	0	0.0	0	0	0	0	0									
May					0	0	0	0	0		0	0	0	0	0									
June		16	.389	.472	36	14	3	0	0	0.0	9	1	4	7	2									
July		23	.229	.349	83	19	5	1	1	1.2	16	9	10	19	4									
Aug		21	.197	.424	66	13	4	1	3	4.5	10	6	7	7	2									
Sept/Oct		24	.218	.327	55	12	3	0	1	1.8	8	4	12	6	0									
Day		23	.286	.429	63	18	3	0	2	3.2	14	10	10	13	2									
Night		64	.226	.367	177	40	12	2	3	1.7	29	10	23	26	6									
vs. Left			.290	.480	100	29	11	1	2	2.0	22	6	13	12	3									
vs. Right			.207	.314	140	29	4	1	3	2.1	21	14	20	27	5									
On Grass		35	.255	.340	94	24	5	0	1	1.1	17	11	12	19	2									
On Turf		52	.233	.411	146	34	10	2	4	2.7	26	9	21	20	6									
Home		38	.206	.363	102	21	5	1	3	2.9	19	7	14	15	5									
Road		49	.268	.399	138	37	10	1	2	1.4	24	13	19	24	3									
Division Rivals																								
vs. CAL		11	.259	.296	27	7	1	0	0	0.0	3	1	3	5	0									
vs. CHI		6	.278	.444	18	5	1	1	0	0.0	2	1	3	3	1									
vs. MIN		7	.278	.333	18	5	1	0	0	0.0	3	0	3	2	0									
vs. OAK		5	.071	.143	14	1	1	0	0	0.0	0	0	0	1	0									
vs. SEA		9	.296	.630	27	8	3	0	2	7.4	6	2	3	4	1									
vs. TEX		6	.200	.200	10	2	0	0	0	0.0	2	1	2	2	1									
On 3B < 2 Out			.250	.417	12	3	2	0	0	0.0	0	5	3	1										
1986	KC A	12	.207	.276	29	6	2	0	0	0.0	3	2	3	3	0	0	0	7	31	1	1	3.3	.974	3B-12, SS-2
1987		66	.276	.378	156	43	5	1	3	1.9	22	14	15	25	5	7	0	67	135	6	28	3.2	.971	SS-36, 3B-17, 2B-15
1988		90	.208	.275	178	37	3	3	1	0.6	25	15	18	34	7	1	1	98	145	6	25	2.8	.976	SS-41, 3B-21, 1B-11, OF-9, DH-4, 2B-3, C-1
1989		65	.205	.410	83	17	4	2	3	3.6	21	5	7	9	5	0	0	50	79	2	14	2.0	.985	SS-29, OF-15, 2B-12, 3B-7, 1B-4, DH-1
1990		87	.242	.383	240	58	15	2	5	2.0	43	20	33	39	8	2	0	160	195	5	44	4.4	.986	2B-50, SS-21, 3B-11, OF-6, 1B-4, DH-2
5 yrs.		320	.235	.353	686	161	29	8	12	1.7	114	56	76	110	25	10	1	382	585	20	112	3.1	.980	SS-129, 2B-80, 3B-68, OF-30, 1B-19, DH-7, C-1

Notes